Official 2011
National Football League

Record
& Fact Book

NATIONAL FOOTBALL LEAGUE
280 Park Avenue, New York, N.Y. 10017 (212) 450-2000. NFL Internet Address: http://www.NFL.com

Compiled by the NFL Communications Department and Seymour Siwoff, Elias Sports Bureau.
Statistics by Elias Sports Bureau.

Edited by Jon Zimmer, NFL Communications Department, and Matt Marini. Layout by William Tham. Cover design by NFL Creative.
Produced by NFL Communications Department.

Time Inc. Home Entertainment
1271 Avenue of the Americas, New York, N.Y. 10020
Manufactured in the United States of America.
First printing, July 2011.
10 9 8 7 6 5 4 3 2 1

JUL 25 2011

TABLE OF CONTENTS

All times local. Dates and times subject to change.
Nationally televised games indicated by network in parentheses.

| | Sunday, August 7 | Hall of Fame Game at Canton, Ohio | |
| | | Chicago _____ vs. St. Louis _____ | (NBC) 8:00 |

PRESEASON/WEEK 1

Thursday, August 11	Seattle _____ at San Diego_____	(ESPN) 5:00
	Jacksonville _____ at New England _____	7:30
	Baltimore _____ at Philadelphia _____	7:30
	Denver _____ at Dallas _____	7:30
	Arizona_____ at Oakland _____	5:00
Friday, August 12	Tampa Bay _____ at Kansas City _____	(FOX) 8:00
	Miami _____ at Atlanta _____	7:30
	Cincinnati _____ at Detroit _____	7:30
	Pittsburgh _____ at Washington _____	7:30
	San Francisco _____ at New Orleans _____	7:00
Saturday, August 13	Green Bay _____ at Cleveland _____	7:30
	New York Giants _____ at Carolina _____	8:00
	Buffalo _____ at Chicago _____	7:00
	Indianapolis _____ at St. Louis _____	7:00
	Minnesota _____ at Tennessee _____	7:00
Monday, August 15	New York Jets _____ at Houston _____	(ESPN) 7:00

PRESEASON/WEEK 2

Thursday, August 18	Philadelphia _____ at Pittsburgh _____	(FOX) 8:00
	New England _____ at Tampa Bay _____	7:30
Friday, August 19	Atlanta _____ at Jacksonville _____	(FOX) 8:00
	Washington _____ at Indianapolis _____	7:00
	Kansas City _____ at Baltimore _____	7:30
	Detroit _____ at Cleveland _____	7:30
	Carolina _____ at Miami _____	7:30
	Arizona _____ at Green Bay _____	7:00
Saturday, August 20	San Diego _____ at Dallas _____	7:00
	New Orleans _____ at Houston _____	7:00
	Tennessee _____ at St. Louis _____	7:00
	Oakland _____ at San Francisco _____	5:00
	Buffalo _____ at Denver _____	6:30
	Minnesota _____ at Seattle _____	7:00
Sunday, August 21	Cincinnati _____ at New York Jets _____	7:00
Monday, August 22	Chicago _____ at New York Giants _____	(ESPN) 8:00

PRESEASON/WEEK 3

Thursday, August 25	Washington _____ at Baltimore _____	(ESPN) 8:00
	Carolina _____ at Cincinnati _____	7:00
	Cleveland _____ at Philadelphia _____	7:30
Friday, August 26	Green Bay _____ at Indianapolis _____	(CBS) 8:00
	Miami _____ at Tampa Bay _____	7:30
	St. Louis _____ at Kansas City _____	7:00
Saturday, August 27	New England _____ at Detroit ___	(CBS) 8:00
	Jacksonville _____ at Buffalo _____	7:00
	New York Jets _____ at New York Giants _____	7:00
	Atlanta _____ at Pittsburgh _____	7:30
	Dallas _____ at Minnesota _____	7:00
	Houston _____ at San Francisco _____	5:00
	Chicago _____ at Tennessee _____	7:00
	Seattle _____ at Denver _____	7:00
	San Diego _____ at Arizona _____	7:00
Sunday, August 28	New Orleans _____ at Oakland _____	(NBC) 5:00

PRESEASON/WEEK 4

Thursday, September 1
Detroit _____ at Buffalo _____	6:30
Indianapolis _____ at Cincinnati _____	7:00
Kansas City _____ at Green Bay _____	7:00
Baltimore _____ at Atlanta _____	7:30
St. Louis _____ at Jacksonville _____	7:30
Dallas _____ at Miami _____	7:30
New York Giants _____ at New England _____	7:30
Philadelphia _____ at New York Jets _____	7:30
Tampa Bay _____ at Washington _____	7:30
Cleveland _____ at Chicago _____	7:00
Houston _____ at Minnesota _____	7:00
Tennessee _____ at New Orleans _____	7:00
Pittsburgh _____ at Carolina _____	8:00
Denver _____ at Arizona _____	7:00
San Francisco _____ at San Diego _____	7:00

Friday, September 2 Oakland _____ at Seattle _____ 7:30

KICKOFF WEEKEND

Thursday, September 8 New Orleans _____ at Green Bay _____ (NBC) 7:30
Sunday, September 11 Pittsburgh _____ at Baltimore _____ 1:00
FOX-TV National Weekend
Atlanta _____ at Chicago _____	12:00
Cincinnati _____ at Cleveland _____	1:00
Indianapolis _____ at Houston _____	12:00
Tennessee _____ at Jacksonville _____	1:00
Buffalo _____ at Kansas City _____	12:00
Philadelphia _____ at St. Louis _____	12:00
Detroit _____ at Tampa Bay _____	1:00
Carolina _____ at Arizona _____	1:15
Minnesota _____ at San Diego _____	1:15
Seattle _____ at San Francisco _____	1:15
New York Giants _____ at Washington _____	4:15
Dallas _____ at New York Jets _____	(NBC) 8:20

Monday, September 12 New England _____ at Miami _____ (ESPN) 7:00
Oakland _____ at Denver _____ (ESPN) 8:15

SECOND WEEK

Sunday, September 18
CBS-TV National Weekend
Oakland _____ at Buffalo _____	1:00
Green Bay _____ at Carolina _____	1:00
Kansas City _____ at Detroit _____	1:00
Cleveland _____ at Indianapolis _____	1:00
Tampa Bay _____ at Minnesota _____	12:00
Chicago _____ at New Orleans _____	12:00
Jacksonville _____ at New York Jets _____	1:00
Seattle _____ at Pittsburgh _____	1:00
Baltimore _____ at Tennessee _____	12:00
Arizona _____ at Washington _____	1:00
Dallas _____ at San Francisco _____	1:05
Cincinnati _____ at Denver _____	2:15
Houston _____ at Miami _____	4:15
San Diego _____ at New England _____	4:15
Philadelphia _____ at Atlanta _____	(NBC) 8:20

Monday, September 19 St. Louis _____ at New York Giants _____ (ESPN) 8:30

THIRD WEEK

Sunday, September 25
FOX-TV National Weekend
New England _____ at Buffalo _____	1:00
Jacksonville _____ at Carolina _____	1:00
San Francisco _____ at Cincinnati _____	1:00
Miami _____ at Cleveland _____	1:00
Detroit _____ at Minnesota _____	12:00
Houston _____ at New Orleans _____	12:00
N.Y. Giants _____ at Philadelphia _____	1:00
Denver _____ at Tennessee _____	12:00
N.Y. Jets _____ at Oakland _____	1:05
Baltimore _____ at St. Louis _____	3:05
Kansas City _____ at San Diego _____	1:05
Green Bay _____ at Chicago _____	3:15
Arizona _____ at Seattle _____	1:15
Atlanta _____ at Tampa Bay _____	4:15
Pittsburgh _____ at Indianapolis _____	(NBC) 8:20

Monday, September 26 Washington _____ at Dallas _____ (ESPN) 7:30

FOURTH WEEK

Sunday, October 2	Carolina _____ at Chicago _____	12:00
CBS-TV National Weekend	Buffalo _____ at Cincinnati _____	1:00
	Tennessee _____ at Cleveland _____	1:00
	Detroit _____ at Dallas _____	12:00
	Pittsburgh _____ at Houston _____	12:00
	New Orleans _____ at Jacksonville _____	1:00
	Minnesota _____ at Kansas City _____	12:00
	San Francisco _____ at Philadelphia _____	1:00
	Washington _____ at St. Louis _____	12:00
	New York Giants _____ at Arizona _____	1:05
	Atlanta _____ at Seattle _____	1:05
	Denver _____ at Green Bay _____	3:15
	New England _____ at Oakland _____	1:15
	Miami _____ at San Diego _____	1:15
	New York Jets _____ at Baltimore _____	(NBC) 8:20
Monday, October 3	Indianapolis _____ at Tampa Bay _____	(ESPN) 8:30

FIFTH WEEK
Open Date: Baltimore, Cleveland, Dallas, Miami, St. Louis, Washington

Sunday, October 9	Philadelphia _____ at Buffalo _____	1:00
CBS-TV National Weekend	New Orleans _____ at Carolina _____	1:00
	Oakland _____ at Houston _____	12:00
	Kansas City _____ at Indianapolis _____	1:00
	Cincinnati _____ at Jacksonville _____	1:00
	Arizona _____ at Minnesota _____	12:00
	Seattle _____ at New York Giants _____	1:00
	Tennessee _____ at Pittsburgh _____	1:00
	Tampa Bay _____ at San Francisco _____	1:05
	San Diego _____ at Denver _____	2:15
	New York Jets _____ at New England _____	4:15
	Green Bay _____ at Atlanta _____	(NBC) 8:20
Monday, October 10	Chicago _____ at Detroit _____	(ESPN) 8:30

SIXTH WEEK
Open Date: Arizona, Denver, Kansas City, San Diego, Seattle, Tennessee

Sunday, October 16	Carolina _____ at Atlanta _____	1:00
FOX-TV National Weekend	Indianapolis _____ at Cincinnati _____	1:00
	San Francisco _____ at Detroit _____	1:00
	St. Louis _____ at Green Bay _____	12:00
	Buffalo _____ at New York Giants _____	1:00
	Jacksonville _____ at Pittsburgh _____	1:00
	Philadelphia _____ at Washington _____	1:00
	Houston _____ at Baltimore _____	4:05
	Cleveland _____ at Oakland _____	1:05
	Dallas _____ at New England _____	4:15
	New Orleans _____ at Tampa Bay _____	4:15
	Minnesota _____ at Chicago _____	(NBC) 7:20
Monday, October 17	Miami _____ at New York Jets _____	(ESPN) 8:30

SEVENTH WEEK
Open Date: Buffalo, Cincinnati, New England, New York Giants, Philadelphia, San Francisco

Sunday, October 23	Washington _____ at Carolina _____	1:00
FOX-TV National Weekend	Seattle _____ at Cleveland _____	1:00
	Atlanta _____ at Detroit _____	1:00
	Denver _____ at Miami _____	1:00
	San Diego _____ at New York Jets _____	1:00
	Chicago _____ at Tampa Bay (London) _____	6:00
	Houston _____ at Tennessee _____	12:00
	Pittsburgh _____ at Arizona _____	1:05
	Kansas City _____ at Oakland _____	1:05
	St. Louis _____ at Dallas _____	3:15
	Green Bay _____ at Minnesota _____	3:15
	Indianapolis _____ at New Orleans _____	(NBC) 7:20
Monday, October 24	Baltimore _____ at Jacksonville _____	(ESPN) 8:30

EIGHTH WEEK
Open Date: Atlanta, Chicago,
Green Bay, New York Jets,
Oakland, Tampa Bay

Sunday, October 30	Arizona _____ at Baltimore _____	1:00
CBS-TV National Weekend	Minnesota _____ at Carolina _____	1:00
	Jacksonville _____ at Houston _____	12:00
	Miami _____ at New York Giants _____	1:00
	New Orleans _____ at St. Louis _____	12:00
	Indianapolis _____ at Tennessee _____	12:00
	Washington _____ at Buffalo (Toronto) _____	4:05
	Detroit _____ at Denver _____	2:05
	New England _____ at Pittsburgh _____	4:15
	Cleveland _____ at San Francisco _____	1:15
	Cincinnati _____ at Seattle _____	1:15
	Dallas _____ at Philadelphia _____	(NBC) 8:20
Monday, October 31	San Diego _____ at Kansas City _____	(ESPN) 7:30

NINTH WEEK
Open Date: Carolina, Detroit,
Jacksonville, Minnesota

Sunday, November 6	New York Jets _____ at Buffalo _____	1:00
FOX-TV National Weekend	Seattle _____ at Dallas _____	12:00
	Cleveland _____ at Houston _____	12:00
	Atlanta _____ at Indianapolis _____	1:00
	Miami _____ at Kansas City _____	12:00
	Tampa Bay _____ at New Orleans _____	12:00
	San Francisco _____ at Washington _____	1:00
	Denver _____ at Oakland _____	1:05
	Cincinnati _____ at Tennessee _____	3:05
	St. Louis _____ at Arizona _____	2:15
	New York Giants _____ at New England _____	4:15
	Green Bay _____ at San Diego _____	1:15
	Baltimore _____ at Pittsburgh _____	(NBC) 8:20
Monday, November 7	Chicago _____ at Philadelphia _____	(ESPN) 8:30

TENTH WEEK

Thursday, November 10	Oakland _____ at San Diego _____	(NFLN) 5:20
Sunday, November 13	New Orleans _____ at Atlanta _____	1:00
FOX-TV National Weekend	Tennessee _____ at Carolina _____	1:00
	Detroit _____ at Chicago _____	12:00
	Pittsburgh _____ at Cincinnati _____	1:00
	St. Louis _____ at Cleveland _____	1:00
	Buffalo _____ at Dallas _____	12:00
	Jacksonville _____ at Indianapolis _____	1:00
	Denver _____ at Kansas City _____	12:00
	Washington _____ at Miami _____	1:00
	Arizona _____ at Philadelphia _____	1:00
	Houston _____ at Tampa Bay _____	1:00
	Baltimore _____ at Seattle _____	1:05
	New York Giants _____ at San Francisco _____	1:15
	New England _____ at New York Jets * _____	(NBC) 8:20
Monday, November 14	Minnesota _____ at Green Bay _____	(ESPN) 7:30

Sunday Night Games In Weeks 10-15 Subject to Change

ELEVENTH WEEK
Open Date: Houston, Indianapolis,
New Orleans, Pittsburgh

Thursday, November 17	New York Jets _____ at Denver _____	(NFLN) 6:20
Sunday, November 20	Tennessee _____ at Atlanta _____	1:00
CBS-TV National Weekend	Cincinnati _____ at Baltimore _____	1:00
	Jacksonville _____ at Cleveland _____	1:00
	Carolina _____ at Detroit _____	1:00
	Tampa Bay _____ at Green Bay _____	12:00
	Buffalo _____ at Miami _____	1:00
	Oakland _____ at Minnesota _____	12:00
	Dallas _____ at Washington _____	1:00
	Seattle _____ at St. Louis _____	3:05
	Arizona _____ at San Francisco _____	1:05
	San Diego _____ at Chicago _____	3:15
	Philadelphia _____ at New York Giants * _____	(NBC) 8:20
Monday, November 21	Kansas City _____ at New England _____	(ESPN) 8:30

Sunday Night Games In Weeks 10-15 Subject to Change

TWELFTH WEEK

NFL **THANKSGIVING** 2011

Thursday, November 24	Green Bay _____ at Detroit _____	(FOX) 12:30
	Miami _____ at Dallas _____	(CBS) 3:15
	San Francisco _____ at Baltimore _____	(NFLN) 8:20
Sunday, November 27	Minnesota _____ at Atlanta _____	1:00
CBS-TV National Weekend	Cleveland _____ at Cincinnati _____	1:00
	Carolina _____ at Indianapolis _____	1:00
	Houston _____ at Jacksonville _____	1:00
	Buffalo _____ at New York Jets _____	1:00
	Arizona _____ at St. Louis _____	12:00
	Tampa Bay _____ at Tennessee _____	12:00
	Chicago _____ at Oakland _____	1:05
	Washington _____ at Seattle _____	1:05
	New England _____ at Philadelphia _____	4:15
	Denver _____ at San Diego _____	1:15
	Pittsburgh _____ at Kansas City * _____	(NBC) 7:20
Monday, November 28	New York Giants _____ at New Orleans _____	(ESPN) 7:30

Sunday Night Games In Weeks 10-15 Subject to Change

THIRTEENTH WEEK

Thursday, December 1	Philadelphia _____ at Seattle _____	(NFLN) 5:20
Sunday, December 4	Tennessee _____ at Buffalo _____	1:00
FOX-TV National Weekend	Kansas City _____ at Chicago _____	12:00
	Baltimore _____ at Cleveland _____	1:00
	Atlanta _____ at Houston _____	12:00
	Oakland _____ at Miami _____	1:00
	Detroit _____ at New Orleans _____	12:00
	Cincinnati _____ at Pittsburgh _____	1:00
	Carolina _____ at Tampa Bay _____	1:00
	New York Jets _____ at Washington _____	1:00
	Denver _____ at Minnesota _____	3:05
	Dallas _____ at Arizona _____	2:15
	Green Bay _____ at New York Giants _____	4:15
	St. Louis _____ at San Francisco _____	1:15
	Indianapolis _____ at New England * _____	(NBC) 8:20
Monday, December 5	San Diego _____ at Jacksonville _____	(ESPN) 8:30

Sunday Night Games In Weeks 10-15 Subject to Change

FOURTEENTH WEEK

Thursday, December 8	Cleveland _____ at Pittsburgh _____	(NFLN) 8:20
Sunday, December 11	Indianapolis _____ at Baltimore _____	1:00
CBS-TV National Weekend	Atlanta _____ at Carolina _____	1:00
	Houston _____ at Cincinnati _____	1:00
	Minnesota _____ at Detroit _____	1:00
	Oakland _____ at Green Bay _____	12:00
	Tampa Bay _____ at Jacksonville _____	1:00
	Philadelphia _____ at Miami _____	1:00
	Kansas City _____ at New York Jets _____	1:00
	New Orleans _____ at Tennessee _____	12:00
	New England _____ at Washington _____	1:00
	San Francisco _____ at Arizona _____	2:05
	Chicago _____ at Denver _____	2:05
	Buffalo _____ at San Diego _____	1:15
	New York Giants _____ at Dallas * _____	(NBC) 7:20
Monday, December 12	St. Louis _____ at Seattle _____	(ESPN) 5:30

Sunday Night Games In Weeks 10-15 Subject to Change

FIFTEENTH WEEK

Thursday, December 15	Jacksonville _____ at Atlanta _____	(NFLN) 8:20
Saturday, December 17	Dallas _____ at Tampa Bay _____	(NFLN) 8:20
Sunday, December 18	Miami _____ at Buffalo _____	1:00
CBS-TV National Weekend	Seattle _____ at Chicago _____	12:00
	Carolina _____ at Houston _____	12:00
	Tennessee _____ at Indianapolis _____	1:00
	Green Bay _____ at Kansas City _____	12:00
	New Orleans _____ at Minnesota _____	12:00
	Washington _____ at N.Y. Giants _____	1:00
	Cincinnati _____ at St. Louis _____	12:00
	Detroit _____ at Oakland _____	1:05
	Cleveland _____ at Arizona _____	2:15
	New England _____ at Denver _____	2:15
	New York Jets _____ at Philadelphia _____	4:15
	Baltimore _____ at San Diego * _____	(NBC) 5:20
Monday, December 19	Pittsburgh _____ at San Francisco _____	(ESPN) 5:30

Sunday Night Games In Weeks 10-15 Subject to Change

SIXTEENTH WEEK

Thursday, December 22	Houston _____ at Indianapolis _____	(NFLN) 8:20
Saturday, December 24	Cleveland _____ at Baltimore _____	1:00
FOX-TV National Weekend	Denver _____ at Buffalo _____	1:00
	Tampa Bay _____ at Carolina _____	1:00
	Arizona _____ at Cincinnati _____	1:00
	Oakland _____ at Kansas City _____	12:00
	Miami _____ at New England _____	1:00
	New York Giants _____ at New York Jets _____	1:00
	St. Louis _____ at Pittsburgh _____	1:00
	Jacksonville _____ at Tennessee _____	12:00
	Minnesota _____ at Washington _____	1:00
	San Diego _____ at Detroit _____	4:05
	Philadelphia _____ at Dallas _____	3:15
	San Francisco _____ at Seattle _____	1:15
Sunday, December 25	Chicago _____ at Green Bay _____	(NBC) 7:20
Monday, December 26	Atlanta _____ at New Orleans _____	(ESPN) 7:30

SEVENTEENTH WEEK

Sunday, January 1	Tampa Bay _____ at Atlanta _____	1:00
CBS-TV and FOX-TV National Weekend	Baltimore _____ at Cincinnati _____	1:00
	Pittsburgh _____ at Cleveland _____	1:00
	Detroit _____ at Green Bay _____	12:00
	Tennessee _____ at Houston _____	12:00
	Indianapolis _____ at Jacksonville _____	1:00
	New York Jets _____ at Miami _____	1:00
	Chicago _____ at Minnesota _____	12:00
	Buffalo _____ at New England _____	1:00
	Carolina _____ at New Orleans _____	12:00
	Dallas _____ at New York Giants _____	1:00
	Washington _____ at Philadelphia _____	1:00
	San Francisco _____ at St. Louis _____	12:00
	Seattle _____ at Arizona _____	2:15
	Kansas City _____ at Denver _____	2:15
	San Diego _____ at Oakland _____	1:15

Sunday Night Game In Week 17 TBD

PLAYOFFS

Wild Card Playoff Games
Site Priorities
Two Wild Card teams (division non-champions with best two records) from each conference and the division champions with the third and fourth-best record in each conference will enter the first round of the playoffs. The division champion with the third-best record will play host to the Wild Card team with the second-best record. The division champion with the fourth-best record will play host to the Wild Card team with the best record. There are no restrictions on intra-division games.

Saturday, January 7, 2012 American Football Conference

_____ at _____ (NBC)

National Football Conference

_____ at _____ (NBC)

Sunday, January 8, 2012 American Football Conference

_____ at _____ (CBS)

National Football Conference

_____ at _____ (FOX)

Divisional Playoff Games
Site Priorities
In each conference, the two division champions with the highest won-lost-tied percentage during the regular season will play host to the Wild Card winners. The division champion with the best record in each conference is assured of playing the lowest seeded Wild Card survivor. There are no restrictions on intra-division games.

Saturday, January 14, 2012 American Football Conference

_____ at _____ (CBS)

National Football Conference

_____ at _____ (FOX)

Sunday, January 15, 2012 American Football Conference

_____ at _____ (CBS)

National Football Conference

_____ at _____ (FOX)

Championship Games
Site Priorities for Championship Games
The home teams will be the surviving playoff winners with the highest seeds. A Wild Card team cannot play host unless two Wild Card teams are in the game, in which case the Wild Card team that was seeded highest in the first round of the playoffs will be the home team.

Sunday, January 22, 2012 American Football Conference

_____ at _____ (CBS)

National Football Conference

_____ at _____ (FOX)

AFC-NFC Pro Bowl

Sunday, January 29, 2012 AFC-NFC Pro Bowl at Aloha Stadium, Honolulu, Hawaii

AFC_____ vs. NFC _____ (NBC)

Super Bowl XLVI

Sunday, February 5, 2012 Super Bowl XLVI at Lucas Oil Stadium, Indianapolis, Indiana

_____ vs. _____ (NBC)

2011 NATIONALLY TELEVISED PRIMETIME GAMES

All times ET

Thursday, Sept. 8	New Orleans at Green Bay (NBC)	8:30
Sunday, Sept. 11	Dallas at New York Jets (NBC)	8:20
Monday, Sept. 12	New England at Miami (ESPN)	7:00
	Oakland at Denver (ESPN)	10:15
Sunday, Sept. 18	Philadelphia at Atlanta (NBC)	8:20
Monday, Sept. 19	St. Louis at New York Giants (ESPN)	8:30
Sunday, Sept. 25	Pittsburgh at Indianapolis (NBC)	8:20
Monday, Sept. 26	Washington at Dallas (ESPN)	8:30
Sunday, Oct. 2	New York Jets at Baltimore (NBC)	8:20
Monday, Oct. 3	Indianapolis at Tampa Bay (ESPN)	8:30
Sunday, Oct. 9	Green Bay at Atlanta (NBC)	8:20
Monday, Oct. 10	Chicago at Detroit (ESPN)	8:30
Sunday, Oct. 16	Minnesota at Chicago (NBC)	8:20
Monday, Oct. 17	Miami at New York Jets (ESPN)	8:30
Sunday, Oct. 23	Indianapolis at New Orleans (NBC)	8:20
Monday, Oct. 24	Baltimore at Jacksonville (ESPN)	8:30
Sunday, Oct. 30	Dallas at Philadelphia (NBC)	8:20
Monday, Oct. 31	San Diego at Kansas City (ESPN)	8:30
Sunday, Nov. 6	Baltimore at Pittsburgh (NBC)	8:20
Monday, Nov. 7	Chicago at Philadelphia (ESPN)	8:30
Thursday, Nov. 10	Oakland at San Diego (NFL Network)	8:20
Sunday, Nov. 13	New England at New York Jets (NBC)*	8:20
Monday, Nov. 14	Minnesota at Green Bay (ESPN)	8:30
Thursday, Nov. 17	New York Jets at Denver (NFL Network)	8:20
Sunday, Nov. 20	Philadelphia at New York Giants (NBC)*	8:20
Monday, Nov. 21	Kansas City at New England (ESPN)	8:30
Thursday, Nov. 24	Green Bay at Detroit (FOX)	12:30
	Miami at Dallas (CBS)	4:15
	San Francisco at Baltimore (NFL Network)	8:20
Sunday, Nov. 27	Pittsburgh at Kansas City (NBC)*	8:20
Monday, Nov. 28	New York Giants at New Orleans (ESPN)	0:30
Thursday, Dec. 1	Philadelphia at Seattle (NFL Network)	8:20
Sunday, Dec. 4	Indianapolis at New England (NBC)*	8:20
Monday, Dec. 5	San Diego at Jacksonville (ESPN)	8:30
Thursday, Dec. 8	Cleveland at Pittsburgh (NFL Network)	8:20
Sunday, Dec. 11	New York Giants at Dallas (NBC)*	8:20
Monday, Dec. 12	St. Louis at Seattle (ESPN)	0:30
Thursday, Dec. 15	Jacksonville at Atlanta (NFL Network)	8:20
Saturday, Dec. 17	Dallas at Tampa Bay (NFL Network)	8:20
Sunday, Dec. 18	Baltimore at San Diego (NBC)*	8:20
Monday, Dec. 19	Pittsburgh at San Francisco (ESPN)	8:30
Thursday, Dec. 22	Houston at Indianapolis (NFL Network)	8:20
Sunday, Dec. 25	Chicago at Green Bay (NBC)	8:20
Monday, Dec. 26	Atlanta at New Orleans (ESPN)	8:30
Sunday, Jan. 1	To be determined (NBC)*	8:20

PLAYOFFS

POSTSEASON GAMES

Saturday, January 7	AFC and NFC Wild Card Playoffs (NBC)
Sunday, January 8	AFC and NFC Wild Card Playoffs (CBS and FOX)
Saturday, January 14	AFC and NFC Divisional Playoffs (CBS and FOX)
Sunday, January 15	AFC and NFC Divisional Playoffs (CBS and FOX)
Sunday, January 22	AFC and NFC Championship Games (CBS and FOX)
Sunday, January 29	AFC-NFC Pro Bowl in Hawaii (NBC)
Sunday, February 5	Super Bowl XLVI in Indianapolis (NBC)

*The NFL again will utilize "flexible scheduling" in 2011.

Flexible scheduling moves will be announced at least 12 days before games in Weeks 10-15. In Week 17, the flexible scheduling move will be announced at least six days before the game. Flexible scheduling will ensure quality matchups on Sunday night in those weeks and give "surprise" teams a chance to play their way on to primetime.

IMPORTANT DATES

2011

August 5-7	Hall of Fame Weekend.
August 7	Pro Football Hall of Fame Game, Canton, Ohio: Chicago vs. St. Louis
August 11-15	First Preseason Weekend.
September 8-12	Regular Season opens.

2012

January 7-8	Wild Card Playoff Games.
January 14-15	Divisional Playoff Games.
January 22	AFC and NFC Championship Games.
January 29	AFC-NFC Pro Bowl, Aloha Stadium, Honolulu, Hawaii.
February 5	Super Bowl XLVI, Lucas Oil Stadium, Indianapolis, Indiana.

2013

February 3*	Super Bowl XLVII, Louisiana Superdome, New Orleans, Louisiana.

2014

February 2*	Super Bowl XLVIII, New Meadowlands Stadium, New York-New Jersey.

Tentative date.

The following procedures will be used to break standings ties for postseason playoffs and to determine regular-season schedules.

Note: Tie games count as one-half win and one-half loss for both clubs.

TO BREAK A TIE WITHIN A DIVISION

If, at the end of the regular season, two or more clubs in the same division finish with the best won-lost-tied percentage, the following steps will be taken until a champion is determined:

TWO CLUBS

1. Head-to-head (best won-lost-tied percentage in games between the clubs.)
2. Best won-lost-tied percentage in games played within the division.
3. Best won-lost-tied percentage in common games.
4. Best won-lost-tied percentage in games played within the conference.
5. Strength of victory.
6. Strength of schedule.
7. Best combined ranking among conference teams in points scored and points allowed.
8. Best combined ranking among all teams in points scored and points allowed.
9. Best net points in common games.
10. Best net points in all games.
11. Best net touchdowns in all games.
12. Coin toss.

THREE OR MORE CLUBS

(Note: If two clubs remain tied after a third club is eliminated during any step, tie-breaker reverts to Step 1 of the two-club format.)

1. Head-to-head (best won-lost-tied percentage in games among the clubs.)
2. Best won-lost-tied percentage in games played within the division.
3. Best won-lost-tied percentage in common games.
4. Best won-lost-tied percentage in games played within the conference.
5. Strength of victory.
6. Strength of schedule.
7. Best combined ranking among conference teams in points scored and points allowed.
8. Best combined ranking among all teams in points scored and points allowed.
9. Best net points in common games.
10. Best net points in all games.
11. Best net touchdowns in all games.
12. Coin toss.

TO BREAK A TIE FOR THE WILD-CARD TEAM

If it is necessary to break ties to determine the two Wild Card clubs from each conference, the following steps will be taken:

A. If all the tied clubs are from the same division, apply division tie-breaker.

B. If the tied clubs are from different divisions, apply the following steps:

TWO CLUBS

1. Head-to-head, if applicable.
2. Best won-lost-tied percentage in the games played within the conference.
3. Best won-lost-tied percentage in common games, minimum of four.
4. Strength of victory.
5. Strength of schedule.
6. Best combined ranking among conference teams in points scored and points allowed.
7. Best combined ranking among all teams in points scored and points allowed.
8. Best net points in conference games.
9. Best net points in all games.
10. Best net touchdowns in all games.
11. Coin toss.

THREE OR MORE CLUBS

1. Apply division tie-breaker to eliminate all but highest ranked club in each division prior to proceeding to Step 2. The original seeding within a division upon application of the division tie-breaker remains the same for all subsequent applications of the procedure that are necessary to identify the Wild Card participants.
2. Head-to-head sweep (apply only if one club has defeated each of the others or one club has lost to each of the others).
3. Best won-lost-tied percentage in games played within the conference.
4. Best won-lost-tied percentage in common games, minimum of four.
5. Strength of victory.
6. Strength of schedule.
7. Best combined ranking among conference teams in points scored and points allowed.
8. Best combined ranking among all teams in points scored and points allowed.
9. Best net points in conference games.
10. Best net points in all games.
11. Best net touchdowns in all games.
12. Coin toss.

When the first Wild Card team has been identified, the procedure is repeated to name the second Wild Card (i.e., eliminate all but the highest ranked club in each division prior to proceeding to Step 2.) In situations where three teams from the same division are involved in the procedure, the original seeding of the teams remains the same for subsequent applications of the tie-breaker if the top-ranked team in that division qualifies for a Wild Card berth.

OTHER TIE-BREAKING PROCEDURES

1. Only one club advances to the playoffs in any tie-breaking step. Remaining tied clubs revert to the first step of the applicable division or Wild Card tie-breakers. As an example, if two clubs remain tied in any tie-breaker step after all other clubs have been eliminated, the procedure reverts to Step 1 of the two-club format to determine the winner. When one club wins the tie-breaker, all other clubs revert to Step 1 of the applicable two-club or three-club format.
2. In comparing records against common opponents among tied teams, the best won-lost-tied percentage is the deciding factor since teams may have played an unequal number of games.
3. To determine home-field priority among division-titlists, apply Wild Card tie-breakers.
4. To determine home-field priority for Wild Card qualifiers, apply division tie-breakers (if teams are from the same division) or Wild Card tie-breakers (if teams are from different divisions).
5. To determine the best combined ranking among conference teams in points scored and points allowed, add a team's position in the two categories, and the lowest score wins. For example, if Team A is first in points scored and second in points allowed, its combined ranking is "3." If Team B is third in points scored and first in points allowed, its combined ranking is "4." Team A then wins the tiebreaker. If two teams are tied for a position, both teams are awarded the ranking as if they held it solely. For example, if Team A and Team B are tied for first in points scored, each team is assigned a ranking of "1" in that category, and if Team C is third, its ranking will still be "3."

TIE-BREAKING PROCEDURE FOR SELECTION MEETING

1. Clubs not participating in the playoffs shall select in the first through 20th positions in reverse standings order.
2. The Super Bowl winner is last and Super Bowl loser is next-to-last.
3. The losers of the Conference Championship games shall select 29th and 30th based on won-lost-tied percentage.
4. The losers of the Divisional playoff games shall select 25th through 28th based on won-lost-tied percentage.
5. The losers of the Wild Card games shall select 21st through 24th based on won-lost-tied percentage.

If ties exist in any grouping except (2) above, such ties shall be broken by strength-of-schedule. If any ties cannot be broken by strength-of-schedule, the divisional or conference tie-breakers, if applicable, shall be applied. Any ties that still exist shall be broken by a coin flip.

The NFL is online to provide fans and media quick and easy access to all the latest professional football information.

NFL.COM—(http://NFL.com)

NFL.com, the league's year-round home page on the Internet, enters its 15th season in cyberspace. The site provides NFL information during the regular season, postseason, and offseason, including:

NEWS/STATS: Up-to-the-minute NFL news, plus game previews, injury reports, and player and team stats.

GAMEDAY COVERAGE: Live game coverage with play-by-play, scores, and statistics, including graphical drive charts and comprehensive scoreboard that reloads automatically with the latest information.

VIDEO HIGHLIGHTS: The site showcases NFL Films video highlights of the previous week's games as well as upcoming matchups. Video also supports feature stories and team highlight clips from every game last season. In addition, exclusive NFL Network programming is featured as well as original video content.

TEAM AREAS: Customized areas for all 32 clubs, featuring updated rosters, depth charts, and all the latest team news.

SUPERBOWL.COM—(http://SuperBowl.com)

Look for SuperBowl.com in late December for complete coverage of the playoffs and Super Bowl XLVI. The multimedia site follows all postseason action and features audio and video clips of past Super Bowls.

During the week leading up to Super Bowl XLVI, the site will go "live" from Indianapolis, providing coverage of events, press conferences, and chats with Super Bowl players and coaches. On Super Bowl Sunday, SuperBowl.com will showcase a live Internet cybercast, complete with online commentators calling the action. The site also features digital photos from the game, live public address audio and press box announcements, and live audio from foreign broadcasts.

NFL.COM/ESPANOL POWERED BY UNIVISION.COM— (http://NFL.COM/ESPANOL)

The official Spanish-language site of the NFL provides in depth information on teams and players, and offers highlights of every NFL game in Spanish. The site includes Hispanic player diaries, live radio broadcasts, up-to-date stats, fantasy football, and more.

NFLHEALTHANDSAFETY.COM—(http://nflhealthandsafety.com)

NFLHEALTHANDSAFETY.com outlines the ways the NFL is addressing player health and safety issues. The site houses information on the partnerships, programs and initiatives the NFL supports to protect the health of current and former NFL players and to promote safe play and healthy lifestyles at all levels of football and other sports. The site provides information to promote health and safety at all playing levels, including partnerships with USA Football and the Centers for Disease Control and Prevention.

NFLFLAG.COM—(http://nflflag.com)

NFLFLAG.com focuses on the NFL FLAG Program, which is also part of NFL PLAY 60. Boys and girls ages 5-17 nationwide have the opportunity to display their skills in a non-contact environment by playing against their peers in five-on-five flag football games. Our website is a resource for league organizers, coaches, parents and youth organizations who want to start or find a local NFL FLAG league in their area as well as promote a positive experience for their youth participants.

NFLRUSH.COM—(http://www.NFLRUSH.com)

NFLRUSH.com, which is targeted to kids 6-15, is the official kids' website of the National Football League, offering unique customizable content, games, fantasy football for kids, contests, videos, fun daily features on NFL players and information on the NFL's Youth Football programs. NFLRUSH.com also features fun and interactive fitness information as part of the NFL PLAY 60 campaign, which encourages kids to be active for 60 minutes a day. The NFLRUSH ZONE, a role playing game on NFLRUSH.com, is an immersive virtual world where kids are able to create avatars, join their favorite team, play games, chat, watch the *RUSH ZONE: Guardians of the Core* animated series and compete with friends in safe and fun environment.

USAFOOTBALL.COM—(http://usafootball.com)

USA Football is an independent, non-profit organization which is leading the growth and development of youth, high school and international amateur football. USA Football helps youth and amateur football organizations keep the sport fun, safe, and accessible by offering resources focused on coaching education, league enhancement, officiating development and health and safety awareness. The organization also serves as the designated United States representatives to the International Federation of American Football. Based Indianapolis, USA Football was endowed by the NFL and NFLPA in 2002.

JOINTHETEAM.COM—(http://JoinTheTeam.com)

JoinTheTeam.com is the official website dedicated to the off-the-field community service initiatives of the NFL and the 32 member clubs. The site provides news, information, and history of the NFL's philanthropic endeavors and serves as a useful tool for individuals in search of community service opportunities. While the NFL's philanthropic endeavors span a wide range of topics, its three primary service themes include: reversing childhood obesity trends (NFL PLAY 60), the global fight against breast cancer (A Crucial Catch), and honoring the men and women of the US armed forces (United Service Organizations). The NFL also takes pride in recognizing its active and former athletes and their philanthropic efforts through the annual presentations of the Walter Payton NFL Man of the Year and NFL Teacher of the Year awards.

PROFOOTBALLHOF.COM—(http://profootballhof.com)

Profootballhof.com is the official site of the Pro Football Hall of Fame in Canton, Ohio. In addition to a complete visitor's guide to the Hall, the site features bios, stories and Q & A's with Hall of Fame inductees, a detailed archive of football history, and information on appearances by members of the Hall.

OFFICIAL NFL TEAM SITES

In addition to a dedicated area on NFL.com, all 32 teams have their own Websites, which have separate URLs, and are linked from NFL.com.

Arizona Cardinals (www.azcardinals.com)
Atlanta Falcons (www.atlantafalcons.com)
Baltimore Ravens (www.baltimoreravens.com)
Buffalo Bills (www.buffalobills.com)
Carolina Panthers (www.panthers.com)
Chicago Bears (www.chicagobears.com)
Cincinnati Bengals (www.bengals.com)
Cleveland Browns (www.clevelandbrowns.com)
Dallas Cowboys (www.dallascowboys.com)
Denver Broncos (www.denverbroncos.com)
Detroit Lions (www.detroitlions.com)
Green Bay Packers (www.packers.com)
Houston Texans (www.houstontexans.com)
Indianapolis Colts (www.colts.com)
Jacksonville Jaguars (www.jaguars.com)
Kansas City Chiefs (www.kcchiefs.com)
Miami Dolphins (www.miamidolphins.com)
Minnesota Vikings (www.vikings.com)
New England Patriots (www.patriots.com)
New Orleans Saints (www.neworleanssaints.com)
New York Giants (www.giants.com)
New York Jets (www.newyorkjets.com)
Oakland Raiders (www.raiders.com)
Philadelphia Eagles (www.philadelphiaeagles.com)
Pittsburgh Steelers (www.steelers.com)
St. Louis Rams (www.stlouisrams.com)
San Diego Chargers (www.chargers.com)
San Francisco 49ers (www.sf49ers.com)
Seattle Seahawks (www.seahawks.com)
Tampa Bay Buccaneers (www.buccaneers.com)
Tennessee Titans (www.titansonline.com)
Washington Redskins (www.redskins.com)

NFL Network provides fans with a network to call their own. Seven days a week, 24 hours a day, 365 days a year, fans turn to NFL Network to receive information and insight straight from the field, team headquarters, league offices and everywhere the NFL is making news.

NFL Network gives fans unprecedented year-round inside access to all NFL events, including the Super Bowl, Playoffs, regular season, preseason, Pro Bowl, Pro Football Hall of Fame induction weekend, NFL Draft, Scouting Combine, Senior Bowl, league meetings, minicamps and training camps.

In addition, NFL Network is the only place on television for fans to view NFL games outside their initial live airings. From original broadcast versions of past Super Bowls, in-week replays of current games, original network telecasts of classic NFL regular season and postseason games, to every preseason game, and regular season *Thursday Night Football* games—NFL Network is truly the year-round destination for football fans. NFL Network is available on cable, telcos and satellite television through your local service provider, as well as on NFL Mobile only on Verizon. If your provider doesn't currently offer NFL Network, please call (866) NFL-NETWORK.

KEY PROGRAMMING

EXCLUSIVE LIVE PRIMETIME GAMES
NFL Network's eight-game, regular-season Thursday Night primetime schedule kicks off in high definition on November 10. Each game, at 8:00 PM ET, will be preceded by a two-hour pregame show and followed by a live post-game show.

NFL TOTAL ACCESS
NFL Network's signature show is the football show of record. *NFL Total Access* is uniquely structured to see the game through the participants' eyes, airing at 7:00 PM ET Monday through Saturday.

Covering all 32 teams, *NFL Total Access* features interviews with players, coaches and other key league personnel. Using "Team Cams" at every facility, *NFL Total Access* has the ability to go live to any NFL team headquarters at any time.

NFL GAMEDAY MORNING
The Emmy-nominated *NFL GameDay Morning* is the first NFL pregame show on the air Sundays at 9:00 AM ET during the regular season and playoffs, providing fans with the earliest news and notes as well as live reports from around the league.

NFL GAMEDAY SCOREBOARD
After Sunday's early games conclude, *NFL GameDay Scoreboard* takes viewers around the league for post-game press conferences and game highlights. *NFL GameDay Scoreboard* airs at 4:00 PM ET on Sundays and continues through the Sunday afternoon games.

NFL GAMEDAY HIGHLIGHTS
Following the late afternoon games, *NFL GameDay Highlights* analysts Deion Sanders and Steve Mariucci join host Rich Eisen to analyze the events of the day. Includes highlights from all completed games, insider commentary, on-field interviews and postgame press conferences.

NFL GAMEDAY FINAL
After each Sunday's final game, the 90-minute *NFL GameDay Final* delivers comprehensive coverage of the day's action. Host Fran Charles is joined by Steve Mariucci, Deion Sanders and Michael Irvin. *NFL GameDay Final* kicks off at 11:30 PM ET and features highlights, post-game press conferences, on-field interviews, analysis and more in wrapping up each NFL Sunday.

NFL REPLAY
NFL games will be re-aired with the original television announcers and cameras. This offering features the most exciting games each week in an abbreviated format (eliminating halftime and other non-critical elements). Enhancements to each broadcast include additional camera angles, sideline sound and post-game interviews.

In addition, *NFL Replay Real-Time* gives fans a unique minute by minute look at what happened in the previous afternoon's games as they unfolded in real time.

PLAYBOOK
NFL Network uses the "all 22" game film watched each week by coaches and players to present football's ultimate chalkboard show. *Playbook*, produced at NFL Films, offers 60-minute strategy sessions with NFL Network analysts, who focus on each week's key matchups and discuss technique and game planning with coaches and players.

THE TOP 100: PLAYERS OF 2011
The Top 100: Players of 2011 is a new annual series airing every offseason on NFL Network. Current players vote for their peers to compile a list of the top 100 playmakers today, counting down from 100 to 1. With 10 players featured in each episode, each player on the list is saluted by an individual close to the subject, from a coach to a rival on the field.

AMERICA'S GAME
The Sports Emmy-winning original series continues its profiles of Super Bowl champions with the 2010 Green Bay Packers.

NFL'S TOP 10
Putting a fresh twist on the countdown genre, *NFL's Top 10* is a fast-paced series that provides an irreverent look at some of the most intriguing subjects in the NFL, creating and debating a top ten list for each category. Each 60-minute episode counts down from No. 10 to the top ranking in each category.

SOUND FX
The sounds of the game that only NFL Films can capture – with exclusive on-field and sideline microphone access – will be featured on the Emmy award-winning *Sound FX*.

PRESEASON GAMES
NFL Network is the only place on television where fans can view all 65 NFL preseason games in high-definition, including encores of the 11 live national preseason telecasts.

SCHEDULING FORMULA

The NFL expanded to 32 teams in 2002 with the addition of the Houston Texans. In addition, the NFL realigned for the first time since 1970—into eight divisions of four teams each—and the scheduling formula that was introduced guarantees for the first time that all teams play each other on a regular, rotating basis. Although the number of teams has increased to 32, the number of playoff teams remains the same at 12.

Under the NFL scheduling formula, every team within a division plays 16 games as follows:

- Home and away against its three division opponents (6 games).
- The four teams from another division within its conference on a rotating three-year cycle (4 games).
- The four teams from a division in the other conference on a rotating four-year cycle (4 games).
- Two intraconference games based on the prior year's standings (2 games). These games will match a first-place team against the first-place teams in the two same-conference divisions the team is not scheduled to play that season. The second-place, third-place, and fourth-place teams in a conference will be matched in the same way each year.

The schedule format takes each team through a cycle of games—home and away—against every other team in the league. From 2002-2009, every team played every other team at least twice—once home and once away. After the 2008 season, a decision was made to continue with the same rotation in 2010 and beyond. Divisional match-ups have tentatively been set for the 2012 season. Home and away pairings for 2012 have yet to be determined.

In determining how to begin the divisional rotation in 2002, the displacement of teams from their old divisions in the new alignment was taken into account. Preference was given to scheduling games with former division rivals and other regional opponents for clubs realigned from otherwise intact divisions.

FUTURE SCHEDULING ROTATION

		2011	2012*
AFC EAST	Intraconference	AFCW	AFCS
	Interconference	NFCE	NFCW
AFC NORTH	Intraconference	AFCS	AFCW
	Interconference	NFCW	NFCE
AFC SOUTH	Intraconference	AFCN	AFCE
	Interconference	NFCS	NFCN
AFC WEST	Intraconference	AFCE	AFCN
	Interconference	NFCN	NFCS
NFC EAST	Intraconference	NFCW	NFCS
	Interconference	AFCE	AFCN
NFC NORTH	Intraconference	NFCS	NFCW
	Interconference	AFCW	AFCS
NFC SOUTH	Intraconference	NFCN	NFCE
	Interconference	AFCS	AFCW
NFC WEST	Intraconference	NFCE	NFCN
	Interconference	AFCN	AFCE

Tentative

AFC EAST NON-DIVISIONAL OPPONENTS 2011

	BUFFALO BILLS			MIAMI DOLPHINS	
	Home	Away		Home	Away
Intraconference by Division	DEN	KC		DEN	KC
	OAK	SD		OAK	SD
Interconference by Division	PHIL	DALL		PHIL	DALL
	WASH	NYG		WASH	NYG
Intraconference by Position	AFCS	AFCN		AFCS	AFCN

	NEW ENGLAND PATRIOTS			NEW YORK JETS	
	Home	Away		Home	Away
Intraconference by Division	KC	DEN		KC	DEN
	SD	OAK		SD	OAK
Interconference by Division	DALL	PHIL		DALL	PHIL
	NYG	WASH		NYG	WASH
Intraconference by Position	AFCS	AFCN		AFCS	AFCN

AFC NORTH NON-DIVISIONAL OPPONENTS 2011

	BALTIMORE RAVENS			CINCINNATI BENGALS	
	Home	Away		Home	Away
Intraconference by Division	HOU	JAX		HOU	JAX
	IND	TENN		IND	TENN
Interconference by Division	ARIZ	STL		ARIZ	STL
	SF	SEA		SF	SEA
Intraconference by Position	AFCE	AFCW		AFCE	AFCW

	CLEVELAND BROWNS			PITTSBURGH STEELERS	
	Home	Away		Home	Away
Intraconference by Division	JAX	HOU		JAX	HOU
	TENN	IND		TENN	IND
Interconference by Division	STL	ARIZ		STL	ARIZ
	SEA	SF		SEA	SF
Intraconference by Position	AFCE	AFCW		AFCE	AFCW

AFC SOUTH NON-DIVISIONAL OPPONENTS 2011

	HOUSTON TEXANS			INDIANAPOLIS COLTS	
	Home	Away		Home	Away
Intraconference by Division	CLE	BALT		CLE	BALT
	PITT	CIN		PITT	CIN
Interconference by Division	ATL	NO		ATL	NO
	CAR	TB		CAR	TB
Intraconference by Position	AFCW	AFCE		AFCW	AFCE

	JACKSONVILLE JAGUARS			TENNESSEE TITANS	
	Home	Away		Home	Away
Intraconference by Division	BALT	CLE		BALT	CLE
	CIN	PITT		CIN	PITT
Interconference by Division	NO	ATL		NO	ATL
	TB	CAR		TB	CAR
Intraconference by Position	AFCW	AFCE		AFCW	AFCE

AFC WEST NON-DIVISIONAL OPPONENTS 2011

	DENVER BRONCOS			KANSAS CITY CHIEFS	
	Home	Away		Home	Away
Intraconference by Division	NE	BUFF		BUFF	NE
	NYJ	MIA		MIA	NYJ
Interconference by Division	CHI	GB		GB	CHI
	DET	MINN		MINN	DET
Intraconference by Position	AFCN	AFCS		AFCN	AFCS

	OAKLAND RAIDERS			SAN DIEGO CHARGERS	
	Home	Away		Home	Away
Intraconference by Division	NE	BUFF		BUFF	NE
	NYJ	MIA		MIA	NYJ
Interconference by Division	CHI	GB		GB	CHI
	DET	MINN		MINN	DET
Intraconference by Position	AFCN	AFCS		AFCN	AFCS

NFC EAST NON-DIVISIONAL OPPONENTS 2011

	DALLAS COWBOYS		NEW YORK GIANTS	
	Home	Away	Home	Away
Intraconference by Division	STL	ARIZ	STL	ARIZ
	SEA	SF	SEA	SF
Interconference by Division	BUFF	NE	BUFF	NE
	MIA	NYJ	MIA	NYJ
Intraconference by Position	NFCN	NFCS	NFCN	NFCS

	PHILADELPHIA EAGLES		WASHINGTON REDSKINS	
	Home	Away	Home	Away
Intraconference by Division	ARIZ	STL	ARIZ	STL
	SF	SEA	SF	SEA
Interconference by Division	NE	BUFF	NE	BUFF
	NYJ	MIA	NYJ	MIA
Intraconference by Position	NFCN	NFCS	NFCN	NFCS

NFC NORTH NON-DIVISIONAL OPPONENTS 2011

	CHICAGO BEARS		DETROIT LIONS	
	Home	Away	Home	Away
Intraconference by Division	ATL	NO	ATL	NO
	CAR	TB	CAR	TB
Interconference by Division	KC	DEN	KC	DEN
	SD	OAK	SD	OAK
Intraconference by Position	NFCW	NFCE	NFCW	NFCE

	GREEN BAY PACKERS		MINNESOTA VIKINGS	
	Home	Away	Home	Away
Intraconference by Division	NO	ATL	NO	ATL
	TB	CAR	TB	CAR
Interconference by Division	DEN	KC	DEN	KC
	OAK	SD	OAK	SD
Intraconference by Position	NFCW	NFCE	NFCW	NFCE

NFC SOUTH NON-DIVISIONAL OPPONENTS 2011

	ATLANTA FALCONS		CAROLINA PANTHERS	
	Home	Away	Home	Away
Intraconference by Division	GB	CHI	GB	CHI
	MINN	DET	MINN	DET
Interconference by Division	JAX	HOU	JAX	HOU
	TENN	IND	TENN	IND
Intraconference by Position	NFCE	NFCW	NFCE	NFCW

	NEW ORLEANS SAINTS		TAMPA BAY BUCCANEERS	
	Home	Away	Home	Away
Intraconference by Division	CHI	GB	CHI	GB
	DET	MINN	DET	MINN
Interconference by Division	HOU	JAX	HOU	JAX
	IND	TENN	IND	TENN
Intraconference by Position	NFCE	NFCW	NFCE	NFCW

NFC WEST NON-DIVISIONAL OPPONENTS 2011

	ARIZONA CARDINALS		ST. LOUIS RAMS	
	Home	Away	Home	Away
Intraconference by Division	DALL	PHIL	PHIL	DALL
	NYG	WASH	WASH	NYG
Interconference by Division	CLE	BALT	BALT	CLE
	PITT	CIN	CIN	PITT
Intraconference by Position	NFCS	NFCN	NFCS	NFCN

	SAN FRANCISCO 49ERS		SEATTLE SEAHAWKS	
	Home	Away	Home	Away
Intraconference by Division	DALL	PHIL	PHIL	DALL
	NYG	WASH	WASH	NYG
Interconference by Division	CLE	BALT	BALT	CLE
	PITT	CIN	CIN	PITT
Intraconference by Position	NFCS	NFCN	NFCS	NFCN

TOP ACTIVE PASSERS
1,000 or more attempts

		Yrs.	Att.	Comp.	Pct. Comp.	Yards	TD	Pct. TD	Had Int.	Pct. Int.	Ratings Pts.
1.	Aaron Rodgers	6	1,611	1,038	64.4	12,723	87	5.4	32	2.0	98.4
2.	Philip Rivers	7	2,455	1,564	63.7	19,661	136	5.5	58	2.4	97.2
3.	Tony Romo	7	2,070	1,326	64.1	16,650	118	5.7	62	3.0	95.5
4.	Tom Brady	11	4,710	2,996	63.6	34,744	261	5.5	103	2.2	95.2
5.	Peyton Manning	13	7,210	4,682	64.9	54,828	399	5.5	198	2.7	94.9
6.	Ben Roethlisberger	7	2,800	1,766	63.1	22,502	144	5.1	86	3.1	92.5
7.	Drew Brees	10	4,822	3,145	65.2	35,266	235	4.9	132	2.7	91.7
8.	Matt Schaub	7	1,987	1,288	64.8	15,457	83	4.2	52	2.6	91.5
9.	Chad Pennington	11	2,471	1,632	66.0	17,823	102	4.1	64	2.6	90.1
10.	Joe Flacco	3	1,416	878	62.0	10,206	60	4.2	34	2.4	87.9
11.	Carson Palmer	7	3,217	2,024	62.9	22,694	154	4.8	100	3.1	86.9
12.	Matt Ryan	3	1,456	885	60.8	10,061	66	4.5	34	2.3	86.9
13.	David Garrard	9	2,281	1,406	61.6	16,003	89	3.9	54	2.4	85.8
14.	Donovan McNabb	12	5,218	3,076	58.9	36,250	230	4.4	115	2.2	85.7
15.	Marc Bulger	9	3,171	1,969	62.1	22,814	122	3.8	93	2.9	84.4
16.	Jay Cutler	5	2,207	1,359	61.6	15,964	104	4.7	79	3.6	84.3
17.	Mark Brunell	17	4,637	2,760	59.5	32,045	184	4.0	108	2.3	84.0
18.	Matt Cassel	6	1,498	882	58.9	9,986	66	4.4	36	2.4	83.6
19.	Jason Campbell	5	1,966	1,196	60.8	13,247	68	3.5	46	2.3	82.6
20.	Matt Hasselbeck	12	4,279	2,572	60.1	29,579	176	4.1	128	3.0	82.2
21.	Jake Delhomme	10	2,904	1,723	59.3	20,764	125	4.3	101	3.5	81.2
22.	Eli Manning	7	3,332	1,932	58.0	22,646	156	4.7	113	3.4	80.2
23.	Michael Vick	8	2,115	1,169	55.3	14,609	93	4.4	58	2.7	80.2
24.	Byron Leftwich	8	1,552	905	58.3	10,260	58	3.7	41	2.6	79.7
25.	Kyle Orton	5	1,952	1,134	58.1	12,774	71	3.6	48	2.5	79.6

TOP ACTIVE SCORERS
(number in parentheses represents 2-point conversions scored)

		Yrs.	TD	FG	PAT	TP
1.	Jason Hanson	19	0	439	573	1,890
2.	John Kasay	20	0	433	524	1,823
3.	Adam Vinatieri	15	0	364	565(1)	1,659
4.	Ryan Longwell	14	0	339	566	1,583
5.	Olindo Mare	14	0	328	436	1,420
6.	David Akers	13	0	294	443	1,325
7.	Sebastian Janikowski	11	0	262	356	1,142
8.	Kris Brown	12	0	256	355	1,123
9.	Jay Feely	10	1	255	349	1,120
10.	Joe Nedney	15	0	256	345	1,113
11.	Rian Lindell	11	0	249	337	1,084
12.	Phil Dawson	12	1	252	301	1,063
13.	Neil Rackers	11	0	232	333	1,029
14.	Jeff Reed	9	0	213	320	959
15.	LaDainian Tomlinson	10	159	0	0	954
16.	Terrell Owens	15	156	0	0(3)	942
17.	Shayne Graham	10	0	208	315	939
18.	Randy Moss	13	154	0	0(4)	932
19.	Josh Brown	8	0	199	284	881
20.	Nate Kaeding	7	0	173	343	862
21.	Matt Bryant	9	0	173	235	754
22.	Rob Bironas	6	0	160	205	685
	Robbie Gould	6	0	159	208	685
24.	Lawrence Tynes	7	0	138	268	682
25.	Josh Scobee	7	0	144	230	662

TOP ACTIVE SCORERS (TOUCHDOWNS)

		Yrs.	Rush	Rec.	Ret.	Tot.
1.	LaDainian Tomlinson	10	144	15	0	159
2.	Terrell Owens	15	3	153	0	156
3.	Randy Moss	13	0	153	1	154
4.	Tony Gonzalez	14	0	88	0	88
5.	Hines Ward	13	1	83	0	84
6.	Clinton Portis	9	75	5	0	80
7.	Fred Taylor	13	66	8	0	74
8.	Brian Westbrook	9	41	30	2	73
9.	Ricky Williams	10	64	8	0	72
10.	Thomas Jones	11	68	3	0	71
11.	Antonio Gates	8	0	69	0	69
	Derrick Mason	14	0	66	3	69
	Reggie Wayne	10	0	69	0	69
14.	Chad Ochocinco	10	0	66	0	66
15.	Larry Fitzgerald	7	0	65	0	65
16.	Maurice Jones-Drew	5	54	7	2	63
17.	Steve Smith	10	2	52	6	60
18.	Willis McGahee	7	55	4	0	59
19.	Chris Chambers	10	0	58	0	58
20.	Santana Moss	10	0	52	3	55
21.	Donald Driver	12	1	53	0	54
	Steven Jackson	7	47	7	0	54
	Adrian Peterson	4	52	2	0	54
24.	Marion Barber	6	47	6	0	53
25.	Anquan Boldin	8	1	51	0	52
	Brandon Jacobs	6	49	3	0	52

TOP ACTIVE RUSHERS

		Yrs.	Att.	Yards	TD
1.	LaDainian Tomlinson	10	3,099	13,404	144
2.	Fred Taylor	13	2,534	11,695	66
3.	Thomas Jones	11	2,525	10,113	68
4.	Clinton Portis	9	2,230	9,923	75
5.	Ricky Williams	10	2,323	9,565	64
6.	Steven Jackson	7	1,878	7,948	47
7.	Frank Gore	6	1,371	6,414	35
8.	Brian Westbrook	9	1,385	6,335	41
9.	Willis McGahee	7	1,541	6,167	55
10.	Adrian Peterson	4	1,198	5,782	52
11.	Maurice Jones-Drew	5	1,141	5,248	54
12.	Michael Turner	7	1,116	5,198	45
13.	Julius Jones	7	1,280	5,068	22
14.	Ronnie Brown	6	1,128	4,815	36
15.	Cedric Benson	6	1,256	4,702	25
16.	Chester Taylor	9	1,140	4,663	25
17.	Michael Vick	8	653	4,630	32
18.	Chris Johnson	3	925	4,598	34
19.	Marion Barber	6	1,042	4,358	47
20.	Brandon Jacobs	6	926	4,278	49
21.	DeAngelo Williams	5	841	4,211	31
22.	Joseph Addai	5	977	4,020	38
23.	Michael Bennett	10	842	3,703	13
24.	Cadillac Williams	6	968	3,677	20
25.	Kevin Faulk	12	847	3,550	16

TOP ACTIVE PASS RECEIVERS

		Yrs.	No.	Yards	TD
1.	Terrell Owens	15	1,078	15,934	153
2.	Tony Gonzalez	14	1,069	12,463	88
3.	Randy Moss	13	954	14,858	153
	Hines Ward	13	954	11,702	83
5.	Derrick Mason	14	924	11,891	66
6.	Reggie Wayne	10	787	10,748	69
7.	Chad Ochocinco	10	751	10,783	66
8.	Donald Driver	12	698	9,615	53
9.	Andre Johnson	8	673	9,164	50
10.	Anquan Boldin	8	650	8,357	51
11.	Steve Smith	10	620	8,884	52
12.	Jason Witten	8	617	6,967	36
13.	T.J. Houshmandzadeh	10	616	7,091	43
14.	Larry Fitzgerald	7	613	8,204	65
15.	Santana Moss	10	593	8,558	52
16.	LaDainian Tomlinson	10	582	4,323	15
17.	Chris Chambers	10	540	7,648	58
18.	Antonio Gates	8	529	7,005	69
19.	Wes Welker	7	528	5,657	23
20.	Jeremy Shockey	9	510	5,688	33
21.	Todd Heap	10	467	5,492	41
22.	Deion Branch	9	451	5,797	34
23.	Brian Westbrook	9	442	3,940	30
24.	Roddy White	6	430	6,078	37
25.	Kevin Faulk	12	424	3,667	15

TOP ACTIVE SCRIMMAGE YARDS LEADERS

		Yrs.	Rush	Rec	Total	TD
1.	LaDainian Tomlinson	10	13,404	4,323	17,727	159
2.	Terrell Owens	15	251	15,934	16,185	156
3.	Randy Moss	13	159	14,858	15,017	153
4.	Fred Taylor	13	11,695	2,384	14,079	74
5.	Tony Gonzalez	14	14	12,463	12,477	88
6.	Hines Ward	13	428	11,702	12,130	84
7.	Thomas Jones	11	10,113	1,980	12,093	71
8.	Ricky Williams	10	9,565	2,523	12,088	72
9.	Clinton Portis	9	9,923	2,018	11,941	80
10.	Derrick Mason	14	3	11,891	11,894	66
11.	Chad Ochocinco	10	175	10,783	10,958	66
12.	Reggie Wayne	10	0	10,748	10,748	69
13.	Steven Jackson	11	7,948	2,670	10,618	54
14.	Brian Westbrook	9	6,335	3,940	10,275	71
15.	Donald Driver	12	217	9,615	9,832	54
16.	Andre Johnson	8	46	9,164	9,210	50
17.	Steve Smith	10	304	8,884	9,188	54
18.	Santana Moss	10	248	8,558	8,806	52
19.	Frank Gore	6	6,414	2,283	8,697	44
20.	Anquan Boldin	8	211	8,357	8,568	52
21.	Larry Fitzgerald	7	55	8,204	8,259	65
22.	Chris Chambers	10	373	7,648	8,021	58
23.	Maurice Jones-Drew	5	5,248	2,099	7,347	61
24.	T.J. Houshmandzadeh	10	142	7,091	7,233	44
25.	Kevin Faulk	12	3,550	3,667	7,217	31

TOP ACTIVE INTERCEPTORS

		Yrs.	No.	Yards	TD
1.	Darren Sharper	14	63	1,412	11
2.	Ed Reed	9	54	1,438	6
3.	Champ Bailey	12	48	446	4
4.	Charles Woodson	13	47	833	10
5.	Asante Samuel	8	42	564	4
6.	Ronde Barber	14	40	751	7
7.	Brian Dawkins	15	37	513	2
8.	Nate Clements	10	33	482	5
9.	DeAngelo Hall	7	32	681	3
10.	Ray Lewis	15	30	499	3
11.	Deon Grant	10	29	267	0
	Rashean Mathis	8	29	511	3
13.	Terence Newman	8	28	265	2
14.	Troy Polamalu	8	27	328	2
	Charles Tillman	8	27	469	3
16.	Lawyer Milloy	15	25	205	1
	Adrian Wilson	10	25	493	2
18.	Chris Gamble	7	24	283	2
19.	Antoine Winfield	12	23	219	2
20.	Oshiomogho Atogwe	6	22	340	1
21.	Sheldon Brown	9	21	399	3
	Keith Bulluck	11	21	199	1
	Nick Collins	6	21	507	4
24.	Phillip Buchanon	9	20	432	5
	Marcus Trufant	8	20	355	2
	Nathan Vasher	7	20	368	2
	Roy Williams	9	20	307	3

TOP ACTIVE PUNT RETURNERS
40 or more punt returns

		Yrs.	No.	Yards	Avg.	TD
1.	Devin Hester	5	178	2,200	12.4	10
2.	Roscoe Parrish	6	130	1,576	12.1	3
3.	Danny Amendola	2	71	812	11.4	0
4.	Santana Moss	10	112	1,268	11.3	3
5.	DeSean Jackson	3	99	1,112	11.2	4
6.	Eddie Royal	3	69	773	11.2	1
7.	Eric Weems	4	45	500	11.1	1
8.	Domenik Hixon	4	48	530	11.0	1
9.	Stefan Logan	2	60	642	10.7	0
10.	Josh Cribbs	6	123	1,309	10.6	2
11.	Ted Ginn	4	60	633	10.6	2
12.	Jim Leonhard	6	73	737	10.1	0
13.	Wes Welker	7	208	2,092	10.1	0
14.	Jacoby Jones	4	130	1,302	10.0	2
15.	Quan Cosby	2	70	699	10.0	0
16.	Nate Clements	10	82	816	10.0	2
17.	Captain Munnerlyn	2	61	605	9.9	0
18.	Mike Thomas	2	48	476	9.9	1
19.	Leon Washington	5	86	848	9.9	0
20.	Davone Bess	3	74	724	9.8	0
21.	Nate Burleson	8	156	1,523	9.8	3
22.	Tramon Williams	4	60	579	9.7	1
23.	Patrick Crayton	7	113	1,089	9.6	2
24.	Mewelde Moore	7	83	792	9.5	2
25.	Adam Jones	4	89	840	9.4	4

TOP ACTIVE KICKOFF RETURNERS
40 or more kickoff returns

		Yrs.	No.	Yards	Avg.	TD
1.	Johnny Knox	2	40	1,109	27.7	1
2.	Danieal Manning	5	101	2,711	26.8	1
3.	Brad Smith	5	74	1,968	26.6	3
4.	Ellis Hobbs	6	141	3,739	26.5	3
5.	Stefan Logan	2	110	2,914	26.5	1
6.	Terrence McGee	8	207	5,450	26.3	5
7.	Eric Weems	4	89	2,333	26.2	1
8.	Leodis McKelvin	3	71	1,854	26.1	1
9.	Maurice Jones-Drew	5	79	2,054	26.0	2
10.	Laurence Maroney	5	41	1,062	25.9	0
11.	Brandon Tate	2	45	1,163	25.8	2
12.	Josh Cribbs	6	305	7,863	25.8	8
13.	LaRod Stephens-Howling	2	109	2,805	25.7	3
14.	Leon Washington	5	174	4,447	25.6	7
15.	Marc Mariani	1	60	1,530	25.5	1
16.	Jerious Norwood	5	121	3,084	25.5	0
17.	Percy Harvin	2	82	2,089	25.5	3
18.	Quintin Demps	3	58	1,469	25.3	1
19.	Micheal Spurlock	4	71	1,797	25.3	2
20.	Michael Turner	7	44	1,111	25.3	0
21.	Adam Jones	4	77	1,937	25.2	0
22.	Brandon Banks	1	46	1,155	25.1	1
23.	Darren Sproles	6	258	6,469	25.1	2
24.	Deji Karim	1	50	1,248	25.0	0
25.	Courtney Roby	5	121	3,007	24.9	1

TOP ACTIVE PUNTERS
50 or more punts

		Yrs.	No.	Avg.	LG
1.	Shane Lechler	11	855	47.3	73
2.	Donnie Jones	7	543	45.5	80
3.	Mat McBriar	7	436	45.5	75
4.	Andy Lee	7	645	45.1	82
5.	Brandon Fields	4	299	44.9	71
6.	Matt Dodge	1	72	44.8	69
7.	Thomas Morstead	2	115	44.7	64
8.	Brett Kern	3	187	44.7	68
9.	Britton Colquitt	6	86	44.6	63
10.	Jon Ryan	5	388	44.5	72
11.	Mike Scifres	8	445	44.5	71
12.	Ben Graham	6	429	44.2	69
13.	Chris Kluwe	6	474	44.2	70
14.	Dustin Colquitt	6	485	44.1	81
15.	Tim Masthay	1	71	43.9	62
16.	Sam Koch	5	402	43.7	74
17.	Brian Moorman	10	775	43.5	84
18.	Daniel Sepulveda	3	196	43.4	62
19.	Zoltan Mesko	1	58	43.2	65
20.	Pat McAfee	2	129	43.2	66
21.	Steve Weatherford	5	363	42.9	66
22.	Sav Rocca	4	299	42.9	65
23.	Josh Bidwell	11	742	42.7	68
24.	Jason Baker	10	732	42.7	70
25.	Kevin Huber	2	157	42.7	72

TOP ACTIVE QUARTERBACK SACKERS

		Yrs.	No.
1.	Jason Taylor	14	132.5
2.	John Abraham	11	102.5
3.	Joey Porter	12	97.0
4.	Dwight Freeney	9	94.0
5.	Trevor Pryce	4	91.0
6.	Julius Peppers	9	89.0
7.	Jared Allen	7	83.0
8.	DeMarcus Ware	6	80.0
9.	Robert Mathis	8	74.0
10.	Shaun Ellis	11	72.5
11.	Terrell Suggs	8	68.5
12.	Andre Carter	10	66.0
13.	Justin Smith	10	65.0
14.	Vonnie Holliday	13	62.5
15.	Phillip Daniels	15	62.0
16.	Osi Umenyiora	7	60.0
17.	Aaron Kampman	9	58.0
18.	Trent Cole	6	57.0
	James Hall	11	57.0
	Mike Vrabel	14	57.0
21.	Shaun Phillips	7	56.5
22.	Will Smith	7	55.0
23.	Julian Peterson	11	51.5
24.	Kevin Williams	8	49.5
25.	James Harrison	8	49.0

ACTIVE COACHES' CAREER RECORDS (Order Based on Career Victories)
Start of 2011 Season

Coach	Team(s)	Regular Season					Postseason			Career			
		Yrs.	Won	Lost	Tied	Pct.	Won	Lost	Pct.	Won	Lost	Tied	Pct.
Bill Belichick	Cleveland Browns, New England Patriots	16	162	94	0	.633	15	6	.714	177	100	0	.639
Mike Shanahan	Los Angeles Raiders, Denver Broncos, Washington Redskins	17	152	108	0	.585	8	5	.615	160	113	0	.586
Tom Coughlin	Jacksonville Jaguars, New York Giants	15	133	107	0	.554	8	7	.533	141	114	0	.553
Andy Reid	Philadelphia Eagles	12	118	73	1	.617	10	9	.526	128	82	1	.609
Norv Turner	Washington Redskins, Oakland Raiders, San Diego Chargers	13	99	105	1	.485	4	4	.500	103	109	1	.486
John Fox	Carolina Panthers, Denver Broncos	9	73	71	0	.507	5	3	.625	78	74	0	.513
Lovie Smith	Chicago Bears	7	63	49	0	.563	3	3	.500	66	52	0	.559
Jack Del Rio	Jacksonville Jaguars	8	65	63	0	.508	1	2	.333	66	65	0	.504
Marvin Lewis	Cincinnati Bengals	8	60	67	1	.473	0	2	.000	60	69	1	.465
Sean Payton	New Orleans Saints	5	49	31	0	.613	4	2	.667	53	33	0	.616
Mike McCarthy	Green Bay Packers	5	48	32	0	.600	5	2	.714	53	34	0	.609
Mike Tomlin	Pittsburgh Steelers	4	43	21	0	.672	5	2	.714	48	23	0	.676
Pete Carroll	New York Jets, New England Patriots, Seattle Seahawks	5	40	40	0	.500	2	3	.400	42	43	0	.494
Gary Kubiak	Houston Texans	5	37	43	0	.463	0	0	---	37	43	0	.463
John Harbaugh	Baltimore Ravens	3	32	16	0	.667	4	3	.571	36	19	0	.655
Ken Whisenhunt	Arizona Cardinals	4	32	32	0	.500	4	2	.667	36	34	0	.514
Mike Smith	Atlanta Falcons	3	33	15	0	.688	0	2	.000	33	17	0	.660
Jim Caldwell	Indianapolis Colts	2	24	8	0	.750	2	2	.500	26	10	0	.722
Tony Sparano	Miami Dolphins	3	25	23	0	.521	0	1	.000	25	24	0	.510
Rex Ryan	New York Jets	2	20	12	0	.625	4	2	.667	24	14	0	.632
Chan Gailey	Dallas Cowboys, Buffalo Bills	3	22	26	0	.458	0	2	.000	22	28	0	.440
Todd Haley	Kansas City Chiefs	2	14	18	0	.438	0	1	.000	14	19	0	.424
Raheem Morris	Tampa Bay Buccaneers	2	13	19	0	.406	0	0	---	13	19	0	.406
Jim Schwartz	Detroit Lions	2	8	24	0	.250	0	0	---	8	24	0	.250
Steve Spagnuolo	St. Louis Rams	2	8	24	0	.250	0	0	---	8	24	0	.250
Jason Garrett	Dallas Cowboys	1	5	3	0	.625	0	0	---	5	3	0	.625
Leslie Frazier	Minnesota Vikings	1	3	3	0	.500	0	0	---	3	3	0	.500
Jim Harbaugh	San Francisco 49ers	0	0	0	0	---	0	0	---	0	0	0	--
Hue Jackson	Oakland Raiders	0	0	0	0	---	0	0	---	0	0	0	---
Mike Munchak	Tennessee Titans	0	0	0	0	---	0	0	---	0	0	0	---
Ron Rivera	Carolina Panthers	0	0	0	0	---	0	0	---	0	0	0	--
Pat Shurmur	Cleveland Browns	0	0	0	0	---	0	0	---	0	0	0	---

COACHES WITH 100 CAREER VICTORIES (Order Based on Career Victories)
Start of 2011 Season

	Coach	Team(s)	Yrs.	Won	Lost	Tied	Pct.	Won	Lost	Pct.	Won	Lost	Tied	Pct.
				Regular Season				Postseason			Career			
1.	Don Shula	Baltimore Colts, Miami Dolphins	33	328	156	6	.677	19	17	.528	347	173	6	.666
2.	George Halas	Chicago Bears	40	318	148	31	.682	6	3	.667	324	151	31	.682
3.	Tom Landry	Dallas Cowboys	29	250	162	6	.607	20	16	.556	270	178	6	.603
4.	Earl (Curly) Lambeau	Green Bay Packers, Chicago Cardinals, Washington Redskins	33	226	132	22	.631	3	2	.600	229	134	22	.631
5.	Chuck Noll	Pittsburgh Steelers	23	193	148	1	.566	16	8	.667	209	156	1	.572
6.	Marty Schottenheimer	Cleveland Browns, Kansas City Chiefs, Washington Redskins, San Diego Chargers	21	200	126	1	.613	5	13	.278	205	139	1	.596
7.	Dan Reeves	Denver Broncos, New York Giants, Atlanta Falcons	23	190	165	2	.535	11	9	.550	201	174	2	.536
8.	Chuck Knox	Los Angeles Rams, Buffalo Bills, Seattle Seahawks	22	186	147	1	.558	7	11	.389	193	158	1	.550
9.	Bill Parcells	New York Giants, New England Patriots, New York Jets, Dallas Cowboys	19	172	130	1	.569	11	8	.579	183	138	1	.570
10.	Bill Belichick	Cleveland Browns, New England Patriots	16	162	94	0	.633	15	6	.714	177	100	0	.639
11.	Mike Holmgren	Green Bay Packers, Seattle Seahawks	17	161	111	0	.592	13	11	.542	174	122	0	.588
12.	Joe Gibbs	Washington Redskins	16	154	94	0	.621	17	7	.708	171	101	0	.629
13.	Paul Brown	Cleveland Browns, Cincinnati Bengals	21	166	100	6	.624	4	8	.333	170	108	6	.612
14.	Bud Grant	Minnesota Vikings	18	158	96	5	.621	10	12	.455	168	108	5	.608
15.	Bill Cowher	Pittsburgh Steelers	15	149	90	1	.623	12	9	.571	161	99	1	.619
16.	Mike Shanahan	Los Angeles Raiders, Denver Broncos, Washington Redskins	17	152	108	0	.585	8	5	.615	160	113	0	.586
17.	Marv Levy	Kansas City Chiefs, Buffalo Bills	17	143	112	0	.561	11	8	.579	154	120	0	.562
18.	Steve Owen	New York Giants	23	151	100	17	.602	2	8	.200	153	108	17	.586
19.	Tony Dungy	Tampa Bay Buccaneers, Indianapolis Colts	13	139	69	0	.668	9	10	.474	148	79	0	.652
20.	Jeff Fisher	Houston/Tennessee Oilers, Tennessee Titans	16	142	120	0	.542	5	6	.455	147	126	0	.539
21.	Tom Coughlin	Jacksonville Jaguars, New York Giants	15	133	107	0	.554	8	7	.533	141	114	0	.553
22.	Hank Stram	Kansas City Chiefs, New Orleans Saints	17	131	97	10	.574	5	3	.625	136	100	10	.576
23.	Weeb Ewbank	Baltimore Colts, New York Jets	20	130	129	7	.502	4	1	.800	134	130	7	.508
24.	Andy Reid	Philadelphia Eagles	12	118	73	1	.617	10	9	.526	128	82	1	.609
25.	Mike Ditka	Chicago Bears, New Orleans Saints	14	121	95	0	.560	6	6	.500	127	101	0	.557
26.	Dick Vermeil	Philadelphia Eagles, St. Louis Rams, Kansas City Chiefs	15	120	109	0	.524	6	5	.545	126	114	0	.525
27.	Jim Mora	New Orleans Saints, Indianapolis Colts	15	125	106	0	.541	0	6	.000	125	112	0	.527
28.	George Seifert	San Francisco 49ers, Carolina Panthers	11	114	62	0	.648	10	5	.667	124	67	0	.649
29.	Sid Gillman	Los Angeles Rams, Los Angeles-San Diego Chargers, Houston Oilers	18	122	99	7	.552	1	5	.167	123	104	7	.542
30.	George Allen	Los Angeles Rams, Washington Redskins	12	116	47	5	.712	2	7	.222	118	54	5	.686
31.	Dennis Green	Minnesota Vikings, Arizona Cardinals	13	113	94	0	.546	4	8	.333	117	102	0	.534
32.	Don Coryell	St. Louis Cardinals, San Diego Chargers	14	111	83	1	.572	3	6	.333	114	89	1	.561
33.	John Madden	Oakland Raiders	10	103	32	7	.759	9	7	.563	112	39	7	.739
34.	Ray (Buddy) Parker	Chicago Cardinals, Detroit Lions, Pittsburgh Steelers	15	104	75	9	.581	3	1	.750	107	76	9	.585
35.	Vince Lombardi	Green Bay Packers, Washington Redskins	10	96	34	6	.739	9	1	.900	105	35	6	.750
36.	Tom Flores	Oakland-Los Angeles Raiders, Seattle Seahawks	12	97	87	0	.527	8	3	.727	105	90	0	.538
37.	Norv Turner	Washington Redskins, Oakland Raiders, San Diego Chargers	13	99	105	1	.485	4	4	.500	103	109	1	.486
38.	Bill Walsh	San Francisco 49ers	10	92	59	1	.609	10	4	.714	102	63	1	.617
39.	Jon Gruden	Oakland Raiders, Tampa Bay Buccaneers	11	95	81	0	.540	5	4	.556	100	85	0	.541

Active coaches in bold.
From 1920-71, tie games were not included in winning percentage.

The **Green Bay Packers** need seven total victories to become the second team in NFL history with 700 total victories. Green Bay (693-540-36 all-time record) would join Chicago (721-530-42) as the only teams to accomplish the feat.

The **Arizona Cardinals** need six victories to reach 500 total victories. Arizona's all-time record is 494-698-39.

The **Detroit Lions** need four regular-season victories to reach 500 total regular-season victories. Detroit's all-time regular-season record is 496-593-32.

The **San Diego Chargers** need six victories to reach 400 total victories. San Diego's all-time record is 394-393-11.

The **Tennessee Titans** need nine victories to reach 400 total victories. Tennessee's all-time record is 391-408-6.

The **Atlanta Falcons** need five victories to reach 300 total victories. Atlanta's all-time record is 295-403-6.

The **Cincinnati Bengals** need nine victories to reach 300 total victories. Cincinnati's all-time record is 291-381-2.

The **New Orleans Saints** need nine victories to reach 300 total victories. New Orleans' all-time record is 291-390-5.

The **Indianapolis Colts** need to qualify for the 2011 postseason to become the first team in NFL history to advance to the playoffs in 10 consecutive seasons. Indianapolis and Dallas (1975-1983) are the only teams with nine consecutive playoff appearances.

Bill Belichick, New England, needs seven victories to surpass Bill Parcells (183) for ninth place all-time in career victories. In 16 seasons, Belichick has 177 career victories.

Mike Shanahan, Washington, needs 12 victories to surpass Bill Cowher (161), Bud Grant (168), Paul Brown (170) and Joe Gibbs (171) for 12th place all-time in career victories. In 17 seasons, Shanahan has 160 career victories.

Tom Coughlin, New York Giants, needs nine victories to become the 19th coach in history to win 150 games. In 15 seasons, Coughlin has 141 career victories.

Peyton Manning needs 4,000 passing yards to become the first player in NFL history with 12 4,000-yard seasons. Manning is the only quarterback to accomplish the feat in 11 seasons.

Manning needs 25 touchdown passes to become the first player in NFL history to throw 25 touchdown passes in 14 consecutive seasons. Manning is the only player to have 13 consecutive seasons with 25 touchdown passes.

Manning has passed for 3,000 yards in each of the past 13 seasons and owns the second-longest streak of consecutive 3,000-yard seasons (Brett Favre, 18). Manning is the only player in NFL history to start a career with 13 consecutive 3,000-yard seasons.

Manning needs 22 touchdown passes to surpass Dan Marino (420) for second place all-time. In 13 seasons, Manning has thrown 399 touchdown passes.

Manning needs 286 pass completions to surpass Dan Marino (4,967) for second place all-time. In 13 seasons, Manning has 4,682 completions.

Manning has 22 games with four or more touchdown passes and needs two such games to surpass Brett Favre (23) for the most games with four touchdown passes in NFL history.

Manning has led the league in touchdown passes three times in his career and can tie Len Dawson, Brett Favre, Johnny Unitas and Steve Young (4) for the most seasons leading the league in touchdown passes (see Brady note).

Manning has passed for 300 yards in a game 63 times in his career, tied with Dan Marino for the most all-time. Manning needs one 300-yard passing game to attain sole possession of first place.

Tom Brady has led the league in touchdown passes three times in his career and can tie Len Dawson, Brett Favre, Johnny Unitas and Steve Young (4) for the most seasons leading the league in touchdown passes (see Manning note).

Philip Rivers has led the league in average yards per pass in each of the past three seasons and can join Steve Young (4) and Sid Luckman (5) as the only players to do so in four consecutive seasons.

LaDainian Tomlinson needs one touchdown to become the third player with 160 touchdowns (see Moss and Owens notes). Tomlinson would join Jerry Rice (208) and Emmitt Smith (175) as the only players to accomplish the feat. In 10 seasons, Tomlinson has scored 159 touchdowns.

Tomlinson needs six rushing touchdowns to become the second player with 150 rushing touchdowns. Tomlinson has scored 144 rushing touchdowns and would join Emmitt Smith (164) as the only players to accomplish the feat.

Tomlinson has four 200-yard rushing games in his career. Tomlinson needs two 200-yard games to surpass Tiki Barber (5) and tie O.J. Simpson (6) for the most all-time.

Tomlinson needs 698 rushing yards to surpass Jerome Bettis (13,662) and Curtis Martin (14,101) for fourth place all-time. In 10 seasons, Tomlinson has rushed for 13,404 yards.

Tomlinson needs 1,000 rushing yards to become the fifth player in NFL history with nine 1,000-yard rushing seasons. Only Walter Payton (10), Barry Sanders (10), Curtis Martin (10) and Emmitt Smith (11) have accomplished the feat.

Tomlinson needs 464 scrimmage yards to surpass Barry Sanders (18,190) for fifth place all-time. In 10 seasons, Tomlinson has 17,727 scrimmage yards.

Terrell Owens needs 25 receptions to surpass Tim Brown (1,094), Cris Carter (1,101) and Marvin Harrison (1,102) for second place all-time (see Gonzalez note). In 15 seasons, Owens has 1,078 receptions.

Owens needs 66 receiving yards to become the second player in NFL history with 16,000 receiving yards. Owens would join Jerry Rice (22,895) as the only players to accomplish the feat. In 15 seasons, Owens has 15,934 receiving yards.

Owens needs seven receiving touchdowns to become the second player in NFL history with 160 receiving TDs. Owens can join Jerry Rice (197) as the only other player in NFL history with 160 receiving touchdowns (see Moss note). In 15 seasons, Owens has 153 touchdown receptions.

Owens needs four touchdowns to become the third player with 160 touchdowns. Owens would join Jerry Rice (208) and Emmitt Smith (175) as the only players to accomplish the feat (see Moss and Tomlinson notes). In 15 seasons, Owens has scored 156 touchdowns.

Owens has recorded 1,000 receiving yards in a season nine times in his 15-year NFL career. Owens can join Jerry Rice (14) and Randy Moss (10) as the only players in NFL history with 10 seasons with 1,000 receiving yards (see Moss note).

Owens needs 50 receptions to join Jerry Rice (17) as the only players in NFL history with 14 50-reception seasons (see Gonzalez note).

Tony Gonzalez needs 34 receptions to surpass Terrell Owens (1,078), Tim Brown (1,094), Cris Carter (1,101) and Marvin Harrison (1,102) for second place all-time (see Owens note). In 14 seasons, Gonzalez has 1,069 receptions – the most ever by a tight end.

Gonzalez needs 50 receptions to join Jerry Rice (17) as the only players in NFL history with 14 50-reception seasons (see Owens note). Gonzalez is the only player in NFL history with 13 consecutive 50-reception seasons.

Randy Moss needs seven receiving touchdowns to become the second player in NFL history with 160 receiving TDs. Moss can join Jerry Rice (197) as the only other player in NFL history with 160 receiving touchdowns (see Owens note). In 13 seasons, Moss has 153 touchdown receptions.

Moss needs six touchdowns to become the third player with 160 touchdowns. Moss would join Jerry Rice (208) and Emmitt

Smith (175) as the only players to accomplish the feat (see Owens and Tomlinson notes). In 13 seasons, Moss has scored 154 touchdowns.

Moss needs 351 receiving yards to surpass Tim Brown (14,934) and Isaac Bruce (15,208) for third place all-time. In 13 seasons, Moss has 14,858 receiving yards.

Moss needs 46 receptions to become the eighth player in NFL history with 1,000 receptions. In 13 seasons, Moss has 954 receptions (see Mason and Ward notes).

Moss has recorded 1,000 receiving yards in a season 10 times in his 13-year NFL career. Moss can join Jerry Rice (14) as the only players in NFL history with 11 seasons with 1,000 receiving yards.

Moss has led the league in touchdown receptions five times in his career and can tie Jerry Rice (6) for the second-most seasons leading the league in touchdown receptions (Don Hutson, 9).

Hines Ward needs 46 receptions to become the eighth player in NFL history with 1,000 receptions (see Mason and Moss notes). In 13 seasons, Ward has 954 receptions.

Derrick Mason needs 76 receptions to become the eighth player in NFL history with 1,000 receptions (see Moss and Ward notes). In 14 seasons, Mason has 924 receptions.

Andre Johnson needs 100 receptions to become the third player in NFL history with four 100-catch seasons. Johnson can join Marvin Harrison and Jerry Rice as the only players with four 100-reception seasons (see Marshall, Wayne and Welker notes).

Johnson needs 1,500 receiving yards to join Marvin Harrison (3) and Jerry Rice (4) as the only players with three 1,500-yard seasons.

Johnson needs two games with 10 receptions and 100 receiving yards to become the NFL's all-time career leader. Johnson has 14 games with at least 10 catches and 100 receiving yards in his career and can surpass Marvin Harrison (14) and Jerry Rice (15) for the most such games in NFL history.

Brandon Marshall needs 100 receptions to become the third player in NFL history with four 100-catch seasons. Marshall can join Marvin Harrison and Jerry Rice as the only players with four 100-reception seasons (see Johnson, Wayne and Welker notes).

Reggie Wayne needs 100 receptions to become the third player in NFL history with four 100-catch seasons. Wayne can join Marvin Harrison and Jerry Rice as the only players with four 100-reception seasons (see Johnson, Marshall and Welker notes).

Wes Welker needs 100 receptions to become the third player in NFL history with four 100-catch seasons. Welker can join Marvin Harrison and Jerry Rice as the only players with four 100-reception seasons (see Johnson, Marshall and Wayne notes).

Ray Lewis needs 1.5 sacks to become the first player in NFL history to record 40 sacks and 30 interceptions in his career. In 15 seasons, Lewis has 38.5 sacks and 30 interceptions.

Jason Taylor needs 9.5 sacks to surpass Leslie O'Neal (132.5), Lawrence Taylor (132.5), John Randle (137.5), Richard Dent (137.5) and Michael Strahan (141.5) to move into fifth place all-time. In 14 seasons, Taylor has 132.5 sacks.

Darren Sharper needs two interception-return touchdowns to surpass Rod Woodson (12) for the most all-time (see C. Woodson note). In 14 seasons, Sharper has 11 interception-return touchdowns.

Sharper needs 72 interception-return yards to surpass Ed Reed (1,438) and Rod Woodson (1,483) for the most all-time (see Reed note). In 14 seasons, Sharper has 1,412 interception-return yards.

Sharper needs six interceptions to surpass Ronnie Lott (63), Ken Riley (65), and Dick "Night Train" Lane (68) to move into fourth place all-time. In 14 seasons, Sharper has 63 interceptions.

Charles Woodson needs three interception-return touchdowns to surpass Darren Sharper (11) and Rod Woodson (12) for the most all-time (see Sharper note). In 13 seasons, Woodson has 10 interception-return touchdowns.

Ed Reed needs 46 interception-return yards to surpass Rod Woodson (1,483) for the most all-time (see Sharper note). In nine seasons, Reed has 1,438 interception-return yards.

Reed is tied with Everson Walls (3) for the most seasons leading the league in interceptions and can become the first player in history to lead the league in INTs four times.

DeMarcus Ware has led the league in sacks twice in his career and can become the first player to lead the league three times since the sack became an official statistic in 1982.

Devin Hester is tied with Eric Metcalf (10) for the most punt-return touchdowns in history and needs one punt-return TD to become the all-time leader. In five seasons, Hester has 10 punt-return touchdowns.

Joshua Cribbs needs two kickoff-return touchdowns to become the first player in history with 10 kickoff return TDs (see Washington note). In six seasons, Cribbs is the all-time leader with eight kickoff return touchdowns.

Leon Washington needs two kickoff-return touchdowns to surpass Joshua Cribbs (8) for the most all-time (see Cribbs note). In five seasons, Washington has seven kickoff return TDs.

DRAFT LIST FOR 2011

76th Annual NFL Draft, April 28-30, 2011
+Denotes Compensatory Selection
#Denotes Underclassman Selection

ARIZONA CARDINALS
1. # Patrick Peterson—5, DB, Louisiana State
2. # Ryan Williams—38, RB, Virginia Tech
3. Rob Housler—69, TE, Florida Atlantic
4. Sam Acho—103, LB, Texas
5. Anthony Sherman—136, RB, Connecticut
6. Quan Sturdivant—171, LB, North Carolina
   David Carter—184, DT, UCLA,
           from TAMPA BAY through PHILADELPHIA
7. +DeMarco Sampson—249, WR, San Diego State

ATLANTA FALCONS
1. #Julio Jones—6, WR, Alabama, from CLEVELAND
3. Akeem Dent—91, LB, Georgia
5. #Jacquizz Rodgers—145, RB, Oregon State, from ST. LOUIS
6. Matt Bosher—192, P, Miami
7. Andrew Jackson—210, G, Fresno State, from DETROIT
   Cliff Matthews—230, DE, South Carolina,
           from NEW ENGLAND

BALTIMORE RAVENS
1. Jimmy Smith—27, DB, Colorado
2. #Torrey Smith—58, WR, Maryland
3. Jah Reid—85, T, Central Florida, from PHILADELPHIA
4. #Tandon Doss—123, WR, Indiana
5. +Chykie Brown—164, DB, Texas
   + Pernell McPhee—165, DE, Mississippi State
6. Tyrod Taylor—180, QB, Virginia Tech, from ST. LOUIS
7. Anthony Allen—225, RB, Georgia Tech,
           from PHILADELPHIA

BUFFALO BILLS
1. #Marcell Dareus—3, DT, Alabama
2. #Aaron Williams—34, DB, Texas
3. Kelvin Sheppard—68, LB, Louisiana State
4. Da'Norris Searcy—100, DB, North Carolina
   Chris Hairston—122, T, Clemson, from SEATTLE
5. Johnny White—133, RB, North Carolina
6. Chris White—169, LB, Mississippi State
7. Justin Rogers—206, DB, Richmond
   + Michael Jasper—245, DT, Bethel (TN)

CAROLINA PANTHERS
1. #Cam Newton—1, QB, Auburn
3. Terrell McClain—65, DT, South Florida
   + Sione Fua—97, DT, Stanford
4. Brandon Hogan—98, DB, West Virginia
5. Kealoha Pilares—132, WR, Hawaii
6. Lawrence Wilson—166, LB, Connecticut
   + Zack Williams—203, C, Washington State
7. +Lee Ziemba—244, T, Auburn

CHICAGO BEARS
1. Gabe Carimi—29, T, Wisconsin
2. Stephen Paea—53, DT, Oregon State,
           from INDIANAPOLIS through WASHINGTON
3. Chris Conte—93, DB, California
5. Nathan Enderle—160, QB, Idaho
6. J.T. Thomas—195, LB, West Virginia
7. Choice Exercised in 2010 Supplemental Draft
           for Harvey Unga, RB, Brigham Young

CINCINNATI BENGALS
1. #A.J. Green—4, WR, Georgia
2. Andy Dalton—35, QB, Texas Christian
3. Dontay Moch—66, LB, Nevada
4. Clint Boling—101, G, Georgia
5. #Robert Sands—134, DB, West Virginia
6. Ryan Whalen—167, WR, Stanford
7. Korey Lindsey—207, DB, Southern Illinois
   + Jay Finley—246, RB, Baylor

CLEVELAND BROWNS
1. Phil Taylor—21, DT, Baylor
2. Jabaal Sheard—37, DE, Pittsburgh
   # Greg Little—59, WR, North Carolina, from ATLANTA
4. Jordan Cameron—102, TE, Southern California
   Owen Marecic—124, RB, Stanford, from ATLANTA
5. Buster Skrine—137, DB, Chattanooga
   Jason Pinkston—150, T, Pittsburgh,
           from NEW YORK GIANTS through MINNESOTA
7. +Eric Hagg—248, DB, Nebraska

DALLAS COWBOYS
1. #Tyron Smith—9, T, Southern California
2. Bruce Carter—40, LB, North Carolina
3. DeMarco Murray—71, RB, Oklahoma
4. David Arkin—110, G, Missouri State
5. Josh Thomas—143, DB, Buffalo
6. Dwayne Harris—176, WR, East Carolina
7. Choice Exercised in 2010 Supplemental Draft
           for Josh Price-Brent, NT, Illinois
   Shaun Chapas—220, RB, Georgia, from SAN DIEGO
   + Bill Nagy—252, C, Wisconsin

DENVER BRONCOS
1. Von Miller—2, LB, Texas A&M
2. #Rahim Moore—45, DB, UCLA, from SAN FRANCISCO
   Orlando Franklin—46, T, Miami, from MIAMI
3. Nate Irving—67, LB, North Carolina State
4. Quinton Carter—108, DB, Oklahoma,
           from SAN FRANCISCO
   Julius Thomas—129, TE, Portland State, from GREEN BAY
6. Mike Mohamed—189, LB, California,
           from NEW ORLEANS through NEW ENGLAND
7. Virgil Green—204, TE, Nevada,
           from CAROLINA through GREEN BAY
   + Jeremy Beal—247, DE, Oklahoma

DETROIT LIONS
1. #Nick Fairley—13, DT, Auburn
2. Titus Young—44, WR, Boise State
   # Mikel Leshoure—57, RB, Illinois, from SEATTLE
5. Doug Hogue—157, LB, Syracuse,
           from BALTIMORE through SEATTLE
7. Johnny Culbreath—209, T, South Carolina State
           from CLEVELAND through SEATTLE

GREEN BAY PACKERS
1. Derek Sherrod—32, T, Mississippi State
2. #Randall Cobb—64, WR, Kentucky
3. Alex Green—96, RB, Hawaii
4. +Davon House—131, DB, New Mexico State
5. D.J. Williams—141, TE, Arkansas,
       from SAN FRANCISCO through DENVER
6. Caleb Schlauderaff—179, G, Utah, from MIAMI
    D.J. Smith—186, LB, Appalachian State,
       from PHILADELPHIA through DETROIT
       and DENVER
    Ricky Elmore—197, LB, Arizona
7. Ryan Taylor—218, TE, North Carolina,
       from JACKSONVILLE through MIAMI
+ Guy Lawrence—233, DT, Arizona State

HOUSTON TEXANS
1. #J.J. Watt—11, DE, Wisconsin
2. Brooks Reed—42, LB, Arizona
  # Brandon Harris—60, DB, Miami, from NEW ENGLAND
4. Rashad Carmichael—127, DB, Virginia Tech,
       from CHICAGO through WASHINGTON
5. Shiloh Keo—144, DB, Idaho, from WASHINGTON
    T.J. Yates—152, QB, North Carolina,
       from INDIANAPOLIS through WASHINGTON
7. Derek Newton—214, T, Arkansas State
+ Cheta Ozougwu—254, LB, Rice

INDIANAPOLIS COLTS
1. Anthony Castonzo—22, T, Boston College
2. Ben Ijalana—49, T, Villanova,
       from JACKSONVILLE through WASHINGTON
3. Drake Nevis—87, DT, Louisiana State
4. Delone Carter—119, RB, Syracuse
6. Chris Rucker—188, DB, Michigan State

JACKSONVILLE JAGUARS
1. #Blaine Gabbert—10, QB, Missouri, from WASHINGTON
3. Will Rackley—76, G, Lehigh, from SAN FRANCISCO
4. Cecil Shorts—114, WR, Mount Union
    Chris Prosinski—121, DB, Wyoming, from NEW ORLEANS
5. Rod Issac—147, DB, Middle Tennessee

KANSAS CITY CHIEFS
1. #Jonathan Baldwin—26, WR, Pittsburgh,
       from ATLANTA through CLEVELAND
2. Rodney Hudson—55, C, Florida State
3. #Justin Houston—70, LB, Georgia, from CLEVELAND
    Allen Bailey—86, DE, Miami
4. Jalil Brown—118, DB, Colorado
5. Ricky Stanzi—135, QB, Iowa,
       from DENVER through TAMPA BAY
    Gabe Miller—140, LB, Oregon State, from DETROIT
6. +Jerrell Powe—199, NT, Mississippi
7. Shane Bannon—223, RB, Yale

MIAMI DOLPHINS
1. Mike Pouncey—15, C, Florida
2. Daniel Thomas—62, RB, Kansas State,
       from CHICAGO through WASHINGTON
4. Edmond Gates—111, WR, Abilene Christian
6. Charles Clay—174, RB, Tulsa,
       from SAN FRANCISCO through GREEN BAY
7. Frank Kearse—231, DT, Alabama A&M,
       from NEW YORK JETS through DETROIT,
       SAN FRANCISCO and GREEN BAY
+ Jimmy Wilson—235, DB, Montana

MINNESOTA VIKINGS
1. Christian Ponder—12, QB, Florida State
2. #Kyle Rudolph—43, TE, Notre Dame
4. Christian Ballard—106, DT, Iowa
5. #Brandon Burton—139, DB, Utah
6. DeMarcus Love—168, T, Arkansas,
       from DENVER through CLEVELAND
    Mistral Raymond—170, DB, South Florida,
       from CLEVELAND
    Brandon Fusco—172, C, Slippery Rock
+ Ross Homan—200, LB, Ohio State
7. D'Aundre Reed—215, DE, Arizona
+ Stephen Burton—236, WR, West Texas A&M

NEW ENGLAND PATRIOTS
1. Nate Solder—17, T, Colorado, from OAKLAND
2. Ras-I Dowling—33, DB, Virginia, from CAROLINA
  # Shane Vereen—56, RB, California, from NEW ORLEANS
3. #Stevan Ridley—73, RB, Louisiana State, from HOUSTON
  # Ryan Mallett—74, QB, Arkansas, from MINNESOTA
5. Marcus Cannon—138, T, Texas Christian, from HOUSTON
    Lee Smith—159, TE, Marshall
6. Markell Carter—194, LB, Central Arkansas,
       from NEW YORK JETS through PHILADELPHIA
7. Malcolm Williams—219, DB, Texas Christian,
       from OAKLAND

NEW ORLEANS SAINTS
1. Cameron Jordan—24, DE, California
  # Mark Ingram—28, RB, Alabama, from NEW ENGLAND
3. #Martez Wilson—72, LB, Illinois
    Johnny Patrick—88, DB, Louisville
7. Greg Romeus—226, DE, Pittsburgh
+ Nate Bussey—243, LB, Illinois

NEW YORK GIANTS
1. Prince Amukamara—19, DB, Nebraska
2. #Marvin Austin—52, DT, North Carolina
3. Jerrel Jernigan—83, WR, Troy
4. James Brewer—117, T, Indiana
6. Greg Jones—185, LB, Michigan State
+ #Tyler Sash—198, DB, Iowa
+ Jacquian Williams—202, LB, South Florida
7. Da'Rel Scott—221, RB, Maryland

NEW YORK JETS
1. #Muhammad Wilkerson—30, DT, Temple
3. Kenrick Ellis—94, DT, Hampton
4. Bilal Powell—126, RB, Louisville
5. Jeremy Kerley—153, WR, Texas Christian,
       from PHILADELPHIA
7. Greg McElroy—208, QB, Alabama, from ARIZONA
    Scotty McKnight—227, WR, Colorado,
       from SEATTLE through PHILADELPHIA

OAKLAND RAIDERS
2. Stefen Wisniewski—48, C, Penn State
3. DeMarcus Van Dyke—81, DB, Miami
   Joe Barksdale—92, T, Louisiana State,
      from NEW ENGLAND
4. Chimdi Chekwa—113, DB, Ohio State
   # Taiwan Jones—125, RB, Eastern Washington
5. Denarius Moore—148, WR, Tennessee
6. Richard Gordon—181, TE, Miami
7.+David Ausberry—241, WR, Southern California

PHILADELPHIA EAGLES
1. Danny Watkins—23, G, Baylor
2. Jaiquawn Jarrett—54, DB, Temple
3. Curtis Marsh—90, DB, Utah State, from BALTIMORE
4. Casey Matthews—116, LB, Oregon, from TAMPA BAY
   Alex Henery—120, K, Nebraska
5.#Dion Lewis—149, RB, Pittsburgh, from SAN DIEGO
   Julian Vandervelde—161, G, Iowa, from NEW YORK JETS
6. Jason Kelce—191, C, Cincinnati, from BALTIMORE
   Brian Rolle—193, LB, Ohio State, from NEW ENGLAND
7.+Greg Lloyd—237, LB, Connecticut
 + Stanley Havili—240, RB, Southern California

PITTSBURGH STEELERS
1. Cameron Heyward—31, DE, Ohio State
2. Marcus Gilbert—63, T, Florida
3. Curtis Brown—95, DB, Texas
4. Cortez Allen—128, DB, The Citadel
5. Chris Carter—162, LB, Fresno State
6. Keith Williams—196, G, Nebraska
7. Baron Batch—232, RB, Texas Tech

ST. LOUIS RAMS
1.#Robert Quinn—14, DE, North Carolina
2. Lance Kendricks—47, TE, Wisconsin
3. Austin Pettis—78, WR, Boise State
4. Greg Salas—112, WR, Hawaii
5. Jermale Hines—158, DB, Ohio State, from ATLANTA
7. Mikail Baker—216, DB, Baylor
   Jabara Williams—228, LB, Stephen F. Austin,
      from BALTIMORE
   Jonathan Nelson—229, DB, Oklahoma, from ATLANTA

SAN DIEGO CHARGERS
1.#Corey Liuget—18, DE, Illinois
2. Marcus Gilchrist—50, DB, Clemson
   Jonas Mouton—61, LB, Michigan, from NEW YORK JETS
3. Vincent Brown—82, WR, San Diego State
   Shareece Wright—89, DB, Southern California,
      from SEATTLE
6.#Jordan Todman—183, RB, Connecticut
 + Stephen Schilling—201, T, Michigan
7.+Andrew Gachkar—234, LB, Missouri

SAN FRANCISCO 49ERS
1.#Aldon Smith—7, LB, Missouri
2. Colin Kaepernick—36, QB, Nevada, from DENVER
3. Chris Culliver—80, DB, South Carolina,
      from JACKSONVILLE
4. Kendall Hunter—115, RB, Oklahoma State,
      from SAN DIEGO
5. Daniel Kilgore—163, G, Appalachian State,
      from GREEN BAY
6. Ronald Johnson—182, WR, Southern California,
      from JACKSONVILLE
   Colin Jones—190, DB, Texas Christian, from SEATTLE
7. Bruce Miller—211, RB, Central Florida
 + Mike Person—239, G, Montana State
 + Curtis Holcomb—250, DB, Florida A&M

SEATTLE SEAHAWKS
1. James Carpenter—25, T, Alabama
3. John Moffitt—75, G, Wisconsin, from DETROIT
4. K.J. Wright—99, LB, Mississippi State,
      from DENVER through NEW ENGLAND
   Kris Durham—107, WR, Georgia, from DETROIT
5. Richard Sherman—154, DB, Stanford,
      from KANSAS CITY through DETROIT
   Mark LeGree—156, DB, Appalachian State
6. Byron Maxwell—173, DB, Clemson, from DETROIT
7. Lazarius Levingston—205, DE, Louisiana State,
      from DENVER through DETROIT
 + Malcolm Smith—242, LB, Southern California

TAMPA BAY BUCCANEERS
1. Adrian Clayborn—20, DE, Iowa
2.#Da'Quan Bowers—51, DE, Clemson
3. Mason Foster—84, LB, Washington
4. Luke Stocker—104, TE, Tennessee,
      from WASHINGTON through PHILADELPHIA
5. Ahmad Black—151, DB, Florida
6. Allen Bradford—187, RB, Southern California,
      from KANSAS CITY
7. Anthony Gaitor—222, DB, Florida International
 + Daniel Hardy—238, TE, Idaho

TENNESSEE TITANS
1. Jake Locker—8, QB, Washington
2.#Akeem Ayers—39, LB, UCLA
3.#Jurrell Casey—77, DT, Southern California
4. Colin McCarthy—109, LB, Miami
 +#Jamie Harper—130, RB, Clemson
5. Karl Klug—142, DT, Iowa
6. Byron Stingily—175, T, Louisville
7. Zach Clayton—212, DT, Auburn
 + Tommie Campbell—251, DB, California (PA)

WASHINGTON REDSKINS
1. Ryan Kerrigan—16, LB, Purdue, from JACKSONVILLE
2. Jarvis Jenkins—41, DE, Clemson
3. Leonard Hankerson—79, WR, Miami, from MIAMI
4. Roy Helu—105, RB, Nebraska, from HOUSTON
5. DeJon Gomes—146, DB, Nebraska, from MIAMI
   Niles Paul—155, WR, Nebraska, from NEW ORLEANS
6. Evan Royster—177, RB, Penn State
   Aldrick Robinson—178, WR, Southern Methodist,
      from HOUSTON
7. Brandyn Thompson—213, DB, Boise State
   Maurice Hurt—217, G, Florida, from MIAMI
   Markus White—224, LB, Florida State, from INDIANAPOLIS
 + Chris Neild—253, NT, West Virginia

NUMBER OF PLAYERS DRAFTED—2011

BY POSITION:

Defensive Backs	53
Linebackers	40
Running Backs	31
Wide Receivers	28
Tackles	21
Defensive Tackles	18
Defensive Ends	16
Guards	12
Quarterbacks	12
Tight Ends	12
Centers	7
Nose Tackles	2
Kicker	1
Punters	1

BY COLLEGE:

North Carolina	9
Southern California	9
Miami	8
Nebraska	7
Clemson	6
Georgia	6
Iowa	6
Louisiana State	6
Alabama	5
Ohio State	5
Pittsburgh	5
Texas Christian	5
Wisconsin	5
Auburn	4
Baylor	4
California	4
Colorado	4
Connecticut	4
Florida	4
Illinois	4
Mississippi State	4
Oklahoma	4
Stanford	4
Texas	4
West Virginia	4
Appalachian State	3
Arizona	3
Arkansas	3
Boise State	3
Florida State	3
Hawaii	3
Idaho	3
Louisville	3
Missouri	3
Nevada	3
Oregon State	3
South Florida	3
UCLA	3
Virginia Tech	3
Central Florida	2
Fresno State	2
Indiana	2
Maryland	2
Michigan	2
Michigan State	2
Penn State	2
San Diego State	2
South Carolina	2
Syracuse	2
Temple	2
Tennessee	2
Utah	2
Washington	2
Abilene Christian	1
Alabama A&M	1
Arizona State	1
Arkansas State	1
Bethel (TN)	1
Boston College	1
Buffalo	1
California (PA)	1
Central Arkansas	1
Chattanooga	1
Cincinnati	1
The Citadel	1
East Carolina	1
Eastern Washington	1
Florida A&M	1
Florida Atlantic	1
Florida International	1
Georgia Tech	1
Hampton	1
Kansas State	1
Kentucky	1
Lehigh	1
Marshall	1
Middle Tennessee	1
Mississippi	1
Missouri State	1
Montana	1
Montana State	1
Mount Union	1
New Mexico State	1
North Carolina State	1
Notre Dame	1
Oklahoma State	1
Oregon	1
Portland State	1
Purdue	1
Rice	1
Richmond	1
Slippery Rock	1
South Carolina State	1
Southern Illinois	1
Southern Methodist	1
Stephen F. Austin	1
Texas A&M	1
Texas Tech	1
Troy	1
Tulsa	1
Utah State	1
Villanova	1
Virginia	1
Washington State	1
West Texas A&M	1
Wyoming	1
Yale	1

BY CONFERENCE:

Southeastern	38
Atlantic Coast	35
Pacific 10	31
Big 12	30
Big Ten	29
Big East	22
Western Athletic	16
Mountain West	10
Conference USA	7
Southern	5
Sun Belt	5
Big Sky	4
Mid-American	3
Mid-Eastern Athletic	3
Colonial Athletic	2
Lone Star	2
Missouri Valley Football	2
Pennsylvania State Athletic	2
Southland	2
Independent	1
Ivy	1
Mid-South	1
Ohio Athletic	1
Patriot	1
Southwestern Athletic	1

UNDERCLASSMEN IN THE DRAFT

Year	D1-FBS	Drafted	In Top 10
1990	28	18	5
1991	23	19	1
1992	30	21	5
1993	34	24	5
1994	31	25	6
1995	33	22	2
1996	24	16	4
1997	34	25	6
1998	32	19	3
1999	31	22	5
2000	26	20	4
2001	35	27	5
2002	38	26	2
2003	47	32	5
2004	43	35	5
2005	51	37	4
2006	52	33	6
2007	40	29	5
2008	53	39	4
2009	46	41	5
2010	53	46	5
2011	56	43	8

The NFL uses a system of Referee Replay Review to aid officiating.

Prior to the two-minute warning of each half, a Coaches' Challenge System will be in effect, except for plays when the on-field ruling results in a score for either team. After the two-minute warning, throughout any overtime period, and after all scoring plays, a Referee Review will be initiated by a Replay Official from a Replay Booth.

The following procedures will be used:

Reviews by Referee: All Replay Reviews will be conducted by the Referee on a field-level monitor after consultation with the other covering official(s), prior to review. A decision will be reversed only when the Referee has *indisputable visual evidence* available to him that warrants the change.

Coaches' Challenge: In each game, a team will be permitted two challenges that will initiate Referee Replay reviews, except for scoring plays, after the two-minute warning of each half, and throughout any overtime period. Each challenge will require the use of a team time out. If a challenge is upheld, the time out will be restored to the challenging team. If both challenges are upheld, a third challenge will be awarded to the challenging team. No challenges will be recognized from a team that has exhausted its time outs.

Replay Official's Request for Review: After the two-minute warning of each half, throughout any overtime period, and after all scoring plays, any review will be initiated by a Replay Official. There is no limit to the number of reviews that may be initiated by the Replay Official. His ability to initiate a review will be unrelated to the number of time outs that either team has remaining, and no time out will be charged for any review initiated by the Replay Official.

Time Limit: Each review will be a maximum of 60 seconds in length, timed from when the Referee begins his review of the replay at the field-level monitor.

Reviewable Plays: The Replay System will cover the following play situations only:

A) **Plays Governed by Sideline, Goal Line, End Zone, End Line, and Goal Posts:**
   1. Scoring plays, including a runner breaking the plane of the goal line.
   2. Pass complete/incomplete/intercepted at sideline, goal line, end zone, and end line.
   3. Runner/receiver in or out of bounds.
   4. Recovery of loose ball in or out of bounds.

B) **Passing Plays:**
   1. Pass ruled complete/incomplete/intercepted in the field of play.
   2. Touching of a forward pass by an ineligible receiver.
   3. Touching of a forward pass by a defensive player.
   4. Quarterback (Passer) forward pass or fumble.
   5. Illegal forward pass beyond line of scrimmage.
   6. Illegal forward pass after change of possession.
   7. Forward or backward pass thrown from behind line of scrimmage.

C) **Other Reviewable Plays:**
   1. Runner ruled not down by defensive contact.
   2. Runner ruled down by defensive contact and there is a recovery by defense.
   3. Forward progress with respect to first down.
   4. Touching of a kick.
   5. Number of players on the field.
   6. Recovery of loose ball in the field of play, including those ruled to have hit sideline.
   7. A field goal or try attempt when it is lower than the top of the uprights.
   8. Illegal forward handoff.

INSTANT REPLAY HISTORY

From 1986-1991, a limited system of Instant Replay was used on a year-by-year basis. Replay also was experimented with during the 1996 and 1998 preseasons. For the 1999 season, the NFL introduced a system of Referee Replay Review to aid officiating. That system was extended on a one-year basis for the 2000 season and then approved for the next three years through 2003. The system was extended on a five-year basis in March 2004 and was later installed permanently in March 2007.

Following are the results of the different systems:

REGULAR SEASON, 1986-1991

Year	Games	Plays Closely Reviewed	Reversals
1986	224	374	38
1987	210	490	57
1988	224	537	53
1989	224	492	65
1990	224	504	73
1991	224	570	90
TOTAL	1,330	2,967	376

PRESEASON, 1996, 1998

Year	Games	Challenges	Reversals
1996	10	13	3
1998	10	10	3
TOTAL	20	23	6

REGULAR SEASON, 1999-2010

Year	Games	Total Replay Reviews	Challenges	Reversals
1999	248	195	133	57
2000	248	247	179	84
2001	248	258	191	89
2002	256	294	208	94
2003	256	255	184	66
2004	256	283	233	88
2005	256	295	223	92
2006	256	311	237	107
2007	256	327	250	122
2008	256	315	229	117
2009	256	328	228	126
2010	256	361	252	133
TOTAL	3,048	3,469	2,547	1,175

PRESEASON AND REGULAR SEASON – SUDDEN DEATH

The sudden death system of determining the winner shall prevail when the score is tied at the end of the regulation playing time of preseason and regular-season NFL games. The team scoring first during overtime play shall be the winner and the game automatically ends upon any score (by safety, field goal, or touchdown) or when a score is awarded by Referee for a palpably unfair act.

- At the end of regulation time the Referee will immediately toss coin at center of field in accordance with rules pertaining to the usual pregame toss. The captain of the visiting team will call the toss prior to the coin being flipped.

- Following a three-minute intermission after the end of the regulation game, play will continue for one 15-minute period or until there is a score. Each team has two time outs. General timing provisions that apply for the fourth quarter will prevail. Try is not attempted if touchdown scored. Disqualified players are not allowed to return.

- **Instant Replay:** No challenges. Reviews to be initiated by the replay assistant.

POSTSEASON – MODIFIED SUDDEN DEATH

NFL owners voted in 2010 to install a modified sudden death system to determine the winner when the score is tied at the end of regulation playing time of postseason NFL games. The system guarantees each team a possession or the opportunity to possess, unless the team that receives the opening kickoff scores a touchdown on its initial possession.

- At the end of regulation time the Referee will immediately toss coin at center of field in accordance with rules pertaining to the usual pregame toss. The captain of the visiting team will call the toss prior to the coin being flipped.

- Following a three-minute intermission after the end of the regulation game, play will be continued in 15-minute periods until a winner is declared. Each team must possess or have the opportunity to possess the ball unless the team that has the ball first scores a touchdown on its initial possession. Play continues in sudden death until a winner is determined, and the game automatically ends upon any score (by safety, field goal, or touchdown) or when a score is awarded by Referee for a palpably unfair act. Each team has three time outs per half and all general timing provisions apply as during a regular game. Try is not attempted if touchdown scored. Disqualified players are not allowed to return.

- **Instant Replay:** No challenges. Reviews to be initiated by the replay assistant.

Key Definitions:

Possession: Actual possession of the ball with complete control. The defense gains possession when it catches, intercepts, or recovers a loose ball.

Opportunity to possess: The opportunity to possess occurs only during kicking plays. A kickoff is an opportunity to possess for the receiving team. If the kicking team legally recovers the kick, the receiving team is considered to have had its opportunity. A punt or a field goal that crosses the line of scrimmage and is muffed by the receiving team is considered to be an opportunity to possess for the receivers. Normal touching rules by the kicking team apply.

The AFC

**American Football Conference
North Division
Team Colors:** Black, Purple, and Metallic
Gold
**1 Winning Drive
Owings Mills, Maryland 21117
Telephone:** (410) 701-4000

2011 SCHEDULE
PRESEASON
Aug. 11 at Philadelphia 7:30
Aug. 19 **Kansas City** 7:30
Aug. 25 **Washington** 8:00
Sep. 1   at Atlanta...........................7:30

REGULAR SEASON
Sep. 11 **Pittsburgh** 1:00
Sep. 18 at Tennessee 1:00
Sep. 25 at St. Louis 4:05
Oct. 2   **New York Jets** 8:20
Oct. 9   BYE
Oct. 16 **Houston** 4:05
Oct. 24 at Jacksonville (Mon) 8:30
Oct. 30 **Arizona** 1:00
Nov. 6   at Pittsburgh 8:20
Nov. 13 at Seattle 4:05
Nov. 20 **Cincinnati** 1:00
Nov. 24 **San Francisco** (Thu) 8:20
Dec. 4   at Cleveland 1:00
Dec. 11 **Indianapolis** 1:00
Dec. 18 at San Diego * 8:20
Dec. 24 **Cleveland** (Sat)................. 1:00
Jan. 1   at Cincinnati 1:00
*All times ET; Sunday night games in
Weeks 11-15, 17 subject to change*
Stadium: M&T Bank Stadium
(opened in 1998)
• **Capacity:** 71,008
1101 Russell Street
Baltimore, Maryland 21230
Playing Surface: Sportexe Momentum
Training Camp: McDaniel College
2 College Hill
Westminster, MD 21157

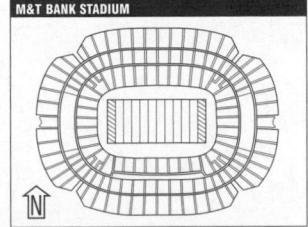
M&T BANK STADIUM

CLUB OFFICIALS
Owner: Steve Bisciotti
President: Dick Cass
Executive Vice President/General
    Manager: Ozzie Newsome
Senior Vice President/Public and
    Community Relations: Kevin Byrne
Vice President of Football Administration:
    Pat Moriarty
Vice President, Corporate Sales and
    Development: Mark Burdett
Vice President and Chief Financial
    Officer: Jeff Goering
Vice President, Regional Partnerships
    and Sales: Ed Burchell
Vice President, Marketing:
    Gabrielle Dow
Vice President, Operations: Bob Eller
Vice President, Information Technology:
    Bill Jankowski
Vice President, Ticket Sales and
    Operations: Baker Koppelman
Vice President, National Partnerships and
    Sales: Kevin Rochlitz
Vice President, Broadcasting:
    Larry Rosen
Vice President, Stadium Operations:
    Roy Sommerhof
Vice President of Digital Media:
    Michelle Andres
Director of Player Personnel:
    Eric DeCosta
Director of College Scouting: Joe Hortiz
Director of Pro Personnel:
    Vincent Newsome
Senior Personnel Assistant:
    George Kokinis
Assistant Director of Pro Personnel:
    Chad Alexander
Director of Player Development:
    O.J. Brigance
Director of Media Relations:
    Chad Steele
Assistant Director of Player Development:
    Harry Swayne
Scouts: Mark Azevedo, Joe Douglas,
    Jack Glowik, Milt Hendrickson,
    Andrew Weidl, Lonnie Young
Equipment Manager: Ed Carroll
Head Athletic Trainer: Mark Smith
Director of Football Video Operations:
    Jon Dubé
Assistant Director of Football Video
    Operations: Mark Bienvenu
Senior Director, Fields & Grounds/Head
    Groundskeeper: Don Follett
Director of Premium Services/Suites:
    Theresa Abato
Controller: Jim Coller
Director, Broadcasting Administration:
    Don DiRaddo
Director, Information Technology:
    Nick Fusee
Director, Human Resources:
    Elizabeth Jackson
Director of Community Relations:
    Melanie LeGrande
Director, Security: Darren Sanders

COACHING HISTORY
(137-117-1)
Records include postseason games
1996-98   Ted Marchibroda 16-31-1
1999-2007 Brian Billick................85-67-0
2008-2010 John Harbaugh 36-19-0

PAID ATTENDANCE
Home 557,354   Away 541,536
Total 1,098,890
Single-game home record,
    71,382 (12/03/07)
Single-season home record, 557,792
    (2008)

2011 DRAFT CHOICES
Round	Name	Pos.	College
1	Jimmy Smith	DB	Colorado
2	Torrey Smith	WR	Maryland
3	Jah Reid	T	Central Florida
4	Tandon Doss	WR	Indiana
5	Chykie Brown	DB	Texas
	Pernell McPhee	DE	Mississippi St.
6	Tyrod Taylor	QB	Virginia Tech
7	Anthony Allen	RB	Georgia Tech

2010 TEAM RECORD

PRESEASON (3-1)

Date	Result	Opponent
8/12	W 17-12	Carolina
8/21	W 23-3	at Washington
8/28	W 24-10	New York Giants
9/2	L 21-27	at St. Louis

REGULAR SEASON (12-4)

Date	Result	Opponent
9/13	W 10-9	at New York Jets
9/19	L 10-15	at Cincinnati
9/26	W 24-17	Cleveland
10/3	W 17-14	at Pittsburgh
10/10	W 31-17	Denver
10/17	L 20-23	at New England (OT)
10/24	W 37-34	Buffalo (OT)
11/7	W 26-10	Miami
11/11	L 21-26	at Atlanta
11/21	W 37-13	at Carolina
11/28	W 17-10	Tampa Bay
12/5	L 10-13	Pittsburgh
12/13	W 34-28	at Houston (OT)
12/19	W 30-24	New Orleans
12/26	W 20-10	at Cleveland
1/2	W 13-7	Cincinnati

POSTSEASON (1-1)

1/9	W 30-7	at Kansas City
1/15	L 24-31	at Pittsburgh

(OT) Overtime

SCORE BY PERIODS

Ravens	61	132	75	80	9 —	357
Opponents	51	73	24	119	3 —	270

2010 TEAM STATISTICS

	Ravens	Opp.
Total First Downs	303	284
Rushing	97	79
Passing	175	187
Penalty	31	18
3rd Down: Made/Att	82/210	87/229
3rd Down Pct.	39.0	38.0
4th Down: Made/Att	4/10	6/12
4th Down Pct.	40.0	50.0
Possession Avg.	30:42	29:18
Total Net Yards	5166	5102
Avg. Per Game	322.9	318.9
Total Plays	1018	1007
Avg. Per Play	5.1	5.1
Net Yards Rushing	1831	1503
Avg. Per Game	114.4	93.9
Total Rushes	487	384
Net Yards Passing	3335	3599
Avg. Per Game	208.4	224.9
Sacked/Yards Lost	40/294	27/190
Gross Yards	3629	3789
Att./Completions	491/308	596/349
Completion Pct.	62.7	58.6
Had Intercepted	10	19
Punts/Average	81/43.6	89/43.5
Net Punting Avg.	81/39.2	89/39.1
Penalties/Yards	90/673	117/984
Fumbles/Ball Lost	22/10	25/8
Touchdowns	40	27
Rushing	11	5
Passing	25	22
Returns	4	0

2010 INDIVIDUAL STATISTICS

PASSING

	Att.	Comp.	Yds.	Pct.	TD	Int.	Tkld.	Rate
Flacco	489	306	3622	62.6	25	10	40/294	93.6
Boldin	1	1	-6	100.0	0	0	0/0	79.2
Koch	1	1	13	100.0	0	0	0/0	118.8
Ravens	491	308	3629	62.7	25	10	40/294	93.6
Opponents	596	349	3789	58.6	22	19	27/190	76.4

SCORING

	TD R	TD P	TD Rt	PAT	FG	Saf	PTS
Cundiff	0	0	0	39/39	26/29	0	117
Boldin	0	7	0	0/0	0/0	0	42
Mason	0	7	0	0/0	0/0	0	42
McGahee	5	1	0	0/0	0/0	0	36
Rice	5	1	0	0/0	0/0	0	36
Heap	0	5	0	0/0	0/0	0	30
Houshmandzadeh	0	3	0	0/0	0/0	0	18
Dickson	0	1	0	0/0	0/0	0	6
Flacco	1	0	0	0/0	0/0	0	6
Landry	0	0	1	0/0	0/0	0	6
Lewis	0	0	1	0/0	0/0	0	6
D. Reed	0	0	1	0/0	0/0	0	6
Wilson	0	0	1	0/0	0/0	0	6
Ravens	11	25	4	39/39	26/29	0	357
Opponents	5	22	0	25/25	27/32	0	270

2-Pt Conversions: Ravens 0-0, Opponents 1-2.

RUSHING

	No.	Yds	Avg	LG	TD
Rice	307	1220	4.0	50	5
McGahee	100	380	3.8	30t	5
L. McClain	28	85	3.0	16	0
Flacco	43	84	2.0	14	1
Stallworth	5	45	9.0	19	0
D. Reed	1	15	15.0	15	0
Boldin	2	2	1.0	3	0
Koch	1	0	0.0	0	0
Ravens	487	1831	3.8	50	11
Opponents	384	1503	3.9	48	5

RECEIVING

	No.	Yds	Avg	LG	TD
Boldin	64	837	13.1	61	7
Rice	63	556	8.8	34	1
Mason	61	802	13.1	42	7
Heap	40	599	15.0	65t	5
Houshmandzadeh	30	398	13.3	56t	3
L. McClain	21	134	6.4	19	0
McGahee	14	55	3.9	32t	1
Dickson	11	152	13.8	58	1
Stallworth	2	82	41.0	67	0
Williams	1	13	13.0	13	0
Pitta	1	1	1.0	1	0
Ravens	308	3629	11.8	67	25
Opponents	349	3789	10.9	88t	22

INTERCEPTIONS

	No.	Yds	Avg	LG	TD
E. Reed	8	183	22.9	44	0
Wilson	3	12	4.0	12t	1
Webb	2	32	16.0	32	0
Lewis	2	26	13.0	24t	0
Carr	2	13	6.5	12	0
Hamlin	1	0	0.0	0	0
Redding	1	0	0.0	0	0
Landry	0	23	—	23t	1
Ravens	19	289	15.2	44	3
Opponents	10	191	19.1	66	0

PUNTING

	No.	Yds.	Avg.	In 20	LG
Koch	81	3530	43.6	39	60
Ravens	81	3530	43.6	39	60
Opponents	89	3875	43.5	26	65

PUNT RETURNS

	Ret	FC	Yds	Avg	LG	TD
Webb	21	12	199	9.5	35	0
Zbikowski	16	8	101	6.3	20	0
Carr	3	0	8	2.7	10	0
E. Reed	3	6	11	3.7	9	0
Ravens	43	26	319	7.4	35	0
Opponents	34	22	275	8.1	32	0

KICKOFF RETURNS

	No.	Yds	Avg	LG	TD
Parmele	24	562	23.4	39	0
D. Reed	21	616	29.3	103t	1
Wilson	6	117	19.5	26	0
Zbikowski	3	48	16.0	20	0
Carr	1	14	14.0	14	0
Nakamura	0	0	—	—	0
Ravens	55	1357	24.7	103t	1
Opponents	38	987	26.0	64	0

FIELD GOALS

	1-19	20-29	30-39	40-49	50+
Cundiff	0/0	11/11	8/9	7/8	0/1
Ravens	0/0	11/11	8/9	7/8	0/1
Opponents	2/2	8/9	8/8	7/10	2/3

SACKS

	No.
Suggs	11.0
Ngata	5.5
Redding	3.0
Lewis	2.0
Johnson	1.5
Ellerbe	1.0
Kruger	1.0
Landry	1.0
J. McClain	1.0
Ravens	27.0
Opponents	40.0

RECORD HOLDERS
INDIVIDUAL RECORDS—CAREER

Category	Name	Performance
Rushing (Yds.)	Jamal Lewis, 2000-06	7,801
Passing (Yds.)	Joe Flacco, 2008-2010	10,206
Passing (TDs)	Joe Flacco, 2008-2010	60
Receiving (No.)	Derrick Mason, 2005-2010	471
Receiving (Yds.)	Derrick Mason, 2005-2010	5,777
Interceptions	Ed Reed, 2002-2010	54
Punting (Avg.)	Sam Koch, 2006-2010	43.7
Punt Return (Avg.)	Jermaine Lewis, 1996-2001	11.8
Kickoff Return (Avg.)	Corey Harris, 1998-2001	24.0
Field Goals	Matt Stover, 1996-2008	354
Touchdowns (Tot.)	Jamal Lewis, 2000-06	47
Points	Matt Stover, 1996-2008	1,464
*Sacks	Peter Boulware, 1997-2005	70.0

INDIVIDUAL RECORDS—SINGLE SEASON

Category	Name	Performance
Rushing (Yds.)	Jamal Lewis, 2003	2,066
Passing (Yds.)	Vinny Testaverde, 1996	4,177
Passing (TDs)	Vinny Testaverde, 1996	33
Receiving (No.)	Derrick Mason, 2007	103
Receiving (Yds.)	Michael Jackson, 1996	1,201
Interceptions	Ed Reed, 2004, 2008	9
Punting (Avg.)	Sam Koch, 2008	45.0
Punt Return (Avg.)	Jermaine Lewis, 2000	16.1
Kickoff Return (Avg.)	Corey Harris, 1998	27.6
Field Goals	Matt Stover, 2000	35
Touchdowns (Tot.)	Michael Jackson, 1996	14
	Jamal Lewis, 2003	14
	Willis McGahee, 2009	14
Points	Matt Stover, 2000	135
*Sacks	Peter Boulware, 2001	15.0

INDIVIDUAL RECORDS—SINGLE GAME

Category	Name	Performance
Rushing (Yds.)	Jamal Lewis, 9-14-03	295
Passing (Yds.)	Vinny Testaverde, 10-27-96	429
Passing (TDs)	Tony Banks, 9-10-00	5
Receiving (No.)	Priest Holmes, 10-11-98	13
Receiving (Yds.)	Qadry Ismail, 12-12-99	268
Interceptions	Many times	2
	Last time by Ed Reed, 1-2-11	
Field Goals	Matt Stover, 9-21-97, 12-26-99, 10-28-00, 10-14-07	5
	Billy Cundiff, 11-22-09	5
Touchdowns (Tot.)	Marcus Robinson, 11-23-03	4
Points	Marcus Robinson, 11-23-03	24
*Sacks	Michael McCrary, 11-8-98	4.0
	Peter Boulware, 1-7-02	4.0

Sacks became an official statistic in 1982.

VETERAN ROSTER AS OF MARCH 3, 2011

No.	Name	Pos.	Ht.	Wt.	Birthdate	^NFL Exp.	College	Hometown	How Acq.	'10 Games/ Starts
51	Ayanbadejo, Brendon	LB	6-1	225	9/6/76	9	UCLA	Santa Cruz, Calif.	UFA(Chi)-'08	10/0
77	Birk, Matt	C	6-4	310	7/23/76	14	Harvard	St. Paul, Minn.	UFA(Minn)-'09	16/16
81	Boldin, Anquan	WR	6-1	223	10/3/80	9	Florida State	Pahokee, Fla.	T(Ariz)-'10	16/16
10	Bulger, Marc	QB	6-3	208	4/5/77	11	West Virginia	Pittsburgh, Pa.	FA-'10	0*
25	Carr, Chris	CB/RS	5-10	182	4/30/83	7	Boise State	Reno, Nev.	UFA(Tenn)-'09	16/16
65	Chester, Chris	G/C	6-3	315	1/12/83	6	Oklahoma	Tustin, Calif.	D2-'06	14/14
62	Cody, Terrence	DT	6-4	349	6/28/88	2	Alabama	Fort Meyers, Fla.	D2b-'10	13/1
64	Cousins, Oniel	T	6-4	315	6/29/84	4	Texas-El Paso	Fullerton, Calif.	D3c-'08	16/1
46	Cox, Morgan	LS	6-4	241	4/26/86	2	Tennessee	Collierville, Tenn.	FA-'10	15/0
7	Cundiff, Billy	K	6-1	212	3/30/80	7	Drake	Harlan, Iowa	FA-'09	16/0
83	Dickson, Ed	TE	6-4	250	7/25/87	2	Oregon	Bellflower, Calif.	D3-'10	15/3
96	Divens, Lamar	DT	6-3	343	11/12/85	4	Tennessee State	Fayetteville, Tenn.	FA-'08	2/0
59	Ellerbe, Dannell	LB	6-1	243	11/29/85	3	Georgia	Hamlet, N.C.	FA-'09	11/1
5	Flacco, Joe	QB	6-6	238	1/16/85	4	Delaware	Audubon, N.J.	D1-'08	16/16
24	Foxworth, Domonique	CB	5-11	180	3/27/83	7	Maryland	Randallstown, Md.	UFA(Atl)-'09	0*
71	Gaither, Jared	T	6-9	340	3/18/86	5	Maryland	White Plains, Md.	SD5-'07	0*
56	Gooden, Tavares	ILB	6-1	242	10/7/84	4	Miami	Fort Lauderdale, Fla.	D3a-'08	10/0
36	Gorrer, Danny	DB	6-0	185	6/1/86	2	Texas A&M	Port Arthur, Texas	FA-'10	0*
97	Gregg, Kelly	DT	6-0	320	11/1/76	12	Oklahoma	Edmond, Okla.	FA-'00	16/16
66	Grubbs, Ben	G	6-3	310	3/10/84	5	Auburn	Eclectic, Ala.	D1-'07	16/16
13	Hardy, James	WR	6-5	220	12/24/85	2	Indiana	Fort Wayne, Ind.	FA-'11	0*
78	Harewood, Ramon	T	6-6	340	2/3/87	2	Morehouse	St. Michael, Barbados	D6-'10	0*
87	Harper, Justin	WR	6-3	226	2/24/85	3	Virginia Tech	Catawba, N.C.	D7a-'08	0*
86	Heap, Todd	TE	6-5	247	3/16/80	11	Arizona State	Mesa, Ariz.	D1-'01	13/13
70	Houser, Kevin	LS	6-2	255	8/23/77	11	Ohio State	Westlake, Ohio	FA-'10	1/0
84	Houshmandzadeh, T.J.	WR	6-2	203	9/26/77	11	Oregon State	Barstow, Calif.	FA-'10	16/2
95	Johnson, Jarret	DE	6-3	265	8/14/81	9	Alabama	Cedar Key, Fla.	D4a-'03	16/16
61	Jones, Arthur	DT	6-3	313	6/3/86	2	Syracuse	Endicott, N.Y.	D5b-'10	2/0
17	Jones, Brandon	WR	6-1	212	10/6/82	5	Oklahoma	Texarkana, Texas	FA-'11	0*
4	Koch, Sam	P	6-1	216	8/13/82	6	Nebraska	Seward, Neb.	D6a-'06	16/0
99	Kruger, Paul	DE	6-4	268	2/15/86	3	Utah	Orem, Utah	D2-'09	11/0
26	Landry, Dawan	S	6-0	210	12/30/82	6	Georgia Tech	Ama, La.	D5a-'06	16/16
32	Lawrence, Matt	RB	6-1	209	5/5/85	3	Massachusetts	Bloomfield, Conn.	FA-'08	0*
52	Lewis, Ray	ILB	6-1	250	5/15/75	16	Miami	Lakeland, Fla.	D1b-'96	16/16
85	Mason, Derrick	WR	5-10	197	1/17/74	15	Michigan State	Detroit, Mich.	FA-'05	16/15
72	Mattison, Bryan	OL	6-3	313	5/15/84	2	Iowa	Mishawaka, Ind.	FA-'08	2/0
53	McClain, Jameel	LB	6-1	250	7/25/85	4	Syracuse	Philadelphia, Pa.	FA-'08	16/15
33	McClain, Le'Ron	FB	6-0	260	12/27/84	5	Alabama	Northport, Ala.	D4b-'07	15/13
23	McGahee, Willis	RB	6-0	235	10/21/81	9	Miami	Miami, Fla.	T(Buff)-'07	15/2
38	McKie, Jason	FB	5-11	247	5/22/80	8	Temple	Gulf Breeze, Fla.	FA-'10	0*
91	McKinney, Brandon	NT	6-2	350	8/24/83	6	Michigan State	Dayton, Ohio	FA-'08	11/4
79	Moll, Tony	G/T	6-5	315	8/23/83	6	Nevada	Sonoma, Calif.	T(GB)-'09	16/3
43	Nakamura, Haruki	S	5-10	200	4/18/86	4	Cincinnati	Cleveland, Ohio	D6-'08	16/0
92	Ngata, Haloti	DT	6-4	350	1/21/84	6	Oregon	Salt Lake City, Utah	D1-'06	16/15
74	Oher, Michael	T	6-4	313	5/28/86	3	Mississippi	Memphis, Tenn.	D1-'09	16/16
34	Parmele, Jalen	RB	5-11	222	12/30/85	4	Toledo	Midland, Mich.	FA-'08	16/0
30	Paschal, Marcus	S	6-0	206	8/31/84	3	Iowa	Largo, Fla.	FA-'09	0*
58	Phillips, Jason	ILB	6-1	242	2/14/86	3	Texas Christian	Waller, Texas	D5a-'09	9/0
88	Pitta, Dennis	TE	6-4	245	6/29/85	2	Brigham Young	Moorpark, Calif.	D4-'10	11/0
93	Redding, Cory	DE	6-4	298	11/15/80	9	Texas	Houston, Texas	FA-'10	15/11
16	Reed, David	WR/RS	6-0	190	3/22/87	2	Utah	New Britain, Conn.	D5a-'10	13/0
20	Reed, Ed	S	5-11	200	9/11/78	10	Miami	St. Rose, La.	D1-'02	10/10
27	Rice, Ray	RB	5-8	212	1/22/87	4	Rutgers	New Rochelle, N.Y.	D2-'08	16/14
11	Smith, Marcus	WR	6-1	225	1/11/85	4	New Mexico	San Diego, Calif.	D4a-'08	14/0
18	Stallworth, Donte'	WR	6-0	204	11/10/80	9	Tennessee	Del Paso Heights, Calif.	FA-'10	8/0
55	Suggs, Terrell	OLB	6-3	260	10/11/82	9	Arizona State	Chandler, Ariz.	D1a-'03	16/16
98	Talavou, Kelly	NT	6-4	350	10/4/84	4	Utah	Fountain Valley, Calif.	FA-'08	0*
31	Washington, Fabian	CB	5-11	175	6/9/83	7	Nebraska	Bradenton, Fla.	T(Oak)-'08	14/8
21	Webb, Lardarius	CB/RS	5-10	182	10/12/85	3	Nicholls State	Opelika, Ala.	D3-'09	15/0
29	Williams, Cary	CB	6-1	182	12/23/84	3	Washburn	Hollywood, Fla.	FA-'09	13/0
37	Wilson, Josh	CB	5-9	192	3/11/85	5	Maryland	Upper Marlboro, Md.	T(Sea)-'10	14/9
73	Yanda, Marshal	G/T	6-3	315	9/15/84	5	Iowa	Anamosa, Iowa	D3b-'07	16/16
28	Zbikowski, Tom	S	5-11	200	5/22/85	4	Notre Dame	Arlington Heights, Ill.	D3b-'08	8/6

* Bulger did not play in 16 games; Foxworth missed '10 season because of injury; Gaither missed '10 season because of injury; Gorrer last active with St. Louis in '09; Hardy last active with Buffalo in '09; Harewood missed '10 season because of injury; Harper spent '10 season on Baltimore practice squad, last active with Baltimore in '09; B. Jones last active with San Francisco in '09; Lawrence missed '10 season because of injury; McKie inactive for 5 games; Paschal last active with Baltimore in '09; Talavou missed '10 season because of injury.

Also played with Ravens in '10—LB Prescott Burgess (16 games), LB/DE Edgar Jones (5).

^ "NFL Exp." as of 2011 Kickoff Weekend. For full explanation of how a player's NFL Experience is measured, refer to explanation underneath the First-Year Roster listed below.

FIRST-YEAR ROSTER

Name	Pos.	Ht.	Wt.	Birthdate	College	Hometown	How Acq.
Allen, Anthony	RB	6-1	230	8/6/88	Georgia Tech	Tampa, Fla.	D7
Bond, Brady (1)	T	6-6	300	6/4/86	Oklahoma State	Garber, Okla.	FA-'10
Brown, Chykie	CB	5-11	190	12/26/86	Texas	Houston, Texas	D5a
Cantwell, Hunter (1)	QB	6-4	236	12/30/85	Louisville	Paducah, Ky.	FA-'10
Doss, Tandon	WR	6-2	200	9/22/89	Indiana	Indianapolis, Ind.	D4
Drew, Davon (1)	TE	6-4	255	12/9/85	East Carolina	New Bern, N.C.	D5b-'09
Kindle, Sergio (1)	OLB	6-3	250	9/20/87	Texas	Dallas, Texas	D2a-'10
McClellan, Albert (1)	OLB	6-2	255	6/4/86	Marshall	Lakeland, Fla.	FA-'10
McPhee, Pernell	DE	6-3	280	12/17/88	Mississippi State	Pahokee, Fla.	D5b
Ramsey, Andre (1)	T	6-5	322	7/24/87	Ball State	Cordele, Ga.	FA-'10
Reid, Jah	T	6-7	330	7/21/88	Central Florida	Haines City, Fla.	D3
Smith, Jimmy	CB	6-2	210	7/26/88	Colorado	Colton, Calif.	D1
Smith, Torrey	WR	6-0	205	1/26/89	Maryland	Falmouth, Va.	D2
Steele, Curtis (1)	RB	6-0	200	3/24/87	Memphis	Franklin, Tenn.	FA-'10
Taylor, Tyrod	QB	6-1	217	8/3/89	Virginia Tech	Hampton, Va.	D6
Vanden Heuvel, Eric	T	6-7	303	6/15/87	Wisconsin	Hudson, Wisc.	FA

The term NFL Rookie is defined as a player who is in his first season of professional football and has not been on the roster of another professional football team for any regular-season or postseason games. A Rookie is designated by an "R" on NFL rosters. Players who have been active in another professional football league or players who have NFL experience, including either preseason training camp or being on an Active List or Inactive List, or on Reserve/Injured or Reserve/Physically Unable to Perform for fewer than six regular-season games, are termed NFL First-Year Players. An NFL First-Year Player is designated by a "1" on NFL rosters. Thereafter, a player is credited with an additional year of experience for each season in which he accumulates six games on the Active List or Inactive List, or on Reserve/Injured or Reserve/Physically Unable to Perform.

Log on to www.baltimoreravens.com for an up-to-date roster.

COACHING STAFF

Head Coach,
John Harbaugh

Pro Career: John Harbaugh was hired as the third head coach in Baltimore Ravens history on January 19, 2008. In three full seasons, Baltimore earned three consecutive postseason appearances for the first time. In 2010, after compiling a 12-4 regular season mark, Harbaugh became the first coach in NFL history to win a playoff game in each of his first three seasons when the Ravens captured a Wild Card win at Kansas City. With that victory, Baltimore also became the only team to win at least one playoff game in each of the past three seasons. During the 2009 campaign, Harbaugh's Ravens posted a 9-7 regular season record prior to earning a Wild Card victory at New England. In 2008, his initial campaign with the team, Harbaugh led Baltimore to an 11-5 record and a berth in the AFC Championship game. Baltimore set an NFL record that season for most total wins (13) by a team with both a rookie head coach and a rookie starting quarterback (Joe Flacco). Under Harbaugh, the Ravens' three playoff defeats have all come at the hands of teams that represented the AFC in each season's respective Super Bowl. Harbaugh spent his first 10 NFL seasons (1998-2007) with the Philadelphia Eagles. He was the team's secondary coach in 2007, after nine seasons as its special teams coordinator. Following the 2001 campaign, he was voted the NFL's Special Teams Coach of the Year by his coaching peers. Harbaugh was also named *The Dallas Morning News* Special Teams Coach of the Year that season. Career record: 36-19.

Background: Played defensive back at Miami (Ohio) from 1980-83, earned degree in political science. Coached collegiately at Western Michigan (1984-86), Pittsburgh (1987), Morehead State (1988), Cincinnati (1989-1996), and Indiana (1997).

Personal: Born in Perrysburg, Ohio on September 23, 1962, Harbaugh and his wife, Ingrid, have a daughter, Alison. He is the son of longtime college coach Jack Harbaugh, and his brother, Jim, the current 49ers head coach, played for the Ravens in 1998. John's brother-in-law, Tom Crean, Indiana University's basketball coach, is married to his sister, Joani.

ASSISTANT COACHES

Roy Anderson, defensive assistant/secondary; born October 5, 1979, Tallahassee, Fla. Quarterback Howard 1997-2001. No pro playing experience. Pro coach: Joined Ravens in 2009.

Teryl Austin, secondary; born March 3, 1965, Sharon, Pa. Defensive back Pittsburgh 1984-87. Pro defensive back Montreal Machine (WLAF) 1991. College coach: Penn State 1991-92, Wake Forest 1993-95, Syracuse 1996-98, Michigan

1999-2002, Florida 2010. Pro coach: Seattle Seahawks 2003-06, Arizona Cardinals 2007-09, joined Ravens in 2011.

Clarence Brooks, defensive line; born May 20, 1951, New York, N.Y. Guard Massachusetts 1970-73. No pro playing experience. College coach: Massachusetts 1976-1980, Syracuse 1981-89, Arizona 1990-92. Pro coach: Chicago Bears 1993-98, Cleveland Browns 1999, Miami Dolphins 2000-04, joined Ravens in 2005.

Jason Brooks, offensive quality control; born Jan. 19, 1978, Amherst, Mass. Attended Middle Tennessee State 2005-06. College coach: Middle Tennessee State 2006, Massachusetts 2007, Norwich 2008. Pro coach: Miami Dolphins 2007, joined Ravens in 2009.

Cam Cameron, offensive coordinator; born February 6, 1961, Chapel Hill, N.C. Quarterback Indiana 1980-83. No pro playing experience. College coach: Michigan 1984-1993, Indiana 1997-2001 (head coach). Pro coach: Washington Redskins 1994-96, San Diego Chargers 2002-06, Miami Dolphins 2007 (head coach), joined Ravens in 2008.

John Dunn, asst. strength and conditioning; born July 22, 1965, Great Barrington, Mass. Guard Penn State 1974-77. No pro playing experience. College coach: Penn State 1978. Pro coach: Washington Redskins 1984-86, Los Angeles Raiders 1987-89, San Diego Chargers 1990-96, New York Giants 1997-2003, Washington Redskins 2004-05, joined Ravens in 2008.

Wade Harman, tight ends; born October 1, 1963, Corydon, Iowa. Linebacker Drake 1985, Utah State 1986. No pro playing experience. College coach: Utah State 1987-1991, Pacific 1992-95, Morningside 1996. Pro coach: Minnesota Vikings 1997-98, joined Ravens in 1999.

Jim Hostler, wide receivers; born November 11, 1966, Pittsburgh. Defensive back Indiana (Pa.) 1986-89. No pro playing experience. College coach: Indiana (Pa.) 1990-92, 1994-99, Juniata (Pa.) 1993. Pro coach: Kansas City Chiefs 2000, New Orleans Saints 2001-02, New York Jets 2003-04, San Francisco 49ers 2005-07, joined Ravens in 2008.

Marwan Maalouf, asst. special teams; born November 26, 1976, Beirut, Lebanon. Guard Baldwin-Wallace 1997-99. No pro playing experience. College coach: Baldwin-Wallace 2000, Fordham 2001, Rutgers 2002-03. Pro coach: Cleveland Browns 2004-06, joined Ravens in 2008.

Andy Moeller, offensive line; June 15, 1964, Grand Rapids, Mich. Linebacker Michigan 1983-86. No pro playing experience. College coach: Indiana 1987, Army 1988-1993, Missouri 1994-99, Michigan 2000-07. Pro coach: joined Ravens in 2008.

Ted Monachino, outside linebackers; born October 15, 1966, Council Bluffs, Iowa. Defensive lineman Missouri 1988-1990. No pro playing experience. College coach: Texas Christian 1996-97, James Madison

1998, Southwest Missouri State 1999, Boise State 2000, Arizona State 2001-05. Pro coach: Jacksonville Jaguars 2006-09, joined Ravens in 2010.

Wilbert Montgomery, running backs; born September 16, 1954, Greenville, Miss. Running back Abilene Christian 1973-76. Pro running back Philadelphia Eagles 1977-1984, Detroit Lions 1985. Pro Coach: St. Louis Rams 1997-2005, Detroit Lions 2006-07, joined Ravens in 2008.

Chuck Pagano, defensive coordinator; born October 2, 1960, Boulder, Colo. Safety Wyoming 1980-83. No pro playing experience. College coach: Southern California 1984-85, Miami 1986, Boise State 1987-88, East Carolina 1989, Nevada-Las Vegas 1990-91, East Carolina 1992-94, Miami 1995-2000, North Carolina 2007. Pro coach: Cleveland Browns 2001-04, Oakland Raiders 2005-06, joined Ravens in 2008.

Dean Pees, linebackers; born September 4, 1949, Dunkirk, Ohio. Attended Bowling Green State. No college or pro playing experience. College coach: Findlay 1979-1982, Miami (Ohio) 1983-86, Naval Academy 1987-89, Toledo 1990-93, Notre Dame 1994, Michigan State 1995-97, Kent State 1998-2003. Pro coach: New England Patriots 2004-09, joined Ravens in 2010.

Bob Rogucki, strength and conditioning; born September 27, 1953, Clarksburg, W.Va. No college or pro playing experience. College coach: Penn State 1981, Weber State 1982, Army 1983-89. Pro coach: Arizona Cardinals 1990-2003, Jacksonville Jaguars 2004, Philadelphia Eagles 2006-07, joined Ravens in 2008.

Jerry Rosburg, special teams coordinator/asst. head coach; born November 24, 1955, Fairmont, Minn. Linebacker North Dakota State 1974-77. No pro playing experience. College coach: Northern Michigan 1981-86, Western Michigan 1987-1991, Cincinnati 1992-95, Minnesota 1996, Boston College 1997-98, Notre Dame 1999-2000. Pro coach: Cleveland Browns 2001-06, Atlanta Falcons 2007, joined Ravens in 2008.

Craig Ver Steeg, offensive assistant/quarterbacks; born September 11, 1960, Inglewood, Calif. No college or pro playing experience. College coach: Southern California 1984-85, Utah 1986-89, Cincinnati 1990-93, Harvard 1994-95, Illinois 1998-2000, Utah 2001-02, Rutgers 2003-07. Pro coach: Chicago Bears 1996-97, joined Ravens in 2008.

Todd Washington, asst. offensive line; born July 19, 1976, Nassawadox, Va. Guard/center Virginia Tech 1993-97. Pro guard/center Tampa Bay 1998-2002, Houston 2003-05. College coach: San Diego 2007-09. Pro coach: Hartford Colonials (UFL) 2010, joined Ravens in 2011.

Matt Weiss, head coach's assistant; born March 1, 1983, New Haven, Conn. Punter Vanderbilt 2001-02. No pro playing experience. College coach: Stanford 2008. Pro coach: Joined Ravens in 2009.

**American Football Conference
East Division
Team Colors:** Dark Navy, Red, Royal,
and Nickel

**One Bills Drive
Orchard Park, New York 14127-2296
Telephone:** (716) 648-1800

2011 SCHEDULE
PRESEASON

Aug. 13	at Chicago	8:00
Aug. 20	at Denver	8:30
Aug. 27	**Jacksonville**	7:00
Sep. 1	**Detroit**	7:30

REGULAR SEASON

Sep. 11	at Kansas City	1:00
Sep. 18	**Oakland**	1:00
Sep. 25	**New England**	1:00
Oct. 2	at Cincinnati	1:00
Oct. 9	**Philadelphia**	1:00
Oct. 16	at New York Giants	1:00
Oct. 23	BYE	
Oct. 30	**Washington** (Toronto)	4:05
Nov. 6	**New York Jets**	1:00
Nov. 13	at Dallas	1:00
Nov. 20	at Miami	1:00
Nov. 27	at New York Jets	1:00
Dec. 4	**Tennessee**	1:00
Dec. 11	at San Diego	4:15
Dec. 18	**Miami**	1:00
Dec. 24	**Denver** (Sat)	1:00
Jan. 1	at New England	1:00

All times ET

Stadium: Ralph Wilson Stadium
(opened in 1973)
• **Capacity:** 73,967
One Bills Drive
Orchard Park, New York
14127-2296
Playing Surface: A-Turf Titan
Training Camp: St. John Fisher College
Rochester, N.Y. 14618

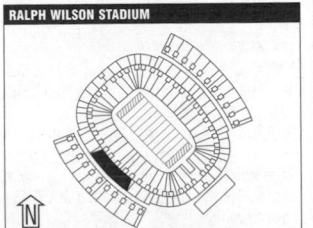

RALPH WILSON STADIUM

CLUB OFFICIALS
Owner and President:
Ralph C. Wilson, Jr.
Chief Executive Officer: Russ Brandon
Treasurer: Jeffrey C. Littmann
Executive Vice President/
General Manager: Buddy Nix
Executive Vice President of Strategic
Planning: Mary Owen
Senior Vice President of
Communications: Scott Berchtold
Senior Vice President of Marketing and
Broadcasting: Marc Honan
Senior Vice President of Government
Relations and External Affairs:
Bill Munson
Senior Vice President of Football
Administration: Jim Overdorf
Senior Vice President of Business
Development: Bruce Popko
Senior Vice President of Business
Operations: Dave Wheat
Vice President of Community Relations:
Gretchen Geltter
Consultant: Christy Wilson Hofmann
Assistant General Manager/Director of
Player Personnel: Doug Whaley
Director of Pro Personnel: Tom Gibbons
Director of College Scouting: Chuck Cook
Executive Director of Information
Technology: Dan Evans
Director of Security: Chris Clark
Director of Stadium Operations: Perry Dix
Director of Merchandise: Tim Kehoe
Director of Player Programs:
Paul Lancaster
Controller: Frank Wojnicki
Equipment Manager: Dave Hojnowski,
Jeff Mazurek
Assistant Equipment Managers:
Randy Ribbeck, Spencer Haws
Head Athletic Trainer: Bud Carpenter
Athletic Trainers: Chris Fischetti,
Shone Gipson, Greg McMillen
Video Director: Greg Estes
Video System Analyst: Wes Burnard
Video Assistant: Dexter Carlo
Coordinator of College Scouting:
Doug Majeski
Scouts: Brian Fisher, Brad Forsyth,
Matt Hand, Shawn Heilen,
CJ Leak (BLESTO), Darrell Moody,
Tom Roth, (emeritus) David G. Smith,
(emeritus) David W. Smith

COACHING HISTORY
(372-421-8)
Records include postseason games

1960-61	Buster Ramsey	11-16-1
1962-65	Lou Saban	38-18-3
1966-68	Joe Collier*	13-17-1
1968	Harvey Johnson	1-10-1
1969-1970	John Rauch	7-20-1
1971	Harvey Johnson	1-13-0
1972-76	Lou Saban**	32-29-1
1976-77	Jim Ringo	3-20-0
1978-1982	Chuck Knox	38-38-0
1983-85	Kay Stephenson***	10-26-0
1985-86	Hank Bullough****	4-17-0
1986-1997	Marv Levy	123-78-0
1998-2000	Wade Phillips	29-21-0
2001-03	Gregg Williams	17-31-0
2004-05	Mike Mularkey	14-18-0
2006-09	Dick Jauron#	24-33-0
2009	Perry Fewell	3-4-0
2010	Chan Gailey	4-12-0

*Released after two games in 1968
**Resigned after five games in 1976
***Released after four games in 1985
****Released after nine games in 1986
#Released after nine games in 2009

PAID ATTENDANCE
Home 473,253   Away 528,229
Total 1,001,482
Single-game home record,
80,368 (10/4/92)
Single-season home record,
635,889 (1991)

2011 DRAFT CHOICES

Round	Name	Pos.	College
1	Marcell Dareus	DT	Alabama
2	Aaron Williams	DB	Texas
3	Kelvin Sheppard	LB	Louisiana State
4	Da'Norris Searcy	DB	North Carolina
	Chris Hairston	T	Clemson
5	Johnny White	RB	North Carolina
6	Chris White	LB	Mississippi St.
7	Justin Rogers	DB	Richmond
	Michael Jasper	DT	Bethel (TN)

2010 TEAM RECORD

PRESEASON (2-2)

Date	Result	Opponent
8/13	L 17-42	at Washington
8/19	W 34-21	Indianapolis
8/28	W 35-20	Cincinnati
9/2	L 23-28	at Detroit

REGULAR SEASON (4-12)

Date	Result	Opponent
9/12	L 10-15	Miami
9/19	L 7-34	at Green Bay
9/26	L 30-38	at New England
10/3	L 14-38	New York Jets
10/10	L 26-36	Jacksonville
10/24	L 34-37	at Baltimore (OT)
10/31	L 10-13	at Kansas City (OT)
11/7	L 19-22	Chicago
11/14	W 14-12	Detroit
11/21	W 49-31	at Cincinnati
11/28	L 16-19	Pittsburgh (OT)
12/5	L 14-38	at Minnesota
12/12	W 13-6	Cleveland
12/19	W 17-14	at Miami
12/26	L 3-34	New England
1/2	L 7-38	at New York Jets

(OT) Overtime

SCORE BY PERIODS

Bills	40	88	65	90	0 —	283
Opponents	70	166	98	82	9 —	425

2010 TEAM STATISTICS

	Bills	Opp.
Total First Downs	263	335
Rushing	82	138
Passing	166	179
Penalty	15	18
3rd Down: Made/Att	80/211	98/227
3rd Down Pct.	37.9	43.2
4th Down: Made/Att	11/24	7/10
4th Down Pct.	45.8	70.0
Possession Avg.	27:40	32:20
Total Net Yards	4878	5786
Avg. Per Game	304.9	361.6
Total Plays	954	1071
Avg. Per Play	5.1	5.4
Net Yards Rushing	1720	2714
Avg. Per Game	107.5	169.6
Total Rushes	401	571
Net Yards Passing	3158	3072
Avg. Per Game	197.4	192.0
Sacked/Yards Lost	34/213	27/181
Gross Yards	3371	3253
Att./Completions	519/296	473/294
Completion Pct.	57.0	62.2
Had Intercepted	21	11
Punts/Average	75/42.4	71/42.1
Net Punting Avg.	75/36.6	71/35.6
Penalties/Yards	82/633	85/634
Fumbles/Ball Lost	33/18	20/11
Touchdowns	34	48
Rushing	6	18
Passing	24	28
Returns	4	2

2010 INDIVIDUAL STATISTICS

PASSING

	Att.	Comp.	Yds.	Pct.	TD	Int.	Tkld.	Rate
Fitzpatrick	441	255	3000	57.8	23	15	24/145	81.8
T. Edwards	52	29	241	55.8	1	2	7/63	58.3
Brohm	23	10	106	43.5	0	3	3/5	17.9
Levi Brown	3	2	24	66.7	0	1	0/0	51.4
Bills	519	296	3371	57.0	24	21	34/213	75.2
Opponents	473	294	3253	62.2	28	11	27/181	92.6

SCORING

	TD R	TD P	TD Rt	PAT	FG	Saf	PTS
Lindell	0	0	0	31/32	16/21	0	79
St. Johnson	0	10	0	0/0	0/0	0	60
F. Jackson	5	2	0	0/0	0/0	0	42
Evans	0	4	0	0/0	0/0	0	24
D. Nelson	0	3	0	0/0	0/0	0	18
Florence	0	0	2	0/0	0/0	0	12
Parrish	0	2	0	0/0	0/0	0	12
Spiller	0	1	1	0/0	0/0	0	12
Byrd	0	0	1	0/0	0/0	0	6
Jones	0	1	0	0/0	0/0	0	6
Martin	0	1	0	0/0	0/0	0	6
McIntyre	1	0	0	0/0	0/0	0	6
Bills	6	24	4	31/32	16/21	0	283
Opponents	18	28	2	46/46	29/39	1	425

2-Pt Conversions: Bills 0-2, Opponents 1-2.

RUSHING

	No.	Yds	Avg	LG	TD
F. Jackson	222	927	4.2	39	5
Spiller	74	283	3.8	20	0
Fitzpatrick	40	269	6.7	22	0
Lynch	37	164	4.4	17	0
T. Edwards	5	24	4.8	8	0
Parrish	3	23	7.7	13	0
Ganther	9	18	2.0	11	0
McIntyre	4	5	1.3	2	1
Roosevelt	1	3	3.0	3	0
Caulcrick	1	2	2.0	2	0
Jones	3	1	0.3	2	0
Moorman	2	1	0.5	1	0
Bills	401	1720	4.3	39	6
Opponents	571	2714	4.8	43t	18

RECEIVING

	No.	Yds	Avg	LG	TD
St. Johnson	82	1073	13.1	45	10
Evans	37	578	15.6	54	4
Parrish	33	400	12.1	37	2
D. Nelson	31	353	11.4	37	3
F. Jackson	31	215	6.9	65t	2
Spiller	24	157	6.5	41	1
Jones	18	213	11.8	40	1
Stupar	12	111	9.3	35	0
Roosevelt	9	139	15.4	30	0
Martin	7	43	6.1	15	1
McIntyre	4	32	8.0	14	0
S. Nelson	3	25	8.3	12	0
Ganther	2	9	4.5	8	0
Chandler	1	8	8.0	8	0
Hubbard	1	8	8.0	8	0
Lynch	1	7	7.0	7	0
Bills	296	3371	11.4	65t	24
Opponents	294	3253	11.1	52t	28

INTERCEPTIONS

	No.	Yds	Avg	LG	TD
Florence	3	42	14.0	40t	1
Wilson	2	65	32.5	56	0
McKelvin	2	10	5.0	10	0
Byrd	1	37	37.0	37t	1
Whitner	1	37	37.0	37	0
Davis	1	11	11.0	11	0
D. Edwards	1	8	8.0	8	0
Bills	11	210	19.1	56	2
Opponents	21	330	15.7	41	2

PUNTING

	No.	Yds.	Avg.	In 20	LG
Moorman	75	3181	42.4	17	61
Bills	75	3181	42.4	17	61
Opponents	71	2986	42.1	24	62

PUNT RETURNS

	Ret	FC	Yds	Avg	LG	TD
Parrish	12	7	131	10.9	33	0
Spiller	12	8	175	14.6	34	0
McKelvin	6	3	24	4.0	25	0
Florence	1	0	6	6.0	6	0
Scott	1	0	0	0.0	0	0
Bills	32	18	336	10.5	34	0
Opponents	32	17	299	9.3	25	0

KICKOFF RETURNS

	No.	Yds	Avg	LG	TD
Spiller	44	1014	23.0	95t	1
McKelvin	14	265	18.9	49	0
Jones	6	120	20.0	31	0
Roosevelt	2	31	15.5	16	0
Caulcrick	2	28	14.0	17	0
Ellis	1	0	0.0	0	0
Bills	69	1458	21.1	95t	1
Opponents	57	1238	21.7	51	0

FIELD GOALS

	1-19	20-29	30-39	40-49	50+
Lindell	1/1	6/6	5/6	2/3	2/5
Bills	1/1	6/6	5/6	2/3	2/5
Opponents	3/3	6/6	6/8	14/20	0/2

SACKS

	No.
K. Williams	5.5
Kelsay	3.5
Scott	3.0
Stroud	3.0
Moats	2.5
Sp. Johnson	2.0
Posluszny	2.0
Byrd	1.0
Carrington	1.0
Corner	1.0
D. Edwards	1.0
Ellis	1.0
Whitner	0.5
Bills	27.0
Opponents	34.0

RECORD HOLDERS
INDIVIDUAL RECORDS—CAREER

Category	Name	Performance
Rushing (Yds.)	Thurman Thomas, 1988-1999	11,938
Passing (Yds.)	Jim Kelly, 1986-1996	35,467
Passing (TDs)	Jim Kelly, 1986-1996	237
Receiving (No.)	Andre Reed, 1985-1999	941
Receiving (Yds.)	Andre Reed, 1985-1999	13,095
Interceptions	George (Butch) Byrd, 1964-1970	40
Punting (Avg.)	Brian Moorman, 2001-2010	43.5
Punt Return (Avg.)	Roscoe Parrish, 2005-2010	12.1
Kickoff Return (Avg.)	O.J. Simpson, 1969-1977	30.0
Field Goals	Steve Christie, 1992-2000	234
Touchdowns (Tot.)	Andre Reed, 1985-1999	87
	Thurman Thomas, 1988-1999	87
Points	Steve Christie, 1992-2000	1,011
*Sacks	Bruce Smith, 1985-1999	**171.0

INDIVIDUAL RECORDS—SINGLE SEASON

Category	Name	Performance
Rushing (Yds.)	O.J. Simpson, 1973	2,003
Passing (Yds.)	Drew Bledsoe, 2002	4,359
Passing (TDs)	Jim Kelly, 1991	33
Receiving (No.)	Eric Moulds, 2002	100
Receiving (Yds.)	Eric Moulds, 1998	1,368
Interceptions	Billy Atkins, 1961	10
	Tom Janik, 1967	10
Punting (Avg.)	Brian Moorman, 2009	46.6
Punt Return (Avg.)	Roscoe Parrish, 2007	16.3
Kickoff Return (Avg.)	Terrence McGee, 2005	30.24
Field Goals	Steve Christie, 1998	33
Touchdowns (Tot.)	O.J. Simpson, 1975	23
Points	Steve Christie, 1998	140
*Sacks	Bruce Smith, 1990	19.0

INDIVIDUAL RECORDS—SINGLE GAME

Category	Name	Performance
Rushing (Yds.)	O.J. Simpson, 11-25-76	273
Passing (Yds.)	Drew Bledsoe, 9-15-02	463
Passing (TDs)	Jim Kelly, 9-8-91	6
Receiving (No.)	Andre Reed, 11-20-94	15
Receiving (Yds.)	Lee Evans, 11-19-06	265
Interceptions	Many times	3
	Last time by Nate Clements, 10-20-02	
Field Goals	Steve Christie, 10-20-96	6
Touchdowns (Tot.)	Cookie Gilchrist, 12-8-63	5
Points	Cookie Gilchrist, 12-8-63	30
*Sacks	Cornelius Bennett, 12-27-87	4.0
	Bruce Smith, 12-9-90, 9-18-94	4.0

*Sacks became an official statistic in 1982.
**NFL Record

VETERAN ROSTER AS OF MARCH 3, 2011

No.	Name	Pos.	Ht.	Wt.	Birthdate	^NFL Exp.	College	Hometown	How Acq.	'10 Games/ Starts
50	Ayodele, Akin	LB	6-2	255	9/17/79	10	Purdue	Irving, Texas	FA-'10	15/10
77	Bell, Demetrius	T	6-5	307	5/3/84	3	Northwestern State	Summerfield, La.	D7a-'08	16/16
4	Brohm, Brian	QB	6-3	223	9/23/85	4	Louisville	Louisville, Ky.	FA-'09	1/1
31	Byrd, Jairus	FS	5-10	200	10/7/86	3	Oregon	Clayton, Mo.	D2a-'09	16/14
92	Carrington, Alex	DE	6-5	284	6/19/87	2	Arkansas State	Tupelo, Miss.	D3-'10	9/0
30	Caulcrick, Jehuu	RB	6-0	260	8/6/83	2	Michigan State	Findley Lake, N.Y.	FA-'10	2/0
84	Chandler, Scott	TE	6-7	272	7/23/85	3	Iowa	Bedford, Texas	FA-'10	4/1
59	Coleman, Antonio	LB	6-1	248	9/1/86	2	Auburn	Mobile, Ala.	FA-'10	8/0
27	Corner, Reggie	CB	5-9	175	11/17/83	4	Akron	Canton, Ohio	D4a-'08	16/2
33	Corto, Jon	SS	6-0	220	9/3/84	4	Sacred Heart	Orchard Park, N.Y.	FA-'08	11/0
54	Davis, Andra	LB	6-1	251	12/23/78	10	Florida	Live Oak, Fla.	FA-'10	6/4
98	Edwards, Dwan	DE	6-3	290	5/16/81	7	Oregon State	Columbus, Mont.	UFA(Balt)-'10	11/11
56	Ellison, Keith	LB	6-0	229	2/6/84	6	Oregon State	Redondo Beach, Calif.	D6-'06	8/2
83	Evans, Lee	WR	5-10	197	3/11/81	8	Wisconsin	Bedford, Ohio	D1a-'04	13/13
14	Fitzpatrick, Ryan	QB	6-2	225	11/24/82	7	Harvard	Gilbert, Ariz.	UFA(Cin)-'09	13/13
29	Florence, Drayton	CB	6-0	195	12/19/80	9	Tuskegee	Ocala, Fla.	FA-'09	16/16
25	Ganther, Quinton	RB	5-9	220	7/15/84	6	Utah	Richmond, Calif.	FA-'10	11/1*
63	Hangartner, Geoff	C	6-5	301	4/22/82	7	Texas A&M	New Braunfels, Texas	UFA(Car)-'09	12/12
68	Howard, Cordaro	G	6-4	314	7/2/87	2	Georgia Tech	Phoenix City, Ala.	FA-'10	10/4
17	Hubbard, Paul	WR	6-2	225	6/12/85	2	Wisconsin	Colorado Springs, Colo.	FA-'10	1/1
15	Huggins, Felton	WR	6-2	186	2/15/83	2	Southeastern Louisiana	Zachary, La.	FA-'10	0*
22	Jackson, Fred	RB	6-1	215	2/20/81	5	Coe College	Fort Worth, Texas	FA-'06	16/13
91	Johnson, Spencer	DE	6-3	286	12/12/81	8	Auburn	Silas, Ala.	UFA(Minn)-'08	14/6
13	Johnson, Stevie	WR	6-2	202	7/22/86	4	Kentucky	San Francisco, Calif.	D7b-'08	16/13
19	Jones, Donald	WR	6-0	214	12/17/87	2	Youngstown State	Plainfield, N.J.	FA-'10	15/5
90	Kelsay, Chris	LB	6-4	261	10/31/79	9	Nebraska	Auburn, Neb.	D2-'03	16/16
67	Levitre, Andy	G	6-2	305	5/15/86	3	Oregon State	Los Gatos, Calif.	D2b-'09	16/16
9	Lindell, Rian	K	6-3	233	1/20/77	12	Washington State	Vancouver, Wash.	FA-'03	16/0
80	Martin, David	TE	6-4	265	3/13/79	10	Tennessee	Norfolk, Va.	FA-'10	16/9
58	Maybin, Aaron	LB	6-4	250	4/6/88	3	Penn State	Ellicott City, Md.	D1a-'09	11/1
97	McCargo, John	DE	6-2	307	8/19/83	6	North Carolina State	Drakes Branch, Va.	D1b-'06	1/0
24	McGee, Terrence	CB	5-9	198	10/14/80	9	Northwestern State	Athens, Texas	D4a-'03	9/3
38	McIntyre, Corey	FB	6-0	245	1/25/79	7	West Virginia	Indiantown, Fla.	FA-'08	16/7
28	McKelvin, Leodis	CB	5-10	184	9/1/85	4	Troy	Waycross, Ga.	D1-'08	16/14
55	Merriman, Shawne	LB	6-4	265	5/25/84	7	Maryland	Washington, D.C.	FA-'10	3/1*
52	Moats, Arthur	LB	6-2	250	3/14/88	2	James Madison	Portsmouth, Va.	D6a-'10	15/4
8	Moorman, Brian	P	6-0	172	2/5/76	11	Pittsburg State	Sedgwick, Kan.	FA-'01	16/0
86	Nelson, David	WR	6-5	217	11/7/86	2	Florida	Wichita Falls, Texas	FA-'10	15/3
89	Nelson, Shawn	TE	6-5	240	10/5/85	3	Southern Mississippi	Gonzales, La.	D4-'09	5/1
11	Parrish, Roscoe	WR	5-9	178	7/16/82	7	Miami	Miami, Fla.	D2-'05	8/6
79	Pears, Erik	T	6-8	305	6/25/82	7	Colorado State	Price, Utah	FA-'10	2/1
51	Posluszny, Paul	LB	6-1	238	10/10/84	5	Penn State	Aliquippa, Pa.	D2-'07	14/14
76	Rinehart, Chad	G	6-5	307	5/4/85	4	Northern Iowa	Boone, Iowa	FA-'10	4/3
18	Roosevelt, Naaman	WR	6-0	189	12/24/87	2	Buffalo	Buffalo, N.Y.	FA-'10	6/1
65	Sanborn, Garrison	LS	6-1	253	7/31/85	3	Florida State	Tampa, Fla.	FA-'09	16/0
43	Scott, Bryan	SS	6-1	219	4/13/81	9	Penn State	Doylestown, Pa.	FA-'07	15/1
21	Spiller, C.J.	RB	5-11	196	8/5/87	2	Clemson	Lake Butler, Fla.	D1-'10	14/1
88	Stupar, Jonathan	TE	6-4	254	7/24/84	3	Virginia	State College, Pa.	FA-'09	16/3
53	Torbor, Reggie	LB	6-2	250	1/25/81	8	Auburn	Baton Rouge, La.	FA-'10	10/7
96	Troup, Torell	NT	6-3	315	6/23/88	2	Central Florida	Conyers, Ga.	D2-'10	15/2
60	Urbik, Kraig	G	6-5	323	9/23/85	2	Wisconsin	Hudson, Wisc.	FA-'10	10/2
71	Wang, Ed	T	6-5	301	3/12/87	2	Virginia Tech	Ashburn, Va.	D5-'10	6/0
20	Whitner, Donte	SS	5-10	208	7/24/85	6	Ohio State	Cleveland, Ohio	D1a-'06	16/16
95	Williams, Kyle	NT	6-1	306	6/10/83	6	Louisiana State	Ruston, La.	D5a-'06	16/16
37	Wilson, George	FS	6-0	212	3/14/81	6	Arkansas	Paducah, Ky.	FA-'04	16/2
70	Wood, Eric	G	6-4	315	3/18/86	3	Louisville	Cincinnati, Ohio	D1b-'09	14/14
61	Wrotto, Mansfield	OL	6-3	310	10/12/84	4	Georgia Tech	Snellville, Ga.	FA-'10	13/7*
26	Youboty, Ashton	CB	5-11	189	7/7/84	6	Ohio State	Klein, Texas	D3-'06	13/0

* Ganther played 3 games with Seattle and 8 games with Buffalo in '10; Huggins missed '10 season because of injury; Merriman played 3 games with San Diego; Wrotto played 2 games with Seattle and 11 games with Buffalo.

Also played with Bills in '10—RB Andre' Anderson (2 games), LB Mike Balogun (2), T Levi Brown (1), QB Trent Edwards (2), LB Chris Ellis (5), T Cornell Green (5), CB Cary Harris (2), DE Marcus Stroud (15).

Traded—RB Marshawn Lynch (4 games in '10) to Seattle.

^ "NFL Exp." as of 2011 Kickoff Weekend. For full explanation of how a player's NFL Experience is measured, refer to explanation underneath the First-Year Roster listed below.

FIRST-YEAR ROSTER

Name	Pos.	Ht.	Wt.	Birthdate	College	Hometown	How Acq.
Batten, Danny (1)	LB	6-4	250	12/8/87	South Dakota State	Gilbert, Ariz.	D6b-'10
Brown, Colin (1)	G	6-7	335	8/29/85	Missouri	Braymer, Mo.	FA-'10
Brown, Levi (1)	QB	6-4	225	3/11/87	Troy	Mt. Juliet, Tenn.	FA-'10
Caussin, Mike (1)	TE	6-5	252	2/26/87	James Madison	Springfield, Va.	FA-'10
Dareus, Marcell	DL	6-3	319	11/18/89	Alabama	Huffman, Ala.	D1
Easley, Marcus (1)	WR	6-2	207	11/2/87	Connecticut	Stratford, Conn.	D4-'10
Hairston, Chris	T	6-6	326	4/26/89	Clemson	Winston-Salem, N.C.	D4b
Heard, Kellen (1)	DT	6-6	355	10/17/85	Memphis	Wharton, Texas	FA-'10
Jasper, Michael	NT	6-4	394	10/8/86	Bethel	Mt. Juliet, Tenn.	D7b
Kirlew, Jammie (1)	LB	6-3	264	5/12/87	Indiana	Cypress Creek, Fla.	FA-'10
Rogers, Justin	DB	5-11	180	1/16/88	Richmond	Baton Rouge, La.	D7a
Searcy, Da'Norris	DB	5-11	223	11/16/88	North Carolina	Decatur, Ga.	D4a
Sheppard, Kelvin	LB	6-2	250	1/2/88	Louisiana State	Stone Mountain, Ga.	D3
Watkins, Jason (1)	T	6-6	325	6/10/85	Florida	New Orleans, La.	FA-'09
White, Chris	LB	6-3	240	1/15/89	Mississippi State	Vancleave, Miss.	D6
White, Johnny	RB	5-10	209	2/3/88	North Carolina	Asheville, N.C.	D5
Williams, Aaron	DB	6-0	204	4/23/90	Texas	Round Rock, Texas	D2

The term NFL Rookie is defined as a player who is in his first season of professional football and has not been on the roster of another professional football team for any regular-season or postseason games. A Rookie is designated by an "R" on NFL rosters. Players who have been active in another professional football league or players who have NFL experience, including either preseason training camp or being on an Active List or Inactive List, or on Reserve/Injured or Reserve/Physically Unable to Perform for fewer than six regular-season games, are termed NFL First-Year Players. An NFL First-Year Player is designated by a "1" on NFL rosters. Thereafter, a player is credited with an additional year of experience for each season in which he accumulates six games on the Active List or Inactive List, or on Reserve/Injured or Reserve/Physically Unable to Perform.

Log on to www.buffalobills.com for an up-to-date roster.

COACHING STAFF
Head Coach,
Chan Gailey

Pro Career: Gailey was named Buffalo's fifteenth head coach on January 19, 2010. Gailey has over three decades of coaching experience, including head coaching experience in college, World League and the NFL. Gailey served as head coach of the Dallas Cowboys from 1998-99, leading the Cowboys to playoff berths in each season. With the Cowboys, in 1998, Gailey became the first coach in NFC Eastern Division history to lead his team to a perfect 8-0 record in division play and a 10-6 overall record. In 1999, Gailey followed that with an 8-8 campaign and his second consecutive playoff appearance. Also has four stints as offensive coordinator in the NFL with Denver (1989-1990), Pittsburgh (1996-97), Miami (2000-01) and Kansas City (2008). Has spent 10 of his 16 NFL seasons as either a head coach or offensive coordinator. During those 10 seasons, his teams have made the playoffs seven times and boasted a 1,000-yard rusher on seven different occasions. In total, he has made playoff appearances in 11 of his 16 seasons in NFL coaching. Résumé also boasts four Super Bowl berths, including one with Pittsburgh (XXX) and three with Denver (XXI, XXII and XXIV). Posted 44-33 record as the head coach at Georgia Tech (2002-07), becoming the first coach in school history to lead the Yellow Jackets to bowl appearance in his first six seasons. Began his NFL career as an assistant with Denver (1985-1990). Career record: 22-28.
Background: Gailey was a three-year letter-winner at quarterback for Florida. He coached collegiately at Florida (1974-75), Troy State (1976-78), Air Force (1979-1982). Gailey was an all-state quarterback at Americus High School in Americus, Ga.
Personal: Born January 5, 1952, Gainesville, Ga. Chan and his wife, Laurie, have two sons, Tate and Andrew, and two grandsons.

ASSISTANT COACHES

Bob Bicknell, tight ends; born November, 13, 1969, Holliston, Mass. Tight end Boston College 1988-1991. No pro playing experience. College coach: Boston University 1993-97, Temple 2006. Pro coach: Frankfurt Galaxy (NFLE) 1998-99, Berlin Thunder 2000-03 (NFLE), Cologne Centurions (NFLE) 2004-05, Kansas City Chiefs 2007-09, joined Bills in 2010.
George Catavolos, defensive backs; born May 8, 1945, Chicago. Defensive back Purdue 1964-67. No pro playing experience. College coach: Purdue 1967-68, 1971-76, Middle Tennessee State 1969, Louisville 1970, Kentucky 1977-1981, Tennessee 1982-83. Pro coach: Indianapolis Colts 1984-1994, 1998-2001, Carolina Panthers 1995-97, Washington Redskins 2002-03, Detroit Lions 2004-05, joined Bills in 2006.
Eric Ciano, co-head strength and condi-

tioning; born August 8, 1973, Waltham, Mass. Offensive line Springfield (Mass.) College 1993-97. No pro playing experience. College coach: Tennessee 1997-99, Louisiana Tech 2000-02, Tennessee 2002-04, Georgia Tech 2005-09. Pro coach: Joined Bills in 2010.
George Cortez, quarterbacks; born February 11, 1951, Port Arthur, Texas. No college or pro playing experience. College coach: Rice 1979-1982, Lamar 1987-89, Southern Methodist 1995-96, California 2002-05. Pro coach: Montreal Alouettes (CFL) 1984-86, Ottawa Roughriders (CFL) 1990-91, Calgary Stampeders (CFL) 1992-94, 1997-2001, 2007-09, joined Bills in 2010.
Joe D'Alessandris, offensive line; born April, 29, 1954, Aliquippa, Pa. Guard Western Carolina 1972-76. No pro playing experience. College coach: Western Carolina 1977-78, Livingston 1979-1983, Memphis 1984-85, Tennessee-Chattanooga 1986-89, Samford 1993, Texas A&M 1994, Pittsburgh 1996, Duke 1997-2001, Georgia Tech 2002-07. Pro coach: Ottawa Rough Riders (CFL) 1990, Birmingham Fire (WLAF) 1991-92, Memphis (AFL) 1995, Kansas City Chiefs 2008-09, joined Bills in 2010.
Daryl Daye, asst. to the head coach; born February 1, 1963, Las Cruces, N.M. Linebacker Louisiana State 1981-85. No pro playing experience. College coach: Louisiana State 1986-88, Southern Mississippi 1989-1990, Liberty 1991-98, Nicholls State 1999-2003, Louisiana State 2004, Southern 2005, Missouri Southern State 2006-09. Pro coach: Joined Bills in 2010.
Bruce DeHaven, special teams coordinator; born September 6, 1948, Trousdale, Kan. Attended Southwestern (Kan.) College. No college or pro playing experience. College coach: Kansas 1979-1981, New Mexico State 1982. Pro coach: New Jersey Generals (USFL) 1983, Pittsburgh Maulers (USFL) 1984, Orlando Renegades (USFL) 1985, Buffalo Bills 1987-1999, San Francisco 49ers 2000-02, Dallas Cowboys 2003-06, Seattle Seahawks 2007-09, re-joined Bills in 2010.
George Edwards, defensive coordinator; born January 16, 1967, Siler City, N.C. Linebacker Duke 1985-89. No pro playing experience. College coach: Florida 1990-91, Appalachian State 1992-95, Duke 1996, Georgia 1997. Pro coach: Dallas Cowboys 1998-2001, Washington Redskins 2002-03, Cleveland Browns 2004, Miami Dolphins 2005-09, joined Bills in 2010.
John Gamble, co-head strength and conditioning; born June 26, 1957, Richmond, Va. Linebacker Hampton 1975-78. No pro playing experience. College coach: Virginia 1982-1993. Pro coach: Miami Dolphins 1994-2005, joined Bills in 2010.
Stan Hixon, wide receivers; born July 24, 1957, Lakeland, Fla. Wide receiver Iowa State 1975-78. No pro playing experience. College coach: Morehead State 1980-82, Appalachian State 1983-88, South Carolina

1989-1992, Wake Forest 1993-94, Georgia Tech 1995-99, Louisiana State 2000-03. Pro coach: Washington Redskins 2004-09, joined Bills in 2010.
Bobby Johnson, asst. offensive line; born February 28, 1963, Akron, Ohio. Offensive line Miami (Ohio) 1992-94. No pro playing experience. College coach: Akron 1995-98, Miami (Ohio) 1999-2004, Indiana 2005-09. Pro coach: Joined Bills in 2010.
Stan Kwan, asst. special teams; born November 2, 1967, Phoenix. Attended South Mountain (Ariz.) C.C., San Diego State. No college or pro playing experience. Pro coach: San Diego Chargers 1991-96, Detroit Lions 1997-2000, Arizona Cardinals 2001-03, Detroit Lions 2004-09, joined Bills in 2010.
Curtis Modkins, offensive coordinator/running backs; born November 15, 1970, Marlin, Texas. Running back Texas Christian 1989-1992. No pro playing experience. College coach: Texas Christian 1995-97, New Mexico 1998-2001, Georgia Tech 2002-07. Pro coach: Kansas City Chiefs 2008, Arizona Cardinals 2009, joined Bills in 2010.
Kevin Patullo, offensive quality control; born July 14, 1981, Hillsborough, N.J. Quarterback/wide receiver South Florida 1999-2001. College coach: South Florida 2002-03, Arizona 2004-06. Pro coach: Kansas City Chiefs 2007-2008, joined Bills in 2010.
Bob Sanders, outside linebackers; born December 5, 1953, Jacksonville, N.C. Linebacker Davidson College 1973-75. No pro playing experience. College coach: Georgia Tech 1978, East Carolina 1980-82, Richmond 1983-84, Duke 1985-89, Florida 1990-2000. Pro coach: Miami Dolphins 2001-04, Green Bay Packers 2005-08, joined Bills in 2009.
Giff Smith, defensive line; born October 23, 1968, Atlanta. Defensive end Georgia Southern 1986-1990. No pro playing experience. Attended College coach: Arkansas 1991-93, Georgia 1994-1995, Georgia Southern 1996-98, Tulane 1999-2003, Georgia Tech 2004-09. Pro coach: Joined Bills in 2010.
Dave Wannstedt, asst. head coach/inside linebackers; born May, 21, 1952, Baldwin, Pa. Tackle Pittsburgh 1970-73. No pro playing experience. College coach: Pittsburgh 1975-78, 2005-2010 (head coach 2005-2010), Oklahoma State 1979-1982, Southern California 1983-85, Miami 1986-88. Pro coach: Dallas Cowboys 1989-1992, Chicago Bears 1993-98 (head coach), Miami Dolphins 1999-2004 (head coach 2000-04), joined Bills in 2011.
Adrian White, defensive quality control; born April 6, 1964, Orange Park, Fla. Defensive back Southern Illinois 1983, Florida 1985-86. Pro defensive back: N.Y. Giants 1987-1991, Green Bay Packers 1992, New England Patriots 1993. Pro coach: Rhein Fire (NFLE) 2001-07, joined Bills in 2008.

**American Football Conference
North Division
Team Colors:** Black, Orange, and White
**One Paul Brown Stadium
Cincinnati, Ohio 45202-3492
Telephone:** (513) 621-3550
Ticket Office (513) 621-TDTD (8383)

2011 SCHEDULE
PRESEASON
Aug. 12	at Detroit	7:30
Aug. 21	at New York Jets	7:00
Aug. 25	**Carolina**	7:00
Sep. 1	**Indianapolis**	7:00

REGULAR SEASON
Sep. 11	at Cleveland	1:00
Sep. 18	at Denver	4:15
Sep. 25	**San Francisco**	1:00
Oct. 2	**Buffalo**	1:00
Oct. 9	at Jacksonville	1:00
Oct. 16	**Indianapolis**	1:00
Oct. 23	BYE	
Oct. 30	at Seattle	4:15
Nov. 6	at Tennessee	4:05
Nov. 13	**Pittsburgh**	1:00
Nov. 20	at Baltimore	1:00
Nov. 27	**Cleveland**	1:00
Dec. 4	at Pittsburgh	1:00
Dec. 11	**Houston**	1:00
Dec. 18	at St. Louis	1:00
Dec. 24	**Arizona** (Sat)	1:00
Jan. 1	**Baltimore**	1:00

*All times ET

Stadium: Paul Brown Stadium
(opened in 2000)
• **Capacity:** 65,515
One Paul Brown Stadium
Cincinnati, Ohio 45202-3492
Playing Surface: Synthetic
Training Camp: Georgetown College
Georgetown, KY 40324

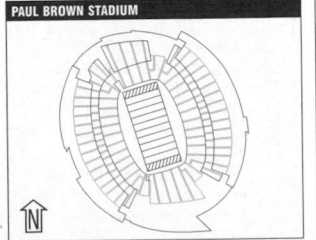

PAUL BROWN STADIUM

CLUB OFFICIALS
President: Mike Brown
Senior Vice President: Pete Brown
Executive Vice President: Katie Blackburn
Vice President: Paul Brown
Vice President: John Sawyer
Vice President: Troy Blackburn
Business Manager: Bill Connelly
Chief Financial Officer: Bill Scanlon
Director of Business Development:
  Bob Bedinghaus
Managing Director of Paul Brown
  Stadium: Eric Brown
Directors of Technology: Michael Kayes,
  Jo Ann Ralstin
Bengals.com Editor: Geoff Hobson
Director of Security: Rusty Guy
Director of Sales and Public Affairs:
  Jeff Berding
Director of Corporate Sales and
  Marketing: TBD
Ticket Manager: Tim Kelly
Director of Player Relations: Eric Ball
Director of Football Operations:
  Jim Lippincott
Director of Player Personnel: Duke Tobin
Public Relations Director: Jack Brennan
Athletic Trainer: Paul Sparling
Equipment Manager: Jeff Brickner
Video Director: Travis Brammer

COACHING HISTORY
(291-381-2)
Records include postseason games
1968-1975	Paul Brown	55-59-1
1976-78	Bill Johnson*	18-15-0
1978-79	Homer Rice	8-19-0
1980-83	Forrest Gregg	34-27-0
1984-1991	Sam Wyche	64-68-0
1992-96	Dave Shula**	19-52-0
1996-2000	Bruce Coslet***	21-39-0
2000-02	Dick LeBeau	12-33-0
2003-2010	Marvin Lewis	60-69-1

  * Resigned after five games in 1978
 ** Released after seven games in 1996
*** Resigned after three games in 2000

PAID ATTENDANCE
Home 467,577   Away 541,917
Total 1,009,494
Single-game home record,
  66,188 (10/28/07)
Single-season home record, 516,154
  (2006)

2011 DRAFT CHOICES
Round	Name	Pos.	College
1	A.J. Green	WR	Georgia
2	Andy Dalton	QB	Texas Christian
3	Dontay Moch	LB	Nevada
4	Clint Boling	G	Georgia
5	Robert Sands	DB	West Virginia
6	Ryan Whalen	WR	Stanford
7	Korey Lindsey	DB	Southern Illinois
	Jay Finley	RB	Baylor

2010 TEAM RECORD
PRESEASON (3-2)

Date	Result	Opponent
8/8	L 7-16	vs Dallas
		in Canton, OH
8/18	W 33-24	Denver
8/20	W 22-9	Philadelphia
8/28	L 20-35	at Buffalo
9/2	W 30-28	at Indianapolis

REGULAR SEASON (4-12)

Date	Result	Opponent
9/12	L 24-38	at New England
9/19	W 15-10	Baltimore
9/26	W 20-7	at Carolina
10/3	L 20-23	at Cleveland
10/10	L 21-24	Tampa Bay
10/24	L 32-39	at Atlanta
10/31	L 14-22	Miami
11/8	L 21-27	Pittsburgh
11/14	L 17-23	at Indianapolis
11/21	L 31-49	Buffalo
11/25	L 10-26	at New York Jets
12/5	L 30-34	New Orleans
12/12	L 7-23	at Pittsburgh
12/19	W 19-17	Cleveland
12/26	W 34-20	San Diego
1/2	L 7-13	at Baltimore

SCORE BY PERIODS

Bengals	45	102	57	118	0	—	322
Opponents	63	113	93	126	0	—	395

2010 TEAM STATISTICS

	Bengals	Opp.
Total First Downs	317	290
Rushing	85	97
Passing	206	170
Penalty	26	23
3rd Down: Made/Att	87/224	75/198
3rd Down Pct.	38.8	37.9
4th Down: Made/Att	13/19	2/7
4th Down Pct.	68.4	28.6
Possession Avg.	31:14	28:46
Total Net Yards	5289	5312
Avg. Per Game	330.6	332.0
Total Plays	1046	957
Avg. Per Play	5.1	5.6
Net Yards Rushing	1522	1843
Avg. Per Game	95.1	115.2
Total Rushes	428	416
Net Yards Passing	3767	3469
Avg. Per Game	235.4	216.8
Sacked/Yards Lost	28/221	27/179
Gross Yards	3988	3648
Att./Completions	590/365	514/326
Completion Pct.	61.9	63.4
Had Intercepted	20	16
Punts/Average	72/41.6	76/41.3
Net Punting Avg.	72/38.2	76/36.6
Penalties/Yards	90/725	95/776
Fumbles/Ball Lost	21/14	20/10
Touchdowns	36	44
Rushing	8	15
Passing	26	21
Returns	2	8

2010 INDIVIDUAL STATISTICS

PASSING	Att.	Comp.	Yds.	Pct.	TD	Int.	Tkld.	Rate
C. Palmer	586	362	3970	61.8	26	20	26/201	82.4
J. Palmer	3	3	18	100.0	0	0	2/20	91.7
Ochocinco	1	0	0	0.0	0	0	0/0	39.6
Bengals	590	365	3988	61.9	26	20	28/221	82.4
Opponents	514	326	3648	63.4	21	16	27/179	85.2

SCORING	TD R	TD P	TD Rt	PAT	FG	Saf	PTS
Nugent	0	0	0	17/17	15/19	0	62
Owens	0	9	0	0/0	0/0	0	54
Benson	7	1	0	0/0	0/0	0	50
Stitser	0	0	0	8/10	7/8	0	29
Gresham	0	4	0	0/0	0/0	0	26
Ochocinco	0	4	0	0/0	0/0	0	24
Shipley	0	3	0	0/0	0/0	0	18
Simpson	0	3	0	0/0	0/0	0	18
Pettrey	0	0	0	5/5	2/4	0	11
A. Jones	0	0	1	0/0	0/0	0	6
Joseph	0	0	1	0/0	0/0	0	6
Leonard	0	1	0	0/0	0/0	0	6
Scott	1	0	0	0/0	0/0	0	6
Whitworth	0	1	0	0/0	0/0	0	6
Bengals	8	26	2	30/32	24/31	0	322
Opponents	15	21	8	43/43	28/33	1	395

2-Pt Conversions: Benson, Gresham.
Bengals 2-4, Opponents 1-1.

RUSHING	No.	Yds	Avg	LG	TD
Benson	321	1111	3.5	26	7
Scott	61	299	4.9	18	1
Leonard	9	61	6.8	42	0
C. Palmer	32	50	1.6	9	0
Simpson	1	2	2.0	2	0
Peerman	2	1	0.5	1	0
Pressley	1	0	0.0	0	0
Caldwell	1	-2	-2.0	-2	0
Bengals	428	1522	3.6	42	8
Opponents	416	1843	4.4	61	15

RECEIVING	No.	Yds	Avg	LG	TD
Owens	72	983	13.7	78t	9
Ochocinco	67	831	12.4	42	4
Shipley	52	600	11.5	64t	3
Gresham	52	471	9.1	27	4
Benson	28	178	6.4	24	1
Caldwell	25	345	13.8	53	0
Simpson	20	277	13.9	59t	3
Leonard	20	137	6.9	20	1
Scott	11	60	5.5	25	0
Kelly	10	42	4.2	9	0
Coffman	3	30	10.0	14	0
Cosby	2	16	8.0	11	0
Peerman	1	11	11.0	11	0
Pressley	1	6	6.0	6	0
Whitworth	1	1	1.0	1t	1
Bengals	365	3988	10.9	78t	26
Opponents	326	3648	11.2	54	21

INTERCEPTIONS	No.	Yds	Avg	LG	TD
Hall	4	19	4.8	22	0
Joseph	3	38	12.7	21t	1
R. Nelson	2	63	31.5	56	0
Maualuga	2	58	29.0	47	0
B. Johnson	1	12	12.0	12	0
A. Jones	1	10	10.0	10	0
Ndukwe	1	0	0.0	0	0
Trent	1	0	0.0	0	0
R. Williams	1	0	0.0	0	0
Bengals	16	200	12.5	56	1
Opponents	20	424	21.2	59t	5

PUNTING	No.	Yds.	Avg.	In 20	LG
Huber	71	2992	42.1	28	72
Bengals	72	2992	41.6	28	72
Opponents	76	3137	41.3	29	61

PUNT RETURNS	Ret	FC	Yds	Avg	LG	TD
Cosby	30	21	225	7.5	20	0
A. Jones	5	0	33	6.6	27	0
Caldwell	1	0	0	0.0	0	0
Bengals	36	21	258	7.2	27	0
Opponents	26	14	124	4.8	20	0

KICKOFF RETURNS	No.	Yds	Avg	LG	TD
Scott	56	1257	22.4	60	0
A. Jones	7	134	19.1	29	0
Caldwell	3	79	26.3	32	0
Cosby	3	44	14.7	18	0
Hall	1	29	29.0	29	0
Kelly	1	8	8.0	8	0
Bengals	71	1551	21.8	60	0
Opponents	64	1504	23.5	97t	2

FIELD GOALS	1-19	20-29	30-39	40-49	50+
Nugent	0/0	5/5	7/7	1/3	2/4
Stitser	0/0	4/5	2/2	1/1	0/0
Pettrey	1/1	1/2	0/0	0/1	0/0
Bengals	1/1	10/12	9/9	2/5	2/4
Opponents	0/0	12/12	8/9	6/9	2/3

SACKS	No.
Dunlap	9.5
Atkins	3.0
M. Johnson	2.5
Sims	2.5
Crocker	2.0
Geathers	1.0
D. Jones	1.0
Maualuga	1.0
Rivers	1.0
Rucker	1.0
R. Williams	1.0
B. Johnson	0.5
Ndukwe	0.5
Peko	0.5
Bengals	27.0
Opponents	28.0

RECORD HOLDERS
INDIVIDUAL RECORDS—CAREER

Category	Name	Performance
Rushing (Yds.)	Corey Dillon, 1997-2003	8,061
Passing (Yds.)	Ken Anderson, 1971-1986	32,838
Passing (TDs)	Ken Anderson, 1971-1986	197
Receiving (No.)	Chad Ochocinco, 2001-2010	751
Receiving (Yds.)	Chad Ochocinco, 2001-2010	10,783
Interceptions	Ken Riley, 1969-1983	65
Punting (Avg.)	Dave Lewis, 1970-73	43.8
Punt Return (Avg.)	Quan Cosby, 2009-2010	10.0
Kickoff Return (Avg.)	Lemar Parrish, 1970-77	24.7
Field Goals	Jim Breech, 1980-1992	225
Touchdowns (Tot.)	Pete Johnson, 1977-1983	70
Points	Jim Breech, 1980-1992	1,151
*Sacks	Eddie Edwards, 1977-1988	47.5

INDIVIDUAL RECORDS—SINGLE SEASON

Category	Name	Performance
Rushing (Yds.)	Rudi Johnson, 2005	1,458
Passing (Yds.)	Carson Palmer, 2007	4,131
Passing (TDs)	Carson Palmer, 2005	32
Receiving (No.)	T.J. Houshmandzadeh, 2007	112
Receiving (Yds.)	Chad Ochocinco, 2007	1,440
Interceptions	Deltha O'Neal, 2005	10
Punting (Avg.)	Dave Lewis, 1970	46.2
Punt Return (Avg.)	Lemar Parrish, 1974	18.8
Kickoff Return (Avg.)	Tremain Mack, 1999	27.1
Field Goals	Shayne Graham, 2007	31
Touchdowns (Tot.)	Carl Pickens, 1995	17
Points	Shayne Graham, 2005	131
*Sacks	Eddie Edwards, 1983	13.0

INDIVIDUAL RECORDS—SINGLE GAME

Category	Name	Performance
Rushing (Yds.)	Corey Dillon, 10-22-00	278
Passing (Yds.)	Boomer Esiason, 10-7-90	490
Passing (TDs)	Carson Palmer, 9-16-07	6
Receiving (No.)	Carl Pickens, 10-11-98	13
Receiving (Yds.)	Chad Ochocinco, 11-12-06	260
Interceptions	Many times	3
	Last time by Leon Hall, 12-21-08	
Field Goals	Shayne Graham, 11-11-07	7
Touchdowns (Tot.)	Larry Kinnebrew, 10-28-84	4
	Corey Dillon, 12-4-97	4
Points	Larry Kinnebrew, 10-28-84	24
	Corey Dillon, 12-4-97	24
*Sacks	Antwan Odom, 9-20-09	5.0

Sacks became an official statistic in 1982.

VETERAN ROSTER AS OF MARCH 3, 2011

No.	Name	Pos.	Ht.	Wt.	Birthdate	^NFL Exp.	College	Hometown	How Acq.	'10 Games/ Starts
95	Adeyanju, Victor	DE	6-4	284	2/11/83	6	Indiana	Chicago, Ill.	FA-'10	0*
97	Atkins, Geno	DT	6-1	290	3/28/88	2	Georgia	Pembroke Pines, Fla.	D4a-'10	16/1
23	Bennett, Fred	CB	6-1	200	12/31/83	5	South Carolina	Manning, S.C.	FA-'10	9/0*
32	Benson, Cedric	HB	5-11	227	12/28/82	7	Texas	Midland, Texas	FA-'08	16/16
87	Caldwell, Andre	WR	6-0	195	4/15/85	4	Florida	Tampa, Fla.	D3b-'08	15/5
72	Chambers, Kirk	T	6-7	315	3/19/79	7	Stanford	Provo, Utah	FA-'10	0*
80	Coffman, Chase	TE	6-6	250	11/10/86	3	Missouri	Peculiar, Mo.	D3b-'09	6/0
73	Collins, Anthony	T	6-5	324	11/2/85	4	Kansas	Beaumont, Texas	D4-'08	9/3
64	Cook, Kyle	C	6-3	316	7/25/83	4	Michigan State	Macomb, Mich.	FA-'07	16/16
12	Cosby, Quan	WR	5-9	190	12/23/82	3	Texas	Mart, Texas	FA-'09	16/0
42	Crocker, Chris	S	5-11	202	3/9/80	9	Marshall	Chesapeake, Va.	FA-'08	9/9
96	Dunlap, Carlos	DE	6-6	285	2/28/89	2	Florida	North Charleston, S.C.	D2-'10	12/0
68	Fanene, Jonathan	DE	6-4	292	3/19/82	7	Utah	Pago Pago, American Samoa	D7-'05	2/0
75	Gardner, Andrew	T	6-6	305	4/4/86	2	Georgia Tech	Tyrone, Ga.	FA-'10	0*
91	Geathers, Robert	DE	6-3	280	8/11/83	8	Georgia	Georgetown, S.C.	D4b-'04	16/16
21	Ghee, Brandon	CB	6-0	190	6/6/87	2	Wake Forest	Fayetteville, N.C.	D3b-'10	6/0
84	Gresham, Jermaine	TE	6-5	260	6/16/88	2	Oklahoma	Ardmore, Okla.	D1-'10	15/10
29	Hall, Leon	CB	5-11	195	12/9/84	5	Michigan	Vista, Calif.	D1-'07	16/16
46	Harris, Clark	LS/TE	6-5	260	7/10/84	3	Rutgers	Manahawkin, N.J.	FA-'09	16/0
10	Huber, Kevin	P	6-1	210	7/16/85	3	Cincinnati	Cincinnati, Ohio	D5-'09	16/0
59	Johnson, Brandon	LB	6-5	240	4/5/83	6	Louisville	Birmingham, Ala.	FA-'08	16/3
93	Johnson, Michael	DE/LB	6-7	268	2/7/87	3	Georgia Tech	Selma, Ala.	D3a-'09	16/10
99	Johnson, Tank	DT	6-3	315	12/7/81	8	Washington	Tempe, Ariz.	UFA(Dall)-'09	7/7
24	Jones, Adam	CB	5-10	188	9/30/83	5	West Virginia	Atlanta, Ga.	FA-'10	5/1
57	Jones, Dhani	LB	6-1	236	2/22/78	12	Michigan	Potomac, Md.	FA-'07	16/16
22	Joseph, Johnathan	CB	5-11	190	4/16/84	6	South Carolina	Rock Hill, S.C.	D1-'06	12/12
82	Kelly, Reggie	TE	6-4	257	2/22/77	13	Mississippi State	Aberdeen, Miss.	UFA(Atl)-'03	16/14
8	LeFevour, Dan	QB	6-3	230	3/19/87	2	Central Michigan	Downers Grove, Ill.	W(Chi)-'10	0*
40	Leonard, Brian	HB	6-1	225	2/3/84	5	Rutgers	Gouverneur, N.Y.	T(StL)-'09	11/0
62	Livings, Nate	G	6-5	332	3/16/82	4	Louisiana State	Lake Charles, La.	FA-'06	16/16
66	Mathis, Evan	G	6-5	302	11/1/81	7	Alabama	Homewood, Ala.	FA-'08	12/0
58	Maualuga, Rey	LB	6-2	255	1/20/87	3	Southern California	Eureka, Calif.	D2-'09	16/15
69	McDonald, Clinton	DT	6-2	297	1/6/87	2	Memphis	Jacksonville, Ark.	D7b-'09	8/0
45	Miles, Jeromy	S	6-2	215	7/20/87	2	Massachusetts	Sicklerville, N.J.	FA-'10	6/0
86	Mills, Garrett	TE	6-1	235	10/12/83	6	Tulsa	Jenks, Okla.	W(Phil)-'10	7/3*
76	Mitchell, Andrew	T	6-5	311	5/12/84	2	Oklahoma State	Choctaw, Okla.	FA-'10	0*
56	Muckelroy, Roddrick	LB	6-2	240	10/27/86	2	Texas	Hallsville, Texas	D4b-'10	14/0
44	Murray, Rico	CB	5-11	200	8/21/87	2	Kent State	Cincinnati, Ohio	FA-'09	4/0
41	Ndukwe, Chinedum	S	6-2	224	3/4/85	5	Notre Dame	Powell, Ohio	D7b-'07	12/6
20	Nelson, Reggie	S	5-11	206	9/21/83	5	Florida	Melbourne, Fla.	T(Jac)-'10	16/6
43	Nelson, Tom	S	5-11	200	12/4/86	3	Illinois State	Arlington Heights, Ill.	FA-'09	8/0
2	Nugent, Mike	K	5-10	186	3/2/82	7	Ohio State	Centerville, Ohio	FA-'10	9/0
85	Ochocinco, Chad	WR	6-1	192	1/9/78	11	Oregon State	Miami, Fla.	D2-'01	14/12
98	Odom, Antwan	DE	6-5	275	9/24/81	8	Alabama	Bayou La Batre, Ala.	UFA(Tenn)-'08	4/3
81	Owens, Terrell	WR	6-3	224	12/7/73	16	Tennessee-Chattanooga	Alexander City, Ala.	UFA(Buff)-'10	14/11
9	Palmer, Carson	QB	6-5	236	12/27/79	9	Southern California	Mission Viejo, Calif.	D1-'03	16/16
5	Palmer, Jordan	QB	6-5	232	5/30/84	4	Texas-El Paso	Mission Viejo, Calif.	FA-'08	1/0
30	Peerman, Cedric	HB	5-10	212	10/10/86	2	Virginia	Gladys, Va.	W(Det)-'10	7/0
94	Peko, Domata	DT	6-3	320	11/27/84	6	Michigan State	Pago Pago (American Samoa)	D4-'06	16/16
36	Pressley, Chris	FB	5-11	260	8/8/86	3	Wisconsin	Woodbury, N.J.	PS(Cin)-'10	7/0*
34	Ratliff, Keiwan	CB	5-11	188	4/19/81	7	Florida	Columbus, Ohio	FA-'10	3/0
55	Rivers, Keith	LB	6-2	242	5/5/86	4	Southern California	Lake Mary, Fla.	D1-'08	15/13
74	Roland, Dennis	T	6-9	320	3/10/83	4	Georgia	Bolivar, Mo.	FA-'08	16/12
92	Rucker, Frostee	DE	6-3	280	9/14/83	6	Southern California	Tustin, Calif.	D3-'06	9/3
28	Scott, Bernard	HB	5-10	197	2/10/84	3	Abilene Christian	Vernon, Texas	D6b-'09	16/0
11	Shipley, Jordan	WR	6-0	190	12/23/85	2	Texas	Burnet, Texas	D3a-'10	15/4
70	Shirley, Jason	G	6-5	345	9/30/85	2	Fresno State	Fontana, Calif.	D5-'08	0*
89	Simpson, Jerome	WR	6-2	195	2/4/86	4	Coastal Carolina	Reidsville, N.C.	D2-'08	5/3
90	Sims, Pat	DT	6-2	325	11/29/85	4	Auburn	Fort Lauderdale, Fla.	D3a-'08	14/8
51	Skuta, Dan	LB	6-2	252	4/21/86	3	Grand Valley State	Flint, Mich.	FA-'09	16/1
71	Smith, Andre	T/G	6-4	345	1/25/87	3	Alabama	Birmingham, Ala.	D1-'09	7/4
61	Stephens, Reggie	C	6-3	320	8/28/87	2	Iowa State	Rowlett, Texas	D7-'10	0*
25	Trent, Morgan	CB	6-1	193	12/14/85	3	Michigan	San Diego, Calif.	D6a-'09	8/1
37	Vakapuna, Fui	FB	6-0	257	3/9/84	3	Brigham Young	Glendale, Utah	PS(Ariz)-'09	0*
26	Wade, Jonathan	CB	5-11	200	3/27/84	5	Tennessee	Shreveport, La.	FA-'10	12/7*
47	White, Marvin	S	6-1	205	12/5/83	4	Texas Christian	Port Barre, La.	FA-'10	3/0

VETERAN ROSTER AS OF MARCH 3, 2011 (CONTINUED)

No.	Name	Pos.	Ht.	Wt.	Birthdate	^NFL Exp.	College	Hometown	How Acq.	'10 Games/ Starts
77	Whitworth, Andrew	T	6-7	335	12/12/81	6	Louisiana State	West Monroe, La.	D2-'06	16/16
63	Williams, Bobbie	G	6-4	345	9/25/76	12	Arkansas	Jefferson, Texas	UFA(Phil)-'04	16/16
31	Williams, Roy	S	6-0	222	8/14/80	10	Oklahoma	Union City, Calif.	FA-'09	12/11
27	Wilson, Gibril	S	6-0	210	11/12/81	8	Tennessee	San Jose, Calif.	FA-'10	0*

* Adeyanju inactive for 6 games with Cincinnati; Bennett played 4 games with San Diego and 5 games with Cincinnati in '10; Chambers did not play in 1 game and was inactive for 6 games; Gardner last active with Miami in '09; LeFevour inactive (designated third quarterback) for 16 games; Mills played 7 games with Philadelphia; Mitchell missed '10 season because of injury; Pressley played 3 games with Tampa Bay and 4 games with Cincinnati; Shirley missed '10 season on the Reserve/Non-Football Injury list; Stephens inactive for 16 games; Vakapuna missed '10 season because of injury; Wade played 8 games with Detroit and 4 games with Cincinnati; Wilson missed '10 season because of injury.

Also played with Bengals in '10—TE Daniel Coats (6 games), TE J.P. Foschi (2), K Aaron Pettrey (2), LB Vincent Rey (2), K Clint Stitser (5).

^ "NFL Exp." as of 2011 Kickoff Weekend. For full explanation of how a player's NFL Experience is measured, refer to explanation underneath the First-Year Roster listed below.

FIRST-YEAR ROSTER

Name	Pos.	Ht.	Wt.	Birthdate	College	Hometown	How Acq.
Boling, Clint	G	6-5	308	5/9/89	Georgia	Alpharetta, Ga.	D4
Dalton, Andy	QB	6-2	215	10/29/87	Texas Christian	Katy, Texas	D2
Develin, James (1)	FB	6-3	260	7/23/88	Brown	Gilbertsville, Pa.	FA-'10
Finley, Jay	HB	5-11	203	5/15/88	Baylor	Corsicana, Texas	D7b
Green, A.J.	WR	6-4	211	7/31/88	Georgia	Summerville, S.C.	D1
Hodge, Shay (1)	WR	6-2	218	10/18/87	Mississippi	Morton, Miss.	FA-'10
Hudson, Otis (1)	G	6-5	320	7/19/86	Eastern Illinois	Barrington, Ill.	D5-'10
Lindsey, Korey	CB	5-10	194	2/3/89	Southern Illinois	Baton Rouge, La.	D7a
Moch, Dontay	LB	6-1	248	7/19/88	Nevada	Chandler, Ariz.	D3
Pender, David (1)	CB	6-0	180	12/4/87	Purdue	Folkston, Ga.	W(Ind)-'10
Rey, Vincent (1)	LB	6-2	244	9/6/87	Duke	Far Rockaway, N.Y.	FA-'10
Ruffin, James (1)	DE	6-4	263	2/6/87	Northern Iowa	Burnsville, Minn.	FA-'10
Sands, Robert	S	6-4	217	11/3/89	West Virginia	Carol City, Fla.	D5
Stitser, Clint (1)	K	6-1	200	5/19/85	Fresno State	Reno, Nev.	FA-'10
Whalen, Ryan	WR	6-1	202	7/26/89	Stanford	Alamo, Calif.	D6

The term NFL Rookie is defined as a player who is in his first season of professional football and has not been on the roster of another professional football team for any regular-season or postseason games. A Rookie is designated by an "R" on NFL rosters. Players who have been active in another professional football league or players who have NFL experience, including either preseason training camp or being on an Active List or Inactive List, or on Reserve/Injured or Reserve/Physically Unable to Perform for fewer than six regular-season games, are termed NFL First-Year Players. An NFL First-Year Player is designated by a "1" on NFL rosters. Thereafter, a player is credited with an additional year of experience for each season in which he accumulates six games on the Active List or Inactive List, or on Reserve/Injured or Reserve/Physically Unable to Perform.

Log on to www.bengals.com for an up-to-date roster.

COACHING STAFF

Head Coach,
Marvin Lewis

Pro Career: In 2011, Marvin Lewis is in his ninth season as Bengals head coach, establishing the longest head coaching tenure in franchise history. He breaks the record of eight seasons he had shared with club founder Paul Brown (1968-1975) and Sam Wyche (1984-1991). Lewis' Bengals won AFC North Division championships in 2005 and 2009, and Cincinnati is among a minority of NFL teams (14 of 32) to have won more than one division crown in the last six years. After establishing himself as a record-setting NFL defensive coordinator, Lewis was named the ninth head coach in Bengals history on January 14, 2003. His 2009 AFC North champions posted the franchise's first-ever unbeaten record (6-0) in division play, and he was the consensus winner in votes for NFL Coach of the Year awards, credited with keeping the team on course in the face of three tragic off-field events during the regular season. Those events included the death of WR Chris Henry in an auto accident, the sudden death of Vikki Zimmer, wife of defensive coordinator Mike Zimmer, and a tsunami in Samoa that affected several players with ties to the area. Lewis has posted 60 wins in his first eight seasons, and he could pass Wyche (64) into first place in franchise history with five wins in 2011. Prior to joining the Bengals, Lewis was Washington Redskins defensive coordinator (2002), serving as assistant head coach in addition to his coordinator's role. He spent six seasons (1996-2001) as defensive coordinator with the Baltimore Ravens, a tenure that included a Super Bowl victory in the 2000 season. In 2000, Lewis' defense set the NFL record for fewest points allowed in a 16-game campaign (165), and the unit has been widely considered as one of the best NFL defenses of all time. Prior to Baltimore, Lewis spent four seasons (1992-95) with the Pittsburgh Steelers as linebackers coach, guiding the careers of Pro Bowl selections Chad Brown, Kevin Greene, Levon Kirkland and Gregg Lloyd. Career record: 60-69-1.

Background: Earned All-Big Sky Conference honors as a linebacker at Idaho State (1978-1980), and saw action at quarterback and free safety. Received his bachelor's degree in physical education from Idaho State in 1981, and earned his Master's degree in athletic administration in 1982. Inducted into Idaho State's Hall of Fame in 2001. Began his coaching career at Idaho State (1981-84). The team finished 12-1 during his first season and won the NCAA Division I-AA championship. Was also the linebackers coach at Long Beach State (1985-86), New Mexico (1987-89), and Pittsburgh (1990-91).

Personal: Born September 23, 1958, McDonald, Pa. Lewis and his wife, Peggy, have two children—Whitney and Marcus.

ASSISTANT COACHES

Paul Alexander, asst. head coach/ offensive line; born February 12, 1960, Rochester, N.Y. Tackle Cortland State 1979-1981. No pro playing experience. College coach: Penn State 1982-84, Michigan 1985-86, Central Michigan 1987-1991. Pro coach: New York Jets 1992-93, joined Bengals in 1994.

Jim Anderson, running backs; born March 27, 1948, Harrisburg, Pa. Linebacker/defensive end California Western 1967-69. No pro playing experience. College coach: California Western 1970-71, Scottsdale (Ariz.) C.C. 1973, Nevada-Las Vegas 1974-75, Southern Methodist 1976-1980, Stanford 1981-83. Pro coach: Joined Bengals in 1984.

Kyle Caskey, offensive quality control; born Dec. 7, 1978, Daingerfield, Texas. Tight end Texas A&M 1997-98. No pro playing experience. College coach: Louisiana-Monroe 2004-05, Indiana State 2006-08, Mississippi 2009. Pro coach: Joined Bengals in 2010.

Kevin Coyle, defensive backs; born January 14, 1956, Staten Island, N.Y. Defensive back Massachusetts 1975-77. No pro playing experience. College coach: Cincinnati 1978-79, Arkansas 1980, U.S. Merchant Marine Academy 1981, Holy Cross 1982-1990, Syracuse 1991-93, Maryland 1994-96, Fresno State 1997-2000. Pro coach: Joined Bengals in 2001.

Jeff FitzGerald, linebackers; born April 18, 1960, Burbank, Calif. Linebacker Oregon State 1980. No pro playing experience. College coach: Cincinnati 1985, Alabama 1986-89, San Diego State 1994-97. Pro coach: Tampa Bay Buccaneers 1990-93, Washington Redskins 1998-99, Arizona Cardinals 2000-03, Baltimore Ravens 2004-07, joined Bengals in 2008.

Jeff Friday, asst. strength and conditioning; born Oct. 11, 1966, Milwaukee, Wis. Attended Wisconsin-Milwaukee. No college or pro playing experience. College coach: Illinois State 1990-91, Northwestern 1992-95. Pro coach: Minnesota Vikings 1996-98, Baltimore Ravens 1999-2007, joined Bengals in 2010.

Jay Gruden, offensive coordinator; born March 4, 1967, Tiffin, Ohio. Quarterback Louisville 1985-88. Pro quarterback Barcelona Dragons (WLAF) 1990, Sacramento Surge (WLAF) 1990, Tampa Bay Storm (AFL) 1991-96, Orlando Predators (AFL) 2002-03. Pro coach: Nashville Katz (AFL) 1997, Orlando Predators (AFL) 1998-2001 (head coach) and 2004-08 (head coach), Tampa Bay Buccaneers 2002-08, Florida Tuskers (UFL) 2009-10 (head coach 2010), joined Bengals in 2011.

Paul Guenther, asst. special teams/asst. linebackers; born Nov. 22, 1971, Richboro, Pa. Linebacker Ursinus College 1990-93. No pro playing experience. College coach: Western Maryland 1994-

95, Ursinus College 1996, 1997-2001 (head coach 1997-2001), Jacksonville 1997. Pro coach: Washington Redskins 2002-03, joined Bengals in 2005.

Jay Hayes, defensive line; born March 3, 1960, South Fayette, Pa. Defensive end Idaho 1978-1981. Pro defensive end/ linebacker Michigan Panthers (USFL) 1984, Memphis Showboats (USFL) 1985. College coach: Notre Dame 1988-1991, California 1992-94, Wisconsin 1995-98. Pro coach: Pittsburgh Steelers 1999-2001, Minnesota Vikings 2002, joined Bengals in 2003.

Jonathan Hayes, tight ends; born Aug. 11, 1962, South Fayette, Pa. Linebacker/ tight end Iowa 1981-84. Pro tight end Kansas City Chiefs 1985-1993, Pittsburgh Steelers 1994-96. College coach: Oklahoma 1999-2002. Pro coach: Joined Bengals in 2003.

David Lippincott, defensive quality control; born July 6, 1977, Cincinnati. Attended Dayton. No college or pro playing experience. College coach: Bluffton 2000-02, Minnesota 2003-04, Richmond 2005-07. Pro coach: Joined Bengals in 2011.

Chip Morton, strength and conditioning; born November 27, 1962, Hamden, Conn. Attended North Carolina. No college or pro playing experience. College coach: Ohio State 1985-86, Penn State 1987-1991. Pro coach: San Diego Chargers 1992-94, Carolina Panthers 1995-98, Baltimore Ravens 1999-2001, Washington Redskins 2002, joined Bengals in 2003.

Darrin Simmons, special teams; born April 9, 1973, Elkhart, Kan. Punter Kansas 1993-95. No pro playing experience. College coach: Kansas 1996, Minnesota 1997. Pro coach: Baltimore Ravens 1998, Carolina Panthers 1999-2002, joined Bengals in 2003.

James Urban, wide receivers; born Dec. 1, 1973, Mechanicsburg, Pa. Wide receiver Washington and Lee 1993-96. No pro playing experience. College coach: Clarion 1997-98, Pennsylvania 1999-2003. Pro coach: Philadelphia Eagles 2004-10, joined Bengals in 2011.

Ken Zampese, quarterbacks; born July 19, 1967, Santa Maria, Calif. Wide receiver San Diego 1985-88. No pro playing experience. College coach: San Diego 1989, Southern California 1990-91, Northern Arizona 1992-95, Miami (Ohio) 1996-97. Pro coach: Philadelphia Eagles 1998, Green Bay Packers 1999, St. Louis Rams 2000-02, joined Bengals in 2003.

Mike Zimmer, defensive coordinator; born June 5, 1956, Peoria, Ill. Quarterback/linebacker Illinois State 1974-76. No pro playing experience. College coach: Missouri 1979-1980, Weber State 1981-88, Washington State 1989-1993. Pro coach: Dallas Cowboys 1994-2006, Atlanta Falcons 2007, joined Bengals in 2008.

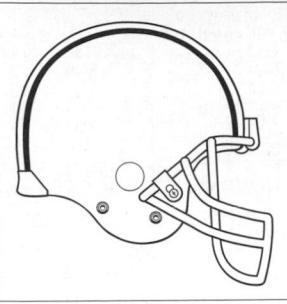

**American Football Conference
North Division
Team Colors:** Brown, Orange, and White
76 Lou Groza Blvd.
Berea, Ohio 44017
Telephone: (440) 891-5000

2011 SCHEDULE
PRESEASON
Aug. 13	Green Bay	7:30
Aug. 19	Detroit	7:30
Aug. 25	at Philadelphia	7:30
Sep. 1	at Chicago	8:00

REGULAR SEASON
Sep. 11	**Cincinnati**	1:00
Sep. 18	at Indianapolis	1:00
Sep. 25	**Miami**	1:00
Oct. 2	**Tennessee**	1:00
Oct. 9	BYE	
Oct. 16	at Oakland	4:05
Oct. 23	**Seattle**	1:00
Oct. 30	at San Francisco	4:15
Nov. 6	at Houston	1:00
Nov. 13	**St. Louis**	1:00
Nov. 20	**Jacksonville**	1:00
Nov. 27	at Cincinnati	1:00
Dec. 4	**Baltimore**	1:00
Dec. 8	at Pittsburgh (Thu)	8:20
Dec. 18	at Arizona	4:15
Dec. 24	at Baltimore (Sat)	1:00
Jan. 1	**Pittsburgh**	1:00

*All times ET
Stadium: Cleveland Browns Stadium
(opened in 1999)
  •**Capacity:** 73,300
  100 Alfred Lerner Way
  Cleveland, Ohio 44114
Playing Surface: Grass
Headquarters/Training Camp:
  76 Lou Groza Boulevard
  Berea, Ohio 44017

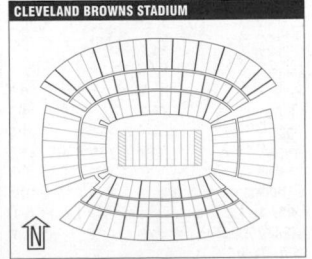

CLEVELAND BROWNS STADIUM

CLUB OFFICIALS
Owner: Randolph D. Lerner
President: Mike Holmgren
General Manager: Tom Heckert
Head Coach: Pat Shurmur
Executive Vice President, Business Operations: Bryan Wiedmeier
Senior Advisor to the President: Gil Haskell
Senior Advisor to the President: Fred Nance
Senior Vice President, Finance & Administration: David A. Jenkins
Senior Vice President, Security: Lew Merletti
Senior Vice President, Business Development: Jim Ross
Vice President, Tickets Sales & Service: Chris Gallagher
Vice President, Media Relations: Neal Gulkis
Vice President, Security: Carl Meyer
Vice President, Corporate Sales & Services: John Penhollow
Vice President, Marketing: Brett Reynolds
Vice President, Football Operations: Mark Schiefelbein
Vice President, Football Administration: Matt Thomas
Director, Stadium Operations: Todd Argust
Director, Content & Production: Reagan Berube
Director, Video: Chad Bogard
Director, Player Development: Jerry Butler
Director, Information Technology: Brandon Covert
Director, Club Level Sales: Jason England
Director, Operations: Phil Dangerfield
Director, Community Outreach: Renee Harvey
Director, Season & Group Ticket Sales: Eric Lapointe
Director, Corporate Sales: Paul Mocho
Director, Creative Services: George Muller
Director, Media Sales: Dana Nagel
Director, Administration: Mike Nikolaus
Director, Client Services: Nicole Peters
Controller: Laurie Rice
Director, Legal Affairs: Megan Rogers
Director, Finance: Gregory Rush
Director, Player Personnel: Jon Sandusky
Director, Ticket Operations: John Schulze
Director, College Scouting: John Spytek
Director, Guest Relations: Lauren Voorhies
Head Athletic Trainer: Joe Sheehan
Head Equipment Manager: Brad Melland
Head Groundskeeper: Chris Powell

COACHING HISTORY
(449-414-10)
Records include postseason games
1950-1962	Paul Brown	115-49-5
1963-1970	Blanton Collier	79-38-2
1971-74	Nick Skorich	30-26-2
1975-77	Forrest Gregg*	18-23-0
1977	Dick Modzelewski	0-1-0
1978-1984	Sam Rutigliano**	47-52-0
1984-88	Marty Schottenheimer	46-31-0
1989-1990	Bud Carson***	12-14-1
1990	Jim Shofner	1-6-0
1991-95	Bill Belichick	37-45-0
1999-2000	Chris Palmer	5-27-0
2001-04	Butch Davis****	24-36-0
2004	Terry Robiskie	1-4-0
2005-08	Romeo Crennel	24-40-0
2009-2010	Eric Mangini	10-22-0

*Resigned after 13 games in 1977
**Released after eight games in 1984
***Released after nine games in 1990
****Resigned after 11 games in 2004

PAID ATTENDANCE
Home 529,458   Away 467,106
Total 996,564
Single-game home record,
  85,073 (9/21/70)
Single-season home record, 620,496
(1980)

2011 DRAFT CHOICES
Round	Name	Pos.	College
1	Phil Taylor	DT	Baylor
2	Jabaal Sheard	DE	Pittsburgh
	Greg Little	WR	North Carolina
4	Jordan Cameron	TE	Southern California
	Owen Marecic	RB	Stanford
5	Buster Skrine	DB	Chattanooga
	Jason Pinkston	T	Pittsburgh
7	Eric Hagg	DB	Nebraska

CLEVELAND BROWNS

2010 TEAM RECORD
PRESEASON (2-2)

Date	Result	Opponent
8/14	W 27-24	at Green Bay
8/21	L 17-19	St. Louis
8/28	L 27-35	at Detroit
9/2	W 13-10	Chicago

REGULAR SEASON (5-11)

Date	Result	Opponent
9/12	L 14-17	at Tampa Bay
9/19	L 14-16	Kansas City
9/26	L 17-24	at Baltimore
10/3	W 23-20	Cincinnati
10/10	L 10-20	Atlanta
10/17	L 10-28	at Pittsburgh
10/24	W 30-17	at New Orleans
11/7	W 34-14	New England
11/14	L 20-26	New York Jets (OT)
11/21	L 20-24	at Jacksonville
11/28	W 24-23	Carolina
12/5	W 13-10	at Miami
12/12	L 6-13	at Buffalo
12/19	L 17-19	at Cincinnati
12/26	L 10-20	Baltimore
1/2	L 9-41	Pittsburgh

(OT) Overtime

SCORE BY PERIODS

Browns	77	91	37	66	0	—	271
Opponents	40	134	47	105	6	—	332

2010 TEAM STATISTICS

	Browns	Opp.
Total First Downs	265	317
Rushing	87	102
Passing	154	195
Penalty	24	20
3rd Down: Made/Att	75/202	96/224
3rd Down Pct.	37.1	42.9
4th Down: Made/Att	5/7	11/15
4th Down Pct.	71.4	73.3
Possession Avg.	27:55	32:05
Total Net Yards	4635	5601
Avg. Per Game	289.7	350.1
Total Plays	927	1041
Avg. Per Play	5.0	5.4
Net Yards Rushing	1646	2070
Avg. Per Game	102.9	129.4
Total Rushes	413	505
Net Yards Passing	2989	3531
Avg. Per Game	186.8	220.7
Sacked/Yards Lost	36/214	29/178
Gross Yards	3203	3709
Att./Completions	478/296	507/309
Completion Pct.	61.9	60.9
Had Intercepted	18	19
Punts/Average	78/43.9	64/44.0
Net Punting Avg.	78/39.0	64/37.8
Penalties/Yards	78/675	85/741
Fumbles/Ball Lost	29/11	16/9
Touchdowns	29	36
Rushing	13	7
Passing	13	26
Returns	3	3

2010 INDIVIDUAL STATISTICS

PASSING

	Att.	Comp.	Yds.	Pct.	TD	Int.	Tkld.	Rate
McCoy	222	135	1576	60.8	6	9	23/132	74.5
Delhomme	149	93	872	62.4	2	7	6/49	63.4
Wallace	101	64	694	63.4	4	2	6/33	88.5
Cribbs	3	2	19	66.7	0	0	1/0	84.0
Hillis	2	1	13	50.0	0	0	0/0	70.8
Massaquoi	1	1	29	100.0	1	0	0/0	158.3
Browns	478	296	3203	61.9	13	18	36/214	75.0
Opponents	507	309	3709	60.9	26	19	29/178	84.8

SCORING

	TD R	TD P	TD Rt	PAT	FG	Saf	PTS
Dawson	0	0	0	28/28	23/28	0	97
Hillis	11	2	0	0/0	0/0	0	78
Robiskie	0	3	0	0/0	0/0	0	18
Watson	0	3	0	0/0	0/0	0	18
Bowens	0	0	2	0/0	0/0	0	12
Massaquoi	0	2	0	0/0	0/0	0	12
Cribbs	0	1	0	0/0	0/0	0	6
Elam	0	0	1	0/0	0/0	0	6
McCoy	1	0	0	0/0	0/0	0	6
Moore	0	1	0	0/0	0/0	0	6
Royal	0	1	0	0/0	0/0	0	6
Stuckey	1	0	0	0/0	0/0	0	6
Browns	13	13	3	28/28	23/28	0	271
Opponents	7	26	3	35/35	27/36	0	332

2-Pt Conversions: Browns 0-1, Opponents 0-0.

RUSHING

	No.	Yds	Avg	LG	TD
Hillis	270	1177	4.4	48	11
McCoy	28	136	4.9	18	1
Harrison	31	91	2.9	39	0
Bell	31	71	2.3	11	0
Hodges	1	68	68.0	68	0
Cribbs	20	66	3.3	19	0
Vickers	5	11	2.2	3	0
Davis	4	9	2.3	4	0
C. Mitchell	1	9	9.0	9	0
Stuckey	3	9	3.0	11t	1
Wallace	7	9	1.3	6	0
Clayton	1	0	0.0	0	0
Watson	1	-1	-1.0	-1	0
Delhomme	8	-2	-.3	2	0
Massaquoi	1	-3	-3.0	-3	0
Figurs	1	-4	-4.0	-4	0
Browns	413	1646	4.0	68	13
Opponents	505	2070	4.1	55	7

RECEIVING

	No.	Yds	Avg	LG	TD
Watson	68	763	11.2	44	3
Hillis	61	477	7.8	47	2
Stuckey	40	346	8.7	25	0
Massaquoi	36	483	13.4	41t	2
Robiskie	29	310	10.7	46t	3
Cribbs	23	292	12.7	65t	1
Moore	16	322	20.1	49	1
Bell	6	62	10.3	28	0
Royal	5	56	11.2	20t	1
Harrison	4	42	10.5	23	0
Vickers	4	15	3.8	10	0
McCoy	1	13	13.0	13	0
Wallace	1	9	9.0	9	0
Aiken	1	7	7.0	7	0
A. Smith	1	6	6.0	6	0
Browns	296	3203	10.8	65t	13
Opponents	309	3709	12.0	78t	26

INTERCEPTIONS

	No.	Yds	Avg	LG	TD
Haden	6	101	16.8	62	0
Bowens	2	94	47.0	64t	2
M. Adams	2	51	25.5	26	0
Ward	2	39	19.5	23	0
Elam	2	18	9.0	18	0
S. Brown	2	0	0.0	0	0
Fujita	1	16	16.0	16	0
Rubin	1	1	1.0	1	0
E. Wright	1	0	0.0	0	0
Browns	19	320	16.8	64t	2
Opponents	18	267	14.8	64	3

PUNTING

	No.	Yds.	Avg.	In 20	LG
Hodges	78	3424	43.9	29	59
Browns	78	3424	43.9	29	59
Opponents	64	2817	44.0	27	61

PUNT RETURNS

	Ret	FC	Yds	Avg	LG	TD
Cribbs	20	6	168	8.4	17	0
C. Smith	0	2	0	—	—	0
Stuckey	2	3	5	2.5	5	0
E. Wright	0	0	62	—	62	0
Browns	22	11	235	10.7	69	0
Opponents	40	13	285	7.1	33	0

KICKOFF RETURNS

	No.	Yds	Avg	LG	TD
Cribbs	40	814	20.4	37	0
C. Smith	5	92	18.4	26	0
Bell	5	55	11.0	31	0
Haden	4	96	24.0	32	0
Ventrone	4	47	11.8	17	0
Harrison	4	32	8.0	10	0
Benard	4	26	6.5	11	0
Vickers	2	13	6.5	10	0
Davis	1	11	11.0	11	0
Gocong	1	5	5.0	5	0
Browns	70	1191	17.0	37	0
Opponents	54	959	17.8	32	0

FIELD GOALS

	1-19	20-29	30-39	40-49	50+
Dawson	3/3	7/7	10/10	3/5	0/3
Browns	3/3	7/7	10/10	3/5	0/3
Opponents	1/1	11/12	6/7	8/14	1/2

SACKS

	No.
Benard	7.5
Fujita	3.5
Roth	3.5
Coleman	2.5
Elam	2.0
Gocong	2.0
Rogers	2.0
Rubin	2.0
M. Adams	1.0
Haden	1.0
Trusnik	1.0
Bowens	0.5
D. Robinson	0.5
Browns	29.0
Opponents	36.0

RECORD HOLDERS
INDIVIDUAL RECORDS—CAREER

Category	Name	Performance
Rushing (Yds.)	Jim Brown, 1957-1965	12,312
Passing (Yds.)	Brian Sipe, 1974-1983	23,713
Passing (TDs)	Brian Sipe, 1974-1983	154
Receiving (No.)	Ozzie Newsome, 1978-1990	662
Receiving (Yds.)	Ozzie Newsome, 1978-1990	7,980
Interceptions	Thom Darden, 1972-74, 1976-1981	45
Punting (Avg.)	Dave Zastudil, 2006-2010	44.1
Punt Return (Avg.)	Greg Pruitt, 1973-1981	11.8
Kickoff Return (Avg.)	Greg Pruitt, 1973-1981	26.3
Field Goals	Phil Dawson, 1999-2010	252
Touchdowns (Tot.)	Jim Brown, 1957-1965	126
Points	Lou Groza, 1950-59, 1961-67	1,349
*Sacks	Clay Matthews, 1978-1993	62.0

INDIVIDUAL RECORDS—SINGLE SEASON

Category	Name	Performance
Rushing (Yds.)	Jim Brown, 1963	1,863
Passing (Yds.)	Brian Sipe, 1980	4,132
Passing (TDs)	Brian Sipe, 1980	30
Receiving (No.)	Ozzie Newsome, 1983	89
	Ozzie Newsome, 1984	89
	Kellen Winslow, 2006	89
Receiving (Yds.)	Braylon Edwards, 2007	1,289
Interceptions	Thom Darden, 1978	10
	Anthony Honry, 2001	10
Punting (Avg.)	Gary Collins, 1965	46.7
Punt Return (Avg.)	Leroy Kelly, 1965	15.6
Kickoff Return (Avg.)	Billy Lefear, 1975	31.7
Field Goals	Phil Dawson, 2008	30
Touchdowns (Tot.)	Jim Brown, 1965	21
Points	Jim Brown, 1965	126
*Sacks	Reggie Camp, 1984	14.0

INDIVIDUAL RECORDS—SINGLE GAME

Category	Name	Performance
Rushing (Yds.)	Jerome Harrison, 12-20-09	286
Passing (TDs)	Frank Ryan, 12-12-64	5
	Bill Nelsen, 11-2-69	5
	Brian Sipe, 10-7-79	5
	Kelly Holcomb, 11-28-04	5
	Derek Anderson, 9-16-07	5
Receiving (No.)	Ozzie Newsome, 10-14-84	14
Receiving (Yds.)	Ozzie Newsome, 10-14-84	191
Interceptions	Many times	3
	Last time by Anthony Henry, 11-18-01	
Field Goals	Phil Dawson, 11-5-06	6
Touchdowns (Tot.)	Dub Jones, 11-25-51	**6
Points	Dub Jones, 11-25-51	36
*Sacks	Andra Davis, 11-9-03	4.0

*Sacks became an official statistic in 1982.
**NFL Record

VETERAN ROSTER AS OF MARCH 3, 2011

No.	Name	Pos.	Ht.	Wt.	Birthdate	^NFL Exp.	College	Hometown	How Acq.	'10 Games/ Starts
20	Adams, Mike	DB	5-11	200	3/24/81	8	Delaware	Paterson, N.J.	UFA(SF)-'07	15/2
62	Adams, Titus	DL	6-4	305	1/28/83	3	Nebraska	Omaha, Neb.	W(NE)-'10	0*
57	Alexander, Eric	LB	6-2	240	2/8/82	6	Louisiana State	Tyler, Texas	FA-'10	9/0*
22 t-	Bell, Mike	RB	6-0	225	4/23/83	6	Arizona	Tolleson, Ariz.	T(Phil)-'10	16/1*
58	Benard, Marcus	LB	6-2	256	7/26/85	3	Jackson State	Adrian, Mich.	FA-'09	15/2
24	Brown, Sheldon	DB	5-10	200	3/19/79	10	South Carolina	Fort Lawn, S.C.	T(Phil)-'10	16/16
59	Brown, Titus	LB	6-3	250	3/27/86	2	Mississippi State	Tuscaloosa, Ala.	FA-'10	13/0
54	Costanzo, Blake	LB	6-1	235	4/14/84	5	Lafayette	Franklin Lakes, N.J.	W(Buff)-'09	10/0
16	Cribbs, Joshua	WR	6-1	215	6/9/83	7	Kent State	Washington, D.C.	FA-'05	15/5
4	Dawson, Phil	K	5-11	200	1/23/75	13	Texas	Dallas, Texas	FA-'99	16/0
17	Delhomme, Jake	QB	6-2	215	1/10/75	13	Louisiana-Lafayette	Breaux Bridge, La.	FA-'10	5/4
85	DeVree, Tyson	TE	6-6	245	11/12/84	2	Colorado	Hudsonville, Mich.	FA-'10	0*
26	Elam, Abram	DB	6-0	207	10/15/81	6	Kent State	Riviera Beach, Fla.	T(NYJ)-'09	16/15
87	Estandia, Greg	TE	6-8	266	11/18/82	5	Nevada-Las Vegas	Moorpark, Calif.	W(Jax)-'09	0*
36	Francies, Coye	DB	6-0	185	11/15/86	2	San Jose State	Sacramento, Calif.	D6b-'09	2/0
99	Fujita, Scott	LB	6-5	250	4/28/79	10	California	Ventura, Calif.	UFA(NO)-'10	9/9
51	Gocong, Chris	LB	6-2	263	11/16/83	6	Cal Poly San Luis Obispo	Santa Barbara, Calif.	T(Phil)-'10	16/16
23	Haden, Joe	DB	5-11	190	4/14/89	2	Florida	Fort Washington, Md.	D1-'10	16/7
86	Haggerty, Johnathan	WR	6-1	195	2/5/88	2	SW Oklahoma State	Dallas, Texas	FA-'10	0*
31	Hardesty, Montario	RB	6-0	225	2/1/87	2	Tennessee	New Bern, N.C.	D2b-'10	0*
40	Hillis, Peyton	RB	6-2	250	1/21/86	4	Arkansas	Conway, Ark.	T(Den)-'10	16/14
2	Hodges, Reggie	P	6-0	220	1/26/82	5	Ball State	Champaign, Ill	FA-'09	16/0
52	Jackson, D'Qwell	LB	6-0	240	9/26/83	6	Maryland	Largo, Fla.	D2-'06	0*
66	Lauvao, Shawn	OL	6-3	315	10/26/87	2	Arizona State	Honolulu, Hawai'i	D3b-'10	10/1
55	Mack, Alex	OL	6-4	311	11/19/85	3	California	Santa Barbara, Calif.	D1-'09	16/16
56	Maiava, Kaluka	LB	6-0	229	12/27/86	3	Southern California	Wailuku, Hawai'i	D4-'09	2/0
11	Massaquoi, Mohamed	WR	6-2	207	11/24/86	3	Georgia	Charlotte, N.C.	D2b-'09	15/14
12	McCoy, Colt	QB	6-1	215	9/5/86	2	Texas	Tuscola, Texas	D3a-'10	8/8
18	Mitchell, Carlton	WR	6-3	215	4/6/88	2	South Florida	Gainesville, Fla.	D6a-'10	5/0
97 t-	Mitchell, Jayme	DL	6-6	285	3/15/84	6	Mississippi	Jackson, Miss.	T(Minn)-'10	2/0*
89	Moore, Evan	TE	6-6	250	1/3/85	3	Stanford	Brea, Calif.	FA-'09	12/4
95	Octavien, Steve	LB	6-0	255	11/25/84	2	Nebraska	Naples, Fla.	FA-'10	2/0
79	Pashos, Tony	OL	6-6	325	8/3/80	9	Illinois	Palos Heights, Ill.	UFA(SF)-'10	6/3
69	Paxson, Scott	DL	6-4	290	2/3/83	2	Penn State	Philadelphia, Pa.	FA-'11	0*
28	Piscitelli, Sabby	DB	6-3	225	8/24/83	5	Oregon State	Boca Raton, Fla.	W(TB)-'10	16/0*
64	Pontbriand, Ryan	LS	6-2	255	10/1/79	9	Rice	Houston, Texas	D5a-'03	16/0
67	Robinson, Derreck	DL	6-4	295	3/3/82	5	Iowa	Minneapolis, Minn.	FA-'09	14/0
38	Robinson, Ramzee	DB	5-10	190	2/20/84	4	Alabama	Huntsville, Ala.	FA-'11	0*
80	Robiskie, Brian	WR	6-3	209	12/3/87	3	Ohio State	Cleveland, Ohio	D2a-'09	14/11
53	Roth, Matt	LB	6-4	275	10/14/82	7	Iowa	Villa Park, Ill.	W(Mia)-'09	16/16
71	Rubin, Ahtyba	DL	6-2	330	7/25/86	4	Iowa State	Pensacola, Fla.	D6a-'08	16/16
70	Sanford, Brian	DL	6-2	280	9/12/87	2	Temple	Hartford, Conn.	FA-'10	0*
91	Schaefering, Brian	DL	6-4	295	8/20/83	2	Lindenwood	St. Louis, Mo.	FA-'09	16/9
81	Smith, Alex	TE	6-4	258	5/22/82	7	Stanford	Denver, Colo.	FA-'10	3/1
25	Smith, DeAngelo	DB	5-11	200	7/17/86	2	Cincinnati	Columbus, Ohio	FA-'10	0*
98	Smith, Robaire	DL	6-5	310	11/15/77	12	Michigan State	Flint, Mich.	UFA(Tenn)-'07	5/5
27	Sorensen, Nick	DB	6-3	210	7/31/78	11	Virginia Tech	Vienna, Va.	FA-'07	15/0
65	Steinbach, Eric	OL	6-6	295	4/4/80	9	Iowa	Lockport, Ill.	UFA(Cin)-'07	16/16
83	Stuckey, Chansi	WR	6-0	196	10/4/83	5	Clemson	Warner Robins, Ga.	T(NYJ)-'09	16/5
73	Thomas, Joe	OL	6-6	312	12/4/84	5	Wisconsin	Brookfield, Wisc.	D1a-'07	16/16
72	Trautwein, Phil	OL	6-6	310	4/15/86	2	Florida	Voorhees, N.J.	FA-'10	0*
93	Trusnik, Jason	LB	6-4	250	6/6/84	5	Ohio Northern	Macedonia, Ohio	T(NYJ)-'09	16/5
60	Vallos, Steve	OL	6-3	310	12/28/83	5	Wake Forest	Boardman, Ohio	W(Sea)-'10	7/0
41	Ventrone, Ray	DB	5-10	200	10/21/82	6	Villanova	Pittsburgh, Pa.	FA-'09	16/0
47	Vickers, Lawrence	FB	6-0	250	5/8/83	6	Colorado	Houston, Texas	D6a-'06	16/4
6	Wallace, Seneca	QB	5-11	205	8/6/80	9	Iowa State	Sacramento, Calif.	T(Sea)-'10	8/4
43	Ward, T.J.	DB	5-10	200	12/12/86	2	Oregon	San Francisco, Calif.	D2a-'10	16/16
82	Watson, Benjamin	TE	6-3	255	12/18/80	8	Georgia	Rock Hill, S.C.	UFA(NE)-'10	16/16
88	Williams, Demetrius	WR	6-2	202	3/28/83	6	Oregon	Concord, Calif.	FA-'10	2/0
77	Womack, Floyd	OL	6-4	328	11/15/78	11	Mississippi State	Cleveland, Miss.	UFA(Sea)-'09	16/15
21	Wright, Eric	DB	5-10	190	7/24/85	5	Nevada-Las Vegas	San Francisco, Calif.	D2-'07	13/10
68	Yates, Billy	OL	6-2	305	4/15/80	8	Texas A&M	Fort Worth, Texas	FA-'10	9/3

* T. Adams missed '10 season because of injury; Alexander played 4 games with Jacksonville and 5 games with Cleveland in '10; Bell played 5 games with Philadelphia; DeVree last active with New England in '08; Estandia missed '10 season because of injury; Haggerty missed '10 season because of injury; Hardesty missed '10 season because of injury; D. Jackson missed '10 season because of injury; J. Mitchell played 2 games with Minnesota; Paxson last active with Pittsburgh in '08; Piscitelli played 11 games with Tampa Bay and 5 games with Cleveland; R. Robinson last active with Cleveland in '09; Sanford inactive for 8 games; D. Smith last active with Detroit in '09; Trautwein last active with St. Louis in '09.

t- Browns traded for M. Bell (Phil) and J. Mitchell (Minn).

   Traded—Jerome Harrison (4 games in '10) to Philadelphia.

   Also played with Browns in '10—WR Sam Aiken (3 games), LB Eric Barton (16), LB David Bowens (15), RB Thomas Clayton (2), DL Kenyon Coleman (16), RB James Davis (4), WR Yamon Figurs (1), DB Eric King (4), DB Derrick Roberson (2), DL Shaun Rogers (15), TE Robert Royal (15), RB Clifton Smith (2), OL John St. Clair (11).

^ "NFL Exp." as of 2011 Kickoff Weekend. For full explanation of how a player's NFL Experience is measured, refer to explanation underneath the First-Year Roster listed below.

FIRST-YEAR ROSTER

Name	Pos.	Ht.	Wt.	Birthdate	College	Hometown	How Acq.
Braxton, Branndon (1)	OL	6-6	315	12/10/85	Oklahoma	Youngstown, Ohio	FA-'10
Brown, Jarrett (1)	QB	6-3	225	9/21/87	West Virginia	Palm Beach, Fla.	FA
Cameron, Jordan	TE	6-5	245	8/8/88	Southern California	Newbury Park, Calif.	D4a
Clutts, Tyler (1)	FB	6-2	260	11/9/84	Fresno State	Clovis, Calif.	FA-'10
English, Auston (1)	LB	6-3	250	3/10/87	Oklahoma	Canadian, Texas	FA
Hagg, Eric	DB	6-1	205	9/15/89	Nebraska	Peoria, Ariz.	D7
Ivey, Travis (1)	DL	6-4	325	12/22/86	Maryland	Upper Marlboro, Md.	W(Mia)-'10
Little, Greg	WR	6-2	220	5/30/89	North Carolina	Durham, N.C.	D2b
Marecic, Owen	FB	6-0	245	10/4/88	Stanford	Portland, Ore.	D4b
Murray, Pat (1)	OL	6-3	316	10/31/84	Truman State	Fort Dodge, Iowa	FA-'09
Norwood, Jordan (1)	WR	5-11	180	9/29/86	Penn State	State College, Pa.	FA-'10
Pinkston, Jason	OL	6-4	305	9/5/87	Pittsburgh	Pittsburgh, Pa.	D5b
Porter, Quinn (1)	RB	6-0	205	2/2/86	Stillman	Quartz Hill, Calif.	FA-'10
Quaye, Ko (1)	DL	6-1	305	5/11/87	South Dakota	Brooklyn Park, Minn.	FA-'10
Sheard, Jabaal	DL	6-2	255	5/10/89	Pittsburgh	Hollywood, Hills, Fla.	D2a
Skrine, Buster	DB	5-9	185	4/26/89	Chattanooga	Woodstock, Ga.	D5a
Taylor, Phil	DL	6-3	335	4/7/88	Baylor	Clinton, Md.	D1
Windsor, Rod (1)	WR	6-2	205	4/24/85	Western New Mexico	Bessemer, Ala.	FA

The term NFL Rookie is defined as a player who is in his first season of professional football and has not been on the roster of another professional football team for any regular-season or postseason games. A Rookie is designated by an "R" on NFL rosters. Players who have been active in another professional football league or players who have NFL experience, including either preseason training camp or being on an Active List or Inactive List, or on Reserve/Injured or Reserve/Physically Unable to Perform for fewer than six regular-season games, are termed NFL First-Year Players. An NFL First-Year Player is designated by a "1" on NFL rosters. Thereafter, a player is credited with an additional year of experience for each season in which he accumulates six games on the Active List or Inactive List, or on Reserve/Injured or Reserve/Physically Unable to Perform.

Log on to www.clevelandbrowns.com for an up-to-date roster.

COACHING STAFF
Head Coach,
Pat Shurmur

Pro Career: Pat Shurmur was named the 13th full-time head coach in Browns history on January 13, 2011. In 12 seasons as an NFL assistant, he has been a part of teams that have qualified for the playoffs seven times, won five division crowns, and appeared in one Super Bowl. Spent the 2009-10 seasons as St. Louis' offensive coordinator, where he helped shape quarterback Sam Bradford. Spent 10 seasons with the Philadelphia Eagles (1999-2008), the first three seasons as the tight ends coach and last seven as the quarterbacks coach. Coached collegiately at Michigan State (1988-1997) and Stanford (1998). Career record: 0-0.

Background: Shurmur earned All-Big Ten conference honors and All-America honorable mention as a center for Michigan State in 1987. Was the school's first graduate student football player, with a master's degree in financial administration.

Personal: Born April 14, 1965, Dearborn, Mich. He and his wife, Jennifer, have four children, daughters Allyson, Erica and Claire, and a son, Kyle. His uncle, the late Fritz Shurmur, coached in the NFL for 24 years and was the Green Bay Packers' defensive coordinator from 1994-98.

ASSISTANT COACHES

Chris Beake, offensive assistant; born September 10, 1972, Kansas City, Mo. Quarterback Air Force 1991-92. No pro playing experience. College coach: Air Force 1994. Pro coach: San Francisco 49ers 1999-2003, Atlanta Falcons 2004-06, Seattle Seahawks 2008-09, San Francisco 49ers 2010, joined Browns in 2011.

Dwaine Board, defensive line; born November 29, 1956, Rocky Mount, Va. Defensive lineman North Carolina A&T 1974-77. Pro defensive lineman San Francisco 49ers 1979-1987, New Orleans Saints 1988. Pro coach: San Francisco 49ers 1990-2002, Seattle Seahawks 2003-08, Oakland Raiders 2009, joined Browns in 2011.

Gary Brown, running backs; born July 1, 1969, Williamsport, Pa. Running back Penn State 1987-1990. Pro running back Houston Oilers 1991-95, San Diego Chargers 1997, New York Giants 1998-99. College coach: Lycoming 2003-05, Susquehanna 2006-07, Rutgers 2008. Pro coach: Joined Browns in 2009.

Chuck Bullough, defensive assistant; born March 3, 1968, East Lansing, Mich. Linebacker Michigan State 1988-1991. Pro linebacker: Miami Dolphins 1993-95. College coach: Michigan State 1997-98, Lake Forest 2004, Western Michigan 2005, UCLA 2006-2010. Pro coach: Chicago Bears 1999-2003, joined Browns in 2011.

Bill Davis, linebackers; born November 5, 1965, Youngstown, Ohio. Quarterback Cincinnati 1984-88. College coach:

Michigan State 1990-91. Pro coach: Pittsburgh Steelers 1992-94, Carolina Panthers 1995-98, Cleveland Browns 1999, Green Bay Packers 2000, Atlanta Falcons 2001-03, New York Giants 2004, San Francisco 49ers 2005-06, Arizona Cardinals 2007-10, re-joined Browns in 2011.

Keith Gilbertson, senior assistant-offense; born May 15, 1948, Snohomish, Wash. Defensive lineman Central Washington 1967, Columbia Basin (Wash.) J.C. 1968, Hawaii 1969-1970. No pro playing experience. College coach: Idaho State 1971-74, Western Washington 1975, 1989-1991, Washington 1976, 1994-2004 (head coach), Utah State 1977-1981, Idaho 1982, 1986-88, California 1992-95 (head coach). Pro coach: L.A. Express (USFL) 1983-85, Seattle Seahawks 1996-98, 2005-08, joined Browns in 2010.

Steve Hagen, tight ends; born September 15, 1961, Forest City, Iowa. Wide receiver Cal Lutheran 1979-1982. No pro playing experience. College coach: Illinois 1984, Kansas 1985-86, Northern Arizona 1987-88, Notre Dame 1989-1990, Kent State 1991, Nevada 1992-93, Nevada-Las Vegas 1994-95, Wartburg 1996, San Jose State 1997-98, California 1999-2000, Fresno State 2006, North Carolina 2007-08. Pro coach: Cleveland Browns 2001-04, re-joined Browns in 2009.

Jerome Henderson, defensive backs; born August 8, 1969, Portsmouth, Va. Defensive back Clemson 1987-1990. Pro cornerback New England Patriots 1991-93, 1996, Buffalo Bills 1993-94, Philadelphia Eagles 1995, New York Jets 1997-98. Pro coach: New York Jets 2007-08, joined Browns in 2009.

Dick Jauron, defensive coordinator; born October 7, 1950. Running back Yale, 1970-72. Pro safety Detroit Lions 1973-77, Cincinnati Bengals 1978-1980. Pro coach: Buffalo Bills 1985, Green Bay Packers 1986-1994, Jacksonville Jaguars 1995-98, Chicago Bears 1999-2003 (head coach), Detroit Lions 2004-05 (head coach 2005), Buffalo Bills 2006-09 (head coach), Philadelphia Eagles 2010, joined Browns in 2011.

Kent Johnston, strength and conditioning; born February 21, 1966, Mexia, Texas. Defensive back Stephen F. Austin 1974- 77. No pro playing experience. College coach: Northwestern Louisiana 1981, Alabama 1985-86, 2004-05. Pro coach: Tampa Bay Buccaneers 1987-1991, Green Bay Packers 1992-98, Seattle Seahawks 1999-2003, joined Browns in 2010.

Rick Lyle, asst. strength and conditioning; born February 26, 1971, Monroe, La. Defensive lineman Missouri 1989-1993. Pro defensive lineman Cleveland Browns 1994-95, Baltimore Ravens 1996, New York Jets 1997-2001, New England Patriots 2002-03. Pro coach: New York Jets 2006-08, joined Browns in 2009.

Shawn Mennenga, special teams assistant; born January 8, 1971, Melbourne,

Iowa. Defensive back Missouri 1992. No pro playing experience. College coach: Southwest Baptist 1994-96, Western Kentucky 1997, Hutchinson (Kan.) C.C. 1998-2000, Culver-Stockton 2001-04 (head coach 2002-04), Fort Hays State 2005-08, South Dakota State 2009-10. Pro coach: Joined Browns in 2011.

Ray Rhodes, senior assistant-defense; born October 20, 1950, Mexia, Texas. Running back Texas Christian 1969-1970, wide receiver/defensive back/kick returner Tulsa 1972-73. Pro wide receiver/defensive back New York Giants 1974-79, San Francisco 49ers 1980. Pro coach: San Francisco 49ers 1981-1991, 1994, Green Bay Packers 1992-93, 1999 (head coach 1999), Philadelphia Eagles 1995-98 (head coach), Washington Redskins 2000, Denver Broncos 2001-02, Seattle Seahawks 2003-07, Houston Texans 2008-10, joined Browns in 2011.

Luke Steckel, assistant to the head coach; born April 28, 1985, Brentwood, Tenn. Linebacker Princeton 2003-06. No pro playing experience. Pro coach: Joined Browns in 2009.

Chris Tabor, special teams coordinator; born March 4, 1971, St. Joseph, Mo. Quarterback Benedictine College 1989-1992. No pro playing experience. College coach: Hutchinson (Kan.) C.C. 1994, Central Methodist College 1995-96, Missouri 1997-2000, Culver-Stockton College 2001 (head coach), Utah State 2002-05, Western Michigan 2006-07. Pro coach: Chicago Bears 2008-10, joined Browns in 2011.

George Warhop, offensive line; born September 19, 1961, Riverside, Calif. Guard/center Mt. San Jacinto (Calif.) J.C. 1979-1980, Cincinnati 1981-82. No pro playing experience. College coach: Cincinnati 1983, Kansas 1984-86, Vanderbilt 1987-89, New Mexico 1990, Southern Methodist 1993, Boston College 1994-95. Pro coach: London Monarchs (World League) 1991-92, St. Louis Rams 1996-97, Arizona Cardinals 1998-2002, Dallas Cowboys 2003-04, San Francisco 49ers 2005-08, joined Browns in 2009.

Mark Whipple, quarterbacks; born April 1, 1957, Tarrytown, N.Y. Quarterback Brown 1976-78. No pro playing experience. College coach: St. Lawrence 1980, Union 1981-82, Brown 1983, New Hampshire 1986-87, New Haven 1988-1993 (head coach), Brown 1994-97 (head coach), Massachusetts 1998-2003 (head coach), Miami 2009-10. Pro coach: Arizona Wranglers (USFL) 1984, Pittsburgh Steelers 2004-06, Philadelphia Eagles 2007, joined Browns in 2011.

Mike Wilson, wide receivers; born December 19, 1958; Los Angeles. Wide receiver Washington State 1978-80. Pro wide receiver San Francisco 49ers 1981-90. College coach: Stanford 1992-94, Southern California 1997-99. Pro coach: Oakland Raiders 1995-96, Arizona Cardinals 2004-06, Las Vegas Locomotives (UFL) 2009-10, joined Browns in 2011.

American Football Conference
West Division
Team Colors: Orange,
Broncos Navy Blue, and White
13655 Broncos Parkway
Englewood, Colorado 80112
Telephone: (303) 649-9000

2011 SCHEDULE
PRESEASON
Aug. 11	at Dallas	6:30
Aug. 20	Buffalo	6:30
Aug. 27	Seattle	7:00
Sep. 1	at Arizona	8:00

REGULAR SEASON
Sep. 12	Oakland (Mon)	8:15
Sep. 18	Cincinnati	2:15
Sep. 25	at Tennessee	11:00
Oct. 2	at Green Bay	2:15
Oct. 9	San Diego	2:15
Oct. 16	BYE	
Oct. 23	at Miami	11:00
Oct. 30	Detroit	2.05
Nov. 6	at Oakland	2:05
Nov. 13	at Kansas City	11:00
Nov. 17	New York Jets (Thu)	6:20
Nov. 27	at San Diego	2:15
Dec. 4	at Minnesota	2:05
Dec. 11	Chicago	2:05
Dec. 18	New England	2:15
Dec. 24	at Buffalo (Sat)	11.00
Jan. 1	Kansas City	2:15

All times MT

Stadium: INVESCO Field at Mile High
(opened in 2001)
•**Capacity:** 76,125
1701 Bryant Street
Denver, Colorado 80204
Playing Surface: DD Grassmaster
Training Camp: 13655 Broncos Parkway
Englewood, Colorado
80112

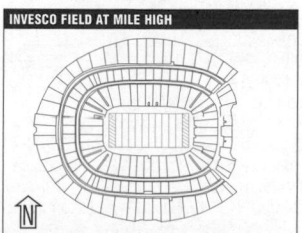

INVESCO FIELD AT MILE HIGH

CLUB OFFICIALS
Owner and CEO: Pat Bowlen
President: Joe Ellis
Executive VP of Football Operations:
John Elway
Head Coach: John Fox
FOOTBALL STAFF
General Manager: Brian Xanders
Director of Pro Personnel: Keith Kidd
Director of Football Administration:
Mike Bluem
Head Athletic Trainer: Steve Antonopulos
BUSINESS STAFF
General Counsel/Executive Vice
President: Rich Slivka
Vice President of Corporate
Communications: Jim Saccomano
Vice President of Community
Development: Cindy Kellogg
Executive Director of Media Relations:
Patrick Smyth
Executive Director of Ticket Operations
and Administration: Kirk Dyer
STADIUM MANAGEMENT COMPANY
Senior Vice President of Business
Development: Mac Freeman

COACHING HISTORY
(415-379-10)
Records include postseason games
1960-61	Frank Filchock	7-20-1
1962-64	Jack Faulkner*	9-22-1
1964-66	Mac Speedie**	6-19-1
1966	Ray Malavasi	4-8-0
1967-1971	Lou Saban***	20-42-3
1971	Jerry Smith	2-3-0
1972-76	John Ralston	34-33-3
1977-1980	Robert (Red) Miller	42-25-0
1981-1992	Dan Reeves	117-79-1
1993-94	Wade Phillips	16-17-0
1995-2008	Mike Shanahan	146-91-0
2009-2010	Josh McDaniels****	11-17-0
2010	Eric Studesville	1-3-0

*Released after four games in 1964
**Resigned after two games in 1966
***Resigned after nine games in 1971
****Released after 12 games in 2010

PAID ATTENDANCE
Home 588,328   Away 516,409
Total 1,104,737
Single-game home record,
76,716 (11/9/09)
Single-season home record, 597,984
(2007)

2011 DRAFT CHOICES
Round	Name	Pos.	College
1	Von Miller	LB	Texas A&M
2	Rahim Moore	DB	UCLA
	Orlando Franklin	T	Miami
3	Nate Irving	LB	North Carolina St.
4	Quinton Carter	DB	Oklahoma
	Julius Thomas	TE	Portland State
6	Mike Mohamed	LB	California
7	Virgil Groon	TE	Nevada
	Jeremy Beal	DE	Oklahoma

2010 TEAM RECORD
PRESEASON (1-3)

Date	Result	Opponent
8/15	L 24-33	at Cincinnati
8/21	L 20-25	Detroit
8/29	W 34-17	Pittsburgh
9/2	L 24-31	at Minnesota

REGULAR SEASON (4-12)

Date	Result	Opponent
9/12	L 17-24	at Jacksonville
9/19	W 31-14	Seattle
9/26	L 13-27	Indianapolis
10/3	W 26-20	at Tennessee
10/10	L 17-31	at Baltimore
10/17	L 20-24	New York Jets
10/24	L 14-59	Oakland
10/31	L 16-24	at San Francisco
11/14	W 49-29	Kansas City
11/22	L 14-35	at San Diego
11/28	L 33-36	St. Louis
12/5	L 6-10	at Kansas City
12/12	L 13-43	at Arizona
12/19	L 23-39	at Oakland
12/26	W 24-23	Houston
1/2	L 28-33	San Diego

SCORE BY PERIODS

Broncos	69	77	78	120	0	344
Opponents	85	143	104	139	0	471

2010 TEAM STATISTICS

	Broncos	Opp.
Total First Downs	309	334
Rushing	81	126
Passing	204	184
Penalty	24	24
3rd Down: Made/Att	67/207	80/209
3rd Down Pct.	32.4	38.3
4th Down: Made/Att	6/19	10/16
4th Down Pct.	31.6	62.5
Possession Avg.	28:09	31:51
Total Net Yards	5582	6253
Avg. Per Game	348.9	390.8
Total Plays	1018	1056
Avg. Per Play	5.5	5.9
Net Yards Rushing	1544	2473
Avg. Per Game	96.5	154.6
Total Rushes	398	531
Net Yards Passing	4038	3780
Avg. Per Game	252.4	236.3
Sacked/Yards Lost	40/269	23/156
Gross Yards	4307	3936
Att./Completions	580/334	502/297
Completion Pct.	57.6	59.2
Had Intercepted	12	10
Punts/Average	86/44.6	73/43.4
Net Punting Avg.	86/36.6	73/37.1
Penalties/Yards	98/944	98/921
Fumbles/Ball Lost	29/15	22/8
Touchdowns	40	55
Rushing	13	26
Passing	25	26
Returns	2	3

2010 INDIVIDUAL STATISTICS

PASSING	Att.	Comp.	Yds.	Pct.	TD	Int.	Tkld.	Rate
Orton	498	293	3653	58.8	20	9	34/243	87.5
Tebow	82	41	654	50.0	5	3	6/26	82.1
Broncos	580	334	4307	57.6	25	12	40/269	86.8
Opponents	502	297	3936	59.2	26	10	23/156	93.0

SCORING	TD R	TD P	TD Rt	PAT	FG	Saf	PTS
Prater	0	0	0	28/29	16/18	0	76
Lloyd	0	11	0	0/0	0/0	0	66
Moreno	5	3	0	0/0	0/0	0	48
Tebow	6	0	0	0/0	0/0	0	36
Hauschka	0	0	0	10/10	6/7	0	28
Buckhalter	2	2	0	0/0	0/0	0	24
Royal	0	3	0	0/0	0/0	0	18
Gaffney	0	2	0	0/0	0/0	0	12
D. Thomas	0	2	0	0/0	0/0	0	12
Decker	0	1	0	0/0	0/0	0	6
Hunter	0	0	1	0/0	0/0	0	6
Larsen	0	1	0	0/0	0/0	0	6
Vaughn	0	0	1	0/0	0/0	0	6
Broncos	13	25	2	38/39	22/25	0	344
Opponents	26	26	3	52/53	29/36	1	471

2-Pt Conversions: Broncos 0-1, Opponents 0-2.

RUSHING	No.	Yds	Avg	LG	TD
Moreno	182	779	4.3	35	5
Tebow	43	227	5.3	40t	6
Ball	41	158	3.9	19	0
Buckhalter	59	147	2.5	13	2
Orton	22	98	4.5	14	0
Maroney	36	74	2.1	13	0
Royal	6	61	10.2	20	0
Larsen	3	18	6.0	14	0
D. Thomas	2	1	0.5	1	0
Colquitt	1	0	0.0	0	0
A. Brown	2	-1	-0.5	0	0
Lloyd	1	-18	-18.0	-18	0
Broncos	398	1544	3.9	40t	13
Opponents	531	2473	4.7	71t	26

RECEIVING	No.	Yds	Avg	LG	TD
Lloyd	77	1448	18.8	71	11
Gaffney	65	875	13.5	50	2
Royal	59	627	10.6	41	3
Moreno	37	372	10.1	45	3
Buckhalter	28	240	8.6	23t	2
D. Thomas	22	283	12.9	31	2
Graham	18	148	8.2	28	0
Gronkowski	8	65	8.1	13	0
Decker	6	106	17.7	38	1
Larsen	5	51	10.2	29	1
Maroney	4	50	12.5	28	0
Ball	3	16	5.3	13	0
Willis	1	17	17.0	17	0
R. Quinn	1	9	9.0	9	0
Broncos	334	4307	12.9	71	25
Opponents	297	3936	13.3	73t	26

INTERCEPTIONS	No.	Yds	Avg	LG	TD
Hill	2	67	33.5	36	0
Thompson	2	20	10.0	18	0
Bailey	2	0	0.0	0	0
Cox	1	15	15.0	15	0
Hunter	1	14	14.0	14	0
Vickerson	1	4	4.0	4	0
Dawkins	1	-2	-2.0	-2	0
Broncos	10	118	11.8	36	0
Opponents	12	255	21.3	44	1

PUNTING	No.	Yds.	Avg.	In 20	LG
Colquitt	86	3835	44.6	19	63
Broncos	86	3835	44.6	19	63
Opponents	73	3169	43.4	27	61

PUNT RETURNS	Ret	FC	Yds	Avg	LG	TD
Royal	25	12	298	11.9	33	0
Thompson	3	2	18	6.0	10	0
Cox	3	1	7	2.3	4	0
Broncos	31	15	323	10.4	33	0
Opponents	50	17	550	11.0	63	0

KICKOFF RETURNS	No.	Yds	Avg	LG	TD
Decker	22	556	25.3	51	0
D. Thomas	16	398	24.9	65	0
Cox	9	172	19.1	30	0
Royal	5	107	21.4	33	0
Larsen	3	44	14.7	19	0
Vaughn	2	125	62.5	97t	1
Ball	2	33	16.5	18	0
Broncos	59	1435	24.3	97t	1
Opponents	51	1259	24.7	98t	1

FIELD GOALS	1-19	20-29	30-39	40-49	50+
Prater	0/0	3/3	7/7	4/5	2/3
Hauschka	0/0	1/1	3/3	2/3	0/0
Broncos	0/0	4/4	10/10	6/8	2/3
Opponents	0/0	3/3	10/11	11/13	5/9

SACKS	No.
D. Williams	5.5
Haggan	5.0
Hunter	3.0
Dawkins	2.0
Vickerson	2.0
Ayers	1.5
Bailey	1.0
Bannan	1.0
M. Thomas	1.0
Woodyard	1.0
Broncos	23.0
Opponents	40.0

RECORD HOLDERS
INDIVIDUAL RECORDS—CAREER

Category	Name	Performance
Rushing (Yds.)	Terrell Davis, 1995-2002	7,607
Passing (Yds.)	John Elway, 1983-1998	51,475
Passing (TDs)	John Elway, 1983-1998	300
Receiving (No.)	Rod Smith, 1995-2007	849
Receiving (Yds.)	Rod Smith, 1995-2007	11,389
Interceptions	Steve Foley, 1976-1986	44
Punting (Avg.)	Jim Fraser, 1962-64	45.2
Punt Return (Avg.)	Darrien Gordon, 1997-98	12.5
Kickoff Return (Avg.)	Abner Haynes, 1965-66	26.3
Field Goals	Jason Elam, 1993-2007	395
Touchdowns (Tot.)	Rod Smith, 1995-2007	71
Points	Jason Elam, 1993-2007	1,786
*Sacks	Simon Fletcher, 1985-1995	97.5

INDIVIDUAL RECORDS—SINGLE SEASON

Category	Name	Performance
Rushing (Yds.)	Terrell Davis, 1998	2,008
Passing (Yds.)	Jay Cutler, 2008	4,526
Passing (TDs)	John Elway, 1997	27
	Jake Plummer, 2004	27
Receiving (No.)	Rod Smith, 2001	113
Receiving (Yds.)	Rod Smith, 2000	1,602
Interceptions	Goose Gonsoulin, 1960	11
Punting (Avg.)	Tom Rouen, 1998	46.9
Punt Return (Avg.)	Floyd Little, 1967	16.9
Kickoff Return (Avg.)	Bill Thompson, 1969	28.5
Field Goals	Jason Elam, 1995, 2001	31
Touchdowns (Tot.)	Terrell Davis, 1998	23
Points	Terrell Davis, 1998	138
*Sacks	Elvis Dumervil, 2009	17.0

INDIVIDUAL RECORDS—SINGLE GAME

Category	Name	Performance
Rushing (Yds.)	Mike Anderson, 12-3-00	251
Passing (Yds.)	Jake Plummer, 10-31-04	499
Passing (TDs)	Frank Tripucka, 10-20-62	5
	John Elway, 11-18-84	5
	Gus Frerotte, 11-19-00	5
Receiving (No.)	Brandon Marshall, 12-13-09	**21
Receiving (Yds.)	Shannon Sharpe, 10-20-02	214
Interceptions	Goose Gonsoulin, 9-18-60	**4
	Willie Brown, 11-15-64	**4
	Deltha O'Neal, 10-7-01	**4
Field Goals	Gene Mingo, 10-6-63	5
	Rich Karlis, 11-20-83	5
	Jason Elam, 9-3-95, 10-13-02	5
Touchdowns (Tot.)	Clinton Portis, 12-7-03	5
Points	Clinton Portis, 12-7-03	30
*Sacks	Karl Mecklenburg, 9-15-85, 12-1-85	4.0
	Simon Fletcher, 11-4-90	4.0
	Elvis Dumervil, 9-20-09	4.0

*Sacks became an official statistic in 1982.
**NFL Record

VETERAN ROSTER AS OF MARCH 3, 2011

No.	Name	Pos.	Ht.	Wt.	Birthdate	^NFL Exp.	College	Hometown	How Acq.	'10 Games/ Starts
56	Ayers, Robert	DE	6-3	274	9/6/85	3	Tennessee	Bennettsville, S.C.	D1b-'09	11/10
24	Bailey, Champ	CB	6-0	192	6/22/78	13	Georgia	Folkston, Ga.	T(Wash)-'04	15/15
35	Ball, Lance	RB	5-9	220	6/2/85	3	Maryland	Teaneck, N.J.	FA-'10	10/0
68	Beadles, Zane	G	6-4	305	11/19/86	2	Utah	Sandy, Utah	D2-'10	16/14
30	Bruton, David	FS	6-2	211	7/23/87	3	Notre Dame	Miamisburg, Ohio	D4a-'09	16/2
28	Buckhalter, Correll	RB	6-0	223	10/6/78	11	Nebraska	Collins, Miss.	UFA(Phil)-'09	15/0
63	Byers, Jeff	G	6-4	301	9/7/85	2	Southern California	Loveland, Colo.	W(Sea)-'10	0*
78	Clady, Ryan	T	6-6	325	9/6/86	4	Boise State	Rialto, Calif.	D1-'08	16/16
75	Clark, Chris	T	6-5	315	10/1/85	2	Southern Mississippi	New Orleans, La.	W(Minn)-'10	8/0
85	Coats, Daniel	TE	6-3	264	4/16/84	5	Brigham Young	Layton, Utah	FA-'10	4/0
4	Colquitt, Britton	P	6-3	205	3/20/85	3	Tennessee	Knoxville, Tenn.	FA-'09	16/0
32	Cox, Perrish	CB	6-0	198	1/10/87	2	Oklahoma State	Waco, Texas	D5-'10	15/9
64	Daniels, Stanley	G	6-4	320	11/30/84	2	Washington	San Diego, Calif.	FA-'10	7/4
17	Davis, Britt	WR	6-3	205	4/23/86	2	Northern Illinois	Broadview, Ill.	FA-'10	3/0
20	Dawkins, Brian	S	6-0	210	10/13/73	16	Clemson	Jacksonville, Fla.	UFA(Phil)-'09	11/11
87	Decker, Eric	WR	6-3	220	3/15/87	2	Minnesota	Cold Spring, Minn.	D3b-'10	14/0
58	Douglas, Dominic	LB	6-1	229	1/13/87	3	Mississippi State	Clinton, Miss.	FA-'10	0*
92	Dumervil, Elvis	DE	5-11	248	1/19/84	6	Louisville	Miami, Fla.	D4b-'06	0*
10	Gaffney, Jabar	WR	6-2	200	12/1/80	10	Florida	Jacksonville, Fla.	UFA(NE)-'09	16/11
21	Goodman, André	CB	5-10	184	8/11/78	10	South Carolina	Greenville, S.C.	UFA(Mia)-'09	8/8
82	Gronkowski, Dan	TE	6-5	255	1/21/85	3	Maryland	Williamsville, N.Y.	T(Det)-'10	12/4
57	Haggan, Mario	LB	6-3	267	3/3/80	9	Mississippi State	Clarksdale, Miss.	FA-'08	16/16
3	Hauschka, Steven	K	6-4	210	6/29/85	4	North Carolina St.	Needham, Mass.	FA -'10	4/0
23	Hill, Renaldo	S	5-11	205	11/12/78	11	Michigan State	Detroit, Mich.	UFA(Mia)-'09	16/16
71	Hochstein, Russ	G	6-4	305	10/7/77	11	Nebraska	Hartington, Neb.	T(NE)-'09	16/6
52	Hunter, Jason	DE	6-4	271	8/28/83	6	Appalachian State	Fayetteville, N.C.	FA-'10	16/12
29	Jackson, Chevis	CB	5-11	193	12/11/85	4	Louisiana State	Mobile, Ala.	W(NE) -'10	0*
37	Johnson, Jeremiah	RB	5-9	218	2/15/87	2	Oregon	Los Angeles, Calif.	FA-'10	0*
33	Jones, Nate	CB	5-10	185	6/15/82	8	Rutgers	Scotch Plains, N.J.	UFA(Mia)-'10	16/3
48	Kelley, Braxton	LB	6-0	242	10/24/86	3	Kentucky	LaGrange, Ga.	FA-'09	0*
73	Kuper, Chris	G	6-4	303	12/19/82	6	North Dakota	Anchorage, Alaska	D5-'06	15/15
46	Larsen, Spencer	FB	6-2	243	3/4/84	4	Arizona	Gilbert, Ariz.	D6-'08	11/5
94	Leonard, Louis	DT	6-4	325	7/16/84	5	Fresno State	Compton, Calif.	FA-'10	0*
84	Lloyd, Brandon	WR	6-0	194	7/5/81	9	Illinois	Blue Springs, Mo.	FA-'09	16/11
51	Mays, Joe	LB	5-11	246	7/6/85	4	North Dakota State	Chicago, Ill.	T(Phil)-'10	12/5
31	McBath, Darcel	S	6-1	198	10/28/85	3	Texas Tech	Gainesville, Texas	D2b-'09	7/1
34	McCarthy, Kyle	S	6-1	210	9/30/86	2	Notre Dame	Youngstown, Ohio	FA-'10	8/0
	McLaughlin, Mike	RB	6-0	245	5/11/87	2	Boston College	Woburn, Mass.	FA-'11	0*
27	Moreno, Knowshon	RB	5-11	210	7/16/87	3	Georgia	Middletown, N.J.	D1a-'09	13/13
	Murphy, Shawn	G	6-4	315	12/17/82	4	Utah State	Highland, Utah	FA-'11	0*
69	Olsen, Eric	G	6-3	305	6/16/88	2	Notre Dame	Brooklyn, N.Y.	D6-'10	1/0
8	Orton, Kyle	QB	6-4	225	11/14/82	7	Purdue	Runnels, Iowa	T(Chi)-'09	13/13
66	Paxton, Lonie	LS	6-2	265	3/13/78	12	Sacramento State	Corona, Calif.	UFA(NE)-'09	16/0
9	Quinn, Brady	QB	6-3	235	10/27/84	5	Notre Dame	Dublin, Ohio	T(Cle)-'10	0*
81	Quinn, Richard	TE	6-4	255	9/6/86	3	North Carolina	Maple Heights, Ohio	D2c-'09	14/4
	Ramirez, Manny	G	6-3	326	2/13/83	5	Texas Tech	Houston, Texas	FA-'11	0*
54	Robinson, Lee	LB	6-2	256	4/23/87	2	Alcorn State	Liberty, Miss.	FA-'10	2/0
19	Royal, Eddie	WR	5-10	180	5/21/86	4	Virginia Tech	Chantilly, Va.	D2-'08	16/10
	Taylor, Herb	T	6-3	295	9/22/84	5	Texas Christian	Sugar Land, Texas	FA-'11	0*
15	Tebow, Tim	QB	6-3	245	8/14/87	2	Florida	Jacksonville, Fla.	D1b-'10	9/3
88	Thomas, Demaryius	WR	6-3	229	12/25/87	2	Georgia Tech	Montrose, Ga.	D1a-'10	10/2
22	Thompson, Syd'Quan	CB	5-9	191	2/7/87	2	California	Sacramento, Calif.	D7a-'10	13/0
41	Vaughn, Cassius	CB	5-11	195	11/3/87	2	Mississippi	Memphis, Tenn.	FA-'10	13/0
90	Veikune, David	DE	6-2	257	12/12/85	3	Hawaii	Ewa Beach, Hawaii	FA-'10	4/0
99	Vickerson, Kevin	DT	6-5	321	1/8/83	6	Michigan State	Detroit, Mich.	FA-'10	15/12
50	Walton, J.D.	C	6-3	305	3/24/87	2	Baylor	Allen, Texas	D3a-'10	16/16
25	White, LenDale	RB	6-1	235	12/20/84	6	Southern California	Denver, Colo.	FA-'10	0*
55	Williams, D.J.	LB	6-1	242	7/20/82	8	Miami	Concord, Calif.	D1-'04	16/15
12	Willis, Matthew	WR	6-0	190	4/13/84	4	UCLA	Anaheim, Calif.	FA-'08	6/0

* Byers inactive for 2 games in '10; Douglas spent 2 games on Denver practice squad, last active with St. Louis in '09; Dumervil missed '10 season because of injury; Jackson inactive for 2 games; Johnson spent 6 games on Denver practice squad, missed '09 season because of injury with Houston; Kelley missed '10 season because of injury; Leonard inactive for 1 game; McLaughlin missed '10 season because of injury with Baltimore; Murphy last active with Tampa Bay in '09; Quinn did not play in 4 games and was inactive for 12 games; Ramirez inactive for 4 games with Detroit; Taylor inactive with Denver for 1 game in '09; White missed '10 season because of injury.

Also played with Broncos in '10—LB/DE Kevin Alexander (8 games), RB Lance Ball (10), T D'Anthony Batiste (5), LB Diyral Briggs (1), RB Andre Brown (3), DL Ronald Fields (16), TE Daniel Graham (16), T Ryan Harris (11), RB Laurence Maroney (4), DE Ryan McBain (16), LB/DE Jarvis Moss (9), K Matt Prater (12), DL Le Kevin Smith (1), DT Marcus Thomas (16), NT Jamal Williams (16), LB Wesley Woodyard (11).

^ "NFL Exp." as of 2011 Kickoff Weekend. For full explanation of how a player's NFL Experience is measured, refer to explanation underneath the First-Year Roster listed below.

FIRST-YEAR ROSTER

Name	Pos.	Ht.	Wt.	Birthdate	College	Hometown	How Acq.
Beal, Jeremy	DE	6-3	267	12/2/87	Oklahoma	Carrollton, Texas	D7b
Carter, Quinton	S	6-1	200	7/20/88	Oklahoma	Las Vegas, Nev.	D4a
Franklin, Orlando	T	6-7	312	12/16/87	Miami	Delray Beach, Fla.	D2b
Green, Virgil	TE	6-5	240	8/3/88	Nevada	Tulare, Calif.	D7a
Irving, Nate	LB	6-1	231	7/12/88	North Carolina State	Wallace, N.C.	D3
Miller, Von	LB	6-3	243	3/26/89	Texas A&M	DeSoto, Texas	D1
Minor, Brandon (1)	RB	6-1	214	7/24/88	Michigan	Richmond, Va.	FA-'10
Mohamed, Mike	LB	6-3	245	3/11/88	California	Brawley, Calif.	D6
Moore, Rahim	S	6-1	196	2/11/90	UCLA	Los Angeles, Calif.	D2a
Polk, Nick (1)	S	6-0	216	10/6/86	Indiana	Milwaukee, Wisc.	FA-'10
Riley, Eron (1)	WR	6-3	210	8/5/87	Duke	Savannah, Ga.	FA-'10
Thomas, Julius	TE	6-5	240	6/27/88	Portland State	Lodi, Calif.	D4b
Unrein, Mitch (1)	DT	6-4	300	3/25/87	Wyoming	Eaton, Colo.	FA-'10

The term NFL Rookie is defined as a player who is in his first season of professional football and has not been on the roster of another professional football team for any regular-season or postseason games. A Rookie is designated by an "R" on NFL rosters. Players who have been active in another professional football league or players who have NFL experience, including either preseason training camp or being on an Active List or Inactive List, or on Reserve/Injured or Reserve/Physically Unable to Perform for fewer than six regular-season games, are termed NFL First-Year Players. An NFL First-Year Player is designated by a "1" on NFL rosters. Thereafter, a player is credited with an additional year of experience for each season in which he accumulates six games on the Active List or Inactive List, or on Reserve/Injured or Reserve/Physically Unable to Perform.

Log on to www.denverbroncos.com for an up-to-date roster.

DENVER BRONCOS

COACHING STAFF
Head Coach,
John Fox

Pro Career: John Fox was named the 14th head coach in Denver Broncos history on January 13, 2011. He joined the Broncos after spending the previous nine seasons (2002-2010) as the head coach of the Carolina Panthers. In 22 NFL seasons, he has appeared in two Super Bowls and three conference championship games as a head coach or coordinator. During that span, he has coached 21 players to a total of 43 Pro Bowl selections, including Pro Football Hall of Fame cornerback Rod Woodson and perennial All-Pros such as defensive ends Michael Strahan and Julius Peppers. A proven leader who consistently produces stout defenses and thrives off a productive running game, Fox ranks third among active NFL head coaches with 78 overall wins since 2002. He compiled a 73-71 (.507) regular-season record with the Panthers that included three 11-win campaigns, two NFC South Division titles and three playoff appearances. Carolina went 5-3 in the postseason under Fox, appearing in two NFC Championship Games and one Super Bowl (XXXVIII in 2003). His four postseason road victories rank third in NFL history behind Tom Landry (7) and Joe Gibbs (5). Prior to joining Denver, he served as the head coach for Carolina (2002-10) and the defensive coordinator for the N.Y. Giants (1997-2001). In 2000, Fox helped the Giants reach Super Bowl XXXV, including posting the first shutout in a conference title game since 1986. Before joining the Giants, was a consultant for the Rams (1996), defensive coordinator for the Raiders (1994-95), defensive backs coach for the Chargers (1992-93) and Steelers (1989-1991), and secondary coach for the USFL's Los Angeles Express (1985). Career record: 78-74.

Background: Defensive back at San Diego State (1976-77). Coached at San Diego State (1978), U.S. International (1979) Boise State (1980), Long Beach State (1981), Utah (1982), Kansas (1983), Iowa State (1984), and Pittsburgh (1986-88). Received bachelor's degree in physical education and earned a teaching credential from San Diego State.

Personal: Born February 8, 1955, in Virginia Beach, Va. He and his wife, Robin, have four children—Mathew, Mark, Cody, and Halle.

ASSISTANT COACHES

Dennis Allen, defensive coordinator; born Sept. 22, 1972, Atlanta. Safety Texas A&M 1992-95. No pro playing experience. College coach: Texas A&M 1996-99, Tulsa 2000-01. Pro coach: Atlanta Falcons 2002-05, New Orleans Saints 2006-2010, joined Broncos in 2011.

Clancy Barone, tight ends; born July 26, 1963, San Andreas, Calif. Offensive lineman Cal State-Sacramento 1981-82, Nevada 1985-86. No pro playing experience. College coach: American River (Calif.) J.C. 1987-89, Cal State-Sacramento 1990-92, Texas A&M 1993, Eastern Illinois 1994-96, Wyoming 1997-99, Houston 2000-02, Texas State 2003. Pro coach: Atlanta Falcons 2004-06, San Diego Chargers 2007-08, joined Broncos in 2009.

Keith Burns, asst. special teams; born May 16, 1972, Greeleyville, S.C. Linebacker Oklahoma State 1991-94. Pro linebacker Denver Broncos 1994-98, 2000-03, 2005-06, Chicago Bears 1999, Tampa Bay Buccaneers 2004. Pro coach: Joined Broncos in 2007.

Brian Callahan, quality control-offense; born June 10, 1984, Champaign, Ill. Quarterback UCLA 2002-06. No pro playing experience. College coach: UCLA 2006-07. Pro coach: Joined Broncos in 2010.

Sam Garnes, asst. secondary; born July 12, 1974, Bronx, N.Y. Safety Cincinnati 1992-96. Pro safety N.Y. Giants 1997-2001, N.Y. Jets 2002-03. Pro coach: Cologne Centurions (NFL Europe) 2006, Las Vegas Locomotives (UFL) 2009, Carolina Panthers 2010, joined Broncos in 2011.

Adam Gase, quarterbacks; born March 29, 1978, Ypsilanti, Mich. Attended Michigan State. No college or pro playing experience. College coach: Louisiana State 2000-02. Pro coach: Detroit Lions 2003-07, San Francisco 49ers 2008, joined Broncos in 2009.

Justin Lovett, strength and conditioning assistant; born January 8, 1977, Dayton, Ohio. Wide receiver Findlay 1995-96. No pro playing experience. College coach: Texas-El Paso 2008. Pro coach: Joined Broncos in 2010.

Dave Magazu, offensive line; born June 10, 1957, Taunton, Mass. Defensive tackle Springfield College 1976-79. No pro playing experience. College coach: Ithaca 1980, Western Michigan 1981, Eastern Michigan 1982, Michigan 1983, Northern Illinois 1984, Ball State 1985-86, Navy 1987-89, Indiana State 1990-91, Colorado State 1992-94, Kentucky 1995-96, Memphis 1997-98, Boston College 1999-2002. Pro coach: Carolina Panthers 2003-10, joined Broncos in 2011.

Mike McCoy, offensive coordinator; born April 1, 1972, San Francisco. Quarterback Long Beach State 1990-91, Utah 1992-94. Pro quarterback Amsterdam Admirals (NFLE) 1997, Calgary Stampeders (CFL) 1999. Pro coach: Carolina Panthers 1999-2008, joined Broncos in 2009.

Ron Milus, secondary; born November 25, 1963, Tacoma, Wash. Cornerback Washington 1982-85. College coach: Washington 1991-98, Texas A&M 1999. Pro coach: Denver Broncos 2000-02, Arizona Cardinals 2003, New York Giants 2004-05, St. Louis Rams 2006-08, Carolina Panthers 2009-2010, re-joined Broncos in 2011.

Wayne Nunnely, defensive line, born March 29, 1952, Los Angeles. Fullback Nevada-Las Vegas 1972-75. No pro playing experience. College coach: Nevada-Las Vegas 1976, 1982-89 (head coach 1986-89), Cal Poly-Pomona 1977-78, Cal State-Fullerton 1979, Pacific 1980-81, Southern California 1991-92, UCLA 1993-94. Pro coach: New Orleans Saints 1995-96, San Diego Chargers 1997-2008, joined Broncos in 2009.

Jay Rodgers, quality control defense; born August 29, 1976, St. Paul, Minn. Quarterback Indiana 1996-98, Missouri State 1999. No pro playing experience. College coach: Missouri State 2004, Stephen F. Austin 2005-06, Iowa State 2007-08. Pro coach: Joined Broncos in 2009.

Jeff Rodgers, special teams coordinator; born January 12, 1978, St. Paul, Minn. Linebacker North Texas 1996-99. College coach: Arizona 2001-02, Kansas State 2008. Pro coach: San Francisco 49ers 2003-07, Carolina Panthers 2009-2010, joined Broncos in 2011.

Greg Saporta, asst. strength and conditioning; born February 2, 1957, New York, N.Y. Wide receiver Buffalo State 1977-79. No pro playing experience. College coach: Florida 1981-88, 1993-94, North Carolina 1989-1992. Pro coach: Joined Broncos in 1995.

Richard Smith, linebackers; born October 17, 1955, Los Angeles. Offensive lineman Rio Hondo (Calif.) J.C. 1975-76, Fresno State 1977-78. College coach: Rio Hondo (Calif.) J.C. 1979-1980, Cal State-Fullerton 1981-83, California 1984-86, Arizona 1987. Pro coach: Houston Oilers 1988-1992, Denver Broncos 1993-96, San Francisco 49ers 1997-2002, Detroit Lions 2003-04, Miami Dolphins 2005, Houston Texans 2006-08, Carolina Panthers 2009-2010, re-joined Broncos 2011.

Eric Studesville, running backs; born May 29, 1967, Madison, Wisc. Defensive back Wisconsin-Whitewater 1985-88. No pro playing experience. College coach: Wingate 1994, Kent State 1995-96. Pro coach: Chicago Bears 1997-2000, New York Giants 2001-03, Buffalo Bills 2004-2009, joined Broncos in 2010 (interim head coach, four games in 2010).

Tyke Tolbert, wide receivers; born September 15, 1967, Conroe, Texas. Wide receiver Louisiana State 1988-1990. No pro playing experience. College coach: Louisiana State 1994, Ohio 1995, Northeast Louisiana 1995-97, Auburn 1998, Louisiana-Lafayette 1999-2001, Florida 2002. Pro coach: Arizona Cardinals 2003, Buffalo Bills 2004-09, Carolina Panthers 2010, joined Broncos in 2011.

Rich Tuten, strength and conditioning; born December 30, 1953, Columbia, S.C. Nose guard Clemson 1976-78. No pro playing experience. College coach: Florida 1979-1988, 1993-94, North Carolina 1989-1992. Pro coach: Joined Broncos in 1995.

American Football Conference
South Division
Team Colors: Deep Steel Blue, Battle
Red, and Liberty White
Two Reliant Park
Houston, Texas 77054
Telephone: (832) 667-2000

2011 SCHEDULE
PRESEASON
Aug. 15 **New York Jets** 7:00
Aug. 20 **New Orleans**.......................7:00
Aug. 27 at San Francisco.................7:00
Sep. 1 at Minnesota 7:00

REGULAR SEASON
Sep. 11 **Indianapolis** 12:00
Sep. 18 at Miami 3:15
Sep. 25 at New Orleans 12:00
Oct. 2 **Pittsburgh** 12:00
Oct. 9 **Oakland** 12:00
Oct. 16 at Baltimore 3:05
Oct. 23 at Tennessee 12:00
Oct. 30 **Jacksonville** 12:00
Nov. 6 **Cleveland** 12:00
Nov. 13 at Tampa Bay 12:00
Nov. 20 BYE
Nov. 27 at Jacksonville 12:00
Dec. 4 **Atlanta** 12:00
Dec. 11 at Cincinnati 12:00
Dec. 18 **Carolina** 12:00
Dec. 22 at Indianapolis (Thu).......... 7:20
Jan. 1 **Tennessee** 12:00
All times CT

Stadium: Reliant Stadium
(opened in 2002)
•**Capacity:** 71,054
Houston, Texas 77054
Playing Surface: Grass
Training Camp: Methodist Training
Center

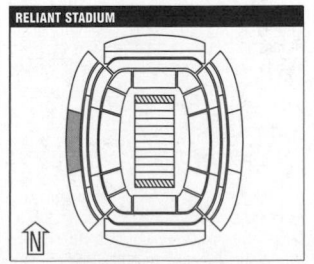

RELIANT STADIUM

CLUB OFFICIALS
Chairman and CEO: Robert C. McNair
Vice Chairman: Philip J. Burguiéres
Vice Chairman: D. Cal McNair
General Manager: Rick Smith
President: Jamey Rootes
Senior Vice President, Treasurer and
CFO: Scott Schwinger
Senior Vice President, General Counsel
and CAO: Suzie Thomas
Vice President and Controller:
Marilan Logan
Vice President, Football Administration:
Chris Olsen
Vice President of Security: Ryan Reichert
Sr. Vice President, Ticketing and Event
Management: John Schriever
Vice President, Finance: Greg Watson
Director of Football Operations:
Doug West
Director of Player Development:
Sean Washington
Director of College Scouting: Dale Strahm
Director of Pro Personnel: Brian Gardner
Associate Director of Pro Scouting:
Bobby Grier
Pro Scout: Kevin Murphy, Larry Wright
Coordinator of College Scouting:
Mike Maccagnan
National College Scout: Ed Lambert
College Scouts: Mike Ackerley, Jon Carr,
Ryan Cavanaugh, Mike Martin,
Bob Merritt, Nathan Trott
Director of Sports Medicine/Head Athletic
Trainer: Geoff Kaplan
Coordinator of Rehabilitation:
Roland Ramirez
Assistant Athletic Trainer: Reggie Barnes
Director of Equipment Services:
Jay Brunetti
Equipment Services Assistants:
Mike Parson, Christian Snell
Director of Video Operations: Joe Malota
Assistant Director of Video Operations:
Bob Ford
Video Operations Assistant: Tim Brog
Sr. Director of Communications:
Kevin Cooper
Sr. Director of Corporate Development:
Greg Grissom
Risk Manager: Jan Kelly
Corporate Counsel: Greg Kondritz
Director of Human Resources:
Glenda Morrison
Sr. Director of Event Operations and
Guest Services: Diane Crossey
Director of Marketing: Jennifer Davenport
Director of Integrated Media:
Nick Schenck
Director of Information Technology:
Jeff Schmitz
Assistant Treasurer: Jon Southern
Director of Premium Seating:
Brian Varnadoe
Director of Ticket and Event Sales:
Derek Beeman
Director of Accounting: Tamala Theeck

COACHING HISTORY
(55-89-0)
2002-05   Dom Capers................18-46-0
2006-2010 Gary Kubiak 37-43-0

PAID ATTENDANCE
Home 556,213   Away 509,771
Total 1,065,984
Single-game home record,
71,456 (9/26/10)
Single-season home record,
556,213 (2010)

2011 DRAFT CHOICES

Round	Name	Pos.	College
1	J.J. Watt	DE	Wisconsin
2	Brooks Reed	LB	Arizona
	Brandon Harris	DB	Miami
4	Rashad Carmichael	DB	Virginia Tech
5	Shiloh Keo	DB	Idaho
	T.J. Yates	QB	North Carolina
7	Derek Newton	T	Arkansas State
	Cheta Ozougwu	LB	Rice

2010 TEAM RECORD
PRESEASON (1-3)

Date	Result	Opponent
8/14	L 16-19	at Arizona
8/21	L 20-38	at New Orleans
8/28	W 23-7	Dallas
9/2	L 17-24	Tampa Bay

REGULAR SEASON (6-10)

Date	Result	Opponent
9/12	W 34-24	Indianapolis
9/19	W 30-27	at Washington (OT)
9/26	L 13-27	Dallas
10/3	W 31-24	at Oakland
10/10	L 10-34	New York Giants
10/17	W 35-31	Kansas City
11/1	L 17-30	at Indianapolis
11/7	L 23-29	San Diego
11/14	L 24-31	at Jacksonville
11/21	L 27-30	at New York Jets
11/28	W 20-0	Tennessee
12/2	L 24-34	at Philadelphia
12/13	L 28-34	Baltimore (OT)
12/19	L 17-31	at Tennessee
12/26	L 23-24	at Denver
1/2	W 34-17	Jacksonville

(OT) Overtime

SCORE BY PERIODS

Texans	53	98	108	128	3 —	390
Opponents	96	139	75	111	6 —	427

2010 TEAM STATISTICS

	Texans	Opp.
Total First Downs	360	352
Rushing	118	113
Passing	222	211
Penalty	20	28
3rd Down: Made/Att	79/192	77/195
3rd Down Pct.	41.1	39.5
4th Down: Made/Att	9/19	11/13
4th Down Pct.	47.4	84.6
Possession Avg.	29:03	30:57
Total Net Yards	6186	6031
Avg. Per Game	386.6	376.9
Total Plays	1029	1010
Avg. Per Play	6.0	6.0
Net Yards Rushing	2042	1751
Avg. Per Game	127.6	109.4
Total Rushes	423	433
Net Yards Passing	4144	4280
Avg. Per Game	259.0	267.5
Sacked/Yards Lost	32/226	30/219
Gross Yards	4370	4499
Att./Completions	574/365	547/354
Completion Pct.	63.6	64.7
Had Intercepted	12	13
Punts/Average	63/42.1	67/43.7
Net Punting Avg.	63/36.8	67/38.1
Penalties/Yards	90/690	105/851
Fumbles/Ball Lost	15/6	16/5
Touchdowns	44	52
Rushing	20	16
Passing	24	33
Returns	0	3

2010 INDIVIDUAL STATISTICS

PASSING

	Att.	Comp.	Yds.	Pct.	TD	Int.	Tkld.	Rate
Schaub	574	365	4370	63.6	24	12	32/226	92.0
Texans	574	365	4370	63.6	24	12	32/226	92.0
Opponents	547	354	4499	64.7	33	13	30/219	100.5

SCORING

	TD R	TD P	TD Rt	PAT	FG	Saf	PTS
Rackers	0	0	0	43/43	27/30	0	124
Foster	16	2	0	0/0	0/0	0	108
Johnson	0	8	0	0/0	0/0	0	48
Walter	0	5	0	0/0	0/0	0	30
Dreessen	0	4	0	0/0	0/0	0	24
Ward	4	0	0	0/0	0/0	0	24
Jones	0	3	0	0/0	0/0	0	20
Daniels	0	2	0	0/0	0/0	0	12
Texans	20	24	0	43/43	27/30	0	390
Opponents	16	33	3	50/50	21/27	0	427

2-Pt Conversions: Jones.
Texans 1-1, Opponents 1-1.

RUSHING

	No.	Yds	Avg	LG	TD
Foster	327	1616	4.9	74t	16
Ward	50	315	6.3	38t	4
Slaton	19	93	4.9	23	0
Schaub	22	28	1.3	8	0
Johnson	2	10	5.0	7	0
Jones	2	7	3.5	10	0
Turk	1	-27	-27.0	-27	0
Texans	423	2042	4.8	74t	20
Opponents	433	1751	4.0	42	16

RECEIVING

	No.	Yds	Avg	LG	TD
Johnson	86	1216	14.1	60	8
Foster	66	604	9.2	50	2
Walter	51	621	12.2	35	5
Jones	51	562	11.0	47	3
Daniels	38	471	12.4	31	2
Dreessen	36	518	14.4	43t	4
D. Anderson	11	117	10.6	35	0
Casey	8	98	12.3	33	0
Leach	8	91	11.4	21	0
Ward	7	61	8.7	12	0
Slaton	3	11	3.7	12	0
Texans	365	4370	12.0	60	24
Opponents	354	4499	12.7	73t	33

INTERCEPTIONS

	No.	Yds	Avg	LG	TD
Nolan	3	35	11.7	20	0
Quin	3	12	4.0	10	0
Allen	3	1	0.3	1	0
Jackson	2	23	11.5	23	0
Bentley	1	18	18.0	18	0
McManis	1	1	1.0	1	0
Texans	13	90	6.9	23	0
Opponents	12	107	8.9	25t	2

PUNTING

	No.	Yds.	Avg.	In 20	LG
Turk	63	2650	42.1	19	60
Texans	63	2650	42.1	19	60
Opponents	67	2930	43.7	31	59

PUNT RETURNS

	Ret	FC	Yds	Avg	LG	TD
Jones	29	15	204	7.0	39	0
D. Anderson	4	1	26	6.5	17	0
Molden	1	0	0	0.0	0	0
Pollard	1	0	5	5.0	5	0
Texans	35	16	235	6.7	39	0
Opponents	29	14	233	8.0	30	0

KICKOFF RETURNS

	No.	Yds	Avg	LG	TD
Slaton	39	767	19.7	50	0
Jones	23	494	21.5	35	0
Leach	3	40	13.3	26	0
McManis	1	25	25.0	25	0
Mitchell	1	0	0.0	0	0
Texans	67	1326	19.8	50	0
Opponents	72	1741	24.2	103t	1

FIELD GOALS

	1-19	20-29	30-39	40-49	50+
Rackers	0/0	8/8	11/11	5/7	3/4
Texans	0/0	8/8	11/11	5/7	3/4
Opponents	0/0	6/7	9/10	6/8	0/2

SACKS

	No.
M. Williams	8.5
M. Anderson	4.0
A. Smith	4.0
Okoye	3.0
Pollard	2.5
Cushing	1.5
Jamison	1.0
Lewis	1.0
Mitchell	1.0
Nolan	1.0
Ryans	1.0
Sharpton	1.0
Nading	0.5
Texans	30.0
Opponents	32.0

RECORD HOLDERS
INDIVIDUAL RECORDS—CAREER

Category	Name	Performance
Rushing (Yds.)	Domanick Williams, 2003-06	3,195
Passing (Yds.)	Matt Schaub, 2007-2010	14,424
Passing (TDs)	Matt Schaub, 2007-2010	77
Receiving (No.)	Andre Johnson, 2003-2010	673
Receiving (Yds.)	Andre Johnson, 2003-2010	9,164
Interceptions	Dunta Robinson, 2004-09	13
Punting (Avg.)	Chad Stanley, 2002-06	41.0
Punt Return (Avg.)	Jacoby Jones, 2007-2010	10.0
Kickoff Return (Avg.)	André Davis, 2007-09	25.4
Field Goals	Kris Brown, 2002-09	172
Touchdowns (Tot.)	Andre Johnson, 2003-2010	50
Points	Kris Brown, 2002-09	767
*Sacks	Mario Williams, 2006-2010	48.0

INDIVIDUAL RECORDS—SINGLE SEASON

Category	Name	Performance
Rushing (Yds.)	Arian Foster, 2010	1,616
Passing (Yds.)	Matt Schaub, 2009	4,770
Passing (TDs)	Matt Schaub, 2009	29
Receiving (No.)	Andre Johnson, 2008	115
Receiving (Yds.)	Andre Johnson, 2008	1,575
Interceptions	Marcus Coleman, 2003	7
Punting (Avg.)	Matt Turk, 2009	42.7
Punt Return (Avg.)	Jacoby Jones, 2008	12.1
Kickoff Return (Avg.)	André Davis, 2007	30.3
Field Goals	Kris Brown, 2008	29
Touchdowns (Tot.)	Arian Foster, 2010	18
Points	Kris Brown, 2008	124
	Neil Rackers, 2010	124
*Sacks	Mario Williams, 2007	14.0

INDIVIDUAL RECORDS—SINGLE GAME

Category	Name	Performance
Rushing (Yds.)	Arian Foster, 9-12-10	231
Passing (Yds.)	Matt Schaub, 9-19-10	497
Passing (TDs)	Sage Rosenfels, 10-21-07	4
	Matt Schaub, 9-20-09, 10-18-09	4
Receiving (No.)	Andre Johnson, 10-10-04, 11-27-05, 9-19-10	12
	Kevin Walter, 10-14-07	12
Receiving (Yds.)	Andre Johnson, 12-14-08	207
Interceptions	Glover Quin, 10-28-10	3
Field Goals	Kris Brown, 9-7-03, 12-4-05, 10-7-07	5
Touchdowns (Tot.)	Ryan Moats, 11-1-09	3
	Arian Foster, 9-12-10	3
Points	Ryan Moats, 11-1-09	18
	Arian Foster, 9-12-10	18
*Sacks	Mario Williams, 12-13-07	3.5

Sacks became an official statistic in 1982.

VETERAN ROSTER AS OF MARCH 3, 2011

No.	Name	Pos.	Ht.	Wt.	Birthdate	^NFL Exp.	College	Hometown	How Acq.	'10 Games/Starts
52	Adibi, Xavier	LB	6-2	242	10/18/84	4	Virginia Tech	Hampton, Va.	D4-'08	11/3
30	Allen, Jason	CB	6-1	200	7/5/83	6	Tennessee	Muscle Shoals, Ala.	W(Mia)-'10	15/7*
89	Anderson, David	WR	5-10	192	7/28/83	6	Colorado State	Thousand Oaks, Calif.	D7-'06	12/1
96	Anderson, Mark	DE	6-4	255	5/26/83	6	Alabama	Tulsa, Okla.	FA-'10	15/3*
34	Barber, Dominique	SS	6-0	213	8/2/86	4	Minnesota	Wayzata, Minn.	D6-'08	8/1
98	Barwin, Connor	DE	6-4	260	10/15/86	3	Cincinnati	Detroit, Mich.	D2-'09	1/0
57	Bentley, Kevin	LB	6-0	252	12/29/79	10	Northwestern	North Hills, Calif.	UFA(Sea)-'08	13/8
65	Brisiel, Mike	G	6-5	302	3/14/83	4	Colorado State	Fayetteville, Ark.	FA-'06	12/9
76	Brown, Duane	T	6-4	312	8/30/85	4	Virginia Tech	Richmond, Va.	D1-'08	12/12
93	Bulman, Tim	DE	6-4	273	10/31/82	5	Boston College	Dorchester, Mass.	FA-'06	0*
78	Butler, Rashad	T	6-4	309	2/10/83	6	Miami	West Palm Beach, Fla.	W(Car)-'07	16/4
62	Caldwell, Antoine	G	6-3	311	4/19/86	3	Alabama	Montgomery, Ala.	D3-'09	12/7
86	Casey, James	TE	6-3	240	9/22/84	3	Rice	Azle, Texas	D5-'09	16/4
95	Cody, Shaun	DT	6-4	304	1/22/83	7	Southern California	Hacienda Heights, Calif.	UFA(Det)-'09	16/16
56	Cushing, Brian	LB	6-3	259	1/24/87	3	Southern California	Park Ridge, N.J.	D1-'09	12/12
81	Daniels, Owen	TE	6-3	242	11/9/82	6	Wisconsin	Naperville, Ill.	D4-'06	11/10
39	Demps, Quintin	SS	5-11	206	6/29/85	4	Texas-El Paso	San Antonio, Texas	FA-'10	2/0
19	Dickerson, Dorin	WR	6-2	227	3/31/88	2	Pittsburgh	Imperial, Pa.	D7-'10	7/0
54	Diles, Zac	LB	6-2	238	6/11/85	5	Kansas State	Tulare, Calif.	D7-'07	15/10
85	Dreessen, Joel	TE	6-4	245	7/26/82	6	Colorado State	Fort Morgan, Colo.	FA-'07	16/10
23	Foster, Arian	RB	6-1	227	8/24/86	3	Tennessee	San Diego, Calif.	FA-'09	16/13
88	Graham, Garrett	TE	6-3	240	8/4/86	2	Wisconsin	Brick, N.J.	D4b-'10	6/0
77	Green, Jarvis	DE	6-3	285	1/12/79	10	Louisiana State	Thibodaux, La.	FA-'10	0*
87	Hill, Anthony	TE	6-6	278	1/2/85	3	North Carolina State	Houston, Texas	D4b-'09	0*
16	Holliday, Trindon	WR	5-5	169	4/27/86	2	Louisiana State	Zachary, La.	D6b-'10	0*
25	Jackson, Kareem	CB	5-10	195	4/10/88	2	Alabama	Macon, Ga.	D1-'10	16/16
77	Jamison, Tim	DE	6-3	273	2/26/86	3	Michigan	Harvey, Ill.	FA-'09	10/1
80	Johnson, Andre	WR	6-3	223	7/11/81	9	Miami	Miami, Fla.	D1-'03	13/13
12	Jones, Jacoby	WR	6-2	210	7/11/84	5	Lane College	New Orleans, La.	D3-'07	15/7
53	Keglar, Stanford	LB	6-2	250	7/4/85	4	Purdue	Indianapolis, Ind.	FA-'10	10/0
44	Leach, Vonta	FB	6-0	255	11/6/81	8	East Carolina	Rowland, N.C.	FA-'06	16/5
9	Leinart, Matt	QB	6-5	232	5/11/83	6	Southern California	Santa Ana, Calif.	FA-'10	0*
97	Lewis, Damione	DT	6-2	301	3/1/78	11	Miami	Sulphur Springs, Texas	FA-'10	10/0
21	McCain, Brice	CB	5-9	184	12/10/86	3	Utah	Terrell, Texas	D6-'09	12/3
22	McManis, Sherrick	CB	6-1	193	12/19/87	2	Northwestern	Peoria, Ill.	D5-'10	14/0
92	Mitchell, Earl	DT	6-3	291	9/25/87	2	Arizona	Galena Park, Texas	D3-'10	15/0
28	Molden, Antwaun	CB	6-1	200	1/23/85	4	Eastern Kentucky	Cleveland, Ohio	D3a-'08	14/0
55	Myers, Chris	C	6-4	296	9/15/81	7	Miami	Miami, Fla.	T(Den)-'08	16/16
72	Nading, Jesse	DE	6-5	261	7/3/85	3	Colorado State	Highlands Ranch, Colo.	FA-'08	5/0
33	Nolan, Troy	SS	6-2	206	9/7/86	3	Arizona State	Woodland Hills, Calif.	D7-'09	16/3
27	Ogbonnaya, Chris	RB	6-0	225	5/20/86	2	Texas	Houston, Texas	FA-'10	0*
91	Okoye, Amobi	DT	6-2	292	6/10/87	5	Louisville	Huntsville, Ala.	D1-'07	16/16
7	Orlovsky, Dan	QB	6-5	230	8/18/83	7	Connecticut	Shelton, Conn.	UFA(Det)-'09	1/0
24	Paymah, Karl	CB	6-0	195	11/29/82	7	Washington State	Culver City, Calilf.	FA-'10	2/0
31	Pollard, Bernard	SS	6-1	225	12/23/84	6	Purdue	Fort Wayne, Ind.	FA-'09	15/15
29	Quin, Glover	CB	6-0	203	1/15/86	3	New Mexico	Summit, Miss.	D4a-'09	16/16
4	Rackers, Neil	K	6-1	215	8/16/76	12	Illinois	St. Louis, Mo.	UFA(Ariz)-'10	16/0
59	Ryans, DeMeco	LB	6-1	248	7/28/84	6	Alabama	Bessemer, Ala.	D2-'06	6/6
8	Schaub, Matt	QB	6-5	239	6/25/81	8	Virginia	West Chester, Pa.	T(Atl)-'07	16/16
51	Sharpton, Darryl	LB	5-11	248	1/1/88	2	Miami	Coral Gables, Fla.	D4a-'10	12/6
20	Slaton, Steve	RB	5-9	206	1/4/86	4	West Virginia	Levittown, Pa.	D3b-'08	12/1
94	Smith, Antonio	DE	6-4	275	10/21/81	8	Oklahoma State	Oklahoma City, Okla.	UFA(Ariz)-'09	16/16
71	Smith, Shelley	G	6-4	299	5/21/87	2	Colorado State	Phoenix, Ariz.	D6a-'10	0*
74	Smith, Wade	G	6-4	309	4/26/81	8	Memphis	Dallas, Texas	UFA(KC)-'10	16/16
64	Studdard, Kasey	G	6-3	304	7/1/84	5	Texas	Lone Tree, Colo.	D6-'07	4/0
43	Tate, Ben	RB	5-11	219	8/21/88	2	Auburn	Salisbury, Md.	D2-'10	0*
1	Turk, Matt	P	6-5	248	6/16/68	16	Wisconsin-Whitewater	Greenfield, Wisc.	FA-'07	16/0
79	Wallace, Cody	C	6-4	300	11/26/84	3	Texas A&M	Cuero, Texas	FA-'10	0*
83	Walter, Kevin	WR	6-3	218	8/4/81	9	Eastern Michigan	Vernon Hills, Ill.	RFA(Cin)-'06	16/16
32	Ward, Derrick	RB	5-11	228	8/30/80	8	Ottawa (KS)	Moreno Valley, Calif.	FA-'10	16/0
46	Weeks, Jon	LS	5-10	254	2/17/86	2	Baylor	Bethpage, N.Y.	FA-'10	16/0
90	Williams, Mario	DE	6-6	290	1/31/85	6	North Carolina State	Richlands, N.C.	D1-'o6	13/13
17	Williams, Paul	WR	6-1	196	12/2/83	3	Fresno State	Hanford, Calif.	FA-'10	0*
42	Williams, Torri	S	6-2	210	8/29/86	2	Purdue	Leander, Texas	FA-'10	1/0
73	Winston, Eric	T	6-7	316	11/17/83	6	Miami	Midland, Texas	D3b-'06	16/16

* Allen played 8 games for Miami and 7 games for Houston in '10; M. Anderson played 4 games for Chicago and 11 games for Houston; Bulman missed '10 season because of injury; Green did not play in 1 game, inactive for 2 games; Hill inactive for 5 games; Holliday missed '10 season because of injury; Leinart inactive (designated third quarterback) for 16 games; Ogbonnaya spent '10 season on Houston practice squad, last active with St. Louis in '09; S. Smith inactive for 8 games; Tate missed '10 season because of injury; Wallace spent 8 games during '10 season on Houston practice squad; P. Williams spent 12 games during '10 season on Houston practice squad, last active with Tennessee in '08.

Also played with Texans in '10—DE Ryan Denney (2 games), LB Isaiah Greenhouse (2), LB David Nixon (3), DE Adewale Ogunleye (4), DT Frank Okam (5), T Ephraim Salaam (4), CB Malcolm Sheppard (1), WR Derrick Townsel (1), DB Jamar Wall (1), FS Eugene Wilson (14).

^ "NFL Exp." as of 2011 Kickoff Weekend. For full explanation of how a player's NFL Experience is measured, refer to explanation underneath the First-Year Roster listed below.

FIRST-YEAR ROSTER

Name	Pos.	Ht.	Wt.	Birthdate	College	Hometown	How Acq.
Baker, Antonio (1)	S	5-11	210	11/23/87	Louisiana Tech	Amite, La.	FA-'10
Carmichael, Roc	CB	5-10	182	9/9/88	Virginia Tech	Clinton, Md.	D4
Harris, Brandon	CB	5-10	191	1/24/90	Miami	Miami, Fla.	D2b
Keo, Shiloh	S	5-11	219	12/17/87	Idaho	Everett, Wash.	D5
Newton, Derek	T	6-6	314	11/16/87	Arkansas State	Utica, Miss.	D7a
Ozougwu, Cheta	LB	6-2	255	11/18/88	Rice	Houston, Texas	D7b
Pemberton, Cole (1)	T	6-7	306	7/1/87	Colorado State	Highlands Ranch, Colo.	FA-'10
Reed, Brooks	LB	6-3	263	2/28/87	Arizona	Tucson, Ariz.	D2a
Townsel, Derrick (1)	WR	5-9	175	7/12/88	Murray State	Memphis, Tenn.	FA-'10
Watt, J.J.	DE	6-5	290	3/22/89	Wisconsin	Pewaukee, Wisc.	D1
Yates, T.J.	QB	6-4	220	5/28/87	North Carolina	Marietta, Ga.	D5b

The term NFL Rookie is defined as a player who is in his first season of professional football and has not been on the roster of another professional football team for any regular-season or postseason games. A Rookie is designated by an "R" on NFL rosters. Players who have been active in another professional football league or players who have NFL experience, including either preseason training camp or being on an Active List or Inactive List, or on Reserve/Injured or Reserve/Physically Unable to Perform for fewer than six regular-season games, are termed NFL First-Year Players. An NFL First-Year Player is designated by a "1" on NFL rosters. Thereafter, a player is credited with an additional year of experience for each season in which he accumulates six games on the Active List or Inactive List, or on Reserve/Injured or Reserve/Physically Unable to Perform.

Log on to www.houstontexans.com for an up-to-date roster.

COACHING STAFF

Head Coach,
Gary Kubiak

Pro Career: Gary Kubiak was introduced as the second head coach in Houston Texans history on January 26, 2006. Kubiak returned to Houston after spending 20 of the previous 23 years in the Denver area. Kubiak's record as Texans head coach is 37-43, making him the franchise's winningest head coach. The Texans ranked among the NFL's top five offenses for the third straight year in 2010 and set team records for rushing, total offense, and scoring. Arian Foster claimed the 2010 NFL rushing title, making Kubiak the only head coach since 2006 to produce a rushing, receiving and passing yardage champion. He guided the Texans to a 9-7 record in 2009, highlighted by a season-ending four-game win streak to capture the franchise's first winning season. Houston narrowly missed its first-ever playoff berth, losing a tie-breaker for the final spot. A franchise-record five players earned trips to the Pro Bowl, led by Pro Bowl MVP Matt Schaub. In 2008, the Texans overcame an 0-4 start that was due in part to the damage inflicted by Hurricane Ike and finished 8-8. Houston became just the ninth squad in NFL history to finish .500 or better after an 0-4 start. In 2007, the Texans broke even for the first time, finishing at 8-8. Houston went 7-3 outside of the AFC West and set a franchise record with a 6-2 mark at home. It was the first time the Texans posted a winning mark at Reliant Stadium. In his first year as a head coach, Kubiak guided the Texans to a 6-10 record, tripling the team's win total of the year before. Prior to joining the Texans, Kubiak spent the previous 11 years (1995-2005) as Denver's offensive coordinator, helping guide the Broncos to back-to-back World Championships in Super Bowls XXXII and XXXIII and three AFC West Division titles. Kubiak tutored Hall of Fame QB John Elway from 1995-98 and RB Terrell Davis was named NFL Most Valuable Player in 1998. In Kubiak's 11 years in Denver, the Broncos had 28 Pro Bowl players on the offensive side of the ball. Kubiak began his coaching career as the running backs coach at Texas A&M (1992-93). Kubiak started his NFL coaching career with the San Francisco 49ers as the quarterbacks coach, winning Super Bowl XXIX in his only season (1994). Kubiak is a veteran of six Super Bowls—three as a player and three as a coach. Career record: 37-43.

Background: Kubiak starred at quarterback for Texas A&M from 1979-1982, earning all-Southwest Conference honors as a senior. He played for the Broncos from 1983-1991 as John Elway's backup. Kubiak played in 119 career games, tossed 14 touchdowns, and was a part of three teams that reached the Super Bowl.

Personal: Born August 15, 1961 in Houston. He and his wife, Rhonda, have three sons—Klint, Klay, and Klein.

ASSISTANT COACHES

John Benton, offensive line; born December 13, 1963, Los Angeles. Offensive lineman Colorado State 1986-1990. No pro playing experience. College coach: California University (Pa.) 1990-94, Colorado State 1996-2003. Pro coach: St. Louis Rams 2004-05, joined Texans in 2006.

Perry Carter, defensive assistant; born August 15, 1971, McComb, Miss. Defensive back Southern Mississippi 1989-1993. Pro defensive back Arizona Cardinals 1994, Kansas City Chiefs 1995, Oakland Raiders 1996-98, Edmonton Eskimos (CFL) 2000-01, Montreal Alouettes (CFL) 2002, British Columbia Lions (CFL) 2003-04. College coach: Texas A&M-Commerce 2004. Pro coach: Hamburg Sea Devils (NFLEL) 2006, joined Texans in 2006.

Rick Dennison, offensive coordinator; born June 22, 1958, Kalispell, Mont. Tight end Colorado State 1976-79. Pro linebacker Denver Broncos 1982-1990. Pro coach: Denver Broncos 1995-2009, joined Texans in 2010.

Chick Harris, running backs; born September 21, 1945, Durham, N.C. Running back Northern Arizona 1966-69. No pro playing experience. College coach: Colorado State 1970-71, Long Beach State 1972-73, Washington 1975-1980. Pro coach: Detroit Wheels (WFL) 1974, Buffalo Bills 1981-82, Seattle Seahawks 1983-1991, Los Angeles Rams 1992-94, Carolina Panthers 1995-2001, joined Texans in 2002.

Reggie Herring, linebackers; born July 3, 1959, Myrtle Beach, S.C. Linebacker Florida State 1978-1980. No pro playing experience. College coach: Oklahoma State 1981-85, Auburn 1986-1991, Texas Christian 1992-93, Clemson 1994-2001, North Carolina State 2004, Arkansas 2005-07 (interim head coach 2007). Pro coach: Houston Texans 2002-03, Dallas Cowboys 2008-2010, re-joined Texans in 2011.

Vance Joseph, defensive backs; born September 20, 1972, Marrero, La. Defensive back Colorado 1990-94. Pro defensive back New York Jets 1995, Indianapolis Colts 1996. College coach: Colorado 1999-2001, 2002-03, Wyoming 2002, Bowling Green State 2004. Pro coach: San Francisco 49ers 2005-2010, joined Texans in 2011.

Bobby King, defensive assistant; born June 29, 1978, Louisville, Ky. Defensive line Texas El-Paso 1998-2000. No pro playing experience. College coach: Texas El-Paso 2002-03, West Texas A&M 2005, 2008-09, Baylor 2006-07. Pro coach: Dallas Cowboys 2010, joined Texans in 2011.

Larry Kirksey, wide receivers; born January 6, 1951, Harlan, Ky. Wide receiver Eastern Kentucky 1970-73. No pro playing experience. College coach: Miami (Ohio) 1974-76, Kentucky 1977-1981, Kansas 1982, Kentucky State 1983 (head coach), Florida 1984-88, Pittsburgh 1989, Alabama 1990-93, Texas A&M 2006, South Middle Tennessee State 2006. Pro coach: San Francisco 49ers 1994-99, Detroit Lions 2001-02,

Jacksonville Jaguars 2003, Denver Broncos 2004, joined Texans in 2007.

Greg Knapp, quarterbacks; born March 5, 1963, Long Beach, Calif. Quarterback San Diego State 1982-85. No pro playing experience. College coach: Sacramento State 1986-1994. Pro coach: San Francisco 49ers 1995-2003, Atlanta Falcons 2004-06, Oakland Raiders 2007-08, Seattle Seahawks 2009, joined Texans in 2010.

Bill Kollar, asst. head coach/defensive line; born November 27, 1952, Warren, Ohio. Defensive end Montana State 1971-73. Pro defensive end Cincinnati Bengals 1974-76, Tampa Bay Buccaneers 1977-1981. College coach: Illinois 1985-87, Purdue 1988-89. Pro coach: Tampa Bay Buccaneers 1984, Atlanta Falcons 1990-2000, St. Louis Rams 2001-05, Buffalo Bills 2006-08, joined Texans in 2009.

Marc Lubick, offensive assistant; born November 13, 1977, Bozeman, Mont. Defensive back Montana State 1996-99. No pro playing experience. College coach: Colorado State 2000-02, 2005-09. Pro coach: St. Louis Rams 2003-04 (scout), joined Texans in 2010.

Joe Marciano, special teams coordinator; born February 10, 1954, Dunmore, Pa. Quarterback Temple 1972-75. No pro playing experience. College coach: East Stroudsburg State 1977, Rhode Island 1978-79, Villanova 1980, Penn State 1981, Temple 1982. Pro coach: Philadelphia/Baltimore Stars (USFL) 1983-85, New Orleans Saints 1986-1995, Tampa Bay Buccaneers 1996-2001, joined Texans in 2002.

Brian Pariani, tight ends; born July 2, 1965, San Francisco. No college or pro playing experience. College coach: UCLA 1989, Syracuse 2005. Pro coach: San Francisco 49ers 1991-94, Denver Broncos 1994-2004, joined Texans in 2006.

Wade Phillips, defensive coordinator; born June 21, 1947, Orange, Texas. Linebacker Houston 1966-68. No pro playing experience. College coach: Houston 1969, Oklahoma State 1973-74, Kansas 1975. Pro coach: Houston Oilers 1976-1980, New Orleans Saints 1981-85 (interim head coach for four games 1985), Philadelphia Eagles 1986-88, Denver Broncos 1989-1994 (head coach 1993-94), Buffalo Bills 1995-2000 (head coach 1998-2000), Atlanta Falcons 2002-03 (interim head coach for three games in 2003), San Diego Chargers 2004-06, Dallas Cowboys 2007-10 (head coach), joined Texans in 2011.

Frank Pollack, asst. offensive line; born November 5, 1967, Camp Springs, Md. Offensive lineman Northern Arizona 1985-89. Pro offensive lineman San Francisco 49ers 1990-97. College coach: Northern Arizona 2005-06. Pro coach: Joined Texans in 2007.

Jim Ryan, offensive assistant; born May 18, 1957, Bellmawr, N.J. Linebacker William & Mary 1974-78. Linebacker Denver Broncos 1979-1988. Pro coach: Denver Broncos 2005-08, Omaha Nighthawks (UFL) 2010, joined Texans in 2011.

American Football Conference
South Division
Team Colors: Royal Blue and White
P.O. Box 535000
Indianapolis, Indiana 46253
Telephone: (317) 297-2658

2011 SCHEDULE
PRESEASON
Aug. 13 at St. Louis...........................8:00
Aug. 19 **Washington** 7:00
Aug. 26 **Green Bay**........................8:00
Sep. 1 at Cincinnati 7:00

REGULAR SEASON
Sep. 11 at Houston 1:00
Sep. 18 **Cleveland** 1:00
Sep. 25 **Pittsburgh** 8:20
Oct. 3 at Tampa Bay (Mon).......... 8.30
Oct. 9 **Kansas City** 1:00
Oct. 16 at Cincinnati 1:00
Oct. 23 at New Orleans 8:20
Oct. 30 at Tennessee 1:00
Nov. 6 **Atlanta** 1:00
Nov. 13 **Jacksonville** 1.00
Nov. 20 BYE
Nov. 27 **Carolina** 1:00
Dec. 4 at New England * 8:20
Dec. 11 at Baltimore 1:00
Dec. 18 **Tennessee** 1:00
Dec. 22 **Houston** (Thu).................. 8:20
Jan. 1 at Jacksonville 1:00
*All times ET, Sunday night games in
    Weeks 11-15, 17 subject to change
Stadium: Lucas Oil Stadium (opened in
        2008) •**Capacity:** 63,000
        500 South Capitol Avenue
        Indianapolis, Indiana 46225
Playing Surface: FieldTurf
Training Camp: Anderson University
        1100 East Fifth Street
        Anderson, IN 46012

LUCAS OIL STADIUM

CLUB OFFICIALS
Owner and CEO: James Irsay
Vice Chairman: Bill Polian
Vice President and General Manager:
    Chris Polian
Head Coach: Jim Caldwell
Vice President: Carlie Irsay-Gordon
Vice President: Casey Irsay Foyt
Vice President: Kalen Irsay
Chief Operating Officer: Pete Ward
Senior Vice President of Sales and
    Marketing: Tom Zupancic
Vice President-Finance: Kurt Humphrey
Vice President-Ticket Operations/Guest
    Services: Larry Hall
Vice President-Public Relations:
    Craig Kelley
Vice President of Sponsorship Sales:
    Jay Souers
Vice President of Premium Seating and
    Ticket Sales: Greg Hylton
Director of Football Administration:
    Steve Champlin
Director of Player Personnel: Tom Telesco
Director of Pro Player Personnel:
    Clyde Powers
Associate Director of Pro Personnel:
    Kevin Rogers
Equipment Manager: Jon Scott
Video Director: TBD
Head Athletic Trainer: Dave Hammer
Director of Rehabilitation: Erin Barill
Assistant Equipment Managers:
    Mike Mays, Sean Sullivan,
    Brian Seabrooks
Assistant Trainers: Dave Walston,
    Bryant Baugh
Assistant Video Director: John Starliper

COACHING HISTORY
Baltimore 1953-1983
(470-416-7)
Records include postseason games
1953	Keith Molesworth	3-9-0
1954-1962	Weeb Ewbank	61-52-1
1963-69	Don Shula	73-26-4
1970-72	Don McCafferty*	26-11-1
1972	John Sandusky	4-5-0
1973-74	Howard Schnellenberger**	4-13-0
1974	Joe Thomas	2-9-0
1975-79	Ted Marchibroda	41-36-0
1980-81	Mike McCormack	9-23-0
1982-84	Frank Kush***	11-28-1
1984	Hal Hunter	0-1-0
1985-86	Rod Dowhower****	5-24-0
1986-1991	Ron Meyer#	36-36-0
1991	Rick Venturi	1-10-0
1992-95	Ted Marchibroda	32-35-0
1996-97	Lindy Infante	12-21-0
1998-2001	Jim Mora	32-34-0
2002-08	Tony Dungy	92-33-0
2009-2010	Jim Caldwell	26-10-0

*Released after five games in 1972
**Released after three games in 1974
***Resigned after 15 games in 1984
****Released after 13 games in 1986
#Released after five games in 1991

PAID ATTENDANCE
Home 520,687   Away 542,967
Total 1,063,654
Single-game home record,
    67,650 (1/24/10)
Single-season home record,
    520,687 (2010)

2011 DRAFT CHOICES
Round	Name	Pos.	College
1	Anthony Castonzo	T	Boston College
2	Ben Ijalana	G	Villanova
3	Drake Nevis	DT	Louisiana State
4	Delone Carter	RB	Syracuse
6	Chris Rucker	DB	Michigan State

2010 TEAM RECORD
PRESEASON (0-4)

Date	Result	Opponent
8/15	L 17-37	San Francisco
8/19	L 21-34	at Buffalo
8/26	L 24-59	at Green Bay
9/2	L 28-30	Cincinnati

REGULAR SEASON (10-6)

Date	Result	Opponent
9/12	L 24-34	at Houston
9/19	W 38-14	New York Giants
9/26	W 27-13	at Denver
10/3	L 28-31	at Jacksonville
10/10	W 19-9	Kansas City
10/17	W 27-24	at Washington
11/1	W 30-17	Houston
11/7	L 24-26	at Philadelphia
11/14	W 23-17	Cincinnati
11/21	L 28-31	at New England
11/28	L 14-36	San Diego
12/5	L 35-38	Dallas (OT)
12/9	W 30-28	at Tennessee
12/19	W 34-24	Jacksonville
12/26	W 31-26	at Oakland
1/2	W 23-20	Tennessee

POSTSEASON (0-1)

1/8	L 16-17	New York Jets
(OT) Overtime		

SCORE BY PERIODS

Colts	78	160	68	129	0 —	435
Opponents	70	89	115	111	3 —	388

2010 TEAM STATISTICS

	Colts	Opp.
Total First Downs	366	314
Rushing	87	111
Passing	253	190
Penalty	26	13
3rd Down: Made/Att	91/204	78/200
3rd Down Pct.	44.6	39.0
4th Down: Made/Att	5/8	8/18
4th Down Pct.	62.5	44.4
Possession Avg.	29:41	30:19
Total Net Yards	6092	5465
Avg. Per Game	380.8	341.6
Total Plays	1088	1010
Avg. Per Play	5.6	5.4
Net Yards Rushing	1483	2032
Avg. Per Game	92.7	127.0
Total Rushes	393	445
Net Yards Passing	4609	3433
Avg. Per Game	288.1	214.6
Sacked/Yards Lost	16/91	30/194
Gross Yards	4700	3627
Att./Completions	679/450	535/356
Completion Pct.	66.3	66.5
Had Intercepted	17	10
Punts/Average	69/42.2	67/44.4
Net Punting Avg.	69/35.5	67/41.0
Penalties/Yards	79/709	95/812
Fumbles/Ball Lost	14/8	24/11
Touchdowns	51	42
Rushing	13	14
Passing	33	22
Returns	5	6

2010 INDIVIDUAL STATISTICS

PASSING	Att.	Comp.	Yds.	Pct.	TD	Int.	Tkld.	Rate
Manning	679	450	4700	66.3	33	17	16/91	91.9
Colts	679	450	4700	66.3	33	17	16/91	91.9
Opponents	535	356	3627	66.5	22	10	30/194	91.7

SCORING	TD R	TD P	TD Rt	PAT	FG	Saf	PTS
Vinatieri	0	0	0	51/51	26/28	0	129
Collie	0	8	0	0/0	0/0	0	48
Garcon	0	6	0	0/0	0/0	0	36
J. James	6	0	0	0/0	0/0	0	36
Wayne	0	6	0	0/0	0/0	0	36
White	0	5	0	0/0	0/0	0	30
Addai	4	0	0	0/0	0/0	0	24
Tamme	0	4	0	0/0	0/0	0	24
Clark	0	3	0	0/0	0/0	0	18
D. Brown	2	0	0	0/0	0/0	0	12
Hayden	0	0	2	0/0	0/0	0	12
Hagler	0	0	1	0/0	0/0	0	6
Hart	1	0	0	0/0	0/0	0	6
Moala	0	0	1	0/0	0/0	0	6
Robinson	0	1	0	0/0	0/0	0	6
Smith	0	0	1	0/0	0/0	0	6
Colts	13	33	5	51/51	26/28	0	435
Opponents	14	22	6	41/41	31/36	0	388

2-Pt Conversions: Colts 0-0, Opponents 1-1.

RUSHING	No.	Yds	Avg	LG	TD
D. Brown	129	497	3.9	49	2
Addai	116	495	4.3	46	4
Hart	43	185	4.3	35	1
Rhodes	37	172	4.6	15	0
J. James	46	112	2.4	11	6
Manning	18	18	1.0	27	0
Garcon	2	6	3.0	11	0
D. Moore	2	-2	-1.0	1	0
Colts	393	1483	3.8	49	13
Opponents	445	2032	4.6	62	14

RECEIVING	No.	Yds	Avg	LG	TD
Wayne	111	1355	12.2	50	6
Garcon	67	784	11.7	57t	6
Tamme	67	631	9.4	30	4
Collie	58	649	11.2	73t	8
Clark	37	347	9.4	50t	3
White	36	355	9.9	33	5
D. Brown	20	205	10.3	25	0
Addai	19	124	6.5	15	0
J. James	9	63	7.0	11	0
B. James	6	40	6.7	17	0
Hart	6	25	4.2	10	0
Gonzalez	5	67	13.4	34	0
Eldridge	5	39	7.8	10	0
Robinson	3	12	4.0	6	1
Rhodes	1	4	4.0	4	0
Colts	450	4700	10.4	73t	33
Opponents	356	3627	10.2	61	22

INTERCEPTIONS	No.	Yds	Avg	LG	TD
Hayden	2	56	28.0	31t	2
Powers	2	11	5.5	11	0
Francisco	2	10	5.0	11	0
Lacey	1	44	44.0	44	0
Hagler	1	35	35.0	35	0
Bethea	1	31	31.0	31	0
Bullitt	1	19	19.0	19	0
Colts	10	206	20.6	44	2
Opponents	17	277	16.3	47	4

PUNTING	No.	Yds.	Avg.	In 20	LG
McAfee	65	2731	42.0	21	66
Kapinos	4	178	44.5	2	55
Colts	69	2909	42.2	23	66
Opponents	67	2978	44.4	23	65

PUNT RETURNS	Ret	FC	Yds	Avg	LG	TD
White	10	14	80	8.0	18	0
Powers	8	4	63	7.9	13	0
B. James	7	3	35	5.0	14	0
K. Moore	6	3	36	6.0	16	0
Colts	31	24	214	6.9	18	0
Opponents	28	22	299	10.7	78t	1

KICKOFF RETURNS	No.	Yds	Avg	LG	TD
Tryon	14	299	21.4	39	0
B. James	14	229	16.4	26	0
D. Moore	12	257	21.4	33	0
Rhodes	12	252	21.0	27	0
C. Brown	5	102	20.4	23	0
K. Moore	5	102	20.4	27	0
J. James	3	16	5.3	16	0
Hagler	1	41	41.0	41t	1
Foster	1	12	12.0	12	0
Colts	67	1310	19.6	41t	1
Opponents	73	1880	25.8	99t	1

FIELD GOALS	1-19	20-29	30-39	40-49	50+
Vinatieri	0/0	8/8	9/10	9/10	0/0
Colts	0/0	8/8	9/10	9/10	0/0
Opponents	0/0	9/9	10/10	7/9	5/8

SACKS	No.
Mathis	11.0
Freeney	10.0
Foster	3.5
Angerer	1.0
Hagler	1.0
Session	1.0
(group)	1.0
Bethea	0.5
Brackett	0.5
A. Johnson	0.5
Colts	30.0
Opponents	16.0

RECORD HOLDERS
INDIVIDUAL RECORDS—CAREER

Category	Name	Performance
Rushing (Yds.)	Edgerrin James, 1999-2005	9,226
Passing (Yds.)	Peyton Manning, 1998-2010	54,828
Passing (TDs)	Peyton Manning, 1998-2010	399
Receiving (No.)	Marvin Harrison, 1996-2008	1,102
Receiving (Yds.)	Marvin Harrison, 1996-2008	14,580
Interceptions	Bob Boyd, 1960-68	57
Punting (Avg.)	Chris Gardocki, 1995-98	44.8
Punt Return (Avg.)	Ron Gardin, 1970-71	13.5
Kickoff Return (Avg.)	Jim Duncan, 1969-1971	32.6
Field Goals	Mike Vanderjagt, 1998-2005	217
Touchdowns (Tot.)	Marvin Harrison, 1996-2008	128
Points	Mike Vanderjagt, 1998-2005	995
*Sacks	Dwight Freeney, 2002-2010	94.0

INDIVIDUAL RECORDS—SINGLE SEASON

Category	Name	Performance
Rushing (Yds.)	Edgerrin James, 2000	1,709
Passing (Yds.)	Peyton Manning, 2010	4,700
Passing (TDs)	Peyton Manning, 2004	49
Receiving (No.)	Marvin Harrison, 2002	**143
Receiving (Yds.)	Marvin Harrison, 2002	1,722
Interceptions	Tom Keane, 1953	11
Punting (Avg.)	Rohn Stark, 1985	45.9
Punt Return (Avg.)	T.J. Rushing, 2007	13.1
Kickoff Return (Avg.)	Jim Duncan, 1970	35.4
Field Goals	Mike Vanderjagt, 2003	37
Touchdowns (Tot.)	Lenny Moore, 1964	20
Points	Mike Vanderjagt, 2003	157
*Sacks	Dwight Freeney, 2004	16.0

INDIVIDUAL RECORDS—SINGLE GAME

Category	Name	Performance
Rushing (Yds.)	Edgerrin James, 10-15-00	219
Passing (Yds.)	Peyton Manning, 10-31-04	472
Passing (TDs)	Peyton Manning, 9-28-03, 11-25-04	6
Receiving (No.)	Reggie Wayne, 10-3-10	15
Receiving (Yds.)	Raymond Berry, 11-10-57	224
Interceptions	Many times	3
	Last time by Mike Prior, 12-20-92	
Field Goals	Many times	5
	Last time by Mike Vanderjagt, 12-7-03	
Touchdowns (Tot.)	Many times	4
	Last time by Joseph Addai, 11-26-06	
Points	Many times	24
	Last time by Joseph Addai, 11-26-06	
*Sacks	Johnie Cooks, 11-25-84	4.5

*Sacks became an official statistic in 1982.
**NFL Record

VETERAN ROSTER AS OF MARCH 3, 2011

No.	Name	Pos.	Ht.	Wt.	Birthdate	^ NFL Exp.	College	Hometown	How Acq.	'10 Games/ Starts
29	Addai, Joseph	RB	5-11	214	5/3/83	6	Louisiana State	Houston, Texas	D1-'06	8/7
23	Afalava, Al	DB	5-11	212	1/20/87	3	Oregon State	Laie, Hawai'i	FA-'10	4/0
51	Angerer, Pat	LB	6-0	235	1/31/87	2	Iowa	Bettendorf, Iowa	D2-'10	16/11
41	Bethea, Antoine	DB	5-11	203	7/27/84	6	Howard	Newport News, Va.	D6b-'06	16/16
58	Brackett, Gary	LB	5-11	235	5/23/80	9	Rutgers	Glassboro, N.J.	FA-'03	12/12
39	Brown, Cornelius	DB	5-11	198	2/26/88	2	Texas-El Paso	Houston, Texas	FA-'10	10/0
31	Brown, Donald	RB	5-10	210	4/11/87	2	Connecticut	Atlantic Highlands, N.J.	D1-'09	13/8
33	Bullitt, Melvin	DB	6-1	201	11/13/84	5	Texas A&M	Bryan, Texas	FA-'07	4/3
44	Clark, Dallas	TE	6-3	252	6/12/79	9	Iowa	Livermore, Iowa	D1-'03	6/6
17	Collie, Austin	WR	6-0	200	11/11/85	3	Brigham Young	El Dorado Hills, Calif.	D4a-'09	9/6
53	Conner, Kavell	LB	6-0	242	2/23/87	2	Clemson	Richmond, Va.	D7b-'10	12/9
96	Dawson, Keyunta	DE	6-3	254	9/13/85	5	Texas Tech	Shreveport, La.	D7-'07	16/0
66	DeVan, Kyle	G	6-2	306	2/10/85	3	Oregon State	Vacaville, Calif.	FA-'09	16/12
71	Diem, Ryan	T	6-6	320	7/1/79	11	Northern Illinois	Carol Stream, Ill.	D4-'01	16/16
81	Eldridge, Brody	TE	6-5	265	3/31/87	2	Oklahoma	La Cygne, Kan.	D5-'10	14/8
68	Foster, Eric	DT	6-2	265	4/5/85	4	Rutgers	Homestead, Fla.	FA-'08	16/0
43	Francisco, Aaron	DB	6-2	207	7/5/83	7	Brigham Young	Laie, Hawai'i	FA-'10	12/12
93	Freeney, Dwight	DE	6-1	268	2/19/80	10	Syracuse	Hartford, Conn.	D1-'02	16/16
85	Garcon, Pierre	WR	6-0	210	8/8/86	4	Mount Union	West Palm Beach, Fla.	D6d-'08	14/14
52	Glenn, Cody	LB	6-0	240	10/6/86	3	Nebraska	Rusk, Texas	FA-'09	10/0
11	Gonzalez, Anthony	WR	6-0	193	9/18/84	5	Ohio State	Cleveland, Ohio	D1-'07	2/0
56	Hagler, Tyjuan	LB	6-0	236	12/3/81	6	Cincinnati	Kankakee, Ill.	D5c-'05	13/2
35	Hamlin, Ken	DB	6-2	208	1/20/81	9	Arkansas	Memphis, Tenn.	FA-'10	9/0*
32	Hart, Mike	RB	5-9	206	4/9/86	4	Michigan	Syracuse, N.Y.	D6c-'08	7/1
26	Hayden, Kelvin	DB	6-0	195	7/23/83	7	Illinois	Chicago, Ill.	D2-'05	11/11
92	Hughes, Jerry	DE	6-2	255	8/13/88	2	Texas Christian	Sugar Land, Texas	D1-'10	12/0
42	James, Javarris	RB	6-0	215	9/18/87	2	Miami	Immokalee, Fla.	FA-'10	10/0
99	Johnson, Antonio	DT	6-3	310	12/8/84	5	Mississippi State	Leland, Miss.	FA-'08	14/2
74	Johnson, Charlie	T	6-4	305	5/2/84	6	Oklahoma State	Sherman, Texas	D6a-'06	15/15
37	King, Brandon	DB	5-10	194	1/28/87	2	Purdue	Warner Robins, Ga.	FA-'10	4/0
27	Lacey, Jacob	DB	5-10	177	5/28/87	3	Oklahoma State	Garland, Texas	FA-'09	12/8
72	Linkenbach, Jeff	T	6-6	311	6/9/87	2	Cincinnati	Sandusky, Ohio	FA-'10	16/4
18	Manning, Peyton	QB	6-5	230	3/24/76	14	Tennessee	New Orleans, La.	D1-'98	16/16
91	Mathews, Ricardo	DT	6-3	294	7/30/87	2	Cincinnati	Jacksonville, Fla.	D7a-'10	8/0
98	Mathis, Robert	DE	6-2	245	2/26/81	9	Alabama A&M	Atlanta, Ga.	D5a-'03	16/16
1	McAfee, Pat	P	6-1	220	5/2/87	3	West Virginia	Plum, Pa.	D7a-'09	15/0
65	McClendon, Jacques	G	6-3	324	1/30/87	2	Tennessee	Cleveland, Tenn.	D4-'10	4/0
95	Moala, Fili	DT	6-4	303	6/23/85	3	Southern California	Buena Park, Calif.	D2a-'09	16/16
45	Moore, Devin	RB	5-9	190	11/6/85	2	Wyoming	Indianapolis, Ind.	FA-'10	4/0
90	Muir, Dan	DT	6-2	312	9/12/83	5	Kent State	Riverdale, Md.	W(GB)-'08	14/14
38	Newton, Mike	DB	5-10	197	11/11/87	2	Buffalo	Pasadena, Md.	FA-'10	12/0
7	Painter, Curtis	QB	6-4	230	6/24/85	3	Purdue	Yorktown, Ind.	D6-'09	0*
78	Pollak, Mike	G	6-3	301	2/16/85	4	Arizona State	Scottsdale, Ariz.	D2-'08	16/13
25	Powers, Jerraud	DB	5-10	192	7/19/87	3	Auburn	Decatur, Ala.	D3-'09	10/10
	Pressley, DeMario	DT	6-3	301	11/3/85	4	North Carolina State	Greensboro, N.C.	W(Hou)-'11	1/0*
30	Rhodes, Dominic	RB	5-9	203	1/17/79	10	Midwestern State	Waco, Texas	FA-'10	3/0
61	Richard, Jamey	G	6-5	295	10/9/84	4	Buffalo	Weston, Conn.	D7-'08	14/4
37	Richardson, Mike	DB	5-11	190	2/18/84	4	Notre Dame	Warner Robins, Ga.	W(KC)-'10	1/0
47	Robinson, Gijon	TE	6-1	255	10/12/84	4	Missouri Western State	Waynesville, Mo.	FA-'10	11/2
86	Santi, Tom	TE	6-3	250	11/22/85	4	Virginia	Nashville, Tenn.	D6a-'08	0*
63	Saturday, Jeff	C	6-2	295	6/18/75	13	North Carolina	Tucker, Ga.	FA-'99	16/16
55	Session, Clint	LB	6-0	235	9/22/84	5	Pittsburgh	Pompano Beach, Fla.	D4c-'07	5/5
40	Silva, Jamie	DB	5-11	204	12/14/84	4	Boston College	East Providence, R.I.	FA-'10	0*
10	Smith, Taj	WR	6-0	192	9/30/83	2	Syracuse	Newark, N.J.	FA-'10	5/0
48	Snow, Justin	TE	6-3	240	12/21/76	12	Baylor	Abilene, Texas	FA-'00	16/0
84	Tamme, Jacob	TE	6-3	236	3/15/85	4	Kentucky	Danville, Ky.	D4-'08	16/8
73	Thomas, Jaimie	G	6-4	330	8/24/86	2	Maryland	Harrisburg, Pa.	D7b-'09	8/0
28	Thomas, Kevin	DB	6-0	192	9/20/86	2	Southern California	Oxnard, Calif.	D3-'10	0*
75	Toudouze, Michael	T	6-6	303	4/27/83	4	Texas Christian	San Antonio, Texas	FA-'10	1/0
54	Triplett, Nate	LB	6-3	247	3/15/87	2	Minnesota	Delano, Minn.	FA-'10	5/0
20	Tryon, Justin	DB	5-9	183	5/29/84	4	Arizona State	Palmdale, Calif.	T(Wash)-'10	12/6
49	Vaughn, Cassius	DB	6-2	221	10/26/85	3	Wake Forest	Fairfax, Va.	FA-'10	3/0
4	Vinatieri, Adam	K	6-0	202	12/28/72	16	South Dakota State	Rapid City, S.D.	UFA(NE)-'06	16/0
87	Wayne, Reggie	WR	6-0	198	11/17/78	11	Miami	New Orleans, La.	D1b-'01	16/16
50	Wheeler, Philip	LB	6-2	240	12/12/84	4	Georgia Tech	Columbus, Ga.	D3-'08	16/6
15	White, Blair	WR	6-2	205	2/20/87	2	Michigan State	Saginaw, Mich.	FA-'10	13/4

* Hamlin played 7 games with Baltimore and 2 games with Indianapolis in '10; Painter did not play in 16 games; Pressley played 1 game with Houston; Santi missed '10 season because of injury; Silva missed '10 season because of injury; J. Thomas missed '10 season because of injury.

Also played with Colts in '10—RB Joique Bell (5 games), WR Chris Brooks (1), RB Andre Brown (1), LB Ramon Humber (2), WR Brandon James (3), P Jeremy Kapinos (1), DT Mitch King (4), WR Kenny Moore (2), DB DaJuan Morgan (2), DB David Pender (3), DB Bob Sanders (1), DB Deshea Townsend (8).

^ "NFL Exp." as of 2011 Kickoff Weekend. For full explanation of how a player's NFL Experience is measured, refer to explanation underneath the First-Year Roster listed below.

FIRST-YEAR ROSTER

Name	Pos.	Ht.	Wt.	Birthdate	College	Hometown	How Acq.
Bender, Casey (1)	T	6-5	295	12/22/86	South Dakota State	Lindsay, Neb.	FA
Brooks, Chris (1)	WR	6-2	210	2/5/87	Nebraska	St. Louis, Mo.	FA
Caldwell, David (1)	DB	5-11	212	5/19/87	William & Mary	Montclair, N.J.	FA
Carter, Delone	RB	5-9	225	6/22/87	Syracuse	Copley, Ohio	D4
Castonzo, Anthony	T	6-7	305	8/9/88	Boston College	Hawthorn Woods, Ill.	D1
Chick, John (1)	DE	6-4	250	11/20/82	Utah State	Gillette, Wyo.	FA
Heckendorf, Kole (1)	WR	6-2	191	11/20/85	North Dakota State	Mosinee, Wisc.	FA
Hemby, Jordan (1)	DB	5-11	190	7/21/87	North Carolina	Raleigh, N.C.	FA
Ijalana, Ben	G	6-4	317	8/6/89	Villanova	Hainesport, N.J.	D2
Johnson, Terrence (1)	DB	5-9	190	7/5/86	California (PA)	Braddock, Pa.	FA
Myers, Rob (1)	TE	6-4	239	4/9/86	Utah State	Houston, Texas	FA
Nevis, Drake	DT	6-1	294	5/8/89	Louisiana State	Harvey, La.	D3
Reitz, Joe (1)	T	6-7	320	6/9/87	Western Michigan	Indianapolis, Ind.	FA
Rucker, Chris	DB	6-1	195	10/12/88	Michigan State	Warren, Ohio	D6
Swenson, Brett (1)	K	5-8	173	2/10/88	Michigan State	Pompano Beach, Fla.	FA
Tepper, Mike (1)	T	6-6	323	12/11/85	California	Cypress, Calif.	FA
Williams, James (1)	T	6-5	295	7/3/88	Harvard	Chestnut Hill, Mass.	FA

The term NFL Rookie is defined as a player who is in his first season of professional football and has not been on the roster of another professional football team for any regular-season or postseason games. A Rookie is designated by an "R" on NFL rosters. Players who have been active in another professional football league or players who have NFL experience, including either preseason training camp or being on an Active List or Inactive List, or on Reserve/Injured or Reserve/Physically Unable to Perform for fewer than six regular-season games, are termed NFL First-Year Players. An NFL First-Year Player is designated by a "1" on NFL rosters. Thereafter, a player is credited with an additional year of experience for each season in which he accumulates six games on the Active List or Inactive List, or on Reserve/Injured or Reserve/Physically Unable to Perform.

Log on to www.colts.com for an up-to-date roster.

COACHING STAFF

Head Coach,
Jim Caldwell

Pro Career: Jim Caldwell was named head coach of the club on January 13, 2009 and enters his third season as head coach of the Colts. In first season, Caldwell guided the Colts to 14 consecutive victories to start the season, the longest winning streak for a coach beginning his career in NFL history. The season culminated with the Colts making their fourth-ever Super Bowl appearance. Prior to his head-coaching promotion, Caldwell had served with Indianapolis from 2002-08. He was elevated to associate head coach with the club on January 21, 2008. Caldwell spent his first three seasons as quarterbacks coach before earning the expanded title of assistant head coach prior to the 2005 season. In 2010, the club made its ninth consecutive playoff appearance, a span that includes Caldwell's tenure in Indianapolis. The Colts extended their streak of double-digit victory seasons to nine, the second-longest streak in NFL history. Caldwell joined Indianapolis from Tampa Bay, where he was quarterbacks coach during the 2001 season. He spent 1993-2000 as head coach at Wake Forest and served as an assistant coach at Southern Illinois (1978-1980), Northwestern (1981), Colorado (1982-84), Louisville (1985) and Penn State (1986-1992). Career record: 26-10.

Background: Caldwell was a four-year starter (1973-76) as a defensive back at Iowa and worked as a graduate assistant for the Hawkeyes in 1977. He holds a bachelor's degree from Iowa.

Personal: Born January 16, 1955 in Beloit, Wis. Jim and his wife, Cheryl, have four children: Jimmy, Jermaine, Jared, and Natalie.

ASSISTANT COACHES

Clyde Christensen, offensive coordinator; born January 28, 1956, Covina, Calif. Quarterback Fresno City College 1975, North Carolina 1976-78. No pro playing experience. College coach: Mississippi 1979, East Tennessee State 1980-82, Temple 1983-85, East Carolina 1986-88, Holy Cross 1989-1990, South Carolina 1991, Maryland 1992-93, Clemson 1994-95. Pro coach: Tampa Bay Buccaneers 1996-2001, joined Colts in 2002.

Jim Bob Cooter, asst. to the offensive coordinator; born July 3, 1984, Huntsville, Ala. Quarterback Tennessee 2002-06. No pro playing experience. College coach: Tennessee 2007-08. Pro coach: Joined Colts in 2009.

Larry Coyer, defensive coordinator; born April 19, 1943, Huntington, W.Va. Quarterback Marshall 1961-64. No pro playing experience. College coach: Marshall 1965-67, Bowling Green 1968-1973, Iowa 1974-77, Oklahoma State

1978, Iowa State 1979-1982, 1995-96, UCLA 1987-89, Houston 1990, Ohio State 1991-92, East Carolina 1993, Pittsburgh 1997-99. Pro coach: Michigan Panthers (USFL) 1983-84, Memphis Showboats (USFL) 1985, New York Jets 1994, Denver Broncos 2000-06, Tampa Bay Buccaneers 2007-08, joined Colts in 2009.

Devin Fitzsimmons, coaching assistant; born October 18, 1982, Folsom, La. Quarterback/Wide receiver Bucknell 2001-05. No pro playing experience. College coach: Shaw (N.C.) 2005, Bucknell 2006, Kansas State 2007-08, Virginia 2009, Richmond 2010. Pro coach: Joined Colts in 2011.

Richard Howell, asst. strength and conditioning; born February 19, 1972, Bladenboro, N.C. Quarterback Davidson 1990-93. No pro playing experience. College coach: Davidson 1994-98, North Carolina 1998-99. Pro coach: Barcelona Dragons (NFLE) 1999, joined Colts in 2000.

Pete Metzelaars, offensive line; born May 24, 1960, Three Rivers, Mich. Tight end Wabash College 1978-1981. Pro tight end Seattle Seahawks 1982-84, Buffalo Bills 1985-1994, Carolina Panthers 1995, Detroit Lions 1996-97. College coach: Wingate 2003. Pro coach: Barcelona Dragons (NFLE) 2003, joined Colts in 2004.

Mike Murphy, linebackers; born September 25, 1944, New York, N.Y. Guard/linebacker Huron (S.D.) 1963-66. No pro playing experience. College coach: Vermont 1970-73, Idaho State 1974-76, Western Illinois 1977-78. Pro coach: Saskatchewan Roughriders (CFL) 1979-1983, Chicago Blitz (USFL) 1984, Detroit Lions 1985-89, Arizona Cardinals 1990-93, Seattle Seahawks 1995-97, joined Colts in 1998.

Rod Perry, special assistant to the defense; born September 11, 1953, Fresno, Calif. Defensive back Colorado 1972-74. Pro cornerback Los Angeles Rams 1975-1982, Cleveland Browns 1983-84. College coach: Columbia 1985, Fresno City College 1986, Fresno State 1987-88. Pro coach: Seattle Seahawks 1989-1991, Los Angeles Rams 1992-94, Houston Oilers 1995-96, San Diego Chargers 1997-2001, Carolina Panthers 2002-06, joined Colts in 2007.

Ron Prince, asst. offensive line; born September 18, 1969, Omaha, Neb. Offensive lineman Dodge City (Kan.) C.C. 1988-89, Appalachian State 1990-91. No pro playing experience. College coach: Dodge City C.C. 1992, Alabama A&M 1993, South Carolina State 1994, James Madison 1995-97, Cornell 1998-2000, Virginia 2001-05, 2009, Kansas State 2006-08 (head coach). Pro coach: Joined Colts in 2010.

Frank Reich, wide receivers; born December 4, 1961, Freeport, N.Y. Quarterback Maryland 1981-84. Pro

quarterback Buffalo Bills 1985-1994, Carolina Panthers 1995, New York Jets 1996, Detroit Lions 1997-98. Pro coach: Joined Colts in 2008.

Ray Rychleski, special teams; born September 27, 1957, Old Forge, Pa. Attended Millersville (Pa.) State College. No college or pro playing experience. College coach: Temple 1981-88, Northeastern 1989-1990, Penn State 1991, East Stroudsburg 1992, Wake Forest 1993-2000, Maryland 2001-07, South Carolina 2008. Pro coach: Joined Colts in 2009.

Bill Teerlinck, defensive assistant; born July 23, 1978, Champaign, Ill. Defensive end Chadron State 2000-02. No pro playing experience. College coach: Indiana 2003-04, Illinois State 2005-06. Pro coach: Joined Colts in 2007.

John Teerlinck, defensive line; born April 9, 1951, Rochester, N.Y. Defensive lineman Western Illinois 1970-73. Pro defensive tackle San Diego Chargers 1974-77. College coach: Iowa Lakes J.C. 1977, Eastern Illinois 1978-79, Illinois 1980-82. Pro coach: Chicago Blitz (USFL) 1983-84, Arizona Wranglers/Outlaws (USFL) 1985-86, Cleveland Browns 1989-1990, Los Angeles Rams 1991, Minnesota Vikings 1992-94, Detroit Lions 1995-96, Denver Broncos 1997-2001, joined Colts in 2002.

Ricky Thomas, tight ends; born March 29, 1965, London, England. Safety Alabama 1983-86. No pro playing experience. College coach: Kentucky 1996, Gardner-Webb 1997. Pro coach: Tampa Bay Buccaneers 1997-2001, joined Colts in 2002.

Jon Torine, strength and conditioning; born November 16, 1973, Livingston, N.J. Linebacker Springfield (Mass.) College 1991. No pro playing experience. Pro coach: Buffalo Bills 1995-97, joined Colts in 1998.

Ron Turner, quarterbacks; born December 5, 1953, Martinez, Calif. Wide receiver Diablo Valley (Calif.) C.C. 1973-74, Pacific 1975-76. No pro playing experience. College coach: Pacific 1977, Arizona 1978-1980, Northwestern 1981-82, Pittsburgh 1983-84, Southern California 1985-87, Texas A&M 1988, Stanford 1989-1991, San Jose State 1992 (head coach), Illinois 1997-2004 (head coach). Pro coach: Chicago Bears 1993-94, 2005-09, joined Colts in 2010.

David Walker, running backs; born December 4, 1969, Rochester, N.Y. Running back Syracuse 1989-1992. No pro playing experience. College coach: Syracuse 1995-2004, Pittsburgh 2005-2010. Pro coach: Joined Colts in 2011.

Alan Williams, defensive backs; born November 4, 1969, Norfolk, Va. Running back William & Mary 1988-1991. No pro playing experience. College coach: William & Mary 1996-2000. Pro coach: Tampa Bay Buccaneers 2001, joined Colts in 2002.

American Football Conference
South Division
Team Colors: Teal, Black, and Gold
EverBank Field
One EverBank Field Drive
Jacksonville, Florida 32202
Telephone: (904) 633-6000

2011 SCHEDULE
PRESEASON
Aug. 11 at New England 7:30
Aug. 19 **Atlanta**..............................8:00
Aug. 27 at Buffalo 7:00
Sep. 1 **St. Louis** 7:30

REGULAR SEASON
Sep. 11 **Tennessee** 1:00
Sep. 18 at New York Jets 1:00
Sep. 25 at Carolina 1:00
Oct. 2 **New Orleans** 1:00
Oct. 9 **Cincinnati** 1:00
Oct. 16 at Pittsburgh 1:00
Oct. 24 **Baltimore** (Mon) 8:30
Oct. 30 at Houston 1:00
Nov. 6 BYE
Nov. 13 at Indianapolis 1:00
Nov. 20 at Cleveland 1:00
Nov. 27 **Houston** 1:00
Dec. 5 **San Diego** (Mon) 8:30
Dec. 11 **Tampa Bay** 1:00
Dec. 15 at Atlanta (Thu) 8:20
Dec. 24 at Tennessee (Sat)............ 1:00
Jan. 1 **Indianapolis** 1:00
All times ET
Stadium: EverBank Field
(opened in 1995)
• Capacity: 67,246
One EverBank Field Drive
Jacksonville, Florida 32202
Playing Surface: Grass
Training Camp: EverBank Field
One EverBank Field Drive
Jacksonville, Florida 32202

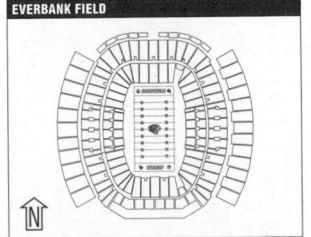

CLUB OFFICIALS
Chairman and Chief Executive Officer:
  Wayne Weaver
Senior Vice President/Football
  Operations: Paul Vance
Senior Vice President/Chief Financial
  Officer: Bill Prescott
Senior Vice President/Communications
  and Media: Dan Edwards
Senior Vice President/Sales and
  Marketing: Macky Weaver

General Manager/Senior Vice President,
  Player Personnel: Gene Smith
Director, Player Personnel:
  Terry McDonough
Assistant Director, College Personnel:
  Tim Mingey
Assistant Director, Pro Personnel:
  Louis Clark
National Scout: Andy Dengler
Regional Scouts: Jason DesJarlais,
  Marty Miller, Chris Prescott,
  Brian Simmons
Pro Scout: Chris Driggers
BLESTO Scout: Jake Peetz
Scouting Assistant, College and Pro
  Personnel: Patrick Mularkey

Executive Director of Football Operations:
  Skip Richardson
Executive Director of Information
  Technology: Bruce Swindell
Director of Ticket Operations: Tim Bishko
Associate General Counsel: Sashi Brown
Director of Football Administration:
  Tim Walsh
Head Athletic Trainer: Michael Ryan
Video Director: Mike Perkins
Equipment Manager: Drew Hampton
Manager, Communications:
  Ryan Robinson
Executive Assistant to Senior VP,
  Communications and Media:
  Alisa Abbott

Chair & Chief Executive Officer, Jaguars
  Foundation: Delores Barr Weaver
Executive Director: Peter Racine

COACHING HISTORY
(138-129-0)
Records include postseason games
1995-2002 Tom Coughlin 72-64-0
2003-2010 Jack Del Rio 66-65-0

PAID ATTENDANCE
Home 467,289   Away 532,075
Total 999,364
Single-game home record,
  74,143 (12/28/98)
Single-season home record,
  561,472 (1998)

2011 DRAFT CHOICES
Round	Name	Pos.	College
1	Blaine Gabbert	QB	Missouri
3	Will Rackley	G/C	Lehigh
4	Cecil Shorts III	WR	Mount Union
	Chris Prosinski	DB	Wyoming
5	Rod Issac	DB	Middle Tennessee

2010 TEAM RECORD
PRESEASON (2-2)

Date	Result		Opponent
8/13	L	27-28	at Philadelphia
8/21	L	26-27	Miami
8/28	W	19-13	at Tampa Bay
9/2	W	13-9	Atlanta

REGULAR SEASON (8-8)

Date	Result		Opponent
9/12	W	24-17	Denver
9/19	L	13-38	at San Diego
9/26	L	3-28	Philadelphia
10/3	W	31-28	Indianapolis
10/10	W	36-26	at Buffalo
10/18	L	3-30	Tennessee
10/24	L	20-42	at Kansas City
10/31	W	35-17	at Dallas
11/14	W	31-24	Houston
11/21	W	24-20	Cleveland
11/28	L	20-24	at New York Giants
12/5	W	17-6	at Tennessee
12/12	W	38-31	Oakland
12/19	L	24-34	at Indianapolis
12/26	L	17-20	Washington (OT)
1/2	L	17-34	at Houston

(OT) Overtime

SCORE BY PERIODS

Jaguars	43	129	86	95	0	—	353
Opponents	88	92	102	134	3	—	419

2010 TEAM STATISTICS

	Jaguars	Opp.
Total First Downs	330	316
Rushing	148	98
Passing	161	197
Penalty	21	21
3rd Down: Made/Att	81/203	78/189
3rd Down Pct.	39.9	41.3
4th Down: Made/Att	16/25	8/18
4th Down Pct.	64.0	44.4
Possession Avg.	31:43	28:17
Total Net Yards	5460	5949
Avg. Per Game	341.3	371.8
Total Plays	1019	948
Avg. Per Play	5.4	6.3
Net Yards Rushing	2395	1945
Avg. Per Game	149.7	121.6
Total Rushes	512	416
Net Yards Passing	3065	4004
Avg. Per Game	191.6	250.3
Sacked/Yards Lost	38/291	26/189
Gross Yards	3356	4193
Att./Completions	469/291	506/329
Completion Pct.	62.0	65.0
Had Intercepted	21	13
Punts/Average	57/43.8	64/42.4
Net Punting Avg.	57/39.2	64/36.5
Penalties/Yards	83/675	85/748
Fumbles/Ball Lost	23/12	12/5
Touchdowns	41	50
Rushing	14	19
Passing	26	28
Returns	1	3

2010 INDIVIDUAL STATISTICS

PASSING

	Att.	Comp.	Yds.	Pct.	TD	Int.	Tkld.	Rate
Garrard	366	236	2734	64.5	23	15	33/253	90.8
Edwards	49	26	280	53.1	1	3	4/32	51.4
Bouman	34	18	222	52.9	2	2	1/6	68.5
McCown	19	11	120	57.9	0	0	0/0	76.6
Jones-Drew	1	0	0	0.0	0	1	0/0	0.0
Jaguars	469	291	3356	62.0	26	21	38/291	83.4
Opponents	506	329	4193	65.0	28	13	26/189	98.5

SCORING

	TD R	TD P	TD Rt	PAT	FG	Saf	PTS
Scobee	0	0	0	41/41	22/28	0	107
Lewis	0	10	0	0/0	0/0	0	60
Jones-Drew	5	2	0	0/0	0/0	0	42
Sims-Walker	0	7	0	0/0	0/0	0	42
Garrard	5	0	0	0/0	0/0	0	30
M. Thomas	0	4	1	0/0	0/0	0	30
Jennings	4	0	0	0/0	0/0	0	24
J. Hill	0	1	0	0/0	0/0	0	6
Miller	0	1	0	0/0	0/0	0	6
Osgood	0	1	0	0/0	0/0	0	6
Jaguars	14	26	1	41/41	22/28	0	353
Opponents	19	28	3	48/48	23/25	0	419

2-Pt Conversions: Jaguars 0-0, Opponents 1-2.

RUSHING

	No.	Yds	Avg	LG	TD
Jones-Drew	299	1324	4.4	37	5
Jennings	84	459	5.5	74t	4
Garrard	66	279	4.2	25t	5
Karim	35	160	4.6	15	0
M. Thomas	12	114	9.5	33	0
Edwards	9	34	3.8	14	0
Miller	2	9	4.5	8	0
Bouman	2	8	4.0	6	0
G. Jones	2	4	2.0	3	0
McCown	1	4	4.0	4	0
Jaguars	512	2395	4.7	74t	14
Opponents	416	1945	4.7	70	19

RECEIVING

	No.	Yds	Avg	LG	TD
M. Thomas	66	820	12.4	50t	4
Lewis	58	700	12.1	42t	10
Sims-Walker	43	562	13.1	39	7
Jones-Drew	34	317	9.3	75	2
Jennings	26	223	8.6	25	0
Miller	20	216	10.8	52t	1
J. Hill	11	248	22.5	48t	1
G. Jones	11	47	4.3	12	0
Underwood	8	111	13.9	22	0
Osgood	6	60	10.0	24t	1
Potter	3	24	8.0	10	0
Karim	3	10	3.3	7	0
Bolen	1	15	15.0	15	0
Wilford	1	3	3.0	3	0
Jaguars	291	3356	11.5	75	26
Opponents	329	4193	12.7	67t	28

INTERCEPTIONS

	No.	Yds	Avg	LG	TD
D. Cox	4	14	3.5	14	0
A. Smith	1	47	47.0	47	0
Mathis	1	24	24.0	24	0
Greene	1	8	8.0	8	0
Da. Smith	1	8	8.0	8	0
Carey	1	7	7.0	7	0
Middleton	1	2	2.0	2	0
D. Jones	1	0	0.0	0	0
Considine	1	-2	-2.0	-2	0
Knighton	1	-3	-3.0	-3	0
Jaguars	13	105	8.1	47	0
Opponents	21	263	12.5	38	1

PUNTING

	No.	Yds.	Avg.	In 20	LG
Podlesh	57	2496	43.8	26	63
Jaguars	57	2496	43.8	26	63
Opponents	64	2714	42.4	16	66

PUNT RETURNS

	Ret	FC	Yds	Avg	LG	TD
M. Thomas	34	7	358	10.5	78t	1
Brackenridge	1	0	1	1.0	1	0
Osgood	1	0	0	0.0	0	0
Mathis	0	1	0	—	—	0
Jaguars	36	8	359	10.0	78t	1
Opponents	19	15	123	6.5	13	0

KICKOFF RETURNS

	No.	Yds	Avg	LG	TD
Karim	50	1248	25.0	65	0
Underwood	24	561	23.4	53	0
J. Hill	1	30	30.0	30	0
Miller	1	22	22.0	22	0
Owens	1	22	22.0	22	0
Potter	1	15	15.0	15	0
Bolen	1	5	5.0	5	0
Wilford	1	0	0.0	0	0
Jaguars	80	1903	23.8	65	0
Opponents	59	1266	21.5	46	1

FIELD GOALS

	1-19	20-29	30-39	40-49	50+
Scobee	2/2	3/3	6/7	9/14	2/2
Jaguars	2/2	3/3	6/7	9/14	2/2
Opponents	0/0	9/9	10/10	3/3	1/3

SACKS

	No.
Mincey	5.0
Kampman	4.0
Knighton	4.0
Alualu	3.5
Da. Smith	3.5
Harvey	2.5
Hart	1.5
Considine	1.0
Middleton	1.0
Jaguars	26.0
Opponents	38.0

RECORD HOLDERS

INDIVIDUAL RECORDS—CAREER

Category	Name	Performance
Rushing (Yds.)	Fred Taylor, 1998-2008	11,271
Passing (Yds.)	Mark Brunell, 1995-2003	25,698
Passing (TDs)	Mark Brunell, 1995-2003	144
Receiving (No.)	Jimmy Smith, 1995-2005	862
Receiving (Yds.)	Jimmy Smith, 1995-2005	12,287
Interceptions	Rashean Mathis, 2003-2010	29
Punting (Avg.)	Bryan Barker, 1995-2000	43.5
Punt Return (Avg.)	Bobby Shaw, 2002	12.4
Kickoff Return (Avg.)	Maurice Jones-Drew, 2006-2010	26.0
Field Goals	Mike Hollis, 1995-2001	175
Touchdowns (Tot.)	Fred Taylor, 1998-2008	70
Points	Mike Hollis, 1995-2001	764
*Sacks	Tony Brackens, 1996-2003	55.0

INDIVIDUAL RECORDS—SINGLE SEASON

Category	Name	Performance
Rushing (Yds.)	Fred Taylor, 2003	1,572
Passing (Yds.)	Mark Brunell, 1996	4,367
Passing (TDs)	David Garrard, 2010	23
Receiving (No.)	Jimmy Smith, 1999	116
Receiving (Yds.)	Jimmy Smith, 1999	1,636
Interceptions	Rashean Mathis, 2006	8
Punting (Avg.)	Bryan Barker, 1998	45.0
Punt Return (Avg.)	Reggie Barlow, 1998	12.9
Kickoff Return (Avg.)	Maurice Jones-Drew, 2006	27.7
Field Goals	Mike Hollis, 1997, 1999	31
Touchdowns (Tot.)	Fred Taylor, 1998	17
Points	Mike Hollis, 1997	134
*Sacks	Tony Brackens, 1999	12.0

INDIVIDUAL RECORDS—SINGLE GAME

Category	Name	Performance
Rushing (Yds.)	Fred Taylor, 11-19-00	234
Passing (Yds.)	Mark Brunell, 9-22-96	432
Passing (TDs)	Mark Brunell, 11-29-98	4
	Quinn Gray, 12-30-07	4
	David Garrard, 10-31-10	4
Receiving (No.)	Keenan McCardell, 10-20-96	16
Receiving (Yds.)	Jimmy Smith, 9-10-00	291
Interceptions	Many times	2
	Last time by Rashean Mathis, 11-5-06	
Field Goals	Mike Hollis, 12-1-96, 11-30-97, 9-10-00	5
	Josh Scobee, 11-25-07, 10-10-10	5
Touchdowns (Tot.)	James Stewart, 10-12-97	5
Points	James Stewart, 10-12-97	30
*Sacks	Kelvin Pritchett, 10-5-97	3.0
	John Henderson, 10-6-02	3.0
	Paul Spicer, 9-25-05	3.0

*Sacks became an official statistic in 1982.

VETERAN ROSTER AS OF MARCH 3, 2011

No.	Name	Pos.	Ht.	Wt.	Birthdate	^NFL Exp.	College	Hometown	How Acq.	'10 Games/Starts
50	Allen, Russell	LB	6-3	234	5/5/86	3	San Diego State	Oceanside, Calif.	FA-'09	16/4
93	Alualu, Tyson	DT	6-3	304	5/12/87	2	California	Honolulu, Hawai'i	D1-'10	16/16
44	Bolen, Brock	FB	6-0	233	3/24/85	2	Louisville	Germantown, Ohio	FA-'09	4/0
51	Bosworth, Kyle	LB	6-1	236	11/21/86	2	UCLA	Plano, Texas	FA-'10	0*
4	Bouman, Todd	QB	6-2	236	8/1/72	11	St. Cloud State	Ruthton, Minn.	FA-'10	1/1
54	Bowen, Alvin	LB	6-1	222	12/24/83	2	Iowa State	East Orange, N.J.	FA-'10	2/0
41	Brackenridge, Tyron	DB	5-11	189	6/30/84	4	Washington State	Pasadena, Calif.	W(NYJ)-'09	16/0
73	Britton, Eben	T	6-6	310	10/14/87	3	Arizona	Brooklyn, N.Y.	D2-'09	7/7
48	Cain, Jeremy	LS	6-1	245	3/24/80	5	Massachusetts	Fort Lauderdale, Fla.	W(Wash)-'09	16/0
22	Carey, Don	DB	5-11	192	2/14/87	3	Norfolk State	Norfolk, Va.	W(Cle)-'09	15/10
98	Collins, Nate	DT	6-2	296	12/14/87	2	Virginia	Port Chester, N.Y.	PS(NYG)-'10	1/0
37	Considine, Sean	S	6-0	212	12/17/82	7	Iowa	Byron, Ill.	UFA(Phil)-'09	14/5
21	Cox, Derek	CB	6-1	190	9/22/86	3	William & Mary	Greenville, N.C.	D3b-'09	13/11
58	Cutrera, Jacob	LB	6-3	238	5/18/88	2	Louisiana State	Lafayette, La.	FA-'10	8/0
87	Dillard, Jarett	WR	5-10	187	12/21/85	3	Rice	San Antonio, Texas	D5-'09	0*
69	Douzable, Leger	DT	6-4	284	5/31/86	3	Central Florida	Tampa, Fla.	FA-'10	15/0
56	Durant, Justin	LB	6-1	240	9/21/85	5	Hampton	Florence, S.C.	D2-'07	10/9
5	Edwards, Trent	QB	6-4	231	10/30/83	5	Stanford	Los Gatos, Calif.	W(Buff)-'10	5/3*
62	Estes, John	C	6-2	302	3/25/87	2	Hawai'i	Stockton, Calif.	FA-'10	0*
9	Garrard, David	QB	6-1	236	2/14/78	10	East Carolina	Durham, N.C.	D4-'02	14/14
36	Greene, Courtney	S	6-0	212	11/23/86	3	Rutgers	New Rochelle, N.Y.	FA-'09	14/11
25	Hamlin, Michael	S	6-2	213	11/21/85	3	Clemson	Lamar, S.C.	FA-'10	6/0*
59	Hart, Larry	DE	6-0	248	7/16/87	2	Central Arkansas	Madison, Miss.	D5a-'10	14/0
91	Harvey, Derrick	DE	6-5	268	11/9/86	4	Florida	Greenbelt, Md.	D1-'08	15/7
72	Haslam, Kevin	OL	6-5	304	11/8/86	2	Rutgers	Mahwah, N.J.	FA-'10	5/0
83	Hill, Jason	WR	6-0	202	2/20/85	5	Washington State	San Francisco, Calif.	W(SF)-'10	8/1*
16	Hughes, Nate	WR	6-2	195	1/18/85	3	Alcorn State	Starkville, Miss.	FA-'08	0*
23	Jennings, Rashad	RB	6-1	228	3/26/85	2	Liberty	Forest, Va.	D7a-'09	13/3
31	Jones, David	CB	6-0	197	9/19/85	5	Wingate	Greenville, S.C.	T(Cin)-'10	16/5
33	Jones, Greg	FB/RB	6-1	254	5/9/81	8	Florida State	Beaufort, S.C.	D2b-'04	16/13
32	Jones-Drew, Maurice	RB	5-7	208	3/23/85	6	UCLA	Antioch, Calif.	D2-'06	14/14
74	Kampman, Aaron	DE	6-4	260	11/30/79	10	Iowa	Kesley, Iowa	UFA(GB)-'10	8/8
35	Karim, Deji	RB/KR	5-8	209	11/18/86	2	Southern Illinois	Oklahoma City, Okla.	D6a-'10	11/0
96	Knighton, Terrance	DT	6-3	336	7/4/86	3	Temple	Hartford, Conn.	D3a-'09	16/16
92	Lane, Austen	DE	6-5	274	11/9/87	2	Murray State	Iola, Wis.	D5b-'10	11/9
89	Lewis, Marcedes	TE	6-6	275	5/19/84	6	UCLA	Long Beach, Calif.	D1-'06	16/16
67	Manuwai, Vince	G	6-2	333	7/12/80	9	Hawai'i	Honolulu, Hawai'i	D3-'03	16/11
27	Mathis, Rashean	CB	6-1	193	8/27/80	9	Bethune-Cookman	Jacksonville, Fla.	D2-'03	16/16
17	Matthews, John	WR	6-0	200	7/19/86	2	San Diego	Littleton, Colo.	W(Ind)-'10	3/0
12	McCown, Luke	QB	6-4	217	7/12/81	8	Louisiana Tech	Jacksonville, Texas	T(TB)-'09	1/0
30	McGee, Scotty	RS	5-8	182	12/4/86	2	James Madison	Virginia Beach, Va.	D6b-'10	0*
63	Meester, Brad	C	6-3	302	3/23/77	12	Northern Iowa	Parkersburg, Iowa	D2-'00	16/16
29	Middleton, William	CB	5-11	194	7/28/86	3	Furman	Marist, Ga.	PS(Atl)-'09	16/3
86	Miller, Zach	TE	6-4	245	10/4/84	3	Nebraska-Omaha	Weston, Neb.	D6-'09	15/5
94	Mincey, Jeremy	DL	6-3	270	12/14/83	4	Florida	Statesboro, Ga.	FA-'10	15/8
75	Monroe, Eugene	T	6-5	308	4/18/87	3	Virginia	Plainfield, N.J.	D1-'09	15/15
97	Morgan, Aaron	DE	6-4	238	12/30/88	2	Louisiana-Monroe	Amite, La.	FA-'10	7/0
55	Morrison, Kirk	LB	6-2	240	2/19/82	7	San Diego State	Oakland, Calif.	T(Oak)-'10	16/16
90	Mosley, C.J.	DL	6-3	305	8/6/83	7	Missouri	Fort Knox, Ky.	FA-'10	8/0
53	Norris, Slade	LB	6-2	232	10/25/85	2	Oregon State	Portland, Ore.	FA-'10	5/0
77	Nwaneri, Uche	G/C	6-3	318	3/20/84	5	Purdue	Garland, Texas	D5a-'07	16/16
81	Osgood, Kassim	WR	6-5	220	5/20/80	9	San Diego State	Salinas, Calif.	UFA(SD)-'10	16/3
24	Owens, Montell	FB	5-10	225	5/4/84	6	Maine	Wilmington, Del.	FA-'06	16/0
3	Podlesh, Adam	P	5-11	200	8/11/83	5	Maryland	Pittsford, N.Y.	D4a-'07	16/0
88	Potter, Zach	TE	6-7	280	5/4/86	2	Nebraska	Omaha, Neb.	FA-'09	13/1
10	Scobee, Josh	K	6-1	210	6/23/82	8	Louisiana Tech	Longview, Texas	D5a-'04	16/0
11	Sims-Walker, Mike	WR	6-2	214	11/21/84	5	Central Florida	Orlando, Fla.	D3-'07	14/13
66	Smiley, Justin	G	6-3	310	11/11/81	8	Alabama	Ellabell, Ga.	T(Mia)-'10	5/5
95	Smith, D'Anthony	DT	6-2	298	6/9/88	2	Louisiana Tech	Pickering, La.	D3-10	0*
52	Smith, Daryl	LB	6-2	249	3/14/82	8	Georgia Tech	Albany, Ga.	D2a-'04	16/16
80	Thomas, Mike	WR	5-8	198	6/4/87	3	Arizona	DeSoto, Texas	D4-'09	16/11
19	Underwood, Tiquan	WR	6-1	183	2/17/87	3	Rutgers	New Brunswick, N.J.	D7b-'09	10/0
20	Wheatley, Terrence	CB	5-9	185	5/5/85	4	Colorado	Plano, Texas	FA-'10	1/0
68	Whimper, Guy	T	6-5	302	5/21/83	6	East Carolina	Havelock, N.C.	FA-'10	6/1
43	Whitehead, Terrell	FS	6-1	194	9/18/88	2	Norfolk State	Virginia Beach, Va.	FA-'10	0*

* Bosworth missed '10 season because of injury; Dillard missed '10 season because of injury; Edwards played 2 games with Buffalo and 3 games with Jacksonville in '10; Estes missed '10 season because of injury; Hamlin played 2 games with Dallas and 4 games with Jacksonville; Hill played 2 games with San Francisco and 6 games with Jacksonville; Hughes missed '10 season because of injury; McGee missed '10 season because of injury; D'A. Smith missed '10 season because of injury; Whitehead missed '10 season because of injury.

Also played with Jaguars in '10—LB Eric Alexander (4 games), S Gerald Alexander (3), T Daniel Baldridge (1), T Jordan Black (15), DB Michael Coe (2), DT Landon Cohen (2), CB Chevis Jackson (2), S Anthony Smith (3), TE Ernest Wilford (2).

^ "NFL Exp." as of 2011 Kickoff Weekend. For full explanation of how a player's NFL Experience is measured, refer to explanation underneath the First-Year Roster listed below.

FIRST-YEAR ROSTER

Name	Pos.	Ht.	Wt.	Birthdate	College	Hometown	How Acq.
Baldridge, Daniel (1)	T	6-8	311	10/21/85	Marshall	Opelousas, La.	FA-'10
Gabbert, Blaine	QB	6-5	233	10/15/89	Missouri	Ballwin, Mo.	D1
Issac, Rod	CB	5-11	196	2/20/89	Middle Tennessee State	Miami, Fla.	D5
Prosinski, Chris	S	6-1	201	4/28/87	Wyoming	Buffalo, Wyo.	D4b
Rackley, Will	G/C	6-3	309	10/11/89	Lehigh	Riverdale, Ga.	D3
Shorts III, Cecil	WR/RS	6-0	193	12/22/87	Mount Union	Cleveland, Ohio	D4a
Vierling, Bradley (1)	C	6-3	290	5/18/86	Vanderbilt	Warminster, Pa.	FA-'10

The term NFL Rookie is defined as a player who is in his first season of professional football and has not been on the roster of another professional football team for any regular-season or postseason games. A Rookie is designated by an "R" on NFL rosters. Players who have been active in another professional football league or players who have NFL experience, including either preseason training camp or being on an Active List or Inactive List, or on Reserve/Injured or Reserve/Physically Unable to Perform for fewer than six regular-season games, are termed NFL First-Year Players. An NFL First-Year Player is designated by a "1" on NFL rosters. Thereafter, a player is credited with an additional year of experience for each season in which he accumulates six games on the Active List or Inactive List, or on Reserve/Injured or Reserve/Physically Unable to Perform.

Log on to www.jaguars.com for an up-to-date roster.

COACHING STAFF

Head Coach,
Jack Del Rio

Pro Career: Jack Del Rio is in his ninth season as Jaguars head coach. He ranks seventh among active coaches in career wins and is one of eight current head coaches with eight or more seasons as an NFL head coach. The 2011 season is Del Rio's 15th as an NFL coach and his 26th year in the league. Over his eight seasons (2003-2010) the Jaguars' defense ranks 10th in the NFL in yards allowed (316.9 per game) and seventh in rushing (104.0), while the offense ranks third in rushing yards (130.5) and fourth in fewest turnovers (179). In 2010, with the league's third-ranked rushing attack, the Jaguars shared first place in the AFC South in five of the final six weeks. Three Jaguars were selected for the AFC Pro Bowl squad, the most in ten years. In 2007 the Jaguars posted an 11-5 record and got the franchise's first playoff win since 1999. Jacksonville finished with a 12-4 record in 2005 and earned its first postseason appearance since 1999. Del Rio was the defensive coordinator for Carolina in 2002 after serving as linebackers coach for Baltimore (1999-2001) en route to a Super Bowl XXXV win. He previously coached in New Orleans (1997-98) after spending 11 years as an NFL linebacker. In 1995 he was a third-round choice of New Orleans. Del Rio also played for Kansas City (1987-88), Dallas (1989-1991), and Minnesota (1992-95). Career record: 66-65.

Background: Four-year starter (1981-84) at linebacker at Southern California, and earned consensus All-America honors as a senior. Drafted by baseball's Toronto Blue Jays in 1981, he batted .340 while playing catcher on USC's baseball team. Has a political science degree from Kansas.

Personal: Born April 4, 1963 in Castro Valley, Calif. Jack and his wife, Linda, live in Jacksonville, and have three daughters, Lauren, Hope, and Aubrey, and a son, Luke.

ASSISTANT COACHES

Craig Aukerman, defensive assistant; born November 22, 1976, McComb, Ohio. Defensive back/wide receiver Findlay 1995-98. No pro playing experience. College coach: Findlay 2000, Miami (Ohio) 2001-02, Western Kentucky 2003-04, Kent State 2009. Pro coach: Denver Broncos 2010, joined Jaguars in 2011.

Brandon Blaney, defensive quality control; born November 3, 1975, Joplin, Mo. Attended Youngstown State. No college or pro playing experience. College coach: Youngstown State 1995-98, Oklahoma 1999-2000, Ohio State 2001, Kansas 2002-09. Pro coach: Joined Jaguars in 2011.

Rob Boras, tight ends; born September 30, 1970, Glen Ellyn, Ill. Center DePauw 1988-1991. No pro playing experience. College coach: DePauw 1992-93, Texas 1994-97, Benedictine 1998 (head coach), Nevada-

Las Vegas 1999-2003. Pro coach: Chicago Bears 2004-09, joined Jaguars in 2010.

Earnest Byner, running backs; born September 15, 1962, Milledgeville, Ga. Running back East Carolina 1980-83. Pro running back Cleveland Browns 1984-88, 1994-95, Washington Redskins 1989-1993, Baltimore Ravens 1996-97. Pro coach: Washington Redskins 2004-07, Tennessee Titans 2008-09, joined Jaguars in 2010.

Johnny Cox, wide receivers; born February 5, 1972, Denver. Wide receiver Fort Lewis College 1990-93. No pro playing experience. College coach: Fort Lewis College 1994, North Dakota State 1996, Texas 1997-98, Fort Lewis College 1999, North Dakota State 2000-02, Holy Cross 2007. Pro coach: Tampa Bay Buccaneers 2008, joined Jaguars in 2009.

Joe Cullen, defensive line; born December 15, 1967, Quincy, Mass. Nose guard Massachusetts 1986-89. No pro playing experience. College coach: Massachusetts 1990-91, Richmond 1992-98, 2000, Louisiana State 1999, Memphis 2001, Indiana 2002-04, Illinois 2005, Idaho State 2009. Pro coach: Detroit Lions 2006-08, joined Jaguars in 2010.

Mark Duffner, linebackers; born July 19, 1953, Annandale, Va. Defensive lineman William & Mary 1972-74. No pro playing experience. College coach: Ohio State 1975-76, Cincinnati 1977-1980, Holy Cross 1981-1991 (head coach 1986-1991), Maryland 1992-1996 (head coach). Pro coach: Cincinnati Bengals 1997-2002, Green Bay Packers 2003-2005, joined Jaguars in 2006.

Jason George, asst. strength and conditioning; born October 3, 1968, Winnipeg, Manitoba, Canada. Safety Manitoba 1991-1992. No pro playing experience. College coach: Kansas 1997-98, Fordham 1998-2008. Pro coach: Joined Jaguars in 2009.

Matt Griffin, offensive quality control; born May 9, 1968, Gardner, Mass. Quarterback New Hampshire 1987-1991. No pro playing experience. College coach: Plymouth State 1992-93, Richmond 1994, Northeastern 1995-96, Tennessee-Martin 1997-98, 2003-05 (head coach 2003-05), Maine 1999-2002, Murray State 2006-09 (head coach). Pro coach: Joined Jaguars in 2010.

Andy Heck, offensive line; born January 1, 1967, Fargo, N.D. Tackle Notre Dame 1985-88. Pro tackle Seattle 1989-1993, Chicago 1994-98, Washington 1999-2000. College coach: Virginia 2001-03. Pro coach: Joined Jaguars in 2003.

Ron Heller, offensive staff assistant; born August 25, 1962, East Meadow, N.Y. Offensive tackle Penn State 1980-83. Pro offensive tackle Tampa Bay Buccaneers 1984-87, Philadelphia Eagles 1988-1992, Miami Dolphins 1993-95. Pro coach: Amsterdam Admirals (NFLE) 2004, 2006-07, Toronto Argonauts (CFL) 2009, joined Jaguars in 2010.

Nate Kaczor, asst. special teams; born April 8, 1967, Scott City, Kan. Center Utah State 1986-89. No pro playing experience. College

coach: Utah State 1991-99, Nebraska-Kerney 2000-03, Idaho 2004-05, Louisiana-Monroe 2006-07. Pro coach: Joined Jaguars in 2008.

Thom Kaumeyer, asst. defensive backs; born March 17, 1967, LaJolla, Calif. Safety Palomar (JC) College 1985-86, Oregon 1987-88. Pro safety Seattle Seahawks 1989-1990, New York Giants 1991-92. College coach: Palomar College 1991-94, 1998-2000, Onward Kashiyama Ltd. (head coach, Japan) 1995-96, San Diego State 2002-06, Tulane 2007, Kentucky 2008. Pro coach: Atlanta Falcons 2001-02, joined Jaguars in 2008.

Dirk Koetter, offensive coordinator; born February 5, 1959, Pocatello, Idaho. Quarterback Idaho State 1978-1981. No pro playing experience. College coach: San Francisco State 1985, Texas El-Paso 1986-88, Missouri 1989-1993, Boston College 1994-95, Oregon 1996-97, Boise State 1998-2000 (head coach), Arizona State 2001-06 (head coach). Pro coach: Joined Jaguars in 2007.

Russ Purnell, special teams coordinator; born June 12, 1948, Chicago. Center Orange Coast (Calif.) J.C. 1966-67, Whittier College 1968-69. No pro playing experience. College coach: Whittier College 1970-71, Southern California 1982-85. Pro coach: Seattle Seahawks 1986-1994, Houston Oilers/Tennessee Titans 1995-98, Baltimore Ravens 1999-2001, Indianapolis Colts 2002-2008, joined Jaguars in 2009.

Luke Richesson, strength and conditioning; born April 29, 1974, Kansas City, Missouri. Defensive back Kansas 1992-96. No pro playing experience. College coach: Wyoming 1998, Arizona State 1999-2000. Pro coach: Joined Jaguars in 2009.

Mike Sheppard, quarterbacks; born October 29, 1951, Tulsa, Okla. Wide receiver California Lutheran 1969-1972. No pro playing experience. College coach: California Lutheran 1974-76, Brigham Young 1977-78, U.S. International 1979, Idaho State 1980-81, Long Beach State 1982, 1984-86, Kansas 1983, New Mexico 1987-1991, California 1992. Pro coach: Cleveland Browns 1993-95, Baltimore Ravens 1996, San Diego Chargers 1997-98, Seattle Seahawks 1999-2000, Buffalo Bills 2001, New Orleans Saints 2002-05, Cincinnati Bengals 2007-10, joined Jaguars in 2011.

Mel Tucker, defensive coordinator; born January 4, 1972, Cleveland. Defensive back Wisconsin 1992-95. No pro playing experience. College coach: Michigan State 1997-98, Miami (Ohio) 1999, Louisiana State 2000, Ohio State 2001-04. Pro coach: Cleveland Browns 2005-08, joined Jaguars in 2009.

Cory Undlin, defensive backs; born June 29, 1971, St. Cloud, Minn. Defensive back California Lutheran 1990-94. No pro playing experience. College coach: California Lutheran 1998-2001, Fresno State 2002-03. Pro coach: New England Patriots 2004, Cleveland Browns 2005-08, joined Jaguars in 2009.

American Football Conference
West Division
Team Colors: Red, Gold, and White
One Arrowhead Drive
Kansas City, Missouri 64129
Telephone: (816) 920-9300

2011 SCHEDULE
PRESEASON
Aug. 12 **Tampa Bay**.........................7:00
Aug. 19 at Baltimore........................6:30
Aug. 26 **St. Louis** 7:00
Sep. 1 at Green Bay 6:00

REGULAR SEASON
Sep. 11 **Buffalo** 12:00
Sep. 18 at Detroit 12:00
Sep. 25 at San Diego 3:05
Oct. 2 **Minnesota** 12:00
Oct. 9 at Indianapolis 12:00
Oct. 16 BYE
Oct. 23 at Oakland 3:05
Oct. 31 **San Diego** (Mon) 7:30
Nov. 6 **Miami** 12:00
Nov. 13 **Denver** 12:00
Nov. 21 at New England (Mon)....... 7:30
Nov. 27 **Pittsburgh** *.....................7:20
Dec. 4 at Chicago 12:00
Dec. 11 at New York Jets 12:00
Dec. 18 **Green Bay** 12:00
Dec. 24 **Oakland** (Sat).................12:00
Jan. 1 at Denver 3:15
*All times CT; Sunday night games in
    Weeks 11-15, 17 subject to change
Stadium: Arrowhead Stadium
            (opened in 1972,
            fully renovated in 2010)
            •**Capacity:** 76,416
            One Arrowhead Drive
            Kansas City, Missouri 64129
Playing Surface: Grass
Training Camp: Missouri Western St. Univ.
            St. Joseph, MO 64507

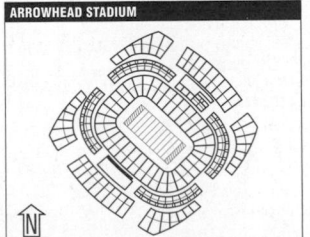

ARROWHEAD STADIUM

CLUB OFFICIALS
Chairman & CEO: Clark Hunt
General Manager: Scott Pioli
President: Mark Donovan
Assistant General Manager: Joel Collier
Chief Financial Officer: Dan Crumb
Director of College Scouting: Phil Emery
Director of Pro Personnel: Ray Farmer
Director of Football Administration:
    Trip MacCracken
Director of Player Development:
    Katie Douglass
Vice President of Sales and Marketing:
    Tammy Fruits
Vice President of Media and Marketing:
    Rob Alberino
Vice President of Stadium Operations:
    David Young
Director of Security: Jason Stone
Director of Facilities: Brandon Hamilton
Director of Special Events: Gary Spani
Director of Human Resources:
    Kirsten Krug
Director of Information Technology:
    Bob Stirton
Equipment Manager: Allen Wright
Asst. Equipment Managers:
    Chris Shropshire, Kyle Crumbaugh,
    Jimmy White
Head Athletic Trainer: David Price
Assistant Athletic Trainers: David Glover,
    Jimmy Ntelekos, Nick Potter
Director of Video Operations: Pat Brazil
Assistant Director Video Operations:
    Ken Radino
Video Assistant: Josh Schmidt

COACHING HISTORY
Dallas Texans 1960-62
(403-379-12)
Records include postseason games
1960-1974 Hank Stram 129-79-10
1975-77   Paul Wiggin* 11-24-0
1977   Tom Bettis 1-6-0
1978-1982 Marv Levy 31-42-0
1983-86   John Mackovic 30-35-0
1987-88   Frank Gansz....................8-22-1
1989-1998 Marty Schottenheimer...104-65-1
1999-2000 Gunther Cunningham 16-16-0
2001-05   Dick Vermeil..................44-37-0
2006-08   Herm Edwards..............15-34-0
2009-2010 Todd Haley 14-19-0
*Released after seven games in 1977

PAID ATTENDANCE
Home 511,321   Away 516,906
Total 1,028,227
Single-game home record,
    *82,893 (10/2/00)
Single-season home record,
    620,560 (1000)
*Arrowhead Stadium attendance: 78,502
    Kauffman Stadium attendance: 4,391

2011 DRAFT CHOICES

Round	Name	Pos.	College
1	Jonathan Baldwin	WR	Pittsburgh
2	Rodney Hudson	C	Florida State
3	Justin Houston	LB	Georgia
	Allen Bailey	DE	Miami
4	Jalil Brown	DB	Colorado
5	Ricky Stanzi	QB	Iowa
	Gabe Miller	LB	Oregon State
6	Jerrell Powe	NT	Mississippi
7	Shane Bannon	RB	Yale

2010 TEAM RECORD

PRESEASON (1-3)

Date	Result	Opponent
8/13	L 10-20	at Atlanta
8/21	L 15-20	at Tampa Bay
8/27	L 17-20	Philadelphia
9/2	W 17-13	Green Bay

REGULAR SEASON (10-6)

Date	Result	Opponent
9/13	W 21-14	San Diego
9/19	W 16-14	at Cleveland
9/26	W 31-10	San Francisco
10/10	L 9-19	at Indianapolis
10/17	L 31-35	at Houston
10/24	W 42-20	Jacksonville
10/31	W 13-10	Buffalo (OT)
11/7	L 20-23	at Oakland (OT)
11/14	L 29-49	at Denver
11/21	W 31-13	Arizona
11/28	W 42-24	at Seattle
12/5	W 10-6	Denver
12/12	L 0-31	at San Diego
12/19	W 27-13	at St. Louis
12/26	W 34-14	Tennessee
1/2	L 10-31	Oakland

POSTSEASON (0-1)

1/9	L 7-30	Baltimore

(OT) Overtime

SCORE BY PERIODS

Chiefs	55	137	77	94	3	—	366
Opponents	57	88	72	106	3	—	326

2010 TEAM STATISTICS

	Chiefs	Opp.
Total First Downs	319	293
Rushing	129	88
Passing	167	186
Penalty	23	19
3rd Down: Made/Att	83/226	84/223
3rd Down Pct.	36.7	37.7
4th Down: Made/Att	10/23	7/20
4th Down Pct.	43.5	35.0
Possession Avg.	31:04	28:56
Total Net Yards	5595	5283
Avg. Per Game	349.7	330.2
Total Plays	1063	1028
Avg. Per Play	5.3	5.1
Net Yards Rushing	2627	1764
Avg. Per Game	164.2	110.3
Total Rushes	556	408
Net Yards Passing	2968	3519
Avg. Per Game	185.5	219.9
Sacked/Yards Lost	32/221	39/258
Gross Yards	3189	3777
Att./Completions	475/274	581/319
Completion Pct.	57.7	54.9
Had Intercepted	8	14
Punts/Average	90/43.8	89/45.2
Net Punting Avg.	90/37.3	89/36.4
Penalties/Yards	90/771	111/922
Fumbles/Ball Lost	15/6	23/9
Touchdowns	44	38
Rushing	13	11
Passing	27	23
Returns	4	4

2010 INDIVIDUAL STATISTICS

PASSING

	Att.	Comp.	Yds.	Pct.	TD	Int.	Tkld.	Rate
Cassel	450	262	3116	58.2	27	7	26/182	93.0
Croyle	19	8	38	42.1	0	1	4/29	27.7
Palko	6	4	35	66.7	0	0	2/10	81.9
Chiefs	475	274	3189	57.7	27	8	32/182	90.1
Opponents	581	319	3777	54.9	23	14	39/258	78.1

SCORING

	TD R	TD P	TD Rt	PAT	FG	Saf	PTS
Succop	0	0	0	42/42	20/26	0	102
Bowe	0	15	0	0/0	0/0	0	90
Charles	5	3	0	0/0	0/0	0	48
Jones	6	0	0	0/0	0/0	0	36
Moeaki	0	3	0	0/0	0/0	0	18
McCluster	0	1	1	0/0	0/0	0	12
Pope	0	2	0	0/0	0/0	0	12
Battle	1	0	0	0/0	0/0	0	6
Berry	0	0	1	0/0	0/0	0	6
Chambers	0	1	0	0/0	0/0	0	6
Flowers	0	0	1	0/0	0/0	0	6
D. Johnson	0	0	1	0/0	0/0	0	6
Smith	1	0	0	0/0	0/0	0	6
Tucker	0	1	0	0/0	0/0	0	6
Vrabel	0	1	0	0/0	0/0	0	6
Chiefs	13	27	4	42/42	20/26	0	366
Opponents	11	23	4	38/38	20/24	0	326

2-Pt Conversions: Chiefs 0-2, Opponents 0-0.

RUSHING

	No.	Yds	Avg	LG	TD
Charles	230	1467	6.4	80	5
Jones	245	896	3.7	70	6
Cassel	33	125	3.8	23	0
McCluster	18	71	3.9	20	0
Battle	20	50	2.5	7	1
Arenas	1	5	5.0	5	0
Palko	2	5	2.5	6	0
Bowe	1	4	4.0	4	0
Castille	5	3	0.6	3	0
Smith	1	1	1.0	1t	1
Chiefs	556	2627	4.7	80	13
Opponents	408	1764	4.3	38t	11

RECEIVING

	No.	Yds	Avg	LG	TD
Bowe	72	1162	16.1	75t	15
Moeaki	47	556	11.8	34	3
Charles	45	468	10.4	31	3
Chambers	22	213	9.7	26	1
McCluster	21	209	10.0	31t	1
Copper	18	157	8.7	20	0
Jones	14	122	8.7	20	0
Pope	10	76	7.6	14	2
Castille	10	43	4.3	14	0
Tucker	6	114	19.0	38	1
Cox	4	27	6.8	13	0
O'Connell	3	31	10.3	18	0
Battle	1	9	9.0	9	0
Vrabel	1	2	2.0	2t	1
Chiefs	274	3189	11.6	75t	27
Opponents	319	3777	11.8	87t	23

INTERCEPTIONS

	No.	Yds	Avg	LG	TD
Berry	4	102	25.5	54t	1
Lewis	3	46	15.3	23	0
Flowers	2	33	16.5	33t	1
McGraw	2	4	2.0	4	0
D. Johnson	1	15	15.0	15t	1
Daniels	1	4	4.0	4	0
Carr	1	0	0.0	0	0
Chiefs	14	204	14.6	54t	3
Opponents	8	57	7.1	22t	1

PUNTING

	No.	Yds.	Avg.	In 20	LG
Colquitt	88	3908	44.4	33	72
Succop	1	33	33.0	0	33
Chiefs	90	3941	43.8	33	72
Opponents	89	4025	45.2	20	60

PUNT RETURNS

	Ret	FC	Yds	Avg	LG	TD
Arenas	39	7	322	8.3	36	0
McCluster	13	2	202	15.5	94t	1
Chiefs	52	9	524	10.1	94t	1
Opponents	42	20	361	8.6	49	0

KICKOFF RETURNS

	No.	Yds	Avg	LG	TD
McCluster	26	527	20.3	36	0
Arenas	24	509	21.2	35	0
Tucker	4	73	18.3	24	0
Copper	2	26	13.0	17	0
O'Connell	1	5	5.0	5	0
Battle	1	0	0.0	0	0
Chiefs	58	1140	19.7	36	0
Opponents	66	1336	20.2	94t	1

FIELD GOALS

	1-19	20-29	30-39	40-49	50+
Succop	0/0	6/6	7/9	6/8	1/3
Chiefs	0/0	6/6	7/9	6/8	1/3
Opponents	1/1	5/5	5/5	7/9	2/4

SACKS

	No.
Hali	14.5
Gilberry	7.0
Arenas	3.0
Studebaker	2.5
Berry	2.0
Dorsey	2.0
Edwards	2.0
Belcher	1.0
Jackson	1.0
D. Johnson	1.0
Smith	1.0
D. Williams	1.0
Chiefs	38.0
Opponents	32.0

RECORD HOLDERS
INDIVIDUAL RECORDS—CAREER

Category	Name	Performance
Rushing (Yds.)	Priest Holmes, 2001-07	6,070
Passing (Yds.)	Len Dawson, 1962-1975	28,507
Passing (TDs)	Len Dawson, 1962-1975	237
Receiving (No.)	Tony Gonzalez, 1997-2008	916
Receiving (Yds.)	Tony Gonzalez, 1997-2008	10,940
Interceptions	Emmitt Thomas, 1966-1978	58
Punting (Avg.)	Dustin Colquitt, 2005-2010	44.1
Punt Return (Avg.)	Noland Smith, 1967-69	11.1
Kickoff Return (Avg.)	Noland Smith, 1967-69	26.8
Field Goals	Nick Lowery, 1980-1993	329
Touchdowns (Tot.)	Priest Holmes, 2001-07	83
Points	Nick Lowery, 1980-1993	1,466
*Sacks	Derrick Thomas, 1989-1999	126.5

INDIVIDUAL RECORDS—SINGLE SEASON

Category	Name	Performance
Rushing (Yds.)	Larry Johnson, 2006	1,789
Passing (Yds.)	Trent Green, 2004	4,591
Passing (TDs)	Len Dawson, 1964	30
Receiving (No.)	Tony Gonzalez, 2004	102
Receiving (Yds.)	Derrick Alexander, 2000	1,391
Interceptions	Emmitt Thomas, 1974	12
Punting (Avg.)	Jerrel Wilson, 1973	45.5
Punt Return (Avg.)	Dante Hall, 2003	16.3
Kickoff Return (Avg.)	Dave Grayson, 1962	29.7
Field Goals	Nick Lowery, 1990	34
Touchdowns (Tot.)	Priest Holmes, 2003	27
Points	Priest Holmes, 2003	162
*Sacks	Derrick Thomas, 1990	20.0

INDIVIDUAL RECORDS—SINGLE GAME

Category	Name	Performance
Rushing (Yds.)	Jamaal Charles, 1-3-10	259
Passing (Yds.)	Elvis Grbac, 11-5-00	504
Passing (TDs)	Len Dawson, 11-1-64	6
Receiving (No.)	Tony Gonzalez, 1-2-05	14
Receiving (Yds.)	Stephone Paige, 12-22-85	309
Interceptions	Bobby Ply, 12-16-62	**4
	Bobby Hunt, 10-4-64	**4
	Deron Cherry, 9-29-85	**4
Field Goals	Many times	5
	Last time by Nick Lowery, 9-20-93	
Touchdowns (Tot.)	Abner Haynes, 11-26-61	5
Points	Abner Haynes, 11-26-61	30
*Sacks	Derrick Thomas, 11-11-90	**7.0

Sacks became an official statistic in 1982.
**NFL Record*

VETERAN ROSTER AS OF MARCH 3, 2011

No.	Name	Pos.	Ht.	Wt.	Birthdate	^ NFL Exp.	College	Hometown	How Acq.	'10 Games/ Starts
76	Albert, Branden	T	6-5	316	11/4/84	4	Virginia	Glen Burnie, Md.	D1b-'08	15/15
52	Anderson, Charlie	LB	6-4	250	12/8/81	8	Mississippi	Jackson, Miss.	FA-'10	2/0
21	Arenas, Javier	CB	5-9	197	10/28/87	2	Alabama	Tampa, Fla.	D2b-'10	16/2
73	Asamoah, Jon	G/C	6-4	305	7/21/88	2	Illinois	Park Forest, Ill.	D3a-'10	16/1
41	Bates, Jackie	CB	5-10	180	10/12/86	2	Hampton	Benicia, Calif.	FA-'10	2/1
26	Battle, Jackie	RB	6-2	238	10/1/83	4	Houston	Humble, Texas	FA-'10	16/0
59	Belcher, Jovan	LB	6-2	228	7/24/87	3	Maine	West Babylon, N.Y.	FA-'09	16/15
29	Berry, Eric	S	6-0	211	12/29/88	2	Tennessee	Fairburn, Ga.	D1-'10	16/16
82	Bowe, Dwayne	WR	6-2	221	9/21/84	5	Louisiana State	Miami, Fla.	D1-'07	16/16
39	Carr, Brandon	CB	6-0	207	5/19/86	4	Grand Valley State	Flint, Mich.	D5-'08	16/16
7	Cassel, Matt	QB	6-4	230	5/17/82	7	Southern California	Northridge, Calif.	T(NE)-'09	15/15
46	Castille, Tim	RB	5-11	238	5/29/84	5	Alabama	Birmingham, Ala	FA-'09	10/4
84	Chambers, Chris	WR	5-11	210	8/12/78	11	Wisconsin	Cleveland, Ohio	UFA(KC)-'10	13/7
25	Charles, Jamaal	RB	5-11	199	12/27/86	4	Texas	Port Arthur, Texas	D3a-'08	16/6
57	Cole, Justin	LB	6-3	242	11/22/87	2	San Jose State	Chino Hills, Calif.	FA-'11	0*
2	Colquitt, Dustin	P	6-3	210	5/6/82	7	Tennessee	Knoxville, Tenn.	D3-'05	16/0
10	Copper, Terrance	WR	6-0	207	3/12/82	8	East Carolina	Washington, N.C.	UFA(KC)-'10	16/3
87	Cottam, Brad	TE	6-7	269	11/28/84	4	Tennessee	Germantown, Tenn.	D3b-'08	0*
42	Cox, Mike	FB	6-0	252	7/11/85	4	Georgia Tech	Woodbury, Pa.	FA-'08	7/2
12	Croyle, Brodie	QB	6-2	206	2/6/83	6	Alabama	Rainbow City, Ala.	D3-'06	2/1
17	Curtis, Kevin	WR	6-0	186	7/17/78	8	Utah State	South Jordan, Utah	FA-'10	2/0*
34	Daniels, Travis	CB	6-1	195	9/8/82	7	Louisiana State	Hollywood, Fla.	FA-'09	16/0
72	Dorsey, Glenn	DE	6-1	297	8/1/85	4	Louisiana State	Gonzales, La.	D1a-'08	16/16
95	Edwards, Ron	DT	6-3	315	7/12/79	11	Texas A&M	Columbus, Ohio	UFA(Buff)-'06	16/15
24	Flowers, Brandon	CB	5-9	187	2/18/86	4	Virginia Tech	Delray Beach, Fla.	D2-'08	15/15
43	Gafford, Thomas	LS	6-2	250	1/29/83	4	Houston	Webster, Texas	FA-'09	16/0
92	Gilberry, Wallace	DE	6-2	268	12/5/84	4	Alabama	Bay Minette, Ala.	FA-'08	16/2
93	Greenwood, Cory	LB	6-2	235	6/5/85	2	Concordia	Kingston, Ontario, Canada	FA-'10	16/0
91	Hali, Tamba	LB	6-3	275	11/3/83	6	Penn State	Ghanga, Liberia	D1-'06	16/16
94	Jackson, Tyson	DE	6-4	296	6/6/86	3	Louisiana State	New Orleans, La.	D1-'09	12/3
56	Johnson, Derrick	LB	6-3	242	11/22/82	7	Texas	Waco, Texas	D1-'05	16/16
38	Johnson, Tervaris	RB	6-2	248	6/14/88	2	Miami	Miami, Fla.	FA-'10	0*
20	Jones, Thomas	RB	5-10	212	8/19/78	12	Virginia	Big Stone Gap, Va.	FA-'10	16/10
48	Langford, Reshard	S	6-1	213	2/6/86	2	Vanderbilt	Tanner, Ala.	FA-'09	6/0
14	Lawrence, Quinten	WR	6-0	184	9/21/84	2	McNeese State	Carencro, La.	D6-'09	0*
31	Leggett, Maurice	CB/S	5-11	188	10/2/86	4	Valdosta State	Pittsburgh, Pa.	FA-'08	0*
23	Lewis, Kendrick	S	6-0	198	6/16/88	2	Mississippi	New Orleans, La.	D5a-'10	12/10
65	Lilja, Ryan	G	6-2	290	10/15/81	8	Kansas State	Kansas City, Mo.	FA-'10	15/15
51	Mays, Corey	LB	6-1	245	11/27/83	6	Notre Dame	Chicago, Ill.	FA-'09	14/0
22	McCluster, Dexter	WR	5-8	170	8/25/88	2	Mississippi	Largo, Fla.	D2a-'10	11/7
47	McGraw, Jon	S	6-3	208	4/2/79	10	Kansas State	Louisville, Kent.	UFA(Det)-'07	12/5
81	Moeaki, Tony	TE	6-3	252	6/8/87	2	Iowa	Warrenville, Ill.	D3b-'10	15/15
64	Niswanger, Rudy	C	6-5	301	11/9/82	6	Louisiana State	Monroe, La.	FA-'06	10/0
75	O'Callaghan, Ryan	T	6-7	330	7/19/83	6	California	Redding, Ca.	W(NE)-'09	11/1
85	O'Connell, Jake	TE	6-3	250	11/6/85	3	Miami (OH)	Naples, Fla.	D7b-'09	15/2
45	Pope, Leonard	TE	6-8	264	9/16/83	6	Georgia	Americus, Ga.	FA-'09	16/6
35	Price, Ricky	S	6-1	195	9/16/87	2	Oklahoma State	Houston, Texas	FA-'09	7/0
67	Richardson, Barry	T	6-6	319	5/15/86	4	Clemson	Mt. Pleasant, S.C.	D6a-'08	16/16
55	Sheffield, Cameron	LB	6-2	257	2/12/88	2	Troy	Portal, Ga.	D5b-'10	0*
99	Simoneau, Mark	LB	6-0	245	1/16/77	12	Kansas State	Smith Center, Kan.	FA-'10	1/0
90	Smith, Shaun	DT	6-2	325	8/19/81	7	South Carolina	Brooklyn, N.Y.	FA-'10	16/10
96	Studebaker, Andy	LB	6-3	248	9/16/85	4	Wheaton	Congerville, Ill.	FA-'08	16/0
6	Succop, Ryan	K	6-2	218	9/19/86	3	South Carolina	Hickory, N.C.	D7c-'09	16/0
98	Toribio, Anthony	DT	6-1	315	3/1/85	2	Carson-Newman	Miami, Fla.	W(GB)-'10	5/0
15	Tucker, Verran	WR	6-1	204	6/26/88	2	California	Los Angeles, Calif.	FA-'10	11/2
50	Vrabel, Mike	LB	6-4	261	8/14/75	15	Ohio State	Akron, Ohio	T(NE)-'09	16/16
83	Urban, Jerheme	WR	6-3	207	11/26/80	7	Trinity (TX)	Victoria, Tex.	FA-'10	0*
97	Walters, Pierre	LB	6-5	269	3/25/86	2	Eastern Illinois	Maywood, Ill.	FA-'11	0*
27	Washington, Donald	S/CB	6-1	197	7/28/86	3	Ohio State	Indianapolis, Ind.	D4-'09	12/2
54	Waters, Brian	G	6-3	320	2/18/77	12	North Texas	Waxahachie, Texas	FA-'00	16/16
62	Wiegmann, Casey	C	6-2	285	7/20/73	16	Iowa	Parkersburg, Iowa	FA-'10	16/16
8	Williams, Chandler	WR	5-11	176	8/9/85	2	Florida International	Miami, Fla.	FA-'10	0*
53	Williams, Demorrio	LB	6-1	232	7/6/80	8	Nebraska	Carthage, Texas	UFA(Atl)-'08	16/0

* Cole inactive for 11 games; Cottam missed '10 season because of injury; Curtis played 2 games with Miami in '10; T. Johnson missed '10 because of injury; Lawrence inactive for 2 games; Leggett missed '10 season because of injury; Sheffield missed '10 season because of injury; Urban missed '10 season because of injury; Walters last active with Kansas City in '09; C. Williams missed '10 season because of injury.

Traded—DE Alex Magee (2 games in '10) to Tampa Bay.

Also played with Chiefs in '10—WR Jeremy Horne (3 games), QB Tyler Palko (2).

^ "NFL Exp." as of 2011 Kickoff Weekend. For full explanation of how a player's NFL Experience is measured, refer to explanation underneath the First-Year Roster listed below.

FIRST-YEAR ROSTER

Name	Pos.	Ht.	Wt.	Birthdate	College	Hometown	How Acq.
Bailey, Allen	DL	6-3	288	3/25/89	Miami	Sapelo, Ga.	D3b
Bakhtiari, Eric (1)	LB	6-3	250	12/2/84	San Diego	Burlingame, Ca.	FA
Baldwin, Jonathan	WR	6-4	230	8/10/89	Pittsburgh	Aliquippa, Pa.	D1
Bannon, Shane	FB	6-3	267	4/20/89	Yale	Southbury, Conn.	D7
Brown, Jalil	DB	6-1	204	10/14/87	Colorado	Phoenix, Ariz.	D4
Gales, Dion (1)	DE/DT	6-5	310	8/17/85	Troy	New Orleans, La.	FA
Greenwood, Bobby (1)	T	6-5	278	3/2/87	Alabama	Prattville, Ala.	FA
Harris, Darryl (1)	G	6-4	300	1/14/85	Mississippi	Clarksdale, Miss.	FA
Horne, Jeremy (1)	WR	6-2	193	10/25/86	Massachusetts	New Berlin, N.Y.	FA
Houston, Justin	LB	6-3	268	1/12/89	Georgia	Statesboro, Ga.	D3a
Hudson, Rodney	OL	6-2	299	7/12/89	Florida State	Mobile, Ala.	D2
Johnson, Micah (1)	LB	6-2	258	6/22/88	Kentucky	Ft. Campbell, Ky.	FA
Miller, Gabe	LB	6-3	257	12/5/87	Oregon State	Lake Oswego, Ore.	D5b
Palko, Tyler (1)	QB	6-1	215	8/9/83	Pittsburgh	Imperial, Pa.	FA-'10
Powe, Jerrell	DL	6-2	331	3/15/87	Mississippi	Waynesboro, Miss.	D6
Slate, Cody (1)	TE	6-4	229	8/14/87	Marshall	Chatham, Va.	FA
Stanzi, Ricky	QB	6-4	228	9/3/87	Iowa	Mentor, Ohio	D5a

The term NFL Rookie is defined as a player who is in his first season of professional football and has not been on the roster of another professional football team for any regular-season or postseason games. A Rookie is designated by an "R" on NFL rosters. Players who have been active in another professional football league or players who have NFL experience, including either preseason training camp or being on an Active List or Inactive List, or on Reserve/Injured or Reserve/Physically Unable to Perform for fewer than six regular-season games, are termed NFL First-Year Players. An NFL First-Year Player is designated by a "1" on NFL rosters. Thereafter, a player is credited with an additional year of experience for each season in which he accumulates six games on the Active List or Inactive List, or on Reserve/Injured or Reserve/Physically Unable to Perform.

Log on to www.kcchiefs.com for an up-to-date roster.

COACHING STAFF
Head Coach,
Todd Haley
Pro Career: Todd Haley was named head coach of the Kansas City Chiefs on February 6, 2009. He is entering his 17th season in the National Football League and his 15th campaign in a coaching capacity in 2011. He led the Chiefs to their sixth AFC West title in 2010 as the team finished with a 10-6 mark. Haley became only the second coach in Chiefs history to guide the club to a double-digit victory tally in his second season with Kansas City. The Chiefs made a six-game leap in the win column from 2009 (4-12) to 2010 (10-6), the biggest leap in team history. Kansas City improved in 39 different statistical categories in Haley's second campaign compared to his inaugural season in 2009. Haley has been on the coaching staff of five different franchises that have reached the playoffs (Kansas City, Arizona, Dallas, Chicago and N.Y. Jets) serving under head coach Bill Parcells in both Dallas and with the Jets. He joined the Chiefs after a two-year stint as the offensive coordinator of the Arizona Cardinals (2007-08). In 2008, Haley helped the Cardinals claim their first division crown since 1975 as Arizona earned a berth in Super Bowl XLIII. The Cardinals offense tied for third in the league in scoring, registering a franchise-record 427 points (26.7 ppg), while ranking fourth in total offense (365.8 ypg). Under Haley in 2007, the Cardinals set a single-season franchise record with 32 TD passes. Served three seasons as Passing Game Coordinator/Wide Receivers coach for Dallas (2004-06). Haley was wide receivers coach for Chicago (2001-03) and the N.Y. Jets (1999-2000) after serving as their offensive assistant/quality control coach from 1997-98. Haley began his NFL career with the Jets as an assistant in the scouting department in 1995. Career record: 14-19.
Background: Haley earned a degree in communications from North Florida in 1991 and received that school's 2009 Distinguished Alumni Achievement Award. Haley is the son of longtime NFL personnel man Dick Haley, one of the architects of the great Steelers teams of the 1970s.
Personal: Born on February 28, 1967 in Atlanta, Georgia. He and his wife, Chrissy, have four daughters: Taylor, Peyton, Kady, and Ella and one son, Richard Todd, Jr.

ASSISTANT COACHES
Richie Anderson, wide receivers; born September 13, 1971, Sandy Springs, Md. Running back Penn State 1989-1992. Pro running back New York Jets 1993-2002, Dallas Cowboys 2003-04. Pro coach: New York Jets 2006, joined Chiefs in 2010.
Maurice Carthon, asst. head coach; born April 24, 1961, Chicago. Running back Arkansas State 1979-1982. Pro running back New Jersey Generals (USFL) 1983-85, New York Giants 1985-1991, Indianapolis Colts 1992. Pro coach: New England Patriots 1994-96, New York Jets 1997-2000, Detroit Lions 2001-02, Dallas Cowboys 2003-04, Cleveland Browns 2005-06, Arizona Cardinals 2007-08, joined Chiefs in 2009.
Mike Clark, strength and conditioning; born August 22, 1954, Wichita, Kan. Center Ottawa 1973-76. No pro playing experience. College coach: Kansas 1977-78, 1982, Wyoming 1981, Oregon 1983-87, Southern California 1988-89, Texas A&M 1990-2003. Pro coach: Seattle Seahawks 2004-09, joined Chiefs in 2010.
Romeo Crennel, defensive coordinator; born June 18, 1947, Lynchburg, Va. Defensive lineman Western Kentucky 1966-69. No pro playing experience. College coach: Western Kentucky 1970-74, Texas Tech 1975-77, Mississippi 1978-79, Georgia 1980. Pro coach: New York Giants 1981-1992, New England Patriots 1993-96, 2001-04, New York Jets 1997-99, Cleveland Browns 2000, 2005-08 (head coach), joined Chiefs in 2010.
Gary Gibbs, linebackers; born August 13, 1952, Beaumont, Texas. Linebacker Oklahoma 1972-74. No pro playing experience. College coach: Oklahoma 1975-1994 (head coach 1989-1994), Georgia 2000, Louisiana State 2001. Pro coach: Dallas Cowboys 2002-04, New Orleans Saints 2006-08, joined Chiefs in 2009.
Steve Hoffman, special teams; born September 8, 1958, Camden, N.J. Quarterback/running back/wide receiver Dickinson College 1977-1980. Pro punter Washington Federals (USFL) 1983. College coach: Miami 1985-87. Pro coach: Dallas Cowboys 1989-2004, Atlanta Falcons 2006, Miami Dolphins 2007-08, joined Chiefs in 2009.
Bill Muir, offensive coordinator/offensive line; born October 26, 1942, Pittsburgh. Tackle Susquehanna 1962-64. No pro playing experience. College coach: Susquehanna 1965, Delaware Valley 1966-67, Rhode Island 1970-71, Idaho State 1972-73, Southern Methodist 1976-77. Pro coach: Orlando (Continental Football League) 1968-69, Houston/Shreveport Steamer (WFL) 1974-75, New England Patriots 1982-84, Detroit Lions 1985-88, Indianapolis Colts 1989-1991, Philadelphia Eagles 1992-94, New York Jets 1995-2001, Tampa Bay Buccaneers 2002-08, joined Chiefs in 2009.
Bernie Parmalee, tight ends; born September 16, 1967, Jersey City, N.J. Running back Ball State 1988-1991. Pro running back Miami Dolphins 1992-98, New York Jets 1999-2000. College coach: Notre Dame 2005-09. Pro coach: Miami Dolphins 2002-04, joined Chiefs in 2010.
Pat Perles, asst. offensive line; born October 2, 1963, Detroit. Defensive tackle Michigan State 1982-85. No pro playing experience. College coach: Toledo 1989-

1991, Michigan State 2000-02, North Dakota State 2003-08. Pro coach: L.A. Rams 1992-93, Saskatchewan Roughriders (CFL) 1994-96, Winnipeg Blue Bombers (CFL) 1997, Hamilton Tigercats (CFL) 1998-99, joined Chiefs in 2009.
Anthony Pleasant, defensive line; born January 27, 1968, Century, Fla. Defensive end Tennessee State 1987-89. Pro defensive end Cleveland Browns 1990-95, Baltimore Ravens 1996, Atlanta Falcons 1997, New York Jets 1998-99, San Francisco 49ers 2000, New England Patriots 2001-03. Pro coach: Joined Chiefs in 2009.
Brent Salazar, asst. strength and conditioning; born May 22, 1980, Denver. Attended New Mexico. No college or pro playing experience. College coach: New Mexico 2002-03, Nevada-Las Vegas 2004, Pacific 2006. Pro coach: Joined Chiefs in 2007.
Nick Sirianni, offensive quality control; born June 15, 1981, Jamestown, N.Y. Wide receiver Mount Union 2000-03. No pro playing experience. College coach: Mount Union 2004-05, Indiana (Pa.) 2006-08. Pro coach: Joined Chiefs in 2009.
Otis Smith, defensive quality control; born October 22, 1965, New Orleans. Defensive back Taft (CA) Junior College 1986-87, Missouri 1988-89. Pro defensive back Philadelphia Eagles 1991-94, New York Jets 1995-96, 1997-99, New England Patriots 1996, 2000-02, Detroit Lions 2003. Pro coach: Philadelphia Eagles 2008, joined Chiefs in 2010.
Emmitt Thomas, defensive backs; born June 3, 1943, Angleton, Tex. Quarterback/wide receiver Bishop (TX) College 1963-65. Pro defensive back Kansas City Chiefs 1966-1978. Inducted into Pro Football Hall of Fame 2008. College coach: Central Missouri State 1979-1980. Pro coach: St. Louis Cardinals 1981-85, Washington Redskins 1986-1994, Philadelphia Eagles 1995-98, Green Bay Packers 1999, Minnesota Vikings 2000-01, Atlanta Falcons 2002-09 (interim head coach 2007), re-joined Chiefs in 2010.
Adam Zimmer, defensive assistant/asst. linebackers; born January 13, 1984, Ogden, Utah. Defensive back Trinity (Texas) 2002-05. No pro playing experience. Pro coach: New Orleans Saints 2006-09, joined Chiefs in 2010.
Jim Zorn, quarterbacks; born May 10, 1953, Whittier, Calif. Quarterback Cal Poly Pomona 1973-74. Pro quarterback Seattle Seahawks 1976-1984, Green Bay Packers 1985, Winnipeg Blue Bombers (CFL) 1986, Tampa Bay Buccaneers 1987. College coach: Boise State 1989-1991, Utah State 1992-94, Minnesota 1995-96. Pro coach: Seattle Seahawks 1997, 2001-07, Detroit Lions 1998-2000, Washington Redskins 2008-09 (head coach), Baltimore Ravens 2010, joined Chiefs in 2011.

**American Football Conference
East Division**
Team Colors: Aqua, Coral, Blue, and
White
7500 S.W. 30th Street
Davie, Florida 33314
Telephone: (954) 452-7000

2011 SCHEDULE
PRESEASON
Aug. 12 at Atlanta.............................7:30
Aug. 19 **Carolina**.............................7:30
Aug. 26 at Tampa Bay 7:30
Sep. 1 **Dallas**.................................7:30

REGULAR SEASON
Sep. 12 **New England** (Mon).......... 7:00
Sep. 18 **Houston** 4:15
Sep. 25 at Cleveland 1:00
Oct. 2 at San Diego 4:15
Oct. 9 BYE
Oct. 17 at New York Jets (Mon) 8:30
Oct. 23 **Denver** 1:00
Oct. 30 at New York Giants 1:00
Nov. 6 at Kansas City 1:00
Nov. 13 **Washington** 1:00
Nov. 20 **Buffalo** 1:00
Nov. 24 at Dallas (Thu) 4:15
Dec. 4 **Oakland** 1:00
Dec. 11 **Philadelphia** 1:00
Dec. 18 at Buffalo 1:00
Dec. 24 at New England (Sat)......... 1:00
Jan. 1 **New York Jets** 1:00
All times ET

Stadium: Sun Life Stadium
(opened in 1987)
•**Capacity:** 75,192
2269 Dan Marino Blvd.
Miami Gardens, Florida 33056
Playing Surface: Grass (PAT)
Training Camp: Nova Southeastern Univ.
7500 S.W. 30th Street
Davie, Florida 33314

SUN LIFE STADIUM

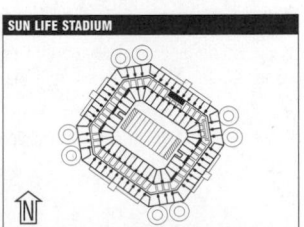

CLUB OFFICIALS
Chairman of the Board/Managing General
Partner: Stephen M. Ross
Chief Executive Officer: Mike Dee
General Manager: Jeff Ireland
Chief Administrative Officer:
Harold Talisman
Senior Vice President of Football
Operations: Dawn Aponte
Senior Vice President-Operations:
Bill Galante
Senior Vice President-Media Relations:
Harvey Greene
Senior Vice President-Public Affairs:
Adam Grossman
Senior Vice President-Chief Technology
Officer: Tery Howard
Senior Vice President-Corporate
Partnerships and Integrated Media:
Jim Rushton
Senior Vice President-Finance and
Administration: Jill R. Strafaci
Senior Vice President-Sales and Ticket
Operations: Mark Tilson
Vice President/Special Advisor:
Nat Moore
Director of Player Personnel:
Brian Gaine
Director of College Scouting: Chris Grier
Player Personnel Coordinator: Chris Shea
Head Athletic Trainer: Kevin O'Neill
Equipment Manager: Joe Cimino
Video Director: Bob Hack
Director of Player Development:
Kaleb Thornhill
Senior Director of Internet and
Publications: Scott Stone
Director of Media Relations:
Jason Jenkins
Director of Communications: Fitz Ollison
Senior Director of Programming and
Production: Jeff Griffith
Senior Director of Cheerleaders and
Entertainment: Dorie Grogan
Cheerleader Coordinator: Emily Snow
Director of Records and Archives:
Kristin Hingston
Senior Director of Community Relations:
Ilona Wolpin
Director of Youth Programs: Twan Russell
Director of Security: Stuart Weinstein

COACHING HISTORY
(414-310-4)
Records include postseason games
1966-69 George Wilson.............15-39-2
1970-1995 Don Shula 274-147-2
1996-99 Jimmy Johnson...........38-31-0
2000-04 Dave Wannstedt* 43-33-0
2004 Jim Bates........................3-4-0
2005-06 Nick Saban.................15-17-0
2007 Cam Cameron 1-15-0
2008-2010 Tony Sparano 25-24-0
*Resigned after nine games in 2004

PAID ATTENDANCE
Home 541,959   Away 520,803
Total 1,062,762
Single-game home record,
75,283 (10/27/96)
Single-season home record, 592,161
(1999)

2011 DRAFT CHOICES
Round	Name	Pos.	College
1	Mike Pouncey	C	Florida
2	Daniel Thomas	RB	Kansas State
4	Edmond Gates	WR	Abilene Christian
6	Charles Clay	RB	Tulsa
7	Frank Kearse	DT	Alabama A&M
	Jimmy Wilson	DB	Montana

2010 TEAM RECORD

PRESEASON (2-2)

Date	Result	Opponent
8/14	W 10-7	Tampa Bay
8/21	W 27-26	at Jacksonville
8/27	L 6-16	Atlanta
9/2	L 25-27	at Dallas

REGULAR SEASON (7-9)

Date	Result	Opponent
9/12	W 15-10	at Buffalo
9/19	W 14-10	at Minnesota
9/26	L 23-31	New York Jets
10/4	L 14-41	New England
10/17	W 23-20	at Green Bay (OT)
10/24	L 22-23	Pittsburgh
10/31	W 22-14	at Cincinnati
11/7	L 10-26	at Baltimore
11/14	W 29-17	Tennessee
11/18	L 0-16	Chicago
11/28	W 33-17	at Oakland
12/5	L 10-13	Cleveland
12/12	W 10-6	at New York Jets
12/19	L 14-17	Buffalo
12/26	L 27-34	Detroit
1/2	L 7-38	at New England

(OT) Overtime

SCORE BY PERIODS

Dolphins	70	72	60	68	3 —	273
Opponents	68	89	97	79	0 —	333

2010 TEAM STATISTICS

	Dolphins	Opp.
Total First Downs	300	264
Rushing	91	84
Passing	189	166
Penalty	20	14
3rd Down: Made/Att	92/230	84/226
3rd Down Pct.	40.0	37.2
4th Down: Made/Att	3/10	8/22
4th Down Pct.	30.0	36.4
Possession Avg.	30:42	29:18
Total Net Yards	5170	4949
Avg. Per Game	323.1	309.3
Total Plays	1040	988
Avg. Per Play	5.0	5.0
Net Yards Rushing	1643	1601
Avg. Per Game	102.7	100.1
Total Rushes	445	447
Net Yards Passing	3527	3348
Avg. Per Game	220.4	209.3
Sacked/Yards Lost	38/228	39/225
Gross Yards	3755	3573
Att./Completions	557/335	502/288
Completion Pct.	60.1	57.4
Had Intercepted	21	11
Punts/Average	75/44.9	77/42.3
Net Punting Avg.	75/37.8	77/37.2
Penalties/Yards	72/595	85/730
Fumbles/Ball Lost	24/10	22/8
Touchdowns	26	36
Rushing	8	8
Passing	17	22
Returns	1	6

2010 INDIVIDUAL STATISTICS

PASSING	Att.	Comp.	Yds.	Pct.	TD	Int.	Tkld.	Rate
Henne	490	301	3301	61.4	15	19	30/178	75.4
Thigpen	62	33	435	53.2	2	2	8/50	73.0
R. Brown	2	0	0	0.0	0	0	0/0	39.6
Pennington	2	1	19	50.0	0	0	0/0	83.3
Marshall	1	0	0	0.0	0	0	0/0	39.6
Dolphins	557	335	3755	60.1	17	21	38/228	74.8
Opponents	502	288	3573	57.4	22	11	39/225	85.0

SCORING	TD R	TD P	TD Rt	PAT	FG	Saf	PTS
D. Carpenter	0	0	0	25/25	30/41	0	115
Bess	0	5	0	0/0	0/0	0	30
R. Brown	5	0	0	0/0	0/0	0	30
Fasano	0	4	0	0/0	0/0	0	24
Marshall	0	3	0	0/0	0/0	0	18
Williams	2	1	0	0/0	0/0	0	18
Cobbs	0	2	0	0/0	0/0	0	12
B. Hartline	0	1	0	0/0	0/0	0	6
Misi	0	0	1	0/0	0/0	0	6
Moore	0	1	0	0/0	0/0	0	6
Polite	1	0	0	0/0	0/0	0	6
Dolphins	8	17	1	25/25	30/41	1	273
Opponents	8	22	6	36/36	27/31	0	333

2-Pt Conversions: Dolphins 0-1, Opponents 0-0.

RUSHING	No.	Yds	Avg	LG	TD
R. Brown	200	734	3.7	51	5
Williams	159	673	4.2	45t	2
Thigpen	13	73	5.6	12	0
Polite	26	62	2.4	4t	1
Henne	35	52	1.5	10	0
B. Hartline	2	27	13.5	30	0
Moore	1	16	16.0	16	0
Curtis	1	6	6.0	6	0
Marshall	2	3	1.5	4	0
Cobbs	4	0	0.0	4	0
Bess	2	-3	-1.5	0	0
Dolphins	445	1643	3.7	51	8
Opponents	447	1601	3.6	30	8

RECEIVING	No.	Yds	Avg	LG	TD
Marshall	86	1014	11.8	46	3
Bess	79	820	10.4	29	5
B. Hartline	43	615	14.3	54	1
Fasano	39	528	13.5	31	4
R. Brown	33	242	7.3	24	0
Williams	19	141	7.4	28t	1
Polite	12	61	5.1	14	0
Cobbs	8	91	11.4	29t	2
Moore	6	128	21.3	57t	1
Wallace	6	62	10.3	19	0
Shuler	2	44	22.0	28	0
Curtis	1	6	6.0	6	0
Hilliard	1	3	3.0	3	0
Dolphins	335	3755	11.2	57t	17
Opponents	288	3573	12.4	86t	22

INTERCEPTIONS	No.	Yds	Avg	LG	TD
J. Allen	3	17	5.7	17	0
Sapp	2	9	4.5	9	0
Bell	1	21	21.0	21	0
S. Smith	1	18	18.0	18	0
Carroll	1	1	1.0	1	0
Clemons	1	0	0.0	0	0
V. Davis	1	0	0.0	0	0
Jones	1	0	0.0	0	0
Dolphins	11	66	6.0	21	0
Opponents	21	201	9.6	51t	2

PUNTING	No.	Yds.	Avg.	In 20	LG
Fields	73	3369	46.2	31	69
Dolphins	75	3369	44.9	31	69
Opponents	77	3255	42.3	24	61

PUNT RETURNS	Ret	FC	Yds	Avg	LG	TD
Bess	25	20	284	11.4	47	0
C. Smith	2	2	9	4.5	6	0
Amaya	1	0	0	0.0	0	0
Dolphins	28	22	293	10.5	47	0
Opponents	43	15	454	10.6	94t	1

KICKOFF RETURNS	No.	Yds	Avg	LG	TD
Carroll	27	655	24.3	46	0
Cobbs	22	431	19.6	40	0
C. Smith	3	52	17.3	19	0
Moore	2	51	25.5	34	0
Polite	2	10	5.0	10	0
Dolphins	56	1199	21.4	46	0
Opponents	53	1303	24.6	103t	2

FIELD GOALS	1-19	20-29	30-39	40-49	50+
D. Carpenter	1/1	9/9	5/5	11/18	4/8
Dolphins	1/1	9/9	5/5	11/18	4/8
Opponents	1/1	11/11	8/9	5/6	2/4

SACKS	No.
Wake	14.0
Misi	4.5
Dansby	3.0
Langford	3.0
Starks	3.0
McDaniel	2.5
Soliai	2.0
Bell	1.5
Clemons	1.5
Dobbins	1.0
Jones	1.0
Moses	1.0
(group)	1.0
Dolphins	39.0
Opponents	38.0

RECORD HOLDERS
INDIVIDUAL RECORDS—CAREER

Category	Name	Performance
Rushing (Yds.)	Larry Csonka, 1968-1974, 1979	6,737
Passing (Yds.)	Dan Marino, 1983-1999	61,361
Passing (TDs)	Dan Marino, 1983-1999	420
Receiving (No.)	Mark Clayton, 1983-1992	550
Receiving (Yds.)	Mark Duper, 1982-1992	8,869
Interceptions	Jake Scott, 1970-75	35
Punting (Avg.)	Brandon Fields, 2007-2010	44.9
Punt Return (Avg.)	Jeff Ogden, 2000-01	13.7
Kickoff Return (Avg.)	Mercury Morris, 1969-1975	26.5
Field Goals	Olindo Mare, 1997-2006	245
Touchdowns (Tot.)	Mark Clayton, 1983-1992	82
Points	Olindo Mare, 1997-2006	1,048
*Sacks	Jason Taylor, 1997-2007, 2009	124.0

INDIVIDUAL RECORDS—SINGLE SEASON

Category	Name	Performance
Rushing (Yds.)	Ricky Williams, 2002	1,853
Passing (Yds.)	Dan Marino, 1984	**5,084
Passing (TDs)	Dan Marino, 1984	48
Receiving (No.)	O.J. McDuffie, 1998	90
Receiving (Yds.)	Mark Clayton, 1984	1,389
Interceptions	Dick Westmoreland, 1967	10
Punting (Avg.)	John Kidd, 1996	46.3
Punt Return (Avg.)	Jeff Ogden, 2000	17.0
Kickoff Return (Avg.)	Duriel Harris, 1976	32.9
Field Goals	Olindo Mare, 1999	39
Touchdowns (Tot.)	Mark Clayton, 1984	18
Points	Olindo Mare, 1999	144
*Sacks	Jason Taylor, 2002	18.5

INDIVIDUAL RECORDS—SINGLE GAME

Category	Name	Performance
Rushing (Yds.)	Ricky Williams, 12-1-02	228
Passing (Yds.)	Dan Marino, 10-23-88	521
Passing (TDs)	Bob Griese, 11-24-77	6
	Dan Marino, 9-21-86	6
Receiving (No.)	Chris Chambers, 12-4-05	15
Receiving (Yds.)	Chris Chambers, 12-4-05	238
Interceptions	Dick Anderson, 12-3-73	**4
Field Goals	Olindo Mare, 10-17-99	6
Touchdowns (Tot.)	Paul Warfield, 12-15-73	4
	Mark Ingram, 11-27-94	4
	Ronnie Brown, 9-21-08	4
Points	Paul Warfield, 12-15-73	24
	Mark Ingram, 11-27-94	24
	Ronnie Brown, 9-21-08	24
*Sacks	Doug Betters, 9-4-83	4.0
	E.J. Junior, 10-6-91	4.0
	Joey Porter, 9-21-08	4.0

*Sacks became an official statistic in 1982.
**NFL Record

VETERAN ROSTER AS OF MARCH 3, 2011

No.	Name	Pos.	Ht.	Wt.	Birthdate	^ NFL Exp.	College	Hometown	How Acq.	'10 Games/ Starts
59	Alama-Francis, Ikaika	DE	6-5	290	12/4/84	5	Hawai'i	Kailua, Hawai'i	FA-'09	11/0
25	Allen, Will	CB	5-10	195	8/5/78	11	Syracuse	Syracuse, N.Y.	UFA(NYG)-'06	0*
40	Amaya, Jonathon	DB	6-2	190	11/25/88	2	Nevada	Diamond Bar, Calif.	FA-'10	10/0
95	Baker, Chris	DT	6-2	329	10/8/87	3	Hampton	Windsor, Conn.	FA-'10	1/0
90	Baker, Ryan	DE	6-5	295	11/25/84	3	Purdue	Indianapolis, Ind.	FA-'09	9/0
73	Barbre, Allen	T	6-4	305	6/22/84	5	Missouri Southern State	Granby, Mo.	FA-'10	0*
37	Bell, Yeremiah	S	6-0	205	3/3/78	8	Eastern Kentucky	Winchester, Ky.	D6c-'03	16/16
67	Berger, Joe	C	6-5	315	5/25/82	7	Michigan Tech	Newaygo, Mich.	UFA(Dall)-'09	15/14
15	Bess, Davone	WR	5-10	190	9/13/85	4	Hawai'i	Oakland, Calif.	FA-'08	16/8
3	Brandstater, Tom	QB	6-5	223	10/21/84	2	Fresno State	Turlock, Calif.	FA-'11	0*
23	Brown, Ronnie	RB	6-0	230	12/12/81	7	Auburn	Cartersville, Ga.	D1-'05	16/16
72	Carey, Vernon	T	6-5	340	7/31/81	8	Miami	Miami, Fla.	D1-'04	12/12
5	Carpenter, Dan	K	6-2	225	11/25/85	4	Montana	Helena, Mont.	FA-'08	16/0
28	Carroll, Nolan	CB	6-1	202	1/18/87	2	Maryland	Green Grove Spring, Fla.	D5a-'10	13/1
30	Clemons, Chris	FS	6-1	210	9/15/85	3	Clemson	Arcadia, Fla.	D5b-'09	15/14
38	Cobbs, Patrick	RB	5-8	205	1/31/83	6	North Texas	Tecumseh, Okla.	FA-'06	16/1
52	Crowder, Channing	LB	6-2	250	12/2/83	7	Florida	Atlanta, Ga.	D3-'05	11/11
29	Culver, Tyrone	S	6-1	210	7/6/83	6	Fresno State	Palmdale, Calif.	FA-'08	15/0
58	Dansby, Karlos	LB	6-4	250	11/3/81	8	Auburn	Birmingham, Ala.	UFA(Ariz)-'10	14/13
21	Davis, Vontae	CB	5-11	203	5/27/88	3	Illinois	Washington, D.C.	D1-'09	16/15
92	Denney, John	LS	6-5	255	12/13/78	7	Brigham Young	Thornton, Colo.	FA-'05	16/0
51	Dobbins, Tim	LB	6-1	246	12/10/82	6	Iowa State	Nashville, Tenn.	T(SD)-'10	16/6
	Dotson, Lionel	DT	6-4	290	2/11/85	4	Arizona	Houston, Texas	D7-'08	3/0
49	Edds, A.J.	LB	6-4	246	9/18/87	2	Iowa	Greenwood, Ind.	D4-'10	0*
81	Epps, Dedrick	TE	6-3	250	6/19/88	2	Miami	Richmond, Va.	FA-'10	3/0
80	Fasano, Anthony	TE	6-4	255	4/20/84	6	Notre Dame	Verona, N.J.	T(Dall)-'08	15/15
2	Fields, Brandon	P	6-5	245	5/21/84	5	Michigan State	Toledo, Ohio	D7b-'07	16/0
75	Garner, Nate	T	6-7	325	1/18/85	4	Arkansas	Roland, Ark.	W(NYJ)-'08	0*
82	Hartline, Brian	WR	6-2	195	11/22/86	3	Ohio State	North Canton, Ohio	D4-'09	12/11
81	Haynos, Joey	TE	6-8	270	8/28/84	4	Maryland	Rockville, Md.	FA-'08	0*
7	Henne, Chad	QB	6-3	230	7/2/85	4	Michigan	Wyomissing, Pa.	D2b-'08	15/14
26	Hilliard, Lex	RB	5-11	240	7/30/84	3	Montana	Kalispell, Mont.	D6c-'08	16/0
68	Incognito, Richie	G	6-3	324	7/5/83	7	Nebraska	Englewood, N.J.	UFA(Buff)-'10	16/16
74	Jerry, John	G	6-5	328	6/14/86	2	Mississippi	Batesville, Miss.	D3-'10	12/10
20	Jones, Reshad	S	6-1	214	2/25/88	2	Georgia	Atlanta, Ga.	D5b-'10	13/2
61	Kopa, Matt	T	6-6	303	2/25/87	2	Stanford	Elk Grove, Calif.	FA-'10	0*
70	Langford, Kendall	DE	6-6	295	1/27/86	4	Hampton	Petersburg, Va.	D3-'08	16/16
77	Long, Jake	T	6-7	317	5/9/85	4	Michigan	Lapeer, Mich.	D1-'08	16/16
19	Marshall, Brandon	WR	6-4	230	3/23/84	6	Central Florida	Winter Park, Fla.	T(Den)-'10	14/14
71	Marten, James	T	6-8	310	4/18/84	3	Boston College	Indianapolis, Ind.	FA-'11	0*
88	Mastrud, Jeron	TE	6-6	253	12/17/87	2	Kansas State	Beaverton, Ore.	FA-'10	8/2
78	McDaniel, Tony	DT	6-7	305	1/20/85	6	Tennessee	Columbia, S.C.	T(Jax) -'09	15/1
79	McQuistan, Pat	OL	6-6	319	1/20/85	6	Weber State	Lebanon, Ore.	T(Dall) -'10	16/8
97	Merling, Phillip	DE	6-4	295	4/19/85	4	Clemson	St. Matthews, S.C.	D2a-'08	5/0
55	Misi, Koa	LB	6-3	251	1/17/87	2	Utah	Santa Rosa, Calif.	D2-'10	16/11
14	Moore, Marlon	WR	6-0	190	9/3/87	2	Fresno State	Sacramento, Calif.	FA-'10	9/0
93	Moses, Quentin	LB	6-5	260	11/18/83	5	Georgia	Athens, Ga.	FA-'07	15/0
76	Murtha, Lydon	T	6-7	315	11/13/85	3	Nebraska	Hutchinson, Minn.	FA-'09	8/4
32	Ness, Nate	CB	6-1	190	9/5/86	2	Arizona	Gardenia, Calif.	FA-'09	3/0
98	Odrick, Jared	DE	6-5	304	12/31/87	2	Penn State	Lebanon County, Pa.	D1-'10	1/1
10	Pennington, Chad	QB	6-3	230	6/26/76	12	Marshall	Knoxville, Tenn.	FA-'08	1/1
36	Polite, Lousaka	FB	6-0	245	9/14/81	7	Pittsburgh	Pittsburgh, Pa.	FA-'08	16/0
71	Procter, Cory	LB	6-4	311	10/18/82	7	Montana	Gig Harbor, Wash.	FA-'10	10/1
27	Sapp, Benny	CB	5-9	190	1/20/81	6	Northern Iowa	Fort Lauderdale, Fla.	T(Minn)-'10	16/6
22	Sheets, Kory	RB	5-11	206	3/31/85	3	Purdue	Bloomfield, Conn.	FA-'09	0*
86	Shuler, Mickey	TE	6-4	251	10/9/86	2	Penn State	Enola, Pa.	W(Minn)-'10	6/2
24	Smith, Sean	CB	6-3	214	7/14/87	3	Utah	Pasadena, Calif.	D2b-'09	15/8
96	Soliai, Paul	DT	6-4	355	12/30/83	5	Utah	Pago Pago, American Samoa	D4-'07	16/14
53	Spitler, Austin	LB	6-2	243	10/26/86	2	Ohio State	Bellbrook, Ohio	D7b-'10	12/0
94	Starks, Randy	DT	6-3	305	12/14/83	8	Maryland	Waldorf, Md.	UFA(Tenn)-'08	16/16
16	Thigpen, Tyler	QB	6-1	224	4/14/84	4	Coastal Carolina	Winnsboro, S.C.	T(KC)-'09	5/1
91	Wake, Cameron	LB	6-3	250	1/30/82	3	Penn State	Hyattsville, Md.	FA-'09	16/16
18	Wallace, Roberto	WR	6-4	225	5/10/86	2	San Diego State	Oceanside, Calif.	FA-'10	12/0
34	Williams, Ricky	RB	5-10	230	5/21/77	11	Texas	San Diego, Calif.	T(NO)-'02	16/0

* Allen missed '10 season because of injury; Barbre played 3 games with Seattle in '10, inactive for 1 game with Miami; Brandstater spent '10 season on Miami practice squad, was inactive third quarterback for Denver in '09; Edds missed '10 season because of injury; Garner missed '10 season because of injury; Haynos missed '10 season because of injury; Kopa did not play in 1 game, inactive for 7 games; Marten spent '10 season on Miami practice squad, last active with Oakland in '08; Sheets missed '10 season because of injury.

Also played with Dolphins in '10—CB Jason Allen (8 games), LB Bobby Carpenter (5), WR Kevin Curtis (2), G Ray Feinga (3), DE Clifton Geathers (1), CB Al Harris (3), LB Micah Johnson (1), TE John Nalbone (2), CB Evan Oglesby (1), RB Clifton Smith (2).

^ "NFL Exp." as of 2011 Kickoff Weekend. For full explanation of how a player's NFL Experience is measured, refer to explanation underneath the First-Year Roster listed below.

FIRST-YEAR ROSTER

Name	Pos.	Ht.	Wt.	Birthdate	College	Hometown	How Acq.
Carter, Patrick (1)	WR	6-3	215	2/6/85	Louisville	St. Petersburg, Fla.	FA
Clay, Charles	FB/TE	6-3	239	2/13/89	Tulsa	Little Rock, Ark.	D6
Feinga, Ray (1)	G	6-4	337	5/8/86	Brigham Young	West Valley City, Utah	FA-'10
Foster, Brooks (1)	WR	6-1	205	6/9/86	North Carolina	Boiling Springs, S.C.	FA
Gates, Edmond	WR	5-11	197	6/13/86	Abilene Christian	Vernon, Texas	D4
Kearse, Frank	DT	6-5	325	10/28/88	Alabama A&M	Savannah, Ga.	D7a
Pouncey, Mike	G/C	6-5	303	7/24/89	Florida	Lakeland, Fla.	D1
Pruitt, Julius (1)	WR	6-2	206	12/30/85	Ouachita Baptist	Newport, Ark.	FA-'10
Restelli, Mark (1)	LB	6-2	215	3/4/86	Cal Poly	Santa Margarita, Calif.	FA
Rivera, Mike (1)	LB	6-2	252	1/10/86	Kansas	Shawnee Mission, Kan.	FA-'10
Rose, Robert (1)	DT	6-4	297	12/24/87	Ohio State	Cleveland, Ohio	FA
Thomas, Daniel	RB	6-1	228	10/27/87	Kansas State	Hilliard, Fla.	D2
Wilson, Jimmy	CB	5-11	185	7/30/86	Montana	San Diego, Calif.	D7b

The term NFL Rookie is defined as a player who is in his first season of professional football and has not been on the roster of another professional football team for any regular-season or postseason games. A Rookie is designated by an "R" on NFL rosters. Players who have been active in another professional football league or players who have NFL experience, including either preseason training camp or being on an Active List or Inactive List, or on Reserve/Injured or Reserve/Physically Unable to Perform for fewer than six regular-season games, are termed NFL First-Year Players. An NFL First-Year Player is designated by a "1" on NFL rosters. Thereafter, a player is credited with an additional year of experience for each season in which he accumulates six games on the Active List or Inactive List, or on Reserve/Injured or Reserve/Physically Unable to Perform.

Log on to www.miamidolphins.com for an up-to-date roster.

COACHING STAFF

Head Coach,
Tony Sparano

Pro Career: Became the eighth head coach in Dolphins history on January 16, 2008. In his first season led the Dolphins to the greatest turnaround in NFL history as Miami posted an 11-5 regular season record while capturing the teams first AFC East Division title since 2000. Sparano had spent the previous five seasons (2003-07) on the staff of the Dallas Cowboys, during which time the team made three playoff appearances. He tutored the Cowboys' offensive line the last three years while also holding the title of assistant head coach the past two seasons. He coached the team's tight ends his first two seasons in Dallas. Prior to joining the Cowboys, Sparano had NFL stops in Cleveland (1999-2000), Washington (2001) and Jacksonville (2002). Career record: 25-24.

Background: Sparano was a four-year letterman as a center at the University of New Haven, where he earned his degree in criminal law. He began his coaching career at his alma mater in 1984 before moving on to Boston University as offensive coordinator in 1989. He returned to New Haven as the school's head coach in 1994, and manned that spot for the next five years.

Personal: Born October 7, 1961 in West Haven, Conn. He and his wife, Jeanette, have two sons, Tony and Andrew, and one daughter, Ryan Leigh.

ASSISTANT COACHES

Todd Bowles, asst. head coach/secondary; born November 18, 1963, Elizabeth, N.J. Defensive back Temple 1982-85. Pro defensive back Washington Redskins 1986-1990, 1992-93, San Francisco 49ers 1991. College coach: Morehouse College 1997, Grambling State 1998-99. Pro coach: New York Jets 2000, Cleveland Browns 2001-04, Dallas Cowboys 2005-07, joined Dolphins in 2008.

Steve Bush, wide receivers; born December 21, 1959, Denville, N.J. Defensive back Southern Connecticut State 1978-1981. No pro playing experience. College coach: Southern Connecticut State 1982-83, Springfield College 1984-85, New Haven 1986-87, Boston University 1988-89, Syracuse 2000-04. Pro coach: Joined Dolphins in 2008.

Dan Campbell, tight ends; born April 13, 1976, Clifton, Texas. Tight end Texas A&M 1994-98. Pro tight end New York Giants 1999-2002, Dallas Cowboys 2003-05, Detroit Lions 2006-08, New Orleans Saints 2009. Pro coach: Joined Dolphins in 2010.

David Corrao, defensive quality control; born June 11, 1974. Running back University of San Diego 1992. No pro playing experience. College coach: Syracuse 2000-03, Northeastern 2004, Mississippi 2005-07. Pro coach: Joined Dolphins in 2008.

Bryan Cox, defensive line; born February 17, 1968, East St. Louis, Mo. Linebacker Western Illinois 1987-1990. Pro linebacker Miami Dolphins 1991-95, Chicago Bears 1996-97, New York Jets 1998-2000, New England Patriots 2001, New Orleans Saints 2002. Pro coach: New York Jets 2006-08, Cleveland Browns 2009-2010, joined Dolphins in 2011.

Brian Daboll, offensive coordinator; born April 14, 1975, Welland, Ontario, Canada. Safety Rochester 1995-97. No pro playing experience. College coach: William & Mary 1997, Michigan State 1998-99. Pro coach: New England Patriots 2000-06, New York Jets 2007-08, Cleveland Browns 2009-2010, joined Dolphins 2011.

Joe Danna, defensive assistant; born April 3, 1977, Midland, Mich. Wide receiver Central Michigan 1995-98. No pro playing experience. College coach: Central Michigan 1999-2000, 2002-05, Georgia 2001, Georgia Southern 2006, James Madison 2007. Pro coach: Atlanta Falcons 2008-09, joined Dolphins in 2010.

Dave DeGuglielmo, offensive line; born July 15, 1968, Cambridge, Mass. Attended Boston University. No college or pro playing experience. College coach: Boston College 1991-92, Boston University 1993-96, Connecticut 1997-98, South Carolina 1999-2003. Pro coach: New York Giants 2004–08, joined Dolphins in 2009.

Karl Dorrell, quarterbacks; born December 18, 1968, Alameda, Calif. Wide receiver UCLA 1982-86. No pro playing experience. College coach: UCLA 1988, 2003-07 (head coach 2003-07), Central Florida 1989, Northern Arizona 1990-91, Colorado 1992-93, 1995-98, Arizona State 1994, Washington 1999. Pro coach: Denver Broncos 2000-02, joined Dolphins in 2008.

Dave Fipp, asst. special teams; born August 8, 1974, Albuquerque, N.M. Safety Arizona 1994-97. No pro playing experience. College coach: Holy Cross 1998-99, Arizona 2000, Cal Poly 2001-03, Nevada 2004, San Jose State 2005-07. Pro coach: San Francisco 49ers 2008-2010, joined Dolphins in 2011.

Ike Hilliard, asst. wide receivers; born April 5, 1976, Patterson, La. Wide receiver Florida 1994-96. Pro wide receiver New York Giants 1997-2004, Tampa Bay Buccaneers 2005-08. Pro coach: Florida Tuskers (UFL) 2009-2010, joined Dolphins in 2011.

Darren Krein, head strength & conditioning; born July 7, 1971, Aurora, Colo. Linebacker/defensive end Miami 1989-1993. Pro linebacker San Diego Chargers 1994, Barcelona Dragons (NFLE) 1996.

Pro coach: Seattle Seahawks 1997-98, 2002-09, joined Dolphins in 2011.

Jeff Nixon, special teams quality control; born October 16, 1974, Rochester, Pa. Running back West Virginia 1993-94, Penn State 1996. No pro playing experience. College coach: Penn State 1997, Princeton 1998, Shippensburg 1999-2002, Tennessee-Chattanooga 2003-05, Temple 2006. Pro coach: Philadelphia Eagles 2007-2010, joined Dolphins in 2011.

Mike Nolan, defensive coordinator; born March 7, 1965, Haverhill, Mass. Safety Oregon 1978-1980. No pro playing experience. College coach: Oregon 1981, Stanford 1982-83, Rice 1984-85, Louisiana State 1986. Pro coach: Denver Broncos 1987-1992, 2009, New York Giants 1993-96, Washington Redskins 1997-99, New York Jets 2000, Baltimore Ravens 2001-04, San Francisco 49ers 2005-08 (head coach), joined Dolphins in 2010.

Dave Puloka, asst. strength and conditioning; born January 12, 1979, Arlington, Mass. Linebacker Holy Cross 1997-2000. No pro playing experience College coach: Stevens Institute of Technology 2005, Virginia 2006. Pro coach: Atlanta Falcons 2007, joined Dolphins in 2008.

Darren Rizzi, special teams coordinator; born July 21, 1970, Hillsdale, N.J. Tight end Rhode Island 1988-1991. College coach: Rhode Island 1992, Colgate 1993, New Haven 1993-97, Northeastern 1998, New Haven 1999-2001 (head coach), Rutgers 2002-07, Rhode Island 2008 (head coach). Pro coach: Joined Dolphins in 2009.

Kacy Rodgers, defensive line; born June 24, 1969, Humboldt, Tennessee. Linebacker/defensive end Tennessee 1988-1991. Pro linebacker Shreveport Pirates (CFL) 1994. College coach: Tennessee-Martin 1997, Louisiana-Monroe 1998, Middle Tennessee State 1999-2001, Arkansas 2002. Pro coach: Dallas Cowboys 2003-07, joined Dolphins in 2008.

Bill Sheridan, linebackers; born January 27, 1959, Detroit. Linebacker Grand Valley State 1979-1982. No pro playing experience. College coach: Michigan 1985-86, Maine 1987-88, Cincinnati 1989-1991, Army 1992-97, Michigan State 1998-2000, Notre Dame 2001, Michigan 2002-04. Pro coach: New York Giants 2005-09, joined Dolphins in 2010.

Tony Sparano Jr., offensive quality control; born October 22, 1986, Colleyville, Texas. Defensive end Albany 2006-08. No pro playing experience. Pro coach: Hartford Colonials (UFL) 2010, joined Dolphins in 2011.

**American Football Conference
East Division
Team Colors:** Blue, Red, Silver, and White
**Gillette Stadium
One Patriot Place
Foxborough, Massachusetts 02035
Telephone:** (508) 543-8200

2011 SCHEDULE
PRESEASON
Aug. 11 **Jacksonville**........................7:30
Aug. 18 at Tampa Bay 7:30
Aug. 27 at Detroit............................8:00
Sep. 1 **New York Giants** 7:30

REGULAR SEASON
Sep. 12 at Miami (Mon) 7:00
Sep. 18 **San Diego** 4:15
Sep. 25 at Buffalo 1:00
Oct. 2 at Oakland 4:15
Oct. 9 **New York Jets** 4:15
Oct. 16 **Dallas** 4:15
Oct. 23 BYE
Oct. 30 at Pittsburgh 4:15
Nov. 6 **New York Giants**.............. 4:15
Nov. 13 at New York Jets * 8:20
Nov. 21 **Kansas City** (Mon)........... 8:30
Nov. 27 at Philadelphia 4:15
Dec. 4 **Indianapolis** * 8:20
Dec. 11 at Washington 1:00
Dec. 18 at Denver 4:15
Dec. 24 **Miami** (Sat) 1:00
Jan. 1 **Buffalo** 1:00
* *All times ET; Sunday night games in
  Weeks 11-15, 17 subject to change*
Stadium: Gillette Stadium
  (opened in 2002)
  •**Capacity:** 68,756
  One Patriot Place
  Foxborough, Massachusetts 02035
Playing Surface: FieldTurf
Training Camp: Gillette Stadium
                Foxborough, MA 02035

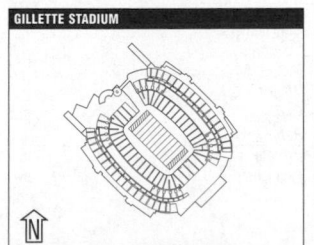

GILLETTE STADIUM

CLUB OFFICIALS
Chairman & CEO: Robert K. Kraft
President: Jonathan A. Kraft
Vice President of Retail Operations:
  Brian Bilello
Vice President of Human Resources:
  Robin Boudreau
Chief Operating Officer of TeamOps
  Security: Mark Briggs
Equipment Manager: Don Brocher
Director of Player Personnel:
  Nick Caserio
Vice President of Information
  Technology: Pat Curley
Video Director: Jimmy Dee
Senior Vice President of Marketing and
  Brand Development: Jennifer Ferron
Vice President of Customer Marketing
  and Strategy: Jessica Gelman
Senior Advisor: Robyn Glaser
Vice President of Media and Community
  Relations: Stacey James
Publisher / Editor-in-Chief and Director of
  Interactive Media: Fred Kirsch
Vice President of Sales: Murray Kohl
President of New England Patriots
  Charitable Foundation: Josh Kraft
Director of Research: Richard Miller
Vice President of Stadium Business
  Development and External Affairs:
  Dan Murphy
Director of Football / Head Coach
  Administration: Berj Najarian
Senior Vice President of Finance,
  Administrative and Operations:
  James Nolan
Vice President of Marketing Integration
  and Events: David Pearlstein
Vice President of Food and Beverage:
  David Wheeler
Senior Football Advisor: Floyd Reese
Executive Producer of Broadcast
  Production: Matt Smith
Director of Cheerleaders: Tracy Sormanti
Executive Director of Community Affairs:
  Andre Tippett
Head Athletic Trainer: Jim Whalen
Vice President of Finance: Jim Wilson

COACHING HISTORY
**Boston 1960-1970
(422-377-9)**
Records include postseason games
1960-61   Lou Saban*....................7-12-0
1961-68   Mike Holovak 53-47-9
1969-1970 Clive Rush**..................5-16-0
1970-72   John Mazur*** 9-21-0
1972   Phil Bengtson...................1-4-0
1973-78   Chuck Fairbanks**** 46-41-0
1978   Hank Bullough-Ron Erhardt#...0-1-0
1979-1981 Ron Erhardt 21-27-0
1982-84   Ron Meyer## 18-16-0
1984-89   Raymond Berry 51-41-0
1990   Rod Rust.........................1-15-0
1991-92   Dick MacPherson 8-24-0
1993-96   Bill Parcells 34-34-0
1997-99   Pete Carroll 28-23-0
2000-2010 Bill Belichick...............140-55-0
         *Released after five games in 1961
       **Released after seven games in 1970
     ***Resigned after nine games in 1972
   ****Suspended for final regular-season game in 1978
         #Co-coaches
       ##Released after eight games in 1984

PAID ATTENDANCE
Home 545,704   Away 517,357
Total 1,063,061
Single-game home record,
  71,768 (11/30/08)
Single-season home record,
  579,182 (2007)

2011 DRAFT CHOICES

Round	Name	Pos.	College
1	Nate Solder	T	Colorado
2	Ras-I Dowling	DB	Virginia
	Shane Vereen	RB	California
3	Stevan Ridley	RB	Louisiana State
	Ryan Mallet	QB	Arkansas
5	Marcus Cannon	T	Texas Christian
	Lee Smith	TE	Marshall
6	Markell Carter	LB	Central Arkansas
7	Malcolm Williams	DB	Texas Christian

2010 TEAM RECORD
PRESEASON (2-2)

Date	Result	Opponent
8/12	W 27-24	New Orleans
8/19	W 28-10	at Atlanta
8/26	L 35-36	St. Louis
9/2	L 17-20	at New York Giants

REGULAR SEASON (14-2)

Date	Result	Opponent
9/12	W 38-24	Cincinnati
9/19	L 14-28	at New York Jets
9/26	W 38-30	Buffalo
10/4	W 41-14	at Miami
10/17	W 23-20	Baltimore (OT)
10/24	W 23-20	at San Diego
10/31	W 28-18	Minnesota
11/7	L 14-34	at Cleveland
11/14	W 39-26	at Pittsburgh
11/21	W 31-28	Indianapolis
11/25	W 45-24	at Detroit
12/6	W 45-3	New York Jets
12/12	W 36-7	at Chicago
12/19	W 31-27	Green Bay
12/26	W 34-3	at Buffalo
1/2	W 38-7	Miami

POSTSEASON (0-1)

Date	Result	Opponent
1/16	L 21-28	New York Jets

(OT) Overtime

SCORE BY PERIODS

Patriots	103	152	138	122	3	—	518
Opponents	39	91	77	106	0	—	313

2010 TEAM STATISTICS

	Patriots	Opp.
Total First Downs	335	348
Rushing	119	99
Passing	196	226
Penalty	20	23
3rd Down: Made/Att	95/197	99/210
3rd Down Pct.	48.2	47.1
4th Down: Made/Att	7/14	12/20
4th Down Pct.	50.0	60.0
Possession Avg.	29:00	31:00
Total Net Yards	5820	5864
Avg. Per Game	363.8	366.5
Total Plays	986	1056
Avg. Per Play	5.9	5.6
Net Yards Rushing	1973	1728
Avg. Per Game	123.3	108.0
Total Rushes	454	409
Net Yards Passing	3847	4136
Avg. Per Game	240.4	258.5
Sacked/Yards Lost	25/175	36/212
Gross Yards	4022	4348
Att./Completions	507/331	611/388
Completion Pct.	65.3	63.5
Had Intercepted	5	25
Punts/Average	58/43.2	58/41.8
Net Punting Avg.	58/38.4	58/34.2
Penalties/Yards	83/766	84/687
Fumbles/Ball Lost	9/5	20/13
Touchdowns	65	36
Rushing	19	10
Passing	37	25
Returns	9	1

2010 INDIVIDUAL STATISTICS

PASSING

	Att.	Comp.	Yds.	Pct.	TD	Int.	Tkld.	Rate
Brady	492	324	3900	65.9	36	4	25/175	111.0
Hoyer	15	7	122	46.7	1	1	0/0	69.3
Patriots	507	331	4022	65.3	37	5	25/175	109.8
Opponents	611	388	4348	63.5	25	25	36/212	81.2

SCORING

	TD R	TD P	TD Rt	PAT	FG	Saf	PTS
Green-Ellis	13	0	0	0/0	0/0	0	78
Graham	0	0	0	35/37	12/12	0	71
Gronkowski	0	10	0	0/0	0/0	0	60
Gostkowski	0	0	0	26/26	10/13	0	56
Welker	0	7	0	1/1	0/0	0	43
Hernandez	0	6	0	0/0	0/0	0	36
Woodhead	5	1	0	0/0	0/0	0	36
Branch	0	5	0	0/0	0/0	0	30
Tate	0	3	2	0/0	0/0	0	30
Moss	0	3	0	0/0	0/0	0	18
Arrington	0	0	2	0/0	0/0	0	12
Crumpler	0	2	0	0/0	0/0	0	12
Guyton	0	0	2	0/0	0/0	0	12
Brady	1	0	0	0/0	0/0	0	6
Chung	0	0	1	0/0	0/0	0	6
Edelman	0	0	1	0/0	0/0	0	6
Sanders	0	0	1	0/0	0/0	0	6
Patriots	19	37	9	62/64	22/25	0	518
Opponents	10	25	1	32/32	19/26	0	313

2-Pt Conversions: Patriots 0-1, Opponents 4-4.

RUSHING

	No.	Yds	Avg	LG	TD
Green-Ellis	229	1008	4.4	33t	13
Woodhead	97	547	5.6	36t	5
F. Taylor	43	155	3.6	24	0
Tate	5	62	12.4	22	0
Morris	20	56	2.8	9	0
Hernandez	3	47	15.7	18	0
Faulk	8	45	5.6	11	0
Brady	31	30	1.0	9	1
Clayton	6	17	2.8	5	0
Edelman	2	14	7.0	13	0
Hoyer	10	-8	-0.8	1	0
Patriots	454	1973	4.3	36t	19
Opponents	409	1728	4.2	36	10

RECEIVING

	No.	Yds	Avg	LG	TD
Welker	86	848	9.9	35	7
Branch	48	706	14.7	79t	5
Hernandez	45	563	12.5	46	6
Gronkowski	42	546	13.0	28	10
Woodhead	34	379	11.1	50	1
Tate	24	432	18.0	65t	3
Green-Ellis	12	85	7.1	16	0
Moss	9	139	15.4	35t	3
Edelman	7	86	12.3	40	0
Morris	7	77	11.0	22	0
Faulk	6	62	10.3	21	0
Crumpler	6	52	8.7	27	2
Price	3	41	13.7	18	0
F. Taylor	2	6	3.0	7	0
Patriots	331	4022	12.2	79t	37
Opponents	388	4348	11.2	66t	25

PUNTING

	No.	Yds.	Avg.	In 20	LG
Mesko	58	2505	43.2	19	65
Patriots	58	2505	43.2	19	65
Opponents	58	2422	41.8	23	61

INTERCEPTIONS

	No.	Yds	Avg	LG	TD
McCourty	7	110	15.7	50	0
Chung	3	96	32.0	51t	1
Sanders	3	60	20.0	32t	1
Meriweather	3	39	13.0	39	0
Guyton	2	72	36.0	59t	1
Ninkovich	2	1	0.5	1	0
Page	2	0	0.0	0	0
Arrington	1	36	36.0	36t	1
Spikes	1	5	5.0	5	0
Fletcher	1	0	0.0	0	0
Patriots	25	419	16.8	59t	4
Opponents	5	12	2.4	12	0

PUNT RETURNS

	Ret	FC	Yds	Avg	LG	TD
Edelman	21	6	321	15.3	94t	1
Welker	5	7	36	7.2	22	0
Tate	1	0	4	4.0	4	0
Faulk	0	1	0	—	—	0
Patriots	27	14	361	13.4	94t	1
Opponents	25	14	179	7.2	18	0

KICKOFF RETURNS

	No.	Yds	Avg	LG	TD
Tate	41	1057	25.8	103t	2
Crumpler	5	18	3.6	7	0
Morris	5	66	13.2	23	0
Connolly	3	90	30.0	71	0
Fletcher	1	0	0.0	0	0
Green-Ellis	1	0	0.0	0	0
Patriots	56	1231	22.0	103t	2
Opponents	81	1826	22.5	95t	1

FIELD GOALS

	1-19	20-29	30-39	40-49	50+
Gostkowski	0/0	2/2	6/7	2/3	0/1
Graham	1/1	5/5	5/5	1/1	0/0
Patriots	1/1	7/7	11/12	3/4	0/1
Opponents	1/1	6/7	9/9	2/4	1/5

SACKS

	No.
Wright	5.5
Banta-Cain	5.0
Ninkovich	4.0
G. Warren	3.5
Guyton	3.0
Deaderick	2.0
Fletcher	2.0
Mayo	2.0
Moore	2.0
Wilfork	2.0
Cunningham	1.0
Love	1.0
McCourty	1.0
Woods	1.0
Crable	0.5
Pryor	0.5
Patriots	36.0
Opponents	25.0

RECORD HOLDERS
INDIVIDUAL RECORDS—CAREER

Category	Name	Performance
Rushing (Yds.)	Sam Cunningham, 1973-79, 1981-82	5,453
Passing (Yds.)	Tom Brady, 2000-2010	34,744
Passing (TDs)	Tom Brady, 2000-2010	261
Receiving (No.)	Troy Brown, 1993-2007	557
Receiving (Yds.)	Stanley Morgan, 1977-1989	10,352
Interceptions	Raymond Clayborn, 1977-1989	36
	Ty Law, 1995-2004	36
Punting (Avg.)	Tom Tupa, 1996-98	44.7
Punt Return (Avg.)	Julian Edelman, 2009-2010	14.2
Kickoff Return (Avg.)	Ellis Hobbs, 2005-08	27.7
Field Goals	Adam Vinatieri, 1996-2005	263
Touchdowns (Tot.)	Stanley Morgan, 1977-1989	68
Points	Adam Vinatieri, 1996-2005	1,158
*Sacks	Andre Tippett, 1982-1993	100.0

INDIVIDUAL RECORDS—SINGLE SEASON

Category	Name	Performance
Rushing (Yds.)	Corey Dillon, 2004	1,635
Passing (Yds.)	Tom Brady, 2007	4,806
Passing (TDs)	Tom Brady, 2007	**50
Receiving (No.)	Wes Welker, 2009	123
Receiving (Yds.)	Randy Moss, 2007	1,493
Interceptions	Ron Hall, 1964	11
Punting (Avg.)	Tom Tupa, 1997	45.8
Punt Return (Avg.)	Julian Edelman, 2010	15.3
Kickoff Return (Avg.)	Raymond Clayborn, 1977	31.0
Field Goals	Stephen Gostkowski, 2008	36
Touchdowns (Tot.)	Randy Moss, 2007	23
Points	Gino Cappelletti, 1964	155
*Sacks	Andre Tippett, 1984	18.5

INDIVIDUAL RECORDS—SINGLE GAME

Category	Name	Performance
Rushing (Yds.)	Tony Collins, 9-18-83	212
Passing (Yds.)	Drew Bledsoe, 11-13-94	426
Passing (TDs)	Tom Brady, 10-21-07, 10-18-09	6
Receiving (No.)	Troy Brown, 9-22-02	16
Receiving (Yds.)	Terry Glenn, 10-3-99	214
Interceptions	Many times	3
	Last time by Leigh Bodden 11-22-09	
Field Goals	Gino Cappelletti, 10-4-64	6
Touchdowns (Tot.)	Randy Moss, 11-18-07	4
Points	Gino Cappelletti, 12-18-65	24
*Sacks	Andre Tippett, 10-26-86	3.5
	Chris Slade, 11-20-94	3.5

*Sacks became an official statistic in 1982.
**NFL Record

VETERAN ROSTER AS OF MARCH 3, 2011

No.	Name	Pos.	Ht.	Wt.	Birthdate	^NFL Exp.	College	Hometown	How Acq.	'10 Games/ Starts
27	Arrington, Kyle	CB	5-10	196	8/12/86	3	Hofstra	Accokeek, Md.	FA-'09	16/14
95	Banta-Cain, Tully	LB	6-2	250	8/28/80	9	California	Sunnyvale, Calif.	FA-'09	15/6
	Barrett, Josh	S	6-2	225	11/22/84	4	Arizona State	Reno, Nev.	W(Den)-'10	0*
23	Bodden, Leigh	CB	6-1	193	9/24/81	9	Duquesne	Hyattsville, Md.	FA-'09	0*
97	Brace, Ron	DL	6-3	330	12/18/86	3	Boston College	Worcester, Mass.	D2b-'09	13/5
12	Brady, Tom	QB	6-4	225	8/3/77	12	Michigan	San Mateo, Calif.	D6b-'00	16/16
84 t-	Branch, Deion	WR	5-9	195	7/18/79	10	Louisville	Albany, Ga.	T(Sea)-'10	15/12*
38	Brown, Sergio	S	6-2	210	5/22/88	2	Notre Dame	Maywood, Ill.	FA-'10	11/0
28	Butler, Darius	CB	5-10	190	3/18/86	3	Connecticut	Ft. Lauderdale, Fla.	D2c-'09	15/3
29	Carter, Tony	CB	5-9	175	5/24/86	3	Florida State	Jacksonville, Fla.	FA-'10	2/0
25	Chung, Patrick	S	5-11	212	8/19/87	3	Oregon	Rancho Cucamonga, Calif.	D2a-'09	14/13
22	Clayton, Thomas	RB	5-11	220	4/26/84	3	Kansas State	Alexandria, Va.	W(Cle)-'10	3/0*
66	Cohen, Landon	DL	6-3	300	8/3/86	4	Ohio	Spartanburg, S.C.	FA-'10	4/1*
63	Connolly, Dan	OL	6-4	313	9/2/82	6	Southeast Missouri St.	St. Louis, Mo.	FA-'08	14/13
82	Crumpler, Alge	TE	6-2	275	12/23/77	11	North Carolina	Wilmington, N.C.	FA-'10	16/10
96	Cunningham, Jermaine	LB	6-3	260	4/24/88	2	Florida	Stone Mountain, Ga.	D2b-'10	15/11
71	Deaderick, Brandon	DL	6-4	305	8/19/87	2	Alabama	Elizabethtown, Ky.	D7b-'10	10/4
11	Edelman, Julian	WR	5-10	198	5/22/86	3	Kent State	Redwood City, Calif.	D7a-'09	15/3
33	Faulk, Kevin	RB	5-8	202	6/5/76	13	Louisiana State	Carencro, La.	D2-'99	2/2
52	Fletcher, Dane	LB	6-2	244	9/14/86	2	Montana State	Bozeman, Mont.	FA-'10	13/0
3	Gostkowski, Stephen	K	6-1	215	1/28/84	6	Memphis	Madison, Miss.	D4b-'06	8/0
5	Graham, Shayne	K	6-0	214	12/9/77	11	Virginia Tech	Radford, Va.	FA-'10	9/0*
42	Green-Ellis, BenJarvus	RB	5-11	215	7/2/85	4	Mississippi	New Orleans, La.	FA-'08	16/11
87	Gronkowski, Rob	TE	6-6	265	5/14/89	2	Arizona	Pittsburgh, Pa.	D2a-'10	16/11
59	Guyton, Gary	LB	6-3	245	11/14/85	4	Georgia Tech	Hinesville, Ga.	FA-'08	16/8
85	Hernandez, Aaron	TE	6-1	245	11/6/89	2	Florida	Bristol, Conn.	D4-'10	14/7
8	Hoyer, Brian	QB	6-2	215	10/13/85	3	Michigan State	North Olmsted, Ohio	FA-'09	5/0
77	Kaczur, Nick	T	6-4	315	7/28/79	7	Toledo	Brantford, Ontario	D3b-'05	0*
48	Katula, Matt	LS	6-6	265	8/22/82	7	Wisconsin	Waukesha, Wisc.	FA-'10	8/0
67	Koppen, Dan	C	6-2	296	9/12/79	9	Boston College	Whitehall, Pa.	D5-'03	16/16
64	LeVoir, Mark	T	6-7	310	7/29/82	5	Notre Dame	Eden Prairie, Minn.	W(StL)-'08	6/0
72	Light, Matt	T	6-4	305	6/23/78	11	Purdue	Greenville, Ohio	D2-'01	16/16
26	Lockett, Bret	DB	6-1	220	10/7/86	3	UCLA	Diamond Bar, Calif.	W(Cle)-'09	0*
74	Love, Kyle	DL	6-1	310	11/18/86	2	Mississippi State	Fairburn, Ga.	FA-'10	9/1
70	Mankins, Logan	G	6-4	310	3/10/82	7	Fresno State	Catheys Valley, Calif.	D1-'05	9/9
51	Mayo, Jerod	LB	6-1	245	2/23/86	4	Tennessee	Hampton, Va.	D1-'08	16/16
32	McCourty, Devin	CB	5-10	193	8/13/87	2	Rutgers	Montvale, N.J.	D1-'10	16/16
30	McGowan, Brandon	S	5-11	210	9/26/83	7	Maine	Jersey City, N.J.	UFA(Chi)-'09	0*
31	Meriweather, Brandon	S	5-11	200	1/14/84	5	Miami	Apopka, Fla.	D1-'07	16/13
14	Mesko, Zoltan	P	6-5	231	3/16/86	2	Michigan	Twinsburg, Ohio	D5-'10	16/0
98	Moore, Eric	DL	6-4	268	2/28/81	6	Florida State	Pahokee, Fla.	FA-'10	4/3
34	Morris, Sammy	RB	6-0	220	3/23/77	12	Texas Tech	San Antonio, Texas	UFA(Mia)-'07	16/0
53	Murrell, Marques	LB	6-2	250	3/20/85	5	Appalachian State	Fayetteville, N.C.	FA-'10	1/0
50	Ninkovich, Rob	LB	6-2	255	2/1/84	6	Purdue	Blue Island, Ill.	FA-'09	16/10
60	Ohrnberger, Rich	OL	6-2	300	2/14/86	3	Penn State	East Meadow, N.Y.	D4-'09	2/0
69	Ojinnaka, Quinn	OL	6-5	295	4/23/84	6	Syracuse	Seabrook, Md.	T(Atl)-'10	8/0
44	Page, Jarrad	S	6-0	225	10/19/84	6	UCLA	San Leandro, Calif.	T(KC)-'10	10/1
17	Price, Taylor	WR	6-0	205	10/8/87	2	Ohio	Hilliard, Ohio	D3-'10	1/0
91	Pryor, Myron	DL	6-1	310	6/13/86	3	Kentucky	Louisville, Ky.	D6b-'09	9/2
90	Richard, Darryl	DL	6-4	295	6/17/86	2	Georgia Tech	Destrehan, La.	D7b-'09	0*
36	Sanders, James	S	5-10	210	11/11/83	7	Fresno State	Porterville, Calif.	D4-'05	15/9
18	Slater, Matthew	WR	6-0	200	9/9/85	4	UCLA	Anaheim, Calif.	D5-'08	15/0
55	Spikes, Brandon	LB	6-2	250	9/3/87	2	Florida	Shelby, N.C.	D2c-'10	12/8
	Stroud, Marcus	DL	6-6	310	6/25/78	11	Georgia	Thomasville, Ga.	FA-'11	15/14*
19	Tate, Brandon	WR	6-1	195	10/5/87	3	North Carolina	Burlington, N.C.	D3a-'09	16/10
21	Taylor, Fred	RB	6-1	228	1/27/76	14	Florida	Belle Glade, Fla.	FA-'09	7/0
76	Vollmer, Sebastian	OL	6-8	315	7/10/84	3	Houston	Kaarst, Germany	D2d-'09	16/16
92	Warren, Gerard	DL	6-4	325	7/25/78	11	Florida	Lake Butler, Fla.	FA-'10	16/10
94	Warren, Ty	DL	6-5	300	2/6/81	9	Texas A&M	Bryan, Texas	D1-'03	0*
83	Welker, Wes	WR	5-9	185	5/1/81	8	Texas Tech	Oklahoma City, Okla.	T(Mia)-'07	15/11
62	Wendell, Ryan	OL	6-2	290	3/4/86	3	Fresno State	Diamond Bar, Calif.	FA-'08	15/2
66	Weston, Kade	DL	6-5	315	11/29/86	2	Georgia	Red Bank, N.J.	D7c-'10	0*
58	White, Tracy	LB	6-0	230	4/14/81	9	Howard	St. Stephen, S.C.	T(Phil)-'10	16/0
75	Wilfork, Vince	NT	6-2	325	11/4/81	8	Miami	Boynton Beach, Fla.	D1a-'04	16/16
24	Wilhite, Jonathan	CB	5-11	185	2/23/84	4	Auburn	Monroe, La.	D4-'08	9/1
39	Woodhead, Danny	RB	5-8	195	1/25/85	4	Chadron State	North Platte, Neb.	FA-'10	15/3*
99	Wright, Mike	DL	6-4	295	3/1/82	7	Cincinnati	Cincinnati, Ohio	FA-'05	10/5

* Barrett missed '10 season because of injury; Bodden missed '10 season because of injury; Branch played 4 games with Seattle and 11 games with New England; Clayton played 2 games with Cleveland and 1 game with New England; Cohen played 2 games with Jacksonville and 2 games with New England; Graham played 1 game with New York Giants and 8 games with New England; Kaczur missed '10 season because of injury; Lockett missed '10 season because of injury; McGowan missed '10 season because of injury; Richard missed '10 season because of injury; Stroud played 15 games with Buffalo; Warren missed '10 season because of injury; Weston missed '10 season because of injury; Woodhead played 1 game with New York Jets and 14 games with New England.

t- Patriots traded for Branch (Sea).

Traded—WR Randy Moss (4 games in '10) to Minnesota.

Also played with Patriots in '10—LB Shawn Crable (6 games), LS Jake Ingram (8), DL Louis Leonard (1), G Stephen Neal (8), LB Pierre Woods (2).

^ "NFL Exp." as of 2011 Kickoff Weekend. For full explanation of how a player's NFL Experience is measured, refer to explanation underneath the First-Year Roster listed below.

FIRST-YEAR ROSTER

Name	Pos.	Ht.	Wt.	Birthdate	College	Hometown	How Acq.
Austin, Thomas (1)	OL	6-4	310	11/14/86	Clemson	Camden, S.C.	FA
Barnes, Tyree (1)	WR	6-0	196	4/15/86	Navy	Hampton, Va.	FA
Butler, Carson (1)	TE	6-4	260	8/21/87	Michigan	Detroit, Mich.	FA
Cannon, Marcus	OL	6-5	358	5/6/88	Texas Christian	Odessa, Texas	D5a
Carter, Markell	LB	6-4	248	12/21/89	Central Arkansas	Bartlesville, Okla.	D6
Crompton, Jonathan (1)	QB	6-3	222	7/25/87	Tennessee	Waynesville, N.C.	FA
Dowling, Ras-I	CB	6-1	198	5/9/88	Virginia	Chesapeake, Va.	D2a
Farnham, Buddy (1)	WR	6-0	185	5/22/87	Brown	Andover, Mass.	FA
Favorite, Marlon (1)	DL	6-1	317	6/22/86	Louisiana State	Harvey, La.	FA
Jenkins, Darnell (1)	WR	5-10	191	12/31/82	Miami	Miami, Fla.	FA
Kettani, Eric (1)	RB	5-11	235	3/26/87	Navy	Kirtland, Ohio	FA
Mallett, Ryan	QB	6-6	238	6/5/88	Arkansas	Texarkana, Texas	D3b
Maneri, Steve (1)	T	6-6	290	3/20/88	Temple	Saddle Brook, N.J.	FA
Ridley, Stevan	RB	5-11	225	1/27/89	Louisiana State	Natchez, Miss.	D3a
Smith, Lee	TE	6-6	269	11/21/87	Marshall	Powell, Tenn.	D5b
Solder, Nate	T	6-8	319	4/12/88	Colorado	Buena Vista, Colo.	D1
Turner, Thad (1)	CB	5-11	188	4/30/87	Ohio	Marietta, Ga.	FA
Ventrone, Ross (1)	DB	5-8	190	9/27/86	Villanova	Pittsburgh, Pa.	FA
Vereen, Shane	RB	5-9	205	5/9/89	California	Valencia, Calif.	D2b
White, Shun (1)	WR	5-8	195	12/9/85	Navy	Memphis, Tenn.	FA
Williams, Malcolm	DB	5-11	200	11/22/87	Texas Christian	Grand Prairie, Texas	D7

The term NFL Rookie is defined as a player who is in his first season of professional football and has not been on the roster of another professional football team for any regular-season or postseason games. A Rookie is designated by an "R" on NFL rosters. Players who have been active in another professional football league or players who have NFL experience, including either preseason training camp or being on an Active List or Inactive List, or on Reserve/Injured or Reserve/Physically Unable to Perform for fewer than six regular-season games, are termed NFL First-Year Players. An NFL First-Year Player is designated by a "1" on NFL rosters. Thereafter, a player is credited with an additional year of experience for each season in which he accumulates six games on the Active List or Inactive List, or on Reserve/Injured or Reserve/Physically Unable to Perform.

Log on to www.patriots.com for an up-to-date roster.

COACHING STAFF
Head Coach,
Bill Belichick
Pro Career: Bill Belichick is in his 37th season as an NFL coach and is the only head coach in NFL history to win three Super Bowl titles in a four-year span. He has won more regular-season games (121) and more games overall (135) during a 10-year stretch (2001-2010) than any other head coach in NFL history. Belichick is currently ranked 10th on the NFL's all-time list with 177 total victories. Hired by Chairman and CEO Robert Kraft on January 27, 2000, Belichick is in his 12th season as New England's head coach. Through 11 seasons, Belichick has delivered three Super Bowl championships, four conference titles, eight division crowns and 14 playoff victories, while posting an overall record of 140-55. Belichick directed the Patriots to victories in Super Bowls XXXVI (2001), XXXVIII (2003) and XXXIX (2004), and in 2007 he became the first NFL head coach to guide his team to a 16-0 regular season. Only one coach (Pittsburgh's Chuck Noll, 4) has won more Super Bowls than Belichick, and his three Super Bowl titles tie Washington's Joe Gibbs and San Francisco's Bill Walsh for second place on the NFL's all-time list. Belichick has led the Patriots to a winning record in each of the last 10 seasons, making the Patriots the only NFL franchise to accomplish that feat from 2001-2010. The only other NFL coach to have 10 consecutive winning seasons with one team since the 1970 merger was Tom Landry, who led the Dallas Cowboys to 16 consecutive winning seasons (1970-1985). In 2010, Belichick guided the Patriots to a 14-2 record. Belichick is the first head coach to ever win at least 14 regular-season games in four separate seasons. Only four other coaches – San Francisco's George Seifert (3), Washington's Joe Gibbs (2), Chicago's Mike Ditka (2) and Miami's Don Shula (2) – have more than one 14-win season. Belichick's Patriots teams own the all-time NFL records for consecutive victories, including the postseason (21 from 2003-04) and consecutive playoff victories (10 from 2001-05). Belichick owns the third-best postseason record in NFL history (15-6) and is the winningest NFL head coach since 2001 (135-44). Over a 100-game span from 2003-08, he directed the Patriots to an 82-18 record – the best record for any 100-game span in NFL history. Belichick (.639) has the third highest winning percentage among coaches with at least 150 wins, trailing only Hall of Famers George Halas (.682) and Don Shula (.666). Belichick's recent accomplishments are the latest triumphs in a career during which he has helped produce five Super Bowl titles, seven conference championships and 15 division titles since entering the NFL in 1975. He won his first two Super Bowls as the defensive coordinator for the New York Giants in 1986 and 1990 before claiming three Super Bowl championships with the Patriots. George Seifert is the only other man to have won multiple Super Bowls both as a head coach and as an assistant coach. Belichick launched his career in 1975 as a special assistant with the Baltimore Colts, then became an assistant special teams coach with Detroit (1976-77), Denver (1978) and the New York Giants (1979-1990). Belichick was named head coach of the Cleveland Browns in 1991, becoming the youngest head coach in the NFL at age 38. By 1994, Belichick brought the Browns back to the playoffs, finishing 11-5 and advancing to the second round of the playoffs, while allowing a league-low 204 total points. In 1996, Belichick joined New England and was a key contributor to the Patriots first division title in 10 years en route to the Patriots' appearance in Super Bowl XXXI. Belichick then spent three seasons with the New York Jets from 1997 to 1999, helping New York improve from a 1-15 season in 1996 to an appearance in the AFC Championship Game in 1998. Career record: 177-100.

Background: Belichick was a center/tight end at Wesleyan 1971-74.

Personal: Born April 16, 1952, Nashville.

ASSISTANT COACHES
Josh Boyer, defensive backs; born January 21, 1977, Heath, Ohio. Wide receiver/defensive back Muskingum College 1996-99. No pro playing experience. College coach: King's College (Pa.) 2000, Dayton 2001, Kent State 2002-03, Bryant University 2004, South Dakota School of Mines and Technology 2005. Pro coach: Joined Patriots in 2006.

Moses Cabrera, asst. strength and conditioning; born August 20, 1978, Deming, N.M. Oral Roberts 1996-2000. No pro playing experience. College coach: Fresno State 2004-09, Colorado 2010. Pro coach: Joined Patriots in 2010.

Ivan Fears, running backs; born November 15, 1954, Portsmouth, Va. Running back William & Mary 1973-75. No pro playing experience. College coach: William & Mary 1977-79, Syracuse 1980-1990. Pro coach: New England Patriots 1991-92, Chicago Bears 1993-98, re-joined Patriots in 1999.

Brian Ferentz, tight ends; born March 28, 1983, Iowa City, Iowa. Offensive lineman Iowa 2001-05. No pro playing experience. Pro coach: Joined Patriots in 2009.

Brian Flores, defensive assistant; born February 24, 1981, Brooklyn, N.Y. Linebacker Boston College 1999-2003. No pro playing experience. Pro coach: Joined Patriots in 2008.

George Godsey, offensive assistant; born January 1, 1979, Tampa. Quarterback Georgia Tech 1998-2001. Pro quarterback Tampa Bay Storm (AFL) 2003. College coach: Central Florida 2004-2010. Pro coach: Joined Patriots in 2011.

Patrick Graham, linebackers; born January 24, 1979, Des Plaines, Ill. Defensive line Yale 1997-2001. College coach: Wagner College 2002-03, Richmond 2004-06, Notre Dame 2007-08. Pro coach: Joined Patriots in 2009.

Pepper Johnson, defensive line; born July 29, 1964, Detroit. Linebacker Ohio State 1982-85. Pro linebacker New York Giants 1986-1992, Cleveland Browns 1993-95, Detroit Lions 1996, New York Jets 1997-98. Pro coach: Joined Patriots in 2001.

Harold Nash, strength and conditioning; born May 5, 1970, New Orleans. Defensive back Louisiana-Lafayette 1988-1993. Pro defensive back Shreveport Pirates (CFL) 1994-95, Montreal Alouettes (CFL) 1996-99, Winnipeg Blue Bombers (CFL) 1999-2003, Edmonton Eskimos (CFL) 2004. Pro coach: Joined Patriots in 2005.

Bill O'Brien, offensive coordinator/quarterbacks; born October 23, 1969, Andover, Mass. Defensive end/linebacker Brown 1990-92. No pro playing experience. College coach: Brown 1993-94, Georgia Tech 1995-2002, Maryland 2003-04, Duke 2005-06. Pro coach: Joined Patriots in 2007.

Scott O'Brien, special teams; born June 25, 1957, Superior, Wisc. Linebacker Wisconsin-Superior 1975-78. No pro playing experience. College coach: Wisconsin-Superior 1980-82, Nevada-Las Vegas 1983-85, Rice 1986, Pittsburgh 1987-1990. Pro coach: Cleveland Browns 1991-95, Baltimore Ravens 1996-98, Carolina Panthers 1999-2004, Miami Dolphins 2005-06, Denver Broncos 2007-08, joined Patriots in 2009.

Chad O'Shea, receivers; born December 18, 1972, Houston. Quarterback Marshall 1991-93, Houston 1994-95. No pro playing experience. College coach: Houston 1996-99, Southern Mississippi 2000-02. Pro coach: Kansas City Chiefs 2003-05, Minnesota Vikings 2006-08, joined Patriots in 2009.

Matt Patricia, safeties; born September 13, 1974, Sherrill, N.Y. Center-guard Rensselaer 1992-96. No pro playing experience. College coach: Rensselaer 1996, Amherst 1999-2000, Syracuse 2001-03. Pro coach: Joined Patriots in 2004.

Dante Scarnecchia, asst. head coach/offensive line; born February 15, 1948, Los Angeles. Center/guard California Western 1968-1970. No pro playing experience. College coach: California Western 1970-72, Iowa State 1973-74, Southern Methodist 1975-76, Pacific 1977-78, Northern Arizona 1979, Southern Methodist 1980-81. Pro coach: New England Patriots 1982-88, Indianapolis Colts 1989-1990, re-joined Patriots in 1991.

American Football Conference
East Division
Team Colors: Green and White
1 Jets Drive
Florham Park, New Jersey 07932
Telephone (973) 549-4800

2011 SCHEDULE
PRESEASON
Aug. 15	at Houston	8:00
Aug. 21	**Cincinnati**	7:00
Aug. 27	at New York Giants	7:00
Sep. 1	**Philadelphia**	7:30

REGULAR SEASON
Sep. 11	**Dallas**	8:20
Sep. 18	**Jacksonville**	1:00
Sep. 25	at Oakland	4:05
Oct. 2	at Baltimore	8:20
Oct. 9	at New England	4:15
Oct. 17	**Miami** (Mon)	8:30
Oct. 23	**San Diego**	1:00
Oct. 30	BYE	
Nov. 6	at Buffalo	1:00
Nov. 13	**New England** *	8:20
Nov. 17	at Denver (Thu)	8:20
Nov. 27	**Buffalo**	1:00
Dec. 4	at Washington	1:00
Dec. 11	**Kansas City**	1:00
Dec. 18	at Philadelphia	4:15
Dec. 24	**New York Giants** (Sat)	1:00
Jan. 1	at Miami	1:00

*All times ET; Sunday night games in
Weeks 11-15, 17 subject to change*

Stadium: New Meadowlands Stadium
(opened in 2010)
•**Capacity:** 82,500
East Rutherford, New Jersey
07073
Playing Surface: FieldTurf
Training Camp: SUNY Cortland
Cortland, New York 13045

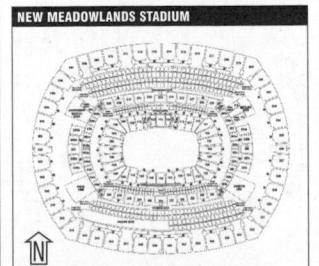

NEW MEADOWLANDS STADIUM

CLUB OFFICIALS
Chairman and CEO:
Robert Wood Johnson IV
Executive V.P., Business Operations:
Matt Higgins
Executive V.P., Finance & Stadium
Development: Thad Sheely
Executive V.P./General Manager:
Mike Tannenbaum
Assistant General Manager: Scott Cohen
Chief Financial Officer: Brian Friedman
Associate General Counsel/ Director,
Legal Affairs: Hymie Elhai
V.P., College Scouting: Joey Clinkscales
Senior V.P., Broadcasting & Production:
Bob Parente
V.P., Corporate Sales: Marc Riccio
V.P., Consumer Sales & Service:
Robert Sullivan
V.P., Security: Steve Yarnell
Senior Personnel Executive:
Terry Bradway
Assistant Director, Player Personnel:
JoJo Wooden
Director, Pro Personnel:
Brendan Prophett
Assistant, Pro Personnel: Cole Hufnagel
Assistant Director, College Scouting:
Michael Davis
Coordinator, College Scouting:
Dan Zbojovsky
National Scouts: Jim Cochran,
Brock Sunderland
Personnel Scouts: Jeff Bauer,
Matt Bazirgan, Joe Bommarito,
Jay Mandolesi
Assistant, Player Personnel:
Kathryn Smith
Director, Football Administration:
Ari Nissim
Manager, Football Administration:
Jacqueline Davidson
Senior Director, Athletic Training:
John Mellody
Assistant Athletic Trainers: Josh Koch,
Dave Zuffelato
Senior Director, Sales: Bob Brennfleck
Senior Director, Multimedia & Production:
Rich Gentile
Senior Director, Ticket Operations:
Jeff Hecker
Senior Director, Corporate Partnerships:
Jennifer Linn
Senior Director, IT: Tom Murphy
Senior Director, Merchandising:
Chris Pierce
Senior Director, Media Relations:
Bruce Speight
Senior Director, Marketing:
Victoria Vitarelli
Director, Equipment: Gus Granneman
Manager, Equipment: Vito Contento
Assistant Manager, Equipment:
Jim Gallione
Assistant, Equipment: Brendan Burger
Director, Community Relations:
Jesse Linder
Director, Events & Game Operations:
Brian Mulligan
Director, Player Development: David Szott
Director, Video: Tim Tubito

COACHING HISTORY
New York Titans 1960-62
(363-426-8)
Records include postseason games
1960-61	Sammy Baugh	14-14-0
1962	Clyde (Bulldog) Turner	5-9-0
1963-1973	Weeb Ewbank	73-78-6
1974-75	Charley Winner*	9-14-0
1975	Ken Shipp	1-4-0
1976	Lou Holtz**	3-10-0
1976	Mike Holovak	0-1-0
1977-1982	Walt Michaels	41-49-1
1983-89	Joe Walton	54-59-1
1990-93	Bruce Coslet	26-39-0
1994	Pete Carroll	6-10-0
1995-96	Rich Kotite	4-28-0
1997-99	Bill Parcells	30-20-0
2000	Al Groh	9-7-0
2001-05	Herman Edwards	41-44-0
2006-08	Eric Mangini	23-26-0
2009-2010	Rex Ryan	24-14-0

*Released after nine games in 1975
**Resigned after 13 games in 1976

PAID ATTENDANCE
Home 581,348   Away 531,391
Total 1,112,739
Single-game home record,
79,572 (11/19/06)
Single-season home record,
628,773 (2002)

2011 DRAFT CHOICES
Round	Name	Pos.	College
1	Muhammad Wilkerson	DT	Temple
3	Kenrick Ellis	DT	Hampton
4	Bilal Powell	RB	Louisville
5	Jeremy Kerley	WR	Texas Christian
7	Greg McElroy	QB	Alabama
	Scotty McKnight	WR	Colorado

2010 TEAM RECORD
PRESEASON (2-2)

Date	Result	Opponent
8/16	L 16-31	New York Giants
8/21	W 9-3	at Carolina
8/27	L 11-16	Washington
9/2	W 21-17	at Philadelphia

REGULAR SEASON (11-5)

Date	Result	Opponent
9/13	L 9-10	Baltimore
9/19	W 28-14	New England
9/26	W 31-23	at Miami
10/3	W 38-14	at Buffalo
10/11	W 29-20	Minnesota
10/17	W 24-20	at Denver
10/31	L 0-9	Green Bay
11/7	W 23-20	at Detroit (OT)
11/14	W 26-20	at Cleveland (OT)
11/21	W 30-27	Houston
11/25	W 26-10	Cincinnati
12/6	L 3-45	at New England
12/12	L 6-10	Miami
12/19	W 22-17	at Pittsburgh
12/26	L 34-38	at Chicago
1/2	W 38-7	Buffalo

POSTSEASON (2-1)

Date	Result	Opponent
1/8	W 17-16	at Indianapolis
1/16	W 28-21	at New England
1/23	L 19-24	at Pittsburgh

(OT) Overtime

SCORE BY PERIODS

Jets	36	127	90	105	9	—	367
Opponents	57	89	75	83	0	—	304

2010 TEAM STATISTICS

	Jets	Opp.
Total First Downs	307	272
Rushing	118	70
Passing	171	169
Penalty	18	33
3rd Down: Made/Att	93/235	81/219
3rd Down Pct.	39.6	37.0
4th Down: Made/Att	5/14	4/6
4th Down Pct.	35.7	66.7
Possession Avg.	32:03	27:57
Total Net Yards	5616	4664
Avg. Per Game	351.0	291.5
Total Plays	1087	979
Avg. Per Play	5.2	4.8
Net Yards Rushing	2374	1454
Avg. Per Game	148.4	90.9
Total Rushes	534	408
Net Yards Passing	3242	3210
Avg. Per Game	202.6	200.6
Sacked/Yards Lost	28/178	40/244
Gross Yards	3420	3454
Att./Completions	525/288	531/269
Completion Pct.	54.9	50.7
Had Intercepted	14	12
Punts/Average	84/42.6	97/45.2
Net Punting Avg.	84/38.1	97/39.0
Penalties/Yards	103/934	74/679
Fumbles/Ball Lost	23/7	25/18
Touchdowns	39	36
Rushing	14	11
Passing	20	24
Returns	5	1

2010 INDIVIDUAL STATISTICS

PASSING

	Att.	Comp.	Yds.	Pct.	TD	Int.	Tkld.	Rate
Sanchez	507	278	3291	54.8	17	13	27/171	75.3
Brunell	13	7	117	53.8	2	1	1/7	92.0
B. Smith	3	2	6	66.7	1	0	0/0	109.7
Clemens	2	1	6	50.0	0	0	0/0	56.3
Jets	525	288	3420	54.9	20	14	28/178	76.5
Opponents	531	269	3454	50.7	24	12	40/244	77.1

SCORING

	TD R	TD P	TD Rt	PAT	FG	Saf	PTS
Folk	0	0	0	37/37	30/39	0	127
Edwards	0	7	0	0/0	0/0	0	44
Holmes	0	6	0	0/0	0/0	0	36
Tomlinson	6	0	0	0/0	0/0	0	36
Keller	0	5	0	0/0	0/0	0	30
Sanchez	3	0	0	0/0	0/0	0	18
B. Smith	1	0	2	0/0	0/0	0	18
Cotchery	0	2	0	0/0	0/0	0	12
Greene	2	0	0	0/0	0/0	0	12
Lowery	0	0	2	0/0	0/0	0	12
Clemens	1	0	0	0/0	0/0	0	6
Cole	0	0	1	0/0	0/0	0	6
Conner	1	0	0	0/0	0/0	0	6
Pryce	0	0	0	0/0	0/0	1	2
J. Taylor	0	0	0	0/0	0/0	1	2
Jets	14	20	5	37/37	30/39	2	367
Opponents	11	24	1	34/35	18/23	0	304

2-Pt Conversions: Edwards.

Jets 1-1, Opponents 0-1.

RUSHING

	No.	Yds	Avg	LG	TD
Tomlinson	219	914	4.2	31	6
Greene	185	766	4.1	36	2
B. Smith	38	299	7.9	53t	1
McKnight	39	189	4.8	18	0
Sanchez	30	105	3.5	20	3
Conner	8	44	5.5	16t	1
Holmes	2	17	8.5	14	0
Weatherford	1	17	17.0	17	0
Richardson	5	13	2.6	4	0
Clemens	2	9	4.5	10t	1
Edwards	1	4	4.0	4	0
Cotchery	4	-3	-.8	4	0
Jets	534	2374	4.4	53t	14
Opponents	408	1454	3.6	32	11

RECEIVING

	No.	Yds	Avg	LG	TD
Keller	55	687	12.5	41	5
Edwards	53	904	17.1	74t	7
Holmes	52	746	14.3	52	6
Tomlinson	52	368	7.1	21	0
Cotchery	41	433	10.6	49	2
Greene	16	120	7.5	15	0
Richardson	5	31	6.2	14	0
B. Smith	4	44	11.0	23	0
McKnight	3	20	6.7	9	0
P. Turner	2	26	13.0	21	0
Conner	2	9	4.5	7	0
Clowney	1	22	22.0	22	0
Hartsock	1	7	7.0	7	0
Cumberland	1	3	3.0	3	0
Jets	288	3420	11.9	74t	20
Opponents	269	3454	12.8	50	24

PUNTING

	No.	Yds.	Avg.	In 20	LG
Weatherford	84	3581	42.6	42	61
Jets	84	3581	42.6	42	61
Opponents	97	4388	45.2	26	69

INTERCEPTIONS

	No.	Yds	Avg	LG	TD
Lowery	3	87	29.0	41	2
Cromartie	3	75	25.0	66	0
Cole	2	49	24.5	35t	1
Leonhard	1	2	2.0	2	0
Pace	1	1	1.0	1	0
Coleman	1	0	0.0	0	0
Pool	1	0	0.0	0	0
Jets	12	214	17.8	66	3
Opponents	14	134	9.6	37t	1

PUNT RETURNS

	Ret	FC	Yds	Avg	LG	TD
Leonhard	21	19	238	11.3	32	0
Wilson	15	2	111	7.4	18	0
Cotchery	8	4	66	8.3	19	0
Cromartie	5	0	36	7.2	16	0
Holmes	4	0	40	10.0	14	0
McKnight	2	0	43	21.5	25	0
Cole	1	0	-5	-5.0	-5	0
Jets	56	25	529	9.4	32	0
Opponents	27	27	299	11.1	38	0

KICKOFF RETURNS

	No.	Yds	Avg	LG	TD
B. Smith	50	1432	28.6	97t	2
Conner	3	35	11.7	18	0
McKnight	3	60	20.0	28	0
Lowery	2	26	13.0	14	0
Wilson	2	22	11.0	15	0
Cromartie	1	-6	-6.0	-6	0
Mulligan	1	8	8.0	8	0
R. Turner	1	11	11.0	11	0
Jets	63	1588	25.2	97t	2
Opponents	73	1428	19.6	44	0

FIELD GOALS

	1-19	20-29	30-39	40-49	50+
Folk	1/1	10/11	14/16	3/6	2/5
Jets	1/1	10/11	14/16	3/6	2/5
Opponents	0/0	6/7	3/5	7/9	2/2

SACKS

	No.
Thomas	6.0
Pace	5.5
J. Taylor	5.0
Ellis	4.5
Coleman	4.0
Harris	3.0
Ihedigbo	3.0
Lowery	2.0
Pouha	2.0
Dixon	1.0
Pool	1.0
Pryce	1.0
Scott	1.0
E. Smith	1.0
Jets	40.0
Opponents	28.0

RECORD HOLDERS
INDIVIDUAL RECORDS—CAREER

Category	Name	Performance
Rushing (Yds.)	Curtis Martin, 1998-2005	10,302
Passing (Yds.)	Joe Namath, 1965-1976	27,057
Passing (TDs)	Joe Namath, 1965-1976	170
Receiving (No.)	Don Maynard, 1960-1972	627
Receiving (Yds.)	Don Maynard, 1960-1972	11,732
Interceptions	Bill Baird, 1963-69	34
Punting (Avg.)	Ben Graham, 2005-08	43.7
Punt Return (Avg.)	Dick Christy, 1961-63	16.2
Kickoff Return (Avg.)	Leon Burton, 1960	28.7
Field Goals	Pat Leahy, 1974-1991	304
Touchdowns (Tot.)	Don Maynard, 1960-1972	88
Points	Pat Leahy, 1974-1991	1,470
*Sacks	Mark Gastineau, 1979-1988	74.0

INDIVIDUAL RECORDS—SINGLE SEASON

Category	Name	Performance
Rushing (Yds.)	Curtis Martin, 2004	1,697
Passing (Yds.)	Joe Namath, 1967	4,007
Passing (TDs)	Vinny Testaverde, 1998	29
Receiving (No.)	Al Toon, 1988	93
Receiving (Yds.)	Don Maynard, 1967	1,434
Interceptions	Dainard Paulson, 1964	12
Punting (Avg.)	Curley Johnson, 1965	45.3
Punt Return (Avg.)	Dick Christy, 1961	21.3
Kickoff Return (Avg.)	Bobby Humphery, 1984	30.7
Field Goals	Jim Turner, 1968	34
Touchdowns (Tot.)	Thomas Jones, 2008	15
Points	Jim Turner, 1968	145
*Sacks	Mark Gastineau, 1984	22.0

INDIVIDUAL RECORDS—SINGLE GAME

Category	Name	Performance
Rushing (Yds.)	Thomas Jones, 10-18-09	210
Passing (Yds.)	Joe Namath, 9-24-72	496
Passing (TDs)	Joe Namath, 9-24-72	6
	Brett Favre, 9-28-08	6
Receiving (No.)	Clark Gaines, 9-21-80	17
Receiving (Yds.)	Don Maynard, 11-17-68	228
Interceptions	Many times	3
	Last time by Ty Law, 1-1-06	
Field Goals	Jim Turner, 11-3-68	6
	Bobby Howfield, 12-3-72	6
Touchdowns (Tot.)	Wesley Walker, 9-21-86	4
Points	Wesley Walker, 9-21-86	24
*Sacks	Mark Gastineau, 11-6-83, 9-2-84	4.0
	John Abraham, 11-4-01	4.0

Sacks became an official statistic in 1982.

VETERAN ROSTER AS OF MARCH 3, 2011

No.	Name	Pos.	Ht.	Wt.	Birthdate	^NFL Exp.	College	Hometown	How Acq.	'10 Games/ Starts
3	Ainge, Erik	QB	6-5	221	6/12/86	3	Tennessee	Hillsboro, Ore.	D5-'08	0*
51	Brown, Cody	LB	6-3	252	11/9/86	2	Connecticut	Coral Springs, Fla.	FA-'10	0*
8	Brunell, Mark	QB	6-1	215	9/17/70	19	Washington	Santa Maria, Calif.	FA-'10	2/0
11	Clemens, Kellen	QB	6-2	220	6/7/83	6	Oregon	Burns, Ore.	D2-'06	1/0
34	Cole, Marquice	CB	5-10	192	11/13/83	3	Northwestern	Hazel Crest, Ill.	FA-'09	12/1
30	Coleman, Drew	CB	5-9	180	4/22/83	6	Texas Christian	Henderson, Texas	D6-'06	16/4
38	Conner, John	FB	5-11	245	6/8/87	2	Kentucky	West Chester, Ohio	D5-'10	16/0
27	Cook, Emanuel	S	5-10	202	1/20/88	2	South Carolina	Riviera Beach, Fla.	FA-'10	4/0
89	Cotchery, Jerricho	WR	6-0	203	6/16/82	8	North Carolina State	Birmingham, Ala.	D4a-'04	14/5
31	Cromartie, Antonio	CB	6-2	210	4/15/84	6	Florida State	Tallahassee, Fla.	T(SD)-'10	15/15
86	Cumberland, Jeff	TE	6-4	260	5/2/87	2	Illinois	Columbus, Ohio	FA-'10	1/0
70	DeVito, Mike	DE	6-3	305	6/10/84	5	Maine	Wellfleet, Mass.	FA-'07	16/11
94	Dixon, Marcus	DT	6-4	295	9/16/84	2	Hampton	Rome, Ga.	W(Dall)-'10	3/1
62	Ducasse, Vladimir	OL	6-5	325	10/15/87	2	Massachusetts	Stamford, Conn.	D2-'10	2/0
17	Edwards, Braylon	WR	6-3	214	2/21/83	7	Michigan	Detroit, Mich.	T(Cle)-'09	16/15
92	Ellis, Shaun	DE	6-5	290	6/24/77	12	Tennessee	Anderson, S.C.	D1a-'00	15/15
60	Ferguson, D'Brickashaw	T	6-6	310	12/10/83	6	Virginia	Freeport, N.Y.	D1a-'06	16/16
2	Folk, Nick	K	6-1	222	11/5/84	5	Arizona	Hollywood, Calif.	FA-'10	16/0
71	Gilbert, Jarron	DT	6-5	285	10/30/86	3	San Jose State	New Orleans, La.	FA-'10	1/0
23	Greene, Shonn	RB	5-11	226	8/21/85	3	Iowa	Sicklerville, N.J.	D3-'09	15/2
52	Harris, David	LB	6-2	250	1/21/84	5	Michigan	Grand Rapids, Mich.	D2-'07	16/16
10	Holmes, Santonio	WR	5-11	192	3/3/84	6	Ohio State	Belle Glade, Fla.	T(Pitt)-'10	12/10
78	Hunter, Wayne	T	6-5	318	7/2/81	8	Hawai'i	Honolulu, Hawai'i	FA-'07	14/4
44	Ihedigbo, James	S	6-1	214	12/3/83	5	Massachusetts	Amherst, Mass.	FA-'08	14/0
	Jennings, Chris	RB	5-10	218	12/12/85	2	Arizona	Huntington, W. Va.	FA-'11	0*
81	Keller, Dustin	TE	6-2	250	9/25/84	4	Purdue	Lafayette, Ind.	D1b-'08	16/13
98	Kroul, Matt	DL	6-3	300	2/25/86	2	Iowa	Mount Vernon, Iowa	FA-'08	6/0
	Lankster, Ellis	CB	5-9	190	6/3/87	2	West Virginia	Whistler, Ala.	FA-'11	0*
	LaRocque, Joey	LB	6-2	228	3/15/86	2	Oregon State	Valencia, Calif.	FA-'11	0*
56	Laury, Lance	LB	6-2	242	1/17/82	6	South Carolina	Hopkins, S.C.	FA-'10	16/0
36	Leonhard, Jim	S	5-8	188	10/27/82	7	Wisconsin	Ladysmith, Wisc.	UFA(Balt)-'09	11/11
26	Lowery, Dwight	CB	5-11	198	1/23/86	4	San Jose State	Santa Cruz, Calif.	D4-'08	14/3
74	Mangold, Nick	C	6-4	307	1/13/84	6	Ohio State	Centerville, Ohio	D1b-'06	16/16
53	Mauga, Josh	LB	6-1	245	6/20/87	2	Nevada	Fallon, Nev.	FA-'08	8/0
25	McKnight, Joe	RB	5-11	205	4/16/88	2	Southern California	River Ridge, La.	D4-'10	9/1
65	Moore, Brandon	G	6-3	305	6/3/80	9	Illinois	Gary, Ind.	FA-'03	16/16
82	Mulligan, Matthew	TE	6-4	265	1/18/85	3	Maine	West Enfield, Maine	W(Tenn)-'09	13/1
	Novak, Nick	K	6-0	198	8/21/81	4	Maryland	Charlottesville, Va.	FA-'11	0*
7	O'Connell, Kevin	QB	6-5	225	5/25/85	4	San Diego State	Carlsbad, Calif.	T(Det)-'09	0*
97	Pace, Calvin	LB	6-4	265	10/28/80	9	Wake Forest	Douglasville, Ga.	UFA(Ariz)-'08	12/11
18	Payne, Logan	WR	6-2	205	1/21/85	2	Minnesota	Lutz, Fla.	FA-'10	0*
79	Pitoitua, Ropati	DE	6-8	315	4/6/85	3	Washington State	Spanaway, Wash.	FA-'08	0*
22	Pool, Brodney	S	6-2	214	5/24/84	7	Oklahoma	Corpus Christi, Texas	FA-'10	15/12
91	Pouha, Sione	DT	6-3	325	2/3/79	7	Utah	Salt Lake City, Utah	D3-'05	16/15
93	Pryce, Trevor	DE	6-5	290	8/3/75	15	Clemson	Brooklyn, N.Y.	FA-'10	13/0*
46	Purdum, Tanner	LS	6-3	270	8/15/84	2	Baker	Enid, Okla.	FA-'09	16/0
24	Revis, Darrelle	CB	5-11	198	7/14/85	5	Pittsburgh	Aliquippa, Pa.	D1-'07	13/13
49	Richardson, Tony	FB	6-1	240	12/17/71	17	Auburn	Daleville, Ala.	UFA(Minn)-'08	16/10
6	Sanchez, Mark	QB	6-2	225	11/11/86	3	Southern California	Mission Viejo, Calif.	D1-'09	16/16
57	Scott, Bart	LB	6-2	242	8/18/80	10	Southern Illinois	Detroit, Mich.	UFA(Balt)-'09	16/16
68	Slauson, Matt	G	6-5	315	2/18/86	3	Nebraska	Colorado Springs, Colo.	D6-'09	16/16
16	Smith, Brad	WR	6-2	212	12/28/83	6	Missouri	Youngstown, Ohio	D4a-'06	16/2
33	Smith, Eric	S	6-1	207	3/17/83	6	Michigan State	Groveport, Ohio	D3b-06	13/6
58	Thomas, Bryan	LB	6-4	265	6/7/79	10	Alabama-Birmingham	Birmingham, Ala.	D1-'02	16/12
21	Tomlinson, LaDainian	RB	5-10	215	6/23/79	11	Texas Christian	Rosebud, Texas	FA-'10	15/13
88	Turner, Patrick	WR	6-5	220	5/19/87	3	Southern California	Nashville, Tenn.	W(Mia)-'10	5/0
75	Turner, Robert	OL	6-4	308	8/20/84	4	New Mexico	Austin, Texas	FA-'07	16/0
9	Weatherford, Steve	P	6-3	215	12/17/82	6	Illinois	Terre Haute, Ind.	FA-'09	16/0
55	Westerman, Jamaal	LB	6-3	255	2/21/85	3	Rutgers	Brampton, Ontario, Canada	FA-'09	6/0
20	Wilson, Kyle	CB	5-10	190	5/30/87	2	Boise State	Piscataway, N.J.	D1-'10	16/6

* Ainge missed '10 season on the non-football injury list; C. Brown spent '10 season on the Jets practice squad, missed '09 season because of an injury with Arizona; Jennings last active with Cleveland in '09; Lankster last active with Buffalo in '09; LaRocque last active with Chicago in '08; Novak last active with Kansas City in '08; O'Connell missed '10 season because of injury; Payne spent '10 season on the Jets practice squad; Pitoitua missed '10 season because of an injury; Pryce played 3 games with Baltimore and 10 games for New York Jets.

Also played with Jets in '10—WR David Clowney (3 games), LB Kenwin Cummings (5), DE Vernon Gholston (16), DT Howard Green (2), TE Ben Hartsock (16), DT Kris Jenkins (1), LB Jason Taylor (16), CB Isaiah Trufant (1), RB Danny Woodhead (1), T Damien Woody (13).

^ "NFL Exp." as of 2011 Kickoff Weekend. For full explanation of how a player's NFL Experience is measured, refer to explanation underneath the First-Year Roster listed below.

FIRST-YEAR ROSTER

Name	Pos.	Ht.	Wt.	Birthdate	College	Hometown	How Acq.
Billingsley, Will (1)	DB	5-10	195	4/23/84	North Carolina A&T	Fort Wayne, Ind.	FA
Brown, Carlos (1)	RB	6-0	210	4/28/88	Michigan	Franklin, Ga.	FA
Conley, T.J. (1)	P	6-3	220	8/29/85	Idaho	Walla Walla, Wash.	FA
Davis, Marlon (1)	G	6-3	305	11/5/86	Alabama	Columbus, Ga.	FA
Ellis, Kenrick	DT	6-4	346	12/10/87	Hampton	Greenacres, Fla.	D3
Felix, Robby (1)	C	6-3	295	6/3/86	Texas-El Paso	Corona, Calif.	FA
Kerley, Jeremy	WR	5-9	188	11/8/88	Texas Christian	Hutto, Texas	D5
Landolt, Dennis (1)	G	6-4	306	10/15/86	Penn State	Burlington, N.J.	FA
Long, Brandon (1)	LB	6-3	254	9/6/86	Michigan State	Canton, Ohio	FA
McElroy, Greg	QB	6-2	225	5/10/88	Alabama	Southlake, Texas	D7a
McIntyre, Garrett (1)	LB	6-3	270	11/26/84	Fresno State	South Lake Tahoe, Calif.	FA
McKnight, Scotty	WR	5-11	185	2/11/88	Colorado	Coto de Caza, Calif.	D7b
Powell, Bilal	RB	5-10	204	10/27/88	Louisville	Lakeland, Fla.	D4
Powell, Carlton (1)	DT	6-2	312	8/14/85	Virginia Tech	Chesapeake, Va.	FA
Satele, Brashton (1)	LB	6-0	248	11/8/87	Hawai'i	Mililani, Hawai'i	FA
Taylor, Richard (1)	DB	5-11	190	11/5/85	Maryland	Centreville, Va.	FA
Tevaseu, Martin (1)	DT	6-2	325	10/7/87	Nevada-Las Vegas	Oakland, Calif.	FA
Toal, Brian (1)	LB	6-0	238	3/8/85	Boston College	Wyckoff, N.J.	FA
Washington, Lorenzo (1)	DE	6-4	296	12/2/86	Alabama	Loganville, Ga.	FA
Wilkerson, Muhammad	DL	6-4	315	10/29/89	Temple	Linden, N.J.	D1
Willy, Drew (1)	QB	6-3	217	11/13/86	Buffalo	Randolph, N.J.	FA

The term NFL Rookie is defined as a player who is in his first season of professional football and has not been on the roster of another professional football team for any regular-season or postseason games. A Rookie is designated by an "R" on NFL rosters. Players who have been active in another professional football league or players who have NFL experience, including either preseason training camp or being on an Active List or Inactive List, or on Reserve/Injured or Reserve/Physically Unable to Perform for fewer than six regular-season games, are termed NFL First-Year Players. An NFL First-Year Player is designated by a "1" on NFL rosters. Thereafter, a player is credited with an additional year of experience for each season in which he accumulates six games on the Active List or Inactive List, or on Reserve/Injured or Reserve/Physically Unable to Perform.

Log on to www.newyorkjets.com for an up-to-date roster.

COACHING STAFF

Head Coach,
Rex Ryan

Pro Career: Named the 15th full-time head coach of the New York Jets on January 19, 2009. In 2010, directed team to 11 regular season victories and became second coach in NFL history to guide team to the conference championship game in his first two seasons after inheriting a team that did not reach the playoffs the year prior to him becoming head coach. The defense ranked third in the league in total yards and rushing yards allowed. In 2009, led team to 9-7 record and AFC Championship game with offense that ranked first in the NFL in rushing yards per game and defense that finished first in total defense, points allowed and passing defense. Ryan spent 10 seasons with the Baltimore Ravens, including 2008 as the assistant head coach/defensive coordinator. Since becoming defensive coordinator in 2005, the Ravens never finished lower than sixth in total defense. From 1999-2008, the Ravens ranked first in the NFL for fewest points allowed, fewest rushing yards allowed, most takeaways, most interceptions and most interceptions returned for touchdowns. Ravens allowed fewest points in NFL history for 16-game season (165) in 2000 en route to winning Super Bowl XXXV. Began NFL career with Arizona under his father, Buddy Ryan, as coach for defensive line (1994) and linebackers (1995). Career record: 24-14.

Background: Coached at Eastern Kentucky (1987-88), New Mexico Highlands (1989), Morehead State (1990-93), Cincinnati (1996-97) and Oklahoma (1998). Played defensive end at Southwestern Oklahoma State with his twin brother, Rob, who is currently the Cleveland defensive coordinator. Earned his Bachelor's and Master's Degree in Physical Education at Eastern Kentucky.

Personal: Born December 13, 1963, Ardmore, Okla. Ryan and his wife Michelle have two sons, Payton and Seth.

ASSISTANT COACHES

Bill Callahan, asst. head coach/offensive line; born July, 31 1956, Chicago. Quarterback Benedictine 1975-77. No pro playing experience. College coach: Illinois 1980-86, Northern Arizona 1987-88, Southern Illinois 1989, Wisconsin 1990-94, Nebraska 2004-2007 (head coach). Pro coach: Philadelphia Eagles 1995-97, Oakland Raiders 1998-2003 (head coach 2002-03), joined Jets in 2008.

Mark Carrier, defensive line; born April 28, 1968, Lake Charles, La. Defensive back Southern California 1987-89. Pro defensive back Chicago Bears 1990-96, Detroit Lions 1997-99, Washington Redskins 2000. College coach: Arizona State 2004-05. Pro coach: Baltimore Ravens 2006-09, joined Jets in 2010.

Matt Cavanaugh, quarterbacks; born October 27, 1956, Youngstown, Ohio. Quarterback Pittsburgh 1974-77. Pro quarterback New England Patriots 1978-1982, San Francisco 49ers 1983-85, Philadelphia Eagles 1986-89, New York Giants 1990-91. College coach: Pittsburgh 1991-93, 2005-08. Pro coach: Arizona Cardinals 1994-95, San Francisco 49ers 1996, Chicago Bears 1997-98, Baltimore Ravens 1999-2004, joined Jets in 2009.

Bryan Dermody, asst. strength and conditioning; born April 4, 1979, Greenfield, Wisc. Outside linebacker Lakeland College 1997-2001. No pro playing experience. College coach: Iowa 2002-05, Drake 2006, Louisville 2006-2009. Pro coach: Joined Jets in 2010.

Mike Devlin, tight ends/asst. offensive line; born November 16, 1969, Blacksburg, Va. Offensive line Iowa 1989-1992. Pro offensive lineman Buffalo Bills 1993-95, Arizona Cardinals 1996-99. College coach: Toledo 2004-05. Pro coach: Arizona Cardinals 2000-03, joined Jets in 2006.

Henry Ellard, wide receivers; born July 21, 1961, Fresno, Calif. Wide receiver Fresno State 1979-1982. Pro wide receiver/punt returner Los Angeles Rams 1983-1993, Washington Redskins 1994-98, New England Patriots 1998. College coach: Fresno State 2000. Pro coach: St. Louis Rams 2001-08, joined Jets in 2009.

Bill Hughan, head strength and conditioning; born February 8, 1975, Oxford, Conn. Attended Springfield College. No college or pro playing experience. College coach: Yale 1997-98, Columbia 1999-2000, Missouri 2001-03. Pro coach: Oakland Raiders 2004-07, Atlanta Falcons 2008-10, joined Jets in 2010.

Ben Kotwica, asst. special teams; born December 8, 1974, Tinley Park, Ill. Linebacker Army 1995-97. No pro playing experience. Pro coach: Joined Jets in 2007.

Anthony Lynn, running backs; born December 21, 1968, McKinney, Texas. Running back Texas Tech 1987-1991. Pro running back Denver Broncos 1993, 1997-99, San Francisco 49ers 1995-96. Pro coach: Denver Broncos 2000-02, Jacksonville Jaguars 2003-04, Dallas Cowboys 2005-06, Cleveland Browns 2007-08, joined Jets in 2009.

Jim O'Neil, asst. defensive backs; born Oct. 26, 1978, Philadelphia. Defensive end Towson University 1997-2000. No pro playing experience. College coach: SUNY-Albany 2001, Pennsylvania 2002, Northwestern 2003-04, Towson University 2005, Eastern Michigan 2006-08. Pro coach: Joined Jets in 2009.

Mike Pettine, defensive coordinator; born September 25, 1966, Doylestown, Pa. Safety Virginia 1984-87. No pro playing experience. College coach: Pittsburgh 1993-94. Pro coach: Baltimore Ravens

2003-08, joined Jets in 2009.

Brian Schottenheimer, offensive coordinator; born October 16, 1973, Denver. Quarterback Kansas 1992, Florida 1993-96. No pro playing experience. College coach: Syracuse 1999, Southern California 2000. Pro coach: St. Louis Rams 1997, Kansas City Chiefs 1998, Washington Redskins 2001, San Diego Chargers 2002-05, joined Jets in 2006.

Bob Sutton, senior defensive assistant/linebackers; born January 28, 1951, Ypsilanti, Mich. Attended Eastern Michigan. No college or pro playing experience. College coach: Michigan 1972-73, Syracuse 1974, Western Michigan 1975-76, 1980-81, Illinois 1977-79, North Carolina State 1982, Army 1983-1999 (head coach 1991-99). Pro coach: Joined Jets in 2000.

Lance Taylor, quality control/offense; born July 17, 1981, Mobile, Ala. Wide receiver Alabama 2000-2003. No pro playing experience. College coach: Alabama 2008, Appalachian State 2009. Pro Coach: Joined Jets in 2010.

Dennis Thurman, defensive backs; born April 13, 1956, Los Angeles, Calif. Defensive back Southern California 1974-77. Pro defensive back Dallas Cowboys 1978-1985, St. Louis Cardinals 1986, Phoenix Cardinals 1988-89. College coach: Southern California 1993-2000. Pro coach: Ohio Glory (WLAF) 1992, Baltimore Ravens 2002-07, joined Jets in 2009.

Jeff Weeks, outside linebackers; born May 30, 1962, Denver. Wide receiver Southwest Oklahoma State 1982-84, Northwest Oklahoma State 1985. No pro playing experience. College coach: Western Kentucky 1987-88, Morehead State 1990-91, Phoenix CC 1996, Oklahoma 1999, Fort Scott (Kan.) C.C. 2001-04, Southeast Oklahoma State 2005, Texas A&M- Kingsville 2006. Pro coach: Oakland Raiders 2008, joined Jets in 2009.

Mike Westhoff, special teams coordinator; born January 10, 1948, Pittsburgh. Linebacker Wyoming 1965, center/linebacker Wichita State 1967-69. No pro playing experience. College coach: Indiana 1974-75, Dayton 1976, Indiana State 1977, Northwestern 1978-1980, Texas Christian 1981. Pro coach: Baltimore Colts 1982-83, Indianapolis Colts 1984, Arizona Outlaws (USFL) 1985, Miami Dolphins 1986-2000, joined Jets in 2001.

**American Football Conference
West Division**
Team Colors: Silver and Black
**1220 Harbor Bay Parkway
Alameda, California 94502**
Telephone: (510) 864-5000

2011 SCHEDULE
PRESEASON
Aug. 11	**Arizona**	8:00
Aug. 20	at San Francisco	5:00
Aug. 28	**New Orleans**	5:00
Sep. 2	at Seattle	7:30

REGULAR SEASON
Sep. 12	at Denver (Mon)	7:15
Sep. 18	at Buffalo	10:00a
Sep. 25	**New York Jets**	1:05
Oct. 2	**New England**	1:15
Oct. 9	at Houston	10:00a
Oct. 16	**Cleveland**	1:05
Oct. 23	**Kansas City**	1:05
Oct. 30	BYE	
Nov. 6	**Denver**	1:05
Nov. 10	at San Diego (Thu)	5:20
Nov. 20	at Minnesota	10:00a
Nov. 27	**Chicago**	1:05
Dec. 4	at Miami	10:00a
Dec. 11	at Green Bay	10:00a
Dec. 18	**Detroit**	1:05
Dec. 24	at Kansas City (Sat)	10:00a
Jan. 1	**San Diego**	1:15

All times CT

Stadium: Oakland Coliseum
(opened in 1966)
• **Capacity:** 63,132
7000 Coliseum Way
Oakland, CA 94621-1917
Playing Surface: Grass
Training Camp: Napa Valley Marriott
Napa, California 94558

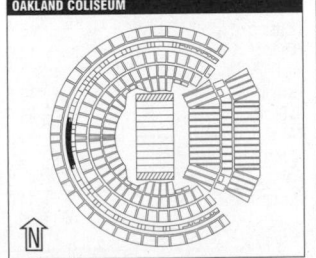

OAKLAND COLISEUM

CLUB OFFICIALS
Owner: Al Davis
Chief Executive: Amy Trask
Legal: Jeff Birren, Dan Ventrelle
Finance: Marc Badain, Tom Blanda,
Derek Person, Ed Villanueva
Special Projects: Willie Brown, Jim Otto
Public Relations: John Herrera, Will Kiss,
Mike Taylor
Tickets, Suites & Premium Seats:
Mark Shearer
Internet: Jerry Knaak
Sponsorships: Airikuh Anderson,
Farnoush Ansari, Morris Bradshaw,
Robert Kinnard
Community Relations: Scott Fink
Youth Initiatives: Rosie Bone
Raiderettes: Jeanette Thompson
Trainers: Chris Cortez, H. Rod Martin,
Scott Touchet
Equipment: Danny Molina,
Bob Romanski, Richard Romanski
Video Operations: Dave Nash, Jim Otten,
John Otten
Broadcasting: Vittorio DeBartolo,
Brad Phinney, Jeanette Thompson
Computer Operations: Benny Hong,
Matthew Pasco, Shawn Testa

COACHING HISTORY
Oakland 1960-1981
Los Angeles 1982-1994
(443-361-11)
Records include postseason games
1960-61	Eddie Erdelatz*	6-10-0
1961-62	Marty Feldman**	2-15-0
1962	Red Conkright	1-8-0
1963-65	Al Davis	23-16-3
1966-68	John Rauch	35-10-1
1969-1978	John Madden	112-39-7
1979-1987	Tom Flores	91-56-0
1988-89	Mike Shanahan***	8-12-0
1989-1994	Art Shell	56-41-0
1995-96	Mike White	15-17-0
1997	Joe Bugel	4-12-0
1998-2001	Jon Gruden	40-28-0
2002-03	Bill Callahan	17-18-0
2004-05	Norv Turner	9-23-0
2006	Art Shell	2-14-0
2007-08	Lane Kiffin****	5-15-0
2008-2010	Tom Cable	17-27-0

* Released after two games in 1961
** Released after five games in 1962
*** Released after four games in 1989
**** Released after four games in 2008

PAID ATTENDANCE
Home 355,297   Away 520,972
Total 876,269
Single-game home record,
62,660 (11/3/02)
Single-season home record,
471,151 (2002)

2011 DRAFT CHOICES
Round	Name	Pos.	College
2	Stefen Wisniewski	C	Penn State
3	DeMarcus Van Dyke	DB	Miami
	Joe Barksdale	T	Louisiana State
4	Chimdi Chekwa	DB	Ohio State
	Taiwan Jones	RB	Eastern Washington
5	Denarius Moore	WR	Tennessee
6	Richard Gordon	TE	Miami
7	David Ausberry	WR	Southern California

2010 TEAM RECORD
PRESEASON (3-1)

Date	Result	Opponent
8/12	W 17-9	at Dallas
8/21	W 32-17	at Chicago
8/28	L 24-28	San Francisco
9/2	W 27-24	Seattle

REGULAR SEASON (8-8)

Date	Result	Opponent
9/12	L 13-38	at Tennessee
9/19	W 16-14	St. Louis
9/26	L 23-24	at Arizona
10/3	L 24-31	Houston
10/10	W 35-27	San Diego
10/17	L 9-17	at San Francisco
10/24	W 59-14	at Denver
10/31	W 33-3	Seattle
11/7	W 23-20	Kansas City (OT)
11/21	L 3-35	at Pittsburgh
11/28	L 17-33	Miami
12/5	W 28-13	at San Diego
12/12	L 31-38	at Jacksonville
12/19	W 39-23	Denver
12/26	L 26-31	Indianapolis
1/2	W 31-10	at Kansas City

(OT) Overtime

SCORE BY PERIODS

Raiders	117	90	78	122	3	—	410
Opponents	68	112	99	92	0	—	371

2010 TEAM STATISTICS

	Raiders	Opp.
Total First Downs	306	292
Rushing	113	98
Passing	159	150
Penalty	34	44
3rd Down: Made/Att	75/220	76/218
3rd Down Pct.	34.1	34.9
4th Down: Made/Att	8/20	3/11
4th Down Pct.	40.0	27.3
Possession Avg.	31:07	28:53
Total Net Yards	5674	5165
Avg. Per Game	354.6	322.8
Total Plays	1039	991
Avg. Per Play	5.5	5.2
Net Yards Rushing	2494	2138
Avg. Per Game	155.9	133.6
Total Rushes	504	474
Net Yards Passing	3180	3027
Avg. Per Game	198.8	189.2
Sacked/Yards Lost	44/291	47/292
Gross Yards	3471	3319
Att./Completions	491/279	470/249
Completion Pct.	56.8	53.0
Had Intercepted	16	12
Punts/Average	78/46.8	94/43.8
Net Punting Avg.	78/40.7	94/38.2
Penalties/Yards	148/1276	117/1161
Fumbles/Ball Lost	32/10	21/12
Touchdowns	44	44
Rushing	19	14
Passing	18	29
Returns	7	1

2010 INDIVIDUAL STATISTICS

PASSING	Att.	Comp.	Yds.	Pct.	TD	Int.	Tkld.	Rate
J. Campbell	329	194	2387	59.0	13	8	33/208	84.5
Gradkowski	157	83	1059	52.9	5	7	10/77	66.3
Boller	4	2	25	50.0	0	1	1/6	30.2
D. McFadden	1	0	0	0.0	0	0	0/0	39.6
Raiders	491	279	3471	56.8	18	16	44/291	77.5
Opponents	470	249	3319	53.0	29	12	47/292	85.6

	TD	TD	TD					
SCORING	R	P	Rt	PAT	FG	Saf	PTS	
Janikowski	0	0	0	43/43	33/41	0	142	
D. McFadden	7	3	0	0/0	0/0	0	60	
Bush	8	0	0	0/0	0/0	0	48	
Ford	2	2	3	0/0	0/0	0	42	
Z. Miller	0	5	0	0/0	0/0	0	30	
Reece	1	3	0	0/0	0/0	0	24	
Murphy	0	2	0	0/0	0/0	0	12	
Barnes	0	1	0	0/0	0/0	0	6	
Branch	0	1	0	0/0	0/0	0	6	
J. Campbell	1	0	0	0/0	0/0	0	6	
Eugene	0	0	1	0/0	0/0	0	6	
Heyward-Bey	0	1	0	0/0	0/0	0	6	
Johnson	0	0	1	0/0	0/0	0	6	
Routt	0	0	1	0/0	0/0	0	6	
Schilens	0	1	0	0/0	0/0	0	6	
Cartwright	0	0	0	0/0	0/0	1	2	
Groves	0	0	0	0/0	0/0	1	2	
Raiders	19	18	7	43/43	33/41	2	410	
Opponents	14	29	1	44/44	21/28	0	371	

2-Pt Conversions: Raiders 0-1, Opponents 0-0.

RUSHING	No.	Yds	Avg	LG	TD
D. McFadden	223	1157	5.2	57t	7
Bush	158	655	4.1	30	8
J. Campbell	47	222	4.7	24	1
Ford	10	155	15.5	71t	2
Reece	30	122	4.1	31	1
Heyward-Bey	4	48	12.0	30	0
Murphy	1	43	43.0	43	0
Gradkowski	12	41	3.4	12	0
Cartwright	9	22	2.4	10	0
Boller	7	18	2.6	15	0
Bennett	2	11	5.5	6	0
Satele	1	0	0.0	0	0
Raiders	504	2494	4.9	71t	19
Opponents	474	2138	4.5	76t	14

RECEIVING	No.	Yds	Avg	LG	TD
Z. Miller	60	685	11.4	43t	5
D. McFadden	47	507	10.8	67t	3
Murphy	41	609	14.9	70	2
Heyward-Bey	26	366	14.1	69t	1
Ford	25	470	18.8	52	2
Reece	25	333	13.3	73t	3
Bush	18	194	10.8	55	0
Myers	12	80	6.7	16	0
Higgins	10	103	10.3	26	0
Schilens	5	40	8.0	11	1
N. Miller	3	40	13.3	32	0
Figurs	2	17	8.5	11	0
Bennett	2	9	4.5	6	0
Barnes	2	8	4.0	6	1
Cartwright	1	10	10.0	10	0
Raiders	279	3471	12.4	73t	18
Opponents	249	3319	13.3	57t	29

INTERCEPTIONS	No.	Yds	Avg	LG	TD
Huff	3	32	10.7	17	0
Johnson	2	30	15.0	30t	1
Routt	2	22	11.0	22t	1
Branch	1	15	15.0	15	0
McClain	1	10	10.0	10	0
Mitchell	1	0	0.0	0	0
Ware	1	0	0.0	0	0
Groves	1	-4	-4.0	-4	0
Raiders	12	105	8.8	30t	2
Opponents	16	204	12.8	38	0

PUNTING	No.	Yds.	Avg.	In 20	LG
Lechler	77	3618	47.0	27	68
Janikowski	1	33	33.0	0	33
Raiders	78	3651	46.8	27	68
Opponents	94	4114	43.8	31	63

PUNT RETURNS	Ret	FC	Yds	Avg	LG	TD
N. Miller	35	7	257	7.3	46	0
Higgins	17	4	123	7.2	53	0
Branch	1	0	-4	-4.0	-4	0
Figurs	1	0	10	10.0	10	0
Myers	1	0	0	0.0	0	0
Raiders	55	11	386	7.0	53	0
Opponents	46	11	400	8.7	47	0

KICKOFF RETURNS	No.	Yds	Avg	LG	TD
Ford	53	1280	24.2	101t	3
Cartwright	6	103	17.2	28	0
Figurs	5	105	21.0	25	0
N. Miller	2	37	18.5	27	0
Huff	1	0	0.0	0	0
Reece	1	7	7.0	7	0
Raiders	68	1532	22.5	101t	3
Opponents	61	1412	23.1	102t	1

FIELD GOALS	1-19	20-29	30-39	40-49	50+
Janikowski	0/0	8/8	13/14	8/12	4/7
Raiders	0/0	8/8	13/14	8/12	4/7
Opponents	1/1	4/5	7/8	9/11	0/3

SACKS	No.
Wimbley	9.0
Kelly	7.0
Shaughnessy	7.0
Seymour	5.5
Houston	5.0
Branch	4.0
Huff	4.0
Bryant	2.5
T. Scott	1.5
Moss	1.0
McClain	0.5
Raiders	47.0
Opponents	44.0

RECORD HOLDERS
INDIVIDUAL RECORDS—CAREER

Category	Name	Performance
Rushing (Yds.)	Marcus Allen, 1982-1992	8,545
Passing (Yds.)	Ken Stabler, 1970-79	19,078
Passing (TDs)	Ken Stabler, 1970-79	150
Receiving (No.)	Tim Brown, 1988-2003	1,070
Receiving (Yds.)	Tim Brown, 1988-2003	14,734
Interceptions	Willie Brown, 1967-1978	39
	Lester Hayes, 1977-1986	39
Punting (Avg.)	Shane Lechler, 2000-2010	**47.3
Punt Return (Avg.)	Claude Gibson, 1963-65	12.6
Kickoff Return (Avg.)	Jack Larscheid, 1960-61	28.4
Field Goals	Sebastian Janikowski, 2000-2010	262
Touchdowns (Tot.)	Tim Brown, 1988-2003	104
Points	Sebastian Janikowski, 2000-2010	1,142
*Sacks	Greg Townsend, 1983-1993, 1997	107.5

INDIVIDUAL RECORDS—SINGLE SEASON

Category	Name	Performance
Rushing (Yds.)	Marcus Allen, 1985	1,759
Passing (Yds.)	Rich Gannon, 2002	4,689
Passing (TDs)	Daryle Lamonica, 1969	34
Receiving (No.)	Tim Brown 1997	104
Receiving (Yds.)	Tim Brown, 1997	1,408
Interceptions	Lester Hayes, 1980	13
Punting (Avg.)	Shane Lechler, 2009	51.1
Punt Return (Avg.)	Claude Gibson, 1964	14.4
Kickoff Return (Avg.)	Harold Hart, 1975	30.5
Field Goals	Jeff Jaeger, 1993	35
Touchdowns (Tot.)	Marcus Allen, 1984	18
Points	Sebastian Janikowski, 2010	142
*Sacks	Derrick Burgess, 2005	16.0

INDIVIDUAL RECORDS—SINGLE GAME

Category	Name	Performance
Rushing (Yds.)	Napoleon Kaufman, 10-19-97	227
Passing (Yds.)	Cotton Davidson, 10-25-64	427
Passing (TDs)	Tom Flores, 12-22-63	6
	Daryle Lamonica, 10-19-69	6
Receiving (No.)	Tim Brown, 12-21-97	14
Receiving (Yds.)	Art Powell, 12-22-63	247
Interceptions	Many times	3
	Last time by Rod Woodson, 9-29-02	
Field Goals	Jeff Jaeger, 12-11-94	5
	Sebastian Janikowski, 10-29-00, 10-5-03, 11-18-07	5
Touchdowns (Tot.)	Art Powell, 12-22-63	4
	Marcus Allen, 9-24-84	4
	Harvey Williams, 11-16-97	4
	Darren McFadden, 10-24-10	4
Points	Art Powell, 12-22-63	24
	Marcus Allen, 9-24-84	24
	Harvey Williams, 11-16-97	24
	Darren McFadden, 10-24-10	24
*Sacks	Howie Long, 10-2-83	5.0

*Sacks became an official statistic in 1982.
**NFL Record

VETERAN ROSTER AS OF MARCH 3, 2011

No.	Name	Pos.	Ht.	Wt.	Birthdate	NFL Exp.	College	Hometown	How Acq.	'10 Games/ Starts
21	Asomugha, Nnamdi	CB	6-2	210	7/6/81	9	California	Los Angeles, Calif.	D1-'03	14/14
69	Barnes, Khalif	T	6-5	325	4/21/82	7	Washington	Spring Valley, Calif.	UFA(Jax)-'09	16/3
32	Bennett, Michael	RB	5-9	205	8/13/78	11	Wisconsin	Milwaukee, Wisc.	FA-'10	7/0
10	Bodiford, Shaun	WR	5-11	185	5/4/82	4	Portland State	Federal Way, Wash.	FA-'10	0*
7	Boller, Kyle	QB	6-3	220	6/17/81	9	California	Newhall, Calif.	UFA(StL)-'10	5/0
33	Branch, Tyvon	S	6-0	205	12/11/86	4	Connecticut	Cicero, N.Y.	D4-'08	16/16
57	Brown, Ricky	LB	6-2	235	12/27/83	6	Boston College	Cincinnati, Ohio	FA-'06	14/1
27	Brown, Stevie	S	5-11	215	7/17/87	2	Michigan	Columbus, Ind.	D7-'10	15/1
90	Bryant, Desmond	DT	6-5	290	12/15/85	3	Harvard	Elizabethtown, N.C.	FA-'09	15/0
29	Bush, Michael	RB	6-1	245	6/16/84	4	Louisville	Louisville, Ky.	D4-'07	14/3
74	Campbell, Bruce	G	6-6	315	5/25/88	2	Maryland	Hamden, Conn.	D4-'10	10/0
8	Campbell, Jason	QB	6-5	230	12/31/81	7	Auburn	Taylorsville, Miss.	T(Wash)-'10	13/12
66	Carlisle, Cooper	G	6-5	295	8/11/77	12	Florida	McComb, Miss.	UFA(Den)-'07	16/16
25	Cartwright, Rock	RB	5-8	215	12/3/79	10	Kansas State	Conroe, Texas	FA-'10	16/0
59	Condo, Jon	LS/LB	6-3	250	8/26/81	6	Maryland	Philipsburg, Pa.	FA-'06	16/0
58	Davis, Bruce	LB	6-3	250	9/2/85	3	UCLA	League City, Texas	FA-'10	6/0
31	Eugene, Hiram	S	6-2	200	11/24/80	6	Louisiana Tech	Jeanerette, La.	FA-'06	14/0
12	Ford, Jacoby	WR	5-9	185	7/27/87	2	Clemson	Royal Palm Beach, Fla.	D4-'10	16/9
3	Frye, Charlie	QB	6-4	220	8/28/81	7	Akron	Willard, Ohio	UFA(Sea)-'09	0*
76	Gallery, Robert	G	6-7	325	7/26/80	8	Iowa	Masonville, Iowa	D1-'04	12/12
50	Goethel, Travis	LB	6-2	240	7/27/87	2	Arizona State	Vista, Calif.	D6-'10	8/0
5	Gradkowski, Bruce	QB	6-1	220	1/27/83	6	Toledo	Pittsburgh, Pa.	W(Cle)-'09	6/4
52	Groves, Quentin	LB	6-3	265	7/5/84	4	Auburn	Greenville, Miss.	T(Jax)-'10	15/12
79	Henderson, John	DT	6-7	335	1/9/79	10	Tennessee	Nashville, Tenn.	UFA(Jax)-'10	9/2
75	Henderson, Mario	T	6-7	300	10/29/84	5	Florida State	Lehigh Acres, Fla.	D3-'07	16/7
85	Heyward-Bey, Darrius	WR	6-2	210	2/26/87	3	Maryland	Owings Mills, Md.	D1-'09	15/14
15	Higgins, Johnnie Lee	WR	5-11	185	9/8/83	5	Texas-El Paso	Sweeny, Texas	D3-'07	13/1
99	Houston, Lamarr	DE	6-3	305	6/24/87	2	Texas	Colorado Springs, Colo.	D2-'10	16/15
53	Howard, Thomas	LB	6-3	240	7/14/83	6	Texas-El Paso	Lubbock, Texas	D2-'06	12/0
24	Huff, Michael	S	6-1	205	3/6/83	6	Texas	Irving, Texas	D1-'06	16/15
11	Janikowski, Sebastian	K	6-2	250	3/2/78	12	Florida State	Daytona Beach, Fla.	D1-'00	16/0
37	Johnson, Chris	CB	6-1	200	9/25/79	8	Louisville	Longview, Texas	UFA(KC)-'07	12/4
93	Kelly, Tommy	DT	6-6	300	12/27/80	8	Mississippi State	Jackson, Miss.	FA-'04	16/16
9	Lechler, Shane	P	6-2	225	8/7/76	12	Texas A&M	Sealy, Texas	D5-'00	16/0
60	Loper, Daniel	G	6-6	320	1/15/82	7	Texas Tech	Houston, Texas	UFA(Det)-'10	10/4
55	McClain, Rolando	LB	6-3	255	7/14/89	2	Alabama	Decatur, Ala.	D1-'10	15/15
20	McFadden, Darren	RB	6-2	210	8/27/87	4	Arkansas	North Little Rock, Ark.	D1-'08	13/13
22	McFadden, Walter	CB	5-10	180	1/21/87	2	Auburn	Pompano Beach, Fla.	D5-'10	4/0
89	Miller, Nick	WR	5-9	180	3/29/87	3	Southern Utah	Mesa, Ariz.	FA-'09	9/0
80	Miller, Zach	TE	6-5	255	12/11/85	5	Arizona State	Phoenix, Ariz.	D2-'07	15/15
34	Mitchell, Mike	S	6-1	220	6/10/87	3	Ohio	Ft. Thomas, Ky.	D2-'09	16/3
94	Moss, Jarvis	DE	6-7	260	8/3/84	5	Florida	Denton, Texas	W(Den)-'10	5/0
18	Murphy, Louis	WR	6-2	200	5/11/87	3	Florida	St. Petersburg, Fla.	D4-'09	14/9
83	Myers, Brandon	TE	6-4	250	9/4/85	3	Iowa	Prairie City, Iowa	D6-'09	15/3
13	O'Sullivan, J.T.	QB	6-2	230	8/25/79	9	U.C. Davis	Sacramento, Calif.	FA-'10	0*
4	Pakulak, Glenn	P	6-3	220	4/9/80	3	Kentucky	Lapeer, Mich.	FA-'11	0*
30	Rankin, Louis	RB	6-1	205	5/4/85	3	Washington	Stockton, Calif.	FA-'11	0*
45	Reece, Marcel	FB	6-3	240	6/23/85	3	Washington	Hesperia, Calif.	FA-'08	16/10
26	Routt, Stanford	CB	6-1	195	7/26/83	7	Houston	Austin, Texas	D2-'05	16/15
64	Satele, Samson	C	6-3	300	11/29/84	5	Hawai'i	Kailua, Hawai'i	T(Mia)-'09	16/15
81	Schilens, Chaz	WR	6-4	225	11/7/85	4	San Diego State	Mesa, Ariz.	D7-'08	5/0
67	Schuening, Roy	G	6-3	315	4/8/84	2	Oregon State	Pendleton, Ore.	FA-'11	0*
91	Scott, Trevor	DE	6-5	255	8/30/84	4	Buffalo	Potsdam, N.Y.	D6-'08	10/10
92	Seymour, Richard	DT/DE	6-6	310	10/6/79	11	Georgia	Gadsden, S.C.	T(NE)-'09	13/13
77	Shaughnessy, Matt	DE	6-5	270	9/23/86	3	Wisconsin	Norwich, Conn.	D3-'09	16/8
68	Veldheer, Jared	T	6-8	315	6/14/87	2	Hillsdale	Grand Rapids, Mich.	D3-'10	16/11
70	Walker, Langston	T	6-8	360	9/3/79	10	California	Oakland, Calif.	FA-'09	15/15
23	Ware, Jeremy	CB	5-10	185	9/18/86	2	Michigan State	Fort Myers, Fla.	D7-'10	8/0
54	Williams, Sam	LB	6-5	260	7/28/80	9	Fresno State	Clayton, Calif.	D3-'03	16/0
96	Wimbley, Kamerion	LB	6-4	255	10/13/83	6	Florida State	Wichita, Kan.	T(Cle)-'10	16/14

* Bodiford last active with Green Bay in '07; Frye missed '10 because of injury; O'Sullivan inactive for 5 games; Pakulak last active with Washington in '09; Rankin last active with Seattle in '09; Schuening inactive with Detroit for 3 games and Oakland for 1 game in '09.

Also played with Raiders in '10—DT Jay Alford (4 games), WR Yamon Figurs (1).

^ "NFL Exp." as of 2011 Kickoff Weekend. For full explanation of how a player's NFL Experience is measured, refer to explanation underneath the First-Year Roster listed below.

FIRST-YEAR ROSTER

Name	Pos.	Ht.	Wt.	Birthdate	College	Hometown	How Acq.
Adeniji, Damola (1)	WR	6-3	215	6/16/87	Oregon State	Eugene, Ore.	FA-'10
Ausberry, David	WR	6-4	245	9/25/87	Southern California	Lemoore, Calif.	D7
Barksdale, Joe	T	6-4	325	1/1/88	Louisiana State	Detroit, Mich.	D3
Brock, Kevin (1)	TE	6-5	260	4/9/86	Rutgers	Hackensack, N.J.	FA-'10
Boyd, Jerome (1)	S	6-2	225	5/26/86	Oregon	Los Angeles, Calif.	FA-'09
Chekwa, Chimdi	CB	6-0	190	9/7/88	Ohio State	Clermont, Fla.	D4
Gordon, Richard	TE	6-4	265	6/7/87	Miami	Miami, Fla.	D6
Hill, Tommie (1)	DE	6-6	245	11/28/85	Colorado State	Littleton, Colo.	FA
Jones, Taiwan	RB	6-0	195	7/26/88	Eastern Washington	Antioch, Calif.	D4
Moore, Denarius	WR	6-0	195	12/9/88	Tennessee	Tatum, Texas	D5
Parsons, Alex (1)	OL	6-4	300	9/14/87	Southern California	Irvine, Calif.	FA-'10
Porter, Joe (1)	CB	5-10	205	11/27/85	Rutgers	Franklin, N.J.	FA
Scott, Quentin (1)	LB	6-3	220	5/31/88	Northern Iowa	Des Moines, Iowa	FA-'10
Tonga, Manase (1)	FB	5-11	245	2/28/84	Brigham Young	San Mateo, Calif.	FA-'10
Van Dyke, DeMarcus	CB	6-1	180	1/17/89	Miami	Miami, Fla.	D3
Wisniewski, Stefen	C	6-3	315	3/22/89	Penn State	Pittsburgh, Pa.	D2

The term NFL Rookie is defined as a player who is in his first season of professional football and has not been on the roster of another professional football team for any regular-season or postseason games. A Rookie is designated by an "R" on NFL rosters. Players who have been active in another professional football league or players who have NFL experience, including either preseason training camp or being on an Active List or Inactive List, or on Reserve/Injured or Reserve/Physically Unable to Perform for fewer than six regular-season games, are termed NFL First-Year Players. An NFL First-Year Player is designated by a "1" on NFL rosters. Thereafter, a player is credited with an additional year of experience for each season in which he accumulates six games on the Active List or Inactive List, or on Reserve/Injured or Reserve/Physically Unable to Perform.

Log on to www.raiders.com for an up-to-date roster.

COACHING STAFF
Head Coach,
Hue Jackson

Pro Career: Named 18th head coach in Raiders history January 17, 2011. Jackson was offensive coordinator for the Oakland Raiders in 2010. Jackson has 25 years of coaching experience in college and professional football and has been an offensive coordinator at both levels. Last year, Jackson coordinated an Oakland Raiders offense that finished fourth in the AFC and sixth in the NFL in scoring (25.6 points per game). The Raiders more than doubled their scoring output from the previous year, totaling 410 points in 2010. Under Jackson's guidance, the Raiders also finished fifth in the AFC and 10th in the NFL in total offense (354.6 yards per game) and second in the NFL and AFC in rushing (155.9 yards per game). Prior to joining the Raiders, Jackson spent two seasons as Baltimore's quarterbacks coach and helped the Ravens advance to the postseason in 2008 and 2009. In 2008, Jackson tutored Joe Flacco, who became the first rookie QB to win two playoff games in NFL history, as the Ravens advanced to the AFC Championship game. In 2007, Jackson was an NFL offensive coordinator for the second time when he served in that capacity for the Atlanta Falcons, having previously served in the capacity for the Washington Redskins in 2003. As the Bengals' receivers coach (2004-06), Chad Ochocinco and T.J. Houshmandzadeh became one of the most prolific wide receiving tandems in NFL history. Ochocinco led the NFL in receiving yards and for the fourth consecutive season, he topped the AFC in yardage. It marked the first time a player had led his conference in receiving yards in four straight seasons. He established an NFL record for most receiving yards in consecutive games (450). In 2005, the Bengals won the AFC North title and secured a playoff berth or the first time in a decade. In Washington, Jackson was promoted to offensive coordinator by Steve Spurrier in 2003 and handled team's offensive play-calling, becoming the only coach to perform that duty other than Spurrier. He was the Redskins' running backs coach in 2001-02. Jackson was a minority fellowship coaching intern in training camp with the Washington Redskins in 1995, the Arizona Cardinals in 1992 and the Los Angeles Rams in 1990. He was a running backs/wide receivers/special teams coach for the London Monarchs of the World League of American Football in the spring. Career record: 0-0.

Background: Jackson was offensive coordinator at University of Southern California (1997-2000) and the University of California (1996). He coached running backs at Arizona State from 1992-95.

From 1990-91, Jackson was running backs coach and special teams coordinator at Cal State Fullerton. Jackson launched his coaching career as a running backs coach at Pacific from 1987-89. As a quarterback at Pacific from 1985-86, Jackson threw for 2,544 yards and 19 TDs. He also lettered in basketball in 1986 and earned his degree in Physical Education. Jackson is a Los Angeles native who was a star quarterback at Dorsey High School in his hometown, where he also lettered in basketball.

Personal: Born October 22, 1965, in Los Angeles. Jackson and his wife Michelle have three daughters.

ASSISTANT COACHES

Greg Biekert, linebackers, born March 14, 1969, Iowa City, Iowa. Linebacker Colorado 1990-93. Pro linebacker Los Angeles/Oakland Raiders 1993-2001, Minnesota Vikings 2002-03. Pro coach: Joined Raiders in 2010.

Chuck Bresnahan, defensive coordinator; born September 8, 1960, Springfield, Mass. Linebacker Navy 1979-1982. No pro playing experience. College coach: Navy 1983, 1986, Georgia Tech 1987-1991, Maine 1992-93. Pro coach: Cleveland Browns 1994-95, Indianapolis Colts 1996-97, Oakland Raiders 1998-2003, Cincinnati Bengals 2004-07, Florida Tuskers (UFL) 2009-2010, re-joined Raiders in 2011.

John Fassel, special teams coordinator; born January 10, 1974, Anaheim, Calif. Wide receiver/quarterback Pacific 1994-95, Weber State 1996-98. No pro playing experience. College coach: Bucknell 1999, 2001, Idaho State 2000, New Mexico Highlands 2002-03. Pro coach: Amsterdam Admirals (NFLE) 2000, Baltimore Ravens 2005-07; joined Raiders in 2008.

Adam Henry, tight ends; born April 27, 1972, Beaumont, Texas. Wide receiver McNeese State 1992-93. Pro receiver New Orleans Saints 1995. College coach: McNeese State 1996-2006. Pro coach: Joined Raiders in 2007.

Sanjay Lal, wide receivers; born July 23, 1969, London, England. Wide receiver UCLA 1989, Washington 1990-92. Pro wide receiver St. Louis Rams 1998, Scottish Claymores (NFLE) 1999. College coach: Los Medanos (Calif.) College 2003, Saint Mary's College 2004, California 2005-06, joined Raiders in 2007.

Brad Roll, strength & conditioning; July 4, 1958, Houston. Center Blinn (Tex.) J.C. 1976-77, Stephen F. Austin 1978-79. No pro playing experience. College coach: Stephen F. Austin 1980, Southwestern Louisiana 1981-86, Kansas 1987-88, Miami 1989-1992. Pro coach: Tampa Bay Buccaneers 1993-95, Miami Dolphins 1996-2003, Buffalo Bills 2004-05, St. Louis Rams 2006-07, joined Raiders in 2008.

Kevin Ross, defensive backs; born January 16, 1962, Camden, N.J. Defensive back Temple 1980-83. Pro defensive back Kansas City Chiefs 1984-1993, 1997, Atlanta Falcons 1994-95, San Diego Chargers 1996. Pro coach: Minnesota Vikings 2003-05, San Diego Chargers 2007-08, joined Raiders in 2010.

Al Saunders, offensive coordinator; born February 1, 1947, London, England. Defensive back San Jose State 1966-68. No pro playing experience. College coach: Southern California 1970-71, Missouri 1972, Utah State 1973-75, California 1976-1981, Tennessee 1982. Pro coach: San Diego Chargers 1983-88 (head coach 1986-88), Kansas City Chiefs 1989-1998, St. Louis Rams 1999-2000, 2008, Kansas City Chiefs 2001-05, Washington Redskins 2006-07, Baltimore Ravens 2009-2010, joined Raiders in 2011.

Kelly Skipper, tight ends; born July 25, 1967, Brawley, Calif. Running back Fresno State 1985-88. No pro playing experience. College coach: Fresno State 1989-1997, UCLA 1998-2002, Washington State 2003-06. Pro coach: Joined Raiders in 2007.

Mike Waufle, defensive line; born June 27, 1954, Hornell, N.Y. U.S. Marines 1972-75. Defensive lineman Bakersfield (Calif.) J.C. 1975-76, Utah State 1977-78. No pro playing experience. College coach: Alfred 1979, Utah State 1980-84, Fresno State 1985-88, UCLA 1989, Oregon State 1990-91, California 1992-97. Pro coach: Oakland Raiders 1998-2003, New York Giants 2004-09, re-joined Raiders in 2010.

Steve Wisniewski, asst. offensive line; born April 7, 1967, Rutland, Ver. Offensive lineman Penn State 1985-88. Pro offensive lineman Los Angeles/Oakland Raiders 1989-2001. College coach: Stanford 2010. Pro coach: Joined Raiders in 2011.

Rod Woodson, defensive backs; born March 10, 1965, Fort Wayne, Ind. Defensive back Purdue 1983-86 Pro defensive back Pittsburgh Steelers 1987-1996, San Francisco 49ers 1997, Baltimore Ravens 1998-2001, Oakland Raiders 2002-03. Inducted into Pro Football Hall of Fame 2009. Pro coach: Joined Raiders in 2011.

Bob Wylie, offensive line; born February 16, 1951, West Warwick, R.I. Linebacker Colorado 1969-1971. No pro playing experience. College coach: Brown 1980-82, Holy Cross 1983-84, Ohio 1985-87, Colorado State 1988-89, Cincinnati 1996, Syracuse 2005-06. Pro coach: New York Jets 1990-91, Tampa Bay Buccaneers 1992-95, Cincinnati Bengals 1997-98, Chicago Bears 1999-2003, Arizona Cardinals 2004, Winnipeg Blue Bombers (CFL) 2007-08, Saskatchewan Roughriders (CFL) 2009, Denver Broncos 2010, joined Raiders in 2011.

American Football Conference
North Division
Team Colors: Black and Gold
3400 South Water Street
Pittsburgh, Pennsylvania 15203
Telephone: (412) 432-7800

2011 SCHEDULE
PRESEASON
Aug. 12 at Washington 7:30
Aug. 18 **Philadelphia** 8:00
Aug. 27 **Atlanta** 7:30
Sep. 1   at Carolina..........................8:00

REGULAR SEASON
Sep. 11 at Baltimore 1:00
Sep. 18 **Seattle** 1:00
Sep. 25 at Indianapolis 8:20
Oct. 2   at Houston 1:00
Oct. 9   **Tennessee** 1:00
Oct. 16 **Jacksonville** 1:00
Oct. 23 at Arizona 4:05
Oct. 30 **New England** 4:15
Nov. 6   **Baltimore** 8:20
Nov. 13 at Cincinnati 1:00
Nov. 20 BYE
Nov. 27 at Kansas City * 8:20
Dec. 4   **Cincinnati** 1:00
Dec. 8   **Cleveland** (Thu) 8:20
Dec. 19 at San Francisco (Mon) 8:30
Dec. 24 **St. Louis** (Sat) 1:00
Jan. 1   at Cleveland 1:00
*All times ET, Sunday night games in
    Weeks 11-15, 17 subject to change
Stadium: Heinz Field (opened in 2001)
    •**Capacity:** 65,500
    100 Art Rooney Avenue
    Pittsburgh, Pennsylvania 15212
Playing Surface: DD GrassMaster
Training Camp: St. Vincent College
            Latrobe, PA 15650

HEINZ FIELD

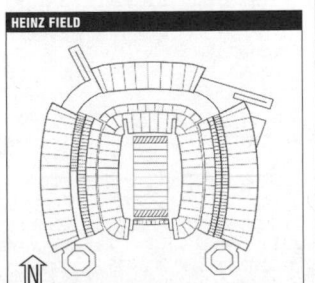

CLUB OFFICIALS
Chairman: Daniel M. Rooney
President: Arthur J. Rooney II
Vice President: John R. McGinley
Vice President: Arthur J. Rooney Jr.
Administration Advisor: Charles H. Noll
Director of Planning & Development:
    Mark Hart
Director of Finance: Bob Tyler
Director of Business & Administration:
    Omar Khan
Director of Football Operations:
    Kevin Colbert
College Scouting Coordinator:
    Ron Hughes
Pro Scouting Coordinator: Brandon Hunt
Head Athletic Trainer: John Norwig
Director of Marketing: Tony Quatrini
Public Relations/Media Manager:
    Burt Lauten
Director of Stadium Management:
    Jim Sacco
Video Coordinator: Bob McCartney
Human Relations/Office Coordinator:
    Geraldine Glenn
Ticket Manager: Ben Lentz

COACHING HISTORY
Pittsburgh Pirates 1933-39
(579-533-21)
Records include postseason games
1933   Forrest (Jap) Douds 3-6-2
1934   Luby DiMelio 2-10-0
1935-36   Joe Bach.......................10-14-0
1937-39   Johnny (Blood) McNally* ..6-19-0
1939-1940 Walt Kiesling 3-13-3
1941   Bert Bell** 0-2-0
           Aldo (Buff) Donelli*** 0-5-0
1941-44   Walt Kiesling**** 13-20-2
1945   Jim Leonard 2-8-0
1946-47   Jock Sutherland..........13-10-1
1948-1951 Johnny Michelosen 20-26-2
1952-53   Joe Bach.......................11-13-0
1954-56   Walt Kiesling 14-22-0
1957-1964 Raymond (Buddy) Parker .51-47-6
1965   Mike Nixon 2-12-0
1966-68   Bill Austin......................11-28-3
1969-1991 Chuck Noll 209-156-1
1992-2006 Bill Cowher 161-99-1
2007-2010 Mike Tomlin..................48-23-0
    *Released after three games in 1939
    **Resigned after two games in 1941
    ***Released after five games in 1941
    ****Co-coach with Earle (Greasy) Neale in
    Philadelphia-Pittsburgh merger in 1943 and
    with Phil Handler in Chicago Cardinals-
    Pittsburgh merger in 1944

PAID ATTENDANCE
Home 517,450   Away 531,350
Total 1,048,800
Single-game home record,
    66,662 (1/23/11)
Single-season home record,
    517,599 (2009)

2011 DRAFT CHOICES

Round	Name	Pos.	College
1	Cameron Heyward	DE	Ohio State
2	Marcus Gilbert	T	Florida
3	Curtis Brown	DB	Texas
4	Cortez Allen	DB	The Citadel
5	Chris Carter	LB	Fresno State
6	Keith Williams	G	Nebraska
7	Baron Batch	RB	Texas Tech

2010 TEAM RECORD
PRESEASON (3-1)

Date	Result	Opponent
8/14	W 23-7	Detroit
8/21	W 24-17	at New York
8/29	L 17-34	at Denver
9/2	W 19-3	Carolina

REGULAR SEASON (12-4)

Date	Result	Opponent
9/12	W 15-9	Atlanta (OT)
9/19	W 19-11	at Tennessee
9/26	W 38-13	at Tampa Bay
10/3	L 14-17	Baltimore
10/17	W 28-10	Cleveland
10/24	W 23-22	at Miami
10/31	L 10-20	at New Orleans
11/8	W 27-21	at Cincinnati
11/14	L 26-39	New England
11/21	W 35-3	Oakland
11/28	W 19-16	at Buffalo (OT)
12/5	W 13-10	at Baltimore
12/12	W 23-7	Cincinnati
12/19	L 17-22	New York Jets
12/23	W 27-3	Carolina
1/2	W 41-9	at Cleveland

POSTSEASON (2-1)

Date	Result	Opponent
1/15	W 31-24	Baltimore
1/23	W 24-19	New York Jets
2/6	L 25-31	vs. Green Bay at North Texas

(OT) Overtime

SCORE BY PERIODS

Steelers	58	148	43	117	9 —	375
Opponents	49	42	39	102	0 —	232

2010 TEAM STATISTICS

	Steelers	Opp.
Total First Downs	295	272
Rushing	106	61
Passing	175	182
Penalty	14	29
3rd Down: Made/Att	94/218	70/209
3rd Down Pct.	43.1	33.5
4th Down: Made/Att	2/5	10/16
4th Down Pct.	40.0	62.5
Possession Avg.	31:53	28:07
Total Net Yards	5525	4429
Avg. Per Game	345.3	276.8
Total Plays	993	974
Avg. Per Play	5.6	4.5
Net Yards Rushing	1924	1004
Avg. Per Game	120.3	62.8
Total Rushes	471	333
Net Yards Passing	3601	3425
Avg. Per Game	225.1	214.1
Sacked/Yards Lost	43/289	48/319
Gross Yards	3890	3744
Att./Completions	479/298	593/363
Completion Pct.	62.2	61.2
Had Intercepted	9	21
Punts/Average	74/44.3	81/40.4
Net Punting Avg.	74/37.3	81/36.4
Penalties/Yards	100/903	86/716
Fumbles/Ball Lost	22/9	28/14
Touchdowns	41	22
Rushing	15	5
Passing	22	15
Returns	4	2

2010 INDIVIDUAL STATISTICS

PASSING

	Att.	Comp.	Yds.	Pct.	TD	Int.	Tkld.	Rate
Roethlisberger	389	240	3200	61.7	17	5	32/220	97.0
Batch	49	29	352	59.2	3	3	4/21	76.2
Dixon	32	22	254	68.8	0	1	5/41	79.4
Leftwich	7	5	42	71.4	0	0	2/7	86.6
Randle El	2	2	42	100.0	2	0	0/0	158.3
Steelers	479	298	3890	62.2	22	9	43/289	95.2
Opponents	593	363	3744	61.2	15	21	48/319	73.1

SCORING

	TD R	TD P	TD Rt	PAT	FG	Saf	PTS
Mendenhall	13	0	0	0/0	0/0	0	78
Reed	0	0	0	19/19	15/22	0	64
Suisham	0	0	0	19/19	14/15	0	61
Wallace	0	10	0	0/0	0/0	0	60
Ward	0	5	0	0/0	0/0	0	30
Miller	0	2	0	0/0	0/0	0	12
Redman	0	2	0	0/0	0/0	0	12
Roethlisberger	2	0	0	0/0	0/0	0	12
Sanders	0	2	0	0/0	0/0	0	12
Brown	0	0	1	0/0	0/0	0	6
Keisel	0	0	1	0/0	0/0	0	6
Polamalu	0	0	1	0/0	0/0	0	6
Spaeth	0	1	0	0/0	0/0	0	6
Woodley	0	0	1	0/0	0/0	0	6
Moore	0	0	0	0/0	0/0	0	4
Steelers	15	22	4	38/38	29/37	0	375
Opponents	5	15	2	18/19	26/30	1	232

2-Pt Conversions: Moore 2.
Steelers 2-2, Opponents 1-3.

RUSHING

	No.	Yds	Avg	LG	TD
Mendenhall	324	1273	3.9	50t	13
Redman	52	247	4.8	23	0
Roethlisberger	34	176	5.2	31	2
Moore	33	99	3.0	18	0
Wallace	5	39	7.8	19	0
Dixon	5	32	6.4	21	0
Batch	7	30	4.3	24	0
Dwyer	9	28	3.1	7	0
Randle El	1	2	2.0	2	0
Ward	1	-2	-2.0	-2	0
Steelers	471	1924	4.1	50t	15
Opponents	333	1004	3.0	24	5

RECEIVING

	No.	Yds	Avg	LG	TD
Wallace	60	1257	21.0	56t	10
Ward	59	755	12.8	43	5
Miller	42	512	12.2	36	2
Sanders	28	376	13.4	35	2
Moore	26	205	7.9	29	0
Mendenhall	23	167	7.3	24	0
Randle El	22	253	11.5	34	0
Brown	16	167	10.4	26	0
Spaeth	9	80	8.9	13	1
Redman	9	72	8.0	16t	2
Johnson	4	46	11.5	25	0
Steelers	298	3890	13.1	56t	22
Opponents	363	3744	10.3	67	15

INTERCEPTIONS

	No.	Yds	Avg	LG	TD
Polamalu	7	101	14.4	45t	1
Clark	2	34	17.0	23	0
Woodley	2	22	11.0	14t	1
I. Taylor	2	9	4.5	9	0
Timmons	2	5	2.5	5	0
Harrison	2	2	1.0	2	0
McFadden	2	-3	-1.5	0	0
Keisel	1	79	79.0	79t	1
Madison	1	-1	-1.0	-1	0
Steelers	21	248	11.8	79t	3
Opponents	9	122	13.6	62	1

PUNTING

	No.	Yds.	Avg.	In 20	LG
Sepulveda	56	2550	45.5	16	62
Kapinos	14	576	41.1	5	59
Suisham	3	115	38.3	1	39
Roethlisberger	1	35	35.0	0	35
Steelers	74	3276	44.3	22	62
Opponents	81	3275	40.4	36	67

PUNT RETURNS

	Ret	FC	Yds	Avg	LG	TD
Brown	19	1	110	5.8	21	0
Randle El	14	17	56	4.0	15	0
Sanders	4	1	60	15.0	38	0
Steelers	37	19	226	6.1	38	0
Opponents	32	25	294	9.2	38	0

KICKOFF RETURNS

	No.	Yds	Avg	LG	TD
Sanders	25	628	25.1	48	0
Brown	17	397	23.4	89t	1
Redman	4	81	20.3	21	0
Moore	3	47	15.7	17	0
Steelers	49	1153	23.5	97t	1
Opponents	77	1540	20.0	97t	1

FIELD GOALS

	1-19	20-29	30-39	40-49	50+
Reed TM	2/2	6/7	5/5	0/4	2/4
Suisham	1/1	4/4	1/1	8/9	0/0
Steelers	3/3	10/11	6/6	8/13	2/4
Opponents	1/1	10/10	10/10	5/8	0/1

SACKS

	No.
Harrison	10.5
Woodley	10.0
Farrior	6.0
Hood	3.0
Keisel	3.0
Timmons	3.0
Gay	2.0
McFadden	2.0
Worilds	2.0
Eason	1.5
Foote	1.0
Hampton	1.0
Madison	1.0
Polamalu	1.0
I. Taylor	1.0
Steelers	48.0
Opponents	43.0

RECORD HOLDERS
INDIVIDUAL RECORDS—CAREER

Category	Name	Performance
Rushing (Yds.)	Franco Harris, 1972-1983	11,950
Passing (Yds.)	Terry Bradshaw, 1970-1983	27,989
Passing (TDs)	Terry Bradshaw, 1970-1983	212
Receiving (No.)	Hines Ward, 1998-2010	954
Receiving (Yds.)	Hines Ward, 1998-2010	11,702
Interceptions	Mel Blount, 1970-1983	57
Punting (Avg.)	Bobby Joe Green, 1960-61	45.7
Punt Return (Avg.)	Bobby Gage, 1949-1950	14.9
Kickoff Return (Avg.)	Lynn Chandnois, 1950-56	29.6
Field Goals	Gary Anderson, 1982-1994	309
Touchdowns (Tot.)	Franco Harris, 1972-1983	100
Points	Gary Anderson, 1982-1994	1,343
*Sacks	Jason Gildon, 1994-2003	77.0

INDIVIDUAL RECORDS—SINGLE SEASON

Category	Name	Performance
Rushing (Yds.)	Barry Foster, 1992	1,690
Passing (Yds.)	Ben Roethlisberger, 2009	4,328
Passing (TDs)	Ben Roethlisberger, 2007	32
Receiving (No.)	Hines Ward, 2002	112
Receiving (Yds.)	Yancey Thigpen, 1997	1,398
Interceptions	Mel Blount, 1975	11
Punting (Avg.)	Bobby Joe Green, 1961	47.0
Punt Return (Avg.)	Bobby Gage, 1949	16.0
Kickoff Return (Avg.)	Lynn Chandnois, 1952	35.2
Field Goals	Norm Johnson, 1995	34
Touchdowns (Tot.)	Willie Parker, 2006	16
Points	Norm Johnson, 1995	141
*Sacks	James Harrison, 2008	16.0

INDIVIDUAL RECORDS—SINGLE GAME

Category	Name	Performance
Rushing (Yds.)	Willie Parker, 12-7-06	223
Passing (Yds.)	Ben Roethlisberger, 12-20-09	503
Passing (TDs)	Terry Bradshaw, 11-15-81	5
	Mark Malone, 9-8-85	5
	Ben Roethlisberger, 11-5-07	5
Receiving (No.)	Courtney Hawkins, 11-1-98	14
Receiving (Yds.)	Plaxico Burress, 11-10-02	253
Interceptions	Jack Butler, 12-13-53	**4
Field Goals	Gary Anderson, 10-23-88	6
	Jeff Reed, 12-1-02	6
Touchdowns (Tot.)	Ray Mathews, 10-17-54	4
	Roy Jefferson, 11-3-68	4
Points	Ray Mathews, 10-17-54	24
	Roy Jefferson, 11-3-68	24
*Sacks	Chad Brown, 10-13-96	4.5

*Sacks became an official statistic in 1982.
**NFL Record

VETERAN ROSTER AS OF MARCH 3, 2011

No.	Name	Pos.	Ht.	Wt.	Birthdate	^ NFL Exp.	College	Hometown	How Acq.	'10 Games/ Starts
71	Adams, Flozell	T	6-7	338	5/18/75	14	Michigan State	Chicago, Ill.	FA-'10	16/16
26	Allen, Will	S	6-1	200	6/17/82	8	Ohio State	Dayton, Ohio	FA-'10	14/0
47	Atkins, Baraka	LB	6-4	271	9/28/84	4	Miami	Sarasota, Fla.	FA-'10	0*
16	Batch, Charlie	QB	6-2	216	12/5/74	14	Eastern Michigan	Homestead, Pa.	FA-'02	3/2
81	Battle, Arnaz	WR	6-1	208	2/22/80	9	Notre Dame	Dallas, Texas	FA-'10	15/0
84	Brown, Antonio	WR	5-10	186	7/10/88	2	Central Michigan	Miami, Fla.	D6b-'10	9/0
28	Butler, Crezdon	CB	6-0	191	5/26/87	2	Clemson	Asheville, N.C.	D5b-'10	4/0
25	Clark, Ryan	S	5-11	205	10/12/79	10	Louisiana State	Marrero, La.	UFA(Wash)-'06	16/15
74	Colon, Willie	T	6-3	315	4/9/83	5	Hofstra	Bronx, N.Y.	D4a-'06	0*
10	Dixon, Dennis	QB	6-3	209	1/11/85	4	Oregon	San Leandro, Calif.	D5-'08	2/2
27	Dwyer, Jonathan	RB	5-11	229	7/26/89	2	Georgia Tech	Marietta, Ga.	D6a-'10	1/0
93	Eason, Nick	DE	6-3	305	5/29/80	9	Clemson	Lyons, Ga.	FA-'07	16/5
90	Ellis, Chris	LB	6-4	267	2/11/85	3	Virginia Tech	Hampton, Va.	FA-'10	5/1*
79	Essex, Trai	G	6-5	324	12/5/82	7	Northwestern	Fort Wayne, Ind.	D3-'05	12/5
51	Farrior, James	LB	6-2	243	1/6/75	15	Virginia	Ettrick, Va.	UFA(NYJ)-'02	16/16
50	Foote, Larry	LB	6-1	239	6/12/80	10	Michigan	Detroit, Mich.	FA-'09	16/0
73	Foster, Ramon	G	6-6	325	1/7/86	3	Tennessee	Henning, Tenn.	FA-'09	12/8
57	Fox, Keyaron	LB	6-3	235	1/24/82	8	Georgia Tech	Atlanta, Ga.	UFA(KC)-'08	16/0
22	Gay, William	CB	5-10	190	1/1/85	5	Louisville	Tallahassee, Fla.	D5b-'07	16/4
98	Hampton, Casey	NT	6-1	325	9/3/77	11	Texas	Galveston, Texas	D1-'01	15/14
31	Harris, Tuff	S	6-0	198	1/23/83	4	Montana	Colstrip, Mont.	FA-'09	0*
92	Harrison, James	LB	6-0	242	5/4/78	8	Kent State	Akron, Ohio	FA-'04	16/16
66	Hills, Tony	T	6-5	304	11/4/84	4	Texas	Houston, Texas	D4-'08	4/0
76	Hoke, Chris	NT	6-2	305	4/6/76	10	Brigham Young	Long Beach, Calif.	FA-'01	15/1
96	Hood, Ziggy	DE	6-3	300	2/16/87	3	Missouri	Amarillo, Texas	D1-'09	16/9
85	Johnson, David	TE	6-2	260	8/26/87	3	Arkansas State	Pine Bluff, Ark.	D7b-'09	16/5
13	Kapinos, Jeremy	P	6-1	233	8/23/84	4	Penn State	West Point, N.Y.	FA-'10	5/0*
99	Keisel, Brett	DE	6-5	285	9/19/78	10	Brigham Young	Greybull, Wyo.	D7b-'02	11/11
68	Kemoeatu, Chris	G	6-3	344	1/4/83	7	Utah	Kahuka, Hawaii	D6-'05	15/15
4	Leftwich, Byron	QB	6-5	250	1/14/80	9	Marshall	Washington, D.C.	T(TB)-'10	1/0
64	Legursky, Doug	C	6-1	315	6/9/86	3	Marshall	Frankfurt, Germany	FA-'08	16/4
23	Lewis, Keenan	CB	6-0	208	5/17/86	3	Oregon State	New Orleans, La.	D3c-'09	9/0
37	Madison, Anthony	CB	5-9	180	10/8/81	6	Alabama	Thomasville, Ala.	FA-'09	16/1
20	McFadden, Bryant	CB	6-0	190	11/21/81	7	Florida State	Hollywood, Fla.	T(Ariz)-'10	16/16
69	McLendon, Steve	DT	6-4	280	1/3/86	2	Troy	Ozark, Ala.	FA-'09	7/0
34	Mendenhall, Rashard	RB	5-10	225	6/19/87	4	Illinois	Skokie, Ill.	D1-'08	16/16
83	Miller, Heath	TE	6-5	256	10/22/82	7	Virginia	Swords Creek, Va.	D1-'05	14/14
21	Moore, Mewelde	RB	5-11	209	7/24/82	8	Tulane	Hammond, La.	UFA(Minn)-'08	15/0
29	Mundy, Ryan	S	6-1	209	2/11/85	3	West Virginia	Pittsburgh, Pa.	D6 -'08	16/2
43	Polamalu, Troy	S	5-10	207	4/19/81	9	Southern California	Tenmile, Ore.	D1-'03	14/14
53	Pouncey, Maurkice	C	6-4	304	7/24/89	2	Florida	Lakeland, Fla.	D1-'10	16/16
82	Randle El, Antwaan	WR	5-10	185	8/17/79	10	Indiana	Riverdale, Ill.	FA-'10	16/0
33	Redman, Isaac	RB	6-0	230	11/10/84	2	Bowie State	Paulsboro, N.J.	FA-'09	16/0
7	Roethlisberger, Ben	QB	6-5	241	3/2/82	8	Miami (OH)	Cory Rawson, Ohio	D1-'04	12/12
88	Sanders, Emmanuel	WR	5-11	180	3/17/87	2	Southern Methodist	Bellville, Texas	D3-'10	13/1
61	Scott, Chris	T	6-4	319	8/4/87	2	Tennessee	Riverdale, Ga.	D5a-'10	0*
72	Scott, Jonathan	T	6-6	318	1/10/83	6	Texas	Dallas, Texas	FA-'10	16/9
9	Sepulveda, Daniel	P	6-3	230	1/12/84	5	Baylor	Austin, Texas	D4a-'07	12/0
91	Smith, Aaron	DE	6-5	298	4/19/76	13	Northern Colorado	Colorado Springs, Colo.	D4-'99	6/6
89	Spaeth, Matt	TE	6-7	270	11/24/83	5	Minnesota	St. Michael, Minn.	D3-'07	14/13
78	Starks, Max	T	6-8	345	1/10/82	8	Florida	Orlando, Fla.	D3-'04	7/7
6	Suisham, Shaun	K	6-0	200	12/29/81	7	Bowling Green	Wallaceburg, Ontario, Canada	FA-'10	7/0
80	Sweed, Limas	WR	6-4	220	12/25/84	3	Texas	Brenham, Texas	D2-'08	0*
55	Sylvester, Stevenson	LB	6-2	231	7/18/88	2	Utah	Las Vegas, Nev.	D5c-'10	16/0
24	Taylor, Ike	CB	6-2	195	5/5/80	9	Louisiana-Lafayette	Gretna, La.	D4-'03	16/15
94	Timmons, Lawrence	LB	6-1	234	5/14/86	5	Florida State	Florence, S.C.	D1-'07	16/15
17	Wallace, Mike	WR	6-0	199	8/1/86	3	Mississippi	New Orleans, La.	D3b-'09	16/16
86	Ward, Hines	WR	6-0	205	3/8/76	14	Georgia	Forest Park, Ga.	D3b-'98	16/15
60	Warren, Greg	LS	6-3	252	10/18/81	7	North Carolina	Goldsboro, N.C.	FA-'05	16/0
56	Woodley, LaMarr	LB	6-2	265	11/3/84	5	Michigan	Saginaw, Mich.	D2-'07	16/16
97	Worilds, Jason	LB	6-2	262	3/3/88	2	Virginia Tech	Carteret, N.J.	D2-'10	14/0

* Atkins last active with Seattle in '08; Colon missed '10 season because of injury; Ellis played 5 games with Buffalo in '10; T. Harris missed '10 season because of injury; Kapinos played 1 game with Indianapolis and 4 games with Pittsburgh; C. Scott inactive for 8 games; Sweed missed '10 season because of injury.

Also played with Steelers in '10—K Jeff Reed (9 games).

^ "NFL Exp." as of 2011 Kickoff Weekend. For full explanation of how a player's NFL Experience is measured, refer to explanation underneath the First-Year Roster listed below.

FIRST-YEAR ROSTER

Name	Pos.	Ht.	Wt.	Birthdate	College	Hometown	How Acq.
Allen, Cortez	CB	6-1	196	10/29/88	The Citadel	Ocala, Fla.	D4
Batch, Baron	RB	5-10	210	12/21/87	Texas A&M	Midland, Texas	D7
Bright, Eugene (1)	TE	6-4	268	4/18/85	Purdue	Bryn Mawr, Pa.	FA-'09
Brooks, Dorian (1)	G	6-2	306	4/16/87	James Madison	Richmond, Va.	FA-'10
Brown, Curtis	CB	6-0	185	9/24/88	Texas	Longview, Texas	D3
Carter, Chris	LB	6-1	248	4/6/87	Fresno State	Fontana, Calif.	D5
Cromartie-Smith, Da'Mon (1)	S	6-2	210	2/19/87	Texas-El Paso	Riverside, Calif.	FA-'10
Gilbert, Marcus	T	6-6	330	2/15/85	Florida	Fort Lauderdale, Fla.	D2
Grisham, Tyler (1)	WR	5-11	180	6/11/87	Clemson	Birmingham, Ala.	FA-'09
Harris, Sunny (1)	DE	6-5	300	8/26/86	Oregon	Pensacola, Fla.	FA-'10
Heyward, Cameron	DE	6-5	288	5/6/86	Ohio State	Pittsburgh, Pa.	D1
Ivy, Mortty (1)	LB	6-1	239	4/26/86	West Virginia	Monroeville, Pa.	FA-'10
Johnson, James (1)	RB	5-11	197	8/6/84	Kansas State	Baton Rouge, La.	FA-'10
Jolly, Kyle (1)	T	6-6	300	7/22/87	North Carolina	Powhatan, Va.	FA-'10
Lyons, Wes (1)	WR	6-8	233	9/12/87	West Virginia	North Braddock, Pa.	FA
McCaskill, Nevin (1)	G	6-3	309	12/29/83	Hampton	Tallahassee, Fla.	FA-'10
McCoy, Chris (1)	LB	6-3	261	11/26/86	Middle Tennessee State	Villa Rica, Ga.	FA
McCoy, Jamie (1)	TE	6-3	240	7/21/87	Texas A&M	Midland, Texas	FA-'10
Warren, Donovan (1)	CB	5-11	193	1/31/89	Michigan	Long Beach, Calif.	FA-'10
Waters, Swayze (1)	K	5-11	181	5/18/87	Alabama-Birmingham	Jackson, Miss.	FA
Williams, Keith	G	6-5	310	4/8/88	Nebraska	Florissant, Mo.	D6

The term NFL Rookie is defined as a player who is in his first season of professional football and has not been on the roster of another professional football team for any regular-season or postseason games. A Rookie is designated by an "R" on NFL rosters. Players who have been active in another professional football league or players who have NFL experience, including either preseason training camp or being on an Active List or Inactive List, or on Reserve/Injured or Reserve/Physically Unable to Perform for fewer than six regular-season games, are termed NFL First-Year Players. An NFL First-Year Player is designated by a "1" on NFL rosters. Thereafter, a player is credited with an additional year of experience for each season in which he accumulates six games on the Active List or Inactive List, or on Reserve/Injured or Reserve/Physically Unable to Perform.

Log on to www.steelers.com for an up-to-date roster.

COACHING STAFF

Head Coach,
Mike Tomlin

Pro Career: Named the sixteenth head coach in Steelers history when he replaced Bill Cowher on January 22, 2007. Became the youngest coach (36 years, 323 days) in NFL history to win a Super Bowl when the Steelers defeated the Arizona Cardinals, 27-23, in Super Bowl XLIII on February 1, 2009. The only coach in Steelers' history to win division titles each of his first two seasons, in 2010 Tomlin's club won its third division title in in a four-year span. In 2008, Tomlin directed the Steelers to a 12-4 record, winning his second-consecutive AFC North title. That season culminated with a Super Bowl triumph, making Tomlin one of only seven coaches in league history to win a Super Bowl within his first two seasons as an NFL head coach. In his first season, Tomlin guided the Steelers to a 10-6 record and their first AFC North title since 2004. Tomlin was the Minnesota Vikings defensive coordinator in 2006 after spending the previous five seasons (2001-05) as defensive backs coach for the Tampa Bay Buccaneers. Tomlin coached one of the top defensive backfields in the NFL for the Buccaneers, culminating with its performance in Super Bowl XXXVII. The secondary recorded four interceptions, returning two for touchdowns to help Tampa Bay capture the franchise's first Super Bowl title. Tomlin served two seasons as the defensive backs coach at the University of Cincinnati (1999-2000) before going to Tampa Bay. Prior to joining the Cincinnati staff, Tomlin had a short stint on the coaching staff at Tennessee-Martin and then spent two seasons at Arkansas State. He spent the 1996 season as a graduate assistant at Memphis. Tomlin began his coaching career in 1995 as wide receivers coach at Virginia Military Institute. Career record: 48-23.

Background: Was a three-year starter at wide receiver at William & Mary (1990-94) and finished his career with 101 receptions for 2,046 yards and a school-record 20 touchdown receptions. A first-team All-Yankee Conference selection in 1994, he established a school record with a 20.2 yards per catch average. Tomlin was a teammate of current Viking Pro Bowl safety Darren Sharper at William and Mary. Graduated in 1994 with a degree in sociology.

Personal: Born in Hampton, Va., on March 15, 1972. He and his wife, Kiya, have two sons, Dino and Mason, and a daughter Harlyn Quinn.

ASSISTANT COACHES

Bruce Arians, offensive coordinator; born October 3, 1952, Paterson, N.J.. Quarterback Virginia Tech 1970-74. No pro playing experience. College coach: Virginia Tech 1975-77, Mississippi State 1978-1980, Alabama 1981-82, Temple 1983-88 (head coach), Mississippi State 1993-95, Alabama 1997. Pro coach: Kansas City Chiefs 1989-1992, New Orleans Saints 1996, Indianapolis Colts 1998-2000, Cleveland Browns 2001-03, joined Steelers in 2004.

Keith Butler, linebackers; born May 16, 1956, Anniston, Ala. Linebacker Memphis 1974-77. Pro linebacker Seattle Seahawks 1978-1987. College coach: Memphis 1990-97, Arkansas State 1998. Pro coach: Cleveland Browns 1999-2002, joined Steelers in 2003.

James Daniel, tight ends; born January 17, 1953, Wetumpka, Ala. Guard Alabama State 1970-73. No pro playing experience. College coach: Auburn 1981-1992. Pro coach: New York Giants 1993-96, Atlanta Falcons 1997-2003, joined Steelers in 2004.

Al Everest, special teams; born August 22, 1950, Santa Barbara, Calif. Safety Southern Methodist 1970-71. No pro playing experience. College coach: Southern Methodist 1972, North Texas 1973-74, Cameron University 1974-75. Pro coach: Arizona Cardinals 1996-99, New Orleans Saints 2000-05, San Francisco 49ers 2007-09, joined Steelers in 2010.

Randy Fichtner, quarterbacks; born November 7, 1963, Cleveland. Defensive back Purdue 1982-85. No pro playing experience. College coach: Michigan 1986-87, Southern California 1988, Nevada-Las Vegas 1989, Memphis 1990-93, Purdue 1994-96, Arkansas State 1997-2000, Memphis 2001-06. Pro coach: Joined Steelers in 2007.

Amos Jones, asst. special teams; born December 31, 1959, Tallahassee, Fla.. Safety/running back Alabama 1978-1980. No pro playing experience. College coach: Alabama 1981-82, Temple 1983-88, Alabama 1990-91, Pittsburgh 1992, Tulane 1995-96, Cincinnati 1999-2002, James Madison 2003, Mississippi State 2004-06. Pro coach: British Columbia (CFL) 1997, joined Steelers in 2007.

Sean Kugler, offensive line; born August 9, 1966, Lockport, N.Y. Offensive line Texas-El Paso 1985-89. No pro playing experience. College coach: Texas-El Paso 1993-2000, Boise State 2006. Pro coach: Detroit Lions 2001-05, Buffalo Bills 2007-09, joined Steelers in 2010.

Carnell Lake, defensive backs; born July 15, 1967, Salt Lake City, Utah. Outside linebacker UCLA 1985-1988. Pro defensive back Pittsburgh Steelers 1989-1998, Jacksonville Jaguars 1999-2000, Baltimore Ravens 2001. College coach: UCLA 2009. Pro coach: Joined Steelers in 2011.

Dick LeBeau, defensive coordinator; born September 9, 1937, London, Ohio. Defensive back Ohio State 1955-58. Pro cornerback Detroit Lions 1959-1972. Pro coach: Philadelphia Eagles 1973-75, Green Bay Packers 1976-79, Cincinnati Bengals 1980-1991, 1997-2002 (head coach 2000-02), Pittsburgh Steelers 1992-96, Buffalo Bills 2003, re-joined Steelers in 2004.

John Mitchell, defensive line; born October 14, 1951, Mobile, Ala. Defensive end Eastern Arizona J.C. 1969-1970, Alabama 1971-72. No pro playing experience. College coach: Alabama 1973-76, Arkansas 1977-1982, Temple 1986, Louisiana State 1987-1990. Pro coach: Birmingham Stallions (USFL) 1983-85, Cleveland Browns 1991-93, joined Steelers in 1994.

Scottie Montgomery, wide receivers; born May 26, 1978, Shelby, N.C. Wide receiver Duke 1996-99. Pro wide receiver Carolina Panthers 2000, Denver Broncos 2000-02, Oakland Raiders 2003, Georgia Force (AFL) 2005. College coach: Duke 2006-09. Pro coach: Joined Steelers in 2010.

Kirby Wilson, running backs; born August 24, 1961, Los Angeles. Running back/wide receiver Pasadena (Calif.) C.C. 1979-1980, Illinois 1981-82. Pro cornerback Winnipeg Blue Bombers (CFL) 1983, Toronto Argonauts (CFL) 1984. College coach: Pasadena (Calif.) C.C. 1989-1990, Southern Illinois 1991-92, Wyoming 1993-94, Iowa State 1995-96, Southern California 2001. Pro coach: New England Patriots 1997-99, Washington Redskins 2000, Tampa Bay Buccaneers 2002-03, Arizona Cardinals 2004-06, joined Steelers in 2007.

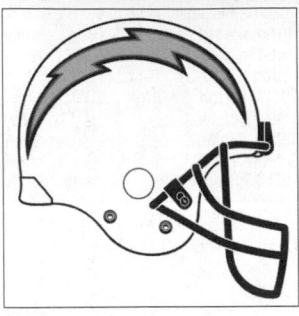

American Football Conference
West Division
Team Colors: Navy Blue, Powder Blue,
White, and Gold
P.O. Box 609609
San Diego, California 92160-9609
Telephone: (858) 874-4500

2011 SCHEDULE
PRESEASON
Aug. 11 **Seattle** 5:00
Aug. 20 at Dallas 5:00
Aug. 27 at Arizona...........................7:00
Sep. 1 **San Francisco** 7:00

REGULAR SEASON
Sep. 11 **Minnesota** 1:15
Sep. 18 at New England 1:15
Sep. 25 **Kansas City** 1:05
Oct. 2 **Miami** 1:15
Oct. 9 at Denver 1:15
Oct. 16 BYE
Oct. 23 at New York Jets............10:00a
Oct. 31 at Kansas City (Mon)......... 5:30
Nov. 6 **Green Bay** 1:15
Nov. 10 **Oakland** (Thu).................. 5:20
Nov. 20 at Chicago 1:15
Nov. 27 **Denver** 1:15
Dec. 5 at Jacksonville (Mon) 5:30
Dec. 11 **Buffalo** 1:15
Dec. 18 **Baltimore** * 5:20
Dec. 24 at Detroit (Sat) 1:05
Jan. 1 at Oakland 1:15
*All times PT; Sunday night games in
Weeks 11-15, 17 subject to change*

Stadium: Qualcomm Stadium
(opened in 1967)
• **Capacity:** 70,000 (app.)
9449 Friars Road
San Diego, California 92108
Playing Surface: Grass
Training Camp: Chargers Park
4020 Murphy Canyon Rd.
San Diego, CA 92123

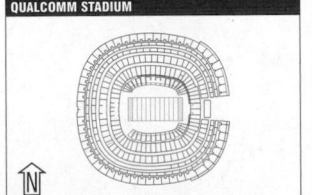

QUALCOMM STADIUM

CLUB OFFICIALS
Owner: Alex G. Spanos
President/CEO: Dean A. Spanos
Executive Vice President:
Michael A. Spanos
Executive Vice President-Executive
Officer: A.G. Spanos
Executive Vice President-General
Manager: A.J. Smith
Executive Vice President of Football
Operations-Assistant General
Manager: Ed McGuire
Executive Vice President-Chief Financial
Officer: Jeanne M. Bonk
Senior Vice President-Chief Marketing
Officer: Ken Derrett
Director of Player Personnel:
Jimmy Raye
Director of College Scouting:
John Spanos
Director of Pro Scouting:
Dennis Abraham
Senior Executive: Randy Mueller
Head Athletic Trainer: James Collins
Director of Video Operations:
Brian Duddy
Equipment Manager: Bob Wick
Director of Player Development:
Arthur Hightower
Vice President of Marketing Partnerships:
Dennis O'Leary
Senior Director of Ticket Sales and
Service: Todd Poulsen
Director of Business Operations:
John Hinek
Director of Public Relations: Bill Johnston
Director of Public Affairs &
Corporate/Community Relations:
Kimberley Layton
Director of Security: Dick Lewis
Director of Stadium/Game Operations &
Events: Sean O'Connor
Controller: Marsha Wells
Director of Ticket Operations:
Michael L. Dougherty

COACHING HISTORY
Los Angeles 1960
(394-393-11)
Records include postseason games
1960-69 Sid Gillman* 83-51-6
1969-1970 Charlie Waller 9-7-3
1971 Sid Gillman** 4-6-0
1971-73 Harland Svare*** 7-17-2
1973 Ron Waller.....................1-5-0
1974-78 Tommy Prothro**** ...21-39-0
1978-1986 Don Coryell# 72-60-0
1986-88 Al Saunders 17-22-0
1989-1991 Dan Henning..............16-32-0
1992-96 Bobby Ross...............50-36-0
1997-98 Kevin Gilbride...............6-16-0
1998 June Jones 3-7-0
1999-2001 Mike Riley...................14-34-0
2002-06 Marty Schottenheimer.47-35-0
2007-2010 Norv Turner................44-26-0
*Retired after nine games in 1969
**Resigned after 10 games in 1971
***Resigned after eight games in 1973
****Resigned after four games in 1978
#Resigned after eight games in 1986
##Released after six games in 1998

PAID ATTENDANCE
Home 524,312   Away 490,068
Total 1,014,380
Single-game home record,
69,288 (11/7/99)
Single-season home record,
547,937 (2005)

2011 DRAFT CHOICES

Round	Name	Pos.	College
1	Corey Liuget	DE	Illinois
2	Marcus Gilchrist	DB	Clemson
	Jonas Mouton	LB	Michigan
3	Vincent Brown	WR	San Diego St.
	Shareece Wright	DB	Southern California
6	Jordan Todman	RB	Connecticut
	Stephen Schilling	T	Michigan
7	Andrew Gachkar	LB	Missouri

2010 TEAM RECORD
PRESEASON (1-3)

Date	Result	Opponent
8/14	W 25-10	Chicago
8/21	L 14-16	Dallas
8/27	L 21-36	at New Orleans
9/2	L 14-17	at San Francisco

REGULAR SEASON (9-7)

Date	Result	Opponent
9/13	L 14-21	at Kansas City
9/19	W 38-13	Jacksonville
9/26	L 20-27	at Seattle
10/3	W 41-10	Arizona
10/10	L 27-35	at Oakland
10/17	L 17-20	at St. Louis
10/24	L 20-23	New England
10/31	W 33-25	Tennessee
11/7	W 29-23	at Houston
11/22	W 35-14	Denver
11/28	W 36-14	at Indianapolis
12/5	L 13-28	Oakland
12/12	W 31-0	Kansas City
12/16	W 34-7	San Francisco
12/26	L 20-34	at Cincinnati
1/2	W 33-28	at Denver

(OT) Overtime

SCORE BY PERIODS

Chargers	76	128	107	130	0 —	441
Opponents	96	94	31	101	0 —	322

2010 TEAM STATISTICS

	Chargers	Opp.
Total First Downs	357	247
Rushing	94	77
Passing	236	153
Penalty	27	17
3rd Down: Made/Att	92/205	70/208
3rd Down Pct.	44.9	33.7
4th Down: Made/Att	5/13	12/28
4th Down Pct.	38.5	42.9
Possession Avg.	33:03	26:57
Total Net Yards	6329	4345
Avg. Per Game	395.6	271.6
Total Plays	1039	939
Avg. Per Play	6.1	4.6
Net Yards Rushing	1810	1500
Avg. Per Game	113.1	93.8
Total Rushes	457	404
Net Yards Passing	4519	2845
Avg. Per Game	282.4	177.8
Sacked/Yards Lost	38/227	47/290
Gross Yards	4746	3135
Att./Completions	544/359	488/285
Completion Pct.	66.0	58.4
Had Intercepted	13	16
Punts/Average	56/43.4	81/42.1
Net Punting Avg.	56/30.8	81/36.2
Penalties/Yards	84/677	97/769
Fumbles/Ball Lost	25/16	13/7
Touchdowns	51	39
Rushing	18	14
Passing	30	18
Returns	3	7

2010 INDIVIDUAL STATISTICS

PASSING

	Att.	Comp.	Yds.	Pct.	TD	Int.	Tkld.	Rate
Rivers	541	357	4710	66.0	30	13	38/227	101.8
Crayton	1	0	0	0.0	0	0	0/0	39.6
Scifres	1	1	28	100.0	0	0	0/0	118.8
Volek	1	1	8	100.0	0	0	0/0	100.0
Chargers	544	359	4746	66.0	30	13	38/227	101.9
Opponents	488	285	3135	58.4	18	16	47/290	76.2

SCORING

	TD R	TD P	TD Rt	PAT	FG	Saf	PTS
Kaeding	0	0	0	40/40	23/28	0	109
Tolbert	11	0	0	0/0	0/0	0	68
Gates	0	10	0	0/0	0/0	0	60
Mathews	7	0	0	0/0	0/0	0	42
Floyd	0	6	0	0/0	0/0	0	36
Brown	0	0	0	8/8	4/5	0	20
Jackson	0	3	0	0/0	0/0	0	18
Ajirotutu	0	2	0	0/0	0/0	0	12
McMichael	0	2	0	0/0	0/0	0	12
Sproles	0	2	0	0/0	0/0	0	12
Naanee	0	1	0	0/0	0/0	0	8
Burnett	0	0	1	0/0	0/0	0	6
Crayton	0	1	0	0/0	0/0	0	6
Davis	0	1	0	0/0	0/0	0	6
Hester	0	1	0	0/0	0/0	0	6
Phillips	0	0	1	0/0	0/0	0	6
Washington	0	1	0	0/0	0/0	0	6
Weddle	0	0	1	0/0	0/0	0	6
Siler	0	0	0	0/0	0/0	1	2
Chargers	18	30	3	48/48	27/33	1	441
Opponents	14	18	7	36/37	16/16	2	322

2-Pt Conversions: Naanee, Tolbert.
Chargers 2-3, Opponents 0-2.

RUSHING

	No.	Yds	Avg	LG	TD
Tolbert	182	735	4.0	36	11
Mathews	158	678	4.3	31t	7
Sproles	50	267	5.3	34	0
Hester	26	60	2.3	6	0
Rivers	29	52	1.8	14	0
Jackson	1	14	14.0	14	0
Brinkley	2	11	5.5	9	0
Naanee	3	-2	-.7	5	0
Volek	6	-5	-.8	0	0
Chargers	457	1810	4.0	36	18
Opponents	404	1500	3.7	56t	14

RECEIVING

	No.	Yds	Avg	LG	TD
Sproles	59	520	8.8	57t	2
Gates	50	782	15.6	48t	10
Floyd	37	717	19.4	55	6
Crayton	28	514	18.4	49	1
Tolbert	25	216	8.6	28	0
Naanee	23	371	16.1	59t	1
Hester	22	145	6.6	21	1
Mathews	22	145	6.6	17	0
Davis	21	259	12.3	49	1
McMichael	20	221	11.1	28	2
Jackson	14	248	17.7	58t	3
Ajirotutu	13	262	20.2	55t	2
Washington	13	173	13.3	36	1
Kr. Wilson	6	73	12.2	37	0
Sperry	4	73	18.3	35	0
Goodman	1	25	25.0	25	0
Banks	1	2	2.0	2	0
Chargers	359	4746	13.2	59t	30
Opponents	285	3135	11.0	71t	18

INTERCEPTIONS

	No.	Yds	Avg	LG	TD
Cason	4	51	12.8	28	0
Weddle	2	64	32.0	41t	1
Gregory	2	41	20.5	41	0
Burnett	2	31	15.5	29t	1
Jammer	2	5	2.5	5	0
Phillips	1	31	31.0	31t	1
Oliver	1	15	15.0	15	0
Cooper	1	2	2.0	2	0
Siler	1	0	0.0	0	0
Chargers	16	240	15.0	41t	3
Opponents	13	167	12.8	47	0

PUNTING

	No.	Yds.	Avg.	In 20	LG
Scifres	52	2430	46.7	13	67
Chargers	56	2430	43.4	13	67
Opponents	81	3414	42.1	28	63

PUNT RETURNS

	Ret	FC	Yds	Avg	LG	TD
Sproles	24	11	166	6.9	16	0
Cason	14	4	231	16.5	62	0
Crayton	2	2	23	11.5	13	0
Weddle	0	2	0	--	--	0
Chargers	40	19	420	10.5	62	0
Opponents	28	7	528	18.9	94t	1

KICKOFF RETURNS

	No.	Yds	Avg	LG	TD
Sproles	51	1257	24.6	45	0
Hester	3	25	8.3	13	0
Brinkley	1	29	29.0	29	0
Crayton	1	31	31.0	31	0
Chargers	56	1342	24.0	45	0
Opponents	84	1880	22.4	101t	3

FIELD GOALS

	1-19	20-29	30-39	40-49	50+
Kaeding	0/0	6/6	7/8	9/10	1/4
Brown	0/0	1/1	3/3	0/0	0/1
Chargers	0/0	7/7	10/11	9/10	1/5
Opponents	0/0	6/6	4/4	4/4	2/2

SACKS

	No.
Phillips	11.0
Burnett	6.0
Garay	5.5
Barnes	4.5
Applewhite	3.0
English	3.0
Castillo	2.5
Thomas	2.0
Cesaire	1.5
Cooper	1.0
T. Johnson	1.0
Lang	1.0
Martin	1.0
Siler	1.0
Strickland	1.0
Tucker	1.0
Nwagbuo	0.5
Weddle	0.5
Chargers	47.0
Opponents	37.0

RECORD HOLDERS
INDIVIDUAL RECORDS—CAREER

Category	Name	Performance
Rushing (Yds.)	LaDainian Tomlinson, 2001-09	12,490
Passing (Yds.)	Dan Fouts, 1973-1987	43,040
Passing (TDs)	Dan Fouts, 1973-1987	254
Receiving (No.)	Charlie Joiner, 1976-1986	586
Receiving (Yds.)	Lance Alworth, 1962-1970	9,584
Interceptions	Gill Byrd, 1983-1992	42
Punting (Avg.)	Mike Scifres, 2003-2010	44.5
Punt Return (Avg.)	Darrien Gordon, 1993-96	13.7
Kickoff Return (Avg.)	Leslie (Speedy) Duncan, 1964-1970	25.3
Field Goals	John Carney, 1990-2000	261
Touchdowns (Tot.)	LaDainian Tomlinson, 2001-09	153
Points	John Carney, 1990-2000	1,076
*Sacks	Leslie O'Neal, 1986-1995	105.5

INDIVIDUAL RECORDS—SINGLE SEASON

Category	Name	Performance
Rushing (Yds.)	LaDainian Tomlinson, 2006	1,815
Passing (Yds.)	Dan Fouts, 1981	4,802
Passing (TDs)	Philip Rivers, 2008	34
Receiving (No.)	LaDainian Tomlinson, 2003	100
Receiving (Yds.)	Lance Alworth, 1965	1,602
Interceptions	Antonio Cromartie, 2007	10
Punting (Avg.)	Mike Scifres, 2010	46.7
Punt Return (Avg.)	Leslie (Speedy) Duncan, 1965	15.5
Kickoff Return (Avg.)	Keith Lincoln, 1962	28.4
Field Goals	John Carney, 1994	34
Touchdowns (Tot.)	LaDainian Tomlinson, 2006	**31
Points	LaDainian Tomlinson, 2006	**186
*Sacks	Leslie O'Neal, 1992	17.0
	Shawne Merriman, 2006	17.0

INDIVIDUAL RECORDS—SINGLE GAME

Category	Name	Performance
Rushing (Yds.)	LaDainian Tomlinson, 12-28-03	243
Passing (Yds.)	Philip Rivers, 9-26-10	455
Passing (TDs)	Dan Fouts, 11-22-81	6
Receiving (No.)	Kellen Winslow, 10-7-84	15
Receiving (Yds.)	Wes Chandler, 12-20-82	260
Interceptions	Many times	3
	Last time by Antonio Cromartie, 11-11-07	
Field Goals	John Carney, 9-5-93, 9-18-93	6
	Greg Davis, 10-5-97	6
Touchdowns (Tot.)	Kellen Winslow, 11-22-81	5
Points	Kellen Winslow, 11-22-81	30
*Sacks	Leslie O'Neal, 11-16-86	5.0

*Sacks became an official statistic in 1982.
**NFL Record

VETERAN ROSTER AS OF MARCH 3, 2011

No.	Name	Pos.	Ht.	Wt.	Birthdate	^NFL Exp.	College	Hometown	How Acq.	'10 Games/ Starts
89	Ajirotutu, Seyi	WR	6-3	211	6/12/87	2	Fresno State	El Dorado Hills, Calif.	FA-'10	10/0
90	Applewhite, Antwan	OLB	6-3	258	12/31/85	4	San Diego State	Los Angeles, Calif.	FA-'07	16/3
98	Barnes, Antwan	OLB	6-1	251	10/19/84	5	Florida International	Miami, Fla.	FA-'10	13/0*
50	Binn, David	LS	6-3	228	2/6/72	18	California	San Mateo, Calif.	FA-'94	1/0
44	Brinkley, Curtis	RB	5-9	208	9/20/85	2	Syracuse	Philadelphia, Pa.	FA-'10	3/0
99	Burnett, Kevin	ILB	6-3	240	12/24/82	7	Tennessee	Compton, Calif.	FA-'09	16/16
51	Butler, Donald	ILB	6-1	248	10/17/88	2	Washington	Sacramento, Calif.	D3-'10	0*
31	Carter, Tyrone	S	5-9	200	3/31/76	12	Minnesota	Pompano Beach, Fla.	FA-'10	7/0
20	Cason, Antoine	CB	6-1	198	7/9/86	4	Arizona	Long Beach, Calif.	D1-'08	16/15
93	Castillo, Luis	DE	6-3	290	8/4/83	7	Northwestern	Garfield, N.J.	D1b-'05	16/16
74	Cesaire, Jacques	DE	6-2	295	8/30/80	9	So. Connecticut State	Gardner, Mass.	FA-'03	16/16
66	Clary, Jeromey	T	6-6	320	11/5/83	5	Kansas State	Mansfield, Texas	D6a-'06	16/16
54	Cooper, Stephen	ILB	6-1	235	6/19/79	9	Maine	Wareham, Mass.	FA-'03	12/11
12	Crayton, Patrick	WR	6-0	205	4/7/79	8	Northwestern Okla. St.	DeSoto, Texas	T(Dall)-'10	9/2
84	Davis, Buster	WR	6-1	210	10/2/85	5	Louisiana State	New Orleans, La.	D1-'07	7/1
58	Dearth, James	LS	6-4	265	1/22/76	11	Tarleton State	Scurry, Texas	FA-'10	0*
68	Dielman, Kris	G	6-4	320	2/3/81	9	Indiana	Troy, Ohio	FA-'03	15/15
62	Dombrowski, Brandyn	G/T	6-5	323	4/3/85	3	San Diego State	Henderson, Nev.	FA-'08	16/5
52	English, Larry	OLB	6-2	255	1/22/86	3	Northern Illinois	Aurora, Ill.	D1-'09	8/2
80	Floyd, Malcom	WR	6-5	225	9/8/81	6	Wyoming	Sacramento, Calif.	FA-'04	11/9
71	Garay, Antonio	DT	6-4	320	11/30/79	5	Boston College	Rahway, N.J.	FA-'09	16/15
85	Gates, Antonio	TE	6-4	260	6/18/80	9	Kent State	Detroit, Mich.	FA-'03	10/10
69	Green, Tyronne	G/T	6-2	316	4/6/86	3	Auburn	Pensacola, Fla.	D4b-'09	12/7
28	Gregory, Steve	SS	5-11	195	1/8/83	6	Syracuse	Staten Island, N.Y.	FA-'06	9/9
61	Hardwick, Nick	C	6-4	305	9/2/81	8	Purdue	Indianapolis, Ind.	D3b-'04	16/16
22	Hester, Jacob	FB	5-11	235	5/8/85	4	Louisiana State	Shreveport, La.	D3-'08	15/7
53	Holt, James	LB	6-2	223	11/24/86	3	Kansas	Altus, Okla.	FA-'09	3/0
24	Hughes, Dante	CB	5-10	190	8/21/85	5	California	Los Angeles, Calif.	FA-'09	12/1
83	Jackson, Vincent	WR	6-5	230	1/14/83	7	Northern Colorado	Colorado Springs, Colo.	D2-'05	5/5
23	Jammer, Quentin	CB	6-0	204	6/19/79	10	Texas	Angleton, Texas	D1-'02	16/16
96	Johnson, Travis	DE/DT	6-3	311	4/26/82	7	Florida State	Sherman Oaks, Calif.	T(HOU)-'09	9/0
10	Kaeding, Nate	K	6-0	187	3/26/82	8	Iowa	Coralville, Iowa	D3a-'04	13/0
57	Lang, Brandon	LB	6-3	266	6/18/86	2	Troy	Tucker, Ga.	FA-'10	10/0
92	Martin, Vaughn	DE/DT	6-4	330	4/18/86	3	Western Ontario	London, Ontario, Canada	D4a-'09	10/0
24	Mathews, Ryan	RB	6-0	218	10/10/87	2	Fresno State	Bakersfield, Calif.	D1-'10	12/9
81	McMichael, Randy	TE	6-3	248	6/28/79	10	Georgia	Fort Valley, Ga.	FA-'10	16/11
73	McNeill, Marcus	T	6-7	336	11/16/83	6	Auburn	Ellenwood, Ga.	D2-'06	11/11
49	Moore, Brandon	LB	6-1	240	1/16/79	7	Oklahoma	Baldwin, N.Y.	FA-'10	2/0
63	Mruczkowski, Scott	C	6-5	310	4/5/82	7	Bowling Green	Garfield Heights, Ohio	D7-'05	15/0
11	Naanee, Legedu	WR	6-2	220	9/16/83	5	Boise State	Portland, Ore.	D5-'07	10/9
58	Neill, Ryan	LS	6-3	253	12/12/82	5	Rutgers	Wayne, N.J.	FA-'10	2/0
91	Nwagbuo, Ogemdi	DE/DT	6-4	312	12/24/85	3	Michigan State	Spring Valley, Calif.	FA-'08	15/0
27	Oliver, Paul	S	5-11	210	3/30/84	5	Georgia	Kennesaw, Ga.	D4(Supp)-'07	16/8
95	Phillips, Shaun	OLB	6-3	250	5/13/81	8	Purdue	Willingboro, N.J.	D4-'04	16/16
17	Rivers, Philip	QB	6-5	228	12/8/81	8	North Carolina State	Athens, Ala.	T(NYG)-'04	16/16
5	Scifres, Mike	P	6-2	221	10/8/80	9	Western Illinois	Destrehan, La.	D5-'03	16/0
59	Siler, Brandon	ILB	6-2	239	12/5/85	5	Florida	Orlando, Fla.	D7-'07	12/5
82	Sperry, Kory	TE	6-5	250	4/10/85	3	Colorado State	Vineland, Colo.	FA-'10	7/1
43	Sproles, Darren	RB/KR	5-6	190	6/20/83	7	Kansas State	Olathe, Kan.	D4-'05	16/3
30	Strickland, Donald	CB	5-10	185	11/27/80	8	Colorado	San Francisco, Calif.	FA-'10	16/0
25	Stuckey, Darrell	S	5-11	208	6/16/87	2	Kansas	Kansas City, Kan.	D4-'10	1/0
36	Teal, Quinton	S	6-0	205	3/8/84	5	Coastal Carolina	Bennettsville, S.C.	FA-'10	13/0
76	Thomas, Cam	DT	6-4	335	12/12/86	2	North Carolina	Robbins, N.C.	D5A-'10	6/0
35	Tolbert, Mike	RB	5-9	243	11/23/85	4	Coastal Carolina	Douglasville, Ga.	FA-'08	15/4
94	Tucker, Jyles	OLB	6-3	258	9/18/83	5	Wake Forest	Dover, N.J.	FA-'07	3/0
65	Vasquez, Louis	G	6-5	335	4/11/87	3	Texas Tech	Corsicana, Tex.	D3-'09	10/10
7	Volek, Billy	QB	6-2	214	4/28/76	12	Fresno State	Fresno, Calif.	T(Tenn)-'06	3/0
	Wallace, C.J.	S	6-0	205	4/17/85	4	Washington	Sacramento, Calif.	FA-'11	0*
87	Washington, Kelley	WR	6-3	217	8/21/79	9	Tennessee	Stephens City, Va.	FA-'10	8/0
26	Watkins, Pat	S	6-5	220	12/18/82	6	Florida State	Tallahassee, Fla.	FA-'10	4/0
32	Weddle, Eric	S	5-11	200	1/4/85	5	Utah	Alta Loma, Calif.	D2-'07	16/16
42	Wilson, Kion	FB/LB	6-0	240	10/24/86	2	South Florida	Jacksonville, Fla.	FA-'10	3/0
88	Wilson, Kris	TE	6-2	245	8/22/81	8	Pittsburgh	Lancaster, Pa.	FA-'08	14/7
47	Windt, Mike	LS	6-1	252	5/29/86	2	Cincinnati	Cincinnati, Ohio	FA-'10	11/0

* Barnes played 2 games with Philadelphia and 11 games with San Diego in '10; Butler missed '10 season because of injury; Dearth missed '10 season because of injury; Wallace last active with Seattle in '09.

Also played with Chargers in '10—LS Ethan Albright (2 games), WR Gary Banks (2), ILB Darry Beckwith (1), DE Alfonso Boone (3), K Kris Brown (3), WR Richard Goodman (3), LB David Herron (2), FB Billy Latsko (1), LB Shawne Merriman (3), LB Cyril Obiozor (2), S C.J. Spillman (5), T Adam Terry (2).

^ "NFL Exp." as of 2011 Kickoff Weekend. For full explanation of how a player's NFL Experience is measured, refer to explanation underneath the First-Year Roster listed below.

FIRST-YEAR ROSTER

Name	Pos.	Ht.	Wt.	Birthdate	College	Hometown	How Acq.
Banks, Gary (1)	WR	6-0	193	11/4/81	Troy	Melvin, Ala.	FA-'08
Beckwith, Darry (1)	ILB	6-0	234	5/15/87	Louisiana State	Baton Rouge, La.	FA-'09
Brown, Vincent	WR/KR	5-11	184	1/25/89	San Diego State	Rancho Cucamonga, Calif.	D3a
Gachkar, Andrew	LB	6-3	228	11/4/88	Missouri	Overland Park, Kan.	D7
Gilchrist, Marcus	CB/KR	5-10	193	12/8/88	Clemson	High Point, N.C.	D2a
Goodman, Richard (1)	WR	6-0	192	4/23/87	Florida State	Ft. Lauderdale, Fla.	FA-'10
Ihenacho, Carl	DE	6-3	245	5/28/88	San Jose State	Gardena, Calif.	FA
Latsko, Billy (1)	FB	5-10	233	2/16/84	Florida	Gainesville, Fla.	FA-'08
Leman, Jeremy (1)	LB	6-2	240	3/1/85	Illinois	Champaign, Ill.	FA-'10
Liuget, Corey	DE	6-2	300	3/18/90	Illinois	Miami, Fla.	D1
Morris, Dennis	TE	6-2	260	2/15/87	Louisiana Tech	Shreveport, La.	FA
Mouton, Jonas	LB	6-2	240	3/17/88	Michigan	Los Angeles, Calif.	D2b
Otterson, Ryan (1)	T	6-5	291	11/29/86	Wyoming	Brighton, Colo.	FA-'10
Richmond, Nick (1)	T	6-8	309	5/1/87	Texas Christian	Garland, Texas	FA-'10
Schilling, Stephen	T	6-5	308	7/21/88	Michigan	Bellevue, Wash.	D6b
Schmitt, Ricky (1)	P	6-3	215	8/17/85	Shepherd	Virginia Beach, Va.	FA
Simmons, Traye (1)	CB	5-9	180	1/18/87	Minnesota	Marietta, Ga.	FA-'10
Summers, Frank (1)	FB	5-10	255	9/6/85	Nevada-Las Vegas	Oakland, Calif.	FA
Todman, Jordan	RB	5-9	193	2/24/90	Connecticut	North Dartmouth, Mass.	D6a
Walters, Bryan (1)	WR	6-0	190	11/4/87	Cornell	Bothell, Wash.	FA-'10
Wright, Shareece	CB	5-11	182	4/8/87	Southern California	Colton, Calif.	D3b
Young, Eric (1)	T	6-3	304	11/22/83	Tennessee	Union, S.C.	FA-'10

The term NFL Rookie is defined as a player who is in his first season of professional football and has not been on the roster of another professional football team for any regular-season or postseason games. A Rookie is designated by an "R" on NFL rosters. Players who have been active in another professional football league or players who have NFL experience, including either preseason training camp or being on an Active List or Inactive List, or on Reserve/Injured or Reserve/Physically Unable to Perform for fewer than six regular-season games, are termed NFL First-Year Players. An NFL First-Year Player is designated by a "1" on NFL rosters. Thereafter, a player is credited with an additional year of experience for each season in which he accumulates six games on the Active List or Inactive List, or on Reserve/Injured or Reserve/Physically Unable to Perform.

Log on to www.chargers.com for an up-to-date roster.

COACHING STAFF

Head Coach,
Norv Turner

Pro Career: A veteran coach of 26 NFL seasons, Turner became the 14th head coach in team history on February 19, 2007. Entering the 2011 season, Turner has the top overall winning percentage (44-26, .629) and top regular season winning percentage (41-23, .641) in team history. In his first three seasons, Turner led the Chargers to three-straight AFC West titles. In the postseason, he led the Chargers to the 2007 AFC Championship Game and the 2008 and 2009 Divisional Playoffs. A two-time Super Bowl champion as an offensive coordinator with the Dallas Cowboys, Turner was the offensive coordinator for the San Francisco 49ers in 2006. A Bay Area native from Martinez, California, this is Turner's second stint with the Chargers. He spent the 2001 season as the Bolts' offensive coordinator. Turner's 26 years of coaching experience include 13 as a head coach—seven for the Washington Redskins (1994-2000), two with the Oakland Raiders (2004-05), and four with the Chargers (2007-2010). In 1999, he led the Redskins to a division title. He spent 13 seasons as an NFL assistant coach, including seven as an offensive coordinator with the Cowboys (1991-93), Chargers (2001), Dolphins (2002-03), and 49ers (2006). Turner began his NFL coaching career as an assistant with the Rams in 1985. He coached wide receivers from 1985-86 before adding the responsibility of the team's tight ends from 1987-1990. Turner made his coaching mark during his three seasons in Dallas as the Cowboys won back-to-back Super Bowls (XXVII and XXVIII) following the 1992 and 1993 seasons. Career record: 103-109-1.

Background: Turner played quarterback at Oregon, spending two seasons behind former Charger and NFL Hall of Fame quarterback Dan Fouts. Turner coached at Oregon (1975) and Southern California (1976-1984). During his nine-year tenure at USC, the Trojans played in four Rose Bowls, winning all four. One of those was a win over Michigan after the 1978 season that capped a 12-1 season and gave USC the National Championship.

Personal: Born in LeJeune, N.C., May 17, 1952. Turner and his wife, Nancy, have three children—Scott, Stephanie, and Drew.

ASSISTANT COACHES

Rich Bisaccia, special teams; born June 3, 1960, Yonkers, N.Y. Defensive back Yankton College 1979-1982. Pro defensive back Philadelphia Stars (USFL) 1983. College coach: Wayne State College 1983-87, South Carolina 1988-1993, Clemson 1994-98, Mississippi 1999-2001. Pro coach: Tampa Bay Buccaneers 2002-2010, joined Chargers in 2011.

Cris Dishman, asst. secondary; born August 13, 1965, Louisville, Kentucky. Cornerback Purdue 1984-87. Pro cornerback Houston Oilers 1988-1996, Washington Redskins 1997-98, Kansas City Chiefs 1999, Minnesota Vikings 2000. College coach: Menlo College 2006-08. Pro coach: Joined Chargers in 2009.

Hal Hunter, offensive line; born July 8, 1959, Canonsburg, Pa. Linebacker Northwestern 1978. College coach: William & Mary 1982, Pittsburgh 1983-84, Columbia 1985, Indiana (Pa.) 1986, Akron 1987-1990, Vanderbilt 1991-94, Louisiana State 1995-99, Indiana 2000-01, North Carolina 2002-05. Pro coach: Joined Chargers in 2006.

Jeff Hurd, strength and conditioning; born April 24, 1958, Pomona, Calif. No college or pro playing experience. College coach: Fort Hays State 1984, Delta State 1985-86, Clemson 1986-87, Western Michigan 1987-1992, Tulsa 1994. Pro coach: Jacksonville Jaguars 1995-97, Kansas City Chiefs 1998-2006, joined Chargers in 2007.

Don Johnson, defensive line; born November 3, 1954, Newark, N.J. Linebacker Jersey City State 1973-76. College coach: Jersey City State 1984-85. Riverside (Calif.) C.C. 1987-1990, Cal State-Fullerton 1991-92, Nevada 1995-98, UCLA 1999-2004. Pro coach: Chicago Bears 2005-06, Oakland Raiders 2007-08, joined Chargers in 2009.

Charlie Joiner, receivers; born October 14, 1947, Many, La. Wide receiver Grambling State 1965-68. Pro defensive back/wide receiver Houston Oilers 1969-1972, Cincinnati Bengals 1972-75, San Diego Chargers 1976-1986. Inducted into Pro Football Hall of Fame 1996. Pro coach: San Diego Chargers 1987-1991, Buffalo Bills 1992-2000, Kansas City Chiefs 2001-07, re-joined Chargers in 2008.

Greg Manusky, defensive coordinator; born August 12, 1966, Wilkes-Barre, Pa. Linebacker Colgate 1983-87. Pro linebacker Washington Redskins 1988-1990, Minnesota Vikings 1991-93, Kansas City Chiefs 1994-99. Pro coach: Washington Redskins 2001, San Diego Chargers 2002-06, San Francisco 49ers 2007-2010, re-joined Chargers in 2011.

Jason Michael, tight ends; born October 15, 1978, Portsmouth, Ohio. Quarterback Western Kentucky 1999-2002. No pro playing experience. College coach: Tennessee 2003-04, 2008. Pro coach: Oakland Raiders 2005, New York Jets 2006-07, San Francisco 49ers 2009-2010, joined Chargers in 2011.

John Pagano, linebackers; born March 30, 1967, Boulder, Colo. Linebacker Mesa State College 1985-88. No pro playing experience. College coach: Mesa State College 1989, Nevada-Las Vegas 1990-91, Louisiana Tech 1994, Mississippi

1995. Pro coach: New Orleans Saints 1996-97, Indianapolis Colts 1998-2001, joined Chargers in 2002.

John Ramsdell, quarterbacks; born August 16, 1954, Lafayette, Ind. Running back Springfield (Mass.) College 1972-75. No pro playing experience. College coach: San Francisco State 1976-77, Long Beach State 1978, Pacific 1979-1982, Oregon 1983-1994. Pro coach: St. Louis Rams 1995-2005, joined Chargers in 2006.

Clarence Shelmon, offensive coordinator; born September 17, 1952, Bossier City, La. Running back Houston 1971-75. No pro playing experience. College coach: Army 1978-1980, Indiana 1981-83, Arizona 1984-86, Southern California 1987-1990. Pro coach: Los Angeles Rams 1991, Seattle Seahawks 1992-97, Dallas Cowboys 1998-2001, joined Chargers in 2002.

Vernon Stephens, asst. strength and conditioning; born November 30, 1974, Jacksonville. No college or pro playing experience. College coach: North Florida 1999-2002, Colorado 2003-06. Pro coach: Jacksonville Jaguars 2002-03, joined Chargers in 2007.

Mike Sullivan, offensive line; born December 2, 1967, Chicago. Offensive lineman Miami 1986-90. Pro offensive lineman Dallas Cowboys 1991, Tampa Bay Buccaneers 1992-95. College coach: Miami 2000, Western Michigan 2005-06. Pro coach: Cleveland Browns 2001-04, 2007-08, joined Chargers in 2009.

Steve Wilks, asst. head coach/secondary; born August 8, 1969, Charlotte. Defensive back Appalachian State 1987-1991. Pro defensive back/wide receiver Charlotte Rage (AFL) 1993. College coach: Johnson C. Smith 1995-96, Savannah State 1997-99, Illinois State 2000, Appalachian State 2001, East Tennessee State 2002, Bowling Green State 2003, Notre Dame 2004, Washington 2005. Pro coach: Chicago Bears 2006-08, joined Chargers in 2009.

Greg Williams, asst. linebackers; born March 12, 1976, Chicago. Wide receiver/defensive back North Carolina 1994-97. Pro defensive back Amsterdam Admirals (NFL Europe) 1999-2000, San Francisco Demons (XFL) 2001, Indiana Firebirds (AFL) 2001-03, Chicago Rush (AFL) 2004. College coach: Arizona State 2003, College of DuPage 2004-05, Arkansas Tech 2006-07, Pittsburgh 2008. Pro coach: Joined Chargers in 2009.

Ollie Wilson, running backs; born March 3, 1951, Worcester, Mass. Wide receiver Springfield 1971-73. No pro playing experience. College coach: Springfield 1975, Northeastern 1976-1982, California 1983-1990. Pro coach: Atlanta Falcons 1991-96, 2002-07, San Diego Chargers 1997-2001, re-joined Chargers in 2008.

American Football Conference
South Division
Team Colors: Navy, Titans Blue, Red, Silver
460 Great Circle Road
Nashville, Tennessee 37228
Telephone: (615) 565-4000

2011 SCHEDULE
PRESEASON
Aug. 13	Minnesota	7:00
Aug. 20	at St. Louis	7:00
Aug. 27	Chicago	7:00
Sep. 1	at New Orleans	7:00

REGULAR SEASON
Sep. 11	at Jacksonville	12:00
Sep. 18	Baltimore	12:00
Sep. 25	Denver	12:00
Oct. 2	at Cleveland	12:00
Oct. 9	at Pittsburgh	12:00
Oct. 16	BYE	
Oct. 23	Houston	12:00
Oct. 30	Indianapolis	12:00
Nov. 6	Cincinnati	3.05
Nov. 13	at Carolina	12:00
Nov. 20	at Atlanta	12:00
Nov. 27	Tampa Bay	12:00
Dec. 4	at Buffalo	12:00
Dec. 11	New Orleans	12:00
Dec. 18	at Indianapolis	12:00
Dec. 24	Jacksonville (Sat)	12:00
Jan. 1	at Houston	12:00

All times CT

Stadium: LP Field
(opened in 1999)
 • **Capacity:** 69,143
One Titans Way
Nashville, Tennessee 37213
Playing Surface: Natural Grass
Training Camp: Baptist Sports Park
460 Great Circle Road
Nashville, TN 37228

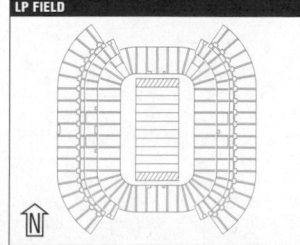

LP FIELD

CLUB OFFICIALS
Founder/Owner/Chairman of the
   Board/CEO/ President:
   K.S. "Bud" Adams, Jr.
Senior Executive V.P./General
   Counsel/Executive Asst. to Chairman
   of the Board: Steve Underwood
Executive V.P. of Administration/Facilities:
   Don MacLachlan
Executive V.P./General Manager:
   Mike Reinfeldt
Vice President/Asst. General Counsel:
   Elza Bullock
Vice President/Community Relations:
   Bob Hyde
Vice President/CFO: Jenneen Kaufman
Vice President/Marketing:
   Ralph Ockenfels
Vice President/Business Operations and
   Sales: Stuart Spears
Vice President/Player Personnel:
   Ruston Webster
Vice President/Football Administration:
   Vincent Marino
Vice President/Football Operations:
   Lake Dawson
Head Coach: Mike Munchak
Director of Player Development:
   Tina Tuggle
Equipment Manager: Paul Noska
Asst. Equipment Manager: Joey Barranco
Video Director: Anthony Pastrana
Asst. Video Director: Craig Patterson
Head Athletic Trainer: Brad Brown
Asst. Athletic Trainers: Don Moseley,
   Casey Carter
National Supervisor of College Scouting:
   C.O. Brocato
Scouting Coordinator: Blake Beddingfield
College Scouts: Ray Biggs,
   Johnny Meads, Phil Neri, Cole Proctor,
   Jon Salge, Richard Shelton,
   Marvin Sunderland
Pro Personnel Assistants: Trey Koziol,
   Brandon Taylor
Operations Manager: Brent Akers
Marketing Manager: Brad McClanahan
Director of Broadcasting: Mike Keith
Director of Information Systems:
   Russ Hudson
Asst. Dir. of Information Systems:
   Craig Pelat
Director of Internet
   Operations/Publications: Gary Glenn
Internet Coordinator: Jeff Harding
Community Relations Coordinator:
   Jerry Blessing
Manager of Community Relations:
   Tresa Halbrooks
Asst. General Counsel: Blu Whipple
Director of Security: Steve Berk
Director of Cheerleading: Stacie Kinder
Mascot Coordinator: Pete Nelson
Director of Media Relations:
   Robbie Bohren
Asst. Director of Media Relations:
   Dwight Spradlin
Media Relations Assistant: Jared Puffer
Senior Director of Ticketing:
   Marty Collins
Asst. Dir. Of Ticket Operations:
   Tim Zenner
Asst. Ticket Manager: Josh Ward
Ticketing/Hospitality Club Member
   Manager: Anthony Hall
Director of Suite Sales and Services:
   Bill Wainwright
General Manager of LP Field:
   Walter Overton
Head Groundskeeper: Terry Porch

COACHING HISTORY
Houston 1960-1996
(391-408-6)
Records include postseason games
1960-61	Lou Rymkus*	12-7-1
1961	Wally Lemm	10-0-0
1962-63	Frank (Pop) Ivy	17-12-0
1964	Sammy Baugh	4-10-0
1965	Hugh Taylor	4-10-0
1966-1970	Wally Lemm	28-40-4
1971	Ed Hughes	4-9-1
1972-73	Bill Peterson**	1-18-0
1973-74	Sid Gillman	8-15-0
1975-1980	O.A. (Bum) Phillips	59-38-0
1981-83	Ed Biles***	8-23-0
1983	Chuck Studley	2-8-0
1984-85	Hugh Campbell****	8-22-0
1985-89	Jerry Glanville	35-35-0
1990-94	Jack Pardee#	44-35-0
1994-2010	Jeff Fisher	147-126-0

  * Released after five games in 1961
 ** Released after five games in 1973
*** Resigned after six games in 1983
**** Released after 14 games in 1985
 # Released after 10 games in 1994

PAID ATTENDANCE
Home 530,478   Away 536,222
Total 1,066,700
Single-game home record,
   69,149, many times (last: 12/18/05)
Single-season home record,
   553,192 (2005)

2011 DRAFT CHOICES
Round	Name	Pos.	College
1	Jake Locker	QB	Washington
2	Akeem Ayers	LB	UCLA
3	Jurrell Casey	DT	Southern California
4	Colin McCarthy	LB	Miami
	Jamie Harper	RB	Clemson
5	Karl Klug	DT	Iowa
6	Byron Stingily	T	Louisville
7	Zach Clayton	DT	Auburn
	Tommie Campbell	DB	California (PA)

2010 TEAM RECORD

PRESEASON (2-2)

Date	Result		Opponent
8/14	L	18-20	at Seattle
8/23	W	24-10	Arizona
8/28	L	7-15	at Carolina
9/2	W	27-24	New Orleans

REGULAR SEASON (6-10)

Date	Result		Opponent
9/12	W	38-13	Oakland
9/19	L	11-19	Pittsburgh
9/26	W	29-10	at New York Giants
10/3	L	20-26	Denver
10/10	W	34-27	at Dallas
10/18	W	30-3	at Jacksonville
10/24	W	37-19	Philadelphia
10/31	L	25-33	at San Diego
11/14	L	17-29	at Miami
11/21	L	16-19	Washington (OT)
11/28	L	0-20	at Houston
12/5	L	6-17	Jacksonville
12/9	L	28-30	Indianapolis
12/19	W	31-17	Houston
12/26	L	14-34	at Kansas City
1/2	L	20-23	at Indianapolis

(OT) Overtime

SCORE BY PERIODS

Titans	79	92	83	102	0	—	356
Opponents	65	130	65	76	3	—	339

2010 TEAM STATISTICS

	Titans	Opp.
Total First Downs	252	356
Rushing	73	107
Passing	155	214
Penalty	24	35
3rd Down: Made/Att	71/204	104/242
3rd Down Pct.	34.8	43.0
4th Down: Made/Att	8/14	9/22
4th Down Pct.	57.1	40.9
Possession Avg.	25:54	34:06
Total Net Yards	4834	5883
Avg. Per Game	302.1	367.7
Total Plays	907	1139
Avg. Per Play	5.3	5.2
Net Yards Rushing	1727	1851
Avg. Per Game	107.9	115.7
Total Rushes	406	474
Net Yards Passing	3107	4032
Avg. Per Game	194.2	252.0
Sacked/Yards Lost	27/171	40/272
Gross Yards	3278	4304
Att./Completions	474/273	625/410
Completion Pct.	57.6	65.6
Had Intercepted	15	17
Punts/Average	77/42.9	61/42.9
Net Punting Avg.	77/39.1	61/34.6
Penalties/Yards	128/1040	114/1039
Fumbles/Ball Lost	22/14	25/8
Touchdowns	40	32
Rushing	13	7
Passing	24	23
Returns	3	2

2010 INDIVIDUAL STATISTICS

PASSING	Att.	Comp.	Yds.	Pct.	TD	Int.	Tkld.	Rate
K. Collins	278	160	1823	57.6	14	8	13/91	82.2
Young	156	93	1255	59.6	10	3	13/80	98.6
Smith	40	20	200	50.0	0	4	1/0	25.0
Titans	474	273	3278	57.6	24	15	27/171	82.6
Opponents	625	410	4304	65.6	23	17	40/272	86.4

SCORING	TD R	TD P	TD Rt	PAT	FG	Saf	PTS
Bironas	0	0	0	38/38	24/26	0	110
C. Johnson	11	1	0	0/0	0/0	0	72
Britt	0	9	0	0/0	0/0	0	56
Washington	0	6	0	0/0	0/0	0	36
Scaife	0	4	0	0/0	0/0	0	24
Mariani	0	0	2	0/0	0/0	0	12
Ringer	2	0	0	0/0	0/0	0	12
Stevens	0	2	0	0/0	0/0	0	12
Cook	0	1	0	0/0	0/0	0	6
Finnegan	0	0	1	0/0	0/0	0	6
Gage	0	1	0	0/0	0/0	0	6
Schommer	0	0	0	0/0	0/0	1	2
Titans	13	24	3	38/38	24/26	2	356
Opponents	7	23	2	30/30	39/48	0	339

2-Pt Conversions: Britt.
Titans 1-2, Opponents 0-2.

RUSHING	No.	Yds	Avg	LG	TD
C. Johnson	316	1364	4.3	76t	11
Ringer	51	239	4.7	54	2
Young	25	125	5.0	20	0
Williams	1	5	5.0	5	0
K. Collins	10	1	0.1	4	0
Hall	1	1	1.0	1	0
Kern	1	0	0.0	0	0
Washington	1	-8	-8.0	-8	0
Titans	406	1727	4.3	76t	13
Opponents	474	1851	3.9	37	7

RECEIVING	No.	Yds	Avg	LG	TD
C. Johnson	44	245	5.6	25	1
Britt	42	775	18.5	80t	9
Washington	42	687	16.4	71t	6
Scaife	36	318	8.8	30	4
Cook	29	361	12.4	36	1
Gage	20	266	13.3	30	1
Williams	16	219	13.7	39	0
Hall	15	100	6.7	19	0
Stevens	11	122	11.1	28	2
Ringer	7	44	6.3	9	0
Moss	6	80	13.3	26	0
L. Hawkins	5	61	12.2	24	0
Titans	273	3278	12.0	80t	24
Opponents	410	4304	10.5	75t	23

INTERCEPTIONS	No.	Yds	Avg	LG	TD
Griffin	4	50	12.5	28	0
Verner	3	41	13.7	19	0
Finnegan	2	41	20.5	41t	1
McCourty	2	11	5.5	11	0
Witherspoon	2	11	5.5	9	0
Hope	1	32	32.0	32	0
Tulloch	1	18	18.0	18	0
Fuller	1	0	0.0	0	0
Marks	1	-6	-6.0	-6	0
Titans	17	198	11.6	41t	1
Opponents	15	120	8.0	54t	1

PUNTING	No.	Yds.	Avg.	In 20	LG
Kern	77	3302	42.9	24	68
Titans	77	3302	42.9	24	68
Opponents	61	2618	42.9	15	68

PUNT RETURNS	Ret	FC	Yds	Avg	LG	TD
Mariani	27	17	329	12.2	87t	1
Titans	27	17	329	12.2	87t	1
Opponents	35	16	214	6.1	29	0

KICKOFF RETURNS	No.	Yds	Avg	LG	TD
Mariani	60	1530	25.5	98t	1
Hall	2	21	10.5	15	0
Cook	1	3	3.0	3	0
Gage	1	2	2.0	2	0
Titans	64	1556	24.3	98t	1
Opponents	56	1389	24.8	97t	1

FIELD GOALS	1-19	20-29	30-39	40-49	50+
Bironas	0/0	6/6	8/9	8/8	2/3
Titans	0/0	6/6	8/9	8/8	2/3
Opponents	1/1	10/10	15/15	11/17	2/5

SACKS	No.
Babin	12.5
Ball	7.0
T. Brown	3.5
Jones	3.5
Ford	3.0
Witherspoon	3.0
Hayes	1.5
McRath	1.5
Morgan	1.5
Finnegan	1.0
Hope	1.0
Tulloch	1.0
Titans	40.0
Opponents	27.0

RECORD HOLDERS
INDIVIDUAL RECORDS—CAREER

Category	Name	Performance
Rushing (Yds.)	Eddie George, 1996-2003	10,009
Passing (Yds.)	Warren Moon, 1984-1993	33,685
Passing (TDs)	Warren Moon, 1984-1993	196
Receiving (No.)	Ernest Givins, 1986-1994	542
Receiving (Yds.)	Ernest Givins, 1986-1994	7,935
Interceptions	Jim Norton, 1960-68	45
Punting (Avg.)	Greg Montgomery, 1988-1993	43.6
Punt Return (Avg.)	Billy Johnson, 1974-1980	13.2
Kickoff Return (Avg.)	Bobby Jancik, 1962-67	26.5
Field Goals	Al Del Greco, 1991-2000	246
Touchdowns (Tot.)	Eddie George, 1996-2003	74
Points	Al Del Greco, 1991-2000	1,060
*Sacks	Ray Childress, 1985-1995	75.5

INDIVIDUAL RECORDS—SINGLE SEASON

Category	Name	Performance
Rushing (Yds.)	Chris Johnson, 2009	2,006
Passing (Yds.)	Warren Moon, 1991	4,690
Passing (TDs)	George Blanda, 1961	36
Receiving (No.)	Charley Hennigan, 1964	101
Receiving (Yds.)	Charley Hennigan, 1961	1,746
Interceptions	Fred Glick, 1963	12
	Mike Reinfeldt, 1979	12
Punting (Avg.)	Craig Hentrich, 1998	47.2
Punt Return (Avg.)	Billy Johnson, 1977	15.4
Kickoff Return (Avg.)	Ken Hall, 1960	31.3
Field Goals	Al Del Greco, 1998	36
Touchdowns (Tot.)	Earl Campbell, 1979	19
Points	Al Del Greco, 1998	136
*Sacks	William Fuller, 1991	15.0

INDIVIDUAL RECORDS—SINGLE GAME

Category	Name	Performance
Rushing (Yds.)	Chris Johnson, 11-1-09	228
Passing (Yds.)	Warren Moon, 12-16-90	527
Passing (TDs)	George Blanda, 11-19-61	**7
Receiving (No.)	Charley Hennigan, 10-13-61	13
	Haywood Jeffires, 10-13-91	13
	Drew Bennett, 12-19-04	13
Receiving (Yds.)	Charley Hennigan, 10-13-61	272
Interceptions	Many times	3
	Last time by Keith Bulluck, 9-24-07	
Field Goals	Rob Bironas, 10-21-07	**8
Touchdowns (Tot.)	Billy Cannon, 12-10-61	5
Points	Billy Cannon, 12-10-61	30
*Sacks	William Fuller, 11-28-93	4.0

*Sacks became an official statistic in 1982.
**NFL Record

TENNESSEE TITANS

VETERAN ROSTER AS OF MARCH 3, 2011

No.	Name	Pos.	Ht.	Wt.	Birthdate	^NFL Exp.	College	Hometown	How Acq.	'10 Games/ Starts
56	Allred, Colin	LB	6-1	242	4/15/83	4	Baylor	Dallas, Texas	FA-'07	5/0
54	Amano, Eugene	G/C	6-3	300	3/1/82	8	SE Missouri State	San Diego, Calif.	D7-'04	13/13
58	Amato, Ken	LB/LS	6-2	240	5/18/77	9	Montana State	Miami, Fla.	FA-'03	16/0
93	Babin, Jason	DE	6-3	260	5/24/80	8	Western Michigan	Paw Paw, Mich.	UFA(Phil)-'10	16/16
57	Bailey, Patrick	LB	6-4	235	11/19/85	4	Duke	Elmendorf, Texas	W(Pitt)-'10	16/0
98	Ball, Dave	DE	6-5	255	1/4/81	7	UCLA	Dixon, Calif.	FA-'08	11/11
2	Bironas, Rob	K	6-0	210	1/29/78	7	Georgia Southern	Louisville, Ky.	FA-'05	16/0
18	Britt, Kenny	WR	6-3	215	9/19/88	3	Rutgers	Bayonne, N.J.	D1-'09	12/76
	Brown, Kareem	DL	6-4	285	1/30/84	4	Miami	Miami, Fla.	FA-'09	0*
97	Brown, Tony	DT	6-3	305	9/29/80	7	Memphis	Chattanooga, Tenn.	FA-'06	11/11
5	Collins, Kerry	QB	6-5	247	12/30/72	17	Penn State	Lebanon, Pa.	UFA(Oak)-'06	10/7
89	Cook, Jared	TE	6-5	248	4/7/87	3	South Carolina	Suwanee, Ga.	D3a-'09	16/1
53	Curran, Rennie	LB	5-11	230	11/10/88	2	Georgia	Snellville, Ga.	D3b-'10	9/0
99	Douglas, Marques	DT	6-2	292	3/15/77	11	Howard	Greensboro, N.C.	FA-'10	6/2
77	Durand, Ryan	G	6-5	301	11/17/85	2	Syracuse	Walpole, N.H.	D7a-'09	1/0
	Figurs, Yamon	WR	5-11	175	1/10/82	4	Kansas State	Fort Pierce, Fla.	FA-'11	2/0*
31	Finnegan, Cortland	CB	5-10	188	2/2/84	6	Samford	Milton, Fla.	D7a-'06	16/16
78	Ford, Jacob	DE	6-4	252	7/20/83	5	Central Arkansas	Memphis, Tenn.	D6b-'07	14/5
22	Fuller, Vincent	S	6-1	192	8/3/82	7	Virginia Tech	Baltimore, Md.	D4a-'05	12/3
12	Gage, Justin	WR	6-4	204	1/24/81	9	Missouri	Jefferson City, Mo.	UFA(Chi)-'07	11/4
33	Griffin, Michael	S	6-0	203	1/4/85	5	Texas	Austin, Texas	D1-'07	16/16
45	Hall, Ahmard	FB	5-11	241	11/13/79	6	Texas	Angleton, Texas	FA-'06	16/4
64	Harris, Leroy	G/C	6-3	303	6/6/84	5	N.C. State	Raleigh, N.C.	D4a-'07	15/15
87	Hawkins, Lavelle	WR	5-11	194	7/12/86	4	California	Stockton, Calif.	D4b-'08	6/0
75	Haye, Jovan	DT	6-2	277	6/21/82	7	Vanderbilt	Fort Lauderdale, Fla.	UFA(TB)-'09	14/1
95	Hayes, William	DE	6-3	272	5/2/85	4	Winston-Salem State	High Point, N.C.	D4a-'08	14/0
37	Hood, Rod	CB	5-11	201	10/3/81	9	Auburn	Columbus, Ga.	FA-'09	0*
24	Hope, Chris	S	6-0	204	9/29/80	10	Florida State	Rock Hill, S.C.	UFA(Pitt)-'06	16/16
	Howard, Marcus	DE	6-0	244	10/12/85	3	Georgia	Huger, S.C.	FA-'10	0*
	Ingram, Jake	LS	6-3	240	10/23/85	3	Hawai'i	Albuquerque, N.M.	FA-'11	9/0*
28	Johnson, Chris	RB	5-11	191	9/23/85	4	East Carolina	Orlando, Fla.	D1-'08	16/16
32	Johnson, Robert	S	6-2	206	2/13/87	2	Utah	Los Angeles, Calif.	D5-'10	0*
26	Johnson, Stafon	RB	5-11	222	2/6/88	2	Southern California	Bellflower, Calif.	FA-'10	0*
91	Jones, Jason	DT	6-5	276	5/23/86	4	Eastern Michigan	Southfield, Mich.	D2-'08	15/15
6	Kern, Brett	P	6-2	217	2/17/86	4	Toledo	Grand Island, N.Y.	W(Den)-'09	16/0
70	Kropog, Troy	T/G	6-6	308	7/31/86	3	Tulane	Metairie, La.	D4b-'09	5/0
83	Mariani, Marc	WR	6-1	190	5/2/87	2	Montana	Havre, Mont.	D7a-'10	16/0
94	Marks, Sen'Derrick	DT	6-2	294	2/23/87	2	Auburn	Mobile, Ala.	D2-'09	12/3
30	McCourty, Jason	CB	6-0	188	8/13/87	3	Rutgers	Nyack, N.Y.	D6a-'09	12/6
51	McRath, Gerald	LB	6-3	228	6/16/86	3	Southern Mississippi	Powder Springs, Ga.	D4a-'09	12/7
90	Morgan, Derrick	DE	6-3	278	1/6/89	2	Georgia Tech	Coatesville, Pa.	D1-'10	4/0
84	Moss, Randy	WR	6-4	210	2/13/77	14	Marshall	Rand, W. Va.	W(Minn)-'10	16/11*
29	Mouton, Ryan	CB	5-9	184	9/23/86	3	Hawai'i	Houston, Texas	D3b-'09	9/0
23	Nickey, Donnie	S	6-3	226	4/25/80	9	Ohio State	Plain City, Ohio	D5-'03	16/0
66	Otto, Mike	T	6-5	310	7/24/83	4	Purdue	Kokomo, Ind.	D7-'07	11/1
	Ratliff, Brett	QB	6-4	224	8/8/85	2	Utah	Chico, Calif.	FA-'11	0*
21	Ringer, Javon	RB	5-9	207	2/2/87	3	Michigan State	Dayton, Ohio	D5-'09	16/0
71	Roos, Michael	T	6-7	320	10/5/82	7	Eastern Washington	Vancouver, Wash.	D2-'05	16/16
80	Scaife, Bo	TE	6-3	249	1/6/81	7	Texas	Denver, Colo.	D6-'05	14/13
39	Schommer, Nick	S	6-0	204	1/3/86	2	North Dakota State	Prescott, Wisc.	D7b-'09	13/0
73	Scott, Jake	G	6-5	292	4/16/81	8	Idaho	Lewiston, Idaho	UFA(Ind)-'10	16/16
59	Shaw, Tim	LB	6-1	236	3/27/84	4	Penn State	Livonia, Mich.	W(Chi)-'10	16/1
96	Sheppard, Malcolm	DT	6-2	289	2/13/88	2	Arkansas	Bainbridge, Ga.	FA-'10	3/0*
7	Simms, Chris	QB	6-4	231	8/29/80	9	Texas	Ramapo, N.J.	FA-'10	0*
11	Smith, Rusty	QB	6-5	226	1/28/87	2	Florida Atlantic	Jacksonville, Fla.	D6a-'10	2/1
88	Stevens, Craig	TE	6-3	268	9/1/84	4	California	San Pedro, Calif.	D3-'08	15/13
76	Stewart, David	T	6-7	315	8/28/82	7	Mississippi State	Moulton, Ala.	D4b-'05	16/16
50	Thornton, David	LB	6-2	233	11/1/78	10	North Carolina	Goldsboro, N.C.	UFA(Ind)-'06	0*
55	Tulloch, Stephen	LB	5-11	240	1/1/85	6	North Carolina State	Miami, Fla.	D4b-'06	16/16
61	Velasco, Fernando	C/G	6-4	312	2/22/85	2	Georgia	Wrens, Ga.	FA-'08	16/3
20	Verner, Alterraun	CB	5-10	187	12/13/88	2	UCLA	Carson, Calif.	D4-'10	16/12
85	Washington, Nate	WR	6-1	177	8/28/83	7	Tiffin	Toledo, Ohio	UFA(Pitt)-'09	16/16
17	Williams, Damian	WR	6-1	199	5/26/88	2	Southern California	Springdale, Ark.	D3a-'10	16/1
52	Winborn, Jamie	LB	5-11	230	5/14/79	10	Vanderbilt	Wetumpka, Ala.	FA-'09	6/3
92	Witherspoon, Will	LB	6-1	240	8/19/80	10	Georgia	Panama City, Fla.	FA-'10	16/16
10	Young, Vince	QB	6-5	232	5/18/83	6	Texas	Houston, Texas	D1-'06	9/8

* K. Brown missed '10 season because of injury; Figurs played 1 game with Oakland and 1 game with Cleveland; Hood missed '10 season because of injury; Howard missed '10 season because of injury; Ingram played 8 games with New England and 1 game with New Orleans; R. Johnson inactive for 16 games; S. Johnson missed '10 season because of injury; Moss played 4 games with New England, 4 games with Minnesota, and 8 games with Tennessee; Ratliff did not play in 3 games with Cleveland; Sheppard played 1 game with Houston and 3 games with Tennessee; Simms did not play in 5 games and inactive in 1 game; Thornton missed '10 season because of injury.

Also played with Titans in '10—DE Hall Davis (1 game), DT Amon Gordon (3), CB Pete Ittersagen (3), C Kevin Matthews (3).

^ "NFL Exp." as of 2011 Kickoff Weekend. For full explanation of how a player's NFL Experience is measured, refer to explanation underneath the First-Year Roster listed below.

FIRST-YEAR ROSTER

Name	Pos.	Ht.	Wt.	Birthdate	College	Hometown	How Acq.
Ayers, Akeem	LB	6-3	254	7/10/89	UCLA	Los Angeles, Calif.	D2
Campbell, Tommie	DB	6-3	205	9/19/87	California (PA)	Aliquippa, Pa.	D7b
Casey, Jurrell	DT	6-1	300	12/5/89	Southern California	Long Beach, Calif.	D3
Clayton, Zach	DT	6-2	299	1/1/88	Auburn	Opelika, Ala.	D7a
Davis, Hall (1)	DE	6-6	262	3/2/87	Louisiana-Lafayette	Baton Rouge, La.	FA-'10
Donaldson, Herb (1)	RB	5-11	221	12/13/85	Western Illinois	St. Louis, Mo.	FA-'10
Egboh, Pannel (1)	DE	6-6	287	3/23/86	Stanford	Mesquite, Texas	FA-'10
Geer, Riar (1)	TE/FB	6-4	250	12/19/86	Colorado	Newscastle, Wyo.	FA-'10
Hansen, Jeff (1)	G	6-4	301	9/24/86	Montana State	Great Falls, Mont.	FA-'10
Harper, Jamie	RB	5-11	233	9/11/89	Clemson	Jacksonville, Fla.	D4b
Hawkins, Chris (1)	CB	6-1	184	4/12/86	Louisiana State	Baton Rouge, La.	FA-'10
Ittersagen, Pete (1)	CB	5-10	191	9/28/85	Wheaton	Wheaton, Ill.	FA-'10
Klug, Karl	DL	6-3	275	3/31/88	Iowa	Caledonia, Minn.	D5
Lindsay, Dominique (1)	RB	5-10	201	12/8/86	East Carolina	Charlotte, N.C.	FA-'10
Locker, Jake	QB	6-3	234	6/15/88	Washington	Ferndale, Wash.	D1
Malast, Kevin (1)	LB	6-2	235	6/6/86	Rutgers	Manchester, N.J.	FA
Matthews, Kevin (1)	C	6-3	302	2/4/87	Texas A&M	Houston, Texas	FA-'10
McCarthy, Colin	LB	6-1	238	5/30/88	Miami	Tampa, Fla.	D4a
Rolle, Myron (1)	S	6-2	219	10/30/86	Florida State	Galloway, N.J.	D6b-'10
Stingily, Byron	T	6-5	313	9/9/88	Louisville	Country Club Hills, Ill.	D6
Tronzo, Joe (1)	RB	5-11	240	6/10/87	Louisville	Louisville, Ky.	FA

The term NFL Rookie is defined as a player who is in his first season of professional football and has not been on the roster of another professional football team for any regular-season or postseason games. A Rookie is designated by an "R" on NFL rosters. Players who have been active in another professional football league or players who have NFL experience, including either preseason training camp or being on an Active List or Inactive List, or on Reserve/Injured or Reserve/Physically Unable to Perform for fewer than six regular-season games, are termed NFL First-Year Players. An NFL First-Year Player is designated by a "1" on NFL rosters. Thereafter, a player is credited with an additional year of experience for each season in which he accumulates six games on the Active List or Inactive List, or on Reserve/Injured or Reserve/Physically Unable to Perform.

Log on to www.titansonline.com for an up-to-date roster.

COACHING STAFF

Head Coach,
Mike Munchak

Pro Career: Munchak became the 16th head coach in franchise history on February 7, 2011, after spending the previous 29 seasons with the team as a player and coach. He spent three seasons as an offensive assistant/quality control coach (1994-96). In 1997, he became the offensive line coach and held that position for 14 years. Four of his offensive linemen totaled 10 Pro Bowl invitations, and his offensive lines paved the way for five different running backs to total 11 1,000-yard rushing seasons. His offensive line allowed the second fewest sacks (28.3 sacks per season) in the NFL since he assumed control of the group in 1997. Additionally, the Titans ranked seventh in the league in rushing yards (124.5 yards per game) during his tenure. During a 12-year playing career as a guard for the Houston Oilers (1982-1993), Munchak started 156 games (seventh in franchise history) and earned nine Pro Bowl invitations. He was selected to the NFL's "All-Decade" team for the 1980s. In 1996, his No. 63 jersey was retired by the club, and in 2001, he became the fifth franchise player to be inducted into the Pro Football Hall of Fame. Career record: 0-0.

Background: Played at Penn State (1979-81) for Joe Paterno. He graduated with a degree in business administration in May 1982. The Oilers made him the eighth overall pick and the first offensive lineman selected in the 1982 NFL Draft.

Personal: Born March 5, 1960, in Scranton, Pa. Munchak and his wife, Marci, have two daughters, Alexandra and Julie.

ASSISTANT COACHES

Frank Bush, linebackers; born January 10, 1963, Athens, Ga. Linebacker North Carolina State 1981-84. Pro linebacker Houston Oilers 1985-86. Pro coach: Houston Oilers 1987-1991 (scout), 1992-94, Denver Broncos 1995-2003, Arizona Cardinals 2004-06, Houston Texans 2007-09, joined Titans in 2011.

Curtis Fuller, secondary assistant; born July 5, 1978, Fort Worth, Texas. Defensive back Tyler (Texas) J.C. 1997, Texas Christian 1998-2000. Pro defensive back Seattle Seahawks 2001-02, Green Bay Packers 2003-04, Carolina Panthers 2004. Pro coach: Oakland Raiders 2007, Green Bay Packers 2009-2010, joined Titans in 2011.

Jerry Gray, defensive coordinator; born December 16, 1962, Lubbock, Texas. Safety Texas 1981-84. Pro defensive back Los Angeles Rams 1985-1991, Houston Oilers 1992, Tampa Bay Buccaneers 1993. College coach: Southern Methodist 1995-96. Pro coach: Tennessee Titans 1997-2000, Buffalo Bills 2001-05, Washington Redskins 2006-09, Seattle

Seahawks 2010, joined Titans in 2011.

Dowell Loggains, quarterbacks/passing game; born October 1, 1980, Newport, Ark. Quarterback Arkansas 2000-04. No pro playing experience. Pro coach: Dallas Cowboys 2005, joined Titans in 2006.

Charles London, offensive assistant/quality control; born August 12, 1975, Dunwoody, Ga. Running back Duke 1994-96. No pro playing experience. College coach: Duke 2004-06. Pro coach: Chicago Bears 2007-09, joined Titans in 2011.

Alan Lowry, special teams; born November 21, 1950, Miami, Okla. Defensive back/quarterback Texas 1970-72. No pro playing experience. College coach: Virginia Tech 1974, Wyoming 1975, Texas 1977-1981. Pro coach: Dallas Cowboys 1982-1990, Tampa Bay Buccaneers 1991, San Francisco 49ers 1992-95, joined Titans/Oilers in 1996.

Bruce Matthews, offensive line; born August 8, 1961, Raleigh, N.C. Offensive lineman Southern California, 1979-1982. Pro offensive lineman Houston Oilers/Tennessee Titans 1983-2001. Inducted into Pro Football Hall of Fame in 2007. Pro coach: Houston Texans 2009-2010, joined Titans in 2011.

Dave McGinnis, senior assistant; born August 7, 1951, Independence, Kan. Defensive back Texas Christian 1970-72. No pro playing experience. College coach: Texas Christian 1973-74, 1982, Missouri 1975-77, Indiana State 1978, 1980-81, Kansas State 1983-85. Pro coach: Chicago Bears 1986-1995, Arizona Cardinals 1996-2003 (head coach 2000-2003), joined Titans in 2004.

Chris Palmer, offensive coordinator; born September 23, 1949, Brewster, N.Y. Quarterback Southern Connecticut State 1968-1971. No pro playing experience. College coach: Connecticut 1972-74, Lehigh 1975, Colgate 1976-1982, New Haven 1986-87 (head coach), Boston 1988-89 (head coach). Pro coach: Montreal Concordes (CFL) 1983, New Jersey Generals (USFL) 1984-85, Houston Oilers 1990-92, New England Patriots 1993-96, Jacksonville Jaguars 1997-98, Cleveland Browns 1999-2000 (head coach), Houston Texans 2001-05, Dallas Cowboys 2006, New York Giants 2007-09, Hartford Colonials (UFL, head coach) 2010, joined Titans in 2011.

Chet Parlavecchio, special teams assistant; born February 14, 1960, Irvington, N.J. Linebacker Penn State 1978-1981. Pro linebacker Green Bay Packers 1982-83, St. Louis Cardinals 1983. College coach: Temple 1992-93. Pro coach: Joined Titans in 2011.

Dave Ragone, wide receivers; born October 3, 1979, Middleburg Heights, Ohio. Quarterback Louisville 1999-2002. Pro quarterback Houston Texans 2003-05. Pro coach: Hartford Colonels (UFL) 2010, joined Titans in 2011.

Marcus Robertson, secondary; born October 2, 1969, Pasadena, Calif. Defensive back Iowa State 1987-1990. Pro safety Houston Oilers/Tennessee Titans 1991-2000, Seattle Seahawks 2001-02. Pro coach: Joined Titans in 2007.

Tracy Rocker, defensive line; born April 9, 1966, Atlanta. Defensive tackle Auburn 1984-88. Pro defensive tackle Washington Redskins 1989-1990, Orlando Thunder (WFL) 1991. College coach: West Alabama 1994-96, Troy 1997-2001, Cincinnati 2002, Arkansas 2003-07, Ole Miss 2008, Auburn 2009-2010. Pro coach: Joined Titans in 2011.

Jim Skipper, running backs; born January 23, 1949, Breaux Bridge, La. Defensive back Whittier College 1971-72. No pro playing experience. College coach: Cal Poly-Pomona 1974-76, San Jose State 1977-78, Pacific 1979, Oregon 1980-82. Pro coach: Philadelphia/Baltimore Stars (USFL) 1983-85, New Orleans Saints 1986-1995, Arizona Cardinals 1996, New York Giants 1997-2000, San Francisco Demons (XFL) 2001 (head coach), Carolina Panthers 2002-2010, joined Titans in 2011.

Arthur Smith, defensive assistant/quality control; born May 27, 1982, Memphis, Tenn. Offensive lineman North Carolina 2001-05. No pro playing experience. College coach: North Carolina 2006. Pro coach: Washington Redskins 2007-08, joined Titans in 2011.

Art Valero, offensive line; born May 12, 1958, La Mirada, Calif. Guard Boise State 1979-1980. No pro playing experience. College coach: Boise State 1981-82, Iowa State 1983, Long Beach State 1984-86, New Mexico 1987-89, Idaho 1990-94, Utah State 1995-97, Louisville 1998-2001. Pro coach: Tampa Bay Buccaneers 2002-07, St. Louis Rams 2008-09, Seattle Seahawks 2010, joined Titans in 2011.

Steve Watterson, asst. head coach/strength & conditioning; born November 27, 1956, Newport, R.I. Attended Rhode Island. No college or pro playing experience. Pro coach: Philadelphia Eagles 1984-85, joined Titans/Oilers in 1986.

John Zernhelt, tight ends; born January 4, 1954, Pottsville, Pa. Offensive lineman Maryland 1974-77. No pro playing experience. College coach: Ferrum 1977-1980, Marshall 1981, East Carolina 1982-86, Maryland 1987-1991, Rice 1992-93, Duke 1994-95, South Carolina 1996-98, James Madison 1999-2002, The Citadel 2003-04 (head coach 2004). Pro coach: New York Jets 2005, joined Titans in 2006.

The NFC

National Football Conference
West Division
Team Colors: Cardinal Red, Black, and
White
8701 S. Hardy Drive
Tempe, Arizona 85284
Telephone: (602) 379-0101

2011 SCHEDULE
PRESEASON
Aug. 11 at Oakland 8:00
Aug. 19 at Green Bay 5:00
Aug. 27 **San Diego** 7:00
Sep. 1 **Denver** 7:00

REGULAR SEASON
Sep. 11 **Carolina** 1:15
Sep. 18 at Washington 10:00a
Sep. 25 at Seattle 1:15
Oct. 2 **New York Giants** 1:05
Oct. 9 at Minnesota 10:00a
Oct. 16 BYE
Oct. 23 **Pittsburgh** 1:05
Oct. 30 at Baltimore 10:00a
Nov. 6 **St. Louis** 2:15
Nov. 13 at Philadelphia 11:00a
Nov. 20 at San Francisco 2:05
Nov. 27 at St. Louis 11:00a
Dec. 4 **Dallas** 2:15
Dec. 11 **San Francisco** 2:05
Dec. 18 **Cleveland** 2:15
Dec. 24 at Cincinnati (Sat)..........11:00a
Jan. 1 **Seattle** 2:15
All times MDT/PST
Stadium: University of Phoenix Stadium
(opened in 2006)
• **Capacity:** 65,000
1 Cardinals Drive
Glendale, Arizona 85305
Playing Surface: Grass
Training Camp: Northern Arizona University
Flagstaff, Arizona 86011

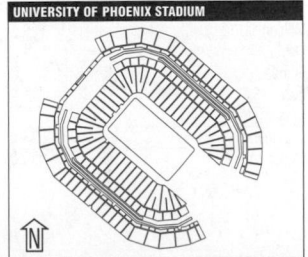

UNIVERSITY OF PHOENIX STADIUM

CLUB OFFICIALS
Owner: William V. Bidwill
President: Michael Bidwill
General Manager: Rod Graves
Executive Vice President/Chief Operating
Officer: Ron Minegar
Chief Financial Officer: Greg Lee
General Counsel: David Koeninger
Vice President, Media Relations:
Mark Dalton
Vice President, Marketing: Lisa Manning
Vice President, Business Development:
Steve Ryan
Vice President, Information Technology:
Mark Feller
Vice President, Security: Rick Knight
Vice President, Stadium Operations:
John Drum
Senior Director, Player Programs:
Anthony Edwards
Senior Director, Community Relations:
Luis Zendejas
Senior Director, Ticketing: Steve Bomar
Senior Director, Ticket Sales:
Ron Campbell
Director, Player Personnel: Steve Keim
Director, Pro Personnel: T.J. McCreight
Director, Football Administration:
Reggie Terry
Director, Broadcasting/Executive
Producer: Tim DeLaney
Director, Cheerleading: Heather Karberg
Website Manager: Darren Urban
Video Director: Rob Brakel
Head Athletic Trainer: Tom Reed
Assistant Athletic Trainers:
Jim Shearer, Jeff Herndon,
Chad Cook
Equipment Manager: Mark Ahlemeier
Assistant Equipment Manager:
Steve Christensen

COACHING HISTORY
Chicago 1920-1959, St. Louis 1960-1987
(494-698-39)
Records include postseason games
1920-22	John (Paddy) Driscoll	17-8-4
1923-24	Arnold Horween	13-8-1
1925-26	Norman Barry	16-8-2
1927	Guy Chamberlin	3-7-1
1928	Fred Gillies	1-5-0
1929	Dewey Scanlon	6-6-1
1930	Ernie Nevers	5-6-2
1931	LeRoy Andrews*	0-1-0
1931	Ernie Nevers	5-3-0
1932	Jack Chevigny	2-6-2
1933-34	Paul Schissler	6-15-1
1935-38	Milan Creighton	16-26-4
1939	Ernie Nevers	1-10-0
1940-42	Jimmy Conzelman	8-22-3
1943-45	Phil Handler**	1-29-0
1946-48	Jimmy Conzelman	27-10-0
1949	Phil Handler-Buddy Parker***	2-4-0
1949	Raymond (Buddy) Parker	4-1-1
1950-51	Earl (Curly) Lambeau****	7-15-0
1951	Phil Handler-Cecil Isbell#	1-1-0
1952	Joe Kuharich	4-8-0
1953-54	Joe Stydahar	3-20-1
1955-57	Ray Richards	14-21-1
1958-1961	Frank (Pop) Ivy##	15-31-2
1961	Chuck Drulis-Ray Prochaska-	
	Ray Willsey###	2-0-0
1962-65	Wally Lemm	27-26-3
1966-1970	Charley Winner	35-30-5
1971-72	Bob Hollway	8-18-2
1973-77	Don Coryell	42-29-1
1978-79	Bud Wilkinson####	9-20-0
1979	Larry Wilson	2-1-0
1980-85	Jim Hanifan	39-50-1
1986-89	Gene Stallings@	23-34-1
1989	Hank Kuhlmann	0-5-0
1990-93	Joe Bugel	20-44-0
1994-95	Buddy Ryan	12-20-0
1996-2000	Vince Tobin@@	29-44-0
2000-03	Dave McGinnis	17-40-0
2004-06	Dennis Green	16-32-0
2007-2010	Ken Whisenhunt	36-34-0

```
       * Resigned after one game in 1931
      ** Co-coach with Walt Kiesling in Chicago
         Cardinals-Pittsburgh merger in 1944
     *** Co-coaches for first six games in 1949
    **** Resigned after 10 games in 1951
       # Co-coaches
      ## Resigned after 12 games in 1961
     ### Co-coaches
    #### Released after 13 games in 1979
       @ Released after 11 games in 1989
      @@ Released after seven games in 2000
```

PAID ATTENDANCE
Home 487,334   Away 500,221
Total 987,555
Single-game home record, 73,025*
(9/19/93)
Single-season home record, 516,646 (2007)
*Team also had attendance of 103,467 for regular-
season home game at Azteca Stadium, Mexico City,
Mexico

2011 DRAFT CHOICES
Round	Name	Pos.	College
1	Patrick Peterson	DB	Louisiana St.
2	Ryan Williams	RB	Virginia Tech
3	Rob Housler	TE	Florida Atlantic
4	Sam Acho	LB	Texas
5	Anthony Sherman	FB	Connecticut
6	Quan Sturdivant	LB	North Carolina
	David Carter	DE	UCLA
7	DeMarco Sampson	WR	San Diego St.

2010 TEAM RECORD

PRESEASON (3-1)

Date	Result	Opponent
8/14	W 19-16	Houston
8/23	L 10-24	at Tennessee
8/28	W 14-9	at Chicago
9/2	W 20-10	Washington

REGULAR SEASON (5-11)

Date	Result	Opponent
9/12	W 17-13	at St. Louis
9/19	L 7-41	at Atlanta
9/26	W 24-23	Oakland
10/3	L 10-41	at San Diego
10/10	W 30-20	New Orleans
10/24	L 10-22	at Seattle
10/31	L 35-38	Tampa Bay
11/7	L 24-27	at Minnesota (OT)
11/14	L 18-36	Seattle
11/21	L 13-31	at Kansas City
11/29	L 6-27	San Francisco
12/5	L 6-19	St. Louis
12/12	W 43-13	Denver
12/19	L 12-19	at Carolina
12/25	W 27-26	Dallas
1/2	L 7-38	at San Francisco

(OT) Overtime

SCORE BY PERIODS

Cardinals	53	98	44	94	0 —	289
Opponents	87	149	102	93	3 —	434

2010 TEAM STATISTICS

	Cardinals	Opp.
Total First Downs	241	339
Rushing	67	123
Passing	154	178
Penalty	20	38
3rd Down: Made/Att	58/209	87/233
3rd Down Pct.	27.8	37.3
4th Down: Made/Att	7/18	9/17
4th Down Pct.	38.9	52.9
Possession Avg.	26:14	33:46
Total Net Yards	4309	5977
Avg. Per Game	269.3	373.6
Total Plays	931	1092
Avg. Per Play	4.6	5.5
Net Yards Rushing	1388	2323
Avg. Per Game	86.8	145.2
Total Rushes	320	526
Net Yards Passing	2921	3654
Avg. Per Game	182.6	228.4
Sacked/Yards Lost	50/343	33/227
Gross Yards	3264	3881
Att./Completions	561/285	533/324
Completion Pct.	50.8	60.8
Had Intercepted	19	17
Punts/Average	94/43.4	64/47.9
Net Punting Avg.	94/36.6	64/41.4
Penalties/Yards	108/870	108/894
Fumbles/Ball Lost	33/16	22/13
Touchdowns	31	45
Rushing	9	19
Passing	10	22
Returns	12	4

2010 INDIVIDUAL STATISTICS

PASSING

PASSING	Att.	Comp.	Yds.	Pct.	TD	Int.	Tkld.	Rate
Anderson	327	169	2065	51.7	7	10	25/176	65.9
Skelton	126	60	662	47.6	2	2	9/65	62.3
M. Hall	78	39	370	50.0	1	6	14/90	35.7
Bartel	28	16	150	57.1	0	1	2/12	57.1
Breaston	2	1	17	50.0	0	0	0/0	79.2
Cardinals	561	285	3264	50.8	10	19	50/343	60.5
Opponents	533	324	3881	60.8	22	17	33/227	83.5

SCORING

SCORING	TD R	TD P	TD Rt	PAT	FG	Saf	PTS
Feely	1	0	0	29/29	24/27	0	107
Fitzgerald	0	6	0	0/0	0/0	0	38
Hightower	5	0	0	0/0	0/0	0	30
Stephens-Howling	1	0	2	0/0	0/0	0	18
Breaston	0	1	1	0/0	0/0	0	12
Rhodes	0	0	2	0/0	0/0	0	12
Roberts	0	2	0	0/0	0/0	0	12
Rodgers-Cromartie	0	0	2	0/0	0/0	0	12
Wells	2	0	0	0/0	0/0	0	12
Adams	0	0	1	0/0	0/0	0	6
L. Brown	0	0	1	0/0	0/0	0	6
Dockett	0	0	1	0/0	0/0	0	6
Doucet	0	1	0	0/0	0/0	0	6
Hayes	0	0	1	0/0	0/0	0	6
Toler	0	0	1	0/0	0/0	0	6
Washington	0	0	0	0/0	0/0	0	0
Cardinals	9	10	12	29/29	24/27	0	289
Opponents	19	22	4	44/45	40/51	0	434

2-Pt Conversions: Fitzgerald.
Cardinals 1-2, Opponents 0-0.

RUSHING

RUSHING	No.	Yds	Avg	LG	TD
Hightower	153	736	4.8	80t	5
Wells	116	397	3.4	24	2
Stephens-Howling	23	113	4.9	30t	1
Skelton	10	49	4.9	16	0
Breaston	3	35	11.7	17	0
Wright	6	28	4.7	10	0
Anderson	5	25	5.0	11	0
Doucet	2	5	2.5	3	0
Feely	1	5	5.0	5t	0
M. Hall	1	-5	-5.0	-5	0
Cardinals	320	1388	4.3	80t	9
Opponents	526	2323	4.4	48	19

RECEIVING

RECEIVING	No.	Yds	Avg	LG	TD
Fitzgerald	90	1137	12.6	41	6
Breaston	47	718	15.3	37	1
Doucet	26	291	11.2	36	1
Roberts	24	307	12.8	74t	2
Hightower	21	136	6.5	20	0
Stephens-Howling	16	111	6.9	13	0
Patrick	15	123	8.2	21	0
Komar	12	117	9.8	20	0
S. Williams	9	101	11.2	17	0
Wright	8	42	5.3	9	0
Spach	7	40	5.7	14	0
Wells	5	74	14.8	43	0
Dray	3	47	15.7	24	0
Maui'a	2	20	10.0	10	0
Cardinals	285	3264	11.5	74t	10
Opponents	324	3881	12.0	70	22

INTERCEPTIONS

INTERCEPTIONS	No.	Yds	Avg	LG	TD
Rhodes	4	174	43.5	66	0
Rodgers-Cromartie	3	86	28.7	32t	2
Toler	2	66	33.0	66t	1
Adams	2	36	18.0	36	0
Lenon	2	12	6.0	10	0
Wilson	2	4	2.0	4	0
Washington	1	39	39.0	39	0
R. Johnson	1	7	7.0	7	0
Cardinals	17	424	24.9	66t	3
Opponents	19	389	20.5	62t	4

PUNTING

PUNTING	No.	Yds.	Avg.	In 20	LG
Graham	94	4080	43.4	29	65
Cardinals	94	4080	43.4	29	65
Opponents	64	3064	47.9	21	67

PUNT RETURNS

PUNT RETURNS	Ret	FC	Yds	Avg	LG	TD
Feely	0/0	8/8	6/6	8/10	2/3	
Cardinals	0/0	8/8	6/6	8/10	2/3	
Opponents	2/2	17/19	10/14	7/10	4/6	

KICKOFF RETURNS

KICKOFF RETURNS	No.	Yds	Avg	LG	TD
Stephens-Howling	57	1548	27.2	102t	2
Roberts	14	326	23.3	47	0
Breaston	7	162	23.1	27	0
Spach	2	26	13.0	15	0
Wright	2	8	4.0	8	0
S. Williams	1	14	14.0	14	0
Obiozor	1	0	0.0	0	0
Cardinals	84	2084	24.8	102t	2
Opponents	51	1234	24.2	51	0

FIELD GOALS

FIELD GOALS	1-19	20-29	30-39	40-49	50+
Feely	0/0	8/8	6/6	8/10	2/3
Cardinals	0/0	8/8	6/6	8/10	2/3
Opponents	2/2	17/19	10/14	7/10	4/6

SACKS

SACKS	No.
Campbell	6.0
Dockett	5.0
Haggans	5.0
Porter	5.0
Branch	2.0
Lenon	2.0
Schofield	2.0
Wilson	2.0
Davis	1.0
Rhodes	1.0
Toler	1.0
Washington	1.0
Cardinals	33.0
Opponents	50.0

RECORD HOLDERS
INDIVIDUAL RECORDS—CAREER

Category	Name	Performance
Rushing (Yds.)	Ottis Anderson, 1979-1986	7,999
Passing (Yds.)	Jim Hart, 1966-1983	34,639
Passing (TDs)	Jim Hart, 1966-1983	209
Receiving (No.)	Larry Fitzgerald, 2004-2010	613
Receiving (Yds.)	Roy Green, 1979-1990	8,497
Interceptions	Larry Wilson, 1960-1972	52
Punting (Avg.)	Jerry Norton, 1959-1961	44.9
Punt Return (Avg.)	Charley Trippi, 1947-1955	13.7
Kickoff Return (Avg.)	Ollie Matson, 1952, 1954-58	28.5
Field Goals	Jim Bakken, 1962-1978	282
Touchdowns (Tot.)	Roy Green, 1979-1990	70
Points	Jim Bakken, 1962-1978	1,380
*Sacks	Freddie Joe Nunn, 1985-1993	66.5

INDIVIDUAL RECORDS—SINGLE SEASON

Category	Name	Performance
Rushing (Yds.)	Ottis Anderson, 1979	1,605
Passing (Yds.)	Neil Lomax, 1984	4,614
Passing (TDs)	Kurt Warner, 2008	30
Receiving (No.)	Larry Fitzgerald, 2005	103
Receiving (Yds.)	David Boston, 2001	1,598
Interceptions	Bob Nussbaumer, 1949	12
Punting (Avg.)	Ben Graham, 2009	47.0
Punt Return (Avg.)	John (Red) Cochran, 1949	20.9
Kickoff Return (Avg.)	Ollie Matson, 1958	35.5
Field Goals	Neil Rackers, 2005	**40
Touchdowns (Tot.)	John David Crow, 1962	17
Points	Neil Rackers, 2005	140
*Sacks	Simeon Rice, 1999	16.5

INDIVIDUAL RECORDS—SINGLE GAME

Category	Name	Performance
Rushing (Yds.)	LeShon Johnson, 9-22-96	214
Passing (Yds.)	Boomer Esiason, 11-10-96 (OT)	522
Passing (TDs)	Jim Hardy, 10-2-50	6
	Charley Johnson, 9-26-65, 11-2-69	6
Receiving (No.)	Sonny Randle, 11-4-62	16
Receiving (Yds.)	Sonny Randle, 11-4-62	256
Interceptions	Bob Nussbaumer, 11-13-49	**4
	Jerry Norton, 11-20-60	**4
	Kwamie Lassiter, 12-27-98	**4
Field Goals	Jim Bakken, 9-24-67	7
Touchdowns (Tot.)	Ernie Nevers, 11-28-29	**6
Points	Ernie Nevers, 11-28-29	**40
*Sacks	Curtis Greer, 12-18-83	4.5

*Sacks became an official statistic in 1982.
**NFL Record

VETERAN ROSTER AS OF MARCH 3, 2011

No.	Name	Pos.	Ht.	Wt.	Birthdate	^NFL Exp.	College	Hometown	How Acq.	'10 Games/ Starts
21	Abdullah, Hamza	SS	6-2	216	8/20/83	7	Washington State	Los Angeles, Calif.	FA-'09	6/0
27	Adams, Michael	CB	5-8	181	6/17/85	5	Louisiana-Lafayette	Dallas, Texas	FA-'07	16/4
42	Ali, Charles	FB	6-2	255	8/23/84	3	Arkansas-Pine Bluff	St. Louis, Mo.	FA-'11	0*
3	Anderson, Derek	QB	6-6	235	6/15/83	7	Oregon State	Scappoose, Ore.	FA-'10	12/9
2	Bartel, Richard	QB	6-3	230	2/3/83	3	Tarleton State	Grapevine, Texas	FA-'10	1/0
74	Batiste, D'Anthony	T	6-4	314	3/29/82	6	Louisiana-Lafayette	Marksville, La.	FA-'10	1/0
78	Branch, Alan	DT	6-6	338	12/29/84	5	Michigan	Rio Rancho, N.M.	D2-'07	16/3
15	Breaston, Steve	WR	6-0	189	8/20/83	5	Michigan	North Braddock, Pa.	D5-'07	13/11
73	Bridges, Jeremy	T	6-5	318	4/19/80	9	Southern Mississippi	South Pike, Miss.	FA-'09	16/7
32	Broughton, Nehemiah	FB	6-0	255	11/4/82	5	The Citadel	Charleston, S.C.	FA-'09	0*
75	Brown, Levi	T	6-6	324	3/16/84	5	Penn State	Norfolk, Va.	D1-'07	16/16
93	Campbell, Calais	DE	6-8	300	9/1/86	4	Miami	Aurora, Colo.	D2-'08	15/15
62	Claxton, Ben	C	6-3	300	7/30/80	4	Mississippi	Dublin, Ga.	FA-'09	0*
59	Davis, Will	LB	6-2	257	6/2/86	3	Illinois	Greenbelt, Md.	D6-'09	10/3
90	Dockett, Darnell	DT	6-4	290	5/27/81	8	Florida State	Burtonsville, Md.	D3-'04	15/15
80	Doucet, Early	WR	6-0	212	10/28/85	4	Louisiana State	St. Martinville, La.	D3-'08	10/5
81	Dray, Jim	TE	6-5	255	12/31/86	2	Stanford	Paramus, N.J.	D7-'10	16/3
94	Dykes, Keilen	DT	6-3	305	9/6/84	3	West Virginia	Youngstown, Ohio	FA-'08	0*
4	Feely, Jay	K	5-10	208	5/23/76	11	Michigan	Tampa, Fla.	UFA(NYJ)-'10	16/0
11	Fitzgerald, Larry	WR	6-3	218	8/31/83	8	Pittsburgh	Minneapolis, Minn.	D1-'04	16/15
57	Gatewood, Curtis	LB	6-3	250	5/18/85	2	Vanderbilt	Memphis, Tenn.	FA-'10	1/0
5	Graham, Ben	P	6-5	236	11/2/73	7	Deakin (Australia)	Geelong, Australia	FA-'08	16/0
30	Green, Marshay	CB	5-10	175	1/14/86	2	Mississippi	Bastrop, La.	FA-'10	0*
70	Hadnot, Rex	G/C	6-2	310	1/28/82	8	Houston	Lufkin, Texas	UFA(Cle)-'10	11/1
53	Haggans, Clark	LB	6-4	243	1/10/77	12	Colorado State	Torrance, Calif.	UFA(Pitt)-'08	13/13
6	Hall, Max	QB	6-1	205	10/1/85	2	Brigham Young	Mesa, Ariz.	FA-'10	6/3
54	Hayes, Gerald	LB	6-1	250	10/10/80	9	Pittsburgh	Paterson, N.J.	D3-'03	6/4
34	Hightower, Tim	RB	6-1	222	5/23/86	4	Richmond	Alexandria, Va.	D5-'08	16/13
91	Iwebema, Kenny	DE	6-4	280	2/6/85	4	Iowa	Arlington, Texas	D4-'08	7/0
20	Jefferson, A.J.	CB	6-1	190	4/4/88	2	Fresno State	Bakersfield, Calif.	FA-'10	2/0
49	Johnson, Rashad	S	5-11	204	1/2/86	3	Alabama	Sulligent, Ala.	D3-'09	16/1
72	Keith, Brandon	T	6-5	335	11/21/84	4	Northern Iowa	McAlester, Okla.	D7-'08	9/9
18	Komar, Max	WR	5-11	202	4/30/87	2	Idaho	Auburn, Wash.	FA-'10	8/0
82	Leach, Mike	LS	6-2	235	10/18/76	12	William & Mary	Jefferson Township, N.J.	FA-'09	16/0
51	Lenon, Paris	LB	6-2	240	11/26/77	10	Richmond	Lynchburg, Va.	UFA(StL)-'10	16/16
76	Lutui, Deuce	G	6-4	338	5/5/83	6	Southern California	Mesa, Ariz.	D2-'06	16/16
45	Maui'a, Reagan	FB	6-0	265	7/6/84	4	Hawai'i	Stockton, Calif.	FA-'10	15/4
23	McBride, Trumaine	CB	5-9	185	9/24/85	5	Mississippi	Clarksdale, Miss.	FA-'10	14/0
69	Navarre, Jeremy	DL	6-3	279	3/16/87	2	Maryland	Joppatowne, Md.	FA-'10	0*
52	Obiozor, Cyril	LB	6-4	249	7/26/86	3	Texas A&M	Houston, Texas	FA-'10	6/0
89	Patrick, Ben	TE	6-3	264	8/23/84	5	Delaware	Savannah, Ga.	D7-'07	15/7
55	Porter, Joey	LB	6-3	248	3/22/77	13	Colorado State	Bakersfield, Calif.	FA-'10	14/14
25	Rhodes, Kerry	FS	6-3	212	8/2/82	7	Louisville	Bessemer, Ala.	T(NYJ)-'10	16/16
12	Roberts, Andre	WR	5-11	195	1/9/88	2	The Citadel	Columbia, S.C.	D3-'10	15/2
97	Robinson, Bryan	DT	6-4	305	6/22/74	15	Fresno State	Toledo, Ohio	UFA(Cin)-'08	16/16
29	Rodgers-Cromartie, Dominique	CB	6-2	182	4/7/86	4	Tennessee State	Bradenton, Fla.	D1-'08	16/16
50	Schofield, O'Brien	LB	6-3	242	4/3/87	2	Wisconsin	Great Lakes, Ill.	D4-'10	10/0
63	Sendlein, Lyle	C	6-3	308	3/16/84	5	Texas	Scottsdale, Ariz.	FA-'07	16/16
19	Skelton, John	QB	6-6	244	3/17/88	2	Fordham	El Paso, Texas	D5-'10	5/4
46	Smith, Alfonso	RB	6-1	208	1/23/87	2	Kentucky	Louisville, Ky.	FA-'10	1/0
83	Spach, Stephen	TE	6-4	260	7/18/82	6	Fresno State	Clovis, Calif.	FA-'08	15/11
36	Stephens-Howling, LaRod	RB	5-7	185	4/26/87	3	Pittsburgh	Johnstown, Pa.	D7a-'09	13/2
95	Togafau, Pago	LB	5-11	240	1/10/84	4	Idaho State	Long Beach, Calif.	FA-'10	0*
28	Toler, Greg	CB	6-0	192	1/2/85	3	Saint Paul's (VA)	Washington, D.C.	D4-'09	14/13
56	Walker, Reggie	LB	6-0	244	12/15/86	3	Kansas State	Sacramento, Calif.	FA-'09	11/0
22	Ware, Matt	S	6-3	218	12/2/82	8	UCLA	Santa Monica, Calif.	W(Phil)-'06	14/0
58	Washington, Daryl	LB	6-2	230	10/9/86	2	Texas Christian	Irving, Texas	D2-'10	16/11
98	Watson, Gabe	DT	6-4	338	9/24/83	6	Michigan	Southfield, Mich.	D4-'06	7/0
26	Wells, Beanie	RB	6-2	229	8/7/88	3	Ohio State	Akron, Ohio	D1-'09	13/2
92	Williams, Dan	DT	6-3	327	6/1/87	2	Tennessee	Memphis, Tenn.	D1-'10	15/0
14	Williams, Stephen	WR	6-5	208	6/29/86	2	Toledo	Houston, Texas	FA-'10	11/3
24	Wilson, Adrian	SS	6-3	230	10/12/79	11	North Carolina State	High Point, N.C.	D3-'01	16/16
31	Wright, Jason	RB	5-10	212	7/12/82	8	Northwestern	Diamond Bar, Calif.	UFA(Cle)-'09	15/1

* Ali last active with Cleveland in '08; Broughton missed '10 season because of injury; Claxton inactive for 16 games; Dykes missed '10 season because of injury; Green inactive for 6 games; Navarre last active with Jacksonville in '09; Togafau last active with Arizona in '09.

Also played with Cardinals in '10—G Alan Faneca (16 games), RB Jerome Johnson (1), DB Brandon McDonald (2).

^ "NFL Exp." as of 2011 Kickoff Weekend. For full explanation of how a player's NFL Experience is measured, refer to explanation underneath the First-Year Roster listed below.

FIRST-YEAR ROSTER

Name	Pos.	Ht.	Wt.	Birthdate	College	Hometown	How Acq.
Acho, Sam	LB	6-1	257	9/6/88	Texas	Dallas, Texas	D4
Carter, David	DE	6-5	300	12/10/87	UCLA	Fontana, Calif.	D6b
Housler, Rob	TE	6-5	250	3/17/88	Florida Atlantic	Converse, Texas	D3
Louis, Cliff (1)	T	6-8	315	8/24/84	Morgan State	Brooklyn, N.Y.	FA-'10
Pestock, Tom (1)	G	6-6	318	9/13/84	Northwest Missouri State	Lenexa, Kan.	FA-'09
Peterson, Patrick	CB	6-1	219	7/11/90	Louisiana State	Pompano Beach, Fla.	D1
Sampson, DeMarco	WR	6-2	204	12/19/85	San Diego State	Chula Vista, Calif.	D7
Sharpe, Brandon (1)	LB	6-2	254	12/11/86	Texas Tech	Lyons, Ga.	FA-'10
Sherman, Anthony	FB	5-10	242	12/11/88	Connecticut	North Attleboro, Mass.	D5
Sturdivant, Quan	LB	6-1	241	12/5/88	North Carolina	Oakboro, N.C.	D6a
Talley, Ronald (1)	DE	6-3	286	2/21/86	Delaware	Detroit, Mich.	FA-'10
Williams, Isaiah (1)	WR	6-3	200	1/30/87	Maryland	Montclair, N.J.	FA-'10
Williams, Ryan	RB	5-9	207	4/9/90	Virginia Tech	Manassas, Va.	D2

The term NFL Rookie is defined as a player who is in his first season of professional football and has not been on the roster of another professional football team for any regular-season or postseason games. A Rookie is designated by an "R" on NFL rosters. Players who have been active in another professional football league or players who have NFL experience, including either preseason training camp or being on an Active List or Inactive List, or on Reserve/Injured or Reserve/Physically Unable to Perform for fewer than six regular-season games, are termed NFL First-Year Players. An NFL First-Year Player is designated by a "1" on NFL rosters. Thereafter, a player is credited with an additional year of experience for each season in which he accumulates six games on the Active List or Inactive List, or on Reserve/Injured or Reserve/Physically Unable to Perform.

Log on to www.azcardinals.com for an up-to-date roster.

COACHING STAFF
Head Coach,
Ken Whisenhunt

Pro Career: Became an NFL head coach for the first time when hired by Arizona on January 14, 2007. After improving the team's won-loss record in each of his first three seasons, was rewarded with an extension on February 25, 2010 that will keep him under contract with the Cardinals through 2013 with a team option for 2014. With 36 victories in four seasons, ranks third among the franchise's all-time coaches (Jim Hanifan 39, Don Coryell 42). His 4-2 career postseason record is among the league leaders in winning percentage. Led the Cardinals to NFC West titles in 2008 and 2009, the team's first back-to-back division crowns since 1974-75. Arizona's 8-8 mark in his first season of 2007 was the team's best record since going 9-7 in 1998. The 2008 season brought the franchise's first postseason appearance since 1998, first division crown since 1975, and first home playoff game since 1947. It ended with the team's first-ever conference title and Super Bowl appearance. Arizona's 12 total wins in 2008 were the most in team history. In 2009, led Cardinals to 10 regular season wins for first time since 1976 and posted 6 road victories, the franchise's most since 1963. Prior to joining the Cardinals, Whisenhunt spent the previous six seasons as an assistant on Bill Cowher's staff with the Pittsburgh Steelers, the first three as tight ends coach and the last three as offensive coordinator. Whisenhunt took over as Pittsburgh's offensive coordinator in 2004, the same year the team drafted quarterback Ben Roethlisberger, who went on to set an NFL record with wins in his first 13 career starts en route to Offensive Rookie of the Year honors. The next season he became the youngest quarterback in NFL history to win a Super Bowl and finished third in the league in passer rating (98.6). In Whisenhunt's first year as coordinator, the Steelers rushing attack improved from thirty-first to second and the overall offense ranked sixteenth. His second year ended with an NFL title after the Steelers offense averaged 26.8 points per game in the playoffs. He joined the Steelers in January of 2001 as tight ends coach. Whisenhunt previously coached at the pro level with the New York Jets (tight ends, 2000), Cleveland Browns (special teams, 1999) and Baltimore Ravens (tight ends, 1997-98). He began his coaching career in the collegiate ranks with Vanderbilt for two seasons (1995-96). Whisenhunt was selected in the 12th round of the 1985 NFL Draft by the Atlanta Falcons out of Georgia Tech. He went on to play nine NFL seasons with the Falcons (1985-88), Washington Redskins (1989-1990), and New York Jets (1991-93). In 74 career

games (37 starts), he caught 62 passes for 601 yards and 6 touchdowns. Career record: 36-34.

Background: After going to Georgia Tech as a walk-on, he played four seasons as a tight end/H-back. He finished his Yellow Jackets' career ranked second on the receiving yardage list (1,264 yards) and fourth in receptions (82). As a senior in 1984, He was a consensus All-ACC and honorable mention All-America selection when he averaged 19.1 yards-per-catch.

Personal: Born February 28, 1962 in Atlanta. Whisenhunt earned a degree in civil engineering from Georgia Tech. Ken and his wife, Alice, have two children—Kenneth, Jr. and Mary Ashley.

ASSISTANT COACHES

Ron Aiken, defensive line; born August 18, 1955, Moncks Corner, S.C. Guard/center North Carolina A&T 1973-76. No pro playing experience. College coach: Bethany College 1979-1981, Tarkio College 1982-84, Rensselaer Polytechnic Institute 1985, Langston 1986-89, New Mexico 1990-94, Vanderbilt 1995-96, Texas 1997, San Diego State 1998, Iowa 1999-2006. Pro coach: Joined Cardinals in 2007.

Pete Alosi, asst. strength and conditioning; born July 31, 1982. Linebacker Salisbury University 2000-02. No pro playing experience. Pro coach: Joined Cardinals in 2010.

Louie Cioffi, defensive backs; born September 21, 1973, Greenlawn, N.Y. Attended SUNY-Stony Brook. No college or pro playing experience. College coach: C.W. Post 1995-96. Pro coach: New York Jets 1993-94, Cincinnati Bengals 1997-2010, joined Cardinals in 2011.

Chad Grimm, offensive quality control; born May 18, 1985, Fairfax, Va. Linebacker Virginia Tech 2003-06. No pro playing experience. Pro coach: Joined Cardinals in 2009.

Russ Grimm, asst. head coach/offensive line; born May 2, 1959, Scottdale, Pa. Center Pittsburgh 1977-1980. Pro guard Washington Redskins 1981-1991. Inducted into Pro Football Hall of Fame in 2010. Pro coach: Washington Redskins 1992-2000, Pittsburgh Steelers 2001-06, joined Cardinals in 2007.

Ray Horton, defensive coordinator; born April 12, 1960, Tacoma, Wash. Cornerback Washington 1979-1982. Pro cornerback Cincinnati Bengals 1983-88, Dallas Cowboys 1989-1992. Pro coach: Washington Redskins 1994-96, Cincinnati Bengals 1997-2001, Detroit Lions 2002-03, Pittsburgh Steelers 2004-2010, joined Cardinals in 2011.

Freddie Kitchens, tight ends; born November 29, 1974, Gadsden, Ala. Quarterback Alabama 1994-97. No pro playing experience. College coach: Glenville State College 1999, Louisiana State 2000, North Texas 2001-03, Mississippi State 2004-05. Pro coach: Dallas Cowboys 2006, joined Cardinals in 2007.

John Lott, strength and conditioning; born May 9, 1964, Denton, Texas. Offensive lineman North Texas 1983-86. Pro offensive lineman Pittsburgh Steelers 1987. College coach: North Texas 1989-1990, Houston 1991-96. Pro coach: New York Jets 1997-2004, Cleveland Browns 2005-06, joined Cardinals in 2007.

John McNulty, wide receivers; born May 29, 1968, Scranton, Pa. Safety Penn State 1988-1990. No pro playing experience. College coach: Michigan 1991-94, Connecticut 1995-97, Rutgers 2004-08. Pro coach: Jacksonville Jaguars 1998-2002, Dallas Cowboys 2003, joined Cardinals in 2009.

Chris Miller, quarterbacks; born August 9, 1965, Pomona, Calif. Quarterback Oregon 1983-86. Pro quarterback Atlanta Falcons 1987-1993, St. Louis Rams 1994-95, Denver Broncos 1999. Pro coach: Joined Cardinals in 2009.

Mike Miller, offensive coordinator; born April 9, 1970, Plum Borough, Pa. Attended Clarion. No college or pro playing experience. College coach: Robert Morris 1997-98, 2006. Pro coach: Pittsburgh Steelers 1999-2003, Buffalo Bills 2004-05, Berlin Thunder (NFLE) 2006, joined Cardinals in 2007.

Matt Raich, linebackers; born August 16, 1970, Monaca, Pa. Middle linebacker Westminster College 1989-1992. No pro playing experience. College coach: Westminster 1993-94, Robert Morris 1996-98, 2000-02, Glenville State 1999. Pro coach: Pittsburgh Steelers 2004-06, joined Cardinals in 2007.

Tommie Robinson, running backs; born April 4, 1963, Columbus, Ga. Safety Troy State 1982-85. No pro playing experience. College coach: Arkansas 1991, Utah State 1992-93, TCU 1994-97, Nevada-Las Vegas 1998, Oklahoma State 2001, Georgia Tech 2002-05, Memphis 2006, Miami 2007-09. Pro coach: Dallas Cowboys 1998-2000, joined Cardinals in 2010.

Ryan Slowik, defensive quality control; born Dec. 27, 1980, Chicago. Safety Wisconsin-Oshkosh 2002-03. No pro playing experience. College coach: Wisconsin-Oshkosh 2004. Pro coach: Denver Broncos 2005-08, joined Cardinals in 2009.

Kevin Spencer, special teams; born November 2, 1953, Queens, N.Y. Outside linebacker Springfield College 1971. No pro playing experience. College coach: SUNY-Cortland 1975-76, Cornell 1979-1980, Ithaca 1981-86, Wesleyan 1987-1991. Pro coach: Cleveland Browns 1991-94, Oakland Raiders 1995-97, Indianapolis Colts 1998-2001, Pittsburgh Steelers 2002-06, joined Cardinals in 2007.

Deshea Townsend, asst. defensive backs; born September 8, 1975, Batesville, Miss. Cornerback Alabama 1994-97. Pro cornerback Pittsburgh Steelers 1998-2009, Indianapolis Colts 2010. Pro coach: Joined Cardinals in 2011.

National Football Conference
South Division
Team Colors: Black, Red, Silver, and White
4400 Falcon Parkway
Flowery Branch, Georgia 30542
Telephone: (770) 965-3115

2011 SCHEDULE
PRESEASON
Aug. 12 **Miami**.................................7:30
Aug. 19 at Jacksonville...................8:00
Aug. 27 at Pittsburgh......................7:30
Sep. 1 **Baltimore**..........................7:30

REGULAR SEASON
Sep. 11 at Chicago 1:00
Sep. 18 **Philadelphia** 8:20
Sep. 25 at Tampa Bay 4:15
Oct. 2 at Seattle 4:05
Oct. 9 **Green Bay** 8:20
Oct. 16 **Carolina** 1:00
Oct. 23 at Detroit 1:00
Oct. 30 BYE
Nov. 6 at Indianapolis 1:00
Nov. 13 **New Orleans** 1:00
Nov. 20 **Tennessee** 1:00
Nov. 27 **Minnesota** 1:00
Dec. 4 at Houston 1:00
Dec. 11 at Carolina 1:00
Dec. 15 **Jacksonville** (Thu) 8:20
Dec. 26 at New Orleans (Mon) 8:30
Jan. 1 **Tampa Bay** 1:00
All times ET

Stadium: Georgia Dome
(opened in 1992)
•**Capacity:** 71,228
One Georgia Dome Drive
Atlanta, Georgia 30313
Playing Surface: FieldTurf
Training Camp: Atlanta Falcons
4400 Falcon Parkway
Flowery Branch, GA 30542

GEORGIA DOME

CLUB OFFICIALS
Owner & CEO: Arthur M. Blank
President: Rich McKay
General Manager: Thomas Dimitroff
Head Coach: Mike Smith
Director of Human Resources:
Karen Walters
Senior Vice President & CFO:
Greg Beadles
Controller: Rob Geoffroy
Vice President of Football
Communications: Reggie Roberts
Vice President of Information
Technology: Danny Branch
Chief Marketing Officer: Jim Smith
Vice President of Sales: Dave Cohen
Vice President of Sponsorship Sales:
Tim Zulawski
Senior Director of Media Relations:
Frank Kleha
Senior Director of Player Development:
Kevin Winston
Director of Logistics and Facilities:
Spencer Treadwell
Director of Ticket Operations:
Mike Gilsenan
Director of Community Relations:
Kendyl Baugh Moss
Director of Event Marketing: Roddy White
Director of Football Administration:
Nick Polk
Director of Player Personnel: Les Snead
Director of College Scouting:
David Caldwell
Assistant Director of Player Personnel:
Lionel Vital
Eastern Regional Scout: Marvin Allen
Western Regional Scout: Mark Olson
Area Scouts: Bob Harrison,
Shepley Heard, Bob Kronenberg,
Taylor Morton, Robinson Payne,
Steve Sabo
Pro Scouts: Ran Carthon,
DeJuan Polk
Scouting Assistant: Anthony Robinson
Head Athletic Trainer: Marty Lauzon
Assistant Athletic Trainer: Danny Long
Video Director: Mike Crews
Video Assistants: Phil Tieman,
Daniel Wayne
Equipment Manager: Brian Boigner
Director of New Media: Dan Levak
Football Communications Coordinator:
Brian Cearns
Football Communications Coordinator:
Matt Haley

COACHING HISTORY
(295-403-6)
Records include postseason games

1966-68	Norb Hecker*	4-26-1
1968-1974	Norm Van Brocklin**	..37-49-3
1974-76	Marion Campbell***	6-19-0
1976	Pat Peppler	3-6-0
1977-1982	Leeman Bennett	47-44-0
1983-86	Dan Henning	22-41-1
1987-89	Marion Campbell****	.11-32-0
1989	Jim Hanifan	0-4-0
1990-93	Jerry Glanville	28-38-0
1994-96	June Jones	19-30-0
1997-2003	Dan Reeves#	52-61-1
2003	Wade Phillips	2-1-0
2004-06	Jim Mora	27-23-0
2007	Bobby Petrino##	3-10-0
2007	Emmitt Thomas	1-2-0
2008-2010	Mike Smith	33-17-0

*Released after three games in 1968
**Released after eight games in 1974
***Released after five games in 1976
****Retired after 12 games in 1989
\#Released after 13 games in 2003
\#\#Resigned after 13 games in 2007

PAID ATTENDANCE
Home 529,270   Away 496,566
Total 1,025,836
Single-game home record,
71,151 (10/22/06)
Single-season home record,
553,979 (1992)

2011 DRAFT CHOICES
Round	Name	Pos.	College
1	Julio Jones	WR	Alabama
3	Akeem Dent	LB	Georgia
5	Jacquizz Rodgers	RB	Oregon State
6	Matt Bosher	P	Miami
7	Andrew Jackson	G	Fresno State
	Cliff Matthews	DE	South Carolina

2010 TEAM RECORD

PRESEASON (2-2)

Date	Result	Opponent
8/13	W 20-10	Kansas City
8/19	L 10-28	New England
8/27	W 16-6	at Miami
9/2	L 9-13	at Jacksonville

REGULAR SEASON (13-3)

Date	Result	Opponent
9/12	L 9-15	at Pittsburgh (OT)
9/19	W 41-7	Arizona
9/26	W 27-24	at New Orleans (OT)
10/3	W 16-14	San Francisco
10/10	W 20-10	at Cleveland
10/17	L 17-31	at Philadelphia
10/24	W 39-32	Cincinnati
11/7	W 27-21	Tampa Bay
11/11	W 26-21	Baltimore
11/21	W 34-17	at St. Louis
11/28	W 20-17	Green Bay
12/5	W 28-24	at Tampa Bay
12/12	W 31-10	at Carolina
12/19	W 34-18	at Seattle
12/27	L 14-17	New Orleans
1/2	W 31-10	Carolina

POSTSEASON (0-1)

1/15	L 21-48	Green Bay
(OT) Overtime		

SCORE BY PERIODS

Falcons	69	148	83	111	3	—	414
Opponents	75	55	83	69	6	—	288

2010 TEAM STATISTICS

	Falcons	Opp.
Total First Downs	353	284
Rushing	111	87
Passing	200	183
Penalty	42	14
3rd Down: Made/Att	112/240	79/201
3rd Down Pct.	46.7	39.3
4th Down: Made/Att	11/15	9/17
4th Down Pct.	73.3	52.9
Possession Avg.	32:15	27:45
Total Net Yards	5458	5319
Avg. Per Game	341.1	332.4
Total Plays	1097	957
Avg. Per Play	5.0	5.6
Net Yards Rushing	1891	1694
Avg. Per Game	118.2	105.9
Total Rushes	497	366
Net Yards Passing	3567	3625
Avg. Per Game	222.9	226.6
Sacked/Yards Lost	23/158	31/221
Gross Yards	3725	3846
Att./Completions	577/361	560/364
Completion Pct.	62.6	65.0
Had Intercepted	9	22
Punts/Average	75/40.2	73/45.5
Net Punting Avg.	75/35.6	73/40.7
Penalties/Yards	58/598	116/1003
Fumbles/Ball Lost	12/8	23/9
Touchdowns	47	35
Rushing	14	9
Passing	28	23
Returns	5	3

2010 INDIVIDUAL STATISTICS

PASSING

	Att.	Comp.	Yds.	Pct.	TD	Int.	Tkld.	Rate
Ryan	571	357	3705	62.5	28	9	23/158	91.0
Redman	6	4	20	66.7	0	0	0/0	71.5
Falcons	577	361	3725	62.6	28	9	23/158	90.8
Opponents	560	364	3846	65.0	23	22	31/221	82.2

SCORING

	TD R	TD P	TD Rt	PAT	FG	Saf	PTS
M. Bryant	0	0	0	44/44	28/31	0	128
Turner	12	0	0	0/0	0/0	0	72
White	0	10	0	0/0	0/0	0	64
Gonzalez	0	6	0	0/0	0/0	0	36
Snelling	2	3	0	0/0	0/0	0	30
Finneran	0	3	0	0/0	0/0	0	18
Jenkins	0	2	0	0/0	0/0	0	12
Weems	0	0	2	0/0	0/0	0	12
Babineaux	0	0	1	0/0	0/0	0	6
Biermann	0	0	1	0/0	0/0	0	6
Davis	0	0	1	0/0	0/0	0	6
Douglas	0	1	0	0/0	0/0	0	6
Mughelli	0	1	0	0/0	0/0	0	6
Palmer	0	1	0	0/0	0/0	0	6
Peelle	0	1	0	0/0	0/0	0	6
Falcons	14	28	5	44/44	28/31	0	414
Opponents	9	23	3	31/31	15/23	0	288

2-Pt Conversions: White 2.
Falcons 2-3, Opponents 1-3.

RUSHING

	No.	Yds	Avg	LG	TD
Turner	334	1371	4.1	55	12
Snelling	87	324	3.7	30	2
Ryan	46	122	2.7	20	0
G. Johnson	10	36	3.6	23	0
Mughelli	13	36	2.8	6	0
Norwood	2	8	4.0	6	0
White	1	3	3.0	3	0
Redman	1	-1	-1.0	-1	0
Smith	1	-3	-3.0	-3	0
Douglas	2	-5	-2.5	0	0
Falcons	497	1891	3.8	55	14
Opponents	366	1694	4.6	80t	9

RECEIVING

	No.	Yds	Avg	LG	TD
White	115	1389	12.1	46	10
Gonzalez	70	656	9.4	34	6
Snelling	44	303	6.9	28t	3
Jenkins	41	505	12.3	43	2
Douglas	22	294	13.4	46	1
Finneran	19	166	8.7	21	3
Mughelli	13	126	9.7	18	1
Turner	12	85	7.1	19	0
Peelle	10	96	9.6	15	1
Weems	6	61	10.2	18	0
Palmer	5	29	5.8	11	1
G. Johnson	3	6	2.0	10	0
Norwood	1	9	9.0	9	0
Falcons	361	3725	10.3	46	28
Opponents	364	3846	10.6	83t	23

INTERCEPTIONS

	No.	Yds	Avg	LG	TD
Moore	5	117	23.4	34	0
Grimes	5	84	16.8	36	0
Peterson	2	18	9.0	17	0
Franks	1	40	40.0	40	0
Biermann	1	31	31.0	31t	1
Davis	1	26	26.0	26t	1
Owens	1	13	13.0	13	0
Abraham	1	6	6.0	6	0
Lofton	1	2	2.0	2	0
Babineaux	1	0	0.0	0	0
DeCoud	1	0	0.0	0	0
Nicholas	1	0	0.0	0	0
Robinson	1	0	0.0	0	0
Falcons	22	337	15.3	40	2
Opponents	9	123	13.7	39	0

PUNTING

	No.	Yds.	Avg.	In 20	LG
Koenen	74	3014	40.7	29	61
Falcons	75	3014	40.2	29	61
Opponents	73	3323	45.5	20	64

PUNT RETURNS

	Ret	FC	Yds	Avg	LG	TD
Weems	18	19	230	12.8	55t	1
DeCoud	1	0	0	0.0	0	0
Falcons	19	19	230	12.1	55t	1
Opponents	28	24	241	8.6	72	0

KICKOFF RETURNS

	No.	Yds	Avg	LG	TD
Weems	40	1100	27.5	102t	1
Norwood	4	97	24.3	34	0
Finneran	1	18	18.0	18	0
Mughelli	1	6	6.0	6	0
Falcons	46	1221	26.5	102t	1
Opponents	64	1362	21.3	89t	1

FIELD GOALS

	1-19	20-29	30-39	40-49	50+
M. Bryant	0/0	11/11	8/9	8/10	1/1
Falcons	0/0	11/11	8/9	8/10	1/1
Opponents	1/1	3/4	8/10	0/2	3/6

SACKS

	No.
Abraham	13.0
Babineaux	4.0
Biermann	3.0
Anderson	2.0
Jerry	2.0
Lofton	2.0
Davis	1.0
Peters	1.0
Peterson	1.0
Weatherspoon	1.0
Williams	1.0
Falcons	31.0
Opponents	23.0

RECORD HOLDERS
INDIVIDUAL RECORDS—CAREER

Category	Name	Performance
Rushing (Yds.)	Gerald Riggs, 1982-88	6,631
Passing (Yds.)	Steve Bartkowski, 1975-1985	23,470
Passing (TDs)	Steve Bartkowski, 1975-1985	154
Receiving (No.)	Terance Mathis, 1994-2001	573
Receiving (Yds.)	Terance Mathis, 1994-2001	7,349
Interceptions	Rolland Lawrence, 1973-1980	39
Punting (Avg.)	Rick Donnelly, 1985-89	42.6
Punt Return (Avg.)	Darrien Gordon, 2001	14.1
Kickoff Return (Avg.)	Darrick Vaughn, 2000-01	25.7
Field Goals	Morten Andersen, 1995-2000, 2006-07	184
Touchdowns (Tot.)	Terance Mathis, 1994-2001	57
Points	Morten Andersen, 1995-2000, 2006-07	806
Sacks*	Chuck Smith, 1992-99	58.5

INDIVIDUAL RECORDS—SINGLE SEASON

Category	Name	Performance
Rushing (Yds.)	Jamal Anderson, 1998	1,846
Passing (Yds.)	Jeff George, 1995	4,143
Passing (TDs)	Steve Bartkowski, 1980	31
Receiving (No.)	Roddy White, 2010	115
Receiving (Yds.)	Roddy White, 2010	1,389
Interceptions	Scott Case, 1988	10
Punting (Avg.)	Billy Lothridge, 1968	44.3
Punt Return (Avg.)	Darrien Gordon, 2001	14.1
Kickoff Return (Avg.)	Darrick Vaughn, 2000	27.7
Field Goals	Jay Feely, 2002	32
Touchdowns (Tot.)	Michael Turner, 2008	17
Points	Jay Feely, 2002	138
Sacks*	John Abraham, 2008	16.5

INDIVIDUAL RECORDS—SINGLE GAME

Category	Name	Performance
Rushing (Yds.)	Michael Turner, 9-7-08	220
Passing (Yds.)	Chris Chandler, 12-23-01	431
Passing (TDs)	Wade Wilson, 12-13-92	5
Receiving (No.)	William Andrews, 11-15-81	15
Receiving (Yds.)	Roddy White, 10-11-09	210
Interceptions	Many times	2
	Last time by Brent Grimes, 12-20-09	
Field Goals	Norm Johnson, 11-13-94	6
Touchdowns (Tot.)	T.J. Duckett, 12-12-04	4
	Michael Turner, 11-23-08	4
Points	T.J. Duckett, 12-12-04	24
	Michael Turner, 11-23-08	24
Sacks*	Chuck Smith, 10-12-97	5.0

Sacks became an official statistic in 1982.

VETERAN ROSTER AS OF MARCH 3, 2011

No.	Name	Pos.	Ht.	Wt.	Birthdate	^NFL Exp.	College	Hometown	How Acq.	'10 Games/ Starts
55	Abraham, John	DE	6-4	263	5/6/78	12	South Carolina	Timmonsville, S.C.	T(NYJ)-'06	15/13
59	Adkins, Spencer	LB	5-11	236	5/16/87	3	Miami	Naples, Fla.	D6-'09	9/0
98	Anderson, Jamaal	DE	6-6	291	2/6/86	5	Arkansas	Little Rock, Ark.	D1-'07	16/3
95	Babineaux, Jonathan	DT	6-2	300	10/12/81	7	Iowa	Port Arthur, Texas	D2-'05	15/15
72	Baker, Sam	T	6-5	301	5/30/85	4	Southern California	Tustin, Calif.	D1b-'08	16/16
71	Biermann, Kroy	DE	6-3	255	9/12/85	4	Montana	Hardin, Mont.	D5b-'08	16/14
63	Blalock, Justin	G	6-4	326	12/20/83	5	Texas	Dallas, Texas	D2a-'07	16/16
3	Bryant, Matt	K	5-9	203	5/29/75	10	Baylor	Orange, Texas	FA-'09	16/0
77	Clabo, Tyson	T	6-6	329	10/17/81	7	Wake Forest	Knoxville, Tenn.	FA-'06	16/16
73	Dahl, Harvey	G	6-5	303	6/24/81	5	Nevada-Reno	Fallon, Nev.	FA-'07	16/16
92	Davis, Chauncey	DE	6-2	271	1/27/83	7	Florida State	Bartow, Fla.	D4-'05	16/2
28	DeCoud, Thomas	S	6-2	192	3/19/85	4	California	Vallejo, Calif.	D3c-'08	16/16
83	Douglas, Harry	WR	6-0	183	9/16/84	3	Louisville	Jonesboro, Ga.	D3b-'08	16/4
86	Finneran, Brian	WR	6-5	213	1/31/76	11	Villanova	Mission Viejo, Calif.	FA-'00	16/1
24	Franks, Dominique	CB	6-0	197	10/8/87	2	Oklahoma	Tulsa, Okla.	D5a-'10	2/0
88	Gonzalez, Tony	TE	6-5	247	2/27/76	15	California	Torrance, Calif.	T(KC)-'09	16/16
20	Grimes, Brent	CB	5-10	183	7/19/83	4	Shippensburg	Philadelphia, Pa.	FA-'07	16/16
61	Hawley, Joe	C	6-3	302	10/22/88	2	Nevada-Las Vegas	Yorba Linda, Calif.	D4-'10	15/0
12	Jenkins, Michael	WR	6-4	214	6/18/82	8	Ohio State	Tampa, Fla.	D1b-'04	11/9
94	Jerry, Peria	DT	6-2	295	8/23/84	3	Mississippi	Batesville, Miss.	D1-'09	16/0
27	Johnson, Gartrell	RB	5-10	219	6/21/86	2	Colorado State	Miami, Fla.	FA-'10	9/0
79	Johnson, Mike	G	6-6	304	4/2/87	2	Alabama	Pensacola, Fla.	D3b-'10	0*
93	Johnson, Thomas	DT	6-2	304	6/24/81	4	Middle Tennessee State	Memphis, Tenn.	FA-'09	0*
9	Koenen, Michael	P	5-11	197	7/13/82	7	Western Washington	Ferndale, Wash.	FA-'05	16/0
97	Lewis, Trey	DT	6-3	312	5/23/85	4	Washburn	Topeka, Kan.	D6a-'07	1/1
50	Lofton, Curtis	LB	6-0	241	6/2/86	4	Oklahoma	Kingfisher, Okla.	D2-'08	16/16
62	McClure, Todd	C	6-1	296	2/16/77	13	Louisiana State	Baton Rouge, La.	D7a-'99	16/16
80	Meier, Kerry	WR	6-3	220	11/12/86	2	Kansas	Pittsburg, Kan.	D5b-'10	0*
25	Moore, William	S	6-0	221	5/18/85	3	Missouri	Hayti, Mo.	D2-'09	16/15
34	Mughelli, Ovie	FB	6-1	250	6/10/80	9	Wake Forest	Boston, Mass.	UFA(Balt)-'07	16/6
54	Nicholas, Stephen	LB	6-3	236	5/1/83	5	South Florida	Jacksonville, Fla.	D4a-'07	16/11
32	Norwood, Jerious	RB	5-11	208	7/29/83	6	Mississippi State	Jackson, Miss.	D3-'06	2/0
21	Owens, Christopher	CB	5-9	180	12/1/86	3	San Jose State	Los Angeles, Calif.	D3-'09	16/3
81	Palmer, Michael	TE	6-5	252	1/18/88	2	Clemson	Stone Mountain, Ga.	FA-'10	14/1
87	Peelle, Justin	TE	6-4	251	3/15/79	10	Oregon	Fresno, Calif.	FA-'08	13/8
91	Peters, Corey	DT	6-3	3-5	6/8/88	2	Kentucky	Louisville, Ky.	D3a-'10	16/15
53	Peterson, Mike	LB	6-1	226	6/17/76	13	Florida	Gainesville, Fla.	UFA(Jax)-'09	16/13
8	Redman, Chris	QB	6-3	225	7/7/77	9	Louisville	Louisville, Ky.	FA-'07	2/0
75	Reynolds, Garrett	T	6-7	310	7/1/87	3	North Carolina	Knoxville, Tenn.	D5b-'09	0*
23	Robinson, Dunta	CB	5-10	183	4/11/82	8	South Carolina	Athens, Ga.	FA-'10	15/15
2	Ryan, Matt	QB	6-4	217	5/17/85	4	Boston College	Exton, Pa.	D1a-'08	16/16
39	Schillinger, Shann	S	6-0	200	5/22/86	2	Montana	Baker, Mont.	D6-'10	15/0
90	Sidbury, Lawrence	DE	6-3	261	2/6/86	3	Richmond	Cheltenham, Md.	D4-'09	6/0
35	Smith, Antone	RB	5-9	192	9/17/85	2	Florida State	Pahokee, Fla.	FA-'09	9/0
44	Snelling, Jason	RB	5-11	234	12/29/83	5	Virginia	Chester, Va.	D7-'07	14/0
74	Svitek, Will	T	6-6	308	1/8/82	6	Stanford	Prague, Czech Republic	FA-'09	16/0
33	Turner, Michael	RB	5-10	247	2/13/82	8	Northern Illinois	Waukegan, Ill.	UFA(SD)-'08	16/15
99	Walker, Vance	DT	6-2	304	4/26/87	3	Georgia Tech	Fort Mill, S.C.	D7-'09	16/1
56	Weatherspoon, Sean	LB	6-2	244	12/29/87	2	Missouri	Jasper, Texas	D1-'10	11/5
14	Weems, Eric	WR	5-9	195	7/4/85	4	Bethune-Cookman	Ormond Beach, Fla.	FA-'07	16/4
84	White, Roddy	WR	6-0	211	11/2/81	7	Alabama-Birmingham	James Island, S.C.	D1-'05	16/16
29	Williams, Brian	CB	5-11	208	7/2/79	10	North Carolina State	High Point, N.C.	FA-'09	16/1
4	Wilson, John Parker	QB	6-2	215	10/17/85	2	Alabama	Hoover, Ala.	FA-'09	0*
52	Wire, Coy	LB	6-2	225	11/7/78	10	Stanford	Camp Hill, Pa.	FA-'08	15/0
82	Zelenka, Joe	LS	6-3	266	3/9/76	13	Wake Forest	Cleveland, Ohio	FA-'09	16/0

* M. Johnson inactive for 16 games; T. Johnson missed '10 season because of injury; Meier missed '10 season because of injury; Reynolds inactive for 16 games; Wilson inactive third quarterback for 16 games.

Also played with the Falcons in '10—C Rob Bruggeman (1 game), S Erik Coleman (12).

^ "NFL Exp." as of 2011 Kickoff Weekend. For full explanation of how a player's NFL Experience is measured, refer to explanation below the First-Year Roster on the next page.

FIRST-YEAR ROSTER

Name	Pos.	Ht.	Wt.	Birthdate	College	Hometown	How Acq.
Agnone, Robbie (1)	TE	6-6	260	10/2/85	Delaware	Etters, Pa.	FA-'10
Bosher, Matt (1)	K/P	6-0	208	10/18/87	Miami	Jupiter, Fla.	D6-'10
Branson, Marquez (1)	TE	6-3	247	2/14/87	Central Arkansas	Starkville, Miss.	FA-'10
Bruggeman, Rob (1)	C	6-4	293	3/21/86	Iowa	Cedar Rapids, Iowa	FA-'09
Buckley, Tim (1)	WR	6-1	185	8/19/88	Alcorn State	Madison, Miss.	FA-'10
Bush, Rafael (1)	S	5-11	180	5/12/87	South Carolina State	Williston, S.C.	FA-'10
Dent, Akeem	LB	6-1	239	9/27/87	Georgia	Atlanta, Ga.	D3
Harvey, Brandyn (1)	WR	6-4	205	11/6/87	Villanova	Spring Valley, Calif.	FA-'10
Jackson, Andrew	G	6-5	299	10/18/88	Fresno State	Grass Valley, Calif.	D7a
James, Robert (1)	LB	5-11	224	12/26/83	Arizona State	Glendale, Ariz.	FA-'10
Jones, Julio	WR	6-3	220	2/3/89	Alabama	Foley, Ala.	D1
Matthews, Cliff	DE	6-4	268	8/5/89	South Carolina	Cheraw, S.C.	D7b
Parrish, Ken	P	6-2	210	6/22/84	East Stroudsburg	East Stroudsburg, Pa.	FA
Priest, Rafael	S	5-10	181	3/11/87	Texas Christian	Dallas, Texas	FA
Rodgers, Jacquizz	RB	5-6	196	2/6/90	Oregon State	Richmond, Texas	D5
Stephens, Emmanuel (1)	DE	6-3	255	2/17/87	Mississippi	Houston, Texas	FA-'10
Strickland, Andy (1)	WR	6-0	197	9/2/87	Wofford	Gaffney, S.C.	FA-'09
Valdez, Jose (1)	G	6-6	324	12/13/86	Arkansas	St. Francis, Wisc.	FA-'09
Woods, Bear	LB	6-0	245	1/22/87	Troy	MacClenny, Fla.	FA

The term NFL Rookie is defined as a player who is in his first season of professional football and has not been on the roster of another professional football team for any regular-season or postseason games. A Rookie is designated by an "R" on NFL rosters. Players who have been active in another professional football league or players who have NFL experience, including either preseason training camp or being on an Active List or Inactive List, or on Reserve/Injured or Reserve/Physically Unable to Perform for fewer than six regular-season games, are termed NFL First-Year Players. An NFL First-Year Player is designated by a "1" on NFL rosters. Thereafter, a player is credited with an additional year of experience for each season in which he accumulates six games on the Active List or Inactive List, or on Reserve/Injured or Reserve/Physically Unable to Perform.

Log on to www.atlantafalcons.com for an up-to-date roster.

COACHING STAFF
Head Coach,
Mike Smith

Pro Career: Mike Smith was named the 14th head coach in Atlanta Falcons franchise history on January 23, 2008. In three seasons with the team, he has compiled a 33-15 record, third-best mark among all NFL head coaches, two playoff appearances and three straight winning seasons for the first time in franchise history. His .688 winning percentage is the best in team history over a three-year period. Smith's 33 wins are easily the most victories by a Falcons head coach in his first three years on the job. His team boasts a 20-4 home record and .833 winning percentage since 2008, the second-best mark in the NFL. Smith's club posted the NFC's top record at 13-3 in 2010, the number one seed in the conference and was the second-most wins in a season in team annals. Smith's charges also captured the NFC South title last season for only the fourth Division crown in franchise history (and first since 2004) and the eight consecutive victories in 2010 was the second longest streak ever. Under Smith's direction last year, the Falcons were the only team to rank in the top 5 in both scoring offense and scoring defense. In 2008, Smith guided the Falcons to an 11-5 record, marking a seven-win turnaround from the previous season. For his efforts, he was named the Associated Press and *Sporting News* NFL Coach of the Year. From 2003-07, Smith served as the defensive coordinator for the Jacksonville Jaguars following a four-year stint with the Baltimore Ravens from 1999-2002, which included the team's 2000 Super Bowl season. Prior to the NFL, Smith coached at San Diego State (1982-85), Morehead State (1986), and Tennessee Tech (1987-1998). Career record: 33-17.

Background: Played linebacker for the CFL's Winnipeg Blue Bombers (1982). He played at East Tennessee (1977-1981) and named defensive MVP twice at his position. Led team with 186 tackles as a senior.

Personal: Born November 30, 1959 in Chicago. Native of Daytona Beach, Florida. He and his wife Julie have one daughter, Logan, who is eight years old.

ASSISTANT COACHES

Keith Armstrong, special teams coordinator; born December 15, 1963, Levittown, Pa. Running back Temple 1983-86. No pro playing experience. College coach: Temple 1987, Miami 1988, Akron 1989, Oklahoma State 1990-92, Notre Dame 1993. Pro coach: Atlanta Falcons 1994-96, Chicago Bears 1997-2000, Miami Dolphins 2001-2007, re-joined Falcons 2008.

Jonas Beauchemin, strength and conditioning assistant; born October 11, 1984, Burlington, Vt. Attended Keene State. No college or pro playing experience. Pro coach: Joined Falcons in 2009.

Paul Boudreau, offensive line; born December 30, 1949, Arlington, Mass. Guard Boston College 1970-73. No pro playing experience. Pro coach: New Orleans Saints 1987-1993, Detroit Lions 1994-96, New England Patriots 1997-98, Miami Dolphins 1999-2000, Carolina Panthers 2001-02, Jacksonville Jaguars 2003-05, St. Louis Rams 2006-07, joined Falcons in 2008.

Bob Bratkowski, quarterbacks; born December 2, 1955, San Angelo, Texas. Wide receiver Washington State 1975-77. No pro playing experience. College coach: Missouri 1978-1980, Weber State 1981-85, Wyoming 1986, Washington State 1987-88, Miami 1989-1991, Pro coach: Seattle Seahawks 1992-98, Pittsburgh Steelers 1999-2000, Cincinnati Bengals 2001-2010, joined Falcons in 2011.

Gerald Brown, running backs; born September 4, 1959, Sweetwater, Tenn. Attended Memphis State. No college or pro playing experience. College coach: Tennessee Tech 1991-2000, Indiana 2002-07. Pro coach: Joined Falcons in 2008.

Mark Collins, defensive assistant; born August 30, 1975, Sault Ste. Marie, Mich. Defensive end/outside linebacker East Tennessee State 1995-98. No pro playing experience. College coach: East Tennessee State 1999-2002, Michigan 2003-04, Elon, 2005, Georgia Southern 2006, Georgia 2007, Louisiana-Monroe 2009. Pro coach: Joined Falcons in 2010.

Paul Dunn, asst. offensive line; born July 7, 1960, Philadelphia. Offensive lineman Pittsburgh 1978-1982. No pro playing experience. College coach: Pittsburgh 1983, 2005-07, Penn State 1984-85, Edinboro 1986-88, Rutgers 1989, Maine 1990-93, Cincinnati 1994-95, Vanderbilt 1996-97, Kansas State 1998-2002, Kentucky 2003-04. Pro coach: Joined Falcons in 2008.

Jeff Fish, director of athletic performance; born June 6, 1966, Ithaca, N.Y. Wide receiver Western Carolina 1985-88. No pro playing experience. College coach: Western Michigan 1989, Clemson 1991-92, Kent State 1993-94, Tulsa 1995-97, Missouri 2001-03. Pro coach: Tampa Bay Buccaneers 1997, Kansas City Chiefs 1998-2000, Oakland Raiders 2004-07, joined Falcons in 2008.

Ray Hamilton, defensive line; born January 20, 1951, Omaha, Neb. Nose tackle Oklahoma 1969-1972. Pro defensive lineman New England Patriots 1973-1981. College coach: Tennessee 1992. Pro coach: New England Patriots 1985-89, Tampa Bay Buccaneers 1991, Los Angeles Raiders 1993-94, New York Jets 1994-96, 2000, New England Patriots 1997-99, Cleveland Browns 2001-02, Jacksonville Jaguars 2003-07, joined Falcons in 2008.

Tim Lewis, secondary; born December 18, 1961, Quakertown, Pa. Cornerback Pittsburgh 1979-1982. Pro cornerback Green Bay Packers 1983-86. Pro coach: Pittsburgh Steelers 1995-2003, New York Giants 2004-06, Carolina Panthers 2007-08, Seattle Seahawks 2009, joined Falcons in 2010.

Mike Mularkey, offensive coordinator; born November 19, 1961, Ft. Lauderdale, Fla. Tight end Florida 1979-1982. Pro tight end Minnesota Vikings 1983-88, Pittsburgh Steelers 1989-1991. College coach: Concordia 1993. Pro coach: Tampa Bay Buccaneers 1994-1995, Pittsburgh Steelers 1996-2003, Buffalo Bills 2004-05 (head coach), Miami Dolphins 2006-07, joined Falcons in 2008.

Glenn Pires, linebackers; born September 13, 1958, New Bedford, Mass. Offensive lineman Springfield College 1976-79. No pro playing experience. College coach: Dartmouth 1985-88, Syracuse 1989-1994, Michigan State 1995. Pro coach: Arizona Cardinals 1996-2000, Detroit Lions 2001-02, Miami Dolphins 2003-07, joined Falcons in 2008.

Alvin Reynolds, defensive backs; born June 24, 1959, Pineville, La. Safety Indiana State 1978-1981. No pro playing experience. College coach: Indiana State 1982-1992. Pro coach: Denver Broncos 1993-95, Baltimore Ravens 1996-98, Carolina Panthers 1999-2002, Jacksonville Jaguars 2003-07, joined Falcons in 2008.

Terry Robiskie, wide receivers; born November 12, 1954, New Orleans. Running back Louisiana State 1973-76. Pro running back Oakland Raiders 1977-79, Miami Dolphins 1980-81. Pro coach: Los Angeles Raiders 1982-1993, Washington Redskins 1994-2000 (interim head coach 2000), Cleveland Browns 2001-06 (interim head coach 2004), Miami Dolphins 2007, joined Falcons in 2008.

Chris Scelfo, tight ends; born September 30, 1963, New Iberia, La. Center Northeast Louisiana 1981-84. No pro playing experience. College coach: Northeast Louisiana 1986-87, Oklahoma 1988-89, Marshall 1990-95, Georgia 1996-98, Tulane 1998-2006. Pro coach: Joined Falcons in 2008.

Eric Sutulovich, asst. special teams; born February 28, 1974, Kansas City, Kan. Tight end Louisiana Tech 1993-95. No pro playing experience. College coach: Louisiana Tech 1997-99, Pittsburgh 2000, Kansas 2006. Pro coach: Houston Texans 2002-05, Detroit Lions 2008, joined Falcons in 2009.

Glenn Thomas, offensive assistant; born September 22, 1977, Eastland, Texas. Attended Texas Tech. No college or pro playing experience. College coach: Texas Tech 1998-2001, Midwestern State 2001-07. Pro coach: Joined Falcons in 2008.

Brian VanGorder, defensive coordinator; born April 17, 1959, Jackson, Mich. Linebacker Wayne State 1979-1980. No pro playing experience. College coach: Grand Valley State 1989-1991, Wayne State 1992-94 (head coach), Central Florida 1995-97, Central Michigan 1998-99, Western Illinois 2000, Georgia 2001-04, Georgia Southern 2006 (head coach). Pro coach: Jacksonville Jaguars 2005, joined Falcons in 2007.

**National Football Conference
South Division
Team Colors:** Black, Panther Blue, and
Silver
**800 South Mint Street
Charlotte, North Carolina 28202-1502
Telephone:** (704) 358-7000

2011 SCHEDULE
PRESEASON
Aug. 13 **New York Giants** 7:00
Aug. 19 at Miami 7:30
Aug. 25 at Cincinnati 7:00
Sep. 1 **Pittsburgh** 8:00

REGULAR SEASON
Sep. 11 at Arizona 4:15
Sep. 18 **Green Bay** 1:00
Sep. 25 **Jacksonville** 1:00
Oct. 2 at Chicago 1:00
Oct. 9 **New Orleans** 1:00
Oct. 16 at Atlanta 1:00
Oct. 23 **Washington** 1:00
Oct. 30 **Minnesota** 1:00
Nov. 6 BYE
Nov. 13 **Tennessee** 1:00
Nov. 20 at Detroit 1:00
Nov. 27 at Indianapolis 1:00
Dec. 4 at Tampa Bay 1:00
Dec. 11 **Atlanta** 1:00
Dec. 18 at Houston 1:00
Dec. 24 **Tampa Bay** (Sat) 1:00
Jan. 1 at New Orleans 1:00
All times ET
Stadium: Bank of America Stadium
(opened in 1996)
•**Capacity:** 73,504
Charlotte, North Carolina
28202-1502
Playing Surface: Grass
Training Camp: Wofford College
Spartanburg,
South Carolina 29303

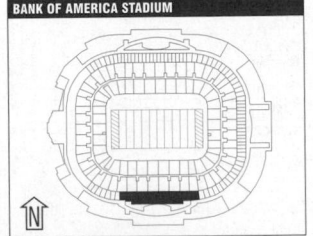

BANK OF AMERICA STADIUM

CLUB OFFICIALS
Owner/Founder: Jerry Richardson
President, Panthers Football LLC:
Danny Morrison
General Manager: Marty Hurney
General Counsel: Richard Thigpen
Chief Financial Officer: Dave Olsen
Controller: Mike Dudan
Director of Human Resources:
Jackie Jeffries
Director of Pro Scouting: Mark Koncz
Director of College Scouting:
Don Gregory
College Scouts: Matt Allen, Jeff Beathard,
Ryan Cowden, Khary Darlington,
Robert Haines, Jeff Morrow,
John Peterson, Mike Szabo
Director of Communications:
Charlie Dayton
Media Relations Manager:
Steven Drummond
Director of Ticket Operations:
Phil Youtsey
Director of Community Relations and
Cheerleader/Mascot Programs:
Riley Fields
Director of Sponsor Sales and Services:
John Berger
Director of Broadcast Administration:
Henry Thomas
Executive Producer-Television:
Greg Brannon
Executive Producer-Radio: David Langton
Director of Team Administration:
Rob Rogers
Director of Team Operations:
Brandon Beane
Video Director: Mark Hobbs
Assistant Video Director: Jeff Mueller
Head Trainer: Ryan Vermillion
Assistant Trainer: Mark Shermansky
Equipment Manager: Jackie Miles
Assistant Equipment Manager: Don Toner
Director of Security: Gene Brown
Stadium Operations Manager: Scott Paul
Director of Entertainment and
PantherVision: Kyle Ritchie
Facility Manager: Matthew Getz
Head Groundskeeper: Tom Vaughan

COACHING HISTORY
(125-141-0)
Records include postseason games
1995-98 Dom Capers 31-35-0
1999-2001 George Seifert 16-32-0
2002-2010 John Fox....................78-74-0

PAID ATTENDANCE
Home 565,833   Away 494,730
Total 1,060,563
Single-game home record,
76,136 (12/10/95)
Single-season home record, 579,192
(2006)

2011 DRAFT CHOICES
Round	Name	Pos.	College
1	Cam Newton	QB	Auburn
3	Terrell McClain	DT	South Florida
	Sione Fua	DT	Stanford
4	Brandon Hogan	DB	West Virginia
5	Kealoha Pilares	WR	Hawaii
6	Lawrence Wilson	LB	Connecticut
	Zack Williams	C	Washington St.
7	Lee Ziemba	T	Auburn

2010 TEAM RECORD

PRESEASON (1-3)

Date	Result		Opponent
8/12	L	12-17	at Baltimore
8/21	L	3-9	New York Jets
8/28	W	15-7	Tennessee
9/2	L	3-19	at Pittsburgh

REGULAR SEASON (2-14)

Date	Result		Opponent
9/12	L	18-31	at New York Giants
9/19	L	7-20	Tampa Bay
9/26	L	7-20	Cincinnati
10/3	L	14-16	at New Orleans
10/10	L	6-23	Chicago
10/24	W	23-20	San Francisco
10/31	L	10-20	at St. Louis
11/7	L	3-34	New Orleans
11/14	L	16-31	at Tampa Bay
11/21	L	13-37	Baltimore
11/28	L	23-24	at Cleveland
12/5	L	14-31	at Seattle
12/12	L	10-31	Atlanta
12/19	W	19-12	Arizona
12/23	L	3-27	at Pittsburgh
1/2	L	10-31	at Atlanta

SCORE BY PERIODS

Panthers	35	67	52	42	0	—	196
Opponents	114	111	74	109	0	—	408

2010 TEAM STATISTICS

	Panthers	Opp.
Total First Downs	225	328
Rushing	78	121
Passing	125	176
Penalty	22	31
3rd Down: Made/Att	69/227	81/213
3rd Down Pct.	30.4	38.0
4th Down: Made/Att	10/23	4/9
4th Down Pct.	43.5	44.4
Possession Avg.	27:24	32:36
Total Net Yards	4135	5374
Avg. Per Game	258.4	335.9
Total Plays	962	1060
Avg. Per Play	4.3	5.1
Net Yards Rushing	1846	1981
Avg. Per Game	115.4	123.8
Total Rushes	428	503
Net Yards Passing	2289	3393
Avg. Per Game	143.1	212.1
Sacked/Yards Lost	50/346	31/224
Gross Yards	2635	3617
Att./Completions	484/256	526/326
Completion Pct.	52.9	62.0
Had Intercepted	21	17
Punts/Average	95/43.1	76/43.5
Net Punting Avg.	95/36.5	76/36.5
Penalties/Yards	106/918	90/765
Fumbles/Ball Lost	31/16	22/12
Touchdowns	17	46
Rushing	7	20
Passing	9	19
Returns	1	7

2010 INDIVIDUAL STATISTICS

PASSING

	Att.	Comp.	Yds.	Pct.	TD	Int.	Tkld.	Rate
Clausen	299	157	1558	52.5	3	9	33/223	58.4
Moore	143	79	857	55.2	5	10	13/90	55.6
St. Pierre	28	13	173	46.4	1	2	3/23	48.7
Pike	12	6	47	50.0	0	0	1/10	60.1
Edwards	1	1	0	100.0	0	0	0/0	79.2
LaFell	1	0	0	0.0	0	0	0/0	39.6
Panthers	484	256	2635	52.9	9	21	50/346	57.0
Opponents	526	326	3617	62.0	19	17	31/224	81.0

SCORING

	TD R	TD P	TD Rt	PAT	FG	Saf	PTS
Kasay	0	0	0	17/17	25/29	0	92
Gettis	0	3	0	0/0	0/0	0	18
Goodson	3	0	0	0/0	0/0	0	18
Stewart	2	1	0	0/0	0/0	0	18
King	0	2	0	0/0	0/0	0	12
Smith	0	2	0	0/0	0/0	0	12
LaFell	0	1	0	0/0	0/0	0	6
Munnerlyn	0	0	1	0/0	0/0	0	6
Vaughan	1	0	0	0/0	0/0	0	6
D. Williams	1	0	0	0/0	0/0	0	6
Hardy	0	0	0	0/0	0/0	1	2
Panthers	7	9	1	17/17	25/29	1	196
Opponents	20	19	7	45/45	29/32	0	408

2-Pt Conversions: Panthers 0-0, Opponents 0-1.

RUSHING

	No.	Yds	Avg	LG	TD
Stewart	178	770	4.3	48	2
Goodson	103	452	4.4	45	3
D. Williams	87	361	4.1	39t	1
Sutton	13	71	5.5	32	0
LaFell	1	60	60.0	60	0
Clausen	23	57	2.5	11	0
Moore	5	25	5.0	8	0
Fiammetta	7	22	3.1	11	0
Smith	1	9	9.0	9	0
Edwards	1	7	7.0	7	0
Vaughan	3	7	2.3	6	1
Senn	1	5	5.0	5	0
Gettis	3	2	0.7	19	0
Baker	1	0	0.0	0	0
Rosario	1	-2	-2.0	-2	0
Panthers	428	1846	4.3	60	7
Opponents	503	1981	3.9	68t	20

RECEIVING

	No.	Yds	Avg	LG	TD
Smith	46	554	12.0	39	2
Goodson	40	310	7.8	32	0
LaFell	38	468	12.3	44	1
Gettis	37	508	13.7	88t	3
Rosario	32	264	8.3	26	0
King	19	121	6.4	16t	2
Sutton	12	70	5.8	14	0
D. Williams	11	61	5.5	14	0
Stewart	8	103	12.9	55t	1
Clowney	6	102	17.0	31	0
Fiammetta	5	34	6.8	11	0
Jarrett	2	40	20.0	21	0
Panthers	256	2635	10.3	88t	9
Opponents	326	3617	11.1	56t	19

PUNTING

	No.	Yds.	Avg.	In 20	LG
Baker	95	4097	43.1	22	60
Panthers	95	4097	43.1	22	60
Opponents	76	3309	43.5	26	63

INTERCEPTIONS

	No.	Yds	Avg	LG	TD
Godfrey	5	112	22.4	38	0
Marshall	3	91	30.3	66	0
Munnerlyn	3	37	12.3	37t	1
S. Martin	1	34	34.0	34	0
Beason	1	7	7.0	7	0
E. Johnson	1	5	5.0	5	0
Anderson	1	1	1.0	1	0
E. Brown	1	0	0.0	0	0
Pugh	1	-2	-2.0	-2	0
Panthers	17	285	16.8	66	1
Opponents	21	270	12.9	42t	5

PUNT RETURNS

	Ret	FC	Yds	Avg	LG	TD
Munnerlyn	30	6	327	10.9	37	0
Smith	6	0	46	7.7	32	0
Edwards	2	0	0	0.0	0	0
Jam. Williams	1	0	0	0.0	0	0
Panthers	39	6	373	9.6	37	0
Opponents	54	16	488	9.0	84	1

KICKOFF RETURNS

	No.	Yds	Avg	LG	TD
Goodson	48	1048	21.8	46	0
Pugh	9	218	24.2	32	0
Gettis	8	145	18.1	28	0
Thomas	3	63	21.0	26	0
Munnerlyn	2	87	43.5	64	0
Sutton	2	30	15.0	18	0
Norwood	1	17	17.0	17	0
King	1	11	11.0	11	0
Panthers	74	1619	21.9	64	0
Opponents	45	1064	23.6	84	0

FIELD GOALS

	1-19	20-29	30-39	40-49	50+
Kasay	0/0	9/9	2/2	11/14	3/4
Panthers	0/0	9/9	2/2	11/14	3/4
Opponents	0/0	9/9	13/13	5/7	2/3

SACKS

	No.
C. Johnson	11.5
Anderson	3.5
E. Brown	3.5
Hardy	3.0
Landri	3.0
Harris	1.5
Beason	1.0
Connor	1.0
Hayden	1.0
Marshall	1.0
Norwood	1.0
Panthers	31.0
Opponents	50.0

RECORD HOLDERS
INDIVIDUAL RECORDS—CAREER

Category	Name	Performance
Rushing (Yds.)	DeAngelo Williams, 2006-2010	4,211
Passing (Yds.)	Jake Delhomme, 2003-09	19,258
Passing (TDs)	Jake Delhomme, 2003-09	120
Receiving (No.)	Muhsin Muhammad, 1996-2004, 2008-09	696
Receiving (Yds.)	Muhsin Muhammad, 1996-2004, 2008-09	9,255
Interceptions	Eric Davis, 1996-2000	25
Punting (Avg.)	Todd Sauerbrun, 2001-04	45.5
Punt Return (Avg.)	Winslow Oliver, 1996-98	10.7
Kickoff Return (Avg.)	Michael Bates, 1996-2000	25.7
Field Goals	John Kasay, 1995-2010	351
Touchdowns (Tot.)	Steve Smith, 2001-2010	60
Points	John Kasay, 1995-2010	1,482
*Sacks	Julius Peppers, 2002-09	81.0

INDIVIDUAL RECORDS—SINGLE SEASON

Category	Name	Performance
Rushing (Yds.)	DeAngelo Williams, 2008	1,515
Passing (Yds.)	Steve Beuerlein, 1999	4,436
Passing (TDs)	Steve Beuerlein, 1999	36
Receiving (No.)	Steve Smith, 2005	103
Receiving (Yds.)	Steve Smith, 2005	1,563
Interceptions	Doug Evans, 2001	8
Punting (Avg.)	Todd Sauerbrun, 2001	47.5
Punt Return (Avg.)	Winslow Oliver, 1996	11.5
Kickoff Return (Avg.)	Michael Bates, 1996	30.2
Field Goals	John Kasay, 1996	37
Touchdowns (Tot.)	DeAngelo Williams, 2008	20
Points	John Kasay, 1996	145
*Sacks	Kevin Greene, 1998	15.0

INDIVIDUAL RECORDS—SINGLE GAME

Category	Name	Performance
Rushing (Yds.)	DeAngelo Williams, 12-8-08	186
Passing (Yds.)	Chris Weinke, 12-10-06	423
Passing (TDs)	Steve Beuerlein, 1-2-00	5
Receiving (No.)	Steve Smith, 11-20-05	14
Receiving (Yds.)	Steve Smith, 10-30-05	201
Interceptions	Deon Grant, 9-22-02	3
Field Goals	John Kasay, 12-5-04	6
Touchdowns (Tot.)	DeAngelo Williams, 11-30-08, 12-21-08	4
Points	DeAngelo Williams, 11-30-08, 12-21-08	24
*Sacks	Many times	3.0
	Julius Peppers, 11-9-08	

Sacks became an official statistic in 1982.

VETERAN ROSTER AS OF MARCH 3, 2011

No.	Name	Pos.	Ht.	Wt.	Birthdate	^NFL Exp.	College	Hometown	How Acq.	'10 Games/ Starts
50	Anderson, James	LB	6-2	235	9/26/83	6	Virginia Tech	Chesapeake, Va.	D3a-'06	16/15
7	Baker, Jason	P	6-2	205	5/17/78	11	Iowa	Fort Wayne, Ind.	T(Den)-'05	16/0
82	Barnidge, Gary	TE	6-5	247	9/22/85	4	Louisville	Middleburg, Fla.	D5-'08	16/3
52	Beason, Jon	LB	6-0	237	1/14/85	5	Miami	Miramar, Fla.	D1-'07	16/16
78	Bender, Jacob	T	6-6	316	4/25/85	3	Nicholls State	Mayo, Md.	FA-'11	0*
73	Bernadeau, Mackenzy	G	6-4	308	1/3/86	4	Bentley	Waltham, Mass.	D7c-'08	16/12
96	Brayton, Tyler	DE	6-6	280	11/20/79	9	Colorado	Pasco, Wash.	UFA(Oak)-'08	15/14
91	Brown, Everette	DE	6-1	256	8/7/87	3	Florida State	Stantonsburg, N.C.	D2a-'09	13/2
2	Clausen, Jimmy	QB	6-2	222	9/21/87	2	Notre Dame	Thousand Oaks, Calif.	D2-'10	13/10
87	Clowney, David	WR	6-0	188	7/7/85	4	Virginia Tech	Amityville, N.Y.	W(NYJ)-'10	13/0*
55	Connor, Dan	LB	6-2	231	11/2/85	4	Penn State	Wallingford, Pa.	D3b-'08	8/8
71	Davis, C.J.	G	6-2	308	2/2/87	3	Pittsburgh	Imperial, Pa.	FA-'09	7/0
58	Davis, Thomas	LB	6-0	240	3/22/83	7	Georgia	Shellman, Ga.	D1-'05	0*
10	Edwards, Armanti	WR	5-11	182	3/8/88	2	Appalachian State	Greenwood, S.C.	D3b-'10	3/0
42	Fiammetta, Tony	FB	6-0	242	8/22/86	3	Syracuse	Walkersville, Md.	D4a-'09	14/9
20	Gamble, Chris	CB	6-1	200	3/11/83	8	Ohio State	Sunrise, Fla.	D1-'04	11/10
12	Gettis, David	WR	6-3	216	8/27/87	2	Baylor	Los Angeles, Calif.	D6b-'10	15/13
30	Godfrey, Charles	S	5-11	205	11/15/85	4	Iowa	Baytown, Texas	D3a-'08	16/16
33	Goodson, Mike	RB	6-0	212	5/23/87	3	Texas A&M	Klein, Texas	D4b-'09	16/3
69	Gross, Jordan	T	6-4	305	7/20/80	9	Utah	Fruitland, Idaho	D1-'03	16/16
76	Hardy, Greg	DE	6-4	277	7/28/88	2	Mississippi	Memphis, Tenn.	D6a-'10	15/0
59	Harris, Nic	LB	6-2	232	10/6/86	3	Oklahoma	Alexandria, La.	FA-'10	15/4
98	Hayden, Nick	DT	6-4	292	2/4/86	3	Wisconsin	Hartland, Wis.	D6-'08	14/10
25	Hudson, Marcus	S	6-2	200	11/15/82	6	North Carolina State	Homestead, Fla.	UFA(SF)-'10	14/0
60	Irvin, Corvey	DT	6-3	302	5/3/85	2	Georgia	Augusta, Ga.	D3-'09	2/0
44	Jansen, J.J.	LS	6-2	256	1/20/86	4	Notre Dame	Phoenix, Ariz.	T(GB)-'09	16/0
95	Johnson, Charles	DE	6-2	275	7/10/86	5	Georgia	Hawkinsville, Ga.	D3-'07	16/16
99	Johnson, Ed	DT	6-2	296	12/18/83	3	Penn State	Detroit, Mich.	FA-'10	12/6
67	Kalil, Ryan	C	6-2	295	3/29/85	5	Southern California	Corona, Calif.	D2b-'07	16/16
4	Kasay, John	K	5-10	210	10/27/69	21	Georgia	Athens, Ga.	UFA(Sea)-'95	16/0
47	King, Jeff	TE	6-3	260	2/19/83	6	Virginia Tech	Pulaski, Va.	D5-'06	16/16
11	LaFell, Brandon	WR	6-2	211	11/4/86	2	Louisiana State	Houston, Texas	D3a-'10	14/2
61	Landri, Derek	DT	6-2	290	9/21/83	5	Notre Dame	Concord, Calif.	FA-'09	16/16
8	Lloyd, Rhys	K	5-11	231	6/5/82	5	Minnesota	Dover, England	FA-'10	15/0
31	Marshall, Richard	CB	5-11	189	12/12/84	6	Fresno State	Los Angeles, Calif.	D2-'06	16/16
83	Martin, Charly	WR	6-1	212	3/20/84	3	West Texas A&M	Farmington, N.M.	FA-'09	1/0
23	Martin, Sherrod	S	6-1	198	10/12/84	3	Troy	Griffin, Ga.	D2b-'09	15/15
36	McClain, Robert	CB	5-9	195	7/22/88	2	Connecticut	Lusby, Md.	D7b-'10	16/2
3	Moore, Matt	QB	6-3	202	8/9/84	5	Oregon State	Valencia, Calif.	W(Dall)-'07	6/5
41	Munnerlyn, Captain	CB	5-8	186	4/10/88	3	South Carolina	Mobile, Ala.	D7-'09	16/5
68	Neblett, Andre	DT	6-0	295	6/7/88	2	Temple	Rahway, N.J.	FA-'10	7/1
92	Norwood, Eric	DE/LB	6-1	241	5/24/88	2	South Carolina	Kennesaw, Ga.	D4-'10	15/0
9	Null, Keith	QB	6-4	220	9/24/85	2	West Texas A&M	Lampasas, Texas	FA-'10	0*
79	Otah, Jeff	T	6-6	330	6/17/86	4	Pittsburgh	New Castle, Del.	D1b-'08	0*
16	Pike, Tony	QB	6-6	222	3/10/86	2	Cincinnati	Cincinnati, Ohio	D6d-'10	1/0
29	Pugh, Jordan	S	5-11	196	1/29/88	2	Texas A&M	Plano, Texas	D6c-'10	15/2
72	Robinson, Duke	G	6-5	330	10/10/86	3	Oklahoma	Atlanta, Ga.	D6-'09	0*
88	Rosario, Dante	TE	6-4	250	10/25/84	5	Oregon	Dayton, Ore.	D5a-'07	16/6
74	Schwartz, Geoff	T	6-6	331	7/11/86	3	Oregon	Los Angeles, Calif.	D7b-'07	16/16
57	Senn, Jordan	LB	5-11	224	6/11/84	4	Portland State	Beaverton, Ore.	FA-'09	14/0
80	Shockey, Jeremy	TE	6-5	251	8/18/80	10	Miami	Ada, Okla.	UFA(NO)-'11	13/11*
89	Smith, Steve	WR	5-9	185	5/12/79	11	Utah	Los Angeles, Calif.	D3-'01	14/14
28	Stewart, Jonathan	RB	5-10	235	3/21/87	4	Oregon	Fort Lewis, Wash.	D7-'07	14/7
22	Sutton, Tyrell	RB	5-8	213	12/19/86	3	Northwestern	Akron, Ohio	FA-'10	9/0
97	Taylor, Hilee	DE	6-2	250	7/18/86	4	North Carolina	Laurinburg, N.C.	D7a-'08	0*
70	Wharton, Travelle	G	6-4	312	5/19/81	8	South Carolina	Simpsonville, S.C.	D3-'04	9/9
34	Williams, DeAngelo	RB	5-9	217	4/25/83	6	Memphis	Wynne, Ark.	D1-'06	6/6
65	Williams, Garry	T	6-3	296	8/20/86	3	Kentucky	Louisville, Ky.	FA-'09	16/11
54	Williams, Jason	LB	6-1	244	2/21/86	3	Western Illinois	Chicago, Ill.	W(Dall)-'10	9/2*
94	Williams, Thomas	LB	6-1	240	12/25/84	2	Southern California	Vacaville, Calif.	FA-'10	2/0*
27	Wilson, C.J.	CB	6-1	195	4/2/85	4	Baylor	Terrell, Texas	D7b-'07	8/0
15	Wright, Wallace	WR	6-1	197	2/1/84	5	North Carolina	Fayetteville, N.C.	FA-'10	0*

* Bender last active with New York Jets in '07; Clowney played 3 games with New York Jets and 10 games with Carolina; T. Davis missed '10 season because of injury; Null did not play in 1 game, inactive for 4 other games; Otah missed '10 season because of injury; Robinson missed '10 season because of injury; Shockey played 13 games with New Orleans in '10; Taylor missed '10 season because of injury; J. Williams played 5 games with Dallas and 4 games with Carolina; T. Williams played 2 games with Buffalo and inactive for 1 game with Carolina; Wright missed '10 season because of injury.

Also played with Panthers in '10—S Gerald Alexander (2 games), K Todd Carter (1), G Tim Duckworth (5), LB Abdul Hodge (5), WR Dwayne Jarrett (3), DT Louis Leonard (2), C Chris Morris (4), T Rob Petitti (5), QB Brian St. Pierre (1), WR Devin Thomas (1), LB Jamar Williams (3).

^ "NFL Exp." as of 2011 Kickoff Weekend. For full explanation of how a player's NFL Experience is measured, refer to explanation underneath the First-Year Roster listed below.

FIRST-YEAR ROSTER

Name	Pos.	Ht.	Wt.	Birthdate	College	Hometown	How Acq.
Duhart, Tommie (1)	DT	6-3	318	12/30/85	Valdosta State	Belle Glade, Fla.	FA-'10
Fua, Sione	DT	6-2	308	6/15/88	Stanford	Encino, Calif.	D3b
Guy, Trent (1)	WR	5-8	171	8/22/87	Louisville	Charlotte, N.C.	FA-'10
Hogan, Brandon	CB	5-10	192	4/1/88	West Virginia	Manassas, Va.	D4
Jackson, Rashawn (1)	FB	6-1	239	1/15/87	Virginia	Jersey City, N.J.	FA-'10
McClain, Terrell	DT	6-2	291	7/20/88	South Florida	Pensacola, Fla.	D3a
Newton, Cam	QB	6-5	248	5/11/89	Auburn	College Park, Ga.	D1
Pilares, Kealoha	WR	5-10	201	2/20/88	Hawai'i	Honolulu, Hawai'i	D5
Stanford, R.J. (1)	CB	5-10	183	5/6/88	Utah	Chino, Calif.	D7a-'10
Vaughan, Josh (1)	RB	6-0	232	12/3/86	Richmond	Richmond, Va.	FA-'10
Ware, Sean (1)	LB	6-2	237	1/31/87	New Hampshire	Bristol, Conn.	FA-'10
Williams, Zack	C/G	6-3	309	12/27/88	Washington State	Pasadena, Calif.	D6b
Wilson, Lawrence	LB	6-1	229	11/16/87	Connecticut	Tuscaloosa, Ala.	D6a
Ziemba, Lee	T	6-6	318	3/29/89	Auburn	Rogers, Ark.	D7

The term NFL Rookie is defined as a player who is in his first season of professional football and has not been on the roster of another professional football team for any regular-season or postseason games. A Rookie is designated by an "R" on NFL rosters. Players who have been active in another professional football league or players who have NFL experience, including either preseason training camp or being on an Active List or Inactive List, or on Reserve/Injured or Reserve/Physically Unable to Perform for fewer than six regular-season games, are termed NFL First-Year Players. An NFL First-Year Player is designated by a "1" on NFL rosters. Thereafter, a player is credited with an additional year of experience for each season in which he accumulates six games on the Active List or Inactive List, or on Reserve/Injured or Reserve/Physically Unable to Perform.

Log on to www.panthers.com for an up-to-date roster.

COACHING STAFF

Head Coach,
Ron Rivera

Pro Career: Became the fourth coach in Carolina Panthers history on January 11, 2011. Before joining the Panthers, Rivera worked with the San Diego Chargers from 2007-10, coaching inside linebackers before taking over as defensive coordinator midway through the 2008 season. In 2010, San Diego led the NFL with an average of 271.6 total yards allowed per game and gave up a league-low 177.8 passing yards per game. In 2009, the team ranked 16th in total defense and 11th against the pass. From 2004-06, Rivera oversaw the Chicago Bears defense, guiding the unit to two top-five finishes in the league. In 2006, the Bears defense led the NFL with 44 take-aways and finished fifth in total defense and third in scoring defense, helping propel Chicago to an appearance in Super Bowl XLI. In 2005, Rivera's defensive unit ranked second in the NFL in total defense and first in scoring defense. The Bears went 43 consecutive quarters without allowing more than seven points – the longest streak in the NFL since 1969. Prior to serving as defensive coordinator with the Bears, Rivera was linebackers coach for the Eagles (1999-2003) and defensive quality control coach for the Bears (1997-98). He is just the third Latino head coach in NFL history, joining Tom Flores with the Oakland Raiders (1979-1987) and Seattle Seahawks (1992-94) and Tom Fears with the New Orleans Saints (1967-1970). A second-round draft choice in 1984 by Chicago, Rivera played nine seasons with the Bears. Primarily an outside linebacker, he was a member of the Super Bowl XX championship team in 1985. Career record: 0-0.

Background: Linebacker at California (1980-83).

Personal: Born January 7, 1962 in Fort Ord, Calif. He and his wife, Stephanie, have two children—Christopher and Courtney.

ASSISTANT COACHES

Warren Belin, linebackers; born October 20, 1967, Marshville, N.C. Linebacker Wake Forest 1987-1990. No pro playing experience. College coach: Cornell 1991, 1993-94, East Tennessee State 1992, William & Mary 1995-96, Southern Methodist 1997-2001, Vanderbilt 2002-09, Georgia 2010. Pro coach: Joined Panthers in 2011.

Ray Brown, asst. offensive line; born December 12, 1962, Marion, Ark. Offensive lineman/tight end Arkansas State 1983-85. Pro offensive lineman St. Louis/Phoenix Cardinals 1986-88, Washington Redskins 1989-1995, 2004-05, San Francisco 49ers 1996-2001, Detroit Lions 2002-03. Pro coach: Washington Redskins 2006, Buffalo Bills 2008-09, San Francisco 49ers 2010, joined Panthers in 2011.

Rod Chudzinski, offensive coordinator; born May 12, 1968, Toledo, Ohio. Tight end Miami 1986-1990. No pro playing experience. College coach: Miami 1994-2003. Pro coach: Cleveland Browns 2004, 2007-08, San Diego Chargers 2005-06, 2009-2010, joined Panthers in 2011.

Adam Feit, asst. strength and conditioning; born August 7, 1985, Springfield, Mass. Offensive lineman Springfield College 2003-06. No pro playing experience. College coach: Arizona State 2007 (winter/spring), The Citadel 2007, Louisville 2008-09, Eastern Michigan 2010. Pro coach: Joined Panthers in 2011.

Fred Graves, wide receivers; born March 2, 1950, Los Angeles. Halfback/split end Utah 1969-1971. No pro playing experience. College coach: Northeast Missouri State 1975-76, Western Illinois 1977-78, New Mexico State 1979-1981, Utah 1982-2000. Pro coach: Buffalo Bills 2001-03, Cleveland Browns 2004, Detroit Lions 2005, Tennessee Titans 2007-2010, joined Panthers in 2011.

Pete Hoener, tight ends; born June 14, 1954, Peoria, Ill. Tight end/defensive end Bradley 1969-1970. No pro playing experience. College coach: Missouri 1975-76, Illinois State 1977, Indiana State 1978-1984, Illinois 1987-88, Purdue 1989-1991, Texas Christian 1992-97, Iowa State 1998-99, Texas A&M 2000. Pro coach: St. Louis/Arizona Cardinals 1985-86, 2001-03, Chicago Bears 2004, San Francisco 49ers 2005-2010, joined Panthers in 2011.

Joe Kenn, strength and conditioning; born October 13, 1966, Far Rockaway, N.Y. Guard Wake Forest 1987-88. No pro playing experience. College coach: Wake Forest 1991 (winter/spring), Boise State 1991-98, Utah 1999-2000, Arizona State 2001-07, Louisville 2008-09. Pro coach: Joined Panthers in 2011.

John Matsko, offensive line; born February 2, 1951, Cleveland. Fullback Kent State 1970-72. No pro playing experience. College coach: Miami (Ohio) 1974-75, 1977, North Carolina 1978-1984, Navy 1985, Arizona 1986, Southern California 1987-1991. Pro coach: Phoenix Cardinals 1992-93, New Orleans Saints 1994-96, New York Giants 1997-98, St. Louis Rams 1999-2005, Kansas City Chiefs 2006-07, Baltimore Ravens 2008-2010, joined Panthers in 2011.

Sean McDermott, defensive coordinator; born March 21, 1974, Omaha, Neb. Safety William & Mary 1994-97. No pro playing experience. College coach: William & Mary 1998. Pro coach: Philadelphia Eagles 1999-2010, joined Panthers in 2011.

Ron Meeks, defensive backfield; born August 27, 1954, Jacksonville. Defensive back Arkansas State 1972-76. Pro defensive back Hamilton Tiger-Cats (CFL) 1977-79, Ottawa Rough Riders (CFL) 1979, Toronto Argonauts (CFL) 1980-81. College coach: Arkansas State 1984-85, Miami

1986-87, New Mexico State 1988, Fresno State 1989-1990. Pro coach: Dallas Cowboys 1991, Cincinnati Bengals 1992-96, Atlanta Falcons 1997-99, Washington Redskins 2000, St. Louis Rams 2001, Indianapolis Colts 2002-08, joined Panthers in 2009.

Sam Mills III, defensive quality control/asst. defensive line; born May 20, 1978, Long Branch, N.J. Defensive back Montclair State 1997-1999. No pro playing experience. Pro coach: Joined Panthers in 2005.

Brian Murphy, special teams coordinator; born July 17, 1969, Elmwood Park, Ill. Defensive lineman Lehigh 1988-1991. No pro playing experience. College coach: Benedictine 1992, Wisconsin 1994-96, 2002-05, Baylor 1997, San Diego 1998, Lehigh 1999. Pro coach: Minnesota Vikings 2006-2010, joined Panthers in 2011.

Ricky Proehl, offensive consultant; born March 7, 1968, Bronx, N.Y. Wide receiver Wake Forest 1986-89. Pro wide receiver Phoenix/Arizona Cardinals 1990-94, Seattle Seahawks 1995-96, Chicago Bears 1997, St. Louis Rams 1998-2002, Carolina Panthers 2003-05, Indianapolis Colts 2006. Pro coach: Joined Panthers in 2011.

John Settle, running backs; born June 2, 1965, Reidsville, N.C. Running back Appalachian State 1983-86. Pro running back Atlanta Falcons 1987-1990, Washington Redskins 1991-92. College coach: Appalachian State 1994, Fresno State 1998-2005, Wisconsin 2006-2010. Pro coach: Cleveland Browns/Baltimore Ravens 1995-97, joined Panthers in 2011.

Mike Shula, quarterbacks; born June 3, 1965, Baltimore. Quarterback Alabama 1984-86. Pro quarterback Tampa Bay Buccaneers 1987. College coach: Alabama 2003-06 (head coach). Pro coach: Tampa Bay Buccaneers 1988-1990, 1996-99, Miami Dolphins 1991-92, 2000-02, Chicago Bears 1993-95, Jacksonville Jaguars 2007-2010, joined Panthers in 2011.

Scott Turner, offensive quality control; born August 7, 1982, Englewood, Calif. Quarterback Nevada-Las Vegas 2002-04. No pro playing experience. College coach: Oregon State 2005, Pittsburgh 2008-2010. Pro coach: Joined Panthers in 2011.

Eric Washington, defensive line; born October 29, 1969, Shreveport, La. Tight end Grambling State 1989-1990. No pro playing experience. College coach: Texas A&M 1997, Ohio 2001-03, Northwestern 2004-07. Pro coach: Chicago Bears 2008-2010, joined Panthers in 2011.

National Football Conference
North Division
Team Colors: Navy Blue, Orange, and
White
Halas Hall at Conway Park
1920 Football Drive
Lake Forest, Illinois 60045
Telephone: (847) 295-6600

2011 SCHEDULE
PRESEASON
Aug. 7 vs. St. Louis (Canton, OH)..7:00
Aug. 14 Buffalo................................7:00
Aug. 22 at New York Giants 7:00
Aug. 27 at Tennessee 7:00
Sep. 1 Cleveland 7:00

REGULAR SEASON
Sep. 11 **Atlanta** 12:00
Sep. 18 at New Orleans 12:00
Sep. 25 **Green Bay** 3:15
Oct. 2 **Carolina** 12:00
Oct. 10 at Detroit (Mon)................. 7:30
Oct. 16 **Minnesota** 7:20
Oct. 23 at Tampa Bay (London) 12:00
Oct. 30 BYE
Nov. 7 at Philadelphia (Mon) 7:30
Nov. 13 **Detroit** 12:00
Nov. 20 **San Diego** 3:15
Nov. 27 at Oakland 3:05
Dec. 4 **Kansas City** 12:00
Dec. 11 at Denver 3:05
Dec. 18 **Seattle** 12:00
Dec. 25 at Green Bay 7:20
Jan. 1 at Minnesota 12:00
All times CT
Stadium: Soldier Field
(opened in 1924)
• **Capacity:** 61,500
1410 S. Museum Campus Dr.
Chicago, Illinois 60605
Playing Surface: Natural Grass
Training Camp: Olivet-Nazarene Univ.
Bourbonnais, Illinois
60901

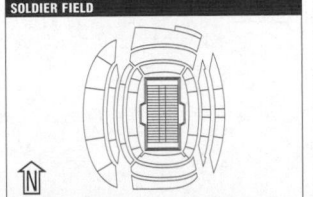
SOLDIER FIELD

CLUB OFFICIALS
Chairman of the Board:
George H. McCaskey
Secretary: Virginia H. McCaskey
President and CEO: Ted Phillips
General Manager: Jerry Angelo
Senior Director of Special Projects:
Pat McCaskey
Senior Director of Business Development
& Alumni Relations: Brian McCaskey
Senior Director of Administration:
John Bostrom
Senior Director of Finance & Treasurer:
Karen Murphy
Senior Director of Corporate Sales &
Marketing: Chris Hibbs
Senior Director of Corporate
Communications: Scott Hagel
Senior Director of Ticket Operations:
Lee Twarling
Senior Director of Football Administration
and General Counsel: Cliff Stein
Director of Pro Personnel: Tim Ruskell
Assistant Director of Pro Personnel:
Kevin Turks
Pro Scout: Dennard Wilson
Director of Player Development:
Isaiah Harris
Director of Video Services:
Dave Hendrickson
Assistant Video Director: Dean Pope
College Video Coordinator: Dan Tuohy
Video Assistant: Jack Dowling
Head Athletic Trainer: Tim Bream
Assistant Trainers: Chris Hanks,
Jeremy Smith
Director of Rehabilitation: Bobby Slater
Head Equipment Manager: Tony Medlin
Assistant Equipment Managers:
Carl Piekarski, John Perkins,
Joseph Shaw
Scouts: Chris Ballard, Marty Barrett,
Rex Hogan, Ted Monago,
Mark Sadowski, Jeff Shiver
Director of Community Relations:
Caroline Guip Schrenker
Director of Broadcasting & Scoreboard
Operations: Greg Miller
Media Services Manager: Jim Christman
Media Relations Coordinator: Mike Corbo
Media Relations Assistant: Cary Dohman

COACHING HISTORY
Decatur Staleys 1920,
Chicago Staleys 1921
(721-530-42)
Records include postseason games

Years	Coach	Record
1920-29	George Halas	84-31-19
1930-32	Ralph Jones	24-10-7
1933-1942	George Halas*	88-24-4
1942-45	Hunk Anderson-Luke Johnsos**	24-12-2
1946-1955	George Halas	76-43-2
1956-57	John (Paddy) Driscoll	14-10-1
1958-1967	George Halas	76-53-6
1968-1971	Jim Dooley	20-36-0
1972-74	Abe Gibron	11-30-1
1975-77	Jack Pardee	20-23-0
1978-1981	Neill Armstrong	30-35-0
1982-1992	Mike Ditka	112-68-0
1993-98	Dave Wannstedt	41-57-0
1999-2003	Dick Jauron	35-46-0
2004-2010	Lovie Smith	66-52-0

*Retired after five games to enter U.S. Navy
**Co-coaches

PAID ATTENDANCE
Home 484,282   Away 513,797
Total 998,079
Single-game home record,
66,900 (9/5/93)
Single-season home record, 527,769
(1999)

2011 DRAFT CHOICES
Round	Name	Pos.	College
1	Gabe Carimi	T	Wisconsin
2	Stephen Paea	DT	Oregon State
3	Chris Conte	DB	California
5	Nathan Enderle	QB	Idaho
6	J.T. Thomas	LB	West Virginia

2010 TEAM RECORD

PRESEASON (0-4)

Date	Result		Opponent
8/14	L	10-25	at San Diego
8/21	L	17-32	Oakland
8/28	L	9-14	Arizona
9/2	L	10-13	at Cleveland

REGULAR SEASON (11-5)

Date	Result		Opponent
9/12	W	19-14	Detroit
9/19	W	27-20	at Dallas
9/27	W	20-17	Green Bay
10/3	L	3-17	at New York Giants
10/10	W	23-6	at Carolina
10/17	L	20-23	Seattle
10/24	L	14-17	Washington
11/7	W	22-19	at Buffalo
11/14	W	27-13	Minnesota
11/18	W	16-0	at Miami
11/28	W	31-26	Philadelphia
12/5	W	24-20	at Detroit
12/12	L	7-36	New England
12/20	W	40-14	at Minnesota
12/26	W	38-34	New York Jets
1/2	L	3-10	at Green Bay

POSTSEASON (1-1)

Date	Result		Opponent
1/16	W	35-24	Seattle
1/23	L	14-21	Green Bay

SCORE BY PERIODS

Bears	88	95	84	67	0	—	334
Opponents	68	111	54	53	0	—	286

2010 TEAM STATISTICS

	Bears	Opp.
Total First Downs	263	282
Rushing	76	88
Passing	163	183
Penalty	24	11
3rd Down: Made/Att	64/195	75/216
3rd Down Pct.	32.8	34.7
4th Down: Made/Att	2/7	6/13
4th Down Pct.	28.6	46.2
Possession Avg.	29:31	30:29
Total Net Yards	4631	5029
Avg. Per Game	289.4	314.3
Total Plays	936	1002
Avg. Per Play	4.9	5.0
Net Yards Rushing	1616	1441
Avg. Per Game	101.0	90.1
Total Rushes	414	386
Net Yards Passing	3015	3588
Avg. Per Game	188.4	224.2
Sacked/Yards Lost	56/382	34/232
Gross Yards	3397	3820
Att./Completions	466/276	582/363
Completion Pct.	59.2	62.4
Had Intercepted	21	21
Punts/Average	83/40.1	88/40.6
Net Punting Avg.	83/35.2	88/32.6
Penalties/Yards	91/768	93/790
Fumbles/Ball Lost	19/10	37/14
Touchdowns	37	32
Rushing	10	14
Passing	23	14
Returns	4	4

2010 INDIVIDUAL STATISTICS

PASSING

	Att.	Comp.	Yds.	Pct.	TD	Int.	Tkld.	Rate
Cutler	432	261	3274	60.4	23	16	52/352	86.3
Collins	27	10	68	37.0	0	5	2/15	5.9
Hanie	7	5	55	71.4	0	0	2/15	94.3
Bears	466	276	3397	59.2	23	21	56/382	79.5
Opponents	582	363	3820	62.4	14	21	34/232	74.4

SCORING

	TD R	TD P	TD Rt	PAT	FG	Saf	PTS
Gould	0	0	0	35/35	25/30	0	110
Forté	6	3	0	0/0	0/0	0	56
Hester	0	4	3	0/0	0/0	0	42
Knox	0	5	0	0/0	0/0	0	30
Olsen	0	5	0	0/0	0/0	0	30
Bennett	0	3	0	0/0	0/0	0	18
Taylor	3	0	0	0/0	0/0	0	18
Cutler	1	0	0	0/0	0/0	0	6
K. Davis	0	1	0	0/0	0/0	0	6
R. Davis	0	1	0	0/0	0/0	0	6
Manumaleuna	0	1	0	0/0	0/0	0	6
D. Moore	0	0	1	0/0	0/0	0	6
Bears	10	23	4	35/35	25/30	0	334
Opponents	14	14	4	29/31	21/27	1	286

2-Pt Conversions: Forté.
Bears 1-2, Opponents 0-1.

RUSHING

	No.	Yds	Avg	LG	TD
Forté	237	1069	4.5	68t	6
Taylor	112	267	2.4	24	3
Cutler	50	232	4.6	25	1
Hester	7	30	4.3	11	0
Bennett	2	9	4.5	5	0
Wolfe	4	8	2.0	7	0
Knox	1	2	2.0	2	0
Hanie	1	-1	-1.0	-1	0
Bears	414	1616	3.9	68t	10
Opponents	386	1441	3.7	45	14

RECEIVING

	No.	Yds	Avg	LG	TD
Knox	51	960	18.8	67t	5
Forté	51	547	10.7	89t	3
Bennett	46	561	12.2	48	3
Olsen	41	404	9.9	39t	5
Hester	40	475	11.9	39	4
Taylor	20	139	7.0	18	0
Aromashodu	10	149	14.9	34	0
R. Davis	9	84	9.3	21	1
Manumaleuna	5	43	8.6	16	1
K. Davis	1	19	19.0	19t	1
Clark	1	12	12.0	12	0
C. Williams	1	4	4.0	4	0
Bears	276	3397	12.3	89t	23
Opponents	363	3820	10.5	59t	14

INTERCEPTIONS

	No.	Yds	Avg	LG	TD
Tillman	5	127	25.4	56	0
C. Harris	5	69	13.8	39	0
D. Moore	4	95	23.8	54t	1
Briggs	2	1	0.5	1	0
Peppers	2	1	0.5	1	0
Jennings	1	39	39.0	39	0
Manning	1	0	0.0	0	0
Urlacher	1	0	0.0	0	0
Bears	21	332	15.8	56	1
Opponents	21	247	11.8	92t	2

PUNTING

	No.	Yds.	Avg.	In 20	LG
Maynard	83	3326	40.1	24	56
Bears	83	3326	40.1	24	56
Opponents	88	3569	40.6	30	58

PUNT RETURNS

	Ret	FC	Yds	Avg	LG	TD
Hester	33	10	564	17.1	89t	3
Bears	33	10	564	17.1	89t	3
Opponents	39	10	303	7.8	62t	1

KICKOFF RETURNS

	No.	Yds	Avg	LG	TD
Manning	33	816	24.7	62	0
Hester	12	427	35.6	79	0
Knox	8	182	22.8	42	0
R. Davis	5	70	14.0	32	0
K. Davis	1	2	2.0	2	0
Bears	59	1497	25.4	79	0
Opponents	59	1404	23.8	60	0

FIELD GOALS

	1-19	20-29	30-39	40-49	50+
Gould	1/1	9/9	8/9	4/7	3/4
Bears	1/1	9/9	8/9	4/7	3/4
Opponents	0/0	9/9	7/11	3/4	2/3

SACKS

	No.
Idonije	8.0
Peppers	8.0
Urlacher	4.0
Melton	2.5
Adams	2.0
Briggs	2.0
Toeaina	2.0
T. Harris	1.5
Iwuh	1.0
D. Moore	1.0
Tinoisamoa	1.0
Wootton	1.0
Bears	34.0
Opponents	56.0

RECORD HOLDERS
INDIVIDUAL RECORDS—CAREER

Category	Name	Performance
Rushing (Yds.)	Walter Payton, 1975-1987	16,726
Passing (Yds.)	Sid Luckman, 1939-1950	14,686
Passing (TDs)	Sid Luckman, 1939-1950	137
Receiving (No.)	Walter Payton, 1975-1987	492
Receiving (Yds.)	Johnny Morris, 1958-1967	5,059
Interceptions	Gary Fencik, 1976-1987	38
Punting (Avg.)	George Gulyanics, 1947-1952	44.5
Punt Return (Avg.)	George McAfee, 1940-41, 1945-1950	**12.8
Kickoff Return (Avg.)	Gale Sayers, 1965-1971	**30.6
Field Goals	Kevin Butler, 1985-1995	243
Touchdowns (Tot.)	Walter Payton, 1975-1987	125
Points	Kevin Butler, 1985-1995	1,116
*Sacks	Richard Dent, 1983-1993, 1995	124.5

INDIVIDUAL RECORDS—SINGLE SEASON

Category	Name	Performance
Rushing (Yds.)	Walter Payton, 1977	1,852
Passing (Yds.)	Erik Kramer, 1995	3,838
Passing (TDs)	Erik Kramer, 1995	29
Receiving (No.)	Marty Booker, 2001	100
Receiving (Yds.)	Marcus Robinson, 1999	1,400
Interceptions	Mark Carrier, 1990	10
Punting (Avg.)	Bobby Joe Green, 1963	46.5
Punt Return (Avg.)	Devin Hester, 2010	17.1
Kickoff Return (Avg.)	Gale Sayers, 1967	37.7
Field Goals	Robbie Gould, 2006	32
Touchdowns (Tot.)	Gale Sayers, 1965	22
Points	Kevin Butler, 1985	144
*Sacks	Richard Dent, 1984	17.5

INDIVIDUAL RECORDS—SINGLE GAME

Category	Name	Performance
Rushing (Yds.)	Walter Payton, 11-20-77	275
Passing (Yds.)	Johnny Lujack, 12-11-49	468
Passing (TDs)	Sid Luckman, 11-14-43	**7
Receiving (No.)	Jim Keane, 10-23-49	14
Receiving (Yds.)	Harlon Hill, 10-31-54	214
Interceptions	Many times	3
	Last time by Mark Carrier, 12-9-90	
Field Goals	Roger LeClerc, 12-3-61	5
	Mac Percival, 10-20-68	5
Touchdowns (Tot.)	Gale Sayers, 12-12-65	**6
Points	Gale Sayers, 12-12-65	36
*Sacks	Richard Dent, 11-4-84, 12-27-87	4.5

*Sacks became an official statistic in 1982.
**NFL Record

VETERAN ROSTER AS OF MARCH 3, 2011

No.	Name	Pos.	Ht.	Wt.	Birthdate	^NFL Exp.	College	Hometown	How Acq.	'10 Games/ Starts
95	Adams, Anthony	DT	6-0	310	6/18/80	9	Penn State	Detroit, Mich.	UFA(SF)-'07	16/16
19	Aromashodu, Devin	WR	6-2	201	5/23/84	5	Auburn	Miami, Fla.	FA-'08	14/2
32	Bell, Kahlil	RB	5-11	212	12/10/86	3	UCLA	Ft. Collins, Colo.	FA-'09	0*
80	Bennett, Earl	WR	6-0	204	3/23/87	4	Vanderbilt	Birmingham, Ala.	D3a-'08	14/3
35	Bowman, Zackary	CB	6-1	193	11/18/84	4	Nebraska	Anchorage, Alaska	D5a-'08	13/3
55	Briggs, Lance	LB	6-1	242	11/12/80	9	Arizona	Sacramento, Calif.	D3-'03	15/15
36	Bullocks, Josh	S	6-0	207	2/28/83	7	Nebraska	Chattanooga, Tenn.	UFA(NO)-'09	16/0
88	Clark, Desmond	TE	6-3	249	4/20/77	13	Wake Forest	Lakeland, Fla.	UFA(Mia)-'03	5/0
10	Collins, Todd	QB	6-4	223	11/5/71	17	Michigan	Walpole, Mass.	FA-'10	2/1
6	Cutler, Jay	QB	6-3	233	4/29/83	6	Vanderbilt	Santa Claus, Ind.	T(Den)-'09	15/15
87	Davis, Kellen	TE	6-7	262	10/11/85	4	Michigan State	Adrian, Mich.	D5b-'08	16/3
81	Davis, Rashied	WR	5-9	187	7/24/79	7	San Jose State	Granada Hills, Calif.	FA-'05	16/0
22	Forté, Matt	RB	6-2	218	12/10/85	4	Tulane	Slidell, La.	D2-'08	16/16
63	Garza, Roberto	G/C	6-2	310	3/26/79	11	Texas A&M-Kingsville	Rio Hondo, Texas	UFA(Atl)-'05	14/14
24	Gerard, K.J.	S	6-1	192	4/22/86	2	Northern Arizona	Fountain Valley, Calif.	FA-'10	0*
9	Gould, Robbie	K	6-0	185	12/30/81	7	Penn State	Lock Haven, Pa.	FA-'05	16/0
21	Graham, Corey	CB	6-0	198	7/25/85	5	New Hampshire	Buffalo, N.Y.	D5b-'07	16/0
8	Gutierrez, Matt	QB	6-4	230	6/9/84	4	Idaho State	Concord, Calif.	FA-'10	0*
12	Hanie, Caleb	QB	6-2	225	9/11/85	4	Colorado State	Forney, Texas	FA-'08	2/0
46	Harris, Chris	S	6-0	207	8/6/82	7	Louisiana-Monroe	Little Rock, Ark.	T(Car)-'10	16/16
99	Harrison, Marcus	DT	6-3	312	7/10/84	4	Arkansas	Little Rock, Ark.	D3b-'08	5/0
23	Hester, Devin	WR	5-11	190	11/4/82	6	Miami	Riviera Beach, Fla.	D2b-'06	16/13
71	Idonije, Israel	DL	6-6	270	11/17/80	8	Manitoba	Lagos, Nigeria	FA-'03	16/15
52	Iwuh, Brian	LB	6-0	239	3/8/84	6	Colorado	Houston, Texas	FA-'10	16/1
26	Jennings, Tim	CB	5-8	185	12/24/83	6	Georgia	Orangeburg, S.C.	UFA(Ind)-'10	16/13
67	Johnson, Herman	G	6-7	360	1/29/85	2	Louisiana State	Denton, Texas	FA-'10	0*
13	Knox, Johnny	WR	6-0	185	11/3/86	3	Abilene Christian	Houston, Texas	D5a-'09	16/16
57	Kreutz, Olin	C	6-2	292	6/9/77	14	Washington	Honolulu, Hawai'i	D3-'98	16/16
60	Louis, Lance	G	6-3	305	4/24/85	3	San Diego State	New Orleans, La.	D7a-'09	16/4
65	Mannelly, Patrick	LS	6-5	265	4/18/75	14	Duke	Atlanta, Ga.	D6b-'98	16/0
38	Manning, Danieal	S	5-11	202	8/9/82	6	Abilene Christian	Corsicana, Texas	D2a-'06	16/16
86	Manumaleuna, Brandon	TE	6-2	295	1/4/80	11	Arizona	Los Angeles, Calif.	UFA(SD)-'10	16/13
4	Maynard, Brad	P	6-1	188	2/9/74	15	Ball State	Sheridan, Ind.	UFA(NYG)-'01	16/0
69	Melton, Henry	DE	6-3	260	10/11/86	3	Texas	Grapevine, Texas	D4a-'09	16/0
30	Moore, D.J.	CB	5-9	183	3/22/87	3	Vanderbilt	Spartanburg, S.C.	D4b-'09	16/0
31	Moore, Joshua	CB	5-11	188	8/20/88	2	Kansas State	Ft. Lauderdale, Fla.	D5-'10	3/0
82	Olsen, Greg	TE	6-5	255	3/11/85	5	Miami	Wayne, N.J.	D1-'07	16/13
68	Omiyale, Frank	T/G	6-4	315	11/23/82	7	Tennessee Tech	Whites Creek, Tenn.	UFA(Car)-'09	16/16
90	Peppers, Julius	DE	6-7	283	1/18/80	10	North Carolina	Bailey, N.C.	UFA(Car)-'10	16/16
97	Reed, Nick	DE	6-1	248	9/1/87	2	Oregon	Trabuco Canyon, Calif.	FA-'11	0*
53	Roach, Nick	LB	6-1	234	6/16/85	5	Northwestern	Milwaukee, Wisc.	FA-'07	15/6
20	Steltz, Craig	S	6-1	210	5/7/86	4	Louisiana State	Metairie, La.	D4-'08	9/0
29	Taylor, Chester	RB	5-11	213	9/22/79	10	Toledo	River Rouge, Mich.	UFA(Minn)-'10	16/1
33	Tillman, Charles	CB	6-1	198	2/23/81	9	Louisiana-Lafayette	Copperas Cove, Texas	D2-'03	16/16
59	Tinoisamoa, Pisa	LB	6-1	230	7/15/81	9	Hawai'i	Vista, Calif.	FA-'09	12/10
75	Toeaina, Matt	DT	6-2	308	10/9/84	4	Oregon	Utulei, American Samoa	FA-'07	16/10
94	Tyler, Tank	DT	6-2	306	2/14/85	4	North Carolina State	Fayetteville, N.C.	FA-'11	0*
45	Unga, Harvey	RB	6-0	237	1/18/87	2	Brigham Young	Provo, Utah	S7-'10	0*
54	Urlacher, Brian	LB	6-4	258	5/25/78	12	New Mexico	Lovington, N.M.	D1-'00	16/16
73	Webb, J'Marcus	T	6-7	328	8/8/88	2	West Texas A&M	Mesquite, Texas	D7-'10	14/12
74	Williams, Chris	T	6-6	315	8/26/85	4	Vanderbilt	Glynn, La.	D1-'08	13/13
43	Williams, Eddie	FB	6-1	249	8/22/87	2	Idaho	San Mateo, Calif.	FA-'10	0*
70	Williams, Edwin	G/C	6-3	313	12/10/86	2	Maryland	Washington D.C.	FA-'10	5/3
58	Wilson, Rod	LB	6-1	230	11/12/81	6	South Carolina	Cross, S.C.	FA-'10	15/0
25	Wolfe, Garrett	RB	5-7	185	8/17/84	5	Northern Illinois	Chicago, Ill.	D3a-'07	16/0
98	Wootton, Corey	DE	6-6	270	6/22/87	2	Northwestern	Rutherford, N.J.	D4-'10	6/0
27	Wright, Major	S	5-11	206	7/1/88	2	Florida	Miramar, Fla.	D3-'10	11/0

* Bell inactive for 16 games in '10; Gerard last active with Baltimore in '09; Gutierrez last active with Kansas City in '09; Johnson inactive for 4 games games; Reed last active with Seattle in '09; Tyler last active with Carolina in '09; Unga missed '10 season because of injury; Edd. Williams spent '10 season on Chicago practice squad, was inactive for 3 games with Washington in '09.

Also played with Bears in '10—DE Mark Anderson (4 games), DT Tommie Harris (15), LB Hunter Hillenmeyer (1), T Kevin Shaffer (16), DE Barry Turner (2).

^ "NFL Exp." as of 2011 Kickoff Weekend. For full explanation of how a player's NFL Experience is measured, refer to explanation below the First-Year Roster on the next page.

FIRST-YEAR ROSTER

Name	Pos.	Ht.	Wt.	Birthdate	College	Hometown	How Acq.
Asiata, Johan (1)	G	6-4	300	12/19/85	Nevada-Las Vegas	Kalihi, Hawai'i	FA-'09
Carimi, Gabe	T	6-7	314	6/13/88	Wisconsin	Cottage Grove, Wisc.	D1
Conte, Chris	S	6-2	197	2/23/89	California	Los Angeles, Calif.	D3
Enderle, Nathan	QB	6-4	240	1/12/88	Idaho	North Platte, Neb.	D5
Fantuz, Andy (1)	WR	6-1	220	12/18/83	Western Ontario	Chatham, Ontario, Canada	FA
Horn, Levi (1)	T	6-6	320	10/2/86	Montana	Spokane, Wash.	FA-'10
Johnson, Chris (1)	LB	6-2	230	12/10/86	South Dakota State	Council Bluffs, Iowa	FA-'10
Jones, Onrea (1)	WR	6-0	202	12/22/83	Hampton	Williamsburg, Va.	FA
McGee, Richmond (1)	P	6-4	203	4/25/83	Texas	Garland, Texas	FA-'09
Paea, Stephen	DT	6-1	303	5/11/88	Oregon State	Los Altos, Calif.	D2
Thomas, J.T.	LB	6-1	241	8/15/88	West Virginia	Ft. Lauderdale, Fla.	D6
Trahan, Patrick (1)	LB	6-2	236	11/7/86	Mississippi	New Orleans, La.	FA

The term NFL Rookie is defined as a player who is in his first season of professional football and has not been on the roster of another professional football team for any regular-season or postseason games. A Rookie is designated by an "R" on NFL rosters. Players who have been active in another professional football league or players who have NFL experience, including either preseason training camp or being on an Active List or Inactive List, or on Reserve/Injured or Reserve/Physically Unable to Perform for fewer than six regular-season games, are termed NFL First-Year Players. An NFL First-Year Player is designated by a "1" on NFL rosters. Thereafter, a player is credited with an additional year of experience for each season in which he accumulates six games on the Active List or Inactive List, or on Reserve/Injured or Reserve/Physically Unable to Perform.

Log on to www.chicagobears.com for an up-to-date roster.

COACHING STAFF
Head Coach,
Lovie Smith
Pro Career: Named the thirteenth head coach in Chicago Bears history on January 15, 2004. Smith enters his eighth season as the head coach of the Chicago Bears after winning his third NFC North crown in 2010, most in the division since 2004. Smith's 63 regular season wins (63-49) are third most in franchise history, trailing only Hall of Famers George Halas and Mike Ditka. Smith also has a 3-3 postseason record, including two NFC Championship game appearances, an NFC Championship and the Bears first Super Bowl appearance in 21 years (2006). With an 11-5 record in 2010, Smith has led the Bears to three 11-win seasons during his tenure, including a career-high 13 wins in 2006 when he led Chicago to home-field advantage in the NFC Playoffs and the team's first NFC Championship since its Super Bowl season of 1985. A year earlier, Smith earned the 2005 AP NFL Coach of the Year Award after turning a 1-3 start to the season into 11 victories, the most by a second-year coach in club annals, and the second seed in the NFC Playoffs. Fueled by an eight-game win streak, Smith led a worst-to-first revival in the NFC North division as the Bears six-win improvement from the previous season was tied for the biggest in the NFL in 2005. In Smith's first season, Chicago posted a 5-11 record. The Bears rank second in the NFL from 2004-07 with 140 takeaways and 14 touchdowns scored via defensive return. Smith came to Chicago from St. Louis (2001-03), where he served as defensive coordinator. In 2001 he helped the Rams return to the Super Bowl after missing the playoffs the previous season. Smith previously coached the linebackers for the Tampa Bay Buccaneers (1996-2000). Career record: 66-52.
Background: Played at Tulsa (1976-79), where he was a linebacker before moving to strong safety and earning two-time All-America and three-time All-Missouri Conference defensive back honors. Began his coaching career at his hometown high school (Big Sandy, Texas) in 1980 before moving to Cascia Hall Prep in Tulsa the following year. Two years later Smith began coaching collegiately at Tulsa (1983-86), Wisconsin (1987), Arizona State (1988-1991), Kentucky (1992), Tennessee (1993-94), and Ohio State (1995).
Personal: Born May 8, 1958, Gladewater, Texas. Lovie and his wife MaryAnne have three sons—Mikal, Matthew and Miles and twin grandsons—Malachi and Noah.

ASSISTANT COACHES
Jim Arthur, strength and conditioning assistant; born July 12, 1978. Attended Springfield (Mass.) College. No college or pro playing experience. College coach: Springfield (Mass.) College 2000, Louisiana Tech 2001, Boston College 2002. Pro coach: Joined Bears in 2005.
Bob Babich, linebackers; born February 20, 1961, Aliquippa, Pa. Linebacker Mesa (Colo.) C.C. 1979-1980, Tulsa 1981-82. No pro playing experience. College coach: Tulsa 1984-87, 1990, Wisconsin 1988-89, Bowling Green 1991, East Carolina 1992-93, Pittsburgh 1994-96, North Dakota State 1997-2002 (head coach). Pro coach: St. Louis Rams 2003, joined Bears in 2004.
Gill Byrd, asst. defensive backs/safeties; born February 20, 1961, San Francisco. Cornerback San Jose State 1979-1982. Pro cornerback San Diego Chargers 1983-1992. Pro coach: St. Louis Rams 2003-05, joined Bears in 2006.
Shane Day, quarterbacks; born September 27, 1974, Manhattan, Kan. Attended Kansas State. Wide receiver Rhodes College 1995-96. No pro playing experience. College coach: Michigan 2005-06. Pro coach: San Francisco 49ers 2007-09, joined Bears in 2010.
Mike DeBord, tight ends; born February 7, 1956, Muncie, Ind. Offensive line Manchester College 1974-77. No pro playing experience. College coach: Franklin 1982-83, Fort Hays State 1984-86, Eastern Illinois 1987-88, Ball State 1989, Colorado State 1990-91, Northwestern 1992, Michigan 1992-99, 2004-07, Central Michigan 2000-03 (head coach). Pro coach: Seattle Seahawks 2008-09, joined Bears in 2010.
Darryl Drake, wide receivers; born December 11, 1956, Louisville, Ky. Wide receiver Western Kentucky 1975-78. Pro wide receiver Washington Redskins 1979, Ottawa Rough Riders (CFL) 1981, Cincinnati Bengals 1983. College coach: Western Kentucky 1983-1991, Georgia 1992-96, Baylor 1997, Texas 1998-2003. Pro coach: Joined Bears in 2004.
Andrew Hayes-Stoker, offensive quality control; born January 9, 1979, Arlington, Texas. Running back Texas Christian 1999-2001. No pro playing experience. Pro coach: Joined Bears in 2010.
Jon Hoke, defensive backs; born January 24, 1957, Kettering, Ohio. Defensive back Ball State 1976-79. Pro defensive back Chicago Bears 1980. College coach: Bowling Green 1983-86, San Diego State 1987-88, Kent State 1989-1993, Missouri 1994-98, Florida 1999-2001. Pro coach: Houston Texans 2002-08, joined Bears in 2009.
Rusty Jones, director of physical development; born August 14, 1953. Attended Springfield (Mass.) College. No college or pro playing experience. College coach: Springfield (Mass.) College 1979-1982. Pro coach: Buffalo Bills 1985-2004, joined Bears in 2005.
Rod Marinelli, defensive coordinator/asst. head coach; born July 13, 1949, Rosemead, Calif. Offensive/defensive tackle Utah 1968, offensive tackle

California Lutheran 1970-72. No pro playing experience. College coach: Utah State 1976, California 1983-1991, Arizona State 1992-94, Southern California 1995. Pro coach: Tampa Bay Buccaneers 1996-2005, Detroit Lions 2006-08 (head coach), joined Bears in 2009.
Mike Martz, offensive coordinator; born May 13, 1951, Sioux Falls, S.D. Tight end Fresno State 1972. No pro playing experience. College coach: San Diego Mesa C.C. 1974, 1976-77, San Jose State 1975, Santa Ana College 1978, Fresno State 1979, Pacific 1980-81, Minnesota 1982, Arizona State 1983-1991. Pro coach: L.A./St. Louis Rams 1992-96, 1999-2005 (head coach 2000-05), Washington Redskins 1997-98, Detroit Lions 2006-07, San Francisco 49ers 2008, joined Bears in 2010.
Kevin O'Dea, asst. special teams; born June 9, 1960, Williamsport, Pa. Wide receiver/defensive back Lock Haven 1984-85. No pro playing experience. College coach: Lock Haven 1986, Cornell 1987, Virginia 1988-1990, Penn State 1991-93. Pro coach: San Diego Chargers 1994-95, Tampa Bay Buccaneers 1996-2001, Detroit Lions 2002-03, Arizona Cardinals 2004-05, Chicago Bears 2006-07, N.Y. Jets 2008-09, joined Bears in 2011.
Mike Phair, defensive line; born November 8, 1969, Mesa, Ariz. Linebacker Mesa (Ariz.) C.C. 1988-89, Arizona State 1990-91. No pro playing experience. College coach: Arizona State 1999-2000, Tiffin University 2001. Pro coach: Seattle Seahawks 2008-2010, joined Bears in 2011.
Mikal Smith, defensive quality control; born November 16, 1976, Dallas. Safety Arizona 1995-97. No pro playing experience. College coach: Trinity International 2006-07. Pro coach: Joined Bears in 2010.
Tim Spencer, running backs; born December 10, 1960, Martin Ferry, Ohio. Running back Ohio State 1979-1982. Pro running back Chicago Blitz (USFL) 1983, Arizona Wranglers (USFL) 1984, Memphis Showboats (USFL) 1985, San Diego Chargers 1985-1990. College coach: Ohio State 1994-2003. Pro coach: Joined Bears in 2004.
Mike Tice, offensive line; born February 2, 1959, Bay Shore, N.Y. Quarterback Maryland 1977-1980. Pro tight end Seattle Seahawks 1981-88, 1990-91, Washington Redskins 1989, Minnesota Vikings 1992-93, 1995. Pro coach: Minnesota Vikings 1996-2005 (head coach 2001-05), Jacksonville Jaguars 2006-09, joined Bears in 2010.
Dave Toub, special teams coordinator; born June 1, 1962, Ossining, N.Y. Offensive lineman Springfield College 1980-81, Texas-El Paso 1983-84. No pro playing experience. College coach: Texas El-Paso 1987-89, Missouri 1989-2000. Pro coach: Philadelphia Eagles 2001-03, joined Bears in 2004.

National Football Conference
East Division
Team Colors: Royal Blue, Metallic Silver
        Blue, and White
Cowboys Center, One Cowboys Parkway
Irving, Texas 75063
Telephone: (972) 556-9900

2011 SCHEDULE
PRESEASON
Aug. 11	**Denver**	7:30
Aug. 20	**San Diego**	7:00
Aug. 27	at Minnesota	7:00
Sep. 1	at Miami	6:30

REGULAR SEASON
Sep. 11	at New York Jets	7:20
Sep. 18	at San Francisco	3:05
Sep. 26	**Washington** (Mon)	7:30
Oct. 2	**Detroit**	12:00
Oct. 9	BYE	
Oct. 16	at New England	3:15
Oct. 23	**St. Louis**	3:15
Oct. 30	at Philadelphia	7:20
Nov. 6	**Seattle**	12:00
Nov. 13	**Buffalo**	12:00
Nov. 20	at Washington	12:00
Nov. 24	**Miami** (Thu)	3:15
Dec. 4	at Arizona	3:15
Dec. 11	**New York Giants** *	7:20
Dec. 17	at Tampa Bay (Sat)	7:20
Dec. 24	**Philadelphia** (Sat)	3:15
Jan. 1	at New York Giants	12:00

*All times CT; Sunday night games in
Weeks 11-15, 17 subject to change*

Stadium: Cowboys Stadium (opened in 2009)
  •**Capacity:** 80,000 (expandable to
100,000 for special events)
One Legends Way
Arlington, Texas 76011
Playing Surface: Sportfield Softtop
Training Camp: TBA

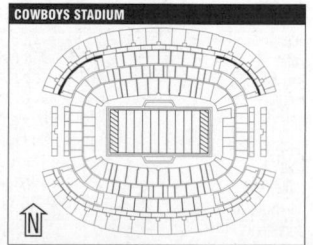

COWBOYS STADIUM

CLUB OFFICIALS
Owner/President/General Manager:
  Jerry Jones
Chief Operating Officer/Executive Vice
  President/Director of Player Personnel:
  Stephen Jones
Executive Vice President/VP of Brand
  Management/President Charity
  Foundation: Charlotte Anderson
Executive Vice President/Chief Sales and
  Marketing Officer: Jerry Jones Jr.
CFO: David Frey
Senior Vice President, Sales and
  Marketing: Greg McElroy
Senior Vice President and General
  Counsel: Alec Scheiner
Vice President Public Relations/
  Communications: Rich Dalrymple
Director of Corporate Communications:
  Brett Daniels
Director of Community Relations and
  Alumni Affairs: Emily Robbins
Director of College and Pro Scouting:
  Tom Ciskowski
Director of Operations: Bruce Mays
Director of Player Development:
  Bryan Wansley
Director of Information Technology:
  Bill Haggard
Director of Broadcasting: Scott Purcel
Internet Director: Derek Eagleton
Director of Ticket Operations:
  Ann Bihari
Head Athletic Trainer: Jim Maurer
Equipment Manager: Mike McCord
Video Director: Robert Blackwell
Cheerleader Director: Kelli Finglass

COACHING HISTORY
(473-349-6)
Records include postseason games
1960-1988	Tom Landry	270-178-6
1989-1993	Jimmy Johnson	51-37-0
1994-97	Barry Switzer	45-26-0
1998-99	Chan Gailey	18-16-0
2000-02	Dave Campo	15-33-0
2003-06	Bill Parcells	34-32-0
2007-2010	Wade Phillips*	35-24-0
2010	Jason Garrett	5-3-0

*Released after eight games in 2010

PAID ATTENDANCE
Home 614,256	Away 568,091

Total 1,182,347
Single-game home record,
  105,121 (9/20/09)
Single-season home record,
  629,749 (2009)

2011 DRAFT CHOICES
Round	Name	Pos.	College
1	Tyron Smith	T	Southern California
2	Bruce Carter	LB	North Carolina
3	DeMarco Murray	RB	Oklahoma
4	David Arkin	G	Missouri State
5	Josh Thomas	DB	Buffalo
6	Dwayne Harris	WR	East Carolina
7	Shaun Chapas	RB	Georgia
	Bill Nagy	C	Wisconsin

2010 TEAM RECORD
PRESEASON (3-2)

Date	Result	Opponent
8/8	W 16-7	vs. Cincinnati in Canton, OH
8/12	L 9-17	Oakland
8/21	W 16-14	at San Diego
8/28	L 7-23	at Houston
9/2	W 27-25	Miami

REGULAR SEASON (6-10)

Date	Result	Opponent
9/12	L 7-13	at Washington
9/19	L 20-27	Chicago
9/26	W 27-13	at Houston
10/10	L 27-34	Tennessee
10/17	L 21-24	at Minnesota
10/25	L 35-41	New York Giants
10/31	L 17-35	Jacksonville
11/7	L 7-45	at Green Bay
11/14	W 33-20	at New York Giants
11/21	W 35-19	Detroit
11/25	L 27-30	New Orleans
12/5	W 38-35	at Indianapolis (OT)
12/12	L 27-30	Philadelphia
12/19	W 33-30	Washington
12/25	L 26-27	at Arizona
1/2	W 14-13	at Philadelphia

(OT) Overtime

SCORE BY PERIODS

Cowboys	70	104	106	111	3 —	394
Opponents	85	130	95	126	0 —	436

2010 TEAM STATISTICS

	Cowboys	Opp.
Total First Downs	327	309
Rushing	104	84
Passing	201	200
Penalty	22	25
3rd Down: Made/Att	86/211	81/204
3rd Down Pct.	40.8	39.7
4th Down: Made/Att	13/22	4/9
4th Down Pct.	59.1	44.4
Possession Avg.	31:11	28:49
Total Net Yards	5828	5628
Avg. Per Game	364.3	351.8
Total Plays	1035	977
Avg. Per Play	5.6	5.8
Net Yards Rushing	1786	1734
Avg. Per Game	111.6	108.4
Total Rushes	428	402
Net Yards Passing	4042	3894
Avg. Per Game	252.6	243.4
Sacked/Yards Lost	31/166	35/257
Gross Yards	4208	4151
Att./Completions	576/379	540/348
Completion Pct.	65.8	64.4
Had Intercepted	19	20
Punts/Average	66/47.2	70/43.1
Net Punting Avg.	66/41.7	70/35.4
Penalties/Yards	109/863	79/641
Fumbles/Ball Lost	28/11	20/10
Touchdowns	46	51
Rushing	10	11
Passing	29	33
Returns	7	7

2010 INDIVIDUAL STATISTICS

PASSING	Att.	Comp.	Yds.	Pct.	TD	Int.	Tkld.	Rate
Kitna	318	209	2365	65.7	16	12	21/100	88.9
Romo	213	148	1605	69.5	11	7	7/41	94.9
McGee	44	22	238	50.0	2	0	3/25	81.4
Barber	1	0	0	0.0	0	0	0/0	39.6
Cowboys	576	379	4208	65.8	29	19	31/166	90.4
Opponents	540	348	4151	64.4	33	20	35/257	92.8

SCORING	TD R	TD P	TD Rt	PAT	FG	Saf	PTS
Buehler	0	0	0	42/44	24/32	0	114
Witten	0	9	0	0/0	0/0	0	56
Austin	1	7	0	0/0	0/0	0	48
Bryant	0	6	2	0/0	0/0	0	48
R. Williams	0	5	0	0/0	0/0	0	32
Barber	4	0	0	0/0	0/0	0	24
Choice	3	0	0	0/0	0/0	0	18
Jones	1	1	0	0/0	0/0	0	12
McCann	0	0	2	0/0	0/0	0	12
Gronkowski	0	1	0	0/0	0/0	0	6
Kitna	1	0	0	0/0	0/0	0	6
Lee	0	0	1	0/0	0/0	0	6
Scandrick	0	0	1	0/0	0/0	0	6
Ware	0	0	1	0/0	0/0	0	6
Cowboys	10	29	7	42/44	24/32	0	394
Opponents	11	33	7	49/49	25/27	1	436

2-Pt Conversions: R. Williams, Witten.
Cowboys 2-2, Opponents 2-2

RUSHING	No.	Yds	Avg	LG	TD
Jones	185	800	4.3	34	1
Barber	113	374	3.3	25	4
Choice	66	243	3.7	26	3
Kitna	31	147	4.7	29t	1
Austin	7	93	13.3	60t	1
McGee	13	74	5.7	14	0
Romo	6	38	6.3	14	0
Gronkowski	5	17	3.4	8	0
Bryant	1	0	0.0	0	0
McBriar	1	0	0.0	0	0
Cowboys	428	1786	4.2	60t	10
Opponents	402	1734	4.3	56	11

RECEIVING	No.	Yds	Avg	LG	TD
Witten	94	1002	10.7	33	9
Austin	69	1041	15.1	69t	7
Jones	48	450	9.4	71t	1
Bryant	45	561	12.5	46	6
R. Williams	37	530	14.3	63t	5
Bennett	33	260	7.9	32	0
Choice	17	109	6.4	17	0
Hurd	14	120	8.6	13	0
Barber	11	49	4.5	15	0
Gronkowski	7	35	5.0	12	1
Ogletree	3	34	11.3	19	0
Johnson	1	6	6.0	6	0
Romo	0	11	—	11	0
Cowboys	379	4208	11.1	71t	29
Opponents	348	4151	11.9	91t	33

INTERCEPTIONS	No.	Yds	Avg	LG	TD
Sensabaugh	5	26	5.2	10	0
Newman	5	16	3.2	30	0
Lee	2	44	22.0	31t	1
Ball	2	27	13.5	27	0
McCann	1	101	101.0	101t	1
Brooking	1	41	41.0	41	0
Scandrick	1	40	40.0	40t	1
James	1	11	11.0	11	0
McCray	1	0	0.0	0	0
Jenkins	1	-4	-4.0	-4	0
Cowboys	20	302	15.1	101t	3
Opponents	19	277	14.6	66t	3

PUNTING	No.	Yds.	Avg.	In 20	LG
McBriar	65	3115	47.9	22	65
Cowboys	66	3115	47.2	22	65
Opponents	70	3020	43.1	26	69

PUNT RETURNS	Ret	FC	Yds	Avg	LG	TD
Bryant	15	0	215	14.3	93t	2
McCann	8	10	165	20.6	97t	1
Holley	1	0	2	2.0	2	0
Owusu-Ansah	0	4	0	—	—	0
Cowboys	24	14	382	15.9	97t	3
Opponents	33	7	205	6.2	16	0

KICKOFF RETURNS	No.	Yds	Avg	LG	TD
Owusu-Ansah	25	543	21.7	41	0
McCann	23	507	22.0	38	0
Bryant	12	293	24.4	43	0
Ogletree	6	109	18.2	31	0
Choice	3	61	20.3	27	0
Gronkowski	2	23	11.5	13	0
Rucker	1	16	16.0	16	0
Chandler	1	11	11.0	11	0
Newman	1	9	9.0	9	0
Cowboys	74	1572	21.2	43	0
Opponents	56	1363	24.3	95t	1

FIELD GOALS	1-19	20-29	30-39	40-49	50+
Buehler	0/0	8/8	4/7	8/11	4/6
Cowboys	0/0	8/8	4/7	8/11	4/6
Opponents	0/0	8/8	4/4	9/10	4/5

SACKS	No.
Ware	15.5
Spencer	5.0
Ratliff	3.5
Scandrick	2.5
Butler	2.0
Sensabaugh	2.0
Bowen	1.5
Brooking	1.0
Hatcher	1.0
Ball	0.5
Lissemore	0.5
Cowboys	35.0
Opponents	31.0

RECORD HOLDERS
INDIVIDUAL RECORDS—CAREER

Category	Name	Performance
Rushing (Yds.)	Emmitt Smith, 1990-2002	**17,162
Passing (Yds.)	Troy Aikman, 1989-2000	32,942
Passing (TDs)	Troy Aikman, 1989-2000	165
Receiving (No.)	Michael Irvin, 1988-1999	750
Receiving (Yds.)	Michael Irvin, 1988-1999	11,904
Interceptions	Mel Renfro, 1964-1977	52
Punting (Avg.)	Mat McBriar, 2004-2010	45.5
Punt Return (Avg.)	Deion Sanders, 1995-99	13.3
Kickoff Return (Avg.)	Mel Renfro, 1964-1977	26.4
Field Goals	Rafael Septien, 1978-1986	162
Touchdowns (Tot.)	Emmitt Smith, 1990-2002	164
Points	Emmitt Smith, 1990-2002	986
*Sacks	Jim Jeffcoat, 1983-1994	94.5

INDIVIDUAL RECORDS—SINGLE SEASON

Category	Name	Performance
Rushing (Yds.)	Emmitt Smith, 1995	1,773
Passing (Yds.)	Tony Romo, 2009	4,483
Passing (TDs)	Tony Romo, 2007	36
Receiving (No.)	Michael Irvin, 1995	111
Receiving (Yds.)	Michael Irvin, 1995	1,603
Interceptions	Everson Walls, 1981	11
Punting (Avg.)	Mat McBriar, 2006	48.2
Punt Return (Avg.)	Bob Hayes, 1968	20.8
Kickoff Return (Avg.)	Mel Renfro, 1965	30.0
Field Goals	Richie Cunningham, 1997	34
Touchdowns (Tot.)	Emmitt Smith, 1995	25
Points	Emmitt Smith, 1995	150
*Sacks	DeMarcus Ware, 2008	20.0

INDIVIDUAL RECORDS—SINGLE GAME

Category	Name	Performance
Rushing (Yds.)	Emmitt Smith, 10-31-93	237
Passing (Yds.)	Don Meredith, 11-10-63	460
Passing (TDs)	Many times	5
	Last time by Tony Romo, 11-23-06	
Receiving (No.)	Jason Witten, 12-9-07	15
Receiving (Yds.)	Miles Austin, 10-11-09	250
Interceptions	Many times	3
	Last time by Terence Newman, 12-14-03	
Field Goals	Chris Boniol, 11-18-96	7
	Billy Cundiff, 9-15-03	7
Touchdowns (Tot.)	Many times	4
	Last time by Terrell Owens, 11-18-07	
Points	Many times	24
	Last time by Terrell Owens, 11-18-07	
*Sacks	Jim Jeffcoat, 11-10-85	5.0

*Sacks became an official statistic in 1982.
**NFL Record

VETERAN ROSTER AS OF MARCH 3, 2011

No.	Name	Pos.	Ht.	Wt.	Birthdate	^NFL Exp.	College	Hometown	How Acq.	'10 Games/ Starts
19	Austin, Miles	WR	6-2	215	6/30/84	6	Monmouth	Garfield, N.J.	FA-'06	16/16
20	Ball, Alan	S/CB	6-2	195	3/29/85	4	Illinois	Detroit, Mich.	D7b-'07	16/16
24	Barber, Marion	RB	5-11	218	6/10/83	7	Minnesota	Wayzata, Minn.	D4a-'05	13/10
71	Barron, Alex	T	6-8	316	9/28/82	7	Florida State	Orangeburg, S.C.	T(StL)-'10	11/1
80	Bennett, Martellus	TE	6-6	267	3/10/87	4	Texas A&M	Alief, Texas	D2-'08	16/11
72	Bowen, Stephen	DE	6-5	306	3/28/84	6	Hofstra	Wheatley Heights, N.Y.	FA-'06	16/9
92	Brent, Josh	NT	6-2	315	1/30/88	2	Illinois	Bloomington, Ill.	S7-'10	16/0
79	Brewster, Robert	T	6-4	320	7/30/86	2	Ball State	Cincinnati, Ohio	D3-'09	1/0
51	Brooking, Keith	LB	6-2	242	10/30/75	14	Georgia Tech	Senoia, Ga.	UFA(Atl)-'09	16/16
5	Brown, Kris	K	5-11	211	12/23/76	13	Nebraska	Southlake, Texas	FA-'10	3/0*
88	Bryant, Dez	WR	6-2	217	11/4/88	2	Oklahoma State	Lufkin, Texas	D1-'10	12/2
18	Buehler, David	K	6-2	225	2/5/87	3	Southern California	Anaheim, Calif.	D5c-'09	16/0
57	Butler, Victor	LB	6-2	246	7/29/87	3	Oregon State	Rialto, Calif.	D4b-'09	15/0
23	Choice, Tashard	RB	5-10	212	11/20/84	4	Georgia Tech	Riverdale, Ga.	D4-'08	16/0
42	Church, Barry	S	6-2	218	2/11/88	2	Toledo	Pittsburgh, Pa.	FA-'10	15/0
75	Colombo, Marc	T	6-8	320	10/8/78	10	Boston College	Bridgewater, Mass.	FA-'05	15/15
67	Costa, Phil	C	6-3	316	7/11/87	2	Maryland	Moorestown, N.J.	FA-'10	4/1
54	Cummings, Kenwin	LB	6-3	250	7/23/86	3	Wingate	Pembroke, N.C.	FA-'10	5/0*
70	Davis, Leonard	G	6-6	355	9/5/78	11	Texas	Wortham, Texas	UFA(Ari)-'07	16/16
68	Free, Doug	T	6-6	320	1/6/84	5	Northern Illinois	Manitowoc, Wisc.	D4b-'07	16/16
44	Gronkowski, Chris	FB	6-2	245	12/26/86	2	Arizona	Amherst, N.Y.	FA-'10	14/7
65	Gurode, Andre	C	6-4	318	3/6/79	10	Colorado	Houston, Texas	D2a-'02	16/16
97	Hatcher, Jason	DE	6-6	311	7/13/82	6	Grambling State	Jena, La.	D3b-'06	13/1
64	Holland, Montrae	G	6-2	326	5/21/80	9	Florida State	Ore, Texas	FA-'10	14/2
16	Holley, Jesse	WR	6-2	211	1/8/84	2	North Carolina	Roselle, N.J.	FA-'09	12/0
17	Hurd, Sam	WR	6-3	209	4/24/85	6	Northern Illinois	San Antonio, Texas	FA-'06	15/1
56	James, Bradie	LB	6-2	245	1/17/81	9	Louisiana State	Monroe, La.	D4-'03	16/16
21	Jenkins, Mike	CB	5-10	200	3/22/85	4	South Florida	Bradenton, Fla.	D1b-'08	16/16
15	Johnson, Manuel	WR	5-11	200	10/14/86	2	Oklahoma	Gilmer, Texas	D7b-'09	2/0
28	Jones, Felix	RB	5-10	220	5/8/87	4	Arkansas	Tulsa, Okla.	D1a-'08	16/7
3	Kitna, Jon	QB	6-2	230	9/21/72	15	Central Washington	Tacoma, Wash.	T(Det)-'09	10/9
63	Kosier, Kyle	G	6-5	309	11/27/78	10	Arizona State	Peoria, Ariz.	UFA(Det)-'06	13/13
91	Ladouceur, Louis-Philippe	LS	6-5	256	3/13/81	7	California	Pointe-Claire, Quebec, Canada	FA-'05	16/0
50	Lee, Sean	LB	6-2	242	7/22/86	2	Penn State	Pittsburgh, Pa.	D2-'10	14/0
95	Lissemore, Sean	DE	6-4	306	9/11/87	2	William & Mary	Dumont, N.J.	D7-'10	2/0
1	McBriar, Mat	P	6-0	217	7/8/79	8	Hawai'i	East Brighton, Australia	FA-'04	16/0
37	McCann, Bryan	CB	5-10	189	9/29/87	2	Southern Methodist	Oklahoma City, Ok.	FA-'10	9/0
40	McCray, Danny	S	6-1	214	3/10/88	2	Louisiana State	Houston, Texas	FA-'10	16/0
7	McGee, Stephen	QB	6-3	222	9/27/85	3	Texas A&M	Burnet, Texas	D4a-'09	2/1
41	Newman, Terence	CB	5-10	193	9/24/78	9	Kansas State	Salina, Kan.	D1-'03	16/16
85	Ogletree, Kevin	WR	6-1	198	8/5/87	3	Virginia	Queens, N.Y.	FA-'09	6/0
99	Olshansky, Igor	DE	6-5	315	5/3/82	8	Oregon	San Francisco, Calif.	UFA(SD)-'09	16/14
27	Owusu-Ansah, Akwasi	S	6-0	208	4/10/88	2	Indiana (PA)	Columbus, Ohio	D4-'10	7/0
78	Parnell, Jermey	T	6-6	307	7/20/86	2	Mississippi	Blytheville, Ark.	FA-'10	0*
89	Phillips, John	TE	6-5	265	6/11/87	2	Virginia	Warm Springs, Va.	D6b-'09	0*
49	Pociask, Jason	TE	6-3	259	2/9/83	5	Wisconsin	Indianapolis, Ind.	FA-'10	0*
90	Ratliff, Jay	NT	6-4	303	8/29/81	7	Auburn	Valdosta, Ga.	D7-'05	16/16
9	Romo, Tony	QB	6-2	223	4/21/80	9	Eastern Illinois	Burlington, Wisc.	FA-'03	6/6
83	Rucker, Martin	TE	6-5	255	5/4/85	4	Missouri	St. Joseph, Mo.	FA-'10	5/1
32	Scandrick, Orlando	CB	5-10	194	2/10/87	4	Boise State	Los Alamitos, Calif.	D5-'08	16/3
36	Sendejo, Andrew	S	6-1	225	9/9/87	2	Rice	San Antonio, Texas	FA-'10	2/0
43	Sensabaugh, Gerald	S	6-1	210	6/13/83	7	North Carolina	Kingsport, Tenn.	UFA(Jac)-'09	16/14
58	Smith, Kelvin	LB	6-2	240	3/20/84	3	Syracuse	Thiells, N.Y.	FA-'10	0*
96	Spears, Marcus	DE	6-4	311	3/8/83	7	Louisiana State	Baton Rouge, La.	D1b-'05	8/7
93	Spencer, Anthony	LB	6-3	260	1/23/84	5	Purdue	Fort Wayne, Ind.	D1-'07	16/16
94	Ware, DeMarcus	LB	6-4	262	7/31/82	7	Troy	Auburn, Ala.	D1a-'05	16/16
59	Williams, Brandon	LB	6-3	246	6/21/88	3	Texas Tech	Fort Worth, Texas	D4c-'09	6/0
52	Williams, Leon	LB	6-3	248	7/30/83	5	Miami	Brooklyn, N.Y.	FA-'10	11/0
11	Williams, Roy	WR	6-3	215	12/20/81	8	Texas	Odessa, Texas	T(Det)-'08	15/9
82	Witten, Jason	TE	6-6	263	5/6/82	9	Tennessee	Elizabethton, Tenn.	D3-'03	16/16
76	Young, Sam	T	6-8	322	6/24/87	2	Notre Dame	Coral Springs, Fla.	D6a-'10	2/0

* Brown played 3 games with San Diego in '10; Cummings played 3 games with New York Jets; Parnell inactive for 12 games; Phillips missed '10 season because of injury; Pociask last active with New York Jets in '07; Smith last active with Carolina in '09.

Also played with Cowboys in '10—FB Deon Anderson (1 game), TE Scott Chandler (9), DE Jeremy Clark (2), S Michael Hamlin (2), NT Jimmy Saddler-McQueen (1), LB Jason Williams (5).

^ "NFL Exp." as of 2011 Kickoff Weekend. For full explanation of how a player's NFL Experience is measured, refer to explanation underneath the First-Year Roster listed below.

FIRST-YEAR ROSTER

Name	Pos.	Ht.	Wt.	Birthdate	College	Hometown	How Acq.
Arkin, David	G	6-5	302	10/7/87	Missouri State	Wichita, Kan.	D4
Balogun, Mike (1)	LB	6-0	215	6/30/84	Oklahoma	District Heights, Md.	FA
Bergeron, Troy (1)	WR	6-2	195	12/3/83	None	Columbus, Ga.	FA-'10
Bright, Travis (1)	G	6-4	322	1/5/83	Brigham Young	Queen Creek, Ariz.	FA-'09
Carter, Bruce	LB	6-3	233	2/19/88	North Carolina	Havelock, N.C.	D2
Chapas, Shaun	FB	6-2	236	5/2/88	Georgia	St. Augustine, Fla.	D7a
Daniels, Alex (1)	DE	6-4	259	11/27/86	Cincinnati	Columbus, Ohio	FA
Geathers, Clifton (1)	DE	6-7	300	12/11/87	South Carolina	Georgetown, S.C.	W(Sea)-'10
Greenhouse, Isaiah (1)	LB	6-2	239	7/15/87	Northwestern State	Marksville, La.	FA
Harris, Dwayne	WR	5-10	200	9/16/87	East Carolina	Stone Mountain, Ga.	D6
Miller, Lonyae (1)	RB	6-0	222	4/29/88	Fresno State	Fontana, Calif.	FA-'10
Moturi, Jeff (1)	WR	5-11	186	4/4/86	Texas-El Paso	Irving, Texas	FA-'10
Murray, DeMarco	RB	6-0	214	2/12/88	Oklahoma	Los Angeles, Calif.	D3
Nagy, Bill	C	6-3	318	10/26/87	Wisconsin	Hudson, Ohio	D7b
Ryan, Titus (1)	WR	6-0	190	5/19/84	Concordia College	Tuscaloosa, Ala.	FA
Smith, Tyron	T	6-5	307	12/12/90	Southern California	Moreno Valley, Calif.	D1
Thomas, Josh	CB	5-11	198	5/3/89	Buffalo	Cedar Hill, Texas	D5
Weaver, Ross (1)	CB	6-1	203	1/29/87	Michigan State	Southfield, Mich.	FA-'10
Williams, Teddy (1)	WR	6-3	198	7/3/88	Texas-San Antonio	Tyler, Texas	FA-'10

The term NFL Rookie is defined as a player who is in his first season of professional football and has not been on the roster of another professional football team for any regular-season or postseason games. A Rookie is designated by an "R" on NFL rosters. Players who have been active in another professional football league or players who have NFL experience, including either preseason training camp or being on an Active List or Inactive List, or on Reserve/Injured or Reserve/Physically Unable to Perform for fewer than six regular-season games, are termed NFL First-Year Players. An NFL First-Year Player is designated by a "1" on NFL rosters. Thereafter, a player is credited with an additional year of experience for each season in which he accumulates six games on the Active List or Inactive List, or on Reserve/Injured or Reserve/Physically Unable to Perform.

Log on to www.dallascowboys.com for an up-to-date roster.

COACHING STAFF

Head Coach,
Jason Garrett

Pro Career: Named the eighth head coach in Dallas Cowboys history on January 5, 2011 and became the first former Cowboys player to become the team's head coach. Named the club's interim head coach at the midpoint of the 2010 and went on to guide a Dallas team that had started the season with a 1-7 record to a 5-3 mark down the stretch. In the season's second half, three of the Cowboys five victories were against teams that posted 10 regular season wins, while the three Dallas defeats were decided by a combined total of seven points. Since the 2007 season Garrett had been the Cowboys offensive coordinator, and in 2008, he was assigned the additional duties of being the club's assistant head coach. Under Garrett, the Dallas offense finished among the NFL's top-10 in total offense in three of his four years at the helm: 2010 (10th), 2009 (2nd), and 2007 (2nd). From the start of the 2007 season, the club has averaged 24.6 points-per-game and 368.5 total yards-per-outing. From 2007 to 2009 the cumulative numbers for total net yards (17,753), gross yards (12,761) and passing yards (12,181) represented the best totals over a three-year span in the history of the organization. En route to winning the 2009 NFC Eastern Division title, Dallas established club records for total offensive yards (6,390), net passing yards (4,287) and pass completions (347). Dallas won the NFC East in 2007 with a team-record tying 13 victories and finished second in the NFL in scoring. The 455 points scored in 2007 marked the second-highest figure in club history behind only the 1983 club (479 points). Garrett was named *Pro Football Weekly's* NFL's Assistant Coach of the Year in March of 2008. Career record: 5-3.

Background: Played quarterback at Princeton (1987-88) and was named the Ivy League's Player of the Year and honorable mention All American as a senior. Played professionally in World League and Canadian Football League (both 1991) before joining Dallas (1992-99), Giants (2000-03), Buccaneers (2004) and Dolphins (also 2004). Key reserve on three Super Bowl teams with the Cowboys and one with the Giants. Began his coaching career as quarterbacks coach with Dolphins for Nick Saban.

Personal: Born March 28, 1966, in Abington, Pa. He and his wife Brill reside in Dallas.

ASSISTANT COACHES

Brian Baker, defensive line; born June 20, 1962, Baltimore. Linebacker Maryland 1981-83. No pro playing experience. College coach: Maryland 1984-85, Army 1986, Georgia Tech 1987-1995. Pro coach: San Diego Chargers 1996, Detroit Lions 1997-2000, Minnesota Vikings 2001-05, St. Louis Rams 2006-2008, Carolina Panthers 2009-2010, joined Cowboys in 2011.

Ben Bloom, defensive quality control/linebackers; born October 17, 1982, Wellesley, Mass. Offensive line Tufts 2001-04. No pro playing experience. College coach: Tufts 2005-07, Harvard 2008. Pro coach: Cleveland Browns 2010, joined Cowboys in 2011.

Chris Boniol, asst. special teams/kickers; born December 9, 1971, Alexandria, La. Kicker Louisiana Tech 1990-93. Pro kicker Dallas Cowboys 1994-96, Philadelphia Eagles 1997-98, Chicago Bears 1999. Pro coach: Joined Cowboys in 2010.

Dave Campo, secondary; born July 18, 1947, Groton, Conn. Defensive back Central Connecticut State 1967-1970. No pro playing experience. College coach: Central Connecticut State 1971-72, Albany 1973, Bridgeport 1974, Pittsburgh 1975, Washington State 1976, Boise State 1977-79, Oregon State 1980, Weber State 1981-82, Iowa State 1983, Syracuse 1984-86, Miami 1987-88. Pro coach: Dallas Cowboys 1989-2002 (head coach 2000-02), Cleveland Browns 2003-04, Jacksonville Jaguars 2005-07, re-joined Cowboys in 2008.

Joe DeCamillis, special teams coordinator; born June 29, 1965, Arvada, Colo. Attended Wyoming. No college or pro playing experience. Pro coach: Denver Broncos 1988-1992, New York Giants 1993-96, Atlanta Falcons 1997-2006, Jacksonville Jaguars 2007-08, joined Cowboys in 2009.

Matt Eberflus, linebackers; born May 17, 1970, Toledo, Ohio. Linebacker Toledo 1988-1991. No pro playing experience. College coach: Toledo 1992-2000, Missouri 2001-08. Pro coach: Cleveland Browns 2009-2010, joined Cowboys in 2011.

John Garrett, passing game coordinator/tight ends; born March 2, 1965, Danville, Pa. Wide receiver Columbia 1983-85, Princeton 1986-87. Pro wide receiver Cincinnati Bengals 1989, Buffalo Bills 1991, San Antonio Riders (World League) 1991. College coach: Virginia 2004-06. Pro coach: Cincinnati Bengals 1995-98, 2001-02, Arizona Cardinals 1999-2000, joined Cowboys in 2007.

Hudson Houck, running game coordinator/offensive line; born January 7, 1943, Los Angeles. Center Southern California 1962-64. No pro playing experience. College coach: Southern California 1970-72, 1976-1982, Stanford 1973-75. Pro coach: Los Angeles Rams 1983-1991, Seattle Seahawks 1992, Dallas Cowboys 1993-2001, San Diego Chargers 2002-04, Miami Dolphins 2005-07, re-joined Cowboys in 2008.

Brett Maxie, secondary/safeties; born January 13, 1962, Dallas. Safety Texas Southern 1982-84. Pro safety New Orleans Saints 1985-1993, Atlanta Falcons 1994, Carolina Panthers 1995-96, San Francisco 49ers 1997. Pro coach: Carolina Panthers 1998, San Francisco 49ers 1999-2003, Miami Dolphins 2007, joined Cowboys in 2008.

Keith O'Quinn, offensive quality control/wide receivers; born July 28, 1973, Pensacola, Fla. Safety North Texas 1991-96. No pro playing experience. College coach: Hardin-Simmons 2000-02, Abilene Christian 2003-04. Pro coach: Joined Cowboys in 2010.

Skip Peete, running backs; born January 30, 1963, Mesa, Ariz. Wide receiver Arizona 1981-82, Kansas 1984-85. Pro wide receiver New York Jets 1987. College coach: Pittsburgh 1988-1992, Michigan State 1993-94, Rutgers 1995, UCLA 1996-97. Pro coach: Oakland Raiders 1998-2006, joined Cowboys in 2007.

Wes Phillips, asst. offensive line; born February 17, 1979, Houston. Quarterback Texas-El Paso 1997-2001. Pro quarterback San Diego Riptide (AFL2) 2002-03. College coach: Texas-El Paso 2003, West Texas A&M 2004-05, Baylor 2006. Pro coach: Joined Cowboys in 2007.

Jimmy Robinson, asst. head coach/wide receivers; born January 3, 1953, Atlanta. Wide receiver Georgia Tech 1972-74. Pro wide receiver N.Y. Giants 1976-79, San Francisco 49ers 1980, Denver Broncos 1981. College coach: Georgia Tech 1987-89. Pro coach: Memphis Showboats (USFL) 1984-85, Atlanta Falcons 1990-93, Indianapolis Colts 1994-97, New York Giants 1998-2003, New Orleans Saints 2004-05, Green Bay Packers 2006-2010, joined Cowboys in 2011.

Rob Ryan, defensive coordinator; born December 13, 1962, Ardmore, Okla. Linebacker Oklahoma State 1984-86, Southwestern Oklahoma State 1985-86. No pro playing experience. College coach: Western Kentucky 1987, Ohio State 1988, Tennessee State 1989-1993, Hutchinson (Kan.) C.C. 1996, Oklahoma State 1997-99. Pro coach: Arizona Cardinals 1994-95, New England Patriots 2000-03, Oakland Raiders 2004-08, Cleveland Browns 2009-2010, joined Cowboys in 2011.

Wade Wilson, quarterbacks; born February 1, 1959, Commerce, Texas. Quarterback East Texas State 1977-1980. Pro quarterback Minnesota Vikings 1981-1991, Atlanta Falcons 1992, New Orleans Saints 1993-94, Dallas Cowboys 1995-97, Oakland Raiders 1998-99. Pro coach: Dallas Cowboys 2000-02, Chicago Bears 2004-06, re-joined Cowboys in 2007.

Mike Woicik, strength and conditioning; born September 26, 1956, Baltimore. Attended Boston College. No college or pro playing experience. College coach: Springfield College 1978-1980, Syracuse 1980-89. Pro coach: Dallas Cowboys 1990-96, New Orleans Saints 1997-99, New England Patriots 2000-10, re-joined Cowboys in 2011.

**National Football Conference
North Division
Team Colors:** Honolulu Blue and Silver
**222 Republic Drive
Allen Park, Michigan 48101
Telephone:** (313) 216-4000

2011 SCHEDULE
PRESEASON

Aug. 12	**Cincinnati**	7:30
Aug. 19	at Cleveland	7:30
Aug. 27	**New England**	8:00
Sep. 1	at Buffalo	6:30

REGULAR SEASON

Sep. 11	at Tampa Bay	1:00
Sep. 18	**Kansas City**	1:00
Sep. 25	at Minnesota	1:00
Oct. 2	at Dallas	1:00
Oct. 10	**Chicago** (Mon)	8:30
Oct. 16	**San Francisco**	1:00
Oct. 23	**Atlanta**	1:00
Oct. 30	at Denver	4:05
Nov. 6	BYE	
Nov. 13	at Chicago	1:00
Nov. 20	**Carolina**	1:00
Nov. 24	**Green Bay** (Thu)	12:30
Dec. 4	at New Orleans	1:00
Dec. 11	**Minnesota**	1:00
Dec. 18	at Oakland	4:05
Dec. 24	**San Diego** (Sat)	4:05
Jan. 1	at Green Bay	1:00

*All times ET

Stadium: Ford Field (opened in 2002)
 • **Capacity:** 64,500
 2000 Brush Street
 Detroit, Michigan 48226
Playing Surface: FieldTurf
Training Camp: 222 Republic Drive
 Allen Park, Michigan
 48101

FORD FIELD

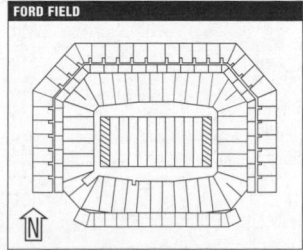

CLUB OFFICIALS
Chairman and Owner: William Clay Ford
Vice Chairman: William Clay Ford, Jr.
President: Tom Lewand
Senior Vice President & General
 Manager: Martin Mayhew

Senior Vice President of
 Communications: Bill Keenist
Senior Vice President & CFO: Luis Perez
Corporate Secretary: David Hempstead
Senior Personnel Executive: James Harris
Vice President of Pro Personnel:
 Sheldon White
Vice President of Football Operations:
 Cedric Saunders
Director of College Scouting:
 Scott McEwen
Player Personnel: Cary Conklin,
 Dennis Gentry, Chad Henry,
 Rob Lohman, Miller McCalmon,
 Silas McKinnie, Lance Newmark,
 Charlie Sanders, Dave Sears,
 Dave Uyrus.
Director of Community Affairs: TBD
Director of Media Relations:
 Matt Barnhart
Director of Broadcasting and Production:
 Bryan Bender
Director of Ticket Operations:
 Mark Graham
Coordinator of Athletic Medicine/Athletic
 Trainer: Dean Kleinschmidt
Athletic Trainer: Al Bellamy
Equipment Manager: Tim O'Neill
Video Director: Robert Yanagi

COACHING HISTORY
**Portsmouth Spartans 1930-33
(503-603-32)**
Records include postseason games

1930	Hal (Tubby) Griffen	5-6-3
1931-36	George (Potsy) Clark	49-20-6
1937-38	Earl (Dutch) Clark	14-8-0
1939	Elmer (Gus) Henderson	6-5-0
1940	George (Potsy) Clark	5-5-1
1941-42	Bill Edwards*	4-9-1
1942	John Karcis	0-8-0
1943-47	Charles (Gus) Dorais	20-31-2
1948-1950	Alvin (Bo) McMillin	12-24-0
1951-56	Raymond (Buddy) Parker	50-24-2
1957-1964	George Wilson	55-45-6
1965-66	Harry Gilmer	10-16-2
1967-1972	Joe Schmidt	43-35-7
1973	Don McCafferty	6-7-1
1974-76	Rick Forzano**	15-17-0
1976-77	Tommy Hudspeth	11-13-0
1978-1984	Monte Clark	43-63-1
1985-88	Darryl Rogers***	18-40-0
1988-1996	Wayne Fontes	67-71-0
1997-2000	Bobby Ross****	27-32-0
2000	Gary Moeller	4-3-0
2001-02	Marty Mornhinweg	5-27-0
2003-05	Steve Mariucci#	15-28-0
2005	Dick Jauron	1-4-0
2006-08	Rod Marinelli	10-38-0
2009-2010	Jim Schwartz	8-24-0

 *Released after three games in 1942
 **Resigned after four games in 1976
 ***Released after 11 games in 1988
 ****Resigned after nine games in 2000
 # Released after 11 games in 2005

PAID ATTENDANCE
Home 436,687   Away 507,606
Total 944,293
Single-game home record,
 80,444 (12/20/81)
Single-season home record, 644,904
 (1980)

2011 DRAFT CHOICES

Round	Name	Pos.	College
1	Nick Fairley	DT	Auburn
2	Titus Young	WR	Boise State
	Mikel Leshoure	RB	Illinois
5	Doug Hogue	LB	Syracuse
7	Johnny Culbreath	T	South Carolina St.

2010 TEAM RECORD
PRESEASON (3-1)

Date	Result	Opponent
8/14	L 7-23	at Pittsburgh
8/21	W 25-20	at Denver
8/28	W 35-27	Cleveland
9/2	W 28-23	Buffalo

REGULAR SEASON (6-10)

Date	Result	Opponent
9/12	L 14-19	at Chicago
9/19	L 32-35	Philadelphia
9/26	L 10-24	at Minnesota
10/3	L 26-28	at Green Bay
10/10	W 44-6	St. Louis
10/17	L 20-28	at New York Giants
10/31	W 37-25	Washington
11/7	L 20-23	New York Jets (OT)
11/14	L 12-14	at Buffalo
11/21	L 19-35	at Dallas
11/25	L 24-45	New England
12/5	L 20-24	Chicago
12/12	W 7-3	Green Bay
12/19	W 23-20	at Tampa Bay (OT)
12/26	W 34-27	at Miami
1/2	W 20-13	Minnesota

(OT) Overtime

SCORE BY PERIODS

Lions	62	118	62	117	3 —	362
Opponents	54	127	86	99	3 —	369

2010 TEAM STATISTICS

	Lions	Opp.
Total First Downs	304	320
Rushing	83	98
Passing	199	187
Penalty	22	35
3rd Down: Made/Att	97/242	77/198
3rd Down Pct.	40.1	38.9
4th Down: Made/Att	10/16	5/12
4th Down Pct.	62.5	41.7
Possession Avg.	29:34	30:26
Total Net Yards	5423	5497
Avg. Per Game	338.9	343.6
Total Plays	1064	1005
Avg. Per Play	5.1	5.5
Net Yards Rushing	1613	1999
Avg. Per Game	100.8	124.9
Total Rushes	404	443
Net Yards Passing	3810	3498
Avg. Per Game	238.1	218.6
Sacked/Yards Lost	27/191	44/288
Gross Yards	4001	3786
Att./Completions	633/383	518/330
Completion Pct.	60.5	63.7
Had Intercepted	16	14
Punts/Average	90/44.6	83/43.8
Net Punting Avg.	90/35.8	83/37.5
Penalties/Yards	136/1018	106/854
Fumbles/Ball Lost	20/9	31/15
Touchdowns	41	45
Rushing	11	18
Passing	26	23
Returns	4	4

2010 INDIVIDUAL STATISTICS

PASSING

PASSING	Att.	Comp.	Yds.	Pct.	TD	Int.	Tkld.	Rate
Sh. Hill	416	257	2686	61.8	16	12	17/113	81.3
Stanton	119	69	780	58.0	4	3	6/42	78.4
Stafford	96	57	535	59.4	6	1	4/36	91.3
Best	1	0	0	0.0	0	0	0/0	39.6
Logan	1	0	0	0.0	0	0	0/0	39.6
Lions	633	383	4001	60.5	26	16	27/191	82.0
Opponents	518	330	3786	63.7	23	14	44/288	89.2

SCORING

SCORING	TD R	TD P	TD Rt	PAT	FG	Saf	PTS
C. Johnson	0	12	0	0/0	0/0	0	74
Hanson	0	0	0	19/19	12/14	0	55
Rayner	0	0	0	16/16	13/16	0	55
Best	4	2	0	0/0	0/0	0	36
Burleson	0	6	0	0/0	0/0	0	36
Morris	5	0	0	0/0	0/0	0	30
Pettigrew	0	4	0	0/0	0/0	0	24
Heller	0	1	0	0/0	0/0	0	6
Levy	0	0	1	0/0	0/0	0	6
Logan	0	0	1	0/0	0/0	0	6
Scheffler	0	1	0	0/0	0/0	0	6
A. Smith	0	0	1	0/0	0/0	0	6
Stafford	1	0	0	0/0	0/0	0	6
Stanton	1	0	0	0/0	0/0	0	6
Suh	0	0	1	0/1	0/0	0	6
B. Johnson	0	0	0	0/0	0/0	2	2
Lions	11	26	4	35/36	25/30	1	362
Opponents	18	23	4	42/42	19/20	0	369

2-Pt Conversions: B. Johnson, C. Johnson.
Lions 2-5, Opponents 0-3.

RUSHING

RUSHING	No.	Yds	Avg	LG	TD
Best	171	555	3.2	45	4
Morris	90	336	3.7	26	5
K. Smith	34	133	3.9	15	0
Sh. Hill	22	123	5.6	40	0
Stanton	18	113	6.3	20	1
Logan	15	95	6.3	21	0
Burleson	7	81	11.6	25	0
Felton	22	76	3.5	9	0
A. Brown	17	58	3.4	9	0
C. Johnson	4	32	8.0	15	0
Stafford	4	11	2.8	9	1
Lions	404	1613	4.0	45	11
Opponents	443	1999	4.5	80t	18

RECEIVING

RECEIVING	No.	Yds	Avg	LG	TD
C. Johnson	77	1120	14.5	87t	12
Pettigrew	71	722	10.2	35	4
Best	58	487	8.4	75t	2
Burleson	55	625	11.4	58	6
Scheffler	45	378	8.4	25	1
Morris	25	170	6.8	16	0
B. Johnson	18	210	11.7	24	0
K. Smith	11	123	11.2	27	0
Felton	8	54	6.8	19	0
A. Brown	8	45	5.6	10	0
Heller	4	37	9.3	13t	0
D. Williams	3	30	10.0	17	0
Lions	383	4001	10.4	87t	26
Opponents	330	3786	11.5	89t	23

INTERCEPTIONS

INTERCEPTIONS	No.	Yds	Avg	LG	TD
A. Smith	5	48	9.6	42t	1
Levy	2	41	20.5	30t	1
Spievey	2	35	17.5	26	0
C. Williams	1	27	27.0	27	0
Berry	1	23	23.0	23	0
Suh	1	20	20.0	20	0
Houston	1	0	0.0	0	0
Vasher	1	0	0.0	0	0
Lions	14	194	13.9	42t	2
Opponents	16	239	14.9	50	2

PUNTING

PUNTING	No.	Yds.	Avg.	In 20	LG
Harris	90	4018	44.6	24	66
Lions	90	4018	44.6	24	66
Opponents	83	3636	43.8	35	63

PUNT RETURNS

PUNT RETURNS	Ret	FC	Yds	Avg	LG	TD
Logan	30	21	362	12.1	71	0
Lions	30	21	362	12.1	71	0
Opponents	54	17	633	11.7	97t	1

KICKOFF RETURNS

KICKOFF RETURNS	No.	Yds	Avg	LG	TD
Logan	55	1448	26.3	105t	1
Felton	2	59	29.5	37	0
Fluellen	1	4	4.0	4	0
McBride	1	8	8.0	8	0
Burleson	1	0	0.0	0	0
Scheffler	1	0	0.0	0	0
Ciurciu	0	—	—	0	0
Lions	61	1519	24.9	105t	1
Opponents	72	1487	20.7	96t	1

FIELD GOALS

FIELD GOALS	1-19	20-29	30-39	40-49	50+
Rayner	0/0	3/3	3/3	5/8	2/2
Hanson	0/0	1/1	4/4	4/5	3/4
Lions	0/0	4/4	7/7	9/13	5/6
Opponents	1/1	6/6	7/7	4/5	1/1

SACKS

SACKS	No.
Suh	10.0
Avril	8.5
Jackson	6.0
McBride	5.0
Vanden Bosch	4.0
Sa. Hill	2.5
Delmas	2.0
C. Williams	2.0
Fluellen	1.0
Palmer	1.0
Peterson	1.0
(group)	1.0
Lions	44.0
Opponents	27.0

RECORD HOLDERS
INDIVIDUAL RECORDS—CAREER

Category	Name	Performance
Rushing (Yds.)	Barry Sanders, 1989-1998	15,269
Passing (Yds.)	Bobby Layne, 1950-58	15,710
Passing (TDs)	Bobby Layne, 1950-58	118
Receiving (No.)	Herman Moore, 1991-2001	670
Receiving (Yds.)	Herman Moore, 1991-2001	9,174
Interceptions	Dick LeBeau, 1959-1972	62
Punting (Avg.)	Yale Lary, 1952-53, 1956-1964	44.3
Punt Return (Avg.)	Jack Christiansen, 1951-58	12.8
Kickoff Return (Avg.)	Pat Studstill, 1961-67	25.7
Field Goals	Jason Hanson, 1992-2010	439
Touchdowns (Tot.)	Barry Sanders, 1989-1998	109
Points	Jason Hanson, 1992-2010	1,890
*Sacks	Robert Porcher, 1992-2003	95.5

INDIVIDUAL RECORDS—SINGLE SEASON

Category	Name	Performance
Rushing (Yds.)	Barry Sanders, 1997	2,053
Passing (Yds.)	Scott Mitchell, 1995	4,338
Passing (TDs)	Scott Mitchell, 1995	32
Receiving (No.)	Herman Moore, 1995	123
Receiving (Yds.)	Herman Moore, 1995	1,686
Interceptions	Don Doll, 1950	12
	Jack Christiansen, 1953	12
Punting (Avg.)	Yale Lary, 1963	48.9
Punt Return (Avg.)	Pat Studstill, 1962	15.8
Kickoff Return (Avg.)	Mel Gray, 1994	28.4
Field Goals	Jason Hanson, 1993	34
Touchdowns (Tot.)	Barry Sanders, 1991	17
Points	Jason Hanson, 1995	132
*Sacks	Robert Porcher, 1999	15.0

INDIVIDUAL RECORDS—SINGLE GAME

Category	Name	Performance
Rushing (Yds.)	Barry Sanders, 11-13-94	237
Passing (Yds.)	Charlie Batch, 11-18-01	436
Passing (TDs)	Gary Danielson, 12-9-78	5
	Matthew Stafford, 11-9-09	5
Receiving (No.)	Herman Moore, 12-4-95	14
Receiving (Yds.)	Cloyce Box, 12-3-50	302
Interceptions	Don Doll, 10-23-49	**4
Field Goals	Garo Yepremian, 11-13-66	6
	Jason Hanson, 10-17-99	6
Touchdowns (Tot.)	Dutch Clark, 10-22-34	4
	Cloyce Box, 12-3-50	4
	Barry Sanders, 11-24-91	4
Points	Dutch Clark, 10-22-34	24
	Cloyce Box, 12-3-50	24
	Barry Sanders, 11-24-91	24
*Sacks	Bill Gay, 9-4-83	5.5

*Sacks became an official statistic in 1982.
**NFL Record

VETERAN ROSTER AS OF MARCH 3, 2011

No.	Name	Pos.	Ht.	Wt.	Birthdate	^NFL Exp.	College	Hometown	How Acq.	'10 Games/ Starts
92	Avril, Cliff	DE	6-3	260	4/8/86	4	Purdue	Green Cove Springs, Fla.	D3c-'08	13/13
76	Backus, Jeff	T	6-5	305	9/21/77	11	Michigan	Norcross, Ga.	D1-'01	16/16
32	Berry, Aaron	CB	5-11	180	6/25/88	2	Pittsburgh	Harrisburg, Pa.	FA-'10	1/1
44	Best, Jahvid	RB	5-10	199	1/30/89	2	California	Richmond, Calif.	D1b-'10	16/9
	Bosworth, Korey	DE	6-1	242	11/21/86	2	UCLA	Irving, Texas	FA-'10	0*
21	Brown, Aaron	RB	6-1	205	10/10/85	3	Texas Christian	Katy, Texas	D6-'09	6/0
39	Brown, C.C.	S	6-0	208	1/27/83	7	Louisiana-Lafayette	Greenwood, Miss.	FA-'10	15/8
13	Burleson, Nate	WR	6-0	198	8/19/81	9	Nevada	Seattle, Wash.	UFA(Sea)-'10	14/14
59	Carpenter, Bobby	LB	6-2	249	8/1/83	6	Ohio State	Lancaster, Ohio	FA-'10	15/4*
77	Cherilus, Gosder	T	6-7	325	6/28/84	4	Boston College	Somerville, Mass.	D1-'08	12/12
52	Ciurciu, Vinny	LB	6-0	240	5/2/80	9	Boston College	Montvale, N.J.	FA-'10	10/0
87	Clark, Brian	WR	6-2	204	12/26/83	6	North Carolina State	Tampa, Fla.	FA-'10	4/0
	Coleman, Erik	S	5-10	207	5/6/82	9	Washington State	Spokane, Wash.	FA-'11	12/1*
26	Delmas, Louis	S	5-11	202	4/12/87	3	Western Michigan	North Miami Beach, Fla.	D2-'09	15/15
95	DeVries, Jared	DE	6-4	275	6/11/76	13	Iowa	Aplington, Iowa	D3-'99	0*
	Dickson, Richard	TE	6-2	245	11/17/87	2	Louisiana State	Ocean Springs, Miss.	FA-'10	0*
57	Dizon, Jordon	LB	6-0	232	1/16/86	4	Colorado	Kauai, Hawai'i	D2-'08	0*
50	Ekejiuba, Isaiah	LB	6-4	240	10/5/81	7	Virginia	Queens, N.Y.	FA-'10	9/0
45	Felton, Jerome	FB	6-0	246	7/3/86	4	Furman	Madisonville, Tenn.	D5b-'08	16/2
96	Fluellen, Andre	DT	6-2	302	3/7/85	4	Florida State	Cartersville, Ga.	D3b-'08	16/0
49	Follett, Zack	LB	6-1	236	7/3/87	3	California	Clovis, Calif.	D7-'09	5/2
70	Fox, Jason	T	6-6	314	5/2/88	2	Miami	Fort Worth, Texas	D4-'10	4/0
65	Gandy, Dylan	C	6-3	295	3/8/82	6	Texas Tech	Harlingen, Texas	FA-'09	16/0
4	Hanson, Jason	K	6-0	190	6/17/70	20	Washington State	Spokane, Wash.	D2b-'92	8/0
2	Harris, Nick	P	6-2	218	7/23/78	11	California	Avondale, Ariz.	W(Cin)-'03	16/0
89	Heller, Will	TE	6-6	275	2/28/81	10	Georgia Tech	Dunwoody, Ga.	UFA(Sea)-'09	16/5
91	Hill, Sammie	DT	6-4	329	11/8/86	3	Stillman	West Blocton, Ala.	D4-'09	15/0
14	Hill, Shaun	QB	6-3	220	1/9/80	10	Maryland	Parsons, Kan.	T(SF)-'10	11/10
24	Hill, Tye	CB	5-10	185	6/3/82	6	Clemson	Dorchester, S.C.	FA-'10	4/1
78	Hilliard, Corey	T	6-6	300	4/26/85	5	Oklahoma State	New Orleans, La.	FA-'09	16/4
23	Houston, Chris	CB	5-11	178	10/18/84	5	Arkansas	Austin, Texas	T(Atl)-'10	15/15
94	Jackson, Lawrence	DE	6-4	271	8/30/85	4	Southern California	Inglewood, Calif.	T(Sea)-'10	11/0
80	Johnson, Bryant	WR	6-3	215	3/7/81	9	Penn State	Baltimore City, Md.	UFA(SF)-'09	14/7
81	Johnson, Calvin	WR	6-5	236	9/29/85	5	Georgia Tech	Tyrone, Ga.	D1-'07	15/15
55	Johnson, Landon	LB	6-2	232	3/13/81	8	Purdue	Lubbock, Texas	FA-'10	12/8
43	King, Eric	CB	5-10	190	5/10/82	6	Wake Forest	Owing Mills, Md.	W(Cle)-'10	7/0*
54	Levy, DeAndre	LB	6-2	238	3/26/87	3	Wisconsin	Milwaukee, Wisc.	D3a-'09	11/11
11	Logan, Stefan	WR	5-6	180	6/2/81	3	South Dakota	Miami, Fla.	W(Pitt)-'10	16/0
75	McBride, Turk	DE	6-2	278	5/30/85	5	Tennessee	Camden, N.J.	W(KC)-'09	15/8
33	McDonald, Brandon	CB	5-10	185	8/26/85	5	Memphis	Collins, Miss.	W(Ariz)-'10	6/2
38	Miller, Prince	CB	5-9	198	1/14/88	2	Georgia	Duncan, S.C.	FA-'10	4/0
28	Morris, Maurice	RB	5-11	216	12/1/79	10	Oregon	Chester, S.C.	UFA(Sea)-'09	14/7
48	Muhlbach, Don	LS	6-4	265	8/17/81	8	Texas A&M	Lufkin, Texas	FA-'04	16/0
47	Nordin, Jake	FB	6-3	262	7/8/84	4	Northern Illinois	Lake Lillian, Minn.	FA-'10	0*
58	Palmer, Ashlee	LB	6-1	236	4/7/86	3	Mississippi	Compton, Calif.	W(Buff)-'10	16/5
66	Peterman, Stephen	G	6-4	323	1/11/82	7	Louisiana State	Waveland, Miss.	FA-'06	16/16
84	Pettigrew, Brandon	TE	6-5	265	2/23/85	3	Oklahoma State	Tyler, Texas	D1b-'09	16/16
51	Raiola, Dominic	C	6-1	295	12/30/78	11	Nebraska	Honolulu, Hawai'i	D2a-'01	16/16
3	Rayner, Dave	K	6-2	215	10/26/82	5	Michigan State	Oxford, Mich.	FA-'10	8/0
16	Robinson, Zac	QB	6-3	218	9/29/86	2	Oklahoma State	Littleton, Colo.	W(Sea)-'10	0*
85	Scheffler, Tony	TE	6-5	255	2/15/83	6	Western Michigan	Chelsea, Mich.	T(Den)-'10	15/4
67	Sims, Rob	G	6-3	312	12/6/83	6	Ohio State	Macedonia, Ohio	T(Sea)-'10	16/16
27	Smith, Alphonso	CB	5-9	190	10/20/85	3	Wake Forest	Pahokee, Fla.	T(Den)-'10	12/10
34	Smith, Kevin	RB	6-1	217	12/17/86	4	Central Florida	Miami, Fla.	D3-'08	6/0
42	Spievey, Amari	CB	5-11	195	4/15/88	2	Iowa	Middleton, Conn.	D3-'10	15/9
9	Stafford, Matthew	QB	6-3	232	2/7/88	3	Georgia	Highland Park, Texas	D1a-'09	3/3
5	Stanton, Drew	QB	6-3	230	5/7/84	5	Michigan State	Farmington Hills, Mich.	D2a-'07	6/3
90	Suh, Ndamukong	DT	6-4	307	1/6/87	2	Nebraska	Portland, Ore.	D1a-'10	16/16
74	Thomas, Donald	G	6-4	310	9/25/85	4	Connecticut	New Haven, Conn.	FA-'10	0*
62	Turner, Barry	DE	6-3	265	1/7/87	2	Nebraska	Nashville, Tenn.	W(Chi)-'10	1/0*
71	Ugoh, Tony	T	6-5	301	11/17/83	5	Arkansas	Houston, Texas	FA-'10	0*
93	Vanden Bosch, Kyle	DE	6-4	278	11/17/78	11	Nebraska	Larchwood, Iowa	UFA(Tenn)-'10	11/11
30	Vasher, Nathan	CB	5-11	185	11/17/81	8	Texas	Texarkana, Texas	FA-'10	14/5
29	Wendling, John	S	6-1	222	6/4/83	5	Wyoming	Rock Springs, Wyo.	FA-'10	16/0
99	Williams, Corey	DT	6-4	320	8/17/80	8	Arkansas State	Camden, Ark.	T(Cle)-'10	16/16
12	Williams, Derrick	WR	5-11	197	7/6/86	3	Penn State	Greenbelt, Md.	D3b-'09	7/1
31	Williams, Jack	CB	5-9	183	3/27/85	4	Kent State	Norfolk, Va.	W(Den)-'09	0*
79	Young, Willie	DE	6-4	251	9/19/85	2	North Carolina State	Palm Beach Gardens, Fla.	D7a-'10	2/0

* Bosworth missed '10 season because of injury; B. Carpenter played 5 games with Dallas and 10 games with Detroit in '10; Coleman played 12 games with Atlanta; DeVries missed '10 season because of injury; Dickson missed '10 season because of injury; Dizon missed '10 season because of injury; King played 4 games with Cleveland and 3 games with Detroit; Nordin missed '10 season because of injury; Robinson did not play in 2 games, inactive for 6 games; Thomas inactive for 6 games; Turner played 1 game with Chicago; Ugoh inactive for 4 games; J. Williams missed '10 season because of injury.

Also played with Lions in '10—TE Spencer Havner (5 games), LB Julian Peterson (15), CB Jonathan Wade (8), CB Dante Wesley (3).

^ "NFL Exp." as of 2011 Kickoff Weekend. For full explanation of how a player's NFL Experience is measured, refer to explanation underneath the First-Year Roster listed below.

FIRST-YEAR ROSTER

Name	Pos.	Ht.	Wt.	Birthdate	College	Hometown	How Acq.
Callaway, Robert (1)	DT	6-5	312	2/14/88	Saginaw Valley State	Mt. Morris, Mich.	FA-'10
Campbell, Caleb (1)	LB	6-2	237	6/19/86	Army	Perryton, Texas	FA-'10
Clapp, Matt (1)	FB	6-2	246	12/6/86	Oklahoma	Phoenix, Ariz.	FA-'10
Culbreath, Johnny	T	6-5	322	5/18/88	South Carolina State	Monroe, Ga.	D7
Fairley, Nick	DT	6-3	291	1/23/88	Auburn	Mobile, Ala.	D1
Finley, Joe Jon (1)	TE	6-6	251	1/30/85	Oklahoma	Arlington, Texas	FA-'10
Gerberry, Dan (1)	C	6-3	302	11/10/85	Ball State	Austintown, Ohio	FA-'09
Hogue, Doug	LB	6-2	235	2/1/89	Syracuse	Yonkers, N.Y.	D5
Johnson, Ian (1)	RB	5-11	212	9/25/85	Boise State	San Dimas, Calif.	FA-'10
Leshoure, Mikel	RB	6-0	227	3/30/90	Illinois	Champaign, Ill.	D2b
Moore, Michael (1)	WR	6-2	210	4/6/86	Georgia	Coconut Creek, Fla.	FA-'10
Phillips, Randy (1)	S	6-1	210	9/14/86	Miami	Belle Grade, Fla.	FA-'10
Pratt, Paul (1)	CB	5-10	185	5/1/85	Nevada-Reno	Woodland Hills, CA	FA-'09
Toone, Tim (1)	WR	5-10	185	2/14/85	Weber State	Peoria, Ariz.	D7b-'10
Young, Titus	WR	5-11	174	8/21/89	Boise State	Los Angeles, Calif.	D2a

The term NFL Rookie is defined as a player who is in his first season of professional football and has not been on the roster of another professional football team for any regular-season or postseason games. A Rookie is designated by an "R" on NFL rosters. Players who have been active in another professional football league or players who have NFL experience, including either preseason training camp or being on an Active List or Inactive List, or on Reserve/Injured or Reserve/Physically Unable to Perform for fewer than six regular-season games, are termed NFL First-Year Players. An NFL First-Year Player is designated by a "1" on NFL rosters. Thereafter, a player is credited with an additional year of experience for each season in which he accumulates six games on the Active List or Inactive List, or on Reserve/Injured or Reserve/Physically Unable to Perform.

Log on to www.detroitlions.com for an up-to-date roster.

COACHING STAFF

Head Coach,
Jim Schwartz

Pro Career: Named Lions' twenty-fifth head coach on January 16, 2009. Schwartz enters his third season in Detroit after helping the team finish the 2010 season on a four-game winning streak. He came to Detroit following 10 seasons with the Tennessee Titans, including the past eight as defensive coordinator. As the Titans' defensive coordinator since 2001, Schwartz's defensive unit held firm in two major defensive categories that factored significantly in the team's overall success; rushing defense and third-down conversion. From 2001-08, Tennessee ranked fifth in rushing yards allowed per game (103.5) and sixth in third-down conversion percentage (36.1). Before joining the Titans in 1999, he spent three years (1996-98) as a defensive assistant/quality control coach with the Baltimore Ravens. During his tenure in Baltimore, he also coached the team's outside linebackers. After the Cleveland Browns moved to Baltimore following the 1995 season, Schwartz made the transition from player personnel to coaching. From 1993-95, he worked in the Browns' player personnel department, serving as both a college and pro scout. Career record: 8-24.

Background: Schwartz worked on the college level for four years before moving onto the NFL. He began his coaching career as a graduate assistant coach at the University of Maryland, tutoring the Terrapins' linebackers in 1989 and then served as graduate assistant at the University of Minnesota (1990). He became a position coach in the secondary at North Carolina Central (1991) before moving to Colgate (1992) as linebackers coach. Played collegiately at Georgetown University where he lettered four years at linebacker. In 1988 he earned numerous honors that include Division III CoSIDA/GTE Academic All-America, All-America and team captain.

Personal: Born June 2, 1966, in Baltimore, Md. He and his wife, Kathy, have twins Christian and Allison along with a younger daughter Maria. He earned a degree in economics at Georgetown as well as Distinguished Economics Graduate honors.

ASSISTANT COACHES

Jason Arapoff, director of physical development; born July 8, 1965, Weymouth, Mass. Defensive back Springfield College 1985-88. No pro playing experience. Pro coach: Washington Redskins 1992-2000, joined Lions in 2001.

Bradford Banta, asst. special teams; born December 14, 1979, Baton Rouge, La. Tight end Southern California 1990-93, Pro tight end/long snapper Indianapolis Colts 1993-99, New York Jets 2000, Detroit Lions 2001-03, Buffalo Bills 2004.

College coach: Tennessee-Chattanooga 2007. Pro coach: Joined Lions in 2008.

Matt Burke, linebackers; born March 25, 1976, Hudson, Mass. Safety Dartmouth 1994-97. No pro playing experience. College coach: Boston College 2000-02, Harvard 2003. Pro coach: Tennessee Titans 2006-08, joined Lions in 2009.

Don Clemons, defensive quality control; born February 15, 1954, Newark, N.J. Defensive end Muhlenberg (Pa.) 1973-76. No pro playing experience. College coach: Kutztown State 1977-78, New Mexico 1979, Arizona State 1980-84. Pro coach: Joined Lions in 1985.

Danny Crossman, special teams: born January 17, 1967, El Paso, Texas. Defensive back Kansas 1985, Pittsburgh 1987-89. Pro defensive back Washington Redskins 1990, Detroit Lions 1991-92. College coach: U.S. Coast Guard Academy 1993, Western Kentucky 1994-96, Central Florida 1997-98, Georgia Tech 1999-2001, Michigan State 2002. Pro coach: Carolina Panthers 2003-09, joined Lions in 2010.

Gunther Cunningham, defensive coordinator; born June 19, 1946, Munich, Germany. Linebacker/placekicker Oregon 1966-68. No pro playing experience. College coach: Oregon 1969-1971, Arkansas 1972, Stanford 1973-76, California 1977-1980. Pro coach: Hamilton Tiger-Cats (CFL) 1981, Baltimore/Indianapolis Colts 1982-84, San Diego Chargers 1985-1990, L.A. Raiders 1991-94, Kansas City Chiefs 1995-2000, 2004-08 (head coach 1999-2000), Tennessee Titans 2001-03, joined Lions in 2009.

Todd Downing, asst. quarterbacks; born July 22, 1980, Eden Prairie, Minn. Attended Minnesota. No college or pro playing experience. Pro coach: Minnesota Vikings 2003-05, St. Louis Rams 2006-08, joined Lions in 2009.

Sam Gash, running backs; born March 7, 1969, Henderson, N.C. Fullback Penn State 1987-1991. Pro fullback New England Patriots 1992-97, Buffalo Bills 1998-99, 2003, Baltimore Ravens 2000-02. Pro coach: New York Jets 2005-06, joined Lions in 2007.

Shawn Jefferson, wide receivers; born February 22, 1969, Jacksonville. Wide receiver Central Florida 1988-1990. Pro wide receiver San Diego Chargers 1991-95, New England Patriots 1996-99, Atlanta Falcons 2000-02, Detroit Lions 2003. Pro coach: Joined Lions in 2005.

Kris Kocurek, defensive line; born November 15, 1978. Defensive tackle Texas Tech 1997-2000. Pro defensive tackle Seattle Seahawks 2001, Tennessee Titans 2002. College coach: Texas Tech 2003, Texas A&M-Kingsville 2004-05, Texas A&M-Commerce 2006, West Texas A&M 2007, Stephen F. Austin State 2008. Pro coach: Joined Lions in 2009.

Tim Lappano, tight ends: born October

14, 1956, Spokane, Wash. Running back Idaho 1978-1981. No pro playing experience. College coach: Idaho 1982-85, Wyoming 1986, Washington State 1987-1991, California 1992-95, Wyoming 1996, Purdue 1997, Oregon State 2000-02, Washington 2005-08. Pro coach: Seattle Seahawks 1998, San Francisco 49ers 2003-04, joined Lions in 2009.

Scott Linehan, offensive coordinator; born September 17, 1963, Sunnyside, Wash. Quarterback Idaho 1982-86. No pro playing experience. College coach: Idaho 1989-1990, 1992-93, Nevada-Las Vegas 1991, Washington 1994-98, Louisville 1999-2001. Pro coach: Minnesota Vikings 2002-04, Miami Dolphins 2005, St Louis Rams 2006-08 (head coach), joined Lions in 2009.

Ted Rath, strength and conditioning assistant: born November 22, 1983. Linebacker Toledo 2003-06. No pro playing experience. College coach: Toledo 2007-09. Pro coach: Joined Lions in 2009.

Tim Walton, secondary; born March 11, 1971. Defensive back Ohio State 1990-94. No pro playing experience. College coach: Bowling Green 1995-99, Memphis 2000-01, 2008, Syracuse 2002, Louisiana State 2003, Miami 2004-07. Pro coach: Joined Lions in 2009.

George Yarno, offensive line; born August 12, 1957, Spokane, Wash. Offensive line Washington State 1975-78. Pro offensive line Tampa Bay Buccaneers 1979-1983, 1985-87, Denver Gold (USFL) 1984-85, Atlanta Falcons 1988, Houston Oilers 1989, Green Bay Packers 1990. College coach: Louisiana State 2001-02, Washington State 2003-07. Pro coach: Tampa Bay Buccaneers 2008, joined Lions in 2009.

National Football Conference
North Division
Team Colors: Dark Green, Gold, and White
Lambeau Field Atrium
1265 Lombardi Avenue
Green Bay, Wisconsin 54304
Telephone: (920) 569-7500

2011 SCHEDULE
PRESEASON
Aug. 13 at Cleveland 6:30
Aug. 19 **Arizona** 7:00
Aug. 26 at Indianapolis 7:00
Sep. 1 **Kansas City** 7:00

REGULAR SEASON
Sep. 8 **New Orleans** (Thu) 7:30
Sep. 18 at Carolina 12:00
Sep. 25 at Chicago 3:15
Oct. 2 **Denver** 3:15
Oct. 9 at Atlanta 7:20
Oct. 16 **St. Louis** 12:00
Oct. 23 at Minnesota 3:15
Oct. 30 BYE
Nov. 6 at San Diego 3:15
Nov. 14 **Minnesota** (Mon) 7:30
Nov. 20 **Tampa Bay** 12:00
Nov. 24 at Detroit (Thu) 11:30a
Dec. 4 at New York Giants 3:15
Dec. 11 **Oakland** 12:00
Dec. 18 at Kansas City 12:00
Dec. 25 **Chicago** 7:20
Jan. 1 **Detroit** 12:00
All times CT

Stadium: Lambeau Field (opened in 1957)
  •**Capacity:** 72,928
   1265 Lombardi Avenue
   Green Bay, Wisconsin 54304
Playing Surface: DD GrassMaster
Training Camp: St. Norbert College
   De Pere, Wisconsin 54115

LAMBEAU FIELD

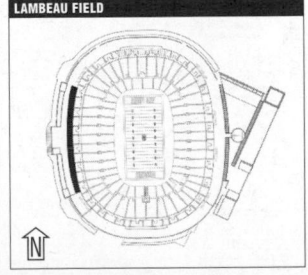

CLUB OFFICIALS
President and Chief Executive Officer:
  Mark Murphy
Executive Vice President/General
  Manager/Director of Football
  Operations: Ted Thompson
Vice President of Football Administration/
  Player Finance: Russ Ball
Vice President of Finance: Paul Baniel
Vice President of Sales and Marketing:
  Tim Connolly
Vice President of Organizational/Staff
  Development: Betsy Mitchell
Vice President of Administration/
  General Counsel: Jason Wied
Director of College Scouting:
  John Dorsey
Director-Football Operations:
  Reggie McKenzie
Director of Player Development:
  Rob Davis
Interim Director of Public Relations:
  Aaron Popkey
Assistant Director of Public Relations:
  Sarah Quick
Communications Manager: Tom Fanning
Public Relations Coordinator:
  Jonathan Butnick
Director of Ticket Operations:
  Mark Wagner
Director of Marketing and Corporate
  Sales: Craig Benzel
Director of Premium Sales and Guest
  Services: Jennifer Ark
Director of Retail Operations:
  Kate Hogan
Director of Information Technology:
  Wayne Wichlacz
Director of Facility Operations:
  Ted Eisenreich
Director of Corporate Security/Risk
  Management: Doug Collins
Manager of Community Outreach &
  Player/Alumni Relations:
  Cathy Dworak
Director of Packers Media Group:
  Joan Malcheski
Internet Coordinator: Duke Bobber
Assistant Director of College Scouting:
  Shaun Herock
College Scouts: Lee Gissendaner,
  Brian Gutekunst, Alonzo Highsmith,
  Sam Seale, Jon-Eric Sullivan,
  Richmond Williams
Scouting Coordinator: Danny Mock
Scouting Assistant: Chad Brinker
Assistant Directors of Pro Personnel:
  Tim Terry, Eliot Wolf
Director of Research and Development:
  Mike Eayrs
Coaching Administrator: Jason Simmons
Strength and Conditioning Assistants:
  Thadeus Jackson, Zac Woodfin
Football Administration Coordinator:
  Matt Klein
Video Director: Bob Eckberg
Head Athletic Trainer: Pepper Burruss
Equipment Manager: Gordon (Red) Batty

COACHING HISTORY
(693-540-36)
Records include postseason games
1921-1949 Earl (Curly) Lambeau .212-106-21
1950-53 Gene Ronzani* 14-31-1
1953 Hugh Devore-
  Ray (Scooter) McLean**..0-2-0
1954-57 Lisle Blackbourn...........17-31-0
1958 Ray (Scooter) McLean....1-10-1
1959-1967 Vince Lombardi 98-30-4
1968-1970 Phil Bengtson 20-21-1
1971-74 Dan Devine..................25-28-4
1975-1983 Bart Starr 53-77-3
1984-87 Forrest Gregg 25-37-1
1988-1991 Lindy Infante...............24-40-0
1992-98 Mike Holmgren 84-42-0
1999 Ray Rhodes....................8-8-0
2000-05 Mike Sherman 59-43-0
2006-2010 Mike McCarthy............53-34-0
  *Resigned after 10 games in 1953
  **Co-coaches

PAID ATTENDANCE
Home 566,362   Away 539,294
Total 1,105,656
Single-game home record,
  71,213 (11/1/09)
Single-season home record,
  566,418 (2007)

2011 DRAFT CHOICES

Round	Name	Pos.	College
1	Derek Sherrod	T	Mississippi State
2	Randall Cobb	WR	Kentucky
3	Alex Green	RB	Hawaii
4	Davon House	DB	New Mexico St.
5	D.J. Williams	TE	Arkansas
6	Caleb Schlauderaff	G	Utah
	D.J. Smith	LB	Appalachian St.
	Ricky Elmore	LB	Arizona
7	Ryan Taylor	TE	North Carolina
	Lawrence Guy	DT	Arizona State

2010 TEAM RECORD

PRESEASON (2-2)

Date	Result	Opponent
8/14	L 24-27	Cleveland
8/21	W 27-24	at Seattle
8/26	W 59-24	Indianapolis
9/2	L 13-17	at Kansas City

REGULAR SEASON (10-6)

Date	Result	Opponent
9/12	W 27-20	at Philadelphia
9/19	W 34-7	Buffalo
9/27	L 17-20	at Chicago
10/3	W 28-26	Detroit
10/10	L 13-16	at Washington (OT)
10/17	L 20-23	Miami (OT)
10/24	W 28-24	Minnesota
10/31	W 9-0	at New York Jets
11/7	W 45-7	Dallas
11/21	W 31-3	at Minnesota
11/28	L 17-20	at Atlanta
12/5	W 34-16	San Francisco
12/12	L 3-7	at Detroit
12/19	L 27-31	at New England
12/26	W 45-17	New York Giants
1/2	W 10-3	Chicago

POSTSEASON (4-0)

Date	Result	Opponent
1/9	W 21-16	at Philadelphia
1/15	W 48-21	at Atlanta
1/23	W 21-14	at Chicago
2/6	W 31-25	vs. Pittsburgh at North Texas

(OT) Overtime

SCORE BY PERIODS

Packers	74	120	110	84	0 —	388
Opponents	33	92	36	73	6 —	240

2010 TEAM STATISTICS

	Packers	Opp.
Total First Downs	312	270
Rushing	88	82
Passing	204	163
Penalty	20	25
3rd Down: Made/Att	85/205	77/213
3rd Down Pct.	41.5	36.2
4th Down: Made/Att	5/13	6/20
4th Down Pct.	38.5	30.0
Possession Avg.	31:36	28:24
Total Net Yards	5730	4945
Avg. Per Game	358.1	309.1
Total Plays	1000	969
Avg. Per Play	5.7	5.1
Net Yards Rushing	1606	1838
Avg. Per Game	100.4	114.9
Total Rushes	421	395
Net Yards Passing	4124	3107
Avg. Per Game	257.8	194.2
Sacked/Yards Lost	38/231	47/333
Gross Yards	4355	3440
Att./Completions	541/352	527/296
Completion Pct.	65.1	56.2
Had Intercepted	13	24
Punts/Average	71/43.9	78/44.8
Net Punting Avg.	71/37.6	78/39.1
Penalties/Yards	78/617	98/758
Fumbles/Ball Lost	20/9	22/8
Touchdowns	46	24
Rushing	11	6
Passing	31	16
Returns	4	2

2010 INDIVIDUAL STATISTICS

PASSING

	Att.	Comp.	Yds.	Pct.	TD	Int.	Tkld.	Rate
Rodgers	475	312	3922	65.7	28	11	31/193	101.2
Flynn	66	40	433	60.6	3	2	7/38	82.4
Packers	541	352	4355	65.1	31	13	38/231	98.9
Opponents	527	296	3440	56.2	16	24	47/333	67.2

SCORING

	TD R	TD P	TD Rt	PAT	FG	Saf	PTS
Crosby	0	0	0	46/46	22/28	0	112
Jennings	0	12	0	0/0	0/0	0	72
Kuhn	4	2	0	0/0	0/0	0	36
J. Jones	0	5	0	0/0	0/0	0	30
Driver	0	4	0	0/0	0/0	0	24
B. Jackson	3	1	0	0/0	0/0	0	24
Rodgers	4	0	0	0/0	0/0	0	24
D. Lee	0	3	0	0/0	0/0	0	18
Nelson	0	2	0	0/0	0/0	0	12
Bishop	0	0	1	0/0	0/0	0	6
Collins	0	0	1	0/0	0/0	0	6
Finley	0	1	0	0/0	0/0	0	6
Matthews	0	0	1	0/0	0/0	0	6
Quarless	0	1	0	0/0	0/0	0	6
Woodson	0	0	1	0/0	0/0	0	6
Packers	11	31	4	46/46	22/28	0	388
Opponents	6	16	2	24/24	24/29	0	240

2-Pt Conversions: Packers 0-0, Opponents 0-0.

RUSHING

	No.	Yds	Avg	LG	TD
B. Jackson	190	703	3.7	71	3
Rodgers	64	356	5.6	27	4
Kuhn	84	281	3.3	18	4
Starks	29	101	3.5	16	0
Nance	36	95	2.6	11	0
Grant	8	45	5.6	18	0
Flynn	9	26	2.9	12	0
Jennings	1	-1	-1.0	-1	0
Packers	421	1606	3.8	71	11
Opponents	395	1838	4.7	40	6

RECEIVING

	No.	Yds	Avg	LG	TD
Jennings	76	1265	16.6	86t	12
Driver	51	565	11.1	61t	4
J. Jones	50	679	13.6	66t	5
Nelson	45	582	12.9	80t	2
B. Jackson	43	342	8.0	37	1
Finley	21	301	14.3	34	1
Quarless	21	238	11.3	23	1
Kuhn	15	97	6.5	12	2
D. Lee	11	73	6.6	17	3
Swain	6	72	12.0	31	0
Crabtree	4	61	15.3	33	0
Nance	3	30	10.0	14	0
Q. Johnson	3	26	8.7	11	0
Starks	2	15	7.5	12	0
Hall	1	9	9.0	9	0
Packers	352	4355	12.4	86t	31
Opponents	296	3440	11.6	85t	16

INTERCEPTIONS

	No.	Yds	Avg	LG	TD
T. Williams	6	87	14.5	64	0
Collins	4	34	8.5	24	0
Hawk	3	31	10.3	21	0
Woodson	2	48	24.0	48t	1
Peprah	2	0	0.0	0	0
Shields	2	0	0	0	0
Matthews	1	62	62.0	62t	1
\Bishop	1	32	32.0	32t	1
Martin	1	15	15.0	15	0
Chillar	1	9	9.0	9	0
Burnett	1	0	0.0	0	0
Packers	24	318	13.3	64	3
Opponents	13	148	11.4	42	1

PUNTING

	No.	Yds.	Avg.	In 20	LG
Masthay	71	3114	43.9	25	62
Packers	71	3114	43.9	25	62
Opponents	78	3496	44.8	24	65

PUNT RETURNS

	Ret	FC	Yds	Avg	LG	TD
T. Williams	41	19	326	8.0	52	0
Shields	0	0	-1	—	-1	0
Packers	41	19	325	7.9	52	0
Opponents	31	18	341	11.0	62t	1

KICKOFF RETURNS

	No.	Yds	Avg	LG	TD
Nelson	22	496	22.5	51	0
Shields	21	452	21.5	49	0
P. Lee	13	265	20.4	30	0
Starks	2	25	12.5	17	0
Kuhn	1	8	8.0	8	0
Wilhelm	1	3	3.0	3	0
Driver	1	0	0.0	0	0
Simpkins	1	0	0.0	0	0
Packers	62	1249	20.1	51	0
Opponents	76	1658	21.8	71	0

FIELD GOALS

	1-19	20-29	30-39	40-49	50+
Crosby	1/1	7/8	4/5	8/10	2/4
Packers	1/1	7/8	4/5	8/10	2/4
Opponents	1/1	8/8	6/7	7/9	2/4

SACKS

	No.
Matthews	13.5
Jenkins	7.0
Raji	6.5
Zombo	4.0
Bishop	3.0
Walden	3.0
Woodson	2.0
Wynn	1.5
Chillar	1.0
Neal	1.0
Pickett	1.0
Poppinga	1.0
T. Williams	1.0
Wilson	1.0
Hawk	0.5
Packers	47.0
Opponents	38.0

RECORD HOLDERS
INDIVIDUAL RECORDS—CAREER

Category	Name	Performance
Rushing (Yds.)	Ahman Green, 2000-06, 2009	8,322
Passing (Yds.)	Brett Favre, 1992-2007	**61,655
Passing (TDs)	Brett Favre, 1992-2007	**442
Receiving (No.)	Donald Driver, 1999-2010	698
Receiving (Yds.)	James Lofton, 1978-1986	9,656
Interceptions	Bobby Dillon, 1952-59	52
Punting (Avg.)	Craig Hentrich, 1994-97	42.8
Punt Return (Avg.)	Desmond Howard, 1996, 1999	13.8
Kickoff Return (Avg.)	Travis Williams, 1967-1970	26.7
Field Goals	Ryan Longwell, 1997-2005	226
Touchdowns (Tot.)	Don Hutson, 1935-1945	105
Points	Ryan Longwell, 1997-2005	1,054
*Sacks	Kabeer Gbaja-Biamila, 2000-08	74.5

INDIVIDUAL RECORDS—SINGLE SEASON

Category	Name	Performance
Rushing (Yds.)	Ahman Green, 2003	1,883
Passing (Yds.)	Lynn Dickey, 1983	4,458
Passing (TDs)	Brett Favre, 1996	39
Receiving (No.)	Sterling Sharpe, 1993	112
Receiving (Yds.)	Robert Brooks, 1995	1,497
Interceptions	Irv Comp, 1943	10
Punting (Avg.)	Craig Hentrich, 1997	45.0
Punt Return (Avg.)	Billy Grimes, 1950	19.1
Kickoff Return (Avg.)	Travis Williams, 1967	**41.1
Field Goals	Chester Marcol, 1972	33
	Ryan Longwell, 2000	33
Touchdowns (Tot.)	Ahman Green, 2003	20
Points	Paul Hornung, 1960	176
*Sacks	Tim Harris, 1989	19.5

INDIVIDUAL RECORDS—SINGLE GAME

Category	Name	Performance
Rushing (Yds.)	Ahman Green, 12-28-03	218
Passing (Yds.)	Lynn Dickey, 10-12-80	418
Passing (TDs)	Many times	5
	Last time by Brett Favre, 9-27-98	
Receiving (No.)	Don Hutson, 11-22-42	14
Receiving (Yds.)	Billy Howton, 10-21-56	257
Interceptions	Bobby Dillon, 11-26-53	**4
	Willie Buchanon, 9-24-78	**4
Field Goals	Chris Jacke, 11-11-90, 10-14-96	5
	Ryan Longwell, 9-24-00	5
Touchdowns (Tot.)	Paul Hornung, 12-12-65	5
Points	Paul Hornung, 10-8-61	33
*Sacks	Vonnie Holliday, 12-22-02	5.0

*Sacks became an official statistic in 1982.
**NFL Record

VETERAN ROSTER AS OF MARCH 3, 2011

No.	Name	Pos.	Ht.	Wt.	Birthdate	^NFL Exp.	College	Hometown	How Acq.	'10 Games/ Starts
56	Barnett, Nick	LB	6-2	236	5/27/81	9	Oregon State	Fontana, Calif.	D1-'03	4/4
	Bell, Josh	CB	5-11	177	1/8/85	4	Baylor	Dallas, Texas	FA-'09	0*
20	Bigby, Atari	S	5-11	213	9/19/81	6	Central Florida	Miami, Fla.	FA-'05	4/0
55	Bishop, Desmond	LB	6-2	238	7/24/84	5	California	Fairfield, Calif.	D6b-'07	15/12
53	Briggs, Diyral	LB	6-3	248	10/31/85	3	Bowling Green	Mt. Healthy, Ohio	FA-'10	7/0*
75	Bulaga, Bryan	T	6-5	314	3/21/89	2	Iowa	Woodstock, Ill.	D1-'10	16/12
42	Burnett, Morgan	S	6-1	209	1/13/89	2	Georgia Tech	College Park, Ga.	D3-'10	4/4
24	Bush, Jarrett	CB/S	6-0	200	5/21/84	6	Utah State	Vacaville, Calif.	W(Car)-'06	16/1
54	Chillar, Brandon	LB	6-3	237	10/21/82	8	UCLA	Carlsbad, Calif.	UFA(StL)-'08	8/1
76	Clifton, Chad	T	6-5	320	6/26/76	12	Tennessee	Martin, Tenn.	D2-'00	16/16
73	Colledge, Daryn	G	6-4	308	2/11/82	6	Boise State	North Pole, Alaska	D2a-'06	16/16
36	Collins, Nick	S	5-11	207	8/16/83	7	Bethune-Cookman	Cross City, Fla.	D2a-'05	16/16
83	Crabtree, Tom	TE	6-4	245	11/4/85	2	Miami (OH)	Carroll, Ohio	FA-'09	16/1
2	Crosby, Mason	K	6-1	207	9/3/84	5	Colorado	Georgetown, Texas	D6c-'07	16/0
62	Dietrich-Smith, Evan	C/G	6-2	308	7/19/86	2	Idaho State	Salinas, Calif.	FA-'10	0*
80	Driver, Donald	WR	6-0	194	2/2/75	13	Alcorn State	Houston, Texas	D7b-'99	15/15
88	Finley, Jermichael	TE	6-5	247	3/26/87	4	Texas	Diboll, Texas	D3-'08	5/5
10	Flynn, Matt	QB	6-2	225	6/20/85	4	Louisiana State	Tyler, Texas	D7a-'08	7/1
49	Francois, Robert	LB	6-2	255	5/14/85	2	Boston College	Byfield, Mass.	FA-'09	8/1
61	Goode, Brett	LS	6-1	255	11/2/84	4	Arkansas	Fort Smith, Ark.	FA-'08	16/0
25	Grant, Ryan	RB	6-1	222	12/9/82	5	Notre Dame	Ramsey, N.J.	T(NYG)-'07	1/1
95	Green, Howard	DE	6-2	340	1/12/79	7	Louisiana State	Donaldsonville, La.	W(NYJ)-'10	11/3*
35	Hall, Korey	FB	6-0	236	8/5/83	5	Boise State	Glenns Ferry, Idaho	D6a-'07	12/6
91	Harrell, Justin	DE	6-4	315	2/14/84	5	Tennessee	Martin, Tenn.	D1-'07	1/0
41	Havner, Spencer	TE	6-3	250	2/2/83	3	UCLA	Grass Valley, Calif.	FA-'10	1/0
50	Hawk, A.J.	LB	6-1	247	1/6/84	6	Ohio State	Centerville, Ohio	D1-'06	16/15
32	Jackson, Brandon	RB	5-10	216	10/2/85	5	Nebraska	Horn Lake, Miss.	D2-'07	16/13
77	Jenkins, Cullen	DE	6-2	305	1/20/81	8	Central Michigan	Belleville, Mich.	FA-'04	11/8
85	Jennings, Greg	WR	5-11	198	9/21/83	6	Western Michigan	Kalamazoo, Mich.	D2b-'06	16/16
45	Johnson, Quinn	FB	6-1	263	9/30/86	3	Louisiana State	Edgard, La.	D5a-'09	11/4
59	Jones, Brad	LB	6-3	242	4/1/86	3	Colorado	East Lansing, Mich.	D7-'09	6/5
89	Jones, James	WR	6-1	208	3/31/84	5	San Jose State	San Jose, Calif.	D3a-'07	16/3
30	Kuhn, John	RB	6-0	250	9/9/82	6	Shippensburg	York, Pa.	W(Pitt)-'07	16/2
70	Lang, T.J.	T/G	6-4	318	9/20/87	3	Eastern Michigan	Birmingham, Mich.	D4-'09	12/0
22	Lee, Pat	CB	6-0	196	2/20/84	4	Auburn	Miami, Fla.	D2c-'08	11/1
8	Masthay, Tim	P	6-1	200	3/16/87	2	Kentucky	Murray, Ky.	FA-'10	16/0
52	Matthews, Clay	LB	6-3	255	5/14/86	3	Southern California	Agoura Hills, Calif.	D1b-'09	15/15
67	McDonald, Nick	C/G	6-4	316	6/27/87	2	Grand Valley State	Sterling Heights, Mich.	FA-'10	0*
23	Nance, Dimitri	RB	5-10	219	2/18/88	2	Arizona State	Euless, Texas	PS(Atl)-'10	12/0
96	Neal, Mike	DE	6-3	294	6/26/87	2	Purdue	Merrillville, Ind.	D2-'10	2/0
87	Nelson, Jordy	WR	6-3	217	5/31/85	4	Kansas State	Riley, Kan.	D2a-'08	16/4
74	Newhouse, Marshall	G/T	6-4	319	9/29/88	2	Texas Christian	Dallas, Texas	D5b-'10	0*
26	Peprah, Charlie	S	5-11	203	2/24/83	6	Alabama	Plano, Texas	FA-'10	14/11
79	Pickett, Ryan	DE	6-2	340	10/8/79	11	Ohio State	Zephyrhills, Fla.	UFA(StL)-'06	14/12
51	Poppinga, Brady	LB	6-3	250	9/21/79	7	Brigham Young	Evanston, Wyo.	D4b-'05	6/1
81	Quarless, Andrew	TE	6-4	252	10/6/88	2	Penn State	Uniondale, N.Y.	D5a-'10	13/3
90	Raji, B.J.	NT	6-2	337	7/11/86	3	Boston College	Washington Township, N.J.	D1a-'09	16/16
12	Rodgers, Aaron	QB	6-2	225	12/2/83	7	California	Chico, Calif.	D1-'05	15/15
37	Shields, Sam	CB	5-11	184	12/8/87	2	Miami	Sarasota, Fla.	FA-'10	14/6
71	Sitton, Josh	G	6-3	318	6/6/86	4	Central Florida	Pensacola, Fla.	D4b-'08	16/16
27	Smith, Anthony	S	6-0	200	9/20/83	6	Syracuse	Hubbard, Ohio	T(Jax)-'10	7/3*
72	Spitz, Jason	C/G	6-3	305	12/19/82	6	Louisville	Jacksonville, Fla.	D3b-'06	16/0
44	Starks, James	RB	6-2	218	2/25/86	2	Buffalo	Niagara Falls, N.Y.	D6-'10	3/0
16	Swain, Brett	WR	6-0	200	6/21/85	3	San Diego State	Carlsbad, Calif.	D7b-'08	16/1
65	Tauscher, Mark	T	6-3	320	6/17/77	12	Wisconsin	Auburndale, Wis.	D7a-'00	4/4
28	Underwood, Brandon	CB	6-1	191	6/24/86	3	Cincinnati	Hamilton, Ohio	D6b-'09	12/0
93	Walden, Erik	LB	6-2	250	8/21/85	4	Middle Tennessee State	Dublin, Ga.	FA-'10	11/2*
63	Wells, Scott	C	6-2	300	1/7/81	8	Tennessee	Brentwood, Tenn.	D7-'04	16/16
57	Wilhelm, Matt	LB	6-4	247	2/2/81	9	Ohio State	Elyria, Ohio	FA-'10	7/0
38	Williams, Tramon	CB	5-11	191	3/16/83	5	Louisiana Tech	Napoleonville, La.	FA-'06	16/16
98	Wilson, C.J.	DE	6-3	290	3/30/87	2	East Carolina	Pinetown, N.C.	D7-'10	15/2
21	Woodson, Charles	CB	6-1	202	10/7/76	14	Michigan	Fremont, Ohio	UFA(Oak)-'06	16/16
94	Wynn, Jarius	DE	6-3	285	8/29/86	3	Georgia	Lincolnton, Ga.	D6a-'09	9/0
58	Zombo, Frank	LB	6-3	254	3/5/87	2	Central Michigan	Sterling Heights, Mich.	FA-'10	13/8

* Bell missed '10 season because of injury; Briggs played 1 game with San Francisco, 1 game with Denver and 5 games with Green Bay in '10; Dietrich-Smith inactive for 4 games with Seattle and 1 game with Green Bay; Green played 2 games with New York Jets and 9 games with Green Bay; McDonald inactive for 16 games; Newhouse inactive for 15 games and on injured reserve for 1 game; Smith played 3 games with Jacksonville and 4 games with Green Bay; Walden played 2 games with Miami and 9 games with Green Bay.

Also played with Packers in '10—TE Donald Lee (15 games), S Derrick Martin (5), DE Michael Montgomery (2), LB Maurice Simpkins (2).

^ "NFL Exp." as of 2011 Kickoff Weekend. For full explanation of how a player's NFL Experience is measured, refer to explanation underneath the First-Year Roster listed below.

FIRST-YEAR ROSTER

Name	Pos.	Ht.	Wt.	Birthdate	College	Hometown	How Acq.
Battles, Adrian (1)	G	6-3	318	10/30/86	Minnesota State	Milwaukee, Wisc.	FA-'10
Campbell, Chris (1)	T	6-5	328	9/22/86	Eastern Illinois	Chicago, Ill.	FA-'10
Cobb, Randall	WR	5-10	192	8/22/90	Kentucky	Alcoa, Tenn.	D2
Elmore, Ricky	LB	6-4	256	2/1/88	Arizona	Simi Valley, Calif.	D6c
Gordy, Josh (1)	CB	5-11	195	2/9/87	Central Michigan	Sandersville, Ga.	FA-'10
Greco, Michael (1)	S	6-3	224	2/26/87	Central Florida	Ft. Lauderdale, Fla.	FA-'10
Green, Alex	RB	6-0	225	6/23/88	Hawai'i	Portland, Ore.	D3
Guy, Lawrence	DE	6-4	304	3/17/90	Arizona State	Las Vegas, Nev.	D7b
Harrell, Graham (1)	QB	6-2	215	5/22/85	Texas Tech	Ennis, Texas	FA-'10
House, Davon	CB	6-0	195	7/10/89	New Mexico State	Palmdale, Calif.	D4
Jackson, Cardia (1)	LB	6-1	236	10/13/88	Louisiana-Monroe	Monroe, La.	FA-'10
Levine, Anthony (1)	S	5-11	199	3/27/87	Tennessee State	Winston-Salem, N.C.	FA-'10
Robinson, Antonio (1)	WR	6-1	195	11/30/87	Nicholls State	Miami, Fla.	FA-'10
Ross, Jay (1)	NT	6-3	302	10/3/87	East Carolina	Wilmington, N.C.	FA-'10
Schlauderaff, Caleb	G	6-4	302	11/7/87	Utah	Shelton, Wash.	D6a
Sherrod, Derek	T	6-5	321	4/23/89	Mississippi State	Columbus, Miss.	D1
Smith, D.J.	LB	5-11	239	2/24/89	Appalachian State	Charlotte, N.C.	D6b
Taylor, Ryan	TE	6-3	254	11/16/87	North Carolina	Winston-Salem, N.C.	D7a
West, Chastin (1)	WR	6-1	216	5/1/87	Fresno State	Moorpark, Calif.	FA-'10
Williams, D.J.	TE	6-2	245	9/10/88	Arkansas	Little Rock, Ark.	D5
Young, Curtis (1)	LB/DE	6-1	270	1/8/87	Cincinnati	Cleveland, Ohio	FA-'10

The term NFL Rookie is defined as a player who is in his first season of professional football and has not been on the roster of another professional football team for any regular-season or postseason games. A Rookie is designated by an "R" on NFL rosters. Players who have had NFL experience, including either preseason training camp or being on an Active List or Inactive List, or on Reserve/Injured or Reserve/Physically Unable to Perform for fewer than six regular-season games, are termed NFL First-Year Players. An NFL First-Year Player is designated by a "1" on NFL rosters. Thereafter, a player is credited with an additional year of experience for each season in which he accumulates six games on the Active List or Inactive List, or on Reserve/Injured or Reserve/Physically Unable to Perform.

Log on to www.packers.com for an up-to-date roster.

COACHING STAFF
Head Coach,
Mike McCarthy

Pro Career: Named the fourteenth head coach in team history January 12, 2006. Having led Green Bay to the playoffs in three of his five seasons as head coach, he joined Vince Lombardi and Mike Holmgren as the only coaches to guide the Packers to a Super Bowl title with a win over Pittsburgh in Super Bowl XLV. Joined Pittsburgh's Bill Cowher (2005) as the only Super Bowl-winning coaches to lead their respective teams to three road wins as the No. 6 seed in the postseason en route to a world title. Including playoffs, Green Bay's 25 wins over the past two seasons rank third in the NFL behind only New Orleans and Indianapolis. His .714 winning percentage (5-2) in the playoffs is tied for first among active NFL coaches, matching the mark of Bill Belichick (15-6) and Mike Tomlin (5-2). The offense has ranked in the top 10 in total yards each of his five seasons as head coach, accumulating most points (461), fewest turnovers (16) and third-most yards (6,065) in team history in 2009. Named Motorola Coach of the Year, matched a franchise record with 13 wins, and won NFC North Division title in 2007. Became the first coach since Lombardi to lead Packers to a championship game in his second season. Had returned to Green Bay after serving as the team's quarterbacks coach in 1999. Was then a highly successful offensive coordinator for the New Orleans Saints (2000-04). With McCarthy calling plays, he was named NFC Assistant Coach of the Year by *USA Today* in 2000, and New Orleans led the league with 432 points and 49 touchdowns in 2002. The list of quarterbacks he has coached includes Joe Montana, Elvis Grbac, Rich Gannon, Brett Favre, Aaron Rodgers, Matt Hasselbeck, Aaron Brooks, Jake Delhomme, Marc Bulger, Steve Bono, and Jeff Blake—a collection that has combined for 36 career Pro Bowl selections and 10 Super Bowl starts. Career record: 53-34.

Background: Graduated with business administration degree from Baker University. Was an all-conference tight end (1985-86), helping the school to a NAIA Division II runner-up finish as a senior captain. Coached collegiately at Fort Hays State (1987-88) and Pittsburgh (1989-1992), before moving to the NFL with the Chiefs (1993-98), Packers (1999), Saints (2000-04) and 49ers (2005).

Personal: Born November 10, 1963, in Pittsburgh. Family includes daughters Alexandra and Gabrielle, wife Jessica and boys Jack and George.

ASSISTANT COACHES

Edgar Bennett, wide receivers; born February 15, 1969, Jacksonville. Running back Florida State 1987, 1989-1991. Pro running back Green Bay Packers 1992-96, Chicago Bears 1998-99. Pro coach: Joined Packers in 2001.

James Campen, offensive line; born June 11, 1964, Sacramento, Calif. Center Sacramento City (Calif.) J.C. 1982-83, Tulane 1984-85. Pro center New Orleans Saints 1987-88, Green Bay Packers 1989-1993. Pro coach: Joined Packers in 2004.

Dom Capers, defensive coordinator; born August 7, 1950, Cambridge, Ohio. Defensive back Mount Union 1968-1971. No pro playing experience. College coach: Kent State 1972-74, Hawaii 1975-76, San Jose State 1977, California 1978-79, Tennessee 1980-81, Ohio State 1982-83. Pro coach: Philadelphia/Baltimore Stars (USFL) 1984-85, New Orleans Saints 1986-1991, Pittsburgh Steelers 1992-94, Carolina Panthers 1995-98 (head coach), Jacksonville Jaguars 1999-2000, Houston Texans 2001-05 (head coach), Miami Dolphins 2006-07, New England Patriots 2008, joined Packers in 2009.

Tom Clements, quarterbacks; born June 18, 1953, McKees Rocks, Pa. Quarterback Notre Dame 1972-74. Pro quarterback Ottawa Rough Riders (CFL) 1975-78, Hamilton Tiger-Cats (CFL) 1979, 1981-82, Kansas City Chiefs 1980, Winnipeg Blue Bombers (CFL) 1983-87. College coach: Notre Dame 1992-95. Pro coach: New Orleans Saints 1997-99, Kansas City Chiefs 2000, Pittsburgh Steelers 2001-03, Buffalo Bills 2004-05, joined Packers in 2006.

Jerry Fontenot, running backs; born November 21, 1966, Lafayette, La. Guard Texas A&M 1985-88. Pro center Chicago Bears 1989-1996, New Orleans Saints 1997-2003, Cincinnati Bengals 2004. Pro coach: Joined Packers in 2006.

Kevin Greene, outside linebackers; born July 31, 1962, Schenectady, N.Y. Linebacker Auburn 1980-85. Pro linebacker Los Angeles Rams 1985-1992, Pittsburgh Steelers 1993-95, Carolina Panthers 1996, San Francisco 49ers 1997, Carolina Panthers 1998-99. Pro coach: Joined Packers in 2009.

Joel Hilgenberg, offensive quality control; born July 10, 1962, Iowa City, Iowa. Center Iowa 1980-83. Pro center/guard New Orleans Saints 1984-1993. Pro coach: Joined Packers in 2011.

Mark Lovat, strength & conditioning coordinator; born Oct. 9, 1969, Pocatello, Idaho. Attended Butler. No college or pro playing experience. Pro coach: Joined Packers in 1999.

Ben McAdoo, tight ends; born July 7, 1977, Homer City, Pa. Attended Indiana University (Pa.). No college or pro playing experience. College coach: Michigan State 2001, Fairfield 2002, Pittsburgh 2003, Akron 2004, Stanford 2005. Pro coach: New Orleans Saints 2004, San Francisco 49ers 2005, joined Packers in 2006.

Scott McCurley, defensive quality control; born August 1, 1980, New Castle, Pa.

Linebacker Pittsburgh 1998-2002. No pro playing experience. College coach: Pittsburgh 2003-05. Pro coach: Joined Packers in 2006.

Chad Morton, special teams assistant; born April 4, 1977, Torrance, Calif. Running back Southern California 1995-99. Pro running back New Orleans Saints 2000, N.Y. Jets 2001-02, Washington Redskins 2003-04, New York Giants 2005-06. Pro coach: Joined Packers in 2009.

Winston Moss, asst. head coach/inside linebackers; born December 24, 1965, Miami. Linebacker Miami 1983-86. Pro linebacker Tampa Bay Buccaneers 1987-1990, Los Angeles Raiders 1991-94, Seattle Seahawks 1995-97. Pro coach: Seattle Seahawks 1998, New Orleans Saints 2000-05, joined Packers in 2006.

Darren Perry, secondary-safeties; born December 29, 1968, Norfolk, Va. Safety Penn State 1989-1991. Pro safety Pittsburgh Steelers 1992-98, San Diego Chargers 1999, New Orleans Saints 2000. Pro coach: Cincinnati Bengals 2002, Pittsburgh Steelers 2003-06, Oakland Raiders 2007-08, joined Packers in 2009.

Joe Philbin, offensive coordinator; born July 2, 1961, Springfield, Mass. Tight end Washington & Jefferson 1980. No pro playing experience. College coach: Tulane 1984-85, Worcester Tech 1986-87, U.S. Merchant Marine Academy 1988-89, Allegheny 1990-93, Ohio University 1994, Northeastern 1995-96, Harvard 1997-98, Iowa 1999-2002. Pro coach: Joined Packers in 2003.

John Rushing, asst. wide receivers/special teams; born February 26, 1972, Merced, Calif. Defensive back Washington State 1991-94. No pro playing experience. College coach: Willamette (Ore.) 1996-97, Boise State 1998-99, Montana State 2000-02, Utah State 2003-08. Pro coach: Joined Packers in 2009.

Shawn Slocum, special teams coordinator; born February 21, 1965, Bryan, Texas. Linebacker Texas A&M 1983-84. No pro playing experience. College coach: Texas A&M 1989, 1991-97, 2000-02, Pittsburgh 1990, Southern California 1998-99, Mississippi 2005. Pro coach: Joined Packers in 2006.

Mike Trgovac, defensive line; born February 27, 1959, Youngstown, Ohio. Defensive lineman Michigan 1977-1980. No pro playing experience. College coach: Michigan 1984-85, Ball State 1986-88, Navy 1989, Colorado State 1990-91, Notre Dame 1992-94. Pro coach: Philadelphia Eagles 1995-98, Green Bay Packers 1999, Washington Redskins 2000-01, Carolina Panthers 2002-08, re-joined Packers in 2009.

Joe Whitt Jr., secondary-cornerbacks; born July 19, 1978, Auburn, Ala. Wide receiver Auburn 1997-99. No pro playing experience. College coach: Auburn 2000-01, The Citadel 2002, Louisville 2003-06. Pro coach: Atlanta Falcons 2007, joined Packers in 2008.

National Football Conference
North Division
Team Colors: Purple, Gold, and White
9520 Viking Drive
Eden Prairie, Minnesota 55344
Telephone: (952) 828-6500

2011 SCHEDULE
PRESEASON
Aug. 13 at Tennessee 7:00
Aug. 20 at Seattle..............................9:00
Aug. 27 **Dallas**................................7:00
Sep. 1 **Houston** 7:00

REGULAR SEASON
Sep. 11 at San Diego 3:15
Sep. 18 **Tampa Bay** 12:00
Sep. 25 **Detroit** 12:00
Oct. 2 at Kansas City 12:00
Oct. 9 **Arizona** 12:00
Oct. 16 at Chicago 7:20
Oct. 23 **Green Bay** 3:15
Oct. 30 at Carolina 12:00
Nov. 6 BYE
Nov. 14 at Green Bay (Mon) 7:30
Nov. 20 **Oakland** 12:00
Nov. 27 at Atlanta 12:00
Dec. 4 **Denver** 3:05
Dec. 11 at Detroit 12:00
Dec. 18 **New Orleans** 12:00
Dec. 24 at Washington (Sat)........12:00
Jan. 1 **Chicago** 12:00
All times CT
Stadium: Mall of America Field at
Hubert H. Humphrey Metrodome
(opened in 1982)
• **Capacity:** 64,111
425 Chicago Avenue
Minneapolis, Minnesota 55415
Playing Surface: Sportexe Momentum
Training Camp: Minnesota State-Mankato
Mankato, Minnesota
56001

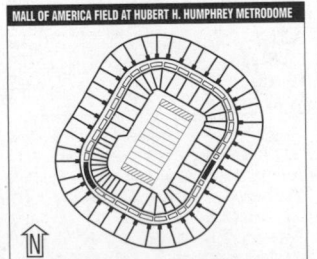

MALL OF AMERICA FIELD AT HUBERT H. HUMPHREY METRODOME

CLUB OFFICIALS
Owner/Chairman: Zygi Wilf
Owner/President: Mark Wilf
Owner/Vice Chairman: Leonard Wilf
Ownership Partners: Reggie Fowler,
Alan Landis, David Mandelbaum
Vice President of Public Affairs/Stadium
Development: Lester Bagley
Vice President of Football Operations:
Rob Brzezinski
Vice President of Sales and Marketing:
Steve LaCroix
Vice President of Finance: Steve Poppen
Vice President of Player Personnel:
Rick Spielman
Vice President of Operations and Legal
Counsel: Kevin Warren
Director of College Scouting:
Scott Studwell
Director of Public Relations: Bob Hagan
Director of Community Relations:
Brad Madson
Director of Operations/Team Travel:
Luther Hippe
Director of Operations & Facilities:
Chad Lundeen
Director of Ticketing and Hospitality:
Phil Huebner
Director of Video: Bob Marcus
Executive Director of Player
Development/Legal: Les Pico
Director of Security: Kim Klawiter
Head Athletic Trainer: Eric Sugarman
Equipment Manager: Dennis Ryan
Director of Marketing & Business
Development: Dannon Hulskotter
Director of Corporate Sales: Mike Slates
Director of Civic and Business Affairs:
Kimberly Fields

COACHING HISTORY
(432-362-9)
Records include postseason games
1961-66 Norm Van Brocklin 29-51-4
1967-1983 Bud Grant 161-99-5
1984 Les Steckel 3-13-0
1985 Bud Grant 7-9-0
1986-1991 Jerry Burns...............55-46-0
1992-2001 Dennis Green* 101-70-0
2001-05 Mike Tice 33-34-0
2006-2010 Brad Childress** 40-37-0
2010 Leslie Frazier.................3-3-0
*Resigned after 15 games in 2001
**Released after 10 games in 2010

PAID ATTENDANCE
Home 413,213   Away 545,025
Total 958,238
Single-game home record,
64,482 (11/2/03)
Single-season home record,
510,741 (1998)

2011 DRAFT CHOICES

Round	Name	Pos.	College
1	Christian Ponder	QB	Florida State
2	Kyle Rudolph	TE	Notre Dame
4	Christian Ballard	DT	Iowa
5	Brandon Burton	DB	Utah
6	DeMarcus Love	T	Arkansas
	Mistral Raymond	DB	South Florida
	Brandon Fusco	C	Slippery Rock
	Ross Homan	LB	Ohio State
7	D'Aundre Reed	DE	Arizona
	Stephen Burton	WR	West Texas A&M

2010 TEAM RECORD

PRESEASON (3-1)

Date	Result	Opponent
8/14	W 28-7	at St. Louis
8/22	L 10-15	at San Francisco
8/28	W 24-13	Seattle
9/2	W 31-24	Denver

REGULAR SEASON (6-10)

Date	Result	Opponent
9/9	L 9-14	at New Orleans
9/19	L 10-14	Miami
9/26	W 24-10	Detroit
10/11	L 20-29	at New York Jets
10/17	W 24-21	Dallas
10/24	L 24-28	at Green Bay
10/31	L 18-28	at New England
11/7	W 27-24	Arizona (OT)
11/14	L 13-27	at Chicago
11/21	L 3-31	Green Bay
11/28	W 17-13	at Washington
12/5	W 38-14	Buffalo
12/13	L 3-21	New York Giants
12/20	L 14-40	Chicago
12/28	W 24-14	at Philadelphia
1/2	L 13-20	at Detroit

(OT) Overtime

SCORE BY PERIODS

Vikings	51	81	85	61	3 —	281
Opponents	69	106	98	75	0 —	348

2010 TEAM STATISTICS

	Vikings	Opp.
Total First Downs	289	276
Rushing	104	87
Passing	159	178
Penalty	26	11
3rd Down: Made/Att	71/205	87/213
3rd Down Pct.	34.6	40.8
4th Down: Made/Att	8/17	5/10
4th Down Pct.	47.1	50.0
Possession Avg.	30:15	29:45
Total Net Yards	5039	5002
Avg. Per Game	314.9	312.6
Total Plays	982	977
Avg. Per Play	5.1	5.1
Net Yards Rushing	1942	1635
Avg. Per Game	121.4	102.2
Total Rushes	441	417
Net Yards Passing	3097	3367
Avg. Per Game	193.6	210.4
Sacked/Yards Lost	36/230	31/177
Gross Yards	3327	3544
Att./Completions	505/305	529/333
Completion Pct.	60.4	62.9
Had Intercepted	26	15
Punts/Average	83/43.0	85/44.1
Net Punting Avg.	83/38.9	85/38.9
Penalties/Yards	100/769	98/786
Fumbles/Ball Lost	20/11	17/11
Touchdowns	33	42
Rushing	16	10
Passing	14	25
Returns	3	7

2010 INDIVIDUAL STATISTICS

Passing	Att.	Comp.	Yds.	Pct.	TD	Int.	Tkld.	Rate
Favre	358	217	2509	60.6	11	19	22/139	69.9
Webb	89	54	477	60.7	0	3	8/48	60.9
Jackson	58	34	341	58.6	3	4	6/43	63.9
Vikings	505	305	3327	60.4	14	26	36/230	67.7
Opponents	529	333	3544	62.9	25	15	31/177	86.4

SCORING	TD R	TD P	TD Rt	PAT	FG	Saf	PTS
Longwell	0	0	0	30/31	17/18	0	81
Peterson	12	1	0	0/0	0/0	0	78
Harvin	1	5	1	0/0	0/0	0	44
Moss	0	2	0	0/0	0/0	0	12
Rice	0	2	0	0/0	0/0	0	12
Shiancoe	0	2	0	0/0	0/0	0	12
Webb	2	0	0	0/0	0/0	0	12
J. Allen	0	0	1	0/0	0/0	0	6
Camarillo	0	1	0	0/0	0/0	0	6
Gerhart	1	0	0	0/0	0/0	0	6
Tahi	1	0	0	0/0	0/0	0	6
Winfield	0	0	1	0/0	0/0	0	6
Vikings	16	14	3	30/31	17/18	0	281
Opponents	10	25	7	42/42	18/23	0	348

2-Pt Conversions: Harvin.
Vikings 1-2, Opponents 0-0.

RUSHING	No.	Yds	Avg	LG	TD
Peterson	283	1298	4.6	80t	12
Gerhart	81	322	4.0	21	1
Webb	18	120	6.7	16	2
Harvin	18	107	5.9	17t	1
Jackson	7	63	9.0	33	0
Young	13	29	2.2	6	0
Favre	17	8	0.5	10	0
Dugan	2	2	1.0	2	0
Tahi	1	1	1.0	1	0
Berrian	1	-8	-8.0	-8	0
Vikings	441	1942	4.4	80t	16
Opponents	417	1635	3.9	73	10

RECEIVING	No.	Yds	Avg	LG	TD
Harvin	71	868	12.2	53t	5
Shiancoe	47	530	11.3	33	2
Peterson	36	341	9.5	34	1
Berrian	28	252	9.0	30	0
Gerhart	21	167	8.0	23	0
Camarillo	20	240	12.0	31	1
Rice	17	280	16.5	46	2
Lewis	17	197	11.6	33	0
Kleinsasser	17	148	8.7	20	0
Moss	13	174	13.4	37t	2
Tahi	6	39	6.5	11	1
Booker	5	32	6.4	7	0
Dugan	4	30	7.5	10	0
Young	2	11	5.5	13	0
Baskett	1	18	18.0	18	0
Vikings	305	3327	10.9	53t	14
Opponents	333	3544	10.6	67t	25

INTERCEPTIONS	No.	Yds	Avg	LG	TD
E.J. Henderson	3	10	3.3	10	0
Abdullah	3	5	1.7	5	0
Winfield	2	41	20.5	41	0
J. Allen	2	40	20.0	36t	1
A. Allen	2	27	13.5	27	0
Leber	1	19	19.0	19	0
Walker	1	10	10.0	10	0
M. Williams	1	0	0.0	0	0
Vikings	15	152	10.1	41	1
Opponents	26	427	16.4	66	3

PUNTING	No.	Yds.	Avg.	In 20	LG
Kluwe	83	3569	43.0	32	59
Vikings	83	3569	43.0	32	59
Opponents	85	3748	44.1	28	60

PUNT RETURNS	Ret	FC	Yds	Avg	LG	TD
Camarillo	39	20	359	9.2	52	0
Berrian	3	2	2	0.7	2	0
Vikings	42	22	361	8.6	52	0
Opponents	32	22	241	7.5	64t	1

KICKOFF RETURNS	No.	Yds	Avg	LG	TD
Harvin	40	933	23.3	95t	1
Booker	18	429	23.8	49	0
Dugan	2	8	4.0	5	0
Webb	1	30	30.0	30	0
Young	1	25	25.0	25	0
Brinkley	1	2	2.0	2	0
Kennedy	1	0	0.0	0	0
Vikings	64	1427	22.3	95t	1
Opponents	61	1455	23.9	96t	1

FIELD GOALS	1-19	20-29	30-39	40-49	50+
Longwell	0/0	7/7	8/9	2/2	0/0
Vikings	0/0	7/7	8/9	2/2	0/0
Opponents	0/0	6/6	7/8	3/6	2/3

SACKS	No.
J. Allen	11.0
Edwards	8.0
Guion	2.0
Robison	2.0
Winfield	2.0
Greenway	1.0
E.J. Henderson	1.0
Mitchell	1.0
Sanford	1.0
K. Williams	1.0
Kennedy	0.5
M. Williams	0.5
Vikings	31.0
Opponents	36.0

RECORD HOLDERS
INDIVIDUAL RECORDS—CAREER

Category	Name	Performance
Rushing (Yds.)	Robert Smith, 1993-2000	6,818
Passing (Yds.)	Fran Tarkenton, 1961-66, 1972-78	33,098
Passing (TDs)	Fran Tarkenton, 1961-66, 1972-78	239
Receiving (No.)	Cris Carter, 1990-2001	1,004
Receiving (Yds.)	Cris Carter, 1990-2001	12,383
Interceptions	Paul Krause, 1968-1979	53
Punting (Avg.)	Chris Kluwe, 2005-2010	44.2
Punt Return (Avg.)	Mewelde Moore, 2004-07	10.4
Kickoff Return (Avg.)	Charlie West, 1968-1973	25.5
Field Goals	Fred Cox, 1963-1977	282
Touchdowns (Tot.)	Cris Carter, 1990-2001	110
Points	Fred Cox, 1963-1977	1,365
*Sacks	John Randle, 1990-2000	114.0

INDIVIDUAL RECORDS—SINGLE SEASON

Category	Name	Performance
Rushing (Yds.)	Adrian Peterson, 2008	1,760
Passing (Yds.)	Daunte Culpepper, 2004	4,717
Passing (TDs)	Daunte Culpepper, 2004	39
Receiving (No.)	Cris Carter, 1994, 1995	122
Receiving (Yds.)	Randy Moss, 2003	1,632
Interceptions	Paul Krause, 1975	10
Punting (Avg.)	Chris Kluwe, 2008	47.6
Punt Return (Avg.)	David Palmer, 1995	13.2
Kickoff Return (Avg.)	Aundrae Allison, 2007	28.7
Field Goals	Gary Anderson, 1998	35
Touchdowns (Tot.)	Chuck Foreman, 1975	22
Points	Gary Anderson, 1998	164
*Sacks	Chris Doleman, 1989	21.0

INDIVIDUAL RECORDS—SINGLE GAME

Category	Name	Performance
Rushing (Yds.)	Adrian Peterson, 11-4-07	**296
Passing (Yds.)	Tommy Kramer, 11-2-86	490
Passing (TDs)	Joe Kapp, 9-28-69	**7
Receiving (No.)	Rickey Young, 12-16-79	15
Receiving (Yds.)	Sammy White, 11-7-76	210
Interceptions	Many Times	3
	Last time by Darren Sharper, 11-13-05	
Field Goals	Rich Karlis, 11-5-89	7
Touchdowns (Tot.)	Chuck Foreman, 12-20-75	4
	Ahmad Rashad, 9-2-79	4
Points	Chuck Foreman, 12-20-75	24
	Ahmad Rashad, 9-2-79	24
*Sacks	Randy Holloway, 9-16-84	5.0

*Sacks became an official statistic in 1982.
**NFL Record

VETERAN ROSTER AS OF MARCH 3, 2011

No.	Name	Pos.	Ht.	Wt.	Birthdate	^NFL Exp.	College	Hometown	How Acq.	'10 Games/ Starts
39	Abdullah, Husain	S	6-0	204	7/27/85	4	Washington State	Pomona, Calif.	FA-'08	15/15
21	Allen, Asher	CB	5-9	194	1/22/88	3	Georgia	Tucker, Ga.	D3-'09	14/11
69	Allen, Jared	DE	6-6	270	4/3/82	8	Idaho State	Los Gatos, Calif.	T(KC)-'08	16/16
67	Awasom, Adrian	DE	6-4	270	10/25/83	3	North Texas	Stafford, Texas	FA-'11	0*
19	Baskett, Hank	WR	6-3	212	9/4/82	6	New Mexico	Clovis, N.M.	FA-'10	6/0
87	Berrian, Bernard	WR	6-1	185	12/27/80	8	Fresno State	Winton, Calif.	UFA(Chi)-'08	14/9
27	Booker, Lorenzo	RB	5-10	201	6/14/84	4	Florida State	Ventura, Calif.	FA-'10	4/0
54	Brinkley, Jasper	LB	6-1	252	7/12/85	3	South Carolina	Thomson, Ga.	D5-'09	16/0
79	Brown, Pat	T	6-5	310	12/25/86	2	Central Florida	St. Charles, Ill.	FA-'10	0*
85	Camarillo, Greg	WR	6-2	200	4/18/82	6	Stanford	Atherton, Calif	T(Mia)-'10	16/1
22	Castille, Simeon	DB	6-0	190	10/12/85	2	Alabama	Birmingham, Ala.	FA-'10	0*
31	Cook, Chris	CB	6-2	212	2/15/87	2	Virginia	Lynchburg, Va.	D2a-'10	6/5
62	Cook, Ryan	G	6-6	328	5/8/83	6	New Mexico	Albuquerque, N.M.	D2b-'06	16/7
68	Cooper, Jon	C	6-2	291	10/1/86	3	Oklahoma	Fort Collins, Colo.	FA-'09	12/1
72	DeGeare, Chris	G	6-4	335	2/17/87	2	Wake Forest	Kernersville, N.C.	D5a-'10	8/5
83	Dugan, Jeff	TE	6-4	258	4/8/81	8	Maryland	Pittsburgh, Pa.	D7-'04	16/4
91	Edwards, Ray	DE	6-5	268	1/1/85	6	Purdue	Cincinnati, Ohio	D4-'06	14/14
90	Evans, Fred	DT	6-4	305	11/6/83	6	Texas St.-San Marcos	Morgan Park, Ill.	FA-'07	8/0
59	Farwell, Heath	LB	6-0	235	12/31/81	7	San Diego State	Corona, Calif.	FA-'05	16/0
37	Frampton, Eric	S	5-11	205	2/6/84	5	Washington State	San Jose, Calif.	W(Det)-'07	14/0
32	Gerhart, Toby	RB	6-0	231	3/28/87	2	Stanford	Norco, Calif.	D2b-'10	15/1
52	Greenway, Chad	LB	6-2	242	1/12/83	6	Iowa	Mt. Vernon, S.D.	D1-'06	16/16
97	Griffen, Everson	DE	6-3	273	12/22/87	2	Southern California	Avondale, Ariz.	D4-'10	11/0
23	Griffin, Cedric	CB	6-0	203	11/11/82	6	Texas	San Antonio, Texas	D2a-'06	2/2
98	Guion, Letroy	DT	6-4	303	6/21/87	4	Florida State	Starke, Fla.	D5b-'08	15/0
12	Harvin, Percy	WR	5-11	184	5/28/88	3	Florida	Virginia Beach, Va.	D1-'09	14/13
56	Henderson, E.J.	LB	6-1	245	8/3/80	9	Maryland	Aberdeen, Md.	D2-'03	16/16
50	Henderson, Erin	LB	6-3	244	7/1/86	4	Maryland	Aberdeen, Md.	FA-'08	9/0
64	Herrera, Anthony	G	6-2	315	6/14/80	8	Tennessee	Naples, Fla.	FA-'04	10/10
76	Hutchinson, Steve	G	6-5	313	11/1/77	11	Michigan	Ft. Lauderdale, Fla.	RFA(Sea)-'06	11/11
7	Jackson, Tarvaris	QB	6-2	225	4/21/83	6	Alabama State	Montgomery, Ala.	D2c-'06	3/1
11	Johnson, Jaymar	WR	6-0	176	7/10/84	2	Jackson State	Gary, Ind.	D6b-'08	0*
25	Johnson, Tyrell	S	6-0	207	5/19/85	4	Arkansas State	Rison, Ark.	D2-'08	7/2
73	Kennedy, Jimmy	DT	6-5	320	11/15/79	9	Penn State	Yonkers, N.Y.	FA(Jax)-'08	9/0
40	Kleinsasser, Jim	TE	6-3	272	1/31/77	13	North Dakota	Carrington, N.D.	D2-'99	16/7
5	Kluwe, Chris	P	6-4	215	12/24/81	7	UCLA	Los Alamitos, Calif.	W(Sea)-'05	16/0
51	Leber, Ben	LB	6-3	244	12/7/78	10	Kansas State	Vermillion, S.D.	UFA(SD)-'06	16/10
17	Lewis, Greg	WR	6-0	185	2/12/80	9	Illinois	Matteson, Ill.	FA-'09	13/5
71	Loadholt, Phil	T	6-8	343	1/21/86	3	Oklahoma	Fountain, Colo.	D2-'09	16/16
46	Loeffler, Cullen	LS	6-5	241	1/27/81	8	Texas	Ingram, Texas	FA-'04	16/0
8	Longwell, Ryan	K	6-0	200	8/16/74	15	California	Bend, Ore.	UFA(GB)-'06	16/0
74	McKinnie, Bryant	T	6-8	335	9/23/79	10	Miami	Woodbury, N.J.	D1-'02	16/16
78	Olsen, Seth	G	6-5	312	12/17/85	2	Iowa	Omaha, Neb.	FA-'10	0*
55	Onatolu, Kenny	LB	6-2	225	10/8/82	3	Nebraska-Omaha	Papillion, Neb.	FA-'09	16/0
28	Peterson, Adrian	RB	6-1	217	3/21/85	5	Oklahoma	Palestine, Texas	D1-'07	15/15
9	Ramsey, Patrick	QB	6-3	240	2/14/79	9	Tulane	Ruston, La.	FA-'10	0*
18	Rice, Sidney	WR	6-4	202	9/1/86	5	South Carolina	Gaffney, S.C.	D2-'07	6/5
96	Robison, Brian	DE	6-3	259	4/27/83	5	Texas	Splendora, Texas	D4-'07	16/2
33	Sanford, Jamarca	S	5-10	200	8/27/85	3	Mississippi	Batesville, Miss.	D7-'09	12/2
29	Sheppard, Lito	CB	5-10	194	4/8/81	10	Florida	Jacksonville, Fla.	FA-'10	13/2
81	Shiancoe, Visanthe	TE	6-4	250	6/18/80	9	Morgan State	Laurel, Md.	UFA(NYG)-'07	16/9
65	Sullivan, John	C	6-4	301	8/8/85	4	Notre Dame	Old Greenwich, Conn.	D6a-'08	14/14
38	Tahi, Naufahu	FB	6-0	254	10/30/81	6	Brigham Young	West Valley City, Utah	PS(Cin)-'06	15/7
41	Walker, Frank	CB	5-11	194	8/6/81	9	Tuskegee	Tuskegee, Ala.	FA'10	11/2
14	Webb, Joe	QB	6-4	220	11/14/86	2	Alabama-Birmingham	Birmingham, Ala.	D6-'10	5/2
93	Williams, Kevin	DT	6-5	311	8/16/80	9	Oklahoma State	Fordyce, Ark.	D1-'03	16/16
20	Williams, Madieu	S	6-1	203	10/18/81	8	Maryland	Lanham, Md.	UFA(Cin)-'08	14/13
94	Williams, Pat	DT	6-3	317	10/24/72	15	Texas A&M	Monroe, La.	UFA(Buff)-'05	16/16
26	Winfield, Antoine	CB	5-9	180	6/24/77	13	Ohio State	Akron, Ohio	UFA(Buff)-'04	16/16
34	Young, Albert	RB	5-10	209	2/25/85	3	Iowa	Moorestown, N.J.	FA-'08	3/0

* Awasom last active with Giants '07; Brown did not play in 5 games, inactive for 1 game; Castille spent 2 game during missed '10 season on Minnesota practice squad, last active with San Diego in '09; J. Johnson missed '10 season because of injury; Olsen spent '10 season on Minnesota practice squad, last active with Denver in '09; Ramsey did not play in 2 games, inactive for 1 game.

Also played with Vikings in '10—DE Jayme Mitchell (2 games), WR Randy Moss (4), CB Marcus Sherels (1).

^ "NFL Exp." as of 2011 Kickoff Weekend. For full explanation of how a player's NFL Experience is measured, refer to explanation underneath the First-Year Roster listed below.

FIRST-YEAR ROSTER

Name	Pos.	Ht.	Wt.	Birthdate	College	Hometown	How Acq.
Arceneaux, Emmanuel	WR	6-2	215	9/17/87	Alcorn State	Alexandria, La.	FA
Ballard, Christian	DT	6-4	283	1/3/89	Iowa	Lawrence, Kan.	D4
Bomar, Rhett (1)	QB	6-2	225	7/2/85	Sam Houston State	Groesbeck, Texas	FA-'10
Brown, Freddie (1)	WR	6-4	204	6/24/86	Utah	La Verne, Calif.	FA-'10
Burton, Brandon	CB	5-11	190	7/31/89	Utah	Houston, Texas	D5
Burton, Stephen	WR	6-1	224	12/11/89	West Texas A&M	Lakewood, Calif.	D7b
D'Imperio, Ryan (1)	FB	6-3	240	8/15/87	Rutgers	Sewell, N.J.	D7b-'10
Fusco, Brandon	C	6-4	306	7/26/88	Slippery Rock	Cranberry Township, Pa.	D6c
Homan, Ross	LB	6-0	240	3/5/87	Ohio State	Coldwater, Ohio	D6d
Iglesias, Juaquin (1)	WR	6-1	202	8/22/87	Oklahoma	Killeen, Texas	PS(Chi)-'10
Johnson, Tremaine (1)	DT	6-2	285	9/26/85	Louisiana State	Galena Park, Texas	FA-'09
Love, DeMarcus	T	6-4	315	3/7/88	Arkansas	Lancaster, Texas	D6a
Parks, Cord (1)	DB	5-11	182	11/12/86	Northeastern	Stone Mountain, Ga.	FA-'10
Ponder, Christian	QB	6-2	229	2/25/88	Florida State	Colleyville, Texas	D1
Raymond, Mistral	S	6-1	194	9/7/87	South Florida	Palmetto, Fla.	D6b
Reed, D'Aundre	DE	6-4	260	1/1/88	Arizona	Moreno Valley, Calif.	D7a
Rudolph, Kyle	TE	6-6	258	11/9/89	Notre Dame	Cincinnati, Ohio	D2
Sherels, Marcus (1)	CB	5-10	175	9/30/87	Minnesota	Rochester, Minn.	FA-'10
Welch, Thomas (1)	T	6-6	300	6/19/87	Vanderbilt	Brentwood, Tenn.	FA-'10

The term NFL Rookie is defined as a player who is in his first season of professional football and has not been on the roster of another professional football team for any regular-season or postseason games. A Rookie is designated by an "R" on NFL rosters. Players who have been active in another professional football league or players who have NFL experience, including either preseason training camp or being on an Active List or Inactive List, or on Reserve/Injured or Reserve/Physically Unable to Perform for fewer than six regular-season games, are termed NFL First-Year Players. An NFL First-Year Player is designated by a "1" on NFL rosters. Thereafter, a player is credited with an additional year of experience for each season in which he accumulates six games on the Active List or Inactive List, or on Reserve/Injured or Reserve/Physically Unable to Perform.

Log on to www.vikings.com for an up-to-date roster.

COACHING STAFF
Head Coach,
Leslie Frazier

Pro Career: Named the eighth head coach in Vikings' history on January 3, 2011 after serving as the club's interim head coach for the final six games of the 2010 season. He guided the Vikings to a 3-3 record, picking up two road victories, despite having to move two home games off-site after the Metrodome roof collapsed due to a major Twin Cities snow storm. Before coming head coach of the Vikings, Frazier led one of the NFL's top defenses from 2007-10 in Minnesota. For the past three seasons (2008-2010) Frazier's defensive units ranked in the top 10 in total defense, a feat that hasn't been accomplished in Minnesota since 1992-94. Frazier enjoyed back-to-back NFC North division titles in 2008 and 2009 where his defense was first and second in the NFL against the run, respectively. Frazier's rush defense set the standard in 2007 as they allowed a measly 3.1 yards per carry that was tops in the league. Frazier won Super Bowl as a player (starting cornerback with the 1985 Chicago Bears in Super Bowl XX) and coach (Super Bowl XLI as a defensive backs coach with the Indianapolis Colts). In his 12 seasons as an NFL coach, and 11 years of collegiate experience prior to that, Frazier has suffered a losing season only twice (Philadelphia in 1999 and Vikings in 2010). He has coached on seven playoff teams in his 12 NFL seasons and been a part of six division championships. Career record: 3-3.
Background: Coached at Trinity (1988-1996) and Illinois (1997-98). Coached professionally with the Philadelphia Eagles (1999-2002), Cincinnati Bengals (2003-04), and Indianapolis Colts (2005-06) before joining the Minnesota Vikings as their assistant head coach/defensive coordinator in 2007. Played defensive back collegiately at Alcorn State (1977-1980) and professionally with the Chicago Bears (1981-86).
Personal: Born April 3, 1959 in Columbus, Miss. He and wife Gayle have three children: Kieron, Chantel and Corey, who plays defensive back at Rice. Frazier earned degree in business administration.

ASSISTANT COACHES
Juney Barnett, asst. strength and conditioning; born January 11, 1979, Philadelphia. Defensive back Bloomsburg 1997-2000. College coach: Bloomsburg 2001, Army 2005. Pro coach: Rhein Fire (NFLE) 2004-05, joined Vikings in 2006.
Jeff Davidson, offensive line; born October 3, 1967, Akron, Ohio. Offensive line Ohio State 1986-89. Pro offensive lineman Denver Broncos 1990-92, New Orleans Saints 1994. Pro coach: New Orleans Saints 1995-96, New England Patriots 1997-2004, Cleveland Browns 2005-06, Carolina Panthers 2007-10, joined Vikings in 2011.
Karl Dunbar, defensive line; born May 18, 1967, Plaisance, La. Defensive lineman Louisiana State 1986-89. Pro defensive lineman Pittsburgh Steelers 1990, New Orleans Saints 1992-93, Arizona Cardinals 1994-95. College coach: Nicholls State 1998-99, Louisiana State

2000-01, 2005, Oklahoma State 2002-03. Pro coach: Chicago Bears 2004, joined Vikings in 2006.
Ryan Ficken, asst. wide receivers; born February 20, 1980, Aurora, Colo. Wide receiver Arizona State 1998-99. No pro playing experience. College coach: UCLA 2004-06. Pro coach: Joined Vikings in 2007.
Jeff Imamura, defensive assistant/linebackers; born May 22, 1974, Lubbock, Texas. Attended Texas Christian. No college or pro playing experience. College coach: Texas Christian 1997-99, Northern Arizona 2000-02, Saginaw Valley State 2003. Pro coach: Joined Vikings in 2006.
Craig Johnson, quarterbacks; born March 3, 1960, Rome, N.Y. Quarterback Wyoming 1979-1982. No pro playing experience. College coach: Wyoming 1983, Arkansas 1984, Army 1985, Rutgers 1986-88, Virginia Military Institute 1989-1991, Northwestern 1992-96, Maryland 1997-99. Pro coach: Tennessee Titans 2000-10, joined Vikings in 2011.
Jimmie Johnson, tight ends; born October 6, 1966, Augusta, Ga. Tight end Howard 1985-88. Pro tight end Washington Redskins 1989-1991, Detroit Lions 1992-93, Kansas City Chiefs 1994, Philadelphia Eagles 1995-98. College coach: South Carolina State 2001, Shaw 2002-03, Texas Southern 2004-05. Pro coach: Joined Vikings in 2006.
Tom Kanavy, strength and conditioning; born April 8, 1970, Archbald, Pa. Attended Penn State. No college or pro playing experience. College coach: Miami 1993, Penn State 1993-95. Pro coach: Philadelphia Eagles 1995-2005, joined Vikings in 2006.
Bill Musgrave, offensive coordinator; born November 11, 1967, Grand Junction, Colo. Quarterback Oregon 1987-1990. Pro quarterback San Francisco 49ers 1991-94, Denver Broncos 1995-96. College coach: Virginia 2001-02. Pro coach: Oakland Raiders 1997, Philadelphia Eagles 1998, Carolina Panthers 1999-2000, Jacksonville Jaguars 2003-04, Washington Redskins 2005, Atlanta Falcons 2006-2010, joined Vikings in 2011.
Fred Pagac, defensive coordinator; born April 26, 1952, Richeyville, Pa. Tight end Ohio State 1971-73. Pro tight end Chicago Bears 1974, Tampa Bay Buccaneers 1976. College coach: Ohio State 1978-2000. Pro coach: Oakland Raiders 2001-03, Kansas City Chiefs 2004-05, joined Vikings in 2006.
Mike Priefer, special teams coordinator; born August 21, 1966, Cleveland. Quarterback/wide receiver Navy 1985-88. No pro playing experience. College coach: Navy 1994-96, Youngstown State 1997-98, Virginia Military Institute 1999, Northern Illinois 2000-01. Pro coach: Jacksonville Jaguars 2002, N.Y. Giants 2003-05, Kansas City Chiefs 2006-08, Denver Broncos 2009-10, joined Vikings in 2011.
Diron Reynolds, asst. defensive line; born February 23, 1971, Aiken, S.C. Linebacker Wake Forest 1990-93. No pro playing experience. College coach: Wake Forest 1997-2000, Indiana 2001. Pro coach: Indianapolis Colts 2002-06, Miami Dolphins 2007, joined Vikings in 2009.

James Saxon, running backs; born March 23, 1966, Beaufort, S.C. Running back American River (Calif.) C.C. 1984-85, San Jose State 1986-87. Pro running back Kansas City Chiefs 1988-1991, Miami Dolphins 1992-94, Philadelphia Eagles 1995. College coach: Rutgers 1997-98, Menlo 1999. Pro coach: Buffalo Bills 2000, Kansas City Chiefs 2001-07, Miami Dolphins 2008-10, joined Vikings in 2011.
Matt Sheldon, asst. defensive backs; born February 26, 1969, Berwyn, Ill. Cornerback Minnesota 1987-1991. No pro playing experience. College coach: Wisconsin 1997-99. Pro coach: St. Louis Rams 2001-2005, Buffalo Bills 2006-09, joined Vikings in 2010.
Ryan Silverfield, asst. offensive line; born August 4, 1980, Jacksonville, Fla. Attended Hampden-Sydney. No college or pro playing experience. College coach: Hampden-Sydney 2000-03, Jacksonville 2005, Central Florida 2006-07. Pro coach: Joined Vikings in 2008.
Mike Singletary, special asst. to head coach/linebackers; born October 9, 1958, Houston. Linebacker Baylor 1977-1980. Pro linebacker Chicago Bears 1981-1992. Pro coach: Baltimore Ravens 2003-04, San Francisco 49ers 2005-2010, joined Vikings in 2011.
Kevin Stefanski, asst. quarterbacks; born May 8, 1982, Philadelphia. Safety Pennsylvania 2000-04. College coach: Pennsylvania 2005. Pro coach: Joined Vikings in 2006.
George Stewart, wide receivers; born December 29, 1958, Little Rock, Ark. Guard Arkansas 1977-1980. No pro playing experience. College coach: Minnesota 1984-85, Notre Dame 1986-88. Pro coach: Pittsburgh Steelers 1989-1991, Tampa Bay Buccaneers 1992-95, San Francisco 49ers 1996-2002, Atlanta Falcons 2003-06, joined Vikings in 2006.
Martin Streight, asst. strength and conditioning; born June 20, 1969, Trenton, N.J. Attended Indiana (Penn.). No college or pro playing experience. College coach: Penn State 1994, Princeton 1995-96. Pro coach: Philadelphia Eagles 1995-96, Arizona Cardinals 1997-2003, Scottish Claymores (NFLE) 2003, Berlin Thunder (NFLE) 2004-05, joined Vikings in 2006.
Cameron Turner, asst. to head coach; born July 29, 1987, Huntington Beach, Calif. Quarterback/wide receiver The Citadel 2006-09. No pro playing experience. College coach: The Citadel 2010. Pro coach: Joined Vikings in 2011.
Chris White, asst. special teams; born June 29, 1967, Haverhill, Mass. Quarterback Colby College 1986-89. No pro playing experience. College coach: Syracuse 1990-92, 2000-08, Arkansas State 1992-93, Holy Cross 1993-94, UNLV 1996-98, Cal Poly-San Luis Obispo 1999. Pro coach: Joined Vikings in 2009.
Joe Woods, defensive backs; born June 25, 1970, Natrona Heights, Pa. Safety Illinois State 1988-1991. College coach: Muskingum 1992, Eastern Michigan 1993, Northwestern (La.) State 1994, Grand Valley State 1994-96, Kent State 1997, Hofstra 1998-2000, Western Michigan 2001-03. Pro coach: Tampa Bay Buccaneers 2004-05, joined Vikings in 2006.

National Football Conference
South Division
Team Colors: Old Gold, Black, and White
5800 Airline Drive
Metairie, Louisiana 70003
Telephone: (504) 733-0255

2011 SCHEDULE
PRESEASON
Aug. 12 **San Francisco** 7:00
Aug. 20 at Houston 7:00
Aug. 28 at Oakland 7:00
Sep. 1 **Tennessee** 7:00

REGULAR SEASON
Sep. 8   at Green Bay (Thu) 7:30
Sep. 18 **Chicago** 12:00
Sep. 25 **Houston** 12:00
Oct. 2   at Jacksonville 12:00
Oct. 9   at Carolina 12:00
Oct. 16 at Tampa Bay 3:15
Oct. 23 **Indianapolis** 7:20
Oct. 30 at St. Louis 12:00
Nov. 6 **Tampa Bay** 12:00
Nov. 13 at Atlanta 12:00
Nov. 20 BYE
Nov. 28 **New York Giants** (Mon) 7:30
Dec. 4 **Detroit** 12:00
Dec. 11 at Tennessee 12:00
Dec. 18 at Minnesota 12:00
Dec. 26 **Atlanta** (Mon) 7:30
Jan. 1 **Carolina** 12:00
All times CT
Stadium: Louisiana Superdome
(opened in 1975)
  • **Capacity:** 68,000
1500 Poydras Street
New Orleans, Louisiana 70112
Playing Surface: UBU Speed Series-S5-M
Training Camp: New Orleans Saints
Metairie, Louisiana 70003

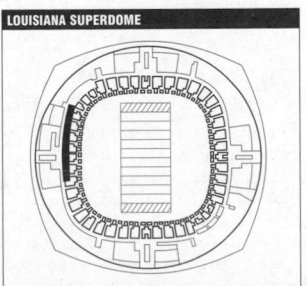

LOUISIANA SUPERDOME

CLUB OFFICIALS
Owner/President: Tom Benson
Owner/Executive Vice President:
  Rita Benson LeBlanc
Executive Vice President/General
  Manager: Mickey Loomis
Executive Vice President/Chief Financial
  Officer: Dennis Lauscha
Vice President of Communications:
  Greg Bensel
Vice President of Marketing and
  Business Development: Ben Hales
Vice President/General Counsel:
  Vicky Neumeyer
Vice President of Ticket and Suite Sales:
  Mike Stanfield
Director of Football Administration:
  Khai Harley
Director of Operations: James Nagaoka
Pro Scouting Director: Ryan Pace
Pro Scouts: Terry Fontenot, Ryan Powell
Director of College Scouting:
  Rick Reiprish
Assistant Director of College Scouting:
  Brian Adams
College Scouting Coordinator:
  Jason Mitchell
Area Scouts: Mike Baugh,
  Dwaune Jones, Josh Lucas,
  Jim Monos, Mike Neu, Terry Wooden
Combine Scout: Ryan Hollern
Salary Cap Analyst/Player Personnel:
  Joseph Laine
Equipment Manager: Dan Simmons
Assistant Equipment Manager:
  Glennon (Silky) Powell
Assistant Equipment Assistant:
  John Baumgartner
Head Athletic Trainer: Scottie B. Patton
Assistant Athletic Trainers:
  Duane Brooks, Kevin Mangum
Video Director: Dave Desposito
Director of Player Development:
  Fred McAfee
Senior Director of Communications:
  Doug Miller
Communications Manager:
  Justin Macione
Director of Photography:
  Michael C. Hebert
Information Technology/Network
  Manager: Jeff Huffman
Facilities Manager: Terry Ashburn
Administrative Director: Jay Romig

COACHING HISTORY
(291-390-5)
Records include postseason games
1967-70	Tom Fears*	13-34-2
1970-72	J.D. Roberts	7-25-3
1973-75	John North**	11-23-0
1975	Ernie Hefferle	1-7-0
1976-77	Hank Stram	7-21-0
1978-80	Dick Nolan***	15-29-0
1980	Dick Stanfel	1-3-0
1981-85	O.A. (Bum) Phillips****	27-42-0
1985	Wade Phillips	1-3-0
1986-96	Jim Mora#	93-78-0
1996	Rick Venturi	1-7-0
1997-99	Mike Ditka	15-33-0
2000-05	Jim Haslett	46-52-0
2006-2010	Sean Payton	53-33-0

  *Released after seven games in 1970
 **Released after six games in 1975
***Released after 12 games in 1980
****Resigned after 12 games in 1985
 #Resigned after eight games in 1996

PAID ATTENDANCE
Home 526,609   Away 527,985
Total 1,054,594
Single-game home record,
  70,940 (9/2/79)
Single-season home record,
  573,876 (2008)

2011 DRAFT CHOICES
Round	Name	Pos.	College
1	Cameron Jordan	DE	California
	Mark Ingram	RB	Alabama
3	Martez Wilson	LB	Illinois
	Johnny Patrick	DB	Louisville
7	Greg Romeus	DE	Pittsburgh
	Nate Bussey	LB	Illinois

2010 TEAM RECORD
PRESEASON (2-2)

Date	Result	Opponent
8/12	L 24-27	at New England
8/21	W 38-20	Houston
8/27	W 36-21	San Diego
9/2	L 24-27	at Tennessee

REGULAR SEASON (11-5)

Date	Result	Opponent
9/9	W 14-9	Minnesota
9/20	W 25-22	at San Francisco
9/26	L 24-27	Atlanta (OT)
10/3	W 16-14	Carolina
10/10	L 20-30	at Arizona
10/17	W 31-6	at Tampa Bay
10/24	L 17-30	Cleveland
10/31	W 20-10	Pittsburgh
11/7	W 34-3	at Carolina
11/21	W 34-19	Seattle
11/25	W 30-27	at Dallas
12/5	W 34-30	at Cincinnati
12/12	W 31-13	St. Louis
12/19	L 24-30	at Baltimore
12/27	W 17-14	at Atlanta
1/2	L 13-23	Tampa Bay

POSTSEASON (0-1)

Date	Result	Opponent
1/8	L 36-41	at Seattle

(OT) Overtime

SCORE BY PERIODS

Saints	112	93	74	105	0	—	384
Opponents	33	112	53	106	3	—	307

2010 TEAM STATISTICS

	Saints	Opp.
Total First Downs	351	273
Rushing	94	94
Passing	236	150
Penalty	21	29
3rd Down: Made/Att	106/217	70/203
3rd Down Pct.	48.8	34.5
4th Down: Made/Att	5/11	15/23
4th Down Pct.	45.5	65.2
Possession Avg.	31:39	28:21
Total Net Yards	5960	4900
Avg. Per Game	372.5	306.3
Total Plays	1067	948
Avg. Per Play	5.6	5.2
Net Yards Rushing	1519	1797
Avg. Per Game	94.9	112.3
Total Rushes	380	421
Net Yards Passing	4441	3103
Avg. Per Game	277.6	193.9
Sacked/Yards Lost	26/195	33/250
Gross Yards	4636	3353
Att./Completions	661/450	494/306
Completion Pct.	68.1	61.9
Had Intercepted	22	9
Punts/Average	57/45.9	67/44.7
Net Punting Avg.	57/38.4	67/40.6
Penalties/Yards	90/884	88/701
Fumbles/Ball Lost	23/9	34/16
Touchdowns	44	32
Rushing	9	13
Passing	33	13
Returns	2	6

2010 INDIVIDUAL STATISTICS

PASSING	Att.	Comp.	Yds.	Pct.	TD	Int.	Tkld.	Rate
Brees	658	448	4620	68.1	33	22	25/185	90.9
Daniel	3	2	16	66.7	0	0	1/10	79.9
Saints	661	450	4636	68.1	33	22	26/195	90.8
Opponents	494	306	3353	61.9	13	9	33/250	83.2

SCORING	TD R	TD P	TD Rt	PAT	FG	Saf	PTS
Hartley	0	0	0	40/40	20/25	0	100
Moore	0	8	0	0/0	0/0	0	48
Colston	0	7	0	0/0	0/0	0	42
Graham	0	5	0	0/0	0/0	0	30
Ivory	5	0	0	0/0	0/0	0	30
Meachem	0	5	0	0/0	0/0	0	30
Carney	0	0	0	3/3	5/6	0	18
Shockey	0	3	0	0/0	0/0	0	18
Betts	2	0	0	0/0	0/0	0	12
P. Thomas	2	0	0	0/0	0/0	0	12
D. Thomas	0	2	0	0/0	0/0	0	12
Bush	0	1	0	0/0	0/0	0	6
H. Evans	0	1	0	0/0	0/0	0	6
Greer	0	0	1	0/0	0/0	0	6
Henderson	0	1	0	0/0	0/0	0	6
Jenkins	0	0	1	0/0	0/0	0	6
Saints	9	33	2	43/43	25/31	1	384
Opponents	13	13	6	27/29	28/34	0	307

2-Pt Conversions: Saints 0-1, Opponents 2-3.

RUSHING	No.	Yds	Avg	LG	TD
Ivory	137	716	5.2	55t	5
P. Thomas	83	269	3.2	16	2
J. Jones	48	193	4.0	54	0
Betts	45	150	3.3	12	2
Bush	36	150	4.2	23	0
Daniel	2	16	8.0	16	0
Meachem	4	14	3.5	8	0
Henderson	3	8	2.7	9	0
Graham	1	3	3.0	3	0
H. Evans	2	2	1.0	2	0
Colston	1	1	1.0	1	0
Brees	18	-3	-.2	7	0
Saints	380	1519	4.0	55t	9
Opponents	421	1797	4.3	68	13

RECEIVING	No.	Yds	Avg	LG	TD
Colston	84	1023	12.2	43	7
Moore	66	763	11.6	80t	8
Meachem	44	638	14.5	55	5
Shockey	41	408	10.0	31	3
Henderson	34	464	13.6	57	1
Bush	34	208	6.1	20	1
Graham	31	356	11.5	52	5
D. Thomas	30	219	7.3	22	2
P. Thomas	29	201	6.9	23	0
Betts	23	141	6.1	25	0
J. Jones	17	59	3.5	13	0
Arrington	7	79	11.3	17	0
H. Evans	7	41	5.9	18	1
Ivory	1	17	17.0	17	0
Humphrey	1	12	12.0	12	0
Brees	1	7	7.0	7	0
Saints	450	4636	10.3	80t	33
Opponents	306	3353	11.0	68	13

INTERCEPTIONS	No.	Yds	Avg	LG	TD
Jenkins	2	105	52.5	96t	1
Greer	2	50	25.0	26	1
Torrence	1	21	21.0	21	0
Harper	1	6	6.0	6	0
Porter	1	5	5.0	5	0
Vilma	1	5	5.0	5	0
Smith	1	4	4.0	4	0
Saints	9	196	21.8	96t	2
Opponents	22	344	15.6	66	4

PUNTING	No.	Yds.	Avg.	In 20	LG
Morstead	57	2618	45.9	21	64
Saints	57	2618	45.9	21	64
Opponents	67	2993	44.7	26	59

PUNT RETURNS	Ret	FC	Yds	Avg	LG	TD
Bush	14	2	92	6.6	43	0
Moore	11	16	112	10.2	72	0
Porter	2	0	6	3.0	4	0
Saints	27	18	210	7.8	72	0
Opponents	26	10	310	11.9	69	0

KICKOFF RETURNS	No.	Yds	Avg	LG	TD
Roby	33	785	23.8	39	0
P. Thomas	7	154	22.0	32	0
Henderson	6	142	23.7	27	0
H. Evans	4	45	11.3	13	0
Bush	1	32	32.0	32	0
Betts	1	23	23.0	23	0
Saints	52	1181	22.7	39	0
Opponents	66	1592	24.1	69	0

FIELD GOALS	1-19	20-29	30-39	40-49	50+
Hartley	1/1	4/6	7/9	6/7	2/2
Carney	0/0	1/2	4/4	0/0	0/0
Saints	1/1	5/8	11/13	6/7	2/2
Opponents	1/1	11/11	5/5	10/14	1/3

SACKS	No.
Ellis	6.0
Smith	5.5
Vilma	4.0
Charleston	3.0
Harper	3.0
A. Brown	2.0
Wilkerson	2.0
Ayodele	1.0
Dunbar	1.0
Hargrove	1.0
Jenkins	1.0
M. Mitchell	1.0
Torrence	1.0
Young	1.0
Prioleau	0.5
Saints	33.0
Opponents	26.0

RECORD HOLDERS
INDIVIDUAL RECORDS—CAREER

Category	Name	Performance
Rushing (Yds.)	Deuce McAllister, 2001-09	6,096
Passing (Yds.)	Drew Brees, 2006-2010	22,918
Passing (TDs)	Drew Brees, 2006-2010	155
Receiving (No.)	Eric Martin, 1985-1993	532
Receiving (Yds.)	Eric Martin, 1985-1993	7,854
Interceptions	Dave Waymer, 1980-89	37
Punting (Avg.)	Mark Royals, 1997-98	45.8
Punt Return (Avg.)	Mel Gray, 1986-88	13.4
Kickoff Return (Avg.)	Walt Roberts, 1967	26.3
Field Goals	Morten Andersen, 1982-1994	302
Touchdowns (Tot.)	Deuce McAllister, 2001-09	55
Points	Morten Andersen, 1982-1994	1,318
*Sacks	Rickey Jackson, 1981-1993	115.0

INDIVIDUAL RECORDS—SINGLE SEASON

Category	Name	Performance
Rushing (Yds.)	George Rogers, 1981	1,674
Passing (Yds.)	Drew Brees, 2008	5,069
Passing (TDs)	Drew Brees, 2008, 2009	34
Receiving (No.)	Marques Colston, 2007	98
Receiving (Yds.)	Joe Horn, 2004	1,399
Interceptions	Dave Whitsell, 1967	10
Punting (Avg.)	Thomas Morstead, 2010	45.9
Punt Return (Avg.)	Mel Gray, 1987	14.7
Kickoff Return (Avg.)	John Gilliam, 1967	30.1
Field Goals	Morten Andersen, 1985	31
	John Carney, 2002	31
Touchdowns (Tot.)	Dalton Hilliard, 1989	18
Points	John Carney, 2002	130
*Sacks	Pat Swilling, 1991	17.0
	La'Roi Glover, 2000	17.0

INDIVIDUAL RECORDS—SINGLE GAME

Category	Name	Performance
Rushing (Yds.)	George Rogers, 9-4-83	206
Passing (Yds.)	Drew Brees, 11-19-06	510
Passing (TDs)	Billy Kilmer, 11-2-69	6
	Drew Brees, 9-13-09	6
Receiving (No.)	Tony Galbreath, 9-10-78	14
Receiving (Yds.)	Wes Chandler, 9-2-79	205
Interceptions	Tommy Myers, 9-3-78	3
	Dave Waymer, 10-6-85	3
	Reggie Sutton, 10-18-87	3
	Gene Atkins, 12-22-91	3
	Sammy Knight, 9-9-01	3
Field Goals	Many times	5
	Last time by John Carney, 9-26-04	
Touchdowns (Tot.)	Joe Horn, 12-14-03	4
	Reggie Bush, 12-3-06	4
Points	Joe Horn, 12-14-03	24
	Reggie Bush, 12-3-06	24
*Sacks	Many times	4.0
	Last time by Wayne Martin, 9-21-97	

Sacks became an official statistic in 1982.

VETERAN ROSTER AS OF MARCH 3, 2011

No.	Name	Pos.	Ht.	Wt.	Birthdate	^ NFL Exp.	College	Hometown	How Acq.	'10 Games/Starts
70	Allen, Roger	G/T	6-3	323	2/10/86	2	Missouri Western	Raytown, Mo.	FA-'10	0*
53	Arnoux, Stanley	LB	6-0	232	9/9/86	3	Wake Forest	Sunrise, Fla.	D4b-'09	9/0
87	Arrington, Adrian	WR	6-3	192	11/7/85	2	Michigan	Cedar Rapids, Iowa	FA-'10	1/0
92	Ayodele, Remi	DT	6-2	318	4/22/83	5	Oklahoma	Grand Prairie, Texas	FA-'08	16/16
43	Bell, Joique	RB	5-11	220	8/4/86	2	Wayne State	Benton Harbor, Mich.	FA-'11	8/0*
46	Betts, Ladell	RB	5-11	224	8/27/79	10	Iowa	Blue Springs, Mo.	FA-'10	8/1
9	Brees, Drew	QB	6-0	209	1/15/79	11	Purdue	Austin, Texas	UFA(SD)-'06	16/16
96	Brown, Alex	DE	6-3	260	6/4/79	10	Florida	White Springs, Fla.	FA-'10	16/16
71	Brown, Charles	T	6-5	297	4/10/87	2	Southern California	Chino Hills, Calif.	D2-'10	3/0
25	Bush, Reggie	RB	6-0	203	3/2/85	6	Southern California	Spring Valley, Calif.	D1-'06	8/6
74	Bushrod, Jermon	T	6-5	315	8/19/84	5	Towson	King George, Va.	D4b-'07	16/16
52	Casillas, Jonathan	LB	6-1	227	6/3/87	3	Wisconsin	New Brunswick, N.J.	FA-'09	0*
97	Charleston, Jeff	DE	6-4	265	1/19/83	5	Idaho State	Oregon City, Ore.	FA-'08	16/1
55	Clark, Danny	LB	6-2	245	5/9/77	12	Illinois	Country Club Hills, Ill.	FA-'10	14/10
12	Colston, Marques	WR	6-4	225	6/5/83	6	Hofstra	Harrisburg, Pa.	D7b-'06	15/11
10	Daniel, Chase	QB	6-0	225	10/7/86	3	Missouri	Southlake, Texas	FA-'09	13/0
60	de la Puente, Brian	G	6-3	306	5/13/85	2	California	San Clemente, Calif.	FA-'10	0*
47	Drescher, Justin	LS	6-1	230	1/1/88	2	Colorado	Southlake, Texas	FA-'10	6/0
56	Dunbar, Jo-Lonn	LB	6-0	226	3/13/85	4	Boston College	Syracuse, N.Y.	FA-'08	13/8
98	Ellis, Sedrick	DT	6-1	307	7/9/85	4	Southern California	Chino, Calif.	D1-'08	16/16
44	Evans, Heath	FB	6-0	250	12/30/78	11	Auburn	West Palm Beach, Fla.	UFA(NE)-'09	16/6
73	Evans, Jahri	G	6-4	318	8/22/83	6	Bloomsburg	Philadelphia, Pa.	D4-'06	16/16
93	Galette, Junior	DE	6-2	258	3/27/88	2	Stillman	Spring Valley, N.Y.	FA-'10	4/0
20	Gay, Randall	CB	5-11	190	5/5/82	8	Louisiana State	Brusly, La.	UFA(NE)-'08	4/0
37	Giordano, Matt	S	5-11	207	10/16/82	7	California	Fresno, Calif.	FA-'10	9/0
76	Goodwin, Jonathan	C	6-3	318	12/2/78	10	Michigan	Richland, S.C.	UFA(NYJ)-'06	16/16
80	Graham, Jimmy	TE	6-6	260	11/24/86	2	Miami	Goldsboro, N.C.	D3-'10	15/5
33	Greer, Jabari	CB	5-11	180	2/11/82	8	Tennessee	Jackson, Tenn.	UFA(Buff)-'09	14/13
30	Hamilton, Lynell	RB	6-0	235	8/5/85	3	San Diego State	Stockton, Calif.	FA-'08	0*
69	Hargrove, Anthony	DL	6-3	272	7/20/83	7	Georgia Tech	Punta Gorda, Fla.	UFA(Buff)-'09	14/0
41	Harper, Roman	S	6-1	200	12/11/82	6	Alabama	Prattville, Ala.	D2-'06	15/15
5	Hartley, Garrett	K	5-8	196	5/16/86	4	Oklahoma	Southlake, Texas	FA-'08	14/0
19	Henderson, Devery	WR	5-11	200	3/26/82	8	Louisiana State	Opelousas, La.	D2a-'04	16/11
54	Humber, Ramon	LB	5-11	232	8/10/87	3	North Dakota State	Brooklyn Park, Minn.	FA-'10	5/0*
84	Humphrey, Tory	TE	6-2	255	1/20/83	5	Central Michigan	Saginaw, Mich.	FA-'10	6/2
29	Ivory, Chris	RB	6-0	222	3/22/88	2	Tiffin	Longview, Texas	FA-'10	12/4
27	Jenkins, Malcolm	S	6-0	204	12/20/87	3	Ohio State	Piscataway, N.J.	D1-'09	15/15
21	Jones, Julius	RB	5-10	208	8/14/81	8	Notre Dame	Big Stone Gap, Va.	FA-'10	12/2*
75	King, Mitch	DT	6-2	280	5/5/86	2	Iowa	Burlington, Iowa	FA-'10	4/0*
57	Kyle, Jason	LS	6-3	242	5/12/72	17	Arizona State	Tempe, Ariz.	FA-'09	9/0
17	Meachem, Robert	WR	6-2	210	9/28/84	5	Tennessee	Tulsa, Okla.	D1-'07	16/7
94	Mitchell, Kawika	LB	6-1	253	10/10/79	9	South Florida	Water Springs, Fla.	FA-'10	1/0
50	Mitchell, Marvin	LB	6-3	249	10/21/84	5	Tennessee	Norfolk, Va.	D7-'07	16/0
16	Moore, Lance	WR	5-9	190	8/31/83	6	Toledo	Westerville, Ohio	FA-'07	16/1
6	Morstead, Thomas	P	6-4	225	3/7/86	3	Southern Methodist	Pearland, Texas	D5-'09	16/0
77	Nicks, Carl	G	6-5	343	5/14/85	4	Nebraska	Salinas, Calif.	D5b-'08	16/16
38	Parson, Mark	CB	5-10	192	5/9/86	2	Ohio	Richmond, Va.	FA-'10	0*
31	Prioleau, Pierson	S	5-11	188	8/6/77	13	Virginia Tech	Alvin, S.C.	UFA(Jax)-'09	15/1
39	Reis, Chris	S	6-1	215	9/19/83	5	Georgia Tech	Roswell, Ga.	FA-'07	2/0
34	Robinson, Patrick	CB	5-11	191	9/7/87	2	Florida State	Miami, Fla.	D1-'10	11/4
15	Roby, Courtney	WR	6-0	189	1/10/83	6	Indiana	Indianapolis, Ind.	FA-'09	13/0
90	Rogers, Shaun	DT	6-4	350	3/12/79	11	Texas	LaPorte, Texas	FA-'11	15/1*
58	Shanle, Scott	LB	6-2	245	11/23/79	9	Nebraska	St. Edward, Neb.	T(Dall)-'06	14/14
42	Sharper, Darren	S	6-2	210	11/3/75	15	William & Mary	Richmond, Va.	UFA(Minn)-'09	8/1
91	Smith, Will	DE	6-3	282	7/4/81	8	Ohio State	Utica, N.Y.	D1-'04	15/15
78	Stinchcomb, Jon	T	6-5	315	8/27/79	9	Georgia	Lilburn, Ga.	D2-'03	16/16
64	Strief, Zach	T	6-7	320	9/22/83	6	Northwestern	Milford, Ohio	D7a-'06	14/2
36	Taylor, Chris	RB	6-0	224	11/7/83	4	Indiana	Memphis, Tenn.	FA-'10	0*
65	Tennant, Matt	C/G	6-4	300	3/19/87	2	Boston College	Cincinnati, Ohio	D5-'10	16/0
85	Thomas, David	TE	6-3	248	7/5/83	6	Texas	Plainview, Texas	T(NE)-'09	13/8
23	Thomas, Pierre	RB	5-11	215	12/18/84	5	Illinois	Lynwood, Ill.	FA-'07	6/3
24	Torrence, Leigh	CB	5-11	179	1/4/82	6	Stanford	Atlanta, Ga.	FA-'10	13/0
51	Vilma, Jonathan	LB	6-1	230	4/16/82	8	Miami	Coral Gables, Fla.	T(NYJ)-'08	16/16
59	Waters, Anthony	LB	6-3	238	7/25/84	4	Clemson	Lake View, S.C.	FA-'09	10/0
99	Wilkerson, Jimmy	DL	6-2	270	1/4/81	9	Oklahoma	Naples, Texas	UFA(TB)-'10	16/0
35	Wynn, DeShawn	RB	5-10	232	10/9/83	5	Florida	Reading, Ohio	FA-'11	7/0*
28	Young, Usama	S	6-0	200	5/8/85	5	Kent State	Largo, Md.	D3a-'07	11/3

* Allen spent '10 season on New Orleans practice squad, last active with Rams in '09; Bell played 3 games with Philadelphia and 5 games with Indianapolis in '10; Casillas missed '10 season because of injury; de la Puente spent 1 game in '10 season on Seattle practice squad and 11 games on New Orleans practice squad, inactive with Kansas City in '08; Hamilton missed '10 season because of injury; Humber played 3 games with New Orleans and 2 games with Indianapolis; Jones played 2 games with Seattle and 10 games with New Orleans; King played 4 games with Indianapolis; Parson spent 9 games in '10 season on New Orleans practice squad, inactive with Houston in '09; Rogers played 15 games with Cleveland; Taylor spent 7 games in '10 season on New Orleans practice squad, last active with Houston in '08; Wynn played 3 games with San Francisco and 4 games with New Orleans.

Also played with Saints in '10—LB K.C. Asiodu (1 game), K John Carney (2), LS Jake Ingram (1), TE Jeremy Shockey (13).

^ "NFL Exp." as of 2011 Kickoff Weekend. For full explanation of how a player's NFL Experience is measured, refer to explanation underneath the First-Year Roster listed below.

FIRST-YEAR ROSTER

Name	Pos.	Ht.	Wt.	Birthdate	College	Hometown	How Acq.
Billings, Montez (1)	WR	6-1	181	6/15/86	Auburn	Pelham, Ala.	FA-'10
Bussey, Nate	LB	6-2	220	2/20/89	Illinois	Washington, D.C.	D7b
Butler, Ezra (1)	LB	6-2	248	11/20/84	Nevada	Calabasas, Calif.	FA
Canfield, Sean (1)	QB	6-4	223	11/12/86	Oregon State	Carlsbad, Calif.	D7-'10
Collins, Jed (1)	FB	6-1	255	3/3/86	Washington State	Mission Viejo, Calif.	FA-'10
Ingram, Mark	RB	5-9	215	12/21/89	Alabama	Flint, Mich.	D1b
Johnson, Tom (1)	DT	6-3	288	8/30/84	Southern Mississippi	Moss Point, Miss.	FA
Jordan, Cameron	DE	6-4	287	7/10/89	California	Chandler, Ariz.	D1a
Lorenzen, Tyler (1)	TE	6-5	234	12/24/85	Connecticut	Fremont, Iowa	FA-'10
Miller, Swanson (1)	DT	6-4	310	3/24/86	Oklahoma State	Alachua, Fla.	FA-'10
Patrick, Johnny	CB	5-11	191	8/17/88	Louisville	DeLand, Fla.	D3b
Romeus, Greg	DE	6-5	267	4/29/88	Pittsburgh	Coral Springs, Fla.	D7a
Tanner, Andy (1)	WR	6-0	183	5/16/88	Midwestern State	Rockwall, Texas	FA-'10
Wilson, Martez	LB	6-4	252	9/21/88	Illinois	Chicago, Ill.	D3a

The term NFL Rookie is defined as a player who is in his first season of professional football and has not been on the roster of another professional football team for any regular-season or postseason games. A Rookie is designated by an "R" on NFL rosters. Players who have been active in another professional football league or players who have NFL experience, including either preseason training camp or being on an Active List or Inactive List, or on Reserve/Injured or Reserve/Physically Unable to Perform for fewer than six regular-season games, are termed NFL First-Year Players. An NFL First-Year Player is designated by a "1" on NFL rosters. Thereafter, a player is credited with an additional year of experience for each season in which he accumulates six games on the Active List or Inactive List, or on Reserve/Injured or Reserve/Physically Unable to Perform.

Log on to www.neworleanssaints.com for an up-to-date roster.

COACHING STAFF

Head Coach,
Sean Payton

Pro Career: Named the fourteenth head coach in Saints history on Jan. 18, 2006 and twice in his first four seasons led the Saints to NFC South division titles, NFC Championship Game appearances and their first Super Bowl appearance and victory in Super Bowl XLIV. Earned unanimous NFL coach of the year honors in his first season in 2006 and received the same honors from some outlets in 2009. Considered one of the NFL's brightest offensive minds, the Saints have ranked among the league's most productive offenses season since his arrival, including finishing first in the NFL in 2009, 2008 and 2006, ranking fourth in 2007 and sixth in 2010. With Dallas Cowboys (2003-05), served as the assistant head coach/passing game coordinator in 2005 after spending his first two seasons as assistant head coach/quarterbacks. Coached four years with the New York Giants (1999-2002), the last three seasons as offensive coordinator, and was quarterbacks coach for the Philadelphia Eagles (1997-98). Career record: 53-33.

Background: Earned a degree in communications at Eastern Illinois, where he departed with a school-record 10,665 passing yards, then the third-highest total in NCAA Division I-AA history. A three-time All-American, Payton had brief playing stops with Chicago of the Arena League, the CFL's Ottawa Rough Riders and the Chicago Bears in 1987. Payton coached collegiately at San Diego State (1988-89, 1992-93), Indiana State (1990-91), and Miami (Ohio) in 1994-95.

Personal: Born Dec. 29, 1963 in San Mateo, Calif. and raised in Naperville, Ill, Payton and his wife, Beth, have a daughter, Meghan, and a son, Connor.

ASSISTANT COACHES

John Bonamego, asst. special teams; born August 14, 1963, Waynesboro, Pa. Wide receiver/quarterback Central Michigan 1985-86. No pro playing experience. College coach: Maine 1988-1991, Lehigh 1992, Army 1993-98. Pro coach: Jacksonville Jaguars 1999-2002, Green Bay Packers 2003-05, New Orleans Saints 2006-07, Miami Dolphins 2008-10, re-joined Saints in 2011.

Charles Byrd, asst. strength and conditioning; born June 24, 1981, Oxford, Ohio. Defensive back Morehead State 2001-04. Pro defensive back Las Vegas Gladiators (AFL) 2006. College coach: Miami (Ohio) 2006-07. Pro coach: Joined Saints in 2008.

Pete Carmichael Jr., offensive coordinator; born October 6, 1971, Framingham, Mass. Attended Boston College. No college or pro playing experience. College coach: New Hampshire 1994, Louisiana Tech 1995-99. Pro coach: Cleveland Browns 2000, Washington Redskins 2001, San Diego Chargers 2002-05, joined Saints in 2006.

Dan Dalrymple, head strength and conditioning; born Aug. 26, 1965, Cleveland. Offensive lineman Miami (Ohio) 1983-86. No pro playing experience. College coach: Miami (Ohio) 1987-2005. Pro coach: Joined Saints in 2006.

Bret Ingalls, running backs; born Aug. 19, 1960, San Jose, Calif. Running back Wichita State 1979-1981. No pro playing experience. College coach: Idaho 1982-88, San Diego State 1989-1993, Eastern Michigan 1994, Louisville 1995-96, Northern Iowa 1997-99, Idaho 2000-03, Indiana State 2004, Miami (Ohio) 2005, Northwestern 2006-08. Pro coach: Joined Saints in 2009.

Bill Johnson, defensive line; born June 23, 1955, Monroe, La. Defensive lineman Northwestern (La.) State 1976-79. No pro playing experience. College coach: Northwestern (La.) 1980-84, McNeese State 1985-86, Miami 1987, Louisiana Tech 1988-89, Arkansas 1990-91, 2000, Texas A&M 1992-99. Pro coach: Atlanta Falcons 2001-06, Denver Broncos 2007-08, joined Saints in 2009.

Curtis Johnson, wide receivers; born November 5, 1961, New Orleans. Wide receiver Idaho 1979-1983. No pro playing experience. College coach: Idaho 1987-88, San Diego State 1989-1993, Southern Methodist 1994, California 1995, Miami 1996-2005. Pro coach: Joined Saints in 2006.

Travis Jones, asst. defensive line; born June 6, 1972, Milledgeville, Ga. Linebacker Georgia 1991-94. Pro linebacker Baltimore Stallions (CFL) 1995. College coach: Georgia 1997, Appalachian State 1998-2000, Kansas 2001-02, Louisiana State 2003-04. Pro coach: Miami Dolphins 2005-07, joined Saints in 2008.

Aaron Kromer, offensive line/running game; born April 30, 1967, Sandusky, Ohio. Offensive tackle Miami (Ohio) 1986-89. No pro playing experience. College coach: Miami (Ohio) 1990-98, Northwestern 1999-2000. Pro coach: Oakland Raiders 2001-04, Tampa Bay Buccaneers 2005-07, joined Saints in 2008.

Joe Lombardi, quarterbacks; born June 6, 1971, Seattle. Tight end Air Force 1992-94. No pro playing experience. College coach: Dayton 1996-98, Virginia Military Institute 1999, Bucknell 2000, Mercyhurst 2002-05. Pro coach: New York/New Jersey Hitmen (XFL) 2001, Atlanta Falcons 2006, joined Saints in 2007.

Mike Mallory, asst. secondary; born Nov. 16, 1962, Bowling Green, Ohio. Linebacker Michigan 1982-85. No pro playing experience. College coach: Indiana 1986-87, Kent State 1989-1990, Eastern Illinois 1991-92, Rhode Island 1993-95, Northern Illinois 1996-99, Maryland 2000, Illinois 2001-05, Kansas 2006, Louisville 2007. Pro coach: Joined Saints in 2008.

Terry Malone, tight ends; born February 26, 1960, Buffalo. Tight end Holy Cross

1978-1982. No pro playing experience. College coach: Arizona 1983-84, Holy Cross 1985, Bowling Green 1986-1995, Boston College 1996, Michigan 1997-2005. Pro coach: Joined Saints in 2006.

Greg McMahon, special teams coordinator; born Jan. 2, 1960, Rantoul, Ill. Defensive back Eastern Illinois 1978-1981. No pro playing experience. College coach: Eastern Illinois 1982, Minnesota 1983-84, North Alabama 1985-87, Southern Illinois 1988, Valdosta State 1989, Nevada Las-Vegas 1990-91, Illinois 1992-2004, East Carolina 2005. Pro coach: Joined Saints in 2006.

Tony Oden, secondary; born June 30, 1973, Cleveland. Linebacker Baldwin-Wallace College 1991-95. No pro playing experience. College coach: Millersville (Penn.) 1996, Boston College 1997, Army 1998-99, East Carolina 2000-02, Eastern Michigan 2003. Pro coach: Houston Texans 2004-05, joined Saints in 2006.

Carter Sheridan, offensive assistant/ wide receivers; born Nov. 20, 1977, New Orleans. Defensive back Florida A&M 1996-98. No pro playing experience. Pro coach: Joined Saints in 2006.

Frank Smith, coaching assistant; born February 21, 1981, Milwaukee. Offensive lineman Miami (Ohio) 1999-2003. No pro playing experience. College coach: Miami (Ohio) 2004-05, Butler 2006-09. Pro coach: Joined Saints in 2010.

Marcus Ungaro, coaching assistant; born October 9, 1984, Seattle. Defensive back Southwestern College 2004-05. No pro playing experience. Pro coach: Joined Saints in 2010.

Joe Vitt, asst. head coach/linebackers; born August 23, 1954, Syracuse, N.Y. Linebacker Towson State 1974-78. No pro playing experience. Pro coach: Baltimore Colts 1979-1981, Seattle Seahawks 1982-1991, Los Angeles Rams 1992-94, Philadelphia Eagles 1995-98, Green Bay Packers 1999, Kansas City Chiefs 2000-03, St. Louis Rams 2004-05 (head coach, final 11 games of 2005), joined Saints in 2006.

Blake Williams, coaching assistant; born Dec. 30, 1984, Independence, Mo. Defensive back Princeton 2003-07. No pro playing experience. Pro coach: Washington Redskins 2006-07, Jacksonville Jaguars 2008, joined Saints in 2009.

Gregg Williams, defensive coordinator; born July 15, 1958, Excelsior Springs, Mo. Quarterback Northeastern Missouri State 1976-79. No pro playing experience. College coach: Houston 1988-89. Pro coach: Houston Oilers/Tennessee Titans 1990-2000, Buffalo Bills 2001-03 (head coach), Washington Redskins 2004-07, Jacksonville Jaguars 2008, joined Saints in 2009.

Brian Young, coaching assistant; born July 8, 1977, Lawton, Okla. Defensive tackle Texas El-Paso 1996-99. Pro defensive tackle St. Louis Rams 2000-03, New Orleans Saints 2004-08. Pro coach: Joined Saints in 2009.

National Football Conference
East Division
Team Colors: Blue, Red, and White
Timex Performance Center
1925 Giants Drive
East Rutherford, New Jersey 07073
Telephone: (201) 935-8111

2011 SCHEDULE
PRESEASON
Aug. 14	at Carolina	8:00
Aug. 22	**Chicago**	8:00
Aug. 27	**New York Jets**	7:00
Sep. 1	at New England	7:30

REGULAR SEASON
Sep. 11	at Washington	4:15
Sep. 19	**St. Louis** (Mon)	8:30
Sep. 25	at Philadelphia	1:00
Oct. 2	at Arizona	4:05
Oct. 9	**Seattle**	1:00
Oct. 16	**Buffalo**	1:00
Oct. 23	BYE	
Oct. 30	**Miami**	1:00
Nov. 6	at New England	4:15
Nov. 13	at San Francisco	4:15
Nov. 20	**Philadelphia** *	8:20
Nov. 28	at New Orleans (Mon)	8:30
Dec. 4	**Green Bay**	4:15
Dec. 11	at Dallas *	8:20
Dec. 18	**Washington**	1:00
Dec. 24	at New York Jets (Sat)	1:00
Jan. 1	**Dallas**	1:00

*All times ET; Sunday night games in
Weeks 11-15, 17 subject to change*
Stadium: New Meadowlands Stadium
(opened in 2010)
•Capacity: 82,500
East Rutherford, New Jersey 07073
Playing Surface: FieldTurf
Training Camp: University at Albany
1400 Washington Avenue
Albany, New York 12222

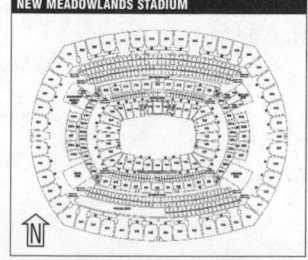

NEW MEADOWLANDS STADIUM

CLUB OFFICIALS
President/CEO: John K. Mara
Chairman/EVP: Steve Tisch
Treasurer: Jonathan Tisch
Senior Vice President-General Manager:
Jerry Reese
Senior Vice President and Chief
Marketing Officer: Michael Stevens
Senior Vice President and General
Counsel: William J. Heller, Esq.
Vice President-Player Evaluations:
Chris Mara
Vice President and Chief Financial
Officer: Christine Procops
Senior Vice President-Marketing:
John Maguire
Vice President-Marketing: Rusty Hawley
VP/Medical Services: Ronnie Barnes
Vice President-Communications:
Pat Hanlon
Vice President, Media and Partnerships:
Dan Lynch
Vice President and Executive Producer,
Giants Entertainment: Don Sperling
Vice President Business Development:
Doug Smoyer
Assistant General Manager:
Kevin Abrams
Director of Pro Player Personnel:
David Gettleman
Assistant Director of Pro Player
Personnel: Ken Sternfeld
Director of College Scouting: Marc Ross
Director of Player Development:
Charles Way
Pro Personnel Assistants:
Patrick Hanscomb, Matthew Shauger
College Scouts: Joe Collins, Jeremiah
Davis, Jerry Shay, Steve Verderosa,
Steve Devine, Donnie Etheridge,
Ryan Jones, Steve Malin, Chris Pettit,
Jeremy Breit, Chris Watts
Director of Promotions: Frank Mara
Ticket Manager: John Gorman
Director of Administration: Jim Phelan
Controller: Steven Hamrahi
Director of Community Relations:
Allison Stangeby
Director of Creative Services:
Doug Murphy
Director of Public/Media Relations:
Peter John-Baptiste
Assistant Director of Communications:
Avis Roper
Head Athletic Trainer: Ronnie Barnes
Assistant Athletic Trainers:
Steve Kennelly, Byron Hansen,
Leigh Weiss
Equipment/Locker Room Manager:
Ed Wagner, Jr.
Equipment Director: Joseph Skiba
Assistant Equipment Managers:
Ed Skiba, Tim Slaman
Video Director: Dave Maltese
Assistant Video Directors:
Carmen Pizzano, Ed Triggs,
Steve Venditti
Assistant Director of Community
Relations: Jen Conley
Directors of Information Technology:
Julie Glisky, Justin Warren
Director of Marketing Services:
Ethan Medley
Manager, Client Services: Nicole Rivera
Director of Facility Construction:
Gary Meyer

COACHING HISTORY
(656-548-33)
Records include postseason games
1925	Bob Folwell	8-4-0
1926	Joe Alexander	8-4-1
1927-28	Earl Potteiger	15-8-3
1929-1930	LeRoy Andrews*	24-5-1
1930	Benny Friedman-Steve Owen	2-0-0
1931-1953	Steve Owen	153-108-17
1954-1960	Jim Lee Howell	55-29-4
1961-68	Allie Sherman	57-54-4
1969-1973	Alex Webster	29-40-1
1974-76	Bill Arnsparger**	7-28-0
1976-78	John McVay	14-23-0
1979-1982	Ray Perkins	24-35-0
1983-1990	Bill Parcells	85-52-1
1991-92	Ray Handley	14-18-0
1993-96	Dan Reeves	32-34-0
1997-2003	Jim Fassel	60-56-1
2004-2010	Tom Coughlin	69-50-0

*Released after 15 games in 1930
**Released after seven games in 1976

PAID ATTENDANCE
Home 628,816   Away 501,845
Total 1,130,661
Single-game home record,
81,034 (12/19/10)
Single-season home record,
629,874 (2004)

2011 DRAFT CHOICES
Round	Name	Pos.	College
1	Prince Amukamara	CB	Nebraska
2	Marvin Austin	DT	North Carolina
3	Jerrel Jernigan	WR	Troy
4	James Brewer	T	Indiana
6	Greg Jones	LB	Michigan State
	Tyler Sash	DB	Iowa
	Jacquian Williams	LB	South Florida
7	Da'Rel Scott	RB	Maryland

2010 TEAM RECORD

PRESEASON (2-2)

Date	Result	Opponent
8/16	W 31-16	at New York
8/21	L 17-24	Pittsburgh
8/28	L 10-24	at Baltimore
9/2	W 20-17	New England

REGULAR SEASON (10-6)

Date	Result	Opponent
9/12	W 31-18	Carolina
9/19	L 14-38	at Indianapolis
9/26	L 10-29	Tennessee
10/3	W 17-3	Chicago
10/10	W 34-10	at Houston
10/17	W 28-20	Detroit
10/25	W 41-35	at Dallas
11/7	W 41-7	at Seattle
11/14	L 20-33	Dallas
11/21	L 17-27	at Philadelphia
11/28	W 24-20	Jacksonville
12/5	W 31-7	Washington
12/13	W 21-3	at Minnesota
12/19	L 31-38	Philadelphia
12/26	L 17-45	at Green Bay
1/2	W 17-14	at Washington

SCORE BY PERIODS

Giants	89	133	102	70	0	—	394
Opponents	67	99	64	117	0	—	347

2010 TEAM STATISTICS

	Giants	Opp.
Total First Downs	331	263
Rushing	112	88
Passing	192	159
Penalty	27	16
3rd Down: Made/Att	74/206	66/208
3rd Down Pct.	35.9	31.7
4th Down: Made/Att	3/11	9/17
4th Down Pct.	27.3	52.9
Possession Avg.	32:32	27:28
Total Net Yards	6085	4972
Avg. Per Game	380.3	310.8
Total Plays	1035	974
Avg. Per Play	5.9	5.1
Net Yards Rushing	2200	1620
Avg. Per Game	137.5	101.3
Total Rushes	480	389
Net Yards Passing	3885	3352
Avg. Per Game	242.8	209.5
Sacked/Yards Lost	16/117	46/316
Gross Yards	4002	3668
Att./Completions	539/339	539/308
Completion Pct.	62.9	57.1
Had Intercepted	25	16
Punts/Average	73/44.1	86/43.5
Net Punting Avg.	73/34.3	86/38.8
Penalties/Yards	92/777	107/899
Fumbles/Ball Lost	26/17	42/23
Touchdowns	48	39
Rushing	17	11
Passing	31	24
Returns	0	4

2010 INDIVIDUAL STATISTICS

PASSING	Att.	Comp.	Yds.	Pct.	TD	Int.	Tkld.	Rate
Manning	539	339	4002	62.9	31	25	16/117	85.3
Giants	539	339	4002	62.9	31	25	16/117	85.3
Opponents	539	308	3668	57.1	24	16	46/316	80.5

	TD	TD	TD				
SCORING	R	P	Rt	PAT	FG	Saf	PTS
Tynes	0	0	0	43/43	19/23	0	100
Nicks	0	11	0	0/0	0/0	0	66
Jacobs	9	0	0	0/0	0/0	0	54
Manningham	0	9	0	0/0	0/0	0	54
Bradshaw	8	0	0	0/0	0/0	0	50
Boss	0	5	0	0/0	0/0	0	30
Smith	0	3	0	0/0	0/0	0	18
Beckum	0	2	0	0/0	0/0	0	12
Hagan	0	1	0	0/0	0/0	0	6
Graham	0	0	0	4/4	0/0	0	4
Giants	17	31	0	47/47	19/23	0	394
Opponents	11	24	4	36/37	23/27	2	347

2-Pt Conversions: Bradshaw.

Giants 1-1, Opponents 2-2.

RUSHING	No.	Yds	Avg	LG	TD
Bradshaw	276	1235	4.5	48t	8
Jacobs	147	823	5.6	73	9
Ware	20	73	3.7	14	0
Manning	32	70	2.2	16	0
Manningham	1	2	2.0	2	0
Dodge	1	0	0.0	0	0
Rosenfels	3	-3	-1.0	0	0
Giants	480	2200	4.6	73	17
Opponents	389	1620	4.2	50t	11

RECEIVING	No.	Yds	Avg	LG	TD
Nicks	79	1052	13.3	46t	11
Manningham	60	944	15.7	92t	9
Smith	48	529	11.0	45	3
Bradshaw	47	314	6.7	18	0
Boss	35	531	15.2	54	5
Hagan	24	223	9.3	17	1
Beckum	13	116	8.9	29	2
Pascoe	9	72	8.0	12	0
Ware	7	67	9.6	18	0
Jacobs	7	59	8.4	22	0
Barden	5	64	12.8	26	0
Clayton	2	19	9.5	14	0
Hedgecock	2	8	4.0	7	0
Calhoun	1	4	4.0	4	0
Giants	339	4002	11.8	92t	31
Opponents	308	3668	11.9	87t	24

INTERCEPTIONS	No.	Yds	Avg	LG	TD
T. Thomas	5	56	11.2	28	0
Webster	4	11	2.8	13	0
Grant	3	0	0.0	0	0
Bulluck	2	7	3.5	6	0
Rolle	1	36	36.0	36	0
Phillips	1	0	0.0	0	0
Giants	16	110	6.9	36	0
Opponents	25	307	12.3	101t	1

PUNTING	No.	Yds.	Avg.	In 20	LG
Dodge	72	3222	44.8	20	69
Giants	73	3222	44.1	20	69
Opponents	86	3744	43.5	28	61

PUNT RETURNS	Ret	FC	Yds	Avg	LG	TD
Reynaud	23	5	132	5.7	20	0
Blackmon	14	7	94	6.7	22	0
Ross	6	1	37	6.2	14	0
Giants	43	13	263	6.1	22	0
Opponents	36	7	535	14.9	93t	2

KICKOFF RETURNS	No.	Yds	Avg	LG	TD
Ware	21	432	20.6	37	0
Reynaud	21	386	18.4	31	0
Blackmon	13	238	18.3	42	0
Nicks	1	14	14.0	14	0
Pierre-Paul	1	12	12.0	12	0
Giants	57	1082	19.0	42	0
Opponents	77	1515	19.7	58	0

FIELD GOALS	1-19	20-29	30-39	40-49	50+
Tynes	0/0	12/12	2/4	3/4	2/3
Giants	0/0	12/12	2/4	3/4	2/3
Opponents	0/0	9/9	6/8	5/7	3/3

SACKS	No.
Tuck	11.5
Umenyiora	11.5
Pierre-Paul	4.5
Cofield	4.0
Kiwanuka	4.0
Bernard	2.0
Canty	1.5
Boley	1.0
Goff	1.0
Grant	1.0
Ross	1.0
T. Thomas	1.0
(group)	1.0
Rolle	0.5
Tollefson	0.5
Giants	46.0
Opponents	16.0

RECORD HOLDERS
INDIVIDUAL RECORDS—CAREER

Category	Name	Performance
Rushing (Yds.)	Tiki Barber, 1997-2006	10,449
Passing (Yds.)	Phil Simms, 1979-1993	33,462
Passing (TDs)	Phil Simms, 1979-1993	199
Receiving (No.)	Amani Toomer, 1996-2008	668
Receiving (Yds.)	Amani Toomer, 1996-2008	9,497
Interceptions	Emlen Tunnell, 1948-1958	74
Punting (Avg.)	Don Chandler, 1956-1964	43.8
Punt Return (Avg.)	Ward Cuff, 1941-45	12.1
Kickoff Return (Avg.)	Rocky Thompson, 1971-73	27.2
Field Goals	Pete Gogolak, 1966-1974	126
Touchdowns (Tot.)	Frank Gifford, 1952-1964	78
Points	Pete Gogolak, 1966-1974	646
*Sacks	Michael Strahan, 1993-2007	141.5

INDIVIDUAL RECORDS—SINGLE SEASON

Category	Name	Performance
Rushing (Yds.)	Tiki Barber, 2005	1,860
Passing (Yds.)	Kerry Collins, 2002	4,073
Passing (TDs)	Y.A. Tittle, 1963	36
Receiving (No.)	Steve Smith, 2009	107
Receiving (Yds.)	Amani Toomer, 2002	1,343
Interceptions	Otto Schnellbacher, 1951	11
	Jim Patton, 1958	11
Punting (Avg.)	Don Chandler, 1959	46.6
Punt Return (Avg.)	Merle Hapes, 1942	15.5
Kickoff Return (Avg.)	John Salscheider, 1949	31.6
Field Goals	Ali Haji-Sheikh, 1983	35
	Jay Feely, 2005	35
	John Carney, 2008	35
Touchdowns (Tot.)	Joe Morris, 1985	21
Points	Jay Feely, 2005	148
*Sacks	Michael Strahan, 2001	**22.5

INDIVIDUAL RECORDS—SINGLE GAME

Category	Name	Performance
Rushing (Yds.)	Tiki Barber, 12-30-06	234
Passing (Yds.)	Phil Simms, 10-13-85	513
Passing (TDs)	Y.A. Tittle, 10-28-62	**7
Receiving (No.)	Tiki Barber, 1-2-00	13
Receiving (Yds.)	Del Shofner, 10-28-62	269
Interceptions	Many times	3
	Last time by Terry Kinard, 9-20-87	
Field Goals	Joe Danelo, 10-18-81	6
Touchdowns (Tot.)	Ron Johnson, 10-2-72	4
	Earnest Gray, 9-7-80	4
	Rodney Hampton, 9-24-95	4
Points	Ron Johnson, 10-2-72	24
	Earnest Gray, 9-7-80	24
	Rodney Hampton, 9-24-95	24
*Sacks	Osi Umenyiora, 9-30-07	6.0

*Sacks became an official statistic in 1982.
**NFL Record

VETERAN ROSTER AS OF MARCH 3, 2011

No.	Name	Pos.	Ht.	Wt.	Birthdate	^NFL Exp.	College	Hometown	How Acq.	'10 Games/ Starts
73	Andrews, Shawn	OL	6-4	335	12/25/82	8	Arkansas	Camden, Ark.	FA-'10	13/7
48	Ballard, Jake	TE	6-6	256	12/21/87	2	Ohio State	Springboro, Ohio	FA-'10	1/0
13	Barden, Ramses	WR	6-6	227	1/1/86	3	Cal Poly	La Canada Flintridge, Calif.	D3-'09	6/0
65	Beatty, Will	T	6-6	307	3/2/85	3	Connecticut	York, Pa.	D2-'09	8/2
47	Beckum, Travis	TE	6-3	239	1/24/87	3	Wisconsin	Milwaukee, Wisc.	D3-'09	16/2
95	Bernard, Rocky	DT	6-3	308	4/19/79	10	Texas A&M	Baytown, Texas	UFA(Sea)-'09	14/0
57	Blackburn, Chase	LB	6-3	247	6/10/83	7	Akron	Marysville, Ohio	FA-'05	14/0
59	Boley, Michael	LB	6-3	223	8/24/82	7	Southern Mississippi	Elkmont, Ala.	UFA(Atl)-'09	16/15
77	Boothe, Kevin	G	6-5	315	7/5/83	6	Cornell	Fort Lauderdale, Fla.	W(Oak)-'07	8/5
89	Boss, Kevin	TE	6-6	253	1/11/84	5	Western Oregon	Philomath, Ore.	D5-'07	15/13
44	Bradshaw, Ahmad	RB	5-9	198	3/19/86	5	Marshall	Bluefield, Va.	D7b-'07	16/11
53	Bulluck, Keith	LB	6-3	235	4/4/77	12	Syracuse	New City, N.Y.	FA-'10	13/8
84	Calhoun, Duke	WR	6-4	205	9/1/87	2	Memphis	Memphis, Tenn.	FA-'10	9/0
99	Canty, Chris	DT	6-7	304	11/10/82	7	Virginia	Charlotte, N.C.	UFA(Dall)-'09	16/16
83	Clayton, Michael	WR	6-4	215	10/13/82	8	Louisiana State	Baton Rouge, La.	FA-'10	6/0
37	Coe, Michael	DB	6-0	190	12/17/83	4	Alabama State	Memphis, Tenn.	FA-'10	4/0
96	Cofield, Barry	DT	6-4	306	3/19/84	6	Northwestern	Cleveland Heights, Ohio	D4a-'06	16/16
80	Cruz, Victor	WR	6-1	200	11/11/86	2	Massachusetts	Paterson, N.J.	FA-'10	3/0
51	DeOssie, Zak	LS	6-4	249	5/24/84	5	Brown	No. Andover, Mass.	D4-'07	16/0
66	Diehl, David	T	6-5	319	9/15/80	9	Illinois	Oak Lawn, Ill.	D5-'03	12/12
55	Dillard, Phillip	LB	6-0	245	12/10/86	2	Nebraska	Tulsa, Okla.	D4-'10	7/0
6	Dodge, Matt	P	6-1	224	5/30/87	2	East Carolina	Morehead City, N.C.	D7-'10	16/0
2	Giguere, Samuel	WR	5-11	215	7/11/85	2	Sherbrooke (Quebec)	Quebec, Canada	FA-'10	0*
54	Goff, Jonathan	LB	6-2	236	12/12/85	4	Vanderbilt	Lynn, Mass.	D5-'08	16/16
34	Grant, Deon	S	6-2	215	3/14/79	12	Tennessee	Augusta, Ga.	FA-'10	16/8
85	Hagan, Derek	WR	6-2	215	9/21/84	6	Arizona State	Palmdale, Calif.	FA-'10	7/4
93	Hall, Alex	DE	6-4	250	8/17/85	4	St. Augustine's	Glenarden, Md.	FA-'10	2/0
39	Hedgecock, Madison	FB	6-3	266	8/27/81	7	North Carolina	Wallburg, N.C.	W(StL)-'07	4/3
87	Hixon, Domenik	WR	6-2	182	10/8/84	6	Akron	Columbus, Ohio	W(Den)-'07	0*
22	Jackson, Brian	DB	6-0	198	5/4/87	2	Oklahoma	DeSoto, Texas	FA-'10	12/0
27	Jacobs, Brandon	RB	6-4	264	7/6/82	7	Southern Illinois	Napoleonville, La.	D4-'05	16/5
25	Johnson, Bruce	CB	5-11	182	12/18/87	3	Miami	Live Oak, Fla.	FA-'09	6/0
20	Johnson, Michael	S	6-2	207	6/9/84	5	Arizona	Pflugerville, Texas	D7-'07	2/0
35	Jones, Chad	S	6-2	221	10/5/88	2	Louisiana State	Baton Rouge, La.	D3-'10	0*
97	Joseph, Linval	DT	6-4	319	10/10/88	2	East Carolina	Gainesville, Fla.	D2-'10	6/0
94	Kiwanuka, Mathias	DE	6-5	265	3/8/83	6	Boston College	Indianapolis, Ind.	D1-'06	3/1
61	Koets, Adam	OL	6-5	300	1/7/84	5	Oregon State	Santa Ana, Calif.	D6-'07	8/4
10	Manning, Eli	QB	6-4	225	1/3/81	8	Mississippi	New Orleans, La.	T(SD)-'04	16/16
82	Manningham, Mario	WR	5-11	183	5/25/86	4	Michigan	Warren, Ohio	D3-'08	16/8
67	McKenzie, Kareem	T	6-6	327	5/24/79	11	Penn State	Willingboro, N.J.	UFA(NYJ)-'05	16/16
79	Meredith, Jamon	T	6-5	304	5/11/86	3	South Carolina	Simpsonville, S.C.	W(Det)-'10	5/0*
	Ndukwe, Ikechuku	OL	6-4	325	7/17/82	5	Northwestern	Dublin, Ohio	FA-'11	0*
88	Nicks, Hakeem	WR	6-0	215	1/14/88	3	North Carolina	Charlotte, N.C.	D1-'09	13/12
60	O'Hara, Shaun	C	6-3	303	6/23/77	12	Rutgers	Hillsborough, N.J.	UFA(Cle)-'04	6/6
86	Pascoe, Bear	TE	6-5	251	2/23/86	3	Fresno State	Porterville, Calif.	FA-'09	15/11
62	Petrus, Mitch	G	6-3	307	5/11/87	2	Arkansas	Carlisle, Ark.	D5-'10	11/0
21	Phillips, Kenny	S	6-2	210	11/24/86	4	Miami	Miami, Fla.	D1-'07	16/16
90	Pierre-Paul, Jason	DE	6-5	270	1/1/89	2	South Florida	Deerfield Beach, Fla.	D1-'10	16/0
15	Reynaud, Darius	WR	5-9	201	12/29/84	4	West Virginia	Luling, La.	T(Minn)-'10	9/0
26	Rolle, Antrel	S	6-0	208	12/16/82	6	Miami	Homestead, Fla.	FA-'10	16/16
18	Rosenfels, Sage	QB	6-4	225	3/16/78	11	Iowa State	Maquoketa, Iowa	T(Minn)-'10	12/0
31	Ross, Aaron	CB	6-0	197	9/15/82	5	Texas	Tyler, Texas	D1-'07	15/1
69	Seubert, Rich	G	6-3	310	3/30/79	11	Western Illinois	Marshfield, Wisc.	FA-'01	16/16
52	Sintim, Clint	LB	6-2	256	2/21/86	3	Virginia	Woodbridge, Va.	D2-'09	13/1
12	Smith, Steve	WR	5-11	195	5/6/85	5	Southern California	Woodland Hills, Calif.	D2-'07	9/7
76	Snee, Chris	G	6-3	317	1/18/82	8	Boston College	Montrose, Pa.	D2-'04	16/16
19	Sorgi, Jim	QB	6-5	196	12/3/80	8	Wisconsin	Fraser, Mich.	UFA(Ind)-'10	0*
81	Thomas, Devin	WR	6-2	218	11/15/86	4	Michigan State	Ann Arbor, Mich.	W(Car)-'10	4/0
24	Thomas, Terrell	CB	6-0	199	1/8/85	4	Southern California	Alto Loma, Calif.	D2-'08	16/15
71	Tollefson, Dave	DE	6-4	255	7/10/82	5	Northwest Missouri St.	Concord, Calif.	FA-'07	13/0
98	Tracy, Adrian	LB	6-2	248	4/6/87	2	William & Mary	Sterling, Va.	D6-'10	0*
91	Tuck, Justin	DE	6-5	274	3/29/83	7	Notre Dame	Kellyton, Ala.	D3-'05	16/16
9	Tynes, Lawrence	K	6-1	202	5/3/78	8	Troy	Milton, Fla.	T(KC)-'07	15/0
72	Umenyiora, Osi	DE	6-3	261	11/16/81	9	Troy	Auburn, Ala.	D2-'03	16/16
28	Ware, D.J.	RB	6-0	234	2/18/85	5	Georgia	Rockmart, Ga.	FA-'07	14/0
	Watkins, Todd	WR	6-3	195	6/22/83	3	Brigham Young	San Diego, Calif.	FA-'11	0*

VETERAN ROSTER AS OF MARCH 3, 2011 (CONTINUED)

No.	Name	Pos.	Ht.	Wt.	Birthdate	^NFL Exp.	College	Hometown	How Acq.	'10 Games/ Starts
23	Webster, Corey	CB	6-0	202	3/2/82	7	Louisiana State	Vacherie, La.	D2-'05	15/15
58	Wilkinson, Gerris	LB	6-3	231	4/5/83	6	Georgia Tech	Oakland, Calif.	D3-'06	12/0
29	Witherspoon, Brian	DB	5-10	180	6/5/85	3	Stillman	Butler, Ala.	FA-'10	1/0

* Giguere played 1 game with Indianapolis in '10; Hixon missed '10 season because of injury; C. Jones missed '10 season because of injury; Meredith played 2 games with Buffalo and 3 games with Giants; Ndukwe last active with Kansas City in '09; Sorgi missed '10 season because of injury; Tracy missed '10 season because of injury; Watkins last active with Oakland in '09.

Also played with Giants in '10—K Shayne Graham (1 game), DB D.J. Johnson (7), LB Bryan Kehl (1).

^ "NFL Exp." as of 2011 Kickoff Weekend. For full explanation of how a player's NFL Experience is measured, refer to explanation underneath the First-Year Roster listed below.

FIRST-YEAR ROSTER

Name	Pos.	Ht.	Wt.	Birthdate	College	Hometown	How Acq.
Amukamara, Prince	CB	6-0	206	6/6/89	Nebraska	Glendale, Ariz.	D1
Austin, Marvin	DT	6-2	312	1/1/89	North Carolina	Washington, D.C.	D2
Brewer, James Jr.	T	6-6	323	12/23/87	Indiana	Indianapolis, Ind.	D4
Burnett, Joe	DB	5-9	198	11/28/86	Central Florida	Eustis, Fla.	FA
Cordle, Jim (1)	C	6-4	297	8/22/87	Ohio State	Lancaster, Ohio	FA-'10
Harris, Cary	DB	5-11	187	3/22/87	Southern California	Pacoima, Calif.	FA
Hendricks, Dwayne (1)	DT	6-4	300	3/17/86	Miami	Millville, N.J.	FA-'10
Ingram, Kenny (1)	LB	6-6	229	2/27/86	Florida State	Edgewater, Fla.	FA-'10
Jernigan, Jerrel	WR	5-8	181	6/14/89	Troy	Eufaula, Ala.	D3
Jones, Greg	LB	5-11	240	10/5/88	Michigan State	Cincinnati, Ohio	D6
Mallett, Martell	RB	6-0	210	5/13/86	Arkansas-Pine Bluff	Pine Bluff, Ark.	FA
Okpokowuruk, Ayanga (1)	DE	6-3	250	6/19/87	Duke	Chattanooga, Tenn.	FA-'10
Perrilloux, Ryan	QB	6-3	223	1/1/87	Jacksonville State	Reserve, La.	FA
Sash, Tyler	S	6-0	211	5/27/88	Iowa	Oskaloosa, Iowa	D6
Scott, Charles (1)	RB	5-11	238	8/8/88	Louisiana State	Saline, La.	FA-'10
Scott, Da'Rel	RB	5-11	205	5/26/88	Maryland	Conshohocken, Pa.	D7
Turenne, Woodny (1)	DB	6-0	184	1/25/87	Louisville	Ft. Lauderdale, Fla.	FA-'10
Williams, Jacquian	LB	6-3	216	7/20/88	South Florida	Apopka, Fla.	D6

The term NFL Rookie is defined as a player who is in his first season of professional football and has not been on the roster of another professional football team for any regular-season or postseason games. A Rookie is designated by an "R" on NFL rosters. Players who have been active in another professional football league or players who have NFL experience, including either preseason training camp or being on an Active List or Inactive List, or on Reserve/Injured or Reserve/Physically Unable to Perform for fewer than six regular-season games, are termed NFL First-Year Players. An NFL First-Year Player is designated by a "1" on NFL rosters. Thereafter, a player is credited with an additional year of experience for each season in which he accumulates six games on the Active List or Inactive List, or on Reserve/Injured or Reserve/Physically Unable to Perform.

Log on to www.giants.com for an up-to-date roster.

COACHING STAFF

Head Coach,
Tom Coughlin

Pro Career: Was named the sixteenth head coach in Giants history on January 6, 2004. This season marks Coughlin's eighth with the Giants and sixteenth as an NFL head coach. In 2010, the Giants posted a record of 10-6. The Giants finished the 2009 season with an 8-8 record. In the 2008 season the Giants finished with a 12-4 record, which won the NFC East division. Coughlin directed the Giants 17-14 win over the New England Patriots in Super Bowl XLII on February 3, 2008, the third championship in the teams history. Coached the Giants to an 11-5 record, the NFC East title and the playoffs in 2005-06, his second and third seasons with the team. Coughlin previously spent eight years (1995-2002) with the Jacksonville Jaguars. Under Coughlin, the Jaguars had the most victories of any NFL expansion team in its first seven seasons. They were also the only expansion team in NFL history to advance to the playoffs four times in their first five seasons. Coughlin's team went 9-7 in 1996 and an NFL-best 14-2 in 1999, both times reaching the AFC Championship Game. Coughlin previously coached the Philadelphia Eagles (1984-85), Green Bay Packers (1986-87), and Giants (1988-1990). He was a member of the Giants' Super Bowl XXV champion coaching staff. Career record: 141-114.

Background: Served as head coach at Boston College (1991-93), and coached at Syracuse (1969, 1974-1980), Rochester Institute of Technology 1970-73 (head coach), and Boston College (1981-83). Played wingback for Syracuse (1965-67).

Personal: Born August 31, 1946, Waterloo, N.Y. Tom and his wife Judy have two daughters, Keli and Katie; two son-in-laws named Chris; two sons, Brian and Tim; two daughters-in-law, Andrea (Tim's wife) and Susie (Brian's wife); and five grandchildren, Emma Rose, Dylan, Shea, Cooper, and Caroline.

ASSISTANT COACHES

Jack Bicknell, Jr., asst. offensive line; born Feb 7, 1963, North Plainfield, N.J. Center Boston College 1981-85. No pro playing experience. College coach: Boston College 1985-87, 2007-08, New Hampshire 1987-1996, Louisiana Tech 1997-2006 (head coach 1999-2006). Pro coach: Joined Giants in 2009.

Perry Fewell, defensive coordinator; born September 7, 1962, Gastonia, N.C. Defensive back Lenoir-Rhyne 1981-84. No pro playing experience. College coach: North Carolina 1985-86, Army 1987, 1992-94, Kent State 1988-1991, Vanderbilt 1995-97. Pro coach: Jacksonville Jaguars 1998-2002, St. Louis Rams 2003-04, Chicago Bears 2005, Buffalo Bills 2006-09, joined Giants in 2010.

Pat Flaherty, offensive line; born April 27, 1956, Hanover, Pa. Center East Stroudsburg 1974-77. No pro playing experience. College coach: East Stroudsburg 1980-81, Penn State 1982-83, Rutgers 1984-1991, East Carolina 1992, Wake Forest 1993-98, Iowa 1999. Pro coach: Washington Redskins 2000, Chicago Bears 2001-03, joined Giants in 2004.

Kevin Gilbride, offensive coordinator; born August 27, 1951, New Haven, Conn. Quarterback/tight end Southern Connecticut State 1971-73. No pro playing experience. College coach: Idaho State 1974-75, Tufts 1976-77, American International 1978-79. Southern Connecticut State 1980-84, East Carolina 1987-88. Pro coach: Ottawa Rough Riders (CFL) 1985-86, Houston Oilers 1989-1994, Jacksonville Jaguars 1995-96, San Diego Chargers 1997-98 (head coach), Pittsburgh Steelers 1999-2000, Buffalo Bills 2002-2003, joined Giants in 2004.

Kevin Gilbride, Jr., offensive quality control; born December 14, 1979, Jacksonville. Quarterback, Hawaii 2000. No pro playing experience. College coach: Syracuse 2004-05, Georgetown 2006, Temple 2007-09. Pro coach: Joined Giants in 2010.

Peter Giunta, secondary/corners; born August 11, 1956, Salem, Mass. Running back/defensive back Northeastern 1974-77. No pro playing experience. College coach: Penn State 1981-83, Brown 1984-87, Lehigh 1988-1990. Pro coach: Philadelphia Eagles 1991-94, N.Y. Jets 1995-96, St. Louis Rams 1997-2000, Kansas City Chiefs 2001-2005, joined Giants in 2006.

Jim Hermann, linebackers; born December 8, 1960, Hollywood, Calif. Linebacker Michigan 1979-1982. No pro playing experience. College coach: Michigan 1983, 1986-2005. Pro coach: New York Jets 2006-2008, joined Giants in 2009.

Al Holcomb, defensive quality control; born October 22, 1970, Queens, N.Y. Attended West Virginia. No college or pro playing experience. College coach: Temple 1995-96, Colby College 1997, Bloomsburg 1998-2003, Kutztown 2004-05, Lafayette 2006-08. Pro coach: Joined Giants in 2009.

Jerald Ingram, running backs; born December 24, 1960, Dayton, Ohio. Fullback Michigan 1979-1983. College coach: Michigan 1984, Ball State 1985-1990, Boston College 1991-93. Pro coach: Jacksonville Jaguars 1994-2002, joined Giants in 2004.

Larry Izzo, asst. special teams; born September 26, 1974, Fort Belvoir, Va. Linebacker Rice 1992-95. Pro linebacker/special teamer Miami Dolphins 1996-2000, New England Patriots 2001-08, New York Jets 2009. Pro coach: Joined Giants in 2011.

David Merritt Sr., secondary/safeties;

born September 8, 1971, Raleigh, N.C. Linebacker North Carolina State 1989-1992. Pro linebacker Miami Dolphins 1993, Arizona Cardinals 1993-96, Rhein Fire (NFLE) 1997. College coach: Chattanooga 1997, Virginia Military Institute 1998-2000. Pro coach: New York Jets 2001-2003, joined Giants in 2004.

Robert Nunn, defensive line; born June 10, 1965, Apache, Okla. Linebacker Oklahoma State 1984-87. No pro playing experience. College coach: Northeastern Oklahoma 1988, Tennessee 1989-1990, Georgia Military 1991-99. Pro coach: Miami Dolphins 2000-02, 2004, Washington Redskins 2003, Green Bay Packers 2005-08, Tampa Bay Buccaneers 2009, joined Giants in 2010.

Jerry Palmieri, strength and conditioning; born October 30, 1958, Englewood, N.J. Attended Montclair State. No college or pro playing experience. College coach: North Carolina 1982-83, Oklahoma State 1984-86, Kansas State 1987-1992, Boston College 1993-94. Pro coach: Jacksonville Jaguars 1995-2002, New Orleans Saints 2003, joined Giants in 2004.

Marcus Paul, asst. strength and conditioning; born April 1, 1966, Orlando, Fla. Safety Syracuse 1984-88. Pro safety Chicago Bears 1989-1993, Tampa Bay Buccaneers 1993. Pro coach: New Orleans Saints 1998-99, New England Patriots 2000-04, New York Jets 2005-2006, joined Giants in 2007.

Michael Pope, tight ends; born March 15, 1942, Monroe, N.C. Quarterback Lenoir-Rhyne 1962-64. No pro playing experience. College coach: Florida State 1970-74, Texas Tech 1975-77, Mississippi 1978-1982. Pro coach: New York Giants 1983-1991, Cincinnati Bengals 1992-93, New England Patriots 1994-96, Washington Redskins 1997-99, re-joined Giants in 2000.

Tom Quinn, special teams coordinator; born January 27, 1968, Pasadena, Calif. Linebacker Arizona 1986-1990. No pro playing experience. College coach: Davidson College 1991, James Madison 1992-94, Boston 1995, Holy Cross 1996-98, San Jose State 1999-2001, Stanford 2002-05. Pro coach: Joined Giants in 2006.

Sean Ryan, wide receivers; born May 1, 1972, Glenn Falls, N.Y. Defensive back Hamilton College 1994. No pro playing experience. College coach: Albany 1998-99, Colgate 2000, Boston College 2001-02, Columbia 2003-04, Harvard 2006. Pro coach: Joined Giants in 2007.

Mike Sullivan, quarterbacks; born January 28, 1967, Santa Maria, Calif. Defensive back Army 1987-88. No pro playing experience. College coach: Mt. San Jacinto (Calif.) J.C. 1993, Humboldt State 1993-94, Army 1995-96, 1999-2000, Youngstown State 1997-98, Ohio 2001. Pro coach: Jacksonville Jaguars 2002-03, joined Giants in 2004.

National Football Conference
East Division
Team Colors: Midnight Green, Silver, Black, and White

NovaCare Complex
One NovaCare Way
Philadelphia, Pennsylvania 19145
Telephone: (215) 463-2500

2011 SCHEDULE
PRESEASON
Aug. 11	**Baltimore**	7:30
Aug. 18	at Pittsburgh	8:00
Aug. 25	**Cleveland**	7:30
Sep. 1	at New York Jets	7:30

REGULAR SEASON
Sep. 11	at St. Louis	1:00
Sep. 18	at Atlanta	8:20
Sep. 25	**New York Giants**	1:00
Oct. 2	**San Francisco**	1:00
Oct. 9	at Buffalo	1:00
Oct. 16	at Washington	1:00
Oct. 23	BYE	
Oct. 30	**Dallas**	8:20
Nov. 7	**Chicago** (Mon)	8:30
Nov. 13	**Arizona**	1:00
Nov. 20	at New York Giants *	8:20
Nov. 27	**New England**	4:15
Dec. 1	at Seattle (Thu)	8:20
Dec. 11	at Miami	1:00
Dec. 18	**New York Jets**	4:15
Dec. 24	at Dallas (Sat)	4:15
Jan. 1	**Washington**	1:00

All times ET; Sunday night games in Weeks 11-15, 17 subject to change
Stadium: Lincoln Financial Field
(opened in 2003)
• **Capacity:** 69,144
One Lincoln Financial Field Way
Philadelphia, Pennsylvania 19148
Playing Surface: Natural Grass
Training Camp: Lehigh University
Bethlehem, PA 18015

LINCOLN FINANCIAL FIELD

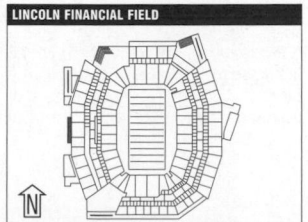

CLUB OFFICIALS
Chairman/Chief Executive Officer:
Jeffrey Lurie
President: Joe Banner
Head Coach/Executive Vice President of
Football Operations: Andy Reid
General Manager: Howie Roseman
Director of Player Personnel:
Ryan Grigson
Chief Operating Officer: Don Smolenski
Senior Vice President/Business:
Ari Roitman
Executive Director of Eagles Youth
Partnership: Sarah Martinez-Helfman
Director of Pro Personnel: Louis Riddick
Director of Football Media Relations:
Derek Boyko
Senior Vice President/Chief Marketing
Officer: Tim McDermott
Director of Human Resources:
Kristie Pappal
Manager of Community Relations:
Julie Hirshey
Director of Events: Leonard Bonacci
Director of Ticket Operations:
Laini Delawter
Director of Ticket Client Relations:
Leo Carlin
Director of Merchandise:
Brendan McQuillen
Director of Team Security: David Young
Head Athletic Trainer: Rick Burkholder
Asst. Athletic Trainers: Steve Condon,
Chris Peduzzi
Video Director: Mike Dougherty
Head Equipment Manager: John Hatfield

COACHING HISTORY
(528-561-26)
Records include postseason games
1933-35	Lud Wray	9-21-1
1936-1940	Bert Bell	10-44-2
1941-1950	Earle (Greasy) Neale*	66-44-5
1951	Alvin (Bo) McMillin**	2-0-0
1951	Wayne Millner	2-8-0
1952-55	Jim Trimble	25-20-3
1956-57	Hugh Devore	7-16-1
1958-1960	Lawrence (Buck) Shaw	20-16-1
1961-63	Nick Skorich	15-24-3
1964-68	Joe Kuharich	28-41-1
1969-1971	Jerry Williams***	7-22-2
1971-72	Ed Khayat	8-15-2
1973-75	Mike McCormack	16-25-1
1976-1982	Dick Vermeil	57-51-0
1983-85	Marion Campbell****	17-29-1
1985	Fred Bruney	1-0-0
1986-1990	Buddy Ryan	43-38-1
1991-94	Rich Kotite	37-29-0
1995-98	Ray Rhodes	30-36-1
1999-2010	Andy Reid	128-82-1

*Co-coach with Walt Kiesling in Philadelphia-
Pittsburgh merger in 1943
**Retired after two games in 1951
***Released after three games in 1971
****Released after 15 games in 1985

PAID ATTENDANCE
Home 538,799   Away 551,629
Total 1,090,428
Single-game home record,
72,111 (11/1/81)
Single-season home record,
557,325 (1980)

2011 DRAFT CHOICES
Round	Name	Pos.	College
1	Danny Watkins	G	Baylor
2	Jaiquawn Jarrett	DB	Temple
3	Curtis Marsh	DB	Utah State
4	Casey Matthews	LB	Oregon
	Alex Henery	K	Nebraska
5	Dion Lewis	RB	Pittsburgh
	Julian Vandervelde	G	Iowa
6	Jason Kelce	C	Cincinnati
	Brian Rolle	LB	Ohio State
7	Greg Lloyd	LB	Connecticut
	Stanley Havili	RB	Southern California

2010 TEAM RECORD

PRESEASON (2-2)

Date	Result	Opponent
8/13	W 28-27	Jacksonville
8/20	L 9-22	at Cincinnati
8/27	W 20-17	at Kansas City
9/2	L 17-21	New York Jets

REGULAR SEASON (10-6)

Date	Result	Opponent
9/12	L 20-27	Green Bay
9/19	W 35-32	at Detroit
9/26	W 28-3	at Jacksonville
10/3	L 12-17	Washington
10/10	W 27-24	at San Francisco
10/17	W 31-17	Atlanta
10/24	L 19-37	at Tennessee
11/7	W 26-24	Indianapolis
11/15	W 59-28	at Washington
11/21	W 27-17	New York Giants
11/28	L 26-31	at Chicago
12/2	W 34-24	Houston
12/12	W 30-27	at Dallas
12/19	W 38-31	at New York Giants
12/28	L 14-24	Minnesota
1/2	L 13-14	Dallas

POSTSEASON (0-1)

Date	Result	Opponent
1/9	L 16-21	Green Bay

SCORE BY PERIODS

Eagles	110	123	68	138	0 —	439
Opponents	59	128	78	112	0 —	377

2010 TEAM STATISTICS

	Eagles	Opp.
Total First Downs	322	309
Rushing	116	91
Passing	189	185
Penalty	17	33
3rd Down: Made/Att	85/214	80/209
3rd Down Pct.	39.7	38.3
4th Down: Made/Att	9/13	5/12
4th Down Pct.	69.2	41.7
Possession Avg.	31:15	28:45
Total Net Yards	6230	5235
Avg. Per Game	389.4	327.2
Total Plays	1038	998
Avg. Per Play	6.0	5.2
Net Yards Rushing	2324	1766
Avg. Per Game	145.3	110.4
Total Rushes	428	423
Net Yards Passing	3906	3469
Avg. Per Game	244.1	216.8
Sacked/Yards Lost	49/309	39/292
Gross Yards	4215	3761
Att./Completions	561/348	536/309
Completion Pct.	62.0	57.6
Had Intercepted	13	23
Punts/Average	73/43.8	82/43.9
Net Punting Avg.	73/39.0	82/37.0
Penalties/Yards	129/1101	87/724
Fumbles/Ball Lost	33/12	18/11
Touchdowns	49	46
Rushing	18	12
Passing	28	31
Returns	3	3

2010 INDIVIDUAL STATISTICS

PASSING

	Att.	Comp.	Yds.	Pct.	TD	Int.	Tkld.	Rate
Vick	372	233	3018	62.6	21	6	34/210	100.2
Kolb	189	115	1197	60.8	7	7	15/99	76.1
Eagles	561	348	4215	62.0	28	13	49/309	92.1
Opponents	536	309	3761	57.6	31	23	39/292	80.8

SCORING

	TD R	TD P	TD Rt	PAT	FG	Saf	PTS
Akers	0	0	0	47/47	32/38	0	143
Maclin	0	10	0	0/0	0/0	0	60
McCoy	7	2	0	0/0	0/0	0	54
Vick	9	0	0	0/0	0/0	0	54
D. Jackson	1	6	1	0/0	0/0	0	48
Celek	0	4	0	0/0	0/0	0	24
Avant	0	1	0	0/0	0/0	0	8
R. Cooper	0	1	0	0/0	0/0	0	6
Hall	0	1	0	0/0	0/0	0	6
Harbor	0	1	0	0/0	0/0	0	6
Harrison	1	0	0	0/0	0/0	0	6
Herremans	0	1	0	0/0	0/0	0	6
Mikell	0	0	1	0/0	0/0	0	6
D. Patterson	0	0	1	0/0	0/0	0	6
Schmitt	0	1	0	0/0	0/0	0	6
Eagles	18	28	3	47/47	32/38	0	439
Opponents	12	31	3	45/45	18/21	0	377

2-Pt Conversions: Avant.
Eagles 1-2, Opponents 1-1.

RUSHING

	No.	Yds	Avg	LG	TD
McCoy	207	1080	5.2	62	7
Vick	100	676	6.8	35	9
Harrison	40	239	6.0	50t	1
D. Jackson	16	104	6.5	31t	1
Buckley	21	67	3.2	13	0
Kolb	15	65	4.3	19	0
Maclin	3	36	12.0	14	0
Hall	9	29	3.2	8	0
M. Bell	16	28	1.8	9	0
Weaver	1	0	0.0	0	0
Eagles	428	2324	5.4	62	18
Opponents	423	1766	4.2	61	12

RECEIVING

	No.	Yds	Avg	LG	TD
McCoy	78	592	7.6	40	2
Maclin	70	964	13.8	83t	10
Avant	51	573	11.2	34	1
D. Jackson	47	1056	22.5	91t	6
Celek	42	511	12.2	65t	4
Schmitt	19	136	7.2	18	1
Hall	11	115	10.5	48	1
Harbor	9	72	8.0	24	1
Harrison	8	43	5.4	15	0
R. Cooper	7	116	16.6	37	1
Mills	2	19	9.5	14	0
Buckley	1	10	10.0	10	0
M. Bell	1	5	5.0	5	0
Herremans	1	2	2.0	2t	1
McGlynn	1	1	1.0	1	0
Eagles	348	4215	12.1	91t	28
Opponents	309	3761	12.2	80t	31

PUNT RETURNS

	Ret	FC	Yds	Avg	LG	TD
D. Jackson	20	8	231	11.6	65t	1
Calvin	12	4	125	10.4	44	0
Hall	3	2	31	10.3	14	0
Maclin	3	5	17	5.7	9	0
Eagles	38	19	404	10.6	65t	1
Opponents	34	21	309	9.1	53	0

INTERCEPTIONS

	No.	Yds	Avg	LG	TD
Samuel	7	70	10.0	33	0
D. Patterson	4	40	10.0	40t	1
Allen	3	27	9.0	16	0
Mikell	3	0	0.0	0	0
Hanson	1	17	17.0	17	0
Laws	1	13	13.0	13	0
Lindley	1	8	8.0	8	0
Coleman	1	7	7.0	7	0
Bradley	1	0	0.0	0	0
Hobbs	1	0	0.0	0	0
Eagles	23	182	7.9	40t	1
Opponents	13	169	13.0	41t	1

PUNTING

	No.	Yds.	Avg.	In 20	LG
Rocca	73	3195	43.8	28	63
Eagles	73	3195	43.8	28	63
Opponents	82	3599	43.9	17	68

KICKOFF RETURNS

	No.	Yds	Avg	LG	TD
Calvin	32	692	21.6	41	0
Hobbs	16	345	21.6	46	0
Hall	4	65	16.3	21	0
Lawson	2	48	24.0	28	0
Schmitt	2	18	9.0	18	0
Maclin	1	22	22.0	22	0
Buckley	1	20	20.0	20	0
Harbor	1	19	19.0	19	0
D. Patterson	1	14	14.0	14	0
Celek	1	12	12.0	12	0
M. Bell	1	8	8.0	8	0
R. Cooper	0	—	—	9	0
Eagles	62	1272	20.5	46	0
Opponents	69	1502	21.8	61	0

FIELD GOALS

	1-19	20-29	30-39	40-49	50+
Akers	0/0	12/12	10/12	9/11	1/3
Eagles	0/0	12/12	10/12	9/11	1/3
Opponents	0/0	5/5	4/4	5/7	4/5

SACKS

	No.
T. Cole	10.0
Parker	6.0
Laws	4.0
Graham	3.0
Tapp	3.0
Allen	2.0
Dixon	2.0
M. Patterson	2.0
Sims	2.0
Bradley	1.0
Fokou	1.0
Mikell	1.0
D. Patterson	1.0
Te'o-Nesheim	1.0
Eagles	39.0
Opponents	49.0

RECORD HOLDERS
INDIVIDUAL RECORDS—CAREER

Category	Name	Performance
Rushing (Yds.)	Wilbert Montgomery, 1977-1984	6,538
Passing (Yds.)	Donovan McNabb, 1999-2009	32,873
Passing (TDs)	Donovan McNabb, 1999-2009	216
Receiving (No.)	Harold Carmichael, 1971-1983	589
Receiving (Yds.)	Harold Carmichael, 1971-1983	8,978
Interceptions	Bill Bradley, 1969-1976	34
	Eric Allen, 1988-1994	34
	Brian Dawkins, 1996-2008	34
Punting (Avg.)	Joe Muha, 1946-1950	42.9
Punt Return (Avg.)	Ernie Steele, 1942-48	16.8
Kickoff Return (Avg.)	Steve Van Buren, 1944-1951	26.7
Field Goals	David Akers, 1999-2010	294
Touchdowns (Tot.)	Harold Carmichael, 1971-1983	79
Points	David Akers, 1999-2010	1,323
*Sacks	Reggie White, 1985-1992	124.0

INDIVIDUAL RECORDS—SINGLE SEASON

Category	Name	Performance
Rushing (Yds.)	Wilbert Montgomery, 1979	1,512
Passing (Yds.)	Donovan McNabb, 2008	3,916
Passing (TDs)	Sonny Jurgensen, 1961	32
Receiving (No.)	Brian Westbrook, 2007	90
Receiving (Yds.)	Mike Quick, 1983	1,409
Interceptions	Bill Bradley, 1971	11
Punting (Avg.)	Joe Muha, 1948	47.2
Punt Return (Avg.)	Steve Van Buren, 1944	15.3
Kickoff Return (Avg.)	Al Nelson, 1972	29.1
Field Goals	David Akers, 2008	33
Touchdowns (Tot.)	Steve Van Buren, 1945	18
Points	David Akers, 2008	144
*Sacks	Reggie White, 1987	21.0

INDIVIDUAL RECORDS—SINGLE GAME

Category	Name	Performance
Rushing (Yds.)	Steve Van Buren, 11-27-49	205
Passing (Yds.)	Donovan McNabb, 12-5-04	464
Passing (TDs)	Adrian Burk, 10-17-54	**7
Receiving (No.)	Don Looney, 12-1-40	14
	Brian Westbrook, 11-4-07	14
Receiving (Yds.)	Tommy McDonald, 12-10-60	237
Interceptions	Russ Craft, 9-24-50	**4
Field Goals	Tom Dempsey, 11-12-72	6
Touchdowns (Tot.)	Many times	4
	Last time by Brian Westbrook, 11-27-08	
Points	Bobby Walston, 10-17-54	25
*Sacks	Clyde Simmons, 9-15-91	4.5
	Hugh Douglas, 10-18-98	4.5

*Sacks became an official statistic in 1982.
**NFL Record

VETERAN ROSTER AS OF MARCH 3, 2011

No.	Name	Pos.	Ht.	Wt.	Birthdate	^NFL Exp.	College	Hometown	How Acq.	'10 Games/ Starts
95	Abiamiri, Victor	DE	6-4	267	1/14/86	5	Notre Dame	Baltimore, Md.	D2b-'07	0*
45	Adams, Jamar	S	6-2	215	11/29/85	2	Michigan	Matthews, N.C.	FA-'10	1/1
2	Akers, David	K	5-10	200	12/9/74	13	Louisville	Lexington, Ky.	FA-99	16/0
29	Allen, Nate	S	6-1	210	11/30/87	2	South Florida	Cape Coral, Fla.	D2-'10	13/13
30	Anderson, Colt	S	5-10	194	10/25/85	2	Montana	Butte, Mont.	FA(Minn)-'10	8/2
81	Avant, Jason	WR	6-0	212	4/20/83	6	Michigan	Chicago, Ill.	D4b-'06	16/3
55	Bradley, Stewart	LB	6-4	258	11/2/83	5	Nebraska	Salt Lake City, Utah	D3a-'07	12/12
34	Buckley, Eldra	RB	5-9	207	6/23/85	3	Tennessee-Chattanooga	Charleston, Miss.	W(SD)-'09	16/0
97	Bunkley, Brodrick	DT	6-2	306	11/23/83	6	Florida State	Tampa, Fla.	D1-'06	14/5
38	Calvin, Jorrick	CB	5-11	192	7/17/87	2	Troy	Baton Rouge, La.	T(Ariz)-'10	12/0
87	Celek, Brent	TE	6-4	255	1/25/85	5	Cincinnati	Cincinnati, Ohio	D5b-'07	16/15
51	Chaney, Jamar	LB	6-0	242	10/11/86	2	Mississippi State	St. Lucie, Fla.	D7a-'10	14/2
63	Clark, Jeremy	DT	6-3	295	9/6/83	2	Alabama	Daphne, Ala.	FA-'10	3/1*
57	Clayton, Keenan	LB	6-1	229	6/19/87	2	Oklahoma	Sulphur Springs, Texas	D4b-'10	7/1
59	Cole, Nick	G/C	6-0	339	7/28/84	6	New Mexico State	Lawton, Okla.	FA-'06	13/7
58	Cole, Trent	DE	6-3	270	10/5/82	7	Cincinnati	Xenia, Ohio	D5a-'05	15/15
42	Coleman, Kurt	S	5-11	195	7/1/88	2	Ohio State	Clayton, Ohio	D7c-'10	15/2
14	Cooper, Riley	WR	6-3	222	9/9/87	2	Florida	Clearwater, Fla.	D5b-'10	13/2
90	Dixon, Antonio	DT	6-3	322	7/17/85	3	Miami	Miami, Fla.	W(Wash)-'09	15/10
46	Dorenbos, Jon	LS	6-0	250	7/21/80	9	Texas-El Paso	Garden Grove, Calif.	FA-'06	16/0
65	Dunlap, King	T	6-9	330	9/14/85	4	Auburn	Brentwood, Tenn.	D7-'08	14/5
53	Fokou, Moise	LB	6-1	236	8/28/85	3	Maryland	Potomac, Md.	D7b-'09	16/11
96	Gaither, Omar	LB	6-2	235	3/18/84	6	Tennessee	Charlotte, N.C.	D5b-'06	14/2
54	Graham, Brandon	DE	6-2	268	4/3/88	2	Michigan	Detroit, Mich.	D1-'10	13/6
16	Hall, Chad	WR	5-8	187	5/23/86	2	Air Force	Atlanta, Ga.	FA-'10	8/1
21	Hanson, Joselio	CB	5-9	185	8/13/81	7	Texas Tech	Playa del Rey, Calif.	FA-'06	15/6
82	Harbor, Clay	TE	6-3	252	7/2/87	2	Missouri State	Dwight, Ill.	D4d-'10	9/6
83	Harper, Rod	WR	6-0	209	3/26/85	2	Murray State	Bradenton, Fla.	FA-'10	0*
41	Harris, Antoine	S	5-10	202	4/8/82	5	Louisville	Columbus, Ohio	FA-'10	0*
33 t-	Harrison, Jerome	RB	5-9	205	2/26/83	6	Washington State	Kalamazoo, Mich.	T(Cle)-'10	12/2*
79	Herremans, Todd	G/T	6-6	321	10/13/82	7	Saginaw Valley State	Ravenna, Mich.	D4b-'05	16/15
31	Hobbs, Ellis	CB	5-9	195	5/16/83	7	Iowa State	DeSoto, Texas	T(NE)-'09	8/7
68	Howard, Austin	T	6-7	333	3/22/87	2	Northern Iowa	Davenport, Iowa	FA-'10	4/1
24	Hughes, Brandon	CB	5-11	188	5/23/86	3	Oregon State	Bloomington, Ill.	FA(NYG)-'10	1/0
88	Ingram, Cornelius	TE	6-4	250	6/10/85	2	Florida	Hawthorne, Fla.	D5a-'09	0*
10	Jackson, DeSean	WR	5-10	175	12/1/86	4	California	Long Beach, Calif.	D2b-'08	14/14
67	Jackson, Jamaal	C	6-4	325	5/8/80	8	Delaware State	Miami, Fla.	FA-'03	1/1
28	Jackson, Marlin	DB	6-0	196	6/30/83	7	Michigan	Sharon, Pa.	FA(Ind)-'10	0*
62	Jean-Gilles, Max	G	6-3	358	11/19/83	6	Georgia	Miami, Fla.	D4a-'06	13/10
	Jeanty, Rashad	LB	6-2	243	4/17/83	5	Central Florida	Miami, Fla.	FA-'11	0*
56	Jordan, Akeem	LB	6-1	230	8/17/85	5	James Madison	Harrisonburg, Va.	FA-'07	16/3
74	Justice, Winston	T	6-6	320	9/14/84	6	Southern California	Long Beach, Calif.	D2-'06	13/13
3	Kafka, Mike	QB	6-3	225	7/25/87	2	Northwestern	Chicago, Ill.	D4c-'10	0*
4	Kolb, Kevin	QB	6-3	218	8/24/84	5	Houston	Stephenville, Texas	D2a-'07	7/5
93	Laws, Trevor	DT	6-1	304	6/14/85	4	Notre Dame	Apple Valley, Minn.	D2a-'08	15/1
47	Lawson, Gerard	CB	5-10	195	1/12/85	3	Oregon State	Las Vegas, Nev.	FA-'10	1/0
35	Lindley, Trevard	CB	6-0	183	2/2/86	2	Kentucky	Hiram, Ga.	D4a-'10	11/1
18	Maclin, Jeremy	WR	6-0	198	5/11/88	3	Missouri	Kirkwood, Mo.	D1-'09	16/16
25	McCoy, LeSean	RB	5-11	208	7/12/88	3	Pittsburgh	Harrisburg, Pa.	D2-'09	15/13
73	McCray, Bobby	DE	6-6	260	8/8/81	7	Florida	Homestead, Fla.	FA-'10	1/0
77	McGlynn, Mike	G	6-4	315	3/8/85	4	Pittsburgh	Austintown, Ohio	D4a-'08	16/14
27	Mikell, Quintin	S	5-10	203	9/16/80	9	Boise State	Eugene, Ore.	FA-'03	15/15
	Moss, Sinorice	WR	5-8	185	12/28/83	6	Miami	Miami, Fla.	FA-'11	0*
	Nalbone, John	TE	6-4	255	5/14/86	2	Monmouth	Lawrenceville, N.J.	FA-'11	2/0*
75	Parker, Juqua	DE	6-2	250	5/15/78	11	Oklahoma State	Houston, Texas	FA-'05	13/10
23	Patterson, Dimitri	CB	5-10	200	6/18/83	6	Tuskegee	Orlando, Fla.	FA-'09	16/9
98	Patterson, Mike	DT	6-1	300	9/1/83	7	Southern California	Los Alamitos, Calif.	D1-'05	15/14
71	Peters, Jason	T	6-4	340	1/22/82	8	Arkansas	Queen City, Texas	T(Buff)-'09	13/13
6	Rocca, Sav	P	6-5	265	11/20/73	5	None	Lakeside, Australia	FA-'07	16/0
22	Samuel, Asante	CB	5-10	185	1/6/81	9	Central Florida	Lauderdale Lakes, Fla.	UFA(NE)-'08	11/10
94	Sapp, Ricky	LB/DE	6-4	252	11/14/86	2	Clemson	Bamberg, S.C.	D5a-'10	0*
32	Schmitt, Owen	FB	6-2	245	2/13/85	4	West Virginia	Fairfax, Va.	FA-'10	15/5
50	Sims, Ernie	LB	6-0	230	12/23/84	6	Florida State	Tallahassee, Fla.	T(Det)-'10	15/15
91	Tapp, Darryl	DE	6-1	270	9/13/84	6	Virginia Tech	Chesapeake, Va.	T(Sea)-'10	14/1
52	Te'o-Nesheim, Daniel	DE	6-3	263	6/12/87	2	Washington	Waikoloa, Hawai'i	D3-'10	6/1
78	Tupou, Fenuki	G/T	6-5	323	5/2/85	2	Oregon	Antelope, Calif.	D5c-'09	0*

VETERAN ROSTER AS OF MARCH 3, 2011 (CONTINUED)

No.	Name	Pos.	Ht.	Wt.	Birthdate	^ NFL Exp.	College	Hometown	How Acq.	'10 Games/ Starts
7	Vick, Michael	QB	6-0	215	6/26/80	10	Virginia Tech	Newport News, Va.	FA-'09	12/12
43	Weaver, Leonard	FB	6-0	250	9/23/82	7	Carson-Newman	Satellite, Fla.	FA(Sea)-'09	1/0
76	Wells, Reggie	G	6-4	318	11/3/80	9	Clarion	Library, Pa.	T(Ariz)-'10	8/1

* Abiamiri missed '10 season because of injury; Clark played in 1 game with Philadelphia and 2 games with Dallas in '10; Harper spent most of the '10 season on the Eagles practice squad; Harris missed '10 season because of injury; Harrison played in 8 games with Philadelphia and 4 games with Cleveland; Ingram spent most of '10 season on Eagles practice squad; M. Jackson missed '10 season because of injury; Jeanty last active with Cincinnati in '09; Kafka did not play in 5 games; Moss missed '10 because of injury with New York Giants; Nalbone played 2 games with Miami; Sapp missed '10 because of injury; Tupou spent '10 season on Eagles practice squad.

t- Eagles traded for Harrison (Cle).

Traded—RB Mike Bell (5 games in '10) to Cleveland.

Also played with Eagles in '10—DE Antwan Barnes (2 games), WR Hank Baskett (2), RB Joique Bell (3), DE/LB Derrick Burgess (1), TE Garrett Mills (7), S Jamar Wall (1).

^ "NFL Exp." as of 2011 Kickoff Weekend. For full explanation of how a player's NFL Experience is measured, refer to explanation underneath the First-Year Roster listed below.

FIRST-YEAR ROSTER

Name	Pos.	Ht.	Wt.	Birthdate	College	Hometown	How Acq.
Havili, Stanley	FB	6-0	230	11/14/87	Southern California	Salt Lake City, Utah	D7b
Henery, Alex	K/P	6-1	177	8/18/87	Nebraska	Omaha, Neb.	D4b
Hunt, Phillip (1)	DE	6-0	248	1/10/86	Houston	Fort Worth, Texas	FA
Jarrett, Jaiquawn	S	6-0	196	9/21/89	Temple	Brooklyn, N.Y.	D2
Kelce, Jason	G/C	6-3	282	11/5/87	Cincinnati	Cleveland, Ohio	D6a
Lloyd, Greg	LB	6-1	247	2/10/89	Connecticut	Clermont, Fla.	D7a
Lewis, Dion	RB	5-8	195	9/27/90	Pittsburgh	Blairstown, N.J.	D5a
Marsh, Curtis	CB	6-0	197	3/1/88	Utah State	Simi Valley, Calif.	D3
Matthews, Casey	LB	6-1	232	1/16/89	Oregon	Westlake Village, Calif.	D4a
Owens, Jeff (1)	DT	6-1	304	10/14/86	Georgia	Sunrise, Fla.	D7b-'10
Reynolds, Dallas (1)	G/C	6-4	320	4/23/84	Brigham Young	Provo, Utah	FA-'09
Rolle, Brian	LB	5-10	227	11/20/88	Ohio State	Immokalee, Fla.	D6b
Shipley, A.Q. (1)	C	6-1	315	5/22/86	Penn State	Coraopolis, Pa.	FA-'10
Trufant, Isaiah (1)	CB	5-8	170	12/9/82	Eastern Washington	Tacoma, Wash.	W(NYJ)
Vandervelde, Julian	G	6-2	300	10/7/87	Iowa	Davenport, Iowa	D5b
Wall, Jamar (1)	CB	5-10	202	1/10/88	Texas Tech	Plainview, Texas	FA-'10
Watkins, Danny	G	6-3	310	11/6/84	Baylor	Kelowna, B.C., Canada	D1
Williams, Jeremy (1)	WR	6-0	203	1/23/87	Tulane	Baytown, Texas	FA-'10

The term NFL Rookie is defined as a player who is in his first season of professional football and has not been on the roster of another professional football team for any regular-season or postseason games. A Rookie is designated by an "R" on NFL rosters. Players who have been active in another professional football league or players who have NFL experience, including either preseason training camp or being on an Active List or Inactive List, or on Reserve/Injured or Reserve/Physically Unable to Perform for fewer than six regular-season games, are termed NFL First-Year Players. An NFL First-Year Player is designated by a "1" on NFL rosters. Thereafter, a player is credited with an additional year of experience for each season in which he accumulates six games on the Active List or Inactive List, or on Reserve/Injured or Reserve/Physically Unable to Perform.

Log on to www.philadelphiaeagles.com for an up-to-date roster.

COACHING STAFF

Head Coach/Executive Vice President of Football Operations,
Andy Reid

Pro Career: Reid has earned NFL coach of the year honors twice, compiled the best win total (128), winning percentage (.609) and playoff victory total (10) in team history. He has captured six division titles and five trips to the NFC Championship game. Since he was hired in 1999, no other franchise has earned more divisional playoff round appearances (7) or conference championships appearances (5) than Philadelphia. Reid is one of 11 coaches in NFL history to win 60% or more of 200-plus games. In his 19-year NFL coaching career, Reid's teams have made the playoffs 15 times (19-14 record). He has coaches in the Super Bowl three times, the NFC Championship game nine times, and the Pro Bowl five times. Reid became the 20th head coach in franchise history on January 11, 1999, and was promoted to head coach/executive vice president of football operations in 2001. He was named NFL coach of the year in 2000 and 2002. He joined the Eagles after a seven-year stint as an assistant coach with Green Bay (1992-98) under Mike Holmgren. With Green Bay, Reid helped the Packers earn a Super Bowl XXXI victory over New England. Career record: 128-82-1.

Background: Coached at Brigham Young (1982), San Francisco State (1983-85), Northern Arizona (1986), Texas-El Paso (1987-88), and Missouri (1989-1991). Reid first met Holmgren, who was a member of BYU's coaching staff, when Reid was an offensive tackle and guard on three Cougar Holiday Bowl teams. Reid graduated with a bachelor's degree in physical education. He also received a master's degree in professional leadership in physical education and athletics.

Personal: Born in Los Angeles on March 19, 1958, Reid and his wife Tammy have five children—Garrett, Britt, Crosby, Drew Ann, and Spencer.

ASSISTANT COACHES

Bobby April, special teams coordinator; born April 15, 1963. Linebacker/defensive end Nicholls State 1972-75. No pro playing experience. College coach: Southern Mississippi 1978, Tulane 1979, Arizona 1980-86, Southern California 1987-1990. Pro coach: Atlanta Falcons 1991-93, Pittsburgh Steelers 1994-95, New Orleans Saints 1996-99, St. Louis Rams 2001-02, Buffalo Bills 2004-09, joined Eagles in 2010.

Bobby April III, defensive quality control; born August 15, 1981, Tucson, Ariz. Attended Louisiana-Lafayette. No college or pro playing experience. College coach: Tulane 2005-06, Portland State 2007-09, Nicholls State 2010. Pro coach: Joined Eagles in 2011

Mike Caldwell, linebackers; born August 31, 1971. Linebacker Middle Tennessee State 1989-1992. Pro linebacker Cleveland Browns 1993-95, Baltimore Ravens 1996, Arizona Cardinals 1997, Philadelphia Eagles 1998-2001, Chicago Bears 2002, Carolina Panthers 2003. Pro coach: Joined Eagles in 2008.

Juan Castillo, defensive coordinator; born October 8, 1959, Port Isabel, Texas. Linebacker Texas A&I (now Texas A&M-Kingsville) 1978-1980. Pro linebacker San Antonio Gunslingers (USFL) 1984-85. College coach: Texas A&I/Texas A&M-Kingsville 1982-85, 1990-94. Pro coach: Joined Eagles in 1995.

David Culley, wide receivers; born September 17, 1955, Sparta, Tenn. Quarterback Vanderbilt 1973-77. No pro playing experience. College coach: Austin Peay 1978, Vanderbilt 1979-1981, Middle Tennessee State 1982, Tennessee-Chattanooga 1983, Western Kentucky 1984, Southwestern Louisiana 1985-88, Texas-El Paso 1989-1990, Texas A&M 1991-93. Pro coach: Tampa Bay Buccaneers 1994-95, Pittsburgh Steelers 1996-1998, joined Eagles in 1999.

Johnnie Lynn, secondary/cornerbacks; born December 19, 1956, Los Angeles, Calif. Defensive back UCLA 1975-78. Pro defensive back New York Jets 1979-1986. College coach: Arizona 1988-1993. Pro coach: Tampa Bay Buccaneers 1994-95, San Francisco 49ers 1996, New York Giants 1997-2003, Baltimore Ravens 2004-05, San Francisco 49ers 2006-10, joined Eagles in 2011.

Tom Melvin, tight ends; born October 1, 1961, Redwood City, Calif. Offensive lineman San Francisco State 1982-83. No pro playing experience. College coach: San Francisco State 1984-85, Northern Arizona 1986-87, California-Santa Barbara 1988-1990, Occidental College 1991-98. Pro coach: Joined Eagles in 1999.

Marty Mornhinweg, asst. head coach/offensive coordinator; born March 29, 1962, Edmond, Okla. Quarterback Montana 1981-84. Pro quarterback Denver Dynamite (AFL) 1987. College coach: Montana 1985, Texas-El Paso 1986-87, Northern Arizona 1988, 1994, Southeast Missouri State 1989-1990, Missouri 1991. Pro coach: Green Bay Packers 1995-96, San Francisco 49ers 1997-2000, Detroit Lions 2001-02 (head coach), joined Eagles in 2003.

Howard Mudd, offensive line; born February 10, 1942, Midland, Mich. Guard Hillsdale (Mich.) College 1960-63. Pro offensive lineman San Francisco 49ers 1964-69, Chicago Bears 1969-1971. College coach: California 1972-73. Pro coach: San Diego Chargers 1974-76, San Francisco 49ers 1977, Seattle Seahawks 1978-1982, 1993-97, Cleveland Browns 1983-88, Kansas City Chiefs 1989-1992,

Eagles in 2011

Mike Caldwell, linebackers; born August 31, 1971. Linebacker Middle Tennessee State 1989-1992. Pro linebacker Cleveland Browns 1993-95, Baltimore Ravens 1996, Arizona Cardinals 1997, Philadelphia Eagles 1998-2001, Chicago Bears 2002, Carolina Panthers 2003. Pro coach: Joined Eagles in 2008.

Indianapolis Colts 1998-2009, joined Eagles in 2011.

Matt Nagy, offensive quality control; born April 24, 1978, Plainfield, N.J. Quarterback Delaware 1996-2000. Pro quarterback New York Dragons (AFL) 2002, Carolina Cobras (AFL) 2004, Georgia Force (AFL) 2005-06, Columbus Destroyers (AFL) 2007-08. Pro coach: Joined Eagles in 2011.

Doug Pederson, quarterbacks; born January 31, 1968, Bellingham, Wash. Quarterback Louisiana-Monroe 1987-1990. Pro experience: Miami Dolphins 1993-95, Green Bay Packers 1995-98, 2001-04, Philadelphia Eagles 1999, Cleveland Browns 2000. Pro coach: Joined Eagles in 2009.

Barry Rubin, strength and conditioning; born June 25, 1957. Running back/punter Louisiana State 1976-77, tight end/punter Northwestern (La.) State 1978-1980. No pro playing experience. College coach: Northeast Louisiana 1981-83, 1987-1990, 1994, Louisiana State 1984-85. Pro coach: Green Bay Packers 1995-2005, joined Eagles in 2008.

Duce Staley, special teams quality control; born February 27, 1975, Tampa. Running back South Carolina 1995-96. Pro running back Philadelphia Eagles 1997-2003, Pittsburgh Steelers 2004-06. Pro coach: Joined Eagles in 2011.

Jim Washburn, defensive line; born December 2, 1949, Shelby, N.C. Offensive lineman Gardner-Webb 1969-1973. No pro playing experience. College coach: Southern Methodist 1976, Lees McRae (N.C.) J.C. 1977-78, Livingston 1979, New Mexico 1980-82, South Carolina 1983-88, Purdue 1989, Arkansas 1994-97, Houston 1998. Pro coach: London Monarchs (WLAF) 1991, Charlotte Rage (AFL) 1993, Tennessee Titans 1999-2010, joined Eagles in 2011.

Ted Williams, running backs; born November 17, 1943, Lyons, Texas. Attended Cal Poly-Pomona. No college or pro playing experience. College coach: UCLA 1980-89, Washington State 1991-93, Arizona 1994. Pro coach: Joined Eagles in 1995.

Michael Zordich, secondary/safeties; born October 12, 1963;. Safety Penn State 1982-85. Pro safety New York Jets 1987-88, Phoenix Cardinals 1989-1993, Philadelphia Eagles 1994-98. Pro coach: Joined Eagles in 2009.

National Football Conference
West Division
Team Colors: New Century Gold,
Millennium Blue, and White

One Rams Way
St. Louis, Missouri 63045
Telephone: (314) 982-7267

2011 SCHEDULE
PRESEASON
Aug. 7   vs. Chicago (Canton, OH) ...7:00
Aug. 13 **Indianapolis** 7:00
Aug. 20 **Tennessee** 7:00
Aug. 26 at Kansas City 7:00
Sep. 1   at Jacksonville 6:30

REGULAR SEASON
Sep. 11 **Philadelphia** 12:00
Sep. 19 at New York Giants (Mon).. 7:30
Sep. 25 **Baltimore** 3:05
Oct. 2   **Washington** 12:00
Oct. 9   BYE
Oct. 16 at Green Bay 12:00
Oct. 23 at Dallas 3:15
Oct. 30 **New Orleans** 12:00
Nov. 6   at Arizona 3:15
Nov. 13 at Cleveland 12:00
Nov. 20 **Seattle** 3:05
Nov. 27 **Arizona** 12:00
Dec. 4   at San Francisco 3:15
Dec. 12 at Seattle (Mon) 7:30
Dec. 18 **Cincinnati** 12:00
Dec. 24 at Pittsburgh (Sat) 12:00
Jan. 1   **San Francisco** 12:00
All times CT

Stadium: Edward Jones Dome
(opened in 1995)
•**Capacity:** 66,000
901 N. Broadway
St. Louis, Missouri 63101
Playing Surface: FieldTurf
Training Camp: Russell Training Center
1 Rams Way
St. Louis, Missouri 63045

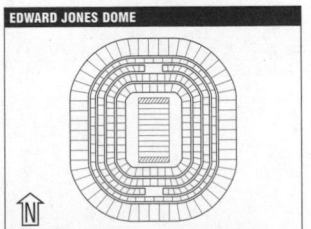

EDWARD JONES DOME

CLUB OFFICIALS
Owner/Chairman: Stan Kroenke
General Manager: Billy Devaney
Executive Vice President Of Football
Operations/Chief Operating Officer:
Kevin Demoff
Director of Player Personnel:
Lawrence McCutcheon
Treasurer: Jeff Brewer
Executive Vice President of Marketing
and Sales: Bob Reif
Vice President of Finance:
Michael T. Naughton
Vice President of Operations:
John Oswald
Vice President of Ticketing: Mike O'Keefe
Senior Director of Communications:
Ted Crews
Director of Media Relations:
Artis Twyman
Director of Corporate Sales:
Chad Watson
Vice President of Corporate
Communications and Civic Affairs:
Molly Higgins
Director of Community Relations:
Michael Yarbrough
Vice President of Player Personnel:
Mike Williams
Director of College Scouting:
John Mancini
Head Trainer: Reggie Scott
Assistant Trainers: James Lomax,
Tyler Williams, Byron Cunningham
Assistant Equipment Manager:
Jim Lake
Scouts: Ray Agnew, Russ Bolinger,
Drew Casani, Luke Driscoll,
Brad Holmes, Steve Kazor,
Brandon Schwab

COACHING HISTORY
Cleveland 1937-1945,
Los Angeles 1946-1994
(530-516-20)
Records include postseason games

Year	Coach	Record
1937-38	Hugo Bezdek*	1-13-0
1938	Art Lewis	4-4-0
1939-1942	Earl (Dutch) Clark	16-26-2
1944	Aldo (Buff) Donelli	4-6-0
1945-46	Adam Walsh	16-5-1
1947	Bob Snyder	6-6-0
1948-49	Clark Shaughnessy	14-8-3
1950-52	Joe Stydahar**	19-9-0
1952-54	Hamp Pool	23-11-2
1955-59	Sid Gillman	28-32-1
1960-62	Bob Waterfield***	9-24-1
1962-65	Harland Svare	14-31-3
1966-1970	George Allen	49-19-4
1971-72	Tommy Prothro	14-12-2
1973-77	Chuck Knox	57-20-1
1978-1982	Ray Malavasi	43-36-0
1983-1991	John Robinson	79-74-0
1992-94	Chuck Knox	15-33-0
1995-96	Rich Brooks	13-19-0
1997-99	Dick Vermeil	25-26-0
2000-05	Mike Martz****	56-36-0
2005	Joe Vitt	4-7-0
2006-08	Scott Linehan#	11-25-0
2008	Jim Haslett	2-10-0
2009-2010	Steve Spagnuolo	8-24-0

* Released after three games in 1938
** Resigned after one game in 1952
*** Resigned after eight games in 1962
**** Took medical leave after five games in 2005
# Released after four games in 2008

PAID ATTENDANCE
Home 408,761   Away 465,688
Total 874,449
Single-game home record,
66,273 (12/10/00)
Single-season home record,
520,926 (1999)

2011 DRAFT CHOICES
Round	Name	Pos.	College
1	Robert Quinn	DE	North Carolina
2	Lance Kendricks	TE	Wisconsin
3	Austin Pettis	WR	Boise State
4	Greg Salas	WR	Hawaii
5	Jermale Hines	DB	Ohio State
7	Mikail Baker	DB	Baylor
	Jabara Williams	LB	Stephen F. Austin
	Jonathan Nelson	DB	Oklahoma

2010 TEAM RECORD
PRESEASON (3-1)

Date	Result		Opponent
8/14	L	7-28	Minnesota
8/21	W	19-17	at Cleveland
8/26	W	36-35	at New England
9/2	W	27-21	Baltimore

REGULAR SEASON (7-9)

Date	Result		Opponent
9/12	L	13-17	Arizona
9/19	L	14-16	at Oakland
9/26	W	30-16	Washington
10/3	W	20-3	Seattle
10/10	L	6-44	at Detroit
10/17	W	20-17	San Diego
10/24	L	17-18	at Tampa Bay
10/31	W	20-10	Carolina
11/14	L	20-23	at San Francisco (OT)
11/21	L	17-34	Atlanta
11/28	W	36-33	at Denver
12/5	W	19-6	at Arizona
12/12	L	13-31	at New Orleans
12/19	L	13-27	Kansas City
12/26	W	25-17	San Francisco
1/2	L	6-16	at Seattle

(OT) Overtime

SCORE BY PERIODS

Rams	69	104	51	65	0 —	289
Opponents	53	113	53	106	3 —	328

2010 TEAM STATISTICS

	Rams	Opp.
Total First Downs	292	304
Rushing	84	88
Passing	179	191
Penalty	29	25
3rd Down: Made/Att	78/235	74/221
3rd Down Pct.	33.2	33.5
4th Down: Made/Att	8/15	6/12
4th Down Pct.	53.3	50.0
Possession Avg.	30:51	29:09
Total Net Yards	4846	5388
Avg. Per Game	302.9	336.8
Total Plays	1053	1017
Avg. Per Play	4.6	5.3
Net Yards Rushing	1578	1810
Avg. Per Game	98.6	113.1
Total Rushes	429	404
Net Yards Passing	3268	3578
Avg. Per Game	204.3	223.6
Sacked/Yards Lost	34/244	43/290
Gross Yards	3512	3868
Att./Completions	590/354	570/328
Completion Pct.	60.0	57.5
Had Intercepted	15	14
Punts/Average	94/45.5	82/44.8
Net Punting Avg.	94/40.0	82/37.1
Penalties/Yards	102/877	126/1008
Fumbles/Ball Lost	14/6	30/12
Touchdowns	27	32
Rushing	9	7
Passing	18	21
Returns	0	4

2010 INDIVIDUAL STATISTICS

PASSING	Att.	Comp.	Yds.	Pct.	TD	Int.	Tkld.	Rate
Bradford	590	354	3512	60.0	18	15	34/244	76.5
Rams	590	354	3512	60.0	18	15	34/244	76.5
Opponents	570	328	3868	57.5	21	14	43/290	80.4

SCORING	TD R	TD P	TD Rt	PAT	FG	Saf	PTS
Jo. Brown	0	0	0	26/27	33/39	0	125
Jackson	6	0	0	0/0	0/0	0	36
Amendola	0	3	0	0/0	0/0	0	18
Darby	2	1	0	0/0	0/0	0	18
Hoomanawanui	0	3	0	0/0	0/0	0	18
Bajema	0	2	0	0/0	0/0	0	12
Clayton	0	2	0	0/0	0/0	0	12
Fells	0	2	0	0/0	0/0	0	12
B. Gibson	0	2	0	0/0	0/0	0	12
Robinson	0	2	0	0/0	0/0	0	12
Alexander	0	1	0	0/0	0/0	0	6
Bradford	1	0	0	0/0	0/0	0	6
Sims	0	0	0	0/0	0/0	1	2
Rams	9	18	0	26/27	33/39	1	289
Opponents	7	21	4	29/29	35/38	0	328

2-Pt Conversions: Rams 0-0, Opponents 1-3.

RUSHING	No.	Yds	Avg	LG	TD
Jackson	330	1241	3.8	42t	6
Darby	34	107	3.1	13	2
Amendola	7	81	11.6	30	0
Bradford	27	63	2.3	17	1
Toston	19	54	2.8	10	0
B. Gibson	3	28	9.3	14	0
Karney	6	12	2.0	4	0
Clayton	1	6	6.0	6	0
Robinson	2	-14	-7.0	-5	0
Rams	429	1578	3.7	42t	9
Opponents	404	1810	4.5	80	7

RECEIVING	No.	Yds	Avg	LG	TD
Amendola	85	689	8.1	36	3
B. Gibson	53	620	11.7	41	2
Jackson	46	383	8.3	49	0
Fells	41	391	9.5	36	2
Robinson	34	344	10.1	32	2
Clayton	23	306	13.3	39	2
Alexander	20	306	15.3	46	1
Bajema	14	145	10.4	26t	2
Hoomanawanui	13	146	11.2	36t	3
Darby	10	61	6.1	21t	1
Gilyard	6	63	10.5	21	0
Karney	5	14	2.8	4	0
Toston	2	29	14.5	23	0
Onobun	2	15	7.5	8	0
Rams	354	3512	9.9	49	18
Opponents	328	3868	11.8	65	21

INTERCEPTIONS	No.	Yds	Avg	LG	TD
Fletcher	4	41	10.3	28	0
Atogwe	3	53	17.7	34	0
Dahl	2	23	11.5	23	0
J. Butler	2	13	6.5	16	0
Murphy	1	19	19.0	19	0
Dockery	1	8	8.0	8	0
Laurinaitis	1	4	4.0	4	0
Rams	14	161	11.5	34	0
Opponents	15	287	19.1	96t	2

PUNTING	No.	Yds.	Avg.	In 20	LG
D. Jones	94	4276	45.5	32	63
Rams	94	4276	45.5	32	63
Opponents	82	3671	44.8	27	72

PUNT RETURNS	Ret	FC	Yds	Avg	LG	TD
Amendola	40	18	452	11.3	42	0
Gilyard	0	1	0	—	—	0
Rams	40	19	452	11.3	42	0
Opponents	45	21	435	9.7	78t	1

KICKOFF RETURNS	No.	Yds	Avg	LG	TD
Amendola	50	1142	22.8	84	0
Gilyard	16	356	22.3	34	0
Toston	4	75	18.8	20	0
Ah You	1	16	16.0	16	0
Grant	1	8	8.0	8	0
Karney	1	17	17.0	17	0
B. Miller	1	0	0.0	0	0
Rams	74	1614	21.8	84	0
Opponents	65	1538	23.7	105t	1

FIELD GOALS	1-19	20-29	30-39	40-49	50+
Jo. Brown	0/0	11/12	12/14	7/9	3/4
Rams	0/0	11/12	12/14	7/9	3/4
Opponents	0/0	11/11	9/10	13/15	2/2

SACKS	No.
Hall	10.5
Long	8.5
Robbins	6.0
Ah You	4.0
Laurinaitis	3.0
Atogwe	2.0
Grant	2.0
Vobora	2.0
Selvie	1.5
Dahl	1.0
M. Lewis	1.0
Stewart	1.0
Cudjo	0.5
Rams	43.0
Opponents	34.0

RECORD HOLDERS
INDIVIDUAL RECORDS—CAREER

Category	Name	Performance
Rushing (Yds.)	Steven Jackson, 2004-2010	7,948
Passing (Yds.)	Jim Everett, 1986-1993	23,758
Passing (TDs)	Roman Gabriel, 1962-1972	154
Receiving (No.)	Isaac Bruce, 1994-2007	942
Receiving (Yds.)	Isaac Bruce, 1994-2007	14,109
Interceptions	Ed Meador, 1959-1970	46
Punting (Avg.)	Danny Villanueva, 1960-64	44.3
Punt Return (Avg.)	Az-Zahir Hakim, 1998-2001	11.4
Kickoff Return (Avg.)	Ron Brown, 1984-89, 1991	26.3
Field Goals	Jeff Wilkins, 1997-2007	265
Touchdowns (Tot.)	Marshall Faulk, 1999-2005	85
Points	Jeff Wilkins, 1997-2007	1,223
*Sacks	Leonard Little, 1998-2008	81.0

INDIVIDUAL RECORDS—SINGLE SEASON

Category	Name	Performance
Rushing (Yds.)	Eric Dickerson, 1984	**2,105
Passing (Yds.)	Kurt Warner, 2001	4,830
Passing (TDs)	Kurt Warner, 1999	41
Receiving (No.)	Isaac Bruce, 1995	119
Receiving (Yds.)	Isaac Bruce, 1995	1,781
Interceptions	Dick (Night Train) Lane, 1952	**14
Punting (Avg.)	Donnie Jones, 2008	50.0
Punt Return (Avg.)	Woodley Lewis, 1952	18.5
Kickoff Return (Avg.)	Verda (Vitamin T) Smith, 1950	33.7
Field Goals	Jeff Wilkins, 2003	39
Touchdowns (Tot.)	Marshall Faulk, 2000	26
Points	Jeff Wilkins, 2003	163
*Sacks	Kevin Carter, 1999	17.0

INDIVIDUAL RECORDS—SINGLE GAME

Category	Name	Performance
Rushing (Yds.)	Willie Ellison, 12-5-71	247
Passing (Yds.)	Norm Van Brocklin, 9-28-51	**554
Passing (TDs)	Many times	5
	Last time by Kurt Warner, 10-10-99	
Receiving (No.)	Tom Fears, 12-3-50	18
Receiving (Yds.)	Willie Anderson, 11-26-89	**336
Interceptions	Many times	3
	Last time by Keith Lyle, 12-15-96	
Field Goals	Bob Waterfield, 12-9-51	5
	Jeff Wilkins, 10-1-00	5
Touchdowns (Tot.)	Many times	4
	Last time by Marshall Faulk, 10-20-02	
Points	Many times	24
	Last time by Marshall Faulk, 10-20-02	
*Sacks	Gary Jeter, 9-18-88	5.0

*Sacks became an official statistic in 1982.
**NFL Record

VETERAN ROSTER AS OF MARCH 3, 2011

No.	Name	Pos.	Ht.	Wt.	Birthdate	^NFL Exp.	College	Hometown	How Acq.	'10 Games/ Starts
99	Ah You, C.J.	DE	6-4	270	7/7/82	3	Oklahoma	Highland, Utah	FA-'07	16/0
84	Alexander, Danario	WR	6-5	215	8/7/88	2	Missouri	Marlin, Texas	FA'10	8/2
16	Amendola, Danny	WR	5-11	186	11/2/85	3	Texas Tech	The Woodlands, Texas	FA-'09	16/6
17	Avery, Donnie	WR	5-11	183	6/12/84	4	Houston	Alief, Texas	D2-'08	0*
47	Bajema, Billy	TE	6-4	259	10/31/82	7	Oklahoma State	Oklahoma City, Okla.	UFA(SF)-'09	13/8
24	Bartell, Ron	CB	6-1	206	2/22/82	7	Howard	Detroit, Mich.	D2-'05	15/13
63	Bell, Jacob	G	6-5	300	3/2/81	8	Miami (OH)	Cleveland, Ohio	UFA(Tenn)-'08	16/16
8	Bradford, Sam	QB	6-4	228	11/8/87	2	Oklahoma	Oklahoma City, Okla.	D1-'10	16/16
60	Brown, Jason	C	6-3	328	5/5/83	7	North Carolina	Henderson, N.C.	UFA(Balt)-'09	16/16
3	Brown, Josh	K	6-0	4/29/79		9	Nebraska	Foyil, Okla.	UFA(Sea)-'08	16/0
37	Butler, James	S	6-3	209	9/7/82	7	Georgia Tech	Bainbridge, Ga.	UFA(NYG)-'09	14/4
36	Butler, Quincy	CB	6-1	188	11/25/83	4	Texas Christian	San Antonio, Texas	FA-'10	6/1
57	Chamberlain, Chris	LB	6-1	230	9/30/85	4	Tulsa	Bethany, Okla.	D7a-'08	11/6
89	Clayton, Mark	WR	5-10	190	7/2/82	7	Oklahoma	Arlington, Texas	T(Balt)-'10	5/5
93	Cudjo, Jermelle	DT	6-2	299	9/28/86	2	Central Oklahoma	Lawton, Okla.	FA-'10	10/0
15	Curry, Dominique	WR	6-2	224	8/16/87	2	California (PA)	Philadelphia, Pa.	FA-'10	2/0
43	Dahl, Craig	S	6-1	209	6/17/85	5	North Dakota State	Mankato, Minn.	FA-'09	15/13
53	Diggs, Na'il	LB	6-4	240	7/8/78	12	Ohio State	Los Angeles, Calif.	FA-'10	12/12
34	Darby, Kenneth	RB	5-10	219	12/26/82	4	Alabama	Huntsville, Ala.	FA-'08	14/0
35	Dockery, Kevin	CB	5-8	188	1/8/84	6	Mississippi State	Hernando, Miss.	FA-'10	10/3
4	Feeley, A.J.	QB	6-3	220	5/16/77	11	Oregon	Caldwell, Idaho	UFA(Car)-'10	0*
46	Fells, Daniel	TE	6-4	272	9/23/83	5	California-Davis	Fullerton, Calif.	FA-'08	16/6
32	Fletcher, Bradley	CB	6-0	198	6/25/86	3	Iowa	Youngstown, Ohio	D3-'09	16/15
70	Foster, Renardo	T	6-7	333	7/15/84	3	Louisville	Ripley, Tenn.	FA-'10	10/1
65	Fraley, Hank	C/G	6-3	310	9/21/77	12	Robert Morris	Gaithersburg, Md.	FA-'10	7/0
11	Gibson, Brandon	WR	6-0	210	8/13/87	3	Washington State	Puyallup, Wash.	T(Phil)-'09	14/12
71	Gibson, Gary	DT	6-3	300	5/5/82	6	Rutgers	Lafayette, N.Y.	FA-'09	16/16
81	Gilyard, Mardy	WR	5-11	194	12/2/86	2	Cincinnati	Bunnell, Fla.	D4-'10	11/2
73	Goldberg, Adam	G	6-7	309	8/12/80	8	Wyoming	Edina, Minn.	T(Minn)-'06	16/16
59	Grant, Larry	LB	6-1	251	2/16/85	3	Ohio State	Sacramento, Calif.	FA-'08	16/8
79	Greco, John	G	6-4	329	3/24/85	4	Toledo	Youngstown, Ohio	D3-'08	6/0
96	Hall, James	DE	6-2	281	2/4/77	12	Michigan	New Orleans, La.	T(Det)-'07	16/16
86	Hoomanawanui, Michael	TE	6-4	265	7/4/88	2	Illinois	Bloomington, Ill.	D5a-'10	8/3
93	Hovan, Chris	DT	6-2	296	5/12/78	12	Boston College	Rocky River, Ohio	FA-'10	0*
56	Hull, Josh	LB	6-3	239	5/21/87	2	Penn State	Millheim, Pa.	D7c-'10	1/0
39	Jackson, Steven	RB	6-2	236	7/22/83	8	Oregon State	Las Vegas, Nev.	D1-'04	16/16
52	Johnson, Curtis	LB	6-2	242	2/16/85	4	Clark Atlanta	Syracuse, N.Y.	FA-'10	0*
5	Jones, Donnie	P	6-2	225	7/5/80	8	Louisiana State	Baton Rouge, La.	RFA(Mia)-'07	16/0
50	Kehl, Bryan	LB	6-2	237	6/16/84	4	Brigham Young	Salt Lake City, Utah	FA'10	14/1
31	King, Justin	CB	5-11	188	5/11/87	4	Penn State	Pittsburgh, Pa.	D4a-'08	8/0
55	Laurinaitis, James	LB	6-2	247	12/3/86	3	Ohio State	Plymouth, Minn.	D2-'09	16/16
22	Lewis, Michael	S	6-1	222	4/29/80	10	Colorado	Richmond, Texas	FA-'10	2/0
91	Long, Chris	DE	6-3	276	3/28/85	4	Virginia	Charlottesville, Va.	D1-'08	16/16
45	Massey, Chris	LS	6-0	237	8/21/79	10	Marshall	Chesapeake, W. Va.	D7-'02	16/0
83	McRae, Brandon	WR	6-3	207	3/5/86	2	Mississippi State	Chester, Va.	FA-'10	0*
49	Miller, Brit	FB	6-1	250	9/15/86	2	Illinois	Decatur, Ill.	FA-'10	9/2
23	Murphy, Jerome	CB	6-0	200	1/13/87	2	South Florida	Elizabeth, N.J.	D3-10	14/0
51	Nixon, David	LB	6-3	225	3/16/85	3	Brigham Young	College Station, Texas	FA-'10	1/0
48	Onobun, Fendi	TE	6-6	249	11/17/86	2	Houston	Houston, Texas	D6A-'10	3/0
98	Robbins, Fred	DT	6-4	325	3/26/77	12	Wake Forest	Pensacola, Fla.	UFA(NYG)-'10	16/16
19	Robinson, Laurent	WR	6-2	197	5/20/85	5	Illinois State	Rockledge, Fla.	T(Atl)-'09	14/11
76	Saffold, Rodger	T	6-5	323	6/6/88	2	Indiana	Bedford, Ohio	D2-'10	16/16
88	Schouman, Derek	TE	6-2	223	3/11/85	5	Boise State	Sandy, Utah	FA-'10	4/0
97	Scott, Darell	DT	6-3	315	3/15/86	3	Clemson	Columbia, S.C.	D4-'09	9/0
90	Selvie, George	DE	6-4	251	3/6/87	2	South Florida	Pensacola, Fla.	D7b-'10	16/0
66	Setterstrom, Mark	G	6-4	318	3/3/84	6	Minnesota	Northfield, Minn.	D7b-'06	0*
92	Sims, Eugene	DE	6-6	250	3/18/86	2	West Texas A&M	Mt. Olive, Miss.	D6b-'10	9/0
77	Smith, Jason	T	6-5	307	4/30/86	3	Baylor	Dallas, Texas	D1-'09	15/15
20	Stewart, Darian	S	5-11	215	8/4/88	2	South Carolina	Huntsville, Ala.	FA-'10	13/0
38	Toston, Keith	RB	5-11	214	5/6/87	2	Oklahoma State	Angleton, Texas	FA-'10	16/0
58	Vobora, David	LB	6-1	239	4/8/86	4	Idaho	Eugene, Ore.	D7b-'08	14/5
33	Washington, Chauncey	RB	5-11	215	4/29/86	2	Southern California	Carson, Calif.	FA-'10	1/0

* Avery missed '10 season because of injury; Feeley did not play in 16 games; Hovan missed '10 season because of injury; Johnson inactive for 3 games; McRae missed '10 season because of injury; Setterstrom spent '10 season on the Physically Unable to Perform list.

Also played with Rams in '10—S Oshiomogho Atogwe (16 games), TE Darcy Johnson (4), DB Marquis Johnson (2), FB Mike Karney (12), DT Clifton Ryan (1).

^ "NFL Exp." as of 2011 Kickoff Weekend. For full explanation of how a player's NFL Experience is measured, refer to explanation underneath the First-Year Roster listed below.

FIRST-YEAR ROSTER

Name	Pos.	Ht.	Wt.	Birthdate	College	Hometown	How Acq.
Baker, Mikail	CB	6-0	211	6/19/87	Baylor	Dallas, Texas	D7a
Hines, Jermale	S	6-01	219	11/11/87	Ohio State	Cleveland, Ohio	D5
Johnson, Marquis (1)	DB	5-11	205	5/18/88	Alabama	Sarasota, Fla.	FA-'10
Kendricks, Lance	TE	6-2	241	1/30/88	Wisconsin	Milwaukee, Wisc.	D2
Lewis, Thaddeus (1)	QB	6-0	219	2/1/88	Duke	Opa Locka, Fla.	FA-'10
Mathews, Greg (1)	WR	6-3	209	1/28/88	Michigan	Honolulu, Hawai'i	FA-'10
McKee, Ryan (1)	T	6-6	291	11/4/86	Southern Mississippi	Daphne, Ala.	W(NYJ)-'09
Miller, Drew (1)	C	6-5	303	7/6/85	Florida	Paducah, Ky.	FA-'09
Nelson, Jonathan	DB	5-11	188	5/6/88	Oklahoma	Arlington, Texas	D7c
Pettis, Austin	WR	6-2	202	5/7/88	Boise State	Orange, Calif.	D3
Quinn, Robert	DE	6-4	268	5/18/90	North Carolina	Ladson, S.C.	D1
Saddler-McQueen, Jimmy (1)	DT	6-3	298	8/4/87	Texas A&M-Kingsville	Forest Brook, Texas	FA-'10
Salas, Greg	WR	6-1	210	8/25/88	Hawai'i	Chino, Calif.	D4
Simpkins, Maurice (1)	LB	6-0	236	4/29/83	Coastal Carolina	Leesville, S.C.	FA-'10
West, Joe (1)	WR	6-1	208	2/1/84	Texas-El Paso	Garland, Texas	FA-'10
Williams, Jabara	LB	6-3	210	7/6/89	Stephen F. Austin	Nacogdoches, Texas	D7b

The term NFL Rookie is defined as a player who is in his first season of professional football and has not been on the roster of another professional football team for any regular-season or postseason games. A Rookie is designated by an "R" on NFL rosters. Players who have been active in another professional football league or players who have NFL experience, including either preseason training camp or being on an Active List or Inactive List, or on Reserve/Injured or Reserve/Physically Unable to Perform for fewer than six regular-season games, are termed NFL First-Year Players. An NFL First-Year Player is designated by a "1" on NFL rosters. Thereafter, a player is credited with an additional year of experience for each season in which he accumulates six games on the Active List or Inactive List, or on Reserve/Injured or Reserve/Physically Unable to Perform.

Log on to www.stlouisrams.com for an up-to-date roster.

COACHING STAFF

Head Coach,
Steve Spagnuolo

Pro Career: Named the twenty-fifth head coach in franchise history on January 19, 2009. In 2010, the Rams made a six-game improvement from 2009, finishing in second place in the NFC West. The six-game swing marked the second best turn-around in the NFL from 2009 to 2010. The Rams finished with a 5-3 home record, the first home winning record since 2004. Spagnuolo was defensive coordinator of the New York Giants from 2007-08. In 2007, the Giants' defense ranked seventh in the NFL in yards allowed after ranking 25th in 2006. The Giants were in the NFL's top 10 in eight statistical categories and led the league with 53 quarterback sacks. The Giants beat the undefeated New England Patriots 17-14 in Super Bowl XLII. The Giants' defense held the Patriots to nearly 130 yards less than their season average. New England scored 14 points in the Super Bowl after averaging more than 36 points per game in the regular season. In 2008, Spagnuolo's defense improved from seventh to fifth in the NFL in total defense as the Giants won the NFC East. Spagnuolo spent eight seasons (1999-2006) with the Philadelphia Eagles, serving as defensive assistant/safeties from 1999-2000, defensive backs coach from 2001-03 and linebackers coach from 2004-06. From 1999-2005, the Eagles played in four NFC Championship games and one Super Bowl. Spagnuolo served as defensive line/special teams coach with the Barcelona Dragons of the WLAF in 1992 and was defensive coordinator/linebackers coach for NFL Europe's Frankfurt Galaxy in 1998. Spagnuolo worked as pro personnel intern with the Washington Redskins in 1983 and as a scout with the San Diego Chargers in 1993. Career record: 8-24.

Background: Wide receiver at Springfield (Mass.) College (1978-1981). Coached collegiately at Massachusetts (1982-83), Lafayette (1984-86), Connecticut (1987-1991), Maine (1993-94), Rutgers (1994-95), and Bowling Green (1996-97).

Personal: Born December 21, 1959 in Whitinsville, Mass. He is married to wife, Maria.

ASSISTANT COACHES

Nolan Cromwell, wide receivers; born January 30, 1955, Smith Center, Kan. Defensive back/quarterback Kansas 1973-76. Pro safety Los Angeles Rams 1977-1987. College coach: Texas A&M 2008-09. Pro coach: Los Angeles Rams 1991, Green Bay Packers 1992-98, Seattle Seahawks 1999-2007, re-joined Rams in 2010.

Sylvester Croom, running backs; born September 25, 1954, Tuscaloosa, Ala. Linebacker/tight end/center Alabama 1971-74. Pro center New Orleans Saints 1975. College coach: Alabama 1976-1986, Mississippi State 2004-08 (head coach). Pro coach: Tampa Bay Buccaneers 1987-1990, Indianapolis Colts 1991, San Diego Chargers 1992-96, Detroit Lions 1997-2000, Green Bay Packers 2001-03, joined Rams in 2009.

Andre Curtis, secondary/safeties; born December 8, 1976, Beaverdam, Va. Linebacker Virginia Military Institute 1996-99. No pro playing experience. College coach: Virginia Military Institute 2000-03, Georgia Southern 2004-05. Pro coach: New York Giants 2006-08, joined Rams in 2009.

Brendan Daly, defensive line; born September 10, 1975, Springfield, Ill. Tight End Drake 1993-96. No pro playing experience. College coach: Drake 1998, Villanova 1999, 2005, Maryland 2000, Oklahoma State 2001-2003, Illinois State 2004. Pro coach: Minnesota Vikings 2006-08, joined Rams in 2009.

Paul Ferraro, linebackers; born April 30, 1959, Ridgewood, N.J. Safety Springfield College 1978-1981. No pro playing experience. College coach: Massachusetts 1982, Syracuse 1983, Villanova 1984-86, Dartmouth 1987, Catholic University 1988, Maine 1989, Ohio University 1990, Bowling Green 1991-98, Georgia Tech 1999-2000, Rutgers 2001-04. Pro coach: Carolina Panthers 2005, Minnesota Vikings 2006-08, joined Rams in 2009.

Ken Flajole, defensive coordinator; born October 4, 1954, Seattle. Linebacker Carroll College 1972, Wenatchee Valley Community College 1973, Pacific Lutheran 1974-75. No pro playing experience. College coach: Pacific Lutheran 1977-78, Washington 1979, Montana 1980-85, Texas-El Paso 1986-88, Missouri 1989-1993, Richmond 1994, Hawaii 1995, Nevada 1996-97. Pro coach: Green Bay Packers 1998, Seattle Seahawks 1999-2002, Carolina Panthers 2003-08, joined Rams in 2009.

Rock Gullickson, strength; born April 11, 1955, Moorhead, Minn. Guard Moorhead State 1973-76. No pro playing experience. College coach: Moorhead State 1978, Maryville State (N.D.) 1979-1980, South Dakota State 1981, Montana State 1982-89, Rutgers 1990-92, Texas 1993-97, Louisville 1998-99. Pro coach: New Orleans Saints 2000-05, Green Bay Packers 2006-08, joined Rams in 2009.

Matt House, defensive quality control; born May 17, 1978, Harrison, Mich. No pro playing experience. College coach: Michigan State 2001-02, North Carolina 2003-04, Gardner-Webb 2005, Buffalo 2006-07. Pro coach: Carolina Panthers 2008, joined Rams in 2009.

Frank Leonard, tight ends; born April 5, 1958, Wethersfield, Conn. Cornerback Central Connecticut State 1976, 1978-1980. No pro playing experience. College coach: Western Connecticut 1982-84, Central Connecticut State 1985-86, Western Connecticut 1987-89, Connecticut 1990-93, Richmond 1994-2003, Kansas State 2007-08. Pro coach: Joined Rams in 2009.

Steve Loney, offensive line; born April 26, 1952, Marshalltown, Iowa. Guard Iowa State 1971-72. No pro playing experience. College coach: Iowa State 1974, 1995-97, Missouri Western 1975-76, Morehead State 1979-1983, Citadel 1984-86, Colorado State 1989-1992, Connecticut 1994, Minnesota 1998-99, Iowa State 2000-01, Drake 2007. Pro coach: Arizona Cardinals 1993, Minnesota Vikings 2002-05, Arizona Cardinals 2006, joined Rams in 2008.

Clayton Lopez, secondary/cornerbacks; born May 26, 1970, Los Angeles. Defensive back Nevada 1991-94. No pro playing experience. College coach: Nevada 1995-98. Pro coach: Seattle Seahawks 1999-2003, Oakland Raiders 2004-05, Detroit Lions 2006-08, joined Rams in 2009.

Josh McDaniels, offensive coordinator, born April 22, 1976, Canton, Ohio. No playing experience. College coach: 1999-2000. Pro coach: New England Patriots 2001-2008, Denver Broncos, 2009-2010 (head coach), joined Rams in 2011.

Tom McMahon, special teams coordinator; born July 12, 1969, Helena, Mont. Corner Carroll College 1988-1992. No pro playing experience. College coach: Carroll College 1992, 1994, Utah State 1995-2005, Louisville 2006. Pro coach: Atlanta Falcons 2007-08, joined Rams in 2009.

Andy Sugarman, quality control/offense; born May 23, 1972, Lafayette, Calif. No college or pro playing experience. College coach: California-Berkeley 1991-97. Pro coach: San Francisco 49ers 1998-2002, Detroit Lions 2003-05, Atlanta Falcons 2007, joined Rams in 2009.

Derius Swinton, quality control special teams; born April 26, 1985, Newport News, Va. Safety Hampton 2003-06. No pro playing experience. College coach: Tennessee 2007-08. Pro coach: Joined Rams in 2009.

National Football Conference
West Division
Team Colors: 49ers Gold and 49ers Red
4949 Centennial Boulevard
Santa Clara, California 95054
Telephone: (408) 562-4949

2011 SCHEDULE
PRESEASON
Aug. 12 at New Orleans 5:00
Aug. 20 **Oakland**..............................5:00
Aug. 27 **Houston**............................5:00
Sep. 1 at San Diego..........................7:00

REGULAR SEASON
Sep. 11 **Seattle** 1:15
Sep. 18 **Dallas** 1:05
Sep. 25 at Cincinnati 10:00a
Oct. 2 at Philadelphia 10:00a
Oct. 9 **Tampa Bay** 1:05
Oct. 16 at Detroit 10:00a
Oct. 23 BYE
Oct. 30 **Cleveland** 1:15
Nov. 6 at Washington 10:00a
Nov. 13 **New York Giants** 1:15
Nov. 20 **Arizona** 1:05
Nov. 24 at Baltimore (Thu) 5:20
Dec. 4 **St. Louis** 1:15
Dec. 11 at Arizona 1:05
Dec. 19 **Pittsburgh** (Mon) 5:30
Dec. 24 at Seattle (Sat) 1:15
Jan. 1 at St. Louis 10:00a
All times PT

Stadium: Candlestick Park
(opened in 1960)
•**Capacity:** 69,732
San Francisco, California 94124
Playing Surface: Natural Grass
Training Camp: Marie P. DeBartolo
Sports Center
4949 Centennial Boulevard
Santa Clara, CA 95054

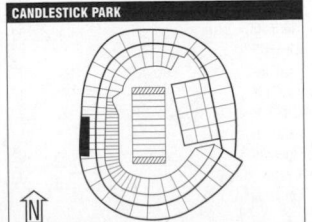

CANDLESTICK PARK

CLUB OFFICIALS
OWNERSHIP
Co-Chairman/Owner:
Denise DeBartolo York
Co-Chairman/Owner: John York
Team President/CEO: Jed York
Limited Partner: The Franklin Mieuli Trust
Limited Partner: Rick and Carla Morabito
MANAGEMENT
General Manager: Trent Baalke
Chief Operating Officer: Paraag Marathe
Chief Financial Officer: Larry MacNeil
Chief Sales Officer: John Vidalin
Chief Strategy Officer: Gideon Yu
Executive Vice President, Stadium
Project: Patty Inglis
Vice President of Ticketing & Suites:
Jamie Brandt
Vice President of Corporate Sales:
Ethan Casson
Vice President of Stadium Operations &
Security: Jim Mercurio
Vice President of Football Affairs:
Keena Turner
Director of Player Personnel:
Tom Gamble
Director of College Scouting: Joel Patten
Director of Public Relations: Bob Lange
Director of Football Operations and
Sports Medicine: Jeff Ferguson
Equipment Manager: Steve Urbaniak
Video Operations Coordinator:
Mike Bracken
Director of Football Administration:
Brian Hampton
Director of Broadcasting & Corporate
Sales: Bob Sargent
Director of Marketing: Ali Towle
Director of Stadium Operations:
Larry Minasian
Director of Finance: Scott Sabatino
Controller: Debye Whelchel
Director of Security: Fred Formosa
Director of Information Technology:
Alexander Ignacio
Director of Alumni Relations:
Guy McIntrye
Senior Manager of Ticket Office:
Lynn Carrozzi
Senior Human Resources Manager:
Tina De Vora Rojas
Director of Community Relations/49ers
Foundation: Joanne Pasternack
Director of Special Projects: Josh Proctor

COACHING HISTORY
(489-414-13)
Records include postseason games

Year	Coach	Record
1950-54	Lawrence (Buck) Shaw	33-25-2
1955	Norman (Red) Strader	4-8-0
1956-58	Frankie Albert	19-17-1
1959-1963	Howard (Red) Hickey*	27-27-1
1963-67	Jack Christiansen	26-38-3
1968-1975	Dick Nolan	56-56-5
1976	Monte Clark	8-6-0
1977	Ken Meyer	5-9-0
1978	Pete McCulley**	1-8-0
1978	Fred O'Connor	1-6-0
1979-1988	Bill Walsh	102-63-1
1989-1996	George Seifert	108-35-0
1997-2002	Steve Mariucci	60-43-0
2003-04	Dennis Erickson	9-23-0
2005-08	Mike Nolan***	18-37-0
2008-2010	Mike Singletary****	19-22-0
2010	Jim Tomsula	1-0-0

* Resigned after three games in 1963
** Released after nine games in 1978
*** Released after seven games in 2008
**** Released after 15 games in 2010

PAID ATTENDANCE
Home 538,773   Away 511,596
Total 1,050,369
Single-game home record,
69,014 (11/13/94)
Single-season home record,
544,228 (1999)

2011 DRAFT CHOICES
Round	Name	Pos.	College
1	Aldon Smith	LB	Missouri
2	Colin Kaepernick	QB	Nevada
3	Chris Culliver	DB	South Carolina
4	Kendall Hunter	RB	Oklahoma St.
5	Daniel Kilgore	G	Appalachian St.
6	Ronald Johnson	WR	Southern California
	Colin Jones	DB	Texas Christian
7	Bruce Miller	RB	Central Florida
	Mike Person	G	Montana State
	Curtis Holcomb	DB	Florida A&M

2010 TEAM RECORD
PRESEASON (4-0)

Date	Result	Opponent
8/15	W 37-17	at Indianapolis
8/22	W 15-10	Minnesota
8/28	W 28-24	at Oakland
9/2	W 17-14	San Diego

REGULAR SEASON (6-10)

Date	Result	Opponent
9/12	L 6-31	at Seattle
9/20	L 22-25	New Orleans
9/26	L 10-31	at Kansas City
10/3	L 14-16	at Atlanta
10/10	L 24-27	Philadelphia
10/17	W 17-9	Oakland
10/24	L 20-23	at Carolina
10/31	W 24-16	Denver
11/14	W 23-20	St. Louis (OT)
11/21	L 0-21	Tampa Bay
11/29	W 27-6	at Arizona
12/5	L 16-34	at Green Bay
12/12	W 40-21	Seattle
12/16	L 7-34	at San Diego
12/26	L 17-25	at St. Louis
1/2	W 38-7	Arizona

(OT) Overtime

SCORE BY PERIODS

49ers	75	79	51	97	3	—	305
Opponents	51	105	93	97	0	—	346

2010 TEAM STATISTICS

	49ers	Opp.
Total First Downs	251	299
Rushing	85	86
Passing	149	188
Penalty	17	25
3rd Down: Made/Att	68/213	84/217
3rd Down Pct.	31.9	38.7
4th Down: Made/Att	8/16	3/13
4th Down Pct.	50.0	23.1
Possession Avg.	28:37	31:23
Total Net Yards	5013	5244
Avg. Per Game	313.3	327.8
Total Plays	945	1033
Avg. Per Play	5.3	5.1
Net Yards Rushing	1657	1547
Avg. Per Game	103.6	96.7
Total Rushes	401	447
Net Yards Passing	3356	3697
Avg. Per Game	209.8	231.1
Sacked/Yards Lost	44/257	36/244
Gross Yards	3613	3941
Att./Completions	500/282	550/358
Completion Pct.	56.4	65.1
Had Intercepted	15	15
Punts/Average	91/46.2	84/42.5
Net Punting Avg.	91/38.2	84/37.4
Penalties/Yards	112/933	97/839
Fumbles/Ball Lost	22/8	18/7
Touchdowns	34	37
Rushing	10	9
Passing	19	25
Returns	5	3

2010 INDIVIDUAL STATISTICS

PASSING	Att.	Comp.	Yds.	Pct.	TD	Int.	Tkld.	Rate
A. Smith	342	204	2370	59.6	14	10	25/140	82.1
T. Smith	145	73	1176	50.3	5	4	18/112	77.8
Carr	13	5	67	38.5	0	1	1/5	23.6
49ers	500	282	3613	56.4	19	15	44/257	79.4
Opponents	550	358	3941	65.1	25	15	36/244	90.0

SCORING	TD R	TD P	TD Rt	PAT	FG	Saf	PTS
Nedney	0	0	0	17/17	11/13	0	50
V. Davis	0	7	0	0/0	0/0	0	44
Reed	0	0	0	13/13	9/10	0	40
Crabtree	0	6	0	0/0	0/0	0	36
Gore	3	2	0	0/0	0/0	0	30
Westbrook	4	1	0	0/0	0/0	0	30
Dixon	2	0	0	0/0	0/0	0	12
Ginn	0	1	1	0/0	0/0	0	12
Morgan	0	2	0	0/0	0/0	0	12
Andrus	0	0	0	3/3	2/4	0	9
T. Brown	0	0	1	0/0	0/0	0	6
Goldson	0	0	1	0/0	0/0	0	6
Mays	0	0	1	0/0	0/0	0	6
McDonald	0	0	1	0/0	0/0	0	6
T. Smith	1	0	0	0/0	0/0	0	6
49ers	10	19	5	33/33	22/27	0	305
Opponents	9	25	3	36/37	28/33	2	346

2-Pt Conversions: V. Davis.
49ers 1-1, Opponents 0-0.

RUSHING	No.	Yds	Avg	LG	TD
Gore	203	853	4.2	64	3
Westbrook	77	340	4.4	30	4
Dixon	70	237	3.4	34	2
T. Smith	23	121	5.3	16	1
A. Smith	18	60	3.3	12	0
Del. Walker	3	18	6.0	10	0
Morgan	2	17	8.5	13	0
Ginn	2	11	5.5	9	0
Norris	3	0	0.0	1	0
49ers	401	1657	4.1	64	10
Opponents	447	1547	3.5	43	9

RECEIVING	No.	Yds	Avg	LG	TD
V. Davis	56	914	16.3	66t	7
Crabtree	55	741	13.5	60t	6
Gore	46	452	9.8	41	2
Morgan	44	698	15.9	65	2
Del. Walker	29	331	11.4	38	0
Westbrook	16	150	9.4	62t	1
Ginn	12	163	13.6	37t	1
Zeigler	9	98	10.9	20	0
Byham	5	27	5.4	9	0
Dixon	5	11	2.2	8	0
Norris	4	20	5.0	8	0
Kyle Williams	1	8	8.0	8	0
49ers	282	3613	12.8	66t	19
Opponents	358	3941	11.0	71	25

INTERCEPTIONS	No.	Yds	Avg	LG	TD
Clements	3	46	15.3	39	0
Spikes	3	9	3.0	6	0
Spencer	3	0	0.0	0	0
T. Brown	1	62	62.0	62t	1
Goldson	1	39	39.0	39t	1
Brooks	1	32	32.0	32	0
McDonald	1	31	31.0	31t	1
R. Smith	1	20	20.0	20	0
Lawson	1	0	0.0	0	0
49ers	15	239	15.9	62t	3
Opponents	15	182	12.1	41	1

PUNTING	No.	Yds.	Avg.	In 20	LG
Lee	91	4203	46.2	34	64
49ers	91	4203	46.2	34	64
Opponents	84	3571	42.5	29	65

PUNT RETURNS	Ret	FC	Yds	Avg	LG	TD
Ginn	24	18	321	13.4	78t	1
Adams	4	0	29	7.3	16	0
Kyle Williams	3	6	16	5.3	9	0
R. Smith	0	1	0	—	—	0
49ers	31	25	366	11.8	78t	1
Opponents	54	12	483	8.9	43	0

KICKOFF RETURNS	No.	Yds	Avg	LG	TD
Ginn	47	992	21.1	61	0
Del. Walker	5	70	14.0	20	0
Kyle Williams	4	82	20.5	30	0
Morgan	2	19	9.5	13	0
Crabtree	1	0	0.0	0	0
Norris	1	12	12.0	12	0
Wragge	1	12	12.0	12	0
49ers	61	1187	19.5	61	0
Opponents	67	1485	22.2	92t	1

FIELD GOALS	1-19	20-29	30-39	40-49	50+
Nedney	0/0	6/6	2/2	1/2	2/3
Reed	0/0	3/3	3/4	3/3	0/0
Andrus	0/0	1/1	1/2	0/1	0/0
49ers	0/0	10/10	6/8	4/6	2/3
Opponents	1/1	5/6	13/14	8/10	1/2

SACKS	No.
J. Smith	8.5
Willis	6.0
Brooks	5.0
LaBoy	5.0
Haralson	4.0
Lawson	2.5
Sopoaga	1.5
Clements	1.0
Goldson	1.0
Jean-Francois	1.0
Spencer	0.5
49ers	36.0
Opponents	44.0

RECORD HOLDERS
INDIVIDUAL RECORDS—CAREER

Category	Name	Performance
Rushing (Yds.)	Joe Perry, 1950-1960, 1963	7,344
Passing (Yds.)	Joe Montana, 1979-1992	35,124
Passing (TDs)	Joe Montana, 1979-1992	244
Receiving (No.)	Jerry Rice, 1985-2000	1,281
Receiving (Yds.)	Jerry Rice, 1985-2000	19,247
Interceptions	Ronnie Lott, 1981-1990	51
Punting (Avg.)	Andy Lee, 2004-2010	45.1
Punt Return (Avg.)	Dana McLemore, 1982-87	10.8
Kickoff Return (Avg.)	Abe Woodson, 1958-1964	29.4
Field Goals	Ray Wersching, 1977-1987	190
Touchdowns (Tot.)	Jerry Rice, 1985-2000	187
Points	Jerry Rice, 1985-2000	1,130
*Sacks	Bryant Young, 1994-2007	89.5

INDIVIDUAL RECORDS—SINGLE SEASON

Category	Name	Performance
Rushing (Yds.)	Frank Gore, 2006	1,695
Passing (Yds.)	Jeff Garcia, 2000	4,278
Passing (TDs)	Steve Young, 1998	36
Receiving (No.)	Jerry Rice, 1995	122
Receiving (Yds.)	Jerry Rice, 1995	**1,848
Interceptions	Dave Baker, 1960	10
	Ronnie Lott, 1986	10
Punting (Avg.)	Andy Lee, 2008	47.8
Punt Return (Avg.)	Jimmy Williams, 2002	16.8
Kickoff Return (Avg.)	Joe Arenas, 1953	34.4
Field Goals	Jeff Wilkins, 1996	30
Touchdowns (Tot.)	Jerry Rice, 1987	23
Points	Jerry Rice, 1987	138
*Sacks	Fred Dean, 1983	17.5

INDIVIDUAL RECORDS—SINGLE GAME

Category	Name	Performance
Rushing (Yds.)	Frank Gore, 11-19-06	212
Passing (Yds.)	Joe Montana, 10-14-90	476
Passing (TDs)	Joe Montana, 10-14-90	6
Receiving (No.)	Terrell Owens, 12-17-00	**20
Receiving (Yds.)	Jerry Rice, 12-18-95	289
Interceptions	Dave Baker, 12-4-60	**4
Field Goals	Ray Wersching, 10-16-83	6
	Jeff Wilkins, 9-29-96	6
Touchdowns (Tot.)	Jerry Rice, 10-14-90	5
Points	Jerry Rice, 10-14-90	30
*Sacks	Fred Dean, 11-13-83	6.0

*Sacks became an official statistic in 1982.
**NFL Record

VETERAN ROSTER AS OF MARCH 3, 2011

No.	Name	Pos.	Ht.	Wt.	Birthdate	^ NFL Exp.	College	Hometown	How Acq.	'10 Games/ Starts
35	Adams, Phillip	CB	5-11	192	7/20/88	2	South Carolina State	Rock Hill, S.C.	D7-'10	15/0
64	Baas, David	G	6-4	330	9/28/81	7	Michigan	Sarasota, Fla.	D2-'05	16/16
75	Boone, Alex	T	6-7	328	5/4/87	2	Ohio State	Lakewood, Ohio	FA-'09	1/0
53	Bowman, NaVorro	LB	6-0	242	5/28/88	2	Penn State	District Heights, Md.	D3-'10	16/1
26	Brock, Tramaine	CB	5-10	197	8/20/88	2	Belhaven	Gulfport, Miss.	FA-'10	3/0
55	Brooks, Ahmad	LB	6-3	259	3/14/84	6	Virginia	Fairfax, Va.	W(Cin)-'08	15/1
25	Brown, Tarell	CB	5-10	193	1/6/85	5	Texas	Mesquite, Texas	D5-'07	15/0
82	Byham, Nate	TE	6-4	264	6/27/88	2	Pittsburgh	Franklin, Pa.	D6b-'10	14/3
5	Carr, David	QB	6-3	216	7/21/79	10	Fresno State	Bakersfield, Calif.	UFA(NYG)-'10	1/0
22	Clements, Nate	CB	6-0	205	12/12/79	11	Ohio State	Shaker Heights, Ohio	UFA(Buff)-'07	16/16
15	Crabtree, Michael	WR	6-1	214	9/14/87	3	Texas Tech	Dallas, Texas	D1-'09	16/15
76	Davis, Anthony	T	6-5	323	10/11/89	2	Rutgers	Piscataway, N.J.	D1a-'10	16/16
85	Davis, Vernon	TE	6-3	250	1/31/84	6	Maryland	Washington, D.C.	D1a-'06	16/16
24	Dixon, Anthony	RB	6-1	233	9/24/87	2	Mississippi State	Jackson, Miss.	D6a-'10	16/0
93	Evans, Demetric	DT	6-4	275	9/3/79	10	Georgia	Haynesville, La.	UFA(Wash)-'09	16/0
92	Franklin, Aubrayo	NT	6-1	317	8/27/80	9	Tennessee	Johnson City, Tenn.	UFA(Balt)-'07	16/16
59	Gibson, Thaddeus	LB	6-2	243	10/21/87	2	Ohio State	Euclid, Ohio	W(Pitt)-'10	2/0
19	Ginn, Ted	WR	5-11	180	4/12/85	5	Ohio State	Cleveland, Ohio	T(Mia)-'10	13/0
38	Goldson, Dashon	S	6-2	200	9/18/84	5	Washington	Carson, Calif.	D4b-'07	16/16
21	Gore, Frank	RB	5-9	217	5/14/83	7	Miami	Coral Gables, Fla.	D3a-'05	11/11
98	Haralson, Parys	LB	6-0	255	1/24/84	6	Tennessee	Flora, Miss.	D5-'06	15/15
66	Heitmann, Eric	C	6-3	312	2/24/80	10	Stanford	Katy, Texas	D7a-'02	0*
77	Iupati, Mike	G	6-5	331	5/12/87	2	Idaho	American Samoa	D1b-'10	16/16
31	James, William	CB	6-0	200	6/15/79	11	Western Illinois	Uniontown, Pa.	UFA(Det)-'10	5/0
95	Jean Francois, Ricky	DT	6-3	295	11/23/86	3	Louisiana State	Miami, Fla.	D7b-'09	16/0
86	Jennings, Brian	TE/LS	6-5	242	10/14/76	12	Arizona State	Phoenix, Ariz.	D7b-'00	16/0
57	Kristick, Keaton	LB	6-3	234	4/25/88	2	Oregon State	Naperville, Ill.	FA-'10	6/0
54	LaBoy, Travis	LB	6-3	250	8/20/81	7	Hawai'i	Honolulu, Hawai'i	FA-'10	14/0
99	Lawson, Manny	LB	6-5	240	7/3/84	6	North Carolina State	Goldsboro, N.C.	D1b-'06	16/16
4	Lee, Andy	P	6-2	180	8/11/82	8	Pittsburgh	Westminster, S.C.	D6a-'04	16/0
18	Long, Lance	WR	5-11	186	5/4/85	2	Mississippi State	Macomb, Mich.	FA-'10	0*
40	Maragos, Chris	S	5-10	200	1/6/87	2	Wisconsin	Racine, Wis.	FA-'10	3/0
23	Mays, Taylor	S	6-3	230	2/7/88	2	Southern California	Seattle, Wash.	D2-'10	16/6
91	McDonald, Ray	DT	6-3	290	9/2/84	5	Florida	Belle Glade, Fla.	D3b-'07	16/0
56	McKillop, Scott	LB	6-1	244	3/4/86	3	Pittsburgh	Export, Pa.	D5a-'09	0*
84	Morgan, Josh	WR	6-0	219	6/20/85	4	Virginia Tech	Washington, D.C.	D6-'08	16/11
6	Nedney, Joe	K	6-5	220	3/22/73	16	San Jose State	San Jose, Calif.	FA-'05	9/0
44	Norris, Moran	FB	6-1	250	6/16/78	11	Kansas	Houston, Texas	UFA(Det)-'09	16/11
33	Omon, Xavier	RB	5-11	227	2/15/85	3	Northwest Missouri State	Beatrice, Neb.	FA-'10	0*
61	Patrick, Chris	T	6-5	305	8/22/84	3	Nebraska	Ithaca, Mich.	FA-'09	0*
62	Rachal, Chilo	T/G	6-5	323	3/15/86	4	Southern California	Compton, Calif.	D2-'08	15/14
3	Reed, Jeff	K	5-11	225	4/9/79	10	North Carolina	Charlotte, N.C.	FA-'10	5/0
65	Sims, Barry	T	6-5	300	12/1/74	13	Utah	Park City, Utah	FA-'08	8/7
11	Smith, Alex	QB	6-4	217	5/7/84	7	Utah	San Diego, Calif.	D1-'05	11/10
94	Smith, Justin	DT	6-4	285	9/30/79	11	Missouri	Jefferson City, Mo.	UFA(Cin)-'08	16/16
30	Smith, Reggie	S	6-1	200	9/3/86	4	Oklahoma	Edmond, Okla.	D3-'08	16/7
1	Smith, Troy	QB	6-0	217	7/20/84	5	Ohio State	Cleveland, Ohio	FA-'10	6/6
68	Snyder, Adam	T/G	6-6	325	1/30/82	7	Oregon	Whittier, Calif.	D3b-'05	15/2
90	Sopoaga, Isaac	DT	6-2	330	9/4/81	8	Hawai'i	Fagasa, American Samoa	D4a-'04	16/16
36	Spencer, Shawntae	CB	6-1	190	2/22/82	8	Pittsburgh	Rankin, Pa.	D2b-'04	16/16
51	Spikes, Takeo	LB	6-2	242	12/17/76	14	Auburn	Augusta, Ga.	FA-'08	16/16
27	Spillman, C.J.	S	6-0	199	5/6/86	3	Marshall	Louisville, Ky.	W(SD)-'10	11/0
74	Staley, Joe	T	6-5	315	8/30/84	5	Central Michigan	Rockford, Mich.	D1b-'07	9/9
28	Taylor, Curtis	S	6-2	209	7/13/85	3	Louisiana State	Bogalusa, La.	D7a-'09	5/0
46	Walker, Delanie	TE	6-0	242	8/12/84	6	Central Missouri	Pomona, Calif.	D6a-'06	14/8
20	Westbrook, Brian	RB	5-10	203	9/2/79	10	Villanova	Fort Washington, Md.	FA-'10	14/5
10	Williams, Kyle	WR	5-10	186	7/19/88	2	Arizona State	San Jose, Calif.	D6c-'10	5/0
52	Willis, Patrick	LB	6-1	240	1/25/85	5	Mississippi	Bruceton, Tenn.	D1a-'07	15/15
69	Wragge, Tony	G	6-4	310	8/14/79	7	New Mexico State	Bloomfield, Neb.	FA-'05	15/0
17	Zeigler, Dominique	WR	6-3	185	10/11/84	3	Baylor	Kalamazoo, Mich.	FA-'07	11/0

* Heitmann missed '10 season because of injury; Long spent '10 season on San Francisco practice squad, last active with Kansas City in '09; McKillop missed '10 season because of injury; Omon spent '10 season on San Francisco practice squad, last active with Buffalo in '09; Patrick missed '10 season because of injury.

Also played with 49ers in '10—K Shane Andrus (2 games), LB Diyral Briggs (1), WR Jason Hill (2), S Michael Lewis (3), RB DeShawn Wynn (3).

^ "NFL Exp." as of 2011 Kickoff Weekend. For full explanation of how a player's NFL Experience is measured, refer to explanation underneath the First-Year Roster listed below.

FIRST-YEAR ROSTER

Name	Pos.	Ht.	Wt.	Birthdate	College	Hometown	How Acq.
Cloherty, Colin (1)	TE	6-2	245	9/16/87	Brown	Bethesda, Md.	FA-'10
Culliver, Chris	CB	6-0	199	8/17/88	South Carolina	Philadelphia, Pa.	D3
Holcomb, Curtis	CB	5-10	190	9/3/88	Florida A&M	Miami, Fla.	D7c
Howell, Nick (1)	G	6-5	295	10/10/86	Southern California	Fresno, Calif.	FA-'10
Hunter, Kendall	RB	5-7	199	9/16/88	Oklahoma State	Tyler, Texas	D4
Johnson, Ronald	WR	5-10	185	8/3/88	Southern California	Muskegon, Mich.	D6a
Jones, Colin	S	6-0	208	10/27/87	Texas Christian	Bridgeport, Texas	D6b
Joseph, Alex (1)	LB	6-2	240	7/6/88	Temple	Stamford, Conn.	FA-'10
Jurovich, Kevin (1)	WR	6-0	183	6/30/86	San Jose State	Santa Clara, Calif.	FA-'10
Kaepernick, Colin	QB	6-4	230	11/3/87	Nevada	Milwaukee, Wis.	D2
Kilgore, Daniel	G	6-3	308	12/18/87	Appalachian State	Kingsport, Tenn.	D5
Miller, Bruce	FB	6-2	248	8/6/87	Central Florida	Canton, Ga.	D7a
Person, Mike	G	6-4	299	6/17/88	Montana State	Glendive, Mont.	D7b
Scaccia, Fabrizio (1)	K	6-1	210	8/21/84	Indian River State College	Port St. Lucie, Fla.	FA-'10
Smith, Aldon	OLB	6-4	258	9/25/89	Missouri	Kansas City, Mo.	D1
Tukuafu, Will (1)	DT	6-4	293	1/3/84	Oregon	Salt Lake City, Utah	FA-'10

The term NFL Rookie is defined as a player who is in his first season of professional football and has not been on the roster of another professional football team for any regular-season or postseason games. A Rookie is designated by an "R" on NFL rosters. Players who have been active in another professional football league or players who have NFL experience, including either preseason training camp or being on an Active List or Inactive List, or on Reserve/Injured or Reserve/Physically Unable to Perform for fewer than six regular-season games, are termed NFL First-Year Players. An NFL First-Year Player is designated by a "1" on NFL rosters. Thereafter, a player is credited with an additional year of experience for each season in which he accumulates six games on the Active List or Inactive List, or on Reserve/Injured or Reserve/Physically Unable to Perform.

Log on to www.sf49ers.com for an up-to-date roster.

COACHING STAFF

Head Coach,
Jim Harbaugh

Pro Career: Named the seventeenth head coach in 49ers history on January 7, 2011, Jim Harbaugh enters his first season at the helm of the San Francisco 49ers. Harbaugh is in his third season as an NFL coach after a 15-year playing career with the Bears, Colts, Ravens, Chargers and Panthers. Prior to being named head coach of the 49ers, Harbaugh was the head coach at Stanford University from 2007-2010 where he led the Cardinal to its first BCS game appearance and victory in the Orange Bowl, in 2010. Harbaugh was head coach at the University of San Diego from 2004-06. He started in the NFL as an offensive assistant with the Oakland Raiders from 2002-03. His first coaching job came from his father, Jack Harbaugh, at Western Kentucky where he served as a volunteer assistant coach. A first-round draft pick by the Bears in 1987, Harbaugh ranks in the NFL's top-50 in two career passing categories: completions (41st) and pass attempts (45th). He appeared in one Pro Bowl and was placed in the Colts Ring of Honor in 2005. Career record: 0-0.
Background: Harbaugh earned first team All-America and Big Ten Player of the Year honors as a senior at Michigan, finishing third in the Heisman Trophy balloting.
Personal: Born December 23, 1963, Toledo, Ohio. He has five children and is married to Sarah.

ASSISTANT COACHES

Michael Christianson, director of football technology/offensive quality control; born April 7, 1965, Boise, Idaho. Western Oregon. No pro playing experience. College coach: Western Oregon 1992-94, Lewis & Clark College 1995, Portland State 1995-99, Montana State 2000-01, Nebraska 2004-05, San Diego 2006. Pro coach: Tampa Bay Buccaneers 2002, joined 49ers in 2011.
Geep Chryst, quarterbacks; born June 25, 1962, Madison, Wisc. Linebacker Princeton 1981-84. Pro linebacker Orlando Thunder (World League) 1992. College coach: Wisconsin-Platteville 1987, Wisconsin 1988, Wyoming 1989-1990. Pro coach: Orlando Thunder (World League) 1991, Chicago Bears 1991-95, Arizona Cardinals 1996-98, San Diego Chargers 1999-2000, Arizona Cardinals 2001-03, Carolina Panthers 2006-2010, joined 49ers in 2011.
Reggie Davis, tight ends; born September 3, 1976, Long Beach, Calif. Linebacker/tight end Washington 1994-98. Pro tight end San Diego Chargers 1999-2000. College coach: San Diego State 2004, UNLV 2005-07, Oregon State 2008-2010. Pro coach: Joined 49ers in 2011.
Ed Donatell, secondary; born February 4, 1957, Akron, Ohio. Defensive back Glenville (W. Va.) State 1975-78. No pro playing experience. College coach: Kent State 1979-1980, Washington 1981-82, 2008, Pacific 1983-85, Idaho 1986-88, Cal State Fullerton 1989. Pro coach: New York Jets 1990-94, Denver Broncos 1995-99, Green Bay Packers 2000-03, Atlanta Falcons 2004-06, New York Jets 2007, Denver Broncos 2009-2010, joined 49ers in 2011.
Tim Drevno, offensive line; born April 20, 1969, Torrance, Calif. Offensive lineman El Camino (Calif.) J.C. 1987-88, Cal State Fullerton 1989-1991. No pro playing experience. College coach: Cal State Fullerton 1991-92, Montana State 1993-97, UNLV 1998, San Jose State 1999, Idaho 2000-02, San Diego 2003-06, Stanford 2007-2010. Pro coach: Joined 49ers in 2011.
Bobby Engram, offensive assistant; born January 7, 1973, Camden, S.C. Wide receiver Penn State 1992-95. Pro wide receiver Chicago Bears 1996-2000, Seattle Seahawks 2001-08, Kansas City Chiefs 2009. Pro coach: Joined 49ers in 2011.
Ejiro Evero, quality control; born January 6, 1981, Colchester, England. Safety California-Davis 2000-03. No pro playing experience. College coach: California-Davis 2005-06, Redlands 2010. Pro coach: Tampa Bay Buccaneers 2007-09, joined 49ers in 2011.
Vic Fangio, defensive coordinator; born August 22, 1958, Dunmore, Pa. Attended East Stroudsburg State. No pro playing experience. College coach: North Carolina 1983, Stanford 2010. Pro coach: Philadelphia/Baltimore Stars (USFL) 1984-85, New Orleans Saints 1986-1994, Carolina Panthers 1995-98, Indianapolis Colts 1999-2001, Houston Texans 2002-05, Baltimore Ravens 2006-09, joined 49ers in 2011.
Peter Hansen, defensive assistant/quality control; born May 30, 1979, Palo Alto, Calif. Tight end/quarterback Arizona 1997-2001. Pro player Cannes Iron Mask (France) 2003. College coach: Stanford 2008-2010. Pro coach: Joined 49ers in 2011.
Greg Jackson, asst. secondary; born August 20, 1966, Hialeah, Fla. College safety Louisiana State 1985-88. Pro safety New York Giants 1989-1993, Philadelphia Eagles 1994-95, New Orleans Saints 1996, San Diego Chargers 1997-2000. College coach: Idaho 2003, Louisiana-Monroe 2004-2006, Tulane 2007-09, Wisconsin 2010. Pro coach: Joined 49ers in 2011.
Jim Leavitt, linebackers; born December 5, 1956, Harlingen, Texas. No college or pro playing experience. College coach: Missouri 1978-79, Dubuque 1980-81, Morning Side 1983-87, Iowa 1988-89, Kansas State 1990-95, South Florida 1995-2009. Pro Coach: Joined 49ers in 2011.
John Morton, wide receivers; born Sept. 24, 1969, Rochester Hills, Mich. Wide receiver Western Michigan 1991-92. Pro wide receiver Toronto Argonauts (CFL) 1995-96, Frankfurt Galaxy (World League) 1997. College coach: San Diego 2005, Southern California 2007-2010. Pro coach: Oakland Raiders 2002-04, New Orleans Saints 2006, joined 49ers in 2011.
Tom Rathman, running backs; born October 7, 1962, Grand Island, Neb. Running back Nebraska 1983-85. Pro running back San Francisco 49ers 1986-1993, Los Angeles Raiders 1994. College coach: Menlo College 1996. Pro coach: San Francisco 1997-2002, Detroit Lions 2003-05, Oakland Raiders 2007-08, re-joined 49ers in 2009.
Greg Roman, offensive coordinator; born August 19, 1972, Atlantic City, N.J. Defensive line/linebacker John Carroll 1990-94. No pro playing experience. College coach: Stanford 2009-2010. Pro coach: Carolina Panthers 1995-2001, Houston Texans 2002-05, Baltimore Ravens 2006-07, joined 49ers in 2011.
Brad Seely, special teams coordinator/asst. head coach; born September 6, 1956, Vinton, Iowa. Offensive lineman South Dakota State 1974-77. No pro playing experience. College coach: South Dakota State 1978, Colorado State 1980, Southern Methodist 1981, North Carolina State 1982, Pacific 1983, Oklahoma State 1984-88. Pro coach: Indianapolis Colts 1989-1993, New York Jets 1994, Carolina Panthers 1995-98, New England Patriots 1999-2008, Cleveland Browns 2009-2010, joined 49ers in 2011.
Mike Solari, offensive line, born January 16, 1955, Daly City, Calif. Offensive lineman San Diego State 1972-75. No pro playing experience. College coach: Mira Costa (Calif.) J.C. 1978, U.S. International 1979, Boise State 1980, Cincinnati 1981-82, Kansas 1983-85, Pittsburgh 1986, Alabama 1990-91. Pro coach: Dallas Cowboys 1987-88, Phoenix Cardinals 1989, San Francisco 49ers 1992-1996, Kansas City Chiefs 1997-2007, Seattle Seahawks 2008-09, rejoined 49ers in 2010.
Kevin Tolbert, asst. strength and conditioning; born September 11, 1958. Fullback Naval Academy 1978-1980. No pro playing experience. College coach: Miami 1998-2000, Michigan 2001-07, Stanford 2009-2010. Pro coach: Philadelphia Eagles 1996-97, Detroit Lions 2008, joined 49ers in 2011.
Jim Tomsula, defensive line; born April 14, 1967, Homestead, Pa. Middle Tennessee State 1985-86, Catawba College 1987-1990. No pro playing experience. College coach: Charleston Southern 1997. Pro coach: England Monarchs (NFL Europe) 1998, Scottish Claymores (NFL Europe) 1999-2003, Berlin Thunder (NFL Europe) 2004-05, Rhein Fire (NFL Europa) 2006 (head coach), joined 49ers in 2007 (interim head coach, one game, 2010).
Mark Uyeyama, head strength and conditioning; born December 2, 1975, Vancouver, B.C. Nose Guard Butte (Mont.) C.C. 1994-95, Northern State 1996-97. No pro playing experience. College coach: Arizona State 2001-03, Utah State 2004-07. Pro coach: Joined 49ers in 2008.

National Football Conference
West Division
Team Colors: Seahawks Blue, Seahawks
Navy, Seahawks Bright Green
Virginia Mason Athletic Center
12 Seahawks Way
Renton, Washington 98056
Telephone: (425) 203-8000

2011 SCHEDULE
PRESEASON
Aug. 11 at San Diego 5:00
Aug. 20 **Minnesota** 7:00
Aug. 27 at Denver............................6:00
Sep. 2   **Oakland** 7:30

REGULAR SEASON
Sep. 11 at San Francisco 1:15
Sep. 18 at Pittsburgh 10:00
Sep. 25 **Arizona** 1:15
Oct. 2   **Atlanta** 1:05
Oct. 9   at New York Giants 10:00a
Oct. 16 BYE
Oct. 23 at Cleveland 10:00a
Oct. 30 **Cincinnati** 1:15
Nov. 6   at Dallas 10:00a
Nov. 13 **Baltimore** 1:05
Nov. 20 at St. Louis 1:05
Nov. 27 **Washington** 1:05
Dec. 1   **Philadelphia** (Thu)............ 5:20
Dec. 12 **St. Louis** (Mon)................. 5:30
Dec. 18 at Chicago 10:00a
Dec. 24 **San Francisco** (Sat).......... 1:15
Jan. 1   at Arizona 1:15
All times PT
Stadium: Qwest Field
(opened in 2002)
• **Capacity:** 67,000
Playing Surface: FieldTurf
Training Camp: VMAC
Renton, WA 98056

QWEST FIELD

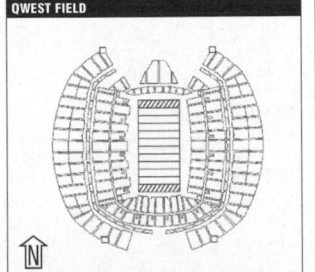

CLUB OFFICIALS
Chairman: Paul Allen
CEO: Peter McLoughlin
Executive Vice President of Football
Operations & Head Coach: Pete Carroll
General Manager: John Schneider
COO: John Rizzardini
CFO & VP/Finance: Karen Harrison
VP/Ticket and Retail Sales & Service:
Chuck Arnold
VP/Community Outreach: Mike Flood
VP/Football Administration: John Idzik
VP/Corporate Partnerships: Ron Jenkins
VP/Football Operations: Will Lewis
VP/General Counsel: Lance Lopes
VP/Communications & Broadcasting:
Dave Pearson
Sr. Personnel Executive:
Scot McCloughan
Director of Corp. Hospitality, Suite Sales
& Service: Amy Sprangers
Director of Pro Personnel: Tag Ribary
Director of Communications:
Lane Gammel
Director of Community Outreach:
Sandy Gregory
Gameday Presentation: Rick Crawford
Video Director Football: Thom Fermstad
Head Athletic Trainer: Sam Ramsden
Equipment Manager: Erik Kennedy
Team Travel: Jeremy Young

COACHING HISTORY
(270-297-0)
Records include postseason games
1976-1982 Jack Patera*...............35-59-0
1982   Mike McCormack 4-3-0
1983-1991 Chuck Knox.................83-67-0
1992-94   Tom Flores..................14-34-0
1995-98   Dennis Erickson...........31-33-0
1999-2008 Mike Holmgren 90-80-0
2009   Jim Mora.....................5-11-0
2010   Pete Carroll..................8-10-0
*Released after two games in 1982

PAID ATTENDANCE
Home 522,371   Away 453,231
Total 975,602
Single-game home record,
68,681 (12/16/00)
Single-season home record,
533,657 (2007)

2011 DRAFT CHOICES
Round	Name	Pos.	College
1	James Carpenter	T	Alabama
3	John Moffitt	G	Wisconsin
4	K.J. Wright	LB	Mississippi St.
	Kris Durham	WR	Georgia
5	Richard Sherman	DB	Stanford
	Mark LeGree	DB	Appalachian St.
6	Byron Maxwell	DB	Clemson
7	Lazarius Levingston	DE	Louisiana St.
	Malcolm Smith	LB	Southern California

SEATTLE SEAHAWKS

2010 TEAM RECORD

PRESEASON (1-3)

Date	Result	Opponent
8/14	W 20-18	Tennessee
8/21	L 24-27	Green Bay
8/28	L 13-24	at Minnesota
9/2	L 24-27	at Oakland

REGULAR SEASON (7-9)

Date	Result	Opponent
9/12	W 31-6	San Francisco
9/19	L 14-31	at Denver
9/26	W 27-20	San Diego
10/3	L 3-20	at St. Louis
10/17	W 23-20	at Chicago
10/24	W 22-10	Arizona
10/31	L 3-33	at Oakland
11/7	L 7-41	New York Giants
11/14	W 36-18	at Arizona
11/21	L 19-34	at New Orleans
11/28	L 24-42	Kansas City
12/5	W 31-14	Carolina
12/12	L 21-40	at San Francisco
12/19	L 18-34	Atlanta
12/26	L 15-38	at Tampa Bay
1/2	W 16-6	St. Louis

POSTSEASON (1-1)

1/8	W 41-36	New Orleans
1/16	L 24-35	at Chicago

SCORE BY PERIODS

Seahawks	55	73	86	96	0 —	310
Opponents	89	141	93	84	0 —	407

2010 TEAM STATISTICS

	Seahawks	Opp.
Total First Downs	260	313
Rushing	81	91
Passing	159	206
Penalty	20	16
3rd Down: Made/Att	76/214	94/238
3rd Down Pct.	35.5	39.5
4th Down: Made/Att	6/17	8/19
4th Down Pct.	35.3	42.1
Possession Avg.	27:33	32:27
Total Net Yards	4765	5897
Avg. Per Game	297.8	368.6
Total Plays	964	1074
Avg. Per Play	4.9	5.5
Net Yards Rushing	1424	1903
Avg. Per Game	89.0	118.9
Total Rushes	385	452
Net Yards Passing	3341	3994
Avg. Per Game	208.8	249.6
Sacked/Yards Lost	35/195	37/246
Gross Yards	3536	4240
Att./Completions	544/324	585/339
Completion Pct.	59.6	57.9
Had Intercepted	20	12
Punts/Average	78/41.7	81/43.5
Net Punting Avg.	78/37.3	81/36.0
Penalties/Yards	101/890	91/706
Fumbles/Ball Lost	18/11	22/10
Touchdowns	33	47
Rushing	13	13
Passing	14	31
Returns	6	3

2010 INDIVIDUAL STATISTICS

PASSING

PASSING	Att.	Comp.	Yds.	Pct.	TD	Int.	Tkld.	Rate
Hasselbeck	444	266	3001	59.9	12	17	29/175	73.2
Whitehurst	99	57	507	57.6	2	3	5/13	65.5
M. Robinson	1	1	28	100.0	0	0	0/0	118.8
Washington	0	0	0	—	0	0	1/7	—
Seahawks	544	324	3536	59.6	14	20	35/195	72.1
Opponents	585	339	4240	57.9	31	12	37/246	89.7

SCORING

SCORING	TD R	TD P	TD Rt	PAT	FG	Saf	PTS
Mare	0	0	0	31/31	25/30	0	106
Lynch	6	0	0	0/0	0/0	0	36
Obomanu	0	4	0	0/0	0/0	0	28
Butler	0	4	0	0/0	0/0	0	24
Washington	1	0	3	0/0	0/0	0	24
Hasselbeck	3	0	0	0/0	0/0	0	18
Forsett	2	0	0	0/0	0/0	0	12
M. Williams	0	2	0	0/0	0/0	0	12
Baker	0	1	0	0/0	0/0	0	6
Branch	0	1	0	0/0	0/0	0	6
Carlson	0	1	0	0/0	0/0	0	6
Martin	0	1	0	0/0	0/0	0	6
Tatupu	0	0	1	0/0	0/0	0	6
Thomas	0	0	1	0/0	0/0	0	6
Trufant	0	0	1	0/0	0/0	0	6
Whitehurst	1	0	0	0/0	0/0	0	6
Babineaux	0	0	0	0/0	0/0	1	2
Seahawks	13	14	6	31/31	25/30	1	310
Opponents	13	31	3	44/44	25/30	1	407

2-Pt Conversions: Obomanu 2.
Seahawks 2-2, Opponents 2-3.

RUSHING

RUSHING	No.	Yds	Avg	LG	TD
Lynch	165	573	3.5	39	6
Forsett	118	523	4.4	32	2
Washington	27	100	3.7	21	1
M. Robinson	12	77	6.4	17	0
Hasselbeck	23	60	2.6	20t	3
Whitehurst	20	43	2.2	9	1
Jones	12	30	2.5	6	0
Obomanu	2	17	8.5	13	0
Butler	2	6	3.0	4	0
Tate	2	4	2.0	3	0
M. Williams	1	0	0.0	0	0
Ryan	1	-9	-9.0	-9	0
Seahawks	385	1424	3.7	39	13
Opponents	452	1903	4.2	53	13

RECEIVING

RECEIVING	No.	Yds	Avg	LG	TD
M. Williams	65	751	11.6	68	2
Butler	36	385	10.7	63t	4
Forsett	33	252	7.6	21	0
Stokley	31	354	11.4	36	0
Carlson	31	318	10.3	37	1
Obomanu	30	494	16.5	87t	4
Tate	21	227	10.8	52	0
Lynch	21	138	6.6	22	0
Branch	13	112	8.6	41	1
Morrah	9	117	13.0	36	0
Baker	9	116	12.9	44	1
Washington	9	79	8.8	28	0
M. Robinson	8	37	4.6	13	0
Martin	7	158	22.6	61	1
Gibson	1	-2	-2.0	-2	0
Seahawks	324	3536	10.9	87t	14
Opponents	339	4240	12.5	69t	31

INTERCEPTIONS

INTERCEPTIONS	No.	Yds	Avg	LG	TD
Thomas	5	68	13.6	34	0
Babineaux	2	37	18.5	20	0
Trufant	1	32	32.0	32t	1
Tatupu	1	26	26.0	26t	1
Hawthorne	1	5	5.0	5	0
Herring	1	0	0.0	0	0
Jennings	1	0	0.0	0	0
Seahawks	12	168	14.0	34	2
Opponents	20	261	13.1	39t	1

PUNTING

PUNTING	No.	Yds.	Avg.	In 20	LG
Ryan	78	3254	41.7	27	63
Seahawks	78	3254	41.7	27	63
Opponents	81	3521	43.5	30	63

PUNT RETURNS

PUNT RETURNS	Ret	FC	Yds	Avg	LG	TD
Washington	22	8	249	11.3	84	0
Tate	16	6	202	12.6	63	0
Forsett	3	0	17	5.7	12	0
Thurmond	1	0	0	0.0	0	0
Seahawks	42	14	468	11.1	84	0
Opponents	35	23	327	9.3	89t	1

KICKOFF RETURNS

KICKOFF RETURNS	No.	Yds	Avg	LG	TD
Washington	57	1461	25.6	101t	3
Morrah	5	76	15.2	30	0
Forsett	1	8	8.0	8	0
A. McCoy	1	3	3.0	3	0
Tate	1	10	10.0	10	0
Seahawks	65	1558	24.0	101t	3
Opponents	50	1099	22.0	79	0

FIELD GOALS

FIELD GOALS	1-19	20-29	30-39	40-49	50+
Mare	2/2	10/12	7/7	5/7	1/2
Seahawks	2/2	10/12	7/7	5/7	1/2
Opponents	0/0	14/15	8/8	3/6	0/1

SACKS

SACKS	No.
Clemons	11.0
Brock	9.0
Milloy	4.0
Curry	3.5
Babineaux	1.5
Bryant	1.0
Chancellor	1.0
Cole	1.0
D. Davis	1.0
Herring	1.0
Lewis	1.0
Mebane	1.0
Tatupu	1.0
Seahawks	37.0
Opponents	35.0

RECORD HOLDERS
INDIVIDUAL RECORDS—CAREER

Category	Name	Performance
Rushing (Yds.)	Shaun Alexander, 2000-07	9,429
Passing (Yds.)	Matt Hasselbeck, 2001-2010	29,434
Passing (TDs)	Dave Krieg, 1980-1991	195
Receiving (No.)	Steve Largent, 1976-1989	819
Receiving (Yds.)	Steve Largent, 1976-1989	13,089
Interceptions	Dave Brown, 1976-1986	50
Punting (Avg.)	Jon Ryan, 2008-2010	44.6
Punt Return (Avg.)	Charlie Rogers, 1999-2001	12.7
Kickoff Return (Avg.)	Josh Wilson, 2007-09	25.8
Field Goals	Norm Johnson, 1982-1990	159
Touchdowns (Tot.)	Shaun Alexander, 2000-07	112
Points	Norm Johnson, 1982-1990	810
*Sacks	Jacob Green, 1980-1991	97.5

INDIVIDUAL RECORDS—SINGLE SEASON

Category	Name	Performance
Rushing (Yds.)	Shaun Alexander, 2005	1,880
Passing (Yds.)	Matt Hasselbeck, 2007	3,966
Passing (TDs)	Dave Krieg, 1984	32
Receiving (No.)	Bobby Engram, 2007	94
Receiving (Yds.)	Steve Largent, 1985	1,287
Interceptions	John Harris, 1981	10
	Kenny Easley, 1984	10
Punting (Avg.)	Jon Ryan, 2009	46.2
Punt Return (Avg.)	Charlie Rogers, 1999	14.5
Kickoff Return (Avg.)	Steve Broussard, 1998	26.9
Field Goals	Todd Peterson, 1999	34
Touchdowns (Tot.)	Shaun Alexander, 2005	28
Points	Shaun Alexander, 2005	168
*Sacks	Michael Sinclair, 1998	16.5

INDIVIDUAL RECORDS—SINGLE GAME

Category	Name	Performance
Rushing (Yds.)	Shaun Alexander, 11-11-01	266
Passing (Yds.)	Matt Hasselbeck, 12-29-02	449
Passing (TDs)	Dave Krieg, 12-2-84, 9-15-85, 11-28-88	5
	Warren Moon, 10-26-97	5
	Matt Hasselbeck, 11-23-03, 9-24-06	5
Receiving (No.)	Steve Largent, 10-18-87	15
Receiving (Yds.)	Steve Largent, 10-18-87	261
Interceptions	Kenny Easley, 9-3-84	3
	Eugene Robinson, 12-6-92	3
	Darryl Williams, 9-21-97	3
	Lofa Tatupu, 12-2-07	3
	Marcus Trufant, 12-9-07	3
Field Goals	Norm Johnson, 9-20-87, 12-18-88	5
	Olindo Mare, 10-24-10, 11-14-10	5
Touchdowns (Tot.)	Shaun Alexander, 9-29-02	5
Points	Shaun Alexander, 9-29-02	30
*Sacks	Many times	4.0
	Last time by Darryl Tapp, 10-21-07	

*Sacks became an official statistic in 1982.

VETERAN ROSTER AS OF MARCH 3, 2011

No.	Name	Pos.	Ht.	Wt.	Birthdate	^NFL Exp.	College	Hometown	How Acq.	'10 Games/ Starts
69	Alford, Jay	DT	6-3	304	5/28/83	4	Penn State	Orange, N.J.	FA-'11	4/0*
77	Andrews, Stacy	T	6-7	340	6/2/81	8	Mississippi	Camden, Ark.	T(Phil)-'10	13/12
27	Babineaux, Jordan	SS	6-0	210	8/31/82	8	Southern Arkansas	Port Arthur, Texas	FA-'04	16/0
95	Balmer, Kentwan	DT	6-5	315	10/15/86	4	North Carolina	Weldon, N.C.	T(SF)-'10	16/11
98	Brock, Raheem	DE	6-4	274	6/10/78	10	Temple	Philadelphia, Pa.	FA-'10	16/0
32	Brown, Marcus	CB	6-1	190	1/27/87	2	Arkansas State	Marianna, Ark.	FA-'10	1/0
79	Bryant, Red	DE	6-4	323	4/18/84	4	Texas A&M	Jasper, Texas	D4-'08	7/7
11	Butler, Deon	WR	5-10	182	1/4/86	3	Penn State	Woodbridge, Va.	D3-'09	13/8
45	Byrd, Dominique	TE	6-3	255	2/7/84	3	Southern California	Minneapolis, Minn.	FA-'11	0*
89	Carlson, John	TE	6-5	251	5/12/84	4	Notre Dame	Litchfield, Minn.	D2-'08	15/13
31	Chancellor, Kam	SS	6-3	232	4/3/88	2	Virginia Tech	Norfolk, Va.	D5-'10	16/0
91	Clemons, Chris	DE	6-3	254	10/30/81	8	Georgia	Griffin, Ga.	T(Phil)-'10	16/16
90	Cole, Colin	DT	6-2	328	6/24/80	9	Iowa	Ft. Lauderdale, Fla.	UFA(GB)-'09	11/11
39	Cox, Kennard	CB	6-0	191	8/17/85	4	Pittsburgh	Miami, Fla.	FA-'10	11/0
59	Curry, Aaron	LB	6-2	255	4/6/86	3	Wake Forest	Fayetteville, N.C.	D1-'09	16/16
58	Davis, Dexter	DE	6-1	244	11/10/86	2	Arizona State	Phoenix, Ariz.	D7a-'10	15/0
18	Edison, Dominique	WR	6-2	204	7/16/86	2	Stephen F. Austin	San Augustine, Texas	FA-'10	0*
66	Fanaika, Paul	G	6-5	327	4/9/86	3	Arizona State	San Mateo, Calif.	PS(Cle)-'10	0*
20	Forsett, Justin	RB	5-8	198	10/14/85	4	California	Arlington, Texas	D7a-'08	16/5
68	Giacomini, Breno	T	6-7	318	9/27/85	4	Louisville	Cambridge, Mass.	FA-'10	0*
64	Gibson, Mike	G	6-3	298	11/18/85	4	California	Napa, Calif.	PS(Phil)-'09	14/8
97	Gordon, Amon	DT	6-2	305	10/13/81	7	Stanford	Queens, N.Y.	FA-'10	1/0
49	Gresham, Clint	LS	6-3	240	8/24/86	2	Texas Christian	Corpus Christi, Texas	FA-'10	16/0
8	Hasselbeck, Matt	QB	6-4	225	9/25/75	13	Boston College	Westwood, Mass.	T(GB)-'01	14/14
57	Hawthorne, David	LB	6-0	246	5/14/85	4	Texas Christian	Corsicana, Texas	FA-'08	16/16
40	Henry, Chris	RB	5-11	234	6/6/85	5	Arizona	Oakland, Calif.	FA-'10	1/0
54	Herring, Will	LB	6-3	241	8/28/83	5	Auburn	Opelika, Ala.	D5-'07	15/0
53	Heygood, Anthony	LB	6-1	232	4/3/86	3	Purdue	Chester, Pa.	FA-'09	0*
56	Hill, Leroy	LB	6-1	238	9/14/82	7	Clemson	Haddock, Ga.	D3b-'05	1/0
21	Jennings, Kelly	CB	5-11	180	11/30/82	6	Miami	Live Oak, Fla.	D1-'06	14/14
46	Konz, Jameson	TE	6-3	234	7/2/86	2	Kent State	Uniontown, Ohio	D7b-'10	0*
34	Lewis, Roy	CB	5-10	190	5/19/85	4	Washington	Los Angeles, Calif.	FA-'09	14/0
75	Locklear, Sean	T	6-4	310	5/29/81	8	North Carolina State	Lumberton, N.C.	D3-'04	16/15
7	Losman, J.P.	QB	6-2	217	3/12/81	8	Tulane	Venice, Calif.	FA-'10	0*
24 t-	Lynch, Marshawn	RB	5-11	215	4/22/86	5	California	Oakland, Calif.	T(Buff)-'10	16/14*
10	Mare, Olindo	K	5-11	192	6/6/73	16	Syracuse	Cooper City, Fla.	FA-'08	16/0
82	Martin, Ruvell	WR	6-4	220	8/10/82	7	Saginaw Valley State	Muskegon, Mich.	UFA(StL)-'10	5/0
85	McCoy, Anthony	TE	6-5	259	12/28/87	2	Southern California	Fresno, Calif.	D6-'10	2/0
52	McCoy, Matt	LB	6-0	232	10/14/82	7	San Diego State	Tustin, Calif.	UFA(TB)-'10	14/0
67	McQuistan, Paul	T	6-6	315	4/30/83	7	Weber State	San Diego, Calif.	FA-'11	0*
92	Mebane, Brandon	DT	6-1	311	1/15/85	5	California	Los Angeles, Calif.	D3-'07	12/12
36	Milloy, Lawyer	S	6-0	211	11/14/73	16	Washington	Tacoma, Wash.	FA-'10	16/16
88	Morrah, Cameron	TE	6-3	251	3/18/87	3	California	Claremont, Calif.	D7c-'09	15/3
87	Obomanu, Ben	WR	6-1	204	10/30/83	6	Auburn	Selma, Ala.	D7b-'06	15/6
76	Okung, Russell	T	6-5	310	10/7/87	2	Oklahoma State	Houston, Texas	D1a-'10	10/10
55	Pawelek, Joe	LB	6-2	237	12/8/86	2	Baylor	San Antonio, Texas	FA-'10	1/0
69	Pitts, Chester	T/G	6-4	308	6/26/79	10	San Diego State	Inglewood, Calif.	UFA(Hou)-'10	7/5
78	Polumbus, Tyler	T	6-8	300	4/10/85	4	Colorado	Denver, Colo.	T(Det)-'10	15/7
99	Richardson, Jay	DE	6-6	280	1/27/84	5	Ohio State	Dublin, Ohio	FA-'10	7/0
26	Robinson, Michael	RB	6-1	223	2/6/83	6	Penn State	Richmond, Va.	FA-'10	11/4
73	Robinson, William	T	6-5	297	12/20/84	4	San Diego State	Pomona, Calif.	PS(Wash)-'10	0*
9	Ryan, Jon	P	6-0	217	11/26/81	6	Regina	Regina, Saskatchewan	FA-'08	16/0
47	Schable, A.J.	DE	6-3	281	5/18/84	3	South Dakota	Ida Grove, Iowa	FA-'11	0*
94	Siavii, Junior	DT	6-5	315	11/14/78	5	Oregon	Pago Pago, Amer. Samoa	FA-'10	14/6
65	Spencer, Chris	C	6-3	309	3/28/82	7	Mississippi	Madison, Miss.	D1-'05	16/16
14	Stanback, Isaiah	WR	6-2	208	8/16/84	5	Washington	Seattle, Wash.	W(NE)-'10	0*
15	Stokley, Brandon	WR	6-0	192	6/23/76	13	Southwestern Louisiana	Lafayette, La.	FA-'10	11/0
81	Tate, Golden	WR	5-10	202	8/2/88	2	Notre Dame	Hendersonville, Tenn.	D2-'10	11/0
51	Tatupu, Lofa	LB	6-0	250	11/15/82	7	Southern California	Wrentham, Mass.	D2-'05	16/16
93	Terrill, Craig	DT	6-2	296	6/27/80	8	Purdue	Lebanon, Ind.	D6-'04	12/1
29	Thomas, Earl	FS	5-10	202	5/7/89	2	Texas	Orange, Texas	D1b-'10	16/16
28	Thurmond, Walter	CB	5-11	190	8/12/87	2	Oregon	West Covina, Calif.	D4a-'10	14/1
23	Trufant, Marcus	CB	5-11	197	12/25/80	9	Washington State	Tacoma, Wash.	D1-'03	16/16
60	Unger, Max	G	6-5	305	4/14/86	3	Oregon	Kailua-Kona, Hawai'i	D2-'09	1/1
70	Walker, Derek	DE	6-4	270	9/16/86	2	Illinois	Glendale Heights, Ill.	FA-'09	0*
33	Washington, Leon	RB	5-8	203	8/29/82	6	Florida State	Jacksonville, Fla.	T(NYJ)-'10	16/0

VETERAN ROSTER AS OF MARCH 3, 2011 (CONTINUED)

No.	Name	Pos.	Ht.	Wt.	Birthdate	^NFL Exp.	College	Hometown	How Acq.	'10 Games/ Starts
63	White, Chris	C	6-2	295	2/28/83	7	Southern Mississippi	Winona, Miss.	FA-'10	6/0
6	Whitehurst, Charlie	QB	6-5	225	8/6/82	6	Clemson	Alpharetta, Ga.	T(SD)-'10	6/2
17	Williams, Mike	WR	6-5	235	1/4/84	5	Southern California	Tampa, Fla.	FA-'10	14/13
74	Willis, Ray	T	6-6	304	8/13/82	7	Florida State	Angleton, Texas	D4-'05	0*

* Alford played 4 games with Oakland in '10; Byrd last played with St. Louis in '07; Edison last active with Tennessee in '09; Fanaika inactive for 3 games; Giacomini did not play in 1 game, inactive for 6 games; Heygood missed '10 season because of injury; Konz missed '10 season because of injury; Losman inactive for 8 games; Lynch played 4 games with Buffalo and 12 games with Seattle; McQuistan played 0 games with Cleveland; W. Robinson inactive for 6 games; Schable last played with Arizona in '06; Stanback missed '10 season because of injury; Walker spent '10 season on San Francisco practice squad, was inactive with Seattle in '09; Willis missed '10 season because of injury.

t- Seahawks traded for Lynch (Buff).

Traded—WR Deion Branch (NE; 4 games in '10).

Also played with Seahawks in '10—TE Chris Baker (16 games), G Allen Barbre (3), FB Quinton Ganther (3), G Ben Hamilton (7), RB Julius Jones (2), CB Nate Ness (1), DE E.J. Wilson (2), G Mansfield Wrotto (2).

^ "NFL Exp." as of 2011 Kickoff Weekend. For full explanation of how a player's NFL Experience is measured, refer to explanation underneath the First-Year Roster listed below.

FIRST-YEAR ROSTER

Name	Pos.	Ht.	Wt.	Birthdate	College	Hometown	How Acq.
Anderson, Andre (1)	RB	6-0	212	5/1/88	Tulane	Stone Mountain, Ga.	FA-'10
Brindley, James (1)	FS	5-11	191	2/1/88	Utah State	Grass Valley, Calif.	FA-'10
Browner, Brandon (1)	CB	6-4	221	8/2/84	Oregon State	Sylmar, Calif.	FA
Carpenter, James	T	6-5	321	3/22/89	Alabama	Augusta, Ga.	D1
Carter, Chris (1)	WR	5-11	191	6/14/87	California-Davis	Danville, Calif.	FA
Durham, Kris	WR	6-5	216	3/17/88	Georgia	Calhoun, Ga.	D4b
Fountain, Maurice (1)	DE	6-3	268	9/22/82	Clemson	Camden, S.C.	FA-'10
Jeanpierre, Lemuel (1)	G	6-3	301	5/19/87	South Carolina	Orlando, Fla.	FA-'10
Johnson, Michael (1)	LB	6-0	254	9/8/86	North Alabama	Panama City, Fla.	FA-'10
LeGree, Mark	FS	6-0	211	7/8/89	Appalachian State	Columbus, Ga.	D5b
Levingston, Pep	DE	6-4	292	11/16/87	Louisiana State	Ruston, La.	D7a
Maxwell, Byron	CB	6-1	207	2/23/88	Clemson	Charleston, S.C.	D6
Moen, Barrett (1)	DT	6-4	282	8/11/87	Minnesota	Bloomington, Minn.	FA
Moffitt, John	G	6-4	319	10/28/86	Wisconsin	Guilford, Conn.	D3
Pinkard, Josh (1)	CB	6-1	218	4/2/86	Southern California	Oxnard, Calif.	FA-'10
Piurowski, Caz (1)	TE	6-7	271	10/11/87	Florida State	Land O' Lakes, Fla.	FA
Sherman, Richard	CB	6-3	195	3/30/88	Stanford	Compton, Calif.	D5a
Smith, Malcolm	LB	6-0	226	7/5/89	Southern California	Northridge, Calif.	D7b
Tuihalamaka, Vuna (1)	LB	6-0	230	2/28/87	Arizona	Inglewood, Calif.	FA-'10
Williams, Pat (1)	WR	6-1	204	1/13/86	Colorado	DeSoto, Texas	FA-'10
Wright, K.J.	LB	6-4	246	7/23/89	Mississippi State	Olive Branch, Miss.	D4a

The term NFL Rookie is defined as a player who is in his first season of professional football and has not been on the roster of another professional football team for any regular-season or postseason games. A Rookie is designated by an "R" on NFL rosters. Players who have been active in another professional football league or players who have NFL experience, including either preseason training camp or being on an Active List or Inactive List, or on Reserve/Injured or Reserve/Physically Unable to Perform for fewer than six regular-season games, are termed NFL First-Year Players. An NFL First-Year Player is designated by a "1" on NFL rosters. Thereafter, a player is credited with an additional year of experience for each season in which he accumulates six games on the Active List or Inactive List, or on Reserve/Injured or Reserve/Physically Unable to Perform.

Log on to www.seahawks.com for an up-to-date roster.

COACHING STAFF

Head Coach,
Pete Carroll

Pro Career: Named as Seattle's eighth head coach on January 11, 2010. Began his NFL career as defensive backs coach for the Buffalo Bills (1984) and Minnesota Vikings (1985-89), before becoming the N.Y. Jets defensive coordinator (1990-93) and head coach (1994). He spent two years as the San Francisco 49ers defensive coordinator (1995-96) before leading the New England Patriots to a 27-21 record and two playoff appearances as head coach (1997-99). Carroll's overall head coaching record is 33-31 in the regular season and 1-2 in the postseason. He returned to the NFL after spending nine years (2001-09) as head coach at USC, where he won seven consecutive Pac-10 titles (2002-08), two national championships and led the Trojans to a 97-19 record. Career record: 42-43.

Background: Two-time All-Pacific Coast Conference safety at Pacific (1971-72). Earned degree in business administration (1973) and secondary teaching credential and master's degree in physical education (1976) from Pacific. College coach: Pacific 1974-76, 1983, Arkansas 1977, Iowa State 1978, Ohio State 1979, North Carolina State 1980-82, USC 2001-09.

Personal: Born September 15, 1951 in San Francisco. He and his wife, Glena, have three children: Brennan, Nate, Jaime, and one grandson: Dillon.

ASSISTANT COACHES

Darrell Bevell, offensive coordinator; born January 6, 1970, Yuma, Ariz. Quarterback Northern Arizona 1989, Wisconsin 1992-95. No pro playing experience. College coach: Westmar 1996, Iowa State 1997, Connecticut 1998-99. Pro coach: Green Bay Packers 2000-05, Minnesota Vikings 2006-2010, joined Seahawks in 2011.

Casey (Gus) Bradley, defensive coordinator; born July 5, 1966, Zumbrota, Minn. Safety/punter North Dakota State 1984-88. No pro playing experience. College coach: North Dakota State 1990-91, 1996-2005, Fort Lewis College 1992-96. Pro coach: Tampa Bay Buccaneers 2006-2008, joined Seahawks in 2009.

Kippy Brown, wide receivers; born March 6, 1955, Sweetwater, Tenn. Quarterback Memphis State 1974-77. No pro playing experience. College coach: Memphis State 1978-1980, Louisville 1982, Tennessee 1983-89, 1993-94, 2009. Pro coach: New York Jets 1990-92, Tampa Bay Buccaneers 1995, Miami Dolphins 1996-99, Green Bay Packers 2000, Houston Texans 2002-05, Detroit Lions 2006-08, joined Seahawks in 2010.

Luke Butkus, quality control/offensive line; born June 26, 1979, Steger, Ill. Center Illinois 1998-2001. Pro center Rhein Fire (NFL Europe) 2003, Cologne Centurions (NFL Europe) 2004. College coach:

Oregon 2005-06. Pro coach: Chicago Bears 2007-09, joined Seahawks in 2010.

Tom Cable, asst. head coach/offensive line; born November 26, 1964, Merced, Calif. Offensive lineman Idaho 1982-86. Pro lineman Indianapolis Colts 1987. College coach: Idaho 1987-88, San Diego State 1989, Cal State-Fullerton 1990, UNLV 1991, California 1992-97, Idaho 2000-03, UCLA 2004-05. Pro coach: Atlanta Falcons 2006, Oakland Raiders 2007-10 (head coach 2008-2010), joined Seahawks in 2011.

Dave Canales, quality control/offense; born May 7, 1981, Carson, Calif. Wide receiver Azusa Pacific 2000-03. No pro playing experience. College coach: El Camino (Calif.) J.C. 2006-08, Southern California 2009. Pro coach: Joined Seahawks in 2010.

Chris Carlisle, head strength & conditioning; born August 7, 1962, Mason City, Iowa. Offensive lineman North Iowa Area Community College 1980-81, Chadron (Neb.) State College 1982-83. No pro playing experience. College coach: Arkansas 1992-93, Trinity Valley (Texas) C.C. 1997, Tennessee 1998-2000, Southern California 2001-09. Pro coach: Joined Seahawks in 2010.

Mondray Gee, asst. strength & conditioning; born June 15, 1976, Detroit. Attended Michigan State. No college or pro playing experience. College coach: Michigan State 2000-01. Pro coach: Detroit Lions 2001-07, Green Bay Packers 2008-09, joined Seahawks in 2010.

Pat McPherson, tight ends; born April 15, 1969, Santa Clara, Calif. Linebacker Santa Clara 1991-92. No pro playing experience. Pro coach: San Francisco 49ers 1996, Denver Broncos 1998-2008, joined Seahawks in 2010.

Ken Norton, Jr., linebackers; born September 29, 1966, Lincoln, Ill. Linebacker UCLA 1984-87. Pro linebacker Dallas Cowboys 1988-1993, San Francisco 49ers 1994-2000. College coach: Southern California 2004-09. Pro coach: Joined Seahawks in 2010.

Kris Richard, defensive backs/cornerbacks; born October 28, 1978, Carson, Calif. Defensive back Southern California 1998-2001. Pro defensive back Seattle Seahawks 2002-04, San Francisco 49ers 2005. College coach: Southern California 2008-09. Pro coach: Joined Seahawks in 2010.

Pat Ruel, asst. offensive line; born December 5, 1950, Coral Gables, Fla. Offensive lineman Miami 1971-72. No pro playing experience. College coach: Miami 1974-76, Arkansas 1977, Washington State 1978-1981, Texas A&M 1982-84, Northern Illinois 1985-87, Kansas 1988-1996, Michigan State 1998-99, USC 2005-09. Pro coach: Detroit Lions 2000, Green Bay Packers 2001-02, Buffalo Bills 2003, New York Giants 2004, joined Seahawks in 2010.

Robert Saleh, quality control/defense; born January 31, 1979, Dearborn, Mich. Tight end Northern Michigan 1997-2000. No pro playing experience. College coach: Michigan State 2002-03, Central Michigan 2004. Pro coach: Houston Texans 2005-2010, joined Seahawks in 2011.

Brian Schneider, special teams coordinator; born May 16, 1971, San Diego. Linebacker Colorado State 1989-1993. No pro playing experience. College coach: Colorado State 1994-2002, UCLA 2003-05, Iowa State 2006, Air Force 2007, Southern California 2009. Pro coach: Oakland Raiders 2007-08, joined Seahawks in 2010.

Rocky Seto, asst. defensive backs/safeties; born March 12, 1976, Arcadia, Calif. Linebacker Southern California 1997-98. No pro playing experience. College coach: Southern California 1999-2009. Pro coach: Joined Seahawks in 2010.

Carl Smith, quarterbacks; born April 26, 1948, Wasco, Calif. Quarterback Bakersfield 1966-67, defensive back Cal Poly-San Luis Obispo 1969-1970. No pro playing experience. College coach: Cal Poly-San Luis Obispo 1971, Colorado 1972-73, Southwestern Louisiana 1974-78, Lamar 1979-1981, North Carolina State 1982, Southern California 2004. Pro coach: Philadelphia/Baltimore Stars 1983-85, New Orleans Saints 1986-1996, New England Patriots 1997-99, Cleveland Browns 2001-03, 2009-2010, Jacksonville Jaguars 2005-06, joined Seahawks in 2011.

Sherman Smith, running backs; born November 1, 1954, Youngstown, Ohio. Quarterback Miami (Ohio) 1972-75. Pro running back Seattle Seahawks 1976-1982, San Diego Chargers 1983-84. College coach: Miami (Ohio) 1990-91, Illinois 1992-94. Pro coach: Houston Oilers/Tennessee Titans 1995-2007, Washington Redskins 2008-09, joined Seahawks in 2010.

Jeff Ulbrich, special teams assistant; born February 17, 1977, San Jose, Calif. Linebacker Hawaii 1996-99. Pro linebacker San Francisco 49ers 2000-09. Pro coach: Joined Seahawks in 2010.

Todd Wash, defensive line; born July 19, 1968, Miles City, Mont. Linebacker North Dakota State 1988-1991. No pro playing experience. College coach: Fort Lewis College 1996-99, Nebraska-Kearney 2000-01, North Dakota State 2002-03, 2005-06, Missouri Southern State 2004. Pro coach: Tampa Bay Buccaneers 2006-2010, joined Seahawks in 2011.

Jamie Yanchar, asst. strength & conditioning, born December 29, 1963, Cleveland. Attended Louisville. No college or pro playing experience. College coach: Southern California 1990-2009. Pro coach: Joined Seahawks in 2010.

National Football Conference
South Division
Team Colors: Buccaneer Red, Pewter,
Black, and Orange
One Buccaneer Place
Tampa, Florida 33607
Telephone: (813) 870-2700

2011 SCHEDULE
PRESEASON
Aug. 12 at Kansas City 8:00
Aug. 18 **New England** 7:30
Aug. 26 **Miami**..............................7:30
Sep. 1   at Washington 7:30

REGULAR SEASON
Sep. 11 **Detroit** 1:00
Sep. 18 at Minnesota 1:00
Sep. 25 **Atlanta** 4:15
Oct. 3   **Indianapolis** (Mon) 8:30
Oct. 9   at San Francisco 4:05
Oct. 16 **New Orleans** 4:15
Oct. 23 **Chicago** (London) 1:00
Oct. 30 BYE
Nov. 6   at New Orleans 1:00
Nov. 13 **Houston** 1:00
Nov. 20 at Green Bay 1:00
Nov. 27 at Tennessee 1:00
Dec. 4   **Carolina** 1:00
Dec. 11 at Jacksonville 1:00
Dec. 17 **Dallas** (Sat) 8:20
Dec. 24 at Carolina (Sat) 1:00
Jan. 1   at Atlanta 1.00
All times ET

Stadium: Raymond James Stadium
(opened in 1998)
•**Capacity:** 65,908
Tampa, Florida 33607
Playing Surface: Grass
Training Camp: One Buccaneer Place
Tampa, Florida 33607

RAYMOND JAMES STADIUM

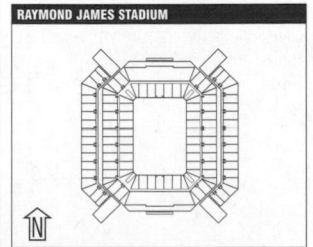

CLUB OFFICIALS
Owner/President: Malcolm Glazer
Co-Chairman: Bryan Glazer
Co-Chairman: Joel Glazer
Co-Chairman: Edward Glazer
General Manager: Mark Dominik
Vice President of Business
Administration: Brian Ford
Director of College Scouting:
Dennis Hickey
Director of Player Development:
Eric Vance
Director of Football Technology:
Chris Wells
Coordinator of Pro Scouting:
Shelton Quarles
Coordinator of Football Administration:
Mike Greenberg
National Scout: Jim Abrams
College Scouts: Andre Forde, Brian
Hudspeth, Byron Kiefer, Tony Kinkela,
Jared Kirksey, Justin Sheridan,
Seth Turner, Mike Yowarsky
Assistant to the Head Coach: Jay Kaiser
Senior Director of Business
Administration: Jason Layton
Chief Financial Officer: Joe Fada
Chief Legal Officer: Steve Johnston
Director of Communications:
Jonathan Grella
Director of Community Relations:
Miray Holmes
Director of Creative Services:
Darren Morgan
Director of Marketing and Business
Development: Jeff Ajluni
Director of Sales: Ben Milsom
Director of Security and Facilities:
Andres Trescastro
Director of Special Events and Team
Operations: Killeen Mullen
Director of Sports Medicine and
Performance: Todd Toriscelli
Director of Rehabilitation:
Shannon Merrick
Team Nutritionist : Kevin Luhrs
Head Equipment Manager: James Sorenson
Asst. Equipment Manager: Mike Myrick
Video Director: Dave Levy
Asst. Video Director: Chris Bryan
Broadcasting Operations Manager:
Jeff Ryan
Cheerleading Manager: Catherine Boyd
Human Resources Generalist:
Raeni Ware
Player Benefits and Alumni Program
Manager: Jill Hobbs
IT Manager: Ed Johnston
Public Relations Manager: Jason Wahlers
Purchasing Manager: Brian Mathiews
Special Events and Team Operations
Manager: Jim Mackes
Ticket Operations Manager: TBD
Video Production Manager: Ed Bottger
Website Manager: Scott Smith

COACHING HISTORY
(224-338-1)
Records include postseason games
1976-1984 John McKay.................45-91-1
1985-86   Leeman Bennett.............4-28-0
1987-1990 Ray Perkins*...............19-41-0
1990-91   Richard Williamson 4-15-0
1992-95   Sam Wyche 23-41-0
1996-2001 Tony Dungy.................56-46-0
2002-08   Jon Gruden.................60-57-0
2009-2010 Raheem Morris 13-19-0
*Released after 13 games in 1990

PAID ATTENDANCE
Home 359,154   Away 540,178
Total 899,332
Single-game home record,
73,523 (12/7/97)
Single-season home record,
545,980 (1979)

2011 DRAFT CHOICES
Round	Name	Pos.	College
1	Adrian Clayborn	DE	Iowa
2	Da'Quan Bowers	DE	Clemson
3	Mason Foster	LB	Washington
4	Luke Stocker	TE	Tennessee
5	Ahmad Black	DB	Florida
6	Allen Bradford	RB	Southern California
7	Anthony Gaitor	DB	Florida International
	Daniel Hardy	TE	Idaho

2010 TEAM RECORD

PRESEASON (2-2)

Date	Result	Opponent
8/14	L 7-10	at Miami
8/21	W 20-15	Kansas City
8/28	L 13-19	Jacksonville
9/2	W 24-17	at Houston

REGULAR SEASON (10-6)

Date	Result	Opponent
9/12	W 17-14	Cleveland
9/19	W 20-7	at Carolina
9/26	L 13-38	Pittsburgh
10/10	W 24-21	at Cincinnati
10/17	L 6-31	New Orleans
10/24	W 18-17	St. Louis
10/31	W 38-35	at Arizona
11/7	L 21-27	at Atlanta
11/14	W 31-16	Carolina
11/21	W 21-0	at San Francisco
11/28	L 10-17	at Baltimore
12/5	L 24-28	Atlanta
12/12	W 17-16	at Washington
12/19	L 20-23	Detroit (OT)
12/26	W 38-15	Seattle
1/2	W 23-13	at New Orleans

(OT) Overtime

SCORE BY PERIODS

Buccaneers	43	127	70	101	0 —	341
Opponents	73	126	53	63	3 —	318

2010 TEAM STATISTICS

	Buccaneers	Opp.
Total First Downs	288	307
Rushing	97	118
Passing	172	171
Penalty	19	18
3rd Down: Made/Att	89/211	92/213
3rd Down Pct.	42.2	43.2
4th Down: Made/Att	10/14	9/17
4th Down Pct.	71.4	52.9
Possession Avg.	30:39	29:21
Total Net Yards	5362	5323
Avg. Per Game	335.1	332.7
Total Plays	955	991
Avg. Per Play	5.6	5.4
Net Yards Rushing	2001	2107
Avg. Per Game	125.1	131.7
Total Rushes	431	444
Net Yards Passing	3361	3216
Avg. Per Game	210.1	201.0
Sacked/Yards Lost	30/203	26/143
Gross Yards	3564	3359
Att./Completions	494/306	521/307
Completion Pct.	61.9	58.9
Had Intercepted	6	19
Punts/Average	76/40.2	72/40.5
Net Punting Avg.	76/35.5	72/35.9
Penalties/Yards	100/837	79/676
Fumbles/Ball Lost	25/13	17/9
Touchdowns	39	38
Rushing	9	12
Passing	26	23
Returns	4	3

2010 INDIVIDUAL STATISTICS

PASSING

	Att.	Comp.	Yds.	Pct.	TD	Int.	Tkld.	Rate
Freeman	474	291	3451	61.4	25	6	28/195	95.9
J. Johnson	16	14	111	87.5	0	0	2/8	95.6
Spurlock	3	0	0	0.0	0	0	0/0	39.6
Graham	1	1	2	100.0	1	0	0/0	118.8
Buccaneers	494	306	3564	61.9	26	6	30/203	96.2
Opponents	521	307	3359	58.9	23	19	26/143	77.6

SCORING

	TD R	TD P	TD Rt	PAT	FG	Saf	PTS
Barth	0	0	0	36/36	23/28	0	105
M. Williams	0	11	0	0/0	0/0	0	66
Blount	6	0	0	0/0	0/0	0	36
Winslow	0	5	0	0/0	0/0	0	30
Spurlock	0	2	1	0/0	0/0	0	18
C. Williams	2	1	0	0/0	0/0	0	18
Benn	0	2	0	0/0	0/0	0	12
Graham	1	1	0	0/0	0/0	0	12
Briscoe	0	1	0	0/0	0/0	0	6
Gilmore	0	1	0	0/0	0/0	0	6
Grimm	0	0	1	0/0	0/0	0	6
Hayes	0	0	1	0/0	0/0	0	6
Penn	0	1	0	0/0	0/0	0	6
Stovall	0	1	0	0/0	0/0	0	6
Talib	0	0	1	0/0	0/0	0	6
Freeman	0	0	0	0/0	0/0	0	2
Buccaneers	9	26	4	36/36	23/28	0	341
Opponents	12	23	3	35/35	17/21	0	318

2-Pt Conversions: Freeman.
Buccaneers 1-3, Opponents 2-3.

RUSHING

	No.	Yds	Avg	LG	TD
Blount	201	1007	5.0	53	6
C. Williams	125	437	3.5	45t	2
Freeman	68	364	5.4	33	0
Graham	20	99	5.0	61	1
J. Johnson	4	39	9.8	14	0
Benn	6	35	5.8	17	0
Huggins	4	11	2.8	7	0
Parker	1	7	7.0	7	0
Stroughter	1	2	2.0	2	0
Lumpkin	1	0	0.0	0	0
Buccaneers	431	2001	4.6	61	9
Opponents	444	2107	4.7	54	12

RECEIVING

	No.	Yds	Avg	LG	TD
Winslow	66	730	11.1	41t	5
M. Williams	65	964	14.8	58t	11
C. Williams	46	355	7.7	20	1
Benn	25	395	15.8	64	2
Stroughter	24	239	10.0	27	0
Spurlock	17	250	14.7	43	2
Graham	16	130	8.1	46	1
Gilmore	13	160	12.3	30	1
Stovall	7	81	11.6	38	1
Briscoe	6	93	15.5	54	1
Purvis	5	38	7.6	12	0
Blount	5	14	2.8	7	0
Parker	4	42	10.5	21	0
Stevens	3	43	14.3	22	0
Lumpkin	1	12	12.0	12	0
Lorig	1	10	10.0	10	0
Huggins	1	7	7.0	7	0
Penn	1	1	1.0	1t	1
Buccaneers	306	3564	11.6	64	26
Opponents	307	3359	10.9	65t	23

INTERCEPTIONS

	No.	Yds	Avg	LG	TD
Talib	6	91	15.2	45t	1
Barber	3	98	32.7	64	0
Grimm	2	24	12.0	13	1
Jones	1	45	45.0	31	0
Hayes	1	41	41.0	41t	1
Piscitelli	1	31	31.0	31	0
Asante	1	4	4.0	4	0
Black	1	4	4.0	4	0
Ruud	1	1	1.0	1	0
Biggers	1	0	0.0	0	0
Lynch	1	0	0.0	0	0
Buccaneers	19	339	17.8	64	3
Opponents	6	153	25.5	79t	0

PUNTING

	No.	Yds.	Avg.	In 20	LG
Malone	52	2160	41.5	17	64
Bryan	23	860	37.4	7	57
Barth	1	33	33.0	0	33
Buccaneers	76	3053	40.2	24	64
Opponents	72	2917	40.5	25	72

PUNT RETURNS

	Ret	FC	Yds	Avg	LG	TD
Spurlock	28	16	193	6.9	23	0
Mack	1	0	0	0.0	0	0
Stroughter	1	0	0	0.0	0	0
Buccaneers	30	16	193	6.4	23	0
Opponents	32	17	232	7.3	37	0

KICKOFF RETURNS

	No.	Yds	Avg	LG	TD
Spurlock	44	1129	25.7	89t	1
Parker	10	178	17.8	37	0
Stroughter	3	79	26.3	30	0
Buccaneers	57	1386	24.3	89t	1
Opponents	75	1554	20.7	102t	1

FIELD GOALS

	1-19	20-29	30-39	40-49	50+
Barth	0/0	6/6	10/10	6/10	1/2
Buccaneers	0/0	6/6	10/10	6/10	1/2
Opponents	0/0	6/7	5/7	6/6	0/1

SACKS

	No.
White	4.5
Hayes	4.0
Crowder	3.0
McCoy	3.0
Black	2.0
Magee	2.0
Ruud	2.0
Barber	1.0
Bennett	1.0
Hayward	1.0
Jones	1.0
Miller	1.0
Woods	0.5
Buccaneers	26.0
Opponents	30.0

RECORD HOLDERS
INDIVIDUAL RECORDS—CAREER

Category	Name	Performance
Rushing (Yds.)	James Wilder, 1981-89	5,957
Passing (Yds.)	Vinny Testaverde, 1987-1992	14,820
Passing (TDs)	Vinny Testaverde, 1987-1992	77
Receiving (No.)	James Wilder, 1981-89	430
Receiving (Yds.)	Mark Carrier, 1987-1992	5,018
Interceptions	Ronde Barber, 1997-2010	40
Punting (Avg.)	Josh Bidwell, 2004-08	44.0
Punt Return (Avg.)	Clifton Smith, 2008	14.1
Kickoff Return (Avg.)	Aaron Stecker, 2000-03	23.8
Field Goals	Martín Gramatica, 1999-2004	137
Touchdowns (Tot.)	Mike Alstott, 1996-2006	71
Points	Martín Gramatica, 1999-2004	592
*Sacks	Warren Sapp, 1995-2003	77.0

INDIVIDUAL RECORDS—SINGLE SEASON

Category	Name	Performance
Rushing (Yds.)	James Wilder, 1984	1,544
Passing (Yds.)	Brad Johnson, 2003	3,811
Passing (TDs)	Brad Johnson, 2003	26
Receiving (No.)	Keyshawn Johnson, 2001	106
Receiving (Yds.)	Mark Carrier, 1989	1,422
Interceptions	Ronde Barber, 2001	10
Punting (Avg.)	Josh Bidwell, 2005	45.6
Punt Return (Avg.)	Karl Williams, 1996	21.1
Kickoff Return (Avg.)	Sammie Stroughter, 2009	29.5
Field Goals	Martín Gramatica, 2002	32
	Matt Bryant, 2008	32
Touchdowns (Tot.)	James Wilder, 1984	13
Points	Matt Bryant, 2008	131
*Sacks	Warren Sapp, 2000	16.5

INDIVIDUAL RECORDS—SINGLE GAME

Category	Name	Performance
Rushing (Yds.)	James Wilder, 11-6-83	219
Passing (Yds.)	Doug Williams, 11-16-80	486
Passing (TDs)	Steve DeBerg, 9-13-87	5
	Brad Johnson, 11-3-02	5
	Josh Freeman, 12-26-10	5
Receiving (No.)	James Wilder, 9-15-85	13
	Earnest Graham, 10-21-07	13
Receiving (Yds.)	Mark Carrier, 12-6-87	212
Interceptions	Ronde Barber, 12-23-01, 12-4-05	3
	Aqib Talib, 9-21-08	3
Field Goals	Martín Gramatica, 12-29-02	5
Touchdowns (Tot.)	Jimmie Giles, 10-20-85	4
Points	Jimmie Giles, 10-20-85	24
*Sacks	Marcus Jones, 10-19-00	4.0
	Simeon Rice, 10-12-03	4.0

*Sacks became an official statistic in 1982.

VETERAN ROSTER AS OF MARCH 3, 2011

No.	Name	Pos.	Ht.	Wt.	Birthdate	^NFL Exp.	College	Hometown	How Acq.	'10 Games/Starts
20	Barber, Ronde	CB	5-10	184	4/7/75	15	Virginia	Roanoke, Va.	D3b-'97	16/16
61	Barker, Will	T	6-7	325	7/3/87	2	Virginia	Bryn Mawr, Pa.	FA-'10	3/0
10	Barth, Connor	K	5-11	193	4/11/86	4	North Carolina	Wilmington, N.C.	FA-'09	16/0
17	Benn, Arrelious	WR	6-2	220	9/8/88	2	Illinois	Washington, D.C.	D2b-'10	15/9
71	Bennett, Michael	DL	6-4	274	11/13/85	3	Texas A&M	Alief, Texas	W(Sea)-'09	13/2
31	Biggers, E.J.	CB	6-0	180	6/13/87	3	Western Michigan	North Miami Beach, Fla.	D7a-'09	16/6
58	Black, Quincy	LB	6-2	240	2/28/84	5	New Mexico	Chicago, Ill.	D3-'07	11/10
27	Blount, LeGarrette	RB	6-0	247	12/5/86	2	Oregon	Perry, Fla.	W(Tenn)-'10	13/7
12	Carpenter, Rudy	QB	6-2	212	4/15/86	3	Arizona State	Westlake Village, Calif.	FA-'09	0*
96	Crowder, Tim	DE	6-4	260	6/30/85	5	Texas	Tyler, Texas	FA-'09	16/9
69	Dotson, Demar	T	6-9	315	10/11/85	3	Southern Mississippi	Alexandria, La.	FA-'09	0*
48	Economos, Andrew	LS	6-1	250	6/24/82	6	Georgia Tech	Atlanta, Ga.	FA-'06	16/0
52	Faine, Jeff	C	6-3	291	4/6/81	9	Notre Dame	Sanford, Fla.	UFA(NO)-'08	8/8
5	Freeman, Josh	QB	6-6	248	1/13/88	3	Kansas State	Kansas City, Mo.	D1-'09	16/16
2	Gilbeaux, Brandon	DE	6-3	270	6/9/87	2	Delaware	Washington, D.C.	FA-'10	0*
88	Gilmore, John	TE	6-5	257	9/21/79	10	Penn State	West Lawn, Pa.	UFA(Chi)-'08	16/11
34	Graham, Earnest	RB	5-9	225	1/15/80	8	Florida	Ft. Myers, Fla.	FA-'03	12/7
35	Grimm, Cody	S	5-11	210	2/26/87	2	Virginia Tech	Fairfax, Va.	D7a-'10	11/9
73	Hardman, Derek	T	6-6	300	9/13/86	2	Eastern Kentucky	Spencer, W. Va.	FA-'10	9/4
54	Hayes, Geno	LB	6-1	226	8/10/87	4	Florida State	Greenville, Fla.	D6-'08	16/16
57	Hayward, Adam	LB	6-1	240	6/23/84	5	Portland State	Westminster, Calif.	D6-'07	16/3
32	Huggins, Kareem	RB	5-9	198	5/24/86	2	Hofstra	Irvington, N.J.	FA-'09	3/0
36	Jackson, Tanard	S	6-0	200	7/21/85	4	Syracuse	Potomac, Md.	D4-'07	2/2
29	Johnson, D.J.	CB	6-1	191	11/7/85	3	Jackson State	LaMarque, Texas	FA-'10	7/0*
11	Johnson, Josh	QB	6-3	205	5/15/86	4	San Diego	Oakland, Calif.	D5-'08	11/0
26	Jones, Sean	S	6-1	220	3/2/82	8	Georgia	Atlanta, Ga.	UFA(Phil)-'10	16/16
75	Joseph, Davin	G	6-3	313	11/22/83	6	Oklahoma	Hallandale, Fla.	D1-'06	11/11
53	Koutouvides, Niko	LB	6-2	238	3/25/81	8	Purdue	Plainville, Conn.	FA-'09	14/0
62	Larsen, Ted	C/G	6-2	305	6/13/87	2	North Carolina State	Palm Beach, Fla.	W(NE)-'10	12/11
77	Lee, James	T	6-4	305	8/17/85	4	South Carolina State	Belle Glade, Fla.	W(Cle)-'08	15/9
23	Lewis, Myron	CB	6-2	203	11/24/87	2	Vanderbilt	Pompano Beach, Fla.	D3-'10	10/1
44	Lorig, Erik	FB/TE	6-4	275	11/17/86	2	Stanford	Palos Verdes, Calif.	D7c-'10	9/1
28	Lumpkin, Kregg	RB	5-11	228	5/5/84	3	Georgia	Albany, Ga.	W(GB)-'10	11/0
41	Lynch, Corey	S	6-0	206	5/7/85	4	Appalachian State	Ft. Myers, Fla.	FA-'09	16/5
33	Mack, Elbert	CB	5-10	175	7/14/86	4	Troy	Wichita, Kan.	FA-'08	12/0
97	t- Magee, Alex	DE	6-3	298	4/28/87	3	Purdue	Oswego, Ill.	T(KC)-'10	10/0*
1	Malone, Robert	P	6-2	215	2/4/88	2	Fresno State	Riverside, Calif.	FA-'10	12/0
93	McCoy, Gerald	DT	6-4	295	2/25/88	2	Oklahoma	Oklahoma City, Okla.	D1-'10	13/13
50	McKenzie, Tyrone	LB	6-2	245	12/11/85	2	South Florida	Riverview, Fla.	FA-'10	3/0
90	Miller, Roy	DT	6-2	310	7/9/87	3	Texas	Killeen, Texas	D3-'09	16/16
94	Moore, Kyle	DE/DT	6-5	272	10/25/86	3	Southern California	Warner Robins, Ga.	D4-'09	7/7
98	Okam, Frank	DT	6-5	350	10/16/85	4	Texas	Dallas, Texas	FA-'10	8/3*
87	Parker, Preston	WR	6-0	200	2/13/87	2	North Alabama	Delray Beach, Fla.	FA-'10	9/0
70	Penn, Donald	T	6-5	305	4/27/83	6	Utah State	Playa del Rey, Calif.	FA-'06	16/16
92	Price, Brian	DT	6-1	303	4/10/89	2	UCLA	Los Angeles, Calif.	D2a-'10	5/0
80	Purvis, Ryan	TE	6-4	260	5/8/86	2	Boston College	Reinholds, Pa.	FA-'09	10/2
51	Ruud, Barrett	LB	6-2	241	5/20/83	7	Nebraska	Lincoln, Neb.	D2-'05	16/16
81	Spurlock, Micheal	WR	5-11	200	1/31/83	4	Mississippi	Indianola, Miss.	FA-'09	16/1
85	Stovall, Maurice	WR	6-5	220	2/21/85	6	Notre Dame	Philadelphia, Pa.	D3-'06	12/1
18	Stroughter, Sammie	WR	5-10	189	1/3/86	3	Oregon State	Sacramento, Calif.	D7b-'09	12/4
25	Talib, Aqib	CB	6-1	205	2/13/86	4	Kansas	Richardson, Texas	D1-'08	11/11
65	Trueblood, Jeremy	T	6-8	320	5/10/83	6	Boston College	Indianapolis, Ind.	D2-'06	14/7
56	Watson, Dekoda	LB	6-2	240	3/3/88	2	Florida State	Aiken, S.C.	D7b-'10	15/1
91	White, Stylez G.	DE	6-3	270	7/25/79	6	Minnesota	Newark, N.J.	FA-'07	16/13
24	Williams, Carnell	RB	5-11	217	4/21/82	7	Auburn	Attalla, Ala.	D1-'05	16/9
19	Williams, Mike	WR	6-2	212	5/18/87	2	Syracuse	Buffalo, N.Y.	D4-'10	16/16
78	Wilson, E.J.	DE	6-3	289	10/28/87	2	North Carolina	Lawrenceville, Va.	FA-'10	2/0*
82	Winslow, Kellen	TE	6-4	240	7/21/83	8	Miami	San Diego, Calif.	T(Cle)-'09	16/11
95	Woods, Al	DT	6-4	307	3/25/87	2	Louisiana State	Elton, La.	FA-'10	9/0
76	Zuttah, Jeremy	G	6-4	308	6/1/86	4	Rutgers	Edison, N.J.	D3-'08	15/9

*   Carpenter inactive for 16 games; Dotson missed '10 season because of injury; Gilbeaux missed '10 season because of injury;
  D.J. Johnson played 7 games with New York Giants in '10; Magee played 2 games with Kansas City and 8 games with Tampa Bay;
  Okam played 5 games with Houston and 3 games with Tampa Bay; Wilson played 2 games with Seattle.

t-   Buccaneers traded for Magee (KC).

Also played with Buccaneers in '10—P Chris Bryan (4 games), S Sabby Piscitelli (11), FB Chris Pressley (3), C Donovan Raiola (1), DT Ryan Sims (6), TE Jerramy Stevens (5), G Keydrick Vincent (5).

^ "NFL Exp." as of 2011 Kickoff Weekend. For full explanation of how a player's NFL Experience is measured, refer to explanation underneath the First-Year Roster listed below.

FIRST-YEAR ROSTER

Name	Pos.	Ht.	Wt.	Birthdate	College	Hometown	How Acq.
Anderson, Vince (1)	S	6-2	205	12/8/84	Webber International (FL)	Lake City, Fla.	FA-'10
Asante, Larry (1)	S	6-0	210	3/7/88	Nebraska	Alexandria, Va.	FA-'10
Black, Ahmad	S	5-9	184	12/12/89	Florida	Lakeland, Fla.	D5
Bowers, Da'Quan	DE	6-4	277	2/23/90	Clemson	Bamberg, S.C.	D2
Bradford, Allen	RB	5-11	235	8/31/88	Southern California	San Bernardino, Calif.	D6
Briscoe, Dezmon (1)	WR	6-2	210	8/31/89	Kansas	Dallas, Texas	FA-'10
Carter, Brandon (1)	G	6-6	319	9/10/86	Texas Tech	Longview, Texas	FA-'10
Clayborn, Adrian	DE	6-3	287	7/6/88	Iowa	St. Louis, Mo.	D1
Dile, Marc (1)	OL	6-4	300	5/5/86	South Florida	Miami, Fla.	FA-'09
Folsom, J.D. (1)	LB	6-3	230	8/19/84	Weber State	Salmon, Idaho	FA-'10
Foster, Mason	LB	6-1	241	3/1/89	Washington	Seaside, Calif.	D3
Gaitor, Anthony	CB	5-10	178	10/9/88	Florida International	Miami, Fla.	D7a
Gant, Ed (1)	WR	6-3	200	1/24/87	North Alabama	Cape Coral, Fla.	FA-'10
Hardy, Daniel	TE	6-4	249	9/7/87	Idaho	Anchorage, Alaska	D7b
Harris, Dominique (1)	S	6-2	213	4/14/87	Temple	Washington, D.C.	FA-'10
Johnson, George (1)	DE	6-4	265	12/11/87	Rutgers	Glassboro, N.J.	FA-'10
Lawrence, Simoni (1)	LB	6-1	221	2/1/89	Minnesota	Upper Darby, Pa.	FA-'10
Malecki, John (1)	C/G	6-2	298	5/26/88	Pittsburgh	Murrysville, Pa.	FA-'10
Overbay, Nathan (1)	TE	6-5	270	1/4/87	Eastern Washington	Chehalis, Wash.	FA-'10
Stocker, Luke	TE	6-5	253	7/17/88	Tennessee	Berea, Ky.	D4
Taylor, Rendrick (1)	FB	6-2	265	4/3/87	Clemson	Clio, S.C.	FA-'10
Worthington, Doug (1)	DT	6-5	292	8/10/87	Ohio State	Athol Springs, N.Y.	FA-'10

The term NFL Rookie is defined as a player who is in his first season of professional football and has not been on the roster of another professional football team for any regular-season or postseason games. A Rookie is designated by an "R" on NFL rosters. Players who have been active in another professional football league or players who have NFL experience, including either preseason training camp or being on an Active List or Inactive List, or on Reserve/Injured or Reserve/Physically Unable to Perform for fewer than six regular-season games, are termed NFL First-Year Players. An NFL First-Year Player is designated by a "1" on NFL rosters. Thereafter, a player is credited with an additional year of experience for each season in which he accumulates six games on the Active List or Inactive List, or on Reserve/Injured or Reserve/Physically Unable to Perform.

Log on to www.buccaneers.com for an up-to-date roster.

COACHING STAFF
Head Coach,
Raheem Morris
Pro Career: Morris was named the eighth head coach in Buccaneers history on January 17, 2009. Prior to being named the head coach, he worked as the Buccaneers defensive backs coach from 2007-08, as assistant defensive back coach from 2004-05, as defensive assistant in 2003 and as a defensive quality control coach in 2002. After Tampa Bay fell to 19th in the NFL in pass defense in 2006, Morris led a resurgence in his return as he guided the Buccaneers pass defense to the league's top ranking en route to the NFC South division title in 2007. In five of his seasons with Tampa Bay, the Bucs ranked in the top five in the NFL in total defense, including No. 1 rankings in 2005 and 2002, when the club captured its first world title in Super Bowl XXXVII. He spent time with the New York Jets serving a defensive minority internship in 2001. Career record: 13-19.
Background: Safety at Hofstra (1994-97), graduating with a degree in physical education. Coached collegiately at Hofstra (1998, 2000-01), Cornell (1999) and Kansas State (2006).
Personal: Born September 3, 1976 in Irvington, New Jersey.

ASSISTANT COACHES
Joe Baker, linebackers; born June 29, 1969, Glen Ridge, N.J. Wide receiver Princeton 1987-1990. No pro playing experience. College coach: East Stroudsburg 1991, Samford 1993, Wisconsin 1999. Pro coach: Birmingham Fire (WFL) 1992, Jacksonville Jaguars 1995-96, New Orleans Saints 2000-04, Green Bay Packers 2006, St. Louis Rams 2006, Denver Broncos 2007-08, joined Buccaneers in 2009.
Tim Berbenich, asst. wide receivers; born December 19, 1979, Huntington, N.Y. Wide receiver Hamilton College 1998-2001. No pro playing experience. Pro coach: New York Jets 2003-05, joined Buccaneers in 2006.
Tim Holt, asst. offensive line; born November 29, 1973, Dighton, Mass. Offensive line Southern Connecticut State 1991-94. No pro playing experience. College coach: Southern Connecticut State 1995-96, 2004-07, Lehigh 1997-98, Cornell 1999-2000, American International 2001-03, Stonehill 2008. Pro coach: Joined Buccaneers in 2009.
Chris Keenan, asst. strength and conditioning; born November 3, 1980, Creston, Iowa. Fullback Drake 1999-2001. No pro playing experience. College coach: Iowa State 2003, Tulane 2006-2008. Pro coach: Minnesota Vikings 2004-05, Tampa Bay Buccaneers 2006, re-joined Buccaneers in 2009.
Jimmy Lake, defensive backs; born December 17, 1976, San Francisco.

Safety Eastern Washington 1995-98. No pro playing experience. College coach: Eastern Washington 1999-2003, Washington 2004, Montana State 2005. Pro coach: Tampa Bay Buccaneers 2006-07, Detroit Lions 2008, re-joined Buccaneers in 2010.
Steve Logan, running backs; born February 3, 1953, Lawton, Okla. No college or pro playing experience. College coach: Oklahoma State 1980, Hutchinson J.C. 1981-82, Tulsa 1983-84, Colorado 1985-86, Mississippi State 1987-88, East Carolina 1989-2002, Boston College 2007-08. Pro coach: Berlin Thunder (NFL Europe) 2004-05, Rhein Fire (NFL Europe) 2006, joined Buccaneers in 2009.
Keith Millard, defensive line; born March 18, 1962, Pleasanton, Calif. Defensive lineman Washington State 1980-84. Pro defensive lineman Jacksonville Bulls (USFL) 1985, Minnesota Vikings 1985-1991, Seattle Seahawks 1992, Green Bay Packers 1992, Philadelphia Eagles 1993. College coach: Fort Lewis 1996, Menlo College 1997-2000. Pro coach: San Francisco Demons (XFL), Denver Broncos 2002-04, Oakland Raiders 2005-08, joined Buccaneers in 2011.
Pat Morris, offensive line; born April 7, 1954, Cleveland. Offensive lineman Southern California 1972-75. No pro playing experience. College coach: Southern California 1976-1977, 1983-86, Northern Arizona 1978, Minnesota 1979-1982, Michigan State 1987-1994, Stanford 1995-96. Pro coach: San Francisco 49ers 1997-2003, Detroit Lions 2004-05, Minnesota Vikings 2006-2010, joined Buccaneers in 2011.
Greg Olson, offensive coordinator; born March 1, 1963, Richland, Wash. Quarterback, Spokane Falls (Wash.) J.C. 1981-82. No pro playing experience. College coach: Washington State 1987-1989, Central Washington 1990-1993, Idaho 1994-1996, Purdue 1997-2000, 2002. Pro coach: San Francisco 49ers 2001, Chicago Bears 2003, Detroit Lions 2004-2005, St. Louis Rams 2006-2007, joined Buccaneers in 2008.
Tyrone Pettaway, defensive quality control; born October 10, 1983, Monterey, Calif. Linebacker St. Augustine 2002-05. No pro playing experience. College coach: Fort Valley State 2006-07, Christopher Newport 2008, Tennessee 2009, Southern California 2010. Pro coach: Joined Buccaneers in 2011.
Alfredo Roberts, tight ends; born March 17, 1965, Fort Lauderdale, Fla. Tight end Miami 1983-87. Pro tight end Kansas City Chiefs 1988-1990, Dallas Cowboys 1991-93. College coach: Florida Atlantic 1999-2002. Pro coach: Jacksonville Jaguars 2003-06, Cleveland Browns 2007-08, joined Buccaneers in 2009.
Kurtis Shultz, head strength and conditioning; born March 10, 1972, Baltimore.

Attended Maryland. No college or pro playing experience. College coach: Loyola (Md.) 1995-98, Maryland and Johns Hopkins 1999-2002. Pro coach: Cincinnati Bengals 2003, Minnesota Vikings 2004-05, joined Buccaneers in 2006.
Byron Storer, asst. special teams; born May 1, 1984, Modesto, Calif. Fullback California 2002-06. Pro fullback Tampa Bay Buccaneers 2007-09. Pro coach: Joined Buccaneers in 2009.
Grady Stretz, defensive line; born November 8, 1972, Chicago. Defensive lineman UCLA 1991-95. No pro playing experience. College coach: UCLA 1996-97, New Mexico 1998-2005, Arizona State 2006-2010. Pro coach: Joined Buccaneers 2011.
Dwayne Stukes, special teams coordinator; born January 24, 1977, Portsmith, Va. Cornerback/safety Virginia 1996-1999. Pro safety Berlin Thunder (NFL Europe) 2001-2002, Colorado Crush (AFL) 2004. Pro coach: Joined Buccaneers in 2006.
Alex Van Pelt, quarterbacks; born May 1, 1970, Pittsburgh. Quarterback Pittsburgh 1989-1992. Pro quarterback Buffalo Bills 1995-2003. College coach: Buffalo 2005. Pro coach: Frankfurt Galaxy (NFLE) 2005, Buffalo Bills 2006-09, joined Buccaneers in 2010.
Eric Yarber, wide receivers; born September 22, 1963, Chicago. Wide receiver Idaho 1984-85. Pro wide receiver Washington Redskins 1986-88. College coach: Idaho 1996, Nevada-Las Vegas 1997, Oregon State 1999-2002, Washington 2005-06, Arizona State 2007-09. Pro coach: Seattle Seahawks 1998, San Francisco 49ers 2003-04, joined Buccaneers in 2010.

**National Football Conference
East Division
Team Colors:** Burgundy and Gold
**Redskins Park
21300 Redskins Park Drive
Ashburn, Virginia 20147
Telephone:** (703) 726-7000

2011 SCHEDULE

PRESEASON

Aug. 12	Pittsburgh	7:30
Aug. 19	at Indianapolis	7:00
Aug. 25	at Baltimore	8:00
Sep. 1	Tampa Bay	7:30

REGULAR SEASON

Sep. 11	**New York Giants**	4:15
Sep. 18	**Arizona**	1:00
Sep. 26	at Dallas (Mon)	8:30
Oct. 2	at St. Louis	1:00
Oct. 9	BYE	
Oct. 16	**Philadelphia**	1:00
Oct. 23	at Carolina	1:00
Oct. 30	at Buffalo (Toronto)	4:05
Nov. 6	**San Francisco**	1:00
Nov. 13	at Miami	1:00
Nov. 20	**Dallas**	1:00
Nov. 27	at Seattle	4:05
Dec. 4	**New York Jets**	1:00
Dec. 11	**New England**	1:00
Dec. 18	at New York Giants	1:00
Dec. 24	**Minnesota** (Sat)	1:00
Jan. 1	at Philadelphia	1:00

All times ET

Stadium: FedExField (opened in 1997)
• **Capacity:** 91,704
1600 FedEx Way
Landover, Maryland 20785
Playing Surface: Natural Grass
Training Camp: Redskins Park
Ashburn, Virginia 20147

FEDEXFIELD

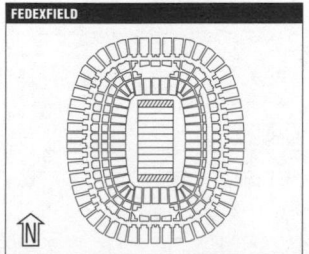

CLUB OFFICIALS

Owner: Daniel M. Snyder
Chief Operating Officer: Dave Donovan
Chief Financial Officer: Nico Foris
Executive Vice President/
    General Manager: Bruce Allen
Executive Vice President/Head Coach:
    Mike Shanahan
Senior Vice President: Tony Wyllie
Chief Marketing Officer: Mitch Gershman
Senior Vice President, Stadium
    Operations: Lon Rosenberg
Director of Player Personnel:
    Scott Campbell
Director of Pro Personnel:
    Morocco Brown
Pro Scouts: Richard Mann II, Alex Santos
College Scouts: Bill Baker, Chip Flanagan,
    Tim Gribble, Shemy Schembechler,
    Jim Zeches
Vice President, Football Administration:
    Eric Schaffer
Leadership Council/Community Affairs:
    BJ Corriveau
Director of Football Administration:
    Paul Kelly
Video Director: Mike Bracken
Video Department: Zachary Kennedy
Head Athletic Trainer: Larry Hess
Assistant Athletic Trainers: Eric Steward,
    Elliott Jermyn, Eli Bisnett-Cobb
Equipment Manager: Brad Berlin
Assistant Equipment Manager:
    Anders Beutel, Chris Collins

COACHING HISTORY

**Boston 1932-36
(570-533-27)**
Records include postseason games

1932	Lud Wray	4-4-2
1933-34	William (Lone Star) Dietz	11-11-2
1935	Eddie Casey	2-8-1
1936-1942	Ray Flaherty	56-23-3
1943	Arthur (Dutch) Bergman	7-4-1
1944-45	Dudley DeGroot	14-6-1
1946-48	Glen (Turk) Edwards	16-18-1
1949	John Whelchel*	3-3-1
1949-1951	Herman Ball**	4-16-0
1951	Dick Todd	5-4-0
1952-53	Earl (Curly) Lambeau	10-13-1
1954-58	Joe Kuharich	26-32-2
1959-1960	Mike Nixon	4-18-2
1961-65	Bill McPeak	21-46-3
1966-68	Otto Graham	17-22-3
1969	Vince Lombardi	7-5-2
1970	Bill Austin	6-8-0
1971-77	George Allen	69-35-1
1978-1980	Jack Pardee	24-24-0
1981-1992	Joe Gibbs	140-65-0
1993	Richie Petitbon	4-12-0
1994-2000	Norv Turner***	50-60-1
2000	Terry Robiskie	1-2-0
2001	Marty Schottenheimer	8-8-0
2002-03	Steve Spurrier	12-20-0
2004-07	Joe Gibbs	31-36-0
2008-09	Jim Zorn	12-20-0
2010	Mike Shanahan	6-10-0

*Released after seven games in 1949
**Released after three games in 1951
***Released after 13 games in 2000

PAID ATTENDANCE

Home 680,966   Away 506,953
Total 1,187,919
Single-game home record,
    90,910 (12/30/07)
Single-season home record,
    * 711,471 (2007)
NFL Record

2011 DRAFT CHOICES

Round	Name	Pos.	College
1	Ryan Kerrigan	LB	Purdue
2	Jarvis Jenkins	DE	Clemson
3	Leonard Hankerson	WR	Miami
4	Roy Helu	RB	Nebraska
5	DeJon Gomes	DB	Nebraska
	Niles Paul	WR	Nebraska
6	Evan Royster	RB	Penn State
	Aldrick Robinson	WR	Southern Methodist
7	Brandyn Thompson	DB	Boise State
	Maurice Hurt	G	Florida
	Markus White	LB	Florida State
	Chris Neild	NT	West Virginia

2010 TEAM RECORD
PRESEASON (2-2)

Date	Result	Opponent
8/13	W 42-17	Buffalo
8/21	L 3-23	Baltimore
8/27	W 16-11	at New York
9/2	L 10-20	at Arizona

REGULAR SEASON (6-10)

Date	Result	Opponent
9/12	W 13-7	Dallas
9/19	L 27-30	Houston (OT)
9/26	L 16-30	at St. Louis
10/3	W 17-12	at Philadelphia
10/10	W 16-13	Green Bay (OT)
10/17	L 24-27	Indianapolis
10/24	W 17-14	at Chicago
10/31	L 25-37	at Detroit
11/15	L 28-59	Philadelphia
11/21	W 19-16	at Tennessee (OT)
11/28	L 13-17	Minnesota
12/5	L 7-31	at New York Giants
12/12	L 16-17	Tampa Bay
12/19	L 30-33	at Dallas
12/26	W 20-17	at Jacksonville (OT)
1/2	L 14-17	New York Giants

(OT) Overtime

SCORE BY PERIODS

Redskins	61	97	51	84	9 —	302
Opponents	104	94	101	75	3 —	377

2010 TEAM STATISTICS

	Redskins	Opp.
Total First Downs	295	326
Rushing	72	106
Passing	194	207
Penalty	29	13
3rd Down: Made/Att	61/208	75/214
3rd Down Pct.	29.3	35.0
4th Down: Made/Att	6/12	7/10
4th Down Pct.	50.0	70.0
Possession Avg.	28:01	31:59
Total Net Yards	5374	6228
Avg. Per Game	335.9	389.3
Total Plays	1002	1051
Avg. Per Play	5.4	5.9
Net Yards Rushing	1461	2041
Avg. Per Game	91.3	127.6
Total Rushes	351	444
Net Yards Passing	3913	4187
Avg. Per Game	244.6	261.7
Sacked/Yards Lost	46/348	29/176
Gross Yards	4261	4363
Att./Completions	605/349	578/367
Completion Pct.	57.7	63.5
Had Intercepted	19	14
Punts/Average	94/40.2	86/43.1
Net Punting Avg.	94/33.7	86/36.0
Penalties/Yards	90/647	104/839
Fumbles/Ball Lost	29/12	24/13
Touchdowns	33	42
Rushing	9	15
Passing	21	23
Returns	3	4

2010 INDIVIDUAL STATISTICS

PASSING

	Att.	Comp.	Yds.	Pct.	TD	Int.	Tkld.	Rate
McNabb	472	275	3377	58.3	14	15	37/271	77.1
Grossman	133	74	884	55.6	7	4	9/77	81.2
Redskins	605	349	4261	57.7	21	19	46/348	78.0
Opponents	578	367	4363	63.5	23	14	29/176	89.6

SCORING

	TD R	TD P	TD Rt	PAT	FG	Saf	PTS
Gano	0	0	0	28/28	24/35	0	100
Moss	0	6	0	0/0	0/0	0	36
Torain	4	2	0	0/0	0/0	0	36
K. Williams	3	2	0	0/0	0/0	0	30
Cooley	0	3	0	0/0	0/0	0	20
Armstrong	0	3	0	0/0	0/0	0	18
F. Davis	0	3	0	0/0	0/0	0	18
Hall	0	0	2	0/0	0/0	0	12
Portis	2	0	0	0/0	0/0	0	12
Banks	0	0	1	0/0	0/0	0	6
Paulsen	0	1	0	0/0	0/0	0	6
Young	0	1	0	0/0	0/0	0	6
Sellers	0	0	0	0/0	0/0	2	2
Redskins	9	21	3	28/28	24/35	0	302
Opponents	15	23	4	37/37	28/38	0	377

2-Pt Conversions: Cooley, Sellers.
Redskins 2-5, Opponents 2-5.

RUSHING

	No.	Yds	Avg	LG	TD
Torain	164	742	4.5	54	4
K. Williams	65	261	4.0	32t	3
Portis	54	227	4.2	27	2
McNabb	29	151	5.2	36	0
J. Davis	15	51	3.4	14	0
Young	4	19	4.8	16	0
Banks	2	6	3.0	3	0
Grossman	3	6	2.0	5	0
L. Johnson	5	2	0.4	7	0
Sellers	4	2	0.5	1	0
Bidwell	1	0	0.0	0	0
Moss	5	-6	-1.2	7	0
Redskins	351	1461	4.2	54	9
Opponents	444	2041	4.6	71	15

RECEIVING

	No.	Yds	Avg	LG	TD
Moss	93	1115	12.0	56	6
Cooley	77	849	11.0	35	3
Armstrong	44	871	19.8	76	3
K. Williams	39	309	7.9	36	2
F. Davis	21	316	15.0	71	3
Sellers	20	224	11.2	28	0
Torain	18	125	6.9	20	2
Galloway	12	173	14.4	62	0
R. Williams	8	109	13.6	34	0
Portis	5	55	11.0	14	0
J. Davis	4	45	11.3	28	0
Austin	3	47	15.7	28	0
Banks	2	10	5.0	15	0
Paulsen	2	10	5.0	9	1
Young	1	3	3.0	3t	1
Redskins	349	4261	12.2	76	21
Opponents	367	4363	11.9	92t	23

INTERCEPTIONS

	No.	Yds	Avg	LG	TD
Hall	6	92	15.3	92t	1
Buchanon	2	51	25.5	43	0
Rogers	2	43	21.5	38	0
Barnes	1	8	8.0	8	0
Ka. Moore	1	5	5.0	5	0
Fletcher	1	0	0.0	0	0
Landry	1	0	0.0	0	0
Redskins	14	199	14.2	92t	1
Opponents	19	216	11.4	64	2

PUNTING

	No.	Yds.	Avg.	In 20	LG
Smith	57	2310	40.5	17	56
Paulescu	17	700	41.2	2	52
Bidwell	15	625	41.7	3	52
Gano	4	141	35.3	1	42
Redskins	94	3776	40.2	23	56
Opponents	86	3704	43.1	29	59

PUNT RETURNS

	Ret	FC	Yds	Avg	LG	TD
Banks	38	10	431	11.3	53	0
Buchanon	2	3	1	0.5	1	0
Redskins	40	13	432	10.8	53	0
Opponents	45	17	568	12.6	87t	1

KICKOFF RETURNS

	No.	Yds	Avg	LG	TD
Banks	46	1155	25.1	96t	1
Thomas	12	336	28.0	42	0
Sellers	7	82	11.7	18	0
Wilson	3	27	9.0	15	0
Simpson	2	59	29.5	32	0
Westbrook	2	6	3.0	6	0
Austin	1	15	15.0	15	0
Redskins	73	1680	23.0	96t	1
Opponents	61	1160	19.0	38	0

FIELD GOALS

	1-19	20-29	30-39	40-49	50+
Gano	1/1	8/10	4/7	11/14	0/3
Redskins	1/1	8/10	4/7	11/14	0/3
Opponents	0/0	8/9	11/15	8/12	1/2

SACKS

	No.
Orakpo	8.5
Carter	2.5
Fletcher	2.5
Haynesworth	2.5
Holliday	2.5
Daniels	2.0
McIntosh	2.0
Alexander	1.5
Carriker	1.5
Doughty	1.0
Jackson	1.0
Landry	1.0
Jarmon	0.5
Redskins	29.0
Opponents	46.0

RECORD HOLDERS
INDIVIDUAL RECORDS—CAREER

Category	Name	Performance
Rushing (Yds.)	John Riggins, 1976-79, 1981-85	7,472
Passing (Yds.)	Joe Theismann, 1974-1985	25,206
Passing (TDs)	Sammy Baugh, 1937-1952	187
Receiving (No.)	Art Monk, 1980-1993	888
Receiving (Yds.)	Art Monk, 1980-1993	12,028
Interceptions	Darrell Green, 1983-2001	54
Punting (Avg.)	Sammy Baugh, 1937-1952	45.1
Punt Return (Avg.)	Johnny Williams, 1952-53	12.8
Kickoff Return (Avg.)	Bobby Mitchell, 1962-68	28.5
Field Goals	Mark Moseley, 1974-1986	263
Touchdowns (Tot.)	Charley Taylor, 1964-1977	90
Points	Mark Moseley, 1974-1986	1,206
*Sacks	Dexter Manley, 1981-89	91.0

INDIVIDUAL RECORDS—SINGLE SEASON

Category	Name	Performance
Rushing (Yds.)	Clinton Portis, 2005	1,516
Passing (Yds.)	Jay Schroeder, 1986	4,109
Passing (TDs)	Sonny Jurgensen, 1967	31
Receiving (No.)	Art Monk, 1984	106
Receiving (Yds.)	Santana Moss, 2005	1,483
Interceptions	Dan Sandifer, 1948	13
Punting (Avg.)	Sammy Baugh, 1940	**51.4
Punt Return (Avg.)	Johnny Williams, 1952	15.3
Kickoff Return (Avg.)	Mike Nelms, 1981	29.7
Field Goals	Mark Moseley, 1983	33
Touchdowns (Tot.)	John Riggins, 1983	24
Points	Mark Moseley, 1983	161
*Sacks	Dexter Manley, 1986	18.5

INDIVIDUAL RECORDS—SINGLE GAME

Category	Name	Performance
Rushing (Yds.)	Gerald Riggs, 9-17-89	221
Passing (Yds.)	Sammy Baugh, 10-31-43	446
Passing (TDs)	Sammy Baugh, 10-31-43, 11-23-47	6
	Mark Rypien, 11-10-91	6
Receiving (No.)	Art Monk, 12-15-85, 11-4-90	13
	Kelvin Bryant, 12-7-86	13
Receiving (Yds.)	Anthony Allen, 10-4-87	255
Interceptions	Sammy Baugh, 11-14-43	**4
	Dan Sandifer, 10-31-48	**4
	DeAngelo Hall, 10-24-10	**4
Field Goals	Many times	5
	Last time by Shaun Suisham, 11-4-07	
Touchdowns (Tot.)	Dick James, 12-17-61	4
	Larry Brown, 12-16-73	4
Points	Dick James, 12-17-61	24
	Larry Brown, 12-16-73	24
*Sacks	Dexter Manley, 10-2-88	4.0
	Ken Harvey, 11-23-97	4.0
	Phillip Daniels, 12-18-05	4.0
	Brian Orakpo, 12-13-09	4.0

*Sacks became an official statistic in 1982.
**NFL Record

VETERAN ROSTER AS OF MARCH 3, 2011

No.	Name	Pos.	Ht.	Wt.	Birthdate	^NFL Exp.	College	Hometown	How Acq.	'10 Games/ Starts
97	Alexander, Lorenzo	LB	6-1	275	5/31/83	5	California	Berkeley, Calif.	FA-'07	16/12
13	Armstrong, Anthony	WR	5-11	183	3/23/83	2	West Texas A&M	Carrollton, Texas	FA-'09	15/11
	Atogwe, Oshiomogho	S	5-11	205	6/23/81	7	Stanford	Windsor, Ontario, Canada	FA-'11	16/15*
18	Austin, Terrence	WR	5-11	175	8/24/88	2	UCLA	Long Beach, Calif.	D7a-'10	5/0
16	Banks, Brandon	WR	5-7	155	12/21/87	2	Kansas State	Garner, N.C.	FA-'10	13/0
25	Barnes, Kevin	CB	6-1	188	9/15/86	3	Maryland	Glen Burnie, Md.	D3-'09	10/2
3	Beck, John	QB	6-2	215	8/21/81	5	Brigham Young	Hayward, Calif.	T(Balt)-'10	0*
	Bidwell, Josh	P	6-3	220	3/13/73	12	Oregon	Winston, Ore.	UFA(TB)-'10	4/0
54	Blades, H.B.	LB	5-10	242	5/31/83	5	Pittsburgh	Plantation, Fla.	D6a-'07	16/1
40	Brown, Andre	RB	6-0	224	12/15/86	3	North Carolina State	Greenville, N.C.	FA-'10	0*
77	Brown, Jammal	T	6-6	313	3/30/81	7	Oklahoma	Lawton, Okla.	T(NO)-'10	15/14
76	Bryant, Anthony	DL	6-3	360	11/6/81	5	Alabama	Greensboro, Ala	FA-'10	6/3
31	Buchanon, Phillip	CB	5-11	186	9/19/80	10	Miami	Ft. Myers, Fla.	FA-'10	16/5
94	Carriker, Adam	DL	6-6	315	5/6/84	5	Nebraska	Kennewick, Wash.	T(StL)-'10	16/16
	Carter, Andre	LB	6-4	253	5/12/79	11	California	San Jose, Calif.	UFA(SF)-'06	16/5
47	Cooley, Chris	TE	6-3	255	7/11/82	7	Utah State	Logan, Utah	D3-'04	16/15
93	Daniels, Phillip	DL	6-6	311	3/4/73	16	Georgia	Donalsonville, Ga.	UFA(Chi)-'04	14/1
86	Davis, Fred	TE	6-4	257	1/15/86	4	Southern California	Toledo, Ohio	D2b-'08	16/9
24	Davis, James	RB	5-11	218	1/1/86	3	Clemson	Atlanta, Ga.	FA-'10	3/0
	Dockery, Derrick	G	6-6	326	9/7/80	9	Texas	Lakeview, Texas	FA-'09	5/2
37	Doughty, Reed	S	6-1	205	11/4/82	6	Northern Colorado	Johnstown, Colo.	D6a-'06	15/9
59	Fletcher, London	LB	5-10	245	5/19/75	14	John Carroll	Cleveland, Ohio	UFA(Buff)-'07	16/16
4	Gano, Graham	K	6-2	200	4/9/87	2	Florida State	Pensacola, Fla.	FA-'09	16/0
64	Golston, Kedric	DL	6-4	310	5/30/83	6	Georgia	Tyrone, Ga.	D6b-'06	13/13
8	Grossman, Rex	QB	6-1	217	8/23/80	9	Florida	Bloomington, Ind.	UFA(Hou)-'10	4/3
23	Hall, DeAngelo	CB	5-10	195	11/19/83	8	Virginia Tech	Chesapeake, Va.	FA-'08	16/16
20	Harris, Macho	S	6-0	200	2/16/86	3	Virginia Tech	Highland Springs, Va.	FA-'10	3/1
92	Haynesworth, Albert	DL	6-6	350	6/17/81	10	Tennessee	Hartsville, S.C.	UFA(Tenn)-'09	8/0
51	Henson, Robert	LB	6-0	245	1/27/86	3	Texas Christian	Longview, Texas	D6-'09	0*
74	Heyer, Stephon	T	6-6	330	1/16/84	5	Maryland	Lawrenceville, Ga.	FA-'07	12/5
75	Hicks, Artis	T/G	6-4	318	11/28/78	10	Memphis	Jackson, Tenn.	UFA(Minn)-'10	15/10
79	Holliday, Vonnie	DL	6-5	288	12/11/75	14	North Carolina	Camden, S.C.	UFA(Den)-'10	15/2
48	Horton, Chris	S	6-1	211	12/29/84	4	UCLA	New Orleans. La.	D7b-'08	7/0
50	Jackson, Rob	LB	6-4	255	11/3/85	2	Kansas State	West Haven, Conn.	D7a-'09	2/0
90	Jarmon, Jeremy	DL	6-3	286	11/20/87	3	Kentucky	Collierville, Tenn.	SD3-'09	5/0
	Jones, Edgar	LB	6-3	262	12/1/84	5	Southeast Missouri State	Rayville, La.	FA-'11	5/0*
12	Kelly, Malcolm	WR	6-4	227	12/30/86	4	Oklahoma	Longview, Texas	D2c-'08	0*
96	Kemoeatu, Maake	DL	6-5	350	1/10/79	10	Utah	Kahuku, Hawai'i	UFA(Car)-'10	14/12
30	Landry, LaRon	S	6-0	220	10/14/84	5	Louisiana State	Ama, La.	D1-'07	9/9
78	Lichtensteiger, Kory	CB	6-2	292	3/22/85	3	Bowling Green	Van Wert, Ohio	FA-'10	16/14
52	McIntosh, Rocky	LB	6-2	238	11/15/82	6	Miami	Gaffney, S.C.	D2-'06	15/15
5	McNabb, Donovan	QB	6-2	240	11/25/76	13	Syracuse	Chicago, Ill.	T(Phil)-'10	13/13
63	Montgomery, Will	G	6-3	305	2/13/83	5	Virginia Tech	Clifton, Va.	FA-'08	13/6
41	Moore, Kareem	S	5-11	215	8/13/84	4	Nicholls State	Okolona, Miss.	D6b-'08	12/11
89	Moss, Santana	WR	5-10	200	6/1/79	11	Miami	Miami, Fla.	T(NYJ)-'05	16/16
68	Oldenburg, Clint	T	6-5	302	9/9/83	2	Colorado State	Campbell County, Wyo.	FA-'09	0*
98	Orakpo, Brian	LB	6-4	260	7/31/86	3	Texas	Houston, Texas	D1-'09	15/15
1	Paulescu, Sam	P	6-0	190	4/18/84	4	Oregon State	La Habra, Calif.	FA-'10	3/0
82	Paulsen, Logan	TE	6-5	265	2/26/87	2	UCLA	Northridge, Calif.	FA-'10	11/0
	Portis, Clinton	RB	5-11	221	9/1/81	10	Miami	Gainesville, Fla.	T(Den)-'04	5/5
61	Rabach, Casey	C	6-4	295	9/24/77	11	Wisconsin	Sturgeon Bay, Wisc.	UFA(Balt)-'05	16/16
38	Rashad, Sh'reff	S	6-0	198	10/6/86	1	Central Florida	Jacksonville, Fla.	FA-'10	1/0
53	Riley, Perry	LB	6-0	240	5/3/88	2	Louisiana State	Ellenwood, Ga.	D4-'10	8/0
22	Rogers, Carlos	CB	6-0	190	7/2/81	7	Auburn	Augusta, Ga.	D1a-'05	12/12
32	Russell, Anderson	S	6-0	205	5/30/87	2	Ohio State	Atlanta, Ga.	FA-'10	2/0
72	Scott, Darrion	DL	6-3	289	10/25/81	6	Ohio State	Charleston, W. Va.	FA-'10	2/0
45	Sellers, Mike	FB	6-3	272	7/21/75	12	Walla Walla (WA) C.C.	North Thurston, Wash.	FA-'04	16/9
29	Simpson, Chad	RB	5-9	216	8/22/85	4	Morgan State	Miami, Fla.	FA-'10	3/0
57	Sundberg, Nick	LS	6-0	245	7/29/87	2	California	Phoenix, Ariz.	FA-'10	16/0
46	Torain, Ryan	RB	6-1	225	8/10/86	3	Arizona State	Topeka, Kan.	FA-'10	10/8
34	Westbrook, Byron	CB	5-10	198	12/26/84	3	Salisbury	Washington, D.C.	FA-'07	16/0
35	Williams, Keiland	RB	5-11	223	8/14/86	2	Louisiana State	Lafayette, La.	FA-'10	15/3
	Williams, Mike	G	6-7	337	1/11/80	6	Texas	Dallas, Texas	FA-'09	0*
87	Williams, Roydell	WR	6-0	187	3/14/81	5	Tulane	New Orleans. La.	FA-'10	16/0
71	Williams, Trent	T	6-5	318	7/19/88	2	Oklahoma	Longview, Texas	D1-'10	14/13
95	Wilson, Chris	LB	6-4	247	7/10/82	5	Northwood	Flint, Mich.	FA-'07	16/0
36	Young, Darrel	FB	5-11	245	4/8/87	2	Villanova	Amityville, N.Y.	FA-'09	16/0

* Atogwe played 16 games with St. Louis in '10; Beck did not play in 2 games, inactive for 14 games; A. Brown inactive for 6 games; Henson missed '10 season because of injury; Jones played 5 games with Baltimore; Kelly missed '10 season because of injury; Oldenburg missed '10 season because of injury; M. Williams missed '10 season because of injury.

Also played with Redskins in '10—WR Joey Galloway (10 games), RB Larry Johnson (2), P Hunter Smith (9), WR Devin Thomas (4).

^ "NFL Exp." as of 2011 Kickoff Weekend. For full explanation of how a player's NFL Experience is measured, refer to explanation underneath the First-Year Roster listed below.

FIRST-YEAR ROSTER

Name	Pos.	Ht.	Wt.	Birthdate	College	Hometown	How Acq.
Capers, Selvish (1)	T	6-5	315	11/13/85	West Virginia	Kenner, La.	D7c-'10
Cook, Erik (1)	C	6-6	320	7/5/87	New Mexico	Albuquerque, N.M.	D7b-'10
Duncan, Rashad (1)	DL	6-2	315	12/10/86	Pittsburgh	Belle Glade, Fla.	FA-'10
Fulton, Xavier (1)	T	6-5	301	4/18/86	Illinois	Flossmoori, Ill.	FA-'10
Hankerson, Leonard	WR	6-2	205	5/7/88	Miami	Fort Lauderdale, Fla.	D3
Helu, Roy	RB	5-11	216	12/7/88	Nebraska	Danville, Calif.	D4
Gomes, DeJon	S	6-0	208	11/17/89	Nebraska	Hayward, Calif.	D5a
Hurt, Maurice	G	6-3	320	9/8/87	Florida	Milledgeville, Ga.	D7b
Jenkins, Jarvis	DL	6-4	310	4/24/88	Clemson	Clemson, S.C.	D2
Johnson, Taurus (1)	WR	6-1	205	4/13/86	South Florida	Cape Coral, Fla.	FA-'10
Jones, Reggie (1)	CB	6-0	193	3/15/86	Portland State	Federal Way, Wash.	FA-'10
Joseph, Joe (1)	DL	6-3	315	10/20/85	Miami	Orlando, Fla.	FA-'10
Kerrigan, Ryan	LB	6-4	265	8/16/88	Purdue	Muncie, Ind.	D1
McNeal, Shawnbrey (1)	RB	5-9	190	10/17/88	Southern Methodist	Dallas, Texas	FA-'10
Neild, Chris	DL	6-2	319	12/1/87	West Virginia	Stroudsburg, Pa.	D7d
Paul, Niles	WR	6-1	224	8/9/89	Nebraska	Omaha, Neb.	D5b
Price, Maurice (1)	WR	6-1	197	9/11/85	Charleston Southern	Orlando, Fla.	FA-'10
Robinson, Aldrick	WR	5-10	185	9/24/88	Southern Methodist	Waxahachie, Texas	D6b
Royster, Evan	RB	6-1	215	11/26/87	Penn State	Fairfax, Va.	D6a
Stehle, Jeff (1)	DL	6-6	310	4/4/87	Wisconsin	Constantia, N.Y.	FA-'10
Thompson, Brandyn	CB	5-10	185	10/30/89	Boise State	Elk Grove, Calif.	D7a
White, Markus	LB	6-4	265	11/25/87	Florida State	West Palm Beach, Fla.	D7c

The term NFL Rookie is defined as a player who is in his first season of professional football and has not been on the roster of another professional football team for any regular-season or postseason games. A Rookie is designated by an "R" on NFL rosters. Players who have been active in another professional football league or players who have NFL experience, including either preseason training camp or being on an Active List or Inactive List, or on Reserve/Injured or Reserve/Physically Unable to Perform for fewer than six regular-season games, are termed NFL First-Year Players. An NFL First-Year Player is designated by a "1" on NFL rosters. Thereafter, a player is credited with an additional year of experience for each season in which he accumulates six games on the Active List or Inactive List, or on Reserve/Injured or Reserve/Physically Unable to Perform.

Log on to www.washingtonredskins.com for an up-to-date roster.

COACHING STAFF
Head Coach,
Mike Shanahan
Pro Career: Became the 28th coach in franchise history when he replaced Jim Zorn on January 6, 2010. Mike Shanahan joined the Redskins after spending 14 seasons as head coach of the Denver Broncos (1995-2008). Shanahan led the Broncos to back-to-back Super Bowl championships in 1997 and 1998, becoming just the fifth head coach to accomplish that feat, and is the only coach to win seven consecutive postseason games in a two-year period. During his NFL career, Shanahan has been a part of teams that have played in nine conference championship games and six Super Bowls. In 31 seasons as a pro and college coach, Shanahan's teams have participated in postseason or bowl games 22 times. Under Shanahan's guidance, Denver set then-NFL records by posting the most victories in both a two-year (33, 1997-98) and three-year (46, 1996-98) span. In 17 years (14 with Denver and three as offensive coordinator with the San Francisco 49ers), Shanahan's offenses have finished number one in the NFL four times, second three times and third twice. Shanahan was an assistant with Denver (1984-87, 1989-1991) and San Francisco (1992-94). Returned to Denver as quarterbacks coach on October 6, 1989, after posting 8-12 record as the Los Angeles Raiders' head coach. Career record: 160-113.
Background: Shanahan coached at Oklahoma (1975-76), Northern Arizona (1977), Eastern Illinois (1978), Minnesota (1979), and Florida (1980-83).
Personal: Born in Oak Park, Illinois, on August 24, 1952. He was a wishbone quarterback/defensive back at Eastern Illinois. Mike and his wife, Peggy, have two children—Kyle and Krystal.

ASSISTANT COACHES
Jacob Burney, defensive line; born January 24, 1959, Chattanooga, Tenn. Defensive tackle Tennessee-Chattanooga 1977-1980. No pro playing experience. College coach: New Mexico 1983-86, Tulsa 1987, Mississippi State 1988, Wisconsin 1989, UCLA 1990-92, Tennessee 1993. Pro coach: Cleveland Browns/Baltimore Ravens 1994-98, Carolina Panthers 1999-2001, Denver Broncos 2002-08, joined Redskins in 2010.
Chad Englehart, asst. strength and conditioning; born June 5, 1981, New Orleans, La. Attended Southeastern Louisiana. No college or pro playing experience. College coach: New Orleans 2006. Pro coach: Florida Tuskers (UFL) 2009, joined Redskins in 2010.
Richmond Flowers, coaching assistant; born May 4, 1978, Birmingham, Ala. Wide receiver Duke 1996, 1998-99, Tennessee-Chattanooga 2000. Pro wide receiver Dallas Cowboys 2001, Washington Redskins 2002. Pro coach: joined Redskins in 2010.
Chris Foerster, offensive line; born October 12, 1961, Milwaukee, Wis. Center Colorado State 1979-1982. No pro playing experience. College coach: Colorado State 1983-87, Stanford 1988-1991, Minnesota 1992. Pro coach: Minnesota Vikings 1993-95, Tampa Bay Buccaneers 1996-2001, Indianapolis Colts 2002-03, Miami Dolphins 2004, Baltimore Ravens 2005-07, San Francisco 49ers 2008-09, joined Redskins in 2010.
Jim Haslett, defensive coordinator; born December 9, 1955, Pittsburgh. Defensive end Indiana (Pa.) 1975-78. Pro linebacker Buffalo Bills 1979-1986, N.Y. Jets 1987. College coach: Buffalo 1988-1990. Pro coach: Sacramento Surge (NFLE) 1991-92, Los Angeles Raiders 1993-94, New Orleans Saints 1995-96, Pittsburgh Steelers 1997-99, New Orleans Saints 2000-05 (head coach), St. Louis Rams 2006-08 (head coach 2008), Florida Tuskers (UFL head coach 2009), joined Redskins in 2010.
Richard Hightower, special teams assistant; born September 15, 1980, Houston. Wide receiver/defensive back Texas 1998-2002. No pro playing experience. College coach: Minnesota 2009. Pro coach: Houston Texans 2006-08, joined Redskins 2010.
Steve Jackson, safeties; born April 8, 1969, Houston. Defensive back Purdue 1987-1990. Pro defensive back Houston Oilers/Tennessee Titans 1991-99. Pro coach: Buffalo Bills 2001-03, joined Redskins in 2004.
Matt LeFleur, quarterbacks; born November 3, 1979, Mt. Pleasant, Mich. Quarterback/wide receiver Western Michigan 1998-99, Saginaw Valley State 2000-02. Pro quarterback Omaha Beef (NIFL) 2002, Billings Outlaws (NIFL) 2002. College coach: Saginaw Valley State 2003, Central Michigan 2004-05, Northern Michigan 2006, Ashland 2007. Pro coach: Houston Texans 2006-08, joined Redskins in 2010.
Keenan McCardell, wide receivers; born January 6, 1970, Houston. Wide receiver Nevada-Las Vegas 1987-1990. Pro wide receiver Washington Redskins 1991, 2007, Cleveland Browns 1992-95, Jacksonville Jaguars 1996-2001, Tampa Bay Buccaneers 2002-03, San Diego Chargers 2004-06. Pro coach: Joined Redskins in 2010.
Mike McDaniel, offensive assistant; born March 6, 1983, Greeley, Colo. Wide receiver Yale 2001-04. No pro playing experience. Pro coach: Houston Texans 2006-08, California Redwoods (UFL) 2009, Sacramento Mountain Lions (UFL) 2010, joined Redskins in 2011.
Sean McVay, tight ends; born January 24, 1986, Marietta, Ga. Wide receiver Miami (Ohio) 2004-07. No pro playing experience. Pro coach: Tampa Bay Buccaneers 2008, Florida Tuskers (UFL) 2009, joined Redskins in 2010.
Chris Morgan, asst. offensive line; born September 24 1976, Killeen, Texas. Offensive lineman Colorado 1996-99. No pro playing experience. College coach: Idaho 2003. Pro coach: Oakland Raiders 2009-2010, joined Redskins in 2011.
Kyle Shanahan, offensive coordinator; born December 14, 1979, Minneapolis. Wide receiver Duke 1998-99, Texas 2000-02. No pro playing experience. College coach: UCLA 2003. Pro coach: Tampa Bay Buccaneers 2004-05, Houston Texans 2006-09, joined Redskins in 2010.
Bob Slowik, defensive backs; born May 16, 1954, Pittsburgh. Defensive back Delaware 1973-76. No pro playing experience. College coach: Delaware 1977-78, Florida 1979-1982, Drake 1983, Rutgers 1984-89, East Carolina 1990-91. Pro coach: Dallas Cowboys 1992, Chicago Bears 1993-98, Cleveland Browns 1999, Green Bay Packers 2000-04, Denver Broncos 2005-2008, joined Redskins 2010.
Bobby Slowik, defensive assistant; born June 7, 1987, Princeton, N.J. Wide receiver Michigan Tech 2005-09. No pro playing experience. Pro coach: Joined Redskins in 2011.
Danny Smith, special teams; born September 7, 1953, Pittsburgh. Defensive back Edinboro State 1972-75. No pro playing experience. College coach: Edinboro State 1976, Clemson 1979, William & Mary 1980-83, Citadel 1984-86, Georgia Tech 1987-1994. Pro coach: Philadelphia Eagles 1995-98, Detroit Lions 1999-2000, Buffalo Bills 2001-03, joined Redskins in 2004.
Lou Spanos, linebackers; born March 27, 1971, Pittsburgh. Center Tulsa 1989-1992. No pro playing experience. College coach: Tulsa 1993. Pro coach: Pittsburgh Steelers 1994-2009, joined Redskins in 2010.
Bobby Turner, asst. head coach/running backs; born May 6, 1949, East Chicago, Ind. Defensive back Indiana State 1968-1971. No pro playing experience. College coach: Indiana State 1975-1982, Fresno State 1983-88, Ohio State 1989-1990, Purdue 1991-94. Pro coach: Denver Broncos 1995-2009, joined Redskins in 2010.
Ray Wright, strength and conditioning; born December 30, 1971, Fort Worth, Texas. Running back/wide receiver Duke 1990-95. No pro playing experience. College coach: Cornell 2000, Maryland 2001. Pro coach: Houston Texans 2002-09, joined Washington in 2010.

2010 Season in Review

2010 TRADES (since May 1)

Linebacker **Bobby Carpenter** from Dallas to St. Louis for tackle **Alex Barron**. (5/10)

Guard **Justin Smiley** from Miami to Jacksonville for an unannounced selection. (5/25)

Wide receiver **Isaac Bruce** from San Francisco to St. Louis for an unannounced selection. (6/7)

Tackle **Jammal Brown** and Saints' unannounced selection from New Orleans to Washington for an unannounced selection. (6/21)

Linebacker **Joe Mays** from Denver to Philadelphia for running back **J.J. Arrington** and an unannounced selection. (7/31)

Quarterback **John Beck** from Baltimore to Washington for defensive back **Doug Dutch**. (8/2)

Defensive end **Kentwan Balmer** from San Francisco to Seattle for an unannounced selection. (8/17)

Defensive end **Lawrence Jackson** from Seattle to Detroit for an unannounced selection. (8/18)

Guard **Quinn Ojinnaka** from Atlanta to New England for an unannounced selection. (8/23)

Wide receiver **Greg Camarillo** from Miami to Minnesota for defensive back **Benny Sapp**. (8/25)

Defensive back **Jorrick Calvin** from Arizona to Philadelphia for running back **Charles Scott**. (8/30)

Tight end **Dennis Morris** from Washington to St. Louis for an unannounced selection. (8/30)

Defensive end **Hall Davis** from St. Louis to Washington for an unannounced selection. (8/30)

Tackle **Tyler Polumbus** from Detroit to Seattle for an unannounced selection. (8/31)

Defensive back **Josh Wilson** from Seattle to Baltimore for an unannounced selection. (9/1)

Guard **Reggie Wells** from Arizona to Philadelphia for an unannounced selection. (9/3)

Tackle **Pat McQuistan** and an unannounced selection from Dallas to Miami for an unannounced selection. (9/4)

Wide receiver **Patrick Crayton** from Dallas to San Diego for an unannounced selection. (9/4)

Wide receiver **Sage Rosenfels** and wide receiver **Darius Reynaud** from Minnesota to the New York Giants for an unannounced selection. (9/4)

Defensive back **Justin Tryon** from Washington to Indianapolis for an unannounced selection. (9/4)

Linebacker **Antwan Barnes** from Baltimore to Philadelphia for an unannounced selection. (9/4)

Defensive back **Alphonso Smith** and an unannounced selection from Denver to Detroit for tight end **Dan Gronkowski** and an unannounced selection. (9/4)

Defensive back **Jarrad Page** from Kansas City to New England for an unannounced selection. (9/4)

Linebacker **Tracy White** and an unannounced selection from Philadelphia to New England for an unannounced selection. (9/4)

Guard **Stacy Andrews** from Philadelphia to Seattle for an unannounced selection. (9/5)

Defensive back **Reggie Nelson** from Jacksonville to Cincinnati for defensive back **David Jones**. (9/4)

Wide receiver **Mark Clayton** and an unannounced selection from Baltimore to St. Louis for an unannounced selection. (9/7)

Running back **Laurence Maroney** and an unannounced selection from New England to Denver for an unannounced selection. (9/15)

Defensive end **Jayme Mitchell** from Minnesota to Cleveland for an unannounced selection. (10/5)

Running back **Marshawn Lynch** from Buffalo to Seattle for an unannounced selection. (10/5)

Wide receiver **Randy Moss** and an unannounced selection from New England to Minnesota for an unannounced selection. (10/6)

Wide receiver **Deion Branch** from Seattle to New England for an unannounced selection. (10/12)

Running back **Jerome Harrison** from Cleveland to Philadelphia for running back **Mike Bell**. (10/18)

Defensive back **Anthony Smith** from Jacksonville to Green Bay for an unannounced selection. (10/18)

Defensive end **Alex Magee** and an unannounced selection from Kansas City to Tampa Bay for an unannounced selection. (10/19)

Draft choice number is listed if club later traded the pick.

2011 TRADES

Atlanta trades Falcons' 2011 first-round selection (#27), second-round selection (WR **Greg Little**), fourth-round selection (RB **Owen Marecic**), and 2012 first- and fourth-round selections to Cleveland for Browns' 2011 first-round selection (WR **Julio Jones**). (4/28)

Jacksonville trades Jaguars' 2011 first-round selection (LB **Ryan Kerrigan**) and second-round selection (#49) to Washington for Redskins' 2011 first-round selection (QB **Blaine Gabbert**). (4/28)

Cleveland trades Falcons' 2011 first-round selection (WR **Jonathan Baldwin**) and Browns' 2011 third-round selection (LB **Justin Houston**) from Cleveland to Kansas City for the Chiefs' 2011 first-round selection (DT **Phil Taylor**). (4/28)

New England trades Patriots' 2011 first-round selection (RB **Mark Ingram**) from New England to New Orleans for the Saints' 2011 second-round selection (RB **Shane Vereen**) and first-round selection in 2012. (4/28)

Denver trades Broncos' 2011 second-round selection (QB **Colin Kaepernick**) from Denver to San Francisco for the 49ers' 2011 second-round selection (DB **Rahim Moore**), fourth-round selection (DB **Quinton Carter**), and fifth-round selection (#141). (4/29)

Washington trades Jaguars' second-round selection (T **Ben Ijalana**) from Washington to Indianapolis for Colts' 2011 second-round selection (#53) and 2011 fifth-round selection (#152). (4/29)

Washington trades Colts' 2011 second-round selection (DT **Stephen Paea**) from Washington to Chicago for Bears' 2011 second-round selection (#62) and fourth-round selection (#127). (4/29)

Detroit trades Lions' 2011 third-round selection (G **John Moffitt**) and fourth-round selection (WR **Kris Durham**), Chiefs' 2011 fifth-round selection (DB **Richard Sherman**), and Broncos' 2011 seventh-round selection (DE **Lazarius Levingston**) from Detroit to Seattle for Seahawks' 2011 second-round selection (RB **Mikel Leshoure**), Ravens' 2011 fifth-round selection (LB **Doug Hogue**), and Browns' 2011 seventh-round selection (T **Johnny Culbreath**). (4/29)

New England trades Patriots' 2011 second-round selection (DB **Brandon Harris**) from New England to Houston for Texans' 2011 third-round selection (RB **Stevan Ridley**) and fifth-round selection (T **Marcus Cannon**). (4/29)

Washington trades Bears' 2011 second-round selection (RB **Daniel Thomas**) from Washington to Miami for Dolphins' 2011 third-round selection (WR **Leonard Hankerson**), fifth-round selection (DB **DeJon Gomes**), and seventh-round selection (G **Maurice Hurt**). (4/29)

San Francisco trades 49ers' 2011 third-round selection (G **Will Rackley**) from San Francisco to Jacksonville for Jaguars' 2011 third-round selection (DB **Chris Culliver**) and sixth-round selection (WR **Ronald Johnson**). (4/29)

New England trades Patriots' 2011 third-round selection (T **Joe Barksdale**) and fourth-round selection (RB **Taiwan Jones**) from New England to Oakland for Raiders' 2011 seventh-round selection (DB **Malcolm Williams**) and 2012 second-round selection. (4/29)

Philadelphia trades Eagles' 2011 third-round selection (T **Jah Reid**) from Philadelphia to Baltimore for Ravens' 2011 third-round selection (DB **Curtis Marsh**) and sixth-round selection (C **Jason Kelce**). (4/29)

Philadelphia trades Redskins' 2011 fourth-round selection (TE **Luke Stocker**) from Philadelphia to Tampa Bay for Buccaneers' 2011 fourth-round selection (LB **Casey Matthews**) and 2012 fourth-round selection. (4/30)

Houston trades Texans' 2011 fourth-round selection (RB **Roy Helu**) and sixth-round selection (WR **Aldrick Robinson**) from Houston to Washington for Bears' 2011 fourth-round selection (DB **Rashad Carmichael**), Redskins' fifth-round selection (DB **Shiloh Keo**), and Colts' 2011 fifth-round selection (QB **T.J. Yates**). (4/30)

Denver trades 49ers' 2011 fifth-round selection (TE **D.J. Williams**) and Lions' 2011 sixth-round selection (LB **D.J. Smith**) from Denver to Green Bay for Packers' 2011 fourth-round selection (TE **Julius Thomas**) and Panthers' 2011 seventh-round selection (TE **Virgil Green**). (4/30)

St. Louis trades Rams' 2011 fifth-round selection (RB **Jacquizz Rodgers**) from St. Louis to Atlanta for Falcons' 2011 fifth-round selection (DB **Jermale Hines**) and seventh-round selection (DB **Jonathan Nelson**). (4/30)

Cleveland trades Broncos' 2011 sixth-round selection (T **DeMarcus Love**) and Browns' 2011 sixth-round selection (DB **Mistral Raymond**) from Cleveland to Minnesota for Giants' 2011 fifth-round selection (T **Jason Pinkston**). (4/30)

New York Jets trade Jets' 2011 fifth-round selection (G **Julian Vandervelde**) and sixth-round selection (#194) from New York Jets to Philadelphia for Eagles' 2011 fifth-round selection (WR **Jeremy Kerley**) and Seahawks' seventh-round selection (WR **Scotty McKnight**). (4/30)

Green Bay trades Packers' 2011 fifth-round selection (G **Daniel Kilgore**) from Green Bay to San Francisco for 49ers' 2011 sixth-round selection (#174) and Jets' seventh-round selection (#231). (4/30)

New England trades Patriots' 2011 sixth-round selection (LB **Brian Rolle**) from New England to Philadelphia for the Jets' 2011 sixth-round selection (LB **Markell Carter**). (4/30)

Green Bay trades 49ers' 2011 sixth-round selection (RB **Charles Clay**) and Jets' 2011 seventh-round selection (DT **Frank Kearse**) from Green Bay to Miami for Dolphins' 2011 sixth-round selection (G **Caleb Schlauderaff**) and Jaguars' 2011 seventh-round selection (TE **Ryan Taylor**). (4/30)

* Draft choice number is listed if club later traded the pick.

PRESEASON STANDINGS
AMERICAN FOOTBALL CONFERENCE
East Division

	W	L	T	Pct.	Pts.	OP
Buffalo	2	2	0	.500	109	111
Miami	2	2	0	.500	68	76
New England	2	2	0	.500	107	90
New York Jets	2	2	0	.500	57	67

North Division

	W	L	T	Pct.	Pts.	OP
Baltimore	3	1	0	.750	85	52
Pittsburgh	3	1	0	.750	83	61
Cincinnati	3	2	0	.600	112	112
Cleveland	2	2	0	.500	84	88

South Division

	W	L	T	Pct.	Pts.	OP
Jacksonville	2	2	0	.500	85	77
Tennessee	2	2	0	.500	76	69
Houston	1	3	0	.250	76	88
Indianapolis	0	4	0	.000	90	160

West Division

	W	L	T	Pct.	Pts.	OP
Oakland	3	1	0	.750	100	78
Denver	1	3	0	.250	102	106
Kansas City	1	3	0	.250	59	73
San Diego	1	3	0	.250	74	79

AFC PRESEASON RECORDS—TEAM BY TEAM

East Division

BUFFALO (2-2)

17	at Washington	42
34	Indianapolis	21
35	Cincinnati	20
23	at Detroit	28
109		111

MIAMI (2-2)

10	Tampa Bay	7
27	at Jacksonville	26
6	Atlanta	16
25	at Dallas	27
68		76

NEW ENGLAND (2-2)

27	New Orleans	24
28	at Atlanta	10
35	St. Louis	36
17	at New York Giants	20
107		90

N.Y. JETS (2-2)

16	New York Giants	31
9	at Carolina	3
11	Washington	16
21	at Philadelphia	17
57		67

North Division

BALTIMORE (3-1)

17	Carolina	12
23	at Washington	3
24	New York Giants	10
21	at St. Louis	27
85		52

CINCINNATI (3-2)

7	Dallas (a)	16
33	Denver	24
22	Philadelphia	9
20	at Buffalo	35
30	at Indianapolis	28
112		112

CLEVELAND (2-2)

27	at Green Bay	24
17	St. Louis	19
27	at Detroit	35
13	Chicago	10
84		88

PITTSBURGH (3-1)

23	Detroit	7
24	at New York Giants	17
17	at Denver	34
19	Carolina	3
83		61

South Division

HOUSTON (1-3)

16	at Arizona	19
20	at New Orleans	38
23	Dallas	7
17	Tampa Bay	24
76		88

INDIANAPOLIS (0-4)

17	San Francisco	37
21	at Buffalo	34
24	at Green Bay	59
28	Cincinnati	30
90		160

JACKSONVILLE (2-2)

27	at Philadelphia	28
26	Miami	27
19	at Tampa Bay	13
13	Atlanta	9
85		77

TENNESSEE (2-2)

18	at Seattle	20
24	Arizona	10
7	at Carolina	15
27	New Orleans	24
76		69

West Division

DENVER (1-3)

24	at Cincinnati	33
20	Detroit	25
34	Pittsburgh	17
24	at Minnesota	31
102		106

KANSAS CITY (1-3)

10	at Atlanta	20
15	at Tampa Bay	20
17	Philadelphia	20
17	Green Bay	13
59		73

OAKLAND (3-1)

17	at Dallas	9
32	at Chicago	17
24	San Francisco	28
27	Seattle	24
100		78

SAN DIEGO (1-3)

25	Chicago	10
14	Dallas	16
21	at New Orleans	36
14	at San Francisco	17
74		79

(a) Pro Football Hall of Fame Game at Canton, Ohio

NFC PRESEASON RECORDS—TEAM BY TEAM

East Division

DALLAS (3-2)

16	Cincinnati (a)	7
9	Oakland	17
16	at San Diego	14
7	at Houston	23
27	Miami	25
75		86

N.Y. GIANTS (2-2)

31	at New York Jets	16
17	Pittsburgh	24
10	at Baltimore	24
20	New England	17
78		81

PHILADELPHIA (2-2)

28	Jacksonville	27
9	at Cincinnati	22
20	at Kansas City	17
17	New York Jets	21
74		87

WASHINGTON (2-2)

42	Buffalo	17
3	Baltimore	23
16	at New York Jets	11
10	at Arizona	20
71		71

North Division

CHICAGO (0-4)

10	at San Diego	25
17	Oakland	32
9	Arizona	14
10	at Cleveland	13
46		84

DETROIT (3-1)

7	at Pittsburgh	23
25	at Denver	20
35	Cleveland	27
28	Buffalo	23
95		93

GREEN BAY (2-2)

24	Cleveland	27
27	at Seattle	24
59	Indianapolis	24
13	at Kansas City	17
123		92

MINNESOTA (3-1)

28	at St. Louis	7
10	at San Francisco	15
24	Seattle	13
31	Denver	24
93		59

South Division

ATLANTA (2-2)

20	Kansas City	10
10	New England	28
16	at Miami	6
9	at Jacksonville	13
55		57

CAROLINA (1-3)

12	at Baltimore	17
3	New York Jets	9
15	Tennessee	7
3	at Pittsburgh	19
33		52

NEW ORLEANS (2-2)

24	at New England	27
38	Houston	20
36	San Diego	21
24	at Tennessee	27
122		95

TAMPA BAY (2-2)

7	at Miami	10
20	Kansas City	15
13	Jacksonville	19
24	at Houston	17
64		61

West Division

ARIZONA (3-1)

19	Houston	16
10	at Tennessee	24
14	at Chicago	9
20	Washington	10
63		59

ST. LOUIS (3-1)

7	Minnesota	28
19	at Cleveland	17
36	at New England	35
27	Baltimore	21
89		101

SAN FRANCISCO (4-0)

37	at Indianapolis	17
15	Minnesota	10
28	at Oakland	24
17	San Diego	14
97		65

SEATTLE (1-3)

20	Tennessee	18
24	Green Bay	27
13	at Minnesota	24
24	at Oakland	27
81		96

PRESEASON STANDINGS
NATIONAL FOOTBALL CONFERENCE

East Division

	W	L	T	Pct.	Pts.	OP
Dallas	3	2	0	.600	75	86
New York Giants	2	2	0	.500	78	81
Philadelphia	2	2	0	.500	74	87
Washington	2	2	0	.500	71	71

North Division

	W	L	T	Pct.	Pts.	OP
Detroit	3	1	0	.750	95	93
Minnesota	3	1	0	.750	93	59
Green Bay	2	2	0	.500	123	92
Chicago	0	4	0	.000	46	84

South Division

	W	L	T	Pct.	Pts.	OP
Atlanta	2	2	0	.500	55	57
New Orleans	2	2	0	.500	122	95
Tampa Bay	2	2	0	.500	64	61
Carolina	1	3	0	.250	33	52

West Division

	W	L	T	Pct.	Pts.	OP
San Francisco	4	0	0	1.000	97	65
Arizona	3	1	0	.750	63	59
St. Louis	3	1	0	.750	89	101
Seattle	1	3	0	.250	81	96

(a) Pro Football Hall of Fame Game at Canton, Ohio

AMERICAN FOOTBALL CONFERENCE

BALTIMORE RAVENS (12-4)
10	at New York Jets	9
10	at Cincinnati	15
24	Cleveland	17
17	at Pittsburgh	14
31	Denver	17
20	at New England (OT)	23
37	Buffalo (OT)	34
26	Miami	10
21	at Atlanta	26
37	at Carolina	13
17	Tampa Bay	10
10	Pittsburgh	13
34	at Houston (OT)	28
30	New Orleans	24
20	at Cleveland	10
13	Cincinnati	7
357		**270**

BUFFALO BILLS (4-12)
10	Miami	15
7	at Green Bay	34
30	at New England	38
14	New York Jets	38
26	Jacksonville	36
34	at Baltimore (OT)	37
10	at Kansas City (OT)	13
19	Chicago	22
14	Detroit	12
49	at Cincinnati	31
16	Pittsburgh (OT)	19
14	at Minnesota	38
13	Cleveland	6
17	at Miami	14
3	New England	34
7	at New York Jets	38
283		**425**

CINCINNATI BENGALS (4-12)
24	at New England	38
15	Baltimore	10
20	at Carolina	7
20	at Cleveland	23
21	Tampa Bay	24
32	at Atlanta	39
14	Miami	22
21	Pittsburgh	27
17	at Indianapolis	23
31	Buffalo	49
10	at New York Jets	26
30	New Orleans	34
7	at Pittsburgh	23
19	Cleveland	17
34	San Diego	20
7	at Baltimore	13
322		**395**

CLEVELAND BROWNS (5-11)
14	at Tampa Bay	17
14	Kansas City	16
17	at Baltimore	24
23	Cincinnati	20
10	Atlanta	20
10	at Pittsburgh	28
30	at New Orleans	17
34	New England	14
20	New York Jets (OT)	26
20	at Jacksonville	24
24	Carolina	23
13	at Miami	10
6	at Buffalo	13
17	at Cincinnati	19
10	Baltimore	20
9	Pittsburgh	41
271		**332**

DENVER BRONCOS (4-12)
17	at Jacksonville	24
31	Seattle	14
13	Indianapolis	27
26	at Tennessee	20
17	at Baltimore	31
20	New York Jets	24
14	Oakland	59
16	at San Francisco	24
49	Kansas City	29
14	at San Diego	35
33	St. Louis	36
6	at Kansas City	10
13	at Arizona	43
23	at Oakland	39
24	Houston	23
28	San Diego	33
344		**471**

HOUSTON TEXANS (6-10)
34	Indianapolis	24
30	at Washington (OT)	27
13	Dallas	27
31	at Oakland	24
10	New York Giants	34
35	Kansas City	31
17	at Indianapolis	30
23	San Diego	29
24	at Jacksonville	31
27	at New York Jets	30
20	Tennessee	0
24	at Philadelphia	34
28	Baltimore (OT)	34
17	at Tennessee	31
23	at Denver	24
34	Jacksonville	17
390		**427**

INDIANAPOLIS COLTS (10-6)
24	at Houston	34
38	New York Giants	14
27	at Denver	13
28	at Jacksonville	31
19	Kansas City	9
27	at Washington	24
30	Houston	17
24	at Philadelphia	26
23	Cincinnati	17
28	at New England	31
14	San Diego	36
35	Dallas (OT)	38
30	at Tennessee	28
34	Jacksonville	24
31	at Oakland	26
23	Tennessee	20
435		**388**

JACKSONVILLE JAGUARS (8-8)
24	Denver	17
13	at San Diego	38
3	Philadelphia	28
31	Indianapolis	28
36	at Buffalo	26
3	Tennessee	30
20	at Kansas City	42
35	at Dallas	17
31	Houston	24
24	Cleveland	20
20	at New York Giants	24
17	at Tennessee	6
38	Oakland	31
24	at Indianapolis	34
17	Washington (OT)	20
17	at Houston	34
353		**419**

KANSAS CITY CHIEFS (10-6)
21	San Diego	14
16	at Cleveland	14
31	San Francisco	10
9	at Indianapolis	19
31	at Houston	35
42	Jacksonville	20
13	Buffalo (OT)	10
20	at Oakland (OT)	23
29	at Denver	49
31	Arizona	13
42	at Seattle	24
10	Denver	6
0	at San Diego	31
27	at St. Louis	13
34	Tennessee	14
10	Oakland	31
366		**326**

MIAMI DOLPHINS (7-9)
15	at Buffalo	10
14	at Minnesota	10
23	New York Jets	31
14	New England	41
23	at Green Bay (OT)	20
22	Pittsburgh	23
22	at Cincinnati	14
10	at Baltimore	26
29	Tennessee	17
0	Chicago	16
33	at Oakland	17
10	Cleveland	13
10	at New York Jets	6
14	Buffalo	17
27	Detroit	34
7	at New England	38
273		**333**

NEW ENGLAND PATRIOTS (14-2)
38	Cincinnati	24
14	at New York Jets	28
38	Buffalo	30
41	at Miami	14
23	Baltimore (OT)	20
23	at San Diego	20
28	Minnesota	18
14	at Cleveland	34
39	at Pittsburgh	26
31	Indianapolis	28
45	at Detroit	24
45	New York Jets	3
36	at Chicago	7
31	Green Bay	27
34	at Buffalo	3
38	Miami	7
518		**313**

NEW YORK JETS (11-5)
9	Baltimore	10
28	New England	14
31	at Miami	23
38	at Buffalo	14
29	Minnesota	20
24	at Denver	20
0	Green Bay	9
23	at Detroit (OT)	20
26	at Cleveland (OT)	20
30	Houston	27
26	Cincinnati	10
3	at New England	45
6	Miami	10
22	at Pittsburgh	17
34	at Chicago	38
38	Buffalo	7
367		**304**

OAKLAND RAIDERS (8-8)
13	at Tennessee	38
16	St. Louis	14
23	at Arizona	24
24	Houston	31
35	San Diego	27
9	at San Francisco	17
59	at Denver	14
33	Seattle	3
23	Kansas City (OT)	20
3	at Pittsburgh	35
17	Miami	33
28	at San Diego	13
31	at Jacksonville	38
39	Denver	23
26	Indianapolis	31
31	at Kansas City	10
410		**371**

PITTSBURGH STEELERS (12-4)
15	Atlanta (OT)	9
19	at Tennessee	11
38	at Tampa Bay	13
14	Baltimore	17
28	Cleveland	10
23	at Miami	22
10	at New Orleans	20
27	at Cincinnati	21
26	New England	39
35	Oakland	3
19	at Buffalo (OT)	16
13	at Baltimore	10
23	Cincinnati	7
17	New York Jets	22
27	Carolina	3
41	at Cleveland	9
375		**232**

SAN DIEGO CHARGERS (9-7)
14	at Kansas City	21
38	Jacksonville	13
20	at Seattle	27
41	Arizona	10
27	at Oakland	35
17	at St. Louis	20
20	New England	23
33	Tennessee	25
29	at Houston	23
35	Denver	14
36	at Indianapolis	14
13	Oakland	28
31	Kansas City	0
34	San Francisco	7
20	at Cincinnati	34
33	at Denver	28
441		**322**

TENNESSEE TITANS (6-10)
38	Oakland	13
11	Pittsburgh	19
29	at New York Giants	10
20	Denver	26
34	at Dallas	27
30	at Jacksonville	3
37	Philadelphia	19
25	at San Diego	33
17	at Miami	29
16	Washington (OT)	19
0	at Houston	20
6	Jacksonville	17
28	Indianapolis	30
31	Houston	17
14	at Kansas City	34
20	at Indianapolis	23
356		**339**

NATIONAL FOOTBALL CONFERENCE

ARIZONA CARDINALS (5-11)
17	at St. Louis	13
7	at Atlanta	41
24	Oakland	23
10	at San Diego	41
30	New Orleans	20
10	at Seattle	22
35	Tampa Bay	38
24	at Minnesota (OT)	27
18	Seattle	36
13	at Kansas City	31
6	San Francisco	27
6	St. Louis	19
43	Denver	13
12	at Carolina	19
27	Dallas	26
7	at San Francisco	38
289		434

ATLANTA FALCONS (13-3)
9	at Pittsburgh (OT)	15
41	Arizona	7
27	at New Orleans (OT)	24
16	San Francisco	14
20	at Cleveland	10
17	at Philadelphia	31
39	Cincinnati	32
27	Tampa Bay	21
26	Baltimore	21
34	at St. Louis	17
20	Green Bay	17
28	at Tampa Bay	24
31	at Carolina	10
34	at Seattle	18
14	New Orleans	17
31	Carolina	10
414		288

CAROLINA PANTHERS (2-14)
18	at New York Giants	31
7	Tampa Bay	20
7	Cincinnati	20
14	at New Orleans	16
6	Chicago	23
23	San Francisco	20
10	at St. Louis	20
3	New Orleans	34
16	at Tampa Bay	31
13	Baltimore	37
23	at Cleveland	24
14	at Seattle	31
10	Atlanta	31
19	Arizona	12
3	at Pittsburgh	27
10	at Atlanta	31
196		408

CHICAGO BEARS (11-5)
19	Detroit	14
27	at Dallas	20
20	Green Bay	17
3	at New York Giants	17
23	at Carolina	6
20	Seattle	23
14	Washington	17
22	at Buffalo	19
27	Minnesota	13
16	at Miami	0
31	Philadelphia	26
24	at Detroit	20
7	New England	36
40	at Minnesota	14
38	New York Jets	34
3	at Green Bay	10
334		286

DALLAS COWBOYS (6-10)
7	at Washington	13
20	Chicago	27
27	at Houston	13
27	Tennessee	34
21	at Minnesota	24
35	New York Giants	41
17	Jacksonville	35
7	at Green Bay	45
33	at New York Giants	20
35	Detroit	19
27	New Orleans	30
38	at Indianapolis (OT)	35
27	Philadelphia	30
33	Washington	30
26	at Arizona	27
14	at Philadelphia	13
394		436

DETROIT LIONS (6-10)
14	at Chicago	19
32	Philadelphia	35
10	at Minnesota	24
26	at Green Bay	28
44	St. Louis	6
20	at New York Giants	28
37	Washington	25
20	New York Jets (OT)	23
12	at Buffalo	14
19	at Dallas	35
24	New England	45
20	Chicago	24
7	Green Bay	3
23	at Tampa Bay (OT)	20
34	at Miami	27
20	Minnesota	13
362		369

GREEN BAY PACKERS (10-6)
27	at Philadelphia	20
34	Buffalo	7
17	at Chicago	20
28	Detroit	26
13	at Washington (OT)	16
20	Miami (OT)	23
28	Minnesota	24
9	at New York Jets	0
45	Dallas	7
31	at Minnesota	3
17	at Atlanta	20
34	San Francisco	16
3	at Detroit	7
27	at New England	31
45	New York Giants	17
10	Chicago	3
388		240

MINNESOTA VIKINGS (6-10)
9	at New Orleans	14
10	Miami	14
24	Detroit	10
20	at New York Jets	29
24	Dallas	21
24	at Green Bay	28
18	at New England	28
27	Arizona (OT)	24
13	at Chicago	27
3	Green Bay	31
17	at Washington	13
38	Buffalo	14
3	New York Giants	21
14	Chicago	40
24	at Philadelphia	14
13	at Detroit	20
281		348

NEW ORLEANS SAINTS (11-5)
14	Minnesota	9
25	at San Francisco	22
24	Atlanta (OT)	27
16	Carolina	14
20	at Arizona	30
31	at Tampa Bay	6
17	Cleveland	30
20	Pittsburgh	10
34	at Carolina	3
34	Seattle	19
30	at Dallas	27
34	at Cincinnati	30
31	St. Louis	13
24	at Baltimore	30
17	at Atlanta	14
13	Tampa Bay	23
384		307

NEW YORK GIANTS (10-6)
31	Carolina	18
14	at Indianapolis	38
10	Tennessee	29
17	Chicago	3
34	at Houston	10
28	Detroit	20
41	at Dallas	35
41	at Seattle	7
20	Dallas	33
17	at Philadelphia	27
24	Jacksonville	20
31	Washington	7
21	at Minnesota	3
31	Philadelphia	38
17	at Green Bay	45
17	at Washington	14
394		347

PHILADELPHIA EAGLES (10-6)
20	Green Bay	27
35	at Detroit	32
28	at Jacksonville	3
12	Washington	17
27	at San Francisco	24
31	Atlanta	17
19	at Tennessee	37
26	Indianapolis	24
59	at Washington	28
27	New York Giants	17
26	at Chicago	31
34	Houston	24
30	at Dallas	27
38	at New York Giants	31
14	Minnesota	24
13	Dallas	14
439		377

ST. LOUIS RAMS (7-9)
13	Arizona	17
14	at Oakland	16
30	Washington	16
20	Seattle	3
6	at Detroit	44
20	San Diego	17
17	at Tampa Bay	18
20	Carolina	10
20	at San Francisco (OT)	23
17	Atlanta	34
36	at Denver	33
19	at Arizona	6
13	at New Orleans	31
13	Kansas City	27
25	San Francisco	17
6	at Seattle	16
289		328

SAN FRANCISCO 49ERS (6-10)
6	at Seattle	31
22	New Orleans	25
10	at Kansas City	31
14	at Atlanta	16
24	Philadelphia	27
17	Oakland	9
20	at Carolina	23
24	Denver	16
23	St. Louis (OT)	20
0	Tampa Bay	21
27	at Arizona	6
16	at Green Bay	34
40	Seattle	21
7	at San Diego	34
17	at St. Louis	25
38	Arizona	7
305		346

SEATTLE SEAHAWKS (7-9)
31	San Francisco	6
14	at Denver	31
27	San Diego	20
3	at St. Louis	20
23	at Chicago	20
22	Arizona	10
3	at Oakland	33
7	New York Giants	41
36	at Arizona	18
19	at New Orleans	34
24	Kansas City	42
31	Carolina	14
21	at San Francisco	40
18	Atlanta	34
15	at Tampa Bay	38
16	St. Louis	6
310		407

TAMPA BAY BUCCANEERS (10-6)
17	Cleveland	14
20	at Carolina	7
13	Pittsburgh	38
24	at Cincinnati	21
6	New Orleans	31
18	St. Louis	17
38	at Arizona	35
21	at Atlanta	27
31	Carolina	16
21	at San Francisco	0
10	at Baltimore	17
24	Atlanta	28
17	at Washington	16
20	Detroit (OT)	23
38	Seattle	15
23	at New Orleans	13
341		318

WASHINGTON REDSKINS (6-10)
13	Dallas	7
27	Houston (OT)	30
16	at St. Louis	30
17	at Philadelphia	12
16	Green Bay (OT)	13
24	Indianapolis	27
17	at Chicago	14
25	at Detroit	37
28	Philadelphia	59
19	at Tennessee (OT)	16
13	Minnesota	17
7	at New York Giants	31
16	Tampa Bay	17
30	at Dallas	33
20	at Jacksonville (OT)	17
14	New York Giants	17
302		377

FINAL STANDINGS

AMERICAN FOOTBALL CONFERENCE

East Division	W	L	T	Pct.	Pts.	OP
* New England	14	2	0	.875	518	313
# New York Jets	11	5	0	.688	367	304
Miami	7	9	0	.438	273	333
Buffalo	4	12	0	.250	283	425

North Division	W	L	T	Pct.	Pts.	OP
* Pittsburgh	12	4	0	.750	375	232
# Baltimore	12	4	0	.750	357	270
Cleveland	5	11	0	.313	271	332
Cincinnati	4	12	0	.250	322	395

South Division	W	L	T	Pct.	Pts.	OP
* Indianapolis	10	6	0	.625	435	388
Jacksonville	8	8	0	.500	353	419
Houston	6	10	0	.375	390	427
Tennessee	6	10	0	.375	356	339

West Division	W	L	T	Pct.	Pts.	OP
* Kansas City	10	6	0	.625	366	326
San Diego	9	7	0	.563	441	322
Oakland	8	8	0	.500	410	371
Denver	4	12	0	.250	344	471

NATIONAL FOOTBALL CONFERENCE

East Division	W	L	T	Pct.	Pts.	OP
* Philadelphia	10	6	0	.625	439	377
New York Giants	10	6	0	.625	394	347
Dallas	6	10	0	.375	394	436
Washington	6	10	0	.375	302	377

North Division	W	L	T	Pct.	Pts.	OP
* Chicago	11	5	0	.688	334	286
# Green Bay	10	6	0	.625	388	240
Detroit	6	10	0	.375	362	369
Minnesota	6	10	0	.375	281	348

South Division	W	L	T	Pct.	Pts.	OP
* Atlanta	13	3	0	.813	414	288
# New Orleans	11	5	0	.688	384	307
Tampa Bay	10	6	0	.625	341	318
Carolina	2	14	0	.125	196	408

West Division	W	L	T	Pct.	Pts.	OP
* Seattle	7	9	0	.438	310	407
St. Louis	7	9	0	.438	289	328
San Francisco	6	10	0	.375	305	346
Arizona	5	11	0	.313	289	434

* Division champion
# Wild Card team

Pittsburgh finished ahead of Baltimore based on better division record (5-1 to 4-2). Indianapolis finished ahead of Kansas City based on head-to-head victory. Houston finished ahead of Tennessee based on better division record (3-3 to 2-4). Philadelphia finished ahead of the Giants based on head-to-head sweep. Dallas finished ahead of Washington based on better division record (3-3 to 2-4). Green Bay finished ahead of the Giants and Tampa Bay based on best strength of victory Green Bay .475; Giants .400; Tampa Bay .344). Detroit finished ahead of Minnesota based on better division record (2-4 to 1-5). Seattle finished ahead of St. Louis based on better division record (4-2 to 3-3).

WILD-CARD PLAYOFFS

AFC
N.Y. Jets 17, INDIANAPOLIS 16
Baltimore 30, KANSAS CITY 7

NFC
SEATTLE 41, New Orleans 36
Green Bay 21, PHILADELPHIA 16

DIVISIONAL PLAYOFFS

AFC
PITTSBURGH 31, Baltimore 24
N.Y. Jets 28, NEW ENGLAND 21

NFC
Green Bay 48, ATLANTA 21
CHICAGO 35, Seattle 24

CHAMPIONSHIP GAMES

AFC
PITTSBURGH 24, N.Y. Jets 19

NFC
Green Bay 21, CHICAGO 14

AFC-NFC PRO BOWL
NFC 55, AFC 41
at Aloha Stadium, Honolulu, Hawaii

SUPER BOWL XLV
Green Bay (NFC) 31, Pittsburgh (AFC) 25
at Cowboys Stadium, North Texas

Home teams in playoff games are indicated in CAPS.

FIRST WEEK STANDINGS
American Football Conference

East Division	W	L	T	Pct.	Pts.	OP
Miami	1	0	0	1.000	15	10
New England	1	0	0	1.000	38	24
Buffalo	0	1	0	.000	10	15
New York Jets	0	1	0	.000	9	10
North Division	**W**	**L**	**T**	**Pct.**	**Pts.**	**OP**
Baltimore	1	0	0	1.000	10	9
Pittsburgh	1	0	0	1.000	15	9
Cincinnati	0	1	0	.000	24	38
Cleveland	0	1	0	.000	14	17
South Division	**W**	**L**	**T**	**Pct.**	**Pts.**	**OP**
Houston	1	0	0	1.000	34	24
Jacksonville	1	0	0	1.000	24	17
Tennessee	1	0	0	1.000	38	13
Indianapolis	0	1	0	.000	24	34
West Division	**W**	**L**	**T**	**Pct.**	**Pts.**	**OP**
Kansas City	1	0	0	1.000	21	14
Denver	0	1	0	.000	17	24
Oakland	0	1	0	.000	13	38
San Diego	0	1	0	.000	14	21

National Football Conference

East Division	W	L	T	Pct.	Pts.	OP
New York Giants	1	0	0	1.000	31	18
Washington	1	0	0	1.000	13	7
Dallas	0	1	0	.000	7	13
Philadelphia	0	1	0	.000	20	27
North Division	**W**	**L**	**T**	**Pct.**	**Pts.**	**OP**
Chicago	1	0	0	1.000	19	14
Green Bay	1	0	0	1.000	27	20
Detroit	0	1	0	.000	14	19
Minnesota	0	1	0	.000	9	14
South Division	**W**	**L**	**T**	**Pct.**	**Pts.**	**OP**
New Orleans	1	0	0	1.000	14	9
Tampa Bay	1	0	0	1.000	17	14
Atlanta	0	1	0	.000	9	15
Carolina	0	1	0	.000	18	31
West Division	**W**	**L**	**T**	**Pct.**	**Pts.**	**OP**
Arizona	1	0	0	1.000	17	13
Seattle	1	0	0	1.000	31	6
St. Louis	0	1	0	.000	13	17
San Francisco	0	1	0	.000	6	31

WEEK 1 RESULTS
Thursday, September 9
NEW ORLEANS 14, Minnesota 9

Sunday, September 12
Miami 15, BUFFALO 10
CHICAGO 19, Detroit 14
HOUSTON 34, Indianapolis 24
JACKSONVILLE 24, Denver 17
NEW ENGLAND 38, Cincinnati 24
NEW YORK GIANTS 31, Carolina 18
PITTSBURGH 15, Atlanta 9 (OT)
TAMPA BAY 17, Cleveland 14
TENNESSEE 38, Oakland 13
Green Bay 27, PHILADELPHIA 20
Arizona 17, ST. LOUIS 13
SEATTLE 31, San Francisco 6
WASHINGTON 13, Dallas 7

Monday, September 13
Baltimore 10, NEW YORK JETS 9
KANSAS CITY 21, San Diego 14

In the 2010 Week By Week section, home teams are indicated by ALL CAPS.

For game recaps, box scores, and video highlights, please visit www.NFL.com/scores.

SECOND WEEK STANDINGS
American Football Conference

East Division	W	L	T	Pct.	Pts.	OP
Miami	2	0	0	1.000	29	20
New England	1	1	0	.500	52	52
New York Jets	1	1	0	.500	37	24
Buffalo	0	2	0	.000	17	49
North Division	**W**	**L**	**T**	**Pct.**	**Pts.**	**OP**
Pittsburgh	2	0	0	1.000	34	20
Baltimore	1	1	0	.500	20	24
Cincinnati	1	1	0	.500	39	48
Cleveland	0	2	0	.000	28	33
South Division	**W**	**L**	**T**	**Pct.**	**Pts.**	**OP**
Houston	2	0	0	1.000	64	51
Indianapolis	1	1	0	.500	62	48
Jacksonville	1	1	0	.500	37	55
Tennessee	1	1	0	.500	49	32
West Division	**W**	**L**	**T**	**Pct.**	**Pts.**	**OP**
Kansas City	2	0	0	1.000	37	28
Denver	1	1	0	.500	34	38
Oakland	1	1	0	.500	29	52
San Diego	1	1	0	.500	52	34

National Football Conference

East Division	W	L	T	Pct.	Pts.	OP
New York Giants	1	1	0	.500	45	56
Philadelphia	1	1	0	.500	55	59
Washington	1	1	0	.500	40	37
Dallas	0	2	0	.000	27	40
North Division	**W**	**L**	**T**	**Pct.**	**Pts.**	**OP**
Chicago	2	0	0	1.000	46	34
Green Bay	2	0	0	1.000	61	27
Detroit	0	2	0	.000	46	54
Minnesota	0	2	0	.000	19	28
South Division	**W**	**L**	**T**	**Pct.**	**Pts.**	**OP**
New Orleans	2	0	0	1.000	39	31
Tampa Bay	2	0	0	1.000	37	21
Atlanta	1	1	0	.500	50	22
Carolina	0	2	0	.000	25	51
West Division	**W**	**L**	**T**	**Pct.**	**Pts.**	**OP**
Arizona	1	1	0	.500	24	54
Seattle	1	1	0	.500	45	37
St. Louis	0	2	0	.000	27	33
San Francisco	0	2	0	.000	28	50

WEEK 2 RESULTS
Sunday, September 19
ATLANTA 41, Arizona 7
Tampa Bay 20, CAROLINA 7
CINCINNATI 15, Baltimore 10
Kansas City 16, CLEVELAND 14
CHICAGO 27, DALLAS 20
Philadelphia 35, DETROIT 32
GREEN BAY 34, Buffalo 7
Miami 14, MINNESOTA 10
Pittsburgh 19, TENNESSEE 11
DENVER 31, Seattle 14
OAKLAND 16, St. Louis 14
NEW YORK JETS 28, New England 14
SAN DIEGO 38, Jacksonville 13
Houston 30, WASHINGTON 27 (OT)
INDIANAPOLIS 38, New York Giants 14

Monday, September 20
New Orleans 25, SAN FRANCISCO 22

THIRD WEEK STANDINGS
American Football Conference

East Division	W	L	T	Pct.	Pts.	OP
Miami	2	1	0	.667	52	51
New England	2	1	0	.667	90	82
New York Jets	2	1	0	.667	68	47
Buffalo	0	3	0	.000	47	87
North Division	**W**	**L**	**T**	**Pct.**	**Pts.**	**OP**
Pittsburgh	3	0	0	1.000	72	33
Baltimore	2	1	0	.667	44	41
Cincinnati	2	1	0	.667	59	55
Cleveland	0	3	0	.000	45	57
South Division	**W**	**L**	**T**	**Pct.**	**Pts.**	**OP**
Houston	2	1	0	.667	77	78
Indianapolis	2	1	0	.667	89	61
Tennessee	2	1	0	.667	78	42
Jacksonville	1	2	0	.333	40	83
West Division	**W**	**L**	**T**	**Pct.**	**Pts.**	**OP**
Kansas City	3	0	0	1.000	68	38
Denver	1	2	0	.333	61	65
Oakland	1	2	0	.333	52	76
San Diego	1	2	0	.333	72	61

National Football Conference

East Division	W	L	T	Pct.	Pts.	OP
Philadelphia	2	1	0	.667	83	62
Dallas	1	2	0	.333	54	53
New York Giants	1	2	0	.333	55	85
Washington	1	2	0	.333	56	67
North Division	**W**	**L**	**T**	**Pct.**	**Pts.**	**OP**
Chicago	3	0	0	1.000	66	51
Green Bay	2	1	0	.667	78	47
Minnesota	1	2	0	.333	43	38
Detroit	0	3	0	.000	56	78
South Division	**W**	**L**	**T**	**Pct.**	**Pts.**	**OP**
Atlanta	2	1	0	.667	77	46
New Orleans	2	1	0	.667	63	58
Tampa Bay	2	1	0	.667	50	59
Carolina	0	3	0	.000	32	71
West Division	**W**	**L**	**T**	**Pct.**	**Pts.**	**OP**
Arizona	2	1	0	.667	48	77
Seattle	2	1	0	.667	72	57
St. Louis	1	2	0	.333	57	49
San Francisco	0	3	0	.000	38	87

WEEK 3 RESULTS
Sunday, September 26
BALTIMORE 24, Cleveland 17
Cincinnati 20, CAROLINA 7
Dallas 27, HOUSTON 13
KANSAS CITY 31, San Francisco 10
MINNESOTA 24, Detroit 10
NEW ENGLAND 38, Buffalo 30
Atlanta 27, NEW ORLEANS 24 (OT)
Tennessee 29, NEW YORK GIANTS 10
Pittsburgh 38, TAMPA BAY 13
Philadelphia 28, JACKSONVILLE 3
ST. LOUIS 30, Washington 16
ARIZONA 24, Oakland 23
Indianapolis 27, DENVER 13
SEATTLE 27, San Diego 20
New York Jets 31, MIAMI 23

Monday, September 27
CHICAGO 20, Green Bay 17

FOURTH WEEK STANDINGS
American Football Conference

East Division	W	L	T	Pct.	Pts.	OP
New England	3	1	0	.750	131	96
New York Jets	3	1	0	.750	106	61
Miami	2	2	0	.500	66	92
Buffalo	0	4	0	.000	61	125
North Division	W	L	T	Pct.	Pts.	OP
Baltimore	3	1	0	.750	61	55
Pittsburgh	3	1	0	.750	86	50
Cincinnati	2	2	0	.500	79	78
Cleveland	1	3	0	.250	68	77
South Division	W	L	T	Pct.	Pts.	OP
Houston	3	1	0	.750	108	102
Indianapolis	2	2	0	.500	117	92
Jacksonville	2	2	0	.500	71	111
Tennessee	2	2	0	.500	98	68
West Division	W	L	T	Pct.	Pts.	OP
Kansas City	3	0	0	1.000	68	38
Denver	2	2	0	.500	87	85
San Diego	2	2	0	.500	113	71
Oakland	1	3	0	.250	76	107

National Football Conference

East Division	W	L	T	Pct.	Pts.	OP
New York Giants	2	2	0	.500	72	88
Philadelphia	2	2	0	.500	95	79
Washington	2	2	0	.500	73	79
Dallas	1	2	0	.333	54	53
North Division	W	L	T	Pct.	Pts.	OP
Chicago	3	1	0	.750	69	68
Green Bay	3	1	0	.750	106	73
Minnesota	1	2	0	.333	43	38
Detroit	0	4	0	.000	82	106
South Division	W	L	T	Pct.	Pts.	OP
Atlanta	3	1	0	.750	93	60
New Orleans	3	1	0	.750	79	72
Tampa Bay	2	1	0	.667	50	59
Carolina	0	4	0	.000	46	87
West Division	W	L	T	Pct.	Pts.	OP
Arizona	2	2	0	.500	58	118
St. Louis	2	2	0	.500	77	52
Seattle	2	2	0	.500	75	77
San Francisco	0	4	0	.000	52	103

WEEK 4 RESULTS
Sunday, October 3

ATLANTA 16, San Francisco 14
New York Jets 38, BUFFALO 14
CLEVELAND 23, Cincinnati 20
GREEN BAY 28, Detroit 26
NEW ORLEANS 16, Carolina 14
Baltimore 17, PITTSBURGH 14
ST. LOUIS 20, Seattle 3
Denver 26, TENNESSEE 20
JACKSONVILLE 31, Indianapolis 28
Houston 31, OAKLAND 24
Washington 17, PHILADELPHIA 12
SAN DIEGO 41, Arizona 10
NEW YORK GIANTS 17, Chicago 3

Monday, October 4
New England 41, MIAMI 14

Byes: Dallas, Kansas City, Minnesota, Tampa Bay

FIFTH WEEK STANDINGS
American Football Conference

East Division	W	L	T	Pct.	Pts.	OP
New York Jets	4	1	0	.800	135	81
New England	3	1	0	.750	131	96
Miami	2	2	0	.500	66	92
Buffalo	0	5	0	.000	87	161
North Division	W	L	T	Pct.	Pts.	OP
Baltimore	4	1	0	.800	92	72
Pittsburgh	3	1	0	.750	86	50
Cincinnati	2	3	0	.400	100	102
Cleveland	1	4	0	.200	78	97
South Division	W	L	T	Pct.	Pts.	OP
Houston	3	2	0	.600	118	136
Indianapolis	3	2	0	.600	136	101
Jacksonville	3	2	0	.600	107	137
Tennessee	3	2	0	.600	132	95
West Division	W	L	T	Pct.	Pts.	OP
Kansas City	3	1	0	.750	77	57
Denver	2	3	0	.400	104	116
Oakland	2	3	0	.400	111	134
San Diego	2	3	0	.400	140	106

National Football Conference

East Division	W	L	T	Pct.	Pts.	OP
New York Giants	3	2	0	.600	106	98
Philadelphia	3	2	0	.600	122	103
Washington	3	2	0	.600	89	92
Dallas	1	3	0	.250	81	87
North Division	W	L	T	Pct.	Pts.	OP
Chicago	4	1	0	.800	92	74
Green Bay	3	2	0	.600	119	89
Minnesota	1	3	0	.250	63	67
Detroit	1	4	0	.200	126	112
South Division	W	L	T	Pct.	Pts.	OP
Atlanta	4	1	0	.800	113	70
Tampa Bay	3	1	0	.750	74	80
New Orleans	3	2	0	.600	99	102
Carolina	0	5	0	.000	52	110
West Division	W	L	T	Pct.	Pts.	OP
Arizona	3	2	0	.600	88	138
Seattle	2	2	0	.500	75	77
St. Louis	2	3	0	.400	83	96
San Francisco	0	5	0	.000	76	130

WEEK 5 RESULTS
Sunday, October 10

BALTIMORE 31, Denver 17
Jacksonville 36, BUFFALO 26
Chicago 23, CAROLINA 6
Tampa Bay 24, CINCINNATI 21
Atlanta 20, CLEVELAND 10
DETROIT 44, St. Louis 6
INDIANAPOLIS 19, Kansas City 9
New York Giants 34, HOUSTON 10
WASHINGTON 16, Green Bay 13 (OT)
ARIZONA 30, New Orleans 20
Tennessee 34, DALLAS 27
OAKLAND 35, San Diego 27
Philadelphia 27, SAN FRANCISCO 24

Monday, October 11
NEW YORK JETS 29, Minnesota 20

Byes: Miami, New England, Pittsburgh, Seattle

SIXTH WEEK STANDINGS
American Football Conference

East Division	W	L	T	Pct.	Pts.	OP
New York Jets	5	1	0	.833	159	101
New England	4	1	0	.800	154	116
Miami	3	2	0	.600	89	112
Buffalo	0	5	0	.000	87	161
North Division	W	L	T	Pct.	Pts.	OP
Pittsburgh	4	1	0	.800	114	60
Baltimore	4	2	0	.667	112	95
Cincinnati	2	3	0	.400	100	102
Cleveland	1	5	0	.167	88	125
South Division	W	L	T	Pct.	Pts.	OP
Houston	4	2	0	.667	153	167
Indianapolis	4	2	0	.667	163	125
Tennessee	4	2	0	.667	162	98
Jacksonville	3	3	0	.500	110	167
West Division	W	L	T	Pct.	Pts.	OP
Kansas City	3	2	0	.600	108	92
Denver	2	4	0	.333	124	140
Oakland	2	4	0	.333	120	151
San Diego	2	4	0	.333	157	126

National Football Conference

East Division	W	L	T	Pct.	Pts.	OP
New York Giants	4	2	0	.667	134	118
Philadelphia	4	2	0	.667	153	120
Washington	3	3	0	.500	113	119
Dallas	1	4	0	.200	102	111
North Division	W	L	T	Pct.	Pts.	OP
Chicago	4	2	0	.667	112	97
Green Bay	3	3	0	.500	139	112
Minnesota	2	3	0	.400	87	88
Detroit	1	5	0	.167	146	140
South Division	W	L	T	Pct.	Pts.	OP
Atlanta	4	2	0	.667	130	101
New Orleans	4	2	0	.667	130	108
Tampa Bay	3	2	0	.600	80	111
Carolina	0	5	0	.000	52	110
West Division	W	L	T	Pct.	Pts.	OP
Arizona	3	2	0	.600	88	138
Seattle	3	2	0	.600	98	97
St. Louis	3	3	0	.500	103	113
San Francisco	1	5	0	.167	93	139

WEEK 6 RESULTS
Sunday, October 17

Seattle 23, CHICAGO 20
Miami 23, GREEN BAY 20 (OT)
HOUSTON 35, Kansas City 31
NEW ENGLAND 23, Baltimore 20 (OT)
NEW YORK GIANTS 28, Detroit 20
PHILADELPHIA 31, Atlanta 17
PITTSBURGH 28, Cleveland 10
ST. LOUIS 20, San Diego 17
New Orleans 31, TAMPA BAY 6
New York Jets 24, DENVER 20
SAN FRANCISCO 17, Oakland 9
MINNESOTA 24, Dallas 21
Indianapolis 27, WASHINGTON 24

Monday, October 18
Tennessee 30, JACKSONVILLE 3

Byes: Arizona, Buffalo, Carolina, Cincinnati

SEVENTH WEEK STANDINGS
American Football Conference

East Division	W	L	T	Pct.	Pts.	OP
New England	5	1	0	.833	177	136
New York Jets	5	1	0	.833	159	101
Miami	3	3	0	.500	111	135
Buffalo	0	6	0	.000	121	198

North Division	W	L	T	Pct.	Pts.	OP
Pittsburgh	5	1	0	.833	137	82
Baltimore	5	2	0	.714	149	129
Cincinnati	2	4	0	.333	132	141
Cleveland	2	5	0	.286	118	142

South Division	W	L	T	Pct.	Pts.	OP
Tennessee	5	2	0	.714	199	117
Houston	4	2	0	.667	153	167
Indianapolis	4	2	0	.667	163	125
Jacksonville	3	4	0	.429	130	209

West Division	W	L	T	Pct.	Pts.	OP
Kansas City	4	2	0	.667	150	112
Oakland	3	4	0	.429	179	165
Denver	2	5	0	.286	138	199
San Diego	2	5	0	.286	177	149

National Football Conference

East Division	W	L	T	Pct.	Pts.	OP
New York Giants	5	2	0	.714	175	153
Philadelphia	4	3	0	.571	172	157
Washington	4	3	0	.571	130	133
Dallas	1	5	0	.167	137	152

North Division	W	L	T	Pct.	Pts.	OP
Chicago	4	3	0	.571	126	114
Green Bay	4	3	0	.571	167	136
Minnesota	2	4	0	.333	111	116
Detroit	1	5	0	.167	146	140

South Division	W	L	T	Pct.	Pts.	OP
Atlanta	5	2	0	.714	169	133
Tampa Bay	4	2	0	.667	98	128
New Orleans	4	3	0	.571	147	138
Carolina	1	5	0	.167	75	130

West Division	W	L	T	Pct.	Pts.	OP
Seattle	4	2	0	.667	120	107
Arizona	3	3	0	.500	98	160
St. Louis	3	4	0	.429	120	131
San Francisco	1	6	0	.143	113	162

WEEK 7 RESULTS
Sunday, October 24
ATLANTA 39, Cincinnati 32
BALTIMORE 37, Buffalo 34 (OT)
CAROLINA 23, San Francisco 20
Washington 17, CHICAGO 14
KANSAS CITY 42, Jacksonville 20
Pittsburgh 23, MIAMI 22
Cleveland 30, NEW ORLEANS 17
TAMPA BAY 18, St. Louis 17
TENNESSEE 37, Philadelphia 19
SEATTLE 22, Arizona 10
New England 23, SAN DIEGO 20
Oakland 59, DENVER 14
GREEN BAY 28, Minnesota 24

Monday, October 25
New York Giants 41, DALLAS 35

Byes: Detroit, Houston
Indianapolis, New York Jets

EIGHTH WEEK STANDINGS
American Football Conference

East Division	W	L	T	Pct.	Pts.	OP
New England	6	1	0	.857	205	154
New York Jets	5	2	0	.714	159	110
Miami	4	3	0	.571	133	149
Buffalo	0	7	0	.000	131	211

North Division	W	L	T	Pct.	Pts.	OP
Baltimore	5	2	0	.714	149	129
Pittsburgh	5	2	0	.714	147	102
Cincinnati	2	5	0	.286	146	163
Cleveland	2	5	0	.286	118	142

South Division	W	L	T	Pct.	Pts.	OP
Indianapolis	5	2	0	.714	193	142
Tennessee	5	3	0	.625	224	150
Houston	4	3	0	.571	170	197
Jacksonville	4	4	0	.500	165	226

West Division	W	L	T	Pct.	Pts.	OP
Kansas City	5	2	0	.714	163	122
Oakland	4	4	0	.500	212	168
San Diego	3	5	0	.375	210	174
Denver	2	6	0	.250	154	223

National Football Conference

East Division	W	L	T	Pct.	Pts.	OP
New York Giants	5	2	0	.714	175	153
Philadelphia	4	3	0	.571	172	157
Washington	4	4	0	.500	155	170
Dallas	1	6	0	.143	154	187

North Division	W	L	T	Pct.	Pts.	OP
Green Bay	5	3	0	.625	176	136
Chicago	4	3	0	.571	126	114
Detroit	2	5	0	.286	183	165
Minnesota	2	5	0	.286	129	144

South Division	W	L	T	Pct.	Pts.	OP
Atlanta	5	2	0	.714	169	133
Tampa Bay	5	2	0	.714	136	163
New Orleans	5	3	0	.625	167	148
Carolina	1	6	0	.143	85	150

West Division	W	L	T	Pct.	Pts.	OP
Seattle	4	3	0	.571	123	140
St. Louis	4	4	0	.500	140	141
Arizona	3	4	0	.429	133	198
San Francisco	2	6	0	.250	137	178

WEEK 8 RESULTS
Sunday, October 31
Miami 22, CINCINNATI 14
Jacksonville 35, DALLAS 17
DETROIT 37, Washington 25
KANSAS CITY 13, Buffalo 10 (OT)
Green Bay 9, NEW YORK JETS 0
ST. LOUIS 20, Carolina 10
SAN FRANCISCO 24, Denver 16 (London)
SAN DIEGO 33, Tennessee 25
NEW ENGLAND 28, Minnesota 18
OAKLAND 33, Seattle 3
Tampa Bay 38, ARIZONA 35
NEW ORLEANS 20, Pittsburgh 10

Monday, November 1
INDIANAPOLIS 30, Houston 17

Byes: Atlanta, Baltimore,
Chicago, Cleveland,
New York Giants, Philadelphia

NINTH WEEK STANDINGS
American Football Conference

East Division	W	L	T	Pct.	Pts.	OP
New England	6	2	0	.750	219	188
New York Jets	6	2	0	.750	182	130
Miami	4	4	0	.500	143	175
Buffalo	0	8	0	.000	150	233

North Division	W	L	T	Pct.	Pts.	OP
Baltimore	6	2	0	.750	175	139
Pittsburgh	6	2	0	.750	174	123
Cleveland	3	5	0	.375	152	156
Cincinnati	2	6	0	.250	167	190

South Division	W	L	T	Pct.	Pts.	OP
Indianapolis	5	3	0	.625	217	168
Tennessee	5	3	0	.625	224	150
Houston	4	4	0	.500	193	226
Jacksonville	4	4	0	.500	165	226

West Division	W	L	T	Pct.	Pts.	OP
Kansas City	5	3	0	.625	183	145
Oakland	5	4	0	.556	235	188
San Diego	4	5	0	.444	239	197
Denver	2	6	0	.250	154	223

National Football Conference

East Division	W	L	T	Pct.	Pts.	OP
New York Giants	6	2	0	.750	216	160
Philadelphia	5	3	0	.625	198	181
Washington	4	4	0	.500	155	170
Dallas	1	7	0	.125	161	232

North Division	W	L	T	Pct.	Pts.	OP
Green Bay	6	3	0	.667	221	143
Chicago	5	3	0	.625	148	133
Minnesota	3	5	0	.375	156	168
Detroit	2	6	0	.250	203	188

South Division	W	L	T	Pct.	Pts.	OP
Atlanta	6	2	0	.750	196	154
New Orleans	6	3	0	.667	201	151
Tampa Bay	5	3	0	.625	157	190
Carolina	1	7	0	.125	88	184

West Division	W	L	T	Pct.	Pts.	OP
St. Louis	4	4	0	.500	140	141
Seattle	4	4	0	.500	130	181
Arizona	3	5	0	.375	157	225
San Francisco	2	6	0	.250	137	178

WEEK 9 RESULTS
Sunday, November 7
ATLANTA 27, Tampa Bay 21
BALTIMORE 26, Miami 10
Chicago 22, BUFFALO 19 (Toronto)
New Orleans 34, CAROLINA 3
CLEVELAND 34, New England 14
New York Jets 23, DETROIT 20 (OT)
San Diego 29, HOUSTON 23
MINNESOTA 27, Arizona 24 (OT)
New York Giants 41, SEATTLE 7
PHILADELPHIA 26, Indianapolis 24
OAKLAND 23, Kansas City 20 (OT)
GREEN BAY 45, Dallas 7

Monday, November 8
Pittsburgh 27, CINCINNATI 21

Byes: Denver, Jacksonville,
St. Louis, San Francisco,
Tennessee, Washington

TENTH WEEK STANDINGS
American Football Conference

East Division	W	L	T	Pct.	Pts.	OP
New England	7	2	0	.778	258	214
New York Jets	7	2	0	.778	208	150
Miami	5	4	0	.556	172	192
Buffalo	1	8	0	.111	164	245
North Division	**W**	**L**	**T**	**Pct.**	**Pts.**	**OP**
Baltimore	6	3	0	.667	196	165
Pittsburgh	6	3	0	.667	200	162
Cleveland	3	6	0	.333	172	182
Cincinnati	2	7	0	.222	184	213
South Division	**W**	**L**	**T**	**Pct.**	**Pts.**	**OP**
Indianapolis	6	3	0	.667	240	185
Jacksonville	5	4	0	.556	196	250
Tennessee	5	4	0	.556	241	179
Houston	4	5	0	.444	217	257
West Division	**W**	**L**	**T**	**Pct.**	**Pts.**	**OP**
Kansas City	5	4	0	.556	212	194
Oakland	5	4	0	.556	235	188
San Diego	4	5	0	.444	239	197
Denver	3	6	0	.333	203	252

National Football Conference

East Division	W	L	T	Pct.	Pts.	OP
New York Giants	6	3	0	.667	236	193
Philadelphia	6	3	0	.667	257	209
Washington	4	5	0	.444	183	229
Dallas	2	7	0	.222	194	252
North Division	**W**	**L**	**T**	**Pct.**	**Pts.**	**OP**
Chicago	6	3	0	.667	175	146
Green Bay	6	3	0	.667	221	143
Minnesota	3	6	0	.333	169	195
Detroit	2	7	0	.222	215	202
South Division	**W**	**L**	**T**	**Pct.**	**Pts.**	**OP**
Atlanta	7	2	0	.778	222	175
New Orleans	6	3	0	.667	201	151
Tampa Bay	6	3	0	.667	188	206
Carolina	1	8	0	.111	104	215
West Division	**W**	**L**	**T**	**Pct.**	**Pts.**	**OP**
Seattle	5	4	0	.556	166	199
St. Louis	4	5	0	.444	160	164
Arizona	3	6	0	.333	175	261
San Francisco	3	6	0	.333	160	198

WEEK 10 RESULTS
Thursday, November 11
ATLANTA 26, Baltimore 21

Sunday, November 14
BUFFALO 14, Detroit 12
CHICAGO 27, Minnesota 13
New York Jets 26, CLEVELAND 20 (OT)
INDIANAPOLIS 23, Cincinnati 17
JACKSONVILLE 31, Houston 24
MIAMI 29, Tennessee 17
TAMPA BAY 31, Carolina 16
DENVER 49, Kansas City 29
Dallas 33, NEW YORK GIANTS 20
Seattle 36, ARIZONA 18
SAN FRANCISCO 23, St. Louis 20 (OT)
New England 39, PITTSBURGH 26

Monday, November 15
Philadelphia 59, WASHINGTON 28

Byes: Green Bay, New Orleans
Oakland, San Diego

ELEVENTH WEEK STANDINGS
American Football Conference

East Division	W	L	T	Pct.	Pts.	OP
New England	8	2	0	.800	289	242
New York Jets	8	2	0	.800	238	177
Miami	5	5	0	.500	172	208
Buffalo	2	8	0	.200	213	276
North Division	**W**	**L**	**T**	**Pct.**	**Pts.**	**OP**
Baltimore	7	3	0	.700	233	178
Pittsburgh	7	3	0	.700	235	165
Cleveland	3	7	0	.300	192	206
Cincinnati	2	8	0	.200	215	262
South Division	**W**	**L**	**T**	**Pct.**	**Pts.**	**OP**
Indianapolis	6	4	0	.600	268	216
Jacksonville	6	4	0	.600	220	270
Tennessee	5	5	0	.500	257	198
Houston	4	6	0	.400	244	287
West Division	**W**	**L**	**T**	**Pct.**	**Pts.**	**OP**
Kansas City	6	4	0	.600	243	207
Oakland	5	5	0	.500	238	223
San Diego	5	5	0	.500	274	211
Denver	3	7	0	.300	217	287

National Football Conference

East Division	W	L	T	Pct.	Pts.	OP
Philadelphia	7	3	0	.700	284	226
New York Giants	6	4	0	.600	253	220
Washington	5	5	0	.500	202	245
Dallas	3	7	0	.300	229	271
North Division	**W**	**L**	**T**	**Pct.**	**Pts.**	**OP**
Chicago	7	3	0	.700	191	146
Green Bay	7	3	0	.700	252	146
Minnesota	3	7	0	.300	172	226
Detroit	2	8	0	.200	234	237
South Division	**W**	**L**	**T**	**Pct.**	**Pts.**	**OP**
Atlanta	8	2	0	.800	256	192
New Orleans	7	3	0	.700	235	170
Tampa Bay	7	3	0	.700	209	206
Carolina	1	9	0	.100	117	252
West Division	**W**	**L**	**T**	**Pct.**	**Pts.**	**OP**
Seattle	5	5	0	.500	185	233
St. Louis	4	6	0	.400	177	198
Arizona	3	7	0	.300	188	292
San Francisco	3	7	0	.300	160	219

WEEK 11 RESULTS
Thursday, November 18
Chicago 16, MIAMI 0

Sunday, November 21
Baltimore 37, CAROLINA 13
Buffalo 49, CINCINNATI 31
DALLAS 35, Detroit 19
JACKSONVILLE 24, Cleveland 20
KANSAS CITY 31, Arizona 13
Green Bay 31, MINNESOTA 3
NEW YORK JETS 30, Houston 27
PITTSBURGH 35, Oakland 3
Washington 19, TENNESSEE 16 (OT)
NEW ORLEANS 34, Seattle 19
Atlanta 34, ST. LOUIS 17
Tampa Bay 21, SAN FRANCISCO 0
NEW ENGLAND 31, Indianapolis 28
PHILADELPHIA 27, New York Giants 17

Monday, November 22
SAN DIEGO 35, Denver 14

TWELFTH WEEK STANDINGS
American Football Conference

East Division	W	L	T	Pct.	Pts.	OP
New England	9	2	0	.818	334	266
New York Jets	9	2	0	.818	264	187
Miami	6	5	0	.545	205	225
Buffalo	2	9	0	.182	229	295
North Division	**W**	**L**	**T**	**Pct.**	**Pts.**	**OP**
Baltimore	8	3	0	.727	250	188
Pittsburgh	8	3	0	.727	254	181
Cleveland	4	7	0	.364	216	229
Cincinnati	2	9	0	.182	225	288
South Division	**W**	**L**	**T**	**Pct.**	**Pts.**	**OP**
Indianapolis	6	5	0	.545	282	252
Jacksonville	6	5	0	.545	240	294
Houston	5	6	0	.455	264	287
Tennessee	5	6	0	.455	257	218
West Division	**W**	**L**	**T**	**Pct.**	**Pts.**	**OP**
Kansas City	7	4	0	.636	285	231
San Diego	6	5	0	.545	310	225
Oakland	5	6	0	.455	255	256
Denver	3	8	0	.273	250	323

National Football Conference

East Division	W	L	T	Pct.	Pts.	OP
New York Giants	7	4	0	.636	277	240
Philadelphia	7	4	0	.636	310	257
Washington	5	6	0	.455	215	262
Dallas	3	8	0	.273	256	301
North Division	**W**	**L**	**T**	**Pct.**	**Pts.**	**OP**
Chicago	8	3	0	.727	222	172
Green Bay	7	4	0	.636	269	166
Minnesota	4	7	0	.364	189	239
Detroit	2	9	0	.182	258	282
South Division	**W**	**L**	**T**	**Pct.**	**Pts.**	**OP**
Atlanta	9	2	0	.818	276	209
New Orleans	8	3	0	.727	265	197
Tampa Bay	7	4	0	.636	219	223
Carolina	1	10	0	.091	140	276
West Division	**W**	**L**	**T**	**Pct.**	**Pts.**	**OP**
St. Louis	5	6	0	.455	213	231
Seattle	5	6	0	.455	209	275
San Francisco	4	7	0	.364	187	225
Arizona	3	8	0	.273	194	319

WEEK 12 RESULTS
Thursday, November 25
New England 45, DETROIT 24
New Orleans 30, DALLAS 27
NEW YORK JETS 26, Cincinnati 10

Sunday, November 28
ATLANTA 20, Green Bay 17
BALTIMORE 17, Tampa Bay 10
Pittsburgh 19, BUFFALO 16 (OT)
CHICAGO 31, Philadelphia 26
CLEVELAND 24, Carolina 23
HOUSTON 20, Tennessee 0
NEW YORK GIANTS 24, Jacksonville 20
Minnesota 17, WASHINGTON 13
Kansas City 42, SEATTLE 24
Miami 33, OAKLAND 17
St. Louis 36, DENVER 33
San Diego 36, INDIANAPOLIS 14

Monday, November 29
San Francisco 27, ARIZONA 6

THIRTEENTH WEEK STANDINGS

American Football Conference

East Division	W	L	T	Pct.	Pts.	OP
New England	10	2	0	.833	379	269
New York Jets	9	3	0	.750	267	232
Miami	6	6	0	.500	215	238
Buffalo	2	10	0	.167	243	333
North Division	**W**	**L**	**T**	**Pct.**	**Pts.**	**OP**
Pittsburgh	9	3	0	.750	267	191
Baltimore	8	4	0	.667	260	201
Cleveland	5	7	0	.417	229	239
Cincinnati	2	10	0	.167	255	322
South Division	**W**	**L**	**T**	**Pct.**	**Pts.**	**OP**
Jacksonville	7	5	0	.583	257	300
Indianapolis	6	6	0	.500	317	290
Houston	5	7	0	.417	288	321
Tennessee	5	7	0	.417	263	235
West Division	**W**	**L**	**T**	**Pct.**	**Pts.**	**OP**
Kansas City	8	4	0	.667	295	237
Oakland	6	6	0	.500	283	269
San Diego	6	6	0	.500	323	253
Denver	3	9	0	.250	256	333

National Football Conference

East Division	W	L	T	Pct.	Pts.	OP
New York Giants	8	4	0	.667	308	247
Philadelphia	8	4	0	.667	344	281
Washington	5	7	0	.417	222	293
Dallas	4	8	0	.333	294	336
North Division	**W**	**L**	**T**	**Pct.**	**Pts.**	**OP**
Chicago	9	3	0	.750	246	192
Green Bay	8	4	0	.667	303	182
Minnesota	5	7	0	.417	227	253
Detroit	2	10	0	.167	278	306
South Division	**W**	**L**	**T**	**Pct.**	**Pts.**	**OP**
Atlanta	10	2	0	.833	304	233
New Orleans	9	3	0	.750	299	227
Tampa Bay	7	5	0	.583	243	251
Carolina	1	11	0	.083	154	307
West Division	**W**	**L**	**T**	**Pct.**	**Pts.**	**OP**
St. Louis	6	6	0	.500	232	237
Seattle	6	6	0	.500	240	289
San Francisco	4	8	0	.333	203	259
Arizona	3	9	0	.250	200	338

WEEK 13 RESULTS

Thursday, December 2
PHILADELPHIA 34, Houston 24

Sunday, December 5
New Orleans 34, CINCINNATI 30
Chicago 24, DETROIT 20
GREEN BAY 34, San Francisco 16
KANSAS CITY 10, Denver 6
Cleveland 13, MIAMI 10
MINNESOTA 38, Buffalo 14
NEW YORK GIANTS 31, Washington 7
Jacksonville 17, TENNESSEE 6
Oakland 28, SAN DIEGO 13
St. Louis 19, ARIZONA 6
Dallas 38, INDIANAPOLIS 35 (OT)
SEATTLE 31, Carolina 14
Atlanta 28, TAMPA BAY 24
Pittsburgh 13, BALTIMORE 10

Monday, December 6
NEW ENGLAND 45, New York Jets 3

FOURTEENTH WEEK STANDINGS

American Football Conference

East Division	W	L	T	Pct.	Pts.	OP
New England#	11	2	0	.846	415	276
New York Jets	9	4	0	.692	273	242
Miami	7	6	0	.538	225	244
Buffalo	3	10	0	.231	256	339
North Division	**W**	**L**	**T**	**Pct.**	**Pts.**	**OP**
Pittsburgh	10	3	0	.769	290	198
Baltimore	9	4	0	.692	294	229
Cleveland	5	8	0	.385	235	252
Cincinnati	2	11	0	.154	262	345
South Division	**W**	**L**	**T**	**Pct.**	**Pts.**	**OP**
Jacksonville	8	5	0	.615	295	331
Indianapolis	7	6	0	.538	347	318
Houston	5	8	0	.385	316	355
Tennessee	5	8	0	.385	291	265
West Division	**W**	**L**	**T**	**Pct.**	**Pts.**	**OP**
Kansas City	8	5	0	.615	295	268
San Diego	7	6	0	.538	354	253
Oakland	6	7	0	.462	314	307
Denver	3	10	0	.231	269	376

National Football Conference

East Division	W	L	T	Pct.	Pts.	OP
New York Giants	9	4	0	.692	329	250
Philadelphia	9	4	0	.692	374	308
Washington	5	8	0	.385	238	310
Dallas	4	9	0	.308	321	366
North Division	**W**	**L**	**T**	**Pct.**	**Pts.**	**OP**
Chicago	9	4	0	.692	253	228
Green Bay	8	5	0	.615	306	189
Minnesota	5	8	0	.385	230	274
Detroit	3	10	0	.231	285	309
South Division	**W**	**L**	**T**	**Pct.**	**Pts.**	**OP**
Atlanta	11	2	0	.846	335	243
New Orleans	10	3	0	.769	330	240
Tampa Bay	8	5	0	.615	260	267
Carolina	1	12	0	.077	164	338
West Division	**W**	**L**	**T**	**Pct.**	**Pts.**	**OP**
St. Louis	6	7	0	.462	245	268
Seattle	6	7	0	.462	261	329
San Francisco	5	8	0	.385	243	280
Arizona	4	9	0	.308	243	351

#Clinched playoff berth

WEEK 14 RESULTS

Thursday, December 9
Indianapolis 30, TENNESSEE 28

Sunday, December 12
BUFFALO 13, Cleveland 6
Atlanta 31, CAROLINA 10
DETROIT 7, Green Bay 3
JACKSONVILLE 38, Oakland 31
PITTSBURGH 23, Cincinnati 7
Tampa Bay 17, WASHINGTON 16
NEW ORLEANS 31, St. Louis 13
SAN FRANCISCO 40, Seattle 21
ARIZONA 43, Denver 13
New England 36, CHICAGO 7
Miami 10, NEW YORK JETS 6
SAN DIEGO 31, Kansas City 0
Philadelphia 30, DALLAS 27

Monday, December 13
New York Giants 21, MINNESOTA 3 (Detroit)
Baltimore 34, HOUSTON 28 (OT)

FIFTEENTH WEEK STANDINGS

American Football Conference

East Division	W	L	T	Pct.	Pts.	OP
New England#	12	2	0	.857	446	303
New York Jets	10	4	0	.714	295	259
Miami	7	7	0	.500	239	261
Buffalo	4	10	0	.286	273	353
North Division	**W**	**L**	**T**	**Pct.**	**Pts.**	**OP**
Pittsburgh#	10	4	0	.714	307	220
Baltimore	10	4	0	.714	324	253
Cleveland	5	9	0	.357	252	271
Cincinnati	3	11	0	.214	281	362
South Division	**W**	**L**	**T**	**Pct.**	**Pts.**	**OP**
Indianapolis	8	6	0	.571	381	342
Jacksonville	8	6	0	.571	319	365
Tennessee	6	8	0	.429	322	282
Houston	5	9	0	.357	333	386
West Division	**W**	**L**	**T**	**Pct.**	**Pts.**	**OP**
Kansas City	9	5	0	.643	322	281
San Diego	8	6	0	.571	388	260
Oakland	7	7	0	.500	353	330
Denver	3	11	0	.214	292	415

National Football Conference

East Division	W	L	T	Pct.	Pts.	OP
Philadelphia	10	4	0	.714	412	339
New York Giants	9	5	0	.643	360	288
Dallas	5	9	0	.357	354	396
Washington	5	9	0	.357	268	343
North Division	**W**	**L**	**T**	**Pct.**	**Pts.**	**OP**
Chicago*	10	4	0	.714	293	242
Green Bay	8	6	0	.571	333	220
Minnesota	5	9	0	.357	244	314
Detroit	4	10	0	.286	308	329
South Division	**W**	**L**	**T**	**Pct.**	**Pts.**	**OP**
Atlanta#	12	2	0	.857	369	261
New Orleans	10	4	0	.714	354	270
Tampa Bay	8	6	0	.571	280	290
Carolina	2	12	0	.143	183	350
West Division	**W**	**L**	**T**	**Pct.**	**Pts.**	**OP**
St. Louis	6	8	0	.429	258	295
Seattle	6	8	0	.429	279	363
San Francisco	5	9	0	.357	250	314
Arizona	4	10	0	.286	255	370

*Clinched division title
#Clinched playoff berth

WEEK 15 RESULTS

Thursday, December 16
SAN DIEGO 34, San Francisco 7

Sunday, December 19
BALTIMORE 30, New Orleans 24
CAROLINA 19, Arizona 12
CINCINNATI 19, Cleveland 17
DALLAS 33, Washington 30
INDIANAPOLIS 34, Jacksonville 24
Buffalo 17, MIAMI 14
Philadelphia 38, NEW YORK GIANTS 31
Kansas City 27, ST. LOUIS 13
Detroit 23, TAMPA BAY 20 (OT)
TENNESSEE 31, Houston 17
Atlanta 34, SEATTLE 18
OAKLAND 39, Denver 23
New York Jets 22, PITTSBURGH 17
NEW ENGLAND 31, Green Bay 27

Monday, December 20
Chicago 40, MINNESOTA 14 (TCF Bank Stadium)

SIXTEENTH WEEK STANDINGS
American Football Conference

East Division	W	L	T	Pct.	Pts.	OP
New England*	13	2	0	.867	480	306
New York Jets#	10	5	0	.667	329	297
Miami	7	8	0	.467	266	295
Buffalo	4	11	0	.267	276	387
North Division	**W**	**L**	**T**	**Pct.**	**Pts.**	**OP**
Pittsburgh#	11	4	0	.733	334	223
Baltimore#	11	4	0	.733	344	263
Cleveland	5	10	0	.333	262	291
Cincinnati	4	11	0	.267	315	382
South Division	**W**	**L**	**T**	**Pct.**	**Pts.**	**OP**
Indianapolis	9	6	0	.600	412	368
Jacksonville	8	7	0	.533	336	385
Tennessee	6	9	0	.400	336	316
Houston	5	10	0	.333	356	410
West Division	**W**	**L**	**T**	**Pct.**	**Pts.**	**OP**
Kansas City*	10	5	0	.667	356	295
San Diego	8	7	0	.533	408	294
Oakland	7	8	0	.467	379	361
Denver	4	11	0	.267	316	438

National Football Conference

East Division	W	L	T	Pct.	Pts.	OP
Philadelphia*	10	5	0	.667	426	363
New York Giants	9	6	0	.600	377	333
Washington	6	9	0	.400	288	360
Dallas	5	10	0	.333	380	423
North Division	**W**	**L**	**T**	**Pct.**	**Pts.**	**OP**
Chicago*	11	4	0	.733	331	276
Green Bay	9	6	0	.600	378	237
Minnesota	6	9	0	.400	268	328
Detroit	5	10	0	.333	342	356
South Division	**W**	**L**	**T**	**Pct.**	**Pts.**	**OP**
Atlanta*	12	3	0	.800	383	278
New Orleans#	11	4	0	.733	371	284
Tampa Bay	9	6	0	.600	318	305
Carolina	2	13	0	.133	186	377
West Division	**W**	**L**	**T**	**Pct.**	**Pts.**	**OP**
St. Louis	7	8	0	.467	283	312
Seattle	6	9	0	.400	294	401
Arizona	5	10	0	.333	282	396
San Francisco	5	10	0	.333	267	339

*Clinched division title
#Clinched playoff berth

WEEK 16 RESULTS
Thursday, December 23
PITTSBURGH 27, Carolina 3

Saturday, December 25
ARIZONA 27, Dallas 26

Sunday, December 26
New England 34, BUFFALO 3
CHICAGO 38, New York Jets 34
Baltimore 20, CLEVELAND 10
Washington 20, JACKSONVILLE 17 (OT)
KANSAS CITY 34, Tennessee 14
Detroit 34, MIAMI 27
ST. LOUIS 25, San Francisco 17
CINCINNATI 34, San Diego 20
GREEN BAY 45, New York Giants 17
Indianapolis 31, OAKLAND 26
DENVER 24, Houston 23
TAMPA BAY 38, Seattle 15

Monday, December 27
New Orleans 17, ATLANTA 14

Tuesday, December 28
Minnesota 24, PHILADELPHIA 14

SEVENTEENTH WEEK STANDINGS
American Football Conference

East Division	W	L	T	Pct.	Pts.	OP
New England*	14	2	0	.875	518	313
New York Jets#	11	5	0	.688	367	304
Miami	7	9	0	.438	273	333
Buffalo	4	12	0	.250	283	425
North Division	**W**	**L**	**T**	**Pct.**	**Pts.**	**OP**
Pittsburgh*	12	4	0	.750	375	232
Baltimore#	12	4	0	.750	357	270
Cleveland	5	11	0	.313	271	332
Cincinnati	4	12	0	.250	322	395
South Division	**W**	**L**	**T**	**Pct.**	**Pts.**	**OP**
Indianapolis*	10	6	0	.625	435	388
Jacksonville	8	8	0	.500	353	419
Houston	6	10	0	.375	390	427
Tennessee	6	10	0	.375	356	339
West Division	**W**	**L**	**T**	**Pct.**	**Pts.**	**OP**
Kansas City*	10	6	0	.625	366	326
San Diego	9	7	0	.563	441	322
Oakland	8	8	0	.500	410	371
Denver	4	12	0	.250	344	471

National Football Conference

East Division	W	L	T	Pct.	Pts.	OP
Philadelphia*	10	6	0	.625	439	377
New York Giants	10	6	0	.625	394	347
Dallas	6	10	0	.375	394	436
Washington	6	10	0	.375	302	377
North Division	**W**	**L**	**T**	**Pct.**	**Pts.**	**OP**
Chicago*	11	5	0	.688	334	286
Green Bay#	10	6	0	.625	388	240
Detroit	6	10	0	.375	362	369
Minnesota	6	10	0	.375	281	348
South Division	**W**	**L**	**T**	**Pct.**	**Pts.**	**OP**
Atlanta*	13	3	0	.813	414	288
New Orleans#	11	5	0	.688	384	307
Tampa Bay	10	6	0	.625	341	318
Carolina	2	14	0	.125	196	408
West Division	**W**	**L**	**T**	**Pct.**	**Pts.**	**OP**
Seattle*	7	9	0	.438	310	407
St. Louis	7	9	0	.438	289	328
San Francisco	6	10	0	.375	305	346
Arizona	5	11	0	.313	289	434

*Clinched division title
#Clinched wild-card berth

WEEK 17 RESULTS
Sunday, January 2, 2011
ATLANTA 31, Carolina 10
BALTIMORE 13, Cincinnati 7
Pittsburgh 41, CLEVELAND 9
DETROIT 20, Minnesota 13
Oakland 31, KANSAS CITY 10
NEW ENGLAND 38, Miami 7
Tampa Bay 23, NEW ORLEANS 13
NEW YORK JETS 38, Buffalo 7
San Diego 33, DENVER 28
GREEN BAY 10, Chicago 3
HOUSTON 34, Jacksonville 17
INDIANAPOLIS 23, Tennessee 20
Dallas 14, PHILADELPHIA 13
SAN FRANCISCO 38, Arizona 7
New York Giants 17, WASHINGTON 14
SEATTLE 16, St. Louis 6

2010 NFL PAID ATTENDANCE BREAKDOWN

Games	Attendance	Average
NFL Preseason Total		
65	3,737,171	57,495
NFL Regular-Season Total		
255 *	16,569,514	64,978
NFL Postseason Total		
12	800,426	66,702
NFL All Games		
332	21,107,111	63,576

*The Week 14 N.Y. Giants at Minnesota game is not included. The game was moved to Detroit due to the Minneapolis blizzard. Original game tickets were cross-honored at Ford Field. Remaining tickets were distributed at no charge.

1.1-MILLION CLUB

During the 2010 season, six teams drew more than 1.1 million paid attendance home and away during the regular season. The Washington Redskins led the NFL in regular-season paid attendance (1,187,919). The Redskins also led the league in home paid attendance (680,966) for the 11th consecutive year.

Team	Total Paid Home Attendance	Total Paid Visiting Attendance	Total Paid Cumulative Attendance
Washington	680,966	506,953	1,187,919
Dallas	614,256	568,091	1,182,347
New York Giants	628,816	501,845	1,130,661
New York Jets	581,348	531,391	1,112,739
Green Bay	566,362	539,294	1,105,656
Denver	588,328	516,409	1,104,737

For complete year-by-year attendance records, see pages 529-530.

2010 AFC PLAYERS OF THE WEEK

	Offense		Defense		Special Teams	
Week 1	RB	Arian Foster, Houston	LB	Daryl Smith, Jacksonville	PR-WR	Dexter McCluster, Kansas City
Week 2	WR	Andre Johnson, Houston	LB	James Harrison, Pittsburgh	K	Mike Nugent, Cincinnati
Week 3	WR	Anquan Boldin, Baltimore	LB	Tamba Hali, Kansas City	KR-RB	C.J. Spiller, Buffalo
Week 4	RB	LaDainian Tomlinson, N.Y. Jets	LB	Shaun Phillips, San Diego	K	Josh Scobee, Jacksonville
Week 5	RB	Chris Johnson, Tennessee	S	Michael Huff, Oakland	K	Nick Folk, N.Y. Jets
Week 6	QB	Matt Schaub, Houston	LB	Lawrence Timmons, Pittsburgh	K	Dan Carpenter, Miami
Week 7	RB	Darren McFadden, Oakland	LB	David Bowens, Cleveland	KR-WR	Emmanuel Sanders, Pittsburgh
Week 8	QB	David Garrard, Jacksonville	DE	Dwight Freeney, Indianapolis	K	Dan Carpenter, Miami
Week 9	RB	Peyton Hillis, Cleveland	DT	Haloti Ngata, Baltimore	KR-WR	Jacoby Ford, Oakland
Week 10	QB	Kyle Orton, Denver	S	James Sanders, New England	K	Adam Vinatieri, Indianapolis
Week 11	QB	Mark Sanchez, N.Y. Jets	CB	Drayton Florence, Buffalo	KR-PR	Marc Mariani, Tennessee
Week 12	QB	Tom Brady, New England	CB	Glover Quin, Houston	KR-WR	Brad Smith, N.Y. Jets
Week 13	QB	Tom Brady, New England	S	Troy Polamalu, Pittsburgh	P	Reggie Hodges, Cleveland
Week 14	QB	Peyton Manning, Indianapolis	S	Troy Polamalu, Pittsburgh	KR	David Reed, Baltimore
Week 15	RB	Ray Rice, Baltimore	LB	Derrick Johnson, Kansas City	G	Dan Connolly, New England
Week 16	WR	Dwayne Bowe, Kansas City	S	Ed Reed, Baltimore	KR-WR	Jacoby Ford, Oakland
Week 17	QB	Ben Roethlisberger, Pittsburgh	LB	Kamerion Wimbley, Oakland	K	Adam Vinatieri, Indianapolis

2010 AFC PLAYERS OF THE MONTH

	Offense		Defense		Special Teams	
September	RB	Arian Foster, Houston	DE	Robert Mathis, Indianapolis	K	Mike Nugent, Cincinnati
October	QB	Philip Rivers, San Diego	S	Michael Griffin, Tennessee	K	Dan Carpenter, Miami
November	QB	Matt Cassel, Kansas City	LB	Terrell Suggs, Baltimore	KR	Jacoby Ford, Oakland
December	QB	Tom Brady, New England	S	Ed Reed, Baltimore	KR	Brad Smith, N.Y. Jets

2010 NFC PLAYERS OF THE WEEK

	Offense		Defense		Special Teams	
Week 1	RB	Matt Forté, Chicago	S	Adrian Wilson, Arizona	K	Mason Crosby, Green Bay
Week 2	RB	Jason Snelling, Atlanta	LB	Clay Matthews, Green Bay	K	Garrett Hartley, New Orleans
Week 3	RB	Adrian Peterson, Minnesota	LB	DeMarcus Ware, Dallas	KR-RB	Leon Washington, Seattle
Week 4	RB	Ahmad Bradshaw, N.Y. Giants	CB	Charles Woodson, Green Bay	K	Matt Bryant, Atlanta
Week 5	QB	Josh Freeman, Tampa Bay	S	LaRon Landry, Washington	KR-PR	Stefan Logan, Detroit
Week 6	QB	Kevin Kolb, Philadelphia	DE	Chris Long, St. Louis	KR-WR	Percy Harvin, Minnesota
Week 7	WR	Roddy White, Atlanta	CB	DeAngelo Hall, Washington	K	Olindo Mare, Seattle
Week 8	WR	Calvin Johnson, Detroit	CB	Aqib Talib, Tampa Bay	P	Tim Masthay, Green Bay
Week 9	QB	Michael Vick, Philadelphia	LB	Clay Matthews, Green Bay	P	Chris Kluwe, Minnesota
Week 10	QB	Michael Vick, Philadelphia	CB	Bryan McCann, Dallas	PR-KR-WR	Devin Hester, Chicago
Week 11	WR	Greg Jennings, Green Bay	DE	Julius Peppers, Chicago	PR-CB	Bryan McCann, Dallas
Week 12	QB	Jay Cutler, Chicago	S	Malcolm Jenkins, New Orleans	K	Matt Bryant, Atlanta
Week 13	QB	Aaron Rodgers, Green Bay	LB	Sean Lee, Dallas	KR-PR	Eric Weems, Atlanta
Week 14	WR	DeSean Jackson, Philadelphia	S	Malcolm Jenkins, New Orleans	K	Jay Feely, Arizona
Week 15	QB	Michael Vick, Philadelphia	CB	Brent Grimes, Atlanta	PR-KR-WR	Devin Hester, Chicago
Week 16	QB	Aaron Rodgers, Green Bay	CB	Antoine Winfield, Minnesota	K	Graham Gano, Washington
Week 17	QB	Josh Freeman, Tampa Bay	LB	Erik Walden, Green Bay	P	Jon Ryan, Seattle

2010 NFC PLAYERS OF THE MONTH

	Offense		Defense		Special Teams	
September	QB	Michael Vick, Philadelphia	LB	Clay Matthews, Green Bay	KR-ST	Courtney Roby, New Orleans
October	WR	Roddy White, Atlanta	DE	Osi Umenyiora, N.Y. Giants	KR-PR-ST	Stefan Logan, Detroit
November	QB	Matt Ryan, Atlanta	DE	Julius Peppers, Chicago	K	David Akers, Philadelphia
December	QB	Aaron Rodgers, Green Bay	LB	Brian Urlacher, Chicago	KR-PR-ST	Eric Weems, Atlanta

2010 NFL ROOKIES OF THE MONTH

	Offense (College)		Defense (College)	
September	RB	Jahvid Best, Detroit (California)	S	Nate Allen, Philadelphia (South Florida)
October	QB	Sam Bradford, St. Louis (Oklahoma)	DT	Ndamukong Suh, Detroit (Nebraska)
November	QB	Sam Bradford, St. Louis (Oklahoma)	CB	Joe Haden, Cleveland (Florida)
December	RB	LeGarrette Blount, Tampa Bay (Oregon)	S	Eric Berry, Kansas City (Tennessee)

2010 PRO FOOTBALL AWARDS

ASSOCIATED PRESS
Most Valuable Player	Tom Brady
Offensive Player of the Year	Tom Brady
Defensive Player of the Year	Troy Polamalu
Offensive Rookie of the Year	Sam Bradford
Defensive Rookie of the Year	Ndamukong Suh
Coach of the Year	Bill Belichick
Comeback Player of the Year	Michael Vick

THE SPORTING NEWS
Offensive Player of the Year	Tom Brady
Defensive Player of the Year	Clay Matthews
Rookie of the Year	Ndamukong Suh
Coach of the Year	Mike Smith

PRO FOOTBALL WEEKLY/PFWA
Executive of the Year	Scott Pioli
Most Valuable Player	Tom Brady
Defensive Player of the Year	Clay Matthews
Offensive Rookie of the Year	Sam Bradford
Defensive Rookie of the Year	Ndamukong Suh
Coach of the Year	Bill Belichick
Assistant Coach of the Year	Marty Mornhinweg
Golden Toe	Billy Cundiff
Comeback Player of the Year	Michael Vick
Most Improved	Arian Foster

SPORTS ILLUSTRATED
Most Valuable Player	Tom Brady
Offensive Rookie of the Year	Sam Bradford
Defensive Rookie of the Year	Ndamukong Suh
Coach of the Year	Bill Belichick

MAXWELL CLUB PLAYER OF THE YEAR
Bert Bell Trophy	Michael Vick

MAXWELL CLUB COACH OF THE YEAR
Earle "Greasy" Neale Trophy	Andy Reid

DIET PEPSI ROOKIE OF THE YEAR
Rookie of the Year	Ndamukong Suh

FEDEX AIR & GROUND NFL PLAYERS OF THE YEAR
FedEx Air NFL Player of the Year	Aaron Rodgers
FedEx Ground NFL Player of the Year	Jamaal Charles

GMC NEVER SAY NEVER MOMENT OF THE YEAR
Moment of the Year Award	DeSean Jackson

MADDEN MOST VALUABLE PROTECTORS AWARD
PRESENTED BY PRILOSEC OTC
New England Patriots Offensive Line

WALTER PAYTON/ NFL MAN OF THE YEAR
Man of the Year	Madieu Williams
Man of the Year Finalist	Nnamdi Asomugha
Man of the Year Finalist	Israel Idonije

SUPER BOWL XLV MOST VALUABLE PLAYER
Pete Rozelle Trophy	Aaron Rodgers

AFC-NFC 2011 PRO BOWL MOST VALUABLE PLAYER
Pro Bowl MVP	DeAngelo Hall

2010 ALL-PRO TEAMS

2010 PFW/PFWA ALL-PRO TEAM
Selected by *Pro Football Weekly* and the Professional Football Writers of America

Offense:
Tom Brady, New England	Quarterback
Arian Foster, Houston	Running Back
Jamaal Charles, Kansas City	Running Back
Jason Witten, Dallas	Tight End
Roddy White, Atlanta	Wide Receiver
Reggie Wayne, Indianapolis	Wide Receiver
Joe Thomas, Cleveland	Tackle
Jake Long, Miami	Tackle
Jahri Evans, New Orleans	Guard
Chris Snee, N.Y. Giants	Guard
Nick Mangold, N.Y. Jets	Center

Defense:
Julius Peppers, Chicago	End
Justin Tuck, N.Y. Giants	End
Haloti Ngata, Baltimore	Tackle
Ndamukong Suh, Detroit	Tackle
Clay Matthews, Green Bay	Outside Linebacker
James Harrison, Pittsburgh	Outside Linebacker
Jerod Mayo, New England	Middle Linebacker
Asante Samuel, Philadelphia	Cornerback
Darrelle Revis, N.Y. Jets	Cornerback
Troy Polamalu, Pittsburgh	Safety
Ed Reed, Baltimore	Safety

Special Teams:
Billy Cundiff, Baltimore	Kicker
Shane Lechler, Oakland	Punter
Leon Washington, Seattle	Kick Returner
Devin Hester, Chicago	Punt Returner
Eric Weems, Atlanta	Special Teams Player

2010 ASSOCIATED PRESS ALL-PRO TEAM
Selected by the Associated Press

Offense:
Tom Brady, New England	Quarterback
Arian Foster, Houston	Running Back
Jamaal Charles, Kansas City	Running Back
Vonta Leach, Houston	Fullback
Jason Witten, Dallas	Tight End
Roddy White, Atlanta	Wide Receiver
Reggie Wayne, Indianapolis	Wide Receiver
Joe Thomas, Cleveland	Tackle
Jake Long, Miami	Tackle
Jahri Evans, New Orleans	Guard
Logan Mankins, New England	Guard
Nick Mangold, N.Y. Jets	Center

Defense:
Julius Peppers, Chicago	End
John Abraham, Atlanta	End
Haloti Ngata, Baltimore	Tackle
Ndamukong Suh, Detroit	Tackle
Clay Matthews, Green Bay	Outside Linebacker
James Harrison, Pittsburgh	Outside Linebacker
Patrick Willis, San Francisco	Inside Linebacker
Jerod Mayo, New England	Inside Linebacker
Nnamdi Asomugha, Oakland	Cornerback
Darrelle Revis, N.Y. Jets	Cornerback
Troy Polamalu, Pittsburgh	Safety
Ed Reed, Baltimore	Safety

Special Teams:
Billy Cundiff, Baltimore	Kicker
Shane Lechler, Oakland	Punter
Devin Hester, Chicago	Kick Returner

2010 ALL-NFL TEAM

Selected by the Associated Press, *Pro Football Weekly*, and the Professional Football Writers of America

Offense:

Tom Brady, New England (PFW, AP)	Quarterback
Arian Foster, Houston (PFW, AP)	Running Back
Jamaal Charles, Kansas City (PFW, AP)	Running Back
Vonta Leach, Houston (AP)	Fullback
Jason Witten, Dallas (PFW, AP)	Tight End
Roddy White, Atlanta (PFW, AP)	Wide Receiver
Reggie Wayne, Indianapolis (PFW, AP)	Wide Receiver
Joe Thomas, Cleveland (PFW, AP)	Tackle
Jake Long, Miami (PFW, AP)	Tackle
Jahri Evans, New Orleans (PFW, AP)	Guard
Chris Snee, N.Y. Giants (PFW)	Guard
Logan Mankins, New England (AP)	Guard
Nick Mangold, N.Y. Jets (PFW, AP)	Center

Defense:

Julius Peppers, Chicago (PFW, AP)	End
Justin Tuck, N.Y. Giants (PFW)	End
John Abraham, Atlanta (AP)	End
Haloti Ngata, Baltimore (PFW, AP)	Tackle
Ndamukong Suh, Detroit (PFW, AP)	Tackle
Clay Matthews, Green Bay (PFW, AP)	Outside Linebacker
James Harrison, Pittsburgh (PFW, AP)	Outside Linebacker
Jerod Mayo, New England (PFW, AP)	Middle Linebacker
Patrick Willis, San Francisco (AP)	Inside Linebacker
Asante Samuel, Philadelphia (PFW)	Cornerback
Nnamdi Asomugha, Oakland (AP)	Cornerback
Darrelle Revis, N.Y. Jets (PFW, AP)	Cornerback
Troy Polamalu, Pittsburgh (PFW, AP)	Safety
Ed Reed, Baltimore (PFW, AP)	Safety

Special Teams:

Billy Cundiff, Baltimore (PFW, AP)	Kicker
Shane Lechler, Oakland (PFW, AP)	Punter
Leon Washington, Seattle (PFW)	Kick Returner
Devin Hester, Chicago (PFW, AP)	Punt Returner
Eric Weems, Atlanta (PFW)	Special Teams Player

2010 PFW/PFWA ALL-ROOKIE TEAM

Selected by *Pro Football Weekly* and the Professional Football Writers of America

Offense:

Sam Bradford, St. Louis	Quarterback
LeGarrette Blount, Tampa Bay	Running Back
Chris Ivory, New Orleans	Running Back
Rob Gronkowski, New England	Tight End
Mike Williams, Tampa Bay	Wide Receiver
Dez Bryant, Dallas	Wide Receiver
Rodger Saffold, St. Louis	Tackle
Bryan Bulaga, Green Bay	Tackle
Mike Iupati, San Francisco	Guard
John Jerry, Miami	Guard
Maurkice Pouncey, Pittsburgh	Center

Defense:

Ndamukong Suh, Detroit	Defensive Lineman
Carlos Dunlap, Cincinnati	Defensive Lineman
Lamarr Houston, Oakland	Defensive Lineman
Tyson Alualu, Jacksonville	Defensive Lineman
Rolando McClain, Oakland	Outside Linebacker
Koa Misi, Miami	Outside Linebacker
Pat Angerer, Indianapolis	Middle Linebacker
Devin McCourty, New England	Cornerback
Joe Haden, Cleveland	Cornerback
Eric Berry, Kansas City	Safety
T.J. Ward, Cleveland	Safety

Special Teams:

Clint Stitser, Cincinnati	Kicker
Zoltan Mesko, New England	Punter
Marc Mariani, Tennessee	Punt Returner
Jacoby Ford, Oakland	Kick Returner
I.J. Brown, Cleveland	Special Teams Player

2010 BEST PERFORMANCES

TEN BEST RUSHING PERFORMANCES, 2010

	Att.	Yards	TD
1. Arian Foster Houston vs. Indianapolis, Sept. 12	33	231	3
2. Maurice Jones-Drew Jacksonville vs. Tennessee, Dec. 5	31	186	0
3. Peyton Hillis Cleveland vs. New England, Nov. 7	29	184	2
4. Arian Foster Houston vs. Jacksonville, Jan. 2	31	180	2
5. Jamaal Charles Kansas City vs. Buffalo, Oct. 31	22	177	0
6. Jamaal Charles Kansas City vs. Seattle, Nov. 28	22	173	1
7. Ryan Torain Washington vs. Tampa Bay, Dec. 12	24	172	0
8. Matt Forté Chicago vs. Carolina, Oct. 10	22	166	2
9. Darren McFadden Oakland vs. Denver, Oct. 24	16	165	3
10. LeGarrette Blount Tampa Bay vs. Seattle, Dec. 26	18	164	0

There were 124 100-yard rushing performances in 2010.

MOST 100-YARD RUSHING PERFORMANCES, 2010

Player, Team	100-Yd. Games
Arian Foster, Houston	8
Chris Johnson, Tennessee	8
Maurice Jones-Drew, Jacksonville	7
Michael Turner, Atlanta	7
Darren McFadden, Oakland	6
Peyton Hillis, Cleveland	5
Adrian Peterson, Minnesota	5
LeGarrette Blount, Tampa Bay	4
Ahmad Bradshaw, New York Giants	4
Jamaal Charles, Kansas City	4
Frank Gore, San Francisco	4
Steven Jackson, St. Louis	4
Cedric Benson, Cincinnati	3
Matt Forté, Chicago	3
Fred Jackson, Buffalo	3
LeSean McCoy, Philadelphia	3
Rashard Mendenhall, Pittsburgh	3
Mike Tolbert, San Diego	3
Ryan Torain, Washington	3
Michael Bush, Oakland	2
Mike Goodson, Carolina	2
BenJarvus Green-Ellis, New England	2
Tim Hightower, Arizona	2
Chris Ivory, New Orleans	2
Brandon Jacobs, New York Giants	2
Rashad Jennings, Jacksonville	2
Thomas Jones, Kansas City	2
Knowshon Moreno, Denver	2
Ray Rice, Baltimore	2
Jonathan Stewart, Carolina	2
Michael Vick, Philadelphia	2
13 players tied with	1

100-YARD RUSHING, 2010 POSTSEASON

Wild Card
Marshawn Lynch, Seattle — 131 yards vs. New Orleans
James Starks, Green Bay — 123 yards vs. Philadelphia
Divisional
None
Championship
Rashard Mendenhall, Pittsburgh — 121 yards vs. New York Jets
Super Bowl XLV
None

TEN BEST PASSING PERFORMANCES, 2010

	Att.	Comp.	Yds.	TD
1. Matt Schaub Houston vs. Washington, Sept. 19	38	52	497	3
2. Kyle Orton Denver vs. Indianapolis, Sept. 26	37	57	476	1
3. Matt Cassel Kansas City vs. Denver, Nov. 14	33	53	469	4
4. Philip Rivers San Diego vs. Seattle, Sept. 26	29	53	455	2
5. Brett Favre Minnesota vs. Arizona, Nov. 7	36	47	446	2
6. Peyton Manning Indianapolis vs. Houston, Sept. 12	40	57	433	3
7. Philip Rivers San Diego vs. Oakland, Oct. 10	27	42	431	2
8. Donovan McNabb Washington vs. Houston, Sept. 19	28	38	426	1
9. Carson Palmer Cincinnati vs. Atlanta, Oct. 24	36	50	412	3
10. Tony Romo Dallas vs. Tennessee, Oct. 10	31	46	406	3

There were 96 300-yard passing performances in 2010.

MOST 300-YARD PASSING PERFORMANCES, 2010

Player, Team	300-Yd. Games
Drew Brees, New Orleans	7
Peyton Manning, Indianapolis	7
Matt Schaub, Houston	7
Kyle Orton, Denver	6
Philip Rivers, San Diego	6
Aaron Rodgers, Green Bay	5
Tom Brady, New England	4
Jon Kitna, Dallas	4
Eli Manning, New York Giants	4
Carson Palmer, Cincinnati	4
Chad Henne, Miami	3
Shaun Hill, Detroit	3
Donovan McNabb, Washington	3
Ben Roethlisberger, Pittsburgh	3
Michael Vick, Philadelphia	3
Jason Campbell, Oakland	2
Matt Cassel, Kansas City	2
Ryan Fitzpatrick, Buffalo	2
Rex Grossman, Washington	2
Matt Hasselbeck, Seattle	2
Tony Romo, Dallas	2
Mark Sanchez, New York Jets	2
13 players tied with	1

300-YARD PASSING, 2010 POSTSEASON

Wild Card
Drew Brees, New Orleans — 404 yards vs. Seattle
Divisional
Aaron Rodgers, Green Bay — 366 yards vs. Atlanta
Championship
None
Super Bowl XLV
Aaron Rodgers, Green Bay — 304 yards vs. Pittsburgh

TEN BEST RECEIVING PERFORMANCES, 2010

	No.	Yards	TD
1. Kenny Britt	7	225	3
Tennessee vs. Philadelphia, Oct. 24			
2. Terrell Owens	10	222	1
Cincinnati vs. Cleveland, Oct. 3			
3. Malcom Floyd	8	213	1
San Diego vs. Oakland, Oct. 10			
4. DeSean Jackson	4	210	1
Philadelphia vs. Dallas, Dec. 12			
5. Roddy White	11	201	2
Atlanta vs. Cincinnati, Oct. 24			
6. Reggie Wayne	14	200	1
Indianapolis vs. Dallas, Dec. 5			
7. Reggie Wayne	15	196	0
Indianapolis vs. Jacksonville, Oct. 3			
8. Dwayne Bowe	13	186	2
Kansas City vs. Denver, Nov. 14			
9. Austin Collie	12	171	2
Indianapolis vs. Denver, Sept. 26			
10. Dwayne Bowe	13	170	3
Kansas City vs. Seattle, Nov. 28			

There were 181 100-yard receiving performances in 2010.

MOST 100-YARD RECEIVING PERFORMANCES, 2010

Player, Team	100-Yd. Games
Mike Wallace, Pittsburgh	7
Andre Johnson, Houston	6
Brandon Lloyd, Denver	6
Miles Austin, Dallas	5
Dwayne Bowe, Kansas City	5
Greg Jennings, Green Bay	5
Roddy White, Atlanta	5
DeSean Jackson, Philadelphia	4
Calvin Johnson, Detroit	4
Brandon Marshall, Miami	4
Hakeem Nicks, New York Giants	4
Hines Ward, Pittsburgh	4
Reggie Wayne, Indianapolis	4
Marques Colston, New Orleans	3
Larry Fitzgerald, Arizona	3
Antonio Gates, San Diego	3
Percy Harvin, Minnesota	3
Steve Johnson, Buffalo	3
Mario Manningham, New York Giants	3
Santana Moss, Washington	3
Terrell Owens, Cincinnati	3
Mike Williams, Seattle	3
Anquan Boldin, Baltimore	2
Deion Branch, New England	2
Steve Breaston, Arizona	2
Kenny Britt, Tennessee	2
Austin Collie, Indianapolis	2
Michael Crabtree, San Francisco	2
Patrick Crayton, San Diego	2
Vernon Davis, San Francisco	2
Jermichael Finley, Green Bay	2
Jacoby Ford, Oakland	2
Santonio Holmes, New York Jets	2
James Jones, Green Bay	2
Jeremy Maclin, Philadelphia	2
Robert Meachem, New Orleans	2
Chad Ochocinco, Cincinnati	2
Jerome Simpson, Cincinnati	2
Mike Sims-Walker, Jacksonville	2
Steve Smith, New York Giants	2
Nate Washington, Tennessee	2
53 players tied with	1

100-YARD RECEIVING, 2010 POSTSEASON

Wild Card
Pierre Garcon, Indianapolis	112 yards vs. New York Jets
Todd Heap, Baltimore	108 yards vs. Kansas City

Divisional
Greg Olsen, Chicago	113 yards vs. Seattle
Greg Jennings, Green Bay	101 yards vs. Atlanta

Championship
Greg Jennings, Green Bay	130 yards vs. Chicago

Super Bowl XLV
Jordy Nelson, Green Bay	140 yards vs. Pittsburgh

TOP QUARTERBACK SACK PERFORMANCES, 2010

	No.
1. Shaun Phillips	4.0
San Diego vs. Arizona, Oct. 3	
2. Clay Matthews	3.0
Green Bay vs. Philadelphia, Sept. 12; vs. Buffalo, Sept. 19	
Mario Williams	3.0
Houston vs. Washington, Sept. 19	
DeMarcus Ware	3.0
Dallas vs. Houston, Sept. 19; vs. Philadelphia, Jan. 2	
Tamba Hali	3.0
Kansas City vs. San Francisco, Sept. 26	
Justin Tuck	3.0
N.Y. Giants vs. Chicago, Oct. 3; vs. Philadelphia, Nov. 21	
Osi Umenyiora,	3.0
N.Y. Giants vs. Chicago, Oct. 3	
Cameron Wake	3.0
Miami vs. Green Bay, Oct. 17	
Mario Haggan	3.0
Denver vs. Kansas City, Nov. 14	
Julius Peppers	3.0
Chicago vs. Miami, Nov. 18	
Cliff Avril	3.0
Detroit vs. Chicago, Dec. 5	
Wallace Gilberry	3.0
Kansas City vs. St. Louis, Dec. 19	
Kamerion Wimbley	3.0
Oakland vs. Kansas City, Jan. 2	
Erik Walden	3.0
Green Bay vs. Chicago, Jan. 2	
Justin Smith	3.0
San Francisco vs. Arizona, Jan. 2	

There were 18 3.0-plus sack performances in 2010.

MOST 3.0-PLUS SACK PERFORMANCES, 2010

Player, Team	3.0-Sack Games
Clay Matthews, Green Bay	2
Justin Tuck, New York Giants	2
DeMarcus Ware, Dallas	2
12 players tied with	1

3.0 SACK PERFORMANCES, 2010 POSTSEASON

Wild Card
None

Divisional
James Harrison, Pittsburgh	3.0 vs. Baltimore
Terrell Suggs, Baltimore	3.0 vs. Pittsburgh

Championship
None

Super Bowl XLV
None

For week-by-week listings of top performances from 1970 to the present, please visit www.NFL.com/stats/topperformers.

AMERICAN FOOTBALL CONFERENCE OFFENSE

	Balt.	Buff.	Cin.	Cle.	Den.	Hou.	Ind.	Jax.	KC	Mia.	NE	NYJ	Oak.	Pitt.	SD	Tenn.
First Downs	303	263	317	265	309	360	366	330	319	300	335	307	306	295	357	252
Rushing	97	82	85	87	81	118	87	148	129	91	119	118	113	106	94	73
Passing	175	166	206	154	204	222	253	161	167	189	196	171	159	175	236	155
Penalty	31	15	26	24	24	20	26	21	23	20	20	18	34	14	27	24
Rushes	487	401	428	413	398	423	393	512	556	445	454	534	504	471	457	406
Net Yds. Gained	1831	1720	1522	1646	1544	2042	1483	2395	2627	1643	1973	2374	2494	1924	1810	1727
Avg. Gain	3.8	4.3	3.6	4.0	3.9	4.8	3.8	4.7	4.7	3.7	4.3	4.4	4.9	4.1	4.0	4.3
Avg. Yds. per Game	114.4	107.5	95.1	102.9	96.5	127.6	92.7	149.7	164.2	102.7	123.3	148.4	155.9	120.3	113.1	107.9
Passes Attempted	491	519	590	478	580	574	679	469	475	557	507	525	491	479	544	474
Completed	308	296	365	296	334	365	450	291	274	335	331	288	279	298	359	273
% Completed	62.7	57.0	61.9	61.9	57.6	63.6	66.3	62.0	57.7	60.1	65.3	54.9	56.8	62.2	66.0	57.6
Total Yds. Gained	3629	3371	3988	3203	4307	4370	4700	3356	3189	3755	4022	3420	3471	3890	4746	3278
Times Sacked	40	34	28	36	40	32	16	38	32	38	25	28	44	43	38	27
Yds. Lost	294	213	221	214	269	226	91	291	221	228	175	178	291	289	227	171
Net Yds. Gained	3335	3158	3767	2989	4038	4144	4609	3065	2968	3527	3847	3242	3180	3601	4519	3107
Avg. Yds. per Game	208.4	197.4	235.4	186.8	252.4	259.0	288.1	191.6	185.5	220.4	240.4	202.6	198.8	225.1	282.4	194.2
Net Yds. per Pass Play	6.28	5.71	6.10	5.82	6.51	6.84	6.63	6.05	5.85	5.93	7.23	5.86	5.94	6.90	7.76	6.20
Yds. Gained per Comp.	11.78	11.39	10.93	10.82	12.90	11.97	10.44	11.53	11.64	11.21	12.15	11.88	12.44	13.05	13.22	12.01
Combined Net Yds. Gained	5166	4878	5289	4635	5582	6186	6092	5460	5595	5170	5820	5616	5674	5525	6329	4834
% Total Yds. Rushing	35.4	35.3	28.8	35.5	27.7	33.0	24.3	43.9	47.0	31.8	33.9	42.3	44.0	34.8	28.6	35.7
% Total Yds. Passing	64.6	64.7	71.2	64.5	72.3	67.0	75.7	56.1	53.0	68.2	66.1	57.7	56.0	65.2	71.4	64.3
Avg. Yds. per Game	322.9	304.9	330.6	289.7	348.9	386.6	380.8	341.3	349.7	323.1	363.8	351.0	354.6	345.3	395.6	302.1
Ball Control Plays	1018	954	1046	927	1018	1029	1088	1019	1063	1040	986	1087	1039	993	1039	907
Avg. Yds. per Play	5.1	5.1	5.1	5.0	5.5	6.0	5.6	5.4	5.3	5.0	5.9	5.2	5.5	5.6	6.1	5.3
Avg. Time of Poss.	30:42	27:40	31:14	27:55	28:09	29:03	29:41	31:43	31:04	30:42	29:00	32:03	31:07	31:53	33:03	25:54
Third Down Efficiency	39.0	37.9	38.8	37.1	32.4	41.1	44.6	39.9	36.7	40.0	48.2	39.6	34.1	43.1	44.9	34.8
Had Intercepted	10	21	20	18	12	12	17	21	8	21	5	14	16	9	13	15
Yds. Opp. Returned	191	330	424	267	255	107	277	263	57	201	12	134	204	122	167	120
Ret. by Opp. for TD	0	2	5	3	1	2	4	1	1	2	0	1	0	1	0	1
Punts	81	75	72	78	86	63	69	57	90	75	58	84	78	74	56	77
Yds. Punted	3530	3181	2992	3424	3835	2650	2909	2496	3941	3369	2505	3581	3651	3276	2430	3302
Avg. Yds. per Punt	43.6	42.4	41.6	43.9	44.6	42.1	42.2	43.8	43.8	44.9	43.2	42.6	46.8	44.3	43.4	42.9
Punt Returns	43	32	36	22	31	35	31	36	52	28	27	56	55	37	40	27
Yds. Returned	319	336	258	235	323	235	214	359	524	293	361	529	386	226	420	329
Avg. Yds. per Return	7.4	10.5	7.2	10.7	10.4	6.7	6.9	10.0	10.1	10.5	13.4	9.4	7.0	6.1	10.5	12.2
Returned for TD	0	0	0	0	0	0	0	1	0	1	1	0	0	0	0	1
Kickoff Returns	55	69	71	70	59	67	67	80	58	56	56	63	68	49	56	64
Yds. Returned	1357	1458	1551	1191	1435	1326	1310	1903	1140	1199	1231	1588	1532	1153	1342	1556
Avg. Yds. per Return	24.7	21.1	21.8	17.0	24.3	19.8	19.6	23.8	19.7	21.4	22.0	25.2	22.5	23.5	24.0	24.3
Returned for TD	1	1	0	0	1	0	1	0	0	0	2	2	3	1	0	1
Fumbles	22	33	21	29	29	15	14	23	15	24	9	23	32	22	25	22
Lost	10	18	14	11	15	6	8	12	6	10	5	7	10	9	16	14
Out of Bounds	3	6	0	0	2	0	2	2	0	1	0	3	2	2	0	1
Own Rec. for TD	0	0	0	0	0	0	0	0	0	0	0	0	0	0	0	0
Opp. Rec. by	8	11	10	9	8	5	11	5	9	8	13	18	12	14	6	8
Opp. Rec. for TD	0	1	1	1	1	0	1	0	0	1	1	0	1	0	0	0
Penalties	90	82	90	78	98	90	79	83	90	72	83	103	148	100	84	128
Yds. Penalized	673	633	725	675	944	690	709	675	771	595	766	934	1276	903	677	1040
Total Points Scored	357	283	322	271	344	390	435	353	366	273	518	367	410	375	441	356
Total TDs	40	34	36	29	40	44	51	41	44	26	65	39	44	41	51	40
TDs Rushing	11	6	8	13	13	20	13	14	13	8	19	14	19	15	18	13
TDs Passing	25	24	26	13	25	24	33	26	27	17	37	20	18	22	30	24
TDs on Ret. and Rec.	4	4	2	3	2	0	5	1	4	1	9	5	7	4	3	3
Extra Point Kicks	39	31	30	28	38	43	51	41	42	25	62	37	43	38	48	38
Extra Point Kicks Att.	39	32	32	28	39	43	51	41	42	25	64	37	43	38	48	38
2Pt Conversions	0	0	2	0	0	1	0	0	0	0	0	1	0	0	2	1
2Pt Conversions Att.	0	2	4	1	1	1	0	0	2	1	1	1	1	2	3	2
Safeties	0	0	0	0	0	0	0	0	1	0	2	2	0	1	2	2
Field Goals Made	26	16	24	23	22	27	26	22	20	30	22	30	33	29	27	24
Field Goals Attempted	29	21	31	28	25	30	28	28	26	41	25	39	41	37	33	26
% Successful	89.7	76.2	77.4	82.1	88.0	90.0	92.9	78.6	76.9	73.2	88.0	76.9	80.5	78.4	81.8	92.3

AMERICAN FOOTBALL CONFERENCE DEFENSE

	Balt.	Buff.	Cin.	Cle.	Den.	Hou.	Ind.	Jax.	KC	Mia.	NE	NYJ	Oak.	Pitt.	SD	Tenn.
First Downs	284	335	290	317	334	352	314	316	293	264	348	272	292	272	247	356
Rushing	79	138	97	102	126	113	111	98	88	84	99	70	98	61	77	107
Passing	187	179	170	195	184	211	190	197	186	166	226	169	150	182	153	214
Penalty	18	18	23	20	24	28	13	21	19	14	23	33	44	29	17	35
Rushes	384	571	416	505	531	433	445	416	408	447	409	408	474	333	404	474
Net Yds. Gained	1503	2714	1843	2070	2473	1751	2032	1945	1764	1601	1728	1454	2138	1004	1500	1851
Avg. Gain	3.9	4.8	4.4	4.1	4.7	4.0	4.6	4.7	4.3	3.6	4.2	3.6	4.5	3.0	3.7	3.9
Avg. Yds. per Game	93.9	169.6	115.2	129.4	154.6	109.4	127.0	121.6	110.3	100.1	108.0	90.9	133.6	62.8	93.8	115.7
Passes Attempted	596	473	514	507	502	547	535	506	581	502	611	531	470	593	488	625
Completed	349	294	326	309	297	354	356	329	319	288	388	269	249	363	285	410
% Completed	58.6	62.2	63.4	60.9	59.2	64.7	66.5	65.0	54.9	57.4	63.5	50.7	53.0	61.2	58.4	65.6
Total Yds. Gained	3789	3253	3648	3709	3936	4499	3627	4193	3777	3573	4348	3454	3319	3744	3135	4304
Times Sacked	27	27	27	29	23	30	30	26	39	39	36	40	47	48	47	40
Yds. Lost	190	181	179	178	156	219	194	189	258	225	212	244	292	319	290	272
Net Yds. Gained	3599	3072	3469	3531	3780	4280	3433	4004	3519	3348	4136	3210	3027	3425	2845	4032
Avg. per Game	224.9	192.0	216.8	220.7	236.3	267.5	214.6	250.3	219.9	209.3	258.5	200.6	189.2	214.1	177.8	252.0
Net Yds. per Pass Play	5.78	6.14	6.41	6.59	7.20	7.42	6.08	7.53	5.68	6.19	6.39	5.62	5.85	5.34	5.32	6.06
Yds. Gained per Comp.	10.86	11.06	11.19	12.00	13.25	12.71	10.19	12.74	11.84	12.41	11.21	12.84	13.33	10.31	11.00	10.50
Combined Net																
Yds. Gained	5102	5786	5312	5601	6253	6031	5465	5949	5283	4949	5864	4664	5165	4429	4345	5883
% Total Yds. Rushing	29.5	46.9	34.7	37.0	39.6	29.0	37.2	32.7	33.4	32.3	29.5	31.2	41.4	22.7	34.5	31.5
% Total Yds. Passing	70.5	53.1	65.3	63.0	60.5	71.0	62.8	67.3	66.6	67.7	70.5	68.8	58.6	77.3	65.5	68.5
Avg. Yds. per Game	318.9	361.6	332.0	350.1	390.8	376.9	341.6	371.8	330.2	309.3	366.5	291.5	322.8	276.8	271.6	367.7
Ball Control Plays	1007	1071	957	1041	1056	1010	1010	948	1028	988	1056	979	991	974	939	1139
Avg. Yds. per Play	5.1	5.4	5.6	5.4	5.9	6.0	5.4	6.3	5.1	5.0	5.6	4.8	5.2	4.5	4.6	5.2
Avg. Time of Poss.	29:18	32:20	28:46	32:05	31:51	30:57	30:19	28:17	28:56	29:18	31:00	27:57	28:53	28:07	26:57	34:06
Third Down Efficiency	38.0	43.2	37.9	42.9	38.3	39.5	39.0	41.3	37.7	37.2	47.1	37.0	34.9	33.5	33.7	43.0
Intercepted By	19	11	16	19	10	13	10	13	14	11	25	12	12	21	16	17
Yds. Returned By	289	210	200	320	118	90	206	105	204	66	419	214	105	248	240	198
Returned for TD	3	2	1	2	0	0	2	0	3	0	4	3	2	3	3	1
Punts	89	71	76	64	73	67	67	64	89	77	58	97	94	81	81	61
Yds. Punted	3875	2986	3137	2817	3169	2930	2978	2714	4025	3255	2422	4388	4114	3275	3414	2618
Avg. Yds. per Punt	43.5	42.1	41.3	44.0	43.4	43.7	44.4	42.4	45.2	42.3	41.8	45.2	43.8	40.4	42.1	42.9
Punt Returns	34	32	26	40	50	29	28	19	42	43	25	27	46	32	28	35
Yds. Returned	275	299	124	285	550	233	299	123	361	454	179	299	400	294	528	214
Avg. Yds. per Return	8.1	9.3	4.8	7.1	11.0	8.0	10.7	6.5	8.6	10.6	7.2	11.1	8.7	9.2	18.9	6.1
Returned for TD	0	0	0	0	0	0	1	0	0	1	0	0	0	0	1	0
Kickoff Returns	38	57	64	54	51	72	73	59	66	53	81	73	61	77	84	56
Yds. Returned	987	1238	1504	959	1259	1741	1880	1266	1336	1303	1820	1428	1412	1540	1880	1389
Avg. Yds. per Return	26.0	21.7	23.5	17.8	24.7	24.2	25.8	21.5	20.2	24.6	22.5	19.6	23.1	20.0	22.4	24.8
Returned for TD	0	0	2	0	1	1	1	1	1	2	1	0	1	1	3	1
Fumbles	25	20	20	16	22	16	24	12	23	22	20	25	21	28	13	25
Lost	8	11	10	9	8	5	11	5	9	8	13	18	12	14	7	8
Out of Bounds	1	2	1	3	0	0	2	2	1	3	1	0	0	1	1	3
Own Rec. for TD	0	0	0	0	1	0	0	0	0	0	0	0	0	0	0	0
Opp. Rec. by	10	18	14	11	15	6	8	12	6	10	5	7	10	9	6	14
Opp. Rec. for TD	0	0	1	0	0	0	0	1	1	0	0	0	0	0	2	0
Penalties	117	85	95	85	98	105	95	85	111	85	84	74	117	86	97	114
Yds. Penalized	984	634	776	741	921	851	812	748	922	730	687	679	1161	716	769	1039
Total Points Scored	270	425	395	332	471	427	388	419	326	333	313	304	371	232	322	339
Total TDs	27	48	44	36	55	52	42	50	38	36	36	36	44	22	39	32
TDs Rushing	5	18	15	7	26	16	14	19	11	8	10	11	14	5	14	7
TDs Passing	22	28	21	26	26	33	22	28	23	22	25	24	29	15	18	23
TDs on Ret. and Rec.	0	2	8	3	3	3	6	3	4	6	1	1	1	2	7	2
Extra Point Kicks	25	46	43	35	52	50	41	48	38	36	32	34	44	18	36	30
Extra Point Kicks Att.	25	46	43	35	53	50	41	48	38	36	32	35	44	19	37	30
2Pt Conversions	1	1	1	0	0	1	1	1	0	0	4	0	0	1	0	0
2Pt Conversions Att.	2	2	1	0	2	1	1	2	0	0	4	1	0	3	2	2
Safeties	0	1	1	0	1	0	0	0	0	0	0	0	0	1	2	0
Field Goals Made	27	29	28	27	29	21	31	23	20	27	19	18	21	26	16	39
Field Goals Attempted	32	39	33	36	36	27	36	25	24	31	26	23	28	30	16	48
% Successful	84.4	74.4	84.8	75.0	80.6	77.8	86.1	92.0	83.3	87.1	73.1	78.3	75.0	86.7	100.0	81.3

NATIONAL FOOTBALL CONFERENCE OFFENSE

	Ariz.	Atl.	Car.	Chi.	Dall.	Det.	GB	Minn.	NO	NYG	Phil.	StL	SF	Sea.	TB	Wash.
First Downs	241	353	225	263	327	304	312	289	351	331	322	292	251	260	288	295
Rushing	67	111	78	76	104	83	88	104	94	112	116	84	85	81	97	72
Passing	154	200	125	163	201	199	204	159	236	192	189	179	149	159	172	194
Penalty	20	42	22	24	22	22	20	26	21	27	17	29	17	20	19	29
Rushes	320	497	428	414	428	404	421	441	380	480	428	429	401	385	431	351
Net Yds. Gained	1388	1891	1846	1616	1786	1613	1606	1942	1519	2200	2324	1578	1657	1424	2001	1461
Avg. Gain	4.3	3.8	4.3	3.9	4.2	4.0	3.8	4.4	4.0	4.6	5.4	3.7	4.1	3.7	4.6	4.2
Avg. Yds. per Game	86.8	118.2	115.4	101.0	111.6	100.8	100.4	121.4	94.9	137.5	145.3	98.6	103.6	89.0	125.1	91.3
Passes Attempted	561	577	484	466	576	633	541	505	661	539	561	590	500	544	494	605
Completed	285	361	256	276	379	383	352	305	450	339	348	354	282	324	306	349
% Completed	50.8	62.6	52.9	59.2	65.8	60.5	65.1	60.4	68.1	62.9	62.0	60.0	56.4	59.6	61.9	57.7
Total Yds. Gained	3264	3725	2635	3397	4208	4001	4355	3327	4636	4002	4215	3512	3613	3536	3564	4261
Times Sacked	50	23	50	56	31	27	38	36	26	16	49	34	44	35	30	46
Yds. Lost	343	158	346	382	166	191	231	230	195	117	309	244	257	195	203	348
Net Yds. Gained	2921	3567	2289	3015	4042	3810	4124	3097	4441	3885	3906	3268	3356	3341	3361	3913
Avg. Yds. per Game	182.6	222.9	143.1	188.4	252.6	238.1	257.8	193.6	277.6	242.8	244.1	204.3	209.8	208.8	210.1	244.6
Net Yds. per Pass Play	4.78	5.95	4.29	5.78	6.66	5.77	7.12	5.72	6.46	7.00	6.40	5.24	6.17	5.77	6.41	6.01
Yds. Gained per Comp.	11.45	10.32	10.29	12.31	11.10	10.45	12.37	10.91	10.30	11.81	12.11	9.92	12.81	10.91	11.65	12.21
Combined Net Yds. Gained	4309	5458	4135	4631	5828	5423	5730	5039	5960	6085	6230	4846	5013	4765	5362	5374
% Total Yds. Rushing	32.2	34.6	44.6	34.9	30.6	29.7	28.0	38.5	25.5	36.2	37.3	32.6	33.1	29.9	37.3	27.2
% Total Yds. Passing	67.8	65.4	55.4	65.1	69.4	70.3	72.0	61.5	74.5	63.8	62.7	67.4	66.9	70.1	62.7	72.8
Avg. Yds. per Game	269.3	341.1	258.4	289.4	364.3	338.9	358.1	314.9	372.5	380.3	389.4	302.9	313.3	297.8	335.1	335.9
Ball Control Plays	931	1097	962	936	1035	1064	1000	982	1067	1035	1038	1053	945	964	955	1002
Avg. Yds. per Play	4.6	5.0	4.3	4.9	5.6	5.1	5.7	5.1	5.6	5.9	6.0	4.6	5.3	4.9	5.6	5.4
Avg. Time of Poss.	26:14	32:15	27:24	29:31	31:11	29:34	31:36	30:15	31:39	32:32	31:15	30:51	28:37	27:33	30:39	28:01
Third Down Efficiency	27.8	46.7	30.4	32.8	40.8	40.1	41.5	34.6	48.8	35.9	39.7	33.2	31.9	35.5	42.2	29.3
Had Intercepted	19	9	21	21	19	16	13	26	22	25	13	15	15	20	6	19
Yds. Opp. Returned	389	123	270	247	277	239	148	427	344	307	169	287	182	261	153	216
Ret. by Opp. for TD	4	0	5	2	3	2	1	3	4	1	1	2	1	1	1	2
Punts	94	75	95	83	66	90	71	83	57	73	73	94	91	78	76	94
Yds. Punted	4080	3014	4097	3326	3115	4018	3114	3569	2618	3222	3195	4276	4203	3254	3053	3776
Avg. Yds. per Punt	43.4	40.2	43.1	40.1	47.2	44.6	43.9	43.0	45.9	44.1	43.8	45.5	46.2	41.7	40.2	40.2
Punt Returns	42	19	39	33	24	30	41	42	27	43	38	40	31	42	30	40
Yds. Returned	294	230	373	564	382	362	325	361	210	263	404	452	366	468	193	432
Avg. Yds. per Return	7.0	12.1	9.6	17.1	15.9	12.1	7.9	8.6	7.8	6.1	10.6	11.3	11.8	11.1	6.4	10.8
Returned for TD	0	1	0	3	3	0	0	0	0	0	1	0	1	0	0	0
Kickoff Returns	84	46	74	59	74	61	62	64	52	57	62	74	61	65	57	73
Yds. Returned	2084	1221	1619	1497	1572	1519	1249	1427	1181	1082	1272	1614	1187	1558	1386	1680
Avg. Yds. per Return	24.8	26.5	21.9	25.4	21.2	24.9	20.1	22.3	22.7	19.0	20.5	21.8	19.5	24.0	24.3	23.0
Returned for TD	2	1	0	0	0	1	0	1	0	0	0	0	0	3	1	1
Fumbles	33	12	31	19	28	20	20	20	23	26	33	14	22	18	25	29
Lost	16	8	16	10	11	9	9	11	9	17	12	6	8	11	13	12
Out of Bounds	3	1	0	1	2	0	2	0	2	1	3	0	2	2	1	4
Own Rec. for TD	3	0	0	0	0	0	0	0	0	0	0	0	0	0	0	0
Opp. Rec. by	13	9	12	14	10	15	8	10	16	23	11	12	7	10	9	13
Opp. Rec. for TD	4	1	0	0	1	1	1	1	0	0	1	0	0	0	0	1
Penalties	108	58	106	91	109	136	78	100	90	92	129	102	112	101	100	90
Yds. Penalized	870	598	918	768	863	1018	617	769	884	777	1101	877	933	890	837	647
Total Points Scored	289	414	196	334	394	362	388	281	384	394	439	289	305	310	341	302
Total TDs	31	47	17	37	46	41	46	33	44	48	49	27	34	33	39	33
TDs Rushing	9	14	7	10	10	11	11	16	9	17	18	9	10	13	9	9
TDs Passing	10	28	9	23	29	26	31	14	33	31	28	18	19	14	26	21
TDs on Ret. and Rec.	12	5	1	4	7	4	4	3	2	0	3	0	5	6	4	3
Extra Point Kicks	29	44	17	35	42	35	46	30	43	47	47	26	33	31	36	28
Extra Point Kicks Att.	29	44	17	35	44	36	46	31	43	47	47	27	33	31	36	28
2Pt Conversions	1	2	0	1	2	2	0	1	0	1	1	0	1	2	1	2
2Pt Conversions Att.	2	3	0	2	2	5	0	2	1	1	2	0	1	2	3	5
Safeties	0	0	1	0	0	1	0	1	0	0	1	0	1	0	0	0
Field Goals Made	24	28	25	25	24	25	22	17	25	19	32	33	22	25	23	24
Field Goals Attempted	27	31	29	30	32	30	28	18	31	23	38	39	27	30	28	35
% Successful	88.9	90.3	86.2	83.3	75.0	83.3	78.6	94.4	80.6	82.6	84.2	84.6	81.5	83.3	82.1	68.6

NATIONAL FOOTBALL CONFERENCE DEFENSE

	Ariz.	Atl.	Car.	Chi.	Dall.	Det.	GB	Minn.	NO	NYG	Phil.	StL	SF	Sea.	TB	Wash.
First Downs	339	284	328	282	309	320	270	276	273	263	309	304	299	313	307	326
Rushing	123	87	121	88	84	98	82	87	94	88	91	88	86	91	118	106
Passing	178	183	176	183	200	187	163	178	150	159	185	191	188	206	171	207
Penalty	38	14	31	11	25	35	25	11	29	16	33	25	25	16	18	13
Rushes	526	366	503	386	402	443	395	417	421	389	423	404	447	452	444	444
Net Yds. Gained	2323	1694	1981	1441	1734	1999	1838	1635	1797	1620	1766	1810	1547	1903	2107	2041
Avg. Gain	4.4	4.6	3.9	3.7	4.3	4.5	4.7	3.9	4.3	4.2	4.2	4.5	3.5	4.2	4.7	4.6
Avg. Yds. per Game	145.2	105.9	123.8	90.1	108.4	124.9	114.9	102.2	112.3	101.3	110.4	113.1	96.7	118.9	131.7	127.6
Passes Attempted	533	560	526	582	540	518	527	529	494	539	536	570	550	585	521	578
Completed	324	364	326	363	348	330	296	333	306	308	309	328	358	339	307	367
% Completed	60.8	65.0	62.0	62.4	64.4	63.7	56.2	62.9	61.9	57.1	57.6	57.5	65.1	57.9	58.9	63.5
Total Yds. Gained	3881	3846	3617	3820	4151	3786	3440	3544	3353	3668	3761	3868	3941	4240	3359	4363
Times Sacked	33	31	31	34	35	44	47	31	33	46	39	43	36	37	26	29
Yds. Lost	227	221	224	232	257	288	333	177	250	316	292	290	244	246	143	176
Net Yds. Gained	3654	3625	3393	3588	3894	3498	3107	3367	3103	3352	3469	3578	3697	3994	3216	4187
Avg. Yds. per Game	228.4	226.6	212.1	224.3	243.4	218.6	194.2	210.4	193.9	209.5	216.8	223.6	231.1	249.6	201.0	261.7
Net Yds. per Pass Play	6.46	6.13	6.09	5.82	6.77	6.22	5.41	6.01	5.89	5.73	6.03	5.84	6.31	6.42	5.88	6.90
Yds. Gained per Comp.	11.98	10.57	11.10	10.52	11.93	11.47	11.62	10.64	10.96	11.91	12.17	11.79	11.01	12.51	10.94	11.89
Combined Net Yds. Gained	5977	5319	5374	5029	5628	5497	4945	5002	4900	4972	5235	5388	5244	5897	5323	6228
% Total Yds. Rushing	38.9	31.8	36.9	28.7	30.8	36.4	37.2	32.7	36.7	32.6	32.6	33.7	33.6	29.5	32.3	39.6
% Total Yds. Passing	61.1	68.2	63.1	71.3	69.2	63.6	62.8	67.3	63.3	67.4	66.3	66.4	70.5	67.7	60.4	67.2
Avg. Yds. per Game	373.6	332.4	335.9	314.3	351.8	343.6	309.1	312.6	306.3	310.8	327.2	336.8	327.8	368.6	332.7	389.3
Ball Control Plays	1092	957	1060	1002	977	1005	969	977	948	974	998	1017	1033	1074	991	1051
Avg. Yds. per Play	5.5	5.6	5.1	5.0	5.8	5.5	5.1	5.1	5.2	5.1	5.2	5.3	5.1	5.5	5.4	5.9
Avg. Time of Poss.	33:46	27:45	32:36	30:29	28:49	30:26	28:24	29:45	28:21	27:28	28:45	29:09	31:23	32:27	29:21	31:59
Third Down Efficiency	37.3	39.3	38.0	34.7	39.7	38.9	36.2	40.8	34.5	31.7	38.3	33.5	38.7	39.5	43.2	35.0
Intercepted By	17	22	17	21	20	14	24	15	9	16	23	14	15	12	19	14
Yds. Returned By	424	337	285	332	302	194	318	152	196	110	182	161	239	168	339	199
Returned for TD	3	2	1	1	3	2	3	1	2	0	1	0	3	2	3	1
Punts	64	73	76	88	70	83	78	85	67	86	82	82	84	81	72	86
Yds. Punted	3064	3323	3309	3569	3020	3636	3406	3748	2993	3744	3599	3071	3571	3521	2917	3704
Avg. Yds. per Punt	47.9	45.5	43.5	40.6	43.1	43.8	44.8	44.1	44.7	43.5	43.9	44.8	42.5	43.5	40.5	43.1
Punt Returns	35	28	54	39	33	54	31	32	26	36	34	45	54	35	32	45
Yds. Returned	458	241	488	303	205	633	341	241	310	535	309	435	483	327	232	568
Avg. Yds. per Return	13.1	8.6	9.0	7.8	6.2	11.7	11.0	7.5	11.9	14.9	9.1	9.7	8.9	9.3	7.3	12.6
Returned for TD	0	0	1	1	0	1	1	0	0	2	0	1	0	1	0	1
Kickoff Returns	51	64	45	59	56	72	76	61	66	77	69	65	67	50	75	61
Yds. Returned	1234	1362	1064	1404	1363	1487	1658	1455	1592	1515	1502	1538	1485	1099	1554	1160
Avg. Yds. per Return	24.2	21.3	23.6	23.8	24.3	20.7	21.8	23.9	24.1	19.7	21.8	23.7	22.2	22.0	20.7	10.0
Returned for TD	0	1	0	0	1	1	0	1	0	0	0	1	1	0	1	0
Fumbles	22	23	22	37	20	31	22	17	34	42	18	30	18	22	17	24
Lost	13	9	12	14	10	15	8	11	16	23	11	12	7	10	9	13
Out of Bounds	1	3	1	1	2	2	4	2	2	0	1	2	2	1	2	1
Own Rec. for TD	0	0	1	0	0	0	0	0	1	0	0	0	0	0	0	0
Opp. Rec. by	15	8	16	10	11	9	9	11	9	17	12	6	8	10	13	12
Opp. Rec. for TD	0	1	0	1	2	0	0	2	1	1	2	0	1	1	1	1
Penalties	108	116	90	93	79	106	98	98	88	107	87	126	97	91	79	104
Yds. Penalized	894	1003	765	790	641	854	758	786	701	899	724	1008	839	706	676	839
Total Points Scored	434	288	408	286	436	369	240	348	307	347	377	328	346	407	318	377
Total TDs	45	35	46	32	51	45	24	42	32	39	46	32	37	47	38	42
TDs Rushing	19	9	20	14	11	18	6	10	13	11	12	7	9	13	12	15
TDs Passing	22	23	19	14	33	23	16	25	13	24	31	21	25	31	23	23
TDs on Ret. and Rec.	4	3	7	4	7	4	2	7	6	4	3	4	3	3	3	4
Extra Point Kicks	44	31	45	29	49	42	24	42	27	36	45	29	36	44	35	37
Extra Point Kicks Att.	45	31	45	31	49	42	24	42	29	37	45	29	37	44	35	37
2Pt Conversions	0	1	0	0	2	0	0	0	2	2	1	1	0	2	2	2
2Pt Conversions Att.	0	3	1	1	2	3	0	0	3	2	1	3	0	3	3	5
Safeties	0	0	0	1	1	0	0	0	0	2	0	0	2	1	0	0
Field Goals Made	40	15	29	21	25	19	24	18	28	23	18	35	28	25	17	28
Field Goals Attempted	51	23	32	27	27	20	29	23	34	27	21	38	33	30	21	38
% Successful	78.4	65.2	90.6	77.8	92.6	95.0	82.8	78.3	82.4	85.2	85.7	92.1	84.8	83.3	81.0	73.7

AFC, NFC, AND NFL SUMMARY

	AFC Offense Total	AFC Offense Average	AFC Defense Total	AFC Defense Average	NFC Offense Total	NFC Offense Average	NFC Defense Total	NFC Defense Average	NFL Total	NFL Average
First Downs	4984	311.5	4886	305.4	4704	294.0	4802	300.1	9688	302.8
Rushing	1628	101.8	1548	96.8	1452	90.8	1532	95.8	3080	96.3
Passing	2989	186.8	2959	184.9	2875	179.7	2905	181.6	5864	183.3
Penalty	367	22.9	379	23.7	377	23.6	365	22.8	744	23.3
Rushes	7282	455.1	7058	441.1	6638	414.9	6862	428.9	13920	435.0
Net Yds. Gained	30755	1922.2	29371	1835.7	27852	1740.8	29236	1827.3	58607	1831.5
Avg. Gain	—	4.2	—	4.2	—	4.2	—	4.3	—	4.2
Avg. Yds. per Game	—	120.1	—	114.7	—	108.8	—	114.2	—	114.5
Passes Attempted	8432	527.0	8581	536.3	8837	552.3	8688	543.0	17269	539.7
Completed	5142	321.4	5185	324.1	5349	334.3	5306	331.6	10491	327.8
% Completed	—	61.0	—	60.4	—	60.5	—	61.1	—	60.8
Total Yds. Gained	60695	3793.4	60308	3769.3	60251	3765.7	60638	3789.9	120946	3779.6
Times Sacked	539	33.7	555	34.7	591	36.9	575	35.9	1130	35.3
Yds. Lost	3599	224.9	3598	224.9	3915	244.7	3916	244.8	7514	234.8
Net Yds. Gained	57096	3568.5	56710	3544.4	56336	3521.0	56722	3545.1	113432	3544.8
Avg. Yds. per Game	—	223.0	—	221.5	—	220.1	—	221.6	—	221.5
Net Yds. per Pass Play	—	6.36	—	6.21	—	5.98	—	6.12	—	6.17
Yds. Gained per Comp.	—	11.80	—	11.63	—	11.26	—	11.43	—	11.53
Combined Net Yds. Gained	87851	5490.7	86081	5380.1	84188	5261.8	85958	5372.4	172039	5376.2
% Total Yds. Rushing	—	35.0	—	34.1	—	33.1	—	34.0	—	34.1
% Total Yds. Passing	—	65.0	—	65.9	—	66.9	—	66.0	—	65.9
Avg. Yds. per Game	—	343.2	—	336.3	—	328.9	—	335.8	—	336.0
Ball Control Plays	16253	1015.8	16194	1012.1	16066	1004.1	16125	1007.8	32319	1010.0
Avg. Yds. per Play	—	5.4	—	5.3	—	5.2	—	5.3	—	5.3
Third Down Efficiency	—	39.5	—	39.0	—	37.1	—	37.5	—	38.2
Interceptions	232	14.5	239	14.9	279	17.4	272	17.0	511	16.0
Yds. Returned	3131	195.7	3232	202.0	4039	252.4	3938	246.1	7170	224.1
Returned for TD	24	1.5	29	1.8	33	2.1	28	1.8	57	1.8
Punts	1173	73.3	1209	75.6	1293	80.8	1257	78.6	2466	77.1
Yds. Punted	51072	3192.0	52117	3257.3	55930	3495.6	54885	3430.3	107002	3343.8
Avg. Yds. per Punt	—	43.5	—	43.1	—	43.3	—	43.7	—	43.4
Punt Returns	588	36.8	536	33.5	561	35.1	613	38.3	1149	35.9
Yds. Returned	5347	334.2	4917	307.3	5679	354.9	6109	381.8	11026	344.6
Avg. Yds. per Return	—	9.1	—	9.2	—	10.1	—	10.0	—	9.6
Returned for TD	4	0.3	3	0.2	9	0.6	10	0.6	13	0.4
Kickoff Returns	1008	63.0	1019	63.7	1025	64.1	1014	63.4	2033	63.5
Yds. Returned	22272	1392.0	22948	1434.3	23148	1446.8	22472	1404.5	45420	1419.4
Avg. Yds. per Return	—	22.1	—	22.5	—	22.6	—	22.2	—	22.3
Returned for TD	13	0.8	16	1.0	10	0.6	7	0.4	23	0.7
Fumbles	358	22.4	332	20.8	373	23.3	399	24.9	731	22.8
Lost	171	10.7	156	9.8	178	11.1	193	12.1	349	10.9
Out of Bounds	24	1.5	21	1.3	24	1.5	27	1.7	48	1.5
Own Rec. for TD	0	0.0	1	0.1	3	0.2	2	0.1	3	0.1
Opp. Rec.	155	9.7	171	10.7	192	12.0	176	11.0	347	10.8
Opp. Rec. for TD	8	0.5	5	0.3	11	0.7	14	0.9	19	0.6
Penalties	1498	93.6	1533	95.8	1602	100.1	1567	97.9	3100	96.9
Yds. Penalized	12686	792.9	13170	823.1	13367	835.4	12883	805.2	26053	814.2
Total Points Scored	5861	366.3	5667	354.2	5422	338.9	5616	351.0	11283	352.6
Total TDs	665	41.6	637	39.8	605	37.8	633	39.6	1270	39.7
TDs Rushing	217	13.6	200	12.5	182	11.4	199	12.4	399	12.5
TDs Passing	391	24.4	385	24.1	360	22.5	366	22.9	751	23.5
TDs on Ret. and Rec.	57	3.6	52	3.3	63	3.9	68	4.3	120	3.8
Extra Point Kicks	634	39.6	608	38.0	569	35.6	595	37.2	1203	37.6
Extra Point Kicks Att.	640	40.0	612	38.3	574	35.9	602	37.6	1214	37.9
2Pt Conversions	9	0.6	11	0.7	17	1.1	15	0.9	26	0.8
2Pt Conversions Att.	22	1.4	23	1.4	31	1.9	30	1.9	53	1.7
Safeties	8	0.5	6	0.4	5	0.3	7	0.4	13	0.4
Field Goals Made	401	25.1	401	25.1	393	24.6	393	24.6	794	24.8
Field Goals Attempted	488	30.5	490	30.6	476	29.8	474	29.6	964	30.1
% Successful	—	82.2	—	81.8	—	82.6	—	82.9	—	82.4

CLUB LEADERS

	Offense	Defense
First Downs	Indianapolis 366	San Diego 247
Rushing	Jacksonville 148	Pittsburgh 61
Passing	Indianapolis 253	New Orleans &
		Oakland 150
Penalty	Atlanta 42	Chicago &
		Minnesota 11
Rushes	Kansas City 556	Pittsburgh 333
Net Yds. Gained	Kansas City 2627	Pittsburgh 1004
Avg. Gain	Philadelphia 5.4	Pittsburgh 3.0
Passes Attempted	Indianapolis 679	Oakland 470
Completed	Indianapolis &	Oakland 249
	New Orleans 450	
% Completed	New Orleans 68.1	N.Y. Jets 50.7
Total Yds. Gained	San Diego 4746	San Diego 3135
Times Sacked	Indianapolis &	Pittsburgh 48
	N.Y. Giants 16	
Yds. Lost	Indianapolis 91	Green Bay 333
Net Yds. Gained	Indianapolis 4609	San Diego 2845
Net Yds. per Pass Play	San Diego 7.8	San Diego 5.3
Yds. Gained per Comp.	San Diego 13.2	Indianapolis 10.2
Combined Net Yds. Gained	San Diego 6329	San Diego 4345
% Total Yds. Rushing	Kansas City 47.0	Pittsburgh 22.7
% Total Yds. Passing	Indianapolis 75.7	Buffalo 53.1
Ball Control Plays	Atlanta 1097	San Diego 939
Avg. Yds. per Play	San Diego 6.1	Pittsburgh 4.5
Avg. Time of Poss.	San Diego 33:03	—
Third Down Efficiency	New Orleans 48.8	N.Y. Giants 31.7
Interceptions	—	New England 25
Yds. Returned	—	Arizona 424
Returned for TD	—	New England 4
Punts	Carolina 95	—
Yds. Punted	St. Louis 4276	—
Avg. Yds. per Punt	Dallas 47.2	—
Punt Returns	N.Y. Jets 56	Jacksonville 19
Yds. Returned	Chicago 564	Jacksonville 123
Avg. Yds. per Return	Chicago 17.1	Cincinnati 4.8
Returned for TD	Chicago & Dallas 3	—
Kickoff Returns	Arizona 84	Baltimore 38
Yds. Returned	Arizona 2084	Cleveland 959
Avg. Yds. per Return	Atlanta 26.5	Cleveland 17.8
Returned for TD	Oakland & Seattle 3	—
Total Points Scored	New England 518	Pittsburgh 232
Total TDs	New England 65	Pittsburgh 22
TDs Rushing	Houston 20	Baltimore &
		Pittsburgh 5
TDs Passing	New England 37	New Orleans 13
TDs on Ret. and Rec.	Arizona 12	Baltimore 0
Extra Point Kicks	New England 62	Pittsburgh 18
2-Point Conversions	Atlanta & Cincinnati &	
	Dallas & Detroit &	
	Pittsburgh &	
	San Diego	
	& Seattle &	
	Washington 2	—
Safeties	N.Y. Jets & Oakland &	
	Tennessee 2	—
Field Goals Made	Oakland & St. Louis 33	Atlanta 15
Field Goals Attempted	Miami & Oakland 41	San Diego 16
% Successful	Minnesota 94.4	Atlanta 65.2

NFL CLUB RANKINGS BY YARDS

	Offense			Defense		
	Total	Rush	Pass	Total	Rush	Pass
Arizona	31	32	31	29	30	23
Atlanta	16	12	15	16	10	22
Baltimore	22	14	20	10	5	21
Buffalo	25	18	24	24	32	3
Carolina	32	13	32	18	23	11
Chicago	30	22	28	9	2	20
Cincinnati	20	27	13	15	19	14T
Cleveland	29	20	29	22	27	18
Dallas	7	16	6	23	12	26
Denver	13	26	7	32	31	25
Detroit	17	23	12	21	24	16
Green Bay	9	24	5	5	18	5
Houston	3	7	4	30	13	32
Indianapolis	4	29	*1	20	25	13
Jacksonville	15	3	27	28	22	28
Kansas City	12	*1	30	14	14	17
Miami	21	21	16	6	7	8
Minnesota	23	10	26	8	9	10
New England	8	9	11	25	11	30
New Orleans	6	26	3	4	16	4
New York Giants	5	6	10	7	8	9
New York Jets	11	4	22	3	3	6
Oakland	10	2	23	11	29	2
Philadelphia	2	5	9	12	15	14T
Pittsburgh	14	11	14	2	*1	12
St. Louis	26	25	21	19	17	19
San Diego	*1	15	2	*1	4	*1
San Francisco	24	19	18	13	6	24
Seattle	28	31	19	27	21	27
Tampa Bay	19	8	17	17	28	7
Tennessee	27	17	25	26	20	29
Washington	18	30	8	31	26	31

T = Tied for position * = League Leader

AFC TAKEAWAYS/GIVEAWAYS

	Takeaways			Giveaways			Net
	Int	Fum	Total	Int	Fum	Total	Diff.
New England	25	13	38	5	5	10	+28
Pittsburgh	21	14	35	9	9	18	+17
Kansas City	14	9	23	8	6	14	+9
N.Y. Jets	12	18	30	14	7	21	+9
Baltimore	19	8	27	10	10	20	+7
Houston	13	5	18	12	6	18	0
Cleveland	19	9	28	18	11	29	-1
Oakland	12	12	24	16	10	26	-2
Indianapolis	10	11	21	17	8	25	-4
Tennessee	17	8	25	15	14	29	-4
San Diego	16	7	23	13	16	29	-6
Cincinnati	16	10	26	20	14	34	-8
Denver	10	8	18	12	15	27	-9
Miami	11	8	19	21	10	31	-12
Jacksonville	13	5	18	21	12	33	-15
Buffalo	11	11	22	21	18	39	-17
Totals	239	156	395	232	171	403	-8

NFC TAKEAWAYS/GIVEAWAYS

	Takeaways			Giveaways			Net
	Int	Fum	Total	Int	Fum	Total	Diff.
Atlanta	22	9	31	9	8	17	+14
Green Bay	24	8	32	13	9	22	+10
Philadelphia	23	11	34	13	12	25	+9
Tampa Bay	19	9	28	6	13	19	+9
St. Louis	14	12	26	15	6	21	+5
Chicago	21	14	35	21	10	31	+4
Detroit	14	15	29	16	9	25	+4
Dallas	20	10	30	19	11	30	0
San Francisco	15	7	22	15	8	23	-1
N.Y. Giants	16	23	39	25	17	42	-3
Washington	14	13	27	19	12	31	-4
Arizona	17	13	30	19	16	35	-5
New Orleans	9	16	25	22	9	31	-6
Carolina	17	12	29	21	16	37	-8
Seattle	12	10	22	20	11	31	-9
Minnesota	15	11	26	26	11	37	-11
Totals	272	193	465	279	178	457	+8

SCORING
POINTS
NFC:	143	David Akers, Philadelphia
AFC:	142	Sebastian Janikowski, Oakland

TOUCHDOWNS
AFC:	18	Arian Foster, Houston
NFC:	13	Adrian Peterson, Minnesota

EXTRA POINT KICKS
AFC:	51	Adam Vinatieri, Indianapolis
NFC:	47	David Akers, Philadelphia

TWO-POINT EXTRA POINT PLAYS
AFC:	2	Mewelde Moore, Pittsburgh
NFC:	2	Ben Obomanu, Seattle
	2	Roddy White, Atlanta

FIELD GOALS
AFC:	33	Sebastian Janikowski, Oakland
NFC:	33	Josh Brown, St. Louis

FIELD GOAL ATTEMPTS
AFC:	41	Dan Carpenter, Miami
	41	Sebastian Janikowski, Oakland
NFC:	39	Josh Brown, St. Louis

LONGEST FIELD GOAL
AFC:	60	Dan Carpenter, Miami vs. Cleveland, December 5
NFC:	56	Mason Crosby, Green Bay at Philadelphia, September 12

MOST POINTS, GAME
NFC:	25	Jay Feely, Arizona vs. Denver, December 12 (1 TD, 5-6 FG, 4-4 PAT)
AFC:	24	Darren McFadden, Oakland at Denver, October 24 (4 TD)

TEAM LEADERS, POINTS
AFC: BALTIMORE, 117, Billy Cundiff; BUFFALO, 79, Rian Lindell; CINCINNATI, 62, Mike Nugent; CLEVELAND, 97, Phil Dawson; DENVER, 76, Matt Prater; HOUSTON, 124, Neil Rackers; INDIANAPOLIS, 129, Adam Vinatieri; JACKSONVILLE, 107, Josh Scobee; KANSAS CITY, 102, Ryan Succop; MIAMI, 115, Dan Carpenter; NEW ENGLAND, 78, BenJarvus Green-Ellis; N.Y. JETS, 127, Nick Folk; OAKLAND, 142, Sebastian Janikowski; PITTSBURGH, 78, Rashard Mendenhall; SAN DIEGO, 109, Nate Kaeding; TENNESSEE, 110, Rob Bironas

NFC: ARIZONA, 107, Jay Feely; ATLANTA, 128, Matt Bryant; CAROLINA, 92, John Kasay; CHICAGO, 110, Robbie Gould; DALLAS, 114, David Buehler; DETROIT, 74, Calvin Johnson; GREEN BAY, 112, Mason Crosby; MINNESOTA, 81, Ryan Longwell; NEW ORLEANS, 100, Garrett Hartley; N.Y. GIANTS, 100, Lawrence Tynes; PHILADELPHIA, 143, David Akers; ST. LOUIS, 125, Josh Brown; SAN FRANCISCO, 50, Joe Nedney; SEATTLE, 106, Olindo Mare; TAMPA BAY, 105, Connor Barth; WASHINGTON, 100, Graham Gano

TEAM CHAMPION
AFC:	518	New England
NFC:	439	Philadelphia

NFL TOP TEN SCORERS—KICKERS
	XP	XPA	FG	FGA	PTS
Akers, David, Phi.	47	47	32	38	143
Janikowski, Sebastian, Oak.	43	43	33	41	142
Vinatieri, Adam, Ind.	51	51	26	28	129
Bryant, Matt, Atl.	44	44	28	31	128
Folk, Nick, NYJ	37	37	30	39	127
Brown, Josh, St.L	26	27	33	39	125
Rackers, Neil, Hou.	43	43	27	30	124
Cundiff, Billy, Bal.	39	39	26	29	117
Carpenter, Dan, Mia.	25	25	30	41	115
Buehler, David, Dal.	42	44	24	32	114

NFL TOP TEN SCORERS—NONKICKERS
	TD	TDR	TDP	TDM	2-PT.	PTS
Foster, Arian, Hou.	18	16	2	0	0	108
Bowe, Dwayne, K.C.	15	0	15	0	0	90
Green-Ellis, BenJarvus, N.E.	13	13	0	0	0	78
Hillis, Peyton, Cle.	13	11	2	0	0	78
Mendenhall, Rashard, Pit.	13	13	0	0	0	78
Peterson, Adrian, Min.	13	12	1	0	0	78
Johnson, Calvin, Det.	12	0	12	0	1	74
Jennings, Greg, G.B.	12	0	12	0	0	72
Johnson, Chris, Ten.	12	11	1	0	0	72
Turner, Michael, Atl.	12	12	0	0	0	72

AFC—INDIVIDUAL SCORERS
KICKERS
	XP	XPA	FG	FGA	PTS
Janikowski, Sebastian, Oak.	43	43	33	41	142
Vinatieri, Adam, Ind.	51	51	26	28	129
Folk, Nick, NYJ	37	37	30	39	127
Rackers, Neil, Hou.	43	43	27	30	124
Cundiff, Billy, Bal.	39	39	26	29	117
Carpenter, Dan, Mia.	25	25	30	41	115
Bironas, Rob, Ten.	38	38	24	26	110
Kaeding, Nate, S.D.	40	40	23	28	109
Scobee, Josh, Jac.	41	41	22	28	107
Succop, Ryan, K.C.	42	42	20	26	102
Dawson, Phil, Cle.	28	28	23	28	97
Lindell, Rian, Buf.	31	32	16	21	79
Prater, Matt, Den.	28	29	16	18	76
Graham, Shayne, NY-G-N.E.	39	41	12	12	75
Nugent, Mike, Cin.	17	17	15	19	62
Suisham, Shaun, Pit.	19	19	14	15	61
Gostkowski, Stephen, N.E.	26	26	10	13	56
Welker, Wes, N.E.	1	1	0	0	43
* Stitser, Clint, Cin.	8	10	7	8	29
Hauschka, Steven, Den.	10	10	6	7	28
Brown, Kris, S.D.	8	8	4	5	20
* Pettrey, Aaron, Cin.	5	5	2	4	11

* Player that was a rookie in 2010

NONKICKERS

Name	TD	TDR	TDP	TDM	2-PT.	PTS
Foster, Arian, Hou.	18	16	2	0	0	108
Bowe, Dwayne, K.C.	15	0	15	0	0	90
Green-Ellis, BenJarvus, N.E.	13	13	0	0	0	78
Hillis, Peyton, Cle.	13	11	2	0	0	78
Mendenhall, Rashard, Pit.	13	13	0	0	0	78
Johnson, Chris, Ten.	12	11	1	0	0	72
Tolbert, Mike, S.D.	11	11	0	0	1	68
Lloyd, Brandon, Den.	11	0	11	0	0	66
Gates, Antonio, S.D.	10	0	10	0	0	60
* Gronkowski, Rob, N.E.	10	0	10	0	0	60
Johnson, Steve, Buf.	10	0	10	0	0	60
Lewis, Marcedes, Jac.	10	0	10	0	0	60
McFadden, Darren, Oak.	10	7	3	0	0	60
Wallace, Mike, Pit.	10	0	10	0	0	60
Britt, Kenny, Ten.	9	0	9	0	1	56
Owens, Terrell, Cin.	9	0	9	0	0	54
Benson, Cedric, Cin.	8	7	1	0	1	50
Bush, Michael, Oak.	8	8	0	0	0	48
Charles, Jamaal, K.C.	8	5	3	0	0	48
Collie, Austin, Ind.	8	0	8	0	0	48
Johnson, Andre, Hou.	8	0	8	0	0	48
Moreno, Knowshon, Den.	8	5	3	0	0	48
Edwards, Braylon, NYJ	7	0	7	0	1	44
Welker, Wes, N.E.	7	0	7	0	0	#43
Boldin, Anquan, Bal.	7	0	7	0	0	42
* Ford, Jacoby, Oak.	7	2	2	3	0	42
Jackson, Fred, Buf.	7	5	2	0	0	42
Jones-Drew, Maurice, Jac.	7	5	2	0	0	42
Mason, Derrick, Bal.	7	0	7	0	0	42
* Mathews, Ryan, S.D.	7	7	0	0	0	42
Sims-Walker, Mike, Jac.	7	0	7	0	0	42
Branch, Deion, Sea.-N.E.	6	0	6	0	0	36
Floyd, Malcom, S.D.	6	0	6	0	0	36
Garcon, Pierre, Ind.	6	0	6	0	0	36
* Hernandez, Aaron, N.E.	6	0	6	0	0	36
Holmes, Santonio, NYJ	6	0	6	0	0	36
^ James, Javarris, Ind.	6	6	0	0	0	36
Jones, Thomas, K.C.	6	6	0	0	0	36
McGahee, Willis, Bal.	6	5	1	0	0	36
Rice, Ray, Bal.	6	5	1	0	0	36
* Tebow, Tim, Den.	6	6	0	0	0	36
Tomlinson, LaDainian, NYJ	6	6	0	0	0	36
Washington, Nate, Ten.	6	0	6	0	0	36
Wayne, Reggie, Ind.	6	0	6	0	0	36
Woodhead, Danny, N.E.	6	5	1	0	0	36
Bess, Davone, Mia.	5	0	5	0	0	30
Brown, Ronnie, Mia.	5	5	0	0	0	30
Garrard, David, Jac.	5	5	0	0	0	30
Heap, Todd, Bal.	5	0	5	0	0	30
Keller, Dustin, NYJ	5	0	5	0	0	30
Miller, Zach, Oak.	5	0	5	0	0	30
Tate, Brandon, N.E.	5	0	3	2	0	30
Thomas, Mike, Jac.	5	0	4	1	0	30
Walter, Kevin, Hou.	5	0	5	0	0	30
Ward, Hines, Pit.	5	0	5	0	0	30
* White, Blair, Ind.	5	0	5	0	0	30
* Gresham, Jermaine, Cin.	4	0	4	0	1	26
Addai, Joseph, Ind.	4	4	0	0	0	24
Buckhalter, Correll, Den.	4	2	2	0	0	24
Dreessen, Joel, Hou.	4	0	4	0	0	24
Evans, Lee, Buf.	4	0	4	0	0	24
Fasano, Anthony, Mia.	4	0	4	0	0	24
Jennings, Rashad, Jac.	4	4	0	0	0	24
Ochocinco, Chad, Cin.	4	0	4	0	0	24
Reece, Marcel, Oak.	4	1	3	0	0	24
Scaife, Bo, Ten.	4	0	4	0	0	24
Tamme, Jacob, Ind.	4	0	4	0	0	24
Ward, Derrick, Hou.	4	4	0	0	0	24
Jones, Jacoby, Hou.	3	0	3	0	1	20
Clark, Dallas, Ind.	3	0	3	0	0	18
Houshmandzadeh, T.J., Bal.	3	0	3	0	0	18
Jackson, Vincent, S.D.	3	0	3	0	0	18
Marshall, Brandon, Mia.	3	0	3	0	0	18
* Moeaki, Tony, K.C.	3	0	3	0	0	18
* Nelson, David, Buf.	3	0	3	0	0	18
Robiskie, Brian, Cle.	3	0	3	0	0	18
Royal, Eddie, Den.	3	0	3	0	0	18
Sanchez, Mark, NYJ	3	3	0	0	0	18
* Shipley, Jordan, Cin.	3	0	3	0	0	18
Simpson, Jerome, Cin.	3	0	3	0	0	18
Smith, Brad, NYJ	3	1	0	2	0	18
Watson, Benjamin, Cle.	3	0	3	0	0	18
Williams, Ricky, Mia.	3	2	1	0	0	18
* Ajirotutu, Seyi, S.D.	2	0	2	0	0	12
Arrington, Kyle, N.E.	2	0	0	2	0	12
Bowens, David, Cle.	2	0	0	2	0	12
Brown, Donald, Ind.	2	2	0	0	0	12
Cobbs, Patrick, Mia.	2	0	2	0	0	12
Cotchery, Jerricho, NYJ	2	0	2	0	0	12
Crumpler, Alge, N.E.	2	0	2	0	0	12
Daniels, Owen, Hou.	2	0	2	0	0	12
Florence, Drayton, Buf.	2	0	0	2	0	12
Gaffney, Jabar, Den.	2	0	2	0	0	12
Greene, Shonn, NYJ	2	2	0	0	0	12
Guyton, Gary, N.E.	2	0	0	2	0	12
Hayden, Kelvin, Ind.	2	0	0	2	0	12
Lowery, Dwight, NYJ	2	0	0	2	0	12
* Mariani, Marc, Ten.	2	0	2	0	0	12
Massaquoi, Mohamed, Cle.	2	0	2	0	0	12
* McCluster, Dexter, K.C.	2	0	1	1	0	12
McMichael, Randy, S.D.	2	0	2	0	0	12
Miller, Heath, Pit.	2	0	2	0	0	12
Murphy, Louis, Oak.	2	0	2	0	0	12
Parrish, Roscoe, Buf.	2	0	2	0	0	12
Pope, Leonard, K.C.	2	0	2	0	0	12
Redman, Isaac, Pit.	2	0	2	0	0	12
Ringer, Javon, Ten.	2	2	0	0	0	12
Roethlisberger, Ben, Pit.	2	2	0	0	0	12
* Sanders, Emmanuel, Pit.	2	0	2	0	0	12
* Spiller, C.J., Buf.	2	0	1	1	0	12
Sproles, Darren, S.D.	2	0	2	0	0	12
Stevens, Craig, Ten.	2	0	2	0	0	12
* Thomas, Demaryius, Den.	2	0	2	0	0	12
Naanee, Legedu, S.D.	1	0	1	0	1	8
Barnes, Khalif, Oak.	1	0	1	0	0	6
Battle, Jackie, K.C.	1	1	0	0	0	6
* Berry, Eric, K.C.	1	0	0	1	0	6
Brady, Tom, N.E.	1	1	0	0	0	6
Branch, Tyvon, Oak.	1	0	0	1	0	6
* Brown, Antonio, Pit.	1	0	0	1	0	6
Burnett, Kevin, S.D.	1	0	0	1	0	6
Byrd, Jairus, Buf.	1	0	0	1	0	6
Campbell, Jason, Oak.	1	1	0	0	0	6
Chambers, Chris, K.C.	1	0	1	0	0	6
Chung, Pat, N.E.	1	0	0	1	0	6
Clemens, Kellen, NYJ	1	1	0	0	0	6
Cole, Marquice, NYJ	1	0	0	1	0	6
* Conner, John, NYJ	1	1	0	0	0	6
Cook, Jared, Ten.	1	0	1	0	0	6
Crayton, Patrick, S.D.	1	0	1	0	0	6
Cribbs, Josh, Cle.	1	0	1	0	0	6
Davis, Buster, S.D.	1	0	1	0	0	6
* Decker, Eric, Den.	1	0	1	0	0	6
* Dickson, Ed, Bal.	1	0	1	0	0	6
Edelman, Julian, N.E.	1	0	0	1	0	6

	TD	TDR	TDP	TDM	2-PT.	PTS
Elam, Abram, Cle.	1	0	0	1	0	6
Eugene, Hiram, Oak.	1	0	0	1	0	6
Finnegan, Cortland, Ten.	1	0	0	1	0	6
Flacco, Joe, Bal.	1	1	0	0	0	6
Flowers, Brandon, K.C.	1	0	0	1	0	6
Gage, Justin, Ten.	1	0	1	0	0	6
Hagler, Tyjuan, Ind.	1	0	0	1	0	6
Hart, Mike, Ind.	1	1	0	0	0	6
Hartline, Brian, Mia.	1	0	1	0	0	6
Hester, Jacob, S.D.	1	0	1	0	0	6
Heyward-Bey, Darrius, Oak.	1	0	1	0	0	6
Hill, Jason, Jac.	1	0	1	0	0	6
Hunter, Jason, Den.	1	0	0	1	0	6
Johnson, Chris, Oak.	1	0	0	1	0	6
Johnson, Derrick, K.C.	1	0	0	1	0	6
Jones, Adam, Cin.	1	0	0	1	0	6
* Jones, Donald, Buf.	1	0	1	0	0	6
Joseph, Johnathan, Cin.	1	0	0	1	0	6
Keisel, Brett, Pit.	1	0	0	1	0	6
Landry, Dawan, Bal.	1	0	0	1	0	6
Larsen, Spencer, Den.	1	0	1	0	0	6
Leonard, Brian, Cin.	1	0	1	0	0	6
Lewis, Ray, Bal.	1	0	0	1	0	6
Martin, David, Buf.	1	0	1	0	0	6
* McCoy, Colt, Cle.	1	1	0	0	0	6
McIntyre, Corey, Buf.	1	1	0	0	0	6
Miller, Zach, Jac.	1	0	1	0	0	6
* Misi, Koa, Mia.	1	0	0	1	0	6
Moala, Fili, Ind.	1	0	0	1	0	6
Moore, Evan, Cle.	1	0	1	0	0	6
* Moore, Marlon, Mia.	1	0	1	0	0	6
Osgood, Kassim, Jac.	1	0	1	0	0	6
Phillips, Shaun, S.D.	1	0	0	1	0	6
Polamalu, Troy, Pit.	1	0	0	1	0	6
Polite, Lousaka, Mia.	1	1	0	0	0	6
* Reed, David, Bal.	1	0	0	1	0	6
Robinson, Gijon, Ind.	1	0	1	0	0	6
Routt, Stanford, Oak.	1	0	0	1	0	6
Royal, Robert, Cle.	1	0	1	0	0	6
Sanders, James, N.E.	1	0	0	1	0	6
Schilens, Chaz, Oak.	1	0	1	0	0	6
Scott, Bernard, Cin.	1	1	0	0	0	6
Smith, Shaun, K.C.	1	1	0	0	0	6
Smith, Taj, Ind.	1	0	0	1	0	6
Spaeth, Matt, Pit.	1	0	1	0	0	6
Stuckey, Chansi, Cle.	1	1	0	0	0	6
* Tucker, Verran, K.C.	1	0	1	0	0	6
* Vaughn, Cassius, Den.	1	0	0	1	0	6
Vrabel, Mike, K.C.	1	0	1	0	0	6
Washington, Kelley, S.D.	1	0	1	0	0	6
Weddle, Eric, S.D.	1	0	0	1	0	6
Whitworth, Andrew, Cin.	1	0	1	0	0	6
Wilson, Josh, Bal.	1	0	0	1	0	6
Woodley, LaMarr, Pit.	1	0	0	1	0	6
Moore, Mewelde, Pit.	0	0	0	0	2	4
Cartwright, Rock, Was.	0	0	0	0	0	^2
Groves, Quentin, Oak.	0	0	0	0	0	^2
Pryce, Trevor, NYJ	0	0	0	0	0	^2
Schommer, Nick, Ten.	0	0	0	0	0	^2
Siler, Brandon, S.D.	0	0	0	0	0	^2
Taylor, Jason, NYJ	0	0	0	0	0	^2

^ Safety
Team safety credited to Tennessee and Miami.

NFC—INDIVIDUAL SCORERS

KICKERS

	XP	XPA	FG	FGA	PTS
Akers, David, Phi.	47	47	32	38	143
Bryant, Matt, Atl.	44	44	28	31	128
Brown, Josh, St.L	26	27	33	39	125
Buehler, David, Dal.	42	44	24	32	114
Crosby, Mason, G.B.	46	46	22	28	112
Gould, Robbie, Chi.	35	35	25	30	110
Feely, Jay, Ariz	29	29	24	27~	107
Mare, Olindo, Sea.	31	31	25	30	106
Barth, Connor, T.B.	36	36	23	28	105
Reed, Jeff, Pit.-S.F.	32	32	24	32	104
Gano, Graham, Was.	28	28	24	35	100
Hartley, Garrett, N.O.	40	40	20	25	100
Tynes, Lawrence, NY-G	43	43	19	23	100
Kasay, John, Car.	17	17	25	29	92
Longwell, Ryan, Min.	30	31	17	18	81
Hanson, Jason, Det.	19	19	12	14	55
Rayner, Dave, Det.	16	16	13	16	55
Nedney, Joe, S.F.	17	17	11	13	50
Carney, John, N.O.	3	3	5	6	18
Andrus, Shane, S.F.	3	3	2	4	9
* Suh, Ndamukong, Det.	0	1	0	0	6

NONKICKERS

	TD	TDR	TDP	TDM	X2G	PTS
Feely, Jay, Ariz	1	1	0	0	0	#107
Peterson, Adrian, Min.	13	12	1	0	0	78
Johnson, Calvin, Det.	12	0	12	0	1	74
Jennings, Greg, G.B.	12	0	12	0	0	72
Turner, Michael, Atl.	12	12	0	0	0	72
Nicks, Hakeem, NY-G	11	0	11	0	0	66
* Williams, Mike, T.B.	11	0	11	0	0	66
White, Roddy, Atl.	10	0	10	0	2	64
Maclin, Jeremy, Phi.	10	0	10	0	0	60
Forté, Matt, Chi.	9	6	3	0	1	56
Witten, Jason, Dal.	9	0	9	0	1	56
Jacobs, Brandon, NY-G	9	9	0	0	0	54
Manningham, Mario, NY-G	9	0	9	0	0	54
McCoy, LeSean, Phi.	9	7	2	0	0	54
Vick, Michael, Phi.	9	9	0	0	0	54
Bradshaw, Ahmad, NY-G	8	8	0	0	1	50
Austin, Miles, Dal.	8	1	7	0	0	48
* Bryant, Dez, Dal.	8	0	6	2	0	48
Jackson, DeSean, Phi.	8	1	6	1	0	48
Moore, Lance, N.O.	8	0	8	0	0	48
Davis, Vernon, S.F.	7	0	7	0	1	44
Harvin, Percy, Min.	7	1	5	1	1	44
Colston, Marques, N.O.	7	0	7	0	0	42
Hester, Devin, Chi.	7	0	4	3	0	42
Fitzgerald, Larry, Ariz	6	0	6	0	1	38
* Best, Jahvid, Det.	6	4	2	0	0	36
* Blount, LeGarrette, T.B.	6	6	0	0	0	36
Burleson, Nate, Det.	6	0	6	0	0	36
Crabtree, Michael, S.F.	6	0	6	0	0	36
Gonzalez, Tony, Atl.	6	0	6	0	0	36
Jackson, Steven, St.L	6	6	0	0	0	36
Kuhn, John, G.B.	6	4	2	0	0	36
Lynch, Marshawn, Sea.	6	6	0	0	0	36
Moss, Santana, Was.	6	0	6	0	0	36
Torain, Ryan, Was.	6	4	2	0	0	36
Williams, Roy, Dal.	5	0	5	0	1	32
Boss, Kevin, NY-G	5	0	5	0	0	30
Gore, Frank, S.F.	5	3	2	0	0	30
* Graham, Jimmy, N.O.	5	0	5	0	0	30
Hightower, Tim, Ariz	5	5	0	0	0	30
* Ivory, Chris, N.O.	5	5	0	0	0	30
Jones, James, G.B.	5	0	5	0	0	30

	TD	TDR	TDP	TDM	2-PT	PTS
Knox, Johnny, Chi.	5	0	5	0	0	30
Meachem, Robert, N.O.	5	0	5	0	0	30
Morris, Maurice, Det.	5	5	0	0	0	30
Moss, Randy, N.E.-Min.	5	0	5	0	0	30
Olsen, Greg, Chi.	5	0	5	0	0	30
Snelling, Jason, Atl.	5	2	3	0	0	30
Westbrook, Brian, S.F.	5	4	1	0	0	30
* Williams, Keiland, Was.	5	3	2	0	0	30
Winslow, Kellen, T.B.	5	0	5	0	0	30
Obomanu, Ben, Sea.	4	0	4	0	2	28
Barber, Marion, Dal.	4	4	0	0	0	24
Butler, Deon, Sea.	4	0	4	0	0	24
Celek, Brent, Phi.	4	0	4	0	0	24
Driver, Donald, G.B.	4	0	4	0	0	24
Jackson, Brandon, G.B.	4	3	1	0	0	24
Pettigrew, Brandon, Det.	4	0	4	0	0	24
Rodgers, Aaron, G.B.	4	4	0	0	0	24
Washington, Leon, Sea.	4	1	0	3	0	24
Cooley, Chris, Was.	3	0	3	0	1	20
Amendola, Danny, St.L	3	0	3	0	0	18
Armstrong, Anthony, Was.	3	0	3	0	0	18
Bennett, Earl, Chi.	3	0	3	0	0	18
Choice, Tashard, Dal.	3	3	0	0	0	18
Darby, Kenneth, St.L	3	2	1	0	0	18
Davis, Fred, Was.	3	0	3	0	0	18
Finneran, Brian, Atl.	3	0	3	0	0	18
* Gettis, David, Car.	3	0	3	0	0	18
Goodson, Mike, Car.	3	3	0	0	0	18
Hasselbeck, Matt, Sea.	3	3	0	0	0	18
* Hoomanawanui, Michael, St.L	3	0	3	0	0	18
Lee, Donald, G.B.	3	0	3	0	0	18
Shockey, Jeremy, N.O.	3	0	3	0	0	18
Smith, Steve, NY-G	3	0	3	0	0	18
Spurlock, Micheal, T.B.	3	0	2	1	0	18
Stephens-Howling, LaRod, Ariz	3	1	0	2	0	18
Stewart, Jonathan, Car.	3	2	1	0	0	18
Taylor, Chester, Chi.	3	3	0	0	0	18
Williams, Cadillac, T.B.	3	2	1	0	0	18
Bajema, Billy, St.L	2	0	2	0	0	12
Beckum, Travis, NY-G	2	0	2	0	0	12
* Benn, Arrelious, T.B.	2	0	2	0	0	12
Betts, Ladell, N.O.	2	2	0	0	0	12
Breaston, Steve, Ariz	2	0	1	1	0	12
Clayton, Mark, St.L	2	0	2	0	0	12
* Dixon, Anthony, S.F.	2	2	0	0	0	12
Fells, Daniel, St.L	2	0	2	0	0	12
Forsett, Justin, Sea.	2	2	0	0	0	12
Gibson, Brandon, St.L	2	0	2	0	0	12
Ginn, Ted, S.F.	2	0	1	1	0	12
Graham, Earnest, T.B.	2	1	1	0	0	12
Hall, DeAngelo, Was.	2	0	0	2	0	12
Jenkins, Michael, Atl.	2	0	2	0	0	12
Jones, Felix, Dal.	2	1	1	0	0	12
King, Jeff, Car.	2	0	2	0	0	12
* McCann, Bryan, Dal.	2	0	0	2	0	12
Morgan, Josh, S.F.	2	0	2	0	0	12
Nelson, Jordy, G.B.	2	0	2	0	0	12
Portis, Clinton, Was.	2	2	0	0	0	12
Rhodes, Kerry, Ariz	2	0	0	2	0	12
Rice, Sidney, Min.	2	0	2	0	0	12
* Roberts, Andre, Ariz	2	0	2	0	0	12
Robinson, Laurent, St.L	2	0	2	0	0	12
Rodgers-Cromartie, Domin., Ariz	2	0	0	2	0	12
Shiancoe, Visanthe, Min.	2	0	2	0	0	12
Smith, Steve, Car.	2	0	2	0	0	12
Thomas, Pierre, N.O.	2	2	0	0	0	12
Thomas, David, N.O.	2	0	2	0	0	12
* Webb, Joe, Min.	2	2	0	0	0	12

	TD	TDR	TDP	TDM	2-PT	PTS
Weems, Eric, Atl.	2	0	0	2	0	12
Wells, Beanie, Ariz	2	2	0	0	0	12
Williams, Mike, Sea.	2	0	2	0	0	12
Avant, Jason, Phi.	1	0	1	0	1	8
Adams, Michael, Ariz	1	0	0	1	0	6
* Alexander, Danario, St.L	1	0	1	0	0	6
Allen, Jared, Min.	1	0	0	1	0	6
Babineaux, Jonathan, Atl.	1	0	0	1	0	6
Baker, Chris, Sea.	1	0	1	0	0	6
* Banks, Brandon, Was.	1	0	0	1	0	6
Biermann, Kroy, Atl.	1	0	0	1	0	6
Bishop, Desmond, G.B.	1	0	0	1	0	6
* Bradford, Sam, St.L	1	1	0	0	0	6
* Briscoe, Dezmon, T.B.	1	0	1	0	0	6
Brown, Levi, Ariz	1	0	0	1	0	6
Brown, Tarell, S.F.	1	0	0	1	0	6
Bush, Reggie, N.O.	1	0	1	0	0	6
Camarillo, Greg, Min.	1	0	1	0	0	6
Carlson, John, Sea.	1	0	1	0	0	6
Collins, Nick, G.B.	1	0	0	1	0	6
* Cooper, Riley, Phi.	1	0	1	0	0	6
Cutler, Jay, Chi.	1	1	0	0	0	6
Davis, Chauncey, Atl.	1	0	0	1	0	6
Davis, Kellen, Chi.	1	0	1	0	0	6
Davis, Rashied, Chi.	1	0	1	0	0	6
Dockett, Darnell, Ariz	1	0	0	1	0	6
Doucet, Early, Ariz	1	0	1	0	0	6
Douglas, Harry, Atl.	1	0	1	0	0	6
Evans, Heath, N.O.	1	0	1	0	0	6
Finley, Jermichael, G.B.	1	0	1	0	0	6
* Gerhart, Toby, Min.	1	1	0	0	0	6
Gilmore, John, T.B.	1	0	1	0	0	6
Goldson, Dashon, S.F.	1	0	0	1	0	6
Greer, Jabari, N.O.	1	0	0	1	0	6
* Grimm, Cody, T.B.	1	0	0	1	0	6
* Gronkowski, Chris, Dal.	1	0	1	0	0	6
Hagan, Derek, NY-G	1	0	1	0	0	6
Hall, Chad, Phi.	1	0	1	0	0	6
* Harbor, Clay, Phi.	1	0	1	0	0	6
Harrison, Jerome, Phi.	1	1	0	0	0	6
Hayes, Geno, T.B.	1	0	0	1	0	6
Hayes, Gerald, Ariz	1	0	0	1	0	6
Heller, Will, Det.	1	0	1	0	0	6
Henderson, Devery, N.O.	1	0	1	0	0	6
Herremans, Todd, Phi.	1	0	1	0	0	6
Jenkins, Malcolm, N.O.	1	0	0	1	0	6
Kitna, Jon, Dal.	1	1	0	0	0	6
* LaFell, Brandon, Car.	1	0	1	0	0	6
* Lee, Sean, Dal.	1	0	0	1	0	6
Levy, DeAndre, Det.	1	0	0	1	0	6
Logan, Stefan, Det.	1	0	1	0	0	6
Manumaleuna, Brandon, Chi.	1	0	1	0	0	6
Martin, Ruvell, Sea.	1	0	1	0	0	6
Matthews, Clay, G.B.	1	0	0	1	0	6
* Mays, Taylor, S.F.	1	0	0	1	0	6
McDonald, Ray, S.F.	1	0	0	1	0	6
Mikell, Quintin, Phi.	1	0	0	1	0	6
Moore, D.J., Chi.	1	0	0	1	0	6
Mughelli, Ovie, Atl.	1	0	1	0	0	6
Munnerlyn, Captain, Car.	1	0	0	1	0	6
* Palmer, Michael, Atl.	1	0	1	0	0	6
Patterson, Dimitri, Phi.	1	0	0	1	0	6
* Paulsen, Logan, Was.	1	0	1	0	0	6
Peelle, Justin, Atl.	1	0	1	0	0	6
Penn, Donald, T.B.	1	0	1	0	0	6
* Quarless, Andrew, G.B.	1	0	1	0	0	6
Scandrick, Orlando, Dal.	1	0	0	1	0	6
Scheffler, Tony, Det.	1	0	1	0	0	6

	TD	TDR	TDP	TDM	2-PT.	PTS		TD	TDR	TDP	TDM	2-PT.	PTS
Schmitt, Owen, Phi.	1	0	1	0	0	6	Williams, DeAngelo, Car.	1	1	0	0	0	6
Smith, Alphonso, Det.	1	0	0	1	0	6	Winfield, Antoine, Min.	1	0	0	1	0	6
Smith, Troy, S.F.	1	1	0	0	0	6	Woodson, Charles, G.B.	1	0	0	1	0	6
Stafford, Matthew, Det.	1	1	0	0	0	6	Young, Darrel, Was.	1	0	1	0	0	6
Stanton, Drew, Det.	1	1	0	0	0	6	Babineaux, Jordan, Sea.	0	0	0	0	0	^2
Stovall, Maurice, T.B.	1	0	1	0	0	6	Freeman, Josh, T.B.	0	0	0	0	1	2
* Suh, Ndamukong, Det.	1	0	0	1	0	6	* Hardy, Greg, Car.	0	0	0	0	0	^2
Tahi, Naufahu, Min.	1	0	1	0	0	6	Johnson, Bryant, Det.	0	0	0	0	1	2
Talib, Aqib, T.B.	1	0	0	1	0	6	Sellers, Mike, Was.	0	0	0	0	1	2
Tatupu, Lofa, Sea.	1	0	0	1	0	6	* Sims, Eugene, St.L	0	0	0	0	0	^2
* Thomas, Earl, Sea.	1	0	0	1	0	6							
Toler, Greg, Ariz	1	0	0	1	0	6	^ Safety						
Trufant, Marcus, Sea.	1	0	0	1	0	6	* Player that was a rookie in 2010						
Vaughan, Josh, Car.	1	1	0	0	0	6	~ Scored touchdown						
Ware, DeMarcus, Dal.	1	0	0	1	0	6	# Scored kicking extra point						
Whitehurst, Charlie, Sea.	1	1	0	0	0	6	Team safety credited to Detroit and New Orleans.						

AMERICAN FOOTBALL CONFERENCE—SCORING

	TD	TDR	TDP	TDM	XKG	XKAtt	X2G	X2Att	FG	FGA	SAF	POINTS
New England	65	19	37	9	62	64	0	1	22	25	0	518
San Diego	51	18	30	3	48	48	2	3	27	33	1	441
Indianapolis	51	13	33	5	51	51	0	0	26	28	0	435
Oakland	44	19	18	7	43	43	0	1	33	41	2	410
Houston	44	20	24	0	43	43	1	1	27	30	0	390
Pittsburgh	41	15	22	4	38	38	2	2	29	37	0	375
N.Y. Jets	39	14	20	5	37	37	1	1	30	39	2	367
Kansas City	44	13	27	4	42	42	0	2	20	26	0	366
Baltimore	40	11	25	4	39	39	0	0	26	29	0	357
Tennessee	40	13	24	3	38	38	1	2	24	26	2	356
Jacksonville	41	14	26	1	41	41	0	0	22	28	0	353
Denver	40	13	25	2	38	39	0	1	22	25	0	344
Cincinnati	36	8	26	2	30	32	2	4	24	31	0	322
Buffalo	34	6	24	4	31	32	0	2	16	21	0	283
Miami	26	8	17	1	25	25	0	1	30	41	1	273
Cleveland	29	13	13	3	28	28	0	1	23	28	0	271
AFC Total	665	217	391	57	634	640	9	22	401	488	8	5861
AFC Average	41.6	13.6	24.4	3.6	39.6	40.0	0.6	1.4	25.1	30.5	0.5	366.3

NATIONAL FOOTBALL CONFERENCE—SCORING

	TD	TDR	TDP	TDM	XKG	XKAtt	X2G	X2Att	FG	FGA	SAF	POINTS
Philadelphia	49	18	28	3	47	47	1	2	32	38	0	439
Atlanta	47	14	28	5	44	44	2	3	28	31	0	414
Dallas	46	10	29	7	42	44	2	2	24	32	0	394
N.Y. Giants	48	17	31	0	47	47	1	1	19	23	0	394
Green Bay	46	11	31	4	46	46	0	1	22	28	0	388
New Orleans	44	9	33	2	43	43	0	1	25	31	1	384
Detroit	41	11	26	4	35	36	2	5	25	30	1	362
Tampa Bay	39	9	26	4	36	36	1	3	23	28	0	341
Chicago	37	10	23	4	35	35	1	2	25	30	0	334
Seattle	33	13	14	6	31	31	2	2	25	30	1	310
San Francisco	34	10	19	5	33	33	1	1	22	27	0	305
Washington	33	9	21	3	28	28	2	5	24	35	0	302
Arizona	31	9	10	12	29	29	1	2	24	27	0	289
St. Louis	27	9	18	0	26	27	0	0	33	39	1	289
Minnesota	33	16	14	3	30	31	1	2	17	18	0	281
Carolina	17	7	9	1	17	17	0	0	25	29	1	196
NFC Total	605	182	360	63	569	574	17	31	393	476	5	5422
NFC Average	37.8	11.4	22.5	3.9	35.6	35.9	1.1	1.9	24.6	29.8	0.3	338.9
NFL Total	1270	399	751	120	1203	1214	26	53	794	964	13	11283
NFL Average	39.7	12.5	23.5	3.8	37.6	37.9	0.8	1.7	24.8	30.1	0.4	352.6

FIELD GOALS

FIELD GOAL PERCENTAGE
NFC: .944 Ryan Longwell, Minnesota
AFC: .929 Adam Vinatieri, Indianapolis

FIELD GOALS
AFC: 33 Sebastian Janikowski, Oakland
NFC: 33 Josh Brown, St. Louis

FIELD GOAL ATTEMPTS
AFC: 41 Dan Carpenter, Miami
41 Sebastian Janikowski, Oakland
NFC: 39 Josh Brown, St. Louis

FIELD GOALS, GAME
AFC: 5 Mike Nugent, Cincinnati vs. Baltimore, September 19 (5 attempts)
5 Josh Scobee, Jacksonville at Buffalo, October 10 (5 attempts)
5 Nick Folk, N.Y. Jets vs. Minnesota, October 11 (5 attempts)
5 Dan Carpenter, Miami vs. Pittsburgh, October 24 (5 attempts)
5 Dan Carpenter, Miami at Cincinnati, October 31 (5 attempts)
5 Nate Kaeding, San Diego at Indianapolis, November 28 (5 attempts)
NFC: 5 Olindo Mare, Seattle vs. Arizona, October 24 (5 attempts)
5 Olindo Mare, Seattle at Arizona, November 14 (6 attempts)
5 Jay Feely, Arizona vs. Denver, December 12 (6 attempts)

LONGEST FIELD GOAL
AFC: 60 Dan Carpenter, Miami vs. Cleveland, December 5
NFC: 56 Mason Crosby, Green Bay at Philadelphia, September 12

AVERAGE YARDS MADE
NFC: 39.8 Dave Rayner, Detroit
AFC: 38.2 Josh Scobee, Jacksonville

AMERICAN FOOTBALL CONFERENCE—FIELD GOALS

	FG	FGA	Pct	Long
Indianapolis	26	28	.929	48
Tennessee	24	26	.923	55
Houston	27	30	.900	57
Baltimore	26	29	.897	49
Denver	22	25	.880	59
New England	22	25	.880	43
Cleveland	23	28	.821	48
San Diego	27	33	.818	50
Oakland	33	41	.805	59
Jacksonville	22	28	.786	59
Pittsburgh	29	37	.784	53
Cincinnati	24	31	.774	54
Kansas City	20	26	.769	53
N.Y. Jets	30	39	.769	56
Buffalo	16	21	.762	51
Miami	30	41	.732	60
AFC Total	401	488	—	60
AFC Average	25.1	30.5	.822	--

NATIONAL FOOTBALL CONFERENCE—FIELD GOALS

	FG	FGA	Pct	Long
Minnesota	17	18	.944	48
Atlanta	28	31	.903	51
Arizona	24	27	.889	55
Carolina	25	29	.862	55
St. Louis	33	39	.846	53
Philadelphia	32	38	.842	50
Chicago	25	30	.833	54
Detroit	25	30	.833	55
Seattle	25	30	.833	51
N.Y. Giants	19	23	.826	53
Tampa Bay	23	28	.821	53
San Francisco	22	27	.815	51
New Orleans	25	31	.806	52
Green Bay	22	28	.786	56
Dallas	24	32	.750	53
Washington	24	35	.686	49
NFC Total	393	476	—	56
NFC Average	24.6	29.8	.826	--
League Total	794	964	—	60
League Average	24.8	30.1	.824	--

AFC—INDIVIDUAL FIELD GOALS

	1-19 Yards	20-29 Yards	30-39 Yards	40-49 Yards	50 or Longer	Totals	Avg Yds Att	Avg Yds Made	Avg Yds Miss	Long
Vinatieri, Adam, Ind.	0-0 —	8-8 1.000	9-10 .900	9-10 .900	0-0 —	26-28 .929	35.6	35.1	43.0	48
Bironas, Rob, Ten.	0-0 —	6-6 1.000	8-9 .889	8-8 1.000	2-3 .667	24-26 .923	36.7	35.7	48.0	55
Rackers, Neil, Hou.	0-0 —	8-8 1.000	11-11 1.000	5-7 .714	3-4 .750	27-30 .900	37.0	35.7	48.3	57
Cundiff, Billy, Bal.	0-0 —	11-11 1.000	8-9 .889	7-8 .875	0-1 .000	26-29 .897	34.7	33.6	44.7	49
Prater, Matt, Den.	0-0 —	3-3 1.000	7-7 1.000	4-5 .800	2-3 .667	16-18 .889	39.7	38.0	53.5	59
Dawson, Phil, Cle.	3-3 1.000	7-7 1.000	10-10 1.000	3-5 .600	0-3 .000	23-28 .821	33.8	30.2	50.6	48
Kaeding, Nate, S.D.	0-0 —	6-6 1.000	7-8 .875	9-10 .900	1-4 .250	23-28 .821	38.9	36.8	48.4	50
Janikowski, Sebastian, Oak.	0-0 —	8-8 1.000	13-14 .929	8-12 .667	4-7 .571	33-41 .805	38.4	36.3	47.0	59
Nugent, Mike, Cin.	0-0 —	5-5 1.000	7-7 1.000	1-3 .333	2-4 .500	15-19 .789	36.8	33.8	48.3	54
Scobee, Josh, Jac.	2-2 1.000	3-3 1.000	6-7 .857	9-14 .643	2-2 1.000	22-28 .786	39.6	38.2	44.8	59
Folk, Nick, NYJ	1-1 1.000	10-11 .909	14-16 .875	3-6 .500	2-5 .400	30-39 .769	35.6	33.1	44.1	56
Succop, Ryan, K.C.	0-0 —	6-6 1.000	7-9 .778	6-8 .750	1-3 .333	20-26 .769	37.4	35.1	45.2	53
Lindell, Rian, Buf.	1-1 1.000	6-6 1.000	5-6 .833	2-3 .667	2-5 .400	16-21 .762	37.3	33.9	48.2	51
Carpenter, Dan, Mia.	1-1 1.000	9-9 1.000	5-5 1.000	11-18 .611	4-8 .500	30-41 .732	40.0	36.8	48.7	60
(Nonqualifiers)										
Suisham, Shaun, Pit.	1-1 1.000	4-4 1.000	1-1 1.000	8-9 .889	0-0 —	14-15 .933	36.4	36.1	41.0	48
Gostkowski, Stephen, N.E.	0-0 —	2-2 1.000	6-7 .857	2-3 .667	0-1 .000	10-13 .769	36.5	33.5	46.7	43
Graham, Shayne, N.E.	1-1 1.000	5-5 1.000	5-5 1.000	1-1 1.000	0-0 —	12-12 1.000	30.2	30.2	—	41
* Stitser, Clint, Cin.	0-0 —	4-5 .800	2-2 1.000	1-1 1.000	0-0 —	7-8 .875	30.8	31.0	29.0	47
Hauschka, Steven, Den.	0-0 —	1-1 1.000	3-3 1.000	2-3 .667	0-0 —	6-7 .857	36.4	35.8	40.0	46
Brown, Kris, S.D.	0-0 —	1-1 1.000	3-3 1.000	0-0 —	0-1 .000	4-5 .800	36.0	32.5	50.0	36
* Pettrey, Aaron, Cin.	1-1 1.000	1-2 .500	0-0 —	0-1 .000	0-0 —	2-4 .500	29.3	23.5	35.0	28
AFC Totals	13-13 1.000	120-124 .968	142-154 .922	99-139 .712	27-58 .466	401-488 .822	36.8	34.7	46.3	60
NFL Totals	19-19 1.000	257-270 .952	251-283 .887	208-284 .732	59-108 .546	794-964 .824	36.5	34.9	44.4	60

Leader based on overall percentage, minimum 16 field goals

NFC—INDIVIDUAL FIELD GOALS

	1-19 Yards	20-29 Yards	30-39 Yards	40-49 Yards	50 or Longer	Totals	Avg Yds Att	Avg Yds Made	Avg Yds Miss	Long
Longwell, Ryan, Min.	0-0 —	7-7 1.000	8-9 .889	2-2 1.000	0-0 —	17-18 .944	31.8	31.4	39.0	48
Bryant, Matt, Atl.	0-0 —	11-11 1.000	8-9 .889	8-10 .800	1-1 1.000	28-31 .903	34.9	34.5	39.0	51
Feely, Jay, Ariz	0-0 —	8-8 1.000	6-6 1.000	8-10 .800	2-3 .667	24-27 .889	38.1	36.6	50.7	55
Kasay, John, Car.	0-0 —	9-9 1.000	2-2 1.000	11-14 .786	3-4 .750	25-29 .862	38.6	37.6	44.8	55
Brown, Josh, St.L	0-0 —	11-12 .917	12-14 .857	7-9 .778	3-4 .750	33-39 .846	36.0	35.5	38.8	53
Akers, David, Phi.	0-0 —	12-12 1.000	10-12 .833	9-11 .818	1-3 .333	32-38 .842	35.9	34.2	45.0	50
Gould, Robbie, Chi.	1-1 1.000	9-9 1.000	8-9 .889	4-7 .571	3-4 .750	25-30 .833	35.3	33.5	44.6	54
Mare, Olindo, Sea.	2-2 1.000	10-12 .833	7-7 1.000	5-7 .714	1-2 .500	25-30 .833	32.4	30.9	39.8	51
Tynes, Lawrence, NY-G	0-0 —	12-12 1.000	2-4 .500	3-4 .750	2-3 .667	19-23 .826	33.5	31.4	43.5	53
Barth, Connor, T.B.	0-0 —	6-6 1.000	10-10 1.000	6-10 .600	1-2 .500	23-28 .821	36.6	34.9	44.2	53
Rayner, Dave, Det.	0-0 —	3-3 1.000	3-3 1.000	5-8 .625	2-2 1.000	13-16 .813	41.3	39.8	47.7	55
Hartley, Garrett, N.O.	1-1 1.000	4-6 .667	7-9 .778	6-7 .857	2-2 1.000	20-25 .800	35.9	36.6	33.4	52
Crosby, Mason, G.B.	1-1 1.000	7-8 .875	4-5 .800	8-10 .800	2-4 .500	22-28 .786	37.2	35.2	44.3	56
Buehler, David, Dal.	0-0 —	8-8 1.000	4-7 .571	8-11 .727	4-6 .667	24-32 .750	38.6	36.9	43.8	53
Reed, Jeff, Pit.-S.F.	2-2 1.000	9-10 .900	8-9 .889	3-7 .429	2-4 .500	24-32 .750	35.2	32.5	43.3	53
Gano, Graham, Was.	1-1 1.000	8-10 .800	4-7 .571	11-14 .786	0-3 .000	24-35 .686	37.1	35.6	40.5	49
(Nonqualifiers)										
Hanson, Jason, Det.	0-0 —	1-1 1.000	4-4 1.000	4-5 .800	3-4 .750	12-14 .857	43.0	41.9	49.5	52
Nedney, Joe, S.F.	0-0 —	6-6 1.000	2-2 1.000	1-2 .500	2-3 .667	11-13 .846	35.5	33.6	46.0	51
Carney, John, N.O.	0-0 —	1-2 .500	4-4 1.000	0-0 —	0-0 —	5-6 .833	30.2	30.4	29.0	32
Andrus, Shane, S.F.	0-0 —	1-1 1.000	1-2 .500	0-1 .000	0-0 —	2-4 .500	37.0	32.0	42.0	38
NFC Totals	6-6 1.000	137-146 .938	109-129 .845	109-145 .752	32-50 .640	393-476 .826	36.3	35.0	42.4	56
NFL Totals	19-19 1.000	257-270 .952	251-283 .887	208-284 .732	59-108 .546	794-964 .824	36.5	34.9	44.4	60

Leader based on overall percentage, minimum 16 field goals
* Player that was a rookie in 2010

RUSHING

YARDS
AFC:	1616	Arian Foster, Houston
NFC:	1371	Michael Turner, Atlanta

YARDS, GAME
AFC:	231	Arian Foster, Houston vs. Indianapolis, September 12 (33 attempts, 3 TD)
NFC:	172	Ryan Torain, Washington vs. Tampa Bay, December 12 (24 attempts, 0 TD)

LONGEST
AFC:	80	Jamaal Charles, Kansas City at St. Louis, December 19
NFC:	80	Tim Hightower, Arizona at Atlanta, September 19 - TD
	80	Adrian Peterson, Minnesota vs. Detroit, September 26 - TD

ATTEMPTS
NFC:	334	Michael Turner, Atlanta
AFC:	327	Arian Foster, Houston

ATTEMPTS, GAME
AFC:	36	Rashard Mendenhall, Pittsburgh at Buffalo, November 28 (151 yards, 1 TD) - (OT)
NFC:	30	Michael Turner, Atlanta at New Orleans, September 26 (114 yards, 1 TD) - (OT)

YARDS PER ATTEMPT
NFC:	6.8	Michael Vick, Philadelphia
AFC:	6.4	Jamaal Charles, Kansas City

TOUCHDOWNS
AFC:	16	Arian Foster, Houston
NFC:	12	Adrian Peterson, Minnesota
	12	Michael Turner, Atlanta

TEAM LEADERS, YARDS

AFC: BALTIMORE, 1220, Ray Rice; BUFFALO, 927, Fred Jackson; CINCINNATI, 1111, Cedric Benson; CLEVELAND, 1177, Peyton Hillis; DENVER, 779, Knowshon Moreno; HOUSTON, 1616, Arian Foster; INDIANAPOLIS, 497, Donald Brown; JACKSONVILLE, 1324, Maurice Jones-Drew; KANSAS CITY, 1467, Jamaal Charles; MIAMI, 734, Ronnie Brown; NEW ENGLAND, 1008, BenJarvus Green-Ellis; N.Y. JETS, 914, LaDainian Tomlinson; OAKLAND, 1157, Darren McFadden; PITTSBURGH, 1273, Rashard Mendenhall; SAN DIEGO, 735, Mike Tolbert; TENNESSEE, 1364, Chris Johnson

NFC: ARIZONA, 736, Tim Hightower; ATLANTA, 1371, Michael Turner; CAROLINA, 770, Jonathan Stewart; CHICAGO, 1069, Matt Forté; DALLAS, 800, Felix Jones; DETROIT, 555, *Jahvid Best; GREEN BAY, 703, Brandon Jackson; MINNESOTA, 1298, Adrian Peterson; NEW ORLEANS, 716, *Chris Ivory; N.Y. GIANTS, 1235, Ahmad Bradshaw; PHILADELPHIA, 1080, LeSean McCoy; ST. LOUIS, 1241, Steven Jackson; SAN FRANCISCO, 853, Frank Gore; SEATTLE, 573, Marshawn Lynch; TAMPA BAY, 1007, *LeGarrette Blount; WASHINGTON, 742, Ryan Torain

TEAM CHAMPION
AFC:	2627	Kansas City
NFC:	2324	Philadelphia

Player that was a rookie in 2010

NFL TOP TEN RUSHERS
	Att	Yards	Avg	Long	TD
Foster, Arian, Hou.	327	1616	4.9	74t	16
Charles, Jamaal, K.C.	230	1467	6.4	80	5
Turner, Michael, Atl.	334	1371	4.1	55	12
Johnson, Chris, Ten.	316	1364	4.3	76t	11
Jones-Drew, Maurice, Jac.	299	1324	4.4	37	5
Peterson, Adrian, Min.	283	1298	4.6	80t	12
Mendenhall, Rashard, Pit.	324	1273	3.9	50t	13
Jackson, Steven, St.L	330	1241	3.8	42t	6
Bradshaw, Ahmad, NY-G	276	1235	4.5	48t	8
Rice, Ray, Bal.	307	1220	4.0	50	5

AFC—INDIVIDUAL RUSHERS
	Att	Yards	Avg	Long	TD
Foster, Arian, Hou.	327	1616	4.9	74t	16
Charles, Jamaal, K.C.	230	1467	6.4	80	5
Johnson, Chris, Ten.	316	1364	4.3	76t	11
Jones-Drew, Maurice, Jac.	299	1324	4.4	37	5
Mendenhall, Rashard, Pit.	324	1273	3.9	50t	13
Rice, Ray, Bal.	307	1220	4.0	50	5
Hillis, Peyton, Cle.	270	1177	4.4	48	11
McFadden, Darren, Oak.	223	1157	5.2	57t	7
Benson, Cedric, Cin.	321	1111	3.5	26	7
Green-Ellis, BenJarvus, N.E.	229	1008	4.4	33t	13
Jackson, Fred, Buf.	222	927	4.2	39	5
Tomlinson, LaDainian, NYJ	219	914	4.2	31	6
Jones, Thomas, K.C.	245	896	3.7	70	6
Moreno, Knowshon, Den.	182	779	4.3	35	5
Greene, Shonn, NYJ	185	766	4.1	23t	2
Tolbert, Mike, S.D.	182	735	4.0	36	11
Brown, Ronnie, Mia.	200	734	3.7	51	5
* Mathews, Ryan, S.D.	158	678	4.3	31t	7
Williams, Ricky, Mia.	159	673	4.2	45t	2
Bush, Michael, Oak.	158	655	4.1	30	8
Woodhead, Danny, N.E.	97	547	5.6	36t	5
Brown, Donald, Ind.	129	497	3.9	49	2
Addai, Joseph, Ind.	116	495	4.3	46	4
Jennings, Rashad, Jac.	84	459	5.5	74t	4
McGahee, Willis, Bal.	100	380	3.8	30t	5
Ward, Derrick, Hou.	50	315	6.3	38t	4
Scott, Bernard, Cin.	61	299	4.9	18	1
Smith, Brad, NYJ	38	299	7.9	53t	1
* Spiller, C.J., Buf.	74	283	3.8	20	0
Garrard, David, Jac.	66	279	4.2	25t	5
Fitzpatrick, Ryan, Buf.	40	269	6.7	22	0
Sproles, Darren, S.D.	50	267	5.3	34	0
Redman, Isaac, Pit.	52	247	4.8	23	0
Ringer, Javon, Ten.	51	239	4.7	54	2
* Tebow, Tim, Den.	43	227	5.3	40t	6
Campbell, Jason, Oak.	47	222	4.7	24	1
* McKnight, Joe, NYJ	39	189	4.8	18	0
Hart, Mike, Ind.	43	185	4.3	35	1
Roethlisberger, Ben, Pit.	34	176	5.2	31	2
Rhodes, Dominic, Ind.	37	172	4.6	15	0
* Karim, Deji, Jac.	35	160	4.6	15	0
Ball, Lance, Den.	41	158	3.9	19	0
* Ford, Jacoby, Oak.	10	155	15.5	71t	2
Taylor, Fred, N.E.	43	155	3.6	24	0
Buckhalter, Correll, Den.	59	147	2.5	13	2
* McCoy, Colt, Cle.	28	136	4.9	18	1
Cassel, Matt, K.C.	33	125	3.8	23	0
Young, Vince, Ten.	25	125	5.0	20	0
Reece, Marcel, Oak.	30	122	4.1	31	1
Thomas, Mike, Jac.	12	114	9.5	33	0
* James, Javarris, Ind.	46	112	2.4	11	6
Sanchez, Mark, NYJ	30	105	3.5	20	3
Bell, Mike, Phi.-Cle.	47	99	2.1	11	0
Moore, Mewelde, Pit.	33	99	3.0	18	0

	Att	Yards	Avg	Long	TD
Orton, Kyle, Den.	22	98	4.5	14	0
Slaton, Steve, Hou.	19	93	4.9	23	0
McClain, Le'Ron, Bal.	28	85	3.0	16	0
Flacco, Joe, Bal.	43	84	2.0	14	1
Maroney, Laurence, Den.	36	74	2.1	13	0
Thigpen, Tyler, Mia.	13	73	5.6	12	0
* McCluster, Dexter, K.C.	18	71	3.9	20	0
Hodges, Reggie, Cle.	1	68	68.0	68	0
Cribbs, Josh, Cle.	20	66	3.3	19	0
Polite, Lousaka, Mia.	26	62	2.4	4t	1
Tate, Brandon, N.E.	5	62	12.4	22	0
Leonard, Brian, Cin.	9	61	6.8	42	0
Royal, Eddie, Den.	6	61	10.2	20	0
Hester, Jacob, S.D.	26	60	2.3	6	0
Edwards, Trent, Buf.-Jac.	14	58	4.1	14	0
Morris, Sammy, N.E.	20	56	2.8	9	0
Henne, Chad, Mia.	35	52	1.5	10	0
Rivers, Philip, S.D.	29	52	1.8	14	0
Battle, Jackie, K.C.	20	50	2.5	7	1
Palmer, Carson, Cin.	32	50	1.6	9	0
Heyward-Bey, Darrius, Oak.	4	48	12.0	30	0
* Hernandez, Aaron, N.E.	3	47	15.7	18	0
Faulk, Kevin, N.E.	8	45	5.6	11	0
Stallworth, Donte', Bal.	5	45	9.0	19	0
* Conner, John, NYJ	8	44	5.5	16t	1
Murphy, Louis, Oak.	1	43	43.0	43	0
Gradkowski, Bruce, Oak.	12	41	3.4	12	0
Wallace, Mike, Pit.	5	39	7.8	19	0
Dixon, Dennis, Pit.	5	32	6.4	21	0
Batch, Charlie, Pit.	7	30	4.3	24	0
Brady, Tom, N.E.	31	30	1.0	9	1
* Dwyer, Jonathan, Pit.	9	28	3.1	7	0
Schaub, Matt, Hou.	22	28	1.3	8	0
Hartline, Brian, Mia.	2	27	13.5	30	0
Parrish, Roscoe, Buf.	3	23	7.7	13	0
Cartwright, Rock, Oak.	9	22	2.4	10	0
Boller, Kyle, Oak.	7	18	2.6	15	0
Ganther, Quinton, Buf.	9	18	2.0	11	0
Larsen, Spencer, Den.	3	18	6.0	14	0
Manning, Peyton, Ind.	18	18	1.0	27	0
Clayton, Thomas, Cle.-N.E.	7	17	2.4	5	0
Holmes, Santonio, NYJ	2	17	8.5	14	0
Weatherford, Steve, NYJ	1	17	17.0	17	0
* Moore, Marlon, Mia.	1	16	16.0	16	0
* Reed, David, Bal.	1	15	15.0	15	0
Edelman, Julian, N.E.	2	14	7.0	13	0
Jackson, Vincent, S.D.	1	14	14.0	14	0
Richardson, Tony, NYJ	5	13	2.6	4	0
Bennett, Michael, Oak.	2	11	5.5	6	0
Brinkley, Curtis, S.D.	2	11	5.5	9	0
Vickers, Lawrence, Cle.	5	11	2.2	3	0
Johnson, Andre, Hou.	2	10	5.0	7	0
Clemens, Kellen, NYJ	2	9	4.5	10t	1
Miller, Zach, Jac.	2	9	4.5	8	0
* Mitchell, Carlton, Cle.	1	9	9.0	9	0
Stuckey, Chansi, Cle.	3	9	3.0	11t	1
Wallace, Seneca, Cle.	7	9	1.3	6	0
Bouman, Todd, Jac.	2	8	4.0	6	0
Jones, Jacoby, Hou.	2	7	3.5	10	0
Curtis, Kevin, Mia.	1	6	6.0	6	0
Garcon, Pierre, Ind.	2	6	3.0	11	0
* Arenas, Javier, K.C.	1	5	5.0	5	0
McIntyre, Corey, Buf.	4	5	1.3	2	1
Palko, Tyler, K.C.	2	5	2.5	6	0
* Williams, Damian, Ten.	1	5	5.0	5	0
Bowe, Dwayne, K.C.	1	4	4.0	4	0
Edwards, Braylon, NYJ	1	4	4.0	4	0
Jones, Greg, Jac.	2	4	2.0	3	0

	Att	Yards	Avg	Long	TD
McCown, Luke, Jac.	1	4	4.0	4	0
Castille, Tim, K.C.	5	3	0.6	3	0
Marshall, Brandon, Mia.	2	3	1.5	4	0
* Roosevelt, Naaman, Buf.	1	3	3.0	3	0
Boldin, Anquan, Bal.	2	2	1.0	3	0
Caulcrick, Jehuu, Buf.	1	2	2.0	2	0
Randle El, Antwaan, Pit.	1	2	2.0	2	0
Simpson, Jerome, Cin.	1	2	2.0	2	0
Collins, Kerry, Ten.	10	1	0.1	4	0
Hall, Ahmard, Ten.	1	1	1.0	1	0
* Jones, Donald, Buf.	3	1	0.3	2	0
Moorman, Brian, Buf.	2	1	0.5	1	0
Peerman, Cedric, Cin.	2	1	0.5	1	0
Smith, Shaun, K.C.	1	1	1.0	1t	1
* Thomas, Demaryius, Den.	2	1	0.5	1	0
Cobbs, Patrick, Mia.	4	0	0.0	4	0
Colquitt, Britton, Den.	1	0	0.0	0	0
Kern, Brett, Ten.	1	0	0.0	0	0
Koch, Sam, Bal.	1	0	0.0	0	0
Pressley, Chris, Cin.	1	0	0.0	0	0
Satele, Samson, Oak.	1	0	0.0	0	0
Brown, Andre, Den.	2	-1	-0.5	0	0
Watson, Benjamin, Cle.	1	-1	-1.0	-1	0
Caldwell, Andre, Cin.	1	-2	-2.0	-2	0
Delhomme, Jake, Cle.	8	-2	-0.3	2	0
Moore, Devin, Ind.	2	-2	-1.0	1	0
Naanee, Legedu, S.D.	3	-2	-0.7	5	0
Ward, Hines, Pit.	1	-2	-2.0	-2	0
Bess, Davone, Mia.	2	-3	-1.5	0	0
Cotchery, Jerricho, NYJ	4	-3	-0.8	4	0
Massaquoi, Mohamed, Cle.	1	-3	-3.0	-3	0
Figurs, Yamon, Cle.	1	-4	-4.0	-4	0
Volek, Billy, S.D.	6	-5	-0.8	0	0
Hoyer, Brian, N.E.	10	-8	-0.8	1	0
Washington, Nate, Ten.	1	-8	-8.0	-8	0
Lloyd, Brandon, Den.	1	-18	-18.0	-18	0
Turk, Matt, Hou.	1	27	27.0	27	0

t = Touchdown
Leader based on most yards gained
* Player that was a rookie in 2010

NFC—INDIVIDUAL RUSHERS

	Att	Yards	Avg	Long	TD
Turner, Michael, Atl.	334	1371	4.1	55	12
Peterson, Adrian, Min.	283	1298	4.6	80t	12
Jackson, Steven, St.L	330	1241	3.8	42t	6
Bradshaw, Ahmad, NY-G	276	1235	4.5	48t	8
McCoy, LeSean, Phi.	207	1080	5.2	62	7
Forté, Matt, Chi.	237	1069	4.5	68t	6
* Blount, LeGarrette, T.B.	201	1007	5.0	53	6
Gore, Frank, S.F.	203	853	4.2	64	3
Jacobs, Brandon, NY-G	147	823	5.6	73	9
Jones, Felix, Dal.	185	800	4.3	34	1
Stewart, Jonathan, Car.	178	770	4.3	48	2
Torain, Ryan, Was.	164	742	4.5	54	4
Lynch, Marshawn, Buf.-Sea.	202	737	3.6	39	6
Hightower, Tim, Ariz	153	736	4.8	80t	5
* Ivory, Chris, N.O.	137	716	5.2	55t	5
Jackson, Brandon, G.B.	190	703	3.7	71	3
Vick, Michael, Phi.	100	676	6.8	35	9
* Best, Jahvid, Det.	171	555	3.2	45	4
Forsett, Justin, Sea.	118	523	4.4	32	2
Goodson, Mike, Car.	103	452	4.4	45	3
Williams, Cadillac, T.B.	125	437	3.5	45t	2
Wells, Beanie, Ariz	116	397	3.4	24	2
Barber, Marion, Dal.	113	374	3.3	25	4
Freeman, Josh, T.B.	68	364	5.4	33	0

	Att	Yards	Avg	Long	TD		Att	Yards	Avg	Long	TD
Williams, DeAngelo, Car.	87	361	4.1	39t	1	Hall, Chad, Phi.	9	29	3.2	8	0
Rodgers, Aaron, G.B.	64	356	5.6	27	4	Young, Albert, Min.	13	29	2.2	6	0
Westbrook, Brian, S.F.	77	340	4.4	30	4	Gibson, Brandon, St.L	3	28	9.3	14	0
Morris, Maurice, Det.	90	336	3.7	26	5	Wright, Jason, Ariz	6	28	4.7	10	0
Harrison, Jerome, Cle.-Phi.	71	330	4.6	50t	1	Flynn, Matt, G.B.	9	26	2.9	12	0
Snelling, Jason, Atl.	87	324	3.7	30	2	Anderson, Derek, Ariz	5	25	5.0	11	0
* Gerhart, Toby, Min.	81	322	4.0	21	1	Moore, Matt, Car.	5	25	5.0	8	0
Kuhn, John, G.B.	84	281	3.3	18	4	Fiammetta, Tony, Car.	7	22	3.1	11	0
Thomas, Pierre, N.O.	83	269	3.2	16	2	Young, Darrel, Was.	4	19	4.8	16	0
Taylor, Chester, Chi.	112	267	2.4	24	3	Walker, Delanie, S.F.	3	18	6.0	10	0
* Williams, Keiland, Was.	65	261	4.0	32t	3	* Gronkowski, Chris, Dal.	5	17	3.4	8	0
Choice, Tashard, Dal.	66	243	3.7	26	3	Morgan, Josh, S.F.	2	17	8.5	13	0
* Dixon, Anthony, S.F.	70	237	3.4	34	2	Obomanu, Ben, Sea.	2	17	8.5	13	0
Cutler, Jay, Chi.	50	232	4.6	25	1	Daniel, Chase, N.O.	2	16	8.0	16	0
Portis, Clinton, Was.	54	227	4.2	27	2	Meachem, Robert, N.O.	4	14	3.5	8	0
Jones, Julius, Sea.-N.O.	60	223	3.7	54	0	Karney, Mike, St.L	6	12	2.0	4	0
McNabb, Donovan, Was.	29	151	5.2	36	0	Ginn, Ted, S.F.	2	11	5.5	9	0
Betts, Ladell, N.O.	45	150	3.3	12	2	Huggins, Kareem, T.B.	4	11	2.8	7	0
Bush, Reggie, N.O.	36	150	4.2	23	0	Stafford, Matthew, Det.	4	11	2.8	9	1
Kitna, Jon, Dal.	31	147	4.7	29t	1	Bennett, Earl, Chi.	2	9	4.5	5	0
Smith, Kevin, Det.	34	133	3.9	15	0	Smith, Steve, Car.	1	9	9.0	9	0
Hill, Shaun, Det.	22	123	5.6	40	0	Favre, Brett, Min.	17	8	0.5	10	0
Ryan, Matt, Atl.	46	122	2.7	20	0	Henderson, Devery, N.O.	3	8	2.7	9	0
Smith, Troy, S.F.	23	121	5.3	16	1	Norwood, Jerious, Atl.	2	8	4.0	6	0
* Webb, Joe, Min.	18	120	6.7	16	2	Wolfe, Garrett, Chi.	4	8	2.0	7	0
Stanton, Drew, Det.	18	113	6.3	20	1	* Edwards, Armanti, Car.	1	7	7.0	7	0
Stephens-Howling, LaRod, Ariz	23	113	4.9	30t	1	* Parker, Preston, T.B.	1	7	7.0	7	0
Darby, Kenneth, St.L	34	107	3.1	13	2	Vaughan, Josh, Car.	3	7	2.3	6	1
Harvin, Percy, Min.	18	107	5.9	17t	1	* Banks, Brandon, Was.	2	6	3.0	3	0
Jackson, DeSean, Phi.	16	104	6.5	31t	1	Butler, Deon, Sea.	2	6	3.0	4	0
* Starks, James, G.B.	29	101	3.5	16	0	Clayton, Mark, St.L	1	6	6.0	6	0
Washington, Leon, Sea.	27	100	3.7	21	1	Grossman, Rex, Was.	3	6	2.0	5	0
Graham, Earnest, T.B.	20	99	5.0	61	1	Doucet, Early, Ariz	2	5	2.5	3	0
Logan, Stefan, Det.	15	95	6.3	21	0	Feely, Jay, Ariz	1	5	5.0	5t	1
* Nance, Dimitri, G.B.	36	95	2.6	11	0	Senn, Jordan, Car.	1	5	5.0	5	0
Austin, Miles, Dal.	7	93	13.3	60t	1	* Tate, Golden, Sea.	2	4	2.0	3	0
Amendola, Danny, St.L	7	81	11.6	30	0	* Graham, Jimmy, N.O.	1	3	3.0	3	0
Burleson, Nate, Det.	7	81	11.6	25	0	White, Roddy, Atl.	1	3	3.0	3	0
Robinson, Michael, Sea.	12	77	6.4	17	0	Dugan, Jeff, Min.	2	2	1.0	2	0
Felton, Jerome, Det.	22	76	3.5	9	0	Evans, Heath, N.O.	2	2	1.0	2	0
McGee, Stephen, Dal.	13	74	5.7	14	0	* Gettis, David, Car.	3	2	0.7	19	0
Ware, Danny, NY-G	20	73	3.7	14	0	Johnson, Larry, Was.	5	2	0.4	7	0
Sutton, Tyrell, Car.	13	71	5.5	32	0	Knox, Johnny, Chi.	1	2	2.0	2	0
Manning, Eli, NY-G	32	70	2.2	16	0	Manningham, Mario, NY-G	1	2	2.0	2	0
Buckley, Eldra, Phi.	21	67	3.2	13	0	Sellers, Mike, Was.	4	2	0.5	1	0
Kolb, Kevin, Phi.	15	65	4.3	19	0	Stroughter, Sammie, T.B.	1	2	2.0	2	0
* Bradford, Sam, St.L	27	63	2.3	17	1	Colston, Marques, N.O.	1	1	1.0	1	0
Jackson, Tarvaris, Min.	7	63	9.0	33	0	Tahi, Naufahu, Min.	1	1	1.0	1	0
Davis, James, Cle.-Was.	19	60	3.2	14	0	Baker, Jason, Car.	1	0	0.0	0	0
Hasselbeck, Matt, Sea.	23	60	2.6	20t	3	Bidwell, Josh, Was.	1	0	0.0	0	0
* LaFell, Brandon, Car.	1	60	60.0	60	0	* Bryant, Dez, Dal.	1	0	0.0	0	0
Smith, Alex, S.F.	18	60	3.3	12	0	* Dodge, Matt, NY-G	1	0	0.0	0	0
Brown, Aaron, Det.	17	58	3.4	9	0	Lumpkin, Kregg, T.B.	1	0	0.0	0	0
* Clausen, Jimmy, Car.	23	57	2.5	11	0	McBriar, Mat, Dal.	1	0	0.0	0	0
* Toston, Keith, St.L	19	54	2.8	10	0	Norris, Moran, S.F.	3	0	0.0	1	0
* Skelton, John, Ariz	10	49	4.9	16	0	Weaver, Leonard, Phi.	1	0	0.0	0	0
Grant, Ryan, G.B.	8	45	5.6	18	0	Williams, Mike, Sea.	1	0	0.0	0	0
Whitehurst, Charlie, Sea.	20	43	2.2	9	1	Hanie, Caleb, Chi.	1	-1	-1.0	-1	0
Johnson, Josh, T.B.	4	39	9.8	14	0	Jennings, Greg, G.B.	1	-1	-1.0	-1	0
Romo, Tony, Dal.	6	38	6.3	14	0	Redman, Chris, Atl.	1	-1	-1.0	-1	0
Johnson, Gartrell, Atl.	10	36	3.6	23	0	Rosario, Dante, Car.	1	-2	-2.0	-2	0
Maclin, Jeremy, Phi.	3	36	12.0	14	0	Brees, Drew, N.O.	18	-3	-0.2	7	0
Mughelli, Ovie, Atl.	13	36	2.8	6	0	Rosenfels, Sage, NY-G	3	-3	-1.0	0	0
* Benn, Arrelious, T.B.	6	35	5.8	17	0	Smith, Antone, Atl.	1	-3	-3.0	-3	0
Breaston, Steve, Ariz	3	35	11.7	17	0	Douglas, Harry, Atl.	2	-5	-2.5	0	0
Johnson, Calvin, Det.	4	32	8.0	15	0	* Hall, Max, Ariz	1	-5	-5.0	-5	0
Hester, Devin, Chi.	7	30	4.3	11	0	Moss, Santana, Was.	5	-6	-1.2	7	0

	Att	Yards	Avg	Long	TD
Berrian, Bernard, Min.	1	-8	-8.0	-8	0
Ryan, Jon, Sea.	1	-9	-9.0	-9	0
Robinson, Laurent, St.L	2	-14	-7.0	-5	0

t = Touchdown
Leader based on most yards gained
* Player that was a rookie in 2010

AMERICAN FOOTBALL CONFERENCE—RUSHING

	Att	Yards	Avg	Long	TD
Kansas City	556	2627	4.7	80	13
Oakland	504	2494	4.9	71t	19
Jacksonville	512	2395	4.7	74t	14
N.Y. Jets	534	2374	4.4	53t	14
Houston	423	2042	4.8	74t	20
New England	454	1973	4.3	36t	19
Pittsburgh	471	1924	4.1	50t	15
Baltimore	487	1831	3.8	50	11
San Diego	457	1810	4.0	36	18
Tennessee	406	1727	4.3	76t	13
Buffalo	401	1720	4.3	39	6
Cleveland	413	1646	4.0	68	13
Miami	445	1643	3.7	51	8
Denver	398	1544	3.9	40t	13
Cincinnati	428	1522	3.6	42	8
Indianapolis	393	1483	3.8	49	13
AFC Total	7282	30755	4.2	80	217
AFC Average	455.1	1922.2	4.2	—	13.6

NATIONAL FOOTBALL CONFERENCE—RUSHING

	Att	Yards	Avg	Long	TD
Philadelphia	428	2324	5.4	62	18
N.Y. Giants	480	2200	4.6	73	17
Tampa Bay	431	2001	4.6	61	9
Minnesota	441	1942	4.4	80t	16
Atlanta	497	1891	3.8	55	14
Carolina	428	1846	4.3	60	7
Dallas	428	1786	4.2	60t	10
San Francisco	401	1657	4.1	64	10
Chicago	414	1616	3.9	68t	10
Detroit	404	1613	4.0	45	11
Green Bay	421	1606	3.8	71	11
St. Louis	429	1578	3.7	42t	9
New Orleans	380	1519	4.0	55t	9
Washington	351	1461	4.2	54	9
Seattle	385	1424	3.7	39	13
Arizona	320	1388	4.3	80t	9
NFC Total	6638	27852	4.2	80t	182
NFC Average	414.9	1740.8	4.2	—	11.4
League Total	13920	58607	—	80	399
League Average	435.0	1831.5	4.2	—	12.5

PASSING

HIGHEST RATING
AFC:	111.0	Tom Brady, New England
NFC:	101.2	Aaron Rodgers, Green Bay

COMPLETION PERCENTAGE
NFC:	68.1	Drew Brees, New Orleans
AFC:	66.3	Peyton Manning, Indianapolis

ATTEMPTS
AFC:	679	Peyton Manning, Indianapolis
NFC:	658	Drew Brees, New Orleans

COMPLETIONS
AFC:	450	Peyton Manning, Indianapolis
NFC:	448	Drew Brees, New Orleans

YARDS
AFC:	4710	Philip Rivers, San Diego
NFC:	4620	Drew Brees, New Orleans

YARDS, GAME
AFC:	497	Matt Schaub, Houston at Washington, September 19 (38-52, 3 TD) - (OT)
NFC:	446	Brett Favre, Minnesota vs. Arizona, November 7 (36-47, 2 TD) - (OT)

LONGEST
NFC:	92	Eli Manning (to Mario Manningham), N.Y. Giants at Washington, January 2 - TD
AFC:	80	Kerry Collins (to Kenny Britt), Tennessee vs. Philadelphia, October 24 - TD

YARDS PER ATTEMPT
AFC:	8.71	Philip Rivers, San Diego
NFC:	8.26	Aaron Rodgers, Green Bay

TOUCHDOWN PASSES
AFC:	36	Tom Brady, New England
NFC:	33	Drew Brees, New Orleans

TOUCHDOWN PASSES, GAME
NFC:	5	Josh Freeman, Tampa Bay vs. Seattle, December 26 (21-26, 237 yards)
AFC:	4	Ryan Fitzpatrick, Buffalo at Baltimore, October 24 (29-43, 382 yards) - (OT)
	4	David Garrard, Jacksonville at Dallas, October 31 (17-21, 260 yards)
	4	Philip Rivers, San Diego at Houston, November 7 (17-23, 295 yards)
	4	Matt Cassel, Kansas City at Denver, November 14 (33-53, 469 yards)
	4	Kyle Orton, Denver vs. Kansas City, November 14 (22-34, 296 yards)
	4	Ryan Fitzpatrick, Buffalo at Cincinnati, November 21 (21-34, 316 yards)
	4	Peyton Manning, Indianapolis at New England, November 21 (38-52, 396 yards)
	4	Philip Rivers, San Diego vs. Denver, November 22 (15-24, 233 yards)
	4	Tom Brady, New England at Detroit, November 25 (21-27, 341 yards)
	4	Matt Cassel, Kansas City at Seattle, November 28 (22-32, 233 yards)
	4	Tom Brady, New England vs. N.Y. Jets, December 6 (21-29, 326 yards)
	4	Carson Palmer, Cincinnati vs. San Diego, December 26 (16-21, 269 yards)

LOWEST INTERCEPTION PERCENTAGE
NFC:	1.3	Josh Freeman, Tampa Bay
AFC:	0.8	Tom Brady, New England

TEAM CHAMPION (MOST NET YARDS)
AFC:	4609	Indianapolis
NFC:	4441	New Orleans

NFL TOP TEN PASSERS

	Att	Comp	Pct Comp	Yds	Avg Gain	TD	Pct TD	Long	Int	Pct Int	Sack	Yds Lost	Rating Points
Brady, Tom, N.E.	492	324	65.9	3900	7.93	36	7.3	79t	4	0.8	25	175	111.0
Rivers, Philip, S.D.	541	357	66.0	4710	8.71	30	5.5	59t	13	2.4	38	227	101.8
Rodgers, Aaron, G.B.	475	312	65.7	3922	8.26	28	5.9	86t	11	2.3	31	193	101.2
Vick, Michael, Phi.	372	233	62.6	3018	8.11	21	5.6	91t	6	1.6	34	210	100.2
Roethlisberger, Ben, Pit.	389	240	61.7	3200	8.23	17	4.4	56t	5	1.3	32	220	97.0
Freeman, Josh, T.B.	474	291	61.4	3451	7.28	25	5.3	64	6	1.3	28	195	95.9
Flacco, Joe, Bal.	489	306	62.6	3622	7.41	25	5.1	67	10	2.0	40	294	93.6
Cassel, Matt, K.C.	450	262	58.2	3116	6.92	27	6.0	75t	7	1.6	26	182	93.0
Schaub, Matt, Hou.	574	365	63.6	4370	7.61	24	4.2	60	12	2.1	32	226	92.0
Manning, Peyton, Ind.	679	450	66.3	4700	6.92	33	4.9	73t	17	2.5	16	91	91.9

AMERICAN FOOTBALL CONFERENCE—PASSING

	Att	Comp	Pct Comp	Gross Yards	Sacked	Yds Lost	Net Yards	Yds/ Att	Yards/ Comp	TD	Pct TD	Long	Int	Pct Int
San Diego	544	359	66.0	4746	38	227	4519	8.72	13.22	30	5.51	59t	13	2.4
Indianapolis	679	450	66.3	4700	16	91	4609	6.92	10.44	33	4.86	73t	17	2.5
Houston	574	365	63.6	4370	32	226	4144	7.61	11.97	24	4.18	60	12	2.1
Denver	580	334	57.6	4307	40	269	4038	7.43	12.90	25	4.31	71	12	2.1
New England	507	331	65.3	4022	25	175	3847	7.93	12.15	37	7.30	79t	5	1.0
Cincinnati	590	365	61.9	3988	28	221	3767	6.76	10.93	26	4.41	78t	20	3.4
Pittsburgh	479	298	62.2	3890	43	289	3601	8.12	13.05	22	4.59	56t	9	1.9
Miami	557	335	60.1	3755	38	228	3527	6.74	11.21	17	3.05	57t	21	3.8
Baltimore	491	308	62.7	3629	40	294	3335	7.39	11.78	25	5.09	67	10	2.0
Oakland	491	279	56.8	3471	44	291	3180	7.07	12.44	18	3.67	73t	16	3.3
N.Y. Jets	525	288	54.9	3420	28	178	3242	6.51	11.88	20	3.81	74t	14	2.7
Buffalo	519	296	57.0	3371	34	213	3158	6.50	11.39	24	4.62	65t	21	4.0
Jacksonville	469	291	62.0	3356	38	291	3065	7.16	11.53	26	5.54	75	21	4.5
Tennessee	474	273	57.6	3278	27	171	3107	6.92	12.01	24	5.06	80t	15	3.2
Cleveland	478	296	61.9	3203	36	214	2989	6.70	10.82	13	2.72	65t	18	3.8
Kansas City	475	274	57.7	3189	32	221	2968	6.71	11.64	27	5.68	75t	8	1.7
AFC Total	8432	5142	—	60695	539	3599	57096	—	—	391	—	80t	232	—
AFC Average	527.0	321.4	61.0	3793.4	33.7	224.0	3568.5	7.20	11.90	24.4	4.6	—	14.5	2.8

NATIONAL FOOTBALL CONFERENCE—PASSING

	Att	Comp	Pct Comp	Gross Yards	Sacked	Yds Lost	Net Yards	Yds/ Att	Yards/ Comp	TD	Pct TD	Long	Int	Pct Int
New Orleans	661	450	68.1	4636	26	195	4441	7.01	10.30	33	4.99	80t	22	3.3
Green Bay	541	352	65.1	4355	38	231	4124	8.05	12.37	31	5.73	86t	13	2.4
Washington	605	349	57.7	4261	46	348	3913	7.04	12.21	21	3.47	76	19	3.1
Philadelphia	561	348	62.0	4215	49	309	3906	7.51	12.11	28	4.99	91t	13	2.3
Dallas	576	379	65.8	4042	31	166	4042	7.31	11.10	29	5.03	71t	19	3.3
N.Y. Giants	539	339	62.9	4002	16	117	3885	7.42	11.81	31	5.75	92t	25	4.6
Detroit	633	383	60.5	4001	27	191	3810	6.32	10.45	26	4.11	87t	16	2.5
Atlanta	577	361	62.6	3725	23	158	3567	6.46	10.32	28	4.85	46	9	1.6
San Francisco	500	282	56.4	3613	44	257	3356	7.23	12.81	19	3.80	66t	15	3.0
Tampa Bay	494	306	61.9	3564	30	203	3361	7.21	11.65	26	5.26	64	6	1.2
Seattle	544	324	59.6	3536	35	195	3341	6.50	10.91	14	2.57	87t	20	3.7
St. Louis	590	354	60.0	3512	34	244	3268	5.95	9.92	18	3.05	49	15	2.5
Chicago	466	276	59.2	3397	56	382	3015	7.29	12.31	23	4.94	89t	14	4.5
Minnesota	505	305	60.4	3327	36	230	3097	6.59	10.91	14	2.77	53t	26	5.1
Arizona	561	285	50.8	3264	50	343	2921	5.82	11.45	10	1.78	74t	19	3.4
Carolina	484	256	52.9	2635	50	346	2289	5.44	10.29	9	1.06	88t	21	4.3
NFC Total	8837	5349	—	60251	591	3915	56336	—	—	360	—	92t	279	—
NFC Average	552.3	334.3	60.5	3765.7	36.9	244.7	3521.0	6.82	11.26	22.5	4.1	—	17.4	3.2
League Total	17269	10491	—	120946	1130	7514	113432	—	—	751	—	92t	511	—
League Average	539.7	327.8	60.8	3779.6	35.3	234.8	3544.8	7.00	11.53	23.5	4.3	—	16.0	3.0

AFC—INDIVIDUAL PASSERS

	Att	Comp	Pct Comp	Yds	Avg Gain	TD	Pct TD	Long	Int	Pct Int	Sack	Yds Lost	Rating Points
Brady, Tom, N.E.	492	324	65.9	3900	7.93	36	7.3	79t	4	0.8	25	175	111.0
Rivers, Philip, S.D.	541	357	66.0	4710	8.71	30	5.5	59t	13	2.4	38	227	101.8
Roethlisberger, Ben, Pit.	389	240	61.7	3200	8.23	17	4.4	56t	5	1.3	32	220	97.0
Flacco, Joe, Bal.	489	306	62.6	3622	7.41	25	5.1	67	10	2.0	40	294	93.6
Cassel, Matt, K.C.	450	262	58.2	3116	6.92	27	6.0	75t	7	1.6	26	182	93.0
Schaub, Matt, Hou.	574	365	63.6	4370	7.61	24	4.2	60	12	2.1	32	226	92.0
Manning, Peyton, Ind.	679	450	66.3	4700	6.92	33	4.9	73t	17	2.5	16	91	91.9
Garrard, David, Jac.	366	236	64.5	2734	7.47	23	6.3	75	15	4.1	33	253	90.8
Orton, Kyle, Den.	498	293	58.8	3653	7.34	20	4.0	71	9	1.8	34	243	87.5
Campbell, Jason, Oak.	329	194	59.0	2387	7.26	13	4.0	73t	8	2.4	33	208	84.5
Palmer, Carson, Cin.	586	362	61.8	3970	6.77	26	4.4	78t	20	3.4	26	201	82.4
Collins, Kerry, Ten.	278	160	57.6	1823	6.56	14	5.0	80t	8	2.9	13	91	82.2
Fitzpatrick, Ryan, Buf.	441	255	57.8	3000	6.80	23	5.2	65t	15	3.4	24	145	81.8
Henne, Chad, Mia.	490	301	61.4	3301	6.74	15	3.1	57t	19	3.9	30	178	75.4
Sanchez, Mark, NYJ	507	278	54.8	3291	6.49	17	3.4	74t	13	2.6	27	171	75.3
(Nonqualifiers)													
Young, Vince, Ten.	156	93	59.6	1255	8.04	10	6.4	71t	3	1.9	13	80	98.6
Brunell, Mark, NYJ	13	7	53.8	117	9.00	2	15.4	52t	1	7.7	1	7	92.0
Wallace, Seneca, Cle.	101	64	63.4	694	6.87	4	4.0	65t	2	2.0	6	33	88.5
* Tebow, Tim, Den.	82	41	50.0	654	7.98	5	6.1	50	3	3.7	6	26	82.1
Dixon, Dennis, Pit.	32	22	68.8	254	7.94	0	0.0	52	1	3.1	5	41	79.4
McCown, Luke, Jac.	19	11	57.9	120	6.32	0	0.0	25	0	0.0	0	0	76.6
Batch, Charlie, Pit.	49	29	59.2	352	7.18	3	6.1	46t	3	6.1	4	21	76.2
* McCoy, Colt, Cle.	222	135	60.8	1576	7.10	6	2.7	47	9	4.1	23	132	74.5
Thigpen, Tyler, Mia.	62	33	53.2	435	7.02	2	3.2	35	2	3.2	8	50	73.0
Hoyer, Brian, N.E.	15	7	46.7	122	8.13	1	6.7	42t	1	6.7	0	0	69.3
Bouman, Todd, Jac.	34	18	52.9	222	6.53	2	5.9	29	2	5.9	1	6	68.5
Gradkowski, Bruce, Oak.	157	83	52.9	1059	6.75	5	3.2	70	7	4.5	10	77	66.3
Delhomme, Jake, Cle.	149	93	62.4	872	5.85	2	1.3	49	7	4.7	6	49	63.4
Edwards, Trent, Buf.-Jac.	101	55	54.5	521	5.16	2	2.0	44	5	5.0	11	95	54.9
Croyle, Brodie, K.C.	19	8	42.1	38	2.00	0	0.0	16	1	5.3	4	29	27.7
* Smith, Rusty, Ten.	40	20	50.0	200	5.00	0	0.0	52	4	10.0	1	0	25.0
Brohm, Brian, Buf.	23	10	43.5	106	4.61	0	0.0	33	3	13.0	3	5	17.9
(Fewer than 10 attempts)													
Boldin, Anquan, Bal.	1	1	100.0	-6	-6.00	0	0.0	-6	0	0.0	0	0	79.2
Boller, Kyle, Oak.	4	2	50.0	25	6.25	0	0.0	20	1	25.0	1	6	30.2
* Brown, Levi, Buf.	3	2	66.7	24	8.00	0	0.0	16	1	33.3	0	0	51.4
Brown, Ronnie, Mia.	2	0	0.0	0	0.00	0	0.0	—	0	0.0	0	0	39.6
Clemens, Kellen, NYJ	2	1	50.0	6	3.00	0	0.0	6	0	0.0	0	0	56.3
Crayton, Patrick, S.D.	1	0	0.0	0	0.00	0	0.0	—	0	0.0	0	0	39.6
Cribbs, Josh, Cle.	3	2	66.7	19	6.33	0	0.0	10	0	0.0	1	0	84.0
Hillis, Peyton, Cle.	2	1	50.0	13	6.50	0	0.0	13	0	0.0	0	0	70.8
Jones-Drew, Maurice, Jac.	1	0	0.0	0	0.00	0	0.0	—	1	100.0	0	0	0.0
Koch, Sam, Bal.	1	1	100.0	13	13.00	0	0.0	13	0	0.0	0	0	118.8
Leftwich, Byron, Pit.	7	5	71.4	42	6.00	0	0.0	14	0	0.0	2	7	86.6
Marshall, Brandon, Mia.	1	0	0.0	0	0.00	0	0.0	—	0	0.0	0	0	39.6
Massaquoi, Mohamed, Cle.	1	1	100.0	29	29.00	1	100.0	29t	0	0.0	0	0	158.3
McFadden, Darren, Oak.	1	0	0.0	0	0.00	0	0.0	—	0	0.0	0	0	39.6
Ochocinco, Chad, Cin.	1	0	0.0	0	0.00	0	0.0	—	0	0.0	0	0	39.6
Palko, Tyler, K.C.	6	4	66.7	35	5.83	0	0.0	18	0	0.0	2	10	81.9
Palmer, Jordan, Cin.	3	3	100.0	18	6.00	0	0.0	7	0	0.0	2	20	91.7
Pennington, Chad, Mia.	2	1	50.0	19	9.50	0	0.0	19	0	0.0	0	0	83.3
Randle El, Antwaan, Pit.	2	2	100.0	42	21.00	2	100.0	39t	0	0.0	0	0	158.3
Scifres, Mike, S.D.	1	1	100.0	28	28.00	0	0.0	28	0	0.0	0	0	118.8
Smith, Brad, NYJ	3	2	66.7	6	2.00	1	33.3	3t	0	0.0	0	0	109.7
Volek, Billy, S.D.	1	1	100.0	8	8.00	0	0.0	8	0	0.0	0	0	100.0

t = Touchdown
Leader based on rating points, minimum 224 attempts
* *Player that was a rookie in 2010*

NFC—INDIVIDUAL PASSERS

	Att	Comp	Pct Comp	Yds	Avg Gain	TD	Pct TD	Long	Int	Pct Int	Sack	Yds Lost	Rating Points
Rodgers, Aaron, G.B.	475	312	65.7	3922	8.26	28	5.9	86t	11	2.3	31	193	101.2
Vick, Michael, Phi.	372	233	62.6	3018	8.11	21	5.6	91t	6	1.6	34	210	100.2
Freeman, Josh, T.B.	474	291	61.4	3451	7.28	25	5.3	64	6	1.3	28	195	95.9
Ryan, Matt, Atl.	571	357	62.5	3705	6.49	28	4.9	46	9	1.6	23	158	91.0
Brees, Drew, N.O.	658	448	68.1	4620	7.02	33	5.0	80t	22	3.3	25	185	90.9
Kitna, Jon, Dal.	318	209	65.7	2365	7.44	16	5.0	71t	12	3.8	21	100	88.9
Cutler, Jay, Chi.	432	261	60.4	3274	7.58	23	5.3	89t	16	3.7	52	352	86.3
Manning, Eli, NY-G	539	339	62.9	4002	7.42	31	5.8	92t	25	4.6	16	117	85.3
Smith, Alex, S.F.	342	204	59.6	2370	6.93	14	4.1	62t	10	2.9	25	140	82.1
Hill, Shaun, Det.	416	257	61.8	2686	6.46	16	3.8	75t	12	2.9	17	113	81.3
McNabb, Donovan, Was.	472	275	58.3	3377	7.15	14	3.0	76	15	3.2	37	271	77.1
* Bradford, Sam, St.L	590	354	60.0	3512	5.95	18	3.1	49	15	2.5	34	244	76.5
Hasselbeck, Matt, Sea.	444	266	59.9	3001	6.76	12	2.7	87t	17	3.8	29	175	73.2
Favre, Brett, Min.	358	217	60.6	2509	7.01	11	3.1	53t	19	5.3	22	139	69.9
Anderson, Derek, Ariz	327	169	51.7	2065	6.31	7	2.1	43	10	3.1	25	176	65.9
* Clausen, Jimmy, Car.	299	157	52.5	1558	5.21	3	1.0	55t	9	3.0	33	223	58.4
(Nonqualifiers)													
Johnson, Josh, T.B.	16	14	87.5	111	6.94	0	0.0	22	0	0.0	2	8	95.6
Romo, Tony, Dal.	213	148	69.5	1605	7.54	11	5.2	69t	7	3.3	7	41	94.9
Stafford, Matthew, Det.	96	57	59.4	535	5.57	6	6.3	36	1	1.0	4	36	91.3
Flynn, Matt, G.B.	66	40	60.6	433	6.56	3	4.5	66t	2	3.0	7	38	82.4
McGee, Stephen, Dal.	44	22	50.0	238	5.41	2	4.5	37t	0	0.0	3	25	81.4
Grossman, Rex, Was.	133	74	55.6	884	6.65	7	5.3	64t	4	3.0	9	77	81.2
Stanton, Drew, Det.	119	69	58.0	780	6.55	4	3.4	87t	3	2.5	6	42	78.4
Smith, Troy, S.F.	145	73	50.3	1176	8.11	5	3.4	66t	4	2.8	18	112	77.8
Kolb, Kevin, Phi.	189	115	60.8	1197	6.33	7	3.7	83t	7	3.7	15	99	76.1
Whitehurst, Charlie, Sea.	99	57	57.6	507	5.12	2	2.0	61	3	3.0	5	13	65.5
Jackson, Tarvaris, Min.	58	34	58.6	341	5.88	3	5.2	46	4	6.9	6	43	63.9
* Skelton, John, Ariz	126	60	47.6	662	5.25	2	1.6	74t	2	1.6	9	65	62.3
* Webb, Joe, Min.	89	54	60.7	477	5.36	0	0.0	46	3	3.4	8	48	60.9
* Pike, Tony, Car.	12	6	50.0	47	3.92	0	0.0	22	0	0.0	1	10	60.1
Bartel, Richard, Ariz	28	16	57.1	150	5.36	0	0.0	31	1	3.6	2	12	57.1
Moore, Matt, Car.	143	79	55.2	857	5.99	5	3.5	39	10	7.0	13	90	55.6
St. Pierre, Brian, Car.	28	13	46.4	173	6.18	1	3.6	88t	2	7.1	3	23	48.7
* Hall, Max, Ariz	78	39	50.0	370	4.74	1	1.3	26	6	7.7	14	90	35.7
Carr, David, S.F.	13	5	38.5	67	5.15	0	0.0	22	1	7.7	1	5	23.6
Collins, Todd, Chi.	27	10	37.0	68	2.52	0	0.0	19	5	18.5	2	15	5.9
(Fewer than 10 attempts)													
Barber, Marion, Dal.	1	0	0.0	0	0.00	0	0.0	—	0	0.0	0	0	39.6
* Best, Jahvid, Det.	1	0	0.0	0	0.00	0	0.0	—	0	0.0	0	0	39.6
Breaston, Steve, Ariz	2	1	50.0	17	8.50	0	0.0	17	0	0.0	0	0	79.2
Daniel, Chase, N.O.	3	2	66.7	16	5.33	0	0.0	9	0	0.0	1	10	79.9
* Edwards, Armanti, Car.	1	1	100.0	0	0.00	0	0.0	0	0	0.0	0	0	79.2
Graham, Earnest, T.B.	1	1	100.0	2	2.00	1	100.0	2t	0	0.0	0	0	118.8
Hanie, Caleb, Chi.	7	5	71.4	55	7.86	0	0.0	26	0	0.0	2	15	94.3
* LaFell, Brandon, Car.	1	0	0.0	0	0.00	0	0.0	—	0	0.0	0	0	39.6
Logan, Stefan, Det.	1	0	0.0	0	0.00	0	0.0	—	0	0.0	0	0	39.6
Redman, Chris, Atl.	6	4	66.7	20	3.33	0	0.0	14	0	0.0	0	0	71.5
Robinson, Michael, Sea.	1	1	100.0	28	28.00	0	0.0	28	0	0.0	0	0	118.8
Spurlock, Micheal, T.B.	3	0	0.0	0	0.00	0	0.0	—	0	0.0	1	0	39.6
Washington, Leon, Sea.	0	0	—	0	—	0	—	—	0	—	1	7	—

t = Touchdown
Leader based on rating points, minimum 224 attempts
* Player that was a rookie in 2010

PASS RECEIVING

RECEPTIONS
NFC:	115	Roddy White, Atlanta
AFC:	111	Reggie Wayne, Indianapolis

RECEPTIONS, GAME
AFC:	15	Reggie Wayne, Indianapolis at Jacksonville, October 3 (196 yards, 0 TD)
NFC:	13	Roddy White, Atlanta at Pittsburgh, September 12 (111 yards, 0 TD) - (OT)

YARDS
AFC:	1448	Brandon Lloyd, Denver
NFC:	1389	Roddy White, Atlanta

YARDS, GAME
AFC:	225	Kenny Britt, Tennessee vs. Philadelphia, October 24 (7 receptions, 3 TD)
NFC:	210	DeSean Jackson, Philadelphia at Dallas, December 12 (4 receptions, 1 TD)

LONGEST
NFC:	92	Mario Manningham (from Eli Manning), N.Y. Giants at Washington, January 2 - TD
AFC:	80	Kenny Britt (from Kerry Collins), Tennessee vs. Philadelphia, October 24 - TD

YARDS PER RECEPTION
NFC:	22.5	DeSean Jackson, Philadelphia
AFC:	21.0	Mike Wallace, Pittsburgh

TOUCHDOWNS
AFC:	15	Dwayne Bowe, Kansas City
NFC:	12	Greg Jennings, Green Bay
	12	Calvin Johnson, Detroit

TEAM LEADERS, RECEPTIONS
AFC: BALTIMORE, 64, Anquan Boldin; BUFFALO, 82, Steve Johnson; CINCINNATI, 72, Terrell Owens; CLEVELAND, 68, Benjamin Watson; DENVER, 77, Brandon Lloyd; HOUSTON, 86, Andre Johnson; INDIANAPOLIS, 111, Reggie Wayne; JACKSONVILLE, 66, Mike Thomas; KANSAS CITY, 72, Dwayne Bowe; MIAMI, 86, Brandon Marshall; NEW ENGLAND, 86, Wes Welker; N.Y. JETS, 55, Dustin Keller; OAKLAND, 60, Zach Miller; PITTSBURGH, 60, Mike Wallace; SAN DIEGO, 59, Darren Sproles; TENNESSEE, 44, Chris Johnson

NFC: ARIZONA, 90, Larry Fitzgerald; ATLANTA, 115, Roddy White; CAROLINA, 46, Steve Smith; CHICAGO, 51, Matt Forté, Johnny Knox; DALLAS, 94, Jason Witten; DETROIT, 77, Calvin Johnson; GREEN BAY, 76, Greg Jennings; MINNESOTA, 71, Percy Harvin; NEW ORLEANS, 84, Marques Colston; N.Y. GIANTS, 79, Hakeem Nicks; PHILADELPHIA, 78, LeSean McCoy; ST. LOUIS, 85, Danny Amendola; SAN FRANCISCO, 56, Vernon Davis; SEATTLE, 65, Mike Williams; TAMPA BAY, 66, Kellen Winslow; WASHINGTON, 93, Santana Moss

NFL TOP TEN PASS RECEIVERS
	No	Yards	Avg	Long	TD
White, Roddy, Atl.	115	1389	12.1	46	10
Wayne, Reggie, Ind.	111	1355	12.2	50	6
Witten, Jason, Dal.	94	1002	10.7	33	9
Moss, Santana, Was.	93	1115	12.0	56	6
Fitzgerald, Larry, Ariz	90	1137	12.6	41	6
Johnson, Andre, Hou.	86	1216	14.1	60	8
Marshall, Brandon, Mia.	86	1014	11.8	46	3
Welker, Wes, N.E.	86	848	9.9	35	7
Amendola, Danny, St.L	85	689	8.1	36	3
Colston, Marques, N.O.	84	1023	12.2	43	7

NFL TOP TEN RECEIVERS BY YARDS
	Yards	No	Avg	Long	TD
Lloyd, Brandon, Den.	1448	77	18.8	71	11
White, Roddy, Atl.	1389	115	12.1	46	10
Wayne, Reggie, Ind.	1355	111	12.2	50	6
Jennings, Greg, G.B.	1265	76	16.6	86t	12
Wallace, Mike, Pit.	1257	60	21.0	56t	10
Johnson, Andre, Hou.	1216	86	14.1	60	8
Bowe, Dwayne, K.C.	1162	72	16.1	75t	15
Fitzgerald, Larry, Ariz	1137	90	12.6	41	6
Johnson, Calvin, Det.	1120	77	14.5	87t	12
Moss, Santana, Was.	1115	93	12.0	56	6

AFC—INDIVIDUAL RECEIVERS
	No	Yards	Avg	Long	TD
Wayne, Reggie, Ind.	111	1355	12.2	50	6
Johnson, Andre, Hou.	86	1216	14.1	60	8
Marshall, Brandon, Mia.	86	1014	11.8	46	3
Welker, Wes, N.E.	86	848	9.9	35	7
Johnson, Steve, Buf.	82	1073	13.1	45	10
Bess, Davone, Mia.	79	820	10.4	29	5
Lloyd, Brandon, Den.	77	1448	18.8	71	11
Bowe, Dwayne, K.C.	72	1162	16.1	75t	15
Owens, Terrell, Cin.	72	983	13.7	78t	9
Watson, Benjamin, Cle.	68	763	11.2	44	3
Ochocinco, Chad, Cin.	67	831	12.4	42	4
Garcon, Pierre, Ind.	67	784	11.7	57t	6
Tamme, Jacob, Ind.	67	631	9.4	30	4
Thomas, Mike, Jac.	66	820	12.4	50t	4
Foster, Arian, Hou.	66	604	9.2	50	2
Gaffney, Jabar, Den.	65	875	13.5	50	2
Boldin, Anquan, Bal.	64	837	13.1	61	7
Rice, Ray, Bal.	63	556	8.8	34	1
Branch, Deion, Sea.-N.E.	61	818	13.4	79t	6
Mason, Derrick, Bal.	61	802	13.1	42	7
Hillis, Peyton, Cle.	61	477	7.8	47	2
Wallace, Mike, Pit.	60	1257	21.0	56t	10
Miller, Zach, Oak.	60	685	11.4	43t	5
Ward, Hines, Pit.	59	755	12.8	43	5
Royal, Eddie, Den.	59	627	10.6	41	3
Sproles, Darren, S.D.	59	520	8.8	57t	2
Lewis, Marcedes, Jac.	58	700	12.1	42t	10
Collie, Austin, Ind.	58	649	11.2	73t	8
Keller, Dustin, NYJ	55	687	12.5	41	5
Edwards, Braylon, NYJ	53	904	17.1	74t	7
Holmes, Santonio, NYJ	52	746	14.3	52	6
* Shipley, Jordan, Cin.	52	600	11.5	64t	3
* Gresham, Jermaine, Cin.	52	471	9.1	27	4
Tomlinson, LaDainian, NYJ	52	368	7.1	21	0
Walter, Kevin, Hou.	51	621	12.2	35	5
Jones, Jacoby, Hou.	51	562	11.0	47	3
Gates, Antonio, S.D.	50	782	15.6	48t	10
* Moeaki, Tony, K.C.	47	556	11.8	34	3
McFadden, Darren, Oak.	47	507	10.8	67t	3
* Hernandez, Aaron, N.E.	45	563	12.5	46	6
Charles, Jamaal, K.C.	45	468	10.4	31	3
Johnson, Chris, Ten.	44	245	5.6	25	1
Hartline, Brian, Mia.	43	615	14.3	54	1

	No	Yards	Avg	Long	TD		No	Yards	Avg	Long	TD
Sims-Walker, Mike, Jac.	43	562	13.1	39	7	Hall, Ahmard, Ten.	15	100	6.7	19	0
Britt, Kenny, Ten.	42	775	18.5	80t	9	Jackson, Vincent, S.D.	14	248	17.7	58t	3
Washington, Nate, Ten.	42	687	16.4	71t	6	Jones, Thomas, K.C.	14	122	8.7	20	0
* Gronkowski, Rob, N.E.	42	546	13.0	28	10	McGahee, Willis, Bal.	14	55	3.9	32t	1
Miller, Heath, Pit.	42	512	12.2	36	2	* Ajirotutu, Seyi, S.D.	13	262	20.2	55t	2
Murphy, Louis, Oak.	41	609	14.9	70	2	Washington, Kelley, S.D.	13	173	13.3	36	1
Cotchery, Jerricho, NYJ	41	433	10.6	49	2	Stupar, Jonathan, Buf.	12	111	9.3	35	0
Heap, Todd, Bal.	40	599	15.0	65t	5	Green-Ellis, BenJarvis, N.E.	12	85	7.1	16	0
Stuckey, Chansi, Cle.	40	346	8.7	25	0	Myers, Brandon, Oak.	12	80	6.7	16	0
Fasano, Anthony, Mia.	39	528	13.5	31	4	Polite, Lousaka, Mia.	12	61	5.1	14	0
Daniels, Owen, Hou.	38	471	12.4	31	2	Hill, Jason, Jac.	11	248	22.5	48t	1
Floyd, Malcom, S.D.	37	717	19.4	55	6	* Dickson, Ed, Bal.	11	152	13.8	58	1
Evans, Lee, Buf.	37	578	15.6	54	4	Stevens, Craig, Ten.	11	122	11.1	28	2
Moreno, Knowshon, Den.	37	372	10.1	45	3	Anderson, David, Hou.	11	117	10.6	35	0
Clark, Dallas, Ind.	37	347	9.4	50t	3	Scott, Bernard, Cin.	11	60	5.5	25	0
Dreessen, Joel, Hou.	36	518	14.4	43t	4	Jones, Greg, Jac.	11	47	4.3	12	0
Massaquoi, Mohamed, Cle.	36	483	13.4	41t	2	Higgins, Johnnie Lee, Oak.	10	103	10.3	26	0
* White, Blair, Ind.	36	355	9.9	33	5	Pope, Leonard, K.C.	10	76	7.6	14	2
Scaife, Bo, Ten.	36	318	8.8	30	4	Castille, Tim, K.C.	10	43	4.3	14	0
Woodhead, Danny, N.E.	34	379	11.1	50	1	Kelly, Reggie, Cin.	10	42	4.2	9	0
Jones-Drew, Maurice, Jac.	34	317	9.3	75	2	* Roosevelt, Naaman, Buf.	9	139	15.4	30	0
Parrish, Roscoe, Buf.	33	400	12.1	37	2	Spaeth, Matt, Pit.	9	80	8.9	13	1
Brown, Ronnie, Mia.	33	242	7.3	24	0	Redman, Isaac, Pit.	9	72	8.0	16t	2
* Nelson, David, Buf.	31	353	11.4	37	3	* James, Javarris, Ind.	9	63	7.0	11	0
Jackson, Fred, Buf.	31	215	6.9	65t	2	Underwood, Tiquan, Jac.	8	111	13.9	22	0
Houshmandzadeh, T.J., Bal.	30	398	13.3	56t	3	Casey, James, Hou.	8	98	12.3	33	0
Cook, Jared, Ten.	29	361	12.4	36	1	Cobbs, Patrick, Mia.	8	91	11.4	29t	2
Robiskie, Brian, Cle.	29	310	10.7	46t	3	Leach, Vonta, Hou.	8	91	11.4	21	0
Crayton, Patrick, S.D.	28	514	18.4	49	1	Gronkowski, Dan, Den.	8	65	8.1	13	0
Moss, Randy, N.E.-Min.-Ten.	28	393	14.0	37t	5	Edelman, Julian, N.E.	7	86	12.3	40	0
* Sanders, Emmanuel, Pit.	28	376	13.4	35	2	Morris, Sammy, N.E.	7	77	11.0	22	0
Buckhalter, Correll, Den.	28	240	8.0	23t	2	Bell, Mike, Phi.-Cle.	7	67	9.0	28	0
Benson, Cedric, Cin.	28	178	6.4	24	1	Ward, Derrick, Hou.	7	61	8.7	12	0
Heyward-Bey, Darrius, Oak.	26	366	14.1	69t	1	Ringer, Javon, Ten.	7	44	6.3	9	0
Jennings, Rashad, Jac.	26	223	8.6	25	0	Martin, David, Buf.	7	43	6.1	15	1
Moore, Mewelde, Pit.	26	205	7.9	29	0	* Moore, Marlon, Mia.	6	128	21.3	57t	1
* Ford, Jacoby, Oak.	25	470	18.8	52	2	* Tucker, Verran, K.C.	6	114	19.0	38	1
Caldwell, Andre, Cin.	25	345	13.8	53	0	* Decker, Eric, Den.	6	106	17.7	38	1
Reece, Marcel, Oak.	25	333	13.3	73t	3	Wilson, Kris, S.D.	6	73	12.2	37	0
Tolbert, Mike, S.D.	25	216	8.6	28	0	Faulk, Kevin, N.E.	6	62	10.3	21	0
Tate, Brandon, N.E.	24	432	18.0	65t	3	* Wallace, Roberto, Mia.	6	62	10.3	19	0
* Spiller, C.J., Buf.	24	157	6.5	41	1	Osgood, Kassim, Jac.	6	60	10.0	24t	1
Naanee, Legedu, S.D.	23	371	16.1	59t	1	Crumpler, Alge, N.E.	6	52	8.7	27	2
Cribbs, Josh, Cle.	23	292	12.7	65t	1	* James, Brandon, Ind.	6	40	6.7	17	0
Mendenhall, Rashard, Pit.	23	167	7.3	24	0	Hart, Mike, Ind.	6	25	4.2	10	0
* Thomas, Demaryius, Den.	22	283	12.9	31	2	Gonzalez, Anthony, Ind.	5	67	13.4	34	0
Randle El, Antwaan, Pit.	22	253	11.5	34	0	Hawkins, Lavelle, Ten.	5	61	12.2	24	0
Chambers, Chris, K.C.	22	213	9.7	26	1	Royal, Robert, Cle.	5	56	11.2	20t	1
Hester, Jacob, S.D.	22	145	6.6	21	1	Larsen, Spencer, Den.	5	51	10.2	29	1
* Mathews, Ryan, S.D.	22	145	6.6	17	0	Schilens, Chaz, Oak.	5	40	8.0	11	1
Davis, Buster, S.D.	21	259	12.3	49	1	* Eldridge, Brody, Ind.	5	39	7.8	10	0
* McCluster, Dexter, K.C.	21	209	10.0	31t	1	Richardson, Tony, NYJ	5	31	6.2	14	0
McClain, Le'Ron, Bal.	21	134	6.4	19	0	Sperry, Kory, S.D.	4	73	18.3	35	0
Simpson, Jerome, Cin.	20	277	13.9	59t	3	Maroney, Laurence, Den.	4	50	12.5	28	0
Gage, Justin, Ten.	20	266	13.3	30	1	Johnson, David, Pit.	4	46	11.5	25	0
McMichael, Randy, S.D.	20	221	11.1	28	2	Smith, Brad, NYJ	4	44	11.0	23	0
Miller, Zach, Jac.	20	216	10.8	52t	1	McIntyre, Corey, Buf.	4	32	8.0	14	0
Brown, Donald, Ind.	20	205	10.3	25	0	Cox, Mike, K.C.	4	27	6.8	13	0
Leonard, Brian, Cin.	20	137	6.9	20	1	Vickers, Lawrence, Cle.	4	15	3.8	10	0
Williams, Ricky, Mia.	19	141	7.4	28t	1	* Price, Taylor, N.E.	3	41	13.7	18	0
Addai, Joseph, Ind.	19	124	6.5	15	0	Miller, Nick, Oak.	3	40	13.3	32	0
* Jones, Donald, Buf.	18	213	11.8	40	1	O'Connell, Jake, K.C.	3	31	10.3	18	0
Bush, Michael, Oak.	18	194	10.8	55	0	Coffman, Chase, Cin.	3	30	10.0	14	0
Copper, Terrance, K.C.	18	157	8.7	20	0	Nelson, Shawn, Buf.	3	25	8.3	12	0
Graham, Daniel, Den.	18	148	8.2	28	0	Potter, Zach, Jac.	3	24	8.0	10	0
Moore, Evan, Cle.	16	322	20.1	49	1	* McKnight, Joe, NYJ	3	20	6.7	9	0
* Williams, Damian, Ten.	16	219	13.7	39	0	Ball, Lance, Den.	3	16	5.3	13	0
* Brown, Antonio, Pit.	16	167	10.4	26	0	Robinson, Gijon, Ind.	3	12	4.0	6	1
Greene, Shonn, NYJ	16	120	7.5	15	0	Slaton, Steve, Hou.	3	11	3.7	12	0

	No	Yards	Avg	Long	TD
* Karim, Deji, Jac.	3	10	3.3	7	0
Stallworth, Donte', Bal.	2	82	41.0	67	0
* Shuler, Mickey, Mia.	2	44	22.0	28	0
Turner, Patrick, NYJ	2	26	13.0	21	0
Figurs, Yamon, Oak.	2	17	8.5	11	0
Cosby, Quan, Cin.	2	16	8.0	11	0
Bennett, Michael, Oak.	2	9	4.5	6	0
* Conner, John, NYJ	2	9	4.5	7	0
Ganther, Quinton, Buf.	2	9	4.5	8	0
Barnes, Khalif, Oak.	2	8	4.0	6	1
Taylor, Fred, N.E.	2	6	3.0	7	0
* Goodman, Richard, S.D.	1	25	25.0	25	0
Willis, Matt, Den.	1	17	17.0	17	0
Bolen, Brock, Jac.	1	15	15.0	15	0
* McCoy, Colt, Cle.	1	13	13.0	13	0
Williams, Cary, Bal.	1	13	13.0	13	0
Peerman, Cedric, Cin.	1	11	11.0	11	0
Cartwright, Rock, Oak.	1	10	10.0	10	0
Battle, Jackie, K.C.	1	9	9.0	9	0
Quinn, Richard, Den.	1	9	9.0	9	0
Wallace, Seneca, Cle.	1	9	9.0	9	0
Chandler, Scott, Buf.	1	8	8.0	8	0
Hubbard, Paul, Buf.	1	8	8.0	8	0
Aiken, Sam, Cle.	1	7	7.0	7	0
Hartsock, Ben, NYJ	1	7	7.0	7	0
Curtis, Kevin, Mia.	1	6	6.0	6	0
Pressley, Chris, Cin.	1	6	6.0	6	0
Smith, Alex, Cle.	1	6	6.0	6	0
Rhodes, Dominic, Ind.	1	4	4.0	4	0
* Cumberland, Jeff, NYJ	1	3	3.0	3	0
Hilliard, Lex, Mia.	1	3	3.0	3	0
Wilford, Ernest, Jac.	1	3	3.0	3	0
Banks, Gary, S.D.	1	2	2.0	2	0
Vrabel, Mike, K.C.	1	2	2.0	2t	1
* Pitta, Dennis, Bal.	1	1	1.0	1	0
Whitworth, Andrew, Cin.	1	1	1.0	1t	1

t = Touchdown; * Player that was a rookie in 2010
Leader based on receptions

NFC—INDIVIDUAL RECEIVERS

	No	Yards	Avg	Long	TD
White, Roddy, Atl.	115	1389	12.1	46	10
Witten, Jason, Dal.	94	1002	10.7	33	9
Moss, Santana, Was.	93	1115	12.0	56	6
Fitzgerald, Larry, Ariz	90	1137	12.6	41	6
Amendola, Danny, St.L	85	689	8.1	36	3
Colston, Marques, N.O.	84	1023	12.2	43	7
Nicks, Hakeem, NY-G	79	1052	13.3	46t	11
McCoy, LeSean, Phi.	78	592	7.6	40	2
Johnson, Calvin, Det.	77	1120	14.5	87t	12
Cooley, Chris, Was.	77	849	11.0	35	3
Jennings, Greg, G.B.	76	1265	16.6	86t	12
Harvin, Percy, Min.	71	868	12.2	53t	5
Pettigrew, Brandon, Det.	71	722	10.2	35	4
Maclin, Jeremy, Phi.	70	964	13.8	83t	10
Gonzalez, Tony, Atl.	70	656	9.4	34	6
Austin, Miles, Dal.	69	1041	15.1	69t	7
Moore, Lance, N.O.	66	763	11.6	80t	8
Winslow, Kellen, T.B.	66	730	11.1	41t	5
* Williams, Mike, T.B.	65	964	14.8	58t	11
Williams, Mike, Sea.	65	751	11.6	68	2
Manningham, Mario, NY-G	60	944	15.7	92t	9
* Best, Jahvid, Det.	58	487	8.4	75t	2
Davis, Vernon, S.F.	56	914	16.3	66t	7
Crabtree, Michael, S.F.	55	741	13.5	60t	6
Burleson, Nate, Det.	55	625	11.4	58	6
Gibson, Brandon, St.L	53	620	11.7	41	2
Knox, Johnny, Chi.	51	960	18.8	67t	5

	No	Yards	Avg	Long	TD
Avant, Jason, Phi.	51	573	11.2	34	0
Driver, Donald, G.B.	51	565	11.1	61t	4
Forté, Matt, Chi.	51	547	10.7	89t	3
Jones, James, G.B.	50	679	13.6	66t	5
Smith, Steve, NY-G	48	529	11.0	45	3
Jones, Felix, Dal.	48	450	9.4	71t	1
Jackson, DeSean, Phi.	47	1056	22.5	91t	6
Breaston, Steve, Ariz	47	718	15.3	37	1
Shiancoe, Visanthe, Min.	47	530	11.3	33	2
Bradshaw, Ahmad, NY-G	47	314	6.7	18	0
Bennett, Earl, Chi.	46	561	12.2	48	3
Smith, Steve, Car.	46	554	12.0	39	2
Gore, Frank, S.F.	46	452	9.8	41	2
Jackson, Steven, St.L	46	383	8.3	49	0
Williams, Cadillac, T.B.	46	355	7.7	20	1
Nelson, Jordy, G.B.	45	582	12.9	80t	2
* Bryant, Dez, Dal.	45	561	12.5	46	6
Scheffler, Tony, Det.	45	378	8.4	25	1
Armstrong, Anthony, Was.	44	871	19.8	76	3
Morgan, Josh, S.F.	44	698	15.9	65	2
Meachem, Robert, N.O.	44	638	14.5	55	5
Snelling, Jason, Atl.	44	303	6.9	28t	1
Jackson, Brandon, G.B.	43	342	8.0	37	1
Celek, Brent, Phi.	42	511	12.2	65t	4
Jenkins, Michael, Atl.	41	505	12.3	43	2
Shockey, Jeremy, N.O.	41	408	10.0	31	3
Olsen, Greg, Chi.	41	404	9.9	39t	5
Fells, Daniel, St.L	41	391	9.5	36	2
Hester, Devin, Chi.	40	475	11.9	39	4
Goodson, Mike, Car.	40	310	7.8	32	0
* Williams, Keiland, Was.	39	309	7.9	36	2
* LaFell, Brandon, Car.	38	468	12.3	44	1
Williams, Roy, Dal.	37	530	14.3	63t	5
* Gettis, David, Car.	37	508	13.7	88t	3
Butler, Deon, Sea.	36	385	10.7	63t	4
Peterson, Adrian, Min.	36	341	9.5	34	1
Boss, Kevin, NY-G	35	531	15.2	54	5
Henderson, Devery, N.O.	34	464	13.6	57	1
Robinson, Laurent, St.L	34	344	10.1	32	2
Bush, Reggie, N.O.	34	208	6.1	20	1
Bennett, Martellus, Dal.	33	260	7.9	32	0
Forsett, Justin, Sea.	33	252	7.6	21	0
Rosario, Dante, Car.	32	264	8.3	26	0
* Graham, Jimmy, N.O.	31	356	11.5	52	5
Stokley, Brandon, Sea.	31	354	11.4	36	0
Carlson, John, Sea.	31	318	10.3	37	1
Obomanu, Ben, Sea.	30	494	16.5	87t	4
Thomas, David, N.O.	30	219	7.3	22	2
Walker, Delanie, S.F.	29	331	11.4	38	0
Thomas, Pierre, N.O.	29	201	6.9	23	0
Berrian, Bernard, Min.	28	252	9.0	30	0
Doucet, Early, Ariz	26	291	11.2	36	1
* Benn, Arrelious, T.B.	25	395	15.8	64	2
Morris, Maurice, Det.	25	170	6.8	16	0
* Roberts, Andre, Ariz	24	307	12.8	74t	2
Stroughter, Sammie, T.B.	24	239	10.0	27	0
Hagan, Derek, NY-G	24	223	9.3	17	1
Clayton, Mark, St.L	23	306	13.3	39	2
Betts, Ladell, N.O.	23	141	6.1	25	0
Douglas, Harry, Atl.	22	294	13.4	46	1
Lynch, Marshawn, Buf.-Sea.	22	145	6.6	22	0
Davis, Fred, Was.	21	316	15.0	71	3
Finley, Jermichael, G.B.	21	301	14.3	34	1
* Quarless, Andrew, G.B.	21	238	11.3	23	1
* Tate, Golden, Sea.	21	227	10.8	52	0
* Gerhart, Toby, Min.	21	167	8.0	23	0
Hightower, Tim, Ariz	21	136	6.5	20	0
* Alexander, Danario, St.L	20	306	15.3	46	1
Camarillo, Greg, Min.	20	240	12.0	31	1

	No	Yards	Avg	Long	TD		No	Yards	Avg	Long	TD
Sellers, Mike, Was.	20	224	11.2	28	0	Portis, Clinton, Was.	5	55	11.0	14	0
Taylor, Chester, Chi.	20	139	7.0	18	0	Manumaleuna, Brandon, Chi.	5	43	8.6	16	1
Finneran, Brian, Atl.	19	166	8.7	21	3	Purvis, Ryan, T.B.	5	38	7.6	12	0
Schmitt, Owen, Phi.	19	136	7.2	18	1	Fiammetta, Tony, Car.	5	34	6.8	11	0
King, Jeff, Car.	19	121	6.4	16t	2	Booker, Lorenzo, Min.	5	32	6.4	7	0
Johnson, Bryant, Det.	18	210	11.7	24	0	* Palmer, Michael, Atl.	5	29	5.8	11	1
Torain, Ryan, Was.	18	125	6.9	20	2	* Byham, Nate, S.F.	5	27	5.4	9	0
Rice, Sidney, Min.	17	280	16.5	46	2	* Blount, LeGarrette, T.B.	5	14	2.8	7	0
Spurlock, Micheal, T.B.	17	250	14.7	43	2	Karney, Mike, St.L	5	14	2.8	4	0
Lewis, Greg, Min.	17	197	11.6	33	0	* Dixon, Anthony, S.F.	5	11	2.2	8	0
Kleinsasser, Jimmy, Min.	17	148	8.7	20	0	Crabtree, Tom, G.B.	4	61	15.3	33	0
Choice, Tashard, Dal.	17	109	6.4	17	0	Davis, James, Was.	4	45	11.3	28	0
Jones, Julius, N.O.	17	59	3.5	13	0	* Parker, Preston, T.B.	4	42	10.5	21	0
Westbrook, Brian, S.F.	16	150	9.4	62t	1	Heller, Will, Det.	4	37	9.3	13t	1
Graham, Earnest, T.B.	16	130	8.1	46	1	Dugan, Jeff, Min.	4	30	7.5	10	0
Stephens-Howling, LaRod, Ariz	16	111	6.9	13	0	Norris, Moran, S.F.	4	20	5.0	8	0
Patrick, Ben, Ariz	15	123	8.2	21	0	* Austin, Terrence, Was.	3	47	15.7	28	0
Kuhn, John, G.B.	15	97	6.5	12	2	* Dray, Jim, Ariz	3	47	15.7	24	0
Bajema, Billy, St.L	14	145	10.4	26t	2	Stevens, Jerramy, T.B.	3	43	14.3	22	0
Hurd, Sam, Dal.	14	120	8.6	13	0	Ogletree, Kevin, Dal.	3	34	11.3	19	0
Gilmore, John, T.B.	13	160	12.3	30	1	* Nance, Dimitri, G.B.	3	30	10.0	14	0
* Hoomanawanui, Michael, St.L	13	146	11.2	36t	3	Williams, Derrick, Det.	3	30	10.0	17	0
Mughelli, Ovie, Atl.	13	126	9.7	18	1	Johnson, Quinn, G.B.	3	26	8.7	11	0
Beckum, Travis, NY-G	13	116	8.9	29	2	Johnson, Gartrell, Atl.	3	6	2.0	10	0
Galloway, Joey, Was.	12	173	14.4	62	0	Jarrett, Dwayne, Car.	2	40	20.0	21	0
Ginn, Ted, S.F.	12	163	13.6	37t	1	* Toston, Keith, St.L	2	29	14.5	23	0
* Komar, Max, Ariz	12	117	9.8	20	0	Maui'a, Reagan, Ariz	2	20	10.0	10	0
Harrison, Jerome, Cle.-Phi.	12	85	7.1	23	0	Clayton, Michael, NY-G	2	19	9.5	14	0
Turner, Michael, Atl.	12	85	7.1	19	0	Mills, Garrett, Phi.	2	19	9.5	14	0
Sutton, Tyrell, Car.	12	70	5.8	14	0	* Onobun, Fendi, St.L	2	15	7.5	8	0
Smith, Kevin, Det.	11	123	11.2	27	0	* Starks, James, G.B.	2	15	7.5	12	0
Hall, Chad, Phi.	11	115	10.5	48	1	Young, Albert, Min.	2	11	5.5	13	0
Lee, Donald, G.B.	11	73	6.6	17	3	* Banks, Brandon, Was.	2	10	5.0	15	0
Williams, DeAngelo, Car.	11	61	5.5	14	0	* Paulsen, Logan, Was.	2	10	5.0	9	1
Barber, Marion, Dal.	11	49	4.5	15	0	Hedgecock, Madison, NY-G	2	8	4.0	7	0
Aromashodu, Devin, Chi.	10	149	14.9	34	0	Davis, Kellen, Chi.	1	19	19.0	19t	1
Peelle, Justin, Atl.	10	96	9.6	15	1	Baskett, Hank, Min.	1	18	18.0	18	0
Darby, Kenneth, St.L	10	61	6.1	21t	1	* Ivory, Chris, N.O.	1	17	17.0	17	0
Morrah, Cameron, Sea.	9	117	13.0	36	0	Clark, Desmond, Chi.	1	12	12.0	12	0
Baker, Chris, Sea.	9	116	12.9	44	1	Humphrey, Tory, N.O.	1	12	12.0	12	0
* Williams, Stephen, Ariz	9	101	11.2	17	0	Lumpkin, Kregg, T.B.	1	12	12.0	12	0
Zeigler, Dominique, S.F.	9	98	10.9	20	0	Buckley, Eldra, Phi.	1	10	10.0	10	0
Davis, Rashied, Chi.	9	84	9.3	21	1	* Lorig, Erik, T.B.	1	10	10.0	10	0
Washington, Leon, Sea.	9	79	8.8	28	0	Hall, Korey, G.B.	1	9	9.0	9	0
* Harbor, Clay, Phi.	9	72	8.0	24	1	Norwood, Jerious, Atl.	1	9	9.0	9	0
Pascoe, Bear, NY-G	9	72	8.0	12	0	* Williams, Kyle, S.F.	1	8	8.0	8	0
Williams, Roydell, Was.	9	100	10.0	61	0	Drees, Drew, N.O.	1	7	7.0	7	0
Stewart, Jonathan, Car.	8	103	12.9	55t	1	Huggins, Kareem, T.B.	1	7	7.0	7	0
Felton, Jerome, Det.	8	54	6.8	19	0	Johnson, Manuel, Dal.	1	6	6.0	6	0
Brown, Aaron, Det.	8	45	5.6	10	0	* Calhoun, Duke, NY-G	1	4	4.0	4	0
Wright, Jason, Ariz	8	42	5.3	9	0	Williams, Chris, Chi.	1	4	4.0	4	0
Robinson, Michael, Sea.	8	37	4.6	13	0	Young, Darrel, Was.	1	3	3.0	3t	1
Martin, Ruvell, Sea.	7	158	22.6	61	1	Herremans, Todd, Phi.	1	2	2.0	2t	1
Clowney, David, NYJ-Car.	7	124	17.7	31	0	McGlynn, Mike, Phi.	1	1	1.0	1	0
* Cooper, Riley, Phi.	7	116	16.6	37	1	Penn, Donald, T.B.	1	1	1.0	1t	1
Stovall, Maurice, T.B.	7	81	11.6	38	1	Gibson, Mike, Sea.	1	-2	-2.0	-2	0
Arrington, Adrian, N.O.	7	79	11.3	17	0	Romo, Tony, Dal.	0	11	—	11	0
Ware, Danny, NY-G	7	67	9.6	18	0						
Jacobs, Brandon, NY-G	7	59	8.4	22	0	t = Touchdown; * Player that was a rookie in 2010					
Evans, Heath, N.O.	7	41	5.9	18	1	Leader based on receptions					
Spach, Stephen, Ariz	7	40	5.7	14	0						
* Gronkowski, Chris, Dal.	7	35	5.0	12	1						
* Briscoe, Dezmon, T.B.	6	93	15.5	54	1						
Swain, Brett, G.B.	6	72	12.0	31	0						
* Gilyard, Mardy, St.L	6	63	10.5	21	0						
Weems, Eric, Atl.	6	61	10.2	18	0						
Tahi, Naufahu, Min.	6	39	6.5	11	1						
Wells, Beanie, Ariz	5	74	14.8	43	0						
Barden, Ramses, NY-G	5	64	12.8	26	0						

INTERCEPTIONS

INTERCEPTIONS

AFC:	8	Ed Reed, Baltimore
NFC:	7	Asante Samuel, Philadelphia

INTERCEPTIONS, GAME

NFC:	4	DeAngelo Hall, Washington at Chicago, October 24 (92 yards, 1 TD)
AFC:	3	Glover Quin, Houston vs. Tennessee, November 28 (12 yards, 0 TD)

YARDS

AFC:	183	Ed Reed, Baltimore
NFC:	174	Kerry Rhodes, Arizona

LONGEST

NFC:	101	* Bryan McCann, Dallas at N.Y. Giants, November 14 - TD
AFC:	79	Brett Keisel, Pittsburgh at Tampa Bay, September 26 - TD

TOUCHDOWNS

AFC:	2	David Bowens, Cleveland
	2	Kelvin Hayden, Indianapolis
	2	Dwight Lowery, N.Y. Jets
NFC:	2	Dominique Rodgers-Cromartie, Arizona

TEAM LEADERS, INTERCEPTIONS

AFC: BALTIMORE, 8, Ed Reed; BUFFALO, 3, Drayton Florence; CINCINNATI, 4, Leon Hall; CLEVELAND, 6, *Joe Haden; DENVER, 2, Champ Bailey, Renaldo Hill; *Syd'Quan Thompson; HOUSTON, 3, Jason Allen, Troy Nolan, Glover Quin; INDIANAPOLIS, 2, Aaron Francisco, Kelvin Hayden, Jerraud Powers; JACKSONVILLE, 4, Derek Cox; KANSAS CITY, 4, *Eric Berry; MIAMI, 3, Jason Allen; NEW ENGLAND, 7, *Devin McCourty; N.Y. JETS, 3, Antonio Cromartie, Dwight Lowery; OAKLAND, 3, Michael Huff; PITTSBURGH, 7, Troy Polamalu; SAN DIEGO, 4, Antoine Cason; TENNESSEE, 4, Michael Griffin

NFC: ARIZONA, 4, Kerry Rhodes; ATLANTA, 5, Brent Grimes, William Moore; CAROLINA, 5, Charles Godfrey; CHICAGO, 5, Chris Harris, Charles Tillman; DALLAS, 5, Terence Newman, Gerald Sensabaugh; DETROIT, 5, Alphonso Smith; GREEN BAY, 6, Tramon Williams; MINNESOTA, 3, Husain Abdullah, E.J. Henderson; NEW ORLEANS, 2, Jabari Greer, Malcolm Jenkins; N.Y. GIANTS, 5, Terrell Thomas; PHILADELPHIA, 7, Asante Samuel; ST. LOUIS, 4, Bradley Fletcher; SAN FRANCISCO, 3, Nate Clements, Shawntae Spencer, Takeo Spikes; SEATTLE, 5, *Earl Thomas; TAMPA BAY, 6, Aqib Talib; WASHINGTON, 6, DeAngelo Hall

TEAM CHAMPION

AFC:	25	New England
NFC:	24	Green Bay

NFL TOP TEN INTERCEPTORS

	No	Yards	Avg	Long	TD
Reed, Ed, Bal.	8	183	22.9	44	0
* McCourty, Devin, N.E.	7	110	15.7	50	0
Polamalu, Troy, Pit.	7	101	14.4	45t	1
Samuel, Asante, Phi.	7	70	10.0	33	0
Allen, Jason, Mia.-Hou.	6	18	3.0	17	0
* Haden, Joe, Cle.	6	101	16.8	62	0
Hall, DeAngelo, Was.	6	92	15.3	92t	1
Talib, Aqib, T.B.	6	91	15.2	45t	1
Williams, Tramon, G.B.	6	87	14.5	64	0
Godfrey, Charles, Car.	5	112	22.4	38	0

	No	Yards	Avg	Long	TD
Grimes, Brent, Atl.	5	84	16.8	36	0
Harris, Chris, Chi.	5	69	13.8	39	0
Moore, William, Atl.	5	117	23.4	34	0
Newman, Terence, Dal.	5	16	3.2	30	0
Sensabaugh, Gerald, Dal.	5	26	5.2	10	0
Smith, Alphonso, Det.	5	48	9.6	42t	1
* Thomas, Earl, Sea.	5	68	13.6	34	0
Thomas, Terrell, NY-G	5	56	11.2	28	0
Tillman, Charles, Chi.	5	127	25.4	56	0

AFC—INDIVIDUAL INTERCEPTORS

	No	Yards	Avg	Long	TD
Reed, Ed, Bal.	8	183	22.9	44	0
* McCourty, Devin, N.E.	7	110	15.7	50	0
Polamalu, Troy, Pit.	7	101	14.4	45t	1
* Haden, Joe, Cle.	6	101	16.8	62	0
Allen, Jason, Mia.-Hou.	6	18	3.0	17	0
* Berry, Eric, K.C.	4	102	25.5	54t	1
Cason, Antoine, S.D.	4	51	12.8	28	0
Griffin, Michael, Ten.	4	50	12.5	28	0
Hall, Leon, Cin.	4	19	4.8	22	0
Cox, Derek, Jac.	4	14	3.5	14	0
Chung, Pat, N.E.	3	96	32.0	51t	1
Lowery, Dwight, NYJ	3	87	29.0	41	2
Cromartie, Antonio, NYJ	3	75	25.0	66	0
Sanders, James, N.E.	3	60	20.0	32t	1
* Lewis, Kendrick, K.C.	3	46	15.3	23	0
Florence, Drayton, Buf.	3	42	14.0	40t	1
* Verner, Alterraun, Ten.	3	41	13.7	19	0
Meriweather, Brandon, N.E.	3	39	13.0	39	0
Joseph, Johnathan, Cin.	3	38	12.7	21t	1
Nolan, Troy, Hou.	3	35	11.7	20	0
Huff, Michael, Oak.	3	32	10.7	17	0
Quin, Glover, Hou.	3	12	4.0	10	0
Wilson, Josh, Bal.	3	12	4.0	12t	1
Bowens, David, Cle.	2	94	47.0	64t	2
Guyton, Gary, N.E.	2	72	36.0	59t	1
Hill, Renaldo, Den.	2	67	33.5	36	0
Wilson, George, Buf.	2	65	32.5	56	0
Weddle, Eric, S.D.	2	64	32.0	41t	1
Nelson, Reggie, Cin.	2	63	31.5	56	0
Maualuga, Rey, Cin.	2	58	29.0	47	0
Hayden, Kelvin, Ind.	2	56	28.0	31t	2
Adams, Mike, Cle.	2	51	25.5	26	0
Cole, Marquice, NYJ	2	49	24.5	35t	1
Finnegan, Cortland, Ten.	2	41	20.5	41t	1
Gregory, Steve, S.D.	2	41	20.5	41	0
* Ward, T.J., Cle.	2	39	19.5	23	0
Clark, Ryan, Pit.	2	34	17.0	23	0
Flowers, Brandon, K.C.	2	33	16.5	33t	1
Webb, Lardarius, Bal.	2	32	16.0	32	0
Burnett, Kevin, S.D.	2	31	15.5	29t	1
Johnson, Chris, Oak.	2	30	15.0	30t	1
Lewis, Ray, Bal.	2	26	13.0	24t	1
* Jackson, Kareem, Hou.	2	23	11.5	23	0
Routt, Stanford, Oak.	2	22	11.0	22t	1
Woodley, LaMarr, Pit.	2	22	11.0	14t	1
* Thompson, Syd'Quan, Den.	2	20	10.0	18	0
Elam, Abram, Cle.	2	18	9.0	18	0
Carr, Chris, Bal.	2	13	6.5	12	0
McCourty, Jason, Ten.	2	11	5.5	11	0
Powers, Jerraud, Ind.	2	11	5.5	11	0
Witherspoon, Will, Ten.	2	11	5.5	9	0
Francisco, Aaron, Ind.	2	10	5.0	11	0
McKelvin, Leodis, Buf.	2	10	5.0	10	0
Sapp, Benny, Mia.	2	9	4.5	9	0
Taylor, Ike, Pit.	2	9	4.5	9	0
Jammer, Quentin, S.D.	2	5	2.5	5	0
Timmons, Lawrence, Pit.	2	5	2.5	5	0

	No	Yards	Avg	Long	TD
McGraw, Jon, K.C.	2	4	2.0	4	0
Harrison, James, Pit.	2	2	1.0	2	0
Ninkovich, Rob, N.E.	2	1	0.5	1	0
Bailey, Champ, Den.	2	0	0.0	0	0
Brown, Sheldon, Cle.	2	0	0.0	0	0
Page, Jarrad, N.E.	2	0	0.0	0	0
McFadden, Bryant, Pit.	2	-3	-1.5	0	0
Keisel, Brett, Pit.	1	79	79.0	79t	1
Lacey, Jacob, Ind.	1	44	44.0	44	0
Byrd, Jairus, Buf.	1	37	37.0	37t	1
Whitner, Donte, Buf.	1	37	37.0	37	0
Arrington, Kyle, N.E.	1	36	36.0	36t	1
Hagler, Tyjuan, Ind.	1	35	35.0	35	0
Hope, Chris, Ten.	1	32	32.0	32	0
Bethea, Antoine, Ind.	1	31	31.0	31	0
Phillips, Shaun, S.D.	1	31	31.0	31t	1
Mathis, Rashean, Jac.	1	24	24.0	24	0
Bell, Yeremiah, Mia.	1	21	21.0	21	0
Bullitt, Melvin, Ind.	1	19	19.0	19	0
Bentley, Kevin, Hou.	1	18	18.0	18	0
Smith, Sean, Mia.	1	18	18.0	18	0
Tulloch, Stephen, Ten.	1	18	18.0	18	0
Fujita, Scott, Cle.	1	16	16.0	16	0
Branch, Tyvon, Oak.	1	15	15.0	15	0
* Cox, Perrish, Den.	1	15	15.0	15	0
Johnson, Derrick, K.C.	1	15	15.0	15t	1
Oliver, Paul, S.D.	1	15	15.0	15	0
Hunter, Jason, Den.	1	14	14.0	14	0
Johnson, Brandon, Cin.	1	12	12.0	12	0
Davis, Andra, Buf.	1	11	11.0	11	0
Jones, Adam, Cin.	1	10	10.0	10	0
* McClain, Rolando, Oak.	1	10	10.0	10	0
Edwards, Dwan, Buf.	1	8	8.0	8	0
Greene, Courtney, Jac.	1	8	8.0	8	0
Smith, Daryl, Jac.	1	8	8.0	8	0
Carey, Don, Jac.	1	7	7.0	7	0
* Spikes, Brandon, N.E.	1	5	5.0	5	0
Daniels, Travis, K.C.	1	4	4.0	4	0
Vickerson, Kevin, Den.	1	4	4.0	4	0
Cooper, Stephen, S.D.	1	2	2.0	2	0
Leonhard, Jim, NYJ	1	2	2.0	2	0
Middleton, William, Jac.	1	2	2.0	2	0
* Carroll, Nolan, Mia.	1	1	1.0	1	0
* McManis, Sherrick, Hou.	1	1	1.0	1	0
Pace, Calvin, NYJ	1	1	1.0	1	0
Rubin, Ahtyba, Cle.	1	1	1.0	1	0
Carr, Brandon, K.C.	1	0	0.0	0	0
Clemons, Chris, Mia.	1	0	0.0	0	0
Coleman, Drew, NYJ	1	0	0.0	0	0
Davis, Vontae, Mia.	1	0	0.0	0	0
* Fletcher, Dane, N.E.	1	0	0.0	0	0
Fuller, Vincent, Ten.	1	0	0.0	0	0
Hamlin, Ken, Bal.	1	0	0.0	0	0
* Jones, Reshad, Mia.	1	0	0.0	0	0
Mitchell, Mike, Oak.	1	0	0.0	0	0
Ndukwe, Chinedum, Cin.	1	0	0.0	0	0
Pool, Brodney, NYJ	1	0	0.0	0	0
Redding, Cory, Bal.	1	0	0.0	0	0
Siler, Brandon, S.D.	1	0	0.0	0	0
Trent, Morgan, Cin.	1	0	0.0	0	0
* Ware, Jeremy, Oak.	1	0	0.0	0	0
Williams, Roy, Cin.	1	0	0.0	0	0
Wright, Eric, Cle.	1	0	0.0	0	0
Madison, Anthony, Pit.	1	-1	-1.0	-1	0
Considine, Sean, Jac.	1	-2	-2.0	-2	0
Dawkins, Brian, Den.	1	-2	-2.0	-2	0
Knighton, Terrance, Jac.	1	-3	-3.0	-3	0
Groves, Quentin, Oak.	1	-4	-4.0	-4	0

	No	Yards	Avg	Long	TD
Marks, Sen'Derrick, Ten.	1	-6	-6.0	-6	0
Landry, Dawan, Bal.	0	23	—	23t	1

t = Touchdown; *Player that was a rookie in 2010
Leader based on interceptions

NFC—INDIVIDUAL INTERCEPTORS

	No	Yards	Avg	Long	TD
Samuel, Asante, Phi.	7	70	10.0	33	0
Hall, DeAngelo, Was.	6	92	15.3	92t	1
Talib, Aqib, T.B.	6	91	15.2	45t	1
Williams, Tramon, G.B.	6	87	14.5	64	0
Tillman, Charles, Chi.	5	127	25.4	56	0
Moore, William, Atl.	5	117	23.4	34	0
Godfrey, Charles, Car.	5	112	22.4	38	0
Grimes, Brent, Atl.	5	84	16.8	36	0
Harris, Chris, Chi.	5	69	13.8	39	0
* Thomas, Earl, Sea.	5	68	13.6	34	0
Thomas, Terrell, NY-G	5	56	11.2	28	0
Smith, Alphonso, Det.	5	48	9.6	42t	1
Sensabaugh, Gerald, Dal.	5	26	5.2	10	0
Newman, Terence, Dal.	5	16	3.2	30	0
Rhodes, Kerry, Ariz	4	174	43.6	66	0
Moore, D.J., Chi.	4	95	23.8	54t	1
Fletcher, Bradley, St.L	4	41	10.3	28	0
Patterson, Dimitri, Phi.	4	40	10.0	40t	1
Collins, Nick, G.B.	4	34	8.5	24	0
Webster, Corey, NY-G	4	11	2.8	13	0
Barber, Ronde, T.B.	3	98	32.7	64	0
Marshall, Richard, Car.	3	91	30.3	66	0
Rodgers-Cromartie, Domin, Ariz	3	86	28.7	32t	2
Atogwe, Oshiomogho, St.L	3	53	17.7	34	0
Clements, Nate, S.F.	3	46	15.3	39	0
Munnerlyn, Captain, Car.	3	37	12.3	37t	1
Hawk, A.J., G.B.	3	31	10.3	21	0
* Allen, Nate, Phi.	3	27	9.0	16	0
Henderson, E.J., Min.	3	10	3.3	10	0
Spikes, Takeo, S.F.	3	9	3.0	6	0
Abdullah, Husain, Min.	3	5	1.7	5	0
Grant, Deon, NY-G	3	0	0.0	0	0
Mikell, Quintin, Phi.	3	0	0.0	0	0
Spencer, Shawntae, S.F.	3	0	0.0	0	0
Jenkins, Malcolm, N.O.	2	105	52.5	96t	1
Toler, Greg, Ariz	2	66	33.0	66t	1
Buchanon, Phillip, Was.	2	51	25.5	43	0
Greer, Jabari, N.O.	2	50	25.0	26	1
Woodson, Charles, G.B.	2	48	24.0	48t	1
* Lee, Sean, Dal.	2	44	22.0	31t	1
Rogers, Carlos, Was.	2	43	21.5	38	0
Levy, DeAndre, Det.	2	41	20.5	30t	1
Winfield, Antoine, Min.	2	41	20.5	41	0
Allen, Jared, Min.	2	40	20.0	36t	1
Babineaux, Jordan, Sea.	2	37	18.5	20	0
Adams, Michael, Ariz	2	36	18.0	36	0
* Spievey, Amari, Det.	2	35	17.5	26	0
Allen, Asher, Min.	2	27	13.5	27	0
Ball, Alan, Dal.	2	27	13.5	27	0
* Grimm, Cody, T.B.	2	24	12.0	13	1
Dahl, Craig, St.L	2	23	11.5	23	0
Peterson, Mike, Atl.	2	18	9.0	17	0
Butler, James, St.L	2	13	6.5	16	0
Lenon, Paris, Ariz	2	12	6.0	10	0
Bulluck, Keith, NY-G	2	7	3.5	6	0
Wilson, Adrian, Ariz	2	4	2.0	4	0
Briggs, Lance, Chi.	2	1	0.5	1	0
Peppers, Julius, Chi.	2	1	0.5	1	0
Peprah, Charlie, G.B.	2	0	0.0	0	0
* Shields, Sam, G.B.	2	0	0.0	0	0
* McCann, Bryan, Dal.	1	101	101.0	101t	1

	No	Yards	Avg	Long	TD
Brown, Tarell, S.F.	1	62	62.0	62t	1
Matthews, Clay, G.B.	1	62	62.0	62t	1
Smith, Anthony, Jac.-G.B.	1	47	47.0	47	0
Jones, Sean, T.B.	1	45	45.0	31	0
Brooking, Keith, Dal.	1	41	41.0	41	0
Hayes, Geno, T.B.	1	41	41.0	41t	1
* Franks, Dominique, Atl.	1	40	40.0	40	0
Scandrick, Orlando, Dal.	1	40	40.0	40t	1
Goldson, Dashon, S.F.	1	39	39.0	39t	1
Jennings, Tim, Chi.	1	39	39.0	39	0
* Washington, Daryl, Ariz	1	39	39.0	39	0
Rolle, Antrel, NY-G	1	36	36.0	36	0
Martin, Sherrod, Car.	1	34	34.0	34	0
Bishop, Desmond, G.B.	1	32	32.0	32t	1
Brooks, Ahmad, S.F.	1	32	32.0	32	0
Trufant, Marcus, Sea.	1	32	32.0	32t	1
Biermann, Kroy, Atl.	1	31	31.0	31t	1
McDonald, Ray, S.F.	1	31	31.0	31t	1
Piscitelli, Sabby, T.B.	1	31	31.0	31	0
Williams, Corey, Det.	1	27	27.0	27	0
Davis, Chauncey, Atl.	1	26	26.0	26t	1
Tatupu, Lofa, Sea.	1	26	26.0	26t	1
* Berry, Aaron, Det.	1	23	23.0	23	0
Torrence, Leigh, N.O.	1	21	21.0	21	0
Smith, Reggie, S.F.	1	20	20.0	20	0
* Suh, Ndamukong, Det.	1	20	20.0	20	0
Leber, Ben, Min.	1	19	19.0	19	0
* Murphy, Jerome, St.L	1	19	19.0	19	0
Hanson, Joselio, Phi.	1	17	17.0	17	0
Martin, Derrick, G.B.	1	15	15.0	15	0
Laws, Trevor, Phi.	1	13	13.0	13	0
Owens, Chris, Atl.	1	13	13.0	13	0
James, Bradie, Dal.	1	11	11.0	11	0
Walker, Frank, Min.	1	10	10.0	10	0
Chillar, Brandon, G.B.	1	9	9.0	9	0
Barnes, Kevin, Was.	1	8	8.0	8	0
Dockery, Kevin, St.L	1	8	8.0	8	0
* Lindley, Trevard, Phi.	1	8	8.0	8	0
Beason, Jon, Car.	1	7	7.0	7	0
* Coleman, Kurt, Phi.	1	7	7.0	7	0
Johnson, Rashad, Ariz	1	7	7.0	7	0
Abraham, John, Atl.	1	6	6.0	6	0
Harper, Roman, N.O.	1	6	6.0	6	0
Hawthorne, David, Sea.	1	5	5.0	5	0
Johnson, Ed, Car.	1	5	5.0	5	0
Moore, Kareem, Was.	1	5	5.0	5	0
Porter, Tracy, N.O.	1	5	5.0	5	0
Vilma, Jonathan, N.O.	1	5	5.0	5	0
* Asante, Larry, T.B.	1	4	4.0	4	0
Black, Quincy, T.B.	1	4	4.0	4	0
Laurinaitis, James, St.L	1	4	4.0	4	0
Smith, Will, N.O.	1	4	4.0	4	0
Lofton, Curtis, Atl.	1	2	2.0	2	0
Anderson, James, Car.	1	1	1.0	1	0
Ruud, Barrett, T.B.	1	1	1.0	1	0
Babineaux, Jonathan, Atl.	1	0	0.0	0	0
Biggers, E.J., T.B.	1	0	0.0	0	0
Bradley, Stewart, Phi.	1	0	0.0	0	0
Brown, Everette, Car.	1	0	0.0	0	0
* Burnett, Morgan, G.B.	1	0	0.0	0	0
DeCoud, Thomas, Atl.	1	0	0.0	0	0
Fletcher, London, Was.	1	0	0.0	0	0
Herring, Will, Sea.	1	0	0.0	0	0
Hobbs, Ellis, Phi.	1	0	0.0	0	0
Houston, Chris, Det.	1	0	0.0	0	0
Jennings, Kelly, Sea.	1	0	0.0	0	0
Landry, LaRon, Was.	1	0	0.0	0	0
Lawson, Manny, S.F.	1	0	0.0	0	0
Lynch, Corey, T.B.	1	0	0.0	0	0

	No	Yards	Avg	Long	TD
Manning, Danieal, Chi.	1	0	0.0	0	0
* McCray, Danny, Dal.	1	0	0.0	0	0
Nicholas, Stephen, Atl.	1	0	0.0	0	0
Phillips, Kenny, NY-G	1	0	0.0	0	0
Robinson, Dunta, Atl.	1	0	0.0	0	0
Urlacher, Brian, Chi.	1	0	0.0	0	0
Vasher, Nathan, Det.	1	0	0.0	0	0
Williams, Madieu, Min.	1	0	0.0	0	0
* Pugh, Jordan, Car.	1	-2	-2.0	-2	0
Jenkins, Mike, Dal.	1	-4	-4.0	-4	0

t = Touchdown; Leader based on interceptions
* Player that was a rookie in 2010

AMERICAN FOOTBALL CONFERENCE—INTERCEPTIONS

	No	Yards	Avg	Long	TD
New England	25	419	16.8	59t	4
Pittsburgh	21	248	11.8	79t	3
Baltimore	19	289	15.2	44	3
Cleveland	19	320	16.8	64t	2
Tennessee	17	198	11.6	41t	1
Cincinnati	16	200	12.5	56	1
San Diego	16	240	15.0	41t	3
Kansas City	14	204	14.6	54t	3
Houston	13	90	6.9	23	0
Jacksonville	13	105	8.1	47	0
N.Y. Jets	12	214	17.8	66	3
Oakland	12	105	8.8	30t	2
Buffalo	11	210	19.1	56	2
Miami	11	66	6.0	21	0
Denver	10	118	11.8	36	0
Indianapolis	10	206	20.6	44	2
AFC Total	239	3232	13.5	79t	29
AFC Average	14.9	202.0	13.5	—	1.8

NATIONAL FOOTBALL CONFERENCE—INTERCEPTIONS

	No	Yards	Avg	Long	TD
Green Bay	24	318	13.3	64	3
Philadelphia	23	182	7.9	40t	1
Atlanta	22	337	15.3	40	2
Chicago	21	332	15.8	56	1
Dallas	20	302	15.1	101t	3
Tampa Bay	19	339	17.8	64	3
Arizona	17	424	24.9	66t	3
Carolina	17	285	16.8	66	1
N.Y. Giants	16	110	6.9	36	0
Minnesota	15	152	10.1	41	1
San Francisco	15	239	15.9	62t	3
Detroit	14	194	13.9	42t	2
St. Louis	14	161	11.5	34	0
Washington	14	199	14.2	92t	1
Seattle	12	168	14.0	34	2
New Orleans	9	196	21.8	96t	2
NFC Total	272	3938	14.5	101t	28
NFC Average	17.0	246.1	14.5	—	1.8
League Total	511	7170	—	101t	57
League Average	16.0	224.1	14.0	—	1.8

KICKOFF RETURNS

YARDS PER RETURN
AFC: 29.3* David Reed, Baltimore
NFC: 27.5 Eric Weems, Atlanta

YARDS
NFC: 1548 LaRod Stephens-Howling, Arizona
AFC: 1530 * Marc Mariani, Tennessee

YARDS, GAME
NFC: 253 Leon Washington, Seattle vs. San Diego, September 26 (4 returns, 2 TD)
AFC: 233 * David Reed, Baltimore at Houston, December 13 (6 returns, 1 TD) - (OT)

LONGEST
NFC: 105 Stefan Logan, Detroit vs. St. Louis, October 10 - TD
AFC: 103 Brandon Tate, New England at Miami, October 4 - TD
103 * David Reed, Baltimore at Houston, December 13 - TD - (OT)

RETURNS
AFC: 60 * Marc Mariani, Tennessee
NFC: 57 LaRod Stephens-Howling, Arizona
57 Leon Washington, Seattle

RETURNS, GAME
AFC: 9 * Brandon James, Indianapolis vs. San Diego, November 28 (150 yards, 0 TD)
NFC: 8 Lorenzo Booker, Minnesota vs. Chicago, December 20 (157 yards, 0 TD)

TOUCHDOWNS
AFC: 3 * Jacoby Ford, Oakland
NFC: 3 Leon Washington, Seattle

TEAM CHAMPION
NFC: 26.5 Atlanta
AFC: 25.2 N.Y. Jets

NFL TOP TEN KICKOFF RETURNERS

	No	Yards	Avg	Long	TD
* Reed, David, Bal.	21	616	29.3	103t	1
Smith, Brad, NYJ	50	1432	28.6	97t	2
Weems, Eric, Atl.	40	1100	27.5	102t	1
Stephens-Howling, LaRod, Ariz	57	1548	27.2	102t	2
Logan, Stefan, Det.	55	1448	26.3	105t	1
Tate, Brandon, N.E.	41	1057	25.8	103t	2
Spurlock, Micheal, T.B.	44	1129	25.7	89t	1
Washington, Leon, Sea.	57	1461	25.6	101t	3
* Mariani, Marc, Ten.	60	1530	25.5	98t	1
* Decker, Eric, Den.	22	556	25.3	51	0

AFC—INDIVIDUAL KICKOFF RETURNERS

	No	Yards	Avg	Long	TD
* Reed, David, Bal.	21	616	29.3	103t	1
Smith, Brad, NYJ	50	1432	28.6	97t	2
Tate, Brandon, N.E.	41	1057	25.8	103t	2
* Mariani, Marc, Ten.	60	1530	25.5	98t	1
* Decker, Eric, Den.	22	556	25.3	51	0
* Sanders, Emmanuel, Pit.	25	628	25.1	48	0
* Karim, Deji, Jac.	50	1248	25.0	65	0
Sproles, Darren, S.D.	51	1257	24.6	45	0
* Carroll, Nolan, Mia.	27	655	24.3	46	0
* Ford, Jacoby, Oak.	53	1280	24.2	101t	3

	No	Yards	Avg	Long	TD
Parmele, Jalen, Bal.	24	562	23.4	39	0
Underwood, Tiquan, Jac.	24	561	23.4	53	0
* Spiller, C.J., Buf.	44	1014	23.0	95t	1
Scott, Bernard, Cin.	56	1257	22.4	60	0
Jones, Jacoby, Hou.	23	494	21.5	35	0
* Arenas, Javier, K.C.	24	509	21.2	35	0
Cribbs, Josh, Cle.	40	814	20.4	37	0
* McCluster, Dexter, K.C.	26	527	20.3	36	0
Slaton, Steve, Hou.	39	767	19.7	50	0
Cobbs, Patrick, Mia.	22	431	19.6	40	0
(Nonqualifiers)					
* Brown, Antonio, Pit.	17	397	23.4	89t	1
* Thomas, Demaryius, Den.	16	398	24.9	65	0
Tryon, Justin, Ind.	14	299	21.4	39	0
McKelvin, Leodis, Buf.	14	265	18.9	49	0
* James, Brandon, Ind.	14	229	16.4	26	0
Moore, Devin, Ind.	12	257	21.4	33	0
Rhodes, Dominic, Ind.	12	252	21.0	27	0
* Cox, Perrish, Den.	9	172	19.1	30	0
Smith, Clifton, Mia.-Cle.	8	144	18.0	26	0
Jones, Adam, Cin.	7	134	19.1	29	0
* Jones, Donald, Buf.	6	120	20.0	31	0
Wilson, Josh, Bal.	6	117	19.5	26	0
Cartwright, Rock, Oak.	6	103	17.2	28	0
Bell, Mike, Phi.-Cle.	6	63	10.5	31	0
Royal, Eddie, Den.	5	107	21.4	33	0
Figurs, Yamon, Oak.	5	105	21.0	25	0
* Brown, Cornelius, Ind.	5	102	20.4	23	0
Moore, Kenny, Ind.	5	102	20.4	27	0
Morris, Sammy, N.E.	5	66	13.2	23	0
Crumpler, Alge, N.E.	5	18	3.6	7	0
* Haden, Joe, Cle.	4	96	24.0	32	0
Redman, Isaac, Pit.	4	81	20.3	21	0
* Tucker, Verran, K.C.	4	73	18.3	24	0
Ventrone, Raymond, Cle.	4	47	11.8	17	0
Harrison, Jerome, Cle.	4	32	8.0	10	0
Benard, Marcus, Cle.	4	26	6.5	11	0
Connolly, Dan, N.E.	3	90	30.0	71	0
Caldwell, Andre, Cin.	3	79	26.3	32	0
* McKnight, Joe, NYJ	3	60	20.0	28	0
Zbikowski, Tom, Bal.	3	48	16.0	20	0
Moore, Mewelde, Pit.	3	47	15.7	17	0
Cosby, Quan, Cin.	3	44	14.7	18	0
Larsen, Spencer, Den.	3	44	14.7	19	0
Leach, Vonta, Hou.	3	40	13.3	26	0
* Conner, John, NYJ	3	35	11.7	18	0
Hester, Jacob, S.D.	3	25	8.3	13	0
* James, Javarris, Ind.	3	16	5.3	16	0
* Vaughn, Cassius, Den.	2	125	62.5	97t	1
* Moore, Marlon, Mia.	2	51	25.5	34	0
Miller, Nick, Oak.	2	37	18.5	27	0
Ball, Lance, Den.	2	33	16.5	18	0
* Roosevelt, Naaman, Buf.	2	31	15.5	16	0
Caulcrick, Jehuu, Buf.	2	28	14.0	17	0
Copper, Terrance, K.C.	2	26	13.0	17	0
Lowery, Dwight, NYJ	2	26	13.0	14	0
* Wilson, Kyle, NYJ	2	22	11.0	15	0
Hall, Ahmard, Ten.	2	21	10.5	15	0
Vickers, Lawrence, Cle.	2	13	6.5	10	0
Polite, Lousaka, Mia.	2	10	5.0	10	0
Hagler, Tyjuan, Ind.	1	41	41.0	41t	1
Crayton, Patrick, S.D.	1	31	31.0	31	0
Hill, Jason, Jac.	1	30	30.0	30	0
Brinkley, Curtis, S.D.	1	29	29.0	29	0
Hall, Leon, Cin.	1	29	29.0	29	0
* McManis, Sherrick, Hou.	1	25	25.0	25	0
Miller, Zach, Jac.	1	22	22.0	22	0

	No	Yards	Avg	Long	TD
Owens, Montell, Jac.	1	22	22.0	22	0
Potter, Zach, Jac.	1	15	15.0	15	0
Carr, Chris, Bal.	1	14	14.0	14	0
Foster, Eric, Ind.	1	12	12.0	12	0
Davis, James, Cle.	1	11	11.0	11	0
Turner, Robert, NYJ	1	11	11.0	11	0
Kelly, Reggie, Cin.	1	8	8.0	8	0
Mulligan, Matthew, NYJ	1	8	8.0	8	0
Reece, Marcel, Oak.	1	7	7.0	7	0
Bolen, Brock, Jac.	1	5	5.0	5	0
Gocong, Chris, Cle.	1	5	5.0	5	0
O'Connell, Jake, K.C.	f1	5	5.0	5	0
Cook, Jared, Ten.	1	3	3.0	3	0
Gage, Justin, Ten.	1	2	2.0	2	0
Battle, Jackie, K.C.	1	0	0.0	0	0
Ellis, Chris, Buf.	1	0	0.0	0	0
* Fletcher, Dane, N.E.	1	0	0.0	0	0
Green-Ellis, BenJarvus, N.E.	1	0	0.0	0	0
Huff, Michael, Oak.	1	0	0.0	0	0
* Mitchell, Earl, Hou.	1	0	0.0	0	0
Wilford, Ernest, Jac.	1	0	0.0	0	0
Cromartie, Antonio, NYJ	1	-6	-6.0	-6	0
Marshall, Brandon, Mia.	f0	0	—	—	0
Nakamura, Haruki, Bal.	f0	0	—	—	0

t = Touchdown; f = Fair Catch
Leader based on average return, minimum 20 returns
* Player that was a rookie in 2010

NFC—INDIVIDUAL KICKOFF RETURNERS

	No	Yards	Avg	Long	TD
Weems, Eric, Atl.	40	1100	27.5	102t	1
Stephens-Howling, LaRod, Ariz	57	1548	27.2	102t	2
Logan, Stefan, Det.	55	1448	26.3	105t	1
Spurlock, Micheal, T.B.	44	1129	25.7	89t	1
Washington, Leon, Sea.	57	1461	25.6	101t	3
* Banks, Brandon, Was.	46	1155	25.1	96t	1
Manning, Danieal, Chi.	33	816	24.7	62	0
Roby, Courtney, N.O.	33	785	23.8	39	0
Harvin, Percy, Min.	40	933	23.3	95t	1
Amendola, Danny, St.L	50	1142	22.8	84	0
Nelson, Jordy, G.B.	22	496	22.5	51	0
* McCann, Bryan, Dal.	23	507	22.0	38	0
Goodson, Mike, Car.	48	1048	21.8	46	0
* Owusu-Ansah, Akwasi, Dal.	25	543	21.7	41	0
* Calvin, Jorrick, Phi.	32	692	21.6	41	0
* Shields, Sam, G.B.	21	452	21.5	49	0
Ginn, Ted, S.F.	47	992	21.1	61	0
Ware, Danny, NY-G	21	432	20.6	37	0
Reynaud, Darius, NY-G	21	386	18.4	31	0
(Nonqualifiers)					
Booker, Lorenzo, Min.	18	429	23.8	49	0
* Gilyard, Mardy, St.L	16	356	22.3	34	0
Hobbs, Ellis, Phi.	16	345	21.6	46	0
Thomas, Devin, Was.-Car.	15	399	26.6	42	0
* Roberts, Andre, Ariz	14	326	23.3	47	0
Lee, Pat, G.B.	13	265	20.4	30	0
Blackmon, Will, NY-G	13	238	18.3	42	0
Hester, Devin, Chi.	12	427	35.6	79	0
* Bryant, Dez, Dal.	12	293	24.4	43	0
* Parker, Preston, T.B.	10	178	17.8	37	0
* Pugh, Jordan, Car.	9	218	24.2	32	0
Knox, Johnny, Chi.	8	182	22.8	42	0
* Gettis, David, Car.	8	145	18.1	28	0
Breaston, Steve, Ariz	7	162	23.1	27	0
Thomas, Pierre, N.O.	7	154	22.0	32	0
Sellers, Mike, Was.	7	82	11.7	18	0

	No	Yards	Avg	Long	TD
Henderson, Devery, N.O.	6	142	23.7	27	0
Ogletree, Kevin, Dal.	6	109	18.2	31	0
Morrah, Cameron, Sea.	5	76	15.2	30	0
Davis, Rashied, Chi.	5	70	14.0	32	0
Walker, Delanie, S.F.	5	70	14.0	20	0
Norwood, Jerious, Atl.	4	97	24.3	34	0
* Williams, Kyle, S.F.	4	82	20.5	30	0
* Toston, Keith, St.L	4	75	18.8	20	0
Hall, Chad, Phi.	4	65	16.3	21	0
Evans, Heath, N.O.	4	45	11.3	13	0
Stroughter, Sammie, T.B.	3	79	26.3	30	0
Choice, Tashard, Dal.	3	61	20.3	27	0
Wilson, Chris, Was.	3	27	9.0	15	0
Munnerlyn, Captain, Car.	2	87	43.5	64	0
Felton, Jerome, Det.	2	59	29.5	37	0
Simpson, Chad, Was.	2	59	29.5	32	0
Lawson, Gerard, Phi.	2	48	24.0	28	0
Sutton, Tyrell, Car.	2	30	15.0	18	0
Spach, Stephen, Ariz	2	26	13.0	15	0
* Starks, James, G.B.	2	25	12.5	17	0
* Gronkowski, Chris, Dal.	2	23	11.5	13	0
Morgan, Josh, S.F.	2	19	9.5	13	0
Schmitt, Owen, Phi.	f2	18	9.0	18	0
Dugan, Jeff, Min.	2	8	4.0	5	0
Wright, Jason, Ariz	2	8	4.0	8	0
Westbrook, Byron, Was.	2	6	3.0	6	0
Bush, Reggie, N.O.	1	32	32.0	32	0
* Webb, Joe, Min.	1	30	30.0	30	0
Young, Albert, Min.	1	25	25.0	25	0
Betts, Ladell, N.O.	1	23	23.0	23	0
Maclin, Jeremy, Phi.	1	22	22.0	22	0
Buckley, Eldra, Phi.	1	20	20.0	20	0
* Harbor, Clay, Phi.	1	19	19.0	19	0
Finneran, Brian, Atl.	1	18	18.0	18	0
Karney, Mike, St.L	1	17	17.0	17	0
* Norwood, Eric, Car.	1	17	17.0	17	0
Ah You, C.J., St.L	1	16	16.0	16	0
Rucker, Martin, Dal.	1	16	16.0	16	0
* Austin, Terrence, Was.	1	15	15.0	15	0
Nicks, Hakeem, NY-G	1	14	14.0	14	0
Patterson, Dimitri, Phi.	1	14	14.0	14	0
* Williams, Stephen, Ariz	1	14	14.0	14	0
Celek, Brent, Phi.	1	12	12.0	12	0
Norris, Moran, S.F.	1	12	12.0	12	0
* Pierre-Paul, Jason, NY-G	1	12	12.0	12	0
Wragge, Tony, S.F.	1	12	12.0	12	0
Chandler, Scott, Dal.	1	11	11.0	11	0
King, Jeff, Car.	1	11	11.0	11	0
* Tate, Golden, Sea.	1	10	10.0	10	0
Newman, Terence, Dal.	1	9	9.0	9	0
Forsett, Justin, Sea.	1	8	8.0	8	0
Grant, Larry, St.L	1	8	8.0	8	0
Kuhn, John, G.B.	1	8	8.0	8	0
McBride, Turk, Det.	1	8	8.0	8	0
Mughelli, Ovie, Atl.	1	6	6.0	6	0
Fluellen, Andre, Det.	1	4	4.0	4	0
* McCoy, Anthony, Sea.	1	3	3.0	3	0
Wilhelm, Matt, G.B.	1	3	3.0	3	0
Brinkley, Jasper, Min.	1	2	2.0	2	0
Davis, Kellen, Chi.	1	2	2.0	2	0
Burleson, Nate, Det.	1	0	0.0	0	0
Crabtree, Michael, S.F.	1	0	0.0	0	0
Driver, Donald, G.B.	1	0	0.0	0	0
Kennedy, Jimmy, Min.	1	0	0.0	0	0
Miller, Brit, St.L	1	0	0.0	0	0
Obiozor, Cyril, Ariz	1	0	0.0	0	0
Scheffler, Tony, Det.	1	0	0.0	0	0

	No	Yards	Avg	Long	TD
Simpkins, Maurice, G.B.	1	0	0.0	0	0
* Cooper, Riley, Phi.	0	9	—	9	0
Jennings, Tim, Chi.	f0	0	—	—	0
Kleinsasser, Jimmy, Min.	f0	0	—	—	0

t = Touchdown; f = Fair Catch
Leader based on average return, minimum 20 returns
* *Player that was a rookie in 2010*

AMERICAN FOOTBALL CONFERENCE—KICKOFF RETURNS

	No	Yards	Avg	Long	TD
N.Y. Jets	63	1588	25.2	97t	2
Baltimore	55	1357	24.7	103t	1
Denver	59	1435	24.3	97t	1
Tennessee	64	1556	24.3	98t	1
San Diego	56	1342	24.0	45	0
Jacksonville	80	1903	23.8	65	0
Pittsburgh	49	1153	23.5	97t	1
Oakland	68	1532	22.5	101t	3
New England	56	1231	22.0	103t	2
Cincinnati	71	1551	21.8	60	0
Miami	56	1199	21.4	46	0
Buffalo	69	1458	21.1	95t	1
Houston	67	1326	19.8	50	0
Kansas City	58	1140	19.7	36	0
Indianapolis	67	1310	19.6	41t	1
Cleveland	70	1191	17.0	37	0
AFC Total	1008	22272	22.1	103t	13
AFC Average	63.0	1392.0	22.1	—	0.8

NATIONAL FOOTBALL CONFERENCE—KICKOFF RETURNS

	No	Yards	Avg	Long	TD
Atlanta	46	1221	26.5	102t	1
Chicago	59	1497	25.4	79	0
Detroit	61	1519	24.9	105t	1
Arizona	84	2084	24.8	102t	2
Tampa Bay	57	1386	24.3	89t	1
Seattle	65	1558	24.0	101t	3
Washington	73	1680	23.0	96t	1
New Orleans	52	1181	22.7	39	0
Minnesota	64	1427	22.3	95t	1
Carolina	74	1619	21.9	64	0
St. Louis	74	1614	21.8	84	0
Dallas	74	1572	21.2	43	0
Philadelphia	62	1272	20.5	46	0
Green Bay	62	1249	20.1	51	0
San Francisco	61	1187	19.5	61	0
N.Y. Giants	57	1082	19.0	42	0
NFC Total	1025	23148	22.6	105t	10
NFC Average	64.1	1446.8	22.6	—	0.6
League Total	2033	45420	—	105t	23
League Average	63.5	1419.4	22.3	—	0.7

PUNTING

NFC:	47.9	Mat McBriar, Dallas
AFC:	47.0	Shane Lechler, Oakland

NET AVERAGE YARDS PER PUNT

NFC:	41.7	Mat McBriar, Dallas
AFC:	40.8	Shane Lechler, Oakland

LONGEST

AFC:	72	Kevin Huber, Cincinnati vs. Tampa Bay, October 10
	72	Dustin Colquitt, Kansas City at St. Louis, December 19
NFC:	69	* Matt Dodge, N.Y. Giants at Dallas, October 25

PUNTS

NFC:	95	Jason Baker, Carolina
AFC:	88	Dustin Colquitt, Kansas City

PUNTS, GAME

AFC:	10	Brandon Fields, Miami at N.Y. Jets, December 12 (564 yards)
NFC:	10	Jon Ryan, Seattle at Chicago, October 17 (397 yards)
	10	Donnie Jones, St. Louis at San Francisco, November 14 (437 yards) - (OT)
	10	Chris Kluwe, Minnesota vs. N.Y. Giants, December 13 (458 yards)

TEAM CHAMPION

NFC:	47.2	Dallas
AFC:	46.8	Oakland

AMERICAN FOOTBALL CONFERENCE—PUNTING

	Total Punts	Yards	Long	Avg	TB	Blk	Opp Ret	Return Yards	In 20	Net Avg
Oakland	78	3651	68	46.8	4	0	46	400	27	40.7
Miami	75	3369	69	44.9	4	2	43	454	31	37.8
Denver	86	3835	63	44.6	7	0	50	550	19	36.6
Pittsburgh	74	3276	62	44.3	11	0	32	294	22	37.3
Cleveland	78	3424	59	43.9	5	0	40	285	29	39.0
Jacksonville	57	2496	63	43.8	7	0	19	123	26	39.2
Kansas City	90	3941	72	43.8	11	1	42	361	33	37.3
Baltimore	81	3530	60	43.6	4	0	34	275	39	39.2
San Diego	56	2430	67	43.4	9	4	28	528	13	30.8
New England	58	2505	65	43.2	5	0	25	179	19	38.4
Tennessee	77	3302	68	42.9	4	0	35	214	24	39.1
N.Y. Jets	84	3581	61	42.6	4	0	27	299	42	38.1
Buffalo	75	3181	61	42.4	7	0	32	299	17	36.6
Indianapolis	69	2909	66	42.2	8	0	28	299	23	35.5
Houston	63	2650	60	42.1	5	0	29	233	19	36.8
Cincinnati	72	2992	72	41.6	6	1	26	124	28	38.2
AFC Total	1173	51072	72	—	101	8	536	4917	411	—
AFC Average	73.3	3192.0	—	43.5	6.3	0.5	33.5	307.3	25.7	37.6

NATIONAL FOOTBALL CONFERENCE—PUNTING

	Total Punts	Yards	Long	Avg	TB	Blk	Opp Ret	Return Yards	In 20	Net Avg
Dallas	66	3115	65	47.2	8	1	33	205	22	41.7
San Francisco	91	4203	64	46.2	12	0	54	483	34	38.2
New Orleans	57	2618	64	45.9	6	0	26	310	21	38.4
St. Louis	94	4276	63	45.5	4	0	45	435	32	40.0
Detroit	90	4018	66	44.6	8	0	54	633	24	35.8
N.Y. Giants	73	3222	69	44.1	9	1	36	535	20	34.3
Green Bay	71	3114	62	43.9	5	0	31	341	25	37.6
Philadelphia	73	3195	63	43.8	2	0	34	309	28	39.0
Arizona	94	4080	65	43.4	9	0	35	458	29	36.6
Carolina	95	4097	60	43.1	7	0	54	488	22	36.5
Minnesota	83	3569	59	43.0	5	0	32	241	32	38.9
Seattle	78	3254	63	41.7	1	0	35	327	27	37.3
Atlanta	75	3014	61	40.2	5	1	28	241	29	35.6
Tampa Bay	76	3053	64	40.2	6	0	32	232	24	35.5
Washington	94	3776	56	40.2	2	1	45	568	23	33.7
Chicago	83	3326	56	40.1	5	0	39	303	24	35.2
NFC Total	1293	55930	69	—	94	4	613	6109	416	—
NFC Average	80.8	3495.6	--	43.3	5.9	0.3	38.3	381.8	26.0	37.1
NFL Total	2466	107002	72	—	195	12	1149	11026	827	—
NFL Average	77.1	3343.8	--	43.4	6.1	0.4	35.9	344.6	25.8	37.3

NFL TOP TEN PUNTERS

	No	Yards	Long	Avg	Total Punts	TB	Blk	Opp Ret	Return Yards	In 20	Net Avg
McBriar, Mat, Dal.	65	3115	65	47.9	66	8	1	33	205	22	41.7
Lechler, Shane, Oak.	77	3618	68	47.0	77	4	0	45	400	27	40.8
Scifres, Mike, S.D.	52	2430	67	46.7	56	9	4	28	528	13	30.8
Lee, Andy, S.F.	91	4203	64	46.2	91	12	0	54	483	34	38.2
Fields, Brandon, Mia.	73	3369	69	46.2	75	4	2	43	454	31	37.8
Morstead, Thomas, N.O.	57	2618	64	45.9	57	6	0	26	310	21	38.4
Sepulveda, Daniel, Pit.	56	2550	62	45.5	56	8	0	23	198	16	39.1
Jones, Donnie, St.L	94	4276	63	45.5	94	4	0	45	435	32	40.0
Dodge, Matt, NY-G	72	3222	69	44.8	73	9	1	36	535	20	34.3
Harris, Nick, Det.	90	4018	66	44.6	90	8	0	54	633	24	35.8

AFC—INDIVIDUAL PUNTERS

	No	Yards	Long	Avg	Total Punts	TB	Blk	Opp Ret	Return Yards	In 20	Net Avg
Lechler, Shane, Oak.	77	3618	68	47.0	77	4	0	45	400	27	40.8
Scifres, Mike, S.D.	52	2430	67	46.7	56	9	4	28	528	13	30.8
Fields, Brandon, Mia.	73	3369	69	46.2	75	4	2	43	454	31	37.8
Sepulveda, Daniel, Pit.	56	2550	62	45.5	56	8	0	23	198	16	39.1
Colquitt, Britton, Den.	86	3835	63	44.6	86	7	0	50	550	19	36.6
Colquitt, Dustin, K.C.	88	3908	72	44.4	89	10	1	42	361	33	37.6
Hodges, Reggie, Cle.	78	3424	59	43.9	78	5	0	40	285	29	39.0
Podlesh, Adam, Jac.	57	2490	63	43.8	57	7	0	19	123	26	39.2
Koch, Sam, Bal.	81	3530	60	43.6	81	4	0	34	275	39	39.2
* Mesko, Zoltan, N.E.	58	2505	65	43.2	58	5	0	25	179	19	38.4
Kern, Brett, Ten.	77	3302	68	42.9	77	4	0	35	214	24	39.1
Weatherford, Steve, NYJ	84	3581	61	42.6	84	4	0	27	299	42	38.1
Moorman, Brian, Buf.	75	3181	61	42.4	75	7	0	32	299	17	36.6
Huber, Kevin, Cin.	71	2992	72	42.1	72	6	1	26	124	28	38.2
Turk, Matt, Hou.	63	2650	60	42.1	63	5	0	29	233	19	36.8
McAfee, Pat, Ind.	65	2731	66	42.0	65	7	0	25	289	21	35.4
(Nonqualifiers)											
Kapinos, Jeremy, Ind.-Pit.	18	754	59	41.9	18	3	0	10	94	7	33.3
Suisham, Shaun, Pit.	3	115	39	38.3	3	0	0	2	12	1	34.3
Roethlisberger, Ben, Pit.	1	35	35	35.0	1	1	0	0	0	0	15.0
Janikowski, Sebastian, Oak.	1	33	33	33.0	1	0	0	1	0	0	33.0
Succop, Ryan, K.C.	1	33	33	33.0	1	1	0	0	0	0	13.0

Leader based on average, minimum 40 punts

NFC—INDIVIDUAL PUNTERS

	No	Yards	Long	Avg	Total Punts	TB	Blk	Opp Ret	Return Yards	In 20	Net Avg
McBriar, Mat, Dal.	65	3115	65	47.9	66	8	1	33	205	22	41.7
Lee, Andy, S.F.	91	4203	64	46.2	91	12	0	54	483	34	38.2
Morstead, Thomas, N.O.	57	2618	64	45.9	57	6	0	26	310	21	38.4
Jones, Donnie, St.L	94	4276	63	45.5	94	4	0	45	435	32	40.0
* Dodge, Matt, NY-G	72	3222	69	44.8	73	9	1	36	535	20	34.3
Harris, Nick, Det.	90	4018	66	44.6	90	8	0	54	633	24	35.8
Masthay, Tim, G.B.	71	3114	62	43.9	71	5	0	31	341	25	37.6
Rocca, Sav, Phi.	73	3195	63	43.8	73	2	0	34	309	28	39.0
Graham, Ben, Ariz	94	4080	65	43.4	94	9	0	35	458	29	36.6
Baker, Jason, Car.	95	4097	60	43.1	95	7	0	54	488	22	36.5
Kluwe, Chris, Min.	83	3569	59	43.0	83	5	0	32	241	32	38.9
Ryan, Jon, Sea.	78	3254	63	41.7	78	1	0	35	327	27	37.3
* Malone, Robert, T.B.	52	2160	64	41.5	52	5	0	22	160	17	36.5
Koenen, Michael, Atl.	74	3014	61	40.7	75	5	1	28	241	29	35.6
Smith, Hunter, Was.	57	2310	56	40.5	57	1	0	25	371	17	33.7
Maynard, Brad, Chi.	83	3326	56	40.1	83	5	0	39	303	24	35.2
(Nonqualifiers)											
* Bryan, Chris, T.B.	23	860	57	37.4	23	0	0	10	72	7	34.3
Paulescu, Sam, Was.	17	700	52	41.2	17	1	0	11	117	2	33.1
Bidwell, Josh, Was.	15	625	52	41.7	15	0	0	7	59	3	37.7
Gano, Graham, Was.	4	141	42	35.3	5	0	1	2	21	1	24.0
Barth, Connor, T.B.	1	33	33	33.0	1	1	0	0	0	0	13.0

Leader based on average, minimum 40 punts
* Player that was a rookie in 2010

PUNT RETURNS

YARDS PER RETURN
NFC:	17.1	Devin Hester, Chicago
AFC:	15.3	Julian Edelman, New England

YARDS
NFC:	564	Devin Hester, Chicago
AFC:	358	Mike Thomas, Jacksonville

YARDS, GAME
AFC:	112	Julian Edelman, New England vs. Miami, January 2 (4 returns, 1 TD)
NFC:	97	* Bryan McCann, Dallas vs. Detroit, November 21 (1 returns, 1 TD)
	97	Ted Ginn, San Francisco at St. Louis, December 26 (3 returns, 1 TD)

LONGEST
NFC:	97	* Bryan McCann, Dallas vs. Detroit, November 21 - TD
AFC:	94	* Dexter McCluster, Kansas City vs. San Diego, September 13 - TD
	94	Julian Edelman, New England vs. Miami, January 2 - TD

RETURNS
NFC:	41	Tramon Williams, Green Bay
AFC:	39	* Javier Arenas, Kansas City

RETURNS, GAME
AFC:	7	* Antonio Brown, Pittsburgh vs. Oakland, November 21 (66 yards, 0 TD)
NFC:	7	Greg Camarillo, Minnesota vs. Arizona, November 7 (86 yards, 0 TD) - (OT)

FAIR CATCHES
AFC:	21	Quan Cosby, Cincinnati
NFC:	21	Stefan Logan, Detroit

TOUCHDOWNS
NFC:	3	Devin Hester, Chicago
AFC:	1	Julian Edelman, New England
	1	* Marc Mariani, Tennessee
	1	* Dexter McCluster, Kansas City
	1	Mike Thomas, Jacksonville

TEAM CHAMPION
NFC:	17.1	Chicago
AFC:	13.4	New England

NFL TOP TEN PUNT RETURNERS
	No	FC	Yards	Avg	Long	TD
Hester, Devin, Chi.	33	10	564	17.1	89t	3
Edelman, Julian, N.E.	21	6	321	15.3	94t	1
Ginn, Ted, S.F.	24	18	321	13.4	78t	1
* Mariani, Marc, Ten.	27	17	329	12.2	87t	1
Logan, Stefan, Det.	30	21	362	12.1	71	0
Royal, Eddie, Den.	25	12	298	11.9	33	0
Jackson, DeSean, Phi.	20	8	231	11.6	65t	1
Bess, Davone, Mia.	25	20	284	11.4	47	0
* Banks, Brandon, Was.	38	10	431	11.3	53	0
Leonhard, Jim, NYJ	21	19	238	11.3	32	0

AFC—INDIVIDUAL PUNT RETURNERS
	No	FC	Yards	Avg	Long	TD
Edelman, Julian, N.E.	21	6	321	15.3	94t	1
* Mariani, Marc, Ten.	27	17	329	12.2	87t	1
Royal, Eddie, Den.	25	12	298	11.9	33	0
Bess, Davone, Mia.	25	20	284	11.4	47	0
Leonhard, Jim, NYJ	21	19	238	11.3	32	0
Thomas, Mike, Jac.	34	7	358	10.5	78t	1
Webb, Lardarius, Bal.	21	12	199	9.5	35	0
Cribbs, Josh, Cle.	20	6	168	8.4	17	0
* Arenas, Javier, K.C.	39	7	322	8.3	36	0
Cosby, Quan, Cin.	30	21	225	7.5	20	0
Miller, Nick, Oak.	35	7	257	7.3	46	0
Jones, Jacoby, Hou.	29	15	204	7.0	39	0
Sproles, Darren, S.D.	24	11	166	6.9	16	0
(Nonqualifiers)						
* Brown, Antonio, Pit.	19	1	110	5.8	21	0
Higgins, Johnnie Lee, Oak.	17	4	123	7.2	53	0
Zbikowski, Tom, Bal.	16	8	101	6.3	20	0
* Wilson, Kyle, NYJ	15	2	111	7.4	18	0
Cason, Antoine, S.D.	14	4	231	16.5	62	0
Randle El, Antwaan, Pit.	14	17	56	4.0	15	0
* McCluster, Dexter, K.C.	13	2	202	15.5	94t	1
* Spiller, C.J., Buf.	12	8	175	14.6	34	0
Parrish, Roscoe, Buf.	12	7	131	10.9	33	0
* White, Blair, Ind.	10	14	80	8.0	18	0
Cotchery, Jerricho, NYJ	8	4	66	8.3	19	0
Powers, Jerraud, Ind.	8	4	63	7.9	13	0
* James, Brandon, Ind.	7	3	35	5.0	14	0
Moore, Kenny, Ind.	6	3	36	6.0	16	0
McKelvin, Leodis, Buf.	6	3	24	4.0	25	0
Cromartie, Antonio, NYJ	5	0	36	7.2	16	0
Welker, Wes, N.E.	5	7	36	7.2	22	0
Jones, Adam, Cin.	5	0	33	6.6	27	0
* Sanders, Emmanuel, Pit.	4	1	60	15.0	38	0
Holmes, Santonio, NYJ	4	0	40	10.0	14	0
Anderson, David, Hou.	4	1	26	6.5	17	0
* Thompson, Syd'Quan, Den.	3	2	18	6.0	10	0
Reed, Ed, Bal.	3	6	11	3.7	9	0
Carr, Chris, Bal.	3	0	8	2.7	10	0
* Cox, Perrish, Den.	3	1	7	2.3	4	0
* McKnight, Joe, NYJ	2	0	43	21.5	25	0
Crayton, Patrick, S.D.	2	2	23	11.5	13	0
Smith, Clifton, Mia.	2	4	9	4.5	6	0
Stuckey, Chansi, Cle.	2	3	5	2.5	5	0
Figurs, Yamon, Oak.	1	0	10	10.0	10	0
Florence, Drayton, Buf.	1	0	6	6.0	6	0
Pollard, Bernard, Hou.	1	0	5	5.0	5	0
Tate, Brandon, N.E.	1	0	4	4.0	4	0
Brackenridge, Tyron, Jac.	1	0	1	1.0	1	0
* Amaya, Jonathon, Mia.	1	0	0	0.0	0	0
Caldwell, Andre, Cin.	1	0	0	0.0	0	0
Molden, Antwaun, Hou.	1	0	0	0.0	0	0
Myers, Brandon, Oak.	1	0	0	0.0	0	0
Osgood, Kassim, Jac.	1	0	0	0.0	0	0
Scott, Bryan, Buf.	1	0	0	0.0	0	0
Branch, Tyvon, Oak.	1	0	-4	-4.0	-4	0

Cole, Marquice, NYJ	1	0	-5	-5.0	-5	0
Wright, Eric, Cle.	0	0	62	—	62	0
Faulk, Kevin, N.E.	0	1	0	—	—	0
Mathis, Rashean, Jac.	0	1	0	—	—	0
Weddle, Eric, S.D.	0	2	0	—	—	0

t = Touchdown
Leader based on average return, minimum 20 returns
* Player that was a rookie in 2010

NFC—INDIVIDUAL PUNT RETURNERS

	No	FC	Yards	Avg	Long	TD
Hester, Devin, Chi.	33	10	564	17.1	89t	3
Ginn, Ted, S.F.	24	18	321	13.4	78t	1
Logan, Stefan, Det.	30	21	362	12.1	71	0
Jackson, DeSean, Phi.	20	8	231	11.6	65t	1
* Banks, Brandon, Was.	38	10	431	11.3	53	0
Washington, Leon, Sea.	22	8	249	11.3	84	0
Amendola, Danny, St.L	40	18	452	11.3	42	0
Munnerlyn, Captain, Car.	30	6	327	10.9	37	0
Camarillo, Greg, Min.	39	20	359	9.2	52	0
Williams, Tramon, G.B.	41	19	326	8.0	52	0
* Roberts, Andre, Ariz	35	8	263	7.5	25	0
Spurlock, Micheal, T.B.	28	16	193	6.9	23	0
Reynaud, Darius, NY-G	23	5	132	5.7	20	0
(Nonqualifiers)						
Weems, Eric, Atl.	18	19	230	12.8	55t	1
* Tate, Golden, Sea.	16	6	202	12.6	63	0
* Bryant, Dez, Dal.	15	0	215	14.3	93t	2
Blackmon, Will, NY-G	14	7	94	6.7	22	0
Bush, Reggie, N.O.	14	2	92	6.6	43	0
* Calvin, Jorrick, Phi.	12	4	125	10.4	44	0
Moore, Lance, N.O.	11	16	112	10.2	72	0
* McCann, Bryan, Dal.	8	10	165	20.6	97t	1
Smith, Steve, Car.	6	0	46	7.7	32	0
Ross, Aaron, NY-G	6	1	37	6.2	14	0
* Komar, Max, Ariz	5	0	31	6.2	9	0
* Adams, Phillip, S.F.	4	0	29	7.3	16	0
Hall, Chad, Phi.	3	2	31	10.3	14	0
Forsett, Justin, Sea.	3	0	17	5.7	12	0
Maclin, Jeremy, Phi.	3	5	17	5.7	9	0
* Williams, Kyle, S.F.	3	6	16	5.3	9	0
Berrian, Bernard, Min.	3	2	2	0.7	2	0
Porter, Tracy, N.O.	2	0	6	3.0	4	0
Buchanon, Phillip, Was.	2	3	1	0.5	1	0
* Edwards, Armanti, Car.	2	0	0	0.0	0	0
Holley, Jesse, Dal.	1	0	2	2.0	2	0
DeCoud, Thomas, Atl.	1	0	0	0.0	0	0
Mack, Elbert, T.B.	1	0	0	0.0	0	0
Rodgers-Cromartie, Dominique, Ariz	1	0	0	0.0	0	0
Stroughter, Sammie, T.B.	1	0	0	0.0	0	0
* Thurmond, Walter, Sea.	1	0	0	0.0	0	0
Ware, Matt, Ariz	1	0	0	0.0	0	0
Williams, Jamar, Car.	1	0	0	0.0	0	0
* Gilyard, Mardy, St.L	0	1	0	—	—	0
* Owusu-Ansah, Akwasi, Dal.	0	4	0	—	—	0
Smith, Reggie, S.F.	0	1	0	—	—	0
* Shields, Sam, G.B.	0	0	-1	—	-1	0

t = Touchdown
Leader based on average return, minimum 20 returns
* Player that was a rookie in 2010

AMERICAN FOOTBALL CONFERENCE—PUNT RETURNS

	No	FC	Yards	Avg	Long	TD
New England	27	14	361	13.4	94t	1
Tennessee	27	17	329	12.2	87t	1
Cleveland	22	11	235	10.7	69	0
Buffalo	32	18	336	10.5	34	0
San Diego	40	19	420	10.5	62	0
Miami	28	22	293	10.5	47	0
Denver	31	15	323	10.4	33	0
Kansas City	52	9	524	10.1	94t	1
Jacksonville	36	8	359	10.0	78t	1
N.Y. Jets	56	25	529	9.4	32	0
Baltimore	43	26	319	7.4	35	0
Cincinnati	36	21	258	7.2	27	0
Oakland	55	11	386	7.0	53	0
Indianapolis	31	24	214	6.9	18	0
Houston	35	16	235	6.7	39	0
Pittsburgh	37	19	226	6.1	38	0
AFC Total	588	275	5347	9.1	94t	4
AFC Average	36.8	17.2	334.2	9.1	—	0.3

NATIONAL FOOTBALL CONFERENCE—PUNT RETURNS

	No	FC	Yards	Avg	Long	TD
Chicago	33	10	564	17.1	89t	3
Dallas	24	14	382	15.9	97t	3
Atlanta	19	19	230	12.1	55t	1
Detroit	30	21	362	12.1	71	0
San Francisco	31	25	366	11.8	78t	1
St. Louis	40	19	452	11.3	42	0
Seattle	42	14	468	11.1	84	0
Washington	40	13	432	10.8	53	0
Philadelphia	38	19	404	10.6	65t	1
Carolina	39	6	373	9.6	37	0
Minnesota	42	22	361	8.6	52	0
Green Bay	41	19	325	7.9	52	0
New Orleans	27	18	210	7.8	72	0
Arizona	42	8	294	7.0	25	0
Tampa Bay	30	16	193	6.4	23	0
N.Y. Giants	43	13	263	6.1	22	0
NFC Total	561	256	5679	10.1	97t	9
NFC Average	35.1	16.0	354.9	10.1	—	0.6
League Total	1149	531	11026	—	97t	13

SACKS

MOST SACKS

NFC: 15.5 DeMarcus Ware, Dallas

AFC: 14.5 Tamba Hali, Kansas City

MOST SACKS, GAME

AFC: 4.0 Shaun Phillips, San Diego vs. Arizona, October 3

NFC: 3.0 Clay Matthews, Green Bay at Philadelphia, September 12

3.0 Clay Matthews, Green Bay vs. Buffalo, September 19

3.0 DeMarcus Ware, Dallas at Houston, September 26

3.0 Justin Tuck, N.Y. Giants vs. Chicago, October 3

3.0 Osi Umenyiora, N.Y. Giants vs. Chicago, October 3

3.0 Julius Peppers, Chicago at Miami, November 18

3.0 Justin Tuck, N.Y. Giants at Philadelphia, November 21

3.0 Cliff Avril, Detroit vs. Chicago, December 5

3.0 DeMarcus Ware, Dallas at Philadelphia, January 2

3.0 Erik Walden, Green Bay vs. Chicago, January 2

3.0 Justin Smith, San Francisco vs. Arizona, January 2

TEAM LEADERS, SACKS

AFC: BALTIMORE, 11, Terrell Suggs; BUFFALO, 5.5, Kyle Williams; CINCINNATI, 9.5, *Carlos Dunlap; CLEVELAND, 7.5, Marcus Benard; DENVER, 5.5, D.J. Williams; HOUSTON, 8.5, Mario Williams; INDIANAPOLIS, 11, Robert Mathis; JACKSONVILLE, 5, Jeremy Mincey; KANSAS CITY, 14.5, Tamba Hali; MIAMI, 14, Cameron Wake; NEW ENGLAND, 5.5, Mike Wright; N.Y. JETS, 6, Bryan Thomas; OAKLAND, 9, Kamerion Wimbley; PITTSBURGH, 10.5, James Harrison; SAN DIEGO, 11, Shaun Phillips; TENNESSEE, 12.5, Jason Babin

NFC: ARIZONA, 6, Calais Campbell; ATLANTA, 13, John Abraham; CAROLINA, 11.5, Charles Johnson; CHICAGO, 8, Israel Idonije, Julius Peppers; DALLAS, 15.5, DeMarcus Ware; DETROIT, 10, *Ndamukong Suh; GREEN BAY, 13.5, Clay Matthews; MINNESOTA, 11, Jared Allen; NEW ORLEANS, 6, Sedrick Ellis; N.Y. GIANTS, 11.5, Justin Tuck, Osi Umenyiora; PHILADELPHIA, 10, Trent Cole; ST. LOUIS, 10.5, James Hall; SAN FRANCISCO, 8.5, Justin Smith; SEATTLE, 11, Chris Clemons; TAMPA BAY, 4.5, Stylez G. White; WASHINGTON, 8.5, Brian Orakpo

TEAM CHAMPION

AFC: 48 Pittsburgh

NFC: 47 Green Bay

NFL TOP TEN LEADERS—SACKS

	Sacks
Ware, DeMarcus, Dal.	15.5
Hali, Tamba, K.C.	14.5
Wake, Cameron, Mia.	14.0
Matthews, Clay, G.B.	13.5
Abraham, John, Atl.	13.0
Babin, Jason, Ten.	12.5
Johnson, Charles, Car.	11.5
Tuck, Justin, NY-G	11.5
Umenyiora, Osi, NY-G	11.5
Allen, Jared, Min.	11.0
Clemons, Chris, Sea.	11.0
Mathis, Robert, Ind.	11.0
Phillips, Shaun, S.D.	11.0
Suggs, Terrell, Bal.	11.0

AMERICAN FOOTBALL CONFERENCE—SACKS

	Sacks	Yards
Pittsburgh	48	319
Oakland	47	292
San Diego	47	290
N.Y. Jets	40	244
Tennessee	40	272
Miami	39	225
Kansas City	38	258
New England	36	212
Houston	30	219
Indianapolis	30	194
Cleveland	29	178
Baltimore	27	190
Buffalo	27	181
Cincinnati	27	179
Jacksonville	26	189
Denver	23	156
AFC Total	554	3598
AFC Average	34.6	224.9

NATIONAL FOOTBALL CONFERENCE—SACKS

	Sacks	Yards
Green Bay	47	333
N.Y. Giants	46	316
Detroit	44	288
St. Louis	43	290
Philadelphia	39	292
Seattle	37	246
San Francisco	36	244
Dallas	35	257
Chicago	34	232
Arizona	33	227
New Orleans	33	250
Atlanta	31	221
Carolina	31	224
Minnesota	31	177
Washington	29	176
Tampa Bay	26	143
NFC Total	575	3916
NFC Average	35.9	244.8
League Total	1129	7514
League Average	35.3	234.8

AFC—INDIVIDUAL SACKS

	Sacks		Sacks		Sacks
Hali, Tamba, K.C.	14.5	Starks, Randy, Mia.	3.0	Geathers, Robert, Cin.	1.0
Wake, Cameron, Mia.	14.0	Stroud, Marcus, Buf.	3.0	* Haden, Joe, Cle.	1.0
Babin, Jason, Ten.	12.5	Timmons, Lawrence, Pit.	3.0	Hagler, Tyjuan, Ind.	1.0
Mathis, Robert, Ind.	11.0	Witherspoon, Will, Ten.	3.0	Hampton, Casey, Pit.	1.0
Phillips, Shaun, S.D.	11.0	Bryant, Desmond, Oak.	2.5	Hope, Chris, Ten.	1.0
Suggs, Terrell, Bal.	11.0	Castillo, Luis, S.D.	2.5	Jackson, Tyson, K.C.	1.0
Harrison, James, Pit.	10.5	Coleman, Kenyon, Cle.	2.5	Jamison, Tim, Hou.	1.0
Freeney, Dwight, Ind.	10.0	Harvey, Derrick, Jac.	2.5	Johnson, Derrick, K.C.	1.0
Woodley, LaMarr, Pit.	10.0	Johnson, Michael, Cin.	2.5	Johnson, Travis, S.D.	1.0
* Dunlap, Carlos, Cin.	9.5	McDaniel, Tony, Mia.	2.5	Jones, Dhani, Cin.	1.0
Wimbley, Kamerion, Oak.	9.0	* Moats, Arthur, Buf.	2.5	* Jones, Reshad, Mia.	1.0
Williams, Mario, Hou.	8.5	Pollard, Bernard, Hou.	2.5	Kruger, Paul, Bal.	1.0
Benard, Marcus, Cle.	7.5	Sims, Pat, Cin.	2.5	Landry, Dawan, Bal.	1.0
Ball, Dave, Ten.	7.0	Studebaker, Andy, K.C.	2.5	* Lang, Brandon, S.D.	1.0
Gilberry, Wallace, K.C.	7.0	* Berry, Eric, K.C.	2.0	Lewis, Damione, Hou.	1.0
Kelly, Tommy, Oak.	7.0	Crocker, Chris, Cin.	2.0	* Love, Kyle, N.E.	1.0
Shaughnessy, Matt, Oak.	7.0	Dawkins, Brian, Den.	2.0	Madison, Anthony, Pit.	1.0
Burnett, Kevin, S.D.	6.0	* Deaderick, Brandon, N.E.	2.0	Martin, Vaughn, S.D.	1.0
Farrior, James, Pit.	6.0	Dorsey, Glenn, K.C.	2.0	Maualuga, Rey, Cin.	1.0
Thomas, Bryan, NYJ	6.0	Edwards, Ron, K.C.	2.0	McClain, Jameel, Bal.	1.0
Garay, Antonio, S.D.	5.5	Elam, Abram, Cle.	2.0	* McCourty, Devin, N.E.	1.0
Ngata, Haloti, Bal.	5.5	* Fletcher, Dane, N.E.	2.0	Middleton, William, Jac.	1.0
Pace, Calvin, NYJ	5.5	Gay, William, Pit.	2.0	* Mitchell, Earl, Hou.	1.0
Seymour, Richard, Oak.	5.5	Gocong, Chris, Cle.	2.0	Moses, Quentin, Mia.	1.0
Williams, D.J., Den.	5.5	Johnson, Spencer, Buf.	2.0	Moss, Jarvis, Oak.	1.0
Williams, Kyle, Buf.	5.5	Lewis, Ray, Bal.	2.0	Nolan, Troy, Hou.	1.0
Wright, Mike, N.E.	5.5	Lowery, Dwight, NYJ	2.0	Polamalu, Troy, Pit.	1.0
Banta-Cain, Tully, N.E.	5.0	Mayo, Jerod, N.E.	2.0	Pool, Brodney, NYJ	1.0
Haggan, Mario, Den.	5.0	McFadden, Bryant, Pit.	2.0	Pryce, Trevor, NYJ	1.0
* Houston, Lamarr, Oak.	5.0	Moore, Eric, N.E.	2.0	Rivers, Keith, Cin.	1.0
Mincey, Jeremy, Jac.	5.0	Posluszny, Paul, Buf.	2.0	Rucker, Frostee, Cin.	1.0
Taylor, Jason, NYJ	5.0	Pouha, Sione, NYJ	2.0	Ryans, DeMeco, Hou.	1.0
Barnes, Antwan, S.D.	4.5	Rogers, Shaun, Cle.	2.0	Scott, Bart, NYJ	1.0
Ellis, Shaun, NYJ	4.5	Rubin, Ahtyba, Cle.	2.0	Session, Clint, Ind.	1.0
* Misi, Koa, Mia.	4.5	Soliai, Paul, Mia.	2.0	* Sharpton, Darryl, Hou.	1.0
Anderson, Mark, Hou.	4.0	* Thomas, Cam, S.D.	2.0	Siler, Brandon, S.D.	1.0
Branch, Tyvon, Oak.	4.0	Vickerson, Kevin, Den.	2.0	Smith, Eric, NYJ	1.0
Coleman, Drew, NYJ	4.0	Wilfork, Vince, N.E.	2.0	Smith, Shaun, K.C.	1.0
Huff, Michael, Oak.	4.0	* Worilds, Jason, Pit.	2.0	Strickland, Donald, S.D.	1.0
Kampman, Aaron, Jac.	4.0	Ayers, Robert, Den.	1.5	Taylor, Ike, Pit.	1.0
Knighton, Terrance, Jac.	4.0	Bell, Yeremiah, Mia.	1.5	Thomas, Marcus, Den.	1.0
Ninkovich, Rob, N.E.	4.0	Cesaire, Jacques, S.D.	1.5	Trusnik, Jason, Cle.	1.0
Smith, Antonio, Hou.	4.0	Clemons, Chris, Mia.	1.5	Tucker, Jyles, S.D.	1.0
* Alualu, Tyson, Jac.	3.5	Cushing, Brian, Hou.	1.5	Tulloch, Stephen, Ten.	1.0
Brown, Tony, Ten.	3.5	Eason, Nick, Pit.	1.5	Williams, Demorrio, K.C.	1.0
Foster, Eric, Ind.	3.5	* Hall, Larry, Jac.	1.5	Williams, Roy, Cin.	1.0
Fujita, Scott, Cle.	3.5	Hayes, William, Ten.	1.5	Woods, Pierre, N.E.	1.0
Jones, Jason, Ten.	3.5	Johnson, Jarret, Bal.	1.5	Woodyard, Wesley, Den.	1.0
Kelsay, Chris, Buf.	3.5	McRath, Gerald, Ten.	1.5	Bethea, Antoine, Ind.	0.5
Roth, Matt, Cle.	3.5	* Morgan, Derrick, Ten.	1.5	Bowens, David, Cle.	0.5
Smith, Daryl, Jac.	3.5	Scott, Trevor, Oak.	1.5	Brackett, Gary, Ind.	0.5
Warren, Gerard, N.E.	3.5	Adams, Mike, Cle.	1.0	Crable, Shawn, N.E.	0.5
Applewhite, Antwan, S.D.	3.0	* Angerer, Pat, Ind.	1.0	Johnson, Antonio, Ind.	0.5
* Arenas, Javier, K.C.	3.0	Bailey, Champ, Den.	1.0	Johnson, Brandon, Cin.	0.5
* Atkins, Geno, Cin.	3.0	Bannan, Justin, Den.	1.0	* McClain, Rolando, Oak.	0.5
Dansby, Karlos, Mia.	3.0	Belcher, Jovan, K.C.	1.0	Nading, Jesse, Hou.	0.5
English, Larry, S.D.	3.0	Byrd, Jairus, Buf.	1.0	Ndukwe, Chinedum, Cin.	0.5
Ford, Jacob, Ten.	3.0	* Carrington, Alex, Buf.	1.0	Nwagbuo, Ogemdi, S.D.	0.5
Guyton, Gary, N.E.	3.0	Considine, Sean, Jac.	1.0	Peko, Domata, Cin.	0.5
Harris, David, NYJ	3.0	Cooper, Stephen, S.D.	1.0	Pryor, Myron, N.E.	0.5
Hood, Ziggy, Pit.	3.0	Corner, Reggie, Buf.	1.0	Robinson, Derreck, Cle.	0.5
Hunter, Jason, Den.	3.0	* Cunningham, Jermaine, N.E.	1.0	Weddle, Eric, S.D.	0.5
Ihedigbo, James, NYJ	3.0	Dixon, Marcus, NYJ	1.0	Whitner, Donte, Buf.	0.5
Keisel, Brett, Pit.	3.0	Dobbins, Tim, Mia.	1.0		
Langford, Kendall, Mia.	3.0	Edwards, Dwan, Buf.	1.0	*Player that was a rookie in 2010*	
Okoye, Amobi, Hou.	3.0	Ellerbe, Dannell, Bal.	1.0		
Redding, Cory, Bal.	3.0	Ellis, Chris, Buf.	1.0		
Scott, Bryan, Buf.	3.0	Finnegan, Cortland, Ten.	1.0		
		Foote, Larry, Pit.	1.0		

NFC—INDIVIDUAL SACKS

Player	Sacks
Ware, DeMarcus, Dal.	15.5
Matthews, Clay, G.B.	13.5
Abraham, John, Atl.	13.0
Johnson, Charles, Car.	11.5
Tuck, Justin, NY-G	11.5
Umenyiora, Osi, NY-G	11.5
Allen, Jared, Min.	11.0
Clemons, Chris, Sea.	11.0
Hall, James, St.L	10.5
Cole, Trent, Phi.	10.0
* Suh, Ndamukong, Det.	10.0
Brock, Raheem, Sea.	9.0
Avril, Cliff, Det.	8.5
Long, Chris, St.L	8.5
Orakpo, Brian, Was.	8.5
Smith, Justin, S.F.	8.5
Edwards, Ray, Min.	8.0
Idonije, Israel, Chi.	8.0
Peppers, Julius, Chi.	8.0
Jenkins, Cullen, G.B.	7.0
Raji, B.J., G.B.	6.5
Campbell, Calais, Ariz	6.0
Ellis, Sedrick, N.O.	6.0
Jackson, Lawrence, Det.	6.0
Parker, Juqua, Phi.	6.0
Robbins, Fred, St.L	6.0
Willis, Patrick, S.F.	6.0
Smith, Will, N.O.	5.5
Brooks, Ahmad, S.F.	5.0
Dockett, Darnell, Ariz	5.0
Haggans, Clark, Ariz	5.0
LaBoy, Travis, S.F.	5.0
McBride, Turk, Det.	5.0
Porter, Joey, Ariz	5.0
Spencer, Anthony, Dal.	5.0
* Pierre-Paul, Jason, NY-G	4.5
White, Stylez G., T.B.	4.5
Ah You, C.J., St.L	4.0
Babineaux, Jonathan, Atl.	4.0
Cofield, Barry, NY-G	4.0
Haralson, Parys, S.F.	4.0
Hayes, Geno, T.B.	4.0
Kiwanuka, Mathias, NY-G	4.0
Laws, Trevor, Phi.	4.0
Milloy, Lawyer, Sea.	4.0
Urlacher, Brian, Chi.	4.0
Vanden Bosch, Kyle, Det.	4.0
Vilma, Jonathan, N.O.	4.0
* Zombo, Frank, G.B.	4.0
Anderson, James, Car.	3.5
Brown, Everette, Car.	3.5
Curry, Aaron, Sea.	3.5
Ratliff, Jay, Dal.	3.5
Biermann, Kroy, Atl.	3.0
Bishop, Desmond, G.B.	3.0
Charleston, Jeff, N.O.	3.0
Crowder, Tim, T.B.	3.0
* Graham, Brandon, Phi.	3.0
* Hardy, Greg, Car.	3.0
Harper, Roman, N.O.	3.0
Landri, Derek, Car.	3.0
Laurinaitis, James, St.L	3.0
* McCoy, Gerald, T.B.	3.0
Tapp, Darryl, Phi.	3.0
Walden, Erik, G.B.	3.0
Carter, Andre, Was.	2.5
Fletcher, London, Was.	2.5
Haynesworth, Albert, Was.	2.5

Player	Sacks
Hill, Sammie Lee, Det.	2.5
Holliday, Vonnie, Was.	2.5
Lawson, Manny, S.F.	2.5
Melton, Henry, Chi.	2.5
Scandrick, Orlando, Dal.	2.5
Adams, Anthony, Chi.	2.0
* Allen, Nate, Phi.	2.0
Anderson, Jamaal, Atl.	2.0
Atogwe, Oshiomogho, St.L	2.0
Bernard, Rocky, NY-G	2.0
Black, Quincy, T.B.	2.0
Branch, Alan, Ariz	2.0
Briggs, Lance, Chi.	2.0
Brown, Alex, N.O.	2.0
Butler, Victor, Dal.	2.0
Daniels, Phillip, Was.	2.0
Delmas, Louis, Det.	2.0
Dixon, Antonio, Phi.	2.0
Grant, Larry, St.L	2.0
Guion, Letroy, Min.	2.0
Jerry, Peria, Atl.	2.0
Lenon, Paris, Ariz	2.0
Lofton, Curtis, Atl.	2.0
Magee, Alex, T.B.	2.0
McIntosh, Rocky, Was.	2.0
Patterson, Mike, Phi.	2.0
Robison, Brian, Min.	2.0
Ruud, Barrett, T.B.	2.0
* Schofield, O'Brien, Ariz	2.0
Sensabaugh, Gerald, Dal.	2.0
Sims, Ernie, Phi.	2.0
Toeaina, Matt, Chi.	2.0
Vobora, David, St.L	2.0
Wilkerson, Jimmy, N.O.	2.0
Williams, Corey, Det.	2.0
Wilson, Adrian, Ariz	2.0
Winfield, Antoine, Min.	2.0
Woodson, Charles, G.B.	2.0
Alexander, Lorenzo, Was.	1.5
Babineaux, Jordan, Sea.	1.5
Bowen, Stephen, Dal.	1.5
Canty, Chris, NY-G	1.5
Carriker, Adam, Was.	1.5
Harris, Nic, Car.	1.5
Harris, Tommie, Chi.	1.5
* Selvie, George, St.L	1.5
Sopoaga, Isaac, S.F.	1.5
Wynn, Jarius, G.B.	1.5
Ayodele, Remi, N.O.	1.0
Barber, Ronde, T.B.	1.0
Beason, Jon, Car.	1.0
Bennett, Michael, T.B.	1.0
Boley, Michael, NY-G	1.0
Bradley, Stewart, Phi.	1.0
Brooking, Keith, Dal.	1.0
Bryant, Red, Sea.	1.0
* Chancellor, Kam, Sea.	1.0
Chillar, Brandon, G.B.	1.0
Clements, Nate, S.F.	1.0
Cole, Colin, Sea.	1.0
Connor, Dan, Car.	1.0
Dahl, Craig, St.L	1.0
Davis, Chauncey, Atl.	1.0
* Davis, Dexter, Sea.	1.0
Davis, Will, Ariz	1.0
Doughty, Reed, Was.	1.0
Dunbar, Jo-Lonn, N.O.	1.0
Fluellen, Andre, Det.	1.0
Fokou, Moise, Phi.	1.0

Player	Sacks
Goff, Jonathan, NY-G	1.0
Goldson, Dashon, S.F.	1.0
Grant, Deon, NY-G	1.0
Greenway, Chad, Min.	1.0
Hargrove, Anthony, N.O.	1.0
Hatcher, Jason, Dal.	1.0
Hayden, Nick, Car.	1.0
Hayward, Adam, T.B.	1.0
Henderson, E.J., Min.	1.0
Herring, Will, Sea.	1.0
Iwuh, Brian, Chi.	1.0
Jackson, Rob, Was.	1.0
Jean-Francois, Ricky, S.F.	1.0
Jenkins, Malcolm, N.O.	1.0
Jones, Sean, T.B.	1.0
Landry, LaRon, Was.	1.0
Lewis, Michael, St.L	1.0
Lewis, Roy, Sea.	1.0
Marshall, Richard, Car.	1.0
Mebane, Brandon, Sea.	1.0
Mikell, Quintin, Phi.	1.0
Miller, Roy, T.B.	1.0
Mitchell, Jayme, Min.	1.0
Mitchell, Marvin, N.O.	1.0
Moore, D.J., Chi.	1.0
* Neal, Mike, G.B.	1.0
* Norwood, Eric, Car.	1.0
Palmer, Ashlee, Det.	1.0
Patterson, Dimitri, Phi.	1.0
* Peters, Corey, Atl.	1.0
Peterson, Julian, Det.	1.0
Peterson, Mike, Atl.	1.0
Pickett, Ryan, G.B.	1.0
Poppinga, Brady, G.B.	1.0
Rhodes, Kerry, Ariz	1.0
Ross, Aaron, NY-G	1.0
Sanford, Jamarca, Min.	1.0
* Stewart, Darian, St.L	1.0
Tatupu, Lofa, Sea.	1.0
* Te'o-Nesheim, Daniel, Phi.	1.0
Thomas, Terrell, NY-G	1.0
Tinoisamoa, Pisa, Chi.	1.0
Toler, Greg, Ariz	1.0
Torrence, Leigh, N.O.	1.0
* Washington, Daryl, Ariz	1.0
* Weatherspoon, Sean, Atl.	1.0
Williams, Brian, Atl.	1.0
Williams, Kevin, Min.	1.0
Williams, Tramon, G.B.	1.0
* Wilson, C.J., G.B.	1.0
Wootton, Corey, Chi.	1.0
Young, Usama, N.O.	1.0
Ball, Alan, Dal.	0.5
* Cudjo, Jermelle, St.L	0.5
Hawk, A.J., G.B.	0.5
Jarmon, Jeremy, Was.	0.5
Kennedy, Jimmy, Min.	0.5
* Lissemore, Sean, Dal.	0.5
Prioleau, Pierson, N.O.	0.5
Rolle, Antrel, NY-G	0.5
Spencer, Shawntae, S.F.	0.5
Tollefson, Dave, NY-G	0.5
Williams, Madieu, Min.	0.5
* Woods, Al, T.B.	0.5

Player that was a rookie in 2010

MOST FUMBLES
AFC: 11 David Garrard, Jacksonville
NFC: 11 Michael Vick, Philadelphia

MOST FUMBLES, GAME
AFC: 4 Mark Sanchez, N.Y. Jets vs. Miami, December 12
NFC: 4 Michael Vick, Philadelphia at Chicago, November 28

OWN FUMBLES RECOVERED
NFC: 8 Donovan McNabb, Washington
AFC: 5 Jason Campbell, Oakland

OWN FUMBLES RECOVERED, GAME
AFC: 2 Mark Sanchez, N.Y. Jets at Detroit, November 7 (0 yards, 0 TD) - (OT)
2 Chad Henne, Miami at Baltimore, November 7 (0 yards, 0 TD)
2 David Garrard, Jacksonville at N.Y. Giants, November 28 (0 yards, 0 TD)
NFC: 2 * Max Komar, Arizona at St. Louis, September 12 (0 yards, 0 TD)
2 * Jimmy Clausen, Carolina vs. Chicago, October 10 (0 yards, 0 TD)
2 Donovan McNabb, Washington at Chicago, October 24 (0 yards, 0 TD)
2 Felix Jones, Dallas at Green Bay, November 7 (0 yards, 0 TD)
2 Mike Goodson, Carolina vs. Baltimore, November 21 (0 yards, 0 TD)
2 Jon Kitna, Dallas vs. New Orleans, November 25 (0 yards, 0 TD)
2 Michael Vick, Philadelphia at Chicago, November 28 (0 yards, 0 TD)
2 Tarvaris Jackson, Minnesota vs. N.Y. Giants, December 13 (0 yards, 0 TD)
2 Josh Freeman, Tampa Bay vs. Seattle, December 26 (0 yards, 0 TD)
2 Troy Smith, San Francisco at St. Louis, December 26 (0 yards, 0 TD)

OPPONENTS' FUMBLES RECOVERED
NFC: 5 Justin Tuck, N.Y. Giants
AFC: 3 Kenyon Coleman, Cleveland
3 Hiram Eugene, Oakland
3 Ray Lewis, Baltimore
3 Jerod Mayo, New England
3 Rob Ninkovich, New England
3 Sione Pouha, N.Y. Jets
3 Roy Williams, Cincinnati

OPPONENTS' FUMBLES RECOVERED, GAME
AFC: 2 Sione Pouha, N.Y. Jets vs. Baltimore, September 13 (2 yards, 0 TD)
2 Kenyon Coleman, Cleveland vs. Cincinnati, October 3 (0 yards, 0 TD)
2 Ray Lewis, Baltimore vs. Cincinnati, January 2 (0 yards, 0 TD)
NFC: 2 Red Bryant, Seattle vs. San Diego, September 26 (0 yards, 0 TD)
2 Stefan Logan, Detroit at Green Bay, October 3 (4 yards, 0 TD)
2 James Anderson, Carolina at New Orleans, October 3 (0 yards, 0 TD)
2 Quintin Mikell, Philadelphia at San Francisco, October 10 (52 yards, 1 TD)
2 Brian Robison, Minnesota vs. Buffalo, December 5 (0 yards, 0 TD)

2 Kenny Phillips, N.Y. Giants vs. Philadelphia, December 19 (25 yards, 0 TD)

YARDS
AFC: 76 Tyvon Branch, Oakland
NFC: 69 Kerry Rhodes, Arizona

LONGEST
AFC: 75 Jason Hunter, Denver vs. Kansas City, November 14 - TD
NFC: 52 Quintin Mikell, Philadelphia at San Francisco, October 10 - TD

AFC—TOUCHDOWNS ON FUMBLE RECOVERIES
Branch, Tyvon, Oak.	1
Elam, Abram, Cle.	1
Florence, Drayton, Buf.	1
Guyton, Gary, N.E.	1
Hunter, Jason, Den.	1
Jones, Adam, Cin.	1
* Misi, Koa, Mia.	1
Moala, Fili, Ind.	1

NFC—TOUCHDOWNS ON FUMBLE RECOVERIES
Rhodes, Kerry, Ariz	2
Adams, Michael, Ariz	1
Babineaux, Jonathan, Atl.	1
Breaston, Steve, Ariz	1
Brown, Levi, Ariz	1
Collins, Nick, G.B.	1
Dockett, Darnell, Ariz	1
Hall, DeAngelo, Was.	1
Hayes, Gerald, Ariz	1
Mikell, Quintin, Phi.	1
* Suh, Ndamukong, Det.	1
Ware, DeMarcus, Dal.	1
Winfield, Antoine, Min.	1

AFC FUMBLES—INDIVIDUAL
	Fum	Own Rec	Opp Rec	Yards	Tot Rec
Adams, Flozell, Pit.	0	1	0	0	1
Addai, Joseph, Ind.	2	1	0	0	1
Albert, Branden, K.C.	0	1	0	0	1
Alexander, Gerald, Jac.	.0	0	1	43	1
Allen, Will, Pit.	0	0	1	0	1
Amano, Eugene, Ten.	1	0	0	-10	0
Amato, Ken, Ten.	1	0	0	-25	0
* Amaya, Jonathon, Mia.	1	1	0	0	1
* Arenas, Javier, K.C.	2	0	0	0	0
Ball, Dave, Ten.	0	0	1	5	1
Ball, Lance, Den.	1	1	0	0	1
Barton, Eric, Cle.	0	0	1	1	1
Batch, Charlie, Pit.	2	1	0	-3	1
Bell, Mike, Phi.-Cle.	2	2	0	0	2
Bell, Yeremiah, Mia.	0	0	1	4	1
Benson, Cedric, Cin.	7	1	0	0	1
Bentley, Kevin, Hou.	0	0	1	8	1
Bess, Davone, Mia.	3	1	0	0	1
Birk, Matt, Bal.	0	1	0	0	1
Boldin, Anquan, Bal.	1	0	0	0	0
Boller, Kyle, Oak.	1	0	0	0	0
Bowe, Dwayne, K.C.	1	1	0	0	1
Brady, Tom, N.E.	3	1	0	-5	1
Branch, Tyvon, Oak.	0	0	2	76	2
Britt, Kenny, Ten.	1	0	0	0	0
Brohm, Brian, Buf.	1	0	0	0	1
* Brown, Antonio, Pit.	1	0	0	0	0
Brown, Ricky, Oak.	0	2	0	0	2
Brown, Ronnie, Mia.	3	0	0	0	0
* Brown, Sergio, N.E.	0	0	1	0	1

	Fum	Own Rec	Opp Rec	Yards	Tot Rec		Fum	Own Rec	Opp Rec	Yards	Tot Rec
Bruton, David, Den.	0	2	0	0	2	Greene, Shonn, NYJ	3	0	0	0	0
Buckhalter, Correll, Den.	1	0	0	0	0	* Gresham, Jermaine, Cin.	2	0	0	0	0
Burnett, Kevin, S.D.	0	0	1	0	1	Griffin, Michael, Ten.	0	0	2	20	2
Bush, Michael, Oak.	0	1	0	0	1	* Gronkowski, Rob, N.E.	1	0	0	0	0
Butler, Darius, N.E.	0	1	0	0	1	Groves, Quentin, Oak.	0	0	2	0	2
Butler, Rashad, Hou.	0	1	0	0	1	Guyton, Gary, N.E.	0	0	1	35	1
Byrd, Jairus, Buf.	0	0	2	0	2	* Haden, Joe, Cle.	1	0	0	0	0
Caldwell, Andre, Cin.	1	0	0	0	0	Haggan, Mario, Den.	0	0	1	0	1
Campbell, Jason, Oak.	9	5	0	-15	5	Hagler, Tyjuan, Ind.	0	0	1	0	1
Carlisle, Cooper, Oak.	0	1	0	0	1	Hali, Tamba, K.C.	0	0	2	2	2
Carr, Brandon, K.C.	0	1	1	23	2	Hamlin, Ken, Bal.	0	0	1	0	1
Cartwright, Rock, Oak.	0	1	0	0	1	Hardwick, Nick, S.D.	0	1	0	0	1
Cassel, Matt, K.C.	3	0	0	-2	0	Harris, David, NYJ	0	0	1	0	1
Castillo, Luis, S.D.	0	0	1	10	1	Harris, Ryan, Den.	0	1	0	0	1
Charles, Jamaal, K.C.	3	3	0	0	3	Harrison, James, Pit.	0	0	1	0	1
Chester, Chris, Bal.	0	1	0	0	1	Hartline, Brian, Mia.	1	1	0	0	1
Clark, Ryan, Pit.	0	0	1	5	1	Heap, Todd, Bal.	1	0	0	0	0
Clemons, Chris, Mia.	0	0	1	0	1	Henne, Chad, Mia.	5	3	0	-22	3
Cobbs, Patrick, Mia.	1	0	0	0	0	Hester, Jacob, S.D.	0	0	2	0	2
Cole, Marquice, NYJ	1	1	0	0	1	Heyward-Bey, Darrius, Oak.	1	0	0	0	0
Coleman, Kenyon, Cle.	0	0	3	0	3	Higgins, Johnnie Lee, Oak.	0	1	0	0	1
Collie, Austin, Ind.	1	0	0	0	0	Hill, Renaldo, Den.	0	0	1	0	1
Collins, Kerry, Ten.	5	1	0	-8	1	Hillis, Peyton, Cle.	8	3	0	0	3
Condo, Jon, Oak.	0	0	1	0	1	Hoke, Chris, Pit.	0	0	1	0	1
* Conner, John, NYJ	0	1	0	0	1	Holmes, Santonio, NYJ	2	0	0	0	0
* Conner, Kavell, Ind.	0	0	1	5	1	Hope, Chris, Ten.	0	0	1	0	1
Considine, Sean, Jac.	0	0	1	0	1	Houshmandzadeh, T.J., Bal.	1	0	0	0	0
Cook, Jared, Ten.	0	1	0	2	1	* Houston, Lamarr, Oak.	0	0	2	0	2
Costanzo, Blake, Cle.	0	1	0	0	1	Hunter, Jason, Den.	0	0	2	75	2
Cotchery, Jerricho, NYJ	0	1	0	0	1	Ihedigbo, James, NYJ	0	0	1	0	1
* Cox, Perrish, Den.	1	0	0	0	0	Incognito, Richie, Mia.	2	0	0	-15	0
Cribbs, Josh, Cle.	7	4	0	0	4	Jackson, Fred, Buf.	5	1	0	0	1
Cromartie, Antonio, NYJ	0	0	1	0	1	Jackson, Vincent, S.D.	0	1	0	-6	1
Dawson, Keyunta, Ind.	0	0	1	0	1	* James, Javarris, Ind.	1	0	0	0	0
* Decker, Eric, Den.	3	0	0	0	0	Johnson, Andre, Hou.	1	1	0	0	1
Delhomme, Jake, Cle.	3	0	0	0	0	Johnson, Antonio, Ind.	0	0	1	0	1
Dielman, Kris, S.D.	0	1	0	0	1	Johnson, Chris, Ten.	3	1	0	0	1
Dixon, Dennis, Pit.	2	0	0	-4	0	Johnson, Chris, Oak.	1	0	0	0	0
Dorsey, Glenn, K.C.	0	0	1	0	1	Johnson, Derrick, K.C.	0	0	1	0	1
Dreessen, Joel, Hou.	1	0	0	0	0	Johnson, Michael, Cin.	0	0	1	0	1
* Dunlap, Carlos, Cin.	0	0	1	0	1	Johnson, Spencer, Buf.	0	0	1	0	1
Durant, Justin, Jac.	0	0	1	0	1	Johnson, Steve, Buf.	1	0	0	0	0
Edelman, Julian, N.E.	1	0	0	0	0	Jones, Adam, Cin.	0	0	2	59	2
Edwards, Braylon, NYJ	1	0	0	0	0	Jones, Jacoby, Hou.	1	1	0	0	1
Elam, Abram, Cle.	0	0	2	18	2	* Jones, Reshad, Mia.	0	0	1	0	1
Ellis, Chris, Buf.	1	0	0	0	0	Jones, Thomas, K.C.	3	0	0	0	0
Eugene, Hiram, Oak.	0	0	3	0	3	Jones-Drew, Maurice, Jac.	2	2	0	0	2
Evans, Lee, Buf.	2	1	0	0	1	* Karim, Deji, Jac.	4	1	0	0	1
Farrior, James, Pit.	0	0	1	8	1	Kelly, Reggie, Cin.	0	1	0	0	1
Ferguson, D'Brickashaw, NYJ	0	1	0	0	1	* King, Brandon, Ind.	0	1	0	0	1
Figurs, Yamon, Oak.	1	0	0	0	0	Koch, Sam, Bal.	1	1	0	-10	1
Fitzpatrick, Ryan, Buf.	8	3	0	0	3	Landry, Dawan, Bal.	0	0	1	0	1
Flacco, Joe, Bal.	9	1	0	-8	1	Laury, Lance, NYJ	0	0	1	0	1
* Fletcher, Dane, N.E.	0	0	1	0	1	Leonhard, Jim, NYJ	0	0	1	-1	1
Florence, Drayton, Buf.	0	1	1	27	2	Lewis, Marcedes, Jac.	2	0	0	0	0
Floyd, Malcom, S.D.	1	0	0	0	0	Lewis, Ray, Bal.	0	0	3	1	3
* Ford, Jacoby, Oak.	3	1	0	0	1	Long, Jake, Mia.	0	1	0	0	1
Foster, Arian, Hou.	3	1	0	1	1	Loper, Daniel, Oak.	0	2	0	3	2
Foster, Eric, Ind.	0	0	2	0	2	Lowery, Dwight, NYJ	0	0	2	2	2
Fox, Keyaron, Pit.	0	0	2	0	2	Madison, Anthony, Pit.	0	1	0	0	1
Gaffney, Jabar, Den.	1	0	0	0	0	Manning, Peyton, Ind.	3	1	0	-2	1
Gafford, Thomas, K.C.	0	0	1	0	1	* Mariani, Marc, Ten.	3	1	0	0	1
Garrard, David, Jac.	11	3	0	-19	3	Maroney, Laurence, Den.	1	0	0	0	0
Geathers, Robert, Cin.	0	0	1	5	1	Marshall, Brandon, Mia.	2	1	0	0	1
Gilberry, Wallace, K.C.	0	0	2	0	2	Massaquoi, Mohamed, Cle.	1	0	0	0	0
Gocong, Chris, Cle.	0	1	1	0	2	* Mathews, Ryan, S.D.	5	1	0	0	1
* Goodman, Richard, S.D.	1	0	0	0	0	Mathis, Robert, Ind.	0	0	1	1	1
Gradkowski, Bruce, Oak.	3	1	0	0	1	Mayo, Jerod, N.E.	0	0	3	-2	3
Graham, Daniel, Den.	1	1	0	0	1	McBean, Ryan, Den.	0	0	1	1	1
Greene, Courtney, Jac.	0	0	1	0	1	McClain, Jameel, Bal.	0	0	1	9	1

Player	Fum	Own Rec	Opp Rec	Yards	Tot Rec
* McCluster, Dexter, K.C.	2	1	0	0	1
* McCoy, Colt, Cle.	1	1	0	0	1
McFadden, Darren, Oak.	4	0	0	-7	0
McGahee, Willis, Bal.	2	0	0	0	0
McIntyre, Corey, Buf.	1	1	0	0	1
McKelvin, Leodis, Buf.	3	0	0	0	0
McLendon, Steve, Pit.	0	0	1	0	1
McQuistan, Pat, Mia.	0	1	0	0	1
Mendenhall, Rashard, Pit.	2	0	0	0	0
Meriweather, Brandon, N.E.	0	0	1	0	1
Miller, Heath, Pit.	1	0	0	0	0
Miller, Nick, Oak.	2	1	0	0	1
Miller, Zach, Oak.	1	0	0	0	0
* Misi, Koa, Mia.	0	0	2	0	2
Mitchell, Mike, Oak.	0	1	1	12	2
Moala, Fili, Ind.	0	0	1	1	1
Monroe, Eugene, Jac.	0	1	0	0	1
Moore, Brandon, NYJ	0	2	0	0	2
Moore, Devin, Ind.	2	0	0	0	0
Moore, Eric, N.E.	0	0	1	0	1
Moore, Evan, Cle.	1	0	0	0	0
Moore, Kenny, Ind.	2	0	0	0	0
Moore, Mewelde, Pit.	0	1	0	0	1
Moreno, Knowshon, Den.	3	0	0	0	0
Morris, Sammy, N.E.	1	0	0	0	0
Moses, Quentin, Mia.	0	0	1	0	1
Murphy, Louis, Oak.	2	1	0	0	1
Myers, Brandon, Oak.	1	0	0	0	0
Naanee, Legedu, S.D.	1	0	0	0	0
Ndukwe, Chinedum, Cin.	0	0	1	0	1
Nelson, Reggie, Cin.	1	0	0	0	0
Nelson, Shawn, Buf.	1	0	0	0	0
* Newton, Mike, Ind.	0	0	1	0	1
Ngata, Haloti, Bal.	0	0	1	0	1
Ninkovich, Rob, N.E.	0	0	3	63	3
Nolan, Troy, Hou.	0	0	1	0	1
Nwagbuo, Ogemdi, S.D.	0	0	1	0	1
Ochocinco, Chad, Cin.	0	1	0	6	1
Oher, Michael, Bal.	0	1	0	0	1
Okoye, Amobi, Hou.	0	0	1	0	1
Oliver, Paul, S.D.	0	0	2	23	2
Orton, Kyle, Den.	4	0	0	-1	0
Osgood, Kassim, Jac.	0	1	0	-1	1
Owens, Montell, Jac.	0	0	1	0	1
Palmer, Carson, Cin.	7	3	0	-5	3
Parmele, Jalen, Bal.	1	0	0	0	0
Parrish, Roscoe, Buf.	1	1	0	4	1
Paxton, Lonie, Den.	1	0	0	-13	0
Phillips, Shaun, S.D.	0	0	1	0	1
* Pitta, Dennis, Bal.	0	1	0	0	1
Polamalu, Troy, Pit.	0	0	1	0	1
Pool, Brodney, NYJ	0	0	1	6	1
Pouha, Sione, NYJ	0	0	3	2	3
* Pouncey, Maurkice, Pit.	0	2	0	0	2
Prater, Matt, Den.	0	1	0	0	1
Quin, Glover, Hou.	0	0	2	3	2
Randle El, Antwaan, Pit.	2	2	0	0	2
Redman, Isaac, Pit.	1	1	0	0	1
Reece, Marcel, Oak.	1	1	0	0	1
Reed, Ed, Bal.	2	1	0	0	1
Revis, Darrelle, NYJ	0	0	2	10	2
Rhodes, Dominic, Ind.	1	0	0	0	0
Rivers, Philip, S.D.	7	2	0	-18	2
Robinson, Lee, Den.	0	1	0	0	1
Roethlisberger, Ben, Pit.	7	1	0	-12	1
Royal, Eddie, Den.	4	2	0	0	2
Sanborn, Garrison, Buf.	1	0	1	-1	1
Sanchez, Mark, NYJ	9	3	0	-6	3
* Sanders, Emmanuel, Pit.	2	0	0	0	0
Sanders, James, N.E.	0	0	1	0	1
Sapp, Benny, Mia.	1	1	0	0	1
Satele, Samson, Oak.	1	0	0	0	0
Saturday, Jeff, Ind.	0	1	0	0	1
Scaife, Bo, Ten.	2	1	0	0	1
Schaub, Matt, Hou.	9	1	0	-15	1
Scifres, Mike, S.D.	1	1	0	0	1
Scott, Bernard, Cin.	1	0	0	0	0
Scott, Bart, NYJ	0	0	1	0	1
Scott, Bryan, Buf.	1	0	2	17	2
Seymour, Richard, Oak.	0	0	1	13	1
Shaw, Tim, Ten.	0	0	1	0	1
Simpson, Jerome, Cin.	2	0	0	0	0
Sims-Walker, Mike, Jac.	1	0	0	0	0
Smith, Brad, NYJ	1	0	0	0	0
Smith, Clifton, Cle.	1	1	0	0	1
Smith, Taj, Ind.	0	0	1	0	1
Smith, Wade, Hou.	0	1	0	0	1
Soliai, Paul, Mia.	0	0	1	0	1
Sorensen, Nick, Cle.	0	1	0	0	1
* Spiller, C.J., Buf.	5	0	0	0	0
Sproles, Darren, S.D.	3	0	0	0	0
Stallworth, Donte', Bal.	1	0	0	0	0
Starks, Randy, Mia.	0	0	1	0	1
St. Clair, John, Cle.	0	1	0	0	1
Stuckey, Chansi, Cle.	3	0	0	0	0
Stupar, Jonathan, Buf.	1	0	0	0	0
Tate, Brandon, N.E.	1	0	0	0	0
Taylor, Jason, NYJ	0	0	2	0	2
* Tebow, Tim, Den.	1	1	0	-1	1
Thigpen, Tyler, Mia.	1	1	0	-9	1
Thomas, Bryan, NYJ	0	0	1	16	1
* Thomas, Demaryius, Den.	3	1	0	0	1
Thomas, Mike, Jac.	3	1	0	0	1
* Thompson, Syd'Quan, Den.	3	1	0	0	1
Timmons, Lawrence, Pit.	0	0	2	0	2
Tolbert, Mike, S.D.	5	0	0	0	0
Tomlinson, LaDainian, NYJ	4	2	0	0	2
Trent, Morgan, Cin.	0	0	1	0	1
Tryon, Justin, Ind.	0	0	1	0	1
* Tucker, Verran, K.C.	0	0	1	0	1
Tulloch, Stephen, Ten.	0	0	1	0	1
* Vaughn, Cassius, Den.	0	0	2	0	2
Velasco, Fernando, Ten.	0	1	0	0	1
* Veldheer, Jared, Oak.	1	1	0	0	1
Ventrone, Raymond, Cle.	0	0	1	0	1
* Verner, Alterraun, Ten.	0	0	2	0	2
Vickers, Lawrence, Cle.	0	1	0	0	1
Wallace, Mike, Pit.	1	1	0	0	1
Wallace, Seneca, Cle.	1	1	0	-17	1
* Walton, J.D., Den.	1	0	0	-13	1
Ward, Derrick, Hou.	0	1	0	0	1
Ward, Hines, Pit.	1	0	0	0	0
Wayne, Reggie, Ind.	1	0	0	0	0
Webb, Lardarius, Bal.	2	2	0	0	2
Welker, Wes, N.E.	1	2	0	0	2
Westerman, Jamaal, NYJ	0	0	1	0	1
* White, Blair, Ind.	1	0	0	0	0
Whitner, Donte, Buf.	0	0	1	0	1
Whitworth, Andrew, Cin.	0	1	0	0	1
Wiegmann, Casey, K.C.	1	2	0	-6	2
Wilfork, Vince, N.E.	0	0	1	0	1
Williams, Ricky, Mia.	4	2	0	0	2
Williams, D.J., Den.	0	0	1	0	1
Williams, Kyle, Buf.	0	0	2	11	2
Williams, Roy, Cin.	0	0	3	1	3
Wilson, George, Buf.	0	0	1	0	1
Wilson, Josh, Bal.	1	0	1	0	1
Wilson, Kris, S.D.	1	0	0	0	0
* Wilson, Kyle, NYJ	2	1	0	0	1
Winston, Eric, Hou.	0	2	0	0	2

	Fum	Own Rec	Opp Rec	Yards	Tot Rec
Womack, Floyd, Cle.	0	2	0	0	2
Wood, Eric, Buf.	0	1	0	0	1
Woodhead, Danny, N.E.	1	0	0	0	0
Woodley, LaMarr, Pit.	0	0	2	19	2
Woody, Damien, NYJ	0	1	0	0	1
* Worilds, Jason, Pit.	0	0	1	0	1
Wright, Eric, Cle.	0	0	1	11	1
Young, Vince, Ten.	6	1	0	-2	1

Yards includes aborted plays, own recoveries and opponents' recoveries.

* *Player that was a rookie in 2010*

NFC FUMBLES—INDIVIDUAL

	Fum	Own Rec	Opp Rec	Yards	Tot Rec
Adams, Michael, Ariz	0	0	1	30	1
* Adams, Phillip, S.F.	1	0	0	0	0
Alexander, Lorenzo, Was.	0	0	1	0	1
Allen, Jared, Min.	0	0	1	0	1
Amendola, Danny, St.L	2	0	0	0	0
Anderson, Derek, Ariz	6	1	0	0	1
Anderson, James, Car.	0	0	3	2	3
Andrews, Stacy, Sea.	0	1	0	0	1
Armstrong, Anthony, Was.	1	1	0	0	1
Austin, Miles, Dal.	1	1	0	0	1
Avant, Jason, Phi.	0	1	0	0	1
Avril, Cliff, Det.	0	0	1	10	1
Baas, David, S.F.	2	0	0	-24	0
Babineaux, Jonathan, Atl.	0	0	1	0	1
Backus, Jeff, Det.	0	1	0	0	1
Bajema, Billy, St.L	1	1	0	0	1
* Banks, Brandon, Was.	2	2	0	0	2
Bell, Jacob, St.L	0	1	0	0	1
* Benn, Arrelious, T.B.	1	0	0	0	0
Bennett, Earl, Chi.	1	1	0	0	1
Bennett, Martellus, Dal.	1	1	0	5	1
Berrian, Bernard, Min.	2	2	0	0	2
* Best, Jahvid, Det.	1	2	0	0	2
Betts, Ladell, N.O.	1	0	0	0	0
Bidwell, Josh, Was.	1	1	0	-12	1
Bigby, Atari, G.B.	0	0	1	0	1
Black, Quincy, T.B.	0	0	1	1	1
Blackburn, Chase, NY-G	0	2	0	0	2
Blackmon, Will, NY-G	2	0	0	0	0
* Blount, LeGarrette, T.B.	4	0	0	0	0
Booker, Lorenzo, Min.	1	0	0	0	0
Boss, Kevin, NY-G	1	0	0	0	0
Bowman, Zack, Chi.	0	0	1	0	1
* Bradford, Sam, St.L	7	3	0	-2	3
Bradshaw, Ahmad, NY-G	7	0	0	0	0
Branch, Deion, Sea.	1	0	0	0	0
Brayton, Tyler, Car.	0	0	2	1	2
Breaston, Steve, Ariz	0	2	0	0	2
Brees, Drew, N.O.	9	5	0	0	5
Briggs, Lance, Chi.	0	0	1	0	1
Brock, Raheem, Sea.	0	0	1	0	1
Brown, Alex, N.O.	0	0	1	0	1
Brown, Jason, St.L	1	0	0	0	0
Brown, Levi, Ariz	0	3	0	-1	3
* Bryant, Dez, Dal.	1	1	0	0	1
Bryant, Red, Sea.	0	0	2	0	2
Buchanon, Phillip, Was.	1	0	1	0	1
Buckley, Eldra, Phi.	1	0	0	0	0
Bulluck, Keith, NY-G	0	0	1	10	1
Burleson, Nate, Det.	2	0	0	0	0
Bush, Jarrett, G.B.	0	0	1	0	1
Bush, Reggie, N.O.	2	2	0	0	2
Butler, James, St.L	0	0	1	49	1
* Calhoun, Duke, NY-G	0	1	0	0	1

	Fum	Own Rec	Opp Rec	Yards	Tot Rec
* Calvin, Jorrick, Phi.	2	1	0	0	1
Campbell, Calais, Ariz	0	0	1	0	1
Carriker, Adam, Was.	0	0	1	0	1
Carter, Andre, Was.	0	0	1	0	1
Charleston, Jeff, N.O.	0	0	1	0	1
Choice, Tashard, Dal.	1	0	0	0	0
Ciurciu, Vinny, Det.	0	1	0	0	1
Clabo, Tyson, Atl.	0	1	0	0	1
* Clausen, Jimmy, Car.	9	3	0	-28	3
Clemens, Nate, S.F.	1	0	0	0	0
Clemons, Chris, Sea.	0	0	1	0	1
Cofield, Barry, NY-G	0	0	1	0	1
Collins, Nick, G.B.	0	0	2	26	2
Cooley, Chris, Was.	3	0	0	0	0
Cox, Kennard, Sea.	0	0	1	0	1
Crowder, Tim, T.B.	0	0	1	0	1
Cutler, Jay, Chi.	10	1	0	0	1
Dahl, Craig, St.L	0	0	1	0	1
Dahl, Harvey, Atl.	0	0	1	0	1
Daniel, Chase, N.O.	1	0	0	-11	0
* Davis, Anthony, S.F.	0	3	0	0	3
Davis, Chauncey, Atl.	0	0	1	0	1
* Davis, Dexter, Sea.	0	0	1	0	1
Davis, Rashied, Chi.	1	0	0	0	0
DeCoud, Thomas, Atl.	1	0	0	0	0
* DeGeare, Chris, Min.	0	0	2	-4	2
Delmas, Louis, Det.	0	0	2	-4	2
Diehl, David, NY-G	0	1	0	0	1
Diggs, Na'il, St.L	0	0	1	3	1
* Dixon, Anthony, S.F.	0	1	0	0	1
Dockett, Darnell, Ariz	0	1	2	0	3
* Dodge, Matt, NY-G	1	0	0	-7	0
Driver, Donald, G.B.	1	0	0	0	0
Dunbar, Jo-Lonn, N.O.	0	0	1	0	1
* Edwards, Armanti, Car.	1	1	0	0	1
Faine, Jeff, T.B.	1	0	0	0	0
Faneca, Alan, Ariz	0	1	0	0	1
Favre, Brett, Min.	7	2	0	-29	2
Felton, Jerome, Det.	1	0	0	0	0
Finneran, Brian, Atl.	0	0	1	0	1
Fitzgerald, Larry, Ariz	0	1	0	0	1
Fletcher, Bradley, St.L	0	0	1	43	1
Fletcher, London, Was.	0	0	3	-3	3
Flynn, Matt, G.B.	1	0	0	0	0
Forté, Matt, Chi.	3	1	0	0	1
Franklin, Aubrayo, S.F.	0	0	1	0	1
Freeman, Josh, T.B.	8	5	0	0	5
* Gerhart, Toby, Min.	3	0	0	0	0
* Gilyard, Mardy, St.L	1	0	0	0	0
Ginn, Ted, S.F.	1	1	0	0	1
Goff, Jonathan, NY-G	0	0	1	22	1
Goldberg, Adam, St.L	0	1	0	0	1
Goodson, Mike, Car.	6	2	0	-13	2
Goodwin, Jonathan, N.O.	0	1	0	0	1
Gore, Frank, S.F.	4	1	0	0	1
Graham, Earnest, T.B.	1	0	0	0	1
* Graham, Jimmy, N.O.	1	1	0	20	1
Grant, Deon, NY-G	0	0	3	0	3
Grant, Larry, St.L	0	0	1	0	1
Greenway, Chad, Min.	0	0	1	0	1
Greer, Jabari, N.O.	0	0	1	0	1
Gross, Jordan, Car.	0	1	0	0	1
Grossman, Rex, Was.	4	0	0	0	0
Gurode, Andre, Dal.	3	0	0	-20	0
Hall, DeAngelo, Was.	0	0	2	32	2
Hall, Korey, G.B.	0	1	0	0	1
* Hall, Max, Ariz	5	1	0	0	1
Haralson, Parys, S.F.	0	0	2	0	2
* Harbor, Clay, Phi.	0	1	0	0	1
Harper, Roman, N.O.	0	0	1	0	1

	Fum	Own Rec	Opp Rec	Yards	Tot Rec		Fum	Own Rec	Opp Rec	Yards	Tot Rec
Harris, Chris, Chi.	0	0	2	0	2	Manning, Eli, NY-G	7	2	0	-4	2
Harris, Nic, Car.	0	0	1	0	1	Manningham, Mario, NY-G	1	0	0	0	0
Harris, Tommie, Chi.	0	0	2	9	2	Marshall, Richard, Car.	0	0	1	0	1
Harrison, Jerome, Cle.-Phi.	2	0	0	0	0	Martin, Sherrod, Car.	0	0	1	0	1
Harvin, Percy, Min.	1	0	0	0	0	Maynard, Brad, Chi.	1	1	0	0	1
Hasselbeck, Matt, Sea.	7	1	0	0	1	McBriar, Mat, Dal.	1	0	0	-8	0
Hatcher, Jason, Dal.	0	0	1	0	1	McBride, Turk, Det.	0	0	1	0	1
Hawk, A.J., G.B.	0	0	1	0	1	* McCann, Bryan, Dal.	6	2	0	0	2
Hawthorne, David, Sea.	0	0	1	0	1	McClure, Todd, Atl.	1	0	0	-4	0
Hayes, Gerald, Ariz	0	0	1	21	1	McCoy, LeSean, Phi.	2	1	0	0	1
Hayward, Adam, T.B.	0	0	2	0	2	McDonald, Brandon, Det.	0	0	1	-5	1
Henderson, E.J., Min.	0	0	1	0	1	McGee, Stephen, Dal.	1	1	0	-4	1
Henderson, Erin, Min.	0	0	1	3	1	McGlynn, Mike, Phi.	0	2	0	0	2
Herremans, Todd, Phi.	0	1	0	0	1	McNabb, Donovan, Was.	10	8	0	-27	8
Heyer, Stephon, Was.	0	1	0	0	1	Melton, Henry, Chi.	0	0	1	0	1
Hightower, Tim, Ariz	5	0	0	0	0	Mikell, Quintin, Phi.	0	0	3	52	3
Hill, Sammie Lee, Det.	0	0	1	0	1	* Miller, Lonyae, Dal.	0	1	0	0	1
Hill, Shaun, Det.	3	1	0	-2	1	Mitchell, Marvin, N.O.	0	0	2	2	2
Hobbs, Ellis, Phi.	1	0	0	0	0	Moore, Kareem, Was.	0	0	2	13	2
Hutchinson, Steve, Min.	0	1	0	0	1	Moore, Kyle, T.B.	0	0	2	5	2
* Ivory, Chris, N.O.	4	0	0	0	0	Moore, Lance, N.O.	2	0	0	0	0
Jackson, Brandon, G.B.	1	3	0	0	3	Moore, Matt, Car.	4	0	0	0	0
Jackson, DeSean, Phi.	4	1	0	0	1	Moore, William, Atl.	0	0	1	0	1
Jackson, Lawrence, Det.	0	0	1	0	1	Morgan, Josh, S.F.	2	0	0	0	0
Jackson, Steven, St.L	1	1	0	0	1	Morris, Maurice, Det.	1	1	0	0	1
Jackson, Tarvaris, Min.	1	2	0	-15	2	Moss, Santana, Was.	3	0	0	0	0
Jacobs, Brandon, NY-G	2	0	0	0	0	Munnerlyn, Captain, Car.	2	1	0	0	1
James, Bradie, Dal.	0	0	2	0	2	* Murphy, Jerome, St.L	0	0	1	0	1
Jansen, J.J., Car.	1	0	0	-10	0	Nelson, Jordy, G.B.	3	1	0	3	1
Jenkins, Malcolm, N.O.	0	0	2	0	2	Newman, Terence, Dal.	0	0	1	1	1
Jennings, Greg, G.B.	2	0	0	0	0	Nicks, Hakeem, NY-G	1	0	0	0	0
Jennings, Tim, Chi.	0	0	1	0	1	Okam, Frank, T.B.	0	0	1	0	1
Johnson, Calvin, Det.	1	0	0	0	0	Olsen, Greg, Chi.	2	1	0	0	1
Johnson, Gartrell, Atl.	1	0	0	0	0	Parker, Juqua, Phi.	0	0	1	0	1
Johnson, Landon, Det.	0	0	1	0	1	Patrick, Ben, Ariz	1	0	0	0	0
Jones, Felix, Dal.	2	3	0	0	3	Patterson, Dimitri, Phi.	1	0	0	0	0
Jones, James, G.B.	3	0	0	0	0	Patterson, Mike, Phi.	0	0	1	0	1
Jones, Julius, N.O.	1	0	0	0	0	Penn, Donald, T.B.	0	1	0	0	1
Jones, Sean, T.B.	0	0	1	0	1	Peterson, Adrian, Min.	1	0	0	0	0
Justice, Winston, Phi.	0	2	0	0	2	Peterson, Julian, Det.	0	1	1	0	2
Kennedy, Jimmy, Min.	1	0	0	0	0	Peterson, Mike, Atl.	0	0	2	0	2
King, Jeff, Car.	0	2	0	0	2	Phillips, Kenny, NY-G	0	0	3	25	3
Kitna, Jon, Dal.	7	5	0	-6	5	Pickett, Ryan, G.B.	0	0	1	0	1
Kleinsasser, Jimmy, Min.	0	1	0	0	1	* Pierre-Paul, Jason, NY-G	0	0	2	0	2
Knox, Johnny, Chi.	1	0	0	0	0	Porter, Tracy, N.O.	0	1	1	2	2
Koets, Adam, NY-G	1	0	0	-5	0	* Quarless, Andrew, G.B.	1	0	0	0	0
Kolb, Kevin, Phi.	6	1	0	0	1	Raiola, Dominic, Det.	1	1	0	0	1
* Komar, Max, Ariz	3	2	0	0	2	Ratliff, Jay, Dal.	0	0	2	0	2
Kreutz, Olin, Chi.	0	1	0	0	1	Reynaud, Darius, NY-G	1	0	0	0	0
Kuhn, John, G.B.	1	2	0	0	2	Rhodes, Kerry, Ariz	1	0	4	69	4
Kyle, Jason, N.O.	0	0	1	0	1	Robbins, Fred, St.L	0	0	2	1	2
LaBoy, Travis, S.F.	0	0	1	0	1	* Roberts, Andre, Ariz	2	0	0	0	0
* LaFell, Brandon, Car.	0	1	0	0	1	Robinson, Dunta, Atl.	0	0	1	0	1
Landri, Derek, Car.	0	0	1	0	1	Robison, Brian, Min.	0	0	2	0	2
Landry, LaRon, Was.	0	0	1	0	1	Roby, Courtney, N.O.	1	0	2	0	2
Laurinaitis, James, St.L	0	0	1	0	1	Rodgers, Aaron, G.B.	4	1	0	-2	1
Laws, Trevor, Phi.	1	0	0	0	0	Rodgers-Cromartie, Domin, Ariz	1	0	0	0	0
Lawson, Manny, S.F.	0	0	1	5	1	Rolle, Antrel, NY-G	0	0	2	4	2
Lawson, Gerard, Phi.	0	0	1	0	1	Rosario, Dante, Car.	0	0	1	0	1
Leber, Ben, Min.	0	0	1	0	1	Ross, Aaron, NY-G	1	0	0	0	0
Lee, Donald, G.B.	1	0	0	0	0	Ryan, Clifton, St.L	1	0	0	18	1
Levy, DeAndre, Det.	0	0	2	0	2	Ryan, Matt, Atl.	4	0	0	0	0
Lewis, Roy, Sea.	0	0	1	0	1	Samuel, Asante, Phi.	1	0	1	1	1
* Lindley, Trevard, Phi.	0	1	0	0	1	Sanford, Jamarca, Min.	0	0	1	0	1
Logan, Stefan, Det.	3	0	2	4	2	Scheffler, Tony, Det.	1	0	0	0	0
Long, Chris, St.L	0	0	1	0	1	Schmitt, Owen, Phi.	0	1	0	0	1
Louis, Lance, Chi.	0	1	0	0	1	* Schofield, O'Brien, Ariz	0	0	1	0	1
Lynch, Marshawn, Buf.-Sea.	4	0	0	0	0	Schwartz, Geoff, Car.	0	1	0	0	1
Mack, Elbert, T.B.	1	0	0	0	0	Sendlein, Lyle, Ariz	2	1	1	-3	2
Maclin, Jeremy, Phi.	1	0	0	0	0	Seubert, Rich, NY-G	1	1	1	-13	2

	Fum	Own Rec	Opp Rec	Yards	Tot Rec
Shanle, Scott, N.O.	0	0	1	0	1
Sharper, Darren, N.O.	0	0	1	11	1
Sims, Ernie, Phi.	0	0	1	0	1
* Sims, Eugene, St.L	0	1	0	0	1
* Skelton, John, Ariz	3	1	0	-14	1
Smith, Alex, S.F.	4	0	0	0	0
Smith, Alphonso, Det.	1	0	1	9	1
Smith, Kevin, Det.	0	1	0	0	1
Smith, Steve, Car.	3	1	0	0	1
Smith, Troy, S.F.	6	3	0	-6	3
Smith, Will, N.O.	1	0	0	0	0
Snelling, Jason, Atl.	2	0	0	0	0
Snyder, Adam, S.F.	0	1	0	0	1
Spencer, Anthony, Dal.	0	0	1	0	1
Spencer, Shawntae, S.F.	0	0	1	0	1
Spikes, Takeo, S.F.	0	0	1	8	1
Spurlock, Micheal, T.B.	2	1	0	0	1
Stafford, Matthew, Det.	2	0	0	-5	0
Stanton, Drew, Det.	3	1	0	0	1
Stephens-Howling, LaRod, Ariz	0	0	1	0	1
* Stewart, Darian, St.L	0	0	1	0	1
Stewart, Jonathan, Car.	4	0	0	0	0
Stinchcomb, Jonathan, N.O.	0	1	0	0	1
Stroughter, Sammie, T.B.	1	0	0	0	0
* Suh, Ndamukong, Det.	0	0	1	17	1
Sullivan, John, Min.	2	0	0	-14	0
Tapp, Darryl, Phi.	0	0	3	0	3
* Tate, Golden, Sea.	1	1	0	0	1
Thomas, David, N.O.	0	1	0	0	1
Thomas, Terrell, NY-G	0	1	1	0	2
* Thurmond, Walter, Sea.	1	0	0	0	0
Tillman, Charles, Chi.	0	0	2	-8	2
Toeaina, Matt, Chi.	0	0	1	0	1
Toler, Greg, Ariz	0	0	1	0	1
Torain, Ryan, Was.	2	0	0	0	0
Trueblood, Jeremy, T.B.	0	1	0	0	1
Trufant, Marcus, Sea.	0	0	2	0	2
Tuck, Justin, NY-G	0	0	5	4	5
Turner, Michael, Atl.	2	0	0	0	0
Umenyiora, Osi, NY-G	0	0	1	0	1
Urlacher, Brian, Chi.	0	0	3	0	3
Vick, Michael, Phi.	11	4	0	-4	4
Vilma, Jonathan, N.O.	0	0	1	0	1
Vincent, Keydrick, T.B.	0	1	0	0	1
Wade, Jonathan, Det.	0	1	0	10	1
Walker, Frank, Min.	0	0	1	0	1
Walker, Delanie, S.F.	1	0	0	0	0
Ware, Danny, NY-G	0	0	1	0	1
Ware, DeMarcus, Dal.	0	0	2	22	2
Ware, Matt, Ariz	1	0	0	0	0
* Washington, Daryl, Ariz	1	0	0	0	0
Washington, Leon, Sea.	3	1	0	0	1
* Webb, Joe, Min.	1	0	0	0	0
Webster, Corey, NY-G	0	0	1	1	1
Wells, Beanie, Ariz	1	1	0	0	1
Westbrook, Brian, S.F.	0	1	0	0	1
Westbrook, Byron, Was.	0	0	1	0	1
Wharton, Travelle, Car.	0	1	0	0	1
White, Roddy, Atl.	1	1	0	0	1
Whitehurst, Charlie, Sea.	2	2	0	-16	2
Williams, Brian, Atl.	0	0	1	12	1
Williams, Cadillac, T.B.	1	0	0	0	0
Williams, Chris, Chi.	0	1	0	0	1
Williams, DeAngelo, Car.	1	0	0	0	0
Williams, Garry, Car.	0	1	0	0	1
Williams, Jason, Car.	0	0	1	7	1
* Williams, Keiland, Was.	1	0	0	0	0
* Williams, Kyle, S.F.	0	1	0	-7	1
Williams, Leon, Dal.	0	0	1	0	1
* Williams, Mike, T.B.	3	1	0	0	1

	Fum	Own Rec	Opp Rec	Yards	Tot Rec
Williams, Roy, Dal.	3	0	0	0	0
Williams, Tramon, G.B.	2	1	2	5	3
Wilson, Chris, Was.	1	0	0	0	0
Wilson, C.J., Car.	0	0	1	0	1
Winfield, Antoine, Min.	0	0	1	45	1
Winslow, Kellen, T.B.	1	0	0	0	0
Wire, Coy, Atl.	0	0	1	0	1
Witten, Jason, Dal.	1	0	0	0	0
Wright, Jason, Ariz	1	0	0	0	0
Zuttah, Jeremy, T.B.	1	1	0	-2	1

Yards includes aborted plays, own recoveries and opponents' recoveries.

* Player that was a rookie in 2010

AMERICAN FOOTBALL CONFERENCE—FUMBLES

	Fum	Own Rec	Fum OB	TD	Opp Rec	TD	Fum Yards	Tot Rec
New England	9	4	0	0	13	1	91	17
Indianapolis	14	4	2	0	11	1	5	15
Houston	15	9	0	0	5	0	-3	14
Kansas City	15	9	0	0	9	0	17	18
Cincinnati	21	7	0	0	10	1	66	17
Baltimore	22	9	3	0	8	0	-8	17
Pittsburgh	22	11	2	0	14	0	13	25
Tennessee	22	7	1	0	8	0	-18	15
Jacksonville	23	9	2	0	5	0	23	14
N.Y. Jets	23	13	3	0	18	0	29	31
Miami	24	13	0	0	8	1	-42	21
San Diego	25	9	0	0	6	0	9	15
Cleveland	29	18	0	0	9	1	13	27
Denver	29	12	2	0	8	1	48	20
Oakland	32	20	2	0	12	1	82	32
Buffalo	33	9	6	0	11	1	58	20
AFC Total	358	163	24	0	155	8	383	318
AFC Average	22.4	10.2	1.5	0.0	9.7	0.5	23.9	19.9

NATIONAL FOOTBALL CONFERENCE—FUMBLES

	Fum	Own Rec	Fum OB	TD	Opp Rec	TD	Fum Yards	Tot Rec
Atlanta	12	3	1	0	9	1	8	12
St. Louis	14	8	0	0	12	0	112	20
Seattle	18	6	2	0	10	0	-16	16
Chicago	19	8	1	0	14	0	1	22
Detroit	20	11	0	0	15	1	34	26
Green Bay	20	9	2	0	8	1	32	17
Minnesota	20	9	0	0	10	1	-10	19
San Francisco	22	12	2	0	7	0	-24	19
New Orleans	23	12	2	0	16	0	24	28
Tampa Bay	25	11	1	0	9	0	4	20
N.Y. Giants	26	8	1	0	23	0	37	31
Dallas	28	15	2	0	10	1	-10	25
Washington	29	13	4	0	13	1	3	26
Carolina	31	15	0	0	12	0	-41	27
Arizona	33	15	3	3	13	4	102	28
Philadelphia	33	18	3	0	11	1	49	29
NFC Total	373	173	24	3	192	11	305	365
NFC Average	23.3	10.8	1.5	0.2	12.0	0.7	19.1	22.8
NFL Total	731	336	48	3	347	19	688	683
NFL Average	22.8	10.5	1.5	0.1	10.8	0.6	21.5	21.3

Inside the Numbers

GREATEST COMEBACKS IN NFL HISTORY
(Most Points Overcome To Win Game)

REGULAR SEASON GAMES

FROM 28 POINTS BEHIND TO WIN:
December 7, 1980, at San Francisco

New Orleans	14	21	0	0	0	—	35
San Francisco	0	7	14	14	3	—	38

- NO — Harris 33 pass from Manning (Ricardo kick)
- NO — Childs 21 pass from Manning (Ricardo kick)
- NO — Holmes 1 run (Ricardo kick)
- SF — Solomon 57 punt return (Wersching kick)
- NO — Holmes 1 run (Ricardo kick)
- NO — Harris 41 pass from Manning (Ricardo kick)
- SF — Montana 1 run (Wersching kick)
- SF — Clark 71 pass from Montana (Wersching kick)
- SF — Solomon 14 pass from Montana (Wersching kick)
- SF — Elliott 7 run (Wersching kick)
- SF — FG Wersching 36

FROM 26 POINTS BEHIND TO WIN:
September 21, 1997, at Buffalo

Indianapolis	14	12	0	9	—	35
Buffalo	0	10	6	21	—	37

- Ind — Bailey 10 pass from Harbaugh (Blanchard kick)
- Ind — Faulk 10 run (Blanchard kick)
- Ind — FG Blanchard 39
- Ind — FG Blanchard 36
- Ind — FG Blanchard 49
- Ind — FG Blanchard 22
- Buff — Johnson 16 pass from Collins (Christie kick)
- Buff — FG Christie 27
- Buff — A. Smith 15 run (2-pt attempt failed)
- Ind — FG Blanchard 25
- Buff — Early 4 pass from Collins (Christie kick)
- Buff — A. Smith 1 run (Christie kick)
- Buff — A. Smith 54 run (Christie kick)
- Ind — Harrison 2 pass from Justin (2-pt attempt failed)

FROM 25 POINTS BEHIND TO WIN:
November 8, 1987, at St. Louis

Tampa Bay	7	7	14	0	—	28
St. Louis	3	0	28	—	31	

- TB — Carrier 5 pass from DeBerg (Igwebuike kick)
- TB — Carter 3 pass from DeBerg (Igwebuike kick)
- StL — FG Gallery 31
- TB — Smith 34 pass from DeBerg (Igwebuike kick)
- TB — Smith 3 run (Igwebuike kick)
- StL — Awalt 4 pass from Lomax (Gallery kick)
- StL — Noga 23 fumble recovery (Gallery kick)
- StL — J. Smith 11 pass from Lomax (Gallery kick)
- StL — J. Smith 17 pass from Lomax (Gallery kick)

FROM 24 POINTS BEHIND TO WIN:
October 27, 1946, at Washington

Philadelphia	0	0	14	14	—	28
Washington	10	14	0	0	—	24

- Wash — Rosato 2 run (Poillon kick)
- Wash — FG Poillon 28
- Wash — Rosato 4 run (Poillon kick)
- Wash — Lapka recovered fumble in end zone (Poillon kick)
- Phil — Steele 1 run (Lio kick)
- Phil — Pritchard 45 pass from Thompson (Lio kick)
- Phil — Steinke 7 pass from Thompson (Lio kick)
- Phil — Ferrante 30 pass from Thompson (Lio kick)

FROM 24 POINTS BEHIND TO WIN:
October 20, 1957, at Detroit

Baltimore	7	14	6	0	—	27
Detroit	0	3	7	21	—	31

- Balt — Mutscheller 15 pass from Unitas (Rechichar kick)
- Det — FG Martin 47
- Balt — Moore 72 pass from Unitas (Rechichar kick)
- Balt — Mutscheller 52 pass from Unitas (Rechichar kick)
- Balt — Moore 4 run from Unitas (kick failed)
- Det — Junker 14 pass from Rote (Layne kick)
- Det — Cassady 26 pass from Layne (Layne kick)
- Det — Johnson 1 run (Layne kick)
- Det — Cassady 29 pass from Layne (Layne kick)

FROM 24 POINTS BEHIND TO WIN:
October 25, 1959, at Minneapolis

Philadelphia	0	0	21	7	—	28
Chicago Cardinals	7	10	7	0	—	24

- Cardinals — Crow 10 pass from Roach (Conrad kick)
- Cardinals — J. Hill 77 blocked field goal return (Conrad kick)
- Cardinals — FG Conrad 15
- Cardinals — Lane 37 interception return (Conrad kick)
- Phil — Barnes 1 run (Walston kick)
- Phil — McDonald 29 pass from Van Brocklin (Walston kick)
- Phil — Barnes 2 run (Walston kick)
- Phil — McDonald 22 pass from Van Brocklin (Walston kick)

FROM 24 POINTS BEHIND TO WIN:
October 23, 1960, at Denver

Boston	10	7	7	0	—	24
Denver	0	0	14	17	—	31

- Bos — FG Cappelletti 12
- Bos — Colclough 10 pass from Songin (Cappelletti kick)
- Bos — Wells 6 pass from Songin (Cappelletti kick)
- Bos — Miller 47 pass from Songin (Cappelletti kick)
- Den — Carmichael 21 pass from Tripucka (Mingo kick)
- Den — Jessup 19 pass from Tripucka (Mingo kick)
- Den — Carmichael 35 lateral from Taylor, pass from Tripucka (Mingo kick)
- Den — Taylor 8 pass from Tripucka (Mingo kick)
- Den — FG Mingo 9

FROM 24 POINTS BEHIND TO WIN:
December 15, 1974, at Miami

New England	21	3	0	3	—	27
Miami	0	17	7	10	—	34

- NE — Hannah recovered fumble in end zone (J. Smith kick)
- NE — Sanders 23 interception return (J. Smith kick)
- NE — Herron 4 pass from Plunkett (J. Smith kick)
- NE — FG J. Smith 46
- Mia — Nottingham 1 run (Yepremian kick)
- Mia — Baker 37 pass from Morrall (Yepremian kick)
- Mia — FG Yepremian 28
- Mia — Baker 46 pass from Morrall (Yepremian kick)
- NE — FG J. Smith 34
- Mia — Nottingham 2 run (Yepremian kick)
- Mia — FG Yepremian 40

FROM 24 POINTS BEHIND TO WIN:
December 4, 1977, at Minnesota

San Francisco	0	10	14	3	—	27
Minnesota	0	0	7	21	—	28

- SF — Delvin Williams 2 run (Wersching kick)
- SF — FG Wersching 31
- SF — Dave Williams 80 kickoff return (Wersching kick)
- SF — Delvin Williams 5 run (Wersching kick)
- Minn — McClanahan 15 pass from Lee (Cox kick)
- Minn — Rashad 8 pass from Kramer (Cox kick)
- Minn — Tucker 9 pass from Kramer (Cox kick)
- SF — FG Wersching 31
- Minn — S. White 69 pass from Kramer (Cox kick)

FROM 24 POINTS BEHIND TO WIN:
September 23, 1979, at Denver

Seattle	10	10	14	0	—	34
Denver	0	10	21	6	—	37

- Sea — FG Herrera 28
- Sea — Doornink 5 run (Herrera kick)
- Den — FG Turner 27
- Sea — Doornink 5 run (Herrera kick)
- Den — Armstrong 2 run (Turner kick)
- Sea — FG Herrera 22
- Sea — McCullum 13 pass from Zorn (Herrera kick)
- Sea — Smith 1 run (Herrera kick)
- Den — Studdard 2 pass from Morton (Turner kick)
- Den — Moses 11 pass from Morton (Turner kick)
- Den — Upchurch 35 pass from Morton (Turner kick)

Den — Lytle 1 run (kick failed)

FROM 24 POINTS BEHIND TO WIN:
September 23, 1979, at Cincinnati

Houston	0	10	17	0	3	— 30
Cincinnati	14	10	0	3	0	— 27

Cin — Johnson 1 run (Bahr kick)
Cin — Alexander 2 run (Bahr kick)
Cin — Johnson 1 run (Bahr kick)
Cin — FG Bahr 52
Hou — Burrough 35 pass from Pastorini (Fritsch kick)
Hou — FG Fritsch 33
Hou — Campbell 8 run (Fritsch kick)
Hou — Caster 22 pass from Pastorini (Fritsch kick)
Hou — FG Fritsch 47
Cin — FG Bahr 55
Hou — FG Fritsch 29

FROM 24 POINTS BEHIND TO WIN:
November 22, 1982, at Los Angeles

San Diego	10	14	0	0	— 24
L.A. Raiders	0	7	14	7	— 28

SD — FG Benirschke 19
SD — Scales 29 pass from Fouts (Benirschke kick)
SD — Muncie 2 run (Benirschke kick)
SD — Muncie 1 run (Benirschke kick)
Raiders — Christensen 1 pass from Plunkett (Bahr kick)
Raiders — Allen 3 run (Bahr kick)
Raiders — Allen 6 run (Bahr kick)
Raiders — Hawkins 1 run (Bahr kick)

FROM 24 POINTS BEHIND TO WIN:
September 26, 1988, at Denver

L.A. Raiders	0	0	14	13	3 — 30
Denver	7	17	0	3	0 — 27

Den — Dorsett 1 run (Karlis kick)
Den — Dorsett 1 run (Karlis kick)
Den — Sewell 7 pass from Elway (Karlis kick)
Den — FG Karlis 39
Raiders — Smith 40 pass from Schroeder (Bahr kick)
Raiders — Smith 42 pass from Schroeder (Bahr kick)
Raiders — FG Bahr 28
Raiders — Allen 4 run (Bahr kick)
Den — FG Karlis 25
Raiders — FG Bahr 44
Raiders — FG Bahr 35

FROM 24 POINTS BEHIND TO WIN:
December 6, 1992, at Tampa

L.A. Rams	0	3	21	7	— 31
Tampa Bay	6	21	0	0	— 27

TB — FG Murray 34
TB — FG Murray 47
TB — Armstrong 81 pass from Testaverde (Murray kick)
TB — Jones 26 fumble recovery (Murray kick)
Rams — FG Zendejas 18
TB — Carrier 10 pass from Testaverde (Murray kick)
Rams — Anderson 40 pass from Everett (Zendejas kick)
Rams — Chadwick 27 pass from Everett (Zendejas kick)
Rams — Lang 1 run (Zendejas kick)

Rams — Carter 8 pass from Everett (Zendejas kick)

POSTSEASON GAMES

FROM 32 POINTS BEHIND TO WIN:
AFC First-Round Playoff Game
January 3, 1993, at Buffalo

Houston	7	21	7	3	0 — 38
Buffalo	3	0	28	7	3 — 41

Hou — Jeffires 3 pass from Moon (Del Greco kick)
Buff — FG Christie 36
Hou — Slaughter 7 pass from Moon (Del Greco kick)
Hou — Duncan 26 pass from Moon (Del Greco kick)
Hou — Jeffires 27 pass from Moon (Del Greco kick)
Hou — McDowell 58 interception return (Del Greco kick)
Buff — Davis 1 run (Christie kick)
Buff — Beebe 38 pass from Reich (Christie kick)
Buff — Reed 26 pass from Reich (Christie kick)
Buff — Reed 18 pass from Reich (Christie kick)
Buff — Reed 17 pass from Reich (Christie kick)
Hou — FG Del Greco 26
Buff — FG Christie 32

FROM 24 POINTS BEHIND TO WIN:
NFC First-Round Playoff Game
January 5, 2003, at San Francisco

N.Y. Giants	7	21	10	0	— 38
San Francisco	7	7	8	17	— 39

SF — Owens 76 pass from Garcia (Chandler kick)
NYG — Toomer 12 pass from Collins (Bryant kick)
NYG — Shockey 2 pass from Collins (Bryant kick)
SF — Barlow 1 run (Chandler kick)
NYG — Toomer 8 pass from Collins (Bryant kick)
NYG — Toomer 24 pass from Collins (Bryant kick)
NYG — Barber 6 run (Bryant kick)
NYG — FG Bryant 21
SF — Owens 26 pass from Garcia (Owens from Garcia)
SF — Garcia 14 run (Owens from Garcia)
SF — Garcia 14 run (Owens from Garcia)
SF — FG Chandler 25
SF — Streets 13 pass from Garcia (2-pt attempt failed)

FROM 20 POINTS BEHIND TO WIN:
Western Conference Playoff Game
December 22, 1957, at San Francisco

Detroit	0	7	14	10	— 31
San Francisco	14	10	3	0	— 27

SF — Owens 34 pass from Tittle (Soltau kick)
SF — McElhenny 47 pass from Tittle (Soltau kick)
Det — Junker 4 pass from Rote (Martin kick)
SF — Wilson 12 pass from Tittle (Soltau kick)
SF — FG Soltau 25

SF — FG Soltau 10
Det — Tracy 2 run (Martin kick)
Det — Tracy 58 run (Martin kick)
Det — Gedman 3 run (Martin kick)
Det — FG Martin 14

FROM 18 POINTS BEHIND TO WIN:
NFC Divisional Playoff Game
December 23, 1972, at San Francisco

Dallas	3	10	0	17	— 30
San Francisco	7	14	7	0	— 28

SF — Washington 97 kickoff return (Gossett kick)
Dall — FG Fritsch 37
SF — Schreiber 1 run (Gossett kick)
SF — Schreiber 1 run (Gossett kick)
Dall — FG Fritsch 45
Dall — Alworth 28 pass from Morton (Fritsch kick)
SF — Schreiber 1 run (Gossett kick)
Dall — FG Fritsch 27
Dall — Parks 20 pass from Staubach (Fritsch kick)
Dall — Sellers 10 pass from Staubach (Fritsch kick)

FROM 18 POINTS BEHIND TO WIN:
AFC Divisional Playoff Game
January 4, 1986, at Miami

Cleveland	7	7	7	0	— 21
Miami	3	0	14	7	— 24

Mia — FG Reveiz 51
Cle — Newsome 16 pass from Kosar (Bahr kick)
Cle — Byner 21 run (Bahr kick)
Cle — Byner 66 run (Bahr kick)
Mia — Moore 6 pass from Marino (Reveiz kick)
Mia — Davenport 31 run (Reveiz kick)
Mia — Davenport 1 run (Reveiz kick)

FROM 18 POINTS BEHIND TO WIN:
AFC Divisional Playoff Game
January 21, 2007, at Indianapolis

New England	7	14	7	6	— 34
Indianapolis	3	3	15	17	— 38

NE — Mankins 0 fumble recovery (Gostkowski kick)
Ind — FG Vinatieri 42
NE — Dillon 7 run (Gostkowski kick)
NE — Samuel 39 interception return (Gostkowski kick)
Ind — FG Vinatieri 26
Ind — Manning 1 run (Vinatieri kick)
Ind — Klecko 1 pass from Manning (Harrison from Manning)
NE — Gaffney 6 pass from Brady (Gostkowski kick)
Ind — Saturday 0 fumble recovery (Vinatieri kick)
NE — FG Gostkowski 28
Ind — FG Vinatieri 36
NE — FG Gostkowski 43
Ind — Addai 3 run (Vinatieri kick)

RECORDS FOR NFL TEAMS FOR MOST POINTS IN A GAME (REGULAR SEASON ONLY)

Note: When the record has been achieved more than once, only the most recent game is shown; summaries are listed in alphabetical order by conference. Bold face indicates team holding record.

BALTIMORE RAVENS
December 13, 2009, at Baltimore

Detroit	0	3	0	0	— 3
Baltimore	3	17	21	7	— 48

TD: Balt—Willis McGahee 2, Derrick Mason, Le'Ron McClain, Ray Rice, Troy Smith. TD Passes: Balt—Joe Flacco. FG: Balt—Billy Cundiff 2; Det—Jason Hanson.

BUFFALO BILLS
September 18, 1966, at Buffalo

Miami	3	7	0	14	— 24
Buffalo	21	27	3	7	— 58

TD: Buff—Bobby Burnett 2, Butch Byrd 2, Jack Spikes 2, Bobby Crockett, Jack Kemp; Mia—Dave Kocourek, Bo Roberson, John Roderick. TD Passes: Buff—Jack Kemp, Daryle Lamonica; Mia—George Wilson 3. FG: Buff—Booth Lusteg; Mia—Gene Mingo.

CINCINNATI BENGALS
December 17, 1989, at Cincinnati

Houston	0	0	0	7	— 7
Cincinnati	21	10	21	9	— 61

TD: Cin—Eddie Brown 2, Eric Ball, James Brooks, Ira Hillary, Rodney Holman, Tim McGee, Craig Taylor; Hou—Lorenzo White. TD Passes: Cin—Boomer Esiason 4, Erik Wilhelm. FG: Cin—Jim Breech 2.

CLEVELAND BROWNS
November 7, 1954, at Cleveland

Washington	0	3	0	0	— 3
Cleveland	13	14	21	14	— 62

TD: Cle—Darrell Brewster 2, Mo Bassett, Ken Gorgal, Otto Graham, Dub Jones, Dante Lavelli, Curley Morrison. TD Passes: Cle—George Ratterman 3, Otto Graham. FG: Cle—Lou Groza 2; Wash—Vic Janowicz.

DENVER BRONCOS
October 6, 1963, at Denver

San Diego	13	7	0	14	— 34
Denver	3	14	9	24	— 50

TD: Den—Lionel Taylor 2, Goose Gonsoulin, Gene Prebola, Donnie Stone; SD—Keith Lincoln 2, Lance Alworth, Paul Lowe, Jacque MacKinnon. TD Passes: Den—John McCormick 3; SD—Tobin Rote 3, John Hadl 2. FG: Den—Gene Mingo 5.

HOUSTON TEXANS
December 30, 2007 at Houston

Jacksonville	7	7	7	7	— 28
Houston	0	21	14	7	— 42

TD: Jax—Earnest Wilford 2, Matt Jones, Reggie Williams; Hou—Andre Davis 2, Ron Dayne 2, Owen Daniels, Darius Walker. TD Passes: Jax—Quinn Gray 4; Hou—Sage Rosenfels.

INDIANAPOLIS COLTS
December 12, 1976, at Baltimore

Buffalo	3	3	7	7	— 20
Baltimore Colts	7	13	28	10	— 58

TD: Balt—Roger Carr, Raymond Chester, Glenn Doughty, Roosevelt Leaks, Derrel Luce, Lydell Mitchell, Howard Stevens; Buff—Bob Chandler, O.J. Simpson. TD Passes: Balt—Bert Jones 3; Buff—Gary Marangi. FG: Balt—Toni Linhart 3; Buff—George Jakowenko 2.

JACKSONVILLE JAGUARS
December 23, 2007, at Jacksonville

Oakland	0	3	0	8	— 11
Jacksonville	14	14	7	14	— 49

TD: Oak—Zach Miller; Jax—Richard Angulo, David Garrard, Greg Jones, Matt Jones, Maurice Jones-Drew, Fred Taylor, Reggie Williams. TD Passes: Oak—JaMarcus Russell; Jax—David Garrard 2, Quinn Gray 2. FG: Oak—Sebastian Janikowski.

KANSAS CITY CHIEFS
September 7, 1963, at Denver

Kansas City	14	14	21	10	— 59
Denver	0	7	0	0	— 7

TD: KC—Chris Burford 2, Frank Jackson 2, Dave Grayson, Abner Haynes, Sherrill Headrick, Curtis McClinton; Den—Lionel Taylor. TD Passes: KC—Len Dawson 4, Curtis McClinton; Den—Mickey Slaughter. FG: KC—Tommy Brooker.

MIAMI DOLPHINS
November 24, 1977, at St. Louis

Miami	14	14	20	7	— 55
St. Louis Cardinals	7	0	0	7	— 14

TD: Mia—Nat Moore 3, Gary Davis, Duriel Harris, Leroy Harris, Benny Malone, Andre Tillman; StL—Ike Harris, Terry Metcalf. TD Passes: Mia—Bob Griese 6; StL—Jim Hart.

NEW ENGLAND PATRIOTS
October 18, 2009, at New England

Tennessee	0	0	0	0	— 0
New England	10	35	14	0	— 59

TD: NE—Randy Moss 3, Wes Welker 2, Kevin Faulk, Brian Hoyer, Laurence Maroney. TD Passes: NE—Tom Brady 6. FG: NE—Stephen Gostkowski.

NEW YORK JETS
November 17, 1985, at New York

Tampa Bay	14	7	7	0	— 28
New York Jets	17	24	14	7	— 62

TD: NYJ—Mickey Shuler 3, Johnny Hector 2, Tony Paige, Al Toon, Wesley Walker; TB—James Wilder 2, Kevin House, Calvin Magee. TD Passes: NYJ—Ken O'Brien 5; TB—Steve DeBerg 2. FG: NYJ—Pat Leahy 2.

OAKLAND RAIDERS
October 24, 2010, at Denver

Oakland	24	14	21	0	— 59
Denver	0	7	7	0	— 14

TD: Oak—Darren McFadden 4, Michael Bush, Chris Johnson, Zach Miller, Marcel Reese; Den—Knowshon Moreno 2. TD Passes: Oak—Jason Campbell 2; Den—Kyle Orton 2. FG: Oak—Sebastian Janikowski.

PITTSBURGH STEELERS
November 30, 1952, at Pittsburgh

New York Giants	0	0	7	0	— 7
Pittsburgh	14	14	7	28	— 63

TD: Pitt—Lynn Chandnois 2, Dick Hensley 2, Jack Butler, George Hays, Ray Mathews, Ed Modzelewski, Elbie Nickel; NYG—Bill Stribling. TD Passes: Pitt—Jim Finks 4, Gary Kerkorian; NYG—Tom Landry.

SAN DIEGO CHARGERS
December 22, 1963, at San Diego

Denver	7	10	3	0	— 20
San Diego	10	16	10	22	— 58

TD: SD—Paul Lowe 2, Chuck Allen, Bobby Jackson, Dave Kocourek, Keith Lincoln, Jacque MacKinnon; Den—Billy Joe, Donnie Stone. TD Passes: SD—John Hadl, Tobin Rote; Den—Don Breaux. FG: SD—George Blair 3; Den—Gene Mingo 2.

TENNESSEE TITANS
December 9, 1990, at Houston

Cleveland	0	7	7	0	— 14
Houston Oilers	14	31	7	6	— 58

TD: Hou—Lorenzo White 4, Ernest Givins, Leonard Harris, Tony Jones, Terry Kinard; Cle—Eric Metcalf 2. TD Passes: Hou—Warren Moon 2, Cody Carlson; Cle—Bernie Kosar. FG: Hou—Teddy Garcia.

ARIZONA CARDINALS
November 13, 1949, at New York
Chicago Cardinals	7	31	14	13	— 65
New York Bulldogs............	7	0	6	7	— 20

TD: Chi—Red Cochran 2, Pat Harder 2, Bill Dewell, Mel Kutner, Bob Ravensburg, Vic Schwall, Charlie Trippi; NY—Joe Golding, Frank Muehlheuser, Johnny Rauch. TD Passes: Chi—Paul Christman 3, Jim Hardy 3; NY—Bobby Layne. FG: Chi—Pat Harder.

ATLANTA FALCONS
September 16, 1973, at New Orleans
Atlanta	0	24	21	17	— 62
New Orleans	0	0	7	0	— 7

TD: Atl—Ken Burrow 2, Eddie Ray 2, Wes Chesson, Tom Hayes, Art Malone, Joe Profit; NO—Bill Butler. TD Passes: Atl—Dick Shiner 3, Bob Lee; NO—Archie Manning. FG: Atl—Nick Mike-Mayer 2.

CAROLINA PANTHERS
December 8, 2002, at Carolina
Cincinnati	7	10	14	0	— 31
Carolina	9	7	21	15	— 52

TD: Car—Steve Smith 3, Dee Brown, Muhsin Muhammad, Al Wallace, Wesley Walls; Cin—Peter Warrick 2, Jon Kitna, Takeo Spikes. TD Passes: Car—Rodney Peete 3; Cin—Jon Kitna 2. FG: Cin—Neil Rackers.

CHICAGO BEARS
December 7, 1980, at Chicago
Green Bay........................	0	7	0	0	— 7
Chicago............................	0	28	13	20	— 61

TD: Chi—Walter Payton 3, Brian Baschnagel, Robin Earl, Roland Harper, Willie McClendon, Len Walterscheid, Rickey Watts; GB—James Lofton. TD Passes: Chi—Vince Evans 3; GB—Lynn Dickey.

DALLAS COWBOYS
October 12, 1980, at Dallas
San Francisco..................	0	7	0	7	— 14
Dallas	14	24	14	7	— 59

TD: Dall—Drew Pearson 3, Ron Springs 2, Tony Dorsett, Billy Joe DuPree, Robert Newhouse; SF—Dwight Clark 2. TD Passes: Dall—Danny White 4; SF—Steve DeBerg 2. FG: Dall—Rafael Septien.

DETROIT LIONS
November 27, 1997, at Detroit
Chicago............................	14	6	0	0	— 20
Detroit..............................	3	14	17	21	— 55

TD: Det—Herman Moore, Johnnie Morton, Ron Rivers, Barry Sanders 3, Tracy Scroggins; Chi—Raymont Harris, Ricky Proehl. TD Passes: Det—Scott Mitchell 2; Chi—Erik Kramer. FG: Det—Jason Hanson 2; Chi—Jeff Jaeger 2.

GREEN BAY PACKERS
October 7, 1945, at Milwaukee
Detroit	0	7	7	7	— 21
Green Bay........................	0	41	9	7	— 57

TD: GB—Don Hutson 4, Charley Brock, Irv Comp, Ted Fritsch, Clyde Goodnight; Det—Chuck Fenenbock, John Greene, Bob Westfall. TD Passes: GB—Tex McKay 4, Lou Brock, Irv Comp; Det—Dave Ryan.

MINNESOTA VIKINGS
October 18, 1970, at Minnesota
Dallas	3	3	0	7	— 13
Minnesota........................	14	20	17	3	— 54

TD: Minn—Clint Jones 2, Ed Sharockman 2, John Beasley, Dave Osborn; Dall—Calvin Hill. TD Pass: Minn—Gary Cuozzo. FG: Minn—Fred Cox 4; Dall—Mike Clark 2.

NEW ORLEANS SAINTS
November 24, 2008, at New Orleans
Green Bay........................	7	14	0	8	— 29
New Orleans....................	14	10	21	6	— 51

TD: NO—Lance Moore 2, Pierre Thomas 2, Billy Miller, Deuce McAllister, Marques Colston; GB—John Kuhn, Greg Jennings, Ruvell Martin, Aaron Rodgers. TD Pass: NO—Drew Brees 4; GB—Aaron Rodgers 2. FG: NO—Garrett Hartley.

NEW YORK GIANTS
November 26, 1972, at New York
Philadelphia	3	7	0	0	— 10
New York Giants	14	24	10	14	— 62

TD: NYG—Don Herrmann 2, Ron Johnson 2, Bob Tucker 2, Randy Johnson; Phil—Harold Jackson. TD Passes: NYG—Norm Snead 3, Randy Johnson 2; Phil—John Reaves. FG: NYG—Pete Gogolak 2; Phil—Tom Dempsey.

PHILADELPHIA EAGLES
November 6, 1934, at Philadelphia
Cincinnati Reds................	0	0	0	0	— 0
Philadelphia....................	26	6	12	20	— 64

TD: Phil—Joe Carter 3, Swede Hanson 3, Marvin Ellstrom, Roger Kirkman, Ed Matesic, Ed Storm. TD Passes: Phil—Ed Matesic 2, Albert Weiner 2, Marvin Ellstrom.

ST. LOUIS RAMS
October 22, 1950, at Los Angeles
Baltimore	13	0	7	7	— 27
Los Angeles Rams...........	21	14	14	21	— 70

TD: LA—Bob Boyd 2, Vitamin T. Smith 2, Tom Fears, Elroy (Crazylegs) Hirsch, Dick Hoerner, Ralph Pasquariello, Dan Towler, Bob Waterfield; Balt—Chet Mutryn 2, Adrian Burk, Billy Stone. TD Passes: LA—Norm Van Brocklin 2, Bob Waterfield 2, Glenn Davis; Balt—Adrian Burk 3.

SAN FRANCISCO 49ERS
October 18, 1992, at San Francisco
Atlanta	7	3	0	7	— 17
San Francisco.................	21	21	14	0	— 56

TD: SF—Jerry Rice 3, Ricky Watters 3, Brent Jones, Tom Rathman; Atl—Michael Haynes, Jason Phillips. TD Passes: SF—Steve Young 3; Atl—Chris Miller, Wade Wilson. FG: Atl—Norm Johnson.

SEATTLE SEAHAWKS
October 30, 1977, at Seattle
Buffalo	3	0	7	7	— 17
Seattle	14	28	7	7	— 56

TD: Sea—Steve Largent 2, Duke Fergerson, Al Hunter, David Sims, Sherman Smith, Don Testerman, Jim Zorn; Buff—Joe Ferguson, John Kimbrough. TD Passes: Sea—Jim Zorn 4; Buff—Joe Ferguson. FG: Buff—Carson Long.

TAMPA BAY BUCCANEERS
December 23, 2001, at Tampa Bay
New Orleans	0	0	7	14	— 21
Tampa Bay	17	13	3	15	— 48

TD: TB—Mike Alstott, Ronde Barber, Warrick Dunn, Dave Moore, Karl Williams; NO—Joe Horn 2, Eddie Williams. TD Passes: TB—Brad Johnson 3; NO—Aaron Brooks 3. FG: TB—Martin Gramatica 4.

WASHINGTON REDSKINS
November 27, 1966, at Washington
New York Giants	0	14	14	13	— 41
Washington......................	13	21	14	24	— 72

TD: Wash—A.D. Whitfield 3, Brig Owens 2, Charley Taylor 2, Rickie Harris, Joe Don Looney, Bobby Mitchell; NYG—Allen Jacobs, Homer Jones, Dan Lewis, Joe Morrison, Aaron Thomas, Gary Wood. TD Passes: Wash—Sonny Jurgensen 3; NYG—Gary Wood 2, Tom Kennedy. FG: Wash—Charlie Gogolak.

RECORDS OF NFL TEAMS SINCE 1970 AFL-NFL MERGER

AFC	W	L	T	Pct.	Division Titles	Playoff Berths	Postseason Record	Super Bowl Record
Pittsburgh	384	246	2	.609	20	25	33-19	6-2
Miami	379	251	2	.601	13	22	20-20	2-3
Denver	359	267	6	.573	10	17	17-15	2-4
Oakland	341	285	6	.545	12	18	22-15	3-1
Baltimore***	128	111	1	.535	2	7	9-6	1-0
New England	338	294	0	.535	12	17	20-14	3-3
Jacksonville**	133	123	0	.520	2	6	5-6	0-0
Indianapolis	318	312	2	.505	13	19	15-17	2-1
Kansas City	308	317	7	.493	6	12	3-12	0-0
Tennessee	307	323	2	.487	5	16	12-16	0-1
San Diego	298	329	5	.475	10	12	9-12	0-1
Buffalo	292	337	3	.464	7	13	12-13	0-4
N.Y. Jets	282	348	2	.448	2	12	10-12	0-0
Cleveland+	258	323	3	.444	6	11	4-11	0-0
Cincinnati	279	352	1	.442	7	9	5-9	0-2
Houston****	55	89	0	.382	0	0	0-0	0-0

NFC	W	L	T	Pct.	Division Titles	Playoff Berths	Postseason Record	Super Bowl Record
Dallas	373	259	0	.590	17	26	32-21	5-3
Minnesota	361	269	2	.573	16	24	17-24	0-3
San Francisco	351	278	3	.558	17	21	25-16	5-0
Washington	343	287	2	.544	6	16	0-13	3-2
Philadelphia	325	299	8	.521	8	19	15-19	0-2
Green Bay	320	304	8	.513	8	15	17-13	2-1
St. Louis	320	308	4	.510	11	19	16-18	1-2
Chicago	317	314	1	.502	10	14	10-13	1-1
N.Y. Giants	312	317	3	.496	7	14	16-11	3-1
Seattle*	262	286	0	.478	7	11	8-11	0-1
Carolina**	119	137	0	.465	3	4	6-4	0-1
Atlanta	277	350	5	.442	4	10	6-10	0-1
New Orleans	274	354	4	.436	4	8	5-7	1-0
Arizona	256	370	6	.410	4	6	5-6	0-1
Detroit	254	374	4	.405	3	9	1-9	0-0
Tampa Bay*	218	329	1	.399	6	10	6-9	1-0

*Entered NFL in 1976.
**Entered NFL in 1995.
***Entered NFL in 1996.
****Entered NFL in 2002.
+Did not play, 1996-98.
Oakland totals include L.A. Raiders, 1982-1994.
Tennessee totals include Houston, 1970-1996.
Indianapolis totals include Baltimore, 1970-1983.
St. Louis totals include L.A. Rams, 1970-1994.
Arizona totals include St. Louis, 1970-1987, and Phoenix, 1988-1993.
Tie games before 1972 are not calculated in won-lost percentage.

HOME RECORDS OF NFL TEAMS SINCE 1970 AFL-NFL MERGER

AFC	W	L	T	Pct.
Pittsburgh	227	88	1	.720
Denver	218	95	4	.695
Miami	214	100	1	.681
Baltimore***	80	39	1	.671
Jacksonville**	79	49	0	.617
New England	194	122	0	.614
Oakland	189	125	2	.602
Kansas City	187	125	3	.599
Tennessee	175	140	1	.556
San Diego	171	142	2	.546
Cincinnati	172	143	1	.546
Buffalo	170	145	2	.539
Indianapolis	169	145	2	.538
Cleveland+	143	146	2	.495
N.Y. Jets	150	164	1	.478
Houston****	34	38	0	.472

NFC	W	L	T	Pct.
Minnesota	214	102	1	.677
Dallas	212	104	0	.671
Washington	194	119	2	.619
Green Bay	192	119	5	.616
San Francisco	193	121	2	.614
Chicago	187	128	1	.593
Seattle*	158	117	0	.575
Philadelphia	180	134	3	.573
St. Louis	177	137	2	.564
N.Y. Giants	170	146	1	.538
Detroit	166	149	1	.527
Atlanta	166	150	1	.525
Carolina**	66	62	0	.516
Arizona	153	159	3	.490
Tampa Bay*	133	140	1	.487
New Orleans	145	170	1	.460

*Entered NFL in 1976.
**Entered NFL in 1995.
***Entered NFL in 1996.
****Entered NFL in 2002.
+Did not play, 1996-98.
Oakland totals include L.A. Raiders, 1982-1994.
Tennessee totals include Houston, 1970-1996.
Indianapolis totals include Baltimore, 1970-1983.
St. Louis totals include L.A. Rams, 1970-1994.
Arizona totals include St. Louis, 1970-1987, and Phoenix, 1988-1993.
Tie games before 1972 are not calculated in won-lost percentage.

ROAD RECORDS OF NFL TEAMS SINCE 1970 AFL-NFL MERGER

AFC	W	L	T	Pct.
Miami	165	151	1	.522
Pittsburgh	157	158	1	.498
Oakland	152	160	4	.487
Indianapolis	149	167	0	.472
New England	144	172	0	.456
Denver	141	172	2	.451
Jacksonville**	54	74	0	.422
Tennessee	132	183	1	.419
N.Y. Jets	132	184	1	.418
San Diego	127	187	3	.405
Baltimore***	48	72	0	.400
Cleveland+	115	177	1	.394
Buffalo	122	192	1	.389
Kansas City	121	192	4	.388
Cincinnati	107	209	0	.339
Houston****	21	51	0	.292

NFC	W	L	T	Pct.
Dallas	161	155	0	.509
San Francisco	158	157	1	.502
Washington	149	168	0	.470
Minnesota	147	167	1	.400
Philadelphia	145	165	5	.468
St. Louis	143	171	2	.456
N.Y. Giants	142	171	2	.454
Carolina**	53	75	0	.414
New Orleans	129	184	3	.412
Chicago	130	186	0	.411
Green Bay	128	185	3	.410
Seattle*	104	160	0	.381
Atlanta	111	200	4	.357
Arizona	103	211	3	.329
Tampa Bay*	85	189	0	.310
Detroit	88	225	3	.283

*Entered NFL in 1976.
**Entered NFL in 1995.
***Entered NFL in 1996.
****Entered NFL in 2002.
+Did not play, 1996-98.
Oakland totals include L.A. Raiders, 1982-1994.
Tennessee totals include Houston, 1970-1996.
Indianapolis totals include Baltimore, 1970-1983.
St. Louis totals include L.A. Rams, 1970-1994.
Arizona totals include St. Louis, 1970-1987, and Phoenix, 1988-1993.
Tie games before 1972 are not calculated in won-lost percentage.

RECORDS OF TEAMS ON KICKOFF WEEKEND

AFC	W	L	T	Pct.	Longest W Strk.	Longest L Strk.	Current Streak
Denver	32	18	1	.640	4	4	L-1
Jacksonville	10	6	0	.625	6	3	W-1
San Diego	29	22	0	.569	6	6	L-1
Pittsburgh	40	32	4	.556	8	3	W-8
Miami	24	20	1	.545	11	5	W-1
Kansas City	27	24	0	.529	7	4	W-1
New England	27	24	0	.529	7	3	W-7
Tennessee	27	24	0	.529	4	3	W-1
Indianapolis	34	32	1	.515	8	8	L-1
Oakland	24	27	0	.471	5	8	L-8
Baltimore	7	8	0	.467	3	4	W-3
Cleveland	27	31	0	.466	5	6	L-6
Houston	4	5	0	.444	2	3	W-1
Cincinnati	19	24	0	.442	4	4	L-3
N.Y. Jets	22	29	0	.431	3	5	L-1
Buffalo	20	31	0	.392	6	5	L-2

NFC	W	L	T	Pct.	Longest W Strk.	Longest L Strk.	Current Streak
Dallas	34	16	1	.680	17	5	L-1
N.Y. Giants	49	32	5	.605	4	3	W-3
Chicago	51	35	5	.593	9	6	W-1
Green Bay	51	36	3	.586	5	6	W-4
Minnesota	28	21	1	.571	5	3	L-1
Atlanta	24	21	0	.533	5	3	L-1
Detroit	42	37	2	.532	10	4	L-3
St. Louis	38	35	0	.521	5	6	L-4
San Francisco	31	29	1	.517	5	3	L-1
Washington	38	37	4	.507	6	5	W-1
Arizona	36	52	2	.409	0	7	W-1
Philadelphia	31	45	1	.408	5	9	L-1
Tampa Bay	14	21	0	.400	3	5	W-1
Carolina	6	10	0	.375	3	4	L-2
Seattle	13	22	0	.371	3	8	W-3
New Orleans	16	28	0	.364	3	6	W-3

Kansas City totals include Dallas Texans, 1960-62.
Oakland totals include L.A. Raiders, 1982-1994.
San Diego totals include L.A. Chargers, 1960.
Indianapolis totals include Baltimore, 1953-1983.
Tennessee total include Houston, 1960-1996.
New England totals include Boston, 1960-1970.
St. Louis totals include Cleveland, 1937-1942 and 1944-45, and L.A. Rams, 1946-1994.
Detroit totals include Portsmouth, 1930-33.
Arizona totals include Chi. Cardinals, 1920-1959, St. Louis, 1960-1987, and Phoenix, 1988-1993.
Chicago totals include Decatur, 1920.
Washington totals include Boston Braves, 1932 and Boston Redskins, 1933-36.
NOTE: All tied games occurred prior to 1972, when calculation of ties in percentage as half-win.

RECORDS OF NFL TEAMS, 2001-2010

AFC	W	L	T	Pct.	Division Titles	Playoff Berths	Postseason Record	Super Bowl Record
New England	121	39	0	.756	8	8	14-5	3-1
Indianapolis	115	45	0	.719	7	9	9-8	1-1
Pittsburgh	106	53	1	.666	6	7	12-5	2-1
San Diego	93	67	0	.581	5	5	3-5	0-0
Baltimore	92	68	0	.575	2	6	5-6	0-0
Denver	86	74	0	.538	1	3	1-3	0-0
Tennessee	84	76	0	.525	2	4	2-4	0-0
N.Y. Jets	82	78	0	.513	1	6	6-6	0-0
Jacksonville	77	83	0	.481	0	2	1-2	0-0
Miami	75	85	0	.469	1	2	0-2	0-0
Kansas City	73	87	0	.456	2	3	0-3	0-0
Cincinnati	68	91	1	.428	2	2	0-2	0-0
Buffalo	62	98	0	.388	0	0	0-0	0-0
Houston	55	89	0	.382	0	0	0-0	0-0
Cleveland	59	101	0	.369	0	1	0-1	0-0
Oakland	58	102	0	.363	2	2	3-2	0-1

Houston entered NFL in 2002.

NFC	W	L	T	Pct.	Division Titles	Playoff Berths	Postseason Record	Super Bowl Record
Philadelphia	102	57	1	.641	6	8	9-8	0-1
Green Bay	96	64	0	.600	4	7	7-6	1-0
Chicago	87	73	0	.544	4	4	3-4	0-1
N.Y. Giants	86	74	0	.538	2	5	4-4	1-0
Atlanta	84	75	1	.528	2	4	2-4	0-0
New Orleans	84	76	0	.525	2	3	4-2	1-0
Seattle	83	77	0	.519	5	6	5-6	0-1
Dallas	83	77	0	.519	2	4	1-4	0-0
Tampa Bay	79	81	0	.494	3	4	3-3	1-0
Minnesota	79	81	0	.494	2	3	2-3	0-0
Carolina	74	86	0	.463	2	3	5-3	0-1
Washington	68	92	0	.425	0	2	1-2	0-0
St. Louis	68	92	0	.425	2	3	3-3	0-1
San Francisco	68	92	0	.425	1	2	1-2	0-0
Arizona	64	96	0	.400	2	2	4-2	0-1
Detroit	39	121	0	.244	0	0	0-0	0-0

Seattle was in the AFC in 2001.

HOME RECORDS, 2001-2010

AFC	W - L - T	Pct.
New England	66-14-0	.825
Indianapolis	60-20-0	.750
Baltimore	59-21-0	.738
Pittsburgh	58-21-1	.731
San Diego	54-26-0	.675
Denver	51-29-0	.638
Jacksonville	45-35-0	.563
Kansas City	45-35-0	.563
Tennessee	45-35-0	.563
N.Y. Jets	43-37-0	.538
Cincinnati	41-38-1	.519
Miami	41-39-0	.513
Houston	34-38-0	.472
Buffalo	35-45-0	.438
Oakland	33-47-0	.413
Cleveland	32-48-0	.400

Houston entered NFL in 2002.

NFC	W - L - T	Pct.
Green Bay	54-26-0	.675
Seattle	53-27-0	.663
Minnesota	52-28-0	.650
Chicago	51-29-0	.638
Philadelphia	51-29-0	.638
Atlanta	47-33-0	.588
Dallas	47-33-0	.588
San Francisco	44-36-0	.550
Tampa Bay	44-36-0	.550
N.Y. Giants	43-37-0	.538
Arizona	41-39-0	.513
New Orleans	40-40-0	.500
St. Louis	40-40-0	.500
Carolina	39-41-0	.488
Washington	38-42-0	.475
Detroit	29-51-0	.363

Seattle was in the AFC in 2001.

ROAD RECORDS, 2001-2010

AFC	W-L-T	Pct.
Indianapolis	55-25-0	.688
New England	55-25-0	.688
Pittsburgh	48-32-0	.600
N.Y. Jets	39-41-0	.488
San Diego	39-41-0	.488
Tennessee	39-41-0	.488
Denver	35-45-0	.438
Miami	34-46-0	.425
Baltimore	33-47-0	.413
Jacksonville	32-48-0	.400
Kansas City	28-52-0	.350
Cleveland	27-53-0	.338
Buffalo	27-53-0	.338
Cincinnati	27-53-0	.338
Oakland	25-55-0	.313
Houston	21-51-0	.292

Houston entered NFL in 2002.

NFC	W-L-T	Pct.
Philadelphia	51-28-1	.644
New Orleans	44-36-0	.550
N.Y. Giants	43-37-0	.538
Green Bay	42-38-0	.525
Atlanta	37-42-1	.469
Chicago	36-44-0	.450
Dallas	36-44-0	.450
Carolina	35-45-0	.438
Tampa Bay	35-45-0	.438
Seattle	30-50-0	.375
Washington	30-50-0	.375
St. Louis	28-52-0	.350
Minnesota	27-53-0	.338
San Francisco	24-56-0	.300
Arizona	23-57-0	.288
Detroit	10-70-0	.125

Seattle was in the AFC in 2001.

RECORDS BY MONTHS, 2001-2010

AFC	Sept. W-L-T	Oct. W-L-T	Nov. W-L-T	Dec. W-L-T	Total W-L-T	Pct.
New England	21-10-0	31-10-0	29-12-0	40- 7-0	121- 39-0	.756
Indianapolis	26- 6-0	25-10-0	32-12-0	32-17-0	115- 45-0	.719
Pittsburgh	19-13-0	25-12-0	26-15-1	36-13-0	106- 53-1	.666
San Diego	17-16-0	22-18-0	23-16-0	31-17-0	93- 67-0	.581
Baltimore	19-12-0	19-19-0	26-18-0	28-19-0	92- 68-0	.575
Denver	24-10-0	22-18-0	19-19-0	21-27-0	86- 74-0	.538
Tennessee	14-18-0	21-19-0	22-16-0	27-23-0	84- 76-0	.525
N.Y. Jets	15-17-0	18-21-0	24-15-0	25-25-0	82- 78-0	.513
Jacksonville	17-15-0	17-21-0	21-19-0	22-28-0	77- 83-0	.481
Miami	13-19-0	15-22-0	23-19-0	24-25-0	75- 85-0	.469
Kansas City	15-18-0	20-19-0	17-23-0	21-27-0	73- 87-0	.456
Cincinnati	15-18-0	13-26-0	19-20-1	21-27-0	68- 91-1	.428
Buffalo	12-21-0	16-23-0	14-25-0	20-29-0	62- 98-0	.388
Houston	9-20-0	16-18-0	11-26-0	19-25-0	55- 89-0	.382
Cleveland	10-24-0	18-19-0	14-26-0	17-32-0	59-101-0	.369
Oakland	14-18-0	14-25-0	14-26-0	16-33-0	58-102-0	.363

Houston entered the NFL in 2002.
December totals include January.

NFC	Sept. W-L-T	Oct. W-L-T	Nov. W-L-T	Dec. W-L-T	Total W-L-T	Pct.
Philadelphia	20-13-0	22-14-0	27-15-1	33-15-0	102- 57-1	.641
Green Bay	20-14-0	20-16-0	23-19-0	33-15-0	96- 64-0	.600
Chicago	16-16-0	20-17-0	24-18-0	27-22-0	87- 73-0	.544
N.Y. Giants	20-12-0	26-13-0	18-23-0	22-26-0	86- 74-0	.538
Atlanta	18-15-0	20-16-0	24-17-1	22-27-0	84- 75-1	.528
New Orleans	18-14-0	23-18-0	21-17-0	22-27-0	84- 76-0	.525
Dallas	19-13-0	19-20-0	25-17-0	20-27-0	83- 77-0	.519
Seattle	20-12-0	15-21-0	22-21-0	26-23-0	83- 77-0	.519
Minnesota	16-18-0	19-17-0	23-18-0	21-28-0	79- 81-0	.494
Tampa Bay	17-15-0	19-21-0	21-18-0	22-27-0	79- 81-0	.494
Carolina	15-17-0	18-22-0	15-25-0	26-22-0	74- 86-0	.463
St. Louis	11-23-0	20-19-0	16-22-0	21-28-0	68- 92-0	.425
San Francisco	12-20-0	14-25-0	18-22-0	24-25-0	68- 92-0	.425
Washington	15-16-0	17-24-0	14-26-0	22-26-0	68- 92-0	.425
Arizona	11-22-0	16-20-0	15-27-0	22-27-0	64- 96-0	.400
Detroit	9-22-0	10-27-0	8-36-0	12-36-0	39-121-0	.244

Seattle was in the AFC in 2001.
December totals include January.

TAKEAWAYS/GIVEAWAYS, 2001-2010

AFC	Takeaways Int.	Fum.	Total	Giveaways Int.	Fum.	Total	Net.Diff.
New England	197	116	313	121	101	222	+91
Indianapolis	155	130	285	144	86	230	+55
San Diego	173	106	279	136	99	235	+44
Kansas City	156	122	278	149	91	240	+38
N.Y. Jets	160	120	280	157	85	242	+38
Pittsburgh	167	124	291	153	103	256	+35
Baltimore	209	107	316	148	143	291	+25
Tennessee	175	107	282	149	119	268	+14
Jacksonville	157	91	248	123	113	236	+12
Cincinnati	172	121	293	180	105	285	+8
Denver	136	120	256	160	102	262	-6
Miami	155	114	269	177	124	301	-32
Houston	114	89	203	143	103	246	-43
Buffalo	152	104	256	168	134	302	-46
Cleveland	182	94	276	200	124	324	-48
Oakland	138	96	234	158	135	293	-59

Houston entered NFL in 2002.

NFC	Takeaways Int.	Fum.	Total	Giveaways Int.	Fum.	Total	Net.Diff.
Philadelphia	169	132	301	133	118	251	+50
Tampa Bay	199	110	309	150	114	264	+45
Atlanta	167	125	292	146	106	252	+40
Green Bay	201	112	313	168	109	277	+36
Carolina	185	133	318	178	123	301	+17
Chicago	181	139	320	190	125	315	+5
Seattle	154	118	272	161	108	269	+3
N.Y. Giants	145	133	278	167	124	291	-13
San Francisco	162	105	267	160	124	284	-17
New Orleans	146	129	275	168	132	300	-25
Minnesota	161	114	275	171	132	303	-28
Washington	146	96	242	139	134	273	-31
Dallas	145	116	261	185	116	301	-40
Detroit	130	136	266	215	102	317	-51
Arizona	162	117	279	190	141	331	-52
St. Louis	145	134	279	209	135	344	-65

Seattle was in the AFC in 2001.

BEST TAKEAWAY/GIVEAWAY DIFFERENTIAL, SEASON
+43   Washington, 1983
+28   New England, 2010
+26   Kansas City, 1990

HIGH AND LOW SINGLE-GAME YARDAGE TOTALS, 2001-2010
Most Total Yards, Game
645   Pittsburgh vs. Atlanta, Nov. 10, 2002 (OT)
619   New England vs. Tennessee, Oct. 18, 2009
605   Minnesota at New Orleans, Oct. 17, 2004
595   New Orleans vs. Cincinnati, Nov. 19, 2006
592   Philadelphia at Washington, Nov. 15, 2010
Fewest Total Yards, Game
26   Cleveland at Buffalo, Dec. 12, 2004
47   Houston at Pittsburgh, Dec. 8, 2002
67   Kansas City at San Diego, Dec. 12, 2010
72   Cincinnati at N.Y. Jets, Jan. 3, 2010
77   Oakland vs. Atlanta, Nov. 2, 2008
Most Yards Rushing, Game
378   Minnesota vs. San Diego, Nov. 4, 2007
375   Jacksonville vs. Indianapolis, Dec. 10, 2006
351   Cleveland at Kansas City, Dec. 20, 2009
343   Baltimore vs. Cleveland, Sept. 14, 2003
337   St. Louis vs. Carolina, Nov. 11, 2001
Fewest Yards Rushing, Game
-18   Detroit at Arizona, Nov. 11, 2007
-3   Detroit vs. Minnesota, Dec. 10, 2006
1   Dallas at Washington, Dec. 30, 2007
4   Seattle at Minnesota, Nov. 22, 2009
5   New England at Pittsburgh, Oct. 31, 2004

Most Yards Passing, Game
504   New Orleans vs. Cincinnati, Nov. 19, 2006
499   Denver vs. Atlanta, Oct. 31, 2004
472   Indianapolis at Kansas City, Oct. 31, 2004
472   Pittsburgh vs. Green Bay, Dec. 20, 2009
472   Denver vs. Indianapolis, Sept. 26, 2010
Fewest Yards Passing, Game
-7   Tennessee at New England, Oct. 18, 2009
-5   Houston at Oakland, Dec. 3, 2006
-3   Cleveland at Buffalo, Dec. 12, 2004
0   Oakland at San Diego, Dec. 28, 2003
    Cincinnati at N.Y. Jets, Jan. 3, 2010

NFL INDIVIDUAL LEADERS, 2001-2010

Points		Passing Yards	
David Akers	1,191	Peyton Manning	42,541
Jay Feely	1,120	Brett Favre	37,132
Ryan Longwell	1,091	Drew Brees	35,266
Adam Vinatieri	1,084	Tom Brady	34,738
Jason Elam	1,034	Donovan McNabb	31,937

Touchdowns		TD Passes	
LaDainian Tomlinson	159	Peyton Manning	314
Terrell Owens	112	Tom Brady	261
Shaun Alexander	110	Brett Favre	253
Randy Moss	110	Drew Brees	235
Priest Holmes	83	Donovan McNabb	201

Field Goals		Receptions	
David Akers	262	Hines Ward	830
Jay Feely	255	Derrick Mason	814
Sebastian Janikowski	240	Tony Gonzalez	808
Rian Lindell	234	Reggie Wayne	787
Matt Stover	234	Torry Holt	786

Rushes		Reception Yards	
LaDainian Tomlinson	3,099	Terrell Owens	11,176
Thomas Jones	2,413	Torry Holt	10,959
Edgerrin James	2,272	Chad Ochocinco	10,783
Jamal Lewis	2,233	Reggie Wayne	10,748
Clinton Portis	2,230	Randy Moss	10,695

Rushing Yards		Receiving TDs	
LaDainian Tomlinson	13,404	Randy Moss	110
Clinton Portis	9,923	Terrell Owens	110
Thomas Jones	9,740	Marvin Harrison	81
Jamal Lewis	9,243	Hines Ward	72
Shaun Alexander	9,140	Two tied	69

Rushing TDs		Interceptions	
LaDainian Tomlinson	144	Ed Reed	54
Shaun Alexander	98	Darren Sharper	49
Priest Holmes	76	Asante Samuel	42
Clinton Portis	75	Champ Bailey	38
Thomas Jones	66	Two tied	37

Pass Attempts		Sacks	
Peyton Manning	5,531	Jason Taylor	101.5
Brett Favre	5,238	John Abraham	98.0
Drew Brees	4,822	Dwight Freeney	94.0
Tom Brady	4,707	Julius Peppers	89.0
Donovan McNabb	4,433	Joey Porter	84.5

Completions	
Peyton Manning	3,668
Brett Favre	3,303
Drew Brees	3,145
Tom Brady	2,995
Donovan McNabb	2,640

NFL GAMES IN WHICH A TEAM HAS SCORED 60 OR MORE POINTS
(Home team in capitals)

Regular Season
WASHINGTON 72, New York Giants 41 ....November 27, 1966
LOS ANGELES RAMS 70, Baltimore 27 ....October 22, 1950
Chicago Cardinals 65, NEW YORK BULLDOGS 20.......................November 13, 1949
LOS ANGELES RAMS 65, Detroit 24 ....October 29, 1950
PHILADELPHIA 64, Cincinnati 0 ....November 6, 1934
CHICAGO CARDINALS 63, New York Giants 35.............................October 17, 1948
PITTSBURGH 63, New York Giants 7 ....November 30, 1952
AKRON 62, Oorang 0..October 29, 1922
CLEVELAND 62, New York Giants 14 ....December 6, 1953
CLEVELAND 62, Washington 3 ....November 7, 1954
NEW YORK GIANTS 62, Philadelphia 10..November 26, 1972
Atlanta 62, NEW ORLEANS 7 ....September 16, 1973
NEW YORK JETS 62, Tampa Bay 28 ....November 17, 1985
CHICAGO 61, San Francisco 20 ....December 12, 1965
Cincinnati 61, HOUSTON 17...December 17, 1972
CHICAGO 61, Green Bay 7 ....December 7, 1980
CINCINNATI 61, Houston 7 ....December 17, 1989
ROCK ISLAND 60, Evansville 0 ....October 15, 1922
CHICAGO CARDINALS 60, Rochester 0 ....October 7, 1923

Postseason
Chicago Bears 73, WASHINGTON 0 ....December 8, 1940
JACKSONVILLE 62, Miami 7 ....January 15, 2000

YOUNGEST AND OLDEST PLAYERS IN NFL IN 2010

10 Youngest Players

	Birthdate	Games	Starts	Position
Aaron Hernandez, New England	11/6/89	14	7	TE
Anthony Davis, San Francisco	10/11/89	16	16	T
Dezmon Briscoe, Tampa Bay	8/31/89	2	0	WR
Jonathan Dwyer, Pittsburgh	7/26/89	1	0	RB
Maurkice Pouncey, Pittsburgh	7/24/89	16	16	C
Rolando McClain, Oakland	7/14/89	15	15	LB
Rob Gronkowski, New England	5/14/89	16	11	TE
Earl Thomas, Seattle	5/7/89	16	16	FS
Joe Haden, Cleveland	4/14/89	16	7	CB
Brian Price, Tampa Bay	4/10/89	5	0	DT

10 Oldest Players

	Birthdate	Games	Starts	Position
John Carney, New Orleans	4/20/64	2	0	K
Matt Turk, Houston	6/16/68	16	0	P
Brett Favre, Minnesota	10/10/69	13	13	QB
John Kasay, Carolina	10/27/69	16	0	K
Jason Hanson, Detroit	6/17/70	8	0	K
Mark Brunell, N.Y. Jets	9/17/70	2	0	QB
Ethan Albright, San Diego	5/1/71	2	0	LS
Todd Collins, Chicago	11/5/71	2	1	QB
Joey Galloway, Washington	11/20/71	10	4	WR
Tony Richardson, N.Y. Jets	12/17/71	16	10	FB

YOUNGEST AND OLDEST REGULAR STARTERS BY POSITION IN 2010
Minimum: 8 Games Started

	Youngest		Oldest	
QB	1/13/89	Josh Freeman, T.B.	10/10/69	Brett Favre, Min.
RB	1/30/89	Jahvid Best, Det.	12/17/71	Tony Richardson, NY Jets
WR	9/8/88	Arrelious Benn, T.B.	12/7/73	Terrell Owens, Cin.
TE	5/14/89	Rob Gronkowski, N.E.	2/27/76	Tony Gonzalez, Atl.
T	10/11/89	Anthony Davis, S.F.	5/18/75	Flozell Adams, Pit.
G	6/13/87	Ted Larsen, T.B.	9/25/76	Bobbie Williams, Cin.
C	7/24/89	Maurkice Pouncey, Pit.	7/20/73	Casey Wiegmann, K.C.
DE	11/9/87	Austen Lane, Jac.	2/4/77	James Hall, St.L.
DT	6/8/88	Corey Peters, Atl.	10/24/72	Pat Williams, Min.
LB	7/14/89	Rolando McClain, Bal.	1/6/75	James Farrior, Pit.
CB	12/13/88	Alterraun Verner, Ten.	4/7/75	Ronde Barber, T.B.
S	5/7/89	Earl Thomas, Sea.	10/13/73	Brian Dawkins, Den.

OLDEST INDIVIDUAL SINGLE-SEASON OR SINGLE-GAME RECORDS IN NFL RECORD & FACT BOOK
Most Points, Game—40, Ernie Nevers, Chi. Cardinals vs. Chi. Bears, Nov. 28, 1929 (6-td, 4-pat)
Most Touchdowns Rushing, Game—6, Ernie Nevers, Chi. Cardinals vs. Chi. Bears, Nov. 28, 1929
Highest Rushing Average Gain, Season (Qualifiers)—8.44, Beattie Feathers, Chi. Bears, 1934 (119-1,004)
Highest Punting Average, Season (Qualifiers)—51.40, Sammy Baugh, Washington, 1940 (35-1,799)
Highest Punting Average, Rookie, Season (Qualifiers)—45.92, Frank Sinkwich, Detroit, 1943 (12-551)
Highest Punting Average, Game (minimum: 4 punts)—61.75, Bob Cifers, Detroit vs. Chi. Bears, Nov. 24, 1946 (4-247)
Highest Average Gain, Pass Receptions, Season (minimum: 24 receptions)—32.58, Don Currivan, Boston, 1947 (24-782)
Highest Average Gain, Passing, Game (minimum: 20 passes)—18.58, Sammy Baugh, Washington vs. Boston, Oct. 31, 1948 (24-446)
Most Touchdowns, Fumble Recoveries, Game—2, Fred (Dippy) Evans, Chi. Bears vs. Washington, Nov. 28, 1948
Most Yards Gained, Intercepted Passes, Rookie, Season—301, Don Doll, Detroit, 1949
Most Passes Had Intercepted, Game—8, Jim Hardy, Chi. Cardinals vs. Philadelphia, Sept. 24, 1950
Highest Kickoff Return Average, Game (minimum: 3 returns)—73.50, Wally Triplett, Detroit vs. Los Angeles, Oct. 29, 1950 (4-294)
Highest Punt Return Average, Season (Qualifiers)—23.00, Herb Rich, Baltimore, 1950 (12-276)
Highest Punt Return Average, Rookie, Season (Qualifiers)—23.00, Herb Rich, Baltimore, 1950 (12-276)
Most Yards Passing, Game—554, Norm Van Brocklin, Los Angeles vs. N.Y. Yanks, Sept. 28, 1951
Most Touchdowns, Punt Returns, Rookie, Season—4, Jack Christiansen, Detroit, 1951
Most Interceptions By, Season—14, Dick (Night Train) Lane, Los Angeles, 1952
Most Interceptions By, Rookie, Season—14, Dick (Night Train) Lane, Los Angeles, 1952
Highest Average Gain, Passing, Season (Qualifiers)—11.17, Tommy O'Connell, Cleveland, 1957 (110-1,229)
Most Yards Gained, Pass Receptions, Rookie, Season—1,473, Bill Groman, Houston, 1960

NFL INDIVIDUAL LEADERS OVER RECENT SEASONS

Last 2 Seasons		Last 3 Seasons		Last 4 Seasons	
Points					
282	David Akers	426	David Akers	534	David Akers
255	Nate Kaeding	382	Nate Kaeding	509	Mason Crosby
241	Mason Crosby	368	Mason Crosby	500	Nate Kaeding
237	Sebastian Janikowski	355	Rob Bironas	488	Rob Bironas
229	Jay Feely	343	Jeff Reed	466	Stephen Gostkowski
Touchdowns					
31	Adrian Peterson	41	Adrian Peterson	54	Adrian Peterson
28	Chris Johnson	39	Michael Turner	52	Randy Moss
23	Maurice Jones-Drew	38	Chris Johnson	48	LaDainian Tomlinson
22	Michael Turner	37	Maurice Jones-Drew	47	Maurice Jones-Drew
21	Three tied	35	Thomas Jones	41	Larry Fitzgerald
Field Goals					
64	David Akers	97	David Akers	121	David Akers
59	Sebastian Janikowski	83	Josh Brown	115	Rob Bironas
55	Dan Carpenter	83	Sebastian Janikowski	111	Josh Brown
55	Nate Kaeding	82	Nate Kaeding	107	Mason Crosby
54	Jay Feely	80	Rob Bironas	106	Three tied
Rushes					
674	Chris Johnson	960	Adrian Peterson	1,198	Adrian Peterson
654	Steven Jackson	925	Chris Johnson	1,176	Thomas Jones
622	Cedric Benson	907	Steven Jackson	1,144	Steven Jackson
611	Maurice Jones-Drew	888	Michael Turner	1,049	LaDainian Tomlinson
597	Adrian Peterson	866	Thomas Jones	1,032	Cedric Benson
Rushing Yards					
3,370	Chris Johnson	4,598	Chris Johnson	5,782	Adrian Peterson
2,715	Maurice Jones-Drew	4,441	Adrian Peterson	4,729	Thomas Jones
2,681	Adrian Peterson	3,941	Michael Turner	4,701	Steven Jackson
2,657	Steven Jackson	3,699	Steven Jackson	4,598	Chris Johnson
2,587	Jamaal Charles	3,610	Thomas Jones	4,307	Maurice Jones-Drew
Rushing Touchdowns					
30	Adrian Peterson	40	Adrian Peterson	52	Adrian Peterson
25	Chris Johnson	39	Michael Turner	44	LaDainian Tomlinson
22	Michael Turner	34	Chris Johnson	41	Maurice Jones-Drew
20	Three tied	33	Thomas Jones	40	Michael Turner
		28	Maurice Jones-Drew	34	Two tied
Passes					
1,250	Peyton Manning	1,807	Drew Brees	2,459	Drew Brees
1,172	Drew Brees	1,805	Peyton Manning	2,320	Peyton Manning
1,157	Matt Schaub	1,603	Jay Cutler	2,070	Jay Cutler
1,057	Tom Brady	1,552	Aaron Rodgers	2,056	Eli Manning
1,052	Carson Palmer	1,537	Matt Schaub	1,965	Philip Rivers
Completions					
843	Peyton Manning	1,224	Drew Brees	1,664	Drew Brees
811	Drew Brees	1,214	Peyton Manning	1,551	Peyton Manning
761	Matt Schaub	1,012	Matt Schaub	1,279	Brett Favre
695	Tom Brady	1,003	Aaron Rodgers	1,278	Jay Cutler
674	Philip Rivers	986	Philip Rivers	1,263	Philip Rivers
Passing Yards					
9,200	Peyton Manning	14,077	Drew Brees	18,500	Drew Brees
9,140	Matt Schaub	13,202	Peyton Manning	17,242	Peyton Manning
9,008	Drew Brees	12,973	Philip Rivers	16,125	Philip Rivers
8,964	Philip Rivers	12,394	Aaron Rodgers	14,963	Jay Cutler
8,356	Aaron Rodgers	12,183	Matt Schaub	14,597	Eli Manning

Last 2 Seasons

Touchdown Passes
67	Drew Brees
66	Peyton Manning
64	Tom Brady
58	Three tied

Receptions
211	Reggie Wayne
209	Wes Welker
200	Roddy White
188	Jason Witten
187	Three tied

Receiving Yards
2,785	Andre Johnson
2,619	Reggie Wayne
2,542	Roddy White
2,378	Greg Jennings
2,361	Miles Austin

Receiving Touchdowns
21	Roddy White
20	Vernon Davis
19	Dwayne Bowe
19	Larry Fitzgerald
18	Three tied

Interceptions
16	Asante Samuel
11	Brent Grimes
11	Ed Reed
11	Aqib Talib
11	Charles Woodson

Sacks
26.5	DeMarcus Ware
25.5	Jared Allen
23.5	Dwight Freeney
23.5	Clay Matthews
23.5	LaMarr Woodley

Last 3 Seasons

Touchdown Passes
101	Drew Brees
93	Peyton Manning
92	Philip Rivers
86	Aaron Rodgers
79	Eli Manning

Receptions
320	Wes Welker
302	Andre Johnson
293	Reggie Wayne
291	Brandon Marshall
288	Roddy White

Receiving Yards
4,360	Andre Johnson
3,924	Roddy White
3,764	Reggie Wayne
3,670	Greg Jennings
3,660	Larry Fitzgerald

Receiving Touchdowns
31	Larry Fitzgerald
29	Calvin Johnson
29	Randy Moss
28	Roddy White
26	Two tied

Interceptions
20	Ed Reed
20	Asante Samuel
18	Charles Woodson
17	Nick Collins
17	Troy Polamalu

Sacks
46.5	DeMarcus Ware
40.0	Jared Allen
36.5	James Harrison
35.0	John Abraham
35.0	LaMarr Woodley

Last 4 Seasons

Touchdown Passes
129	Drew Brees
124	Peyton Manning
114	Tom Brady
113	Philip Rivers
102	Eli Manning

Receptions
432	Wes Welker
397	Reggie Wayne
393	Brandon Marshall
383	Larry Fitzgerald
371	Roddy White

Receiving Yards
5,274	Reggie Wayne
5,211	Andre Johnson
5,126	Roddy White
5,069	Larry Fitzgerald
4,724	Brandon Marshall

Receiving Touchdowns
52	Randy Moss
41	Larry Fitzgerald
39	Terrell Owens
37	Greg Jennings
35	Antonio Gates

Interceptions
27	Ed Reed
26	Asante Samuel
22	Charles Woodson
20	DeAngelo Hall
18	Three tied

Sacks
60.5	DeMarcus Ware
55.5	Jared Allen
45.0	John Abraham
45.0	James Harrison
44.0	Trent Cole

NFL TEAM LEADERS OVER RECENT SEASONS

Highest Won-Lost Percentage

Last 2 Seasons
.750	Indianapolis
.750	New England
.750	New Orleans
.688	Atlanta
.688	San Diego

Last 3 Seasons
.750	Indianapolis
.729	New England
.688	Atlanta
.688	Pittsburgh
.667	Two tied

Last 4 Seasons
.797	New England
.766	Indianapolis
.672	Pittsburgh
.641	San Diego
.625	Two tied

Most Points

Last 2 Seasons
945	New England
895	San Diego
894	New Orleans
868	Philadelphia
851	Indianapolis

Last 3 Seasons
1,357	New Orleans
1,355	New England
1,334	San Diego
1,284	Philadelphia
1,268	Green Bay

Last 4 Seasons
1,944	New England
1,746	San Diego
1,736	New Orleans
1,703	Green Bay
1,678	Indianapolis

Most Total Yards

Last 2 Seasons
12,421	New Orleans
12,315	Houston
12,218	Dallas
12,177	New England
12,090	San Diego

Last 3 Seasons
18,992	New Orleans
18,428	Houston
18,024	New England
17,730	Dallas
17,674	San Diego

Last 4 Seasons
24,772	New Orleans
24,604	New England
23,765	Houston
23,581	Dallas
23,344	Green Bay

Last 2 Seasons		Last 3 Seasons		Last 4 Seasons	
Most Rushing Yards					
5,130	N.Y. Jets	7,134	N.Y. Jets	8,835	N.Y. Jets
4,556	Kansas City	6,781	Carolina	8,832	Minnesota
4,424	Jacksonville	6,555	N.Y. Giants	8,703	N.Y. Giants
4,344	Carolina	6,518	Tennessee	8,627	Tennessee
4,319	Tennessee	6,407	Baltimore	8,605	Carolina
Most Passing Yards					
9,305	Indianapolis	14,195	New Orleans	18,610	New Orleans
9,252	San Diego	13,647	Houston	17,657	Indianapolis
9,173	Houston	13,485	Indianapolis	17,572	Houston
9,126	New Orleans	13,261	San Diego	17,352	Green Bay
8,847	Green Bay	12,891	Green Bay	17,211	New England
Fewest Turnovers					
32	New England	53	New England	68	New England
38	Green Bay	59	Green Bay	83	Green Bay
41	Kansas City	63	Atlanta	85	Indianapolis
42	Atlanta	63	Baltimore	87	Atlanta
42	Baltimore	65	Kansas City	90	Two tied
Fewest Points Allowed					
531	Baltimore	775	Baltimore	1,048	Pittsburgh
537	Green Bay	779	Pittsburgh	1,159	Baltimore
540	N.Y. Jets	896	N.Y. Jets	1,181	New England
556	Pittsburgh	907	New England	1,208	Green Bay
598	New England	917	Green Bay	1,251	N.Y. Jets
Fewest Total Yards Allowed					
8,701	N.Y. Jets	13,109	Pittsburgh	17,371	Pittsburgh
9,314	Pittsburgh	13,971	N.Y. Jets	18,912	Baltimore
9,496	Green Bay	14,087	Baltimore	19,281	N.Y. Jets
9,577	San Diego	14,569	Minnesota	19,722	N.Y. Giants
9,890	Minnesota	14,761	Philadelphia	19,743	Philadelphia
Fewest Rushing Yards Allowed					
2,442	Pittsburgh	3,726	Pittsburgh	5,164	Pittsburgh
2,995	Baltimore	4,259	Minnesota	5,444	Minnesota
3,029	Minnesota	4,297	Baltimore	5,565	Baltimore
3,032	N.Y. Jets	4,550	N.Y. Jets	6,401	Dallas
3,099	San Francisco	4,808	San Francisco	6,450	Philadelphia
Fewest Passing Yards Allowed					
6,158	N.Y. Jets	9,831	Buffalo	12,965	Tampa Bay
6,390	Buffalo	10,030	Tampa Bay	13,393	Indianapolis
6,704	San Diego	10,163	N.Y. Jets	13,433	Pittsburgh
6,843	Tampa Bay	10,258	Oakland	13,525	N.Y. Jets
6,850	Oakland	10,274	Green Bay	13,576	Oakland
Most Opponents' Turnovers					
72	Green Bay	101	Philadelphia	128	Chicago
72	Philadelphia	100	Green Bay	128	Green Bay
66	Carolina	95	Chicago	122	Tampa Bay
66	New England	93	Baltimore	121	Carolina
64	New Orleans	91	Two tied	120	Two tied

RETIRED UNIFORM NUMBERS IN NFL

AFC

Baltimore	None	
Buffalo	Jim Kelly	12
Cincinnati	Bob Johnson	54
Cleveland	Otto Graham	14
	Jim Brown	32
	Ernie Davis	45
	Don Fleming	46
	Lou Groza	76
Denver	John Elway	7
	Frank Tripucka	18
	Floyd Little	44
Houston	None	
Indianapolis	Johnny Unitas	19
	Buddy Young	22
	Lenny Moore	24
	Art Donovan	70
	Jim Parker	77
	Raymond Berry	82
	Gino Marchetti	89
Jacksonville	None	
Kansas City	Jan Stenerud	3
	Len Dawson	16
	Emmitt Thomas	18
	Abner Haynes	28
	Stone Johnson	33
	Mack Lee Hill	36
	Derrick Thomas	58
	Willie Lanier	63
	Bobby Bell	78
	Buck Buchanan	86
Miami	Bob Griese	12
	Dan Marino	13
	Larry Csonka	39
New England	Gino Cappelletti	20
	Mike Haynes	40
	Steve Nelson	57
	John Hannah	73
	Bruce Armstrong	78
	Jim Lee Hunt	79
	Bob Dee	89
New York Jets	Joe Namath	12
	Don Maynard	13
	Joe Klecko	73
Oakland	None	
Pittsburgh	Ernie Stautner	70
San Diego	Dan Fouts	14
	Lance Alworth	19
Tennessee	Warren Moon	1
	Earl Campbell	34
	Jim Norton	43
	Mike Munchak	63
	Elvin Bethea	65
	Bruce Matthews	74

NFC

Arizona	Larry Wilson	8
	Pat Tillman	40
	Stan Mauldin	77
	J.V. Cain	88
	Marshall Goldberg	99
Atlanta	Steve Bartkowski	10
	William Andrews	31
	Jeff Van Note	57
	Tommy Nobis	60
Carolina	Sam Mills	51
Chicago	Bronko Nagurski	3
	George McAfee	5
	George Halas	7
	Willie Galimore	28
	Walter Payton	34
	Gale Sayers	40
	Brian Piccolo	41
	Sid Luckman	42
	Dick Butkus	51
	Bill Hewitt	56
	Bill George	61
	Bulldog Turner	66
	Red Grange	77
Dallas	None	
Detroit	Dutch Clark	7
	Bobby Layne	22
	Doak Walker	37
	Joe Schmidt	56
	Chuck Hughes	85
Green Bay	Tony Canadeo	3
	Don Hutson	14
	Bart Starr	15
	Ray Nitschke	66
	Reggie White	92
Minnesota	Fran Tarkenton	10
	Mick Tingelhoff	53
	Jim Marshall	70
	Korey Stringer	77
	Cris Carter	80
	Alan Page	88
New Orleans	Jim Taylor	31
	Doug Atkins	81
New York Giants	Ray Flaherty	1
	Tuffy Leemans	4
	Mel Hein	7
	Phil Simms	11
	Y.A. Tittle	14
	Frank Gifford	16
	Al Blozis	32
	Joe Morrison	40
	Charlie Conerly	42
	Ken Strong	50
	Lawrence Taylor	56
Philadelphia	Steve Van Buren	15
	Tom Brookshier	40
	Pete Retzlaff	44
	Chuck Bednarik	60
	Al Wistert	70
	Reggie White	92
	Jerome Brown	99
St. Louis	Bob Waterfield	7
	Eric Dickerson	29
	Merlin Olsen	74
	Deacon Jones	75
	Jackie Slater	78
	Isaac Bruce	80
	Jack Youngblood	85
San Francisco	Steve Young	8
	John Brodie	12
	Joe Montana	16
	Joe Perry	34
	Jimmy Johnson	37
	Hugh McElhenny	39
	Ronnie Lott	42
	Charlie Krueger	70
	Leo Nomellini	73
	Bob St. Clair	79
	Jerry Rice	80
	Dwight Clark	87
Seattle	"Fans/the twelfth man"	12
	Steve Largent	80
Tampa Bay	Lee Roy Selmon	63
Washington	Sammy Baugh	33

The NFL rates its passers for statistical purposes against a fixed performance standard based on statistical achievements of all qualified pro passers since 1960. The current system replaced one that rated passers in relation to their position in a total group based on various criteria. The current system, which was adopted in 1973, removes inequities that existed in the former method and, at the same time, provides a means of comparing passing performances from one season to the next.

It is important to remember that the system is used to rate passers, not quarterbacks. Statistics do not reflect leadership, play-calling, and other intangible factors that go into making a successful professional quarterback. Four categories are used as a basis for compiling a rating:

—Percentage of completions per attempt
—Average yards gained per attempt
—Percentage of touchdown passes per attempt
—Percentage of interceptions per attempt

The average standard is 1.000. The bottom is .000. To earn a 2.000 rating, a passer must perform at exceptional levels, i.e., 70 percent in completions, 10 percent in touchdowns, 1.5 percent in interceptions, and 11 yards average gain per pass attempt. The maximum a passer can receive in any category is 2.375.

For example, to gain a 2.375 in completion percentage, a passer would have to complete 77.5 percent of his passes. The NFL record is 70.55 by Ken Anderson (Cincinnati, 1982). To earn a 2.375 in percentage of touchdowns, a passer would have to achieve a percentage of 11.9. The record is 13.9 by Sid Luckman (Chicago, 1943). To gain 2.375 in percentage of interceptions, a passer would have to go the entire season without an interception. The 2.375 figure in average yards is 12.50, compared with the NFL record of 11.17 by Tommy O'Connell (Cleveland, 1957).

In order to make the rating more understandable, the point rating is then converted into a scale of 100, with 158.3 being the highest rating a passer can achieve. In cases where statistical performance has been superior, it is possible for a passer to sur-

pass a 100 rating. For example, take Peyton Manning's record-setting season in 2004 when he completed 336 of 497 passes for 4,557 yards, 49 touchdowns, and 10 interceptions. The four calculations would be:

—Percentage of Completions—336 of 497 is 67.60 percent. Subtract 30 from the completion percentage (37.60) and multiply the result by 0.05. The result is a point rating of 1.880.
Note: If the result is less than zero (Comp. Pct. less than 30.0), award zero points. If the results are greater than 2.375 (Comp. Pct. greater than 77.5), award 2.375.

—Average Yards Gained Per Attempt—4,557 yards divided by 497 attempts is 9.17. Subtract three yards from yards-per-attempt (6.17) and multiply the result by 0.25. The result is 1.543.
Note: If the result is less than zero (yards per attempt less than 3.0), award zero points. If the result is greater than 2.375 (yards per attempt greater than 12.5), award 2.375 points.

—Percentage of Touchdown Passes—49 touchdowns in 497 attempts is 9.86 percent. Multiply the touchdown percentage by 0.2. The result is 1.972.
Note: If the result is greater than 2.375 (touchdown percentage greater than 11.875), award 2.375.

—Percentage of Interceptions—10 interceptions in 497 attempts is 2.01 percent. Multiply the interception percentage by 0.25 (0.503) and subtract the number from 2.375. The result is 1.872.
Note: If the result is less than zero (interception percentage greater than 9.5), award zero points.

The sum of the four steps is (1.880 + 1.543 + 1.972 + 1.872) 7.267. The sum is then divided by six (1.211) and multiplied by 100. In this case, the result is 121.1. This same formula can be used to determine a passer rating for any player who attempts at least one pass.

Fifty-two qualifying passers have had a single-season passer rating of 100 or higher. The following is a list of the Top 25 single-season passer ratings among qualifying players:

TOP 25 NFL SINGLE-SEASON PASSER RATINGS (QUALIFYING PLAYERS)

Player, Team	Season	Rating	Att.	Comp.	Pct.	Yds.	Yds. Avg.	TD	TD Pct.	Int.	Int. Pct.
Peyton Manning, Indianapolis	2004	*121.1	497	336	67.6	4,557	9.17	49	9.9	10	2.0
Tom Brady, New England	2007	117.2	578	398	68.9	4,806	8.31	*50	8.7	8	1.4
Steve Young, San Francisco	1994	112.8	461	324	70.2	3,969	8.61	35	7.6	10	2.2
Joe Montana, San Francisco	1989	112.4	386	271	70.2	3,521	9.12	26	6.7	8	2.1
Tom Brady, New England	2010	111.0	492	324	65.9	3,900	7.93	36	7.3	4	0.8
Daunte Culpepper, Minnesota	2004	110.9	548	379	69.2	4,717	8.61	39	7.1	11	2.0
Milt Plum, Cleveland	1960	110.4	250	151	60.4	2,297	9.19	21	8.4	5	2.0
Sammy Baugh, Washington	1945	109.9	182	128	70.3	1,669	9.17	11	6.0	4	2.2
Drew Brees, New Orleans	2009	109.6	514	363	*70.6	4,388	8.54	34	6.6	11	2.1
Kurt Warner, St. Louis	1999	109.2	499	325	65.1	4,353	8.72	41	8.2	13	2.6
Dan Marino, Miami	1984	108.9	564	362	64.2	*5,084	9.01	48	8.5	17	3.0
Sid Luckman, Chicago Bears	1943	107.5	202	110	54.5	2,194	10.86	28	13.9	12	5.9
Brett Favre, Minnesota	2009	107.2	531	363	68.4	4,202	7.91	30	5.6	7	1.3
Steve Young, San Francisco	1992	107.0	402	268	66.7	3,465	8.62	25	6.2	7	1.7
Randall Cunningham, Minnesota	1998	106.0	425	259	60.9	3,704	8.72	34	8.0	10	2.4
Philip Rivers, San Diego	2008	105.5	478	312	65.3	4,009	8.39	34	7.1	11	2.3
Bart Starr, Green Bay	1966	105.0	251	156	62.2	2,257	8.99	14	5.6	3	1.2
Drew Brees, San Diego	2004	104.8	400	262	65.5	3,159	7.90	27	6.8	7	1.8
Roger Staubach, Dallas	1971	104.8	211	126	59.7	1,882	8.92	15	7.1	4	1.9
Y.A. Tittle, N.Y. Giants	1963	104.8	367	221	60.2	3,145	8.57	36	9.8	14	3.8
Donovan McNabb, Philadelphia	2004	104.7	469	300	64.0	3,875	8.06	31	6.6	8	1.7
Steve Young, San Francisco	1997	104.7	356	241	67.7	3,029	8.51	19	5.3	6	1.7
Philip Rivers, San Diego	2009	104.4	486	317	65.2	4,254	8.75	28	5.7	9	1.9
Bart Starr, Green Bay	1968	104.3	171	109	63.7	1,617	9.46	15	8.8	8	4.7
Chad Pennington, N.Y. Jets	2002	104.2	399	275	68.9	3,120	7.82	22	5.5	6	1.5

*NFL Record

HIGHEST NFL POSTSEASON PASSER RATINGS (MINIMUM: 150 ATTEMPTS)

Player	Games	Att.	Cmp.	Pct.	Yards	Avg. Gain	TD	Int.	Rating
Aaron Rodgers	6	174	118	67.8	1,517	8.72	13	3	112.6
Bart Starr	10	213	130	61.0	1,753	8.23	15	3	104.8
Kurt Warner	13	462	307	66.5	3,952	8.55	31	14	102.8
Drew Brees	7	285	189	66.3	2,052	7.20	15	2	102.0
Joe Montana	23	734	460	62.7	5,772	7.86	45	21	95.6
Mark Sanchez	6	157	95	60.5	1,155	7.36	9	3	94.3
Ken Anderson	6	166	110	66.3	1,321	7.96	9	6	93.5
Joe Theismann	10	211	128	60.7	1,782	8.45	11	7	91.4
Peyton Manning	19	718	453	63.1	5,389	7.51	29	19	88.4
Troy Aikman	16	502	320	63.7	3,849	7.67	23	17	88.3

HIGHEST NFL POSTSEASON PASSER RATINGS, ACTIVE PLAYERS (MINIMUM: 150 ATTEMPTS)

Player	Games	Att.	Cmp.	Pct.	Yards	Avg. Gain	TD	Int.	Rating
Aaron Rodgers	5	174	118	67.8	1,517	8.72	13	3	112.6
Drew Brees	7	285	189	66.3	2,052	7.20	15	2	102.0
Mark Sanchez	6	157	95	60.5	1,155	7.36	9	3	94.3
Peyton Manning	19	718	453	63.1	5,389	7.51	29	19	88.4
Tom Brady	19	682	424	62.2	4,407	6.46	30	16	85.7
Ben Roethlisberger	13	369	226	61.3	2,861	7.75	19	16	84.5
Matt Hasselbeck	11	406	237	58.4	2,741	6.75	18	9	84.4
Jake Delhomme	8	226	130	57.5	1,847	8.17	12	10	83.3
Donovan McNabb	16	577	341	59.1	3,752	6.50	24	17	80.0
Philip Rivers	7	229	134	58.5	1,820	7.95	8	9	79.2

ALL-TIME RANKINGS OF PLAYERS IN FOUR CATEGORIES THAT DETERMINE NFL PASSER RATING
Minimum: 1,500 Attempts

COMPLETION PERCENTAGE

	Pct.	Att.	Comp.
Chad Pennington	66.05	2,471	1,632
Kurt Warner	65.50	4,070	2,666
Drew Brees	65.22	4,822	3,145
Peyton Manning	64.94	7,210	4,682
Matt Schaub	64.82	1,987	1,288
Aaron Rodgers	64.43	1,611	1,038
Steve Young	64.28	4,149	2,667
Tony Romo	64.06	2,070	1,326
Philip Rivers	63.71	2,455	1,564
Tom Brady	63.61	4,710	2,996

TOUCHDOWN PERCENTAGE

	Pct.	Att.	TD
Sid Luckman	7.86	1,744	137
Frank Ryan	6.99	2,133	149
Len Dawson	6.39	3,741	239
Daryle Lamonica	6.31	2,601	164
Sammy Baugh	6.24	2,995	187
Charlie Conerly	6.11	2,833	173
Bob Waterfield	6.00	1,617	97
Earl Morrall	5.99	2,689	161
Sonny Jurgensen	5.98	4,262	255
Norm Van Brocklin	5.98	2,895	173

AVERAGE YARDS PER PASS

	Avg.	Att.	Yards
Otto Graham	8.63	1,565	13,499
Sid Luckman	8.42	1,744	14,686
Norm Van Brocklin	8.16	2,895	23,611
Tony Romo	8.04	2,070	16,650
Ben Roethlisberger	8.04	2,800	22,502
Philip Rivers	8.01	2,455	19,661
Steve Young	7.98	4,149	33,124
Kurt Warner	7.95	4,070	32,344
Aaron Rodgers	7.90	1,611	12,723
Ed Brown	7.85	1,987	15,600

INTERCEPTION PERCENTAGE

	Pct.	Att.	Int.
Aaron Rodgers	1.99	1,611	32
Neil O'Donnell	2.11	3,229	68
Tom Brady	2.19	4,710	103
Donovan McNabb	2.20	5,218	115
Jeff Garcia	2.26	3,676	83
Mark Brunell	2.33	4,637	108
Jason Campbell	2.34	1,966	46
Philip Rivers	2.36	2,455	58
David Garrard	2.37	2,281	54
Kyle Orton	2.46	1,952	48

STARTING RECORDS OF ACTIVE NFL QUARTERBACKS

Minimum: 10 starts

	W - L - T	Pct.
Tom Brady	111-32-0	.776
Matt Ryan	33-13-0	.717
Ben Roethlisberger	69-29-0	.704
Philip Rivers	55-25-0	.688
Peyton Manning	141-67-0	.678
Joe Flacco	32-16-0	.667
Tony Romo	39-22-0	.639
Vince Young	30-17-0	.638
Donovan McNabb	97-57-1	.629
Mark Sanchez	19-12-0	.613
Michael Vick	46-31-1	.596
Rex Grossman	20-14-0	.588
Jake Delhomme	56-40-0	.583
Eli Manning	60-43-0	.583
Drew Brees	79-58-0	.577
Aaron Rodgers	27-20-0	.574
Chad Pennington	44-37-0	.543
Matt Moore	7- 6-0	.538
Matt Cassel	24-21-0	.533
Matt Hasselbeck	69-62-0	.527
Kyle Orton	32-29-0	.525
Todd Collins	11-10-0	.524
Josh Freeman	13-12-0	.520
Mark Brunell	78-73-0	.517
David Garrard	39-37-0	.513
Jay Cutler	34-34-0	.500
Shaun Hill	13-13-0	.500
Tarvaris Jackson	10-10-0	.500
Sage Rosenfels	6- 6-0	.500
Byron Leftwich	24-25-0	.490
Chad Henne	13-14-0	.481
Carson Palmer	46-51-0	.474
A.J. Feeley	7- 8-0	.467
Kerry Collins	81-96-0	.458
Matt Schaub	25-31-0	.446
Charlie Batch	23-29-0	.442
Sam Bradford	7- 9-0	.438
Chris Simms	7- 9-0	.438
Kyle Boller	20-26-0	.435
Marc Bulger	41-54-0	.432
Trent Edwards	14-19-0	.424
Jason Campbell	27-37-0	.422
Derek Anderson	18-25-0	.419
Patrick Ramsey	10-14-0	.417
Matt Leinart	7-10-0	.412
Jon Kitna	50-74-0	.403
Alex Smith	19-31-0	.380
Ryan Fitzpatrick	12-23-1	.347
Chris Redman	4- 8-0	.333
Seneca Wallace	6-12-0	.333
Charlie Frye	7-16-0	.304
J.P. Losman	10-23-0	.303
Bruce Gradkowski	6-14-0	.300
Billy Volek	3- 7-0	.300
David Carr	23-56-0	.291
Brady Quinn	3- 9-0	.250
Matthew Stafford	3-10-0	.231
Jimmy Clausen	1- 9-0	.100
Tyler Thigpen	1-11-0	.083
Brodie Croyle	0-10-0	.000

MOST GAME-WINNING DRIVES IN FOURTH QUARTER OR OVERTIME SINCE 1970

47	Dan Marino, Miami, 1983-1999
45	Peyton Manning, Indianapolis, 1998-2010
43	Brett Favre, Atlanta, 1991; Green Bay, 1992-2007; N.Y. Jets, 2008; Minnesota, 2009-2010
40	John Elway, Denver, 1983-1998
35	Warren Moon, Houston, 1984-1993; Minnesota, 1994-96; Seattle, 1997-98; Kansas City, 1999-2000

TEAMS THAT FINISHED IN FIRST PLACE IN THEIR DIVISION THE SEASON AFTER FINISHING IN LAST PLACE

Season	Team	Record	Prior Season
1967	Houston	9-4-1	*3-11-0
1968	Minnesota	8-6-0	3- 8-3
1970	Cincinnati	8-6-0	4- 9-1
1970	San Francisco	10-3-1	4- 8-2
1972	Green Bay	10-4-0	4- 8-2
1975	Baltimore	10-4-0	2-12-0
1979	Tampa Bay	10-6-0	5-11-0
1981	Cincinnati	12-4-0	6-10-0
1987	Indianapolis	9-6-0	3-13-0
1988	Cincinnati	12-4-0	4-11-0
1990	Cincinnati	9-7-0	8- 8-0
1991	Denver	12-4-0	5-11-0
1992	San Diego	11-5-0	4-12-0
1993	Detroit	10-6-0	5-11-0
1997	N.Y. Giants	10-5-1	6-10-0
1999	Indianapolis	13-3-0	3-13-0
1999	St. Louis	13-3-0	4-12-0
2000	New Orleans	10-6-0	3-13-0
2001	Chicago	13-3-0	5-11-0
2001	New England	11-5-0	5-11-0
2003	Carolina	11-5-0	7- 9-0
2003	Kansas City	13-3-0	*8- 8-0
2004	Atlanta	11-5-0	5-11-0
2004	San Diego	12-4-0	*4-12-0
2005	Chicago	11-5-0	5-11-0
2005	Tampa Bay	11-5-0	5-11-0
2006	Baltimore	13-3-0	*6-10-0
2006	New Orleans	10-6-0	3-13-0
2006	Philadelphia	10-6-0	6-10-0
2007	Tampa Bay	9-7-0	4-12-0
2008	Miami	11-5-0	1-15-0
2009	New Orleans	13-3-0	8-8-0
2010	Kansas City	10-6-0	4-12-0

*tied for last place

LONGEST WINNING STREAKS SINCE 1970

23	Indianapolis, 2008-09	(9 in 2008; 14 in 2009)
21	New England, 2006-08	(3 in 2006, 16 in 2007, 2 in 2008)
18	New England, 2003-04	(12 in 2003, 6 in 2004)
16	Miami, 1971-73	(1 in 1971, 14 in 1972, 1 in 1973)
16	Miami, 1983-84	(5 in 1983, 11 in 1984)
16	Pittsburgh, 2004-05	(14 in 2004, 2 in 2005)
15	San Francisco, 1989-90	(5 in 1989, 10 in 1990)
14	Oakland, 1976-77	(10 in 1976, 4 in 1977)
14	Denver, 1997-98	(1 in 1997, 13 in 1998)
13	Minnesota, 1974-75	(3 in 1974, 10 in 1975)
13	Chicago, 1984-85	(1 in 1984, 12 in 1985)
13	N.Y. Giants, 1989-90	(3 in 1989, 10 in 1990)
13	Indianapolis, 2005	
13	Tennessee, 2007-08	(3 in 2007, 10 in 2008)
13	New Orleans, 2009	
12	Washington, 1990-91	(1 in 1990, 11 in 1991)
11	Pittsburgh, 1975	
11	Baltimore, 1975-76	(9 in 1975, 2 in 1976)
11	Chicago, 1986-87	(7 in 1986, 4 in 1987)
11	Houston, 1993	
11	San Francisco, 1997	
11	Jacksonville, 1999	
11	Indianapolis, 1999	
11	Seattle, 2005	
11	San Diego, 2006-07	(10 in 2006, 1 in 2007)
11	San Diego, 2009	

NFL PLAYOFF APPEARANCES BY SEASONS

Team	Number of Seasons in Playoffs
Dallas	30
N.Y. Giants	30
St. Louis	27
Green Bay	26
Minnesota	26
Pittsburgh	26

Team	Number of Seasons in Playoffs
Chicago	25
Cleveland	24
Indianapolis	24
Philadelphia	23
Miami	22
San Francisco	22
Washington	22
Oakland	21
Tennessee	21
New England	18
Buffalo	17
Denver	17
San Diego	17
Kansas City	16
Detroit	14
N.Y. Jets	14
Seattle	11
Atlanta	10
Tampa Bay	10
Cincinnati	9
Arizona	8
New Orleans	8
Baltimore	7
Jacksonville	6
Carolina	4

Year	W	L	T	Pct
1978	93	130	1	.417
1979	92	132	0	.411
1980	101	122	1	.453
1981	84	139	1	.377
1982	57	68	1	.456
1983	104	119	1	.467
1984	94	129	1	.422
1985	80	144	0	.357
1986	104	118	2	.469
1987	95	114	1	.455
1988	92	131	1	.413
1989	95	128	1	.426
1990	93	131	0	.415
1991	92	132	0	.411
1992	88	136	0	.393
1993	101	123	0	.451
1994	96	128	0	.429
1995	96	144	0	.400
1996	91	149	0	.379
1997	93	145	2	.392
1998	89	151	0	.371
1999	100	148	0	.403
2000	110	138	0	.444
2001	112	136	0	.452
2002	107	148	1	.420
2003	99	157	0	.387
2004	111	145	0	.434
2005	105	151	0	.410
2006	120	136	0	.469
2007	109	147	0	.426
2008	109	146	1	.428
2009	110	146	0	.430
2010	113	143	0	.441

TEAMS IN SUPER BOWL CONTENTION (1978-2010)

	With 3 Weeks to Play	With 2 Weeks to Play	With 1 Week to Play
1978	20	17	12
1979	19	15	13
1980	20	14	12
1981	21	20	16
1982	*27	25	*22
1983	24	19	15
1984	18	14	13
1985	21	18	13
1986	19	17	14
1987	19	19	15
1988	21	18	15
1989	21	18	17
1990	23	20	15
1991	20	18	13
1992	20	16	14
1993	20	18	16
1994	25	22	15
1995	*27	21	18
1996	23	21	13
1997	22	18	14
1998	22	19	14
1999	23	20	16
2000	19	17	16
2001	23	16	13
2002	21	21	19
2003	22	17	14
2004	*27	*26	17
2005	18	17	14
2006	25	24	20
2007	23	16	15
2008	22	19	18
2009	24	19	17
2010	23	20	16

RECORD OF TEAMS ON THE ROAD (1970-2010)

Year	W	L	T	Pct
1970	72	101	9	.420
1971	74	100	8	.429
1972	87	90	5	.492
1973	66	109	7	.382
1974	82	99	1	.453
1975	81	101	0	.445
1976	83	112	1	.426
1977	83	113	0	.423

GAMES DECIDED BY 7 POINTS OR FEWER AND 3 POINTS OR FEWER (1970-2010)

	Games Decided by 7 Points or Fewer	Games Decided by 3 Points or Fewer
1970	59 of 182 (32.4%)	34 of 182 (18.7%)
1971	76 of 182 (41.8%)	35 of 182 (19.2%)
1972	71 of 182 (39.0%)	38 of 182 (20.9%)
1973	60 of 182 (32.9%)	28 of 182 (15.4%)
1974	91 of 182 (50.0%)	37 of 182 (20.3%)
1975	62 of 182 (34.1%)	35 of 182 (19.2%)
1976	73 of 196 (37.2%)	38 of 196 (19.4%)
1977	85 of 196 (43.4%)	36 of 196 (18.4%)
1978	108 of 224 (48.2%)	49 of 224 (21.9%)
1979	104 of 224 (46.4%)	51 of 224 (22.8%)
1980	108 of 224 (48.2%)	58 of 224 (25.9%)
1981	91 of 224 (40.6%)	60 of 224 (26.8%)
1982	61 of 126 (48.4%)	33 of 126 (26.2%)
1983	106 of 224 (47.3%)	54 of 224 (24.1%)
1984	95 of 224 (42.4%)	58 of 224 (25.9%)
1985	87 of 224 (38.8%)	38 of 224 (17.0%)
1986	106 of 224 (47.3%)	48 of 224 (21.4%)
1987	99 of 210 (47.1%)	40 of 210 (19.0%)
1988	113 of 224 (50.4%)	62 of 224 (27.7%)
1989	107 of 224 (47.8%)	55 of 224 (24.6%)
1990	97 of 224 (43.3%)	54 of 224 (24.1%)
1991	112 of 224 (50.0%)	57 of 224 (25.4%)
1992	88 of 224 (39.3%)	48 of 224 (21.4%)
1993	*105 of 224 (46.9%)	53 of 224 (23.7%)
1994	115 of 224 (51.3%)	60 of 224 (26.8%)
1995	115 of 240 (47.9%)	61 of 240 (25.4%)
1996	109 of 240 (45.4%)	47 of 240 (19.6%)
1997	111 of 240 (46.3%)	67 of 240 (27.9%)
1998	113 of 240 (47.1%)	50 of 240 (20.8%)
1999	115 of 248 (46.4%)	**64 of 248 (25.8%)
2000	109 of 248 (44.0%)	61 of 248 (24.6%)
2001	121 of 248 (48.8%)	62 of 248 (25.0%)
2002	126 of 256 (49.2%)	63 of 256 (24.6%)
2003	124 of 256 (48.4%)	60 of 256 (23.4%)
2004	116 of 256 (45.3%)	61 of 256 (23.8%)

	Games Decided by 7 Points or Fewer	Games Decided by 3 Points or Fewer
2005	114 of 256 (44.5%)	60 of 256 (23.4%)
2006	117 of 256 (45.7%)	61 of 256 (23.8%)
2007	110 of 256 (43.0%)	55 of 256 (21.5%)
2008	115 of 256 (44.9%)	50 of 256 (19.5%)
2009	110 of 256 (43.0%)	54 of 256 (21.1%)
2010	121 of 256 (47.3%)	65 of 256 (25.4%)

*Week record: Dec. 11-13, 1993 (Week 15), 12 of 14 games (86%) decided by 7 points or fewer.

**Week record: Oct. 10-11, 1999 (Week 5), 10 of 14 games (71%) decided by 3 points or fewer.

GAMES DECIDED BY 8 PTS. OR FEWER (1994-2010)

1994	121 of 224 (54.0%)	2005	123 of 256 (48.0%)
1995	123 of 240 (51.3%)	2006	126 of 256 (49.2%)
1996	115 of 240 (47.9%)	2007	120 of 256 (46.9%)
1997	120 of 240 (50.0%)	2008	118 of 256 (46.1%)
1998	120 of 240 (50.0%)	2009	120 of 256 (46.9%)
1999	124 of 248 (50.0%)	2010	131 of 256 (51.2%)
2000	119 of 248 (48.0%)	*Week record: Oct. 14-15,	
2001	*128 of 248 (51.6%)	2001 (Week 5), 12 of 14	
2002	137 of 256 (53.5%)	games (86%) decided by 8	
2003	132 of 256 (51.6%)	points or fewer	
2004	121 of 256 (47.3%)		

TWO-POINT CONVERSION RESULTS (1994-2010)

1994	59 of 116 (50.9%)	2003	29 of 66 (43.9%)
1995	40 of 104 (38.5%)	2004	37 of 76 (48.7%)
1996	44 of 92 (47.8%)	2005	27 of 53 (50.9%)
1997	47 of 109 (43.1%)	2006	21 of 41 (51.2%)
1998	41 of 105 (39.1%)	2007	30 of 61 (49.2%)
1999	31 of 84 (36.9%)	2008	28 of 68 (41.2%)
2000	35 of 85 (41.2%)	2009	24 of 60 (40.0%)
2001	40 of 90 (44.4%)	2010	26 of 53 (49.1%)
2002	47 of 98 (48.0%)		

RECORDS AFTER BYE WEEKS (1990-2010)

AFC		NFC	
Baltimore	10- 5	Arizona	10-12
Buffalo	14- 8	Atlanta	12-10
Cincinnati	5-16-1	Carolina	8- 8
Cleveland	7-10	Chicago	14- 8
Denver	16- 6	Dallas	16- 6
Houston	2- 7	Detroit	10-12
Indianapolis	13- 9	Green Bay	13- 9
Jacksonville	8- 8	Minnesota	17- 5
Kansas City	12- 10	New Orleans	10-12
Miami	13- 9	N.Y. Giants	7-15
New England	13- 9	Philadelphia	18- 4
N.Y. Jets	11-11	San Francisco	9-13
Oakland	9-13	Seattle	6-16
Pittsburgh	13- 9	St. Louis	11-11
San Diego	11-10	Tampa Bay	10-12
Tennessee	13- 9	Washington	11-11

2010 RECORDS OF TEAMS IN CLOSE GAMES

AFC	Overall Record	Decided by 8 Pts. or Fewer	Decided By 3 Pts. or Fewer
Baltimore	12-4	8-4	3-2
Buffalo	4-12	3-6	2-4
Cincinnati	4-12	2-8	1-2
Cleveland	5-11	3-7	3-3
Denver	4-12	2-6	1-1
Houston	6-10	3-5	1-2
Indianapolis	10-6	5-4	3-4
Jacksonville	8-8	5-2	1-1
Kansas City	10-6	4-2	2-1
Miami	7-9	5-5	1-3
New England	14-2	5-0	3-0
N.Y. Jets	11-5	6-3	2-1
Oakland	8-8	3-5	2-1
Pittsburgh	12-4	6-2	3-1
San Diego	9-7	3-5	0-2
Tennessee	6-10	1-6	0-3

NFC	Overall Record	Decided by 8 Pts. or Fewer	Decided By 3 Pts. or Fewer
Arizona	5-11	3-3	2-2
Atlanta	13-3	7-2	3-1
Carolina	2-14	2-2	1-2
Chicago	11-5	7-3	2-2
Dallas	6-10	3-8	3-4
Detroit	6-10	4-7	1-4
Green Bay	10-6	4-6	1-4
Minnesota	6-10	3-4	2-0
New Orleans	11-5	6-2	4-1
N.Y. Giants	10-6	4-1	1-0
Philadelphia	10-6	5-4	4-1
San Francisco	6-10	3-5	1-4
Seattle	7-9	2-0	1-0
St. Louis	7-9	3-4	2-3
Tampa Bay	10-6	5-4	5-1
Washington	6-10	6-6	4-5

SUPER BOWL CHAMPIONS THAT DID NOT MAKE PLAYOFFS THE FOLLOWING YEAR

Pittsburgh—Super Bowl XLIII champions did not make playoffs in 2009 season.

Pittsburgh—Super Bowl XL champions did not make playoffs in 2006 season.

Tampa Bay—Super Bowl XXXVII champions did not make playoffs in 2003 season.

New England—Super Bowl XXXVI champions did not make playoffs in the 2002 season.

Denver—Super Bowl XXXIII champions did not make playoffs in the 1999 season.

N.Y. Giants—Super Bowl XXV champions did not make playoffs in the 1991 season.

Washington—Super Bowl XXII champions did not make playoffs in the 1988 season.

N.Y. Giants—Super Bowl XXI champions did not make playoffs in the 1987 season.

San Francisco—Super Bowl XVI champions did not make playoffs in the 1982 season.

Oakland—Super Bowl XV champions did not make playoffs in the 1981 season.

Pittsburgh—Super Bowl XIV champions did not make playoffs in the 1980 season.

Kansas City—Super Bowl IV champions did not make playoffs in the 1970 season.

Green Bay—Super Bowl II champions did not make playoffs in the 1968 season.

NON-DIVISION WINNERS THAT PLAYED IN SUPER BOWL

2010	Green Bay Packers (Defeated Pittsburgh, 31-25)	Super Bowl XLV
2007	New York Giants (Defeated New England, 17-14)	Super Bowl XLII
2005	Pittsburgh Steelers (Defeated Seattle, 21-10)	Super Bowl XL
2000	Baltimore Ravens (Defeated N.Y. Giants, 34-7)	Super Bowl XXXV
1999	Tennessee Titans (Lost to St. Louis, 23-16)	Super Bowl XXXIV
1997	Denver Broncos (Defeated Green Bay, 31-24)	Super Bowl XXXII
1992	Buffalo Bills (Lost to Dallas, 52-17)	Super Bowl XXVII
1985	New England Patriots (Lost to Chicago, 46-10)	Super Bowl XX
1980	Oakland Raiders (Defeated Philadelphia, 27-10)	Super Bowl XV
1975	Dallas Cowboys (Lost to Pittsburgh, 21-17)	Super Bowl X
1969	Kansas City Chiefs (Defeated Minnesota, 23-7)	Super Bowl IV

TEAMS AT OR UNDER .500 IN POSTSEASON PLAY

2010	Seattle Seahawks	7-9
2008	San Diego Chargers	8-8
2006	New York Giants	8-8
2004	Minnesota Vikings	8-8
2004	St. Louis Rams	8-8
1999	Dallas Cowboys	8-8
1999	Detroit Lions	8-8
1991	New York Jets	8-8
1990	New Orleans Saints	8-8
1985	Cleveland Browns	8-8
1982	Cleveland Browns	4-5
1982	Detroit Lions	4-5
1969	Houston Oilers	6-6-2

TEAMS TO BEAT OPPOSING TEAM THREE TIMES IN A SEASON SINCE 1970

Year	Team	Opponent
2009	Dallas Cowboys	Philadelphia Eagles
2008	Pittsburgh Steelers	Baltimore Ravens
2004	St. Louis Rams	Seattle Seahawks
2002	Pittsburgh Steelers	Cleveland Browns
2000	New York Giants	Philadelphia Eagles
1999	Tennessee Titans	Jacksonville Jaguars
1997	Green Bay Packers	Tampa Bay Buccaneers
1997	New England Patriots	Miami Dolphins
1994	Pittsburgh Steelers	Cleveland Browns
1993	Los Angeles Raiders	Denver Broncos
1991	Kansas City Chiefs	Los Angeles Raiders
1986	New York Giants	Washington Redskins
1982	Miami Dolphins	New York Jets

COLDEST NFL GAMES ON RECORD

-13 degrees (-48 degree wind chill)—December 31, 1967, Lambeau Field, Green Bay, Wisconsin, NFL Championship (Green Bay 21, Dallas 17)

-9 degrees (-59 degree wind chill)—January 10, 1982, Riverfront Stadium, Cincinnati, Ohio, AFC Championship (Cincinnati 27, San Diego 7)

-1 degrees (-23 degree wind chill)—January 20, 2008, Lambeau Field, Green Bay, Wisconsin, NFC Championship (N.Y. Giants 23, Green Bay 20 in OT)

TEAM LEADERS

Offense	Most Scored		Fewest Scored	
1st Quarter	117	Oakland	35	Carolina
2nd Quarter	160	Indianapolis	67	Carolina
3rd Quarter	138	New England	37	Cleveland
4th Quarter	138	Philadelphia	42	Carolina
Defense	**Most Scored**		**Fewest Scored**	
1st Quarter	33	N.O. & G.B.	114	Carolina
2nd Quarter	42	Pittsburgh	166	Buffalo
3rd Quarter	24	Baltimore	115	Indianapolis
4th Quarter	53	Chicago	139	Denver

2010 NFL SCORE BY QUARTERS

AFC Offense	1	2	3	4	OT	PTS
New England	103	152	138	122	3	518
San Diego	76	128	107	130	0	441
Indianapolis	78	160	68	129	0	435
Oakland	117	90	78	122	3	410
Houston	53	98	108	128	3	390
Pittsburgh	58	148	43	117	9	375
N.Y. Jets	36	127	90	105	9	367
Kansas City	55	137	77	94	3	366
Baltimore	61	132	75	80	9	357
Tennessee	79	92	83	102	0	356
Jacksonville	43	129	86	95	0	353
Denver	69	77	78	120	0	344
Cincinnati	45	102	57	118	0	322
Buffalo	40	88	65	90	0	283
Miami	70	72	60	68	3	273
Cleveland	77	91	37	66	0	271

NFC Offense	1	2	3	4	OT	PTS
Philadelphia	110	123	68	138	0	439
Atlanta	69	148	83	111	3	414
Dallas	70	104	106	111	3	394
N.Y. Giants	89	133	102	70	0	394
Green Bay	74	120	110	84	0	388
New Orleans	112	93	74	105	0	384
Detroit	62	118	62	117	3	362
Tampa Bay	43	127	70	101	0	341
Chicago	88	95	84	67	0	334
Seattle	55	73	86	96	0	310
San Francisco	75	79	51	97	3	305
Washington	61	97	51	84	9	302
Arizona	53	98	44	94	0	289
St. Louis	69	104	51	65	0	289
Minnesota	51	81	85	61	3	281
Carolina	35	67	52	42	0	196

AFC Defense	1	2	3	4	OT	PTS
Pittsburgh	49	42	39	102	0	232
Baltimore	51	73	24	119	3	270
N.Y. Jets	57	89	75	83	0	304
New England	39	91	77	106	0	313
San Diego	96	94	31	101	0	322
Kansas City	57	88	72	106	3	326
Cleveland	40	134	47	105	6	332
Miami	68	89	97	79	0	333
Tennessee	65	130	65	76	3	339
Oakland	68	112	99	92	0	371
Indianapolis	70	89	115	111	3	388
Cincinnati	63	113	93	126	0	395
Jacksonville	88	92	102	134	3	419
Buffalo	70	166	98	82	9	425
Houston	96	139	75	111	6	427
Denver	85	143	104	139	0	471

NFC Defense	1	2	3	4	OT	PTS
Green Bay	33	92	36	73	6	240
Chicago	68	111	54	53	0	286
Atlanta	75	55	83	69	6	288
New Orleans	33	112	53	106	3	307
Tampa Bay	73	126	53	63	3	318
St. Louis	53	113	53	106	3	328
San Francisco	51	105	93	97	0	346
N.Y. Giants	67	99	64	117	0	347
Minnesota	69	106	98	75	0	348
Detroit	54	127	86	99	3	369
Washington	104	94	101	75	3	377
Philadelphia	59	128	78	112	0	377
Seattle	89	141	93	84	0	407
Carolina	114	111	74	109	0	408
Arizona	87	149	102	93	3	434
Dallas	85	130	95	126	0	436
NFL TOTALS	**2,176**	**3,483**	**2,429**	**3,129**	**66**	**11,283**

2011 TOP 100 TELEVISION MARKETS
(NFL TEAM MARKETS IN BOLD)

RANK	MARKET	TV HOUSEHOLDS	% of U.S.
1	**New York**	**7,515,330**	**6.484**
2	Los Angeles	5,666,900	4.889
3	**Chicago**	**3,502,610**	**3.022**
4	**Philadelphia**	**3,015,820**	**2.602**
5	**Dallas-Ft. Worth**	**2,594,630**	**2.239**
6	**San Francisco-Oak-San Jose**	**2,523,520**	**2.177**
7	**Boston (Manchester)**	**2,460,290**	**2.123**
8	**Atlanta**	**2,407,080**	**2.077**
9	**Washington, DC (Hagrstwn)**	**2,389,710**	**2.062**
10	**Houston**	**2,177,220**	**1.878**
11	**Detroit**	**1,883,840**	**1.625**
12	**Phoenix (Prescott)**	**1,881,310**	**1.623**
13	**Seattle-Tacoma**	**1,874,750**	**1.617**
14	**Tampa-St. Pete (Sarasota)**	**1,795,200**	**1.549**
15	**Minneapolis-St. Paul**	**1,753,780**	**1.513**
16	**Miami-Ft. Lauderdale**	**1,580,580**	**1.364**
17	**Denver**	**1,572,740**	**1.357**
18	**Cleveland-Akron (Canton)**	**1,526,200**	**1.317**
19	Orlando-Daytona Bch-Melbrn	1,453,120	1.254
20	Sacramnto-Stkton-Modesto	1,409,400	1.216
21	**St. Louis**	**1,258,580**	**1.086**
22	Portland, OR	1,197,780	1.033
23	**Charlotte**	**1,166,180**	**1.006**
24	**Pittsburgh**	**1,160,820**	**1.002**
25	Raleigh-Durham (Fayetvlle)	1,131,310	0.976
26	**Baltimore**	**1,108,360**	**0.956**
27	**Indianapolis**	**1,106,420**	**0.955**
28	**San Diego**	**1,089,010**	**0.940**
29	**Nashville**	**1,039,430**	**0.897**
30	Hartford & New Haven	1,018,770	0.879
31	**Kansas City**	**974,820**	**0.841**
32	Salt Lake City	953,950	0.823
33	**Cincinnati**	**923,830**	**0.797**
34	Columbus, OH	915,950	0.790
35	Milwaukee	901,100	0.777
36	Greenvll-Spart-Ashevll-And	878,550	0.758
37	San Antonio	844,910	0.729
38	West Palm Beach-Ft. Pierce	773,890	0.668
39	Harrisburg-Lncstr-Leb-York	749,020	0.646
40	Birmingham (Ann and Tusc)	747,190	0.645
41	Grand Rapids-Kalmzoo-B.Crk	740,230	0.639
42	Las Vegas	718,030	0.619
43	Norfolk-Portsmth-Newpt Nws	716,050	0.618
44	Austin	707,430	0.610
45	Oklahoma City	704,670	0.608
46	Albuquerque-Santa Fe	703,720	0.607
47	Greensboro-H.Point-W.Salem	699,040	0.603
48	Memphis	693,860	0.599
49	**Jacksonville**	**678,430**	**0.585**
50	Louisville	674,940	0.582

2011 TOP 100 TELEVISION MARKETS
(NFL TEAM MARKETS IN BOLD)

RANK	MARKET	TV HOUSEHOLDS	% of U.S.
51	**Buffalo**	**636,320**	**0.549**
52	**New Orleans**	**635,860**	**0.549**
53	Providence-New Bedford	620,600	0.535
54	Wilkes Barre-Scranton	595,480	0.514
55	Fresno-Visalia	581,340	0.502
56	Little Rock-Pine Bluff	573,670	0.495
57	Richmond-Petersburg	558,500	0.482
58	Albany-Schenectady-Troy	557,860	0.481
59	Knoxville	557,040	0.481
60	Mobile-Pensacola (Ft Walt)	539,190	0.465
61	Tulsa	535,820	0.462
62	Dayton	527,030	0.455
63	Lexington	515,320	0.445
64	Charleston-Huntington	505,200	0.436
65	Ft. Myers-Naples	499,410	0.431
66	Roanoke-Lynchburg	464,480	0.401
67	Tucson (Sierra Vista)	461,450	0.398
68	Wichita-Hutchinson Plus	457,000	0.395
69	Flint-Saginaw-Bay City	455,840	0.393
70	Toledo	445,600	0.384
71	**Green Bay-Appleton**	**445,510**	**0.384**
72	Honolulu	433,530	0.374
73	Des Moines-Ames	432,820	0.373
74	Springfield, MO	424,270	0.366
75	Spokane	424,220	0.366
76	Omaha	418,290	0.361
77	Portland-Auburn	410,300	0.354
78	Columbia, SC	405,670	0.350
79	Huntsville-Decatur (Flor)	399,440	0.345
80	Paducah-Cape Girard-Harsbg	398,820	0.344
81	Rochester, NY	392,090	0.338
82	Syracuse	380,970	0.330
83	Shreveport	387,060	0.334
84	Champaign&Sprngfld-Decatur	384,990	0.332
85	Madison	382,700	0.330
86	Chattanooga	376,910	0.325
87	Harlingen-Wslco-Brnsvl-McA	356,010	0.307
88	Cedar Rapids-Wtrlo-IWC&Dub	346,010	0.299
89	Waco-Temple-Bryan	344,020	0.297
90	Jackson, MS	338,030	0.292
91	Tri-Cities TN-VA	337,010	0.291
92	Colorado Springs-Pueblo	336,880	0.291
93	South Bend-Elkhart	336,220	0.290
94	Baton Rouge	334,730	0.289
95	Burlington-Plattsburgh	330,730	0.285
96	Savannah	329,460	0.284
97	El Paso (Las Cruces)	315,130	0.272
98	Charleston, SC	312,770	0.270
99	Davenport-R.Island-Moline	309,800	0.267
100	Ft. Smith-Fay-Sprngdl-Rgrs	304,060	0.262
	TOTAL NFL MARKETS	**54,678,180**	**47.175**
	TOTAL TOP 100 MARKETS	**99,822,240**	**86.124**
	TOTAL MARKETS	**115,905,450**	**100.000**

ALL-TIME REGULAR-SEASON RECORDS OF CURRENT NFL TEAMS

AFC
BALTIMORE RAVENS

Season	All Games W	L	T	Home Games W	L	T	Road Games W	L	T
1996	4	12		4	4		0	8	
1997	6	9	1	3	4	1	3	5	
1998	6	10		4	4		2	6	
1999	8	8		4	4		4	4	
2000	12	4		6	2		6	2	
2001	10	6		6	2		4	4	
2002	7	9		4	4		3	5	
2003	10	6		7	1		3	5	
2004	9	7		6	2		3	5	
2005	6	10		6	2		0	8	
2006	13	3		7	1		6	2	
2007	5	11		4	4		1	7	
2008	11	5		6	2		5	3	
2009	9	7		6	2		3	5	
2010	12	4		7	1		5	3	
	128	111	1	80	39	1	48	72	

BUFFALO BILLS

Season	All Games W	L	T	Home Games W	L	T	Road Games W	L	T
1960	5	8	1	3	4		2	4	1
1961	6	8		2	5		4	3	
1962	7	6	1	3	3	1	4	3	
1963	7	6	1	4	2	1	3	4	
1964	12	2		6	1		6	1	
1965	10	3	1	5	2		5	1	1
1966	9	4	1	4	2	1	5	2	
1967	4	10		2	5		2	5	
1968	1	12	1	1	6		0	6	1
1969	4	10		4	3		0	7	
1970	3	10	1	1	6		2	4	1
1971	1	13		1	6		0	7	
1972	4	9	1	2	4	1	2	5	
1973	9	5		5	2		4	3	
1974	9	5		5	2		4	3	
1975	8	6		3	4		5	2	
1976	2	12		1	6		1	6	
1977	3	11		1	6		2	5	
1978	5	11		4	4		1	7	
1979	7	9		3	5		4	4	
1980	11	5		6	2		5	3	
1981	10	6		7	1		3	5	
1982	4	5		4	1		0	4	
1983	8	8		3	5		5	3	
1984	2	14		2	6		0	8	
1985	2	14		2	6		0	8	
1986	4	12		3	5		1	7	
1987	7	8		4	4		3	4	
1988	12	4		8	0		4	4	
1989	9	7		6	2		3	5	
1990	13	3		8	0		5	3	
1991	13	3		7	1		6	2	
1992	11	5		6	2		5	3	
1993	12	4		6	2		6	2	
1994	7	9		4	4		3	5	
1995	10	6		6	2		4	4	
1996	10	6		7	1		3	5	
1997	6	10		4	4		2	6	
1998	10	6		6	2		4	4	
1999	11	5		6	2		5	3	
2000	8	8		5	3		3	5	
2001	3	13		1	7		2	6	
2002	8	8		5	3		3	5	
2003	6	10		4	4		2	6	

Season	All Games W	L	T	Home Games W	L	T	Road Games W	L	T
2004	9	7		5	3		4	4	
2005	5	11		4	4		1	7	
2006	7	9		4	4		3	5	
2007	7	9		4	4		3	5	
2008	7	9		3	5		4	4	
2009	6	10		3	5		3	5	
2010	4	12		2	6		2	6	
	358	406	8	205	178	4	153	228	4

CINCINNATI BENGALS

Season	All Games W	L	T	Home Games W	L	T	Road Games W	L	T
1968	3	11		2	5		1	6	
1969	4	9	1	4	3		0	6	1
1970	8	6		5	2		3	4	
1971	4	10		3	4		1	6	
1972	8	6		4	3		4	3	
1973	10	4		7	0		3	4	
1974	7	7		4	3		3	4	
1975	11	3		6	1		5	2	
1976	10	4		6	1		4	3	
1977	8	6		5	2		3	4	
1978	4	12		3	5		1	7	
1979	4	12		4	4		0	8	
1980	6	10		3	5		3	5	
1981	12	4		6	2		6	2	
1982	7	2		4	0		3	2	
1983	7	9		4	4		3	5	
1984	8	8		5	3		3	5	
1985	7	9		5	3		2	6	
1986	10	6		6	2		4	4	
1987	4	11		1	7		3	4	
1988	12	4		8	0		4	4	
1989	8	8		5	3		3	5	
1990	9	7		5	3		4	4	
1991	3	13		3	5		0	8	
1992	5	11		3	5		2	6	
1993	3	13		3	5		0	8	
1994	3	13		2	6		1	7	
1995	7	9		3	5		4	4	
1996	8	8		6	2		2	6	
1997	7	9		6	2		1	7	
1998	3	13		1	7		2	6	
1999	4	12		2	6		2	6	
2000	4	12		3	5		1	7	
2001	6	10		4	4		2	6	
2002	2	14		1	7		1	7	
2003	8	8		5	3		3	5	
2004	8	8		5	3		3	5	
2005	11	5		5	3		6	2	
2006	8	8		4	4		4	4	
2007	7	9		5	3		2	6	
2008	4	11	1	3	4	1	1	7	
2009	10	6		6	2		4	4	
2010	4	12		3	5		1	7	
	286	372	2	178	151	1	108	221	1

CLEVELAND BROWNS*

Season	All Games W	L	T	Home Games W	L	T	Road Games W	L	T
1950	10	2		5	1		5	1	
1951	11	1		6	0		5	1	
1952	8	4		4	2		4	2	
1953	11	1		6	0		5	1	
1954	9	3		5	1		4	2	
1955	9	2	1	5	1		4	1	1
1956	5	7		1	5		4	2	
1957	9	2	1	6	0		3	2	1

Season	All Games W	L	T	Home Games W	L	T	Road Games W	L	T
1958	9	3		4	2		5	1	
1959	7	5		3	3		4	2	
1960	8	3	1	4	2		4	1	1
1961	8	5	1	4	3		4	2	1
1962	7	6	1	4	2	1	3	4	
1963	10	4		5	2		5	2	
1964	10	3	1	5	1	1	5	2	
1965	11	3		5	2		6	1	
1966	9	5		5	2		4	3	
1967	9	5		6	1		3	4	
1968	10	4		5	2		5	2	
1969	10	3	1	5	1	1	5	2	
1970	7	7		4	3		3	4	
1971	9	5		4	3		5	2	
1972	10	4		4	3		6	1	
1973	7	5	2	5	1	1	2	4	1
1974	4	10		3	4		1	6	
1975	3	11		3	4		0	7	
1976	9	5		6	1		3	4	
1977	6	8		2	5		4	3	
1978	8	8		5	3		3	5	
1979	9	7		5	3		4	4	
1980	11	5		6	2		5	3	
1981	5	11		3	5		2	6	
1982	4	5		2	3		2	3	
1983	9	7		6	2		3	5	
1984	5	11		2	6		3	5	
1985	8	8		5	3		3	5	
1986	12	4		6	2		6	2	
1987	10	5		5	2		5	3	
1988	10	6		6	2		4	4	
1989	9	6	1	5	2	1	4	4	
1990	3	13		2	6		1	7	
1991	6	10		3	5		3	5	
1992	7	9		4	4		3	5	
1993	7	9		4	4		3	5	
1994	11	5		6	2		5	3	
1995	5	11		3	5		2	6	
1999	2	14		0	8		2	6	
2000	3	13		2	6		1	7	
2001	7	9		4	4		3	5	
2002	9	7		3	5		6	2	
2003	5	11		2	6		3	5	
2004	4	12		3	5		1	7	
2005	6	10		4	4		2	6	
2006	4	12		2	6		2	6	
2007	10	6		7	1		3	5	
2008	4	12		1	7		3	5	
2009	5	11		3	5		2	6	
2010	5	11		3	5		2	6	
	438	394	10	236	179	5	202	215	5

Did not play from 1996-98.

DENVER BRONCOS

Season	All Games W	L	T	Home Games W	L	T	Road Games W	L	T
1960	4	9	1	2	4	1	2	5	
1961	3	11		2	5		1	6	
1962	7	7		3	4		4	3	
1963	2	11	1	2	5		0	6	1
1964	2	11	1	2	4	1	0	7	
1965	4	10		2	5		2	5	
1966	4	10		3	4		1	6	
1967	3	11		1	6		2	5	
1968	5	9		3	4		2	5	
1969	5	8	1	4	2	1	1	6	
1970	5	8	1	3	3	1	2	5	
1971	4	9	1	2	4	1	2	5	
1972	5	9		3	4		2	5	
1973	7	5	2	3	3	1	4	2	1
1974	7	6	1	3	3	1	4	3	
1975	6	8		5	2		1	6	
1976	9	5		6	1		3	4	
1977	12	2		6	1		6	1	
1978	10	6		6	2		4	4	
1979	10	6		6	2		4	4	
1980	8	8		4	4		4	4	
1981	10	6		8	0		2	6	
1982	2	7		1	4		1	3	
1983	9	7		6	2		3	5	
1984	13	3		7	1		6	2	
1985	11	5		6	2		5	3	
1986	11	5		7	1		4	4	
1987	10	4	1	7	1		3	3	1
1988	8	8		6	2		2	6	
1989	11	5		6	2		5	3	
1990	5	11		4	4		1	7	
1991	12	4		7	1		5	3	
1992	8	8		7	1		1	7	
1993	9	7		5	3		4	4	
1994	7	9		4	4		3	5	
1995	8	8		6	2		2	6	
1996	13	3		8	0		5	3	
1997	12	4		8	0		4	4	
1998	14	2		8	0		6	2	
1999	6	10		3	5		3	5	
2000	11	5		6	2		5	3	
2001	8	8		6	2		2	6	
2002	9	7		5	3		4	4	
2003	10	6		6	2		4	4	
2004	10	6		6	2		4	4	
2005	13	3		8	0		5	3	
2006	9	7		4	4		5	3	
2007	7	9		5	3		2	6	
2008	8	8		4	4		4	4	
2009	8	8		4	4		4	4	
2010	4	12		3	5		1	7	
	398	364	10	242	138	7	156	226	3

HOUSTON TEXANS

Season	All Games W	L	T	Home Games W	L	T	Road Games W	L	T
2002	4	12		2	6		2	6	
2003	5	11		3	5		2	6	
2004	7	9		3	5		4	4	
2005	2	14		2	6		0	8	
2006	6	10		4	4		2	6	
2007	8	8		6	2		2	6	
2008	8	8		6	2		2	6	
2009	9	7		4	4		5	3	
2010	6	10		4	4		2	6	
	55	89		34	38		21	51	

INDIANAPOLIS COLTS*

Season	All Games W	L	T	Home Games W	L	T	Road Games W	L	T
1953	3	9		2	4		1	5	
1954	3	9		2	4		1	5	
1955	5	6	1	4	1	1	1	5	
1956	5	7		4	2		1	5	
1957	7	5		4	2		3	3	
1958	9	3		6	0		3	3	
1959	9	3		4	2		5	1	
1960	6	6		4	2		2	4	
1961	8	6		5	2		3	4	
1962	7	7		3	4		4	3	

Season	All Games W	L	T	Home Games W	L	T	Road Games W	L	T
1963	8	6		4	3		4	3	
1964	12	2		7	1		5	1	
1965	10	3	1	5	2		5	1	1
1966	9	5		5	2		4	3	
1967	11	1	2	6	0	1	5	1	1
1968	13	1		6	1		7	0	
1969	8	5	1	4	2	1	4	3	
1970	11	2	1	5	1	1	6	1	
1971	10	4		5	2		5	2	
1972	5	9		2	5		3	4	
1973	4	10		3	4		1	6	
1974	2	12		0	7		2	5	
1975	10	4		5	2		5	2	
1976	11	3		6	1		5	2	
1977	10	4		6	1		4	3	
1978	5	11		2	6		3	5	
1979	5	11		3	5		2	6	
1980	7	9		2	6		5	3	
1981	2	14		1	7		1	7	
1982	0	8	1	0	3	1	0	5	
1983	7	9		3	5		4	4	
1984	4	12		2	6		2	6	
1985	5	11		4	4		1	7	
1986	3	13		1	7		2	6	
1987	9	6		4	4		5	2	
1988	9	7		6	2		3	5	
1989	8	8		6	2		2	6	
1990	7	9		3	5		4	4	
1991	1	15		0	8		1	7	
1992	9	7		4	4		5	3	
1993	4	12		2	6		2	6	
1994	8	8		5	3		3	5	
1995	9	7		5	3		4	4	
1996	9	7		6	2		3	5	
1997	3	13		2	6		1	7	
1998	3	13		3	5		0	8	
1999	13	3		7	1		6	2	
2000	10	6		6	2		4	4	
2001	6	10		3	5		3	5	
2002	10	6		5	3		5	3	
2003	12	4		5	3		7	1	
2004	12	4		7	1		5	3	
2005	14	2		7	1		7	1	
2006	12	4		8	0		4	4	
2007	13	3		6	2		7	1	
2008	12	4		6	2		6	2	
2009	14	2		7	1		7	1	
2010	10	6		6	2		4	4	
	451	396	7	244	179	5	207	217	2

*includes Baltimore Colts (1953-1983).

JACKSONVILLE JAGUARS

Season	All Games W	L	T	Home Games W	L	T	Road Games W	L	T
1995	4	12		2	6		2	6	
1996	9	7		7	1		2	6	
1997	11	5		7	1		4	4	
1998	11	5		7	1		4	4	
1999	14	2		7	1		7	1	
2000	7	9		4	4		3	5	
2001	6	10		3	5		3	5	
2002	6	10		3	5		3	5	
2003	5	11		5	3		0	8	
2004	9	7		4	4		5	3	
2005	12	4		6	2		6	2	
2006	8	8		6	2		2	6	
2007	11	5		6	2		5	3	
2008	5	11		2	6		3	5	
2009	7	9		5	3		2	6	
2010	8	8		5	3		3	5	
	133	123		79	49		54	74	

KANSAS CITY CHIEFS*

Season	All Games W	L	T	Home Games W	L	T	Road Games W	L	T
1960	8	6		5	2		3	4	
1961	6	8		4	3		2	5	
1962	11	3		6	1		5	2	
1963	5	7	2	4	3		1	4	2
1964	7	7		4	3		3	4	
1965	7	5	2	5	2		2	3	2
1966	11	2	1	4	2	1	7	0	
1967	9	5		4	3		5	2	
1968	12	2		6	1		6	1	
1969	11	3		6	1		5	2	
1970	7	5	2	4	1	2	3	4	
1971	10	3	1	7	0		3	3	1
1972	8	6		3	4		5	2	
1973	7	5	2	5	1	1	2	4	1
1974	5	9		1	6		4	3	
1975	5	9		3	4		2	5	
1976	5	9		1	6		4	3	
1977	2	12		1	6		1	6	
1978	4	12		3	5		1	7	
1979	7	9		3	5		4	4	
1980	8	8		3	5		5	3	
1981	9	7		5	3		4	4	
1982	3	6		2	2		1	4	
1983	6	10		5	3		1	7	
1984	8	8		5	3		3	5	
1985	6	10		5	3		1	7	
1986	10	6		6	2		4	4	
1987	4	11		3	4		1	7	
1988	4	11	1	4	4		0	7	1
1989	8	7	1	5	3		3	4	1
1990	11	5		6	2		5	3	
1991	10	6		6	2		4	4	
1992	10	6		7	1		3	5	
1993	11	5		7	1		4	4	
1994	9	7		5	3		4	4	
1995	13	3		8	0		5	3	
1996	9	7		5	3		4	4	
1997	13	3		8	0		5	3	
1998	7	9		5	3		2	6	
1999	9	7		6	2		3	5	
2000	7	9		5	3		2	6	
2001	6	10		3	5		3	5	
2002	8	8		6	2		2	6	
2003	13	3		8	0		5	3	
2004	7	9		4	4		3	5	
2005	10	6		7	1		3	5	
2006	9	7		6	2		3	5	
2007	4	12		2	6		2	6	
2008	2	14		1	7		1	7	
2009	4	12		1	7		3	5	
2010	10	6		7	1		3	5	
	395	365	12	235	146	4	160	219	8

*includes Dallas Texans (1960-62).

MIAMI DOLPHINS

Season	All Games W	L	T	Home Games W	L	T	Road Games W	L	T
1966	3	11		2	5		1	6	
1967	4	10		4	3		0	7	
1968	5	8	1	1	5	1	4	3	
1969	3	10	1	2	4	1	1	6	
1970	10	4		6	1		4	3	
1971	10	3	1	6	1		4	2	1

Season	All Games			Home Games			Road Games		
	W	L	T	W	L	T	W	L	T
1972	14	0		7	0		7	0	
1973	12	2		7	0		5	2	
1974	11	3		7	0		4	3	
1975	10	4		5	2		5	2	
1976	6	8		3	4		3	4	
1977	10	4		6	1		4	3	
1978	11	5		7	1		4	4	
1979	10	6		6	2		4	4	
1980	8	8		5	3		3	5	
1981	11	4	1	6	1	1	5	3	
1982	7	2		4	0		3	2	
1983	12	4		7	1		5	3	
1984	14	2		7	1		7	1	
1985	12	4		8	0		4	4	
1986	8	8		4	4		4	4	
1987	8	7		4	3		4	4	
1988	6	10		4	4		2	6	
1989	8	8		4	4		4	4	
1990	12	4		7	1		5	3	
1991	8	8		5	3		3	5	
1992	11	5		6	2		5	3	
1993	9	7		4	4		5	3	
1994	10	6		6	2		4	4	
1995	9	7		5	3		4	4	
1996	8	8		4	4		4	4	
1997	9	7		6	2		3	5	
1998	10	6		7	1		3	5	
1999	9	7		5	3		4	4	
2000	11	5		5	3		6	2	
2001	11	5		7	1		4	4	
2002	9	7		7	1		2	6	
2003	10	6		4	4		6	2	
2004	4	12		3	5		1	7	
2005	9	7		5	3		4	4	
2006	6	10		4	4		2	6	
2007	1	15		1	7		0	8	
2008	11	5		5	3		6	2	
2009	7	9		4	4		3	5	
2010	7	9		1	7		6	2	
	394	290	4	223	117	3	171	173	1

NEW ENGLAND PATRIOTS*

Season	All Games			Home Games			Road Games		
	W	L	T	W	L	T	W	L	T
1960	5	9		3	4		2	5	
1961	9	4	1	4	2	1	5	2	
1962	9	4	1	6	1		3	3	1
1963	7	6	1	5	1	1	2	5	
1964	10	3	1	4	2	1	6	1	
1965	4	8	2	1	4	2	3	4	
1966	8	4	2	4	2	1	4	2	1
1967	3	10	1	2	4		1	6	1
1968	4	10		2	5		2	5	
1969	4	10		2	5		2	5	
1970	2	12		1	6		1	6	
1971	6	8		5	2		1	6	
1972	3	11		2	5		1	6	
1973	5	9		3	4		2	5	
1974	7	7		3	4		4	3	
1975	3	11		2	5		1	6	
1976	11	3		6	1		5	2	
1977	9	5		6	1		3	4	
1978	11	5		5	3		6	2	
1979	9	7		6	2		3	5	
1980	10	6		6	2		4	4	
1981	2	14		2	6		0	8	
1982	5	4		3	1		2	3	
1983	8	8		5	3		3	5	
1984	9	7		5	3		4	4	
1985	11	5		7	1		4	4	
1986	11	5		4	4		7	1	
1987	8	7		5	3		3	4	
1988	9	7		7	1		2	6	
1989	5	11		3	5		2	6	
1990	1	15		0	8		1	7	
1991	6	10		4	4		2	6	
1992	2	14		1	7		1	7	
1993	5	11		3	5		2	6	
1994	10	6		5	3		5	3	
1995	6	10		3	5		3	5	
1996	11	5		6	2		5	3	
1997	10	6		6	2		4	4	
1998	9	7		6	2		3	5	
1999	8	8		5	3		3	5	
2000	5	11		3	5		2	6	
2001	11	5		6	2		5	3	
2002	9	7		5	3		4	4	
2003	14	2		8	0		6	2	
2004	14	2		8	0		6	2	
2005	10	6		5	3		5	3	
2006	12	4		5	3		7	1	
2007	16	0		8	0		8	0	
2008	11	5		5	3		6	2	
2009	10	6		8	0		2	6	
2010	14	2		8	0		6	2	
	401	362	9	227	152	6	174	210	3

*includes Boston Patriots (1960-1970).

NEW YORK JETS*

Season	All Games			Home Games			Road Games		
	W	L	T	W	L	T	W	L	T
1960	7	7		3	4		4	3	
1961	7	7		5	2		2	5	
1962	5	9		2	5		3	4	
1963	5	8	1	4	2	1	1	6	
1964	5	8	1	5	1	1	0	7	
1965	5	8	1	3	3	1	2	5	
1966	6	6	2	4	3		2	3	2
1967	8	5	1	4	2	1	4	3	
1968	11	3		6	1		5	2	
1969	10	4		5	2		5	2	
1970	4	10		2	5		2	5	
1971	6	8		4	3		2	5	
1972	7	7		4	3		3	4	
1973	4	10		2	4		2	6	
1974	7	7		3	4		4	3	
1975	3	11		1	6		2	5	
1976	3	11		2	5		1	6	
1977	3	11		1	6		2	5	
1978	8	8		4	4		4	4	
1979	8	8		6	2		2	6	
1980	4	12		2	6		2	6	
1981	10	5	1	6	2		4	3	1
1982	6	3		3	1		3	2	
1983	7	9		2	6		5	3	
1984	7	9		3	5		4	4	
1985	11	5		7	1		4	4	
1986	10	6		5	3		5	3	
1987	6	9		4	4		2	5	
1988	8	7	1	5	2	1	3	5	
1989	4	12		1	7		3	5	
1990	6	10		3	5		3	5	
1991	8	8		4	4		4	4	
1992	4	12		3	5		1	7	
1993	8	8		3	5		5	3	
1994	6	10		4	4		2	6	

Season	All Games W	L	T	Home Games W	L	T	Road Games W	L	T
1995	3	13		2	6		1	7	
1996	1	15		0	8		1	7	
1997	9	7		5	3		4	4	
1998	12	4		7	1		5	3	
1999	8	8		4	4		4	4	
2000	9	7		5	3		4	4	
2001	10	6		3	5		7	1	
2002	9	7		5	3		4	4	
2003	6	10		4	4		2	6	
2004	10	6		6	2		4	4	
2005	4	12		4	4		0	8	
2006	10	6		4	4		6	2	
2007	4	12		3	5		1	7	
2008	9	7		5	3		4	4	
2009	9	7		4	4		5	3	
2010	11	5		5	3		6	2	
	351	413	8	191	189	5	160	224	3

includes New York Titans (1960-62).

OAKLAND RAIDERS*

Season	All Games W	L	T	Home Games W	L	T	Road Games W	L	T
1960	6	8		3	4		3	4	
1961	2	12		1	6		1	6	
1962	1	13		1	6		0	7	
1963	10	4		6	1		4	3	
1964	5	7	2	5	2		0	5	2
1965	8	5	1	5	2		3	3	1
1966	8	5	1	3	3	1	5	2	
1967	13	1		7	0		6	1	
1968	12	2		6	1		6	1	
1969	12	1	1	7	0		5	1	1
1970	8	4	2	6	1		2	3	2
1971	8	4	2	5	1	1	3	3	1
1972	10	3	1	5	1	1	5	2	
1973	9	4	1	5	2		4	2	1
1974	12	2		6	1		6	1	
1975	11	3		6	1		5	2	
1976	13	1		7	0		6	1	
1977	11	3		6	1		5	2	
1978	9	7		4	4		5	3	
1979	9	7		6	2		3	5	
1980	11	5		6	2		5	3	
1981	7	9		4	4		3	5	
1982	8	1		4	0		4	1	
1983	12	4		6	2		6	2	
1984	11	5		6	2		5	3	
1985	12	4		7	1		5	3	
1986	8	8		3	5		5	3	
1987	5	10		3	5		2	5	
1988	7	9		3	5		4	4	
1989	8	8		7	1		1	7	
1990	12	4		6	2		6	2	
1991	9	7		5	3		4	4	
1992	7	9		5	3		2	6	
1993	10	6		5	3		5	3	
1994	9	7		4	4		5	3	
1995	8	8		4	4		4	4	
1996	7	9		4	4		3	5	
1997	4	12		2	6		2	6	
1998	8	8		4	4		4	4	
1999	8	8		5	3		3	5	
2000	12	4		7	1		5	3	
2001	10	6		5	3		5	3	
2002	11	5		6	2		5	3	
2003	4	12		4	4		0	8	
2004	5	11		3	5		2	6	
2005	4	12		2	6		2	6	

Season	All Games W	L	T	Home Games W	L	T	Road Games W	L	T
2006	2	14		2	6		0	8	
2007	4	12		2	6		2	6	
2008	5	11		4	4		1	7	
2009	5	11		2	6		3	5	
2010	8	8		5	3		3	5	
	418	343	11	235	148	3	183	195	8

includes Los Angeles Raiders (1982-1994).

PITTSBURGH STEELERS*

Season	All Games W	L	T	Home Games W	L	T	Road Games W	L	T
1933	3	6	2	2	3		1	3	2
1934	2	10		1	5		1	5	
1935	4	8		2	5		2	3	
1936	6	6		4	1		2	5	
1937	4	7		2	4		2	3	
1938	2	9		0	5		2	4	
1939	1	9	1	1	4		0	5	1
1940	2	7	2	1	2	2	1	5	
1941	1	9	1	1	4		0	5	1
1942	7	4		3	2		4	2	
1945	2	8		1	4		1	4	
1946	5	5	1	4	1		1	4	1
1947	8	4		5	1		3	3	
1948	4	8		4	2		0	6	
1949	6	5	1	3	2	1	3	3	
1950	6	6		2	4		4	2	
1951	4	7	1	1	4	1	3	3	
1952	5	7		2	4		3	3	
1953	6	6		3	3		3	3	
1954	5	7		4	2		1	5	
1955	4	8		3	2		1	6	
1956	5	7		3	3		2	4	
1957	6	6		4	2		2	4	
1958	7	4	1	5	1		2	3	1
1959	6	5	1	3	2	1	3	3	
1960	5	6	1	4	2		1	4	1
1961	6	8		4	3		2	5	
1962	9	5		4	3		5	2	
1963	7	4	3	5	0	2	2	4	1
1964	5	9		2	5		3	4	
1965	2	12		1	6		1	6	
1966	5	8	1	3	3	1	2	5	
1967	4	9	1	1	6		3	3	1
1968	2	11	1	1	6		1	5	1
1969	1	13		1	6		0	7	
1970	5	9		4	3		1	6	
1971	6	8		5	2		1	6	
1972	11	3		7	0		4	3	
1973	10	4		7	1		3	3	
1974	10	3	1	5	2		5	1	1
1975	12	2		6	1		6	1	
1976	10	4		6	1		4	3	
1977	9	5		6	1		3	4	
1978	14	2		7	1		7	1	
1979	12	4		8	0		4	4	
1980	9	7		6	2		3	5	
1981	8	8		5	3		3	5	
1982	6	3		4	0		2	3	
1983	10	6		4	4		6	2	
1984	9	7		6	2		3	5	
1985	7	9		5	3		2	6	
1986	6	10		4	4		2	6	
1987	8	7		4	3		4	4	
1988	5	11		4	4		1	7	
1989	9	7		4	4		5	3	
1990	9	7		6	2		3	5	
1991	7	9		5	3		2	6	

Season	All Games W	L	T	Home Games W	L	T	Road Games W	L	T
1992	11	5		7	1		4	4	
1993	9	7		6	2		3	5	
1994	12	4		7	1		5	3	
1995	11	5		6	2		5	3	
1996	10	6		7	1		3	5	
1997	11	5		7	1		4	4	
1998	7	9		5	3		2	6	
1999	6	10		2	6		4	4	
2000	9	7		4	4		5	3	
2001	13	3		7	1		6	2	
2002	10	5	1	5	2	1	5	3	
2003	6	10		4	4		2	6	
2004	15	1		8	0		7	1	
2005	11	5		5	3		6	2	
2006	8	8		5	3		3	5	
2007	10	6		7	1		3	5	
2008	12	4		6	2		6	2	
2009	9	7		6	2		3	5	
2010	12	4		5	3		7	1	
	541	499	20	317	200	9	224	299	11

*includes Pittsburgh Pirates (1933-39).

SAN DIEGO CHARGERS*

Season	All Games W	L	T	Home Games W	L	T	Road Games W	L	T
1960	10	4		5	2		5	2	
1961	12	2		6	1		6	1	
1962	4	10		3	4		1	6	
1963	11	3		6	1		5	2	
1964	8	5	1	4	3		4	2	1
1965	9	2	3	4	1	2	5	1	1
1966	7	6	1	5	2		2	4	1
1967	8	5	1	5	2	1	3	3	
1968	9	5		4	3		5	2	
1969	8	6		5	2		3	4	
1970	5	6	3	2	3	2	3	3	1
1971	6	8		6	1		0	7	
1972	4	9	1	2	5		2	4	1
1973	2	11	1	2	5		0	6	1
1974	5	9		3	4		2	5	
1975	2	12		1	6		1	6	
1976	6	8		3	4		3	4	
1977	7	7		3	4		4	3	
1978	9	7		5	3		4	4	
1979	12	4		7	1		5	3	
1980	11	5		6	2		5	3	
1981	10	6		5	3		5	3	
1982	6	3		3	1		3	2	
1983	6	10		4	4		2	6	
1984	7	9		4	4		3	5	
1985	8	8		6	2		2	6	
1986	4	12		2	6		2	6	
1987	8	7		4	3		4	4	
1988	6	10		3	5		3	5	
1989	6	10		4	4		2	6	
1990	6	10		3	5		3	5	
1991	4	12		3	5		1	7	
1992	11	5		6	2		5	3	
1993	8	8		4	4		4	4	
1994	11	5		5	3		6	2	
1995	9	7		5	3		4	4	
1996	8	8		5	3		3	5	
1997	4	12		2	6		2	6	
1998	5	11		4	4		1	7	
1999	8	8		4	4		4	4	
2000	1	15		1	7		0	8	
2001	5	11		4	4		1	7	
2002	8	8		5	3		3	5	
2003	4	12		2	6		2	6	
2004	12	4		7	1		5	3	
2005	9	7		4	4		5	3	
2006	14	2		8	0		6	2	
2007	11	5		7	1		4	4	
2008	8	8		5	3		3	5	
2009	13	3		6	2		7	1	
2010	9	7		6	2		3	5	
	384	377	11	218	163	5	166	214	6

*includes Los Angeles Chargers (1960).

TENNESSEE TITANS*

Season	All Games W	L	T	Home Games W	L	T	Road Games W	L	T
1960	10	4		6	1		4	3	
1961	10	3	1	6	1		4	2	1
1962	11	3		6	1		5	2	
1963	6	8		4	3		2	5	
1964	4	10		3	4		1	6	
1965	4	10		3	4		1	6	
1966	3	11		3	4		0	7	
1967	9	4	1	5	2		4	2	1
1968	7	7		3	4		4	3	
1969	6	6	2	4	2	1	2	4	1
1970	3	10	1	1	6		2	4	1
1971	4	9	1	3	3	1	1	6	
1972	1	13		1	6		0	7	
1973	1	13		0	7		1	6	
1974	7	7		3	4		4	3	
1975	10	4		5	2		5	2	
1976	5	9		3	4		2	5	
1977	8	6		5	2		3	4	
1978	10	6		5	3		5	3	
1979	11	5		6	2		5	3	
1980	11	5		6	2		5	3	
1981	7	9		5	3		2	6	
1982	1	8		1	4		0	4	
1983	2	14		2	6		0	8	
1984	3	13		2	6		1	7	
1985	5	11		4	4		1	7	
1986	5	11		4	4		1	7	
1987	9	6		5	2		4	4	
1988	10	6		7	1		3	5	
1989	9	7		6	2		3	5	
1990	9	7		6	2		3	5	
1991	11	5		7	1		4	4	
1992	10	6		5	3		5	3	
1993	12	4		7	1		5	3	
1994	2	14		2	6		0	8	
1995	7	9		3	5		4	4	
1996	8	8		2	6		6	2	
1997	8	8		6	2		2	6	
1998	8	8		3	5		5	3	
1999	13	3		8	0		5	3	
2000	13	3		7	1		6	2	
2001	7	9		3	5		4	4	
2002	11	5		6	2		5	3	
2003	12	4		7	1		5	3	
2004	5	11		2	6		3	5	
2005	4	12		3	5		1	7	
2006	8	8		4	4		4	4	
2007	10	6		5	3		5	3	
2008	13	3		7	1		6	2	
2009	8	8		5	3		3	5	
2010	6	10		3	5		3	5	
	377	389	6	218	166	2	159	223	4

*includes Houston (1960-1996) and Tennessee Oilers (1997-98).

NFC
ARIZONA CARDINALS*

Season	All Games W	L	T	Home Games W	L	T	Road Games W	L	T
1920	6	2	2	5	1	1	1	1	1
1921	3	3	2	3	3	1	0	0	1
1922	8	3		8	3		0	0	
1923	8	4		8	3		0	1	
1924	5	4	1	5	3	1	0	1	
1925	11	2	1	11	2		0	0	1
1926	5	6	1	3	3		2	3	1
1927	3	7	1	2	3	1	1	4	
1928	1	5		1	1		0	4	
1929	6	6	1	3	2		3	4	1
1930	5	6	2	3	2		2	4	2
1931	5	4		3	0		2	4	
1932	2	6	2	1	2	1	1	4	1
1933	1	9	1	0	4	1	1	5	
1934	5	6		2	2		3	4	
1935	6	4	2	2	2		4	2	2
1936	3	8	1	3	1	1	0	7	
1937	5	5	1	1	3		4	2	1
1938	2	9		1	4		1	5	
1939	1	10		0	4		1	6	
1940	2	7	2	2	1	1	0	6	1
1941	3	7	1	0	3	1	3	4	
1942	3	8		2	2		1	6	
1943	0	10		0	3		0	7	
1945	1	9		0	3		1	6	
1946	6	5		2	2		4	3	
1947	9	3		5	0		4	3	
1948	11	1		5	1		6	0	
1949	6	5	1	2	3	1	4	2	
1950	5	7		3	3		2	4	
1951	3	9		1	5		2	4	
1952	4	8		2	4		2	4	
1953	1	10	1	0	5	1	1	5	
1954	2	10		2	4		0	6	
1955	4	7	1	3	2	1	1	5	
1956	7	5		4	2		3	3	
1957	3	9		0	6		3	3	
1958	2	9	1	1	4	1	1	5	
1959	2	10		2	4		0	6	
1960	6	5	1	3	2	1	3	3	
1961	7	7		3	4		4	3	
1962	4	9	1	2	4	1	2	5	
1963	9	5		3	4		6	1	
1964	9	3	2	4	1	1	5	2	1
1965	5	9		2	5		3	4	
1966	8	5	1	5	1	1	3	4	
1967	6	7	1	3	3	1	3	4	
1968	9	4	1	4	2	1	5	2	
1969	4	9	1	3	4		1	5	1
1970	8	5	1	6	1		2	4	1
1971	4	9	1	1	5	1	3	4	
1972	4	9	1	2	5		2	4	1
1973	4	9	1	2	4	1	2	5	
1974	10	4		5	2		5	2	
1975	11	3		6	1		5	2	
1976	10	4		6	1		4	3	
1977	7	7		4	3		3	4	
1978	6	10		3	5		3	5	
1979	5	11		3	5		2	6	
1980	5	11		2	6		3	5	
1981	7	9		5	3		2	6	
1982	5	4		1	3		4	1	
1983	8	7	1	4	3	1	4	4	
1984	9	7		5	3		4	4	
1985	5	11		4	4		1	7	
1986	4	11	1	3	5		1	6	1
1987	7	8		4	3		3	5	
1988	7	9		4	4		3	5	
1989	5	11		2	6		3	5	
1990	5	11		3	5		2	6	
1991	4	12		2	6		2	6	
1992	4	12		3	5		1	7	
1993	7	9		4	4		3	5	
1994	8	8		5	3		3	5	
1995	4	12		3	5		1	7	
1996	7	9		5	3		2	6	
1997	4	12		3	5		1	7	
1998	9	7		5	3		4	4	
1999	6	10		4	4		2	6	
2000	3	13		3	5		0	8	
2001	7	9		3	5		4	4	
2002	5	11		3	5		2	6	
2003	4	12		4	4		0	8	
2004	6	10		5	3		1	7	
2005	5	11		3	5		2	6	
2006	5	11		3	5		2	6	
2007	8	8		6	2		2	6	
2008	9	7		6	2		3	5	
2009	10	6		4	4		6	2	
2010	5	11		4	4		1	7	
	488	681	39	286	294	22	202	387	17

*includes Chicago Cardinals (1920-1959), St. Louis Cardinals (1960-1987), and Phoenix Cardinals (1988-1993).

ATLANTA FALCONS

Season	All Games W	L	T	Home Games W	L	T	Road Games W	L	T
1966	3	11		1	6		2	5	
1967	1	12	1	1	5	1	0	7	
1968	2	12		1	6		1	6	
1969	6	8		4	3		2	5	
1970	4	8	2	3	4		1	4	2
1971	7	6	1	4	3		3	3	1
1972	7	7		4	3		3	4	
1973	9	5		4	3		5	2	
1974	3	11		2	5		1	6	
1975	4	10		3	4		1	6	
1976	4	10		3	4		1	6	
1977	7	7		4	3		3	4	
1978	9	7		7	1		2	6	
1979	6	10		3	5		3	5	
1980	12	4		6	2		6	2	
1981	7	9		4	4		3	5	
1982	5	4		2	3		3	1	
1983	7	9		4	4		3	5	
1984	4	12		2	6		2	6	
1985	4	12		3	5		1	7	
1986	7	8	1	2	5	1	5	3	
1987	3	12		2	6		1	6	
1988	5	11		2	6		3	5	
1989	3	13		3	5		0	8	
1990	5	11		5	3		0	8	
1991	10	6		6	2		4	4	
1992	6	10		5	3		1	7	
1993	6	10		4	4		2	6	
1994	7	9		5	3		2	6	
1995	9	7		7	1		2	6	
1996	3	13		2	6		1	7	
1997	7	9		3	5		4	4	
1998	14	2		8	0		6	2	
1999	5	11		4	4		1	7	
2000	4	12		3	5		1	7	
2001	7	9		3	5		4	4	
2002	9	6	1	5	3		4	3	1

Season	All Games W	L	T	Home Games W	L	T	Road Games W	L	T
2003	5	11		2	6		3	5	
2004	11	5		7	1		4	4	
2005	8	8		4	4		4	4	
2006	7	9		3	5		4	4	
2007	4	12		3	5		1	7	
2008	11	5		7	1		4	4	
2009	9	7		6	2		3	5	
2010	13	3		7	1		6	2	
	289	393	6	173	170	2	116	223	4

CAROLINA PANTHERS

Season	All Games W	L	T	Home Games W	L	T	Road Games W	L	T
1995	7	9		5	3		2	6	
1996	12	4		8	0		4	4	
1997	7	9		2	6		5	3	
1998	4	12		2	6		2	6	
1999	8	8		5	3		3	5	
2000	7	9		5	3		2	6	
2001	1	15		0	8		1	7	
2002	7	9		4	4		3	5	
2003	11	5		6	2		5	3	
2004	7	9		3	5		4	4	
2005	11	5		5	3		6	2	
2006	8	8		4	4		4	4	
2007	7	9		2	6		5	3	
2008	12	4		8	0		4	4	
2009	8	8		5	3		3	5	
2010	2	14		2	6		0	8	
	119	137		66	62		53	75	

CHICAGO BEARS*

Season	All Games W	L	T	Home Games W	L	T	Road Games W	L	T
1920	10	1	2	6	0	1	4	1	1
1921	9	1	1	9	1	1	0	0	
1922	9	3		7	1		2	2	
1923	9	2	1	7	1	1	2	1	
1924	6	1	4	5	0	3	1	1	1
1925	9	5	3	7	1	1	2	4	2
1926	12	1	3	10	0	2	2	1	1
1927	9	3	2	7	1	1	2	2	1
1928	7	5	1	6	3		1	2	1
1929	4	9	2	1	5	2	3	4	
1930	9	4	1	5	2	1	4	2	
1931	8	5		6	3		2	2	
1932	7	1	6	6	1	1	1	0	5
1933	10	2	1	6	0		4	2	1
1934	13	0		5	0		8	0	
1935	6	4	2	1	2	2	5	2	
1936	9	3		3	1		6	2	
1937	9	1	1	4	1		5	0	1
1938	6	5		2	3		4	2	
1939	8	3		4	1		4	2	
1940	8	3		5	0		3	3	
1941	10	1		5	1		5	0	
1942	11	0		6	0		5	0	
1943	8	1	1	5	0		3	1	1
1944	6	3	1	4	0	1	2	3	
1945	3	7		2	3		1	4	
1946	8	2	1	4	1	1	4	1	
1947	8	4		4	2		4	2	
1948	10	2		5	1		5	1	
1949	9	3		5	1		4	2	
1950	9	3		6	0		3	3	
1951	7	5		3	3		4	2	
1952	5	7		3	3		2	4	
1953	3	8	1	1	4	1	2	4	
1954	8	4		4	2		4	2	
1955	8	4		5	1		3	3	
1956	9	2	1	6	0		3	2	1
1957	5	7		2	4		3	3	
1958	8	4		5	1		3	3	
1959	8	4		4	2		4	2	
1960	5	6	1	4	2		1	4	1
1961	8	6		5	2		3	4	
1962	9	5		4	3		5	2	
1963	11	1	2	6	0	1	5	1	1
1964	5	9		2	5		3	4	
1965	9	5		5	2		4	3	
1966	5	7	2	4	1	2	1	6	
1967	7	6	1	3	3	1	4	3	
1968	7	7		2	5		5	2	
1969	1	13		1	6		0	7	
1970	6	8		3	4		3	4	
1971	6	8		4	3		2	5	
1972	4	9	1	1	5	1	3	4	
1973	3	11		1	6		2	5	
1974	4	10		4	3		0	7	
1975	4	10		3	4		1	6	
1976	7	7		4	3		3	4	
1977	9	5		5	2		4	3	
1978	7	9		4	4		3	5	
1979	10	6		6	2		4	4	
1980	7	9		5	3		2	6	
1981	6	10		4	4		2	6	
1982	3	6		2	2		1	4	
1983	8	8		5	3		3	5	
1984	10	6		6	2		4	4	
1985	15	1		8	0		7	1	
1986	14	2		7	1		7	1	
1987	11	4		6	2		5	2	
1988	12	4		7	1		5	3	
1989	6	10		4	4		2	6	
1990	11	5		7	1		4	4	
1991	11	5		6	2		5	3	
1992	5	11		4	4		1	7	
1993	7	9		3	5		4	4	
1994	9	7		5	3		4	4	
1995	9	7		5	3		4	4	
1996	7	9		6	2		1	7	
1997	4	12		2	6		2	6	
1998	4	12		3	5		1	7	
1999	6	10		3	5		3	5	
2000	5	11		3	5		2	6	
2001	13	3		7	1		6	2	
2002	4	12		3	5		1	7	
2003	7	9		6	2		1	7	
2004	5	11		2	6		3	5	
2005	11	5		7	1		4	4	
2006	13	3		6	2		7	1	
2007	7	9		4	4		3	5	
2008	9	7		6	2		3	5	
2009	7	9		5	3		2	6	
2010	11	5		5	3		6	2	
	704	512	42	414	213	24	290	299	18

*includes Decatur Staleys (1920) and Chicago Staleys (1921).

DALLAS COWBOYS

Season	All Games W	L	T	Home Games W	L	T	Road Games W	L	T
1960	0	11	1	0	6		0	5	1
1961	4	9	1	2	4	1	2	5	
1962	5	8	1	2	4	1	3	4	
1963	4	10		3	4		1	6	
1964	5	8	1	2	4	1	3	4	

Season	All Games W	L	T	Home Games W	L	T	Road Games W	L	T
1965	7	7		5	2		2	5	
1966	10	3	1	6	1		4	2	1
1967	9	5		5	2		4	3	
1968	12	2		5	2		7	0	
1969	11	2	1	6	0	1	5	2	
1970	10	4		6	1		4	3	
1971	11	3		6	1		5	2	
1972	10	4		5	2		5	2	
1973	10	4		6	1		4	3	
1974	8	6		5	2		3	4	
1975	10	4		5	2		5	2	
1976	11	3		6	1		5	2	
1977	12	2		6	1		6	1	
1978	12	4		7	1		5	3	
1979	11	5		6	2		5	3	
1980	12	4		8	0		4	4	
1981	12	4		8	0		4	4	
1982	6	3		3	2		3	1	
1983	12	4		6	2		6	2	
1984	9	7		5	3		4	4	
1985	10	6		7	1		3	5	
1986	7	9		3	5		4	4	
1987	7	8		3	4		4	4	
1988	3	13		1	7		2	6	
1989	1	15		0	8		1	7	
1990	7	9		5	3		2	6	
1991	11	5		6	2		5	3	
1992	13	3		7	1		6	2	
1993	12	4		6	2		6	2	
1994	12	4		6	2		6	2	
1995	12	4		6	2		6	2	
1996	10	6		6	2		4	4	
1997	6	10		5	3		1	7	
1998	10	6		6	2		4	4	
1999	8	8		7	1		1	7	
2000	5	11		3	5		2	6	
2001	5	11		4	4		1	7	
2002	5	11		4	4		1	7	
2003	10	6		6	2		4	4	
2004	6	10		4	4		2	6	
2005	9	7		5	3		4	4	
2006	9	7		4	4		5	3	
2007	13	3		6	2		7	1	
2008	9	7		6	2		3	5	
2009	11	5		6	2		5	3	
2010	6	10		2	6		4	4	
	440	324	6	248	133	4	192	191	2

DETROIT LIONS*

Season	All Games W	L	T	Home Games W	L	T	Road Games W	L	T
1930	5	6	3	5	1	2	0	5	1
1931	11	3		8	0		3	3	
1932	6	2	4	3	0	2	3	2	2
1933	6	5		4	1		2	4	
1934	10	3		6	2		4	1	
1935	7	3	2	5	0	1	2	3	1
1936	8	4		5	1		3	3	
1937	7	4		4	2		3	2	
1938	7	4		4	3		3	1	
1939	6	5		4	2		2	3	
1940	5	5	1	3	3		2	2	1
1941	4	6	1	3	2		1	4	1
1942	0	11		0	7		0	4	
1943	3	6	1	2	2	1	1	4	
1944	6	3	1	4	2		2	1	1
1945	7	3		4	1		3	2	
1946	1	10		1	5		0	5	

Season	All Games W	L	T	Home Games W	L	T	Road Games W	L	T
1947	3	9		2	4		1	5	
1948	2	10		2	4		0	6	
1949	4	8		2	4		2	4	
1950	6	6		4	2		2	4	
1951	7	4	1	3	3	1	4	1	
1952	9	3		6	1		3	2	
1953	10	2		5	1		5	1	
1954	9	2	1	5	0	1	4	2	
1955	3	9		3	4		0	5	
1956	9	3		5	1		4	2	
1957	8	4		5	1		3	3	
1958	4	7	1	2	4		2	3	1
1959	3	8	1	2	4		1	4	1
1960	7	5		5	1		2	4	
1961	8	5	1	2	5		6	0	1
1962	11	3		7	0		4	3	
1963	5	8	1	3	3	1	2	5	
1964	7	5	2	3	3	1	4	2	1
1965	6	7	1	2	4	1	4	3	
1966	4	9	1	3	4		1	5	1
1967	5	7	2	3	4		2	3	2
1968	4	8	2	1	4	2	3	4	
1969	9	4	1	5	2		4	2	1
1970	10	4		6	1		4	3	
1971	7	6	1	3	4		4	2	1
1972	8	5	1	5	2		3	3	1
1973	6	7	1	4	3		2	4	1
1974	7	7		5	2		2	5	
1975	7	7		4	3		3	4	
1976	6	8		5	2		1	6	
1977	6	8		5	2		1	6	
1978	7	9		5	3		2	6	
1979	2	14		2	6		0	8	
1980	9	7		6	2		3	5	
1981	8	8		7	1		1	7	
1982	4	5		2	3		2	2	
1983	9	7		6	2		3	5	
1984	4	11	1	2	5	1	2	6	
1985	7	9		6	2		1	7	
1986	5	11		1	7		4	4	
1987	4	11		1	6		3	5	
1988	4	12		2	6		2	6	
1989	7	9		4	4		3	5	
1990	6	10		3	5		3	5	
1991	12	4		8	0		4	4	
1992	5	11		3	5		2	6	
1993	10	6		5	3		5	3	
1994	9	7		6	2		3	5	
1995	10	6		7	1		3	5	
1996	5	11		4	4		1	7	
1997	9	7		6	2		3	5	
1998	5	11		4	4		1	7	
1999	8	8		6	2		2	6	
2000	9	7		4	4		5	3	
2001	2	14		2	6		0	8	
2002	3	13		3	5		0	8	
2003	5	11		5	3		0	8	
2004	6	10		3	5		3	5	
2005	5	11		3	5		2	6	
2006	3	13		2	6		1	7	
2007	7	9		5	3		2	6	
2008	0	16		0	8		0	8	
2009	2	14		2	6		0	8	
2010	6	10		4	4		2	6	
	496	593	32	311	246	14	185	347	18

*includes Portsmouth Spartans (1930-33).

GREEN BAY PACKERS

Season	All Games W	L	T	Home Games W	L	T	Road Games W	L	T
1921	3	2	1	2	1		1	1	1
1922	4	3	3	4	1	1	0	2	2
1923	7	2	1	4	2	1	3	0	
1924	7	4		5	0		2	4	
1925	8	5		6	0		2	5	
1926	7	3	3	4	1	2	3	2	1
1927	7	2	1	6	1		1	1	1
1928	6	4	3	2	2	2	4	2	1
1929	12	0	1	5	0		7	0	1
1930	10	3	1	6	0		4	3	1
1931	12	2		8	0		4	2	
1932	10	3	1	5	0	1	5	3	
1933	5	7	1	3	2	1	2	5	
1934	7	6		4	2		3	4	
1935	8	4		5	2		3	2	
1936	10	1	1	5	1		5	0	1
1937	7	4		3	2		4	2	
1938	8	3		4	2		4	1	
1939	9	2		4	1		5	1	
1940	6	4	1	4	2		2	2	1
1941	10	1		4	1		6	0	
1942	8	2	1	4	1		4	1	1
1943	7	2	1	2	1	1	5	1	
1944	8	2		5	0		3	2	
1945	6	4		4	1		2	3	
1946	6	5		2	3		4	2	
1947	6	5	1	4	2		2	3	1
1948	3	9		2	4		1	5	
1949	2	10		1	5		1	5	
1950	3	9		3	3		0	6	
1951	3	9		2	4		1	5	
1952	6	6		3	3		3	3	
1953	2	9	1	1	5		1	4	1
1954	4	8		2	4		2	4	
1955	6	6		5	1		1	5	
1956	4	8		2	4		2	4	
1957	3	9		1	5		2	4	
1958	1	10	1	1	4	1	0	6	
1959	7	5		4	2		3	3	
1960	8	4		4	2		4	2	
1961	11	3		6	1		5	2	
1962	13	1		7	0		6	1	
1963	11	2	1	6	1		5	1	1
1964	8	5	1	4	3		4	2	1
1965	10	3	1	6	1		4	2	1
1966	12	2		6	1		6	1	
1967	9	4	1	4	2	1	5	2	
1968	6	7	1	2	5		4	2	1
1969	8	6		5	2		3	4	
1970	6	8		4	3		2	5	
1971	4	8	2	3	3	1	1	5	1
1972	10	4		4	3		6	1	
1973	5	7	2	3	2	2	2	5	
1974	6	8		4	3		2	5	
1975	4	10		3	4		1	6	
1976	5	9		4	3		1	6	
1977	4	10		2	5		2	5	
1978	8	7	1	5	2	1	3	5	
1979	5	11		4	4		1	7	
1980	5	10	1	4	4		1	6	1
1981	8	8		4	4		4	4	
1982	5	3	1	3	1		2	2	1
1983	8	8		5	3		3	5	
1984	8	8		5	3		3	5	
1985	8	8		5	3		3	5	
1986	4	12		1	7		3	5	
1987	5	9	1	2	5	1	3	4	
1988	4	12		2	6		2	6	
1989	10	6		6	2		4	4	
1990	6	10		3	5		3	5	
1991	4	12		2	6		2	6	
1992	9	7		6	2		3	5	
1993	9	7		6	2		3	5	
1994	9	7		7	1		2	6	
1995	11	5		7	1		4	4	
1996	13	3		8	0		5	3	
1997	13	3		8	0		5	3	
1998	11	5		7	1		4	4	
1999	8	8		5	3		3	5	
2000	9	7		6	2		3	5	
2001	12	4		7	1		5	3	
2002	12	4		8	0		4	4	
2003	10	6		5	3		5	3	
2004	10	6		4	4		6	2	
2005	4	12		3	5		1	7	
2006	8	8		3	5		5	3	
2007	13	3		7	1		6	2	
2008	6	10		4	4		2	6	
2009	11	5		6	2		5	3	
2010	10	6		7	1		3	5	
	664	524	36	383	212	16	281	312	20

MINNESOTA VIKINGS

Season	All Games W	L	T	Home Games W	L	T	Road Games W	L	T
1961	3	11		3	4		0	7	
1962	2	11	1	1	5	1	1	6	
1963	5	8	1	3	4		2	4	1
1964	8	5	1	4	3		4	2	1
1965	7	7		2	5		5	2	
1966	4	9	1	2	5		2	4	1
1967	3	8	3	1	4	2	2	4	1
1968	8	6		4	3		4	3	
1969	12	2		7	0		5	2	
1970	12	2		7	0		5	2	
1971	11	3		5	2		6	1	
1972	7	7		3	4		4	3	
1973	12	2		7	0		5	2	
1974	10	4		4	3		6	1	
1975	12	2		7	0		5	2	
1976	11	2	1	6	0	1	5	2	
1977	9	5		5	2		4	3	
1978	8	7	1	5	3		3	4	1
1979	7	9		5	3		2	6	
1980	9	7		5	3		4	4	
1981	7	9		5	3		2	6	
1982	5	4		4	1		1	3	
1983	8	8		3	5		5	3	
1984	3	13		2	6		1	7	
1985	7	9		4	4		3	5	
1986	9	7		5	3		4	4	
1987	8	7		5	3		3	4	
1988	11	5		7	1		4	4	
1989	10	6		8	0		2	6	
1990	6	10		4	4		2	6	
1991	8	8		4	4		4	4	
1992	11	5		5	3		6	2	
1993	9	7		4	4		5	3	
1994	10	6		6	2		4	4	
1995	8	8		6	2		2	6	
1996	9	7		5	3		4	4	
1997	9	7		5	3		4	4	
1998	15	1		8	0		7	1	
1999	10	6		6	2		4	4	
2000	11	5		7	1		4	4	

Season	All Games W	L	T	Home Games W	L	T	Road Games W	L	T
2001	5	11		5	3		0	8	
2002	6	10		4	4		2	6	
2003	9	7		6	2		3	5	
2004	8	8		5	3		3	5	
2005	9	7		6	2		3	5	
2006	6	10		3	5		3	5	
2007	8	8		5	3		3	5	
2008	10	6		6	2		4	4	
2009	12	4		8	0		4	4	
2010	6	10		4	4		2	6	
	413	336	9	241	135	4	172	201	5

NEW ORLEANS SAINTS

Season	All Games W	L	T	Home Games W	L	T	Road Games W	L	T
1967	3	11		2	5		1	6	
1968	4	9	1	3	4		1	5	1
1969	5	9		3	4		2	5	
1970	2	11	1	2	5		0	6	1
1971	4	8	2	2	4	1	2	4	1
1972	2	11	1	2	5		0	6	1
1973	5	9		5	2		0	7	
1974	5	9		4	3		1	6	
1975	2	12		2	5		0	7	
1976	4	10		2	5		2	5	
1977	3	11		2	5		1	6	
1978	7	9		3	5		4	4	
1979	8	8		3	5		5	3	
1980	1	15		0	8		1	7	
1981	4	12		2	6		2	6	
1982	4	5		2	3		2	2	
1983	8	8		5	3		3	5	
1984	7	9		3	5		4	4	
1985	5	11		3	5		2	6	
1986	7	9		4	4		3	5	
1987	12	3		6	1		6	2	
1988	10	6		5	3		5	3	
1989	9	7		5	3		4	4	
1990	8	8		5	3		3	5	
1991	11	5		6	2		5	3	
1992	12	4		6	2		6	2	
1993	8	8		4	4		4	4	
1994	7	9		3	5		4	4	
1995	7	9		4	4		3	5	
1996	3	13		2	6		1	7	
1997	6	10		3	5		3	5	
1998	6	10		4	4		2	6	
1999	3	13		3	5		0	8	
2000	10	6		3	5		7	1	
2001	7	9		3	5		4	4	
2002	9	7		4	4		5	3	
2003	8	8		5	3		3	5	
2004	8	8		3	5		5	3	
2005	3	13		1	7		2	6	
2006	10	6		4	4		6	2	
2007	7	9		3	5		4	4	
2008	8	8		6	2		2	6	
2009	13	3		6	2		7	1	
2010	11	5		5	3		6	2	
	286	383	5	153	183	1	133	200	4

NEW YORK GIANTS

Season	All Games W	L	T	Home Games W	L	T	Road Games W	L	T
1925	8	4		7	2		1	2	
1926	8	4	1	5	2	1	3	2	
1927	11	1	1	7	1		4	0	1
1928	4	7	2	1	2	2	3	5	
1929	13	1	1	7	1		6	0	1
1930	13	4		6	2		7	2	
1931	7	6	1	4	2	1	3	4	
1932	4	6	2	3	2	1	1	4	1
1933	11	3		7	0		4	3	
1934	8	5		5	1		3	4	
1935	9	3		4	2		5	1	
1936	5	6	1	3	3	1	2	3	
1937	6	3	2	4	2	1	2	1	1
1938	8	2	1	6	1		2	1	1
1939	9	1	1	6	0		3	1	1
1940	6	4	1	4	3		2	1	1
1941	8	3		5	2		3	1	
1942	5	5	1	3	2	1	2	3	
1943	6	3	1	4	2		2	1	1
1944	8	1	1	5	1		3	0	1
1945	3	6	1	2	4		1	2	1
1946	7	3	1	5	1	1	2	2	
1947	2	8	2	2	3	1	0	5	1
1948	4	8		2	4		2	4	
1949	6	6		2	4		4	2	
1950	10	2		5	1		5	1	
1951	9	2	1	5	1		4	1	1
1952	7	5		2	4		5	1	
1953	3	9		2	4		1	5	
1954	7	5		4	2		3	3	
1955	6	5	1	4	1	1	2	4	
1956	8	3	1	4	1	1	4	2	
1957	7	5		3	3		4	2	
1958	9	3		5	1		4	2	
1959	10	2		5	1		5	1	
1960	6	4	2	1	3	2	5	1	
1961	10	3	1	4	2	1	6	1	
1962	12	2		6	1		6	1	
1963	11	3		5	2		6	1	
1964	2	10	2	2	5		0	5	2
1965	7	7		3	4		4	3	
1966	1	12	1	1	6		0	6	1
1967	7	7		5	2		2	5	
1968	7	7		3	4		4	3	
1969	6	8		5	2		1	6	
1970	9	5		5	2		4	3	
1971	4	10		1	6		3	4	
1972	8	6		4	3		4	3	
1973	2	11	1	2	4	1	0	7	
1974	2	12		0	7		2	5	
1975	5	9		2	5		3	4	
1976	3	11		3	4		0	7	
1977	5	9		3	4		2	5	
1978	6	10		5	3		1	7	
1979	6	10		4	4		2	6	
1980	4	12		2	6		2	6	
1981	9	7		4	4		5	3	
1982	4	5		2	3		2	2	
1983	3	12	1	1	7		2	5	1
1984	9	7		6	2		3	5	
1985	10	6		6	2		4	4	
1986	14	2		8	0		6	2	
1987	6	9		5	3		1	6	
1988	10	6		5	3		5	3	
1989	12	4		7	1		5	3	
1990	13	3		7	1		6	2	
1991	8	8		5	3		3	5	
1992	6	10		4	4		2	6	
1993	11	5		6	2		5	3	
1994	9	7		4	4		5	3	
1995	5	11		3	5		2	6	
1996	6	10		3	5		3	5	

Season	All Games W	L	T	Home Games W	L	T	Road Games W	L	T
1997	10	5	1	6	2		4	3	1
1998	8	8		5	3		3	5	
1999	7	9		4	4		3	5	
2000	12	4		5	3		7	1	
2001	7	9		5	3		2	6	
2002	10	6		5	3		5	3	
2003	4	12		1	7		3	5	
2004	6	10		3	5		3	5	
2005	11	5		7	1		4	4	
2006	8	8		3	5		5	3	
2007	10	6		3	5		7	1	
2008	12	4		7	1		5	3	
2009	8	8		4	4		4	4	
2010	10	6		5	3		5	3	
	636	524	33	353	245	16	283	279	17

PHILADELPHIA EAGLES

Season	All Games W	L	T	Home Games W	L	T	Road Games W	L	T
1933	3	5	1	2	3	1	1	2	
1934	4	7		2	4		2	3	
1935	2	9		0	5		2	4	
1936	1	11		1	6		0	5	
1937	2	8	1	0	5	1	2	3	
1938	5	6		2	3		3	3	
1939	1	9	1	1	3	1	0	6	
1940	1	10		1	4		0	6	
1941	2	8	1	1	4	1	1	4	
1942	2	9		0	5		2	4	
1944	7	1	2	3	1	2	4	0	
1945	7	3		6	0		1	3	
1946	6	5		3	2		3	3	
1947	8	4		6	1		2	3	
1948	9	2	1	6	0		3	2	1
1949	11	1		6	0		5	1	
1950	6	6		2	4		4	2	
1951	4	8		1	5		3	3	
1952	7	5		4	2		3	3	
1953	7	4	1	5	0	1	2	4	
1954	7	4	1	5	1		2	3	1
1955	4	7	1	4	2		0	5	1
1956	3	8	1	2	3	1	1	5	
1957	4	8		3	3		1	5	
1958	2	9	1	2	4		0	5	1
1959	7	5		5	1		2	4	
1960	10	2		5	1		5	1	
1961	10	4		5	2		5	2	
1962	3	10	1	2	5		1	5	1
1963	2	10	2	1	5	1	1	5	1
1964	6	8		3	4		3	4	
1965	5	9		2	5		3	4	
1966	9	5		5	2		4	3	
1967	6	7	1	5	2		1	5	1
1968	2	12		1	6		1	6	
1969	4	9	1	2	5		2	4	1
1970	3	10	1	3	3	1	0	7	
1971	6	7	1	3	4		3	3	1
1972	2	11	1	0	6	1	2	5	
1973	5	8	1	4	3		1	5	1
1974	7	7		5	2		2	5	
1975	4	10		2	5		2	5	
1976	4	10		2	5		2	5	
1977	5	9		4	3		1	6	
1978	9	7		5	3		4	4	
1979	11	5		5	3		6	2	
1980	12	4		7	1		5	3	
1981	10	6		6	2		4	4	
1982	3	6		1	4		2	2	

Season	All Games W	L	T	Home Games W	L	T	Road Games W	L	T
1983	5	11		1	7		4	4	
1984	6	9	1	5	3		1	6	1
1985	7	9		4	4		3	5	
1986	5	10	1	2	5	1	3	5	
1987	7	8		4	4		3	4	
1988	10	6		5	3		5	3	
1989	11	5		6	2		5	3	
1990	10	6		6	2		4	4	
1991	10	6		4	4		6	2	
1992	11	5		8	0		3	5	
1993	8	8		3	5		5	3	
1994	7	9		5	3		2	6	
1995	10	6		6	2		4	4	
1996	10	6		5	3		5	3	
1997	6	9	1	6	2		0	7	1
1998	3	13		3	5		0	8	
1999	5	11		4	4		1	7	
2000	11	5		5	3		6	2	
2001	11	5		4	4		7	1	
2002	12	4		7	1		5	3	
2003	12	4		5	3		7	1	
2004	13	3		7	1		6	2	
2005	6	10		4	4		2	6	
2006	10	6		5	3		5	3	
2007	8	8		3	5		5	3	
2008	9	6	1	6	2		3	4	1
2009	11	5		6	2		5	3	
2010	10	6		4	4		6	2	
	504	537	25	284	242	12	220	295	13

ST. LOUIS RAMS*

Season	All Games W	L	T	Home Games W	L	T	Road Games W	L	T
1937	1	10		0	5		1	5	
1938	4	7		2	2		2	5	
1939	5	5	1	3	2	1	2	3	
1940	4	6	1	3	1	1	1	5	
1941	2	9		1	4		1	5	
1942	5	6		3	2		2	4	
1944	4	6		1	2		3	4	
1945	9	1		4	0		5	1	
1946	6	4	1	3	2		3	2	1
1947	6	6		3	3		3	3	
1948	6	5	1	3	2	1	3	3	
1949	8	2	2	5	1		3	1	2
1950	9	3		5	1		4	2	
1951	8	4		5	2		3	2	
1952	9	3		5	1		4	2	
1953	8	3	1	5	1		3	2	1
1954	6	5	1	3	2	1	3	3	
1955	8	3	1	5	1		3	2	1
1956	4	8		4	2		0	6	
1957	6	6		5	1		1	5	
1958	8	4		4	2		4	2	
1959	2	10		0	6		2	4	
1960	4	7	1	2	3	1	2	4	
1961	4	10		4	3		0	7	
1962	1	12	1	0	7		1	5	1
1963	5	9		3	4		2	5	
1964	5	7	2	3	2	2	2	5	
1965	4	10		3	4		1	6	
1966	8	6		5	2		3	4	
1967	11	1	2	5	1	1	6	0	1
1968	10	3	1	5	2		5	1	1
1969	11	3		5	2		6	1	
1970	9	4	1	3	3	1	6	1	
1971	8	5	1	4	2	1	4	3	
1972	6	7	1	4	3		2	4	1

Season	All Games W	L	T	Home Games W	L	T	Road Games W	L	T
1973	12	2		7	0		5	2	
1974	10	4		6	1		4	3	
1975	12	2		6	1		6	1	
1976	10	3	1	5	2		5	1	1
1977	10	4		7	0		3	4	
1978	12	4		6	2		6	2	
1979	9	7		4	4		5	3	
1980	11	5		6	2		5	3	
1981	6	10		4	4		2	6	
1982	2	7		1	4		1	3	
1983	9	7		5	3		4	4	
1984	10	6		5	3		5	3	
1985	11	5		6	2		5	3	
1986	10	6		6	2		4	4	
1987	6	9		3	4		3	5	
1988	10	6		4	4		6	2	
1989	11	5		6	2		5	3	
1990	5	11		2	6		3	5	
1991	3	13		2	6		1	7	
1992	6	10		4	4		2	6	
1993	5	11		3	5		2	6	
1994	4	12		3	5		1	7	
1995	7	9		4	4		3	5	
1996	6	10		4	4		2	6	
1997	5	11		2	6		3	5	
1998	4	12		2	6		2	6	
1999	13	3		8	0		5	3	
2000	10	6		5	3		5	3	
2001	14	2		6	2		8	0	
2002	7	9		6	2		1	7	
2003	12	4		8	0		4	4	
2004	8	8		6	2		2	6	
2005	6	10		3	5		3	5	
2006	8	8		4	4		4	4	
2007	3	13		1	7		2	6	
2008	2	14		1	7		1	7	
2009	1	15		0	8		1	7	
2010	7	9		5	3		2	6	
	511	492	20	284	212	10	227	280	10

*includes Cleveland Rams (1937-1942, 1944-45) and Los Angeles Rams (1946-1994).

Season	All Games W	L	T	Home Games W	L	T	Road Games W	L	T
1973	5	9		3	4		2	5	
1974	6	8		3	4		3	4	
1975	5	9		2	5		3	4	
1976	8	6		4	3		4	3	
1977	5	9		3	4		2	5	
1978	2	14		2	6		0	8	
1979	2	14		2	6		0	8	
1980	6	10		4	4		2	6	
1981	13	3		7	1		6	2	
1982	3	6		0	5		3	1	
1983	10	6		4	4		6	2	
1984	15	1		7	1		8	0	
1985	10	6		5	3		5	3	
1986	10	5	1	6	2		4	3	1
1987	13	2		6	1		7	1	
1988	10	6		4	4		6	2	
1989	14	2		6	2		8	0	
1990	14	2		6	2		8	0	
1991	10	6		7	1		3	5	
1992	14	2		7	1		7	1	
1993	10	6		6	2		4	4	
1994	13	3		7	1		6	2	
1995	11	5		6	2		5	3	
1996	12	4		6	2		6	2	
1997	13	3		8	0		5	3	
1998	12	4		8	0		4	4	
1999	4	12		3	5		1	7	
2000	6	10		4	4		2	6	
2001	12	4		7	1		5	3	
2002	10	6		5	3		5	3	
2003	7	9		6	2		1	7	
2004	2	14		1	7		1	7	
2005	4	12		3	5		1	7	
2006	7	9		4	4		3	5	
2007	5	11		3	5		2	6	
2008	7	9		4	4		3	5	
2009	8	8		6	2		2	6	
2010	6	10		5	3		1	7	
	471	406	13	262	176	7	209	230	6

SAN FRANCISCO 49ERS

Season	All Games W	L	T	Home Games W	L	T	Road Games W	L	T
1950	3	9		3	3		0	6	
1951	7	4	1	5	1		2	3	1
1952	7	5		3	3		4	2	
1953	9	3		5	1		4	2	
1954	7	4	1	4	2		3	2	1
1955	4	8		2	4		2	4	
1956	5	6	1	3	3		2	3	1
1957	8	4		5	1		3	3	
1958	6	6		4	2		2	4	
1959	7	5		4	2		3	3	
1960	7	5		3	3		4	2	
1961	7	6	1	5	1	1	2	5	
1962	6	8		1	6		5	2	
1963	2	12		2	5		0	7	
1964	4	10		3	4		1	6	
1965	7	6	1	4	2	1	3	4	
1966	6	6	2	4	2	1	2	4	1
1967	7	7		3	4		4	3	
1968	7	6	1	3	3	1	4	3	
1969	4	8	2	3	3	1	1	5	1
1970	10	3	1	5	1	1	5	2	
1971	9	5		4	3		5	2	
1972	8	5	1	4	2	1	4	3	

SEATTLE SEAHAWKS

Season	All Games W	L	T	Home Games W	L	T	Road Games W	L	T
1976	2	12		1	6		1	6	
1977	5	9		3	4		2	5	
1978	9	7		5	3		4	4	
1979	9	7		5	3		4	4	
1980	4	12		0	8		4	4	
1981	6	10		5	3		1	7	
1982	4	5		3	2		1	3	
1983	9	7		5	3		4	4	
1984	12	4		7	1		5	3	
1985	8	8		5	3		3	5	
1986	10	6		7	1		3	5	
1987	9	6		6	2		3	4	
1988	9	7		5	3		4	4	
1989	7	9		3	5		4	4	
1990	9	7		5	3		4	4	
1991	7	9		5	3		2	6	
1992	2	14		1	7		1	7	
1993	6	10		4	4		2	6	
1994	6	10		3	5		3	5	
1995	8	8		5	3		3	5	
1996	7	9		4	4		3	5	
1997	8	8		4	4		4	4	
1998	8	8		6	2		2	6	
1999	9	7		5	3		4	4	
2000	6	10		3	5		3	5	

Season	All Games			Home Games			Road Games		
	W	L	T	W	L	T	W	L	T
2001	9	7		6	2		3	5	
2002	7	9		3	5		4	4	
2003	10	6		8	0		2	6	
2004	9	7		5	3		4	4	
2005	13	3		8	0		5	3	
2006	9	7		5	3		4	4	
2007	10	6		7	1		3	5	
2008	4	12		2	6		2	6	
2009	5	11		4	4		1	7	
2010	7	9		5	3		2	6	
	262	286		158	117		104	169	

TAMPA BAY BUCCANEERS

Season	All Games			Home Games			Road Games		
	W	L	T	W	L	T	W	L	T
1976	0	14		0	7		0	7	
1977	2	12		1	6		1	6	
1978	5	11		3	5		2	6	
1979	10	6		5	3		5	3	
1980	5	10	1	2	5	1	3	5	
1981	9	7		6	2		3	5	
1982	5	4		4	1		1	3	
1983	2	14		1	7		1	7	
1984	6	10		6	2		0	8	
1985	2	14		2	6		0	8	
1986	2	14		1	7		1	7	
1987	4	11		2	5		2	6	
1988	5	11		3	5		2	6	
1989	5	11		2	6		3	5	
1990	6	10		4	4		2	6	
1991	3	13		3	5		0	8	
1992	5	11		3	5		2	6	
1993	5	11		3	5		2	6	
1994	6	10		4	4		2	6	
1995	7	9		5	3		2	6	
1996	6	10		5	3		1	7	
1997	10	6		5	3		5	3	
1998	8	8		6	2		2	6	
1999	11	5		7	1		4	4	
2000	10	6		6	2		4	4	
2001	9	7		5	3		4	4	
2002	12	4		6	2		6	2	
2003	7	9		3	5		4	4	
2004	5	11		4	4		1	7	
2005	11	5		6	2		5	3	
2006	4	12		3	5		1	7	
2007	9	7		6	2		3	5	
2008	9	7		6	2		3	5	
2009	3	13		1	7		2	6	
2010	10	6		4	4		6	2	
	218	329	1	133	140	1	85	189	

WASHINGTON REDSKINS*

Season	All Games			Home Games			Road Games		
	W	L	T	W	L	T	W	L	T
1932	4	4	2	2	2	1	2	1	1
1933	5	5	2	4	2		1	3	2
1934	6	6		4	3		2	3	
1935	2	8	1	2	5		0	3	1
1936	7	5		4	3		3	2	
1937	8	3		4	2		4	1	
1938	6	3	2	3	1	1	3	2	1
1939	8	2	1	5	0	1	3	2	
1940	9	2		6	0		3	2	
1941	6	5		4	2		2	3	
1942	10	1		5	1		5	0	
1943	6	3	1	4	2		2	1	1
1944	6	3	1	4	2		2	1	1
1945	8	2		6	0		2	2	
1946	5	5	1	3	2	1	2	3	
1947	4	8		4	2		0	6	
1948	7	5		4	2		3	3	
1949	4	7	1	3	3		1	4	1
1950	3	9		1	5		2	4	
1951	5	7		2	4		3	3	
1952	4	8		1	5		3	3	
1953	6	5	1	3	3		3	2	1
1954	3	9		3	3		0	6	
1955	8	4		3	3		5	1	
1956	6	6		4	2		2	4	
1957	5	6	1	2	3	1	3	3	
1958	4	7	1	3	2	1	1	5	
1959	3	9		2	4		1	5	
1960	1	9	2	1	4	1	0	5	1
1961	1	12	1	1	6		0	6	1
1962	5	7	2	3	4		2	3	2
1963	3	11		1	6		2	5	
1964	6	8		4	3		2	5	
1965	6	8		3	4		3	4	
1966	7	7		4	3		3	4	
1967	5	6	3	2	4	1	3	2	2
1968	5	9		3	4		2	5	
1969	7	5	2	4	2	1	3	3	1
1970	6	8		4	3		2	5	
1971	9	4	1	4	2	1	5	2	
1972	11	3		6	1		5	2	
1973	10	4		7	0		3	4	
1974	10	4		6	1		4	3	
1975	8	6		5	2		3	4	
1976	10	4		5	2		5	2	
1977	9	5		5	2		4	3	
1978	8	8		5	3		3	5	
1979	10	6		6	2		4	4	
1980	6	10		4	4		2	6	
1981	8	8		5	3		3	5	
1982	8	1		3	1		5	0	
1983	14	2		7	1		7	1	
1984	11	5		7	1		4	4	
1985	10	6		5	3		5	3	
1986	12	4		7	1		5	3	
1987	11	4		6	1		5	3	
1988	7	9		4	4		3	5	
1989	10	6		4	4		6	2	
1990	10	6		7	1		3	5	
1991	14	2		7	1		7	1	
1992	9	7		6	2		3	5	
1993	4	12		3	5		1	7	
1994	3	13		0	8		3	5	
1995	6	10		4	4		2	6	
1996	9	7		5	3		4	4	
1997	8	7	1	5	2	1	3	5	
1998	6	10		4	4		2	6	
1999	10	6		6	2		4	4	
2000	8	8		4	4		4	4	
2001	8	8		4	4		4	4	
2002	7	9		5	3		2	6	
2003	5	11		3	5		2	6	
2004	6	10		3	5		3	5	
2005	10	6		6	2		4	4	
2006	5	11		3	5		2	6	
2007	9	7		5	3		4	4	
2008	8	8		4	4		4	4	
2009	4	12		3	5		1	7	
2010	6	10		2	6		4	4	
	547	516	27	315	228	11	232	288	16

*includes Boston Braves (1932) and Boston Redskins (1933-36).

ALL-TIME REGULAR-SEASON RECORDS OF NFL TEAMS

AFC	W	L	T	Pct.
Miami	394	290	4	.576
Oakland	418	343	11	.549
Baltimore	128	111	1	.535
Indianapolis	451	396	7	.532
Cleveland	438	394	10	.526
New England	401	362	9	.526
Denver	398	364	10	.522
Pittsburgh	541	499	20	.520
Kansas City	395	365	12	.520
Jacksonville	133	123	0	.520
San Diego	384	377	11	.505
Tennessee	377	389	6	.492
Buffalo	358	406	8	.469
N.Y. Jets	351	413	8	.460
Cincinnati	286	372	2	.435
Houston	55	89	0	.382

NFC	W	L	T	Pct.
Chicago	704	512	42	.579
Dallas	440	324	6	.576
Green Bay	664	524	36	.559
Minnesota	413	336	9	.551
N.Y. Giants	636	524	33	.548
San Francisco	471	406	13	.537
Washington	547	516	27	.515
St. Louis	511	492	20	.509
Philadelphia	504	537	25	.484
Seattle	262	286	0	.478
Carolina	119	137	0	.465
Detroit	496	593	32	.456
New Orleans	286	383	5	.428
Arizona	488	681	39	.418
Atlanta	289	393	6	.424
Tampa Bay	218	329	1	.399

From 1920-1971, tie games were not included in win percentage.

History

The Professional Football Hall of Fame is located in Canton, Ohio, site of the organizational meeting on September 17, 1920, from which the National Football League evolved. The NFL recognized Canton as the Hall of Fame site on April 27, 1961. Canton area individuals, foundations, and companies donated almost $400,000 in cash and services to provide funds for the construction of the original two-building complex, which was dedicated on September 7, 1963. Since that time, the Hall added three buildings with major expansion projects in 1971, 1978, and 1995.

The Hall has renovated four of its six major exhibition galleries in recent years. The *Lamar Hunt Super Bowl Gallery*, featuring the Super Bowl Theater, opened in summer 2009. The *Moments, Memories & Mementos Gallery* and *Pro Football Today Gallery* were opened—one in 2008 preceded by a brand new *Hall of Fame Gallery*, home to enshrinees bronze busts, in 2003. Other highlights of the Hall include an extensive archive and information center and a large museum store.

Throughout the years, the Pro Football Hall of Fame has become an extremely popular tourist attraction. Since its opening, the Hall has had nearly nine million visitors.

New members of the Pro Football Hall of Fame are elected annually by a 44-member National Board of Selectors, made up of media representatives from every league city, eleven at-large representatives, and a representative of the Pro Football Writers of America. Between four and seven new members are elected each year. An affirmative vote of approximately 80 percent is needed for election.

Any fan may nominate any eligible player or contributor simply by writing to the Pro Football Hall of Fame. Players and coaches must have last played or coached at least five years before he is eligible. Contributors (administrators, owners, *et al.*) may be elected while they are still active.

The charter class of 17 enshrinees was elected in 1963 and the honor roll now stands at 267 (158 living as of May 1, 2011) with the election of a seven-man class in 2011. That class consists of Richard Dent, Marshall Faulk, Chris Hanburger, Les Richter, Ed Sabol, Deion Sanders, and Shannon Sharpe.

ROSTER OF MEMBERS

HERB ADDERLEY
Cornerback. 6-0, 205. Born in Philadelphia, Pennsylvania, June 8, 1939. Michigan State. Inducted in 1980. 1961-69 Green Bay Packers, 1970-72 Dallas Cowboys. **Highlights:** 48 interceptions, 7 touchdowns. Played in four Super Bowls, five Pro Bowls.

TROY AIKMAN
Quarterback. 6-4, 219. Born in West Covina, California, November 21, 1966. Oklahoma, UCLA. Inducted in 2006. 1989-2000 Dallas Cowboys. **Highlights:** His 90 wins in 1990s make him winningest quarterback of any decade. Led Cowboys to three Super Bowl wins. Passed for 32,942 yards, 165 touchdowns. Named to six Pro Bowls.

GEORGE ALLEN
Coach. Born in Detroit, Michigan, April 29, 1918. Died December 31, 1990. Alma College, Eastern Michigan, Marquette, Michigan. Inducted in 2002. 1966-1970 Los Angeles Rams, 1971-77 Washington Redskins. **Highlights:** 118-54-5 overall record. Never suffered a losing season, and ranked tenth in coaching victories at time of retirement.

MARCUS ALLEN
Running back. 6-2, 210. Born in San Diego, California, March 26, 1960. Southern California. Inducted in 2003. 1982-1992 Los Angeles Raiders, 1993-1997 Kansas City Chiefs. **Highlights:** First player in NFL history to tally 10,000 rushing yards and 5,000 receiving yards. MVP, Super Bowl XVIII.

LANCE ALWORTH
Wide receiver. 6-0, 184. Born in Houston, Texas, August 3, 1940. Arkansas. Inducted in 1978. 1962-1970 San Diego Chargers, 1971-72 Dallas Cowboys. **Highlights:** 542 receptions for 10,266 yards, 85 touchdowns. All-AFL seven times, seven All-Star games.

DOUG ATKINS
Defensive end. 6-8, 275. Born in Humboldt, Tennessee, May 8, 1930. Tennessee. Inducted in 1982. 1953-54 Cleveland Browns, 1955-1966 Chicago Bears, 1967-69 New Orleans Saints. **Highlights:** Eight Pro Bowls, All-NFL four times. Played for 17 years, 205 games.

MORRIS (RED) BADGRO
End. 6-0, 190. Born in Orillia, Washington, December 1, 1902. Died July 13, 1998. Southern California. Inducted in 1981. 1927-28 New York Yankees, 1930-35 New York Giants, 1936 Brooklyn Dodgers. **Highlights:** First- or second-team All-NFL four times. Scored first touchdown in NFL Championship Game series.

LEM BARNEY
Cornerback. 6-0, 190. Born in Gulfport, Mississippi, September 8, 1945. Jackson State. Inducted in 1992. 1967-1977 Detroit Lions. **Highlights:** 56 interceptions for 1,077 yards, 11 touchdowns (7 defensive, 4 special teams). Seven Pro Bowls, All-NFL/NFC four times.

CLIFF BATTLES
Halfback. 6-1, 195. Born in Akron, Ohio, May 1, 1910. Died April 28, 1981. West Virginia Wesleyan. Inducted in 1968. 1932 Boston Braves, 1933-36 Boston Redskins, 1937 Washington Redskins. **Highlights:** NFL rushing champion 1932, 1937. First to gain more than 200 yards in a game, 1933.

SAMMY BAUGH
Quarterback. 6-2, 180. Born in Temple, Texas, March 17, 1914. Died December 17, 2008. Texas Christian. Inducted in 1963. 1937-1952 Washington Redskins. **Highlights:** Charter enshrinee. Six-time NFL passing leader. NFL passing, punting, interception champ, 1943.

CHUCK BEDNARIK
Center-linebacker. 6-3, 230. Born in Bethlehem, Pennsylvania, May 1, 1925. Pennsylvania. Inducted in 1967. 1949-1962 Philadelphia Eagles. **Highlights:** Eight Pro Bowls. Missed three games in 14 years. Named NFL all-time center, 1969.

BERT BELL
Team owner. Commissioner. Born in Philadelphia, Pennsylvania, February 25, 1895. Died October 11, 1959. Pennsylvania. Inducted in 1963. 1933-1940 Philadelphia Eagles, 1941-42 Pittsburgh Steelers, 1943 Phil-Pitt, 1944 Card-Pitt, 1945-46 Pittsburgh Steelers. Commissioner, 1946-1959. **Highlights:** Charter enshrinee. Built NFL image as commissioner, 1946-1959. Set up long-term television policies.

BOBBY BELL
Linebacker. 6-4, 225. Born in Shelby, North Carolina, June 17, 1940. Minnesota. Inducted in 1983. 1963-1974 Kansas City Chiefs. **Highlights:** 26 interceptions. All-AFL/AFC eight times. Nine career touchdowns, 1 on onside kick return.

RAYMOND BERRY
End. 6-2, 187. Born in Corpus Christi, Texas, February 27, 1933. Southern Methodist. Inducted in 1973. 1955-1967 Baltimore Colts. **Highlights:** 631 receptions for 9,275 yards, 68 touchdowns. Set NFL title game mark with 12 catches for 178 yards, 1958.

ELVIN BETHEA
Defensive end. 6-2, 260. Born in Trenton, New Jersey, March 1, 1946. North Carolina A&T. Inducted in 2003. 1968-1983 Houston Oilers. **Highlights:** Led team in sacks six times. Elected to eight Pro Bowls. Played for 16 years, 210 games.

CHARLES W. BIDWILL SR.
Team owner. Born in Chicago, Illinois, September 16, 1895. Died April 19, 1947. Loyola of Chicago. Inducted in 1967. 1933-1943 Chicago Cardinals, 1944 Card-Pitt, 1945-47 Chicago Cardinals. **Highlights:** Guiding light for NFL during depression years. Built famous "Dream Backfield."

FRED BILETNIKOFF
Wide receiver. 6-1, 190. Born in Erie, Pennsylvania, February 23, 1943. Florida State. Inducted in 1988. 1965-1978 Oakland Raiders. **Highlights:** 589 receptions for 8,974 yards, 76 touchdowns. 40 catches 10 straight years. MVP, Super Bowl XI.

GEORGE BLANDA
Quarterback-kicker. 6-2, 215. Born in Youngwood, Pennsylvania, September 17, 1927. Died September 27, 2010. Kentucky. Inducted in 1981. 1949-1958 Chicago Bears, 1950 Baltimore Colts, 1960-66 Houston Oilers, 1967-1975 Oakland Raiders. **Highlights:** 2,002 career points. 26-season, 340-game career longest in NFL history at retirement.

MEL BLOUNT
Cornerback. 6-3, 205. Born in Vidalia, Georgia, April 10, 1948. Southern University. Inducted in 1989. 1970-1983 Pittsburgh Steelers. **Highlights:** 57 interceptions for 736 yards. NFL defensive MVP, 1975. Played in five Pro Bowls.

TERRY BRADSHAW
Quarterback. 6-3, 210. Born in Shreveport, Louisiana, September 2, 1948. Louisiana Tech. Inducted in 1989. 1970-1983 Pittsburgh Steelers. **Highlights:** 27,989 yards passing, 212 touchdowns. MVP in Super Bowls XIII, XIV.

BOB (BOOMER) BROWN
Tackle. 6-4, 280. Born in Cleveland, Ohio, December 8, 1941. Nebraska. Inducted in 2004. 1964-68 Philadelphia Eagles, 1969-1970 Los Angeles Rams, 1971-73 Oakland Raiders. **Highlights:** All-NFL seven of 10 seasons, six Pro Bowls. Named to 1960s All-Decade Team.

JIM BROWN
Fullback. 6-2, 228. Born in St. Simons, Georgia, February 17, 1936. Syracuse. Inducted in 1971. 1957-1965 Cleveland Browns. **Highlights:** 12,312 yards rushing, 756 points. Led NFL rushers eight years. Nine consecutive Pro Bowls.

PAUL BROWN
Coach. Born in Norwalk, Ohio, September 7, 1908. Died August 5, 1991. Miami (Ohio). Inducted in 1967. 1946-49 Cleveland Browns (AAFC), 1950-1962 Cleveland Browns. **Highlights:** Built Cleveland dynasty with 167-53-8 record, four AAFC titles, three NFL crowns. Returned to coaching with Cincinnati Bengals after induction, 1968-1975.

ROOSEVELT BROWN
Tackle. 6-3, 255. Born in Charlottesville, Virginia, October 20, 1932. Died June 9, 2004. Morgan State. Inducted in 1975. 1953-1965 New York Giants. **Highlights:** All-NFL eight consecutive years, nine Pro Bowls. NFL's lineman of year, 1956.

WILLIE BROWN
Cornerback. 6-1, 210. Born in Yazoo City, Mississippi, December 2, 1940. Grambling. Inducted in 1984. 1963-66 Denver Broncos, 1967-1978 Oakland Raiders. **Highlights:** 54 interceptions for 472 yards. Scored on 75-yard interception in Super Bowl XI.

BUCK BUCHANAN
Defensive tackle. 6-7, 274. Born in Gainesville, Alabama, September 10, 1940. Died July 16, 1992. Grambling. Inducted in 1990. 1963-1975 Kansas City Chiefs. **Highlights:** Led Chiefs defensive efforts in Super Bowl I, IV. Did not miss a game in 13 years.

NICK BUONICONTI
Linebacker. 5-11, 220. Born in Springfield, Massachusetts, December 15, 1940. Notre Dame. Inducted in 2001. 1962-68 Boston Patriots, 1969-1974, 1976 Miami Dolphins. **Highlights:** All-AFL/AFC eight times. Named to AFL's All-Time Team.

DICK BUTKUS
Linebacker. 6-3, 245. Born in Chicago, Illinois, December 9, 1942. Illinois. Inducted in 1979. 1965-1973 Chicago Bears. **Highlights:** All-NFL six years, eight consecutive Pro Bowls. 27 fumble recoveries.

EARL CAMPBELL
Running back. 5-11, 233. Born in Tyler, Texas, March 29, 1955. Texas. Inducted in 1991. 1978-1984 Houston Oilers, 1984-85 New Orleans Saints. **Highlights:** 9,407 yards rushing, 74 touchdowns. 1,934 yards rushing in 1980, including four games with at least 200 yards.

TONY CANADEO
Halfback. 5-11, 195. Born in Chicago, Illinois, May 5, 1919. Died November 29, 2003. Gonzaga. Inducted in 1974. 1941-44, 1946-1952 Green Bay Packers. **Highlights:** Two-way player. Third player to rush for 1,000 yards in single season, 1949.

JOE CARR
NFL president. Born in Columbus, Ohio, October 23, 1879. Died May 20, 1939. Did not attend college. Inducted in 1963. President, 1921-1939 National Football League. **Highlights:** Charter enshrinee. NFL co-organizer, 1920. Introduced standard player contract.

HARRY CARSON
Linebacker. 6-2, 237. Born in Florence, South Carolina, November 26, 1953. South Carolina State. Inducted in 2006. 1976-1988 New York Giants. **Highlights:** 11 career interceptions. Named to nine Pro Bowls. Named first- or second-team All-NFL six times.

DAVE CASPER
Tight end. 6-4, 240. Born in Bemidji, Minnesota, February 2, 1952. Notre Dame. Inducted in 2002. 1974-1980 Oakland Raiders, 1980-83 Houston Oilers, 1983 Minnesota Vikings, 1984 Los Angeles Raiders. **Highlights:** 378 receptions for 5,216 yards, 52 touchdowns. Five consecutive Pro Bowls.

GUY CHAMBERLIN
End. Coach. 6-2, 196. Born in Blue Springs, Nebraska, January 16, 1894. Died April 4, 1967. Nebraska. Inducted in 1965. 1919 Canton Bulldogs, 1920-21 Decatur Staleys/Chicago Staleys, player-coach 1922-23 Canton Bulldogs, 1924 Cleveland Bulldogs, 1925-26 Frankford Yellow jackets, 1927-28 Chicago Cardinals. **Highlights:** Player-coach of four NFL championship teams. Six-year coaching record of 58-16-7.

JACK CHRISTIANSEN
Safety. 6-1, 185. Born in Sublette, Kansas, December 20, 1928. Died June 29, 1986. Colorado State. Inducted in 1970. 1951-58 Detroit Lions. **Highlights:** 46 interceptions. NFL interception leader, 1953, 1957. Eight punt returns for touchdowns.

EARL (DUTCH) CLARK
Quarterback. 6-0, 185. Born in Fowler, Colorado, October 11, 1906. Died August 5, 1978. Colorado College. Inducted in 1963. 1931-32 Portsmouth Spartans, 1934-38 Detroit Lions. **Highlights:** Charter enshrinee. NFL scoring champion three years. Led Lions to 1935 NFL title.

GEORGE CONNOR
Tackle-linebacker. 6-3, 240. Born in Chicago, Illinois, January 21, 1925. Died March 31, 2003. Holy Cross, Notre Dame. Inducted in 1975. 1948-1955 Chicago Bears. **Highlights:** All-NFL at three positions—T, DT, LB. All-NFL five years. Played in first four Pro Bowls.

JIMMY CONZELMAN
Quarterback. Coach. Team owner. 6-0, 180. Born in St. Louis, Missouri, March 6, 1898. Died July 31, 1970. Washington of St. Louis. Inducted in 1964. 1920 Decatur Staleys, 1921-22 Rock Island Independents, 1922-24 Milwaukee Badgers; owner-coach 1925-26 Detroit Panthers; player-coach 1927-29, coach 1930 Providence Steam Roller; coach 1940-42, 1946-48 Chicago Cardinals. **Highlights:** Player-coach of four NFL teams in 1920's. Coached Cardinals to 1947 NFL crown.

LOU CREEKMUR
Tackle-guard. 6-4, 255. Born in Hopelawn, New Jersey. January 22, 1927. Died July 5, 2009. William & Mary. Inducted in 1996. 1950-59 Detroit Lions. **Highlights:** All-NFL six times, twice at guard and four times at tackle. Selected to eight Pro Bowls and played on three NFL championship teams.

LARRY CSONKA
Running back. 6-3, 235. Born in Stow, Ohio, December 25, 1946. Syracuse. Inducted in 1987. 1968-1974, 1979 Miami Dolphins, 1976-78 New York Giants. **Highlights:** 8,081 yards rushing, 68 touchdowns. MVP Super Bowl VIII. Only 21 fumbles in 1,891 carries and 106 receptions.

AL DAVIS
Team, League Administrator. Born in Brockton, Massachusetts, July 4, 1929. Wittenberg, Syracuse. Inducted in 1992. 1963-1981, 1995-present Oakland Raiders, 1982-1994 Los Angeles Raiders, 1966 American Football League. **Highlights:** Only person to serve in pros as personnel assistant, scout, assistant coach, head coach, general manager, commissioner, team owner/CEO.

WILLIE DAVIS
Defensive end. 6-3, 245. Born in Lisbon, Louisiana, July 24, 1934. Grambling. Inducted in 1981. 1958-59 Cleveland Browns, 1960-69 Green Bay Packers. **Highlights:** All-NFL five seasons, five Pro Bowls. Did not miss game in 12-year career.

LEN DAWSON
Quarterback. 6-0, 190. Born in Alliance, Ohio, June 20, 1935. Purdue. Inducted in 1987. 1957-59 Pittsburgh Steelers, 1960-61 Cleveland Browns, 1962 Dallas Texans, 1963-1975 Kansas City Chiefs. **Highlights:** 28,711 yards passing, 239 touchdowns. Four AFL passing crowns. MVP, Super Bowl IV.

FRED DEAN
Defensive end. 6-3, 230. Born in Arcadia, Louisiana, February 24, 1952. Louisiana Tech. Inducted in 2008. 1975-1981 San Diego Chargers, 1981-85 San Francisco 49ers. **Highlights:** Had career-high 17.5 sacks in 1983. Played on two Super Bowl championship teams with 49ers (Super Bowls XVI, XIX).

JOE DeLAMIELLEURE
Guard. 6-3, 254. Born in Detroit, Michigan, March 16, 1951. Michigan State. Inducted in 2003. 1973-1979, 1985 Buffalo Bills, 1980-1984 Cleveland Browns. **Highlights:** Selected All-Pro and All-AFC six consecutive times, 1975-1980. Named to six Pro Bowls. Played 13 years, 185 games.

RICHARD DENT
Defensive end. 6-5, 265. Born in Atlanta, Georgia, December 13, 1960. Tennessee State. Inducted in 2011. 1983-1993, 1995 Chicago Bears, 1994 San Francisco 49ers, 1996 Indianapolis Colts, 1997 Philadelphia Eagles. **Highlights:** Named MVP of Super Bowl XX. Had double-digit sack totals 10 times. Recorded 137.5 career sacks, third most at time of retirement. Named first- or second-team All-NFL four times, voted to four Pro Bowls.

ERIC DICKERSON
Running back. 6-3, 220. Born in Sealy, Texas, September 2, 1960. Southern Methodist. Inducted in 1999. 1983-87 Los Angeles Rams, 1987-1991 Indianapolis Colts, 1992 Los Angeles Raiders, 1993 Atlanta Falcons. **Highlights:** Rushed for 13,259 career yards, including an NFL record 2,105 yards in 1984. All-Pro five times, six Pro Bowls.

DAN DIERDORF
Tackle. 6-3, 290. Born in Canton, Ohio, June 29, 1949. Michigan. Inducted in 1996. 1971-1983 St. Louis Cardinals. **Highlights:** All-Pro five times, played in six Pro Bowls, named NFL's best blocker three times.

MIKE DITKA
Tight end. 6-3, 225. Born in Carnegie, Pennsylvania, October 18, 1939. Pittsburgh. Inducted in 1988. 1961-66 Chicago Bears, 1967-68 Philadelphia Eagles, 1969-1972 Dallas Cowboys. **Highlights:** 427 receptions for 5,812 yards, 43 touchdowns. First tight end selected to Hall of Fame. Five consecutive Pro Bowls.

ART DONOVAN
Defensive tackle. 6-3, 265. Born in Bronx, New York, June 5, 1925. Boston College. Inducted in 1968. 1950 Baltimore Colts, 1951 New York Yanks, 1952 Dallas Texans, 1953-1961 Baltimore Colts. **Highlights:** Five Pro Bowls. Vital part of Baltimore's climb to powerhouse status in 1950s.

TONY DORSETT
Running back. 5-11, 184. Born in Rochester, Pennsylvania, April 7, 1954. Pittsburgh. Inducted in 1994. 1977-1987 Dallas Cowboys, 1988 Denver Broncos. **Highlights:** 12,739 yards rushing, 398 receptions, 91 touchdowns. Ran record 99 yards for touchdown vs. Minnesota, January, 1983.

JOHN (PADDY) DRISCOLL
Quarterback. 5-11, 160. Born in Evanston, Illinois, January 11, 1896. Died June 29, 1968. Northwestern. Inducted in 1965. 1919 Hammond Pros, 1920 Decatur Staleys, 1920-25 Chicago Cardinals, 1926-29 Chicago Bears. **Highlights:** All-NFL seven times. Dropkicked record 4 field goals in one game, 1925.

BILL DUDLEY
Halfback. 5-10, 182. Born in Bluefield, Virginia, December 24, 1921. Died February 4, 2010. Virginia. Inducted in 1966. 1942, 1945-46 Pittsburgh Steelers, 1947-49 Detroit Lions, 1950-51, 1953 Washington Redskins. **Highlights:** Won NFL rushing, interception, punt return titles, 1946. All-NFL 1942, 1946, and 1947.

ALBERT GLEN (TURK) EDWARDS
Tackle. 6-2, 260. Born in Mold, Washington, September 28, 1907. Died January 12, 1973. Washington State. Inducted in 1969. 1932 Boston Braves, 1933-36 Boston Redskins, 1937-1940 Washington Redskins. **Highlights:** All-NFL 1932-34, 1936, 1937. Steamrolling blocker, smothering tackler.

CARL ELLER
Defensive end. 6-6, 247. Born in Winston-Salem, North Carolina, January 25, 1942. Minnesota. Inducted in 2004. 1964-1978 Minnesota Vikings, 1979 Seattle Seahawks. **Highlights:** Fixture on Vikings' "Purple People Eaters" defensive line, All-Pro five time, elected to six Pro Bowls.

JOHN ELWAY
Quarterback. 6-3, 215. Born in Port Angeles, Washington, June 28, 1960. Stanford. Inducted in 2004. 1983-1998 Denver Broncos. **Highlights:** Passed for 51,475 yards, 300 touchdowns. Named to nine Pro Bowls. NFL MVP, 1987; MVP, Super Bowl XXXIII.

WEEB EWBANK

Coach. Born in Richmond, Indiana, May 6, 1907. Died November 17, 1998. Miami (Ohio). Inducted in 1978. 1954-1962 Baltimore Colts, 1963-1973 New York Jets. **Highlights:** Only coach to win championships in both NFL, AFL. Led both Colts (1958 and 1959) and Jets (1968) to championships.

MARSHALL FAULK

Running back. 5-10, 208. Born in New Orleans, Louisiana, February 26, 1973. San Diego State. Inducted in 2011. 1994-98 Indianapolis Colts, 1999-2005 St. Louis Rams. **Highlights:** Became second player to eclipse 1,000 yards in rushing and receiving same season when he set then-record for yards from scrimmage, 1999. NFL's MVP in 2000. Rushed for 1,000 yards in seven of first eight seasons.

TOM FEARS

End. 6-2, 215. Born in Guadalajara, Mexico, December 3, 1922. Died January 4, 2000. Santa Clara, UCLA. Inducted in 1970. 1948-1956 Los Angeles Rams. **Highlights:** 400 receptions for 5,397 yards, 38 touchdowns. Led NFL receivers first three seasons. Had then-record 18 receptions in single game.

JIM FINKS

Administrator. Born in St. Louis, Missouri, August 31, 1927. Died May 8, 1994. Tulsa. Inducted 1995. 1964-1973 Minnesota Vikings, 1974-1982 Chicago Bears, 1986-1993 New Orleans Saints. **Highlights:** Developed Vikings, Bears, Saints—all teams with losing records—into winners.

RAY FLAHERTY

Coach. Born in Spokane, Washington, September 1, 1903. Died July 19, 1994. Gonzaga. Inducted in 1976. 1936-1942 Boston/Washington Redskins, 1946-48 New York Yankees (AAFC), 1949 Chicago Hornets (AAFC). **Highlights:** 82-41-5 coaching record. Introduced screen pass in 1937 title game and platoon system.

LEN FORD

Defensive end. 6-4, 260. Born in Washington, D.C., February 18, 1926. Died March 14, 1972. Morgan State, Michigan. Inducted in 1976. 1948-49 Los Angeles Dons (AAFC), 1950-57 Cleveland Browns, 1958 Green Bay Packers. **Highlights:** All-NFL five times, four Pro Bowls. Recovered 20 opponents' fumbles.

DAN FORTMANN

Guard. 6-0, 210. Born in Pearl River, New York, April 11, 1916. Died May 23, 1995. Colgate. Inducted in 1965. 1936-1943 Chicago Bears. **Highlights:** At 20, became youngest starter in NFL. First- or second-team All-NFL every season of career.

DAN FOUTS

Quarterback. 6-3, 210. Born in San Francisco, California, June 10, 1951. Oregon. Inducted in 1993. 1973-1987 San Diego Chargers. **Highlights:** 43,040 passing yards, 254 touchdowns. Six Pro Bowls, NFL MVP, 1982.

BENNY FRIEDMAN

Quarterback. 5-10, 183. Born in Cleveland, Ohio, March 18, 1905. Died November 23, 1982. Michigan. Inducted in 2005. 1927 Cleveland Bulldogs, 1928 Detroit Wolverines, 1929-1931 New York Giants, 1932-34 Brooklyn Dodgers. **Highlights:** NFL's first great passer. Set league mark for touchdowns with 20 in 1929. Led NFL in touchdown passes each of his first four seasons.

FRANK GATSKI

Center. 6-3, 240. Born in Farmington, West Virginia, March 18, 1919. Marshall, Auburn. Died November 22, 2005. Inducted in 1985. 1946-49 Cleveland Browns (AAFC), 1950-56 Cleveland Browns, 1957 Detroit Lions. **Highlights:** Never missed game in high school, college, or pro football. Played 11 championship games, winning eight.

BILL GEORGE

Linebacker. 6-2, 230. Born in Waynesburg, Pennsylvania, October 27, 1929. Died September 30, 1982. Wake Forest. Inducted in 1974. 1952-1965 Chicago Bears, 1966 Los Angeles Rams. **Highlights:** All-NFL eight years, eight consecutive Pro Bowls. 14 years of service, longest of any Bears player.

JOE GIBBS

Coach. Born in Mocksville, North Carolina, November 25, 1940. Cerritos (Calif.) J.C., San Diego State. Inducted in 1996. 1981-1992 Washington Redskins. **Highlights:** 124-60-0 record in regular season, 16-5 in postseason, including four Super Bowl appearances—winning three. Won 10 or more games eight times.

FRANK GIFFORD

Halfback. 6-1, 195. Born in Santa Monica, California, August 16, 1930. Southern California. Inducted in 1977. 1952-1960, 1962-64 New York Giants. **Highlights:** Starred on both offense and defense. Named to eight Pro Bowls, 1956 NFL player of the year.

SID GILLMAN

Coach. Born in Minneapolis, Minnesota, October 26, 1911. Died January 3, 2003. Ohio State. Inducted in 1983. 1955-59 Los Angeles Rams, 1960-69, 1971 Los Angeles/San Diego Chargers, 1973-74 Houston Oilers. **Highlights:** 123-104-7 coaching record. First to win division titles in both NFL, AFL.

OTTO GRAHAM

Quarterback. 6-1, 195. Born in Waukegan, Illinois, December 6, 1921. Died December 17, 2003. Northwestern. Inducted in 1965. 1946-49 Cleveland Browns (AAFC), 1950-55 Cleveland Browns. **Highlights:** 23,584 passing yards, 174 touchdowns. Guided Browns to 10 division or league crowns in 10 years.

HAROLD (RED) GRANGE

Halfback. 6-0, 185. Born in Forksville, Pennsylvania, June 13, 1903. Died January 28, 1991. Illinois. Inducted in 1963. 1925, 1929-1934 Chicago Bears, 1926 New York Yankees (AFL), 1927 New York Yankees. **Highlights:** Charter enshrinee. Nicknamed "Galloping Ghost." Name produced first huge pro football crowds.

BUD GRANT

Coach. Born in Superior, Wisconsin, May 20, 1927. Minnesota. Inducted in 1994. 1967-1983, 1985 Minnesota Vikings. **Highlights:** 168-108-5 coaching record. Led Vikings to 11 division championships, four Super Bowls.

DARRELL GREEN

Cornerback. . 5-8, 176. Born in Houston, Texas, February 15, 1960. Texas A&I. Inducted in 2008. 1983-2002 Washington Redskins. **Highlights:** 54 interceptions, 621 yards, 6 TDs. Played 20 seasons. Recorded interception in NFL record 19 straight seasons. Selected to seven Pro Bowls.

JOE GREENE

Defensive tackle. 6-4, 260. Born in Temple, Texas, September 24, 1946. North Texas State. Inducted in 1987. 1969-1981 Pittsburgh Steelers. **Highlights:** NFL defensive player of the year, 1972, 1974. Four-time Super Bowl champion, 10 Pro Bowls.

FORREST GREGG

Tackle. 6-4, 250. Born in Birthright, Texas, October 18, 1933. Southern Methodist. Inducted in 1977. 1956, 1958-1970 Green Bay Packers, 1971 Dallas Cowboys. **Highlights:** Played 188 consecutive games. Nine Pro Bowls. Played on six NFL championship teams, three Super Bowl winners.

BOB GRIESE

Quarterback. 6-1, 190. Born in Evansville, Indiana, February 3, 1945. Purdue. Inducted in 1990. 1967-1980 Miami Dolphins. **Highlights:** 25,092 passing yards, 192 touchdowns. Led Miami to three AFC titles, Super Bowl VII, VIII wins.

RUSS GRIMM

Guard. 6-3, 273. Born in Scottdale, Pennsylvania, May 2, 1959. Pittsburgh. Inducted in 2010. 1981-1991 Washington Redskins. **Highlights:** Member of famed "Hogs" offensive line, All-NFL four times, four Pro Bowls. Member of All-Decade Team 1980s.

LOU GROZA

Tackle-kicker. 6-3, 250. Born in Martins Ferry, Ohio, January 25, 1924. Died November 29, 2000. Ohio State. Inducted in 1974. 1946-49 Cleveland Browns (AAFC), 1950-59, 1961-67 Cleveland Browns. **Highlights:** 1,608 points in 21 years. Nine Pro Bowls, All-NFL six years. NFL player of the year, 1954.

JOE GUYON

Halfback. 6-1, 180. Born on White Earth Indian Reservation, Minnesota, November 26, 1892. Died November 27, 1971. Carlisle, Georgia Tech. Inducted in 1966. 1919-1920 Canton Bulldogs, 1921 Cleveland Indians, 1922-23 Oorang Indians, 1924 Rock Island Independents, 1924-25 Kansas City Cowboys, 1927 New York Giants. **Highlights:** Touchdown pass gave Giants victory over Bears to win 1927 championship.

GEORGE HALAS

End. Coach. Team owner. Born in Chicago, Illinois, February 2, 1895. Died October 31, 1983. Illinois. Inducted in 1963. Player-coach 1920 Decatur Staleys, 1921 Chicago Staleys, 1922-29 Chicago Bears; coach 1933-1942, 1946-1955, 1958-1967 Chicago Bears. **Highlights:** Charter enshrinee. 324 coaching wins. Only person associated with NFL throughout first 50 years. Coached Bears 40 seasons, won six NFL titles.

JACK HAM

Linebacker. 6-1, 225. Born in Johnstown, Pennsylvania, December 23, 1948. Penn State. Inducted in 1988. 1971-1982 Pittsburgh Steelers. **Highlights:** Won four Super Bowls, 21 opponents' fumbles recovered, 32 interceptions. Eight consecutive Pro Bowls.

DAN HAMPTON

Defensive tackle-defensive end. 6-5, 264. Born in Oklahoma City, Oklahoma, September 19, 1957. Arkansas. Inducted in 2002. 1979-1990 Chicago Bears. **Highlights:** A versatile player, he earned all-pro honors at both defensive tackle and defensive end. Named to four Pro Bowls.

CHRIS HANBURGER

Linebacker. 6-2, 218. Born in Fort Bragg, North Carolina, August 13, 1941. North Carolina. Inducted in 2011. 1965-1978 Washington Redskins. **Highlights:** Leader of dominant Redskins defenses. Named first-team All-NFL four times in five-season span. Voted to nine Pro Bowls. Three fumble recoveries for TDs tied for NFL record at time of his retirement.

JOHN HANNAH

Guard. 6-2, 265. Born in Canton, Georgia, April 4, 1951. Alabama. Inducted in 1991. 1973-1985 New England Patriots. **Highlights:** Renowned as premier guard of era. All-Pro 10 years, nine Pro Bowls.

FRANCO HARRIS

Running back. 6-2, 225. Born in Fort Dix, New Jersey, March 7, 1950. Penn State. Inducted in 1990. 1972-1983 Pittsburgh Steelers, 1984 Seattle Seahawks. **Highlights:** 12,120 rushing yards, 100 total touchdowns. 1,556 rushing yards in 19 postseason games. MVP in Super Bowl IX.

BOB HAYES

Wide receiver. 5-11, 185. Born in Jacksonville, Florida, December 20, 1942. Died September 18, 2002. Florida A&M. Inducted in 2009. 1965-1974 Dallas Cowboys, 1975 San Francisco 49ers. **Highlights:** Olympic gold medalist with world class speed led Cowboys in receiving three times. 371 receptions for 7,414 yards, 71 TDs. Three Pro Bowls.

MIKE HAYNES

Cornerback. 6-2, 195. Born in Denison, Texas, July 1, 1953. Arizona State. Inducted in 1997. 1976-1982 New England Patriots, 1983-89 Los Angeles Raiders. **Highlights:** Defensive rookie of the year. Selected to nine Pro Bowls and intercepted 46 passes, plus one pick in Super Bowl XVIII.

ED HEALEY

Tackle. 6-3, 220. Born in Indian Orchard, Massachusetts, December 28, 1894. Died December 9, 1978. Dartmouth. Inducted in 1964. 1920-22 Rock Island Independents, 1922-27 Chicago Bears. **Highlights:** Two-way star. Perennial all-pro with Bears.

MEL HEIN

Center. 6-2, 225. Born in Redding, California, August 22, 1909. Died January 31, 1992. Washington State. Inducted in 1963. 1931-1945 New York Giants. **Highlights:** Charter enshrinee. 60-minute regular for 15 years. All-NFL eight consecutive years.

TED HENDRICKS

Linebacker. 6-7, 235. Born in Guatemala City, Guatemala, November 1, 1947. Miami. Inducted in 1990. 1969-1973 Baltimore Colts, 1974 Green Bay Packers, 1975-1981 Oakland Raiders, 1982-83 Los Angeles Raiders. **Highlights:** 25 blocked field goals, extra points, and punts, 26 interceptions. Played in 215 consecutive games.

WILBUR (PETE) HENRY

Tackle. 6-0, 250. Born in Mansfield, Ohio, October 31, 1897. Died February 7, 1952. Washington & Jefferson. Inducted in 1963. 1920-23, 1925-26 Canton Bulldogs, 1927 New York Giants, 1927-28 Pottsville Maroons. **Highlights:** Charter enshrinee. Largest player of his time at 250 pounds. Bulwark of Canton's championship lines.

ARNIE HERBER

Quarterback. 6-0, 200. Born in Green Bay, Wisconsin, April 2, 1910. Died October 14, 1969. Wisconsin, Regis College. Inducted in 1966. 1930-1940 Green Bay Packers, 1944-45 New York Giants. **Highlights:** NFL passing leader 1932, 1934, 1936. Came out of retirement to lead 1944 Giants to NFL Eastern crown.

BILL HEWITT

End. 5-11, 191. Born in Bay City, Michigan, October 8, 1909. Died January 14, 1947. Michigan. Inducted in 1971. 1932-36 Chicago Bears, 1937-39 Philadelphia Eagles, 1943 Phil-Pitt. **Highlights:** First to be named all-NFL with two teams—1933, 1934, 1936 Bears; 1937 Eagles.

GENE HICKERSON

Guard. 6-3, 248. Born in Trenton, Tennessee, February 15, 1935. Died October 20, 2008. Mississippi. Inducted in 2007. 1958-1973 Cleveland Browns. **Highlights:** Blocked for three Hall of Fame running backs. Voted to six straight Pro Bowls. Named to NFL's All-Decade Team of the 1960s.

CLARKE HINKLE

Fullback. 5-11, 201. Born in Toronto, Ohio, April 10, 1909. Died November 9, 1988. Bucknell. Inducted in 1964. 1932-1941 Green Bay Packers. **Highlights:** 3,860 yards rushing, 379 points. Fullback on offense, linebacker on defense.

ELROY (CRAZYLEGS) HIRSCH

Halfback-end. 6-2, 190. Born in Wausau, Wisconsin, June 17, 1923. Died January 28, 2004. Wisconsin, Michigan. Inducted in 1968. 1946-48 Chicago Rockets (AAFC), 1949-1957 Los Angeles Rams. **Highlights:** 387 receptions for 7,029 yards, 60 touchdowns. Key part of Rams' revolutionary "three end" offense, 1949.

PAUL HORNUNG
Halfback. 6-2, 220. Born in Louisville, Kentucky, December 23, 1935. Notre Dame. Inducted in 1986. 1957-1962, 1964-66 Green Bay Packers. **Highlights:** 760 points. Led NFL scorers three years, including record 176 points, 1960. Record 19 points scored in 1961 NFL title game.

KEN HOUSTON
Safety. 6-3, 198. Born in Lufkin, Texas, November 12, 1944. Prairie View A&M. Inducted in 1986. 1967-1972 Houston Oilers, 1973-1980 Washington Redskins. **Highlights:** 49 interceptions, 898 yards, 9 touchdowns. NFL's premier strong safety of 1970s. 12 Pro Bowls.

ROBERT (CAL) HUBBARD
Tackle. 6-5, 250. Born in Keytesville, Missouri, October 31, 1900. Died October 17, 1977. Centenary, Geneva. Inducted in 1963. 1927-28, 1936 New York Giants, 1929-1933, 1935 Green Bay Packers, 1936 Pittsburgh Pirates. **Highlights:** Charter enshrinee. Most feared lineman of his time. All-NFL six years, 1927-29, 1931-33.

SAM HUFF
Linebacker. 6-1, 230. Born in Morgantown, West Virginia, October 4, 1934. West Virginia. Inducted in 1982. 1956-1963 New York Giants, 1964-67, 1969 Washington Redskins. **Highlights:** 30 interceptions. Played in six NFL title games, five Pro Bowls. Redskins player-coach, 1969.

LAMAR HUNT
Team owner. Born in El Dorado, Arkansas, August 2, 1932. Died December 13, 2006. Southern Methodist. Inducted in 1972. 1960-2006 Dallas Texans/Kansas City Chiefs. **Highlights:** Driving force behind organization of AFL. Spearheaded merger negotiations with NFL, 1966.

DON HUTSON
End. 6-1, 180. Born in Pine Bluff, Arkansas, January 31, 1913. Died June 26, 1997. Alabama. Inducted in 1963. 1935-1945 Green Bay Packers. **Highlights:** Charter enshrinee. 488 receptions for 7,991 yards, 99 touchdowns. NFL receiving champion eight years. NFL MVP, 1941, 1942.

MICHAEL IRVIN
Wide receiver. 6-2, 207. Born in Ft. Lauderdale, Florida, March 5, 1966. Miami. Inducted in 2007. 1988-1999 Dallas Cowboys. **Highlights:** 750 career receptions for 11,904 yards, 65 touchdowns. Had NFL record eleven 100-yard receiving games, 1995.

RICKEY JACKSON
Linebacker. 6-2, 243. Born in Pahokee, Florida, March 20, 1958. Pittsburgh. Inducted in 2010. 1981-1993 New Orleans Saints, 1994-95 San Francisco 49ers. **Highlights:** Recorded double-digit sacks in six seasons. Six Pro Bowls, named All-Pro four times. Finished career as defensive end with 49ers.

JIMMY JOHNSON
Cornerback. 6-2, 187. Born in Dallas, Texas, March 31, 1938. UCLA. Inducted in 1994. 1961-1976 San Francisco 49ers. **Highlights:** 47 interceptions for 615 yards. Five Pro Bowls. Opposing passers avoided throwing in his area.

JOHN HENRY JOHNSON
Fullback. 6-2, 225. Born in Waterproof, Louisiana, November 24, 1929. St. Mary's, Arizona State. Inducted in 1987. 1954-56 San Francisco 49ers, 1957-59 Detroit Lions, 1960-65 Pittsburgh Steelers, 1966 Houston Oilers. **Highlights:** 6,803 yards rushing, 55 total touchdowns. Member of San Francisco's "Million-Dollar" backfield.

CHARLIE JOINER
Wide receiver. 5-11, 180. Born in Many, Louisiana, October 14, 1947. Grambling. Inducted in 1996. 1969-1972 Houston Oilers, 1972-75 Cincinnati Bengals, 1976-1986 San Diego Chargers. **Highlights:** 750 receptions for 12,146 yards and 65 touchdowns. Played 18 seasons, 239 games, most ever for wide receiver at time of retirement.

DAVID (DEACON) JONES
Defensive end. 6-5, 260. Born in Eatonville, Florida, December 9, 1938. South Carolina State, Mississippi Vocational. Inducted in 1980. 1961-1971 Los Angeles Rams, 1972-73 San Diego Chargers, 1974 Washington Redskins. **Highlights:** Specialized in quarterback "sacks," a term he invented. Unanimous all-league five consecutive years.

STAN JONES
Guard-defensive tackle. 6-1, 250. Born in Altoona, Pennsylvania, November 24, 1931. Died May 21, 2010. Maryland. Inducted in 1991. 1954-1965 Chicago Bears, 1966 Washington Redskins. **Highlights:** Seven consecutive Pro Bowls. First to rely on weightlifting for football preparation.

HENRY JORDAN
Defensive tackle, 6-3, 240. Born in Emporia, Virginia, January 26, 1935. Died February 21, 1977. Virginia. Inducted in 1995. 1957-58 Cleveland Browns, 1959-1969 Green Bay Packers. **Highlights:** Fixture at DT during Packers' dynasty. Played in four Pro Bowls, seven NFL title games, Super Bowls I, II.

SONNY JURGENSEN
Quarterback. 6-0, 203. Born in Wilmington, North Carolina, August 23, 1934. Duke. Inducted in 1983. 1957-1963 Philadelphia Eagles, 1964-1974 Washington Redskins. **Highlights:** 32,224 yards passing, 255 touchdowns, 82.63 passer rating. Surpassed 3,000 yards passing in five seasons.

JIM KELLY
Quarterback. 6-3, 225. Born in Pittsburgh, Pennsylvania, February 14, 1960. Miami. Inducted in 2002. 1986-1996 Buffalo Bills. **Highlights:** Passed for more than 3,000 yards eight times. Mastered the no-huddle offense that propelled Bills to four consecutive Super Bowls.

LEROY KELLY
Running back. 6-0, 205. Born in Philadelphia, Pennsylvania, May 20, 1942. Morgan State. Inducted in 1994. 1964-1973 Cleveland Browns. **Highlights:** 7,274 yards rushing, 90 total touchdowns, 1,000-yard rusher first three years as starter. Punt return champion, 1965.

WALT KIESLING
Guard. Coach. 6-2, 245. Born in St. Paul, Minnesota, March 27, 1903. Died March 2, 1962. St. Thomas (Minnesota). Inducted in 1966. 1926-27 Duluth Eskimos, 1928 Pottsville Maroons, 1929-1933 Chicago Cardinals, 1934 Chicago Bears, 1935-36 Green Bay Packers, 1937-38 Pittsburgh Pirates; coach, 1939 Pittsburgh Pirates, 1940-42 Pittsburgh Steelers; co-coach, 1943 Phil-Pitt, 1944 Card-Pitt; coach, 1954-56 Pittsburgh Steelers. **Highlights:** 34-year career as pro player, assistant coach, head coach. Led Steelers to first winning season, 1942.

FRANK (BRUISER) KINARD
Tackle. 6-1, 210. Born in Pelahatchie, Mississippi, October 23, 1914. Died September 7, 1985. Mississippi. Inducted in 1971. 1938-1943 Brooklyn Dodgers, 1944 Brooklyn Tigers, 1946-47 New York Yankees (AAFC). **Highlights:** First man to earn both All-NFL, All-AAFC honors. Out because of injury only once.

PAUL KRAUSE
Safety. 6-3, 200. Born in Flint, Michigan, February 19, 1942. Iowa. Inducted in 1998. 1964-67 Washington Redskins, 1968-1979 Minnesota Vikings. **Highlights:** NFL all-time leader with 81 interceptions. Played in eight Pro Bowls. Starting safety in four Super Bowls.

EARL (CURLY) LAMBEAU
Coach. Born in Green Bay, Wisconsin, April 9, 1898. Died June 1, 1965. Notre Dame. Inducted in 1963. 1919-1949 Green Bay Packers, 1950-51 Chicago Cardinals, 1952-53 Washington Redskins. **Highlights:** Charter enshrinee. 229-134-22 coaching record with six NFL championships. Founded pre-NFL Packers, 1919.

JACK LAMBERT
Linebacker. 6-4, 220. Born in Mantua, Ohio, July 8, 1952. Kent State. Inducted in 1990. 1974-1984 Pittsburgh Steelers. **Highlights:** Leader of 'Steel Curtain.' NFL defensive player of year in 1976, nine Pro Bowls.

TOM LANDRY
Coach. Born in Mission, Texas, September 11, 1924. Died February 12, 2000. Texas. Inducted in 1990. 1960-1988 Dallas Cowboys. **Highlights:** 270-178-6 coaching record. 20 consecutive winning seasons. Innovator on offense and defense.

DICK (NIGHT TRAIN) LANE
Cornerback. 6-2, 210. Born in Austin, Texas, April 16, 1928. Died January 29, 2002. Scottsbluff Junior College. Inducted in 1974. 1952-53 Los Angeles Rams, 1954-59 Chicago Cardinals, 1960-65 Detroit Lions. **Highlights:** 68 interceptions for 1,207 yards, 5 touchdowns. Record 14 interceptions as rookie. Seven Pro Bowls.

JIM LANGER
Center. 6-2, 255. Born in Little Falls, Minnesota, May 16, 1948. South Dakota State. Inducted in 1987. 1970-79 Miami Dolphins, 1980-81 Minnesota Vikings. **Highlights:** Played every offensive down in Dolphins' perfect 1972 season. Six Pro Bowls.

WILLIE LANIER
Linebacker. 6-1, 245. Born in Clover, Virginia, August 21, 1945. Morgan State. Inducted in 1986. 1967-1977 Kansas City Chiefs. **Highlights:** 27 interceptions. Defensive star in Super Bowl IV upset. Nicknamed 'Contact' for ferocious tackling.

STEVE LARGENT
Wide receiver. 5-11, 191. Born in Tulsa, Oklahoma, September 28, 1954, Tulsa. Inducted in 1995. 1976-1989 Seattle Seahawks. **Highlights:** 819 receptions for 13,089 yards, 100 touchdowns. Receptions in 177 consecutive games.

YALE LARY
Safety. 5-11, 189. Born in Fort Worth, Texas, November 24, 1930. Texas A&M. Inducted in 1979. 1952-53, 1956-1964 Detroit Lions. **Highlights:** 50 interceptions. Three NFL punting crowns, three touchdowns on punt returns. Nine Pro Bowls.

DANTE LAVELLI
End. 6-0, 199. Born in Hudson, Ohio, February 23, 1923. Died January 20, 2009. Ohio State. Inducted in 1975. 1946-49 Cleveland Browns (AAFC). 1950-56 Cleveland Browns. **Highlights:** 386 receptions for 6,488 yards, 62 touchdowns. 24 catches in six NFL title games.

BOBBY LAYNE
Quarterback. 6-2, 190. Born in Santa Anna, Texas, December 19, 1926. Died December 1, 1986. Texas. Inducted in 1967. 1948 Chicago Bears, 1949 New York Bulldogs, 1950-58 Detroit Lions, 1958-1962 Pittsburgh Steelers. **Highlights:** 26,768 yards passing, 196 touchdowns, 2,451 yards rushing. Late touchdown pass won 1953 NFL title game.

DICK LeBEAU
Cornerback. 6-1, 185. Born in London, Ohio, September 9, 1937. Ohio State. Inducted in 2010. 1959-1972 Detroit Lions. **Highlights:** Recorded 62 career interceptions for 762 yards, 3 TDs, ranked third all-time in interceptions at retirement. Voted to three Pro Bowls.

ALPHONSE (TUFFY) LEEMANS
Fullback. 6-0, 200. Born in Superior, Wisconsin, November 12, 1912. Died January 19, 1979. Oregon, George Washington. Inducted in 1978. 1936-1943 New York Giants. **Highlights:** 3,132 yards rushing, 2,318 yards passing, 422 yards receiving. Led NFL rushers as rookie, 1936.

MARV LEVY
Coach. Born in Chicago, Illinois, August 3, 1925. Wyoming, Coe College, Harvard. Inducted in 2001. 1978-1982 Kansas City Chiefs, 1986-1997 Buffalo Bills. **Highlights:** Led Bills to unprecedented four consecutive Super Bowls. Had 154-120 record. Coaching victories ranked 10th when retired.

BOB LILLY
Defensive tackle. 6-5, 260. Born in Olney, Texas, July 26, 1939. Texas Christian. Inducted in 1980. 1961-1974 Dallas Cowboys. **Highlights:** Eleven Pro Bowls. Played 196 consecutive games. Foundation of great Dallas defensive units.

FLOYD LITTLE
Running back. 5-10, 196. Born in New Haven, Connecticut, July 4, 1942. Syracuse. Inducted in 2010. 1967-1975 Denver Broncos. **Highlights:** Broncos' first 1,000-yard rusher, won NFL rushing title in 1971. Amassed more than 12,000 career all-purpose yards, 54 TDs, five AFL All-Star Games/Pro Bowls.

LARRY LITTLE
Guard. 6-1, 265. Born in Groveland, Georgia, November 2, 1945. Bethune-Cookman. Inducted in 1993. 1967-68 San Diego Chargers, 1969-1980 Miami Dolphins. **Highlights:** Five Pro Bowls, started in three Super Bowls. Epitome of powerful Dolphins rushing game of 1970s.

JAMES LOFTON
Wide receiver. 6-3, 192. Born in Fort Ord, California, July 5, 1956. Stanford. Inducted in 2003. 1978-1986 Green Bay Packers, 1987-88 Los Angeles Raiders, 1989-1992 Buffalo Bills, 1993 Los Angeles Rams, 1993 Philadelphia Eagles. **Highlights:** Played 16 seasons, 233 games. Caught 764 passes for 75 touchdowns and a then-record 14,004 yards. All-Pro four times, eight Pro Bowls.

VINCE LOMBARDI
Coach. Born in Brooklyn, New York, June 11, 1913. Died September 3, 1970. Fordham. Inducted in 1971. 1959-1967 Green Bay Packers, 1969 Washington Redskins. **Highlights:** 105-35-6 coaching record in 10 years, including five NFL titles and victories in Super Bowls I and II.

HOWIE LONG
Defensive end. 6-5, 268. Born in Somerville, Massachusetts, January 6, 1960. Villanova. Inducted in 2000. 1981-1993 Oakland/Los Angeles Raiders. **Highlights:** All-Pro 1983, 1984, 1985. Named All-AFC four times, 1983-1986. Eight Pro Bowls.

RONNIE LOTT
Cornerback-safety. 6-0, 203. Born in Albuquerque, New Mexico, May 8, 1959. Southern California. Inducted in 2000. 1981-1990 San Francisco 49ers, 1991-92 Los Angeles Raiders, 1993-94 New York Jets. **Highlights:** Ten Pro Bowls, 63 career interceptions, and was named to the NFL's 75th Anniversary Team.

SID LUCKMAN
Quarterback. 6-0, 195. Born in Brooklyn, New York, November 21, 1916. Died July 5, 1998. Columbia. Inducted in 1965. 1939-1950 Chicago Bears. **Highlights:** 137 touchdown passes. All-NFL five times. League MVP in 1943.

WILLIAM ROY (LINK) LYMAN

Tackle. 6-2, 252. Born in Table Rock, Nebraska, November 30, 1898. Died December 28, 1972. Nebraska. Inducted in 1964. 1922-23, 1925 Canton Bulldogs, 1924 Cleveland Bulldogs, 1925 Frankford Yellowjackets, 1926-28, 1930-31, 1933-34 Chicago Bears. **Highlights:** Played for four NFL champions. In 16 seasons of college and pro football, played on one losing team.

TOM MACK

Guard. 6-3, 250. Born in Cleveland, Ohio, November 1, 1943. Michigan. Inducted in 1999. 1966-1978 Los Angeles Rams. **Highlights:** Never missed a game in entire 184-game career. Elected to 11 Pro Bowls.

JOHN MACKEY

Tight end. 6-2, 224. Born in New York, New York, September 24, 1941. Syracuse. Inducted in 1992. 1963-1971 Baltimore Colts, 1972 San Diego Chargers. **Highlights:** 331 receptions for 5,236 yards, 38 touchdowns. Second tight end to enter Hall of Fame.

JOHN MADDEN

Coach. Born in Austin, Minnesota, April 10, 1936. San Mateo Junior College, California Polytechnic College at San Luis Obispo. Inducted in 2006. 1969-1978 Oakland Raiders. **Highlights:** Became one of youngest coaches in history when hired at age 32. 112-39-7 overall record. Owns best regular season winning percentage among coaches with 100 wins.

TIM MARA

Team owner. Born in New York, New York, July 29, 1887. Died February 16, 1959. Did not attend college. Inducted in 1963. 1925-1959 New York Giants. **Highlights:** Charter enshrinee. Founder of New York Giants. Built team into powerhouse winning four NFL titles, 10 division titles.

WELLINGTON MARA

Team owner. Born in New York, New York, August 14, 1916. Died October 25, 2005. Fordham. Inducted in 1997. 1937-2005 New York Giants. **Highlights:** Lifetime contributor to NFL and New York Giants. Worked as Giants' ballboy, secretary, vice-president, president and co-CEO. NFC president 1984-present.

GINO MARCHETTI

Defensive end. 6-4, 245. Born in Smithers, West Virginia, January 2, 1927. San Francisco. Inducted in 1972. 1952 Dallas Texans, 1953-1964, 1966 Baltimore Colts. **Highlights:** Named top defensive end of NFL's first 50 years. 10 consecutive Pro Bowls. All-NFL seven times.

DAN MARINO

Quarterback. 6-4, 218. Born in Pittsburgh, Pennsylvania, September 15, 1961. Pittsburgh. Inducted in 2005. 1983-1999 Miami Dolphins. **Highlights:** Held NFL records for career passing yardage (61,361), completions (4,967), attempts (8,358), and touchdowns (420). Voted to nine Pro Bowls.

GEORGE PRESTON MARSHALL

Team owner. Born in Grafton, West Virginia, October 11, 1896. Died August 9, 1969. Randolph-Macon. Inducted in 1963. 1932 Boston Braves, 1933-36 Boston Redskins, 1937-1969 Washington Redskins. **Highlights:** Charter enshrinee. Sponsored progressive rules changes. Organized first team band, pioneered halftime shows.

OLLIE MATSON

Halfback. 6-2, 220. Born in Trinity, Texas, May 1, 1930. Died February 19, 2011. San Francisco. Inducted in 1972. 1952, 1954-58 Chicago Cardinals, 1959-1962 Los Angeles Rams, 1963 Detroit Lions, 1964-66 Philadelphia Eagles. **Highlights:** Nine touchdowns on kickoff, punt returns. Traded for nine players in 1959.

BRUCE MATTHEWS

Guard-tackle-center. 6-5, 289. Born in Raleigh, North Carolina, August 8, 1961. Southern California. Inducted in 2007. 1983-2001 Houston Oilers/Tennessee Oilers/Tennessee Titans. **Highlights:** Played in 296 games, most ever by positional player at time of his retirement. Named to a record-tying 14 straight Pro Bowls. All-Pro nine times, All-AFC 12 times.

DON MAYNARD

Wide receiver. 6-1, 185. Born in Crosbyton, Texas, January 25, 1935. Texas Western. Inducted in 1987. 1958 New York Giants, 1960-62 New York Titans, 1963-1972 New York Jets, 1973 St. Louis Cardinals. **Highlights:** 633 receptions for 11,834 yards, 88 touchdowns. At least 50 catches and 1,000 yards in five different seasons.

GEORGE McAFEE

Halfback. 6-0, 177. Born in Corbin, Kentucky, March 13, 1918. Died March 4, 2009. Duke. Inducted in 1966. 1940-41, 1945-1950 Chicago Bears. **Highlights:** Two-way star. 25 interceptions, 234 points. Career punt-return average of 12.78 yards per return.

MIKE McCORMACK

Tackle. 6-4, 250. Born in Chicago, Illinois, June 21, 1930. Kansas. Inducted in 1984. 1951 New York Yanks, 1954-1962 Cleveland Browns. **Highlights:** Excelled as offensive right tackle for eight years. Six Pro Bowls.

RANDALL McDANIEL

Guard. 6-3, 276. Born in Phoenix, Arizona, December 19, 1964. Arizona State. Inducted in 2009. 1988-1999 Minnesota Vikings, 2000-01 Tampa Bay Buccaneers. **Highlights:** 12 Pro Bowls, All-Pro nine straight times. Blocked for six different 1,000-yard rushers, five 3,000-yard passers.

TOMMY McDONALD

Wide receiver. 5-9, 175. Born in Roy, New Mexico, July 26, 1934. Oklahoma. Inducted in 1998. 1957-1963 Philadelphia Eagles, 1964 Dallas Cowboys, 1965-66 Los Angeles Rams, 1967 Atlanta Falcons, 1968 Cleveland Browns. **Highlights:** Recorded 495 receptions for 8,410 yards, 84 touchdowns.

HUGH McELHENNY

Halfback. 6-1, 198. Born in Los Angeles, California, December 31, 1928. Washington. Inducted in 1970. 1952-1960 San Francisco 49ers, 1961-62 Minnesota Vikings, 1963 New York Giants, 1964 Detroit Lions. **Highlights:** 5,281 rushing yards, 360 points. Totaled 11,369 yards rushing, receiving, and returning kicks.

JOHNNY (BLOOD) McNALLY

Halfback. 6-0, 185. Born in New Richmond, Wisconsin, November 27, 1903. Died November 28, 1985. Notre Dame, St. John's (Minnesota). Inducted in 1963. 1925-26 Milwaukee Badgers, 1926-27 Duluth Eskimos, 1928 Pottsville Maroons, 1929-1933, 1935-36 Green Bay Packers, 1934 Pittsburgh Pirates; player-coach, 1937-38 Pittsburgh Pirates. **Highlights:** Charter enshrinee. 49 touchdowns, 297 points in 14 seasons with five teams.

MIKE MICHALSKE

Guard. 6-0, 209. Born in Cleveland, Ohio, April 24, 1903. Died October 26, 1983. Penn State. Inducted in 1964. 1926 New York Yankees (AFL), 1927-28 New York Yankees, 1929-1935, 1937 Green Bay Packers. **Highlights:** Anchored Packers' championship lines, 1929-1931. First guard enshrined in Canton.

WAYNE MILLNER

End. 6-0, 191. Born in Roxbury, Massachusetts, January 31, 1913. Died November 19, 1976. Notre Dame. Inducted in 1968. 1936 Boston Redskins, 1937-1941, 1945 Washington Redskins. **Highlights:** Redskins' all-time leader with 124 catches when retired. 55- and 78-yard touchdown receptions in 1937 NFL Championship Game.

BOBBY MITCHELL

Running back-wide receiver. 6-0, 195. Born in Hot Springs, Arkansas, June 6, 1935. Illinois. Inducted in 1983. 1958-1961 Cleveland Browns, 1962-68 Washington Redskins. **Highlights:** 91 touchdowns, including 8 on kickoff and punt returns. 14,078 combined yards.

RON MIX

Tackle. 6-4, 255. Born in Los Angeles, California, March 10, 1938. Southern California. Inducted in 1979. 1960 Los Angeles Chargers, 1961-69 San Diego Chargers, 1971 Oakland Raiders. **Highlights:** All-AFL nine times. Only two holding penalties in 10 years with the Chargers.

ART MONK

Wide receiver. 6-3, 210. Born in White Plains, New York, December 5, 1957. Syracuse. Inducted in 2008. 1980-1993 Washington Redskins, 1994 New York Jets, 1995 Philadelphia Eagles. **Highlights:** 940 receptions, 12,721 yards, 68 TDs. Set then-single season record, 106 catches, 1984. Had 50 or more catches in a season nine times.

JOE MONTANA

Quarterback. 6-2, 200. Born in New Eagle, Pennsylvania, June, 11, 1956. Notre Dame. Inducted in 2000. 1979-1992 San Francisco 49ers, 1993-94 Kansas City Chiefs. **Highlights:** MVP in Super Bowl's XVI, XIX, and XXIV. Eight Pro Bowls and All-NFL three times.

WARREN MOON

Quarterback. 6-3, 212. Born in Los Angeles, California, November 18, 1956. West Los Angeles Junior College, Washington. Inducted in 2006. 1984-1993 Houston Oilers, 1994-1996 Minnesota Vikings, 1997-1998 Seattle Seahawks, 1999-2000 Kansas City Chiefs. **Highlights:** Passed for 49,325 yards and 291 touchdowns in 17 NFL seasons. Elected to nine Pro Bowls including eight straight. Threw for 3,000 yards in nine seasons.

LENNY MOORE

Flanker-running back. 6-1, 198. Born in Reading, Pennsylvania, November 25, 1933. Penn State. Inducted in 1975. 1956-1967 Baltimore Colts. **Highlights:** From 1963-65, scored touchdowns in record 18 consecutive games. 113 career touchdowns. 12,451 combined net yards.

MARION MOTLEY

Fullback. 6-1, 238. Born in Leesburg, Georgia, June 5, 1920. Died June 27, 1999. South Carolina State, Nevada. Inducted in 1968. 1946-49 Cleveland Browns (AAFC), 1950-53 Cleveland Browns, 1955 Pittsburgh Steelers. **Highlights:** AAFC's all-time rushing champion. Led league in rushing in first NFL season.

MIKE MUNCHAK

Guard. 6-3, 281. Born in Scranton, Pennsylvania, March 5, 1960. Penn State. Inducted in 2001. 1982-1993 Houston Oilers. **Highlights:** Devastating blocker, All-AFC seven times, elected to nine Pro Bowls.

ANTHONY MUÑOZ

Tackle. 6-6, 278. Born in Ontario, California, August 19, 1958. Southern California. Inducted in 1998. 1980-1992 Cincinnati Bengals. **Highlights:** All-Pro choice 11 consecutive years, 1981-1991. Selected to 11 straight Pro Bowls.

GEORGE MUSSO

Guard-tackle. 6-2, 270. Born in Collinsville, Illinois. April 8, 1910. Died September 5, 2000. Millikin. Inducted in 1982. 1933-1944 Chicago Bears. **Highlights:** First player to achieve All-NFL status at two positions—tackle in 1935 and guard in 1937.

BRONKO NAGURSKI

Fullback. 6-2, 225. Born in Rainy River, Ontario, Canada, November 3, 1908. Died January 7, 1990. Minnesota. Inducted in 1963. 1930-37, 1943 Chicago Bears. **Highlights:** Charter enshrinee. 2,778 rushing yards in nine seasons. All-NFL five times.

JOE NAMATH

Quarterback. 6-2, 200. Born in Beaver Falls, Pennsylvania, May 31, 1943. Alabama. Inducted in 1985. 1965-1976 New York Jets, 1977 Los Angeles Rams. **Highlights:** First quarterback to pass for more than 4,000 yards in season, 1967. Guaranteed, delivered victory over Colts in Super Bowl III.

EARLE (GREASY) NEALE

Coach. Born in Parkersburg, West Virginia, November 5, 1891. Died November 2, 1973. West Virginia Wesleyan. Inducted in 1969. 1941-42, 1944-1950 Philadelphia Eagles; co-coach, 1943 Phil-Pitt. **Highlights:** Turned Eagles into winners with three consecutive division crowns, NFL championships in 1948 and 1949.

ERNIE NEVERS

Fullback. 6-1, 205. Born in Willow River, Minnesota, June 11, 1903. Died May 3, 1976. Stanford. Inducted in 1963. 1926-27 Duluth Eskimos, 1929-1931 Chicago Cardinals. **Highlights:** Charter enshrinee. Holds NFL's longest-standing record, 40 points in one game in 1929.

OZZIE NEWSOME

Tight end. 6-2, 232. Born in Muscle Shoals, Alabama, March 16, 1956. Alabama. Inducted in 1999. 1978-1990 Cleveland Browns. **Highlights:** Finished career as all-time leader among tight ends with 662 receptions for 7,980 yards.

RAY NITSCHKE

Linebacker. 6-3, 235. Born in Elmwood Park, Illinois, December 29, 1936. Died March 8, 1998. Illinois. Inducted in 1978. 1958-1972 Green Bay Packers. **Highlights:** MVP of 1962 title game. Named NFL's all-time linebacker in 1969.

CHUCK NOLL

Coach. Born in Cleveland, Ohio, January 5, 1932. Dayton. Inducted in 1993. 1969-1991 Pittsburgh Steelers. **Highlights:** Coached for 23 years. Only coach to win four Super Bowl titles (IX, X, XIII, XIV).

LEO NOMELLINI

Defensive tackle. 6-3, 264. Born in Lucca, Italy, June 19, 1924. Died October 17, 2000. Minnesota. Inducted in 1969. 1950-1963 San Francisco 49ers. **Highlights:** Played every 49ers game for 14 seasons. 10 Pro Bowls.

MERLIN OLSEN

Defensive tackle. 6-5, 270. Born in Logan, Utah, September 15, 1940. Died March 11, 2010. Utah State. Inducted in 1982. 1962-1976 Los Angeles Rams. **Highlights:** Member of the Fearsome "Foursome. Named" to 14 consecutive Pro Bowls, Rams' all-time team.

JIM OTTO

Center. 6-2, 255. Born in Wausau, Wisconsin, January 5, 1938. Miami. Inducted in 1980. 1960-1974 Oakland Raiders. **Highlights:** Named AFL's all-time center. Played in 210 games, 12 AFL All-Star Games or Pro Bowls, six AFL/AFC title games.

STEVE OWEN

Tackle. Coach. 6-2, 235. Born in Cleo Springs, Oklahoma, April 21, 1898. Died May 17, 1964. Phillips. Inducted in 1966. 1924-25 Kansas City Cowboys, 1925 Cleveland Bulldogs, 1926-1931, 1933 New York Giants; coach, 1930-1953 New York Giants. **Highlights:** Both player and coach. Coached Giants to record of 155-108-17, eight divisional titles, two NFL championships.

ALAN PAGE

Defensive tackle. 6-4, 225. Born in Canton, Ohio, August 7, 1945. Notre Dame. Inducted in 1988. 1967-1978 Minnesota Vikings, 1978-1981 Chicago Bears. **Highlights:** Dominating defensive tackle played in 238 consecutive games, four Super Bowls. Won league MVP honors in 1971.

CLARENCE (ACE) PARKER
Quarterback. 5-11, 168. Born in Portsmouth, Virginia, May 17, 1912. Duke. Inducted in 1972. 1937-1941 Brooklyn Dodgers, 1945 Boston Yanks, 1946 New York Yankees (AAFC). **Highlights:** Two-way threat. Two-time All-NFL performer, league MVP in 1940.

JIM PARKER
Guard-tackle. 6-3, 273. Born in Macon, Georgia, April 3, 1934. Died July 18, 2005. Ohio State. Inducted in 1973. 1957-1967 Baltimore Colts. **Highlights:** First full-time offensive lineman elected to Hall of Fame. All-NFL eight consecutive years, eight Pro Bowls.

WALTER PAYTON
Running back. 5-10, 202. Born in Columbia, Mississippi, July 25, 1954. Died November 1, 1999. Jackson State. Inducted in 1993. 1975-1987 Chicago Bears. **Highlights:** NFL's all-time leading rusher with 16,726 yards and combined net yardage with 21,803 at time of retirement.

JOE PERRY
Fullback. 6-0, 200. Born in Stevens, Arkansas, January 22, 1927. Died April 25, 2011. Compton Junior College. Inducted in 1969. 1948-49 San Francisco 49ers (AAFC), 1950-1960, 1963 San Francisco 49ers, 1961-62 Baltimore Colts. **Highlights:** First player in NFL history to gain 1,000 yards two consecutive seasons. 12,532 combined yards.

PETE PIHOS
End. 6-1, 210. Born in Orlando, Florida, October 22, 1923. Indiana. Inducted in 1970. 1947-1955 Philadelphia Eagles. **Highlights:** Three-time NFL receiving champion. Caught winning touchdown in 1949 NFL Championship Game.

FRITZ POLLARD
Halfback-Coach. 5-9, 165. Born in Chicago, Illinois, January 27, 1894. Died May 11, 1986. Brown. Inducted in 2005. 1919-1921, 1925-26 Akron Pros/Indians, 1922 Milwaukee Badgers, 1923, 1925 Hammond Pros, 1925 Providence Steam Roller. **Highlights:** True pioneer as one of two African American players in the NFL in 1920 and helped lead Akron to league title that season. In 1921, became the league's first black head coach.

JOHN RANDLE
Defensive tackle. 6-1, 278. Born in Hearne, Texas, December 12, 1967. Trinity Valley Community College; Texas A&I. Inducted in 2010. 1990-2000 Minnesota Vikings, 2001-03 Seattle Seahawks. **Highlights:** Undrafted free agent rookie, record eight straight seasons with 10 or more sacks, had 137.5 career sacks. Voted to seven Pro Bowls, named All-Pro/NFC six consecutive years, All-AFC once.

HUGH (SHORTY) RAY
Supervisor of officials 1938-1952. Born in Highland Park, Illinois, September 21, 1884. Died September 16, 1956. Illinois. Inducted in 1966. **Highlights:** Supervisor of Officials, 1938-1952. Streamlined rules to improve game tempo, player safety.

DAN REEVES
Team owner. Born in New York, New York, June 30, 1912. Died April 15, 1971. Georgetown. Inducted in 1967. 1941-45 Cleveland Rams, 1946-1971 Los Angeles Rams. **Highlights:** Moved Rams to Los Angeles in 1946 and opened up West Coast to pro football. First postwar owner to sign African-American player.

MEL RENFRO
Cornerback-safety. 6-0, 192. Born in Houston, Texas, December 30, 1941. Oregon. Inducted in 1996. 1964-1977 Dallas Cowboys. **Highlights:** 52 interceptions for 626 yards and 3 touchdowns. Also added 842 yards on punt returns, 2,246 yards on kickoff returns. Elected to Pro Bowl first 10 seasons.

JERRY RICE
Wide receiver. 6-2, 200. Born in Starksville, Mississippi, October 13, 1962. Mississippi Valley State. Inducted in 2010. 1985-2000 San Francisco 49ers, 2001-04 Oakland Raiders, 2004 Seattle Seahawks. **Highlights:** NFL's all-time reception leader with 1,549 catches for 22,895 yards, 208 total touchdowns. Had 14 seasons with 1,000 yards receiving; 23,546 combined net yards. All-Pro 11 times, Super Bowl XXIII MVP.

LES RICHTER
Linebacker. 6-3, 238. Born in Fresno, California, October 6, 1930. Died June 12, 2011. California. Inducted in 2011. 1954-1962 Los Angeles Rams. **Highlights:** Second overall pick in 1952 by New York Yanks. Rights traded to Rams in exchange for 11 players. Rugged, fierce competitor. Voted to eight straight Pro Bowls. Recorded 16 career interceptions, also handled Rams' placekicking duties early in career.

JOHN RIGGINS
Running back. 6-2, 240. Born in Seneca, Kansas, August 4, 1949. Kansas. Inducted in 1992. 1971-75 New York Jets, 1976-79, 1981-85 Washington Redskins. **Highlights:** 11,352 rushing yards, 116 total touchdowns. MVP of Super Bowl XVII with 166 rushing yards including game-winning 43-yard touchdown.

JIM RINGO
Center. 6-2, 230. Born in Orange, New Jersey, November 21, 1931. Died November 19, 2007. Syracuse. Inducted in 1981. 1953-1963 Green Bay Packers, 1964-67 Philadelphia Eagles. **Highlights:** Ten-time Pro Bowl selection, seven-time All-NFL selection. Started in then-record 182 consecutive games.

ANDY ROBUSTELLI
Defensive end. 6-0, 230. Born in Stamford, Connecticut, December 6, 1925. Arnold College. Inducted in 1971. 1951-55 Los Angeles Rams, 1956-1964 New York Giants. **Highlights:** Anchored defense in eight championship games. Named NFL's top player in 1962.

ART ROONEY
Team owner. Born in Coulterville, Pennsylvania, January 27, 1901. Died August 25, 1988. Georgetown, Duquesne. Inducted in 1964. 1933-39 Pittsburgh Pirates, 1940-42, 1945-1988 Pittsburgh Steelers, 1943 Phil-Pitt, 1944 Card-Pitt. **Highlights:** Founded Pittsburgh Pirates in 1933 and renamed them Steelers in 1940. Team won four Super Bowls in 1970s.

DAN ROONEY
Team owner. Born in Pittsburgh, Pennsylvania, July, 20, 1932. Duquesne. Inducted in 2000. 1955-present Pittsburgh Steelers. **Highlights:** Has been on the board of directors for the NFL Trust Fund, NFL Films, and Scheduling Committee. Played a key role in the labor agreement reached in 1993 between the NFL owners and players.

PETE ROZELLE
Commissioner. Born in South Gate, California, March 1, 1926. Died December 6, 1996. Compton Junior College, San Francisco. Inducted in 1985. Commissioner, 1960-1989. **Highlights:** Negotiated first league-wide television contract in 1962. Generally recognized as premiere commissioner in all of sports. Credited with making NFL the nation's most popular sport.

BOB ST. CLAIR
Tackle. 6-9, 265. Born in San Francisco, California, February 18, 1931. San Francisco, Tulsa. Inducted in 1990. 1953-1963 San Francisco 49ers. **Highlights:** Exceptional offensive lineman. Also played goal-line defense and had 10 blocked field goals, 1956.

ED SABOL
Founder-President-Chairman. Born in Atlantic City, New Jersey, September 11, 1916. Ohio State. Inducted in 2011. 1964-1995 NFL Films. **Highlights:** Bid and received rights to film 1962 NFL Championship Game. Two years later, founded NFL Films. During his tenure, NFL Films won 52 Emmys. Vision and innovations changed the way in which sports were presented.

BARRY SANDERS
Running back. 5-8, 203. Born in Wichita, Kansas, July 16, 1968. Inducted in 2004. 1989-1998 Detroit Lions. **Highlights:** 15,269 rushing yards, 99 touchdowns. Rushed for 1,000 yards in each of 10 seasons. NFL co-MVP, 1997. Selected to 10 Pro Bowls.

CHARLIE SANDERS
Tight end. 6-4, 230. Born in Richlands, North Carolina, August 25, 1946. Minnesota. Inducted in 2007. 1968-1977 Detroit Lions. **Highlights:** 336 career receptions for 4,817 yards and 31 touchdowns. Selected to seven Pro Bowls. Named to the NFL's All-Decade Team of 1970s.

DEION SANDERS
Cornerback-Kick returner-Punt returner. 6-1, 195. Born in Fort Myers, Florida, August 9, 1967. Florida State. Inducted in 2011. 1989-1993 Atlanta Falcons, 1994 San Francisco 49ers, 1995-99 Dallas Cowboys, 2000 Washington Redskins, 2004-05 Baltimore Ravens. **Highlights:** First-team All-NFL nine times. Voted to the NFL's All-Decade Team of the 1990s at both cornerback and punt returner. 53 career interceptions. Career touchdowns include six on punt returns, three on kickoff returns, nine on interceptions, one fumble recovery, and three receiving.

GALE SAYERS
Running back. 6-0, 200. Born in Wichita, Kansas, May 30, 1943. Kansas. Inducted in 1977. 1965-1971 Chicago Bears. **Highlights:** Broke into league by scoring rookie-record 22 touchdowns. Led league in rushing in 1966, 1969. MVP of three Pro Bowls.

JOE SCHMIDT
Linebacker. 6-0, 222. Born in Pittsburgh, Pennsylvania, January 18, 1932. Pittsburgh. Inducted in 1973. 1953-1965 Detroit Lions. **Highlights:** 24 interceptions. Lions' team captain for nine years. Mastered middle linebacker position that evolved in 1950s.

TEX SCHRAMM
Team president-general manager. Born in San Gabriel, California, June 2, 1920. Died July 15, 2003. Texas. Inducted in 1991. 1947-1956 Los Angeles Rams. 1960-1989 Dallas Cowboys. **Highlights:** Played prominent role in AFL-NFL merger. Chairman of Competition Committee from 1966-1988.

LEE ROY SELMON
Defensive end. 6-3, 250. Born in Eufaula, Oklahoma, October 20, 1954. Oklahoma. Inducted in 1995. 1976-1984 Tampa Bay Buccaneers. **Highlights:** 78½ sacks, 380 quarterback pressures, forced 28 fumbles. Six consecutive Pro Bowl selections.

SHANNON SHARPE
Tight end. 6-2, 230. Born in Chicago, Illinois, June 26, 1968. Savannah State. Inducted in 2011. 1990-99, 2002-03 Denver Broncos, 2000-01 Baltimore Ravens. **Highlights:** Retired as the NFL's all-time leader among tight ends for catches (815), receiving yards (10,060) and TD receptions (62). Selected as first- or second-team All-Pro five times, named to eight Pro Bowls. Played on three Super Bowl championship teams in four seasons.

BILLY SHAW
Guard. 6-2, 258. Born in Natchez, Mississippi, December 15, 1938. Georgia Tech. Inducted in 1999. 1961-69 Buffalo Bills. **Highlights:** First player who played entire career in AFL to be elected to Hall of Fame. Named to AFL's all-time team.

ART SHELL
Tackle. 6-5, 285. Born in Charleston, South Carolina, November 26, 1946. Maryland State-Eastern Shore. Inducted in 1989. 1968-82 Oakland/Los Angeles Raiders. **Highlights:** Cornerstone of Raiders' offensive line in 1970s. 207 regular-season games, 23 postseason games, eight Pro Bowls.

DON SHULA
Coach. Born in Grand River, Ohio, January 4, 1930. John Carroll. Inducted in 1997. 1963-69 Baltimore Colts, 1970-1995 Miami Dolphins. **Highlights:** Won more games (347) than any coach in NFL history. Won two Super Bowl titles, including Super Bowl VII when Dolphins recorded NFL's only perfect season (17-0).

O.J. SIMPSON
Running back. 6-1, 212. Born in San Francisco, California, July 9, 1947. City College (San Francisco), Southern California. Inducted in 1985. 1969-1977 Buffalo Bills, 1978-79 San Francisco 49ers. **Highlights:** In 1973, became first player to rush for 2,000 yards in season. Finished career with four rushing titles, 11,236 yards.

MIKE SINGLETARY
Linebacker. 6-0, 230. Born in Houston, Texas, October 9, 1958. Baylor. Inducted in 1998. 1981-1992 Chicago Bears. **Highlights:** All-Pro choice eight times and All-NFC nine consecutive seasons. Selected to 10 Pro Bowls.

JACKIE SLATER
Tackle. 6-4, 277. Born in Jackson, Mississippi, May 27, 1954. Jackson State. Inducted in 2001. 1976-1995 Los Angeles/St. Louis Rams. **Highlights:** Played 20 seasons, 259 games. Blocked for seven different 1,000-yard rushers. Seven Pro Bowls.

BRUCE SMITH
Defensive end. 6-4, 280. Born in Norfolk, Virginia, June 18, 1963. Virginia Tech. Inducted in 2009. 1985-1999 Buffalo Bills, 2000-03 Washington Redskins. **Highlights:** NFL's all-time leader in sacks with 200. Named All-Pro nine times, 11 Pro Bowls. Selected to NFL's All-Decade Team of 1980s and 1990s.

EMMITT SMITH
Running back. 5-9, 207. Born in Pensacola, Florida, May 15, 1969. Florida. Inducted in 2010. 1990-2002 Dallas Cowboys, 2003-04 Arizona Cardinals. **Highlights:** Won four rushing titles in five years, recorded record 11 straight 1,000-yard seasons. NFL's all-time leading rusher with 18,355 yards, 164 rushing TDs. Won NFL MVP and Super Bowl XXVIII MVP in 1993.

JACKIE SMITH
Tight end. 6-4, 232. Born in Columbia, Mississippi, February 23, 1940. Northwestern State (Louisiana). Inducted in 1994. 1963-1977 St. Louis Cardinals, 1978 Dallas Cowboys. **Highlights:** 480 receptions for 7,918 yards, 40 touchdowns. Third tight end to be elected to Hall of Fame.

JOHN STALLWORTH

Wide receiver. 6-2, 191. Born in Tuscaloosa, Alabama, July 15, 1952. Alabama A&M. Inducted in 2002. 1974-1987 Pittsburgh Steelers. **Highlights:** 537 receptions for 8,723 yards, 63 touchdowns. Scored go-ahead touchdown in Super Bowl XIV on 73-yard reception.

BART STARR

Quarterback. 6-1, 200. Born in Montgomery, Alabama, January 9, 1934. Alabama. Inducted in 1977. 1956-1971 Green Bay Packers. **Highlights:** Quarterbacked Packers to six division titles, five NFL titles, and first two Super Bowls in which he was MVP.

ROGER STAUBACH

Quarterback. 6-3, 202. Born in Cincinnati, Ohio, February 5, 1942. New Mexico Military Institute, Navy. Inducted in 1985. 1969-1979 Dallas Cowboys. **Highlights:** Led Cowboys to four NFC titles and victories in Super Bowls VI, XII. When retired, 83.4 career passer rating was best of all time.

ERNIE STAUTNER

Defensive tackle. 6-2, 235. Born in Prinzing-by-Cham, Bavaria, April 20, 1925. Died February 16, 2006. Boston College. Inducted in 1969. 1950-1963 Pittsburgh Steelers. **Highlights:** Played in nine Pro Bowls and won the best lineman award in 1957. Recorded 3 safeties.

JAN STENERUD

Kicker. 6-2, 190. Born in Fetsund, Norway, November 26, 1942. Montana State. Inducted in 1991. 1967-1979 Kansas City Chiefs, 1980-83 Green Bay Packers, 1984-85 Minnesota Vikings. **Highlights:** 1,699 points on 580 extra points, 373 field goals. First pure placekicker to enter Hall of Fame.

DWIGHT STEPHENSON

Center. 6-2, 255. Born in Murfreesboro, North Carolina, November 20, 1957. Alabama. Inducted in 1998. 1980-87 Miami Dolphins. **Highlights:** Recognized as premier center of his time. All-Pro, All-AFC five straight years. Selected to five Pro Bowls.

HANK STRAM

Coach. Born in Chicago, Illinois, January 3, 1923. Died July 4, 2005. Purdue. Inducted in 2003. 1960-1974 Dallas Texans/Kansas City Chiefs, 1976-1977 New Orleans Saints. **Highlights:** Overall record of 136-100-10. Recorded most wins in AFL history. Guided teams to titles in 1962, 1966, and 1969. Led Chiefs to AFL win in Super Bowl IV.

KEN STRONG

Halfback. 5-11, 210. Born in West Haven, Connecticut, April 21, 1906. Died October 5, 1979. New York University. Inducted in 1967. 1929-1932 Staten Island Stapletons, 1933-35, 1939, 1944-47 New York Giants, 1936-37 New York Yanks (AFL). **Highlights:** Scored 17 points to lead Giants to victory in 1934 'Sneakers' game, led NFL with 64 points, 1933.

JOE STYDAHAR

Tackle. 6-4, 230. Born in Kaylor, Pennsylvania, March 17, 1912. Died March 23, 1977. West Virginia. Inducted in 1967. 1936-1942, 1945-46 Chicago Bears. **Highlights:** One of stalwarts of Bears' 'Monsters of the Midway.' Played on five divisional, three NFL championship teams.

LYNN SWANN

Wide receiver. 5-11, 180. Born in Alcoa, Tennessee, March 7, 1952. Southern California. Inducted in 2001. 1974-1982 Pittsburgh Steelers. **Highlights:** All-AFC three times. Selected to three Pro Bowls. MVP, Super Bowl X.

FRAN TARKENTON

Quarterback. 6-0, 185. Born in Richmond, Virginia, February 3, 1940. Georgia. Inducted in 1986. 1961-66, 1972-78 Minnesota Vikings, 1967-1971 New York Giants. **Highlights:** At retirement, held NFL records for attempts (6,467), completions (3,686), yards (47,003), and touchdowns (342). Four touchdowns passes in first NFL game.

CHARLEY TAYLOR

Running back-wide receiver. 6-3, 210. Born in Grand Prairie, Texas, September 28, 1941. Arizona State. Inducted in 1984. 1964-1975, 1977 Washington Redskins. **Highlights:** Won rookie of year honors as running back. Switched to wide receiver and won receiving titles in 1966, 1967.

JIM TAYLOR

Fullback. 6-0, 216. Born in Baton Rouge, Louisiana, September 20, 1935. Hinds Junior College; Louisiana State. Inducted in 1976. 1958-1966 Green Bay Packers, 1967 New Orleans Saints. **Highlights:** 8,597 rushing yards, 558 points. In 1962, led league in rushing and scoring with 19 touchdowns.

LAWRENCE TAYLOR

Linebacker. 6-3, 237. Born in Williamsburg, Virginia, February 4, 1959. North Carolina. Inducted in 1999. 1981-1993 New York Giants. **Highlights:** Redefined the position of outside linebacker. All-Pro nine times, 10 Pro Bowls. NFL MVP in 1986.

DERRICK THOMAS

Linebacker. 6-3, 243. Born in Miami, Florida, January 1, 1967. Died February 8, 2000. Alabama. Inducted in 2009. 1989-1999 Kansas City Chiefs. **Highlights:** Set NFL record with 7 sacks in one game. Recorded most sacks in NFL during 1990s. Nine Pro Bowls. Named to NFL's All-Decade Team of 1990s.

EMMITT THOMAS

Cornerback. 6-2, 192. Born in Angleton, Texas, June 3, 1943. Bishop. Inducted in 2008. 1966-1978 Kansas City Chiefs. **Highlights:** Undrafted free agent. 58 interceptions, 937 yards, 5 TDs. Ranked fifth all-time in interceptions at retirement. Interception leader —AFL, 1969 and NFL, 1974.

THURMAN THOMAS

Running back. 5-10, 198. Born in Houston, Texas, May 16, 1966. Oklahoma State. Inducted in 2007. 1988-1999 Buffalo Bills, 2000 Miami Dolphins. **Highlights:** Amassed 16,532 total yards including 12,074 yards rushing. Scored 88 touchdowns. Only player in history to lead league in yards from scrimmage four straight seasons.

JIM THORPE

Halfback. 6-1, 190. Born in Prague, Oklahoma, May 28, 1888. Died March 28, 1953. Carlisle. Inducted in 1963. 1915-17, 1919-1920, 1926 Canton Bulldogs, 1921 Cleveland Indians, 1922-23 Oorang Indians, 1924 Rock Island Independents, 1925 New York Giants, 1928 Chicago Cardinals. **Highlights:** Charter enshrinee. First president of American Professional Football Association, 1920. Played for 12 seasons.

ANDRE TIPPETT

Linebacker. 6-3, 240. Born in Birmingham, Alabama, December 27, 1959. Iowa; Ellsworth (IA) Jr. College. Inducted in 2008. 1982-1993 New England Patriots. **Highlights:** Recorded 100 career sacks including personal best 18.5 sacks, 1984. Named to five straight Pro Bowls, 1985-89.

Y.A. TITTLE

Quarterback. 6-0, 200. Born in Marshall, Texas, October 24, 1926. Louisiana State. Inducted in 1971. 1948-49 Baltimore Colts (AAFC), 1950 Baltimore Colts, 1951-1960 San Francisco 49ers, 1961-64 New York Giants. **Highlights:** 33,070 yards, 242 touchdowns. 33 touchdown passes in 1962 and 36 in 1963. Two-time league MVP.

GEORGE TRAFTON
Center. 6-2, 235. Born in Chicago, Illinois, December 6, 1896. Died September 5, 1971. Notre Dame. Inducted in 1964. 1920-1932 Decatur Staleys/Chicago Staleys/Chicago Bears. **Highlights:** First center to snap with one hand. Named top NFL center of 1920s.

CHARLEY TRIPPI
Halfback-quarterback. 6-0, 185. Born in Pittston, Pennsylvania, December 14, 1922. Georgia. Inducted in 1968. 1947-1955 Chicago Cardinals. **Highlights:** One of football's most versatile performers. Played halfback five years, quarterback for two, defense for two.

EMLEN TUNNELL
Safety. 6-1, 200. Born in Bryn Mawr, Pennsylvania, March 29, 1925. Died July 22, 1975. Toledo, Iowa. Inducted in 1967. 1948-1958 New York Giants, 1959-1961 Green Bay Packers. **Highlights:** 79 interceptions. Gained more yards on kickoff, punt, and interception returns (924) in 1952 than that season's NFL rushing leader.

CLYDE (BULLDOG) TURNER
Center. 6-2, 235. Born in Plains, Texas, March 10, 1919. Died October 30, 1998. Hardin-Simmons. Inducted in 1966. 1940-1952 Chicago Bears. **Highlights:** Anchored defense for four NFL championship teams, including 4 interceptions in five title games.

JOHNNY UNITAS
Quarterback. 6-1, 195. Born in Pittsburgh, Pennsylvania, May 7, 1933. Died September 11, 2002. Louisville. Inducted in 1979. 1956-1972 Baltimore Colts, 1973 San Diego Chargers. **Highlights:** 40,239 passing yards, 290 touchdowns. Led Colts to two NFL championships. Passed for at least one touchdown in 47 consecutive games.

GENE UPSHAW
Guard. 6-5, 255. Born in Robstown, Texas, August 15, 1945. Died August 20, 2008. Texas A & I. Inducted in 1987. 1967-1981 Oakland Raiders. **Highlights:** Premier guard of his era played in 10 AFL/AFC Championship Games, three Super Bowls, seven Pro Bowls.

NORM VAN BROCKLIN
Quarterback. 6-1, 190. Born in Eagle Butte, South Dakota, March 15, 1926. Died May 2, 1983. Oregon. Inducted in 1971. 1949-1957 Los Angeles Rams, 1958-1960 Philadelphia Eagles. **Highlights:** NFL-record 554 yards passing in 1951 season opener. Guided Eagles to NFL crown as league's Most Outstanding Player in 1960.

STEVE VAN BUREN
Halfback. 6-1, 200. Born in La Ceiba, Honduras, December 28, 1920. Louisiana State. Inducted in 1965. 1944-1951 Philadelphia Eagles. **Highlights:** Four-time rushing champion. Won 1944 punt-return title and was 1945 kickoff-return champion.

DOAK WALKER
Halfback. 5-11, 173. Born in Dallas, Texas, January 1, 1927. Died September 27, 1998. Southern Methodist. Inducted in 1986. 1950-55 Detroit Lions. **Highlights:** 534 points. Won two NFL scoring titles. Had winning 67-yard scoring run in 1952 title game.

BILL WALSH
Coach. Born in Los Angeles, California, November 30, 1931. Died July 30, 2007. San Jose State. Inducted in 1993. 1979-1988 San Francisco 49ers. **Highlights:** 102-63-1 coaching record. Guided 49ers to three Super Bowl titles (XVI, XIX, XXIII) in 10 years.

PAUL WARFIELD
Wide receiver. 6-0, 188. Born in Warren, Ohio, November 28, 1942. Ohio State. Inducted in 1983. 1964-69, 1976-77 Cleveland Browns, 1970-74 Miami Dolphins. **Highlights:** 8,565 yards receiving, 85 touchdowns. Eight-time Pro Bowl player. Key to both Cleveland and Miami offenses.

BOB WATERFIELD
Quarterback. 6-2, 200. Born in Elmira, New York, July 26, 1920. Died March 25, 1983. UCLA. Inducted in 1965. 1945 Cleveland Rams, 1946-1952 Los Angeles Rams. **Highlights:** NFL MVP as rookie in 1945 and led Rams to NFL title. Grabbed 20 interceptions in limited defensive duties.

MIKE WEBSTER
Center. 6-2, 260. Born in Tomahawk, Wisconsin, March 18, 1952. Died September 24, 2002. Wisconsin. Inducted in 1997. 1974-1988 Pittsburgh Steelers, 1989-1990 Kansas City Chiefs. **Highlights:** Played in 245 games, nine Pro Bowls, and won four Super Bowls during 17-year career.

ROGER WEHRLI
Cornerback. 6-0, 190. Born in New Point, Missouri, November 26, 1947. Missouri. Inducted in 2007. 1969-1982 St. Louis Cardinals. **Highlights:** 40 career interceptions. Named to the NFL's All-Decade Team of 1970s. All-Pro five times, selected to seven Pro Bowls.

ARNIE WEINMEISTER
Defensive tackle. 6-4, 235. Born in Rhein, Saskatchewan, Canada, March 23, 1923. Died June 29, 2000. Washington. Inducted in 1984. 1948-49 New York Yankees (AAFC), 1950-53 New York Giants. **Highlights:** Dominant defensive tackle of his time. Four-time All-NFL selection, four Pro Bowls.

RANDY WHITE
Defensive tackle. 6-4, 265. Born in Pittsburgh, Pennsylvania, January 15, 1953. Maryland. Inducted in 1994. 1975-1988 Dallas Cowboys. **Highlights:** Missed only one game in 14 seasons. Co-MVP of Super Bowl XII. Nine-time Pro Bowl selection.

REGGIE WHITE
Defensive end. 6-5, 291. Born in Chattanooga, Tennessee, December 19, 1961. Died December 26, 2004. Tennessee. Inducted in 2006. 1985-1992 Philadelphia Eagles, 1993-1998 Green Bay Packers, 2000 Carolina Panthers. **Highlights:** Retired as all-time sack leader with 198. Named All-Pro 13 of 15 seasons including 10 as first-team selection. Named to 13 straight Pro Bowls.

DAVE WILCOX
Linebacker. 6-3, 241. Born in Ontario, Oregon, September, 29, 1942. Boise State, Oregon. Inducted in 2000. 1964-1974 San Francisco 49ers. **Highlights:** Seven Pro Bowls, All-NFL five times. Missed only one game because of injury.

BILL WILLIS
Guard. 6-2, 215. Born in Columbus, Ohio, October 5, 1921. Died November 27, 2007. Ohio State. Inducted in 1977. 1946-1953 Cleveland Browns (AAFC/NFL). **Highlights:** Two-way player who excelled on defense. Four-time All-NFL player, played in three Pro Bowls.

LARRY WILSON
Safety. 6-0, 190. Born in Rigby, Idaho, March 24, 1938. Utah. Inducted in 1978. 1960-1972 St. Louis Cardinals. **Highlights:** 52 interceptions. Had interception in seven consecutive games in 1966. Made "safety blitz" famous.

RALPH WILSON, JR.
Owner-founder. Born in Columbus, Ohio, October 17, 1918. Virginia, Michigan. Inducted in 2009. 1960-present Buffalo Bills. **Highlights:** Founded team. Bills teams captured back-to-back AFL titles in mid-1960s. Unprecedented four straight Super Bowl appearances.

KELLEN WINSLOW
Tight end. 6-5, 250. Born in St. Louis, Missouri, November 5, 1957. Missouri. Inducted in 1995. 1979-1987 San Diego Chargers **Highlights:** 541 receptions for 6,741 yards, 45 touchdowns. 13 catches, blocked field goal in 1981 playoff win over Miami.

ALEX WOJCIECHOWICZ
Center. 6-0, 235. Born in South River, New Jersey, August 12, 1915. Died July 13, 1992. Fordham. Inducted in 1968. 1938-1946 Detroit Lions, 1946-1950 Philadelphia Eagles. **Highlights:** One of league's first Iron men. Played both ways for eight years with Lions.

WILLIE WOOD
Safety. 5-10, 190. Born in Washington, D.C., December 23, 1936. Southern California. Inducted in 1989. 1960-1971 Green Bay Packers. **Highlights:** 48 interceptions. Competed in six NFL Championship Games and Super Bowls I and II.

ROD WOODSON
Cornerback-safety. 6-0, 200. Born in Fort Wayne, Indiana, March 10, 1965. Purdue. Inducted in 2009. 1987-1996 Pittsburgh Steelers, 1997 San Francisco 49ers, 1998-2001 Baltimore Ravens, 2002-03 Oakland Raiders. **Highlights:** 71 interceptions returned for 1,483 yards and NFL record 12 TDs. Named NFL Defensive Player of Year, 1993. Member of NFL's 75th Anniversary Team. 11 Pro Bowls.

RAYFIELD WRIGHT
Tackle. 6-6, 255. Born in Griffin, Georgia, August 23, 1945. Fort Valley State. Inducted in 2006. 1967-1979 Dallas Cowboys. **Highlights:** Named first- or second-team All-Pro and voted to Pro Bowl six straight seasons, 1971-76. Played in six NFC championship games and five Super Bowls. Named to NFL's All-Decade Team of 1970s.

RON YARY
Tackle. 6-5, 255. Born in Chicago, Illinois, July 16, 1946. Cerritos (Calif.) J.C., Southern California. Inducted in 2001. 1968-1981 Minnesota Vikings, 1982 Los Angeles Rams. **Highlights:** All-Pro six consecutive seasons, All-NFC eight consecutive years. Named to seven Pro Bowls. Started in four Super Bowls and five NFL/NFC Championship Games.

STEVE YOUNG
Quarterback. 6-2, 205. Born in Salt Lake City, Utah, October 11, 1961. Brigham Young. Inducted in 2005. 1985-86 Tampa Bay Buccaneers, 1987-1999 San Francisco 49ers. **Highlights:** Led the NFL in passing a record-tying six times. Passed for more than 33,000 yards and 232 touchdowns in career. MVP of Super Bowl XXIX. Elected to seven Pro Bowls.

JACK YOUNGBLOOD
Defensive end. 6-4, 247. Born in Jacksonville, Florida, January 26, 1950. Florida. Inducted in 2001. 1971-1984 Los Angeles Rams. **Highlights:** Played in club-record 201 consecutive games. Played in five NFC Championship Games, one Super Bowl. Named All-Pro five times, All-NFC seven times. Elected to seven consecutive Pro Bowls. Lions.

GARY ZIMMERMAN
Tackle. 6-6, 294. Born in Fullerton, California, December 13, 1961. Oregon. Inducted in 2008. 1986-1992 Minnesota Vikings, 1993-97 Denver Broncos. **Highlights:** Named to seven Pro Bowls. One of handful of players to be named to two NFL All-Decade Teams, 1980s and 1990s.

ENSHRINEES BY YEAR OF INDUCTION
*Deceased
(Date of enshrinement in parentheses)

1963 CHARTER CLASS
(September 7, 1963)
Sammy Baugh*
Bert Bell*
Joe Carr*
Earl (Dutch) Clark*
Harold (Red) Grange*
George Halas*
Mel Hein*
Wilbur (Pete) Henry*
Robert (Cal) Hubbard*
Don Hutson*
Earl (Curly) Lambeau*
Tim Mara*
George Preston Marshall*
John (Blood) McNally*
Bronko Nagurski*
Ernie Nevers*
Jim Thorpe*

CLASS OF 1964
(September 6, 1964)
Jimmy Conzelman*
Ed Healey*
Clarke Hinkle*
William Roy (Link) Lyman*
Mike Michalske*
Art Rooney*
George Trafton*

CLASS OF 1965
(September 12, 1965)
Guy Chamberlin*
John (Paddy) Driscoll*
Dan Fortmann*
Otto Graham*
Sid Luckman*
Steve Van Buren
Bob Waterfield*

CLASS OF 1966
(September 17, 1966)
Bill Dudley*
Joe Guyon*
Arnie Herber*
Walt Kiesling*
George McAfee*
Steve Owen*
Hugh (Shorty) Ray*
Clyde (Bulldog) Turner*

CLASS OF 1967
(August 5, 1967)
Chuck Bednarik
Charles W. Bidwill Sr.*
Paul Brown*
Bobby Layne*
Dan Reeves*
Ken Strong*
Joe Stydahar*
Emlen Tunnell*

CLASS OF 1968
(August 3, 1968)
Cliff Battles*
Art Donovan
Elroy (Crazylegs) Hirsch*
Wayne Millner*
Marion Motley*
Charley Trippi
Alex Wojciechowicz*

CLASS OF 1969
(September 13, 1969)
Albert Glen (Turk) Edwards*
Earle (Greasy) Neale*
Leo Nomellini*
Joe Perry*
Ernie Stautner*

CLASS OF 1970
(August 8, 1970)
Jack Christiansen*
Tom Fears*
Hugh McElhenny
Pete Pihos

CLASS OF 1971
(July 31, 1971)
Jim Brown
Bill Hewitt*
Frank (Bruiser) Kinard*
Vince Lombardi*
Andy Robustelli
Y. A. Tittle
Norm Van Brocklin*

CLASS OF 1972
(July 29, 1972)
Lamar Hunt*
Gino Marchetti
Ollie Matson*
Clarence (Ace) Parker

CLASS OF 1973
(July 28, 1973)
Raymond Berry
Jim Parker*
Joe Schmidt

CLASS OF 1974
(July 27, 1974)
Tony Canadeo*
Bill George*
Lou Groza*
Dick (Night Train) Lane*

CLASS OF 1975
(August 2, 1975)
Roosevelt Brown*
George Connor*
Dante Lavelli*
Lenny Moore

CLASS OF 1976
(July 24, 1976)
Ray Flaherty*
Len Ford*
Jim Taylor

CLASS OF 1977
(July 30, 1977)
Frank Gifford
Forrest Gregg
Gale Sayers
Bart Starr
Bill Willis*

CLASS OF 1978
(July 29, 1978)
Lance Alworth
Weeb Ewbank*
Alphonse (Tuffy) Leemans*
Ray Nitschke*
Larry Wilson

CLASS OF 1979
(July 28, 1979)
Dick Butkus
Yale Lary
Ron Mix
Johnny Unitas*

CLASS OF 1980
(August 2, 1980)
Herb Adderley
David (Deacon) Jones
Bob Lilly
Jim Otto

CLASS OF 1981
(August 1, 1981)
Morris (Red) Badgro*
George Blanda*
Willie Davis
Jim Ringo*

CLASS OF 1982
(August 7, 1982)
Doug Atkins
Sam Huff
George Musso*
Merlin Olsen*

CLASS OF 1983
(July 30, 1983)
Bobby Bell
Sid Gillman*
Sonny Jurgensen
Bobby Mitchell
Paul Warfield

CLASS OF 1984
(July 28, 1984)
Willie Brown
Mike McCormack
Charley Taylor
Arnie Weinmeister*

CLASS OF 1985
(August 3, 1985)
Frank Gatski*
Joe Namath
Pete Rozelle*
O. J. Simpson
Roger Staubach

CLASS OF 1986
(August 2, 1986)
Paul Hornung
Ken Houston
Willie Lanier
Fran Tarkenton
Doak Walker*

CLASS OF 1987
(August 8, 1987)
Larry Csonka
Len Dawson
Joe Greene
John Henry Johnson
Jim Langer
Don Maynard
Gene Upshaw*

CLASS OF 1988
(July 30, 1988)
Fred Biletnikoff
Mike Ditka
Jack Ham
Alan Page

CLASS OF 1989
(August 5, 1989)
Mel Blount
Terry Bradshaw
Art Shell
Willie Wood

CLASS OF 1990
(August 4, 1990)
Buck Buchanan*
Bob Griese
Franco Harris
Ted Hendricks
Jack Lambert
Tom Landry*
Bob St. Clair

CLASS OF 1991
(July 27, 1991)
Earl Campbell
John Hannah
Stan Jones*
Tex Schramm*
Jan Stenerud

CLASS OF 1992
(August 1, 1992)
Lem Barney
Al Davis
John Mackey
John Riggins

CLASS OF 1993
(July 31, 1993)
Dan Fouts
Larry Little
Chuck Noll
Walter Payton*
Bill Walsh*

CLASS OF 1994
(July 30, 1994)
Tony Dorsett
Bud Grant
Jimmy Johnson
Leroy Kelly
Jackie Smith
Randy White

CLASS OF 1995
(July 29, 1995)
Jim Finks*
Henry Jordan*
Steve Largent
Lee Roy Selmon
Kellen Winslow

CLASS OF 1996
(July 27, 1996)
Lou Creekmur*
Dan Dierdorf
Joe Gibbs
Charlie Joiner
Mel Renfro

CLASS OF 1997
(July 26, 1997)
Mike Haynes
Wellington Mara*
Don Shula
Mike Webster*

CLASS OF 1998
(August 1, 1998)
Paul Krause
Tommy McDonald
Anthony Muñoz
Mike Singletary
Dwight Stephenson

CLASS OF 1999
(August 7, 1999)
Eric Dickerson
Tom Mack
Ozzie Newsome
Billy Shaw
Lawrence Taylor

CLASS OF 2000
(July 29, 2000)
Howie Long
Ronnie Lott
Joe Montana
Dan Rooney
Dave Wilcox

CLASS OF 2001
(August 4, 2001)
Nick Buoniconti
Marv Levy
Mike Munchak
Jackie Slater
Lynn Swann
Ron Yary
Jack Youngblood

CLASS OF 2002
(August 3, 2002)
George Allen*
Dave Casper
Dan Hampton
Jim Kelly
John Stallworth

CLASS OF 2003
(August 3, 2003)
Marcus Allen
Elvin Bethea
Joe DeLamielleure
James Lofton
Hank Stram*

CLASS OF 2004
(August 8, 2004)
Bob (Boomer) Brown
Carl Eller
John Elway
Barry Sanders

CLASS OF 2005
(August 7, 2005)
Benny Friedman*
Dan Marino
Fritz Pollard*
Steve Young

CLASS OF 2006
(August 6, 2006)
Troy Aikman
Harry Carson
John Madden
Warren Moon
Reggie White*
Rayfield Wright

CLASS OF 2007
(August 4, 2007)
Gene Hickerson*
Michael Irvin
Bruce Matthews
Charlie Sanders
Thurman Thomas
Roger Wehrli

CLASS OF 2008
(August 2, 2008)
Fred Dean
Darrell Green
Art Monk
Emmitt Thomas
Andre Tippett
Gary Zimmerman

CLASS OF 2009
(August 8, 2009)
Bob Hayes*
Randall McDaniel
Bruce Smith
Derrick Thomas*
Ralph Wilson, Jr.
Rod Woodson

CLASS OF 2010
(August 7, 2010)
Russ Grimm
Rickey Jackson
Dick LeBeau
Floyd Little
John Randle
Jerry Rice
Emmitt Smith

CLASS OF 2011
(August 6, 2011)
Richard Dent
Marshall Faulk
Chris Hanburger
Les Richter*
Ed Sabol
Deion Sanders
Shannon Sharpe

PRO FOOTBALL HALL OF FAME GAME (48)

Date	Winner	Loser	Attendance
August 11, 1962	New York Giants 21 (tie)	St. Louis Cardinals 21 (tie)	14,000
September 8, 1963	Pittsburgh Steelers 16	Cleveland Browns 7	18,462
September 6, 1964	Baltimore Colts 48	Pittsburgh Steelers 17	11,479
September 12, 1965	Washington Redskins 20	Detroit Lions 3	14,416
1966	No game was played		
August 5, 1967	Philadelphia Eagles 28	Cleveland Browns 13	17,304
August 3, 1968	Chicago Bears 30	Dallas Cowboys 24	14,578
September 13, 1969	Green Bay Packers 38	Atlanta Falcons 24	17,411
August 8, 1970	New Orleans Saints 14	Minnesota Vikings 13	17,932
July 31, 1971	Los Angeles Rams (NFC) 17	Houston Oilers (AFC) 6	19,384
July 29, 1972	Kansas City Chiefs (AFC) 23	New York Giants (NFC) 17	19,304
July 28, 1973	San Francisco 49ers (NFC) 20	New England Patriots (AFC) 7	19,685
July 27, 1974	St. Louis Cardinals (NFC) 21	Buffalo Bills (AFC) 13	17,286
August 2, 1975	Washington Redskins (NFC) 17	Cincinnati Bengals (AFC) 9	19,360
July 24, 1976	Denver Broncos (AFC) 10	Detroit Lions (NFC) 7	17,639
July 30, 1977	Chicago Bears (NFC) 20	New York Jets (AFC) 6	19,057
July 29, 1978	Philadelphia Eagles (NFC) 17	Miami Dolphins (AFC) 3	19,255
July 28, 1979	Oakland Raiders (AFC) 20	Dallas Cowboys (NFC) 13	20,648
August 2, 1980*	San Diego Chargers (AFC) 0	Green Bay Packers (NFC) 0	19,972
August 1, 1981	Cleveland Browns (AFC) 24	Atlanta Falcons (NFC) 10	23,921
August 7, 1982	Minnesota Vikings (NFC) 30	Baltimore Colts (AFC) 14	23,379
July 30, 1983	Pittsburgh Steelers (AFC) 27	New Orleans Saints (NFC) 14	22,000
July 28, 1984	Seattle Seahawks (AFC) 38	Tampa Bay Buccaneers (NFC) 0	22,250
August 3, 1985	New York Giants (NFC) 21	Houston Oilers (AFC) 20	23,940
August 2, 1986	New England Patriots (AFC) 21	St. Louis Cardinals (NFC) 16	22,739
August 8, 1987	San Francisco 49ers (NFC) 20	Kansas City Chiefs (AFC) 7	23,826
July 30, 1988	Cincinnati Bengals (AFC) 14	Los Angeles Rams (NFC) 7	23,801
August 5, 1989	Washington Redskins (NFC) 31	Buffalo Bills (AFC) 6	23,948
August 4, 1990	Chicago Bears (NFC) 13	Cleveland Browns (AFC) 0	23,952
July 27, 1991	Detroit Lions (NFC) 14	Denver Broncos (AFC) 3	23,815
August 1, 1992	New York Jets (AFC) 41	Philadelphia Eagles (NFC) 14	23,853
July 31, 1993	Los Angeles Raiders (AFC) 19	Green Bay Packers (NFC) 3	23,863
July 30, 1994	Atlanta Falcons (NFC) 21	San Diego Chargers (AFC) 17	23,185
July 29, 1995	Carolina Panthers (NFC) 20	Jacksonville Jaguars (AFC) 14	24,625
July 27, 1996	Indianapolis Colts (AFC) 10	New Orleans Saints (NFC) 3	23,376
July 26, 1997	Minnesota Vikings (NFC) 28	Seattle Seahawks (AFC) 26	23,846
August 1, 1998	Tampa Bay Buccaneers (NFC) 30	Pittsburgh Steelers (AFC) 6	23,875
August 9, 1999	Cleveland Browns (AFC) 20	Dallas Cowboys (NFC) 17 (OT)	25,156
July 31, 2000	New England Patriots (AFC) 20	San Francisco 49ers (NFC) 0	22,840
August 6, 2001	St. Louis Rams (NFC) 17	Miami Dolphins (AFC) 10	22,736
August 5, 2002	New York Giants (NFC) 34	Houston Texans (AFC) 17	22,461
August 4, 2003**	Kansas City Chiefs (AFC) 9	Green Bay Packers (NFC) 0	22,385
August 9, 2004	Washington Redskins (NFC) 20	Denver Broncos (AFC) 17	22,177
August 8, 2005	Chicago Bears (NFC) 27	Miami Dolphins (AFC) 24	22,292
August 6, 2006	Oakland Raiders (AFC) 16	Philadelphia Eagles (NFC) 10	22,000
August 5, 2007	Pittsburgh Steelers (AFC) 20	New Orleans Saints (NFC) 7	22,302
August 3, 2008	Washington Redskins (NFC) 30	Indianapolis Colts (AFC) 16	22,216
August 9, 2009	Tennessee Titans (AFC) 21	Buffalo Bills (AFC) 18	22,153
August 8, 2010	Dallas Cowboys (NFC) 16	Cincinnati Bengals (AFC) 7	22,364

*Game called with 5:29 remaining in the fourth quarter because of severe thunder and lightning.
**Game called with 5:49 remaining in the third quarter because of lightning and torrential rain.

1869

Rutgers and Princeton played a college soccer football game, the first ever, November 6. The game used modified London Football Association rules. During the next seven years, rugby gained favor with the major eastern schools over soccer, and modern football began to develop from rugby.

1876

At the Massasoit convention, the first rules for American football were written. Walter Camp, who would become known as the father of American football, first became involved with the game.

1892

In an era in which football was a major attraction of local athletic clubs, an intense competition between two Pittsburgh-area clubs, the Allegheny Athletic Association (AAA) and the Pittsburgh Athletic Club (PAC), led to the making of the first professional football player. Former Yale All-America guard William (Pudge) Heffelfinger was paid $500 by the AAA to play in a game against the PAC, becoming the first person to be paid to play football, November 12. The AAA won the game 4-0 when Heffelfinger picked up a PAC fumble and ran 35 yards for a touchdown.

1893

The Pittsburgh Athletic Club signed one of its players, probably halfback Grant Dibert, to the first known pro football contract, which covered all of the PAC's games for the year.

1895

John Brallier became the first football player to openly turn pro, accepting $10 and expenses to play for the Latrobe YMCA against the Jeannette Athletic Club.

1896

The Allegheny Athletic Association team fielded the first completely professional team for its abbreviated two-game season.

1897

The Latrobe Athletic Association football team went entirely professional, becoming the first team to play a full season with only professionals.

1898

A touchdown was changed from four points to five.

Chris O'Brien formed a neighborhood team, which played under the name the Morgan Athletic Club, on the south side of Chicago. The team later became known as the Normals, then the Racine (for a street in Chicago) Cardinals, the Chicago Cardinals, the St. Louis Cardinals, the Phoenix Cardinals, and, in 1994, the Arizona Cardinals. The team remains the oldest continuing operation in pro football.

1900

William C. Temple took over the team payments for the Duquesne Country and Athletic Club, becoming the first known individual club owner.

1902

Baseball's Philadelphia Athletics, managed by Connie Mack, and the Philadelphia Phillies formed professional football teams, joining the Pittsburgh Stars in the first attempt at a pro football league, named the National Football League. The Athletics won the first night football game ever played, 39-0 over Kanaweola AC at Elmira, New York, November 21.

All three teams claimed the pro championship for the year, but the league president, Dave Berry, named the Stars the champions. Pitcher Rube Waddell was with the Athletics, and pitcher Christy Mathewson a fullback for Pittsburgh.

The first World Series of pro football, actually a five-team tournament, was played among a team made up of players from both the Athletics and the Phillies, but simply named New York; the New York Knickerbockers; the Syracuse AC; the Warlow AC; and the Orange (New Jersey) AC in New York's original Madison Square Garden. New York and Syracuse played the first indoor football game before 3,000, December 28. Syracuse, with Glen (Pop) Warner at guard, won 6-0 and went on to win the tournament.

1903

The Franklin (Pa.) Athletic Club won the second and last World Series of pro football over the Oreos AC of Asbury Park, New Jersey; the Watertown Red and Blacks; and the Orange AC.

Pro football was popularized in Ohio when the Massillon Tigers, a strong amateur team, hired four Pittsburgh pros to play in the season-ending game against Akron. At the same time, pro football declined in the Pittsburgh area, and the emphasis on the pro game moved west from Pennsylvania to Ohio.

1904

A field goal was changed from five points to four.

Ohio had at least seven pro teams, with Massillon winning the Ohio Independent Championship, that is, the pro title. Talk surfaced about forming a state-wide league to end spiraling salaries brought about by constant bidding for players and to write universal rules for the game. The feeble attempt to start the league failed.

Halfback Charles Follis signed a contract with the Shelby (Ohio) AC, making him the first known black pro football player.

1905

The Canton AC, later to become known as the Bulldogs, became a professional team. Massillon again won the Ohio League championship.

1906

The forward pass was legalized. The first authenticated pass completion in a pro game came on October 25, when George (Peggy) Parratt of Massillon threw a completion to Dan (Bullet) Riley in a victory over a combined Benwood-Moundsville team.

Arch-rivals Canton and Massillon, the two best pro teams in America, played twice, with Canton winning the first game but Massillon winning the second and the Ohio League championship. A betting scandal and the financial disaster wrought upon the two clubs by paying huge salaries caused a temporary decline in interest in pro football in the two cities and, somewhat,

throughout Ohio.

1909

A field goal dropped from four points to three.

1912

A touchdown was increased from five points to six.

Jack Cusack revived a strong pro team in Canton.

1913

Jim Thorpe, a former football and track star at the Carlisle Indian School (Pa.) and a double gold medal winner at the 1912 Olympics in Stockholm, played for the Pine Village Pros in Indiana.

1915

Massillon again fielded a major team, reviving the old rivalry with Canton. Cusack signed Thorpe to play for Canton for $250 a game.

1916

With Thorpe and former Carlisle teammate Pete Calac starring, Canton went 9-0-1, won the Ohio League championship, and was acclaimed the pro football champion.

1917

Despite an upset by Massillon, Canton again won the Ohio League championship.

1919

Canton again won the Ohio League championship, despite the team having been turned over from Cusack to Ralph Hay. Thorpe and Calac were joined in the backfield by Joe Guyon.

Earl (Curly) Lambeau and George Calhoun organized the Green Bay Packers. Lambeau's employer at the Indian Packing Company provided $500 for equipment and allowed the team to use the company field for practices. The Packers went 10-1.

1920

Pro football was in a state of confusion due to three major problems: dramatically rising salaries; players continually jumping from one team to another following the highest offer; and the use of college players still enrolled in school. A league in which all the members would follow the same rules seemed the answer. An organizational meeting, at which the Akron Pros, Canton Bulldogs, Cleveland Indians, and Dayton Triangles were represented, was held at the Jordan and Hupmobile auto showroom in Canton, Ohio, August 20. This meeting resulted in the formation of the American Professional Football Conference.

A second organizational meeting was held in Canton, September 17. The teams were from four states—Akron, Canton, Cleveland, and Dayton from Ohio; the Hammond Pros and Muncie Flyers from Indiana; the Rochester Jeffersons from New York; and the Rock Island Independents, Decatur Staleys, and Racine Cardinals from Illinois. The name of the league was changed to the American Professional Football Association. Hoping to capitalize on his fame, the members elected Thorpe president; Stanley Cofall of Cleveland was elected vice president. A membership fee of $100 per team was charged to give an appearance of respectability, but no team ever paid it. Scheduling was left up to the teams, and there were wide variations, both in the overall number of games played and in the number played against APFA member teams.

Four other teams—the Buffalo All-Americans, Chicago Tigers, Columbus Panhandles, and Detroit Heralds—joined the league sometime during the year. On September 26, the first game featuring an APFA team was played at Rock Island's Douglas Park. A crowd of 800 watched the Independents defeat the St. Paul Ideals 48-0. A week later, October 3, the first game matching two APFA teams was held. At Triangle Park, Dayton defeated Columbus 14-0, with Lou Partlow of Dayton scoring the first touchdown in a game between Association teams. The same day, Rock Island defeated Muncie 45-0.

By the beginning of December, most of the teams in the APFA had abandoned their hopes for a championship, and some of them, including the Chicago Tigers and Detroit Heralds, had finished their seasons, disbanded, and

had their franchises canceled by the Association. Four teams—Akron, Buffalo, Canton, and Decatur—still had championship aspirations, but a series of late-season games among them left Akron as the only undefeated team in the Association. At one of these games, Akron sold tackle Bob Nash to Buffalo for $300 and five percent of the gate receipts—the first APFA player deal.

1921
At the league meeting in Akron, April 30, the championship of the 1920 season was awarded to the Akron Pros. The APFA was reorganized, with Joe Carr of the Columbus Panhandles named president and Carl Storck of Dayton secretary-treasurer. Carr moved the Association's headquarters to Columbus, drafted a league constitution and by-laws, gave teams territorial rights, restricted player movements, developed membership criteria for the franchises, and issued standings for the first time, so that the APFA would have a clear champion.

The Association's membership increased to 22 teams, including the Green Bay Packers, who were awarded to John Clair of the Acme Packing Company.

Thorpe moved from Canton to the Cleveland Indians, but he was hurt early in the season and played very little.

A.E. Staley turned the Decatur Staleys over to player-coach George Halas, who moved the team to Cubs Park in Chicago. Staley paid Halas $5,000 to keep the name Staleys for one more year. Halas made halfback Ed (Dutch) Sternaman his partner.

Player-coach Fritz Pollard of the Akron Pros became the first black head coach.

The Staleys claimed the APFA championship with a 9-1-1 record, as did Buffalo at 9-1-2. Carr ruled in favor of the Staleys, giving Halas his first championship.

1922
After admitting the use of players who had college eligibility remaining during the 1921 season, Clair and the Green Bay management with-

drew from the APFA, January 28. Curly Lambeau promised to obey league rules and then used $50 of his own money to buy back the franchise. Bad weather and low attendance plagued the Packers, and Lambeau went broke, but local merchants arranged a $2,500 loan for the club. A public non-profit corporation was set up to operate the team, with Lambeau as head coach and manager.

The American Professional Football Association changed its name to the National Football League, June 24. The Chicago Staleys became the Chicago Bears.

The NFL fielded 18 teams, including the new Oorang Indians of Marion, Ohio, an all-Indian team featuring Thorpe, Joe Guyon, and Pete Calac, and sponsored by the Oorang dog kennels.

Canton, led by player-coach Guy Chamberlin and tackles Link Lyman and Wilbur (Pete) Henry, emerged as the league's first true powerhouse, going 10-0-2.

1923
For the first time, all of the franchises considered to be part of the NFL fielded teams. Thorpe played his second and final season for the Oorang Indians. Against the Bears, Thorpe fumbled, and Halas picked up the ball and returned it 98 yards for a touchdown, a record that would last until 1972.

Canton had its second consecutive undefeated season, going 11-0-1 for the NFL title.

1924
The league had 18 franchises, including new ones in Kansas City, Kenosha, and Frankford, a section of Philadelphia. League champion Canton, successful on the field but not at the box office, was purchased by the owner of the Cleveland franchise, who kept the Canton franchise inactive, while using the best players for his Cleveland team, which he renamed the Bulldogs. Cleveland won the title with a 7-1-1 record.

1925
Five new franchises were admitted to the NFL—the New York Giants, who were award-

ed to Tim Mara and Billy Gibson for $500; the Detroit Panthers, featuring Jimmy Conzelman as owner, coach, and tailback; the Providence Steam Roller; a new Canton Bulldogs team; and the Pottsville Maroons, who had been perhaps the most successful independent pro team. The NFL established its first player limit, at 16 players.

Late in the season, the NFL made its greatest coup in gaining national recognition. Shortly after the University of Illinois season ended in November, All-America halfback Harold (Red) Grange signed a contract to play with the Chicago Bears. On Thanksgiving Day, a crowd of 36,000—the largest in pro football history—watched Grange and the Bears play the Chicago Cardinals to a scoreless tie at Wrigley Field. At the beginning of December, the Bears left on a barnstorming tour that saw them play eight games in 12 days, in St. Louis, Philadelphia, New York City, Washington, Boston, Pittsburgh, Detroit, and Chicago. A crowd of 73,000 watched the game against the Giants at the Polo Grounds, helping assure the future of the troubled NFL franchise in New York. The Bears then played nine more games in the South and West, including a game in Los Angeles, in which 75,000 fans watched them defeat the Los Angeles Tigers in the Los Angeles Memorial Coliseum.

Pottsville and the Chicago Cardinals were the top contenders for the league title, with Pottsville winning a late-season meeting 21-7. Pottsville scheduled a game against a team of former Notre Dame players for Shibe Park in Philadelphia. Frankford lodged a protest not only because the game was in Frankford's protected territory, but because it was being played the same day as a Yellow Jackets home game. Carr gave three different notices forbidding Pottsville to play the game, but Pottsville played anyway, December 12. That day, Carr fined the club, suspended it from all rights and privileges (including the right to play for the NFL championship), and returned its franchise to the league. The Cardinals, who ended the season with the best record in the league, were named the 1925 champions.

1926

Grange's manager, C.C. Pyle, told the Bears that Grange wouldn't play for them unless he was paid a five-figure salary and given one-third ownership of the team. The Bears refused. Pyle leased Yankee Stadium in New York City, then petitioned for an NFL franchise. After he was refused, he started the first American Football League. It lasted one season and included Grange's New York Yankees and eight other teams. The AFL champion Philadelphia Quakers played a December game against the New York Giants, seventh in the NFL, and the Giants won 31-0. At the end of the season, the AFL folded.

Halas pushed through a rule that prohibited any team from signing a player whose college class had not graduated.

The NFL grew to 22 teams, including the Duluth Eskimos, who signed All-America fullback Ernie Nevers of Stanford, giving the league a gate attraction to rival Grange. The 15-member Eskimos, dubbed the Iron Men of the North, played 29 exhibition and league games, 28 on the road, and Nevers played in all but 29 minutes of them.

Frankford edged the Bears for the championship, despite Halas having obtained John (Paddy) Driscoll from the Cardinals. On December 4, the Yellow Jackets scored in the final two minutes to defeat the Bears 7-6 and move ahead of them in the standings.

1927

At a special meeting in Cleveland, April 23, Carr decided to secure the NFL's future by eliminating the financially weaker teams and consolidating the quality players onto a limited number of more successful teams. The new-look NFL dropped to 12 teams, and the center of gravity of the league left the Midwest, where the NFL had started, and began to emerge in the large cities of the East. One of the new teams was Grange's New

York Yankees, but Grange suffered a knee injury and the Yankees finished in the middle of the pack. The NFL championship was won by the cross-town rival New York Giants, who posted 10 shutouts in 13 games.

1928

Grange and Nevers both retired from pro football, and Duluth disbanded, as the NFL was reduced to only 10 teams. The Providence Steam Roller of Jimmy Conzelman and Pearce Johnson won the championship, playing in the Cycledrome, a 10,000-seat oval that had been built for bicycle races.

1929

Chris O'Brien sold the Chicago Cardinals to David Jones, July 27.

The NFL added a fourth official, the field judge, July 28.

Grange and Nevers returned to the NFL. Nevers scored six rushing touchdowns and four extra points as the Cardinals beat Grange's Bears 40-6, November 28. The 40 points set a record that remains the NFL's oldest.

Providence became the first NFL team to host a game at night under floodlights, against the Cardinals, November 6.

The Packers added back Johnny Blood (McNally), tackle Cal Hubbard, and guard Mike Michalske, and won their first NFL championship, edging the Giants, who featured quarterback Benny Friedman.

1930

Dayton, the last of the NFL's original franchises, was purchased by William B. Dwyer and John C. Depler, moved to Brooklyn, and renamed the Dodgers. The Portsmouth, Ohio, Spartans entered the league.

The Packers edged the Giants for the title, but the most improved team was the Bears. Halas retired as a player and replaced himself as coach of the Bears with Ralph Jones, who refined the T-formation by introducing wide ends and a halfback in motion. Jones also introduced rookie All-America fullback-tackle Bronko Nagurski.

The Giants defeated a team of former Notre Dame players coached by Knute Rockne 22-0 before 55,000 at the Polo Grounds, December 14. The proceeds went to the New York Unemployment Fund to help those suffering because of the Great Depression, and the easy victory helped give the NFL credibility with the press and the public.

1931

The NFL decreased to 10 teams, and halfway through the season the Frankford franchise folded. Carr fined the Bears, Packers, and Portsmouth $1,000 each for using players whose college classes had not graduated.

The Packers won an unprecedented third consecutive title, beating out the Spartans, who were led by rookie backs Earl (Dutch) Clark and Glenn Presnell.

1932

George Preston Marshall, Vincent Bendix, Jay O'Brien, and M. Dorland Doyle were awarded a franchise for Boston, July 9. Despite the presence of two rookies—halfback Cliff Battles and tackle Glen (Turk) Edwards—the new team, named the Braves, lost money and Marshall was left as the sole owner at the end of the year.

NFL membership dropped to eight teams, the lowest in history. Official statistics were kept for the first time. The Bears and the Spartans finished the season in the first-ever tie for first place. After the season finale, the league office arranged for an additional regular-season game to determine the league champion. The game was moved indoors to Chicago Stadium because of bitter cold and heavy snow. The arena allowed only an 80-yard field that came right to the walls. The goal posts were moved from the end lines to the goal lines and, for safety, inbounds lines or hashmarks where the ball would be put in play were drawn 10 yards from the walls that butted against the sidelines. The Bears won 9-0, December 18, scoring the winning touchdown on a two-yard pass from Nagurski to Grange. The Spartans claimed Nagurski's pass was thrown

from less than five yards behind the line of scrimmage, violating the existing passing rule, but the play stood.

1933

The NFL, which long had followed the rules of college football, made a number of significant changes from the college game for the first time and began to develop rules serving its needs and the style of play it preferred. The innovations from the 1932 championship game—inbounds line or hashmarks and goal posts on the goal lines—were adopted. Also the forward pass was legalized from anywhere behind the line of scrimmage, February 25.

Marshall and Halas pushed through a proposal that divided the NFL into two divisions, with the winners to meet in an annual championship game, July 8.

Three new franchises joined the league—the Pittsburgh Pirates of Art Rooney, the Philadelphia Eagles of Bert Bell and Lud Wray, and the Cincinnati Reds. The Staten Island Stapletons suspended operations for a year, but never returned to the league.

Halas bought out Sternaman, became sole owner of the Bears, and reinstated himself as head coach. Marshall changed the name of the Boston Braves to the Redskins. David Jones sold the Chicago Cardinals to Charles W. Bidwill.

In the first NFL Championship Game scheduled before the season, the Western Division champion Bears defeated the Eastern Division champion Giants 23-21 at Wrigley Field, December 17.

1934

G.A. (Dick) Richards purchased the Portsmouth Spartans, moved them to Detroit, and renamed them the Lions.

Professional football gained new prestige when the Bears were matched against the best college football players in the first Chicago College All-Star Game, August 31. The game ended in a scoreless tie before 79,432 at Soldier Field.

The Cincinnati Reds lost their first eight games, then were suspended from the league for defaulting on payments. The St. Louis Gunners, an independent team, joined the NFL by buying the Cincinnati franchise and went 1-2 the last three weeks.

Rookie Beattie Feathers of the Bears became the NFL's first 1,000-yard rusher, gaining 1,004 on 101 carries. The Thanksgiving Day game between the Bears and the Lions became the first NFL game broadcast nationally, with Graham McNamee announcer for NBC radio.

In the championship game, on an extremely cold and icy day at the Polo Grounds, the Giants trailed the Bears 13-3 in the third quarter before changing to basketball shoes for better footing. The Giants won 30-13 in what has come to be known as the Sneakers Game, December 9.

The player waiver rule was adopted, December 10.

1935
The NFL adopted Bert Bell's proposal to hold an annual draft of college players, to begin in 1936, with teams selecting in an inverse order of finish, May 19. The inbounds line or hashmarks were moved nearer the center of the field, 15 yards from the sidelines.

All-America end Don Hutson of Alabama joined Green Bay. The Lions defeated the Giants 26-7 in the NFL Championship Game, December 15.

1936
There were no franchise transactions for the first year since the formation of the NFL. It also was the first year in which all member teams played the same number of games.

The Eagles made University of Chicago halfback and Heisman Trophy winner Jay Berwanger the first player ever selected in the NFL draft, February 8. The Eagles traded his rights to the Bears, but Berwanger never played pro football. The first player selected to actually sign was the number-two pick, Riley Smith of Alabama, who was selected by Boston.

A rival league was formed, and it became the second to call itself the American Football League. The Boston Shamrocks were its champions.

Because of poor atten-

dance, Marshall, the owner of the host team, moved the Championship Game from Boston to the Polo Grounds in New York. Green Bay defeated the Redskins 21-6, December 13.

1937
Homer Marshman was granted a Cleveland franchise, named the Rams, February 12. Marshall moved the Redskins to Washington, D.C., February 13. The Redskins signed TCU All-America tailback Sammy Baugh, who led them to a 28-21 victory over the Bears in the NFL Championship Game, December 12.

The Los Angeles Bulldogs had an 8-0 record to win the AFL title, but then the 2-year-old league folded.

1938
At the suggestion of Halas, Hugh (Shorty) Ray became a technical advisor on rules and officiating to the NFL. A new rule called for a 15-yard penalty for roughing the passer.

Rookie Byron (Whizzer) White of the Pittsburgh Pirates led the NFL in rushing. The Giants defeated the Packers 23-17 for the NFL title, December 11.

Marshall, *Los Angeles Times* sports editor Bill Henry, and promoter Tom Gallery established the Pro Bowl game between the NFL champion and a team of pro all-stars.

1939
The New York Giants defeated the Pro All-Stars 13-10 in the first Pro Bowl, at Wrigley Field, Los Angeles, January 15.

Carr, NFL president since 1921, died in Columbus, May 20. Carl Storck was named acting president, May 25.

An NFL game was televised for the first time when NBC broadcast the Brooklyn Dodgers-Philadelphia Eagles game from Ebbets Field to the approximately 1,000 sets then in New York, October 22.

Green Bay defeated New York 27-0 in the NFL Championship Game, December 10 at Milwaukee. NFL attendance exceeded 1 million in a season for the first time, reaching 1,071,200.

1940
A six-team rival league, the third to call itself the American Football League, was formed, and the Columbus Bullies won its championship.

Halas' Bears, with additional coaching by Clark Shaughnessy of Stanford, defeated the Redskins 73-0 in the NFL Championship Game, December 8. The game, which was the most decisive victory in NFL history, popularized the Bears' T-formation with a man-in-motion. It was the first championship carried on network radio, broadcast by Red Barber to 120 stations of the Mutual Broadcasting System, which paid $2,500 for the rights.

Art Rooney sold the Pittsburgh franchise to Alexis Thompson, December 9, then bought part interest in the Philadelphia Eagles.

Bell and Rooney traded the Eagles to Thompson for the Pirates, then re-named their new team the Steelers.

1941
Elmer Layden was named the first Commissioner of the NFL, March 1; Storck, the acting president, resigned, April 5. NFL headquarters were moved to Chicago.

Homer Marshman sold the Rams to Daniel F. Reeves and Fred Levy, Jr.

The league by-laws were revised to provide for playoffs in case there were ties in division races, and sudden-death overtimes in case a playoff game was tied after four quarters. An official *NFL Record Manual* was published for the first time.

Columbus again won the championship of the AFL, but the two-year-old league then folded.

The Bears and the Packers finished in a tie for the Western Division championship, setting up the first divisional playoff game in league history. The Bears won 33-14, then defeated the Giants 37-9 for the NFL championship, December 21.

1942
Players departing for service in World War II depleted the rosters of NFL teams. Halas left the Bears in midseason to join the Navy, and Luke John-

sos and Heartley (Hunk) Anderson served as co-coaches as the Bears went 11-0 in the regular season. The Redskins defeated the Bears 14-6 in the NFL Championship Game, December 13.

1943
The Cleveland Rams, with co-owners Reeves and Levy in the service, were granted permission to suspend operations for one season, April 6. Levy transferred his stock in the team to Reeves, April 16.

The NFL adopted free substitution, April 7. The league also made the wearing of helmets mandatory and approved a 10-game schedule for all teams.

Philadelphia and Pittsburgh were granted permission to merge for one season, June 19. The team, known as Phil-Pitt (and called the Steagles by fans), divided home games between the two cities, and Earle (Greasy) Neale of Philadelphia and Walt Kiesling of Pittsburgh served as co-coaches. The merger automatically dissolved the last day of the season, December 5.

Ted Collins was granted a franchise for Boston, to become active in 1944.

Sammy Baugh led the league in passing, punting, and interceptions. He led the Redskins to a tie with the Giants for the Eastern Division title, and then to a 28-0 victory in a divisional playoff game. The Bears beat the Redskins 41-21 in the NFL Championship Game, December 26.

1944
Collins, who had wanted a franchise in Yankee Stadium in New York, named his new team in Boston the Yanks. Cleveland resumed operations. The Brooklyn Dodgers changed their name to the Tigers.

Coaching from the bench was legalized, April 20.

The Cardinals and the Steelers were granted permission to merge for one year under the name Card-Pitt, April 21. Phil Handler of the Cardinals and Walt Kiesling of the Steelers served as co-coaches. The merger automatically dissolved the last day of the season, December 3.

In the NFL Championship Game, Green Bay defeated the New York Giants 14-7, December 17.

1945

The inbounds lines or hash-marks were moved from 15 yards away from the sidelines to nearer the center of the field—20 yards from the sidelines.

Brooklyn and Boston merged into a team that played home games in both cities and was known simply as The Yanks. The team was coached by former Boston head coach Herb Kopf. In December, the Brooklyn franchise withdrew from the NFL to join the new All-America Football Conference; all the players on its active and reserve lists were assigned to The Yanks, who once again became the Boston Yanks.

Halas rejoined the Bears late in the season after service with the U.S. Navy. Although Halas took over much of the coaching duties, Anderson and Johnsos remained the coaches of record throughout the season.

Steve Van Buren of Philadelphia led the NFL in rushing, kickoff returns, and scoring.

After the Japanese surrendered ending World War II, a count showed that the NFL service roster, limited to men who had played in league games, totaled 638, 21 of whom had died in action.

Rookie quarterback Bob Waterfield led Cleveland to a 15-14 victory over Washington in the NFL Championship Game, December 16.

1946

The contract of Commissioner Layden was not renewed, and Bert Bell, the co-owner of the Steelers, replaced him, January 11. Bell moved the league headquarters from Chicago to the Philadelphia suburb of Bala-Cynwyd.

Free substitution was withdrawn and substitutions were limited to no more than three men at a time. Forward passes were made automatically incomplete upon striking the goal posts, January 11.

The NFL took on a truly national appearance for the first time when Reeves was granted permission by the league to move his NFL champion Rams to Los Angeles.

Halfback Kenny Washington (March 21) and end Woody Strode (May 7) signed with the Los Angeles Rams to become the first African-Americans to play in the NFL in the modern era. Guard Bill Willis (August 6) and running back Marion Motley (August 9) joined the AAFC with the Cleveland Browns.

The rival All-America Football Conference began play with eight teams. The Cleveland Browns, coached by Paul Brown, won the AAFC's first championship, defeating the New York Yankees 14-9.

Bill Dudley of the Steelers led the NFL in rushing, interceptions, and punt returns, and won the league's most valuable player award.

Backs Frank Filchock and Merle Hapes of the Giants were questioned about an attempt by a New York man to fix the championship game with the Bears. Bell suspended Hapes but allowed Filchock to play; he played well, but Chicago won 24-14, December 15.

1947

The NFL added a fifth official, the back judge.

A bonus choice was made for the first time in the NFL draft. One team each year would select the special choice before the first round began. The Chicago Bears won a lottery and the rights to the first choice and drafted back Bob Fenimore of Oklahoma A&M.

The Cleveland Browns again won the AAFC title, defeating the New York Yankees 14-3.

Charles Bidwill, Sr., owner of the Cardinals, died April 19, but his wife and sons retained ownership of the team. On December 28, the Cardinals won the NFL Championship Game 28-21 over the Philadelphia Eagles, who had beaten Pittsburgh 21-0 in a playoff.

1948

Plastic helmets were prohibited. A flexible artificial tee was permitted at the kickoff. Officials other than the referee were equipped with whistles, not horns, January 14.

Fred Mandel sold the Detroit Lions to a syndicate headed by D. Lyle Fife, January 15.

Halfback Fred Gehrke of the Los Angeles Rams painted horns on the Rams' helmets, the first modern helmet emblems in pro football.

The Cleveland Browns won their third straight championship in the AAFC, going 14-0 and then defeating the Buffalo Bills 49-7.

In a blizzard, the Eagles defeated the Cardinals 7-0 in the NFL Championship Game, December 19.

1949

Alexis Thompson sold the champion Eagles to a syndicate headed by James P. Clark, January 15. The Boston Yanks became the New York Bulldogs, sharing the Polo Grounds with the Giants.

Free substitution was adopted for one year, January 20.

The NFL had two 1,000-yard rushers in the same season for the first time—Steve Van Buren of Philadelphia and Tony Canadeo of Green Bay.

The AAFC played its season with a one-division, seven-team format. On December 9, Bell announced a merger agreement in which three AAFC franchises—Cleveland, San Francisco, and Baltimore—would join the NFL in 1950. The Browns won their fourth consecutive AAFC title, defeating the 49ers 21-7, December 11.

In a heavy rain, the Eagles defeated the Rams 14-0 in the NFL Championship Game, December 18.

1950

Unlimited free substitution was restored, opening the way for the era of two platoons and specialization in pro football, January 20.

Curly Lambeau, founder of the franchise and Green Bay's head coach since 1921, resigned under fire, February 1.

The name National Football League was restored after about three months as the National-American Football League. The American and National conferences were created to replace the Eastern and Western divisions, March 3.

The New York Bulldogs became the Yanks and divided the players of the former AAFC Yankees with the Giants. A special allocation draft was held in which the 13 teams drafted the remaining AAFC players, with special consideration for Baltimore, which received 15 choices compared to 10 for other teams.

The Los Angeles Rams became the first NFL team to have all of its games—both home and away—televised. The Washington Redskins followed the Rams in arranging to televise their games; other teams made deals to put selected games on television.

In the first game of the season, former AAFC champion Cleveland defeated NFL champion Philadelphia 35-10. For the first time, deadlocks occurred in both conferences and playoffs were necessary. The Browns defeated the Giants in the American and the Rams defeated the Bears in the National. Cleveland defeated Los Angeles 30-28 in the NFL Championship Game, December 24.

1951

The Pro Bowl game, dormant since 1942, was revived under a new format matching the all-stars of each conference at the Los Angeles Memorial Coliseum. The American Conference defeated the National Conference 28-27, January 14.

Abraham Watner returned the Baltimore franchise and its player contracts back to the NFL for $50,000. Baltimore's former players were made available for drafting at the same time as college players, January 18.

A rule was passed that no tackle, guard, or center would be eligible to catch a forward pass, January 18.

The Rams reversed their television policy and televised only road games.

The NFL Championship Game was televised coast-to-coast for the first time, December 23. The DuMont Network paid $75,000 for the rights to the game, in which the Rams defeated the Browns 24-17.

1952

Ted Collins sold the New York Yanks' franchise back to the NFL, January 19. A new franchise was awarded to a group in Dallas after it purchased the assets of the Yanks, January 24. The new Texans went 1-11, with the owners turning the franchise back to the league in midseason. For the last five games of the season, the commissioner's office operated the Texans as a road team, using Hershey, Pennsylvania, as a home base. At the end of the season the franchise was canceled, the last time an NFL team failed.

The Pittsburgh Steelers abandoned the Single-Wing for the T-formation, the last pro team to do so.

The Detroit Lions won their first NFL championship in 17 years, defeating the Browns 17-7 in the title game, December 28.

1953

A Baltimore group headed by Carroll Rosenbloom was granted a franchise and was awarded the holdings of the defunct Dallas organization, January 23. The team, named the Colts, put together the largest trade in league history, acquiring 10 players from Cleveland in exchange for five.

The names of the American and National conferences were changed to the Eastern and Western conferences, January 24.

Jim Thorpe died, March 28.

Mickey McBride, founder of the Cleveland Browns, sold the franchise to a syndicate headed by Dave R. Jones, June 10.

The NFL policy of blacking out home games was upheld by Judge Allan K. Grim of the U.S. District Court in Philadelphia, November 12.

The Lions again defeated the Browns in the NFL Championship Game, winning 17-16, December 27.

1954

The Canadian Football League began a series of raids on NFL teams, signing quarterback Eddie LeBaron and defensive end Gene Brito of Washington and defensive tackle Arnie Weinmeister of the Giants, among others.

Fullback Joe Perry of the 49ers became the first player in league history to gain 1,000 yards rushing in consecutive seasons.

Cleveland defeated Detroit 56-10 in the NFL Championship Game, December 26.

1955

The sudden-death overtime rule was used for the first time in a preseason game between the Rams and Giants at Portland, Oregon, August 28. The Rams won 23-17 three minutes into overtime.

A rule change declared the ball dead immediately if the ball carrier touched the ground with any part of his body except his hands or feet while in the grasp of an opponent.

The Baltimore Colts made an 80-cent phone call to Johnny Unitas and signed him as a free agent. Another quarterback, Otto Graham, played his last game as the Browns defeated the Rams 38-14 in the NFL Championship Game, December 26. Graham had quarterbacked the Browns to 10 championship-game appearances in 10 years.

NBC replaced DuMont as the network for the title game, paying a rights fee of $100,000.

1956

The NFL Players Association was founded.

Grabbing an opponent's facemask (other than the ball carrier) was made illegal. Using radio receivers to communicate with players on the field was prohibited. A natural leather ball with white and stripes replaced the white ball with black stripes for night games.

The Giants moved from the Polo Grounds to Yankee Stadium.

Halas retired as coach of the Bears, and was replaced by Paddy Driscoll.

CBS became the first network to broadcast some NFL regular-season games to selected television markets across the nation.

The Giants routed the Bears 47-7 in the NFL Championship Game, December 30.

1957

Pete Rozelle was named general manager of the Rams. Anthony J. Morabito, founder and co-owner of the 49ers, died of a heart attack during a game against the Bears at Kezar Stadium, October 28.

An NFL-record crowd of 102,368 saw the 49ers-Rams game at the Los Angeles Memorial Coliseum, November 10.

The Lions came from 20 points down to post a 31-27 playoff victory over the 49ers, December 22. Detroit defeated Cleveland 59-14 in the NFL Championship Game, December 29.

1958

The bonus selection in the draft was eliminated, January 29. The last selection was quarterback King Hill of Rice by the Chicago Cardinals.

Halas reinstated himself as coach of the Bears.

Jim Brown of Cleveland gained an NFL-record 1,527 yards rushing. In a divisional playoff game, the Giants held Brown to eight yards and defeated Cleveland 10-0.

Baltimore, coached by Weeb Ewbank, defeated the Giants 23-17 in the first sudden-death overtime in an NFL Championship Game, December 28. The game ended when Colts fullback Alan Ameche scored on a one-yard touchdown run after 8:15 of overtime.

1959

Vince Lombardi was named head coach of the Green Bay Packers, January 28. Tim Mara, the co-founder of the Giants, died, February 17.

Lamar Hunt of Dallas announced his intentions to form a second pro football league. The first meeting was held in Chicago, August 14, and consisted of Hunt representing Dallas; Bob Howsam, Denver; K.S. (Bud) Adams, Houston; Barron Hilton, Los Angeles; Max Winter and Bill Boyer, Minneapolis; and Harry Wismer, New York City. They made plans to begin play in 1960.

The new league was named the American Football League, August 22. Buffalo, owned by Ralph Wilson, became the seventh franchise, October 28. Boston, owned by William H. Sullivan, became the eighth team, November 22. The first AFL draft, lasting 33 rounds, was held, November 22. Joe Foss was named AFL Commissioner, November 30. An additional draft of 20 rounds

was held by the AFL, December 2.

NFL Commissioner Bert Bell died of a heart attack suffered at Franklin Field, Philadelphia, during the last two minutes of a game between the Eagles and the Steelers, October 11. Treasurer Austin Gunsel was named president in the office of the commissioner, October 14.

The Colts again defeated the Giants in the NFL Championship Game, 31-16, December 27.

1960

Pete Rozelle was elected NFL Commissioner as a compromise choice on the twenty-third ballot, January 26. Rozelle moved the league offices to New York City.

Hunt was elected AFL president for 1960, January 26. Minneapolis withdrew from the AFL, January 27, and the same ownership was given an NFL franchise for Minnesota (to start in 1961), January 28. Dallas received an NFL franchise for 1960, January 28. Oakland received an AFL franchise, January 30.

The AFL adopted the two-point option on points after touchdown, January 28. A no-tampering verbal pact, relative to players' contracts, was agreed to between the NFL and AFL, February 9.

The NFL owners voted to allow the transfer of the Chicago Cardinals to St. Louis, March 13.

The AFL signed a five-year television contract with ABC, June 9.

The Boston Patriots defeated the Buffalo Bills 28-7 before 16,000 at Buffalo in the first AFL preseason game, July 30. The Denver Broncos defeated the Patriots 13-10 before 21,597 at Boston in the first AFL regular-season game, September 9.

Philadelphia defeated Green Bay 17-13 in the NFL Championship Game, December 26.

1961

The Houston Oilers defeated the Los Angeles Chargers 24-16 before 32,183 in the first AFL Championship Game, January 1.

Detroit defeated Cleveland 17-16 in the first Playoff Bowl, or Bert Bell Benefit Bowl, between second-place teams in each conference in Miami, January 7.

End Willard Dewveall of the Bears played out his option and joined the Oilers, becoming the first player to play out his contract and jump from the NFL to the AFL, January 14.

Ed McGah, Wayne Valley, and Robert Osborne bought out their partners in the ownership of the Raiders, January 17. The Chargers were transferred to San Diego, February 10. Dave R. Jones sold the Browns to a group headed by Arthur B. Modell, March 22. The Howsam brothers sold the Broncos to a group headed by Calvin Kunz and Gerry Phipps, May 26.

NBC was awarded a two-year contract for radio and television rights to the NFL Championship Game for $615,000 annually, $300,000 of which was to go directly into the NFL Player Benefit Plan, April 5.

Canton, Ohio, where the league that became the NFL was formed in 1920, was chosen as the site of the Pro Football Hall of Fame, April 27.

A bill legalizing single-network television contracts by professional sports leagues was introduced in Congress by Representative Emanuel Celler. It passed the House and Senate and was signed into law by President John F. Kennedy, September 30.

Houston defeated San Diego 10-3 for the AFL championship, December 24. Green Bay won its first NFL championship since 1944, defeating the New York Giants 37-0, December 31.

1962
The Western Division defeated the Eastern Division 47-27 in the first AFL All-Star Game, played before 20,973 in San Diego, January 7.

Both leagues prohibited grabbing any player's face-mask. The AFL voted to make the scoreboard clock the official timer of the game.

The NFL entered into a single-network agreement with CBS for telecasting all regular-season games for $4.65 million annually, January 10.

Judge Roszel Thompson of the U.S. District Court in Baltimore ruled against the AFL in its antitrust suit against the NFL, May 21. The AFL had charged the NFL with monopoly and conspiracy in areas of expansion, television, and player signings. The case lasted two and a half years, the trial two months.

McGah and Valley acquired controlling interest in the Raiders, May 24. The AFL assumed financial responsibility for the New York Titans, November 8. With Commissioner Rozelle as referee, Daniel F. Reeves regained the ownership of the Rams, outbidding his partners in sealed-envelope bidding for the team, November 27.

The Dallas Texans defeated the Oilers 20-17 for the AFL championship at Houston after a then record 17 minutes, 54 seconds of overtime on a 25-yard field goal by Tommy Brooker. The game lasted 77 minutes, 54 seconds, December 23.

Judge Edward Weinfeld of the U.S. District Court in New York City upheld the legality of the NFL's television blackout within a 75-mile radius of home games and denied an injunction that would have forced the championship game between the Giants and the Packers to be televised in the New York City area, December 28. The Packers beat the Giants 16-7 for the NFL title, December 30.

1963
Don Shula, who went on to become the winningest head coach in NFL history, replaced Weeb Ewbank as head coach of the Colts, January 8.

Paul Brown, head coach of the Browns since their inception, was fired on January 9 and replaced the following day by Blanton Collier.

The Dallas Texans transferred to Kansas City, becoming the Chiefs, February 8. The New York Titans were sold to a five-man syndicate headed by David (Sonny) Werblin, March 28. Weeb Ewbank became the Titans' new head coach and the team's name was changed to the Jets, April 15. They began play in the Polo Grounds.

NFL Properties, Inc., was founded to serve as the licensing arm of the NFL.

Rozelle indefinitely suspended Green Bay halfback Paul Hornung and Detroit defensive tackle Alex Karras for placing bets on their own teams and on other NFL games; he also fined five other Detroit players $2,000 each for betting on one game in which they did not participate, and the Detroit Lions Football Company $2,000 on each of two counts for failure to report information promptly and for lack of sideline supervision, April 17.

The AFL allowed the Jets and Raiders to select players from other franchises in hopes of giving the league more competitive balance, May 11.

NBC was awarded exclusive network broadcasting rights for the 1963 NFL Championship Game for $926,000, May 23.

The Pro Football Hall of Fame was dedicated at Canton, Ohio, September 7.

The U.S. Fourth Circuit Court of Appeals reaffirmed the lower court's finding for the NFL in the $10-million suit brought by the AFL, ending three and a half years of litigation, November 21.

Jim Brown of Cleveland rushed for an NFL single-season record 1,863 yards.

Boston defeated Buffalo 26-8 in the first divisional playoff game in AFL history, December 28.

The Bears defeated the Giants 14-10 in the NFL Championship Game, a record sixth and last title for Halas in his thirty-sixth season as the Bears' coach, December 29.

1964
The Chargers defeated the Patriots 51-10 in the AFL Championship Game, January 5.

William Clay Ford, the Lions' president since 1961, purchased the team, January 10. A group representing the late James P. Clark sold the Eagles to a group headed by Jerry Wolman, January 21. Carroll Rosenbloom, the majority owner of the Colts since 1953, acquired complete ownership of the team, January 23.

The AFL signed a five-year, $36-million television contract with NBC to begin with the 1965 season, January 29.

Hornung and Karras were reinstated by Rozelle, March 16.

CBS submitted the winning bid of $14.1 million per year for the NFL regular-season television rights for 1964 and 1965, January 24. CBS acquired the rights to the championship games for 1964 and 1965 for $1.8 million per game, April 17.

Pete Gogolak of Cornell signed a contract with Buffalo, becoming the first soccer-style kicker in pro football.

Buffalo defeated San Diego 20-7 in the AFL Championship Game, December 26. Cleveland defeated Baltimore 27-0 in the NFL Championship Game, December 27.

1965
The NFL teams pledged not to sign college seniors until completion of all their games, including bowl games, and empowered the Commissioner to discipline the clubs up to as much as the loss of an entire draft list for a violation of the pledge, February 15.

The NFL added a sixth official, the line judge, February 19. The color of the officials' penalty flags was changed from white to bright gold, April 5.

Commissioner Rozelle negotiated an agreement on behalf of the NFL clubs to purchase Ed Sabol's Blair Motion Pictures, which was renamed NFL Films, April.

Atlanta was awarded an NFL franchise for 1966, with Rankin Smith, Sr., as owner, June 30. Miami was awarded an AFL franchise for 1966, with Joe Robbie and Danny Thomas as owners, August 16.

Field Judge Burl Toler became the first black official in NFL history, September 19.

According to a Harris survey, sports fans chose professional football (41 percent) as their favorite sport, overtaking baseball (38 percent) for the first time, October.

Green Bay defeated Baltimore 13-10 in sudden-death overtime in a Western Conference playoff game. Don Chandler kicked a 25-yard field goal for the Packers after 13 minutes, 39 seconds of overtime, December 26. The Packers then defeated the Browns 23-12 in the NFL Championship Game, January 2.

In the AFL Championship

Game, the Bills defeated the Chargers, 23-0, December 26.

CBS acquired the rights to the NFL regular-season games in 1966 and 1967, with an option for 1968, for $18.8 million per year, December 29.

1966
The AFL-NFL war reached its peak, as the leagues spent a combined $7 million to sign their 1966 draft choices. The NFL signed 75 percent of its 232 draftees, the AFL 46 percent of its 181. Of the 111 common draft choices, 79 signed with the NFL, 28 with the AFL, and 4 went unsigned.

Buddy Young became the first African-American to work in the league office when Commissioner Rozelle named him director of player relations, February 1.

The rights to the 1966 and 1967 NFL Championship Games were sold to CBS for $2 million per game, February 14.

Foss resigned as AFL Commissioner, April 7. Al Davis, the head coach and general manager of the Raiders, was named to replace him, April 8.

Goal posts offset from the goal line, painted bright yellow, and with uprights 20 feet above the cross-bar were made standard in the NFL, May 16.

A series of secret meetings regarding a possible AFL-NFL merger were held in the spring between Hunt of Kansas City and Tex Schramm of Dallas. Rozelle announced the merger, June 8. Under the agreement, the two leagues would combine to form an expanded league with 24 teams, to be increased to 26 in 1968 and to 28 by 1970 or soon thereafter. All existing franchises would be retained, and no franchises would be transferred outside their metropolitan areas. While maintaining separate schedules through 1969, the leagues agreed to play an annual AFL-NFL World Championship Game beginning in January, 1967, and to hold a combined draft, also beginning in 1967. Preseason games would be held between teams of each league starting in 1967. Official regular-season play would start in 1970 when the two leagues would officially merge to form one

league with two conferences. Rozelle was named Commissioner of the expanded league setup.

Davis rejoined the Raiders, and Milt Woodard was named president of the AFL, July 25.

The St. Louis Cardinals moved into newly constructed Busch Memorial Stadium.

Barron Hilton sold the Chargers to a group headed by Eugene Klein and Sam Schulman, August 25.

Congress approved the AFL-NFL merger, passing legislation exempting the agreement itself from antitrust action, October 21.

New Orleans was awarded an NFL franchise to begin play in 1967, November 1. John Mecom, Jr., of Houston was designated majority stockholder and president of the franchise, December 15.

The NFL was realigned for the 1967-69 seasons into the Capitol and Century Divisions in the Eastern Conference and the Central and Coastal Divisions in the Western Conference, December 2. New Orleans and the New York Giants agreed to switch divisions in 1968 and return to the 1967 alignment in 1969.

The rights to the Super Bowl for four years were sold to CBS and NBC for $9.5 million, December 13.

1967
Green Bay earned the right to represent the NFL in the first AFL-NFL World Championship Game by defeating Dallas 34-27, January 1. The same day, Kansas City defeated Buffalo 31-7 to represent the AFL. The Packers defeated the Chiefs 35-10 before 61,946 fans at the Los Angeles Memorial Coliseum in the first game between AFL and NFL teams, January 15. The winning players' share for the Packers was $15,000 each, and the losing players' share for the Chiefs was $7,500 each. The game was televised by both CBS and NBC.

The "sling-shot" goal post and a six-foot-wide border around the field were made standard in the NFL, February 22.

Baltimore made Bubba Smith, a Michigan State defensive lineman, the first choice in the first combined

AFL-NFL draft, March 14.

The AFL awarded a franchise to begin play in 1968 to Cincinnati, May 23. A group with Paul Brown as part owner, general manager, and head coach, was awarded the Cincinnati franchise, September 27.

Arthur B. Modell, the president of the Cleveland Browns, was elected president of the NFL, May 28.

Defensive back Emlen Tunnell of the New York Giants became the first black player to enter the Pro Football Hall of Fame, August 5.

An AFL team defeated an NFL team for the first time, when Denver beat Detroit 13-7 in a preseason game, August 5.

Green Bay defeated Dallas 21-17 for the NFL championship on a last-minute 1-yard quarterback sneak by Bart Starr in 13-below-zero temperature at Green Bay, December 31. The same day, Oakland defeated Houston 40-7 for the AFL championship.

1968
Green Bay defeated Oakland 33-14 in Super Bowl II at Miami, January 14. The game had the first $3-million gate in pro football history.

Vince Lombardi resigned as head coach of the Packers, but remained as general manager, January 28.

Werblin sold his shares in the Jets to his partners Don Lillis, Leon Hess, Townsend Martin, and Phil Iselin, May 21. Lillis assumed the presidency of the club, but then died July 23. Iselin was appointed president, August 6.

Halas retired for the fourth and last time as head coach of the Bears, May 27.

The Oilers left Rice Stadium for the Astrodome and became the first NFL team to play its home games in a domed stadium.

The movie *Heidi* became a footnote in sports history when NBC didn't show the last 50 seconds of the Jets-Raiders game in order to permit the children's special to begin on time. The Raiders scored two touchdowns in the last 42 seconds to win 43-32, November 17.

Ewbank became the first coach to win titles in both the

NFL and AFL when his Jets defeated the Raiders 27-23 for the AFL championship, December 29. The same day, Baltimore defeated Cleveland 34-0.

1969
The AFL established a playoff format for the 1969 season, with the winner in one division playing the runner-up in the other, January 11.

An AFL team won the Super Bowl for the first time, as the Jets defeated the Colts 16-7 at Miami, January 12 in Super Bowl III. The title Super Bowl was recognized by the NFL for the first time.

Vince Lombardi became part owner, executive vice-president, and head coach of the Washington Redskins, February 7.

Wolman sold the Eagles to Leonard Tose, May 1.

Baltimore, Cleveland, and Pittsburgh agreed to join the AFL teams to form the 13-team American Football Conference of the NFL in 1970, May 10. The NFL also agreed on a playoff format that would include one "wild-card" team per conference—the second-place team with the best record.

The NFL announced a three-year agreement with ABC to televise *Monday Night Football*. The new series makes the NFL the first league with a regular series of national telecasts in prime time, May 26.

George Preston Marshall, president emeritus of the Redskins, died at 72, August 9.

The NFL marked its fiftieth year by the wearing of a special patch by each of the 16 teams.

1970
Kansas City defeated Minnesota 23-7 in Super Bowl IV at New Orleans, January 11. The gross receipts of approximately $3.8 million were the largest ever for a one-day sports event.

A special league meeting was held to determine the divisional realignment of the National Football Conference. With no consensus, Rozelle ordered the five most viable plans be written down on sheets of paper. Rozelle's assistant, Thelma Elkjer, picked the winning one out of a vase at random, January 17.

Four-year television contracts, under which CBS would televise all NFC games and NBC all AFC games (except Monday night games) and the two would divide televising the Super Bowl and AFC-NFC Pro Bowl games, were announced, January 26.

Art Modell resigned as president of the NFL, March 12. Milt Woodard resigned as president of the AFL, March 13. Lamar Hunt was elected president of the AFC and George Halas was elected president of the NFC, March 19.

The merged 26-team league adopted rules changes putting names on the backs of players' jerseys, making a point after touchdown worth only one point, and making the scoreboard clock the official timing device of the game, March 18.

The Players Negotiating Committee and the NFL Players Association announced a four-year agreement guaranteeing approximately $4,535,000 annually to player pension and insurance benefits, August 3. The owners also agreed to contribute $250,000 annually to improve or implement items such as disability payments, widows' benefits, maternity benefits, and dental benefits. The agreement also provided for increased preseason game and per diem payments, averaging approximately $2.6 million annually.

The Pittsburgh Steelers moved into Three Rivers Stadium. The Cincinnati Bengals moved to Riverfront Stadium.

Vince Lombardi died of cancer at 57, September 3.

The Super Bowl trophy was renamed the Vince Lombardi trophy, September 10.

Tom Dempsey of New Orleans kicked a game-winning NFL-record 63-yard field goal against Detroit, November 8.

1971

Baltimore defeated Dallas 16-13 on Jim O'Brien's 32-yard field goal with five seconds to go in Super Bowl V at Miami, January 17.

The NFC defeated the AFC 27-6 in the first AFC-NFC Pro Bowl at Los Angeles, January

24.

The Boston Patriots changed their name to the New England Patriots, March 25. Their new stadium, Schaefer Stadium, was dedicated in a 20-14 preseason victory over the Giants.

The Philadelphia Eagles left Franklin Field and played their games at the new Veterans Stadium.

The San Francisco 49ers left Kezar Stadium and moved their games to Candlestick Park.

Daniel F. Reeves, the president and general manager of the Rams, died at 58, April 15.

The Dallas Cowboys moved from the Cotton Bowl into their new home, Texas Stadium, October 24.

Miami defeated Kansas City 27-24 in sudden-death overtime in an AFC Divisional Playoff Game, December 25. Garo Yepremian kicked a 37-yard field goal for the Dolphins after 22 minutes, 40 seconds of overtime, as the game lasted 82 minutes, 40 seconds overall, making it the longest game in history.

1972

Dallas defeated Miami 24-3 in Super Bowl VI at New Orleans, January 16.

The inbounds lines or hashmarks were moved nearer the center of the field, 23 yards, 1 foot, 9 inches from the sidelines, March 23. The method of determining won-lost percentage in standings changed. Tie games, previously not counted in the standings, were made equal to a half-game won and a half-game lost, May 24.

Robert Irsay purchased the Los Angeles Rams and transferred ownership of the club to Carroll Rosenbloom in exchange for the Baltimore Colts, July 13.

William V. Bidwill purchased the stock of his brother Charles (Stormy) Bidwill to become the sole owner of the St. Louis Cardinals, September 2.

The National District Attorneys Association endorsed the position of professional leagues in opposing proposed legalization of gambling on professional team sports, September 28.

Franco Harris' "Immaculate

Reception" gave the Steelers their first postseason win ever, 13-7 over the Raiders, December 23.

1973

Rozelle announced that all Super Bowl VII tickets were sold and that the game would be telecast in Los Angeles, the site of the game, on an experimental basis, January 3.

Miami defeated Washington 14-7 in Super Bowl VII at Los Angeles, completing a 17-0 season, the first perfect-record regular-season and postseason mark in NFL history, January 14.

The AFC defeated the NFC 33-28 in the Pro Bowl in Dallas, the first time since 1942 that the game was played outside Los Angeles, January 21.

A jersey numbering system was adopted, April 5: 1-19 for quarterbacks and specialists, 20-49 for running backs and defensive backs, 50-59 for centers and linebackers, 60-79 for defensive linemen and interior offensive linemen other than centers, and 80-89 for wide receivers and tight ends. Players who had been in the NFL in 1972 could continue to use old numbers.

NFL Charities, a nonprofit organization, was created to derive an income from monies generated from NFL Properties' licensing of NFL trademarks and team names, June 26. NFL Charities was set up to support education and charitable activities and to supply economic support to persons formerly associated with professional football who were no longer able to support themselves.

Congress adopted experimental legislation (for three years) requiring any NFL game that had been declared a sellout 72 hours prior to kickoff to be made available for local televising, September 14. The legislation provided for an annual review to be made by the Federal Communications Commission.

The Buffalo Bills moved their home games from War Memorial Stadium to Rich Stadium in nearby Orchard Park. The Giants tied the Eagles 23-23 in the final game in Yankee Stadium, September 23. The Giants played the rest of their home games at the Yale

Bowl in New Haven, Connecticut.

A rival league, the World Football League, was formed and was reported in operation, October 2. It had plans to start play in 1974.

O.J. Simpson of Buffalo became the first player to rush for more than 2,000 yards in a season, gaining 2,003.

1974

Miami defeated Minnesota 24-7 in Super Bowl VIII at Houston, the second consecutive Super Bowl championship for the Dolphins, January 13.

Rozelle was given a 10-year contract effective January 1, 1973, February 27.

Tampa Bay was awarded the twenty-seventh franchise to begin operation in 1976, April 24.

Sweeping rules changes were adopted to add action and tempo to games: one sudden-death overtime period was added for preseason and regular-season games; the goal posts were moved from the goal line to the end lines; kickoffs were moved from the 40- to the 35-yard line; after missed field goals from beyond the 20, the ball was to be returned to the line of scrimmage; restrictions were placed on members of the punting team to open up return possibilities; roll-blocking and cutting of wide receivers was eliminated; the extent of downfield contact a defender could have with an eligible receiver was restricted; the penalties for offensive holding, illegal use of the hands, and tripping were reduced from 15 to 10 yards; wide receivers blocking back toward the ball within three yards of the line of scrimmage were prevented from blocking below the waist, April 25.

Seattle was awarded the twenty-eighth NFL franchise to begin play in 1976, June 4. Lloyd W. Nordstrom, president of the Seattle Seahawks, and Hugh Culverhouse, president of the Tampa Bay Buccaneers, signed franchise agreements, December 5.

The Birmingham Americans defeated the Florida Blazers 22-21 in the WFL World Bowl, winning the league championship, December 5.

1975

Pittsburgh defeated Minnesota 16-6 in Super Bowl IX at New Orleans, the Steelers' first championship since entering the NFL in 1933, January 12.

The Memphis Southmen of the WFL signed Larry Csonka, Jim Kiick, and Paul Warfield of Miami, March 31.

The divisional winners with the highest won-loss percentage were made the home team for the divisional playoffs, and the surviving winners with the highest percentage made home teams for the championship games. Previously, the home sites were pre-determined by division on a rotating basis, June 26.

Referees were equipped with wireless microphones for all preseason, regular-season, and playoff games.

The Lions moved to the new Pontiac Silverdome. The Giants played their home games in Shea Stadium. The Saints moved into the Louisiana Superdome.

The World Football League folded, October 22.

1976

Pittsburgh defeated Dallas 21-17 in Super Bowl X in Miami. The Steelers joined Green Bay and Miami as the only teams to win two Super Bowls; the Cowboys became the first wild-card team to play in the Super Bowl, January 18.

Lloyd Nordstrom, the president of the Seahawks, died at 66, January 20. His brother Elmer succeeded him as majority representative of the team.

The owners adopted the use of two 30-second clocks for all games, visible to both players and fans to note the official time between the ready-for-play signal and snap of the ball, March 16.

A veteran player allocation was held to stock the Seattle and Tampa Bay franchises with 39 players each, March 30-31. In the college draft, Seattle and Tampa Bay each received eight extra choices, April 8-9.

The Giants moved into new Giants Stadium in East Rutherford, New Jersey.

The Steelers defeated the College All-Stars in a storm-shortened Chicago College

All-Star Game, the last of the series, July 23. St. Louis defeated San Diego 20-10 in a preseason game before 38,000 in Korakuen Stadium, Tokyo, in the first NFL game outside of North America, August 16.

1977

Oakland defeated Minnesota 32-14 in Super Bowl XI at Pasadena, January 9. The paid attendance was a pro record 103,438.

The NFL Players Association and the NFL Management Council ratified a collective bargaining agreement extending until 1982, covering five football seasons while continuing the pension plan—including years 1974, 1975, and 1976—with contributions totaling more than $55 million. The total cost of the agreement was estimated at $107 million. The agreement called for a college draft at least through 1986; contained a no-strike, no-suit clause; established a 43-man active player limit; reduced pension vesting to four years; provided for increases in minimum salaries and preseason and postseason pay; improved insurance, medical, and dental benefits; modified previous practices in player movement and control; and reaffirmed the NFL Commissioner's disciplinary authority. Additionally, the agreement called for the NFL member clubs to make payments totaling $16 million the next 10 years to settle various legal disputes, February 25.

The San Francisco 49ers were sold to Edward J. DeBartolo, Jr., March 28.

A 16-game regular season, 4-game preseason was adopted to begin in 1978, March 29. A second wild-card team was adopted for the playoffs beginning in 1978, with the wild-card teams to play each other and the winners advancing to a round of eight postseason series.

The Seahawks were permanently aligned in the AFC Western Division and the Buccaneers in the NFC Central Division, March 31.

Rules changes were adopted to open up the passing game and to cut down on injuries. Defenders were permitted to make contact with

eligible receivers only once; the head slap was outlawed; offensive linemen were prohibited from thrusting their hands to an opponent's neck, face, or head; and wide receivers were prohibited from clipping, even in the legal clipping zone.

Rozelle negotiated contracts with the three television networks to televise all NFL regular-season and postseason games, plus selected preseason games, for four years beginning with the 1978 season. ABC was awarded yearly rights to 16 Monday night games, four primetime games, the AFC-NFC Pro Bowl, and the Hall of Fame games. CBS received the rights to all NFC regular-season and postseason games (except those in the ABC package) and to Super Bowls XIV and XVI. NBC received the rights to all AFC regular-season and postseason games (except those in the ABC package) and to Super Bowls XIII and XV. Industry sources considered it the largest single television package ever negotiated, October 12.

1978

Dallas defeated Denver 27-10 in Super Bowl XII, held indoors for the first time, at the Louisiana Superdome in New Orleans, January 15. Dallas' victory was the first for the NFC in six years.

According to a Louis Harris Sports Survey, 70 percent of the nation's sports fans said they followed football, compared to 54 percent who followed baseball. Football increased its lead as the country's favorite, 26 percent to 16 percent for baseball, January 19.

A seventh official, the side judge, was added to the officiating crew, March 14.

The NFL continued a trend toward opening up the game. Rules changes permitted a defender to maintain contact with a receiver within five yards of the line of scrimmage, but restricted contact beyond that point. The pass-blocking rule was interpreted to permit the extending of arms and open hands, March 17.

A study on the use of instant replay as an officiating

aid was made during seven nationally televised preseason games.

The NFL played for the first time in Mexico City, with the Saints defeating the Eagles 14-7 in a preseason game, August 5.

Bolstered by the expansion of the regular-season schedule from 14 to 16 weeks, NFL paid attendance exceeded 12 million (12,771,800) for the first time. The per-game average of 57,017 was the third-highest in league history and the most since 1973.

1979

Pittsburgh defeated Dallas 35-31 in Super Bowl XIII at Miami to become the first team ever to win three Super Bowls, January 21.

NFL rules changes emphasized additional player safety. The changes prohibited players on the receiving team from blocking below the waist during kicking kickoffs, punts, and field-goal attempts; prohibited the wearing of torn or altered equipment and exposed pads that could be hazardous; extended the zone in which there could be no crackback blocks; and instructed officials to quickly whistle a play dead when a quarterback was clearly in the grasp of a tackler, March 16.

Carroll Rosenbloom, the president of the Rams, drowned at 72, April 2. His widow, Georgia, assumed control of the club.

1000

Pittsburgh defeated the Los Angeles Rams 31-19 in Super Bowl XIV at Pasadena to become the first team to win four Super Bowls, January 20.

The AFC-NFC Pro Bowl, won 37-27 by the NFC, was played before 48,060 fans at Aloha Stadium in Honolulu, Hawaii. It was the first time in the 30-year history of the Pro Bowl that the game was played in a non-NFL city.

Rules changes placed greater restrictions on contact in the area of the head, neck, and face. Under the heading of "personal foul," players were prohibited from directly striking, swinging, or clubbing on the head, neck, or face. Starting in 1980, a penalty could be called for such contact whether or not the initial contact was made below the neck area.

CBS, with a record bid of $12 million, won the national radio rights to 26 NFL regular-season games, including Monday Night Football, and all 10 postseason games for the 1980-83 seasons.

The Los Angeles Rams moved their home games to Anaheim Stadium in nearby Orange County, California.

The Oakland Raiders joined the Los Angeles Coliseum Commission's antitrust suit against the NFL. The suit contended the league violated antitrust laws in declining to approve a proposed move by the Raiders from Oakland to Los Angeles.

The NFL Draft is televised for the first time by ESPN, April 29.

Television ratings in 1980 were the second-best in NFL history, trailing only the combined ratings of the 1976 season. All three networks posted gains, and NBC's 15.0 rating was its best ever. CBS and ABC had their best ratings since 1977, with 15.3 and 20.8 ratings, respectively. CBS Radio reported a record audience of 7 million for Monday night and special games.

1981

Oakland defeated Philadelphia 27-10 in Super Bowl XV at the Louisiana Superdome in New Orleans, to become the first wild-card team to win a Super Bowl, January 25.

Edgar F. Kaiser, Jr., purchased the Denver Broncos from Gerald and Allan Phipps, February 26.

The owners adopted a disaster plan for re-stocking a team should the club be involved in a fatal accident, March 20.

A CBS-New York Times poll showed that 48 percent of sports fans preferred football to 31 percent for baseball.

The NFL teams hosted 167 representatives from 44 predominantly black colleges during training camps for a total of 289 days. The program was adopted for renewal during each training camp period.

ABC and CBS set all-time rating highs. ABC finished with a 21.7 rating and CBS with a 17.5 rating. NBC was down slightly to 13.9.

1982

San Francisco defeated Cincinnati 26-21 in Super Bowl XVI at the Pontiac Silverdome, in the first Super Bowl held in the North, January 24. The CBS telecast achieved the highest rating of any televised sports event ever, 49.1 with a 73.0 share.

The NFL signed a five-year contract with the three television networks (ABC, CBS, and NBC) to televise all NFL regular-season and postseason games starting with the 1982 season.

A jury ruled against the NFL in the antitrust trial brought by the Los Angeles Coliseum Commission and the Oakland Raiders, May 7. The verdict cleared the way for the Raiders to move to Los Angeles, where they defeated Green Bay 24-3 in their first preseason game, August 29.

The 1982 season was reduced from a 16-game schedule to nine as the result of a 57-day players' strike. The strike was called by the NFLPA at midnight on Monday, September 20, following the Green Bay at New York Giants game. Play resumed November 21-22 following ratification of the Collective Bargaining Agreement by NFL owners, November 17 in New York.

Under the Collective Bargaining Agreement, which was to run through the 1986 season, the NFL draft was extended through 1992 and the veteran free-agent system was left basically unchanged. A minimum salary schedule for years of experience was established; training camp and postseason pay were increased; players' medical, insurance, and retirement benefits were increased; and a severance-pay system was introduced to aid in career transition, a first in professional sports.

Despite the players' strike, the average paid attendance in 1982 was 58,472, the fifth-highest in league history.

1983

Because of the shortened season, the NFL adopted a format of 16 teams competing in a Super Bowl Tournament for the 1982 playoffs. The NFC's

number-one seed, Washington, defeated the AFC's number-two seed, Miami, 27-17 in Super Bowl XVII at the Rose Bowl in Pasadena, January 30.

Super Bowl XVII was the second-highest rated live television program of all time, giving the NFL a sweep of the top 10 live programs in television history.

George Halas, the owner of the Bears and the last surviving member of the NFL's second organizational meeting, died at 88, October 31.

1984

The Los Angeles Raiders defeated Washington 38-9 in Super Bowl XVIII at Tampa Stadium, January 22.

An 11-man group headed by H.R. (Bum) Bright purchased the Dallas Cowboys from Clint Murchison, Jr., March 20. Club president Tex Schramm was designated as managing general partner.

Wellington Mara was named president of the NFC, March 20.

Patrick Bowlen purchased a majority interest in the Denver Broncos from Edgar Kaiser, Jr., March 21.

The Colts relocated to Indianapolis, March 28. Their new home became the Hoosier Dome.

The New York Jets moved their home games to Giants Stadium in East Rutherford, New Jersey.

Alex G. Spanos purchased a majority interest in the San Diego Chargers from Eugene V. Klein, August 28.

Houston defeated Pittsburgh 23-20 to mark the one-hundredth overtime game in regular-season play since overtime was adopted in 1974, December 2.

On the field, many all-time records were set: Dan Marino of Miami passed for 5,084 yards and 48 touchdowns; Eric Dickerson of the Los Angeles Rams rushed for 2,105 yards; Art Monk of Washington caught 106 passes; and Walter Payton of Chicago broke Jim Brown's career rushing mark, finishing the season with 13,309 yards.

According to a CBS Sports/New York Times survey, 53 percent of the nation's sports fans said they most

enjoyed watching football, compared to 18 percent for baseball, December 2-4.

1985

San Francisco defeated Miami 38-16 in Super Bowl XIX at Stanford Stadium in Stanford, California, January 20. President Ronald Reagan, who took his second oath of office before tossing the coin for the game, was one of 115,936,000 viewers. Super Bowl XIX had a direct economic impact of $113.5 million on the San Francisco Bay area.

NBC Radio and the NFL entered into a two-year agreement granting NBC the radio rights to a 37-game package in each of the 1985-86 seasons, March 6. The package included 27 regular-season games and 10 postseason games.

Norman Braman, in partnership with Edward Leibowitz, bought the Philadelphia Eagles from Leonard Tose, April 29.

A group headed by Tom Benson, Jr., was approved to purchase the New Orleans Saints from John W. Mecom, Jr., June 3.

The NFL owners adopted a resolution calling for a series of overseas preseason games, beginning in 1986, with one game to be played in England/Europe and/or one game in Japan each year. The game would be a fifth preseason game for the clubs involved and all arrangements and selection of the clubs would be under the control of the Commissioner, May 23.

The league-wide conversion to videotape from movie film for coaching study was approved.

A Louis Harris poll in December revealed that pro football remained the sport most followed by Americans. Fifty-nine percent of those surveyed followed pro football, compared with 54 percent who followed baseball.

The Chicago-Miami Monday game had the highest rating, 29.6, and share, 46.0, of any primetime game in NFL history, December 2. The game was viewed in more than 25 million homes.

The NFL showed a ratings increase on all three networks for the season, gaining 4 percent on NBC, 10 on CBS, and 16 on ABC.

1986

Chicago defeated New England 46-10 in Super Bowl XX at the Louisiana Superdome, January 26. The Patriots had earned the right to play the Bears by becoming the first wild-card team to win three consecutive games on the road. The NBC telecast replaced the final episode of *M*A*S*H* as the most-viewed television program in history, with an audience of 127 million viewers, according to A.C. Nielsen figures. In addition to drawing a 48.3 rating and a 70 percent share, Super Bowl XX was televised to 59 foreign countries and beamed via satellite to the QE II.

The owners adopted limited use of instant replay as an officiating aid, prohibited players from wearing or otherwise displaying equipment, apparel, or other items that carry commercial names, names of organizations, or personal messages of any type, March 11.

After an 11-week trial, a jury in U.S. District Court in New York awarded the United States Football League one dollar in its $1.7 billion antitrust suit against the NFL. The jury rejected all of the USFL's television-related claims, which were the self-proclaimed heart of the USFL's case. The jury deliberated five days, July 29.

Chicago defeated Dallas 17-6 at Wembley Stadium in London in the first American Bowl. The game drew a sellout crowd of 82,699 and the NBC national telecast in this country produced a 12.4 rating and 36 percent share, making it the highest daytime preseason television audience ever with 10.65-million viewers, August 3.

ABC's *NFL Monday Night Football*, in its seventeenth season, became the longest-running primetime series in the history of the network.

1987

The New York Giants defeated Denver 39-20 in Super Bowl XXI and captured their first NFL title since 1956. The game, played in Pasadena's Rose Bowl, drew a sellout crowd of 101,063, January 25.

New three-year TV contracts with ABC, CBS, and NBC were announced for 1987-89 at the NFL annual meeting in Maui, Hawaii, March 15. Commissioner Rozelle and Broadcast Committee Chairman Art Modell also announced a three-year contract with ESPN to televise 13 primetime games each season. The ESPN contract was the first with a cable network. However, NFL games on ESPN also were scheduled for regular television in the city of the visiting team and in the home city if the game was sold out 72 hours in advance.

A special payment program was adopted to benefit nearly 1,000 former NFL players who participated in the League before the current Bert Bell NFL Pension Plan was created and made retroactive to the 1959 season. Players covered by the new program spent at least five years in the League and played all or part of their career prior to 1959. Each vested player would receive $60 per month for each year of service in the League for life.

NFL and CBS Radio jointly announced agreement granting CBS the radio rights to a 40-game package in each of the next three NFL seasons, 1987-89, April 7.

Over 400 former NFL players from the pre-1959 era received first payments from NFL owners, July 1.

The NFL's debut on ESPN produced the two highest-rated and most-watched sports programs in basic cable history. The Chicago at Miami game on August 16 drew an 8.9 rating in 3.81 million homes. Those records fell two weeks later when the Los Angeles Raiders at Dallas game achieved a 10.2 cable rating in 4.36 million homes.

The 1987 season was reduced from a 16-game season to 15 as the result of a 24-day players' strike. The strike was called by the NFLPA on Tuesday, September 22, following the New England at New York Jets game. Games scheduled for the third weekend were canceled but the games of weeks four, five, and six were played with replacement teams. Striking players returned for the seventh week of the season, October 25.

In a three-team deal involving 10 players and/or draft choices, the Los Angeles Rams traded running back Eric Dickerson to the Indianapolis Colts for six draft choices and two players. Buffalo obtained the rights to linebacker Cornelius Bennett from Indianapolis, sending Greg Bell and three draft choices to the Rams. The Colts added Owen Gill and three draft choices of their own to complete the deal with the Rams, October 31.

The Chicago at Minnesota game became the highest-rated and most-watched sports program in basic cable history when it drew a 14.4 cable rating in 6.5 million homes, December 6.

1988

Washington defeated Denver 42-10 in Super Bowl XXII to earn its second victory this decade in the NFL Championship Game. The game, played for the first time in San Diego Jack Murphy Stadium, drew a sellout crowd of 73,302. Doug Williams, the game's MVP, became the first African-American quarterback to play in a Super Bowl, January 31.

In a unanimous 3-0 decision, the 2nd Circuit Court of Appeals in New York upheld the verdict of the jury that in July, 1986, had awarded the United States Football League one dollar in its $1.7 billion antitrust suit against the NFL. In a 91-page opinion, Judge Ralph K. Winter said the USFL sought through court decree the success it failed to gain among football fans, March 10.

By a 23-5 margin, owners voted to continue the instant replay system for the third consecutive season with the Instant Replay Official to be assigned to a regular seven-man, on-the-field crew. At the NFL annual meeting in Phoenix, Arizona, a 45-second clock was also approved to replace the 30-second clock. For a normal sequence of plays, the interval between plays was changed to 45 seconds from the time the

ball is signaled dead until it is snapped on the succeeding play.

NFL owners approved the transfer of the Cardinals' franchise from St. Louis to Phoenix; approved two supplemental drafts each year—one prior to training camp and one prior to the regular season; and voted to initiate an annual series of games in Japan/Asia as early as the 1989 preseason, March 14-18.

The NFL Annual Selection Meeting returned to a separate two-day format and for the first time originated on a Sunday. ESPN drew a 3.6 rating during their seven-hour coverage of the draft, which was viewed in 1.6 million homes, April 24-25.

Art Rooney, founder and owner of the Steelers, died at 87, August 25.

Johnny Grier became the first African-American referee in NFL history, September 4.

Commissioner Rozelle announced that two teams would play a preseason game as part of the American Bowl series on August 6, 1989, in the Korakuen Tokyo Dome in Japan, December 16.

1989

San Francisco defeated Cincinnati 20-16 in Super Bowl XXIII. The game, played for the first time at Joe Robbie Stadium in Miami, was attended by a sellout crowd of 75,129, January 22.

Commissioner Rozelle announced his retirement, pending the naming of a successor, March 22 at the NFL annual meeting in Palm Desert, California.

Following the announcement, AFC president Lamar Hunt and NFC president Wellington Mara announced the formation of a six-man search committee composed of Art Modell, Robert Parins, Dan Rooney, and Ralph Wilson. Hunt and Mara served as co-chairmen.

By a 24-4 margin, owners voted to continue the instant replay system for the fourth straight season. A strengthened policy regarding anabolic steroids and masking agents was announced by Commissioner Rozelle. NFL clubs called for strong disciplinary measures in cases of feigned injuries and adopted a joint proposal by the Long-Range Planning and Finance committees regarding player personnel rules, March 19-23.

Two hundred twenty-nine unconditional free agents signed with new teams under management's Plan B system, April 1.

Jerry Jones purchased a majority interest in the Dallas Cowboys from H.R. (Bum) Bright, April 18.

Tex Schramm was named president of the new World League of American Football to work with a six-man committee of Dan Rooney, chairman; Norman Braman, Lamar Hunt, Victor Kiam, Mike Lynn, and Bill Walsh, April 18.

NFL and CBS Radio jointly announced agreement extending CBS's radio rights to an annual 40-game package through the 1994 season, April 18.

As of opening day, September 10, of the 229 Plan B free agents, 111 were active and 23 others were on teams' reserve lists. Ninety-two others were waived and three retired.

Art Shell was named head coach of the Los Angeles Raiders making him the NFL's first black head coach since Fritz Pollard coached the Akron Pros in 1921, October 3.

The site of the New England Patriots at San Francisco 49ers game scheduled for Candlestick Park on October 22 was switched to Stanford Stadium in the aftermath of the Bay Area Earthquake of October 17. The change was announced on October 19.

Paul Tagliabue became the seventh chief executive of the NFL on October 26 when he was chosen to succeed Commissioner Pete Rozelle on the sixth ballot of a three-day meeting in Cleveland, Ohio. In all, 12 ballots were required to select Tagliabue. Two were conducted at a meeting in Chicago on July 6, and four at a meeting in Dallas on October 10-11. On the twelfth ballot, with Seattle absent, Tagliabue received more than the 19 affirmative votes required for election from among the 27 clubs present.

The transfer from Commissioner Rozelle to Commissioner Tagliabue took place at 12:01 A.M. on Sunday, November 5.

NFL Charities donated $1 million through United Way to benefit Bay Area earthquake victims, November 6.

1990

San Francisco defeated Denver 55-10 in Super Bowl XXIV at the Louisiana Superdome, January 28. San Francisco joined Pittsburgh as the NFL's only teams to win four Super Bowls.

The NFL announced revisions in its 1990 draft eligibility rules. College juniors became eligible but must renounce their collegiate football eligibility before applying for the NFL Draft, February 16.

Commissioner Tagliabue announced NFL teams will play their 16-game schedule over 17 weeks in 1990-92 and 16 games over 18 weeks in 1993, February 27.

The NFL revised its playoff format to include two additional wild-card teams (one per conference), which raised the total to six wild-card teams.

Commissioner Tagliabue and Broadcast Committee Chairman Art Modell announced a four-year contract with Turner Broadcasting to televise nine Sunday-night games.

New four-year TV agreements were ratified for 1990-93 for ABC, CBS, NBC, ESPN, and TNT at the NFL annual meeting in Orlando, Florida, March 12. The contracts totaled $3.6 billion, the largest in TV history.

The NFL announced plans to expand its American Bowl series of preseason games. In addition to games in London and Tokyo, American Bowl games were scheduled for Berlin, Germany, and Montreal, Canada, in 1990.

For the fifth straight year, NFL owners voted to continue a limited system of Instant Replay. Beginning in 1990, the replay official will have a two-minute time limit to make a decision. The vote was 21-7, March 12.

Commissioner Tagliabue announced the formation of a Committee on Expansion and Realignment, March 13. He also named a Player Advisory Council, comprised of 12 former NFL players, March 14.

One-hundred eighty-four Plan B unconditional free agents signed with new teams, April 2.

Commissioner Tagliabue appointed Dr. John Lombardo as the League's Drug Advisor for Anabolic Steroids, April 25 and named Dr. Lawrence Brown as the League's Advisor for Drugs of Abuse, May 17.

NFL International Week was celebrated with four preseason games in seven days in Tokyo, London, Berlin, and Montreal. More than 200,000 fans on three continents attended the four games, August 4-11.

Commissioner Tagliabue announced the NFL Teacher of the Month program in which the League furnishes grants and scholarships in recognition of teachers who provided a positive influence upon NFL players in elementary and secondary schools, September 20.

For the first time since 1957, every NFL club won at least one of its first four games, October 1.

The Super Bowl Most Valuable Player trophy was renamed the Pete Rozelle trophy, October 8.

1991

The New York Giants defeated Buffalo 20-19 in Super Bowl XXV to capture their second title in five years. The game was played before a sellout crowd of 73,813 at Tampa Stadium and became the first Super Bowl decided by one point, January 26.

New York businessman Robert Tisch purchased a 50 percent interest in the New York Giants from Mrs. Helen Mara Nugent and her children, Tim Mara and Maura Mara Concannon, February 2.

NFL clubs voted to continue a limited system of Instant Replay for the sixth consecutive year. The vote was 21-7, March 19.

The NFL launched the World League of American Football, the first sports league to operate on a weekly basis on two separate continents, March 23.

NFL Charities presented a $250,000 donation to the United Service Organization. The donation was the second largest single grant ever by NFL Charities, April 5.

Commissioner Tagliabue named Harold Henderson as Executive Vice President for Labor Relations and Chairman of the NFL Management Council Executive Committee, April 8.

NFL clubs approved a recommendation by the Expansion and Realignment Committee to add two teams for the 1994 season, resulting in six divisions of five teams each, May 22.

"NFL International Week" featured six 1990 playoff teams playing nationally televised games in London, Berlin, and Tokyo on July 28 and August 3-4. The games drew more than 150,000 fans.

Paul Brown, founder of the Cleveland Browns and Cincinnati Bengals, died at age 82, August 5.

NFL clubs approved a resolution establishing an international division. A three-year financial plan for the World League was approved by NFL clubs at a meeting in Dallas, October 23.

1992

The NFL agreed to provide a minimum of $2.5 million in financial support to the NFL Alumni Association and assistance to NFL Alumni-related programs. The agreement included contributions from NFL Charities to the Pre-59ers and Dire Need Programs for former players, January 25.

The Washington Redskins defeated the Buffalo Bills 37-24 in Super Bowl XXVI to capture their third world championship in 10 years, January 26. The game was played before a sellout crowd of 63,130 at the Hubert H. Humphrey Metrodome in Minneapolis.

The use in officiating of a limited system of Instant Replay was not approved. The vote was 17-11 in favor of approval (21 votes were required). Instant Replay had been used for six consecutive years (1986-1991), March 18.

St. Louis businessman James Orthwein purchased controlling interest in the New

England Patriots from Victor Kiam, May 11.

In a Harris Poll taken during the NFL offseason, professional football again was declared the nation's most popular sport. Professional football finished atop similar surveys conducted by Harris in 1985 and 1989, May 23.

NFL clubs accepted the report of the Expansion Committee at a league meeting in Pasadena. The report names five cities as finalists for the two expansion teams—Baltimore, Charlotte, Jacksonville, Memphis, and St. Louis, May 19.

At a league meeting in Dallas, NFL clubs approved a proposal by the World League Board of Directors to restructure the World League and place future emphasis on its international success, September 17.

The Professional and Amateur Sports Protection Act made it unlawful for a government entity to operate a lottery or other betting scheme based on pro or collegiate games. Four states that already had such betting were grandfathered, October 6.

NFL teams played their 16-game regular-season schedule over 18 weeks for the only time in league history.

1993

The NFL and lawyers for the players announced a settlement of various lawsuits and an agreement on the terms of a seven-year deal that included a new player system to be in place through the 1999 season, January 6.

Commissioner Tagliabue announced the establishment of the "NFL World Partnership Program" to develop amateur football internationally through a series of clinics conducted by former NFL players and coaches, January 14.

As part of Super Bowl XXVII, the NFL announced the creation of the first NFL Youth Education Town, a facility located in south central Los Angeles for inner city youth, January 25.

The Dallas Cowboys defeated the Buffalo Bills 52-17 in Super Bowl XXVII to capture their first NFL title since 1978. The game was played before a crowd of

98,374 at the Rose Bowl in Pasadena, California, January 31.

The NFL and the NFL Players Association officially signed a 7-year Collective Bargaining Agreement in Washington, D.C., which guarantees more than $1 billion in pension, health, and post-career benefits for current and retired players—the most extensive benefits plan in pro sports. It was the NFL's first CBA since the 1982 agreement expired in 1987, June 29.

NFL Enterprises, a newly formed division of the NFL responsible for NFL Films, home video, and special domestic and international television programming was announced, August 19.

NFL announced plans to allow fans, for the first time ever, to join players and coaches in selecting the annual AFC and NFC Pro Bowl teams, October 12.

NFL clubs unanimously awarded the league's twenty-ninth franchise to the Carolina Panthers and owner Jerry Richardson at a meeting in Chicago, October 26.

At the same meeting in Chicago, NFL clubs approved a plan to form a European league with joint venture partners, October 27.

Don Shula became the winningest coach in NFL history when Miami beat Philadelphia to give Shula his 325th victory, one more than George Halas, November 14.

NFL clubs awarded the league's thirtieth franchise to the Jacksonville Jaguars and owner Wayne Weaver at a meeting in Chicago, November 30.

The NFL announced new 4-year television agreements with NBC, ABC, ESPN, TNT, and NFL newcomer FOX, which took over the NFC package from CBS, December 18.

The NFL completed its new TV agreements by announcing that NBC would retain the rights to the AFC package, December 20.

1994

The Dallas Cowboys defeated the Buffalo Bills 30-13 in Super Bowl XXVIII to become the fifth team to win back-to-back Super Bowl titles, Janu-

ary 30.

NFL clubs unanimously approved the transfer of the New England Patriots from James Orthwein to Robert Kraft at a meeting in Orlando, February 22.

In a move to increase offensive production, NFL clubs at the league's annual meeting in Orlando adopted a package of changes, including modifications in line play, chucking rules, and the roughing-the-passer rule, plus the adoption of the two-point conversion and moving the spot of the kickoff back to the 30-yard line, March 22.

NFL clubs approved the transfer of the majority interest in the Miami Dolphins from the Robbie family to H. Wayne Huizenga, March 23.

The NFL and FOX announced the formation of a joint venture to create a six-team World League to begin play in Europe in April, 1995, March 23.

The Carolina Panthers earned the right to select first in the 1995 NFL draft by winning a coin toss with the Jacksonville Jaguars. The Jaguars received the second selection in the 1995 draft, April 24.

NFL clubs approved the transfer of the Philadelphia Eagles from Norman Braman to Jeffrey Lurie, May 6.

The NFL launched "NFL Sunday Ticket," a new season subscription service for satellite television dish owners, June 1.

An all-time NFL record crowd of 112,376 attended the American Bowl game between Dallas and Houston in Mexico City. It concluded the biggest American Bowl series in NFL history with four games attracting a record 256,666 fans, August 15.

The NFL reached agreement on a new seven-year contract with its game officials, September 22.

The NFL Management Council and the NFL Players Association announced an agreement on the formulation and implementation of the most comprehensive drug and alcohol policy in sports, October 28.

At an NFL meeting in Chicago, Commissioner Tagliabue slotted the two new expansion teams into the AFC Central

(Jacksonville Jaguars) and NFC West (Carolina Panthers) for the 1995 season only. He also appointed a special committee on realignment to make recommendations on the 1996 season and beyond, November 2.

1995

The San Francisco 49ers became the first team to win five Super Bowls when they defeated the San Diego Chargers 49-26 in Super Bowl XXIX at Joe Robbie Stadium in Miami, January 29.

Carolina and Jacksonville stocked their expansion rosters with a total of 66 players from other NFL teams in a veteran player allocation draft in New York, February 16.

CBS Radio and the NFL agreed to a new four-year contract for an annual 53-game package of games, continuing a relationship that spanned 15 of the past 17 years, February 22.

NFL clubs approved the transfer of the Tampa Bay Buccaneers from the estate of the late Hugh Culverhouse to South Florida businessman Malcolm Glazer, March 13.

After a two-year hiatus, the World League of American Football returned to action with six teams in Europe, April 8.

The NFL became the first major sports league to establish a site on the Internet system of on-line computer communication, April 10.

The transfer of the Rams from Los Angeles to St. Louis was approved by a vote of the NFL clubs at a meeting in Dallas, April 12.

ABC's *NFL Monday Night Football* finished the 1994-95 television season as the fifth highest-rated show out of 146 with a 17.8 average rating, the highest finish in the 25-year history of the series, April 18.

The Frankfurt Galaxy defeated the Amsterdam Admirals 26-22 to win the 1995 World Bowl before a crowd of 23,847 in Amsterdam's Olympic Stadium, June 23.

The transfer of the Raiders from Los Angeles to Oakland was approved by a vote of the NFL clubs at a meeting in Chicago, July 22.

Jacksonville Municipal Stadium opened in Jacksonville, Florida before a sold-out crowd of more than 70,000 as the St. Louis Rams defeated the Jacksonville Jaguars 27-10 in their first preseason game, August 18.

NFL Charities and 50 NFL players donated $1 million to the United Negro College Fund in honor of the fiftieth anniversary of the UNCF and the integration of the modern NFL, September 15.

The Trans World Dome opened in St. Louis with a sold-out crowd of 65,598 as the Rams defeated the Carolina Panthers 28-17, November 12.

On the field, many significant records and milestones were achieved: Miami's Dan Marino surpassed Pro Football Hall of Famer Fran Tarkenton in four major passing categories—attempts, completions, yards, and touchdowns—to become the NFL's all-time career leader. San Francisco's Jerry Rice became the all-time reception and receiving-yardage leader.

1996

The Dallas Cowboys won their third Super Bowl title in four years when they defeated the Pittsburgh Steelers 27-17 in Super Bowl XXX at Sun Devil Stadium in Tempe, Arizona, January 28.

An agreement between the NFL and the city of Cleveland regarding the Cleveland Browns' relocation was approved by a vote of the NFL clubs, February 9. According to the agreement, the city of Cleveland retained the Browns' heritage and records, including the name, logo, colors, history, playing records, trophies, and memorabilia, and committed to building a new 72,000-seat stadium for a reactivated Browns' franchise to begin play there no later than 1999. Art Modell received approval to move his franchise to Baltimore and rename it.

The transfer of the Oilers from Houston to Nashville for the 1998 season was approved by a vote of the NFL clubs at a meeting in Atlanta, April 30.

The Scottish Claymores defeated the Frankfurt Galaxy 32-27 to win the 1996 World Bowl in front of 38,982 at Murrayfield Stadium in Edinburgh, Scotland, June 23.

The NFL returned to Baltimore when the new Baltimore Ravens defeated the Philadelphia Eagles 17-9 in a preseason game before a crowd of 63,804 at Memorial Stadium, August 3.

Ericsson Stadium opened in Charlotte, North Carolina with a crowd of 65,350 as the Carolina Panthers defeated the Chicago Bears 30-12 in a preseason game, August 3.

Former NFL Commissioner Pete Rozelle died at his home in Rancho Santa Fe, California. Rozelle, regarded as the premiere commissioner in sports history, led the NFL for 29 years, from 1960-1989, December 6.

1997

Indianapolis Colts owner Robert Irsay died from complications related to a stroke he suffered in 1995. Irsay acquired the club in 1972 when he traded his Los Angeles Rams to Carrol Rosenbloom for the Colts. He later moved the Colts from Baltimore to Indianapolis in 1984, January 14.

The Green Bay Packers won their first NFL title in 29 years by defeating the New England Patriots 35-21 in Super Bowl XXXI at the Louisiana Superdome in New Orleans, January 26.

The rules governing cross-ownership were modified, permitting NFL club owners to also own teams in other sports in their home market or markets without NFL teams. The vote was 24-5 (one abstention) in favor of approval, March 11.

Washington Redskins owner Jack Kent Cooke died at his home in Washington, D.C. Cooke became majority owner in 1974 and the Redskins won three Super Bowls under his leadership, April 6.

The Barcelona Dragons defeated the Rhein Fire 38-24 to win the 1997 World Bowl in front of 31,100 fans at Estadi Olimpic de Montjuic in Barcelona, Spain, June 22.

NFL clubs approved the transfer of the Seattle Seahawks from Ken Behring to Paul Allen, August 19.

Jack Kent Cooke Stadium opened in Raljon, Maryland with a crowd of 78,270 as the Washington Redskins defeated the Arizona Cardinals 19-13 in

overtime, September 14.

The 10,000th regular-season game in NFL history was played when the Seattle Seahawks defeated the Tennessee Oilers 16-13 at the Kingdome in Seattle, October 5.

Atlanta Falcons owner Rankin Smith died of heart failure three days prior to his seventy-third birthday. Smith was the founder of the Falcons and was instrumental in bringing Super Bowls XXVIII and XXXIV to Atlanta, October 26.

1998

The NFL reached agreement on record eight-year television contracts with four networks. ABC (NFL Monday Night Football) and FOX (NFC) retained their previous rights, CBS took over the AFC package from NBC, and ESPN won the right to broadcast the entire Sunday night cable package, January 13.

The World League was renamed the NFL Europe League, January 22.

The Denver Broncos won their first Super Bowl by defeating the defending champion Green Bay Packers 31-24 in Super Bowl XXXII at Qualcomm Stadium in San Diego, January 25.

The NFL clubs approved an extension of the Collective Bargaining Agreement through 2003. The extended CBA also created a $100 million fund for youth football, March 22.

The NFL clubs unanimously approved an expansion team for Cleveland to fulfill the commitment to return the Browns to the field in 1999, March 23.

The Rhein Fire defeated the Frankfurt Galaxy 34-10 to win the 1998 World Bowl in front of 47,846 fans in Frankfurt's Waldstadion—the biggest crowd to witness a World Bowl since 1991, June 14.

NFL clubs approved the transfer of the Minnesota Vikings from a 10-man ownership group to Red McCombs, July 28.

The NFL Stadium at Camden Yards opened in Baltimore, Maryland before a crowd of 65,938 as the Baltimore Ravens defeated the Chicago Bears 19-14 in a preseason game, August 8.

Raymond James Stadium opened in Tampa, Florida before a crowd of 62,410 as

the Tampa Bay Buccaneers defeated the Chicago Bears 27-15, September 20.

Tennessee Oilers owner Bud Adams announced the team will change its name to the Tennessee Titans following the 1998 season. The NFL announced that the name Oilers will be retired—a first in league history, November 14.

1999

The Denver Broncos won their second consecutive Super Bowl title by defeating the NFC champion Atlanta Falcons 34-19 in Super Bowl XXXIII at Pro Player Stadium in Miami, January 31.

Jim Pyne, a center allocated by the Detroit Lions, was the first selection of the Cleveland Browns in the 1999 NFL Expansion Draft. The Browns eventually selected 37 players, February 9.

CBS Radio/Westwood One agreed to a 3-year extension of their exclusive national radio rights to NFL games, March 11.

By a vote of 28-3, the owners adopted an instant replay system as an officiating aid for the 1999 season, March 17.

New York Jets owner Leon Hess died from complications of a blood disease. Hess had been involved in the ownership of the Jets since 1963 and was sole owner of the club since 1984, May 9.

A group led by Washington area businessman Daniel Snyder is approved by NFL clubs as the new owner of the Washington Redskins at a league meeting in Atlanta, May 25.

The Frankfurt Galaxy became the first team in NFL Europe League history to win a second World Bowl by defeating the Barcelona Dragons 38-24 at Rheinstadion, in Düsseldorf, Germany, June 27.

The Cleveland Browns returned to the field for the first time since 1995 and defeated the Dallas Cowboys 20-17 in overtime in the annual Hall of Fame Game at Canton, Ohio, August 9.

Cleveland Browns Stadium opened in Cleveland, Ohio before a crowd of 71,398 as the Minnesota Vikings defeated the Browns in a preseason game, 24-17, August 21.

Adelphia Coliseum opened in Nashville, Tennessee before a crowd of 65,729 with the Tennessee Titans defeating the Atlanta Falcons 17-3 in a pre-season game, August 26.

Houston, Texas and owner Robert McNair were awarded the NFL's thirty-second franchise in a vote of the NFL clubs at a league meeting in Atlanta. The team will begin play in 2002. The NFL clubs also voted to realign into eight divisions of four teams each for the 2002 season, October 6.

Walter Payton, the NFL's all-time leading rusher, died of liver cancer at the age of 45. Payton played for the Chicago Bears from 1975-1987 and rushed for an NFL-record 16,726 yards, November 1.

Former NFL Commissioner Pete Rozelle, who guided a still-developing league to its position today as America's most popular sport, was named by *The Sporting News* as the most powerful person in sports in the 20th Century, December 15.

2000

New York businessman Robert Wood Johnson IV was approved by NFL clubs as the new owner of the New York Jets at a league meeting, January 18.

The St. Louis Rams won their first Super Bowl by defeating the AFC champion Tennessee Titans 23-16 in Super Bowl XXXIV at the Georgia Dome in Atlanta, January 30.

For the first time in league history, paid attendance topped 16 million for the regular season and more than 65,000 per game, an increase of 1,300 per game over 1998. Paid attendance for all NFL games increased in 1999 for the third year in a row and was the highest ever in the 80-year history of the league. It marked the first time in league history that the 20-million paid attendance mark was reached for all games in a season, March 27.

The Rhein Fire won their second World Bowl in three years, defeating the Scottish Claymores 13-10 to win World Bowl 2000 in front of 35,680 at Frankfurt's Waldstadion, June 25.

More than 100 of the 136 living members of the Pro Football Hall of Fame gathered to celebrate Pro Football's Greatest Reunion in Canton, Ohio, July 28-31.

Paul Brown Stadium opened in Cincinnati, Ohio with a crowd of 56,180 as the Cincinnati Bengals defeated the Chicago Bears 24-20 in a preseason game, August 19.

Minnesota's Gary Anderson converted a 21-yard field goal against Buffalo to pass George Blanda as the NFL's all-time scoring leader with 2,004 points, October 22.

San Francisco's Terrell Owens set a single-game receiving record with 20 receptions (283 yards) against Chicago, surpassing the previous mark of 18 by Tom Fears of the Los Angeles Rams in 1950, December 17.

2001

NFL clubs approved additional league-wide revenue sharing at a special league meeting in Dallas. The teams agreed to pool the visiting team share of gate receipts for all preseason and regular-season games and divide the pool equally starting in 2002, January 17.

The Baltimore Ravens won their first Super Bowl by defeating the NFC champion New York Giants 34-7 in Super Bowl XXXV at Raymond James Stadium in Tampa Bay, January 28.

The *Sports Business Daily* named NFL Commissioner Paul Tagliabue the 2000 Sports Industrialist of the Year February 28.

NFL owners unanimously approved a realignment plan for the league starting in 2002. With the addition of the Houston Texans, the league's 32 teams will be divided into eight four-team divisions. Seven clubs change divisions, and the Seattle Seahawks change conferences, moving from the AFC to the NFC. A new scheduling format ensures that every team meets every other team in the league at least once every four years, May 22.

The Berlin Thunder won their first World Bowl, defeating the Barcelona Dragons 24-17 to win World Bowl IX in front of 32,116 at Amsterdam ArenA, June 30.

Heinz Field opened in Pittsburgh, Pennsylvania before a crowd of 57,829 with the Pittsburgh Steelers defeating the Detroit Lions 20-7 in a pre-season game; and INVESCO Field at Mile High opened in Denver, Colorado before a crowd of 74,063 with the Denver Broncos defeating the New Orleans Saints 31-24 in a pre-season game, August 25.

President George W. Bush became the first United States President to be involved in an NFL regular-season pregame coin toss as he helped kick off the 2001 season from the White House. Via satellite, President Bush tossed the coin for the 10 regular-season games that started at 1:00 P.M. ET, September 9.

In the wake of the September 11 terrorist attacks, Commissioner Paul Tagliabue postponed the games scheduled for September 16-17, September 13.

The league's 16-game regular season was retained when the postponed Week 2 games were rescheduled for the weekend of January 6-7, September 18.

The NFL and its game officials agreed to a new six-year Collective Bargaining Agreement, ending a two-week lockout of the regular officials, who returned to work on September 23, September 19.

The NFL announced that the league's prohibition of anabolic steroids and related substances had been strengthened to include supplements containing ephedrine and other high-risk supplements, September 27.

The NFL announced that the Super Bowl would be rescheduled from January 27 to February 3 in order to retain the full playoff format for the 2002 season. It will be the first Super Bowl played in February, October 3.

President Bush designated Super Bowl XXXVI as a "National Special Security Event," allowing all security for the game to be coordinated by the Secret Service, November 26.

2002

The NFL and the NFL Players Association agreed to a fourth extension of the 1993 Collective Bargaining Agreement

through 2007, January 7.

In an AFC Wild Card matchup, the Oakland Raiders defeated the New York Jets 38-24 in the NFL's first-ever primetime playoff game, January 12.

In a special meeting in New Orleans, NFL owners voted unanimously to approve the purchase of the Atlanta Falcons to Home Depot co-founder Arthur Blank, February 2.

The New England Patriots won their first Super Bowl by defeating the NFC champion St. Louis Rams 20-17 in Super Bowl XXXVI at the Louisiana Superdome in New Orleans. The game marked the first time in Super Bowl history that the winning points came on the final play, a 48-yard field goal by Patriots kicker Adam Vinatieri, February 3.

Tony Boselli, a five-time Pro Bowl tackle allocated by the Jacksonville Jaguars, was the first selection of the Houston Texans in the 2002 NFL Expansion Draft. The Texans selected 19 players, February 18.

The NFL and Westwood One/CBS Radio Sports announced the renewal of a multiyear agreement for Westwood One/CBS Radio Sports to continue as the exclusive network radio home of the NFL, April 9.

NFL Europe kicked off its tenth season with a record 254 players allocated by NFL clubs, April 13-14.

The Berlin Thunder became the first team to win consecutive World Bowls, defeating the Rhein Fire 26-20 to win World Bowl X in front of 53,109 fans at Rheinstadion, June 22.

Seahawks Stadium opened in Seattle, Washington with an attendance of 52,902 fans as the Indianapolis Colts defeated the Seattle Seahawks 28-10 in a preseason game, August 10.

Gillette Stadium opened in Foxboro, Massachusetts with a crowd of 68,436 fans as the New England Patriots defeated the Philadelphia Eagles 16-15 in a preseason game, August 17.

Reliant Stadium opened in Houston, Texas with 69,432 fans in attendance, the largest non-Super Bowl crowd to ever watch an NFL game in Houston as the Miami Dolphins defeated the Houston Texans 24-3 in a preseason game, August 24.

For the first time, the NFL season kicked off on a Thursday night in prime time as the San Francisco 49ers defeated the New York Giants 16-13 at Giants Stadium. The game was preceded by "NFL Kickoff Live From Times Square," presented by New York City and the NFL, a football and music festival honoring the resilient spirit of New York and America, September 5.

Week 1 of the 2002 season produced the highest-scoring and most competitive Kickoff Weekend in NFL history. The 16 games averaged 49.3 points per game. A total of 788 points and 89 touchdowns were scored, the most in league history for an opening weekend. Eleven of the 16 games were decided by one score (eight points or less), a Kickoff Weekend record, September 5-9.

Johnny Unitas, the legendary quarterback for the Baltimore Colts and a Pro Football Hall of Fame member, died of a heart attack at the age of 69, September 11.

Oakland Raiders wide receiver Jerry Rice became the all-time leader in yards from scrimmage, surpassing Pro Football Hall of Fame running back Walter Payton (21,281 yards), September 29.

Cleveland Browns owner Al Lerner, the NFL Finance Committee Chairman and Chairman and CEO of MBNA Corporation, died at the age of 69, October 23.

Dallas Cowboys running back Emmitt Smith became the NFL's all-time rushing leader, surpassing Pro Football Hall of Fame running back Walter Payton (16,726 yards), October 27.

The NFL and NFLPA announced the creation of USA Football, the first national advocacy organization representing all levels of amateur football, December 5.

The 2002 season concluded with 25 overtime games, the most in NFL history, December 30.

2003
The Tampa Bay Buccaneers

won their first Super Bowl by defeating the AFC champion Oakland Raiders 48-21 in Super Bowl XXXVII at Qualcomm Stadium in San Diego, January 26.

Chicago Bears chairman emeritus Edward W. McCaskey died at the age of 83, April 8.

The Frankfurt Galaxy became the first team to win three World Bowls, defeating the Rhein Fire 35-16 to win World Bowl XI in front of 28,138 fans at Hampden Park, June 14.

Tex Schramm, the legendary team president and general manager of the Dallas Cowboys and a member of the Pro Football Hall of Fame, died at the age of 83, July 15.

Lincoln Financial Field opened in Philadelphia, Pennsylvania with an attendance of 66,279 fans as the New England Patriots defeated the Philadelphia Eagles 24-12 in a preseason game, August 22.

A renovated Lambeau Field opened in Green Bay, Wisconsin with a crowd of 69,831 fans as the Carolina Panthers defeated the Green Bay Packers 20-7 in a preseason game, August 23.

A renovated Soldier Field opened in Chicago, Illinois with an attendance of 61,500 fans as the Green Bay Packers defeated the Chicago Bears 38-23 in a regular season game on ABC's *NFL Monday Night Football*, September 29.

NFL Network, the first 24-hour, year-round television channel dedicated to the NFL and the sport of football, launched on DirecTV, November 4.

2004
The New England Patriots won their second Super Bowl in three years by defeating the NFC champion Carolina Panthers 32-29 in Super Bowl XXXVIII at Reliant Stadium in Houston, February 1.

By a vote of 29-3, NFL owners extended the instant replay system for another five seasons through 2008, March 30.

Steve Bisciotti took over as the controlling owner of the Baltimore Ravens, succeeding Art Modell, who operated the franchise for 43 years, April 8.

Former Arizona Cardinals

safety Pat Tillman was killed in a firefight while on combat patrol with the U.S. Army Rangers in Afghanistan, April 22.

A federal appeals court formally ruled in favor of the NFL's draft eligibility rule in Maurice Clarett's lawsuit, citing federal labor policy in permitting the NFL and the Players Association to set rules for when players can enter the league, May 24.

The Berlin Thunder defeated the Frankfurt Galaxy 30-24 to win World Bowl XII in front of 35,413 fans at Arena AufSchalke, June 12.

The New England Patriots defeated the New York Jets 13-7 for their NFL-record 18th consecutive regular-season victory, October 24.

The NFL reached an agreement on six-year contract extensions with two of its network television partners—CBS and FOX—to run through the 2011 season, November 8.

The NFL and DirecTV announced a five-year extension on the NFL Sunday Ticket subscription television package to run through the 2010 season, November 8.

NFL Europe named the Hamburg Sea Devils as the league's newest team, November 24.

2005
Indianapolis Colts quarterback Peyton Manning set the NFL single-season record with 49 touchdown passes, January 2.

The New England Patriots became the second team in NFL history to win three Super Bowls in four seasons by defeating the Philadelphia Eagles 24-21 in Super Bowl XXXIX at ALLTEL Stadium in Jacksonville, February 6.

The Pat Tillman USO Center opened in Afghanistan. The NFL donated $250,000 to the USO to honor the memory of the former Arizona Cardinals player who died in Afghanistan while serving in the U.S. Army, April 1.

The NFL reached long-term agreements for its Sunday and Monday primetime TV packages. NBC returned to the NFL by acquiring the Sunday night package for six years (2006-2011). ESPN agreed on an

eight-year deal to televise *Monday Night Football* from 2006-2013, April 18.

The NFL strengthened its steroids program by adopting the Olympic testosterone testing standard, tripling the number of times a player can be randomly tested during the offseason from two to six, adding substances to the list of banned substances, and putting new language in the policy to allow for testing of designer drugs and other substances that may have evaded detection, April 27.

NFL owners voted unanimously to approve the sale of the Minnesota Vikings to real-estate developer Zygi Wilf, May 25.

The Amsterdam Admirals defeated the Berlin Thunder 27-21 to win World Bowl XIII in front of 35,134 fans at LTU Arena in Düsseldorf, Germany, June 11.

The NFL designated September 18-19 as "Hurricane Relief Weekend," which concluded with a telethon in conjunction with a Monday Night Football doubleheader on ABC and ESPN. The New York Giants-New Orleans Saints game, originally scheduled for the Louisiana Superdome, was moved to Giants Stadium following Hurricane Katrina. In total, the NFL, its owners, teams, players, and fans contributed $21 million to aid the Hurricane Katrina rebuilding effort, September 19.

An NFL record 103,467 fans attended the Arizona Cardinals' 31-14 victory over the San Francisco 49ers at Mexico City's Azteca Stadium, the first-ever regular-season NFL game played outside the United States, October 2.

Wellington Mara, the New York Giants' president and co-chief executive officer, died at the age of 89, October 25.

Preston Robert Tisch, the Giants' chairman and co-chief executive officer, died at the age of 79, November 15.

2006
The NFL announced that NFL Network would begin airing a "Road To The Playoffs" package of eight primetime regular season NFL games starting in 2006, January 28.

The Pittsburgh Steelers won their fifth Super Bowl,

defeating the Seattle Seahawks 21-10 in Super Bowl XL at Ford Field in Detroit, Michigan, February 5.

The NFL clubs approved an extension of the Collective Bargaining Agreement through 2012, March 8.

Commissioner Tagliabue announced his decision to retire by the end of July. The NFL enjoyed an era of unrivaled prosperity in the Tagliabue Era, including labor peace throughout his 17-year tenure, March 20.

NFL clubs unanimously decided to return the name of the official game ball to "The Duke" in honor of the late New York Giants owner Wellington Mara, March 27.

The Amsterdam Admirals defeated the Berlin Thunder 22-7 to win World Bowl XIV in front of 36,286 fans at LTU Arena in Düsseldorf, Germany, May 27.

Roger Goodell became the eighth chief executive of the NFL on August 8 when he was chosen to succeed Paul Tagliabue as commissioner by a unanimous vote of the clubs at a three-day meeting in Chicago, Illinois. The transfer from Commissioner Tagliabue to Commissioner Goodell took place at 6:00 A.M. on Friday, September 1.

Cardinals Stadium opened in Glendale, Arizona with a crowd of 63,400 fans on August 12 as the Arizona Cardinals defeated the Pittsburgh Steelers 21-13 in a preseason game. The facility was later renamed University of Phoenix Stadium on September 26.

President George W. Bush signed into law HR 4954, which included the Internet Gambling Prohibition and Enforcement Act. The bill prohibits online gamblers from using credit cards, checks and electronic fund transfers to place and settle bets, strengthening enforcement of federal and state gambling laws that had been evaded by overseas gambling operations using the Internet, October 13.

NFL owners approved a resolution to stage a limited number of international regular-season games—up to two per season—beginning in 2007 and continuing through 2011, October 24.

The NFL Network broadcast its first-ever regular-season game as the Kansas City Chiefs defeated the Denver Broncos 19-10 at Arrowhead Stadium on Thanksgiving night, November 23.

San Diego Chargers running back LaDainian Tomlinson set the NFL single-season record for touchdowns 29 on December 10. He finished the season with 31 touchdowns and also set a single-season record for points with 186.

Lamar Hunt, founder of the Kansas City Chiefs and the American Football League, died at the age of 74, December 13.

2007

The Indianapolis Colts won their second Super Bowl, defeating the Chicago Bears 29-17 in Super Bowl XLI at Dolphin Stadium in South Florida, February 4. Both teams were coached by African-Americans: Tony Dungy of the Colts and Lovie Smith of the Bears.

NFL clubs approved additional league-wide revenue sharing at a league meeting in Phoenix, Arizona. The teams agreed to redistribute up to $430 million over a four-year span, retroactive to 2006, March 26.

The NFL announced changes to its long-standing personal conduct policy and programs for players, coaches, and other team and league employees. The modifications focus on expanded educational and support programs in addition to increased levels of discipline for violations of the policy, April 10.

The NFL, NFL Players Association, NFL Retired Players Association, NFL Alumni Association, NFL Charities and Pro Football Hall of Fame formed the first-ever Alliance to coordinate medical support services for former players, May 22.

The Hamburg Sea Devils defeated the Frankfurt Galaxy 37-28 to win World Bowl XV in front of 48,125 fans at Commerzbank-Arena in Frankfurt, Germany, June 23.

The NFL announced it will focus its international business strategy on reaching the widest possible global audience, including the staging of international regular-season games, and discontinued NFL Europa after 15 seasons of operation, June 29.

NFL owners unanimously approved $10 million in additional Alliance funding for retired players to help pay for joint replacement surgeries and other medical assistance, supplementing the initial $7 million committed in July by Alliance members, October 24.

The New York Giants defeated the Miami Dolphins 13-10 at London's in front of 81,176 fans at Wembley Stadium in the first regular-season game played outside of North America, October 28.

On the field in the 2007 season, many significant records and milestones were achieved. Green Bay quarterback Brett Favre surpassed Pro Football Hall of Famer Dan Marino in both passing categories—touchdowns and yards—to become the NFL's all-time career leader. Patriots quarterback Tom Brady set the single-season record with 50 touchdown passes, including 23 to wide receiver Randy Moss—also a record. New England, which became the first team ever to finish 16-0 in the regular season, scored a record 589 points.

2008

The NFL, United States Olympic Committee, United States Anti-Doping Agency and MLB announced a partnership to form a clean competition anti-doping research collaborative, January 10.

Georgia Frontiere, majority owner of the St. Louis Rams, died at the age of 80, January 18.

The NFL announced it will stage a regular-season game in the United Kingdom during each of the next three seasons, beginning with the New Orleans Saints hosting the San Diego Chargers on October 26, 2008 at London's Wembley Stadium, February 1.

The New York Giants scored with 35 seconds remaining to win their third Super Bowl, defeating the New England Patriots 17-14 in Super Bowl XLII at University of Phoenix Stadium in Glendale, Arizona, February 3.

The NFL set an all-time paid attendance record in 2007 for the sixth consecutive season. Attendance for all 2007 games was 22,256,502, an increase of 56,790 over the previous mark. The Washington Redskins set an all-time NFL regular-season home paid attendance record of 711,471 for eight games, breaking their own record of 708,852 in 2006.

NFL clubs voted unanimously to exercise their option to shorten by two years the current Collective Bargaining Agreement, which now will run through the 2010 season and 2011 NFL Draft, May 20.

Lucas Oil Stadium opened in Indianapolis, Indiana with a crowd of 65,333 as the Buffalo Bills defeated the Indianapolis Colts by a score of 20-7 in a preseason game, August 24.

The NFL established a new fan code of conduct to help support a positive fan environment at all NFL stadiums, August 5.

NFLPA Executive Director and Pro Football Hall of Famer Gene Upshaw died at the age of 63, August 20.

For the first time, an NFL game was broadcast on NBC and also streamed live in its entirety to fans on the Internet via NFL.com and NBCSports.com as the Giants beat the Redskins 16-7 in the 2009 NFL Kickoff game, September 4.

Owners approved a restructured ownership plan for the Pittsburgh Steelers that will keep the team under the control of chairman Dan Rooney and team president Art Rooney II, December 17.

The NFL announced that the 2010 Pro Bowl will be played a week prior to Super Bowl XLIV on Sunday, January 31, 2010. Both games will be played in South Florida, December 30.

In the 256 regular-season games of 2008, 44.1 points per game were scored—the highest average since 1970.

2009

Stephen M. Ross purchased an additional 45 percent of the Miami Dolphins from Wayne Huizenga and became the team's managing partner. Coupled with his April 1, 2008 purchase of 50 percent of the franchise, the stadium, and the excess developable land,

Ross now owns 95 percent of the Dolphins and the stadium while Huizenga retains a five percent share of both and remains a 50 percent partner in that land, January 20.

The NFL re-named its minority coaching internship program the Bill Walsh NFL Minority Coaching Fellowship, honoring the Pro Football Hall of Fame coach who conceived of the program, January 29.

The Pittsburgh Steelers scored a touchdown with 42 seconds remaining to claim their NFL-record sixth Super Bowl title, defeating the Arizona Cardinals 27-23 in Super Bowl XLIII at Raymond James Stadium in Tampa Bay, February 1.

The NFL and Westwood One announced a new two-year agreement for Westwood One to continue as the exclusive network radio partner of the NFL, March 12.

The NFLPA selected Washington-based attorney DeMaurice Smith as its new executive director, March 16.

The NFL and DIRECTV announced an agreement to extend DIRECTV's rights to carry NFL Sunday Ticket through the 2014 season, March 23.

The NFL reached an agreement on two-year contract extensions with two of its network television partners – CBS and FOX – to run through the 2013 season, May 19.

The NFL extended by two years its broadcast partnership with NBC to televise the Sunday night package through the 2013 season, August 19.

Cowboys Stadium opened in Arlington, Texas with a crowd of 75,720 as the Dallas Cowboys defeated the Tennessee Titans by a score of 30-10 in a preseason game, August 21.

The NFL announced games that were blacked out in home team markets during the 2009 season would be shown on NFL.com in their entirety on a delayed basis, September 10.

The NFL launched a new "Red Zone Channel," offering fans crucial live action cut-ins of all Sunday afternoon games, September 13.

Pro Football Hall of Fame head coach and broadcaster John Madden was appointed special advisor to Commissioner Goodell, September 10.

NFL appointed former head coach Tony Dungy to lead a new NFL Player Advisory Forum and serve as a special advisor to Commissioner Goodell, November 19.

Commissioner Goodell notified NFL teams of new and expanded guidelines on return-to-play for any player who sustains a concussion, December 2.

2010

For the first time, the Pro Bowl was played in the Super Bowl city the week before the Super Bowl, as the AFC All-Stars beat the NFC All-Stars 41-34 in the 2010 Pro Bowl at Sun Life Stadium in South Florida. The game drew 70,697 fans – the highest attendance for a Pro Bowl since 1959, January 31.

The New Orleans Saints won their first Super Bowl title, defeating the Indianapolis Colts 31-17 in Super Bowl XLIV at Sun Life Stadium in South Florida, February 7.

Dr. Hunt Batjer of Northwestern University Feinberg School of Medicine and Dr. Richard G. Ellenbogen of the University of Washington School of Medicine were named the new co-chairs of the NFL Head, Neck and Spine Medical Committee, March 16.

NFL owners voted to amend postseason overtime rules to a modified sudden death format, guaranteeing at least one possession for each club if the receiving team fails to score a touchdown on its first overtime possession, March 23.

The NFL and NFL Alumni Association announced a new neurological care program for retired players, one of a series of NFL initiatives addressing the quality of life of retired players, March 24.

NFL rules changes emphasized additional player safety. Protection for defenseless players was standardized and expanded, protecting a player who has just completed a catch from blows to the head or neck by an opponent who launches. Additional protection was also given to longsnappers. Play will now stop if a ball carrier's helmet is removed, March 24.

The NFL Draft debuted a new three-day format, with the first two days broadcast in primetime. A record combined total of 45.4 million viewers tuned in to watch the 75th NFL Draft on NFL Network, ESPN and ESPN2, April 22-24.

New Meadowlands Stadium opened in East Rutherford, New Jersey as the New York Giants defeat the New York Jets by a score of 31-16 in a preseason game, August 16.

Stan Kroenke purchased an additional 60 percent of the St. Louis Rams from the Rosenbloom family and became the team's sole owner and chairman, August 25.

A renovated Arrowhead Stadium opened in Kansas City, Missouri as the Philadelphia Eagles defeated the Kansas City Chiefs 20-17 in a preseason game, August 27.

A poster created by the NFL and the Centers for Disease Control and Prevention (CDC) to help educate young athletes on concussions was released to the public. The poster, similar to one on display in NFL locker rooms, stresses the importance of recognizing a concussion, taking time to recover, and not returning to play too soon, October 11.

The NFL, NFL Alumni and Gay Culverhouse Players' Outreach Program announced a partnership to expand services for retired NFL players. The outreach program identifies retired players in need, ensuring they receive comprehensive medical evaluations and assistance in applying for the expanded benefits and services created in recent years by the NFL, October 12.

Commissioner Roger Goodell notified NFL teams that more significant discipline, including suspensions, would be imposed on players that strike an opponent in the head or neck area in violation of the rules, October 20.

The NFL and Westwood One Radio announced the renewal of a multi-year agreement for Westwood One to continue as the exclusive network radio home of the NFL, December 22.

2011

The NFL appointed Pro Football Hall of Famers Ronnie Lott and John Madden as co-chairs of a new Player Safety Advisory Panel. The panel provides recommendations on a variety of safety-related football matters, while taking a long-term view towards making the game safer at every level of the sport, January 4.

The Green Bay Packers won their fourth Super Bowl title, defeating the Pittsburgh Steelers 31-25 in Super Bowl XLV at Cowboys Stadium in North Texas. The game was viewed by 162.9 million people, making it the most-watched program in U.S. television history, February 6.

The NFL Head, Neck and Spine Committee announced a new standardized sideline concussion assessment protocol for team medical personnel. The new protocol includes a symptom checklist, limited neurologic examination and balance assessment, February 25.

NFL COMMISSIONERS AND PRESIDENTS*

1920	Jim Thorpe, President
1921-39	Joe Carr, President
1939-41	Carl Storck, President
1941-46	Elmer Layden, Commissioner
1946-1959	Bert Bell, Commissioner
1960-1989	Pete Rozelle, Commissioner
1989-2006	Paul Tagliabue, Commissioner
2006-present	Roger Goodell, Commissioner

*NFL treasurer Austin Gunsel served as president in the office of the commissioner following the death of Bert Bell (Oct. 11, 1959) until the election of Pete Rozelle (Jan. 26, 1960).

2010

AMERICAN CONFERENCE

East Division

	W	L	T	Pct.	Pts.	OP
New England#	14	2	0	.875	518	313
New York Jets*	11	5	0	.688	367	304
Miami	7	9	0	.438	273	333
Buffalo	4	12	0	.250	283	425

North Division

	W	L	T	Pct.	Pts.	OP
Pittsburgh	12	4	0	.750	375	232
Baltimore *	12	4	0	.750	357	270
Cleveland	5	11	0	.313	271	332
Cincinnati	4	12	0	.250	322	395

South Division

	W	L	T	Pct.	Pts.	OP
Indianapolis	10	6	0	.625	435	388
Jacksonville	8	8	0	.500	353	419
Houston	6	10	0	.375	390	427
Tennessee	6	10	0	.375	356	339

West Division

	W	L	T	Pct.	Pts.	OP
Kansas City	10	6	0	.625	366	326
San Diego	9	7	0	.563	441	322
Oakland	8	8	0	.500	410	371
Denver	4	12	0	.250	344	471

NATIONAL CONFERENCE

East Division

	W	L	T	Pct.	Pts.	OP
Philadelphia	10	6	0	.625	439	377
New York Giants	10	6	0	.625	394	347
Dallas	6	10	0	.375	394	436
Washington	6	10	0	.375	302	377

North Division

	W	L	T	Pct.	Pts.	OP
Chicago	11	5	0	.688	334	286
Green Bay*	10	6	0	.625	388	240
Detroit	6	10	0	.375	362	369
Minnesota	6	10	0	.375	281	348

South Division

	W	L	T	Pct.	Pts.	OP
Atlanta#	13	3	0	.813	414	288
New Orleans*	11	5	0	.688	384	307
Tampa Bay	10	6	0	.625	341	318
Carolina	2	14	0	.125	196	408

West Division

	W	L	T	Pct.	Pts.	OP
Seattle	7	9	0	.438	310	407
St. Louis	7	9	0	.438	209	328
San Francisco	6	10	0	.375	305	346
Arizona	5	11	0	.313	289	434

*Wild Card qualifier for playoffs; #Top playoff seed in conference
Pittsburgh finished ahead of Baltimore based on better division record (5-1 to 4-2). Indianapolis finished ahead of Kansas City based on head-to-head victory. Houston finished ahead of Tennessee based on better division record (3-3 to 2-4). Philadelphia finished ahead of the Giants based on head-to-head sweep. Dallas finished ahead of Washington based on better division record (3-3 to 2-4). Green Bay finished ahead of the Giants and Tampa Bay based on best strength of victory Green Bay .475; Giants .400; Tampa Bay .344). Detroit finished ahead of Minnesota based on better division record (2-4 to 1-5). Seattle finished ahead of St. Louis based on better division record (4-2 to 3-3).

Wild Card Playoff Games: N.Y. Jets 17, INDIANAPOLIS 16; Baltimore 30, KANSAS CITY 7
Divisional Playoff Games: PITTSBURGH 31, Baltimore 24; N.Y. Jets 28, NEW ENGLAND 21
AFC Championship Game: PITTSBURGH 24, N.Y. Jets 19
Wild Card Playoff Games: SEATTLE 41, New Orleans 36; Green Bay 21, PHILADELPHIA 16
Divisional Playoff Games: Green Bay 48, ATLANTA 21; CHICAGO 35, Seattle 24
NFC Championship Game: Green Bay 21, CHICAGO 14
Super Bowl XLV: Green Bay (NFC) 31, Pittsburgh (AFC) 25 at Cowboys Stadium, North Texas

In Past Standings section, home teams in playoff games are indicated by capital letters.

Playoff Seeds

AFC	NFC
1. New England	1. Atlanta
2. Pittsburgh	2. Chicago
3. Indianapolis	3. Philadelphia
4. Kansas City	4. Seattle
5. Baltimore	5. New Orleans
6. N.Y. Jets	**6. Green Bay**

2009

AMERICAN CONFERENCE

East Division

	W	L	T	Pct.	Pts.	OP
New England	10	6	0	.625	427	285
New York Jets*	9	7	0	.563	348	236
Miami	7	9	0	.438	360	390
Buffalo	6	10	0	.375	258	326

North Division

	W	L	T	Pct.	Pts.	OP
Cincinnati	10	6	0	.625	305	291
Baltimore*	9	7	0	.563	391	261
Pittsburgh	9	7	0	.563	368	324
Cleveland	5	11	0	.313	245	375

South Division

	W	L	T	Pct.	Pts.	OP
Indianapolis#	14	2	0	.875	416	307
Houston	9	7	0	.563	388	333
Tennessee	8	8	0	.500	354	402
Jacksonville	7	9	0	.438	290	380

West Division

	W	L	T	Pct.	Pts.	OP
San Diego	13	3	0	.813	454	320
Denver	8	8	0	.500	326	324
Oakland	5	11	0	.313	197	379
Kansas City	4	12	0	.250	294	424

NATIONAL CONFERENCE

East Division

	W	L	T	Pct.	Pts.	OP
Dallas	11	5	0	.688	361	250
Philadelphia*	11	5	0	.688	429	337
New York Giants	8	8	0	.500	402	427
Washington	4	12	0	.250	266	336

North Division

	W	L	T	Pct.	Pts.	OP
Minnesota	12	4	0	.750	470	312
Green Bay*	11	5	0	.688	461	297
Chicago	7	9	0	.438	327	375
Detroit	2	14	0	.125	262	494

South Division

	W	L	T	Pct.	Pts.	OP
New Orleans#	13	3	0	.813	510	341
Atlanta	9	7	0	.563	363	325
Carolina	8	8	0	.500	315	308
Tampa Bay	3	13	0	.188	244	400

West Division

	W	L	T	Pct.	Pts.	OP
Arizona	10	6	0	.625	375	325
San Francisco	8	8	0	.500	330	281
Seattle	5	11	0	.313	280	390
St. Louis	1	15	0	.063	175	436

*Wild Card qualifier for playoffs; #Top playoff seed in conference
New England finished ahead of Cincinnati based on better strength of victory (.450 to Bengals' .438). Baltimore finished ahead of Pittsburgh based on better division record (3-3 to Steelers' 2-4). New York Jets finished ahead of Baltimore for first Wild Card based on better record vs. common opponents (4-1 to Havens' 1-4) and ahead of Houston based on better conference record (7-5 to Texans' 6-6). Baltimore was second Wild Card based on better conference record than Houston (7-5 to Texans' 6-6). Dallas finished ahead of Philadelphia based on head-to-head sweep (2-0). Green Bay was first Wild Card ahead of Philadelphia based on better record vs. common opponents (4-1 to Eagles' 3-2).

Wild Card Playoff: New York Jets 24, CINCINNATI 14; Baltimore 33, NEW ENGLAND 14
Divisional Playoff: INDIANAPOLIS 20, Baltimore 3; New York Jets 17, SAN DIEGO 14
AFC Championship: INDIANAPOLIS 30, New York Jets 17
Wild Card Playoff: DALLAS 34, Philadelphia 14; ARIZONA 51, Green Bay 45 (OT)
Divisional Playoff Games: NEW ORLEANS 45, Arizona 14; MINNESOTA 34, Dallas 3
NFC Championship Game: NEW ORLEANS 31, Minnesota 28 (OT)
Super Bowl XLIV: New Orleans (NFC) 31, Indianapolis (AFC) 17 at Sun Life Stadium, South Florida

Playoff Seeds

AFC	NFC
1. Indianapolis	**1. New Orleans**
2. San Diego	2. Minnesota
3. New England	3. Dallas
4. Cincinnati	4. Arizona
5. New York Jets	5. Green Bay
6. Baltimore	6. Philadelphia

2008

AMERICAN CONFERENCE

East Division

	W	L	T	Pct.	Pts.	OP
Miami	11	5	0	.688	345	317
New England	11	5	0	.688	410	309
New York Jets	9	7	0	.563	405	356
Buffalo	7	9	0	.438	336	342

North Division

	W	L	T	Pct.	Pts.	OP
Pittsburgh	12	4	0	.750	347	223
Baltimore*	11	5	0	.688	385	244
Cincinnati	4	11	1	.281	204	364
Cleveland	4	12	0	.250	232	350

South Division

	W	L	T	Pct.	Pts.	OP
Tennessee#	13	3	0	.813	375	234
Indianapolis*	12	4	0	.750	377	298
Houston	8	8	0	.500	366	394
Jacksonville	5	11	0	.313	302	367

West Division

	W	L	T	Pct.	Pts.	OP
San Diego	8	8	0	.500	439	347
Denver	8	8	0	.500	370	448
Oakland	5	11	0	.313	263	388
Kansas City	2	14	0	.125	291	440

NATIONAL CONFERENCE

East Division

	W	L	T	Pct.	Pts.	OP
New York Giants	12	4	0	.750	427	294
Philadelphia*	9	6	1	.594	416	289
Dallas	9	7	0	.563	362	365
Washington	8	8	0	.500	265	296

North Division

	W	L	T	Pct.	Pts.	OP
Minnesota	10	6	0	.625	379	333
Chicago	9	7	0	.563	375	350
Green Bay	6	10	0	.375	419	380
Detroit	0	16	0	.000	268	517

South Division

	W	L	T	Pct.	Pts.	OP
Carolina	12	4	0	.750	414	329
Atlanta*	11	5	0	.688	391	325
Tampa Bay	9	7	0	.563	361	323
New Orleans	8	8	0	.500	463	393

West Division

	W	L	T	Pct.	Pts.	OP
Arizona	9	7	0	.563	427	426
San Francisco	7	9	0	.438	339	381
Seattle	4	12	0	.250	294	392
St. Louis	2	14	0	.125	232	465

*Wild Card qualifier for playoffs; #Top playoff seed in conference
Miami finished ahead of New England based on better conference record (8-4 to Patriots' 7-5). Baltimore was second Wild Card ahead of New England based on better conference record (8-4 to Patriots' 7-5). San Diego finished ahead of Denver based on better division record (5-1 to Broncos' 3-3). N.Y. Giants finished ahead of Carolina based on head-to-head victory.
Wild Card Playoff: SAN DIEGO 23, Indianapolis 17; Baltimore 27, MIAMI 9
Divisional Playoff: Baltimore 13, TENNESSEE 10; PITTSBURGH 35, San Diego 24
AFC Championship: PITTSBURGH 23, Baltimore 14
Wild Card Playoff: ARIZONA 30, Atlanta 24; Philadelphia 26, MINNESOTA 14
Divisional Playoff: Arizona 33, CAROLINA 13; Philadelphia 23, N.Y. GIANTS 11
NFC Championship: ARIZONA 32, Philadelphia 25
Super Bowl XLIII: Pittsburgh (AFC) 27, Arizona (NFC) 23 at Raymond James Stadium, Tampa, Florida

Playoff Seeds

AFC	NFC
1. Tennessee	1. N.Y. Giants
2. Pittsburgh	2. Carolina
3. Miami	3. Minnesota
4. San Diego	**4. Arizona**
5. Indianapolis	5. Atlanta
6. Baltimore	6. Philadelphia

2007

AMERICAN CONFERENCE

East Division

	W	L	T	Pct.	Pts.	OP
New England#	16	0	0	1.000	589	274
Buffalo	7	9	0	.438	252	354
New York Jets	4	12	0	.250	268	355
Miami	1	15	0	.063	267	437

North Division

	W	L	T	Pct.	Pts.	OP
Pittsburgh	10	6	0	.625	393	269
Cleveland	10	6	0	.625	402	382
Cincinnati	7	9	0	.438	380	385
Baltimore	5	11	0	.313	275	384

South Division

	W	L	T	Pct.	Pts.	OP
Indianapolis	13	3	0	.813	450	262
Jacksonville*	11	5	0	.688	411	304
Tennessee*	10	6	0	.625	301	297
Houston	8	8	0	.500	379	384

West Division

	W	L	T	Pct.	Pts.	OP
San Diego	11	5	0	.688	412	284
Denver	7	9	0	.438	320	409
Kansas City	4	12	0	.250	226	335
Oakland	4	12	0	.250	283	398

NATIONAL CONFERENCE

East Division

	W	L	T	Pct.	Pts.	OP
Dallas#	13	3	0	.813	455	325
New York Giants*	10	6	0	.625	373	351
Washington*	9	7	0	.563	334	310
Philadelphia	8	8	0	.500	336	300

North Division

	W	L	T	Pct.	Pts.	OP
Green Bay	13	3	0	.813	435	291
Minnesota	8	8	0	.500	365	311
Detroit	7	9	0	.438	346	444
Chicago	7	9	0	.438	334	348

South Division

	W	L	T	Pct.	Pts.	OP
Tampa Bay	9	7	0	.563	334	270
Carolina	7	9	0	.438	267	347
New Orleans	7	9	0	.438	379	388
Atlanta	4	12	0	.250	259	414

West Division

	W	L	T	Pct.	Pts.	OP
Seattle	10	6	0	.625	393	291
Arizona	8	8	0	.500	404	399
San Francisco	5	11	0	.313	219	364
St. Louis	3	13	0	.188	263	438

*Wild Card qualifier for playoffs; #Top playoff seed in conference
Pittsburgh finished ahead of Cleveland based on head-to-head sweep (2-0). Tennessee finished ahead of Cleveland based on better record vs. common opponents (4-1 to Browns' 3-2). Kansas City finished ahead of Oakland based on better record vs. common opponents (2-10 to Raiders' 1-11). Dallas finished ahead of Green Bay based on head-to-head victory. Detroit finished ahead of Chicago based on head-to-head sweep (2-0). Carolina finished ahead of New Orleans based on better conference record (7-5 to Saints' 6-6).
Wild Card Playoff: Jacksonville 31, PITTSBURGH 29; SAN DIEGO 17, Tennessee 6
Divisional Playoff: NEW ENGLAND 31, Jacksonville 20; San Diego 28, INDIANAPOLIS 24
AFC Championship: NEW ENGLAND 21, San Diego 12
Wild Card Playoff: SEATTLE 35, Washington 14; N.Y. Giants 24, TAMPA BAY 14
Divisional Playoff: GREEN BAY 42, Seattle 20; N.Y. Giants 21, DALLAS 17
NFC Championship: N.Y. Giants 23, GREEN BAY 20 (OT)
Super Bowl XLII: N.Y. Giants (NFC) 17, New England (AFC) 14 at University of Phoenix Stadium, Glendale, Arizona

Playoff Seeds

AFC	NFC
1. New England	1. Dallas
2. Indianapolis	2. Green Bay
3. San Diego	3. Seattle
4. Pittsburgh	4. Tampa Bay
5. Jacksonville	**5. N.Y. Giants**
6. Tennessee	6. Washington

2006

AMERICAN CONFERENCE

East Division

	W	L	T	Pct.	Pts.	OP
New England	12	4	0	.750	385	237
New York Jets*	10	6	0	.625	316	295
Buffalo	7	9	0	.438	300	311
Miami	6	10	0	.375	260	283

North Division

	W	L	T	Pct.	Pts.	OP
Baltimore	13	3	0	.813	353	201
Cincinnati	8	8	0	.500	373	331
Pittsburgh	8	8	0	.500	353	315
Cleveland	4	12	0	.250	238	356

South Division

	W	L	T	Pct.	Pts.	OP
Indianapolis	12	4	0	.750	427	360
Tennessee	8	8	0	.500	324	400
Jacksonville	8	8	0	.500	371	274
Houston	6	10	0	.375	267	366

West Division

	W	L	T	Pct.	Pts.	OP
San Diego#	14	2	0	.875	492	303
Kansas City*	9	7	0	.563	331	315
Denver	9	7	0	.563	319	305
Oakland	2	14	0	.125	168	332

NATIONAL CONFERENCE

East Division

	W	L	T	Pct.	Pts.	OP
Philadelphia	10	6	0	.625	398	328
Dallas*	9	7	0	.563	425	350
New York Giants*	8	8	0	.500	355	362
Washington	5	11	0	.313	307	376

North Division

	W	L	T	Pct.	Pts.	OP
Chicago#	13	3	0	.813	427	255
Green Bay	8	8	0	.500	301	366
Minnesota	6	10	0	.375	282	327
Detroit	3	13	0	.188	305	398

South Division

	W	L	T	Pct.	Pts.	OP
New Orleans	10	6	0	.625	413	322
Carolina	8	8	0	.500	270	305
Atlanta	7	9	0	.438	292	328
Tampa Bay	4	12	0	.250	211	353

West Division

	W	L	T	Pct.	Pts.	OP
Seattle	9	7	0	.563	335	341
St. Louis	8	8	0	.500	367	381
San Francisco	7	9	0	.438	298	412
Arizona	5	11	0	.313	314	389

*Wild Card qualifier for playoffs; #Top playoff seed in conference
Indianapolis finished ahead of New England based on head-to-head victory. Cincinnati finished ahead of Pittsburgh based on better division record (4-2 to Steelers' 3-3). Tennessee finished ahead of Jacksonville based on better division record (4-2 to Jaguars' 2-4). Kansas City finished ahead of Denver based on better division record (4-2 to Broncos' 3-3). New Orleans finished ahead of Philadelphia based on head-to-head victory. N.Y. Giants finished ahead of Carolina and St. Louis based on better conference record (Giants' 7-5 to Panthers' 6-6 and Rams' 6-6) and ahead of Green Bay based on strength of victory (.422 to Packers' .383).
Wild Card Playoff: INDIANAPOLIS 23, Kansas City 8; NEW ENGLAND 37, N.Y. Jets 16
Divisional Playoff: Indianapolis 15, BALTIMORE 6; New England 24, SAN DIEGO 21
AFC Championship: INDIANAPOLIS 38, New England 34
Wild Card Playoff: SEATTLE 21, Dallas 20; PHILADELPHIA 23, N.Y. Giants 20
Divisional Playoff: NEW ORLEANS 27, Philadelphia 24; CHICAGO 27, Seattle 24 (OT)
NFC Championship: CHICAGO 39, New Orleans 14
Super Bowl XLI: Indianapolis (AFC) 29, Chicago (NFC) 17 at Dolphin Stadium, Miami, Florida

Playoff Seeds

AFC	NFC
1. San Diego	**1. Chicago**
2. Baltimore	2. New Orleans
3. Indianapolis	3. Philadelphia
4. New England	4. Seattle
5. N.Y. Jets	5. Dallas
6. Kansas City	6. N.Y. Giants

2005

AMERICAN CONFERENCE

East Division

	W	L	T	Pct.	Pts.	OP
New England	10	6	0	.625	379	338
Miami	9	7	0	.563	318	317
Buffalo	5	11	0	.313	271	367
N.Y. Jets	4	12	0	.250	240	355

North Division

	W	L	T	Pct.	Pts.	OP
Cincinnati	11	5	0	.688	421	350
Pittsburgh*	11	5	0	.688	389	258
Baltimore	6	10	0	.375	265	299
Cleveland	6	10	0	.375	232	301

South Division

	W	L	T	Pct.	Pts.	OP
Indianapolis#	14	2	0	.875	439	247
Jacksonville*	12	4	0	.750	361	269
Tennessee	4	12	0	.250	299	421
Houston	2	14	0	.125	260	431

West Division

	W	L	T	Pct.	Pts.	OP
Denver	13	3	0	.813	395	258
Kansas City	10	6	0	.625	403	325
San Diego	9	7	0	.563	418	312
Oakland	4	12	0	.250	290	383

NATIONAL CONFERENCE

East Division

	W	L	T	Pct.	Pts.	OP
N.Y. Giants	11	5	0	.688	422	314
Washington*	10	6	0	.625	359	293
Dallas	9	7	0	.563	325	308
Philadelphia	6	10	0	.375	310	388

North Division

	W	L	T	Pct.	Pts.	OP
Chicago	11	5	0	.688	260	202
Minnesota	9	7	0	.563	306	344
Detroit	5	11	0	.313	254	345
Green Bay	4	12	0	.250	298	344

South Division

	W	L	T	Pct.	Pts.	OP
Tampa Bay	11	5	0	.688	300	274
Carolina*	11	5	0	.688	391	259
Atlanta	8	8	0	.500	351	341
New Orleans	3	13	0	.188	235	398

West Division

	W	L	T	Pct.	Pts.	OP
Seattle#	13	3	0	.813	452	271
St. Louis	6	10	0	.375	363	429
Arizona	5	11	0	.313	311	387
San Francisco	4	12	0	.250	239	428

*Wild Card qualifier for playoffs; #Top playoff seed in conference
Cincinnati finished ahead of Pittsburgh based on better division record (5-1 to Steelers' 4-2). Baltimore finished ahead of Cleveland based on better division record (2-4 to Browns' 1-5). Tampa Bay finished ahead of Carolina based on better division record (5-1 to Panthers' 4-2). Chicago finished ahead of Tampa Bay, and Tampa Bay finished ahead of the N.Y. Giants, based on better conference record (Bears' 10-2 to Buccaneers' 9-3 to Giants' 8-4).
Wild Card playoff: NEW ENGLAND 28, Jacksonville 3; Pittsburgh 31, CINCINNATI 17
Divisional playoff: DENVER 27, New England 13; Pittsburgh 21, INDIANAPOLIS 18
AFC Championship: Pittsburgh 34, DENVER 17
Wild Card playoffs: Washington 17, TAMPA BAY 10; Carolina 23, NEW YORK GIANTS 0
Divisional playoff: SEATTLE 20, Washington 10; Carolina 29, CHICAGO 21
NFC Championship: SEATTLE 34, Carolina 14
Super Bowl XL: Pittsburgh (AFC) 21, Seattle (NFC) 10 at Ford Field, Detroit, Michigan

Playoff Seeds

AFC	NFC
1. Indianapolis	**1. Seattle**
2. Denver	2. Chicago
3. Cincinnati	3. Tampa Bay
4. New England	4. New York Giants
5. Jacksonville	5. Carolina
6. Pittsburgh	6. Washington

2004

AMERICAN CONFERENCE

East Division

	W	L	T	Pct.	Pts.	OP
New England	14	2	0	.875	437	260
N.Y. Jets*	10	6	0	.625	333	261
Buffalo	9	7	0	.563	395	284
Miami	4	12	0	.250	275	354

North Division

	W	L	T	Pct.	Pts.	OP
Pittsburgh#	15	1	0	.938	372	251
Baltimore	9	7	0	.563	317	268
Cincinnati	8	8	0	.500	374	372
Cleveland	4	12	0	.250	276	390

South Division

	W	L	T	Pct.	Pts.	OP
Indianapolis	12	4	0	.750	522	351
Jacksonville	9	7	0	.563	261	280
Houston	7	9	0	.438	309	339
Tennessee	5	11	0	.313	344	439

West Division

	W	L	T	Pct.	Pts.	OP
San Diego	12	4	0	.750	446	313
Denver*	10	6	0	.625	381	304
Kansas City	7	9	0	.438	483	435
Oakland	5	11	0	.313	320	442

NATIONAL CONFERENCE

East Division

	W	L	T	Pct.	Pts.	OP
Philadelphia#	13	3	0	.813	386	260
N.Y. Giants	6	10	0	.375	303	347
Dallas	6	10	0	.375	293	405
Washington	6	10	0	.375	240	265

North Division

	W	L	T	Pct.	Pts.	OP
Green Bay	10	6	0	.625	424	380
Minnesota*	8	8	0	.500	405	395
Detroit	6	10	0	.375	296	350
Chicago	5	11	0	.313	231	331

South Division

	W	L	T	Pct.	Pts.	OP
Atlanta	11	5	0	.688	340	337
New Orleans	8	8	0	.500	348	405
Carolina	7	9	0	.438	355	339
Tampa Bay	5	11	0	.313	301	304

West Division

	W	L	T	Pct.	Pts.	OP
Seattle	9	7	0	.563	371	373
St. Louis*	8	8	0	.500	319	392
Arizona	6	10	0	.375	284	322
San Francisco	2	14	0	.125	259	452

*Wild Card qualifier for playoffs; #Top playoff seed in conference Indianapolis finished ahead of San Diego based on head-to-head victory. N.Y. Jets finished ahead of Denver based on better record vs. common opponents (5-0 to Broncos' 3-2). St. Louis finished ahead of New Orleans and Minnesota based on best conference record (7-5 to Saints' 6-6 to Vikings' 5-7), and Minnesota finished ahead of New Orleans based on head-to-head victory. N.Y. Giants finished ahead of Dallas and Washington based on better head-to-head record (3-1 to Cowboys' 2-2 to Redskins' 1-3), and Dallas finished ahead of Washington based on head-to-head sweep (2-0).

Wild Card playoffs: N.Y. Jets 20, SAN DIEGO 17 (OT); INDIANAPOLIS 49, Denver 24

Divisional playoffs: PITTSBURGH 20, N.Y. Jets 17 (OT); NEW ENGLAND 20, Indianapolis 3

AFC Championship: New England 41, PITTSBURGH 27

Wild Card playoffs: St. Louis 27, SEATTLE 20; Minnesota 31, GREEN BAY 17

Divisional playoffs: ATLANTA 47, St. Louis 17; PHILADELPHIA 27, Minnesota 14

NFC Championship: PHILADELPHIA 27, Atlanta 10

Super Bowl XXXIX: New England (AFC) 24, Philadelphia (NFC) 21 at Alltel Stadium, Jacksonville, Florida

Playoff Seeds

AFC	NFC
1. Pittsburgh	1. **Philadelphia**
2. **New England**	2. Atlanta
3. Indianapolis	3. Green Bay
4. San Diego	4. Seattle
5. N.Y. Jets	5. St. Louis
6. Denver	6. Minnesota

2003

AMERICAN CONFERENCE

East Division

	W	L	T	Pct.	Pts.	OP
New England#	14	2	0	.875	348	238
Miami	10	6	0	.625	311	261
Buffalo	6	10	0	.375	243	279
N.Y. Jets	6	10	0	.375	283	299

North Division

	W	L	T	Pct.	Pts.	OP
Baltimore	10	6	0	.625	391	281
Cincinnati	8	8	0	.500	346	384
Pittsburgh	6	10	0	.375	300	327
Cleveland	5	11	0	.313	254	322

South Division

	W	L	T	Pct.	Pts.	OP
Indianapolis	12	4	0	.750	447	336
Tennessee*	12	4	0	.750	435	324
Jacksonville	5	11	0	.313	276	331
Houston	5	11	0	.313	255	380

West Division

	W	L	T	Pct.	Pts.	OP
Kansas City	13	3	0	.813	484	332
Denver*	10	6	0	.625	381	301
Oakland	4	12	0	.250	270	379
San Diego	4	12	0	.250	313	441

NATIONAL CONFERENCE

East Division

	W	L	T	Pct.	Pts.	OP
Philadelphia#	12	4	0	.750	374	287
Dallas*	10	6	0	.625	289	260
Washington	5	11	0	.313	287	372
N.Y. Giants	4	12	0	.250	243	387

North Division

	W	L	T	Pct.	Pts.	OP
Green Bay	10	6	0	.625	442	307
Minnesota	9	7	0	.563	416	353
Chicago	7	9	0	.438	283	346
Detroit	5	11	0	.313	270	379

South Division

	W	L	T	Pct.	Pts.	OP
Carolina	11	5	0	.688	325	304
New Orleans	8	8	0	.500	340	326
Tampa Bay	7	9	0	.438	301	264
Atlanta	5	11	0	.313	299	422

West Division

	W	L	T	Pct.	Pts.	OP
St. Louis	12	4	0	.750	447	328
Seattle*	10	6	0	.625	404	327
San Francisco	7	9	0	.438	384	337
Arizona	4	12	0	.250	225	452

*Wild Card qualifier for playoffs; #Top playoff seed in conference Buffalo finished ahead of N.Y. Jets based on better division record (2-4 to Jets' 1-5). Indianapolis finished ahead of Tennessee based on head-to-head sweep (2-0). Jacksonville finished ahead of Houston based on better division record (2-4 to Texans' 1-5). Denver finished ahead of Miami based on better conference record (9-3 to Dolphins' 7-5). Oakland finished ahead of San Diego based on better conference record (3-9 to Chargers' 2-10). Philadelphia finished ahead of St. Louis based on better conference record (9-3 to Rams' 8-4). Seattle finished ahead of Dallas based on better strength of victory (65-95 to Cowboys' 62-98).

Wild Card playoffs: Tennessee 20, BALTIMORE 17; INDIANAPOLIS 41, Denver 10

Divisional playoffs: NEW ENGLAND 17, Tennessee 14; Indianapolis 38, KANSAS CITY 31

AFC Championship: NEW ENGLAND 24, Indianapolis 14

Wild Card playoffs: CAROLINA 29, Dallas 10; GREEN BAY 33, Seattle 27 (OT)

Divisional playoffs: Carolina 29, ST. LOUIS 23 (2OT); PHILADELPHIA 20, Green Bay 17 (OT)

NFC Championship: Carolina 14, PHILADELPHIA 3

Super Bowl XXXVIII: New England (AFC) 32, Carolina (NFC) 29 at Reliant Stadium, Houston, Texas

Playoff Seeds

AFC	NFC
1. **New England**	1. Philadelphia
2. Kansas City	2. St. Louis
3. Indianapolis	3. **Carolina**
4. Baltimore	4. Green Bay
5. Tennessee	5. Seattle
6. Denver	6. Dallas

2002

AMERICAN CONFERENCE

East Division

	W	L	T	Pct.	Pts.	OP
N.Y. Jets	9	7	0	.563	359	336
New England	9	7	0	.563	381	346
Miami	9	7	0	.563	378	301
Buffalo	8	8	0	.500	379	397

North Division

	W	L	T	Pct.	Pts.	OP
Pittsburgh	10	5	1	.656	390	345
Cleveland*	9	7	0	.563	344	320
Baltimore	7	9	0	.438	316	354
Cincinnati	2	14	0	.125	279	456

South Division

	W	L	T	Pct.	Pts.	OP
Tennessee	11	5	0	.688	367	324
Indianapolis*	10	6	0	.625	349	313
Jacksonville	6	10	0	.375	328	315
Houston	4	12	0	.250	213	356

West Division

	W	L	T	Pct.	Pts.	OP
Oakland#	11	5	0	.688	450	304
Denver	9	7	0	.563	392	344
San Diego	8	8	0	.500	333	367
Kansas City	8	8	0	.500	467	399

NATIONAL CONFERENCE

East Division

	W	L	T	Pct.	Pts.	OP
Philadelphia#	12	4	0	.750	415	241
N.Y. Giants*	10	6	0	.625	320	279
Washington	7	9	0	.438	307	365
Dallas	5	11	0	.313	217	329

North Division

	W	L	T	Pct.	Pts.	OP
Green Bay	12	4	0	.750	398	328
Minnesota	6	10	0	.375	390	442
Chicago	4	12	0	.250	281	379
Detroit	3	13	0	.188	306	451

South Division

	W	L	T	Pct.	Pts.	OP
Tampa Bay	12	4	0	.750	346	196
Atlanta*	9	6	1	.594	402	314
New Orleans	9	7	0	.563	432	388
Carolina	7	9	0	.438	258	302

West Division

	W	L	T	Pct.	Pts.	OP
San Francisco	10	6	0	.625	367	351
St. Louis	7	9	0	.438	316	369
Seattle	7	9	0	.438	355	369
Arizona	5	11	0	.313	262	417

*Wild Card qualifier for playoffs; #Top playoff seed in conference
New York Jets finished ahead of New England based on better record in common games (8-4 to Patriots' 7-5) and Miami based on better division record (4-2 to Dolphins' 2-4). New England finished ahead of Miami based on better division record (4-2 to Dolphins' 2-4). Cleveland finished ahead of Denver and New England based on better conference record (7-5 to Broncos' 5-7 and Patriots' 6-6). Oakland finished ahead of Tennessee based on better head-to-head record (1-0). San Diego finished ahead of Kansas City based on better division record (3-3 to Chiefs' 2-4). Philadelphia finished ahead of Green Bay and Tampa Bay based on better conference record (11-1 to Packers' 9-3 and Buccaneers' 9-3). Tampa Bay finished ahead of Green Bay based on better head-to-head record (1-0). St. Louis finished ahead of Seattle based on better division record (4-2 to Seahawks' 2-4).
Wild Card playoffs: N.Y. JETS 41, Indianapolis 0;
PITTSBURGH 36, Cleveland 33
Divisional playoffs: TENNESSEE 34, Pittsburgh 31 (OT);
OAKLAND 30, N.Y. Jets 10
AFC Championship: OAKLAND 41, Tennessee 24
Wild Card playoffs: Atlanta 27, GREEN BAY 7;
SAN FRANCISCO 39, N.Y. Giants 38
Divisional playoffs: PHILADELPHIA 20, Atlanta 6;
TAMPA BAY 31, San Francisco 6
NFC Championship: Tampa Bay 27, PHILADELPHIA 10
Super Bowl XXXVII: Tampa Bay (NFC) 48, Oakland (AFC) 21
at Qualcomm Stadium, San Diego, California

Playoff Seeds

AFC
1. Oakland
2. Tennessee
3. Pittsburgh
4. N.Y. Jets
5. Indianapolis
6. Cleveland

NFC
1. Philadelphia
2. Tampa Bay
3. Green Bay
4. San Francisco
5. N.Y. Giants
6. Atlanta

2001

AMERICAN CONFERENCE

Eastern Division

	W	L	T	Pct.	Pts.	OP
New England	11	5	0	.688	371	272
Miami*	11	5	0	.688	344	290
N.Y. Jets*	10	6	0	.625	308	295
Indianapolis	6	10	0	.375	413	486
Buffalo	3	13	0	.188	265	420

Central Division

	W	L	T	Pct.	Pts.	OP
Pittsburgh#	13	3	0	.813	352	212
Baltimore*	10	6	0	.625	303	265
Cleveland	7	9	0	.438	285	319
Tennessee	7	9	0	.438	336	388
Jacksonville	6	10	0	.375	294	286
Cincinnati	6	10	0	.375	226	309

Western Division

	W	L	T	Pct.	Pts.	OP
Oakland	10	6	0	.625	399	327
Seattle	9	7	0	.563	301	324
Denver	8	8	0	.500	340	339
Kansas City	6	10	0	.375	320	344
San Diego	5	11	0	.313	332	321

NATIONAL CONFERENCE

Eastern Division

	W	L	T	Pct.	Pts.	OP
Philadelphia	11	5	0	.688	343	208
Washington	8	8	0	.500	256	303
N.Y. Giants	7	9	0	.438	294	321
Arizona	7	9	0	.438	295	343
Dallas	5	11	0	.313	246	338

Central Division

	W	L	T	Pct.	Pts.	OP
Chicago	13	3	0	.813	338	203
Green Bay*	12	4	0	.750	390	266
Tampa Bay*	9	7	0	.563	324	280
Minnesota	5	11	0	.313	290	390
Detroit	2	14	0	.125	270	424

Western Division

	W	L	T	Pct.	Pts.	OP
St. Louis#	14	2	0	.875	503	273
San Francisco*	12	4	0	.750	409	282
New Orleans	7	9	0	.438	333	409
Atlanta	7	9	0	.438	291	377
Carolina	1	15	0	.063	253	410

*Wild Card qualifier for playoffs; #Top playoff seed in conference
New England finished ahead of Miami based on better division record (6-2 to Dolphins' 5-3). Baltimore was second Wild Card ahead of N.Y. Jets based on better record against common opponents (3-2 to Jets' 2-2). Cleveland finished ahead of Tennessee based on better division record (5-5 to Titans' 3-7). Jacksonville finished ahead of Cincinnati based on head-to-head record (2-0). N.Y. Giants finished ahead of Arizona based on head-to-head record (2-0). Green Bay was first Wild Card ahead of San Francisco based on better conference record (9-3 to 49ers' 8-4). New Orleans finished ahead of Atlanta based on better division record (4-4 to Falcons' 3-5).
Wild Card playoffs: OAKLAND 38, N.Y. Jets 24;
Baltimore 20, MIAMI 3
Divisional playoffs: NEW ENGLAND 16, Oakland 13 (OT);
PITTSBURGH 27, Baltimore 10
AFC Championship: New England 24, PITTSBURGH 17
Wild Card playoffs: PHILADELPHIA 31, Tampa Bay 9;
GREEN BAY 25, San Francisco 15
Divisional playoffs: Philadelphia 33, CHICAGO 19;
ST. LOUIS 45, Green Bay 17
NFC Championship: ST. LOUIS 29, Philadelphia 24
Super Bowl XXXVI: New England (AFC) 20, St. Louis (NFC) 17
at Louisiana Superdome, New Orleans, Louisiana

Playoff Seeds

AFC
1. Pittsburgh
2. New England
3. Oakland
4. Miami
5. Baltimore
6. N.Y. Jets

NFC
1. St. Louis
2. Chicago
3. Philadelphia
4. Green Bay
5. San Francisco
6. Tampa Bay

2000

AMERICAN CONFERENCE

Eastern Division

	W	L	T	Pct.	Pts.	OP
Miami	11	5	0	.688	323	226
Indianapolis*	10	6	0	.625	429	326
N.Y. Jets	9	7	0	.563	321	321
Buffalo	8	8	0	.500	315	350
New England	5	11	0	.313	276	338

Central Division

	W	L	T	Pct.	Pts.	OP
Tennessee#	13	3	0	.813	346	191
Baltimore*	12	4	0	.750	333	165
Pittsburgh	9	7	0	.563	321	255
Jacksonville	7	9	0	.438	367	327
Cincinnati	4	12	0	.250	185	359
Cleveland	3	13	0	.188	161	419

Western Division

	W	L	T	Pct.	Pts.	OP
Oakland	12	4	0	.750	479	299
Denver*	11	5	0	.688	485	369
Kansas City	7	9	0	.438	355	354
Seattle	6	10	0	.375	320	405
San Diego	1	15	0	.063	269	440

NATIONAL CONFERENCE

Eastern Division

	W	L	T	Pct.	Pts.	OP
N.Y. Giants#	12	4	0	.750	328	246
Philadelphia*	11	5	0	.688	351	245
Washington	8	8	0	.500	281	269
Dallas	5	11	0	.313	294	361
Arizona	3	13	0	.188	210	443

Central Division

	W	L	T	Pct.	Pts.	OP
Minnesota	11	5	0	.688	397	371
Tampa Bay*	10	6	0	.625	388	269
Green Bay	9	7	0	.563	353	323
Detroit	9	7	0	.563	307	307
Chicago	5	11	0	.313	216	355

Western Division

	W	L	T	Pct.	Pts.	OP
New Orleans	10	6	0	.625	354	305
St. Louis*	10	6	0	.625	540	471
Carolina	7	9	0	.438	310	310
San Francisco	6	10	0	.375	388	422
Atlanta	4	12	0	.250	252	413

*Wild Card qualifier for playoffs; #Top playoff seed in conference
Green Bay finished ahead of Detroit based on better division record (5-3 to Lions' 3-5). New Orleans finished ahead of St. Louis based on better division record (7-1 to Rams' 5-3). Tampa Bay was second Wild Card based on head-to-head victory over St. Louis (1-0).
Wild Card playoffs: MIAMI 23, Indianapolis 17 (OT); BALTIMORE 21, Denver 3
Divisional playoffs: OAKLAND 27, Miami 0; Baltimore 24, TENNESSEE 10
AFC Championship: Baltimore 16, OAKLAND 3
Wild Card playoffs: NEW ORLEANS 31, St. Louis 28; PHILADELPHIA 21, Tampa Bay 3
Divisional playoffs: MINNESOTA 34, New Orleans 16; N.Y. GIANTS 20, Philadelphia 10
NFC Championship: N.Y. GIANTS 41, Minnesota 0
Super Bowl XXXV: Baltimore (AFC) 34, N.Y. Giants (NFC) 7 at Raymond James Stadium, Tampa, Florida

Playoff Seeds

AFC	NFC
1. Tennessee	**1. N.Y. Giants**
2. Oakland	2. Minnesota
3. Miami	3. New Orleans
4. Baltimore	4. Philadelphia
5. Denver	5. Tampa Bay
6. Indianapolis	6. St. Louis

1999

AMERICAN CONFERENCE

Eastern Division

	W	L	T	Pct.	Pts.	OP
Indianapolis	13	3	0	.813	423	333
Buffalo*	11	5	0	.688	320	229
Miami*	9	7	0	.563	326	336
N.Y. Jets	8	8	0	.500	308	309
New England	8	8	0	.500	299	284

Central Division

	W	L	T	Pct.	Pts.	OP
Jacksonville#	14	2	0	.875	396	217
Tennessee*	13	3	0	.813	392	324
Baltimore	8	8	0	.500	324	277
Pittsburgh	6	10	0	.375	317	320
Cincinnati	4	12	0	.250	283	460
Cleveland	2	14	0	.125	217	437

Western Division

	W	L	T	Pct.	Pts.	OP
Seattle	9	7	0	.563	338	298
Kansas City	9	7	0	.563	390	322
San Diego	8	8	0	.500	269	316
Oakland	8	8	0	.500	390	329
Denver	6	10	0	.375	314	318

NATIONAL CONFERENCE

Eastern Division

	W	L	T	Pct.	Pts.	OP
Washington	10	6	0	.625	443	377
Dallas*	8	8	0	.500	352	276
N.Y. Giants	7	9	0	.438	299	358
Arizona	6	10	0	.375	245	382
Philadelphia	5	11	0	.313	272	357

Central Division

	W	L	T	Pct.	Pts.	OP
Tampa Bay*	11	5	0	.688	270	235
Minnesota*	10	6	0	.625	399	335
Detroit*	8	8	0	.500	322	323
Green Bay	8	8	0	.500	357	341
Chicago	6	10	0	.375	272	341

Western Division

	W	L	T	Pct.	Pts.	OP
St. Louis#	13	3	0	.813	526	242
Carolina	8	8	0	.500	421	381
Atlanta	5	11	0	.313	285	380
San Francisco	4	12	0	.250	295	453
New Orleans	3	13	0	.188	260	434

*Wild Card qualifier for playoffs; #Top playoff seed in conference
Miami was third Wild Card ahead of Kansas City based on better record against common opponents (6-1 to Chiefs' 5-3). N.Y. Jets finished ahead of New England based on better division record (4-4 to Patriots' 2-6). Seattle finished ahead of Kansas City based on head-to-head sweep (2-0). San Diego finished ahead of Oakland based on better division record (5-3 to Raiders' 3-5). Dallas was second Wild Card based on better record against common opponents (3-2 to Lions' 3-3) and better conference record than Carolina (7-5 to Panthers' 6-6). Detroit was third Wild Card based on better conference record than Green Bay (7-5 to Packers' 6-6) and head-to-head victory over Carolina.
Wild Card playoffs: TENNESSEE 22, Buffalo 16; Miami 20, SEATTLE 17
Divisional playoffs: JACKSONVILLE 62, Miami 7; Tennessee 19, INDIANAPOLIS 16
AFC Championship: Tennessee 33, JACKSONVILLE 14
Wild Card playoffs: WASHINGTON 27, Detroit 13; MINNESOTA 27, Dallas 10
Divisional playoffs: TAMPA BAY 14, Washington 13; ST. LOUIS 49, Minnesota 37
NFC Championship: ST. LOUIS 11, Tampa Bay 6
Super Bowl XXXIV: St. Louis (NFC) 23, Tennessee (AFC) 16 at Georgia Dome, Atlanta, Georgia

Playoff Seeds

AFC	NFC
1. Jacksonville	**1. St. Louis**
2. Indianapolis	2. Tampa Bay
3. Seattle	3. Washington
4. Tennessee	4. Minnesota
5. Buffalo	5. Dallas
6. Miami	6. Detroit

1998

AMERICAN CONFERENCE

Eastern Division

	W	L	T	Pct.	Pts.	OP
N.Y. Jets	12	4	0	.750	416	266
Miami*	10	6	0	.625	321	265
Buffalo*	10	6	0	.625	400	333
New England*	9	7	0	.563	337	329
Indianapolis	3	13	0	.188	310	444

Central Division

	W	L	T	Pct.	Pts.	OP
Jacksonville	11	5	0	.688	392	338
Tennessee	8	8	0	.500	330	320
Pittsburgh	7	9	0	.438	263	303
Baltimore	6	10	0	.375	269	335
Cincinnati	3	13	0	.188	268	452

Western Division

	W	L	T	Pct.	Pts.	OP
Denver#	14	2	0	.875	501	309
Oakland	8	8	0	.500	288	356
Seattle	8	8	0	.500	372	310
Kansas City	7	9	0	.438	327	363
San Diego	5	11	0	.313	241	342

NATIONAL CONFERENCE

Eastern Division

	W	L	T	Pct.	Pts.	OP
Dallas	10	6	0	.625	381	275
Arizona*	9	7	0	.563	325	378
N.Y. Giants	8	8	0	.500	287	309
Washington	6	10	0	.375	319	421
Philadelphia	3	13	0	.188	161	344

Central Division

	W	L	T	Pct.	Pts.	OP
Minnesota#	15	1	0	.938	556	296
Green Bay*	11	5	0	.688	408	319
Tampa Bay	8	8	0	.500	314	295
Detroit	5	11	0	.313	306	378
Chicago	4	12	0	.250	276	368

Western Division

	W	L	T	Pct.	Pts.	OP
Atlanta	14	2	0	.875	442	289
San Francisco*	12	4	0	.750	479	328
New Orleans	6	10	0	.375	305	359
Carolina	4	12	0	.250	336	413
St. Louis	4	12	0	.250	285	378

*Wild Card qualifier for playoffs; #Top playoff seed in conference
Miami finished ahead of Buffalo based on better net division points (6 to Bills' 0). Oakland finished ahead of Seattle based on head-to-head sweep (2-0). Carolina finished ahead of St. Louis based on head-to-head sweep (2-0).

Wild Card playoffs: MIAMI 24, Buffalo 17; JACKSONVILLE 25, New England 10
Divisional playoffs: DENVER 38, Miami 3; N.Y. JETS 34, Jacksonville 24
AFC Championship: DENVER 23, N.Y. Jets 10
Wild Card playoffs: Arizona 20, DALLAS 7; SAN FRANCISCO 30, Green Bay 27
Divisional playoffs: ATLANTA 20, San Francisco 18; MINNESOTA 41, Arizona 21
NFC Championship: Atlanta 30, MINNESOTA 27 (OT)
Super Bowl XXXIII: Denver (AFC) 34, Atlanta (NFC) 19, at Pro Player Stadium, Miami, Florida

Playoff Seeds

AFC	NFC
1. Denver	1. Minnesota
2. N.Y. Jets	**2. Atlanta**
3. Jacksonville	3. Dallas
4. Miami	4. San Francisco
5. Buffalo	5. Green Bay
6. New England	6. Arizona

1997

AMERICAN CONFERENCE

Eastern Division

	W	L	T	Pct.	Pts.	OP
New England	10	6	0	.625	369	289
Miami*	9	7	0	.563	339	327
N.Y. Jets	9	7	0	.563	348	287
Buffalo	6	10	0	.375	255	367
Indianapolis	3	13	0	.188	313	401

Central Division

	W	L	T	Pct.	Pts.	OP
Pittsburgh	11	5	0	.688	372	307
Jacksonville*	11	5	0	.688	394	318
Tennessee	8	8	0	.500	333	310
Cincinnati	7	9	0	.438	355	405
Baltimore	6	9	1	.406	326	345

Western Division

	W	L	T	Pct.	Pts.	OP
Kansas City#	13	3	0	.813	375	232
Denver*	12	4	0	.750	472	287
Seattle	8	8	0	.500	365	362
Oakland	4	12	0	.250	324	419
San Diego	4	12	0	.250	266	425

NATIONAL CONFERENCE

Eastern Division

	W	L	T	Pct.	Pts.	OP
N.Y. Giants	10	5	1	.656	307	265
Washington	8	7	1	.531	327	289
Philadelphia	6	9	1	.406	317	372
Dallas	6	10	0	.375	304	314
Arizona	4	12	0	.250	283	379

Central Division

	W	L	T	Pct.	Pts.	OP
Green Bay	13	3	0	.813	422	282
Tampa Bay*	10	6	0	.625	299	263
Detroit*	9	7	0	.563	379	306
Minnesota*	9	7	0	.563	354	359
Chicago	4	12	0	.250	263	421

Western Division

	W	L	T	Pct.	Pts.	OP
San Francisco#	13	3	0	.813	375	265
Carolina	7	9	0	.438	265	314
Atlanta	7	9	0	.438	320	361
New Orleans	6	10	0	.375	237	327
St. Louis	5	11	0	.313	299	359

*Wild Card qualifier for playoffs; #Top playoff seed in conference
Miami finished ahead of N.Y. Jets based on head-to-head sweep (2-0). Pittsburgh finished ahead of Jacksonville based on better net division points (78 to Jaguars' 23). Oakland finished ahead of San Diego based on better division record (2-6 to Chargers' 1-7). San Francisco was top playoff seed based on better conference record than Green Bay (11-1 to Packers' 10-2). Detroit finished ahead of Minnesota based on head-to-head sweep (2-0). Carolina finished ahead of Atlanta based on head-to-head sweep (2-0).

Wild Card playoffs: DENVER 42, Jacksonville 17; NEW ENGLAND 17, Miami 3
Divisional playoffs: PITTSBURGH 7, New England 6; Denver 14, KANSAS CITY 10
AFC Championship: Denver 24, PITTSBURGH 21
Wild Card playoffs: Minnesota 23, N.Y. GIANTS 22; TAMPA BAY 20, Detroit 10
Divisional playoffs: SAN FRANCISCO 38, Minnesota 22; GREEN BAY 21, Tampa Bay 7
NFC Championship: Green Bay 23, SAN FRANCISCO 10
Super Bowl XXXII: Denver (AFC) 31, Green Bay (NFC) 24, at Qualcomm Stadium, San Diego, California

Playoff Seeds

AFC	NFC
1. Kansas City	1. San Francisco
2. Pittsburgh	**2. Green Bay**
3. New England	3. N.Y. Giants
4. Denver	4. Tampa Bay
5. Jacksonville	5. Detroit
6. Miami	6. Minnesota

1996

AMERICAN CONFERENCE

Eastern Division

	W	L	T	Pct.	Pts.	OP
New England	11	5	0	.688	418	313
Buffalo*	10	6	0	.625	319	266
Indianapolis*	9	7	0	.563	317	334
Miami	8	8	0	.500	339	325
N.Y. Jets	1	15	0	.063	279	454

Central Division

	W	L	T	Pct.	Pts.	OP
Pittsburgh	10	6	0	.625	344	257
Jacksonville*	9	7	0	.563	325	335
Cincinnati	8	8	0	.500	372	369
Houston	8	8	0	.500	345	319
Baltimore	4	12	0	.250	371	441

Western Division

	W	L	T	Pct.	Pts.	OP
Denver#	13	3	0	.813	391	275
Kansas City	9	7	0	.563	297	300
San Diego	8	8	0	.500	310	376
Oakland	7	9	0	.438	340	293
Seattle	7	9	0	.438	317	376

NATIONAL CONFERENCE

Eastern Division

	W	L	T	Pct.	Pts.	OP
Dallas	10	6	0	.625	286	250
Philadelphia*	10	6	0	.625	363	341
Washington	9	7	0	.563	364	312
Arizona	7	9	0	.438	300	397
N.Y. Giants	6	10	0	.375	242	297

Central Division

	W	L	T	Pct.	Pts.	OP
Green Bay#	13	3	0	.813	456	210
Minnesota*	9	7	0	.563	298	315
Chicago	7	9	0	.438	283	305
Tampa Bay	6	10	0	.375	221	293
Detroit	5	11	0	.313	302	368

Western Division

	W	L	T	Pct.	Pts.	OP
Carolina	12	4	0	.750	367	218
San Francisco*	12	4	0	.750	398	257
St. Louis	6	10	0	.375	303	409
Atlanta	3	13	0	.188	309	461
New Orleans	3	13	0	.188	229	339

*Wild Card qualifier for playoffs; #Top playoff seed in conference
Jacksonville was second Wild Card ahead of Indianapolis and
Kansas City based on better conference record (7-5 to Colts' 6-6
and Chiefs' 5-7). Indianapolis was third Wild Card based on
head-to-head victory over Kansas City (1-0). Cincinnati finished
ahead of Houston based on better net division points (19 to
Oilers' 11). Oakland finished ahead of Seattle based on better
division record (3-5 to Seahawks' 2-6). Dallas finished ahead of
Philadelphia based on better record against common opponents
(7-4 to Eagles' 6-5). Minnesota was third Wild Card based on
better conference record than Washington (8-4 to Redskins'
6-6). Carolina finished ahead of San Francisco based on head-to-
head sweep (2-0). Atlanta finished ahead of New Orleans based
on head-to-head sweep (2-0).

Wild Card playoffs: Jacksonville 30, BUFFALO 27;
PITTSBURGH 42, Indianapolis 14
Divisional playoffs: Jacksonville 30, DENVER 27;
NEW ENGLAND 28, Pittsburgh 3
AFC Championship: NEW ENGLAND 20, Jacksonville 6
Wild Card playoffs: DALLAS 40, Minnesota 15;
SAN FRANCISCO 14, Philadelphia 0
Divisional playoffs: GREEN BAY 35, San Francisco 14;
CAROLINA 26, Dallas 17
NFC Championship: GREEN BAY 30, Carolina 13
Super Bowl XXXI: Green Bay (NFC) 35, New England (AFC) 21,
at Louisiana Superdome, New Orleans, Louisiana

Playoff Seeds

AFC	NFC
1. Denver	**1. Green Bay**
2. New England	2. Carolina
3. Pittsburgh	3. Dallas
4. Buffalo	4. San Francisco
5. Jacksonville	5. Philadelphia
6. Indianapolis	6. Minnesota

1995

AMERICAN CONFERENCE

Eastern Division

	W	L	T	Pct.	Pts.	OP
Buffalo	10	6	0	.625	350	335
Indianapolis*	9	7	0	.563	331	316
Miami*	9	7	0	.563	398	332
New England	6	10	0	.375	294	377
N.Y. Jets	3	13	0	.188	233	384

Central Division

	W	L	T	Pct.	Pts.	OP
Pittsburgh	11	5	0	.688	407	327
Cincinnati	7	9	0	.438	349	374
Houston	7	9	0	.438	348	324
Cleveland	5	11	0	.313	289	356
Jacksonville	4	12	0	.250	275	404

Western Division

	W	L	T	Pct.	Pts.	OP
Kansas City#	13	3	0	.813	358	241
San Diego*	9	7	0	.563	321	323
Seattle	8	8	0	.500	363	366
Denver	8	8	0	.500	388	345
Oakland	8	8	0	.500	348	332

NATIONAL CONFERENCE

Eastern Division

	W	L	T	Pct.	Pts.	OP
Dallas#	12	4	0	.750	435	291
Philadelphia*	10	6	0	.625	318	338
Washington	6	10	0	.375	326	359
N.Y. Giants	5	11	0	.313	290	340
Arizona	4	12	0	.250	275	422

Central Division

	W	L	T	Pct.	Pts.	OP
Green Bay	11	5	0	.688	404	314
Detroit*	10	6	0	.625	436	336
Chicago	9	7	0	.563	392	360
Minnesota	8	8	0	.500	412	385
Tampa Bay	7	9	0	.438	238	335

Western Division

	W	L	T	Pct.	Pts.	OP
San Francisco	11	5	0	.688	457	258
Atlanta*	9	7	0	.563	362	349
St. Louis	7	9	0	.438	309	418
Carolina	7	9	0	.438	289	325
New Orleans	7	9	0	.438	319	348

*Wild Card qualifier for playoffs; #Top playoff seed in conference
Indianapolis finished ahead of Miami based on head-to-head sweep
(2-0). San Diego was first Wild Card based on head-to-head
victory over Indianapolis (1-0). Cincinnati finished ahead of
Houston based on better division record (4-4 to Oilers' 3-5).
Seattle finished ahead of Denver and Oakland based on best
head-to-head record (3-1 to Broncos' 2-2 and Raiders' 1-3).
Denver finished ahead of Oakland based on head-to-head sweep
(2-0). Philadelphia was first Wild Card ahead of Detroit based on
better conference record (9-3 to Lions' 7-5). San Francisco was
second playoff seed over Green Bay based on better
conference record (8-4 to Packers' 7-5). Atlanta was third Wild
Card ahead of Chicago based on better record against common
opponents (4-2 to Bears' 3-3). St. Louis finished ahead of
Carolina and New Orleans based on best head-to-head record
(3-1 to Panthers' 1-3 and Saints' 2-2). Carolina finished ahead of
New Orleans based on better conference record (4-8 to 3-9).

Wild Card playoffs: BUFFALO 37, Miami 22;
Indianapolis 35, SAN DIEGO 20
Divisional playoffs: PITTSBURGH 40, Buffalo 21;
Indianapolis 10, KANSAS CITY 7
AFC Championship: PITTSBURGH 20, Indianapolis 16
Wild Card playoffs: PHILADELPHIA 58, Detroit 37;
GREEN BAY 37, Atlanta 20
Divisional playoffs: Green Bay 27, SAN FRANCISCO 17;
DALLAS 30, Philadelphia 11
NFC Championship: DALLAS 38, Green Bay 27
Super Bowl XXX: Dallas (NFC) 27, Pittsburgh (AFC) 17,
at Sun Devil Stadium, Tempe, Arizona

Playoff Seeds

AFC	NFC
1. Kansas City	**1. Dallas**
2. Pittsburgh	2. San Francisco
3. Buffalo	3. Green Bay
4. San Diego	4. Philadelphia
5. Indianapolis	5. Detroit
6. Miami	6. Atlanta

1994

AMERICAN CONFERENCE
Eastern Division

	W	L	T	Pct.	Pts.	OP
Miami	10	6	0	.625	389	327
New England*	10	6	0	.625	351	312
Indianapolis	8	8	0	.500	307	320
Buffalo	7	9	0	.438	340	356
N.Y. Jets	6	10	0	.375	264	320

Central Division

	W	L	T	Pct.	Pts.	OP
Pittsburgh#	12	4	0	.750	316	234
Cleveland*	11	5	0	.688	340	204
Cincinnati	3	13	0	.188	276	406
Houston	2	14	0	.125	226	352

Western Division

	W	L	T	Pct.	Pts.	OP
San Diego	11	5	0	.688	381	306
Kansas City*	9	7	0	.563	319	298
L.A. Raiders	9	7	0	.563	303	327
Denver	7	9	0	.438	347	396
Seattle	6	10	0	.375	287	323

NATIONAL CONFERENCE
Eastern Division

	W	L	T	Pct.	Pts.	OP
Dallas	12	4	0	.750	414	248
N.Y. Giants	9	7	0	.563	279	305
Arizona	8	8	0	.500	235	267
Philadelphia	7	9	0	.438	308	308
Washington	3	13	0	.188	320	412

Central Division

	W	L	T	Pct.	Pts.	OP
Minnesota	10	6	0	.625	356	314
Green Bay*	9	7	0	.563	382	287
Detroit*	9	7	0	.563	357	342
Chicago*	9	7	0	.563	271	307
Tampa Bay	6	10	0	.375	251	351

Western Division

	W	L	T	Pct.	Pts.	OP
San Francisco#	13	3	0	.813	505	296
New Orleans	7	9	0	.438	348	407
Atlanta	7	9	0	.438	317	385
L.A. Rams	4	12	0	.250	286	365

*Wild Card qualifier for playoffs; #Top playoff seed in conference

Miami finished ahead of New England based on head-to-head sweep (2-0). Kansas City finished ahead of L.A. Raiders based on head-to-head sweep (2-0). Green Bay was first Wild Card based on best head-to-head record (3-1) vs. Detroit (2-2) and Chicago (1-3) and better conference record (8-4) than N.Y. Giants (6-6). Detroit was second Wild Card based on better division record (4-4) than Chicago (3-5) and head-to-head victory over N.Y. Giants (1-0). Chicago was third Wild Card based on better record against common opponents (4-4) than N.Y. Giants (3-5). New Orleans finished ahead of Atlanta based on head-to-head sweep (2-0).

Wild Card playoffs: MIAMI 27, Kansas City 17; CLEVELAND 20, New England 13
Divisional playoffs: PITTSBURGH 29. Cleveland 9; SAN DIEGO 22, Miami 21
AFC Championship: San Diego 17, PITTSBURGH 13
Wild Card playoffs: GREEN BAY 16, Detroit 12; Chicago 35, MINNESOTA 18
Divisional playoffs: SAN FRANCISCO 44, Chicago 15; DALLAS 35, Green Bay 9
NFC Championship: SAN FRANCISCO 38, Dallas 28
Super Bowl XXIX: San Francisco (NFC) 49, San Diego (AFC) 26, at Joe Robbie Stadium, Miami, Florida

Playoff Seeds

AFC	NFC
1. Pittsburgh	**1. San Francisco**
2. San Diego	2. Dallas
3. Miami	3. Minnesota
4. Cleveland	4. Green Bay
5. New England	5. Detroit
6. Kansas City	6. Chicago

1993

AMERICAN CONFERENCE
Eastern Division

	W	L	T	Pct.	Pts.	OP
Buffalo#	12	4	0	.750	329	242
Miami	9	7	0	.563	349	351
N.Y. Jets	8	8	0	.500	270	247
New England	5	11	0	.313	238	286
Indianapolis	4	12	0	.250	189	378

Central Division

	W	L	T	Pct.	Pts.	OP
Houston	12	4	0	.750	368	238
Pittsburgh*	9	7	0	.563	308	281
Cleveland	7	9	0	.438	304	307
Cincinnati	3	13	0	.188	187	319

Western Division

	W	L	T	Pct.	Pts.	OP
Kansas City	11	5	0	.688	328	291
L.A. Raiders*	10	6	0	.625	306	326
Denver*	9	7	0	.563	373	284
San Diego	8	8	0	.500	322	290
Seattle	6	10	0	.375	280	314

NATIONAL CONFERENCE
Eastern Division

	W	L	T	Pct.	Pts.	OP
Dallas#	12	4	0	.750	376	229
N.Y. Giants*	11	5	0	.688	288	205
Philadelphia	8	8	0	.500	293	315
Phoenix	7	9	0	.438	326	269
Washington	4	12	0	.250	230	345

Central Division

	W	L	T	Pct.	Pts.	OP
Detroit	10	6	0	.625	298	292
Minnesota*	9	7	0	.563	277	290
Green Bay*	9	7	0	.563	340	282
Chicago	7	9	0	.438	234	230
Tampa Bay	5	11	0	.313	237	376

Western Division

	W	L	T	Pct.	Pts.	OP
San Francisco	10	6	0	.625	473	295
New Orleans	8	8	0	.500	317	343
Atlanta	6	10	0	.375	316	385
L.A. Rams	5	11	0	.313	221	367

*Wild Card qualifier for playoffs; #Top playoff seed in conference

Buffalo was top playoff seed based on head-to-head victory over Houston (1-0). Denver was second Wild Card ahead of Pittsburgh and Miami based on better conference record (8-4 to Steelers' 7-5 to Dolphins' 6-6). Pittsburgh was third Wild Card ahead of Miami based on head-to-head victory. San Francisco was second playoff seed based on head-to-head victory over Detroit (1-0). Minnesota finished ahead of Green Bay based on head-to-head sweep (2-0).

Wild Card playoffs: KANSAS CITY 27, Pittsburgh 24 (OT); L.A. RAIDERS 42, Denver 24
Divisional playoffs: BUFFALO 29, L.A. Raiders 23; Kansas City 28, HOUSTON 20
AFC Championship: BUFFALO 30, Kansas City 13
Wild Card playoffs: Green Bay 28, DETROIT 24; N.Y. GIANTS 17, Minnesota 10
Divisional playoffs: SAN FRANCISCO 44, N.Y. Giants 3; DALLAS 27, Green Bay 17
NFC Championship: DALLAS 38, San Francisco 21
Super Bowl XXVIII: Dallas (NFC) 30, Buffalo (AFC) 13, at Georgia Dome, Atlanta, Georgia

Playoff Seeds

AFC	NFC
1. Buffalo	**1. Dallas**
2. Houston	2. San Francisco
3. Kansas City	3. Detroit
4. L.A. Raiders	4. N.Y. Giants
5. Denver	5. Minnesota
6. Pittsburgh	6. Green Bay

1992

AMERICAN CONFERENCE
Eastern Division

	W	L	T	Pct.	Pts.	OP
Miami	11	5	0	.688	340	281
Buffalo*	11	5	0	.688	381	283
Indianapolis	9	7	0	.563	216	302
N.Y. Jets	4	12	0	.250	220	315
New England	2	14	0	.125	205	363

Central Division

	W	L	T	Pct.	Pts.	OP
Pittsburgh#	11	5	0	.688	299	225
Houston*	10	6	0	.625	352	258
Cleveland	7	9	0	.438	272	275
Cincinnati	5	11	0	.313	274	364

Western Division

	W	L	T	Pct.	Pts.	OP
San Diego	11	5	0	.688	335	241
Kansas City*	10	6	0	.625	348	282
Denver	8	8	0	.500	262	329
L.A. Raiders	7	9	0	.438	249	281
Seattle	2	14	0	.125	140	312

NATIONAL CONFERENCE
Eastern Division

	W	L	T	Pct.	Pts.	OP
Dallas	13	3	0	.813	409	243
Philadelphia*	11	5	0	.688	354	245
Washington*	9	7	0	.563	300	255
N.Y. Giants	6	10	0	.375	306	367
Phoenix	4	12	0	.250	243	332

Central Division

	W	L	T	Pct.	Pts.	OP
Minnesota	11	5	0	.688	374	249
Green Bay	9	7	0	.563	276	296
Tampa Bay	5	11	0	.313	267	365
Chicago	5	11	0	.313	295	361
Detroit	5	11	0	.313	273	332

Western Division

	W	L	T	Pct.	Pts.	OP
San Francisco#	14	2	0	.875	431	236
New Orleans*	12	4	0	.750	330	202
Atlanta	6	10	0	.375	327	414
L.A. Rams	6	10	0	.375	313	383

*Wild Card qualifier for playoffs; #Top playoff seed in conference
Pittsburgh was top playoff seed, and Miami was second playoff seed ahead of San Diego, based on conference record (10-2 to Dolphins' 9-3 to Chargers' 9-5). Miami finished ahead of Buffalo based on better conference record (9-3 to Bills' 7-5). Houston was second Wild Card based on head-to-head victory over Kansas City (1-0). Washington was third Wild Card based on better conference record than Green Bay (7-5 to Packers' 6-6). Tampa Bay finished ahead of Chicago and Chicago finished ahead of Detroit based on better conference record (5-9 to Bears' 4-8 and Lions' 3-9). Atlanta finished ahead of L.A. Rams based on better record against common opponents (5-7 to Rams' 4-8).
Wild Card playoffs: SAN DIEGO 17, Kansas City 0;
   BUFFALO 41, Houston 38 (OT)
Divisional playoffs: Buffalo 24, PITTSBURGH 3;
   MIAMI 31, San Diego 0
AFC Championship: Buffalo 29, MIAMI 10
Wild Card playoffs: Washington 24, MINNESOTA 7;
   Philadelphia 36, NEW ORLEANS 20
Divisional playoffs: SAN FRANCISCO 20, Washington 13;
   DALLAS 34, Philadelphia 10
NFC Championship: Dallas 30, SAN FRANCISCO 20
Super Bowl XXVII: Dallas (NFC) 52, Buffalo (AFC) 17,
   at Rose Bowl, Pasadena, California

Playoff Seeds

AFC	NFC
1. Pittsburgh	1. San Francisco
2. Miami	**2. Dallas**
3. San Diego	3. Minnesota
4. Buffalo	4. New Orleans
5. Houston	5. Philadelphia
6. Kansas City	6. Washington

1991

AMERICAN CONFERENCE
Eastern Division

	W	L	T	Pct.	Pts.	OP
Buffalo#	13	3	0	.813	458	318
N.Y. Jets*	8	8	0	.500	314	293
Miami	8	8	0	.500	343	349
New England	6	10	0	.375	211	305
Indianapolis	1	15	0	.063	143	381

Central Division

	W	L	T	Pct.	Pts.	OP
Houston	11	5	0	.688	386	251
Pittsburgh	7	9	0	.438	292	344
Cleveland	6	10	0	.375	293	298
Cincinnati	3	13	0	.188	263	435

Western Division

	W	L	T	Pct.	Pts.	OP
Denver	12	4	0	.750	304	235
Kansas City*	10	6	0	.625	322	252
L.A. Raiders*	9	7	0	.563	298	297
Seattle	7	9	0	.438	276	261
San Diego	4	12	0	.250	274	342

NATIONAL CONFERENCE
Eastern Division

	W	L	T	Pct.	Pts.	OP
Washington#	14	2	0	.875	485	224
Dallas*	11	5	0	.688	342	310
Philadelphia	10	6	0	.625	285	244
N.Y. Giants	8	8	0	.500	281	297
Phoenix	4	12	0	.250	196	344

Central Division

	W	L	T	Pct.	Pts.	OP
Detroit	12	4	0	.750	339	295
Chicago*	11	5	0	.688	299	269
Minnesota	8	8	0	.500	301	306
Green Bay	4	12	0	.250	273	313
Tampa Bay	3	13	0	.188	199	365

Western Division

	W	L	T	Pct.	Pts.	OP
New Orleans	11	5	0	.688	341	211
Atlanta*	10	6	0	.625	361	338
San Francisco	10	6	0	.625	393	239
L.A. Rams	3	13	0	.188	234	390

*Wild Card qualifier for playoffs; #Top playoff seed in conference
N.Y. Jets finished ahead of Miami based on head-to-head sweep (2-0). Chicago was first Wild Card based on better conference record than Dallas (9-3 to Cowboys' 8-4). Atlanta finished ahead of San Francisco based on head-to-head sweep (2-0), and was third Wild Card ahead of Philadelphia based on better conference record (7-5 to Eagles' 6-6).
Wild Card playoffs: KANSAS CITY 10, L.A. Raiders 6;
   HOUSTON 17, N.Y. Jets 10
Divisional playoffs: DENVER 26, Houston 24;
   BUFFALO 37, Kansas City 14
AFC Championship: BUFFALO 10, Denver 7
Wild Card playoffs: Atlanta 27, NEW ORLEANS 20;
   Dallas 17, CHICAGO 13
Divisional playoffs: WASHINGTON 24, Atlanta 7;
   DETROIT 38, Dallas 6
NFC Championship: WASHINGTON 41, Detroit 10
Super Bowl XXVI: Washington (NFC) 37, Buffalo (AFC) 24,
   at Hubert H. Humphrey Metrodome, Minneapolis, Minnesota

Playoff Seeds

AFC	NFC
1. Buffalo	**1. Washington**
2. Denver	2. Detroit
3. Houston	3. New Orleans
4. Kansas City	4. Chicago
5. L.A. Raiders	5. Dallas
6. N.Y. Jets	6. Atlanta

1990

AMERICAN CONFERENCE

Eastern Division

	W	L	T	Pct.	Pts.	OP
Buffalo#	13	3	0	.813	428	263
Miami*	12	4	0	.750	336	242
Indianapolis	7	9	0	.438	281	353
N.Y. Jets	6	10	0	.375	295	345
New England	1	15	0	.063	181	446

Central Division

	W	L	T	Pct.	Pts.	OP
Cincinnati	9	7	0	.563	360	352
Houston*	9	7	0	.563	405	307
Pittsburgh	9	7	0	.563	292	240
Cleveland	3	13	0	.188	228	462

Western Division

	W	L	T	Pct.	Pts.	OP
L.A. Raiders	12	4	0	.750	337	268
Kansas City*	11	5	0	.688	369	257
Seattle	9	7	0	.563	306	286
San Diego	6	10	0	.375	315	281
Denver	5	11	0	.313	331	374

NATIONAL CONFERENCE

Eastern Division

	W	L	T	Pct.	Pts.	OP
N.Y. Giants	13	3	0	.813	335	211
Philadelphia*	10	6	0	.625	396	299
Washington*	10	6	0	.625	381	301
Dallas	7	9	0	.438	244	308
Phoenix	5	11	0	.313	268	396

Central Division

	W	L	T	Pct.	Pts.	OP
Chicago	11	5	0	.688	348	280
Tampa Bay	6	10	0	.375	264	367
Detroit	6	10	0	.375	373	413
Green Bay	6	10	0	.375	271	347
Minnesota	6	10	0	.375	351	326

Western Division

	W	L	T	Pct.	Pts.	OP
San Francisco#	14	2	0	.875	353	239
New Orleans*	8	8	0	.500	274	275
L.A. Rams	5	11	0	.313	345	412
Atlanta	5	11	0	.313	348	365

*Wild Card qualifier for playoffs; #Top playoff seed in conference
Cincinnati finished ahead of Houston and Pittsburgh based on best head-to-head record (3-1 to Oilers' 2-2 to Steelers' 1-3). Houston was Wild Card based on better conference record (8-4) than Seattle (7-5) and Pittsburgh (6-6). Philadelphia finished ahead of Washington based on better division record (5-3 to Redskins' 4-4). Tampa Bay was second in NFC Central based on best head-to-head record (3-1 against Detroit (2-4), Green Bay (3-3), and Minnesota (2-4). Detroit finished third based on best net division points (minus 8) against Green Bay (minus 40). Green Bay finished ahead of Minnesota based on better conference record (5-7 to Vikings' 4-8). The L.A. Rams finished ahead of Atlanta based on net points in division (plus 1 to Falcons' minus 31).
Wild Card playoffs: MIAMI 17, Kansas City 16;
  CINCINNATI 41, Houston 14
Divisional playoffs: BUFFALO 44, Miami 34;
  L.A. RAIDERS 20, Cincinnati 10
AFC Championship: BUFFALO 51, L.A. Raiders 3
Wild Card playoffs: Washington 20, PHILADELPHIA 6;
  CHICAGO 16, New Orleans 6
Divisional playoffs: SAN FRANCISCO 28, Washington 10;
  N.Y. GIANTS 31, Chicago 3
NFC Championship: N.Y. Giants 15, SAN FRANCISCO 13
Super Bowl XXV: N.Y. Giants (NFC) 20, Buffalo (AFC) 19,
  at Tampa Stadium, Tampa, Florida

Playoff Seeds

AFC	NFC
1. Buffalo	1. San Francisco
2. L.A. Raiders	**2. N.Y. Giants**
3. Cincinnati	3. Chicago
4. Miami	4. Philadelphia
5. Kansas City	5. Washington
6. Houston	6. New Orleans

1989

AMERICAN CONFERENCE

Eastern Division

	W	L	T	Pct.	Pts.	OP
Buffalo	9	7	0	.563	409	317
Indianapolis	8	8	0	.500	298	301
Miami	8	8	0	.500	331	379
New England	5	11	0	.313	297	391
N.Y. Jets	4	12	0	.250	253	411

Central Division

	W	L	T	Pct.	Pts.	OP
Cleveland	9	6	1	.594	334	254
Houston*	9	7	0	.563	365	412
Pittsburgh*	9	7	0	.563	265	326
Cincinnati	8	8	0	.500	404	285

Western Division

	W	L	T	Pct.	Pts.	OP
Denver#	11	5	0	.688	362	226
Kansas City	8	7	1	.531	318	286
L.A. Raiders	8	8	0	.500	315	297
Seattle	7	9	0	.438	241	327
San Diego	6	10	0	.375	266	290

NATIONAL CONFERENCE

Eastern Division

	W	L	T	Pct.	Pts.	OP
N.Y. Giants	12	4	0	.750	348	252
Philadelphia*	11	5	0	.688	342	274
Washington	10	6	0	.625	386	308
Phoenix	5	11	0	.313	258	377
Dallas	1	15	0	.063	204	393

Central Division

	W	L	T	Pct.	Pts.	OP
Minnesota	10	6	0	.625	351	275
Green Bay	10	6	0	.625	362	356
Detroit	7	9	0	.438	312	364
Chicago	6	10	0	.375	358	377
Tampa Bay	5	11	0	.313	320	419

Western Division

	W	L	T	Pct.	Pts.	OP
San Francisco#	14	2	0	.875	442	253
L.A. Rams*	11	5	0	.688	426	344
New Orleans	9	7	0	.563	386	301
Atlanta	3	13	0	.188	279	437

*Wild Card qualifier for playoffs; #Top playoff seed in conference
Indianapolis finished ahead of Miami based on better conference record (7-5 vs. Dolphins' 6-8). Houston finished ahead of Pittsburgh based on head-to-head sweep (2-0). The L.A. Rams did not play San Francisco in the divisional playoffs because, from 1970-1989, two teams from the same division could not meet prior to the conference championship game. Philadelphia was first Wild Card ahead of L.A. Rams based on better record against common opponents (7-3 to Rams' 5-4). Minnesota finished ahead of Green Bay based on better division record (6-2 vs. Packers' 5-3).
Wild Card playoff: Pittsburgh 26, HOUSTON 23 (OT)
Divisional playoffs: CLEVELAND 34, Buffalo 30;
  DENVER 24, Pittsburgh 23
AFC Championship: DENVER 37, Cleveland 21
Wild Card playoff: L.A. Rams 21, PHILADELPHIA 7
Divisional playoffs: L.A. Rams 19, N.Y. GIANTS 13 (OT);
  SAN FRANCISCO 41, Minnesota 13
NFC Championship: SAN FRANCISCO 30, L.A. Rams 3
Super Bowl XXIV: San Francisco (NFC) 55, Denver (AFC) 10,
  at Louisiana Superdome, New Orleans, Louisiana

1988

AMERICAN CONFERENCE

Eastern Division

	W	L	T	Pct.	Pts.	OP
Buffalo	12	4	0	.750	329	237
Indianapolis	9	7	0	.563	354	315
New England	9	7	0	.563	250	284
N.Y. Jets	8	7	1	.531	372	354
Miami	6	10	0	.375	319	380

Central Division

	W	L	T	Pct.	Pts.	OP
Cincinnati#	12	4	0	.750	448	329
Cleveland*	10	6	0	.625	304	288
Houston*	10	6	0	.625	424	365
Pittsburgh	5	11	0	.313	336	421

Western Division

	W	L	T	Pct.	Pts.	OP
Seattle	9	7	0	.563	339	329
Denver	8	8	0	.500	327	352
L.A. Raiders	7	9	0	.438	325	369
San Diego	6	10	0	.375	231	332
Kansas City	4	11	1	.281	254	320

NATIONAL CONFERENCE

Eastern Division

	W	L	T	Pct.	Pts.	OP
Philadelphia	10	6	0	.625	379	319
N.Y. Giants	10	6	0	.625	359	304
Washington	7	9	0	.438	345	387
Phoenix	7	9	0	.438	344	398
Dallas	3	13	0	.188	265	381

Central Division

	W	L	T	Pct.	Pts.	OP
Chicago#	12	4	0	.750	312	215
Minnesota*	11	5	0	.688	406	233
Tampa Bay	5	11	0	.313	261	350
Detroit	4	12	0	.250	220	313
Green Bay	4	12	0	.250	240	315

Western Division

	W	L	T	Pct.	Pts.	OP
San Francisco	10	6	0	.625	369	294
L.A. Rams*	10	6	0	.625	407	293
New Orleans	10	6	0	.625	312	283
Atlanta	5	11	0	.313	244	315

*Wild Card qualifier for playoffs; #Top playoff seed in conference
Cincinnati was top playoff seed ahead of Buffalo based on head-to-head victory (1-0). Indianapolis finished ahead of New England based on better record against common opponents (7-5 to Patriots' 6-6). Cleveland finished ahead of Houston based on better division record (4-2 to Oilers' 3-3). Houston did not play Cincinnati, and Minnesota did not play Chicago in the divisional playoffs because, from 1970-1989, two teams from the same division could not meet prior to the conference championship game. Philadelphia finished first in NFC East based on head-to-head sweep of N.Y. Giants (2-0). Washington finished third in NFC East based on better division record (4-4) than Phoenix (3-5). Detroit finished fourth in NFC Central based on head-to-head sweep of Green Bay (2-0). San Francisco finished first in NFC West based on better head-to-head record (3-1) against L.A. Rams (2-2) and New Orleans (1-3). San Francisco finished with second playoff seed ahead of Philadelphia based on better record against common opponents (5-3 to Eagles' 5-4). L.A. Rams finished second in NFC West based on better division record (4-2) than New Orleans (3-3) and earned Wild-Card position based on better conference record (8-4) than N.Y. Giants (9-5) and New Orleans (6-6).
Wild Card playoff: Houston 24, CLEVELAND 23
Divisional playoffs: CINCINNATI 21, Seattle 13; BUFFALO 17, Houston 10
AFC Championship: CINCINNATI 21, Buffalo 10
Wild Card playoff: MINNESOTA 28, L.A. Rams 17
Divisional playoffs: CHICAGO 20, Philadelphia 12; SAN FRANCISCO 34, Minnesota 9
NFC Championship: San Francisco 28, CHICAGO 3
Super Bowl XXIII: San Francisco (NFC) 20, Cincinnati (AFC) 16, at Joe Robbie Stadium, Miami, Florida

1987

AMERICAN CONFERENCE

Eastern Division

	W	L	T	Pct.	Pts.	OP
Indianapolis	9	6	0	.600	300	238
New England	8	7	0	.533	320	293
Miami	8	7	0	.533	362	335
Buffalo	7	8	0	.467	270	305
N.Y. Jets	6	9	0	.400	334	360

Central Division

	W	L	T	Pct.	Pts.	OP
Cleveland	10	5	0	.667	390	239
Houston*	9	6	0	.600	345	349
Pittsburgh	8	7	0	.533	285	299
Cincinnati	4	11	0	.267	285	370

Western Division

	W	L	T	Pct.	Pts.	OP
Denver#	10	4	1	.700	379	288
Seattle*	9	6	0	.600	371	314
San Diego	8	7	0	.533	253	317
L.A. Raiders	5	10	0	.333	301	289
Kansas City	4	11	0	.267	273	388

NATIONAL CONFERENCE

Eastern Division

	W	L	T	Pct.	Pts.	OP
Washington	11	4	0	.733	379	285
Dallas	7	8	0	.467	340	348
St. Louis	7	8	0	.467	362	368
Philadelphia	7	8	0	.467	337	380
N.Y. Giants	6	9	0	.400	280	312

Central Division

	W	L	T	Pct.	Pts.	OP
Chicago	11	4	0	.733	356	282
Minnesota*	8	7	0	.533	336	335
Green Bay	5	9	1	.367	255	300
Tampa Bay	4	11	0	.267	286	360
Detroit	4	11	0	.267	269	384

Western Division

	W	L	T	Pct.	Pts.	OP
San Francisco#	13	2	0	.867	459	253
New Orleans*	12	3	0	.800	422	283
L.A. Rams	6	9	0	.400	317	361
Atlanta	3	12	0	.200	205	436

*Wild Card qualifier for playoffs; #Top playoff seed in conference
New England finished ahead of Miami based on head-to-head sweep (2-0). Houston was first Wild Card ahead of Seattle based on better conference record (7-4 to Seahawks' 5-6). Chicago was second playoff seed ahead of Washington based on better conference record (9-2 to Redskins' 9-3). Dallas finished ahead of St. Louis and Philadelphia based on better division record (4-4 to Cardinals' 3-5 and Eagles' 3-5). St. Louis finished ahead of Philadelphia based on better conference record (7-7 to Eagles' 4-7). Tampa Bay finished ahead of Detroit based on better division record (3-4 to Lions' 2-5).
Wild Card playoff: HOUSTON 23, Seattle 20 (OT)
Divisional playoffs: CLEVELAND 38, Indianapolis 21; DENVER 34, Houston 10
AFC Championship: DENVER 38, Cleveland 33
Wild Card playoff: Minnesota 44, NEW ORLEANS 10
Divisional playoffs: Minnesota 36, SAN FRANCISCO 24; Washington 21, CHICAGO 17
NFC Championship: WASHINGTON 17, Minnesota 10
Super Bowl XXII: Washington (NFC) 42, Denver (AFC) 10, at San Diego Jack Murphy Stadium, San Diego, California
Note: 1987 regular season was reduced from 16 to 15 games for each team due to players' strike.

1986

AMERICAN CONFERENCE
Eastern Division

	W	L	T	Pct.	Pts.	OP
New England	11	5	0	.688	412	307
N.Y. Jets*	10	6	0	.625	364	386
Miami	8	8	0	.500	430	405
Buffalo	4	12	0	.250	287	348
Indianapolis	3	13	0	.188	229	400

Central Division

	W	L	T	Pct.	Pts.	OP
Cleveland#	12	4	0	.750	391	310
Cincinnati	10	6	0	.625	409	394
Pittsburgh	6	10	0	.375	307	336
Houston	5	11	0	.313	274	329

Western Division

	W	L	T	Pct.	Pts.	OP
Denver	11	5	0	.688	378	327
Kansas City*	10	6	0	.625	358	326
Seattle	10	6	0	.625	366	293
L.A. Raiders	8	8	0	.500	323	346
San Diego	4	12	0	.250	335	396

NATIONAL CONFERENCE
Eastern Division

	W	L	T	Pct.	Pts.	OP
N.Y. Giants#	14	2	0	.875	371	236
Washington*	12	4	0	.750	368	296
Dallas	7	9	0	.438	346	337
Philadelphia	5	10	1	.344	256	312
St. Louis	4	11	1	.281	218	351

Central Division

	W	L	T	Pct.	Pts.	OP
Chicago	14	2	0	.875	352	187
Minnesota	9	7	0	.563	398	273
Detroit	5	11	0	.313	277	326
Green Bay	4	12	0	.250	254	418
Tampa Bay	2	14	0	.125	239	473

Western Division

	W	L	T	Pct.	Pts.	OP
San Francisco	10	5	1	.656	374	247
L.A. Rams*	10	6	0	.625	309	267
Atlanta	7	8	1	.469	280	280
New Orleans	7	9	0	.438	288	287

*Wild Card qualifier for playoffs; #Top playoff seed in conference
Denver was second playoff seed ahead of New England based on
head-to-head victory (1-0). N.Y. Jets were first Wild Card based
on better conference record (8-4) than Kansas City (9-5), Seattle
(7-5), and Cincinnati (7-5). Kansas City was second Wild Card
based on better conference record (9-5) than Seattle (7-5) and
Cincinnati (7-5). N.Y. Giants were top playoff seed based on
better conference record than Chicago (11-1 to Bears' 10-2).
Washington did not play the N.Y. Giants in the divisional playoffs
because, from 1970-1989, two teams from the same division
could not meet prior to the conference championship game.
Wild Card playoff: N.Y. JETS 35, Kansas City 15
Divisional playoffs: CLEVELAND 23, N.Y. Jets 20 (OT);
    DENVER 22, New England 17
AFC Championship: Denver 23, CLEVELAND 20 (OT)
Wild Card playoff: WASHINGTON 19, L.A. Rams 7
Divisional playoffs: Washington 27, CHICAGO 13
    N.Y. GIANTS 49, San Francisco 3
NFC Championship: N.Y. GIANTS 17, Washington 0
Super Bowl XXI: N.Y. Giants (NFC) 39, Denver (AFC) 20,
    at Rose Bowl, Pasadena, California

1985

AMERICAN CONFERENCE
Eastern Division

	W	L	T	Pct.	Pts.	OP
Miami	12	4	0	.750	428	320
N.Y. Jets*	11	5	0	.688	393	264
New England*	11	5	0	.688	362	290
Indianapolis	5	11	0	.313	320	386
Buffalo	2	14	0	.125	200	381

Central Division

	W	L	T	Pct.	Pts.	OP
Cleveland	8	8	0	.500	287	294
Cincinnati	7	9	0	.438	441	437
Pittsburgh	7	9	0	.438	379	355
Houston	5	11	0	.313	284	412

Western Division

	W	L	T	Pct.	Pts.	OP
L.A. Raiders#	12	4	0	.750	354	308
Denver	11	5	0	.688	380	329
Seattle	8	8	0	.500	349	303
San Diego	8	8	0	.500	467	435
Kansas City	6	10	0	.375	317	360

NATIONAL CONFERENCE
Eastern Division

	W	L	T	Pct.	Pts.	OP
Dallas	10	6	0	.625	357	333
N.Y. Giants*	10	6	0	.625	399	283
Washington	10	6	0	.625	297	312
Philadelphia	7	9	0	.438	286	310
St. Louis	5	11	0	.313	278	414

Central Division

	W	L	T	Pct.	Pts.	OP
Chicago#	15	1	0	.938	456	198
Green Bay	8	8	0	.500	337	355
Minnesota	7	9	0	.438	346	359
Detroit	7	9	0	.438	307	366
Tampa Bay	2	14	0	.125	294	448

Western Division

	W	L	T	Pct.	Pts.	OP
L.A. Rams	11	5	0	.688	340	277
San Francisco*	10	6	0	.625	411	263
New Orleans	5	11	0	.313	294	401
Atlanta	4	12	0	.250	282	452

*Wild Card qualifier for playoffs; #Top playoff seed in conference
L.A. Raiders were top playoff seed ahead of Miami based on better
record against common opponents (5-1 to 4-2). N.Y. Jets were
first Wild Card based on better conference record (9-3) than New
England (8-4) and Denver (8-4). New England was second Wild
Card ahead of Denver based on better record against common
opponents (4-2 to Broncos' 3-3). Cincinnati finished ahead of
Pittsburgh based on head-to-head sweep (2-0). Seattle finished
ahead of San Diego based on head-to-head sweep (2-0). Dallas
finished ahead of N.Y. Giants and Washington based on better
head-to-head record (4-0 to Giants' 1-3 and Redskins' 1-3). N.Y.
Giants were first Wild Card based on better conference record
(8-4) than San Francisco (7-5) and Washington (6-6). San Fran-
cisco was second Wild Card based on head-to-head victory over
Washington (1-0). Minnesota finished ahead of Detroit based on
better division record (3-5 to Lions' 2-6).
Wild Card playoff: New England 26, N.Y. JETS 14
Divisional playoffs: MIAMI 24, Cleveland 21;
    New England 27, L.A. RAIDERS 20
AFC Championship: New England 31, MIAMI 14
Wild Card playoff: N.Y. GIANTS 17, San Francisco 3
Divisional playoffs: L.A. RAMS 20, Dallas 0;
    CHICAGO 21, N.Y. Giants 0
NFC Championship: CHICAGO 24, L.A. Rams 0
Super Bowl XX: Chicago (NFC) 46, New England (AFC) 10,
    at Louisiana Superdome, New Orleans, Louisiana

1984

AMERICAN CONFERENCE
Eastern Division

	W	L	T	Pct.	Pts.	OP
Miami#	14	2	0	.875	513	298
New England	9	7	0	.563	362	352
N.Y. Jets	7	9	0	.438	332	364
Indianapolis	4	12	0	.250	239	414
Buffalo	2	14	0	.125	250	454

Central Division

	W	L	T	Pct.	Pts.	OP
Pittsburgh	9	7	0	.563	387	310
Cincinnati	8	8	0	.500	339	339
Cleveland	5	11	0	.313	250	297
Houston	3	13	0	.188	240	437

Western Division

	W	L	T	Pct.	Pts.	OP
Denver	13	3	0	.813	353	241
Seattle*	12	4	0	.750	418	282
L.A. Raiders*	11	5	0	.688	368	278
Kansas City	8	8	0	.500	314	324
San Diego	7	9	0	.438	394	413

NATIONAL CONFERENCE
Eastern Division

	W	L	T	Pct.	Pts.	OP
Washington	11	5	0	.688	426	310
N.Y. Giants*	9	7	0	.563	299	301
St. Louis	9	7	0	.563	423	345
Dallas	9	7	0	.563	308	308
Philadelphia	6	9	1	.406	278	320

Central Division

	W	L	T	Pct.	Pts.	OP
Chicago	10	6	0	.625	325	248
Green Bay	8	8	0	.500	390	309
Tampa Bay	6	10	0	.375	335	380
Detroit	4	11	1	.281	283	408
Minnesota	3	13	0	.188	276	484

Western Division

	W	L	T	Pct.	Pts.	OP
San Francisco#	15	1	0	.938	475	227
L.A. Rams*	10	6	0	.625	346	316
New Orleans	7	9	0	.438	298	361
Atlanta	4	12	0	.250	281	382

*Wild Card qualifier for playoffs; #Top playoff seed in conference
N.Y. Giants finished ahead of St. Louis and Dallas based on best head-to-head record (3-1 to Cardinals' 2-2 and Cowboys' 1-3). St. Louis finished ahead of Dallas based on better division record (5-3 to Cowboys' 3-5).
Wild Card playoff: SEATTLE 13, L.A. Raiders 7
Divisional playoffs: MIAMI 31, Seattle 10;
    Pittsburgh 24, DENVER 17
AFC Championship: MIAMI 45, Pittsburgh 28
Wild Card playoff: N.Y. Giants 16, L.A. RAMS 13
Divisional playoffs: SAN FRANCISCO 21, N.Y. Giants 10;
    Chicago 23, WASHINGTON 19
NFC Championship: SAN FRANCISCO 23, Chicago 0
Super Bowl XIX: San Francisco (NFC) 38, Miami (AFC) 16,
    at Stanford Stadium, Stanford, California

1983

AMERICAN CONFERENCE
Eastern Division

	W	L	T	Pct.	Pts.	OP
Miami	12	4	0	.750	389	250
New England	8	8	0	.500	274	289
Buffalo	8	8	0	.500	283	351
Baltimore	7	9	0	.438	264	354
N.Y. Jets	7	9	0	.438	313	331

Central Division

	W	L	T	Pct.	Pts.	OP
Pittsburgh	10	6	0	.625	355	303
Cleveland	9	7	0	.563	356	342
Cincinnati	7	9	0	.438	346	302
Houston	2	14	0	.125	288	460

Western Division

	W	L	T	Pct.	Pts.	OP
L.A. Raiders#	12	4	0	.750	442	338
Seattle*	9	7	0	.563	403	397
Denver*	9	7	0	.563	302	327
San Diego	6	10	0	.375	358	462
Kansas City	6	10	0	.375	386	367

NATIONAL CONFERENCE
Eastern Division

	W	L	T	Pct.	Pts.	OP
Washington#	14	2	0	.875	541	332
Dallas*	12	4	0	.750	479	360
St. Louis	8	7	1	.531	374	428
Philadelphia	5	11	0	.313	233	322
N.Y. Giants	3	12	1	.219	267	347

Central Division

	W	L	T	Pct.	Pts.	OP
Detroit	9	7	0	.563	347	286
Green Bay	8	8	0	.500	429	439
Chicago	8	8	0	.500	311	301
Minnesota	8	8	0	.500	316	348
Tampa Bay	2	14	0	.125	241	380

Western Division

	W	L	T	Pct.	Pts.	OP
San Francisco	10	6	0	.625	432	293
L.A. Rams*	9	7	0	.563	361	344
New Orleans	8	8	0	.500	319	337
Atlanta	7	9	0	.438	370	389

*Wild Card qualifier for playoffs; #Top playoff seed in conference
L.A. Raiders were top playoff seed ahead of Miami based on head-to-head victory (1-0). Seattle was first Wild Card ahead of Denver based on better division record (5-3 to Broncos' 3-5) after Cleveland was eliminated from three-way tie based on losing head-to-head to both Seattle and Denver. Seattle did not play the L.A. Raiders in the divisional playoffs because, from 1970-1989, two teams from the same division could not meet prior to the conference championship game. New England finished ahead of Buffalo based on head-to-head sweep (2-0). Baltimore finished ahead of N.Y. Jets based on better conference record (5-9 to Jets' 4-8). San Diego finished ahead of Kansas City based on head-to-head sweep (2-0). Green Bay finished ahead of Chicago based on better record against common opponents (4-4 to Bears' 3-5) after Minnesota was eliminated from three-way tie based on conference record (Chicago 7-7 and Green Bay 6-6 to Vikings' 4-8).
Wild Card playoff: SEATTLE 31, Denver 7
Divisional playoffs: Seattle 27, MIAMI 20;
    L.A. RAIDERS 38, Pittsburgh 10
AFC Championship: L.A. RAIDERS 30, Seattle 14
Wild Card playoff: L.A. Rams 24, DALLAS 17
Divisional playoffs: SAN FRANCISCO 24, Detroit 23;
    WASHINGTON 51, L.A. Rams 7
NFC Championship: WASHINGTON 24, San Francisco 21
Super Bowl XVIII: L.A. Raiders (AFC) 38, Washington (NFC) 9,
    at Tampa Stadium, Tampa, Florida

1982

AMERICAN CONFERENCE

	W	L	T	Pct.	Pts.	OP
L.A. Raiders#	8	1	0	.889	260	200
Miami	7	2	0	.778	198	131
Cincinnati	7	2	0	.778	232	177
Pittsburgh	6	3	0	.667	204	146
San Diego	6	3	0	.667	288	221
N.Y. Jets	6	3	0	.667	245	166
New England	5	4	0	.556	143	157
Cleveland	4	5	0	.444	140	182
Buffalo	4	5	0	.444	150	154
Seattle	4	5	0	.444	127	147
Kansas City	3	6	0	.333	176	184
Denver	2	7	0	.222	148	226
Houston	1	8	0	.111	136	245
Baltimore	0	8	1	.056	113	236

NATIONAL CONFERENCE

	W	L	T	Pct.	Pts.	OP
Washington#	8	1	0	.889	190	128
Dallas	6	3	0	.667	226	145
Green Bay	5	3	1	.611	226	169
Minnesota	5	4	0	.556	187	198
Atlanta	5	4	0	.556	183	199
St. Louis	5	4	0	.556	135	170
Tampa Bay	5	4	0	.556	158	178
Detroit	4	5	0	.444	181	176
New Orleans	4	5	0	.444	129	160
N.Y. Giants	4	5	0	.444	164	160
San Francisco	3	6	0	.333	209	206
Chicago	3	6	0	.333	141	174
Philadelphia	3	6	0	.333	191	195
L.A. Rams	2	7	0	.222	200	250

As the result of a 57-day players' strike, the 1982 NFL regular season schedule was reduced from 16 weeks to 9. At the conclusion of the regular season, the NFL conducted a 16-team postseason Super Bowl Tournament. Eight teams from each conference were seeded 1-8 based on their records during the season.

#Top playoff seed in conference

Miami finished ahead of Cincinnati based on better conference record (6-1 to Bengals' 6-2). Pittsburgh finished ahead of San Diego based on better record against common opponents (3-1 to Chargers' 2-1) after N.Y. Jets were eliminated from three-way tie based on conference record (Pittsburgh and San Diego 5-3 to Jets' 2-3). Cleveland finished ahead of Buffalo and Seattle based on better conference record (4-3 to Bills' 3-3 to Seahawks' 3-5). Buffalo finished ahead of Seattle based on better conference record (3-3 to Seahawks' 3-5). Minnesota (4-1), Atlanta (4-3), St. Louis (5-4), Tampa Bay (3-3) seeds were determined by best won-lost record in conference games. Detroit finished ahead of New Orleans and the N.Y. Giants based on best conference record (4-4 to Saints' 3-5 to Giants' 3-5). New Orleans finished ahead of N.Y. Giants based on better record against common opponents (1-3 to Giants' 0-4). San Francisco finished ahead of Chicago, and Chicago finished ahead of Philadelphia, based on conference record (49ers' 2-3 to Bears' 2-5 to Eagles' 1-5).

First round playoff: MIAMI 28, New England 13;
   L.A. RAIDERS 27, Cleveland 10;
   N.Y. Jets 44, CINCINNATI 17;
   San Diego 31, PITTSBURGH 28
Second round playoff: N.Y. Jets 17, L.A. RAIDERS 14;
   MIAMI 34, San Diego 13
AFC Championship: MIAMI 14, N.Y. Jets 0
First round playoff: WASHINGTON 31, Detroit 7;
   GREEN BAY 41, St. Louis 16;
   MINNESOTA 30, Atlanta 24;
   DALLAS 30, Tampa Bay 17
Second round playoff: WASHINGTON 21, Minnesota 7;
   DALLAS 37, Green Bay 26
NFC Championship: WASHINGTON 31, Dallas 17
Super Bowl XVII: Washington (NFC) 27, Miami (AFC) 17,
   at Rose Bowl, Pasadena, California

1981

AMERICAN CONFERENCE

Eastern Division

	W	L	T	Pct.	Pts.	OP
Miami	11	4	1	.719	345	275
N.Y. Jets*	10	5	1	.656	355	287
Buffalo*	10	6	0	.625	311	276
Baltimore	2	14	0	.125	259	533
New England	2	14	0	.125	322	370

Central Division

	W	L	T	Pct.	Pts.	OP
Cincinnati#	12	4	0	.750	421	304
Pittsburgh	8	8	0	.500	356	297
Houston	7	9	0	.438	281	355
Cleveland	5	11	0	.313	276	375

Western Division

	W	L	T	Pct.	Pts.	OP
San Diego	10	6	0	.625	478	390
Denver	10	6	0	.625	321	289
Kansas City	9	7	0	.563	343	290
Oakland	7	9	0	.438	273	343
Seattle	6	10	0	.375	322	388

NATIONAL CONFERENCE

Eastern Division

	W	L	T	Pct.	Pts.	OP
Dallas	12	4	0	.750	367	277
Philadelphia*	10	6	0	.625	368	221
N.Y. Giants*	9	7	0	.563	295	257
Washington	8	8	0	.500	347	349
St. Louis	7	9	0	.438	315	408

Central Division

	W	L	T	Pct.	Pts.	OP
Tampa Bay	9	7	0	.563	315	268
Detroit	8	8	0	.500	397	322
Green Bay	8	8	0	.500	324	361
Minnesota	7	9	0	.438	325	369
Chicago	6	10	0	.375	253	324

Western Division

	W	L	T	Pct.	Pts.	OP
San Francisco#	13	3	0	.813	357	250
Atlanta	7	9	0	.438	426	355
Los Angeles	6	10	0	.375	303	351
New Orleans	4	12	0	.250	207	378

*Wild Card qualifier for playoffs; //Top playoff seed in conference

Baltimore finished ahead of New England based on head-to-head sweep (2-0). San Diego finished ahead of Denver based on better division record (6-2 to Broncos' 5-3). Buffalo was second Wild Card based on head-to-head victory over Denver (1-0). Detroit finished ahead of Green Bay based on better record against common opponents (4-4 to Packers' 3-5).

Wild Card playoff: Buffalo 31, N.Y. JETS 27
Divisional playoffs: San Diego 41, MIAMI 38 (OT);
   CINCINNATI 28, Buffalo 21
AFC Championship: CINCINNATI 27, San Diego 7
Wild Card playoff: N.Y. Giants 27, PHILADELPHIA 21
Divisional playoffs: DALLAS 38, Tampa Bay 0;
   SAN FRANCISCO 38, N.Y. Giants 24
NFC Championship: SAN FRANCISCO 28, Dallas 27
Super Bowl XVI: San Francisco (NFC) 26, Cincinnati (AFC) 21,
   at Silverdome, Pontiac, Michigan

1980

AMERICAN CONFERENCE

Eastern Division

	W	L	T	Pct.	Pts.	OP
Buffalo	11	5	0	.688	320	260
New England	10	6	0	.625	441	325
Miami	8	8	0	.500	266	305
Baltimore	7	9	0	.438	355	387
N.Y. Jets	4	12	0	.250	302	395

Central Division

	W	L	T	Pct.	Pts.	OP
Cleveland	11	5	0	.688	357	310
Houston*	11	5	0	.688	295	251
Pittsburgh	9	7	0	.563	352	313
Cincinnati	6	10	0	.375	244	312

Western Division

	W	L	T	Pct.	Pts.	OP
San Diego#	11	5	0	.688	418	327
Oakland*	11	5	0	.688	364	306
Kansas City	8	8	0	.500	319	336
Denver	8	8	0	.500	310	323
Seattle	4	12	0	.250	291	408

NATIONAL CONFERENCE

Eastern Division

	W	L	T	Pct.	Pts.	OP
Philadelphia	12	4	0	.750	384	222
Dallas*	12	4	0	.750	454	311
Washington	6	10	0	.375	261	293
St. Louis	5	11	0	.313	299	350
N.Y. Giants	4	12	0	.250	249	425

Central Division

	W	L	T	Pct.	Pts.	OP
Minnesota	9	7	0	.563	317	308
Detroit	9	7	0	.563	334	272
Chicago	7	9	0	.438	304	264
Tampa Bay	5	10	1	.344	271	341
Green Bay	5	10	1	.344	231	371

Western Division

	W	L	T	Pct.	Pts.	OP
Atlanta#	12	4	0	.750	405	272
Los Angeles*	11	5	0	.688	424	289
San Francisco	6	10	0	.375	320	415
New Orleans	1	15	0	.063	291	487

*Wild Card qualifier for playoffs; #Top playoff seed in conference
San Diego was top playoff seed based on better conference record than Cleveland and Buffalo (9-3 to Browns' 8-4 and Bills' 8-4). Cleveland was second playoff seed based on better record against common opponents (5-2 to Bills' 5-3). Cleveland finished ahead of Houston based on better conference record (8-4 to Oilers' 7-5). Oakland was first Wild Card based on better conference record than Houston (9-3 to Oilers' 7-5). San Diego finished ahead of Oakland based on better net points in division games (plus 60 net points to Raiders' plus 37). Oakland did not play San Diego in the divisional playoffs because, from 1970-1989, two teams from the same division could not meet prior to the conference championship game. Kansas City finished ahead of Denver based on head-to-head sweep (2-0). Atlanta was top playoff seed based on head-to-head victory over Philadelphia (1-0). Philadelphia finished ahead of Dallas based on better net points in division games (plus 84 net points to Cowboys' plus 50). Minnesota finished ahead of Detroit based on better conference record (8-4 to Lions' 9-5). Tampa Bay finished ahead of Green Bay based on better head-to-head record (1-0-1 to Packers' 0-1-1).
Wild Card playoff: OAKLAND 27, Houston 7
Divisional playoffs: SAN DIEGO 20, Buffalo 14;
  Oakland 14, CLEVELAND 12
AFC Championship: Oakland 34, SAN DIEGO 27
Wild Card playoff: DALLAS 34, Los Angeles 13
Divisional playoffs: PHILADELPHIA 31, Minnesota 16;
  Dallas 30, ATLANTA 27
NFC Championship: PHILADELPHIA 20, Dallas 7
Super Bowl XV: Oakland (AFC) 27, Philadelphia (NFC) 10,
  at Louisiana Superdome, New Orleans, Louisiana

1979

AMERICAN CONFERENCE

Eastern Division

	W	L	T	Pct.	Pts.	OP
Miami	10	6	0	.625	341	257
New England	9	7	0	.563	411	326
N.Y. Jets	8	8	0	.500	337	383
Buffalo	7	9	0	.438	268	279
Baltimore	5	11	0	.313	271	351

Central Division

	W	L	T	Pct.	Pts.	OP
Pittsburgh	12	4	0	.750	416	262
Houston*	11	5	0	.688	362	331
Cleveland	9	7	0	.563	359	352
Cincinnati	4	12	0	.250	337	421

Western Division

	W	L	T	Pct.	Pts.	OP
San Diego#	12	4	0	.750	411	246
Denver*	10	6	0	.625	289	262
Seattle	9	7	0	.563	378	372
Oakland	9	7	0	.563	365	337
Kansas City	7	9	0	.438	238	262

NATIONAL CONFERENCE

Eastern Division

	W	L	T	Pct.	Pts.	OP
Dallas#	11	5	0	.688	371	313
Philadelphia*	11	5	0	.688	339	282
Washington	10	6	0	.625	348	295
N.Y. Giants	6	10	0	.375	237	323
St. Louis	5	11	0	.313	307	358

Central Division

	W	L	T	Pct.	Pts.	OP
Tampa Bay	10	6	0	.625	273	237
Chicago*	10	6	0	.625	306	249
Minnesota	7	9	0	.438	259	337
Green Bay	5	11	0	.313	246	316
Detroit	2	14	0	.125	219	365

Western Division

	W	L	T	Pct.	Pts.	OP
Los Angeles	9	7	0	.563	323	309
New Orleans	8	8	0	.500	370	360
Atlanta	6	10	0	.375	300	388
San Francisco	2	14	0	.125	308	416

*Wild Card qualifier for playoffs; #Top playoff seed in conference
San Diego was top playoff seed based on head-to-head victory over Pittsburgh (1-0). Seattle finished ahead of Oakland based on head-to-head sweep (2-0). Dallas finished ahead of Philadelphia based on better conference record (10-2 to Eagles' 9-3). Philadelphia did not play Dallas in the divisional playoffs because, from 1970-1989, two teams from the same division could not meet prior to the conference championship game. Tampa Bay finished ahead of Chicago based on a better division record (6-2 to Bears' 5-3). Chicago was second Wild Card ahead of Washington based on better net points in all games (57 to Redskins' 53).
Wild Card playoff: HOUSTON 13, Denver 7
Divisional playoffs: Houston 17, SAN DIEGO 14;
  PITTSBURGH 34, Miami 14
AFC Championship: PITTSBURGH 27, Houston 13
Wild Card playoff: PHILADELPHIA 27, Chicago 17
Divisional playoffs: TAMPA BAY 24, Philadelphia 17;
  Los Angeles 21, DALLAS 19
NFC Championship: Los Angeles 9, TAMPA BAY 0
Super Bowl XIV: Pittsburgh (AFC) 31, Los Angeles (NFC) 19,
  at Rose Bowl, Pasadena, California

1978

AMERICAN CONFERENCE
Eastern Division

	W	L	T	Pct.	Pts.	OP
New England	11	5	0	.688	358	286
Miami*	11	5	0	.688	372	254
N.Y. Jets	8	8	0	.500	359	364
Buffalo	5	11	0	.313	302	354
Baltimore	5	11	0	.313	239	421

Central Division

	W	L	T	Pct.	Pts.	OP
Pittsburgh#	14	2	0	.875	356	195
Houston*	10	6	0	.625	283	298
Cleveland	8	8	0	.500	334	356
Cincinnati	4	12	0	.250	252	284

Western Division

	W	L	T	Pct.	Pts.	OP
Denver	10	6	0	.625	282	198
Oakland	9	7	0	.563	311	283
Seattle	9	7	0	.563	345	358
San Diego	9	7	0	.563	355	309
Kansas City	4	12	0	.250	243	327

NATIONAL CONFERENCE
Eastern Division

	W	L	T	Pct.	Pts.	OP
Dallas	12	4	0	.750	384	208
Philadelphia*	9	7	0	.563	270	250
Washington	8	8	0	.500	273	283
St. Louis	6	10	0	.375	248	296
N.Y. Giants	6	10	0	.375	264	298

Central Division

	W	L	T	Pct.	Pts.	OP
Minnesota	8	7	1	.531	294	306
Green Bay	8	7	1	.531	249	269
Detroit	7	9	0	.438	290	300
Chicago	7	9	0	.438	253	274
Tampa Bay	5	11	0	.313	241	259

Western Division

	W	L	T	Pct.	Pts.	OP
Los Angeles#	12	4	0	.750	316	245
Atlanta*	9	7	0	.563	240	290
New Orleans	7	9	0	.438	281	298
San Francisco	2	14	0	.125	219	350

*Wild Card qualifier for playoffs; #Top playoff seed in conference
New England finished ahead of Miami based on better division
record (6-2 to Dolphins' 5-3). Buffalo finished ahead of Baltimore
based on head-to-head sweep (2-0). Oakland finished ahead of
Seattle and San Diego based on better record against common
opponents (6-2 to Seahawks' 5-3 and Chargers' 4-4). Atlanta
was first Wild Card ahead of Philadelphia based on better record
against common opponents (5-2 to Eagles' 5-3). Houston did not
play Pittsburgh, and Atlanta did not play Los Angeles in the
divisional playoffs because, from 1970-1989, two teams from the
same division could not meet prior to the conference
championship game. Los Angeles was top playoff seed based on
head-to-head victory over Dallas (1-0). St. Louis finished ahead
of N.Y. Giants based on better division record (3-5 to Giants'
2-6). Minnesota finished ahead of Green Bay based on better
head-to-head record (1-0-1). Detroit finished ahead of Chicago
based on better division record (4-4 to Bears' 3-5).
Wild Card playoff: Houston 17, MIAMI 9
Divisional playoffs: Houston 31, NEW ENGLAND 14;
   PITTSBURGH 33, Denver 10
AFC Championship: PITTSBURGH 34, Houston 5
Wild Card playoff: ATLANTA 14, Philadelphia 13
Divisional playoffs: DALLAS 27, Atlanta 20;
   LOS ANGELES 34, Minnesota 10
NFC Championship: Dallas 28, LOS ANGELES 0
Super Bowl XIII: Pittsburgh (AFC) 35, Dallas (NFC) 31,
   at Orange Bowl, Miami, Florida

1977

AMERICAN CONFERENCE
Eastern Division

	W	L	T	Pct.	Pts.	OP
Baltimore	10	4	0	.714	295	221
Miami	10	4	0	.714	313	197
New England	9	5	0	.643	278	217
N.Y. Jets	3	11	0	.214	191	300
Buffalo	3	11	0	.214	160	313

Central Division

	W	L	T	Pct.	Pts.	OP
Pittsburgh	9	5	0	.643	283	243
Houston	8	6	0	.571	299	230
Cincinnati	8	6	0	.571	238	235
Cleveland	6	8	0	.429	269	267

Western Division

	W	L	T	Pct.	Pts.	OP
Denver#	12	2	0	.857	274	148
Oakland*	11	3	0	.786	351	230
San Diego	7	7	0	.500	222	205
Seattle	5	9	0	.357	282	373
Kansas City	2	12	0	.143	225	349

NATIONAL CONFERENCE
Eastern Division

	W	L	T	Pct.	Pts.	OP
Dallas#	12	2	0	.857	345	212
Washington	9	5	0	.643	196	189
St. Louis	7	7	0	.500	272	287
Philadelphia	5	9	0	.357	220	207
N.Y. Giants	5	9	0	.357	181	265

Central Division

	W	L	T	Pct.	Pts.	OP
Minnesota	9	5	0	.643	231	227
Chicago*	9	5	0	.643	255	253
Detroit	6	8	0	.429	183	252
Green Bay	4	10	0	.286	134	219
Tampa Bay	2	12	0	.143	103	223

Western Division

	W	L	T	Pct.	Pts.	OP
Los Angeles	10	4	0	.714	302	146
Atlanta	7	7	0	.500	179	129
San Francisco	5	9	0	.357	220	260
New Orleans	3	11	0	.214	232	336

*Wild Card qualifier for playoffs; #Top playoff seed in conference
Baltimore finished ahead of Miami based on better conference
record (9-3 to Dolphins' 8-4). N.Y. Jets finished ahead of Buffalo
based on better point-differential in head-to-head competition
(1 point). Houston finished ahead of Cincinnati based on better
point-differential in head-to-head competition (2 points). Oakland
did not play Denver in the divisional playoffs because, from
1970-1989, two teams from the same division could not meet
prior to the conference championship game. Minnesota finished
ahead of Chicago based on better point-differential in head-to-
head competition (3 points). Chicago won Wild Card ahead of
Washington based on better net points in conference games
(48 to Redskins' 4). Philadelphia finished ahead of N.Y. Giants
based on head-to-head sweep (2-0).
Divisional playoffs: DENVER 34, Pittsburgh 21;
   Oakland 37, BALTIMORE 31 (OT)
AFC Championship: DENVER 20, Oakland 17
Divisional playoffs: DALLAS 37, Chicago 7;
   Minnesota 14, LOS ANGELES 7
NFC Championship: DALLAS 23, Minnesota 6
Super Bowl XII: Dallas (NFC) 27, Denver (AFC) 10,
   at Louisiana Superdome, New Orleans, Louisiana

1976

AMERICAN CONFERENCE

Eastern Division

	W	L	T	Pct.	Pts.	OP
Baltimore	11	3	0	.786	417	246
New England*	11	3	0	.786	376	236
Miami	6	8	0	.429	263	264
N.Y. Jets	3	11	0	.214	169	383
Buffalo	2	12	0	.143	245	363

Central Division

	W	L	T	Pct.	Pts.	OP
Pittsburgh	10	4	0	.714	342	138
Cincinnati	10	4	0	.714	335	210
Cleveland	9	5	0	.643	267	287
Houston	5	9	0	.357	222	273

Western Division

	W	L	T	Pct.	Pts.	OP
Oakland#	13	1	0	.929	350	237
Denver	9	5	0	.643	315	206
San Diego	6	8	0	.429	248	285
Kansas City	5	9	0	.357	290	376
Tampa Bay	0	14	0	.000	125	412

NATIONAL CONFERENCE

Eastern Division

	W	L	T	Pct.	Pts.	OP
Dallas	11	3	0	.786	296	194
Washington*	10	4	0	.714	291	217
St. Louis	10	4	0	.714	309	267
Philadelphia	4	10	0	.286	165	286
N.Y. Giants	3	11	0	.214	170	250

Central Division

	W	L	T	Pct.	Pts.	OP
Minnesota#	11	2	1	.821	305	176
Chicago	7	7	0	.500	253	216
Detroit	6	8	0	.429	262	220
Green Bay	5	9	0	.357	218	299

Western Division

	W	L	T	Pct.	Pts.	OP
Los Angeles	10	3	1	.750	351	190
San Francisco	8	6	0	.571	270	190
New Orleans	4	10	0	.286	253	346
Atlanta	4	10	0	.286	172	312
Seattle	2	12	0	.143	229	429

*Wild Card qualifier for playoffs; #Top playoff seed in conference
Baltimore finished ahead of New England based on better division record (7-1 to Patriots' 6-2). Pittsburgh finished ahead of Cincinnati based on head-to-head sweep (2-0). Washington finished ahead of St. Louis based on head-to-head sweep (2-0). New Orleans finished ahead of Atlanta based on better point-differential in head-to-head competition (27 points).
Divisional playoffs: OAKLAND 24, New England 21; Pittsburgh 40, BALTIMORE 14
AFC Championship: OAKLAND 24, Pittsburgh 7
Divisional playoffs: MINNESOTA 35, Washington 20; Los Angeles 14, DALLAS 12
NFC Championship: MINNESOTA 24, Los Angeles 13
Super Bowl XI: Oakland (AFC) 32, Minnesota (NFC) 14, at Rose Bowl, Pasadena, California

1975

AMERICAN CONFERENCE

Eastern Division

	W	L	T	Pct.	Pts.	OP
Baltimore	10	4	0	.714	395	269
Miami	10	4	0	.714	357	222
Buffalo	8	6	0	.571	420	355
N.Y. Jets	3	11	0	.214	258	433
New England	3	11	0	.214	258	358

Central Division

	W	L	T	Pct.	Pts.	OP
Pittsburgh#	12	2	0	.857	373	162
Cincinnati*	11	3	0	.786	340	246
Houston	10	4	0	.714	293	226
Cleveland	3	11	0	.214	218	372

Western Division

	W	L	T	Pct.	Pts.	OP
Oakland	11	3	0	.786	375	255
Denver	6	8	0	.429	254	307
Kansas City	5	9	0	.357	282	341
San Diego	2	12	0	.143	189	345

NATIONAL CONFERENCE

Eastern Division

	W	L	T	Pct.	Pts.	OP
St. Louis	11	3	0	.786	356	276
Dallas*	10	4	0	.714	350	268
Washington	8	6	0	.571	325	276
N.Y. Giants	5	9	0	.357	216	306
Philadelphia	4	10	0	.286	225	302

Central Division

	W	L	T	Pct.	Pts.	OP
Minnesota#	12	2	0	.857	377	180
Detroit	7	7	0	.500	245	262
Chicago	4	10	0	.286	191	379
Green Bay	4	10	0	.286	226	285

Western Division

	W	L	T	Pct.	Pts.	OP
Los Angeles	12	2	0	.857	312	135
San Francisco	5	9	0	.357	255	286
Atlanta	4	10	0	.286	240	289
New Orleans	2	12	0	.143	165	360

*Wild Card qualifier for playoffs; #Top playoff seed in conference
Baltimore finished ahead of Miami based on head-to-head sweep (2-0). Cincinnati did not play Pittsburgh in the divisional playoffs because, from 1970-1989, two teams from the same division could not meet prior to the conference championship game.
N.Y. Jets finished ahead of New England based on head-to-head sweep (2-0). Minnesota was top playoff seed based on better Point Rating system than Los Angeles (3 to 6). Chicago finished ahead of Green Bay based on better division record (2-4 to Bears' 1-5).
Divisional playoffs: PITTSBURGH 28, Baltimore 10; OAKLAND 31, Cincinnati 28
AFC Championship: PITTSBURGH 16, Oakland 10
Divisional playoffs: LOS ANGELES 35, St. Louis 23; Dallas 17, MINNESOTA 14
NFC Championship: Dallas 37, LOS ANGELES 7
Super Bowl X: Pittsburgh (AFC) 21, Dallas (NFC) 17, at Orange Bowl, Miami, Florida

1974

AMERICAN CONFERENCE

Eastern Division

	W	L	T	Pct.	Pts.	OP
Miami	11	3	0	.786	327	216
Buffalo*	9	5	0	.643	264	244
N.Y. Jets	7	7	0	.500	279	300
New England	7	7	0	.500	348	289
Baltimore	2	12	0	.143	190	329

Central Division

	W	L	T	Pct.	Pts.	OP
Pittsburgh	10	3	1	.750	305	189
Houston	7	7	0	.500	236	282
Cincinnati	7	7	0	.500	283	259
Cleveland	4	10	0	.286	251	344

Western Division

	W	L	T	Pct.	Pts.	OP
Oakland	12	2	0	.857	355	228
Denver	7	6	1	.536	302	294
Kansas City	5	9	0	.357	233	293
San Diego	5	9	0	.357	212	285

NATIONAL CONFERENCE

Eastern Division

	W	L	T	Pct.	Pts.	OP
St. Louis	10	4	0	.714	285	218
Washington*	10	4	0	.714	320	196
Dallas	8	6	0	.571	297	235
Philadelphia	7	7	0	.500	242	217
N.Y. Giants	2	12	0	.143	195	299

Central Division

	W	L	T	Pct.	Pts.	OP
Minnesota	10	4	0	.714	310	195
Detroit	7	7	0	.500	256	270
Green Bay	6	8	0	.429	210	206
Chicago	4	10	0	.286	152	279

Western Division

	W	L	T	Pct.	Pts.	OP
Los Angeles	10	4	0	.714	263	181
San Francisco	6	8	0	.429	226	236
New Orleans	5	9	0	.357	166	263
Atlanta	3	11	0	.214	111	271

*Wild Card qualifier for playoffs

N.Y. Jets finished ahead of New England based on better conference record (5-6 to Patriots' 4-7). Houston finished ahead of Cincinnati based on head-to-head sweep (2-0). Kansas City finished ahead of San Diego based on better point-differential in head-to-head competition (3 points). St. Louis finished ahead of Washington based on head-to-head sweep (2-0).

Divisional playoffs: OAKLAND 28, Miami 26;
   PITTSBURGH 32, Buffalo 14
AFC Championship: Pittsburgh 24, OAKLAND 13
Divisional playoffs: MINNESOTA 30, St. Louis 14;
   LOS ANGELES 19, Washington 10
NFC Championship: MINNESOTA 14, Los Angeles 10
Super Bowl IX: Pittsburgh (AFC) 16, Minnesota (NFC) 6,
   at Tulane Stadium, New Orleans, Louisiana

From 1933-1974, sites for league/conference championship games alternated by division.

1973

AMERICAN CONFERENCE

Eastern Division

	W	L	T	Pct.	Pts.	OP
Miami	12	2	0	.857	343	150
Buffalo	9	5	0	.643	259	230
New England	5	9	0	.357	258	300
N.Y. Jets	4	10	0	.286	240	306
Baltimore	4	10	0	.286	226	341

Central Division

	W	L	T	Pct.	Pts.	OP
Cincinnati	10	4	0	.714	286	231
Pittsburgh*	10	4	0	.714	347	210
Cleveland	7	5	2	.571	234	255
Houston	1	13	0	.071	199	447

Western Division

	W	L	T	Pct.	Pts.	OP
Oakland	9	4	1	.679	292	175
Kansas City	7	5	2	.571	231	192
Denver	7	5	2	.571	354	296
San Diego	2	11	1	.179	188	386

NATIONAL CONFERENCE

Eastern Division

	W	L	T	Pct.	Pts.	OP
Dallas	10	4	0	.714	382	203
Washington*	10	4	0	.714	325	198
Philadelphia	5	8	1	.393	310	393
St. Louis	4	9	1	.321	286	365
N.Y. Giants	2	11	1	.179	226	362

Central Division

	W	L	T	Pct.	Pts.	OP
Minnesota	12	2	0	.857	296	168
Detroit	6	7	1	.464	271	247
Green Bay	5	7	2	.429	202	259
Chicago	3	11	0	.214	195	334

Western Division

	W	L	T	Pct.	Pts.	OP
Los Angeles	12	2	0	.857	388	178
Atlanta	9	5	0	.643	318	224
San Francisco	5	9	0	.357	262	319
New Orleans	5	9	0	.357	163	312

*Wild Card qualifier for playoffs

Cincinnati finished ahead of Pittsburgh based on better conference record (8-3 to Steelers' 7-4). N.Y. Jets finished ahead of Baltimore based on head-to-head sweep (2-0). Kansas City finished ahead of Denver based on better division record (4-2 to Broncos' 3-2-1). Dallas finished ahead of Washington based on better point differential in head-to-head games (13 points). San Francisco finished ahead of New Orleans based on better division record (2-4 to Saints' 1-5).

Divisional playoffs: OAKLAND 33, Pittsburgh 14;
   MIAMI 34, Cincinnati 16
AFC Championship: MIAMI 27, Oakland 10
Divisional playoffs: MINNESOTA 27, Washington 20;
   DALLAS 27, Los Angeles 16
NFC Championship: Minnesota 27, DALLAS 10
Super Bowl VIII: Miami (AFC) 24, Minnesota (NFC) 7,
   at Rice Stadium, Houston, Texas

1972

AMERICAN CONFERENCE

Eastern Division

	W	L	T	Pct.	Pts.	OP
Miami	14	0	0	1.000	385	171
N.Y. Jets	7	7	0	.500	367	324
Baltimore	5	9	0	.357	235	252
Buffalo	4	9	1	.321	257	377
New England	3	11	0	.214	192	446

Central Division

	W	L	T	Pct.	Pts.	OP
Pittsburgh	11	3	0	.786	343	175
Cleveland*	10	4	0	.714	268	249
Cincinnati	8	6	0	.571	299	229
Houston	1	13	0	.071	164	380

Western Division

	W	L	T	Pct.	Pts.	OP
Oakland	10	3	1	.750	365	248
Kansas City	8	6	0	.571	287	254
Denver	5	9	0	.357	325	350
San Diego	4	9	1	.321	264	344

NATIONAL CONFERENCE

Eastern Division

	W	L	T	Pct.	Pts.	OP
Washington	11	3	0	.786	336	218
Dallas*	10	4	0	.714	319	240
N.Y. Giants	8	6	0	.571	331	247
St. Louis	4	9	1	.321	193	303
Philadelphia	2	11	1	.179	145	352

Central Division

	W	L	T	Pct.	Pts.	OP
Green Bay	10	4	0	.714	304	226
Detroit	8	5	1	.607	339	290
Minnesota	7	7	0	.500	301	252
Chicago	4	9	1	.321	225	275

Western Division

	W	L	T	Pct.	Pts.	OP
San Francisco	8	5	1	.607	353	249
Atlanta	7	7	0	.500	269	274
Los Angeles	6	7	1	.464	291	286
New Orleans	2	11	1	.179	215	361

Wild Card qualifier for playoffs

Dallas did not play Washington in the divisional playoffs because, from 1970-1989, two teams from the same division could not meet prior to the conference championship game.

Divisional playoffs: PITTSBURGH 13, Oakland 7; MIAMI 20, Cleveland 14

AFC Championship: Miami 21, PITTSBURGH 17

Divisional playoffs: Dallas 30, SAN FRANCISCO 28; WASHINGTON 16, Green Bay 3

NFC Championship: WASHINGTON 26, Dallas 3

Super Bowl VII: Miami (AFC) 14, Washington (NFC) 7, at Memorial Coliseum, Los Angeles, California

1971

AMERICAN CONFERENCE

Eastern Division

	W	L	T	Pct.	Pts.	OP
Miami	10	3	1	.769	315	174
Baltimore*	10	4	0	.714	313	140
New England	6	8	0	.429	238	325
N.Y. Jets	6	8	0	.429	212	299
Buffalo	1	13	0	.071	184	394

Central Division

	W	L	T	Pct.	Pts.	OP
Cleveland	9	5	0	.643	285	273
Pittsburgh	6	8	0	.429	246	292
Houston	4	9	1	.308	251	330
Cincinnati	4	10	0	.286	284	265

Western Division

	W	L	T	Pct.	Pts.	OP
Kansas City	10	3	1	.769	302	208
Oakland	8	4	2	.667	344	278
San Diego	6	8	0	.429	311	341
Denver	4	9	1	.308	203	275

NATIONAL CONFERENCE

Eastern Division

	W	L	T	Pct.	Pts.	OP
Dallas	11	3	0	.786	406	222
Washington*	9	4	1	.692	276	190
Philadelphia	6	7	1	.462	221	302
St. Louis	4	9	1	.308	231	279
N.Y. Giants	4	10	0	.286	228	362

Central Division

	W	L	T	Pct.	Pts.	OP
Minnesota	11	3	0	.786	245	139
Detroit	7	6	1	.538	341	286
Chicago	6	8	0	.429	185	276
Green Bay	4	8	2	.333	274	298

Western Division

	W	L	T	Pct.	Pts.	OP
San Francisco	9	5	0	.643	300	216
Los Angeles	8	5	1	.615	313	260
Atlanta	7	6	1	.538	274	277
New Orleans	4	8	2	.333	266	347

Wild Card qualifier for playoffs

New England finished ahead of N.Y. Jets based on better point-differential in head-to-head competition (13 points).

Divisional playoffs: Miami 27, KANSAS CITY 24 (OT); Baltimore 20, CLEVELAND 3

AFC Championship: MIAMI 21, Baltimore 0

Divisional playoffs: Dallas 20, MINNESOTA 12; SAN FRANCISCO 24, Washington 20

NFC Championship: DALLAS 14, San Francisco 3

Super Bowl VI: Dallas (NFC) 24, Miami (AFC) 3, at Tulane Stadium, New Orleans, Louisiana

From 1920-1971, tie games were not included in winning percentage.

1970

AMERICAN CONFERENCE
Eastern Division

	W	L	T	Pct.	Pts.	OP
Baltimore	11	2	1	.846	321	234
Miami*	10	4	0	.714	297	228
N.Y. Jets	4	10	0	.286	255	286
Buffalo	3	10	1	.231	204	337
Boston Patriots	2	12	0	.143	149	361

Central Division

	W	L	T	Pct.	Pts.	OP
Cincinnati	8	6	0	.571	312	255
Cleveland	7	7	0	.500	286	265
Pittsburgh	5	9	0	.357	210	272
Houston	3	10	1	.231	217	352

Western Division

	W	L	T	Pct.	Pts.	OP
Oakland	8	4	2	.667	300	293
Kansas City	7	5	2	.583	272	244
San Diego	5	6	3	.455	282	278
Denver	5	8	1	.385	253	264

NATIONAL CONFERENCE
Eastern Division

	W	L	T	Pct.	Pts.	OP
Dallas	10	4	0	.714	299	221
N.Y. Giants	9	5	0	.643	301	270
St. Louis	8	5	1	.615	325	228
Washington	6	8	0	.429	297	314
Philadelphia	3	10	1	.231	241	332

Central Division

	W	L	T	Pct.	Pts.	OP
Minnesota	12	2	0	.857	335	143
Detroit*	10	4	0	.714	347	202
Green Bay	6	8	0	.429	196	293
Chicago	6	8	0	.429	256	261

Western Division

	W	L	T	Pct.	Pts.	OP
San Francisco	10	3	1	.769	352	267
Los Angeles	9	4	1	.692	325	202
Atlanta	4	8	2	.333	206	261
New Orleans	2	11	1	.154	172	347

*Wild Card qualifier for playoffs

Miami did not play Baltimore, and Detroit did not play Minnesota, in the divisional playoffs because, from 1970-1989, two teams from the same division could not meet prior to the conference championship game. Green Bay finished ahead of Chicago based on better division record (2-4 to Bears' 1-5).

Divisional playoffs: BALTIMORE 17, Cincinnati 0, OAKLAND 21, Miami 14
AFC Championship: BALTIMORE 27, Oakland 17
Divisional playoffs: DALLAS 5, Detroit 0; San Francisco 17, MINNESOTA 14
NFC Championship: Dallas 17, SAN FRANCISCO 10
Super Bowl V: Baltimore (AFC) 16, Dallas (NFC) 13, at Orange Bowl, Miami, Florida

1969 NFL

EASTERN CONFERENCE
Capitol Division

	W	L	T	Pct.	Pts.	OP
Dallas	11	2	1	.846	369	223
Washington	7	5	2	.583	307	319
New Orleans	5	9	0	.357	311	393
Philadelphia	4	9	1	.308	279	377

Century Division

	W	L	T	Pct.	Pts.	OP
Cleveland	10	3	1	.769	351	300
N.Y. Giants	6	8	0	.429	264	298
St. Louis	4	9	1	.308	314	389
Pittsburgh	1	13	0	.071	218	404

WESTERN CONFERENCE
Coastal Division

	W	L	T	Pct.	Pts.	OP
Los Angeles	11	3	0	.786	320	243
Baltimore	8	5	1	.615	279	268
Atlanta	6	8	0	.429	276	268
San Francisco	4	8	2	.333	277	319

Central Division

	W	L	T	Pct.	Pts.	OP
Minnesota	12	2	0	.857	379	133
Detroit	9	4	1	.692	259	188
Green Bay	8	6	0	.571	269	221
Chicago	1	13	0	.071	210	339

Conference championships: Cleveland 38, DALLAS 14; MINNESOTA 23, Los Angeles 20
NFL championship: MINNESOTA 27, Cleveland 7
Super Bowl IV: Kansas City (AFL) 23, Minnesota (NFL) 7, at Tulane Stadium, New Orleans, Louisiana

1969 AFL

EASTERN DIVISION

	W	L	T	Pct.	Pts.	OP
N.Y. Jets	10	4	0	.714	353	269
Houston	6	6	2	.500	278	279
Boston Patriots	4	10	0	.286	266	316
Buffalo	4	10	0	.286	230	359
Miami	3	10	1	.231	233	332

WESTERN DIVISION

	W	L	T	Pct.	Pts.	OP
Oakland	12	1	1	.923	377	242
Kansas City	11	3	0	.786	359	177
San Diego	8	6	0	.571	288	276
Denver	5	8	1	.385	297	344
Cincinnati	4	9	1	.308	280	367

Divisional playoffs: Kansas City 13, N.Y. JETS 6; OAKLAND 56, Houston 7
AFL championship: Kansas City 17, OAKLAND 7

1968 NFL

EASTERN CONFERENCE
Capitol Division

	W	L	T	Pct.	Pts.	OP
Dallas	12	2	0	.857	431	186
N.Y. Giants	7	7	0	.500	294	325
Washington	5	9	0	.357	249	358
Philadelphia	2	12	0	.143	202	351

Century Division

	W	L	T	Pct.	Pts.	OP
Cleveland	10	4	0	.714	394	273
St. Louis	9	4	1	.692	325	289
New Orleans	4	9	1	.308	246	327
Pittsburgh	2	11	1	.154	244	397

WESTERN CONFERENCE
Coastal Division

	W	L	T	Pct.	Pts.	OP
Baltimore	13	1	0	.929	402	144
Los Angeles	10	3	1	.769	312	200
San Francisco	7	6	1	.538	303	310
Atlanta	2	12	0	.143	170	389

Central Division

	W	L	T	Pct.	Pts.	OP
Minnesota	8	6	0	.571	282	242
Chicago	7	7	0	.500	250	333
Green Bay	6	7	1	.462	281	227
Detroit	4	8	2	.333	207	241

Conference championships: CLEVELAND 31, Dallas 20; BALTIMORE 24, Minnesota 14
NFL championship: Baltimore 34, CLEVELAND 0
Super Bowl III: N.Y. Jets (AFL) 16, Baltimore (NFL) 7, at Orange Bowl, Miami, Florida

1968 AFL

EASTERN DIVISION

	W	L	T	Pct.	Pts.	OP
N.Y. Jets	11	3	0	.786	419	280
Houston	7	7	0	.500	303	248
Miami	5	8	1	.385	276	355
Boston Patriots	4	10	0	.286	229	406
Buffalo	1	12	1	.077	199	367

WESTERN DIVISION

	W	L	T	Pct.	Pts.	OP
Oakland	12	2	0	.857	453	233
Kansas City	12	2	0	.857	371	170
San Diego	9	5	0	.643	382	310
Denver	5	9	0	.357	255	404
Cincinnati	3	11	0	.214	215	329

Western Division playoff: OAKLAND 41, Kansas City 6
AFL championship: N.Y. JETS 27, Oakland 23

1967 NFL

EASTERN CONFERENCE

Capitol Division

	W	L	T	Pct.	Pts.	OP
Dallas	9	5	0	.643	342	268
Philadelphia	6	7	1	.462	351	409
Washington	5	6	3	.455	347	353
New Orleans	3	11	0	.214	233	379

Century Division

	W	L	T	Pct.	Pts.	OP
Cleveland	9	5	0	.643	334	297
N.Y. Giants	7	7	0	.500	369	379
St. Louis	6	7	1	.462	333	356
Pittsburgh	4	9	1	.308	281	320

WESTERN CONFERENCE

Coastal Division

	W	L	T	Pct.	Pts.	OP
Los Angeles	11	1	2	.917	398	196
Baltimore	11	1	2	.917	394	198
San Francisco	7	7	0	.500	273	337
Atlanta	1	12	1	.077	175	422

Central Division

	W	L	T	Pct.	Pts.	OP
Green Bay	9	4	1	.692	332	209
Chicago	7	6	1	.538	239	218
Detroit	5	7	2	.417	260	259
Minnesota	3	8	3	.273	233	294

Los Angeles finished ahead of Baltimore based on better point differential in head-to-head games (net 24 points).
Conference championships: DALLAS 52, Cleveland 14; GREEN BAY 28, Los Angeles 7
NFL championship: GREEN BAY 21, Dallas 17
Super Bowl II: Green Bay (NFL) 33, Oakland (AFL) 14, at Orange Bowl, Miami, Florida

1967 AFL

EASTERN DIVISION

	W	L	T	Pct.	Pts.	OP
Houston	9	4	1	.692	258	199
N.Y. Jets	8	5	1	.615	371	329
Buffalo	4	10	0	.286	237	285
Miami	4	10	0	.286	219	407
Boston Patriots	3	10	1	.231	280	389

WESTERN DIVISION

	W	L	T	Pct.	Pts.	OP
Oakland	13	1	0	.929	468	233
Kansas City	9	5	0	.643	408	254
San Diego	8	5	1	.615	360	352
Denver	3	11	0	.214	256	409

AFL championship: OAKLAND 40, Houston 7

1966 NFL

EASTERN CONFERENCE

	W	L	T	Pct.	Pts.	OP
Dallas	10	3	1	.769	445	239
Cleveland	9	5	0	.643	403	259
Philadelphia	9	5	0	.643	326	340
St. Louis	8	5	1	.615	264	265
Washington	7	7	0	.500	351	355
Pittsburgh	5	8	1	.385	316	347
Atlanta	3	11	0	.214	204	437
N.Y. Giants	1	12	1	.077	263	501

WESTERN CONFERENCE

	W	L	T	Pct.	Pts.	OP
Green Bay	12	2	0	.857	335	163
Baltimore	9	5	0	.643	314	226
Los Angeles	8	6	0	.571	289	212
San Francisco	6	6	2	.500	320	325
Chicago	5	7	2	.417	234	272
Detroit	4	9	1	.308	206	317
Minnesota	4	9	1	.308	292	304

NFL championship: Green Bay 34, DALLAS 27
Super Bowl I: Green Bay (NFL) 35, Kansas City (AFL) 10, at Memorial Coliseum, Los Angeles, California

1966 AFL

EASTERN DIVISION

	W	L	T	Pct.	Pts.	OP
Buffalo	9	4	1	.692	358	255
Boston Patriots	8	4	2	.677	315	283
N.Y. Jets	6	6	2	.500	322	312
Houston	3	11	0	.214	335	396
Miami	3	11	0	.214	213	362

WESTERN DIVISION

	W	L	T	Pct.	Pts.	OP
Kansas City	11	2	1	.846	448	276
Oakland	8	5	1	.615	315	288
San Diego	7	6	1	.538	335	284
Denver	4	10	0	.286	196	381

AFL championship: Kansas City 31, BUFFALO 7

1965 NFL

EASTERN CONFERENCE

	W	L	T	Pct.	Pts.	OP
Cleveland	11	3	0	.786	363	325
Dallas	7	7	0	.500	325	280
N.Y. Giants	7	7	0	.500	270	338
Washington	6	8	0	.429	257	301
Philadelphia	5	9	0	.357	363	359
St. Louis	5	9	0	.357	296	309
Pittsburgh	2	12	0	.143	202	397

WESTERN CONFERENCE

	W	L	T	Pct.	Pts.	OP
Green Bay	10	3	1	.769	316	224
Baltimore	10	3	1	.769	389	284
Chicago	9	5	0	.643	409	275
San Francisco	7	6	1	.538	421	402
Minnesota	7	7	0	.500	383	403
Detroit	6	7	1	.462	257	295
Los Angeles	4	10	0	.286	269	328

Western Conference playoff: GREEN BAY 13, Baltimore 10 (OT)
NFL championship: GREEN BAY 23, Cleveland 12

1965 AFL

EASTERN DIVISION

	W	L	T	Pct.	Pts.	OP
Buffalo	10	3	1	.769	313	226
N.Y. Jets	5	8	1	.385	285	303
Boston Patriots	4	8	2	.333	244	302
Houston	4	10	0	.286	298	429

WESTERN DIVISION

	W	L	T	Pct.	Pts.	OP
San Diego	9	2	3	.818	340	227
Oakland	8	5	1	.615	298	239
Kansas City	7	5	2	.583	322	285
Denver	4	10	0	.286	303	392

AFL championship: Buffalo 23, SAN DIEGO 0

1964 NFL

EASTERN CONFERENCE

	W	L	T	Pct.	Pts.	OP
Cleveland	10	3	1	.769	415	293
St. Louis	9	3	2	.750	357	331
Philadelphia	6	8	0	.429	312	313
Washington	6	8	0	.429	307	305
Dallas	5	8	1	.385	250	289
Pittsburgh	5	9	0	.357	253	315
N.Y. Giants	2	10	2	.167	241	399

WESTERN CONFERENCE

	W	L	T	Pct.	Pts.	OP
Baltimore	12	2	0	.857	428	225
Green Bay	8	5	1	.615	342	245
Minnesota	8	5	1	.615	355	296
Detroit	7	5	2	.583	280	260
Los Angeles	5	7	2	.417	283	339
Chicago	5	9	0	.357	260	379
San Francisco	4	10	0	.286	236	330

NFL championship: CLEVELAND 27, Baltimore 0

1964 AFL

EASTERN DIVISION

	W	L	T	Pct.	Pts.	OP
Buffalo	12	2	0	.857	400	242
Boston Patriots	10	3	1	.769	365	297
N.Y. Jets	5	8	1	.385	278	315
Houston	4	10	0	.286	310	355

WESTERN DIVISION

	W	L	T	Pct.	Pts.	OP
San Diego	8	5	1	.615	341	300
Kansas City	7	7	0	.500	366	306
Oakland	5	7	2	.417	303	350
Denver	2	11	1	.154	240	438

AFL championship: BUFFALO 20, San Diego 7

1963 NFL

EASTERN CONFERENCE

	W	L	T	Pct.	Pts.	OP
N.Y. Giants	11	3	0	.786	448	280
Cleveland	10	4	0	.714	343	262
St. Louis	9	5	0	.643	341	283
Pittsburgh	7	4	3	.636	321	295
Dallas	4	10	0	.286	305	378
Washington	3	11	0	.214	279	398
Philadelphia	2	10	2	.167	242	381

WESTERN CONFERENCE

	W	L	T	Pct.	Pts.	OP
Chicago	11	1	2	.917	301	144
Green Bay	11	2	1	.846	369	206
Baltimore	8	6	0	.571	316	285
Detroit	5	8	1	.385	326	265
Minnesota	5	8	1	.385	309	390
Los Angeles	5	9	0	.357	210	350
San Francisco	2	12	0	.143	198	391

NFL championship: CHICAGO 14, N.Y. Giants 10

1963 AFL

EASTERN DIVISION

	W	L	T	Pct.	Pts.	OP
Boston Patriots	7	6	1	.538	327	257
Buffalo	7	6	1	.538	304	291
Houston	6	8	0	.429	302	372
N.Y. Jets	5	8	1	.385	249	399

WESTERN DIVISION

	W	L	T	Pct.	Pts.	OP
San Diego	11	3	0	.786	399	255
Oakland	10	4	0	.714	363	282
Kansas City	5	7	2	.417	347	263
Denver	2	11	1	.154	301	473

Eastern Division playoff: Boston 26, BUFFALO 8
AFL championship: SAN DIEGO 51, Boston 10

1962 NFL

EASTERN CONFERENCE	W	L	T	Pct.	Pts.	OP	WESTERN CONFERENCE	W	L	T	Pct.	Pts.	OP
N.Y. Giants	12	2	0	.857	398	283	Green Bay	13	1	0	.929	415	148
Pittsburgh	9	5	0	.643	312	363	Detroit	11	3	0	.786	315	177
Cleveland	7	6	1	.538	291	257	Chicago	9	5	0	.643	321	287
Washington	5	7	2	.417	305	376	Baltimore	7	7	0	.500	293	288
Dallas Cowboys	5	8	1	.385	398	402	San Francisco	6	8	0	.429	282	331
St. Louis	4	9	1	.308	287	361	Minnesota	2	11	1	.154	254	410
Philadelphia	3	10	1	.231	282	356	Los Angeles	1	12	1	.077	220	334

NFL championship: Green Bay 16, N.Y. GIANTS 7

1962 AFL

EASTERN DIVISION	W	L	T	Pct.	Pts.	OP	WESTERN DIVISION	W	L	T	Pct.	Pts.	OP
Houston	11	3	0	.786	387	270	Dallas Texans	11	3	0	.786	389	233
Boston Patriots	9	4	1	.692	346	295	Denver	7	7	0	.500	353	334
Buffalo	7	6	1	.538	309	272	San Diego	4	10	0	.286	314	392
N.Y. Titans	5	9	0	.357	278	423	Oakland	1	13	0	.071	213	370

AFL championship: Dallas Texans 20, HOUSTON 17 (OT)

1961 NFL

EASTERN CONFERENCE	W	L	T	Pct.	Pts.	OP	WESTERN CONFERENCE	W	L	T	Pct.	Pts.	OP
N.Y. Giants	10	3	1	.769	368	220	Green Bay	11	3	0	.786	391	223
Philadelphia	10	4	0	.714	361	297	Detroit	8	5	1	.615	270	258
Cleveland	8	5	1	.615	319	270	Baltimore	8	6	0	.571	302	307
St. Louis	7	7	0	.500	279	267	Chicago	8	6	0	.571	326	302
Pittsburgh	6	8	0	.429	295	287	San Francisco	7	6	1	.538	346	272
Dallas Cowboys	4	9	1	.308	236	380	Los Angeles	4	10	0	.286	263	333
Washington	1	12	1	.077	174	392	Minnesota	3	11	0	.214	285	407

NFL championship: GREEN BAY 37, N.Y. Giants 0

1961 AFL

EASTERN DIVISION	W	L	T	Pct.	Pts.	OP	WESTERN DIVISION	W	L	T	Pct.	Pts.	OP
Houston	10	3	1	.769	513	242	San Diego	12	2	0	.857	396	219
Boston Patriots	9	4	1	.692	413	313	Dallas Texans	6	8	0	.429	334	343
N.Y. Titans	7	7	0	.500	301	390	Denver	3	11	0	.214	251	432
Buffalo	6	8	0	.429	294	342	Oakland	2	12	0	.143	237	458

AFL championship: Houston 10, SAN DIEGO 3

1960 NFL

EASTERN CONFERENCE	W	L	T	Pct.	Pts.	OP	WESTERN CONFERENCE	W	L	T	Pct.	Pts.	OP
Philadelphia	10	2	0	.833	321	246	Green Bay	8	4	0	.667	332	209
Cleveland	8	3	1	.727	362	217	Detroit	7	5	0	.583	239	212
N.Y. Giants	6	4	2	.600	271	261	San Francisco	7	5	0	.583	208	205
St. Louis	6	5	1	.545	288	230	Baltimore	6	6	0	.500	288	234
Pittsburgh	5	6	1	.455	240	275	Chicago	5	6	1	.455	194	299
Washington	1	9	2	.100	178	309	L.A. Rams	4	7	1	.364	265	297
							Dallas Cowboys	0	11	1	.000	177	369

NFL championship: PHILADELPHIA 17, Green Bay 13

1960 AFL

EASTERN CONFERENCE	W	L	T	Pct.	Pts.	OP	WESTERN CONFERENCE	W	L	T	Pct.	Pts.	OP
Houston	10	4	0	.714	379	285	L.A. Chargers	10	4	0	.714	373	336
N.Y. Titans	7	7	0	.500	382	399	Dallas Texans	8	6	0	.571	362	253
Buffalo	5	8	1	.385	296	303	Oakland	6	8	0	.429	319	388
Boston Patriots	5	9	0	.357	286	349	Denver	4	9	1	.308	309	393

AFL championship: HOUSTON 24, L.A. Chargers 16

1959

EASTERN CONFERENCE	W	L	T	Pct.	Pts.	OP	WESTERN CONFERENCE	W	L	T	Pct.	Pts.	OP
N.Y. Giants	10	2	0	.833	284	170	Baltimore	9	3	0	.750	374	251
Cleveland	7	5	0	.583	270	214	Chi. Bears	8	4	0	.667	252	196
Philadelphia	7	5	0	.583	268	278	Green Bay	7	5	0	.583	248	246
Pittsburgh	6	5	1	.545	257	216	San Francisco	7	5	0	.583	255	237
Washington	3	9	0	.250	185	350	Detroit	3	8	1	.273	203	275
Chi. Cardinals	2	10	0	.167	234	324	Los Angeles	2	10	0	.167	242	315

NFL championship: BALTIMORE 31, N.Y. Giants 16

1958

EASTERN CONFERENCE	W	L	T	Pct.	Pts.	OP	WESTERN CONFERENCE	W	L	T	Pct.	Pts.	OP
N.Y. Giants	9	3	0	.750	246	183	Baltimore	9	3	0	.750	381	203
Cleveland	9	3	0	.750	302	217	Chi. Bears	8	4	0	.667	298	230
Pittsburgh	7	4	1	.636	261	230	Los Angeles	8	4	0	.667	344	278
Washington	4	7	1	.364	214	268	San Francisco	6	6	0	.500	257	324
Chi. Cardinals	2	9	1	.182	261	356	Detroit	4	7	1	.364	261	276
Philadelphia	2	9	1	.182	235	306	Green Bay	1	10	1	.091	193	382

Eastern Conference playoff: N.Y. GIANTS 10, Cleveland 0
NFL championship: Baltimore 23, N.Y. GIANTS 17 (OT)

1957

EASTERN CONFERENCE	W	L	T	Pct.	Pts.	OP	WESTERN CONFERENCE	W	L	T	Pct.	Pts.	OP
Cleveland	9	2	1	.818	269	172	Detroit	8	4	0	.667	251	231
N.Y. Giants	7	5	0	.583	254	211	San Francisco	8	4	0	.667	260	264
Pittsburgh	6	6	0	.500	161	178	Baltimore	7	5	0	.583	303	235
Washington	5	6	1	.455	251	230	Los Angeles	6	6	0	.500	307	278
Philadelphia	4	8	0	.333	173	230	Chi. Bears	5	7	0	.417	203	211
Chi. Cardinals	3	9	0	.250	200	299	Green Bay	3	9	0	.250	218	311

Western Conference playoff: Detroit 31, SAN FRANCISCO 27
NFL championship: DETROIT 59, Cleveland 14

1956

EASTERN CONFERENCE	W	L	T	Pct.	Pts.	OP	WESTERN CONFERENCE	W	L	T	Pct.	Pts.	OP
N.Y. Giants	8	3	1	.727	264	197	Chi. Bears	9	2	1	.818	363	246
Chi. Cardinals	7	5	0	.583	240	182	Detroit	9	3	0	.750	300	188
Washington	6	6	0	.500	183	225	San Francisco	5	6	1	.455	233	284
Cleveland	5	7	0	.417	167	177	Baltimore	5	7	0	.417	270	322
Pittsburgh	5	7	0	.417	217	250	Green Bay	4	8	0	.333	264	342
Philadelphia	3	8	1	.273	143	215	Los Angeles	4	8	0	.333	291	307

NFL championship: N.Y. GIANTS 47, Chi. Bears 7

1955

EASTERN CONFERENCE	W	L	T	Pct.	Pts.	OP	WESTERN CONFERENCE	W	L	T	Pct.	Pts.	OP
Cleveland	9	2	1	.818	349	218	Los Angeles	8	3	1	.727	260	231
Washington	8	4	0	.667	246	222	Chi. Bears	8	4	0	.667	294	251
N.Y. Giants	6	5	1	.545	267	223	Green Bay	6	6	0	.500	258	276
Chi. Cardinals	4	7	1	.364	224	252	Baltimore	5	6	1	.455	214	239
Philadelphia	4	7	1	.364	248	231	San Francisco	4	8	0	.333	216	298
Pittsburgh	4	8	0	.333	195	285	Detroit	3	9	0	.250	230	275

NFL championship: Cleveland 38, LOS ANGELES 14

1954

EASTERN CONFERENCE	W	L	T	Pct.	Pts.	OP
Cleveland	9	3	0	.750	336	162
Philadelphia	7	4	1	.636	284	230
N.Y. Giants	7	5	0	.583	293	184
Pittsburgh	5	7	0	.417	219	263
Washington	3	9	0	.250	207	432
Chi. Cardinals	2	10	0	.167	183	347

WESTERN CONFERENCE	W	L	T	Pct.	Pts.	OP
Detroit	9	2	1	.818	337	189
Chi. Bears	8	4	0	.667	301	279
San Francisco	7	4	1	.636	313	251
Los Angeles	6	5	1	.545	314	285
Green Bay	4	8	0	.333	234	251
Baltimore	3	9	0	.250	131	279

NFL championship: CLEVELAND 56, Detroit 10

1953

EASTERN CONFERENCE	W	L	T	Pct.	Pts.	OP
Cleveland	11	1	0	.917	348	162
Philadelphia	7	4	1	.636	352	215
Washington	6	5	1	.545	208	215
Pittsburgh	6	6	0	.500	211	263
N.Y. Giants	3	9	0	.250	179	277
Chi. Cardinals	1	10	1	.091	190	337

WESTERN CONFERENCE	W	L	T	Pct.	Pts.	OP
Detroit	10	2	0	.833	271	205
San Francisco	9	3	0	.750	372	237
Los Angeles	8	3	1	.727	366	236
Chi. Bears	3	8	1	.273	218	262
Baltimore	3	9	0	.250	182	350
Green Bay	2	9	1	.182	200	338

NFL championship: DETROIT 17, Cleveland 16

1952

AMERICAN CONFERENCE	W	L	T	Pct.	Pts.	OP
Cleveland	8	4	0	.667	310	213
N.Y. Giants	7	5	0	.583	234	231
Philadelphia	7	5	0	.583	252	271
Pittsburgh	5	7	0	.417	300	273
Chi. Cardinals	4	8	0	.333	172	221
Washington	4	8	0	.333	240	287

NATIONAL CONFERENCE	W	L	T	Pct.	Pts.	OP
Detroit	9	3	0	.750	344	192
Los Angeles	9	3	0	.750	349	234
San Francisco	7	5	0	.583	285	221
Green Bay	6	6	0	.500	295	312
Chi. Bears	5	7	0	.417	245	326
Dallas Texans	1	11	0	.083	182	427

National Conference playoff: DETROIT 31, Los Angeles 21
NFL championship: Detroit 17, CLEVELAND 7

1951

AMERICAN CONFERENCE	W	L	T	Pct.	Pts.	OP
Cleveland	11	1	0	.917	331	152
N.Y. Giants	9	2	1	.818	254	161
Washington	5	7	0	.417	183	296
Pittsburgh	4	7	1	.364	183	235
Philadelphia	4	8	0	.333	234	264
Chi. Cardinals	3	9	0	.250	210	287

NATIONAL CONFERENCE	W	L	T	Pct.	Pts.	OP
Los Angeles	8	4	0	.667	392	261
Detroit	7	4	1	.636	336	259
San Francisco	7	4	1	.636	255	205
Chi. Bears	7	5	0	.583	286	282
Green Bay	3	9	0	.250	254	375
N.Y. Yanks	1	9	2	.100	241	382

NFL championship: LOS ANGELES 24, Cleveland 17

1950

AMERICAN CONFERENCE	W	L	T	Pct.	Pts.	OP
Cleveland	10	2	0	.833	310	144
N.Y. Giants	10	2	0	.833	268	150
Philadelphia	6	6	0	.500	254	141
Pittsburgh	6	6	0	.500	180	195
Chi. Cardinals	5	7	0	.417	233	287
Washington	3	9	0	.250	232	326

NATIONAL CONFERENCE	W	L	T	Pct.	Pts.	OP
Los Angeles	9	3	0	.750	466	309
Chi. Bears	9	3	0	.750	279	207
N.Y. Yanks	7	5	0	.583	366	367
Detroit	6	6	0	.500	321	285
Green Bay	3	9	0	.250	244	406
San Francisco	3	9	0	.250	213	300
Baltimore	1	11	0	.083	213	462

American Conference playoff: CLEVELAND 8, N.Y. Giants 3
National Conference playoff: LOS ANGELES 24, Chi. Bears 14
NFL championship: CLEVELAND 30, Los Angeles 28

1949

EASTERN DIVISION	W	L	T	Pct.	Pts.	OP
Philadelphia	11	1	0	.917	364	134
Pittsburgh	6	5	1	.545	224	214
N.Y. Giants	6	6	0	.500	287	298
Washington	4	7	1	.364	268	339
N.Y. Bulldogs	1	10	1	.091	153	368

WESTERN DIVISION	W	L	T	Pct.	Pts.	OP
Los Angeles	8	2	2	.800	360	239
Chi. Bears	9	3	0	.750	332	218
Chi. Cardinals	6	5	1	.545	360	301
Detroit	4	8	0	.333	237	259
Green Bay	2	10	0	.167	114	329

NFL championship: Philadelphia 14, LOS ANGELES 0

1948

EASTERN DIVISION	W	L	T	Pct.	Pts.	OP
Philadelphia	9	2	1	.818	376	156
Washington	7	5	0	.583	291	287
N.Y. Giants	4	8	0	.333	297	388
Pittsburgh	4	8	0	.333	200	243
Boston	3	9	0	.250	174	372

WESTERN DIVISION	W	L	T	Pct.	Pts.	OP
Chi. Cardinals	11	1	0	.917	395	226
Chi. Bears	10	2	0	.833	375	151
Los Angeles	6	5	1	.545	327	269
Green Bay	3	9	0	.250	154	290
Detroit	2	10	0	.167	200	407

NFL championship: PHILADELPHIA 7, Chi. Cardinals 0

1947

EASTERN DIVISION	W	L	T	Pct.	Pts.	OP
Philadelphia	8	4	0	.667	308	242
Pittsburgh	8	4	0	.667	240	259
Boston	4	7	1	.364	168	256
Washington	4	8	0	.333	295	367
N.Y. Giants	2	8	2	.200	190	309

WESTERN DIVISION	W	L	T	Pct.	Pts.	OP
Chi. Cardinals	9	3	0	.750	306	231
Chi. Bears	8	4	0	.667	363	241
Green Bay	6	5	1	.545	274	210
Los Angeles	6	6	0	.500	259	214
Detroit	3	9	0	.250	231	305

Eastern Division playoff: Philadelphia 21, PITTSBURGH 0
NFL championship: CHI. CARDINALS 28, Philadelphia 21

1946

EASTERN DIVISION	W	L	T	Pct.	Pts.	OP
N.Y. Giants	7	3	1	.700	236	162
Philadelphia	6	5	0	.545	231	220
Washington	5	5	1	.500	171	191
Pittsburgh	5	5	1	.500	136	117
Boston	2	8	1	.200	189	273

WESTERN DIVISION	W	L	T	Pct.	Pts.	OP
Chi. Bears	8	2	1	.800	289	193
Los Angeles	6	4	1	.600	277	257
Green Bay	6	5	0	.545	148	158
Chi. Cardinals	6	5	0	.545	260	198
Detroit	1	10	0	.091	142	310

NFL championship: Chi. Bears 24, N.Y. GIANTS 14

1945

EASTERN DIVISION	W	L	T	Pct.	Pts.	OP
Washington	8	2	0	.800	209	121
Philadelphia	7	3	0	.700	272	133
N.Y. Giants	3	6	1	.333	179	198
Boston	3	6	1	.333	123	211
Pittsburgh	2	8	0	.200	79	220

WESTERN DIVISION	W	L	T	Pct.	Pts.	OP
Cleveland	9	1	0	.900	244	136
Detroit	7	3	0	.700	195	194
Green Bay	6	4	0	.600	258	173
Chi. Bears	3	7	0	.300	192	235
Chi. Cardinals	1	9	0	.100	98	228

NFL championship: CLEVELAND 15, Washington 14

1944

EASTERN DIVISION	W	L	T	Pct.	Pts.	OP
N.Y. Giants	8	1	1	.889	206	75
Philadelphia	7	1	2	.875	267	131
Washington	6	3	1	.667	169	180
Boston	2	8	0	.200	82	233
Brooklyn	0	10	0	.000	69	166

WESTERN DIVISION	W	L	T	Pct.	Pts.	OP
Green Bay	8	2	0	.800	238	141
Chi. Bears	6	3	1	.667	258	172
Detroit	6	3	1	.667	216	151
Cleveland	4	6	0	.400	188	224
Card-Pitt	0	10	0	.000	108	328

NFL championship: Green Bay 14, N.Y. GIANTS 7

1943

EASTERN DIVISION	W	L	T	Pct.	Pts.	OP	WESTERN DIVISION	W	L	T	Pct.	Pts.	OP
Washington	6	3	1	.667	229	137	Chi. Bears	8	1	1	.889	303	157
N.Y. Giants	6	3	1	.667	197	170	Green Bay	7	2	1	.778	264	172
Phil-Pitt	5	4	1	.556	225	230	Detroit	3	6	1	.333	178	218
Brooklyn	2	8	0	.200	65	234	Chi. Cardinals	0	10	0	.000	95	238

Eastern Division playoff: Washington 28, N.Y. GIANTS 0
NFL championship: CHI. BEARS 41, Washington 21

1942

EASTERN DIVISION	W	L	T	Pct.	Pts.	OP	WESTERN DIVISION	W	L	T	Pct.	Pts.	OP
Washington	10	1	0	.909	227	102	Chi. Bears	11	0	0	1.000	376	84
Pittsburgh	7	4	0	.636	167	119	Green Bay	8	2	1	.800	300	215
N.Y. Giants	5	5	1	.500	155	139	Cleveland	5	6	0	.455	150	207
Brooklyn	3	8	0	.273	100	168	Chi. Cardinals	3	8	0	.273	98	209
Philadelphia	2	9	0	.182	134	239	Detroit	0	11	0	.000	38	263

NFL championship: WASHINGTON 14, Chi. Bears 6

1941

EASTERN DIVISION	W	L	T	Pct.	Pts.	OP	WESTERN DIVISION	W	L	T	Pct.	Pts.	OP
N.Y. Giants	8	3	0	.727	238	114	Chi. Bears	10	1	0	.909	396	147
Brooklyn	7	4	0	.636	158	127	Green Bay	10	1	0	.909	258	120
Washington	6	5	0	.545	176	174	Detroit	4	6	1	.400	121	195
Philadelphia	2	8	1	.200	119	218	Chi. Cardinals	3	7	1	.300	127	197
Pittsburgh	1	9	1	.100	103	276	Cleveland	2	9	0	.182	116	244

Western Division playoff: CHI. BEARS 33, Green Bay 14
NFL championship: CHI. BEARS 37, N.Y. Giants 9

1940

EASTERN DIVISION	W	L	T	Pct.	Pts.	OP	WESTERN DIVISION	W	L	T	Pct.	Pts.	OP
Washington	9	2	0	.818	245	142	Chi. Bears	8	3	0	.727	238	152
Brooklyn	8	3	0	.727	186	120	Green Bay	6	4	1	.600	238	155
N.Y. Giants	6	4	1	.600	131	133	Detroit	5	5	1	.500	138	153
Pittsburgh	2	7	2	.222	60	178	Cleveland	4	6	1	.400	171	191
Philadelphia	1	10	0	.091	111	211	Chi. Cardinals	2	7	2	.222	139	222

NFL championship: Chi. Bears 73, WASHINGTON 0

1939

EASTERN DIVISION	W	L	T	Pct.	Pts.	OP	WESTERN DIVISION	W	L	T	Pct.	Pts.	OP
N.Y. Giants	9	1	1	.900	168	85	Green Bay	9	2	0	.818	233	153
Washington	8	2	1	.800	242	94	Chi. Bears	8	3	0	.727	298	157
Brooklyn	4	6	1	.400	108	219	Detroit	6	5	0	.545	145	150
Philadelphia	1	9	1	.100	105	200	Cleveland	5	5	1	.500	195	164
Pittsburgh	1	9	1	.100	114	216	Chi. Cardinals	1	10	0	.091	84	254

NFL championship: GREEN BAY 27, N.Y. Giants 0

1938

EASTERN DIVISION	W	L	T	Pct.	Pts.	OP	WESTERN DIVISION	W	L	T	Pct.	Pts.	OP
N.Y. Giants	8	2	1	.800	194	79	Green Bay	8	3	0	.727	223	118
Washington	6	3	2	.667	148	154	Detroit	7	4	0	.636	119	108
Brooklyn	4	4	3	.500	131	161	Chi. Bears	6	5	0	.545	194	148
Philadelphia	5	6	0	.455	154	164	Cleveland	4	7	0	.364	131	215
Pittsburgh	2	9	0	.182	79	169	Chi. Cardinals	2	9	0	.182	111	168

NFL championship: N.Y. GIANTS 23, Green Bay 17

1937

EASTERN DIVISION	W	L	T	Pct.	Pts.	OP	WESTERN DIVISION	W	L	T	Pct.	Pts.	OP
Washington	8	3	0	.727	195	120	Chi. Bears	9	1	1	.900	201	100
N.Y. Giants	6	3	2	.667	128	109	Green Bay	7	4	0	.636	220	122
Pittsburgh	4	7	0	.364	122	145	Detroit	7	4	0	.636	180	105
Brooklyn	3	7	1	.300	82	174	Chi. Cardinals	5	5	1	.500	135	165
Philadelphia	2	8	1	.200	86	177	Cleveland	1	10	0	.091	75	207

NFL championship: Washington 28, CHI. BEARS 21

1936

EASTERN DIVISION	W	L	T	Pct.	Pts.	OP	WESTERN DIVISION	W	L	T	Pct.	Pts.	OP
Boston	7	5	0	.583	149	110	Green Bay	10	1	1	.909	248	118
Pittsburgh	6	6	0	.500	98	187	Chi. Bears	9	3	0	.750	222	94
N.Y. Giants	5	6	1	.455	115	163	Detroit	8	4	0	.667	235	102
Brooklyn	3	8	1	.273	92	161	Chi. Cardinals	3	8	1	.273	74	143
Philadelphia	1	11	0	.083	51	206							

NFL championship: Green Bay 21, Boston 6, at Polo Grounds, N.Y.

1935

EASTERN DIVISION	W	L	T	Pct.	Pts.	OP	WESTERN DIVISION	W	L	T	Pct.	Pts.	OP
N.Y. Giants	9	3	0	.750	180	96	Detroit	7	3	2	.700	191	111
Brooklyn	5	6	1	.455	90	141	Green Bay	8	4	0	.667	181	96
Pittsburgh	4	8	0	.333	100	209	Chi. Bears	6	4	2	.600	192	106
Boston	2	8	1	.200	65	123	Chi. Cardinals	6	4	2	.600	99	97
Philadelphia	2	9	0	.182	60	179							

NFL championship: DETROIT 26, N.Y. Giants 7
One game between Boston and Philadelphia was canceled.

1934

EASTERN DIVISION	W	L	T	Pct.	Pts.	OP	WESTERN DIVISION	W	L	T	Pct.	Pts.	OP
N.Y. Giants	8	5	0	.615	147	107	Chi. Bears	13	0	0	1.000	286	86
Boston	6	6	0	.500	107	94	Detroit	10	3	0	.769	238	59
Brooklyn	4	7	0	.364	61	153	Green Bay	7	6	0	.538	156	112
Philadelphia	4	7	0	.364	127	85	Chi. Cardinals	5	6	0	.455	80	84
Pittsburgh	2	10	0	.167	51	206	St. Louis	1	2	0	.333	27	61
							Cincinnati	0	8	0	.000	10	243

NFL championship: N.Y. GIANTS 30, Chi. Bears 13

1933

EASTERN DIVISION	W	L	T	Pct.	Pts.	OP	WESTERN DIVISION	W	L	T	Pct.	Pts.	OP
N.Y. Giants	11	3	0	.786	244	101	Chi. Bears	10	2	1	.833	133	82
Brooklyn	5	4	1	.556	93	54	Portsmouth	6	5	0	.545	128	87
Boston	5	5	2	.500	103	97	Green Bay	5	7	1	.417	170	107
Philadelphia	3	5	1	.375	77	158	Cincinnati	3	6	1	.333	38	110
Pittsburgh	3	6	2	.333	67	208	Chi. Cardinals	1	9	1	.100	52	101

NFL championship: CHI. BEARS 23, N.Y. Giants 21

1932

	W	L	T	Pct.
Chicago Bears	7	1	6	.875
Green Bay Packers	10	3	1	.769
Portsmouth Spartans	6	2	4	.750
Boston Braves	4	4	2	.500
New York Giants	4	6	2	.400
Brooklyn Dodgers	3	9	0	.250
Chicago Cardinals	2	6	2	.250
Staten Island Stapletons	2	7	3	.222

Chicago Bears and Portsmouth finished regularly scheduled games tied for first place. Bears won playoff game, which counted in standings, 9-0.

1931

	W	L	T	Pct.
Green Bay Packers	12	2	0	.857
Portsmouth Spartans	11	3	0	.786
Chicago Bears	8	5	0	.615
Chicago Cardinals	5	4	0	.556
New York Giants	7	6	1	.538
Providence Steam Roller	4	4	3	.500
Staten Island Stapletons	4	6	1	.400
Cleveland Indians	2	8	0	.200
Brooklyn Dodgers	2	12	0	.143
Frankford Yellow Jackets	1	6	1	.143

1930

	W	L	T	Pct.
Green Bay Packers	10	3	1	.769
New York Giants	13	4	0	.765
Chicago Bears	9	4	1	.692
Brooklyn Dodgers	7	4	1	.636
Providence Steam Roller	6	4	1	.600
Staten Island Stapletons	5	5	2	.500
Chicago Cardinals	5	6	2	.455
Portsmouth Spartans	5	6	3	.455
Frankford Yellow Jackets	4	13	1	.222
Minneapolis Red Jackets	1	7	1	.125
Newark Tornadoes	1	10	1	.091

1929

	W	L	T	Pct.
Green Bay Packers	12	0	1	1.000
New York Giants	13	1	1	.929
Frankford Yellow Jackets	10	4	5	.714
Chicago Cardinals	6	6	1	.500
Boston Bulldogs	4	4	0	.500
Staten Island Stapletons	3	4	3	.429
Providence Steam Roller	4	6	2	.400
Orange Tornadoes	3	5	4	.375
Chicago Bears	4	9	2	.308
Buffalo Bisons	1	7	1	.125
Minneapolis Red Jackets	1	9	0	.100
Dayton Triangles	0	6	0	.000

1928

	W	L	T	Pct.
Providence Steam Roller	8	1	2	.889
Frankford Yellow Jackets	11	3	2	.786
Detroit Wolverines	7	2	1	.778
Green Bay Packers	6	4	3	.600
Chicago Bears	7	5	1	.583
New York Giants	4	7	2	.364
New York Yankees	4	8	1	.333
Pottsville Maroons	2	8	0	.200
Chicago Cardinals	1	5	0	.167
Dayton Triangles	0	7	0	.000

1927

	W	L	T	Pct.
New York Giants	11	1	1	.917
Green Bay Packers	7	2	1	.778
Chicago Bears	9	3	2	.750
Cleveland Bulldogs	8	4	1	.667
Providence Steam Roller	8	5	1	.615
New York Yankees	7	8	1	.467
Frankford Yellow Jackets	6	9	3	.400
Pottsville Maroons	5	8	0	.385
Chicago Cardinals	3	7	1	.300
Dayton Triangles	1	6	1	.143
Duluth Eskimos	1	8	0	.111
Buffalo Bisons	0	5	0	.000

1926

	W	L	T	Pct.
Frankford Yellow Jackets	14	1	2	.933
Chicago Bears	12	1	3	.923
Pottsville Maroons	10	2	2	.833
Kansas City Cowboys	8	3	0	.727
Green Bay Packers	7	3	3	.700
Los Angeles Buccaneers	6	3	1	.667
New York Giants	8	4	1	.667
Duluth Eskimos	6	5	3	.545
Buffalo Rangers	4	4	2	.500
Chicago Cardinals	5	6	1	.455
Providence Steam Roller	5	7	1	.417
Detroit Panthers	4	6	2	.400
Hartford Blues	3	7	0	.300
Brooklyn Lions	3	8	0	.273
Milwaukee Badgers	2	7	0	.222
Akron Indians	1	4	3	.200
Dayton Triangles	1	4	1	.200
Racine Tornadoes	1	4	0	.200
Columbus Tigers	1	6	0	.143
Canton Bulldogs	1	9	3	.100
Louisville Colonels	0	4	0	.000

1925

	W	L	T	Pct.
Chicago Cardinals	11	2	1	.846
Pottsville Maroons	10	2	0	.833
Detroit Panthers	8	2	2	.800
New York Giants	8	4	0	.667
Akron Indians	4	2	2	.667
Frankford Yellow Jackets	13	7	0	.650
Chicago Bears	9	5	3	.643
Rock Island Independents	5	3	3	.625
Green Bay Packers	8	5	0	.615
Providence Steam Roller	6	5	1	.545
Canton Bulldogs	4	4	0	.500
Cleveland Bulldogs	5	8	1	.385
Kansas City Cowboys	2	5	1	.286
Hammond Pros	1	4	0	.200
Buffalo Bisons	1	6	2	.143
Duluth Kelleys	0	3	0	.000
Rochester Jeffersons	0	6	1	.000
Milwaukee Badgers	0	6	0	.000
Dayton Triangles	0	7	1	.000
Columbus Tigers	0	9	0	.000

1924

	W	L	T	Pct.
Cleveland Bulldogs	7	1	1	.875
Chicago Bears	6	1	4	.857
Frankford Yellow Jackets	11	2	1	.846
Duluth Kelleys	5	1	0	.833
Rock Island Independents	5	2	2	.714
Green Bay Packers	7	4	0	.636
Racine Legion	4	3	3	.571
Chicago Cardinals	5	4	1	.556
Buffalo Bisons	6	5	0	.545
Columbus Tigers	4	4	0	.500
Hammond Pros	2	2	1	.500
Milwaukee Badgers	5	8	0	.385
Akron Indians	2	6	0	.250
Dayton Triangles	2	6	0	.250
Kansas City Blues	2	7	0	.222
Kenosha Maroons	0	4	1	.000
Minneapolis Marines	0	6	0	.000
Rochester Jeffersons	0	7	0	.000

1923

	W	L	T	Pct.
Canton Bulldogs	11	0	1	1.000
Chicago Bears	9	2	1	.818
Green Bay Packers	7	2	1	.778
Milwaukee Badgers	7	2	3	.778
Cleveland Indians	3	1	3	.750
Chicago Cardinals	8	4	0	.667
Duluth Kelleys	4	3	0	.571
Buffalo All-Americans	4	4	3	.556
Columbus Tigers	5	4	1	.556
Racine Legion	4	4	2	.500
Toledo Maroons	3	3	2	.500
Rock Island Independents	2	3	3	.400
Minneapolis Marines	2	5	2	.286
St. Louis All-Stars	1	4	2	.200
Hammond Pros	1	5	1	.167
Dayton Triangles	1	6	1	.143
Akron Indians	1	6	0	.143
Oorang Indians	1	10	0	.091
Louisville Brecks	0	3	0	.000
Rochester Jeffersons	0	4	0	.000

1922

	W	L	T	Pct.
Canton Bulldogs	10	0	2	1.000
Chicago Bears	9	3	0	.750
Chicago Cardinals	8	3	0	.727
Toledo Maroons	5	2	2	.714
Rock Island Independents	4	2	1	.667
Racine Legion	6	4	1	.600
Dayton Triangles	4	3	1	.571
Green Bay Packers	4	3	3	.571
Buffalo All-Americans	5	4	1	.556
Akron Pros	3	5	2	.375
Milwaukee Badgers	2	4	3	.333
Oorang Indians	3	6	0	.333
Minneapolis Marines	1	3	0	.250
Louisville Brecks	1	3	0	.250
Evansville Crimson Giants	0	3	0	.000
Rochester Jeffersons	0	4	1	.000
Hammond Pros	0	5	1	.000
Columbus Panhandles	0	8	0	.000

1921

	W	L	T	Pct.
Chicago Staleys	9	1	1	.900
Buffalo All-Americans	9	1	2	.900
Akron Pros	8	3	1	.727
Canton Bulldogs	5	2	3	.714
Rock Island Independents	4	2	1	.667
Evansville Crimson Giants	3	2	0	.600
Green Bay Packers	3	2	1	.600
Dayton Triangles	4	4	1	.500
Chicago Cardinals	3	3	2	.500
Rochester Jeffersons	2	3	0	.400
Cleveland Indians	3	5	0	.375
Washington Senators	1	2	0	.333
Cincinnati Celts	1	3	0	.250
Hammond Pros	1	3	1	.250
Minneapolis Marines	1	3	0	.250
Detroit Tigers	1	5	1	.167
Columbus Panhandles	1	8	0	.111
Tonawanda Kardex	0	1	0	.000
Muncie Flyers	0	2	0	.000
Louisville Brecks	0	2	0	.000
New York Giants	0	2	0	.000

1920*

	W	L	T	Pct.
Akron Pros	8	0	3	1.000
Decatur Staleys	10	1	2	.909
Buffalo All-Americans	9	1	1	.900
Chicago Cardinals	6	2	2	.750
Rock Island Independents	6	2	2	.750
Dayton Triangles	5	2	2	.714
Rochester Jeffersons	6	3	2	.667
Canton Bulldogs	7	4	2	.636
Detroit Heralds	2	3	3	.400
Cleveland Tigers	2	4	2	.333
Chicago Tigers	2	5	1	.286
Hammond Pros	2	5	0	.286
Columbus Panhandles	2	6	2	.250
Muncie Flyers	0	1	0	.000

No official standings were maintained for the 1920 season, and the championship was awarded to the Akron Pros in a League meeting on April 30, 1921. Clubs played schedules that included games against nonleague opponents.

RS=REGULAR SEASON
PS=POSTSEASON
*ARIZONA vs. ATLANTA
RS: Cardinals lead series, 14-11
PS: Cardinals lead series, 1-0
1966—Falcons, 16-10 (Atl)
1968—Cardinals, 17-12 (StL)
1971—Cardinals, 26-9 (Atl)
1973—Cardinals, 32-10 (Atl)
1975—Cardinals, 23-20 (StL)
1978—Cardinals, 42-21 (StL)
1980—Falcons, 33-27 (StL) OT
1981—Falcons, 41-20 (Atl)
1982—Cardinals, 23-20 (Atl)
1986—Falcons, 33-13 (Atl)
1987—Cardinals, 34-21 (Atl)
1989—Cardinals, 34-20 (P)
1990—Cardinals, 24-13 (Atl)
1991—Cardinals, 16-10 (P)
1992—Falcons, 20-17 (Atl)
1993—Cardinals, 27-10 (Atl)
1994—Falcons, 10-6 (Atl)
1995—Cardinals, 40-37 (Ariz) OT
1997—Cardinals, 29-26 (Ariz)
1000—Falcons, 37-11 (Atl)
2001—Falcons, 34-14 (Ariz)
2004—Falcons, 6-3 (Atl)
2006—Falcons, 32-10 (Atl)
2007—Cardinals, 30-27 (Ariz) OT
2008—**Cardinals, 30-24 (Ariz)
2010—Falcons, 41-7 (Atl)
(RS Pts.—Falcons 559, Cardinals 538)
(PS Pts.—Cardinals 30, Falcons 24)
Franchise known as Phoenix prior to
1994 and in St. Louis prior to 1988
**NFC First-Round Playoff
*ARIZONA vs. BALTIMORE
RS: Ravens lead series, 3-1
1997—Cardinals, 16-13 (B)
2000—Ravens, 13-7 (A)
2003—Ravens, 26-18 (A)
2007—Ravens, 26-23 (B)
(RS Pts.—Ravens 78, Cardinals 64)
*ARIZONA vs. BUFFALO
RS: Bills lead series, 5-4
1971—Cardinals, 28-23 (B)
1975—Bills, 32-14 (StL)
1981—Cardinals, 24-0 (StL)
1984—Cardinals, 37-7 (StL)
1986—Bills, 17-10 (B)
1990—Bills, 45-14 (B)
1999—Bills, 31-21 (A)
2004—Bills, 38-14 (B)
2008—Cardinals, 41-17 (A)
(RS Pts.—Bills 210, Cardinals 203)
Franchise known as Phoenix prior to
1994 and in St. Louis prior to 1988
ARIZONA vs. CAROLINA
RS: Panthers lead series, 8-2
PS: Cardinals lead series, 1-0
1995—Panthers, 27-7 (C)
2001—Cardinals, 30-7 (C)
2002—Cardinals, 16-13 (C)
2003—Panthers, 20-17 (A)
2004—Panthers, 35-10 (C)
2005—Panthers, 24-20 (A)
2007—Panthers, 25-10 (A)
2008—Panthers, 27-23 (C)
   **Cardinals, 33-13 (C)
2009—Panthers, 34-21 (A)
2010—Panthers, 19-12 (C)

(RS Pts.—Panthers 231, Cardinals 166)
(PS Pts.—Cardinals 33, Panthers 13)
*NFC Divisional Playoff
*ARIZONA vs. **CHICAGO
RS: Bears lead series, 55-27-6
(NP denotes Normal Park;
Wr denotes Wrigley Field;
Co denotes Comiskey Park;
So denotes Soldier Field;
all Chicago)
1920—Cardinals, 7-6 (NP)
   Staleys, 10-0 (Wr)
1921—Tie, 0-0 (Wr)
1922—Cardinals, 6-0 (Co)
   Cardinals, 9-0 (Co)
1923—Bears, 3-0 (Wr)
1924—Bears, 6-0 (Wr)
   Bears, 21-0 (Co)
1925—Cardinals, 9-0 (Co)
   Tie, 0-0 (Wr)
1926—Bears, 16-0 (Wr)
   Bears, 10-0 (So)
   Tie, 0-0 (Wr)
1927—Bears, 9-0 (NP)
   Cardinals, 3-0 (Wr)
1928—Bears, 15-0 (NP)
   Bears, 34-0 (Wr)
1929—Tie, 0-0 (Wr)
   Cardinals, 40-6 (Co)
1930—Bears, 32-6 (Co)
   Bears, 6-0 (Wr)
1931—Bears, 26-13 (Wr)
   Bears, 18-7 (Wr)
1932—Tie, 0-0 (Wr)
   Bears, 34-0 (Wr)
1933—Bears, 12-9 (Wr)
   Bears, 22-6 (Wr)
1934—Bears, 20-0 (Wr)
   Bears, 17-6 (Wr)
1935—Tie, 7-7 (Wr)
   Bears, 13-0 (Wr)
1936—Bears, 7-3 (Wr)
   Cardinals, 14-7 (Wr)
1937—Bears, 16-7 (Wr)
   Bears, 42-28 (Wr)
1938—Bears, 16-13 (So)
   Bears, 34-28 (Wr)
1939—Bears, 44-7 (Wr)
   Bears, 48-7 (Co)
1940—Cardinals, 21-7 (Co)
   Bears, 31-23 (Wr)
1941—Bears, 53-7 (Wr)
   Bears, 34-24 (Co)
1942—Bears, 41-14 (Wr)
   Bears, 21-7 (Co)
1943—Bears, 20-0 (Wr)
   Bears, 35-24 (Co)
1945—Cardinals, 16-7 (Wr)
   Bears, 28-20 (Co)
1946—Bears, 34-17 (Co)
   Cardinals, 35-28 (Wr)
1947—Cardinals, 31-7 (Co)
   Cardinals, 30-21 (Wr)
1948—Bears, 28-17 (Co)
   Cardinals, 24-21 (Wr)
1949—Bears, 17-7 (Co)
   Bears, 52-21 (Wr)
1950—Bears, 27-6 (Wr)
   Cardinals, 20-10 (Co)
1951—Cardinals, 28-14 (Co)
   Cardinals, 24-14 (Wr)

1952—Cardinals, 21-10 (Co)
   Bears, 10-7 (Wr)
1953—Cardinals, 24-17 (Wr)
1954—Bears, 29-7 (Co)
1955—Cardinals, 53-14 (Co)
1956—Bears, 10-3 (Wr)
1957—Bears, 14-6 (Co)
1958—Bears, 30-14 (Wr)
1959—Bears, 31-7 (So)
1965—Bears, 34-13 (Wr)
1966—Cardinals, 24-17 (StL)
1967—Bears, 30-3 (Wr)
1969—Cardinals, 20-17 (StL)
1972—Bears, 27-10 (StL)
1975—Cardinals, 34-20 (So)
1977—Cardinals, 16-13 (StL)
1978—Bears, 17-10 (So)
1979—Bears, 42-6 (So)
1982—Cardinals, 10-7 (So)
1984—Cardinals, 38-21 (StL)
1990—Bears, 31-21 (P)
1994—Bears, 19-16 (A) OT
1998—Cardinals, 20-7 (A)
2001—Bears, 20-13 (C)
2000—Bears, 20-0 (C)
2006—Bears, 24-23 (A)
2009—Cardinals, 41-21 (C)
(RS Pts.—Bears 1,667, Cardinals 1,114)
Franchise known as Phoenix prior to
1994, in St. Louis prior to 1988, and in
Chicago prior to 1960
**Franchise in Decatur prior to 1921 and
known as Staleys prior to 1922
*ARIZONA vs. CINCINNATI
RS: Bengals lead series, 5-4
1973—Bengals, 42-24 (C)
1979—Bengals, 34-28 (C)
1985—Cardinals, 41-27 (StL)
1988—Bengals, 21-14 (C)
1994—Cardinals, 28-7 (A)
1997—Bengals, 24-21 (C)
2000—Bengals, 24-13 (C)
2003—Cardinals, 17-14 (A)
2007—Cardinals, 35-27 (C)
(RS Pts.—Cardinals 221, Bengals 220)
Franchise known as Phoenix prior to
1994 and in St. Louis prior to 1988
*ARIZONA vs. CLEVELAND
RS: Browns lead series, 33-12-3
1950—Browns, 34-24 (Cle)
   Browns, 10-7 (Chi)
1951—Browns, 34-17 (Chi)
   Browns, 49-28 (Cle)
1952—Browns, 28-13 (Cle)
   Browns, 10-0 (Chi)
1953—Browns, 27-7 (Chi)
   Browns, 27-16 (Cle)
1954—Browns, 31-7 (Cle)
   Browns, 35-3 (Chi)
1955—Browns, 26-20 (Chi)
   Browns, 35-24 (Cle)
1956—Cardinals, 9-7 (Chi)
   Cardinals, 24-7 (Cle)
1957—Browns, 17-7 (Chi)
   Browns, 31-0 (Cle)
1958—Browns, 35-28 (Cle)
   Browns, 38-24 (Chi)
1959—Browns, 34-7 (Chi)
   Browns, 17-7 (Cle)
1960—Browns, 28-27 (Cle)
   Tie, 17-17 (StL)

1961—Browns, 20-17 (Cle)
Browns, 21-10 (StL)
1962—Browns, 34-7 (StL)
Browns, 38-14 (Cle)
1963—Cardinals, 20-14 (Cle)
Browns, 24-10 (StL)
1964—Tie, 33-33 (Cle)
Cardinals, 28-19 (StL)
1965—Cardinals, 49-13 (Cle)
Browns, 27-24 (StL)
1966—Cardinals, 34-28 (Cle)
Browns, 38-10 (StL)
1967—Browns, 20-16 (Cle)
Browns, 20-16 (StL)
1968—Cardinals, 27-21 (Cle)
Cardinals, 27-16 (StL)
1969—Tie, 21-21 (Cle)
Browns, 27-21 (StL)
1974—Cardinals, 29-7 (StL)
1979—Browns, 38-20 (StL)
1985—Cardinals, 27-24 (Cle) OT
1988—Browns, 29-21 (P)
1994—Browns, 32-0 (Cle)
2000—Cardinals, 29-21 (A)
2003—Browns, 44-6 (Cle)
2007—Cardinals, 27-21 (A)
(RS Pts.—Browns 1,227, Cardinals 859)
*Franchise known as Phoenix prior to
1994, in St. Louis prior to 1988,
and in Chicago prior to 1960
ARIZONA vs. DALLAS
RS: Cowboys lead series, 55-29-1
PS: Cardinals lead series, 1-0
1960—Cardinals, 12-10 (StL)
1961—Cardinals, 31-17 (D)
Cardinals, 31-13 (StL)
1962—Cardinals, 28-24 (D)
Cardinals, 52-20 (StL)
1963—Cardinals, 34-7 (D)
Cowboys, 28-24 (StL)
1964—Cardinals, 16-6 (D)
Cowboys, 31-13 (StL)
1965—Cardinals, 20-13 (StL)
Cowboys, 27-13 (D)
1966—Tie, 10-10 (StL)
Cowboys, 31-17 (D)
1967—Cowboys, 46-21 (D)
1968—Cowboys, 27-10 (StL)
1969—Cowboys, 24-3 (D)
1970—Cardinals, 20-7 (StL)
Cardinals, 38-0 (D)
1971—Cowboys, 16-13 (StL)
Cowboys, 31-12 (D)
1972—Cowboys, 33-24 (D)
Cowboys, 27-6 (StL)
1973—Cowboys, 45-10 (D)
Cowboys, 30-3 (StL)
1974—Cardinals, 31-28 (StL)
Cowboys, 17-14 (D)
1975—Cowboys, 37-31 (D) OT
Cardinals, 31-17 (StL)
1976—Cardinals, 21-17 (StL)
Cowboys, 19-14 (D)
1977—Cowboys, 30-24 (StL)
Cardinals, 24-17 (D)
1978—Cowboys, 21-12 (D)
Cowboys, 24-21 (StL) OT
1979—Cowboys, 22-21 (StL)
Cowboys, 22-13 (D)
1980—Cowboys, 27-24 (StL)
Cowboys, 31-21 (D)

1981—Cowboys, 30-17 (D)
Cardinals, 20-17 (StL)
1982—Cowboys, 24-7 (StL)
1983—Cowboys, 34-17 (StL)
Cowboys, 35-17 (D)
1984—Cardinals, 31-20 (D)
Cowboys, 24-17 (StL)
1985—Cardinals, 21-10 (StL)
Cowboys, 35-17 (D)
1986—Cowboys, 31-7 (StL)
Cowboys, 37-6 (D)
1987—Cardinals, 24-13 (StL)
Cowboys, 21-16 (D)
1988—Cowboys, 17-14 (P)
Cardinals, 16-10 (D)
1989—Cardinals, 19-10 (D)
Cardinals, 24-20 (P)
1990—Cardinals, 20-3 (P)
Cowboys, 41-10 (D)
1991—Cowboys, 17-9 (P)
Cowboys, 27-7 (D)
1992—Cowboys, 31-20 (D)
Cowboys, 16-10 (P)
1993—Cowboys, 17-10 (P)
Cowboys, 20-15 (D)
1994—Cowboys, 38-3 (D)
Cowboys, 28-21 (A)
1995—Cowboys, 34-20 (D)
Cowboys, 37-13 (A)
1996—Cowboys, 17-3 (D)
Cowboys, 10-6 (A)
1997—Cardinals, 25-22 (A) OT
Cowboys, 24-6 (D)
1998—Cowboys, 38-10 (D)
Cowboys, 35-28 (A)
**Cardinals, 20-7 (D)
1999—Cowboys, 35-7 (D)
Cardinals, 13-9 (A)
2000—Cardinals, 32-31 (A)
Cowboys, 48-7 (D)
2001—Cowboys, 17-3 (D)
Cardinals, 17-10 (A)
2002—Cardinals, 9-6 (A) OT
2003—Cowboys, 24-7 (D)
2005—Cowboys, 34-13 (D)
2006—Cowboys, 27-10 (A)
2008—Cardinals, 30-24 (A) OT
2010—Cardinals, 27-26 (A)
(RS Pts.—Cowboys 1,986, Cardinals 1,464)
(PS Pts.—Cardinals 20, Cowboys 7)
*Franchise known as Phoenix prior to
1994 and in St. Louis prior to 1988
**NFC First-Round Playoff
ARIZONA vs. DENVER
RS: Broncos lead series, 7-1-1
1973—Tie, 17-17 (StL)
1977—Broncos, 7-0 (D)
1989—Broncos, 37-0 (P)
1991—Broncos, 24-19 (D)
1995—Broncos, 38-6 (D)
2001—Broncos, 38-17 (A)
2002—Broncos, 37-7 (D)
2006—Broncos, 37-20 (A)
2010—Cardinals, 43-13 (A)
(RS Pts.—Broncos 248, Cardinals 129)
*Franchise known as Phoenix prior to
1994 and in St. Louis prior to 1988
ARIZONA vs. **DETROIT
RS: Lions lead series, 31-24-5
1930—Tie, 0-0 (Port)
Cardinals, 23-0 (C)

1931—Spartans, 13-3 (Port)
Cardinals, 20-19 (C)
1932—Tie, 7-7 (Port)
1933—Spartans, 7-6 (Port)
1934—Lions, 6-0 (D)
Lions, 17-13 (C)
1935—Tie, 10-10 (D)
Lions, 7-6 (C)
1936—Lions, 39-0 (D)
Lions, 14-7 (C)
1937—Lions, 16-7 (C)
Lions, 16-7 (D)
1938—Lions, 10-0 (D)
Lions, 7-3 (C)
1939—Lions, 21-3 (D)
Lions, 17-3 (C)
1940—Tie, 0-0 (Buffalo)
Lions, 43-14 (C)
1941—Tie, 14-14 (C)
Lions, 21-3 (D)
1942—Cardinals, 13-0 (C)
Cardinals, 7-0 (D)
1943—Lions, 35-17 (D)
Lions, 7-0 (Buffalo)
1945—Lions, 10-0 (Milwaukee)
Lions, 26-0 (D)
1946—Cardinals, 34-14 (C)
Cardinals, 36-14 (D)
1947—Cardinals, 45-21 (C)
Cardinals, 17-7 (D)
1948—Cardinals, 56-20 (C)
Cardinals, 28-14 (D)
1949—Lions, 24-7 (C)
Cardinals, 42-19 (D)
1959—Lions, 45-21 (D)
1961—Lions, 45-14 (StL)
1967—Cardinals, 38-28 (StL)
1969—Lions, 20-0 (D)
1970—Lions, 16-3 (D)
1973—Lions, 20-16 (StL)
1975—Cardinals, 24-13 (D)
1978—Cardinals, 21-14 (StL)
1980—Lions, 20-7 (D)
Cardinals, 24-23 (StL)
1989—Cardinals, 16-13 (D)
1993—Lions, 26-20 (D)
Lions, 21-14 (Phx)
1995—Cardinals, 20-17 (D)
1998—Cardinals, 17-15 (D)
1999—Cardinals, 23-19 (A)
2001—Cardinals, 45-38 (A)
2002—Cardinals, 23-20 (A) OT
2003—Lions, 42-24 (D)
2004—Lions, 26-12 (D)
2005—Lions, 29-21 (D)
2006—Cardinals, 17-10 (A)
2007—Cardinals, 31-21 (A)
2009—Cardinals, 31-24 (D)
(RS Pts.—Lions 1,093, Cardinals 943)
*Franchise known as Phoenix prior to
1994, in St. Louis prior to 1988,
and in Chicago prior to 1960
**Franchise in Portsmouth prior to 1934
and known as the Spartans
ARIZONA vs. GREEN BAY
RS: Packers lead series, 43-22-4
PS: Series tied, 1-1
1921—Tie, 3-3 (C)
1922—Cardinals, 16-3 (C)
1924—Cardinals, 3-0 (C)
1925—Cardinals, 9-6 (C)

1926—Cardinals, 13-7 (GB)
Packers, 3-0 (C)
1927—Packers, 13-0 (GB)
Tie, 6-6 (C)
1928—Packers, 20-0 (GB)
1929—Packers, 9-2 (GB)
Packers, 7-6 (C)
Packers, 12-0 (C)
1930—Packers, 14-0 (GB)
Cardinals, 13-6 (C)
1931—Packers, 26-7 (GB)
Cardinals, 21-13 (C)
1932—Packers, 15-7 (GB)
Packers, 19-9 (C)
1933—Packers, 14-6 (C)
1934—Packers, 15-0 (GB)
Cardinals, 9-0 (Mil)
Cardinals, 6-0 (C)
1935—Cardinals, 7-6 (GB)
Cardinals, 3-0 (Mil)
Cardinals, 9-7 (C)
1936—Packers, 10-7 (GB)
Packers, 24-0 (Mil)
Tie, 0-0 (C)
1937—Cardinals, 14-7 (GB)
Packers, 34-13 (Mil)
1938—Packers, 28-7 (Mil)
Packers, 24-22 (Buffalo)
1939—Packers, 14-10 (GB)
Packers, 27-20 (Mil)
1940—Packers, 31-6 (Mil)
Packers, 28-7 (C)
1941—Packers, 14-13 (Mil)
Packers, 17-9 (GB)
1942—Packers, 17-13 (C)
Packers, 55-24 (GB)
1943—Packers, 28-7 (C)
Packers, 35-14 (Mil)
1945—Packers, 33-14 (GB)
Packers, 19-7 (C)
1946—Cardinals, 24-6 (GB)
1947—Cardinals, 14-10 (GB)
Cardinals, 21-20 (C)
1948—Cardinals, 17-7 (Mil)
Cardinals, 42-7 (C)
1949—Cardinals, 39-17 (Mil)
Cardinals, 41-21 (C)
1955—Packers, 31-14 (GB)
1956—Packers, 24-21 (C)
1962—Packers, 17-0 (Mil)
1963—Packers, 30-7 (StL)
1967—Packers, 31-23 (StL)
1969—Packers, 45-28 (GB)
1971—Tie, 16-16 (StL)
1973—Packers, 25-21 (GB)
1976—Cardinals, 29-0 (StL)
1982—**Packers, 41-16 (GB)
1984—Packers, 24-23 (GB)
1985—Cardinals, 43-28 (StL)
1988—Packers, 26-17 (P)
1990—Packers, 24-21 (P)
1999—Packers, 49-24 (GB)
2000—Packers, 29-3 (A)
2003—Cardinals, 20-13 (A)
2006—Packers, 31-14 (GB)
2009—Packers, 33-7 (A)
**Cardinals, 51-45 (A) OT
(RS Pts.—Packers 1,233, Cardinals 891)
(PS Pts.—Packers 86, Cardinals 67)
*Franchise known as Phoenix prior to
1994, in St. Louis prior to 1988,

and in Chicago prior to 1960
**NFC First-Round Playoff
ARIZONA vs. HOUSTON
RS: Series tied, 1-1
2005—Texans, 30-19 (H)
2009—Cardinals, 28-21 (A)
(RS Pts.—Texans 51, Cardinals 47)
ARIZONA vs. **INDIANAPOLIS
RS: Colts lead series, 8-6
1961—Colts, 16-0 (B)
1964—Colts, 47-27 (B)
1968—Colts, 27-0 (B)
1972—Cardinals, 10-3 (B)
1976—Cardinals, 24-17 (StL)
1978—Colts, 30-17 (StL)
1980—Cardinals, 17-10 (B)
1981—Cardinals, 35-24 (B)
1984—Cardinals, 34-33 (I)
1990—Cardinals, 20-17 (P)
1992—Colts, 16-13 (I)
1996—Colts, 20-13 (I)
2005—Colts, 17-13 (I)
2009—Colts, 31-10 (A)
(RS Pts.—Colts 308, Cardinals 233)
*Franchise known as Phoenix prior to
1994 and in St. Louis prior to 1988
**Franchise in Baltimore prior to 1984
ARIZONA vs. JACKSONVILLE
RS: Jaguars lead series, 2-1
2000—Jaguars, 44-10 (J)
2005—Jaguars, 24-17 (A)
2009—Cardinals, 31-17 (J)
(RS Pts.—Jaguars 85, Cardinals 58)
ARIZONA vs. KANSAS CITY
RS: Chiefs lead series, 8-2-1
1970—Tie, 6-6 (KC)
1974—Chiefs, 17-13 (StL)
1980—Chiefs, 21-13 (StL)
1983—Chiefs, 38-14 (KC)
1986—Cardinals, 23-14 (StL)
1995—Chiefs, 24-3 (A)
1998—Chiefs, 34-24 (KC)
2001—Cardinals, 24-16 (A)
2002—Chiefs, 49-0 (KC)
2006—Chiefs, 23-20 (A)
2010—Cardinals, 31-13 (KC)
(RS Pts.—Chiefs 273, Cardinals 153)
*Franchise known as Phoenix prior to
1994 and in St. Louis prior to 1988
ARIZONA vs. MIAMI
RS: Dolphins lead series, 8-2
1972—Dolphins, 31-10 (M)
1977—Dolphins, 55-14 (StL)
1978—Dolphins, 24-10 (M)
1981—Dolphins, 20-7 (StL)
1984—Dolphins, 36-28 (StL)
1990—Dolphins, 23-3 (M)
1996—Dolphins, 38-10 (A)
1999—Dolphins, 19-16 (M)
2004—Cardinals, 24-23 (M)
2008—Cardinals, 31-10 (A)
(RS Pts.—Dolphins 279, Cardinals 153)
*Franchise known as Phoenix prior to
1994 and in St. Louis prior to 1988
ARIZONA vs. MINNESOTA
RS: Vikings lead series, 11-10
PS: Vikings lead series, 2-0
1963—Cardinals, 56-14 (M)
1967—Cardinals, 34-24 (M)
1969—Vikings, 27-10 (StL)
1972—Cardinals, 19-17 (M)

1974—Vikings, 28-24 (StL)
**Vikings, 30-14 (M)
1977—Cardinals, 27-7 (M)
1979—Cardinals, 37-7 (StL)
1981—Cardinals, 30-17 (StL)
1983—Cardinals, 41-31 (StL)
1991—Vikings, 34-7 (M)
Vikings, 28-0 (P)
1994—Cardinals, 17-7 (A)
1995—Vikings, 30-24 (A) OT
1996—Vikings, 41-17 (M)
1997—Vikings, 20-19 (A)
1998—**Vikings, 41-21 (M)
2000—Vikings, 31-14 (M)
2003—Cardinals, 18-17 (A)
2006—Vikings, 31-26 (M)
2008—Vikings, 35-14 (A)
2009—Cardinals, 30-17 (A)
2010—Vikings, 27-24 (M) OT
(RS Pts.—Vikings 490, Cardinals 488)
(PS Pts.—Vikings 71, Cardinals 35)
*Franchise known as Phoenix prior to
1994 and in St. Louis prior to 1988
**NFC Divisional Playoff
ARIZONA vs. **NEW ENGLAND
RS: Series tied, 6-6
1970—Cardinals, 31-0 (StL)
1975—Cardinals, 24-17 (StL)
1978—Patriots, 16-6 (StL)
1981—Cardinals, 27-20 (NE)
1984—Cardinals, 33-10 (NE)
1990—Cardinals, 34-14 (P)
1991—Cardinals, 24-10 (P)
1993—Patriots, 23-21 (P)
1996—Patriots, 31-0 (NE)
1999—Patriots, 27-3 (A)
2004—Patriots, 23-12 (A)
2008—Patriots, 47-7 (NE)
(RS Pts.—Patriots 238, Cardinals 222)
*Franchise known as Phoenix prior to
1994 and in St. Louis prior to 1988
**Franchise in Boston prior to 1971
ARIZONA vs. NEW ORLEANS
RS: Cardinals lead series, 14-12
PS: Saints lead series, 1-0
1967—Cardinals, 31-20 (StL)
1968—Cardinals, 21-20 (NO)
Cardinals, 31-17 (StL)
1969—Saints, 51-42 (StL)
1970—Cardinals, 24-17 (StL)
1974—Saints, 14-0 (NO)
1977—Cardinals, 49-31 (StL)
1980—Cardinals, 40-7 (NO)
1981—Cardinals, 30-3 (StL)
1982—Cardinals, 21-7 (NO)
1983—Saints, 28-17 (NO)
1984—Saints, 34-24 (NO)
1985—Cardinals, 28-16 (StL)
1986—Saints, 16-7 (StL)
1987—Cardinals, 24-19 (StL)
1990—Saints, 28-7 (NO)
1991—Saints, 27-3 (P)
1992—Saints, 30-21 (P)
1993—Saints, 20-17 (P)
1996—Cardinals, 28-14 (NO)
1997—Cardinals, 27-10 (NO)
1998—Cardinals, 19-17 (A)
2000—Saints, 21-10 (A)
2004—Cardinals, 34-10 (A)
2007—Saints, 31-24 (NO)
2009—**Saints, 45-14 (NO)

2010—Cardinals, 30-20 (A)
(RS Pts.—Cardinals 592, Saints 545)
(PS Pts.—Saints 45, Cardinals 14)
*Franchise known as Phoenix prior to
1994 and in St. Louis prior to 1988
**NFC Divisional Playoff
**ARIZONA vs. N.Y. GIANTS*
RS: Giants lead series, 79-42-2
1926—Giants, 20-0 (NY)
1927—Giants, 28-7 (NY)
1929—Giants, 24-21 (NY)
1930—Giants, 25-12 (NY)
　　　Giants, 13-7 (C)
1935—Cardinals, 14-13 (NY)
1936—Giants, 14-6 (NY)
1938—Giants, 6-0 (NY)
1939—Giants, 17-7 (NY)
1941—Cardinals, 10-7 (NY)
1942—Giants, 21-7 (NY)
1943—Giants, 24-13 (NY)
1946—Giants, 28-24 (NY)
1947—Giants, 35-31 (NY)
1948—Cardinals, 63-35 (NY)
1949—Giants, 41-38 (NY)
1950—Cardinals, 17-3 (C)
　　　Giants, 51-21 (NY)
1951—Giants, 28-17 (NY)
　　　Giants, 10-0 (C)
1952—Cardinals, 24-23 (NY)
　　　Giants, 28-6 (C)
1953—Giants, 21-7 (NY)
　　　Giants, 23-20 (C)
1954—Giants, 41-10 (C)
　　　Giants, 31-17 (NY)
1955—Cardinals, 28-17 (C)
　　　Giants, 10-0 (NY)
1956—Cardinals, 35-27 (C)
　　　Giants, 23-10 (NY)
1957—Giants, 27-14 (NY)
　　　Giants, 28-21 (C)
1958—Giants, 37-7 (Buffalo)
　　　Cardinals, 23-6 (NY)
1959—Giants, 9-3 (NY)
　　　Giants, 30-20 (Minn)
1960—Giants, 35-14 (StL)
　　　Cardinals, 20-13 (NY)
1961—Giants, 21-10 (NY)
　　　Giants, 24-9 (StL)
1962—Giants, 31-14 (StL)
　　　Giants, 31-28 (NY)
1963—Giants, 38-21 (StL)
　　　Cardinals, 24-17 (NY)
1964—Giants, 34-17 (NY)
　　　Tie, 10-10 (StL)
1965—Giants, 14-10 (NY)
　　　Giants, 28-15 (StL)
1966—Cardinals, 24-19 (StL)
　　　Cardinals, 20-17 (NY)
1967—Giants, 37-20 (StL)
　　　Giants, 37-14 (NY)
1968—Cardinals, 28-21 (NY)
1969—Cardinals, 42-17 (StL)
　　　Giants, 49-6 (NY)
1970—Giants, 35-17 (NY)
　　　Giants, 34-17 (StL)
1971—Giants, 21-20 (StL)
　　　Cardinals, 24-7 (NY)
1972—Giants, 27-21 (NY)
　　　Giants, 13-7 (StL)
1973—Cardinals, 35-27 (StL)
　　　Giants, 24-13 (New Haven)

1974—Cardinals, 23-21 (New Haven)
　　　Cardinals, 26-14 (StL)
1975—Cardinals, 26-14 (StL)
　　　Cardinals, 20-13 (NY)
1976—Cardinals, 27-21 (StL)
　　　Cardinals, 17-14 (NY)
1977—Cardinals, 28-0 (StL)
　　　Giants, 27-7 (NY)
1978—Cardinals, 20-10 (StL)
　　　Giants, 17-0 (NY)
1979—Cardinals, 27-14 (NY)
　　　Cardinals, 29-20 (StL)
1980—Giants, 41-35 (StL)
　　　Cardinals, 23-7 (NY)
1981—Giants, 34-14 (NY)
　　　Giants, 20-10 (StL)
1982—Cardinals, 24-21 (StL)
1983—Tie, 20-20 (StL) OT
　　　Cardinals, 10-6 (NY)
1984—Giants, 16-10 (NY)
　　　Cardinals, 31-21 (StL)
1985—Giants, 27-17 (NY)
　　　Giants, 34-3 (StL)
1986—Giants, 13-6 (StL)
　　　Giants, 27-7 (NY)
1987—Giants, 30-7 (NY)
　　　Cardinals, 27-24 (StL)
1988—Cardinals, 24-17 (P)
　　　Giants, 44-7 (NY)
1989—Giants, 35-7 (NY)
　　　Giants, 20-13 (P)
1990—Giants, 20-19 (NY)
　　　Giants, 24-21 (P)
1991—Giants, 20-9 (NY)
　　　Giants, 21-14 (P)
1992—Giants, 31-21 (NY)
　　　Cardinals, 19-0 (P)
1993—Giants, 19-17 (NY)
　　　Cardinals, 17-6 (P)
1994—Giants, 20-17 (A)
　　　Cardinals, 10-9 (NY)
1995—Giants, 27-21 (NY) OT
　　　Giants, 10-6 (A)
1996—Giants, 16-8 (NY)
　　　Cardinals, 31-23 (A)
1997—Giants, 27-13 (A)
　　　Giants, 19-10 (NY)
1998—Giants, 34-7 (NY)
　　　Giants, 23-19 (A)
1999—Cardinals, 14-3 (A)
　　　Cardinals, 34-24 (NY)
2000—Giants, 21-16 (NY)
　　　Giants, 31-7 (A)
2001—Giants, 17-10 (A)
　　　Giants, 17-13 (NY)
2002—Cardinals, 21-7 (A)
2004—Cardinals, 17-14 (A)
2005—Giants, 42-19 (NY)
2008—Giants, 37-29 (A)
2009—Giants, 24-17 (NY)
(RS Pts.—Giants 2,715, Cardinals 2,099)
*Franchise known as Phoenix prior to
1994, in St. Louis prior to 1988,
and in Chicago prior to 1960
**ARIZONA vs. N.Y. JETS*
RS: Jets lead series, 5-2
1971—Cardinals, 17-10 (StL)
1975—Cardinals, 37-6 (NY)
1978—Jets, 23-10 (NY)
1996—Jets, 31-21 (A)
1999—Jets, 12-7 (NY)

2004—Jets, 13-3 (A)
2008—Jets, 56-35 (NY)
(RS Pts.—Jets 151, Cardinals 130)
*Franchise known as Phoenix prior to
1994 and in St. Louis prior to 1988
**ARIZONA vs. **OAKLAND*
RS: Raiders lead series, 5-3
1973—Raiders, 17-10 (StL)
1983—Cardinals, 34-24 (LA)
1989—Raiders, 16-14 (LA)
1998—Raiders, 23-20 (A)
2001—Cardinals, 34-31 (O) OT
2002—Raiders, 41-20 (A)
2006—Raiders, 22-9 (O)
2010—Cardinals, 24-23 (A)
(RS Pts.— Raiders 197, Cardinals 165)
*Franchise known as Phoenix prior to
1994 and in St. Louis prior to 1988
**Franchise in Los Angeles from
1982-1994
**ARIZONA vs. PHILADELPHIA*
RS: Series tied, 53-53-5
PS: Cardinals lead series, 2-1
1935—Cardinals, 12-3 (C)
1936—Cardinals, 13-0 (C)
1937—Tie, 6-6 (P)
1938—Eagles, 7-0 (Erie, Pa.)
1941—Eagles, 21-14 (P)
1945—Eagles, 21-6 (P)
1947—Cardinals, 45-21 (P)
　　　**Cardinals, 28-21 (C)
1948—Cardinals, 21-14 (C)
　　　**Eagles, 7-0 (P)
1949—Eagles, 28-3 (P)
1950—Eagles, 45-7 (C)
　　　Cardinals, 14-10 (P)
1951—Eagles, 17-14 (C)
1952—Eagles, 10-7 (P)
　　　Cardinals, 28-22 (C)
1953—Eagles, 56-17 (C)
　　　Eagles, 38-0 (P)
1954—Eagles, 35-16 (C)
　　　Eagles, 30-14 (P)
1955—Tie, 24-24 (C)
　　　Eagles, 27-3 (P)
1956—Cardinals, 20-6 (P)
　　　Cardinals, 28-17 (C)
1957—Eagles, 38-21 (C)
　　　Cardinals, 31-27 (P)
1958—Tie, 21-21 (C)
　　　Eagles, 49-21 (P)
1959—Eagles, 28-24 (Minn)
　　　Eagles, 27-17 (P)
1960—Eagles, 31-27 (P)
　　　Eagles, 20-6 (StL)
1961—Cardinals, 30-27 (P)
　　　Eagles, 20-7 (StL)
1962—Cardinals, 27-21 (P)
　　　Cardinals, 45-35 (StL)
1963—Cardinals, 28-24 (P)
　　　Cardinals, 38-14 (StL)
1964—Cardinals, 38-13 (P)
　　　Cardinals, 36-34 (StL)
1965—Eagles, 34-27 (P)
　　　Eagles, 28-24 (StL)
1966—Cardinals, 16-13 (StL)
　　　Cardinals, 41-10 (P)
1967—Cardinals, 48-14 (StL)
1968—Cardinals, 45-17 (P)
1969—Eagles, 34-30 (StL)
1970—Cardinals, 35-20 (P)

Cardinals, 23-14 (StL)
1971—Eagles, 37-20 (StL)
Eagles, 19-7 (P)
1972—Tie, 6-6 (P)
Cardinals, 24-23 (StL)
1973—Cardinals, 34-23 (P)
Eagles, 27-24 (StL)
1974—Cardinals, 7-3 (StL)
Cardinals, 13-3 (P)
1975—Cardinals, 31-20 (StL)
Cardinals, 24-23 (P)
1976—Cardinals, 33-14 (StL)
Cardinals, 17-14 (P)
1977—Cardinals, 21-17 (P)
Cardinals, 21-16 (StL)
1978—Cardinals, 16-10 (P)
Eagles, 14-10 (StL)
1979—Cardinals, 24-20 (StL)
Eagles, 16-13 (P)
1980—Cardinals, 24-14 (StL)
Eagles, 17-3 (P)
1981—Eagles, 52-10 (StL)
Eagles, 38-0 (P)
1982—Cardinals, 23-20 (P)
1983—Cardinals, 14-11 (P)
Cardinals, 31-7 (StL)
1984—Cardinals, 34-14 (P)
Cardinals, 17-16 (StL)
1985—Eagles, 30-7 (P)
Eagles, 24-14 (StL)
1986—Cardinals, 13-10 (StL)
Tie, 10-10 (P) OT
1987—Eagles, 28-23 (StL)
Cardinals, 31-19 (P)
1988—Eagles, 31-21 (P)
Eagles, 23-17 (Phx)
1989—Eagles, 17-5 (Phx)
Eagles, 31-14 (P)
1990—Cardinals, 23-21 (P)
Eagles, 23-21 (Phx)
1991—Cardinals, 26-10 (P)
Eagles, 34-14 (Phx)
1992—Eagles, 31-14 (Phx)
Eagles, 7-3 (P)
1993—Eagles, 23-17 (P)
Cardinals, 16-3 (Phx)
1994—Eagles, 17-7 (P)
Cardinals, 12-6 (A)
1995—Eagles, 31-19 (A)
Eagles, 21-20 (P)
1996—Cardinals, 36-30 (A)
Eagles, 29-19 (P)
1997—Eagles, 13-10 (P) OT
Cardinals, 31-21 (A)
1998—Cardinals, 17-3 (A)
Cardinals, 20-17 (P) OT
1999—Cardinals, 25-24 (P)
Cardinals, 21-17 (A)
2000—Eagles, 33-14 (A)
Eagles, 34-9 (P)
2001—Cardinals, 21-20 (P)
Eagles, 21-7 (A)
2002—Eagles, 38-14 (P)
2005—Cardinals, 27-21 (A)
2008—Eagles, 48-20 (P)
***Cardinals, 32-25 (A)
(RS Pts.—Eagles 2,388, Cardinals 2,153)
(PS Pts.—Cardinals 60, Eagles 53)
*Franchise known as Phoenix prior to
1994, in St. Louis prior to 1988,
and in Chicago prior to 1960

**NFL Championship
***NFC Championship
**ARIZONA vs. **PITTSBURGH*
RS: Steelers lead series, 31-23-3
PS: Steelers lead series, 1-0
1933—Pirates, 14-13 (P)
1935—Pirates, 17-13 (P)
1936—Cardinals, 14-6 (C)
1937—Cardinals, 13-7 (P)
1939—Cardinals, 10-0 (P)
1940—Tie, 7-7 (P)
1942—Steelers, 19-3 (P)
1945—Steelers, 23-0 (P)
1946—Steelers, 14-7 (P)
1948—Cardinals, 24-7 (P)
1950—Steelers, 28-17 (C)
Steelers, 28-7 (P)
1951—Steelers, 28-14 (C)
1952—Steelers, 34-28 (C)
Steelers, 17-14 (P)
1953—Steelers, 31-28 (P)
Steelers, 21-17 (C)
1954—Cardinals, 17-14 (C)
Steelers, 20-17 (P)
1955—Steelers, 14-7 (P)
Cardinals, 27-13 (C)
1956—Steelers, 14-7 (P)
Cardinals, 38-27 (C)
1957—Steelers, 29-20 (P)
Steelers, 27-2 (C)
1958—Steelers, 27-20 (C)
Steelers, 38-21 (P)
1959—Cardinals, 45-24 (C)
Steelers, 35-20 (P)
1960—Steelers, 27-14 (P)
Cardinals, 38-7 (StL)
1961—Steelers, 30-27 (P)
Cardinals, 20-0 (StL)
1962—Steelers, 26-17 (StL)
Steelers, 19-7 (P)
1963—Steelers, 23-10 (P)
Cardinals, 24-23 (StL)
1964—Cardinals, 34-30 (StL)
Cardinals, 21-20 (P)
1965—Cardinals, 20-7 (P)
Cardinals, 21-17 (StL)
1966—Steelers, 30-9 (P)
Cardinals, 6-3 (StL)
1967—Cardinals, 28-14 (P)
Tie, 14-14 (StL)
1968—Tie, 28-28 (StL)
Cardinals, 20-10 (P)
1969—Cardinals, 27-14 (P)
Cardinals, 47-10 (StL)
1972—Steelers, 25-19 (StL)
1979—Steelers, 24-21 (StL)
1985—Steelers, 23-10 (P)
1988—Cardinals, 31-14 (Phx)
1994—Cardinals, 20-17 (A) OT
1997—Steelers, 26-20 (A) OT
2003—Steelers, 28-15 (P)
2007—Cardinals, 21-14 (A)
2008—***Steelers, 27-23 (Tampa Bay)
(RS Pts.—Steelers 1,106, Cardinals 1,059)
(PS Pts.—Steelers 27, Cardinals 23)
*Franchise known as Phoenix prior to
1994, in St. Louis prior to 1988,
and in Chicago prior to 1960
**Steelers known as Pirates prior to 1940
***Super Bowl XLIII

*ARIZONA vs. **ST. LOUIS*
RS: Series tied, 31-31-2
PS: Rams lead series, 1-0
1937—Cardinals, 6-0 (Cle)
Cardinals, 13-7 (Chi)
1938—Cardinals, 7-6 (Cle)
Cardinals, 31-17 (Chi)
1939—Rams, 24-0 (Chi)
Rams, 14-0 (Cle)
1940—Rams, 26-14 (Cle)
Cardinals, 17-7 (Chi)
1941—Rams, 10-6 (Cle)
Cardinals, 7-0 (Chi)
1942—Cardinals, 7-0 (Buffalo)
Rams, 7-3 (Cle)
1945—Rams, 21-0 (Cle)
Rams, 35-21 (Chi)
1946—Cardinals, 34-10 (Chi)
Rams, 17-14 (LA)
1947—Rams, 27-7 (LA)
Cardinals, 17-10 (Chi)
1948—Cardinals, 27-22 (LA)
Cardinals, 27-24 (Chi)
1949—Tie, 28-28 (Chi)
Cardinals, 31-27 (LA)
1951—Rams, 45-21 (LA)
1953—Tie, 24-24 (Chi)
1954—Rams, 28-17 (LA)
1958—Rams, 20-14 (Chi)
1960—Cardinals, 43-21 (LA)
1965—Rams, 27-3 (StL)
1968—Rams, 24-13 (StL)
1970—Rams, 34-13 (LA)
1972—Cardinals, 24-14 (StL)
1975—***Rams, 35-23 (LA)
1976—Cardinals, 30-28 (LA)
1979—Rams, 21-0 (LA)
1980—Rams, 21-13 (StL)
1984—Rams, 16-13 (StL)
1985—Rams, 46-14 (LA)
1986—Rams, 16-10 (StL)
1987—Rams, 27-24 (StL)
1988—Cardinals, 41-27 (LA)
1989—Rams, 37-14 (LA)
1991—Cardinals, 24-14 (LA)
1992—Cardinals, 20-14 (LA)
1993 Cardinals, 38 10 (P)
1994—Rams, 14-12 (LA)
1996—Cardinals, 31-28 (A) OT
1998—Cardinals, 20-17 (StL)
2002—Rams, 27-14 (A)
Rams, 30-28 (StL)
2003—Rams, 37-13 (StL)
Rams, 30-27 (A) OT
2004—Rams, 17-10 (StL)
Cardinals, 31-7 (A)
2005—Rams, 17-12 (A)
Cardinals, 38-28 (StL)
2006—Rams, 16-14 (A)
Cardinals, 34-20 (StL)
2007—Cardinals, 34-31 (StL)
Cardinals, 48-19 (A)
2008—Cardinals, 34-13 (StL)
Cardinals, 34-10 (A)
2009—Cardinals, 21-13 (StL)
Cardinals, 31-10 (A)
2010—Cardinals, 17-13 (StL)
Rams, 19-6 (A)
(RS Pts.—Rams 1,269, Cardinals 1,239)
(PS Pts.—Rams 35, Cardinals 23)

*Franchise known as Phoenix prior to 1994, in St. Louis prior to 1988, and in Chicago prior to 1960
**Franchise in Los Angeles prior to 1995 and in Cleveland prior to 1946
***NFC Divisional Playoff

*ARIZONA vs. SAN DIEGO
RS: Chargers lead series, 9-3
1971—Chargers, 20-17 (SD)
1976—Chargers, 43-24 (SD)
1983—Cardinals, 44-14 (StL)
1987—Chargers, 28-24 (SD)
1989—Chargers, 24-13 (P)
1992—Chargers, 27-21 (P)
1995—Chargers, 28-25 (SD)
1998—Cardinals, 16-13 (A)
2001—Cardinals, 20-17 (SD)
2002—Chargers, 23-15 (A)
2006—Chargers, 27-20 (SD)
2010—Chargers, 41-10 (SD)
(RS Pts.—Chargers 305, Cardinals 249)
*Franchise known as Phoenix prior to 1994, in St. Louis prior to 1988,

*ARIZONA vs. SAN FRANCISCO
RS: 49ers lead series, 23-16
1951—Cardinals, 27-21 (SF)
1957—Cardinals, 20-10 (SF)
1962—49ers, 24-17 (StL)
1964—Cardinals, 23-13 (A)
1968—49ers, 35-17 (SF)
1971—49ers, 26-14 (StL)
1974—Cardinals, 34-9 (SF)
1976—Cardinals, 23-20 (StL) OT
1978—Cardinals, 16-10 (SF)
1979—Cardinals, 13-10 (StL)
1980—49ers, 24-21 (SF) OT
1982—49ers, 31-20 (SF)
1983—49ers, 42-27 (StL)
1986—49ers, 43-17 (SF)
1987—49ers, 34-28 (SF)
1988—Cardinals, 24-23 (P)
1991—49ers, 14-10 (SF)
1992—Cardinals, 24-14 (P)
1993—49ers, 28-14 (St)
1999—49ers, 24-10 (A)
2000—49ers, 27-20 (SF)
2002—49ers, 38-28 (SF)
    49ers, 17-14 (A)
2003—Cardinals, 16-13 (A) OT
    49ers, 50-14 (SF)
2004—49ers, 31-28 (SF) OT
    49ers, 31-28 (A) OT
2005—Cardinals, 31-14 (Mex. City)
    Cardinals, 17-10 (SF)
2006—Cardinals, 34-27 (A)
    Cardinals, 26-20 (SF)
2007—49ers, 20-17 (SF)
    49ers, 37-31 (A) OT
2008—Cardinals, 23-13 (SF)
    Cardinals, 29-24 (A)
2009—49ers, 20-16 (A)
    49ers, 24-9 (SF)
2010—49ers, 27-6 (A)
    49ers, 38-7 (SF)
(RS Pts.—49ers 936, Cardinals 793)
*Franchise known as Phoenix prior to 1994, in St. Louis prior to 1988, and in Chicago prior to 1960

*ARIZONA vs. SEATTLE
RS: Cardinals lead series, 13-11
1976—Cardinals, 30-24 (S)

1983—Cardinals, 33-28 (StL)
1989—Cardinals, 34-24 (S)
1993—Cardinals, 30-27 (S) OT
1995—Cardinals, 20-14 (A) OT
1998—Seahawks, 33-14 (S)
2002—Cardinals, 24-13 (S)
    Seahawks, 27-6 (A)
2003—Seahawks, 38-0 (A)
    Seahawks, 28-10 (S)
2004—Cardinals, 25-17 (A)
    Seahawks, 24-21 (S)
2005—Seahawks, 37-12 (S)
    Seahawks, 33-19 (A)
2006—Seahawks, 21-10 (S)
    Cardinals, 27-21 (A)
2007—Cardinals, 23-20 (A)
    Seahawks, 42-21 (S)
2008—Cardinals, 26-20 (S)
    Cardinals, 34-21 (A)
2009—Cardinals, 27-3 (S)
    Cardinals, 31-20 (A)
2010—Seahawks, 22-10 (S)
    Seahawks, 36-18 (A)
(RS Pts.—Seahawks 593, Cardinals 505)
*Franchise known as Phoenix prior to 1994 and in St. Louis prior to 1988

*ARIZONA vs. TAMPA BAY
RS: Buccaneers lead series, 9-8
1977—Buccaneers, 17-7 (TB)
1981—Buccaneers, 20-10 (TB)
1983—Cardinals, 34-27 (TB)
1985—Buccaneers, 16-0 (TB)
1986—Cardinals, 30-19 (TB)
    Cardinals, 21-17 (StL)
1987—Cardinals, 31-28 (StL)
    Cardinals, 31-14 (TB)
1988—Cardinals, 30-24 (TB)
1989—Buccaneers, 14-13 (P)
1992—Buccaneers, 23-7 (TB)
    Buccaneers, 7-3 (P)
1996—Cardinals, 13-9 (A)
1997—Buccaneers, 19-18 (TB)
2004—Cardinals, 12-7 (A)
2007—Buccaneers, 17-10 (TB)
2010—Buccaneers, 38-35 (A)
(RS Pts.—Buccaneers 316, Cardinals 305)
*Franchise known as Phoenix prior to 1994 and in St. Louis prior to 1988

*ARIZONA vs. **TENNESSEE
RS: Cardinals lead series, 5-4
1970—Cardinals, 44-0 (StL)
1974—Cardinals, 31-27 (H)
1979—Cardinals, 24-17 (H)
1985—Oilers, 20-10 (StL)
1988—Oilers, 38-20 (H)
1994—Cardinals, 30-12 (H)
1997—Oilers, 41-14 (A)
2005—Cardinals, 20-10 (A)
2009—Titans, 20-17 (T)
(RS Pts.—Cardinals 210, Titans 185)
*Franchise known as Phoenix prior to 1994 and in St. Louis prior to 1988
**Franchise in Houston prior to 1997; known as Oilers prior to 1999

*ARIZONA vs. **WASHINGTON
RS: Redskins lead series, 73-44-2
1932—Cardinals, 9-0 (B)
    Braves, 8-6 (C)
1933—Redskins, 10-0 (C)
    Tie, 0-0 (B)
1934—Redskins, 9-0 (B)

1935—Cardinals, 6-0 (B)
1936—Redskins, 13-10 (B)
1937—Cardinals, 21-14 (W)
1939—Redskins, 28-7 (W)
1940—Redskins, 28-21 (W)
1942—Redskins, 28-0 (W)
1943—Cardinals, 13-7 (W)
1945—Redskins, 24-21 (W)
1947—Redskins, 45-21 (W)
1949—Cardinals, 38-7 (C)
1950—Cardinals, 38-28 (W)
1951—Redskins, 7-3 (C)
    Redskins, 20-17 (W)
1952—Cardinals, 23-7 (C)
    Cardinals, 17-6 (W)
1953—Redskins, 24-13 (C)
    Redskins, 28-17 (W)
1954—Cardinals, 38-16 (C)
    Redskins, 37-20 (W)
1955—Cardinals, 24-10 (W)
    Redskins, 31-0 (C)
1956—Cardinals, 31-3 (W)
    Redskins, 17-14 (C)
1957—Redskins, 37-14 (C)
    Cardinals, 44-14 (W)
1958—Cardinals, 37-10 (C)
    Redskins, 45-31 (W)
1959—Cardinals, 49-21 (C)
    Redskins, 23-14 (W)
1960—Cardinals, 44-7 (StL)
    Cardinals, 26-14 (W)
1961—Cardinals, 24-0 (W)
    Cardinals, 38-24 (StL)
1962—Redskins, 24-14 (W)
    Tie, 17-17 (StL)
1963—Cardinals, 21-7 (W)
    Cardinals, 24-20 (StL)
1964—Cardinals, 23-17 (W)
    Cardinals, 38-24 (StL)
1965—Cardinals, 37-16 (W)
    Redskins, 24-20 (StL)
1966—Cardinals, 23-7 (StL)
    Redskins, 26-20 (W)
1967—Cardinals, 27-21 (W)
1968—Cardinals, 41-14 (StL)
1969—Redskins, 33-17 (W)
1970—Cardinals, 27-17 (StL)
    Redskins, 28-27 (W)
1971—Cardinals, 24-17 (StL)
    Redskins, 20-0 (W)
1972—Redskins, 24-10 (W)
    Redskins, 33-3 (StL)
1973—Cardinals, 34-27 (StL)
    Redskins, 31-13 (W)
1974—Cardinals, 17-10 (W)
    Cardinals, 23-20 (StL)
1975—Cardinals, 27-17 (W)
    Cardinals, 20-17 (StL) OT
1976—Redskins, 20-10 (W)
    Redskins, 16-10 (StL)
1977—Redskins, 24-14 (W)
    Redskins, 26-20 (StL)
1978—Redskins, 28-10 (StL)
    Cardinals, 27-17 (W)
1979—Redskins, 17-7 (StL)
    Redskins, 30-28 (W)
1980—Cardinals, 23-0 (W)
    Redskins, 31-7 (StL)
1981—Cardinals, 40-30 (StL)
    Redskins, 42-21 (W)
1982—Redskins, 12-7 (StL)

Redskins, 28-0 (W)
1983—Redskins, 38-14 (StL)
Redskins, 45-7 (W)
1984—Cardinals, 26-24 (StL)
Redskins, 29-27 (W)
1985—Redskins, 27-10 (W)
Redskins, 27-16 (StL)
1986—Redskins, 28-21 (W)
Redskins, 20-17 (StL)
1987—Redskins, 28-21 (W)
Redskins, 34-17 (StL)
1988—Cardinals, 30-21 (P)
Redskins, 33-17 (W)
1989—Redskins, 30-28 (W)
Redskins, 29-10 (P)
1990—Redskins, 31-0 (W)
Redskins, 38-10 (P)
1991—Redskins, 34-0 (W)
Redskins, 20-14 (P)
1992—Cardinals, 27-24 (P)
Redskins, 41-3 (W)
1993—Cardinals, 17-10 (W)
Cardinals, 36-6 (P)
1994—Cardinals, 19-16 (W) OT
Cardinals, 17-15 (A)
1995—Redskins, 27-7 (W)
Cardinals, 24-20 (A)
1996—Cardinals, 37-34 (W) OT
Cardinals, 27-26 (A)
1997—Redskins, 19-13 (W) OT
Redskins, 38-28 (A)
1998—Cardinals, 29-27 (A)
Cardinals, 45-42 (W)
1999—Redskins, 24-10 (A)
Redskins, 28-3 (W)
2000—Cardinals, 16-15 (A)
Redskins, 20-3 (W)
2001—Redskins, 20-10 (A)
Redskins, 20-17 (W)
2002—Redskins, 31-23 (W)
2005—Redskins, 17-13 (A)
2007—Redskins, 21-19 (W)
2008—Redskins, 24-17 (W)
(RS Pts.—Redskins 2,645, Cardinals 2,203)
*Franchise known as Phoenix prior to
1994, in St. Louis prior to 1988,
and in Chicago prior to 1960
**Franchise in Boston prior to 1937 and
known as Braves prior to 1933

ATLANTA vs. ARIZONA
RS: Cardinals lead series, 14-11
PS: Cardinals lead series, 1-0;
See Arizona vs. Atlanta

ATLANTA vs. BALTIMORE
RS: Series tied, 2-2
1999—Ravens, 19-13 (A) OT
2002—Falcons, 20-17 (A)
2006—Ravens, 24-10 (B)
2010—Falcons, 26-21 (A)
(RS Pts.—Ravens 81, Falcons 69)

ATLANTA vs. BUFFALO
RS: Falcons lead series, 6-4
1973—Bills, 17-6 (A)
1977—Bills, 3-0 (B)
1980—Falcons, 30-14 (B)
1983—Falcons, 31-14 (A)
1989—Falcons, 30-28 (A)
1992—Bills, 41-14 (B)
1995—Bills, 23-17 (B)
2001—Falcons, 33-30 (A)

2005—Falcons, 24-16 (B)
2009—Falcons, 31-3 (A)
(RS Pts.—Falcons 216, Bills 189)

ATLANTA vs. CAROLINA
RS: Falcons lead series, 20-12
1995—Falcons, 23-20 (A) OT
Panthers, 21-17 (C)
1996—Panthers, 29-6 (C)
Falcons, 20-17 (A)
1997—Panthers, 9-6 (A)
Panthers, 21-12 (C)
1998—Falcons, 19-14 (C)
Falcons, 51-23 (A)
1999—Falcons, 27-20 (A)
Panthers, 34-28 (C)
2000—Falcons, 15-10 (C)
Falcons, 13-12 (A)
2001—Falcons, 24-16 (A)
Falcons, 10-7 (C)
2002—Falcons, 30-0 (A)
Falcons, 41-0 (C)
2003—Panthers, 23-3 (C)
Falcons, 20-14 (A) OT
2004—Falcons, 27-10 (C)
Falcons, 34-31 (A) OT
2005—Panthers, 24-6 (C)
Panthers, 44-11 (A)
2006—Falcons, 20-6 (C)
Panthers, 10-3 (A)
2007—Panthers, 27-20 (A)
Falcons, 20-13 (C)
2008—Panthers, 24-9 (C)
Falcons, 45-28 (A)
2009—Falcons, 28-20 (A)
Panthers, 28-19 (C)
2010—Falcons, 31-10 (A)
Falcons, 31-10 (A)
(RS Pts.—Falcons 669, Panthers 575)

ATLANTA vs. CHICAGO
RS: Series tied, 12-12
1966—Bears, 23-6 (C)
1967—Bears, 23-14 (A)
1968—Falcons, 16-13 (C)
1969—Falcons, 48-31 (A)
1970—Bears, 23-14 (A)
1972—Falcons, 37-21 (C)
1973—Falcons, 46-6 (A)
1974—Falcons, 13-10 (A)
1976—Falcons, 10-0 (A)
1977—Falcons, 16-10 (C)
1978—Bears, 13-7 (C)
1980—Bears, 28-17 (A)
1983—Falcons, 20-17 (C)
1985—Bears, 36-0 (C)
1986—Bears, 13-10 (A)
1990—Bears, 30-24 (A)
1992—Bears, 41-31 (C)
1993—Bears, 6-0 (C)
1998—Falcons, 20-13 (A)
2001—Bears, 31-3 (A)
2002—Bears, 14-13 (A)
2005—Bears, 16-3 (C)
2008—Falcons, 22-20 (A)
2009—Falcons, 21-14 (A)
(RS Pts.—Bears 441, Falcons 422)

ATLANTA vs. CINCINNATI
RS: Bengals lead series, 7-5
1971—Falcons, 9-6 (C)
1975—Bengals, 21-14 (A)
1978—Bengals, 37-7 (C)
1981—Bengals, 30-28 (A)

1984—Bengals, 35-14 (C)
1987—Bengals, 16-10 (A)
1990—Falcons, 38-17 (A)
1993—Bengals, 21-17 (C)
1996—Bengals, 41-31 (C)
2002—Falcons, 30-3 (A)
2006—Falcons, 29-27 (C)
2010—Falcons, 39-32 (A)
(RS Pts.—Bengals 286, Falcons 266)

ATLANTA vs. CLEVELAND
RS: Browns lead series, 10-3
1966—Browns, 49-17 (A)
1968—Browns, 30-7 (C)
1971—Falcons, 31-14 (C)
1976—Browns, 20-17 (A)
1978—Browns, 24-16 (A)
1981—Browns, 28-17 (C)
1984—Browns, 23-7 (A)
1987—Browns, 38-3 (C)
1990—Browns, 13-10 (C)
1993—Falcons, 17-14 (A)
2002—Browns, 24-16 (C)
2006—Browns, 17-13 (A)
2010—Falcons, 20-10 (C)
(RS Pts.—Browns 304, Falcons 191)

ATLANTA vs. DALLAS
RS: Cowboys lead series, 14-8
PS: Cowboys lead series, 2-0
1966—Cowboys, 47-14 (A)
1967—Cowboys, 37-7 (D)
1969—Cowboys, 24-17 (A)
1970—Cowboys, 13-0 (D)
1974—Cowboys, 24-0 (A)
1976—Falcons, 17-10 (A)
1978—*Cowboys, 27-20 (D)
1980—*Cowboys, 30-27 (A)
1985—Cowboys, 24-10 (D)
1986—Falcons, 37-35 (D)
1987—Falcons, 21-10 (D)
1988—Cowboys, 26-20 (D)
1989—Falcons 27-21 (A)
1990—Falcons, 26-7 (A)
1991—Cowboys, 31-27 (D)
1992—Cowboys, 41-17 (A)
1993—Falcons, 27-14 (A)
1995—Cowboys, 28-13 (A)
1996—Cowboys, 32-28 (D)
1999—Cowboys, 24-7 (D)
2001—Falcons, 20-13 (A)
2003—Falcons, 27-13 (D)
2006—Cowboys, 38-28 (A)
2009—Cowboys, 37-21 (D)
(RS Pts.—Cowboys 549, Falcons 411)
(PS Pts.—Cowboys 57, Falcons 47)
*NFC Divisional Playoff

ATLANTA vs. DENVER
RS: Broncos lead series, 8-4
PS: Broncos lead series, 1-0
1970—Broncos, 24-10 (D)
1972—Falcons, 23-20 (A)
1975—Falcons, 35-21 (A)
1979—Broncos, 20-17 (A) OT
1982—Falcons, 34-27 (D)
1985—Broncos, 44-28 (A)
1988—Broncos, 30-14 (D)
1994—Broncos, 32-28 (D)
1997—Broncos, 29-21 (A)
1998—*Broncos, 34-19 (South Florida)
2000—Broncos, 42-14 (D)
2004—Falcons, 41-28 (D)
2008—Broncos, 24-20 (A)

(RS Pts.—Broncos 341, Falcons 285)
(PS Pts.—Broncos 34, Falcons 19)
*Super Bowl XXXIII

ATLANTA vs. DETROIT
RS: Lions lead series, 23-10
1966—Lions, 28-10 (D)
1967—Lions, 24-3 (D)
1968—Lions, 24-7 (A)
1969—Lions, 27-21 (D)
1971—Lions, 41-38 (D)
1972—Lions, 26-23 (A)
1973—Lions, 31-6 (D)
1975—Lions, 17-14 (A)
1976—Lions, 24-10 (D)
1977—Falcons, 17-6 (A)
1978—Falcons, 14-0 (A)
1979—Lions, 24-23 (D)
1980—Falcons, 43-28 (A)
1983—Lions, 30-14 (D)
1984—Lions, 27-24 (A) OT
1985—Lions, 28-27 (A)
1986—Falcons, 20-6 (D)
1987—Lions, 30-13 (A)
1988—Lions, 31-17 (D)
1989—Lions, 31-24 (A)
1990—Lions, 21-14 (D)
1993—Lions, 30-13 (D)
1994—Lions, 31-28 (D) OT
1995—Falcons, 34-22 (A)
1996—Lions, 28-24 (D)
1997—Lions, 28-17 (D)
1998—Falcons, 24-17 (D)
2000—Lions, 13-10 (D)
2002—Falcons, 36-15 (A)
2004—Lions, 17-10 (A)
2005—Falcons, 27-7 (D)
2006—Lions, 30-14 (D)
2008—Falcons, 34-21 (A)
(RS Pts.—Lions 747, Falcons 669)

ATLANTA vs. GREEN BAY
RS: Series tied, 12-12
PS: Packers lead series, 2-1
1966—Packers, 56-3 (Mil)
1967—Packers, 23-0 (Mil)
1968—Packers, 38-7 (A)
1969—Packers, 28-10 (GB)
1970—Packers, 27-24 (GB)
1971—Falcons, 28-21 (A)
1972—Falcons, 10-9 (Mil)
1974—Falcons, 10-3 (A)
1975—Packers, 22-13 (GB)
1976—Packers, 24-20 (A)
1979—Falcons, 25-7 (A)
1981—Falcons, 31-17 (GB)
1982—Packers, 38-7 (A)
1983—Falcons, 47-41 (A) OT
1988—Falcons, 20-0 (A)
1989—Packers, 23-21 (Mil)
1991—Falcons, 35-31 (A)
1992—Falcons, 24-10 (A)
1994—Packers, 21-17 (Mil)
1995—*Packers, 37-20 (GB)
2001—Falcons, 23-20 (GB)
2002—Packers, 37-34 (GB) OT
    *Falcons, 27-7 (GB)
2005—Packers, 33-25 (A)
2008—Falcons, 27-24 (GB)
2010—Falcons, 20-17 (A)
    **Packers, 48-21 (A)
(RS Pts.—Packers 570, Falcons 481)
(PS Pts.—Packers 92, Falcons 68)

*NFC First-Round Playoff
**NFC Divisional Playoff

ATLANTA vs. HOUSTON
RS: Series tied, 1-1
2003—Texans, 17-13 (H)
2007—Falcons, 26-16 (A)
(RS Pts.—Falcons 39, Texans 33)

ATLANTA vs. *INDIANAPOLIS
RS: Colts lead series, 13-1
1966—Colts, 19-7 (A)
1967—Colts, 38-31 (B)
    Colts, 49-7 (A)
1968—Colts, 28-20 (A)
    Colts, 44-0 (B)
1969—Colts, 21-14 (A)
    Colts, 13-6 (B)
1974—Colts, 17-7 (A)
1986—Colts, 28-23 (A)
1989—Colts, 13-9 (I)
1998—Falcons, 28-21 (A)
2001—Colts, 41-27 (I)
2003—Colts, 38-7 (I)
2007—Colts, 31-13 (A)
(RS Pts.—Colts 401, Falcons 199)
*Franchise in Baltimore prior to 1984

ATLANTA vs. JACKSONVILLE
RS: Jaguars lead series, 3-1
1996—Jaguars, 19-17 (J)
1999—Jaguars, 30-7 (A)
2003—Falcons, 21-14 (A)
2007—Jaguars, 13-7 (J)
(RS Pts.—Jaguars 76, Falcons 52)

ATLANTA vs. KANSAS CITY
RS: Chiefs lead series, 5-2
1972—Chiefs, 17-14 (A)
1985—Chiefs, 38-10 (KC)
1991—Chiefs, 14-3 (KC)
1994—Chiefs, 30-10 (A)
2000—Falcons, 29-13 (A)
2004—Chiefs, 56-10 (KC)
2008—Falcons, 38-14 (A)
(RS Pts.—Chiefs 182, Falcons 114)

ATLANTA vs. MIAMI
RS: Dolphins lead series, 7-4
1970—Dolphins, 20-7 (A)
1974—Dolphins, 42-7 (M)
1980—Dolphins, 20-17 (A)
1983—Dolphins, 31-24 (M)
1986—Falcons, 20-14 (M)
1992—Dolphins, 21-17 (M)
1995—Dolphins, 21-20 (M)
1998—Falcons, 38-16 (A)
2001—Dolphins, 21-14 (M)
2005—Falcons, 17-10 (M)
2009—Falcons, 19-7 (A)
(RS Pts.—Dolphins 223, Falcons 200)

ATLANTA vs. MINNESOTA
RS: Vikings lead series, 15-9
PS: Series tied, 1-1
1966—Falcons, 20-13 (M)
1967—Falcons, 21-20 (A)
1968—Vikings, 47-7 (M)
1969—Falcons, 10-3 (A)
1970—Vikings, 37-7 (A)
1971—Vikings, 24-7 (M)
1973—Falcons, 20-14 (A)
1974—Vikings, 23-10 (M)
1975—Vikings, 38-0 (M)
1977—Vikings, 14-7 (A)
1980—Vikings, 24-23 (M)
1981—Falcons, 31-30 (A)

1982—*Vikings, 30-24 (M)
1984—Vikings, 27-20 (M)
1985—Falcons, 14-13 (A)
1987—Vikings, 24-13 (M)
1989—Vikings, 43-17 (M)
1991—Vikings, 20-19 (A)
1996—Vikings, 23-17 (A)
1998—**Falcons, 30-27 (M) OT
1999—Vikings, 17-14 (A)
2002—Falcons, 30-24 (M) OT
2003—Vikings, 39-26 (A)
2005—Vikings, 30-10 (A)
2007—Vikings, 24-3 (M)
2008—Falcons, 24-17 (M)
(RS Pts.—Vikings 568, Falcons 390)
(PS Pts.—Vikings 57, Falcons 54)
*NFC First-Round Playoff
**NFC Championship

ATLANTA vs. NEW ENGLAND
RS: Series tied, 6-6
1972—Patriots, 21-20 (NE)
1977—Patriots, 16-10 (A)
1980—Falcons, 37-21 (NE)
1983—Falcons, 24-13 (A)
1986—Patriots, 25-17 (NE)
1989—Falcons, 16-15 (A)
1992—Falcons, 34-0 (A)
1995—Falcons, 30-17 (A)
1998—Falcons, 41-10 (NE)
2001—Patriots, 24-10 (A)
2005—Patriots, 31-28 (A)
2009—Patriots, 26-10 (NE)
(RS Pts.—Falcons 277, Patriots 219)

ATLANTA vs. NEW ORLEANS
RS: Falcons lead series, 45-38
PS: Falcons lead series, 1-0
1967—Saints, 27-24 (A)
1969—Falcons, 45-17 (A)
1970—Falcons, 14-3 (NO)
    Falcons, 32-14 (A)
1971—Falcons, 28-6 (A)
    Falcons, 24-20 (NO)
1972—Falcons, 21-14 (NO)
    Falcons, 36-20 (A)
1973—Falcons, 62-7 (NO)
    Falcons, 14-10 (A)
1974—Saints, 14-13 (NO)
    Saints, 13-3 (A)
1975—Falcons, 14-7 (A)
    Saints, 23-7 (NO)
1976—Saints, 30-0 (NO)
    Falcons, 23-20 (A)
1977—Saints, 21-20 (NO)
    Falcons, 35-7 (A)
1978—Falcons, 20-17 (NO)
    Falcons, 20-17 (A)
1979—Falcons, 40-34 (NO) OT
    Saints, 37-6 (A)
1980—Falcons, 41-14 (NO)
    Falcons, 31-13 (A)
1981—Falcons, 27-0 (A)
    Falcons, 41-10 (NO)
1982—Falcons, 35-0 (A)
    Saints, 35-6 (NO)
1983—Saints, 19-17 (A)
    Saints, 27-10 (NO)
1984—Falcons, 36-28 (NO)
    Saints, 17-13 (A)
1985—Falcons, 31-24 (A)
    Falcons, 16-10 (NO)
1986—Falcons, 31-10 (NO)

Saints, 14-9 (A)
1987—Saints, 38-0 (A)
1988—Saints, 29-21 (A)
Saints, 10-9 (NO)
1989—Saints, 20-13 (NO)
Saints, 26-17 (A)
1990—Falcons, 28-27 (A)
Saints, 10-7 (NO)
1991—Saints, 27-6 (A)
Falcons, 23-20 (NO) OT
*Falcons, 27-20 (NO)
1992—Saints, 10-7 (A)
Saints, 22-14 (NO)
1993—Saints, 34-31 (A)
Falcons, 26-15 (NO)
1994—Saints, 33-32 (NO)
Saints, 29-20 (A)
1995—Falcons, 27-24 (NO) OT
Falcons, 19-14 (A)
1996—Falcons, 17-15 (A)
Falcons, 31-15 (NO)
1997—Falcons, 23-17 (NO)
Falcons, 20-3 (A)
1998—Falcons, 31-23 (A)
Falcons, 27-17 (NO)
1999—Falcons, 20-17 (NO)
Falcons, 35-12 (A)
2000—Saints, 21-19 (A)
Saints, 23-7 (NO)
2001—Falcons, 20-13 (NO)
Saints, 28-10 (NO)
2002—Falcons, 37-35 (NO)
Falcons, 24-17 (A)
2003—Saints, 45-17 (A)
Saints, 23-20 (NO) OT
2004—Falcons, 24-21 (A)
Saints, 26-13 (NO)
2005—Falcons, 34-31 (San Antonio)
Falcons, 36-17 (A)
2006—Saints, 23-3 (NO)
Saints, 31-13 (A)
2007—Saints, 22-16 (NO)
Saints, 34-14 (A)
2008—Falcons, 34-20 (A)
Saints, 29-25 (NO)
2009—Saints, 35-27 (NO)
Saints, 26-23 (A)
2010—Falcons, 27-24 (NO) OT
Saints, 17-14 (A)
(RS Pts.—Falcons 1,806, Saints 1,667)
(PS Pts.—Falcons 27, Saints 20)
*NFC First-Round Playoff
ATLANTA vs. N.Y. GIANTS
RS: Series tied, 10-10
1966—Falcons, 27-16 (NY)
1968—Falcons, 24-21 (A)
1971—Giants, 21-17 (A)
1974—Falcons, 14-7 (New Haven)
1977—Falcons, 17-3 (A)
1978—Falcons, 23-20 (A)
1979—Giants, 24-3 (NY)
1981—Giants, 27-24 (A) OT
1982—Falcons, 16-14 (NY)
1983—Giants, 16-13 (A) OT
1984—Giants, 19-7 (A)
1988—Giants, 23-16 (A)
1998—Falcons, 34-20 (NY)
2000—Giants, 13-6 (A)
2002—Falcons, 17-10 (NY)
2003—Falcons, 27-7 (NY)
2004—Falcons, 14-10 (NY)

2006—Giants, 27-14 (A)
2007—Giants, 31-10 (A)
2009—Giants, 34-31 (NY) OT
(RS Pts.—Giants 363, Falcons 354)
ATLANTA vs. N.Y. JETS
RS: Falcons lead series, 6-4
1973—Falcons, 28-20 (NY)
1980—Jets, 14-7 (A)
1983—Falcons, 27-21 (NY)
1986—Jets, 28-14 (A)
1989—Jets, 27-7 (NY)
1992—Falcons, 20-17 (A)
1995—Falcons, 13-3 (A)
1998—Jets, 28-3 (NY)
2005—Falcons, 27-14 (A)
2009—Falcons, 10-7 (NY)
(RS Pts.—Jets 179, Falcons 156)
ATLANTA vs. *OAKLAND
RS: Raiders lead series, 7-5
1971—Falcons, 24-13 (A)
1975—Raiders, 37-34 (O) OT
1979—Raiders, 50-19 (O)
1982—Raiders, 38-14 (A)
1985—Raiders, 34-24 (A)
1988—Falcons, 12-6 (LA)
1991—Falcons, 21-17 (A)
1994—Raiders, 30-17 (LA)
1997—Raiders, 36-31 (A)
2000—Raiders, 41-14 (O)
2004—Falcons, 35-10 (A)
2008—Falcons, 24-0 (O)
(RS Pts.—Raiders 312, Falcons 269)
*Franchise in Los Angeles from 1982-1994
ATLANTA vs. PHILADELPHIA
RS: Eagles lead series, 15-10-1
PS: Eagles lead series, 2-1
1966—Eagles, 23-10 (P)
1967—Eagles, 38-7 (A)
1969—Falcons, 27-3 (P)
1970—Tie, 13-13 (P)
1973—Falcons, 44-27 (P)
1976—Falcons, 14-13 (A)
1978—*Falcons, 14-13 (A)
1979—Falcons, 14-10 (P)
1980—Falcons, 20-17 (P)
1981—Eagles, 16-13 (P)
1983—Eagles, 28-24 (A)
1984—Falcons, 26-10 (A)
1985—Eagles, 23-17 (P) OT
1986—Eagles, 16-0 (A)
1988—Falcons, 27-24 (P)
1990—Eagles, 24-23 (A)
1994—Eagles, 28-21 (A)
1996—Eagles, 33-18 (A)
1997—Falcons, 20-17 (A)
1998—Falcons, 17-12 (A)
2000—Eagles, 38-10 (P)
2002—**Eagles, 20-6 (P)
2003—Eagles, 23-16 (A)
2004—***Eagles, 27-10 (P)
2005—Falcons, 14-10 (A)
2006—Eagles, 24-17 (P)
2008—Eagles, 27-14 (P)
2009—Eagles, 34-7 (A)
2010—Eagles, 31-17 (P)
(RS Pts.—Eagles 556, Falcons 456)
(PS Pts.—Eagles 60, Falcons 30)
*NFC First-Round Playoff
**NFC Divisional Playoff
***NFC Championship

ATLANTA vs. PITTSBURGH
RS: Steelers lead series, 12-2-1
1966—Steelers, 57-33 (A)
1968—Steelers, 41-21 (A)
1970—Falcons, 27-16 (A)
1974—Steelers, 24-17 (P)
1978—Steelers, 31-7 (P)
1981—Steelers, 34-20 (A)
1984—Steelers, 35-10 (P)
1987—Steelers, 28-12 (A)
1990—Steelers, 21-9 (P)
1993—Steelers, 45-17 (A)
1996—Steelers, 20-17 (A)
1999—Steelers, 13-9 (P)
2002—Tie, 34-34 (P) OT
2006—Falcons, 41-38 (A) OT
2010—Steelers, 15-9 (P) OT
(RS Pts.—Steelers 452, Falcons 283)
ATLANTA vs. *ST. LOUIS
RS: Rams lead series, 47-26-2
PS: Falcons lead series, 1-0
1966—Rams, 19-14 (A)
1967—Rams, 31-3 (A)
Rams, 20-3 (LA)
1968—Rams, 27-14 (LA)
Rams, 17-10 (A)
1969—Rams, 17-7 (LA)
Rams, 38-6 (A)
1970—Tie, 10-10 (LA)
Rams, 17-7 (A)
1971—Tie, 20-20 (LA)
Rams, 24-16 (A)
1972—Falcons, 31-3 (A)
Rams, 20-7 (LA)
1973—Rams, 31-0 (LA)
Falcons, 15-13 (A)
1974—Rams, 21-0 (LA)
Rams, 30-7 (A)
1975—Rams, 22-7 (LA)
Rams, 16-7 (A)
1976—Rams, 30-14 (A)
Rams, 59-0 (LA)
1977—Falcons, 17-6 (A)
Rams, 23-7 (LA)
1978—Rams, 10-0 (LA)
Falcons, 15-7 (A)
1979—Rams, 20-14 (LA)
Rams, 34-13 (A)
1980—Falcons, 13-10 (A)
Rams, 20-17 (LA) OT
1981—Rams, 37-35 (A)
Rams, 21-16 (LA)
1982—Falcons, 34-17 (A)
1983—Rams, 27-21 (LA)
Rams, 36-13 (A)
1984—Falcons, 30-28 (LA)
Rams, 24-10 (A)
1985—Rams, 17-6 (LA)
Falcons, 30-14 (A)
1986—Falcons, 26-14 (A)
Rams, 14-7 (LA)
1987—Falcons, 24-20 (A)
Rams, 33-0 (LA)
1988—Rams, 33-0 (A)
Rams, 22-7 (LA)
1989—Rams, 31-21 (A)
Rams, 26-14 (LA)
1990—Rams, 44-24 (LA)
Falcons, 20-13 (A)
1991—Falcons, 31-14 (A)
Falcons, 31-14 (LA)

1992—Falcons, 30-28 (A)
    Rams, 38-27 (LA)
1993—Falcons, 30-24 (A)
    Falcons, 13-0 (LA)
1994—Falcons, 31-13 (A)
    Falcons, 8-5 (LA)
1995—Rams, 21-19 (StL)
    Falcons, 31-6 (A)
1996—Rams, 59-16 (StL)
    Rams, 34-27 (A)
1997—Falcons, 34-31 (A)
    Falcons, 27-21 (StL)
1998—Falcons, 37-15 (A)
    Falcons, 21-10 (StL)
1999—Rams, 35-7 (StL)
    Rams, 41-13 (A)
2000—Rams, 41-20 (A)
    Rams, 45-29 (StL)
2001—Rams, 35-6 (A)
    Rams, 31-13 (StL)
2003—Rams, 36-0 (StL)
2004—Falcons, 34-17 (A)
    **Falcons, 47-17 (A)
2007—Rams, 28-16 (StL)
2008—Falcons, 31-27 (A)
2010—Falcons, 34-17 (StL)
(RS Pts.—Rams 1,772, Falcons 1,248)
(PS Pts.—Falcons 47, Rams 17)
Franchise in Los Angeles prior to 1995
**NFC Divisional Playoff*
ATLANTA vs. SAN DIEGO
RS: Falcons lead series, 7-1
1973—Falcons, 41-0 (SD)
1979—Falcons, 28-26 (SD)
1988—Chargers, 10-7 (A)
1991—Falcons, 13-10 (SD)
1994—Falcons, 10-9 (A)
1997—Falcons, 14-3 (SD)
2004—Falcons, 21-20 (A)
2008—Falcons, 22-16 (SD)
(RS Pts.—Falcons 156, Chargers 94)
ATLANTA vs. SAN FRANCISCO
RS: 49ers lead series, 44-29-1
PS: Falcons lead series, 1-0
1966—49ers, 44-7 (A)
1967—49ers, 38-7 (SF)
    49ers, 34-28 (A)
1968—49ers, 28-13 (SF)
    49ers, 14-12 (A)
1969—Falcons, 24-12 (A)
    Falcons, 21-7 (SF)
1970—Falcons, 21-20 (A)
    49ers, 24-20 (SF)
1971—Falcons, 20-17 (A)
    49ers, 24-3 (SF)
1972—49ers, 49-14 (A)
    49ers, 20-0 (SF)
1973—49ers, 13-9 (A)
    Falcons, 17-3 (SF)
1974—49ers, 16-10 (A)
    49ers, 27-0 (SF)
1975—Falcons, 17-3 (SF)
    Falcons, 31-9 (A)
1976—49ers, 15-0 (SF)
    Falcons, 21-16 (A)
1977—Falcons, 7-0 (SF)
    49ers, 10-3 (A)
1978—Falcons, 20-17 (SF)
    Falcons, 21-10 (A)
1979—49ers, 20-15 (SF)
    Falcons, 31-21 (A)

1980—Falcons, 20-17 (SF)
    Falcons, 35-10 (A)
1981—Falcons, 34-17 (A)
    49ers, 17-14 (SF)
1982—Falcons, 17-7 (SF)
1983—49ers, 24-20 (SF)
    Falcons, 28-24 (A)
1984—49ers, 14-5 (SF)
    49ers, 35-17 (A)
1985—49ers, 35-16 (SF)
    49ers, 38-17 (A)
1986—Tie, 10-10 (A) OT
    49ers, 20-0 (SF)
1987—49ers, 25-17 (A)
    49ers, 35-7 (SF)
1988—Falcons, 34-17 (SF)
    49ers, 13-3 (A)
1989—49ers, 45-3 (SF)
    49ers, 23-10 (A)
1990—49ers, 19-13 (SF)
    49ers, 45-35 (A)
1991—Falcons, 39-34 (SF)
    Falcons, 17-14 (A)
1992—49ers, 56-17 (SF)
    49ers, 41-3 (A)
1993—49ers, 37-30 (SF)
    Falcons, 27-24 (A)
1994—49ers, 42-3 (A)
    49ers, 50-14 (SF)
1995—49ers, 41-10 (SF)
    Falcons, 28-27 (A)
1996—49ers, 39-17 (SF)
    49ers, 34-10 (A)
1997—49ers, 34-7 (SF)
    49ers, 35-28 (A)
1998—49ers, 31-20 (SF)
    Falcons, 31-19 (A)
    *Falcons, 20-18 (A)
1999—49ers, 26-7 (SF)
    Falcons, 34-29 (A)
2000—Falcons, 36-28 (A)
    49ers, 16-6 (SF)
2001—49ers, 16-13 (SF) OT
    49ers, 37-31 (A) OT
2004—Falcons, 21-19 (SF)
2007—Falcons, 20-16 (A)
2009—Falcons, 45-10 (SF)
2010—Falcons, 16-14 (A)
(RS Pts.—49ers 1,770, Falcons 1,277)
(PS Pts.—Falcons 20, 49ers 18)
NFC Divisional Playoff
ATLANTA vs. SEATTLE
RS: Seahawks lead series, 8-4
1976—Seahawks, 30-13 (S)
1979—Seahawks, 31-28 (A)
1985—Seahawks, 30-26 (S)
1988—Seahawks, 31-20 (A)
1991—Falcons, 26-13 (A)
1997—Falcons, 24-17 (S)
2000—Seahawks, 30-10 (A)
2002—Seahawks, 30-24 (A) OT
2004—Seahawks, 28-26 (S)
2005—Seahawks, 21-18 (S)
2007—Falcons, 44-41 (A)
2010—Falcons, 34-18 (S)
(RS Pts.—Seahawks 320, Falcons 293)
ATLANTA vs. TAMPA BAY
RS: Buccaneers lead series, 18-17
1977—Falcons, 17-0 (TB)
1978—Buccaneers, 14-9 (TB)
1979—Falcons, 17-14 (A)

1981—Buccaneers, 24-23 (TB)
1984—Buccaneers, 23-6 (TB)
1986—Falcons, 23-20 (TB) OT
1987—Buccaneers, 48-10 (TB)
1988—Falcons, 17-10 (A)
1990—Buccaneers, 23-17 (TB)
1991—Falcons, 43-7 (A)
1992—Falcons, 35-7 (TB)
1993—Buccaneers, 31-24 (A)
1994—Falcons, 34-13 (A)
1995—Falcons, 24-21 (TB)
1997—Buccaneers, 31-10 (A)
1999—Buccaneers, 19-10 (TB)
2000—Buccaneers, 27-14 (A)
2002—Buccaneers, 20-6 (A)
    Buccaneers, 34-10 (TB)
2003—Buccaneers, 31-10 (A)
    Falcons, 30-28 (TB)
2004—Falcons, 24-14 (A)
    Buccaneers, 27-0 (TB)
2005—Buccaneers, 30-27 (A)
    Buccaneers, 27-24 (TB) OT
2006—Falcons, 14-3 (A)
    Falcons, 17-6 (TB)
2007—Buccaneers, 31-7 (A)
    Buccaneers, 37-3 (TB)
2008—Buccaneers, 24-9 (TB)
    Falcons, 13-10 (A) OT
2009—Falcons, 20-17 (A)
    Falcons, 20-10 (TB)
2010—Falcons, 27-21 (A)
    Falcons, 28-24 (TB)
(RS Pts.—Buccaneers 726, Falcons 622)
ATLANTA vs. *TENNESSEE
RS: Titans lead series, 7-5
1972—Falcons, 20-10 (A)
1976—Oilers, 20-14 (H)
1978—Falcons, 20-14 (A)
1981—Falcons, 31-27 (H)
1984—Falcons, 42-10 (A)
1987—Oilers, 37-33 (H)
1990—Falcons, 47-27 (A)
1993—Oilers, 33-17 (H)
1996—Oilers, 23-13 (A)
1999—Titans, 30-17 (T)
2003—Titans, 38-31 (A)
2007—Titans, 20-13 (T)
(RS Pts.—Falcons 298, Titans 289)
Franchise in Houston prior to 1997;
known as Oilers prior to 1999
ATLANTA vs. WASHINGTON
RS: Redskins lead series, 14-6-1
PS: Redskins lead series, 1-0
1966—Redskins, 33-20 (W)
1967—Tie, 20-20 (A)
1969—Redskins, 27-20 (W)
1972—Redskins, 24-13 (W)
1975—Redskins, 30-27 (A)
1977—Redskins, 10-6 (W)
1978—Falcons, 20-17 (A)
1979—Redskins, 16-7 (A)
1980—Falcons, 10-6 (A)
1983—Redskins, 37-21 (W)
1984—Redskins, 27-14 (W)
1985—Redskins, 44-10 (A)
1987—Falcons, 21-20 (A)
1989—Redskins, 31-30 (A)
1991—Redskins, 56-17 (W)
    *Redskins, 24-7 (W)
1992—Redskins, 24-17 (W)
1993—Redskins, 30-17 (W)

1994—Falcons, 27-20 (W)
2003—Redskins, 33-31 (A)
2006—Falcons, 24-14 (W)
2009—Falcons, 31-17 (W)
(RS Pts.—Redskins 536, Falcons 403)
(PS Pts.—Redskins 24, Falcons 7)
*NFC Divisional Playoff

BALTIMORE vs. ARIZONA
RS: Ravens lead series, 3-1;
See Arizona vs. Baltimore
BALTIMORE vs. ATLANTA
RS: Series tied, 2-2;
See Atlanta vs. Baltimore
BALTIMORE vs. BUFFALO
RS: Ravens lead series, 3-2
1999—Bills, 13-10 (Balt)
2004—Ravens, 20-6 (Balt)
2006—Ravens, 19-7 (Balt)
2007—Bills, 19-14 (Buf)
2010—Ravens, 37-34 (Balt) OT
(RS Pts.—Ravens 100, Bills 79)
BALTIMORE vs. CAROLINA
RS: Panthers lead series, 3-1
1996—Panthers, 27-16 (C)
2002—Panthers, 10-7 (C)
2006—Panthers, 23-21 (B)
2010—Ravens, 37-13 (C)
(RS Pts.—Panthers 81, Ravens 73)
BALTIMORE vs. CHICAGO
RS: Series tied, 2-2
1998—Bears, 24-3 (C)
2001—Ravens, 17-6 (B)
2005—Bears, 10-6 (C)
2009—Ravens, 31-7 (C)
(RS Pts.—Ravens 57, Bears 47)
BALTIMORE vs. CINCINNATI
RS: Ravens lead series, 16-15
1996—Bengals, 24-21 (B)
        Bengals, 21-14 (C)
1997—Ravens, 23-10 (B)
        Bengals, 16-14 (C)
1998—Ravens, 31-24 (B)
        Ravens, 20-13 (C)
1999—Ravens, 34-31 (C)
        Ravens, 22-0 (B)
2000—Ravens, 37-0 (B)
        Ravens, 27-7 (C)
2001—Bengals, 21-10 (C)
        Ravens, 16-0 (B)
2002—Ravens, 38-27 (B)
        Ravens, 27-23 (C)
2003—Bengals, 34-26 (C)
        Ravens, 31-13 (B)
2004—Ravens, 23-9 (C)
        Bengals, 27-26 (B)
2005—Ravens, 21-9 (B)
        Bengals, 42-29 (C)
2006—Ravens, 26-20 (B)
        Bengals, 13-7 (C)
2007—Bengals, 27-20 (C)
        Bengals, 21-7 (B)
2008—Ravens, 17-10 (B)
        Ravens, 34-3 (C)
2009—Bengals, 17-14 (B)
        Bengals, 17-7 (C)
2010—Bengals, 15-10 (C)
        Ravens, 13-7 (B)
(RS Pts.—Ravens 633, Bengals 513)
BALTIMORE vs. CLEVELAND
RS: Ravens lead series, 17-7

1999—Ravens, 17-10 (B)
        Ravens, 41-9 (C)
2000—Ravens, 12-0 (C)
        Ravens, 44-7 (B)
2001—Browns, 24-14 (C)
        Browns, 27-17 (B)
2002—Ravens, 26-21 (B)
        Browns, 14-13 (B)
2003—Ravens, 33-13 (B)
        Ravens, 35-0 (C)
2004—Browns, 20-3 (C)
        Ravens, 27-13 (B)
2005—Ravens, 16-3 (B)
        Browns, 20-16 (C)
2006—Ravens, 15-14 (C)
        Ravens, 27-17 (B)
2007—Browns, 27-13 (C)
        Browns, 33-30 (B) OT
2008—Ravens, 28-10 (B)
        Ravens, 37-27 (C)
2009—Ravens, 34-3 (B)
        Ravens, 16-0 (C)
2010—Ravens, 24-17 (B)
        Ravens, 20-10 (C)
(RS Pts.—Ravens 550, Browns 339)
BALTIMORE vs. DALLAS
RS: Ravens lead series, 3-0
2000—Ravens, 27-0 (B)
2004—Ravens, 30-10 (B)
2008—Ravens, 33-24 (D)
(RS Pts.—Ravens 90, Cowboys 34)
BALTIMORE vs. DENVER
RS: Ravens lead series, 5-3
PS: Ravens lead series, 1-0
1996—Broncos, 45-34 (D)
2000—*Ravens, 21-3 (B)
2001—Ravens, 20-13 (D)
2002—Ravens, 34-23 (B)
2003—Ravens, 26-6 (B)
2005—Broncos, 12-10 (D)
2006—Broncos, 13-3 (D)
2009—Ravens, 30-7 (B)
2010—Ravens, 31-17 (B)
(RS Pts.—Ravens 188, Broncos 136)
(PS Pts.—Ravens 21, Broncos 3)
*AFC First-Round Playoff
BALTIMORE vs. DETROIT
RS: Ravens lead series, 2-1
1998—Ravens, 19-10 (B)
2005—Lions, 35-17 (D)
2009—Ravens, 48-3 (B)
(RS Pts.—Ravens 84, Lions 48)
BALTIMORE vs. GREEN BAY
RS: Packers lead series, 3-1
1998—Packers, 28-10 (GB)
2001—Packers, 31-23 (GB)
2005—Ravens, 48-3 (B)
2009—Packers, 27-14 (GB)
(RS Pts.—Ravens 95, Packers 89)
BALTIMORE vs. HOUSTON
RS: Ravens lead series, 4-0
2002—Ravens, 23-19 (H)
2005—Ravens, 16-15 (B)
2008—Ravens, 41-13 (H)
2010—Ravens, 34-28 (H) OT
(RS Pts.—Ravens 114, Texans 75)
BALTIMORE vs. INDIANAPOLIS
RS: Colts lead series, 7-2
PS: Colts lead series, 2-0
1996—Colts, 26-21 (I)
1998—Ravens, 38-31 (B)

2001—Ravens, 39-27 (B)
2002—Colts, 22-20 (I)
2004—Colts, 20-10 (I)
2005—Colts, 24-7 (B)
2006—*Colts, 15-6 (B)
2007—Colts, 44-20 (B)
2008—Colts, 31-3 (I)
2009—Colts, 17-15 (B)
        *Colts, 20-3 (I)
(RS Pts.—Colts 242, Ravens 173)
(PS Pts.—Colts 35, Ravens 9)
*AFC Divisional Playoff
BALTIMORE vs. JACKSONVILLE
RS: Jaguars lead series, 9-7
1996—Jaguars, 30-27 (J)
        Jaguars, 28-25 (B) OT
1997—Jaguars, 28-27 (J)
        Jaguars, 29-27 (J)
1998—Jaguars, 24-10 (J)
        Jaguars, 45-19 (B)
1999—Jaguars, 6-3 (J)
        Jaguars, 30-23 (B)
2000—Ravens, 39-36 (B)
        Ravens, 15-10 (J)
2001—Ravens, 18-17 (B)
        Ravens, 24-21 (J)
2002—Ravens, 17-10 (B)
2003—Ravens, 24-17 (B)
2005—Jaguars, 30-3 (J)
2008—Ravens, 27-7 (B)
(RS Pts.—Jaguars 368, Ravens 328)
BALTIMORE vs. KANSAS CITY
RS: Chiefs lead series, 3-2
PS: Ravens lead series, 1-0
1999—Chiefs, 35-8 (B)
2003—Chiefs, 17-10 (B)
2004—Chiefs, 27-24 (B)
2006—Ravens, 20-10 (KC)
2009—Ravens, 38-24 (B)
2010—*Ravens, 30-7 (KC)
(RS Pts.—Chiefs 113, Ravens 100)
(PS Pts.—Ravens 30, Chiefs 7)
*AFC First-Round Playoff
BALTIMORE vs. MIAMI
RS: Dolphins lead series, 5-3
PS: Ravens lead series, 2-0
1997—Dolphins, 24-13 (B)
2000—Dolphins, 19-6 (M)
2001—*Ravens, 20-3 (M)
2002—Dolphins, 26-7 (M)
2003—Dolphins, 9-6 (M) OT
2004—Ravens, 30-23 (B)
2007—Dolphins, 22-16 (M) OT
2008—Ravens, 27-13 (M)
        *Ravens, 27-9 (M)
2010—Ravens, 26-10 (B)
(RS Pts.—Dolphins 146, Ravens 131)
(PS Pts.—Ravens 47, Dolphins 12)
*AFC First-Round Playoff
BALTIMORE vs. MINNESOTA
RS: Series tied, 2-2
1998—Vikings, 38-28 (B)
2001—Ravens, 19-3 (B)
2005—Ravens, 30-23 (B)
2009—Vikings, 33-31 (M)
(RS Pts.—Ravens 108, Vikings 97)
BALTIMORE vs. NEW ENGLAND
RS: Patriots lead series, 6-0
PS: Ravens lead series, 1-0
1996—Patriots, 46-38 (B)
1999—Patriots, 20-3 (NE)

2004—Patriots, 24-3 (NE)
2007—Patriots, 27-24 (B)
2009—Patriots, 27-21 (NE)
    *Ravens, 33-14 (NE)
2010—Patriots, 23-20 (NE) OT
(RS Pts.—Patriots 167, Ravens 109)
(PS Pts.—Ravens 33, Patriots 14)
*AFC First-Round Playoff

BALTIMORE vs. NEW ORLEANS
RS: Ravens lead series, 4-1
1996—Ravens, 17-10 (B)
1999—Ravens, 31-8 (B)
2002—Saints, 37-25 (B)
2006—Ravens, 35-22 (NO)
2010—Ravens, 30-24 (B)
(RS Pts.—Ravens 138, Saints 101)

BALTIMORE vs. N.Y. GIANTS
RS: Ravens lead series, 2-1
PS: Ravens lead series, 1-0
1997—Ravens, 24-23 (NY)
2000—*Ravens, 34-7 (Tampa)
2004—Ravens, 37-14 (B)
2008—Giants, 30-10 (NY)
(RS Pts.—Ravens 71, Giants 67)
(PS Pts.—Ravens 34, Giants 7)
*Super Bowl XXXV

BALTIMORE vs. N.Y. JETS
RS: Ravens lead series, 6-1
1997—Jets, 19-16 (NY) OT
1998—Ravens, 24-10 (NY)
2000—Ravens, 34-20 (B)
2004—Ravens, 20-17 (NY) OT
2005—Ravens, 13-3 (B)
2007—Ravens, 20-13 (B)
2010—Ravens, 10-9 (NY)
(RS Pts.—Ravens 137, Jets 91)

BALTIMORE vs. OAKLAND
RS: Ravens lead series, 5-1
PS: Ravens lead series, 1-0
1996—Ravens, 19-14 (B)
1998—Ravens, 13-10 (B)
2000—*Ravens, 16-3 (O)
2003—Raiders, 20-12 (O)
2006—Ravens, 28-6 (B)
2008—Ravens, 29-10 (B)
2009—Ravens, 21-13 (O)
(RS Pts.—Ravens 122, Raiders 73)
(PS Pts.—Ravens 16, Raiders 3)
*AFC Championship

BALTIMORE vs. PHILADELPHIA
RS: Series tied, 1-1-1
1997—Tie, 10-10 (B) OT
2004—Eagles, 15-10 (P)
2008—Ravens, 36-7 (B)
(RS Pts.—Ravens 56, Eagles 32)

BALTIMORE vs. PITTSBURGH
RS: Steelers lead series, 18-12
PS: Steelers lead series, 3-0
1996—Steelers, 31-17 (P)
    Ravens, 31-17 (B)
1997—Steelers, 42-34 (B)
    Steelers, 37-0 (P)
1998—Steelers, 20-13 (B)
    Steelers, 16-6 (P)
1999—Steelers, 23-20 (B)
    Ravens, 31-24 (P)
2000—Ravens, 16-0 (P)
    Steelers, 9-6 (B)
2001—Ravens, 13-10 (P)
    Steelers, 26-21 (B)
    *Steelers, 27-10 (P)

2002—Steelers, 31-18 (B)
    Steelers, 34-31 (P)
2003—Steelers, 34-15 (P)
    Ravens, 13-10 (B) OT
2004—Ravens, 30-13 (B)
    Steelers, 20-7 (P)
2005—Steelers, 20-19 (P)
    Ravens, 16-13 (B) OT
2006—Ravens, 27-0 (B)
    Ravens, 31-7 (P)
2007—Steelers, 38-7 (P)
    Ravens, 27-21 (B)
2008—Steelers, 23-20 (P) OT
    Steelers, 13-9 (B)
    **Steelers, 23-14 (P)
2009—Ravens, 20-17 (B) OT
    Steelers, 23-20 (P)
2010—Ravens, 17-14 (P)
    Steelers, 13-10 (B)
    *Steelers, 31-24 (P)
(RS Pts.—Steelers 599, Ravens 545)
(PS Pts.—Steelers 81, Ravens 48)
*AFC Divisional Playoff
**AFC Championship

BALTIMORE vs. ST. LOUIS
RS: Series tied, 2-2
1996—Ravens, 37-31 (B) OT
1999—Rams, 27-10 (StL)
2003—Rams, 33-22 (StL)
2007—Ravens, 22-3 (B)
(RS Pts.—Rams 94, Ravens 91)

BALTIMORE vs. SAN DIEGO
RS: Ravens lead series, 4-3
1997—Chargers, 21-17 (SD)
1998—Chargers, 14-13 (SD)
2000—Ravens, 24-3 (B)
2003—Ravens, 24-10 (SD)
2006—Ravens, 16-13 (B)
2007—Chargers, 32-14 (SD)
2009—Ravens, 31-26 (SD)
(RS Pts.—Ravens 139, Chargers 119)

BALTIMORE vs. SAN FRANCISCO
RS: Ravens lead series, 2-1
1996—49ers, 38-20 (SF)
2003—Ravens, 44-6 (B)
2007—Ravens, 9-7 (SF)
(RS Pts.—Ravens 73, 49ers 51)

BALTIMORE vs. SEATTLE
RS: Ravens lead series, 2-1
1997—Ravens, 31-24 (B)
2003—Ravens, 44-41 (B) OT
2007—Seahawks, 27-6 (S)
(RS Pts.—Seahawks 92, Ravens 81)

BALTIMORE vs. TAMPA BAY
RS: Series tied, 2-2
2001—Buccaneers, 22-10 (TB)
2002—Buccaneers, 25-0 (B)
2006—Ravens, 27-0 (TB)
2010—Ravens, 17-10 (B)
(RS Pts.—Buccaneers 57, Ravens 54)

BALTIMORE vs. *TENNESSEE
RS: Series tied, 8-8
PS: Ravens lead series, 2-1
1996—Oilers, 29-13 (H)
    Oilers, 24-21 (B)
1997—Ravens, 36-10 (T)
    Ravens, 21-19 (B)
1998—Oilers, 12-8 (B)
    Oilers, 16-14 (T)
1999—Titans, 14-11 (T)
    Ravens, 41-14 (B)

2000—Titans, 14-6 (B)
    Ravens, 24-23 (T)
    **Ravens, 24-10 (T)
2001—Ravens, 26-7 (B)
    Ravens, 16-10 (T)
2002—Ravens, 13-12 (B)
2003—***Titans, 20-17 (B)
2005—Titans, 25-10 (T)
2006—Ravens, 27-26 (T)
2008—Titans, 13-10 (B)
    **Ravens, 13-10 (T)
(RS Pts.—Ravens 297, Titans 268)
(PS Pts.—Ravens 54, Titans 40)
*Franchise in Houston prior to 1997;
known as Oilers prior to 1999
**AFC Divisional Playoff
***AFC First-Round Playoff

BALTIMORE vs. WASHINGTON
RS: Ravens lead series, 3-1
1997—Ravens, 20-17 (W)
2000—Redskins, 10-3 (W)
2004—Ravens, 17-10 (W)
2008—Ravens, 24-10 (B)
(RS Pts.—Ravens 64, Redskins 47)

BUFFALO vs. ARIZONA
RS: Bills lead series, 5-4;
See Arizona vs. Buffalo

BUFFALO vs. ATLANTA
RS: Falcons lead series, 6-4;
See Atlanta vs. Buffalo

BUFFALO vs. BALTIMORE
RS: Ravens lead series, 3-2;
See Baltimore vs. Buffalo

BUFFALO vs. CAROLINA
RS: Bills lead series, 4-1
1995—Bills, 31-9 (B)
1998—Bills, 30-14 (C)
2001—Bills, 25-24 (B)
2005—Panthers, 13-9 (B)
2009—Bills, 20-9 (C)
(RS Pts.—Bills 115, Panthers 69)

BUFFALO vs. CHICAGO
RS: Bears lead series, 7-4
1970—Bears, 31-13 (C)
1974—Bills, 16-6 (B)
1979—Bears, 7-0 (B)
1988—Bears, 24-3 (C)
1991—Bills, 35-20 (B)
1994—Bears, 20-13 (C)
1997—Bears, 20-3 (C)
2000—Bills, 20-3 (B)
2002—Bills, 33-27 (B) OT
2006—Bears, 40-7 (C)
2010—Bears, 22-19 (Toronto)
(RS Pts.—Bears 220, Bills 162)

BUFFALO vs. CINCINNATI
RS: Bills lead series, 15-9
PS: Bengals lead series, 2-0
1968—Bengals, 34-23 (C)
1969—Bills, 16-13 (B)
1970—Bengals, 43-14 (B)
1973—Bengals, 16-13 (B)
1975—Bengals, 33-24 (C)
1978—Bills, 5-0 (B)
1979—Bills, 51-24 (B)
1980—Bills, 14-0 (C)
1981—Bengals, 27-24 (C) OT
    *Bengals, 28-21 (C)
1983—Bills, 10-6 (C)
1984—Bengals, 52-21 (C)

1985—Bengals, 23-17 (B)
1986—Bengals, 36-33 (C) OT
1988—Bengals, 35-21 (C)
    **Bengals, 21-10 (C)
1989—Bills, 24-7 (B)
1991—Bills, 35-16 (B)
1996—Bills, 31-17 (B)
1998—Bills, 33-20 (C)
2002—Bills, 27-9 (B)
2003—Bills, 22-16 (B) OT
2004—Bills, 33-17 (C)
2005—Bills, 37-27 (C)
2007—Bills, 33-21 (B)
2010—Bills, 49-31 (C)
(RS Pts.—Bills 610, Bengals 523)
(PS Pts.—Bengals 49, Bills 31)
AFC Divisional Playoff
**AFC Championship*
BUFFALO vs. CLEVELAND
RS: Browns lead series, 10-6
PS: Browns lead series, 1-0
1972—Browns, 27-10 (C)
1974—Bills, 15-10 (C)
1977—Browns, 27-16 (B)
1978—Browns, 41-20 (C)
1981—Bills, 22-13 (B)
1984—Browns, 13-10 (B)
1985—Browns, 17-7 (C)
1986—Browns, 21-17 (B)
1987—Browns, 27-21 (C)
1989—*Browns, 34-30 (C)
1990—Bills, 42-0 (C)
1995—Bills, 22-19 (C)
2004—Bills, 37-7 (B)
2007—Browns, 8-0 (C)
2008—Browns, 29-27 (B)
2009—Browns, 6-3 (B)
2010—Bills, 13-6 (B)
(RS Pts.—Bills 282, Browns 271)
(PS Pts.—Browns 34, Bills 30)
AFC Divisional Playoff
BUFFALO vs. DALLAS
RS: Cowboys lead series, 5-3
PS: Cowboys lead series, 2-0
1971—Cowboys, 49-37 (B)
1976—Cowboys, 17-10 (D)
1981—Cowboys, 27-14 (D)
1984—Bills, 14-3 (B)
1992—*Cowboys, 52-17 (Pasadena)
1993—Bills, 13-10 (D)
    **Cowboys, 30-13 (Atlanta)
1996—Bills, 10-7 (B)
2003—Cowboys, 10-6 (D)
2007—Cowboys, 25-24 (B)
(RS Pts.—Cowboys 148, Bills 128)
(PS Pts.—Cowboys 82, Bills 30)
Super Bowl XXVII
**Super Bowl XXVIII*
BUFFALO vs. DENVER
RS: Bills lead series, 18-15-1
PS: Bills lead series, 1-0
1960—Broncos, 27-21 (B)
    Tie, 38-38 (D)
1961—Broncos, 22-10 (B)
    Bills, 23-10 (D)
1962—Broncos, 23-20 (B)
    Bills, 45-38 (D)
1963—Bills, 30-28 (B)
    Bills, 27-17 (B)
1964—Bills, 30-13 (B)
    Bills, 30-19 (D)

1965—Bills, 30-15 (D)
    Bills, 31-13 (B)
1966—Bills, 38-21 (B)
1967—Bills, 17-16 (D)
    Broncos, 21-20 (B)
1968—Broncos, 34-32 (D)
1969—Bills, 41-28 (B)
1970—Broncos, 25-10 (B)
1975—Bills, 38-14 (B)
1977—Broncos, 26-6 (D)
1979—Broncos, 19-16 (B)
1981—Bills, 9-7 (B)
1984—Broncos, 37-7 (B)
1987—Bills, 21-14 (B)
1989—Broncos, 28-14 (B)
1990—Bills, 29-28 (B)
1991—*Bills, 10-7 (B)
1992—Bills, 27-17 (B)
1994—Bills, 27-20 (B)
1995—Broncos, 22-7 (D)
1997—Broncos, 23-20 (B) OT
2002—Broncos, 28-23 (D)
2005—Broncos, 28-17 (B)
2007—Broncos, 15-14 (B)
2009—Bills, 20-23 (D)
(RS Pts.—Bills 798, Broncos 757)
(PS Pts.—Bills 10, Broncos 7)
AFC Championship
BUFFALO vs. DETROIT
RS: Series tied, 4-4-1
1972—Tie, 21-21 (B)
1976—Lions, 27-14 (D)
1979—Bills, 20-17 (D)
1991—Lions, 17-14 (B) OT
1994—Lions, 35-21 (D)
1997—Bills, 22-13 (B)
2002—Bills, 24-17 (B)
2006—Lions, 20-17 (D)
2010—Bills, 14-12 (B)
(RS Pts.—Lions 179, Bills 167)
BUFFALO vs. GREEN BAY
RS: Bills lead series, 7-4
1974—Bills, 27-7 (GB)
1979—Bills, 19-12 (B)
1982—Packers, 33-21 (Mil)
1988—Bills, 28-0 (B)
1991—Bills, 34-24 (Mil)
1994—Bills 29-20 (B)
1997—Packers, 31-21 (GB)
2000—Bills 27-18 (B)
2002—Packers, 10-0 (GB)
2006—Bills, 24-10 (B)
2010—Packers, 34-7 (GB)
(RS Pts.—Bills 237, Packers 199)
BUFFALO vs. HOUSTON
RS: Bills lead series, 3-2
2002—Bills, 31-24 (H)
2003—Texans, 12-10 (B)
2005—Bills, 22-7 (B)
2006—Bills, 24-21 (H)
2009—Texans, 31-10 (B)
(RS Pts.—Bills 97, Texans 95)
BUFFALO vs. *INDIANAPOLIS
RS: Bills lead series, 35-30-1
1970—Tie, 17-17 (Balt)
    Colts, 20-14 (Buff)
1971—Colts, 43-0 (Buff)
    Colts, 24-0 (Balt)
1972—Colts, 17-0 (Buff)
    Colts, 35-7 (Balt)
1973—Bills, 31-13 (Buff)

    Bills, 24-17 (Balt)
1974—Bills, 27-14 (Balt)
    Bills, 6-0 (Buff)
1975—Bills, 38-31 (Balt)
    Colts, 42-35 (Buff)
1976—Colts, 31-13 (Buff)
    Colts, 58-20 (Balt)
1977—Colts, 17-14 (Balt)
    Colts, 31-13 (Buff)
1978—Bills, 24-17 (Buff)
    Bills, 21-14 (Balt)
1979—Bills, 31-13 (Balt)
    Colts, 14-13 (Buff)
1980—Colts, 17-12 (Buff)
    Colts, 28-24 (Balt)
1981—Bills, 35-3 (Balt)
    Bills, 23-17 (Buff)
1982—Bills, 20-0 (Buff)
1983—Bills, 28-23 (Buff)
    Bills, 30-7 (Balt)
1984—Colts, 31-17 (I)
    Bills, 21-15 (Buff)
1985—Colts, 49-17 (I)
    Bills, 21-9 (Buff)
1986—Bills, 24-13 (Buff)
    Colts, 24-14 (I)
1987—Colts, 47-6 (Buff)
    Bills, 27-3 (I)
1988—Bills, 34-23 (Buff)
    Colts, 17-14 (I)
1989—Colts, 37-14 (I)
    Bills, 30-7 (Buff)
1990—Bills, 26-10 (Buff)
    Bills, 31-7 (I)
1991—Bills, 42-6 (Buff)
    Bills, 35-7 (I)
1992—Bills, 38-0 (Buff)
    Colts, 16-13 (I) OT
1993—Bills, 23-9 (Buff)
    Bills, 30-10 (I)
1994—Colts, 27-17 (Buff)
    Colts, 10-9 (I)
1995—Bills, 20-14 (Buff)
    Bills, 16-10 (I)
1996—Bills, 16-13 (Buff) OT
    Colts, 13-10 (I) OT
1997—Bills, 37-35 (B)
    Bills, 9-6 (I)
1998—Bills, 31-24 (I)
    Bills, 34-11 (B)
1999—Colts, 31-14 (I)
    Bills, 31-6 (B)
2000—Colts, 18-16 (B)
    Colts, 44-20 (I)
2001—Colts, 42-26 (I)
    Colts, 30-14 (B)
2003—Colts, 17-14 (B)
2006—Colts, 17-16 (I)
2009—Bills, 30-7 (I)
(RS Pts.—Bills 1,377, Colts 1,278)
Franchise in Baltimore prior to 1984
BUFFALO vs. JACKSONVILLE
RS: Series tied, 5-5
PS: Jaguars lead series, 1-0
1996—*Jaguars, 30-27 (B)
1997—Jaguars, 20-14 (B)
1998—Bills, 17-16 (B)
2001—Bills, 13-10 (J)
2003—Bills, 38-17 (J)
2004—Jaguars, 13-10 (B)
2006—Bills, 27-24 (B)

2007—Jaguars, 36-14 (J)
2008—Bills, 20-16 (J)
2009—Jaguars, 18-15 (J)
2010—Jaguars, 36-26 (B)
(RS Pts.—Jaguars 206, Bills 194)
(PS Pts.—Jaguars 30, Bills 27)
*AFC First-Round Playoff
BUFFALO vs. *KANSAS CITY
RS: Bills lead series, 21-17-1
PS: Bills lead series, 2-1
1960—Texans, 45-28 (B)
    Texans, 24-7 (D)
1961—Bills, 27-24 (B)
    Bills, 30-20 (D)
1962—Texans, 41-21 (D)
    Bills, 23-14 (B)
1963—Tie, 27-27 (B)
    Bills, 35-26 (KC)
1964—Bills, 34-17 (B)
    Bills, 35-22 (KC)
1965—Bills, 23-7 (KC)
    Bills, 34-25 (B)
1966—Chiefs, 42-20 (B)
    Bills, 29-14 (KC)
    **Chiefs, 31-7 (B)
1967—Chiefs, 23-13 (KC)
1968—Chiefs, 18-7 (B)
1969—Chiefs, 29-7 (B)
    Chiefs, 22-19 (KC)
1971—Chiefs, 22-9 (KC)
1973—Bills, 23-14 (B)
1976—Bills, 50-17 (B)
1978—Bills, 28-13 (B)
    Chiefs, 14-10 (KC)
1982—Bills, 14-9 (B)
1983—Bills, 14-9 (KC)
1986—Chiefs, 20-17 (B)
    Bills, 17-14 (KC)
1991—Chiefs, 33-6 (KC)
    ***Bills, 37-14 (B)
1993—Chiefs, 23-7 (KC)
    ****Bills, 30-13 (B)
1994—Bills, 44-10 (B)
1996—Bills, 20-9 (B)
1997—Chiefs, 22-16 (KC)
2000—Bills, 21-17 (KC)
2002—Chiefs, 17-16 (KC)
2003—Chiefs, 38-5 (KC)
2005—Bills, 14-3 (B)
2008—Bills, 54-31 (KC)
2009—Bills, 16-10 (KC)
2010—Chiefs, 13-10 (KC) OT
(RS Pts.—Bills 830, Chiefs 798)
(PS Pts.—Bills 74, Chiefs 58)
*Franchise in Dallas prior to 1963 and known as Texans
**AFL Championship
***AFC Divisional Playoff
****AFC Championship
BUFFALO vs. MIAMI
RS: Dolphins lead series, 53-36-1
PS: Bills lead series, 3-1
1966—Bills, 58-24 (B)
    Bills, 29-0 (M)
1967—Bills, 35-13 (B)
    Dolphins, 17-14 (M)
1968—Tie, 14-14 (M)
    Dolphins, 21-17 (B)
1969—Dolphins, 24-6 (M)
    Bills, 28-3 (B)
1970—Dolphins, 33-14 (B)

    Dolphins, 45-7 (M)
1971—Dolphins, 29-14 (B)
    Dolphins, 34-0 (M)
1972—Dolphins, 24-23 (M)
    Dolphins, 30-16 (B)
1973—Dolphins, 27-6 (M)
    Dolphins, 17-0 (B)
1974—Dolphins, 24-16 (B)
    Dolphins, 35-28 (M)
1975—Dolphins, 35-30 (B)
    Dolphins, 31-21 (M)
1976—Dolphins, 30-21 (B)
    Dolphins, 45-27 (M)
1977—Dolphins, 13-0 (B)
    Dolphins, 31-14 (M)
1978—Dolphins, 31-24 (M)
    Dolphins, 25-24 (B)
1979—Dolphins, 9-7 (B)
    Dolphins, 17-7 (M)
1980—Bills, 17-7 (B)
    Dolphins, 17-14 (M)
1981—Bills, 31-21 (B)
    Dolphins, 16-6 (M)
1982—Dolphins, 9-7 (B)
    Dolphins, 27-10 (M)
1983—Dolphins, 12-0 (B)
    Bills, 38-35 (M) OT
1984—Dolphins, 21-17 (B)
    Dolphins, 38-7 (M)
1985—Dolphins, 23-14 (B)
    Dolphins, 28-0 (M)
1986—Dolphins, 27-14 (M)
    Dolphins, 34-24 (B)
1987—Bills, 34-31 (M) OT
    Bills, 27-0 (B)
1988—Bills, 9-6 (B)
    Bills, 31-6 (M)
1989—Bills, 27-24 (M)
    Bills, 31-17 (B)
1990—Dolphins, 30-7 (M)
    Bills, 24-14 (B)
    *Bills, 44-34 (B)
1991—Bills, 35-31 (B)
    Bills, 41-27 (M)
1992—Dolphins, 37-10 (B)
    Bills, 26-20 (M)
    **Bills, 29-10 (M)
1993—Dolphins, 22-13 (B)
    Bills, 47-34 (M)
1994—Bills, 21-11 (B)
    Bills, 42-31 (M)
1995—Dolphins, 23-6 (M)
    Bills, 23-20 (B)
    ***Bills, 37-22 (B)
1996—Dolphins, 21-7 (B)
    Dolphins, 16-14 (M)
1997—Bills, 9-6 (B)
    Dolphins, 30-13 (M)
1998—Dolphins, 13-7 (M)
    Bills, 30-24 (B)
    ***Dolphins, 24-17 (M)
1999—Bills, 23-18 (M)
    Bills, 23-3 (B)
2000—Dolphins, 22-13 (M)
    Dolphins, 33-6 (B)
2001—Dolphins, 34-27 (B)
    Dolphins, 34-7 (M)
2002—Bills, 23-10 (M)
    Bills, 38-21 (B)
2003—Dolphins, 17-7 (M)
    Dolphins, 20-3 (B)

2004—Bills, 20-13 (B)
    Bills, 42-32 (M)
2005—Bills, 20-14 (B)
    Dolphins, 24-23 (M)
2006—Bills, 16-6 (M)
    Bills, 21-0 (B)
2007—Bills, 13-10 (M)
    Bills, 38-17 (B)
2008—Dolphins, 25-16 (M)
    Dolphins, 16-3 (Toronto)
2009—Dolphins, 38-10 (M)
    Bills, 31-14 (B)
2010—Dolphins, 15-10 (B)
    Bills, 17-14 (M)
(RS Pts.—Dolphins 1,940, Bills 1,683)
(PS Pts.—Bills 127, Dolphins 90)
*AFC Divisional Playoff
**AFC Championship
***AFC First-Round Playoff
BUFFALO vs. MINNESOTA
RS: Vikings lead series, 8-4
1971—Vikings, 19-0 (M)
1975—Vikings, 35-13 (B)
1979—Vikings, 10-3 (M)
1982—Bills, 23-22 (B)
1985—Vikings, 27-20 (B)
1988—Bills, 13-10 (B)
1994—Vikings, 21-17 (B)
1997—Vikings, 34-13 (B)
2000—Vikings, 31-27 (M)
2002—Bills, 45-39 (M) OT
2006—Bills, 17-12 (B)
2010—Vikings, 38-14 (M)
(RS Pts.—Vikings 298, Bills 205)
BUFFALO vs. *NEW ENGLAND
RS: Patriots lead series, 60-40-1
PS: Patriots lead series, 1-0
1960—Bills, 13-0 (Bos)
    Bills, 38-14 (Buff)
1961—Patriots, 23-21 (Buff)
    Patriots, 52-21 (Bos)
1962—Tie, 28-28 (Buff)
    Patriots, 21-10 (Bos)
1963—Bills, 28-21 (Buff)
    Patriots, 17-7 (Bos)
    **Patriots, 26-8 (Buff)
1964—Patriots, 36-28 (Buff)
    Bills, 24-14 (Bos)
1965—Bills, 24-7 (Buff)
    Bills, 23-7 (Bos)
1966—Patriots, 20-10 (Buff)
    Patriots, 14-3 (Bos)
1967—Patriots, 23-0 (Buff)
    Bills, 44-16 (Bos)
1968—Patriots, 16-7 (Buff)
    Patriots, 23-6 (Bos)
1969—Bills, 23-16 (Buff)
    Patriots, 35-21 (Bos)
1970—Bills, 45-10 (Bos)
    Patriots, 14-10 (Buff)
1971—Patriots, 38-33 (NE)
    Bills, 27-20 (Buff)
1972—Bills, 38-14 (Buff)
    Bills, 27-24 (NE)
1973—Bills, 31-13 (NE)
    Bills, 37-13 (Buff)
1974—Bills, 30-28 (Buff)
    Bills, 29-28 (NE)
1975—Bills, 45-31 (Buff)
    Bills, 34-14 (NE)
1976—Patriots, 26-22 (Buff)

Patriots, 20-10 (NE)
1977—Bills, 24-14 (NE)
Patriots, 20-7 (Buff)
1978—Patriots, 14-10 (Buff)
Patriots, 26-24 (NE)
1979—Patriots, 26-6 (Buff)
Bills, 16-13 (NE) OT
1980—Bills, 31-13 (Buff)
Patriots, 24-2 (NE)
1981—Bills, 20-17 (Buff)
Bills, 19-10 (NE)
1982—Patriots, 30-19 (NE)
1983—Patriots, 31-0 (Buff)
Patriots, 21-7 (NE)
1984—Patriots, 21-17 (Buff)
Patriots, 38-10 (NE)
1985—Patriots, 17-14 (Buff)
Patriots, 14-3 (NE)
1986—Patriots, 23-3 (Buff)
Patriots, 22-19 (NE)
1987—Patriots, 14-7 (NE)
Patriots, 13-7 (Buff)
1988—Bills, 16-14 (NE)
Bills, 23-20 (Buff)
1989—Bills, 31-10 (Buff)
Patriots, 33-24 (NE)
1990—Bills, 27-10 (NE)
Bills, 14-0 (Buff)
1991—Bills, 22-17 (Buff)
Patriots, 16-13 (NE)
1992—Bills, 41-7 (NE)
Bills, 16-7 (Buff)
1993—Bills, 38-14 (Buff)
Bills, 13-10 (NE) OT
1994—Bills, 38-35 (NE)
Patriots, 41-17 (Buff)
1995—Patriots, 27-14 (NE)
Patriots, 35-25 (Buff)
1996—Bills, 17-10 (Buff)
Patriots, 28-25 (NE)
1997—Patriots, 33-6 (NE)
Patriots, 31-10 (Buff)
1998—Bills, 13-10 (Buff)
Patriots, 25-21 (NE)
1999—Bills, 17-7 (Buff)
Bills, 13-10 (NE) OT
2000—Bills, 16-13 (NE) OT
Patriots, 13-10 (Buff) OT
2001—Patriots, 21-11 (NE)
Patriots, 12-9 (Buff) OT
2002—Patriots, 38-7 (Buff)
Patriots, 27-17 (NE)
2003—Bills, 31-0 (Buff)
Patriots, 31-0 (NE)
2004—Patriots, 31-17 (Buff)
Patriots, 29-6 (NE)
2005—Patriots, 21-16 (NE)
Patriots, 35-7 (Buff)
2006—Patriots, 19-17 (NE)
Patriots, 28-6 (Buff)
2007—Patriots, 38-7 (NE)
Patriots, 56-10 (Buff)
2008—Patriots, 20-10 (NE)
Patriots, 13-0 (Buff)
2009—Patriots, 25-24 (NE)
Patriots, 17-10 (Buff)
2010—Patriots, 38-30 (NE)
Patriots, 34-3 (Buff)
(RS Pts.—Patriots 2,126, Bills 1,820)
(PS Pts.—Patriots 26, Bills 8)
*Franchise in Boston prior to 1971

**Division Playoff
BUFFALO vs. NEW ORLEANS
RS: Saints lead series, 5-4
1973—Saints, 13-0 (NO)
1980—Bills, 35-26 (NO)
1983—Bills, 27-21 (B)
1989—Saints, 22-19 (B)
1992—Bills, 20-16 (NO)
1998—Bills, 45-33 (NO)
2001—Saints, 24-6 (B)
2005—Saints, 19-7 (San Antonio)
2009—Saints, 27-7 (B)
(RS Pts.—Saints 201, Bills 166)
BUFFALO vs. N.Y. GIANTS
RS: Bills lead series, 6-4
PS: Giants lead series, 1-0
1970—Giants, 20-6 (NY)
1975—Giants, 17-14 (B)
1978—Bills, 41-17 (B)
1987—Bills, 6-3 (B) OT
1990—Bills, 17-13 (NY)
*Giants, 20-19 (Tampa)
1993—Bills, 17-14 (B)
1996—Bills, 23-20 (NY) OT
1999—Giants, 19-17 (B)
2003—Bills, 24-7 (NY)
2007—Giants, 38-21 (B)
(RS Pts.—Bills 186, Giants 168)
(PS Pts.—Giants 20, Bills 19)
*Super Bowl XXV
BUFFALO vs. *N.Y. JETS
RS: Bills lead series, 53-47
PS: Bills lead series, 1-0
1960—Titans, 27-3 (NY)
Titans, 17-13 (B)
1961—Bills, 41-31 (B)
Titans, 21-14 (NY)
1962—Titans, 17-6 (B)
Bills, 20-3 (NY)
1963—Bills, 45-14 (B)
Bills, 19-10 (NY)
1964—Bills, 34-24 (B)
Bills, 20-7 (NY)
1965—Bills, 33-21 (B)
Jets, 14-12 (NY)
1966—Bills, 33-23 (NY)
Bills, 14-3 (B)
1967—Bills, 20-17 (B)
Jets, 20-10 (NY)
1968—Bills, 37-35 (B)
Jets, 25-21 (NY)
1969—Jets, 33-19 (B)
Jets, 16-6 (NY)
1970—Bills, 34-31 (B)
Bills, 10-6 (NY)
1971—Jets, 28-17 (NY)
Jets, 20-7 (B)
1972—Jets, 41-24 (B)
Jets, 41-3 (NY)
1973—Bills, 9-7 (B)
Bills, 34-14 (NY)
1974—Bills, 16-12 (B)
Jets, 20-10 (NY)
1975—Bills, 42-14 (B)
Bills, 24-23 (NY)
1976—Jets, 17-14 (NY)
Bills, 19-14 (B)
1977—Jets, 24-19 (B)
Bills, 14-10 (NY)
1978—Jets, 21-20 (B)
Jets, 45-14 (NY)

1979—Bills, 46-31 (B)
Bills, 14-12 (NY)
1980—Bills, 20-10 (B)
Bills, 31-24 (NY)
1981—Bills, 31-0 (B)
Jets, 33-14 (NY)
**Bills, 31-27 (NY)
1983—Jets, 34-10 (B)
Bills, 24-17 (NY)
1984—Jets, 28-26 (B)
Jets, 21-17 (NY)
1985—Jets, 42-3 (NY)
Jets, 27-7 (B)
1986—Jets, 28-24 (B)
Jets, 14-13 (NY)
1987—Jets, 31-28 (B)
Bills, 17-14 (NY)
1988—Bills, 37-14 (NY)
Bills, 9-6 (B) OT
1989—Bills, 34-3 (B)
Bills, 37-0 (NY)
1990—Bills, 30-7 (NY)
Bills, 30-27 (B)
1991—Bills, 23-20 (NY)
Bills, 24-13 (B)
1992—Bills, 24-20 (NY)
Jets, 24-17 (B)
1993—Bills, 19-10 (NY)
Bills, 16-14 (B)
1994—Jets, 23-3 (B)
Jets, 22-17 (NY)
1995—Bills, 29-10 (B)
Bills, 28-26 (NY)
1996—Bills, 25-22 (NY)
Bills, 35-10 (B)
1997—Bills, 28-22 (NY)
Bills, 20-10 (B)
1998—Jets, 34-12 (NY)
Jets, 17-10 (B)
1999—Bills, 17-3 (B)
Jets, 17-7 (NY)
2000—Jets, 27-14 (NY)
Bills, 23-20 (B)
2001—Jets, 42-36 (B)
Bills, 14-9 (NY)
2002—Jets, 37-31 (B) OT
Jets, 31-13 (NY)
2003—Jets, 30-3 (NY)
Bills, 17-6 (B)
2004—Jets, 16-14 (NY)
Bills, 22-17 (B)
2005—Bills, 27-17 (B)
Jets, 30-26 (NY)
2006—Jets, 28-20 (B)
Bills, 31-13 (NY)
2007—Bills, 17-14 (B)
Bills, 13-3 (NY)
2008—Jets, 26-17 (B)
Jets, 31-27 (NY)
2009—Bills, 16-13 (NY) OT
Jets, 19-13 (Toronto)
2010—Jets, 38-14 (B)
Jets, 38-7 (NY)
(RS Pts.—Bills 2,016, Jets 2,016)
(PS Pts.—Bills 31, Jets 27)
*Jets known as Titans prior to 1963
**AFC First-Round Playoff
BUFFALO vs. *OAKLAND
RS: Raiders lead series, 19-16
PS: Bills lead series, 2-0
1960—Bills, 38-9 (B)

Raiders, 20-7 (O)
1961—Raiders, 31-22 (B)
Bills, 26-21 (O)
1962—Bills, 14-6 (B)
Bills, 10-6 (O)
1963—Raiders, 35-17 (O)
Bills, 12-0 (B)
1964—Bills, 23-20 (B)
Raiders, 16-13 (O)
1965—Bills, 17-12 (B)
Bills, 17-14 (O)
1966—Bills, 31-10 (O)
1967—Raiders, 24-20 (B)
Raiders, 28-21 (O)
1968—Raiders, 48-6 (B)
Raiders, 13-10 (O)
1969—Raiders, 50-21 (O)
1972—Raiders, 28-16 (O)
1974—Bills, 21-20 (B)
1977—Raiders, 34-13 (O)
1980—Bills, 24-7 (B)
1983—Raiders, 27-24 (B)
1987—Raiders, 34-21 (LA)
1988—Bills, 37-21 (B)
1990—Bills, 38-24 (B)
**Bills, 51-3 (B)
1991—Bills, 30-27 (LA) OT
1992—Raiders, 20-3 (LA)
1993—Raiders, 25-24 (B)
***Bills, 29-23 (B)
1998—Bills, 44-21 (B)
1999—Raiders, 20-14 (B)
2002—Raiders, 49-31 (B)
2004—Raiders, 13-10 (O)
2005—Raiders, 38-17 (O)
2008—Bills, 24-23 (B)
(RS Pts.—Raiders 794, Bills 716)
(PS Pts.—Bills 80, Raiders 26)
*Franchise in Los Angeles from 1982-1994
**AFC Championship
***AFC Divisional Playoff
BUFFALO vs. PHILADELPHIA
RS: Eagles lead series, 6-5
1973—Bills, 27-26 (B)
1981—Eagles, 20-14 (B)
1984—Eagles, 27-17 (B)
1985—Eagles, 21-17 (P)
1987—Eagles, 17-7 (P)
1990—Bills, 30-23 (B)
1993—Bills, 10-7 (P)
1996—Bills, 24-17 (P)
1999—Bills, 26-0 (B)
2003—Bills, 23-13 (B)
2007—Eagles, 17-9 (P)
(RS Pts.—Eagles 198, Bills 194)
BUFFALO vs. PITTSBURGH
RS: Steelers lead series, 12-8
PS: Steelers lead series, 2-1
1970—Steelers, 23-10 (P)
1972—Steelers, 38-21 (B)
1974—*Steelers, 32-14 (P)
1975—Bills, 30-21 (P)
1978—Steelers, 28-17 (B)
1979—Steelers, 28-0 (P)
1980—Bills, 28-13 (B)
1982—Bills, 13-0 (B)
1985—Steelers, 30-24 (P)
1986—Bills, 16-12 (B)
1988—Bills, 36-28 (B)
1991—Bills, 52-34 (B)
1992—Bills, 28-20 (B)

*Bills, 24-3 (P)
1993—Steelers, 23-0 (P)
1994—Steelers, 23-10 (P)
1995—*Steelers, 40-21 (P)
1996—Steelers, 24-6 (P)
1999—Bills, 24-21 (B)
2001—Steelers, 20-3 (B)
2004—Steelers, 29-24 (B)
2007—Steelers, 26-3 (P)
2010—Steelers, 19-16 (B) OT
(RS Pts.—Steelers 460, Bills 361)
(PS Pts.—Steelers 75, Bills 59)
*AFC Divisional Playoff
BUFFALO vs. *ST. LOUIS
RS: Bills lead series, 6-4
1970—Rams, 19-0 (B)
1974—Rams, 19-14 (LA)
1980—Bills, 10-7 (B) OT
1983—Rams, 41-17 (LA)
1989—Bills, 23-20 (B)
1992—Bills, 40-7 (B)
1995—Bills, 45-27 (StL)
1998—Rams, 34-33 (B)
2004—Bills, 37-17 (B)
2008—Bills, 31-14 (StL)
(RS Pts.—Bills 250, Rams 205)
*Franchise in Los Angeles prior to 1995
BUFFALO vs. *SAN DIEGO
RS: Chargers lead series, 20-10-2
PS: Bills lead series, 2-1
1960—Chargers, 24-10 (B)
Bills, 32-3 (LA)
1961—Chargers, 19-11 (B)
Chargers, 28-10 (SD)
1962—Bills, 35-10 (B)
Bills, 40-20 (SD)
1963—Chargers, 14-10 (SD)
Chargers, 23-13 (B)
1964—Bills, 30-3 (B)
Bills, 27-24 (SD)
**Bills, 20-7 (B)
1965—Chargers, 34-3 (B)
Tie, 20-20 (SD)
**Bills, 23-0 (SD)
1966—Chargers, 27-7 (SD)
Tie, 17-17 (B)
1967—Chargers, 37-17 (B)
1968—Chargers, 21-6 (B)
1969—Chargers, 45-6 (B)
1971—Chargers, 20-3 (SD)
1973—Chargers, 34-7 (SD)
1976—Chargers, 34-13 (B)
1979—Chargers, 27-19 (SD)
1980—Bills, 26-24 (SD)
***Chargers, 20-14 (SD)
1981—Bills, 28-27 (SD)
1985—Chargers, 14-9 (B)
Chargers, 40-7 (SD)
1998—Chargers, 16-14 (SD)
2000—Bills, 27-24 (B) OT
2001—Chargers, 27-24 (SD)
2002—Bills, 20-13 (B)
2005—Chargers, 48-10 (SD)
2006—Chargers, 24-21 (B)
2008—Bills, 23-14 (B)
(RS Pts.—Chargers 755, Bills 545)
(PS Pts.—Bills 57, Chargers 27)
*Franchise in Los Angeles prior to 1961
**AFL Championship
***AFC Divisional Playoff
BUFFALO vs. SAN FRANCISCO

RS: Series tied, 5-5
1972—Bills, 27-20 (B)
1980—Bills, 18-13 (SF)
1983—49ers, 23-10 (B)
1989—49ers, 21-10 (SF)
1992—Bills, 34-31 (SF)
1995—49ers, 27-17 (SF)
1998—Bills, 26-21 (B)
2001—49ers, 35-0 (SF)
2004—Bills, 41-7 (SF)
2008—49ers, 10-3 (B)
(RS Pts.—49ers 208, Bills 186)
BUFFALO vs. SEATTLE
RS: Seahawks lead series, 6-5
1977—Seahawks, 56-17 (S)
1984—Seahawks, 31-28 (S)
1988—Bills, 13-3 (S)
1989—Seahawks, 17-16 (S)
1995—Bills, 27-21 (B)
1996—Seahawks, 26-18 (S)
1999—Seahawks, 26-16 (S)
2000—Bills, 42-23 (B)
2001—Seahawks, 23-20 (B)
2004—Bills, 38-9 (S)
2008—Bills, 34-10 (B)
(RS Pts.—Bills 269, Seahawks 245)
BUFFALO vs. TAMPA BAY
RS: Buccaneers lead series, 6-3
1976—Bills, 14-9 (TB)
1978—Buccaneers, 31-10 (TB)
1982—Buccaneers, 24-23 (TB)
1986—Buccaneers, 34-28 (TB)
1988—Buccaneers, 10-5 (TB)
1991—Bills, 17-10 (TB)
2000—Buccaneers, 31-17 (TB)
2005—Buccaneers, 19-3 (TB)
2009—Bills, 33-20 (B)
(RS Pts.—Buccaneers 188, Bills 150)
BUFFALO vs. *TENNESSEE
RS: Titans lead series, 25-14
PS: Bills lead series, 2-1
1960—Bills, 25-24 (B)
Oilers, 31-23 (H)
1961—Bills, 22-12 (H)
Oilers, 28-16 (B)
1962—Bills, 28-23 (B)
Oilers, 17-14 (H)
1963—Oilers, 31-20 (B)
Oilers, 28-14 (H)
1964—Bills, 48-17 (H)
Bills, 24-10 (B)
1965—Oilers, 19-17 (B)
Bills, 29-18 (H)
1966—Bills, 27-20 (B)
Bills, 42-20 (H)
1967—Oilers, 20-3 (B)
Oilers, 10-3 (H)
1968—Oilers, 30-7 (B)
Oilers, 35-6 (H)
1969—Oilers, 17-3 (B)
Oilers, 28-14 (H)
1971—Oilers, 20-14 (B)
1974—Oilers, 21-9 (B)
1976—Oilers, 13-3 (B)
1978—Oilers, 17-10 (H)
1983—Bills, 30-13 (B)
1985—Bills, 20-0 (B)
1986—Oilers, 16-7 (H)
1987—Bills, 34-30 (B)
1988—**Bills, 17-10 (B)
1989—Bills, 47-41 (H) OT

1990—Oilers, 27-24 (H)
1992—Oilers, 27-3 (H)
  ***Bills, 41-38 (B) OT
1993—Bills, 35-7 (B)
1994—Bills, 15-7 (H)
1995—Oilers, 28-17 (B)
1997—Oilers, 31-14 (T)
1999—***Titans, 22-16 (T)
2000—Bills, 16-13 (B)
2003—Titans, 28-26 (T)
2006—Titans, 30-29 (B)
2009—Titans, 41-17 (T)
(RS Pts.—Titans 853, Bills 750)
(PS Pts.—Bills 74, Titans 70)
*Franchise in Houston prior to 1997;
known as Oilers prior to 1999
**AFC Divisional Playoff
***AFC First-Round Playoff
BUFFALO vs. WASHINGTON
RS: Bills lead series, 7-4
PS: Redskins lead series, 1-0
1972—Bills, 24-17 (W)
1977—Redskins, 10-0 (B)
1981—Bills, 21-14 (B)
1984—Redskins, 41-14 (W)
1987—Redskins, 27-7 (B)
1990—Redskins, 29-14 (W)
1991—*Redskins, 37-24 (Minneapolis)
1993—Bills, 24-10 (B)
1996—Bills, 38-13 (B)
1999—Bills, 34-17 (W)
2003—Bills, 24-7 (B)
2007—Bills, 17-16 (W)
(RS Pts.—Bills 217, Redskins 201)
(PS Pts.—Redskins 37, Bills 24)
*Super Bowl XXVI

CAROLINA vs. ARIZONA
RS: Panthers lead series, 8-2
PS: Cardinals lead series, 1-0;
See Arizona vs. Carolina
CAROLINA vs. ATLANTA
RS: Falcons lead series, 20-12;
See Atlanta vs. Carolina
CAROLINA vs. BALTIMORE
RS: Panthers lead series, 3-1;
See Baltimore vs. Carolina
CAROLINA vs. BUFFALO
RS: Bills lead series, 4-1;
See Buffalo vs. Carolina
CAROLINA vs. CHICAGO
RS: Bears lead series, 3-2
PS: Panthers lead series, 1-0
1995—Bears, 31-27 (Chi)
2002—Panthers, 24-14 (Car)
2005—Bears, 13-3 (Chi)
  *Panthers, 29-21 (Chi)
2008—Panthers, 20-17 (Car)
2010—Bears, 23-6 (Car)
(RS Pts.—Bears 98, Panthers 80)
(PS Pts.—Panthers 29, Bears 21)
*NFC Divisional Playoff
CAROLINA vs. CINCINNATI
RS: Series tied, 2-2
1999—Panthers, 27-3 (Car)
2002—Panthers, 52-31 (Car)
2006—Bengals, 17-14 (Cin)
2010—Bengals, 20-7 (Car)
(RS Pts.—Panthers 100, Bengals 71)
CAROLINA vs. CLEVELAND
RS: Panthers lead series, 3-1

1999—Panthers, 31-17 (Cle)
2002—Panthers, 13-6 (Cle)
2006—Panthers, 20-12 (Car)
2010—Browns, 24-23 (Cle)
(RS Pts.—Panthers 87, Browns 59)
CAROLINA vs. DALLAS
RS: Cowboys lead series, 8-1
PS: Panthers lead series, 2-0
1996—*Panthers, 26-17 (C)
1997—Panthers, 23-13 (D)
1998—Cowboys, 27-20 (D)
2000—Cowboys, 16-13 (C) OT
2002—Cowboys, 14-13 (D)
2003—Cowboys, 24-20 (D)
  **Panthers, 29-10 (C)
2005—Cowboys, 24-20 (C)
2006—Cowboys, 35-14 (C)
2007—Cowboys, 20-13 (C)
2009—Cowboys, 21-7 (D)
(RS Pts.—Cowboys 194, Panthers 143)
(PS Pts.—Panthers 55, Cowboys 27)
*NFC Divisional Playoff
*NFC First-Round Playoff
CAROLINA vs. DENVER
RS: Broncos lead series, 2-1
1997—Broncos, 34-0 (D)
2004—Broncos, 20-17 (D)
2008—Panthers, 30-10 (C)
(RS Pts.—Broncos 64, Panthers 47)
CAROLINA vs. DETROIT
RS: Panthers lead series, 4-1
1999—Lions, 24-9 (C)
2002—Panthers, 31-7 (C)
2003—Panthers, 20-14 (C)
2005—Panthers, 21-20 (D)
2008—Panthers, 31-22 (C)
(RS Pts.—Panthers 112, Lions 87)
CAROLINA vs. GREEN BAY
RS: Packers lead series, 6-4
PS: Packers lead series, 1-0
1996—*Packers, 30-13 (GB)
1997—Packers, 31-10 (C)
1998—Packers, 37-30 (C)
1999—Panthers, 33-31 (GB)
2000—Panthers, 31-14 (C)
2001—Panthers, 28-7 (C)
2002—Packers, 17-14 (GB)
2004—Packers, 24-14 (C)
2005—Panthers, 32-29 (C)
2007—Packers, 31-17 (GB)
2008—Panthers, 35-31 (GB)
(RS Pts.—Packers 273, Panthers 223)
(PS Pts.—Packers 30, Panthers 13)
*NFC Championship
CAROLINA vs. HOUSTON
RS: Texans lead series, 2-0
2003—Texans, 14-10 (H)
2007—Texans, 34-21 (C)
(RS Pts.—Texans 48, Panthers 31)
CAROLINA vs. INDIANAPOLIS
RS: Panthers lead series, 3-1
1995—Panthers, 13-10 (C)
1998—Panthers, 27-19 (I)
2003—Panthers, 23-20 (I) OT
2007—Colts, 31-7 (C)
(RS Pts.—Colts 80, Panthers 70)
CAROLINA vs. JACKSONVILLE
RS: Jaguars lead series, 3-1
1996—Jaguars, 24-14 (J)
1999—Jaguars, 22-20 (C)
2003—Panthers, 24-23 (C)

2007—Jaguars, 37-6 (J)
(RS Pts.—Jaguars 106, Panthers 64)
CAROLINA vs. KANSAS CITY
RS: Series tied, 2-2
1997—Chiefs, 35-14 (C)
2000—Chiefs, 15-14 (KC)
2004—Panthers, 28-17 (KC)
2008—Panthers, 34-0 (C)
(RS Pts.—Panthers 90, Chiefs 67)
CAROLINA vs. MIAMI
RS: Dolphins lead series, 4-0
1998—Dolphins, 13-9 (C)
2001—Dolphins, 23-6 (M)
2005—Dolphins, 27-24 (M)
2009—Dolphins, 24-17 (C)
(RS Pts.—Dolphins 87, Panthers 56)
CAROLINA vs. MINNESOTA
RS: Vikings lead series, 5-4
1996—Vikings, 14-12 (M)
1997—Vikings, 21-14 (M)
2000—Vikings, 31-17 (M)
2001—Panthers, 24-13 (M)
2002—Panthers, 21-14 (M)
2005—Panthers, 38-13 (C)
2006—Vikings, 16-13 (M) OT
2008—Vikings, 20-10 (M)
2009—Panthers, 26-7 (C)
(RS Pts.—Panthers 175, Vikings 149)
CAROLINA vs. NEW ENGLAND
RS: Series tied, 2-2
PS: Patriots lead series, 1-0
1995—Panthers, 20-17 (NE) OT
2001 Patriots, 38-6 (C)
2003—*Patriots, 32-29 (Houston)
2005—Panthers, 27-17 (C)
2009—Patriots, 20-10 (NE)
(RS Pts.—Patriots 92, Panthers 63)
(PS Pts.—Patriots 32, Panthers 29)
*Super Bowl XXXVIII
CAROLINA vs. NEW ORLEANS
RS: Panthers lead series, 17-15
1995—Panthers, 20-3 (C)
  Saints, 34-26 (NO)
1996—Panthers, 22-20 (NO)
  Panthers, 19-7 (C)
1997—Panthers, 13-0 (NO)
  Saints, 16-13 (C)
1998 Saints, 19-14 (NO)
  Panthers, 31-17 (C)
1999—Saints, 19-10 (NO)
  Panthers, 45-13 (C)
2000—Panthers, 24-6 (NO)
  Saints, 20-10 (C)
2001—Saints, 27-25 (C)
  Saints, 27-23 (NO)
2002—Saints, 34-24 (C)
  Panthers, 10-6 (NO)
2003—Panthers, 19-13 (C)
  Panthers, 23-20 (NO) OT
2004—Panthers, 32-21 (NO)
  Saints, 21-18 (C)
2005—Saints, 23-20 (C)
  Panthers, 27-10 (Baton Rouge)
2006—Panthers, 21-18 (C)
  Panthers, 31-21 (NO)
2007—Panthers, 16-13 (NO)
  Saints, 31-6 (C)
2008—Panthers, 30-7 (C)
  Panthers, 33-31 (NO)
2009—Saints, 30-20 (NO)
  Panthers, 23-10 (C)

2010—Saints, 16-14 (NO)
    Saints, 34-3 (C)
(RS Pts.—Panthers 647, Saints 605)
CAROLINA vs. N.Y. GIANTS
RS: Series tied, 3-3
PS: Panthers lead series, 1-0
1996—Panthers, 27-17 (C)
2003—Panthers, 37-24 (NY)
2005—*Panthers, 23-0 (NY)
2006—Giants, 27-13 (C)
2008—Giants, 34-28 (NY) OT
2009—Panthers, 41-9 (NY)
2010—Giants, 31-18 (NY)
(RS Pts.—Panthers 164, Giants 142)
(PS Pts.—Panthers 23, Giants 0)
NFC First-Round Playoff
CAROLINA vs. N.Y. JETS
RS: Jets lead series, 3-2
1995—Panthers, 26-15 (C)
1998—Jets, 48-21 (NY)
2001—Jets, 13-12 (C)
2005—Panthers, 30-3 (C)
2009—Jets, 17-6 (NY)
(RS Pts.—Jets 96, Panthers 95)
CAROLINA vs. OAKLAND
RS: Series tied, 2-2
1997—Panthers, 38-14 (C)
2000—Raiders, 52-9 (O)
2004—Raiders, 27-24 (C)
2008—Panthers, 17-6 (O)
(RS Pts.— Raiders 99, Panthers 88)
CAROLINA vs. PHILADELPHIA
RS: Eagles lead series, 5-1
PS: Panthers lead series, 1-0
1996—Eagles, 20-9 (P)
1999—Panthers, 33-7 (C)
2003—Eagles, 25-16 (C)
    *Panthers, 14-3 (P)
2004—Eagles, 30-8 (P)
2006—Eagles, 27-24 (P)
2009—Panthers, 38-10 (C)
(RS Pts.—Eagles 147, Panthers 100)
(PS Pts.—Panthers 14, Eagles 3)
NFC Championship
CAROLINA vs. PITTSBURGH
RS: Steelers lead series, 4-1
1996—Panthers, 18-14 (C)
1999—Steelers, 30-20 (P)
2002—Steelers, 30-14 (P)
2006—Steelers, 37-3 (C)
2010—Steelers, 27-3 (P)
(RS Pts.—Steelers 138, Panthers 58)
CAROLINA vs. ST. LOUIS
RS: Panthers lead series, 10-8
PS: Panthers lead series, 1-0
1995—Rams, 31-10 (C)
    Rams, 28-17 (StL)
1996—Panthers, 45-13 (C)
    Panthers, 20-10 (StL)
1997—Panthers, 16-10 (StL)
    Rams, 30-18 (C)
1998—Panthers, 24-20 (StL)
    Panthers, 20-13 (C)
1999—Rams, 35-10 (StL)
    Rams, 34-21 (C)
2000—Panthers, 27-24 (StL)
    Panthers, 16-3 (C)
2001—Rams, 48-14 (StL)
    Rams, 38-32 (C)
2003—*Panthers, 29-23 (StL) 2OT
2004—Panthers, 20-7 (C)

2006—Panthers, 15-0 (C)
2007—Panthers, 27-13 (StL)
2010—Rams, 20-10 (StL)
(RS Pts.—Rams 377, Panthers 362)
(PS Pts.—Panthers 29, Rams 23)
NFC Divisional Playoff
CAROLINA vs. SAN DIEGO
RS: Panthers lead series, 3-1
1997—Panthers, 26-7 (SD)
2000—Panthers, 30-22 (C)
2004—Chargers, 17-6 (C)
2008—Panthers, 26-24 (SD)
(RS Pts.—Panthers 88, Chargers 70)
CAROLINA vs. SAN FRANCISCO
RS: Panthers lead series, 10-7
1995—Panthers, 13-7 (SF)
    49ers, 31-10 (C)
1996—Panthers, 23-7 (C)
    Panthers, 30-24 (SF)
1997—49ers, 34-21 (C)
    49ers, 27-19 (SF)
1998—49ers, 25-23 (SF)
    49ers, 31-28 (C) OT
1999—Panthers, 31-29 (SF)
    Panthers, 41-24 (C)
2000—Panthers, 38-22 (SF)
    Panthers, 34-16 (C)
2001—49ers, 24-14 (SF)
    49ers, 25-22 (C) OT
2004—Panthers, 37-27 (C)
2007—Panthers, 31-14 (C)
2010—Panthers, 23-20 (C)
(RS Pts.—Panthers 438, 49ers 387)
CAROLINA vs. SEATTLE
RS: Series tied, 2-2
PS: Seahawks lead series, 1-0
2000—Panthers, 26-3 (C)
2004—Seahawks, 23-17 (S)
2005—*Seahawks, 34-14 (S)
2007—Panthers, 13-10 (C)
2010—Seahawks, 31-14 (S)
(RS Pts.—Panthers 70, Seahawks 67)
(PS Pts.—Seahawks 34, Panthers 14)
NFC Championship
CAROLINA vs. TAMPA BAY
RS: Panthers lead series, 12-9
1995—Buccaneers, 20-13 (C)
1996—Panthers, 24-0 (C)
1998—Buccaneers, 16-13 (TB)
2002—Buccaneers, 12-9 (C)
    Buccaneers, 23-10 (TB)
2003—Panthers, 12-9 (TB) OT
    Panthers, 27-24 (C)
2004—Panthers, 21-14 (C)
    Panthers, 37-20 (TB)
2005—Panthers, 34-14 (TB)
    Buccaneers, 20-10 (C)
2006—Panthers, 26-24 (TB)
    Panthers, 24-10 (C)
2007—Buccaneers, 20-7 (C)
    Panthers, 31-23 (TB)
2008—Buccaneers, 27-3 (TB)
    Panthers, 38-23 (C)
2009—Panthers, 28-21 (TB)
    Panthers, 16-6 (C)
2010—Buccaneers, 20-7 (C)
    Buccaneers, 31-16 (TB)
(RS Pts.—Panthers 406, Buccaneers 377)
CAROLINA vs. *TENNESSEE
RS: Titans lead series, 2-1
1996—Panthers, 31-6 (H)

2003—Titans, 37-17 (C)
2006—Panthers, 26-24 (TB)
    Panthers, 24-10 (C)
2007—Titans, 20-7 (T)
(RS Pts.—Titans 63, Panthers 55)
Franchise in Houston prior to 1997; known as Oilers prior to 1999
CAROLINA vs. WASHINGTON
RS: Redskins lead series, 7-2
1995—Redskins, 20-17 (W)
1997—Redskins, 24-10 (C)
1998—Redskins, 28-25 (C)
1999—Redskins, 38-36 (W)
2000—Redskins, 20-17 (W)
2001—Redskins, 17-14 (W) OT
2003—Panthers, 20-17 (C)
2006—Redskins, 17-13 (W)
2009—Panthers, 20-17 (C)
(RS Pts.—Redskins 198, Panthers 172)

CHICAGO vs. ARIZONA
RS: Bears lead series, 55-27-6;
See Arizona vs. Chicago
CHICAGO vs. ATLANTA
RS: Series tied, 12-12;
See Atlanta vs. Chicago
CHICAGO vs. BALTIMORE
RS: Series tied, 2-2;
See Baltimore vs. Chicago
CHICAGO vs. BUFFALO
RS: Bears lead series, 7-4;
See Buffalo vs. Chicago
CHICAGO vs. CAROLINA
RS: Bears lead series, 3-2
PS: Panthers lead series, 1-0;
See Carolina vs. Chicago
CHICAGO vs. CINCINNATI
RS: Bengals lead series, 6-3
1972—Bengals, 13-3 (Chi)
1980—Bengals, 17-14 (Chi) OT
1986—Bears, 44-7 (Cin)
1989—Bears, 17-14 (Chi)
1992—Bengals, 31-28 (Chi) OT
1995—Bengals, 16-10 (Cin)
2001—Bears, 24-0 (Cin)
2005—Bengals, 24-7 (Chi)
2009—Bengals, 45-10 (Cin)
(RS Pts.—Bengals 167, Bears 157)
CHICAGO vs. CLEVELAND
RS: Browns lead series, 9-5
1951—Browns, 42-21 (Cle)
1954—Browns, 39-10 (Chi)
1960—Browns, 42-0 (Cle)
1961—Bears, 17-14 (Chi)
1967—Browns, 24-0 (Cle)
1969—Browns, 28-24 (Chi)
1972—Bears, 17-0 (Cle)
1980—Browns, 27-21 (Cle)
1986—Bears, 41-31 (Chi)
1989—Browns, 27-7 (Cle)
1992—Browns, 27-14 (Cle)
2001—Bears, 27-21 (Chi) OT
2005—Browns, 20-10 (Cle)
2009—Bears, 30-6 (Chi)
(RS Pts.—Browns 348, Bears 239)
CHICAGO vs. DALLAS
RS: Cowboys lead series, 11-9
PS: Cowboys lead series, 2-0
1960—Bears, 17-7 (C)
1962—Bears, 34-33 (D)
1964—Cowboys, 24-10 (C)

1968—Cowboys, 34-3 (C)
1971—Bears, 23-19 (C)
1973—Cowboys, 20-17 (C)
1976—Cowboys, 31-21 (D)
1977—*Cowboys, 37-7 (C)
1979—Cowboys, 24-20 (D)
1981—Cowboys, 10-9 (D)
1984—Cowboys, 23-14 (C)
1985—Bears, 44-0 (D)
1986—Bears, 24-10 (D)
1988—Bears, 17-7 (C)
1991—**Cowboys, 17-13 (C)
1992—Cowboys, 27-14 (D)
1996—Bears, 22-6 (C)
1997—Cowboys, 27-3 (D)
1998—Bears, 13-12 (C)
2004—Cowboys, 21-7 (D)
2007—Cowboys, 34-10 (C)
2010—Bears, 27-20 (D)
(RS Pts.—Cowboys 389, Bears 349)
(PS Pts.—Cowboys 54, Bears 20)
*NFC Divisional Playoff
**NFC First-Round Playoff
CHICAGO vs. DENVER
RS: Bears lead series, 7-6
1971—Broncos, 6-3 (D)
1973—Bears, 33-14 (D)
1976—Broncos, 28-14 (C)
1978—Broncos, 16-7 (D)
1981—Bears, 35-24 (C)
1983—Bears, 31-14 (C)
1984—Bears, 27-0 (C)
1987—Broncos, 31-29 (D)
1990—Bears, 16-13 (D) OT
1993—Broncos, 13-3 (C)
1996—Broncos, 17-12 (D)
2003—Bears, 19-10 (D)
2007—Bears, 37-34 (C) OT
(RS Pts.—Bears 266, Broncos 220)
CHICAGO vs. *DETROIT
RS: Bears lead series, 93-64-5
1930—Spartans, 7-6 (P)
Bears, 14-6 (C)
1931—Bears, 9-6 (C)
Spartans, 3-0 (P)
1932—Tie, 13-13 (C)
Tie, 7-7 (P)
Bears, 9-0 (C)
1933—Bears, 17-14 (C)
Bears, 17-7 (P)
1934—Bears, 19-16 (D)
Bears, 10-7 (C)
1935—Tie, 20-20 (C)
Lions, 14-2 (D)
1936—Bears, 12-10 (C)
Lions, 13-7 (D)
1937—Bears, 28-20 (C)
Bears, 13-0 (D)
1938—Lions, 13-7 (C)
Lions, 14-7 (D)
1939—Lions, 10-0 (C)
Bears, 23-13 (D)
1940—Bears, 7-0 (C)
Lions, 17-14 (D)
1941—Bears, 49-0 (C)
Bears, 24-7 (D)
1942—Bears, 16-0 (C)
Bears, 42-0 (D)
1943—Bears, 27-21 (D)
Bears, 35-14 (C)
1944—Tie, 21-21 (C)

Lions, 41-21 (D)
1945—Lions, 16-10 (D)
Lions, 35-28 (C)
1946—Bears, 42-6 (C)
Bears, 45-24 (D)
1947—Bears, 33-24 (D)
Bears, 34-14 (D)
1948—Bears, 28-0 (C)
Bears, 42-14 (D)
1949—Bears, 27-24 (D)
Bears, 28-7 (D)
1950—Bears, 35-21 (D)
Bears, 6-3 (C)
1951—Bears, 28-23 (D)
Lions, 41-28 (C)
1952—Bears, 24-23 (C)
Lions, 45-21 (D)
1953—Lions, 20-16 (C)
Lions, 13-7 (D)
1954—Lions, 48-23 (D)
Bears, 28-24 (C)
1955—Bears, 24-14 (D)
Bears, 21-20 (C)
1956—Lions, 42-10 (D)
Bears, 38-21 (C)
1957—Bears, 27-7 (D)
Lions, 21-13 (C)
1958—Bears, 20-7 (D)
Bears, 21-16 (C)
1959—Bears, 24-14 (D)
Bears, 25-14 (C)
1960—Bears, 28-7 (C)
Lions, 36-0 (D)
1961—Bears, 31-17 (D)
Lions, 16-15 (C)
1962—Lions, 11-3 (D)
Bears, 3-0 (C)
1963—Bears, 37-21 (D)
Bears, 24-14 (C)
1964—Lions, 10-0 (C)
Bears, 27-24 (D)
1965—Bears, 38-10 (C)
Bears, 17-10 (D)
1966—Lions, 14-3 (D)
Tie, 10-10 (C)
1967—Bears, 14-3 (C)
Bears, 27-13 (D)
1968—Lions, 42-0 (D)
Lions, 28-10 (C)
1969—Lions, 13-7 (D)
Lions, 20-3 (C)
1970—Lions, 28-14 (D)
Lions, 16-10 (C)
1971—Bears, 28-23 (D)
Lions, 28-3 (C)
1972—Lions, 38-24 (C)
Lions, 14-0 (D)
1973—Lions, 30-7 (C)
Lions, 40-7 (D)
1974—Bears, 17-9 (C)
Lions, 34-17 (D)
1975—Lions, 27-7 (D)
Bears, 25-21 (C)
1976—Bears, 10-3 (C)
Lions, 14-10 (D)
1977—Bears, 30-20 (C)
Bears, 31-14 (D)
1978—Bears, 19-0 (D)
Lions, 21-17 (C)
1979—Bears, 35-7 (C)
Lions, 20-0 (D)

1980—Bears, 24-7 (C)
Bears, 23-17 (D) OT
1981—Lions, 48-17 (D)
Lions, 23-7 (C)
1982—Lions, 17-10 (D)
Bears, 20-17 (C)
1983—Lions, 31-17 (D)
Lions, 38-17 (C)
1984—Bears, 16-14 (C)
Bears, 30-13 (D)
1985—Bears, 24-3 (C)
Bears, 37-17 (D)
1986—Bears, 13-7 (C)
Bears, 16-13 (D)
1987—Bears, 30-10 (C)
1988—Bears, 24-7 (D)
Bears, 13-12 (C)
1989—Bears, 47-27 (D)
Lions, 27-17 (C)
1990—Bears, 23-17 (C) OT
Lions, 38-21 (D)
1991—Bears, 20-10 (C)
Lions, 16-6 (D)
1992—Bears, 27-24 (C)
Lions, 16-3 (D)
1993—Bears, 10-6 (D)
Lions, 20-14 (C)
1994—Lions, 21-16 (D)
Bears, 20-10 (C)
1995—Lions, 24-17 (C)
Lions, 27-7 (D)
1996—Lions, 35-16 (D)
Bears, 31-14 (C)
1997—Lions, 32-7 (C)
Lions, 55-20 (D)
1998—Bears, 31-27 (C)
Lions, 26-3 (D)
1999—Lions, 21-17 (D)
Bears, 28-10 (C)
2000—Lions, 21-14 (C)
Bears, 23-20 (D)
2001—Bears, 13-10 (C)
Bears, 24-0 (D)
2002—Lions, 23-20 (D)
Bears, 20-17 (C) OT
2003—Bears, 24-16 (C)
Lions, 12-10 (D)
2004—Lions, 20-16 (C)
Lions, 19-13 (D)
2005—Bears, 38-6 (D)
Bears, 19-13 (D) OT
2006—Bears, 34-7 (C)
Bears, 26-21 (D)
2007—Lions, 37-27 (D)
Lions, 16-7 (C)
2008—Bears, 34-7 (D)
Bears, 27-23 (C)
2009—Bears, 48-24 (C)
Bears, 37-23 (D)
2010—Bears, 19-14 (D)
Bears, 24-20 (D)
(RS Pts.—Bears 3,116, Lions 2,827)
*Franchise in Portsmouth prior to 1934
and known as the Spartans
CHICAGO vs. GREEN BAY
RS: Bears lead series, 91-83-6
PS: Series tied, 1-1
1921—Staleys, 20-0 (C)
1923—Bears, 3-0 (GB)
1924—Bears, 3-0 (C)
1925—Packers, 14-10 (GB)

Bears, 21-0 (C)
1926—Tie, 6-6 (GB)
Bears, 19-13 (C)
Tie, 3-3 (C)
1927—Bears, 7-6 (GB)
Bears, 14-6 (C)
1928—Tie, 12-12 (GB)
Packers, 16-6 (C)
Packers, 6-0 (C)
1929—Packers, 23-0 (GB)
Packers, 14-0 (C)
Packers, 25-0 (C)
1930—Packers, 7-0 (GB)
Packers, 13-12 (C)
Bears, 21-0 (C)
1931—Packers, 7-0 (GB)
Packers, 6-2 (C)
Bears, 7-6 (C)
1932—Tie, 0-0 (GB)
Packers, 2-0 (C)
Bears, 9-0 (C)
1933—Bears, 14-7 (GB)
Bears, 10-7 (C)
Bears, 7-6 (C)
1934—Bears, 24-10 (GB)
Bears, 27-14 (C)
1935—Packers, 7-0 (GB)
Packers, 17-14 (C)
1936—Bears, 30-3 (GB)
Packers, 21-10 (C)
1937—Bears, 14-2 (GB)
Packers, 24-14 (C)
1938—Bears, 2-0 (GB)
Packers, 24-17 (C)
1939—Packers, 21-16 (GB)
Bears, 30-27 (C)
1940—Bears, 41-10 (GB)
Bears, 14-7 (C)
1941—Bears, 25-17 (GB)
Packers, 16-14 (C)
**Bears, 33-14 (C)
1942—Bears, 44-28 (GB)
Bears, 38-7 (C)
1943—Tie, 21-21 (GB)
Bears, 21-7 (C)
1944—Packers, 42-28 (GB)
Bears, 21-0 (C)
1945—Packers, 31-21 (GB)
Bears, 28-24 (C)
1946—Bears, 30-7 (GB)
Bears, 10-7 (C)
1947—Packers, 29-20 (GB)
Bears, 20-17 (C)
1948—Bears, 45-7 (GB)
Bears, 7-6 (C)
1949—Bears, 17-0 (GB)
Bears, 24-3 (C)
1950—Packers, 31-21 (GB)
Bears, 28-14 (C)
1951—Bears, 31-20 (GB)
Bears, 24-13 (C)
1952—Bears, 24-14 (GB)
Packers, 41-28 (C)
1953—Bears, 17-13 (GB)
Tie, 21-21 (C)
1954—Packers, 10-3 (GB)
Bears, 28-23 (C)
1955—Packers, 24-3 (GB)
Bears, 52-31 (C)
1956—Bears, 37-21 (GB)
Bears, 38-14 (C)

1957—Packers, 21-17 (GB)
Bears, 21-14 (C)
1958—Bears, 34-20 (GB)
Bears, 24-10 (C)
1959—Packers, 9-6 (GB)
Bears, 28-17 (C)
1960—Bears, 17-14 (GB)
Packers, 41-13 (C)
1961—Packers, 24-0 (GB)
Packers, 31-28 (C)
1962—Packers, 49-0 (GB)
Packers, 38-7 (C)
1963—Bears, 10-3 (GB)
Bears, 26-7 (C)
1964—Packers, 23-12 (GB)
Packers, 17-3 (C)
1965—Packers, 23-14 (GB)
Bears, 31-10 (C)
1966—Packers, 17-0 (C)
Packers, 13-6 (GB)
1967—Packers, 13-10 (GB)
Packers, 17-13 (C)
1968—Packers, 13-10 (GB)
Packers, 28-27 (C)
1969—Packers, 17-0 (GB)
Packers, 21-3 (C)
1970—Packers, 20-19 (GB)
Bears, 35-17 (C)
1971—Packers, 17-14 (C)
Packers, 31-10 (GB)
1972—Packers, 20-17 (GB)
Packers, 23-17 (C)
1973—Bears, 31-17 (GB)
Packers, 21-0 (C)
1974—Bears, 10-9 (C)
Packers, 20-3 (Mil)
1975—Bears, 27-14 (C)
Packers, 28-7 (GB)
1976—Bears, 24-13 (C)
Bears, 16-10 (GB)
1977—Bears, 26-0 (GB)
Bears, 21-10 (C)
1978—Packers, 24-14 (GB)
Bears, 14-0 (C)
1979—Bears, 6-3 (C)
Bears, 15-14 (GB)
1980—Packers, 12-6 (GB) OT
Bears, 61-7 (C)
1981—Packers, 16-9 (C)
Packers, 21-17 (GB)
1983—Packers, 31-28 (GB)
Bears, 23-21 (C)
1984—Bears, 9-7 (GB)
Packers, 20-14 (C)
1985—Bears, 23-7 (C)
Bears, 16-10 (GB)
1986—Bears, 25-12 (GB)
Bears, 12-10 (C)
1987—Bears, 26-24 (GB)
Bears, 23-10 (C)
1988—Bears, 24-6 (GB)
Bears, 16-0 (C)
1989—Packers, 14-13 (GB)
Packers, 40-28 (C)
1990—Bears, 31-13 (GB)
Bears, 27-13 (C)
1991—Bears, 10-0 (GB)
Bears, 27-13 (C)
1992—Bears, 30-10 (GB)
Packers, 17-3 (C)
1993—Packers, 17-3 (GB)

Bears, 30-17 (C)
1994—Packers, 33-6 (C)
Packers, 40-3 (GB)
1995—Packers, 27-24 (C)
Packers, 35-28 (GB)
1996—Packers, 37-6 (C)
Packers, 28-17 (GB)
1997—Packers, 38-24 (GB)
Packers, 24-23 (C)
1998—Packers, 26-20 (GB)
Packers, 16-13 (C)
1999—Bears, 14-13 (GB)
Packers, 35-19 (C)
2000—Bears, 27-24 (GB)
Packers, 28-6 (C)
2001—Packers, 20-12 (C)
Packers, 17-7 (GB)
2002—Packers, 34-21 (C)
Packers, 30-20 (GB)
2003—Packers, 38-23 (GB)
Packers, 34-21 (C)
2004—Bears, 21-10 (GB)
Packers, 31-14 (C)
2005—Bears, 19-7 (C)
Bears, 24-17 (GB)
2006—Bears, 26-0 (GB)
Packers, 26-7 (C)
2007—Bears, 27-20 (GB)
Bears, 35-7 (C)
2008—Packers, 37-3 (GB)
Bears, 20-17 (C) OT
2009—Packers, 21-15 (GB)
Packers, 21-14 (C)
2010—Bears, 20-17 (C)
Packers, 10-3 (GB)
***Packers, 21-14 (C)
(RS Pts.—Bears 3,060, Packers 2,948)
(PS Pts.—Bears 47, Packers 35)
*Bears known as Staleys prior to 1922
**Division Playoff
***NFC Championship
CHICAGO vs. HOUSTON
RS: Texans lead series, 2-0
2004—Texans, 24-5 (C)
2008—Texans, 31-24 (H)
(RS Pts.—Texans 55, Bears 29)
CHICAGO vs. *INDIANAPOLIS
RS: Colts lead series, 22-18
PS: Colts lead series, 1-0
1953—Colts, 13-9 (B)
Colts, 16-14 (C)
1954—Bears, 28-9 (C)
Bears, 28-13 (B)
1955—Colts, 23-17 (B)
Bears, 38-10 (C)
1956—Colts, 28-21 (B)
Bears, 58-27 (C)
1957—Colts, 21-10 (B)
Colts, 29-14 (C)
1958—Colts, 51-38 (B)
Colts, 17-0 (C)
1959—Bears, 26-21 (B)
Colts, 21-7 (C)
1960—Colts, 42-7 (B)
Bears, 24-20 (C)
1961—Bears, 24-10 (C)
Bears, 21-20 (B)
1962—Bears, 35-15 (C)
Bears, 57-0 (B)
1963—Bears, 10-3 (C)
Bears, 17-7 (B)

1964—Colts, 52-0 (B)
    Colts, 40-24 (C)
1965—Colts, 26-21 (C)
    Bears, 13-0 (B)
1966—Bears, 27-17 (C)
    Colts, 21-16 (B)
1967—Colts, 24-3 (C)
1968—Colts, 28-7 (B)
1969—Colts, 24-21 (C)
1970—Colts, 21-20 (B)
1975—Colts, 35-7 (C)
1983—Colts, 22-19 (B) OT
1985—Bears, 17-10 (C)
1988—Bears, 17-13 (I)
1991—Bears, 31-17 (I)
2000—Bears, 27-24 (C)
2004—Colts, 41-10 (C)
2006—**Colts, 29-17 (South Florida)
2008—Bears, 29-13 (I)
(RS Pts.—Colts 848, Bears 808)
(PS: Pts.—Colts 29, Bears 17)
*Franchise in Baltimore prior to 1984
**Super Bowl XLI

CHICAGO vs. JACKSONVILLE
RS: Bears lead series, 3-2
1995—Bears, 30-27 (J)
1998—Jaguars, 24-23 (C)
2001—Bears, 33-13 (C)
2004—Jaguars, 22-3 (J)
2008—Bears, 23-10 (C)
(RS Pts.—Bears 112, Jaguars 96)
CHICAGO vs. KANSAS CITY
RS: Bears lead series, 6-4
1973—Chiefs, 19-7 (KC)
1977—Bears, 28-27 (C)
1981—Bears, 16-13 (KC) OT
1987—Bears, 31-28 (C)
1990—Chiefs, 21-10 (C)
1993—Bears, 19-17 (KC)
1996—Chiefs, 14-10 (KC)
1999—Bears, 20-17 (C)
2003—Chiefs, 31-3 (KC)
2007—Bears, 20-10 (C)
(RS Pts.—Chiefs 197, Bears 164)
CHICAGO vs. MIAMI
RS: Dolphins lead series, 7-4
1971—Dolphins, 34-3 (M)
1975—Dolphins, 46-13 (C)
1979—Dolphins, 31-16 (M)
1985—Dolphins, 38-24 (M)
1988—Bears, 34-7 (C)
1991—Dolphins, 16-13 (C) OT
1994—Bears, 17-14 (M)
1997—Bears, 36-33 (M) OT
2002—Dolphins, 27-9 (M)
2006—Dolphins, 31-13 (C)
2010—Bears, 16-0 (M)
(RS Pts.—Dolphins 277, Bears 194)
CHICAGO vs. MINNESOTA
RS: Vikings lead series, 52-45-2
PS: Bears lead series, 1-0
1961—Vikings, 37-13 (M)
    Bears, 52-35 (C)
1962—Bears, 13-0 (M)
    Bears, 31-30 (C)
1963—Bears, 28-7 (M)
    Tie, 17-17 (C)
1964—Bears, 34-28 (M)
    Vikings, 41-14 (C)
1965—Bears, 45-37 (M)
    Vikings, 24-17 (C)

1966—Bears, 13-10 (M)
    Bears, 41-28 (C)
1967—Bears, 17-7 (M)
    Tie, 10-10 (C)
1968—Bears, 27-17 (M)
    Bears, 26-24 (C)
1969—Vikings, 31-0 (C)
    Vikings, 31-14 (M)
1970—Vikings, 24-0 (C)
    Vikings, 16-13 (M)
1971—Bears, 20-17 (M)
    Vikings, 27-10 (C)
1972—Bears, 13-10 (C)
    Vikings, 23-10 (M)
1973—Vikings, 22-13 (C)
    Vikings, 31-13 (M)
1974—Vikings, 11-7 (M)
    Vikings, 17-0 (C)
1975—Vikings, 28-3 (M)
    Vikings, 13-9 (C)
1976—Vikings, 20-19 (M)
    Bears, 14-13 (C)
1977—Vikings, 22-16 (M) OT
    Bears, 10-7 (C)
1978—Vikings, 24-20 (C)
    Vikings, 17-14 (M)
1979—Bears, 26-7 (C)
    Vikings, 30-27 (M)
1980—Vikings, 34-14 (C)
    Vikings, 13-7 (M)
1981—Vikings, 24-21 (M)
    Bears, 10-9 (C)
1982—Vikings, 35-7 (M)
1983—Vikings, 23-14 (C)
    Bears, 19-13 (M)
1984—Bears, 16-7 (C)
    Bears, 34-3 (M)
1985—Bears, 33-24 (M)
    Bears, 27-9 (C)
1986—Bears, 23-0 (C)
    Vikings, 23-7 (M)
1987—Bears, 27-7 (C)
    Bears, 30-24 (M)
1988—Vikings, 31-7 (C)
    Vikings, 28-27 (M)
1989—Bears, 38-7 (C)
    Vikings, 27-16 (M)
1990—Bears, 19-16 (C)
    Vikings, 41-13 (M)
1991—Bears, 10-6 (C)
    Bears, 34-17 (M)
1992—Vikings, 21-20 (M)
    Vikings, 38-10 (C)
1993—Vikings, 10-7 (M)
    Vikings, 19-12 (C)
1994—Vikings, 42-14 (C)
    Vikings, 33-27 (M) OT
    *Bears, 35-18 (M)
1995—Bears, 31-14 (C)
    Bears, 14-6 (M)
1996—Vikings, 20-14 (C)
    Bears, 15-13 (M)
1997—Vikings, 27-24 (C)
    Vikings, 29-22 (M)
1998—Vikings, 31-28 (C)
    Vikings, 48-22 (M)
1999—Bears, 24-22 (M)
    Vikings, 27-24 (C) OT
2000—Vikings, 30-27 (M)
    Vikings, 28-16 (C)
2001—Bears, 17-10 (C)

    Bears, 13-6 (M)
2002—Bears, 27-23 (C)
    Vikings, 25-7 (M)
2003—Vikings, 24-13 (M)
    Bears, 13-10 (C)
2004—Vikings, 27-22 (M)
    Bears, 24-14 (C)
2005—Bears, 28-3 (C)
    Vikings, 34-10 (M)
2006—Bears, 19-16 (M)
    Bears, 23-13 (C)
2007—Vikings, 34-31 (C)
    Vikings, 20-13 (M)
2008—Bears, 48-41 (C)
    Vikings, 34-14 (M)
2009—Vikings, 36-10 (M)
    Bears, 36-30 (C) OT
2010—Bears, 27-13 (C)
    Bears, 40-14 (M)
(RS Pts.—Vikings 2,099, Bears 1,908)
(PS Pts.—Bears 35, Vikings 18)
*NFC First-Round Playoff
CHICAGO vs. NEW ENGLAND
RS: Patriots lead series, 8-3
PS: Bears lead series, 1-0
1973—Patriots, 13-10 (C)
1979—Patriots, 27-7 (C)
1982—Bears, 26-13 (C)
1985—Bears, 20-7 (C)
    *Bears, 46-10 (New Orleans)
1988—Patriots, 30-7 (NE)
1994—Patriots, 13-3 (C)
1997—Patriots, 31-3 (NE)
2000—Bears, 24-17 (C)
2002—Patriots, 33-30 (C)
2006—Patriots, 17-13 (NE)
2010—Patriots, 36-7 (C)
(RS Pts.—Patriots 237, Bears 150)
(PS Pts.—Bears 46, Patriots 10)
*Super Bowl XX
CHICAGO vs. NEW ORLEANS
RS: Bears lead series, 13-11
PS: Bears lead series, 2-0
1968—Bears, 23-17 (NO)
1970—Bears, 24-3 (NO)
1971—Bears, 35-14 (C)
1973—Saints, 21-16 (NO)
1974—Bears, 24-10 (C)
1975—Bears, 42-17 (NO)
1977—Saints, 42-24 (C)
1980—Bears, 22-3 (C)
1982—Saints, 10-0 (C)
1983—Saints, 34-31 (NO) OT
1984—Bears, 20-7 (C)
1987—Saints, 19-17 (C)
1990—*Bears, 16-6 (C)
1991—Bears, 20-17 (NO)
1992—Saints, 28-6 (NO)
1994—Bears, 17-7 (C)
1996—Saints, 27-24 (NO)
1997—Saints, 20-17 (C)
1999—Bears, 14-10 (C)
2000—Saints, 31-10 (C)
2002—Saints, 29-23 (C)
2003—Saints, 20-13 (NO)
2005—Bears, 20-17 (Baton Rouge)
2006—**Bears, 39-14 (C)
2007—Saints, 33-25 (C)
2008—Bears, 27-24 (C) OT
(RS Pts.—Bears 502, Saints 452)
(PS Pts.—Bears 55, Saints 20)

*NFC First-Round Playoff
**NFC Championship

CHICAGO vs. N.Y. GIANTS
RS: Bears lead series, 27-19-2
PS: Bears lead series, 5-3
1925—Bears, 19-7 (NY)
　　　Giants, 9-0 (C)
1926—Bears, 7-0 (C)
1927—Giants, 13-7 (NY)
1928—Bears, 13-0 (C)
1929—Giants, 26-14 (C)
　　　Giants, 34-0 (NY)
　　　Giants, 14-9 (C)
1930—Giants, 12-0 (C)
　　　Bears, 12-0 (NY)
1931—Bears, 6-0 (C)
　　　Bears, 12-6 (NY)
　　　Giants, 25-6 (C)
1932—Bears, 28-8 (C)
　　　Bears, 6-0 (C)
1933—Bears, 14-10 (C)
　　　Giants, 3-0 (NY)
　　　*Bears, 23-21 (C)
1934—Bears, 27-7 (C)
　　　Bears, 10-9 (NY)
　　　*Giants, 30-13 (NY)
1935—Bears, 20-3 (NY)
　　　Giants, 3-0 (C)
1936—Bears, 25-7 (NY)
1937—Tie, 3-3 (NY)
1939—Giants, 16-13 (NY)
1940—Bears, 37-21 (NY)
1941—*Bears, 37-9 (C)
1942—Bears, 26-7 (NY)
1943—Bears, 56-7 (NY)
1946—Bears, 14-0 (NY)
　　　*Bears, 24-14 (NY)
1948—Bears, 35-14 (C)
1949—Giants, 35-28 (NY)
1956—Tie, 17-17 (NY)
　　　*Giants, 47-7 (NY)
1962—Giants, 26-24 (C)
1963—*Bears, 14-10 (C)
1965—Bears, 35-14 (NY)
1967—Bears, 34-7 (C)
1969—Giants, 28-24 (NY)
1970—Bears, 24-16 (NY)
1974—Bears, 16-13 (C)
1977—Bears, 12-9 (NY) OT
1985—**Bears, 21-0 (C)
1987—Bears, 34-19 (C)
1990—**Giants, 31-3 (NY)
1991—Bears, 20-17 (C)
1992—Giants, 27-14 (C)
1993—Giants, 26-20 (C)
1995—Bears, 27-24 (NY)
2000—Giants, 14-7 (C)
2004—Bears, 28-21 (NY)
2006—Bears, 38-20 (NY)
2007—Giants, 21-16 (C)
2010—Giants, 17-3 (NY)
(RS Pts.—Bears 826, Giants 649)
(PS Pts.—Giants 162, Bears 142)
*NFL Championship
**NFC Divisional Playoff

CHICAGO vs. N.Y. JETS
RS: Bears lead series, 7-3
1974—Jets, 23-21 (C)
1979—Bears, 23-13 (C)
1985—Bears, 19-6 (NY)
1991—Bears, 19-13 (C) OT

1994—Bears, 19-7 (NY)
1997—Jets, 23-15 (C)
2000—Jets, 17-10 (NY)
2002—Bears, 20-13 (C)
2006—Bears, 10-0 (NY)
2010—Bears, 38-34 (C)
(RS Pts.—Bears 194, Jets 149)

CHICAGO vs. *OAKLAND
RS: Series tied, 6-6
1972—Raiders, 28-21 (O)
1976—Raiders, 28-27 (C)
1978—Raiders, 25-19 (C) OT
1981—Bears, 23-6 (O)
1984—Bears, 17-6 (C)
1987—Bears, 6-3 (LA)
1990—Raiders, 24-10 (LA)
1993—Raiders, 16-14 (C)
1996—Bears, 19-17 (C)
1999—Raiders, 24-17 (O)
2003—Bears, 24-21 (C)
2007—Bears, 17-6 (O)
(RS Pts.—Bears 214, Raiders 204)
*Franchise in Los Angeles from 1982-1994

CHICAGO vs. PHILADELPHIA
RS: Bears lead series, 27-9-1
PS: Eagles lead series, 2-1
1933—Tie, 3-3 (P)
1935—Bears, 39-0 (C)
1936—Bears, 17-0 (C)
　　　Bears, 28-7 (P)
1938—Bears, 28-6 (P)
1939—Bears, 27-14 (C)
1941—Bears, 49-14 (C)
1942—Bears, 45-14 (C)
1944—Bears, 28-7 (P)
1946—Bears, 21-14 (C)
1947—Bears, 40-7 (C)
1948—Eagles, 12-7 (P)
1949—Bears, 38-21 (C)
1955—Bears, 17-10 (C)
1961—Eagles, 16-14 (P)
1963—Bears, 16-7 (C)
1968—Bears, 29-16 (P)
1970—Bears, 20-16 (C)
1972—Bears, 21-12 (P)
1975—Bears, 15-13 (C)
1979—*Eagles, 27-17 (P)
1980—Eagles, 17-14 (P)
1983—Bears, 7-6 (P)
　　　Bears, 17-14 (C)
1986—Bears, 13-10 (C) OT
1987—Bears, 35-3 (P)
1988—**Bears, 20-12 (C)
1989—Bears, 27-13 (C)
1993—Bears, 17-6 (P)
1994—Eagles, 30-22 (P)
1995—Bears, 20-14 (C)
1999—Eagles, 20-16 (C)
2000—Eagles, 13-9 (P)
2001—**Eagles, 33-19 (C)
2002—Eagles, 19-13 (C)
2004—Eagles, 19-9 (C)
2007—Bears, 19-16 (P)
2008—Bears, 24-20 (C)
2009—Eagles, 24-20 (C)
2010—Bears, 31-26 (C)
(RS Pts.—Bears 815, Eagles 479)
(PS Pts.—Eagles 72, Bears 56)
*NFC First-Round Playoff
**NFC Divisional Playoff

CHICAGO vs. *PITTSBURGH
RS: Bears lead series, 17-7-1
1934—Bears, 28-0 (P)
1935—Bears, 23-7 (P)
1936—Bears, 27-9 (P)
　　　Bears, 26-7 (C)
1937—Bears, 7-0 (P)
1939—Bears, 32-0 (P)
1941—Bears, 34-7 (C)
1945—Bears, 28-7 (C)
1947—Bears, 49-7 (C)
1949—Bears, 30-21 (C)
1958—Steelers, 24-10 (P)
1959—Steelers, 27-21 (C)
1963—Tie, 17-17 (P)
1967—Steelers, 41-13 (P)
1969—Bears, 38-7 (C)
1971—Bears, 17-15 (C)
1975—Steelers, 34-3 (C)
1980—Steelers, 38-3 (P)
1986—Bears, 13-10 (C) OT
1989—Bears, 20-0 (P)
1992—Bears, 30-6 (C)
1995—Steelers, 37-34 (C) OT
1998—Steelers, 17-12 (P)
2005—Steelers, 21-9 (P)
2009—Bears, 17-14 (C)
(RS Pts.—Bears 547, Steelers 367)
*Steelers known as Pirates prior to 1940

CHICAGO vs. *ST. LOUIS
RS: Bears lead series, 50-34-3
PS: Series tied, 1-1
1937—Bears, 20-2 (Cle)
　　　Bears, 15-7 (C)
1938—Rams, 14-7 (C)
　　　Rams, 23-21 (Cle)
1939—Bears, 30-21 (C)
　　　Bears, 35-21 (C)
1940—Bears, 21-14 (Cle)
　　　Bears, 47-25 (C)
1941—Bears, 48-21 (C)
　　　Bears, 31-13 (C)
1942—Bears, 21-7 (Cle)
　　　Bears, 47-0 (C)
1944—Rams, 19-7 (Cle)
　　　Bears, 28-21 (C)
1945—Rams, 17-0 (Cle)
　　　Rams, 41-21 (C)
1946—Tie, 28-28 (C)
　　　Bears, 27-21 (LA)
1947—Bears, 41-21 (C)
　　　Rams, 17-14 (C)
1948—Bears, 42-21 (C)
　　　Bears, 21-6 (LA)
1949—Rams, 31-16 (C)
　　　Rams, 27-24 (LA)
1950—Bears, 24-20 (C)
　　　Bears, 24-14 (C)
　　　**Rams, 24-14 (LA)
1951—Rams, 42-17 (C)
1952—Rams, 31-7 (LA)
　　　Rams, 40-24 (C)
1953—Rams, 38-24 (C)
　　　Bears, 24-21 (C)
1954—Rams, 42-38 (LA)
　　　Bears, 24-13 (C)
1955—Bears, 31-20 (LA)
　　　Bears, 24-3 (C)
1956—Bears, 35-24 (LA)
　　　Bears, 30-21 (C)
1957—Bears, 34-26 (C)

Bears, 16-10 (LA)
1958—Bears, 31-10 (C)
Rams, 41-35 (LA)
1959—Rams, 28-21 (C)
Bears, 26-21 (LA)
1960—Bears, 34-27 (C)
Tie, 24-24 (LA)
1961—Bears, 21-17 (LA)
Bears, 28-24 (C)
1962—Bears, 27-23 (LA)
Bears, 30-14 (C)
1963—Bears, 52-14 (LA)
Bears, 6-0 (C)
1964—Bears, 38-17 (C)
Bears, 34-24 (LA)
1965—Rams, 30-28 (LA)
Bears, 31-6 (C)
1966—Rams, 31-17 (LA)
Bears, 17-10 (C)
1967—Rams, 28-17 (C)
1968—Bears, 17-16 (LA)
1969—Rams, 9-7 (C)
1971—Rams, 17-3 (LA)
1972—Tie, 13-13 (C)
1973—Rams, 26-0 (C)
1975—Rams, 38-10 (LA)
1976—Bears, 20-12 (LA)
1977—Bears, 24-23 (C)
1979—Bears, 27-23 (C)
1981—Rams, 24-7 (C)
1982—Bears, 34-26 (LA)
1983—Bears, 21-14 (LA)
1984—Rams, 29-13 (LA)
1985—***Bears, 24-0 (C)
1986—Rams, 20-17 (C)
1988—Rams, 23-3 (LA)
1989—Bears, 20-10 (C)
1990—Bears, 38-9 (C)
1993—Rams, 20-6 (LA)
1994—Bears, 27-13 (C)
1995—Rams, 34-28 (StL)
1996—Bears, 35-9 (C)
1997—Bears, 13-10 (StL)
1998—Rams, 20-12 (C)
1999—Rams, 34-12 (StL)
2002—Rams, 21-16 (StL)
2003—Rams, 23-21 (C)
2006—Bears, 42-27 (StL)
2009—Bears, 27-3 (StL)
2009—Bears, 17-9 (C)
(RS Pts.—Bears 2,020, Rams 1,762)
(PS Pts.—Bears 38, Rams 24)
*Franchise in Los Angeles prior to 1995
and in Cleveland prior to 1946
**Conference Playoff
***NFC Championship
CHICAGO vs. SAN DIEGO
RS: Series tied, 5-5
1970—Chargers, 20-7 (C)
1974—Chargers, 28-21 (SD)
1978—Chargers, 40-7 (SD)
1981—Bears, 20-17 (C) OT
1984—Chargers, 20-7 (SD)
1993—Bears, 16-13 (SD)
1996—Bears, 27-14 (C)
1999—Bears, 23-20 (SD) OT
2003—Bears, 20-7 (C)
2007—Chargers, 14-3 (SD)
(RS Pts.—Chargers 193, Bears 151)
CHICAGO vs. SAN FRANCISCO
RS: Bears lead series, 29-28-1

PS: 49ers lead series, 3-0
1950—Bears, 32-20 (SF)
Bears, 17-0 (C)
1951—Bears, 13-7 (C)
1952—49ers, 40-16 (C)
Bears, 20-17 (SF)
1953—49ers, 35-28 (C)
49ers, 24-14 (C)
1954—49ers, 31-24 (C)
Bears, 31-27 (SF)
1955—49ers, 20-19 (C)
Bears, 34-23 (SF)
1956—Bears, 31-7 (C)
Bears, 38-21 (SF)
1957—49ers, 21-17 (C)
49ers, 21-17 (SF)
1958—Bears, 28-6 (C)
Bears, 27-14 (SF)
1959—49ers, 20-17 (SF)
Bears, 14-3 (C)
1960—Bears, 27-10 (C)
49ers, 25-7 (SF)
1961—Bears, 31-0 (C)
49ers, 41-31 (SF)
1962—Bears, 30-14 (SF)
49ers, 34-27 (C)
1963—49ers, 20-14 (SF)
Bears, 27-7 (C)
1964—49ers, 31-21 (SF)
Bears, 23-21 (C)
1965—49ers, 52-24 (SF)
Bears, 61-20 (C)
1966—Tie, 30-30 (C)
49ers, 41-14 (SF)
1967—Bears, 28-14 (SF)
1968—Bears, 27-19 (C)
1969—49ers, 42-21 (SF)
1970—49ers, 37-16 (C)
1971—Bears, 13-0 (SF)
1972—49ers, 34-21 (C)
1974—49ers, 34-0 (C)
1975—49ers, 31-3 (SF)
1976—Bears, 19-12 (SF)
1978—Bears, 16-13 (SF)
1979—Bears, 28-27 (SF)
1981—49ers, 28-17 (SF)
1983—Bears, 13-3 (C)
1984—*49ers, 23-0 (SF)
1985—Bears, 26-10 (SF)
1987—49ers, 41-0 (SF)
1988—Bears, 10-9 (C)
*49ers, 28-3 (C)
1989—49ers, 26-0 (C)
1991—49ers, 52-14 (SF)
1994—**49ers, 44-15 (SF)
2000—49ers, 17-0 (C)
2001—Bears, 37-31 (C) OT
2003—49ers, 49-7 (SF)
2004—Bears, 23-13 (C)
2005—Bears, 17-9 (C)
2006—Bears, 41-10 (C)
2009—49ers, 10-6 (SF)
(RS Pts.—49ers 1,287, Bears 1,194)
(PS Pts.—49ers 95, Bears 18)
*NFC Championship
**NFC Divisional Playoff
CHICAGO vs. SEATTLE
RS: Seahawks lead series, 8-4
PS: Bears lead series, 2-0
1976—Bears, 34-7 (S)
1978—Seahawks, 31-29 (C)

1982—Seahawks, 20-14 (S)
1984—Seahawks, 38-9 (S)
1987—Seahawks, 34-21 (C)
1990—Bears, 17-0 (C)
1999—Seahawks, 14-13 (C)
2003—Seahawks, 24-17 (S)
2006—Bears, 37-6 (C)
*Bears, 27-24 (C) OT
2007—Seahawks, 30-23 (S)
2009—Bears, 25-19 (S)
2010—Seahawks, 23-20 (C)
*Bears, 35-24 (C)
(RS Pts.—Bears 259, Seahawks 246)
(PS Pts.—Bears 62, Seahawks 48)
*NFC Divisional Playoff
CHICAGO vs. TAMPA BAY
RS: Bears lead series, 35-18
1977—Bears, 10-0 (TB)
1978—Buccaneers, 33-19 (TB)
Bears, 14-3 (C)
1979—Buccaneers, 17-13 (TB)
Bears, 14-0 (TB)
1980—Bears, 23-0 (C)
Bears, 14-13 (TB)
1981—Bears, 28-17 (C)
Buccaneers, 20-10 (TB)
1982—Buccaneers, 26-23 (TB) OT
1983—Bears, 17-10 (C)
Bears, 27-0 (TB)
1984—Bears, 34-14 (C)
Bears, 44-9 (TB)
1985—Bears, 38-28 (C)
Bears, 27-19 (TB)
1986—Bears, 23-3 (TB)
Bears, 48-14 (C)
1987—Bears, 20-3 (C)
Bears, 27-26 (TB)
1988—Bears, 28-10 (C)
Bears, 27-15 (TB)
1989—Buccaneers, 42-35 (TB)
Buccaneers, 32-31 (C)
1990—Bears, 26-6 (TB)
Bears, 27-14 (C)
1991—Bears, 21-20 (TB)
Bears, 27-0 (C)
1992—Bears, 31-14 (C)
Buccaneers, 20-17 (TB)
1993—Bears, 47-17 (C)
Buccaneers, 13-10 (TB)
1994—Bears, 21-9 (C)
Bears, 20-6 (TB)
1995—Bears, 25-6 (TB)
Bears, 31-10 (C)
1996—Bears, 13-10 (C)
Buccaneers, 34-19 (TB)
1997—Bears, 13-7 (C)
Buccaneers, 31-15 (TB)
1998—Buccaneers, 27-15 (TB)
Buccaneers, 31-17 (C)
1999—Buccaneers, 6-3 (TB)
Buccaneers, 20-6 (C)
2000—Buccaneers, 41-0 (TB)
Bears, 13-10 (C)
2001—Bears, 27-24 (TB)
Bears, 27-3 (C)
2002—Buccaneers, 15-0 (C)
2004—Buccaneers, 19-7 (TB)
2005—Bears, 13-10 (TB)
2006—Bears, 34-31 (C) OT
2008—Buccaneers, 27-24 (C) OT
(RS Pts.—Bears 1,143, Buccaneers 835)

CHICAGO vs. *TENNESSEE
RS: Series tied, 5-5
1973—Bears, 35-14 (C)
1977—Oilers, 47-0 (H)
1980—Bears, 10-6 (C)
1986—Bears, 20-7 (H)
1989—Oilers, 33-28 (C)
1992—Oilers, 24-7 (H)
1995—Bears, 35-32 (C)
1998—Bears, 23-20 (T)
2004—Bears, 19-17 (T) OT
2008—Titans, 21-14 (C)
(RS Pts.—Titans 225, Bears 187)
*Franchise in Houston prior to 1997;
known as Oilers prior to 1999

CHICAGO vs. *WASHINGTON
RS: Bears lead series, 20-19-1
PS: Redskins lead series, 4-3
1932—Tie, 7-7 (B)
1933—Bears, 7-0 (C)
     Redskins, 10-0 (B)
1934—Bears, 21-0 (B)
1935—Bears, 30-14 (B)
1936—Bears, 26-0 (B)
1937—**Redskins, 28-21 (C)
1938—Bears, 31-7 (C)
1940—Redskins, 7-3 (W)
     **Bears, 73-0 (W)
1941—Bears, 35-21 (C)
1942—**Redskins, 14-6 (W)
1943—Redskins, 21-7 (W)
     **Bears, 41-21 (C)
1945—Redskins, 28-21 (W)
1946—Bears, 24-20 (C)
1947—Bears, 56-20 (W)
1948—Bears, 48-13 (C)
1949—Bears, 31-21 (W)
1951—Bears, 27-0 (W)
1953—Bears, 27-24 (W)
1957—Redskins, 14-3 (C)
1964—Redskins, 27-20 (W)
1968—Redskins, 38-28 (C)
1971—Bears, 16-15 (C)
1974—Redskins, 42-0 (W)
1976—Bears, 33-7 (C)
1978—Bears, 14-10 (W)
1980—Bears, 35-21 (C)
1981—Redskins, 24-7 (C)
1984—***Bears, 23-19 (W)
1985—Bears, 45-10 (C)
1986—***Redskins, 27-13 (C)
1987—***Redskins, 21-17 (C)
1988—Bears, 34-14 (W)
1989—Redskins, 38-14 (W)
1990—Redskins, 10-9 (W)
1991—Redskins, 20-7 (C)
1996—Redskins, 10-3 (W)
1997—Redskins, 31-8 (C)
1999—Redskins, 48-22 (W)
2001—Bears, 20-15 (W)
2003—Bears, 27-24 (C)
2004—Redskins, 13-10 (C)
2005—Redskins, 9-7 (W)
2007—Redskins, 24-16 (W)
2010—Redskins, 17-14 (C)
(RS Pts.—Bears 793, Redskins 694)
(PS Pts.—Bears 194, Redskins 130)
*Franchise in Boston prior to 1937 and
known as Braves prior to 1933
**NFL Championship
***NFC Divisional Playoff

CINCINNATI vs. ARIZONA
RS: Bengals lead series, 5-4;
See Arizona vs. Cincinnati

CINCINNATI vs. ATLANTA
RS: Bengals lead series, 7-5;
See Atlanta vs. Cincinnati

CINCINNATI vs. BALTIMORE
RS: Ravens lead series, 16-14;
See Baltimore vs. Cincinnati

CINCINNATI vs. BUFFALO
RS: Bills lead series, 15-9
PS: Bengals lead series, 2-0;
See Buffalo vs. Cincinnati

CINCINNATI vs. CAROLINA
RS: Series tied, 2-2;
See Carolina vs. Cincinnati

CINCINNATI vs. CHICAGO
RS: Bengals lead series, 6-3;
See Chicago vs. Cincinnati

CINCINNATI vs. CLEVELAND
RS: Bengals lead series, 39-36
1970—Browns, 30-27 (Cle)
     Bengals, 14-10 (Cin)
1971—Browns, 27-24 (Cin)
     Browns, 31-27 (Cle)
1972—Browns, 27-6 (Cle)
     Browns, 27-24 (Cin)
1973—Browns, 17-10 (Cle)
     Bengals, 34-17 (Cin)
1974—Bengals, 33-7 (Cin)
     Bengals, 34-24 (Cle)
1975—Bengals, 24-17 (Cin)
     Browns, 35-23 (Cle)
1976—Bengals, 45-24 (Cle)
     Bengals, 21-6 (Cin)
1977—Browns, 13-3 (Cin)
     Bengals, 10-7 (Cle)
1978—Browns, 13-10 (Cle) OT
     Bengals, 48-16 (Cin)
1979—Browns, 28-27 (Cle)
     Bengals, 16-12 (Cin)
1980—Browns, 31-7 (Cle)
     Browns, 27-24 (Cin)
1981—Browns, 20-17 (Cin)
     Bengals, 41-21 (Cle)
1982—Bengals, 23-10 (Cin)
1983—Browns, 17-7 (Cle)
     Bengals, 28-21 (Cin)
1984—Bengals, 12-9 (Cin)
     Bengals, 20-17 (Cle) OT
1985—Bengals, 27-10 (Cin)
     Browns, 24-6 (Cle)
1986—Bengals, 30-13 (Cle)
     Browns, 34-3 (Cin)
1987—Browns, 34-0 (Cin)
     Browns, 38-24 (Cle)
1988—Bengals, 24-17 (Cin)
     Browns, 23-16 (Cle)
1989—Bengals, 21-14 (Cin)
     Bengals, 21-0 (Cle)
1990—Bengals, 34-13 (Cle)
     Bengals, 21-14 (Cin)
1991—Browns, 14-13 (Cle)
     Bengals, 23-21 (Cin)
1992—Bengals, 30-10 (Cin)
     Browns, 37-21 (Cle)
1993—Browns, 27-14 (Cle)
     Browns, 28-17 (Cin)
1994—Browns, 28-20 (Cin)
     Browns, 37-13 (Cle)

1995—Browns, 29-26 (Cin) OT
     Browns, 26-10 (Cle)
1999—Bengals, 18-17 (Cle)
     Bengals, 44-28 (Cin)
2000—Browns, 24-7 (Cin)
     Bengals, 12-3 (Cle)
2001—Bengals, 24-14 (Cin)
     Browns, 18-0 (Cle)
2002—Browns, 20-7 (Cle)
     Browns, 27-20 (Cin)
2003—Bengals, 21-14 (Cle)
     Browns, 22-14 (Cin)
2004—Browns, 34-17 (Cle)
     Bengals, 58-48 (Cin)
2005—Bengals, 27-13 (Cle)
     Bengals, 23-20 (Cin)
2006—Bengals, 34-17 (Cin)
     Bengals, 30-0 (Cle)
2007—Browns, 51-45 (Cin)
     Bengals, 19-14 (Cle)
2008—Browns, 20-12 (Cin)
     Bengals, 14-0 (Cle)
2009—Bengals, 23-20 (Cle) OT
     Bengals, 16-7 (Cin)
2010—Browns, 23-20 (Cle)
     Bengals, 19-17 (Cin)
(RS Pts.—Bengals 1,577, Browns 1,523)

CINCINNATI vs. DALLAS
RS: Cowboys lead series, 6-4
1973—Cowboys, 38-10 (D)
1979—Cowboys, 38-13 (D)
1985—Bengals, 50-24 (C)
1988—Bengals, 38-24 (D)
1991—Cowboys, 35-23 (D)
1994—Cowboys, 23-20 (C)
1997—Bengals, 31-24 (C)
2000—Cowboys, 23-6 (D)
2004—Bengals, 26-3 (C)
2008—Cowboys, 31-22 (D)
(RS Pts.—Cowboys 263, Bengals 239)

CINCINNATI vs. DENVER
RS: Broncos lead series, 17-8
1968—Bengals, 24-10 (C)
     Broncos, 10-7 (D)
1969—Bengals, 30-23 (C)
     Broncos, 27-16 (D)
1971—Bengals, 24-10 (C)
1972—Bengals, 21-10 (C)
1973—Broncos, 28-10 (D)
1975—Bengals, 17-16 (D)
1976—Bengals, 17-7 (C)
1977—Broncos, 24-13 (C)
1979—Broncos, 10-0 (D)
1981—Bengals, 38-21 (C)
1983—Broncos, 24-17 (D)
1984—Broncos, 20-17 (D)
1986—Broncos, 34-28 (D)
1991—Broncos, 45-14 (D)
1994—Broncos, 15-13 (D)
1996—Broncos, 14-10 (C)
1997—Broncos, 38-20 (D)
1998—Broncos, 33-26 (C)
2000—Bengals, 31-21 (C)
2003—Broncos, 30-10 (C)
2004—Bengals, 23-10 (C)
2006—Broncos, 24-23 (D)
2009—Broncos, 12-7 (C)
(RS Pts.—Broncos 523, Bengals 449)

CINCINNATI vs. DETROIT
RS: Bengals lead series, 7-3
1970—Lions, 38-3 (D)

1974—Lions, 23-19 (C)
1983—Bengals, 17-9 (C)
1986—Bengals, 24-17 (D)
1989—Bengals, 42-7 (C)
1992—Lions, 19-13 (C)
1998—Bengals, 34-28 (D) OT
2001—Bengals, 31-27 (D)
2005—Bengals, 41-17 (D)
2009—Bengals, 23-13 (C)
(RS Pts.—Bengals 247, Lions 198)

CINCINNATI vs. GREEN BAY
RS: Bengals lead series, 6-5
1971—Packers, 20-17 (GB)
1976—Bengals, 28-7 (C)
1977—Bengals, 17-7 (Mil)
1980—Packers, 14-9 (GB)
1983—Bengals, 34-14 (C)
1986—Bengals, 34-28 (Mil)
1992—Packers, 24-23 (GB)
1995—Packers, 24-10 (GB)
1998—Packers, 13-6 (C)
2005—Bengals, 21-14 (C)
2009—Bengals, 31-24 (GB)
(RS Pts.—Bengals 230, Packers 189)

CINCINNATI vs. HOUSTON
RS: Bengals lead series, 3-2
2002—Bengals, 38-3 (H)
2003—Bengals, 34-27 (C)
2005—Bengals, 16-10 (C)
2008—Texans, 35-6 (H)
2009—Texans, 28-17 (C)
(RS Pts.—Bengals 111, Texans 103)

CINCINNATI vs. *INDIANAPOLIS
RS: Colts lead series, 16-8
PS: Colts lead series, 1-0
1970—**Colts, 17-0 (B)
1972—Colts, 20-19 (C)
1974—Colts, 24-14 (B)
1976—Colts, 28-27 (B)
1979—Colts, 38-28 (B)
1980—Bengals, 34-33 (C)
1981—Bengals, 41-19 (B)
1982—Bengals, 20-17 (B)
1983—Colts, 34-31 (C)
1987—Bengals, 23-21 (I)
1989—Colts, 23-12 (C)
1990—Colts, 34-20 (C)
1992—Colts, 21-17 (C)
1993—Colts, 9-6 (C)
1994—Colts, 17-13 (C)
1995—Bengals, 24-21 (I) OT
1996—Bengals, 31-24 (C)
1997—Bengals, 28-13 (I)
1998—Colts, 39-26 (I)
1999—Colts, 31-10 (I)
2002—Colts, 28-21 (I)
2005—Colts, 45-37 (C)
2006—Colts, 34-16 (I)
2008—Colts, 35-3 (I)
2010—Colts, 23-17 (I)
(RS Pts.—Colts 621, Bengals 528)
(PS Pts.—Colts 17, Bengals 0)
*Franchise in Baltimore prior to 1984
**AFC Divisional Playoff

CINCINNATI vs. JACKSONVILLE
RS: Jaguars lead series, 11-6
1995—Bengals, 24-17 (C)
        Bengals, 17-13 (J)
1996—Bengals, 28-21 (C)
        Jaguars, 30-27 (J)
1997—Jaguars, 21-13 (J)

Bengals, 31-26 (C)
1998—Jaguars, 24-11 (J)
        Jaguars, 34-17 (C)
1999—Jaguars, 41-10 (C)
        Jaguars, 24-7 (J)
2000—Jaguars, 13-0 (J)
        Bengals, 17-14 (C)
2001—Jaguars, 30-13 (J)
        Jaguars, 14-10 (C)
2002—Jaguars, 29-15 (C)
2005—Jaguars, 23-20 (J)
2008—Bengals, 21-19 (C)
(RS Pts.—Jaguars 393, Bengals 281)

CINCINNATI vs. KANSAS CITY
RS: Series tied, 13-13
1968—Chiefs, 13-3 (KC)
        Chiefs, 16-9 (C)
1969—Bengals, 24-19 (C)
        Chiefs, 42-22 (KC)
1970—Chiefs, 27-19 (C)
1972—Bengals, 23-16 (KC)
1973—Bengals, 14-6 (C)
1974—Bengals, 33-6 (C)
1976—Bengals, 27-24 (KC)
1977—Bengals, 27-7 (KC)
1978—Chiefs, 24-23 (C)
1979—Chiefs, 10-7 (C)
1980—Bengals, 20-6 (KC)
1983—Chiefs, 20-15 (KC)
1984—Chiefs, 27-22 (C)
1986—Chiefs, 24-14 (KC)
1987—Bengals, 30-27 (C) OT
1988—Chiefs, 31-28 (KC)
1989—Bengals, 21-17 (KC)
1993—Chiefs, 17-15 (KC)
2003—Bengals, 24-19 (C)
2005—Chiefs, 37-3 (KC)
2006—Bengals, 23-10 (KC)
2007—Chiefs, 27-20 (KC)
2008—Bengals, 16-6 (C)
2009—Bengals, 17-10 (C)
(RS Pts.—Bengals 499, Chiefs 488)

CINCINNATI vs. MIAMI
RS: Dolphins lead series, 13-5
PS: Dolphins lead series, 1-0
1968—Dolphins, 24-22 (C)
        Bengals, 38-21 (M)
1969—Bengals, 27-21 (C)
1971—Dolphins, 23-13 (C)
1973—*Dolphins, 34-16 (M)
1974—Dolphins, 24-3 (M)
1977—Bengals, 23-17 (C)
1978—Dolphins, 21-0 (M)
1980—Dolphins, 17-16 (M)
1983—Dolphins, 38-14 (M)
1987—Dolphins, 20-14 (C)
1989—Dolphins, 20-13 (C)
1991—Dolphins, 37-13 (M)
1994—Dolphins, 23-7 (C)
1995—Dolphins, 26-23 (C)
2000—Dolphins, 31-16 (C)
2004—Bengals, 16-13 (C)
2007—Bengals, 38-25 (M)
2010—Dolphins, 22-14 (C)
(RS Pts.—Dolphins 423, Bengals 310)
(PS Pts.—Dolphins 34, Bengals 16)
*AFC Divisional Playoff

CINCINNATI vs. MINNESOTA
RS: Vikings lead series, 6-5
1973—Bengals, 27-0 (C)
1977—Vikings, 42-10 (M)

1980—Bengals, 14-0 (C)
1983—Vikings, 20-14 (M)
1986—Bengals, 24-20 (C)
1989—Vikings, 29-21 (M)
1992—Vikings, 42-7 (C)
1995—Bengals, 27-24 (C)
1998—Vikings, 24-3 (M)
2005—Bengals, 37-8 (C)
2009—Vikings, 30-10 (M)
(RS Pts.—Vikings 239, Bengals 194)

CINCINNATI vs. *NEW ENGLAND
RS: Patriots lead series, 14-8
1968—Patriots, 33-14 (B)
1969—Patriots, 25-14 (C)
1970—Bengals, 45-7 (C)
1972—Bengals, 31-7 (NE)
1975—Bengals, 27-10 (C)
1978—Patriots, 10-3 (C)
1979—Patriots, 20-14 (C)
1984—Patriots, 20-14 (NE)
1985—Patriots, 34-23 (NE)
1986—Bengals, 31-7 (NE)
1988—Patriots, 27-21 (NE)
1990—Bengals, 41-7 (C)
1991—Bengals, 29-7 (C)
1992—Bengals, 20-10 (C)
1993—Patriots, 7-2 (NE)
1994—Bengals, 31-28 (C)
2000—Patriots, 16-13 (NE)
2001—Bengals, 23-17 (C)
2004—Patriots, 35-28 (NE)
2006—Patriots, 38-13 (C)
2007—Patriots, 34-13 (C)
2010—Patriots, 38-24 (NE)
(RS Pts.—Bengals 471, Patriots 440)
*Franchise in Boston prior to 1971

CINCINNATI vs. NEW ORLEANS
RS: Series tied, 6-6
1970—Bengals, 26-6 (C)
1975—Bengals, 21-0 (NO)
1978—Saints, 20-18 (C)
1981—Saints, 17-7 (NO)
1984—Bengals, 24-21 (NO)
1987—Saints, 41-24 (C)
1990—Saints, 21-7 (C)
1993—Saints, 20-13 (NO)
1996—Bengals, 30-15 (C)
2002—Bengals, 20-13 (C)
2006—Bengals, 31-16 (NO)
2010—Saints, 34-30 (C)
(RS Pts.—Bengals 251, Saints 224)

CINCINNATI vs. N.Y. GIANTS
RS: Bengals lead series, 5-3
1972—Bengals, 13-10 (C)
1977—Bengals, 30-13 (C)
1985—Bengals, 35-30 (C)
1991—Bengals, 27-24 (C)
1994—Giants, 27-20 (NY)
1997—Giants, 29-27 (NY)
2004—Bengals, 23-22 (C)
2008—Giants, 26-23 (NY) OT
(RS Pts.—Bengals 198, Giants 181)

CINCINNATI vs. N.Y. JETS
RS: Jets lead series, 15-7
PS: Jets lead series, 2-0
1968—Jets, 27-14 (NY)
1969—Jets, 21-7 (C)
        Jets, 40-7 (NY)
1971—Jets, 35-21 (NY)
1973—Bengals, 20-14 (C)
1976—Bengals, 42-3 (NY)

1981—Bengals, 31-30 (NY)
1982—*Jets, 44-17 (C)
1984—Jets, 43-23 (NY)
1985—Jets, 29-20 (C)
1986—Bengals, 52-21 (C)
1987—Jets, 27-20 (NY)
1988—Bengals, 36-19 (C)
1990—Bengals, 25-20 (C)
1992—Jets, 17-14 (NY)
1993—Jets, 17-12 (NY)
1997—Jets, 31-14 (C)
2001—Jets, 15-14 (NY)
2004—Jets, 31-24 (NY)
2007—Bengals, 38-31 (C)
2008—Jets, 26-14 (NY)
2009—Jets, 37-0 (NY)
　　　*Jets, 24-14 (C)
2010—Jets, 26-10 (NY)
(RS Pts.—Jets 560, Bengals 458)
(PS Pts.—Jets 68, Bengals 31)
*AFC First-Round Playoff
CINCINNATI vs. *OAKLAND
RS: Raiders lead series, 18-8
PS: Raiders lead series, 2-0
1968—Raiders, 31-10 (O)
　　　Raiders, 34-0 (C)
1969—Bengals, 31-17 (C)
　　　Raiders, 37-17 (O)
1970—Bengals, 31-21 (C)
1971—Raiders, 31-27 (O)
1972—Raiders, 20-14 (C)
1974—Raiders, 30-27 (O)
1975—Bengals, 14-10 (C)
　　　**Raiders, 31-28 (O)
1976—Raiders, 35-20 (O)
1978—Raiders, 34-21 (C)
1980—Raiders, 28-17 (O)
1982—Bengals, 31-17 (C)
1983—Raiders, 20-10 (C)
1985—Raiders, 13-6 (LA)
1988—Bengals, 45-21 (LA)
1989—Raiders, 28-7 (LA)
1990—Raiders, 24-7 (LA)
　　　**Raiders, 20-10 (LA)
1991—Raiders, 38-14 (C)
1992—Bengals, 24-21 (C) OT
1993—Bengals, 16-10 (C)
1995—Raiders, 20-17 (C)
1998—Raiders, 27-10 (O)
2003—Raiders, 23-20 (O)
2006—Bengals, 27-10 (C)
2009—Raiders, 20-17 (O)
(RS Pts.—Raiders 620, Bengals 480)
(PS Pts.—Raiders 51, Bengals 38)
*Franchise in Los Angeles from 1982-1994
**AFC Divisional Playoff
CINCINNATI vs. PHILADELPHIA
RS: Bengals lead series, 7-3-1
1971—Bengals, 37-14 (C)
1975—Bengals, 31-0 (P)
1979—Bengals, 37-13 (C)
1982—Bengals, 18-14 (P)
1988—Bengals, 28-24 (P)
1991—Eagles, 17-10 (P)
1994—Bengals, 33-30 (C)
1997—Eagles, 44-42 (P)
2000—Eagles, 16-7 (P)
2004—Bengals, 38-10 (P)
2008—Tie, 13-13 (C) OT
(RS Pts.—Bengals 294, Eagles 195)

CINCINNATI vs. PITTSBURGH
RS: Steelers lead series, 49-32
PS: Steelers lead series, 1-0
1970—Steelers, 21-10 (P)
　　　Bengals, 34-7 (C)
1971—Steelers, 21-10 (P)
　　　Steelers, 21-13 (C)
1972—Bengals, 15-10 (C)
　　　Steelers, 40-17 (P)
1973—Bengals, 19-7 (C)
　　　Steelers, 20-13 (P)
1974—Bengals, 17-10 (C)
　　　Steelers, 27-3 (P)
1975—Steelers, 30-24 (C)
　　　Steelers, 35-14 (P)
1976—Steelers, 23-6 (P)
　　　Steelers, 7-3 (C)
1977—Steelers, 20-14 (P)
　　　Bengals, 17-10 (C)
1978—Steelers, 28-3 (C)
　　　Steelers, 7-6 (P)
1979—Bengals, 34-10 (C)
　　　Steelers, 37-17 (P)
1980—Bengals, 30-28 (C)
　　　Bengals, 17-16 (P)
1981—Bengals, 34-7 (C)
　　　Bengals, 17-10 (P)
1982—Steelers, 26-20 (P) OT
1983—Steelers, 24-14 (C)
　　　Bengals, 23-10 (P)
1984—Steelers, 38-17 (P)
　　　Bengals, 22-20 (C)
1985—Bengals, 37-24 (P)
　　　Bengals, 26-21 (C)
1986—Bengals, 24-22 (C)
　　　Steelers, 30-9 (P)
1987—Steelers, 23-20 (P)
　　　Steelers, 30-16 (C)
1988—Bengals, 17-12 (P)
　　　Bengals, 42-7 (C)
1989—Bengals, 41-10 (C)
　　　Bengals, 26-16 (P)
1990—Bengals, 27-3 (C)
　　　Bengals, 16-12 (P)
1991—Steelers, 33-27 (C) OT
　　　Steelers, 17-10 (P)
1992—Steelers, 20-0 (P)
　　　Bengals, 21-9 (C)
1993—Steelers, 34-7 (P)
　　　Steelers, 24-16 (C)
1994—Steelers, 14-10 (P)
　　　Steelers, 38-15 (C)
1995—Bengals, 27-9 (P)
　　　Steelers, 49-31 (C)
1996—Steelers, 20-10 (P)
　　　Bengals, 34-24 (C)
1997—Steelers, 26-10 (C)
　　　Steelers, 20-3 (P)
1998—Bengals, 25-20 (C)
　　　Bengals, 25-24 (P)
1999—Steelers, 17-3 (C)
　　　Bengals, 27-20 (P)
2000—Steelers, 15-0 (P)
　　　Steelers, 48-28 (C)
2001—Steelers, 16-7 (P)
　　　Bengals, 26-23 (C) OT
2002—Steelers, 34-7 (C)
　　　Steelers, 29-21 (P)
2003—Steelers, 17-10 (C)
　　　Bengals, 24-20 (P)
2004—Steelers, 28-17 (P)

　　　Steelers, 19-14 (C)
2005—Steelers, 27-13 (C)
　　　Bengals, 38-31 (P)
　　　*Steelers, 31-17 (C)
2006—Bengals, 28-20 (P)
　　　Steelers, 23-17 (C) OT
2007—Steelers, 24-13 (C)
　　　Steelers, 24-10 (P)
2008—Steelers, 38-10 (C)
　　　Steelers, 27-10 (P)
2009—Bengals, 23-20 (C)
　　　Bengals, 18-12 (P)
2010—Steelers, 27-21 (C)
　　　Steelers, 23-7 (P)
(RS Pts.—Steelers 1,755, Bengals 1,435)
(PS Pts.—Steelers 31, Bengals 17)
*AFC First-Round Playoff
CINCINNATI vs. *ST. LOUIS
RS: Bengals lead series, 6-5
1972—Rams, 15-12 (LA)
1976—Bengals, 20-12 (C)
1978—Bengals, 20-19 (LA)
1981—Bengals, 24-10 (C)
1984—Rams, 24-14 (C)
1990—Bengals, 34-31 (LA) OT
1993—Bengals, 15-3 (C)
1996—Rams, 26-16 (StL)
1999—Rams, 38-10 (C)
2003—Rams, 27-10 (StL)
2007—Bengals, 19-10 (C)
(RS Pts.—Rams 215, Bengals 194)
*Franchise in Los Angeles prior to 1995
CINCINNATI vs. SAN DIEGO
RS: Chargers lead series, 19-11
PS: Bengals lead series, 1-0
1968—Chargers, 29-13 (SD)
　　　Chargers, 31-10 (C)
1969—Bengals, 34-20 (C)
　　　Chargers, 21-14 (SD)
1970—Bengals, 17-14 (SD)
1971—Bengals, 31-0 (C)
1973—Bengals, 20-13 (SD)
1974—Chargers, 20-17 (C)
1975—Bengals, 47-17 (C)
1977—Chargers, 24-3 (SD)
1978—Chargers, 22-13 (SD)
1979—Chargers, 26-24 (C)
1980—Chargers, 31-14 (C)
1981—Bengals, 40-17 (SD)
　　　*Bengals, 27-7 (C)
1982—Chargers, 50-34 (SD)
1985—Chargers, 44-41 (C)
1987—Chargers, 10-9 (C)
1988—Bengals, 27-10 (C)
1990—Bengals, 21-16 (SD)
1992—Chargers, 27-10 (SD)
1994—Chargers, 27-10 (SD)
1996—Chargers, 27-14 (SD)
1997—Bengals, 38-31 (C)
1999—Chargers, 34-7 (C)
2001—Chargers, 28-14 (SD)
2002—Chargers, 34-6 (C)
2003—Bengals, 34-27 (SD)
2006—Chargers, 49-41 (C)
2009—Chargers, 27-24 (SD)
2010—Bengals, 34-20 (C)
(RS Pts.—Chargers 746, Bengals 661)
(PS Pts.—Bengals 27, Chargers 7)
*AFC Championship
CINCINNATI vs. SAN FRANCISCO
RS: 49ers lead series, 8-3

PS: 49ers lead series, 2-0
1974—Bengals, 21-3 (SF)
1978—49ers, 28-12 (SF)
1981—49ers, 21-3 (C)
   *49ers, 26-21 (Detroit)
1984—49ers, 23-17 (SF)
1987—49ers, 27-26 (C)
1988—**49ers, 20-16 (South Florida)
1990—49ers, 20-17 (C) OT
1993—49ers, 21-8 (C)
1996—49ers, 28-21 (SF)
1999—Bengals, 44-30 (C)
2003—Bengals, 41-38 (C)
2007—49ers, 20-13 (SF)
(RS Pts.—49ers 259, Bengals 223)
(PS Pts.—49ers 46, Bengals 37)
*Super Bowl XVI
**Super Bowl XXIII
CINCINNATI vs. SEATTLE
RS: Seahawks lead series, 9-8
PS: Bengals lead series, 1-0
1977—Bengals, 42-20 (C)
1981—Bengals, 27-21 (C)
1982—Bengals, 24-10 (C)
1984—Seahawks, 26-6 (C)
1985—Seahawks, 28-24 (C)
1986—Bengals, 34-7 (C)
1987—Bengals, 17-10 (S)
1988—*Bengals, 21-13 (C)
1989—Seahawks, 24-17 (C)
1990—Seahawks, 31-16 (S)
1991—Seahawks, 13-7 (C)
1992—Bengals, 21-3 (S)
1993—Seahawks, 19-10 (C)
1994—Bengals, 20-17 (S) OT
1995—Seahawks, 24-21 (S)
1999—Seahawks, 37-20 (S)
2003—Bengals, 27-24 (C)
2007—Seahawks, 24-21 (S)
(RS Pts.—Bengals 354, Seahawks 338)
(PS Pts.—Bengals 21, Seahawks 13)
*AFC Divisional Playoff
CINCINNATI vs. TAMPA BAY
RS: Buccaneers lead series, 7-3
1976—Bengals, 21-0 (C)
1980—Buccaneers, 17-12 (C)
1983—Bengals, 23-17 (TB)
1989—Bengals, 56-23 (C)
1995—Buccaneers, 19-16 (TB)
1998—Buccaneers, 35-0 (C)
2001—Buccaneers, 16-13 (C) OT
2002—Buccaneers, 35-7 (C)
2006—Buccaneers, 14-13 (TB)
2010—Buccaneers, 24-21 (C)
(RS Pts.— Buccaneers 200, Bengals 182)
CINCINNATI vs. *TENNESSEE
RS: Titans lead series, 39-31-1
PS: Bengals lead series, 1-0
1968—Oilers, 27-17 (C)
1969—Tie, 31-31 (H)
1970—Oilers, 20-13 (C)
   Bengals, 30-20 (H)
1971—Oilers, 10-6 (H)
   Bengals, 28-13 (C)
1972—Bengals, 30-7 (C)
   Bengals, 61-17 (H)
1973—Bengals, 24-10 (C)
   Bengals, 27-24 (H)
1974—Oilers, 34-21 (C)
   Oilers, 20-3 (H)
1975—Bengals, 21-19 (H)

Bengals, 23-19 (C)
1976—Bengals, 27-7 (H)
   Bengals, 31-27 (C)
1977—Bengals, 13-10 (C) OT
   Oilers, 21-16 (H)
1978—Bengals, 28-13 (C)
   Oilers, 17-10 (H)
1979—Oilers, 30-27 (C) OT
   Oilers, 42-21 (H)
1980—Oilers, 13-10 (C)
   Oilers, 23-3 (H)
1981—Oilers, 17-10 (H)
   Bengals, 34-21 (C)
1982—Bengals, 27-6 (C)
   Bengals, 35-27 (H)
1983—Bengals, 55-14 (H)
   Bengals, 38-10 (C)
1984—Bengals, 13-3 (C)
   Bengals, 31-13 (H)
1985—Oilers, 44-27 (H)
   Bengals, 45-27 (C)
1986—Bengals, 31-28 (C)
   Oilers, 32-28 (H)
1987—Oilers, 31-29 (C)
   Oilers, 21-17 (H)
1988—Bengals, 44-21 (C)
   Oilers, 41-6 (H)
1989—Oilers, 26-24 (H)
   Bengals, 61-7 (C)
1990—Oilers, 48-17 (H)
   Bengals, 40-20 (C)
   **Bengals, 41-14 (C)
1991—Oilers, 30-7 (C)
   Oilers, 35-3 (H)
1992—Oilers, 38-24 (C)
   Oilers, 26-10 (H)
1993—Oilers, 28-12 (H)
   Oilers, 38-3 (C)
1994—Oilers, 20-13 (H)
   Bengals, 34-31 (C)
1995—Bengals, 38-28 (C)
   Bengals, 32-25 (H)
1996—Oilers, 30-27 (C) OT
   Bengals, 21-13 (H)
1997—Oilers, 30-7 (C)
   Bengals, 41-14 (C)
1998—Oilers, 23-14 (C)
   Oilers, 44-14 (T)
1999—Titans, 36-35 (T)
   Titans, 24-14 (C)
2000—Titans, 23-14 (C)
   Titans, 35-3 (T)
2001—Titans, 20-7 (C)
   Bengals, 23-21 (T)
2002—Titans, 30-24 (C)
2004—Titans, 27-20 (T)
2005—Bengals, 31-23 (T)
2007—Bengals, 35-6 (C)
2008—Titans, 24-7 (C)
(RS Pts.—Titans 1,663, Bengals 1,636)
(PS Pts.—Bengals 41, Titans 14)
*Franchise in Houston prior to 1997;
known as Oilers prior to 1999
**AFC First-Round Playoff
CINCINNATI vs. WASHINGTON
RS: Series tied, 4-4
1970—Redskins, 20-0 (W)
1974—Bengals, 28-17 (C)
1979—Redskins, 28-14 (W)
1985—Redskins, 27-24 (W)
1988—Bengals, 20-17 (C) OT

1991—Redskins, 34-27 (C)
2004—Bengals, 17-10 (W)
2008—Bengals, 20-13 (C)
(RS Pts.—Redskins 166, Bengals 150)

CLEVELAND vs. ARIZONA
RS: Browns lead series, 33-12-3;
See Arizona vs. Cleveland
CLEVELAND vs. ATLANTA
RS: Browns lead series, 10-3;
See Atlanta vs. Cleveland
CLEVELAND vs. BALTIMORE
RS: Ravens lead series, 17-7;
See Baltimore vs. Cleveland
CLEVELAND vs. BUFFALO
RS: Browns lead series, 10-6
PS: Browns lead series, 1-0;
See Buffalo vs. Cleveland
CLEVELAND vs. CAROLINA
RS: Panthers lead series, 3-1;
See Carolina vs. Cleveland
CLEVELAND vs. CHICAGO
RS: Browns lead series, 9-5;
See Chicago vs. Cleveland
CLEVELAND vs. CINCINNATI
RS: Bengals lead series, 39-36;
See Cincinnati vs. Cleveland
CLEVELAND vs. DALLAS
RS: Browns lead series, 15-11
PS: Browns lead series, 2-1
1960—Browns, 48-7 (D)
1961—Browns, 25-7 (C)
   Browns, 38-17 (D)
1962—Browns, 19-10 (C)
   Cowboys, 45-21 (D)
1963—Browns, 41-24 (D)
   Browns, 27-17 (C)
1964—Browns, 27-6 (C)
   Browns, 20-16 (D)
1965—Browns, 23-17 (C)
   Browns, 24-17 (D)
1966—Browns, 30-21 (C)
   Cowboys, 26-14 (D)
1967—Cowboys, 21-14 (C)
   *Cowboys, 52-14 (D)
1968—Cowboys, 28-7 (D)
   *Browns, 31-20 (C)
1969—Browns, 42-10 (C)
   *Browns, 38-14 (D)
1970—Cowboys, 6-2 (C)
1974—Cowboys, 41-17 (D)
1979—Browns, 26-7 (C)
1982—Cowboys, 31-14 (D)
1985—Cowboys, 20-7 (C)
1988—Browns, 24-21 (C)
1991—Cowboys, 26-14 (C)
1994—Browns, 19-14 (D)
2004—Cowboys, 19-12 (D)
2008—Cowboys, 28-10 (C)
(RS Pts.—Browns 565, Cowboys 502)
(PS Pts.—Cowboys 86, Browns 83)
*Conference Championship
CLEVELAND vs. DENVER
RS: Broncos lead series, 18-5
PS: Broncos lead series, 3-0
1970—Browns, 27-13 (D)
1971—Broncos, 27-0 (C)
1972—Browns, 27-20 (D)
1974—Browns, 23-21 (C)
1975—Broncos, 16-15 (D)
1976—Broncos, 44-13 (D)

1978—Broncos, 19-7 (C)
1980—Broncos, 19-16 (C)
1981—Broncos, 23-20 (D) OT
1983—Broncos, 27-6 (D)
1984—Broncos, 24-14 (C)
1986—*Broncos, 23-20 (C) OT
1987—*Broncos, 38-33 (D)
1988—Broncos, 30-7 (D)
1989—Browns, 16-13 (C)
　　　*Broncos, 37-21 (D)
1990—Browns, 30-29 (D)
1991—Broncos, 17-7 (C)
1992—Broncos, 12-0 (C)
1993—Broncos, 29-14 (C)
1994—Broncos, 26-14 (D)
2000—Broncos, 44-10 (D)
2003—Broncos, 23-20 (D) OT
2006—Broncos, 17-7 (C)
2008—Broncos, 34-30 (C)
2009—Broncos, 27-6 (D)
(RS Pts.—Broncos 554, Browns 329)
(PS Pts.—Broncos 98, Browns 74)
*AFC Championship

CLEVELAND vs. DETROIT
RS: Lions lead series, 14-4
PS: Lions lead series, 3-1
1952—Lions, 17-6 (D)
　　　*Lions, 17-7 (C)
1953—*Lions, 17-16 (D)
1954—Lions, 14-10 (C)
　　　*Browns, 56-10 (C)
1957—Lions, 20-7 (D)
　　　*Lions, 59-14 (D)
1958—Lions, 30-10 (C)
1963—Lions, 38-10 (D)
1964—Browns, 37-21 (C)
1967—Lions, 31-14 (D)
1969—Lions, 28-21 (C)
1970—Lions, 41-24 (C)
1975—Lions, 21-10 (D)
1983—Browns, 31-26 (C)
1986—Browns, 24-21 (C)
1989—Lions, 13-10 (D)
1992—Lions, 24-14 (D)
1995—Lions, 38-20 (D)
2001—Browns, 24-14 (C)
2005—Lions, 13-10 (C)
2009—Lions, 38-37 (D)
(RS Pts.—Lions 448, Browns 319)
(PS Pts.—Lions 103, Browns 93)
*NFL Championship

CLEVELAND vs. GREEN BAY
RS: Packers lead series, 10-7
PS: Packers lead series, 1-0
1953—Browns, 27-0 (Mil)
1955—Browns, 41-10 (C)
1956—Browns, 24-7 (Mil)
1961—Packers, 49-17 (C)
1964—Packers, 28-21 (Mil)
1965—*Packers, 23-12 (GB)
1966—Packers, 21-20 (C)
1967—Packers, 55-7 (Mil)
1969—Browns, 20-7 (C)
1972—Packers, 26-10 (C)
1980—Browns, 26-21 (C)
1983—Packers, 35-21 (Mil)
1986—Packers, 17-14 (C)
1992—Browns, 17-6 (C)
1995—Packers, 31-20 (C)
2001—Packers, 30-7 (GB)
2005—Browns, 26-24 (GB)

2009—Packers, 31-3 (C)
(RS Pts.—Packers 398, Browns 321)
(PS Pts.—Packers 23, Browns 12)
*NFL Championship

CLEVELAND vs. HOUSTON
RS: Series tied, 3-3
2002—Browns, 34-17 (C)
2004—Browns, 22-14 (H)
2005—Texans, 19-16 (H)
2006—Texans, 14-6 (H)
2007—Browns, 27-17 (C)
2008—Texans, 16-6 (C)
(RS Pts.—Browns 111, Texans 97)

CLEVELAND vs. *INDIANAPOLIS
RS: Browns lead series, 13-12
PS: Series tied, 2-2
1956—Colts, 21-7 (C)
1959—Browns, 38-31 (B)
1962—Colts, 36-14 (C)
1964—**Browns, 27-0 (C)
1968—Browns, 30-20 (B)
　　　**Colts, 34-0 (C)
1971—Browns, 14-13 (B)
　　　***Colts, 20-3 (C)
1973—Browns, 24-14 (C)
1975—Colts, 21-7 (B)
1978—Browns, 45-24 (B)
1979—Browns, 13-10 (C)
1980—Browns, 28-27 (B)
1981—Browns, 42-28 (C)
1983—Browns, 41-23 (C)
1986—Browns, 24-9 (I)
1987—Colts, 9-7 (C)
　　　***Browns, 38-21 (C)
1988—Browns, 23-17 (C)
1989—Colts, 23-17 (I) OT
1991—Browns, 31-0 (I)
1992—Colts, 14-3 (I)
1993—Colts, 23-10 (I)
1994—Browns, 21-14 (I)
1999—Colts, 29-28 (C)
2002—Colts, 28-23 (C)
2003—Colts, 9-6 (C)
2005—Colts, 13-6 (I)
2008—Colts, 10-6 (C)
(RS Pts.—Browns 508, Colts 466)
(PS Pts.—Colts 75, Browns 68)
*Franchise in Baltimore prior to 1984
**NFL Championship
***AFC Divisional Playoff

CLEVELAND vs. JACKSONVILLE
RS: Jaguars lead series, 9-4
1995—Jaguars, 23-15 (C)
　　　Jaguars, 24-21 (J)
1999—Jaguars, 24-7 (J)
　　　Jaguars, 24-14 (C)
2000—Jaguars, 27-7 (C)
　　　Jaguars, 48-0 (J)
2001—Browns, 23-14 (J)
　　　Jaguars, 15-10 (C)
2002—Browns, 21-20 (J)
2005—Jaguars, 20-14 (C)
2008—Browns, 23-17 (J)
2009—Browns, 23-17 (C)
2010—Jaguars, 24-20 (J)
(RS Pts.—Jaguars 297, Browns 198)

CLEVELAND vs. KANSAS CITY
RS: Series tied, 10-10-2
1971—Chiefs, 13-7 (KC)
1972—Chiefs, 31-7 (C)
1973—Tie, 20-20 (KC)

1975—Browns, 40-14 (C)
1976—Chiefs, 39-14 (KC)
1977—Browns, 44-7 (C)
1978—Chiefs, 17-3 (KC)
1979—Browns, 27-24 (KC)
1980—Browns, 20-13 (C)
1984—Chiefs, 10-6 (KC)
1986—Browns, 20-7 (C)
1988—Browns, 6-3 (KC)
1989—Tie, 10-10 (C) OT
1990—Chiefs, 34-0 (KC)
1991—Browns, 20-15 (C)
1994—Chiefs, 20-13 (KC)
1995—Browns, 35-17 (C)
2002—Chiefs, 40-39 (C)
2003—Chiefs, 41-20 (KC)
2006—Browns, 31-28 (C) OT
2009—Browns, 41-34 (KC)
2010—Chiefs, 16-14 (C)
(RS Pts.—Chiefs 453, Browns 437)

CLEVELAND vs. MIAMI
RS: Series tied, 7-7
PS: Dolphins lead series, 2-0
1970—Browns, 28-0 (M)
1972—*Dolphins, 20-14 (M)
1973—Dolphins, 17-9 (C)
1976—Browns, 17-13 (C)
1979—Browns, 30-24 (C) OT
1985—*Dolphins, 24-21 (M)
1986—Browns, 26-16 (C)
1988—Dolphins, 38-31 (M)
1989—Dolphins, 13-10 (M) OT
1990—Dolphins, 30-13 (C)
1992—Dolphins, 27-23 (C)
1993—Dolphins, 24-14 (C)
2004—Dolphins, 10-7 (M)
2005—Browns, 22-0 (C)
2007—Browns, 41-31 (C)
2010—Browns, 13-10 (M)
(RS Pts.—Browns 284, Dolphins 253)
(PS Pts.—Dolphins 44, Browns 35)
*AFC Divisional Playoff

CLEVELAND vs. MINNESOTA
RS: Vikings lead series, 10-3
PS: Vikings lead series, 1-0
1965—Vikings, 27-17 (C)
1967—Browns, 14-10 (C)
1969—Vikings, 51-3 (M)
　　　*Vikings, 27-7 (M)
1973—Vikings, 26-3 (M)
1975—Vikings, 42-10 (C)
1980—Vikings, 28-23 (M)
1983—Vikings, 27-21 (C)
1986—Browns, 23-20 (M)
1989—Browns, 23-17 (C) OT
1992—Vikings, 17-13 (M)
1995—Vikings, 27-11 (M)
2005—Vikings, 24-12 (M)
2009—Vikings, 34-20 (C)
(RS Pts.—Vikings 350, Browns 193)
(PS Pts.—Vikings 27, Browns 7)
*NFL Championship

CLEVELAND vs. NEW ENGLAND
RS: Browns lead series, 12-9
PS: Browns lead series, 1-0
1971—Browns, 27-7 (C)
1974—Browns, 21-14 (NE)
1977—Browns, 30-27 (C) OT
1980—Patriots, 34-17 (NE)
1982—Browns, 10-7 (C)
1983—Browns, 30-0 (NE)

1984—Patriots, 17-16 (C)
1985—Browns, 24-20 (C)
1987—Browns, 20-10 (NE)
1991—Browns, 20-0 (NE)
1992—Browns, 19-17 (NE)
1993—Patriots, 20-17 (C)
1994—Browns, 13-6 (C)
　　　*Browns, 20-13 (C)
1995—Patriots, 17-14 (NE)
1999—Patriots, 19-7 (C)
2000—Browns, 19-11 (C)
2001—Patriots, 27-16 (NE)
2003—Patriots, 9-3 (NE)
2004—Patriots, 42-15 (C)
2007—Patriots, 34-17 (NE)
2010—Browns, 34-14 (C)
(RS Pts.—Browns 389, Patriots 352)
(PS Pts.—Browns 20, Patriots 13)
*AFC First-Round Playoff
CLEVELAND vs. NEW ORLEANS
RS: Browns lead series, 12-4
1967—Browns, 42-7 (NO)
1968—Browns, 24-10 (NO)
　　　Browns, 35-17 (C)
1969—Browns, 27-17 (NO)
1971—Browns, 21-17 (NO)
1975—Browns, 17-16 (C)
1978—Browns, 24-16 (NO)
1981—Browns, 20-17 (C)
1984—Saints, 16-14 (C)
1987—Saints, 28-21 (NO)
1990—Saints, 25-20 (NO)
1993—Browns, 17-13 (C)
1999—Browns, 21-16 (NO)
2002—Browns, 24-15 (NO)
2006—Saints, 19-14 (C)
2010—Browns, 30-17 (NO)
(RS Pts.—Browns 371, Saints 266)
CLEVELAND vs. N.Y. GIANTS
RS: Browns lead series, 26-19-2
PS: Series tied, 1-1
1950—Giants, 6-0 (C)
　　　Giants, 17-13 (NY)
　　　*Browns, 8-3 (C)
1951—Browns, 14-13 (C)
　　　Browns, 10-0 (NY)
1952　Giants, 17-9 (C)
　　　Giants, 37-34 (NY)
1953—Browns, 7-0 (NY)
　　　Browns, 62-14 (C)
1954—Browns, 24-14 (C)
　　　Browns, 16-7 (NY)
1955—Browns, 24-14 (C)
　　　Tie, 35-35 (NY)
1956—Giants, 21-9 (C)
　　　Browns, 24-7 (NY)
1957—Browns, 6-3 (C)
　　　Browns, 34-28 (NY)
1958—Giants, 21-17 (C)
　　　Giants, 13-10 (NY)
　　　*Giants, 10-0 (NY)
1959—Giants, 10-6 (C)
　　　Giants, 48-7 (NY)
1960—Giants, 17-13 (C)
　　　Browns, 48-34 (NY)
1961—Giants, 37-21 (C)
　　　Tie, 7-7 (NY)
1962—Browns, 17-7 (C)
　　　Giants, 17-13 (NY)
1963—Browns, 35-24 (NY)
　　　Giants, 33-6 (C)

1964—Browns, 42-20 (C)
　　　Browns, 52-20 (NY)
1965—Browns, 38-14 (NY)
　　　Browns, 34-21 (C)
1966—Browns, 28-7 (NY)
　　　Browns, 49-40 (C)
1967—Giants, 38-34 (NY)
　　　Browns, 24-14 (C)
1968—Browns, 45-10 (C)
1969—Browns, 28-17 (C)
　　　Giants, 27-14 (NY)
1973—Browns, 12-10 (C)
1977—Browns, 21-7 (NY)
1985—Browns, 35-33 (NY)
1991—Giants, 13-10 (NY)
1994—Giants, 16-13 (C)
2000—Giants, 24-3 (C)
2004—Giants, 27-10 (NY)
2008—Browns, 35-14 (C)
(RS Pts.—Browns 1,048, Giants 873)
(PS Pts.—Giants 13, Browns 8)
*Conference Playoff
CLEVELAND vs. N.Y. JETS
RS: Browns lead series, 12-8
PS: Browns lead series, 1-0
1970—Browns, 31-21 (C)
1972—Browns, 26-10 (NY)
1976—Browns, 38-17 (C)
1978—Browns, 37-34 (C) OT
1979—Browns, 25-22 (NY) OT
1980—Browns, 17-14 (C)
1981—Jets, 14-13 (C)
1983—Browns, 10-7 (C)
1984—Jets, 24-20 (C)
1985—Jets, 37-10 (NY)
1986—*Browns, 23-20 (C) OT
1988—Jets, 23-3 (C)
1989—Browns, 38-24 (C)
1990—Jets, 24-21 (NY)
1991—Jets, 17-14 (C)
1994—Browns, 27-7 (C)
2002—Browns, 24-21 (NY)
2004—Jets, 10-7 (C)
2006—Browns, 20-13 (C)
2007—Browns, 24-18 (NY)
2010—Jets, 26-20 (NY) OT
(RS Pts.—Browns 425, Jets 383)
(PS Pts.—Browns 23, Jets 20)
*AFC Divisional Playoff
CLEVELAND vs. *OAKLAND
RS: Raiders lead series, 10-8
PS: Raiders lead series, 2-0
1970—Raiders, 23-20 (O)
1971—Raiders, 34-20 (C)
1973—Browns, 7-3 (O)
1974—Raiders, 40-24 (C)
1975—Raiders, 38-17 (O)
1977—Raiders, 26-10 (C)
1979—Raiders, 19-14 (O)
1980—**Raiders, 14-12 (C)
1982—***Raiders, 27-10 (LA)
1985—Raiders, 21-20 (C)
1986—Raiders, 27-14 (LA)
1987—Browns, 24-17 (LA)
1992—Browns, 28-16 (LA)
1993—Browns, 19-16 (LA)
2000—Raiders, 36-10 (O)
2003—Browns, 13-7 (C)
2005—Browns, 9-7 (O)
2006—Browns, 24-21 (O)
2007—Raiders, 26-24 (O)

2009—Browns, 23-9 (C)
(RS Pts.—Raiders 386, Browns 320)
(PS Pts.—Raiders 41, Browns 22)
*Franchise in Los Angeles from 1982-1994
**AFC Divisional Playoff
***AFC First-Round Playoff
CLEVELAND vs. PHILADELPHIA
RS: Browns lead series, 31-15-1
1950—Browns, 35-10 (P)
　　　Browns, 13-7 (C)
1951—Browns, 20-17 (C)
　　　Browns, 24-9 (P)
1952—Browns, 49-7 (P)
　　　Eagles, 28-20 (C)
1953—Browns, 37-13 (C)
　　　Eagles, 42-27 (P)
1954—Eagles, 28-10 (P)
　　　Browns, 6-0 (C)
1955—Browns, 21-17 (C)
　　　Eagles, 33-17 (P)
1956—Browns, 16-0 (P)
　　　Browns, 17-14 (C)
1957—Browns, 24-7 (C)
　　　Eagles, 17-7 (P)
1958—Browns, 28-14 (C)
　　　Browns, 21-14 (P)
1959—Browns, 28-7 (C)
　　　Browns, 28-21 (P)
1960—Browns, 41-24 (P)
　　　Eagles, 31-29 (C)
1961—Eagles, 27-20 (P)
　　　Browns, 45-24 (C)
1962—Eagles, 35-7 (P)
　　　Tie, 14-14 (C)
1963—Browns, 37-7 (C)
　　　Browns, 23-17 (P)
1964—Browns, 28-20 (P)
　　　Browns, 38-24 (C)
1965—Browns, 35-17 (P)
　　　Browns, 38-34 (C)
1966—Browns, 27-7 (C)
　　　Eagles, 33-21 (P)
1967—Eagles, 28-24 (P)
1968—Browns, 47-13 (C)
1969—Browns, 27-20 (P)
1972—Browns, 27-17 (P)
1976—Browns, 24-3 (C)
1979—Browns, 24-19 (P)
1982—Eagles, 24-21 (C)
1988—Browns, 19-3 (C)
1991—Eagles, 32-30 (C)
1994—Browns, 26-7 (C)
2000—Eagles, 35-24 (C)
2004—Eagles, 34-31 (C) OT
2008—Eagles, 30-10 (P)
(RS Pts.—Browns 1,185, Eagles 884)
CLEVELAND vs. PITTSBURGH
RS: Steelers lead series, 60-56
PS: Steelers lead series, 2-0
1950—Browns, 30-17 (P)
　　　Browns, 45-7 (C)
1951—Browns, 17-0 (C)
　　　Browns, 28-0 (P)
1952—Browns, 21-20 (P)
　　　Browns, 29-28 (C)
1953—Browns, 34-16 (C)
　　　Browns, 20-16 (P)
1954—Steelers, 55-27 (P)
　　　Browns, 42-7 (C)
1955—Browns, 41-14 (C)
　　　Browns, 30-7 (P)

1956—Browns, 14-10 (P)
Steelers, 24-16 (C)
1957—Browns, 23-12 (P)
Browns, 24-0 (C)
1958—Browns, 45-12 (P)
Browns, 27-10 (C)
1959—Steelers, 17-7 (P)
Steelers, 21-20 (C)
1960—Browns, 28-20 (C)
Steelers, 14-10 (P)
1961—Browns, 30-28 (P)
Steelers, 17-13 (C)
1962—Browns, 41-14 (P)
Browns, 35-14 (C)
1963—Browns, 35-23 (C)
Steelers, 9-7 (P)
1964—Steelers, 23-7 (C)
Browns, 30-17 (P)
1965—Browns, 24-19 (C)
Browns, 42-21 (P)
1966—Browns, 41-10 (C)
Steelers, 16-6 (P)
1967—Browns, 21-10 (C)
Browns, 34-14 (P)
1968—Browns, 31-24 (C)
Browns, 45-24 (P)
1969—Browns, 42-31 (C)
Browns, 24-3 (P)
1970—Browns, 15-7 (C)
Steelers, 28-9 (P)
1971—Browns, 27-17 (C)
Steelers, 26-9 (P)
1972—Browns, 26-24 (C)
Steelers, 30-0 (P)
1973—Steelers, 33-6 (P)
Browns, 21-16 (C)
1974—Steelers, 20-16 (P)
Steelers, 26-16 (C)
1975—Steelers, 42-6 (C)
Steelers, 31-17 (P)
1976—Steelers, 31-14 (P)
Browns, 18-16 (C)
1977—Steelers, 28-14 (C)
Steelers, 35-31 (P)
1978—Steelers, 15-9 (P) OT
Steelers, 34-14 (C)
1979—Steelers, 51-35 (C)
Steelers, 33-30 (P) OT
1980—Browns, 27-26 (P)
Steelers, 16-13 (P)
1981—Steelers, 13-7 (P)
Steelers, 32-10 (C)
1982—Browns, 10-9 (C)
Steelers, 37-21 (P)
1983—Steelers, 44-17 (P)
Browns, 30-17 (C)
1984—Browns, 20-10 (C)
Steelers, 23-20 (P)
1985—Browns, 17-7 (C)
Steelers, 10-9 (P)
1986—Browns, 27-24 (P)
Browns, 37-31 (C) OT
1987—Browns, 34-10 (C)
Browns, 19-13 (P)
1988—Browns, 23-9 (P)
Browns, 27-7 (C)
1989—Browns, 51-0 (P)
Steelers, 17-7 (C)
1990—Browns, 13-3 (C)
Steelers, 35-0 (P)
1991—Browns, 17-14 (C)

1992—Browns, 17-9 (C)
Steelers, 23-13 (P)
1993—Browns, 28-23 (C)
Steelers, 16-9 (P)
1994—Steelers, 17-10 (C)
Steelers, 17-7 (P)
*Steelers, 29-9 (P)
1995—Steelers, 20-3 (P)
Steelers, 20-17 (C)
1999—Steelers, 43-0 (C)
Browns, 16-15 (P)
2000—Browns, 23-20 (C)
Steelers, 22-0 (P)
2001—Steelers, 15-12 (C) OT
Steelers, 28-7 (P)
2002—Steelers, 16-13 (P) OT
Steelers, 23-20 (C)
**Steelers, 36-33 (P)
2003—Browns, 33-13 (P)
Steelers, 13-6 (C)
2004—Steelers, 34-23 (P)
Steelers, 24-10 (C)
2005—Steelers, 34-21 (P)
Steelers, 41-0 (C)
2006—Steelers, 24-20 (C)
Steelers, 27-7 (P)
2007—Steelers, 34-7 (C)
Steelers, 31-28 (P)
2008—Steelers, 10-6 (C)
Steelers, 31-0 (P)
2009—Steelers, 27-14 (P)
Browns, 13-6 (C)
2010—Steelers, 28-10 (P)
Steelers, 41-9 (C)
(RS Pts.—Steelers 2,356, Browns 2,287)
(PS Pts.—Steelers 65, Browns 42)
*AFC Divisional Playoff
**AFC First-Round Playoff

CLEVELAND vs. *ST. LOUIS
RS: Series tied, 9-9
PS: Browns lead series, 2-1
1950—**Browns, 30-28 (C)
1951—Browns, 38-23 (LA)
**Rams, 24-17 (LA)
1952—Browns, 37-7 (C)
1955—**Browns, 38-14 (LA)
1957—Browns, 45-31 (C)
1958—Browns, 30-27 (LA)
1963—Browns, 20-6 (C)
1965—Rams, 42-7 (LA)
1968—Rams, 24-6 (C)
1973—Rams, 30-17 (LA)
1977—Rams, 9-0 (C)
1978—Browns, 30-19 (C)
1981—Rams, 27-16 (LA)
1984—Rams, 20-17 (LA)
1987—Rams, 30-17 (C)
1990—Rams, 38-23 (C)
1993—Browns, 42-14 (LA)
1999—Rams, 34-3 (StL)
2003—Rams, 26-20 (C)
2007—Browns, 27-20 (StL)
(RS Pts.—Rams 414, Browns 408)
(PS Pts.—Browns 85, Rams 66)
*Franchise in Los Angeles prior to 1995
**NFL Championship
CLEVELAND vs. SAN DIEGO
RS: Chargers lead series, 14-7-1
1970—Chargers, 27-10 (SD)
1972—Browns, 21-17 (SD)

1973—Tie, 16-16 (C)
1974—Chargers, 36-35 (SD)
1976—Browns, 21-17 (C)
1977—Chargers, 37-14 (SD)
1981—Chargers, 44-14 (C)
1982—Chargers, 30-13 (C)
1983—Browns, 30-24 (SD) OT
1985—Browns, 21-7 (SD)
1986—Browns, 47-17 (C)
1987—Chargers, 27-24 (SD) OT
1990—Chargers, 24-14 (C)
1991—Browns, 30-24 (SD) OT
1992—Chargers, 14-13 (C)
1995—Chargers, 31-13 (SD)
1999—Chargers, 23-10 (SD)
2001—Browns, 20-16 (C)
2003—Chargers, 26-20 (C)
2004—Chargers, 21-0 (C)
2006—Chargers, 32-25 (SD)
2009—Chargers, 30-23 (C)
(RS Pts.—Chargers 540, Browns 434)
CLEVELAND vs. SAN FRANCISCO
RS: Browns lead series, 11-6
1950—Browns, 34-14 (C)
1951—49ers, 24-10 (SF)
1953—Browns, 23-21 (C)
1955—Browns, 38-3 (SF)
1959—49ers, 21-20 (C)
1962—Browns, 13-10 (SF)
1968—Browns, 33-21 (C)
1970—49ers, 34-31 (SF)
1974—Browns, 7-0 (C)
1978—Browns, 24-7 (C)
1981—Browns, 15-12 (SF)
1984—49ers, 41-7 (C)
1987—49ers, 38-24 (SF)
1990—49ers, 20-17 (SF)
1993—Browns, 23-13 (C)
2003—Browns, 13-12 (SF)
2007—Browns, 20-7 (C)
(RS Pts.—Browns 352, 49ers 298)
CLEVELAND vs. SEATTLE
RS: Seahawks lead series, 11-5
1977—Seahawks, 20-19 (S)
1978—Seahawks, 47-24 (S)
1979—Seahawks, 29-24 (C)
1980—Browns, 27-3 (S)
1981—Seahawks, 42-21 (S)
1982—Browns, 21-7 (S)
1983—Seahawks, 24-9 (C)
1984—Seahawks, 33-0 (S)
1985—Seahawks, 31-13 (C)
1988—Seahawks, 16-10 (C)
1989—Browns, 17-7 (S)
1993—Seahawks, 22-5 (S)
1994—Browns, 35-9 (C)
2001—Seahawks, 9-6 (S)
2003—Seahawks, 34-7 (S)
2007—Browns, 33-30 (C) OT
(RS Pts.—Seahawks 363, Browns 271)
CLEVELAND vs. TAMPA BAY
RS: Browns lead series, 5-3
1976—Browns, 24-7 (TB)
1980—Browns, 34-27 (TB)
1983—Browns, 20-0 (C)
1989—Browns, 42-31 (TB)
1995—Browns, 22-6 (C)
2002—Buccaneers 17-3 (TB)
2006—Buccaneers, 22-7 (C)
2010—Buccaneers, 17-14 (TB)
(RS Pts.—Browns 166, Buccaneers 127)

CLEVELAND vs. *TENNESSEE
RS: Browns lead series, 33-27
PS: Titans lead series, 1-0
1970—Browns, 28-14 (C)
　　　Browns, 21-10 (H)
1971—Browns, 31-0 (C)
　　　Browns, 37-24 (H)
1972—Browns, 23-17 (H)
　　　Browns, 20-0 (C)
1973—Browns, 42-13 (C)
　　　Browns, 23-13 (H)
1974—Browns, 20-7 (C)
　　　Oilers, 28-24 (H)
1975—Oilers, 40-10 (C)
　　　Oilers, 21-10 (H)
1976—Browns, 21-7 (H)
　　　Browns, 13-10 (C)
1977—Browns, 24-23 (H)
　　　Oilers, 19-15 (C)
1978—Oilers, 16-13 (C)
　　　Oilers, 14-10 (H)
1979—Oilers, 31-10 (H)
　　　Browns, 14-7 (C)
1980—Oilers, 16-7 (C)
　　　Browns, 17-14 (H)
1981—Oilers, 9-3 (C)
　　　Oilers, 17-13 (H)
1982—Browns, 20-14 (H)
1983—Browns, 25-19 (C) OT
　　　Oilers, 34-27 (H)
1984—Browns, 27-10 (C)
　　　Browns, 27-20 (H)
1985—Browns, 21-6 (H)
　　　Browns, 28-21 (C)
1986—Browns, 23-20 (H)
　　　Browns, 13-10 (C) OT
1987—Oilers, 15-10 (C)
　　　Browns, 40-7 (H)
1988—Oilers, 24-17 (H)
　　　Browns, 28-23 (C)
　　**Oilers, 24-23 (C)
1989—Browns, 28-17 (C)
　　　Browns, 24-20 (H)
1990—Oilers, 35-23 (C)
　　　Oilers, 58-14 (H)
1991—Oilers, 28-24 (H)
　　　Oilers, 17-14 (C)
1992—Browns, 24-14 (H)
　　　Oilers, 17-14 (C)
1993—Oilers, 27-20 (C)
　　　Oilers, 19-17 (H)
1994—Browns, 11-8 (H)
　　　Browns, 34-10 (C)
1995—Browns, 14-7 (H)
　　　Oilers, 37-10 (C)
1999—Titans, 26-9 (T)
　　　Titans, 33-21 (C)
2000—Titans, 24-10 (T)
　　　Titans, 24-0 (C)
2001—Titans, 31-15 (C)
　　　Browns, 41-38 (T)
2002—Browns, 31-28 (T) OT
2005—Browns, 20-14 (C)
2008—Titans, 28-9 (T)
(RS Pts.—Browns 1,182, Titans 1,153)
(PS Pts.—Titans 24, Browns 23)
*Franchise in Houston prior to 1997;
known as Oilers prior to 1999
**AFC First-Round Playoff
CLEVELAND vs. WASHINGTON
RS: Browns lead series, 33-10-1

1950—Browns, 20-14 (C)
　　　Browns, 45-21 (W)
1951—Browns, 45-0 (C)
1952—Browns, 19-15 (C)
　　　Browns, 48-24 (W)
1953—Browns, 30-14 (W)
　　　Browns, 27-3 (C)
1954—Browns, 62-3 (C)
　　　Browns, 34-14 (W)
1955—Redskins, 27-17 (C)
　　　Browns, 24-14 (W)
1956—Redskins, 20-9 (W)
　　　Redskins, 20-17 (C)
1957—Browns, 21-17 (C)
　　　Tie, 30-30 (W)
1958—Browns, 20-10 (W)
　　　Browns, 21-14 (C)
1959—Browns, 34-7 (C)
　　　Browns, 31-17 (W)
1960—Browns, 31-10 (W)
　　　Browns, 27-16 (C)
1961—Browns, 31-7 (C)
　　　Browns, 17-6 (W)
1962—Redskins, 17-16 (C)
　　　Redskins, 17-9 (W)
1963—Browns, 37-14 (C)
　　　Browns, 27-20 (W)
1964—Browns, 27-13 (W)
　　　Browns, 34-24 (C)
1965—Browns, 17-7 (W)
　　　Browns, 24-16 (C)
1966—Browns, 38-14 (W)
　　　Rrowns, 14-3 (C)
1967—Browns, 42-37 (W)
1968—Browns, 24-21 (W)
1969—Browns, 27-23 (C)
1971—Browns, 20-13 (W)
1975—Redskins, 23-7 (C)
1979—Redskins, 13-9 (C)
1985—Redskins, 14-7 (C)
1988—Browns, 17-13 (W)
1991—Redskins, 42-17 (W)
2004—Browns, 17-13 (C)
2008—Redskins, 14-11 (W)
(RS Pts.—Browns 1,101, Redskins 694)

──────────

DALLAS vs. ARIZONA
RS: Cowboys lead series, 55-29-1
PS: Cardinals lead series, 1-0;
See Arizona vs. Dallas
DALLAS vs. ATLANTA
RS: Cowboys lead series, 14-8
PS: Cowboys lead series, 2-0;
See Atlanta vs. Dallas
DALLAS vs. BALTIMORE
RS: Ravens lead series, 3-0;
See Baltimore vs. Dallas
DALLAS vs. BUFFALO
RS: Cowboys lead series, 5-3
PS: Cowboys lead series, 2-0;
See Buffalo vs. Dallas
DALLAS vs. CAROLINA
RS: Cowboys lead series, 8-1
PS: Panthers lead series, 2-0;
See Carolina vs. Dallas
DALLAS vs. CHICAGO
RS: Cowboys lead series, 11-9
PS: Cowboys lead series, 2-0;
See Chicago vs. Dallas
DALLAS vs. CINCINNATI
RS: Cowboys lead series, 6-4;

See Cincinnati vs. Dallas
DALLAS vs. CLEVELAND
RS: Browns lead series, 15-11
PS: Browns lead series, 2-1;
See Cleveland vs. Dallas
DALLAS vs. DENVER
RS: Broncos lead series, 6-4
PS: Cowboys lead series, 1-0
1973—Cowboys, 22-10 (Den)
1977—Cowboys, 14-6 (Dal)
　　　*Cowboys, 27-10 (New Orleans)
1980—Broncos, 41-20 (Den)
1986—Broncos, 29-14 (Den)
1992—Cowboys, 31-27 (Den)
1995—Cowboys, 31-21 (Dal)
1998—Broncos, 42-23 (Den)
2001—Broncos, 26-24 (Dal)
2005—Broncos, 24-21 (Dal) OT
2009—Broncos, 17-10 (Den)
(RS Pts.—Broncos 243, Cowboys 210)
(PS Pts.—Cowboys 27, Broncos 10)
*Super Bowl XII
DALLAS vs. DETROIT
RS: Cowboys lead series, 12-9
PS: Series tied, 1-1
1960—Lions, 23-14 (Det)
1963—Cowboys, 17-14 (Dal)
1968—Cowboys, 59-13 (Dal)
1970—*Cowboys, 5-0 (Dal)
1972—Cowboys, 28-24 (Dal)
1975—Cowboys, 36-10 (Det)
1977—Cowboys, 37-0 (Dal)
1981—Lions, 27-24 (Det)
1985—Lions, 26-21 (Det)
1986—Cowboys, 31-7 (Det)
1987—Lions, 27-17 (Det)
1991—Lions, 34-10 (Det)
　　　*Lions, 38-6 (Det)
1992—Cowboys, 37-3 (Det)
1994—Lions, 20-17 (Dal) OT
2001—Lions, 15-10 (Det)
2002—Lions, 9-7 (Det)
2003—Cowboys, 38-7 (Det)
2004—Cowboys, 31-21 (Dal)
2005—Cowboys, 20-7 (Dal)
2006—Lions, 39-31 (Dal)
2007—Cowboys, 28-27 (Det)
2010—Cowboys, 35-19 (Dal)
(RS Pts.—Cowboys 548, Lions 372)
(PS Pts.—Lions 38, Cowboys 11)
*NFC Divisional Playoff
DALLAS vs. GREEN BAY
RS: Series tied, 12-12
PS: Cowboys lead series, 4-2
1960—Packers, 41-7 (GB)
1964—Packers, 45-21 (D)
1965—Packers, 13-3 (Mil)
1966—*Packers, 34-27 (D)
1967—*Packers, 21-17 (GB)
1968—Packers, 28-17 (D)
1970—Cowboys, 16-3 (D)
1972—Packers, 16-13 (Mil)
1975—Packers, 19-17 (D)
1978—Cowboys, 42-14 (Mil)
1980—Cowboys, 28-7 (Mil)
1982—**Cowboys, 37-26 (D)
1984—Cowboys, 20-6 (D)
1989—Packers, 31-13 (GB)
　　　Packers, 20-10 (D)
1991—Cowboys, 20-17 (Mil)
1993—Cowboys, 36-14 (D)

***Cowboys, 27-17 (D)
1994—Cowboys, 42-31 (D)
  ***Cowboys, 35-9 (D)
1995—Cowboys, 34-24 (D)
  ****Cowboys, 38-27 (D)
1996—Cowboys, 21-6 (D)
1997—Packers, 45-17 (GB)
1999—Cowboys, 27-13 (D)
2004—Packers, 41-20 (GB)
2007—Cowboys, 37-27 (D)
2008—Cowboys, 27-16 (GB)
2009—Packers, 17-7 (GB)
2010—Packers, 45-7 (GB)
(RS Pts.—Packers, 539, Cowboys 502)
(PS Pts.—Cowboys 181, Packers 134)
*NFL Championship
**NFC Second-Round Playoff
***NFC Divisional Playoff
****NFC Championship
DALLAS vs. HOUSTON
RS: Cowboys lead series, 2-1
2002—Texans, 19-10 (H)
2006—Cowboys, 34-6 (D)
2010—Cowboys, 27-13 (H)
(RS Pts.—Cowboys 71, Texans 38)
DALLAS vs. *INDIANAPOLIS
RS: Cowboys lead series, 9-5
PS: Colts lead series, 1-0
1960—Colts, 45-7 (D)
1967—Colts, 23-17 (B)
1969—Cowboys, 27-10 (D)
1970—**Colts, 16-13 (Miami)
1972—Cowboys, 21-0 (B)
1976—Cowboys, 30-27 (D)
1978—Cowboys, 38-0 (D)
1981—Cowboys, 37-13 (B)
1984—Cowboys, 22-3 (D)
1993—Cowboys, 27-3 (I)
1996—Colts, 25-24 (D)
1999—Colts, 34-24 (I)
2002—Colts, 20-3 (I)
2006—Cowboys, 21-14 (D)
2010—Cowboys, 38-35 (I) OT
(RS Pts.—Cowboys 336, Colts 252)
(PS Pts.—Colts 16, Cowboys 13)
*Franchise in Baltimore prior to 1984
**Super Bowl V
DALLAS vs. JACKSONVILLE
RS: Jaguars lead series, 3-2
1997—Cowboys, 26-22 (D)
2000—Jaguars, 23-17 (D) OT
2002—Cowboys, 21-19 (D)
2006—Jaguars, 24-17 (J)
2010—Jaguars, 35-17 (D)
(RS Pts.—Jaguars 123, Cowboys 98)
DALLAS vs. KANSAS CITY
RS: Cowboys lead series, 6-3
1970—Cowboys, 27-16 (KC)
1975—Chiefs, 34-31 (D)
1983—Cowboys, 41-21 (D)
1989—Chiefs, 36-28 (KC)
1992—Cowboys, 17-10 (D)
1995—Cowboys, 24-12 (D)
1998—Chiefs, 20-17 (KC)
2005—Cowboys, 31-28 (D)
2009—Cowboys, 26-20 (KC) OT
(RS Pts.—Cowboys 242, Chiefs 197)
DALLAS vs. MIAMI
RS: Dolphins lead series, 7-4
PS: Cowboys lead series, 1-0
1971—*Cowboys, 24-3 (New Orleans)

1973—Dolphins, 14-7 (D)
1978—Dolphins, 23-16 (M)
1981—Cowboys, 28-27 (D)
1984—Dolphins, 28-21 (M)
1987—Dolphins, 20-14 (D)
1989—Dolphins, 17-14 (D)
1993—Dolphins, 16-14 (D)
1996—Cowboys, 29-10 (M)
1999—Cowboys, 20-0 (D)
2003—Dolphins, 40-21 (D)
2007—Cowboys, 37-20 (M)
(RS Pts.—Cowboys 221, Dolphins 215)
(PS Pts.—Cowboys 24, Dolphins 3)
*Super Bowl VI
DALLAS vs. MINNESOTA
RS: Vikings lead series, 11-10
PS: Cowboys lead series, 4-3
1961—Cowboys, 21-7 (D)
  Cowboys, 28-0 (M)
1966—Cowboys, 28-17 (D)
1968—Cowboys, 20-7 (M)
1970—Vikings, 54-13 (M)
1971—*Cowboys, 20-12 (M)
1973—**Vikings, 27-10 (D)
1974—Vikings, 23-21 (D)
1975—*Cowboys, 17-14 (M)
1977—Cowboys, 16-10 (M) OT
  **Cowboys, 23-6 (D)
1978—Vikings, 21-10 (D)
1979—Cowboys, 36-20 (M)
1982—Vikings, 31-27 (M)
1983—Cowboys, 37-24 (M)
1987—Vikings, 44-38 (D) OT
1988—Vikings, 43-3 (D)
1993—Cowboys, 37-20 (M)
1995—Cowboys, 23-17 (M) OT
1996—***Cowboys, 40-15 (D)
1998—Vikings, 46-36 (D)
1999—Vikings, 27-17 (M)
  ***Vikings, 27-10 (M)
2000—Cowboys, 27-15 (D)
2004—Vikings, 35-17 (M)
2007—Cowboys, 24-14 (D)
2009—*Vikings, 34-3 (M)
2010—Vikings, 24-21 (M)
(RS Pts.—Vikings 511, Cowboys 488)
(PS Pts.—Cowboys 135, Vikings 123)
*NFC Divisional Playoff
**NFC Championship
***NFC First-Round Playoff
DALLAS vs. NEW ENGLAND
RS: Cowboys lead series, 7-3
1971—Cowboys, 44-21 (D)
1975—Cowboys, 34-31 (NE)
1978—Cowboys, 17-10 (D)
1981—Cowboys, 35-21 (NE)
1984—Cowboys, 20-17 (D)
1987—Cowboys, 23-17 (NE) OT
1996—Cowboys, 12-6 (D)
1999—Patriots, 13-6 (NE)
2003—Patriots, 12-0 (NE)
2007—Patriots, 48-27 (D)
(RS Pts.—Cowboys 218, Patriots 196)
DALLAS vs. NEW ORLEANS
RS: Cowboys lead series, 15-9
1967—Cowboys, 14-10 (D)
  Cowboys, 27-10 (NO)
1968—Cowboys, 17-3 (NO)
1969—Cowboys, 21-17 (NO)
  Cowboys, 33-17 (D)
1971—Saints, 24-14 (NO)

1973—Cowboys, 40-3 (D)
1976—Cowboys, 24-6 (NO)
1978—Cowboys, 27-7 (D)
1982—Cowboys, 21-7 (D)
1983—Cowboys, 21-20 (D)
1984—Cowboys, 30-27 (D) OT
1988—Saints, 20-17 (NO)
1989—Saints, 28-0 (NO)
1990—Cowboys, 17-13 (D)
1991—Cowboys, 23-14 (D)
1994—Cowboys, 24-16 (NO)
1998—Saints, 22-3 (NO)
1999—Saints, 31-24 (NO)
2003—Saints, 13-7 (NO)
2004—Saints, 27-13 (D)
2006—Saints, 42-17 (D)
2009—Cowboys, 24-17 (NO)
2010—Saints, 30-27 (D)
(RS Pts.—Cowboys 485, Saints 424)
DALLAS vs. N.Y. GIANTS
RS: Cowboys lead series, 56-39-2
PS: Giants lead series, 1-0
1960—Tie, 31-31 (NY)
1961—Giants, 31-10 (D)
  Cowboys, 17-16 (NY)
1962—Giants, 41-10 (D)
  Giants, 41-31 (NY)
1963—Giants, 37-21 (D)
  Giants, 34-27 (D)
1964—Tie, 13-13 (D)
  Cowboys, 31-21 (NY)
1965—Cowboys, 31-2 (D)
  Cowboys, 38-20 (NY)
1966—Cowboys, 52-7 (D)
  Cowboys, 17-7 (NY)
1967—Cowboys, 38-24 (D)
1968—Giants, 27-21 (D)
  Cowboys, 28-10 (NY)
1969—Cowboys, 25-3 (D)
1970—Cowboys, 28-10 (D)
  Giants, 23-20 (NY)
1971—Cowboys, 20-13 (D)
  Cowboys, 42-14 (NY)
1972—Cowboys, 23-14 (NY)
  Giants, 23-3 (D)
1973—Cowboys, 45-28 (D)
  Cowboys, 23-10 (New Haven)
1974—Giants, 14-6 (D)
  Cowboys, 21-7 (New Haven)
1975—Cowboys, 13-7 (NY)
  Cowboys, 14-3 (D)
1976—Cowboys, 24-14 (NY)
  Cowboys, 9-3 (D)
1977—Cowboys, 41-21 (D)
  Cowboys, 24-10 (NY)
1978—Cowboys, 34-24 (NY)
  Cowboys, 24-3 (D)
1979—Cowboys, 16-14 (NY)
  Cowboys, 28-7 (D)
1980—Cowboys, 24-3 (D)
  Giants, 38-35 (NY)
1981—Cowboys, 18-10 (D)
  Giants, 13-10 (NY) OT
1983—Cowboys, 28-13 (D)
  Cowboys, 38-20 (NY)
1984—Giants, 28-7 (NY)
  Giants, 19-7 (D)
1985—Cowboys, 30-29 (NY)
  Cowboys, 28-21 (D)
1986—Cowboys, 31-28 (D)
  Giants, 17-14 (NY)

1987—Cowboys, 16-14 (NY)
   Cowboys, 33-24 (D)
1988—Giants, 12-10 (D)
   Giants, 29-21 (NY)
1989—Giants, 30-13 (D)
   Giants, 15-0 (NY)
1990—Giants, 28-7 (D)
   Giants, 31-17 (NY)
1991—Cowboys, 21-16 (D)
   Giants, 22-9 (NY)
1992—Cowboys, 34-28 (NY)
   Cowboys, 30-3 (D)
1993—Cowboys, 31-9 (D)
   Cowboys, 16-13 (NY) OT
1994—Cowboys, 38-10 (D)
   Giants, 15-10 (NY)
1995—Giants, 35-0 (NY)
   Cowboys, 21-20 (D)
1996—Cowboys, 27-0 (D)
   Giants, 20-6 (NY)
1997—Giants, 20-17 (NY)
   Giants, 20-7 (D)
1998—Cowboys, 31-7 (NY)
   Cowboys, 16-6 (D)
1999—Giants, 13-10 (NY)
   Cowboys, 26-18 (D)
2000—Giants, 19-14 (NY)
   Giants, 17-13 (D)
2001—Giants, 27-24 (NY) OT
   Cowboys, 20-13 (D)
2002—Giants, 21-17 (D)
   Giants, 37-7 (NY)
2003—Cowboys, 35-32 (NY) OT
   Cowboys, 19-3 (D)
2004—Giants, 26-10 (D)
   Giants, 28-24 (NY)
2005—Cowboys, 16-13 (D) OT
   Giants, 17-10 (NY)
2006—Giants, 36-22 (D)
   Cowboys, 23-20 (NY)
2007—Cowboys, 45-35 (D)
   Cowboys, 31-20 (NY)
   *Giants, 21-17 (D)
2008—Giants, 35-14 (NY)
   Cowboys, 20-8 (D)
2009—Giants, 33-31 (D)
   Giants, 31-24 (NY)
2010—Giants, 41-35 (D)
   Cowboys, 33-20 (NY)
(RS Pts.—Cowboys 2,158, Giants 1,821)
(PS Pts.—Giants 21, Cowboys 17)
*NFC Divisional Playoff

DALLAS vs. N.Y. JETS
RS: Cowboys lead series, 7-2
1971—Cowboys, 52-10 (D)
1975—Cowboys, 31-21 (NY)
1978—Cowboys, 30-7 (NY)
1987—Cowboys, 38-24 (NY)
1990—Jets, 24-9 (NY)
1993—Cowboys, 28-7 (NY)
1999—Jets, 22-21 (D)
2003—Cowboys, 17-6 (NY)
2007—Cowboys, 34-3 (D)
(RS Pts.—Cowboys 260, Jets 124)

DALLAS vs. *OAKLAND
RS: Raiders lead series, 6-4
1974—Raiders, 27-23 (O)
1980—Cowboys, 19-13 (O)
1983—Raiders, 40-38 (D)
1986—Raiders, 17-13 (D)
1992—Cowboys, 28-13 (LA)

1995—Cowboys, 34-21 (O)
1998—Raiders, 13-12 (D)
2001—Raiders, 28-21 (O)
2005—Raiders, 19-13 (O)
2009—Cowboys, 24-7 (D)
(RS Pts.—Cowboys 225, Raiders 198)
*Franchise in Los Angeles from 1982-1994

DALLAS vs. PHILADELPHIA
RS: Cowboys lead series, 56-44
PS: Cowboys lead series, 3-1
1960—Eagles, 27-25 (D)
1961—Eagles, 43-7 (D)
   Eagles, 35-13 (P)
1962—Cowboys, 41-19 (D)
   Eagles, 28-14 (P)
1963—Eagles, 24-21 (P)
   Cowboys, 27-20 (D)
1964—Eagles, 17-14 (D)
   Eagles, 24-14 (P)
1965—Eagles, 35-24 (D)
   Cowboys, 21-19 (P)
1966—Cowboys, 56-7 (D)
   Eagles, 24-23 (P)
1967—Eagles, 21-14 (P)
   Cowboys, 38-17 (D)
1968—Cowboys, 45-13 (D)
   Cowboys, 34-14 (D)
1969—Cowboys, 38-7 (P)
   Cowboys, 49-14 (D)
1970—Cowboys, 17-7 (P)
   Cowboys, 21-17 (D)
1971—Cowboys, 42-7 (P)
   Cowboys, 20-7 (D)
1972—Cowboys, 28-6 (D)
   Cowboys, 28-7 (P)
1973—Eagles, 30-16 (P)
   Cowboys, 31-10 (D)
1974—Eagles, 13-10 (P)
   Cowboys, 31-24 (D)
1975—Cowboys, 20-17 (P)
   Cowboys, 27-17 (D)
1976—Cowboys, 27-7 (D)
   Cowboys, 26-7 (P)
1977—Cowboys, 16-10 (P)
   Cowboys, 24-14 (D)
1978—Cowboys, 14-7 (D)
   Cowboys, 31-13 (P)
1979—Eagles, 31-21 (D)
   Cowboys, 24-17 (P)
1980—Eagles, 17-10 (P)
   Cowboys, 35-27 (D)
   *Eagles, 20-7 (P)
1981—Cowboys, 17-14 (P)
   Cowboys, 21-10 (D)
1982—Eagles, 24-20 (D)
1983—Cowboys, 37-7 (D)
   Cowboys, 27-20 (P)
1984—Cowboys, 23-17 (D)
   Cowboys, 26-10 (D)
1985—Eagles, 16-14 (P)
   Cowboys, 34-17 (D)
1986—Cowboys, 17-14 (P)
   Eagles, 23-21 (D)
1987—Cowboys, 41-22 (D)
   Eagles, 37-20 (P)
1988—Eagles, 24-23 (P)
   Eagles, 23-7 (D)
1989—Eagles, 27-0 (D)
   Eagles, 20-10 (P)
1990—Eagles, 21-20 (D)
   Eagles, 17-3 (P)

1991—Eagles, 24-0 (D)
   Cowboys, 25-13 (P)
1992—Eagles, 31-7 (P)
   Cowboys, 20-10 (D)
   **Cowboys, 34-10 (D)
1993—Cowboys, 23-10 (P)
   Cowboys, 23-17 (D)
1994—Cowboys, 24-13 (D)
   Cowboys, 31-19 (P)
1995—Cowboys, 34-12 (D)
   Eagles, 20-17 (P)
   **Cowboys, 30-11 (D)
1996—Cowboys, 23-19 (P)
   Eagles, 31-21 (D)
1997—Cowboys, 21-20 (D)
   Eagles, 13-12 (P)
1998—Cowboys, 34-0 (P)
   Cowboys, 13-9 (D)
1999—Eagles, 13-10 (P)
   Cowboys, 20-10 (D)
2000—Eagles, 41-14 (D)
   Eagles, 16-13 (P) OT
2001—Eagles, 40-18 (P)
   Eagles, 36-3 (D)
2002—Eagles, 44-13 (P)
   Eagles, 27-3 (D)
2003—Cowboys, 23-21 (D)
   Eagles, 36-10 (P)
2004—Eagles, 49-21 (D)
   Eagles, 12-7 (P)
2005—Cowboys, 33-10 (D)
   Cowboys, 21-20 (P)
2006—Cowboys, 38-24 (P)
   Eagles, 23-7 (D)
2007—Cowboys, 38-17 (P)
   Eagles, 10-6 (D)
2008—Cowboys, 41-37 (D)
   Eagles, 44-6 (P)
2009—Cowboys, 20-16 (P)
   Cowboys, 24-0 (D)
   ***Cowboys, 34-14 (D)
2010—Eagles, 30-27 (D)
   Cowboys, 14-13 (P)
(RS Pts.—Cowboys 2,162, Eagles 1,947)
(PS Pts.—Cowboys 105, Eagles 55)
*NFC Championship
**NFC Divisional Playoff
***NFC First-Round Playoff

DALLAS vs. PITTSBURGH
RS: Cowboys lead series, 14-13
PS: Steelers lead series, 2-1
1960—Steelers, 35-28 (D)
1961—Cowboys, 27-24 (D)
   Steelers, 37-7 (P)
1962—Steelers, 30-28 (D)
   Cowboys, 42-27 (P)
1963—Steelers, 27-21 (P)
   Steelers, 24-19 (D)
1964—Steelers, 23-17 (P)
   Cowboys, 17-14 (D)
1965—Steelers, 22-13 (P)
   Cowboys, 24-17 (D)
1966—Cowboys, 52-21 (D)
   Cowboys, 20-7 (P)
1967—Cowboys, 24-21 (D)
1968—Cowboys, 28-7 (D)
1969—Cowboys, 10-7 (P)
1972—Cowboys, 17-13 (D)
1975—*Steelers, 21-17 (Miami)
1977—Steelers, 28-13 (P)
1978—**Steelers, 35-31 (Miami)

1979—Steelers, 14-3 (P)
1982—Steelers, 36-28 (D)
1985—Cowboys, 27-13 (D)
1988—Steelers, 24-21 (P)
1991—Cowboys, 20-10 (D)
1994—Cowboys, 26-9 (P)
1995—***Cowboys, 27-17 (Tempe)
1997—Cowboys, 37-7 (P)
2004—Steelers, 24-20 (D)
2008—Steelers, 20-13 (P)
(RS Pts.—Cowboys 602, Steelers 541)
(PS Pts.—Cowboys 75, Steelers 73)
*Super Bowl X
**Super Bowl XIII
***Super Bowl XXX

DALLAS vs. *ST. LOUIS
RS: Rams lead series, 11-10
PS: Series tied, 4-4
1960—Rams, 38-13 (D)
1962—Cowboys, 27-17 (LA)
1967—Rams, 35-13 (D)
1969—Rams, 24-23 (LA)
1971—Cowboys, 28-21 (D)
1973—Rams, 37-31 (LA)
        **Cowboys, 27-16 (D)
1975—Cowboys, 18-7 (D)
        ***Cowboys, 37-7 (LA)
1976—**Rams, 14-12 (D)
1978—Rams, 27-14 (LA)
        ***Cowboys, 28-0 (LA)
1979—Cowboys, 30-6 (D)
        **Rams, 21-19 (D)
1980—Rams, 38-14 (LA)
        ****Cowboys, 34-13 (D)
1981—Cowboys, 29-17 (D)
1983—****Rams, 24-17 (D)
1984—Cowboys, 20-13 (LA)
1985—**Rams, 20-0 (LA)
1986—Rams, 29-10 (LA)
1987—Cowboys, 29-21 (LA)
1989—Rams, 35-31 (D)
1990—Cowboys, 24-21 (LA)
1992—Cowboys, 27-23 (D)
2002—Cowboys, 13-10 (StL)
2005—Rams, 20-10 (D)
2007—Cowboys, 35-7 (D)
2008—Rams, 34-14 (StL)
(RS Pts.—Rams 484, Cowboys 449)
(PS Pts.—Cowboys 174, Rams 115)
*Franchise in Los Angeles prior to 1995
**NFC Divisional Playoff
***NFC Championship
****NFC First-Round Playoff

DALLAS vs. SAN DIEGO
RS: Cowboys lead series, 6-3
1972—Cowboys, 34-28 (SD)
1980—Cowboys, 42-31 (D)
1983—Chargers, 24-23 (SD)
1986—Cowboys, 24-21 (SD)
1990—Cowboys, 17-14 (D)
1995—Cowboys, 23-9 (SD)
2001—Chargers, 32-21 (D)
2005—Cowboys, 28-24 (SD)
2009—Chargers, 20-17 (D)
(RS Pts.—Cowboys 229, Chargers 203)

DALLAS vs. SAN FRANCISCO
RS: 49ers lead series, 14-10-1
PS: Cowboys lead series, 5-2
1960—49ers, 26-14 (D)
1963—49ers, 31-24 (SF)
1965—Cowboys, 39-31 (D)

1967—49ers, 24-16 (SF)
1969—Tie, 24-24 (D)
1970—*Cowboys, 17-10 (SF)
1971—*Cowboys, 14-3 (D)
1972—49ers, 31-10 (D)
        **Cowboys, 30-28 (SF)
1974—Cowboys, 20-14 (D)
1977—Cowboys, 42-35 (SF)
1979—Cowboys, 21-13 (SF)
1980—Cowboys, 59-14 (D)
1981—49ers, 45-14 (SF)
        *49ers, 28-27 (SF)
1983—49ers, 42-17 (D)
1985—49ers, 31-16 (SF)
1989—49ers, 31-14 (D)
1990—49ers, 24-6 (D)
1992—*Cowboys, 30-20 (SF)
1993—Cowboys, 26-17 (D)
        *Cowboys, 38-21 (D)
1994—49ers, 21-14 (SF)
        *49ers, 38-28 (SF)
1995—49ers, 38-20 (D)
1996—Cowboys, 20-17 (SF) OT
1997—49ers, 17-10 (SF)
2000—49ers, 41-24 (D)
2001—Cowboys, 27-21 (D)
2002—49ers, 31-27 (D)
2005—Cowboys, 34-31 (SF)
2008—Cowboys, 35-22 (D)
(RS Pts.—49ers 672, Cowboys 573)
(PS Pts.—Cowboys 184, 49ers 148)
*NFC Championship
**NFC Divisional Playoff

DALLAS vs. SEATTLE
RS: Cowboys lead series, 8-4
PS: Seahawks lead series, 1-0
1976—Cowboys, 28-13 (S)
1980—Cowboys, 51-7 (D)
1983—Cowboys, 35-10 (S)
1986—Seahawks, 31-14 (D)
1992—Cowboys, 27-0 (S)
1998—Cowboys, 30-22 (D)
2001—Seahawks, 29-3 (S)
2002—Seahawks, 17-14 (D)
2004—Cowboys, 43-39 (S)
2005—Seahawks, 13-10 (S)
2006—*Seahawks, 21-20 (S)
2008—Cowboys, 34-9 (D)
2009—Cowboys, 38-17 (D)
(RS Pts.—Cowboys 327, Seahawks 207)
(PS Pts.—Seahawks 21, Cowboys 20)
*NFC First-Round Playoff

DALLAS vs. TAMPA BAY
RS: Cowboys lead series, 9-3
PS: Cowboys lead series, 2-0
1977—Cowboys, 23-7 (D)
1980—Cowboys, 28-17 (D)
1981—*Cowboys, 38-0 (D)
1982—Cowboys, 14-9 (D)
        **Cowboys, 30-17 (D)
1983—Cowboys, 27-24 (D) OT
1990—Cowboys, 14-10 (D)
        Cowboys, 17-13 (TB)
2000—Buccaneers, 27-7 (TB)
2001—Buccaneers, 10-6 (D)
2003—Buccaneers, 16-0 (TB)
2006—Cowboys, 38-10 (D)
2008—Cowboys, 13-9 (D)
2009—Cowboys, 34-21 (TB)
(RS Pts.—Cowboys 221, Buccaneers 173)
(PS Pts.—Cowboys 68, Buccaneers 17)

*NFC Divisional Playoff
**NFC First-Round Playoff
DALLAS vs. *TENNESSEE
RS: Cowboys lead series, 7-6
1970—Cowboys, 52-10 (D)
1974—Cowboys, 10-0 (H)
1979—Oilers, 30-24 (D)
1982—Cowboys, 37-7 (H)
1985—Cowboys, 17-10 (H)
1988—Oilers, 25-17 (D)
1991—Oilers, 26-23 (H) OT
1994—Cowboys, 20-17 (D)
1997—Oilers, 27-14 (D)
2000—Titans, 31-0 (T)
2002—Cowboys, 21-13 (D)
2006—Cowboys, 45-14 (T)
2010—Titans, 34-27 (D)
(RS Pts.—Cowboys 307, Titans 244)
*Franchise in Houston prior to 1997;
known as Oilers prior to 1999

DALLAS vs. WASHINGTON
RS: Cowboys lead series, 60-38-2
PS: Redskins lead series, 2-0
1960—Redskins, 26-14 (W)
1961—Tie, 28-28 (D)
        Redskins, 34-24 (W)
1962—Tie, 35-35 (D)
        Cowboys, 38-10 (W)
1963—Redskins, 21-17 (W)
        Cowboys, 35-20 (D)
1964—Cowboys, 24-18 (D)
        Redskins, 28-16 (W)
1965—Cowboys, 27-7 (D)
        Redskins, 34-31 (W)
1966—Cowboys, 31-30 (W)
        Redskins, 34-31 (D)
1967—Cowboys, 17-14 (W)
        Redskins, 27-20 (D)
1968—Cowboys, 44-24 (W)
        Cowboys, 29-20 (D)
1969—Cowboys, 41-28 (W)
        Cowboys, 20-10 (D)
1970—Cowboys, 45-21 (W)
        Cowboys, 34-0 (D)
1971—Redskins, 20-16 (D)
        Cowboys, 13-0 (W)
1972—Redskins, 24-20 (D)
        Cowboys, 34-24 (D)
        *Redskins, 26-3 (W)
1973—Cowboys, 14-7 (W)
        Cowboys, 27-7 (D)
1974—Redskins, 28-21 (W)
        Cowboys, 24-23 (D)
1975—Redskins, 30-24 (W) OT
        Cowboys, 31-10 (D)
1976—Cowboys, 20-7 (W)
        Redskins, 27-14 (D)
1977—Cowboys, 34-16 (D)
        Cowboys, 14-7 (W)
1978—Redskins, 9-5 (W)
        Cowboys, 37-10 (D)
1979—Redskins, 34-20 (W)
        Cowboys, 35-34 (D)
1980—Cowboys, 17-3 (W)
        Cowboys, 14-10 (D)
1981—Cowboys, 26-10 (W)
        Cowboys, 24-10 (D)
1982—Cowboys, 24-10 (W)
        *Redskins, 31-17 (W)
1983—Cowboys, 31-30 (W)
        Redskins, 31-10 (D)

1984—Redskins, 34-14 (W)
    Redskins, 30-28 (D)
1985—Cowboys, 44-14 (D)
    Cowboys, 13-7 (W)
1986—Cowboys, 30-6 (D)
    Redskins, 41-14 (W)
1987—Redskins, 13-7 (D)
    Redskins, 24-20 (W)
1988—Redskins, 35-17 (D)
    Cowboys, 24-17 (W)
1989—Redskins, 30-7 (D)
    Cowboys, 13-3 (W)
1990—Redskins, 19-15 (W)
    Cowboys, 27-17 (D)
1991—Redskins, 33-31 (D)
    Cowboys, 24-21 (W)
1992—Cowboys, 23-10 (D)
    Redskins, 20-17 (W)
1993—Redskins, 35-16 (W)
    Cowboys, 38-3 (D)
1994—Cowboys, 34-7 (W)
    Cowboys, 31-7 (D)
1995—Redskins, 27-23 (W)
    Redskins, 24-17 (D)
1996—Cowboys, 21-10 (D)
    Redskins, 37-10 (W)
1997—Redskins, 21-16 (W)
    Cowboys, 17-14 (D)
1998—Cowboys, 31-10 (W)
    Cowboys, 23-7 (D)
1999—Cowboys, 41-35 (W) OT
    Cowboys, 38-20 (D)
2000—Cowboys, 27-21 (W)
    Cowboys, 32-13 (D)
2001—Cowboys, 9-7 (D)
    Cowboys, 20-14 (W)
2002—Cowboys, 27-20 (D)
    Redskins, 20-14 (W)
2003—Cowboys, 21-14 (D)
    Cowboys, 27-0 (W)
2004—Cowboys, 21-18 (W)
    Cowboys, 13-10 (D)
2005—Redskins, 14-13 (W)
    Redskins, 35-7 (W)
2006—Cowboys, 27-10 (D)
    Redskins, 22-19 (W)
2007 Cowboys, 28-23 (D)
    Redskins, 27-6 (W)
2008—Redskins, 26-24 (D)
    Cowboys, 14-10 (W)
2009—Cowboys, 7-6 (D)
    Cowboys, 17-0 (W)
2010—Redskins, 13-7 (W)
    Cowboys, 33-30 (D)
(RS Pts.—Cowboys 2,280, Redskins 1,881)
(PS Pts.—Redskins 57, Cowboys 20)
*NFC Championship

DENVER vs. ARIZONA
RS: Broncos lead series, 7-1-1;
See Arizona vs. Denver
DENVER vs. ATLANTA
RS: Broncos lead series, 8-4
PS: Broncos lead series, 1-0;
See Atlanta vs. Denver
DENVER vs. BALTIMORE
RS: Ravens lead series, 5-3
PS: Ravens lead series, 1-0;
See Baltimore vs. Denver
DENVER vs. BUFFALO
RS: Bills lead series, 18-15-1

PS: Bills lead series, 1-0;
See Buffalo vs. Denver
DENVER vs. CAROLINA
RS: Broncos lead series, 2-1;
See Carolina vs. Denver
DENVER vs. CHICAGO
RS: Bears lead series, 7-6;
See Chicago vs. Denver
DENVER vs. CINCINNATI
RS: Broncos lead series, 17-8;
See Cincinnati vs. Denver
DENVER vs. CLEVELAND
RS: Broncos lead series, 18-5
PS: Broncos lead series, 3-0;
See Cleveland vs. Denver
DENVER vs. DALLAS
RS: Broncos lead series, 6-4
PS: Cowboys lead series, 1-0;
See Dallas vs. Denver
DENVER vs. DETROIT
RS: Broncos lead series, 6-4
1971—Lions, 24-20 (Den)
1974—Broncos, 31-27 (Det)
1978—Lions, 17-14 (Det)
1981—Broncos, 27-21 (Den)
1984—Broncos, 28-7 (Det)
1987—Broncos, 34-0 (Den)
1990—Lions, 40-27 (Det)
1999—Broncos, 17-7 (Det)
2003—Broncos, 20-16 (Den)
2007—Lions, 44-7 (Det)
(RS Pts.—Broncos 225, Lions 203)
DENVER vs. GREEN BAY
RS: Series tied, 5-5-1
PS: Broncos lead series, 1-0
1971—Packers, 34-13 (Mil)
1975—Broncos, 23-13 (D)
1978—Broncos, 16-3 (D)
1984—Broncos, 17-14 (D)
1987—Tie, 17-17 (Mil) OT
1990—Broncos, 22-13 (D)
1993—Packers, 30-27 (GB)
1996—Packers, 41-6 (GB)
1997—*Broncos, 31-24 (San Diego)
1999—Broncos, 31-10 (D)
2003—Packers, 31-3 (GB)
2007—Packers, 19-13 (D) OT
(RS Pts.—Packers 225, Broncos 188)
(PS Pts.—Broncos 31, Packers 24)
*Super Bowl XXXII
DENVER vs. HOUSTON
RS: Broncos lead series, 2-1
2004—Broncos, 31-13 (D)
2007—Texans, 31-13 (H)
2010—Broncos, 24-23 (D)
(RS Pts.—Broncos 68, Texans 67)
DENVER vs. *INDIANAPOLIS
RS: Broncos lead series, 11-8
PS: Colts lead series, 2-0
1974—Broncos, 17-6 (B)
1977—Broncos, 27-13 (D)
1978—Colts, 7-6 (B)
1981—Broncos, 28-10 (D)
1983—Broncos, 17-10 (B)
    Broncos, 21-19 (D)
1985—Broncos, 15-10 (I)
1988—Colts, 55-23 (I)
1989—Broncos, 14-3 (D)
1990—Broncos, 27-17 (I)
1993—Broncos, 35-13 (D)
2001—Colts, 29-10 (I)

2002—Colts, 23-20 (D) OT
2003—Broncos, 31-17 (I)
    **Colts, 41-10 (I)
2004—Broncos, 33-14 (D)
    **Colts, 49-24 (I)
2006—Colts, 34-31 (D)
2007—Colts, 38-20 (I)
2009—Colts, 28-16 (I)
2010—Colts, 27-13 (D)
(RS Pts.—Broncos 404, Colts 373)
(PS Pts.—Colts 90, Broncos 34)
*Franchise in Baltimore prior to 1984
**AFC First-Round Playoff
DENVER vs. JACKSONVILLE
RS: Jaguars lead series, 5-3
PS: Series tied, 1-1
1995—Broncos, 31-23 (D)
1996—*Jaguars, 30-27 (D)
1997—**Broncos, 42-17 (D)
1998—Broncos, 37-24 (D)
1999—Jaguars, 27-24 (J)
2004—Jaguars, 7-6 (J)
2005—Broncos, 20-7 (J)
2007—Jaguars, 23-14 (D)
2008—Jaguars, 24-17 (D)
2010—Jaguars, 24-17 (J)
(RS Pts.—Broncos 166, Jaguars 159)
(PS Pts.—Broncos 69, Jaguars 47)
*AFC Divisional Playoff
**AFC First-Round Playoff
DENVER vs. *KANSAS CITY
RS: Chiefs lead series, 55-46
PS: Broncos lead series, 1-0
1960—Texans, 17-14 (D)
    Texans, 34-7 (Dal)
1961—Texans, 19-12 (D)
    Texans, 49-21 (Dal)
1962—Texans, 24-3 (D)
    Texans, 17-10 (Dal)
1963—Chiefs, 59-7 (D)
    Chiefs, 52-21 (KC)
1964—Broncos, 33-27 (D)
    Chiefs, 49-39 (KC)
1965—Chiefs, 31-23 (D)
    Chiefs, 45-35 (KC)
1966—Chiefs, 37-10 (KC)
    Chiefs, 56-10 (D)
1967—Chiefs, 52-9 (KC)
    Chiefs, 38-24 (D)
1968—Chiefs, 34-2 (KC)
    Chiefs, 30-7 (D)
1969—Chiefs, 26-13 (D)
    Chiefs, 31-17 (KC)
1970—Broncos, 26-13 (D)
    Chiefs, 16-0 (KC)
1971—Broncos, 16-3 (D)
    Chiefs, 28-10 (KC)
1972—Chiefs, 45-24 (D)
    Chiefs, 24-21 (KC)
1973—Chiefs, 16-14 (KC)
    Broncos, 14-10 (D)
1974—Broncos, 17-14 (KC)
    Chiefs, 42-34 (D)
1975—Broncos, 37-33 (D)
    Chiefs, 26-13 (KC)
1976—Broncos, 35-26 (KC)
    Broncos, 17-16 (D)
1977—Broncos, 23-7 (D)
    Chiefs, 14-7 (KC)
1978—Broncos, 23-17 (KC) OT
    Broncos, 24-3 (D)

1979—Broncos, 24-10 (KC)
    Broncos, 20-3 (D)
1980—Chiefs, 23-17 (D)
    Chiefs, 31-14 (KC)
1981—Chiefs, 28-14 (KC)
    Broncos, 16-13 (D)
1982—Chiefs, 37-16 (D)
1983—Broncos, 27-24 (D)
    Chiefs, 48-17 (KC)
1984—Broncos, 21-0 (D)
    Chiefs, 16-13 (KC)
1985—Broncos, 30-10 (KC)
    Broncos, 14-13 (D)
1986—Broncos, 38-17 (D)
    Chiefs, 37-10 (KC)
1987—Broncos, 26-17 (KC)
    Broncos, 20-17 (D)
1988—Chiefs, 20-13 (KC)
    Broncos, 17-11 (D)
1989—Broncos, 34-20 (D)
    Broncos, 16-13 (KC)
1990—Broncos, 24-23 (D)
    Chiefs, 31-20 (KC)
1991—Broncos, 19-16 (D)
    Broncos, 24-20 (KC)
1992—Broncos, 20-19 (D)
    Chiefs, 42-20 (KC)
1993—Chiefs, 15-7 (KC)
    Broncos, 27-21 (D)
1994—Chiefs, 31-28 (D)
    Broncos, 20-17 (KC) OT
1995—Chiefs, 21-7 (D)
    Chiefs, 20-17 (KC)
1996—Chiefs, 17-14 (KC)
    Broncos, 34-7 (D)
1997—Broncos, 19-3 (D)
    Chiefs, 24-22 (KC)
    **Broncos, 14-10 (KC)
1998—Broncos, 30-7 (KC)
    Broncos, 35-31 (D)
1999—Chiefs, 26-10 (KC)
    Chiefs, 16-10 (D)
2000—Chiefs, 23-22 (D)
    Chiefs, 20-7 (KC)
2001—Broncos, 20-6 (D)
    Chiefs, 26-23 (KC) OT
2002—Broncos, 37-34 (KC) OT
    Broncos, 31-24 (D)
2003—Chiefs, 24-23 (KC)
    Broncos, 45-27 (D)
2004—Broncos, 34-24 (D)
    Chiefs, 45-17 (KC)
2005—Broncos, 30-10 (D)
    Chiefs, 31-27 (KC)
2006—Broncos, 9-6 (D) OT
    Chiefs, 19-10 (KC)
2007—Broncos, 27-11 (KC)
    Broncos, 41-7 (D)
2008—Chiefs, 33-19 (KC)
    Broncos, 24-17 (D)
2009—Broncos, 44-13 (KC)
    Chiefs, 44-24 (D)
2010—Broncos, 49-29 (D)
    Chiefs, 10-6 (KC)
(RS Pts.—Chiefs 2,384, Broncos 2,059)
(PS Pts.—Broncos 14, Chiefs 10)
*Franchise in Dallas prior to 1963 and known as Texans
**AFC Divisional Playoff

DENVER vs. MIAMI
RS: Dolphins lead series, 11-3-1

PS: Broncos lead series, 1-0
1966—Dolphins, 24-7 (M)
    Broncos, 17-7 (D)
1967—Dolphins, 35-21 (M)
1968—Broncos, 21-14 (D)
1969—Dolphins, 27-24 (M)
1971—Tie, 10-10 (D)
1975—Dolphins, 14-13 (M)
1985—Dolphins, 30-26 (D)
1998—Dolphins, 31-21 (M)
    *Broncos, 38-3 (D)
1999—Dolphins, 38-21 (D)
2001—Dolphins, 21-10 (M)
2002—Dolphins, 24-22 (D)
2004—Broncos, 20-17 (D)
2005—Dolphins, 34-10 (M)
2008—Dolphins, 26-17 (D)
(RS Pts.—Dolphins 352, Broncos 260)
(PS Pts.—Broncos 38, Dolphins 3)
*AFC Divisional Playoff

DENVER vs. MINNESOTA
RS: Vikings lead series, 7-5
1972—Vikings, 23-20 (D)
1978—Vikings, 12-9 (M) OT
1981—Broncos, 19-17 (D)
1984—Broncos, 42-21 (D)
1987—Vikings, 34-27 (M)
1990—Vikings, 27-22 (M)
1991—Broncos, 13-6 (M)
1993—Vikings, 26-23 (D)
1996—Broncos, 21-17 (M)
1999—Vikings, 23-20 (D)
2003—Vikings, 28-20 (M)
2007—Broncos, 22-19 (D) OT
(RS Pts.—Broncos 258, Vikings 253)

DENVER vs. *NEW ENGLAND
RS: Broncos lead series, 25-16
PS: Broncos lead series, 2-0
1960—Broncos, 13-10 (B)
    Broncos, 31-24 (D)
1961—Patriots, 45-17 (B)
    Patriots, 28-24 (D)
1962—Patriots, 41-16 (B)
    Patriots, 33-29 (D)
1963—Broncos, 14-10 (D)
    Patriots, 40-21 (B)
1964—Patriots, 39-10 (D)
    Patriots, 12-7 (B)
1965—Broncos, 27-10 (B)
    Patriots, 28-20 (D)
1966—Patriots, 24-10 (D)
    Broncos, 17-10 (B)
1967—Broncos, 26-21 (D)
1968—Patriots, 20-17 (D)
    Broncos, 35-14 (B)
1969—Broncos, 35-7 (D)
1972—Broncos, 45-21 (D)
1976—Patriots, 38-14 (NE)
1979—Broncos, 45-10 (D)
1980—Patriots, 23-14 (NE)
1984—Broncos, 26-19 (D)
1986—Broncos, 27-20 (D)
    **Broncos, 22-17 (D)
1987—Broncos, 31-20 (D)
1988—Broncos, 21-10 (D)
1991—Broncos, 9-6 (NE)
    Broncos, 20-3 (D)
1995—Broncos, 37-3 (NE)
1996—Broncos, 34-8 (NE)
1997—Broncos, 34-13 (D)
1998—Broncos, 27-21 (D)

1999—Patriots, 24-23 (NE)
2000—Patriots, 28-19 (D)
2001—Broncos, 31-20 (D)
2002—Broncos, 24-16 (NE)
2003—Patriots, 30-26 (D)
2005—Broncos, 28-20 (D)
    **Broncos, 27-13 (D)
2006—Broncos, 17-7 (NE)
2008—Patriots, 41-7 (NE)
2009—Broncos, 20-17 (D) OT
(RS Pts.—Broncos 948, Patriots 834)
(PS Pts.—Broncos 49, Patriots 30)
*Franchise in Boston prior to 1971
**AFC Divisional Playoff

DENVER vs. NEW ORLEANS
RS: Broncos lead series, 7-2
1970—Broncos, 31-6 (NO)
1974—Broncos, 33-17 (D)
1979—Broncos, 10-3 (D)
1985—Broncos, 34-23 (D)
1988—Saints, 42-0 (NO)
1994—Saints, 30-28 (D)
2000—Broncos, 38-23 (NO)
2004—Broncos, 34-13 (NO)
2008—Broncos, 34-32 (D)
(RS Pts.—Broncos 242, Saints 189)

DENVER vs. N.Y. GIANTS
RS: Series tied, 5-5
PS: Giants lead series, 1-0
1972—Giants, 29-17 (NY)
1976—Broncos, 14-13 (D)
1980—Broncos, 14-9 (NY)
1986—Broncos, 19-16 (NY)
    *Giants, 39-20 (Pasadena)
1989—Giants, 14-7 (D)
1992—Broncos, 27-13 (D)
1998—Giants, 20-16 (NY)
2001—Broncos, 31-20 (D)
2005—Giants, 24-23 (NY)
2009—Broncos, 26-6 (D)
(RS Pts.—Broncos 191, Giants 167)
(PS Pts.—Giants 39, Broncos 20)
*Super Bowl XXI

DENVER vs. *N.Y. JETS
RS: Broncos lead series, 16-15-1
PS: Broncos lead series, 1-0
1960—Titans, 28-24 (NY)
    Titans, 30-27 (D)
1961—Titans, 35-28 (NY)
    Broncos, 27-10 (D)
1962—Broncos, 32-10 (NY)
    Titans, 46-45 (D)
1963—Tie, 35-35 (NY)
    Jets, 14-9 (D)
1964—Jets, 30-6 (NY)
    Broncos, 20-16 (D)
1965—Broncos, 16-13 (D)
    Jets, 45-10 (NY)
1966—Jets, 16-7 (D)
1967—Jets, 38-24 (D)
    Broncos, 33-24 (NY)
1968—Broncos, 21-13 (NY)
1969—Broncos, 21-19 (D)
1973—Broncos, 40-28 (NY)
1976—Broncos, 46-3 (D)
1978—Jets, 31-28 (D)
1980—Broncos, 31-24 (D)
1986—Jets, 22-10 (NY)
1992—Broncos, 27-16 (D)
1993—Broncos, 26-20 (NY)
1994—Jets, 25-22 (NY) OT

1996—Broncos, 31-6 (D)
1998—**Broncos, 23-10 (D)
1999—Jets, 21-13 (D)
2000—Broncos, 30-23 (NY)
2002—Jets, 19-13 (NY)
2005—Broncos, 27-0 (D)
2008—Broncos, 34-17 (NY)
2010—Jets, 24-20 (D)
(RS Pts.—Broncos 783, Jets 701)
(PS Pts.—Broncos 23, Jets 10)
*Jets known as Titans prior to 1963
**AFC Championship
DENVER vs. *OAKLAND
RS: Raiders lead series, 58-41-2
PS: Series tied, 1-1
1960—Broncos, 31-14 (D)
Raiders, 48-10 (O)
1961—Raiders, 33-19 (O)
Broncos, 27-24 (D)
1962—Broncos, 44-7 (D)
Broncos, 23-6 (O)
1963—Raiders, 26-10 (D)
Raiders, 35-31 (O)
1964—Raiders, 40-7 (O)
Tie, 20-20 (D)
1965—Raiders, 28-20 (D)
Raiders, 24-13 (O)
1966—Raiders, 17-3 (D)
Raiders, 28-10 (O)
1967—Raiders, 51-0 (O)
Raiders, 21-17 (D)
1968—Raiders, 43-7 (D)
Raiders, 33-27 (O)
1969—Raiders, 24-14 (D)
Raiders, 41-10 (O)
1970—Raiders, 35-23 (O)
Raiders, 24-19 (D)
1971—Raiders, 27-16 (D)
Raiders, 21-13 (O)
1972—Broncos, 30-23 (O)
Raiders, 37-20 (D)
1973—Tie, 23-23 (D)
Raiders, 21-17 (O)
1974—Raiders, 28-17 (D)
Broncos, 20-17 (O)
1975—Raiders, 42-17 (D)
Raiders, 17-10 (O)
1976—Raiders, 17-10 (D)
Raiders, 19-6 (O)
1977—Broncos, 30-7 (O)
Raiders, 24-14 (D)
**Broncos, 20-17 (D)
1978—Broncos, 14-6 (D)
Broncos, 21-6 (O)
1979—Raiders, 27-3 (O)
Raiders, 14-10 (D)
1980—Raiders, 9-3 (O)
Raiders, 24-21 (D)
1981—Broncos, 9-7 (D)
Broncos, 17-0 (O)
1982—Raiders, 27-10 (LA)
1983—Raiders, 22-7 (D)
Raiders, 22-20 (LA)
1984—Broncos, 16-13 (D)
Broncos, 22-19 (LA) OT
1985—Raiders, 31-28 (LA) OT
Raiders, 17-14 (D) OT
1986—Broncos, 38-36 (D)
Broncos, 21-10 (LA)
1987—Broncos, 30-14 (D)
Broncos, 23-17 (LA)

1988—Raiders, 30-27 (D) OT
Raiders, 21-20 (LA)
1989—Broncos, 31-21 (D)
Raiders, 16-13 (LA) OT
1990—Raiders, 14-9 (LA)
Raiders, 23-20 (D)
1991—Raiders, 16-13 (LA)
Raiders, 17-16 (D)
1992—Broncos, 17-13 (D)
Raiders, 24-0 (LA)
1993—Raiders, 23-20 (D)
Raiders, 33-30 (LA) OT
***Raiders, 42-24 (LA)
1994—Raiders, 48-16 (D)
Raiders, 23-13 (LA)
1995—Broncos, 27-0 (D)
Broncos, 31-28 (O)
1996—Broncos, 22-21 (D)
Broncos, 24-19 (D)
1997—Raiders, 28-25 (O)
Broncos, 31-3 (D)
1998—Broncos, 34-17 (O)
Broncos, 40-14 (D)
1999—Broncos, 16-13 (O)
Broncos, 27-21 (D) OT
2000—Broncos, 33-24 (D)
Broncos, 27-24 (D)
2001—Raiders, 38-28 (O)
Broncos, 23-17 (D)
2002—Raiders, 34-10 (D)
Raiders, 28-16 (O)
2003—Broncos, 31-10 (D)
Broncos, 22-8 (O)
2004—Broncos, 31-3 (O)
Raiders, 25-24 (D)
2005—Broncos, 31-17 (O)
Broncos, 22-3 (D)
2006—Broncos, 13-3 (D)
Broncos, 17-13 (O)
2007—Broncos, 23-20 (D) OT
Raiders, 34-20 (O)
2008—Broncos, 41-14 (O)
Raiders, 31-10 (D)
2009—Broncos, 23-3 (O)
Raiders, 20-19 (D)
2010—Raiders, 59-14 (D)
Raiders, 39-23 (O)
(RS Pts.—Raiders 2,219, Broncos 1,978)
(PS Pts.—Raiders 59, Broncos 44)
*Franchise in Los Angeles from 1982-1994
**AFC Championship
***AFC First-Round Playoff
DENVER vs. PHILADELPHIA
RS: Eagles lead series, 7-4
1971—Eagles, 17-16 (P)
1975—Broncos, 25-10 (D)
1980—Eagles, 27-6 (P)
1983—Eagles, 13-10 (D)
1986—Broncos, 33-7 (P)
1989—Eagles, 28-24 (D)
1992—Eagles, 30-0 (P)
1995—Eagles, 31-13 (P)
1998—Broncos, 41-16 (D)
2005—Broncos, 49-21 (D)
2009—Eagles, 30-27 (P)
(RS Pts.—Broncos 244, Eagles 230)
DENVER vs. PITTSBURGH
RS: Broncos lead series, 13-7-1
PS: Series tied, 3-3
1970—Broncos, 16-13 (D)
1971—Broncos, 22-10 (P)

1973—Broncos, 23-13 (P)
1974—Tie, 35-35 (D) OT
1975—Steelers, 20-9 (P)
1977—Broncos, 21-7 (D)
*Broncos, 34-21 (D)
1978—Steelers, 21-17 (D)
*Steelers, 33-10 (P)
1979—Steelers, 42-7 (P)
1983—Broncos, 14-10 (P)
1984—*Steelers, 24-17 (P)
1985—Broncos, 31-23 (P)
1986—Broncos, 21-10 (P)
1988—Steelers, 39-21 (P)
1989—Broncos, 34-7 (D)
*Broncos, 24-23 (D)
1990—Steelers, 34-17 (D)
1991—Broncos, 20-13 (D)
1993—Broncos, 37-13 (D)
1997—Steelers, 35-24 (P)
**Broncos, 24-21 (P)
2003—Broncos, 17-14 (D)
2005—**Steelers, 34-17 (D)
2006—Broncos, 31-20 (P)
2007—Broncos, 31-28 (D)
2009—Steelers, 28-10 (D)
(RS Pts.—Broncos 458, Steelers 435)
(PS Pts.—Steelers 156, Broncos 126)
*AFC Divisional Playoff
**AFC Championship
DENVER vs. *ST. LOUIS
RS: Rams lead series, 7-5
1972—Broncos, 16-10 (LA)
1974—Rams, 17-10 (D)
1979—Rams, 13-9 (D)
1982—Broncos, 27-24 (LA)
1985—Rams, 20-16 (LA)
1988—Broncos, 35-24 (D)
1994—Rams, 27-21 (LA)
1997—Broncos, 35-14 (D)
2000—Rams, 41-36 (StL)
2002—Broncos, 23-16 (D)
2006—Rams, 18-10 (StL)
2010—Rams, 36-33 (D)
(RS Pts.—Broncos 271, Rams 260)
*Franchise in Los Angeles prior to 1995
DENVER vs. *SAN DIEGO
RS: Broncos lead series, 54-47-1
1960—Chargers, 23-19 (D)
Chargers, 41-33 (LA)
1961—Chargers, 37-0 (D)
Chargers, 19-16 (D)
1962—Broncos, 30-21 (D)
Broncos, 23-20 (SD)
1963—Broncos, 50-34 (D)
Chargers, 58-20 (SD)
1964—Chargers, 42-14 (SD)
Chargers, 31-20 (D)
1965—Chargers, 34-31 (SD)
Chargers, 33-21 (D)
1966—Chargers, 24-17 (SD)
Broncos, 20-17 (D)
1967—Chargers, 38-21 (D)
Chargers, 24-20 (SD)
1968—Chargers, 55-24 (SD)
Chargers, 47-23 (D)
1969—Broncos, 13-0 (D)
Chargers, 45-24 (SD)
1970—Chargers, 24-21 (SD)
Tie, 17-17 (D)
1971—Broncos, 20-16 (D)
Chargers, 45-17 (SD)

1972—Chargers, 37-14 (SD)
   Broncos, 38-13 (D)
1973—Broncos, 30-19 (D)
   Broncos, 42-28 (SD)
1974—Broncos, 27-7 (D)
   Chargers, 17-0 (SD)
1975—Broncos, 27-17 (SD)
   Broncos, 13-10 (D) OT
1976—Broncos, 26-0 (D)
   Broncos, 17-0 (SD)
1977—Broncos, 17-14 (SD)
   Broncos, 17-9 (D)
1978—Broncos, 27-14 (D)
   Chargers, 23-0 (SD)
1979—Broncos, 7-0 (D)
   Chargers, 17-7 (SD)
1980—Chargers, 30-13 (D)
   Broncos, 20-13 (SD)
1981—Broncos, 42-24 (D)
   Chargers, 34-17 (SD)
1982—Chargers, 23-3 (D)
   Chargers, 30-20 (SD)
1983—Broncos, 14-6 (D)
   Chargers, 31-7 (SD)
1984—Broncos, 16-13 (SD)
   Broncos, 16-13 (D)
1985—Chargers, 30-10 (SD)
   Broncos, 30-24 (D) OT
1986—Broncos, 31-14 (D)
   Chargers, 9-3 (D)
1987—Broncos, 31-17 (SD)
   Broncos, 24-0 (D)
1988—Broncos, 34-3 (D)
   Broncos, 12-0 (SD)
1989—Broncos, 16-10 (D)
   Chargers, 19-16 (SD)
1990—Chargers, 19-7 (SD)
   Broncos, 20-10 (D)
1991—Broncos, 27-19 (D)
   Broncos, 17-14 (SD)
1992—Broncos, 21-13 (D)
   Chargers, 24-21 (SD)
1993—Broncos, 34-17 (D)
   Chargers, 13-10 (SD)
1994—Chargers, 37-34 (D)
   Broncos, 20-15 (SD)
1995—Chargers, 17-6 (SD)
   Broncos, 30-27 (D)
1996—Broncos, 28-17 (D)
   Chargers, 16-10 (SD)
1997—Broncos, 38-28 (SD)
   Broncos, 38-3 (D)
1998—Broncos, 27-10 (D)
   Broncos, 31-16 (SD)
1999—Broncos, 33-17 (SD)
   Chargers, 12-6 (D)
2000—Broncos, 21-7 (SD)
   Broncos, 38-37 (D)
2001—Chargers, 27-10 (SD)
   Broncos, 26-16 (D)
2002—Broncos, 26-9 (D)
   Chargers, 30-27 (SD) OT
2003—Broncos, 37-13 (SD)
   Broncos, 37-8 (D)
2004—Broncos, 23-13 (D)
   Chargers, 20-17 (SD)
2005—Broncos, 20-17 (D)
   Broncos, 23-7 (SD)
2006—Chargers, 35-27 (D)
   Chargers, 48-20 (SD)
2007—Chargers, 41-3 (D)

   Chargers, 23-3 (SD)
2008—Broncos, 39-38 (D)
   Chargers, 52-21 (SD)
2009—Broncos, 34-23 (SD)
   Chargers, 32-3 (D)
2010—Chargers, 35-14 (SD)
   Chargers, 33-28 (D)
(RS Pts.—Chargers 2,223, Broncos 2,153)
*Franchise in Los Angeles prior to 1961
DENVER vs. SAN FRANCISCO
RS: Series tied, 6-6
PS: 49ers lead series, 1-0
1970—49ers, 19-14 (SF)
1973—49ers, 36-34 (D)
1979—Broncos, 38-28 (SF)
1982—Broncos, 24-21 (D)
1985—Broncos, 17-16 (D)
1988—Broncos, 16-13 (SF) OT
1989—*49ers, 55-10 (New Orleans)
1994—49ers, 42-19 (SF)
1997—49ers, 34-17 (SF)
2000—Broncos, 38-9 (D)
2002—Broncos, 24-14 (SF)
2006—49ers, 26-23 (D) OT
2010—49ers, 24-16 (London)
(RS Pts.—49ers 282, Broncos 280)
(PS Pts.—49ers 55, Broncos 10)
*Super Bowl XXIV
DENVER vs. SEATTLE
RS: Broncos lead series, 34-18
PS: Seahawks lead series, 1-0
1977—Broncos, 24-13 (S)
1978—Broncos, 28-7 (D)
   Broncos, 20-17 (S) OT
1979—Broncos, 37-34 (D)
   Seahawks, 28-23 (S)
1980—Broncos, 36-20 (D)
   Broncos, 25-17 (S)
1981—Seahawks, 13-10 (S)
   Broncos, 23-13 (D)
1982—Seahawks, 17-10 (D)
   Seahawks, 13-11 (S)
1983—Seahawks, 27-19 (S)
   Broncos, 38-27 (D)
   *Seahawks, 31-7 (S)
1984—Seahawks, 27-24 (D)
   Broncos, 31-14 (S)
1985—Broncos, 13-10 (D) OT
   Broncos, 27-24 (S)
1986—Broncos, 20-13 (D)
   Seahawks, 41-16 (S)
1987—Broncos, 40-17 (D)
   Seahawks, 28-21 (S)
1988—Seahawks, 21-14 (D)
   Seahawks, 42-14 (S)
1989—Broncos, 24-21 (S) OT
   Broncos, 41-14 (D)
1990—Broncos, 34-31 (D) OT
   Seahawks, 17-12 (S)
1991—Broncos, 16-10 (D)
   Seahawks, 13-10 (S)
1992—Seahawks, 16-13 (S) OT
   Broncos, 10-6 (D)
1993—Broncos, 28-17 (D)
   Broncos, 17-9 (S)
1994—Broncos, 16-9 (S)
   Broncos, 17-10 (D)
1995—Seahawks, 27-10 (S)
   Seahawks, 31-27 (D)
1996—Broncos, 30-20 (S)
   Broncos, 34-7 (D)

1997—Broncos, 35-14 (S)
   Broncos, 30-27 (D)
1998—Broncos, 21-16 (S)
   Broncos, 28-21 (D)
1999—Seahawks, 20-17 (S)
   Broncos, 36-30 (D) OT
2000—Broncos, 38-31 (S)
   Broncos, 31-24 (D)
2001—Seahawks, 34-21 (S)
   Broncos, 20-7 (D)
2002—Broncos, 31-9 (S)
2006—Seahawks, 23-20 (D)
2010—Broncos, 31-14 (D)
(RS Pts.—Broncos 1,222, Seahawks 1,011)
(PS Pts.—Seahawks 31, Broncos 7)
*AFC First-Round Playoff
DENVER vs. TAMPA BAY
RS: Broncos lead series, 5-2
1976—Broncos, 48-13 (D)
1981—Broncos, 24-7 (TB)
1993—Buccaneers, 17-10 (D)
1996—Broncos, 27-23 (D)
1999—Buccaneers, 13-10 (TB)
2004—Broncos, 16-13 (TB)
2008—Broncos, 16-13 (D)
(RS Pts.—Broncos 151, Buccaneers 99)
DENVER vs. *TENNESSEE
RS: Titans lead series, 20-14-1
PS: Broncos lead series, 2-1
1960—Oilers, 45-25 (D)
   Oilers, 20-10 (H)
1961—Oilers, 55-14 (D)
   Oilers, 45-14 (H)
1962—Broncos, 20-10 (D)
   Oilers, 34-17 (H)
1963—Oilers, 20-14 (H)
   Oilers, 33-24 (D)
1964—Oilers, 38-17 (D)
   Oilers, 34-15 (H)
1965—Broncos, 28-17 (D)
   Broncos, 31-21 (H)
1966—Oilers, 45-7 (H)
   Broncos, 40-38 (D)
1967—Oilers, 10-6 (H)
   Oilers, 20-18 (D)
1968—Oilers, 38-17 (H)
1969—Oilers, 24-21 (H)
   Tie, 20-20 (D)
1970—Oilers, 31-21 (H)
1972—Broncos, 30-17 (D)
1973—Broncos, 48-20 (H)
1974—Broncos, 37-14 (D)
1976—Oilers, 17-3 (H)
1977—Broncos, 24-14 (H)
1979—**Oilers, 13-7 (H)
1980—Oilers, 20-16 (D)
1983—Broncos, 26-14 (H)
1985—Broncos, 31-20 (D)
1987—Oilers, 40-10 (D)
   ***Broncos, 34-10 (D)
1991—Oilers, 42-14 (H)
   ***Broncos, 26-24 (D)
1992—Broncos, 27-21 (D)
1995—Oilers, 42-33 (H)
2004—Broncos, 37-16 (T)
2007—Broncos, 34-20 (D)
2010—Broncos, 26-20 (T)
(RS Pts.—Titans 935, Broncos 775)
(PS Pts.—Broncos 67, Titans 47)
*Franchise in Houston prior to 1997;
known as the Oilers prior to 1999

**AFC First-Round Playoff
***AFC Divisional Playoff

DENVER vs. WASHINGTON
RS: Broncos lead series, 6-5
PS: Redskins lead series, 1-0
1970—Redskins, 19-3 (D)
1974—Redskins, 30-3 (W)
1980—Broncos, 20-17 (D)
1986—Broncos, 31-30 (D)
1987—*Redskins, 42-10 (San Diego)
1989—Broncos, 14-10 (W)
1992—Redskins, 34-3 (W)
1995—Broncos, 38-31 (D)
1998—Broncos, 38-16 (W)
2001—Redskins, 17-10 (D)
2005—Broncos, 21-19 (D)
2009—Redskins, 27-17 (W)
(RS Pts.—Redskins 250, Broncos 198)
(PS Pts.—Redskins 42, Broncos 10)
*Super Bowl XXII

DETROIT vs. ARIZONA
RS: Lions lead series, 31-24-5;
See Arizona vs. Detroit
DETROIT vs. ATLANTA
RS: Lions lead series, 23-10;
See Atlanta vs. Detroit
DETROIT vs. BALTIMORE
RS: Ravens lead series, 2-1;
See Baltimore vs. Detroit
DETROIT vs. BUFFALO
RS: Series tied, 4-4-1;
See Buffalo vs. Detroit
DETROIT vs. CAROLINA
RS: Panthers lead series, 4-1;
See Carolina vs. Detroit
DETROIT vs. CHICAGO
RS: Bears lead series, 93-64-5;
See Chicago vs. Detroit
DETROIT vs. CINCINNATI
RS: Bengals lead series, 7-3;
See Cincinnati vs. Detroit
DETROIT vs. CLEVELAND
RS: Lions lead series, 14-4
PS: Lions lead series, 3-1;
See Cleveland vs. Detroit
DETROIT vs. DALLAS
RS: Cowboys lead series, 12-9
PS: Series tied, 1-1;
See Dallas vs. Detroit
DETROIT vs. DENVER
RS: Broncos lead series, 6-4;
See Denver vs. Detroit
*DETROIT vs. GREEN BAY
RS: Packers lead series, 89-65-7
PS: Packers lead series, 2-0
1930—Packers, 47-13 (GB)
Tie, 6-6 (P)
1932—Packers, 15-10 (GB)
Spartans, 19-0 (P)
1933—Packers, 17-0 (GB)
Spartans, 7-0 (P)
1934—Lions, 3-0 (GB)
Packers, 3-0 (D)
1935—Packers, 13-9 (Mil)
Packers, 31-7 (GB)
Lions, 20-10 (D)
1936—Packers, 20-18 (GB)
Packers, 26-17 (D)
1937—Packers, 26-6 (GB)
Packers, 14-13 (D)

1938—Lions, 17-7 (GB)
Packers, 28-7 (D)
1939—Packers, 26-7 (GB)
Packers, 12-7 (D)
1940—Lions, 23-14 (GB)
Packers, 50-7 (D)
1941—Packers, 23-0 (GB)
Packers, 24-7 (D)
1942—Packers, 38-7 (Mil)
Packers, 28-7 (D)
1943—Packers, 35-14 (GB)
Packers, 27-6 (D)
1944—Packers, 27-6 (Mil)
Packers, 14-0 (D)
1945—Packers, 57-21 (Mil)
Lions, 14-3 (D)
1946—Packers, 10-7 (Mil)
Packers, 9-0 (D)
1947—Packers, 34-17 (GB)
Packers, 35-14 (D)
1948—Packers, 33-21 (GB)
Lions, 24-20 (D)
1949—Packers, 16-14 (Mil)
Lions, 21-7 (D)
1950—Packers, 45-7 (GB)
Lions, 24-21 (D)
1951—Lions, 24-17 (GB)
Lions, 52-35 (D)
1952—Packers, 52-17 (GB)
Lions, 48-24 (D)
1953—Lions, 14-7 (GB)
Lions, 34-15 (D)
1954—Lions, 21-17 (GB)
Lions, 28-24 (D)
1955—Packers, 20-17 (GB)
Lions, 24-10 (D)
1956—Lions, 20-16 (GB)
Packers, 24-20 (D)
1957—Lions, 24-14 (GB)
Lions, 18-6 (D)
1958—Tie, 13-13 (GB)
Lions, 24-14 (D)
1959—Packers, 28-10 (GB)
Packers, 24-17 (D)
1960—Packers, 28-9 (GB)
Lions, 23-10 (D)
1961—Lions, 17-13 (Mil)
Packers, 17-9 (D)
1962—Packers, 9-7 (GB)
Lions, 26-14 (D)
1963—Packers, 31-10 (Mil)
Tie, 13-13 (D)
1964—Packers, 14-10 (D)
Packers, 30-7 (GB)
1965—Packers, 31-21 (D)
Lions, 12-7 (GB)
1966—Packers, 23-14 (GB)
Packers, 31-7 (D)
1967—Tie, 17-17 (GB)
Packers, 27-17 (D)
1968—Lions, 23-17 (GB)
Tie, 14-14 (D)
1969—Packers, 28-17 (D)
Lions, 16-10 (GB)
1970—Lions, 40-0 (D)
Lions, 20-0 (GB)
1971—Lions, 31-28 (D)
Tie, 14-14 (Mil)
1972—Packers, 24-23 (D)
Packers, 33-7 (GB)
1973—Tie, 13-13 (GB)

Lions, 34-0 (D)
1974—Packers, 21-19 (Mil)
Lions, 19-17 (D)
1975—Lions, 30-16 (Mil)
Lions, 13-10 (D)
1976—Packers, 24-14 (GB)
Lions, 27-6 (D)
1977—Lions, 10-6 (D)
Packers, 10-9 (GB)
1978—Packers, 13-7 (D)
Packers, 35-14 (Mil)
1979—Packers, 24-16 (Mil)
Packers, 18-13 (D)
1980—Lions, 29-7 (Mil)
Lions, 24-3 (D)
1981—Lions, 31-27 (D)
Packers, 31-17 (GB)
1982—Lions, 30-10 (GB)
Lions, 27-24 (D)
1983—Lions, 38-14 (D)
Lions, 23-20 (Mil) OT
1984—Packers, 41-9 (GB)
Lions, 31-28 (D)
1985—Packers, 43-10 (GB)
Packers, 26-23 (D)
1986—Lions, 21-14 (GB)
Packers, 44-40 (D)
1987—Lions, 19-16 (GB) OT
Packers, 34-33 (D)
1988—Lions, 19-9 (Mil)
Lions, 30-14 (D)
1989—Packers, 23-20 (Mil) OT
Lions, 31-22 (D)
1990—Packers, 24-21 (D)
Lions, 24-17 (GB)
1991—Lions, 23-14 (D)
Lions, 21-17 (GB)
1992—Packers, 27-13 (D)
Packers, 38-10 (Mil)
1993—Packers, 26-17 (Mil)
Lions, 30-20 (D)
**Packers, 28-24 (D)
1994—Packers, 38-30 (Mil)
Lions, 34-31 (D)
**Packers, 16-12 (GB)
1995—Packers, 30-21 (GB)
Lions, 24-16 (D)
1996—Packers, 28-18 (GB)
Packers, 31-3 (D)
1997—Lions, 26-15 (D)
Packers, 20-10 (GB)
1998—Packers, 38-19 (GB)
Lions, 27-20 (D)
1999—Lions, 23-15 (D)
Packers, 26-17 (GB)
2000—Lions, 31-24 (D)
Packers, 26-13 (GB)
2001—Packers, 28-6 (GB)
Packers, 29-27 (D)
2002—Packers, 37-31 (D)
Packers, 40-14 (GB)
2003—Packers, 31-6 (GB)
Lions, 22-14 (D)
2004—Packers, 38-10 (D)
Packers, 16-13 (GB)
2005—Lions, 17-3 (D)
Packers, 16-13 (GB) OT
2006—Packers, 31-24 (D)
Packers, 17-9 (GB)
2007—Packers, 37-26 (D)
Packers, 34-13 (GB)

2008—Packers, 48-25 (D)
    Packers, 31-21 (GB)
2009—Packers, 26-0 (GB)
    Packers, 34-12 (D)
2010—Packers, 28-26 (GB)
    Lions, 7-3 (D)
(RS Pts.—Packers 3,386, Lions 2,889)
(PS Pts.—Packers 44, Lions 36)
*Franchise in Portsmouth prior to 1934
and known as the Spartans*
**NFC First-Round Playoff*

DETROIT vs. HOUSTON
RS: Series tied, 1-1
2004—Lions, 28-16 (D)
2008—Texans, 28-21 (H)
(RS Pts.—Lions 49, Texans 44)

DETROIT vs. *INDIANAPOLIS
RS: Colts lead series, 20-18-2
1953—Lions, 27-17 (B)
    Lions, 17-7 (D)
1954—Lions, 35-0 (D)
    Lions, 27-3 (B)
1955—Colts, 28-13 (B)
    Lions, 24-14 (D)
1956—Lions, 31-14 (B)
    Lions, 27-3 (D)
1957—Colts, 34-14 (B)
    Lions, 31-27 (D)
1958—Colts, 28-15 (B)
    Colts, 40-14 (D)
1959—Colts, 21-9 (B)
    Colts, 31-24 (D)
1960—Lions, 30-17 (D)
    Lions, 20-15 (B)
1961—Lions, 16-15 (B)
    Colts, 17-14 (D)
1962—Lions, 29-20 (B)
    Lions, 21-14 (D)
1963—Colts, 25-21 (D)
    Colts, 24-21 (B)
1964—Colts, 34-0 (D)
    Lions, 31-14 (B)
1965—Colts, 31-7 (B)
    Tie, 24-24 (D)
1966—Colts, 45-14 (B)
    Lions, 20-14 (D)
1967—Colts, 41-7 (B)
1968—Colts, 27-10 (D)
1969—Tie, 17-17 (B)
1973—Colts, 29-27 (D)
1977—Lions, 13-10 (B)
1980—Lions, 10-9 (D)
1985—Colts, 14-6 (I)
1991—Lions, 33-24 (I)
1997—Lions, 32-10 (D)
2000—Colts, 30-18 (I)
2004—Colts, 41-9 (D)
2008—Colts, 31-21 (I)
(RS Pts.—Colts 860, Lions 778)
Franchise in Baltimore prior to 1984

DETROIT vs. JACKSONVILLE
RS: Jaguars lead series, 3-1
1995—Lions, 44-0 (D)
1998—Jaguars, 37-22 (J)
2004—Jaguars, 23-17 (J) OT
2008—Jaguars, 38-14 (D)
(RS Pts.—Jaguars 98, Lions 97)

DETROIT vs. KANSAS CITY
RS: Chiefs lead series, 7-4
1971—Lions, 32-21 (D)
1975—Chiefs, 24-21 (KC) OT

1980—Chiefs, 20-17 (KC)
1981—Lions, 27-10 (D)
1987—Chiefs, 27-20 (D)
1988—Lions, 7-6 (KC)
1990—Chiefs, 43-24 (KC)
1996—Chiefs, 28-24 (D)
1999—Chiefs, 31-21 (KC)
2003—Chiefs, 45-17 (KC)
2007—Lions, 25-20 (D)
(RS Pts.—Chiefs 275, Lions 235)

DETROIT vs. MIAMI
RS: Dolphins lead series, 7-3
1973—Dolphins, 34-7 (M)
1979—Dolphins, 28-10 (D)
1985—Lions, 31-21 (D)
1991—Lions, 17-13 (D)
1994—Dolphins, 27-20 (M)
1997—Dolphins, 33-30 (M)
2000—Dolphins, 23-8 (D)
2002—Dolphins, 49-21 (M)
2006—Dolphins, 27-10 (D)
2010—Lions, 34-27 (M)
(RS Pts.—Dolphins 282, Lions 188)

DETROIT vs. MINNESOTA
RS: Vikings lead series, 66-31-2
1961—Lions, 37-10 (M)
    Lions, 13-7 (D)
1962—Lions, 17-6 (M)
    Lions, 37-23 (D)
1963—Lions, 28-10 (D)
    Vikings, 34-31 (M)
1964—Lions, 24-20 (M)
    Tie, 23-23 (D)
1965—Lions, 31-29 (M)
    Vikings, 29-7 (D)
1966—Lions, 32-31 (M)
    Vikings, 28-16 (D)
1967—Tie, 10-10 (M)
    Lions, 14-3 (D)
1968—Vikings, 24-10 (M)
    Vikings, 13-6 (D)
1969—Vikings, 24-10 (M)
    Vikings, 27-0 (D)
1970—Vikings, 30-17 (D)
    Vikings, 24-20 (M)
1971—Vikings, 16-13 (D)
    Vikings, 29-10 (M)
1972—Vikings, 34-10 (D)
    Vikings, 16-14 (M)
1973—Vikings, 23-9 (D)
    Vikings, 28-7 (M)
1974—Vikings, 7-6 (D)
    Lions, 20-16 (M)
1975—Vikings, 25-19 (M)
    Lions, 17-10 (D)
1976—Vikings, 10-9 (D)
    Vikings, 31-23 (M)
1977—Vikings, 14-7 (M)
    Vikings, 30-21 (D)
1978—Vikings, 17-7 (M)
    Lions, 45-14 (D)
1979—Vikings, 13-10 (D)
    Vikings, 14-7 (M)
1980—Lions, 27-7 (D)
    Vikings, 34-0 (M)
1981—Vikings, 26-24 (M)
    Lions, 45-7 (D)
1982—Vikings, 34-31 (D)
1983—Vikings, 20-17 (M)
    Lions, 13-2 (D)
1984—Vikings, 29-28 (D)

    Lions, 16-14 (M)
1985—Vikings, 16-13 (M)
    Lions, 41-21 (D)
1986—Lions, 13-10 (M)
    Vikings, 24-10 (D)
1987—Vikings, 34-19 (M)
    Vikings, 17-14 (D)
1988—Vikings, 44-17 (M)
    Vikings, 23-0 (D)
1989—Vikings, 24-17 (M)
    Vikings, 20-7 (D)
1990—Lions, 34-27 (M)
    Vikings, 17-7 (D)
1991—Lions, 24-20 (D)
    Lions, 34-14 (M)
1992—Lions, 31-17 (D)
    Vikings, 31-14 (M)
1993—Lions, 30-27 (M)
    Vikings, 13-0 (D)
1994—Vikings, 10-3 (M)
    Lions, 41-19 (D)
1995—Vikings, 20-10 (M)
    Lions, 44-38 (D)
1996—Vikings, 17-13 (M)
    Vikings, 24-22 (D)
1997—Lions, 38-15 (D)
    Lions, 14-13 (M)
1998—Vikings, 29-6 (M)
    Vikings, 34-13 (D)
1999—Lions, 25-23 (D)
    Vikings, 24-17 (M)
2000—Vikings, 31-24 (D)
    Vikings, 24-17 (M)
2001—Vikings, 31-26 (D)
    Lions, 27-24 (D)
2002—Vikings, 31-24 (M)
    Vikings, 38-36 (D)
2003—Vikings, 23-13 (D)
    Vikings, 24-14 (M)
2004—Vikings, 22-19 (M)
    Vikings, 28-27 (D)
2005—Vikings, 27-14 (M)
    Vikings, 21-16 (D)
2006—Vikings, 26-17 (M)
    Vikings, 30-20 (D)
2007—Lions, 20-17 (D) OT
    Vikings, 42-10 (M)
2008—Vikings, 12-10 (M)
    Vikings, 20-16 (D)
2009—Vikings, 27-13 (D)
    Vikings, 27-10 (M)
2010—Vikings, 24-10 (M)
    Lions, 20-13 (D)
(RS Pts.—Vikings 2,152, Lions 1,812)

DETROIT vs. NEW ENGLAND
RS: Patriots lead series, 6-4
1971—Lions, 34-7 (NE)
1976—Lions, 30-10 (D)
1979—Patriots, 24-17 (NE)
1985—Patriots, 23-6 (NE)
1993—Lions, 19-16 (NE) OT
1994—Patriots, 23-17 (D)
2000—Lions, 34-9 (D)
2002—Patriots, 20-12 (D)
2006—Patriots, 28-21 (NE)
2010—Patriots, 45-24 (D)
(RS Pts.—Lions 214, Patriots 205)

DETROIT vs. NEW ORLEANS
RS: Saints lead series, 10-9-1
1968—Tie, 20-20 (D)
1970—Saints, 19-17 (NO)

1972—Lions, 27-14 (D)
1973—Saints, 20-13 (NO)
1974—Lions, 19-14 (D)
1976—Saints, 17-16 (NO)
1977—Lions, 23-19 (D)
1979—Saints, 17-7 (NO)
1980—Lions, 24-13 (D)
1988—Saints, 22-14 (D)
1989—Lions, 21-14 (D)
1990—Lions, 27-10 (NO)
1992—Saints, 13-7 (D)
1993—Saints, 14-3 (NO)
1997—Saints, 35-17 (NO)
2000—Lions, 14-10 (NO)
2002—Lions, 26-21 (D)
2005—Lions, 13-12 (San Antonio)
2008—Saints, 42-7 (D)
2009—Saints, 45-27 (NO)
(RS Pts.—Saints 391, Lions 342)
*DETROIT vs. N.Y. GIANTS
RS: Lions lead series, 20-19-1
PS: Lions lead series, 1-0
1930—Giants, 19-6 (P)
1931—Spartans, 14-6 (P)
Giants, 14-0 (NY)
1932—Spartans, 7-0 (P)
Spartans, 6-0 (NY)
1933—Spartans, 17-7 (P)
Giants, 13-10 (NY)
1934—Lions, 9-0 (D)
1935—**Lions, 26-7 (D)
1936—Giants, 14-7 (NY)
Lions, 38-0 (D)
1937—Lions, 17-0 (NY)
1939—Lions, 18-14 (D)
1941—Giants, 20-13 (NY)
1943—Tie, 0-0 (D)
1945—Lions, 35-14 (NY)
1947—Lions, 35-7 (D)
1949—Lions, 45-21 (NY)
1953—Lions, 27-16 (NY)
1955—Giants, 24-19 (D)
1958—Giants, 19-17 (D)
1962—Giants, 17-14 (NY)
1964—Lions, 26-3 (D)
1967—Lions, 30-7 (NY)
1969—Lions, 24-0 (D)
1972—Lions, 30-16 (D)
1974—Lions, 20-19 (D)
1976—Giants, 24-10 (NY)
1982—Giants, 13-6 (D)
1983—Lions, 15-9 (D)
1988—Giants, 30-10 (NY)
Giants, 13-10 (D) OT
1989—Giants, 24-14 (NY)
1990—Giants, 20-0 (NY)
1994—Lions, 28-25 (NY) OT
1996—Giants, 35-7 (D)
1997—Giants, 26-20 (D) OT
2000—Lions, 31-21 (NY)
2004—Lions, 28-13 (NY)
2007—Giants, 16-10 (D)
2010—Giants, 28-20 (NY)
(RS Pts.—Lions 672, Giants 588)
(PS Pts.—Lions 26, Giants 7)
**Franchise in Portsmouth prior to 1934
and known as the Spartans
**NFL Championship*
DETROIT vs. N.Y. JETS
RS: Series tied, 6-6
1972—Lions, 37-20 (D)

1979—Jets, 31-10 (NY)
1982—Jets, 28-13 (D)
1985—Lions, 31-20 (D)
1988—Jets, 17-10 (D)
1991—Lions, 34-20 (D)
1994—Lions, 18-7 (NY)
1997—Lions, 13-10 (D)
2000—Lions, 10-7 (NY)
2002—Jets, 31-14 (D)
2006—Jets, 31-24 (NY)
2010—Jets, 23-20 (D) OT
(RS Pts.—Jets 245, Lions 234)
DETROIT vs. *OAKLAND
RS: Raiders lead series, 6-4
1970—Lions, 28-14 (D)
1974—Raiders, 35-13 (O)
1978—Raiders, 29-17 (O)
1981—Lions, 16-0 (D)
1984—Raiders, 24-3 (D)
1987—Raiders, 27-7 (LA)
1990—Raiders, 38-31 (D)
1996—Raiders, 37-21 (O)
2003—Lions, 23-13 (D)
2007—Lions, 36-21 (O)
(RS Pts.—Raiders 238, Lions 195)
*Franchise in Los Angeles from 1982-1994
*DETROIT vs. PHILADELPHIA
RS: Eagles lead series, 14-12-2
PS: Eagles lead series, 1-0
1933—Spartans, 25-0 (P)
1934—Lions, 10-0 (P)
1935—Lions, 35-0 (D)
1936—Lions, 23-0 (P)
1938—Eagles, 21-7 (D)
1940—Lions, 21-0 (P)
1941—Lions, 21-17 (D)
1945—Lions, 28-24 (D)
1948—Eagles, 45-21 (P)
1949—Eagles, 22-14 (D)
1951—Lions, 28-10 (P)
1954—Tie, 13-13 (D)
1957—Lions, 27-16 (P)
1960—Eagles, 28-10 (P)
1961—Eagles, 27-24 (D)
1965—Lions, 35-28 (P)
1968—Eagles, 12-0 (D)
1971—Eagles, 23-20 (D)
1974—Eagles, 28-17 (P)
1977—Lions, 17-13 (D)
1979—Eagles, 44-7 (P)
1984—Tie, 23-23 (D) OT
1986—Lions, 13-11 (P)
1995—**Eagles, 58-37 (P)
1996—Eagles, 24-17 (P)
1998—Eagles, 10-9 (P)
2004—Eagles, 30-13 (D)
2007—Eagles, 56-21 (P)
2010—Eagles, 35-32 (D)
(RS Pts.—Eagles 560, Lions 531)
(PS Pts.—Eagles 58, Lions 37)
**Franchise in Portsmouth prior to 1934
and known as the Spartans
**NFC First-Round Playoff*
DETROIT vs. *PITTSBURGH
RS: Steelers lead series, 15-14-1
1934—Lions, 40-7 (D)
1936—Lions, 28-3 (D)
1937—Lions, 7-3 (D)
1938—Lions, 16-7 (D)
1940—Steelers, 10-7 (D)
1942—Steelers, 35-7 (D)

1946—Lions, 17-7 (D)
1947—Steelers, 17-10 (P)
1948—Lions, 17-14 (D)
1949—Steelers, 14-7 (P)
1950—Lions, 10-7 (D)
1952—Lions, 31-6 (P)
1953—Lions, 38-21 (D)
1955—Lions, 31-28 (D)
1956—Lions, 45-7 (D)
1959—Tie, 10-10 (P)
1962—Lions, 45-7 (D)
1966—Steelers, 17-3 (P)
1967—Steelers, 24-14 (D)
1969—Steelers, 16-13 (P)
1973—Steelers, 24-10 (P)
1983—Lions, 45-3 (D)
1986—Steelers, 27-17 (P)
1989—Steelers, 23-3 (D)
1992—Steelers, 17-14 (P)
1995—Steelers, 23-20 (P)
1998—Lions, 19-16 (D) OT
2001—Steelers, 47-14 (P)
2005—Steelers, 35-21 (P)
2009—Steelers, 28-20 (D)
(RS Pts.—Lions 579, Steelers 503)
*Steelers known as Pirates prior to 1940
DETROIT vs. *ST. LOUIS
RS: Rams lead series, 42-38-1
PS: Lions lead series, 1-0
1937—Lions, 28-0 (C)
Lions, 27-7 (D)
1938—Rams, 21-17 (C)
Lions, 6-0 (D)
1939—Lions, 15-7 (D)
Rams, 14-3 (C)
1940—Lions, 6-0 (D)
Rams, 24-0 (C)
1941—Lions, 17-7 (D)
Lions, 14-0 (C)
1942—Rams, 14-0 (D)
Rams, 27-7 (C)
1944—Rams, 20-17 (D)
Lions, 26-14 (C)
1945—Rams, 28-21 (D)
1946—Rams, 35-14 (LA)
Rams, 41-20 (D)
1947—Rams, 27-13 (D)
Rams, 28-17 (LA)
1948—Rams, 44-7 (LA)
Rams, 34-27 (D)
1949—Rams, 27-24 (LA)
Rams, 21-10 (D)
1950—Rams, 30-28 (D)
Rams, 65-24 (LA)
1951—Rams, 27-21 (D)
Lions, 24-22 (LA)
1952—Lions, 17-14 (LA)
Lions, 24-16 (D)
**Lions, 31-21 (D)
1953—Rams, 31-19 (D)
Rams, 37-24 (LA)
1954—Lions, 21-3 (D)
Lions, 27-24 (LA)
1955—Rams, 17-10 (D)
Rams, 24-13 (LA)
1956—Lions, 24-21 (D)
Lions, 16-7 (LA)
1957—Lions, 10-7 (D)
Rams, 35-17 (LA)
1958—Rams, 42-28 (D)
Lions, 41-24 (LA)

1959—Lions, 17-7 (LA)
    Lions, 23-17 (D)
1960—Rams, 48-35 (LA)
    Lions, 12-10 (D)
1961—Lions, 14-13 (D)
    Lions, 28-10 (LA)
1962—Lions, 13-10 (D)
    Lions, 12-3 (LA)
1963—Lions, 23-2 (LA)
    Rams, 28-21 (D)
1964—Tie, 17-17 (LA)
    Lions, 37-17 (D)
1965—Lions, 20-0 (D)
    Lions, 31-7 (LA)
1966—Rams, 14-7 (D)
    Rams, 23-3 (LA)
1967—Rams, 31-7 (D)
1968—Rams, 10-7 (LA)
1969—Lions, 28-0 (D)
1970—Lions, 28-23 (LA)
1971—Rams, 21-13 (D)
1972—Lions, 34-17 (LA)
1974—Rams, 16-13 (LA)
1975—Rams, 20-0 (D)
1976—Rams, 20-17 (D)
1980—Lions, 41-20 (LA)
1981—Rams, 20-13 (LA)
1982—Lions, 19-14 (LA)
1983—Rams, 21-10 (LA)
1986—Rams, 14-10 (LA)
1987—Rams, 37-16 (D)
1988—Rams, 17-10 (LA)
1991—Lions, 21-10 (D)
1993—Lions, 16-13 (LA)
1999—Lions, 31-27 (D)
2001—Rams, 35-0 (D)
2003—Lions, 30-20 (D)
2006—Rams, 41-34 (StL)
2009—Rams, 17-10 (D)
2010—Lions, 44-6 (D)
(RS Pts.—Rams 1,582, Lions 1,489)
(PS Pts.—Lions 31, Rams 21)
*Franchise in Los Angeles prior to 1995
and in Cleveland prior to 1946
**Conference Playoff

DETROIT vs. SAN DIEGO
RS: Chargers lead series, 6-3
1972—Lions, 34-20 (D)
1977—Lions, 20-0 (D)
1978—Lions, 31-14 (D)
1981—Chargers, 28-23 (SD)
1984—Chargers, 27-24 (SD)
1996—Chargers, 27-21 (SD)
1999—Chargers, 20-10 (D)
2003—Chargers, 14-7 (D)
2007—Chargers, 51-14 (SD)
(RS Pts.—Chargers 201, Lions 184)

DETROIT vs. SAN FRANCISCO
RS: 49ers lead series, 34-26-1
PS: Series tied, 1-1
1950—Lions, 24-7 (D)
    49ers, 28-27 (SF)
1951—49ers, 20-10 (D)
    49ers, 21-17 (SF)
1952—49ers, 17-3 (SF)
    49ers, 28-0 (D)
1953—Lions, 24-21 (D)
    Lions, 14-10 (SF)
1954—49ers, 37-31 (SF)
    Lions, 48-7 (D)
1955—49ers, 27-24 (D)

    49ers, 38-21 (SF)
1956—Lions, 20-17 (D)
    Lions, 17-13 (SF)
1957—49ers, 35-31 (SF)
    Lions, 31-10 (D)
    *Lions, 31-27 (SF)
1958—49ers, 24-21 (SF)
    Lions, 35-21 (D)
1959—49ers, 34-13 (D)
    49ers, 33-7 (SF)
1960—49ers, 14-10 (D)
    Lions, 24-0 (SF)
1961—49ers, 49-0 (D)
    Tie, 20-20 (SF)
1962—Lions, 45-24 (D)
    Lions, 38-24 (SF)
1963—Lions, 26-3 (D)
    Lions, 45-7 (SF)
1964—Lions, 26-17 (SF)
    Lions, 24-7 (D)
1965—49ers, 27-21 (D)
    49ers, 17-14 (SF)
1966—49ers, 27-24 (SF)
    49ers, 41-14 (D)
1967—Lions, 45-3 (SF)
1968—49ers, 14-7 (SF)
1969—Lions, 26-14 (SF)
1970—Lions, 28-7 (D)
1971—49ers, 31-27 (SF)
1973—Lions, 30-20 (D)
1974—Lions, 17-13 (D)
1975—Lions, 28-17 (SF)
1977—49ers, 28-7 (SF)
1978—Lions, 33-14 (D)
1980—Lions, 17-13 (D)
1981—Lions, 24-17 (D)
1983—**49ers, 24-23 (SF)
1984—49ers, 30-27 (D)
1985—Lions, 23-21 (D)
1988—49ers, 20-13 (D)
1991—49ers, 35-3 (SF)
1992—49ers, 24-6 (SF)
1993—49ers, 55-17 (D)
1994—49ers, 27-21 (D)
1995—Lions, 27-24 (D)
1996—49ers, 24-14 (D)
1998—49ers, 35-13 (SF)
2001—49ers, 21-13 (SF)
2003—49ers, 24-17 (SF)
2006—49ers, 19-13 (D)
2008—49ers, 31-13 (SF)
2009—49ers, 20-6 (SF)
(RS Pts.—49ers 1,326, Lions 1,264)
(PS Pts.—Lions 54, 49ers 51)
*Conference Playoff
**NFC Divisional Playoff

DETROIT vs. SEATTLE
RS: Seahawks lead series, 7-4
1976—Lions, 41-14 (S)
1978—Seahawks, 28-16 (S)
1984—Seahawks, 38-17 (S)
1987—Seahawks, 37-14 (S)
1990—Seahawks, 30-10 (S)
1993—Lions, 30-10 (D)
1996—Lions, 17-16 (D)
1999—Lions, 28-20 (S)
2003—Seahawks, 35-14 (S)
2006—Seahawks, 9-6 (D)
2009—Seahawks, 32-20 (S)
(RS Pts.—Seahawks 269, Lions 213)

DETROIT vs. TAMPA BAY
RS: Lions lead series, 28-25
PS: Buccaneers lead series, 1-0
1977—Lions, 16-7 (D)
1978—Lions, 15-7 (TB)
    Lions, 34-23 (D)
1979—Buccaneers, 31-16 (TB)
    Buccaneers, 16-14 (D)
1980—Lions, 24-10 (TB)
    Lions, 27-14 (D)
1981—Buccaneers, 28-10 (TB)
    Buccaneers, 20-17 (D)
1982—Buccaneers, 23-21 (TB)
1983—Lions, 11-0 (TB)
    Lions, 23-20 (D)
1984—Buccaneers, 21-17 (TB)
    Lions, 13-7 (D) OT
1985—Lions, 30-9 (D)
    Buccaneers, 19-16 (TB) OT
1986—Buccaneers, 24-20 (D)
    Lions, 38-17 (TB)
1987—Buccaneers, 31-27 (D)
    Lions, 20-10 (TB)
1988—Buccaneers, 23-20 (D)
    Buccaneers, 21-10 (TB)
1989—Lions, 17-16 (TB)
    Lions, 33-7 (D)
1990—Buccaneers, 38-21 (D)
    Buccaneers, 23-20 (TB)
1991—Lions, 31-3 (D)
    Buccaneers, 30-21 (TB)
1992—Buccaneers, 27-23 (D)
    Lions, 38-7 (TB)
1993—Buccaneers, 27-10 (TB)
    Lions, 23-0 (D)
1994—Buccaneers, 24-14 (TB)
    Lions, 14-9 (D)
1995—Lions, 27-24 (D)
    Lions, 37-10 (TB)
1996—Lions, 21-6 (D)
    Lions, 27-0 (TB)
1997—Buccaneers, 24-17 (D)
    Lions, 27-9 (TB)
    *Buccaneers, 20-10 (TB)
1998—Lions, 27-6 (D)
    Lions, 28-25 (TB)
1999—Lions, 20-3 (D)
    Buccaneers, 23-16 (TB)
2000—Buccaneers, 31-10 (D)
    Lions, 28-14 (TB)
2001—Buccaneers, 20-17 (D)
    Buccaneers, 15-12 (TB)
2002—Buccaneers, 23-20 (D)
2005—Buccaneers, 17-13 (D)
2007—Lions, 23-16 (D)
2008—Buccaneers, 38-20 (D)
2010—Lions, 23-20 (TB) OT
(RS Pts—Lions 1,117, Buccaneers 916)
(PS Pts.—Buccaneers 20, Lions 10)
*NFC First-Round Playoff

DETROIT vs. *TENNESSEE
RS: Titans lead series, 7-3
1971—Lions, 31-7 (H)
1975—Oilers, 24-8 (H)
1983—Oilers, 27-17 (H)
1986—Lions, 24-13 (D)
1989—Oilers, 35-31 (H)
1992—Oilers, 24-21 (H)
1995—Lions, 24-17 (H)
2001—Titans, 27-24 (D)
2004—Titans, 24-19 (T)

2008—Titans, 47-10 (D)
(RS Pts.—Titans 245, Lions 209)
*Franchise in Houston prior to 1997;
known as Oilers prior to 1999*
*DETROIT vs. **WASHINGTON
RS: Redskins lead series, 27-12
PS: Redskins lead series, 3-0
1932—Spartans, 10-0 (P)
1933—Spartans, 13-0 (B)
1934—Lions, 24-0 (D)
1935—Lions, 17-7 (B)
    Lions, 14-0 (D)
1938—Redskins, 7-5 (D)
1939—Redskins, 31-7 (W)
1940—Redskins, 20-14 (D)
1942—Redskins, 15-3 (D)
1943—Redskins, 42-20 (W)
1946—Redskins, 17-16 (W)
1947—Lions, 38-21 (D)
1948—Redskins, 46-21 (W)
1951—Lions, 35-17 (D)
1956—Redskins, 18-17 (W)
1965—Lions, 14-10 (D)
1968—Redskins, 14-3 (W)
1970—Redskins, 31-10 (W)
1973—Redskins, 20-0 (D)
1976—Redskins, 20-7 (W)
1978—Redskins, 21-19 (D)
1979—Redskins, 27-24 (D)
1981—Redskins, 33-31 (W)
1982—***Redskins, 31-7 (W)
1983—Redskins, 38-17 (W)
1984—Redskins, 28-14 (W)
1985—Redskins, 24-3 (W)
1987—Redskins, 20-13 (W)
1990—Redskins, 41-38 (D) OT
1991—Redskins, 45-0 (W)
    ****Redskins, 41-10 (W)
1992—Redskins, 13-10 (W)
1995—Redskins, 36-30 (W) OT
1997—Redskins, 30-7 (W)
1999—Lions, 33-17 (D)
    ***Redskins, 27-13 (W)
2000—Lions, 15-10 (D)
2004—Redskins, 17-10 (D)
2007—Redskins, 34-3 (W)
2008—Redskins, 25-17 (D)
2009—Lions, 19-14 (D)
2010—Lions, 37-25 (D)
(RS Pts.—Redskins 834, Lions 628)
(PS Pts.—Redskins 99, Lions 30)
**Franchise in Portsmouth prior to 1934
and known as the Spartans.
**Franchise in Boston prior to 1937
***NFC First-Round Playoff
****NFC Championship*

GREEN BAY vs. ARIZONA
RS: Packers lead series, 43-22-4
PS: Series tied, 1-1;
See Arizona vs. Green Bay
GREEN BAY vs. ATLANTA
RS: Series tied, 12-12
PS: Packers lead series, 2-1;
See Atlanta vs. Green Bay
GREEN BAY vs. BALTIMORE
RS: Packers lead series, 3-1;
See Baltimore vs. Green Bay
GREEN BAY vs. BUFFALO
RS: Bills lead series, 7-4;
See Buffalo vs. Green Bay

GREEN BAY vs. CAROLINA
RS: Packers lead series, 6-4
PS: Packers lead series, 1-0;
See Carolina vs. Green Bay
GREEN BAY vs. CHICAGO
RS: Bears lead series, 91-83-6
PS: Series tied, 1-1;
See Chicago vs. Green Bay
GREEN BAY vs. CINCINNATI
RS: Bengals lead series, 6-5;
See Cincinnati vs. Green Bay
GREEN BAY vs. CLEVELAND
RS: Packers lead series, 10-7
PS: Packers lead series, 1-0;
See Cleveland vs. Green Bay
GREEN BAY vs. DALLAS
RS: Series tied, 12-12
PS: Cowboys lead series, 4-2;
See Dallas vs. Green Bay
GREEN BAY vs. DENVER
RS: Series tied, 5-5-1
PS: Broncos lead series, 1-0;
See Denver vs. Green Bay
GREEN BAY vs. DETROIT
RS: Packers lead series, 89-65-7
PS: Packers lead series, 2-0;
See Detroit vs. Green Bay
GREEN BAY vs. HOUSTON
RS: Series tied, 1-1
2004—Packers, 16-13 (H)
2008—Texans, 24-21 (GB)
(RS Pts.—Packers 37, Texans 37)
GREEN BAY vs. *INDIANAPOLIS
RS: Series tied, 20-20-1
PS: Packers lead series, 1-0
1953—Packers, 37-14 (GB)
    Packers, 35-24 (B)
1954—Packers, 7-6 (B)
    Packers, 24-13 (Mil)
1955—Colts, 24-20 (Mil)
    Colts, 14-10 (B)
1956—Packers, 38-33 (Mil)
    Colts, 28-21 (B)
1957—Colts, 45-17 (Mil)
    Packers, 24-21 (B)
1958—Colts, 24-17 (Mil)
    Colts, 56-0 (B)
1959—Colts, 38-21 (B)
    Colts, 28-24 (Mil)
1960—Packers, 35-21 (GB)
    Colts, 38-24 (B)
1961—Packers, 45-7 (GB)
    Colts, 45-21 (B)
1962—Packers, 17-6 (B)
    Packers, 17-13 (GB)
1963—Packers, 31-20 (GB)
    Packers, 34-20 (B)
1964—Colts, 21-20 (GB)
    Colts, 24-21 (B)
1965—Packers, 20-17 (Mil)
    Packers, 42-27 (B)
    **Packers, 13-10 (GB) OT
1966—Packers, 24-3 (Mil)
    Packers, 14-10 (B)
1967—Colts, 13-10 (B)
1968—Colts, 16-3 (GB)
1969—Colts, 14-6 (B)
1970—Colts, 13-10 (Mil)
1974—Packers, 20-13 (B)
1982—Tie, 20-20 (B) OT
1985—Colts, 37-10 (I)

1988—Colts, 20-13 (GB)
1991—Packers, 14-10 (Mil)
1997—Colts, 41-38 (I)
2000—Packers, 26-24 (GB)
2004—Colts, 45-31 (I)
2008—Packers, 34-14 (GB)
(RS Pts.—Colts 920, Packers 895)
(PS Pts.—Packers 13, Colts 10)
**Franchise in Baltimore prior to 1984
**Conference Playoff*
GREEN BAY vs. JACKSONVILLE
RS: Series tied, 2-2
1995—Packers, 24-14 (J)
2001—Packers, 28-21 (J)
2004—Jaguars, 28-25 (GB)
2008—Jaguars, 20-16 (J)
(RS Pts.—Packers 93, Jaguars 83)
GREEN BAY vs. KANSAS CITY
RS: Chiefs lead series, 6-2-1
PS: Packers lead series, 1-0
1966—*Packers, 35-10 (Los Angeles)
1973—Tie, 10-10 (Mil)
1977—Chiefs, 20-10 (KC)
1987—Packers, 23-3 (KC)
1989—Chiefs, 21-3 (GB)
1990—Chiefs, 17-3 (GB)
1993—Chiefs, 23-16 (KC)
1996—Chiefs, 27-20 (KC)
2003—Chiefs, 40-34 (GB) OT
2007—Packers, 33-22 (KC)
(RS Pts.—Chiefs 183, Packers 152)
(PS Pts.—Packers 35, Chiefs 10)
*Super Bowl I
GREEN BAY vs. MIAMI
RS: Dolphins lead series, 10-3
1971—Dolphins, 27-6 (Mia)
1975—Dolphins, 31-7 (GB)
1979—Dolphins, 27-7 (Mia)
1985—Dolphins, 34-24 (GB)
1988—Dolphins, 24-17 (Mia)
1989—Dolphins, 23-20 (Mia)
1991—Dolphins, 16-13 (Mia)
1994—Dolphins, 24-14 (Mil)
1997—Packers, 23-18 (GB)
2000—Dolphins, 28-20 (Mia)
2002—Packers, 24-10 (GB)
2006—Packers, 34-24 (M)
2010—Dolphins, 23-20 (GB) OT
(RS Pts.—Dolphins 309, Packers 229)
GREEN BAY vs. MINNESOTA
RS: Packers lead series, 51-47-1
PS: Vikings lead series, 1-0
1961—Packers, 33-7 (Minn)
    Packers, 28-10 (Mil)
1962—Packers, 34-7 (GB)
    Packers, 48-21 (Minn)
1963—Packers, 37-28 (Minn)
    Packers, 28-7 (GB)
1964—Vikings, 24-23 (GB)
    Packers, 42-13 (Minn)
1965—Packers, 38-13 (Minn)
    Packers, 24-19 (GB)
1966—Vikings, 20-17 (GB)
    Packers, 28-16 (Minn)
1967—Vikings, 10-7 (Mil)
    Packers, 30-27 (Minn)
1968—Vikings, 26-13 (Mil)
    Vikings, 14-10 (Minn)
1969—Vikings, 19-7 (Minn)
    Vikings, 9-7 (Mil)
1970—Packers, 13-10 (Mil)

Vikings, 10-3 (Minn)
1971—Vikings, 24-13 (GB)
Vikings, 3-0 (Minn)
1972—Vikings, 27-13 (GB)
Packers, 23-7 (Minn)
1973—Vikings, 11-3 (Minn)
Vikings, 31-7 (GB)
1974—Vikings, 32-17 (GB)
Packers, 19-7 (Minn)
1975—Vikings, 28-17 (GB)
Vikings, 24-3 (Minn)
1976—Vikings, 17-10 (Mil)
Vikings, 20-9 (Minn)
1977—Vikings, 19-7 (Minn)
Vikings, 13-6 (GB)
1978—Vikings, 21-7 (Minn)
Tie, 10-10 (GB) OT
1979—Vikings, 27-21 (Minn) OT
Packers, 19-7 (Mil)
1980—Packers, 16-3 (GB)
Packers, 25-13 (Minn)
1981—Vikings, 30-13 (Mil)
Packers, 35-23 (Minn)
1982—Packers, 26-7 (Mil)
1983—Vikings, 20-17 (GB) OT
Packers, 29-21 (Minn)
1984—Packers, 45-17 (Mil)
Packers, 38-14 (Minn)
1985—Packers, 20-17 (Mil)
Packers, 27-17 (Minn)
1986—Vikings, 42-7 (Minn)
Vikings, 32-6 (GB)
1987—Packers, 23-16 (Minn)
Packers, 16-10 (Mil)
1988—Packers, 34-14 (Minn)
Packers, 18-6 (GB)
1989—Vikings, 26-14 (Minn)
Packers, 20-19 (Mil)
1990—Packers, 24-10 (Mil)
Vikings, 23-7 (Minn)
1991—Vikings, 35-21 (GB)
Packers, 27-7 (Minn)
1992—Vikings, 23-20 (GB) OT
Vikings, 27-7 (Minn)
1993—Vikings, 15-13 (Minn)
Vikings, 21-17 (Mil)
1994—Packers, 16-10 (GB)
Vikings, 13-10 (Minn) OT
1995—Packers, 38-21 (GB)
Vikings, 27-24 (Minn)
1996—Vikings, 30-21 (Minn)
Packers, 38-10 (GB)
1997—Packers, 38-32 (GB)
Packers, 27-11 (Minn)
1998—Vikings, 37-24 (GB)
Vikings, 28-14 (Minn)
1999—Packers, 23-20 (GB)
Vikings, 24-20 (Minn)
2000—Packers, 26-20 (GB) OT
Packers, 33-28 (Minn)
2001—Vikings, 35-13 (Minn)
Packers, 24-13 (GB)
2002—Vikings, 31-21 (Minn)
Packers, 26-22 (GB)
2003—Vikings, 30-25 (GB)
Packers, 30-27 (Minn)
2004—Packers, 34-31 (GB)
Packers, 34-31 (Minn)
*Vikings, 31-17 (GB)
2005—Vikings, 23-20 (Minn)
Vikings, 20-17 (GB)

2006—Packers, 23-17 (Minn)
Packers, 9-7 (GB)
2007—Packers, 23-16 (Minn)
Packers, 34-0 (GB)
2008—Packers, 24-19 (GB)
Vikings, 28-27 (Minn)
2009—Vikings, 30-23 (Minn)
Vikings, 38-26 (GB)
2010—Packers, 28-24 (GB)
Packers, 31-3 (Minn)
(RS Pts.—Packers 2,083, Vikings 1,902)
(PS Pts.—Vikings 31, Packers 17)
*NFC First-Round Playoff
GREEN BAY vs. NEW ENGLAND
RS: Patriots lead series, 5-4
PS: Packers lead series, 1-0
1973—Patriots, 33-24 (NE)
1979—Packers, 27-14 (GB)
1985—Patriots, 26-20 (NE)
1988—Packers, 45-3 (Mil)
1994—Patriots, 17-16 (NE)
1996—*Packers, 35-21 (New Orleans)
1997—Packers, 28-10 (NE)
2002—Packers, 28-10 (NE)
2006—Patriots, 35-0 (GB)
2010—Patriots, 31-27 (NE)
(RS Pts.—Packers 215, Patriots 179)
(PS Pts.—Packers 35, Patriots 21)
*Super Bowl XXXI
GREEN BAY vs. NEW ORLEANS
RS: Packers lead series, 14-7
1968—Packers, 29-7 (Mil)
1971—Saints, 29-21 (Mil)
1972—Packers, 30-20 (NO)
1973—Packers, 30-10 (Mil)
1975—Saints, 20-19 (NO)
1976—Packers, 32-27 (Mil)
1977—Packers, 24-20 (NO)
1978—Packers, 28-17 (Mil)
1979—Packers, 28-19 (Mil)
1981—Packers, 35-7 (NO)
1984—Packers, 23-13 (NO)
1985—Packers, 38-14 (Mil)
1986—Saints, 24-10 (NO)
1987—Saints, 33-24 (NO)
1989—Packers, 35-34 (GB)
1993—Packers, 19-17 (NO)
1995—Packers, 34-23 (NO)
2002—Saints, 35-20 (NO)
2005—Packers, 52-3 (GB)
2006—Saints, 34-27 (GB)
2008—Saints, 51-29 (NO)
(RS Pts.—Packers 587, Saints 457)
GREEN BAY vs. N.Y. GIANTS
RS: Packers lead series, 26-21-2
PS: Packers lead series, 4-2
1928—Giants, 6-0 (GB)
Packers, 7-0 (NY)
1929—Packers, 20-6 (NY)
1930—Packers, 14-7 (GB)
Giants, 13-6 (NY)
1931—Packers, 27-7 (GB)
Packers, 14-10 (NY)
1932—Packers, 13-0 (GB)
Giants, 6-0 (NY)
1933—Giants, 10-7 (Mil)
Giants, 17-6 (NY)
1934—Packers, 20-6 (Mil)
Giants, 17-3 (NY)
1935—Packers, 16-7 (GB)
1936—Packers, 26-14 (NY)

1937—Giants, 10-0 (NY)
1938—Giants, 15-3 (NY)
*Giants, 23-17 (NY)
1939—*Packers, 27-0 (Mil)
1940—Giants, 7-3 (NY)
1942—Tie, 21-21 (NY)
1943—Packers, 35-21 (NY)
1944—Giants, 24-0 (NY)
*Packers, 14-7 (NY)
1945—Packers, 23-14 (NY)
1947—Tie, 24-24 (NY)
1948—Giants, 49-3 (Mil)
1949—Giants, 30-10 (GB)
1952—Packers, 17-3 (GB)
1957—Giants, 31-17 (GB)
1959—Giants, 20-3 (NY)
1961—Packers, 20-17 (Mil)
*Packers, 37-0 (GB)
1962—*Packers, 16-7 (NY)
1967—Packers, 48-21 (NY)
1969—Packers, 20-10 (Mil)
1971—Giants, 42-40 (GB)
1973—Packers, 16-14 (New Haven)
1975—Packers, 40-14 (Mil)
1980—Giants, 27-21 (NY)
1981—Packers, 27-14 (NY)
Packers, 26-24 (Mil)
1982—Packers, 27-19 (NY)
1983—Giants, 27-3 (NY)
1985—Packers, 23-20 (GB)
1986—Giants, 55-24 (NY)
1987—Giants, 20-10 (NY)
1992—Giants, 27-7 (NY)
1995—Packers, 14-6 (GB)
1998—Packers, 37-3 (NY)
2001—Packers, 34-25 (NY)
2004—Giants, 14-7 (GB)
2007—Packers, 35-13 (NY)
**Giants, 23-20 (GB) OT
2010—Packers, 45-17 (GB)
(RS Pts.—Packers 862, Giants 824)
(PS Pts.—Packers 131, Giants 60)
*NFL Championship
**NFC Championship Game
GREEN BAY vs. N.Y. JETS
RS: Jets lead series, 8-3
1973—Packers, 23-7 (Mil)
1979—Jets, 27-22 (GB)
1981—Jets, 28-3 (NY)
1982—Jets, 15-13 (NY)
1985—Jets, 24-3 (Mil)
1991—Jets, 19-16 (NY) OT
1994—Packers, 17-10 (GB)
2000—Jets, 20-16 (GB)
2002—Jets, 42-17 (NY)
2006—Jets, 38-10 (GB)
2010—Packers, 9-0 (NY)
(RS Pts.—Jets 230, Packers 149)
GREEN BAY vs. *OAKLAND
RS: Series tied, 5-5
PS: Packers lead series, 1-0
1967—**Packers, 33-14 (Miami)
1972—Raiders, 20-14 (GB)
1976—Raiders, 18-14 (O)
1978—Raiders, 28-3 (GB)
1984—Raiders, 28-7 (LA)
1987—Raiders, 20-0 (GB)
1990—Packers, 29-16 (LA)
1993—Packers, 28-0 (GB)
1999—Packers, 28-24 (GB)
2003—Packers, 41-7 (O)

2007—Packers, 38-7 (GB)
(RS Pts.—Packers 202, Raiders 168)
(PS Pts.—Packers 33, Raiders 14)
*Franchise in Los Angeles from 1982-1994
**Super Bowl II

GREEN BAY vs. PHILADELPHIA
RS: Packers lead series, 24-13
PS: Eagles lead series, 2-1
1933—Packers, 35-9 (GB)
    Packers, 10-0 (P)
1934—Packers, 19-6 (GB)
1935—Packers, 13-6 (GB)
1937—Packers, 37-7 (Mil)
1939—Packers, 23-16 (P)
1940—Packers, 27-20 (GB)
1942—Packers, 7-0 (P)
1946—Packers, 19-7 (P)
1947—Eagles, 28-14 (P)
1951—Packers, 37-24 (GB)
1952—Packers, 12-10 (Mil)
1954—Packers, 37-14 (P)
1958—Packers, 38-35 (GB)
1960—*Eagles, 17-13 (P)
1962—Packers, 49-0 (P)
1968—Packers, 30-13 (GB)
1970—Packers, 30-17 (Mil)
1974—Eagles, 36-14 (P)
1976—Packers, 28-13 (GB)
1978—Eagles, 10-3 (P)
1979—Eagles, 21-10 (GB)
1987—Packers, 16-10 (GB) OT
1990—Eagles, 31-0 (P)
1991—Eagles, 20-3 (GB)
1992—Packers, 27-24 (Mil)
1993—Eagles, 20-17 (GB)
1994—Eagles, 13-7 (P)
1996—Packers, 39-13 (GB)
1997—Eagles, 10-9 (P)
1998—Packers, 24-16 (GB)
2000—Packers, 6-3 (GB)
2003—Eagles, 17-14 (GB)
    **Eagles, 20-17 (P) OT
2004—Eagles, 47-17 (P)
2005—Eagles, 19-14 (P)
2006—Eagles, 31-9 (P)
2007—Packers, 16-13 (GB)
2010—Packers, 27-20 (P)
    ***Packers, 21-16 (P)
(RS Pts.—Packers 737, Eagles 599)
(PS Pts.—Eagles 53, Packers 51)
*NFL Championship
**NFC Divisional Playoff
***NFC First-Round Playoff

GREEN BAY vs. *PITTSBURGH
RS: Packers lead series, 18-14
PS: Packers lead series, 1-0
1933—Packers, 47-0 (GB)
1935—Packers, 27-0 (GB)
    Packers, 34-14 (P)
1936—Packers, 42-10 (Mil)
1938—Packers, 20-0 (GB)
1940—Packers, 24-3 (Mil)
1941—Packers, 54-7 (P)
1942—Packers, 24-21 (Mil)
1946—Packers, 17-7 (GB)
1947—Steelers, 18-17 (Mil)
1948—Steelers, 38-7 (P)
1949—Steelers, 30-7 (Mil)
1951—Packers, 35-33 (Mil)
    Steelers, 28-7 (P)
1953—Steelers, 31-14 (P)

1954—Steelers, 21-20 (GB)
1957—Packers, 27-10 (P)
1960—Packers, 19-13 (P)
1963—Packers, 33-14 (Mil)
1965—Packers, 41-9 (P)
1967—Steelers, 24-17 (GB)
1969—Packers, 38-34 (P)
1970—Packers, 20-12 (P)
1975—Steelers, 16-13 (Mil)
1980—Steelers, 22-20 (P)
1983—Steelers, 25-21 (GB)
1986—Steelers, 27-3 (P)
1992—Packers, 17-3 (GB)
1995—Packers, 24-19 (GB)
1998—Steelers, 27-20 (P)
2005—Steelers, 20-10 (GB)
2009—Steelers, 37-36 (P)
2010—**Packers, 31-25 (North Texas)
(RS Pts.—Packers 755, Steelers 573)
(PS Pts.—Packers 31, Steelers 25)
*Steelers known as Pirates prior to 1940
**Super Bowl XLV

GREEN BAY vs. *ST. LOUIS
RS: Rams lead series, 45-42-2
PS: Series tied, 1-1
1937—Packers, 35-10 (C)
    Packers, 35-7 (GB)
1938—Packers, 26-17 (GB)
    Packers, 28-7 (C)
1939—Rams, 27-24 (GB)
    Packers, 7-6 (C)
1940—Packers, 31-14 (GB)
    Tie, 13-13 (C)
1941—Packers, 24-7 (Mil)
    Packers, 17-14 (C)
1942—Packers, 45-28 (GB)
    Packers, 30-12 (C)
1944—Packers, 30-21 (GB)
    Packers, 42-7 (C)
1945—Rams, 27-14 (GB)
    Rams, 20-7 (C)
1946—Rams, 21-17 (Mil)
    Rams, 38-17 (LA)
1947—Packers, 17-14 (Mil)
    Packers, 30-10 (LA)
1948—Packers, 16-0 (GB)
    Rams, 24-10 (LA)
1949—Rams, 48-7 (GB)
    Rams, 35-7 (LA)
1950—Rams, 45-14 (Mil)
    Rams, 51-14 (LA)
1951—Rams, 28-0 (Mil)
    Rams, 42-14 (LA)
1952—Rams, 30-28 (Mil)
    Rams, 45-27 (LA)
1953—Rams, 38-20 (Mil)
    Rams, 33-17 (LA)
1954—Packers, 35-17 (Mil)
    Rams, 35-27 (LA)
1955—Packers, 30-28 (Mil)
    Rams, 31-17 (LA)
1956—Rams, 42-17 (Mil)
    Rams, 49-21 (LA)
1957—Rams, 31-27 (Mil)
    Rams, 42-17 (LA)
1958—Rams, 20-7 (GB)
    Rams, 34-20 (LA)
1959—Rams, 45-6 (Mil)
    Packers, 38-20 (LA)
1960—Rams, 33-31 (Mil)
    Packers, 35-21 (LA)

1961—Packers, 35-17 (GB)
    Packers, 24-17 (LA)
1962—Packers, 41-10 (Mil)
    Packers, 20-17 (LA)
1963—Packers, 42-10 (GB)
    Packers, 31-14 (LA)
1964—Rams, 27-17 (Mil)
    Tie, 24-24 (LA)
1965—Packers, 6-3 (Mil)
    Rams, 21-10 (LA)
1966—Packers, 24-13 (GB)
    Packers, 27-23 (LA)
1967—Rams, 27-24 (LA)
    **Packers, 28-7 (Mil)
1968—Rams, 16-14 (Mil)
1969—Rams, 34-21 (LA)
1970—Rams, 31-21 (GB)
1971—Rams, 30-13 (LA)
1973—Rams, 24-7 (LA)
1974—Packers, 17-6 (Mil)
1975—Rams, 22-5 (LA)
1977—Rams, 24-6 (Mil)
1978—Rams, 31-14 (LA)
1980—Rams, 51-21 (LA)
1981—Rams, 35-23 (LA)
1982—Packers, 35-23 (Mil)
1983—Packers, 27-24 (Mil)
1984—Packers, 31-6 (Mil)
1985—Rams, 34-17 (LA)
1988—Rams, 34-7 (GB)
1989—Rams, 41-38 (LA)
1990—Packers, 36-24 (GB)
1991—Rams, 23-21 (LA)
1992—Packers, 28-13 (GB)
1993—Packers, 36-6 (Mil)
1994—Packers, 24-17 (GB)
1995—Rams, 17-14 (GB)
1996—Packers, 24-9 (StL)
1997—Packers, 17-7 (GB)
2001—***Rams, 45-17 (StL)
2003—Rams, 34-24 (StL)
2004—Packers, 45-17 (StL)
2006—Rams, 23-20 (GB)
2007—Packers, 33-14 (StL)
2009—Packers, 36-17 (StL)
(RS Pts.—Rams 2,072, Packers 2,016)
(PS Pts.—Rams 52, Packers 45)
*Franchise in Los Angeles prior to 1995
and in Cleveland prior to 1946
**Conference Championship
***NFC Divisional Playoff

GREEN BAY vs. SAN DIEGO
RS: Packers lead series, 8-1
1970—Packers, 22-20 (SD)
1974—Packers, 34-0 (GB)
1978—Packers, 24-3 (SD)
1984—Chargers, 34-28 (SD)
1993—Packers, 20-13 (SD)
1996—Packers, 42-10 (GB)
1999—Packers, 31-3 (SD)
2003—Packers, 38-21 (SD)
2007—Packers, 31-24 (GB)
(RS Pts.—Packers 270, Chargers 128)

GREEN BAY vs. SAN FRANCISCO
RS: Packers lead series, 30-25-1
PS: Packers lead series, 4-1
1950—Packers, 25-21 (GB)
    49ers, 30-14 (SF)
1951—49ers, 31-19 (GB)
1952—49ers, 24-14 (SF)
1953—49ers, 37-7 (Mil)

49ers, 48-14 (SF)
1954—49ers, 23-17 (Mil)
49ers, 35-0 (SF)
1955—Packers, 27-21 (Mil)
Packers, 28-7 (SF)
1956—49ers, 17-16 (GB)
49ers, 38-20 (SF)
1957—49ers, 24-14 (Mil)
49ers, 27-20 (SF)
1958—49ers, 33-12 (Mil)
49ers, 48-21 (SF)
1959—Packers, 21-20 (GB)
Packers, 36-14 (SF)
1960—Packers, 41-14 (Mil)
Packers, 13-0 (SF)
1961—Packers, 30-10 (GB)
49ers, 22-21 (SF)
1962—Packers, 31-13 (Mil)
Packers, 31-21 (SF)
1963—Packers, 28-10 (Mil)
Packers, 21-17 (SF)
1964—Packers, 24-14 (Mil)
49ers, 24-14 (SF)
1965—Packers, 27-10 (GB)
Tie, 24-24 (SF)
1966—49ers, 21-20 (SF)
Packers, 20-7 (Mil)
1967—Packers, 13-0 (GB)
1968—49ers, 27-20 (SF)
1969—Packers, 14-7 (Mil)
1970—49ers, 26-10 (SF)
1972—Packers, 34-24 (Mil)
1973—49ers, 20-6 (SF)
1974—49ers, 7-6 (SF)
1976—49ers, 26-14 (GB)
1977—Packers, 16-14 (Mil)
1980—Packers, 23-16 (Mil)
1981—49ers, 13-3 (Mil)
1986—49ers, 31-17 (Mil)
1987—Packers, 23-12 (GB)
1989—Packers, 21-17 (GB)
1990—49ers, 24-20 (GB)
1995—*Packers, 27-17 (SF)
1996—Packers, 23-20 (GB) OT
*Packers, 35-14 (GB)
1997—**Packers, 23-10 (SF)
1998—Packers, 36-22 (GB)
***49ers, 30-27 (SF)
1999—Packers, 20-3 (GB)
2000—Packers, 31-28 (GB)
2001—***Packers, 25-15 (GB)
2002—Packers, 20-14 (SF)
2003—Packers, 20-10 (GB)
2006—Packers, 30-19 (GB)
2009—Packers, 30-24 (GB)
2010—Packers, 34-16 (GB)
(RS Pts.—Packers 1,143, 49ers 1,136)
(PS Pts.—Packers 137, 49ers 86)
*NFC Divisional Playoff
**NFC Championship
***NFC First-Round Playoff
GREEN BAY vs. SEATTLE
RS: Packers lead series, 8-5
PS: Packers lead series, 2-0
1976—Packers, 27-20 (Mil)
1978—Packers, 45-28 (Mil)
1981—Packers, 34-24 (GB)
1984—Seahawks, 30-24 (Mil)
1987—Seahawks, 24-13 (S)
1990—Seahawks, 20-14 (Mil)
1996—Packers, 31-10 (S)

1999—Seahawks, 27-7 (GB)
2003—Packers, 35-13 (GB)
*Packers, 33-27 (GB) OT
2005—Packers, 23-17 (GB)
2006—Seahawks, 34-24 (S)
2007—**Packers, 42-20 (GB)
2008—Packers, 27-17 (S)
2009—Packers, 48-10 (GB)
(RS Pts.—Packers 352, Seahawks 274)
(PS Pts.—Packers 75, Seahawks 47)
*NFC First-Round Playoff
**NFC Divisional Playoff
GREEN BAY vs. TAMPA BAY
RS: Packers lead series, 29-21-1
PS: Packers lead series, 1-0
1977—Packers, 13-0 (TB)
1978—Packers, 9-7 (GB)
Packers, 17-7 (TB)
1979—Buccaneers, 21-10 (GB)
Buccaneers, 21-3 (TB)
1980—Tie, 14-14 (TB) OT
Buccaneers, 20-17 (Mil)
1981—Buccaneers, 21-10 (GB)
Buccaneers, 37-3 (TB)
1983—Packers, 55-14 (GB)
Packers, 12-9 (TB) OT
1984—Buccaneers, 30-27 (TB) OT
Packers, 27-14 (GB)
1985—Packers, 21-0 (GB)
Packers, 20-17 (TB)
1986—Packers, 31-7 (Mil)
Packers, 21-7 (TB)
1987—Buccaneers, 23-17 (Mil)
1988—Buccaneers, 13-10 (GB)
Buccaneers, 27-24 (TB)
1989—Buccaneers, 23-21 (GB)
Packers, 17-16 (TB)
1990—Buccaneers, 26-14 (TB)
Packers, 20-10 (Mil)
1991—Packers, 15-13 (GB)
Packers, 27-0 (TB)
1992—Buccaneers, 31-3 (TB)
Packers, 19-14 (Mil)
1993—Packers, 37-14 (TB)
Packers, 13-10 (GB)
1994—Packers, 30-3 (GB)
Packers, 34-19 (TB)
1995—Packers, 35-13 (GB)
Buccaneers, 13-10 (TB) OT
1996—Packers, 34-3 (TB)
Packers, 13-7 (GB)
1997—Packers, 21-16 (GB)
Packers, 17-6 (TB)
*Packers, 21-7 (GB)
1998—Packers, 23-15 (GB)
Buccaneers, 24-22 (TB)
1999—Packers, 26-23 (GB)
Buccaneers, 29-10 (TB)
2000—Buccaneers, 20-15 (TB)
Packers, 17-14 (GB) OT
2001—Buccaneers, 14-10 (TB)
Packers, 21-20 (GB)
2002—Buccaneers, 21-7 (TB)
2003—Packers, 20-13 (TB)
2005—Buccaneers, 17-16 (GB)
2008—Buccaneers, 30-21 (TB)
2009—Buccaneers, 38-28 (TB)
(RS Pts.—Packers 977, Buccaneers 824)
(PS Pts.—Packers 21, Buccaneers 7)
*NFC Divisional Playoff

GREEN BAY vs. *TENNESSEE
RS: Titans lead series, 6-4
1972—Packers, 23-10 (H)
1977—Oilers, 16-10 (GB)
1980—Oilers, 22-3 (GB)
1983—Packers, 41-38 (H) OT
1986—Oilers, 31-3 (GB)
1992—Packers, 16-14 (H)
1998—Packers, 30-22 (GB)
2001—Titans, 26-20 (T)
2004—Titans, 48-27 (GB)
2008—Titans, 19-16 (T) OT
(RS Pts.—Titans 246, Packers 189)
*Franchise in Houston prior to 1997;
known as Oilers prior to 1999
GREEN BAY vs. *WASHINGTON
RS: Packers lead series, 17-13-1
PS: Series tied, 1-1
1932—Packers, 21-0 (B)
1933—Tie, 7-7 (GB)
Redskins, 20-7 (B)
1934—Packers, 10-0 (B)
1936—Packers, 31-2 (GB)
Packers, 7-3 (B)
**Packers, 21-6 (New York)
1937—Redskins, 14-6 (W)
1939—Packers, 24-14 (Mil)
1941—Packers, 22-17 (W)
1943—Redskins, 33-7 (Mil)
1946—Packers, 20-7 (W)
1947—Packers, 27-10 (Mil)
1948—Redskins, 23-7 (Mil)
1949—Redskins, 30-0 (W)
1950—Packers, 35-21 (Mil)
1952—Packers, 35-20 (Mil)
1958—Redskins, 37-21 (W)
1959—Packers, 21-0 (GB)
1968—Packers, 27-7 (W)
1972—Redskins, 21-16 (W)
***Redskins, 16-3 (W)
1974—Redskins, 17-6 (GB)
1977—Redskins, 10-9 (W)
1979—Packers, 38-21 (W)
1983—Packers, 48-47 (GB)
1986—Redskins, 16-7 (GB)
1988—Redskins, 20-17 (Mil)
2001—Packers, 37-0 (GB)
2002—Packers, 30-9 (GB)
2004—Packers, 28-14 (W)
2007—Packers, 17-14 (GB)
2010—Redskins, 16-13 (W) OT
(RS Pts.—Packers 584, Redskins 487)
(PS Pts.—Packers 24, Redskins 22)
*Franchise in Boston prior to 1937 and
known as Braves prior to 1933
**NFL Championship
***NFC Divisional Playoff

HOUSTON vs. ARIZONA
RS: Series tied, 1-1;
See Arizona vs. Houston
HOUSTON vs. ATLANTA
RS: Series tied, 1-1;
See Atlanta vs. Houston
HOUSTON vs. BALTIMORE
RS: Ravens lead series, 4-0;
See Baltimore vs. Houston
HOUSTON vs. BUFFALO
RS: Bills lead series, 3-2;
See Buffalo vs. Houston

HOUSTON vs. CAROLINA
RS: Texans lead series, 2-0;
See Carolina vs. Houston
HOUSTON vs. CHICAGO
RS: Texans lead series, 2-0;
See Chicago vs. Houston
HOUSTON vs. CINCINNATI
RS: Bengals lead series, 3-2;
See Cincinnati vs. Houston
HOUSTON vs. CLEVELAND
RS: Series tied, 3-3;
See Cleveland vs. Houston
HOUSTON vs. DALLAS
RS: Cowboys lead series, 2-1;
See Dallas vs. Houston
HOUSTON vs. DENVER
RS: Broncos lead series, 2-1;
See Denver vs. Houston
HOUSTON vs. DETROIT
RS: Series tied, 1-1;
See Detroit vs. Houston
HOUSTON vs. GREEN BAY
RS: Series tied, 1-1;
See Green Bay vs. Houston
HOUSTON vs. INDIANAPOLIS
RS: Colts lead series, 16-2
2002—Colts, 23-3 (H)
　　　Colts, 19-3 (I)
2003—Colts, 30-21 (I)
　　　Colts, 20-17 (H)
2004—Colts, 49-14 (I)
　　　Colts, 23-14 (H)
2005—Colts, 38-20 (H)
　　　Colts, 31-17 (I)
2006—Colts, 43-24 (I)
　　　Texans, 27-24 (H)
2007—Colts, 30-24 (H)
　　　Colts, 38-15 (I)
2008—Colts, 31-27 (H)
　　　Colts, 33-27 (I)
2009—Colts, 20-17 (I)
　　　Colts, 35-27 (H)
2010—Texans, 34-24 (H)
　　　Colts, 30-17 (I)
(RS Pts.—Colts 541, Texans 348)
HOUSTON vs. JACKSONVILLE
RS: Series tied, 9-9
2002—Texans, 21-19 (I)
　　　Jaguars, 24-21 (H)
2003—Texans, 24-20 (H)
　　　Jaguars, 27-0 (J)
2004—Texans, 20-6 (H)
　　　Texans, 21-0 (J)
2005—Jaguars, 21-14 (J)
　　　Jaguars, 38-20 (H)
2006—Texans, 27-7 (H)
　　　Texans, 13-10 (J)
2007—Jaguars, 37-17 (J)
　　　Texans, 42-28 (H)
2008—Jaguars, 30-27 (J) OT
　　　Texans, 30-17 (H)
2009—Jaguars, 31-24 (H)
　　　Jaguars, 23-18 (J)
2010—Jaguars, 31-24 (J)
　　　Texans, 34-17 (H)
(RS Pts.—Texans 397, Jaguars 386)
HOUSTON vs. KANSAS CITY
RS: Texans lead series, 3-2
2003—Chiefs, 42-14 (H)
2004—Texans, 24-21 (KC)
2005—Chiefs, 45-17 (H)

2007—Texans, 20-3 (H)
2010—Texans, 35-31 (H)
(RS Pts.—Chiefs 142, Texans 110)
HOUSTON vs. MIAMI
RS: Texans lead series, 5-0
2003—Texans, 21-20 (M)
2006—Texans, 17-15 (H)
2007—Texans, 22-19 (H)
2008—Texans, 29-28 (H)
2009—Texans, 27-20 (M)
(RS Pts.—Texans 116, Dolphins 102)
HOUSTON vs. MINNESOTA
RS: Vikings lead series, 2-0
2004—Vikings, 34-28 (H) OT
2008—Vikings, 28-21 (M)
(RS Pts.—Vikings 62, Texans 49)
HOUSTON vs. NEW ENGLAND
RS: Patriots lead series, 2-1
2003—Patriots, 23-20 (H) OT
2006—Patriots, 40-7 (NE)
2009—Texans, 34-27 (H)
(RS Pts.—Patriots 90, Texans 61)
HOUSTON vs. NEW ORLEANS
RS: Series tied, 1-1
2003—Saints, 31-10 (NO)
2007—Texans, 23-10 (H)
(RS Pts.—Saints 41, Texans 33)
HOUSTON vs. N.Y. GIANTS
RS: Giants lead series, 2-1
2002—Texans, 16-14 (H)
2006—Giants, 14-10 (NY)
2010—Giants, 34-10 (H)
(RS Pts.　Giants 62, Texans 36)
HOUSTON vs. N.Y. JETS
RS: Jets lead series, 5-0
2003—Jets, 19-14 (H)
2004—Jets, 29-7 (NY)
2006—Jets, 26-11 (NY)
2009—Jets, 24-7 (H)
2010—Jets, 30-27 (NY)
(RS Pts.—Jets 128, Texans 66)
HOUSTON vs. OAKLAND
RS: Texans lead series, 5-1
2004—Texans, 30-17 (H)
2006—Texans, 23-14 (O)
2007—Texans, 24-17 (O)
2008—Raiders, 27-16 (O)
2009—Texans, 29-6 (H)
2010—Texans, 31-24 (O)
(RS Pts.—Texans 153, Raiders 105)
HOUSTON vs. PHILADELPHIA
RS: Eagles lead series, 3-0
2002—Eagles, 35-17 (P)
2006—Eagles, 24-10 (H)
2010—Eagles, 34-24 (P)
(RS Pts.—Eagles 93, Texans 51)
HOUSTON vs. PITTSBURGH
RS: Steelers lead series, 2-1
2002—Texans, 24-6 (P)
2005—Steelers, 27-7 (H)
2008—Steelers, 38-17 (P)
(RS Pts.—Steelers 71, Texans 48)
HOUSTON vs. ST. LOUIS
RS: Series tied, 1-1
2005—Rams, 33-27 (H) OT
2009—Texans, 16-13 (StL)
(RS Pts.—Rams 46, Texans 43)
HOUSTON vs. SAN DIEGO
RS: Chargers lead series, 4-0
2002—Chargers, 24-3 (SD)
2004—Chargers, 27-20 (H)

2007—Chargers, 35-10 (SD)
2010—Chargers, 29-23 (H)
(RS Pts.—Chargers 115, Texans 56)
HOUSTON vs. SAN FRANCISCO
RS: Series tied, 1-1
2005—49ers, 20-17 (SF) OT
2009—Texans, 24-21 (H)
(RS Pts.—Texans 41, 49ers 41)
HOUSTON vs. SEATTLE
RS: Series tied, 1-1
2005—Seahawks, 42-10 (S)
2009—Texans, 34-7 (H)
(RS Pts.—Seahawks 49, Texans 44)
HOUSTON vs. TAMPA BAY
RS: Series tied, 1-1
2003—Buccaneers, 16-3 (TB)
2007—Texans, 28-14 (H)
(RS Pts.—Texans 31, Buccaneers 30)
HOUSTON vs. TENNESSEE
RS: Titans lead series, 13-5
2002—Titans, 17-10 (T)
　　　Titans, 13-3 (H)
2003—Titans, 38-17 (T)
　　　Titans, 27-24 (H)
2004—Texans, 20-10 (T)
　　　Texans, 31-21 (H)
2005—Titans, 34-20 (H)
　　　Titans, 13-10 (T)
2006—Titans, 28-22 (T)
　　　Titans, 26-20 (H) OT
2007—Titans, 38-36 (H)
　　　Titans, 28-20 (T)
2008—Titans, 31-12 (T)
　　　Texans, 13-12 (H)
2009—Texans, 34-31 (T)
　　　Titans, 20-17 (H)
2010—Texans, 20-0 (H)
　　　Titans, 31-17 (T)
(RS Pts.—Titans 418, Texans 346)
HOUSTON vs. WASHINGTON
RS: Redskins lead series, 2-1
2002—Redskins, 26-10 (W)
2006—Redskins, 31-15 (H)
2010—Texans, 30-27 (W) OT
(RS Pts.—Redskins 84, Texans 55)

INDIANAPOLIS vs. ARIZONA
RS: Colts lead series, 8-6;
See Arizona vs. Indianapolis
INDIANAPOLIS vs. ATLANTA
RS: Colts lead series, 13-1;
See Atlanta vs. Indianapolis
INDIANAPOLIS vs. BALTIMORE
RS: Colts lead series, 7-2
PS: Colts lead series, 2-0;
See Baltimore vs. Indianapolis
INDIANAPOLIS vs. BUFFALO
RS: Bills lead series, 35-30-1;
See Buffalo vs. Indianapolis
INDIANAPOLIS vs. CAROLINA
RS: Panthers lead series, 3-1;
See Carolina vs. Indianapolis
INDIANAPOLIS vs. CHICAGO
RS: Colts lead series, 22-18
PS: Colts lead series, 1-0;
See Chicago vs. Indianapolis
INDIANAPOLIS vs. CINCINNATI
RS: Colts lead series, 16-8
PS: Colts lead series, 1-0;
See Cincinnati vs. Indianapolis

INDIANAPOLIS vs. CLEVELAND
RS: Browns lead series, 13-12
PS: Series tied, 2-2;
See Cleveland vs. Indianapolis
INDIANAPOLIS vs. DALLAS
RS: Cowboys lead series, 9-5
PS: Colts lead series, 1-0;
See Dallas vs. Indianapolis
INDIANAPOLIS vs. DENVER
RS: Broncos lead series, 11-8
PS: Colts lead series, 2-0;
See Denver vs. Indianapolis
INDIANAPOLIS vs. DETROIT
RS: Colts lead series, 20-18-2;
See Detroit vs. Indianapolis
INDIANAPOLIS vs. GREEN BAY
RS: Series tied, 20-20-1
PS: Packers lead series, 1-0;
See Green Bay vs. Indianapolis
INDIANAPOLIS vs. HOUSTON
RS: Colts lead series, 16-2;
See Houston vs. Indianapolis
INDIANAPOLIS vs. JACKSONVILLE
RS: Colts lead series, 15-5
1995—Colts, 41-31 (J)
2000—Colts, 43-14 (I)
2002—Colts, 28-25 (J)
    Colts, 20-13 (I)
2003—Colts, 23-13 (I)
    Jaguars, 28-23 (J)
2004—Colts, 24-17 (J)
    Jaguars, 27-24 (I)
2005—Colts, 10-3 (I)
    Colts, 26-18 (J)
2006—Colts, 21-14 (I)
    Jaguars, 44-17 (J)
2007—Colts, 29-7 (J)
    Colts, 28-25 (I)
2008—Jaguars, 23-21 (I)
    Colts, 31-24 (J)
2009—Colts, 14-12 (I)
    Colts, 35-31 (J)
2010—Jaguars, 31-28 (J)
    Colts, 34-24 (I)
(RS Pts.—Colts 520, Jaguars 424)
*INDIANAPOLIS vs. KANSAS CITY
RS: Colts lead series, 10-7
PS: Colts lead series, 3-0
1970—Chiefs, 44-24 (B)
1972—Chiefs, 24-10 (KC)
1975—Colts, 28-14 (B)
1977—Colts, 17-6 (KC)
1979—Chiefs, 14-0 (KC)
    Chiefs, 10-7 (B)
1980—Colts, 31-24 (KC)
    Chiefs, 38-28 (B)
1985—Chiefs, 20-7 (KC)
1990—Colts, 23-19 (I)
1995—**Colts, 10-7 (KC)
1996—Colts, 24-19 (KC)
1999—Colts, 25-17 (I)
2000—Colts, 27-14 (KC)
2001—Colts, 35-28 (KC)
2003—**Colts, 38-31 (KC)
2004—Chiefs, 45-35 (KC)
2006—***Colts, 23-8 (I)
2007—Colts, 13-10 (I)
2010—Colts, 19-9 (I)
(RS Pts.—Chiefs 355, Colts 353)
(PS Pts.—Colts 71, Chiefs 46)
*Franchise in Baltimore prior to 1984

**AFC Divisional Playoff
***AFC First-Round Playoff
*INDIANAPOLIS vs. MIAMI
RS: Dolphins lead series, 44-24
PS: Dolphins lead series, 2-0
1970—Colts, 35-0 (B)
    Dolphins, 34-17 (M)
1971—Dolphins, 17-14 (M)
    Colts, 14-3 (B)
    **Dolphins, 21-0 (M)
1972—Dolphins, 23-0 (B)
    Dolphins, 16-0 (M)
1973—Dolphins, 44-0 (M)
    Colts, 16-3 (B)
1974—Dolphins, 17-7 (M)
    Dolphins, 17-16 (B)
1975—Colts, 33-17 (M)
    Colts, 10-7 (B) OT
1976—Colts, 28-14 (B)
    Colts, 17-16 (M)
1977—Colts, 45-28 (B)
    Dolphins, 17-6 (M)
1978—Dolphins, 42-0 (B)
    Dolphins, 26-8 (M)
1979—Dolphins, 19-0 (M)
    Dolphins, 28-24 (B)
1980—Colts, 30-17 (M)
    Dolphins, 24-14 (B)
1981—Dolphins, 31-28 (B)
    Dolphins, 27-10 (M)
1982—Dolphins, 24-20 (M)
    Dolphins, 34-7 (B)
1983—Dolphins, 21-7 (B)
    Dolphins, 37-0 (M)
1984—Dolphins, 44-7 (M)
    Dolphins, 35-17 (I)
1985—Dolphins, 30-13 (M)
    Dolphins, 34-20 (I)
1986—Dolphins, 30-10 (M)
    Dolphins, 17-13 (I)
1987—Dolphins, 23-10 (I)
    Colts, 40-21 (M)
1988—Colts, 15-13 (I)
    Colts, 31-28 (M)
1989—Dolphins, 19-13 (M)
    Colts, 42-13 (I)
1990—Dolphins, 27-7 (I)
    Dolphins, 23-17 (M)
1991—Dolphins, 17-6 (M)
    Dolphins, 10-6 (I)
1992—Colts, 31-20 (M)
    Dolphins, 28-0 (I)
1993—Dolphins, 24-20 (I)
    Dolphins, 41-27 (M)
1994—Dolphins, 22-21 (M)
    Colts, 10-6 (I)
1995—Colts, 27-24 (M) OT
    Colts, 36-28 (I)
1996—Colts, 10-6 (I)
    Dolphins, 37-13 (M)
1997—Dolphins, 16-10 (M)
    Colts, 41-0 (I)
1998—Dolphins, 24-15 (I)
    Dolphins, 27-14 (M)
1999—Dolphins, 34-31 (I)
    Colts, 37-34 (M)
2000—Dolphins, 17-14 (I)
    Colts, 20-13 (M)
    ***Dolphins 23-17 (M) OT
2001—Dolphins, 27-24 (I)
    Dolphins, 41-6 (M)

2002—Dolphins, 21-13 (I)
2003—Colts, 23-17 (M)
2006—Colts, 27-22 (I)
2009—Colts, 27-23 (M)
(RS Pts.—Dolphins 1,539, Colts 1,170)
(PS Pts.—Dolphins 44, Colts 17)
*Franchise in Baltimore prior to 1984
**AFC Championship
***AFC First-Round Playoff
*INDIANAPOLIS vs. MINNESOTA
RS: Colts lead series, 14-7-1
PS: Colts lead series, 1-0
1961—Colts, 34-33 (B)
    Vikings, 28-20 (M)
1962—Colts, 34-7 (M)
    Colts, 42-17 (B)
1963—Colts, 37-34 (M)
    Colts, 41-10 (B)
1964—Vikings, 34-24 (M)
    Colts, 17-14 (B)
1965—Colts, 35-16 (B)
    Colts, 41-21 (M)
1966—Colts, 38-23 (M)
    Colts, 20-17 (B)
1967—Tie, 20-20 (M)
1968—Colts, 21-9 (B)
    **Colts, 24-14 (B)
1969—Vikings, 52-14 (M)
1971—Vikings, 10-3 (M)
1982—Vikings, 13-10 (M)
1988—Vikings, 12-3 (M)
1997—Vikings, 39-28 (M)
2000—Colts, 31-10 (I)
2004—Colts, 31-28 (I)
2008—Colts, 18-15 (M)
(RS Pts.—Colts 562, Vikings 462)
(PS Pts.—Colts 24, Vikings 14)
*Franchise in Baltimore prior to 1984
**Conference Championship
*INDIANAPOLIS vs. **NEW ENGLAND
RS: Patriots lead series, 43-28
PS: Patriots lead series, 2-1
1970—Colts, 14-6 (Bos)
    Colts, 27-3 (Balt)
1971—Colts, 23-3 (NE)
    Patriots, 21-17 (Balt)
1972—Colts, 24-17 (NE)
    Colts, 31-0 (Balt)
1973—Patriots, 24-16 (NE)
    Colts, 18-13 (Balt)
1974—Patriots, 42-3 (NE)
    Patriots, 27-17 (Balt)
1975—Patriots, 21-10 (NE)
    Colts, 34-21 (Balt)
1976—Colts, 27-13 (NE)
    Patriots, 21-14 (Balt)
1977—Patriots, 17-3 (NE)
    Colts, 30-24 (Balt)
1978—Colts, 34-27 (NE)
    Patriots, 35-14 (Balt)
1979—Colts, 31-26 (Balt)
    Patriots, 50-21 (NE)
1980—Patriots, 37-21 (Balt)
    Patriots, 47-21 (NE)
1981—Colts, 29-28 (NE)
    Colts, 23-21 (Balt)
1982—Patriots, 24-13 (Balt)
1983—Colts, 29-23 (NE) OT
    Colts, 12-7 (Balt)
1984—Patriots, 50-17 (I)
    Patriots, 16-10 (NE)

1985—Patriots, 34-15 (NE)
    Patriots, 38-31 (I)
1986—Patriots, 33-3 (NE)
    Patriots, 30-21 (I)
1987—Colts, 30-16 (I)
    Patriots, 24-0 (NE)
1988—Patriots, 21-17 (NE)
    Colts, 24-21 (I)
1989—Patriots, 23-20 (I) OT
    Patriots, 22-16 (NE)
1990—Patriots, 16-14 (I)
    Colts, 13-10 (NE)
1991—Patriots, 16-7 (I)
    Patriots, 23-17 (NE) OT
1992—Patriots, 37-34 (I) OT
    Colts, 6-0 (NE)
1993—Colts, 9-6 (I)
    Patriots, 38-0 (NE)
1994—Patriots, 12-10 (I)
    Patriots, 28-13 (NE)
1995—Colts, 24-10 (NE)
    Colts, 10-7 (I)
1996—Patriots, 27-9 (I)
    Patriots, 27-13 (NE)
1997—Patriots, 31-0 (I)
    Patriots, 20-17 (NE)
1998—Patriots, 29-6 (NE)
    Patriots, 21-16 (I)
1999—Patriots, 31-28 (NE)
    Colts, 20-15 (I)
2000—Patriots, 24-16 (NE)
    Colts, 30-23 (I)
2001—Patriots, 44-13 (NE)
    Patriots, 38-17 (I)
2003—Patriots, 38-34 (I)
    ***Patriots, 24-14 (NE)
2004—Patriots, 27-24 (NE)
    ****Patriots, 20-3 (NE)
2005—Colts, 40-21 (NF)
2006—Colts, 27-20 (NE)
    ***Colts, 38-34 (I)
2007—Patriots, 24-20 (I)
2008—Colts, 18-15 (I)
2009—Colts, 35-34 (I)
2010—Patriots, 31-28 (NE)
(RS Pts.—Patriots 1,669, Colts 1,334)
(PS Pts.—Patriots 78, Colts 55)
*Franchise in Baltimore prior to 1984
**Franchise in Boston prior to 1971
***AFC Championship
****AFC Divisional Playoff
*INDIANAPOLIS vs. NEW ORLEANS
RS: Series tied, 5-5
PS: Saints lead series, 1-0
1967—Colts, 30-10 (B)
1969—Colts, 30-10 (NO)
1973—Colts, 14-10 (B)
1986—Saints, 17-14 (I)
1989—Saints, 41-6 (NO)
1995—Saints, 17-14 (NO)
1998—Saints, 19-13 (I) OT
2001—Colts, 34-20 (NO)
2003—Colts, 55-21 (NO)
2007—Colts, 41-10 (I)
2009—**Saints 31-17 (South Florida)
(RS Pts.—Colts 237, Saints 189)
(PS Pts.—Saints 31, Colts 17)
*Franchise in Baltimore prior to 1984
**Super Bowl XLIV
*INDIANAPOLIS vs. N.Y. GIANTS
RS: Colts lead series, 8-6

PS: Colts lead series, 2-0
1954—Colts, 20-14 (B)
1955—Giants, 17-7 (NY)
1958—Giants, 24-21 (NY)
    **Colts, 23-17 (NY) OT
1959—**Colts, 31-16 (B)
1963—Giants, 37-28 (B)
1968—Colts, 26-0 (NY)
1971—Colts, 31-7 (NY)
1975—Colts, 21-0 (NY)
1979—Colts, 31-7 (NY)
1990—Giants, 24-7 (I)
1993—Giants, 20-6 (NY)
1999—Colts, 27-19 (NY)
2002—Giants, 44-27 (I)
2006—Colts, 26-21 (NY)
2010—Colts, 38-14 (I)
(RS Pts.—Colts 316, Giants 248)
(PS Pts.—Colts 54, Giants 33)
*Franchise in Baltimore prior to 1984
**NFL Championship
*INDIANAPOLIS vs. N.Y. JETS
RS: Colts lead series, 40-26
PS: Jets lead series, 3-1
1968—**Jets 16-7 (Miami)
1970—Colts, 29-22 (NY)
    Colts, 35-20 (B)
1971—Colts, 22-0 (B)
    Colts, 14-13 (NY)
1972—Jets, 44-34 (B)
    Jets, 24-20 (NY)
1973—Jets, 34-10 (B)
    Jets, 20-17 (NY)
1974—Colts, 35-20 (NY)
    Jets, 45-38 (B)
1975—Colts, 45-28 (NY)
    Colts, 52-19 (B)
1976—Colts, 20-0 (NY)
    Colts, 33-16 (B)
1977—Colts, 20-12 (NY)
    Colts, 33-12 (B)
1978—Jets, 33-10 (B)
    Jets, 24-16 (NY)
1979—Colts, 10-8 (B)
    Jets, 30-17 (NY)
1980—Colts, 17-14 (NY)
    Colts, 35-21 (B)
1981—Jets, 41-14 (B)
    Jets, 25-0 (NY)
1982—Jets, 37-0 (NY)
1983—Colts, 17-14 (NY)
    Jets, 10-6 (B)
1984—Jets, 23-14 (I)
    Colts, 9-5 (NY)
1985—Colts, 25-20 (NY)
    Jets, 35-17 (I)
1986—Jets, 26-7 (I)
    Jets, 31-16 (NY)
1987—Colts, 6-0 (I)
    Colts, 19-14 (NY)
1988—Colts, 38-14 (I)
    Jets, 34-16 (NY)
1989—Colts, 17-10 (NY)
    Colts, 27-10 (I)
1990—Colts, 17-14 (I)
    Colts, 29-21 (NY)
1991—Jets, 17-6 (I)
    Colts, 28-27 (NY)
1992—Colts, 6-3 (I) OT
    Colts, 10-6 (NY)
1993—Jets, 31-17 (I)

    Colts, 9-6 (NY)
1994—Jets, 16-6 (NY)
    Colts, 28-25 (I)
1995—Colts, 27-24 (NY) OT
    Colts, 17-10 (I)
1996—Colts, 21-7 (NY)
    Colts, 34-29 (I)
1997—Jets, 16-12 (I)
    Colts, 22-14 (NY)
1998—Jets, 44-6 (NY)
    Colts, 24-23 (I)
1999—Colts, 16-13 (NY)
    Colts, 13-6 (I)
2000—Colts, 23-15 (I)
    Jets, 27-17 (NY)
2001—Colts, 45-24 (NY)
    Jets, 29-28 (I)
2002—***Jets, 41-0 (NY)
2003—Colts, 38-31 (I)
2006—Colts, 31-28 (NY)
2009—Jets, 29-15 (I)
    ****Colts, 30-17 (I)
2010—***Jets, 17-16 (I)
(RS Pts.—Colts 1,350, Jets 1,348)
(PS Pts.—Jets 91, Colts 53)
*Franchise in Baltimore prior to 1984
**Super Bowl III
***AFC First-Round Playoff
****AFC Championship
*INDIANAPOLIS vs. **OAKLAND
RS: Raiders lead series, 7-5
PS: Series tied, 1-1
1970—***Colts, 27-17 (B)
1971—Colts, 37-14 (O)
1973—Raiders, 34-21 (B)
1975—Raiders, 31-20 (B)
1977—****Raiders, 37-31 (B) OT
1984—Raiders, 21-7 (LA)
1986—Colts, 30-24 (LA)
1991—Raiders, 16-0 (LA)
1995—Raiders, 30-17 (O)
2000—Raiders, 38-31 (I)
2001—Raiders, 23-18 (I)
2004—Colts, 35-14 (I)
2007—Colts, 21-14 (O)
2010—Colts, 31-26 (O)
(RS Pts.—Raiders 286, Colts 268)
(PS Pts.—Colts 58, Raiders 51)
*Franchise in Baltimore prior to 1984
**Franchise in Los Angeles from 1982-1994
***AFC Championship
****AFC Divisional Playoff
*INDIANAPOLIS vs. PHILADELPHIA
RS: Colts lead series, 10-7
1953—Eagles, 45-14 (P)
1965—Colts, 34-24 (B)
1967—Colts, 38-6 (P)
1969—Colts, 24-20 (B)
1970—Colts, 29-10 (B)
1974—Eagles, 30-10 (P)
1978—Eagles, 17-14 (B)
1981—Eagles, 38-13 (P)
1983—Colts, 22-21 (P)
1984—Eagles, 16-7 (P)
1990—Colts, 24-23 (P)
1993—Eagles, 20-10 (I)
1996—Colts, 37-10 (I)
1999—Colts, 44-17 (P)
2002—Colts, 35-13 (P)
2006—Colts, 45-21 (I)

2010—Eagles, 26-24 (P)
(RS Pts.—Colts 424, Eagles 357)
Franchise in Baltimore prior to 1984
*INDIANAPOLIS vs. PITTSBURGH
RS: Steelers lead series, 13-6
PS: Steelers lead series, 5-0
1957—Steelers, 19-13 (B)
1968—Colts, 41-7 (P)
1971—Colts, 34-21 (B)
1974—Steelers, 30-0 (P)
1975—**Steelers, 28-10 (P)
1976—**Steelers, 40-14 (B)
1977—Colts, 31-21 (B)
1978—Steelers, 35-13 (P)
1979—Steelers, 17-13 (P)
1980—Steelers, 20-17 (B)
1983—Steelers, 24-13 (B)
1984—Colts, 17-16 (I)
1985—Steelers, 45-3 (P)
1987—Steelers, 21-7 (P)
1991—Steelers, 21-3 (I)
1992—Steelers, 30-14 (P)
1994—Steelers, 31-21 (P)
1995—***Steelers, 20-16 (P)
1996—****Steelers, 42-14 (P)
1997—Steelers, 24-22 (P)
2002—Steelers, 28-10 (P)
2005—Colts, 26-7 (I)
    **Steelers, 21-18 (I)
2008—Colts, 24-20 (P)
(RS Pts.—Steelers 437, Colts 322)
(PS Pts.—Steelers 151, Colts 72)
Franchise in Baltimore prior to 1984
**AFC Divisional Playoff
***AFC Championship
****AFC First-Round Playoff
*INDIANAPOLIS vs. **ST. LOUIS
RS: Colts lead series, 23-17-2
1953—Rams, 21-13 (B)
    Rams, 45-2 (LA)
1954—Rams, 48-0 (B)
    Colts, 22-21 (LA)
1955—Tie, 17-17 (B)
    Rams, 20-14 (LA)
1956—Colts, 56-21 (B)
    Rams, 31-7 (LA)
1957—Colts, 31-14 (B)
    Rams, 37-21 (LA)
1958—Colts, 34-7 (B)
    Rams, 30-28 (LA)
1959—Colts, 35-21 (B)
    Colts, 45-26 (LA)
1960—Colts, 31-17 (B)
    Rams, 10-3 (LA)
1961—Colts, 27-24 (B)
    Rams, 34-17 (LA)
1962—Colts, 30-27 (B)
    Colts, 14-2 (LA)
1963—Rams, 17-16 (LA)
    Colts, 19-16 (B)
1964—Colts, 35-20 (B)
    Colts, 24-7 (LA)
1965—Colts, 35-20 (B)
    Colts, 20-17 (LA)
1966—Colts, 17-3 (LA)
    Rams, 23-7 (B)
1967—Tie, 24-24 (B)
    Rams, 34-10 (LA)
1968—Colts, 27-10 (B)
    Colts, 28-24 (LA)
1969—Rams, 27-20 (B)

Colts, 13-7 (LA)
1971—Colts, 24-17 (B)
1975—Rams, 24-13 (LA)
1986—Rams, 24-7 (I)
1989—Rams, 31-17 (LA)
1995—Colts, 21-18 (I)
2001—Rams, 42-17 (StL)
2005—Colts, 45-28 (I)
2009—Colts, 42-6 (StL)
(RS Pts.—Colts 928, Rams 912)
Franchise in Baltimore prior to 1984
**Franchise in Los Angeles prior to 1995
*INDIANAPOLIS vs. SAN DIEGO
RS: Chargers lead series, 15-9
PS: Chargers lead series, 2-1
1970—Colts, 16-14 (SD)
1972—Chargers, 23-20 (B)
1976—Colts, 37-21 (SD)
1981—Chargers, 43-14 (B)
1982—Chargers, 44-26 (SD)
1984—Chargers, 38-10 (I)
1986—Chargers, 17-3 (I)
1987—Chargers, 16-13 (I)
    Colts, 20-7 (SD)
1988—Colts, 16-0 (SD)
1989—Colts, 10-6 (I)
1992—Chargers, 34-14 (I)
    Chargers, 26-0 (SD)
1993—Chargers, 31-0 (I)
1995—Chargers, 27-24 (I)
    **Colts, 35-20 (SD)
1996—Chargers, 26-19 (I)
1997—Chargers, 35-19 (SD)
1998—Colts, 17-12 (I)
1999—Colts, 27-19 (SD)
2004—Chargers, 34-31 (I) OT
2005—Chargers, 26-17 (I)
2007—Chargers, 23-21 (SD)
    ***Chargers, 28-24 (I)
2008—Colts, 23-20 (SD)
    **Chargers, 23-17 (SD) OT
2010—Chargers, 36-14 (I)
(RS Pts.—Chargers 575, Colts 414)
(PS Pts.—Colts 76, Chargers 71)
Franchise in Baltimore prior to 1984
**AFC First-Round Playoff
***AFC Divisional Playoff
*INDIANAPOLIS vs. SAN FRANCISCO
RS: Colts lead series, 24-18
1953—49ers, 38-21 (B)
    49ers, 45-14 (SF)
1954—Colts, 17-13 (B)
    49ers, 10-7 (SF)
1955—Colts, 26-14 (B)
    49ers, 35-24 (SF)
1956—49ers, 20-17 (B)
    49ers, 30-17 (SF)
1957—Colts, 27-21 (B)
    49ers, 17-13 (SF)
1958—Colts, 35-27 (B)
    49ers, 21-12 (SF)
1959—Colts, 45-14 (B)
    Colts, 34-14 (SF)
1960—49ers, 30-22 (B)
    49ers, 34-10 (SF)
1961—Colts, 20-17 (B)
    Colts, 27-24 (SF)
1962—49ers, 21-13 (B)
    Colts, 22-3 (SF)
1963—Colts, 20-14 (SF)
    Colts, 20-3 (B)

1964—Colts, 37-7 (B)
    Colts, 14-3 (SF)
1965—Colts, 27-24 (B)
    Colts, 34-28 (SF)
1966—Colts, 36-14 (B)
    Colts, 30-14 (SF)
1967—Colts, 41-7 (B)
    Colts, 26-9 (SF)
1968—Colts, 27-10 (B)
    Colts, 42-14 (SF)
1969—49ers, 24-21 (B)
    49ers, 20-17 (SF)
1972—49ers, 24-21 (SF)
1986—49ers, 35-14 (SF)
1989—49ers, 30-24 (I)
1995—Colts, 18-17 (I)
1998—49ers, 34-31 (SF)
2001—49ers, 40-21 (I)
2005—Colts, 28-3 (SF)
2009—Colts, 18-14 (I)
(RS Pts.—Colts 990, 49ers 836)
Franchise in Baltimore prior to 1984
*INDIANAPOLIS vs. SEATTLE
RS: Colts lead series, 6-4
1977—Colts, 29-14 (S)
1978—Colts, 17-14 (S)
1991—Seahawks, 31-3 (S)
1994—Colts, 17-15 (I)
    Colts, 31-19 (S)
1997—Seahawks, 31-3 (I)
1998—Seahawks, 27-23 (S)
2000—Colts, 37-24 (S)
2005—Seahawks, 28-13 (S)
2009—Colts, 34-17 (I)
(RS Pts.—Seahawks 220, Colts 207)
Franchise in Baltimore prior to 1984
*INDIANAPOLIS vs. TAMPA BAY
RS: Colts lead series, 7-4
1976—Colts, 42-17 (B)
1979—Buccaneers, 29-26 (B) OT
1985—Colts, 31-23 (TB)
1987—Colts, 24-6 (I)
1988—Colts, 35-31 (I)
1991—Buccaneers, 17-3 (TB)
1992—Colts, 24-14 (TB)
1994—Buccaneers, 24-10 (TB)
1997—Buccaneers, 31-28 (I)
2003—Colts, 38-35 (TB) OT
2007—Colts, 33-14 (I)
(RS Pts.—Colts 294, Buccaneers 241)
Franchise in Baltimore prior to 1984
*INDIANAPOLIS vs. **TENNESSEE
RS: Colts lead series, 20-12
PS: Titans lead series, 1-0
1970—Colts, 24-20 (H)
1973—Oilers, 31-27 (B)
1976—Colts, 38-14 (B)
1979—Oilers, 28-16 (B)
1980—Oilers, 21-16 (H)
1983—Colts, 20-10 (B)
1984—Colts, 35-21 (H)
1985—Colts, 34-16 (I)
1986—Oilers, 31-17 (H)
1987—Colts, 51-27 (I)
1988—Oilers, 17-14 (I) OT
1990—Oilers, 24-10 (H)
1992—Oilers, 20-10 (I)
1994—Colts, 45-21 (I)
1999—***Titans, 19-16 (I)
2002—Titans, 23-15 (I)
    Titans, 27-17 (T)

2003—Colts, 33-7 (I)
    Colts, 29-27 (T)
2004—Colts, 31-17 (T)
    Colts, 51-24 (I)
2005—Colts, 31-10 (T)
    Colts, 35-3 (I)
2006—Colts, 14-13 (I)
    Titans, 20-17 (T)
2007—Colts, 22-20 (T)
    Titans, 16-10 (T)
2008—Titans, 31-21 (T)
    Colts, 23-0 (I)
2009—Colts, 31-9 (T)
    Colts, 27-17 (I)
2010—Colts, 30-28 (T)
    Colts, 23-20 (I)
(RS Pts.—Colts 817, Titans 613)
(PS Pts.—Titans 19, Colts 16)
*Franchise in Baltimore prior to 1984
**Franchise in Houston prior to 1997;
known as Oilers prior to 1999
***AFC Divisional Playoff
INDIANAPOLIS vs. WASHINGTON
RS: Colts lead series, 19-10
1953—Colts, 27-17 (B)
1954—Redskins, 24-21 (W)
1955—Redskins, 14-13 (B)
1956—Colts, 19-17 (B)
1957—Colts, 21-17 (W)
1958—Colts, 35-10 (B)
1959—Redskins, 27-24 (W)
1960—Colts, 20-0 (B)
1961—Colts, 27-6 (W)
1962—Colts, 34-21 (B)
1963—Colts, 36-20 (B)
1964—Colts, 45-17 (B)
1965—Colts, 38-7 (W)
1966—Colts, 37-10 (B)
1967—Colts, 17-13 (W)
1969—Colts, 41-17 (B)
1973—Redskins, 22-14 (W)
1977—Colts, 10-3 (B)
1978—Colts, 21-17 (B)
1981—Redskins, 38-14 (W)
1984—Redskins, 35-7 (I)
1990—Colts, 35-28 (I)
1993—Redskins, 30-24 (W)
1994—Redskins, 41-27 (I)
1996—Redskins, 31-16 (W)
1999—Colts, 24-21 (I)
2002—Redskins, 26-21 (W)
2006—Colts, 36-22 (I)
2010—Colts, 27-24 (W)
(RS Pts.—Colts 731, Redskins 575)
*Franchise in Baltimore prior to 1984

JACKSONVILLE vs. ARIZONA
RS: Jaguars lead series, 2-1;
See Arizona vs. Jacksonville
JACKSONVILLE vs. ATLANTA
RS: Jaguars lead series, 3-1;
See Atlanta vs. Jacksonville
JACKSONVILLE vs. BALTIMORE
RS: Jaguars lead series, 9-7;
See Baltimore vs. Jacksonville
JACKSONVILLE vs. BUFFALO
RS: Series tied, 5-5
PS: Jaguars lead series, 1-0;
See Buffalo vs. Jacksonville
JACKSONVILLE vs. CAROLINA
RS: Jaguars lead series, 3-1;

See Carolina vs. Jacksonville
JACKSONVILLE vs. CHICAGO
RS: Bears lead series, 3-2;
See Chicago vs. Jacksonville
JACKSONVILLE vs. CINCINNATI
RS: Jaguars lead series, 11-6;
See Cincinnati vs. Jacksonville
JACKSONVILLE vs. CLEVELAND
RS: Jaguars lead series, 9-4;
See Cleveland vs. Jacksonville
JACKSONVILLE vs. DALLAS
RS: Jaguars lead series, 3-2;
See Dallas vs. Jacksonville
JACKSONVILLE vs. DENVER
RS: Jaguars lead series, 5-3
PS: Series tied, 1-1;
See Denver vs. Jacksonville
JACKSONVILLE vs. DETROIT
RS: Jaguars lead series, 3-1;
See Detroit vs. Jacksonville
JACKSONVILLE vs. GREEN BAY
RS: Series tied, 2-2;
See Green Bay vs. Jacksonville
JACKSONVILLE vs. HOUSTON
RS: Series tied, 9-9;
See Houston vs. Jacksonville
JACKSONVILLE vs. INDIANAPOLIS
RS: Colts lead series, 15-5;
See Indianapolis vs. Jacksonville
JACKSONVILLE vs. KANSAS CITY
RS: Jaguars lead series, 6-3
1997—Jaguars, 24-10 (J)
1998—Jaguars, 21-16 (J)
2001—Chiefs, 30-26 (J)
2002—Jaguars, 23-16 (KC)
2004—Jaguars, 22-16 (J)
2006—Chiefs, 35-30 (KC)
2007—Jaguars, 17-7 (KC)
2009—Jaguars, 24-21 (J)
2010—Chiefs, 42-20 (KC)
(RS Pts.—Jaguars 207, Chiefs 193)
JACKSONVILLE vs. MIAMI
RS: Series tied, 2-2
PS: Jaguars lead series, 1-0
1998—Jaguars, 28-21 (J)
1999—*Jaguars, 62-7 (J)
2003—Dolphins, 24-10 (J)
2006—Jaguars, 24-10 (M)
2009—Dolphins, 14-10 (J)
(RS Pts.—Jaguars 72, Dolphins 69)
(PS Pts.—Jaguars 62, Dolphins 7)
*AFC Divisional Playoff
JACKSONVILLE vs. MINNESOTA
RS: Vikings lead series, 3-1
1998—Vikings, 50-10 (M)
2001—Jaguars, 33-3 (M)
2004—Vikings, 27-16 (M)
2008—Vikings, 30-12 (J)
(RS Pts.—Vikings 110, Jaguars 71)
JACKSONVILLE vs. NEW ENGLAND
RS: Patriots lead series, 5-0
PS: Patriots lead series, 3-1
1996—Patriots, 28-25 (NE) OT
    *Patriots, 20-6 (NE)
1997—Patriots, 26-20 (J)
1998—**Jaguars, 25-10 (J)
2003—Patriots, 27-13 (NE)
2005—**Patriots, 28-3 (NE)
2006—Patriots, 24-21 (J)
2007—***Patriots, 31-20 (NE)
2009—Patriots, 35-7 (NE)

(RS Pts.—Patriots 140, Jaguars 86)
(PS Pts.—Patriots 89, Jaguars 54)
*AFC Championship
**AFC First-Round Playoff
***AFC Divisional Playoff
JACKSONVILLE vs. NEW ORLEANS
RS: Series tied, 2-2
1996—Saints, 17-13 (NO)
1999—Jaguars, 41-23 (J)
2003—Jaguars, 20-19 (J)
2007—Saints, 41-24 (NO)
(RS Pts.—Saints 100, Jaguars 98)
JACKSONVILLE vs. N.Y. GIANTS
RS: Giants lead series, 3-2
1997—Jaguars, 40-13 (J)
2000—Giants, 28-25 (NY)
2002—Giants, 24-17 (NY)
2006—Jaguars, 26-10 (J)
2010—Giants, 24-20 (NY)
(RS Pts.—Jaguars 128, Giants 99)
JACKSONVILLE vs. N.Y. JETS
RS: Jaguars lead series, 6-2
PS: Jets lead series, 1-0
1995—Jets, 27-10 (NY)
1996—Jaguars, 21-17 (J)
1998—*Jets, 34-24 (NY)
1999—Jaguars, 16-6 (NY)
2002—Jaguars, 28-3 (J)
2003—Jets, 13-10 (NY)
2005—Jaguars, 26-20 (NY) OT
2006—Jaguars, 41-0 (J)
2009—Jaguars, 24-22 (NY)
(RS Pts.—Jaguars 176, Jets 108)
(PS Pts.—Jets 34, Jaguars 24)
*AFC Divisional Playoff
JACKSONVILLE vs. OAKLAND
RS: Jaguars lead series, 4-1
1996—Raiders, 17-3 (O)
1997—Jaguars, 20-9 (O)
2004—Jaguars, 13-6 (O)
2007—Jaguars, 49-11 (J)
2010—Jaguars, 38-31 (J)
(RS Pts.—Jaguars 123, Raiders 74)
JACKSONVILLE vs. PHILADELPHIA
RS: Jaguars lead series, 3-1
1997—Jaguars, 38-21 (J)
2002—Jaguars, 28-25 (J)
2006—Jaguars, 13-6 (P)
2010—Eagles, 28-3 (J)
(RS Pts.—Jaguars 82, Eagles 80)
JACKSONVILLE vs. PITTSBURGH
RS: Jaguars lead series, 11-9
PS: Jaguars lead series, 1-0
1995—Jaguars, 20-16 (J)
    Steelers, 24-7 (P)
1996—Jaguars, 24-9 (J)
    Steelers, 28-3 (P)
1997—Jaguars, 30-21 (J)
    Steelers, 23-17 (P) OT
1998—Steelers, 30-15 (P)
    Jaguars, 21-3 (J)
1999—Jaguars, 17-3 (P)
    Jaguars, 20-6 (J)
2000—Steelers, 24-13 (J)
    Jaguars, 34-24 (P)
2001—Jaguars, 21-3 (J)
    Steelers, 20-7 (P)
2002—Steelers, 25-23 (J)
2004—Steelers, 17-16 (J)
2005—Jaguars, 23-17 (P) OT
2006—Jaguars, 9-0 (J)

2007—Jaguars, 29-22 (P)
  *Jaguars, 31-29 (P)
2008—Steelers, 26-21 (J)
(RS Pts.—Jaguars 370, Steelers 341)
(PS Pts.—Jaguars 31, Steelers 29)
*AFC First-Round Playoff
JACKSONVILLE vs. ST. LOUIS
RS: Rams lead series, 2-1
1996—Rams, 17-14 (StL)
2005—Rams, 24-21 (StL)
2009—Jaguars, 23-20 (J) OT
(RS Pts.—Rams 61, Jaguars 58)
JACKSONVILLE vs. SAN DIEGO
RS: Series tied, 2-2
2003—Jaguars, 27-21 (J)
2004—Chargers, 34-21 (SD)
2007—Jaguars, 24-17 (J)
2010—Chargers, 38-13 (SD)
(RS Pts.—Chargers 110, Jaguars 85)
JACKSONVILLE vs. SAN FRANCISCO
RS: Jaguars lead series, 2-1
1999—Jaguars, 41-3 (J)
2005—Jaguars, 10-9 (J)
2009—49ers, 20-3 (SF)
(RS Pts.—Jaguars 54, 49ers 32)
JACKSONVILLE vs. SEATTLE
RS: Seahawks lead series, 4-2
1995—Seahawks, 47-30 (J)
1996—Jaguars, 20-13 (J)
2000—Seahawks, 28-21 (J)
2001—Seahawks, 24-15 (S)
2005—Jaguars, 26-14 (J)
2009—Seahawks, 41-0 (S)
(RS Pts.—Seahawks 167, Jaguars 112)
JACKSONVILLE vs. TAMPA BAY
RS: Jaguars lead series, 3-1
1995—Buccaneers, 17-16 (TB)
1998—Jaguars, 29-24 (J)
2003—Jaguars, 17-10 (J)
2007—Jaguars, 24-23 (TB)
(RS Pts.—Jaguars 86, Buccaneers 74)
JACKSONVILLE vs. *TENNESSEE
RS: Titans lead series, 18-14
PS: Titans lead, 1-0
1995—Oilers, 10-3 (J)
  Jaguars, 17-16 (H)
1996—Oilers, 34-27 (J)
  Jaguars, 23-17 (H)
1997—Jaguars, 30-24 (T)
  Jaguars, 17-9 (J)
1998—Jaguars, 27-22 (T)
  Oilers, 16-13 (J)
1999—Titans, 20-19 (J)
  Titans, 41-14 (T)
  **Titans, 33-14 (J)
2000—Titans, 27-13 (T)
  Jaguars, 16-13 (J)
2001—Jaguars, 13-6 (J)
  Titans, 28-24 (T)
2002—Titans, 23-14 (T)
  Titans, 28-10 (J)
2003—Titans, 30-17 (J)
  Titans, 10-3 (T)
2004—Jaguars, 15-12 (T)
  Titans, 18-15 (J)
2005—Jaguars, 31-28 (T)
  Jaguars, 40-13 (J)
2006—Jaguars, 37-7 (J)
  Titans, 24-17 (T)
2007—Titans, 13-10 (J)
  Jaguars, 28-13 (T)

2008—Titans, 17-10 (T)
  Titans, 24-14 (J)
2009—Jaguars, 37-17 (J)
  Titans, 30-13 (T)
2010—Titans, 30-3 (J)
  Jaguars, 17-6 (T)
(RS Pts.—Titans 626, Jaguars 587)
(PS Pts.—Titans 33, Jaguars 14)
*Franchise in Houston prior to 1997;
known as Oilers prior to 1999
**AFC Championship
JACKSONVILLE vs. WASHINGTON
RS: Redskins lead series, 4-1
1997—Redskins, 24-12 (W)
2000—Redskins, 35-16 (J)
2002—Jaguars, 26-7 (J)
2006—Redskins, 36-30 (W) OT
2010—Redskins, 20-17 (J) OT
(RS Pts.—Redskins 122, Jaguars 101)

KANSAS CITY vs. ARIZONA
RS: Chiefs lead series, 8-2-1;
See Arizona vs. Kansas City
KANSAS CITY vs. ATLANTA
RS: Chiefs lead series, 5-2;
See Atlanta vs. Kansas City
KANSAS CITY vs. BALTIMORE
RS: Chiefs lead series, 3-2
PS: Ravens lead series, 1-0;
See Baltimore vs. Kansas City
KANSAS CITY vs. BUFFALO
RS: Bills lead series, 21-17-1
PS: Bills lead series, 2-1;
See Buffalo vs. Kansas City
KANSAS CITY vs. CAROLINA
RS: Series tied, 2-2;
See Carolina vs. Kansas City
KANSAS CITY vs. CHICAGO
RS: Bears lead series, 6-4;
See Chicago vs. Kansas City
KANSAS CITY vs. CINCINNATI
RS: Series tied, 13-13;
See Cincinnati vs. Kansas City
KANSAS CITY vs. CLEVELAND
RS: Series tied, 10-10-2;
See Cleveland vs. Kansas City
KANSAS CITY vs. DALLAS
RS: Cowboys lead series, 6-3;
See Dallas vs. Kansas City
KANSAS CITY vs. DENVER
RS: Chiefs lead series, 55-46
PS: Broncos lead series, 1-0;
See Denver vs. Kansas City
KANSAS CITY vs. DETROIT
RS: Chiefs lead series, 7-4;
See Detroit vs. Kansas City
KANSAS CITY vs. GREEN BAY
RS: Chiefs lead series, 6-2-1
PS: Packers lead series, 1-0;
See Green Bay vs. Kansas City
KANSAS CITY vs. HOUSTON
RS: Texans lead series, 3-2;
See Houston vs. Kansas City
KANSAS CITY vs. INDIANAPOLIS
RS: Colts lead series, 10-7
PS: Colts lead series, 3-0;
See Indianapolis vs. Kansas City
KANSAS CITY vs. JACKSONVILLE
RS: Jaguars lead series, 6-3;
See Jacksonville vs. Kansas City

KANSAS CITY vs. MIAMI
RS: Series tied, 12-12
PS: Dolphins lead series, 3-0
1966—Chiefs, 34-16 (KC)
  Chiefs, 19-18 (M)
1967—Chiefs, 24-0 (M)
  Chiefs, 41-0 (KC)
1968—Chiefs, 48-3 (M)
1969—Chiefs, 17-10 (KC)
1971—*Dolphins, 27-24 (KC) OT
1972—Dolphins, 20-10 (KC)
1974—Dolphins, 9-3 (M)
1976—Dolphins, 20-17 (M) OT
1981—Dolphins, 17-7 (KC)
1983—Dolphins, 14-6 (M)
1985—Dolphins, 31-0 (M)
1987—Chiefs, 42-0 (M)
1989—Chiefs, 26-21 (KC)
  Chiefs, 27-24 (M)
1990—**Dolphins, 17-16 (M)
1991—Chiefs, 42-7 (KC)
1993—Dolphins, 30-10 (M)
1994—Dolphins, 45-28 (M)
  **Dolphins, 27-17 (M)
1995—Dolphins, 13-6 (M)
1997—Dolphins, 17-14 (M)
2002—Chiefs, 48-30 (KC)
2005—Chiefs, 30-20 (M)
2006—Dolphins, 13-10 (M)
2008—Chiefs, 38-31 (KC)
(RS Pts.—Chiefs 501, Dolphins 455)
(PS Pts.—Dolphins 71, Chiefs 57)
*AFC Divisional Playoff
**AFC First-Round Playoff
KANSAS CITY vs. MINNESOTA
RS: Chiefs lead series, 5-4
PS: Chiefs lead series, 1-0
1969—*Chiefs, 23-7 (New Orleans)
1970—Vikings, 27-10 (M)
1974—Vikings, 35-15 (KC)
1981—Chiefs, 10-6 (M)
1990—Chiefs, 24-21 (KC)
1993—Vikings, 30-10 (M)
1996—Chiefs, 21-6 (M)
1999—Chiefs, 31-28 (KC)
2003—Vikings, 45-20 (M)
2007—Chiefs, 13-10 (KC)
(RS Pts.—Vikings 208, Chiefs 154)
(PS Pts.—Chiefs 23, Vikings 7)
*Super Bowl IV
KANSAS CITY vs. **NEW ENGLAND
RS: Chiefs lead series, 16-12-3
1960—Patriots, 42-14 (B)
  Texans, 34-0 (D)
1961—Patriots, 18-17 (D)
  Patriots, 28-21 (B)
1962—Texans, 42-28 (D)
  Texans, 27-7 (B)
1963—Tie, 24-24 (B)
  Chiefs, 35-3 (KC)
1964—Patriots, 24-7 (B)
  Patriots, 31-24 (KC)
1965—Chiefs, 27-17 (KC)
  Tie, 10-10 (B)
1966—Chiefs, 43-24 (B)
  Tie, 27-27 (KC)
1967—Chiefs, 33-10 (B)
1968—Chiefs, 31-17 (KC)
1969—Chiefs, 31-0 (B)
1970—Chiefs, 23-10 (KC)
1973—Chiefs, 10-7 (NE)

1977—Patriots, 21-17 (NE)
1981—Patriots, 33-17 (NE)
1990—Chiefs, 37-7 (NE)
1992—Chiefs, 27-20 (KC)
1995—Chiefs, 31-26 (KC)
1998—Patriots, 40-10 (NE)
1999—Chiefs, 16-14 (KC)
2000—Patriots, 30-24 (NE)
2002—Patriots, 41-38 (NE) OT
2004—Patriots, 27-19 (KC)
2005—Chiefs, 26-16 (KC)
2008—Patriots, 17-10 (NE)
(RS Pts.—Chiefs 752, Patriots 619)
*Franchise located in Dallas prior to 1963 and known as Texans
**Franchise in Boston prior to 1971
KANSAS CITY vs. NEW ORLEANS
RS: Saints lead series, 5-4
1972—Chiefs, 20-17 (NO)
1976—Saints, 27-17 (KC)
1982—Saints, 27-17 (NO)
1985—Chiefs, 47-27 (NO)
1991—Saints, 17-10 (KC)
1994—Chiefs, 30-17 (NO)
1997—Chiefs, 25-13 (KC)
2004—Saints, 27-20 (NO)
2008—Saints, 30-20 (KC)
(RS Pts.—Chiefs 206, Saints 202)
KANSAS CITY vs. N.Y. GIANTS
RS: Giants lead series, 10-2
1974—Giants, 33-27 (KC)
1978—Giants, 26-10 (NY)
1979—Giants, 21-17 (KC)
1983—Chiefs, 38-17 (KC)
1984—Giants, 28-27 (NY)
1988—Giants, 28-12 (NY)
1992—Giants, 35-21 (NY)
1995—Chiefs, 20-17 (KC) OT
1998—Giants, 28-7 (NY)
2001—Giants, 13-3 (KC)
2005—Giants, 27-17 (NY)
2009—Giants, 27-16 (KC)
(RS Pts.—Giants 300, Chiefs 215)
***KANSAS CITY vs. **N.Y. JETS**
RS: Series tied, 16-16-1
PS: Series tied, 1-1
1960—Titans, 37-35 (D)
    Titans, 41-35 (NY)
1961—Titans, 28-7 (NY)
    Texans, 35-24 (D)
1962—Texans, 20-17 (D)
    Texans, 52-31 (NY)
1963—Jets, 17-0 (NY)
    Chiefs, 48-0 (KC)
1964—Jets, 27-14 (NY)
    Chiefs, 24-7 (KC)
1965—Chiefs, 14-10 (NY)
    Jets, 13-10 (KC)
1966—Chiefs, 32-24 (NY)
1967—Chiefs, 42-18 (KC)
    Chiefs, 21-7 (NY)
1968—Jets, 20-19 (KC)
1969—Chiefs, 34-16 (NY)
    ***Chiefs, 13-6 (NY)
1971—Jets, 13-10 (NY)
1974—Chiefs, 24-16 (KC)
1975—Jets, 30-24 (KC)
1982—Chiefs, 37-13 (KC)
1984—Jets, 17-16 (KC)
    Jets, 28-7 (NY)
1986—****Jets, 35-15 (NY)

1987—Jets, 16-9 (KC)
1988—Tie, 17-17 (NY)
    Chiefs, 38-34 (KC)
1992—Chiefs, 23-7 (NY)
1998—Jets, 20-17 (KC)
2001—Jets, 27-7 (NY)
2002—Chiefs, 29-25 (NY)
2005—Chiefs, 27-7 (KC)
2007—Jets, 13-10 (NY) OT
2008—Jets, 28-24 (NY)
(RS Pts.—Chiefs 761, Jets 648)
(PS Pts.—Jets 41, Chiefs 28)
*Franchise in Dallas prior to 1963 and known as Texans
**Jets known as Titans prior to 1963
***Inter-Divisional Playoff
****AFC First-Round Playoff
***KANSAS CITY vs. **OAKLAND**
RS: Chiefs lead series, 52-47-2
PS: Chiefs lead series, 2-1
1960—Texans, 34-16 (O)
    Raiders, 20-19 (D)
1961—Texans, 42-35 (O)
    Texans, 43-11 (D)
1962—Texans, 20-10 (O)
    Texans, 35-7 (D)
1963—Raiders, 10-7 (O)
    Raiders, 22-7 (KC)
1964—Chiefs, 21-9 (O)
    Chiefs, 42-7 (KC)
1965—Raiders, 37-10 (O)
    Chiefs, 14-7 (KC)
1966—Chiefs, 32-10 (O)
    Raiders, 34-13 (KC)
1967—Raiders, 23-21 (O)
    Raiders, 44-22 (KC)
1968—Raiders, 24-10 (KC)
    Raiders, 38-21 (O)
    ***Raiders, 41-6 (O)
1969—Raiders, 27-24 (KC)
    Raiders, 10-6 (O)
    ****Chiefs, 17-7 (O)
1970—Tie, 17-17 (KC)
    Raiders, 20-6 (O)
1971—Tie, 20-20 (O)
    Chiefs, 16-14 (KC)
1972—Chiefs, 27-14 (KC)
    Raiders, 26-3 (O)
1973—Chiefs, 16-3 (KC)
    Raiders, 37-7 (O)
1974—Raiders, 27-7 (O)
    Raiders, 7-6 (KC)
1975—Chiefs, 42-10 (KC)
    Raiders, 28-20 (O)
1976—Raiders, 24-21 (KC)
    Raiders, 21-10 (O)
1977—Raiders, 37-28 (KC)
    Raiders, 21-20 (O)
1978—Raiders, 28-6 (O)
    Raiders, 20-10 (KC)
1979—Chiefs, 35-7 (KC)
    Chiefs, 24-21 (O)
1980—Raiders, 27-14 (KC)
    Chiefs, 31-17 (O)
1981—Chiefs, 27-0 (KC)
    Chiefs, 28-17 (O)
1982—Raiders, 21-16 (KC)
1983—Raiders, 21-20 (LA)
    Raiders, 28-20 (KC)
1984—Raiders, 22-20 (KC)
    Raiders, 17-7 (LA)

1985—Chiefs, 36-20 (KC)
    Raiders, 19-10 (LA)
1986—Raiders, 24-17 (KC)
    Chiefs, 20-17 (LA)
1987—Raiders, 35-17 (LA)
    Chiefs, 16-10 (KC)
1988—Raiders, 27-17 (KC)
    Raiders, 17-10 (LA)
1989—Chiefs, 24-19 (KC)
    Raiders, 20-14 (LA)
1990—Chiefs, 9-7 (KC)
    Chiefs, 27-24 (LA)
1991—Chiefs, 24-21 (KC)
    Chiefs, 27-21 (LA)
    *****Chiefs, 10-6 (KC)
1992—Chiefs, 27-7 (KC)
    Raiders, 28-7 (LA)
1993—Chiefs, 24-9 (KC)
    Chiefs, 31-20 (LA)
1994—Chiefs, 13-3 (KC)
    Chiefs, 19-9 (LA)
1995—Chiefs, 23-17 (KC) OT
    Chiefs, 29-23 (O)
1996—Chiefs, 19-3 (KC)
    Raiders, 26-7 (O)
1997—Chiefs, 28-27 (O)
    Chiefs, 30-0 (KC)
1998—Chiefs, 28-8 (KC)
    Chiefs, 31-24 (O)
1999—Chiefs, 37-34 (O)
    Raiders, 41-38 (KC) OT
2000—Raiders, 20-17 (KC)
    Raiders, 49-31 (O)
2001—Raiders, 27-24 (KC)
    Raiders, 28-26 (O)
2002—Chiefs, 20-10 (KC)
    Raiders, 24-0 (O)
2003—Chiefs, 17-10 (KC)
    Chiefs, 27-24 (KC)
2004—Chiefs, 34-27 (O)
    Chiefs, 31-30 (KC)
2005—Chiefs, 23-17 (O)
    Chiefs, 27-23 (KC)
2006—Chiefs, 17-13 (KC)
    Chiefs, 20-9 (O)
2007—Chiefs, 12-10 (O)
    Raiders, 20-17 (KC)
2008—Raiders, 23-8 (KC)
    Chiefs, 20-13 (O)
2009—Raiders, 13-10 (KC)
    Chiefs, 16-10 (O)
2010—Raiders, 23-20 (O) OT
    Raiders, 31-10 (KC)
(RS Pts.—Chiefs 2,073, Raiders 1,979)
(PS Pts.—Raiders 54, Chiefs 33)
*Franchise in Dallas prior to 1963 and known as Texans
**Franchise in Los Angeles from 1982-1994
***Division Playoff
****AFC Championship
*****AFC First-Round Playoff
KANSAS CITY vs. PHILADELPHIA
RS: Eagles lead series, 4-2
1972—Eagles, 21-20 (KC)
1992—Chiefs, 24-17 (KC)
1998—Chiefs, 24-21 (P)
2001—Eagles, 23-10 (KC)
2005—Eagles, 37-31 (KC)
2009—Eagles, 34-14 (P)
(RS Pts.—Eagles 153, Chiefs 123)

KANSAS CITY vs. PITTSBURGH
RS: Steelers lead series, 17-9
PS: Chiefs lead series, 1-0
1970—Chiefs, 31-14 (P)
1971—Chiefs, 38-16 (KC)
1972—Steelers, 16-7 (P)
1974—Steelers, 34-24 (KC)
1975—Steelers, 28-3 (P)
1976—Steelers, 45-0 (KC)
1978—Steelers, 27-24 (P)
1979—Steelers, 30-3 (KC)
1980—Steelers, 21-16 (P)
1981—Chiefs, 37-33 (P)
1982—Steelers, 35-14 (P)
1984—Chiefs, 37-27 (P)
1985—Steelers, 36-28 (KC)
1986—Chiefs, 24-19 (P)
1987—Steelers, 17-16 (KC)
1988—Steelers, 16-10 (P)
1989—Steelers, 23-17 (P)
1992—Steelers, 27-3 (KC)
1993—*Chiefs, 27-24 (KC) OT
1996—Steelers, 17-7 (KC)
1997—Chiefs, 13-10 (KC)
1998—Steelers, 20-13 (KC)
1999—Chiefs, 35-19 (KC)
2001—Steelers, 20-17 (KC)
2003—Chiefs, 41-20 (KC)
2006—Steelers, 45-7 (P)
2009—Chiefs, 27-24 (KC) OT
(RS Pts.—Steelers 639, Chiefs 492)
(PS Pts.—Chiefs 27, Steelers 24)
*AFC First-Round Playoff
KANSAS CITY vs. *ST. LOUIS
RS: Chiefs lead series, 6-4
1973—Rams, 23-13 (KC)
1982—Rams, 20-14 (LA)
1985—Rams, 16-0 (KC)
1991—Chiefs, 27-20 (LA)
1994—Rams, 16-0 (KC)
1997—Chiefs, 28-20 (StL)
2000—Chiefs, 54-34 (KC)
2002—Chiefs, 49-10 (KC)
2006—Chiefs, 31-17 (StL)
2010—Chiefs, 27-13 (StL)
(RS Pts.—Chiefs 243, Rams 189)
*Franchise in Los Angeles prior to 1995
KANSAS CITY vs. **SAN DIEGO
RS: Chiefs lead series, 51-49-1
PS: Chargers lead series, 1-0
1960—Chargers, 21-20 (LA)
　　　Texans, 17-0 (D)
1961—Chargers, 26-10 (D)
　　　Chargers, 24-14 (SD)
1962—Chargers, 32-28 (SD)
　　　Texans, 26-17 (D)
1963—Chargers, 24-10 (SD)
　　　Chargers, 38-17 (KC)
1964—Chargers, 28-14 (KC)
　　　Chiefs, 49-6 (SD)
1965—Tie, 10-10 (SD)
　　　Chiefs, 31-7 (KC)
1966—Chiefs, 24-14 (KC)
　　　Chiefs, 27-17 (SD)
1967—Chargers, 45-31 (SD)
　　　Chargers, 17-16 (KC)
1968—Chiefs, 27-20 (KC)
　　　Chiefs, 40-3 (SD)
1969—Chiefs, 27-9 (SD)
　　　Chiefs, 27-3 (KC)
1970—Chiefs, 26-14 (KC)

Chargers, 31-13 (SD)
1971—Chargers, 21-14 (SD)
　　　Chiefs, 31-10 (KC)
1972—Chiefs, 26-14 (SD)
　　　Chargers, 27-17 (KC)
1973—Chiefs, 19-0 (SD)
　　　Chiefs, 33-6 (KC)
1974—Chiefs, 24-14 (KC)
　　　Chiefs, 14-7 (KC)
1975—Chiefs, 12-10 (SD)
　　　Chargers, 28-20 (KC)
1976—Chargers, 30-16 (KC)
　　　Chiefs, 23-20 (SD)
1977—Chargers, 23-7 (KC)
　　　Chiefs, 21-16 (SD)
1978—Chargers, 29-23 (SD) OT
　　　Chiefs, 23-0 (KC)
1979—Chargers, 20-14 (KC)
　　　Chargers, 28-7 (SD)
1980—Chargers, 24-7 (KC)
　　　Chargers, 20-7 (SD)
1981—Chargers, 42-31 (KC)
　　　Chargers, 22-20 (SD)
1982—Chiefs, 19-12 (KC)
1983—Chargers, 17-14 (KC)
　　　Chargers, 41-38 (SD)
1984—Chiefs, 31-13 (KC)
　　　Chiefs, 42-21 (SD)
1985—Chargers, 31-20 (SD)
　　　Chiefs, 38-34 (KC)
1986—Chiefs, 42-41 (KC)
　　　Chiefs, 24-23 (SD)
1987—Chiefs, 20-13 (KC)
　　　Chargers, 42-21 (SD)
1988—Chargers, 24-23 (KC)
　　　Chargers, 24-13 (SD)
1989—Chargers, 21-6 (SD)
　　　Chargers, 20-13 (SD)
1990—Chiefs, 27-10 (KC)
　　　Chiefs, 24-21 (SD)
1991—Chiefs, 14-13 (SD)
　　　Chiefs, 20-17 (KC) OT
1992—Chiefs, 24-10 (SD)
　　　Chiefs, 16-14 (KC)
　　　***Chargers, 17-0 (SD)
1993—Chiefs, 17-14 (SD)
　　　Chiefs, 28-24 (KC)
1994—Chargers, 20-6 (SD)
　　　Chargers, 14-13 (KC)
1995—Chiefs, 29-23 (KC) OT
　　　Chiefs, 22-7 (SD)
1996—Chargers, 22-19 (SD)
　　　Chiefs, 28-14 (KC)
1997—Chiefs, 31-3 (KC)
　　　Chiefs, 29-7 (SD)
1998—Chiefs, 23-7 (KC)
　　　Chiefs, 38-37 (SD)
1999—Chargers, 21-14 (SD)
　　　Chiefs, 34-0 (KC)
2000—Chiefs, 42-10 (KC)
　　　Chargers, 17-16 (SD)
2001—Chiefs, 25-20 (SD)
　　　Chiefs, 20-17 (KC)
2002—Chargers, 35-34 (SD)
　　　Chiefs, 24-22 (KC)
2003—Chiefs, 27-14 (KC)
　　　Chiefs, 28-24 (SD)
2004—Chargers, 34-31 (KC)
　　　Chargers, 24-17 (SD)
2005—Chargers, 28-20 (SD)
　　　Chiefs, 20-7 (KC)

2006—Chiefs, 30-27 (KC)
　　　Chargers, 20-9 (SD)
2007—Chiefs, 30-16 (SD)
　　　Chargers, 24-10 (KC)
2008—Chargers, 20-19 (SD)
　　　Chargers, 22-21 (KC)
2009—Chargers, 37-7 (KC)
　　　Chargers, 43-14 (SD)
2010—Chiefs, 21-14 (KC)
　　　Chargers, 31-0 (SD)
(RS Pts.—Chiefs 2,176, Chargers 2,020)
(PS Pts.—Chargers 17, Chiefs 0)
*Franchise in Dallas prior to 1963 and
known as Texans
**Franchise in Los Angeles prior to 1961
***AFC First-Round Playoff
KANSAS CITY vs. SAN FRANCISCO
RS: 49ers lead series, 6-5
1971—Chiefs, 26-17 (SF)
1975—49ers, 20-3 (KC)
1982—49ers, 26-13 (KC)
1985—49ers, 31-3 (SF)
1991—49ers, 28-14 (SF)
1994—Chiefs, 24-17 (KC)
1997—Chiefs, 44-9 (KC)
2000—49ers, 21-7 (SF)
2002—49ers, 17-13 (SF)
2006—Chiefs, 41-10 (KC)
2010—Chiefs, 31-10 (KC)
(PS Pts.—Chiefs 219, 49ers 196)
KANSAS CITY vs. SEATTLE
RS: Chiefs lead series, 32-18
1977—Seahawks, 34-31 (KC)
1978—Seahawks, 13-10 (KC)
　　　Seahawks, 23-19 (S)
1979—Chiefs, 24-6 (S)
　　　Chiefs, 37-21 (KC)
1980—Seahawks, 17-16 (KC)
　　　Chiefs, 31-30 (S)
1981—Chiefs, 20-14 (S)
　　　Chiefs, 40-13 (KC)
1983—Chiefs, 17-13 (KC)
　　　Seahawks, 51-48 (S) OT
1984—Seahawks, 45-0 (S)
　　　Chiefs, 34-7 (KC)
1985—Chiefs, 28-7 (KC)
　　　Seahawks, 24-6 (S)
1986—Seahawks, 23-17 (S)
　　　Chiefs, 27-7 (KC)
1987—Seahawks, 43-14 (S)
　　　Chiefs, 41-20 (KC)
1988—Seahawks, 31-10 (S)
　　　Chiefs, 27-24 (KC)
1989—Chiefs, 20-16 (S)
　　　Chiefs, 20-10 (KC)
1990—Seahawks, 19-7 (S)
　　　Seahawks, 17-16 (KC)
1991—Chiefs, 20-13 (KC)
　　　Chiefs, 19-6 (S)
1992—Chiefs, 26-7 (KC)
　　　Chiefs, 24-14 (S)
1993—Chiefs, 31-16 (S)
　　　Chiefs, 34-24 (KC)
1994—Chiefs, 38-23 (KC)
　　　Seahawks, 10-9 (S)
1995—Chiefs, 34-10 (S)
　　　Chiefs, 26-3 (KC)
1996—Chiefs, 35-17 (S)
　　　Chiefs, 34-16 (KC)
1997—Chiefs, 20-17 (KC) OT
　　　Chiefs, 19-14 (S)

1998—Chiefs, 17-6 (KC)
    Seahawks, 24-12 (S)
1999—Seahawks, 31-19 (KC)
    Seahawks, 23-14 (S)
2000—Chiefs, 24-17 (KC)
    Chiefs, 24-19 (S)
2001—Chiefs, 19-7 (KC)
    Seahawks, 21-18 (S)
2002—Seahawks, 39-32 (S)
2006—Chiefs, 35-28 (KC)
2010—Chiefs, 42-24 (S)
(RS Pts.—Chiefs 1,185, Seahawks 957)

KANSAS CITY vs. TAMPA BAY
RS: Series tied, 5-5
1976—Chiefs, 28-19 (TB)
1978—Buccaneers, 30-13 (KC)
1979—Buccaneers, 3-0 (TB)
1981—Chiefs, 19-10 (KC)
1984—Chiefs, 24-20 (KC)
1986—Chiefs, 27-20 (KC)
1993—Chiefs, 27-3 (TB)
1999—Buccaneers, 17-10 (TB)
2004—Buccaneers, 34-31 (TB)
2008—Buccaneers, 30-27 (KC) OT
(RS Pts.—Chiefs 206, Buccaneers 100)

*KANSAS CITY vs. **TENNESSEE
RS: Chiefs lead series, 26-20
PS: Chiefs lead series, 2-0
1960—Oilers, 20-10 (H)
    Texans, 24-0 (D)
1961—Texans, 26-21 (D)
    Oilers, 38-7 (H)
1962—Texans, 31-7 (H)
    Oilers, 14-6 (D)
    ***Texans, 20-17 (H) OT
1963—Chiefs, 28-7 (KC)
    Oilers, 28-7 (H)
1964—Chiefs, 28-7 (KC)
    Chiefs, 28-19 (H)
1965—Chiefs, 52-21 (KC)
    Oilers, 38-36 (H)
1966—Chiefs, 48-23 (KC)
    Oilers, 24-19 (KC)
1967—Chiefs, 25-20 (H)
    Oilers, 24-19 (KC)
1968—Chiefs, 26-21 (H)
    Chiefs, 24-10 (KC)
1969—Chiefs, 24-0 (KC)
1970—Chiefs, 24-9 (KC)
1971—Chiefs, 20-16 (H)
1973—Chiefs, 38-14 (KC)
1974—Chiefs, 17-7 (H)
1975—Oilers, 17-13 (KC)
1977—Chiefs, 34-20 (H)
1978—Oilers, 20-17 (KC)
1979—Oilers, 20-6 (H)
1980—Chiefs, 21-20 (KC)
1981—Chiefs, 23-10 (KC)
1983—Chiefs, 13-10 (H) OT
1984—Oilers, 17-16 (KC)
1985—Oilers, 23-20 (H)
1986—Chiefs, 27-13 (KC)
1988—Oilers, 7-6 (H)
1989—Chiefs, 34-0 (KC)
1990—Oilers, 27-10 (KC)
1991—Oilers, 17-7 (H)
1992—Oilers, 23-20 (H) OT
1993—Oilers, 30-0 (H)
    ****Chiefs, 28-20 (H)
1994—Chiefs, 31-9 (KC)
1995—Chiefs, 20-13 (KC)
1996—Chiefs, 20-19 (H)

2000—Titans, 17-14 (T) OT
2004—Chiefs, 49-38 (T)
2007—Titans, 26-17 (KC)
2008—Titans, 34-10 (KC)
2010—Chiefs, 34-14 (KC)
(RS Pts.—Chiefs 996, Titans 822)
(PS Pts.—Chiefs 48, Titans 37)
**Franchise in Dallas prior to 1963 and
known as Texans*
***Franchise in Houston prior to 1997;
known as Oilers prior to 1999*
***AFL Championship
****AFC Divisional Playoff

KANSAS CITY vs. WASHINGTON
RS: Chiefs lead series, 7-1
1971—Chiefs, 27-20 (KC)
1976—Chiefs, 33-30 (W)
1983—Redskins, 27-12 (W)
1992—Chiefs, 35-16 (KC)
1995—Chiefs, 24-3 (KC)
2001—Chiefs, 45-13 (W)
2005—Chiefs, 28-21, (KC)
2009—Chiefs, 14-6 (W)
(RS Pts.—Chiefs 218, Redskins 136)

MIAMI vs. ARIZONA
RS: Dolphins lead series, 8-2;
See Arizona vs. Miami
MIAMI vs. ATLANTA
RS: Dolphins lead series, 7-4;
See Atlanta vs. Miami
MIAMI vs. BALTIMORE
RS: Dolphins lead series, 5-3
PS: Ravens lead series, 2-0;
See Baltimore vs. Miami
MIAMI vs. BUFFALO
RS: Dolphins lead series, 53-36-1
PS: Bills lead series, 3-1;
See Buffalo vs. Miami
MIAMI vs. CAROLINA
RS: Dolphins lead series, 4-0;
See Carolina vs. Miami
MIAMI vs. CHICAGO
RS: Dolphins lead series, 7-4;
See Chicago vs. Miami
MIAMI vs. CINCINNATI
RS: Dolphins lead series, 13-5
PS: Dolphins lead series, 1-0;
See Cincinnati vs. Miami
MIAMI vs. CLEVELAND
RS: Series tied, 7-7
PS: Dolphins lead series, 2-0;
See Cleveland vs. Miami
MIAMI vs. DALLAS
RS: Dolphins lead series, 7-4
PS: Cowboys lead series, 1-0;
See Dallas vs. Miami
MIAMI vs. DENVER
RS: Dolphins lead series, 11-3-1
PS: Broncos lead series, 1-0;
See Denver vs. Miami
MIAMI vs. DETROIT
RS: Dolphins lead series, 7-3;
See Detroit vs. Miami
MIAMI vs. GREEN BAY
RS: Dolphins lead series, 10-3;
See Green Bay vs. Miami
MIAMI vs. HOUSTON
RS: Texans lead series, 5-0;
See Houston vs. Miami

MIAMI vs. INDIANAPOLIS
RS: Dolphins lead series, 44-24
PS: Dolphins lead series, 2-0;
See Indianapolis vs. Miami
MIAMI vs. JACKSONVILLE
RS: Series tied, 2-2
PS: Jaguars lead series, 1-0;
See Jacksonville vs. Miami
MIAMI vs. KANSAS CITY
RS: Series tied, 12-12
PS: Dolphins lead series, 3-0;
See Kansas City vs. Miami
MIAMI vs. MINNESOTA
RS: Dolphins lead series, 6-4
PS: Dolphins lead series, 1-0
1972—Dolphins, 16-14 (Minn)
1973—*Dolphins, 24-7 (Houston)
1976—Vikings, 29-7 (Mia)
1979—Dolphins, 27-12 (Minn)
1982—Dolphins, 22-14 (Mia)
1988—Dolphins, 24-7 (Mia)
1994—Vikings, 38-35 (Minn)
2000—Vikings, 13-7 (Minn)
2002—Vikings, 20-17 (Minn)
2006—Dolphins, 24-20 (Mia)
2010—Dolphins, 14-10 (Minn)
(RS Pts.—Dolphins 193, Vikings 177)
(PS Pts.—Dolphins 24, Vikings 7)
*Super Bowl VIII
MIAMI vs. *NEW ENGLAND
RS: Dolphins lead series, 49-39
PS: Patriots lead series, 2-1
1966—Patriots, 20-14 (M)
1967—Patriots, 41-10 (B)
    Dolphins, 41-32 (M)
1968—Dolphins, 34-10 (B)
    Dolphins, 38-7 (M)
1969—Dolphins, 17-16 (B)
    Patriots, 38-23 (Tampa)
1970—Patriots, 27-14 (B)
    Dolphins, 37-20 (M)
1971—Dolphins, 41-3 (M)
    Patriots, 34-13 (NE)
1972—Dolphins, 52-0 (M)
    Dolphins, 37-21 (NE)
1973—Dolphins, 44-23 (M)
    Dolphins, 30-14 (NE)
1974—Patriots, 34-24 (NE)
    Dolphins, 34-27 (M)
1975—Dolphins, 22-14 (NE)
    Dolphins, 20-7 (M)
1976—Patriots, 30-14 (NE)
    Dolphins, 10-3 (M)
1977—Dolphins, 17-5 (M)
    Patriots, 14-10 (NE)
1978—Patriots, 33-24 (NE)
    Dolphins, 23-3 (M)
1979—Patriots, 28-13 (NE)
    Dolphins, 39-24 (M)
1980—Patriots, 34-0 (NE)
    Dolphins, 16-13 (M) OT
1981—Dolphins, 30-27 (NE) OT
    Dolphins, 24-14 (M)
1982—Patriots, 3-0 (NE)
    **Dolphins, 28-13 (M)
1983—Dolphins, 34-24 (M)
    Patriots, 17-6 (NE)
1984—Dolphins, 28-7 (M)
    Dolphins, 44-24 (NE)
1985—Patriots, 17-13 (NE)
    Dolphins, 30-27 (M)

***Patriots, 31-14 (M)
1986—Patriots, 34-7 (NE)
Patriots, 34-27 (M)
1987—Patriots, 28-21 (NE)
Patriots, 24-10 (M)
1988—Patriots, 21-10 (NE)
Patriots, 6-3 (M)
1989—Dolphins, 24-10 (NE)
Dolphins, 31-10 (M)
1990—Dolphins, 27-24 (NE)
Dolphins, 17-10 (M)
1991—Dolphins, 20-10 (NE)
Dolphins, 30-20 (M)
1992—Dolphins, 38-17 (M)
Dolphins, 16-13 (NE) OT
1993—Dolphins, 17-13 (M)
Patriots, 33-27 (NE) OT
1994—Dolphins, 39-35 (M)
Dolphins, 23-3 (NE)
1995—Dolphins, 20-3 (NE)
Patriots, 34-17 (M)
1996—Dolphins, 24-10 (M)
Patriots, 42-23 (NE)
1997—Patriots, 27-24 (NE)
Patriots, 14-12 (M)
**Patriots, 17-3 (NE)
1998—Dolphins, 12-9 (M) OT
Patriots, 26-23 (NE)
1999—Dolphins, 31-30 (NE)
Dolphins, 27-17 (M)
2000—Dolphins, 10-3 (M)
Dolphins, 27-24 (NE)
2001—Dolphins, 30-10 (M)
Patriots, 20-13 (NE)
2002—Dolphins, 26-13 (M)
Patriots, 27-24 (NE) OT
2003—Patriots, 19-13 (M) OT
Patriots, 12-0 (NE)
2004—Patriots, 24-10 (NE)
Dolphins, 29-28 (M)
2005—Patriots, 23-16 (M)
Dolphins, 28-26 (NE)
2006—Patriots, 20-10 (NE)
Dolphins, 21-0 (M)
2007—Patriots, 49-28 (M)
Patriots, 28-7 (NE)
2008—Dolphins, 38-13 (NE)
Patriots, 48-28 (M)
2009—Patriots, 27-17 (NE)
Dolphins, 22-21 (M)
2010—Patriots, 41-14 (M)
Patriots, 38-7 (NE)
(RS Pts.—Dolphins 1,938, Patriots 1,806)
(PS Pts.—Patriots 61, Dolphins 45)
*Franchise in Boston prior to 1971
**AFC First-Round Playoff
***AFC Championship

MIAMI vs. NEW ORLEANS
RS: Dolphins lead series, 6-4
1970—Dolphins, 21-10 (M)
1974—Dolphins, 21-0 (NO)
1980—Dolphins, 21-16 (M)
1983—Saints, 17-7 (NO)
1986—Dolphins, 31-27 (NO)
1992—Saints, 24-13 (NO)
1995—Saints, 33-30 (NO)
1998—Dolphins, 30-10 (M)
2005—Dolphins, 21-6 (Baton Rouge)
2009—Saints, 46-34 (M)
(RS Pts.—Dolphins 229, Saints 189)

MIAMI vs. N.Y. GIANTS
RS: Giants lead series, 4-2
1972—Dolphins, 23-13 (NY)
1990—Giants, 20-3 (NY)
1993—Giants, 19-14 (M)
1996—Giants, 17-7 (M)
2003—Dolphins, 23-10 (NY)
2007—Giants, 13-10 (London)
(RS Pts.—Giants 92, Dolphins 80)

MIAMI vs. N.Y. JETS
RS: Jets lead series, 47-42-1
PS: Dolphins lead series, 1-0
1966—Jets, 19-14 (M)
Jets, 30-13 (NY)
1967—Jets, 29-7 (NY)
Jets, 33-14 (M)
1968—Jets, 35-17 (NY)
Jets, 31-7 (M)
1969—Jets, 34-31 (NY)
Jets, 27-9 (M)
1970—Dolphins, 20-6 (NY)
Dolphins, 16-10 (M)
1971—Jets, 14-10 (M)
Dolphins, 30-14 (NY)
1972—Dolphins, 27-17 (NY)
Dolphins, 28-24 (M)
1973—Dolphins, 31-3 (M)
Dolphins, 24-14 (NY)
1974—Dolphins, 21-17 (M)
Jets, 17-14 (NY)
1975—Dolphins, 43-0 (NY)
Dolphins, 27-7 (M)
1976—Dolphins, 16-0 (M)
Dolphins, 27-7 (NY)
1977—Dolphins, 21-17 (M)
Dolphins, 14-10 (NY)
1978—Jets, 33-20 (NY)
Jets, 24-13 (M)
1979—Jets, 33-27 (NY)
Jets, 27-24 (M)
1980—Jets, 17-14 (NY)
Jets, 24-17 (M)
1981—Tie, 28-28 (M) OT
Jets, 16-15 (NY)
1982—Dolphins, 45-28 (NY)
Dolphins, 20-19 (M)
*Dolphins, 14-0 (M)
1983—Dolphins, 32-14 (NY)
Dolphins, 34-14 (M)
1984—Dolphins, 31-17 (M)
Dolphins, 28-17 (M)
1985—Jets, 23-7 (NY)
Dolphins, 21-17 (M)
1986—Jets, 51-45 (NY) OT
Dolphins, 45-3 (M)
1987—Jets, 37-31 (NY) OT
Dolphins, 37-28 (M)
1988—Jets, 44-30 (M)
Jets, 38-34 (NY)
1989—Jets, 40-33 (M)
Dolphins, 31-23 (NY)
1990—Dolphins, 20-16 (M)
Dolphins, 17-3 (NY)
1991—Jets, 41-23 (NY)
Jets, 23-20 (M) OT
1992—Jets, 26-14 (M)
Dolphins, 19-17 (M)
1993—Jets, 24-14 (M)
Jets, 27-10 (NY)
1994—Dolphins, 28-14 (M)
Dolphins, 28-24 (NY)

1995—Dolphins, 52-14 (M)
Jets, 17-16 (NY)
1996—Dolphins, 36-27 (M)
Dolphins, 31-28 (NY)
1997—Dolphins, 31-20 (NY)
Dolphins, 24-17 (M)
1998—Jets, 20-9 (NY)
Jets, 21-16 (M)
1999—Jets, 28-20 (NY)
Jets, 38-31 (M)
2000—Jets, 40-37 (NY) OT
Jets, 20-3 (M)
2001—Jets, 21-17 (NY)
Jets, 24-0 (M)
2002—Dolphins, 30-3 (M)
Jets, 13-10 (NY)
2003—Jets, 21-10 (NY)
Dolphins, 23-21 (M)
2004—Jets, 17-9 (M)
Jets, 41-14 (NY)
2005—Jets, 17-7 (NY)
Dolphins, 24-20 (M)
2006—Jets, 20-17 (NY)
Jets, 13-10 (M)
2007—Jets, 31-28 (NY)
Jets, 40-13 (M)
2008—Jets, 20-14 (M)
Dolphins, 24-17 (NY)
2009—Jets, 31-27 (M)
Dolphins, 30-25 (NY)
2010—Jets, 31-23 (M)
Dolphins, 10-6 (NY)
(RS Pts.—Dolphins 1,997, Jets 1,952)
(PS Pts.—Dolphins 14, Jets 0)
*AFC Championship

MIAMI vs. *OAKLAND
RS: Raiders lead series, 16-13-1
PS: Raiders lead series, 3-1
1966—Raiders, 23-14 (M)
Raiders, 21-10 (O)
1967—Raiders, 31-17 (O)
1968—Raiders, 47-21 (M)
1969—Raiders, 20-17 (O)
Tie, 20-20 (M)
1970—Dolphins, 20-13 (M)
**Raiders, 21-14 (O)
1973—Raiders, 12-7 (O)
***Dolphins, 27-10 (M)
1974—**Raiders, 28-26 (O)
1975—Raiders, 31-21 (M)
1978—Dolphins, 23-6 (M)
1979—Raiders, 13-3 (O)
1980—Raiders, 16-10 (O)
1981—Raiders, 33-17 (M)
1983—Raiders, 27-14 (LA)
1984—Raiders, 45-34 (M)
1986—Raiders, 30-28 (M)
1988—Dolphins, 24-14 (LA)
1990—Raiders, 13-10 (M)
1992—Dolphins, 20-7 (M)
1994—Dolphins, 20-17 (M) OT
1996—Raiders, 17-7 (O)
1997—Dolphins, 34-16 (O)
1998—Dolphins, 27-17 (O)
1999—Dolphins, 16-9 (O)
2000—**Raiders, 27-0 (O)
2001—Dolphins, 18-15 (M)
2002—Dolphins, 23-17 (M)
2005—Dolphins, 33-21 (O)
2007—Raiders, 35-17 (M)
2008—Dolphins, 17-15 (M)

2010—Dolphins, 33-17 (O)
(RS Pts.—Raiders 618, Dolphins 575)
(PS Pts.—Raiders 86, Dolphins 67)
*Franchise in Los Angeles from 1982-1994
**AFC Divisional Playoff
***AFC Championship
MIAMI vs. PHILADELPHIA
RS: Dolphins lead series, 7-5
1970—Eagles, 24-17 (P)
1975—Dolphins, 24-16 (M)
1978—Eagles, 17-3 (P)
1981—Dolphins, 13-10 (M)
1984—Dolphins, 24-23 (M)
1987—Dolphins, 28-10 (P)
1990—Dolphins, 23-20 (M) OT
1993—Dolphins, 19-14 (P)
1996—Eagles, 35-28 (P)
1999—Dolphins, 16-13 (M)
2003—Eagles, 34-27 (M)
2007—Eagles, 17-7 (P)
(RS Pts.—Eagles 233, Dolphins 229)
MIAMI vs. PITTSBURGH
RS: Steelers lead series, 12-9
PS: Dolphins lead series, 2-1
1971—Dolphins, 24-21 (M)
1972—*Dolphins, 21-17 (P)
1973—Dolphins, 30-26 (M)
1976—Steelers, 14-3 (P)
1979—**Steelers, 34-14 (P)
1980—Steelers, 23-10 (P)
1981—Dolphins, 30-10 (M)
1984—Dolphins, 31-7 (P)
      *Dolphins, 45-28 (M)
1985—Dolphins, 24-20 (M)
1987—Steelers, 35-24 (M)
1988—Steelers, 40-24 (P)
1989—Steelers, 34-14 (M)
1990—Dolphins, 28-6 (P)
1993—Steelers, 21-20 (M)
1994—Steelers, 16-13 (P) OT
1995—Dolphins, 23-10 (M)
1996—Steelers, 24-17 (M)
1998—Dolphins, 21-0 (M)
2004—Steelers, 13-3 (M)
2006—Steelers, 28-17 (P)
2007—Steelers, 3-0 (P)
2009—Steelers, 30-24 (M)
2010—Steelers, 23-22 (M)
(RS Pts.—Dolphins 110, Steelers 639)
(PS Pts.—Dolphins 80, Steelers 79)
*AFC Championship
**AFC Divisional Playoff
MIAMI vs. *ST. LOUIS
RS: Dolphins lead series, 9-2
1971—Dolphins, 20-14 (LA)
1976—Rams, 31-28 (M)
1980—Dolphins, 35-14 (LA)
1983—Dolphins, 30-14 (M)
1986—Dolphins, 37-31 (LA) OT
1992—Dolphins, 26-10 (M)
1995—Dolphins, 41-22 (StL)
1998—Dolphins, 14-0 (M)
2001—Rams, 42-10 (StL)
2004—Dolphins, 31-14 (M)
2008—Dolphins, 16-12 (StL)
(RS Pts.—Dolphins 288, Rams 204)
*Franchise in Los Angeles prior to 1995
MIAMI vs. SAN DIEGO
RS: Dolphins lead series, 12-11
PS: Series tied, 2-2
1966—Chargers, 44-10 (SD)

1967—Chargers, 24-0 (SD)
      Dolphins, 41-24 (M)
1968—Chargers, 34-28 (SD)
1969—Chargers, 21-14 (M)
1972—Dolphins, 24-10 (M)
1974—Dolphins, 28-21 (SD)
1977—Chargers, 14-13 (M)
1978—Dolphins, 28-21 (SD)
1980—Chargers, 27-24 (M) OT
1981—*Chargers, 41-38 (M) OT
1982—**Dolphins, 34-13 (M)
1984—Chargers, 34-28 (SD) OT
1986—Chargers, 50-28 (SD)
1988—Dolphins, 31-28 (M)
1991—Chargers, 38-30 (SD)
1992—*Dolphins, 31-0 (M)
1993—Chargers, 45-20 (SD)
1994—*Chargers, 22-21 (SD)
1995—Dolphins, 24-14 (SD)
1999—Dolphins, 12-9 (M)
2000—Dolphins, 17-7 (SD)
2002—Dolphins, 30-3 (M)
2003—Dolphins, 26-10 (Ariz)
2005—Dolphins, 23-21 (SD)
2008—Dolphins, 17-10 (M)
2009—Chargers, 23-13 (SD)
(RS Pts.—Chargers 532, Dolphins 509)
(PS Pts.—Dolphins 124, Chargers 76)
*AFC Divisional Playoff
**AFC Second-Round Playoff
MIAMI vs. SAN FRANCISCO
RS: Dolphins lead series, 6-4
PS: 49ers lead series, 1-0
1973—Dolphins, 21-13 (M)
1977—Dolphins, 19-15 (SF)
1980—Dolphins, 17-13 (M)
1983—Dolphins, 20-17 (SF)
1984—*49ers, 38-16 (Stanford)
1986—49ers, 31-16 (M)
1992—49ers, 27-3 (SF)
1995—49ers, 44-20 (M)
2001—49ers, 21-0 (SF)
2004—Dolphins, 24-17 (SF)
2008—Dolphins, 14-9 (M)
(RS Pts.—49ers 207, Dolphins 154)
(PS Pts.—49ers 38, Dolphins 16)
*Super Bowl XIX
MIAMI vs. SEATTLE
RS: Dolphins lead series, 7-3
PS: Dolphins lead series, 2-1
1977—Dolphins, 31-13 (M)
1979—Dolphins, 19-10 (M)
1983—*Seahawks, 27-20 (M)
1984—*Dolphins, 31-10 (M)
1987—Seahawks, 24-20 (S)
1990—Dolphins, 24-17 (M)
1992—Dolphins, 19-17 (S)
1996—Seahawks, 22-15 (M)
1999—**Dolphins, 20-17 (S)
2000—Dolphins, 23-0 (M)
2001—Dolphins, 24-20 (S)
2004—Seahawks, 24-17 (S)
2008—Dolphins, 21-19 (M)
(RS Pts.—Dolphins 213, Seahawks 166)
(PS Pts.—Dolphins 71, Seahawks 54)
*AFC Divisional Playoff
**AFC First-Round Playoff
MIAMI vs. TAMPA BAY
RS: Dolphins lead series, 5-4
1976—Dolphins, 23-20 (TB)
1982—Buccaneers, 23-17 (TB)

1985—Dolphins, 41-38 (M)
1988—Dolphins, 17-14 (TB)
1991—Dolphins, 33-14 (M)
1997—Buccaneers, 31-21 (TB)
2000—Buccaneers, 16-13 (M)
2005—Buccaneers, 27-13 (TB)
2009—Dolphins, 25-23 (M)
(RS Pts.—Buccaneers 206, Dolphins 203)
MIAMI vs. *TENNESSEE
RS: Dolphins lead series, 18-14
PS: Titans lead series, 1-0
1966—Dolphins, 20-13 (H)
      Dolphins, 29-28 (H)
1967—Oilers, 17-14 (H)
      Oilers, 41-10 (M)
1968—Oilers, 24-10 (M)
      Dolphins, 24-7 (H)
1969—Oilers, 22-10 (H)
      Oilers, 32-7 (M)
1970—Dolphins, 20-10 (H)
1972—Dolphins, 34-13 (M)
1975—Oilers, 20-19 (H)
1977—Dolphins, 27-7 (M)
1978—Oilers, 35-30 (H)
      **Oilers, 17-9 (M)
1979—Oilers, 9-6 (M)
1981—Dolphins, 16-10 (H)
1983—Dolphins, 24-17 (H)
1984—Dolphins, 28-10 (H)
1985—Oilers, 26-23 (H)
1986—Dolphins, 28-7 (M)
1989—Oilers, 39-7 (H)
1991—Oilers, 17-13 (M)
1992—Dolphins, 19-16 (M)
1996—Dolphins, 23-20 (H)
1997—Dolphins, 16-13 (M) OT
1999—Dolphins, 17-0 (M)
2001—Dolphins, 31-23 (T)
2003—Titans, 31-7 (T)
2004—Titans, 17-7 (M)
2005—Dolphins, 24-10 (M)
2006—Dolphins, 13-10 (M)
2009—Titans, 27-24 (T) OT
2010—Dolphins, 29-17 (M)
(RS Pts.—Dolphins 609, Titans 588)
(PS Pts.—Titans 17, Dolphins 9)
*Franchise in Houston prior to 1997;
known as Oilers prior to 1999
**AFC First-Round Playoff
MIAMI vs. WASHINGTON
RS: Dolphins lead series, 6-4
PS: Series tied, 1-1
1972—*Dolphins, 14-7 (Los Angeles)
1974—Redskins, 20-17 (W)
1978—Dolphins, 16-0 (W)
1981—Dolphins, 13-10 (W)
1982—**Redskins, 27-17 (Pasadena)
1984—Dolphins, 35-17 (W)
1987—Dolphins, 23-21 (M)
1990—Redskins, 42-20 (W)
1993—Dolphins, 17-10 (M)
1999—Redskins, 21-10 (W)
2003—Dolphins, 24-23 (M)
2007—Redskins, 16-13 (W) OT
(RS Pts.—Dolphins 188, Redskins 180)
(PS Pts.—Redskins 34, Dolphins 31)
*Super Bowl VII
**Super Bowl XVII

MINNESOTA vs. ARIZONA
RS: Vikings lead series, 11-10

PS: Vikings lead series, 2-0;
See Arizona vs. Minnesota

MINNESOTA vs. ATLANTA
RS: Vikings lead series, 15-9
PS: Series tied, 1-1;
See Atlanta vs. Minnesota

MINNESOTA vs. BALTIMORE
RS: Series tied, 2-2;
See Baltimore vs. Minnesota

MINNESOTA vs. BUFFALO
RS: Vikings lead series, 8-4;
See Buffalo vs. Minnesota

MINNESOTA vs. CAROLINA
RS: Vikings lead series, 5-4;
See Carolina vs. Minnesota

MINNESOTA vs. CHICAGO
RS: Vikings lead series, 52-45-2
PS: Bears lead series, 1-0;
See Chicago vs. Minnesota

MINNESOTA vs. CINCINNATI
RS: Vikings lead series, 6-5;
See Cincinnati vs. Minnesota

MINNESOTA vs. CLEVELAND
RS: Vikings lead series, 10-3
PS: Vikings lead series, 1-0;
See Cleveland vs. Minnesota

MINNESOTA vs. DALLAS
RS: Vikings lead series, 11-10
PS: Cowboys lead series, 4-3;
See Dallas vs. Minnesota

MINNESOTA vs. DENVER
RS: Vikings lead series, 7-5;
See Denver vs. Minnesota

MINNESOTA vs. DETROIT
RS: Vikings lead series, 66-31-2;
See Detroit vs. Minnesota

MINNESOTA vs. GREEN BAY
RS: Packers lead series, 51-47-1
PS: Vikings lead series, 1-0;
See Green Bay vs. Minnesota

MINNESOTA vs. HOUSTON
RS: Vikings lead series, 2-0;
See Houston vs. Minnesota

MINNESOTA vs. INDIANAPOLIS
RS: Colts lead series, 14-7-1
PS: Colts lead series, 1-0;
See Indianapolis vs. Minnesota

MINNESOTA vs. JACKSONVILLE
RS: Vikings lead series, 3-1;
See Jacksonville vs. Minnesota

MINNESOTA vs. KANSAS CITY
RS: Chiefs lead series, 5-4
PS: Chiefs lead series, 1-0;
See Kansas City vs. Minnesota

MINNESOTA vs. MIAMI
RS: Dolphins lead series, 6-4
PS: Dolphins lead series, 1-0;
See Miami vs. Minnesota

MINNESOTA vs. *NEW ENGLAND
RS: Patriots lead series, 7-4
1970—Vikings, 35-14 (B)
1974—Patriots, 17-14 (M)
1979—Patriots, 27-23 (NE)
1988—Vikings, 36-6 (M)
1991—Patriots, 26-23 (NE) OT
1994—Patriots, 26-20 (NE) OT
1997—Vikings, 23-18 (M)
2000—Vikings, 21-13 (NE)
2002—Patriots, 24-17 (NE)
2006—Patriots, 31-7 (M)
2010—Patriots, 28-18 (NE)

(RS Pts.—Vikings 237, Patriots 230)
*Franchise in Boston prior to 1971

MINNESOTA vs. NEW ORLEANS
RS: Vikings lead series, 18-8
PS: Vikings lead series, 2-1
1968—Saints, 20-17 (NO)
1970—Vikings, 26-0 (M)
1971—Vikings, 23-10 (NO)
1972—Vikings, 37-6 (M)
1974—Vikings, 29-9 (M)
1975—Vikings, 20-7 (NO)
1976—Vikings, 40-9 (NO)
1978—Saints, 31-24 (NO)
1980—Vikings, 23-20 (NO)
1981—Vikings, 20-10 (M)
1983—Saints, 17-16 (NO)
1985—Saints, 30-23 (M)
1986—Vikings, 33-17 (M)
1987—*Vikings, 44-10 (NO)
1988—Vikings, 45-3 (M)
1990—Vikings, 32-3 (M)
1991—Saints, 26-0 (NO)
1993—Saints, 17-14 (M)
1994—Vikings, 21-20 (M)
1995—Vikings, 43-24 (M)
1998—Vikings, 31-24 (M)
2000—**Vikings, 34-16 (M)
2001—Saints, 28-15 (NO)
2002—Vikings, 32-31 (NO)
2004—Vikings, 38-31 (NO)
2005—Vikings, 33-16 (M)
2008—Vikings, 30-27 (NO)
2009—***Saints, 31-28 (NO) OT
2010—Saints, 14-9 (NO)
(RS Pts.—Vikings 674, Saints 450)
(PS Pts.—Vikings 106, Saints 57)
*NFC First-Round Playoff
**NFC Divisional Playoff
***NFC Championship

MINNESOTA vs. N.Y. GIANTS
RS: Vikings lead series, 13-9
PS: Giants lead series, 2-1
1964—Vikings, 30-21 (NY)
1965—Vikings, 40-14 (M)
1967—Vikings, 27-24 (M)
1969—Giants, 24-23 (NY)
1971—Vikings, 17-10 (NY)
1973—Vikings, 31-7 (New Haven)
1976—Vikings, 24-7 (M)
1986—Giants, 22-20 (M)
1989—Giants, 24-14 (M)
1990—Giants, 23-15 (NY)
1993—*Giants, 17-10 (NY)
1994—Vikings, 27-10 (NY)
1996—Giants, 15-10 (NY)
1997—*Vikings, 23-22 (NY)
1999—Vikings, 34-17 (NY)
2000—**Giants, 41-0 (NY)
2001—Vikings, 28-16 (M)
2002—Giants, 27-20 (M)
2003—Giants, 29-17 (M)
2004—Giants, 34-13 (M)
2005—Vikings, 24-21 (NY)
2007—Vikings, 41-17 (NY)
2008—Vikings, 20-19 (M)
2009—Vikings, 44-7 (M)
2010—Vikings, 21-3 (Detroit)
(RS Pts.—Vikings 522, Giants 409)
(PS Pts.—Giants 80, Vikings 33)
*NFC First-Round Playoff
**NFC Championship

MINNESOTA vs. N.Y. JETS
RS: Jets lead series, 8-1
1970—Jets, 20-10 (M)
1975—Vikings, 29-21 (M)
1979—Jets, 14-7 (NY)
1982—Jets, 42-14 (M)
1994—Jets, 31-21 (M)
1997—Jets, 23-21 (NY)
2002—Vikings, 20-7 (NY)
2006—Jets, 26-13 (M)
2010—Jets, 29-20 (NY)
(RS Pts.—Jets 226, Vikings 142)

MINNESOTA vs. *OAKLAND
RS: Raiders lead series, 8-4
PS: Raiders lead series, 1-0
1973—Vikings, 24-16 (M)
1976—**Raiders, 32-14 (Pasadena)
1977—Raiders, 35-13 (O)
1978—Raiders, 27-20 (O)
1981—Raiders, 36-10 (M)
1984—Raiders, 23-20 (LA)
1987—Vikings, 31-20 (M)
1990—Raiders, 28-24 (M)
1993—Raiders, 24-7 (LA)
1996—Vikings, 16-13 (O) OT
1999—Raiders, 22-17 (M)
2003—Raiders, 28-18 (O)
2007—Vikings, 29-22 (M)
(RS Pts.—Raiders 294, Vikings 229)
(PS Pts.—Raiders 32, Vikings 14)
*Franchise in Los Angeles from 1982-1994
**Super Bowl XI

MINNESOTA vs. PHILADELPHIA
RS: Vikings lead series, 12-9
PS: Eagles lead series, 3-0
1962—Vikings, 31-21 (M)
1963—Vikings, 34-13 (P)
1968—Vikings, 24-17 (P)
1971—Vikings, 13-0 (P)
1973—Vikings, 28-21 (M)
1976—Vikings, 31-12 (P)
1978—Vikings, 28-27 (M)
1980—Eagles, 42-7 (M)
        *Eagles, 31-16 (P)
1981—Vikings, 35-23 (M)
1984—Eagles, 19-17 (P)
1985—Vikings, 28-23 (P)
        Eagles, 37-35 (M)
1988—Vikings, 23-21 (M)
1989—Eagles, 10-9 (P)
1990—Eagles, 32-24 (P)
1992—Eagles, 28-17 (P)
1997—Vikings, 28-19 (M)
2001—Eagles, 48-17 (P)
2004—Eagles, 27-16 (P)
        *Eagles, 27-14 (P)
2007—Eagles, 23-16 (M)
2008—**Eagles, 26-14 (M)
2010—Vikings, 24-14 (P)
(RS Pts.—Vikings 485, Eagles 477)
(PS Pts.—Eagles 84, Vikings 44)
*NFC Divisional Playoff
**NFC First-Round Playoff

MINNESOTA vs. PITTSBURGH
RS: Vikings lead series, 8-7
PS: Steelers lead series, 1-0
1962—Steelers, 39-31 (P)
1964—Vikings, 30-10 (M)
1967—Vikings, 41-27 (P)
1969—Vikings, 52-14 (M)
1972—Steelers, 23-10 (P)

1974—*Steelers, 16-6 (New Orleans)
1976—Vikings, 17-6 (M)
1980—Steelers, 23-17 (M)
1983—Vikings, 17-14 (P)
1986—Vikings, 31-7 (M)
1989—Steelers, 27-14 (P)
1992—Vikings, 6-3 (P)
1995—Vikings, 44-24 (P)
2001—Steelers, 21-16 (P)
2005—Steelers, 18-3 (M)
2009—Steelers, 27-17 (P)
(RS Pts.—Vikings 346, Steelers 283)
(PS Pts.—Steelers 16, Vikings 6)
*Super Bowl IX

MINNESOTA vs. *ST. LOUIS
RS: Vikings lead series, 18-14-2
PS: Vikings lead series, 5-2
1961—Rams, 31-17 (LA)
  Vikings, 42-21 (M)
1962—Vikings, 38-14 (LA)
  Tie, 24-24 (M)
1963—Rams, 27-24 (LA)
  Vikings, 21-13 (M)
1964—Rams, 22-13 (LA)
  Vikings, 34-13 (M)
1965—Vikings, 38-35 (LA)
  Vikings, 24-13 (M)
1966—Vikings, 35-7 (M)
  Rams, 21-6 (LA)
1967—Rams, 39-3 (LA)
1968—Rams, 31-3 (M)
1969—Vikings, 20-13 (LA)
  **Vikings, 23-20 (M)
1970—Vikings, 13-3 (M)
1972—Vikings, 45-41 (LA)
1973—Vikings, 10-9 (LA)
1974—Rams, 20-17 (LA)
  ***Vikings, 14-10 (M)
1976—Tie, 10-10 (M) OT
  ***Vikings, 24-13 (M)
1977—Rams, 35-3 (LA)
  ****Vikings, 14-7 (LA)
1978—Rams, 34-17 (M)
  ****Rams, 34-10 (LA)
1979—Rams, 27-21 (LA) OT
1985—Rams, 13-10 (LA)
1987—Vikings, 21-16 (LA)
1988—*****Vikings, 28-17 (M)
1989—Vikings, 23-21 (M) OT
1991—Vikings, 20-14 (M)
1992—Vikings, 31-17 (LA)
1998—Vikings, 38-31 (StL)
1999—****Rams, 49-37 (StL)
2000—Rams, 40-29 (StL)
2003—Rams, 48-17 (StL)
2005—Vikings, 27-13 (M)
2006—Rams, 41-21 (M)
2009—Vikings, 38-10 (StL)
(RS Pts.—Rams 767, Vikings 753)
(PS Pts.—Rams 150, Vikings 150)
*Franchise in Los Angeles prior to 1995
**Conference Championship
***NFC Championship
****NFC Divisional Playoff
*****NFC First-Round Playoff

MINNESOTA vs. SAN DIEGO
RS: Series tied, 5-5
1971—Chargers, 30-14 (SD)
1975—Vikings, 28-13 (M)
1978—Chargers, 13-7 (M)
1981—Vikings, 33-31 (SD)

1984—Chargers, 42-13 (M)
1985—Vikings, 21-17 (M)
1993—Chargers, 30-17 (M)
1999—Vikings, 35-27 (M)
2003—Chargers, 42-28 (SD)
2007—Vikings, 35-17 (M)
(RS Pts.—Chargers 262, Vikings 231)

MINNESOTA vs. SAN FRANCISCO
RS: Vikings lead series, 20-18-1
PS: 49ers lead series, 4-1
1961—49ers, 38-24 (M)
  49ers, 38-28 (SF)
1962—49ers, 21-7 (SF)
  49ers, 35-12 (M)
1963—Vikings, 24-20 (SF)
  Vikings, 45-14 (M)
1964—Vikings, 27-22 (SF)
  Vikings, 24-7 (M)
1965—Vikings, 42-41 (SF)
  49ers, 45-24 (M)
1966—Tie, 20-20 (SF)
  Vikings, 28-3 (M)
1967—49ers, 27-21 (M)
1968—Vikings, 30-20 (SF)
1969—Vikings, 10-7 (M)
1970—*49ers, 17-14 (M)
1971—49ers, 13-9 (M)
1972—49ers, 20-17 (SF)
1973—Vikings, 17-13 (SF)
1975—Vikings, 27-17 (M)
1976—49ers, 20-16 (SF)
1977—Vikings, 28-27 (M)
1979—Vikings, 28-22 (M)
1983—49ers, 48-17 (M)
1984—49ers, 51-7 (SF)
1985—Vikings, 28-21 (M)
1986—Vikings, 27-24 (SF) OT
1987—*Vikings, 36-24 (SF)
1988—49ers, 24-21 (M)
  *49ers, 34-9 (SF)
1989—*49ers, 41-13 (SF)
1990—49ers, 20-17 (M)
1991—Vikings, 17-14 (M)
1992—49ers, 20-17 (M)
1993—49ers, 38-19 (SF)
1994—Vikings, 21-14 (M)
1995—49ers, 37-30 (SF)
1997—49ers, 28-17 (SF)
  *49ers, 38-22 (SF)
1999—Vikings, 40-16 (M)
2003—Vikings, 35-7 (M)
2006—49ers, 9-3 (SF)
2007—Vikings, 27-7 (SF)
2009—Vikings, 27-24 (M)
(RS Pts.—49ers 892, Vikings 878)
(PS Pts.—49ers 154, Vikings 94)
*NFC Divisional Playoff

MINNESOTA vs. SEATTLE
RS: Seahawks lead series, 6-5
1976—Vikings, 27-21 (M)
1978—Seahawks, 29-28 (S)
1984—Seahawks, 20-12 (M)
1987—Seahawks, 28-17 (S)
1990—Vikings, 24-21 (S)
1996—Seahawks, 42-23 (M)
2002—Seahawks, 48-23 (S)
2003—Vikings, 34-7 (M)
2004—Seahawks, 27-23 (M)
2006—Vikings, 31-13 (S)
2009—Vikings, 35-9 (M)
(RS Pts.—Vikings 277, Seahawks 265)

MINNESOTA vs. TAMPA BAY
RS: Vikings lead series, 31-20
1977—Vikings, 9-3 (TB)
1978—Buccaneers, 16-10 (M)
  Vikings, 24-7 (TB)
1979—Buccaneers, 12-10 (M)
  Vikings, 23-22 (TB)
1980—Vikings, 38-30 (M)
  Vikings, 21-10 (TB)
1981—Buccaneers, 21-13 (TB)
  Vikings, 25-10 (M)
1982—Vikings, 17-10 (M)
1983—Vikings, 19-16 (TB) OT
  Buccaneers, 17-12 (M)
1984—Buccaneers, 35-31 (TB)
  Vikings, 27-24 (M)
1985—Vikings, 31-16 (TB)
  Vikings, 26-7 (M)
1986—Vikings, 23-10 (TB)
  Vikings, 45-13 (M)
1987—Buccaneers, 20-10 (TB)
  Vikings, 23-17 (M)
1988—Vikings, 14-13 (M)
  Vikings, 49-20 (TB)
1989—Vikings, 17-3 (M)
  Vikings, 24-10 (TB)
1990—Buccaneers, 23-20 (M) OT
  Buccaneers, 26-13 (TB)
1991—Vikings, 28-13 (M)
  Vikings, 26-24 (TB)
1992—Vikings, 26-20 (M)
  Vikings, 35-7 (TB)
1993—Vikings, 15-0 (M)
  Buccaneers, 23-10 (TB)
1994—Vikings, 36-13 (TB)
  Buccaneers, 20-17 (M) OT
1995—Buccaneers, 20-17 (TB) OT
  Vikings, 31-17 (M)
1996—Buccaneers, 24-13 (TB)
  Vikings, 21-10 (M)
1997—Buccaneers, 28-14 (M)
  Vikings, 10-6 (TB)
1998—Vikings, 31-7 (M)
  Buccaneers, 27-24 (TB)
1999—Vikings, 21-14 (M)
  Buccaneers, 24-17 (TB)
2000—Vikings, 30-23 (M)
  Buccaneers, 41-13 (TB)
2001—Vikings, 20-16 (M)
  Buccaneers, 41-14 (TB)
2002—Buccaneers, 38-24 (TB)
2005—Buccaneers, 24-13 (M)
2008—Buccaneers, 19-13 (TB)
(RS Pts.—Vikings 1,093, Buccaneers 910)

MINNESOTA vs. *TENNESSEE
RS: Vikings lead series, 7-4
1974—Vikings, 51-10 (M)
1980—Oilers, 20-16 (H)
1983—Vikings, 34-14 (M)
1986—Oilers, 23-10 (H)
1989—Vikings, 38-7 (M)
1992—Oilers, 17-13 (M)
1995—Vikings, 23-17 (M) OT
1998—Vikings, 26-16 (T)
2001—Vikings, 42-24 (M)
2004—Vikings, 20-3 (M)
2008—Titans, 30-17 (T)
(RS Pts.—Vikings 290, Titans 181)
*Franchise in Houston prior to 1997;
known as Oilers prior to 1999

MINNESOTA vs. WASHINGTON
RS: Redskins lead series, 8-7
PS: Redskins lead series, 3-2
1968—Vikings, 27-14 (M)
1970—Vikings, 19-10 (W)
1972—Redskins, 24-21 (M)
1973—*Vikings, 27-20 (M)
1975—Redskins, 31-30 (W)
1976—*Vikings, 35-20 (M)
1980—Vikings, 39-14 (W)
1982—**Redskins, 21-7 (W)
1984—Redskins, 31-17 (M)
1986—Redskins, 44-38 (W) OT
1987—Redskins, 27-24 (M) OT
      ***Redskins, 17-10 (W)
1992—Redskins, 15-13 (M)
      ****Redskins, 24-7 (M)
1993—Vikings, 14-9 (W)
1998—Vikings, 41-7 (M)
2004—Redskins, 21-18 (W)
2006—Vikings, 19-16 (W)
2007—Redskins, 32-21 (M)
2010—Vikings, 17-13 (W)
(RS Pts.—Vikings 358, Redskins 308)
(PS Pts.—Redskins 102, Vikings 86)
*NFC Divisional Playoff
**NFC Second-Round Playoff
***NFC Championship
****NFC First-Round Playoff

NEW ENGLAND vs. ARIZONA
RS: Series tied, 6-6;
See Arizona vs. New England
NEW ENGLAND vs. ATLANTA
RS: Series tied, 6-6;
See Atlanta vs. New England
NEW ENGLAND vs. BALTIMORE
RS: Patriots lead series, 6-0
PS: Ravens lead series, 1-0;
See Baltimore vs. New England
NEW ENGLAND vs. BUFFALO
RS: Patriots lead series, 60-40-1
PS: Patriots lead series, 1-0;
See Buffalo vs. New England
NEW ENGLAND vs. CAROLINA
RS: Series tied, 2-2
PS: Patriots lead series, 1-0;
See Carolina vs. New England
NEW ENGLAND vs. CHICAGO
RS: Patriots lead series, 8-3
PS: Bears lead series, 1-0;
See Chicago vs. New England
NEW ENGLAND vs. CINCINNATI
RS: Patriots lead series, 14-8;
See Cincinnati vs. New England
NEW ENGLAND vs. CLEVELAND
RS: Browns lead series, 12-9
PS: Browns lead series, 1-0;
See Cleveland vs. New England
NEW ENGLAND vs. DALLAS
RS: Cowboys lead series, 7-3;
See Dallas vs. New England
NEW ENGLAND vs. DENVER
RS: Broncos lead series, 25-16
PS: Broncos lead series, 2-0;
See Denver vs. New England
NEW ENGLAND vs. DETROIT
RS: Patriots lead series, 6-4;
See Detroit vs. New England
NEW ENGLAND vs. GREEN BAY
RS: Patriots lead series, 5-4

PS: Packers lead series, 1-0;
See Green Bay vs. New England
NEW ENGLAND vs. HOUSTON
RS: Patriots lead series, 2-1;
See Houston vs. New England
NEW ENGLAND vs. INDIANAPOLIS
RS: Patriots lead series, 43-28
PS: Patriots lead series, 2-1;
See Indianapolis vs. New England
NEW ENGLAND vs. JACKSONVILLE
RS: Patriots lead series, 5-0
PS: Patriots lead series, 3-1;
See Jacksonville vs. New England
NEW ENGLAND vs. KANSAS CITY
RS: Chiefs lead series, 16-12-3;
See Kansas City vs. New England
NEW ENGLAND vs. MIAMI
RS: Dolphins lead series, 49-39
PS: Patriots lead series, 2-1;
See Miami vs. New England
NEW ENGLAND vs. MINNESOTA
RS: Patriots lead series, 7-4;
See Minnesota vs. New England
NEW ENGLAND vs. NEW ORLEANS
RS: Patriots lead series, 8-4
1972—Patriots, 17-10 (NO)
1976—Patriots, 27-6 (NE)
1980—Patriots, 38-27 (NO)
1983—Patriots, 7-0 (NE)
1986—Patriots, 21-20 (NO)
1989—Saints, 28-24 (NE)
1992—Saints, 31-14 (NE)
1995—Saints, 31-17 (NE)
1998—Patriots, 30-27 (NO)
2001—Patriots, 34-17 (NE)
2005—Patriots, 24-17 (NE)
2009—Saints, 38-17 (NO)
(RS Pts.—Patriots 270, Saints 252)
*NEW ENGLAND vs. N.Y. GIANTS
RS: Patriots lead series, 5-3
PS: Giants lead series, 1-0;
1970—Giants, 16-0 (B)
1974—Patriots, 28-20 (New Haven)
1987—Giants, 17-10 (NY)
1990—Giants, 13-10 (NE)
1996—Patriots, 23-22 (NY)
1999—Patriots, 16-14 (NE)
2003—Patriots, 17-6 (NE)
2007—Patriots, 38-35 (NY)
      **Giants, 17-14 (Arizona)
(RS Pts.—Giants 143, Patriots 142)
(PS Pts.—Giants 17, Patriots 14)
*Franchise in Boston prior to 1971
**Super Bowl XLII
*NEW ENGLAND vs. **N.Y. JETS
RS: Jets lead series, 51-49-1
PS: Patriots lead series, 2-1
1960—Patriots, 28-24 (NY)
      Patriots, 38-21 (B)
1961—Titans, 21-20 (B)
      Titans, 37-30 (NY)
1962—Patriots, 43-14 (NY)
      Patriots, 24-17 (B)
1963—Patriots, 38-14 (B)
      Jets, 31-24 (NY)
1964—Patriots, 26-10 (B)
      Jets, 35-14 (NY)
1965—Jets, 30-20 (B)
      Patriots, 27-23 (NY)
1966—Tie, 24-24 (B)
      Jets, 38-28 (NY)

1967—Jets, 30-23 (NY)
      Jets, 29-24 (B)
1968—Jets, 47-31 (Birmingham)
      Jets, 48-14 (NY)
1969—Jets, 23-14 (B)
      Jets, 23-17 (NY)
1970—Jets, 31-21 (B)
      Jets, 17-3 (NY)
1971—Patriots, 20-0 (NE)
      Jets, 13-6 (NY)
1972—Jets, 41-13 (NE)
      Jets, 34-10 (NY)
1973—Jets, 9-7 (NE)
      Jets, 33-13 (NY)
1974—Patriots, 24-0 (NY)
      Jets, 21-16 (NE)
1975—Jets, 36-7 (NY)
      Jets, 30-28 (NE)
1976—Patriots, 41-7 (NE)
      Patriots, 38-24 (NY)
1977—Jets, 30-27 (NY)
      Patriots, 24-13 (NE)
1978—Patriots, 55-21 (NE)
      Patriots, 19-17 (NY)
1979—Patriots, 56-3 (NE)
      Jets, 27-26 (NY)
1980—Patriots, 21-11 (NY)
      Patriots, 34-21 (NE)
1981—Jets, 28-24 (NY)
      Jets, 17-6 (NE)
1982—Jets, 31-7 (NE)
1983—Patriots, 23-13 (NE)
      Jets, 26-3 (NY)
1984—Patriots, 28-21 (NY)
      Patriots, 30-20 (NE)
1985—Patriots, 20-13 (NE)
      Jets, 16-13 (NY) OT
      ***Patriots, 26-14 (NY)
1986—Patriots, 20-6 (NY)
      Jets, 31-24 (NE)
1987—Jets, 43-24 (NY)
      Patriots, 42-20 (NE)
1988—Patriots, 28-3 (NE)
      Patriots, 14-13 (NY)
1989—Patriots, 27-24 (NY)
      Jets, 27-26 (NE)
1990—Jets, 37-13 (NE)
      Jets, 42-7 (NY)
1991—Jets, 28-21 (NE)
      Patriots, 6-3 (NY)
1992—Jets, 30-21 (NY)
      Patriots, 24-3 (NE)
1993—Jets, 45-7 (NY)
      Jets, 6-0 (NE)
1994—Jets, 24-17 (NY)
      Patriots, 24-13 (NE)
1995—Patriots, 20-7 (NY)
      Patriots, 31-28 (NE)
1996—Patriots, 31-27 (NE)
      Patriots, 34-10 (NE)
1997—Patriots, 27-24 (NE) OT
      Jets, 24-19 (NY)
1998—Jets, 24-14 (NE)
      Jets, 31-10 (NE)
1999—Patriots, 30-28 (NY)
      Jets, 24-17 (NE)
2000—Patriots, 20-19 (NY)
      Jets, 34-17 (NE)
2001—Jets, 10-3 (NE)
      Patriots, 17-16 (NY)
2002—Patriots, 44-7 (NY)

Jets, 30-17 (NE)
2003—Patriots, 23-16 (NE)
Patriots, 21-16 (NY)
2004—Patriots, 13-7 (NE)
Patriots, 23-7 (NY)
2005—Patriots, 16-3 (NE)
Patriots, 31-21 (NY)
2006—Patriots, 24-17 (NY)
Jets, 17-14 (NE)
***Patriots, 37-16 (NE)
2007—Patriots, 38-14 (NY)
Patriots, 20-10 (NE)
2008—Patriots, 19-10 (NY)
Jets, 34-31 (NE) OT
2009—Jets, 16-9 (NY)
Patriots, 31-14 (NE)
2010—Jets, 28-14 (NY)
Patriots, 45-3 (NE)
****Jets, 28-21 (NE)
(RS Pts.—Patriots 2,237, Jets 2,138)
(PS Pts.—Patriots 84, Jets 58)
*Franchise in Boston prior to 1971
**Jets known as Titans prior to 1963
***AFC First-Round Playoff
****AFC Divisional Playoff
NEW ENGLAND vs. **OAKLAND
RS: Series tied, 14-14-1
PS: Patriots lead series, 2-1
1960—Raiders, 27-14 (O)
Patriots, 34-28 (B)
1961—Patriots, 20-17 (B)
Patriots, 35-21 (O)
1962—Patriots, 26-16 (B)
Raiders, 20-0 (O)
1963—Patriots, 20-14 (O)
Patriots, 20-14 (B)
1964—Patriots, 17-14 (O)
Tie, 43-43 (B)
1965—Raiders, 24-10 (B)
Raiders, 30-21 (O)
1966—Raiders, 24-21 (B)
1967—Raiders, 35-7 (O)
Raiders, 48-14 (B)
1968—Raiders, 41-10 (O)
1969—Raiders, 38-23 (B)
1971—Patriots, 20-6 (NE)
1974—Raiders, 41-26 (O)
1976—Patriots, 48-17 (NE)
****Raiders, 24-21 (O)
1978—Patriots, 21-14 (O)
1981—Raiders, 27-17 (O)
1985—Raiders, 35-20 (NE)
***Patriots, 27-20 (LA)
1987—Patriots, 26-23 (NE)
1989—Raiders, 24-21 (LA)
1994—Raiders, 21-17 (NE)
2001—***Patriots, 16-13 (NE) OT
2002—Patriots, 27-20 (O)
2005—Patriots, 30-20 (NE)
2008—Patriots, 49-26 (O)
(RS Pts.—Raiders 732, Patriots 653)
(PS Pts.—Patriots 64, Raiders 57)
*Franchise in Boston prior to 1971
**Franchise in Los Angeles from 1982-1994
***AFC Divisional Playoff
NEW ENGLAND vs. PHILADELPHIA
RS: Eagles lead series, 6-4
PS: Patriots lead series, 1-0
1973—Eagles, 24-23 (P)
1977—Patriots, 14-6 (NE)

1978—Patriots, 24-14 (NE)
1981—Eagles, 13-3 (P)
1984—Eagles, 27-17 (P)
1987—Eagles, 34-31 (NE) OT
1990—Eagles, 48-20 (P)
1999—Eagles, 24-9 (P)
2003—Patriots, 31-10 (P)
2004—*Patriots, 24-21 (Jacksonville)
2007—Patriots, 31-28 (NE)
(RS Pts.—Eagles 228, Patriots 203)
(PS Pts.—Patriots 24, Eagles 21)
*Super Bowl XXXIX
NEW ENGLAND vs. PITTSBURGH
RS: Steelers lead series, 13-8
PS: Patriots lead series, 3-1
1972—Steelers, 33-3 (P)
1974—Steelers, 21-17 (NE)
1976—Patriots, 30-27 (P)
1979—Steelers, 16-13 (NE) OT
1981—Steelers, 27-21 (P) OT
1982—Steelers, 37-14 (P)
1983—Patriots, 28-23 (P)
1986—Patriots, 34-0 (P)
1989—Steelers, 28-10 (P)
1990—Steelers, 24-3 (P)
1991—Steelers, 20-6 (P)
1993—Patriots, 17-14 (P)
1995—Steelers, 41-27 (P)
1996—*Patriots, 28-3 (NE)
1997—Steelers, 24-21 (NE) OT
*Steelers, 7-6 (P)
1998—Patriots, 23-9 (P)
2001—**Patriots, 24-17 (P)
2002—Patriots, 30-14 (NE)
2004—Steelers, 34-20 (P)
**Patriots, 41-27 (P)
2005—Patriots, 23-20 (P)
2007—Patriots, 34-13 (NE)
2008—Steelers, 33-10 (NE)
2010—Patriots, 39-26 (P)
(RS Pts.—Steelers 487, Patriots 420)
(PS Pts.—Patriots 99, Steelers 54)
*AFC Divisional Playoff
**AFC Championship
NEW ENGLAND vs. *ST. LOUIS
RS: Series tied, 5-5
PS: Patriots lead series, 1-0
1974—Patriots, 20-14 (NE)
1980—Rams, 17-14 (NE)
1983—Patriots, 21-7 (LA)
1986—Patriots, 30-28 (LA)
1989—Rams, 24-20 (NE)
1992—Rams, 14-0 (LA)
1998—Rams, 32-18 (StL)
2001—Rams, 24-17 (NE)
**Patriots, 20-17 (New Orleans)
2004—Patriots, 40-22 (StL)
2008—Patriots, 23-16 (NE)
(RS Pts.—Patriots 203, Rams 198)
(PS Pts.—Patriots 20, Rams 17)
*Franchise in Los Angeles prior to 1995
**Super Bowl XXXVI
NEW ENGLAND vs. **SAN DIEGO
RS: Patriots lead series, 19-14-2
PS: Patriots lead series, 2-1
1960—Patriots, 35-0 (LA)
Chargers, 45-16 (B)
1961—Chargers, 38-27 (B)
Patriots, 41-0 (B)
1962—Patriots, 24-20 (B)
Patriots, 20-14 (SD)

1963—Chargers, 17-13 (SD)
Chargers, 7-6 (B)
***Chargers, 51-10 (SD)
1964—Patriots, 33-28 (SD)
Chargers, 26-17 (B)
1965—Tie, 10-10 (B)
Patriots, 22-6 (SD)
1966—Chargers, 24-0 (SD)
Patriots, 35-17 (B)
1967—Chargers, 28-14 (SD)
Tie, 31-31 (SD)
1968—Chargers, 27-17 (B)
1969—Chargers, 13-10 (B)
Chargers, 28-18 (SD)
1970—Chargers, 16-14 (B)
1973—Patriots, 30-14 (NE)
1975—Patriots, 33-19 (SD)
1977—Patriots, 24-20 (SD)
1978—Patriots, 28-23 (NE)
1979—Patriots, 27-21 (NE)
1983—Patriots, 37-21 (NE)
1994—Patriots, 23-17 (NE)
1996—Patriots, 45-7 (SD)
1997—Patriots, 41-7 (NE)
2001—Patriots, 29-26 (NE) OT
2002—Chargers, 21-14 (SD)
2005—Chargers, 41-17 (NE)
2006—****Patriots, 24-21 (SD)
2007—Patriots, 38-14 (NE)
*****Patriots, 21-12 (NE)
2008—Chargers, 30-10 (SD)
2010—Patriots, 23-20 (SD)
(RS Pts.—Patriots 825, Chargers 699)
(PS Pts.—Chargers 84, Patriots 55)
*Franchise in Boston prior to 1971
**Franchise in Los Angeles prior to 1961
***AFL Championship
****AFC Divisional Playoff
*****AFC Championship
NEW ENGLAND vs. SAN FRANCISCO
RS: 49ers lead series, 7-4
1971—49ers, 27-10 (SF)
1975—Patriots, 24-16 (NE)
1980—49ers, 21-17 (SF)
1983—49ers, 33-13 (NE)
1986—49ers, 29-24 (NE)
1989—49ers, 37-20 (SF)
1992—49ers, 24-12 (NF)
1995—49ers, 28-3 (SF)
1998—Patriots, 24-21 (NE)
2004—Patriots, 21-7 (NE)
2008—Patriots, 30-21 (SF)
(RS Pts.—49ers 264, Patriots 198)
NEW ENGLAND vs. SEATTLE
RS: Patriots lead series, 8-7
1977—Patriots, 31-0 (NE)
1980—Patriots, 37-31 (NE)
1982—Patriots, 16-0 (S)
1983—Seahawks, 24-6 (S)
1984—Patriots, 38-23 (NE)
1985—Patriots, 20-13 (S)
1986—Seahawks, 38-31 (NE)
1988—Patriots, 13-7 (NE)
1989—Seahawks, 24-3 (NE)
1990—Seahawks, 33-20 (NE)
1992—Seahawks, 10-6 (NE)
1993—Seahawks, 17-14 (NE)
Seahawks, 10-9 (S)
2004—Patriots, 30-20 (NE)
2008—Patriots, 24-21 (S)
(RS Pts.—Patriots 298, Seahawks 271)

NEW ENGLAND vs. TAMPA BAY
RS: Patriots lead series, 5-2
1976—Patriots, 31-14 (TB)
1985—Patriots, 32-14 (TB)
1988—Patriots, 10-7 (NE) OT
1997—Buccaneers, 27-7 (TB)
2000—Buccaneers, 21-16 (NE)
2005—Patriots, 28-0 (NE)
2009—Patriots, 35-7 (London)
(RS Pts.—Patriots 159, Buccaneers 90)

*NEW ENGLAND vs. **TENNESSEE
RS: Patriots lead series, 21-15-1
PS: Series tied, 1-1
1960—Oilers, 24-10 (B)
        Oilers, 37-21 (H)
1961—Tie, 31-31 (B)
        Oilers, 27-15 (H)
1962—Patriots, 34-21 (B)
        Oilers, 21-17 (H)
1963—Patriots, 45-3 (B)
        Patriots, 46-28 (H)
1964—Patriots, 25-24 (B)
        Patriots, 34-17 (H)
1965—Oilers, 31-10 (H)
        Patriots, 42-14 (B)
1966—Patriots, 27-21 (B)
        Patriots, 38-14 (H)
1967—Patriots, 18-7 (B)
        Oilers, 27-6 (H)
1968—Oilers, 16-0 (B)
        Oilers, 45-17 (H)
1969—Oilers, 24-0 (B)
        Oilers, 27-23 (H)
1971—Patriots, 28-20 (NE)
1973—Patriots, 32-0 (H)
1975—Oilers, 7-0 (NE)
1978—Oilers, 26-23 (NE)
        ***Oilers, 31-14 (NE)
1980—Oilers, 38-34 (H)
1981—Patriots, 38-10 (NE)
1982—Patriots, 29-21 (NE)
1987—Patriots, 21-7 (H)
1988—Oilers, 31-6 (H)
1989—Patriots, 23-13 (NE)
1991—Patriots, 24-20 (NE)
1993—Oilers, 28-14 (NE)
1998—Patriots, 27-16 (NE)
2002—Titans, 24-7 (T)
2003—Patriots, 38-30 (NE)
        ***Patriots, 17-14 (NE)
2006—Patriots, 40-23 (T)
2009—Patriots, 59-0 (NE)
(RS Pts.—Patriots 926, Titans 749)
(PS Pts.—Titans 45, Patriots 31)
*Franchise in Boston prior to 1971
**Franchise in Houston prior to 1997;
known as Oilers prior to 1999
***AFC Divisional Playoff

NEW ENGLAND vs. WASHINGTON
RS: Redskins lead series, 6-2
1972—Patriots, 24-23 (NE)
1978—Redskins, 16-14 (NE)
1981—Redskins, 24-22 (W)
1984—Redskins, 26-10 (NE)
1990—Redskins, 25-10 (NE)
1996—Patriots, 27-22 (NE)
2003—Redskins, 20-17 (W)
2007—Patriots, 52-7 (NE)
(RS Pts.—Patriots 171, Redskins 168)

NEW ORLEANS vs. ARIZONA
RS: Cardinals lead series, 14-12
PS: Saints lead series, 1-0;
See Arizona vs. New Orleans

NEW ORLEANS vs. ATLANTA
RS: Falcons lead series, 45-38
PS: Falcons lead series, 1-0;
See Atlanta vs. New Orleans

NEW ORLEANS vs. BALTIMORE
RS: Ravens lead series, 4-1;
See Baltimore vs. New Orleans

NEW ORLEANS vs. BUFFALO
RS: Saints lead series, 5-4;
See Buffalo vs. New Orleans

NEW ORLEANS vs. CAROLINA
RS: Panthers lead series, 17-15;
See Carolina vs. New Orleans

NEW ORLEANS vs. CHICAGO
RS: Bears lead series, 13-11
PS: Bears lead series, 2-0;
See Chicago vs. New Orleans

NEW ORLEANS vs. CINCINNATI
RS: Series tied, 6-6;
See Cincinnati vs. New Orleans

NEW ORLEANS vs. CLEVELAND
RS: Browns lead series, 12-4;
See Cleveland vs. New Orleans

NEW ORLEANS vs. DALLAS
RS: Cowboys lead series, 15-9;
See Dallas vs. New Orleans

NEW ORLEANS vs. DENVER
RS: Broncos lead series, 7-2;
See Denver vs. New Orleans

NEW ORLEANS vs. DETROIT
RS: Saints lead series, 10-9-1;
See Detroit vs. New Orleans

NEW ORLEANS vs. GREEN BAY
RS: Packers lead series, 14-7;
See Green Bay vs. New Orleans

NEW ORLEANS vs. HOUSTON
RS: Series tied, 1-1;
See Houston vs. New Orleans

NEW ORLEANS vs. INDIANAPOLIS
RS: Series tied, 5-5
PS: Saints lead series, 1-0;
See Indianapolis vs. New Orleans

NEW ORLEANS vs. JACKSONVILLE
RS: Series tied, 2-2;
See Jacksonville vs. New Orleans

NEW ORLEANS vs. KANSAS CITY
RS: Saints lead series, 5-4;
See Kansas City vs. New Orleans

NEW ORLEANS vs. MIAMI
RS: Dolphins lead series, 6-4;
See Miami vs. New Orleans

NEW ORLEANS vs. MINNESOTA
RS: Vikings lead series, 18-8
PS: Vikings lead series, 2-1;
See Minnesota vs. New Orleans

NEW ORLEANS vs. NEW ENGLAND
RS: Patriots lead series, 8-4;
See New England vs. New Orleans

NEW ORLEANS vs. N.Y. GIANTS
RS: Giants lead series, 14-11
1967—Giants, 27-21 (NY)
1968—Giants, 38-21 (NY)
1969—Saints, 25-24 (NY)
1970—Saints, 14-10 (NO)
1972—Giants, 45-21 (NY)
1975—Giants, 28-14 (NY)

1978—Saints, 28-17 (NO)
1979—Saints, 24-14 (NO)
1981—Giants, 20-7 (NY)
1984—Saints, 10-3 (NY)
1985—Giants, 21-13 (NO)
1986—Giants, 20-17 (NY)
1987—Saints, 23-14 (NO)
1988—Giants, 13-12 (NO)
1993—Giants, 24-14 (NO)
1994—Saints, 27-22 (NO)
1995—Giants, 45-29 (NY)
1996—Saints, 17-3 (NY)
1997—Giants, 14-9 (NY)
1999—Giants, 31-3 (NY)
2001—Giants, 21-13 (NY)
2003—Saints, 45-7 (NO)
2005—Giants, 27-10 (NY*)
2006—Saints, 30-7 (NY)
2009—Saints, 48-27 (NO)
(RS Pts.—Giants 522, Saints 495)
*Saints home game

NEW ORLEANS vs. N.Y. JETS
RS: Saints lead series, 6-5
1972—Jets, 18-17 (NY)
1977—Jets, 16-13 (NO)
1980—Saints, 21-20 (NY)
1983—Jets, 31-28 (NO)
1986—Jets, 28-23 (NY)
1989—Saints, 29-14 (NO)
1992—Saints, 20-0 (NY)
1995—Saints, 12-0 (NY)
2001—Jets, 16-9 (NO)
2005—Saints, 21-19 (NY)
2009—Saints, 24-10 (NO)
(RS Pts.—Saints 217, Jets 172)

NEW ORLEANS vs. *OAKLAND
RS: Series tied, 5-5-1
1971—Tie, 21-21 (NO)
1975—Raiders, 48-10 (O)
1979—Raiders, 42-35 (NO)
1985—Raiders, 23-13 (LA)
1988—Saints, 20-6 (NO)
1991—Saints, 27-0 (NO)
1994—Raiders, 24-19 (LA)
1997—Saints, 13-10 (O)
2000—Raiders, 31-22 (NO)
2004—Saints, 31-26 (O)
2008—Saints, 34-3 (NO)
(RS Pts.—Saints 245, Raiders 234)
*Franchise in Los Angeles from 1982-1994

NEW ORLEANS vs. PHILADELPHIA
RS: Eagles lead series, 15-10
PS: Series tied, 1-1
1967—Saints, 31-24 (NO)
        Eagles, 48-21 (P)
1968—Eagles, 29-17 (P)
1969—Eagles, 13-10 (P)
        Saints, 26-17 (NO)
1972—Saints, 21-3 (NO)
1974—Saints, 14-10 (NO)
1977—Eagles, 28-7 (P)
1978—Eagles, 24-17 (NO)
1979—Eagles, 26-14 (NO)
1980—Eagles, 34-21 (NO)
1981—Eagles, 31-14 (NO)
1983—Saints, 20-17 (P) OT
1985—Saints, 23-21 (NO)
1987—Eagles, 27-17 (P)
1989—Saints, 30-20 (NO)
1991—Saints, 13-6 (P)
1992—Eagles, 15-13 (P)

*Eagles, 36-20 (NO)
1993—Eagles, 37-26 (P)
1995—Eagles, 15-10 (NO)
2000—Eagles, 21-7 (NO)
2003—Eagles, 33-20 (P)
2006—Saints, 27-24 (NO)
　　**Saints, 27-24 (NO)
2007—Eagles, 38-23 (NO)
2009—Saints, 48-22 (P)
(RS Pts.—Eagles 583, Saints 490)
(PS Pts.—Eagles 60, Saints 47)
*NFC First-Round Playoff
**NFC Divisional Playoff
NEW ORLEANS vs. PITTSBURGH
RS: Series tied, 7-7
1967—Steelers, 14-10 (NO)
1968—Saints, 16-12 (P)
　　Saints, 24-14 (NO)
1969—Saints, 27-24 (NO)
1974—Steelers, 28-7 (NO)
1978—Steelers, 20-14 (P)
1981—Steelers, 20-6 (NO)
1984—Saints, 27-24 (NO)
1987—Saints, 20-16 (P)
1990—Steelers, 9-6 (NO)
1993—Steelers, 37-14 (P)
2002—Saints, 32-29 (NO)
2006—Steelers, 38-31 (P)
2010—Saints, 20-10 (NO)
(RS Pts.—Steelers 295, Saints 254)
NEW ORLEANS vs. *ST. LOUIS
RS: Rams lead series, 38-31
PS: Saints lead series, 1-0
1967—Rams, 27-13 (NO)
1969—Rams, 36-17 (LA)
1970—Rams, 30-17 (NO)
　　Rams, 34-16 (LA)
1971—Saints, 24-20 (NO)
　　Rams, 45-28 (LA)
1972—Rams, 34-14 (LA)
　　Saints, 19-16 (NO)
1973—Rams, 29-7 (LA)
　　Rams, 24-13 (NO)
1974—Rams, 24-0 (LA)
　　Saints, 20-7 (NO)
1975—Rams, 38-14 (LA)
　　Rams, 14-7 (NO)
1976—Rams, 16-10 (NO)
　　Rams, 33-14 (LA)
1977—Rams, 14-7 (LA)
　　Saints, 27-26 (NO)
1978—Rams, 26-20 (NO)
　　Saints, 10-3 (LA)
1979—Rams, 35-17 (NO)
　　Saints, 29-14 (LA)
1980—Rams, 45-31 (LA)
　　Rams, 27-7 (NO)
1981—Saints, 23-17 (NO)
　　Saints, 21-13 (LA)
1983—Rams, 30-27 (LA)
　　Rams, 26-24 (NO)
1984—Rams, 28-10 (NO)
　　Rams, 34-21 (LA)
1985—Rams, 28-10 (LA)
　　Saints, 29-3 (NO)
1986—Saints, 6-0 (NO)
　　Rams, 26-13 (LA)
1987—Saints, 37-10 (NO)
　　Saints, 31-14 (LA)
1988—Rams, 12-10 (NO)
　　Saints, 14-10 (LA)

1989—Saints, 40-21 (LA)
　　Rams, 20-17 (NO) OT
1990—Saints, 24-20 (LA)
　　Saints, 20-17 (NO)
1991—Saints, 24-7 (NO)
　　Saints, 24-17 (LA)
1992—Saints, 13-10 (NO)
　　Saints, 37-14 (LA)
1993—Saints, 37-6 (LA)
　　Rams, 23-20 (NO)
1994—Saints, 37-34 (NO)
　　Saints, 31-15 (LA)
1995—Rams, 17-13 (StL)
　　Saints, 19-10 (NO)
1996—Rams, 26-10 (NO)
　　Rams, 14-13 (StL)
1997—Rams, 38-24 (StL)
　　Rams, 34-27 (NO)
1998—Saints, 24-17 (StL)
　　Saints, 24-3 (NO)
1999—Rams, 43-12 (StL)
　　Rams, 30-14 (NO)
2000—Saints, 31-24 (StL)
　　Rams, 26-21 (NO)
　　**Saints, 31-28 (NO)
2001—Saints, 34-31 (StL)
　　Rams, 34-21 (NO)
2004—Saints, 28-25 (StL) OT
2005—Rams, 28-17 (StL)
2007—Rams, 37-29 (NO)
2009—Saints, 28-23 (StL)
2010—Saints, 31-13 (NO)
(RS Pts.—Rams 1,545, Saints 1,401)
(PS Pts.—Saints 31, Rams 28)
*Franchise in Los Angeles prior to 1995
**NFC First-Round Playoff
NEW ORLEANS vs. SAN DIEGO
RS: Chargers lead series, 7-3
1973—Chargers, 17-14 (SD)
1977—Chargers, 14-0 (NO)
1979—Chargers, 35-0 (NO)
1988—Saints, 23-17 (SD)
1991—Chargers, 24-21 (SD)
1994—Chargers, 36-22 (NO)
1997—Chargers, 20-6 (NO)
2000—Saints, 28-27 (SD)
2004—Chargers, 43-17 (SD)
2008—Saints, 37-32 (London)
(RS Pts.—Chargers 265, Saints 168)
NEW ORLEANS vs. SAN FRANCISCO
RS: 49ers lead series, 45-24-2
1967—49ers, 27-13 (SF)
1969—Saints, 43-38 (NO)
1970—Tie, 20-20 (SF)
　　49ers, 38-27 (NO)
1971—49ers, 38-20 (NO)
　　Saints, 26-20 (SF)
1972—49ers, 37-2 (NO)
　　Tie, 20-20 (SF)
1973—49ers, 40-0 (SF)
　　Saints, 16-10 (NO)
1974—49ers, 17-13 (NO)
　　49ers, 35-21 (SF)
1975—49ers, 35-21 (SF)
　　49ers, 16-6 (NO)
1976—49ers, 33-3 (SF)
　　49ers, 27-7 (NO)
1977—49ers, 10-7 (NO) OT
　　49ers, 20-17 (SF)
1978—Saints, 14-7 (SF)
　　Saints, 24-13 (NO)

1979—Saints, 30-21 (SF)
　　Saints, 31-20 (NO)
1980—49ers, 26-23 (NO)
　　49ers, 38-35 (SF) OT
1981—49ers, 21-14 (SF)
　　49ers, 21-17 (NO)
1982—49ers, 23-20 (SF)
1983—49ers, 32-13 (NO)
　　49ers, 27-0 (SF)
1984—49ers, 30-20 (SF)
　　49ers, 35-3 (NO)
1985—Saints, 20-17 (SF)
　　49ers, 31-19 (NO)
1986—49ers, 26-17 (SF)
　　Saints, 23-10 (NO)
1987—49ers, 24-22 (NO)
　　Saints, 26-24 (SF)
1988—49ers, 34-33 (NO)
　　49ers, 30-17 (SF)
1989—49ers, 24-20 (NO)
　　49ers, 31-13 (SF)
1990—49ers, 13-12 (NO)
　　Saints, 13-10 (SF)
1991—Saints, 10-3 (NO)
　　49ers, 38-24 (SF)
1992—49ers, 16-10 (SF)
　　49ers, 21-20 (SF)
1993—Saints, 16-13 (NO)
　　49ers, 42-7 (SF)
1994—49ers, 24-13 (SF)
　　49ers, 35-14 (NO)
1995—49ers, 24-22 (NO)
　　Saints, 11-7 (SF)
1996—49ers, 27-11 (SF)
　　49ers, 24-17 (NO)
1997—49ers, 33-7 (SF)
　　49ers, 23-0 (NO)
1998—49ers, 31-0 (NO)
　　49ers, 31-20 (SF)
1999—49ers, 28-21 (SF)
　　Saints, 24-6 (NO)
2000—Saints, 31-15 (NO)
　　Saints, 31-27 (SF)
2001—Saints, 28-27 (SF)
　　49ers, 38-0 (NO)
2002—Saints, 35-27 (NO)
2004—Saints, 30-27 (NO)
2006—Saints, 34-10 (NO)
2007—Saints, 31-10 (SF)
2008—Saints, 31-17 (NO)
2010—Saints, 25-22 (SF)
(RS Pts.—49ers 1,713, Saints 1,286)
NEW ORLEANS vs. SEATTLE
RS: Saints lead series, 6-5
PS: Seahawks lead series, 1-0
1976—Saints, 51-27 (S)
1979—Seahawks, 38-24 (S)
1985—Seahawks, 27-3 (NO)
1988—Saints, 20-19 (S)
1991—Saints, 27-24 (NO)
1997—Saints, 20-17 (NO) OT
2000—Seahawks, 20-10 (S)
2003—Seahawks, 27-10 (S)
2004—Seahawks, 21-7 (NO)
2007—Saints, 28-17 (S)
2010—Saints, 34-19 (NO)
　　*Seahawks, 41-36 (S)
(RS Pts.—Seahawks 256, Saints 234)
(PS Pts.—Seahawks 41, Saints 36)
*NFC First-Round Playoff

NEW ORLEANS vs. TAMPA BAY
RS: Saints lead series, 22-16
1977—Buccaneers, 33-14 (NO)
1978—Saints, 17-10 (TB)
1979—Saints, 42-14 (TB)
1981—Buccaneers, 31-14 (NO)
1982—Buccaneers, 13-10 (NO)
1983—Saints, 24-21 (TB)
1984—Saints, 17-13 (NO)
1985—Saints, 20-13 (NO)
1986—Saints, 38-7 (NO)
1987—Saints, 44-34 (NO)
1988—Saints, 13-9 (NO)
1989—Buccaneers, 20-10 (TB)
1990—Saints, 35-7 (NO)
1991—Saints, 23-7 (NO)
1992—Saints, 23-21 (NO)
1994—Saints, 9-7 (TB)
1996—Buccaneers, 13-7 (TB)
1998—Saints, 9-3 (NO)
1999—Buccaneers, 31-16 (NO)
2001—Buccaneers, 48-21 (TB)
2002—Saints, 26-20 (TB) OT
   Saints, 23-20 (NO)
2003—Saints, 17-14 (TB)
   Buccaneers, 14-7 (NO)
2004—Buccaneers, 20-17 (NO)
   Saints, 21-17 (TB)
2005—Buccaneers, 10-3 (Baton Rouge)
   Buccaneers, 27-13 (TB)
2006—Saints, 24-21 (NO)
   Saints, 31-14 (TB)
2007—Buccaneers, 31-14 (TB)
   Buccaneers, 27-23 (NO)
2008—Saints, 24-20 (NO)
   Buccaneers, 23-20 (TB)
2009—Saints, 38-7 (TB)
   Buccaneers, 20-17 (NO) OT
2010—Saints, 31-6 (TB)
   Buccaneers, 23-13 (NO)
(RS Pts.—Saints 768, Buccaneers 689)

NEW ORLEANS vs. *TENNESSEE
RS: Titans lead series, 7-4-1
1971—Tie, 13-13 (H)
1976—Oilers, 31-26 (NO)
1978—Oilers, 17-12 (NO)
1981—Saints, 27-24 (H)
1984—Saints, 27-10 (H)
1987—Saints, 24-10 (NO)
1990—Oilers, 23-10 (H)
1993—Saints, 33-21 (NO)
1996—Oilers, 31-14 (NO)
1999—Titans, 24-21 (NO)
2003—Titans, 27-12 (T)
2007—Titans, 31-14 (NO)
(RS Pts.—Titans 262, Saints 233)
*Franchise in Houston prior to 1997;
known as Oilers prior to 1999

NEW ORLEANS vs. WASHINGTON
RS: Redskins lead series, 15-8
1967—Redskins, 30-10 (NO)
   Saints, 30-14 (W)
1968—Saints, 37-17 (NO)
1969—Redskins, 26-20 (NO)
   Redskins, 17-14 (W)
1971—Redskins, 24-14 (W)
1973—Saints, 19-3 (NO)
1975—Redskins, 41-3 (W)
1979—Saints, 14-10 (W)
1980—Redskins, 22-14 (W)
1982—Redskins, 27-10 (NO)

1986—Redskins, 14-6 (NO)
1988—Redskins, 27-24 (W)
1989—Redskins, 16-14 (NO)
1990—Redskins, 31-17 (W)
1992—Saints, 20-3 (NO)
1994—Redskins, 38-24 (NO)
2001—Redskins, 40-10 (NO)
2002—Saints, 43-27 (W)
2003—Saints, 24-20 (W)
2006—Redskins, 16-10 (NO)
2008—Redskins, 29-24 (W)
2009—Saints, 33-30 (W) OT
(RS Pts.—Redskins 522, Saints 434)

N.Y. GIANTS vs. ARIZONA
RS: Giants lead series, 79-42-2;
See Arizona vs. N.Y. Giants

N.Y. GIANTS vs. ATLANTA
RS: Series tied, 10-10;
See Atlanta vs. N.Y. Giants

N.Y. GIANTS vs. BALTIMORE
RS: Ravens lead series, 2-1
PS: Ravens lead series, 1-0;
See Baltimore vs. N.Y. Giants

N.Y. GIANTS vs. BUFFALO
RS: Bills lead series, 6-4
PS: Giants lead series, 1-0;
See Buffalo vs. N.Y. Giants

N.Y. GIANTS vs. CAROLINA
RS: Series tied, 3-3
PS: Panthers lead series, 1-0;
See Carolina vs. N.Y. Giants

N.Y. GIANTS vs. CHICAGO
RS: Bears lead series, 27-19-2
PS: Bears lead series, 5-3;
See Chicago vs. N.Y. Giants

N.Y. GIANTS vs. CINCINNATI
RS: Bengals lead series, 5-3;
See Cincinnati vs. N.Y. Giants

N.Y. GIANTS vs. CLEVELAND
RS: Browns lead series, 26-19-2
PS: Series tied, 1-1;
See Cleveland vs. N.Y. Giants

N.Y. GIANTS vs. DALLAS
RS: Cowboys lead series, 56-39-2
PS: Giants lead series, 1-0;
See Dallas vs. N.Y. Giants

N.Y. GIANTS vs. DENVER
RS: Series tied, 5-5
PS: Giants lead series, 1-0;
See Denver vs. N.Y. Giants

N.Y. GIANTS vs. DETROIT
RS: Lions lead series, 20-19-1
PS: Lions lead series, 1-0;
See Detroit vs. N.Y. Giants

N.Y. GIANTS vs. GREEN BAY
RS: Packers lead series, 26-21-2
PS: Packers lead series, 4-2;
See Green Bay vs. N.Y. Giants

N.Y. GIANTS vs. HOUSTON
RS: Giants lead series, 2-1;
See Houston vs. N.Y. Giants

N.Y. GIANTS vs. INDIANAPOLIS
RS: Colts lead series, 8-6
PS: Colts lead series, 2-0;
See Indianapolis vs. N.Y. Giants

N.Y. GIANTS vs. JACKSONVILLE
RS: Giants lead series, 3-2;
See Jacksonville vs. N.Y. Giants

N.Y. GIANTS vs. KANSAS CITY
RS: Giants lead series, 10-2;

See Kansas City vs. N.Y. Giants

N.Y. GIANTS vs. MIAMI
RS: Giants lead series, 4-2;
See Miami vs. N.Y. Giants

N.Y. GIANTS vs. MINNESOTA
RS: Vikings lead series, 13-9
PS: Giants lead series, 2-1;
See Minnesota vs. N.Y. Giants

N.Y. GIANTS vs. NEW ENGLAND
RS: Patriots lead series, 5-3
PS: Giants lead series, 1-0;
See New England vs. N.Y. Giants

N.Y. GIANTS vs. NEW ORLEANS
RS: Giants lead series, 14-11;
See New Orleans vs. N.Y. Giants

N.Y. GIANTS vs. N.Y. JETS
RS: Giants lead series, 7-4
1970—Giants, 22-10 (NYJ)
1974—Jets, 26-20 (New Haven) OT
1981—Jets, 26-7 (NYG)
1984—Giants, 20-10 (NYJ)
1987—Giants, 20-7 (NYG)
1988—Jets, 27-21 (NYJ)
1993—Jets, 10-6 (NYG)
1996—Giants, 13-6 (NYJ)
1999—Giants, 41-28 (NYG)
2003—Giants, 31-28 (NYJ) OT
2007—Giants, 35-24 (NYG)
(RS Pts.—Giants 236, Jets 202)

N.Y. GIANTS vs. *OAKLAND
RS: Raiders lead series, 7-4
1973—Raiders, 42-0 (O)
1980—Raiders, 33-17 (NY)
1983—Raiders, 27-12 (LA)
1986—Giants, 14-9 (LA)
1989—Giants, 34-17 (NY)
1992—Raiders, 13-10 (LA)
1995—Raiders, 17-13 (NY)
1998—Raiders, 20-17 (O)
2001—Raiders, 28-10 (NY)
2005—Giants, 30-21 (O)
2009—Giants, 44-7 (NY)
(RS Pts.—Raiders 234, Giants 201)
*Franchise in Los Angeles from 1982-1994

N.Y. GIANTS vs. PHILADELPHIA
RS: Giants lead series, 79-71-2
PS: Series tied, 2-2
1933—Giants, 56-0 (NY)
   Giants, 20-14 (P)
1934—Giants, 17-0 (NY)
   Eagles, 6-0 (P)
1935—Giants, 10-0 (NY)
   Giants, 21-14 (P)
1936—Eagles, 10-7 (P)
   Giants, 21-17 (NY)
1937—Giants, 16-7 (P)
   Giants, 21-0 (NY)
1938—Eagles, 14-10 (P)
   Giants, 17-7 (NY)
1939—Giants, 13-3 (P)
   Giants, 27-10 (NY)
1940—Giants, 20-14 (P)
   Giants, 17-7 (NY)
1941—Giants, 24-0 (P)
   Giants, 16-0 (NY)
1942—Giants, 35-17 (NY)
   Giants, 14-0 (P)
1944—Eagles, 24-17 (NY)
   Tie, 21-21 (P)
1945—Eagles, 38-17 (P)
   Giants, 28-21 (NY)

1946—Eagles, 24-14 (P)
  Giants, 45-17 (NY)
1947—Eagles, 23-0 (P)
  Eagles, 41-24 (NY)
1948—Eagles, 45-0 (P)
  Eagles, 35-14 (NY)
1949—Eagles, 24-3 (NY)
  Eagles, 17-3 (P)
1950—Eagles, 7-3 (NY)
  Giants, 9-7 (P)
1951—Giants, 26-24 (NY)
  Giants, 23-7 (P)
1952—Giants, 31-7 (P)
  Eagles, 14-10 (NY)
1953—Eagles, 30-7 (P)
  Giants, 37-28 (NY)
1954—Giants, 27-14 (NY)
  Eagles, 29-14 (P)
1955—Eagles, 27-17 (P)
  Giants, 31-7 (NY)
1956—Giants, 20-3 (NY)
  Giants, 21-7 (P)
1957—Giants, 24-20 (P)
  Giants, 13-0 (NY)
1958—Eagles, 27-24 (P)
  Giants, 24-10 (NY)
1959—Eagles, 49-21 (NY)
  Giants, 24-7 (NY)
1960—Eagles, 17-10 (NY)
  Eagles, 31-23 (P)
1961—Giants, 38-21 (NY)
  Giants, 28-24 (P)
1962 Giants, 29-13 (P)
  Giants, 19-14 (NY)
1963—Giants, 37-14 (P)
  Giants, 42-14 (NY)
1964—Eagles, 38-7 (P)
  Eagles, 23-17 (NY)
1965—Giants, 16-14 (P)
  Giants, 35-27 (NY)
1966—Eagles, 35-17 (P)
  Eagles, 31-3 (NY)
1967—Giants, 44-7 (NY)
1968—Giants, 34-25 (P)
  Giants, 7-6 (NY)
1969—Eagles, 23-20 (NY)
1970—Giants, 30-23 (NY)
  Eagles, 23-20 (P)
1971—Eagles, 23-7 (P)
  Eagles, 41-28 (NY)
1972—Giants, 27-12 (P)
  Giants, 62-10 (NY)
1973—Tie, 23-23 (NY)
  Eagles, 20-16 (P)
1974—Eagles, 35-7 (P)
  Eagles, 20-7 (New Haven)
1975—Giants, 23-14 (P)
  Eagles, 13-10 (NY)
1976—Eagles, 20-7 (P)
  Eagles, 10-0 (NY)
1977—Eagles, 28-10 (NY)
  Eagles, 17-14 (P)
1978—Eagles, 19-17 (NY)
  Eagles, 20-3 (P)
1979—Eagles, 23-17 (P)
  Eagles, 17-13 (NY)
1980—Eagles, 35-3 (P)
  Eagles, 31-16 (NY)
1981—Eagles, 24-10 (NY)
  Giants, 20-10 (P)
  *Giants, 27-21 (P)

1982—Giants, 23-7 (NY)
  Giants, 26-24 (P)
1983—Eagles, 17-13 (NY)
  Giants, 23-0 (P)
1984—Giants, 28-27 (NY)
  Eagles, 24-10 (P)
1985—Giants, 21-0 (NY)
  Giants, 16-10 (P) OT
1986—Giants, 35-3 (NY)
  Giants, 17-14 (P)
1987—Giants, 20-17 (P)
  Giants, 23-20 (NY) OT
1988—Eagles, 24-13 (P)
  Eagles, 23-17 (NY) OT
1989—Eagles, 21-19 (P)
  Eagles, 24-17 (NY)
1990—Giants, 27-20 (NY)
  Eagles, 31-13 (P)
1991—Eagles, 30-7 (P)
  Eagles, 19-14 (NY)
1992—Eagles, 47-34 (NY)
  Eagles, 20-10 (P)
1993—Giants, 21-10 (NY)
  Giants, 7-3 (P)
1994—Giants, 28-23 (NY)
  Giants, 16-13 (P)
1995—Eagles, 17-14 (NY)
  Eagles, 28-19 (P)
1996—Eagles, 19-10 (NY)
  Eagles, 24-0 (P)
1997—Giants, 31-17 (NY)
  Giants, 31-21 (P)
1998—Giants, 20-0 (NY)
  Giants, 20-10 (P)
1999—Giants, 16-15 (NY)
  Giants, 23-17 (P) OT
2000—Giants, 33-18 (P)
  Giants, 24-7 (NY)
  **Giants, 20-10 (NY)
2001—Eagles, 10-9 (NY)
  Eagles, 24-21 (P)
2002—Eagles, 17-3 (P)
  Giants, 10-7 (NY) OT
2003—Eagles, 14-10 (NY)
  Eagles, 28-10 (P)
2004—Eagles, 31-17 (P)
  Eagles, 27-6 (NY)
2005 Giants, 27-17 (NY)
  Giants, 26-23 (P) OT
2006—Giants, 30-24 (P) OT
  Eagles, 36-22 (NY)
  *Eagles, 23-20 (P)
2007—Giants, 16-3 (NY)
  Giants, 16-13 (P)
2008—Giants, 36-31 (P)
  Eagles, 20-14 (NY)
  **Eagles, 23-11 (NY)
2009—Eagles, 40-17 (P)
  Eagles, 45-38 (NY)
2010—Eagles, 27-17 (P)
  Eagles, 38-31 (NY)
(RS Pts.—Giants 2,909, Eagles 2,817)
(PS Pts.—Giants 78, Eagles 77)
*NFC First-Round Playoff
**NFC Divisional Playoff
N.Y. GIANTS vs. *PITTSBURGH
RS: Giants lead series, 44-28-3
1933—Giants, 23-2 (P)
  Giants, 27-3 (NY)
1934—Giants, 14-12 (P)
  Giants, 17-7 (NY)

1935—Giants, 42-7 (P)
  Giants, 13-0 (NY)
1936—Pirates, 10-7 (P)
1937—Giants, 10-7 (P)
  Giants, 17-0 (NY)
1938—Giants, 27-14 (P)
  Pirates, 13-10 (NY)
1939—Giants, 14-7 (P)
  Giants, 23-7 (NY)
1940—Tie, 10-10 (P)
  Giants, 12-0 (NY)
1941—Giants, 37-10 (P)
  Giants, 28-7 (NY)
1942—Steelers, 13-10 (P)
  Steelers, 17-9 (NY)
1945—Giants, 34-6 (P)
  Steelers, 21-7 (NY)
1946—Giants, 17-14 (P)
  Giants, 7-0 (NY)
1947—Steelers, 38-21 (NY)
  Steelers, 24-7 (P)
1948—Steelers, 34-27 (NY)
  Steelers, 38-28 (P)
1949—Steelers, 28-7 (P)
  Steelers, 21-17 (NY)
1950—Giants, 18-7 (P)
  Steelers, 17-6 (NY)
1951—Tie, 13-13 (P)
  Giants, 14-0 (NY)
1952—Steelers, 63-7 (P)
1953—Steelers, 24-14 (P)
  Steelers, 14-10 (NY)
1954—Giants, 30-6 (P)
  Giants, 24-3 (NY)
1955—Steelers, 30-23 (P)
  Steelers, 19-17 (NY)
1956—Steelers, 38-10 (NY)
  Giants, 17-14 (P)
1957—Giants, 35-0 (NY)
  Steelers, 21-10 (P)
1958—Giants, 17-6 (NY)
  Steelers, 31-10 (P)
1959—Giants, 21-16 (P)
  Steelers, 14-9 (NY)
1960—Giants, 19-17 (P)
  Giants, 27-24 (NY)
1961 Giants, 17-14 (P)
  Giants, 10-21 (NY)
1962—Giants, 31-27 (P)
  Steelers, 20-17 (NY)
1963—Steelers, 31-0 (P)
  Giants, 33-17 (NY)
1964—Steelers, 27-24 (P)
  Steelers, 44-17 (NY)
1965—Giants, 23-13 (P)
  Giants, 35-10 (NY)
1966—Tie, 34-34 (P)
  Steelers, 47-28 (NY)
1967—Giants, 27-24 (P)
  Giants, 28-20 (NY)
1968—Giants, 34-20 (P)
1969—Giants, 10-7 (NY)
  Giants, 21-17 (P)
1971—Steelers, 17-13 (P)
1976—Steelers, 27-0 (NY)
1985—Giants, 28-10 (P)
1991—Giants, 23-20 (P)
1994—Steelers, 10-6 (NY)
2000—Giants, 30-10 (NY)
2004—Steelers, 33-30 (NY)
2008—Giants, 21-14 (P)

(RS Pts.—Giants 1,480, Steelers 1,246)
Steelers known as Pirates prior to 1940
N.Y. GIANTS vs. *ST. LOUIS
RS: Rams lead series, 25-13
PS: Series tied, 1-1
1938—Giants, 28-0 (NY)
1940—Rams, 13-0 (NY)
1941—Giants, 49-14 (NY)
1945—Rams, 21-17 (NY)
1946—Rams, 31-21 (NY)
1947—Rams, 34-10 (LA)
1948—Rams, 52-37 (NY)
1953—Rams, 21-7 (LA)
1954—Rams, 17-16 (NY)
1959—Giants, 23-21 (LA)
1961—Giants, 24-14 (NY)
1966—Rams, 55-14 (LA)
1968—Rams, 24-21 (LA)
1970—Rams, 31-3 (NY)
1973—Rams, 40-6 (LA)
1976—Rams, 24-10 (LA)
1978—Rams, 20-17 (NY)
1979—Giants, 20-14 (LA)
1980—Rams, 28-7 (NY)
1981—Giants, 10-7 (NY)
1983—Rams, 16-6 (NY)
1984—Rams, 33-12 (LA)
      **Giants, 16-13 (LA)
1985—Giants, 24-19 (NY)
1988—Rams, 45-31 (NY)
1989—Rams, 31-10 (LA)
      ***Rams, 19-13 (NY) OT
1990—Giants, 31-7 (LA)
1991—Rams, 19-13 (NY)
1992—Rams, 38-17 (LA)
1993—Giants, 20-10 (NY)
1994—Rams, 17-10 (LA)
1997—Rams, 13-3 (StL)
1999—Rams, 31-10 (StL)
2000—Rams, 38-24 (NY)
2001—Rams, 15-14 (StL)
2002—Rams, 26-21 (StL)
2003—Giants, 23-13 (NY)
2005—Giants, 44-24 (NY)
2008—Giants, 41-13 (StL)
(RS Pts.—Rams 884, Giants 699)
(PS Pts.—Rams 32, Giants 29)
*Franchise in Los Angeles prior to 1995
and in Cleveland prior to 1946*
**NFC First-Round Playoff*
***NFC Divisional Playoff*
N.Y. GIANTS vs. SAN DIEGO
RS: Series tied, 5-5
1971—Giants, 35-17 (NY)
1975—Giants, 35-24 (NY)
1980—Chargers, 44-7 (SD)
1983—Chargers, 41-34 (NY)
1986—Giants, 20-7 (NY)
1989—Giants, 20-13 (SD)
1995—Chargers, 27-17 (NY)
1998—Giants, 34-16 (SD)
2005—Chargers, 45-23 (SD)
2009—Chargers, 21-20 (NY)
(RS Pts.—Chargers 255, Giants 245)
N.Y. GIANTS vs. SAN FRANCISCO
RS: Giants lead series, 14-13
PS: 49ers lead series, 4-3
1952—Giants, 23-14 (NY)
1956—Giants, 38-21 (SF)
1957—49ers, 27-17 (NY)
1960—Giants, 21-19 (SF)

1963—Giants, 48-14 (NY)
1968—49ers, 26-10 (NY)
1972—Giants, 23-17 (SF)
1975—Giants, 26-23 (SF)
1977—Giants, 20-17 (NY)
1978—Giants, 27-10 (NY)
1979—Giants, 32-16 (NY)
1980—49ers, 12-0 (SF)
1981—49ers, 17-10 (SF)
      *49ers, 38-24 (SF)
1984—49ers, 31-10 (NY)
      *49ers, 21-10 (SF)
1985—**Giants, 17-3 (NY)
1986—Giants, 21-17 (SF)
      *Giants, 49-3 (NY)
1987—49ers, 41-21 (NY)
1988—49ers, 20-17 (NY)
1989—49ers, 34-24 (SF)
1990—49ers, 7-3 (SF)
      ***Giants, 15-13 (SF)
1991—Giants, 16-14 (NY)
1992—49ers, 31-14 (NY)
1993—*49ers, 44-3 (SF)
1995—49ers, 20-6 (SF)
1998—49ers, 31-7 (SF)
2002—49ers, 16-13 (NY)
      **49ers, 39-38 (SF)
2005—Giants, 24-6 (SF)
2007—Giants, 33-15 (NY)
2008—Giants, 29-17 (NY)
(RS Pts.—49ers 533, Giants 533)
(PS Pts.—49ers 161, Giants 156)
NFC Divisional Playoff
**NFC First-Round Playoff*
***NFC Championship*
N.Y. GIANTS vs. SEATTLE
RS: Giants lead series, 9-5
1976—Giants, 28-16 (NY)
1980—Giants, 27-21 (S)
1981—Giants, 32-0 (S)
1983—Seahawks, 17-12 (NY)
1986—Seahawks, 17-12 (S)
1989—Giants, 15-3 (NY)
1992—Giants, 23-10 (NY)
1995—Seahawks, 30-28 (S)
2001—Giants, 27-24 (NY)
2002—Giants, 9-6 (NY)
2005—Seahawks, 24-21 (S) OT
2006—Seahawks, 42-30 (S)
2008—Giants, 44-6 (NY)
2010—Giants, 41-7 (S)
(RS Pts.—Giants 349, Seahawks 223)
N.Y. GIANTS vs. TAMPA BAY
RS: Giants lead series, 11-6
PS: Giants lead series, 1-0
1977—Giants, 10-0 (TB)
1978—Giants, 19-13 (TB)
      Giants, 17-14 (NY)
1979—Giants, 17-14 (NY)
      Buccaneers, 31-3 (TB)
1980—Buccaneers, 30-13 (TB)
1984—Giants, 17-14 (NY)
      Buccaneers, 20-17 (TB)
1985—Giants, 22-20 (NY)
1991—Giants, 21-14 (TB)
1993—Giants, 23-7 (NY)
1997—Buccaneers, 20-8 (NY)
1998—Buccaneers, 20-3 (TB)
1999—Giants, 17-13 (TB)
2003—Buccaneers, 19-13 (TB)
2006—Giants, 17-3 (NY)

2007—*Giants, 24-14 (TB)
2009—Giants, 24-0 (TB)
(RS Pts.—Giants 261, Buccaneers 252)
(PS Pts.—Giants 24, Buccaneers 14)
NFC First-Round Playoff
N.Y. GIANTS vs. *TENNESSEE
RS: Series tied, 5-5
1973—Giants, 34-14 (NY)
1982—Giants, 17-14 (NY)
1985—Giants, 35-14 (H)
1991—Giants, 24-20 (NY)
1994—Giants, 13-10 (H)
1997—Oilers, 10-6 (T)
2000—Titans, 28-14 (T)
2002—Titans, 32-29 (NY) OT
2006—Titans, 24-21 (T)
2010—Titans, 29-10 (NY)
(RS Pts.—Giants 203, Titans 195)
*Franchise in Houston prior to 1997;
known as Oilers prior to 1999*
N.Y. GIANTS vs. *WASHINGTON
RS: Giants lead series, 91-61-4
PS: Series tied, 1-1
1932—Braves, 14-6 (B)
      Tie, 0-0 (NY)
1933—Redskins, 21-20 (B)
      Giants, 7-0 (NY)
1934—Giants, 16-13 (B)
      Giants, 3-0 (NY)
1935—Giants, 20-12 (B)
      Giants, 17-6 (NY)
1936—Giants, 7-0 (B)
      Redskins, 14-0 (NY)
1937—Redskins, 13-3 (W)
      Redskins, 49-14 (NY)
1938—Giants, 10-7 (W)
      Giants, 36-0 (NY)
1939—Tie, 0-0 (W)
      Giants, 9-7 (NY)
1940—Redskins, 21-7 (W)
      Giants, 21-7 (NY)
1941—Giants, 17-10 (W)
      Giants, 20-13 (NY)
1942—Giants, 14-7 (W)
      Redskins, 14-7 (NY)
1943—Giants, 14-10 (W)
      Giants, 31-7 (NY)
      **Redskins, 28-0 (NY)
1944—Giants, 16-13 (NY)
      Giants, 31-0 (W)
1945—Redskins, 24-14 (NY)
      Redskins, 17-0 (W)
1946—Redskins, 24-14 (W)
      Giants, 31-0 (NY)
1947—Redskins, 28-20 (W)
      Giants, 35-10 (NY)
1948—Redskins, 41-10 (W)
      Redskins, 28-21 (NY)
1949—Redskins, 45-35 (W)
      Giants, 23-7 (NY)
1950—Giants, 21-17 (W)
      Giants, 24-21 (NY)
1951—Giants, 35-14 (W)
      Giants, 28-14 (NY)
1952—Giants, 14-10 (W)
      Redskins, 27-17 (NY)
1953—Redskins, 13-9 (W)
      Redskins, 24-21 (NY)
1954—Giants, 51-21 (W)
      Giants, 24-7 (NY)
1955—Giants, 35-7 (NY)

Giants, 27-20 (W)
1956—Redskins, 33-7 (W)
Giants, 28-14 (NY)
1957—Giants, 24-20 (W)
Redskins, 31-14 (NY)
1958—Giants, 21-14 (W)
Giants, 30-0 (NY)
1959—Giants, 45-14 (W)
Giants, 24-10 (W)
1960—Tie, 24-24 (NY)
Giants, 17-3 (W)
1961—Giants, 24-21 (W)
Giants, 53-0 (NY)
1962—Giants, 49-34 (NY)
Giants, 42-24 (W)
1963—Giants, 24-14 (W)
Giants, 44-14 (NY)
1964—Giants, 13-10 (NY)
Redskins, 36-21 (W)
1965—Redskins, 23-7 (NY)
Giants, 27-10 (W)
1966—Giants, 13-10 (NY)
Redskins, 72-41 (W)
1967—Redskins, 38-34 (W)
1968—Giants, 48-21 (NY)
Giants, 13-10 (W)
1969—Redskins, 20-14 (W)
1970—Giants, 35-33 (NY)
Giants, 27-24 (W)
1971—Redskins, 30-3 (NY)
Redskins, 23-7 (W)
1972—Redskins, 23-16 (NY)
Redskins, 27-13 (W)
1973—Redskins, 21-3 (New Haven)
Redskins, 27-24 (W)
1974—Redskins, 13-10 (New Haven)
Redskins, 24-3 (W)
1975—Redskins, 49-13 (W)
Redskins, 21-13 (NY)
1976—Redskins, 19-17 (W)
Giants, 12-9 (NY)
1977—Giants, 20-17 (W)
Giants, 17-6 (W)
1978—Giants, 17-6 (W)
Redskins, 16-13 (W) OT
1979—Redskins, 27-0 (W)
Giants, 14-6 (NY)
1980—Redskins, 23-21 (NY)
Redskins, 16-13 (W)
1981—Giants, 17-7 (W)
Redskins, 30-27 (NY) OT
1982—Redskins, 27-17 (NY)
Redskins, 15-14 (W)
1983—Redskins, 33-17 (NY)
Redskins, 31-22 (W)
1984—Redskins, 30-14 (W)
Giants, 37-13 (NY)
1985—Giants, 17-3 (NY)
Redskins, 23-21 (W)
1986—Giants, 27-20 (NY)
Giants, 24-14 (W)
***Giants, 17-0 (NY)
1987—Redskins, 38-12 (NY)
Redskins, 23-19 (W)
1988—Giants, 27-20 (W)
Giants, 24-23 (W)
1989—Giants, 27-24 (W)
Giants, 20-17 (NY)
1990—Giants, 24-20 (W)
Giants, 21-10 (NY)
1991—Redskins, 17-13 (NY)

1992—Giants, 24-7 (W)
Redskins, 28-10 (NY)
1993—Giants, 41-7 (W)
Giants, 20-6 (NY)
1994—Giants, 31-23 (NY)
Giants, 21-19 (W)
1995—Giants, 24-15 (W)
Giants, 20-13 (NY)
1996—Redskins, 31-10 (NY)
Redskins, 31-21 (W)
1997—Tie, 7-7 (W) OT
Giants, 30-10 (NY)
1998—Giants, 31-24 (NY)
Redskins, 21-14 (W)
1999—Redskins, 50-21 (NY)
Redskins, 23-13 (W)
2000—Redskins, 16-6 (NY)
Giants, 9-7 (W)
2001—Giants, 23-9 (NY)
Redskins, 35-21 (W)
2002—Giants, 19-17 (NY)
Giants, 27-21 (W)
2003—Giants, 24-21 (W) OT
Redskins, 20-7 (NY)
2004—Giants, 20-14 (NY)
Redskins, 31-7 (W)
2005—Giants, 36-0 (NY)
Redskins, 35-20 (W)
2006—Giants, 19-3 (NY)
Giants, 34-28 (W)
2007—Giants, 24-17 (W)
Redskins, 22-10 (NY)
2008—Giants, 16-7 (NY)
Giants, 23-7 (W)
2009—Giants, 23-17 (NY)
Giants, 45-12 (W)
2010—Giants, 31-7 (NY)
Giants, 17-14 (W)
(RS Pts.—Giants 3,134, Redskins 2,794)
(PS Pts.—Redskins 28, Giants 17)
*Franchise in Boston prior to 1937 and
known as Braves prior to 1933
**Division Playoff
***NFC Championship

N.Y. JETS vs. ARIZONA
RS: Jets lead series, 5-2;
See Arizona vs. N.Y. Jets
N.Y. JETS vs. ATLANTA
RS: Falcons lead series, 6-4;
See Atlanta vs. N.Y. Jets
N.Y. JETS vs. BALTIMORE
RS: Ravens lead series, 6-1;
See Baltimore vs. N.Y. Jets
N.Y. JETS vs. BUFFALO
RS: Bills lead series, 53-47
PS: Bills lead series, 1-0;
See Buffalo vs. N.Y. Jets
N.Y. JETS vs. CAROLINA
RS: Jets lead series, 3-2;
See Carolina vs. N.Y. Jets
N.Y. JETS vs. CHICAGO
RS: Bears lead series, 7-3;
See Chicago vs. N.Y. Jets
N.Y. JETS vs. CINCINNATI
RS: Jets lead series, 15-7
PS: Jets lead series, 2-0;
See Cincinnati vs. N.Y. Jets
N.Y. JETS vs. CLEVELAND
RS: Browns lead series, 12-8

PS: Browns lead series, 1-0;
See Cleveland vs. N.Y. Jets
N.Y. JETS vs. DALLAS
RS: Cowboys lead series, 7-2;
See Dallas vs. N.Y. Jets
N.Y. JETS vs. DENVER
RS: Broncos lead series, 16-15-1
PS: Broncos lead series, 1-0;
See Denver vs. N.Y. Jets
N.Y. JETS vs. DETROIT
RS: Series tied, 6-6;
See Detroit vs. N.Y. Jets
N.Y. JETS vs. GREEN BAY
RS: Jets lead series, 8-3;
See Green Bay vs. N.Y. Jets
N.Y. JETS vs. HOUSTON
RS: Jets lead series, 5-0;
See Houston vs. N.Y. Jets
N.Y. JETS vs. INDIANAPOLIS
RS: Colts lead series, 40-26
PS: Jets lead series, 3-1;
See Indianapolis vs. N.Y. Jets
N.Y. JETS vs. JACKSONVILLE
RS: Jaguars lead series, 6-2
PS: Jets lead series, 1-0;
See Jacksonville vs. N.Y. Jets
N.Y. JETS vs. KANSAS CITY
RS: Series tied, 16-16-1
PS: Series tied, 1-1;
See Kansas City vs. N.Y. Jets
N.Y. JETS vs. MIAMI
RS: Jets lead series, 47-42-1
PS: Dolphins lead series, 1-0;
See Miami vs. N.Y. Jets
N.Y. JETS vs. MINNESOTA
RS: Jets lead series, 8-1;
See Minnesota vs. N.Y. Jets
N.Y. JETS vs. NEW ENGLAND
RS: Jets lead series, 51-49-1
PS: Patriots lead series, 2-1;
See New England vs. N.Y. Jets
N.Y. JETS vs. NEW ORLEANS
RS: Saints lead series, 6-5;
See New Orleans vs. N.Y. Jets
N.Y. JETS vs. N.Y. GIANTS
RS: Giants lead series, 7-4;
See N.Y. Giants vs. N.Y. Jets
***N.Y. JETS vs. **OAKLAND**
RS: Raiders lead series, 20-15-2
PS: Series tied, 2-2
1960—Raiders, 28-27 (NY)
Titans, 31-28 (O)
1961—Titans, 14-6 (O)
Titans, 23-12 (NY)
1962—Titans, 28-17 (O)
Titans, 31-21 (NY)
1963—Jets, 10-7 (NY)
Raiders, 49-26 (O)
1964—Jets, 35-13 (NY)
Raiders, 35-26 (O)
1965—Tie, 24-24 (NY)
Raiders, 24-14 (O)
1966—Raiders, 24-21 (NY)
Tie, 28-28 (O)
1967—Jets, 27-14 (NY)
Raiders, 38-29 (O)
1968—Raiders, 43-32 (O)
***Jets, 27-23 (NY)
1969—Raiders, 27-14 (NY)
1970—Raiders, 14-13 (NY)
1972—Raiders, 24-16 (O)

1977—Raiders, 28-27 (NY)
1979—Jets, 28-19 (NY)
1982—****Jets, 17-14 (LA)
1985—Raiders, 31-0 (LA)
1989—Raiders, 14-7 (NY)
1993—Raiders, 24-20 (LA)
1995—Raiders, 47-10 (NY)
1996—Raiders, 34-13 (NY)
1997—Jets 23-22 (NY)
1999—Raiders, 24-23 (O)
2000—Raiders, 31-7 (O)
2001—Jets, 24-22 (O)
　　　*****Raiders, 38-24 (O)
2002—Raiders, 26-20 (O)
　　　****Raiders, 30-10 (O)
2003—Jets, 27-24 (O) OT
2005—Jets, 26-10 (NY)
2006—Jets, 23-3 (NY)
2008—Raiders, 16-13 (O) OT
2009—Jets, 38-0 (O)
(RS Pts.—Raiders 851, Jets 798)
(PS Pts.—Raiders 105, Jets 78)
*Jets known as Titans prior to 1963
**Franchise in Los Angeles from
1982-1994
***AFL Championship
****AFC Second-Round Playoff
*****AFC First-Round Playoff
N.Y. JETS vs. PHILADELPHIA
RS: Eagles lead series, 8-0
1973—Eagles, 24-23 (P)
1977—Eagles, 27-0 (P)
1978—Eagles, 17-9 (P)
1987—Eagles, 38-27 (NY)
1993—Eagles, 35-30 (NY)
1996—Eagles, 21-20 (NY)
2003—Eagles, 24-17 (P)
2007—Eagles, 16-9 (NY)
(RS Pts.—Eagles 202, Jets 135)
N.Y. JETS vs. PITTSBURGH
RS: Steelers lead series, 15-4
PS: Steelers lead series, 2-0
1970—Steelers, 21-17 (P)
1973—Steelers, 26-14 (P)
1975—Steelers, 20-7 (NY)
1977—Steelers, 23-20 (NY)
1978—Steelers, 28-17 (NY)
1981—Steelers, 38-10 (P)
1983—Steelers, 34-7 (NY)
1984—Steelers, 23-17 (NY)
1986—Steelers, 45-24 (NY)
1988—Jets, 24-20 (NY)
1989—Steelers, 13-0 (NY)
1990—Steelers, 24-7 (NY)
1992—Steelers, 27-10 (P)
2000—Steelers, 20-3 (NY)
2001—Steelers, 18-7 (P)
2003—Jets, 6-0 (NY)
2004—Steelers, 17-6 (P)
　　　*Steelers, 20-17 (P) OT
2007—Jets, 19-16 (NY) OT
2010—Jets, 22-17 (P)
　　　**Steelers, 24-19 (P)
(RS Pts.—Steelers 430, Jets 237)
(PS Pts.—Steelers 44, Jets 36)
*AFC Divisional Playoff
**AFC Championship
N.Y. JETS vs. *ST. LOUIS
RS: Rams lead series, 9-3
1970—Jets, 31-20 (LA)
1974—Rams, 20-13 (NY)

1980—Rams, 38-13 (LA)
1983—Jets, 27-24 (NY) OT
1986—Rams, 17-3 (NY)
1989—Rams, 38-14 (LA)
1992—Rams, 18-10 (LA)
1995—Rams, 23-20 (NY)
1998—Rams, 30-10 (StL)
2001—Rams, 34-14 (NY)
2004—Rams, 32-29 (StL) OT
2008—Jets, 47-3 (NY)
(RS Pts.—Rams 297, Jets 231)
*Franchise in Los Angeles prior to 1995
N.Y. JETS vs. **SAN DIEGO
RS: Chargers lead series, 19-11-1
PS: Jets lead series, 2-0
1960—Chargers, 21-7 (NY)
　　　Chargers, 50-43 (LA)
1961—Chargers, 25-10 (NY)
　　　Chargers, 48-13 (SD)
1962—Chargers, 40-14 (SD)
　　　Titans, 23-3 (NY)
1963—Chargers, 24-20 (SD)
　　　Chargers, 53-7 (NY)
1964—Tie, 17-17 (NY)
　　　Chargers, 38-3 (SD)
1965—Chargers, 34-9 (NY)
　　　Chargers, 38-7 (SD)
1966—Jets, 17-16 (NY)
　　　Chargers, 42-27 (SD)
1967—Jets, 42-31 (NY)
1968—Jets, 23-20 (NY)
　　　Jets, 37-15 (SD)
1969—Chargers, 34-27 (SD)
1971—Chargers, 49-21 (SD)
1974—Jets, 27-14 (NY)
1975—Chargers, 24-16 (SD)
1983—Jets, 41-29 (SD)
1989—Jets, 20-17 (SD)
1990—Chargers, 39-3 (NY)
　　　Chargers, 38-17 (SD)
1991—Jets, 24-3 (NY)
1994—Chargers, 21-6 (NY)
2002—Jets, 44-13 (SD)
2004—Jets, 34-28 (SD)
　　　***Jets, 20-17 (SD) OT
2005—Chargers, 31-26 (NY)
2008—Chargers, 48-29 (SD)
2009—****Jets, 17-14 (SD)
(RS Pts.—Chargers 903, Jets 654)
(PS Pts.—Jets 37, Chargers 31)
*Jets known as Titans prior to 1963
**Franchise in Los Angeles prior to 1961
***AFC First-Round Playoff
****AFC Divisional Playoff
N.Y. JETS vs. SAN FRANCISCO
RS: 49ers lead series, 9-2
1971—49ers, 24-21 (NY)
1976—49ers, 17-6 (SF)
1980—49ers, 37-27 (NY)
1983—Jets, 27-13 (SF)
1986—49ers, 24-10 (SF)
1989—49ers, 23-10 (NY)
1992—49ers, 31-14 (NY)
1998—49ers, 36-30 (SF) OT
2001—49ers, 19-17 (NY)
2004—Jets, 22-14 (NY)
2008—49ers, 24-14 (SF)
(RS Pts.—49ers 262, Jets 198)
N.Y. JETS vs. SEATTLE
RS: Seahawks lead series, 9-8
1977—Seahawks, 17-0 (NY)

1978—Seahawks, 24-17 (NY)
1979—Seahawks, 30-7 (S)
1980—Seahawks, 27-17 (NY)
1981—Seahawks, 19-3 (NY)
　　　Seahawks, 27-23 (S)
1983—Seahawks, 17-10 (NY)
1985—Jets, 17-14 (NY)
1986—Jets, 38-7 (S)
1987—Jets, 30-14 (NY)
1991—Seahawks, 20-13 (S)
1995—Jets, 16-10 (S)
1997—Jets, 41-3 (S)
1998—Jets, 32-31 (NY)
1999—Jets, 19-9 (NY)
2004—Jets, 37-14 (NY)
2008—Seahawks, 13-3 (S)
(RS Pts.—Jets 323, Seahawks 296)
N.Y. JETS vs. TAMPA BAY
RS: Jets lead series, 9-1
1976—Jets, 34-0 (NY)
1982—Jets, 32-17 (NY)
1984—Buccaneers, 41-21 (TB)
1985—Jets, 62-28 (NY)
1990—Jets, 16-14 (TB)
1991—Jets, 16-13 (NY)
1997—Jets, 31-0 (NY)
2000—Jets, 21-17 (TB)
2005—Jets, 14-12 (NY)
2009—Jets, 26-3 (TB)
(RS Pts.—Jets 273, Buccaneers 145)
N.Y. JETS vs. **TENNESSEE
RS: Titans lead series, 21-17-1
PS: Titans lead series, 1-0
1960—Oilers, 27-21 (H)
　　　Oilers, 42-28 (NY)
1961—Oilers, 49-13 (H)
　　　Oilers, 48-21 (NY)
1962—Oilers, 56-17 (H)
　　　Oilers, 44-10 (NY)
1963—Jets, 24-17 (NY)
　　　Oilers, 31-27 (H)
1964—Jets, 24-21 (NY)
　　　Oilers, 33-17 (H)
1965—Oilers, 27-21 (H)
　　　Jets, 41-14 (NY)
1966—Jets, 52-13 (NY)
　　　Oilers, 24-0 (H)
1967—Tie, 28-28 (NY)
1968—Jets, 20-14 (H)
　　　Jets, 26-7 (NY)
1969—Jets, 26-17 (NY)
　　　Jets, 34-26 (H)
1972—Oilers, 26-20 (H)
1974—Oilers, 27-22 (NY)
1977—Oilers, 20-0 (H)
1979—Oilers, 27-24 (H) OT
1980—Jets, 31-28 (NY) OT
1981—Oilers, 33-17 (NY)
1984—Oilers, 31-20 (NY)
1988—Jets, 45-3 (NY)
1990—Jets, 17-12 (H)
1991—Oilers, 23-20 (NY)
　　　***Oilers, 17-10 (H)
1993—Oilers, 24-0 (H)
1994—Oilers, 24-10 (H)
1995—Oilers, 23-6 (H)
1996—Oilers, 35-10 (NY)
1998—Jets, 24-3 (T)
2003—Jets, 24-17 (NY)
2006—Jets, 23-16 (T)
2007—Titans, 10-6 (T)

2008—Jets, 34-13 (T)
2009—Jets, 24-17 (NY)
(RS Pts.—Titans 934, Jets 843)
(PS Pts.—Titans 17, Jets 10)
*Jets known as Titans prior to 1963
**Franchise in Houston prior to 1997;
known as Oilers prior to 1999
***AFC First-Round Playoff

N.Y. JETS vs. WASHINGTON
RS: Redskins lead series, 8-1
1972—Redskins, 35-17 (NY)
1976—Redskins, 37-16 (NY)
1978—Redskins, 23-3 (W)
1987—Redskins, 17-16 (W)
1993—Jets, 3-0 (W)
1996—Redskins, 31-16 (W)
1999—Redskins, 27-20 (NY)
2003—Redskins, 16-13 (W)
2007—Redskins 23-20 (NY) OT
(RS Pts.—Redskins 209, Jets 124)

OAKLAND vs. ARIZONA
RS: Raiders lead series, 5-3;
See Arizona vs. Oakland
OAKLAND vs. ATLANTA
RS: Raiders lead series, 7-5;
See Atlanta vs. Oakland
OAKLAND vs. BALTIMORE
RS: Ravens lead series, 5-1
PS: Ravens lead series, 1-0;
See Baltimore vs. Oakland
OAKLAND vs. BUFFALO
RS: Raiders lead series, 19-16
PS: Bills lead series, 2-0;
See Buffalo vs. Oakland
OAKLAND vs. CAROLINA
RS: Series tied, 2-2;
See Carolina vs. Oakland
OAKLAND vs. CHICAGO
RS: Series tied, 6-6;
See Chicago vs. Oakland
OAKLAND vs. CINCINNATI
RS: Raiders lead series, 18-8
PS: Raiders lead series, 2-0;
See Cincinnati vs. Oakland
OAKLAND vs. CLEVELAND
RS: Raiders lead series, 10-8
PS: Raiders lead series, 2-0;
See Cleveland vs. Oakland
OAKLAND vs. DALLAS
RS: Raiders lead series, 6-4;
See Dallas vs. Oakland
OAKLAND vs. DENVER
RS: Raiders lead series, 58-41-2
PS: Series tied, 1-1;
See Denver vs. Oakland
OAKLAND vs. DETROIT
RS: Raiders lead series, 6-4;
See Detroit vs. Oakland
OAKLAND vs. GREEN BAY
RS: Series tied, 5-5
PS: Packers lead series, 1-0;
See Green Bay vs. Oakland
OAKLAND vs. HOUSTON
RS: Texans lead series, 5-1;
See Houston vs. Oakland
OAKLAND vs. INDIANAPOLIS
RS: Raiders lead series, 7-5
PS: Series tied, 1-1;
See Indianapolis vs. Oakland

OAKLAND vs. JACKSONVILLE
RS: Jaguars lead series, 4-1;
See Jacksonville vs. Oakland
OAKLAND vs. KANSAS CITY
RS: Chiefs lead series, 52-47-2
PS: Chiefs lead series, 2-1;
See Kansas City vs. Oakland
OAKLAND vs. MIAMI
RS: Raiders lead series, 16-13-1
PS: Raiders lead series, 3-1;
See Miami vs. Oakland
OAKLAND vs. MINNESOTA
RS: Raiders lead series, 8-4
PS: Raiders lead series, 1-0;
See Minnesota vs. Oakland
OAKLAND vs. NEW ENGLAND
RS: Series tied, 14-14-1
PS: Patriots lead series, 2-1;
See New England vs. Oakland
OAKLAND vs. NEW ORLEANS
RS: Series tied, 5-5-1;
See New Orleans vs. Oakland
OAKLAND vs. N.Y. GIANTS
RS: Raiders lead series, 7-4;
See N.Y. Giants vs. Oakland
OAKLAND vs. N.Y. JETS
RS: Raiders lead series, 20-15-2
PS: Series tied, 2-2;
See N.Y. Jets vs. Oakland
*OAKLAND vs. PHILADELPHIA
RS: Series tied, 5-5
PS: Raiders lead series, 1-0
1971—Raiders, 34-10 (O)
1976—Raiders, 26-7 (P)
1980—Eagles, 10-7 (P)
        **Raiders, 27-10 (New Orleans)
1986—Eagles, 33-27 (LA) OT
1989—Eagles, 10-7 (P)
1992—Eagles, 31-10 (P)
1995—Raiders, 48-17 (O)
2001—Raiders, 20-10 (P)
2005—Eagles, 23-20 (P)
2009—Raiders, 13-9 (O)
(RS Pts.—Raiders 212, Eagles 160)
(PS Pts.—Raiders 27, Eagles 10)
*Franchise in Los Angeles from 1982-1994
**Super Bowl XV
*OAKLAND vs. PITTSBURGH
RS: Raiders lead series, 10-9
PS: Series tied, 3-3
1970—Raiders, 31-14 (O)
1972—Steelers, 34-28 (P)
        **Steelers, 13-7 (P)
1973—Steelers, 17-9 (O)
        **Raiders, 33-14 (O)
1974—Raiders, 17-0 (P)
        ***Steelers, 24-13 (O)
1975—***Steelers, 16-10 (P)
1976—Raiders, 31-28 (O)
        ***Raiders, 24-7 (O)
1977—Raiders, 16-7 (P)
1980—Raiders, 45-34 (O)
1981—Raiders, 30-27 (O)
1983—**Raiders, 38-10 (LA)
1984—Steelers, 13-7 (LA)
1990—Raiders, 20-3 (LA)
1994—Steelers, 21-3 (LA)
1995—Steelers, 29-10 (O)
2000—Steelers, 21-20 (P)
2002—Raiders, 30-17 (P)
2003—Steelers, 27-7 (P)

2004—Steelers, 24-21 (P)
2006—Raiders, 20-13 (O)
2009—Raiders, 27-24 (P)
2010—Steelers, 35-3 (P)
(RS Pts.—Steelers 388, Raiders 375)
(PS Pts.—Raiders 125, Steelers 84)
*Franchise in Los Angeles from 1982-1994
**AFC Divisional Playoff
***AFC Championship
*OAKLAND vs. **ST. LOUIS
RS: Raiders lead series, 8-4
1972—Raiders, 45-17 (O)
1977—Rams, 20-14 (LA)
1979—Raiders, 24-17 (LA)
1982—Raiders, 37-31 (LA Raiders)
1985—Raiders, 16-6 (LA Rams)
1988—Rams, 22-17 (LA Raiders)
1991—Raiders, 20-17 (LA Raiders)
1994—Raiders, 20-17 (LA Rams)
1997—Raiders, 35-17 (O)
2002—Rams, 28-13 (StL)
2006—Rams, 20-0 (O)
2010—Raiders, 16-14 (O)
(RS Pts.—Raiders 257, Rams 226)
*Franchise in Los Angeles from 1982-1994
**Franchise in Los Angeles prior to 1995
*OAKLAND vs. **SAN DIEGO
RS: Raiders lead series, 56-44-2
PS: Raiders lead series, 1-0
1960—Chargers, 52-28 (LA)
        Chargers, 41-17 (O)
1961—Chargers, 44-0 (SD)
        Chargers, 41-10 (O)
1962—Chargers, 42-33 (O)
        Chargers, 31-21 (SD)
1963—Raiders, 34-33 (SD)
        Raiders, 41-27 (O)
1964—Chargers, 31-17 (SD)
        Raiders, 21-20 (O)
1965—Chargers, 17-6 (O)
        Chargers, 24-14 (SD)
1966—Chargers, 29-20 (O)
        Raiders, 41-19 (SD)
1967—Raiders, 51-10 (O)
        Raiders, 41-21 (SD)
1968—Chargers, 23-14 (O)
        Raiders, 34-27 (SD)
1969—Raiders, 24-12 (SD)
        Raiders, 21-16 (O)
1970—Tie, 27-27 (SD)
        Raiders, 20-17 (O)
1971—Raiders, 34-0 (SD)
        Raiders, 34-33 (O)
1972—Tie, 17-17 (O)
        Raiders, 21-19 (SD)
1973—Raiders, 27-17 (SD)
        Raiders, 31-3 (O)
1974—Raiders, 14-10 (SD)
        Raiders, 17-10 (O)
1975—Raiders, 6-0 (SD)
        Raiders, 25-0 (O)
1976—Raiders, 27-17 (SD)
        Raiders, 24-0 (O)
1977—Raiders, 24-0 (O)
        Chargers, 12-7 (SD)
1978—Raiders, 21-20 (SD)
        Chargers, 27-23 (O)
1979—Chargers, 30-10 (SD)
        Raiders, 45-22 (O)
1980—Chargers, 30-24 (SD) OT
        Raiders, 38-24 (O)

***Raiders, 34-27 (SD)
1981—Chargers, 55-21 (O)
Chargers, 23-10 (SD)
1982—Raiders, 28-24 (LA)
Raiders, 41-34 (SD)
1983—Raiders, 42-10 (SD)
Raiders, 30-14 (LA)
1984—Raiders, 33-30 (LA)
Raiders, 44-37 (SD)
1985—Raiders, 34-21 (LA)
Chargers, 40-34 (SD) OT
1986—Raiders, 17-13 (LA)
Raiders, 37-31 (SD) OT
1987—Chargers, 23-17 (LA)
Chargers, 16-14 (SD)
1988—Raiders, 24-13 (LA)
Raiders, 13-3 (SD)
1989—Raiders, 40-14 (LA)
Chargers, 14-12 (SD)
1990—Raiders, 24-9 (SD)
Raiders, 17-12 (LA)
1991—Chargers, 21-13 (LA)
Raiders, 9-7 (SD)
1992—Chargers, 27-3 (SD)
Chargers, 36-14 (LA)
1993—Chargers, 30-23 (LA)
Raiders, 12-7 (SD)
1994—Chargers, 26-24 (LA)
Raiders, 24-17 (SD)
1995—Raiders, 17-7 (O)
Chargers, 12-6 (SD)
1996—Chargers, 40-34 (O)
Raiders, 23-14 (SD)
1997—Chargers, 25-10 (O)
Raiders, 38-13 (SD)
1998—Raiders, 7-6 (O)
Raiders, 17-10 (SD)
1999—Raiders, 28-9 (O)
Chargers, 23-20 (SD)
2000—Raiders, 9-6 (O)
Raiders, 15-13 (SD)
2001—Raiders, 34-24 (O)
Raiders, 13-6 (SD)
2002—Chargers, 27-21 (O) OT
Raiders, 27-7 (SD)
2003—Raiders, 34-31 (O) OT
Chargers, 21-14 (SD)
2004—Chargers, 42-14 (SD)
Chargers, 23-17 (O)
2005—Chargers, 27-14 (O)
Chargers, 34-10 (SD)
2006—Chargers, 27-0 (O)
Chargers, 21-14 (SD)
2007—Chargers, 28-14 ((SD)
Chargers, 30-17 (O)
2008—Chargers, 28-18 (O)
Chargers, 34-7 (SD)
2009—Chargers, 24-20 (O)
Chargers, 24-16 (SD)
2010—Raiders, 35-27 (O)
Raiders, 28-13 (SD)
(RS Pts.—Raiders 2,249, Chargers 2,178)
(PS Pts.—Raiders 34, Chargers 27)
*Franchise in Los Angeles from 1982-1994
**Franchise in Los Angeles prior to 1961
***AFC Championship
OAKLAND vs. SAN FRANCISCO
RS: Series tied, 6-6
1970—49ers, 38-7 (O)
1974—Raiders, 35-24 (SF)
1979—Raiders, 23-10 (O)

1982—Raiders, 23-17 (SF)
1985—49ers, 34-10 (LA)
1988—Raiders, 9-3 (SF)
1991—Raiders, 12-6 (LA)
1994—49ers, 44-14 (SF)
2000—Raiders, 34-28 (SF) OT
2002—49ers, 23-20 (O) OT
2006—49ers, 34-20 (SF)
2010—49ers, 17-9 (SF)
(RS Pts.—49ers 278, Raiders 216)
*Franchise in Los Angeles from 1982-1994
OAKLAND vs. SEATTLE
RS: Raiders lead series, 28-23
PS: Series tied, 1-1
1977—Raiders, 44-7 (O)
1978—Seahawks, 27-7 (S)
Seahawks, 17-16 (O)
1979—Seahawks, 27-10 (S)
Seahawks, 29-24 (O)
1980—Raiders, 33-14 (O)
Raiders, 19-17 (S)
1981—Raiders, 20-10 (O)
Raiders, 32-31 (S)
1982—Raiders, 28-23 (LA)
1983—Seahawks, 38-36 (S)
Seahawks, 34-21 (LA)
**Raiders, 30-14 (LA)
1984—Raiders, 28-14 (LA)
Seahawks, 17-14 (S)
***Seahawks, 13-7 (S)
1985—Seahawks, 33-3 (S)
Raiders, 13-3 (LA)
1986—Raiders, 14-10 (LA)
Seahawks, 37-0 (S)
1987—Seahawks, 35-13 (LA)
Raiders, 37-14 (S)
1988—Seahawks, 35-27 (S)
Seahawks, 43-37 (LA)
1989—Seahawks, 24-20 (LA)
Seahawks, 23-17 (S)
1990—Raiders, 17-13 (S)
Raiders, 24-17 (LA)
1991—Raiders, 23-20 (S) OT
Raiders, 31-7 (LA)
1992—Raiders, 19-0 (S)
Raiders, 20-3 (LA)
1993—Raiders, 17-13 (S)
Raiders, 27-23 (LA)
1994—Seahawks, 38-9 (LA)
Raiders, 17-16 (S)
1995—Raiders, 34-14 (O)
Seahawks, 44-10 (S)
1996—Raiders, 27-21 (S)
Seahawks, 28-21 (O)
1997—Seahawks, 45-34 (O)
Seahawks, 22-21 (O)
1998—Raiders, 31-18 (S)
Raiders, 20-17 (O)
1999—Seahawks, 22-21 (S)
Raiders, 30-21 (O)
2000—Raiders, 31-3 (O)
Seahawks, 27-24 (S)
2001—Raiders, 38-14 (O)
Seahawks, 34-27 (S)
2002—Raiders, 31-17 (O)
2006—Seahawks, 16-0 (S)
2010—Raiders, 33-3 (O)
(RS Pts.—Raiders 1,150, Seahawks 1,078)
(PS Pts.—Raiders 37, Seahawks 27)
*Franchise in Los Angeles from 1982-1994
**AFC Championship

***AFC First-Round Playoff
OAKLAND vs. TAMPA BAY
RS: Raiders lead series, 6-1
PS: Buccaneers lead series, 1-0
1976—Raiders, 49-16 (O)
1981—Raiders, 18-16 (O)
1993—Raiders, 27-20 (LA)
1996—Buccaneers, 20-17 (TB) OT
1999—Raiders, 45-0 (O)
2002—**Buccaneers, 48-21 (San Diego)
2004—Raiders, 30-20 (O)
2008—Raiders, 31-24 (TB)
(RS Pts.—Raiders 217, Buccaneers 116)
(PS Pts.—Buccaneers 48, Raiders 21)
*Franchise in Los Angeles from 1982-1994
**Super Bowl XXXVII
OAKLAND vs. **TENNESSEE
RS: Raiders lead series, 23-19
PS: Raiders lead series, 4-0
1960—Oilers, 37-22 (O)
Raiders, 14-13 (H)
1961—Oilers, 55-0 (H)
Oilers, 47-16 (O)
1962—Oilers, 28-20 (O)
Oilers, 32-17 (H)
1963—Raiders, 24-13 (H)
Raiders, 52-49 (O)
1964—Oilers, 42-28 (O)
Raiders, 20-10 (H)
1965—Raiders, 21-17 (O)
Raiders, 33-21 (H)
1966—Oilers, 31-0 (H)
Raiders, 38-23 (O)
1967—Raiders, 19-7 (H)
***Raiders, 40-7 (O)
1968—Raiders, 24-15 (H)
1969—Raiders, 21-17 (O)
****Raiders, 56-7 (O)
1971—Raiders, 41-21 (O)
1972—Raiders, 34-0 (H)
1973—Raiders, 17-6 (H)
1975—Oilers, 27-26 (O)
1976—Raiders, 14-13 (H)
1977—Raiders, 34-29 (H)
1978—Raiders, 21-17 (O)
1979—Oilers, 31-17 (H)
1980—*****Raiders, 27-7 (O)
1981—Oilers, 17-16 (H)
1983—Raiders, 20-6 (LA)
1984—Raiders, 24-14 (H)
1986—Raiders, 28-17 (H)
1988—Oilers, 38-35 (H)
1989—Oilers, 23-7 (H)
1991—Oilers, 47-17 (H)
1994—Raiders, 17-14 (LA)
1997—Oilers, 24-21 (T) OT
1999—Titans, 21-14 (T)
2001—Titans, 13-10 (O)
2002—Raiders, 52-25 (O)
******Raiders, 41-24 (O)
2003—Titans, 25-20 (T)
2004—Raiders, 40-35 (O)
2005—Raiders, 34-25 (T)
2007—Titans, 13-9 (T)
2010—Titans, 38-13 (T)
(RS Pts.—Titans 996, Raiders 950)
(PS Pts.—Raiders 164, Titans 45)
*Franchise in Los Angeles from 1982-1994
**Franchise in Houston prior to 1997;
known as Oilers prior to 1999
***AFL Championship

*****Inter-Divisional Playoff*
*****AFC First-Round Playoff*
******AFC Championship*
*OAKLAND vs. WASHINGTON
RS: Raiders lead series, 7-4
PS: Raiders lead series, 1-0
1970—Raiders, 34-20 (O)
1975—Raiders, 26-23 (W) OT
1980—Raiders, 24-21 (O)
1983—Redskins, 37-35 (W)
　　　**Raiders, 38-9 (Tampa)
1986—Redskins, 10-6 (W)
1989—Raiders, 37-24 (LA)
1992—Raiders, 21-20 (W)
1995—Raiders, 20-8 (W)
1998—Redskins, 29-19 (O)
2005—Raiders, 16-13 (W)
2009—Redskins, 34-13 (O)
(RS Pts.—Raiders 251, Redskins 239)
(PS Pts.—Raiders 38, Redskins 9)
*Franchise in Los Angeles from
1982-1994
**Super Bowl XVIII

PHILADELPHIA vs. ARIZONA
RS: Series tied, 53-53-5
PS: Cardinals lead series, 2-1;
See Arizona vs. Philadelphia
PHILADELPHIA vs. ATLANTA
RS: Eagles lead series, 15-10-1
PS: Eagles lead series, 2-1;
See Atlanta vs. Philadelphia
PHILADELPHIA vs. BALTIMORE
RS: Series tied, 1-1-1;
See Baltimore vs. Philadelphia
PHILADELPHIA vs. BUFFALO
RS: Eagles lead series, 6-5;
See Buffalo vs. Philadelphia
PHILADELPHIA vs. CAROLINA
RS: Eagles lead series, 5-1
PS: Panthers lead series, 1-0;
See Carolina vs. Philadelphia
PHILADELPHIA vs. CHICAGO
RS: Bears lead series, 27-9-1
PS: Eagles lead series, 2-1;
See Chicago vs. Philadelphia
PHILADELPHIA vs. CINCINNATI
RS: Bengals lead series, 7-3-1;
See Cincinnati vs. Philadelphia
PHILADELPHIA vs. CLEVELAND
RS: Browns lead series, 31-15-1;
See Cleveland vs. Philadelphia
PHILADELPHIA vs. DALLAS
RS: Cowboys lead series, 56-44
PS: Cowboys lead series, 3-1;
See Dallas vs. Philadelphia
PHILADELPHIA vs. DENVER
RS: Eagles lead series, 7-4;
See Denver vs. Philadelphia
PHILADELPHIA vs. DETROIT
RS: Eagles lead series, 14-12-2
PS: Eagles lead series, 1-0;
See Detroit vs. Philadelphia
PHILADELPHIA vs. GREEN BAY
RS: Packers lead series, 24-13
PS: Eagles lead series, 2-1;
See Green Bay vs. Philadelphia
PHILADELPHIA vs. HOUSTON
RS: Eagles lead series, 3-0;
See Houston vs. Philadelphia

PHILADELPHIA vs. INDIANAPOLIS
RS: Colts lead series, 10-7;
See Indianapolis vs. Philadelphia
PHILADELPHIA vs. JACKSONVILLE
RS: Jaguars lead series, 3-1;
See Jacksonville vs. Philadelphia
PHILADELPHIA vs. KANSAS CITY
RS: Eagles lead series, 4-2;
See Kansas City vs. Philadelphia
PHILADELPHIA vs. MIAMI
RS: Dolphins lead series, 7-5;
See Miami vs. Philadelphia
PHILADELPHIA vs. MINNESOTA
RS: Vikings lead series, 12-9
PS: Eagles lead series, 3-0;
See Minnesota vs. Philadelphia
PHILADELPHIA vs. NEW ENGLAND
RS: Eagles lead series, 6-4
PS: Patriots lead series, 1-0;
See New England vs. Philadelphia
PHILADELPHIA vs. NEW ORLEANS
RS: Eagles lead series, 15-10
PS; Series tied, 1-1;
See New Orleans vs. Philadelphia
PHILADELPHIA vs. N.Y. GIANTS
RS: Giants lead series, 79-71-2
PS: Series tied, 2-2;
See N.Y. Giants vs. Philadelphia
PHILADELPHIA vs. N.Y. JETS
RS: Eagles lead series, 8-0;
See N.Y. Jets vs. Philadelphia
PHILADELPHIA vs. OAKLAND
RS: Series tied, 5-5
PS: Raiders lead series, 1-0;
See Oakland vs. Philadelphia
PHILADELPHIA vs. *PITTSBURGH
RS: Eagles lead series, 46-27-3
PS: Eagles lead series, 1-0
1933—Eagles, 25-6 (Phila)
1934—Eagles, 17-0 (Pitt)
　　　Pirates, 9-7 (Phila)
1935—Pirates, 17-7 (Phila)
　　　Eagles, 17-6 (Pitt)
1936—Pirates, 17-0 (Pitt)
　　　Pirates, 6-0 (Johnstown, Pa.)
1937—Pirates, 27-14 (Pitt)
　　　Pirates, 16-7 (Pitt)
1938—Eagles, 27-7 (Buffalo)
　　　Eagles, 14-7 (Charleston, W. Va.)
1939—Eagles, 17-14 (Phila)
　　　Pirates, 24-12 (Pitt)
1940—Steelers, 7-3 (Pitt)
　　　Eagles, 7-0 (Phila)
1941—Eagles, 10-7 (Pitt)
　　　Tie, 7-7 (Phila)
1942—Eagles, 24-14 (Pitt)
　　　Steelers, 14-0 (Phila)
1945—Eagles, 45-3 (Pitt)
　　　Eagles, 30-6 (Phila)
1946—Steelers, 10-7 (Pitt)
　　　Eagles, 10-7 (Phila)
1947—Steelers, 35-24 (Pitt)
　　　Eagles, 21-0 (Phila)
　　　**Eagles, 21-0 (Pitt)
1948—Eagles, 34-7 (Pitt)
　　　Eagles, 17-0 (Phila)
1949—Eagles, 38-7 (Pitt)
　　　Eagles, 34-17 (Phila)
1950—Eagles, 17-10 (Phila)
　　　Steelers, 9-7 (Phila)
1951—Eagles, 34-13 (Pitt)

　　　Steelers, 17-13 (Phila)
1952—Eagles, 31-25 (Pitt)
　　　Eagles, 26-21 (Phila)
1953—Eagles, 23-17 (Phila)
　　　Eagles, 35-7 (Pitt)
1954—Eagles, 24-22 (Phila)
　　　Steelers, 17-7 (Pitt)
1955—Steelers, 13-7 (Pitt)
　　　Eagles, 24-0 (Phila)
1956—Eagles, 35-21 (Phila)
　　　Eagles, 14-7 (Phila)
1957—Steelers, 6-0 (Pitt)
　　　Eagles, 7-6 (Phila)
1958—Steelers, 24-3 (Pitt)
　　　Steelers, 31-24 (Phila)
1959—Eagles, 28-24 (Phila)
　　　Steelers, 31-0 (Pitt)
1960—Eagles, 34-7 (Phila)
　　　Steelers, 27-21 (Pitt)
1961—Eagles, 21-16 (Phila)
　　　Eagles, 35-24 (Pitt)
1962—Steelers, 13-7 (Pitt)
　　　Steelers, 26-17 (Phila)
1963—Tie, 21-21 (Phila)
　　　Tie, 20-20 (Pitt)
1964—Eagles, 21-7 (Phila)
　　　Eagles, 34-10 (Pitt)
1965—Steelers, 20-14 (Phila)
　　　Eagles, 47-13 (Pitt)
1966—Eagles, 31-14 (Pitt)
　　　Eagles, 27-23 (Phila)
1967—Eagles, 34-24 (Phila)
1968　Steelers, 6-3 (Pitt)
1969—Eagles, 41-27 (Phila)
1970—Eagles, 30-20 (Phila)
1974—Steelers, 27-0 (Pitt)
1979—Eagles, 17-14 (Phila)
1988—Eagles, 27-26 (Pitt)
1991—Eagles, 23-14 (Phila)
1994—Steelers, 14-3 (Pitt)
1997—Eagles, 23-20 (Phila)
2000—Eagles, 26-23 (Pitt) OT
2004—Steelers, 27-3 (Pitt)
2008—Eagles, 15-6 (Phila)
(RS Pts.—Eagles 1,429, Steelers 1,097)
(PS Pts.—Eagles 21, Steelers 0)
*Steelers known as Pirates prior to 1940
**Division Playoff
PHILADELPHIA vs. *ST. LOUIS
RS: Series tied, 17-17-1
PS: Rams lead series, 2-1
1937—Rams, 21-3 (P)
1939—Rams, 35-13 (Colorado Springs)
1940—Rams, 21-13 (C)
1942—Rams, 24-14 (Akron)
1944—Eagles, 26-13 (P)
1945—Eagles, 28-14 (P)
1946—Eagles, 25-14 (LA)
1947—Eagles, 14-7 (P)
1948—Tie, 28-28 (LA)
1949—Eagles, 38-14 (P)
　　　**Eagles, 14-0 (LA)
1950—Eagles, 56-20 (P)
1955—Rams, 23-21 (P)
1956—Rams, 27-7 (LA)
1957—Rams, 17-13 (LA)
1959—Eagles, 23-20 (P)
1964—Rams, 20-10 (LA)
1967—Rams, 33-17 (LA)
1969—Rams, 23-17 (P)
1972—Rams, 34-3 (P)

1975—Rams, 42-3 (P)
1977—Rams, 20-0 (LA)
1978—Rams, 16-14 (P)
1983—Eagles, 13-9 (P)
1985—Rams, 17-6 (P)
1986—Eagles, 34-20 (P)
1988—Eagles, 30-24 (P)
1989—***Rams, 21-7 (P)
1990—Eagles, 27-21 (LA)
1995—Eagles, 20-9 (P)
1998—Eagles, 17-14 (P)
1999—Eagles, 38-31 (P)
2001—Rams, 20-17 (P) OT
     ****Rams, 29-24 (StL)
2002—Eagles, 10-3 (P)
2004—Rams, 20-7 (StL)
2005—Eagles, 17-16 (StL)
2008—Eagles, 38-3 (P)
(RS Pts.—Rams 693, Eagles 660)
(PS Pts.—Rams 50, Eagles 45)
*Franchise in Los Angeles prior to 1995
and in Cleveland prior to 1946
**NFL Championship
***NFC First-Round Playoff
****NFC Championship

PHILADELPHIA vs. SAN DIEGO
RS: Chargers lead series, 6-4
1974—Eagles, 13-7 (SD)
1980—Chargers, 22-21 (SD)
1985—Chargers, 20-14 (SD)
1986—Eagles, 23-7 (P)
1989—Chargers, 20-17 (SD)
1995—Chargers, 27-21 (P)
1998—Chargers, 13-10 (SD)
2001—Eagles, 24-14 (P)
2005—Eagles, 20-17 (P)
2009—Chargers, 31-23 (SD)
(RS Pts.—Eagles 186, Chargers 178)

PHILADELPHIA vs. SAN FRANCISCO
RS: 49ers lead series, 16-12-1
PS: 49ers lead series, 1-0
1951—Eagles, 21-14 (P)
1953—49ers, 31-21 (SF)
1956—Tie, 10-10 (P)
1958—49ers, 30-24 (P)
1959—49ers, 24-14 (SF)
1964—49ers, 28-24 (P)
1966—Eagles, 35-34 (SF)
1967—Eagles, 28-27 (P)
1969—49ers, 14-13 (SF)
1971—49ers, 31-3 (P)
1973—49ers, 38-28 (SF)
1975—Eagles, 27-17 (P)
1983—Eagles, 22-17 (SF)
1984—49ers, 21-9 (P)
1985—49ers, 24-13 (SF)
1989—49ers, 38-28 (P)
1991—49ers, 23-7 (P)
1992—49ers, 20-14 (SF)
1993—Eagles, 37-34 (SF) OT
1994—Eagles, 40-8 (SF)
1996—*49ers, 14-0 (SF)
1997—49ers, 24-12 (P)
2001—49ers, 13-3 (SF)
2002—Eagles, 38-17 (P)
2003—49ers, 31-28 (P) OT
2005—Eagles, 42-3 (P)
2006—Eagles, 38-24 (SF)
2008—Eagles, 40-26 (P)
2009—Eagles, 27-13 (P)
2010—Eagles, 27-24 (SF)

(RS Pts.—Eagles 672, 49ers 659)
(PS Pts.—49ers 14, Eagles 0)
*NFC First-Round Playoff

PHILADELPHIA vs. SEATTLE
RS: Eagles lead series, 7-5
1976—Eagles, 27-10 (P)
1980—Eagles, 27-20 (S)
1986—Seahawks, 24-20 (S)
1989—Eagles, 31-7 (P)
1992—Eagles, 20-17 (S) OT
1995—Seahawks, 26-14 (S)
1998—Seahawks, 38-0 (P)
2001—Eagles, 27-3 (S)
2002—Eagles, 27-20 (S)
2005—Seahawks, 42-0 (P)
2007—Seahawks, 28-24 (P)
2008—Eagles, 26-7 (S)
(RS Pts.—Eagles 243, Seahawks 242)

PHILADELPHIA vs. TAMPA BAY
RS: Eagles lead series, 6-5
PS: Series tied, 2-2
1977—Eagles, 13-3 (P)
1979—*Buccaneers, 24-17 (TB)
1981—Eagles, 20-10 (P)
1988—Eagles, 41-14 (TB)
1991—Buccaneers, 14-13 (TB)
1995—Buccaneers, 21-6 (P)
1999—Buccaneers, 19-5 (P)
2000—**Eagles, 21-3 (P)
2001—Eagles, 17-13 (TB)
     **Eagles, 31-9 (P)
2002—Eagles, 20-10 (P)
     ***Buccaneers, 27-10 (P)
2003—Buccaneers, 17-0 (P)
2006—Buccaneers, 23-21 (TB)
2009—Eagles, 33-14 (P)
(RS Pts.—Eagles 189, Buccaneers 158)
(PS Pts.—Eagles 79, Buccaneers 63)
*NFC Divisional Playoff
**NFC First-Round Playoff
***NFC Championship

PHILADELPHIA vs. *TENNESSEE
RS: Eagles lead series, 6-4
1972—Eagles, 18-17 (H)
1979—Eagles, 26-20 (H)
1982—Eagles, 35-14 (P)
1988—Eagles, 32-23 (P)
1991—Eagles, 13-6 (H)
1994—Eagles, 21-6 (P)
2000—Titans, 15-13 (P)
2002—Titans, 27-24 (T)
2006—Titans, 31-13 (P)
2010—Titans, 37-19 (T)
(RS Pts.—Eagles 214, Titans 196)
*Franchise in Houston prior to 1997;
known as Oilers prior to 1999

PHILADELPHIA vs. *WASHINGTON
RS: Redskins lead series, 78-68-5
PS: Redskins lead series, 1-0
1934—Redskins, 6-0 (B)
     Redskins, 14-7 (P)
1935—Eagles, 7-6 (B)
1936—Redskins, 26-3 (P)
     Redskins, 17-7 (B)
1937—Eagles, 14-0 (W)
     Redskins, 10-7 (P)
1938—Redskins, 26-23 (P)
     Redskins, 20-14 (W)
1939—Redskins, 7-0 (P)
     Redskins, 7-6 (W)
1940—Redskins, 34-17 (P)

Redskins, 13-6 (W)
1941—Redskins, 21-17 (P)
     Redskins, 20-14 (W)
1942—Redskins, 14-10 (P)
     Redskins, 30-27 (W)
1944—Tie, 31-31 (P)
     Eagles, 37-7 (W)
1945—Redskins, 24-14 (W)
     Eagles, 16-0 (P)
1946—Eagles, 28-24 (W)
     Redskins, 27-10 (P)
1947—Eagles, 45-42 (P)
     Eagles, 38-14 (W)
1948—Eagles, 45-0 (W)
     Eagles, 42-21 (P)
1949—Eagles, 49-14 (P)
     Eagles, 44-21 (W)
1950—Eagles, 35-3 (P)
     Eagles, 33-0 (W)
1951—Redskins, 27-23 (P)
     Eagles, 35-21 (W)
1952—Eagles, 38-20 (P)
     Redskins, 27-21 (W)
1953—Tie, 21-21 (P)
     Redskins, 10-0 (W)
1954—Eagles, 49-21 (W)
     Eagles, 41-33 (P)
1955—Redskins, 31-30 (P)
     Redskins, 34-21 (W)
1956—Eagles, 13-9 (P)
     Redskins, 19-17 (W)
1957—Eagles, 21-12 (P)
     Redskins, 42-7 (W)
1958—Redskins, 24-14 (P)
     Redskins, 20-0 (W)
1959—Eagles, 30-23 (P)
     Eagles, 34-14 (W)
1960—Eagles, 19-13 (P)
     Eagles, 38-28 (W)
1961—Eagles, 14-7 (P)
     Eagles, 27-24 (W)
1962—Redskins, 27-21 (P)
     Eagles, 37-14 (W)
1963—Eagles, 37-24 (W)
     Redskins, 13-10 (P)
1964—Redskins, 35-20 (W)
     Redskins, 21-10 (P)
1965—Redskins, 23-21 (W)
     Eagles, 21-14 (P)
1966—Redskins, 27-13 (P)
     Eagles, 37-28 (W)
1967—Eagles, 35-24 (P)
     Tie, 35-35 (W)
1968—Redskins, 17-14 (W)
     Redskins, 16-10 (P)
1969—Tie, 28-28 (W)
     Redskins, 34-29 (P)
1970—Redskins, 33-21 (P)
     Redskins, 24-6 (W)
1971—Tie, 7-7 (W)
     Redskins, 20-13 (P)
1972—Redskins, 14-0 (W)
     Redskins, 23-7 (P)
1973—Redskins, 28-7 (P)
     Redskins, 38-20 (W)
1974—Redskins, 27-20 (P)
     Redskins, 26-7 (W)
1975—Eagles, 26-10 (P)
     Eagles, 26-3 (W)
1976—Redskins, 20-17 (P) OT
     Redskins, 24-0 (W)

1977—Redskins, 23-17 (W)
    Redskins, 17-14 (P)
1978—Redskins, 35-30 (W)
    Eagles, 17-10 (P)
1979—Eagles, 28-17 (P)
    Redskins, 17-7 (W)
1980—Eagles, 24-14 (P)
    Eagles, 24-0 (W)
1981—Eagles, 36-13 (P)
    Redskins, 15-13 (W)
1982—Redskins, 37-34 (P) OT
    Redskins, 13-9 (W)
1983—Redskins, 23-13 (P)
    Redskins, 28-24 (W)
1984—Redskins, 20-0 (W)
    Eagles, 16-10 (P)
1985—Eagles, 19-6 (P)
    Redskins, 17-12 (P)
1986—Redskins, 41-14 (W)
    Redskins, 21-14 (P)
1987—Redskins, 34-24 (W)
    Eagles, 31-27 (P)
1988—Redskins, 17-10 (P)
    Redskins, 20-19 (P)
1989—Eagles, 42-37 (W)
    Redskins, 10-3 (P)
1990—Redskins, 13-7 (W)
    Eagles, 28-14 (P)
    **Redskins, 20-6 (P)
1991—Redskins, 23-0 (W)
    Eagles, 24-22 (P)
1992—Redskins, 16-12 (W)
    Eagles, 17-13 (P)
1993—Eagles, 34-31 (P)
    Eagles, 17-14 (P)
1994—Eagles, 21-17 (P)
    Eagles, 31-29 (P)
1995—Eagles, 37-34 (P) OT
    Eagles, 14-7 (W)
1996—Eagles, 17-14 (W)
    Redskins, 26-21 (P)
1997—Eagles, 24-10 (P)
    Redskins, 35-32 (W)
1998—Eagles, 17-12 (W)
    Redskins, 28-3 (W)
1999—Eagles, 35-28 (P)
    Redskins, 20-17 (W) OT
2000—Redskins, 17-14 (P)
    Eagles, 23-20 (W)
2001—Redskins, 13-3 (P)
    Eagles, 20-6 (W)
2002—Eagles, 37-7 (W)
    Eagles, 34-21 (P)
2003—Eagles, 27-25 (P)
    Eagles, 31-7 (W)
2004—Eagles, 28-6 (P)
    Eagles, 17-14 (W)
2005—Redskins, 17-10 (W)
    Redskins, 31-20 (P)
2006—Eagles, 27-3 (P)
    Eagles, 21-19 (W)
2007—Redskins, 20-12 (P)
    Eagles, 33-25 (W)
2008—Redskins, 23-17 (P)
    Redskins, 10-3 (P)
2009—Eagles, 27-17 (W)
    Eagles, 27-24 (P)
2010—Redskins, 17-12 (P)
    Eagles, 59-28 (W)
(RS Pts.—Eagles 3,118, Redskins 2,954)
(PS Pts.—Redskins 20, Eagles 6)

Franchise in Boston prior to 1937
**NFC First-Round Playoff*

PITTSBURGH vs. ARIZONA
RS: Steelers lead series, 31-23-3
PS: Steelers lead series, 1-0;
See Arizona vs. Pittsburgh
PITTSBURGH vs. ATLANTA
RS: Steelers lead series, 12-2-1;
See Atlanta vs. Pittsburgh
PITTSBURGH vs. BALTIMORE
RS: Steelers lead series, 18-12
PS: Steelers lead series, 3-0;
See Baltimore vs. Pittsburgh
PITTSBURGH vs. BUFFALO
RS: Steelers lead series, 12-8
PS: Steelers lead series, 2-1;
See Buffalo vs. Pittsburgh
PITTSBURGH vs. CAROLINA
RS: Steelers lead series, 4-1;
See Carolina vs. Pittsburgh
PITTSBURGH vs. CHICAGO
RS: Bears lead series, 17-7-1;
See Chicago vs. Pittsburgh
PITTSBURGH vs. CINCINNATI
RS: Steelers lead series, 49-32
PS: Steelers lead series, 1-0;
See Cincinnati vs. Pittsburgh
PITTSBURGH vs. CLEVELAND
RS: Steelers lead series, 60-56
PS: Steelers lead series, 2-0;
See Cleveland vs. Pittsburgh
PITTSBURGH vs. DALLAS
RS: Cowboys lead series, 14-13
PS: Steelers lead series, 2-1;
See Dallas vs. Pittsburgh
PITTSBURGH vs. DENVER
RS: Broncos lead series, 13-7-1
PS: Series tied, 3-3;
See Denver vs. Pittsburgh
PITTSBURGH vs. DETROIT
RS: Steelers lead series, 15-14-1;
See Detroit vs. Pittsburgh
PITTSBURGH vs. GREEN BAY
RS: Packers lead series, 18-14
PS: Packers lead series, 1-0;
See Green Bay vs. Pittsburgh
PITTSBURGH vs. HOUSTON
RS: Steelers lead series 2-1;
See Houston vs. Pittsburgh
PITTSBURGH vs. INDIANAPOLIS
RS: Steelers lead series, 13-6
PS: Steelers lead series, 5-0;
See Indianapolis vs. Pittsburgh
PITTSBURGH vs. JACKSONVILLE
RS: Jaguars lead series, 11-9
PS: Jaguars lead series, 1-0;
See Jacksonville vs. Pittsburgh
PITTSBURGH vs. KANSAS CITY
RS: Steelers lead series, 17-9
PS: Chiefs lead series, 1-0;
See Kansas City vs. Pittsburgh
PITTSBURGH vs. MIAMI
RS: Steelers lead series, 12-9
PS: Dolphins lead series, 2-1;
See Miami vs. Pittsburgh
PITTSBURGH vs. MINNESOTA
RS: Vikings lead series, 8-7
PS: Steelers lead series, 1-0;
See Minnesota vs. Pittsburgh

PITTSBURGH vs. NEW ENGLAND
RS: Steelers lead series, 13-8
PS: Patriots lead series, 3-1;
See New England vs. Pittsburgh
PITTSBURGH vs. NEW ORLEANS
RS: Series tied, 7-7;
See New Orleans vs. Pittsburgh
PITTSBURGH vs. N.Y. GIANTS
RS: Giants lead series, 44-28-3;
See N.Y. Giants vs. Pittsburgh
PITTSBURGH vs. N.Y. JETS
RS: Steelers lead series, 15-4
PS: Steelers lead series, 2-0;
See N.Y. Jets vs. Pittsburgh
PITTSBURGH vs. OAKLAND
RS: Raiders lead series, 10-9
PS: Series tied, 3-3;
See Oakland vs. Pittsburgh
PITTSBURGH vs. PHILADELPHIA
RS: Eagles lead series, 46-27-3
PS: Eagles lead series, 1-0;
See Philadelphia vs. Pittsburgh
*PITTSBURGH vs. **ST. LOUIS
RS: Rams lead series, 15-6-2
PS: Steelers lead series, 1-0
1938—Rams, 13-7 (New Orleans)
1939—Tie, 14-14 (C)
1941—Rams, 17-14 (Akron)
1947—Rams, 48-7 (P)
1948—Rams, 31-14 (LA)
1949—Tie, 7-7 (P)
1952—Rams, 28-14 (LA)
1955—Rams, 27-26 (LA)
1956—Steelers, 30-13 (P)
1961—Rams, 24-14 (LA)
1964—Rams, 26-14 (P)
1968—Rams, 45-10 (LA)
1971—Rams, 23-14 (P)
1975—Rams, 10-3 (LA)
1978—Rams, 10-7 (LA)
1979—***Steelers, 31-19 (Pasadena)
1981—Steelers, 24-0 (P)
1984—Steelers, 24-14 (P)
1987—Rams, 31-21 (LA)
1990—Steelers, 41-10 (P)
1993—Rams, 27-0 (LA)
1996—Steelers, 42-6 (P)
2003—Rams, 33-21 (P)
2007—Steelers, 41-24 (StL)
(RS Pts.—Rams 481, Steelers 409)
(PS Pts.—Steelers 31, Rams 19)
Steelers known as Pirates prior to 1940
**Franchise in Los Angeles prior to 1995
and in Cleveland prior to 1946*
***Super Bowl XIV*
PITTSBURGH vs. SAN DIEGO
RS: Steelers lead series, 21-6
PS: Chargers lead series, 2-1
1971—Steelers, 21-17 (P)
1972—Steelers, 24-2 (SD)
1973—Steelers, 38-21 (P)
1975—Steelers, 37-0 (SD)
1976—Steelers, 23-0 (P)
1977—Steelers, 10-9 (SD)
1979—Chargers, 35-7 (SD)
1980—Chargers, 26-17 (SD)
1982—*Chargers, 31-28 (P)
1983—Steelers, 26-3 (P)
1984—Steelers, 52-24 (P)
1985—Chargers, 54-44 (SD)
1987—Steelers, 20-16 (SD)

1988—Chargers, 20-14 (SD)
1989—Steelers, 20-17 (P)
1990—Steelers, 36-14 (P)
1991—Steelers, 26-20 (P)
1992—Steelers, 23-6 (SD)
1993—Steelers,.16-3 (P)
1994—Chargers, 37-34 (SD)
    **Chargers, 17-13 (P)
1995—Steelers, 31-16 (P)
1996—Steelers, 16-3 (P)
2000—Steelers, 34-21 (SD)
2003—Steelers, 40-24 (P)
2005—Steelers, 24-22 (SD)
2006—Chargers, 23-13 (SD)
2008—Steelers, 11-10 (P)
    ***Steelers, 35-24 (P)
2009—Steelers, 38-28 (P)
(RS Pts.—Steelers 695, Chargers 471)
(PS Pts.—Steelers 76, Chargers 72)
*AFC First-Round Playoff
**AFC Championship
***AFC Divisional Playoff

PITTSBURGH vs. SAN FRANCISCO
RS: 49ers lead series, 10-9
1951—49ers, 28-24 (P)
1952—Steelers, 24-7 (SF)
1954—49ers, 31-3 (SF)
1958—49ers, 23-20 (SF)
1961—49ers, 20-10 (P)
1965—49ers, 27-17 (SF)
1968—49ers, 45-28 (P)
1973—Steelers, 37-14 (SF)
1977—Steelers, 27-0 (P)
1978—Steelers, 24-7 (SF)
1981—49ers, 17-14 (P)
1984—Steelers, 20-17 (SF)
1987—Steelers, 30-17 (P)
1990—49ers, 27-7 (SF)
1993—49ers, 24-13 (P)
1996—49ers, 25-15 (P)
1999—Steelers, 27-6 (SF)
2003—49ers, 30-14 (SF)
2007—Steelers, 37-16 (P)
(RS Pts.—Steelers 401, 49ers 371)

PITTSBURGH vs. SEATTLE
RS: Seahawks lead series, 8-7
PS: Steelers lead series, 1-0
1977—Steelers, 30-20 (P)
1978—Steelers, 21-10 (P)
1981—Seahawks, 24-21 (S)
1982—Seahawks, 16-0 (S)
1983—Steelers, 27-21 (S)
1986—Seahawks, 30-0 (S)
1987—Steelers, 13-9 (P)
1991—Seahawks, 27-7 (P)
1992—Steelers, 20-14 (P)
1993—Seahawks, 16-6 (S)
1994—Seahawks, 30-13 (S)
1998—Steelers, 13-10 (P)
1999—Seahawks, 29-10 (P)
2003—Seahawks, 23-16 (S)
2005—*Steelers, 21-10 (Detroit)
2007—Steelers, 21-0 (P)
(RS Pts.—Seahawks 279, Steelers 218)
(PS Pts.—Steelers 21, Seahawks 10)
*Super Bowl XL

PITTSBURGH vs. TAMPA BAY
RS: Steelers lead series, 8-1
1976—Steelers, 42-0 (P)
1980—Steelers, 24-21 (TB)
1983—Steelers, 17-12 (P)

1989—Steelers, 31-22 (TB)
1998—Buccaneers, 16-3 (TB)
2001—Steelers, 17-10 (TB)
2002—Steelers, 17-7 (TB)
2006—Steelers, 20-3 (P)
2010—Steelers, 38-13 (TB)
(RS Pts.—Steelers 209, Buccaneers 104)

PITTSBURGH vs. *TENNESSEE
RS: Steelers lead series, 40-29
PS: Steelers lead series, 3-1
1970—Oilers, 19-7 (P)
    Steelers, 7-3 (H)
1971—Steelers, 23-16 (P)
    Oilers, 29-3 (H)
1972—Steelers, 24-7 (P)
    Steelers, 9-3 (H)
1973—Steelers, 36-7 (H)
    Steelers, 33-7 (P)
1974—Steelers, 13-7 (H)
    Oilers, 13-10 (P)
1975—Steelers, 24-17 (P)
    Steelers, 32-9 (H)
1976—Steelers, 32-16 (P)
    Steelers, 21-0 (H)
1977—Oilers, 27-10 (H)
    Steelers, 27-10 (P)
1978—Oilers, 24-17 (P)
    Steelers, 13-3 (H)
    **Steelers, 34-5 (P)
1979—Steelers, 38-7 (P)
    Oilers, 20-17 (H)
    **Steelers, 27-13 (P)
1980—Steelers, 31-17 (P)
    Oilers, 6-0 (H)
1981—Steelers, 26-13 (P)
    Oilers, 21-20 (H)
1982—Steelers, 24-10 (H)
1983—Steelers, 40-28 (H)
    Steelers, 17-10 (P)
1984—Steelers, 35-7 (P)
    Oilers, 23-20 (H) OT
1985—Steelers, 20-0 (P)
    Steelers, 30-7 (H)
1986—Steelers, 22-16 (H) OT
    Steelers, 21-10 (P)
1987—Oilers, 23-3 (P)
    Oilers, 24-16 (H)
1988—Oilers, 34-14 (P)
    Steelers, 37-34 (H)
1989—Oilers, 27-0 (H)
    Oilers, 23-16 (P)
    ***Steelers, 26-23 (H) OT
1990—Steelers, 20-9 (P)
    Oilers, 34-14 (H)
1991—Steelers, 26-14 (P)
    Oilers, 31-6 (H)
1992—Steelers, 29-24 (H)
    Steelers, 21-20 (P)
1993—Oilers, 23-3 (H)
    Oilers, 26-17 (P)
1994—Steelers, 30-14 (P)
    Steelers, 12-9 (H) OT
1995—Steelers, 34-17 (H)
    Steelers, 21-7 (P)
1996—Steelers, 30-16 (P)
    Oilers, 23-13 (H)
1997—Steelers, 37-24 (P)
    Oilers, 16-6 (T)
1998—Oilers, 41-31 (P)
    Oilers, 23-14 (T)
1999—Titans, 16-10 (T)

    Titans, 47-36 (P)
2000—Titans, 23-20 (P)
    Titans, 9-7 (T)
2001—Steelers, 34-7 (P)
    Steelers, 34-24 (T)
2002—Titans, 31-23 (T)
    ****Titans, 34-31 (T) OT
2003—Titans, 30-13 (P)
2005—Steelers, 34-7 (P)
2008—Titans, 31-14 (P)
2009—Steelers, 13-10 (P) OT
2010—Steelers, 19-11 (T)
(RS Pts.—Steelers 1,409, Titans 1,194)
(PS Pts.—Steelers 118, Titans 75)
*Franchise in Houston prior to 1997;
known as Oilers prior to 1999
**AFC Championship
***AFC First-Round Playoff
****AFC Divisional Playoff

*PITTSBURGH vs. **WASHINGTON
RS: Redskins lead series, 42-31-3
1933—Redskins, 21-6 (P)
    Pirates, 16-14 (B)
1934—Redskins, 7-0 (P)
    Redskins, 39-0 (B)
1935—Pirates, 6-0 (P)
    Redskins, 13-3 (B)
1936—Pirates, 10-0 (P)
    Redskins, 30-0 (B)
1937—Redskins, 34-20 (W)
    Pirates, 21-13 (P)
1938—Redskins, 7-0 (P)
    Redskins, 15-0 (W)
1939—Redskins, 44-14 (W)
    Redskins, 21-14 (P)
1940—Redskins, 40-10 (P)
    Redskins, 37-10 (W)
1941—Redskins, 24-20 (P)
    Redskins, 23-3 (W)
1942—Redskins, 28-14 (W)
    Redskins, 14-0 (P)
1945—Redskins, 14-0 (W)
    Redskins, 24-0 (W)
1946—Tie, 14-14 (W)
    Steelers, 14-7 (P)
1947—Redskins, 27-26 (W)
    Steelers, 21-14 (P)
1948—Redskins, 17-14 (W)
    Steelers, 10-7 (P)
1949—Redskins, 27-14 (P)
    Redskins, 27-14 (W)
1950—Steelers, 26-7 (W)
    Redskins, 24-7 (P)
1951—Redskins, 22-7 (P)
    Steelers, 20-10 (W)
1952—Redskins, 28-24 (P)
    Steelers, 24-23 (W)
1953—Redskins, 17-9 (P)
    Steelers, 14-13 (W)
1954—Steelers, 37-7 (P)
    Redskins, 17-14 (W)
1955—Steelers, 23-14 (P)
    Redskins, 28-17 (W)
1956—Steelers, 30-13 (P)
    Steelers, 23-0 (W)
1957—Steelers, 28-7 (P)
    Redskins, 10-3 (W)
1958—Steelers, 24-16 (P)
    Tie, 14-14 (W)
1959—Redskins, 23-17 (P)
    Steelers, 27-6 (W)

1960—Tie, 27-27 (W)
　　　　Steelers, 22-10 (P)
1961—Steelers, 20-0 (P)
　　　　Steelers, 30-14 (W)
1962—Steelers, 23-21 (P)
　　　　Steelers, 27-24 (W)
1963—Steelers, 38-27 (P)
　　　　Steelers, 34-28 (W)
1964—Redskins, 30-0 (P)
　　　　Steelers, 14-7 (W)
1965—Redskins, 31-3 (P)
　　　　Redskins, 35-14 (W)
1966—Redskins, 33-27 (P)
　　　　Redskins, 24-10 (W)
1967—Redskins, 15-10 (P)
1968—Redskins, 16-13 (W)
1969—Redskins, 14-7 (P)
1973—Steelers, 21-16 (P)
1979—Steelers, 38-7 (P)
1985—Redskins, 30-23 (P)
1988—Redskins, 30-29 (W)
1991—Redskins, 41-14 (P)
1997—Steelers, 14-13 (P)
2000—Steelers, 24-3 (P)
2004—Steelers, 10-7 (P)
2008—Steelers, 23-6 (W)
(RS Pts.—Redskins 1,419, Steelers 1,194)
*Steelers known as Pirates prior to 1940
**Franchise in Boston prior to 1937

ST. LOUIS vs. ARIZONA
RS: Series tied, 31-31-2
PS: Rams lead series, 1-0;
See Arizona vs. St. Louis
ST. LOUIS vs. ATLANTA
RS: Rams lead series, 47-26-2
PS: Falcons lead series, 1-0;
See Atlanta vs. St. Louis
ST. LOUIS vs. BALTIMORE
RS: Series tied, 2-2;
See Baltimore vs. St. Louis
ST. LOUIS vs. BUFFALO
RS: Bills lead series, 6-4;
See Buffalo vs. St. Louis
ST. LOUIS vs. CAROLINA
RS: Panthers lead series, 10-8
PS: Panthers lead series, 1-0;
See Carolina vs. St. Louis
ST. LOUIS vs. CHICAGO
RS: Bears lead series, 50-34-3
PS: Series tied, 1-1;
See Chicago vs. St. Louis
ST. LOUIS vs. CINCINNATI
RS: Bengals lead series, 6-5;
See Cincinnati vs. St. Louis
ST. LOUIS vs. CLEVELAND
RS: Series tied, 9-9
PS: Browns lead series, 2-1;
See Cleveland vs. St. Louis
ST. LOUIS vs. DALLAS
RS: Rams lead series, 11-10
PS: Series tied, 4-4;
See Dallas vs. St. Louis
ST. LOUIS vs. DENVER
RS: Rams lead series, 7-5;
See Denver vs. St. Louis
ST. LOUIS vs. DETROIT
RS: Rams lead series, 42-38-1
PS: Lions lead series, 1-0;
See Detroit vs. St. Louis

ST. LOUIS vs. GREEN BAY
RS: Rams lead series, 45-42-2
PS: Series tied, 1-1;
See Green Bay vs. St. Louis
ST. LOUIS vs. HOUSTON
RS: Series tied, 1-1;
See Houston vs. St. Louis
ST. LOUIS vs. INDIANAPOLIS
RS: Colts lead series, 23-17-2;
See Indianapolis vs. St. Louis
ST. LOUIS vs. JACKSONVILLE
RS: Rams lead series, 2-1;
See Jacksonville vs. St. Louis
ST. LOUIS vs. KANSAS CITY
RS: Chiefs lead series; 6-4;
See Kansas City vs. St. Louis
ST. LOUIS vs. MIAMI
RS: Dolphins lead series, 9-2;
See Miami vs. St. Louis
ST. LOUIS vs. MINNESOTA
RS: Vikings lead series, 18-14-2
PS: Vikings lead series, 5-2;
See Minnesota vs. St. Louis
ST. LOUIS vs. NEW ENGLAND
RS: Series tied, 5-5
PS: Patriots lead series, 1-0;
See New England vs. St. Louis
ST. LOUIS vs. NEW ORLEANS
RS: Rams lead series, 38-31
PS: Saints lead series, 1-0;
See New Orleans vs. St. Louis
ST. LOUIS vs. N.Y. GIANTS
RS: Rams lead series, 25-13
PS: Series tied, 1-1;
See N.Y. Giants vs. St. Louis
ST. LOUIS vs. N.Y. JETS
RS: Rams lead series, 9-3;
See N.Y. Jets vs. St. Louis
ST. LOUIS vs. OAKLAND
RS: Raiders lead series, 8-4;
See Oakland vs. St. Louis
ST. LOUIS vs. PHILADELPHIA
RS: Series tied, 17-17-1
PS: Rams lead series, 2-1;
See Philadelphia vs. St. Louis
ST. LOUIS vs. PITTSBURGH
RS: Rams lead series, 15-6-2
PS: Steelers lead series, 1-0;
See Pittsburgh vs. St. Louis
*ST. LOUIS vs. SAN DIEGO
RS: Rams lead series, 6-4
1970—Rams, 37-10 (LA)
1975—Rams, 13-10 (SD) OT
1979—Chargers, 40-16 (LA)
1988—Chargers, 38-24 (LA)
1991—Rams, 30-24 (LA)
1994—Chargers, 31-17 (SD)
2000—Rams, 57-31 (StL)
2002—Rams, 28-24 (StL)
2006—Chargers, 38-24 (SD)
2010—Rams, 20-17 (StL)
(RS Pts.—Rams 266, Chargers 263)
*Franchise in Los Angeles prior to 1995
*ST. LOUIS vs. SAN FRANCISCO
RS: Rams lead series, 61-59-2
PS: 49ers lead series, 1-0
1950—Rams, 35-14 (SF)
　　　　Rams, 28-21 (LA)
1951—49ers, 44-17 (SF)
　　　　Rams, 23-16 (LA)
1952—Rams, 35-9 (LA)

Rams, 34-21 (SF)
1953—49ers, 31-30 (SF)
　　　　49ers, 31-27 (LA)
1954—Tie, 24-24 (LA)
　　　　Rams, 42-34 (SF)
1955—Rams, 23-14 (SF)
　　　　Rams, 27-14 (LA)
1956—49ers, 33-30 (SF)
　　　　Rams, 30-6 (LA)
1957—49ers, 23-20 (SF)
　　　　Rams, 37-24 (LA)
1958—Rams, 33-3 (SF)
　　　　Rams, 56-7 (LA)
1959—49ers, 34-0 (SF)
　　　　49ers, 24-16 (LA)
1960—49ers, 13-9 (SF)
　　　　49ers, 23-7 (LA)
1961—49ers, 35-0 (SF)
　　　　Rams, 17-7 (LA)
1962—Rams, 28-14 (SF)
　　　　49ers, 24-17 (LA)
1963—Rams, 28-21 (LA)
　　　　Rams, 21-17 (SF)
1964—Rams, 42-14 (LA)
　　　　49ers, 28-7 (SF)
1965—49ers, 45-21 (LA)
　　　　49ers, 30-27 (SF)
1966—Rams, 34-3 (LA)
　　　　49ers, 21-13 (SF)
1967—49ers, 27-24 (LA)
　　　　Rams, 17-7 (SF)
1968—Rams, 24-10 (LA)
　　　　Tie, 20-20 (SF)
1969—Rams, 27-21 (SF)
　　　　Rams, 41-30 (LA)
1970—49ers, 20-6 (LA)
　　　　Rams, 30-13 (SF)
1971—Rams, 20-13 (SF)
　　　　Rams, 17-6 (LA)
1972—Rams, 31-7 (LA)
　　　　Rams, 26-16 (SF)
1973—Rams, 40-20 (SF)
　　　　Rams, 31-13 (LA)
1974—Rams, 37-14 (LA)
　　　　Rams, 15-13 (LA)
1975—Rams, 23-14 (SF)
　　　　49ers, 24-23 (LA)
1976—49ers, 16-0 (LA)
　　　　Rams, 23-3 (SF)
1977—Rams, 34-14 (LA)
　　　　Rams, 23-10 (SF)
1978—Rams, 27-10 (LA)
　　　　Rams, 31-28 (SF)
1979—Rams, 27-24 (LA)
　　　　Rams, 26-20 (SF)
1980—Rams, 48-26 (LA)
　　　　Rams, 31-17 (SF)
1981—49ers, 20-17 (SF)
　　　　49ers, 33-31 (LA)
1982—49ers, 30-24 (LA)
　　　　Rams, 21-20 (SF)
1983—Rams, 10-7 (SF)
　　　　49ers, 45-35 (LA)
1984—49ers, 33-0 (LA)
　　　　49ers, 19-16 (SF)
1985—49ers, 28-14 (LA)
　　　　Rams, 27-20 (SF)
1986—Rams, 16-13 (LA)
　　　　49ers, 24-14 (SF)
1987—49ers, 31-10 (LA)
　　　　49ers, 48-0 (SF)

1988—49ers, 24-21 (LA)
Rams, 38-16 (SF)
1989—Rams, 13-12 (SF)
49ers, 30-27 (LA)
**49ers, 30-3 (SF)
1990—49ers, 28-17 (SF)
49ers, 26-10 (LA)
1991—49ers, 27-10 (SF)
49ers, 33-10 (LA)
1992—49ers, 27-24 (SF)
49ers, 27-10 (LA)
1993—49ers, 40-17 (SF)
49ers, 35-10 (LA)
1994—49ers, 34-19 (LA)
49ers, 31-27 (SF)
1995—49ers, 44-10 (StL)
49ers, 41-13 (SF)
1996—49ers, 34-0 (SF)
49ers, 28-11 (StL)
1997—49ers, 15-12 (StL)
49ers, 30-10 (SF)
1998—49ers, 28-10 (SF)
49ers, 38-19 (SF)
1999—Rams, 42-20 (StL)
Rams, 23-7 (SF)
2000—Rams, 41-24 (StL)
Rams, 34-24 (SF)
2001—Rams, 30-26 (SF)
Rams, 27-14 (StL)
2002—49ers, 37-13 (SF)
Rams, 31-20 (StL)
2003—Rams, 27-24 (StL) OT
49ers, 30-10 (SF)
2004—Rams, 24-14 (SF)
Rams, 16-6 (StL)
2005—49ers, 28-25 (SF)
49ers, 24-20 (StL)
2006—49ers, 20-13 (SF)
Rams, 20-17 (StL)
2007—49ers, 17-16 (StL)
Rams, 13-9 (SF)
2008—49ers, 35-16 (SF)
49ers, 17-16 (StL)
2009—49ers, 35-0 (SF)
49ers, 28-6 (StL)
2010—49ers, 23-20 (SF) OT
Rams, 25-17 (StL)
(RS Pts.—49ers 2,702, Rams 2,652)
(PS Pts.—49ers 30, Rams 3)
*Franchise in Los Angeles prior to 1995
**NFC Championship
ST. LOUIS vs. SEATTLE
RS: Seahawks lead series, 15-10
PS: Rams lead series, 1-0
1976—Rams, 45-6 (LA)
1979—Rams, 24-0 (Sea)
1985—Rams, 35-24 (Sea)
1988—Rams, 31-10 (LA)
1991—Seahawks, 23-9 (Sea)
1997—Seahawks, 17-9 (StL)
2000—Rams, 37-34 (Sea)
2002—Rams, 37-20 (StL)
Seahawks, 30-10 (Sea)
2003—Seahawks, 24-23 (Sea)
Rams, 27-22 (StL)
2004—Rams, 33-27 (Sea) OT
Rams, 23-12 (StL)
**Rams, 27-20 (Sea)
2005—Seahawks, 37-31 (StL)
Seahawks, 31-16 (Sea)
2006—Seahawks, 30-28 (StL)

Seahawks, 24-22 (Sea)
2007—Seahawks, 33-6 (Sea)
Seahawks, 24-19 (StL)
2008—Seahawks, 37-13 (Sea)
Seahawks, 23-20 (StL)
2009—Seahawks, 28-0 (Sea)
Seahawks, 27-17 (StL)
2010—Rams, 20-3 (StL)
Seahawks, 16-6 (Sea)
(RS Pts.—Seahawks 562, Rams 541)
(PS Pts.—Rams 27, Seahawks 20)
*Franchise in Los Angeles prior to 1995
**NFC First-Round Playoff
ST. LOUIS vs. TAMPA BAY
RS: Rams lead series, 9-8
PS: Rams lead series, 2-0
1977—Rams, 31-0 (LA)
1978—Rams, 26-23 (LA)
1979—Buccaneers, 21-6 (TB)
**Rams, 9-0 (TB)
1980—Buccaneers, 10-9 (TB)
1984—Rams, 34-33 (TB)
1985—Rams, 31-27 (TB)
1986—Rams, 26-20 (LA) OT
1987—Rams, 35-3 (LA)
1990—Rams, 35-14 (TB)
1992—Rams, 31-27 (TB)
1994—Buccaneers, 24-14 (TB)
1999—**Rams, 11-6 (StL)
2000—Buccaneers, 38-35 (TB)
2001—Buccaneers, 24-17 (StL)
2002—Buccaneers, 26-14 (TB)
2004—Rams, 28-21 (StL)
2007—Buccaneers, 24-3 (TB)
2010—Rams, 18-17 (TB)
(RS Pts.—Rams 392, Buccaneers 353)
(PS Pts.—Rams 20, Buccaneers 6)
*Franchise in Los Angeles prior to 1995
**NFC Championship
ST. LOUIS vs. **TENNESSEE
RS: Rams lead series, 6-4
PS: Rams lead series, 1-0
1973—Rams, 31-26 (H)
1978—Rams, 10-6 (H)
1981—Oilers, 27-20 (LA)
1984—Rams, 27-16 (LA)
1987—Oilers, 20-16 (H)
1990—Rams, 17-13 (LA)
1993—Rams, 28-13 (H)
1999—Titans, 24-21 (T)
***Rams, 23-16 (Atlanta)
2005—Rams, 31-27 (StL)
2009—Titans, 47-7 (T)
(RS Pts.—Titans, 219, Rams 208)
(PS Pts.—Rams 23, Titans 16)
*Franchise in Los Angeles prior to 1995
**Franchise in Houston prior to 1997;
known as Oilers prior to 1999
***Super Bowl XXXIV
ST. LOUIS vs. WASHINGTON
RS: Redskins lead series, 21-9-1
PS: Series tied, 2-2
1937—Redskins, 16-7 (C)
1938—Redskins, 37-13 (W)
1941—Redskins, 17-13 (W)
1942—Redskins, 33-14 (W)
1944—Redskins, 14-10 (W)
1945—**Rams, 15-14 (C)
1948—Rams, 41-13 (W)
1949—Rams, 53-27 (LA)
1951—Redskins, 31-21 (W)

1962—Redskins, 20-14 (W)
1963—Redskins, 37-14 (LA)
1967—Tie, 28-28 (LA)
1969—Rams, 24-13 (W)
1971—Redskins, 38-24 (LA)
1974—Redskins, 23-17 (LA)
***Rams, 19-10 (LA)
1977—Redskins, 17-14 (W)
1981—Redskins, 30-7 (LA)
1983—Redskins, 42-20 (LA)
***Redskins, 51-7 (W)
1986—****Redskins, 19-7 (W)
1987—Rams, 30-26 (W)
1991—Redskins, 27-6 (LA)
1993—Rams, 10-6 (LA)
1994—Redskins, 24-21 (LA)
1995—Redskins, 35-23 (StL)
1996—Redskins, 17-10 (StL)
1997—Rams, 23-20 (W)
2000—Redskins, 33-20 (StL)
2002—Redskins, 20-17 (W)
2005—Redskins, 24-9 (StL)
2006—Rams, 37-31 (StL) OT
2008—Rams, 19-17 (W)
2009—Redskins, 9-7 (W)
2010—Rams, 30-16 (StL)
(RS Pts.—Redskins 741, Rams 596)
(PS Pts.—Redskins 94, Rams 48)
*Franchise in Los Angeles prior to 1995
and in Cleveland prior to 1946
**NFL Championship
***NFC Divisional Playoff
****NFC First-Round Playoff

SAN DIEGO vs. ARIZONA
RS: Chargers lead series, 9-3;
See Arizona vs. San Diego
SAN DIEGO vs. ATLANTA
RS: Falcons lead series, 7-1;
See Atlanta vs. San Diego
SAN DIEGO vs. BALTIMORE
RS: Ravens lead series, 4-3;
See Baltimore vs. San Diego
SAN DIEGO vs. BUFFALO
RS: Chargers lead series, 20-10-2
PS: Bills lead series, 2-1;
See Buffalo vs. San Diego
SAN DIEGO vs. CAROLINA
RS: Panthers lead series, 3-1;
See Carolina vs. San Diego
SAN DIEGO vs. CHICAGO
RS: Series tied, 5-5;
See Chicago vs. San Diego
SAN DIEGO vs. CINCINNATI
RS: Chargers lead series, 19-11
PS: Bengals lead series, 1-0;
See Cincinnati vs. San Diego
SAN DIEGO vs. CLEVELAND
RS: Chargers lead series, 14-7-1;
See Cleveland vs. San Diego
SAN DIEGO vs. DALLAS
RS: Cowboys lead series, 6-3;
See Dallas vs. San Diego
SAN DIEGO vs. DENVER
RS: Broncos lead series, 54-47-1;
See Denver vs. San Diego
SAN DIEGO vs. DETROIT
RS: Chargers lead series, 6-3;
See Detroit vs. San Diego
SAN DIEGO vs. GREEN BAY
RS: Packers lead series, 8-1;

See Green Bay vs. San Diego
SAN DIEGO vs. HOUSTON
RS: Chargers lead series, 4-0;
See Houston vs. San Diego
SAN DIEGO vs. INDIANAPOLIS
RS: Chargers lead series, 15-9
PS: Chargers lead series, 2-1;
See Indianapolis vs. San Diego
SAN DIEGO vs. JACKSONVILLE
RS: Series tied, 2-2;
See Jacksonville vs. San Diego
SAN DIEGO vs. KANSAS CITY
RS: Chiefs lead series, 51-49-1
PS: Chargers lead series, 1-0;
See Kansas City vs. San Diego
SAN DIEGO vs. MIAMI
RS: Dolphins lead series, 12-11
PS: Series tied, 2-2;
See Miami vs. San Diego
SAN DIEGO vs. MINNESOTA
RS: Series tied, 5-5;
See Minnesota vs. San Diego
SAN DIEGO vs. NEW ENGLAND
RS: Patriots lead series, 19-14-2
PS: Patriots lead series, 2-1;
See New England vs. San Diego
SAN DIEGO vs. NEW ORLEANS
RS: Chargers lead series, 7-3;
See New Orleans vs. San Diego
SAN DIEGO vs. N.Y. GIANTS
RS: Series tied, 5-5;
See N.Y. Giants vs. San Diego
SAN DIEGO vs. N.Y. JETS
RS: Chargers lead series, 19-11-1
PS: Jets lead series, 2-0;
See N.Y. Jets vs. San Diego
SAN DIEGO vs. OAKLAND
RS: Raiders lead series, 56-44-2
PS: Raiders lead series, 1-0;
See Oakland vs. San Diego
SAN DIEGO vs. PHILADELPHIA
RS: Chargers lead series, 6-4;
See Philadelphia vs. San Diego
SAN DIEGO vs. PITTSBURGH
RS: Steelers lead series, 21-6
PS: Chargers lead series, 2-1;
See Pittsburgh vs. San Diego
SAN DIEGO vs. ST. LOUIS
RS: Rams lead series, 6-4;
See St. Louis vs. San Diego
SAN DIEGO vs. SAN FRANCISCO
RS: Series tied, 6-6
PS: 49ers lead series, 1-0
1972—49ers, 34-3 (SF)
1976—Chargers, 13-7 (SD) OT
1979—Chargers, 31-9 (SD)
1982—Chargers, 41-37 (SF)
1988—49ers, 48-10 (SD)
1991—49ers, 34-14 (SF)
1994—49ers, 38-15 (SD)
      *49ers, 49-26 (South Florida)
1997—49ers, 17-10 (SF)
2000—49ers, 45-17 (SD)
2002—Chargers, 20-17 (SD) OT
2006—Chargers, 48-19 (SF)
2010—Chargers, 34-7 (SD)
(RS Pts.—49ers 312, Chargers 256)
(PS Pts.—49ers 49, Chargers 26)
*Super Bowl XXIX
SAN DIEGO vs. SEATTLE
RS: Seahawks lead series, 26-23

1977—Chargers, 30-28 (Sea)
1978—Chargers, 24-20 (Sea)
      Chargers, 37-10 (SD)
1979—Chargers, 33-16 (Sea)
      Chargers, 20-10 (SD)
1980—Chargers, 34-13 (Sea)
      Chargers, 21-14 (SD)
1981—Chargers, 24-10 (SD)
      Seahawks, 44-23 (Sea)
1983—Seahawks, 34-31 (Sea)
      Chargers, 28-21 (SD)
1984—Seahawks, 31-17 (Sea)
      Seahawks, 24-0 (SD)
1985—Seahawks, 49-35 (SD)
      Seahawks, 26-21 (Sea)
1986—Seahawks, 33-7 (Sea)
      Seahawks, 34-24 (SD)
1987—Seahawks, 34-3 (Sea)
1988—Chargers, 17-6 (SD)
      Seahawks, 17-14 (Sea)
1989—Seahawks, 17-16 (SD)
      Seahawks, 10-7 (Sea)
1990—Chargers, 31-14 (Sea)
      Seahawks, 13-10 (SD) OT
1991—Seahawks, 20-9 (Sea)
      Chargers, 17-14 (SD)
1992—Chargers, 17-6 (SD)
      Chargers, 31-14 (Sea)
1993—Chargers, 18-12 (SD)
      Seahawks, 31-14 (Sea)
1994—Chargers, 24-10 (Sea)
      Chargers, 35-15 (SD)
1995—Chargers, 14-10 (SD)
      Chargers, 35-25 (Sea)
1996—Chargers, 29-7 (SD)
      Seahawks, 32-13 (Sea)
1997—Seahawks, 26-22 (Sea)
      Seahawks, 37-31 (SD)
1998—Seahawks, 27-20 (SD)
      Seahawks, 38-17 (Sea)
1999—Chargers, 13-10 (SD)
      Chargers, 19-16 (Sea)
2000—Seahawks, 20-12 (SD)
      Seahawks, 17-15 (Sea)
2001—Seahawks, 13-10 (Sea) OT
      Seahawks, 25-22 (SD)
2002—Seahawks, 31-28 (SD) OT
2006—Chargers, 20-17 (Sea)
2010—Chargers, 27-20 (Sea)
(RS Pts.—Seahawks 1,028, Chargers 1,012)
SAN DIEGO vs. TAMPA BAY
RS: Chargers lead series, 8-1
1976—Chargers, 23-0 (TB)
1981—Chargers, 24-23 (TB)
1987—Chargers, 17-13 (TB)
1990—Chargers, 41-10 (SD)
1992—Chargers, 29-14 (SD)
1993—Chargers, 32-17 (TB)
1996—Buccaneers, 25-17 (SD)
2004—Chargers, 31-24 (SD)
2008—Chargers, 41-24 (TB)
(RS Pts.—Chargers 255, Buccaneers 150)
*SAN DIEGO vs. **TENNESSEE
RS: Chargers lead series, 24-13-1
PS: Titans lead series, 3-1
1960—Oilers, 38-28 (H)
      Chargers, 24-21 (LA)
      ***Oilers, 24-16 (H)
1961—Chargers, 34-24 (SD)
      Oilers, 33-13 (H)
      ***Oilers, 10-3 (SD)

1962—Oilers, 42-17 (SD)
      Oilers, 33-27 (H)
1963—Chargers, 27-0 (SD)
      Chargers 20-14 (H)
1964—Chargers, 27-21 (SD)
      Chargers, 20-17 (H)
1965—Chargers, 31-14 (SD)
      Chargers, 37-26 (H)
1966—Chargers, 28-22 (H)
1967—Chargers, 13-3 (SD)
      Oilers, 24-17 (H)
1968—Chargers, 30-14 (SD)
1969—Chargers, 21-17 (H)
1970—Tie, 31-31 (SD)
1971—Oilers, 49-33 (H)
1972—Chargers, 34-20 (SD)
1974—Oilers, 21-14 (H)
1975—Oilers, 33-17 (H)
1976—Chargers, 30-27 (SD)
1978—Chargers, 45-24 (H)
1979—****Oilers, 17-14 (SD)
1984—Chargers, 31-14 (SD)
1985—Oilers, 37-35 (H)
1986—Chargers, 27-0 (SD)
1987—Oilers, 33-18 (H)
1989—Oilers, 34-27 (SD)
1990—Oilers, 17-7 (SD)
1992—Oilers, 27-0 (H)
1993—Chargers, 18-17 (SD)
1998—Chargers, 13-7 (T)
2004—Chargers, 38-17 (SD)
2006—Chargers, 40-7 (SD)
2007—Chargers, 23-17 (T) OT
      *****Chargers, 17-6 (SD)
2009—Chargers, 42-17 (T)
2010—Chargers, 33-25 (SD)
(RS Pts.—Chargers 970, Titans 837)
(PS Pts.—Titans 57, Chargers 50)
*Franchise in Los Angeles prior to 1961
**Franchise in Houston prior to 1997;
known as Oilers prior to 1999
***AFL Championship
****AFC Divisional Playoff
*****AFC First-Round Playoff
SAN DIEGO vs. WASHINGTON
RS: Redskins lead series, 6-3
1973—Redskins, 38-0 (W)
1980—Redskins, 40-17 (W)
1983—Redskins, 27-24 (SD)
1986—Redskins, 30-27 (SD)
1989—Redskins, 26-21 (W)
1998—Redskins, 24-20 (W)
2001—Chargers, 30-3 (SD)
2005—Chargers, 23-17 (W) OT
2009—Chargers, 23-20 (SD)
(RS Pts.—Redskins 225, Chargers 185)

SAN FRANCISCO vs. ARIZONA
RS: 49ers lead series, 23-16;
See Arizona vs. San Francisco
SAN FRANCISCO vs. ATLANTA
RS: 49ers lead series, 44-29-1
PS: Falcons lead series, 1-0;
See Atlanta vs. San Francisco
SAN FRANCISCO vs. BALTIMORE
RS: Ravens lead series, 2-1;
See Baltimore vs. San Francisco
SAN FRANCISCO vs. BUFFALO
RS: Series tied, 5-5;
See Buffalo vs. San Francisco

SAN FRANCISCO vs. CAROLINA
RS: Panthers lead series, 10-7;
See Carolina vs. San Francisco

SAN FRANCISCO vs. CHICAGO
RS: Bears lead series, 29-28-1
PS: 49ers lead series, 3-0;
See Chicago vs. San Francisco

SAN FRANCISCO vs. CINCINNATI
RS: 49ers lead series, 8-3
PS: 49ers lead series, 2-0;
See Cincinnati vs. San Francisco

SAN FRANCISCO vs. CLEVELAND
RS: Browns lead series, 11-6;
See Cleveland vs. San Francisco

SAN FRANCISCO vs. DALLAS
RS: 49ers lead series, 14-10-1
PS: Cowboys lead series, 5-2;
See Dallas vs. San Francisco

SAN FRANCISCO vs. DENVER
RS: Series tied, 6-6
PS: 49ers lead series, 1-0;
See Denver vs. San Francisco

SAN FRANCISCO vs. DETROIT
RS: 49ers lead series, 34-26-1
PS: Series tied, 1-1;
See Detroit vs. San Francisco

SAN FRANCISCO vs. GREEN BAY
RS: Packers lead series, 30-25-1
PS: Packers lead series, 4-1;
See Green Bay vs. San Francisco

SAN FRANCISCO vs. HOUSTON
RS: Series tied, 1-1;
See Houston vs. San Francisco

SAN FRANCISCO vs. INDIANAPOLIS
RS: Colts lead series, 24-18;
See Indianapolis vs. San Francisco

SAN FRANCISCO vs. JACKSONVILLE
RS: Jaguars lead series, 2-1;
See Jacksonville vs. San Francisco

SAN FRANCISCO vs. KANSAS CITY
RS: 49ers lead series, 6-5;
See Kansas City vs. San Francisco

SAN FRANCISCO vs. MIAMI
RS: Dolphins lead series, 6-4
PS: 49ers lead series, 1-0;
See Miami vs. San Francisco

SAN FRANCISCO vs. MINNESOTA
RS: Vikings lead series, 20-18-1
PS: 49ers lead series, 4-1;
See Minnesota vs. San Francisco

SAN FRANCISCO vs. NEW ENGLAND
RS: 49ers lead series, 7-4;
See New England vs. San Francisco

SAN FRANCISCO vs. NEW ORLEANS
RS: 49ers lead series, 45-24-2;
See New Orleans vs. San Francisco

SAN FRANCISCO vs. N.Y. GIANTS
RS: Giants lead series, 14-13
PS: 49ers lead series, 4-3;
See N.Y. Giants vs. San Francisco

SAN FRANCISCO vs. N.Y. JETS
RS: 49ers lead series, 9-2;
See N.Y. Jets vs. San Francisco

SAN FRANCISCO vs. OAKLAND
RS: Series tied, 6-6;
See Oakland vs. San Francisco

SAN FRANCISCO vs. PHILADELPHIA
RS: 49ers lead series, 16-12-1
PS: 49ers lead series, 1-0;
See Philadelphia vs. San Francisco

SAN FRANCISCO vs. PITTSBURGH
RS: 49ers lead series, 10-9;
See Pittsburgh vs. San Francisco

SAN FRANCISCO vs. ST. LOUIS
RS: Rams lead series, 61-59-2
PS: 49ers lead series, 1-0;
See St. Louis vs. San Francisco

SAN FRANCISCO vs. SAN DIEGO
RS: Series tied, 6-6
PS: 49ers lead series, 1-0;
See San Diego vs. San Francisco

SAN FRANCISCO vs. SEATTLE
RS: Seahawks lead series, 13-11
1976—49ers, 37-21 (Sea)
1979—Seahawks, 35-24 (SF)
1985—49ers, 19-6 (SF)
1988—49ers, 38-7 (Sea)
1991—49ers, 24-22 (Sea)
1997—Seahawks, 38-9 (Sea)
2002—49ers, 28-21 (Sea)
    49ers, 31-24 (SF)
2003—Seahawks, 20-19 (Sea)
    Seahawks, 24-17 (SF)
2004—Seahawks, 34-0 (Sea)
    Seahawks, 42-27 (SF)
2005—Seahawks, 27-25 (SF)
    Seahawks, 41-3 (Sea)
2006—49ers, 20-14 (SF)
    49ers, 24-14 (Sea)
2007—Seahawks, 23-3 (SF)
    Seahawks, 24-0 (Sea)
2008—49ers, 33-30 (Sea) OT
    Seahawks, 34-13 (SF)
2009—49ers, 23-10 (SF)
    Seahawks, 20-17 (Sea)
2010—Seahawks, 31-6 (Sea)
    49ers, 40-21 (SF)
(RS Pts.—Seahawks 583, 49ers 480)

SAN FRANCISCO vs. TAMPA BAY
RS: 49ers lead series, 15-4
PS: Buccaneers lead series, 1-0
1977—49ers, 20-10 (SF)
1978—49ers, 6-3 (SF)
1979—49ers, 23-7 (SF)
1980—Buccaneers, 24-23 (SF)
1983—49ers, 35-21 (SF)
1984—49ers, 24-17 (SF)
1986—49ers, 31-7 (TB)
1987—49ers, 24-10 (TB)
1989—49ers, 20-16 (TB)
1990—49ers, 31-7 (SF)
1992—49ers, 21-14 (SF)
1993—49ers, 45-21 (TB)
1994—49ers, 41-16 (SF)
1997—Buccaneers, 13-6 (TB)
2002—*Buccaneers, 31-6 (TB)
2003—49ers, 24-7 (SF)
2004—Buccaneers, 35-3 (TB)
2005—49ers, 15-10 (SF)
2007—49ers, 21-19 (SF)
2010—Buccaneers, 21-0 (SF)
(RS Pts.—49ers 413, Buccaneers 278)
(PS Pts.—Buccaneers 31, 49ers 6)
*NFC Divisional Playoff

SAN FRANCISCO vs. *TENNESSEE
RS: 49ers lead series, 7-5
1970—49ers, 30-20 (H)
1975—Oilers, 27-13 (SF)
1978—Oilers, 20-19 (H)
1981—49ers, 28-6 (SF)
1984—49ers, 34-21 (H)

1987—49ers, 27-20 (SF)
1990—49ers, 24-21 (H)
1993—Oilers, 10-7 (SF)
1996—49ers, 10-9 (H)
1999—49ers, 24-22 (SF)
2005—Titans, 33-22 (T)
2009—Titans, 34-27 (SF)
(RS Pts.—49ers 265, Titans 243)
*Franchise in Houston prior to 1997;
known as Oilers prior to 1999

SAN FRANCISCO vs. WASHINGTON
RS: 49ers lead series, 14-9-1
PS: 49ers lead series, 3-1
1952—49ers, 23-17 (W)
1954—49ers, 41-7 (SF)
1955—Redskins, 7-0 (W)
1961—49ers, 35-3 (SF)
1967—Redskins, 31-28 (W)
1969—Tie, 17-17 (SF)
1970—49ers, 26-17 (SF)
1971—*49ers, 24-20 (SF)
1973—Redskins, 33-9 (W)
1976—Redskins, 24-21 (SF)
1978—Redskins, 38-20 (W)
1981—49ers, 30-17 (W)
1983—**Redskins, 24-21 (W)
1984—49ers, 37-31 (SF)
1985—49ers, 35-8 (W)
1986—Redskins, 14-6 (W)
1988—49ers, 37-21 (SF)
1990—49ers, 26-13 (SF)
    *49ers, 28-10 (SF)
1992—*49ers, 20-13 (SF)
1994—49ers, 37-22 (W)
1996—49ers, 19-16 (W) OT
1998—49ers, 45-10 (W)
1999—Redskins, 26-20 (SF) OT
2002—49ers, 20-10 (SF)
2004—Redskins, 26-16 (SF)
2005—Redskins, 52-17 (W)
2008—49ers, 27-24 (SF)
(RS Pts.—49ers 592, Redskins 484)
(PS Pts.—49ers 93, Redskins 67)
*NFC Divisional Playoff
**NFC Championship

SEATTLE vs. ARIZONA
RS: Cardinals lead series, 13-11;
See Arizona vs. Seattle

SEATTLE vs. ATLANTA
RS: Seahawks lead series, 8-4;
See Atlanta vs. Seattle

SEATTLE vs. BALTIMORE
RS: Ravens lead series, 2-1;
See Baltimore vs. Seattle

SEATTLE vs. BUFFALO
RS: Seahawks lead series, 6-5;
See Buffalo vs. Seattle

SEATTLE vs. CAROLINA
RS: Series tied, 2-2
PS: Seahawks lead series, 1-0;
See Carolina vs. Seattle

SEATTLE vs. CHICAGO
RS: Seahawks lead series, 8-4
PS: Bears lead series, 2-0;
See Chicago vs. Seattle

SEATTLE vs. CINCINNATI
RS: Seahawks lead series, 9-8
PS: Bengals lead series, 1-0;
See Cincinnati vs. Seattle

SEATTLE vs. CLEVELAND
RS: Seahawks lead series, 11-5;
See Cleveland vs. Seattle
SEATTLE vs. DALLAS
RS: Cowboys lead series, 8-4
PS: Seahawks lead series, 1-0;
See Dallas vs. Seattle
SEATTLE vs. DENVER
RS: Broncos lead series, 34-18
PS: Seahawks lead series, 1-0;
See Denver vs. Seattle
SEATTLE vs. DETROIT
RS: Seahawks lead series, 7-4;
See Detroit vs. Seattle
SEATTLE vs. GREEN BAY
RS: Packers lead series, 8-5
PS: Packers lead series, 2-0;
See Green Bay vs. Seattle
SEATTLE vs. HOUSTON
RS: Series tied, 1-1;
See Houston vs. Seattle
SEATTLE vs. INDIANAPOLIS
RS: Colts lead series, 6-4;
See Indianapolis vs. Seattle
SEATTLE vs. JACKSONVILLE
RS: Seahawks lead series, 4-2;
See Jacksonville vs. Seattle
SEATTLE vs. KANSAS CITY
RS: Chiefs lead series, 32-18;
See Kansas City vs. Seattle
SEATTLE vs. MIAMI
RS: Dolphins lead series, 7-3
PS: Dolphins lead series, 2-1;
See Miami vs. Seattle
SEATTLE vs. MINNESOTA
RS: Seahawks lead series, 6-5;
See Minnesota vs. Seattle
SEATTLE vs. NEW ENGLAND
RS: Patriots lead series, 8-7;
See New England vs. Seattle
SEATTLE vs. NEW ORLEANS
RS: Saints lead series, 6-5
PS: Seahawks lead series, 1-0;
See New Orleans vs. Seattle
SEATTLE vs. N.Y. GIANTS
RS: Giants lead series, 9-5;
See N.Y. Giants vs. Seattle
SEATTLE vs. N.Y. JETS
RS: Seahawks lead series, 9-8;
See N.Y. Jets vs. Seattle
SEATTLE vs. OAKLAND
RS: Raiders lead series, 28-23
PS: Series tied, 1-1;
See Oakland vs. Seattle
SEATTLE vs. PHILADELPHIA
RS: Eagles lead series, 7-5;
See Philadelphia vs. Seattle
SEATTLE vs. PITTSBURGH
RS: Seahawks lead series, 8-7
PS: Steelers lead series, 1-0;
See Pittsburgh vs. Seattle
SEATTLE vs. ST. LOUIS
RS: Seahawks lead series, 15-10
PS: Rams lead series, 1-0;
See St. Louis vs. Seattle
SEATTLE vs. SAN DIEGO
RS: Seahawks lead series, 26-23;
See San Diego vs. Seattle
SEATTLE vs. SAN FRANCISCO
RS: Seahawks lead series, 13-11;
See San Francisco vs. Seattle

SEATTLE vs. TAMPA BAY
RS: Seahawks lead series, 7-4
1976—Seahawks, 13-10 (TB)
1977—Seahawks, 30-23 (S)
1994—Seahawks, 22-21 (S)
1996—Seahawks, 17-13 (TB)
1999—Buccaneers, 16-3 (S)
2004—Seahawks, 10-6 (TB)
2006—Seahawks, 23-7 (TB)
2007—Seahawks, 20-6 (S)
2008—Buccaneers, 20-10 (TB)
2009—Buccaneers, 24-7 (S)
2010—Seahawks, 35-15 (TB)
(RS Pts.—Buccaneers 184, Seahawks 170)
SEATTLE vs. *TENNESSEE
RS: Seahawks lead series, 9-5
PS: Titans lead series, 1-0
1977—Oilers, 22-10 (S)
1979—Seahawks, 34-14 (S)
1980—Seahawks, 26-7 (H)
1981—Oilers, 35-17 (H)
1982—Oilers, 23-21 (H)
1987—**Oilers, 23-20 (H) OT
1988—Seahawks, 27-24 (S)
1990—Seahawks, 13-10 (S) OT
1993—Oilers, 24-14 (H)
1994—Seahawks, 16-14 (H)
1996—Seahawks, 23-16 (S)
1997—Seahawks, 16-13 (S)
1998—Seahawks, 20-18 (S)
2005—Seahawks, 28-24 (T)
2009—Titans, 17-13 (S)
(RS Pts.—Seahawks 278, Titans 261)
(PS Pts.—Titans 23, Seahawks 20)
*Franchise in Houston prior to 1997;
known as Oilers prior to 1999
**AFC First-Round Playoff
SEATTLE vs. WASHINGTON
RS: Redskins lead series, 10-4
PS: Seahawks lead series, 2-0
1976—Redskins, 31-7 (W)
1980—Seahawks, 14-0 (W)
1983—Redskins, 27-17 (S)
1986—Redskins, 19-14 (W)
1989—Redskins, 29-0 (S)
1992—Redskins, 16-3 (S)
1994—Seahawks, 28-7 (W)
1996—Seahawks, 27-20 (W)
1998—Seahawks, 24-14 (S)
2001—Redskins, 27-14 (W)
2002—Redskins, 14-3 (S)
2003—Redskins, 27-20 (W)
2005—Redskins, 20-17 (W) OT
*Seahawks, 20-10 (S)
2007—**Seahawks, 35-14 (S)
2008—Redskins, 20-17 (S)
(RS Pts.—Redskins 271, Seahawks 205)
(PS Pts.—Seahawks 55, Redskins 24)
*NFC Divisional Playoff
**NFC First-Round Playoff

TAMPA BAY vs. ARIZONA
RS: Buccaneers lead series, 9-8;
See Arizona vs. Tampa Bay
TAMPA BAY vs. ATLANTA
RS: Buccaneers lead series, 18-17;
See Atlanta vs. Tampa Bay
TAMPA BAY vs. BALTIMORE
RS: Series tied, 2-2;
See Baltimore vs. Tampa Bay

TAMPA BAY vs. BUFFALO
RS: Buccaneers lead series, 6-3;
See Buffalo vs. Tampa Bay
TAMPA BAY vs. CAROLINA
RS: Panthers lead series, 12-9;
See Carolina vs. Tampa Bay
TAMPA BAY vs. CHICAGO
RS: Bears lead series, 35-18;
See Chicago vs. Tampa Bay
TAMPA BAY vs. CINCINNATI
RS: Buccaneers lead series, 7-3;
See Cincinnati vs. Tampa Bay
TAMPA BAY vs. CLEVELAND
RS: Browns lead series, 5-3;
See Cleveland vs. Tampa Bay
TAMPA BAY vs. DALLAS
RS: Cowboys lead series, 9-3
PS: Cowboys lead series, 2-0;
See Dallas vs. Tampa Bay
TAMPA BAY vs. DENVER
RS: Broncos lead series, 5-2;
See Denver vs. Tampa Bay
TAMPA BAY vs. DETROIT
RS: Lions lead series, 20-25
PS: Buccaneers lead series, 1-0;
See Detroit vs. Tampa Bay
TAMPA BAY vs. GREEN BAY
RS: Packers lead series, 29-21-1
PS: Packers lead series, 1-0;
See Green Bay vs. Tampa Bay
TAMPA BAY vs. HOUSTON
RS: Series tied, 1-1;
See Houston vs. Tampa Bay
TAMPA BAY vs. INDIANAPOLIS
RS: Colts lead series, 7-4;
See Indianapolis vs. Tampa Bay
TAMPA BAY vs. JACKSONVILLE
RS: Jaguars lead series, 3-1;
See Jacksonville vs. Tampa Bay
TAMPA BAY vs. KANSAS CITY
RS: Series tied, 5-5;
See Kansas City vs. Tampa Bay
TAMPA BAY vs. MIAMI
RS: Dolphins lead series, 5-4;
See Miami vs. Tampa Bay
TAMPA BAY vs. MINNESOTA
RS: Vikings lead series, 31-20;
See Minnesota vs. Tampa Bay
TAMPA BAY vs. NEW ENGLAND
RS: Patriots lead series, 5-2;
See New England vs. Tampa Bay
TAMPA BAY vs. NEW ORLEANS
RS: Saints lead series, 22-16;
See New Orleans vs. Tampa Bay
TAMPA BAY vs. N.Y. GIANTS
RS: Giants lead series, 11-6
PS: Giants lead series, 1-0;
See N.Y. Giants vs. Tampa Bay
TAMPA BAY vs. N.Y. JETS
RS: Jets lead series, 9-1;
See N.Y. Jets vs. Tampa Bay
TAMPA BAY vs. OAKLAND
RS: Raiders lead series, 6-1
PS: Buccaneers lead series, 1-0;
See Oakland vs. Tampa Bay
TAMPA BAY vs. PHILADELPHIA
RS: Eagles lead series, 6-5
PS: Series tied, 2-2;
See Philadelphia vs. Tampa Bay
TAMPA BAY vs. PITTSBURGH
RS: Steelers lead series, 8-1;

See Pittsburgh vs. Tampa Bay
TAMPA BAY vs. ST. LOUIS
RS: Rams lead series, 9-8
PS: Rams lead series, 2-0;
See St. Louis vs. Tampa Bay
TAMPA BAY vs. SAN DIEGO
RS: Chargers lead series, 8-1;
See San Diego vs. Tampa Bay
TAMPA BAY vs. SAN FRANCISCO
RS: 49ers lead series, 15-4
PS: Buccaneers lead series, 1-0;
See San Francisco vs. Tampa Bay
TAMPA BAY vs. SEATTLE
RS: Seahawks lead series, 7-4;
See Seattle vs. Tampa Bay
TAMPA BAY vs. *TENNESSEE
RS: Titans lead series, 7-2
1976—Oilers, 20-0 (H)
1980—Oilers, 20-14 (H)
1983—Buccaneers, 33-24 (TB)
1989—Oilers, 20-17 (H)
1995—Oilers, 19-7 (H)
1998—Oilers, 31-22 (TB)
2001—Titans, 31-28 (Tenn) OT
2003—Titans, 33-13 (Tenn)
2007—Buccaneers, 13-10 (TB)
(RS Pts.—Titans 208, Buccaneers 147)
*Franchise in Houston prior to 1997;
known as Oilers prior to 1999*
TAMPA BAY vs. WASHINGTON
RS: Buccaneers lead series, 9-8
PS: Series tied, 1-1
1977—Redskins, 10-0 (TB)
1982—Redskins, 21-13 (TB)
1989—Redskins, 32-28 (W)
1993—Redskins, 23-17 (TB)
1994—Buccaneers, 26-21 (TB)
        Buccaneers, 17-14 (W)
1995—Buccaneers, 14-6 (TB)
1996—Buccaneers, 24-10 (TB)
1998—Buccaneers, 20-16 (W)
1999—*Buccaneers, 14-13 (TB)
2000—Buccaneers, 20-17 (W) OT
2003—Buccaneers, 35-13 (W)
2004—Redskins, 16-10 (W)
2005—Buccaneers, 36-35 (TB)
        **Redskins, 17-10 (TB)
2006—Buccaneers, 20-17 (TB)
2007—Buccaneers, 19-13 (TB)
2009—Redskins, 16-13 (W)
2010—Buccaneers, 17-16 (W)
(RS Pts.—Buccaneers 322, Redskins 303)
(PS Pts.—Redskins 30, Buccaneers 24)
NFC Divisional Playoff
**NFC First-Round Playoff*

TENNESSEE VS. ARIZONA
RS: Cardinals lead series, 5-4;
See Arizona vs. Tennessee
TENNESSEE vs. ATLANTA
RS: Titans lead series, 7-5;
See Atlanta vs. Tennessee
TENNESSEE vs. BALTIMORE
RS: Series tied, 8-8
PS: Ravens lead series, 2-1;
See Baltimore vs. Tennessee
TENNESSEE vs. BUFFALO
RS: Titans lead series, 25-14
PS: Bills lead series, 2-1;
See Buffalo vs. Tennessee

TENNESSEE vs. CAROLINA
RS: Titans lead series, 2-1;
See Carolina vs. Tennessee
TENNESSEE vs. CHICAGO
RS: Series tied, 5-5;
See Chicago vs. Tennessee
TENNESSEE vs. CINCINNATI
RS: Titans lead series, 39-31-1
PS: Bengals lead series, 1-0;
See Cincinnati vs. Tennessee
TENNESSEE vs. CLEVELAND
RS: Browns lead series, 33-27
PS: Titans lead series, 1-0;
See Cleveland vs. Tennessee
TENNESSEE vs. DALLAS
RS: Cowboys lead series, 7-6;
See Dallas vs. Tennessee
TENNESSEE vs. DENVER
RS: Titans lead series, 20-14-1
PS: Broncos lead series, 2-1;
See Denver vs. Tennessee
TENNESSEE vs. DETROIT
RS: Titans lead series, 7-3;
See Detroit vs. Tennessee
TENNESSEE vs. GREEN BAY
RS: Titans lead series, 6-4;
See Green Bay vs. Tennessee
TENNESSEE vs. HOUSTON
RS: Titans lead series, 13-5;
See Houston vs. Tennessee
TENNESSEE vs. INDIANAPOLIS
RS: Colts lead series, 20-12
PS: Titans lead series, 1-0;
See Indianapolis vs. Tennessee
TENNESSEE vs. JACKSONVILLE
RS: Titans lead series, 18-14
PS: Titans lead series, 1-0;
See Jacksonville vs. Tennessee
TENNESSEE vs. KANSAS CITY
RS: Chiefs lead series, 26-20
PS: Chiefs lead series, 2-0;
See Kansas City vs. Tennessee
TENNESSEE vs. MIAMI
RS: Dolphins lead series, 18-14
PS: Titans lead series, 1-0;
See Miami vs. Tennessee
TENNESSEE vs. MINNESOTA
RS: Vikings lead series, 7-4;
See Minnesota vs. Tennessee
TENNESSEE vs. NEW ENGLAND
RS: Patriots lead series, 21-15-1
PS: Series tied, 1-1;
See New England vs. Tennessee
TENNESSEE vs. NEW ORLEANS
RS: Titans lead series, 7-4-1;
See New Orleans vs. Tennessee
TENNESSEE vs. N.Y. GIANTS
RS: Series tied, 5-5;
See N.Y. Giants vs. Tennessee
TENNESSEE vs. N.Y. JETS
RS: Titans lead series, 21-17-1
PS: Titans lead series, 1-0;
See N.Y. Jets vs. Tennessee
TENNESSEE vs. OAKLAND
RS: Raiders lead series, 23-19
PS: Raiders lead series, 4-0;
See Oakland vs. Tennessee
TENNESSEE vs. PHILADELPHIA
RS: Eagles lead series, 6-4;
See Philadelphia vs. Tennessee

TENNESSEE vs. PITTSBURGH
RS: Steelers lead series, 40-29
PS: Steelers lead series, 3-1;
See Pittsburgh vs. Tennessee
TENNESSEE vs. ST. LOUIS
RS: Rams lead series, 6-4
PS: Rams lead series, 1-0;
See St. Louis vs. Tennessee
TENNESSEE vs. SAN DIEGO
RS: Chargers lead series, 24-13-1
PS: Titans lead series, 3-1;
See San Diego vs. Tennessee
TENNESSEE vs. SAN FRANCISCO
RS: 49ers lead series, 7-5;
See San Francisco vs. Tennessee
TENNESSEE vs. SEATTLE
RS: Seahawks lead series, 9-5
PS: Titans lead series, 1-0;
See Seattle vs. Tennessee
TENNESSEE vs. TAMPA BAY
RS: Titans lead series, 7-2;
See Tampa Bay vs. Tennessee
TENNESSEE vs. WASHINGTON
RS: Titans lead series, 6-5
1971—Redskins, 22-13 (W)
1975—Oilers, 13-10 (H)
1979—Oilers, 29-27 (W)
1985—Redskins, 16-13 (W)
1988—Oilers, 41-17 (H)
1991—Redskins, 16-13 (W) OT
1997—Oilers, 28-14 (T)
2000—Titans, 27-21 (W)
2002—Redskins, 31-14 (T)
2006—Titans, 25-22 (W)
2010—Redskins, 19-16 (T) OT
(RS—Titans 232, Redskins 215)
*Franchise in Houston prior to 1997;
known as Oilers prior to 1999*

WASHINGTON vs. ARIZONA
RS: Redskins lead series, 73-44-2;
See Arizona vs. Washington
WASHINGTON vs. ATLANTA
RS: Redskins lead series, 14-6-1
PS: Redskins lead series, 1-0;
See Atlanta vs. Washington
WASHINGTON vs. BALTIMORE
RS: Ravens lead series, 3-1;
See Baltimore vs. Washington
WASHINGTON vs. BUFFALO
RS: Bills lead series, 7-4
PS: Redskins lead series, 1-0;
See Buffalo vs. Washington
WASHINGTON vs. CAROLINA
RS: Redskins lead series, 7-2;
See Carolina vs. Washington
WASHINGTON vs. CHICAGO
RS: Bears lead series, 20-19-1
PS: Redskins lead series, 4-3;
See Chicago vs. Washington
WASHINGTON vs. CINCINNATI
RS: Series tied, 4-4;
See Cincinnati vs. Washington
WASHINGTON vs. CLEVELAND
RS: Browns lead series, 33-10-1;
See Cleveland vs. Washington
WASHINGTON vs. DALLAS
RS: Cowboys lead series, 60-38-2
PS: Redskins lead series, 2-0;
See Dallas vs. Washington
WASHINGTON vs. DENVER
RS: Broncos lead series, 6-5

PS: Redskins lead series, 1-0;
See Denver vs. Washington
WASHINGTON vs. DETROIT
RS: Redskins lead series, 27-12
PS: Redskins lead series, 3-0;
See Detroit vs. Washington
WASHINGTON vs. GREEN BAY
RS: Packers lead series, 17-13-1
PS: Series tied, 1-1;
See Green Bay vs. Washington
WASHINGTON vs. HOUSTON
RS: Redskins lead series, 2-1;
See Houston vs. Washington
WASHINGTON vs. INDIANAPOLIS
RS: Colts lead series, 19-10;
See Indianapolis vs. Washington
WASHINGTON vs. JACKSONVILLE
RS: Redskins lead series, 4-1;
See Jacksonville vs. Washington
WASHINGTON vs. KANSAS CITY
RS: Chiefs lead series, 7-1;
See Kansas City vs. Washington
WASHINGTON vs. MIAMI
RS: Dolphins lead series, 6-4
PS: Series tied, 1-1;
See Miami vs. Washington
WASHINGTON vs. MINNESOTA
RS: Redskins lead series, 8-7
PS: Redskins lead series, 3-2;
See Minnesota vs. Washington
WASHINGTON vs. NEW ENGLAND
RS: Redskins lead series, 6-2;
See New England vs. Washington
WASHINGTON vs. NEW ORLEANS
RS: Redskins lead series, 15-8;
See New Orleans vs. Washington
WASHINGTON vs. N.Y. GIANTS
RS: Giants lead series, 91-61-4
PS: Series tied, 1-1;
See N.Y. Giants vs. Washington
WASHINGTON vs. N.Y. JETS
RS: Redskins lead series, 8-1;
See N.Y. Jets vs. Washington
WASHINGTON vs. OAKLAND
RS: Raiders lead series, 7-4
PS: Raiders lead series, 1-0;
See Oakland vs. Washington
WASHINGTON vs. PHILADELPHIA
RS: Redskins lead series, 78-68-5
PS: Redskins lead series, 1-0;
See Philadelphia vs. Washington
WASHINGTON vs. PITTSBURGH
RS: Redskins lead series, 42-31-3;
See Pittsburgh vs. Washington
WASHINGTON vs. ST. LOUIS
RS: Redskins lead series, 21-9-1
PS: Series tied, 2-2;
See St. Louis vs. Washington
WASHINGTON vs. SAN DIEGO
RS: Redskins lead series, 6-3;
See San Diego vs. Washington
WASHINGTON vs. SAN FRANCISCO
RS: 49ers lead series, 14-9-1
PS: 49ers lead series, 3-1;
See San Francisco vs. Washington
WASHINGTON vs. SEATTLE
RS: Redskins lead series, 10-4
PS: Seahawks lead series, 2-0;
See Seattle vs. Washington
WASHINGTON vs. TAMPA BAY
RS: Buccaneers lead series, 9-8
PS: Series tied, 1-1;

See Tampa Bay vs. Washington
WASHINGTON vs. TENNESSEE
RS: Titans lead series, 6-5;
See Tennessee vs. Washington

NFL OPENING KICKOFF GAMES (9)
(Home Team in capitals)

Date	Sites*	Teams
Sept. 5, 2002	Giants Stadium (East Rutherford, New Jersey) Times Square (New York, New York)	San Francisco 16, N.Y. GIANTS 13
Sept. 4, 2003	FedExField (Landover, Maryland) National Mall (Washington, D.C.)	WASHINGTON 16, N.Y. Jets 13
Sept. 9, 2004	Gillette Stadium (Foxboro, Massachusetts) Metropolitan Park (Jacksonville, Florida)	NEW ENGLAND 27, Indianapolis 24
Sept. 8, 2005	Gillette Stadium (Foxboro, Massachusetts) Detroit, Michigan Los Angeles Coliseum (Los Angeles, California)	NEW ENGLAND 30, Oakland 20
Sept. 7, 2006	Heinz Field (Pittsburgh, Pennsylvania) Miami, Florida	PITTSBURGH 28, Miami 17
Sept. 6, 2007	RCA Dome (Indianapolis, Indianapolis)	INDIANAPOLIS 41, New Orleans 10
Sept. 4, 2008	Giants Stadium (East Rutherford, New Jersey) Columbus Circle (New York, New York)	N.Y. GIANTS 16, Washington 7
Sept. 10, 2009	Heinz Field (Pittsburgh, Pennsylvania) Point State Park (Pittsburgh, Pennsylvania)	PITTSBURGH 13, Tennessee 10 (OT)
Sept. 9, 2010	Louisiana Superdome (New Orleans, Louisiana) Jackson Square (New Orleans, Louisiana)	NEW ORLEANS 14, Minnesota 9

The first site listed each year designates location of Thursday Night NFL Kickoff Weekend game; subsequent locations indicate site(s) of NFL Kickoff Weekend concert.

SUPER BOWL COMPOSITE STANDINGS

	W	L	Pct.	Pts.	OP
San Francisco 49ers	5	0	1.000	188	89
Baltimore Ravens	1	0	1.000	34	7
New Orleans Saints	1	0	1.000	31	17
New York Jets	1	0	1.000	16	7
Tampa Bay Buccaneers	1	0	1.000	48	21
Green Bay Packers	4	1	.800	158	101
Pittsburgh Steelers	6	2	.750	193	164
New York Giants	3	1	.750	83	87
Dallas Cowboys	5	3	.625	221	132
Oakland/L.A. Raiders	3	2	.600	132	114
Washington Redskins	3	2	.600	122	103
New England Patriots	3	3	.500	121	165
Indianapolis/Baltimore Colts	2	2	.500	69	77
Chicago Bears	1	1	.500	63	39
Kansas City Chiefs	1	1	.500	33	42
Miami Dolphins	2	3	.400	74	103
Denver Broncos	2	4	.333	115	206
St. Louis/L.A. Rams	1	2	.333	59	67
Arizona Cardinals	0	1	.000	23	27
Atlanta Falcons	0	1	.000	19	34
Carolina Panthers	0	1	.000	29	32
San Diego Chargers	0	1	.000	26	49
Seattle Seahawks	0	1	.000	10	21
Tennessee Titans	0	1	.000	16	23
Cincinnati Bengals	0	2	.000	37	46
Philadelphia Eagles	0	2	.000	31	51
Buffalo Bills	0	4	.000	73	139
Minnesota Vikings	0	4	.000	34	95

SUPER BOWL HOST CITIES

South Florida	10	
New Orleans	9	
Los Angeles	7	(LA Coliseum 2, Rose Bowl 5)
Tampa Bay	4	
San Diego	3	
Arizona	2	
Atlanta	2	
Detroit	2	
Houston	2	
Jacksonville	1	
Minneapolis	1	
North Texas	1	
Stanford	1	

FUTURE SUPER BOWL SITES

Super Bowl XLVI	Feb. 5, 2012	Lucas Oil Stadium, Indianapolis, Indiana
Super Bowl XLVII	Feb. 3, 2013 *	Louisiana Superdome New Orleans, Louisiana
Super Bowl XLVIII	Feb. 2, 2014 *	New Meadowlands Stadium New York-New Jersey

*Tentative date

PETE ROZELLE TROPHY/SUPER BOWL MVPs*

Super Bowl I	— QB Bart Starr, Green Bay
Super Bowl II	— QB Bart Starr, Green Bay
Super Bowl III	— QB Joe Namath, N.Y. Jets
Super Bowl IV	— QB Len Dawson, Kansas City
Super Bowl V	— LB Chuck Howley, Dallas
Super Bowl VI	— QB Roger Staubach, Dallas
Super Bowl VII	— S Jake Scott, Miami
Super Bowl VIII	— RB Larry Csonka, Miami
Super Bowl IX	— RB Franco Harris, Pittsburgh
Super Bowl X	— WR Lynn Swann, Pittsburgh
Super Bowl XI	— WR Fred Biletnikoff, Oakland
Super Bowl XII	— DT Randy White and DE Harvey Martin, Dallas
Super Bowl XIII	— QB Terry Bradshaw, Pittsburgh
Super Bowl XIV	— QB Terry Bradshaw, Pittsburgh
Super Bowl XV	— QB Jim Plunkett, Oakland
Super Bowl XVI	— QB Joe Montana, San Francisco
Super Bowl XVII	— RB John Riggins, Washington
Super Bowl XVIII	— RB Marcus Allen, L.A. Raiders
Super Bowl XIX	— QB Joe Montana, San Francisco
Super Bowl XX	— DE Richard Dent, Chicago
Super Bowl XXI	— QB Phil Simms, N.Y. Giants
Super Bowl XXII	— QB Doug Williams, Washington
Super Bowl XXIII	— WR Jerry Rice, San Francisco
Super Bowl XXIV	— QB Joe Montana, San Francisco
Super Bowl XXV	— RB Ottis Anderson, N.Y. Giants
Super Bowl XXVI	— QB Mark Rypien, Washington
Super Bowl XXVII	— QB Troy Aikman, Dallas
Super Bowl XXVIII	— RB Emmitt Smith, Dallas
Super Bowl XXIX	— QB Steve Young, San Francisco
Super Bowl XXX	— CB Larry Brown, Dallas
Super Bowl XXXI	— KR-PR Desmond Howard, Green Bay
Super Bowl XXXII	— RB Terrell Davis, Denver
Super Bowl XXXIII	— QB John Elway, Denver
Super Bowl XXXIV	— QB Kurt Warner, St. Louis
Super Bowl XXXV	— LB Ray Lewis, Baltimore
Super Bowl XXXVI	— QB Tom Brady, New England
Super Bowl XXXVII	— S Dexter Jackson, Tampa Bay
Super Bowl XXXVIII	— QB Tom Brady, New England
Super Bowl XXXIX	— WR Deion Branch, New England
Super Bowl XL	— WR Hines Ward, Pittsburgh
Super Bowl XLI	— QB Peyton Manning, Indianapolis
Super Bowl XLII	— QB Eli Manning, N.Y. Giants
Super Bowl XLIII	— WR Santonio Holmes, Pittsburgh
Super Bowl XLIV	— QB Drew Brees, New Orleans
Super Bowl XLV	— QB Aaron Rodgers, Green Bay

* Award named Pete Rozelle Trophy since Super Bowl XXV.

SUPER BOWL MVP BY POSITION

Quarterback	24
Running Back	7
Wide Receiver	6
Defensive End	2
Linebacker	2
Safety	2
Cornerback	1
Defensive Tackle	1
Kick Returner-Punt Returner	1

A defensive end and defensive tackle shared the Super Bowl XII MVP award.

RESULTS

NFC leads AFC, 24-21

Super Bowl	Date	Winner (Share)	Loser (Share)	Score	Site	Attendance
XLV	2-6-11	Green Bay ($83,000)	Pittsburgh ($42,000)	31-25	North Texas	91,060
XLIV	2-7-10	New Orleans ($83,000)	Indianapolis ($42,000)	31-17	South Florida	74,059
XLIII	2-1-09	Pittsburgh ($78,000)	Arizona ($40,000)	27-23	Tampa Bay	70,774
XLII	2-3-08	N.Y. Giants ($78,000)	New England ($40,000)	17-14	Arizona	71,101
XLI	2-4-07	Indianapolis ($73,000)	Chicago ($38,000)	29-17	South Florida	74,512
XL	2-5-06	Pittsburgh ($73,000)	Seattle ($38,000)	21-10	Detroit	68,206
XXXIX	2-6-05	New England ($68,000)	Philadelphia ($36,500)	24-21	Jacksonville	78,125
XXXVIII	2-1-04	New England ($68,000)	Carolina ($36,500)	32-29	Houston	71,525
* XXXVII	1-26-03	Tampa Bay ($63,000)	Oakland ($35,000)	48-21	San Diego	67,603
* XXXVI	2-3-02	New England ($63,000)	St. Louis ($34,500)	20-17	New Orleans	72,922
XXXV	1-28-01	Baltimore ($58,000)	N.Y. Giants ($34,500)	34-7	Tampa Bay	71,921
* XXXIV	1-30-00	St. Louis ($58,000)	Tennessee ($33,000)	23-16	Atlanta	72,625
XXXIII	1-31-99	Denver ($53,000)	Atlanta ($32,500)	34-19	South Florida	74,803
XXXII	1-25-98	Denver ($48,000)	Green Bay ($29,000)	31-24	San Diego	68,912
XXXI	1-26-97	Green Bay ($48,000)	New England ($29,000)	35-21	New Orleans	72,301
XXX	1-28-96	Dallas ($42,000)	Pittsburgh ($27,000)	27-17	Arizona	76,347
XXIX	1-29-95	San Francisco ($42,000)	San Diego ($26,000)	49-26	South Florida	74,107
* XXVIII	1-30-94	Dallas ($38,000)	Buffalo ($23,500)	30-13	Atlanta	72,817
XXVII	1-31-93	Dallas ($36,000)	Buffalo ($18,000)	52-17	Pasadena	98,374
XXVI	1-26-92	Washington ($36,000)	Buffalo ($18,000)	37-24	Minneapolis	63,130
* XXV	1-27-91	N.Y. Giants ($36,000)	Buffalo ($18,000)	20-19	Tampa Bay	73,813
XXIV	1-28-90	San Francisco ($36,000)	Denver ($18,000)	55-10	New Orleans	72,919
XXIII	1-22-89	San Francisco ($36,000)	Cincinnati ($18,000)	20-16	South Florida	75,129
XXII	1-31-88	Washington ($36,000)	Denver ($18,000)	42-10	San Diego	73,302
XXI	1-25-87	N.Y. Giants ($36,000)	Denver ($18,000)	39-20	Pasadena	101,063
XX	1-26-86	Chicago ($36,000)	New England ($18,000)	46-10	New Orleans	73,818
XIX	1-20-85	San Francisco ($36,000)	Miami ($18,000)	38-16	Stanford	84,059
XVIII	1-22-84	L.A. Raiders ($36,000)	Washington ($18,000)	38-9	Tampa Bay	72,920
* XVII	1-30-83	Washington ($36,000)	Miami ($18,000)	27-17	Pasadena	103,667
XVI	1-24-82	San Francisco ($18,000)	Cincinnati ($9,000)	26-21	Pontiac	81,270
XV	1-25-81	Oakland ($18,000)	Philadelphia ($9,000)	27-10	New Orleans	76,135
XIV	1-20-80	Pittsburgh ($18,000)	Los Angeles ($9,000)	31-19	Pasadena	103,985
XIII	1-21-79	Pittsburgh ($18,000)	Dallas ($9,000)	35-31	South Florida	79,484
XII	1-15-78	Dallas ($18,000)	Denver ($9,000)	27-10	New Orleans	75,583
XI	1-9-77	Oakland ($15,000)	Minnesota ($7,500)	32-14	Pasadena	103,438
X	1-18-76	Pittsburgh ($15,000)	Dallas ($7,500)	21-17	South Florida	80,187
IX	1-12-75	Pittsburgh ($15,000)	Minnesota ($7,500)	16-6	New Orleans	80,997
VIII	1-13-74	Miami ($15,000)	Minnesota ($7,500)	24-7	Houston	71,882
VII	1-14-73	Miami ($15,000)	Washington ($7,500)	14-7	Los Angeles	90,182
VI	1-16-72	Dallas ($15,000)	Miami ($7,500)	24-3	New Orleans	81,023
V	1-17-71	Baltimore ($15,000)	Dallas ($7,500)	16-13	South Florida	79,204
* IV	1-11-70	Kansas City ($15,000)	Minnesota ($7,500)	23-7	New Orleans	80,562
III	1-12-69	N.Y. Jets ($15,000)	Baltimore ($7,500)	16-7	South Florida	75,389
II	1-14-68	Green Bay ($15,000)	Oakland ($7,500)	33-14	South Florida	75,546
I	1-15-67	Green Bay ($15,000)	Kansas City ($7,500)	35-10	Los Angeles	61,946

* One week between conference championship games and Super Bowl; all others had two weeks between conference championship games and Super Bowl.

For historical Super Bowl game recaps, box scores, and video highlights, please visit www.SuperBowl.com.

SUPER BOWL XLV

Cowboys Stadium, North Texas

February 6, 2011, Attendance: 91,060

GREEN BAY 31, PITTSBURGH 25— Aaron Rodgers passed for 304 yards and three touchdowns, and two interceptions by the Packers' defense resulted in 14 points, as Green Bay won its fourth Super Bowl title. Faced with third-and-one in the middle of the first quarter, Rodgers completed a 29-yard touchdown pass down the right sideline to Jordy Nelson for a 7-0 lead. On the next play from scrimmage, Nick Collins intercepted a pass intended for Mike Wallace and returned it 37 yards for a touchdown. The Packers scored 14 points in 24 seconds. The Steelers responded with a 13-play drive, keyed by an 18-yard scramble on third-and-9 by Roethlisberger followed three plays later by a 13-yard pass to Emmanuel Sanders on third-and-13, that led to Shaun Suisham's 33-yard field goal. Later in the second quarter, Jarrett Bush intercepted a pass near midfield. A 16-yard pass to Nelson and 12-yard run by James Starks led to Rodgers' 21-yard touchdown pass to Greg Jennings for a 21-3 Packers' lead with 2:24 to play in the half. Roethlisberger's 14-yard pass to Hines Ward on third-and-10 kept alive the next drive, and a few plays later Ward caught an 8-yard touchdown pass on first-and-goal with 39 seconds left in the half to trim the deficit to 21-10. The Steelers' defense forced a punt on Green Bay's first drive of the second half, and the offense needed just five plays to cover 50 yards, keyed by a 17-yard run by Rashard Mendenhall and 16-yard run by Isaac Redman, and capped by Mendenhall's 8-yard touchdown run. Down four points, the Steelers' defense forced a three-and-out and drove to the Packers' 29. But a three-yard tackle-for-loss by Desmond

Bishop and a 2-yard sack by Frank Zombo pushed Pittsburgh back to the 34-yard-line and Suisham's 52-yard field-goal attempt sailed wide left. After a flurry of punts, the Steelers regained possession, but on the first play of the fourth quarter, Clay Matthews forced Mendenhall to fumble and Bishop recovered at the Packers' 45. Rodgers then completed a 12-yard pass to James Jones on third-and-7 to keep alive the drive. Three plays later, faced with third-and-10, Rodgers found Nelson short over the middle. Nelson sliced through the defense for 38 yards. Jennings' 8-yard touchdown catch two plays later stretched the Packers' lead to 28-17 with 11:57 to play. The Steelers drove to the Packers' 25. Faced with third-and-3, Roethlisberger completed a pass to Wallace deep down the left side for a 25-yard touchdown. With 7:34 to play and down 28-23, Mike Tomlin chose to go for the 2-point conversion, and it worked as Antwaan Randle El took an option pitch from Roethlisberger and cut the deficit to 28-25. The Packers immediately were faced with a third-and-10 and looked as if they would have to give the ball back to Pittsburgh. But Rodgers completed a 31-yard pass to Jennings deep down the middle. A 14-yard run by Starks and 21-yard pass to Jones set up Mason Crosby's 23-yard field goal with 2:07 remaining for a 31-25 lead. The Steelers reached their own 33-yard line with 1:08 to play, but Roethlisberger's final three pass attempts fell incomplete and the Packers clinched their fourth Super Bowl title in 14 years. Rodgers was 24 of 39 for 304 yards and 3 touchdowns and was named Super Bowl MVP. His main target was Nelson, who had 9 receptions for 140 yards. Defensively, Charlie Peprah had 10 tackles and Bishop registered three tackles for losses. Roethlisberger completed 25 of 40 passes for 263 yards and 2 touchdowns, with 2 interceptions.

Pittsburgh (25)		Green Bay (31)
Offense		
Hines Ward	WR	Greg Jennings
Jonathan Scott	LT	Chad Clifton
Chris Kemoeatu	LG	Daryn Colledge
Doug Legursky	C	Scott Wells
Ramon Foster	RG	Josh Sitton
Flozell Adams	RT	Bryan Bulaga
Heath Miller	TE/WR	James Jones
Matt Spaeth	TE/WR	Donald Driver
Ben Roethlisberger	QB	Aaron Rodgers
Rashard Mendenhall	RB	James Starks
David Johnson	FB/WR	Jordy Nelson
Defense		
Brett Keisel	RDE/LDE	Ryan Pickett
Casey Hampton	NT	B.J. Raji
LaMarr Woodley	LOLB	Clay Matthews
James Farrior	LILB	A.J. Hawk
Lawrence Timmons	RILB	Desmond Bishop
James Harrison	ROLB	Frank Zombo
William Gay	CB/RDE	Howard Green
Bryant McFadden	LCB/DE	C.J. Wilson

Ike Taylor	RCB	Tramon Williams
Troy Polamalu	SS/LCB	Charles Woodson
Ryan Clark	FS	Nick Collins

SUBSTITUTIONS

OFFICIALS

SCORING

Pittsburgh (AFC)	0 10 7 8	— 25
Green Bay (NFC)	14 7 0 10	— 31

GB — Nelson 29 pass from Rodgers (Crosby kick) (3:44)
GB — Collins 37 interception return (Crosby kick) (3:20)
Pitt — FG Suisham 33 (11:08)
GB — Jennings 21 pass from Rodgers (Crosby kick) (2:24)
Pitt — Ward 8 pass from Roethlisberger (Suisham kick) (0:39)
Pitt — Mendenhall 8 run (Suisham kick) (10:19)
GB — Jennings 8 pass from Rodgers (11:57)
Pitt — Wallace 25 pass from Roethlisberger (Randle El run) (7:34)
GB — FG Crosby 23 (2:07)

TEAM STATISTICS	PITT	GB
Total First Downs	19	15
Rushing	8	4
Passing	11	11
Penalty	0	0
Total Net Yardage	387	338
Total Offensive Plays	64	55
Avg. Gain Per Offensive Play	6.0	6.1
Rushes	23	13
Yards Gained Rushing (Net)	126	50
Avg. Yards per Rush	5.5	3.8
Passes Attempted	40	39
Passes Completed	25	24
Had Intercepted	2	0
Tackled Attempting to Pass	1	3
Yards Lost Attempting to Pass	2	16
Yards Gained Passing (Net)	261	288
Punts	3	6
Avg. Distance	51.0	40.5
Punt Returns	4	1
Punt Return Yardage	5	0
Kickoff Returns	6	3
Kickoff Return Yardage	111	63
Interception Return Yardage	0	38
Total Return Yardage (excl. Kickoff)	5	38
Fumbles	1	1
Fumbles Lost	1	0
Own Fumbles Recovered	0	1
Opponent Fumbles Recovered	0	1
Penalties	6	7
Yards Penalized	55	67
Field Goals	1	1
Field Goals Attempted	2	1
Third-Down Efficiency	7/13	6/13
Fourth-Down Efficiency	0/1	0/0
Time of Possession	33:25	26:35

INDIVIDUAL STATISTICS

RUSHING: PITT: Mendenhall 14-63-1, Roethlisberger 4-31-0, Redman 2-19-0, Moore 3-13-0. GB: Starks 11-52-0, Rodgers 2-(-2)-0.
PASSING: PITT: Roethlisberger 40-25-263-2-2. GB: Rodgers 39-24-304-3-0.
RECEIVING: PITT: Wallace 9-89-1, Ward 7-78-1, Randle El 2-50-0, Sanders 2-17-0, Miller 2-12-0, Spaeth 1-9-0, Mendenhall 1-7-0, Brown 1-1-0. GB: Nelson 9-140-1, Jones 5-50-0, Jennings 4-64-2, Driver 2-28-0, Jackson 1-14-0, Quarless 1-5-0, Hall 1-2-0, Crabtree 1-1-0.
KICKOFF RETURNS: PITT: Brown 4-88-0, Redman 1-12-0, Moore 1-11-0. GB: Lee 2-44-0, Nelson 1-19-0.
PUNT RETURNS: PITT: Brown 4-5-0. GB: Williams 1-0-0.
PUNTING: PITT: Kapinos 3-153-51.0. GB: Masthay 6-243-40.5.
INTERCEPTIONS: PITT: None. GB: Collins 1-37-1, Bush 1-1-0.
SACKS: PITT: Harrison 1, Hood 1, Woodley 1. GB: Zombo 1.

AFC CHAMPIONSHIP GAME RESULTS
Includes AFL Championship Games (1960-69)

Season	Date	Winner (Share)	Loser (Share)	Score	Site	Attendance
2010	Jan. 23	Pittsburgh ($38,000)	N.Y. Jets ($38,000)	24-19	Pittsburgh	66,662
2009	Jan. 24	Indianapolis ($38,000)	N.Y. Jets ($38,000)	30-17	Indianapolis	67,650
2008	Jan. 18	Pittsburgh ($37,500)	Baltimore ($37,500)	23-14	Pittsburgh	65,350
2007	Jan. 20	New England ($37,500)	San Diego ($37,500)	21-12	Foxborough	68,756
2006	Jan. 21	Indianapolis ($37,000)	New England ($37,000)	38-34	Indianapolis	57,433
2005	Jan. 22	Pittsburgh ($37,000)	Denver ($37,000)	34-17	Denver	76,775
2004	Jan. 23	New England ($36,500)	Pittsburgh ($36,500)	41-27	Pittsburgh	65,242
2003	Jan. 18	New England ($36,500)	Indianapolis ($36,500)	24-14	Foxborough	68,436
2002	Jan. 19	Oakland ($35,000)	Tennessee ($35,000)	41-24	Oakland	62,544
2001	Jan. 27	New England ($34,500)	Pittsburgh ($34,500)	24-17	Pittsburgh	64,704
2000	Jan. 14	Baltimore ($34,500)	Oakland ($34,500)	16-3	Oakland	62,784
1999	Jan. 23	Tennessee ($33,000)	Jacksonville ($33,000)	33-14	Jacksonville	75,206
1998	Jan. 17	Denver ($32,500)	N.Y. Jets ($32,500)	23-10	Denver	75,482
1997	Jan. 11	Denver ($30,000)	Pittsburgh ($30,000)	24-21	Pittsburgh	61,382
1996	Jan. 12	New England ($29,000)	Jacksonville ($29,000)	20-6	Foxborough	60,190
1995	Jan. 14	Pittsburgh ($27,000)	Indianapolis ($27,000)	20-16	Pittsburgh	61,062
1994	Jan. 15	San Diego ($26,000)	Pittsburgh ($26,000)	17-13	Pittsburgh	61,545
1993	Jan. 23	Buffalo ($23,500)	Kansas City ($23,500)	30-13	Buffalo	76,642
1992	Jan. 17	Buffalo ($18,000)	Miami ($18,000)	29-10	Miami	72,703
1991	Jan. 12	Buffalo ($18,000)	Denver ($18,000)	10-7	Buffalo	80,272
1990	Jan. 20	Buffalo ($18,000)	L.A. Raiders ($18,000)	51-3	Buffalo	80,325
1989	Jan. 14	Denver ($18,000)	Cleveland ($18,000)	37-21	Denver	76,046
1988	Jan. 8	Cincinnati ($18,000)	Buffalo ($18,000)	21-10	Cincinnati	59,747
1987	Jan. 17	Denver ($18,000)	Cleveland ($18,000)	38-33	Denver	76,197
1986	Jan. 11	Denver ($18,000)	Cleveland ($18,000)	23-20*	Cleveland	79,973
1985	Jan. 12	New England ($18,000)	Miami ($18,000)	31-14	Miami	75,662
1984	Jan. 6	Miami ($18,000)	Pittsburgh ($18,000)	45-28	Miami	76,029
1983	Jan. 8	L.A. Raiders ($18,000)	Seattle ($18,000)	30-14	Los Angeles	91,445
1982	Jan. 23	Miami ($18,000)	N.Y. Jets ($18,000)	14-0	Miami	67,396
1981	Jan. 10	Cincinnati ($9,000)	San Diego ($9,000)	27-7	Cincinnati	46,302
1980	Jan. 11	Oakland ($9,000)	San Diego ($9,000)	34-27	San Diego	52,675
1979	Jan. 6	Pittsburgh ($9,000)	Houston ($9,000)	27-13	Pittsburgh	50,475
1978	Jan. 7	Pittsburgh ($9,000)	Houston ($9,000)	34-5	Pittsburgh	50,725
1977	Jan. 1	Denver ($9,000)	Oakland ($9,000)	20-17	Denver	75,044
1976	Dec. 26	Oakland ($8,500)	Pittsburgh ($5,500)	24-7	Oakland	53,821
1975	Jan. 4	Pittsburgh ($8,500)	Oakland ($5,500)	16-10	Pittsburgh	50,609
1974	Dec. 29	Pittsburgh ($8,500)	Oakland ($5,500)	24-13	Oakland	53,800
1973	Dec. 30	Miami ($8,500)	Oakland ($5,500)	27-10	Miami	79,325
1972	Dec. 31	Miami ($8,500)	Pittsburgh ($5,500)	21-17	Pittsburgh	50,845
1971	Jan. 2	Miami ($8,500)	Baltimore ($5,500)	21-0	Miami	76,622
1970	Jan. 3	Baltimore ($8,500)	Oakland ($5,500)	27-17	Baltimore	54,799
1969	Jan. 4	Kansas City ($7,755)	Oakland ($6,252)	17-7	Oakland	53,564
1968	Dec. 29	N.Y. Jets ($7,007)	Oakland ($5,349)	27-23	New York	62,627
1967	Dec. 31	Oakland ($6,321)	Houston ($4,996)	40-7	Oakland	53,330
1966	Jan. 1	Kansas City ($5,309)	Buffalo ($3,799)	31-7	Buffalo	42,080
1965	Dec. 26	Buffalo ($5,189)	San Diego ($3,447)	23-0	San Diego	30,361
1964	Dec. 26	Buffalo ($2,668)	San Diego ($1,738)	20-7	Buffalo	40,242
1963	Jan. 5	San Diego ($2,498)	Boston ($1,596)	51-10	San Diego	30,127
1962	Dec. 23	Dallas ($2,206)	Houston ($1,471)	20-17*	Houston	37,981
1961	Dec. 24	Houston ($1,792)	San Diego ($1,111)	10-3	San Diego	29,556
1960	Jan. 1	Houston ($1,025)	L.A. Chargers ($718)	24-16	Houston	32,183

Sudden death overtime

AFC CHAMPIONSHIP GAME COMPOSITE STANDINGS

	W	L	Pct.	Pts.	OP
Cincinnati Bengals	2	0	1.000	48	17
Buffalo Bills	6	2	.750	180	92
Denver Broncos	6	2	.750	189	166
New England Patriots**	6	2	.750	205	179
Kansas City Chiefs*	3	1	.750	81	61
Miami Dolphins	5	2	.714	152	115
Pittsburgh Steelers	8	7	.533	332	303
Indianapolis Colts#	3	3	.500	125	133
Baltimore Ravens	1	1	.500	30	26
Tennessee Titans###	3	5	.375	133	195
Oakland Raiders###	5	9	.357	272	304
New York Jets	1	4	.200	73	114
San Diego Chargers***	2	7	.222	140	182
Seattle Seahawks	0	1	.000	14	30
Jacksonville Jaguars	0	2	.000	20	53
Cleveland Browns	0	3	.000	74	98

* *One game played when franchise was in Dallas (Texans) (Won 20-17)*
** *One game played when franchise was in Boston (Lost 51-10)*
*** *One game played when franchise was in Los Angeles (Lost 24-16)*
\# *Two games played when franchise was in Baltimore (Won 27-17, lost 21-0)*
\#\# *Six games played when franchise was in Houston and known as Oilers (Won 2, lost 4)*
\#\#\# *Two games played when franchise was in Los Angeles (Won 30-14, lost 51-3)*

2011 AFC CHAMPIONSHIP GAME
Heinz Field, Pittsburgh, Pennsylvania
January 23, 2011, Attendance: 66,662
PITTSBURGH 24, NEW YORK JETS 19—The Steelers jumped out to a 24-0 lead before holding off a furious second-half comeback attempt by the Jets. Pittsburgh won its record eighth AFC title, including its second in three seasons. The Steelers began the game with a 15-play, 66-yard drive, which consumed nine minutes and six seconds, and culminated in Rashard Mendenhall's 1-yard touchdown run. In the second quarter, the Steelers drove to the Jets' 2-yard line before settling for Shaun Suisham's field goal for a 10-0 lead. The Steelers' defense forced a three-and-out, and Ben Roethlisberger completed passes of 24 yards (Heath Miller), 20 yards (Emmanuel Sanders), and 14 yards (Mendenhall) to set up his own 2-yard touchdown scramble for a 17-0 lead. Three plays later, Ike Taylor sacked Mark Sanchez and forced him to fumble. William Gay picked up the ball and returned it 19 yards for a touchdown and 24-0 lead with 1:13 left in the second quarter. Nick Folk kicked a field goal just before halftime, and Sanchez' 45-yard touchdown pass to Santonio Holmes five plays into the third quarter suddenly cut the lead to 24-10. Brodney Pool's interception deep in Steelers territory stopped Pittsburgh's ensuing possession. Late in the third quarter, the Jets began a 17-play, 80-yard drive, but the Steelers stopped Tomlinson for no gain on fourth-and-goal at the 1-yard line with 7:44 to play. The Jets were not done, however, as the Steelers mishandled the snap on the next play. Roethlisberger recovered the ball but was tackled in the end zone by Mike DeVito for a safety, cutting the deficit to 24-12. Following the free kick, the Jets drove 58 yards in 10 plays, capped by Jerricho Cotchery's 4-yard touchdown catch with 3:06 to play, pulling the Jets to within five points. Mendenhall gained one first down and, facing third-and-6 with 2:00 to play, Roethlisberger completed a 14-yard pass to Antonio Brown on third-and-6 to secure the victory. Roethlisberger was 10 of 19 for 133 yards, with 2 interceptions. Mendenhall rushed 27 times for 121 yards. Sanchez completed 20 of 33 for 233 yards and 2 touchdowns.

New York Jets (19)	Offense	Pittsburgh (24)
Ben Hartsock	TE	Max Spaeth
D'Brickashaw Ferguson	LT	Jonathan Scott
Matt Slauson	LG	Chris Kemoeatu
Nick Mangold	C	Maurkice Pouncey
Brandon Moore	RG	Ramon Foster
Wayne Hunter	RT	Flozell Adams
Dustin Keller	TE	Heath Miller
Braylon Edwards	WR	Mike Wallace
Mark Sanchez	QB	Ben Roethlisberger
LaDainian Tomlinson	RB	Rashard Mendenhall
Jerricho Cotchery	WR/FB	David Johnson
	Defense	
Shaun Ellis	DE	Ziggy Hood
Sione Pouha	NT	Casey Hampton
Mike DeVito	DT/DE	Brett Keisel
Bryan Thomas	OLB/LOLB	LaMarr Woodley
Bart Scott	WILL/LILB	James Farrior
David Harris	MIKE/RILB	Lawrence Timmons
Calvin Pace	OLB/ROLB	James Harrison
Darrelle Revis	CB/LCB	Ike Taylor
Antonio Cromartie	CB/RCB	William Gay
Eric Smith	SS/FS	Ryan Clark
Brodney Pool	SS	Troy Polamalu

SUBSTITUTIONS
NEW YORK JETS—Specialists: K—Nick Folk. P—Steve Weatherford. LS—Tanner Purdum. Offense: RB—Shonn Greene, Joe McKnight. FB—Tony Richardson. WR—Santonio Holmes, Brad Smith. OL—Robert Turner. Defense: DT—Martin Tevaseu, DE—Trevor Pryce. LB—Lance Laury, Joshua Mauga, Jason Taylor, Jamaal Westerman. CB—Marquice Cole, Drew Coleman, Dwight Lowery, Kyle Wilson. S—Emanuel Cook, James Ihedigbo. Did Not Play: QB—Mark Brunell. OL—Vladimir Ducasse. Not Active: QB—

Kellen Clemens. FB—John Conner. WR—Patrick Turner. TE—Jeff Cumberland, Matthew Mulligan. DT—Marcus Dixon, Jarron Gilbert. DT—Vernon Gholston.
PITTSBURGH—Specialists: K—Shaun Suisham. P—Jeremy Kapinos. LS—Greg Warren. Offense: RB—Mewelde Moore, Ike Redman. WR—Arnaz Battle, Antonio Brown, Antwaan Randle El, Emmanuel Sanders, Hines Ward. C—Doug Legursky. G—Trai Essex. Defense: DE—Nick Eason. NT—Chris Hoke. LB—Larry Foote, Keyaron Fox, Stevenson Sylvester, Jason Worilds. CB—Keenan Lewis, Anthony Madison, Bryant McFadden. S—Ryan Mundy. DNP: QB—Byron Leftwich. Not Active: QB—Charlie Batch. RB—Jonathan Dwyer. T—Tony Hills, Chris Scott. DT—Steve McLendon. DE—Anthony Smith. CB—Crezdon Butler. S—Will Allen.

OFFICIALS
Referee—Ed Hochuli. Umpire—Garth DeFelice.
Line Judge—Thomas Symonette. Side Judge—Laird Hayes.
Head Linesman—Mark Hittner. Back Judge—Dino Paganelli.
Field Judge—Bob Waggoner.

SCORING

New York Jets	0	3	7	9	—	19
Pittsburgh	7	17	0	0	—	24

Pitt — Mendenhall 1 run (Suisham kick)
Pitt — FG Suisham 20
Pitt — Roethlisberger 2 run (Suisham kick)
Pitt — Gay 19 fumble return (Suisham kick)
NYJ — FG Folk 42
NYJ — Holmes 45 pass from Sanchez (Folk kick)
NYJ — Safety, DeVito tackled Roethlisberger in end zone
NYJ — Cotchery 4 pass from Sanchez (Folk kick)

TEAM STATISTICS	NYJ	PITT
Total First Downs	17	23
Rushing	2	10
Passing	12	9
Penalty	3	4
Total Net Yardage	289	287
Total Offensive Plays	57	64
Average Gain Per Offensive Play	5.1	4.5
Rushes	22	43
Yards Gained Rushing (Net)	70	166
Average Yards per Rush	3.2	3.9
Passes Attempted	33	19
Passes Completed	20	10
Had Intercepted	0	2
Tackled Attempting to Pass	2	2
Yards Lost Attempting to Pass	14	12
Yards Gained Passing (Net)	219	121
Punts	4	1
Average Distance	36.5	38.0
Punt Returns	0	2
Punt Return Yardage	0	10
Kickoff Returns	5	4
Kickoff Return Yardage	51	70
Interception Return Yardage	10	0
Total Return Yardage (not incl. kickoffs)	10	10
Fumbles	2	3
Fumbles Lost	1	0
Own Fumbles Recovered	1	3
Opponent Fumbles Recovered	0	1
Penalties	6	4
Yards Penalized	50	25
Field Goals	1	1
Field Goals Attempted	1	1
Third-Down Efficiency	5/14	6/11
Fourth-Down Efficiency	2/3	0/1
Time of Possession	25:19	34:41

INDIVIDUAL STATISTICS
RUSHING: NYJ: Greene 9-52-0, Tomlinson 9-16-0, Sanchez 3-6-0, Cotchery 1-(-4)-0. PITT: Mendenhall 27-121-1, Redman 4-27-0, Roethlisberger 11-21-1, Moore 1-(-3)-0.

PASSING: NYJ: Sanchez 33-20-233-2-0. PITT: Roethlisberger 19-10-133-0-2. **RECEIVING:** NYJ: Keller 8-64-0, Cotchery 5-33-1, Edwards 3-50-0, Holmes 2-61-1, Smith 2-25-0. PITT: Miller 2-38-0, Mendenhall 2-32-0, Ward 2-14-0, Sanders 1-20-0, Brown 1-14-0, Moore 1-9-0, Wallace 1-6-0.

KICKOFF RETURNS: NYJ: Cotchery 2-23-0, Smith 2-22-0, Turner 1-6-0. PITT: Brown 3-68-0, Spaeth 1-2-0. **PUNT RETURNS:** NYJ: None. PITT: Randle El 2-10-0. **PUNTING:** NYJ: Weatherford 4-146-36.5. PITT: Kapinos 1-38-38.0. **INTERCEPTIONS:** NYJ: Pool 1-9-0, Thomas 1-1-0. PITT: None. **SACKS:** NYJ: Pace 1.0, Pryce 1.0. PITT: Taylor 1.0, Woodley 1.0.

NFC CHAMPIONSHIP GAME RESULTS
Includes NFL Championship Games (1933-1969)

Season	Date	Winner (Share)	Loser (Share)	Score	Site	Attendance
2010	Jan. 23	Green Bay ($38,000)	Chicago ($38,000)	21-14	Chicago	62,377
2009	Jan. 24	New Orleans ($38,000)	Minnesota ($38,000)	31-28*	New Orleans	71,276
2008	Jan. 18	Arizona ($37,500)	Philadelphia ($37,500)	32-25	Glendale	70,650
2007	Jan. 20	N.Y. Giants ($37,500)	Green Bay ($37,500)	23-20*	Green Bay	72,740
2006	Jan. 21	Chicago ($37,000)	New Orleans ($37,000)	39-14	Chicago	61,817
2005	Jan. 22	Seattle ($37,000)	Carolina ($37,000)	34-14	Seattle	67,837
2004	Jan. 23	Philadelphia ($36,500)	Atlanta ($36,500)	27-10	Philadelphia	67,717
2003	Jan. 18	Carolina ($36,500)	Philadelphia ($36,500)	14-3	Philadelphia	67,862
2002	Jan. 19	Tampa Bay ($35,000)	Philadelphia ($35,000)	27-10	Philadelphia	66,713
2001	Jan. 27	St. Louis ($34,500)	Philadelphia ($34,500)	29-24	St. Louis	66,502
2000	Jan. 14	N.Y. Giants ($34,500)	Minnesota ($34,500)	41-0	East Rutherford	79,310
1999	Jan. 23	St. Louis ($33,000)	Tampa Bay ($33,000)	11-6	St. Louis	66,396
1998	Jan. 17	Atlanta ($32,500)	Minnesota ($32,500)	30-27*	Minneapolis	64,060
1997	Jan. 11	Green Bay ($30,000)	San Francisco ($30,000)	23-10	San Francisco	68,987
1996	Jan. 12	Green Bay ($29,000)	Carolina ($29,000)	30-13	Green Bay	60,216
1995	Jan. 14	Dallas ($27,000)	Green Bay ($27,000)	38-27	Dallas	65,135
1994	Jan. 15	San Francisco ($26,000)	Dallas ($26,000)	38-28	San Francisco	69,125
1993	Jan. 23	Dallas ($23,500)	San Francisco ($23,500)	38-21	Dallas	64,902
1992	Jan. 17	Dallas ($18,000)	San Francisco ($18,000)	30-20	San Francisco	64,920
1991	Jan. 12	Washington ($18,000)	Detroit ($18,000)	41-10	Washington	55,585
1990	Jan. 20	N.Y. Giants ($18,000)	San Francisco ($18,000)	15-13	San Francisco	65,750
1989	Jan. 14	San Francisco ($18,000)	L.A. Rams ($18,000)	30-3	San Francisco	65,634
1988	Jan. 8	San Francisco ($18,000)	Chicago ($18,000)	28-3	Chicago	66,946
1987	Jan. 17	Washington ($18,000)	Minnesota ($18,000)	17-10	Washington	55,212
1986	Jan. 11	New York Giants ($18,000)	Washington ($18,000)	17-0	East Rutherford	76,891
1985	Jan. 12	Chicago ($18,000)	L.A. Rams ($18,000)	24-0	Chicago	66,030
1984	Jan. 6	San Francisco ($18,000)	Chicago ($18,000)	23-0	San Francisco	61,336
1983	Jan. 8	Washington ($18,000)	San Francisco ($18,000)	24-21	Washington	55,363
1982	Jan. 22	Washington ($18,000)	Dallas ($18,000)	31-17	Washington	55,045
1981	Jan. 10	San Francisco ($9,000)	Dallas ($9,000)	28-27	San Francisco	60,525
1980	Jan. 11	Philadelphia ($9,000)	Dallas ($9,000)	20-7	Philadelphia	71,522
1979	Jan. 6	Los Angeles ($9,000)	Tampa Bay ($9,000)	9-0	Tampa	72,033
1978	Jan. 7	Dallas ($9,000)	Los Angeles ($9,000)	28-0	Los Angeles	71,086
1977	Jan. 1	Dallas ($9,000)	Minnesota ($9,000)	23-6	Dallas	64,293
1976	Dec. 26	Minnesota ($8,500)	Los Angeles ($5,500)	24-13	Minneapolis	48,379
1975	Jan. 4	Dallas ($8,500)	Los Angeles ($5,500)	37-7	Los Angeles	88,919
1974	Dec. 29	Minnesota ($8,500)	Los Angeles ($5,500)	14-10	Minneapolis	48,444
1973	Dec. 30	Minnesota ($8,500)	Dallas ($5,500)	27-10	Dallas	64,422
1972	Dec. 31	Washington ($8,500)	Dallas ($5,500)	26-3	Washington	53,129
1971	Jan. 2	Dallas ($8,500)	San Francisco ($5,500)	14-3	Dallas	63,409
1970	Jan. 3	Dallas ($8,500)	San Francisco ($5,500)	17-10	San Francisco	59,364
1969	Jan. 4	Minnesota ($7,930)	Cleveland ($5,118)	27-7	Minneapolis	46,503
1968	Dec. 29	Baltimore ($9,306)	Cleveland ($5,963)	34-0	Cleveland	78,410
1967	Dec. 31	Green Bay ($7,950)	Dallas ($5,299)	21-17	Green Bay	50,861
1966	Jan. 1	Green Bay ($9,813)	Dallas ($6,527)	34-27	Dallas	74,152
1965	Jan. 2	Green Bay ($7,819)	Cleveland ($5,288)	23-12	Green Bay	50,777
1964	Dec. 27	Cleveland ($8,052)	Baltimore ($5,571)	27-0	Cleveland	79,544
1963	Dec. 29	Chicago ($5,899)	New York ($4,218)	14-10	Chicago	45,801
1962	Dec. 30	Green Bay ($5,888)	New York ($4,166)	16-7	New York	64,892
1961	Dec. 31	Green Bay ($5,195)	New York ($3,339)	37-0	Green Bay	39,029
1960	Dec. 26	Philadelphia ($5,116)	Green Bay ($3,105)	17-13	Philadelphia	67,325
1959	Dec. 27	Baltimore ($4,674)	New York ($3,083)	31-16	Baltimore	57,545
1958	Dec. 28	Baltimore ($4,718)	New York ($3,111)	23-17*	New York	64,185
1957	Dec. 29	Detroit ($4,295)	Cleveland ($2,750)	59-14	Detroit	55,263
1956	Dec. 30	New York ($3,779)	Chi. Bears ($2,485)	47-7	New York	56,836
1955	Dec. 26	Cleveland ($3,508)	Los Angeles ($2,316)	38-14	Los Angeles	85,693
1954	Dec. 26	Cleveland ($2,478)	Detroit ($1,585)	56-10	Cleveland	43,827
1953	Dec. 27	Detroit ($2,424)	Cleveland ($1,654)	17-16	Detroit	54,577
1952	Dec. 28	Detroit ($2,274)	Cleveland ($1,712)	17-7	Cleveland	50,934
1951	Dec. 23	Los Angeles ($2,108)	Cleveland ($1,483)	24-17	Los Angeles	57,522

Season	Date	Winner (Share)	Loser (Share)	Score	Site	Attendance
1950	Dec. 24	Cleveland ($1,113)	Los Angeles ($686)	30-28	Cleveland	29,751
1949	Dec. 18	Philadelphia ($1,094)	Los Angeles ($739)	14-0	Los Angeles	27,980
1948	Dec. 19	Philadelphia ($1,540)	Chi. Cardinals ($874)	7-0	Philadelphia	36,309
1947	Dec. 28	Chi. Cardinals ($1,132)	Philadelphia ($754)	28-21	Chicago	30,759
1946	Dec. 15	Chi. Bears ($1,975)	New York ($1,295)	24-14	New York	58,346
1945	Dec. 16	Cleveland ($1,469)	Washington ($902)	15-14	Cleveland	32,178
1944	Dec. 17	Green Bay ($1,449)	New York ($814)	14-7	New York	46,016
1943	Dec. 26	Chi. Bears ($1,146)	Washington ($765)	41-21	Chicago	34,320
1942	Dec. 13	Washington ($965)	Chi. Bears ($637)	14-6	Washington	36,006
1941	Dec. 21	Chi. Bears ($430)	New York ($288)	37-9	Chicago	13,341
1940	Dec. 8	Chi. Bears ($873)	Washington ($606)	73-0	Washington	36,034
1939	Dec. 10	Green Bay ($703.97)	New York ($455.57)	27-0	Milwaukee	32,279
1938	Dec. 11	New York ($504.45)	Green Bay ($368.81)	23-17	New York	48,120
1937	Dec. 12	Washington ($225.90)	Chi. Bears ($127.78)	28-21	Chicago	15,870
1936	Dec. 13	Green Bay ($250)	Boston ($180)	21-6	New York	29,545
1935	Dec. 15	Detroit ($313.35)	New York ($200.20)	26-7	Detroit	15,000
1934	Dec. 9	New York ($621)	Chi. Bears ($414.02)	30-13	New York	35,059
1933	Dec. 17	Chi. Bears ($210.34)	New York ($140.22)	23-21	Chicago	26,000

*Sudden death overtime

NFC CHAMPIONSHIP GAME COMPOSITE STANDINGS

	W	L	Pct.	Pts.	OP
Seattle Seahawks	1	0	1.000	34	14
Baltimore Colts	3	1	.750	88	60
Green Bay Packers	11	4	.733	344	214
Detroit Lions	4	2	.667	139	141
Arizona Cardinals**	2	1	.667	60	53
Washington Redskins*	7	5	.583	222	255
Chicago Bears	8	7	.533	339	280
Dallas Cowboys	8	8	.500	361	319
Philadelphia Eagles	5	5	.500	168	160
Atlanta Falcons	1	1	.500	40	54
New Orleans Saints	1	1	.500	45	67
Minnesota Vikings	4	5	.444	163	182
San Francisco 49ers	5	7	.417	245	222
New York Giants	7	11	.389	304	342
Cleveland Browns	4	7	.364	224	253
St. Louis Rams***	5	9	.357	163	300
Carolina Panthers	1	2	.333	41	67
Tampa Bay Buccaneers	1	2	.333	33	30

*One game played when franchise was in Boston (Lost 21-6)
**Both games played when franchise was in Chicago (Won 28-21, lost 7-0)
***One game played when franchise was in Cleveland (Won 15 14), and 11 games when franchise was in Los Angeles (Won 2, lost 9, scored 188 points, allowed 290 points).

2010 NFC CHAMPIONSHIP GAME

Soldier Field, Chicago, Illinois
January 23, 2011, Attendance: 62,377
GREEN BAY 21, CHICAGO 14—Aaron Rodgers passed for 244 yards and ran for a touchdown as the Packers won their first NFC title since 1997. With the game played in 7-degree wind chill, the Packers drove 84 yards with their opening possession, sparked by 22- and 26-yard passes to Greg Jennings, and capped by Rodgers' 1-yard touchdown run. Late in the quarter, Brandon Underwood downed Tim Masthay's punt at the Bears' 3-yard line. The Packers' defense then forced a punt, and the offense only needed 44 yards to score, capped by James Starks' 4-yard scoring run, for a 14-0 lead with 11:13 left in the half. Lance Briggs intercepted a pass at the Bears' 42 with 49 seconds left in the half, but two plays later Sam Shields intercepted Jay Cutler's long pass intended for Johnny Knox to secure Green Bay's 14-0 lead going into the locker room. The Packers drove to the Bears' 6 in the third quarter, but Brian Urlacher intercepted a pass and returned it 39 yards. Todd Collins replaced an injured Cutler for two possessions, and Caleb Hanie replaced Collins late in the third quarter with the score still 14-0. Hanie promptly engineered an 8-

play, 67-yard drive, highlighted by his 32-yard pass to Knox, and culminating with Chester Taylor's 1-yard touchdown run with 12:02 to play. With 6:12 remaining, the Bears had the ball at their own 15-yard line facing third-and-5. Hanie's short pass intended for Matt Forté was intercepted by B.J. Raji, who rumbled 18 yards for a touchdown and 21-7 lead. Undaunted, Hanie needed just four plays, capped by his 35-yard touchdown pass to Earl Bennett, to trim the deficit to 21-14 with 4:43 remaining. The Bears' defense forced a three-and-out, and Chicago's offense drove to the Packers' 29. On fourth-and-5 with 47 seconds to play, Shields nabbed his second interception of the game, thus sending the Packers to the Super Bowl. Rodgers was 17 of 30 for 244 yards, with 2 interceptions. Jennings had 8 catches for 130 yards. Cutler was 6 of 14 for 80 yards, with 1 interception. Hanie was 13 of 20 for 153 yards and 1 touchdown, with 2 interceptions. Forté had 10 receptions for 90 yards.

Green Bay (21)	Offense	Chicago (14)
Greg Jennings	WR	Johnny Knox
Chad Clifton	LT	Frank Omiyale
Daryn Colledge	LG	Chris Williams
Scott Wells	C	Olin Kreutz
Josh Sitton	RG	Roberto Garza
Bryan Bulaga	RT	J'Marcus Webb
Donald Lee	TE	Greg Olsen
Jordy Nelson	WR	Devin Hester
Aaron Rodgers	QB	Jay Cutler
Quinn Johnson	FB/RB	Matt Forté
James Starks	RB/FB	Brandon Manumaleuna
	Defense	
Ryan Pickett	LDE	Israel Idonije
B.J. Raji	NT/DT	Tommie Harris
Howard Green	RDE/NT	Anthony Adams
Clay Matthews	LOLB/RE	Julius Peppers
A.J. Hawk	LILB/WLB	Lance Briggs
Desmond Bishop	RILB/MLB	Brian Urlacher
Erik Walden	ROLB/SLB	Piso Tinoisamoa
Charles Woodson	LCB	Tim Jennings
Tramon Williams	RCB	Charles Tillman
Sam Shields	SS	Danieal Manning
Nick Collins	FS	Chris Harris

SUBSTITUTIONS

GREEN BAY—Specialists: K—Mason Crosby. P—Tom Masthay. LS—Brett Goode. Offense: RB—Brandon Jackson, John Kuhn. FB—Korey Hall. WR—Donald Driver, James Jones, Brett Swain. TE—Tom Crabtree, Andrew Quarless. C/G—Jason Spitz. T/G—T.J. Lang. Defense: DE—Cullen Jenkins, C.J. Wilson. LB—Desmond Briggs, Robert Francois, Matt Wilhelm. CB—Brandon Underwood. CB/S—Jarrett Bush. S—Atari Bigby, Charlie Peprah.

DNP: QB—Matt Flynn. Not Active: QB—Graham Harrell. RB—Dimitri Nance. C/G—Evan Dietrich-Smith. G—Nick McDonald. DE—Jarius Wynn. LB—Frank Zombo. CB—Josh Gordy, Pat Lee. **CHICAGO**—Specialists: K—Robbie Gould. P—Brad Maynard. LS—Patrick Mannelly. Offense: QB—Todd Collins, Caleb Hanie. RB—Chester Taylor, Garrett Wolfe. WR—Earl Bennett, Rashied Davis. TE—Desmond Clark, Kellen Davis. G—Lance Louis. T—Kevin Shaffer. Defense: DT—Matt Toeaina. DE—Henry Melton, Corey Wootton. LB—Brian Iwuh, Nick Roach, Rod Wilson. CB—Zackary Bowman, Corey Graham, D.J. Moore. S—Josh Bullocks, Major Wright. Not Active: RB—Kahlil Bell. WR—Devin Aromashodu. G/C—Eddie Williams. G—Herman Johnson. DT—Marcus Harrison. CB—Joshua Moore. S—Craig Steltz.

OFFICIALS
Referee—Terry McAulay. Umpire—Carl Paganelli. Line Judge—Mark Perlman. Side Judge—Greg Meyer. Head Linesman—George Hayward. Back Judge—Tony Steratore. Field Judge—Steve Zimmer.

SCORING

Green Bay	7	7	0	7	—	21
Chicago	0	0	0	14	—	14

GB	—	Rodgers 1 run (Crosby kick)
GB	—	Starks 4 run (Crosby kick)
Chi	—	Taylor 1 run (Gould kick)
GB	—	Raji 18 interception return (Crosby kick)
Chi	—	Bennett 35 pass from Hanie (Gould kick)

TEAM STATISTICS

	GB	CHI
Total First Downs	23	17
Rushing	9	5
Passing	11	11
Penalty	3	1
Total Net Yardage	356	301
Total Offensive Plays	63	64
Average Gain Per Offensive Play	5.7	4.7
Rushes	32	24
Yards Gained Rushing (Net)	120	83
Average Yards per Rush	43.8	3.5
Passes Attempted	30	38
Passes Completed	17	19
Had Intercepted	2	3
Tackled Attempting to Pass	1	2
Yards Lost Attempting to Pass	8	15
Yards Gained Passing (Net)	236	218
Punts	8	9
Average Distance	41.8	37.1
Punt Returns	3	4
Punt Return Yardage	13	38
Kickoff Returns	3	4
Kickoff Return Yardage	44	63
Interception Return Yardage	58	43
Total Return Yardage (excluding Kickoffs)	71	81
Fumbles	2	1
Fumbles Lost	0	0
Own Fumbles Recovered	2	1
Opponent Fumbles Recovered	0	0
Penalties	6	9
Yards Penalized	40	89
Field Goals	0	0
Field Goals Attempted	0	0
Third-Down Efficiency	2/11	1/13
Fourth-Down Efficiency	0/0	1/2
Time of Possession	34:04	25:56

INDIVIDUAL STATISTICS
RUSHING: GB: Starks 22-74-1, Rodgers 7-39-1, Jackson 2-5-0, Kuhn 1-2-0. CHI: Forté 17-70-0, Cutler 2-10-0, Hanie 1-3-0, Taylor 3-2-1, Bennett 1(-2)-0.
PASSING: GB: Rodgers 30-17-244-0-2. CHI: Cutler 14-6-80-0-1, Collins 4-0-0-0-0, Hanie 20-13-153-1-2.
RECEIVING: GB: Jennings 8-130-0, Nelson 4-67-0, Jackson 1-16-0, Jones 1-10-0, Driver 1-9-0, Kuhn 1-6-0, Starks 1-6-0. CHI: Forté 10-90-0, Bennett 3-45-1, Olsen 3-30-0, Knox 2-56-0, Taylor 1-12-0.
KICKOFF RETURNS: GB: Starks 2-30-0, Woodson 1-14-0. CHI: Hester 1-24-0, R. Davis 1-16-0, Manning 1-15-0, K. Davis 1-8-0.
PUNT RETURNS: GB: Williams 3-13-0. CHI: Hester 3-16-0, Bennett 1-22-0.
PUNTING: GB: Masthay 8-334-41.8. CHI: Maynard 9-334-37.1.
INTERCEPTIONS: GB: Shields 2-40-0, Raji 1-18-1. CHI: Urlacher 1-39-0, Briggs 1-4-0.
SACKS: GB: Shields 1.0, Jenkins 0/5, Matthews 0.5. CHI: Urlacher 1.0.

AFC DIVISIONAL PLAYOFFS RESULTS
Includes Second-Round Playoff Games (1982), AFC Inter-Divisional Games (1969), and special playoff games to break ties for AFL Division Championships (1963, 1968)

Season	Date	Winner (Share)	Loser (Share)	Score	Site	Attendance
2010	Jan. 16	N.Y. Jets ($21,000)	New England ($21,000)	28-21	Foxborough	68,756
	Jan. 15	Pittsburgh ($21,000)	Baltimore ($21,000)	31-24	Pittsburgh	64,879
2009	Jan. 17	N.Y. Jets ($21,000)	San Diego ($21,000)	17-14	San Diego	69,498
	Jan. 16	Indianapolis ($21,000)	Baltimore ($21,000)	20-3	Indianapolis	67,535
2008	Jan. 11	Pittsburgh ($20,000)	San Diego ($20,000)	35-24	Pittsburgh	63,899
	Jan. 10	Baltimore ($20,000)	Tennessee ($20,000)	13-10	Nashville	69,143
2007	Jan. 13	San Diego ($20,000)	Indianapolis ($20,000)	28-24	Indianapolis	56,950
	Jan. 12	New England ($20,000)	Jacksonville ($20,000)	31-20	Foxborough	68,756
2006	Jan. 14	New England ($19,000)	San Diego ($19,000)	24-21	San Diego	68,810
	Jan. 13	Indianapolis ($19,000)	Baltimore ($19,000)	15-6	Baltimore	71,162
2005	Jan. 15	Pittsburgh ($19,000)	Indianapolis ($19,000)	21-18	Indianapolis	57,449
	Jan. 14	Denver ($19,000)	New England ($19,000)	27-13	Denver	76,238
2004	Jan. 16	New England ($18,000)	Indianapolis ($18,000)	20-3	Foxborough	68,756
	Jan. 15	Pittsburgh ($18,000)	N.Y. Jets ($18,000)	20-17*	Pittsburgh	64,915
2003	Jan. 11	Indianapolis ($18,000)	Kansas City ($18,000)	38-31	Kansas City	79,159
	Jan. 10	New England ($18,000)	Tennessee ($18,000)	17-14	Foxborough	68,436
2002	Jan. 12	Oakland ($17,000)	N.Y. Jets ($17,000)	30-10	Oakland	62,207
	Jan. 11	Tennessee ($17,000)	Pittsburgh ($17,000)	34-31*	Nashville	68,809
2001	Jan. 20	Pittsburgh ($17,000)	Baltimore ($17,000)	27-10	Pittsburgh	63,976
	Jan. 19	New England ($17,000)	Oakland ($17,000)	16-13*	Foxborough	60,292
2000	Jan. 7	Baltimore ($16,000)	Tennessee ($16,000)	24-10	Nashville	68,527
	Jan. 6	Oakland ($16,000)	Miami ($16,000)	27-0	Oakland	61,998

Season	Date	Winner (Share)	Loser (Share)	Score	Site	Attendance
1999	Jan. 16	Tennessee ($16,000)	Indianapolis ($16,000)	19-16	Indianapolis	57,097
	Jan. 15	Jacksonville ($16,000)	Miami ($16,000)	62-7	Jacksonville	75,173
1998	Jan. 10	N.Y. Jets ($15,000)	Jacksonville ($15,000)	34-24	East Rutherford	78,817
	Jan. 9	Denver ($15,000)	Miami ($15,000)	38-3	Denver	75,729
1997	Jan. 4	Denver ($15,000)	Kansas City ($15,000)	14-10	Kansas City	76,965
	Jan. 3	Pittsburgh ($15,000)	New England ($15,000)	7-6	Pittsburgh	61,228
1996	Jan. 5	New England ($14,000)	Pittsburgh ($14,000)	28-3	Foxborough	60,188
	Jan. 4	Jacksonville ($14,000)	Denver ($14,000)	30-27	Denver	75,678
1995	Jan. 7	Indianapolis ($13,000)	Kansas City ($13,000)	10-7	Kansas City	77,594
	Jan. 6	Pittsburgh ($13,000)	Buffalo ($13,000)	40-21	Pittsburgh	59,072
1994	Jan. 8	San Diego ($12,000)	Miami ($12,000)	22-21	San Diego	63,381
	Jan. 7	Pittsburgh ($12,000)	Cleveland ($12,000)	29-9	Pittsburgh	58,185
1993	Jan. 16	Kansas City ($12,000)	Houston ($12,000)	28-20	Houston	64,011
	Jan. 15	Buffalo ($12,000)	L.A. Raiders ($12,000)	29-23	Buffalo	61,923
1992	Jan. 10	Miami ($10,000)	San Diego ($10,000)	31-0	Miami	71,224
	Jan. 9	Buffalo ($10,000)	Pittsburgh ($10,000)	24-3	Pittsburgh	60,407
1991	Jan. 5	Buffalo ($10,000)	Kansas City ($10,000)	37-14	Buffalo	80,182
	Jan. 4	Denver ($10,000)	Houston ($10,000)	26-24	Denver	75,301
1990	Jan. 13	L.A. Raiders ($10,000)	Cincinnati ($10,000)	20-10	Los Angeles	92,045
	Jan. 12	Buffalo ($10,000)	Miami ($10,000)	44-34	Buffalo	77,087
1989	Jan. 7	Denver ($10,000)	Pittsburgh ($10,000)	24-23	Denver	75,477
	Jan. 6	Cleveland ($10,000)	Buffalo ($10,000)	34-30	Cleveland	78,921
1988	Jan. 1	Buffalo ($10,000)	Houston ($10,000)	17-10	Buffalo	79,532
	Dec. 31	Cincinnati ($10,000)	Seattle ($10,000)	21-13	Cincinnati	58,560
1987	Jan. 10	Denver ($10,000)	Houston ($10,000)	34-10	Denver	75,440
	Jan. 9	Cleveland ($10,000)	Indianapolis ($10,000)	38-21	Cleveland	79,372
1986	Jan. 4	Denver ($10,000)	New England ($10,000)	22-17	Denver	75,262
	Jan. 3	Cleveland ($10,000)	N.Y. Jets ($10,000)	23-20*	Cleveland	79,720
1985	Jan. 5	New England ($10,000)	L.A. Raiders ($10,000)	27-20	Los Angeles	87,163
	Jan. 4	Miami ($10,000)	Cleveland ($10,000)	24-21	Miami	74,667
1984	Dec. 30	Pittsburgh ($10,000)	Denver ($10,000)	24-17	Denver	74,981
	Dec. 29	Miami ($10,000)	Seattle ($10,000)	31-10	Miami	73,469
1983	Jan. 1	L.A. Raiders ($10,000)	Pittsburgh ($10,000)	38-10	Los Angeles	90,380
	Dec. 31	Seattle ($10,000)	Miami ($10,000)	27-20	Miami	74,136
1982	Jan. 16	Miami ($10,000)	San Diego ($10,000)	34-13	Miami	71,383
	Jan. 15	N.Y. Jets ($10,000)	L.A. Raiders ($10,000)	17-14	Los Angeles	90,038
1981	Jan. 3	Cincinnati ($5,000)	Buffalo ($5,000)	28-21	Cincinnati	55,420
	Jan. 2	San Diego ($5,000)	Miami ($5,000)	41-38*	Miami	73,735
1980	Jan. 4	Oakland ($5,000)	Cleveland ($5,000)	14-12	Cleveland	78,245
	Jan. 3	San Diego ($5,000)	Buffalo ($5,000)	20-14	San Diego	52,253
1979	Dec. 30	Pittsburgh ($5,000)	Miami ($5,000)	34-14	Pittsburgh	50,214
	Dec. 29	Houston ($5,000)	San Diego ($5,000)	17-14	San Diego	51,192
1978	Dec. 31	Houston ($5,000)	New England ($5,000)	31-14	Foxborough	60,735
	Dec. 30	Pittsburgh ($5,000)	Denver ($5,000)	33-10	Pittsburgh	50,230
1977	Dec. 24	Oakland ($5,000)	Baltimore ($5,000)	37-31*	Baltimore	59,925
	Dec. 24	Denver ($5,000)	Pittsburgh ($5,000)	34-21	Denver	75,059
1976	Dec. 19	Pittsburgh [$]	Baltimore [$]	40-14	Baltimore	59,296
	Dec. 18	Oakland [$]	New England [$]	24-21	Oakland	53,050
1975	Dec. 28	Oakland [$]	Cincinnati [$]	31-28	Oakland	53,030
	Dec. 27	Pittsburgh [$]	Baltimore [$]	28-10	Pittsburgh	49,557
1974	Dec. 22	Pittsburgh [$]	Buffalo [$]	32-14	Pittsburgh	49,841
	Dec. 21	Oakland [$]	Miami [$]	28-26	Oakland	53,023
1973	Dec. 23	Miami [$]	Cincinnati [$]	34-16	Miami	78,928
	Dec. 22	Oakland [$]	Pittsburgh [$]	33-14	Oakland	52,646
1972	Dec. 24	Miami [$]	Cleveland [$]	20-14	Miami	78,916
	Dec. 23	Pittsburgh [$]	Oakland [$]	13-7	Pittsburgh	50,327
1971	Dec. 26	Baltimore [$]	Cleveland [$]	20-3	Cleveland	70,734
	Dec. 25	Miami [$]	Kansas City [$]	27-24*	Kansas City	50,374
1970	Dec. 27	Oakland [$]	Miami [$]	21-14	Oakland	52,594
	Dec. 26	Baltimore [$]	Cincinnati [$]	17-0	Baltimore	49,694
1969	Dec. 21	Oakland [$]	Houston [$]	56-7	Oakland	53,539
	Dec. 20	Kansas City [$]	N.Y. Jets [$]	13-6	New York	62,977
1968	Dec. 22	Oakland [$]	Kansas City [$]	41-6	Oakland	53,605
1963	Dec. 28	Boston [$]	Buffalo [$]	26-8	Buffalo	33,044

*Sudden death overtime
$ Players received 1/14 of annual salary for playoff appearances.

2010 AFC DIVISIONAL PLAYOFF GAMES

Gillette Stadium, Foxborough, Massachusetts
January 16, 2011, Attendance: 68,756

NEW YORK JETS 28, NEW ENGLAND 21—Mark Sanchez passed for 3 touchdowns and the Jets' defense sacked Tom Brady five times as the Jets reached the AFC Championship Game for the second consecutive season. The victory was in stark contrast to the game played on the same field less than two months earlier, when the Patriots won 45-3. The Jets trailed 3-0 in the second quarter when Sanchez connected on a 37-yard pass to Braylon Edwards to the Patriots' 8, setting up LaDainian Tomlinson's 7-yard touchdown catch. With 1:14 left in the half and punting from their own 38 on fourth-and-4, Patrick Chung took a direct snap and attempted to run for a first down, but was tackled by Eric Smith. Edwards' 15-yard touchdown catch four plays later staked the Jets to a 14-3 halftime lead. Late in the third quarter, Brady completed a 37-yard pass to Rob Gronkowski to spark an 80-yard touchdown drive. Sammy Morris successfully ran in the two-point conversion to pull the Patriots to within 14-11. Jerricho Cotchery took a short pass and ran 58 yards to the Patriots' 13 to set up Santonio Holmes' 7-yard touchdown catch with 13:00 remaining for a 21-11 lead. The Patriots drove to the Jets' 34, where Brady's fourth-and-13 pass to Deion Branch was incomplete with 5:15 to play. The Patriots forced a punt, and Shayne Graham's 35-yard field goal trimmed the deficit to 21-14 with 1:57 remaining, but Antonio Cromartie recovered the onside kick and returned it 23 yards, setting up Shonn Greene's 16-yard touchdown run with 1:41 to play. Brady completed a touchdown pass to Branch with 24 seconds left, but Smith recovered the onside kick. Sanchez was 16 of 25 for 194 yards and 3 touchdowns. Brady was 29 of 45 for 299 yards and 2 touchdowns, with 1 interception.

New York Jets	0	14	0	14	—	28
New England	3	0	8	10	—	21

NE	—	FG Graham 34
NYJ	—	Tomlinson 7 pass from Sanchez (Folk kick)
NYJ	—	Edwards 15 pass from Sanchez (Folk kick)
NE	—	Crumpler 2 pass from Brady (Morris run)
NYJ	—	Holmes 7 pass from Sanchez (Folk kick)
NE	—	FG Graham 35
NE	—	Greene 16 run (Folk kick)
NE	—	Branch 13 pass from Brady (Graham kick)

Heinz Field, Pittsburgh, Pennsylvania
January 15, 2011, Attendance: 64,879

PITTSBURGH 31, BALTIMORE 24—The Steelers overcame a 14-point second-half deficit, capped by Rashard Mendenhall's 2-yard touchdown run with 1:33 to play, to vault Pittsburgh back into the AFC Championship Game for the fourth time in the past seven years. Despite the 55 points scored, both defense excelled. The Steelers limited Baltimore to 126 total yards and forced three turnovers. The Ravens' defense permitted just 263 yards and recovered two fumbles. Ben Roethlisberger was sacked six times by Baltimore, while Joe Flacco was dropped five times by the Steelers' defense. With the score 7-7 late in the first quarter, Terrell Suggs sacked Roethlisberger. Cory Redding picked up the loose ball and ran 13 yards for a touchdown. Ed Reed recovered a fumble by Mendenhall in the second quarter at the Steelers' 16 to set up Todd Heap's 4-yard touchdown catch for a 21-7 lead. In the third quarter, Ryan Clark forced Ray Rice to fumble. LaMarr Woodley recovered at the Ravens' 23, and Heath Miller's 9-yard touchdown catch two plays later cut the deficit to 21-14. Later in the quarter, Clark intercepted Flacco's pass and returned the ball 17 yards to the Ravens' 25. On third-and-6, Roethlisberger completed an 8-yard touchdown pass to Hines Ward to tie the game with 1:21 left in the third quarter. Flacco mishandled the snap two plays later and Brett Keisel recovered, setting up Shaun Suisham's go-ahead field goal with 12:15 remaining. With 5:55 to play, Lardarius Webb's punt return gave Baltimore the ball at the Steelers' 29, setting up Billy Cundiff's game-tying field goal with 3:54 left. On the Steelers' ensuing drive, Roethlisberger completed a 12-yard pass to Ward on third-and-10 to keep alive the drive, and three plays later found Antonio Brown open for a 58-yard pass to the Raven's 4 with 1:58 left. Mendenhall scored on third down with 1:33 left. The Ravens began their final possession at the Steelers' 48, but two incompletions, a sack by Ziggy Hood, and an incomplete pass on fourth-and-18 clinched the victory for Pittsburgh. Roethlisberger was 19 of 32 for 226 yards and 2 touchdowns. Flacco was 16 of 30 for 125 yards and 1 touchdown, with 1 interception.

Baltimore	14	7	0	3	—	24
Pittsburgh	7	0	14	10	—	31

Pitt	—	Mendenhall 1 run (Suisham kick)
Balt	—	Rice 14 run (Cundiff kick)
Balt	—	Redding 13 fumble return (Cundiff kick)
Balt	—	Heap 4 pass from Flacco (Cundiff kick)
Pitt	—	H. Miller 9 pass from Roethlisberger (Suisham kick)
Pitt	—	Ward 8 pass from Roethlisberger (Suisham kick)
Pitt	—	FG Suisham 35
Balt	—	FG Cundiff 24
Pitt	—	Mendenhall 2 run (Suisham kick)

NFC DIVISIONAL PLAYOFFS RESULTS

Includes Second-Round Playoff Games (1982), NFL Conference Championship Games (1967-69), and special playoff games to break ties for NFL Division or Conference Championships (1941, 1943, 1947, 1950, 1952, 1957, 1958, 1965)

Season	Date	Winner (Share)	Loser (Share)	Score	Site	Attendance
2010	Jan. 16	Chicago ($21,000)	Seattle ($21,000)	35-24	Chicago	62,265
	Jan. 15	Green Bay ($21,000)	Atlanta ($21,000)	48-21	Atlanta	69,210
2009	Jan. 17	Minnesota ($21,000)	Dallas ($21,000)	34-3	Minneapolis	63,547
	Jan. 16	New Orleans ($21,000)	Arizona ($21,000)	45-14	New Orleans	70,149
2008	Jan. 11	Philadelphia ($20,000)	N.Y. Giants ($20,000)	23-11	East Rutherford	79,193
	Jan. 10	Arizona ($20,000)	Carolina ($20,000)	33-13	Charlotte	73,695
2007	Jan. 13	N.Y. Giants ($20,000)	Dallas ($20,000)	21-17	Dallas	63,660
	Jan. 12	Green Bay ($20,000)	Seattle ($20,000)	42-20	Green Bay	72,168
2006	Jan. 14	Chicago ($19,000)	Seattle ($19,000)	27-24*	Chicago	62,184
	Jan. 13	New Orleans ($19,000)	Philadelphia ($19,000)	27-24	New Orleans	70,001
2005	Jan. 15	Carolina ($19,000)	Chicago ($19,000)	29-21	Chicago	62,209
	Jan. 14	Seattle ($19,000)	Washington ($19,000)	20-10	Seattle	67,551
2004	Jan. 16	Philadelphia ($18,000)	Minnesota ($18,000)	27-14	Philadelphia	67,722
	Jan. 15	Atlanta ($18,000)	St. Louis ($18,000)	47-17	Atlanta	70,099
2003	Jan. 11	Philadelphia ($18,000)	Green Bay ($18,000)	20-17*	Philadelphia	67,707
	Jan. 10	Carolina ($18,000)	St. Louis ($18,000)	29-23*	St. Louis	66,165
2002	Jan. 12	Tampa Bay ($17,000)	San Francisco ($17,000)	31-6	Tampa	65,599
	Jan. 11	Philadelphia ($17,000)	Atlanta ($17,000)	20-6	Philadelphia	66,452
2001	Jan. 20	St. Louis ($17,000)	Green Bay ($17,000)	45-17	St. Louis	66,338
	Jan. 19	Philadelphia ($17,000)	Chicago ($17,000)	33-19	Chicago	66,944
2000	Jan. 7	N.Y. Giants ($16,000)	Philadelphia ($16,000)	20-10	East Rutherford	78,765
	Jan. 6	Minnesota ($16,000)	New Orleans ($16,000)	34-16	Minneapolis	63,881

Season	Date	Winner (Share)	Loser (Share)	Score	Site	Attendance
1999	Jan. 16	St. Louis ($16,000)	Minnesota ($16,000)	49-37	St. Louis	66,194
	Jan. 15	Tampa Bay ($16,000)	Washington ($16,000)	14-13	Tampa	65,835
1998	Jan. 10	Minnesota ($15,000)	Arizona ($15,000)	41-21	Minneapolis	63,760
	Jan. 9	Atlanta ($15,000)	San Francisco ($15,000)	20-18	Atlanta	70,264
1997	Jan. 4	Green Bay ($15,000)	Tampa Bay ($15,000)	21-7	Green Bay	60,327
	Jan. 3	San Francisco ($15,000)	Minnesota ($15,000)	38-22	San Francisco	65,018
1996	Jan. 5	Carolina ($14,000)	Dallas ($14,000)	26-17	Charlotte	72,808
	Jan. 4	Green Bay ($14,000)	San Francisco ($14,000)	35-14	Green Bay	60,787
1995	Jan. 7	Dallas ($13,000)	Philadelphia ($13,000)	30-11	Dallas	64,371
	Jan. 6	Green Bay ($13,000)	San Francisco ($13,000)	27-17	San Francisco	69,311
1994	Jan. 8	Dallas ($12,000)	Green Bay ($12,000)	35-9	Dallas	64,745
	Jan. 7	San Francisco ($12,000)	Chicago ($12,000)	44-15	San Francisco	64,644
1993	Jan. 16	Dallas ($12,000)	Green Bay ($12,000)	27-17	Dallas	64,790
	Jan. 15	San Francisco ($12,000)	N.Y. Giants ($12,000)	44-3	San Francisco	67,143
1992	Jan. 10	Dallas ($10,000)	Philadelphia ($10,000)	34-10	Dallas	63,721
	Jan. 9	San Francisco ($10,000)	Washington ($10,000)	20-13	San Francisco	64,991
1991	Jan. 5	Detroit ($10,000)	Dallas ($10,000)	38-6	Detroit	78,290
	Jan. 4	Washington ($10,000)	Atlanta ($10,000)	24-7	Washington	55,181
1990	Jan. 13	N.Y. Giants ($10,000)	Chicago ($10,000)	31-3	East Rutherford	77,025
	Jan. 12	San Francisco ($10,000)	Washington ($10,000)	28-10	San Francisco	65,292
1989	Jan. 7	L.A. Rams ($10,000)	N.Y. Giants ($10,000)	19-13*	East Rutherford	76,526
	Jan. 6	San Francisco ($10,000)	Minnesota ($10,000)	41-13	San Francisco	64,918
1988	Jan. 1	San Francisco ($10,000)	Minnesota ($10,000)	34-9	San Francisco	61,848
	Dec. 31	Chicago ($10,000)	Philadelphia ($10,000)	20-12	Chicago	65,534
1987	Jan. 10	Washington ($10,000)	Chicago ($10,000)	21-17	Chicago	65,268
	Jan. 9	Minnesota ($10,000)	San Francisco ($10,000)	36-24	San Francisco	63,008
1986	Jan. 4	N.Y. Giants ($10,000)	San Francisco ($10,000)	49-3	East Rutherford	75,691
	Jan. 3	Washington ($10,000)	Chicago ($10,000)	27-13	Chicago	65,524
1985	Jan. 5	Chicago ($10,000)	N.Y. Giants ($10,000)	21-0	Chicago	65,670
	Jan. 4	L.A. Rams ($10,000)	Dallas ($10,000)	20-0	Anaheim	66,581
1984	Dec. 30	Chicago ($10,000)	Washington ($10,000)	23-19	Washington	55,431
	Dec. 29	San Francisco ($10,000)	N.Y. Giants ($10,000)	21-10	San Francisco	60,303
1983	Jan. 1	Washington ($10,000)	L.A. Rams ($10,000)	51-7	Washington	54,440
	Dec. 31	San Francisco ($10,000)	Detroit ($10,000)	24-23	San Francisco	59,979
1982	Jan. 16	Dallas ($10,000)	Green Bay ($10,000)	37-26	Dallas	63,972
	Jan. 15	Washington ($10,000)	Minnesota ($10,000)	21-7	Washington	54,593
1981	Jan. 3	San Francisco ($5,000)	N.Y. Giants ($5,000)	38-24	San Francisco	58,360
	Jan. 2	Dallas ($5,000)	Tampa Bay ($5,000)	38-0	Dallas	64,848
1980	Jan. 4	Dallas ($5,000)	Atlanta ($5,000)	30-27	Atlanta	59,793
	Jan. 3	Philadelphia ($5,000)	Minnesota ($5,000)	31-16	Philadelphia	70,178
1979	Dec. 30	Los Angeles ($5,000)	Dallas ($5,000)	21-19	Dallas	64,792
	Dec. 29	Tampa Bay ($5,000)	Philadelphia ($5,000)	24-17	Tampa	71,402
1978	Dec. 31	Los Angeles ($5,000)	Minnesota ($5,000)	34-10	Los Angeles	70,436
	Dec. 30	Dallas ($5,000)	Atlanta ($5,000)	27-20	Dallas	63,406
1977	Dec. 26	Dallas ($5,000)	Chicago ($5,000)	37-7	Dallas	63,260
	Dec. 26	Minnesota ($5,000)	Los Angeles ($5,000)	14-7	Los Angeles	70,203
1976	Dec. 19	Los Angeles [$]	Dallas [$]	14-12	Dallas	63,283
	Dec. 18	Minnesota [$]	Washington [$]	35-20	Minneapolis	47,466
1975	Dec. 28	Dallas [$]	Minnesota [$]	17-14	Minneapolis	48,050
	Dec. 27	Los Angeles [$]	St. Louis [$]	35-23	Los Angeles	73,459
1974	Dec. 22	Los Angeles [$]	Washington [$]	19-10	Los Angeles	77,925
	Dec. 21	Minnesota [$]	St. Louis [$]	30-14	Minneapolis	48,150
1973	Dec. 23	Dallas [$]	Los Angeles [$]	27-16	Dallas	63,272
	Dec. 22	Minnesota [$]	Washington [$]	27-20	Minneapolis	48,040
1972	Dec. 24	Washington [$]	Green Bay [$]	16-3	Washington	52,321
	Dec. 23	Dallas [$]	San Francisco [$]	30-28	San Francisco	59,746
1971	Dec. 26	San Francisco [$]	Washington [$]	24-20	San Francisco	45,327
	Dec. 25	Dallas [$]	Minnesota [$]	20-12	Minneapolis	47,307
1970	Dec. 27	San Francisco [$]	Minnesota [$]	17-14	Minneapolis	45,103
	Dec. 26	Dallas [$]	Detroit [$]	5-0	Dallas	69,613
1969	Dec. 28	Cleveland [$]	Dallas [$]	38-14	Dallas	69,321
	Dec. 27	Minnesota [$]	Los Angeles [$]	23-20	Minneapolis	47,900
1968	Dec. 22	Baltimore [$]	Minnesota [$]	24-14	Baltimore	60,238
	Dec. 21	Cleveland [$]	Dallas [$]	31-20	Cleveland	81,497
1967	Dec. 24	Dallas [$]	Cleveland [$]	52-14	Dallas	70,786
	Dec. 23	Green Bay [$]	Los Angeles [$]	28-7	Milwaukee	49,861
1965	Dec. 26	Green Bay [$]	Baltimore [$]	13-10*	Green Bay	50,484
1958	Dec. 21	N.Y. Giants (#)	Cleveland (#)	10-0	New York	61,274
1957	Dec. 22	Detroit (#)	San Francisco (#)	31-27	San Francisco	60,118
1952	Dec. 21	Detroit (#)	Los Angeles (#)	31-21	Detroit	47,645
1950	Dec. 17	Los Angeles (#)	Chicago Bears (#)	24-14	Los Angeles	83,501
	Dec. 17	Cleveland (#)	N.Y. Giants (#)	8-3	Cleveland	33,054
1947	Dec. 21	Philadelphia (#)	Pittsburgh (#)	21-0	Pittsburgh	35,729
1943	Dec. 19	Washington (¢)	N.Y. Giants (¢)	28-0	New York	42,800
1941	Dec. 14	Chicago Bears (¢)	Green Bay (¢)	33-14	Chicago	43,425

*Sudden death overtime
$ Players received 1/14 of annual salary for playoff appearances.
# Players received 1/12 of annual salary for playoff appearances.
¢ Players received 1/10 of annual salary for playoff appearances.

2010 NFC DIVISIONAL PLAYOFF GAMES

Soldier Field, Chicago, Illinois
January 16, 2011, Attendance: 62,265

CHICAGO 35, SEATTLE 24—Jay Cutler passed for 2 touchdowns and ran for two more as the Bears jumped out to a 28-0 lead en route to victory. The Bears' defense forced the Seahawks to punt on all seven of their first-half possessions. The offense, meanwhile, scored touchdowns on three of its first four possessions, capped by Cutler's 6-yard run with 10:01 left in the second quarter for a 21-0 lead. The Bears outgained Seattle 238-96 yards in the first half. Cutler's 9-yard touchdown run in the third quarter capped an almost eight-minute drive and extended the lead to 28-0 with 4:12 left in the third quarter. Seattle managed a field goal by Olindo Mare, and then Aaron Curry intercepted Matt Forté's halfback-option pass to set up Mike Williams' touchdown catch to cut the deficit to 28-10 with 11:21 to play. After an exchange of punts, Cutler found Kellen Davis open for a 39-yard touchdown pass on third-and-1 with 4:40 remaining for a 35-10 lead. Matt Hasselbeck completed two late touchdown passes, but Johnny Knox recovered the final onside kick with 1:25 to play to secure the victory. Cutler was 15 of 28 for 274 yards and 2 touchdowns. Greg Olsen had three catches for 113 yards. Hasselbeck was 26 of 46 for 258 yards and 3 touchdowns.

Seattle	0	0	3	21	—	24
Chicago	14	7	7	7	—	35

Chi	—	Olsen 58 pass from Cutler (Gould kick)
Chi	—	Taylor 1 run (Gould kick)
Chi	—	Cutler 6 run (Gould kick)
Chi	—	Cutler 9 run (Gould kick)
Sea	—	FG Mare 30
Sea	—	Williams 2 pass from Hasselbeck (Mare kick)
Chi	—	K. Davis 39 pass from Cutler (Gould kick)
Sea	—	Williams 3 pass from Hasselbeck (Mare kick)
Sea	—	Stokley 9 pass from Hasselbeck (Mare kick)

Georgia Dome, Atlanta, Georgia
January 15, 2011, Attendance: 69,210

GREEN BAY 48, ATLANTA 21—Aaron Rodgers passed for 366 yards and 3 touchdowns as the Packers scored 28 unanswered points in a span of 12 minutes, 38 seconds to post their second consecutive road playoff victory. The Packers offense tallied 442 yards, while the defense permitted just 194 yards, registered five sacks, and forced four turnovers. The Packers fumbled on their first drive, but then scored touchdowns on their next five possessions, ultimately scoring on seven of their next eight possessions. The Packers' 28-point second quarter stopped the momentum created by Eric Weems' 102-yard kickoff return touchdown that gave Atlanta an early 14-7 lead. It was 14-14 and Atlanta drove to the Packers' 26, but Tramon Williams intercepted Matt Ryan for a touchback with 2:20 left in the half. Rodgers completed five of six passes on the ensuing drive, capped by James Jones' 20-yard scoring catch, for a 21-14 lead with 42 seconds left in the half. Atlanta drove to the Packers' 35 with 10 seconds left, but Ryan's short pass was intercepted by Williams and returned 70 yards for a momentum-swinging touchdown as the half expired for a 28-14 lead. The Packers drove 80 yards for a touchdown to begin the second half, the defense forced a punt, and John Kuhn capped the next possession with a 7-yard touchdown for a 42-14 lead with 2:41 left in the third quarter. Rodgers was 31 of 36 for 366 yards and 3 touchdowns. Jennings had eight catches for 101 yards.

Green Bay	0	28	14	6	—	48
Atlanta	7	7	0	7	—	21

Atl	—	Turner 12 run (Bryant kick)
GB	—	Nelson 6 pass from Rodgers (Crosby kick)
Atl	—	Weems 102 kickoff return (Bryant kick)
GB	—	Kuhn 1 run (Crosby kick)
GB	—	Jones 20 pass from Rodgers (Crosby kick)
GB	—	Williams 70 interception return (Crosby kick)
GB	—	Rodgers 7 run (Crosby kick)
GB	—	Kuhn 7 pass from Rodgers (Crosby kick)
Atl	—	White 6 pass from Ryan (Bryant kick)
GB	—	FG Crosby 43
GB	—	FG Crosby 32

AFC WILD CARD PLAYOFF GAMES RESULTS

Season	Date	Winner (Share)	Loser (Share)	Score	Site	Attendance
2010	Jan. 9	Baltimore ($19,000)	Kansas City ($21,000)	30-7	Foxborough	72,190
	Jan. 8	N.Y. Jets ($19,000)	Indianapolis ($21,000)	17-16	Indianapolis	65,332
2009	Jan. 10	Baltimore ($19,000)	New England ($21,000)	33-14	Foxborough	68,756
	Jan. 9	N.Y. Jets ($19,000)	Cincinnati ($21,000)	24-14	Cincinnati	63,686
2008	Jan. 4	Baltimore ($18,000)	Miami ($20,000)	27-9	Miami	74,240
	Jan. 3	San Diego ($20,000)	Indianapolis ($18,000)	23-17*	San Diego	68,082
2007	Jan. 6	San Diego ($20,000)	Tennessee ($18,000)	17-6	San Diego	65,640
	Jan. 5	Jacksonville ($18,000)	Pittsburgh ($20,000)	31-29	Pittsburgh	63,629
2006	Jan. 7	New England ($19,000)	N.Y. Jets ($17,000)	37-16	Foxborough	68,756
	Jan. 6	Indianapolis ($19,000)	Kansas City ($17,000)	23-8	Indianapolis	57,215
2005	Jan. 8	Pittsburgh ($17,000)	Cincinnati ($19,000)	31-17	Cincinnati	65,870
	Jan. 7	New England ($19,000)	Jacksonville ($17,000)	28-3	Foxborough	68,756
2004	Jan. 9	Indianapolis ($18,000)	Denver ($15,000)	49-24	Indianapolis	56,609
	Jan. 8	N.Y. Jets ($15,000)	San Diego ($18,000)	20-17*	San Diego	67,536
2003	Jan. 4	Indianapolis ($18,000)	Denver ($15,000)	41-10	Indianapolis	56,586
	Jan. 3	Tennessee ($15,000)	Baltimore ($18,000)	20-17	Baltimore	69,452
2002	Jan. 5	Pittsburgh ($17,000)	Cleveland ($12,500)	36-33	Pittsburgh	62,595
	Jan. 4	N.Y. Jets ($17,000)	Indianapolis ($12,500)	41-0	East Rutherford	78,524
2001	Jan. 13	Baltimore ($12,500)	Miami ($12,500)	20-3	Miami	72,251
	Jan. 12	Oakland ($17,000)	N.Y. Jets ($12,500)	38-24	Oakland	61,503
2000	Dec. 31	Baltimore (12,500)	Denver ($12,500)	21-3	Baltimore	69,638
	Dec. 30	Miami ($16,000)	Indianapolis ($12,500)	23-17*	Miami	73,193
1999	Jan. 9	Miami ($10,000)	Seattle ($16,000)	20-17	Seattle	66,170
	Jan. 8	Tennessee ($10,000)	Buffalo ($10,000)	22-16	Nashville	66,672
1998	Jan. 3	Jacksonville ($15,000)	New England ($10,000)	25-10	Jacksonville	71,139
	Jan. 2	Miami ($10,000)	Buffalo ($10,000)	24-17	Miami	72,698
1997	Dec. 28	New England ($15,000)	Miami ($10,000)	17-3	Foxborough	60,041
	Dec. 27	Denver ($10,000)	Jacksonville ($10,000)	42-17	Denver	74,481

Season	Date	Winner (Share)	Loser (Share)	Score	Site	Attendance
1996	Dec. 29	Pittsburgh ($14,000)	Indianapolis ($10,000)	42-14	Pittsburgh	58,078
	Dec. 28	Jacksonville ($10,000)	Buffalo ($10,000)	30-27	Buffalo	70,213
1995	Dec. 31	Indianapolis ($7,500)	San Diego ($7,500)	35-20	San Diego	61,182
	Dec. 30	Buffalo ($13,000)	Miami ($7,500)	37-22	Buffalo	73,103
1994	Jan. 1	Cleveland ($7,500)	New England ($7,500)	20-13	Cleveland	77,452
	Dec. 31	Miami ($12,000)	Kansas City ($7,500)	27-17	Miami	67,487
1993	Jan. 9	L.A. Raiders ($7,500)	Denver ($7,500)	42-24	Los Angeles	65,314
	Jan. 8	Kansas City ($12,000)	Pittsburgh ($7,500)	27-24*	Kansas City	74,515
1992	Jan. 3	Buffalo ($6,000)	Houston ($6,000)	41-38*	Buffalo	75,141
	Jan. 2	San Diego ($10,000)	Kansas City ($6,000)	17-0	San Diego	58,278
1991	Dec. 29	Houston ($10,000)	N.Y. Jets ($6,000)	17-10	Houston	61,485
	Dec. 28	Kansas City ($6,000)	L.A. Raiders ($6,000)	10-6	Kansas City	75,827
1990	Jan. 6	Cincinnati ($10,000)	Houston ($6,000)	41-14	Cincinnati	60,012
	Jan. 5	Miami ($6,000)	Kansas City ($6,000)	17-16	Miami	67,276
1989	Dec. 31	Pittsburgh ($6,000)	Houston ($6,000)	26-23*	Houston	59,406
1988	Dec. 26	Houston ($6,000)	Cleveland ($6,000)	24-23	Cleveland	75,896
1987	Jan. 3	Houston ($6,000)	Seattle ($6,000)	23-20*	Houston	50,519
1986	Dec. 28	N.Y. Jets ($6,000)	Kansas City ($6,000)	35-15	East Rutherford	75,210
1985	Dec. 28	New England ($6,000)	N.Y. Jets ($6,000)	26-14	East Rutherford	75,945
1984	Dec. 22	Seattle ($6,000)	L.A. Raiders ($6,000)	13-7	Seattle	62,049
1983	Dec. 24	Seattle ($6,000)	Denver ($6,000)	31-7	Seattle	64,275
1982	Jan. 9	N.Y. Jets ($6,000)	Cincinnati ($6,000)	44-17	Cincinnati	57,560
	Jan. 9	San Diego ($6,000)	Pittsburgh ($6,000)	31-28	Pittsburgh	53,546
	Jan. 8	L.A. Raiders ($6,000)	Cleveland ($6,000)	27-10	Los Angeles	56,555
	Jan. 8	Miami ($6,000)	New England ($6,000)	28-13	Miami	68,842
1981	Dec. 27	Buffalo ($3,000)	N.Y. Jets ($3,000)	31-27	New York	57,050
1980	Dec. 28	Oakland ($3,000)	Houston ($3,000)	27-7	Oakland	53,333
1979	Dec. 23	Houston ($3,000)	Denver ($3,000)	13-7	Houston	48,776
1978	Dec. 24	Houston ($3,000)	Miami ($3,000)	17-9	Miami	72,445

*Sudden death overtime

2010 AFC WILD CARD PLAYOFF GAMES

Arrowhead Stadium, Kansas City, Missouri
January 9, 2011, Attendance: 72,190
BALTIMORE 30, KANSAS CITY 7—Joe Flacco passed for 2 touchdowns and the Ravens scored the game's final 27 points en route to a wild-card victory. Baltimore's defense allowed just 161 total yards and forced five turnovers. Late in the first quarter, Tamba Hali sacked Flacco, forced him to fumble, and recovered the ball. Two plays later, Jamaal Charles ran up the middle 41 yards for a touchdown and 7-3 lead. The Chiefs' defense then forced a punt, and Kansas City drove across midfield. But Terrence Cody forced Charles to fumble and Brandon McKinney recovered. Late in the half, Flacco connected on a 13-yard pass to Todd Heap on third-and-13. The play sparked a drive that culminated with Ray Rice's 9-yard touchdown grab with just 19 seconds left in the half for a 10-7 halftime lead. The Chiefs drove to the Ravens' 33 to begin the second half, but Dawan Landry and his teammates stopped Charles on fourth-and-1 to regain possession. Billy Cundiff kicked a field goal to conclude the ensuing possession, and three plays later Ray Lewis forced Dexter McCluster to fumble. Chris Carr recovered at the Chiefs' 17, and Cundiff's third field goal gave Baltimore a 16-7 lead. Two plays later, Landry intercepted Matt Cassel's pass at the Chiefs' 31, and Anquan Boldin's 4-yard touchdown reception increased the lead to 23-7. After forcing a punt, the Ravens drove 80 yards in 15 plays, with Willis McGahee's fourth-and-goal 1-yard touchdown run giving Baltimore a 30-7 lead with 4:26 to play. Flacco was 25 of 34 for 265 yards and 2 touchdowns. Heap had 10 catches for 108 yards. Cassel completed 9 of 18 passes for 70 yards, with 3 interceptions.

Baltimore	3	7	13	7	—	30
Kansas City	7	0	0	0	—	7

Balt	—	FG Cundiff 19
KC	—	Charles 41 run (Succop kick)
Balt	—	Rice 9 pass from Flacco (Cundiff kick)
Balt	—	FG Cundiff 29
Balt	—	FG Cundiff 29
Balt	—	Boldin 4 pass from Flacco (Cundiff kick)
Balt	—	McGahee 25 run (Cundiff kick)

Lucas Oil Stadium, Indianapolis, Indiana
January 8, 2011, Attendance: 65,332
NEW YORK JETS 17, INDIANAPOLIS 16—Nick Folk's 32-yard field goal as time expired lifted the Jets past the Colts. Both teams punted to conclude each of their first four possessions before the Colts broke through. Dominic Rhodes picked up a first down on third-and-1, and on the next play Peyton Manning hit Pierre Garcon for a 57-yard touchdown pass. The Jets reached the Colts' red zone just before halftime, but Justin Tryon intercepted Mark Sanchez's pass, and the Colts took a 7-0 lead to the locker room. The Jets converted two third-down situations to begin the second half, and LaDainian Tomlinson tied the game with a 1-yard touchdown run. The Colts responded with a field goal, but the Jets answered with a 17-play, 87-yard drive that featured two third-down conversions and once again concluded with a Tomlinson 1-yard scoring run for a 14-10 lead with 9:59 remaining. The Colts kicked field goals on their next two possessions, taking a 16-14 lead with Adam Vinatieri's 50-yard boot with 53 seconds to play. Antonio Cromartie returned the ensuing kickoff 47 yards, and Sanchez completed a pair of passes to Braylon Edwards, including an 18-yard catch to the Colts' 14. Folk made the 32-yard field goal as time expired. Sanchez was 18 of 31 for 189 yards, with 1 interception. Manning was 18 of 26 for 225 yards and 1 touchdown. Garcon had 5 receptions for 112 yards.

New York Jets	0	0	7	10	—	17
Indianapolis	0	7	3	6	—	16

Ind	—	Garcon 57 pass from Manning (Vinatieri kick)
NYJ	—	Tomlinson 1 run (Folk kick)
Ind	—	FG Vinatieri 47
NYJ	—	Tomlinson 1 run (Folk kick)
Ind	—	FG Vinatieri 32
Ind	—	FG Vinatieri 50
NYJ	—	FG Folk 32

NFC WILD CARD PLAYOFF GAMES RESULTS

Season	Date	Winner (Share)	Loser (Share)	Score	Site	Attendance
2010	Jan. 9	Green Bay ($19,000)	Philadelphia ($21,000)	21-16	Philadelphia	69,144
	Jan. 8	Seattle ($21,000)	New Orleans ($19,000)	41-36	Seattle	66,336
2009	Jan. 10	Arizona ($21,000)	Green Bay ($19,000)	51-45*	Glendale	61,926
	Jan. 9	Dallas ($21,000)	Philadelphia ($19,000)	34-14	Dallas	92,951
2008	Jan. 4	Philadelphia ($18,000)	Minnesota ($20,000)	26-14	Minneapolis	61,746
	Jan. 3	Arizona ($20,000)	Atlanta ($18,000)	30-24	Glendale	62,848
2007	Jan. 6	N.Y. Giants ($18,000)	Tampa Bay ($20,000)	24-14	Tampa	65,621
	Jan. 5	Seattle ($20,000)	Washington ($18,000)	35-14	Seattle	68,297
2006	Jan. 7	Philadelphia ($19,000)	N.Y. Giants ($17,000)	23-20	Philadelphia	69,094
	Jan. 6	Seattle ($19,000)	Dallas ($17,000)	21-20	Seattle	68,058
2005	Jan. 8	Carolina ($17,000)	N.Y. Giants ($19,000)	23-0	East Rutherford	79,378
	Jan. 7	Washington ($17,000)	Tampa Bay ($19,000)	17-10	Tampa	65,514
2004	Jan. 9	Minnesota ($15,000)	Green Bay ($18,000)	31-17	Green Bay	71,075
	Jan. 8	St. Louis ($15,000)	Seattle ($18,000)	27-20	Seattle	65,397
2003	Jan. 4	Green Bay ($18,000)	Seattle ($15,000)	33-27*	Green Bay	71,457
	Jan. 3	Carolina ($18,000)	Dallas ($15,000)	29-10	Charlotte	73,014
2002	Jan. 5	San Francisco ($17,000)	N.Y. Giants ($12,500)	39-38	San Francisco	66,318
	Jan. 4	Atlanta ($12,500)	Green Bay ($17,000)	27-7	Green Bay	65,358
2001	Jan. 13	Green Bay ($12,500)	San Francisco ($12,500)	25-15	Green Bay	59,825
	Jan. 12	Philadelphia ($17,000)	Tampa Bay ($12,500)	31-9	Philadelphia	65,847
2000	Dec. 31	Philadelphia ($12,500)	Tampa Bay ($12,500)	21-3	Philadelphia	65,813
	Dec. 30	New Orleans ($16,000)	St. Louis ($12,500)	31-28	New Orleans	64,900
1999	Jan. 9	Minnesota ($10,000)	Dallas ($10,000)	27-10	Minneapolis	64,056
	Jan. 8	Washington ($16,000)	Detroit ($10,000)	27-13	Washington	79,411
1998	Jan. 3	San Francisco ($10,000)	Green Bay ($10,000)	30-27	San Francisco	66,506
	Jan. 2	Arizona ($10,000)	Dallas ($15,000)	20-7	Dallas	62,969
1997	Dec. 28	Tampa Bay ($10,000)	Detroit ($10,000)	20-10	Tampa	73,361
	Dec. 27	Minnesota ($10,000)	N.Y. Giants ($15,000)	23-22	East Rutherford	77,497
1996	Dec. 29	San Francisco ($10,000)	Philadelphia ($10,000)	14-0	San Francisco	56,460
	Dec. 28	Dallas ($14,000)	Minnesota ($10,000)	40-15	Dallas	64,682
1995	Dec. 31	Green Bay ($13,000)	Atlanta ($7,500)	37-20	Green Bay	60,453
	Dec. 30	Philadelphia ($7,500)	Detroit ($7,500)	58-37	Philadelphia	66,099
1994	Jan. 1	Chicago ($7,500)	Minnesota ($12,000)	35-18	Minnesota	60,347
	Dec. 31	Green Bay ($7,500)	Detroit ($7,500)	16-12	Green Bay	58,125
1993	Jan. 9	N.Y. Giants ($7,500)	Minnesota ($7,500)	17-10	East Rutherford	75,089
	Jan. 8	Green Bay ($7,500)	Detroit ($12,000)	28-24	Detroit	68,479
1992	Jan. 3	Philadelphia ($6,000)	New Orleans ($6,000)	36-20	New Orleans	68,893
	Jan. 2	Washington ($6,000)	Minnesota ($10,000)	24-7	Minnesota	57,353
1991	Dec. 29	Dallas ($6,000)	Chicago ($6,000)	17-13	Chicago	62,594
	Dec. 28	Atlanta ($6,000)	New Orleans ($10,000)	27-20	New Orleans	68,794
1990	Jan. 6	Chicago ($10,000)	New Orleans ($6,000)	16-6	Chicago	60,767
	Jan. 5	Washington ($6,000)	Philadelphia ($6,000)	20-6	Philadelphia	65,287
1989	Dec. 31	L.A. Rams ($6,000)	Philadelphia ($6,000)	21-7	Philadelphia	65,479
1988	Dec. 26	Minnesota ($6,000)	L.A. Rams ($6,000)	28-17	Minnesota	61,204
1987	Jan. 3	Minnesota ($6,000)	New Orleans ($6,000)	44-10	New Orleans	68,546
1986	Dec. 28	Washington ($6,000)	L.A. Rams ($6,000)	19-7	Washington	54,567
1985	Dec. 29	N.Y. Giants ($6,000)	San Francisco ($6,000)	17-3	East Rutherford	75,131
1984	Dec. 23	N.Y. Giants ($6,000)	L.A. Rams ($6,000)	16-13	Anaheim	67,037
1983	Dec. 26	L.A. Rams ($6,000)	Dallas ($6,000)	24-17	Dallas	62,118
1982	Jan. 9	Dallas ($6,000)	Tampa Bay ($6,000)	30-17	Dallas	65,042
	Jan. 9	Minnesota ($6,000)	Atlanta ($6,000)	30-24	Minnesota	60,560
	Jan. 8	Green Bay ($6,000)	St. Louis ($6,000)	41-16	Green Bay	54,282
	Jan. 8	Washington ($6,000)	Detroit ($6,000)	31-7	Washington	55,045
1981	Dec. 27	N.Y. Giants ($3,000)	Philadelphia ($3,000)	27-21	Philadelphia	71,611
1980	Dec. 28	Dallas ($3,000)	Los Angeles ($3,000)	34-13	Dallas	63,052
1979	Dec. 23	Philadelphia ($3,000)	Chicago ($3,000)	27-17	Philadelphia	69,397
1978	Dec. 24	Atlanta ($3,000)	Philadelphia ($3,000)	14-13	Atlanta	59,403

*Sudden death overtime

2010 NFC WILD CARD PLAYOFF GAMES

Lincoln Financial Field, Philadelphia, Pennsylvania
January 9, 2011, Attendance: 69,144

GREEN BAY 21, PHILADELPHIA 16—Aaron Rodgers passed for 3 touchdowns, James Starks ran for a career-high 123 yards, and Tramon Williams intercepted a pass in the end zone with 44 seconds remaining to give Green Bay a road playoff victory. Omar Gaither recovered a muffed punted two minutes into the game, but David Akers' 41-yard field-goal attempt sailed wide right moments later. The Packers drove 68 yards in 10 plays on their second possession, capped by Tom Crabtree's 7-yard scoring catch, for a 7-0 lead. The Packers' defense forced a punt and the offense methodically drove 57 yards in 12 plays, keyed by Rodgers' 8-yard scramble on third-and-5 that was immediately followed by his 9-yard touchdown pass to James Jones for a 14-0 lead with 5:21 left in the second quarter. The Eagles responded with a field goal and then, early in the second half, Darryl Tapp sacked Rodgers and forced him to fumble. Juqua Parker recovered, and two plays later Michael Vick completed a 24-yard touchdown pass to Jason Avant, trimming the deficit to 14-10.

The Packers then used a 20-yard pass to Donald Driver, 19-yard run by James Starks, and 16-yard pass to John Kuhn to set up Brandon Jackson's 16-yard touchdown catch for a 21-10 lead. Early in the fourth quarter, the Packers' defense stopped LeSean McCoy for no gain on third-and-1, and Akers' 34-yard field-goal attempt again sailed wide right with 13:05 to play. The Eagles' defense forced a punt, and 16-yard catches by McCoy and Brent Celek led to Vick's 1-yard quarterback sneak for a touchdown on fourth-and-goal with 4:02 to play. The Packers' defense stopped Vick's 2-point conversion pass attempt, however, and Green Bay led 21-16. Keenan Clayton's third-down sack of Rodgers forced Packers' punt, and DeSean Jackson's 14-yard return gave the Eagles the ball at their own 34-yard-line with 1:45 remaining. A 28-yard pass to Jackson and 11-yard catch by Riley Cooper put the ball at the Packers' 27 with 44 seconds to play. But on the next play Vick's pass for Cooper in the end zone was intercepted by Williams to clinch the road victory for Green Bay. Rodgers completed 18 of 27 passes for 180 yards and 3 touchdowns. Starks rushed 23 times for 123 yards. Vick was 20 of 36 for 292 yards and 1 touchdown, with 1 interception.

| Green Bay | 7 | 7 | 7 | 0 | — | 21 |
| Philadelphia | 0 | 3 | 7 | 6 | — | 16 |

GB — Crabtree 7 pass from Rodgers (Crosby kick)
GB — Jones 9 pass from Rodgers (Crosby kick)
Phil — FG Akers 29
Phil — Avant 24 pass from Vick (Akers kick)
GB — Jackson 16 pass from Rodgers (Crosby kick)
Phil — Vick 1 run (pass failed)

Qwest Field, Seattle, Washington
January 8, 2011, Attendance: 66,336
SEATTLE 41, NEW ORLEANS 36—Matt Hasselbeck passed for 4 touchdowns and Marshawn Lynch had a remarkable 67-yard touchdown run in the waning moments as the Seahawks defeated the defending Super Bowl champions. The Saints scored on their first three possessions, with Julius Jones' 5-yard touchdown run staking New Orleans to a 17-7 lead with 13:38 left in the second quarter. Seattle wasted little time in responding, keyed by a 39-yard pass to Cameron Morrah, and capped by John Carlson's 7-yard scoring catch, the Seahawks cut the deficit to 17-14. After an exchange of punts, Raheem Brock forced Jones to fumble. David Hawthorne recovered and Olindo Mare kicked a 29-yard field goal to tie the game. Seattle's defense forced another punt, and the offense drove 76 yards in nine plays, capped by Brandon Stokley's 45-yard touchdown grab with 1:15 left in the half. New Orleans drove 77 yards and cut the lead to 24-20 with Garrett Hartley's 22-yard field goal as the half expired. Seattle began the second half with the ball, and once again had success throwing deep, as Ben Obomanu's 18-yard reception set up Mike Williams' 38-yard touchdown catch for a 31-20 lead. After a Saints punt, Mare's second field goal expanded the lead to 34-20 with 5:27 remaining in the third quarter. After an exchange of punts, Jones' second touchdown culminated an 87-yard Saints drive and trimmed the deficit to 34-27 with 13:11 to play. Following a three-and-out, Jones' 33-yard catch led to Garrett Hartley's 21-yard field goal with 9:13 to play. After an exchange of punts, the Seahawks faced second-and-10 from their own 33-yard line with 3:38 remaining. Lynch took the handoff and ran over right tackle. Lynch broke a pair of tackles at the line of scrimmage, two tackles near midfield, and then stiff-armed a defender near the Saints' 35. With a convoy of blockers, Lynch stepped out of another tackle attempt and weaved his way through three more defenders before falling into the end zone. The crowd's reaction to Lynch's 67-yard touchdown run registered on the seismic Richter scale under Qwest Field. Down 11 points with 3:22 to play, Brees engineered a 70-yard scoring drive. Devery Henderson's touchdown catch pulled New Orleans within 41-36 with 1:30 to play, but the Seahawks stopped DeShawn Wynn's 2-point conversion running play, and Carlson recovered the ensuing onside kick to ensure victory. Hasselbeck was 22 of 35 for

272 yards and 4 touchdowns, with 1 interception. Lynch carried 19 times for 131 yards. Brees was 39 of 60 for 404 yards and 2 touchdowns.

| New Orleans | 10 | 10 | 0 | 16 | — | 36 |
| Seattle | 7 | 17 | 10 | 7 | — | 41 |

NO — FG Hartley 26
NO — Evans 1 pass from Brees (Hartley kick)
Sea — Carlson 11 pass from Hasselbeck (Mare kick)
NO — Jones 5 run (Hartley kick)
Sea — Carlson 7 pass from Hasselbeck (Mare kick)
Sea — FG Mare 29
Sea — Stokley 45 pass from Hasselbeck (Mare kick)
NO — FG Hartley 22
Sea — M. Williams 38 pass from Hasselbeck (Mare kick)
Sea — FG Mare 39
NO — Jones 4 run (Hartley kick)
NO — FG Hartley 21
Sea — Lynch 67 run (Mare kick)
NO — Henderson 6 pass from Brees (run failed)

AFC-NFC PRO BOWL RESULTS (1971-2011)

NFC leads series, 21-20

Year	Date	Winner (Share)	Loser (Share)	Score	Site	Attendance
2011	Jan. 30	NFC ($45,000)	AFC ($22,500)	55-41	Honolulu	49,331
2010	Jan. 31	AFC ($45,000)	NFC ($22,500)	41-34	Miami	70,697
2009	Feb. 8	NFC ($45,000)	AFC ($22,500)	30-21	Honolulu	49,958
2008	Feb. 10	NFC ($40,000)	AFC ($20,000)	42-30	Honolulu	50,044
2007	Feb. 10	AFC ($40,000)	NFC ($20,000)	31-28	Honolulu	50,410
2006	Feb. 12	NFC ($40,000)	AFC ($20,000)	23-17	Honolulu	50,190
2005	Feb. 13	AFC ($35,000)	NFC ($17,500)	38-27	Honolulu	50,225
2004	Feb. 8	NFC ($35,000)	AFC ($17,500)	55-52	Honolulu	50,127
2003	Feb. 2	AFC ($30,000)	NFC ($15,000)	45-20	Honolulu	50,125
2002	Feb. 9	AFC ($30,000)	NFC ($15,000)	38-30	Honolulu	50,301
2001	Feb. 4	AFC ($30,000)	NFC ($15,000)	38-17	Honolulu	50,128
2000	Feb. 6	NFC ($25,000)	AFC ($12,500)	51-31	Honolulu	50,112
1999	Feb. 7	AFC ($25,000)	NFC ($12,500)	23-10	Honolulu	50,075
1998	Feb. 1	AFC ($25,000)	NFC ($12,500)	29-24	Honolulu	49,995
1997	Feb. 2	AFC ($20,000)	NFC ($10,000)	26-23 (OT)	Honolulu	50,031
1996	Feb. 4	NFC ($20,000)	AFC ($10,000)	20-13	Honolulu	50,034
1995	Feb. 5	AFC ($20,000)	NFC ($10,000)	41-13	Honolulu	50,529
1994	Feb. 6	NFC ($20,000)	AFC ($10,000)	17-3	Honolulu	50,026
1993	Feb. 7	AFC ($10,000)	NFC ($5,000)	23-20 (OT)	Honolulu	50,007
1992	Feb. 2	NFC ($10,000)	AFC ($5,000)	21-15	Honolulu	50,209
1991	Feb. 3	AFC ($10,000)	NFC ($5,000)	23-21	Honolulu	50,345
1990	Feb. 4	NFC ($10,000)	AFC ($5,000)	27-21	Honolulu	50,445
1989	Jan. 29	NFC ($10,000)	AFC ($5,000)	34-3	Honolulu	50,113
1988	Feb. 7	AFC ($10,000)	NFC ($5,000)	15-6	Honolulu	50,113
1987	Feb. 1	AFC ($10,000)	NFC ($5,000)	10-6	Honolulu	50,101
1986	Feb. 2	NFC ($10,000)	AFC ($5,000)	28-24	Honolulu	50,101
1985	Jan. 27	AFC ($10,000)	NFC ($5,000)	22-14	Honolulu	50,385
1984	Jan. 29	NFC ($10,000)	AFC ($5,000)	45-3	Honolulu	50,445
1983	Feb. 6	NFC ($10,000)	AFC ($5,000)	20-19	Honolulu	49,883
1982	Jan. 31	AFC ($5,000)	NFC ($2,500)	16-13	Honolulu	50,402
1981	Feb. 1	NFC ($5,000)	AFC ($2,500)	21-7	Honolulu	50,360
1980	Jan. 27	NFC ($5,000)	AFC ($2,500)	37-27	Honolulu	49,800
1979	Jan. 29	NFC ($5,000)	AFC ($2,500)	13-7	Los Angeles	46,281
1978	Jan. 23	NFC ($5,000)	AFC ($2,500)	14-13	Tampa	51,337
1977	Jan. 17	AFC ($2,000)	NFC ($1,500)	24-14	Seattle	64,752
1976	Jan. 26	NFC ($2,000)	AFC ($1,500)	23-20	New Orleans	30,546
1975	Jan. 20	NFC ($2,000)	AFC ($1,500)	17-10	Miami	26,484
1974	Jan. 20	AFC ($2,000)	NFC ($1,500)	15-13	Kansas City	66,918
1973	Jan. 21	AFC ($2,000)	NFC ($1,500)	33-28	Dallas	37,091
1972	Jan. 23	AFC ($2,000)	NFC ($1,500)	26-13	Los Angeles	53,647
1971	Jan. 24	NFC ($2,000)	AFC ($1,500)	27-6	Los Angeles	48,222

2011 AFC-NFC PRO BOWL

Aloha Stadium, Honolulu, Hawai'i
January 30, 2011, Attendance: 49,331
NFC 55, AFC 41—The NFC jumped out to a 42-0 lead, scoring six touchdowns in less than 14 minutes, and forced six turnovers en route to victory. After the AFC failed to convert a fourth-and-three from the NFC's 41-yard line, Michael Vick scrambled for a first down on third-and-6, and completed a 23-yard pass to Roddy White on third-and-10 to set up Ovie Mughelli's 1-yard touchdown run with 3:14 left in the first quarter. On the AFC's next play, London Fletcher intercepted Philip Rivers' pass and returned it to the AFC 43. Five plays later, Adrian Peterson scored on a 14-yard run for a 14-0 lead. DeAngelo Hall and Devin McCourty had interceptions on back-to-back plays to give the AFC the ball, but Brent Grimes snared a Peyton Manning pass at the NFC 42. Keyed by a Devin Hester 19-yard run, the NFC took a 21-0 lead on Matt Ryan's 4-yard touchdown pass to Tony Gonzalez with 10:41 remaining in the half. On the next play from scrimmage, Wes Welker fumbled. Hall returned the fumble 34 yards for a touchdown and 28-0 advantage. The NFC defense forced a three-and-out, and Ryan's 25-yard touchdown pass to Larry Fitzgerald four plays later extended the lead. Two plays later, Antoine Winfield intercepted Matt Cassel's pass, and Steven Jackson's 21-yard scoring scamper gave the NFC a 42-0 lead with 4:32 left in the half. The NFC scored six touchdowns in 13 minutes, 42 seconds. The AFC cracked the scoreboard as Jamaal Charles carried five times on a six-play drive, capped by his 8-yard scoring run with 1:54 left in the half. Rivers engineered an eight-play, 69-yard drive to begin the second half, and his 16-yard touchdown pass to Reggie Wayne cut the deficit to 42-14. Hester then fumbled the ensuing kickoff. Montell Owens scooped up the ball for an 8-yard touchdown return for 14 points in five seconds. David Akers then made a field goal. It was his 48th career Pro Bowl point, setting the game's all-time scoring record. Rivers' touchdown pass to Marcedes Lewis cut the deficit to 45-28, and the AFC drove into NFC territory on its next drive, but failed to convert on fourth-and-seven with 8:10 to play. Akers made his second field goal, and three plays later Jon Beason intercepted a pass by Cassel and returned it 49 yards for a touchdown and 55-28 lead with 3:33 remaining. Cassel threw two touchdowns in the final 1:55, including a 67-yard pass play that included laterals by Dwyane Bowe and Owens to center Alex Mack, who took the ball the final 40 yards. With a fumble return for a touchdown, along with an interception, Hall was named MVP, only the second defensive player in 21 years so honored.

AFC (41)	Offense	NFC (55)
Brandon Lloyd (Denver)	WR	Roddy White (Atlanta)
D'Brickashaw Ferguson (N.Y. Jets)	LT	Tyson Clabo (Atlanta)
Kris Dielman (San Diego)	LG	Jahri Evans (New Orleans)
Jeff Saturday (Indianapolis)	C	Andre Gurode (Dallas)
Logan Mankins (New England)	RG	Chris Snee (N.Y. Giants)
Joe Thomas (Cleveland)	RT	Jordan Gross (Carolina)
Marcedes Lewis (Jacksonville)	TE	Jason Witten (Dallas)
Reggie Wayne (Indianapolis)	WR	Calvin Johnson (Detroit)
Philip Rivers (San Diego)	QB	Michael Vick (Philadelphia)
Vonta Leach (Houston)	FB	Ovie Mughelli (Atlanta)
Arian Foster (Houston)	RB	Michael Turner (Atlanta)

Defense

Jason Babin (Tennessee)	DE	Julius Peppers (Chicago)
Haloti Ngata (Baltimore)	UT	Justin Smith (San Francisco)
Vince Wilfork (New England)	NT	Jay Ratliff (Dallas)
Robert Mathis (Indianapolis)	DE	John Abraham (Atlanta)
Terrell Suggs (Baltimore)	SLB	Brian Orakpo (Washington)
Ray Lewis (Baltimore)	MLB	Jonathan Vilma (New Orleans)
Cameron Wake (Miami)	WLB	DeMarcus Ware (Dallas)
Devin McCourty (New England)	CB	DeAngelo Hall (Washington)
Darrelle Revis (N.Y. Jets)	CB	Brent Grimes (Atlanta)
Michael Griffin (Tennessee)	FS	Antrel Rolle (N.Y. Giants)
Brandon Meriweather (New England)	SS	Adrian Wilson (Arizona)

SUBSTITUTIONS

AFC—Specialists: K—Billy Cundiff (Baltimore). P—Shane Lechler (Oakland). KR—Marc Mariani (Tennessee). LS—John Denney (Miami). ST—Montell Owens (Jacksonville). Offense: QB—Matt Cassel (Kansas City), Peyton Manning (Indianapolis). RB—Jamaal Charles (Kansas City), Chris Johnson (Tennessee). TE—Zach Miller (Oakland). WR—Dwayne Bowe (Kansas City), Wes Welker (New England). G—Brian Waters (Kansas City). T—Matt Light (New England). C—Alex Mack (Cleveland), Nick Mangold (N.Y. Jets). Defense: DE—Randy Starks (Miami). DL—Kyle Williams (Buffalo). LB—Jerod Mayo (New England), Shaun Phillips (San Diego). CB—Champ Bailey (Denver). S—Eric Berry (Kansas City), Ed Reed (Baltimore). Not Active: QB—Tom Brady (New England). RB—Maurice Jones-Drew (Jacksonville). WR—Andre Johnson (Houston). TE—Antonio Gates (San Diego). T—Jake Long

(Miami). C—Maurkice Pouncey (Pittsburgh). DE—Dwight Freeney (Indianapolis), Brett Keisel (Pittsburgh). DL—Richard Seymour (Oakland). LB—James Harrison (Pittsburgh). CB—Nnamdi Asomugha (Oakland). S—Troy Polamalu (Pittsburgh).

NFC—Specialists: K—David Akers (Philadelphia). P—Mat McBriar (Dallas). KR—Devin Hester (Chicago). LS—Zak DeOssie (N.Y. Giants). ST—Eric Weems (Atlanta). Offense: QB—Drew Brees (New Orleans), Matt Ryan (Atlanta). RB—Steven Jackson (St. Louis), Adrian Peterson (Minnesota). WR—Miles Austin (Dallas), Larry Fitzgerald (Arizona). TE—Tony Gonzalez (Atlanta). T—Donald Penn (Tampa Bay). C—Ryan Kalil (Carolina). Defense: DE—Justin Tuck (N.Y. Giants). DL—Darnell Dockett (Arizona). LB—Jon Beason (Carolina), London Fletcher (Washington). CB—Antoine Winfield (Minnesota). S—Roman Harper (New Orleans). Not Active: WR—Donald Driver (Green Bay), DeSean Jackson (Philadelphia), Greg Jennings (Green Bay). T—Chad Clifton (Green Bay), Jason Peters (Philadelphia). C—Shaun O'Hara (N.Y. Giants). DT—Ndamukong Suh (Detroit). LB—Lance Briggs (Chicago), A.J. Hawk (Green Bay), E.J. Henderson (Minnesota), Clay Matthews (Green Bay), Brian Urlacher (Chicago), Patrick Willis (San Francisco). CB—Asante Samuel (Philadelphia), Tramon Williams (Green Bay), Charles Woodson (Green Bay). S—Nick Collins (Green Bay).

HEAD COACHES

AFC—Bill Belichick (New England)
NFC—Mike Smith (Atlanta)

OFFICIALS

Referee—Tony Corrente. Umpire—Jeff Rice. Side Judge—Larry Rose. Field Judge—Greg Gautreaux. Head Linesman—Tom Stabile. Back Judge—Terrence Miles. Line Judge—Byron Boston.

AFC	0	7	21	13	— 41
NFC	14	28	3	10	— 55

NFC — Mughelli 1 run (Akers kick)
NFC — Peterson 14 run (Akers kick)
NFC — Gonzalez 4 pass from Ryan (Akers kick)
NFC — Hall 34 fumble return (Akers kick)
NFC — Fitzgerald 25 pass from Ryan (Akers kick)
NFC — Jackson 21 run (Akers kick)
AFC — Charles 8 run (Cundiff kick)
AFC — Wayne 16 pass from Rivers (Cundiff kick)
AFC — Owens 8 fumble return (Cundiff kick)
NFC — FG Akers 41
AFC — M. Lewis 28 pass from Rivers (Cundiff kick)
NFC — FG Akers 38
NFC — Beason 49 interception return (Akers kick)
AFC — Owens 7 pass from Cassel (Cundiff kick)

AFC — Mack 67 pass play from Cassel (pass failed)

TEAM STATISTICS

	AFC	NFC
Total First Downs	23	24
Rushing	8	8
Passing	13	16
Penalty	2	0
Total Net Yardage	425	429
Total Offensive Plays	66	67
Avg. Gain Per Offensive Play	6.4	6.4
Rushes	22	37
Yards Gained Rushing (Net)	132	184
Avg. Yards per Rush	6.0	5.0
Passes Attempted	43	29
Passes Completed	24	18
Had Intercepted	5	1
Tackled Attempting to Pass	1	1
Yards Lost Attempting to Pass	6	0
Yards Gained Passing (Net)	293	245
Punts	1	1
Avg. Distance	36.0	70.0
Punt Returns	1	0
Punt Return Yardage	1	0
Kickoff Returns	9	6
Kickoff Return Yardage	326	112
Interception Return Yardage	0	111
Total Return Yardage (KO excluded)	1	111
Fumbles	2	1
Fumbles Lost	1	1
Own Fumbles Recovered	1	0
Opponent Fumbles Recovered	1	1
Penalties	0	3
Yards Penalized	0	30
Field Goals	0	2
Field Goals Attempted	0	3
Third-Down Efficiency	3/10	5/10
Fourth-Down Efficiency	2/4	0/1
Time of Possession	27.52	32.08

INDIVIDUAL STATISTICS

RUSHING: AFC: Charles 10-72-1, Ch. Johnson 6-33-0, Foster 3-13-0, Mariani 2-11-0, Owens 1-3-0. NFC: Peterson 14-80-1, Turner 8-53-0, S. Jackson 6-33-1, Hester 2-21-0, Mughelli 2-3-1, Brees 5-(-6)-0.

PASSING: AFC: Rivers 26-17-192-2-2, Cassel 12-8-95-2-2, Manning 5-2-12-0-1, Foster 0-0-0-0-0. NFC: Ryan 13-9-118-2-1, Vick 10-5-59-0-0, Brees 6-4-68-0-0.

RECEIVING: AFC: Wayne 5-86-1, Welker 5-34-0, Bowe 4-54-0, Owens 2-22-1, Ch. Johnson 2-9-0, Foster 2-9-0, Charles 2-0-0, M. Lewis 1-28-1, Lloyd 1-15-0, Mack 0-40-0. NFC: White 5-69-0, Gonzalez 3-42-1, Hester 2-27-0, Mughelli 2-23-0, Fitzgerald 1-25-1, Witten 1-18-0, Ca. Johnson 1-11-0, Turner 1-11-0, Jackson 1-11-0, Austin 1-8-0.

KICKOFF RETURNS: AFC: Mariani 9-326-0. NFC: Hester 5-100-0, Peterson 1-12-0.

PUNT RETURNS: AFC: Mariani 1-1-0. NFC: None.

PUNTING: AFC: Lechler 1-36-36.0. NFC: McBriar 1-70-70.0.

INTERCEPTIONS: AFC: McCourty 1-0. NFC: Beason 1-49, Hall 1-29, Winfield 1-19, Fletcher 1-14, Grimes 1-0.

SACKS: AFC: Starks 1. NFC: Peppers 1.

Includes AFL All-Star Game played after the 1961-69 seasons.

Date	Result/Honored players	Site (attendance)
Jan. 15, 1939	New York Giants 13, Pro All-Stars 10	Wrigley Field, Los Angeles (20,000)
Jan. 14, 1940	Green Bay 16, NFL All-Stars 7	Gilmore Stadium, Los Angeles (18,000)
Dec. 29, 1940	Chicago Bears 28, NFL All-Stars 14	Gilmore Stadium, Los Angeles (21,624)
Jan. 4, 1942	Chicago Bears 35, NFL All-Stars 24	Polo Grounds, New York (17,725)
Dec. 27, 1942	NFL All-Stars 17, Washington 14	Shibe Park, Philadelphia (18,671)
Jan. 14, 1951	American Conf. 28, National Conf. 27	Los Angeles Memorial Coliseum (53,676)
	Otto Graham, Cleveland, player of the game	
Jan. 12, 1952	National Conf. 30, American Conf. 13	Los Angeles Memorial Coliseum (19,400)
	Dan Towler, Los Angeles, player of the game	
Jan. 10, 1953	National Conf. 27, American Conf. 7	Los Angeles Memorial Coliseum (34,208)
	Don Doll, Detroit, player of the game	
Jan. 17, 1954	East 20, West 9	Los Angeles Memorial Coliseum (44,214)
	Chuck Bednarik, Philadelphia, player of the game	
Jan. 16, 1955	West 26, East 19	Los Angeles Memorial Coliseum (43,972)
	Billy Wilson, San Francisco, player of the game	
Jan. 15, 1956	East 31, West 30	Los Angeles Memorial Coliseum (37,867)
	Ollie Matson, Chi. Cardinals, player of the game	
Jan. 13, 1957	West 19, East 10	Los Angeles Memorial Coliseum (44,177)
	Bert Rechichar, Baltimore, outstanding back	
	Ernie Stautner, Pittsburgh, outstanding lineman	
Jan. 12, 1958	West 26, East 7	Los Angeles Memorial Coliseum (66,634)
	Hugh McElhenny, San Francisco, outstanding back	
	Gene Brito, Washington, outstanding lineman	
Jan. 11, 1959	East 28, West 21	Los Angeles Memorial Coliseum (72,250)
	Frank Gifford, N.Y. Giants, outstanding back	
	Doug Atkins, Chi. Bears, outstanding lineman	
Jan. 17, 1960	West 38, East 21	Los Angeles Memorial Coliseum (56,876)
	Johnny Unitas, Baltimore, outstanding back	
	Gene (Big Daddy) Lipscomb, Baltimore, outstanding lineman	
Jan. 15, 1961	West 35, East 31	Los Angeles Memorial Coliseum (62,971)
	Johnny Unitas, Baltimore, outstanding back	
	Sam Huff, N.Y. Giants, outstanding lineman	
Jan. 7, 1962	AFL West 47, East 27	Balboa Stadium, San Diego (20,973)
	Cotton Davidson, Dallas Texans, player of the game	
Jan. 14, 1962	NFL West 31, East 30	Los Angeles Memorial Coliseum (57,409)
	Jim Brown, Cleveland, outstanding back	
	Henry Jordan, Green Bay, outstanding lineman	
Jan. 13, 1963	AFL West 21, East 14	Balboa Stadium, San Diego (27,641)
	Curtis McClinton, Dallas Texans, outstanding offensive player	
	Earl Faison, San Diego, outstanding defensive player	
Jan. 13, 1963	NFL East 30, West 20	Los Angeles Memorial Coliseum (61,374)
	Jim Brown, Cleveland, outstanding back	
	Gene (Big Daddy) Lipscomb, Pittsburgh, outstanding lineman	
Jan. 12, 1964	NFL West 31, East 17	Los Angeles Memorial Coliseum (67,242)
	Johnny Unitas, Baltimore, player of the game	
	Gino Marchetti, Baltimore, outstanding lineman	
Jan. 19, 1964	AFL West 27, East 24	Balboa Stadium, San Diego (20,016)
	Keith Lincoln, San Diego, outstanding offensive player	
	Archie Matsos, Oakland, outstanding defensive player	
Jan. 10, 1965	NFL West 34, East 14	Los Angeles Memorial Coliseum (60,598)
	Fran Tarkenton, Minnesota, outstanding back	
	Terry Barr, Detroit, outstanding lineman	
Jan. 16, 1965	AFL West 38, East 14	Jeppesen Stadium, Houston (15,446)
	Keith Lincoln, San Diego, outstanding offensive player	
	Willie Brown, Denver, outstanding defensive player	
Jan. 15, 1966	AFL All-Stars 30, Buffalo 19	Rice Stadium, Houston (35,572)
	Joe Namath, N.Y. Jets, most valuable player, offense	
	Frank Buncom, San Diego, most valuable player, defense	
Jan. 15, 1966	NFL East 36, West 7	Los Angeles Memorial Coliseum (60,124)
	Jim Brown, Cleveland, outstanding back	
	Dale Meinert, St. Louis, outstanding lineman	
Jan. 21, 1967	AFL East 30, West 23	Oakland-Alameda County Coliseum (18,876)
	Babe Parilli, Boston, outstanding offensive player	
	Verlon Biggs, N.Y. Jets, outstanding defensive player	
Jan. 22, 1967	NFL East 20, West 10	Los Angeles Memorial Coliseum (15,062)
	Gale Sayers, Chicago, outstanding back	
	Floyd Peters, Philadelphia, outstanding lineman	

Jan. 21, 1968 AFL East 25, West 24 .... Gator Bowl, Jacksonville, Fla. (40,103)
    Joe Namath and Don Maynard, N.Y. Jets, out. off. players
    Leslie (Speedy) Duncan, San Diego, out. def. player
Jan. 21, 1968 NFL West 38, East 20 .... Los Angeles Memorial Coliseum (53,289)
    Gale Sayers, Chicago, outstanding back
    Dave Robinson, Green Bay, outstanding lineman
Jan. 19, 1969 AFL West 38, East 25 .... Gator Bowl, Jacksonville, Fla. (41,058)
    Len Dawson, Kansas City, outstanding offensive player
    George Webster, Houston, outstanding defensive player
Jan. 19, 1969 NFL West 10, East 7 .... Los Angeles Memorial Coliseum (32,050)
    Roman Gabriel, Los Angeles, outstanding back
    Merlin Olsen, Los Angeles, outstanding lineman
Jan. 17, 1970 AFL West 26, East 3 .... Astrodome, Houston (30,170)
    John Hadl, San Diego, player of the game
Jan. 18, 1970 NFL West 16, East 13 .... Los Angeles Memorial Coliseum (57,786)
    Gale Sayers, Chicago, outstanding back
    George Andrie, Dallas, outstanding lineman
Jan. 24, 1971 NFC 27, AFC 6 .... Los Angeles Memorial Coliseum (48,222)
    Mel Renfro, Dallas, outstanding back
    Fred Carr, Green Bay, outstanding lineman
Jan. 23, 1972 AFC 26, NFC 13 .... Los Angeles Memorial Coliseum (53,647)
    Jan Stenerud, Kansas City, outstanding offensive player
    Willie Lanier, Kansas City, outstanding defensive player
Jan. 21, 1973 AFC 33, NFC 28 .... Texas Stadium, Irving (37,091)
    O.J. Simpson, Buffalo, player of the game
Jan. 20, 1974 AFC 15, NFC 13 .... Arrowhead Stadium, Kansas City (66,918)
    Garo Yepremian, Miami, player of the game
Jan. 20, 1975 NFC 17, AFC 10 .... Orange Bowl, Miami (26,484)
    James Harris, Los Angeles, player of the game
Jan. 26, 1976 NFC 23, AFC 20 .... Louisiana Superdome, New Orleans (30,546)
    Billy Johnson, Houston, player of the game
Jan. 17, 1977 AFC 24, NFC 14 .... Kingdome, Seattle (64,752)
    Mel Blount, Pittsburgh, player of the game
Jan. 23, 1978 NFC 14, AFC 13 .... Tampa Stadium (51,337)
    Walter Payton, Chicago, player of the game
Jan. 29, 1979 NFC 13, AFC 7 .... Los Angeles Memorial Coliseum (46,281)
    Ahmad Rashad, Minnesota, player of the game
Jan. 27, 1980 NFC 37, AFC 27 .... Aloha Stadium, Honolulu (49,800)
    Chuck Muncie, New Orleans, player of the game
Feb. 1, 1981 NFC 21, AFC 7 .... Aloha Stadium, Honolulu (50,360)
    Eddie Murray, Detroit, player of the game
Jan. 31, 1982 AFC 16, NFC 13 .... Aloha Stadium, Honolulu (50,402)
    Kellen Winslow, San Diego, and Lee Roy Selmon, Tampa Bay, players of the game
Feb. 6, 1983 NFC 20, AFC 19 .... Aloha Stadium, Honolulu (49,883)
    Dan Fouts, San Diego, and John Jefferson, Green Bay, players of the game
Jan. 29, 1984 NFC 45, AFC 3 .... Aloha Stadium, Honolulu (50,445)
    Joe Theismann, Washington, player of the game
Jan. 27, 1985 AFC 22, NFC 14 .... Aloha Stadium, Honolulu (50,385)
    Mark Gastineau, N.Y. Jets, player of the game
Feb. 2, 1986 NFC 28, AFC 24 .... Aloha Stadium, Honolulu (50,101)
    Phil Simms, N.Y. Giants, player of the game
Feb. 1, 1987 AFC 10, NFC 6 .... Aloha Stadium, Honolulu (50,101)
    Reggie White, Philadelphia, player of the game
Feb. 7, 1988 AFC 15, NFC 6 .... Aloha Stadium, Honolulu (50,113)
    Bruce Smith, Buffalo, player of the game
Jan. 29, 1989 NFC 34, AFC 3 .... Aloha Stadium, Honolulu (50,113)
    Randall Cunningham, Philadelphia, player of the game
Feb. 4, 1990 NFC 27, AFC 21 .... Aloha Stadium, Honolulu (50,445)
    Jerry Gray, L.A. Rams, player of the game
Feb. 3, 1991 AFC 23, NFC 21 .... Aloha Stadium, Honolulu (50,345)
    Jim Kelly, Buffalo, player of the game
Feb. 2, 1992 NFC 21, AFC 15 .... Aloha Stadium, Honolulu (50,209)
    Michael Irvin, Dallas, player of the game
Feb. 7, 1993 AFC 23, NFC 20 (OT) .... Aloha Stadium, Honolulu (50,007)
    Steve Tasker, Buffalo, player of the game
Feb. 6, 1994 NFC 17, AFC 3 .... Aloha Stadium, Honolulu (50,026)
    Andre Rison, Atlanta, player of the game
Feb. 5, 1995 AFC 41, NFC 13 .... Aloha Stadium, Honolulu (50,529)
    Marshall Faulk, Indianapolis, player of the game

Feb. 4, 1996   NFC 20, AFC 13...Aloha Stadium, Honolulu (50,034)
          Jerry Rice, San Francisco, player of the game

Feb. 2, 1997   AFC 26, NFC 23 (OT)...Aloha Stadium, Honolulu (50,031)
          Mark Brunell, Jacksonville, player of the game

Feb. 1, 1998   AFC 29, NFC 24 ....Aloha Stadium, Honolulu (49,995)
          Warren Moon, Seattle, player of the game

Feb. 7, 1999   AFC 23, NFC 10 ....Aloha Stadium, Honolulu (50,075)
          Keyshawn Johnson, N.Y. Jets and Ty Law, New England, co-players of the game

Feb. 6, 2000   NFC 51, AFC 31 ....Aloha Stadium, Honolulu (50,112)
          Randy Moss, Minnesota, player of the game

Feb. 4, 2001   AFC 38, NFC 17 ....Aloha Stadium, Honolulu (50,128)
          Rich Gannon, Oakland, player of the game

Feb. 9, 2002   AFC 38, NFC 30 ....Aloha Stadium, Honolulu (50,301)
          Rich Gannon, Oakland, player of the game

Feb. 2, 2003   AFC 45, NFC 20 ....Aloha Stadium, Honolulu (50,125)
          Ricky Williams, Miami, player of the game

Feb. 8, 2004   NFC 55, AFC 52 ....Aloha Stadium, Honolulu (50,127)
          Marc Bulger, St. Louis, player of the game

Feb. 13, 2005   AFC 38, NFC 27 ....Aloha Stadium, Honolulu (50,225)
          Peyton Manning, Indianapolis, player of the game

Feb. 12, 2006   NFC 23, AFC 17 ....Aloha Stadium, Honolulu (50,190)
          Derrick Brooks, Tampa Bay, player of the game

Feb. 10, 2007   AFC 31, NFC 28 ....Aloha Stadium, Honolulu (50,410)
          Carson Palmer, Cincinnati, player of the game

Feb. 10, 2008   NFC 42, AFC 30 ....Aloha Stadium, Honolulu (50,044)
          Adrian Peterson, Minnesota, most valuable player

Feb. 8, 2009   NFC 30, AFC 21 ....Aloha Stadium, Honolulu (49,958)
          Larry Fitzgerald, Arizona, most valuable player

Jan. 31, 2010   AFC 41, NFC 34...Sun Life Stadium, South Florida (70,697)
          Matt Schaub, Houston, most valuable player

Jan. 30, 2011   NFC 55, AFC 41 ....Aloha Stadium, Honolulu (49,331)
          DeAngelo Hall, Washington, most valuable player

2010 PRIMETIME GAMES
(Home Team in capitals, games listed in chronological order.)

SUNDAY NIGHT FOOTBALL
WASHINGTON 13, Dallas 7
INDIANAPOLIS 38, New York Giants 14
New York Jets 31, MIAMI 23
NEW YORK GIANTS 17, Chicago 3
Philadelphia 27, SAN FRANCISCO 24
Indianapolis 27, WASHINGTON 24
GREEN BAY 28, Minnesota 24
NEW ORLEANS 20, Pittsburgh 10
GREEN BAY 45, Dallas 7
New England 39, PITTSBURGH 26
PHILADELPHIA 27, New York Giants 17
San Diego 36, INDIANAPOLIS 14
Pittsburgh 13, BALTIMORE 10
Philadelphia 30, DALLAS 27
NEW ENGLAND 31, Green Bay 27
GREEN BAY 45, New York Giants 17
SEATTLE 16, St. Louis 9

MONDAY NIGHT FOOTBALL
Baltimore 10, NEW YORK JETS 9
KANSAS CITY 21, San Diego 14
New Orleans 25, SAN FRANCISCO 22
CHICAGO 20, Green Bay 17
New England 41, MIAMI 14
NEW YORK JETS 29, Minnesota 20
Tennessee 30, JACKSONVILLE 3
New York Giants 41, DALLAS 35
INDIANAPOLIS 30, Houston 17
Pittsburgh 27, CINCINNATI 21
Philadelphia 59, WASHINGTON 28
SAN DIEGO 35, Denver 14
San Francisco 27, ARIZONA 6
NEW ENGLAND 45, New York Jets 3
New York Giants 21, MINNESOTA 3
Baltimore 34, HOUSTON 28 (OT)
Chicago 40, MINNESOTA 14
New Orleans 17, ATLANTA 14

THURSDAY-SATURDAY NIGHT FOOTBALL
NEW ORLEANS 14, Minnesota 9 (Thurs.)
ATLANTA 26, Baltimore 21 (Thurs.)
Chicago 16, MIAMI 0 (Thurs.)
NEW YORK JETS 26, Cincinnati 10 (Thurs.)
PHILADELPHIA 34, Houston 24 (Thurs.)
INDIANAPOLIS 30, Tennessee 28 (Thurs.)
SAN DIEGO 34, San Francisco 7 (Thurs.)
PITTSBURGH 27, Carolina 3 (Thurs.)
ARIZONA 27, Dallas 26 (Sat.)

SUNDAY NIGHT WON-LOST RECORDS, 1978-2010
AMERICAN FOOTBALL CONFERENCE

	Balt.	Buff.	Cin.	Clev.	Den.	Hou.	Ind.	Jax.	K.C.	Mia.	N.E.	N.Y.J.	Oak.	Pitt.	S.D.	Tenn.
Total	9-9	10-10	3-10	1-9	18-15	1-3	18-17	5-6	10-4	19-8	17-14	9-11	16-18	16-16	15-15	11-9
2010	0-1						2-1			0-1	2-0	1-0		1-2	1-0	
2009	1-0		0-1		3-0						0-1	1-0		1-1	0-1	
2008	1-0			0-1			2-1	0-1			0-2			2-0	2-1	0-1
2007	0-1	0-1	0-1	1-0			1-2				3-0			1-1	1-1	1-0
2006				2-2	3-0				0-1		0-2		0-1	0-1	3-0	
2005	1-1	0-1	0-1	0-1		0-2	1-0	1-0	2-0		1-0	0-1	0-2	1-0	2-0	
2004	2-1	0-1	1-0	0-2	1-1	0-1	1-0	0-1	0-1	1-2	1-0		2-0	2-0		
2003	1-1	0-2	1-0	1-0			1-1	1-0	1-0	2-0	1-0		0-1	0-2		1-0
2002	1-0		0-1	0-1	0-2	1-0	1-1	0-1		1-1	0-2	2-0	2-0	0-1		
2001	0-1	0-1		2-0	0-2					1-0	0-1	2-0	1-1	1-0		0-1
2000	1-1	1-0					1-0			1-0	0-2	2-0	0-1		0-1	0-1
1999		2-0	0-1	0-1	1-1		1-0	1-0	1-0	2-0	0-1	0-1	1-0			0-1
1998	1-0	1-0	0-1		1-0		0-1	0-1	2-0	0-1	1-0	1-0	1-1		0-1	1-0
1997	0-1		1-0		0-1						1-1	1-0	0-1	2-0	0-2	
1996	0-1	1-1	0-1	1-1	1-0		1-0		1-0		2-0	0-1	0-1		1-1	1-0
1995		0-2		2-1				0-1	1-0	1-0	0-1	0-1	1-1		0-1	0-1
1994		1-0	0-1	0-1			0-1		2-0	2-1	1-0	0-1	1-1	0-1	1-0	
1993		1-0	0-1	0-1			0-3		0-1	1-0	0-1	1-1	1-0	0-1	0-2	2-1
1992		1-1	1-0	2-0			0-1		1-1	1-0	0-1	1-1	0-2	1-0	1-0	1-1
1991		1-0	0-1	2-0			0-2			1-0		0-1	2-0	1-1	0-1	2-0
1990		1-0	1-1	0-2						1-0			0-1	1-2	0-1	1-1
1989							1-0				1-0	0-1	0-1	0-2	1-0	
1988		0-1									0-1	1-0	1-0	1-0	0-1	1-1
1987			0-1	0-1							2-0	0-1	0-1	1-0		
1986																
1985														0-1	1-0	
1984			0-1	1-0												
1983														1-0		
1982																
1981																
1980															0-1	
1979																
1978					1-0						1-0		0-2	0-1		

SUNDAY NIGHT FOOTBALL ALL-TIME STANDINGS
AMERICAN FOOTBALL CONFERENCE

East	W	L	T	Pct.
Miami	19	8	0	.704
New England	17	14	0	.548
Buffalo	10	10	0	.500
New York Jets	9	11	0	.450

North	W	L	T	Pct.
Pittsburgh	16	16	0	.500
Baltimore	9	9	0	.500
Cincinnati	3	10	0	.231
Cleveland	1	9	0	.100

South	W	L	T	Pct.
Tennessee	11	9	0	.550
Indianapolis	18	17	0	.514
Jacksonville	5	6	0	.455
Houston	1	3	0	.250

West	W	L	T	Pct.
Kansas City	10	4	0	.714
Denver	18	15	0	.545
San Diego	15	15	0	.500
Oakland	16	18	0	.471

SUNDAY NIGHT WON-LOST RECORDS, 1978-2010
NATIONAL FOOTBALL CONFERENCE

	Ariz.	Atl.	Car.	Chi.	Dall.	Det.	G.B.	Minn.	N.O.	N.Y.G.	Phil.	St. L.	S.F.	Sea.	T.B.	Wash.
Total	7-13	7-7	5-7	13-17	20-19	5-7	17-5	15-15	12-12	15-21-1	15-12	10-12	11-9	16-11	6-11	15-15-1
2010				0-1	0-3		3-1	0-1	1-0	1-3	3-0	0-1	0-1	1-0		1-1
2009	2-1	1-0	1-0	0-3	2-1		1-0	0-2		1-2	2-1					0-1
2008			0-1	2-1	3-0		0-1	1-0		2-1	0-2			0-1	1-0	0-2
2007				1-1	3-0		0-1	0-1	1-0	1-2	0-3			0-1		2-0
2006			0-1	2-1	2-1		1-0		1-0	0-2	0-1			1-1		0-1
2005	1-0	0-1		1-0	0-1	0-1	1-0	0-1	1-0	0-1	0-1	1-0	0-1	1-0		1-0
2004				1-0	0-1		1-0	1-0	0-1	1-0	1-0	1-0	0-2		0-1	0-2
2003		1-0	0-1	0-1	0-1		1-0	1-1	1-1	0-1		1-0	0-1	1-0	0-1	0-1
2002		1-0		0-1	0-1		1-0	0-2	1-0	1-0		1-0		1-0	1-1	1-0
2001	0-1		0-1	1-0	0-1			0-1	0-2		2-0	1-0	2-0	1-1	0-1	1-0
2000	1-1	0-1	1-0	0-2	0-2		1-0	1-0		2-1	1-0	0-1				1-0
1999	0-2	0-1	1-0		0-1	1-0	1-0	0-1	0-1	0-1			0-1	2-0	0-2	2-0
1998	1-0	1-0	0-1	0-2	1-0	1-0		2-0	0-1	0-1	0-1		1-0	0-2	0-1	0-1
1997	1-0	0-1	1-1	1-1	0-1	0-2	1-0	1-0	1-0	0-0-1	0-1	0-1	0-1	1-0	1-0	1-0-1
1996	0-1	0-1	1-0			0-1	1-0	2-0	0-1	0-2	1-0	0-1	1-0	0-1	1-0	1-0
1995	0-1	0-2	0-1		1-0			1-1	0-1	1-0	1-0	2-0	1-0	1-0	1-0	0-1
1994	1-1		1-0		1-1				1-0	1-0	1-0	0-1	1-0	0-1	0-1	0-1
1993	0-1		1-0	1-0	1-0	2-0	1-2	1-0	0-1	1-0			1-0	0-1	1-0	1-0
1992	0-1		0-1			1-0			1-1	1-1	1-0	1-1	1-0	0-1	0-1	0-1
1991	0-1	1-0		1-0	0-1		1-1	1-1	0-1			0-2		1-1	0-1	2-0
1990	0-1	1-0		1-1	0-1	1-1	0-1	2-0		1-0	0-2	0-1	1-0	2-0	1-0	1-0
1989			0-1	1-0			1-0	0-1				1-0		1-0		0-1
1988				0-1				1-0	0-1	1-0		1-0	0-1	1-0		0-1
1987			1-0	0-1				0-1		1-0		0-1	2-0	1-0		0-1
1986				0-1								1-0				
1985				1-0						0-1						
1984				1-0					0-1							
1983				0-1												
1982		1-0														
1981					1-0								0-1			
1980					1-0											
1979					1-0								0-1			
1978													1-0			

SUNDAY NIGHT FOOTBALL ALL-TIME STANDINGS
NATIONAL FOOTBALL CONFERENCE

East	W	L	T	Pct.	South	W	L	T	Pct.
Philadelphia	15	12	0	.556	New Orleans	12	12	0	.500
Dallas	20	19	0	.513	Atlanta	7	7	0	.500
Washington	15	15	1	.500	Carolina	5	7	0	.417
New York Giants	15	21	1	.419	Tampa Bay	6	11	0	.353

North	W	L	T	Pct.	West	W	L	T	Pct.
Green Bay	17	5	0	.773	Seattle	16	11	0	.593
Minnesota	15	15	0	.500	San Francisco	11	9	0	.550
Chicago	13	17	0	.433	St. Louis	10	12	0	.455
Detroit	5	7	0	.417	Arizona	7	13	0	.350

MONDAY NIGHT WON-LOST RECORDS, 1970-2010

AMERICAN FOOTBALL CONFERENCE

	Balt.	Buff.	Cin.	Cle.	Den.	Hou.	Ind.	Jax.	K.C.	Mia.	N.E.	N.Y.J.	Oak.	Pitt.	S.D.	Tenn.
Total	7-8	17-23	9-19	15-14	27-34-1	1-3	21-11	7-6	21-15	40-36	19-22	18-25	36-25-1	39-22	19-16	20-16
2010	2-0		0-1		0-1	0-2	1-0	0-1	1-0		0-1	2-0	1-2	1-0	1-1	1-0
2009	1-1	0-1		0-1	1-1	0-1	1-0			1-1	1-1	0-1	0-1	1-0	1-1	1-0
2008	0-1	0-1		2-1	1-1	1-0	0-1	0-1			1-0		0-1	0-1	2-0	1-0	1-0
2007	0-3	0-1	1-1		1-2		1-0	0-1	0-1	2-0				2-0	1-0	1-1
2006	0-1		0-1		1-0		1-0	2-0	0-1	0-1	1-0	1-0	0-2	0-1	1-0	
2005	1-1			1-0			3-0		0-1		1-1	0-2		2-1	0-1	
2004	0-1		1-0	0-1	1-0		2-1		1-1	1-1	1-0					1-1
2003			0-1	1-1	1-0		1-0		1-1	1-0	1-0		0-3	0-1	0-1	0-1
2002	1-0			0-2	0-1				1-1	1-1		0-1	2-0	2-1		1-0
2001	2-0			1-1	0-1	0-1			1-0			0-1	1-0	1-0		0-2
2000		0-1		1-1	2-0	0-2	1-1		1-1	1-1	2-0	0-1				3-0
1999		1-0		1-2			2-0		1-2	0-1	2-1		0-1	1-0		
1998				2-1			2-0	0-2	1-2	1-2	1-0			2-1		
1997		1-1		2-1		0-1	1-0	2-0	1-2	1-2				0-2	0-2	
1996		0-2		1-0	1-0				0-2	1-2			2-1	3-0	1-1	
1995		1-1	0-2	1-0					1-1	2-1	1-0		0-2	1-1	1-1	
1994		1-1		0-2					1-1	1-0			1-1	2-0	0-1	0-3
1993		2-1	1-0	0-2		0-1			2-0	1-2			1-0	3-0	2-0	0-1
1992		2-0	0-1	0-1	0-2				1-0	2-1		0-1	0-2	1-0		1-0
1991		2-1	0-2						2-1	1-1		0-1	0-2	0-1		1-1
1990		1-1	1-1	1-1	1-1		0-1		0-1			0-1	0-1	2-0	1-0	1-0
1989		1-2	1-2	1-1	2-0								0-1	1-0		1-0
1988		2-0		1-2	0-2		1-1			1-1		0-1	1-1			1-0
1987				1-0	2-1						1-1	1-1	2-1	1-1		
1986		1-0	1-0	1-1					1-2	1-0	1-1		0-1	0-2	0-1	
1985		1-0	1-0	1-0					2-1	0-1			1-0	0-2	0-1	
1984		0-1	0-1	1-0						3-0		0-1	2-1	1-1	1-2	
1983		0-1	0-2						0-1	1-1		2-0	1-0	1-0	1-1	
1982		0-1	0-1							1-1	1-0		1-0	1-0	1-1	0-1
1981	1-1		0-1	1-0						1-1	0-1		2-1	1-1	2-1	0-1
1980		1-1		1-2					1-1	1-2	1-0		3-0	0-2	1-0	2-0
1979				1-0	0-2				0-2	0-2	1-1		2-0	2-1	1-0	2-0
1978		1-2		1-1	2-1				2-1	0-2			1-0	1-1	1-0	2-0
1977		0-1	0-1	1-0			1-1		0-1	1-0	0-1		2-0	2-0		
1976		0-2	1-1				2-0		0-1	1-1	1-0	0-1	2-0	0-1		0-1
1975		0-2	1-0		1-1				1-0	1-1	0-1	0-1	2-0	1-0	1-0	0-1
1974	1-0	0-1		0-2					1-0	2-0			0-1	0-1	2-0	
1973	1-0		0-1	0-0-1					1-1	2-0			0-1	0-0-1	1-1	
1972	1-0				1-0		1-0		1-0	0-1	0-1		2-0		0-1	0-1
1971			0-1		1-1				2-0	1-0			0-1	1-0	1-0	
1970			0-1	2-0	1-1		1-0		1-0	1-0			0-1	1-0	1-0	0-1

MONDAY NIGHT FOOTBALL ALL-TIME STANDINGS

AMERICAN FOOTBALL CONFERENCE

East	W	L	T	Pct.
Miami	40	36	0	.526
New England	19	22	0	.463
Buffalo	17	23	0	.425
New York Jets	18	25	0	.419

South	W	L	T	Pct.
Indianapolis	21	11	0	.656
Tennessee	20	16	0	.556
Jacksonville	7	6	0	.538
Houston	1	3	0	.250

North	W	L	T	Pct.
Pittsburgh	39	22	0	.639
Cleveland	15	14	0	.517
Baltimore	7	8	0	.467
Cincinnati	9	19	0	.321

West	W	L	T	Pct.
Oakland	36	25	1	.589
Kansas City	21	15	0	.583
San Diego	19	16	0	.543
Denver	27	34	1	.444

From 1970-71, tie games were not included in winning percentage.

MONDAY NIGHT WON-LOST RECORDS, 1970-2010
NATIONAL FOOTBALL CONFERENCE

	Ariz.	Atl.	Car.	Chi.	Dall.	Det.	G.B.	Minn.	N.O.	N.Y.G.	Phil.	St.L.	S.F.	Sea.	T.B.	Wash.
Total	6-14-1	9-23	5-4	22-33	42-30	11-13-1	27-29-1	26-28	14-16	21-31-1	27-22	26-27	40-25	16-8	8-9	26-33
2010	0-1	0-1		2-0	0-1		0-1	0-3	2-0	2-0	1-0		1-1			0-1
2009	0-1	0-1	0-1	1-0	1-0		1-1	1-1	2-0	1-0	1-0		1-0			0-2
2008	1-0		1-0	1-0	1-0		1-2	1-1	1-1	0-1	1-1		0-1		0-1	0-1
2007	0-1	0-2		0-1	1-0		1-0	1-0	2-0	1-0	0-1		1-1	1-0		1-0
2006	0-1		1-1	2-0	0-1		0-2	1-1	1-0	1-1	2-0	0-1		2-0	0-1	0-1
2005		3-0	1-0	1-1			0-3	1-0	0-2	1-0	0-3	0-1		1-0		1-0
2004		0-1		2-1			2-1	0-2		2-1	2-1			0-1	0-1	0-1
2003		0-1	0-1	1-0			2-1		0-2	2-1	2-0	1-0			2-1	
2002			0-3				2-0		0-1	3-0	2-1	1-2		0-1	1-1	0-1
2001				1-0	0-1		2-0	1-1	0-1	0-3	1-0	2-1	1-0		1-0	0-2
2000			1-0	1-1			1-1	1-1				1-2		0-1	1-1	1-2
1999	0-1	1-2		1-2			1-2	2-1		1-0		1-2	1-0	1-0		
1998				2-0	1-1		0-3	1-0		0-2	0-1	3-0			1-1	0-1
1997		1-1	1-1	1-2			3-0	0-1		0-2		3-0				1-0
1996		0-1	2-0	2-1	0-2		2-1	0-1		0-2		2-1				
1995	0-1		1-2	3-0	2-0		1-0	0-2	0-1	0-1		2-1				
1994				0-2	2-1	1-0	1-0	2-0	0-2	1-2	2-0	2-1				
1993		0-1		0-1	1-1		0-1	1-0	0-2	1-0	1-1	1-2				1-2
1992		0-2		0-3	2-1	0-1		1-0	1-0	1-0			2-0	1-0		1-2
1991				2-1	0-1			0-1	1-0	2-1	2-1	0-1	2-1			2-0
1990					0-1			0-1	1-1	1-1	2-0	0-3	3-0	1-0		0-1
1989				1-1				1-1	1-1	2-1	0-2	0-2	3-0	1-0		0-2
1988	0-1			1-2	1-1			1-0	1-0	1-1	1-0	1-0	1-1	1-0		0-2
1987				1-2	2-1		1-0			0-3		1-2	2-0	0-2		1-1
1986	0-1			2-1	2-0	0-1	0-1			2-1		1-0	0-2	2-0		1-1
1985	1-1			1-1	1-1		0-1			0-1		2-1	1-2	0-2		2-1
1984		0-2		0-1	1-1	0-1	0-1		1-0	0-1		1-1	2-0	2-0		1-1
1983	0-0-1	0-1		1-1	2-0	2-1	0-1	0-1	1-1-1			1-0	1-0		0-1	1-2
1982				1-2	0-1	1-0	1-0		0-1						1-0	
1981		1-2		0-2	2-0	1-0	0-3				1-1	2-0	1-0			
1980		1-1		1-1					0-1	0-1	1-0	2-0		0-1	0-1	0-2
1979		1-2		0-2		1-0	0-1	0-1	0-1	1-1	1-0			2-0		1-0
1978		1-0		0-3	1-1		2-0					0-2	0-1			1-1
1977	2-0			1-0	1-1		0-1	0-1	0-1			1-1	0-2			1-1
1976	0-1			1-0			1-1			0-1		0-2	2-0			2-0
1975	0-1			0-1	1-1	0-1	0-1	1-0	1-0	0-1	1-0					1-0
1974	0-1	0-1		1-0	0-1	1-0	0-1	1-0	0-1		1-0	1-1	0-2			2-0
1973		1-1		0-1	1-1	1-0	1-1	0-1	0-1	0-1		1-0	1-0			1-1
1972	0-1	0-1		1-0	1-0	0-2	1-0	0-2	0-1	1-0	0-1	1-0	0-1			2-0
1971	1-1	1-0		0-1	1-0	0-1-1	0-1-1	2-0	0-1			0-2	0-1			1-0
1970	1-0	0-1		0-1	0-1		2-0	1-1	1-0	0-1		1-0	0-2			0-1

MONDAY NIGHT FOOTBALL ALL-TIME STANDINGS
NATIONAL FOOTBALL CONFERENCE

East	W	L	T	Pct.	South	W	L	T	Pct.
Dallas	42	30	0	.583	Carolina	5	4	0	.556
Philadelphia	27	22	0	.551	Tampa Bay	8	9	0	.471
Washington	26	33	0	.441	New Orleans	14	16	0	.467
New York Giants	21	31	1	.406	Atlanta	9	23	0	.281

North	W	L	T	Pct.	West	W	L	T	Pct.
Green Bay	27	29	1	.482	Seattle	16	8	0	.667
Minnesota	26	28	0	.481	San Francisco	40	25	0	.615
Detroit	11	13	1	.458	St. Louis	26	27	0	.491
Chicago	22	33	0	.400	Arizona	6	14	1	.310

From 1970-71, tie games were not included in winning percentage.

Compiled by Elias Sports Bureau
*NFL record.

MONDAY NIGHT RECORDS

SCORING
TOUCHDOWNS
Most Touchdowns, Career
- 36 Jerry Rice, San Francisco, 1985-2000; Oakland, 2001-04; Seattle 2004
- 24 Emmitt Smith, Dallas, 1990-2002; Arizona 2003-04
- 20 Terrell Owens, San Francisco, 1996-2003; Philadelphia, 2004-05; Dallas, 2006-08; Buffalo, 2009; Cincinnati, 2010

Most Touchdowns, Game
- 4 Ron Johnson, N.Y. Giants at Philadelphia, Oct. 2, 1972
  Earl Campbell, Houston vs. Miami, Nov. 20, 1978
  Marcus Allen, L.A. Raiders vs. San Diego, Sept. 24, 1984
  Eric Dickerson, Indianapolis vs. Denver, Oct. 31, 1988
  Emmitt Smith, Dallas at N.Y. Giants, Sept. 4, 1995
  Marshall Faulk, St. Louis at Tampa Bay, Dec. 18, 2000

FIELD GOALS
Most Field Goals, Career
- 51 Gary Anderson, Pittsburgh, 1982-1994; Philadelphia, 1995-96; San Francisco, 1997; Minnesota, 1998-2002; Tennessee, 2003-04
- 50 Jason Elam, Denver, 1993-2007; Atlanta, 2008-09
- 42 Ryan Longwell, Green Bay, 1997-2005; Minnesota, 2006-2010

Most Field Goals, Game
- 7 Chris Boniol, Dallas vs. Green Bay, Nov. 18, 1996*
  Billy Cundiff, Dallas at N.Y. Giants, Sept. 15, 2003 (OT)*
- 5 Tim Mazzetti, Atlanta vs. Los Angeles, Oct. 30, 1978
  Roger Ruzek, Dallas at L.A. Rams, Dec. 21, 1987
  Rich Karlis, Minnesota vs. Cincinnati, Dec. 25, 1989
  Nick Lowery, Kansas City vs. Denver, Sept. 20, 1993
  Chris Jacke, Green Bay vs. San Francisco, Oct. 14, 1996 (OT)
  Richie Cunningham, Dallas vs. Philadelphia, Sept. 15, 1997
  Phil Dawson, Cleveland vs. Buffalo, Nov. 17, 2008
  Nick Folk, N.Y. Jets vs. Minnesota, Oct. 11, 2010

RUSHING
YARDS GAINED
Most Yards Gained, Career
- 2,434 Emmitt Smith, Dallas, 1990-2002; Arizona, 2003-04
- 1,897 Tony Dorsett, Dallas, 1977-1987; Denver, 1988
- 1,769 Thurman Thomas, Buffalo, 1988-1999; Miami, 2000

Most Yards Gained, Game
- 221 Bo Jackson, L.A. Raiders at Seattle, Nov. 30, 1987
- 216 Ricky Williams, Miami vs. Chicago, Dec. 9, 2002
- 214 Thurman Thomas, Buffalo at N.Y. Jets, Sept. 24, 1990

Longest Run From Scrimmage, Game
- 99 Tony Dorsett, Dallas at Minnesota, Jan. 3, 1983 (TD)*
- 91 Bo Jackson, L.A. Raiders at Seattle, Nov. 30, 1987 (TD)
- 83 James Lofton, Green Bay at N.Y. Giants, Sept. 20, 1982 (TD)

TOUCHDOWNS
Most Rushing Touchdowns, Career
- 23 Emmitt Smith, Dallas, 1990-2002; Arizona, 2003-04
- 17 Marcus Allen, L.A. Raiders, 1982-1992; Kansas City, 1993-97
- 14 Eric Dickerson, L.A. Rams, 1983-87; Indianapolis, 1987-1991; L.A. Raiders, 1992; Atlanta, 1993

Most Rushing Touchdowns, Game
- 4 Earl Campbell, Houston vs. Miami, Nov. 20, 1978
  Eric Dickerson, Indianapolis vs. Denver, Oct. 31, 1988
  Emmitt Smith, Dallas at N.Y. Giants, Sept. 4, 1995

PASSING
YARDS GAINED
Most Yards Gained, Career
- 9,654 Dan Marino, Miami, 1983-1999
- 9,068 Brett Favre, Atlanta, 1991; Green Bay, 1992-2007; N.Y. Jets, 2008; Minnesota, 2009-2010
- 5,148 Joe Montana, San Francisco, 1979-1992; Kansas City, 1993-94

Most Yards Gained, Game
- 458 Joe Montana, San Francisco at L.A. Rams, Dec. 11, 1989
- 448 Marc Bulger, St. Louis at Green Bay, Nov. 29, 2004
- 447 Ken Anderson, Cincinnati vs. Buffalo, Nov. 17, 1975

Longest Pass Play
- 99 Brett Favre to Robert Brooks, Green Bay at Chicago, Sept. 11, 1995 (TD)*
- 97 Bernie Kosar to Webster Slaughter, Cleveland vs. Chicago, Oct. 23, 1989 (TD)
- 95 Joe Montana to John Taylor, San Francisco at L.A. Rams, Dec. 11, 1989 (TD)

TOUCHDOWNS
Most Touchdown Passes, Career
- 74 Dan Marino, Miami, 1983-1999
- 69 Brett Favre, Atlanta, 1991; Green Bay, 1992-2007; N.Y. Jets, 2008; Minnesota, 2009-2010
- 42 Steve Young, Tampa Bay, 1985-86; San Francisco, 1987-1999

Most Touchdown Passes, Game
- 5 Dave Krieg, Seattle vs. L.A. Raiders, Nov. 28, 1988
  Jim Kelly, Buffalo vs. Cincinnati, Oct. 21, 1991
  Vinny Testaverde, N.Y. Jets vs. Miami, Oct. 23, 2000 (OT)
  Ben Roethlisberger, Pittsburgh vs. Baltimore, Nov. 5, 2007
  Drew Brees, New Orleans vs. New England, Nov. 30, 2009

RECEIVING
PASS RECEPTIONS
Most Pass Receptions, Career
- 254 Jerry Rice, San Francisco, 1985-2000; Oakland, 2001-04; Seattle, 2004
- 124 Andre Reed, Buffalo, 1985-1999; Washington, 2000
- 123 Cris Carter, Philadelphia, 1987-89; Minnesota, 1990-2001; Miami, 2002

Most Pass Receptions, Game
- 14 Herman Moore, Detroit vs. Chicago, Dec. 4, 1995
  Jerry Rice, San Francisco vs. Minnesota, Dec. 18, 1995
- 13 Andre Reed, Buffalo vs. Denver, Sept. 18, 1989
  Terrell Owens, San Francisco vs. Philadelphia, Nov. 25, 2002

YARDS GAINED
Most Yards Gained, Career
- 4,029 Jerry Rice, San Francisco, 1985-2000; Oakland, 2001-04; Seattle, 2004
- 1,783 Andre Reed, Buffalo, 1985-1999; Washington, 2000
- 1,697 Terrell Owens, San Francisco, 1996-2003; Philadelphia, 2004-05; Dallas, 2006-08; Buffalo, 2009; Cincinnati, 2010

Most Yards Gained, Game
- 289   Jerry Rice, San Francisco vs. Minnesota, Dec. 18, 1995
- 286   John Taylor, San Francisco at L.A. Rams, Dec. 11, 1989
- 260   Wes Chandler, San Diego vs. Cincinnati, Dec. 20, 1982

TOUCHDOWN
Most Receiving Touchdowns, Career
- 34   Jerry Rice, San Francisco, 1985-2000; Oakland, 2001-04; Seattle, 2004
- 20   Terrell Owens, San Francisco, 1996-2003; Philadelphia, 2004-05; Dallas, 2006-08; Buffalo, 2009; Cincinnati, 2010
- 17   Randy Moss, Minnesota, 1998-2004; Oakland, 2005-06; New England, 2007-2010; Minnesota, 2010; Tennessee, 2010

Most Receiving Touchdowns, Game
- 3   Ron Johnson, N.Y. Giants at Philadelphia, Oct. 2, 1972
  Wesley Walker, N.Y. Jets at Detroit, Dec. 6, 1982
  Steve Largent, Seattle at San Diego, Oct. 29, 1984
  Mark Clayton, Miami vs. Dallas, Dec. 17, 1984
  Jerry Rice, San Francisco vs. Chicago, Dec. 14, 1987
  Jerry Rice, San Francisco vs. Minnesota, Dec. 18, 1995
  Lamar Thomas, Miami vs. Denver, Dec. 21, 1998
  Ed McCaffrey, Denver vs. Miami, Sept. 13, 1999
  Randy Moss, Minnesota vs. N.Y. Giants, Nov. 19, 2001
  Isaac Bruce, St. Louis at New Orleans, Dec. 17, 2001
  Terrell Owens, Philadelphia at Dallas, Nov. 15, 2004
  Drew Bennett, Tennessee vs. Kansas City, Dec. 13, 2004
  Marvin Harrison, Indianapolis vs. Cincinnati, Dec. 18, 2006

YARDS FROM SCRIMMAGE
Most Scrimmage Yards, Career
- 4,116   Jerry Rice, San Francisco, 1985-2000; Oakland, 2001-04; Seattle, 2004
- 2,836   Emmitt Smith, Dallas, 1990-2002; Arizona, 2003-04
- 2,567   Tony Dorsett, Dallas, 1977-1987; Denver, 1988

INTERCEPTIONS BY
Most Interceptions, Career
- 11   Everson Walls, Dallas, 1981-89; N.Y. Giants, 1990-92; Cleveland, 1992-93
- 9   Merton Hanks, San Francisco, 1991-98; Seattle, 1999
- 8   Emmitt Thomas, Kansas City, 1966-1978
  Darren Sharper, Green Bay, 1997-2004; Minnesota, 2005-08; New Orleans, 2009-2010

Most Interceptions, Game
- 4   Dick Anderson, Miami vs. Pittsburgh, Dec. 3, 1973*
- 3   Johnny Robinson, Kansas City at Baltimore, Sept. 28, 1970
  Charlie Babb, Miami vs. Oakland, Sept. 22, 1975
  Charles Phillips, Oakland vs. Denver, Dec. 8, 1975
  Mark Murphy, Washington at San Diego, Oct. 31, 1983
  Ken Easley, Seattle at San Diego, Oct. 29, 1984
  Dwayne Harper, San Diego vs. Oakland, Nov. 27, 1995
  Marcus Coleman, N.Y. Jets vs. Miami, Oct. 23, 2000 (OT)
  Keith Bulluck, Tennessee vs. New Orleans, Sept. 24, 2007

Longest Interception Return
- 102   Eddie Anderson, L.A. Raiders at Miami, Dec. 14, 1992 (TD)
- 101   Lito Sheppard, Philadelphia at Dallas, Nov. 15, 2004 (TD)
- 98   Marcus Coleman, N.Y. Jets vs. Miami, Dec. 27, 1999 (TD)
  Rod Woodson, Oakland at Denver, Nov. 11, 2002 (TD)
  Brandon McDonald, Cleveland vs. Philadelphia, Dec. 15, 2008

SACKS
Most Sacks, Career
- 24.5   Bruce Smith, Buffalo, 1985-1999; Washington, 2000-03
- 20.0   Richard Dent, Chicago, 1983-1993, 1995; San Francisco, 1994; Indianapolis, 1996; Philadelphia, 1997
- 18.0   Kevin Greene, L.A. Rams, 1985-1992; Pittsburgh, 1993-95; Carolina, 1996, 1998-99; San Francisco, 1997

PUNTING
Highest Punt Average, Career (Minimum: 25 Punts)
- 47.24   Shane Lechler, Oakland, 2000-2010
- 47.17   Mike Scifres, San Diego, 2003-2010
- 47.04   Andy Lee, San Francisco, 2004-2010

Longest Punt
- 90   Rodney Williams, N.Y. Giants at Denver, Sept. 10, 2001
- 83   Bryan Barker, Jacksonville vs. N.Y. Jets, Oct. 11, 1999
- 75   Craig Hentrich, Indianapolis vs. Tennessee, Oct. 27, 2008

PUNT RETURNS
Longest Punt Return
- 95   John Taylor, San Francisco vs. Washington, Nov. 21, 1988 (TD)
- 94   Dennis McKinnon, Chicago vs. N.Y. Giants, Sept. 14, 1987 (TD)
  Dexter McCluster, Kansas City vs. San Diego, Sept. 13, 2010 (TD)
- 93   Dez Bryant, Dallas vs. N.Y. Giants, Oct. 25, 2010 (TD)

KICKOFF RETURNS
Longest Kickoff Return
- 105   Terry Fair, Detroit vs. Tampa Bay, Sept. 28, 1998 (TD)
- 104   Allen Rossum, San Francisco vs. Arizona, Nov. 10, 2008 (TD)
- 103   Terrence McGee, Buffalo vs. Dallas, Oct. 8, 2007 (TD)
  Brandon Tate, New England at Miami, Oct. 4, 2010 (TD)
  David Reed, Baltimore at Houston, Dec. 13, 2010 (TD)

FUMBLES
Longest Fumble Return
- 99   Don Griffin, San Francisco vs. Chicago, Dec. 23, 1991 (TD)
- 96   Joe Lavender, Philadelphia vs. Dallas, Sept. 23, 1974 (TD)
- 93   Adam Archuleta, St. Louis vs. Tampa Bay, Oct. 18, 2004 (TD)

THANKSGIVING DAY FOOTBALL, 1920-2010
(Home Team in capitals, games listed in chronological order.)
(AFL)-American Football League, 1960-69.

Nov. 25, 1920	AKRON PROS 7, Canton Bulldogs 0
	Decatur Staleys 6, CHICAGO TIGERS 0
	ELYRIA (OH) ATHLETICS* 0, Columbus Panhandles 0
	DAYTON TRIANGLES 28, Detroit Heralds 0
	CHICAGO BOOSTERS* 27, Hammond Pros 0
	All-Tonawanda (NY) 14, ROCHESTER JEFFERSONS 3
	* Non league team. Games between league teams and non league teams counted in standings in 1920.

Nov. 24, 1921	Canton Bulldogs 14, AKRON PROS 0
	Buffalo All-Americans 7, CHICAGO STALEYS 6

Nov. 30, 1922	Buffalo All-Americans 21, ROCHESTER JEFFERSONS 0
	CHICAGO CARDINALS 6, Chicago Bears 0
	RACINE LEGION 3, Milwaukee Badgers 0
	Oorang Indians 18, COLUMBUS PANHANDLES 6
	CANTON BULLDOGS 14, Akron Pros 0

Nov. 29, 1923	CANTON BULLDOGS 28, Toledo Maroons 0
	CHICAGO BEARS 3, Chicago Cardinals 0
	GREEN BAY PACKERS 19, Hammond Pros 0
	Milwaukee Badgers 16, RACINE LEGION 0
	AKRON PROS 2, Buffalo All-Americans 0

Nov. 27, 1924	AKRON PROS 22, Buffalo Bisons 0
	Chicago Bears 21, CHICAGO CARDINALS 0
	FRANKFORD YELLOWJACKETS 32, Dayton Triangles 7
	CLEVELAND BULLDOGS 53, Milwaukee Badgers 10 (at Canton, Ohio)
	Green Bay Packers 17, KANSAS CITY BLUES 6

Nov. 26, 1925	CHICAGO BEARS 0, Chicago Cardinals 0
	Kansas City Cowboys 17, CLEVELAND BULLDOGS 0 (at Hartford, Connecticut)
	Rock Island Independents 6, DETROIT PANTHERS 3
	POTTSVILLE MAROONS 31, Green Bay Packers 0

Nov. 25, 1926	New York Giants 17, BROOKLYN LIONS 0
	Los Angeles Buccaneers 9, DETROIT PANTHERS 6
	CHICAGO BEARS 0, Chicago Cardinals 0
	FRANKFORD YELLOWJACKETS 20, Green Bay Packers 14
	POTTSVILLE MAROONS 8, Providence Steam Roller 0
	CANTON BULLDOGS 0, Akron Pros 0

Nov. 24, 1927	Chicago Cardinals 3, CHICAGO BEARS 0
	POTTSVILLE MAROONS 6, Providence Steam Roller 0
	Green Bay Packers 17, FRANKFORD YELLOWJACKETS 9
	Cleveland Bulldogs 30, NEW YORK YANKEES 19

Nov. 29, 1928	Providence Steam Roller 7, POTTSVILLE MAROONS 0
	DETROIT WOLVERINES 33, Dayton Triangles 0
	FRANKFORD YELLOWJACKETS 2, Green Bay Packers 0
	CHICAGO BEARS 34, Chicago Cardinals 0

Nov. 28, 1929	New York Giants 21, STATEN ISLAND STAPLETONS 7
	FRANKFORD YELLOWJACKETS 0, Green Bay Packers 0
	Chicago Cardinals 40, CHICAGO BEARS 6

Nov. 27, 1930	STATEN ISLAND STAPLETONS 7, New York Giants 6
	BROOKLYN DODGERS 33, Providence Steam Roller 12
	Green Bay Packers 25, FRANKFORD YELLOWJACKETS 7
	CHICAGO BEARS 6, Chicago Cardinals 0

Nov. 26, 1931	Green Bay Packers 38, PROVIDENCE STEAM ROLLER 7
	STATEN ISLAND STAPLETONS 9, New York Giants 6
	CHICAGO BEARS 18, Chicago Cardinals 7

Nov. 24, 1932	CHICAGO BEARS 34, Chicago Cardinals 0
	Green Bay Packers 7, BROOKLYN DODGERS 0
	STATEN ISLAND STAPLETONS 13, New York Giants 13

Nov. 30, 1933	Chicago Bears 22, CHICAGO CARDINALS 6
	New York Giants 10, BROOKLYN DODGERS 0

Nov. 29, 1934	CHICAGO CARDINALS 6, Green Bay Packers 0
	Chicago Bears 19, DETROIT LIONS 16
	New York Giants 27, BROOKLYN DODGERS 0

Nov. 28, 1935	New York Giants 21, BROOKLYN DODGERS 0 CHICAGO CARDINALS 9, Green Bay Packers 7 DETROIT LIONS 14, Chicago Bears 2
Nov. 26, 1936	DETROIT LIONS 13, Chicago Bears 7 New York Giants 14, BROOKLYN DODGERS 0
Nov. 25, 1937	Chicago Bears 13, DETROIT LIONS 0 BROOKLYN DODGERS 13, New York Giants 13
Nov. 24, 1938	DETROIT LIONS 14, Chicago Bears 7 BROOKLYN DODGERS 7, New York Giants 7
Nov. 23, 1939#	PHILADELPHIA EAGLES 17, Pittsburgh Steelers 14
Nov. 28, 1940#	PHILADELPHIA EAGLES 7, Pittsburgh Steelers 0

In 1939 and 1940, President Roosevelt moved Thanksgiving one week earlier. Various states celebrated on the date declared by the President, while other states recognized the traditional fourth Thursday of the month. In 1941, Thanksgiving was sanctioned by Congress to be celebrated on the fourth Thursday of November, which it has been ever since.

Nov. 22, 1945	Cleveland Rams 28, DETROIT LIONS 21
Nov. 28, 1946	Boston Yanks 34, DETROIT LIONS 10
Nov. 27, 1947	Chicago Bears 34, DETROIT LIONS 14
Nov. 25, 1948	Chicago Cardinals 28, DETROIT LIONS 14
Nov. 24, 1949	Chicago Bears 28, DETROIT LIONS 7
Nov. 23, 1950	DETROIT LIONS 49, New York Yanks 14 Pittsburgh Steelers 28, CHICAGO CARDINALS 17
Nov. 22, 1951	DETROIT LIONS 52, Green Bay Packers 35
Nov. 27, 1952	DETROIT LIONS 48, Green Bay Packers 24 DALLAS TEXANS 27, Chicago Bears 23 (at Akron, Ohio)
Nov. 26, 1953	DETROIT LIONS 34, Green Bay Packers 15
Nov. 25, 1954	DETROIT LIONS 28, Green Bay Packers 24
Nov. 24, 1955	DETROIT LIONS 24, Green Bay Packers 10
Nov. 22, 1956	Green Bay Packers 24, DETROIT LIONS 20
Nov. 28, 1957	DETROIT LIONS 18, Green Bay Packers 6
Nov. 27, 1958	DETROIT LIONS 24, Green Bay Packers 14
Nov. 26, 1959	Green Bay Packers 24, DETROIT LIONS 17
Nov. 24, 1960	DETROIT LIONS 23, Green Bay Packers 10 (AFL) - NEW YORK TITANS 41, Dallas Texans 35
Nov. 23, 1961	Green Bay Packers 17, DETROIT LIONS 9 (AFL) - NEW YORK TITANS 21, Buffalo Bills 14
Nov. 22, 1962	DETROIT LIONS 26, Green Bay Packers 14 (AFL) - New York Titans 46, DENVER BRONCOS 45
Nov. 28, 1963	DETROIT LIONS 13, Green Bay Packers 13 (AFL) - Oakland Raiders 26, DENVER BRONCOS 10
Nov. 26, 1964	Chicago Bears 27, DETROIT LIONS 24 (AFL) - Buffalo Bills 27, SAN DIEGO CHARGERS 24
Nov. 25, 1965	DETROIT LIONS 24, Baltimore Colts 24 (AFL) - SAN DIEGO CHARGERS 20, Buffalo Bills 20
Nov. 24, 1966	San Francisco 49ers 41, DETROIT LIONS 14 DALLAS COWBOYS 26, Cleveland Browns 14 (AFL) - Buffalo Bills 31, OAKLAND RAIDERS 10
Nov. 23, 1967	Los Angeles Rams 31, DETROIT LIONS 7 DALLAS COWBOYS 46, St. Louis Cardinals 21 (AFL) - Oakland Raiders 44, KANSAS CITY CHIEFS 22 (AFL) - SAN DIEGO CHARGERS 24, Denver Broncos 20

Nov. 28, 1968	Philadelphia Eagles 12, DETROIT LIONS 0
	DALLAS COWBOYS 29, Washington Redskins 20
	(AFL) - OAKLAND RAIDERS 13, Buffalo Bills 10
	(AFL) - KANSAS CITY CHIEFS 24, Houston Oilers 10
Nov. 27, 1969	Minnesota Vikings 27, DETROIT LIONS 0
	DALLAS COWBOYS 24, San Francisco 49ers 24
	(AFL) - KANSAS CITY CHIEFS 31, Denver Broncos 17
	(AFL) - San Diego Chargers 21, HOUSTON OILERS 17
Nov. 26, 1970	DETROIT LIONS 28, Oakland Raiders 14
	DALLAS COWBOYS 16, Green Bay Packers 3
Nov. 25, 1971	DETROIT LIONS 32, Kansas City Chiefs 21
	DALLAS COWBOYS 28, Los Angeles Rams 21
Nov. 23, 1972	DETROIT LIONS 37, New York Jets 20
	San Francisco 49ers 31, DALLAS COWBOYS 10
Nov. 22, 1973	Washington Redskins 20, DETROIT LIONS 0
	Miami Dolphins 14, DALLAS COWBOYS 7
Nov. 28, 1974	Denver Broncos 31, DETROIT LIONS 27
	DALLAS COWBOYS 24, Washington Redskins 23
Nov. 27, 1975	Los Angeles Rams 20, DETROIT LIONS 0
	Buffalo Bills 32, ST. LOUIS CARDINALS 14
Nov. 25, 1976	DETROIT LIONS 27, Buffalo Bills 14
	DALLAS COWBOYS 19, St. Louis Cardinals 14
Nov. 24, 1977	Chicago Bears 31, DETROIT LIONS 14
	Miami Dolphins 55, ST. LOUIS CARDINALS 14
Nov. 23, 1978	DETROIT LIONS 17, Denver Broncos 14
	DALLAS COWBOYS 37, Washington Redskins 10
Nov. 22, 1979	DETROIT LIONS 20, Chicago Bears 0
	Houston Oilers 30, DALLAS COWBOYS 24
Nov. 27, 1980	Chicago Bears 23, DETROIT LIONS 17 (OT)
	DALLAS COWBOYS 51, Seattle Seahawks 7
Nov. 26, 1981	DETROIT LIONS 27, Kansas City Chiefs 10
	DALLAS COWBOYS 10, Chicago Bears 9
Nov. 25, 1982	New York Giants 13, DETROIT LIONS 6
	DALLAS COWBOYS 31, Cleveland Browns 14
Nov. 24, 1983	DETROIT LIONS 45, Pittsburgh Steelers 3
	DALLAS COWBOYS 35, St. Louis Cardinals 17
Nov. 22, 1984	DETROIT LIONS 31, Green Bay Packers 28
	DALLAS COWBOYS 20, New England Patriots 17
Nov. 28, 1985	DETROIT LIONS 31, New York Jets 20
	DALLAS COWBOYS 35, St. Louis Cardinals 17
Nov. 27, 1986	Green Bay Packers 44, DETROIT LIONS 40
	Seattle Seahawks 31, DALLAS COWBOYS 14
Nov. 26, 1987	Kansas City Chiefs 27, DETROIT LIONS 20
	Minnesota Vikings 44, DALLAS COWBOYS 38 (OT)
Nov. 24, 1988	Minnesota Vikings 23, DETROIT LIONS 0
	Houston Oilers 25, DALLAS COWBOYS 17
Nov. 23, 1989	DETROIT LIONS 13, Cleveland Browns 10
	Philadelphia Eagles 27, DALLAS COWBOYS 0
Nov. 22, 1990	DETROIT LIONS 40, Denver Broncos 27
	DALLAS COWBOYS 27, Washington Redskins 17
Nov. 28, 1991	DETROIT LIONS 16, Chicago Bears 6
	DALLAS COWBOYS 20, Pittsburgh Steelers 10
Nov. 26, 1992	Houston Oilers 24, DETROIT LIONS 21
	DALLAS COWBOYS 30, New York Giants 3
Nov. 25, 1993	Chicago Bears 10, DETROIT LIONS 6
	Miami Dolphins 16, DALLAS COWBOYS 14

Nov. 24, 1994	DETROIT LIONS 35, Buffalo Bills 21 DALLAS COWBOYS 42, Green Bay Packers 31
Nov. 23, 1995	DETROIT LIONS 44, Minnesota Vikings 38 DALLAS COWBOYS 24, Kansas City Chiefs 12
Nov. 28, 1996	Kansas City Chiefs 28, DETROIT LIONS 24 DALLAS COWBOYS 21, Washington Redskins 10
Nov. 27, 1997	DETROIT LIONS 55, Chicago Bears 20 Tennessee Titans 27, DALLAS COWBOYS 14
Nov. 26, 1998	DETROIT LIONS 19, Pittsburgh Steelers 16 (OT) Minnesota Vikings 46, DALLAS COWBOYS 36
Nov. 25, 1999	DETROIT LIONS 21, Chicago Bears 17 DALLAS COWBOYS 20, Miami Dolphins 0
Nov. 23, 2000	DETROIT LIONS 34, New England Patriots 9 Minnesota Vikings 27, DALLAS COWBOYS 15
Nov. 22, 2001	Green Bay Packers 29, DETROIT LIONS 27 Denver Broncos 26, DALLAS COWBOYS 24
Nov. 28, 2002	New England Patriots 20, DETROIT LIONS 12 DALLAS COWBOYS 27, Washington Redskins 20
Nov. 27, 2003	DETROIT LIONS 22, Green Bay Packers 14 Miami Dolphins 40, DALLAS COWBOYS 21
Nov. 25, 2004	Indianapolis Colts 41, DETROIT LIONS 9 DALLAS COWBOYS 21, Chicago Bears 7
Nov. 24, 2005	Atlanta Falcons 27, DETROIT LIONS 7 Denver Broncos 24, DALLAS COWBOYS 21 (OT)
Nov. 23, 2006	Miami Dolphins 27, DETROIT LIONS 10 DALLAS COWBOYS 38, Tampa Bay Buccaneers 10 KANSAS CITY CHIEFS 19, Denver Broncos 10
Nov. 22, 2007	Green Bay Packers 37, DETROIT LIONS 26 DALLAS COWBOYS 34, New York Jets 3 Indianapolis Colts 31, ATLANTA FALCONS 13
Nov. 27, 2008	Tennessee Titans 41, DETROIT LIONS 10 DALLAS COWBOYS 34, Seattle Seahawks 9 PHILADELPHIA EAGLES 48, Arizona Cardinals 20
Nov. 26, 2009	Green Bay Packers 34, DETROIT LIONS 12 DALLAS COWBOYS 24, Oakland Raiders 7 DENVER BRONCOS 26, New York Giants 6
Nov. 25, 2010	New England Patriots 45, DETROIT LIONS 24 New Orleans Saints 30, DALLAS COWBOYS 27 NEW YORK JETS 26, Cincinnati Bengals 10

THANKSGIVING DAY RECORDS
*NFL record; stats compiled by Elias Sports Bureau.

SCORING / Most Touchdowns, Game
- 6   Ernie Nevers, Chi. Cardinals vs. Chi. Bears, Nov. 28, 1929*
- 4   Sterling Sharpe, Green Bay at Dallas, Nov. 24, 1994
- 3   By many players

RUSHING / Most Yards Rushing, Game
- 273   O.J. Simpson, Buffalo at Detroit, Nov. 25, 1976
- 198   Bob Hoernschemeyer, Detroit vs. N.Y. Yankees, Nov. 23, 1950
- 195   Earl Campbell, Houston at Dallas, Nov. 22, 1979

PASSING / Most Yards Passing, Game
- 455   Troy Aikman, Dallas vs. Minnesota, Nov. 26, 1998
- 410   Scott Mitchell, Detroit vs. Minnesota, Nov. 23, 1995
- 384   Warren Moon, Minnesota at Detroit, Nov. 23, 1995

PASS RECEIVING
RECEPTIONS / Most Pass Receptions, Game
- 12   Brett Perriman, Detroit vs. Minnesota, Nov. 23, 1995
Marvin Harrison, Indianapolis at Detroit, Nov. 25, 2004
- 11   Daryl Johnston, Dallas vs. Miami, Nov. 25, 1993
Michael Irvin, Dallas vs. Kansas City, Nov. 23, 1995

YARDS GAINED / Most Yards on Pass Receptions, Game
- 303   Jim Benton, Cleveland at Detroit, Nov. 22, 1945
- 185   Lance Alworth, San Diego vs. Buffalo, Nov. 26, 1964
- 184   Anthony Carter, Minnesota at Dallas, Nov. 26, 1987 (OT)

italic * indicates Monday-night game
# indicates Thursday/Saturday/Sunday-night game
+ indicates Thanksgiving Day game

REGULAR SEASON

Sept. 12, 2010—Pittsburgh 15, Atlanta 9, at Pittsburgh; Falcons win toss. Weems returns kickoff 19 yards. Drive begins on Falcons 9 after holding penalty. Drive ends on Atlanta 14. Koenen punts 36 yards. Downed on 50, where drive begins. Mendenhall rushes for 50-yard touchdown at 2:35.

Sept. 19, 2010—Houston 30, Washington 27, at Washington; Texans win toss. Slaton returns kick 7 yards. Drive begins on Houston 12. Drive ends on Washington 49. Turk punts 39 yards for touchback. Drive starts Washington 20. Drive starts on Houston 34. Gano misses field goal wide right. Drive starts on Houston 42. Rackers kicks 35-yard field goal at 11:36.

Sept. 26, 2010—Atlanta 27, New Orleans 24, at New Orleans; Falcons win toss. Weems returns kickoff 35 yards. Drive begins on Atlanta 39. Drive ends on Atlanta 33. Koenen punts 35 yards and Moore makes fair catch at New Orleans 32. Drive ends on Atlanta 11 as Hartley misses 29-yard field goal. Drive ends on Atlanta 20. Bryant kicks 46-yard field goal at 13:05.

Oct. 10, 2010—Washington 16, Green Bay 13, at Washington; Packers win toss. Lee returns kickoff 26 yards. Drive begins on Green Bay 26. Drive ends on Green Bay 16. Masthay punts 44 yards and Banks returns it 20 yards to Washington 40. Drive ends on Washington 46. Smith punts 41 yards and Williams returns it 6 yards to Green Bay 19. Landry intercepts pass at Green Bay 39. Gano kicks 33-yard field goal at 6:54.

Oct. 17, 2010—Miami 23, Green Bay 20, at Green Bay; Dolphins win toss. Carroll returns kickoff 21 yards. Drive begins on Miami 25. Drive ends on Miami 27. Fields punts 50 yards and Williams returns it 7 yards to Green Bay 30. Illegal block above waist called. Drive starts on Green Bay 16. Drive ends on Green Bay 15. Masthay punts 37 yards and Goode makes fair catch at Miami 48. Carpenter kicks 44-yard field goal at 5:59.

Oct. 17, 2010—New England 23, Baltimore 20, at New England; Ravens win toss. Touchback. Drive begins on Baltimore 20. Drive ends on Baltimore 25. Koch punts 43 yards and Welker returns it 3 yards to New England 35. Drive ends on New England 32. Mesko punts 40 yards and Carr returns it 9 yards to Baltimore 37. Illegal block above the waist called. Drive begins on Baltimore 17. Drive ends on New England 48. Koch punts 36 yards and Cox makes fair catch at New England 12. Drive ends on New England 16. Mesko punts 65 yards. Downed on Baltimore 19. Drive ends on Baltimore 19. Koch punts 45 yards and Cox returns it 2 yards to New England 38. Gostkowski kicks 35-yard field goal at 13:04.

Oct. 24, 2010—Baltimore 37, Buffalo 34, at Baltimore; Ravens win toss. Parmele returns kickoff 32 yards. Drive begins on Baltimore 27. Drive ends on Baltimore 29. Koch punts 49 yards and Cox makes fair catch at Buffalo 22. Lewis recovers Nelson's fumble and returns it 1 yard. Drive begins on Buffalo 29 following Bills' unnecessary roughness penalty. Cundiff kicks 38-yard field goal at 4:06.

Oct. 31, 2010—Kansas City 13, Buffalo 10, at Kansas City; Bills win toss. Spiller returns kickoff 22 yards. Drive begins on Buffalo 29. Drive ends on Kansas City 40. Moorman punts 40 yards for touchback. Drive begins on Kansas City 20. Drive ends on Buffalo 49. Colquitt punts 39 yards out of bounds. Drive begins on Buffalo 10. Lindell misses 53-yard field goal. Drive begins on Kansas City 43. Succop misses 39-yard field goal. Drive begins on Buffalo 29. Moorman punts 26 yards out of bounds. Drive begins on Kansas City 31. Succop kicks 35-yard field goal at 15:00.

Nov. 7, 2010—N.Y. Jets 23, Detroit 20, at Detroit; Jets win toss. Smith returns kickoff 24 yards. Drive begins on New York 32. Folk kicks 30-yard field goal at 3:18.

Nov. 7, 2010—Minnesota 27, Arizona 24, at Minnesota; Cardinals win toss. Stephens-Howling returns kickoff 25 yards. Drive begins on Arizona 27. Drive ends on Arizona 21. Graham punts 48 yards out of bounds. Drive begins on Minnesota 31. Longwell kicks 35-yard field goal at 5:18.

Nov. 7, 2010—Oakland 23, Kansas City 20, at Oakland; Chiefs win toss. Arenas returns kickoff 7 yards. Drive begins on Kansas City 10. Drive ends on Kansas City 12. Colquitt

punts 53 yards and Miller returns it 3 yards to Oakland 38. Janikowski kicks 33-yard field goal at 2:53.

Nov. 14, 2010—NY Jets 26, Cleveland Browns 20, at Cleveland; Jets win toss. Smith returns kickoff 19 yards. Drive begins on New York 17. Drive ends on Jets 32. Weatherford punts 37 yards and Stuckey returns it 5 yards to Cleveland 36. Stuckey catches pass from McCoy for 14 yards and fumbles. Fumble recovered by Cromartie at New York 36. Drive ends on Cleveland 29 as Folk misses 47-yard field goal. Drive begins on Cleveland 37. Drive ends on Cleveland 44. Hodges punts 47 yards and ball is downed at New York 9. Haden intercepts pass at Cleveland 3. Drive ends on Cleveland 2. Hodges punts 53 yards and Leonhard returns it 18 yards to Cleveland 37. Sanchez completes 37-yard touchdown pass to Holmes at 14:44.

Nov. 14, 2010—San Francisco 23, St. Louis 20, at San Francisco; Rams win toss. Amendola returns kickoff 25 yards. Drive begins on St. Louis 30. Drive ends on St. Louis 27. Jones punts 39 yards and it is downed at San Francisco 34. Nedney kicks 29-yard field goal at 5:21.

Nov. 21, 2010—Washington 19, Tennessee 16, at Tennessee; Titans win toss. Mariani returns kickoff 30 yards. Drive begins on Titans 33. Drive ends on Titans 48. Kern punts 39 yards and Banks makes fair catch at Redskins 13. Gano kicks 48-yard field goal at 6:43.

Nov. 28, 2010—Pittsburgh 19, Buffalo 16, at Buffalo; Bills win toss. McKelvin returns kickoff 49 yards. Drive begins on Pittsburgh 48. Drive ends on Pittsburgh 41. Moorman punts 37 out of bounds at Pittsburgh 4. Drive ends on Pittsburgh 1. Sepulveda punts 55 yards and McKelvin returns it five yards. Drive ends on Buffalo 34. Drive ends on Pittsburgh 39. Moorman punts 39 yards for a touchback. Drive starts on Pittsburgh 20. Suisham kicks 41-yard field goal at 12:46.

Dec. 5, 2010—Dallas 38, Indianapolis 35, at Indianapolis; Colts win toss. Tryon fields kickoff for touchback. Drive begins on Indianapolis 20. Drive ends on Indianapolis 37. McAfee punts 45 yards and McCann makes fair catch at Dallas 18. Drive ends on Dallas 19. McBriar punts 65 yards and White returns it 11 yards. Drive begins on Indianapolis 27. Lee intercepts pass at Colts 49 and returns it 13 yards. Drive starts at Indianapolis 36. Buehler kicks 38-yard field goal at 7:05.

* **Dec. 13, 2010—Baltimore 34, Houston 28,** at Houston; Ravens win toss. D. Reed fields kickoff for touchback. Drive begins on Baltimore 20. Drive ends on Baltimore 30. Koch punts 58 yards and Cox returns it for a loss of three yards. Drive begins on Houston 9. Wilson intercepts pass at Houston 12 and returns it for a touchdown at 3:05.

Dec. 19, 2010—Detroit 23, Tampa Bay 20, at Tampa Bay; Lions win toss. Logan returns kickoff 18 yards. Drive begins on Detroit 21. Rayner kicks 34-yard field goal at 5:09.

Dec. 26, 2010—Washington 20, Jacksonville 17, at Jacksonville; Jaguars win toss. Karim returns kickoff seven yards. Drive begins on Jacksonville 11. Barnes intercepts pass at Jacksonville 22 and returns it eight yards. Drive begins on Jacksonville 14. Gano kicks 31-yard field goal at 3:47.

POSTSEASON

Dec. 28, 1958—Baltimore 23, New York Giants 17, at New York in NFL Championship Game; Giants win toss. Maynard returns kickoff to Giants' 20. Chandler punts and Taseff returns one yard to Colts' 20. Ameche scores on 1-yard run at 8:15.

Dec. 23, 1962—Dallas Texans 20, Houston Oilers 17, at Houston in AFL Championship Game; Texans win toss and kick off. Jancik returns kickoff to Oilers' 33. Norton punts and Jackson makes fair catch on Texans' 22. Wilson punts and Jancik makes fair catch on Oilers' 45. Robinson intercepts Blanda's pass and returns 13 yards to Oilers' 47. Wilson's punt rolls dead at Oilers' 12. Hull intercepts Blanda's pass and returns 23 yards to midfield. Brooker kicks 25-yard field goal at 17:54.

Dec. 26, 1965—Green Bay 13, Baltimore 10, at Green Bay in NFL Divisional Playoff Game; Packers win toss. Moore returns kickoff to Packers' 22. Chandler punts and Haymond returns nine yards to Colts' 41. Gilburg punts and Wood makes fair catch at Packers' 21. Chandler punts and Haymond returns one yard to Colts' 41. Michaels misses 47-yard field goal. Chandler kicks 25-yard field goal at 13:39.

Dec. 25, 1971—Miami 27, Kansas City 24, at Kansas City in

AFC Divisional Playoff Game; Chiefs win toss. Podolak, after a lateral from Buchanan, returns kickoff to Chiefs' 46. Stenerud's 42-yard field goal is blocked. Seiple punts and Podolak makes fair catch at Chiefs' 17. Wilson punts and Scott returns 18 yards to Dolphins' 39. Yepremian misses 62-yard field goal. Scott intercepts Dawson's pass and returns 13 yards to Dolphins' 46. Seiple punts and Podolak loses one yard to Chiefs' 15. Wilson punts and Scott makes fair catch on Dolphins' 30. Yepremian kicks 37-yard field goal at 22:40.

Dec. 24, 1977—Oakland 37, Baltimore 31, at Baltimore in AFC Divisional Playoff Game; Colts win toss. Raiders start on own 42 following a punt late in the first overtime. Oakland works way into field-goal range on Stabler's 19-yard pass to Branch at Colts' 26. Four plays later, on the second play of the second overtime, Stabler hits Casper with a 10-yard touchdown pass at 15:43.

Jan. 2, 1982—San Diego 41, Miami 38, at Miami in AFC Divisional Playoff Game; Chargers win toss. San Diego drives from its 13 to Miami 8. On second-and-goal, Benirschke misses 27-yard field goal attempt wide left at 9:15. Miami has the ball twice and San Diego twice more before the Dolphins get their third possession. Miami drives from the San Diego 46 to Chargers' 17 and on fourth-and-two, von Schamann's 34-yard field goal attempt is blocked by San Diego's Winslow after 11:27. Fouts then completes four of five passes, including a 39-yarder to Joiner that puts the ball on Dolphins' 10. On first down, Benirschke kicks a 29-yard field goal at 13:52.

Jan. 3, 1987—Cleveland 23, New York Jets 20, at Cleveland in AFC Divisional Playoff Game; Jets win toss. Jets' punt downed at Browns' 26. Moseley's 23-yard field goal attempt is wide right. Teams trade punts. Jets' second punt downed at Browns' 31. First overtime period expires eight plays later with Browns in possession at Jets' 42. Moseley kicks 27-yard field goal four plays into second overtime at 17:02.

Jan. 11, 1987—Denver 23, Cleveland 20, at Cleveland in AFC Championship Game; Browns win toss. Broncos hold Browns on four downs. Browns' punt returned four yards to Denver's 25. Elway completes 22- and 28-yard passes to set up Karlis's 33-yard field goal nine plays into drive at 5:38.

Jan. 3, 1988—Houston 23, Seattle 20, at Houston in AFC Wild Card Game; Seahawks win toss. Rodriguez punts to K. Johnson who returns one yard to Houston 15. Zendejas kicks 32-yard field goal 12 plays later at 8:05.

Dec. 31, 1989—Buffalo 34, Houston 30, at Houston in AFC Wild Card Playoff Game; Steelers win toss. Steelers punt to Oilers. Oilers' fumble recovered by Woodson and returned three yards. Four plays and 13 yards later, Anderson kicks a 50-yard field goal at 3:26.

Jan. 7, 1990—Los Angeles Rams 19, New York Giants 13, at New York in NFC Divisional Game; Rams win toss. Everett completes two passes to move ball to Giants' 48. White called for pass interference; ball spotted on Giants' 25. Everett hits Anderson with a 30-yard touchdown pass at 1:06.

Jan. 3, 1993—Buffalo 41, Houston 38, at Buffalo in AFC Wild Card Game; Oilers win toss. Oilers begin at 20. After 2 plays, Moon's pass is intercepted by Odomes who returns ball 2 yards to Houston 35. After 2 plays, Christie kicks 32-yard field goal at 3:06.

Jan. 8, 1994—Kansas City 27, Pittsburgh 24, at Kansas City in AFC Wild Card Game; Chiefs win toss. Hughes returns kickoff 20 yards to Kansas City 25. After 3 plays, Barker punts 48 yards to Pittsburgh 18 where Woodson returns 8 yards to the 26. After 6 plays, Royals punts 30 yards to Kansas City 20. Kansas City drives to Pittsburgh 14 where Lowery kicks 32-yard field goal at 11:03.

Jan. 17, 1999—Atlanta 30, Minnesota 27, at Minnesota in NFC Championship Game; Vikings win toss. Palmer returns kickoff 30 yards to Minnesota 29. After four plays, Berger punts 51 yards to Atlanta 7 where Dwight returns 8 yards to Atlanta 15. Falcons drive to Atlanta 36. Stryzinski punts 37 yards to Vikings' 27. Palmer calls fair catch. Vikings drive to Minnesota 39. Berger punts 52 yards to Atlanta 9. Downed by Vikings. Atlanta drives to Minnesota 21 where Andersen kicks 38-yard field goal at 11:52.

Dec. 30, 2000—Miami 23, Indianapolis 17, at Miami in AFC Wild Card Game; Dolphins win toss. Williams returns kickoff

18 yards to Miami 20. Offensive holding penalty on Freeman, 10 yards, ball spotted on Miami 10. Dolphins drive to Miami 29 where Turk punts 53 yards to Indianapolis 18. Colts drive to Miami 31 where Vanderjagt misses 49-yard field-goal attempt wide right. Dolphins drive to Indianapolis 17 where Smith rushes for a 17-yard touchdown at 11:16.

Jan. 19, 2002—New England 16, Oakland 13, at New England in AFC Divisional Playoff Game; Patriots win toss. Pass returns kickoff 24 yards to New England 34. Patriots drive to Oakland 5. Vinatieri kicks 23-yard field goal at 8:29.

Jan. 11, 2003—Tennessee 34, Pittsburgh 31, at Tennessee in AFC Divisional Playoff Game; Tennessee wins toss. Reed kicks 60 yards. Returned by Simon 21 yards to Tennessee 31. Titans drive to Pittsburgh 8. Nedney's 26-yard field goal is good at 2:15.

Jan. 4, 2004—Green Bay 33, Seattle 27, at Green Bay in NFC Wild Card Game; Seahawks win toss. Morris returns kick to Seattle 33. Seahawks drive to Seattle 42. Seahawks win 44-yard punt returned by Chatman to Green Bay 26. Packers drive to Green Bay 31. Bidwell punts 35 yards to Seattle 34. Seahawks drive to Seattle 45. Hasselbeck's pass to Bannister intercepted by Packers' Harris and returned 52 yards for touchdown at 4:25.

Jan. 10, 2004—Carolina 29, St. Louis 23, at St. Louis in NFC Divisional Game; Panthers win toss. Smart returns kick to Carolina 32. Panthers drive to St. Louis 27. Kasay's 45-yard field-goal attempt no good. Rams take over at own 35 and drive to Carolina 35. Wilkins' 53-yard field-goal attempt no good. Panthers take over at Carolina 43, drive to Carolina 47. Sauerbrun punts 40 yards to St. Louis 13. Rams drive to Carolina 38. Bulger's pass intercepted by Manning at Carolina 35. Panthers drive to Carolina 31. First overtime ends. On first play of second overtime, Delhomme passes to Smith for 69-yard touchdown at 15:10.

Jan. 11, 2004—Philadelphia 20, Green Bay 17, at Philadelphia in NFC Divisional Game; Eagles win toss. Thrash returns kick to Philadelphia 28. Eagles drive to Philadelphia 24. Johnson punts 49 yards and Packers start at own 32 after holding penalty. Favre's pass intercepted by Dawkins at Philadelphia 31 and returned to Green Bay 34. Eagles drive to Green Bay 13. Akers kicks 31-yard field goal at 4:48.

Jan. 8, 2005—New York Jets 20, San Diego 17, at San Diego in AFC Wild Card Game; Chargers win toss. Dwight returns kick to San Diego 26. Chargers drive to San Diego 35. Scifres punts 39 yards and ball is downed at the New York 26. Jets gain no yards. Gowin punts 41 yards. Parker loses 3 yards on return. San Diego starts on own 30. Chargers drive to New York 22. Kaeding's 40-yard field-goal attempt no good. Jets drive to San Diego 10. Brien kicks 28-yard field goal at 14:55.

Jan. 15, 2005—Pittsburgh 20, New York Jets 17, at Pittsburgh in AFC Divisional Game; Jets win toss. Cotchery returns kick to New York 31. Jets drive to New York 41. Gowin punts 54 yards. Randle El returns 8 yards to Pittsburgh 13. Steelers drive to New York 15. Reed kicks 33-yard field goal at 11:04.

Jan. 14, 2007—Chicago 27, Seattle 24, at Chicago in NFC Divisional Playoff Game; Seahawks win the toss. Burleson returns kickoff 25 yards to Seahawks 30. Plackemeier punts 18 yards. Drive begins at Bears 34. Gould kicks 49-yard field goal at 4:53.

Jan. 20, 2008—New York Giants 23, Green Bay 20, at Green Bay in NFC Championship Game; Packers win toss. K. Robinson returns kick 19 yards to Green Bay 26. Favre pass intercepted by Webster and returned 9 yards to Green Bay 34. Tynes kicks 47-yard field goal at 12:34.

Jan. 3, 2009—San Diego Chargers 23, Indianapolis 17, at San Diego in AFC Wild Card Playoffs; Chargers win toss. Sproles returns kick 31 yards to San Diego 25. Sproles scores on 22-yard touchdown run at 6:12.

Jan. 10, 2010—Arizona Cardinals 51, Green Bay Packers 45, at Arizona in Wild Card Playoffs; Packers win toss. Touchback. Rodgers is sacked and fumbles, recovered by Dansby for 17-yard touchdown at 1:18.

Jan. 24, 2010—New Orleans Saints 31, Minnesota Vikings 28, at New Orleans in NFC Championship; Saints win toss. Thomas returns kick 40 yards. Drive begins at Saints 39. Hartley kicks 40-yard field goal at 4:45.

NFL POSTSEASON OVERTIME GAMES
(BY LENGTH OF GAME)

Date	Game	Time
Dec. 25, 1971	Miami 27, KANSAS CITY 24	82:40
Dec. 23, 1962	Dallas Texans 20, HOUSTON 17	77:54
Jan. 3, 1987	CLEVELAND 23, N.Y. Jets 20	77:02
Dec. 24, 1977	Oakland 37, BALTIMORE 31	75:43
Jan. 10, 2004	Carolina 29, ST. LOUIS 23	75:10
Jan. 8, 2005	N.Y. Jets 20, SAN DIEGO 17	74:55
Jan 2, 1982	San Diego 41, MIAMI 38	73:52
Dec. 26, 1965	GREEN BAY 13, Baltimore 10	73:39
Jan. 17, 1999	Atlanta 30, MINNESOTA 27	71:52
Dec. 30, 2000	MIAMI 23, Indianapolis 17	71:16
Jan. 15, 2005	PITTSBURGH 20, N.Y. Jets 17	71:04
Jan. 8, 1994	KANSAS CITY 27, Pittsburgh 24	71:03
Jan. 19, 2002	NEW ENGLAND 16, Oakland 13	68:29
Dec. 28, 1958	Baltimore 23, N.Y. GIANTS 17	68:15
Jan. 3, 1988	HOUSTON 23, Seattle 20	68:05
Jan. 3, 2009	SAN DIEGO 23, Indianapolis 17	66:12
Jan. 11, 1987	Denver 23, CLEVELAND 20	65:38
Jan. 14, 2007	CHICAGO 27, Seattle 24	64:53
Jan. 11, 2004	PHILADELPHIA 20, Green Bay 17	64:48
Jan. 24, 2010	NEW ORLEANS 31, Minnesota 28	64:45
Jan. 4, 2004	GREEN BAY 33, Seattle 27	64:25
Dec. 31, 1989	Pittsburgh 26, HOUSTON 23	63:26
Jan. 3, 1993	BUFFALO 41, Houston 38	63:06
Jan. 20, 2008	N.Y. Giants 23, GREEN BAY 20	62:26
Jan. 11, 2003	TENNESSEE 34, Pittsburgh 31	62:15
Jan. 10, 2010	ARIZONA 51, Green Bay 45	61:18
Jan. 7, 1990	L.A. Rams 19, N.Y. GIANTS 13	61:06

Home team in CAPS

There have been 27 overtime postseason games dating back to 1958. In 22 cases, both teams had at least one possession. Last time: 1/10/10, ARIZONA 51, Green Bay 45.

OVERTIME WON-LOST RECORDS, 1974-2010
(REGULAR SEASON)

Team	Win	Loss	Tie	Pct.
AFC				
Baltimore	9	7	1	.559
Buffalo	18	12	0	.600
Cincinnati	15	11	1	.574
Cleveland	16	15	1	.516
Denver	22	15	2	.590
Houston	1	7	0	.125
Indianapolis	12	10	1	.543
Jacksonville	7	4	0	.636
Kansas City	12	17	2	.419
Miami	13	19	1	.409
New England	17	20	0	.459
N.Y. Jets	18	16	2	.528
Oakland	15	17	0	.469
Pittsburgh	20	14	2	.583
San Diego	12	17	0	.414
Tennessee	14	18	0	.438
NFC				
Arizona	18	15	2	.543
Atlanta	13	19	2	.412
Carolina	4	9	0	.308
Chicago	22	15	0	.595
Dallas	15	12	0	.556
Detroit	13	16	1	.450
Green Bay	11	15	4	.433
Minnesota	18	17	2	.514
New Orleans	8	11	0	.421
N.Y. Giants	18	14	2	.559
Philadelphia	11	16	4	.419
St. Louis	12	10	1	.543
San Francisco	19	13	1	.591
Seattle	8	17	0	.320
Tampa Bay	14	16	1	.468
Washington	22	13	1	.625

OVERTIME GAMES BY YEAR
(REGULAR SEASON)

2010-19	2000-13	1990-10	1980-13
2009-13	1999-11	1989-11	1979-12
2008-15	1998-7	1988- 9	1978-11
2007-15	1997-17	1987-13	1977-6
2006-11	1996-14	1986-16	1976-5
2005-14	1995-21	1985-10	1975-9
2004-12	1994-16	1984- 9	1974-2
2003-23	1993-7	1983-19	
2002-25*	1992-10	1982- 4	
2001-17	1991-15	1981-10	

*Record

OVERTIME GAME SUMMARY—1974-2010

There have been 464 overtime games in regular season play since the rule was adopted in 1974 (19 in 2010 season). Breakdown follows:

RESULTS

248 (8) times the team which won the toss won the game (53.4%)

199(11) times the team which lost the toss won the game (42.9%)

17 (0) games ended tied (3.7%). Last time: Nov. 16, 2008, Philadelphia 13 at Cincinnati 13.

POSSESSIONS

327(17) times both teams had at least one possession (70.5%)

137 (2) times the team which won the toss drove for winning score (102 FG, 35 TD) (29.5%)

Of the 464 overtime games, there were 13 miscellaneous situations in which non-standard possessions took place:

9 (0) times the defense or special teams won without registering an official possession (5 INT, 2 blocked punts, 1 FR, 1 blocked FG) (1.9%)

1 (0) times the special teams forced a fumble on the opening kickoff and drove for winning score (0.2%)

1 (0) times the punting team recovered a muffed punt and drove for winning score with team muffing punt having no official possessions (0.2%)

2 (0) times the team that won the toss elected to kick and the team receiving the ball drove for winning score (0.4%)

SCORING

328(16) games were decided by a field goal (70.7%)

117 (3) games were decided by a touchdown (25.2%)

2 (0) games were decided by a safety (0.4%)

17 (0) games ended tied (3.7%). Last time: Nov. 16, 2008, Philadelphia 13 at Cincinnati 13.

COIN TOSS

455(19) times the team which won the toss elected to receive (98.1%)

9 (0) times the team which won the toss elected to kick off (4 wins) (1.9%)

Note: The number in parentheses is the 2010 Season Total.

MOST OVERTIME GAMES, SEASON

5	Green Bay Packers, 1983
4	Denver Broncos, 1985, 2007
	Cleveland Browns, 1989
	Minnesota Vikings, 1994, 1995
	Arizona Cardinals, 1995, 1997
	San Francisco 49ers, 2001
	Atlanta Falcons, 2002
	San Diego Chargers, 2002
	Carolina Panthers, 2003
	Washington Redskins, 2010

LONGEST CONSECUTIVE GAME STREAKS
WITHOUT OVERTIME (Current)
51   San Diego Chargers (Last OT Game, 12/9/07 vs.
        Tennessee Titans)
(Record: 110, St. Louis/Phoenix Cardinals, 12/7/86-12/19/93)

There have been 27 overtime postseason games dating back to 1958. In 22 cases, both teams had at least one possession. Last time: 1/10/10, ARIZONA 51, Green Bay 45.

SHORTEST OVERTIME GAMES
0:14   New York Jets 37, BUFFALO 31; 9/8/02
0:16   CHICAGO 37, San Francisco 31; 10/28/01
0:16   Green Bay 19, DENVER 13; 10/29/07
0:17   NEW ORLEANS 20, Seattle 17; 11/16/97
0:21   Chicago 23, DETROIT 17; 11/27/80
0:30   Baltimore 29, NEW ENGLAND 23; 9/4/83
0:34   San Diego 23, WASHINGTON 17; 11/27/05
0:55   New York Giants 16, PHILADELPHIA 10; 9/29/85

LONGEST OVERTIME GAMES
(ALL POSTSEASON GAMES)
22:40   Miami 27, KANSAS CITY 24; 12/25/71
17:54   Dallas Texans 20, HOUSTON 17; 12/23/62
17:02   CLEVELAND 23, New York Jets 20; 1/3/87
15:43   Oakland 37, BALTIMORE 31; 12/24/77
15:10   Carolina 29, ST. LOUIS 23; 1/10/04

OVERTIME SCORING SUMMARY
328   were decided by a field goal
54   were decided by a touchdown pass
32   were decided by a touchdown run
18   were decided by an interception
3   were decided by a fumble recovery (Baltimore 29, New England 23, 9/4/83; Denver 36, Seattle 30, 12/19/99; San Francisco 37, Arizona 31, 11/24/07)
2   were decided on a fake field goal/touchdown pass (Minnesota 22, Chicago 16, 10/16/77; Cleveland 23, Minnesota 17, 12/17/89)
2   were decided by a kickoff return (Chicago 23, Detroit 17, 11/27/80; New York Jets 37, Buffalo 31, 9/8/02)
2   were decided by a safety (Minnesota 23, Los Angeles Rams 21, 11/5/89; Chicago 19, Tennessee 17, 11/14/04)
1   was decided by a punt return (Kansas City 29, San Diego 23, 10/9/95)
1   was decided on a fake field goal/touchdown run (Los Angeles Rams 27, Minnesota 21, 12/2/79)
1   was decided on a blocked field goal (Denver 30, San Diego 24, 11/17/85)
1   was decided on a blocked field goal/recovery by kicker (Green Bay 12, Chicago 6, 9/7/80)
1   was decided on a blocked field goal/recovery by kicking team (Philadelphia 23, New York Giants 17, 11/20/88)
1   was decided by a blocked punt (Arizona 30, Dallas 24, 10/12/08)
17   ended tied

OVERTIME RECORDS
Longest Touchdown Pass
99 Yards — Ron Jaworski to Mike Quick, Philadelphia 23, Atlanta 17 (11/10/85)
82 Yards — Tom Brady to Troy Brown, New England 19, Miami 13 (10/19/03); Brett Favre to Greg Jennings, Green Bay 19, Denver 13 (10/29/07)
76 Yards — Troy Aikman to Raghib Ismail, Dallas 41, Washington 35 (9/12/99)

Longest Touchdown Run
96 Yards — Garrison Hearst, San Francisco 36, New York Jets 30 (9/6/98)
60 Yards — Herschel Walker, Dallas 23, New England 17 (11/15/87)
50 Yards — Rashard Mendenhall, Pittsburgh 15, Atlanta 9 (9/12/10)

Longest Field Goal
57 Yards — Sebastian Janikowski, Oakland 16, New York Jets 13 (10/19/08)
53 Yards — Chris Jacke, Green Bay 23, San Francisco 20 (10/4/96)
52 Yards — Mike Cofer, Indianapolis 27, New York Jets 24 (9/10/95)

Longest Touchdown Plays
99 Yards — (Pass) Ron Jaworski to Mike Quick, Philadelphia 23, Atlanta 17 (11/10/85)
96 Yards — (Run) Garrison Hearst, San Francisco 36, New York Jets 30 (9/6/98)
96 Yards — (Kickoff return) Chad Morton, New York Jets 37, Buffalo 31 (9/8/02)
95 Yards — (Kickoff return) Dave Williams, Chicago 23, Detroit 17 (11/27/80)
86 Yards — (Punt return) Tamarick Vanover, Kansas City 29, San Diego 23 (10/9/95)

ASSOCIATED PRESS NFL MOST OUTSTANDING/VALUABLE PLAYERS

THE FOLLOWING AWARDS WERE NAMED BY ASSOCIATED PRESS IN BALLOTING BY A NATIONWIDE PANEL OF MEDIA.

NFL MOST OUTSTANDING PLAYER AWARD

YEAR	PLAYER	POS.	TEAM	ACCOMPLISHMENTS
1957	Jim Brown	RB	Cleveland Browns	Rushed for league-leading 942 yards and added 9 touchdowns as a rookie.
1958	Jim Brown	RB	Cleveland Browns	Rushed for NFL-record 1,527 yards and added 17 touchdowns. Led Browns to 9-3 record.
1959	Charley Conerly	QB	New York Giants	Passed for 14 touchdowns and only 4 interceptions. Led offense to division-leading 284 points.
1960	Norm Van Brocklin	QB	Philadelphia Eagles	Guided Eagles to first division title since 1949. Passed for 2,471 yards and 24 touchdowns.

NFL MOST VALUABLE PLAYER AWARD

YEAR	PLAYER	POS.	TEAM	ACCOMPLISHMENTS
1961	Paul Hornung	RB	Green Bay Packers	Led league in scoring for second straight season with 146 points (10 TD, 15 FG, 41 PAT).
1962	Jim Taylor	RB	Green Bay Packers	League rushing champion with 1,474 yards. Scored all-time record 19 touchdowns.
1963	Y.A. Tittle	QB	New York Giants	Set all-time season record with 36 touchdown passes. Guided league's top offense (5,024 yards).
1964	Johnny Unitas	QB	Baltimore Colts	Guided Colts to NFL's best record (12-2) and league's top offensive attack (4,779 yards).
1965	Jim Brown	RB	Cleveland Browns	Leader of NFL's top rushing attack. Led league with 1,544 yards, added 21 total touchdowns.
1966	Bart Starr	QB	Green Bay Packers	Passed for 14 touchdowns and only 3 interceptions. Led Packers to league-best 12-2 record.
1967	Johnny Unitas	QB	Baltimore Colts	Passed for 3,428 yards and 20 touchdowns. Led Colts to 11-1-2 record.
1968	Earl Morrall	QB	Baltimore Colts	Guided Colts to NFL-best 13-1 record. Led league with 26 touchdown passes.
1969	Roman Gabriel	QB	Los Angeles Rams	Led NFL with 24 touchdown passes. Guided Rams to 11-3 record.
1970	John Brodie	QB	San Francisco 49ers	Took 49ers to first division title. Threw NFL-best 24 touchdown passes.
1971	Alan Page	DT	Minnesota Vikings	Led defense that allowed NFL-low 139 points. Vikings won fourth straight NFC Central title.
1972	Larry Brown	RB	Washington Redskins	Led conference with 1,216 rushing yards. Redskins had NFC-best 11-3 record.
1973	O.J. Simpson	RB	Buffalo Bills	Rushed for all-time record 2,003 yards, including three 200-yard performances.
1974	Ken Stabler	QB	Oakland Raiders	Led league with 26 touchdown passes and only 12 interceptions. Raiders had NFL-best 12-2 record.
1975	Fran Tarkenton	QB	Minnesota Vikings	Tied for league-best 12-2 record. Led NFC with 91.7 passer rating.
1976	Bert Jones	QB	Baltimore Colts	Threw 24 touchdowns and only 9 interceptions for 102.5 passer rating.
1977	Walter Payton	RB	Chicago Bears	Rushed for league-leading 1,852 yards and 16 total touchdowns.
1978	Terry Bradshaw	QB	Pittsburgh Steelers	Led Steelers to league-leading 14-2 mark. Set club record with 28 touchdown passes.
1979	Earl Campbell	RB	Houston Oilers	Led league with 1,697 rushing yards and 19 touchdowns.
1980	Brian Sipe	QB	Cleveland Browns	NFL-best 91.4 passer rating. Set Browns' records with 30 touchdown passes and 4,132 yards.
1981	Ken Anderson	QB	Cincinnati Bengals	Led Bengals to first division title since 1973. NFL-high 98.5 passer rating.
1982	Mark Moseley	K	Washington Redskins	Converted 20 of 21 FGs. Set consecutive field-goal record at 23 (including last three in '81).
1983	Joe Theismann	QB	Washington Redskins	Leader of offense that scored NFL record 541 points. Redskins had NFL-best 14-2 record.
1984	Dan Marino	QB	Miami Dolphins	Set NFL records with 5,084 yards and 48 touchdown passes. Led Dolphins to AFC-best 14-2 mark.
1985	Marcus Allen	RB	Los Angeles Raiders	Rushed for league-leading 1,759 yards. Tied for AFC lead with 11 rushing touchdowns.
1986	Lawrence Taylor	LB	New York Giants	Recorded league-high 20.5 sacks, and led Giants' second-ranked defense (297.3).
1987	John Elway	QB	Denver Broncos	In 12 games, passed for 19 touchdowns and 3,198 yards, including four 300-yard games.
1988	Boomer Esiason	QB	Cincinnati Bengals	Led NFL with 97.4 passer rating. Tied for AFC lead with 28 TD passes.
1989	Joe Montana	QB	San Francisco 49ers	Set NFL record with 112.4 passer rating, including 70.2 completion percentage.
1990	Joe Montana	QB	San Francisco 49ers	Led 49ers to league-best 14-2 record. Completed NFC-high 61.7 percent of passes.
1991	Thurman Thomas	RB	Buffalo Bills	Recorded league-high 2,038 yards from scrimmage (1,407 rushing, 631 receiving).
1992	Steve Young	QB	San Francisco 49ers	NFL's top passer with 107.0 rating. Led 49ers to NFL-best 14-2 record.

Year	Player	Pos.	Team	Description
1993	Emmitt Smith	RB	Dallas Cowboys	Led league in rushing (1,486 yards) for third straight year despite missing first two games.
1994	Steve Young	QB	San Francisco 49ers	Compiled NFL all-time best 112.8 passer rating. Completed more than 70 percent of his passes.
1995	Brett Favre	QB	Green Bay Packers	Led league with 38 touchdown passes and NFC with 99.5 passer rating.
1996	Brett Favre	QB	Green Bay Packers	Led Packers to top conference record (13-3). Threw NFL-best 39 touchdown passes.
1997*	Brett Favre	QB	Green Bay Packers	Led league with 35 touchdown passes. Led NFC with 3,867 passing yards.
	Barry Sanders	RB	Detroit Lions	Rushed for all-time second-best 2,053 yards, including record 14 straight 100-yard games.
1998	Terrell Davis	RB	Denver Broncos	Rushed for 2,008 yards and scored league-best 23 total touchdowns.
1999	Kurt Warner	QB	St. Louis Rams	Became the second QB in history to have 40 touchdown passes in a season (41).
2000	Marshall Faulk	RB	St. Louis Rams	Set NFL record with 26 touchdowns and led NFC with 2,189 yards from scrimmage.
2001	Kurt Warner	QB	St. Louis Rams	Led NFL with 4,830 passing yards, 36 touchdowns, 68.7 completion percentage, and 101.4 passer rating.
2002	Rich Gannon	QB	Oakland Raiders	Set single-season records with 10 300-yard passing games and 418 completions, and led NFL with 4,689 passing yards.
2003*	Peyton Manning	QB	Indianapolis Colts	Led NFL with 4,267 passing yards, had AFC-best 29 touchdown passes, and posted 99.0 passer rating.
	Steve McNair	QB	Tennessee Titans	Posted NFL-best 100.4 passer rating, passing for 3,215 yards with 24 touchdowns against 7 interceptions.
2004	Peyton Manning	QB	Indianapolis Colts	Set NFL records with 49 touchdown passes and 121.1 passer rating while passing for 4,557 yards.
2005	Shaun Alexander	RB	Seattle Seahawks	Set NFL record with 28 touchdowns and led league with 1,880 rushing yards.
2006	LaDainian Tomlinson	RB	San Diego Chargers	Set NFL record for touchdowns (31) and points scored (186). Rushed for team-record 1,815 yards.
2007	Tom Brady	QB	New England Patriots	Set NFL record with 50 passing touchdowns. Led New England to first 16-0 regular-season record in league history.
2008	Peyton Manning	QB	Indianapolis Colts	Threw for 4,002 yards and 27 touchdowns and 95.0 passer rating. Led Indianapolis to 12-4 record.
2009	Peyton Manning	QB	Indianapolis Colts	Threw for 4,500 yards with 33 touchdowns for 99.9 passer rating while leading Colts to NFL-best 14-2 record.
2010	Tom Brady	QB	New England Patriots	Led league with 111.0 passer rating, throwing for 3,900 yards and 36 touchdowns while guiding Patriots to NFL-best 14-2 record.

Total Associated Press NFL MVPs: 52
Four-time Winner: Peyton Manning
Three-time Winner: Brett Favre
Two-time Winners: Tom Brady, Joe Montana, Johnny Unitas, Kurt Warner, Steve Young
* The award was shared in 1997 and 2003.

ASSOCIATED PRESS MVPs WHO WON SUPER BOWL/NFL CHAMPIONSHIP IN SAME SEASON: 13

1961	Paul Hornung	Green Bay Packers
1962	Jim Taylor	Green Bay Packers
1966	Bart Starr	Green Bay Packers
1968	Earl Morrall	Baltimore Colts
1978	Terry Bradshaw	Pittsburgh Steelers
1982	Mark Moseley	Washington Redskins
1986	Lawrence Taylor	New York Giants
1989	Joe Montana	San Francisco 49ers
1993	Emmitt Smith	Dallas Cowboys
1994	Steve Young	San Francisco 49ers
1996	Brett Favre	Green Bay Packers
1998	Terrell Davis	Denver Broncos
1999	Kurt Warner	St. Louis Rams

ASSOCIATED PRESS NFL MVP BY POSITION

Position	Count	Position	Count
Quarterback:	34	Kicker:	1
Running Back:	15	Linebacker:	1
Defensive Tackle:	1		

ASSOCIATED PRESS MVPs BY TEAM

8 Indianapolis/Baltimore Colts

6 Green Bay Packers

5 San Francisco 49ers

4 St. Louis/Los Angeles Rams

3 Oakland/Los Angeles Raiders
  Washington Redskins

2 Buffalo Bills
  Cincinnati Bengals
  Cleveland Browns
  Denver Broncos
  Houston Oilers/Tennessee Titans
  Minnesota Vikings
  New England Patriots
  New York Giants

1 Chicago Bears
  Dallas Cowboys
  Detroit Lions
  Miami Dolphins
  Pittsburgh Steelers
  San Diego Chargers
  Seattle Seahawks

AP OFFENSIVE PLAYER OF THE YEAR

1973	O.J. Simpson	RB	Buffalo Bills
1974	Ken Stabler	QB	Oakland Raiders
1975	Fran Tarkenton	QB	Minnesota Vikings
1976	Bert Jones	QB	Baltimore Colts
1977	Walter Payton	RB	Chicago Bears
1978	Earl Campbell	RB	Houston Oilers
1979	Earl Campbell	RB	Houston Oilers
1980	Earl Campbell	RB	Houston Oilers
1981	Ken Anderson	QB	Cincinnati Bengals
1982	Dan Fouts	QB	San Diego Chargers
1983	Joe Theismann	QB	Washington Redskins
1984	Dan Marino	QB	Miami Dolphins
1985	Marcus Allen	RB	Los Angeles Raiders
1986	Eric Dickerson	RB	Los Angeles Rams
1987	Jerry Rice	WR	San Francisco 49ers
1988	Roger Craig	RB	San Francisco 49ers
1989	Joe Montana	QB	San Francisco 49ers
1990	Warren Moon	QB	Houston Oilers
1991	Thurman Thomas	RB	Buffalo Bills
1992	Steve Young	QB	San Francisco 49ers
1993	Jerry Rice	WR	San Francisco 49ers
1994	Barry Sanders	RB	Detroit Lions
1995	Brett Favre	QB	Green Bay Packers
1996	Terrell Davis	RB	Denver Broncos
1997	Barry Sanders	RB	Detroit Lions
1998	Terrell Davis	RB	Denver Broncos
1999	Marshall Faulk	RB	St. Louis Rams
2000	Marshall Faulk	RB	St. Louis Rams
2001	Marshall Faulk	RB	St. Louis Rams
2002	Priest Holmes	RB	Kansas City Chiefs
2003	Jamal Lewis	RB	Baltimore Ravens
2004	Peyton Manning	QB	Indianapolis Colts
2005	Shaun Alexander	RB	Seattle Seahawks
2006	LaDainian Tomlinson	RB	San Diego Chargers
2007	Tom Brady	QB	New England Patriots
2008	Drew Brees	QB	New Orleans Saints
2009	Chris Johnson	RB	Tennessee Titans
2010	Tom Brady	QB	New England Patriots

AP OFFENSIVE ROOKIE OF THE YEAR

1957	Jim Brown	RB	Cleveland Browns
1958	Jimmy Orr	WR	Pittsburgh Steelers
1959	Nick Pietrosante	RB	Detroit Lions
1960	Gail Cogdill	WR	Detroit Lions
1961	Mike Ditka	TE	Chicago Bears
1962	Ron Bull	RB	Chicago Bears
1963	Paul Flatley	WR	Minnesota Vikings
1964	Charley Taylor	WR	Washington Redskins
1965	Gale Sayers	RB	Chicago Bears
1966	Johnny Roland	RB	St. Louis Cardinals
1967	Mel Farr	RB	Detroit Lions
1968	Earl McCullouch	WR	Detroit Lions
1969	Calvin Hill	RB	Dallas Cowboys
1970	Duane Thomas	RB	Dallas Cowboys
1971	John Brockington	RB	Green Bay Packers
1972	Franco Harris	RB	Pittsburgh Steelers
1973	Chuck Foreman	RB	Minnesota Vikings
1974	Don Woods	RB	San Diego Chargers
1975	Mike Thomas	RB	Washington Redskins
1976	Sammy White	WR	Minnesota Vikings
1977	Tony Dorsett	RB	Dallas Cowboys
1978	Earl Campbell	RB	Houston Oilers
1979	Ottis Anderson	RB	St. Louis Cardinals
1980	Billy Sims	RB	Detroit Lions
1981	George Rogers	RB	New Orleans Saints
1982	Marcus Allen	RB	Los Angeles Raiders
1983	Eric Dickerson	RB	Los Angeles Rams

1984	Louis Lipps	WR	Pittsburgh Steelers
1985	Eddie Brown	WR	Cincinnati Bengals
1986	Rueben Mayes	RB	New Orleans Saints
1987	Troy Stradford	RB	Miami Dolphins
1988	John Stephens	RB	New England Patriots
1989	Barry Sanders	RB	Detroit Lions
1990	Emmitt Smith	RB	Dallas Cowboys
1991	Leonard Russell	RB	New England Patriots
1992	Carl Pickens	WR	Cincinnati Bengals
1993	Jerome Bettis	RB	Los Angeles Rams
1994	Marshall Faulk	RB	Indianapolis Colts
1995	Curtis Martin	RB	New England Patriots
1996	Eddie George	RB	Houston Oilers
1997	Warrick Dunn	RB	Tampa Bay Buccaneers
1998	Randy Moss	WR	Minnesota Vikings
1999	Edgerrin James	RB	Indianapolis Colts
2000	Mike Anderson	RB	Denver Broncos
2001	Anthony Thomas	RB	Chicago Bears
2002	Clinton Portis	RB	Denver Broncos
2003	Anquan Boldin	WR	Arizona Cardinals
2004	Ben Roethlisberger	QB	Pittsburgh Steelers
2005	Carnell Williams	RB	Tampa Bay Buccaneers
2006	Vince Young	QB	Tennessee Titans
2007	Adrian Peterson	RB	Minnesota Vikings
2008	Matt Ryan	QB	Atlanta Falcons
2009	Percy Harvin	WR	Minnesota Vikings
2010	Sam Bradford	QB	St. Louis Rams

AP DEFENSIVE PLAYER OF THE YEAR

1971	Alan Page	DT	Minnesota Vikings
1972	Joe Greene	DT	Pittsburgh Steelers
1973	Dick Anderson	S	Miami Dolphins
1974	Joe Greene	DT	Pittsburgh Steelers
1975	Mel Blount	CB	Pittsburgh Steelers
1976	Jack Lambert	LB	Pittsburgh Steelers
1977	Harvey Martin	DE	Dallas Cowboys
1978	Randy Gradishar	LB	Denver Broncos
1979	Lee Roy Selmon	DE	Tampa Bay Buccaneers
1980	Lester Hayes	CB	Oakland Raiders
1981	Lawrence Taylor	LB	New York Giants
1982	Lawrence Taylor	LB	New York Giants
1983	Doug Betters	DE	Miami Dolphins
1984	Kenny Easley	S	Seattle Seahawks
1985	Mike Singletary	LB	Chicago Bears
1986	Lawrence Taylor	LB	New York Giants
1987	Reggie White	DT	Philadelphia Eagles
1988	Mike Singletary	LB	Chicago Bears
1989	Keith Millard	DT	Minnesota Vikings
1990	Bruce Smith	DE	Buffalo Bills
1991	Pat Swilling	LB	New Orleans Saints
1992	Cortez Kennedy	DT	Seattle Seahawks
1993	Rod Woodson	CB	Pittsburgh Steelers
1994	Deion Sanders	CB	San Francisco 49ers
1995	Bryce Paup	LB	Buffalo Bills
1996	Bruce Smith	DE	Buffalo Bills
1997	Dana Stubblefield	DT	San Francisco 49ers
1998	Reggie White	DE	Green Bay Packers
1999	Warren Sapp	DT	Tampa Bay Buccaneers
2000	Ray Lewis	LB	Baltimore Ravens
2001	Michael Strahan	DE	New York Giants
2002	Derrick Brooks	LB	Tampa Bay Buccaneers
2003	Ray Lewis	LB	Baltimore Ravens
2004	Ed Reed	S	Baltimore Ravens
2005	Brian Urlacher	LB	Chicago Bears
2006	Jason Taylor	DE	Miami Dolphins
2007	Bob Sanders	S	Indianapolis Colts
2008	James Harrison	LB	Pittsburgh Steelers
2009	Charles Woodson	CB	Green Bay Packers
2010	Troy Polamalu	S	Pittsburgh Steelers

AP DEFENSIVE ROOKIE OF THE YEAR

1967	Lem Barney	CB	Detroit Lions
1968	Claude Humphrey	DE	Atlanta Falcons
1969	Joe Greene	DT	Pittsburgh Steelers
1970	Bruce Taylor	CB	San Francisco 49ers
1971	Isiah Robertson	LB	Los Angeles Rams
1972	Willie Buchanon	CB	Green Bay Packers
1973	Wally Chambers	DT	Chicago Bears
1974	Jack Lambert	LB	Pittsburgh Steelers
1975	Robert Brazile	LB	Houston Oilers
1976	Mike Haynes	S	New England Patriots
1977	A.J. Duhe	DT	Miami Dolphins
1978	Al Baker	DE	Detroit Lions
1979	Jim Haslett	LB	Buffalo Bills
1980*	Buddy Curry	LB	Atlanta Falcons
	Al Richardson	LB	Atlanta Falcons
1981	Lawrence Taylor	LB	New York Giants
1982	Chip Banks	LB	Cleveland Browns
1983	Vernon Maxwell	LB	Baltimore Colts
1984	Bill Maas	NT	Kansas City Chiefs
1985	Duane Bickett	LB	Indianapolis Colts
1986	John Offerdahl	LB	Miami Dolphins
1987	Shane Conlan	LB	Buffalo Bills
1988	Erik McMillan	S	New York Jets
1989	Derrick Thomas	LB	Kansas City Chiefs
1990	Mark Carrier	S	Chicago Bears
1991	Mike Croel	LB	Denver Broncos
1992	Dale Carter	CB	Kansas City Chiefs
1993	Dana Stubblefield	DT	San Francisco 49ers
1994	Tim Bowens	DT	Miami Dolphins
1995	Hugh Douglas	DE	New York Jets
1996	Simeon Rice	DE	Arizona Cardinals
1997	Peter Boulware	LB	Baltimore Ravens
1998	Charles Woodson	CB	Oakland Raiders
1999	Jevon Kearse	DE	Tennessee Titans
2000	Brian Urlacher	LB	Chicago Bears
2001	Kendrell Bell	LB	Pittsburgh Steelers
2002	Julius Peppers	DE	Carolina Panthers
2003	Terrell Suggs	LB	Baltimore Ravens
2004	Jonathan Vilma	LB	New York Jets
2005	Shawne Merriman	LB	San Diego Chargers
2006	DeMeco Ryans	LB	Houston Texans
2007	Patrick Willis	LB	San Francisco 49ers
2008	Jerod Mayo	LB	New England Patriots
2009	Brian Cushing	LB	Houston Texans
2010	Ndamukong Suh	DT	Detroit Lions

The award was shared in 1980.

AP COMEBACK PLAYER OF THE YEAR

1998	Doug Flutie	QB	Buffalo Bills
1999	Bryant Young	DT	San Francisco 49ers
2000	Joe Johnson	DE	New Orleans Saints
2001	Garrison Hearst	RB	San Francisco 49ers
2002	Tommy Maddox	QB	Pittsburgh Steelers
2003	Jon Kitna	QB	Cincinnati Bengals
2004	Drew Brees	QB	San Diego Chargers
2005*	Steve Smith	WR	Carolina Panthers
	Tedy Bruschi	LB	New England Patriots
2006	Chad Pennington	QB	New York Jets
2007	Greg Ellis	DE	Dallas Cowboys
2008	Chad Pennington	QB	Miami Dolphins
2009	Tom Brady	QB	New England Patriots
2010	Michael Vick	QB	Philadelphia Eagles

*The award was shared in 2005.

AP COACH OF THE YEAR

1957	George Wilson	Detroit Lions
1958	Weeb Ewbank	Baltimore Colts
1959	Vince Lombardi	Green Bay Packers
1960	Buck Shaw	Philadelphia Eagles
1961	Allie Sherman	New York Giants
1962	Allie Sherman	New York Giants
1963	George Halas	Chicago Bears
1964	Don Shula	Baltimore Colts
1965	George Halas	Chicago Bears
1966	Tom Landry	Dallas Cowboys
1967*	George Allen	Los Angeles Rams
	Don Shula	Baltimore Colts
1968	Don Shula	Baltimore Colts
1969	Bud Grant	Minnesota Vikings
1970	Paul Brown	Cincinnati Bengals
1971	George Allen	Washington Redskins
1972	Don Shula	Miami Dolphins
1973	Chuck Knox	Los Angeles Rams
1974	Don Coryell	St. Louis Cardinals
1975	Ted Marchibroda	Baltimore Colts
1976	Forrest Gregg	Cleveland Browns
1977	Red Miller	Denver Broncos
1978	Jack Patera	Seattle Seahawks
1979	Jack Pardee	Washington Redskins
1980	Chuck Knox	Buffalo Bills
1981	Bill Walsh	San Francisco 49ers
1982	Joe Gibbs	Washington Redskins
1983	Joe Gibbs	Washington Redskins
1984	Chuck Knox	Seattle Seahawks
1985	Mike Ditka	Chicago Bears
1986	Bill Parcells	New York Giants
1987	Jim Mora	New Orleans Saints
1988	Mike Ditka	Chicago Bears
1989	Lindy Infante	Green Bay Packers
1990	Jimmy Johnson	Dallas Cowboys
1991	Wayne Fontes	Detroit Lions
1992	Bill Cowher	Pittsburgh Steelers
1993	Dan Reeves	New York Giants
1994	Bill Parcells	New England Patriots
1995	Ray Rhodes	Philadelphia Eagles
1996	Dom Capers	Carolina Panthers
1997	Jim Fassel	New York Giants
1998	Dan Reeves	Atlanta Falcons
1999	Dick Vermeil	St. Louis Rams
2000	Jim Haslett	New Orleans Saints
2001	Dick Jauron	Chicago Bears
2002	Andy Reid	Philadelphia Eagles
2003	Bill Belichick	New England Patriots
2004	Marty Schottenheimer	San Diego Chargers
2005	Lovie Smith	Chicago Bears
2006	Sean Payton	New Orleans Saints
2007	Bill Belichick	New England Patriots
2008	Mike Smith	Atlanta Falcons
2009	Marvin Lewis	Cincinnati Bengals
2010	Bill Belichick	New England Patriots

*The award was shared in 1967.

ANNUAL ACTIVE PLAYER LIMITS
NFL

Year(s)	Limit
1991-2010	45**
1985-90	45
1983-84	49
1982	45†-49
1978-81	45
1975-77	43
1974	47
1964-73	40
1963	37
1961-62	36
1960	38
1959	36
1957-58	35
1951-56	33
1949-50	32
1948	35
1947	35*-34
1945-46	33
1943-44	28
1940-42	33
1938-39	30
1936-37	25
1935	24
1930-34	20
1926-29	18
1925	16

** 45 plus a third quarterback
† 45 for first two games
* 35 for first three games

AFL

Year(s)	Limit
1966-69	40
1965	38
1964	34
1962-63	33
1960-61	35

NFL FREE AGENCY MOVEMENT

The following chart details veteran free agents who signed with new teams:

	Unrestricted	Restricted	Transition	Franchise	TOTALS
1993	108	8	4	1	121
1994	121	7	4	0	132
1995	171	6	2	0	179
1996	100	4	2	0	106
1997	86	2	2	0	90
1998	112	4	1	2	119
1999	115	2	1	0	118
2000	107	4	0	0	111
2001	93	4	0	0	97
2002	130	1	0	0	131
2003	111	5	1	0	117
2004	124	1	1	0	126
2005	104	3	0	0	107
2006	149	4	1	0	154
2007	126	4	0	0	130
2008	132	3	0	0	135
2009	128	0	0	0	128
2010	51	1	0	0	52

WALTER PAYTON NFL MAN OF THE YEAR

The Walter Payton NFL Man of the Year Award is the only NFL award that recognizes a player for his community service activities as well as his excellence on the field. Renamed in 1999 for the legendary Chicago Bears Pro Football Hall of Fame running back, the Walter Payton NFL Man of the Year Award has been given annually since 1970.

YEAR	PLAYER	POS.	TEAM
1970	Johnny Unitas	QB	Baltimore Colts
1971	John Hadl	QB	San Diego Chargers
1972	Willie Lanier	LB	Kansas City Chiefs
1973	Len Dawson	QB	Kansas City Chiefs
1974	George Blanda	QB	Oakland Raiders
1975	Ken Anderson	QB	Cincinnati Bengals
1976	Franco Harris	RB	Pittsburgh Steelers
1977	Walter Payton	RB	Chicago Bears
1978	Roger Staubach	QB	Dallas Cowboys
1979	Joe Greene	DT	Pittsburgh Steelers
1980	Harold Carmichael	WR	Philadelphia Eagles
1981	Lynn Swann	WR	Pittsburgh Steelers
1982	Joe Theismann	QB	Washington Redskins
1983	Rolf Benirschke	K	San Diego Chargers
1984	Marty Lyons	T	New York Jets
1985	Dwight Stephenson	C	Miami Dolphins
1986	Reggie Williams	LB	Cincinnati Bengals
1987	Dave Duerson	S	Chicago Bears
1988	Steve Largent	WR	Seattle Seahawks
1989	Warren Moon	QB	Houston Oilers
1990	Mike Singletary	LB	Chicago Bears
1991	Anthony Muñoz	T	Cincinnati Bengals
1992	John Elway	QB	Denver Broncos
1993	Derrick Thomas	LB	Kansas City Chiefs
1994	Junior Seau	LB	San Diego Chargers
1995	Boomer Esiason	QB	New York Jets
1996	Darrell Green	CB	Washington Redskins
1997	Troy Aikman	QB	Dallas Cowboys
1998	Dan Marino	QB	Miami Dolphins
1999	Cris Carter	WR	Minnesota Vikings
2000*	Derrick Brooks	LB	Tampa Bay Buccaneers
	Jim Flanigan	DT	Chicago Bears
2001	Jerome Bettis	RB	Pittsburgh Steelers
2002	Troy Vincent	CB	Philadelphia Eagles
2003	Will Shields	G	Kansas City Chiefs
2004	Warrick Dunn	RB	Atlanta Falcons
2005	Peyton Manning	QB	Indianapolis Colts
2006*	Drew Brees	QB	New Orleans Saints
	LaDainian Tomlinson	RB	San Diego Chargers
2007	Jason Taylor	DE	Miami Dolphins
2008	Kurt Warner	QB	Arizona Cardinals
2009	Brian Waters	G	Kansas City Chiefs
2010	Madieu Williams	S	Minnesota Vikings

* The award was shared in 2000 and 2006.

NUMBER-ONE DRAFT CHOICES

Season	Date	Team	Player	Position	College
2011	April 28-30	Carolina	Cam Newton	QB	Auburn
2010	April 22-24	St. Louis	Sam Bradford	QB	Oklahoma
2009	April 25-26	Detroit	Matthew Stafford	QB	Georgia
2008	April 26-27	Miami	Jake Long	T	Michigan
2007	April 28-29	Oakland	JaMarcus Russell	QB	Louisiana State
2006	April 29-30	Houston	Mario Williams	DE	North Carolina State
2005	April 23-24	San Francisco	Alex Smith	QB	Utah
2004	April 24-25	San Diego	Eli Manning	QB	Mississippi
2003	April 26-27	Cincinnati	Carson Palmer	QB	Southern California
2002	April 20-21	Houston	David Carr	QB	Fresno State
2001	April 21-22	Atlanta	Michael Vick	QB	Virginia Tech
2000	April 15-16	Cleveland	Courtney Brown	DE	Penn State
1999	April 17-18	Cleveland	Tim Couch	QB	Kentucky
1998	April 18-19	Indianapolis	Peyton Manning	QB	Tennessee
1997	April 19-20	St. Louis	Orlando Pace	T	Ohio State
1996	April 20-21	New York Jets	Keyshawn Johnson	WR	Southern California
1995	April 22-23	Cincinnati	Ki-Jana Carter	RB	Penn State
1994	April 24-25	Cincinnati	Dan Wilkinson	DT	Ohio State
1993	April 25-26	New England	Drew Bledsoe	QB	Washington State
1992	April 26-27	Indianapolis	Steve Emtman	DT	Washington
1991	April 21-22	Dallas	Russell Maryland	DT	Miami
1990	April 22-23	Indianapolis	Jeff George	QB	Illinois
1989	April 23-24	Dallas	Troy Aikman	QB	UCLA
1988	April 24-25	Atlanta	Aundray Bruce	LB	Auburn
1987	April 28-29	Tampa Bay	Vinny Testaverde	QB	Miami
1986	April 29-30	Tampa Bay	Bo Jackson	RB	Auburn
1985	April 30-May 1	Buffalo	Bruce Smith	DE	Virginia Tech
1984	May 1-2	New England	Irving Fryar	WR	Nebraska
1983	April 26-27	Baltimore	John Elway	QB	Stanford
1982	April 27-28	New England	Kenneth Sims	DT	Texas
1981	April 28-29	New Orleans	George Rogers	RB	South Carolina
1980	April 29-30	Detroit	Billy Sims	RB	Oklahoma
1979	May 3-4	Buffalo	Tom Cousineau	LB	Ohio State
1978	May 2-3	Houston	Earl Campbell	RB	Texas
1977	May 3-4	Tampa Bay	Ricky Bell	RB	Southern California
1976	April 8-9	Tampa Bay	Lee Roy Selmon	DE	Oklahoma
1975	January 28-29	Atlanta	Steve Bartkowski	QB	California
1974	January 29-30	Dallas	Ed Jones	DE	Tennessee State
1973	January 30-31	Houston	John Matuszak	DE	Tampa
1972	February 1-2	Buffalo	Walt Patulski	DE	Notre Dame
1971	January 28-29	New England	Jim Plunkett	QB	Stanford
1970	January 27-28	Pittsburgh	Terry Bradshaw	QB	Louisiana Tech
1969	January 28-29	Buffalo (AFL)	O.J. Simpson	RB	Southern California
1968	January 30-31	Minnesota	Ron Yary	T	Southern California
1967	March 14	Baltimore	Bubba Smith	DT	Michigan State
1966	November 27, 1965	Atlanta	Tommy Nobis	LB	Texas
	November 28, 1965	Miami (AFL)	Jim Grabowski	RB	Illinois
1965	November 28, 1964	New York Giants	Tucker Frederickson	RB	Auburn
	November 28, 1964	Houston (AFL)	Lawrence Elkins	E	Baylor
1964	December 2, 1963	San Francisco	Dave Parks	E	Texas Tech
	November 30, 1963	Boston (AFL)	Jack Concannon	QB	Boston College
1963	December 3, 1962	Los Angeles	Terry Baker	QB	Oregon State
	December 1, 1962	Kansas City (AFL)	Buck Buchanan	DT	Grambling
1962	December 4, 1961	Washington	Ernie Davis	RB	Syracuse
	December 2, 1961	Oakland (AFL)	Roman Gabriel	QB	North Carolina State
1961	December 27-28, 1960	Minnesota	Tommy Mason	RB	Tulane
	November 23, 1960	Buffalo (AFL)	Ken Rice	G	Auburn
1960	Secret Draft	Los Angeles	Billy Cannon	RB	Louisiana State
	November 22, December 2, 1959	(AFL had no formal first pick)			
1959	December 2, 1958	Green Bay	Randy Duncan	QB	Iowa
1958	December 2, 1957	Chicago Cardinals	King Hill	QB	Rice

Season	Date	Team	Player	Position	College
1957	November 27, 1956	Green Bay	Paul Hornung	HB	Notre Dame
1956	November 29, 1955	Pittsburgh	Gary Glick	DB	Colorado A&M
1955	January 27-28	Baltimore	George Shaw	QB	Oregon
1954	January 28	Cleveland	Bobby Garrett	QB	Stanford
1953	January 22	San Francisco	Harry Babcock	E	Georgia
1952	January 17	Los Angeles	Bill Wade	QB	Vanderbilt
1951	January 18-19	New York Giants	Kyle Rote	HB	Southern Methodist
1950	January 21-22	Detroit	Leon Hart	E	Notre Dame
1949	December 21, 1948	Philadelphia	Chuck Bednarik	C	Pennsylvania
1948	December 19, 1947	Washington	Harry Gilmer	QB	Alabama
1947	December 16, 1946	Chicago Bears	Bob Fenimore	HB	Oklahoma A&M
1946	January 14	Boston	Frank Dancewicz	QB	Notre Dame
1945	April 6	Chicago Cardinals	Charley Trippi	HB	Georgia
1944	April 19	Boston	Angelo Bertelli	QB	Notre Dame
1943	April 8	Detroit	Frank Sinkwich	HB	Georgia
1942	December 22, 1941	Pittsburgh	Bill Dudley	HB	Virginia
1941	December 10, 1940	Chicago Bears	Tom Harmon	HB	Michigan
1940	December 9, 1939	Chicago Cardinals	George Cafego	HB	Tennessee
1939	December 8, 1938	Chicago Cardinals	Ki Aldrich	C	Texas Christian
1938	December 12, 1937	Cleveland	Corbett Davis	FB	Indiana
1937	December 12, 1936	Philadelphia	Sam Francis	FB	Nebraska
1936	February 8	Philadelphia	Jay Berwanger	HB	Chicago

Note: From 1947 through 1958, the first selection in the draft was a Bonus pick, awarded to the winner of a random draw. That club, in turn, forfeited its last-round draft choice. The winner of the Bonus choice was eliminated from future draws. The system was abolished after 1958, by which time all clubs had received a Bonus choice.

NUMBER-ONE DRAFT CHOICES BY POSITION

Quarterbacks:	30
Running Backs:	23
Defensive Linemen:	13
Offensive Linemen:	6
Wide Receivers:	6
Linebackers:	3
Defensive Backs:	1

FIRST-ROUND SELECTIONS

If club had no first-round selection, first player drafted is listed with round in parentheses.

ARIZONA CARDINALS

Year Player, College, Position
1936 Jim Lawrence, Texas Christian, B
1937 Ray Buivid, Marquette, B
1938 Jack Robbins, Arkansas, B
1939 Charles (Ki) Aldrich, TCU, C
1940 George Cafego, Tennessee, B
1941 John Kimbrough, Texas A&M, B
1942 Steve Lach, Duke, B
1943 Glenn Dobbs, Tulsa, B
1944 Pat Harder, Wisconsin, B
1945 Charley Trippi, Georgia, B
1946 Dub Jones, Louisiana State, B
1947 DeWitt (Tex) Coulter, Army, T
1948 Jim Spavital, Oklahoma A&M, B
1949 Bill Fischer, Notre Dame, G
1950 Jack Jennings, Ohio State, T (2)
1951 Jerry Groom, Notre Dame, C
1952 Ollie Matson, San Francisco, B
1953 Johnny Olszewski, California, B
1954 Lamar McHan, Arkansas, B
1955 Max Boydston, Oklahoma, E
1956 Joe Childress, Auburn, B
1957 Jerry Tubbs, Oklahoma, C
1958 King Hill, Rice, B
      John David Crow, Texas A&M, B
1959 Bill Stacy, Mississippi State, B
1960 George Izo, Notre Dame, QB
1961 Ken Rice, Auburn, T
1962 Fate Echols, Northwestern, DT
      Irv Goode, Kentucky, C
1963 Jerry Stovall, Louisiana State, S
      Don Brumm, Purdue, DE
1964 Ken Kortas, Louisville, DT
1965 Joe Namath, Alabama, QB
1966 Carl McAdams, Oklahoma, LB
1967 Dave Williams, Washington, WR
1968 MacArthur Lane, Utah State, RB
1969 Roger Wehrli, Missouri, DB
1970 Larry Stegent, Texas A&M, RB
1971 Norm Thompson, Utah, CB
1972 Ahmad Rashad, Oregon, RB-WR
1973 Dave Butz, Purdue, DT
1974 J.V. Cain, Colorado, TE
1975 Tim Gray, Texas A&M, DB
1976 Mike Dawson, Arizona, DT
1977 Steve Pisarkiewicz, Missouri, QB
1978 Steve Little, Arkansas, K
      Ken Greene, Washington State, DB
1979 Ottis Anderson, Miami, RB
1980 Curtis Greer, Michigan, DE
1981 E.J. Junior, Alabama, LB
1982 Luis Sharpe, UCLA, T
1983 Leonard Smith, McNeese St., DB
1984 Clyde Duncan, Tennessee, WR
1985 Freddie Joe Nunn, Mississippi, LB
1986 Anthony Bell, Michigan State, LB
1987 Kelly Stouffer, Colorado State, QB
1988 Ken Harvey, California, LB
1989 Eric Hill, Louisiana State, LB
      Joe Wolf, Boston College, G
1990 Anthony Thompson, Indiana, RB (2)
1991 Eric Swann, No College, DE
1992 Tony Sacca, Penn State, QB (2)

1993 Garrison Hearst, Georgia, RB
      Ernest Dye, South Carolina, T
1994 Jamir Miller, UCLA, LB
1995 Frank Sanders, Auburn, WR (2)
1996 Simeon Rice, Illinois, DE
1997 Tom Knight, Iowa, DB
1998 Andre Wadsworth, Florida St., DE
1999 David Boston, Ohio State, WR
      L.J. Shelton, Eastern Michigan, T
2000 Thomas Jones, Virginia, RB
2001 Leonard Davis, Texas, T
2002 Wendell Bryant, Wisconsin, DT
2003 Bryant Johnson, Penn State, WR
      Calvin Pace, Wake Forest, DE
2004 Larry Fitzgerald, Pittsburgh, WR
2005 Antrel Rolle, Miami, DB
2006 Matt Leinart, So. California, QB
2007 Levi Brown, Penn State, T
2008 Dominique Rodgers-Cromartie, Tenn. St., DB
2009 Beanie Wells, Ohio State, RB
2010 Dan Williams, Tennessee, DT
2011 Patrick Peterson, Louisiana St., DB

ATLANTA FALCONS

Year Player, College, Position
1966 Tommy Nobis, Texas, LB
      Randy Johnson, Texas A&I, QB
1967 Leo Carroll, San Diego St., DE (2)
1968 Claude Humphrey, Tennessee St., DE
1969 George Kunz, Notre Dame, T
1970 John Small, Citadel, LB
1971 Joe Profit, Northeast Louisiana, RB
1972 Clarence Ellis, Notre Dame, DB
1973 Greg Marx, Notre Dame, DT (2)
1974 Gerald Tinker, Kent State, WR (2)
1975 Steve Bartkowski, California, QB
1976 Bubba Bean, Texas A&M, RB
1977 Warren Bryant, Kentucky, T
      Wilson Faumuina, San Jose St., DT
1978 Mike Kenn, Michigan, T
1979 Don Smith, Miami, DE
1980 Junior Miller, Nebraska, TE
1981 Bobby Butler, Florida State, DB
1982 Gerald Riggs, Arizona State, RB
1983 Mike Pitts, Alabama, DE
1984 Rick Bryan, Oklahoma, DT
1985 Bill Fralic, Pittsburgh, T
1986 Tony Casillas, Oklahoma, NT
      Tim Green, Syracuse, LB
1987 Chris Miller, Oregon, QB
1988 Aundray Bruce, Auburn, LB
1989 Deion Sanders, Florida State, DB
      Shawn Collins, No. Arizona, WR
1990 Steve Broussard, Washington St., RB
1991 Bruce Pickens, Nebraska, DB
      Mike Pritchard, Colorado, WR
1992 Bob Whitfield, Stanford, T
      Tony Smith, So. Mississippi, RB
1993 Lincoln Kennedy, Washington, T
1994 Bert Emanuel, Rice, WR (2)
1995 Devin Bush, Florida State, DB
1996 Shannon Brown, Alabama, DT (3)
1997 Michael Booker, Nebraska, DB
1998 Keith Brooking, Georgia Tech, LB
1999 Patrick Kerney, Virginia, DE
2000 Travis Claridge, So. California, T (2)
2001 Michael Vick, Virginia Tech, QB
2002 T.J. Duckett, Michigan State, RB
2003 Bryan Scott, Penn State, DB (2)

2004 DeAngelo Hall, Virginia Tech, DB
      Michael Jenkins, Ohio State, WR
2005 Roddy White, Ala.-Birmingham, WR
2006 Jimmy Williams, Virginia Tech, DB (2)
2007 Jamaal Anderson, Arkansas, DE
2008 Matt Ryan, Boston College, QB
      Sam Baker, So. California, T
2009 Peria Jerry, Mississippi, DT
2010 Sean Weatherspoon, Missouri, LB
2011 Julio Jones, Alabama, WR

BALTIMORE RAVENS

Year Player, College, Position
1996 Jonathan Ogden, UCLA, T
      Ray Lewis, Miami, LB
1997 Peter Boulware, Florida State, DE
1998 Duane Starks, Miami, DB
1999 Chris McAlister, Arizona, DB
2000 Jamal Lewis, Tennessee, RB
      Travis Taylor, Florida, WR
2001 Todd Heap, Arizona State, TE
2002 Ed Reed, Miami, DB
2003 Terrell Suggs, Arizona State, DE
      Kyle Boller, California, QB
2004 Dwan Edwards, Oregon St., DT (2)
2005 Mark Clayton, Oklahoma, WR
2006 Haloti Ngata, Oregon, DT
2007 Ben Grubbs, Auburn, G
2008 Joe Flacco, Delaware, QB
2009 Michael Oher, Mississippi, T
2010 Sergio Kindle, Texas, LB (2)
2011 Jimmy Smith, Colorado, DB

BUFFALO BILLS

Year Player, College, Position
1960 Richie Lucas, Penn State, QB
1961 Ken Rice, Auburn, T
1962 Ernie Davis, Syracuse, RB
1963 Dave Behrman, Michigan State, C
1964 Carl Eller, Minnesota, DE
1965 Jim Davidson, Ohio State, T
1966 Mike Dennis, Mississippi, RB
1967 John Pitts, Arizona State, S
1968 Haven Moses, San Diego St., WR
1969 O.J. Simpson, So. California, RB
1970 Al Cowlings, So. California, DE
1971 J.D. Hill, Arizona State, WR
1972 Walt Patulski, Notre Dame, DE
1973 Paul Seymour, Michigan, TE
      Joe DeLamielleure, Michigan St., G
1974 Reuben Gant, Oklahoma State, TE
1975 Tom Ruud, Nebraska, LB
1976 Mario Clark, Oregon, DB
1977 Phil Dokes, Oklahoma State, DT
1978 Terry Miller, Oklahoma State, RB
1979 Tom Cousineau, Ohio State, LB
      Jerry Butler, Clemson, WR
1980 Jim Ritcher, North Carolina St., C
1981 Booker Moore, Penn State, RB
1982 Perry Tuttle, Clemson, WR
1983 Tony Hunter, Notre Dame, TE
      Jim Kelly, Miami, QB
1984 Greg Bell, Notre Dame, RB
1985 Bruce Smith, Virginia Tech, DE
      Derrick Burroughs, Memphis St., DB
1986 Ronnie Harmon, Iowa, RB
      Will Wolford, Vanderbilt, T
1987 Shane Conlan, Penn State, LB
1988 Thurman Thomas, Oklahoma St., RB (2)
1989 Don Beebe, Chadron, Neb., WR (3)

1990	James Williams, Fresno State, DB
1991	Henry Jones, Illinois, DB
1992	John Fina, Arizona, T
1993	Thomas Smith, North Carolina, DB
1994	Jeff Burris, Notre Dame, DB
1995	Ruben Brown, Pittsburgh, G
1996	Eric Moulds, Mississippi St., WR
1997	Antowain Smith, Houston, RB
1998	Sam Cowart, Florida State, LB (2)
1999	Antoine Winfield, Ohio State, DB
2000	Erik Flowers, Arizona State, DE
2001	Nate Clements, Ohio State, DB
2002	Mike Williams, Texas, T
2003	Willis McGahee, Miami, RB
2004	Lee Evans, Wisconsin, WR
	J.P. Losman, Tulane, QB
2005	Roscoe Parrish, Miami, WR (2)
2006	Donte' Whitner, Ohio State, DB
	John McCargo, North Carolina St., DT
2007	Marshawn Lynch, California, RB
2008	Leodis McKelvin, Troy, DB
2009	Aaron Maybin, Penn State, DE
	Eric Wood, Louisville, C
2010	C.J. Spiller, Clemson, RB
2011	Marcell Dareus, Alabama, DT

CAROLINA PANTHERS
Year Player, College, Position

1995	Kerry Collins, Penn State, QB
	Tyrone Poole, Ft. Valley State, DB
	Blake Brockermeyer, Texas, T
1996	Tim Biakabutuka, Michigan, RB
1997	Rae Carruth, Colorado, WR
1998	Jason Peter, Nebraska, DT
1999	Chris Terry, Georgia, T (2)
2000	Rashard Anderson, Jackson St., DB
2001	Dan Morgan, Miami, LB
2002	Julius Peppers, North Carolina, DE
2003	Jordan Gross, Utah, T
2004	Chris Gamble, Ohio State, DB
2005	Thomas Davis, Georgia, DB
2006	DeAngelo Williams, Memphis, RB
2007	Jon Beason, Miami, LB
2008	Jonathan Stewart, Oregon, RB
	Jeff Otah, Pittsburgh, T
2009	Everette Brown, Florida St., DE (2)
2010	Jimmy Clausen, Notre Dame, QB (2)
2011	Cam Newton, Auburn, QB

CHICAGO BEARS
Year Player, College, Position

1936	Joe Stydahar, West Virginia, T
1937	Les McDonald, Nebraska, E
1938	Joe Gray, Oregon State, B
1939	Sid Luckman, Columbia, QB
	Bill Osmanski, Holy Cross, B
1940	Clyde (Bulldog) Turner, Hardin-Simmons, C
1941	Tom Harmon, Michigan, B
	Norm Standlee, Stanford, B
	Don Scott, Ohio State, B
1942	Frankie Albert, Stanford, B
1943	Bob Steber, Missouri, B
1944	Ray Evans, Kansas, B
1945	Don Lund, Michigan, B
1946	Johnny Lujack, Notre Dame, QB
1947	Bob Fenimore, Oklahoma State, B
	Don Kindt, Wisconsin, B
1948	Bobby Layne, Texas, QB
	Max Bumgardner, Texas, E
1949	Dick Harris, Texas, C

1950	Chuck Hunsinger, Florida, B
	Fred Morrison, Ohio State, B
1951	Bob Williams, Notre Dame, B
	Billy Stone, Bradley, B
	Gene Schroeder, Virginia, E
1952	Jim Dooley, Miami, B
1953	Billy Anderson, Compton (Calif.) J.C., B
1954	Stan Wallace, Illinois, B
1955	Ron Drzewiecki, Marquette, B
1956	Menan (Tex) Schriewer, Texas, E
1957	Earl Leggett, Louisiana State, T
1958	Chuck Howley, West Virginia, G
1959	Don Clark, Ohio State, B
1960	Roger Davis, Syracuse, G
1961	Mike Ditka, Pittsburgh, E
1962	Ronnie Bull, Baylor, RB
1963	Dave Behrman, Michigan State, C
1964	Dick Evey, Tennessee, DT
1965	Dick Butkus, Illinois, LB
	Gale Sayers, Kansas, RB
	Steve DeLong, Tennessee, T
1966	George Rice, Louisiana State, DT
1967	Loyd Phillips, Arkansas, DE
1968	Mike Hull, Southern California, RB
1969	Rufus Mayes, Ohio State, T
1970	George Farmer, UCLA, WR (3)
1971	Joe Moore, Missouri, RB
1972	Lionel Antoine, Southern Illinois, T
	Craig Clemons, Iowa, DB
1973	Wally Chambers, Eastern Kentucky, DE
1974	Waymond Bryant, Tennessee St., LB
	Dave Gallagher, Michigan, DT
1975	Walter Payton, Jackson State, RB
1976	Dennis Lick, Wisconsin, T
1977	Ted Albrecht, California, T
1978	Brad Shearer, Texas, DT (3)
1979	Dan Hampton, Arkansas, DT
	Al Harris, Arizona State, DE
1980	Otis Wilson, Louisville, LB
1981	Keith Van Horne, So. California, T
1982	Jim McMahon, Brigham Young, QB
1983	Jim Covert, Pittsburgh, T
	Willie Gault, Tennessee, WR
1984	Wilber Marshall, Florida, LB
1985	William Perry, Clemson, DT
1986	Neal Anderson, Florida, RB
1987	Jim Harbaugh, Michigan, QB
1988	Brad Muster, Stanford, RB
	Wendell Davis, Louisiana St., WR
1989	Donnell Woolford, Clemson, DB
	Trace Armstrong, Florida, DE
1990	Mark Carrier, So. California, DB
1991	Stan Thomas, Texas, T
1992	Alonzo Spellman, Ohio State, DE
1993	Curtis Conway, So. California, WR
1994	John Thierry, Alcorn State, DE
1995	Rashaan Salaam, Colorado, RB
1996	Walt Harris, Mississippi State, DB
1997	John Allred, So. California, TE (2)
1998	Curtis Enis, Penn State, RB
1999	Cade McNown, UCLA, QB
2000	Brian Urlacher, New Mexico, LB
2001	David Terrell, Michigan, WR
2002	Marc Colombo, Boston College, T
2003	Michael Haynes, Penn State, DE
	Rex Grossman, Florida, QB
2004	Tommie Harris, Oklahoma, DT
2005	Cedric Benson, Texas, RB
2006	Danieal Manning, Abilene Christian, DB (2)
2007	Greg Olsen, Miami, TE

2008	Chris Williams, Vanderbilt, T
2009	Jarron Gilbert, San Jose State, DT (3)
2010	Major Wright, Florida, DB (3)
2011	Gabe Carimi, Wisconsin, T

CINCINNATI BENGALS
Year Player, College, Position

1968	Bob Johnson, Tennessee, C
1969	Greg Cook, Cincinnati, QB
1970	Mike Reid, Penn State, DT
1971	Vernon Holland, Tennessee St., T
1972	Sherman White, California, DE
1973	Isaac Curtis, San Diego State, WR
1974	Bill Kollar, Montana State, DT
1975	Glenn Cameron, Florida, LB
1976	Billy Brooks, Oklahoma, WR
	Archie Griffin, Ohio State, RB
1977	Eddie Edwards, Miami, DT
	Wilson Whitley, Houston, DT
	Mike Cobb, Michigan State, TE
1978	Ross Browner, Notre Dame, DT
	Blair Bush, Washington, C
1979	Jack Thompson, Washington St., QB
	Charles Alexander, Louisiana St., RB
1980	Anthony Muñoz, So. California, T
1981	David Verser, Kansas, WR
1982	Glen Collins, Mississippi State, DE
1983	Dave Rimington, Nebraska, C
1984	Ricky Hunley, Arizona, LB
	Pete Koch, Maryland, DT
	Brian Blados, North Carolina, T
1985	Eddie Brown, Miami, WR
	Emanuel King, Alabama, LB
1986	Joe Kelly, Washington, LB
	Tim McGee, Tennessee, WR
1987	Jason Buck, Brigham Young, DE
1988	Rickey Dixon, Oklahoma, DB
1989	Eric Ball, UCLA, RB (2)
1990	James Francis, Baylor, LB
1991	Alfred Williams, Colorado, LB
1992	David Klingler, Houston, QB
	Darryl Williams, Miami, DB
1993	John Copeland, Alabama, DE
1994	Dan Wilkinson, Ohio State, DT
1995	Ki-Jana Carter, Penn State, RB
1996	Willie Anderson, Auburn, T
1997	Reinard Wilson, Florida State, LB
1998	Takeo Spikes, Auburn, LB
	Brian Simmons, North Carolina, LB
1999	Akili Smith, Oregon, QB
2000	Peter Warrick, Florida State, WR
2001	Justin Smith, Missouri, DE
2002	Levi Jones, Arizona State, T
2003	Carson Palmer, Southern California, QB
2004	Chris Perry, Michigan, RB
2005	David Pollack, Georgia, LB
2006	Johnathan Joseph, South Carolina, DB
2007	Leon Hall, Michigan, DB
2008	Keith Rivers, So. California, LB
2009	Andre Smith, Alabama, T
2010	Jermaine Gresham, Oklahoma, TE
2011	A.J. Green, Georgia, WR

CLEVELAND BROWNS
Year Player, College, Position

1950	Ken Carpenter, Oregon State, B
1951	Ken Konz, Louisiana State, B
1952	Bert Rechichar, Tennessee, DB
	Harry Agganis, Boston U., QB
1953	Doug Atkins, Tennessee, DE

1954 Bobby Garrett, Stanford, QB
     John Bauer, Illinois, G
1955 Kurt Burris, Oklahoma, C
1956 Preston Carpenter, Arkansas, B
1957 Jim Brown, Syracuse, RB
1958 Jim Shofner, Texas Christian, DB
1959 Rich Kreitling, Illinois, DE
1960 Jim Houston, Ohio State, DE
1961 Bobby Crespino, Mississippi, TE
1962 Gary Collins, Maryland, WR
     Leroy Jackson, Western Illinois, RB
1963 Tom Hutchinson, Kentucky, WR
1964 Paul Warfield, Ohio State, WR
1965 James Garcia, Purdue, T (2)
1966 Milt Morin, Massachusetts, TE
1967 Bob Matheson, Duke, LB
1968 Marvin Upshaw, Trinity, Tex., DT-DE
1969 Ron Johnson, Michigan, RB
1970 Mike Phipps, Purdue, QB
     Bob McKay, Texas, T
1971 Clarence Scott, Kansas State, CB
1972 Thom Darden, Michigan, DB
1973 Steve Holden, Arizona State, WR
     Pete Adams, Southern California, T
1974 Billy Corbett, Johnson C. Smith, T (2)
1975 Mack Mitchell, Houston, DE
1976 Mike Pruitt, Purdue, RB
1977 Robert Jackson, Texas A&M, LB
1978 Clay Matthews, So. California, LB
     Ozzie Newsome, Alabama, TE
1979 Willis Adams, Houston, WR
1980 Charles White, So. California, RB
1981 Hanford Dixon, So. Mississippi, DB
1982 Chip Banks, So. California, LB
1983 Ron Brown, Arizona State, WR (2)
1984 Don Rogers, UCLA, DB
1985 Greg Allen, Florida State, RB (2)
1986 Webster Slaughter, San Diego St., WR (2)
1987 Mike Junkin, Duke, LB
1988 Clifford Charlton, Florida, LB
1989 Eric Metcalf, Texas, RB
1990 Leroy Hoard, Michigan, RB (2)
1991 Eric Turner, UCLA, DB
1992 Tommy Vardell, Stanford, RB
1993 Steve Everitt, Michigan, C
1994 Antonio Langham, Alabama, DB
     Derrick Alexander, Michigan, WR
1995 Craig Powell, Ohio State, LB
1999 Tim Couch, Kentucky, QB
2000 Courtney Brown, Penn State, DE
2001 Gerard Warren, Florida, DT
2002 William Green, Boston College, RB
2003 Jeff Faine, Norte Dame, C
2004 Kellen Winslow, Miami, TE
2005 Braylon Edwards, Michigan, WR
2006 Kamerion Wimbley, Florida St., DE
2007 Joe Thomas, Wisconsin, T
     Brady Quinn, Notre Dame, QB
2008 Beau Bell, Nevada-Las Vegas, LB (4)
2009 Alex Mack, California, C
2010 Joe Haden, Florida, DB
2011 Phil Taylor, Baylor, DT

DALLAS COWBOYS
Year Player, College, Position
1960 None
1961 Bob Lilly, Texas Christian, DT
1962 Sonny Gibbs, TCU, QB (2)
1963 Lee Roy Jordan, Alabama, LB
1964 Scott Appleton, Texas, DT

1965 Craig Morton, California, QB
1966 John Niland, Iowa, G
1967 Phil Clark, Northwestern, DB (3)
1968 Dennis Homan, Alabama, WR
1969 Calvin Hill, Yale, RB
1970 Duane Thomas, West Texas St., RB
1971 Tody Smith, So. California, DE
1972 Bill Thomas, Boston College, RB
1973 Billy Joe DuPree, Michigan St., TE
1974 Ed (Too Tall) Jones, Tennessee St., DE
     Charley Young, North Carolina St., RB
1975 Randy White, Maryland, LB
     Thomas Henderson, Langston, LB
1976 Aaron Kyle, Wyoming, DB
1977 Tony Dorsett, Pittsburgh, RB
1978 Larry Bethea, Michigan State, DE
1979 Robert Shaw, Tennessee, C
1980 Bill Roe, Colorado, LB (3)
1981 Howard Richards, Missouri, T
1982 Rod Hill, Kentucky State, DB
1983 Jim Jeffcoat, Arizona State, DE
1984 Billy Cannon, Jr., Texas A&M, LB
1985 Kevin Brooks, Michigan, DE
1986 Mike Sherrard, UCLA, WR
1987 Danny Noonan, Nebraska, DT
1988 Michael Irvin, Miami, WR
1989 Troy Aikman, UCLA, QB
1990 Emmitt Smith, Florida, RB
1991 Russell Maryland, Miami, DT
     Alvin Harper, Tennessee, WR
     Kelvin Pritchett, Mississippi, DT
1992 Kevin Smith, Texas A&M, DB
     Robert Jones, East Carolina, LB
1993 Kevin Williams, Miami, WR (2)
1994 Shante Carver, Arizona State, DE
1995 Sherman Williams, Alabama, RB (2)
1996 Kavika Pittman, McNeese St., DE (2)
1997 David LaFleur, Louisiana State, TE
1998 Greg Ellis, North Carolina, DE
1999 Ebenezer Ekuban, North Carolina, DE
2000 Dwayne Goodrich, Tennessee, DB (2)
2001 Quincy Carter, Georgia, QB (2)
2002 Roy Williams, Oklahoma, DB
2003 Terence Newman, Kansas State, DB
2004 Julius Jones, Notre Dame, RB (2)
2005 DeMarcus Ware, Troy, DE
     Marcus Spears, Louisiana St., DE
2006 Bobby Carpenter, Ohio State, LB
2007 Anthony Spencer, Purdue, LB
2008 Felix Jones, Arkansas, RB
     Mike Jenkins, South Florida, DB
2009 Jason Williams, Western Illinois, LB (3)
2010 Dez Bryant, Oklahoma State, WR
2011 Tyron Smith, Southern California, T

DENVER BRONCOS
Year Player, College, Position
1960 Roger LeClerc, Trinity, Conn., C
1961 Bob Gaiters, New Mexico St., RB
1962 Merlin Olsen, Utah State, DT
1963 Kermit Alexander, UCLA, CB
1964 Bob Brown, Nebraska, T
1965 Dick Butkus, Illinois, LB (2)
1966 Jerry Shay, Purdue, DT
1967 Floyd Little, Syracuse, RB
1968 Curley Culp, Arizona State, DE (2)
1969 Grady Cavness, Texas-El Paso, DB (2)
1970 Bob Anderson, Colorado, RB
1971 Marv Montgomery, So. California, T
1972 Riley Odoms, Houston, TE

1973 Otis Armstrong, Purdue, RB
1974 Randy Gradishar, Ohio State, LB
1975 Louis Wright, San Jose State, DB
1976 Tom Glassic, Virginia, G
1977 Steve Schindler, Boston College, G
1978 Don Latimer, Miami, DT
1979 Kelvin Clark, Nebraska, T
1980 Rulon Jones, Utah State, DE (2)
1981 Dennis Smith, So. California, DB
1982 Gerald Willhite, San Jose St., RB
1983 Chris Hinton, Northwestern, G
1984 Andre Townsend, Mississippi, DE (2)
1985 Steve Sewell, Oklahoma, RB
1986 Jim Juriga, Illinois, T (4)
1987 Ricky Nattiel, Florida, WR
1988 Ted Gregory, Syracuse, NT
1989 Steve Atwater, Arkansas, DB
1990 Alton Montgomery, Houston, DB (2)
1991 Mike Croel, Nebraska, LB
1992 Tommy Maddox, UCLA, QB
1993 Dan Williams, Toledo, DE
1994 Allen Aldridge, Houston, LB (2)
1995 Jamie Brown, Florida A&M, T (4)
1996 John Mobley, Kutztown, LB
1997 Trevor Pryce, Clemson, DT
1998 Marcus Nash, Tennessee, WR
1999 Al Wilson, Tennessee, LB
2000 Deltha O'Neal, California, DB
2001 Willie Middlebrooks, Minnesota, DB
2002 Ashley Lelie, Hawaii, WR
2003 George Foster, Georgia, T
2004 D.J. Williams, Miami, LB
2005 Darrent Williams, Oklahoma St., DB (2)
2006 Jay Cutler, Vanderbilt, QB
2007 Jarvis Moss, Florida, DE
2008 Ryan Clady, Boise State, T
2009 Knowshon Moreno, Georgia, RB
     Robert Ayers, Tennessee, DE
2010 Demaryius Thomas, Georgia Tech, WR
     Tim Tebow, Florida, QB
2011 Von Miller, Texas A&M, LB

DETROIT LIONS
Year Player, College, Position
1936 Sid Wagner, Michigan State, G
1937 Lloyd Cardwell, Nebraska, B
1938 Alex Wojciechowicz, Fordham, C
1939 John Pingel, Michigan State, B
1940 Doyle Nave, Southern California, B
1941 Jim Thomason, Texas A&M, B
1942 Bob Westfall, Michigan, B
1943 Frank Sinkwich, Georgia, B
1944 Otto Graham, Northwestern, B
1945 Frank Szymanski, Notre Dame, C
1946 Bill Dellastatious, Missouri, B
1947 Glenn Davis, Army, B
1948 Y.A. Tittle, Louisiana State, B
1949 John Rauch, Georgia, B
1950 Leon Hart, Notre Dame, E
     Joe Watson, Rice, C
1951 Dick Stanfel, San Francisco, G (2)
1952 Yale Lary, Texas A&M, B (3)
1953 Harley Sewell, Texas, G
1954 Dick Chapman, Rice, T
1955 Dave Middleton, Auburn, B
1956 Hopalong Cassady, Ohio State, B
1957 Bill Glass, Baylor, G
1958 Alex Karras, Iowa, T
1959 Nick Pietrosante, Notre Dame, B
1960 John Robinson, Louisiana State, S

1961	Danny LaRose, Missouri, T (2)
1962	John Hadl, Kansas, QB
1963	Daryl Sanders, Ohio State, T
1964	Pete Beathard, So. California, QB
1965	Tom Nowatzke, Indiana, RB
1966	Nick Eddy, Notre Dame, RB (2)
1967	Mel Farr, UCLA, RB
1968	Greg Landry, Massachusetts, QB
	Earl McCullouch, So. California, WR
1969	Altie Taylor, Utah State, RB (2)
1970	Steve Owens, Oklahoma, RB
1971	Bob Bell, Cincinnati, DT
1972	Herb Orvis, Colorado, DE
1973	Ernie Price, Texas A&I, DE
1974	Ed O'Neil, Penn State, LB
1975	Lynn Boden, South Dakota St., G
1976	James Hunter, Grambling, DB
	Lawrence Gaines, Wyoming, RB
1977	Walt Williams, New Mexico St., DB (2)
1978	Luther Bradley, Notre Dame, DB
1979	Keith Dorney, Penn State, T
1980	Billy Sims, Oklahoma, RB
1981	Mark Nichols, San Jose State, WR
1982	Jimmy Williams, Nebraska, LB
1983	James Jones, Florida, RB
1984	David Lewis, California, TE
1985	Lomas Brown, Florida, T
1986	Chuck Long, Iowa, QB
1987	Reggie Rogers, Washington, DE
1988	Bennie Blades, Miami, DB
1989	Barry Sanders, Oklahoma St., RB
1990	Andre Ware, Houston, QB
1991	Herman Moore, Virginia, WR
1992	Robert Porcher, South Carolina St., DE
1993	Ryan McNeil, Miami, DB (2)
1994	Johnnie Morton, So. California, WR
1995	Luther Elliss, Utah, DT
1996	Reggie Brown, Texas A&M, LB
	Jeff Hartings, Penn State, G
1997	Bryant Westbrook, Texas, DB
1998	Terry Fair, Tennessee, DB
1999	Chris Claiborne, So. California, LB
	Aaron Gibson, Wisconsin, T
2000	Stockar McDougle, Oklahoma, T
2001	Jeff Backus, Michigan, T
2002	Joey Harrington, Oregon, QB
2003	Charles Rogers, Michigan State, WR
2004	Roy Williams, Texas, WR
	Kevin Jones, Virginia Tech, RB
2005	Mike Williams, So. California, WR
2006	Ernie Sims, Florida State, LB
2007	Calvin Johnson, Georgia Tech, WR
2008	Gosder Cherilus, Boson College, T
2009	Matthew Stafford, Georgia, QB
	Brandon Pettigrew, Oklahoma St., TE
2010	Ndamukong Suh, Nebraska, DT
	Jahvid Best, California, RB
2011	Nick Fairley, Auburn, DT

GREEN BAY PACKERS

Year Player, College, Position

1936	Russ Letlow, San Francisco, G
1937	Eddie Jankowski, Wisconsin, B
1938	Cecil Isbell, Purdue, B
1939	Larry Buhler, Minnesota, B
1940	Harold Van Every, Minnesota, B
1941	George Paskvan, Wisconsin, B
1942	Urban Odson, Minnesota, T
1943	Dick Wildung, Minnesota, T
1944	Merv Pregulman, Michigan, G

1945	Walt Schlinkman, Texas Tech, B
1946	Johnny Strzykalski, Marquette, B
1947	Ernie Case, UCLA, B
1948	Earl (Jug) Girard, Wisconsin, B
1949	Stan Heath, Nevada, B
1950	Clayton Tonnemaker, Minnesota, C
1951	Bob Gain, Kentucky, T
1952	Babe Parilli, Kentucky, QB
1953	Al Carmichael, So. California, B
1954	Art Hunter, Notre Dame, T
	Veryl Switzer, Kansas State, B
1955	Tom Bettis, Purdue, G
1956	Jack Losch, Miami, B
1957	Paul Hornung, Notre Dame, B
	Ron Kramer, Michigan, E
1958	Dan Currie, Michigan State, C
1959	Randy Duncan, Iowa, B
1960	Tom Moore, Vanderbilt, RB
1961	Herb Adderley, Michigan State, CB
1962	Earl Gros, Louisiana State, RB
1963	Dave Robinson, Penn State, LB
1964	Lloyd Voss, Nebraska, DT
1965	Donny Anderson, Texas Tech, RB
	Lawrence Elkins, Baylor, E
1966	Jim Grabowski, Illinois, RB
	Gale Gillingham, Minnesota, T
1967	Bob Hyland, Boston College, C
	Don Horn, San Diego State, QB
1968	Fred Carr, Texas-El Paso, LB
	Bill Lueck, Arizona, G
1969	Rich Moore, Villanova, DT
1970	Mike McCoy, Notre Dame, DT
	Rich McGeorge, Elon, TE
1971	John Brockington, Ohio State, RB
1972	Willie Buchanon, San Diego St., DB
	Jerry Tagge, Nebraska, QB
1973	Barry Smith, Florida State, WR
1974	Barty Smith, Richmond, RB
1975	Bill Bain, So. California, G (2)
1976	Mark Koncar, Colorado, T
1977	Mike Butler, Kansas, DE
	Ezra Johnson, Morris Brown, DE
1978	James Lofton, Stanford, WR
	John Anderson, Michigan, LB
1979	Eddie Lee Ivery, Georgia Tech, RB
1980	Bruce Clark, Penn State, DE
	George Cumby, Oklahoma, LB
1981	Rich Campbell, California, QB
1982	Ron Hallstrom, Iowa, G
1983	Tim Lewis, Pittsburgh, DB
1984	Alphonso Carreker, Florida St., DE
1985	Ken Ruettgers, So. California, T
1986	Kenneth Davis, TCU, RB (2)
1987	Brent Fullwood, Auburn, RB
1988	Sterling Sharpe, South Carolina, WR
1989	Tony Mandarich, Michigan State, T
1990	Tony Bennett, Mississippi, LB
	Darrell Thompson, Minnesota, RB
1991	Vinnie Clark, Ohio State, DB
1992	Terrell Buckley, Florida State, DB
1993	Wayne Simmons, Clemson, LB
	George Teague, Alabama, DB
1994	Aaron Taylor, Notre Dame, T
1995	Craig Newsome, Arizona State, DB
1996	John Michels, Southern California, T
1997	Ross Verba, Iowa, T
1998	Vonnie Holliday, North Carolina, DT
1999	Antuan Edwards, Clemson, DB
2000	Bubba Franks, Miami, TE
2001	Jamal Reynolds, Florida State, DE

2002	Javon Walker, Florida State, WR
2003	Nick Barnett, Oregon State, LB
2004	Ahmad Carroll, Arkansas, DB
2005	Aaron Rodgers, California, QB
2006	A.J. Hawk, Ohio State, LB
2007	Justin Harrell, Tennessee, DT
2008	Jordy Nelson, Kansas State, WR (2)
2009	B.J. Raji, Boston College, DT
	Clay Matthews, So. California, LB
2010	Bryan Bulaga, Iowa, T
2011	Derek Sherrod, Mississippi State, T

HOUSTON TEXANS

Year Player, College, Position

2002	David Carr, Fresno State, QB
2003	Andre Johnson, Miami, WR
2004	Dunta Robinson, South Carolina, DB
	Jason Babin, Western Michigan, LB
2005	Travis Johnson, Florida State, DE
2006	Mario Williams, North Carolina St., DE
2007	Amobi Okoye, Louisville, DT
2008	Duane Brown, Virginia Tech, T
2009	Brian Cushing, So. California, LB
2010	Kareem Jackson, Alabama, DB
2011	J.J. Watt, Wisconsin, DE

INDIANAPOLIS COLTS

Year Player, College, Position

1953	Billy Vessels, Oklahoma, B
1954	Cotton Davidson, Baylor, B
1955	George Shaw, Oregon, B
	Alan Ameche, Wisconsin, FB
1956	Lenny Moore, Penn State, B
1957	Jim Parker, Ohio State, G
1958	Lenny Lyles, Louisville, B
1959	Jackie Burkett, Auburn, C
1960	Ron Mix, Southern California, T
1961	Tom Matte, Ohio State, RB
1962	Wendell Harris, Louisiana State, S
1963	Bob Vogel, Ohio State, T
1964	Marv Woodson, Indiana, CB
1965	Mike Curtis, Duke, LB
1966	Sam Ball, Kentucky, T
1967	Bubba Smith, Michigan State, DT
	Jim Detwiler, Michigan, RB
1968	John Williams, Minnesota, G
1969	Eddie Hinton, Oklahoma, WR
1970	Norman Bulaich, Texas Christian, RB
1971	Don McCauley, North Carolina, RB
	Leonard Dunlap, North Texas St., DB
1972	Tom Drougas, Oregon, T
1973	Bert Jones, Louisiana State, QB
	Joe Ehrmann, Syracuse, DT
1974	John Dutton, Nebraska, DE
	Roger Carr, Louisiana Tech, WR
1975	Ken Huff, North Carolina, G
1976	Ken Novak, Purdue, DT
1977	Randy Burke, Kentucky, WR
1978	Reese McCall, Auburn, TE
1979	Barry Krauss, Alabama, LB
1980	Curtis Dickey, Texas A&M, RB
	Derrick Hatchett, Texas, DB
1981	Randy McMillan, Pittsburgh, RB
	Donnell Thompson, North Carolina, DT
1982	Johnie Cooks, Mississippi St., LB
	Art Schlichter, Ohio State, QB
1983	John Elway, Stanford, QB
1984	Leonard Coleman, Vanderbilt, DB
	Ron Solt, Maryland, G
1985	Duane Bickett, So. California, LB

1986	Jon Hand, Alabama, DE
1987	Cornelius Bennett, Alabama, LB
1988	Chris Chandler, Washington, QB (3)
1989	Andre Rison, Michigan State, WR
1990	Jeff George, Illinois, QB
1991	Shane Curry, Miami, DE (2)
1992	Steve Emtman, Washington, DT
	Quentin Coryatt, Texas A&M, LB
1993	Sean Dawkins, California, WR
1994	Marshall Faulk, San Diego St., RB
	Trev Alberts, Nebraska, LB
1995	Ellis Johnson, Florida, DT
1996	Marvin Harrison, Syracuse, WR
1997	Tarik Glenn, California, T
1998	Peyton Manning, Tennessee, QB
1999	Edgerrin James, Miami, RB
2000	Rob Morris, Brigham Young, LB
2001	Reggie Wayne, Miami, WR
2002	Dwight Freeney, Syracuse, DE
2003	Dallas Clark, Iowa, TE
2004	Bob Sanders, Iowa, DB (2)
2005	Marlin Jackson, Michigan, DB
2006	Joseph Addai, Louisiana State, RB
2007	Anthony Gonzalez, Ohio State, WR
2008	Mike Pollak, Arizona State, G (2)
2009	Donald Brown, Connecticut, RB
2010	Jerry Hughes, Texas Christian, DE
2011	Anthony Castonzo, Boston College, T

JACKSONVILLE JAGUARS

Year	Player, College, Position
1995	Tony Boselli, Southern California, T
	James Stewart, Tennessee, RB
1996	Kevin Hardy, Illinois, LB
1997	Renaldo Wynn, Notre Dame, DT
1998	Fred Taylor, Florida, RB
	Donovin Darius, Syracuse, DB
1999	Fernando Bryant, Alabama, DB
2000	R. Jay Soward, So. California, WR
2001	Marcus Stroud, Georgia, DT
2002	John Henderson, Tennessee, DT
2003	Byron Leftwich, Marshall, QB
2004	Reggie Williams, Washington, WR
2005	Matt Jones, Arkansas, WR
2006	Marcedes Lewis, UCLA, TE
2007	Reggie Nelson, Florida, DB
2008	Derrick Harvey, Florida, DE
2009	Eugene Monroe, Virginia, T
2010	Tyson Alualu, California, DT
2011	Blaine Gabbert, Missouri, QB

KANSAS CITY CHIEFS

Year	Player, College, Position
1960	Don Meredith, So. Methodist, QB
1961	E.J. Holub, Texas Tech, C
1962	Ronnie Bull, Baylor, RB
1963	Buck Buchanan, Grambling, DT
	Ed Budde, Michigan State, G
1964	Pete Beathard, So. California, QB
1965	Gale Sayers, Kansas, RB
1966	Aaron Brown, Minnesota, DE
1967	Gene Trosch, Miami, DE-DT
1968	Mo Moorman, Texas A&M, G
	George Daney, Texas-El Paso, G
1969	Jim Marsalis, Tennessee State, CB
1970	Sid Smith, Southern California, T
1971	Elmo Wright, Houston, WR
1972	Jeff Kinney, Nebraska, RB
1973	Gary Butler, Rice, TE (2)
1974	Woody Green, Arizona State, RB

1975	Elmore Stephens, Kentucky, TE (2)
1976	Rod Walters, Iowa, G
1977	Gary Green, Baylor, DB
1978	Art Still, Kentucky, DE
1979	Mike Bell, Colorado State, DE
	Steve Fuller, Clemson, QB
1980	Brad Budde, Southern California, G
1981	Willie Scott, South Carolina, TE
1982	Anthony Hancock, Tennessee, WR
1983	Todd Blackledge, Penn State, QB
1984	Bill Maas, Pittsburgh, DT
	John Alt, Iowa, T
1985	Ethan Horton, North Carolina, RB
1986	Brian Jozwiak, West Virginia, T
1987	Paul Palmer, Temple, RB
1988	Neil Smith, Nebraska, DE
1989	Derrick Thomas, Alabama, LB
1990	Percy Snow, Michigan State, LB
1991	Harvey Williams, Louisiana St., RB
1992	Dale Carter, Tennessee, DB
1993	Will Shields, Nebraska, G (3)
1994	Greg Hill, Texas A&M, RB
1995	Trezelle Jenkins, Michigan, T
1996	Jerome Woods, Memphis, DB
1997	Tony Gonzalez, California, TE
1998	Victor Riley, Auburn, T
1999	John Tait, Brigham Young, T
2000	Sylvester Morris, Jackson St., WR
2001	Eric Downing, Syracuse, DT (3)
2002	Ryan Sims, North Carolina, DT
2003	Larry Johnson, Penn State, RB
2004	Junior Siavii, Oregon, DT (2)
2005	Derrick Johnson, Texas, LB
2006	Tamba Hali, Penn State, DE
2007	Dwayne Bowe, Louisiana State, WR
2008	Glenn Dorsey, Louisiana State, DT
	Branden Albert, Virginia, T
2009	Tyson Jackson, Louisiana State, DE
2010	Eric Berry, Tennessee, DB
2011	Jonathan Baldwin, Pittsburgh, WR

MIAMI DOLPHINS

Year	Player, College, Position
1966	Jim Grabowski, Illinois, RB
	Rick Norton, Kentucky, QB
1967	Bob Griese, Purdue, QB
1968	Larry Csonka, Syracuse, RB
	Doug Crusan, Indiana, T
1969	Bill Stanfill, Georgia, DE
1970	Jim Mandich, Michigan, TE (2)
1971	Otto Stowe, Iowa State, WR (2)
1972	Mike Kadish, Notre Dame, DT
1973	Chuck Bradley, Oregon, C (2)
1974	Donald Reese, Jackson State, DE
1975	Darryl Carlton, Tampa, T
1976	Larry Gordon, Arizona State, LB
	Kim Bokamper, San Jose State, LB
1977	A.J. Duhe, Louisiana State, DT
1978	Guy Benjamin, Stanford, QB (2)
1979	Jon Giesler, Michigan, T
1980	Don McNeal, Alabama, DB
1981	David Overstreet, Oklahoma, RB
1982	Roy Foster, Southern California, G
1983	Dan Marino, Pittsburgh, QB
1984	Jackie Shipp, Oklahoma, LB
1985	Lorenzo Hampton, Florida, RB
1986	John Offerdahl, Western Michigan, LB (2)
1987	John Bosa, Boston College, DE
1988	Eric Kumerow, Ohio State, DE

1989	Sammie Smith, Florida State, RB
	Louis Oliver, Florida, DB
1990	Richmond Webb, Texas A&M, T
1991	Randal Hill, Miami, WR
1992	Troy Vincent, Wisconsin, DB
	Marco Coleman, Georgia Tech, LB
1993	O.J. McDuffie, Penn State, WR
1994	Tim Bowens, Mississippi, DT
1995	Billy Milner, Houston, T
1996	Daryl Gardener, Baylor, DT
1997	Yatil Green, Miami, WR
1998	John Avery, Mississippi, RB
1999	J.J. Johnson, Mississippi St., RB (2)
2000	Todd Wade, Mississippi, T (2)
2001	Jamar Fletcher, Wisconsin, DB
2002	Seth McKinney, Texas A&M, C (3)
2003	Eddie Moore, Tennessee, LB (2)
2004	Vernon Carey, Miami, T
2005	Ronnie Brown, Auburn, RB
2006	Jason Allen, Tennessee, DB
2007	Ted Ginn, Ohio State, WR
2008	Jake Long, Michigan, T
2009	Vontae Davis, Illinois, DB
2010	Jared Odrick, Penn State, DT
2011	Mike Pouncey, Florida, C

MINNESOTA VIKINGS

Year	Player, College, Position
1961	Tommy Mason, Tulane, RB
1962	Bill Miller, Miami, WR (3)
1963	Jim Dunaway, Mississippi, T
1964	Carl Eller, Minnesota, DE
1965	Jack Snow, Notre Dame, WR
1966	Jerry Shay, Purdue, DT
1967	Clint Jones, Michigan State, RB
	Gene Washington, Michigan St., WR
	Alan Page, Notre Dame, DT
1968	Ron Yary, Southern California, T
1969	Ed White, California, G (2)
1970	John Ward, Oklahoma State, DT
1971	Leo Hayden, Ohio State, RB
1972	Jeff Siemon, Stanford, LB
1973	Chuck Foreman, Miami, RB
1974	Fred McNeill, UCLA, LB
	Steve Riley, Southern California, T
1975	Mark Mullaney, Colorado State, DE
1976	James White, Oklahoma State, DT
1977	Tommy Kramer, Rice, QB
1978	Randy Holloway, Pittsburgh, DE
1979	Ted Brown, North Carolina St., RB
1980	Doug Martin, Washington, DT
1981	Mardye McDole, Mississippi St., WR (2)
1982	Darrin Nelson, Stanford, RB
1983	Joey Browner, So. California, DB
1984	Keith Millard, Washington St., DE
1985	Chris Doleman, Pittsburgh, LB
1986	Gerald Robinson, Auburn, DE
1987	D.J. Dozier, Penn State, RB
1988	Randall McDaniel, Arizona State, G
1989	David Braxton, Wake Forest, LB (2)
1990	Mike Jones, Texas A&M, TE (3)
1991	Carlos Jenkins, Michigan St., LB (3)
1992	Robert Harris, Southern Univ., DE (2)
1993	Robert Smith, Ohio State, RB
1994	DeWayne Washington, N. Carolina St., DB
	Todd Steussie, California, T
1995	Derrick Alexander, Florida St., DE
	Korey Stringer, Ohio State, T
1996	Duane Clemons, California, DE
1997	Dwayne Rudd, Alabama, LB

1998 Randy Moss, Marshall, WR
1999 Daunte Culpepper, Central Florida, QB
     Dimitrius Underwood, Michigan St., DE
2000 Chris Hovan, Boston College, DT
2001 Michael Bennett, Wisconsin, RB
2002 Bryant McKinnie, Miami, T
2003 Kevin Williams, Oklahoma State, DT
2004 Kenechi Udeze, Southern California, DE
2005 Troy Williamson, South Carolina, WR
     Erasmus James, Wisconsin, DE
2006 Chad Greenway, Iowa, LB
2007 Adrian Peterson, Oklahoma, RB
2008 Tyrell Johnson, Arkansas State, DB (2)
2009 Percy Harvin, Florida, WR
2010 Chris Cook, Virginia, DB (2)
2011 Christian Ponder, Florida State, QB

NEW ENGLAND PATRIOTS
Year Player, College, Position
1960 Ron Burton, Northwestern, RB
1961 Tommy Mason, Tulane, RB
1962 Gary Collins, Maryland, WR
1963 Art Graham, Boston College, WR
1964 Jack Concannon, Boston College, QB
1965 Jerry Rush, Michigan State, DE
1966 Karl Singer, Purdue, T
1967 John Charles, Purdue, S
1968 Dennis Byrd, North Carolina St., DE
1969 Ron Sellers, Florida State, WR
1970 Phil Olsen, Utah State, DE
1971 Jim Plunkett, Stanford, QB
1972 Tom Reynolds, San Diego St., WR (2)
1973 John Hannah, Alabama, G
     Sam Cunningham, So. California, RB
     Darryl Stingley, Purdue, WR
1974 Steve Corbett, Boston College, G (2)
1975 Russ Francis, Oregon, TE
1976 Mike Haynes, Arizona State, DB
     Pete Brock, Colorado, C
     Tim Fox, Ohio State, DB
1977 Raymond Clayborn, Texas, DB
     Stanley Morgan, Tennessee, WR
1978 Bob Cryder, Alabama, G
1979 Rick Sanford, South Carolina, DB
1980 Roland James, Tennessee, DB
     Vagas Ferguson, Notre Dame, RB
1981 Brian Holloway, Stanford, T
1982 Kenneth Sims, Texas, DT
     Lester Williams, Miami, DT
1983 Tony Eason, Illinois, QB
1984 Irving Fryar, Nebraska, WR
1985 Trevor Matich, Brigham Young, C
1986 Reggie Dupard, So. Methodist, RB
1987 Bruce Armstrong, Louisville, T
1988 John Stephens, Northwestern St., La., RB
1989 Hart Lee Dykes, Oklahoma St., WR
1990 Chris Singleton, Arizona, LB
     Ray Agnew, North Carolina St., DE
1991 Pat Harlow, Southern California, T
     Leonard Russell, Arizona St., RB
1992 Eugene Chung, Virginia Tech, T
1993 Drew Bledsoe, Washington St., QB
1994 Willie McGinest, So. California, DE
1995 Ty Law, Michigan, DB
1996 Terry Glenn, Ohio State, WR
1997 Chris Canty, Kansas State, DB
1998 Robert Edwards, Georgia, RB
     Tebucky Jones, Syracuse, DB
1999 Damien Woody, Boston College, C
     Andy Katzenmoyer, Ohio State, LB

2000 Adrian Klemm, Hawaii, T (2)
2001 Richard Seymour, Georgia, DT
2002 Daniel Graham, Colorado, TE
2003 Ty Warren, Texas A&M, DT
2004 Vince Wilfork, Miami, DT
     Ben Watson, Georgia, TE
2005 Logan Mankins, Fresno State, G
2006 Laurence Maroney, Minnesota, RB
2007 Brandon Meriweather, Miami, DB
2008 Jerod Mayo, Tennessee, LB
2009 Patrick Chung, Oregon, DB (2)
2010 Devin McCourty, Rutgers, DB
2011 Nate Solder, Colorado, T

NEW ORLEANS SAINTS
Year Player, College, Position
1967 Les Kelley, Alabama, RB
1968 Kevin Hardy, Notre Dame, DE
1969 John Shinners, Xavier, G
1970 Ken Burrough, Texas Southern, WR
1971 Archie Manning, Mississippi, QB
1972 Royce Smith, Georgia, G
1973 Derland Moore, Oklahoma, DE (2)
1974 Rick Middleton, Ohio State, LB
1975 Larry Burton, Purdue, WR
     Kurt Schumacher, Ohio State, T
1976 Chuck Muncie, California, RB
1977 Joe Campbell, Maryland, DE
1978 Wes Chandler, Florida, WR
1979 Russell Erxleben, Texas, P-K
1980 Stan Brock, Colorado, T
1981 George Rogers, South Carolina, RB
1982 Lindsay Scott, Georgia, WR
1983 Steve Korte, Arkansas, G (2)
1984 James Geathers, Wichita State, DE
1985 Alvin Toles, Tennessee, LB
1986 Jim Dombrowski, Virginia, T
1987 Shawn Knight, Brigham Young, DT
1988 Craig Heyward, Pittsburgh, RB
1989 Wayne Martin, Arkansas, DE
1990 Renaldo Turnbull, West Virginia, DE
1991 Wesley Carroll, Miami, WR (2)
1992 Vaughn Dunbar, Indiana, RB
1993 Willie Roaf, Louisiana Tech, T
     Irv Smith, Notre Dame, TE
1994 Joe Johnson, Louisville, DE
1995 Mark Fields, Washington State, LB
1996 Alex Molden, Oregon, DB
1997 Chris Naeole, Colorado, G
1998 Kyle Turley, San Diego State, T
1999 Ricky Williams, Texas, RB
2000 Darren Howard, Kansas St., DE (2)
2001 Deuce McAllister, Mississippi, RB
2002 Donte' Stallworth, Tennessee, WR
     Charles Grant, Georgia, DE
2003 Johnathan Sullivan, Georgia, DT
2004 Will Smith, Ohio State, DE
2005 Jammal Brown, Oklahoma, T
2006 Reggie Bush, So. California, RB
2007 Robert Meachem, Tennessee, WR
2008 Sedrick Ellis, So. California, DT
2009 Malcolm Jenkins, Ohio State, DB
2010 Patrick Robinson, Florida State, DB
2011 Cameron Jordan, California, DE
     Mark Ingram, Alabama, RB

NEW YORK GIANTS
Year Player, College, Position
1936 Art Lewis, Ohio U., T
1937 Ed Widseth, Minnesota, T

1938 George Karamatic, Gonzaga, B
1939 Walt Neilson, Arizona, B
1940 Grenville Lansdell, So. California, B
1941 George Franck, Minnesota, B
1942 Merle Hapes, Mississippi, B
1943 Steve Filipowicz, Fordham, B
1944 Billy Hillenbrand, Indiana, B
1945 Elmer Barbour, Wake Forest, B
1946 George Connor, Notre Dame, T
1947 Vic Schwall, Northwestern, B
1948 Tony Minisi, Pennsylvania, B
1949 Paul Page, Southern Methodist, B
1950 Travis Tidwell, Auburn, B
1951 Kyle Rote, Southern Methodist, B
     Jim Spavital, Oklahoma A&M, B
1952 Frank Gifford, Southern California, B
1953 Bobby Marlow, Alabama, B
1954 Ken Buck, Pacific, C (2)
1955 Joe Heap, Notre Dame, B
1956 Henry Moore, Arkansas, B (2)
1957 Sam DeLuca, South Carolina, T (2)
1958 Phil King, Vanderbilt, B
1959 Lee Grosscup, Utah, B
1960 Lou Cordileone, Clemson, G
1961 Bruce Tarbox, Syracuse, G (2)
1962 Jerry Hillebrand, Colorado, LB
1963 Frank Lasky, Florida, T (2)
1964 Joe Don Looney, Oklahoma, RB
1965 Tucker Frederickson, Auburn, RB
1966 Francis Peay, Missouri, T
1967 Louis Thompson, Alabama, DT (4)
1968 Dick Buzin, Penn State, T (2)
1969 Fred Dryer, San Diego State, DE
1970 Jim Files, Oklahoma, LB
1971 Rocky Thompson, West Texas St., WR
1972 Eldridge Small, Texas A&I, DB
     Larry Jacobson, Nebraska, DE
1973 Brad Van Pelt, Michigan St., LB (2)
1974 John Hicks, Ohio State, G
1975 Al Simpson, Colorado State, T (2)
1976 Troy Archer, Colorado, DE
1977 Gary Jeter, Southern California, DT
1978 Gordon King, Stanford, T
1979 Phil Simms, Morehead State, QB
1980 Mark Haynes, Colorado, DB
1981 Lawrence Taylor, North Carolina, LB
1982 Butch Woolfolk, Michigan, RB
1983 Terry Kinard, Clemson, DB
1984 Carl Banks, Michigan State, LB
     William Roberts, Ohio State, T
1985 George Adams, Kentucky, RB
1986 Eric Dorsey, Notre Dame, DE
1987 Mark Ingram, Michigan State, WR
1988 Eric Moore, Indiana, T
1989 Brian Williams, Minnesota, C-G
1990 Rodney Hampton, Georgia, RB
1991 Jarrod Bunch, Michigan, RB
1992 Derek Brown, Notre Dame, TE
1993 Michael Strahan, Texas Southern, DE (2)
1994 Thomas Lewis, Indiana, WR
1995 Tyrone Wheatley, Michigan, RB
1996 Cedric Jones, Oklahoma, DE
1997 Ike Hilliard, Florida, WR
1998 Shaun Williams, UCLA, DB
1999 Luke Petitgout, Notre Dame, T
2000 Ron Dayne, Wisconsin, RB
2001 Will Allen, Syracuse, DB
2002 Jeremy Shockey, Miami, TE
2003 William Joseph, Miami, DT
2004 Philip Rivers, North Carolina St., QB

2005	Corey Webster, Louisiana St., DB (2)	
2006	Mathias Kiwanuka, Boston College, DE	
2007	Aaron Ross, Texas, DB	
2008	Kenny Phillips, Miami, DB	
2009	Hakeem Nicks, North Carolina, WR	
2010	Jason Pierre-Paul, South Florida, DE	
2011	Prince Amukamara, Nebraska, DB	

NEW YORK JETS
Year Player, College, Position
1960 George Izo, Notre Dame, QB
1961 Tom Brown, Minnesota, G
1962 Sandy Stephens, Minnesota, QB
1963 Jerry Stovall, Louisiana State, S
1964 Matt Snell, Ohio State, RB
1965 Joe Namath, Alabama, QB
     Tom Nowatzke, Indiana, RB
1966 Bill Yearby, Michigan, DT
1967 Paul Seiler, Notre Dame, T
1968 Lee White, Weber State, RB
1969 Dave Foley, Ohio State, T
1970 Steve Tannen, Florida, CB
1971 John Riggins, Kansas, RB
1972 Jerome Barkum, Jackson St., WR
     Mike Taylor, Michigan, LB
1973 Burgess Owens, Miami, DB
1974 Carl Barzilauskas, Indiana, DT
1975 Anthony Davis, So. California, RB (2)
1976 Richard Todd, Alabama, QB
1977 Marvin Powell, So. California, T
1978 Chris Ward, Ohio State, T
1979 Marty Lyons, Alabama, DE
1980 Johnny (Lam) Jones, Texas, WR
1981 Freeman McNeil, UCLA, RB
1982 Bob Crable, Notre Dame, LB
1983 Ken O'Brien, Cal-Davis, QB
1984 Russell Carter, So. Methodist, DB
     Ron Faurot, Arkansas, DE
1985 Al Toon, Wisconsin, WR
1986 Mike Haight, Iowa, T
1987 Roger Vick, Texas A&M, RB
1988 Dave Cadigan, So. California, T
1989 Jeff Lageman, Virginia, LB
1990 Blair Thomas, Penn State, RB
1991 Browning Nagle, Louisville, QB (2)
1992 Johnny Mitchell, Nebraska, TE
1993 Marvin Jones, Florida State, LB
1994 Aaron Glenn, Texas A&M, DB
1995 Kyle Brady, Penn State, TE
     Hugh Douglas, Central St., Ohio, DE
1996 Keyshawn Johnson, So. California, WR
1997 James Farrior, Virginia, LB
1998 Dorian Boose, Washington St., DE (2)
1999 Randy Thomas, Mississippi St., G (2)
2000 Shaun Ellis, Tennessee, DE
     John Abraham, South Carolina, LB
     Chad Pennington, Marshall, QB
     Anthony Becht, West Virginia, TE
2001 Santana Moss, Miami, WR
2002 Bryan Thomas, Ala.-Birmingham, DE
2003 Dewayne Robertson, Kentucky, DT
2004 Jonathan Vilma, Miami, LB
2005 Mike Nugent, Ohio State, K (2)
2006 D'Brickashaw Ferguson, Virginia, T
     Nick Mangold, Ohio State, C
2007 Darrelle Revis, Pittsburgh, DB
2008 Vernon Gholston, Ohio State, LB
     Dustin Keller, Purdue, TE
2009 Mark Sanchez, So. California, QB
2010 Kyle Wilson, Boise State, DB

2011 Muhammad Wilkerson, Temple, DT

OAKLAND RAIDERS
Year Player, College, Position
1960 Dale Hackbart, Wisconsin, CB
1961 Joe Rutgens, Illinois, DT
1962 Roman Gabriel, North Carolina St., QB
1963 George Wilson, Alabama, RB (6)
1964 Tony Lorick, Arizona State, RB
1965 Harry Schuh, Memphis State, T
1966 Rodger Bird, Kentucky, S
1967 Gene Upshaw, Texas A&I, G
1968 Eldridge Dickey, Tennessee St., QB
1969 Art Thoms, Syracuse, DT
1970 Raymond Chester, Morgan St., TE
1971 Jack Tatum, Ohio State, S
1972 Mike Siani, Villanova, WR
1973 Ray Guy, Southern Mississippi, P
1974 Henry Lawrence, Florida A&M, T
1975 Neal Colzie, Ohio State, DB
1976 Charles Philyaw, Texas Southern, DT (2)
1977 Mike Davis, Colorado, DB (2)
1978 Dave Browning, Washington, DE (2)
1979 Willie Jones, Florida State, DE (2)
1980 Marc Wilson, Brigham Young, QB
1981 Ted Watts, Texas Tech, DB
     Curt Marsh, Washington, T
1982 Marcus Allen, So. California, RB
1983 Don Mosebar, So. California, T
1984 Sean Jones, Northeastern, DE (2)
1985 Jessie Hester, Florida State, WR
1986 Bob Buczkowski, Pittsburgh, DE
1987 John Clay, Missouri, T
1988 Tim Brown, Notre Dame, WR
     Terry McDaniel, Tennessee, DB
     Scott Davis, Illinois, DE
1989 Jeff Francis, Tennessee, QB (6)
1990 Anthony Smith, Arizona, DE
1991 Todd Marinovich, So. California, QB
1992 Chester McGlockton, Clemson, DE
1993 Patrick Bates, Texas A&M, DB
1994 Rob Fredrickson, Michigan St., LB
1995 Napoleon Kaufman, Washington, RB
1996 Rickey Dudley, Ohio State, TE
1997 Darrell Russell, Southern California, DT
1998 Charles Woodson, Michigan, DB
     Mo Collins, Florida, T
1999 Matt Stinchcomb, Georgia, T
2000 Sebastian Janikowski, Florida St., K
2001 Derrick Gibson, Florida State, DB
2002 Phillip Buchanon, Miami, DB
     Napoleon Harris, Northwestern, LB
2003 Nnamdi Asomugha, California, DB
     Tyler Brayton, Colorado, DE
2004 Robert Gallery, Iowa, T
2005 Fabian Washington, Nebraska, DB
2006 Michael Huff, Texas, DB
2007 JaMarcus Russell, Louisiana State, QB
2008 Darren McFadden, Arkansas, RB
2009 Darrius Heyward-Bey, Maryland, WR
2010 Rolando McClain, Alabama, LB
2011 Stefan Wisniewski, Penn State, C (2)

PHILADELPHIA EAGLES
Year Player, College, Position
1936 Jay Berwanger, Chicago, B
1937 Sam Francis, Nebraska, B
1938 Jim McDonald, Ohio State, B
1939 Davey O'Brien, Texas Christian, B
1940 George McAfee, Duke, B

1941 Art Jones, Richmond, B (2)
1942 Pete Kmetovic, Stanford, B
1943 Joe Muha, Virginia Military, B
1944 Steve Van Buren, Louisiana St., B
1945 John Yonaker, Notre Dame, E
1946 Leo Riggs, Southern California, B
1947 Neill Armstrong, Oklahoma A&M, E
1948 Clyde (Smackover) Scott, Arkansas, B
1949 Chuck Bednarik, Pennsylvania, C
     Frank Tripucka, Notre Dame, B
1950 Harry (Bud) Grant, Minnesota, E
1951 Ebert Van Buren, Louisiana St., B
     Chet Mutryn, Xavier, B
1952 Johnny Bright, Drake, B
1953 Al Conway, Army, B (2)
1954 Neil Worden, Notre Dame, B
1955 Dick Bielski, Maryland, B
1956 Bob Pellegrini, Maryland, C
1957 Clarence Peaks, Michigan State, B
1958 Walt Kowalczyk, Michigan State, B
1959 J.D. Smith, Rice, T (2)
1960 Ron Burton, Northwestern, RB
1961 Art Baker, Syracuse, RB
1962 Pete Case, Georgia, G (2)
1963 Ed Budde, Michigan State, G
1964 Bob Brown, Nebraska, T
1965 Ray Rissmiller, Georgia, T (2)
1966 Randy Beisler, Indiana, DE
1967 Harry Jones, Arkansas, RB
1968 Tim Rossovich, So. California, DE
1969 Leroy Keyes, Purdue, RB
1970 Steve Zabel, Oklahoma, TE
1971 Richard Harris, Grambling, DE
1972 John Reaves, Florida, QB
1973 Jerry Sisemore, Texas, T
     Charle Young, So. California, TE
1974 Mitch Sutton, Kansas, DT (3)
1975 Bill Capraun, Miami, T (7)
1976 Mike Smith, Florida, DE (4)
1977 Skip Sharp, Kansas, DB (5)
1978 Reggie Wilkes, Georgia Tech, LB (3)
1979 Jerry Robinson, UCLA, LB
1980 Roynell Young, Alcorn State, DB
1981 Leonard Mitchell, Houston, DE
1982 Mike Quick, North Carolina St., WR
1983 Michael Haddix, Mississippi St., RB
1984 Kenny Jackson, Penn State, WR
1985 Kevin Allen, Indiana, T
1986 Keith Byars, Ohio State, RB
1987 Jerome Brown, Miami, DT
1988 Keith Jackson, Oklahoma, TE
1989 Jessie Small, Eastern Kentucky, LB (2)
1990 Ben Smith, Georgia, DB
1991 Antone Davis, Tennessee, T
1992 Siran Stacy, Alabama, RB (2)
1993 Lester Holmes, Jackson State, T
     Leonard Renfro, Colorado, DT
1994 Bernard Williams, Georgia, T
1995 Mike Mamula, Boston College, DE
1996 Jermane Mayberry, Texas A&M-Kingsville, T
1997 Jon Harris, Virginia, DE
1998 Tra Thomas, Florida State, T
1999 Donovan McNabb, Syracuse, QB
2000 Corey Simon, Florida State, DT
2001 Freddie Mitchell, UCLA, WR
2002 Lito Sheppard, Florida, DB
2003 Jerome McDougle, Miami, DE
2004 Shawn Andrews, Arkansas, T
2005 Mike Patterson, So. California, DT
2006 Brodrick Bunkley, Florida State, DT

2007 Kevin Kolb, Houston, QB (2)
2008 Trevor Laws, Notre Dame, DT (2)
2009 Jeremy Maclin, Missouri, WR
2010 Brandon Graham, Michigan, DE
2011 Danny Watkins, Baylor, G

PITTSBURGH STEELERS
Year Player, College, Position
1936 Bill Shakespeare, Notre Dame, B
1937 Mike Basrak, Duquesne, C
1938 Byron (Whizzer) White, Colorado, B
1939 Bill Patterson, Baylor, B (3)
1940 Kay Eakin, Arkansas, B
1941 Chet Gladchuk, Boston College, C (2)
1942 Bill Dudley, Virginia, B
1943 Bill Daley, Minnesota, B
1944 Johnny Podesto, St. Mary's, Calif., B
1945 Paul Duhart, Florida, B
1946 Felix (Doc) Blanchard, Army, B
1947 Hub Bechtol, Texas, E
1948 Dan Edwards, Georgia, E
1949 Bobby Gage, Clemson, B
1950 Lynn Chandnois, Michigan St., B
1951 Butch Avinger, Alabama, B
1952 Ed Modzelewski, Maryland, B
1953 Ted Marchibroda, St. Bonaventure, B
1954 Johnny Lattner, Notre Dame, B
1955 Frank Varrichione, Notre Dame, T
1956 Gary Glick, Colorado A&M, B
      Art Davis, Mississippi State, B
1957 Len Dawson, Purdue, B
1958 Larry Krutko, West Virginia, B (2)
1959 Tom Barnett, Purdue, B (8)
1960 Jack Spikes, Texas Christian, RB
1961 Myron Pottios, Notre Dame, LB (2)
1962 Bob Ferguson, Ohio State, RB
1963 Frank Atkinson, Stanford, T (8)
1964 Paul Martha, Pittsburgh, S
1965 Roy Jefferson, Utah, WR (2)
1966 Dick Leftridge, West Virginia, RB
1967 Don Shy, San Diego State, RB (2)
1968 Mike Taylor, Southern California, T
1969 Joe Greene, North Texas State, DT
1970 Terry Bradshaw, Louisiana Tech, QB
1971 Frank Lewis, Grambling, WR
1972 Franco Harris, Penn State, RB
1973 J.T. Thomas, Florida State, DB
1974 Lynn Swann, So. California, WR
1975 Dave Brown, Michigan, DB
1976 Bennie Cunningham, Clemson, TE
1977 Robin Cole, New Mexico, LB
1978 Ron Johnson, Eastern Michigan, DB
1979 Greg Hawthorne, Baylor, RB
1980 Mark Malone, Arizona State, QB
1981 Keith Gary, Oklahoma, DE
1982 Walter Abercrombie, Baylor, RB
1983 Gabriel Rivera, Texas Tech, DT
1984 Louis Lipps, So. Mississippi, WR
1985 Darryl Sims, Wisconsin, DE
1986 John Rienstra, Temple, G
1987 Rod Woodson, Purdue, DB
1988 Aaron Jones, Eastern Kentucky, DE
1989 Tim Worley, Georgia, RB
      Tom Ricketts, Pittsburgh, T
1990 Eric Green, Liberty, TE
1991 Huey Richardson, Florida, DE
1992 Leon Searcy, Miami, T
1993 Deon Figures, Colorado, DB
1994 Charles Johnson, Colorado, WR
1995 Mark Bruener, Washington, TE

1996 Jamain Stephens, North Carolina A&T, T
1997 Chad Scott, Maryland, DB
1998 Alan Faneca, Louisiana State, G
1999 Troy Edwards, Louisiana Tech, WR
2000 Plaxico Burress, Michigan St., WR
2001 Casey Hampton, Texas, DT
2002 Kendall Simmons, Auburn, G
2003 Troy Polamalu, Southern California, DB
2004 Ben Roethlisberger, Miami (OH), QB
2005 Heath Miller, Virginia, TE
2006 Santonio Holmes, Ohio State, WR
2007 Lawrence Timmons, Florida State, LB
2008 Rashard Mendenhall, Illinois, RB
2009 Evander Hood, Missouri, DE
2010 Maurkice Pouncey, Florida, C
2011 Cameron Heyward, Ohio State, DE

ST. LOUIS RAMS
Year Player, College, Position
1937 Johnny Drake, Purdue, B
1938 Corbett Davis, Indiana, B
1939 Parker Hall, Mississippi, B
1940 Ollie Cordill, Rice, B
1941 Rudy Mucha, Washington, C
1942 Jack Wilson, Baylor, B
1943 Mike Holovak, Boston College, B
1944 Tony Butkovich, Illinois, B
1945 Elroy (Crazylegs) Hirsch, Wisconsin, B
1946 Emil Sitko, Notre Dame, B
1947 Herman Wedemeyer, St. Mary's, Calif., B
1948 Tom Keane, West Virginia, B (2)
1949 Bobby Thomason, Virginia Military, B
1950 Ralph Pasquariello, Villanova, B
      Stan West, Oklahoma, G
1951 Bud McFadin, Texas, G
1952 Bill Wade, Vanderbilt, QB
      Bob Carey, Michigan State, E
1953 Donn Moomaw, UCLA, C
      Ed Barker, Washington State, E
1954 Ed Beatty, Cincinnati, C
1955 Larry Morris, Georgia Tech, C
1956 Joe Marconi, West Virginia, B
      Charles Horton, Vanderbilt, B
1957 Jon Arnett, Southern California, B
      Del Shofner, Baylor, E
1958 Lou Michaels, Kentucky, T
      Jim Phillips, Auburn, E
1959 Dick Bass, Pacific, B
      Paul Dickson, Baylor, T
1960 Billy Cannon, Louisiana State, RB
1961 Marlin McKeever, So. California, E-LB
1962 Roman Gabriel, North Carolina St., QB
      Merlin Olsen, Utah State, DT
1963 Terry Baker, Oregon State, QB
      Rufus Guthrie, Georgia Tech, G
1964 Bill Munson, Utah State, QB
1965 Clancy Williams, Washington St., CB
1966 Tom Mack, Michigan, G
1967 Willie Ellison, Texas Southern, RB (2)
1968 Gary Beban, UCLA, QB (2)
1969 Larry Smith, Florida, RB
      Jim Seymour, Notre Dame, WR
      Bob Klein, Southern California, TE
1970 Jack Reynolds, Tennessee, LB
1971 Isiah Robertson, Southern, LB
      Jack Youngblood, Florida, DE
1972 Jim Bertelsen, Texas, RB (2)
1973 Cullen Bryant, Colorado, DB (2)
1974 John Cappelletti, Penn State, RB

1975 Mike Fanning, Notre Dame, DT
      Dennis Harrah, Miami, T
      Doug France, Ohio State, T
1976 Kevin McLain, Colorado State, LB
1977 Bob Brudzinski, Ohio State, LB
1978 Elvis Peacock, Oklahoma, RB
1979 George Andrews, Nebraska, LB
      Kent Hill, Georgia Tech, T
1980 Johnnie Johnson, Texas, DB
1981 Mel Owens, Michigan, LB
1982 Barry Redden, Richmond, RB
1983 Eric Dickerson, So. Methodist, RB
1984 Hal Stephens, East Carolina, DE (5)
1985 Jerry Gray, Texas, DB
1986 Mike Schad, Queen's Univ., Canada, T
1987 Donald Evans, Winston-Salem, DE (2)
1988 Gaston Green, UCLA, RB
      Aaron Cox, Arizona State, WR
1989 Bill Hawkins, Miami, DE
      Cleveland Gary, Miami, RB
1990 Bern Brostek, Washington, C
1991 Todd Lyght, Notre Dame, DB
1992 Sean Gilbert, Pittsburgh, DE
1993 Jerome Bettis, Notre Dame, RB
1994 Wayne Gandy, Auburn, T
1995 Kevin Carter, Florida, DE
1996 Lawrence Phillips, Nebraska, RB
      Eddie Kennison, Louisiana St., WR
1997 Orlando Pace, Ohio State, T
1998 Grant Wistrom, Nebraska, DE
1999 Torry Holt, North Carolina St., WR
2000 Trung Canidate, Arizona, RB
2001 Damione Lewis, Miami, DT
      Adam Archuleta, Arizona State, DB
      Ryan Pickett, Ohio State, DT
2002 Robert Thomas, UCLA, LB
2003 Jimmy Kennedy, Penn State, DT
2004 Steven Jackson, Oregon State, RB
2005 Alex Barron, Florida State, T
2006 Tye Hill, Clemson, DB
2007 Adam Carriker, Nebraska, DE
2008 Chris Long, Virginia, DE
2009 Jason Smith, Baylor, T
2010 Sam Bradford, Oklahoma, QB
2011 Robert Quinn, North Carolina, DE

SAN DIEGO CHARGERS
Year Player, College, Position
1960 Monty Stickles, Notre Dame, E
1961 Earl Faison, Indiana, DE
1962 Bob Ferguson, Ohio State, RB
1963 Walt Sweeney, Syracuse, G
1964 Ted Davis, Georgia Tech, LB
1965 Steve DeLong, Tennessee, DE
1966 Don Davis, Cal St.-Los Angeles, DT
1967 Ron Billingsley, Wyoming, DE
1968 Russ Washington, Missouri, DT
      Jimmy Hill, Texas A&I, DB
1969 Marty Domres, Columbia, QB
      Bob Babich, Miami, Ohio, LB
1970 Walker Gillette, Richmond, WR
1971 Leon Burns, Long Beach State, RB
1972 Pete Lazetich, Stanford, DE (2)
1973 Johnny Rodgers, Nebraska, WR
1974 Bo Matthews, Colorado, RB
      Don Goode, Kansas, LB
1975 Gary Johnson, Grambling, DT
      Mike Williams, Louisiana State, DB
1976 Joe Washington, Oklahoma, RB
1977 Bob Rush, Memphis State, C

1978 John Jefferson, Arizona State, WR
1979 Kellen Winslow, Missouri, TE
1980 Ed Luther, San Jose State, QB (4)
1981 James Brooks, Auburn, RB
1982 Hollis Hall, Clemson, DB (7)
1983 Billy Ray Smith, Arkansas, LB
     Gary Anderson, Arkansas, WR
     Gill Byrd, San Jose State, DB
1984 Mossy Cade, Texas, DB
1985 Jim Lachey, Ohio State, G
1986 Leslie O'Neal, Oklahoma State, DE
     James FitzPatrick, So. California, T
1987 Rod Bernstine, Texas A&M, TE
1988 Anthony Miller, Tennessee, WR
1989 Burt Grossman, Pittsburgh, DE
1990 Junior Seau, So. California, LB
1991 Stanley Richard, Texas, DB
1992 Chris Mims, Tennessee, DE
1993 Darrien Gordon, Stanford, DB
1994 Isaac Davis, Arkansas, G (2)
1995 Terrance Shaw, Stephen F. Austin, DB (2)
1996 Bryan Still, Virginia Tech, WR (2)
1997 Freddie Jones, North Carolina, TE (2)
1998 Ryan Leaf, Washington State, QB
1999 Jermaine Fazande, Oklahoma, RB (2)
2000 Rogers Beckett, Marshall, DB (2)
2001 LaDainian Tomlinson, TCU, RB
2002 Quentin Jammer, Texas, DB
2003 Sammy Davis, Texas A&M, DB
2004 Eli Manning, Mississippi, QB
2005 Shawne Merriman, Maryland, LB
     Luis Castillo, Northwestern, DT
2006 Antonio Cromartie, Florida State, DB
2007 Craig Davis, Louisiana State, WR
2008 Antoine Cason, Arizona, DB
2009 Larry English, Northern Illinois, LB
2010 Ryan Mathews, Fresno State, RB
2011 Corey Liuget, Illinois, DE

SAN FRANCISCO 49ERS
Year Player, College, Position
1950 Leo Nomellini, Minnesota, T
1951 Y.A. Tittle, Louisiana State, B
1952 Hugh McElhenny, Washington, B
1953 Harry Babcock, Georgia, E
     Tom Stolhandske, Texas, E
1954 Bernie Faloney, Maryland, B
1955 Dickie Moegle, Rice, B
1956 Earl Morrall, Michigan State, B
1957 John Brodie, Stanford, B
1958 Jim Pace, Michigan, B
     Charlie Krueger, Texas A&M, T
1959 Dave Baker, Oklahoma, B
     Dan James, Ohio State, C
1960 Monty Stickles, Notre Dame, E
1961 Jimmy Johnson, UCLA, CB
     Bernie Casey, Bowling Green, WR
     Bill Kilmer, UCLA, QB
1962 Lance Alworth, Arkansas, WR
1963 Kermit Alexander, UCLA, CB
1964 Dave Parks, Texas Tech, WR
1965 Ken Willard, North Carolina, RB
     George Donnelly, Illinois, DB
1966 Stan Hindman, Mississippi, DE
1967 Steve Spurrier, Florida, QB
     Cas Banaszek, Northwestern, T
1968 Forrest Blue, Auburn, C
1969 Ted Kwalick, Penn State, TE
     Gene Washington, Stanford, WR

1970 Cedrick Hardman, North Texas St., DE
     Bruce Taylor, Boston U., DB
1971 Tim Anderson, Ohio State, DB
1972 Terry Beasley, Auburn, WR
1973 Mike Holmes, Texas Southern, DB
1974 Wilbur Jackson, Alabama, RB
     Bill Sandifer, UCLA, DT
1975 Jimmy Webb, Mississippi St., DT
1976 Randy Cross, UCLA, C (2)
1977 Elmo Boyd, Eastern Kentucky, WR (3)
1978 Ken MacAfee, Notre Dame, TE
     Dan Bunz, Cal St.-Long Beach, LB
1979 James Owens, UCLA, WR (2)
1980 Earl Cooper, Rice, RB
     Jim Stuckey, Clemson, DT
1981 Ronnie Lott, So. California, DB
1982 Bubba Paris, Michigan, T (2)
1983 Roger Craig, Nebraska, RB (2)
1984 Todd Shell, Brigham Young, LB
1985 Jerry Rice, Mississippi Valley St., WR
1986 Larry Roberts, Alabama, DE (2)
1987 Harris Barton, North Carolina, T
     Terrence Flagler, Clemson, RB
1988 Danny Stubbs, Miami, DE (2)
1989 Keith DeLong, Tennessee, LB
1990 Dexter Carter, Florida State, RB
1991 Ted Washington, Louisville, DT
1992 Dana Hall, Washington, DB
1993 Dana Stubblefield, Kansas, DT
     Todd Kelly, Tennessee, DE
1994 Bryant Young, Notre Dame, DT
     William Floyd, Florida State, RB
1995 J.J. Stokes, UCLA, WR
1996 Israel Ifeanyi, So.California, DE (2)
1997 Jim Druckenmiller, Virginia Tech, QB
1998 R.W. McQuarters, Oklahoma St., DB
1999 Reggie McGrew, Florida, DT
2000 Julian Peterson, Michigan St., LB
     Ahmed Plummer, Ohio State, DB
2001 Andre Carter, California, DE
2002 Mike Rumph, Miami, DB
2003 Kwame Harris, Stanford, T
2004 Rashaun Woods, Oklahoma St., WR
2005 Alex Smith, Utah, QB
2006 Vernon Davis, Maryland, TE
     Manny Lawson, North Carolina St., DE
2007 Patrick Willis, Mississippi, LB
     Joe Staley, Central Michigan, T
2008 Kentwan Balmer, North Carolina, DT
2009 Michael Crabtree, Texas Tech, WR
2010 Anthony Davis, Rutgers, T
     Mike Iupati, Idaho, G
2011 Aldon Smith, Missouri, LB

SEATTLE SEAHAWKS
Year Player, College, Position
1976 Steve Niehaus, Notre Dame, DT
1977 Steve August, Tulsa, G
1978 Keith Simpson, Memphis St., DB
1979 Manu Tuiasosopo, UCLA, DT
1980 Jacob Green, Texas A&M, DE
1981 Ken Easley, UCLA, DB
1982 Jeff Bryant, Clemson, DE
1983 Curt Warner, Penn State, RB
1984 Terry Taylor, Southern Illinois, DB
1985 Owen Gill, Iowa, RB (2)
1986 John L. Williams, Florida, RB
1987 Tony Woods, Pittsburgh, LB
1988 Brian Blades, Miami, WR (2)
1989 Andy Heck, Notre Dame, T

1990 Cortez Kennedy, Miami, DT
1991 Dan McGwire, San Diego St., QB
1992 Ray Roberts, Virginia, T
1993 Rick Mirer, Notre Dame, QB
1994 Sam Adams, Texas A&M, DT
1995 Joey Galloway, Ohio State, WR
1996 Pete Kendall, Boston College, T
1997 Shawn Springs, Ohio State, DB
     Walter Jones, Florida State, T
1998 Anthony Simmons, Clemson, LB
1999 Lamar King, Saginaw Valley St., DE
2000 Shaun Alexander, Alabama, RB
     Chris McIntosh, Wisconsin, T
2001 Koren Robinson, North Carolina St., WR
     Steve Hutchinson, Michigan, G
2002 Jerramy Stevens, Washington, TE
2003 Marcus Trufant, Washington State, DB
2004 Marcus Tubbs, Texas, DT
2005 Chris Spencer, Mississippi, C
2006 Kelly Jennings, Miami, DB
2007 Josh Wilson, Maryland, DB (2)
2008 Lawrence Jackson, So. California, DE
2009 Aaron Curry, Wake Forest, LB
2010 Russell Okung, Oklahoma State, T
     Earl Thomas, Texas, DB
2011 James Carpenter, Alabama, T

TAMPA BAY BUCCANEERS
Year Player, College, Position
1976 Lee Roy Selmon, Oklahoma, DT
1977 Ricky Bell, Southern California, RB
1978 Doug Williams, Grambling, QB
1979 Greg Roberts, Oklahoma, G (2)
1980 Ray Snell, Wisconsin, G
1981 Hugh Green, Pittsburgh, LB
1982 Sean Farrell, Penn State, G
1983 Randy Grimes, Baylor, C (2)
1984 Keith Browner, So. California, LB (2)
1985 Ron Holmes, Washington, DE
1986 Bo Jackson, Auburn, RB
     Roderick Jones, So. Methodist, DB
1987 Vinny Testaverde, Miami, QB
1988 Paul Gruber, Wisconsin, T
1989 Broderick Thomas, Nebraska, LB
1990 Keith McCants, Alabama, LB
1991 Charles McRae, Tennessee, T
1992 Courtney Hawkins, Michigan St., WR (2)
1993 Eric Curry, Alabama, DE
1994 Trent Dilfer, Fresno State, QB
1995 Warren Sapp, Miami, DT
     Derrick Brooks, Florida State, LB
1996 Regan Upshaw, California, DE
     Marcus Jones, North Carolina, DT
1997 Warrick Dunn, Florida State, RB
     Reidel Anthony, Florida, WR
1998 Jacquez Green, Florida, WR (2)
1999 Anthony McFarland, Louisiana St., DT
2000 Cosey Coleman, Tennessee, G (2)
2001 Kenyatta Walker, Florida, T
2002 Marquise Walker, Michigan, WR (3)
2003 Dewayne White, Louisville, DE (2)
2004 Michael Clayton, Louisiana St., WR
2005 Carnell Williams, Auburn, RB
2006 Davin Joseph, Oklahoma, G
2007 Gaines Adams, Clemson, DE
2008 Aqib Talib, Kansas, DB
2009 Josh Freeman, Kansas State, QB
2010 Gerald McCoy, Oklahoma, DT
2011 Adrian Clayborn, Iowa, DE

TENNESSEE TITANS
Year   Player, College, Position
1960   Billy Cannon, Louisiana State, RB
1961   Mike Ditka, Pittsburgh, E
1962   Ray Jacobs, Howard Payne, DT
1963   Danny Brabham, Arkansas, LB
1964   Scott Appleton, Texas, DT
1965   Lawrence Elkins, Baylor, WR
1966   Tommy Nobis, Texas, LB
1967   George Webster, Michigan St., LB
        Tom Regner, Notre Dame, G
1968   Mac Haik, Mississippi, WR (2)
1969   Ron Pritchard, Arizona State, LB
1970   Doug Wilkerson, N. Carolina Central, G
1971   Dan Pastorini, Santa Clara, QB
1972   Greg Sampson, Stanford, DE
1973   John Matuszak, Tampa, DE
        George Amundson, Iowa State, RB
1974   Steve Manstedt, Nebraska, LB (4)
1975   Robert Brazile, Jackson State, LB
        Don Hardeman, Texas A&I, RB
1976   Mike Barber, Louisiana Tech, TE (2)
1977   Morris Towns, Missouri, T
1978   Earl Campbell, Texas, RB
1979   Mike Stensrud, Iowa State, DE (2)
1980   Angelo Fields, Michigan St., T (2)
1981   Michael Holston, Morgan St., WR (3)
1982   Mike Munchak, Penn State, G
1983   Bruce Matthews, So. California, T
1984   Dean Steinkuhler, Nebraska, T
1985   Ray Childress, Texas A&M, DE
        Richard Johnson, Wisconsin, DB
1986   Jim Everett, Purdue, QB
1987   Alonzo Highsmith, Miami, RB
        Haywood Jeffires, North Carolina St., WR
1988   Lorenzo White, Michigan State, RB
1989   David Williams, Florida, T
1990   Lamar Lathon, Houston, LB
1991   Mike Dumas, Indiana, DB (2)
1992   Eddie Robinson, Alabama St., LB (2)
1993   Brad Hopkins, Illinois, T
1994   Henry Ford, Arkansas, DE
1995   Steve McNair, Alcorn State, QB
1996   Eddie George, Ohio State, RB
1997   Kenny Holmes, Miami, DE
1998   Kevin Dyson, Utah, WR
1999   Jevon Kearse, Florida, DE
2000   Keith Bulluck, Syracuse, LB
2001   Andre Dyson, Utah, DB (2)
2002   Albert Haynesworth, Tennessee, DT
2003   Andre Woolfolk, Oklahoma, DB
2004   Ben Troupe, Florida, TE (2)
2005   Adam Jones, West Virginia, DB
2006   Vince Young, Texas, QB
2007   Michael Griffin, Texas, DB
2008   Chris Johnson, East Carolina, RB
2009   Kenny Britt, Rutgers, WR
2010   Derrick Morgan, Georgia Tech, DE
2011   Jake Locker, Washington, QB

WASHINGTON REDSKINS
Year   Player, College, Position
1936   Riley Smith, Alabama, B
1937   Sammy Baugh, Texas Christian, B
1938   Andy Farkas, Detroit, B
1939   I.B. Hale, Texas Christian, T
1940   Ed Boell, New York U., B
1941   Forest Evashevski, Michigan, B
1942   Orban (Spec) Sanders, Texas, B
1943   Jack Jenkins, Missouri, B

1944   Mike Micka, Colgate, B
1945   Jim Hardy, Southern California, B
1946   Cal Rossi, UCLA, B*
1947   Cal Rossi, UCLA, B
1948   Harry Gilmer, Alabama, B
        Lowell Tew, Alabama, B
1949   Rob Goode, Texas A&M, B
1950   George Thomas, Oklahoma, B
1951   Leon Heath, Oklahoma, B
1952   Larry Isbell, Baylor, B
1953   Jack Scarbath, Maryland, B
1954   Steve Meilinger, Kentucky, E
1955   Ralph Guglielmi, Notre Dame, B
1956   Ed Vereb, Maryland, B
1957   Don Bosseler, Miami, B
1958   Mike Sommer, George
        Washington, B (2)
1959   Don Allard, Boston College, B
1960   Richie Lucas, Penn State, QB
1961   Norman Snead, Wake Forest, QB
        Joe Rutgens, Illinois, DT
1962   Ernie Davis, Syracuse, RB
1963   Pat Richter, Wisconsin, TE
1964   Charley Taylor, Arizona St., RB-WR
1965   Bob Breitenstein, Tulsa, T (2)
1966   Charlie Gogolak, Princeton, K
1967   Ray McDonald, Idaho, RB
1968   Jim Smith, Oregon, DB
1969   Eugene Epps, Texas-El Paso, DB (2)
1970   Bill Bundige, Colorado, DT (2)
1971   Cotton Speyrer, Texas, WR (2)
1972   Moses Denson, Maryland St., RB (8)
1973   Charles Cantrell, Lamar, G (5)
1974   Jon Keyworth, Colorado, TE (6)
1975   Mike Thomas, Nevada-Las Vegas, RB (6)
1976   Mike Hughes, Baylor, G (5)
1977   Duncan McColl, Stanford, DE (4)
1978   Tony Green, Florida, RB (6)
1979   Don Warren, San Diego St., TE (4)
1980   Art Monk, Syracuse, WR
1981   Mark May, Pittsburgh, T
1982   Vernon Dean, San Diego St., DB (2)
1983   Darrell Green, Texas A&I, DB
1984   Bob Slater, Oklahoma, DT (2)
1985   Tory Nixon, San Diego St., DB (2)
1986   Markus Koch, Boise State, DE (2)
1987   Brian Davis, Nebraska, DB (2)
1988   Chip Lohmiller, Minnesota, K (2)
1989   Tracy Rocker, Auburn, DT (3)
1990   Andre Collins, Penn State, LB (2)
1991   Bobby Wilson, Michigan State, DT
1992   Desmond Howard, Michigan, WR
1993   Tom Carter, Notre Dame, DB
1994   Heath Shuler, Tennessee, QB
1995   Michael Westbrook, Colorado, WR
1996   Andre Johnson, Penn State, T
1997   Kenard Lang, Miami, DE
1998   Stephen Alexander, Oklahoma, TE (2)
1999   Champ Bailey, Georgia, DB
2000   LaVar Arrington, Penn State, LB
        Chris Samuels, Alabama, T
2001   Rod Gardner, Clemson, WR
2002   Patrick Ramsey, Tulane, QB
2003   Taylor Jacobs, Florida, WR (2)
2004   Sean Taylor, Miami, DB
2005   Carlos Rogers, Auburn, DB
        Jason Campbell, Auburn, QB
2006   Rocky McIntosh, Miami, LB (2)
2007   LaRon Landry, Louisiana State, DB
2008   Devin Thomas, Michigan State, WR (2)

2009   Brian Orakpo, Texas, DE
2010   Trent Williams, Oklahoma, T
2011   Ryan Kerrigan, Purdue, LB
Choice lost because of ineligibility

NFL'S 10 HIGHEST SCORING WEEKENDS

Point Total	Date	Weekend
837	November 20-24, 2008	12th
788	December 29-30, 2007	17th
788	December 5-6, 2004	13th
788	September 5, 8-9, 2002	1st
779	December 16, 19-20, 2010	15th
762	November 10-11, 1996	11th
761	October 16-17, 1983	7th
753	December 8-9, 2002	14th
752	November 29, December 2-3, 2007	13th
752	December 23, 25-28, 2010	16th

TOP 10 TELEVISED SPORTS EVENTS OF ALL-TIME
(Based on A.C. Nielsen Figures)

Program	Date	Network	Share	Rating
Super Bowl XVI	1/24/82	CBS	73%	49.1
Super Bowl XVII	1/30/83	NBC	69%	48.6
Winter Olympics	2/23/94	CBS	64%	48.5
Super Bowl XX	1/26/86	NBC	70%	48.3
Super Bowl XII	1/15/78	CBS	67%	47.2
Super Bowl XIII	1/21/79	NBC	74%	47.1
Super Bowl XVIII	1/22/84	CBS	71%	46.4
Super Bowl XIX	1/20/85	ABC	63%	46.4
Super Bowl XIV	1/20/80	CBS	67%	46.3
Super Bowl XXX	1/28/96	NBC	68%	46.0

TEN MOST WATCHED TV PROGRAMS & ESTIMATED TOTAL NUMBER OF VIEWERS
(Based on A.C. Nielsen Figures)

Program	Date	Network	*Total Viewers
Super Bowl XLV	Feb. 6, 2011	FOX	162,900,000
Super Bowl XLIV	Feb. 7, 2010	CBS	153,400,000
Super Bowl XLIII	Feb. 1, 2009	NBC	151,600,000
Super Bowl XLII	Feb. 3, 2008	FOX	148,300,000
Super Bowl XXXVIII	Feb. 1, 2004	CBS	144,400,000
Super Bowl XL	Feb. 5, 2006	ABC	141,400,000
Super Bowl XLI	Feb. 4, 2007	CBS	139,800,000
Super Bowl XXXVII	Jan. 26, 2003	ABC	138,900,000
Super Bowl XXX	Jan. 28, 1996	NBC	138,488,000
Super Bowl XXVIII	Jan. 30, 1994	NBC	134,800,000

*Watched some portion of the broadcast

NFL'S TOP FIVE PAID ATTENDANCE TOTALS FOR ALL GAMES

Year	Preseason	Regular Season	Postseason	All Games
2007	4,119,278	17,345,205	792,019	22,256,502
2006	4,083,282	17,340,879	775,551	22,199,712
2008	3,995,942	17,055,982	806,840	21,858,764
2005	3,977,388	17,012,453	802,255	21,792,096
2004	3,918,848	17,000,811	788,965	21,708,624

TEN HIGHEST-RATED *NFL MONDAY NIGHT FOOTBALL* GAMES OF ALL-TIME
(Based on A.C. Nielsen Figures)

Game	Date	Share	Rating
Chicago at Miami	12/2/85	46%	29.6
N.Y. Giants at San Francisco	12/3/90	42%	26.9
Dallas at Washington	10/2/78	43%	26.8
Pittsburgh at San Diego	12/22/80	40%	25.3
Philadelphia at Miami	11/30/81	40%	25.3
Pittsburgh at Houston	12/10/79	40%	25.1
Dallas at Miami	12/17/84	40%	25.1
Pittsburgh at Dallas	9/13/82	42%	24.9
Cincinnati at Oakland	12/6/76	40%	24.7
Dallas at Washington	10/8/73	40%	24.6
Minnesota at Atlanta	11/19/73	40%	24.6

NFL'S 10 BIGGEST SINGLE-GAME ATTENDANCE TOTALS

Date	Site	Game	Teams	Attendance
August 15, 1994	Azteca Stadium	American Bowl (Mexico City)	Cowboys vs. Oilers	112,376
August 17, 1998	Azteca Stadium	American Bowl (Mexico City)	Cowboys vs. Patriots	106,424
August 22, 1947	Soldier Field	College All-Star	Bears vs. All-Stars	105,840
September 20, 2009	Cowboys Stadium	Regular Season	Cowboys vs. Giants	105,121
August 4, 1997	Estadio Guillermo Canedo	American Bowl (Mexico City)	Broncos vs. Dolphins	104,629
January 20, 1980	Rose Bowl	Super Bowl XIV	Steelers vs. Rams	103,985
January 30, 1983	Rose Bowl	Super Bowl XVII	Redskins vs. Dolphins	103,667
October 2, 2005	Azteca Stadium	Regular Season	49ers at Cardinals	103,467
January 9, 1977	Rose Bowl	Super Bowl XI	Raiders vs. Vikings	103,438
November 10, 1957	L.A. Coliseum	Regular Season	49ers at Rams	102,368

NFL'S TOP 10 PAID ATTENDANCE WEEKENDS

Weekend	Games	Attendance
September 8, 11-12, 2005	16	1,115,018
December 6, 9-10, 2007	16	1,113,376
November 20-21, 2005	16	1,112,555
December 27-28, 2003	16	1,106,818
November 19-20, 2006	16	1,106,739
September 23-24, 2007	16	1,103,570
December 24-26, 2005	16	1,102,701
September 7, 10-11, 2006	16	1,102,102
September 9, 12-13, 2004	16	1,101,332
December 7, 10-11, 2006	16	1,099,794

NFL'S TOP 10 TEAM SINGLE-SEASON HOME PAID ATTENDANCE TOTALS

Year	Club	Games	Attendance
2007	Washington Redskins	8	711,471
2008	Washington Redskins	8	710,049
2006	Washington Redskins	8	708,952
2004	Washington Redskins	8	707,920
2005	Washington Redskins	8	707,614
2009	Washington Redskins	8	681,703
2010	Washington Redskins	8	680,966
2003	Washington Redskins	8	667,033
2002	Washington Redskins	8	663,536
2001	Washington Redskins	8	661,970

NFL PAID ATTENDANCE

For detailed 2010 attendance, see page 242.

Year	Regular Season		Average	Postseason	Total
2010	16,569,514	(255 games****)	64,978	800,426 (12)	17,369,940
2009	16,651,126	(256 games)	65,043	823,882 (12)	17,475,008
2008	17,055,982	(256 games)	66,625	806,840 (12)	17,862,822
2007	17,345,205	(256 games)	#67,755	792,019 (12)	#18,137,224
2006	17,340,879	(256 games)	67,738	775,551 (12)	18,116,430
2005	17,012,453	(256 games)	66,455	802,255 (12)	17,814,708
2004	17,000,811	(256 games)	66,409	788,965 (12)	17,789,776
2003	16,913,584	(255 games***)	66,328	805,546 (12)	17,719,130
2002	16,833,310	(256 games)	65,755	781,944 (12)	17,615,254
2001	16,166,258	(248 games)	65,187	766,905 (12)	16,933,163
2000	16,387,289	(248 games)	66,078	809,132 (12)	17,196,421
1999	16,206,640	(248 games)	65,349	793,759 (12)	17,000,399
1998	15,364,873	(240 games)	64,020	822,885 (12)	16,187,758
1997	14,967,314	(240 games)	62,364	801,879 (12)	15,769,193
1996	14,612,417	(240 games)	60,885	769,310 (12)	15,381,727
1995	15,043,502	(240 games)	62,682	790,906 (12)	15,834,408
1994	14,030,435	(224 games)	62,636	779,738 (12)	14,810,173
1993	13,966,843	(224 games)	62,352	814,607 (12)	14,781,450
1992	13,828,887	(224 games)	61,736	815,910 (12)	14,644,797
1991	13,841,459	(224 games)	61,792	813,247 (12)	14,654,706
1990	13,959,896	(224 games)	62,321	847,543 (12)	14,807,439
1989	13,025,002	(224 games)	60,829	685,771 (10)	14,311,433
1988	13,539,848	(224 games)	60,446	658,317 (10)	14,198,165
1987	11,406,166	(210 games**)	54,315	656,977 (10)	12,063,143
1986	13,588,551	(224 games)	60,663	734,002 (10)	14,322,553
1985	13,345,047	(224 games)	59,567	710,768 (10)	14,055,815
1984	13,398,112	(224 games)	59,813	665,194 (10)	14,063,306
1983	13,277,222	(224 games)	59,273	675,513 (10)	13,952,735
1982	7,367,438	(126 games*)	58,472	#1,033,153 (16)	8,400,591
1981	13,606,990	(224 games)	60,745	637,763 (10)	14,244,753
1980	13,392,230	(224 games)	59,787	624,430 (10)	14,016,660
1979	13,182,039	(224 games)	58,848	630,326 (10)	13,812,365
1978	12,771,800	(224 games)	57,017	624,388 (10)	13,396,188
1977	11,018,632	(196 games)	56,218	534,925 (8)	11,553,557
1976	11,070,543	(196 games)	56,482	492,884 (8)	11,563,427
1975	10,213,193	(182 games)	56,116	475,919 (8)	10,689,112
1974	10,236,322	(182 games)	56,244	438,664 (8)	10,674,986
1973	10,730,933	(182 games)	58,961	525,433 (8)	11,256,366
1972	10,445,827	(182 games)	57,395	483,345 (8)	10,929,172
1971	10,076,035	(182 games)	55,363	483,891 (8)	10,559,926
1970	9,533,333	(182 games)	52,381	458,493 (8)	9,991,826
1969	6,096,127	(112 games) NFL	54,430	162,279 (3)	6,258,406
	2,843,373	(70 games) AFL	40,620	167,088 (3)	3,010,461
1968	5,882,313	(112 games) NFL	52,521	215,902 (3)	6,098,215
	2,635,004	(70 games) AFL	37,643	114,438 (2)	2,749,442
1967	5,938,924	(112 games) NFL	53,026	166,208 (3)	6,105,132
	2,295,697	(63 games) AFL	36,439	53,330 (1)	2,349,027
1966	5,337,044	(105 games) NFL	50,829	74,152 (1)	5,411,196
	2,160,369	(63 games) AFL	34,291	42,080 (1)	2,202,449
1965	4,634,021	(98 games) NFL	47,286	100,304 (2)	4,734,325
	1,782,384	(56 games) AFL	31,828	30,361 (1)	1,812,745
1964	4,563,049	(98 games) NFL	46,562	79,544 (1)	4,642,593
	1,447,875	(56 games) AFL	25,855	40,242 (1)	1,488,117

PAID ATTENDANCE

Year	Regular Season			Average	Postseason	Total
1963	4,163,643	(98 games)	NFL	42,486	45,801 (1)	4,209,444
	1,208,697	(56 games)	AFL	21,584	63,171 (2)	1,271,868
1962	4,003,421	(98 games)	NFL	40,851	64,892 (1)	4,068,313
	1,147,302	(56 games)	AFL	20,487	37,981 (1)	1,185,283
1961	3,986,159	(98 games)	NFL	40,675	39,029 (1)	4,025,188
	1,002,657	(56 games)	AFL	17,904	29,556 (1)	1,032,213
1960	3,128,296	(78 games)	NFL	40,106	67,325 (1)	3,195,621
	926,156	(56 games)	AFL	16,538	32,183 (1)	958,339
1959	3,140,000	(72 games)		43,617	57,545 (1)	3,197,545
1958	3,006,124	(72 games)		41,752	123,659 (2)	3,129,783
1957	2,836,318	(72 games)		39,393	119,579 (2)	2,955,897
1956	2,551,263	(72 games)		35,434	56,836 (1)	2,608,099
1955	2,521,836	(72 games)		35,026	85,693 (1)	2,607,529
1954	2,190,571	(72 games)		30,425	43,827 (1)	2,234,398
1953	2,164,585	(72 games)		30,064	54,577 (1)	2,219,162
1952	2,052,126	(72 games)		28,502	97,507 (2)	2,149,633
1951	1,913,019	(72 games)		26,570	57,522 (1)	1,970,541
1950	1,977,753	(78 games)		25,356	136,647 (3)	2,114,400
1949	1,391,735	(60 games)		23,196	27,980 (1)	1,419,715
1948	1,525,243	(60 games)		25,421	36,309 (1)	1,561,552
1947	1,837,437	(60 games)		30,624	66,268 (2)	1,903,705
1946	1,732,135	(55 games)		31,493	58,346 (1)	1,790,481
1945	1,270,401	(50 games)		25,408	32,178 (1)	1,302,579
1944	1,019,649	(50 games)		20,393	46,016 (1)	1,065,665
1943	969,128	(40 games)		24,228	71,315 (2)	1,040,443
1942	887,920	(55 games)		16,144	36,006 (1)	923,926
1941	1,108,615	(55 games)		20,157	55,870 (2)	1,164,485
1940	1,063,025	(55 games)		19,328	36,034 (1)	1,099,059
1939	1,071,200	(55 games)		19,476	32,279 (1)	1,103,479
1938	937,197	(55 games)		17,040	48,120 (1)	985,317
1937	963,039	(55 games)		17,510	15,878 (1)	978,917
1936	816,007	(54 games)		15,111	29,545 (1)	845,552
1935	638,178	(53 games)		12,041	15,000 (1)	653,178
1934	492,684	(60 games)		8,211	35,059 (1)	527,743

Record

*Players' 57-day strike reduced 224-game schedule to 126 games.

**Players' 24-day strike reduced 224-game schedule to 210 games.

***The Week 8 Miami at San Diego game is not included. The game was moved to Arizona due to the San Diego wildfires and tickets were distributed at no charge.

****The Week 14 N.Y. Giants at Minnesota game is not included. The game was moved to Detroit due to the Minneapolis blizzard. Original game tickets were cross-honored at Ford Field. Remaining tickets were distributed at no charge.

NFL INTERNATIONAL GAMES (65)

REGULAR SEASON GAMES (8)
(Home Team in capitals)

Date	Site	Teams
October 2, 2005	Mexico City, Mexico	ARIZONA 31, San Francisco 14
October 28, 2007	London, England	N.Y. Giants 13, MIAMI 10
October 26, 2008	London, England	NEW ORLEANS 37, San Diego 32
December 7, 2008	Toronto, Canada	Miami 16, BUFFALO 3
October 25, 2009	London, England	New England 35, TAMPA BAY 7
December 3, 2009	Toronto, Canada	N.Y. Jets 19, BUFFALO 13
October 31, 2010	London, England	SAN FRANCISCO 24, Denver 16
November 7, 2010	Toronto, Canada	Chicago 22, BUFFALO 19

PRESEASON GAMES (57)

Date	Site	Teams
August 12, 1950	Ottawa, Canada	N.Y. Giants 27, Ottawa Rough Riders 6
August 11, 1951	Ottawa, Canada	N.Y. Giants 41, Ottawa Rough Riders 18
August 5, 1959	Toronto, Canada	Chi. Cardinals 55, Tor. Argonauts 26
August 3, 1960	Toronto, Canada	Pittsburgh 43, Toronto Argonauts 16
August 15, 1960	Toronto, Canada	Chicago 16, N.Y. Giants 7
August 2, 1961	Toronto, Canada	St. Louis 36, Toronto Argonauts 7
August 5, 1961	Montreal, Canada	Chicago 34, Montreal Alouettes 16
August 8, 1961	Hamilton, Canada	Hamilton Tiger-Cats 38, Buffalo 21
August 25, 1969	Montreal, Canada	Detroit 22, Boston 9
September 11, 1969	Montreal, Canada	Pittsburgh 17, N.Y. Giants 13
August 16, 1976	Tokyo, Japan	St. Louis 20, San Diego 10
August 5, 1978	Mexico City, Mexico	New Orleans 14, Philadelphia 7
August 6, 1983	London, England	Minnesota 28, St. Louis 10
* August 3, 1986	London, England	Chicago 17, Dallas 6
* August 9, 1987	London, England	L.A. Rams 28, Denver 27
* July 31, 1988	London, England	Miami 27, San Francisco 21
August 14, 1988	Goteborg, Sweden	Minnesota 28, Chicago 21
August 18, 1988	Montreal, Canada	N.Y. Jets 11, Cleveland 7
* August 5, 1989	Tokyo, Japan	L.A. Rams 16, San Francisco 13 (OT)
* August 6, 1989	London, England	Philadelphia 17, Cleveland 13
* August 4, 1990	Tokyo, Japan	Denver 10, Seattle 7
* August 5, 1990	London, England	New Orleans 17, L.A. Raiders 10
* August 9, 1990	Montreal, Canada	Pittsburgh 30, New England 14
* August 11, 1990	Berlin, Germany	L.A. Rams 19, Kansas City 3
* July 28, 1991	London, England	Buffalo 17, Philadelphia 13
* August 3, 1991	Berlin, Germany	San Francisco 21, Chicago 7
* August 3, 1991	Tokyo, Japan	Miami 19, L.A. Raiders 17
* August 1, 1992	Tokyo, Japan	Houston 34, Dallas 23
* August 15, 1992	Berlin, Germany	Miami 31, Denver 27
* August 16, 1992	London, England	San Francisco 17, Washington 15
* July 31, 1993	Tokyo, Japan	New Orleans 28, Philadelphia 16
* August 1, 1993	Barcelona, Spain	San Francisco 21, Pittsburgh 14
* August 7, 1993	Berlin, Germany	Minnesota 20, Buffalo 6
* August 8, 1993	London, England	Dallas 13, Detroit 13 (OT)
August 14, 1993	Toronto, Canada	Cleveland 12, New England 9
* July 31, 1994	Barcelona, Spain	L.A. Raiders 25, Denver 22
* August 6, 1994	Tokyo, Japan	Minnesota 17, Kansas City 9
* August 13, 1994	Berlin, Germany	N.Y. Giants 28, San Diego 20
* August 15, 1994	Mexico City, Mexico	Houston 6, Dallas 0
* August 5, 1995	Tokyo, Japan	Denver 24, San Francisco 10
* August 12, 1995	Toronto, Canada	Buffalo 9, Dallas 7
* July 27, 1996	Tokyo, Japan	San Diego 20, Pittsburgh 10
* August 5, 1996	Monterrey, Mexico	Kansas City 32, Dallas 6
* July 27, 1997	Dublin, Ireland	Pittsburgh 30, Chicago 17
* August 4, 1997	Mexico City, Mexico	Miami 38, Denver 19
* August 16, 1997	Toronto, Canada	Green Bay 35, Buffalo 3
* August 1, 1998	Tokyo, Japan	Green Bay 27, Kansas City 24 (OT)
* August 15, 1998	Vancouver, Canada	San Francisco 24, Seattle 21
* August 17, 1998	Mexico City, Mexico	New England 21, Dallas 3
* August 7, 1999	Sydney, Australia	Denver 20, San Diego 17
* August 5, 2000	Tokyo, Japan	Atlanta 20, Dallas 9
* August 19, 2000	Mexico City, Mexico	Indianapolis 24, Pittsburgh 23
* August 27, 2001	Mexico City, Mexico	Dallas 21, Oakland 6
* August 3, 2002	Osaka, Japan	Washington 38, San Francisco 7
* August 2, 2003	Tokyo, Japan	Tampa Bay 30, N.Y. Jets 14
* August 6, 2005	Tokyo, Japan	Atlanta 27, Indianapolis 21
August 14, 2008	Toronto, Canada	Buffalo 34, Pittsburgh 21
August 19, 2010	Toronto, Canada	Buffalo 34, Indianapolis 21

* *American Bowl Game*

AFC VS. NFC (REGULAR SEASON), 1970-2010

	Balt	Buff	Cin	Cle	Den	Hou	Ind	Jax	KC	Mia
1970		0-3	1-2	0-3	2-2		3-0		0-2-1	2-1
1971		0-3	1-2	2-1	1-3		2-1		2-1	3-0
1972		2-0-1	2-1	1-2	1-3		0-3		2-1	3-0
1973		2-1	2-1	1-2	0-3-1		2-1		1-1-1	3-0
1974		2-1	2-1	1-2	2-2		1-2		1-2	2-1
1975		1-2	3-0	1-3	2-1		2-1		2-1	3-0
1976		0-2	2-0	2-0	2-0		0-2		1-1	0-2
1977		1-1	2-1	1-1	1-1		1-1		1-1	2-0
1978		1-1	2-2	4-0	2-2		2-2		0-2	3-1
1979		2-2	2-2	3-1	3-1		1-1		0-2	4-0
1980		3-1	2-2	3-1	3-1		1-1		2-0	4-0
1981		1-3	2-2	3-1	3-1		0-4		2-2	3-1
1982		1-2	1-0	0-2	2-1		0-1-1		0-3	1-1
1983		1-3	3-1	2-2	0-2		2-0		2-2	3-1
1984		1-3	2-2	1-3	3-1		0-4		1-1	4-0
1985		0-2	2-2	1-3	3-1		3-1		2-2	3-1
1986		1-1	3-1	2-2	3-1		1-3		1-1	2-2
1987		1-2	1-2	2-2	2-1-1		1-0		1-2	3-0
1988		2-2	4-0	4-0	3-1		2-2		0-2	3-1
1989		1-3	2-2	3-1	2-2		1-3		2-0	2-0
1990		3-1	1-3	1-3	1-3		2-2		4-0	2-2
1991		3-1	1-3	0-4	2-0		0-4		2-2	3-1
1992		4-0	1-3	2-2	1-3		2-0		2-2	2-2
1993		4-0	2-2	3-1	1-3		0-4		2-2	3-1
1994		1-3	1-3	3-1	1-3		0-2		3-1	2-2
1995		3-1	2-2	1-3	2-2		2-2	0-4	3-1	2-2
1996	2-2	4-0	2-2		3-1		3-1	2-2	4-0	1-3
1997	2-1-1	1-3	2-2		3-1		1-3	2-2	4-0	1-3
1998	1-3	3-1	1-3		3-1		0-4	3-1	3-1	3-1
1999	2-1	3-1	1-2	1-2	2-2		4-0	4-0	2-2	2-2
2000	2-1	2-2	1-2	0-3	3-1		2-2	2-2	2-2	2-2
2001	2-2	1-3	1-2	1-2	3-1		1-3	1-2	1-3	2-2
2002	0-4	3-1	1-3	2-2	4-0	2-2	2-2	2-2	2-2	2-2
2003	3-1	2-2	2-2	2-2	1-3	2-2	3-1	2-2	3-1	3-1
2004	3-1	4-0	4-0	1-3	3-1	1-3	4-0	3-1	1-3	2-2
2005	2-2	0-4	4-0	2-2	3-1	1-3	3-1	3-1	1-3	2-2
2006	3-1	2-2	2-2	1-3	1-3	0-4	3-1	3-1	4-0	3-1
2007	3-1	1-3	1-3	3-1	1-3	3-1	4-0	3-1	1-3	0-4
2008	3-1	2-2	1-2-1	1-3	3-1	3-1	2-2	2-2	0-4	3-1
2009	2-2	2-2	3-1	0-4	2-2	3-1	4-0	1-3	1-3	2-2
2010	3-1	1-3	1-3	2-2	1-3	1-3	2-2	1-3	4-0	2-2
Total	**33-24-1**	**72-73-1**	**76-71-1**	**63-75**	**84-68-2**	**16-20**	**69-69-1**	**34-29**	**72-64-2**	**97-52**

AFC VS. NFC (REGULAR SEASON), 1970-2010

	NE	NYJ	Oak	Pitt	SD	Sea	TB	Tenn	TOTALS
1970	0-3	2-1	1-2	0-3	1-2			0-3	12-27-1
1971	0-3	0-3	1-1-1	1-2	2-1			0-2-1	15-23-2
1972	3-0	1-2	3-0	2-1	0-3			0-3	20-19-1
1973	2-1	0-3	2-1	3-0	1-2			0-3	19-19-2
1974	3-0	2-1	3-0	3-0	1-2			0-3	23-17
1975	1-2	0-3	3-0	2-1	0-3			3-0	23-17
1976	1-1	0-2	3-0	1-1	2-0		0-1	2-0	16-12
1977	2-0	1-1	1-1	2-0	1-1	1-0		2-0	19-9
1978	2-2	1-3	4-0	3-1	2-2	3-1		2-2	31-21
1979	3-1	3-1	4-0	3-1	3-1	3-1		2-2	36-16
1980	1-3	1-3	2-2	4-0	2-2	1-3		4-0	33-19
1981	0-4	2-0	2-2	3-1	2-2	0-2		1-3	24-28
1982	0-1	4-0	3-0	1-0	1-0	1-0		0-3	15-14-1
1983	2-2	3-1	2-2	2-2	2-2	1-3		1-3	26-26
1984	0-4	0-2	3-1	3-1	4-0	4-0		0-4	26-26
1985	3-1	2-2	3-1	1-3	1-1	2-2		1-3	27-25
1986	3-1	2-2	1-3	2-2	0-4	3-1		2-2	26-26
1987	0-3	0-4	2-2	2-2	2-0	4-0		2-2	23-22-1
1988	2-2	2-0	1-3	1-3	2-2	1-3		3-1	30-22
1989	0-4	1-3	2-2	3-1	2-2	0-4		3-1	24-28
1990	0-4	2-0	3-1	3-1	1-1	2-2		1-3	26-26
1991	1-1	2-2	2-2	0-4	1-3	1-3		1-3	19-33
1992	0-4	0-4	2-2	1-3	2-0	0-4		3-1	22-30
1993	1-1	2-2	3-1	2-2	2-2	0-2		2-2	27-25
1994	4-0	1-3	3-1	2-2	2-2	2-0		0-4	25-27
1995	0-4	0-4	3-1	2-2	3-1	3-1		1-3	27-33
1996	2-2	1-3	1-3	2-2	1-3	2-2		2-2	32-28
1997	1-3	3-1	2-2	2-2	1-3	2-2		4-0	31-28-1
1998	2-2	2-2	3-1	2-2	1-3	3-1		1-3	31-29
1999	3-1	2-2	3-1	3-0	1-3	2-2		3-1	38-22
2000	0-4	3-1	4-0	1-2	0-4	2-2		4-0	30-30
2001	3-1	2-2	3-1	3-0	2-2	1-3		3-1	30-30
2002	3-1	3-1	2-2	2-1-1	2-2			2-2	34-29-1
2003	3-1	0-4	1-3	1-3	2-2			4-0	34-30
2004	4-0	3-1	2-2	4-0	3-1			2-2	44-20
2005	3-1	1-3	2-2	4-0	2-2			1-3	34-30
2006	4-0	3-1	1-3	3-1	4-0			3-1	40-24
2007	4-0	0-4	0-4	3-1	2-2			3-1	32-32
2008	4-0	2-2	1-3	2-2	1-3			4-0	34-29-1
2009	3-1	2-2	1-3	3-1	4-0			4-0	37-27
2010	4-0	2-2	2-2	3-1	2-2			3-1	34-30
Total	77-69	63-83	90-63-1	90-57-1	70-73	44-44	0-1	79-73-1	1129-1008-11

NFC VS. AFC (REGULAR SEASON), 1970-2010

	Ariz	Atl	Car	Chi	Dall	Det	GB	Minn	NO
1970	2-0-1	1-2		1-2	3-0	3-0	2-1	2-1	0-3
1971	2-1	3-0		1-2	3-0	4-0	2-1	2-1	0-1-2
1972	1-2	2-2		1-2	3-0	2-0-1	2-1	1-2	0-3
1973	0-2-1	2-1		2-2	2-1	0-3	1-1-1	2-1	1-2
1974	2-1	0-3		0-3	2-1	1-2	2-1	2-1	0-3
1975	2-1	1-2		0-3	2-1	1-2	0-3	4-0	0-3
1976	1-1	0-2		0-2	2-0	2-0	0-2	2-0	1-2
1977	0-2	0-2		1-1	1-1	2-0	0-3	1-1	0-2
1978	0-4	1-3		0-4	3-1	2-2	2-2	1-3	1-3
1979	1-3	1-3		2-2	1-3	0-4	1-3	1-3	0-4
1980	1-1	2-2		0-4	3-1	0-2	1-3	1-3	1-3
1981	3-1	1-3		4-0	4-0	2-2	1-1	1-3	2-2
1982		1-1		1-1	2-1	0-1	1-1-1	1-3	1-0
1983	3-1	3-1		1-1	2-2	1-3	2-2	4-0	1-3
1984	3-1	1-3		2-2	2-2	0-4	0-4	0-4	3-1
1985	2-2	0-4		3-1	3-1	2-2	0-4	2-0	0-4
1986	1-1	1-3		4-0	1-3	1-3	1-3	1-3	1-3
1987	0-1	0-4		2-2	2-1	0-4	1-2-1	2-1	4-0
1988	1-3	1-3		3-1	0-4	1-1	1-3	2-2	4-0
1989	1-3	2-2		2-2	0-2	1-3	0-2	2-2	4-0
1990	2-2	2-2		2-2	1-1	1-3	1-3	2-2	2-2
1991	1-1	3-1		2-2	3-1	4-0	1-3	0-2	3-1
1992	0-2	2-2		1-3	4-0	2-2	3-1	3-1	3-1
1993	1-1	1-3		2-2	2-2	2-0	3-1	2-2	2-2
1994	3-1	1-3		3-1	3-1	2-2	1-3	2-2	1-3
1995	1-3	2-2	3-1	2-2	4-0	3-1	4-0	3-1	4-0
1996	0-4	0-4	3-1	2-2	2-2	1-3	3-1	1-3	1-3
1997	1-3	2-2	2-2	2-2	2-2	2-2	3-1	3-1	2-2
1998	1-3	3-1	1-3	2-2	1-3	1-3	3-1	4-0	1-3
1999	0-4	0-4	2-2	2-2	1-3	1-3	2-2	2-2	0-4
2000	1-3	1-3	2-2	2-2	1-3	2-2	1-3	3-1	1-3
2001	3-1	1-3	0-4	3-1	0-4	0-4	3-1	1-3	2-2
2002	0-4	2-1-1	3-1	1-3	2-2	0-4	3-1	1-3	2-2
2003	1-3	1-3	2-2	3-1	2-2	1-3	3-1	2-2	1-3
2004	1-3	3-1	1-3	1-3	1-3	1-3	1-3	3-1	2-2
2005	1-3	3-1	3-1	1-3	2-2	2-2	0-4	1-3	2-2
2006	0-4	2-2	2-2	2-2	3-1	1-3	1-3	0-4	1-3
2007	3-1	1-3	0-4	3-1	3-1	3-1	4-0	2-2	1-3
2008	2-2	3-1	4-0	2-2	2-2	0-4	1-3	2-2	3-1
2009	2-2	3-1	0-4	2-2	2-2	1-3	2-2	3-1	4-0
2010	2-2	3-1	0-4	3-1	2-2	1-3	2-2	1-3	2-2
Total	**52-83-2**	**62-90-1**	**28-36**	**73-78**	**84-64**	**56-89-1**	**65-82-3**	**75-75**	**64-86-2**

NFC VS. AFC (REGULAR SEASON), 1970-2010

	NYG	Phil	StL	SF	Sea	TB	Wash	TOTALS
1970	3-0	2-1	2-1	4-0			2-1	27-12-1
1971	1-2	1-2	1-2	2-1			1-2	23-15-2
1972	1-2	2-1	1-2	2-1			1-2	19-20-1
1973	1-2	2-1	3-0	1-2			2-1	19-19-2
1974	1-2	2-1	3-1	0-3			2-1	17-23
1975	2-1	0-3	3-0	1-2			1-2	17-23
1976	0-2	0-2	1-1	1-1	1-0		1-1	12-16
1977	0-2	1-1	2-0	0-2		0-1	1-1	9-19
1978	1-1	3-1	2-2	1-3		2-0	2-2	21-31
1979	1-1	2-2	2-2	0-4		2-0	2-2	16-36
1980	1-3	3-1	2-2	2-2		1-3	1-3	19-33
1981	1-1	3-1	1-3	3-1		0-4	2-2	28-24
1982	1-0	2-1	1-2	1-3		2-1		14-15-1
1983	0-4	1-1	1-3	2-2		1-3	4-0	26-26
1984	2-0	3-1	3-1	3-1		1-1	3-1	26-26
1985	2-2	1-1	3-1	3-1		0-4	4-0	25-27
1986	3-1	2-2	2-2	4-0		1-1	3-1	26-26
1987	2-1	3-1	1-2	3-1		0-2	2-1	22-23-1
1988	1-1	2-2	2-2	2-2		1-3	1-3	22-30
1989	4-0	3-1	3-1	4-0		0-4	2-2	28-24
1990	3-1	1-3	2-2	4-0		0-2	3-1	26-26
1991	3-1	4-0	1-3	3-1		1-3	4-0	33-19
1992	2-2	3-1	2-2	3-1		0-2	2-2	30-22
1993	2-2	2-2	2-2	2-2		1-3	1-3	25-27
1994	3-1	1-3	2-2	3-1		1-1	1-1	27-25
1995	0-4	1-3	1-3	3-1		2-2	0-4	33-27
1996	2-2	2-2	2-2	4-0		2-2	3-1	28-32
1997	1-3	2-1-1	0-4	2-2		3-1	1-3	28-31-1
1998	3-1	0-4	3-1	2-2		2-2	2-2	29-31
1999	2-2	1-3	3-1	1-3		3-1	2-2	22-38
2000	3-1	3-1	3-1	2-2		3-1	2-2	30-30
2001	2-2	3-1	4-0	4-0		2-2	2-2	30-30
2002	2-2	1-3	2-2	2-2	2-2	3-1	3-1	29-34-1
2003	1-3	3-1	4-0	1-3	2-2	1-3	2-2	30-34
2004	1-3	2-2	1-3	0-4	1-3	1-3	0-4	20-44
2005	3-1	3-1	3-1	1-3	3-1	2-2	0-4	30-34
2006	1-3	1-3	2-2	2-2	2-2	2-2	2-2	24-40
2007	3-1	3-1	0-4	1-3	2-2	1-3	2-2	32-32
2008	3-1	2-1-1	0-4	2-2	1-3	1-3	1-3	29-34-1
2009	2-2	2-2	0-4	1-3	1-3	0-4	2-2	27-37
2010	2-2	3-1	2-2	2-2	1-3	2-2	2-2	30-34
Total	72-68	81-66-2	78-75	84-71	16-21	44-72	74-73	1008-1129-11

2010 INTERCONFERENCE GAMES
(Home Team in capital letters)

AFC 34, NFC 30

AFC VICTORIES
PITTSBURGH 15, Atlanta 9 (OT)
Miami 14, MINNESOTA 10
DENVER 31, Seattle 14
OAKLAND 16, St. Louis 14
Houston 30, WASHINGTON 27 (OT)
INDIANAPOLIS 38, New York Giants 14
Cincinnati 20, CAROLINA 7
KANSAS CITY 31, San Francisco 10
Tennessee 29, NEW YORK GIANTS 10
Pittsburgh 38, TAMPA BAY 13
SAN DIEGO 41, Arizona 10
Tennessee 34, DALLAS 27
NEW YORK JETS 29, Minnesota 20
Miami 23, GREEN BAY 20 (OT)
Indianapolis 27, WASHINGTON 24
Cleveland 30, NEW ORLEANS 17
TENNESSEE 37, Philadelphia 19
Jacksonville 35, DALLAS 17
NEW ENGLAND 28, Minnesota 18
OAKLAND 33, Seattle 3
New York Jets 23, DETROIT 20 (OT)
BUFFALO 14, Detroit 12
Baltimore 37, CAROLINA 13
KANSAS CITY 31, Arizona 13
New England 45, DETROIT 24
CLEVELAND 24, Carolina 23
Kansas City 42, SEATTLE 24
BALTIMORE 17, Tampa Bay 10
New England 36, CHICAGO 7
SAN DIEGO 34, San Francisco 7
BALTIMORE 30, New Orleans 24
Kansas City 27, ST. LOUIS 13
NEW ENGLAND 31, Green Bay 27
PITTSBURGH 27, Carolina 3

NFC VICTORIES
TAMPA BAY 17, Cleveland 14
GREEN BAY 34, Buffalo 7
Dallas 27, HOUSTON 13
Philadelphia 28, JACKSONVILLE 3
ARIZONA 24, Oakland 23
SEATTLE 27, San Diego 20
Tampa Bay 24, CINCINNATI 21
Atlanta 20, CLEVELAND 10
New York Giants 34, HOUSTON 10
ST. LOUIS 20, San Diego 17
SAN FRANCISCO 17, Oakland 9
ATLANTA 39, Cincinnati 32
Green Bay 9, NEW YORK JETS 0
SAN FRANCISCO 24, Denver 16 (London)
NEW ORLEANS 20, Pittsburgh 10
Chicago 22, BUFFALO 19 (Toronto)
PHILADELPHIA 26, Indianapolis 24
ATLANTA 26, Baltimore 21
Chicago 16, MIAMI 0
Washington 19, TENNESSEE 16 (OT)
NEW YORK GIANTS 24, Jacksonville 20
St. Louis 36, DENVER 33
PHILADELPHIA 34, Houston 24
New Orleans 34, CINCINNATI 30
MINNESOTA 38, Buffalo 14
Dallas 38, INDIANAPOLIS 35 (OT)
ARIZONA 43, Denver 13
CHICAGO 38, New York Jets 34
Washington 20, JACKSONVILLE 17 (OT)
Detroit 34, MIAMI 27

REGULAR SEASON INTERCONFERENCE RECORDS, 1970-2010

AMERICAN FOOTBALL CONFERENCE

East	W	L	T	Pct.
Miami	97	52	0	.651
New England	77	69	0	.527
Buffalo	72	73	1	.497
New York Jets	63	83	0	.432
North	**W**	**L**	**T**	**Pct.**
Pittsburgh	90	57	1	.611
Baltimore	33	24	1	.578
Cincinnati	76	71	1	.517
Cleveland	63	75	0	.457
South	**W**	**L**	**T**	**Pct.**
Jacksonville	34	29	0	.540
Tennessee	79	73	1	.520
Indianapolis	69	69	1	.500
Houston	16	20	0	.444
West	**W**	**L**	**T**	**Pct.**
Oakland	90	63	1	.588
Denver	84	68	2	.552
Kansas City	72	64	2	.529
San Diego	70	73	0	.490

NATIONAL FOOTBALL CONFERENCE

East	W	L	T	Pct.
Dallas	84	64	0	.568
Philadelphia	81	66	2	.550
New York Giants	72	68	0	.514
Washington	74	73	0	.503
North	**W**	**L**	**T**	**Pct.**
Minnesota	75	75	0	.500
Chicago	73	78	0	.483
Green Bay	65	82	3	.443
Detroit	56	89	1	.387
South	**W**	**L**	**T**	**Pct.**
Carolina	28	36	0	.438
New Orleans	64	86	0	.427
Atlanta	62	90	1	.408
Tampa Bay*	44	73	0	.376
West	**W**	**L**	**T**	**Pct.**
San Francisco	84	71	0	.542
St. Louis	78	75	0	.510
Seattle* #	60	65	0	.480
Arizona	52	83	2	.386

* Records include one game played between Seattle and Tampa Bay, won by the Seahawks 13-10, in their inaugural season (1976) when Seattle competed in the NFC and Tampa Bay in the AFC.

\# Seattle was a member of the AFC from 1977-2001.
From 1970-71, tie games were not included in winning percentage.

INTERCONFERENCE VICTORIES, 1970-2010

	REGULAR SEASON				PRESEASON		
	AFC	NFC	Tie		AFC	NFC	Tie
1970	12	27	1	1970	21	28	1
1971	15	23	2	1971	28	28	3
1972	20	19	1	1972	27	25	4
1973	19	19	2	1973	23	35	2
1974	23	17	0	1974	35	25	0
1975	23	17	0	1975	30	26	1
1976	16	12	0	1976	30	31	0
1977	19	9	0	1977	38	25	0
1978	31	21	0	1978	20	19	0
1979	36	16	0	1979	25	18	0
1980	33	19	0	1980	22	20	1
1981	24	28	0	1981	18	19	0
1982	15	14	1	1982	25	19	0
1983	26	26	0	1983	15	24	0
1984	26	26	0	1984	16	19	0
1985	27	25	0	1985	10	22	1
1986	26	26	0	1986	22	17	0
1987	23	22	1	1987	22	22	0
1988	30	22	0	1988	23	16	1
1989	24	28	0	1989	16	27	0
1990	26	26	0	1990	15	29	0
1991	19	33	0	1991	19	27	0
1992	22	30	0	1992	30	22	0
1993	27	25	0	1993	17	22	0
1994	25	27	0	1994	22	16	0
1995	27	33	0	1995	19	26	0
1996	32	28	0	1996	27	19	0
1997	31	28	1	1997	26	17	0
1998	31	29	0	1998	34	16	0
1999	38	22	0	1999	22	25	0
2000	30	30	0	2000	34	17	0
2001	30	30	0	2001	28	23	0
2002	34	29	1	2002	25	24	0
2003	34	30	0	2003	25	21	0
2004	44	20	0	2004	21	18	0
2005	34	30	0	2005	21	29	0
2006	40	24	0	2006	27	24	0
2007	32	32	0	2007	27	24	0
2008	34	29	1	2008	21	27	0
2009	37	27	0	2009	24	26	0
2010	34	30	0	2010	25	29	0
Total	1,129	1,008	11		975	943	14

Records

Compiled by Elias Sports Bureau.

The following records reflect all available official information on the National Football League from its formation in 1920 to date. Also included are all applicable records from the American Football League, 1960-69.

Individuals eligible for Rookie records are players who were in their first season of professional football and had not been on the roster of another professional football team, including teams in other leagues, for any regular-season or postseason games in a previous season. Eligible players, therefore, include those who were under contract to a National Football League club for a previous season but were terminated prior to their club's first regular-season game and not re-signed, or who were placed on Reserve/Injured (or another category of the Reserve List) prior to their club's first regular-season game and were not activated during the rest of the regular season or postseason.

INDIVIDUAL RECORDS

SERVICE
Most Seasons
- 26 George Blanda, Chi. Bears, 1949, 1950-58; Baltimore, 1950; Houston, 1960-66; Oakland, 1967-1975
- 25 Morten Andersen, New Orleans, 1982-1994; Atlanta, 1995-2000; N.Y. Giants, 2001; Kansas City, 2002-03; Minnesota, 2004; Atlanta, 2006-07
- 23 Gary Anderson, Pittsburgh, 1982-1994; Philadelphia, 1995-96; San Francisco, 1997; Minnesota, 1998-2002; Tennessee, 2003-04
- John Carney, Tampa Bay, 1988-89; L.A. Rams, 1990: San Diego, 1990-2000; New Orleans, 2001-06; Jacksonville, 2007; Kansas City, 2007; N.Y. Giants, 2008; New Orleans, 2009-2010

Most Seasons, One Club
- 20 Jackie Slater, L.A. Rams, 1976-1994; St. Louis, 1995
- Darrell Green, Washington, 1983-2002
- 19 Jim Marshall, Minnesota, 1961-1979
- Bruce Matthews, Houston, 1983-1996; Tennessee, 1997-2001
- Jason Hanson, Detroit, 1992-2010
- 18 Jim Hart, St. Louis, 1966-1983
- Jeff Van Note, Atlanta, 1969-1986
- Pat Leahy, N.Y. Jets, 1974-1991

Most Games Played, Career
- 382 Morten Andersen, New Orleans, 1982-1994; Atlanta, 1995-2000; N.Y. Giants, 2001; Kansas City, 2002-03; Minnesota, 2004; Atlanta, 2006-07
- 353 Gary Anderson, Pittsburgh, 1982-1994; Philadelphia, 1995-96; San Francisco, 1997; Minnesota, 1998-2002; Tennessee, 2003-04
- 352 Jeff Feagles, New England, 1988-89; Philadelphia, 1990-93; Arizona, 1994-97; Seattle, 1998-2002; N.Y. Giants, 2003-09

Most Consecutive Games Played, Career
- 352 Jeff Feagles, New England, 1988-89; Philadelphia, 1990-93; Arizona, 1994-97; Seattle, 1998-2002; N.Y. Giants, 2003-09
- 299 Brett Favre, Green Bay, 1992-2007; N.Y. Jets, 2008; Minnesota, 2009-2010
- 282 Jim Marshall, Cleveland, 1960; Minnesota, 1961-1979

SCORING
Most Seasons Leading League
- 5 Don Hutson, Green Bay, 1940-44
- Gino Cappelletti, Boston, 1961, 1963-66
- 3 Earl (Dutch) Clark, Portsmouth, 1932; Detroit, 1935-36
- Pat Harder, Chi. Cardinals, 1947-49

Paul Hornung, Green Bay, 1959-1961
- 2 Jack Manders, Chi. Bears, 1934, 1937
- Gordy Soltau, San Francisco, 1952-53
- Doak Walker, Detroit, 1950, 1955
- Gene Mingo, Denver, 1960, 1962
- Jim Turner, N.Y. Jets, 1968-69
- Fred Cox, Minnesota, 1969-1970
- Chester Marcol, Green Bay, 1972, 1974
- John Smith, New England, 1979-1980
- Marshall Faulk, St. Louis, 2000-01

Most Consecutive Seasons Leading League
- 5 Don Hutson, Green Bay, 1940-44
- 4 Gino Cappelletti, Boston, 1963-66
- 3 Pat Harder, Chi. Cardinals, 1947-49
- Paul Hornung, Green Bay, 1959-1961

POINTS
Most Points, Career
- 2,544 Morten Andersen, New Orleans, 1982-1994; Atlanta, 1995-2000; N.Y. Giants, 2001; Kansas City, 2002-03; Minnesota, 2004; Atlanta, 2006-07 (849-pat, 565-fg)
- 2,434 Gary Anderson, Pittsburgh, 1982-1994; Philadelphia 1995-96; San Francisco, 1997; Minnesota, 1998-2002; Tennessee, 2003-04 (820-pat, 538-fg)
- 2,062 John Carney, Tampa Bay, 1988-89; L.A. Rams, 1990; San Diego, 1990-2000; New Orleans, 2001-06; Jacksonville, 2007; Kansas City, 2007; N.Y. Giants, 2008; New Orleans, 2009-2010 (628-pat, 478-fg)

Most Points, Season
- 186 LaDainian Tomlinson, San Diego, 2006 (31-td)
- 176 Paul Hornung, Green Bay, 1960 (15-td, 41-pat, 15-fg)
- 168 Shaun Alexander, Seattle, 2005 (28-td)

Most Point, No Touchdowns, Season
- 164 Gary Anderson, Minnesota, 1998 (59-pat, 35-fg)
- 163 Jeff Wilkins, St. Louis, 2003 (46-pat, 39-fg)
- 161 Mark Moseley, Washington, 1983 (62-pat, 33-fg)

Most Seasons, 100 or More Points
- 16 Jason Elam, Denver, 1993-2007; Atlanta, 2008
- 14 Gary Anderson, Pittsburgh, 1983-85, 1988, 1991-94; Philadelphia 1996; San Francisco, 1997; Minnesota, 1998-2000; Tennessee, 2003
- Morten Andersen, New Orleans, 1985-89, 1991-94; Atlanta, 1995, 1997-98; Kansas City, 2002-03
- Adam Vinatieri, New England, 1996-2005; Indianapolis, 2006-08, 2010
- 12 Matt Stover, Cleveland, 1994-95; Baltimore, 1997, 1999-2001, 2003-08

Most Points, Rookie Season
- 144 Kevin Butler, Chicago, 1985 (51-pat, 31-fg)
- 141 Mason Crosby, Green Bay, 2007 (48-pat, 31-fg)
- 132 Gale Sayers, Chicago, 1965 (22-td)

Most Points, Game
- 40 Ernie Nevers, Chi. Cardinals vs. Chi. Bears, Nov. 28, 1929 (6-td, 4-pat)
- 36 Dub Jones, Cleveland vs. Chi. Bears, Nov. 25, 1951 (6-td)
- Gale Sayers, Chicago vs. San Francisco, Dec. 12, 1965 (6-td)
- 33 Paul Hornung, Green Bay vs. Baltimore, Oct. 8, 1961 (4-td, 6-pat, 1-fg)

Most Consecutive Games Scoring
- 360 Morten Andersen, New Orleans, 1983-1994; Atlanta, 1995-2000; N.Y. Giants, 2001; Kansas City, 2002-03; Minnesota, 2004; Atlanta, 2006-07
- 263 Jason Elam, Denver, 1993-2007; Atlanta, 2008-09
- 186 Jim Breech, Oakland, 1979; Cincinnati, 1980-1992

TOUCHDOWNS

Most Seasons Leading League
- 8 Don Hutson, Green Bay, 1935-38, 1941-44
- 3 Jim Brown, Cleveland, 1958-59, 1963
     Lance Alworth, San Diego, 1964-66
     Emmitt Smith, Dallas, 1992, 1994-95
- 2 By many players

Most Consecutive Seasons Leading League
- 4 Don Hutson, Green Bay, 1935-38, 1941-44
- 3 Lance Alworth, San Diego, 1964-66
- 2 By many players

Most Touchdowns, Career
- 208 Jerry Rice, San Francisco, 1985-2000;
       Oakland, 2001-04;
       Seattle, 2004 (10-r, 197-p, 1-ret)
- 175 Emmitt Smith, Dallas, 1990-2002; Arizona, 2003-04
       (164-r, 11-p)
- 159 LaDainian Tomlinson, San Diego, 2001-09;
       N.Y. Jets, 2010 (144-r, 15-p)

Most Touchdowns, Season
- 31 LaDainian Tomlinson, San Diego, 2006 (28-r, 3-p)
- 28 Shaun Alexander, Seattle, 2005 (27-r, 1-p)
- 27 Priest Holmes, Kansas City, 2003 (27-r)

Most Touchdowns, Rookie, Season
- 22 Gale Sayers. Chicago, 1965 (14-r, 6-p)
- 20 Eric Dickerson, Rams, 1983 (18-r, 2-p)
- 17 Fred Taylor, Jacksonville, 1998 (14-r, 3-p)
      Randy Moss, Minnesota, 1998 (17-p)
      Edgerrin James, Indianapolis, 1999 (13-r, 4-p)
      Clinton Portis, Denver, 2002 (15-r, 2-p)

Most Touchdowns, Game
- 6 Ernie Nevers, Chi. Cardinals vs. Chi. Bears,
     Nov. 28, 1929 (6-r)
     Dub Jones, Cleveland vs. Chi. Bears, Nov. 25, 1951
     (4-r, 2-p)
     Gale Sayers, Chicago vs. San Francisco, Dec. 12, 1965
     (4-r, 1-p, 1-ret)
- 5 Jimmy Conzelman, Rhode Island vs. Evansville,
     Oct. 15, 1922 (5-r)
     Bob Shaw, Chi. Cardinals vs. Baltimore, Oct. 2, 1950
     (5-p)
     Jim Brown, Cleveland vs. Baltimore, Nov. 1, 1959 (5-r)
     Abner Haynes, Dall. Texans vs. Oakland,
     Nov. 26, 1961 (4-r, 1-p)
     Billy Cannon, Houston vs. N.Y. Titans, Dec. 10, 1961
     (3-r, 2-p)
     Cookie Gilchrist, Buffalo vs. N.Y. Jets, Dec. 8, 1963 (5-r)
     Paul Hornung, Green Bay vs. Baltimore,
     Dec. 12, 1965 (3-r, 2-p)
     Kellen Winslow, San Diego vs. Oakland,
     Nov. 22, 1981 (5-p)
     Jerry Rice, San Francisco vs. Atlanta, Oct. 14, 1990
     (5-p)
     James Stewart, Jacksonville vs. Philadelphia,
     Oct. 12, 1997 (5-r)
     Shaun Alexander, Seattle vs. Minnesota,
     Sept. 29, 2002 (4-r, 1-p)
     Clinton Portis, Denver vs. Kansas City, Dec. 7, 2003
     (5-r)
- 4 By many players. Last time:
     Darren McFadden, Oakland vs. Denver,
     Oct. 24, 2010 (3-r, 1-p)

Most Consecutive Games Scoring Touchdowns
- 18 Lenny Moore, Baltimore, 1963-65
      LaDainian Tomlinson, San Diego, 2004-05
- 14 O.J. Simpson, Buffalo, 1975
- 13 John Riggins, Washington, 1982-83
      George Rogers, Washington, 1985-86
      Jerry Rice, San Francisco, 1986-87

POINTS AFTER TOUCHDOWN

Most Seasons Leading League
- 8 George Blanda, Chi. Bears, 1956; Houston,
     1961-62; Oakland, 1967-69, 1972, 1974
- 4 Bob Waterfield, Cleveland, 1945; Los Angeles, 1946,
     1950, 1952
- 3 Earl (Dutch) Clark, Portsmouth, 1932; Detroit,
     1935-36 Jack Manders, Chi. Bears, 1933-35
     Don Hutson, Green Bay, 1941-42, 1945

Most (Kicking) Points After Touchdown Attempted, Career
- 959 George Blanda, Chi. Bears, 1949, 1950-58; Baltimore,
       1950; Houston, 1960-66; Oakland, 1967-1975
- 859 Morten Andersen, New Orleans, 1982-1994;
       Atlanta, 1995-2000; N.Y. Giants, 2001;
       Kansas City, 2002-03; Minnesota, 2004;
       Atlanta, 2006-07
- 827 Gary Anderson, Pittsburgh, 1982-1994; Philadelphia
       1995-96; San Francisco, 1997; Minnesota,
       1998-2002; Tennessee, 2003-04

Most (Kicking) Points After Touchdown Attempted, Season
- 74 Stephen Gostkowski, New England, 2007
- 70 Uwe von Schamann, Miami, 1984
- 65 George Blanda, Houston, 1961

Most (Kicking) Points After Touchdown Attempted, Game
- 10 Charlie Gogolak, Washington vs. N.Y. Giants,
      Nov. 27, 1966
- 9   Pat Harder, Chi. Cardinals vs. N.Y. Giants,
      Oct. 17, 1948; vs. N.Y. Bulldogs, Nov. 13, 1949
      Bob Waterfield, Los Angeles vs. Baltimore,
      Oct. 22, 1950
      Bob Thomas, Chicago vs. Green Bay, Dec. 7, 1980
- 8   By many players

Most (One-Point) Points After Touchdown, Career
- 943 George Blanda, Chi. Bears, 1949, 1950-58; Baltimore,
       1950; Houston, 1960-66; Oakland, 1967-1975
- 849 Morten Andersen, New Orleans, 1982-1994;
       Atlanta, 1995-2000; N.Y. Giants, 2001;
       Kansas City, 2002-03; Minnesota, 2004,
       Atlanta, 2006-07
- 820 Gary Anderson, Pittsburgh, 1982-1994; Philadelphia
       1995-96; San Francisco, 1997; Minnesota,
       1998-2002; Tennessee, 2003-04

Most (One-Point) Points After Touchdown, Season
- 74 Stephen Gostkowski, New England, 2007
- 66 Uwe von Schamann, Miami, 1984
- 64 George Blanda, Houston, 1961
      Jeff Wilkins, St. Louis, 1999

Most (One-Point) Points After Touchdown, Game
- 9   Pat Harder, Chi. Cardinals vs. N.Y. Giants,
      Oct. 17, 1948
      Bob Waterfield, Los Angeles vs. Baltimore,
      Oct. 22, 1950
      Charlie Gogolak, Washington vs. N.Y. Giants,
      Nov. 27, 1966
- 8   By many players

Most Consecutive (Kicking) Points After Touchdown
- 422 Matt Stover, Baltimore, 1996-2008; Indianapolis,
       2009
- 371 Jason Elam, Denver, 1993-2002
       Jeff Wilkins, St. Louis, 1999-2007
- 321 Rian Lindell, Seattle, 2000-02; Buffalo, 2003-2010

Highest (Kicking) Points After Touchdown Percentage, Career
(200 points after touchdown)
- 99.70 Rian Lindell, Seattle, 2000-02; Buffalo, 2003-2010
         (337-338)
- 99.57 Stephen Gostkowski, New England, 2006-2010
         (230-231)
- 99.52 Robbie Gould, Chicago, 2005-2010 (208-209)

Most (Kicking) Points After Touchdown, No Misses, Season
- 74 Stephen Gostkowski, New England, 2007
- 64 Jeff Wilkins, St. Louis, 1999
- 59 Gary Anderson, Minnesota, 1998

Most (Kicking) Points After Touchdown, No Misses, Game
- 9 Pat Harder, Chi. Cardinals vs. N.Y. Giants,
     Oct. 17, 1948
     Bob Waterfield, Los Angeles vs. Baltimore,
     Oct. 22, 1950
- 8 By many players

Most Two-Point Conversions, Career
Two-point conversions include AFL (1960-69) and NFL (since 1994).
- 7 Marshall Faulk, Indianapolis, 1994-98; St. Louis,
     1999-2005
- 6 Terance Mathis, Atlanta, 1994-2001; Pittsburgh, 2002
- 5 Cris Carter, Minnesota, 1994-2001; Miami, 2002
     Rob Moore, N.Y. Jets, 1994; Arizona, 1995-99
     Willie Jackson, Jacksonville, 1995-97; Cincinnati,
       1998-99; New Orleans, 2000-01; Washington,
       2002
     Keenan McCardell, Cleveland, 1994-95; Jacksonville,
       1996-2001; Tampa Bay, 2002-03; San Diego,
       2004-06, Washington, 2007
     Marvin Harrison, Indianapolis, 1996-2008
     Marcus Pollard, Indianapolis, 1995-2004; Detroit,
       2005-06; Seattle, 2007; Atlanta, 2008
     Todd Heap, Baltimore, 2001-2010
     Hines Ward, Pittsburgh, 1998-2010
     Edgerrin James, Indianapolis, 1999-2005;
       Arizona, 2006-08; Seattle, 2009

Most Two-Point Conversions, Season
- 4 Todd Heap, Baltimore, 2003
- 3 Gino Cappelletti, Boston, 1960
     Richie Lucas, Buffalo, 1961
     Ronnie Harmon, San Diego, 1994
     Haywood Jeffires, Houston, 1994
     Tom Tupa, Cleveland, 1994
     Terance Mathis, Atlanta, 1995
     Lamar Smith, Seattle, 1996
     Cris Carter, Minnesota, 1997
     Terrell Davis, Denver, 1997
     James Stewart, Detroit, 2000
     Hines Ward, Pittsburgh, 2002
     Brian Finneran, Atlanta, 2005
     Reggie Bush, New Orleans, 2007
- 2 By many players

Most Two-Point Conversions, Game
- 2 Brett Perriman, Detroit vs. Green Bay, Nov. 6, 1994
     Michael Jackson, Baltimore vs. New England,
       Oct. 6, 1996
     Terrell Davis, Denver vs. Atlanta, Sept. 28, 1997
     Charles Johnson, Pittsburgh vs. Tennessee,
       Nov. 1, 1998
     Marshall Faulk, St. Louis vs. Atlanta, Oct. 15, 2000
     Todd Heap, Baltimore vs. Cincinnati, Oct. 19, 2003
     Reggie Bush, New Orleans vs. St. Louis,
       Nov. 11, 2007
     Tarvaris Jackson, Minnesota vs. Denver,
       Dec. 30, 2007 (ot)
     Mewelde Moore, Pittsburgh vs. New England,
       Nov. 14, 2010

FIELD GOALS
Most Seasons Leading League
- 5 Lou Groza, Cleveland, 1950, 1952-54, 1957
- 4 Jack Manders, Chi. Bears, 1933-34, 1936-37
     Ward Cuff, N.Y. Giants, 1938-39, 1943; Green Bay,
       1947
     Mark Moseley, Washington, 1976-77, 1979, 1982
- 3 Bob Waterfield, Los Angeles, 1947, 1949, 1951

     Gino Cappelletti, Boston, 1961, 1963-64
     Fred Cox, Minnesota, 1965, 1969-1970
     Jan Stenerud, Kansas City, 1967, 1970, 1975

Most Consecutive Seasons Leading League
- 3 Lou Groza, Cleveland, 1952-54
- 2 Jack Manders, Chi. Bears, 1933-34
     Armand Niccolai, Pittsburgh, 1935-36
     Jack Manders, Chi. Bears, 1936-37
     Ward Cuff, N.Y. Giants, 1938-39
     Clark Hinkle, Green Bay, 1940-41
     Cliff Patton, Philadelphia, 1948-49
     Gino Cappelletti, Boston, 1963-64
     Jim Turner, N.Y. Jets, 1968-69
     Fred Cox, Minnesota, 1969-1970
     Mark Moseley, Washington, 1976-77
     Chip Lohmiller, Washington, 1991-92
     Pete Stoyanovich, Miami, 1991-92

Most Field Goals Attempted, Career
- 709 Morten Andersen, New Orleans, 1982-1994; Atlanta,
        1995-2000; N.Y. Giants, 2001; Kansas City,
        2002-03; Minnesota, 2004; Atlanta, 2006-07
- 672 Gary Anderson, Pittsburgh, 1982-1994; Philadelphia,
        1995-96; San Francisco, 1997; Minnesota,
        1998-2002; Tennessee, 2003-04
- 641 George Blanda, Chi. Bears, 1949, 1950-58;
        Baltimore, 1950; Houston, 1960-66; Oakland,
        1967-1975

Most Field Goals Attempted, Season
- 49 Bruce Gossett, Los Angeles, 1966
      Curt Knight, Washington, 1971
- 48 Chester Marcol, Green Bay, 1972
- 47 Jim Turner, N.Y. Jets, 1969
      David Ray, Los Angeles, 1973
      Mark Moseley, Washington, 1983

Most Field Goals Attempted, Game
- 9 Jim Bakken, St. Louis vs. Pittsburgh, Sept. 24, 1967
- 8 Lou Michaels, Pittsburgh vs. St. Louis, Dec. 2, 1962
     Garo Yepremian, Detroit vs. Minnesota, Nov. 13, 1966
     Jim Turner, N.Y. Jets vs. Buffalo, Nov. 3, 1968
     Billy Cundiff, Dallas vs. N.Y. Giants, Sept. 15, 2003 (ot)
     Rob Bironas, Tennessee vs. Houston, Oct. 21, 2007
- 7 By many players

Most Field Goals, Career
- 565 Morten Andersen, New Orleans, 1982-1994; Atlanta,
        1995-2000; N.Y. Giants, 2001; Kansas City,
        2002-03; Minnesota, 2004; Atlanta, 2006-07
- 538 Gary Anderson, Pittsburgh, 1982-1994; Philadelphia,
        1995-96; San Francisco, 1997; Minnesota,
        1998-2002; Tennessee, 2003-04
- 478 John Carney, Tampa Bay, 1988-89; L.A. Rams,
        1990; San Diego, 1990-2000; New Orleans,
        2001-06; Jacksonville, 2007; Kansas City,
        2007; N.Y. Giants, 2008; New Orleans,
        2009-2010

Most Field Goals, Season
- 40 Neil Rackers, Arizona, 2005
- 39 Olindo Mare, Miami, 1999
      Jeff Wilkins, St. Louis, 2003
- 37 John Kasay, Carolina, 1996
      Mike Vanderjagt, Indianapolis, 2003

Most Field Goals, Rookie, Season
- 35 Ali Haji-Sheikh, N.Y. Giants, 1983
- 34 Richie Cunningham, Dallas, 1997
- 33 Chester Marcol, Green Bay, 1972

Most Field Goals, Game
- 8 Rob Bironas, Tennessee vs. Houston, Oct. 21, 2007
- 7 Jim Bakken, St. Louis vs. Pittsburgh, Sept. 24, 1967
     Rich Karlis, Minnesota vs. L.A. Rams, Nov. 5, 1989
       (ot)
     Chris Boniol, Dallas vs. Green Bay, Nov. 18, 1996

Billy Cundiff, Dallas vs. N.Y. Giants, Sept. 15, 2003 (ot)
Shayne Graham, Cincinnati vs. Baltimore, Nov. 11, 2007
6 By many players

Most Field Goals, One Quarter
4 Garo Yepremian, Detroit vs. Minnesota, Nov. 13, 1966
(second quarter)
Curt Knight, Washington vs. N.Y. Giants, Nov. 15, 1970
(second quarter)
Roger Ruzek, Dallas vs. N.Y. Giants, Nov. 2, 1987
(fourth quarter)
Cary Blanchard, Indianapolis vs. Buffalo,
Sept. 21 1997 (second quarter)
Sebastian Janikowski, Oakland vs. Chicago,
Oct. 5, 2003 (second quarter)
Jeff Wilkins, St. Louis vs. Baltimore, Nov. 9, 2003
(fourth quarter)
Lawrence Tynes, Kansas City vs. New England,
Nov. 27, 2005 (second quarter)
Shayne Graham, Cincinnati vs. Baltimore,
Nov. 11, 2007 (fourth quarter)
3 By many players

Most Consecutive Games Scoring Field Goals
38 Matt Stover, Baltimore, 1999-2001
31 Fred Cox, Minnesota, 1968-1970
28 Jim Turner, N.Y. Jets, 1970; Denver, 1971-72
Chip Lohmiller, Washington, 1988-1990

Most Consecutive Field Goals
42 Mike Vanderjagt, Indianapolis, 2002-04
40 Gary Anderson, San Francisco, 1997; Minnesota,
1998
36 Matt Stover, Baltimore, 2005-06

Longest Field Goal
63 Tom Dempsey, New Orleans vs. Detroit, Nov. 8, 1970
Jason Elam, Denver vs. Jacksonville, Oct. 25, 1998
62 Matt Bryant, Tampa Bay vs. Philadelphia,
Oct. 22, 2006
61 Sebastian Janikowski, Oakland vs. Cleveland,
Dec. 27, 2009

Highest Field Goal Pct., Career (100 field goals)
86.50 Nate Kaeding, San Diego, 2004-2010 (173-200)
86.47 Mike Vanderjagt, Indianapolis, 1998-2005; Dallas,
2006 (230-266)
85.95 Shayne Graham, Buffalo, 2001; Carolina, 2002;
Cincinnati, 2003-09; N.Y. Giants, 2010; New
England, 2010 (208-242)

Highest Field Goal Pct., Season (Qualifiers)
100.00 Tony Zendejas, L.A. Rams, 1991 (17-17)
Gary Anderson, Minnesota, 1998 (35-35)
Jeff Wilkins, St. Louis, 2000 (17-17)
Mike Vanderjagt, Indianapolis, 2003 (37-37)
96.43 Chris Boniol, Dallas, 1995 (28-27)
96.30 Norm Johnson, Atlanta, 1993 (27-26)
Pete Stoyanovich, Kansas City, 1997 (27-26)

Most Field Goals, No Misses, Game
8 Rob Bironas, Tennessee vs. Houston, Oct. 21, 2007
7 Rich Karlis, Minnesota vs. L.A. Rams, Nov. 5, 1989
(ot)
Chris Boniol, Dallas vs. Green Bay, Nov. 18, 1996
Shayne Graham, Cincinnati vs. Baltimore,
Nov. 11, 2007
6 By many players

Most Field Goals, 50 or More Yards, Career
45 Jason Hanson, Detroit, 1992-2010
40 Morten Andersen, New Orleans, 1982-1994;
Atlanta, 1995-2000; N.Y. Giants, 2001;
Kansas City, 2002-03; Minnesota, 2004;
Atlanta, 2006-07
John Kasay, Seattle, 1991-94; Carolina, 1995-99,
2001-2010
39 Jason Elam, Denver, 1993-2007; Atlanta, 2008-09

Most Field Goals, 50 or More Yards, Season
8 Morten Andersen, Atlanta, 1995
Jason Hanson, Detroit, 2008
6 Dean Biasucci, Indianapolis, 1988
Chris Jacke, Green Bay, 1993
Tony Zendejas, L.A. Rams, 1993
Mike Vanderjagt, Indianapolis, 1998
Neil Rackers, Arizona, 2005
Sebastian Janikowski, Oakland, 2007
Josh Brown, St. Louis, 2008
Ryan Longwell, Minnesota, 2008
Josh Brown, St. Louis, 2009
Sebastian Janikowski, Oakland, 2009
5 Fred Steinfort, Denver, 1980
Norm Johnson, Seattle, 1986
Kevin Butler, Chicago, 1993
Jason Elam, Denver, 1995, 1999
Cary Blanchard, Indianapolis, 1996
Martin Gramatica, Tampa Bay, 2000, 2002
Paul Edinger, Chicago, 2002
Neil Rackers, Arizona, 2004
Josh Brown, Seattle, 2005
Kris Brown, Houston, 2007
Matt Prater, Denver, 2000
Rob Bironas, Tennessee, 2009

Most Field Goals, 50 or More Yards, Game
3 Morten Andersen, Atlanta vs. New Orleans,
Dec. 10, 1995
Neil Rackers, Arizona vs. Seattle, Oct. 24, 2004
Kris Brown, Houston vs. Miami, Oct. 7, 2007
Conner Barth, Tampa Bay vs. Miami, Nov. 15, 2009
2 By many players. Last time: Sebastian Janikowski,
Oakland vs. Indianapolis, Dec. 26, 2010

SAFETIES
Most Safeties, Career
4 Ted Hendricks, Baltimore, 1969-1973; Green Bay,
1974; Oakland, 1975-1981; L.A. Raiders, 1982-83
Doug English, Detroit, 1975-79, 1981-85
3 Bill McPeak, Pittsburgh, 1949-1957
Charlie Krueger, San Francisco, 1959-1973
Ernie Stautner, Pittsburgh, 1950-1963
Jim Katcavage, N.Y. Giants, 1956-1968
Roger Brown, Detroit, 1960-66; Los Angeles,
1967-69
Bruce Maher, Detroit, 1960-67; N.Y. Giants, 1968-69
Ron McDole, St. Louis, 1961; Houston, 1962;
Buffalo, 1963-1970; Washington, 1971-78
Alan Page, Minnesota, 1967-1978; Chicago,
1979-1981
Lyle Alzado, Denver, 1971-78; Cleveland,
1979-1981; L.A. Raiders, 1982-85
Rulon Jones, Denver, 1980-88
Steve McMichael, New England, 1980; Chicago,
1981-1993; Green Bay, 1994
Kevin Greene, L.A. Rams, 1985-1992; Pittsburgh,
1993-95; Carolina, 1996, 1998-99;
San Francisco, 1997
Burt Grossman, San Diego, 1989-1993;
Philadelphia, 1994
Eric Swann, Phoenix, 1991-93; Arizona, 1994-99;
Carolina, 2000
Dan Saleaumua, Detroit, 1987-88; Kansas City,
1989-1996; Seattle, 1997-98
Derrick Thomas, Kansas City, 1989-1999
Bryant Young, San Francisco, 1994-2007
Jared Allen, Kansas City, 2004-07; Minnesota,
2008-2010
Jason Taylor, Miami, 1997-2007; Washington, 2008;
Miami, 2009; N.Y. Jets, 2010

2 By many players

Most Safeties, Season
2 Tom Nash, Green Bay, 1932
   Roger Brown, Detroit, 1962
   Ron McDole, Buffalo, 1964
   Alan Page, Minnesota, 1971
   Fred Dryer, Los Angeles, 1973
   Benny Barnes, Dallas, 1973
   James Young, Houston, 1977
   Doug English, Detroit, 1983
   Don Blackmon, New England, 1985
   Tim Harris, Green Bay, 1988
   Brian Jordan, Atlanta, 1991
   Burt Grossman, San Diego, 1992
   Rod Stephens, Seattle, 1993
   Bryant Young, San Francisco, 1996
   Jared Allen, Minnesota, 2008
   Jameel McClain, Baltimore, 2008

Most Safeties, Game
2 Fred Dryer, Los Angeles vs. Green Bay,
   Oct. 21, 1973

RUSHING

Most Seasons Leading League
8 Jim Brown, Cleveland, 1957-1961, 1963-65
4 Steve Van Buren, Philadelphia, 1945, 1947-49
   O.J. Simpson, Buffalo, 1972-73, 1975-76
   Eric Dickerson, L.A. Rams, 1983-84, 1986;
      Indianapolis, 1988
   Emmitt Smith, Dallas, 1991-93, 1995
   Barry Sanders, Detroit, 1990, 1994, 1996-97
3 Earl Campbell, Houston, 1978-1980

Most Consecutive Seasons Leading League
5 Jim Brown, Cleveland, 1957-1961
3 Steve Van Buren, Philadelphia, 1947-49
   Jim Brown, Cleveland, 1963-65
   Earl Campbell, Houston, 1978-1980
   Emmitt Smith, Dallas, 1991-93
2 By many players

ATTEMPTS

Most Seasons Leading League
6 Jim Brown, Cleveland, 1958-59, 1961, 1963-65
4 Steve Van Buren, Philadelphia, 1947-1950
   Walter Payton, Chicago, 1976-79
3 Cookie Gilchrist, Buffalo, 1963-64; Denver, 1965
   Jim Nance, Boston, 1966-67, 1969
   O.J. Simpson, Buffalo, 1973-75
   Eric Dickerson, L.A. Rams, 1983, 1986;
      Indianapolis, 1988
   Emmitt Smith, Dallas, 1991, 1994-95

Most Consecutive Seasons Leading League
4 Steve Van Buren, Philadelphia, 1947-1950
   Walter Payton, Chicago, 1976-79
3 Jim Brown, Cleveland, 1963-65
   Cookie Gilchrist, Buffalo, 1963-64; Denver, 1965
   O.J. Simpson, Buffalo, 1973-75
2 By many players

Most Attempts, Career
4,409 Emmitt Smith, Dallas, 1990-2002; Arizona, 2003-04
3,838 Walter Payton, Chicago, 1975-1987
3,518 Curtis Martin, New England, 1995-97; N.Y. Jets,
       1998-2005

Most Attempts, Season
416 Larry Johnson, Kansas City, 2006
410 Jamal Anderson, Atlanta, 1998
407 James Wilder, Tampa Bay, 1984

Most Attempts, Rookie, Season
390 Eric Dickerson, L.A. Rams, 1983
378 George Rogers, New Orleans, 1981

369 Edgerrin James, Indianapolis, 1999

Most Attempts, Game
45 Jamie Morris, Washington vs. Cincinnati,
    Dec. 17, 1988 (ot)
43 Butch Woolfolk, N.Y. Giants vs. Philadelphia,
    Nov. 20, 1983
    James Wilder, Tampa Bay vs. Green Bay,
    Sept. 30, 1984 (ot)
    Rudi Johnson, Cincinnati vs. Houston, Nov. 9, 2003
42 James Wilder, Tampa Bay vs. Pittsburgh,
    Oct. 30, 1983
    Terrell Davis, Denver vs. Buffalo, Oct. 26, 1997 (ot)
    Ricky Williams, Miami vs. Buffalo, Sept. 21, 2003

YARDS GAINED
Most Yards Gained, Career
18,355 Emmitt Smith, Dallas, 1990-2002; Arizona, 2003-04
16,726 Walter Payton, Chicago, 1975-1987
15,269 Barry Sanders, Detroit, 1989-1998

Most Seasons, 1,000 or More Yards Rushing
11 Emmitt Smith, Dallas, 1991-2001
10 Walter Payton, Chicago, 1976-1981, 1983-86
    Barry Sanders, Detroit, 1989-1998
    Curtis Martin, New England, 1995-97; N.Y. Jets,
       1998-2004
8   Franco Harris, Pittsburgh, 1972, 1974-79, 1983
    Tony Dorsett, Dallas, 1977-1981, 1983-85
    Thurman Thomas, Buffalo, 1989-1996
    Jerome Bettis, L.A. Rams, 1993-94; Pittsburgh,
       1996-2001
    LaDainian Tomlinson, San Diego, 2001-08

Most Consecutive Seasons, 1,000 or More Yards Rushing
11 Emmitt Smith, Dallas, 1991-2001
10 Barry Sanders, Detroit, 1989-1998
    Curtis Martin, New England, 1995-97; N.Y. Jets,
       1998-2004
8   Thurman Thomas, Buffalo, 1989-1996
    LaDainian Tomlinson, San Diego, 2001-08

Most Yards Gained, Season
2,105 Eric Dickerson, L.A. Rams, 1984
2,066 Jamal Lewis, Baltimore, 2003
2,053 Barry Sanders, Detroit, 1997

Most Yards Gained, Rookie, Season
1,808 Eric Dickerson, L.A. Rams, 1983
1,674 George Rogers, New Orleans, 1981
1,605 Ottis Anderson, St. Louis, 1979

Most Yards Gained, Game
296 Adrian Peterson, Minnesota vs. San Diego,
     Nov. 4, 2007
295 Jamal Lewis, Baltimore vs. Cleveland,
     Sept. 14, 2003
286 Jerome Harrison, Cleveland vs. Kansas City,
     Dec. 20, 2009

Most Games, 200 or More Yards Rushing, Career
6 O.J. Simpson, Buffalo, 1969-1977; San Francisco,
   1978-79
5 Tiki Barber, N.Y. Giants, 1997-2006
4 Jim Brown, Cleveland, 1957-1965
   Earl Campbell, Houston, 1978-1984; New Orleans,
      1984-85
   Barry Sanders, Detroit, 1989-1998
   LaDainian Tomlinson, San Diego, 2001-09;
      N.Y. Jets, 2010

Most Games, 200 or More Yards Rushing, Season
4 Earl Campbell, Houston, 1980
3 O.J. Simpson, Buffalo, 1973
   Tiki Barber, N.Y. Giants, 2005
2 Jim Brown, Cleveland, 1963
   O.J. Simpson, Buffalo, 1976
   Walter Payton, Chicago, 1977

Eric Dickerson, L.A. Rams, 1984
Greg Bell, L.A. Rams, 1989
Terrell Davis, Denver, 1997
Barry Sanders, Detroit, 1997
Corey Dillon, Cincinnati, 2000
Marshall Faulk, St. Louis, 2000
LaDainian Tomlinson, San Diego, 2002
Ricky Williams, Miami, 2002
Jamal Lewis, Baltimore, 2003
LaDainian Tomlinson, San Diego, 2003
Larry Johnson, Kansas City, 2005
Willie Parker, Pittsburgh, 2006
Adrian Peterson, Minnesota, 2007
Michael Turner, Atlanta, 2008

Most Consecutive Games, 200 or More Yards Rushing
2   O.J. Simpson, Buffalo, 1973, 1976
     Earl Campbell, Houston, 1980
     Ricky Williams, Miami, 2002

Most Games, 100 or more Yards Rushing, Career
78 Emmitt Smith, Dallas, 1990-2002; Arizona, 2003-04
77 Walter Payton, Chicago, 1975-1987
76 Barry Sanders, Detroit, 1989-1998

Most Games, 100 or More Yards Rushing, Season
14 Barry Sanders, Detroit, 1997
12 Eric Dickerson, L.A. Rams, 1984
     Barry Foster, Pittsburgh, 1992
     Jamal Anderson, Atlanta, 1998
     Jamal Lewis, Baltimore, 2003
     Chris Johnson, Tennessee, 2009
11 O.J. Simpson, Buffalo, 1973
     Earl Campbell, Houston, 1979
     Marcus Allen, L.A. Raiders, 1985
     Eric Dickerson, L.A. Rams, 1986
     Emmitt Smith, Dallas, 1995
     Terrell Davis, Denver, 1998
     Shaun Alexander, Seattle, 2005
     Larry Johnson, Kansas City, 2006

Most Consecutive Games, 100 or More Yards Rushing
14 Barry Sanders, Detroit, 1997
12 Chris Johnson, Tennessee, 2009-2010
11 Marcus Allen, L.A. Raiders, 1985-86

Longest Run from Scrimmage
99 Tony Dorsett, Dallas vs. Minnesota, Jan. 3, 1983
     (TD)
98 Ahman Green, Green Bay vs. Denver, Dec. 28, 2003
     (TD)
97 Andy Uram, Green Bay vs. Chi. Cardinals, Oct. 8,
     1939 (TD)
     Bob Gage, Pittsburgh vs. Chi. Bears, Dec. 4, 1949
     (TD)

AVERAGE GAIN
Highest Average Gain, Career (750 attempts)
6.36 Randall Cunningham, Philadelphia, 1985-1995;
       Minnesota, 1997-99; Dallas, 2000; Baltimore,
       2001 (775-4,928)
5.22 Jim Brown, Cleveland, 1957-1965 (2,359-12,312)
5.14 Mercury Morris, Miami, 1969-1975; San Diego,
       1976 (804-1,433)

Highest Average Gain, Season (Qualifiers)
8.45 Michael Vick, Atlanta, 2006 (123-1,039)
8.44 Beattie Feathers, Chi. Bears, 1934 (119-1,004)
7.98 Randall Cunningham, Philadelphia, 1990 (118-942)

Highest Average Gain, Game (10 attempts)
17.30 Michael Vick, Atlanta vs. Minnesota, Dec. 1, 2002
       (10-173)
17.09 Marion Motley, Cleveland vs. Pittsburgh, Oct. 29,
       1950 (11-188)
16.70 Billy Grimes, Green Bay vs. N.Y. Yanks, Oct. 8, 1950
       (10-167)

TOUCHDOWNS
Most Seasons Leading League
5 Jim Brown, Cleveland, 1957-59, 1963, 1965
4 Steve Van Buren, Philadelphia, 1945, 1947-49
3 Abner Haynes, Dall. Texans, 1960-62
   Cookie Gilchrist, Buffalo, 1962-64
   Paul Lowe, L.A. Chargers, 1960; San Diego, 1961,
     1965
   Leroy Kelly, Cleveland, 1966-68
   Emmitt Smith, Dallas, 1992, 1994-95
   LaDainian Tomlinson, San Diego, 2004, 2006-07

Most Consecutive Seasons Leading League
3 Steve Van Buren, Philadelphia, 1947-49
   Jim Brown, Cleveland, 1957-59
   Abner Haynes, Dall. Texans, 1960-62
   Cookie Gilchrist, Buffalo, 1962-64
   Leroy Kelly, Cleveland, 1966-68

Most Touchdowns, Career
164 Emmitt Smith, Dallas, 1990-2002; Arizona, 2003-04
144 LaDainian Tomlinson, San Diego, 2001-09;
      N.Y. Jets, 2010
123 Marcus Allen, L.A. Raiders, 1982-1992; Kansas City,
      1993-97

Most Rushing Touchdowns, Season
28 LaDainian Tomlinson, San Diego, 2006
27 Priest Holmes, Kansas City, 2003
   Shaun Alexander, Seattle, 2005
25 Emmitt Smith, Dallas, 1995

Most Touchdowns, Rookie, Season
18 Eric Dickerson, L.A. Rams, 1983
15 Ickey Woods, Cincinnati, 1988
   Mike Anderson, Denver, 2000
   Clinton Portis, Denver, 2002
14 Gale Sayers, Chicago, 1965
   Barry Sanders, Detroit, 1989
   Curtis Martin, New England, 1995
   Fred Taylor, Jacksonville, 1998

Most Touchdowns, Game
6 Ernie Nevers, Chi. Cardinals vs. Chi. Bears,
    Nov. 28, 1929
5 Jimmy Conzelman, Rhode Island vs. Evansville,
    Oct. 15, 1922
   Jim Brown, Cleveland vs. Baltimore, Nov. 1, 1959
   Cookie Gilchrist, Buffalo vs. N.Y. Jets, Dec. 8, 1963
   James Stewart, Jacksonville vs. Philadelphia,
    Oct. 12, 1997
   Clinton Portis, Denver vs. Kansas City, Dec. 7, 2003
4 By many players

Most Consecutive Games Rushing for Touchdowns
18 LaDainian Tomlinson, San Diego, 2004-05
13 John Riggins, Washington, 1982-83
   George Rogers, Washington, 1985-86
11 Lenny Moore, Baltimore, 1963-64
   Emmitt Smith, Dallas, 1994-95
   Emmitt Smith, Dallas, 1995
   Priest Holmes, Kansas City, 2002

PASSING
Most Seasons Leading League (Passer Rating)
6 Sammy Baugh, Washington, 1937, 1940, 1943,
    1945, 1947, 1949
   Steve Young San Francisco, 1991-94, 1996-97
4 Len Dawson, Dall. Texans; 1962; Kansas City, 1964,
    1966, 1968
   Roger Staubach, Dallas, 1971, 1973, 1978-79
   Ken Anderson, Cincinnati, 1974-75, 1981-82
3 Arnie Herber, Green Bay, 1932, 1934, 1936
   Norm Van Brocklin, Los Angeles, 1950, 1952, 1954
   Bart Starr, Green Bay, 1962, 1964, 1966

Peyton Manning, Indianapolis, 2004-06

Most Consecutive Seasons Leading League (Passer Rating)
- 4   Steve Young, San Francisco, 1991-94
- 3   Peyton Manning, Indianapolis, 2004-06
- 2   Cecil. Isbell, Green Bay, 1941-42
     Milt Plum, Cleveland, 1960-61
     Ken Anderson, Cincinnati, 1974-75, 1981-82
     Roger Staubach, Dallas, 1978-79
     Steve Young, San Francisco, 1996-97

PASSER RATING
Highest Passer Rating, Career (1,500 attempts)
- 98.4   Aaron Rodgers, Green Bay, 2005-2010
- 97.2   Philip Rivers, San Diego, 2004-2010
- 96.8   Steve Young, Tampa Bay, 1985-86; San Francisco, 1987-1999

Highest Passer Rating, Season (Qualifiers)
- 121.1   Peyton Manning, Indianapolis, 2004
- 117.2   Tom Brady, New England, 2007
- 112.8   Steve Young, San Francisco, 1994

Highest Passer Rating, Rookie, Season (Qualifiers)
- 98.1   Ben Roethlisberger, Pittsburgh, 2004
- 96.0   Dan Marino, Miami, 1983
- 88.3   Greg Cook, Cincinnati, 1969

ATTEMPTS
Most Seasons Leading League
- 5   Dan Marino, Miami, 1984, 1986, 1988, 1992, 1997
- 4   Sammy Baugh, Washington, 1937, 1943, 1947-48
     Johnny Unitas, Baltimore, 1957, 1959-1961
     George Blanda, Chi. Bears, 1953; Houston, 1963-65
- 3   Arnie Herber, Green Bay, 1932, 1934, 1936
     Sonny Jurgensen, Washington, 1966-67, 1969
     Drew Bledsoe, New England, 1994-96
     Brett Favre, Green Bay, 1999, 2005-06

Most Consecutive Seasons Leading League
- 3   Johnny Unitas, Baltimore, 1959-1961
     George Blanda, Houston, 1963-65
     Drew Bledsoe, New England, 1994-96
- 2   By many players

Most Passes Attempted, Career
- 10,169   Brett Favre, Atlanta, 1991; Green Bay, 1992-2007; N.Y. Jets, 2008; Minnesota, 2009-2010
- 8,358   Dan Marino, Miami, 1983-1999
- 7,250   John Elway, Denver, 1983-1998

Most Passes Attempted, Season
- 691   Drew Bledsoe, New England, 1994
- 679   Peyton Manning, Indianapolis, 2010
- 658   Drew Brees, New Orleans, 2010

Most Passes Attempted, Rookie, Season
- 590   Sam Bradford, St. Louis, 2010
- 575   Peyton Manning, Indianapolis, 1998
- 540   Chris Weinke, Carolina, 2001

Most Passes Attempted, Game
- 70   Drew Bledsoe, New England vs. Minnesota, Nov. 13, 1994
- 69   Vinny Testaverde, N.Y. Jets vs. Baltimore, Dec. 24, 2000
- 68   George Blanda, Houston vs. Buffalo, Nov. 1, 1964
     Jon Kitna, Cincinnati vs. Pittsburgh, Dec. 30, 2001

COMPLETIONS
Most Seasons Leading League
- 6   Dan Marino, Miami, 1984-86, 1988, 1992, 1997
- 5   Sammy Baugh, Washington, 1937, 1943, 1945, 1947-48
- 4   George Blanda, Chi. Bears, 1953; Houston, 1963-65
     Sonny Jurgensen, Philadelphia, 1961; Washington, 1966-67, 1969

Most Consecutive Seasons Leading League
- 3   George Blanda, Houston, 1963-65
     Dan Marino, Miami, 1984-86
- 2   By many players

Most Passes Completed, Career
- 6,300   Brett Favre, Atlanta, 1991; Green Bay, 1992-2007; N.Y. Jets, 2008, Minnesota, 2009-2010
- 4,967   Dan Marino, Miami, 1983-1999
- 4,682   Peyton Manning, Indianapolis, 1998-2010

Most Passes Completed, Season
- 450   Peyton Manning, Indianapolis, 2010
- 448   Drew Brees, New Orleans, 2010
- 440   Drew Brees, New Orleans, 2007

Most Passes Completed, Rookie, Season
- 354   Sam Bradford, St. Louis, 2010
- 326   Peyton Manning, Indianapolis, 1998
- 293   Chris Weinke, Carolina, 2001

Most Passes Completed, Game
- 45   Drew Bledsoe, New England vs. Minnesota, Nov. 13, 1994 (ot)
- 43   Rich Gannon, Oakland vs. Pittsburgh, Sept. 15, 2002
- 42   Richard Todd, N.Y. Jets vs. San Francisco, Sept. 21, 1980
     Vinny Testaverde, N.Y. Jets vs. Seattle, Dec. 6, 1998

Most Consecutive Passes Completed
- 24   Donovan McNabb, Philadelphia vs. N.Y. Giants (10), Nov. 28, 2004; vs. Green Bay (14), Dec. 5, 2004
- 23   Peyton Manning, Indianapolis vs. Detroit (6), Dec. 14, 2008; vs. Jacksonville (17), Dec. 18, 2008
- 22   Joe Montana, San Francisco vs. Cleveland (5), Nov. 29, 1987; vs. Green Bay (17), Dec. 6, 1987
     Mark Brunell, Washington vs. Houston, Sept. 24, 2006
     David Carr, Houston vs. Buffalo, Nov. 19, 2006

COMPLETION PERCENTAGE
Most Seasons Leading League
- 8   Len Dawson, Dall. Texans, 1962; Kansas City, 1964-69, 1975
- 7   Sammy Baugh, Washington, 1940, 1942-43, 1945, 1947-49
- 5   Joe Montana, San Francisco, 1980-81, 1985, 1987, 1989
     Steve Young, San Francisco, 1992, 1994-97

Most Consecutive Seasons Leading League
- 6   Len Dawson, Kansas City, 1964-69
- 4   Steve Young, San Francisco, 1994-97
- 3   Sammy Baugh, Washington, 1947-49
     Otto Graham, Cleveland, 1953-55
     Milt Plum, Cleveland, 1959-1961
     Kurt Warner, St. Louis, 1999-2001

Highest Completion Percentage, Career (1,500 attempts)
- 66.05   Chad Pennington, N.Y. Jets, 2000-07; Miami, 2008-2010 (2,471-1,632)
- 65.50   Kurt Warner, St. Louis, 1998-2003; N.Y. Giants, 2004; Arizona, 2005-09 (4,070-2,666)
- 65.22   Drew Brees, San Diego, 2001-05; New Orleans, 2006-2010 (4,822-3,145)

Highest Completion Percentage, Season (Qualifiers)
- 70.62   Drew Brees, New Orleans, 2009 (514-363)
- 70.55   Ken Anderson, Cincinnati, 1982 (309-218)
- 70.33   Sammy Baugh, Washington, 1945 (182-128)

Highest Completion Percentage, Rookie, Season (Qualifiers)
- 66.44   Ben Roethlisberger, Pittsburgh, 2004 (295-196)
- 61.06   Matt Ryan, Atlanta, 2008 (434-265)
- 60.05   Joe Flacco, Baltimore, 2008 (428-257)

Highest Completion Percentage, Game (20 attempts)
- 92.31   Kurt Warner, Arizona vs. Jacksonville, Sept. 20, 2009 (26-24)
- 91.30   Vinny Testaverde, Cleveland vs. L.A. Rams, Dec. 26, 1993 (23-21)
- 90.91   Ken Anderson, Cincinnati vs. Pittsburgh, Nov. 10, 1974 (22-20)

YARDS GAINED

Most Seasons Leading League
- 5   Sonny Jurgensen, Philadelphia, 1961-62; Washington, 1966-67, 1969
-    Dan Marino, Miami, 1984-86, 1988, 1992
- 4   Sammy Baugh, Washington, 1937, 1940, 1947-48
-    Johnny Unitas, Baltimore, 1957, 1959-1960, 1963
-    Dan Fouts, San Diego, 1979-1982
- 3   Arnie Herber, Green Bay, 1932, 1934, 1936
-    Sid Luckman, Chi. Bears, 1943, 1945-46
-    John Brodie, San Francisco, 1965, 1968, 1970
-    John Hadl, San Diego, 1965, 1968, 1971
-    Joe Namath, N.Y. Jets, 1966-67, 1972

Most Consecutive Seasons Leading League
- 4   Dan Fouts, San Diego, 1979-1982
- 3   Dan Marino, Miami, 1984-86
- 2   By many players

Most Yards Gained, Career
- 71,838   Brett Favre, Atlanta, 1991; Green Bay, 1992-2007; N.Y. Jets, 2008, Minnesota, 2009-2010
- 61,361   Dan Marino, Miami, 1983-1999
- 54,828   Peyton Manning, Indianapolis, 1998-2010

Most Seasons, 3,000 or More Yards Passing
- 18   Brett Favre, Green Bay, 1992-2007; N.Y. Jets, 2008; Minnesota, 2009
- 13   Dan Marino, Miami, 1984-1992, 1994-95, 1997-98
-    Peyton Manning, Indianapolis, 1998-2010
- 12   John Elway, Denver, 1985-1991, 1993-97

Most Yards Gained, Season
- 5,084   Dan Marino, Miami, 1984
- 5,069   Drew Brees, New Orleans, 2008
- 4,830   Kurt Warner, St. Louis, 2001

Most Yards Gained, Rookie, Season
- 3,739   Peyton Manning, Indianapolis, 1998
- 3,512   Sam Bradford, St. Louis, 2010
- 3,440   Matt Ryan, Atlanta, 2008

Most Yards Gained, Game
- 554   Norm Van Brocklin, Los Angeles vs. N.Y. Yanks, Sept. 28, 1951
- 527   Warren Moon, Houston vs. Kansas City, Dec. 16, 1990
- 522   Boomer Esiason, Arizona vs. Washington, Nov. 10, 1996 (ot)

Most Games, 400 or More Yards Passing, Career
- 13   Dan Marino, Miami, 1983-1999
- 8   Peyton Manning, Indianapolis, 1998-2010
- 7   Joe Montana, San Francisco, 1979-1990, 1992; Kansas City, 1993-94
-    Warren Moon, Houston, 1984-1993; Minnesota, 1994-96; Seattle, 1997-98; Kansas City, 1999-2000

Most Games, 400 or More Yards Passing, Season
- 4   Dan Marino, Miami, 1984
- 3   Dan Marino, Miami, 1986
- 2   By many players

Most Consecutive Games, 400 or More Yards Passing
- 2   Dan Fouts, San Diego, 1982
-    Dan Marino, Miami, 1984
-    Phil Simms, N.Y. Giants, 1985
-    Billy Volek, Tennessee, 2004
-    Matt Cassel, New England, 2008

Most Games, 300 or More Yards Passing, Career
- 63   Dan Marino, Miami, 1983-1999
-    Peyton Manning, Indianapolis, 1998-2010
- 62   Brett Favre, Atlanta, 1991; Green Bay, 1992-2007; N.Y. Jets, 2008; Minnesota, 2009-2010
- 52   Kurt Warner, St. Louis, 1998-2003; N.Y. Giants, 2004; Arizona, 2005-09

Most Games, 300 or More Yards Passing, Season
- 10   Rich Gannon, Oakland, 2002
-    Drew Brees, New Orleans, 2008
- 9   Dan Marino, Miami, 1984
-    Warren Moon, Houston, 1990
-    Kurt Warner, St. Louis, 1999
-    Kurt Warner, St. Louis, 2001
-    Peyton Manning, Indianapolis, 2009
-    Matt Schaub, Houston, 2009
- 8   Dan Fouts, San Diego, 1980
-    Kurt Warner, St. Louis, 2000
-    Trent Green, Kansas City, 2004
-    Marc Bulger, St. Louis, 2006
-    Drew Brees, New Orleans, 2006
-    Tom Brady, New England, 2007
-    Jay Cutler, Denver, 2008
-    Tony Romo, Dallas, 2009

Most Consecutive Games, 300 or More Yards Passing
- 6   Steve Young, San Francisco, 1998
-    Kurt Warner, St. Louis, 2000
-    Rich Gannon, Oakland, 2002
- 5   Joe Montana, San Francisco, 1982
-    Kerry Collins, N.Y. Giants, 2001-02
-    Drew Brees, New Orleans, 2006
-    Kurt Warner, Arizona, 2008
-    Tom Brady, New England, 2009
-    Peyton Manning, Indianapolis, 2009
- 4   Dan Fouts, San Diego, 1979
-    Dan Fouts, San Diego, 1980-81
-    Bill Kenney, Kansas City, 1983
-    Joe Montana, San Francisco, 1985-86
-    Joe Montana, San Francisco, 1990
-    Warren Moon, Houston, 1990
-    Drew Bledsoe, New England, 1993-94
-    Kurt Warner, St. Louis, 1999
-    Brian Griese, Denver, 2002
-    Daunte Culpepper, Minnesota, 2004
-    Trent Green, Kansas City, 2004
-    Drew Brees, New Orleans, 2008-09
-    Kyle Orton, Denver, 2010
-    Matt Schaub, Houston, 2010

Longest Pass Completion (All TDs except as noted)
- 99   Frank Filchock (to Farkas), Washington vs. Pittsburgh, Oct. 15, 1939
-    George Izo (to Mitchell), Washington vs. Cleveland, Sept. 15, 1963
-    Karl Sweetan (to Studstill), Detroit vs. Baltimore, Oct. 16, 1966
-    Sonny Jurgensen (to Allen), Washington vs. Chicago, Sept. 15, 1968
-    Jim Plunkett (to Branch), L.A. Raiders vs. Washington, Oct. 2, 1983
-    Ron Jaworski (to Quick), Philadelphia vs. Atlanta, Nov. 10, 1985
-    Stan Humphries (to Martin), San Diego vs. Seattle, Sept. 18, 1994
-    Brett Favre (to Brooks), Green Bay vs. Chicago, Sept. 11, 1995
-    Trent Green (to Boerigter), Kansas City vs. San Diego, Dec. 22, 2002
-    Jeff Garcia (to Davis), Cleveland vs. Cincinnati, Oct. 17, 2004

Gus Frerotte (to Berrian), Minnesota vs. Chicago,
Nov. 30, 2008

98 Doug Russell (to Tinsley), Chi. Cardinals vs.
Cleveland, Nov. 27, 1938
Ogden Compton (to Lane), Chi. Cardinals vs.
Green Bay, Nov. 13, 1955
Bill Wade (to Farrington), Chicago Bears vs. Detroit,
Oct. 8, 1961
Jacky Lee (to Dewveall), Houston vs. San Diego,
Nov. 25, 1962
Earl Morrall (to Jones), N.Y. Giants vs. Pittsburgh,
Sept. 11, 1966
Jim Hart (to Rashad), St. Louis vs. Los Angeles,
Dec. 10, 1972 (no TD)
Bobby Hebert (to Haynes), Atlanta vs. New Orleans,
Sept. 12, 1993
Charlie Batch (to Morton), Detroit vs. Chicago,
Oct. 4, 1998
Ryan Fitzpatrick (to Owens), Buffalo vs. Jacksonville,
Nov. 22, 2009

97 Pat Coffee (to Tinsley), Chi. Cardinals vs. Chi. Bears,
Dec. 5, 1937
Bobby Layne (to Box), Detroit vs. Green Bay,
Nov. 26, 1953
George Shaw (to Tarr), Denver vs. Boston,
Sept. 21, 1962
Bernie Kosar (to Slaughter), Cleveland vs. Chicago,
Oct. 23, 1989
Steve Young (to Taylor), San Francisco vs. Atlanta,
Nov. 3, 1991

AVERAGE GAIN
Most Seasons Leading League
7   Sid Luckman, Chi. Bears, 1939-1943, 1946-47
5   Steve Young, San Francisco, 1991-94, 1997
3   Arnie Herber, Green Bay, 1932, 1934, 1936
Norm Van Brocklin, Los Angeles, 1950, 1952, 1954
Len Dawson, Dall. Texans, 1962; Kansas City, 1966,
1968
Bart Starr, Green Bay, 1966-68
Kurt Warner, St. Louis, 1999-2001
Philip Rivers, San Diego, 2008-2010

Most Consecutive Seasons Leading League
5   Sid Luckman, Chi. Bears, 1939-1943
4   Steve Young, San Francisco, 1991-94
3   Bart Starr, Green Bay, 1966-68
Kurt Warner, St. Louis, 1999-2001
Philip Rivers, San Diego, 2008-2010

Highest Average Gain, Career (1,500 Attempts)
8.63 Otto Graham, Cleveland, 1950-55 (1,565-13,499)
8.42 Sid Luckman, Chi. Bears, 1939-1950 (1,744-
14,686)
8.16 Norm Van Brocklin, Los Angeles, 1949-1957;
Philadelphia, 1958-1960 (2,895-23,611)

Highest Average Gain, Season (Qualifiers)
11.17 Tommy O'Connell, Cleveland, 1957 (110-1,229)
10.86 Sid Luckman, Chi. Bears, 1943 (202-2,194)
10.55 Otto Graham, Cleveland, 1953 (258-2,722)

Highest Average Gain, Rookie, Season (Qualifiers)
9.411 Greg Cook, Cincinnati, 1969 (197-1,854)
9.409 Bob Waterfield, Cleveland, 1945 (171-1,609)
8.88 Ben Roethlisberger, Pittsburgh, 2004 (295-2,621)

Highest Average Gain, Game (20 attempts)
18.58 Sammy Baugh, Washington vs. Boston,
Oct. 31, 1948 (24-446)
18.50 Johnny Unitas, Baltimore vs. Atlanta, Nov. 12, 1967
(20-370)
17.71 Joe Namath, N.Y. Jets vs. Baltimore, Sept. 24, 1972
(28-496)

TOUCHDOWNS
Most Seasons Leading League
4   Johnny Unitas, Baltimore, 1957-1960
Len Dawson, Dall. Texans, 1962; Kansas City, 1963,
1965-66
Steve Young, San Francisco, 1992-94, 1998
Brett Favre, Green Bay, 1995-97, 2003
3   Arnie Herber, Green Bay, 1932, 1934, 1936
Sid Luckman, Chi. Bears, 1943, 1945-46
Y.A. Tittle, San Francisco, 1955; N.Y. Giants, 1962-63
Dan Marino, Miami, 1984-86
Peyton Manning, Indianapolis, 2000, 2004, 2006
Tom Brady, New England, 2002, 2007, 2010
2   By many players

Most Consecutive Seasons Leading League
4   Johnny Unitas, Baltimore, 1957-1960
3   Dan Marino, Miami, 1984-86
Steve Young, San Francisco, 1992-94
Brett Favre, Green Bay, 1995-97
2   By many players

Most Touchdown Passes, Career
508 Brett Favre, Atlanta, 1991; Green Bay, 1992-2007;
N.Y. Jets, 2008, Minnesota, 2009-2010
420 Dan Marino, Miami, 1983-1999
399 Peyton Manning, Indianapolis, 1998-2010

Most Touchdown Passes, Season
50 Tom Brady, New England, 2007
49 Peyton Manning, Indianapolis, 2004
48 Dan Marino, Miami, 1984

Most Touchdown Passes, Rookie, Season
26 Peyton Manning, Indianapolis, 1998
22 Charlie Conerly, N.Y. Giants, 1948
20 Dan Marino, Miami, 1983

Most Touchdown Passes, Game
7   Sid Luckman, Chi. Bears vs. N.Y. Giants,
Nov. 14, 1943
Adrian Burk, Philadelphia vs. Washington,
Oct. 17, 1954
George Blanda, Houston vs. N.Y. Titans,
Nov. 19, 1961
Y.A. Tittle, N.Y. Giants vs. Washington, Oct. 28, 1962
Joe Kapp, Minnesota vs. Baltimore, Sept. 28, 1969
6   By many players. Last time:
Tom Brady, New England vs. Tennessee,
Oct. 18, 2009

Most Games, Four or More Touchdown Passes, Career
23 Brett Favre, Atlanta, 1991; Green Bay, 1992-2007;
N.Y. Jets, 2008; Minnesota, 2009-2010
22 Peyton Manning, Indianapolis, 1998-2010
21 Dan Marino, Miami, 1983-1999

Most Games, Four or More Touchdown Passes, Season
6   Dan Marino, Miami, 1984
Peyton Manning, Indianapolis, 2004
5   Dan Marino, Miami, 1986
Brett Favre, Green Bay, 1996
Donovan McNabb, Philadelphia, 2004
Tom Brady, New England, 2007
4   George Blanda, Houston, 1961
Vince Ferragamo, Los Angeles, 1980
Steve Young, San Francisco, 1994
Randall Cunningham, Minnesota, 1998
Daunte Culpepper, Minnesota, 2004
Tony Romo, Dallas, 2007
Peyton Manning, Indianapolis, 2009

Most Consecutive Games, Four or More Touchdown Passes
5   Peyton Manning, Indianapolis, 2004
4   Dan Marino, Miami, 1984
2   By many players

Most Consecutive Games, Touchdown Passes
- 47   Johnny Unitas, Baltimore, 1956-1960
- 36   Brett Favre, Green Bay, 2002-2004
- 30   Dan Marino, Miami, 1985-87

HAD INTERCEPTED

Most Consecutive Passes Attempted, None Intercepted
- 335   Tom Brady, New England, 2010 (current)
- 308   Bernie Kosar, Cleveland, 1990-91
- 294   Bart Starr, Green Bay, 1964-65

Most Passes Had Intercepted, Career
- 336   Brett Favre, Atlanta, 1991; Green Bay, 1992-2007; N.Y. Jets, 2008; Minnesota, 2009-2010
- 277   George Blanda, Chi. Bears, 1949, 1950-58; Baltimore, 1950; Houston, 1960-66; Oakland, 1967-1975
- 268   John Hadl, San Diego, 1962-1972; Los Angeles, 1973-74; Green Bay, 1974-75; Houston, 1976-77

Most Passes Had Intercepted, Season
- 42   George Blanda, Houston, 1962
- 35   Vinny Testaverde, Tampa Bay, 1988
- 34   Frank Tripucka, Denver, 1960

Most Passes Had Intercepted, Game
- 8   Jim Hardy, Chi. Cardinals vs. Philadelphia, Sept. 24, 1950
- 7   Parker Hall, Cleveland vs. Green Bay, Nov. 8, 1942
    Frank Sinkwich, Detroit vs. Green Bay, Oct. 24, 1943
    Bob Waterfield, Los Angeles vs. Green Bay, Oct. 17, 1948
    Zeke Bratkowski, Chicago vs. Baltimore, Oct. 2, 1960
    Tommy Wade, Pittsburgh vs. Philadelphia, Dec. 12, 1965
    Ken Stabler, Oakland vs. Denver, Oct. 16, 1977
    Steve DeBerg, Tampa Bay vs. San Francisco, Sept. 7, 1986
    Ty Detmer, Detroit vs. Cleveland, Sept. 23, 2001
- 6   By many players

Most Attempts, No Interceptions, Game
- 70   Drew Bledsoe, New England vs. Minnesota, Nov. 13, 1994 (ot)
- 63   Rich Gannon, Minnesota vs. New England, Oct. 20, 1991 (ot)
- 60   Davey O'Brien, Philadelphia vs. Washington, Dec. 1, 1940

LOWEST PERCENTAGE, PASSES HAD INTERCEPTED

Most Seasons Leading League, Lowest Percentage, Passes Had Intercepted
- 5   Sammy Baugh, Washington, 1940, 1942, 1944-45, 1947
- 3   Charlie Conerly, N.Y. Giants, 1950, 1956, 1959
    Bart Starr, Green Bay, 1962, 1964, 1966
    Roger Staubach, Dallas, 1971, 1977, 1979
    Ken Anderson, Cincinnati, 1972, 1981-82
    Ken O'Brien, N.Y. Jets, 1985, 1987-88
- 2   By many players

Lowest Pct., Passes Had Intercepted, Career (1,500 attempts)
- 1.99   Aaron Rodgers, Green Bay, 2005-2010 (1,611-32)
- 2.11   Neil O'Donnell, Pittsburgh, 1991-95; N.Y. Jets, 1996-97; Cincinnati, 1998; Tennessee, 1999-2003 (3,229-68)
- 2.19   Tom Brady, New England, 2000-2010 (4,710-103)

Lowest Pct., Passes Had Intercepted, Season (Qualifiers)
- 0.41   Damon Huard, Kansas City, 2006 (244-1)
- 0.66   Joe Ferguson, Buffalo, 1976 (151-1)
- 0.81   Tom Brady, New England, 2010 (492-4)

Lowest Pct., Passes Had Intercepted, Rookie, Season (Qualifiers)
- 1.98   Charlie Batch, Detroit, 1998 (303-6)

- 2.03   Dan Marino, Miami, 1983 (296-6)
- 2.10   Gary Wood, N.Y. Giants, 1964 (143-3)

TIMES SACKED

Times Sacked has been compiled since 1963.

Most Times Sacked, Career
- 525   Brett Favre, Atlanta, 1991; Green Bay, 1992-2007; N.Y. Jets, 2008; Minnesota, 2009-2010
- 516   John Elway, Denver, 1983-1998
- 494   Dave Krieg, Seattle, 1980-1991; Kansas City, 1992-93; Detroit, 1994; Arizona, 1995; Chicago, 1996; Tennessee, 1997-98

Most Times Sacked, Season
- 76   David Carr, Houston, 2002
- 72   Randall Cunningham, Philadelphia, 1986
- 68   David Carr, Houston, 2005

Most Times Sacked, Game
- 12   Bert Jones, Baltimore vs. St. Louis, Oct. 26, 1980
    Warren Moon, Houston vs. Dallas, Sept. 29, 1985
    Donovan McNabb, Philadelphia vs. N.Y. Giants, Sept. 30, 2007
- 11   Charley Johnson, St. Louis vs. N.Y. Giants, Nov. 1, 1964
    Bart Starr, Green Bay vs. Detroit, Nov. 7, 1965
    Jack Kemp, Buffalo vs. Oakland, Oct. 15, 1967
    Bob Berry, Atlanta vs. St. Louis, Nov. 24, 1968
    Greg Landry, Detroit vs. Dallas, Oct. 6, 1975
    Ron Jaworski, Philadelphia vs. St. Louis, Dec. 18, 1983
    Paul McDonald, Cleveland vs. Kansas City, Sept. 30, 1984
    Archie Manning, Minnesota vs. Chicago, Oct. 28, 1984
    Steve Pelluer, Dallas vs. San Diego, Nov. 16, 1986
    Randall Cunningham, Philadelphia vs. L.A. Raiders, Nov. 30, 1986 (ot)
    David Norrie, N.Y. Jets vs. Dallas, Oct. 4, 1987
    Troy Aikman, Dallas vs. Philadelphia, Sept. 15, 1991
    Bernie Kosar, Cleveland vs. Indianapolis, Sept. 6, 1992
- 10   By many players

RECEIVING

Most Seasons Leading League
- 8   Don Hutson, Green Bay, 1936-37, 1939, 1941-45
- 5   Lionel Taylor, Denver, 1960-63, 1965
- 3   Tom Fears, Los Angeles, 1948-1950
    Pete Pihos, Philadelphia, 1953-55
    Billy Wilson, San Francisco, 1954, 1956-57
    Raymond Berry, Baltimore, 1958-1960
    Lance Alworth, San Diego, 1966, 1968-69
    Sterling Sharpe, Green Bay, 1989, 1992-93

Most Consecutive Seasons Leading League
- 5   Don Hutson, Green Bay, 1941-45
- 4   Lionel Taylor, Denver, 1960-63
- 3   Tom Fears, Los Angeles, 1948-1950
    Pete Pihos, Philadelphia, 1953-55
    Raymond Berry, Baltimore, 1958-1960

Most Pass Receptions, Career
- 1,549   Jerry Rice, San Francisco, 1985-2000; Oakland, 2001-04; Seattle, 2004
- 1,102   Marvin Harrison, Indianapolis, 1996-2008
- 1,101   Cris Carter, Philadelphia, 1987-89; Minnesota, 1990-2001; Miami, 2002

Most Seasons, 50 or More Pass Receptions
- 17   Jerry Rice, San Francisco, 1986-1996, 1998-2000; Oakland, 2001-03
- 13   Andre Reed, Buffalo, 1986-1994, 1996-99
    Tony Gonzalez, Kansas City, 1998-2008; Atlanta, 2009-2010

      Terrell Owens, San Francisco, 1997-2003;
        Philadelphia, 2004; Dallas, 2006-08;
        Buffalo, 2009; Cincinnati, 2010
  12 Isaac Bruce, St. Louis, 1995-97, 1999-2004,
        2006-07; San Francisco, 2008
      Marvin Harrison, Indianapolis, 1996-2006, 2008

Most Pass Receptions, Season
- 143 Marvin Harrison, Indianapolis, 2002
- 123 Herman Moore, Detroit, 1995
      Wes Welker, New England, 2009
- 122 Cris Carter, Minnesota, 1994
      Jerry Rice, San Francisco, 1995
      Cris Carter, Minnesota, 1995

Most Pass Receptions, Rookie, Season
- 101 Anquan Boldin, Arizona, 2003
- 91 Eddie Royal, Denver, 2008
- 90 Terry Glenn, New England, 1996

Most Pass Receptions, Game
- 21 Brandon Marshall, Denver vs. Indianapolis, Dec. 13, 2009
- 20 Terrell Owens, San Francisco vs. Chicago, Dec. 17, 2000
- 18 Tom Fears, Los Angeles vs. Green Bay, Dec. 3, 1950
      Brandon Marshall, Denver vs. San Diego, Sept. 14, 2008

Most Consecutive Games, Pass Receptions
- 274 Jerry Rice, San Francisco, 1985-2000; Oakland, 2001-04
- 190 Marvin Harrison, Indianapolis, 1996-2008
- 186 Hines Ward, Pittsburgh, 1998-2010

YARDS GAINED
Most Seasons Leading League
- 7 Don Hutson, Green Bay, 1936, 1938-39, 1941-44
- 6 Jerry Rice, San Francisco, 1986, 1989-1990, 1993-95
- 3 Raymond Berry, Baltimore, 1957, 1959-1960
    Lance Alworth, San Diego, 1965-66, 1968

Most Consecutive Seasons Leading League
- 4 Don Hutson, Green Bay, 1941-44
- 3 Jerry Rice, San Francisco, 1993-95
- 2 By many players

Most Yards Gained, Career
- 22,895 Jerry Rice, San Francisco, 1985-2000; Oakland, 2001-04; Seattle, 2004
- 15,934 Terrell Owens, San Francisco, 1996-2003; Philadelphia, 2004-05; Dallas, 2006-08; Buffalo, 2009; Cincinnati, 2010
- 15,208 Isaac Bruce, L.A. Rams, 1994; St. Louis, 1995-2007; San Francisco, 2008-09

Most Seasons, 1,000 or More Yards, Pass Receiving
- 14 Jerry Rice, San Francisco, 1986-1996, 1998; Oakland, 2001-02
- 10 Randy Moss, Minnesota, 1998-2003; Oakland, 2005; New England, 2007-09
- 9 Tim Brown, L.A. Raiders, 1993-94; Oakland, 1995-2001
    Jimmy Smith, Jacksonville, 1996-2002, 2004-05
    Terrell Owens, San Francisco, 1998, 2000-03; Philadelphia, 2004; Dallas, 2006-08

Most Yards Gained, Season
- 1,848 Jerry Rice, San Francisco, 1995
- 1,781 Isaac Bruce, St. Louis, 1995
- 1,746 Charley Hennigan, Houston, 1961

Most Yards Gained, Rookie, Season
- 1,473 Bill Groman, Houston, 1960
- 1,377 Anquan Boldin, Arizona, 2003
- 1,313 Randy Moss, Minnesota, 1998

Most Yards Gained, Game
- 336 Flipper Anderson, L.A. Rams vs. New Orleans, Nov. 26, 1989
- 309 Stephone Paige, Kansas City vs. San Diego, Dec. 22, 1985
- 303 Jim Benton, Cleveland vs. Detroit, Nov. 22, 1945

Most Games, 200 or More Yards Pass Receiving, Career
- 5 Lance Alworth, San Diego, 1962-1970; Dallas, 1971-72
- 4 Don Hutson, Green Bay, 1935-45
    Charley Hennigan, Houston, 1960-66
    Jerry Rice, San Francisco, 1985-2000; Oakland, 2001-04; Seattle, 2004
- 3 Don Maynard, N.Y. Giants, 1958; N.Y. Jets, 1960-1972; St. Louis, 1973
    Wes Chandler, New Orleans, 1978-1981; San Diego, 1981-87; San Francisco, 1988
    Isaac Bruce, L.A. Rams, 1994; St. Louis, 1995-2007; San Francisco, 2008
    Terrell Owens, San Francisco, 1996-2003; Philadelphia, 2004-05; Dallas, 2006-08; Buffalo, 2009; Cincinnati, 2010

Most Games, 200 or More Yards Pass Receiving, Season
- 3 Charley Hennigan, Houston, 1961
- 2 Don Hutson, Green Bay, 1942
    Gene Roberts, N.Y. Giants, 1949
    Lance Alworth, San Diego, 1963
    Don Maynard, N.Y. Jets, 1968

Most Games, 100 or More Yards Pass Receiving, Career
- 76 Jerry Rice, San Francisco, 1985-2000; Oakland, 2001-04; Seattle, 2004
- 64 Randy Moss, Minnesota, 1998-2004; Oakland, 2005-06; New England, 2007-2010; Minnesota, 2010; Tennessee, 2010
- 59 Marvin Harrison, Indianapolis, 1996-2008

Most Games, 100 or More Yards Pass Receiving, Season
- 11 Michael Irvin, Dallas, 1995
- 10 Charley Hennigan, Houston, 1961
    Herman Moore, Detroit, 1995
    Marvin Harrison, Indianapolis, 2002
    Torry Holt, St. Louis, 2003
- 9 Elroy (Crazylegs) Hirsch, Los Angeles, 1951
    Bill Groman, Houston, 1960
    Lance Alworth, San Diego, 1965
    Don Maynard, N.Y. Jets, 1967
    Stanley Morgan, New England, 1986
    Mark Carrier, Tampa Bay, 1989
    Robert Brooks, Green Bay, 1995
    Isaac Bruce, St. Louis, 1995
    Jerry Rice, San Francisco, 1995
    Marvin Harrison, Indianapolis, 1999
    Jimmy Smith, Jacksonville, 1999
    David Boston, Arizona, 2001
    Steve Smith, Carolina, 2005
    Randy Moss, New England, 2007

Most Consecutive Games, 100 or More Yards Pass Receiving
- 7 Charley Hennigan, Houston, 1961
    Michael Irvin, Dallas, 1995
- 6 Raymond Berry, Baltimore, 1960
    Bill Groman, Houston, 1961
    Pat Studstill, Detroit, 1966
    Isaac Bruce, St. Louis, 1995
- 5 Elroy (Crazylegs) Hirsch, Los Angeles, 1951
    Bob Boyd, Los Angeles, 1954
    Terry Barr, Detroit, 1963
    Lance Alworth, San Diego, 1966
    Don Maynard, N.Y. Jets, 1968-69
    Harold Jackson, Philadelphia, 1971-72
    Patrick Jeffers, Carolina, 1999
    Terrell Owens, Philadelphia, 2004

Anquan Boldin, Arizona, 2005

Longest Pass Reception (All TDs except as noted)

99 Andy Farkas (from Filchock), Washington vs. Pittsburgh, Oct. 15, 1939

Bobby Mitchell (from Izo), Washington vs. Cleveland, Sept. 15, 1963

Pat Studstill (from Sweetan), Detroit vs. Baltimore, Oct. 16, 1966

Gerry Allen (from Jurgensen), Washington vs. Chicago, Sept. 15, 1968

Cliff Branch (from Plunkett), L.A. Raiders vs. Washington, Oct. 2, 1983

Mike Quick (from Jaworski), Philadelphia vs. Atlanta, Nov. 10, 1985

Tony Martin (from Humphries), San Diego vs. Seattle, Sept. 18, 1994

Robert Brooks (from Favre), Green Bay vs. Chicago, Sept. 11, 1995

Marc Boerigter (from Green), Kansas City vs. San Diego, Dec. 22, 2002

Andre Davis (from Garcia), Cleveland vs. Cincinnati, Oct. 17, 2004

Bernard Berrian (from Frerotte), Minnesota vs. Chicago, Nov. 30, 2008

98 Gaynell Tinsley (from Russell), Chi. Cardinals vs. Cleveland, Nov. 17, 1938

Dick (Night Train) Lane (from Compton), Chi. Cardinals vs. Green Bay, Nov. 13, 1955

John Farrington (from Wade), Chicago vs. Detroit, Oct. 8, 1961

Willard Dewveall (from Lee), Houston vs. San Diego, Nov. 25, 1962

Homer Jones (from Morrall), N.Y. Giants vs. Pittsburgh, Sept. 11, 1966

Ahmad Rashad (from Hart), St. Louis vs. Los Angeles, Dec. 10, 1972 (no TD)

Michael Haynes (from Hebert), Atlanta vs. New Orleans, Sept. 12, 1993

Johnnie Morton (from Batch), Detroit vs. Chicago, Oct. 4, 1998

Terrell Owens (from Fitzpatrick), Buffalo vs. Jacksonville, Nov. 22, 2009

97 Gaynell Tinsley (from Coffee), Chi. Cardinals vs. Chi. Bears, Dec. 5, 1937

Cloyce Box (from Layne), Detroit vs. Green Bay, Nov. 26, 1953

Jerry Tarr (from Shaw), Denver vs. Boston, Sept. 21, 1962

Webster Slaughter (from Kosar), Cleveland vs. Chicago, Oct. 23, 1989

John Taylor (from Young), San Francisco vs. Atlanta, Nov. 3, 1991

AVERAGE GAIN

Highest Avg. Gain, Career (200 receptions)

22.26 Homer Jones, N.Y. Giants, 1964-69; Cleveland, 1970 (224-4,986)

20.83 Buddy Dial, Pittsburgh, 1959-1963; Dallas, 1964-66 (261-5,436)

20.24 Harlon Hill, Chi. Bears, 1954-1961; Pittsburgh, 1962; Detroit, 1962 (233-4,717)

Highest Avg. Gain, Season (24 receptions)

32.58 Don Currivan, Boston, 1947 (24-782)

31.44 Bucky Pope, Los Angeles, 1964 (25-786)

28.60 Bobby Duckworth, San Diego, 1984 (25-715)

Highest Average Gain, Game (3 receptions)

63.00 Torry Holt, St. Louis vs. Atlanta, Sept. 24, 2000 (3-189)

60.67 Bill Groman, Houston vs. Denver, Nov. 20, 1960 (3-182)

Homer Jones, N.Y. Giants vs. Washington, Dec. 12, 1965 (3-182)

60.33 Don Currivan, Boston vs. Washington, Nov. 30, 1947 (3-181)

TOUCHDOWNS

Most Seasons Leading League

9 Don Hutson, Green Bay, 1935-38, 1940-44

6 Jerry Rice, San Francisco, 1986-87, 1989-1991, 1993

5 Randy Moss, Minnesota, 1998, 2000, 2003; New England, 2007, 2009

Most Consecutive Seasons Leading League

5 Don Hutson, Green Bay, 1940-44

4 Don Hutson, Green Bay, 1935-38

3 Lance Alworth, San Diego, 1964-66

Jerry Rice, San Francisco, 1989-1991

Most Touchdowns, Career

197 Jerry Rice, San Francisco, 1985-2000; Oakland, 2001-04; Seattle, 2004

153 Randy Moss, Minnesota, 1998-2004; Oakland, 2005-06; New England, 2007-2010; Minnesota, 2010; Tennessee, 2010

Terrell Owens, San Francisco, 1996-2003; Philadelphia, 2004-05; Dallas, 2006-08; Buffalo, 2009; Cincinnati, 2010

130 Cris Carter, Philadelphia, 1987-89; Minnesota, 1990-2001; Miami, 2002

Most Touchdowns, Season

23 Randy Moss, New England, 2007

22 Jerry Rice, San Francisco, 1987

18 Mark Clayton, Miami, 1984

Sterling Sharpe, Green Bay, 1994

Most Touchdowns, Rookie, Season

17 Randy Moss, Minnesota, 1998

13 Bill Howton, Green Bay, 1952

John Jefferson, San Diego, 1978

12 Harlon Hill, Chi. Bears, 1954

Bill Groman, Houston, 1960

Mike Ditka, Chicago, 1961

Bob Hayes, Dallas, 1965

Most Touchdowns, Game

5 Bob Shaw, Chi. Cardinals vs. Baltimore, Oct. 2, 1950

Kellen Winslow, San Diego vs. Oakland, Nov. 22, 1981

Jerry Rice, San Francisco vs. Atlanta, Oct. 14, 1990

4 By many players. Last time: Randy Moss, New England vs. Buffalo, Nov. 18, 2007

Terrell Owens, Dallas vs. Washington, Nov. 18, 2007

Most Consecutive Games, Touchdowns

13 Jerry Rice, San Francisco, 1986-87

11 Elroy (Crazylegs) Hirsch, Los Angeles, 1950-51

Buddy Dial, Pittsburgh, 1959-1960

10 Carl Pickens, Cincinnati, 1994-95

Randy Moss, Minnesota, 2003-04

YARDS FROM SCRIMMAGE

Most Scrimmage Yards, Career

23,540 Jerry Rice, San Francisco 1985-2000; Oakland, 2001-04; Seattle, 2004

21,579 Emmitt Smith, Dallas, 1990-2002; Arizona, 2003-04

21,264 Walter Payton, Chicago, 1975-1987

Most Scrimmage Yards, Season

2,509 Chris Johnson, Tennessee, 2009

2,429 Marshall Faulk, St. Louis, 1999

2,390 Tiki Barber, N.Y. Giants, 2005

Most Scrimmage Yards, Rookie, Season

2,212 Eric Dickerson, L.A. Rams, 1983

2,139 Edgerrin James, Indianapolis, 1999

1,924 Billy Sims, Detroit, 1980

Most Scrimmage Yards, Game
- 336   Flipper Anderson, L.A. Rams vs. New Orleans, Nov. 26, 1989 (ot)
- 330   Billy Cannon, Houston vs. N.Y. Titans, Dec. 10, 1961
- 315   Adrian Peterson, Minnesota vs. San Diego, Nov. 4, 2007

INTERCEPTIONS BY
Most Seasons Leading League
- 3   Everson Walls, Dallas, 1981-82, 1985
     Ed Reed, Baltimore, 2004, 2008, 2010
- 2   Dick (Night Train) Lane, Los Angeles, 1952; Chi. Cardinals, 1954
     Jack Christiansen, Detroit, 1953, 1957
     Milt Davis, Baltimore, 1957, 1959
     Dick Lynch, N.Y. Giants, 1961, 1963
     Johnny Robinson, Kansas City, 1966, 1970
     Bill Bradley, Philadelphia, 1971-72
     Emmitt Thomas, Kansas City, 1969, 1974
     Ronnie Lott, San Francisco, 1986; L.A. Raiders, 1991
     Rod Woodson, Baltimore, 1999; Oakland, 2002
     Ty Law, New England, 1998; N.Y. Jets, 2005
     Darren Sharper, Green Bay, 2000; New Orleans, 2009
     Asante Samuel, New England, 2006; Philadelphia, 2009

Most Interceptions By, Career
- 81   Paul Krause, Washington, 1964-67; Minnesota, 1968-1979
- 79   Emlen Tunnell, N.Y. Giants, 1948-1958; Green Bay, 1959-1961
- 71   Rod Woodson, Pittsburgh, 1987-1996; San Francisco, 1997; Baltimore, 1998-2001; Oakland, 2002-03

Most Interceptions By, Season
- 14   Dick (Night Train) Lane, Los Angeles, 1952
- 13   Dan Sandifer, Washington, 1948
     Orban (Spec) Sanders, N.Y. Yanks, 1950
     Lester Hayes, Oakland, 1980
- 12   By nine players

Most Interceptions By, Rookie, Season
- 14   Dick (Night Train) Lane, Los Angeles, 1952
- 13   Dan Sandifer, Washington, 1948
- 12   Woodley Lewis, Los Angeles, 1950
     Paul Krause, Washington, 1964

Most Interceptions By, Game
- 4   Sammy Baugh, Washington vs. Detroit, Nov. 14, 1943
     Dan Sandifer, Washington vs. Boston, Oct. 31, 1948
     Don Doll, Detroit vs. Chi. Cardinals, Oct. 23, 1949
     Bob Nussbaumer, Chi. Cardinals vs. N.Y. Bulldogs, Nov. 13, 1949
     Russ Craft, Philadelphia vs. Chi. Cardinals, Sept. 24, 1950
     Bobby Dillon, Green Bay vs. Detroit, Nov. 26, 1953
     Jack Butler, Pittsburgh vs. Washington, Dec. 13, 1953
     Austin (Goose) Gonsoulin, Denver vs. Buffalo, Sept. 18, 1960
     Jerry Norton, St. Louis vs. Washington, Nov. 20, 1960; vs. Pittsburgh, Nov. 26, 1961
     Dave Baker, San Francisco vs. L.A. Rams, Dec. 4, 1960
     Bobby Ply, Dall. Texans vs. San Diego, Dec. 16, 1962
     Bobby Hunt, Kansas City vs. Houston, Oct. 4, 1964
     Willie Brown, Denver vs. N.Y. Jets, Nov. 15, 1964
     Dick Anderson, Miami vs. Pittsburgh, Dec. 3, 1973
     Willie Buchanon, Green Bay vs. San Diego, Sept. 24, 1978
     Deron Cherry, Kansas City vs. Seattle, Sept. 29, 1985
     Kwamie Lassiter, Arizona vs. San Diego, Dec. 27, 1998
     Deltha O'Neal, Denver vs. Kansas City, Oct. 7, 2001
     DeAngelo Hall, Washington vs. Chicago, Oct. 24, 2010

Most Consecutive Games, Passes Intercepted By
- 8   Tom Morrow, Oakland, 1962-63
- 7   Tom Landry, N.Y. Giants, 1950-51
     Paul Krause, Washington, 1964
     Larry Wilson, St. Louis, 1966
     Ben Davis, Cleveland, 1968
- 6   By many players.
       Last time: Brian Russell, Minnesota, 2003

YARDS GAINED
Most Seasons Leading League
- 3   Darren Sharper, Green Bay, 2002; Minnesota, 2005; New Orleans, 2009
- 2   Dick (Night Train) Lane, Los Angeles, 1952; Chi. Cardinals, 1954
     Herb Adderley, Green Bay, 1965, 1969
     Dick Anderson, Miami, 1968, 1970
     Ed Reed, Baltimore, 2004, 2010

Most Yards Gained, Career
- 1,483   Rod Woodson, Pittsburgh, 1987-1996; San Francisco, 1997; Baltimore, 1998-2001; Oakland, 2002-03
- 1,438   Ed Reed, Baltimore, 2002-2010
- 1,412   Darren Sharper, Green Bay, 1997-2004; Minnesota, 2005-08; New Orleans, 2009-2010

Most Yards Gained, Season
- 376   Darren Sharper, New Orleans, 2009
- 358   Ed Reed, Baltimore, 2004
- 349   Charlie McNeil, San Diego, 1961

Most Yards Gained, Rookie, Season
- 301   Don Doll, Detroit, 1949
- 298   Dick (Night Train) Lane, Los Angeles, 1952
- 275   Woodley Lewis, Los Angeles, 1950

Most Yards Gained, Game
- 177   Charlie McNeil, San Diego vs. Houston, Sept. 24, 1961
- 170   Louis Oliver, Miami vs. Buffalo, Oct. 4, 1992
- 167   Dick Jauron, Detroit vs. Chicago, Nov. 18, 1973

Longest Return (All TDs)
- 107   Ed Reed, Baltimore vs. Philadelphia, Nov. 23, 2008
- 106   Ed Reed, Baltimore vs. Cleveland, Nov. 7, 2004
- 103   Vencie Glenn, San Diego vs. Denver, Nov. 29, 1987
     Louis Oliver, Miami vs. Buffalo, Oct. 4, 1992

TOUCHDOWNS
Most Touchdowns, Career
- 12   Rod Woodson, Pittsburgh, 1987-1996; San Francisco, 1997; Baltimore, 1998-2001; Oakland, 2002-03
- 11   Darren Sharper, Green Bay, 1997-2004; Minnesota, 2005-08; New Orleans, 2009-2010
- 10   Charles Woodson, Oakland, 1998-2005; Green Bay, 2006-2010

Most Touchdowns, Season
- 4   Ken Houston, Houston, 1971
     Jim Kearney, Kansas City, 1972
     Eric Allen, Philadelphia, 1993
- 3   Dick Harris, San Diego, 1961
     Dick Lynch, N.Y. Giants, 1963
     Herb Adderley, Green Bay, 1965
     Lem Barney, Detroit, 1967
     Miller Farr, Houston, 1967
     Monte Jackson, Los Angeles, 1976
     Rod Perry, Los Angeles, 1978
     Ronnie Lott, San Francisco, 1981
     Lloyd Burruss, Kansas City, 1986
     Wayne Haddix, Tampa Bay, 1990
     Robert Massey, Phoenix, 1992
     Ray Buchanan, Indianapolis, 1994
     Deion Sanders, San Francisco, 1994
     Mark McMillian, Kansas City, 1997

Otis Smith, N.Y. Jets, 1997
Jimmy Hitchcock, Minnesota, 1998
Eric Allen, Oakland, 2000
Derrick Brooks, Tampa Bay, 2002
Antrel Rolle, Arizona, 2007
Nick Collins, Green Bay, 2008
Darren Sharper, New Orleans, 2009
Charles Woodson, Green Bay, 2009
  2 By many players

Most Touchdowns, Rookie, Season
  3 Lem Barney, Detroit, 1967
      Ronnie Lott, San Francisco, 1981
  2 By many players

Most Touchdowns, Game
  2 Bill Blackburn, Chi. Cardinals vs. Boston,
      Oct. 24, 1948
      Dan Sandifer, Washington vs. Boston, Oct. 31, 1948
      Bob Franklin, Cleveland vs. Chicago, Dec. 11, 1960
      Bill Stacy, St. Louis vs. Dall. Cowboys, Nov. 5, 1961
      Jerry Norton, St. Louis vs. Pittsburgh, Nov. 26, 1961
      Miller Farr, Houston vs. Buffalo, Dec. 7, 1968
      Ken Houston, Houston vs. San Diego, Dec. 19, 1971
      Jim Kearney, Kansas City vs. Denver, Oct. 1, 1972
      Lemar Parrish, Cincinnati vs. Houston, Dec. 17, 1972
      Dick Anderson, Miami vs. Pittsburgh, Dec. 3, 1973
      Prentice McCray, New England vs. N.Y. Jets,
      Nov. 21, 1976
      Kenny Johnson, Atlanta vs. Green Bay,
      Nov. 27, 1983 (ot)
      Mike Kozlowski, Miami vs. N.Y. Jets, Dec. 16, 1983
      Dave Brown, Seattle vs. Kansas City, Nov. 4, 1984
      Lloyd Burruss, Kansas City vs. San Diego,
      Oct. 19, 1986
      Henry Jones, Buffalo vs. Indianapolis, Sept. 20, 1992
      Robert Massey, Phoenix vs. Washington, Oct. 4, 1992
      Eric Allen, Philadelphia vs. New Orleans,
      Dec. 26, 1993
      Ken Norton, San Francisco vs. St. Louis,
      Oct. 22, 1995
      Otis Smith, N.Y. Jets vs. Tampa Bay, Dec. 14, 1997
      Dewayne Washington, Pittsburgh vs. Jacksonville,
      Nov. 22, 1998
      Aaron Glenn, Houston vs. Pittsburgh, Dec. 8, 2002
      Ronde Barber, Tampa Bay vs. Philadelphia,
      Oct. 22, 2006
      Antrel Rolle, Arizona vs. Cincinnati, Nov. 18, 2007
      Derrick Johnson, Kansas City vs. Denver,
      Jan. 3, 2010
      David Bowens, Cleveland vs. New Orleans,
      Oct. 24, 2010

PUNTING

Most Punts, Career
1,713 Jeff Feagles, New England, 1988-89; Philadelphia,
       1990-93; Arizona, 1994-97; Seattle, 1998-
       2002; N.Y. Giants, 2003-09
1,401 Sean Landeta, N.Y. Giants, 1985-1993; L.A. Rams,
       1993-94; St. Louis, 1995-96; Tampa Bay, 1997;
       Green Bay, 1998; Philadelphia, 1999-2002;
       St. Louis, 2003-04; Philadelphia, 2005
1,258 Brad Maynard, N.Y. Giants, 1997-2000; Chicago,
       2001-2010

Most Punts, Season
 114 Bob Parsons, Chicago, 1981
      Chad Stanley, Houston, 2002
 111 Brad Maynard, N.Y. Giants, 1997
 109 John James, Atlanta, 1978

Most Punts, Rookie, Season
 111 Brad Maynard, N.Y. Giants, 1997
 108 John Teltschik, Philadelphia, 1986

 101 Daniel Pope, Kansas City, 1999

Most Punts, Game
 16 Leo Araguz, Oakland vs. San Diego, Oct. 11, 1998
 15 John Teltschik, Philadelphia vs. N.Y. Giants,
     Dec. 6, 1987 (ot)
 14 Dick Nesbitt, Chi. Cardinals vs. Chi. Bears,
     Nov. 30, 1933
     Keith Molesworth, Chi. Bears vs. Green Bay,
     Dec. 10, 1933
     Sammy Baugh, Washington vs. Philadelphia,
     Nov. 5, 1939
     Carl Kinscherf, N.Y. Giants vs. Detroit, Nov. 7, 1943
     George Taliaferro, N.Y. Yanks vs. Los Angeles,
     Sept. 28, 1951

Longest Punt
 98 Steve O'Neal, N.Y. Jets vs. Denver, Sept. 21, 1969
 94 Joe Lintzenich, Chi. Bears vs. N.Y. Giants, Nov. 16, 1931
 93 Shawn McCarthy, New England vs. Buffalo,
     Nov. 3, 1991

AVERAGE YARDAGE
Highest Average, Punting, Career (250 punts)
47.29 Shane Lechler, Oakland, 2000-2010 (855-40,429)
45.54 Donnie Jones, Seattle, 2004; Miami, 2005-06;
      St. Louis, 2007-2010 (543-24,727)
45.47 Mat McBriar, Dallas, 2004-2010 (436-19,827)

Highest Avg. Punting, Season (Qualifiers)
51.40 Sammy Baugh, Washington, 1940 (35-1,799)
51.14 Shane Lechler, Oakland, 2009 (96-4,909)
50.00 Donnie Jones, St. Louis, 2008 (82-4,100)

Highest Avg. Punting, Rookie, Season
46.74 Brett Kern, Denver, 2008 (46-2,150)
45.92 Frank Sinkwich, Detroit, 1943 (12-551)
45.91 Shane Lechler, Oakland, 2000 (65-2,984)

Highest Avg. Punting, Game (4 punts)
61.75 Bob Cifers, Detroit vs. Chi. Bears, Nov. 24, 1946
      (4-247)
61.60 Roy McKay, Green Bay vs. Chi. Cardinals, Oct. 28,
      1945 (5-308)
59.50 Darren Bennett, San Diego vs. Pittsburgh, Oct. 1,
      1995 (4-238)
      Mike Scifres, San Diego vs. St. Louis, Oct. 17, 2010
      (6-357)

NET AVERAGE
Net average has been compiled since 1976.

Highest Net Average, Punting, Career (250 punts)
39.18 Donnie Jones, Seattle, 2004; Miami, 2005-06;
      St. Louis, 2007-2010 (545-21,352)
38.68 Dustin Colquitt, Kansas City, 2005-2010
      (488-18,875)
38.65 Shane Lechler, Oakland, 2000-2010 (858-33,164)

Highest Net Average, Punting, Season (Qualifiers)
43.85 Shane Lechler, Oakland, 2009 (96-4,210)
41.69 Donnie Jones, St. Louis, 2009 (90-3,752)
41.67 Mat McBriar, Dallas, 2010 (66-2,750)

Highest Net Average, Punting, Rookie, Season (Qualifiers)
38.38 Zoltan Mesko, New England, 2010 (58-2,226)
38.00 Dale Hatcher, L.A. Rams, 1985 (88-3,344)
37.95 Shane Lechler, Oakland, 2000 (66-2,505)

Highest Net Average, Punting, Game (4 punts)
59.50 Rohn Stark, Indianapolis vs. Houston,
      Sept. 13, 1992 (4-238)
53.00 Brian Moorman, Buffalo vs. Kansas City, Dec. 13,
      2009 (4-212)
52.80 Mike Horan, Denver vs. L.A. Raiders, Sept. 26, 1988
      (ot) (5-264)
      David Zastudil, Cleveland vs. Pittsburgh, Sept. 14,
      2008 (5-264)

PUNTS HAD BLOCKED
Most Consecutive Punts, None Blocked
- 1,177 Chris Gardocki, Chicago, 1992-94; Indianapolis, 1995-98; Cleveland, 1999-2003; Pittsburgh, 2004-06
- 878 Bryan Barker, Kansas City, 1993; Philadelphia, 1994; Jacksonville, 1995-2000; Washington, 2001-03; Green Bay, 2004; St. Louis, 2005
- 694 Brian Moorman, Buffalo, 2002-2010 (current)

Most Punts Had Blocked, Career
- 14 Herman Weaver, Detroit, 1970-76; Seattle, 1977-1980
  Harry Newsome, Pittsburgh, 1985-89; Minnesota, 1990-93
- 12 Jerrel Wilson, Kansas City, 1963-1977; New England, 1978
  Tom Blanchard, N.Y. Giants, 1971-73; New Orleans, 1974-78; Tampa Bay, 1979-1981
  Jeff Feagles, New England, 1988-89; Philadelphia, 1990-93; Arizona, 1994-97; Seattle, 1998-2002; N.Y. Giants, 2003-09
- 11 David Lee, Baltimore, 1966-1978

Most Punts Had Blocked, Season
- 6 Harry Newsome, Pittsburgh, 1988
- 4 Bryan Wagner, Cleveland, 1990
  Mike Scifres, San Diego, 2010
- 3 By many players

PUNTS INSIDE THE 20
Punts Inside the 20 have been compiled since 1976.
Most Punts Inside the 20, Career
- 554 Jeff Feagles, New England, 1988-89; Philadelphia, 1990-93; Arizona, 1994-97; Seattle, 1998-2002; N.Y. Giants, 2003-09
- 407 Brad Maynard, N.Y. Giants, 1997-2000; Chicago, 2001-2010
- 399 Craig Hentrich, Green Bay, 1994-97; Tennessee, 1998-2009

Most Punts Inside the 20, Season
- 42 Andy Lee, San Francisco, 2007
  Ben Graham, Arizona, 2009
  Steve Weatherford, N.Y. Jets, 2010
- 41 Dustin Colquitt, Kansas City, 2009
- 40 Brad Maynard, Chicago, 2008

Most Punts Inside the 20, Game
- 8 Mark Royals, Pittsburgh vs. Houston, Nov. 6, 1994 (ot)
  Bryan Barker, Jacksonville vs. Baltimore, Nov. 14, 1999
- 7 Josh Miller, Pittsburgh vs. Cincinnati, Dec. 20, 1998
  David Zastudil. Cleveland vs. Buffalo, Oct. 11, 2009
  Thomas Morstead, New Orleans vs. Carolina, Jan. 3, 2010
- 6 By many players

PUNT RETURNS
Most Seasons Leading League
- 3 Les (Speedy) Duncan, San Diego, 1965-66; Washington, 1971
  Rick Upchurch, Denver, 1976, 1978, 1982
- 2 Dick Christy, N.Y. Titans, 1961-62
  Claude Gibson, Oakland, 1963-64
  Billy (White Shoes) Johnson, Houston, 1975, 1977
  Mel Gray, New Orleans, 1987; Detroit, 1991
  Jermaine Lewis, Baltimore, 1997, 2000
  Roscoe Parrish, Buffalo, 2007-08

PUNT RETURNS
Most Punt Returns, Career
- 463 Brian Mitchell, Washington, 1990-99; Philadelphia, 2000-02; N.Y. Giants, 2003

- 351 Eric Metcalf, Cleveland, 1989-1994; Atlanta, 1995-96; San Diego, 1997; Arizona, 1998; Carolina, 1999; Washington, 2001; Green Bay, 2002
- 349 David Meggett, N.Y. Giants, 1989-1994; New England, 1995-97; N.Y. Jets, 1998

Most Punt Returns, Season
- 70 Danny Reece, Tampa Bay, 1979
- 62 Fulton Walker, Miami-L.A. Raiders, 1985
- 58 J.T. Smith, Kansas City, 1979
  Greg Pruitt, L.A. Raiders, 1983
  Leo Lewis, Minnesota, 1988
  Desmond Howard, Green Bay, 1996
  Nate Burleson, Seattle, 2007

Most Punt Returns, Rookie, Season
- 57 Lew Barnes, Chicago, 1986
- 55 B.J. Sams, Baltimore, 2004
- 54 James Jones, Dallas, 1980

Most Punt Returns, Game
- 11 Eddie Brown, Washington vs. Tampa Bay, Oct. 9, 1977
- 10 Theo Bell, Pittsburgh vs. Buffalo, Dec. 16, 1979
  Mike Nelms, Washington vs. New Orleans, Dec. 26, 1982
  Ronnie Harris, New England vs. Pittsburgh, Dec. 5, 1993
- 9 Rodger Bird, Oakland vs. Denver, Sept. 10, 1967
  Ralph McGill, San Francisco vs. Atlanta, Oct. 29, 1972
  Ed Podolak, Kansas City vs. San Diego, Nov. 10, 1974
  Anthony Leonard, San Francisco vs. New Orleans, Oct. 17, 1976
  Butch Johnson, Dallas vs. Buffalo, Nov. 15, 1976
  Larry Marshall, Philadelphia vs. Tampa Bay, Sept. 18, 1977
  Nesby Glasgow, Baltimore vs. Kansas City, Sept. 2, 1979
  Mike Nelms, Washington vs. St. Louis, Dec. 21, 1980
  Leon Bright, N.Y. Giants vs. Philadelphia, Dec. 11, 1982
  Pete Shaw, N.Y. Giants vs. Philadelphia, Nov. 20, 1983
  Cleotha Montgomery, L.A. Raiders vs. Detroit, Dec. 10, 1984
  Phil McConkey, N.Y. Giants vs. Philadelphia, Dec. 6, 1987 (ot)
  Andre Hastings, Pittsburgh vs. Cleveland, Nov. 13, 1995
  Steve Smith, Carolina vs. Detroit, Sept. 15, 2002
  Reggie Swinton, Arizona vs. Philadelphia, Dec. 24, 2005

FAIR CATCHES
Most Fair Catches, Career
- 231 Brian Mitchell, Washington, 1990-99; Philadelphia, 2000-02; N.Y. Giants, 2003
- 162 Tim Brown, L.A. Raiders, 1988-1994; Oakland, 1995-2003; Tampa Bay, 2004
- 144 Glyn Milburn, Denver, 1993-95; Detroit, 1996-97; Chicago, 1998-2001; San Diego, 2001

Most Fair Catches, Season
- 33 Brian Mitchell, Philadelphia, 2000
- 29 Wes Welker, Miami, 2006
- 27 Leo Lewis, Minnesota, 1989
  Antonio Chatman, Green Bay, 2004

Most Fair Catches, Game
- 7 Bake Turner, N.Y. Jets vs. Miami, Nov. 20, 1966
  Lem Barney, Detroit vs. Chicago, Nov. 21, 1976
  Bobby Morse, Philadelphia vs. Buffalo, Dec. 27, 1987
  Chris Carr, Tennessee vs. Jacksonville, Nov. 16, 2008

 6   Jake Scott, Miami vs. Buffalo, Dec. 20, 1970
     Greg Pruitt, L.A. Raiders vs. Seattle, Oct. 7, 1984
     Phil McConkey, San Diego vs. Kansas City,
       Dec. 17, 1989
     Gerald McNeil, Houston vs. Pittsburgh,
       Sept. 16, 1990
     Bobby Engram, Chicago vs. Minnesota,
       Sept. 15, 1996
     Eddie Kennison, New Orleans vs. Baltimore,
       Dec. 19, 1999
     R.W. McQuarters, N.Y. Giants vs. Atlanta,
       Oct. 15, 2007
 5   By many players

YARDS GAINED
Most Seasons Leading League
 3   Alvin Haymond, Baltimore, 1965-66; Los Angeles, 1969
 2   Bill Dudley, Pittsburgh, 1942, 1946
     Emlen Tunnell, N.Y. Giants, 1951-52
     Dick Christy, N.Y. Titans, 1961-62
     Claude Gibson, Oakland, 1963-64
     Rodger Bird, Oakland, 1966-67
     J.T. Smith, Kansas City, 1979-1980
     Vai Sikahema, St. Louis, 1986-87
     David Meggett, N.Y. Giants, 1989-1990
     Tamarick Vanover, Kansas City, 1995, 1999
     Devin Hester, Chicago, 2006, 2010

Most Yards Gained, Career
4,999   Brian Mitchell, Washington, 1990-99; Philadelphia, 2000-02; N.Y. Giants, 2003
3,708   Dave Meggett, N.Y. Giants, 1989-1994; New England, 1995-97; N.Y. Jets, 1998
3,601   Darrien Gordon, San Diego, 1993-94, 1996; Denver, 1997-98; Oakland, 1999-2000; Atlanta, 2001; Green Bay, 2002

Most Yards Gained, Season
 875   Desmond Howard, Green Bay, 1996
 692   Fulton Walker, Miami-L.A. Raiders, 1985
 666   Greg Pruitt, L.A. Raiders, 1983

Most Yards Gained, Rookie, Season
 656   Louis Lipps, Pittsburgh, 1984
 655   Neal Colzie, Oakland, 1975
 619   Leon Johnson, N.Y. Jets, 1997

Most Yards Gained, Game
 207   LeRoy Irvin, Los Angeles vs. Atlanta, Oct. 11, 1981
 205   George Atkinson, Oakland vs. Buffalo, Sept. 15, 1968
 199   Eddie Drummond, Detroit vs. Jacksonville, Nov. 14, 2004 (ot)

Longest Punt Return (All TDs)
 103   Robert Bailey, L.A. Rams vs. New Orleans, Oct. 23, 1994
 98   Gil LeFebvre, Cincinnati vs. Brooklyn, Dec. 3, 1933
     Charlie West, Minnesota vs. Washington, Nov. 3, 1968
     Dennis Morgan, Dallas vs. St. Louis, Oct. 13, 1974
     Terance Mathis, N.Y. Jets vs. Dallas, Nov. 4, 1990
 97   Greg Pruitt, L.A. Raiders vs. Washington, Oct. 2, 1983
     Bryan McCann, Dallas vs. Detroit, Nov. 21, 2010

AVERAGE YARDAGE
Highest Average, Career (75 returns)
 12.78   George McAfee, Chi. Bears, 1940-41, 1945-1950 (112-1,431)
 12.75   Jack Christiansen, Detroit, 1951-58 (85-1,084)
 12.55   Claude Gibson, San Diego, 1961-62; Oakland, 1963-65 (110-1,381)

Highest Average, Season (Qualifiers)
 23.00   Herb Rich, Baltimore, 1950 (12-276)

 21.47   Jack Christiansen, Detroit, 1952 (15-322)
 21.28   Dick Christy, N.Y. Titans, 1961 (18-383)
Highest Average, Rookie, Season (Qualifiers)
 23.00   Herb Rich, Baltimore, 1950 (12-276)
 20.88   Jerry Davis, Chi. Cardinals, 1948 (16-334)
 20.73   Frankie Sinkwich, Detroit, 1943 (11-228)
Highest Average, Game
 51.00   Steve Smith, Carolina vs. Cincinnati, Dec. 8, 2002 (3-153)
 47.67   Chuck Latourette, St. Louis vs. New Orleans, Sept. 29, 1968 (3-143)
 47.33   Johnny Roland, St. Louis vs. Philadelphia, Oct. 2, 1966 (3-142)

TOUCHDOWNS
Most Touchdowns, Career
 10   Eric Metcalf, Cleveland, 1989-1994; Atlanta, 1995-96; San Diego, 1997; Arizona, 1998; Carolina, 1999; Washington, 2001; Green Bay, 2002
     Devin Hester, Chicago, 2006-2010
 9   Brian Mitchell, Washington, 1990-99; Philadelphia 2000-02; N.Y. Giants, 2003
 8   Jack Christiansen, Detroit, 1951-58
     Rick Upchurch, Denver, 1975-1983
     Desmond Howard, Washington, 1992-94; Jacksonville, 1995; Green Bay, 1996, 1999; Oakland, 1997-98; Detroit, 1999-2002

Most Touchdowns, Season
 4   Jack Christiansen, Detroit, 1951
     Rick Upchurch, Denver, 1976
     Devin Hester, Chicago, 2007
 3   Emlen Tunnell, N.Y. Giants, 1951
     Billy (White Shoes) Johnson, Houston, 1975
     LeRoy Irvin, Los Angeles, 1981
     Desmond Howard, Green Bay, 1996
     Darrien Gordon, Denver, 1997
     Eric Metcalf, San Diego, 1997
     Devin Hester, Chicago, 2006
     Adam Jones, Tennessee, 2006
     Reggie Bush, New Orleans, 2008
     Johnnie Lee Higgins, Oakland, 2008
     Devin Hester, Chicago, 2010
 2   By many players

Most Touchdowns, Rookie, Season
 4   Jack Christiansen, Detroit, 1951
 3   Devin Hester, Chicago, 2006
 2   By many players

Most Touchdowns, Game
 2   Jack Christiansen, Detroit vs. Los Angeles, Oct. 14, 1951; vs. Green Bay, Nov. 22, 1951
     Dick Christy, N.Y. Titans vs. Denver, Sept. 24, 1961
     Rick Upchurch, Denver vs. Cleveland, Sept. 26, 1976
     LeRoy Irvin, Los Angeles vs. Atlanta, Oct. 11, 1981
     Vai Sikahema, St. Louis vs. Tampa Bay, Dec. 21, 1986
     Todd Kinchen, L.A. Rams vs. Atlanta, Dec. 27, 1992
     Eric Metcalf, Cleveland vs. Pittsburgh, Oct. 24, 1993; San Diego vs. Cincinnati, Nov. 2, 1997
     Darrien Gordon, Denver vs. Carolina, Nov. 9, 1997
     Jermaine Lewis, Baltimore vs. Seattle, Dec. 7, 1997
     Baltimore vs. N.Y. Jets, Dec. 24, 2000
     Steve Smith, Carolina vs. Cincinnati, Dec. 8, 2002
     Eddie Drummond, Detroit vs. Jacksonville, Nov. 14, 2004 (ot)
     Reggie Bush, New Orleans vs. Minnesota, Oct. 6, 2008

KICKOFF RETURNS
Most Seasons Leading League
 3   Abe Woodson, San Francisco, 1959, 1962-63

     2 Lynn Chandnois, Pittsburgh, 1951-52
        Bobby Jancik, Houston, 1962-63
        Travis Williams, Green Bay, 1967; Los Angeles, 1971
        Mel Gray, Detroit, 1991, 1994
        Michael Bates, Carolina, 1996-97

KICKOFF RETURNS
Most Kickoff Returns, Career
   607 Brian Mitchell, Washington, 1990-99; Philadelphia,
        2000-02; N.Y. Giants, 2003
   514 Allen Rossum, Philadelphia, 1998-99; Green Bay,
        2000-01; Atlanta, 2002-06; Pittsburgh, 2007;
        San Francisco, 2008-09; Dallas, 2009
   426 Dante Hall, Kansas City, 2000-06; St. Louis,
        2007-08
Most Kickoff Returns, Season
    82 MarTay Jenkins, Arizona, 2000
    73 Josh Scobey, Arizona, 2003
        Chris Carr, Oakland, 2005
    70 Tyrone Hughes, New Orleans, 1996
        Michael Lewis, New Orleans, 2002
Most Kickoff Returns, Rookie, Season
    73 Josh Scobey, Arizona, 2003
        Chris Carr, Oakland, 2005
    67 Ronney Jenkins, San Diego, 2000
    64 Tab Perry, Cincinnati, 2005
Most Kickoff Returns, Game
    10 Desmond Howard, Oakland vs. Seattle, Oct. 26, 1997
        Richard Alston, Cleveland vs. Cincinnati,
        Nov. 28, 2004
     9 Noland Smith, Kansas City vs. Oakland, Nov. 23, 1967
        Dino Hall, Cleveland vs. Pittsburgh, Oct. 7, 1979
        Paul Palmer, Kansas City vs. Seattle, Sept. 20, 1987
        Eric Metcalf, Atlanta vs. San Francisco,
        Sept. 29, 1996; vs. St. Louis, Nov. 10, 1996
        Michael Bates, Carolina vs. Atlanta, Oct. 4, 1998
        Nate Jacquet, Minnesota vs. Philadelphia,
        Nov. 11, 2001
        Ahmad Merritt, Chicago vs. San Francisco,
        Sept. 7, 2003
        Josh Scobey, Arizona vs. Cleveland, Nov. 16, 2003
        Maurice Hicks, San Francisco vs. San Diego,
        Oct. 15, 2006
        Aveion Cason, Detroit vs. San Diego, Dec. 16, 2007
        Allen Rossum, San Francisco vs. Philadelphia,
        Oct. 12, 2008
        Steve Breaston, Arizona vs. New England,
        Dec. 21, 2008
        Danny Amendola, St. Louis vs. Tennessee,
        Dec. 13, 2009
        Brandon James, Indianapolis vs. San Diego,
        Nov. 28, 2010
     8 By many players

YARDS GAINED
Most Seasons Leading League
     3 Bruce Harper, N.Y. Jets, 1977-79
        Tyrone Hughes, New Orleans, 1994-96
     2 Marshall Goldberg, Chi. Cardinals, 1941-42
        Woodley Lewis, Los Angeles, 1953-54
        Al Carmichael, Green Bay, 1956-57
        Timmy Brown, Philadelphia, 1961, 1963
        Bobby Jancik, Houston, 1963, 1966
        Ron Smith, Atlanta, 1966-67
        Chris Carr, Oakland, 2005-06
Most Yards Gained, Career
 14,014 Brian Mitchell, Washington, 1990-99; Philadelphia,
        2000-02; N.Y. Giants, 2003

 11,947 Allen Rossum, Philadelphia, 1998-99; Green Bay,
        2000-01; Atlanta, 2002-06; Pittsburgh, 2007;
        San Francisco, 2008-09; Dallas, 2009
 10,250 Mel Gray, New Orleans, 1986-88; Detroit, 1989-
        1994; Houston, 1995-96; Tennessee, 1997;
        Philadelphia, 1997
Most Yards Gained, Season
  2,186 MarTay Jenkins, Arizona, 2000
  1,809 Josh Cribbs, Cleveland, 2007
  1,807 Michael Lewis, New Orleans, 2002
Most Yards Gained, Rookie, Season
  1,752 Chris Carr, Oakland, 2005
  1,684 Josh Scobey, Arizona, 2003
  1,577 Justin Miller, N.Y. Jets, 2005
Most Yards Gained, Game
    304 Tyrone Hughes, New Orleans vs. L.A. Rams,
        Oct. 23, 1994
    299 Ted Ginn, Jr., Miami vs. N.Y. Jets, Nov. 1, 2009
    294 Wally Triplett, Detroit vs. Los Angeles, Oct. 29, 1950
Longest Kickoff Return (All TDs)
    108 Ellis Hobbs, New England, vs. N.Y. Jets,
        Sept. 9, 2007
    106 Al Carmichael, Green Bay vs. Chi. Bears, Oct. 7, 1956
        Noland Smith, Kansas City vs. Denver, Dec. 17, 1967
        Roy Green, St. Louis vs. Dallas, Oct. 21, 1979
        Brad Smith, N.Y. Jets vs. Indianapolis, Dec. 27, 2009
    105 Frank Seno, Chi. Cardinals vs. N.Y. Giants,
        Oct. 20, 1946
        Ollie Matson, Chi. Cardinals vs. Washington,
        Oct. 14, 1956
        Abe Woodson, San Francisco vs. Los Angeles,
        Nov. 8, 1959
        Timmy Brown, Philadelphia vs. Cleveland,
        Sept. 17, 1961
        Jon Arnett, Los Angeles vs. Detroit, Oct. 29, 1961
        Eugene (Mercury) Morris, Miami vs. Cincinnati,
        Sept. 14, 1969
        Travis Williams, Los Angeles vs. New Orleans,
        Dec. 5, 1971
        Terry Fair, Detroit vs. Tampa Bay, Sept. 28, 1998
        Stefan Logan, Detroit vs. St. Louis, Oct. 10, 2010

AVERAGE YARDAGE
Highest Average, Career (75 returns)
    30.56 Gale Sayers, Chicago, 1965-1971 (91-2,781)
    29.57 Lynn Chandnois, Pittsburgh, 1950-56 (92-2,720)
    28.69 Abe Woodson, San Francisco, 1958-1964; St. Louis,
        1965-66 (193-5,538)
Highest Average, Season (Qualifiers)
    41.06 Travis Williams, Green Bay, 1967 (18-739)
    37.69 Gale Sayers, Chicago, 1967 (16-603)
    35.50 Ollie Matson, Chi. Cardinals, 1958 (14-497)
Highest Average, Rookie, Season (Qualifiers)
    41.06 Travis Williams, Green Bay, 1967 (18-739)
    33.08 Tom Moore, Green Bay, 1960 (12-397)
    32.88 Duriel Harris, Miami, 1976 (17-559)
Highest Average, Game (3 returns)
    73.50 Wally Triplett, Detroit vs. Los Angeles, Oct. 29, 1950
        (4-294)
    67.33 Lenny Lyles, San Francisco vs. Baltimore, Dec. 18,
        1960 (3-202)
    65.33 Ken Hall, Houston vs. N.Y. Titans, Oct. 23, 1960
        (3-196)

TOUCHDOWNS
Most Touchdowns, Career
     8 Josh Cribbs, Cleveland, 2005-2010
     7 Leon Washington, N.Y. Jets, 2006-09; Seattle, 2010

6   Ollie Matson, Chi. Cardinals, 1952, 1954-58;
L.A. Rams, 1959-1962; Detroit, 1963;
Philadelphia, 1964
Gale Sayers, Chicago, 1965-1971
Travis Williams, Green Bay, 1967-1970;
Los Angeles, 1971
Mel Gray, New Orleans, 1986-88; Detroit,
1989-1994; Houston, 1995-96; Tennessee,
1997; Philadelphia, 1997
Dante Hall, Kansas City, 2000-06; St. Louis, 2007-08

Most Touchdowns, Season

4   Travis Williams, Green Bay, 1967
Cecil Turner, Chicago, 1970
3   Verda (Vitamin T) Smith, Los Angeles, 1950
Abe Woodson, San Francisco, 1963
Gale Sayers, Chicago, 1967
Raymond Clayborn, New England, 1977
Ron Brown, L.A. Rams, 1985
Mel Gray, Detroit, 1994
Darrick Vaughn, Atlanta, 2000
Terrence McGee, Buffalo, 2004
André Davis, Houston, 2007
Leon Washington, N.Y. Jets, 2007
Josh Cribbs, Cleveland, 2009
Jacoby Ford, Oakland, 2010
Leon Washington, Seattle, 2010
2   By many players

Most Touchdowns, Rookie, Season

4   Travis Williams, Green Bay, 1967
3   Raymond Clayborn, New England, 1977
Darrick Vaughn, Atlanta, 2000
Jacoby Ford, Oakland, 2010
2   By many players

Most Touchdowns, Game

2   Timmy Brown, Philadelphia vs. Dallas, Nov. 6, 1966
Travis Williams, Green Bay vs. Cleveland,
Nov. 12, 1967
Ron Brown, L.A. Rams vs. Green Bay, Nov. 24, 1985
Tyrone Hughes, New Orleans vs. L.A. Rams,
Oct. 23, 1994
Chad Morton, N.Y. Jets vs. Buffalo, Sept. 8, 2002 (ot)
Devin Hester, Chicago vs. St. Louis, Dec. 11, 2006
André Davis, Houston vs. Jacksonville, Dec. 30, 2007
Ted Ginn, Jr., Miami vs. N.Y. Jets, Nov. 1, 2009
Josh Cribbs, Cleveland vs. Kansas City, Dec. 20, 2009
Leon Washington, Seattle vs. San Diego,
Sept. 26, 2010

COMBINED KICK RETURNS

Most Combined Kick Returns, Career

1,070   Brian Mitchell, Washington, 1990-99; Philadelphia,
2000-02; N.Y. Giants, 2003 (p-463, k-607)
821   Allen Rossum, Philadelphia, 1998-99; Green Bay,
2000-01; Atlanta, 2002-06; Pittsburgh, 2007;
San Francisco, 2008-09; Dallas, 2009
(p-307, k-514)
711   Glyn Milburn, Denver, 1993-95; Detroit, 1996-97;
Chicago, 1998-2001; San Diego, 2001 (p-304,
k-407)

Most Combined Kick Returns, Season

114   Michael Lewis, New Orleans, 2002 (p-44, k-70)
B.J. Sams, Baltimore, 2004 (p-55, k-59)
107   Chris Carr, Oakland, 2005 (p-34, k-73)
Dante Hall, Kansas City, 2005 (p-42, k-65)
105   Reggie Swinton, Arizona, 2005 (p-42, k-63)

Most Combined Kick Returns, Game

13   Stump Mitchell, St. Louis vs. Atlanta, Oct. 18, 1981
(p-6, k-7)
Ronnie Harris, New England vs. Pittsburgh,
Dec. 5, 1993 (p-10, k-3)

12   Mel Renfro, Dallas vs. Green Bay, Nov. 29, 1964
(p-4, k-8)
Larry Jones, Washington vs. Dallas, Dec. 13, 1975
(p-6, k-6)
Eddie Brown, Washington vs. Tampa Bay,
Oct. 9, 1977 (p-11, k-1)
Nesby Glasgow, Baltimore vs. Denver, Sept. 2, 1979
(p-9, k-3)
Tim Dwight, Atlanta vs. Detroit, Nov. 12, 2000
(p-8, k-4)
Wes Welker, Miami vs. Buffalo, Dec. 5, 2004
(p-6, k-6)
Reggie Swinton, Arizona vs. Philadelphia,
Dec. 24, 2005 (p-9, k-3)
Devin Hester, Chicago vs. Detroit, Sept. 30, 2007
(p-5, k-7)
Brandon James, Indianapolis vs. San Diego,
Nov. 28, 2010 (p-3, k-9)
11   By many players

YARDS GAINED

Most Yards Returned, Career

19,013   Brian Mitchell, Washington, 1990-99; Philadelphia,
2000-02; N.Y. Giants, 2003 (p-4,999; k-14,014)
15,003   Allen Rossum, Philadelphia, 1998-99; Green Bay,
2000-01; Atlanta, 2002-06; Pittsburgh, 2007;
San Francisco, 2008-09; Dallas, 2009
(p-3,056; k-11,947)
13,003   Mel Gray, New Orleans, 1986-88; Detroit, 1989-
1994; Houston, 1995-96; Tennessee, 1997;
Philadelphia, 1997 (p-2,753; k-10,250)

Most Yards Returned, Season

2,432   Michael Lewis, New Orleans, 2002 (p-625; k-1,807)
2,214   Josh Cribbs, Cleveland, 2007 (p-405; k-1,809)
2,187   MarTay Jenkins, Arizona, 2000 (pr-1; k-2,186)

Most Yards Returned, Game

347   Tyrone Hughes, New Orleans vs. L.A. Rams,
Oct. 23, 1994 (p-43; k-304)
314   Devin Hester, Chicago vs. Detroit, Sept. 30, 2007
(p-95; k-219)
306   Josh Cribbs, Cleveland vs. Baltimore, Nov. 18, 2007
(p-61; k-245) (ot)

TOUCHDOWNS

Most Touchdowns, Career

14   Devin Hester, Chicago, 2006-2010 (p-10, k-4)
13   Brian Mitchell, Washington, 1990-99; Philadelphia,
2000-02; N.Y. Giants, 2003 (p-9, k-4)
12   Eric Metcalf, Cleveland, 1989-1994; Atlanta,
1995-96; San Diego, 1997; Arizona, 1998;
Carolina, 1999; Washington, 2001; Green Bay,
2002 (p-10, k-2)
Dante Hall, Kansas City, 2000-06;
St. Louis, 2007-08 (p-6, k-6)

Most Touchdowns, Season

6   Devin Hester, Chicago, 2007 (p-4, k-2)
5   Devin Hester, Chicago, 2006 (p-3, k-2)
4   Jack Christiansen, Detroit, 1951 (p-4)
Emlen Tunnell, N.Y. Giants, 1951 (p-3, k-1)
Gale Sayers, Chicago, 1967 (p-1, k-3)
Travis Williams, Green Bay, 1967 (k-4)
Cecil Turner, Chicago, 1970 (k-4)
Billy Johnson, Houston, 1975 (p-3, k-1)
Rick Upchurch, Denver, 1976 (p-4)
Dante Hall, Kansas City, 2003 (p-2, r-2)
Eddie Drummond, Detroit, 2004 (p-2, k-2)
Josh Cribbs, Cleveland, 2009 (p-1, k-3)

Most Touchdowns, Game

2   Jack Christiansen, Detroit vs. Los Angeles,
    Oct. 14, 1951 (p-2); vs. Green Bay,
    Nov. 22, 1951 (p-2)
  Jim Patton, N.Y. Giants vs. Washington,
    Oct. 30, 1955 (p-1, k-1)
  Bobby Mitchell, Cleveland vs. Philadelphia,
    Nov. 23, 1958 (p-1, k-1)
  Dick Christy, N.Y. Titans vs. Denver, Sept. 24, 1961
    (p-2)
  Al Frazier, Denver vs. Boston, Dec. 3, 1961 (p-1, k-1)
  Timmy Brown, Philadelphia vs. Dallas, Nov. 6, 1966
    (k-2)
  Travis Williams, Green Bay vs. Cleveland,
    Nov. 12, 1967 (k-2); vs. Pittsburgh,
    Nov. 2, 1969 (p-1, k-1)
  Gale Sayers, Chicago vs. San Francisco,
    Dec. 3, 1967 (p-1, k-1)
  Rick Upchurch, Denver vs. Cleveland,
    Sept. 26, 1976 (p-2)
  Eddie Payton, Detroit vs. Minnesota, Dec. 17, 1977
    (p-1, k-1)
  LeRoy Irvin, Los Angeles vs. Atlanta, Oct. 11, 1981
    (p-2)
  Ron Brown, L.A. Rams vs. Green Bay,
    Nov. 24, 1985 (k-2)
  Vai Sikahema, St. Louis vs. Tampa Bay,
    Dec. 21, 1986 (p-2)
  Todd Kinchen, L.A. Rams vs. Atlanta, Dec. 27, 1992
    (p-2)
  Eric Metcalf, Cleveland vs. Pittsburgh, Oct. 24, 1993
    (p-2); San Diego vs. Cincinnati, Nov. 2, 1997
    (p-2)
  Tyrone Hughes, New Orleans vs. L.A. Rams,
    Oct. 23, 1994 (k-2)
  Darrien Gordon, Denver vs. Carolina, Nov. 9, 1997
    (p-2)
  Jermaine Lewis, Baltimore vs. Seattle, Dec. 7, 1997
    (p-2); Baltimore vs. N.Y. Jets, Dec. 24, 2000
    (p-2)
  Chad Morton, N.Y. Jets vs. Buffalo, Sept. 8, 2002
    (ot) (k-2)
  Michael Lewis, New Orleans vs. Washington,
    Oct. 13, 2002 (p-1, k-1)
  Dante Hall, Kansas City vs. St. Louis, Dec. 8, 2002
    (p-1, k-1)
  Steve Smith, Carolina vs. Cincinnati, Dec. 8, 2002
    (p-2)
  Eddie Drummond, Detroit vs. Jacksonville,
    Nov. 14, 2004 (ot) (p-2)
  Devin Hester, Chicago vs. St. Louis, Dec. 11, 2006
    (k-2)
  Darren Sproles, San Diego vs. Indianapolis,
    Nov. 11, 2007 (p-1, k-1)
  Devin Hester, Chicago vs. Denver, Nov. 25, 2007
    (p-1, k-1)
  André Davis, Houston vs. Jacksonville,
    Dec. 30, 2007 (k-2)
  Reggie Bush, New Orleans vs. Minnesota,
    Oct. 6, 2008
  Eddie Royal, Denver vs. San Diego, Oct. 19, 2009
    (p-1, k-1)
  Ted Ginn, Jr., Miami vs. N.Y. Jets, Nov. 1, 2009
    (k-2)
  Josh Cribbs, Cleveland vs. Kansas City,
    Dec. 20, 2009 (k-2)
  Leon Washington, Seattle vs. San Diego,
    Sept. 26, 2010 (k-2)

FUMBLES

Most Fumbles, Career

166   Brett Favre, Atlanta, 1991; Green Bay, 1992-2007;
    N.Y. Jets, 2008; Minnesota, 2009-2010
161   Warren Moon, Houston, 1984-1993; Minnesota,
    1994-96; Seattle, 1997-98; Kansas City,
    1999-2000
153   Dave Krieg, Seattle, 1980-1991; Kansas City,
    1992-93; Detroit, 1994; Arizona, 1995;
    Chicago, 1996; Tennessee, 1997-98

Most Fumbles, Season

23   Kerry Collins, N.Y. Giants, 2001
    Daunte Culpepper, Minnesota, 2002
21   Tony Banks, St. Louis, 1996
    David Carr, Houston, 2002
18   Dave Krieg, Seattle, 1989
    Warren Moon, Houston, 1990

Most Fumbles, Game

7   Len Dawson, Kansas City vs. San Diego,
    Nov. 15, 1964
6   Sam Etcheverry, St. Louis vs. N.Y. Giants,
    Sept. 17, 1961
  Dave Krieg, Seattle vs. Kansas City, Nov. 5, 1989
  Brett Favre, Green Bay vs. Tampa Bay, Dec. 7, 1998
  Kurt Warner, St. Louis vs. N.Y. Giants, Sept. 7, 2003
  Chad Pennington, N.Y. Jets vs. Kansas City,
    Sept. 11, 2005
5   Paul Christman, Chi. Cardinals vs. Green Bay,
    Nov. 10, 1946
  Joe Perry, San Francisco vs. Cleveland,
    Nov. 12, 1950
  Charlie Conerly, N.Y. Giants vs. San Francisco,
    Dec. 1, 1957
  Tom Yewcic, Boston vs. Oakland, Dec. 16, 1962
  Jack Kemp, Buffalo vs. Houston, Oct. 29, 1967
  Roman Gabriel, Philadelphia vs. Oakland,
    Nov. 21, 1976
  Randall Cunningham, Philadelphia vs. L.A. Raiders,
    Nov. 30, 1986 (ot)
  Willie Totten, Buffalo vs. Indianapolis, Oct. 4, 1987
  Dave Walter, Cincinnati vs. Seattle, Oct. 11, 1987
  Dave Krieg, Seattle vs. San Diego, Nov. 25, 1990 (ot)
  Andre Ware, Detroit vs. Green Bay, Dec. 6, 1992
  Steve Beuerlein, Carolina vs. San Francisco,
    Nov. 8, 1998
  Patrick Ramsey, Washington vs. Green Bay,
    Oct. 20, 2002
  Eli Manning, N.Y. Giants vs. Buffalo, Dec. 23, 2007
  Josh Johnson, Tampa Bay vs. Carolina,
    Oct. 18, 2009

FUMBLES RECOVERED

Most Fumbles Recovered, Career, Own and Opponents'

56   Warren Moon, Houston, 1984-1993; Minnesota,
    1994-96; Seattle, 1997-98; Kansas City,
    1999-2000 (56 own)
47   Dave Krieg, Seattle, 1980-1991; Kansas City,
    1992-93; Detroit, 1994; Arizona, 1995; Chica-
    go, 1996; Tennessee, 1997-98 (47 own)
45   Boomer Esiason, Cincinnati, 1984-1992, 1997;
    N.Y. Jets, 1993-95; Arizona, 1996 (45 own)

Most Fumbles Recovered, Season, Own and Opponents'

12   David Carr, Houston, 2002 (12 own)
9   Don Hultz, Minnesota, 1963 (9 opp)
  Dave Krieg, Seattle, 1989 (9 own)
  Brian Griese, Denver, 1999 (9 own)
  Jon Kitna, Seattle, 2000 (9 own)
8   Paul Christman, Chi. Cardinals, 1945 (8 own)
  Joe Schmidt, Detroit, 1955 (8 opp)

Bill Butler, Minnesota, 1963 (8 own)
Kermit Alexander, San Francisco, 1965
   (4 own, 4 opp)
Jack Lambert, Pittsburgh, 1976 (1 own, 7 opp)
Danny White, Dallas, 1981 (8 own)
Dan Marino, Miami, 1988 (7 own, 1 opp)
Tony Banks, St. Louis, 1998 (8 own)
Ryan Fitzpatrick, Cincinnati, 2008 (8 own)
Donovan McNabb, Washington, 2010 (8 own)

Most Fumbles Recovered, Game, Own and Opponents'
4   Otto Graham, Cleveland vs. N.Y. Giants,
     Oct. 25, 1953 (4 own)
    Sam Etcheverry, St. Louis vs. N.Y. Giants,
     Sept. 17, 1961 (4 own)
    Roman Gabriel, Los Angeles vs. San Francisco,
     Oct. 12, 1969 (4 own)
    Randall Cunningham, Philadelphia vs. L.A. Raiders,
     Nov. 30, 1986 (ot) (4 own)
    Joe Ferguson, Buffalo vs. Miami, Sept. 18, 1977
     (4 own)
3   By many players

OWN FUMBLES RECOVERED
Most Own Fumbles Recovered, Career
56 Warren Moon, Houston, 1984-1993; Minnesota,
     1994-96; Seattle, 1997-98; Kansas City,
     1999-2000
47 Dave Krieg, Seattle, 1980-1991; Kansas City,
     1992-93; Detroit, 1994; Arizona, 1995;
     Chicago, 1996; Tennessee, 1997-98
45 Boomer Esiason, Cincinnati, 1984-1992, 1997;
     N.Y. Jets, 1993-95; Arizona, 1996

Most Own Fumbles Recovered, Season
12 David Carr, Houston, 2002
9   Dave Krieg, Seattle, 1989
    Brian Griese, Denver, 1999
    Jon Kitna, Seattle, 2000
8   Paul Christman, Chi. Cardinals, 1945
    Bill Butler, Minnesota, 1963
    Danny White, Dallas, 1981
    Tony Banks, St. Louis, 1998
    Ryan Fitzpatrick, Cincinnati, 2008
    Donovan McNabb, Washington, 2010

Most Own Fumbles Recovered, Game
4   Otto Graham, Cleveland vs. N.Y. Giants, Oct. 25, 1953
    Sam Etcheverry, St. Louis vs. N.Y. Giants,
     Sept. 17, 1961
    Roman Gabriel, Los Angeles vs. San Francisco,
     Oct. 12, 1969
    Joe Ferguson, Buffalo vs. Miami, Sept. 18, 1977
    Randall Cunningham, Philadelphia vs. L.A. Raiders,
     Nov. 30, 1986 (ot)
3   By many players

OPPONENTS' FUMBLES RECOVERED
Most Opponents' Fumbles Recovered, Career
29 Jim Marshall, Cleveland, 1960; Minnesota, 1961-1979
28 Jason Taylor, Miami, 1997-2007; Washington, 2008;
     Miami, 2009; N.Y. Jets, 2010
28 Rickey Jackson, New Orleans, 1981-1993;
     San Francisco, 1994-95
26 Kevin Greene, L.A. Rams, 1985-1992; Pittsburgh,
     1993-95; Carolina, 1996; San Francisco, 1997;
     Carolina, 1998-99
    Cornelius Bennett, Buffalo, 1987-1995; Atlanta,
     1996-98; Indianapolis, 1999-2000

Most Opponents' Fumbles Recovered, Season
9   Don Hultz, Minnesota, 1963
8   Joe Schmidt, Detroit, 1955
7   Alan Page, Minnesota, 1970

Jack Lambert, Pittsburgh, 1976
Ray Childress, Houston, 1988
Rickey Jackson, New Orleans, 1990

Most Opponents' Fumbles Recovered, Game
3   Corwin Clatt, Chi. Cardinals vs. Detroit, Nov. 6, 1949
    Vic Sears, Philadelphia vs. Green Bay, Nov. 2, 1952
    Ed Beatty, San Francisco vs. Los Angeles,
     Oct. 7, 1956
    Ron Carroll, Houston vs. Cincinnati, Oct. 27, 1974
    Maurice Spencer, New Orleans vs. Atlanta,
     Oct. 10, 1976
    Steve Nelson, New England vs. Philadelphia,
     Oct. 8, 1978
    Charles Jackson, Kansas City vs. Pittsburgh,
     Sept. 6, 1981
    Willie Buchanon, San Diego vs. Denver,
     Sept. 27, 1981
    Joey Browner, Minnesota vs. San Francisco,
     Sept. 8, 1985
    Ray Childress, Houston vs. Washington, Oct. 30, 1988
    John Thierry, Chicago vs. Houston, Oct. 22, 1995
    Stephen Boyd, Detroit vs. Chicago, Oct. 4, 1998
    Darryl Williams, Seattle vs. Kansas City, Oct. 4, 1998
    Rod Woodson, Oakland vs. Pittsburgh, Sept. 15, 2002
    Brian Young, St. Louis vs. Baltimore, Nov. 9, 2003
2   By many players

YARDS RETURNING FUMBLES
Longest Fumble Run (All TDs)
104 Jack Tatum, Oakland vs. Green Bay, Sept. 24, 1972
     Aeneas Williams, Arizona vs. Washington,
     Nov. 5, 2000
102 Travis Davis, Pittsburgh vs. Carolina, Dec. 26, 1999
100 Chris Martin, Kansas City vs. Miami, Oct. 13, 1991

TOUCHDOWNS
Most Touchdowns, Career (Total)
6   Jason Taylor, Miami, 1997-2007; Washington, 2008;
     Miami, 2009; N.Y. Jets, 2010
5   Jessie Tuggle, Atlanta, 1987-2000
4   Bill Thompson, Denver, 1969-1981
    Derrick Thomas, Kansas City, 1989-1999
    Keith Bulluck, Tennessee, 2000-09;
     N.Y. Giants, 2010
    Ronde Barber, Tampa Bay, 1997-2010

Most Touchdowns, Season (Total)
2   Harold McPhail, Boston, 1934
    Harry Ebding, Detroit, 1937
    John Morelli, Boston, 1944
    Frank Maznicki, Boston, 1947
    Fred (Dippy) Evans, Chi. Bears, 1948
    Ralph Heywood, Boston, 1948
    Art Tait, N.Y. Yanks, 1951
    John Dwyer, Los Angeles, 1952
    Leo Sugar, Chi. Cardinals, 1957
    Doug Cline, Houston, 1961
    Jim Bradshaw, Pittsburgh, 1964
    Royce Berry, Cincinnati, 1970
    Ahmad Rashad, Buffalo, 1974
    Tim Gray, Kansas City, 1977
    Charles Phillips, Oakland, 1978
    Kenny Johnson, Atlanta, 1981
    George Martin, N.Y. Giants, 1981
    Del Rodgers, Green Bay, 1982
    Mike Douglass, Green Bay, 1983
    Shelton Robinson, Seattle, 1983
    Erik McMillan, N.Y. Jets, 1989
    Les Miller, San Diego, 1990
    Seth Joyner, Philadelphia, 1991
    Robert Goff, New Orleans, 1992

Willie Clay, Detroit, 1993
Tyrone Hughes, New Orleans, 1994
Chad Brown, Seattle, 1997
Marcus Robertson, Tennessee, 1997
Dwayne Rudd, Minnesota, 1998
Keith McKenzie, Green Bay, 1999
Ronde Barber, Tampa Bay, 2004
Leonard Little, St. Louis, 2004
Antwan Odom, Tennessee, 2005
Adalius Thomas, Baltimore, 2005
Kevin Curtis, Philadelphia, 2007
Kerry Rhodes, Arizona, 2010

Most Touchdowns, Career (Own recovered)
2   Ken Kavanaugh, Chi. Bears, 1940-41, 1945-1950
    Mike Ditka, Chicago, 1961-66; Philadelphia,
        1967-68; Dallas, 1969-1972
    Gail Cogdill, Detroit, 1960-68; Baltimore, 1968;
        Atlanta, 1969-1970
    Ahmad Rashad, St. Louis, 1972-73; Buffalo, 1974;
        Minnesota, 1976-1982
    Jim Mitchell, Atlanta, 1969-1979
    Drew Pearson, Dallas, 1973-1983
    Del Rodgers, Green Bay, 1982, 1984; San Francisco,
        1987-88
    Alan Ricard, Baltimore, 2001-05
    Kevin Curtis, St. Louis, 2003-06; Philadelphia,
        2007-09; Miami, 2010

Most Touchdowns, Season (Own recovered)
2   Ahmad Rashad, Buffalo, 1974
    Del Rodgers, Green Bay, 1982
    Kevin Curtis, Philadelphia, 2007
1   By many players

Most Touchdowns, Career (Opponents' recovered)
6   Jason Taylor, Miami, 1997-2007; Washington, 2008;
        Miami, 2009; N.Y. Jets, 2010
5   Jessie Tuggle, Atlanta, 1987-2000
4   Derrick Thomas, Kansas City, 1989-1999
    Keith Bulluck, Tennessee, 2000-09;
        N.Y. Giants, 2010
    Ronde Barber, Tampa Bay, 1997-2010

Most Touchdowns, Season (Opponents' recovered)
2   Harold McPhail, Boston, 1934
    Harry Ebding, Detroit, 1937
    John Morelli, Boston, 1944
    Frank Maznicki, Boston, 1947
    Fred (Dippy) Evans, Chi. Bears, 1948
    Ralph Heywood, Boston, 1948
    Art Tait, N.Y. Yanks, 1951
    John Dwyer, Los Angeles, 1952
    Leo Sugar, Chi. Cardinals, 1957
    Doug Cline, Houston, 1961
    Jim Bradshaw, Pittsburgh, 1964
    Royce Berry, Cincinnati, 1970
    Tim Gray, Kansas City, 1977
    Charles Phillips, Oakland, 1978
    Kenny Johnson, Atlanta, 1981
    George Martin, N.Y. Giants, 1981
    Mike Douglass, Green Bay, 1983
    Shelton Robinson, Seattle, 1983
    Erik McMillan, N.Y. Jets, 1989
    Les Miller, San Diego, 1990
    Seth Joyner, Philadelphia, 1991
    Robert Goff, New Orleans, 1992
    Willie Clay, Detroit, 1993
    Tyrone Hughes, New Orleans, 1994
    Chad Brown, Seattle, 1997
    Marcus Robertson, Tennessee, 1997
    Dwayne Rudd, Minnesota, 1998
    Keith McKenzie, Green Bay, 1999
    Ronde Barber, Tampa Bay, 2004

Leonard Little, St. Louis, 2004
Antwan Odom, Tennessee, 2005
Adalius Thomas, Baltimore, 2005
Kerry Rhodes, Arizona, 2010

Most Touchdowns, Game (Opponents' recovered)
2   Fred (Dippy) Evans, Chi. Bears vs. Washington,
        Nov. 28, 1948

COMBINED NET YARDS GAINED
Rushing, receiving, interception returns, punt returns, kickoff
returns, and fumble returns

Most Seasons Leading League
5   Jim Brown, Cleveland, 1958-1961, 1964
4   Brian Mitchell, Washington, 1994-96, 1998
3   Cliff Battles, Boston, 1932-33; Washington, 1937
    Gale Sayers, Chicago, 1965-67
    Eric Dickerson, L.A. Rams, 1983-84, 1986
    Thurman Thomas, Buffalo, 1989, 1991-92

Most Consecutive Seasons Leading League
4   Jim Brown, Cleveland, 1958-1961
3   Gale Sayers, Chicago, 1965-67
    Brian Mitchell, Washington, 1994-96
2   Cliff Battles, Boston, 1932-33
    Charley Trippi, Chi. Cardinals, 1948-49
    Timmy Brown, Philadelphia, 1962-63
    Floyd Little, Denver, 1967-68
    James Brooks, San Diego, 1981-82
    Eric Dickerson, L.A. Rams, 1983-84
    Thurman Thomas, Buffalo, 1991-92
    Dante Hall, Kansas City, 2003-04

ATTEMPTS
Most Attempts, Career
4,939   Emmitt Smith. Dallas, 1990-2002; Arizona, 2003-04
4,368   Walter Payton, Chicago, 1975-1987
4,016   Curtis Martin, New England, 1995-97; N.Y. Jets,
            1998-2005

Most Attempts, Season
496   James Wilder, Tamp Bay, 1984
458   Larry Johnson, Kansas City, 2006
455   Eddie George, Tennessee, 2000

Most Attempts, Rookie, Season
442   Eric Dickerson, L.A. Rams, 1983
433   Edgerrin James, Indianapolis, 1999
401   Curtis Martin, New England, 1995

Most Attempts, Game
48   James Wilder, Tampa Bay vs. Pittsburgh, Oct. 30, 1983
     LaDainian Tomlinson, San Diego vs. Denver,
         Dec. 1, 2002 (ot)
47   James Wilder, Tampa Bay vs. Green Bay,
         Sept. 30, 1984 (ot)
     Terrell Davis, Denver vs. Buffalo, Oct. 26, 1997 (ot)
46   Gerald Riggs, Atlanta vs. L.A. Rams, Nov. 17, 1985

YARDS GAINED
Most Yards Gained, Career
23,546   Jerry Rice, San Francisco, 1985-2000; Oakland,
             2001-04; Seattle, 2004
23,330   Brian Mitchell, Washington, 1990-99; Philadelphia,
             2000-02; N.Y. Giants, 2003
21,803   Walter Payton, Chicago, 1975-1987

Most Yards Gained, Season
2,690   Derrick Mason, Tennessee, 2000
2,647   Michael Lewis, New Orleans, 2002
2,535   Lionel James, San Diego, 1985

Most Yards Gained, Rookie, Season
2,317   Tim Brown, L.A. Raiders, 1988
2,272   Gale Sayers, Chicago, 1965
2,250   Maurice Jones-Drew, Jacksonville, 2006

Most Yards Gained, Game
- 404   Glyn Milburn, Denver vs. Seattle, Dec. 10, 1995
- 373   Billy Cannon, Houston vs. N.Y. Titans, Dec. 10. 1961
- 361   Adrian Peterson, Minnesota vs. Chicago, Oct. 14, 2007

SACKS
Sacks have been compiled since 1982.

Most Seasons Leading League
- 2   Mark Gastineau, N.Y. Jets, 1983-84
  Reggie White, Philadelphia, 1987-88
  Kevin Greene, Pittsburgh, 1994; Carolina, 1996
  Michael Strahan, N.Y. Giants, 2001, 2003
  DeMarcus Ware, Dallas, 2008, 2010

Most Sacks, Career
- 200.0   Bruce Smith, Buffalo, 1985-1999; Washington, 2000-03
- 198.0   Reggie White, Philadelphia, 1985-1992; Green Bay, 1993-98; Carolina, 2000
- 160.0   Kevin Greene, L.A. Rams, 1985-1992; Pittsburgh, 1993-95; Carolina, 1996, 1998-99; San Francisco, 1997

Most Sacks, Season
- 22.5   Michael Strahan, N.Y. Giants, 2001
- 22.0   Mark Gastineau, N.Y. Jets, 1984
- 21.0   Reggie White, Philadelphia, 1987
  Chris Doleman, Minnesota, 1989

Most Sacks, Rookie, Season
- 14.5   Jevon Kearse, Tennessee, 1999
- 13.0   Dwight Freeney, Indianapolis, 2002
- 12.5   Leslie O'Neal, San Diego, 1986
  Simeon Rice, Arizona, 1996

Most Sacks, Game
- 7.0   Derrick Thomas, Kansas City vs. Seattle, Nov. 11, 1990
- 6.0   Fred Dean, San Francisco vs. New Orleans, Nov. 13, 1983
  Derrick Thomas, Kansas City vs. Oakland, Sept. 6, 1998
  Osi Umenyiora, N.Y. Giants vs. Philadelphia, Sept. 30, 2007
- 5.5   William Gay, Detroit vs. Tampa Bay, Sept. 4, 1983

Most Seasons, 10 or More Sacks
- 13   Bruce Smith, Buffalo, 1986-1990, 1992-98; Washington, 2000
- 12   Reggie White, Philadelphia, 1985-1992; Green Bay, 1993, 1995, 1997-98
- 10   Kevin Greene, L.A. Rams, 1988-1990, 1992; Pittsburgh, 1993-94; Carolina, 1996, 1998-99; San Francisco, 1997

Most Consecutive Seasons, 10 or More Sacks
- 9   Reggie White, Philadelphia, 1985-1992; Green Bay, 1993
- 8   John Randle, Minnesota, 1992-99
- 7   Lawrence Taylor, N.Y. Giants, 1984-1990
  Bruce Smith, Buffalo, 1992-98

Most Consecutive Games, Sack
- 10   Simon Fletcher, Denver, Nov. 15, 1992-Sept. 20, 1993
  DeMarcus Ware, Dallas, Dec. 16, 2007-Oct. 19, 2008
- 9   Bruce Smith, Buffalo, Nov. 16, 1986-Oct. 25, 1987
  Kevin Greene, San Francisco-Carolina, Dec. 7, 1997-Oct. 18, 1998
  Dwight Freeney, Indianapolis, Dec. 18, 2008-Nov. 8, 2009
- 8   By many players

MISCELLANEOUS
Longest Return of Missed Field Goal (All TDs)
- 109   Antonio Cromartie, San Diego vs. Minnesota, Nov. 4, 2007

- 108   Nathan Vasher, Chicago vs. San Francisco, Nov. 13, 2005
  Devin Hester, Chicago vs. N.Y. Giants, Nov. 12, 2006
- 107   Chris McAlister, Baltimore vs. Denver, Sept. 30, 2002

TEAM RECORDS

CHAMPIONSHIPS
Most Seasons League Champion
- 13   Green Bay, 1929-1931, 1936, 1939, 1944, 1961-62, 1965-67, 1996, 2010
- 9   Chi. Bears, 1921, 1932-33, 1940-41, 1943, 1946, 1963, 1985
- 7   N.Y. Giants, 1927, 1934, 1938, 1956, 1986, 1990, 2007

Most Consecutive Seasons League Champion
- 3   Green Bay, 1929-1931
  Green Bay, 1965-67
- 2   Canton, 1922-23
  Chi. Bears, 1932-33
  Chi. Bears, 1940-41
  Philadelphia, 1948-49
  Detroit, 1952-53
  Cleveland, 1954-55
  Baltimore, 1958-59
  Houston, 1960-61
  Green Bay, 1961-62
  Buffalo, 1964-65
  Miami, 1972-73
  Pittsburgh, 1974-75
  Pittsburgh, 1978-79
  San Francisco, 1988-89
  Dallas, 1992-93
  Denver, 1997-98
  New England, 2003-04

Most Times Finishing First, Regular Season
- 22   N.Y. Giants, 1927, 1933-35, 1938-39, 1941, 1944, 1946, 1956, 1958-59, 1961-63, 1986, 1989-1990, 1997, 2000, 2005, 2008
  Chi. Bears, 1921, 1932-34, 1937, 1940-43, 1946, 1956, 1963, 1984-88, 1990, 2001, 2005-06, 2010
- 21   Green Bay, 1929-1931, 1936, 1938-39, 1944, 1960-62, 1965-67, 1972, 1995-97, 2002-04, 2007
  Dallas, 1966-1971, 1973, 1976-79, 1981, 1985, 1992-96, 1998, 2007, 2009
- 20   Pittsburgh, 1972, 1974-79, 1983-84, 1992, 1994-97, 2001-02, 2004, 2007-08, 2010

Most Consecutive Times Finishing First, Regular Season
- 7   Los Angeles, 1973-79
- 6   Cleveland, 1950-55
  Dallas, 1966-1971
  Minnesota, 1973-78
  Pittsburgh, 1974-79
- 5   Oakland, 1972-76
  Chicago, 1984-88
  San Francisco, 1986-1990
  Dallas, 1992-96
  Indianapolis, 2003-07
  New England, 2003-07

GAMES WON
Most Consecutive Games Won
- 23   Indianapolis, 2008-09
- 21   New England, 2006-08
- 18   New England, 2003-04

Most Consecutive Games Without Defeat
- 25   Canton, 1921-23 (won 22, tied 3)
- 24   Chi. Bears, 1941-43 (won 23, tied 1)

23   Green Bay, 1928-1930 (won 21, tied 2)
    Indianapolis, 2009 (won 23)
Most Games Won, Season
16   New England, 2007
15   San Francisco, 1984
    Chicago, 1985
    Minnesota, 1998
    Pittsburgh, 2004
14   By many teams
Most Consecutive Games Won, Season
16   New England, 2007, entire season
14   Miami, 1972, entire season
    Pittsburgh, 2004
    Indianapolis, 2009
13   Chi. Bears, 1934, entire season
    Denver, 1998
    Indianapolis, 2005
    New Orleans, 2009
Most Consecutive Games Won, Start of Season
16   New England, 2007, entire season
14   Miami, 1972, entire season
    Indianapolis, 2009
13   Chi. Bears, 1934, entire season
    Denver, 1998
    Indianapolis, 2005
    New Orleans, 2009
Most Consecutive Games Won, End of Season
16   New England, 2007, entire season
14   Miami, 1972, entire season
    Pittsburgh, 2004
13   Chi. Bears, 1934, entire season
Most Consecutive Games Without Defeat, Season
16   New England, 2007 (won 16), entire season
14   Miami, 1972 (won 14), entire season
    Pittsburgh, 2004 (won 14)
    Indianapolis, 2009 (won 14)
13   Chi. Bears, 1926 (won 11, tied 2)
    Green Bay, 1929 (won 12, tied 1)
    Chi. Bears, 1934 (won 13), entire season
    Baltimore, 1967 (won 11, tied 2)
    Denver, 1998 (won 13)
    Indianapolis, 2005 (won 13)
    New Orleans, 2009 (won 13)
Most Consecutive Games Without Defeat, Start of Season
16   New England, 2007 (won 16), entire season
14   Miami, 1972 (won 14), entire season
    Indianapolis, 2009 (won 14)
13   Chi. Bears, 1926 (won 11, tied 2)
    Green Bay, 1929 (won 12, tied 1), entire season
    Chi. Bears, 1934 (won 13), entire season
    Baltimore, 1967 (won 11, tied 2)
    Denver, 1998 (won 13)
    Indianapolis, 2005 (won 13)
    New Orleans, 2009 (won 13)
Most Consecutive Games Without Defeat, End of Season
16   New England, 2007 (won 16), entire season
14   Miami, 1972 (won 14), entire season
    Pittsburgh, 2004 (won 14)
13   Green Bay, 1929 (won 12, tied 1), entire season
    Chi. Bears, 1934 (won 13), entire season
Most Consecutive Home Games Won
27   Miami, 1971-74
25   Green Bay, 1995-98
24   Denver, 1996-98
Most Consecutive Home Games Without Defeat
29   Green Bay, 1928-1933 (won 26, tied 3)
27   Miami, 1971-74 (won 27)
25   Green Bay, 1995-98 (won 25)
Most Consecutive Road Games Won
18   San Francisco, 1988-1990

12   New England, 2006-08
11   L.A. Chargers/San Diego, 1960-61
    San Francisco, 1987-88
    Pittsburgh, 2004-05
    Indianapolis, 2008-09
Most Consecutive Road Games Without Defeat
18   San Francisco, 1988-1990 (won 18)
13   Chi. Bears, 1941-43 (won 12, tied 1)
12   Green Bay, 1928-1930 (won 10, tied 2)
    New England, 2006-08 (won 12)
Most Shutout Games Won or Tied, Season
10   Pottsville, 1926 (won 9, tied 1)
    N.Y. Giants, 1927 (won 9, tied 1)
9   Akron, 1921 (won 8, tied 1)
    Canton, 1922 (won 7, tied 2)
    Frankford, 1926 (won 9)
    Frankford, 1929 (won 6, tied 3)
Most Consecutive Shutout Games Won or Tied
13   Akron, 1920-21 (won 10, tied 3)
7   Pottsville, 1926 (won 6, tied 1)
    Detroit, 1934 (won 7)
6   Buffalo, 1920-21 (won 5, tied 1)
    Frankford, 1926 (won 6)
    Detroit, 1926 (won 4, tied 2)
    N.Y. Giants, 1926-27 (won 5, tied 1)

GAMES LOST
Most Consecutive Games Lost
26   Tampa Bay, 1976-1977
19   Chi. Cardinals, 1942-43, 1945
    Oakland, 1961-62
    Detroit, 2007-09
18   Houston, 1972-73
Most Consecutive Games Without Victory
26   Tampa Bay, 1976-77 (lost 26)
23   Rochester, 1922-25 (lost 21, tied 2)
    Washington, 1960-61 (lost 20, tied 3)
19   Dayton, 1927-29 (lost 18, tied 1)
    Chi. Cardinals, 1942-43, 1945 (lost 19)
    Oakland, 1961-62 (lost 19)
    Detroit, 2007-09 (lost 19)
Most Games Lost, Season
16   Detroit, 2008
15   New Orleans, 1980
    Dallas, 1989
    New England, 1990
    Indianapolis, 1991
    N.Y. Jets, 1996
    San Diego, 2000
    Carolina, 2001
    Miami, 2007
    St. Louis, 2009
14   By many teams
Most Consecutive Games Lost, Season
16   Detroit, 2008, entire season
15   Carolina, 2001
14   Tampa Bay, 1976
    New Orleans, 1980
    Baltimore, 1981
    New England, 1990
Most Consecutive Games Lost, Start of Season
16   Detroit, 2008, entire season
14   Tampa Bay, 1976, entire season
    New Orleans, 1980
13   Oakland, 1962
    Indianapolis, 1986
    Miami, 2007
Most Consecutive Games Lost, End of Season
16   Detroit, 2008, entire season
15   Carolina, 2001

14 Tampa Bay, 1976, *entire season*
New England, 1990

Most Consecutive Games Without Victory, Season
16 Detroit, 2008 (lost 16), *entire season*
15 Carolina, 2001 (lost 15)
14 Tampa Bay, 1976 (lost 14), *entire season*
New Orleans, 1980 (lost 14)
Baltimore, 1981 (lost 14)
New England, 1990 (lost 14)

Most Consecutive Games Without Victory, Start of Season
16 Detroit, 2008 (lost 16), *entire season*
14 Tampa Bay, 1976 (lost 14), *entire season*
New Orleans, 1980 (lost 14)
13 Washington, 1961 (lost 12, tied 1)
Oakland, 1962 (lost 13)
Indianapolis, 1986 (lost 13)
Miami, 2007 (lost 13)

Most Consecutive Games Without Victory, End of Season
16 Detroit, 2008 (lost 16), *entire season*
15 Carolina, 2001
14 Tampa Bay, 1976, (lost 14), *entire season*
New England, 1990 (lost 14)

Most Consecutive Home Games Lost
14 Dallas, 1988-89
St. Louis, 2008-2010
13 Houston, 1972-73
Tampa Bay, 1976-77
N.Y. Jets, 1995-97
11 Oakland, 1961-62
Los Angeles, 1961-63
Cincinnati, 1998-99

Most Consecutive Home Games Without Victory
14 Dallas, 1988-89 (lost 14)
St. Louis, 2008-2010 (lost 14)
13 Houston, 1972-73 (lost 13)
Tampa Bay, 1976-77 (lost 13)
N.Y. Jets, 1995-97 (lost 13)
Philadelphia, 1936-38 (lost 12, tied 1)

Most Consecutive Road Games Lost
26 Detroit, 2007-2010
24 Detroit, 2001-03
23 Houston, 1981-84

Most Consecutive Road Games Without Victory
26 Detroit, 2007-2010 (lost 26)
24 Detroit, 2001-03 (lost 24)
23 Houston, 1981-84 (lost 23)

Most Shutout Games Lost or Tied, Season
8 Frankford, 1927 (lost 6, tied 2)
Brooklyn, 1931 (lost 8)
7 Dayton, 1925 (lost 6, tied 1)
Orange, 1929 (lost 4, tied 3)
Frankford, 1931 (lost 6, tied 1)
6 By many teams

Most Consecutive Shutout Games Lost or Tied
8 Rochester, 1922-24 (lost 8)
7 Hammond, 1922-23 (lost 6, tied 1)
6 Providence, 1926-27 (lost 5, tied 1)
Brooklyn, 1942-43 (lost 6)

TIE GAMES

Most Tie Games, Season
6 Chi. Bears, 1932
5 Frankford, 1929
4 Chi. Bears, 1924
Orange, 1929
Portsmouth, 1932

Most Consecutive Tie Games
3 Chi. Bears, 1932
2 By many teams

SCORING

Most Seasons Leading League
10 Chi. Bears, 1932, 1934-35, 1939, 1941-43,
1946-47, 1956
9 San Francisco, 1953, 1965, 1970, 1987, 1989,
1992-95
L.A./St. Louis Rams, 1950-52, 1957, 1967, 1973,
1999-2001
7 Green Bay, 1931, 1936-38, 1961-62, 1996

Most Consecutive Seasons Leading League
4 San Francisco, 1992-1995
3 Green Bay, 1936-38
Chi. Bears, 1941-43
Los Angeles, 1950-52
Oakland, 1967-69
St. Louis, 1999-2001
2 By many teams

POINTS

Most Points, Season
589 New England, 2007
556 Minnesota, 1998
541 Washington, 1983

Fewest Points, Season (Since 1932)
37 Cincinnati/St. Louis, 1934
38 Cincinnati, 1933
Detroit, 1942
51 Pittsburgh, 1934
Philadelphia, 1936

Most Points, Game
72 Washington vs. N.Y. Giants, Nov. 27, 1966
70 Los Angeles vs. Baltimore, Oct. 22, 1950
66 Rochester vs. *Fort Porter, Oct. 10, 1920
*Not a member of the American Professional
Football Association

Most Points, Both Teams, Game
113 Washington (72) vs. N.Y. Giants (41), Nov. 27, 1966
106 Cincinnati (58) vs. Cleveland (48), Nov. 28, 2004
101 Oakland (52) vs. Houston (49), Dec. 22, 1963

Fewest Points, Both Teams, Game
0 In many games. Last time: N.Y. Giants vs. Detroit,
Nov. 7, 1943

Most Points, Shutout Victory Game
66 Rochester vs. *Fort Porter, Oct. 10, 1920
*Not a member of the American Professional
Football Association
64 Philadelphia vs. Cincinnati, Nov. 6, 1934
62 Akron vs. Oorang, Oct. 29, 1922

Most Consecutive Games Scoring
420 San Francisco, 1977-2004
293 Denver, 1992-2010 (current)
274 Cleveland, 1950-1971

Fewest Points, Shutout Victory, Game
2 Akron vs. Buffalo, Nov. 29, 1923
Kansas City vs. Buffalo, Nov. 21, 1926
Frankford vs. Green Bay, Nov. 29, 1928
Green Bay vs. Chi. Bears, Oct. 16, 1932
Chi. Bears vs. Green Bay, Sept. 18, 1938

Most Points Overcome to Win Game
28 San Francisco vs. New Orleans, Dec. 7, 1980 (ot)
(trailed 7-35, won 38-35)
26 Buffalo vs. Indianapolis, Sept., 21, 1997
(trailed 0-26, won 37-35)
25 St. Louis vs. Tampa Bay, Nov. 8, 1987
(trailed 3-28, won 31-28)

Most Points Overcome to Tie Game
31 Denver vs. Buffalo, Nov. 27, 1960
(trailed 7-38, tied 38-38)

28 Los Angeles vs. Philadelphia, Oct. 3, 1948
      (trailed 0-28, tied 28-28)

Most Points, Each Half
1st: 49 Green Bay vs. Tampa Bay, Oct. 2, 1983
   48 Buffalo vs. Miami, Sept. 18, 1966
   45 Green Bay vs. Cleveland, Nov. 12, 1967
      Indianapolis vs. Denver, Oct. 31, 1988
      Houston vs. Cleveland, Dec. 9, 1990
      Seattle vs. Minnesota, Sept. 29, 2002
      New England vs. Tennessee, Oct. 18, 2009
      Philadelphia vs. Washington, Nov. 15, 2010
2nd: 49 Chi. Bears vs. Philadelphia, Nov. 30, 1941
   48 Chi. Cardinals vs. Baltimore, Oct. 2, 1960
      N.Y. Giants vs. Baltimore, Nov. 19, 1950
   45 Cincinnati vs. Houston, Dec. 17, 1972

Most Points, Both Teams, Each Half
1st: 70 Houston (35) vs. Oakland (35), Dec. 22, 1963
   63 Philadelphia (42) vs. Detroit (21), Sept. 23, 2007
   62 N.Y. Jets (41) vs. Tampa Bay (21), Nov. 17, 1985
      Indianapolis (35) vs. Cincinnati (27), Nov. 20, 2005
2nd: 66 Cleveland (35) vs. Cincinnati (31), Nov. 28, 2004
   65 Washington (38) vs. N.Y. Giants (27), Nov. 27, 1966
   62 L.A. Raiders (31) vs. San Diego (31), Jan. 2, 1983
      Baltimore (38) vs. Seattle (24), Nov. 23, 2003

Most Points, One Quarter
41 Green Bay vs. Detroit, Oct. 7, 1945 (second quarter)
      Los Angeles vs. Detroit, Oct. 29, 1950
      (third quarter)
37 Los Angeles vs. Green Bay, Sept. 21, 1980
      (second quarter)
35 Chi. Cardinals vs. Boston, Oct. 24, 1948
      (third quarter)
      Green Bay vs. Cleveland, Nov. 12, 1967 (first quarter)
      Green Bay vs. Tampa Bay, Oct. 2, 1983
      (second quarter)
      New England vs. Tennessee, Oct. 18, 2009
      (second quarter)

Most Points, Both Teams, One Quarter
49 Oakland (28) vs. Houston (21), Dec. 22, 1963
      (second quarter)
48 Green Bay (41) vs. Detroit (7), Oct. 7, 1945
      (second quarter)
      Los Angeles (41) vs. Detroit (7), Oct. 29, 1950
      (third quarter)
      Detroit (34) vs. Chicago (14), Sept. 30, 2007
      (fourth quarter)
47 St. Louis (27) vs. Philadelphia (20), Dec. 13, 1964
      (second quarter)

Most Points, Each Quarter
1st: 35 Green Bay vs. Cleveland, Nov. 12, 1967
   31 Buffalo vs. Kansas City, Sept. 13, 1964
   28 By nine teams
2nd: 41 Green Bay vs. Detroit, Oct. 7, 1945
   37 Los Angeles vs. Green Bay, Sept. 21, 1980
   35 Green Bay vs. Tampa Bay, Oct. 2, 1983
      New England vs. Tennessee, Oct. 18, 2009
3rd: 41 Los Angeles vs. Detroit, Oct. 29, 1950
   35 Chi. Cardinals vs. Boston, Oct. 24, 1948
   28 By 10 teams
4th: 34 Detroit vs. Chicago, Sept. 30, 2007
   31 Oakland vs. Denver, Dec. 17, 1960
      Oakland vs. San Diego, Dec. 8, 1963
      Atlanta vs. Green Bay, Sept. 13, 1981
   30 N.Y. Jets vs. Miami, Oct. 23, 2000

Most Points, Both Teams, Each Quarter
1st: 42 Green Bay (35) vs. Cleveland (7), Nov. 12, 1967
   41 Tennessee (24) vs. Indianapolis (17), Dec. 5, 2004
   35 Dall. Texans (21) vs. N.Y. Titans (14), Nov. 11, 1962
      Dallas (28) vs. Philadelphia (7), Oct. 19, 1969
      Kansas City (21) vs. Seattle (14), Dec. 11, 1977

      Detroit (21) vs. L.A. Raiders (14), Dec. 10, 1990
      Dallas (21) vs. Atlanta (14), Dec. 22, 1991
      Indianapolis (21) vs. Green Bay (14), Sept 26, 2004
      Miami (21) vs. Buffalo (14), Dec. 5, 2004
      Philadelphia (21) vs. New Orleans (14), Dec. 23, 2007
2nd: 49 Oakland (28) vs. Houston (21), Dec. 22, 1963
   48 Green Bay (41) vs. Detroit (7), Oct. 7, 1945
   47 St. Louis (27) vs. Philadelphia (20), Dec. 13, 1964
3rd: 48 Los Angeles (41) vs. Detroit (7), Oct. 29, 1950
   42 Washington (28) vs. Philadelphia (14), Oct. 1, 1955
   41 Green Bay (21) vs. N.Y. Yanks (20), Oct. 8, 1950
4th: 48 Detroit (34) vs. Chicago (14), Sept. 30, 2007
   43 Atlanta (28) vs. Carolina (15), Nov. 23, 2008
   42 Chi. Cardinals (28) vs. Philadelphia (14), Dec. 7, 1947
      Green Bay (28) vs. Chi. Bears (14), Nov. 6, 1955
      N.Y. Jets (28) vs. Boston (14), Oct. 27, 1968
      Pittsburgh (21) vs. Cleveland (21), Oct. 18, 1969
      New England (21) vs. Kansas City (21),
        Sept. 22, 2002

TOUCHDOWNS

Most Seasons Leading League, Touchdowns
13 Chi. Bears, 1932, 1934-35, 1939, 1941-44,
     1946-48, 1956, 1965
  7 Dallas, 1966, 1968, 1971, 1973, 1977-78, 1980
     San Francisco, 1953, 1970, 1987, 1992-95
     L.A./St. Louis Rams, 1949-1952, 1999-2001
     San Diego, 1963, 1965, 1979, 1981-82, 1985,
     2006
  6 Oakland, 1967-69, 1972, 1974, 1977
     Green Bay, 1932, 1937-38, 1961-62, 1996
     Baltimore/Indianapolis Colts, 1957-59, 1964, 1976,
     2004

Most Consecutive Seasons Leading League, Touchdowns
4 Chi. Bears, 1941-44
    Los Angeles, 1949-1952
    San Francisco, 1992-95
3 Chi. Bears, 1946-48
    Baltimore, 1957-59
    Oakland, 1967-69
    St. Louis, 1999-2001
2 By many teams

Most Touchdowns, Season
75 New England, 2007
70 Miami, 1984
67 St. Louis, 2000

Fewest Touchdowns, Season (Since 1932)
3 Cincinnati, 1933
4 Cincinnati/St. Louis, 1934
5 Detroit, 1942

Most Touchdowns, Game
10 Rochester vs. *Fort Porter, Oct. 10, 1920
    *Not a member of the American Professional
    Football Association
    Philadelphia vs. Cincinnati, Nov. 6, 1934
    Los Angeles vs. Baltimore, Oct. 22, 1950
    Washington vs. N.Y. Giants, Nov. 27, 1966
  9 Rock Island vs. Evansville, Oct. 15, 1922
    Akron vs. Oorang, Oct. 29, 1922
    Racine vs. Louisville, Nov. 5, 1922
    Chi. Cardinals vs. Rochester, Oct. 7, 1923
    Chi. Cardinals vs. Milwaukee, Dec. 10, 1925
    Chi. Cardinals vs. N.Y. Giants, Oct. 17, 1948
    Chi. Cardinals vs. N.Y. Bulldogs, Nov. 13, 1949
    Los Angeles vs. Detroit, Oct. 29, 1950
    Pittsburgh vs. N.Y. Giants, Nov. 30, 1952
    Chicago vs. San Francisco, Dec. 12, 1965
    Chicago vs. Green Bay, Dec. 7, 1980
  8 By many teams

Most Touchdowns, Both Teams, Game
- 16 Washington (10) vs. N.Y. Giants (6), Nov. 27, 1966
- 14 Chi. Cardinals (9) vs. N.Y. Giants (5), Oct. 17, 1948
  - Los Angeles (10) vs. Baltimore (4), Oct. 22, 1950
  - Houston (7) vs. Oakland (7), Dec. 22, 1963
- 13 New Orleans (7) vs. St. Louis (6), Nov. 2, 1969
  - Kansas City (7) vs. Seattle (6), Nov. 27, 1983 (ot)
  - San Diego (8) vs. Pittsburgh (5), Dec. 8, 1985
  - N.Y. Jets (7) vs. Miami (6), Sept. 21, 1986 (ot)
  - Cincinnati (7) vs. Cleveland (6), Nov. 28, 2004

Most Consecutive Games Scoring Touchdowns
- 166 Cleveland, 1957-1969
- 133 San Diego, 2002-2010 (current)
- 127 Indianapolis, 2003-2010 (current)

POINTS AFTER TOUCHDOWN

Most (One-Point) Points After Touchdown, Season
- 74 New England, 2007
- 66 Miami, 1984
- 65 Houston, 1961

Fewest (One-Point) Points After Touchdown, Season
- 2 Chi. Cardinals, 1933
- 3 Cincinnati, 1933
  - Pittsburgh, 1934
- 4 Cincinnati/St. Louis, 1934

Most (One-Point) Points After Touchdown, Game
- 10 Los Angeles vs. Baltimore, Oct. 22, 1950
- 9 Chi. Cardinals vs. N.Y. Giants, Oct. 17, 1948
  - Pittsburgh vs. N.Y. Giants, Nov. 30, 1952
  - Washington vs. N.Y. Giants, Nov. 27, 1966
- 8 By many teams

Most (One-Point) Points After Touchdown, Both Teams, Game
- 14 Chi. Cardinals (9) vs. N.Y. Giants (5), Oct. 17, 1948
  - Houston (7) vs. Oakland (7), Dec. 22, 1963
  - Washington (9) vs. N.Y. Giants (5), Nov. 27, 1966
- 13 Los Angeles (10) vs. Baltimore (3), Oct. 22, 1950
  - Cincinnati (7) vs. Cleveland (6), Nov. 28, 2004
- 12 In many games

Most Two-Point Conversions, Season
- 6 Miami, 1994
  - Minnesota, 1997
- 5 Arizona, 1995
  - Baltimore, 1996
  - Jacksonville, 1996
  - Chicago, 1997
  - San Francisco, 1998
  - Pittsburgh, 2002
- 4 By many teams

Most Two-Point Conversions, Game
- 4 St. Louis vs. Atlanta, Oct. 15, 2000
- 3 Baltimore vs. New England, Oct. 6, 1996
  - Pittsburgh vs. Tennessee, Nov. 1, 1998
- 2 By many teams

Most Two-Point Conversions, Both Teams, Game
- 5 Baltimore (3) vs. New England (2), Oct. 6, 1996
  - St. Louis (4) vs. Atlanta (1), Oct. 15, 2000
- 3 Seattle (2) vs. Kansas City (1), Oct. 23, 1994
  - Minnesota (2) vs. Seattle (1), Nov. 10, 1996
  - Pittsburgh (3) vs. Tennessee (0), Nov. 1, 1998
- 2 In many games

FIELD GOALS

Most Seasons Leading League, Field Goals
- 11 Green Bay, 1935-36, 1940-43, 1946-47, 1955, 1972, 1974
- 9 L.A./St. Louis Rams, 1949, 1951, 1958, 1966, 1973, 1978, 2003, 2006, 2010
- 8 Washington, 1945, 1956, 1971, 1976-77, 1979, 1982, 1992

N.Y. Giants, 1933, 1937, 1939, 1941, 1944, 1959, 1983, 2008

Most Consecutive Seasons Leading League, Field Goals
- 4 Green Bay, 1940-43
- 3 Cleveland, 1952-54
- 2 By many teams

Most Field Goals Attempted, Season
- 49 Los Angeles, 1966
  - Washington, 1971
- 48 Green Bay, 1972
- 47 N.Y. Jets, 1969
  - Los Angeles, 1973
  - Washington, 1983

Fewest Field Goals Attempted, Season (Since 1938)
- 0 Chi. Bears, 1944
- 2 Cleveland, 1939
  - Card-Pitt, 1944
  - Boston, 1946
  - Chi. Bears, 1947
- 3 Chi. Bears, 1945
  - Cleveland, 1945

Most Field Goals Attempted, Game
- 9 St. Louis vs. Pittsburgh, Sept. 24, 1967
- 8 Pittsburgh vs. St. Louis, Dec. 2, 1962
  - Detroit vs. Minnesota, Nov. 13, 1966
  - N.Y. Jets vs. Buffalo, Nov. 3, 1968
  - Dallas vs. N.Y. Giants, Sept. 15, 2003 (ot)
  - Tennessee vs. Houston, Oct. 21, 2007
- 7 By many teams

Most Field Goals Attempted, Both Teams, Game
- 11 St. Louis (6) vs. Pittsburgh (5), Nov. 13, 1966
  - Washington (6) vs. Chicago (5), Nov. 14, 1971
  - Green Bay (6) vs. Detroit (5), Sept. 29, 1974
  - Washington (6) vs. N.Y. Giants (5), Nov. 14, 1976
- 10 In many games

Most Field Goals, Season
- 43 Arizona, 2005
- 39 Miami, 1999
  - St. Louis, 2003
- 37 Carolina, 1996
  - Indianapolis, 2003

Fewest Field Goals, Season (Since 1932)
- 0 Boston, 1932, 1935
  - Chi. Cardinals, 1932, 1945
  - Green Bay, 1932, 1944
  - N.Y. Giants, 1932
  - Brooklyn, 1944
  - Card-Pitt, 1944
  - Chi. Bears, 1944, 1947
  - Boston, 1946
  - Baltimore, 1950
  - Dallas, 1952

Most Field Goals, Game
- 8 Tennessee vs. Houston, Oct. 21, 2007
- 7 St. Louis vs. Pittsburgh, Sept. 24, 1967
  - Minnesota vs. L.A. Rams, Nov. 5, 1989 (ot)
  - Dallas vs. Green Bay, Nov. 18, 1996
  - Dallas vs. N.Y. Giants, Sept. 15, 2003 (ot)
  - Cincinnati vs. Baltimore, Nov. 11, 2007
- 6 By many teams

Most Field Goals, Both Teams, Game
- 9 San Diego (5) vs. Kansas City (4), Sept. 29, 1996
  - Miami (6) vs. New England (3), Oct. 17, 1999
  - Houston (5) vs. Miami (4), Oct. 7, 2007
- 8 Cleveland (4) vs. St. Louis (4), Sept. 20, 1964
  - Chicago (5) vs. Philadelphia (3), Oct. 20, 1968
  - Washington (5) vs. Chicago (3), Nov. 14, 1971
  - Kansas City (5) vs. Buffalo (3), Dec. 19, 1971
  - Detroit (4) vs. Green Bay (4), Sept. 29, 1974
  - Cleveland (5) vs. Denver (3), Oct. 19, 1975

New England (4) vs. San Diego (4), Nov. 9, 1975
San Francisco (6) vs. New Orleans (2), Oct. 16, 1983
Seattle (5) vs. L.A. Raiders (3), Dec. 18, 1988
Atlanta (6) vs. New Orleans (2), Nov. 13, 1994
Indianapolis (4) vs. San Diego (4), Nov. 3, 1996
Dallas (7) vs. N.Y. Giants (1), Sept. 15, 2003 (ot)
Oakland (5) vs. Chicago (3), Oct. 5, 2003
Buffalo (5) vs. Tennessee (3), Dec. 24, 2006
Tennessee (8) vs. Houston (0), Oct. 21, 2007
Buffalo (5) vs. Washington (3), Dec. 2, 2007
Kansas City (4) vs. Denver (4), Sept. 28, 2008
San Francisco (4) vs. Philadelphia (4), Oct. 12, 2008
Pittsburgh (4) vs. Cincinnati (4), Nov. 15, 2009
Miami (5) vs. Pittsburgh (3), Oct. 24, 2010
  7 In many games

Most Consecutive Games Scoring Field Goals
  38 Baltimore, 1999-2001
  31 Minnesota, 1968-1970
  28 Washington, 1988-1990

SAFETIES

Most Safeties, Season
  4 Cleveland, 1927
     Detroit, 1962
     Seattle, 1993
     San Francisco, 1996
     Tennessee, 1999
  3 By many teams

Most Safeties, Game
  3 L.A. Rams vs. N.Y. Giants, Sept. 30, 1984
  2 N.Y. Giants vs. Pottsville, Oct. 30, 1927
     Chi. Bears vs. Pottsville, Nov. 13, 1927
     Detroit vs. Brooklyn, Dec. 1, 1935
     N.Y. Giants vs. Pittsburgh, Sept. 17, 1950
     N.Y. Giants vs. Washington, Nov. 5, 1961
     Chicago vs. Pittsburgh, Nov. 9, 1969
     Dallas vs. Philadelphia, Nov. 19, 1972
     Los Angeles vs. Green Bay, Oct. 21, 1973
     Oakland vs. San Diego, Oct. 26, 1975
     Denver vs. Seattle, Jan. 2, 1983
     New Orleans vs. Cleveland, Sept. 13, 1987
     Buffalo vs. Denver, Nov. 8, 1987
     San Francisco vs. St. Louis, Sept. 8, 1996
     Jacksonville vs. Pittsburgh, Oct. 3, 1999
     Minnesota vs. Atlanta, Oct. 5, 2003
     Dallas vs. Arizona, Oct. 5, 2003
     Buffalo vs. Houston, Nov. 16, 2003
     Minnesota vs. Green Bay, Nov. 9, 2008

Most Safeties, Both Teams, Game
  3 L.A. Rams (3) vs. N.Y. Giants (0), Sept. 30, 1984
  2 Chi. Cardinals (1) vs. Frankford (1), Nov. 19, 1927
     Chi. Cardinals (1) vs. Cincinnati (1), Nov. 12, 1933
     Chi. Bears (1) vs. San Francisco (1), Oct. 19, 1952
     Cincinnati (1) vs. Los Angeles (1), Oct. 22, 1972
     Chi. Bears (1) vs. San Francisco (1), Sept. 19, 1976
     Baltimore (1) vs. Miami (1), Oct. 29, 1978
     Atlanta (1) vs. Detroit (1), Oct. 5, 1980
     Houston (1) vs. Philadelphia (1), Oct. 2, 1988
     Cleveland (1) vs. Seattle (1), Nov. 14, 1993
     Arizona (1) vs. Houston (1), Dec. 4, 1994
     (Also see previous record)

FIRST DOWNS

Most Seasons Leading League
  9 Chi. Bears, 1935, 1939, 1941, 1943, 1945,
     1947-49, 1955
  7 San Diego, 1965, 1969, 1980-83, 1985
     L.A./St. Louis Rams, 1946, 1950-51, 1954, 1957,
     1973, 2001

Baltimore/Indianapolis Colts, 1958-59, 1967, 2003,
     2005-06, 2010
  6 San Francisco, 1965, 1987, 1989, 1993-94, 1998

Most Consecutive Seasons Leading League
  4 San Diego, 1980-83
  3 Chi. Bears, 1947-49
     New England, 2007-09
  2 By many teams

Most First Downs, Season
  398 Kansas City, 2004
  393 New England, 2007
  387 Miami, 1984

Fewest First Downs, Season
  51 Cincinnati, 1933
  64 Pittsburgh, 1935
  67 Philadelphia, 1937

Most First Downs, Game
  39 N.Y. Jets vs. Miami, Nov. 27, 1988
     Washington vs. Detroit, Nov. 4, 1990 (ot)
  38 Los Angeles vs. N.Y. Giants, Nov. 13, 1966
  37 Green Bay vs. Philadelphia, Nov. 11, 1962

Fewest First Downs, Game
  0 N.Y. Giants vs. Green Bay, Oct. 1, 1933
     Pittsburgh vs. Boston, Oct. 29, 1933
     Philadelphia vs. Detroit, Sept. 20, 1935
     N.Y. Giants vs. Washington, Sept. 27, 1942
     Denver vs. Houston, Sept. 3, 1966

Most First Downs, Both Teams, Game
  64 Seattle (32) vs. Kansas City (32), Nov. 24, 2002
  62 San Diego (32) vs. Seattle (30), Sept. 15, 1985
     Oakland (31) vs. Kansas City (31), Nov. 5, 2000
  59 Miami (31) vs. Buffalo (28), Oct. 9, 1983 (ot)
     Seattle (33) vs. Kansas City (26), Nov. 27, 1983 (ot)
     N.Y. Jets (32) vs. Miami (27), Sept. 21, 1986 (ot)
     N.Y. Jets (39) vs. Miami (20), Nov. 27, 1988
     Oakland (31) vs. San Francisco (28), Oct. 8, 2000 (ot)

Fewest First Downs, Both Teams, Game
  7 Chi. Cardinals (2) vs. Detroit (5), Sept. 15, 1940
  9 Pittsburgh (1) vs. Boston (8), Oct. 27, 1935
     Boston (4) vs. Brooklyn (5), Nov. 24, 1935
     N.Y. Giants (3) vs. Detroit (6), Nov. 7, 1943
     Pittsburgh (4) vs. Chi. Cardinals (5), Nov. 11, 1945
     N.Y. Bulldogs (1) vs. Philadelphia (8), Sept. 22, 1949
  10 Philadelphia (4) vs. Brooklyn (6), Nov. 5, 1944
     N.Y. Giants (4) vs. Washington (6), Dec. 11, 1960

Most First Downs, Rushing, Season
  181 New England, 1978
  177 Los Angeles, 1973
  176 Chicago, 1985

Fewest First Downs, Rushing, Season
  36 Cleveland, 1942
     Boston, 1944
  39 Brooklyn, 1943
  40 Philadelphia, 1940
     Detroit, 1945

Most First Downs, Rushing, Game
  25 Philadelphia vs. Washington, Dec. 2, 1951
  23 St. Louis vs. New Orleans, Oct. 5, 1980
  21 Cleveland vs. Philadelphia, Dec. 13, 1959
     Green Bay vs. Philadelphia, Nov. 11, 1962
     Los Angeles vs. New Orleans, Nov. 25, 1973
     Pittsburgh vs. Kansas City, Nov. 7, 1976
     New England vs. Denver, Nov. 28, 1976
     Oakland vs. Green Bay, Sept. 17, 1978
     Buffalo vs. Washington, Nov. 3, 1996
     San Francisco vs. Detroit, Dec. 14, 1998
     Kansas City vs. Atlanta, Oct. 24, 2004

Fewest First Downs, Rushing, Game
  0 By many teams. Last time:
     San Diego vs. Oakland, Dec. 5, 2010

Most First Downs, Rushing, Both Teams, Game
- 36 Philadelphia (25) vs. Washington (11), Dec. 2, 1951
- 31 Detroit (18) vs. Washington (13), Sept. 30, 1951
- 30 Los Angeles (17) vs. Minnesota (13), Nov. 5, 1961
      New Orleans (17) vs. Green Bay (13), Sept. 9, 1979
      New Orleans (16) vs. San Francisco (14), Nov. 11, 1979
      New England (16) vs. Kansas City (14), Oct. 4, 1981
      Indianapolis (18) vs. Denver (12), Sept. 30, 2007

Fewest First Downs, Rushing, Both Teams, Game
- 1 Oakland (0) vs. Tennessee (1), Sept. 7, 2003
     Carolina (0) vs. Detroit (1), Oct. 16, 2005
- 2 Houston (0) vs. Denver (2), Dec. 2, 1962
     N.Y. Jets, (1) vs. St. Louis (1), Dec. 3, 1995
     Miami (1) vs. San Diego (1), Dec. 19, 1999
     New Orleans (0) vs. Baltimore (2), Dec. 19, 1999
     Baltimore (0) vs. Tennessee (2), Sept. 18, 2005
     Pittsburgh (1) vs. Baltimore (1), Nov. 5, 2007
     Arizona (1) vs. San Francisco (1), Sept. 13, 2009
- 3 In many games

Most First Downs, Passing, Season
- 259 San Diego, 1985
- 253 Indianapolis, 2010
- 251 Houston, 1990

Fewest First Downs, Passing, Season
- 18 Pittsburgh, 1941
- 23 Brooklyn, 1942
      N.Y. Giants, 1944
- 24 N.Y. Giants, 1943

Most First Downs, Passing, Game
- 29 N.Y. Giants vs. Cincinnati, Oct. 13, 1985
- 28 Tennessee vs. Oakland, Dec. 19, 2004
- 27 San Diego vs. Seattle, Sept. 15, 1985

Fewest First Downs, Passing, Game
- 0 By many teams. Last time:
     Pittsburgh vs. Tennessee, Sept. 19, 2010

Most First Downs, Passing, Both Teams, Game
- 43 San Diego (23) vs. Cincinnati (20), Dec. 20, 1982
     Miami (24) vs. N.Y. Jets (19), Sept. 21, 1986 (ot)
     Tennessee (28) vs. Oakland (15), Dec. 19, 2004
- 42 San Francisco (22) vs. San Diego (20), Dec. 11, 1982
     Seattle (22) vs. Cleveland (20), Nov. 4, 2007 (ot)
     Pittsburgh (22) vs. New England (20),
        Nov. 14, 2010
- 41 San Diego (27) vs. Seattle (14), Sept. 15, 1985
     Miami (26) vs. Cleveland (15), Dec. 12, 1988
     Kansas City (23) vs. Oakland (18), Nov. 5, 2000
     Kansas City (24) vs. Denver (17), Nov. 14, 2010

Fewest First Downs, Passing, Both Teams, Game
- 0 Brooklyn vs. Pittsburgh, Nov. 29, 1942
- 1 Green Bay (0) vs. Cleveland (1), Sept. 21, 1941
     Pittsburgh (0) vs. Brooklyn (1), Oct. 11, 1942
     N.Y. Giants (0) vs. Detroit (1), Nov. 7, 1943
     Pittsburgh (0) vs. Chi. Cardinals (1), Nov. 11, 1945
     N.Y. Bulldogs (0) vs. Philadelphia (1), Sept. 22, 1949
     Chicago (0) vs. Buffalo (1), Oct. 7, 1979
- 2 In many games

Most First Downs, Penalty, Season
- 47 Buffalo, 2002
      Indianapolis, 2004
- 44 Dallas, 2005
- 43 Denver, 1994

Fewest First Downs, Penalty, Season
- 2 Brooklyn, 1940
- 4 Chi. Cardinals, 1940
     N.Y. Giants, 1942, 1944
     Washington, 1944
     Cleveland, 1952
     Kansas City, 1969
- 5 Brooklyn, 1939
     Chi. Bears, 1939

Detroit, 1953
Los Angeles, 1953
Houston, 1982

Most First Downs, Penalty, Game
- 11 Denver vs. Houston, Oct. 6, 1985
- 9 Chi. Bears vs. Cleveland, Nov. 25, 1951
    Baltimore vs. Pittsburgh, Oct. 30, 1977
    N.Y. Jets vs. Houston, Sept. 18, 1988
    Dallas vs. Detroit, Nov. 20, 2005
- 8 Philadelphia vs. Detroit, Dec. 2, 1979
    Cincinnati vs. N.Y. Jets, Oct. 6, 1985
    Buffalo vs. Houston, Sept. 20, 1987
    Houston vs. Atlanta, Sept. 9, 1990
    Kansas City vs. L.A. Raiders, Oct. 3, 1993
    San Francisco vs. New Orleans, Oct. 11, 1998
    Oakland vs. San Francisco, Oct. 8, 2000 (ot)
    Philadelphia vs. Chicago, Nov. 3, 2002
    Detroit vs. Baltimore, Oct. 9, 2005
    Atlanta vs. Arizona, Sept. 19, 2010

Most First Downs, Penalty, Both Teams, Game
- 12 Buffalo (7) vs. San Francisco (5), Oct. 4, 1998
     Detroit (8) vs. Baltimore (4), Oct. 9, 2005
- 11 Chi. Bears (9) vs. Cleveland (2), Nov. 25, 1951
     Cincinnati (8) vs. N.Y. Jets (3), Oct. 6, 1985
     Denver (11) vs. Houston (0), Oct. 6, 1985
     Detroit (6) vs. Dallas (5), Nov. 8, 1987
     N.Y. Jets (9) vs. Houston (2), Sept. 18, 1988
     Kansas City (8) vs. L.A. Raiders (3), Oct. 3, 1993
     Detroit (6) vs. San Diego (5), Nov. 11, 1996
     Philadelphia (8) vs. Chicago (3), Nov. 3, 2002
     Arizona (6) vs. St. Louis (5), Dec. 3, 2006
     Indianapolis (6) vs. Green Bay (5), Oct. 19, 2008
- 10 In many games

NET YARDS GAINED RUSHING AND PASSING
Most Seasons Leading League
- 12 Chi. Bears, 1932, 1934-35, 1939, 1941-44, 1947,
         1949, 1955-56
- 9 L.A./St. Louis Rams, 1946, 1950-51, 1954, 1957,
        1973, 1999-2001
- 8 San Diego, 1963, 1965, 1980-83, 1985, 2010

Most Consecutive Seasons Leading League
- 4 Chi. Bears, 1941-44
     San Diego, 1980-83
- 3 Baltimore, 1958-1960
     Houston, 1960-62
     Oakland, 1968-1970
     St. Louis, 1999-2001
- 2 By many teams

Most Yards Gained, Season
- 7,075 St. Louis, 2000
- 6,936 Miami, 1984
- 6,800 San Francisco, 1998

Fewest Yards Gained, Season
- 1,150 Cincinnati, 1933
- 1,443 Chi. Cardinals, 1934
- 1,486 Chi. Cardinals, 1933

Most Yards Gained, Game
- 735 Los Angeles vs. N.Y. Yanks, Sept. 28, 1951
- 683 Pittsburgh vs. Chi. Cardinals, Dec. 13, 1958
- 682 Chi. Bears vs. N.Y. Giants, Nov. 14, 1943

Fewest Yards Gained, Game
- −7 Seattle vs. Los Angeles, Nov. 4, 1979
- −5 Denver vs. Oakland, Sept. 10, 1967
- 14 Chi. Cardinals vs. Detroit, Sept. 15, 1940

Most Yards Gained, Both Teams, Game
- 1,133 Los Angeles (636) vs. N.Y. Yanks (497), Nov. 19,
            1950
- 1.102 San Diego (661) vs. Cincinnati (441), Dec. 20, 1982

1,095   Kansas City (590) vs. Indianapolis (505),
       Oct. 31, 2004

Fewest Yards Gained, Both Teams, Game
- 30   Chi. Cardinals (14) vs. Detroit (16), Sept. 15, 1940
- 136   Chi. Cardinals (50) vs. Green Bay (86), Nov. 18, 1934
- 154   N.Y. Giants (51) vs. Washington (103), Dec. 11, 1960

Most Consecutive Games, 400 or More Yards Gained
- 11   San Diego, 1982-83
- 9   New England, 2006-07
- 8   St. Louis, 1999-2000

Most Consecutive Games, 300 or More Yards Gained
- 36   Minnesota, 2002-04
- 30   Minnesota, 1999-2000
       St. Louis, 2000-02
- 29   Los Angeles, 1949-1951
       New Orleans, 2008-09

RUSHING

Most Seasons Leading League
- 16   Chi. Bears, 1932, 1934-35, 1939-1942, 1951,
       1955-56, 1968, 1977, 1983-86
- 7   Buffalo, 1962, 1964, 1973, 1975, 1982, 1991-92
- 6   Cleveland, 1958-59, 1963, 1965-67
       San Francisco, 1952-54, 1987, 1998-99
       Dall. Texans/K.C. Chiefs, 1961, 1966, 1968-69,
       1995, 2010

Most Consecutive Seasons Leading League
- 4   Chi. Bears, 1939-1942
       Chi. Bears, 1983-86
- 3   Detroit, 1936-38
       San Francisco, 1952-54
       Cleveland, 1965-67
       Atlanta, 2004-06
- 2   By many teams

ATTEMPTS

Most Rushing Attempts, Season
- 681   Oakland, 1977
- 674   Chicago, 1984
- 671   New England, 1978

Fewest Rushing Attempts, Season
- 211   Philadelphia, 1982
- 219   San Francisco, 1982
- 225   Houston, 1982

Most Rushing Attempts, Game
- 72   Chi. Bears vs. Brooklyn, Oct. 20, 1935
- 70   Chi. Cardinals vs. Green Bay, Dec. 5, 1948
- 69   Chi. Cardinals vs. Green Bay, Dec. 6, 1936
       Kansas City vs. Cincinnati, Sept. 3, 1978

Fewest Rushing Attempts, Game
- 6   Chi. Cardinals vs. Boston, Oct. 29, 1933
       New England vs. Pittsburgh, Oct. 31, 2004
       Arizona vs. Minnesota, Nov. 26, 2006
- 7   Oakland vs. Buffalo, Oct. 5, 1963
       Houston vs. N.Y. Giants, Dec. 8, 1985
       Seattle vs. L.A. Raiders, Nov. 17, 1991
       Green Bay vs. Miami, Sept. 11, 1994
       Detroit vs. Minnesota, Dec. 2, 2007
       Arizona vs. Minnesota, Dec. 14, 2008
- 8   Denver vs. Oakland, Dec. 17, 1960
       Buffalo vs. St. Louis, Sept. 9, 1984
       Detroit vs. San Francisco, Oct. 20, 1991
       Atlanta vs. Detroit, Sept. 5, 1993
       St. Louis vs. San Francisco, Nov. 2, 2003
       N.Y. Jets vs. Denver, Nov. 20, 2005
       St. Louis vs. Carolina, Nov. 19, 2006
       Detroit vs. Arizona, Nov. 11, 2007
       San Diego vs. Pittsburgh, Oct. 4, 2009
       San Diego vs. Oakland, Dec. 5, 2010

Most Rushing Attempts, Both Teams, Game
- 108   Chi. Bears (70) vs. Green Bay (38), Dec. 5, 1948
- 105   Oakland (62) vs. Atlanta (43), Nov. 30, 1975 (ot)
- 104   Chi. Bears (64) vs. Pittsburgh (40), Oct. 18, 1936

Fewest Rushing Attempts, Both Teams, Game
- 16   Chi. Cardinals (6) vs. Boston (10), Oct. 22, 1933
- 30   Minnesota (15) vs. New England (15), Oct. 30, 2006
- 31   Green Bay (12) vs. Pittsburgh (19), Dec. 20, 2009

YARDS GAINED

Most Yards Gained Rushing, Season
- 3,165   New England, 1978
- 3,088   Buffalo, 1973
- 2,986   Kansas City, 1978

Fewest Yards Gained Rushing, Season
- 298   Philadelphia, 1940
- 467   Detroit, 1946
- 471   Boston, 1944

Most Yards Gained Rushing, Game
- 426   Detroit vs. Pittsburgh, Nov. 4, 1934
- 423   N.Y. Giants vs. Baltimore, Nov. 19, 1950
- 420   Boston vs. N.Y. Giants, Oct. 8, 1933

Fewest Yards Gained Rushing, Game
- −53   Detroit vs. Chi. Cardinals, Oct. 17, 1943
- −36   Philadelphia vs. Chi. Bears, Nov. 19, 1939
- −33   Brooklyn vs. Phil-Pitt, Oct. 2, 1943

Most Yards Gained Rushing, Both Teams, Game
- 595   Los Angeles (371) vs. N.Y. Yankees (224), Nov. 18,
       1951
- 574   Chi. Bears (396) vs. Pittsburgh (178), Oct. 10, 1934
- 558   Boston (420) vs. N.Y. Giants (138), Oct. 8, 1933

Fewest Yards Gained Rushing, Both Teams, Game
- −15   Detroit (−53) vs. Chi. Cardinals (38), Oct. 17, 1943
- 4   Detroit (−10) vs. Chi. Cardinals (14), Sept. 15, 1940
- 45   San Diego (21) vs. Philadelphia (24), Oct. 23, 2005

AVERAGE GAIN

Highest Average Gain, Rushing, Season
- 5.74   Cleveland, 1963
- 5.65   San Francisco, 1954
- 5.56   San Diego, 1963

Lowest Average Gain, Rushing, Season
- 0.94   Philadelphia, 1940
- 1.45   Boston, 1944
- 1.55   Pittsburgh, 1935

TOUCHDOWNS

Most Touchdowns, Rushing, Season
- 36   Green Bay, 1962
- 33   Pittsburgh, 1976
- 32   Kansas City, 2003

Fewest Touchdowns, Rushing, Season
- 1   Brooklyn, 1934
- 2   Chi. Cardinals, 1933
       Cincinnati, 1933
       Pittsburgh, 1934
       Philadelphia, 1935
       Philadelphia, 1936
       Philadelphia, 1937
       Philadelphia, 1938
       Pittsburgh, 1940
       Philadelphia, 1972
       N.Y. Jets, 1995
       Arizona, 2005
- 3   By many teams

Most Touchdowns, Rushing, Game
- 9   Rock Island vs. Evansville, Oct. 15, 1922
       Racine vs. Louisville, Nov. 5, 1922
- 8   Chi. Cardinals vs. Rochester, Oct. 7, 1923
       Kansas City vs. Atlanta, Oct. 24, 2004

7 By many teams
Most Touchdowns, Rushing, Both Teams, Game
  9 Rock Island (9) vs. Evansville (0), Oct. 15, 1922
    Racine (9) vs. Louisville (0), Nov. 5, 1922
  8 Chi. Cardinals (8) vs. Rochester (0), Oct. 7, 1923
    Canton (7) vs. Cleveland (1), Nov. 25, 1923
    Los Angeles (6) vs. N.Y. Yanks (2), Nov. 18, 1951
    Chi. Bears (5) vs. Green Bay (3), Nov. 6, 1955
    Denver (5) vs. Kansas City (3), Dec. 7, 2003
    Kansas City (8) vs. Atlanta (0), Oct. 24, 2004
  7 In many games

PASSING

ATTEMPTS
Most Passes Attempted, Season
  709 Minnesota, 1981
  699 New England, 1994
  686 New England, 1995
Fewest Passes Attempted, Season
  102 Cincinnati, 1933
  106 Boston, 1933
  120 Detroit, 1937
Most Passes Attempted, Game
  70 New England vs. Minnesota, Nov. 13, 1994 (ot)
  69 N.Y. Jets vs. Baltimore, Dec. 24, 2000
  68 Houston vs. Buffalo, Nov 1, 1964
    Cincinnati vs. Pittsburgh, Dec. 30, 2001 (ot)
Fewest Passes Attempted, Game
  0 Green Bay vs. Portsmouth, Oct. 8, 1933
    Detroit vs. Cleveland, Sept. 10, 1937
    Pittsburgh vs. Brooklyn, Nov. 16, 1941
    Pittsburgh vs. Los Angeles, Nov. 13, 1949
    Cleveland vs. Philadelphia, Dec. 3, 1950
Most Passes Attempted, Both Teams, Game
  112 New England (70) vs. Minnesota (42),
      Nov. 13, 1994 (ot)
  104 Miami (55) vs. N.Y. Jets (49), Oct. 18. 1987 (ot)
    N.Y. Jets (58) vs. San Francisco (46),
      Sept. 6, 1998 (ot)
  103 Cincinnati (68) vs. Pittsburgh (35), Dec. 30, 2001 (ot)
    Seattle (53) vs. San Diego (50), Dec. 29, 2002 (ot)
Fewest Passes Attempted, Both Teams, Game
  4 Chi. Cardinals (1) vs. Detroit (3), Nov. 3, 1935
    Detroit (0) vs. Cleveland (4), Sept. 10, 1937
  6 Chi. Cardinals (2) vs. Detroit (4), Sept. 15, 1940
  8 Brooklyn (2) vs. Philadelphia (6). Oct. 1, 1939

COMPLETIONS
Most Passes Completed, Season
  450 Indianapolis, 2010
    New Orleans, 2010
  440 New Orleans, 2007
  432 San Francisco, 1995
Fewest Passes Completed, Season
  25 Cincinnati, 1933
  33 Boston, 1933
  34 Chi. Cardinals, 1934
Most Passes Completed, Game
  45 New England vs. Minnesota, Nov. 13, 1994 (ot)
  43 Washington vs. Detroit, Nov. 4, 1990 (ot)
    Oakland vs. Pittsburgh, Sept. 15, 2002
  42 N.Y. Jets vs. San Francisco, Sept. 21, 1980
    N.Y. Jets vs. Seattle, Dec. 6, 1998
Fewest Passes Completed, Game
  0 By many teams. Last time: Buffalo vs. N.Y. Jets,
      Sept. 29, 1974
Most Passes Completed, Both Teams, Game
  71 New England (45) vs. Minnesota (26),
      Nov. 13, 1994 (ot)

68 San Francisco (37) vs. Atlanta (31), Oct. 6, 1985
    Denver (34) vs. Oakland (34), Nov. 11, 2002
66 Cincinnati (40) vs. San Diego (26), Dec. 20, 1982
    Indianapolis (34) vs. Houston (32), Nov. 8, 2009
    Houston (38) vs. Washington (28),
      Sept. 19, 2010 (OT)
Fewest Passes Completed, Both Teams, Game
  1 Chi. Cardinals (0) vs. Philadelphia (1), Nov. 8, 1936
    Detroit (0) vs. Cleveland (1), Sept. 10, 1937
    Chi. Cardinals (0) vs. Detroit (1), Sept. 15, 1940
    Brooklyn (0) vs. Pittsburgh (1), Nov. 29, 1942
  2 Chi. Cardinals (0) vs. Detroit (2), Nov. 3, 1935
    Buffalo (0) vs. N.Y. Jets (2), Sept. 29, 1974
    Chi. Cardinals (0) vs. Green Bay (2), Nov. 18, 1934
  3 In seven games

YARDS GAINED
Most Seasons Leading League, Passing Yardage
  10 San Diego, 1965, 1968, 1971, 1978-1983, 1985
  8 Chi. Bears, 1932, 1939, 1941, 1943, 1945, 1949,
      1954, 1964
    Washington, 1938, 1940, 1944, 1947-48, 1967,
      1974, 1989
    Balt./Indianapolis, 1957, 1959, 1960, 1963, 1976,
      2003-04, 2010
  7 Houston, 1960-61, 1963-64, 1990-92
    L.A./St. Louis Rams, 1946, 1950-51, 1956,
      1999-2001
Most Consecutive Seasons Leading League, Passing Yardage
  6 San Diego, 1978-1983
  4 Green Bay, 1934-37
  3 Miami, 1986-88
    Houston, 1990-92
    St. Louis, 1999-2001
Most Yards Gained, Passing, Season
  5,232 St. Louis, 2000
  5,018 Miami, 1984
  4,977 New Orleans, 2008
Fewest Yards Gained, Passing, Season
  302 Chi. Cardinals, 1934
  357 Cincinnati, 1933
  459 Boston, 1934
Most Yards Gained Passing, Game
  554 Los Angeles vs. N.Y. Yankees, Sept. 28, 1951
  530 Minnesota vs. Baltimore, Sept. 28, 1969
  521 Miami vs. N.Y. Jets, Oct. 23, 1988
Fewest Yards Gained, Passing, Game
  –53 Denver vs. Oakland, Sept. 10, 1967
  –52 Cincinnati vs. Houston, Oct. 31, 1971
  –39 Atlanta vs. San Francisco, Oct. 23, 1976
Most Yards Gained, Passing, Both Teams, Game
  884 N.Y. Jets (449) vs. Miami (435), Sept. 21, 1986 (ot)
  883 San Diego (486) vs. Cincinnati (397), Dec. 20, 1982
  874 Miami (456) vs. New England (418), Sept. 4, 1994
Fewest Yards Gained, Passing, Both Teams, Game
  –11 Green Bay (–10) vs. Dallas (–1), Oct. 24, 1965
  1 Chi. Cardinals (0) vs. Philadelphia (1), Nov. 8, 1936
  7 Brooklyn (0) vs. Pittsburgh (7), Nov. 29, 1942

TIMES SACKED
Most Seasons Leading League, Fewest Times Sacked
  10 Miami, 1973, 1982-1990
  6 Indianapolis, 1999-2000, 2004-06, 2009
  5 N.Y. Jets, 1965-66, 1968, 1993, 2000
Most Consecutive Seasons Leading League, Fewest Times Sacked
  9 Miami, 1982-1990
  3 St. Louis, 1974-76
    Indianapolis, 2004-06
  2 By many teams

Most Times Sacked, Season
- 104   Philadelphia, 1986
- 78   Arizona, 1997
- 76   Houston, 2002

Fewest Times Sacked, Season
- 7   Miami, 1988
- 8   San Francisco, 1970
  -    St. Louis, 1975
- 9   N.Y. Jets, 1966
  -    Washington, 1991

Most Times Sacked, Game
- 12   Pittsburgh vs. Dallas, Nov. 20, 1966
  -    Baltimore vs. St. Louis, Oct. 26, 1980
  -    Detroit vs. Chicago, Dec. 16, 1984
  -    Houston vs. Dallas, Sept. 29, 1985
  -    Philadelphia vs. N.Y. Giants, Sept. 30, 2007
- 11   St. Louis vs. N.Y. Giants, Nov. 1, 1964
  -    Los Angeles vs. Baltimore, Nov. 22, 1964
  -    Denver vs. Buffalo, Dec. 13, 1964
  -    Green Bay vs. Detroit, Nov. 7, 1965
  -    Buffalo vs. Oakland, Oct. 15, 1967
  -    Denver vs. Oakland, Nov. 5, 1967
  -    Atlanta vs. St. Louis, Nov. 24, 1968
  -    Detroit vs. Dallas, Oct. 6, 1975
  -    Philadelphia vs. St. Louis, Dec. 18, 1983
  -    Cleveland vs. Kansas City, Sept. 30, 1984
  -    Minnesota vs. Chicago, Oct. 28, 1984
  -    Atlanta vs. Cleveland, Nov. 18, 1984
  -    Dallas vs. San Diego, Nov. 16, 1986
  -    Philadelphia vs. Detroit, Nov. 16, 1986
  -    Philadelphia vs. L.A. Raiders, Nov. 30, 1986 (ot)
  -    L.A. Raiders vs. Seattle, Dec. 8, 1986
  -    N.Y. Jets vs. Dallas, Oct. 4, 1987
  -    Philadelphia vs. Chicago, Oct. 4, 1987
  -    Dallas vs. Philadelphia, Sept. 15, 1991
  -    Cleveland vs. Indianapolis, Sept. 6, 1992
- 10   By many teams

Most Times Sacked, Both Teams, Game
- 18   Green Bay (10) vs. San Diego (8), Sept. 24, 1978
- 17   Buffalo (10) vs. N.Y. Titans (7), Nov. 23, 1961
  -    Pittsburgh (12) vs. Dallas (5), Nov. 20, 1966
  -    Atlanta (9) vs. Philadelphia (8), Dec. 16, 1984
  -    Philadelphia (11) vs. L.A. Raiders (6), Nov. 30, 1986 (ot)
- 16   Los Angeles (11) vs. Baltimore (5), Nov. 22, 1964
  -    Buffalo (11) vs. Oakland (5), Oct. 15, 1967

COMPLETION PERCENTAGE

Most Seasons Leading League, Completion Percentage
- 14   San Francisco, 1952, 1957-58, 1965, 1981, 1983, 1987, 1989, 1992-97
- 11   Washington, 1937, 1939-1940, 1942-45, 1947-48, 1969-1970
- 8   Green Bay, 1936, 1941, 1961-62, 1964, 1966, 1968, 1998

Most Consecutive Seasons Leading League, Completion Percentage
- 6   San Francisco, 1992-97
- 4   Washington, 1942-45
  -    Kansas City, 1966-69
- 3   Cleveland, 1953-55
  -    St. Louis, 1999-2001

Highest Completion Percentage, Season
- 70.65   Cincinnati, 1982 (310-219)
- 70.25   San Francisco, 1994 (511-359)
- 70.19   San Francisco, 1989 (483-339)

Lowest Completion Percentage, Season
- 22.9   Philadelphia, 1936 (170-39)
- 24.5   Cincinnati, 1933 (102-25)
- 25.0   Pittsburgh, 1941 (168-42)

TOUCHDOWNS

Most Touchdowns, Passing, Season
- 51   Indianapolis, 2004
- 50   New England, 2007
- 49   Miami, 1984

Fewest Touchdowns, Passing, Season
- 0   Cincinnati, 1933
  -    Pittsburgh, 1945
- 1   Boston, 1932
  -    Boston, 1933
  -    Chi. Cardinals, 1934
  -    Cincinnati/St. Louis, 1934
  -    Detroit, 1942
- 2   Chi. Cardinals, 1932
  -    Stapleton, 1932
  -    Chi. Cardinals, 1935
  -    Brooklyn, 1936
  -    Pittsburgh, 1942

Most Touchdowns, Passing, Game
- 7   Chi. Bears vs. N.Y. Giants, Nov. 14, 1943
  -    Philadelphia vs. Washington, Oct. 17, 1954
  -    Houston vs. N.Y. Titans, Nov. 19, 1961
  -    Houston vs. N.Y. Titans, Oct. 14, 1962
  -    N.Y. Giants vs. Washington, Oct. 28, 1962
  -    Minnesota vs. Baltimore, Sept. 28, 1969
  -    San Diego vs. Oakland, Nov. 22, 1981
- 6   By many teams

Most Touchdowns, Passing, Both Teams, Game
- 12   New Orleans (6) vs. St. Louis (6), Nov. 2, 1969
- 11   N.Y. Giants (7) vs. Washington (4), Oct. 28, 1962
  -    Oakland (6) vs. Houston (5), Dec. 22, 1963
  -    Cincinnati (6) vs. Cleveland, (5), Sept. 16, 2007
- 10   San Diego (5) vs. Seattle (5), Sept. 15, 1985
  -    Miami (6) vs. N.Y. Jets (4), Sept. 21, 1986 (ot)
  -    San Francisco (6) vs. Atlanta (4), Oct. 14, 1990

PASSES HAD INTERCEPTED

Most Passes Had Intercepted, Season
- 48   Houston, 1962
- 45   Denver, 1961
- 41   Card-Pitt, 1944

Fewest Passes Had Intercepted, Season
- 5   Cleveland, 1960
  -    Green Bay, 1966
  -    Kansas City, 1990
  -    N.Y. Giants, 1990
  -    New England, 2010
- 6   Green Bay, 1964
  -    St. Louis, 1982
  -    Dallas, 1993
  -    Jacksonville, 2005
  -    Washington, 2008
  -    Tampa Bay, 2010
- 7   Los Angeles, 1969
  -    Denver, 2005
  -    Miami, 2008
  -    Minnesota, 2009

Most Passes Had Intercepted, Game
- 9   Detroit vs. Green Bay, Oct. 24, 1943
  -    Pittsburgh vs. Philadelphia, Dec. 12, 1965
- 8   Green Bay vs. N.Y. Giants, Nov. 21, 1948
  -    Chi. Cardinals vs. Philadelphia, Sept. 24, 1950
  -    N.Y. Yanks vs. N.Y. Giants, Dec. 16, 1951
  -    Denver vs. Houston, Dec. 2, 1962
  -    Chi. Bears vs. Detroit, Sept. 22, 1968
  -    Baltimore vs. N.Y. Jets, Sept. 23, 1973
- 7   By many teams. Last time: Detroit vs. Cleveland, Sept. 23, 2001

Most Passes Had Intercepted, Both Teams, Game
- 13   Denver (8) vs. Houston (5), Dec. 2, 1962

11   Philadelphia (7) vs. Boston (4), Nov. 3, 1935
     Boston (6) vs. Pittsburgh (5), Dec. 1, 1935
     Cleveland (7) vs. Green Bay (4), Oct. 30, 1938
     Green Bay (7) vs. Detroit (4), Oct. 20, 1940
     Detroit (7) vs. Chi. Bears (4), Nov. 22, 1942
     Detroit (7) vs. Cleveland (4), Nov. 26, 1944
     Chi. Cardinals (8) vs. Philadelphia (3), Sept. 24, 1950
     Washington (7) vs. N.Y. Giants (4), Dec. 8, 1963
     Pittsburgh (9) vs. Philadelphia (2), Dec 12, 1965
10   In many games

PUNTING

Most Seasons Leading League (Average Distance)
8   Oakland, 1974-75, 1977-78, 2003-04, 2007, 2009
7   Denver 1962-64, 1966-67, 1982, 1999
6   Washington, 1940-43, 1945, 1958
     Kansas City, 1968, 1971-73, 1979, 1984
     L.A. Rams, 1946, 1949, 1955-56, 1994, 2008

**Most Consecutive Seasons Leading League
(Average Distance)**
4   Washington, 1940-43
3   Cleveland, 1950-52
     Denver, 1962-64
     Kansas City, 1971-73

Most Punts, Season
116   Houston, 2002
114   Chicago, 1981
113   Boston, 1934
     Brooklyn, 1934
     Dallas, 2002

Fewest Punts, Season
23   San Diego, 1982
31   Cincinnati, 1982
32   Chi. Bears, 1941

Most Punts, Game
17   Chi. Bears vs. Green Bay, Oct. 22, 1933
     Cincinnati vs. Pittsburgh, Oct. 22, 1933
16   Cincinnati vs. Portsmouth, Sept. 17, 1933
     Chi. Cardinals vs. Chi. Bears, Nov. 30, 1933
     Chi. Cardinals vs. Detroit, Sept. 15, 1940
     Oakland vs. San Diego, Oct. 11, 1998
15   Chi. Cardinals vs. Cincinnati, Nov. 12, 1933
     N.Y. Giants vs. Chi. Bears, Nov. 17, 1935
     Philadelphia vs. N.Y. Giants, Dec. 6, 1987 (ot)

Fewest Punts, Game
0   By many teams. Last time:
     Baltimore vs. Miami, Nov. 7, 2010

Most Punts, Both Teams, Game
31   Chi. Bears (17) vs. Green Bay (14), Oct. 22, 1933
     Cincinnati (17), vs. Pittsburgh (14), Oct. 22, 1933
29   Chi. Cardinals (15) vs. Cincinnati (14), Nov. 12, 1933
     Chi. Cardinals (16) vs. Chi. Bears (13), Nov. 30, 1933
     Chi. Cardinals (16) vs. Detroit (13), Sept. 15, 1940
28   Philadelphia (14) vs. Washington (14), Nov. 5, 1939

Fewest Punts, Both Teams, Game
0   Buffalo vs. San Francisco, Sept. 13, 1992
1   Baltimore (0) vs. Cleveland (1), Nov. 1, 1959
     Dall. Cowboys (0) vs. Cleveland (1), Dec. 3, 1961
     Chicago (0) vs. Detroit (1), Oct. 1, 1972
     San Francisco (0) vs. N.Y. Giants (1), Oct. 15, 1972
     Green Bay (0) vs. Buffalo (1), Dec. 5, 1982
     Miami (0) vs. Buffalo (1), Oct. 12, 1986
     Green Bay (0) vs. Chicago (1), Dec. 17, 1989
     Oakland (0) vs. Seattle (1), Dec. 5, 1999
     Tampa Bay (0) vs. Minnesota (1), Oct. 29, 2000
     New Orleans (0) vs. San Francisco (1), Oct. 20, 2002
2   In many games

AVERAGE YARDAGE

Highest Avg. Distance, Punting, Season
51.1   Oakland, 2009
49.6   St. Louis, 2008
49.1   Oakland, 2007

Lowest Average Distance, Punting, Season
32.7   Card-Pitt, 1944 (60-1,964)
33.8   Cincinnati, 1986 (59-1,996)
33.9   Detroit, 1969 (74-2,510)

PUNT RETURNS

Most Seasons Leading League (Average Return)
9   Detroit, 1943-45, 1951-52, 1962, 1966, 1969, 1991
7   Chi. Cardinals/St. Louis, 1948-49, 1955-56, 1959, 1986-87
6   Green Bay, 1950, 1953-54, 1961, 1972, 1996
     Dallas/Kansas City, 1960, 1968, 1970, 1979-1980, 2003

Most Consecutive Seasons Leading League (Average Return)
3   Detroit, 1943-45
2   By many teams

Most Punt Returns, Season
71   Pittsburgh, 1976
     Tampa Bay, 1979
     L.A. Raiders, 1985
67   Pittsburgh, 1974
     Los Angeles, 1978
     L.A. Raiders, 1984
65   San Francisco, 1976

Fewest Punt Returns, Season
12   Baltimore, 1981
     San Diego, 1982
14   Los Angeles, 1961
     Philadelphia, 1962
     Baltimore, 1982
15   Houston, 1960
     Washington, 1960
     Oakland, 1961
     N.Y. Giants, 1969
     Philadelphia, 1973
     Kansas City, 1982

Most Punt Returns, Game
12   Philadelphia vs. Cleveland, Dec. 3, 1950
11   Chi. Bears vs. Chi. Cardinals, Oct. 8, 1950
     Washington vs. Tampa Bay, Oct. 9, 1977
10   Philadelphia vs. N.Y. Giants, Nov. 26, 1950
     Philadelphia vs. Tampa Bay, Sept. 18, 1977
     Pittsburgh vs. Buffalo, Dec. 16, 1979
     Washington vs. New Orleans, Dec. 26, 1982
     Philadelphia vs. Seattle, Dec. 13, 1992 (ot)
     New England vs. Pittsburgh, Dec. 5, 1993

Most Punt Returns, Both Teams, Game
17   Philadelphia (12) vs. Cleveland (5), Dec. 3, 1950
16   N.Y. Giants (9) vs. Philadelphia (7), Dec. 12, 1954
     Washington (11) vs. Tampa Bay (5), Oct. 9, 1977
     Oakland (8) vs. San Diego (8), Oct. 11, 1998
15   Detroit (8) vs. Cleveland (7), Sept. 27, 1942
     Los Angeles (8) vs. Baltimore (7), Nov. 27, 1966
     Pittsburgh (8) vs. Houston (7), Dec. 1, 1974
     Philadelphia (10) vs. Tampa Bay (5), Sept. 18, 1977
     Baltimore (9) vs. Kansas City (6), Sept. 2, 1979
     Washington (10) vs. New Orleans (5), Dec. 26, 1982
     L.A. Raiders (8) vs. Cleveland (7), Nov. 16, 1986

FAIR CATCHES

Most Fair Catches, Season
34   Baltimore, 1971
33   Philadelphia, 2000
32   San Diego, 1969
     Oakland, 2001

Fewest Fair Catches, Season
- 0 San Diego, 1975
  - New England, 1976
  - Tampa Bay, 1976
  - Pittsburgh, 1977
  - Dallas, 1982
- 1 Cleveland, 1974
  - San Francisco, 1975
  - Kansas City, 1976
  - St. Louis, 1976
  - San Diego, 1976
  - L.A. Rams, 1982
  - St. Louis, 1982
  - Tampa Bay, 1982
  - Arizona, 2001
- 2 By many teams

Most Fair Catches, Game
- 7 Minnesota vs. Dallas, Sept. 25, 1966
  - N.Y. Jets vs. Miami, Nov. 20, 1966
  - Detroit vs. Chicago, Nov. 21, 1976
  - Philadelphia vs. Buffalo, Dec. 27, 1987
  - Tennessee vs. Jacksonville, Nov. 16, 2008
- 6 By many teams

YARDS GAINED
Most Yards, Punt Returns, Season
- 875 Green Bay, 1996
- 785 L.A. Raiders, 1985
- 781 Chi. Bears, 1948

Fewest Yards, Punt Returns, Season
- 27 St. Louis, 1965
- 35 N.Y. Giants, 1965
- 37 New England, 1972

Most Yards, Punt Returns, Game
- 231 Detroit vs. San Francisco, Oct. 6, 1963
- 225 Oakland vs. Buffalo, Sept. 15, 1968
- 219 L.A. Rams vs. Atlanta, Oct. 11, 1981

Fewest Yards, Punt Returns, Game
- -28 Washington vs. Dallas, Dec. 11, 1966
- -23 N.Y. Giants vs. Buffalo, Oct. 20, 1975
  - Pittsburgh vs. Houston, Sept. 20, 1970
- -20 New Orleans vs. Pittsburgh, Oct. 20, 1968

Most Yards, Punt Returns, Both Teams, Game
- 282 L.A. Rams (219) vs. Atlanta (63), Oct. 11, 1981
- 245 Detroit (231) vs. San Francisco (14), Oct. 6, 1963
- 244 Oakland (225) vs. Buffalo (19), Sept. 15, 1968

Fewest Yards, Punt Returns, Both Teams, Game
- -18 Buffalo (-18) vs. Pittsburgh (0), Oct. 29, 1972
- -14 Miami (-14) vs. Boston (0), Nov. 30, 1969
  - Tennessee (-14) vs. New Orleans (0),
    Sept. 21, 2003
- -13 N.Y. Giants (-13) vs. Cleveland (0), Nov. 14, 1965

AVERAGE YARDS RETURNING PUNTS
Highest Average, Punt Returns, Season
- 20.2 Chi. Bears, 1941
- 19.1 Chi. Cardinals, 1948
- 18.2 Chi. Cardinals, 1949

Lowest Average, Punt Returns, Season
- 1.2 St. Louis, 1965 (23-27)
- 1.5 N.Y. Giants, 1965 (24-35)
- 1.7 Washington, 1970 (27-45)

TOUCHDOWNS RETURNING PUNTS
Most Touchdowns, Punt Returns, Season
- 5 Chi. Cardinals, 1959
- 4 Chi. Cardinals, 1948
  - Detroit, 1951
  - N.Y. Giants, 1951

- Denver, 1976
- Chicago, 2007
- 3 Washington, 1941
  - Detroit, 1952
  - Pittsburgh, 1952
  - Houston, 1975
  - Los Angeles, 1981
  - Cleveland, 1993
  - Green Bay, 1996
  - Denver, 1997
  - San Diego, 1997
  - Chicago, 2006
  - Tennessee, 2006
  - New Orleans, 2008
  - Oakland, 2008
  - Chicago, 2010
  - Dallas, 2010

Most Touchdowns, Punt Returns, Game
- 2 Detroit vs. Los Angeles, Oct. 14, 1951
  - Detroit vs. Green Bay, Nov. 22, 1951
  - Chi. Cardinals vs. Pittsburgh, Nov. 1, 1959
  - Chi. Cardinals vs. N.Y. Giants, Nov. 22, 1959
  - N.Y. Titans vs. Denver, Sept. 24, 1961
  - Denver vs. Cleveland, Sept. 26, 1976
  - Los Angeles vs. Atlanta, Oct. 11, 1981
  - St. Louis vs. Tampa Bay, Dec. 21, 1986
  - L.A. Rams vs. Atlanta, Dec. 27, 1992
  - Cleveland vs. Pittsburgh, Oct. 24, 1993
  - San Diego vs. Cincinnati, Nov. 2, 1997
  - Denver vs. Carolina, Nov. 9, 1997
  - Baltimore vs. Seattle, Dec. 7, 1997
  - Baltimore vs. N.Y. Jets, Dec. 24, 2000
  - Oakland vs. Tennessee, Sept. 29, 2002
  - Carolina vs. Cincinnati, Dec. 8, 2002
  - Detroit vs. Jacksonville, Nov. 14, 2004 (ot)
  - New Orleans vs. Minnesota, Oct. 6, 2008

Most Touchdowns, Punt Returns, Both Teams, Game
- 2 Philadelphia (1) vs. Washington (1), Nov. 9, 1952
  - Kansas City (1) vs. Buffalo (1), Sept. 11, 1966
  - Baltimore (1) vs. New England (1), Nov. 18, 1979
  - L.A. Raiders (1) vs. Philadelphia (1),
    Nov. 30, 1986 (ot)
  - Cincinnati (1) vs. Green Bay (1), Sept. 20, 1992
  - Oakland (1) vs. Seattle (1), Nov. 15, 1998
  - Atlanta (1) vs. Tennessee (1), Nov. 23, 2003
  - San Diego (1) vs. Denver (1), Oct. 19, 2009
(Also see previous record)

KICKOFF RETURNS
Most Seasons Leading League (Average Return)
- 8 Washington, 1942, 1947, 1962-63, 1973-74, 1981,
    1995
- 6 Chicago Bears, 1943, 1948, 1958, 1966, 1972, 1985
  - N.Y. Giants, 1944, 1946, 1949, 1951, 1953, 2004
- 5 Green Bay, 1954, 1964, 1967, 1993, 1998
  - New England, 1977, 1980, 1982, 1997, 2006
  - Hou. Oilers/ Tenn. Titans, 1960, 1962-63, 1968, 2008

Most Consecutive Seasons Leading League (Average Return)
- 3 Denver, 1965-67
- 2 By many teams

Most Kickoff Returns, Season
- 96 Detroit, 2009
- 89 Cleveland, 1999
- 88 New Orleans, 1980

Fewest Kickoff Returns, Season
- 17 N.Y. Giants, 1944
- 20 N.Y. Giants, 1941, 1943
  - Chi. Bears, 1942
- 23 Washington, 1942

Most Kickoff Returns, Game
- 12   N.Y. Giants vs. Washington, Nov. 27, 1966
- 11   Kansas City vs. Buffalo, Nov. 23, 2008
- 10   By many teams

Most Kickoff Returns, Both Teams, Game
- 19   N.Y. Giants (12) vs. Washington (7), Nov. 27, 1966
-      Cleveland (10) vs. Cincinnati (9), Nov. 28, 2004
- 18   Houston (10) vs. Oakland (8), Dec. 22, 1963
- 17   Washington (9) vs. Green Bay (8), Oct. 17, 1983
-      San Diego (9) vs. Pittsburgh (8), Dec. 8, 1985
-      Detroit (9) vs. Green Bay (8), Nov. 27, 1986
-      L.A. Raiders (9) vs. Seattle (8), Dec. 18, 1988
-      Oakland (10) vs. Seattle (7), Oct. 26, 1997
-      Buffalo (9) vs. Minnesota (8), Sept. 15, 2002 (ot)
-      Cincinnati (10) vs. Cleveland (7), Sept. 16, 2007
-      Kansas City (11) vs. Buffalo (6), Nov. 23, 2008

YARDS GAINED

Most Yards, Kickoff Returns, Season
- 2,296   Arizona, 2000
- 2,084   Arizona, 2010
- 2,173   Houston, 2005

Fewest Yards, Kickoff Returns, Season
- 282   N.Y. Giants, 1940
- 381   Green Bay, 1940
- 424   Chicago, 1963

Most Yards, Kickoff Returns, Game
- 367   Baltimore vs. Minnesota, Dec. 13, 1998
- 362   Detroit vs. Los Angeles, Oct. 29, 1950
- 304   Chi. Bears vs. Green Bay, Nov. 9, 1952
-      New Orleans vs. L.A. Rams, Oct. 23, 1994

Most Yards, Kickoff Returns, Both Teams, Game
- 560   Detroit (362) vs. L.A. Rams (198), Oct. 29, 1950
- 511   Baltimore (367) vs. Minnesota (144), Dec. 13, 1998
- 501   New Orleans (304) vs. L.A. Rams (197), Oct. 23, 1994

AVERAGE YARDAGE

Highest Average, Kickoff Returns, Season
- 29.4   Chicago, 1972
- 28.9   Pittsburgh, 1952
- 28.2   Washington, 1962

Lowest Average, Kickoff Returns, Season
- 14.7   N.Y. Jets, 1993 (46-675)
- 15.8   N.Y. Giants, 1993 (32-507)
- 15.9   Tampa Bay, 1993 (58-922)

TOUCHDOWNS

Most Touchdowns, Kickoff Returns, Season
- 4   Green Bay, 1967
-    Chicago, 1970
-    Detroit, 1994
-    Houston, 2007
- 3   Los Angeles, 1950
-    Chi. Cardinals, 1954
-    San Francisco, 1963
-    Denver, 1966
-    Chicago, 1967
-    New England, 1977
-    L.A. Rams, 1985
-    Atlanta, 2000
-    Buffalo, 2004
-    N.Y. Jets, 2007
-    Cleveland, 2009
-    Oakland, 2010
-    Seattle, 2010
- 2   By many teams

Most Touchdowns, Kickoff Returns, Game
- 2   Chi. Bears vs. Green Bay, Sept. 22, 1940
-    Chi. Bears vs. Green Bay, Nov. 9, 1952

     Philadelphia vs. Dallas, Nov. 6, 1966
     Green Bay vs. Cleveland, Nov. 12, 1967
     L.A. Rams vs. Green Bay, Nov. 24, 1985
     New Orleans vs. L.A. Rams, Oct. 23, 1994
     Baltimore vs. Minnesota, Dec. 13, 1998
     N.Y. Jets vs. Buffalo, Sept. 8, 2002 (ot)
     Chicago vs. St. Louis, Dec. 11, 2006
     Houston vs. Jacksonville, Dec. 30, 2007
     Miami vs. N.Y. Jets, Nov. 1, 2009
     Cleveland vs. Kansas City, Dec. 20, 2009
     Seattle vs. San Diego, Sept. 26, 2010

Most Touchdowns, Kickoff Returns, Both Teams, Game
- 3   Baltimore (2) vs. Minnesota (1), Dec. 13, 1998
- 2   In many games

FUMBLES

Most Fumbles, Season
- 56   Chi. Bears, 1938
-    San Francisco, 1978
- 54   Philadelphia, 1946
- 51   New England, 1973

Fewest Fumbles, Season
- 7   Kansas City, 2002
- 8   Cleveland, 1959
- 9   New England, 2010

Most Fumbles, Game
- 10   Phil-Pitt vs. N.Y. Giants, Oct. 9, 1943
-      Detroit vs. Minnesota, Nov. 12, 1967
-      Kansas City vs. Houston, Oct. 12, 1969
-      San Francisco vs. Detroit, Dec. 17, 1978
- 9   Philadelphia vs. Green Bay, Oct. 13, 1946
-    Boston at Oakland, Dec. 16, 1962
-    Kansas City vs. San Diego, Nov. 15, 1964
-    N.Y. Giants vs. Buffalo, Oct. 20, 1975
-    St. Louis vs. Washington, Oct. 25, 1976
-    San Diego vs. Green Bay, Sept. 24, 1978
-    Pittsburgh vs. Cincinnati, Oct. 14, 1979
-    Cleveland vs. Seattle, Dec. 20, 1981
-    Cleveland vs. Pittsburgh, Dec. 23, 1990
-    Oakland vs. Seattle, Dec. 22, 1996
- 8   By many teams

Most Fumbles, Both Teams, Game
- 14   Chi. Bears (7) vs. Cleveland (7), Nov. 24, 1940
-      St. Louis (8) vs. N.Y. Giants (6), Sept. 17, 1961
-      Kansas City (10) vs. Houston (4), Oct. 12, 1969
- 13   Washington (8) vs. Pittsburgh (5), Nov. 14, 1937
-      Philadelphia (7) vs. Boston (6), Dec. 8, 1946
-      N.Y. Giants (7) vs. Washington (6), Nov. 5, 1950
-      Kansas City (9) vs. San Diego (4), Nov. 15, 1964
-      Buffalo (7) vs. Denver (6), Dec. 13, 1964
-      N.Y. Jets (7) vs. Houston (6), Sept. 12, 1965
-      Cleveland (7) vs. New Orleans (6), Dec. 12, 1971
-      Houston (8) vs. Pittsburgh (5), Dec. 9, 1973
-      St. Louis (9) vs. Washington (4), Oct. 25, 1976
-      Cleveland (9) vs. Seattle (4), Dec. 20, 1981
-      Green Bay (7) vs. Detroit (6), Oct. 6, 1985
- 12   In many games

FUMBLES LOST

Most Fumbles Lost, Season
- 36   Chi. Cardinals, 1959
- 31   Green Bay, 1952
- 29   Chi. Cardinals, 1946
-    Pittsburgh, 1950
-    Cleveland, 1978

Fewest Fumbles Lost, Season
- 2   Kansas City, 2002
- 3   Philadelphia, 1938
-    Minnesota, 1980
-    N.Y. Giants, 2008

4   San Francisco, 1960
    Kansas City, 1982
    Minnesota, 1998
    Detroit, 2003
Most Fumbles Lost, Game
8   St. Louis vs. Washington, Oct. 25, 1976
    Cleveland vs. Pittsburgh, Dec. 23, 1990
7   Cincinnati vs. Buffalo, Nov. 30, 1969
    Pittsburgh vs. Cincinnati, Oct. 14, 1979
    Cleveland vs. Seattle, Dec. 20, 1981
6   By many teams

FUMBLES RECOVERED

Most Fumbles Recovered, Season, Own and Opponents'
58 Minnesota, 1963 (27 own, 31 opp)
51 Chi. Bears, 1938 (37 own, 14 opp)
    San Francisco, 1978 (24 own, 27 opp)
50 Philadelphia, 1987 (23 own, 27 opp)
Fewest Fumbles Recovered, Season, Own and Opponents'
9   San Francisco, 1982 (5 own, 4 opp)
10 Jacksonville, 2006 (6 own, 4 opp)
11 Cincinnati, 1982 (5 own, 6 opp)
    Denver, 2008 (4 own, 7 opp)
    Washington, 2008 (6 own, 5 opp)
Most Fumbles Recovered, Game, Own and Opponents'
10 Denver vs. Buffalo, Dec. 13, 1964 (5 own, 5 opp)
    Pittsburgh vs. Houston, Dec. 9, 1973 (5 own, 5 opp)
    Washington vs. St. Louis, Oct. 25, 1976
      (2 own, 8 opp)
9   St. Louis vs. N.Y. Giants, Sept. 17, 1961
      (6 own, 3 opp)
    Houston vs. Cincinnati, Oct. 27, 1974 (4 own, 5 opp)
    Kansas City vs. Dallas, Nov. 10, 1975 (4 own, 5 opp)
    Green Bay vs. Detroit, Oct. 6, 1985 (5 own, 4 opp)
    Pittsburgh vs. Cleveland, Dec. 23, 1990
      (1 own, 8 opp)
8   By many teams
Most Own Fumbles Recovered, Season
37 Chi. Bears, 1938
28 Pittsburgh, 1987
27 Philadelphia, 1946
    Minnesota, 1963
Fewest Own Fumbles Recovered, Season
1   Indianapolis, 2006
    Philadelphia, 2008
2   Washington, 1958
    Miami, 2000
3   Detroit, 1956
    Cleveland, 1959
    Houston, 1982
    New Orleans, 2005
    Atlanta, 2010
Most Opponents' Fumbles Recovered, Season
31 Minnesota, 1963
29 Cleveland, 1951
28 Green Bay, 1946
    Houston, 1977
    Seattle, 1983
Fewest Opponents' Fumbles Recovered, Season
3   Los Angeles, 1974
    Green Bay, 1995
4   Philadelphia, 1944
    San Francisco, 1982
    Jacksonville, 2006
    Jacksonville, 2008
5   Baltimore, 1982
    Arizona, 1997
    Baltimore, 1998
    Chicago, 2003
    Oakland, 2006

N.Y. Giants, 2008
Washington, 2008
Buffalo, 2009
Houston, 2010
Jacksonville, 2010
Most Opponents' Fumbles Recovered, Game
8   Washington vs. St. Louis, Oct. 25, 1976
    Pittsburgh vs. Cleveland, Dec. 23, 1990
7   Buffalo vs. Cincinnati, Nov. 30, 1969
    Cincinnati vs. Pittsburgh, Oct. 14, 1979
    Seattle vs. Cleveland, Dec. 20, 1981
6   By many teams

TOUCHDOWNS

**Most Touchdowns, Fumbles Recovered, Season,
Own and Opponents'**
7   Arizona, 2010 (3 own, 4 opp)
5   Chi. Bears, 1942 (1 own, 4 opp)
    Los Angeles, 1952 (1 own, 4 opp)
    San Francisco, 1965 (1 own, 4 opp)
    Oakland, 1978 (2 own, 3 opp)
4   Chi. Bears, 1948 (1 own, 3 opp)
    Boston, 1948 (4 opp)
    Denver, 1979 (1 own, 3 opp)
    Atlanta, 1981 (1 own, 3 opp)
    Denver, 1984 (4 opp)
    St. Louis, 1987 (4 opp)
    Minnesota, 1989 (4 opp)
    Atlanta, 1991 (4 opp)
    Philadelphia, 1995 (4 opp)
    Atlanta, 1998 (4 opp)
    New Orleans, 1998 (4 opp)
    Kansas City, 1999 (4 opp)
Most Touchdowns, Own Fumbles Recovered, Season
3   Arizona, 2010
2   Chi. Bears, 1953
    New England, 1973
    Buffalo, 1974
    Denver, 1975
    Oakland, 1978
    Green Bay, 1982
    New Orleans, 1983
    Cleveland, 1986
    Green Bay, 1989
    Miami, 1996
    Buffalo, 2000
    Philadelphia, 2007
Most Touchdowns, Opponents' Fumbles Recovered, Season
4   Detroit, 1937
    Chi. Bears, 1942
    Boston, 1948
    Los Angeles, 1952
    San Francisco, 1965
    Denver, 1984
    St. Louis, 1987
    Minnesota, 1989
    Atlanta, 1991
    Philadelphia, 1995
    Atlanta, 1998
    New Orleans, 1998
    Kansas City, 1999
    Arizona, 2010
3   By many teams
**Most Touchdowns, Fumbles Recovered, Game,
Own and Opponents'**
2   By many teams
**Most Touchdowns, Fumbles Recovered, Game, Both Teams,
Own and Opponents'**
3   Detroit (2) vs. Minnesota (1), Dec. 9, 1962
      (2 own, 1 opp)

Green Bay (2) vs. Dallas (1), Nov. 29, 1964 (3 opp)
Oakland (2) vs. Buffalo (1), Dec. 24, 1967 (3 opp)
Oakland (2) vs. Philadelphia (1), Sept. 24, 1995
   (3 opp)
Tennessee (2) vs. Pittsburgh (1), Jan. 2, 2000
   (3 opp)

Most Touchdowns, Own Fumbles Recovered, Game
2 Miami vs. New England, Sept.1, 1996

Most Touchdowns, Opponents' Fumbles Recovered, Game
2 Many times. Last time:
    San Francisco vs. St. Louis, Oct. 4, 2009

Most Touchdowns, Opponents' Fumbles Recovered, Game, Both Teams
3 Green Bay (2) vs. Dallas (1), Nov. 29, 1964
   Oakland (2) vs. Buffalo (1), Dec. 24, 1967
   Oakland (2) vs. Philadelphia (1), Sept. 24, 1995
   Tennessee (2) vs. Pittsburgh (1), Jan. 2, 2000

TURNOVERS
(Number of times losing the ball on interceptions and fumbles.)

Most Turnovers, Season
65 Denver, 1961
63 San Francisco, 1978
58 Chi. Bears, 1947
   Pittsburgh, 1950
   N.Y. Giants, 1983

Fewest Turnovers, Season
10 New England, 2010
12 Kansas City, 1982
13 Miami, 2008
   N.Y. Giants, 2008

Most Turnovers, Game
12 Detroit vs. Chi. Bears, Nov. 22, 1942
   Chi. Cardinals vs. Philadelphia, Sept. 24, 1950
   Pittsburgh vs. Philadelphia, Dec. 12, 1965
11 San Diego vs. Green Bay, Sept. 24, 1978
10 Washington vs. N.Y. Giants, Dec. 4, 1938
   Pittsburgh vs. Green Bay, Nov. 23, 1941
   Detroit vs. Green Bay, Oct. 24, 1943
   Chi. Cardinals vs. Green Bay, Nov. 10, 1946
   Chi. Cardinals vs. N.Y. Giants, Nov. 2, 1952
   Minnesota vs. Detroit, Dec. 9, 1962
   Houston vs. Oakland, Sept. 7, 1963
   Washington vs. N.Y. Giants, Dec. 8, 1963
   Chicago vs. Detroit, Sept. 22, 1968
   St. Louis vs. Washington, Oct. 25, 1976
   N.Y. Jets vs. New England, Nov. 21, 1976
   San Francisco vs. Dallas, Oct. 12, 1980
   Cleveland vs. Seattle, Dec. 20, 1981
   Detroit vs. Denver, Oct. 7, 1984

Most Turnovers, Both Teams, Game
17 Detroit (12) vs. Chi. Bears (5), Nov. 22, 1942
   Boston (9) vs. Philadelphia (8), Dec. 8, 1946
16 Chi. Cardinals (12) vs. Philadelphia (4),
    Sept. 24, 1950
   Chi. Cardinals (8) vs. Chi. Bears (8), Dec. 7, 1958
   Minnesota (10) vs. Detroit (6), Dec. 9, 1962
   Houston (9) vs. Kansas City (7), Oct. 12, 1969
15 Philadelphia (8) vs. Chi. Cardinals (7), Oct. 3, 1954
   Denver (9) vs. Houston (6), Dec. 2, 1962
   Washington (10) vs. N.Y. Giants (5), Dec. 8, 1963
   St. Louis (9) vs. Kansas City (6), Oct. 2, 1983

PENALTIES

Most Seasons Leading League, Fewest Penalties
13 Miami, 1968, 1976-1984, 1986, 1990-91
9 Pittsburgh, 1946-47, 1950-52, 1954, 1963, 1965,
   1968
8 Boston/New England, 1962, 1964-65, 1973, 1987,
   1989, 1993, 2008

Most Consecutive Seasons Leading League, Fewest Penalties
9 Miami, 1976-1984
3 Pittsburgh, 1950-52
2 By many teams

Most Seasons Leading League, Most Penalties
16 Chi. Bears, 1941-44, 1946-49, 1951, 1959-1961,
    1963, 1965, 1968, 1976
   Oakland/L.A. Raiders, 1963, 1966, 1968-69, 1975,
    1982, 1984, 1991, 1993-96, 2003-05, 2010
7 L.A./St. Louis Rams, 1950, 1952, 1962, 1969,
    1978, 1980, 1997
6 Dallas, 1964, 1971-72, 1988, 1999, 2008

Most Consecutive Seasons Leading League, Most Penalties
4 Chi. Bears, 1941-44, 1946-49
   Oakland/L.A. Raiders, 1993-96
3 Chi. Cardinals, 1954-56
   Chi. Bears, 1959-1961
   Oakland, 2003-05

Fewest Penalties, Season
19 Detroit, 1937
21 Boston, 1935
24 Philadelphia, 1936

Most Penalties, Season
158 Kansas City, 1998
156 L.A. Raiders, 1994
    Oakland, 1996
149 Houston, 1989

Fewest Penalties, Game
0 By many teams. Last time:
   New England vs. New Orleans, Nov. 30, 2009

Most Penalties, Game
22 Brooklyn vs. Green Bay, Sept. 17, 1944
   Chi. Bears vs. Philadelphia, Nov. 26, 1944
   San Francisco vs. Buffalo, Oct. 4, 1998
21 Cleveland vs. Chi. Bears, Nov. 25, 1951
   Baltimore vs. Detroit, Oct. 9, 2005
20 Tampa Bay vs. Seattle, Oct. 17, 1976
   Oakland vs. Denver, Dec. 15, 1996

Fewest Penalties, Both Teams, Game
0 Brooklyn vs. Pittsburgh, Oct. 28, 1934
   Brooklyn vs. Boston, Sept. 28, 1936
   Cleveland vs. Chi. Bears, Oct. 9, 1938
   Pittsburgh vs. Philadelphia, Nov. 10, 1940

Most Penalties, Both Teams, Game
37 Cleveland (21) vs. Chi. Bears (16), Nov. 25, 1951
35 Tampa Bay (20) vs. Seattle (15), Oct. 17, 1976
34 San Francisco (22) vs. Buffalo (12), Oct. 4, 1998

YARDS PENALIZED

Most Seasons Leading League, Fewest Yards Penalized
14 Miami, 1967-68, 1973, 1977-1984, 1990-91, 2010
10 Boston/Washington, 1935, 1953-54, 1956-58,
    1970, 1985, 1995, 1997
8 Boston/New England, 1962, 1964-66, 1987, 1989,
    1993, 2008

Most Consecutive Seasons Leading League, Fewest Yards Penalized
8 Miami, 1977-1984
3 Washington, 1956-58
   Boston, 1964-66
2 By many teams

Most Seasons Leading League, Most Yards Penalized
15 Chi. Bears, 1935, 1937, 1939-1944, 1946-47,
    1949, 1951, 1961-62, 1968
13 Oakland/L.A. Raiders, 1963-64, 1968-69, 1975,
    1982, 1984, 1991, 1993-94, 1996, 2003, 2010
6 Buffalo, 1962, 1967, 1970, 1972, 1981, 1983
   Houston, 1961, 1985-86, 1988-1990

Most Consecutive Seasons Leading League, Most Yards Penalized
- 6   Chi. Bears, 1939-1944
- 3   Houston, 1988-1990
- 2   By many teams

Fewest Yards Penalized, Season
- 139   Detroit, 1937
- 146   Philadelphia, 1937
- 159   Philadelphia, 1936

Most Yards Penalized, Season
- 1,304   Kansas City, 1998
- 1,276   Oakland, 2010
- 1,274   Oakland, 1969

Fewest Yards Penalized, Game
- 0   By many teams. Last time:
  - New England vs. New Orleans, Nov. 30, 2009

Most Yards Penalized, Game
- 212   Tennessee vs. Baltimore, Oct. 10, 1999
- 209   Cleveland vs. Chi. Bears, Nov. 25, 1951
- 191   Philadelphia vs. Seattle, Dec. 13, 1992 (ot)

Fewest Yards Penalized, Both Teams, Game
- 0   Brooklyn vs. Pittsburgh, Oct. 28, 1934
  - Brooklyn vs. Boston, Sept. 28, 1936
  - Cleveland vs. Chi. Bears, Oct. 9, 1938
  - Pittsburgh vs. Philadelphia, Nov. 10, 1940

Most Yards Penalized, Both Teams, Game
- 374   Cleveland (209) vs. Chi. Bears (165), Nov. 25, 1951
- 310   Tampa Bay (190) vs. Seattle (120), Oct. 17, 1976
  - Green Bay (175) vs. Baltimore (135), Dec. 7, 2009
- 309   Green Bay (184) vs. Boston (125), Oct. 21, 1945

DEFENSE

SCORING

Most Seasons Leading League, Fewest Points Allowed
- 11   N.Y. Giants, 1927, 1935, 1938-39, 1941, 1944, 1958-59, 1961, 1990, 1993
  - Chi. Bears, 1932, 1936-37, 1942, 1948, 1963, 1985-86, 1988, 2001, 2005
- 7   Cleveland, 1951, 1953-57, 1994
  - Green Bay, 1929, 1935, 1947, 1962, 1965-66, 1996
- 6   Dallas/Kansas City, 1960, 1962, 1968-69, 1995, 1997
  - Pittsburgh, 1946, 1976, 1978, 2004, 2008, 2010

Most Consecutive Seasons Leading League, Fewest Points Allowed
- 5   Cleveland, 1953-57
- 3   Buffalo, 1964-66
  - Minnesota, 1969-1971
- 2   By many teams

Fewest Points Allowed, Season (Since 1932)
- 44   Chi. Bears, 1932
- 54   Brooklyn, 1933
- 59   Detroit, 1934

Most Points Allowed, Season
- 533   Baltimore, 1981
- 517   Detroit, 2008
- 501   N.Y. Giants, 1966

Fewest TDs Allowed, Season (Since 1932)
- 6   Chi. Bears, 1932
  - Brooklyn, 1933
- 7   Detroit, 1934
- 8   Green Bay, 1932
- 9   St. Louis, 1934
  - N.Y. Giants, 1939
  - N.Y. Giants, 1944

Most Touchdowns Allowed, Season
- 68   Baltimore, 1981
- 66   N.Y. Giants, 1966
- 63   Baltimore, 1950

Detroit, 2008

FIRST DOWNS

Fewest First Downs Allowed, Season
- 77   Detroit, 1935
- 79   Boston, 1935
- 82   Washington, 1937

Most First Downs Allowed, Season
- 406   Baltimore, 1981
- 371   Seattle, 1981
- 368   Cleveland, 1999

Fewest First Downs Allowed, Rushing, Season
- 35   Chi. Bears, 1942
- 40   Green Bay, 1939
- 41   Brooklyn, 1944

Most First Downs Allowed, Rushing, Season
- 179   Detroit, 1985
- 178   New Orleans, 1980
- 175   Seattle, 1981

Fewest First Downs Allowed, Passing, Season
- 33   Chi. Bears, 1943
- 34   Pittsburgh, 1941
  - Washington, 1943
- 35   Detroit, 1940
  - Philadelphia, 1940
  - Philadelphia, 1944

Most First Downs Allowed, Passing, Season
- 230   Atlanta, 1995
- 227   Kansas City, 2002
- 226   New England, 2010

Fewest First Downs Allowed, Penalty, Season
- 1   Boston, 1944
- 3   Philadelphia, 1940
  - Pittsburgh, 1945
  - Washington, 1957
- 4   Cleveland, 1940
  - Green Bay, 1943
  - N.Y. Giants, 1943

Most First Downs Allowed, Penalty, Season
- 56   Kansas City, 1998
- 48   Houston, 1985
- 46   Houston, 1986

NET YARDS ALLOWED RUSHING AND PASSING

Most Seasons Leading League, Fewest Yards Allowed
- 8   Chi. Bears, 1942-43, 1948, 1958, 1963, 1984-86
  - Pittsburgh, 1957, 1974, 1976, 1990, 2001, 2004, 2007-08
- 6   N.Y. Giants, 1938, 1940-41, 1951, 1956, 1959
  - Philadelphia, 1944-45, 1949, 1953, 1981, 1991
  - Minnesota, 1969-1970, 1975, 1988-89, 1993

Most Consecutive Seasons Leading League, Fewest Yards Allowed
- 3   Boston/Washington, 1935-37
  - Chicago, 1984-86
- 2   By many teams

Fewest Yards Allowed, Season
- 1,539   Chi. Cardinals, 1934
- 1,703   Chi. Bears, 1942
- 1,789   Brooklyn, 1933

Most Yards Allowed, Season
- 6,793   Baltimore, 1981
- 6,470   Detroit, 2008
- 6,403   Green Bay, 1983

RUSHING

Most Seasons Leading League, Fewest Yards Allowed
- 10   Chi. Bears, 1937, 1939, 1942, 1946, 1949, 1963, 1984-85, 1987-88

8 Pittsburgh, 1961, 1976, 1982, 1997, 2001-02, 2004, 2010
7 Detroit, 1938, 1950, 1952, 1962, 1970, 1980-81
    Philadelphia, 1944-45, 1947-48, 1953, 1990-91
    Dallas, 1966-69, 1972, 1978, 1992

Most Consecutive Seasons Leading League, Fewest Yards Allowed
4 Dallas, 1966-69
3 Minnesota, 2006-08
2 By many teams

Fewest Yards Allowed, Rushing, Season
519 Chi. Bears, 1942
558 Philadelphia, 1944
762 Pittsburgh, 1982

Most Yards Allowed, Rushing, Season
3,228 Buffalo, 1978
3,106 New Orleans, 1980
3,010 Baltimore, 1978

Fewest Touchdowns Allowed, Rushing, Season
2 Detroit, 1934
   N.Y. Giants, 1944
   Dallas, 1968
   Minnesota, 1971
3 By many teams

Most Touchdowns Allowed, Rushing, Season
36 Oakland, 1961
31 N.Y. Giants, 1980
   Tampa Bay, 1986
   Detroit, 2008
30 Baltimore, 1981

PASSING

Most Seasons Leading League, Fewest Yards Allowed
10 Green Bay, 1947-48, 1962, 1964-68, 1996, 2005
7 Washington, 1939, 1942, 1945, 1952-53, 1980, 1985
   Philadelphia 1934, 1936, 1940, 1949, 1981, 1991, 1998
   Pittsburgh, 1941, 1946, 1951, 1955, 1974, 1990, 2008
6 Chi. Bears, 1938, 1943-44, 1958, 1960, 1963
   Minnesota, 1969-1970, 1972, 1975-76, 1989

Most Consecutive Seasons Leading League, Fewest Yards Allowed
5 Green Bay, 1964-68
2 By many teams

Fewest Yards Allowed Passing, Season
545 Philadelphia, 1934
558 Portsmouth, 1933
585 Chi. Cardinals, 1934

Most Yards Allowed, Passing, Season
4,541 Atlanta, 1995
4.427 San Francisco, 2005
4,389 N.Y. Jets, 1986

Fewest Touchdowns Allowed, Passing, Season
1 Portsmouth, 1932
   Philadelphia, 1934
2 Brooklyn, 1933
   Chi. Bears, 1934
3 Chi. Bears, 1932
   Green Bay, 1932
   Green Bay, 1934
   Chi. Bears, 1936
   New York, 1939
   New York, 1944

Most Touchdowns Allowed, Passing, Season
40 Denver, 1963
38 St. Louis, 1969
37 Washington, 1961
   Baltimore, 1981

SACKS

Most Seasons Leading League
5 Oakland/L.A. Raiders, 1966-68, 1982, 1986
   Dallas, 1966, 1968-69, 1978, 2008
4 New England/Boston, 1961, 1963, 1977, 1979
   Dallas/Kansas City, 1960, 1965, 1969, 1990
   L.A./St. Louis Rams, 1968, 1970, 1988, 1999
   N.Y. Giants, 1963, 1985, 1998, 2007
   Pittsburgh, 1974, 1994, 2001, 2010
3 San Francisco, 1967, 1972, 1976
   N.Y. Giants, 1963, 1985, 1998
   New Orleans, 1992, 1997, 2000
   San Diego, 1962, 1980, 2006

Most Consecutive Seasons Leading League
3 Oakland, 1966-68
2 Dallas, 1968-69

Most Sacks, Season
72 Chicago, 1984
71 Minnesota, 1989
70 Chicago, 1987

Fewest Sacks, Season
10 Kansas City, 2008
11 Baltimore, 1982
12 Buffalo, 1982

Most Sacks, Game
12 Dallas vs. Pittsburgh, Nov. 20, 1966
   St. Louis vs. Baltimore, Oct. 26, 1980
   Chicago vs. Detroit, Dec. 16, 1984
   Dallas vs. Houston, Sept. 29, 1985
   N.Y. Giants vs. Philadelphia, Sept. 30, 2007
11 N.Y. Giants vs. St. Louis, Nov. 1, 1964
   Baltimore vs. Los Angeles, Nov. 22, 1964
   Buffalo vs. Denver, Dec. 13, 1964
   Detroit vs. Green Bay, Nov. 7, 1965
   Oakland vs. Buffalo, Oct. 15, 1967
   Oakland vs. Denver, Nov. 5, 1967
   St. Louis vs. Atlanta, Nov. 24, 1968
   Dallas vs. Detroit, Oct. 6, 1975
   St. Louis vs. Philadelphia, Dec. 18, 1983
   Kansas City vs. Cleveland, Sept. 30, 1984
   Chicago vs. Minnesota, Oct. 28, 1984
   Cleveland vs. Atlanta, Nov. 18, 1984
   Detroit vs. Philadelphia, Nov. 16, 1986
   San Diego vs. Dallas, Nov. 16, 1986
   L.A. Raiders vs. Philadelphia, Nov. 30, 1986 (ot)
   Seattle vs. L.A. Raiders, Dec. 8, 1986
   Chicago vs. Philadelphia, Oct. 4, 1987
   Dallas vs. N.Y. Jets, Oct. 4, 1987
   Philadelphia vs. Dallas, Sept. 15, 1991
   Indianapolis vs. Cleveland, Sept. 6, 1992
10 By many teams

Most Opponents Yards Lost Attempting to Pass, Season
666 Oakland, 1967
583 Chicago, 1984
573 San Francisco, 1976

Fewest Opponents Yards Lost Attempting to Pass, Season
62 Kansas City, 2008
72 Jacksonville, 1995
75 Green Bay, 1956

INTERCEPTIONS BY

Most Seasons Leading League
10 N.Y. Giants, 1933, 1937-39, 1944, 1948, 1951, 1954, 1961, 1997
9 Green Bay, 1940, 1942-43, 1947, 1955, 1957, 1962, 1965, 2009
8 Chi. Bears, 1935-36, 1941-42, 1946, 1963, 1985, 1990

Most Consecutive Seasons Leading League
- 5   Kansas City, 1966-1970
- 3   N.Y. Giants, 1937-39
- 2   By many teams

Most Passes Intercepted, Season
- 49   San Diego, 1961
- 42   Green Bay, 1943
- 41   N.Y. Giants, 1951

Fewest Passes Intercepted By, Season
- 3   Houston, 1982
- 4   Detroit, 2008
- 5   Baltimore, 1982
-    Oakland, 2005

Most Passes Intercepted By, Game
- 9   Green Bay vs. Detroit, Oct. 24, 1943
-    Philadelphia vs. Pittsburgh, Dec. 12, 1965
- 8   N.Y. Giants vs. Green Bay, Nov. 21, 1948
-    Philadelphia vs. Chi. Cardinals, Sept. 24, 1950
-    N.Y. Giants vs. N.Y. Yanks, Dec. 16, 1951
-    Houston vs. Denver, Dec. 2, 1962
-    Detroit vs. Chicago, Sept. 22, 1968
-    N.Y. Jets vs. Baltimore, Sept. 23, 1973
- 7   By many teams. Last time:
-      Cleveland vs. Detroit, Sept. 23, 2001

Most Consecutive Games, One or More Interceptions By
- 46   L.A. Chargers/San Diego, 1960-63
- 37   Detroit, 1960-63
- 36   Boston, 1944-47

Most Yards Returning Interceptions, Season
- 929   San Diego, 1961
- 712   Los Angeles, 1952
- 700   Baltimore, 2004

Fewest Yards Returning Interceptions, Season
- 5   Los Angeles, 1959
- 16   Detroit, 2008
- 25   Washington, 2006

Most Yards Returning Interceptions, Game
- 325   Seattle vs. Kansas City, Nov. 4, 1984
- 314   Los Angeles vs. San Francisco, Oct. 18, 1964
- 245   Houston vs. N.Y. Jets, Oct. 15, 1967

Most Yards Returning Interceptions, Both Teams, Game
- 356   Seattle (325) vs. Kansas City (31), Nov. 4, 1984
- 338   Los Angeles (314) vs. San Francisco (24), Oct. 18, 1964
- 308   Dallas (182) vs. Los Angeles (126), Nov. 2, 1952

Most Touchdowns, Returning Interceptions, Season
- 9   San Diego, 1961
- 8   Seattle, 1998
- 7   Seattle, 1984
-    St. Louis, 1999

Most Touchdowns Returning Interceptions, Game
- 4   Seattle vs. Kansas City, Nov. 4, 1984
- 3   Baltimore vs. Green Bay, Nov. 5, 1950
-    Cleveland vs. Chicago, Dec. 11, 1960
-    Philadelphia vs. Pittsburgh, Dec. 12, 1965
-    Baltimore vs. Pittsburgh, Sept. 29, 1968
-    Buffalo vs. N.Y. Jets, Sept. 29, 1968
-    Houston vs. San Diego, Dec. 19, 1971
-    Cincinnati vs. Houston, Dec. 17, 1972
-    Tampa Bay vs. New Orleans, Dec. 11, 1977
-    Minnesota vs. N.Y. Giants, Nov. 25, 2007
- 2   By many teams

Most Touchdown Returning Interceptions, Both Teams, Game
- 4   Philadelphia (3) vs. Pittsburgh (1), Dec. 12, 1965
-    Seattle (4) vs. Kansas City (0), Nov. 4, 1984
- 3   Los Angeles (2) vs. Detroit (1), Nov. 1, 1953
-    Cleveland (2) vs. N.Y. Giants (1), Dec. 18, 1960
-    Pittsburgh (2) vs. Cincinnati (1), Oct. 10, 1983
-    Kansas City (2) vs. San Diego (1), Oct. 19, 1986

   Arizona (2) vs. St. Louis (1), Dec. 30, 2007
   (Also see previous record)

PUNT RETURNS
Fewest Opponents Punt Returns, Season
- 7   Washington, 1962
-    San Diego, 1982
- 10   Buffalo, 1982
- 11   Boston, 1962
-    New England, 2008

Most Opponents Punt Returns, Season
- 71   Tampa Bay, 1976, 1977
- 69   N.Y. Giants, 1953
-    Cleveland, 2000
- 68   Cleveland, 1974
-    Cleveland, 1999

Fewest Yards Allowed, Punt Returns, Season
- 22   Green Bay, 1967
- 30   Buffalo, 1982
- 34   Washington, 1962

Most Yards Allowed, Punt Returns, Season
- 932   Green Bay, 1949
- 913   Boston, 1947
- 906   New Orleans, 1974

Lowest Avg. Allowed, Punt Returns, Season
- 1.20   Chi. Cardinals, 1954
- 1.22   Cleveland, 1959
- 1.55   Chi. Cardinals, 1953

Highest Average Allowed, Punt Returns, Season
- 18.9   San Diego, 2010 (28-528)
- 18.6   Green Bay, 1949 (50-932)
- 18.0   Cleveland, 1977 (31-558)

Most Touchdowns Allowed, Punt Returns, Season
- 4   Los Angeles, 1951
-    N.Y. Giants, 1959
-    Atlanta, 1992
-    Minnesota, 2008
- 3   Green Bay, 1949
-    Chi. Cardinals, 1951
-    L.A. Rams, 1951, 1994
-    Washington, 1952
-    Dallas, 1952
-    Pittsburgh, 1959, 1993
-    N.Y. Jets, 1968
-    Cleveland, 1977
-    Atlanta, 1986
-    Tampa Bay, 1986
-    Arizona, 2002
-    Cincinnati, 2002
-    Tennessee, 2002
- 2   By many teams

KICKOFF RETURNS
Fewest Opponents Kickoff Returns, Season
- 10   Brooklyn, 1943
- 13   Denver, 1992
- 15   Detroit, 1942
-    Brooklyn, 1944

Most Opponents Kickoff Returns, Season
- 93   Indianapolis, 2003
- 92   Indianapolis, 2004
-    New England, 2007
- 91   Washington, 1983
-    Minnesota, 2009

Fewest Yards Allowed, Kickoff Returns, Season
- 225   Brooklyn, 1943
- 254   Denver, 1992
- 293   Brooklyn, 1944

Most Yards Allowed, Kickoff Returns, Season
- 2,194   St. Louis, 2001

2,115 St. Louis, 1999
2,060 Minnesota, 2009

Lowest Average Allowed, Kickoff Returns, Season
14.3 Cleveland, 1980
14.9 Indianapolis, 1993
15.0 Seattle, 1982

Highest Average Allowed, Kickoff Returns, Season
29.5 N.Y. Jets, 1972 (47-1,386)
29.4 Los Angeles, 1950 (48-1,411)
29.1 New England, 1971 (49-1,427)

Most Touchdowns Allowed, Kickoff Returns, Season
4 Minnesota, 1998
   Pittsburgh, 2009
3 Minnesota, 1963, 1970
   Dallas, 1966
   Detroit, 1980
   Pittsburgh, 1986
   Buffalo, 1997
   Atlanta, 2000
   Arizona, 2005
   Indianapolis, 2007
   San Diego, 2010
2 By many teams

FUMBLES

Fewest Opponents Fumbles, Season
11 Cleveland, 1956
    Baltimore, 1982
    Tennessee, 1998
12 Green Bay, 1995
    Cincinnati, 1998
    Jacksonville, 2006
    Baltimore, 2007
    Jacksonville, 2010
13 Los Angeles, 1956
    Chicago, 1960
    Cleveland, 1963
    Cleveland, 1965
    Detroit, 1967
    San Diego, 1969
    New England, 2005
    Cleveland, 2006
    San Diego, 2010

Most Opponents Fumbles, Season
50 Minnesota, 1963
    San Francisco, 1978
48 N.Y. Giants, 1980
    N.Y. Jets, 1986
47 N.Y. Giants, 1977
    Seattle, 1984

TURNOVERS
(Number of times losing the ball on interceptions and fumbles.)

Fewest Opponents Turnovers, Season
11 Baltimore, 1982
12 Washington, 2006
13 San Francisco, 1982
    Denver, 2008

Most Opponent Turnovers, Season
66 San Diego, 1961
63 Seattle, 1984
61 Washington, 1983
57 Detroit, 1952
    Buffalo, 1965

Most Opponent Turnovers, Game
12 Chi. Bears vs. Detroit, Nov. 22, 1942
    Philadelphia vs. Chi. Cardinals, Sept. 24, 1950
    Philadelphia vs. Pittsburgh, Dec. 12, 1965
11 Green Bay vs. San Diego, Sept. 24, 1978
10 By 14 teams

1,000 YARDS RUSHING IN A SEASON

Year	Player, Team	Att.	Yards	Avg.	Long	TD
2010	Arian Foster, Houston	327	1,616	4.9	74	16
	Jamaal Charles, Kansas City[2]	230	1,467	6.4	80	5
	Michael Turner, Atlanta[2]	334	1,371	4.1	55	12
	Chris Johnson, Tennessee[3]	316	1,364	4.3	76	11
	Maurice Jones-Drew, Jacksonville[2]	299	1,324	4.4	37	5
	Adrian Peterson, Minnesota[4]	283	1,298	4.6	80	12
	Rashard Mendenhall, Pittsburgh[2]	324	1,273	3.9	50	13
	Steven Jackson, St. Louis[6]	330	1,241	3.8	42	6
	Ahmad Bradshaw, N.Y. Giants	276	1,235	4.5	48	8
	Ray Rice, Baltimore[2]	307	1,220	4.0	50	5
	Peyton Hillis, Cleveland	270	1,177	4.4	48	11
	Darren McFadden, Oakland	223	1,157	5.2	57	7
	Cedric Benson, Cincinnati[2]	321	1,111	3.5	26	7
	LeSean McCoy, Philadelphia	207	1,080	5.2	62	7
	Matt Forté, Chicago[2]	237	1,069	4.5	68	6
	BenJarvus Green-Ellis, New England	229	1,008	4.4	33	13
	*LeGarrette Blount, Tampa Bay	201	1,007	5.0	53	6
2009	Chris Johnson, Tennessee[2]	358	2,006	5.6	91	14
	Steven Jackson, St. Louis[5]	324	1,416	4.8	58	4
	Thomas Jones, N.Y. Jets[5]	331	1,402	4.2	71	14
	Maurice Jones-Drew, Jacksonville	312	1,391	4.5	80	15
	Adrian Peterson, Minnesota[3]	314	1,383	4.4	64	18
	Ray Rice, Baltimore	254	1,339	5.3	59	7
	Ryan Grant, Green Bay[2]	282	1,253	4.4	62	11
	Cedric Benson, Cincinnati	301	1,251	4.2	42	6
	Jonathan Stewart, Carolina	221	1,133	5.1	67	10
	Ricky Williams, Miami[5]	241	1,121	4.6	68	11
	Jamaal Charles, Kansas City	190	1,120	5.9	76	7
	Frank Gore, San Francisco[4]	229	1,120	4.9	80	10
	DeAngelo Williams, Carolina[2]	216	1,117	5.2	77	7
	Rashard Mendenhall, Pittsburgh	242	1,108	4.6	60	7
	Fred Jackson, Buffalo	237	1,062	4.5	43	2
2008	Adrian Peterson, Minnesota[2]	363	1,760	4.9	67	10
	Michael Turner, Atlanta	376	1,699	4.5	70	17
	DeAngelo Williams, Carolina	273	1,515	5.6	69	18
	Clinton Portis, Washington[6]	342	1,487	4.4	31	9
	Thomas Jones, N.Y. Jets[4]	290	1,312	4.5	59	13
	*Steve Slaton, Houston	268	1,282	4.8	71	9
	*Matt Forté, Chicago	316	1,238	3.9	50	8
	*Chris Johnson, Tennessee	251	1,228	4.9	66	9
	Ryan Grant, Green Bay	312	1,203	3.9	57	4
	LaDainian Tomlinson, San Diego[8]	292	1,110	3.8	45	11
	Brandon Jacobs, N.Y. Giants[2]	219	1,089	5.0	44	15
	Steven Jackson, St. Louis[4]	253	1,042	4.1	56	7
	Frank Gore, San Francisco[3]	240	1,036	4.3	41	6
	Marshawn Lynch, Buffalo[2]	250	1,036	4.1	50	8
	Derrick Ward, N.Y. Giants	182	1,025	5.6	51	2
	Jamal Lewis, Cleveland[7]	279	1,002	3.6	29	4
2007	LaDainian Tomlinson, San Diego[7]	315	1,474	4.7	49	15
	*Adrian Peterson, Minnesota	238	1,341	5.6	73	12
	Brian Westbrook, Philadelphia[2]	278	1,333	4.8	36	7
	Willie Parker, Pittsburgh[3]	321	1,316	4.1	32	2
	Jamal Lewis, Cleveland[6]	298	1,304	4.4	66	9
	Clinton Portis, Washington[5]	325	1,262	3.9	32	11
	Edgerrin James, Arizona[7]	324	1,222	3.8	27	7
	Willis McGahee, Baltimore[3]	294	1,207	4.1	46	7
	Fred Taylor, Jacksonville[7]	223	1,202	5.4	80	5
	Thomas Jones, N.Y. Jets[3]	310	1,119	3.6	36	1
	*Marshawn Lynch, Buffalo	280	1,115	4.0	56	7
	LenDale White, Tennessee	303	1,110	3.7	28	7
	Frank Gore, San Francisco[2]	260	1,102	4.2	43	5
	Joseph Addai, Indianapolis[2]	261	1,072	4.1	23	12
	Justin Fargas, Oakland	222	1,009	4.6	48	4
	Brandon Jacobs, N.Y. Giants	202	1,009	5.0	43	4
	Steven Jackson, St. Louis[3]	237	1,002	4.2	54	5
2006	LaDainian Tomlinson, San Diego[6]	348	1,815	5.2	85	28
	Larry Johnson, Kansas City[2]	416	1,789	4.3	47	17
	Frank Gore, San Francisco	312	1,695	5.4	72	8

Year	Player, Team	Att.	Yards	Avg.	Long	TD
	Tiki Barber, N.Y. Giants[6]	327	1,662	5.1	55	5
	Steven Jackson, St. Louis[2]	346	1,528	4.4	59	13
	Willie Parker, Pittsburgh[2]	337	1,494	4.4	76	13
	Rudi Johnson, Cincinnati[3]	341	1,309	3.8	22	12
	Brian Westbrook, Philadelphia	240	1,217	5.1	71	7
	Chester Taylor, Minnesota	303	1,216	4.0	95	6
	Travis Henry, Tennessee[3]	270	1,211	4.5	70	7
	Thomas Jones, Chicago[2]	296	1,210	4.1	30	6
	Edgerrin James, Arizona[6]	337	1,159	3.4	18	6
	Ladell Betts, Washington	245	1,154	4.7	26	4
	Fred Taylor, Jacksonville[6]	231	1,146	5.0	76	5
	Warrick Dunn, Atlanta[5]	286	1,140	4.0	90	4
	Jamal Lewis, Baltimore[5]	314	1,132	3.6	52	9
	Julius Jones, Dallas	267	1,084	4.1	77	4
	*Joseph Addai, Indianapolis	226	1,081	4.8	41	7
	Ahman Green, Green Bay[6]	266	1,059	4.0	70	5
	Deuce McAllister, New Orleans[4]	244	1,057	4.3	57	10
	Michael Vick, Atlanta	123	1,039	8.5	51	2
	Tatum Bell, Denver	233	1,025	4.4	51	2
	Ronnie Brown, Miami	241	1,008	4.2	47	5
2005	Shaun Alexander, Seattle[5]	370	1,880	5.1	88	27
	Tiki Barber, N.Y. Giants[5]	357	1,860	5.2	95	9
	Larry Johnson, Kansas City	336	1,750	5.2	40	20
	Clinton Portis, Washington[4]	352	1,516	4.3	47	11
	Edgerrin James, Indianapolis[5]	360	1,506	4.2	33	13
	LaDainian Tomlinson, San Diego[5]	339	1,462	4.3	62	18
	Rudi Johnson, Cincinnati[2]	337	1,458	4.3	33	12
	Warrick Dunn, Atlanta[4]	280	1,416	5.1	65	3
	Thomas Jones, Chicago	314	1,335	4.3	42	9
	Willis McGahee, Buffalo[2]	325	1,247	3.8	27	5
	Reuben Droughns, Cleveland[2]	309	1,232	4.0	75	2
	Willie Parker, Pittsburgh	255	1,202	4.7	80	4
	*Carnell Williams, Tampa Bay	290	1,178	4.1	71	6
	Steven Jackson, St. Louis	254	1,046	4.1	51	8
	LaMont Jordan, Oakland	272	1,025	3.8	26	9
	Mike Anderson, Denver[2]	239	1,014	4.2	44	12
2004	Curtis Martin, N.Y. Jets[10]	371	1,697	4.6	25	12
	Shaun Alexander, Seattle[4]	353	1,696	4.8	44	16
	Corey Dillon, New England[7]	345	1,635	4.7	44	12
	Edgerrin James, Indianapolis[4]	334	1,548	4.6	40	9
	Tiki Barber, N.Y. Giants[4]	322	1,518	4.7	72	13
	Rudi Johnson, Cincinnati	361	1,454	4.0	52	12
	LaDainian Tomlinson, San Diego[4]	339	1,335	3.9	42	17
	Clinton Portis, Washington[3]	343	1,315	3.8	64	5
	Reuben Droughns, Denver	275	1,240	4.5	51	6
	Fred Taylor, Jacksonville[5]	260	1,224	4.7	46	2
	Domanick Davis, Houston[2]	302	1,188	3.9	44	13
	Ahman Green, Green Bay[5]	259	1,163	4.5	90	7
	*Kevin Jones, Detroit	241	1,133	4.7	74	5
	Willis McGahee, Buffalo	284	1,128	4.0	41	13
	Warrick Dunn, Atlanta[3]	265	1,106	4.2	60	9
	Deuce McAllister, New Orleans[3]	269	1,074	4.0	71	9
	Chris Brown, Tennessee	220	1,067	4.9	52	6
	Jamal Lewis, Baltimore[4]	235	1,006	4.3	75	7
2003	Jamal Lewis, Baltimore[3]	387	2,066	5.3	82	14
	Ahman Green, Green Bay[4]	355	1,883	5.3	98	15
	LaDainian Tomlinson, San Diego[3]	313	1,645	5.3	73	13
	Deuce McAllister, New Orleans[2]	351	1,641	4.7	76	8
	Clinton Portis, Denver[2]	290	1,591	5.5	65	14
	Fred Taylor, Jacksonville[4]	345	1,572	4.6	62	6
	Stephen Davis, Carolina[4]	318	1,444	4.5	40	8
	Shaun Alexander, Seattle[3]	326	1,435	4.4	55	14
	Priest Holmes, Kansas City[4]	320	1,420	4.4	31	27
	Ricky Williams, Miami[4]	392	1,372	3.5	45	9
	Travis Henry, Buffalo[2]	331	1,356	4.1	64	10
	Curtis Martin, N.Y. Jets[9]	323	1,308	4.1	56	2
	Edgerrin James, Indianapolis[3]	310	1,259	4.1	43	11
	Tiki Barber, N.Y. Giants[3]	278	1,216	4.4	27	2
	*Domanick Davis, Houston	238	1,031	4.3	51	8

Year	Player, Team	Att.	Yards	Avg.	Long	TD
	Eddie George, Tennessee[7]	312	1,031	3.3	27	5
	Kevan Barlow, San Francisco	201	1,024	5.1	78	6
	Anthony Thomas, Chicago[2]	244	1,024	4.2	67	6
2002	Ricky Williams, Miami[3]	383	1,853	4.8	63	16
	LaDainian Tomlinson, San Diego[2]	372	1,683	4.5	76	14
	Priest Holmes, Kansas City[3]	313	1,615	5.2	56	21
	*Clinton Portis, Denver	273	1,508	5.5	59	15
	Travis Henry, Buffalo	325	1,438	4.4	34	13
	Deuce McAllister, New Orleans	325	1,388	4.3	62	13
	Tiki Barber, N.Y. Giants[2]	304	1,387	4.6	70	11
	Jamal Lewis, Baltimore[2]	308	1,327	4.3	75	6
	Fred Taylor, Jacksonville[3]	287	1,314	4.6	63	8
	Corey Dillon, Cincinnati[6]	314	1,311	4.2	67	7
	Michael Bennett, Minnesota	255	1,296	5.1	85	5
	Ahman Green, Green Bay[3]	286	1,240	4.3	43	7
	Shaun Alexander, Seattle[2]	295	1,175	4.0	58	16
	Eddie George, Tennessee[6]	343	1,165	3.4	35	12
	Curtis Martin, N.Y. Jets[8]	261	1,094	4.2	35	7
	Duce Staley, Philadelphia[3]	269	1,029	3.8	57	5
	James Stewart, Detroit[2]	231	1,021	4.4	56	4
2001	Priest Holmes, Kansas City[2]	327	1,555	4.8	41	8
	Curtis Martin, N.Y. Jets[7]	333	1,513	4.5	47	10
	Stephen Davis, Washington[3]	356	1,432	4.0	32	5
	Ahman Green, Green Bay[2]	304	1,387	4.6	83	9
	Marshall Faulk, St. Louis[7]	260	1,382	5.3	71	12
	Shaun Alexander, Seattle	309	1,318	4.3	88	14
	Corey Dillon, Cincinnati[5]	340	1,315	3.9	96	10
	Ricky Williams, New Orleans[2]	313	1,245	4.0	46	6
	*LaDainian Tomlinson, San Diego	339	1,236	3.6	54	10
	Garrison Hearst, San Francisco[4]	252	1,206	4.8	43	4
	*Anthony Thomas, Chicago	278	1,183	4.3	46	7
	Antowain Smith, New England[2]	287	1,157	4.0	44	12
	*Dominic Rhodes, Indianapolis	233	1,104	4.7	77	9
	Jerome Bettis, Pittsburgh[8]	225	1,072	4.8	48	4
	Emmitt Smith, Dallas[11]	261	1,021	3.9	44	3
2000	Edgerrin James, Indianapolis[2]	387	1,709	4.4	30	13
	Robert Smith, Minnesota[4]	295	1,521	5.2	72	7
	Eddie George, Tennessee[5]	403	1,509	3.7	35	14
	*Mike Anderson, Denver	297	1,487	5.0	80	15
	Corey Dillon, Cincinnati[4]	315	1,435	4.6	80	7
	Fred Taylor, Jacksonville[2]	292	1,399	4.8	71	12
	*Jamal Lewis, Baltimore	309	1,364	4.4	45	6
	Marshall Faulk, St. Louis[6]	253	1,359	5.4	36	18
	Jerome Bettis, Pittsburgh[7]	355	1,341	3.8	30	8
	Stephen Davis, Washington[2]	332	1,318	4.0	50	11
	Ricky Watters, Seattle[7]	278	1,242	4.5	55	7
	Curtis Martin, N.Y. Jets[6]	316	1,204	3.8	55	9
	Emmitt Smith, Dallas[10]	294	1,203	4.1	52	9
	James Stewart, Detroit	339	1,184	3.5	34	10
	Ahman Green, Green Bay	263	1,175	4.5	39	10
	Charlie Garner, San Francisco[2]	258	1,142	4.4	42	7
	Lamar Smith, Miami	309	1,139	3.7	68	14
	Warrick Dunn, Tampa Bay[2]	248	1,133	4.6	70	8
	James Allen, Chicago	290	1,120	3.9	29	2
	Tyrone Wheatley, Oakland	232	1,046	4.5	80	9
	Jamal Anderson, Atlanta[4]	282	1,024	3.6	42	6
	Tiki Barber, N.Y. Giants	213	1,006	4.7	78	8
	Ricky Williams, New Orleans	248	1,000	4.0	26	8
1999	*Edgerrin James, Indianapolis	369	1,553	4.2	72	13
	Curtis Martin, N.Y. Jets[5]	367	1,464	4.0	50	5
	Stephen Davis, Washington	290	1,405	4.8	76	17
	Emmitt Smith, Dallas[9]	329	1,397	4.3	63	11
	Marshall Faulk, St. Louis[5]	253	1,381	5.5	58	7
	Eddie George, Tennessee[4]	320	1,304	4.1	40	9
	Duce Staley, Philadelphia[2]	325	1,273	3.9	29	4
	Charlie Garner, San Francisco	241	1,229	5.1	53	4
	Ricky Watters, Seattle[6]	325	1,210	3.7	45	5
	Corey Dillon, Cincinnati[3]	263	1,200	4.6	50	5
	*Olandis Gary, Denver	276	1,159	4.2	71	7

Year	Player, Team	Att.	Yards	Avg.	Long	TD
	Jerome Bettis, Pittsburgh[6]	299	1,091	3.7	35	7
	Dorsey Levens, Green Bay[2]	279	1,034	3.7	36	9
	Robert Smith, Minnesota[3]	221	1,015	4.6	70	2
1998	Terrell Davis, Denver[4]	392	2,008	5.1	70	21
	Jamal Anderson, Atlanta[3]	410	1,846	4.5	48	14
	Garrison Hearst, San Francisco[3]	310	1,570	5.1	96	7
	Barry Sanders, Detroit[10]	343	1,491	4.3	73	4
	Emmitt Smith, Dallas[8]	319	1,332	4.2	32	13
	Marshall Faulk, Indianapolis[4]	324	1,319	4.1	68	6
	Eddie George, Tennessee[3]	348	1,294	3.7	37	5
	Curtis Martin, N.Y. Jets[4]	369	1,287	3.5	60	8
	Ricky Watters, Seattle[5]	319	1,239	3.9	39	9
	*Fred Taylor, Jacksonville	264	1,223	4.6	77	14
	Robert Smith, Minnesota[2]	249	1,187	4.8	74	6
	Jerome Bettis, Pittsburgh[5]	316	1,185	3.8	42	3
	Corey Dillon, Cincinnati[2]	262	1,130	4.3	66	4
	Antowain Smith, Buffalo	300	1,124	3.7	30	8
	*Robert Edwards, New England	291	1,115	3.8	53	9
	Duce Staley, Philadelphia	258	1,065	4.1	64	5
	Gary Brown, N.Y. Giants[2]	247	1,063	4.3	45	5
	Adrian Murrell, Arizona[3]	274	1,042	3.8	32	8
	Warrick Dunn, Tampa Bay	245	1,026	4.2	50	2
	Priest Holmes, Baltimore	233	1,008	4.3	56	7
1997	Barry Sanders, Detroit[9]	335	2,053	6.1	82	11
	Terrell Davis, Denver[3]	369	1,750	4.7	50	15
	Jerome Bettis, Pittsburgh[4]	375	1,665	4.4	34	7
	Dorsey Levens, Green Bay	329	1,435	4.4	52	7
	Eddie George, Tennessee[2]	357	1,399	3.9	30	6
	Napoleon Kaufman, Oakland	272	1,294	4.8	83	6
	Robert Smith, Minnesota	232	1,266	5.5	78	6
	Curtis Martin, New England[3]	274	1,160	4.2	70	4
	*Corey Dillon, Cincinnati	233	1,129	4.8	71	10
	Ricky Watters, Philadelphia[4]	285	1,110	3.9	28	7
	Adrian Murrell, N.Y. Jets[2]	300	1,086	3.6	43	7
	Emmitt Smith, Dallas[7]	261	1,074	4.1	44	4
	Marshall Faulk, Indianapolis[3]	264	1,054	4.0	45	7
	Raymont Harris, Chicago	275	1,033	3.8	68	10
	Garrison Hearst, San Francisco[2]	234	1,019	4.4	51	4
	Jamal Anderson, Atlanta[2]	290	1,002	3.5	39	7
1996	Barry Sanders, Detroit[8]	307	1,553	5.1	54	11
	Terrell Davis, Denver[2]	345	1,538	4.5	71	13
	Jerome Bettis, Pittsburgh[3]	320	1,431	4.5	50	11
	Ricky Watters, Philadelphia[3]	353	1,411	4.0	56	13
	*Eddie George, Houston	335	1,368	4.1	76	8
	Terry Allen, Washington[4]	347	1,353	3.9	49	21
	Adrian Murrell, N.Y. Jets	301	1,249	4.1	78	6
	Emmitt Smith, Dallas[5]	327	1,204	3.7	42	12
	Curtis Martin, New England[2]	316	1,152	3.6	57	14
	Anthony Johnson, Carolina	300	1,120	3.7	29	6
	*Karim Abdul-Jabbar, Miami	307	1,116	3.6	29	11
	Jamal Anderson, Atlanta	232	1,055	4.5	32	5
	Thurman Thomas, Buffalo[8]	281	1,033	3.7	36	8
1995	Emmitt Smith, Dallas[5]	377	1,773	4.7	60	25
	Barry Sanders, Detroit[7]	314	1,500	4.8	75	11
	*Curtis Martin, New England	368	1,487	4.0	49	14
	Chris Warren, Seattle[4]	310	1,346	4.3	52	15
	Terry Allen, Washington[3]	338	1,309	3.9	28	10
	Ricky Watters, Philadelphia[2]	337	1,273	3.8	57	11
	Errict Rhett, Tampa Bay[2]	332	1,207	3.6	21	11
	Rodney Hampton, N.Y. Giants[5]	306	1,182	3.9	32	10
	*Terrell Davis, Denver	237	1,117	4.7	60	7
	Harvey Williams, Oakland	255	1,114	4.4	60	9
	Craig Heyward, Atlanta	236	1,083	4.6	31	6
	Marshall Faulk, Indianapolis[2]	289	1,078	3.7	40	11
	*Rashaan Salaam, Chicago	296	1,074	3.6	42	10
	Garrison Hearst, Arizona	284	1,070	3.8	38	1
	Edgar Bennett, Green Bay	316	1,067	3.4	23	3
	Thurman Thomas, Buffalo[7]	267	1,005	3.8	49	6
1994	Barry Sanders, Detroit[6]	331	1,883	5.7	85	7

Year	Player, Team	Att.	Yards	Avg.	Long	TD
	Chris Warren, Seattle[3]	333	1,545	4.6	41	9
	Emmitt Smith, Dallas[4]	368	1,484	4.0	46	21
	Natrone Means, San Diego	343	1,350	3.9	25	12
	*Marshall Faulk, Indianapolis	314	1,282	4.1	52	11
	Thurman Thomas, Buffalo[6]	287	1,093	3.8	29	7
	Rodney Hampton, N.Y. Giants[4]	327	1,075	3.3	27	6
	Terry Allen, Minnesota[2]	255	1,031	4.0	45	8
	Jerome Bettis, L.A. Rams[2]	319	1,025	3.2	19	3
	*Errict Rhett, Tampa Bay	284	1,011	3.6	27	7
1993	Emmitt Smith, Dallas[3]	283	1,486	5.3	62	9
	*Jerome Bettis, L.A. Rams	294	1,429	4.9	71	7
	Thurman Thomas, Buffalo[5]	355	1,315	3.7	27	6
	Erric Pegram, Atlanta	292	1,185	4.1	29	3
	Barry Sanders, Detroit[5]	243	1,115	4.6	42	3
	Leonard Russell, New England	300	1,088	3.6	21	7
	Rodney Hampton, N.Y. Giants[3]	292	1,077	3.7	20	5
	Chris Warren, Seattle[2]	273	1,072	3.9	45	7
	*Reggie Brooks, Washington	223	1,063	4.8	85	3
	*Ron Moore, Phoenix	263	1,018	3.9	20	9
	Gary Brown, Houston	195	1,002	5.1	26	6
1992	Emmitt Smith, Dallas[2]	373	1,713	4.6	68	18
	Barry Foster, Pittsburgh	390	1,690	4.3	69	11
	Thurman Thomas, Buffalo[4]	312	1,487	4.8	44	9
	Barry Sanders, Detroit[4]	312	1,352	4.3	55	9
	Lorenzo White, Houston	265	1,226	4.6	44	7
	Terry Allen, Minnesota	266	1,201	4.5	51	13
	Reggie Cobb, Tampa Bay	310	1,171	3.8	25	9
	Harold Green, Cincinnati	265	1,170	4.4	53	2
	Rodney Hampton, N.Y. Giants[2]	257	1,141	4.4	63	14
	Cleveland Gary, L.A. Rams	279	1,125	4.0	63	7
	Herschel Walker, Philadelphia[2]	267	1,070	4.0	38	8
	Chris Warren, Seattle	223	1,017	4.6	52	3
	Ricky Watters, San Francisco	206	1,013	4.9	43	9
1991	Emmitt Smith, Dallas	365	1,563	4.3	75	12
	Barry Sanders, Detroit[3]	342	1,548	4.5	69	16
	Thurman Thomas, Buffalo[3]	288	1,407	4.9	33	7[3]
	Rodney Hampton, N.Y. Giants	256	1,059	4.1	44	10
	Earnest Byner, Washington[3]	274	1,048	3.8	32	5
	Gaston Green, Denver	261	1,037	4.0	63	4
	Christian Okoye, Kansas City[2]	225	1,031	4.6	48	9
1990	Barry Sanders, Detroit[2]	255	1,304	5.1	45	13
	Thurman Thomas, Buffalo[2]	271	1,297	4.8	80	11[2]
	Marion Butts, San Diego	265	1,225	4.6	52	8
	Earnest Byner, Washington[2]	297	1,219	4.1	22	6
	Bobby Humphrey, Denver[2]	288	1,202	4.2	37	7
	Neal Anderson, Chicago[3]	260	1,078	4.1	52	10
	Barry Word, Kansas City	204	1,015	5.0	53	4
	James Brooks, Cincinnati[3]	195	1,004	5.1	56	5
1989	Christian Okoye, Kansas City	370	1,480	4.0	59	12
	*Barry Sanders, Detroit	280	1,470	5.3	34	14
	Eric Dickerson, Indianapolis[7]	314	1,311	4.2	21	7
	Neal Anderson, Chicago[2]	274	1,275	4.7	73	11
	Dalton Hilliard, New Orleans	344	1,262	3.7	40	13
	Thurman Thomas, Buffalo	298	1,244	4.2	38	6
	James Brooks, Cincinnati[2]	221	1,239	5.6	65	7
	*Bobby Humphrey, Denver	294	1,151	3.9	40	7
	Greg Bell, L.A. Rams[3]	272	1,137	4.2	47	15
	Roger Craig, San Francisco[3]	271	1,054	3.9	27	6
	Ottis Anderson, N.Y. Giants[6]	325	1,023	3.1	36	14
1988	Eric Dickerson, Indianapolis[6]	388	1,659	4.3	41	14
	Herschel Walker, Dallas	361	1,514	4.2	38	5
	Roger Craig, San Francisco[2]	310	1,502	4.8	46	9
	Greg Bell, L.A. Rams[2]	288	1,212	4.2	44	16
	*John Stephens, New England	297	1,168	3.9	52	4
	Gary Anderson, San Diego	225	1,119	5.0	36	3
	Neal Anderson, Chicago	249	1,106	4.4	80	12
	Joe Morris, N.Y. Giants[3]	307	1,083	3.5	27	5
	*Ickey Woods, Cincinnati	203	1,066	5.3	56	15
	Curt Warner, Seattle[4]	266	1,025	3.9	29	10

Year	Player, Team	Att.	Yards	Avg.	Long	TD
	John Settle, Atlanta	232	1,024	4.4	62	7
	Mike Rozier, Houston	251	1,002	4.0	28	10
1987	Charles White, L.A. Rams	324	1,374	4.2	58	11
	Eric Dickerson, L.A. Rams-Indianapolis[5]	283	1,288	4.6	57	6
1986	Eric Dickerson, L.A. Rams[4]	404	1,821	4.5	42	11
	Joe Morris, N.Y. Giants[2]	341	1,516	4.4	54	14
	Curt Warner, Seattle[3]	319	1,481	4.6	60	13
	*Rueben Mayes, New Orleans	286	1,353	4.7	50	8
	Walter Payton, Chicago[10]	321	1,333	4.2	41	8
	Gerald Riggs, Atlanta[3]	343	1,327	3.9	31	9
	George Rogers, Washington[4]	303	1,203	4.0	42	18
	James Brooks, Cincinnati	205	1,087	5.3	56	5
1985	Marcus Allen, L.A. Raiders[3]	390	1,759	4.6	61	11
	Gerald Riggs, Atlanta[2]	397	1,719	4.3	50	10
	Walter Payton, Chicago[9]	324	1,551	4.8	40	9
	Joe Morris, N.Y. Giants	294	1,336	4.5	65	21
	Freeman McNeil, N.Y. Jets[2]	294	1,331	4.5	69	3
	Tony Dorsett, Dallas[8]	305	1,307	4.3	60	7
	James Wilder, Tampa Bay[2]	365	1,300	3.6	28	10
	Eric Dickerson, L.A. Rams[3]	292	1,234	4.2	43	12
	Craig James, New England	263	1,227	4.7	65	5
	Kevin Mack, Cleveland	222	1,104	5.0	61	7
	Curt Warner, Seattle[2]	291	1,094	3.8	38	8
	George Rogers, Washington[3]	231	1,093	4.7	35	7
	Roger Craig, San Francisco	214	1,050	4.9	62	9
	Earnest Jackson, Philadelphia[2]	282	1,028	3.6	59	5
	Stump Mitchell, St. Louis	183	1,006	5.5	64	7
	Earnest Byner, Cleveland	244	1,002	4.1	36	8
1984	Eric Dickerson, L.A. Rams[2]	379	2,105	5.6	66	14
	Walter Payton, Chicago[8]	381	1,684	4.4	72	11
	James Wilder, Tampa Bay	407	1,544	3.8	37	13
	Gerald Riggs, Atlanta	353	1,486	4.2	57	13
	Wendell Tyler, San Francisco[3]	246	1,262	5.1	40	7
	John Riggins, Washington[5]	327	1,239	3.8	24	14
	Tony Dorsett, Dallas[7]	302	1,189	3.9	31	6
	Earnest Jackson, San Diego	296	1,179	4.0	32	8
	Ottis Anderson, St. Louis[5]	289	1,174	4.1	24	6
	Marcus Allen, L.A. Raiders[2]	275	1,168	4.2	52	13
	Sammy Winder, Denver	296	1,153	3.9	24	4
	*Greg Bell, Buffalo	262	1,100	4.2	85	7
	Freeman McNeil, N.Y. Jets	229	1,070	4.7	53	5
1983	*Eric Dickerson, L.A. Rams	390	1,808	4.6	85	18
	William Andrews, Atlanta[4]	331	1,567	4.7	27	7
	*Curt Warner, Seattle	335	1,449	4.3	60	13
	Walter Payton, Chicago[7]	314	1,421	4.5	49	6
	John Riggins, Washington[4]	375	1,347	3.6	44	24
	Tony Dorsett, Dallas[6]	289	1,321	4.6	77	8
	Earl Campbell, Houston[5]	322	1,301	4.0	42	12
	Ottis Anderson, St. Louis[4]	296	1,270	4.3	43	5
	Mike Pruitt, Cleveland[4]	293	1,184	4.0	27	10
	George Rogers, New Orleans[2]	256	1,144	4.5	76	5
	Joe Cribbs, Buffalo[3]	263	1,131	4.3	45	3
	Curtis Dickey, Baltimore	254	1,122	4.4	56	4
	Tony Collins, New England	219	1,049	4.8	50	10
	Billy Sims, Detroit[3]	220	1,040	4.7	41	7
	Marcus Allen, L.A. Raiders	266	1,014	3.8	19	9
	Franco Harris, Pittsburgh[8]	279	1,007	3.6	19	5
1981	*George Rogers, New Orleans	378	1,674	4.4	79	13
	Tony Dorsett, Dallas[5]	342	1,646	4.8	75	4
	Billy Sims, Detroit[2]	296	1,437	4.9	51	13
	Wilbert Montgomery, Philadelphia[3]	286	1,402	4.9	41	8
	Ottis Anderson, St. Louis[3]	328	1,376	4.2	28	9
	Earl Campbell, Houston[4]	361	1,376	3.8	43	10
	William Andrews, Atlanta[3]	289	1,301	4.5	29	10
	Walter Payton, Chicago[6]	339	1,222	3.6	39	6
	Chuck Muncie, San Diego[2]	251	1,144	4.6	73	19
	*Joe Delaney, Kansas City	234	1,121	4.8	82	3
	Mike Pruitt, Cleveland[3]	247	1,103	4.5	21	7
	Joe Cribbs, Buffalo[2]	257	1,097	4.3	35	3

Year	Player, Team	Att.	Yards	Avg.	Long	TD
	Pete Johnson, Cincinnati	274	1,077	3.9	39	12
	Wendell Tyler, Los Angeles[2]	260	1,074	4.1	69	12
	Ted Brown, Minnesota	274	1,063	3.9	34	6
1980	Earl Campbell, Houston[3]	373	1,934	5.2	55	13
	Walter Payton, Chicago[5]	317	1,460	4.6	69	6
	Ottis Anderson, St. Louis[2]	301	1,352	4.5	52	9
	William Andrews, Atlanta[2]	265	1,308	4.9	33	4
	*Billy Sims, Detroit	313	1,303	4.2	52	13
	Tony Dorsett, Dallas[4]	278	1,185	4.3	56	11
	*Joe Cribbs, Buffalo	306	1,185	3.9	48	11
	Mike Pruitt, Cleveland[2]	249	1,034	4.2	56	6
1979	Earl Campbell, Houston[2]	368	1,697	4.6	61	19
	Walter Payton, Chicago[4]	369	1,610	4.4	43	14
	*Ottis Anderson, St. Louis	331	1,605	4.8	76	8
	Wilbert Montgomery, Philadelphia[2]	338	1,512	4.5	62	9
	Mike Pruitt, Cleveland	264	1,294	4.9	77	9
	Ricky Bell, Tampa Bay	283	1,263	4.5	49	7
	Chuck Muncie, New Orleans	238	1,198	5.0	69	11
	Franco Harris, Pittsburgh[7]	267	1,186	4.4	71	11
	John Riggins, Washington[3]	260	1,153	4.4	66	9
	Wendell Tyler, Los Angeles	218	1,109	5.1	63	9
	Tony Dorsett, Dallas[3]	250	1,107	4.4	41	6
	*William Andrews, Atlanta	239	1,023	4.3	23	3
1978	*Earl Campbell, Houston	302	1,450	4.8	81	13
	Walter Payton, Chicago[3]	333	1,395	4.2	76	11
	Tony Dorsett, Dallas[2]	290	1,325	4.6	63	7
	Delvin Williams, Miami[2]	272	1,258	4.6	58	8
	Wilbert Montgomery, Philadelphia	259	1,220	4.7	47	9
	Terdell Middleton, Green Bay	284	1,116	3.9	76	11
	Franco Harris, Pittsburgh[6]	310	1,082	3.5	37	8
	Mark van Eeghen, Oakland[3]	270	1,080	4.0	34	9
	*Terry Miller, Buffalo	238	1,060	4.5	60	7
	Tony Reed, Kansas City	206	1,053	5.1	62	5
	John Riggins, Washington[2]	248	1,014	4.1	31	5
1977	Walter Payton, Chicago[2]	339	1,852	5.5	73	14
	Mark van Eeghen, Oakland[2]	324	1,273	3.9	27	7
	Lawrence McCutcheon, Los Angeles[4]	294	1,238	4.2	48	7
	Franco Harris, Pittsburgh[5]	300	1,162	3.9	61	11
	Lydell Mitchell, Baltimore[3]	301	1,159	3.9	64	3
	Chuck Foreman, Minnesota[3]	270	1,112	4.1	51	6
	Greg Pruitt, Cleveland[3]	236	1,086	4.6	78	3
	Sam Cunningham, New England	270	1,015	3.8	31	4
	*Tony Dorsett, Dallas	208	1,007	4.8	84	12
1976	O.J. Simpson, Buffalo[5]	290	1,503	5.2	75	8
	Walter Payton, Chicago	311	1,390	4.5	60	13
	Delvin Williams, San Francisco	248	1,203	4.9	80	7
	Lydell Mitchell, Baltimore[2]	289	1,200	4.2	43	5
	Lawrence McCutcheon, Los Angeles[3]	291	1,168	4.0	40	9
	Chuck Foreman, Minnesota[2]	278	1,155	4.2	46	13
	Franco Harris, Pittsburgh[4]	289	1,128	3.9	30	14
	Mike Thomas, Washington	254	1,101	4.3	28	5
	Rocky Bleier, Pittsburgh	220	1,036	4.7	28	5
	Mark van Eeghen, Oakland	233	1,012	4.3	21	3
	Otis Armstrong, Denver[2]	247	1,008	4.1	31	5
	Greg Pruitt, Cleveland[2]	209	1,000	4.8	64	4
1975	O.J. Simpson, Buffalo[4]	329	1,817	5.5	88	16
	Franco Harris, Pittsburgh[3]	262	1,246	4.8	36	10
	Lydell Mitchell, Baltimore	289	1,193	4.1	70	11
	Jim Otis, St. Louis	269	1,076	4.0	30	5
	Chuck Foreman, Minnesota	280	1,070	3.8	31	13
	Greg Pruitt, Cleveland	217	1,067	4.9	50	8
	John Riggins, N.Y. Jets	238	1,005	4.2	42	8
	Dave Hampton, Atlanta	250	1,002	4.0	22	5
1974	Otis Armstrong, Denver	263	1,407	5.3	43	9
	*Don Woods, San Diego	227	1,162	5.1	56	7
	O.J. Simpson, Buffalo[3]	270	1,125	4.2	41	3
	Lawrence McCutcheon, Los Angeles[2]	236	1,109	4.7	23	3
	Franco Harris, Pittsburgh[2]	208	1,006	4.8	54	5
1973	O.J. Simpson, Buffalo[2]	332	2,003	6.0	80	12

Year	Player, Team	Att.	Yards	Avg.	Long	TD
	John Brockington, Green Bay[3]	265	1,144	4.3	53	3
	Calvin Hill, Dallas[2]	273	1,142	4.2	21	6
	Lawrence McCutcheon, Los Angeles	210	1,097	5.2	37	2
	Larry Csonka, Miami[3]	219	1,003	4.6	25	5
1972	O.J. Simpson, Buffalo	292	1,251	4.3	94	6
	Larry Brown, Washington[2]	285	1,216	4.3	38	8
	Ron Johnson, N.Y. Giants[2]	298	1,182	4.0	35	9
	Larry Csonka, Miami[2]	213	1,117	5.2	45	6
	Marv Hubbard, Oakland	219	1,100	5.0	39	4
	*Franco Harris, Pittsburgh	188	1,055	5.6	75	10
	Calvin Hill, Dallas	245	1,036	4.2	26	6
	Mike Garrett, San Diego[2]	272	1,031	3.8	41	6
	John Brockington, Green Bay[2]	274	1,027	3.7	30	8
	Eugene (Mercury) Morris, Miami	190	1,000	5.3	33	12
1971	Floyd Little, Denver	284	1,133	4.0	40	6
	*John Brockington, Green Bay	216	1,105	5.1	52	4
	Larry Csonka, Miami	195	1,051	5.4	28	7
	Steve Owens, Detroit	246	1,035	4.2	23	8
	Willie Ellison, Los Angeles	211	1,000	4.7	80	4
1970	Larry Brown, Washington	237	1,125	4.7	75	5
	Ron Johnson, N.Y. Giants	263	1,027	3.9	68	8
1969	Gale Sayers, Chicago[2]	236	1,032	4.4	28	8
1968	Leroy Kelly, Cleveland[3]	248	1,239	5.0	65	16
	*Paul Robinson, Cincinnati	238	1,023	4.3	87	8
1967	Jim Nance, Boston[2]	269	1,216	4.5	53	7
	Leroy Kelly, Cleveland[2]	235	1,205	5.1	42	11
	Hoyle Granger, Houston	236	1,194	5.1	67	6
	Mike Garrett, Kansas City	236	1,087	4.6	58	9
1966	Jim Nance, Boston	299	1,458	4.9	65	11
	Gale Sayers, Chicago	229	1,231	5.4	58	8
	Leroy Kelly, Cleveland	209	1,141	5.5	70	15
	Dick Bass, Los Angeles[2]	248	1,090	4.4	50	8
1965	Jim Brown, Cleveland[7]	289	1,544	5.3	67	17
	Paul Lowe, San Diego[2]	222	1,121	5.0	59	7
1964	Jim Brown, Cleveland[6]	280	1,446	5.2	71	7
	Jim Taylor, Green Bay[5]	235	1,169	5.0	84	12
	John Henry Johnson, Pittsburgh[2]	235	1,048	4.5	45	7
1963	Jim Brown, Cleveland[5]	291	1,863	6.4	80	12
	Clem Daniels, Oakland	215	1,099	5.1	74	3
	Jim Taylor, Green Bay[4]	248	1,018	4.1	40	9
	Paul Lowe, San Diego	177	1,010	5.7	66	8
1962	Jim Taylor, Green Bay[3]	272	1,474	5.4	51	19
	John Henry Johnson, Pittsburgh	251	1,141	4.5	40	7
	Cookie Gilchrist, Buffalo	214	1,096	5.1	44	13
	Abner Haynes, Dall. Texans	221	1,049	4.7	71	13
	Dick Bass, Los Angeles	196	1,033	5.3	57	6
	Charlie Tolar, Houston	244	1,012	4.1	25	7
1961	Jim Brown, Cleveland[4]	305	1,408	4.6	38	8
	Jim Taylor, Green Bay[2]	243	1,307	5.4	53	15
1960	Jim Brown, Cleveland[3]	215	1,257	5.8	71	9
	Jim Taylor, Green Bay	230	1,101	4.8	32	11
	John David Crow, St. Louis	183	1,071	5.9	57	6
1959	Jim Brown, Cleveland[2]	290	1,329	4.6	70	14
	J.D. Smith, San Francisco	207	1,036	5.0	73	10
1958	Jim Brown, Cleveland	257	1,527	5.9	65	17
1956	Rick Casares, Chi. Bears	234	1,126	4.8	68	12
1954	Joe Perry, San Francisco[2]	173	1,049	6.1	58	8
1953	Joe Perry, San Francisco	192	1,018	5.3	51	10
1949	Steve Van Buren, Philadelphia[2]	263	1,146	4.4	41	11
	Tony Canadeo, Green Bay	208	1,052	5.1	54	4
1947	Steve Van Buren, Philadelphia	217	1,008	4.6	45	13
1934	*Beattie Feathers, Chi. Bears	119	1,004	8.4	82	8

*First season of professional football.

200 YARDS RUSHING IN A GAME

Date	Player, Team, Opponent	Att.	Yards	TD
Sept. 12, 2010	Arian Foster, Houston vs. Indianapolis	33	231	3
Jan. 3, 2010	Jamaal Charles, Kansas City vs. Denver	25	259	2
Jan. 3, 2010	Fred Jackson, Buffalo vs. Indianapolis	33	212	0

Date	Player, Team, Opponent	Att.	Yards	TD
Dec. 27, 2009	Jonathan Stewart, Carolina vs. N.Y. Giants	28	206	1
Dec. 20, 2009	Jerome Harrison, Cleveland vs. Kansas City	34	286	3
Nov. 1, 2009	Chris Johnson, Tennessee vs. Jacksonville	24	228	2
Oct. 18, 2009	Thomas Jones, N.Y. Jets vs. Buffalo (OT)	22	210	1
Sept. 20, 2009	Frank Gore, San Francisco vs. Seattle	16	207	2
Dec. 28, 2008	Michael Turner, Atlanta vs. St. Louis	25	208	1
Dec. 21, 2008	Derrick Ward, N.Y. Giants vs. Carolina (OT)	15	215	0
Sept. 7, 2008	Michael Turner, Atlanta vs. Detroit	22	220	2
Nov. 4, 2007	*Adrian Peterson, Minnesota vs. San Diego	30	296	3
Oct. 14, 2007	*Adrian Peterson, Minnesota vs. Chicago	20	224	3
Sept. 16, 2007	Jamal Lewis, Cleveland vs. Cincinnati	27	216	1
Dec. 30, 2006	Tiki Barber, N.Y. Giants vs. Washington	23	234	3
Dec. 7, 2006	Willie Parker, Pittsburgh vs. Cleveland	32	223	1
Nov. 27, 2006	Shaun Alexander, Seattle vs. Green Bay	40	201	0
Nov. 19, 2006	Frank Gore, San Francisco vs. Seattle	24	212	0
Nov. 12, 2006	Willie Parker, Pittsburgh vs. New Orleans	22	213	2
Jan. 1, 2006	Larry Johnson, Kansas City vs. Cincinnati	26	201	3
Dec. 31, 2005	Tiki Barber, N.Y. Giants vs. Oakland	28	203	1
Dec. 17, 2005	Tiki Barber, N.Y. Giants vs. Kansas City	29	220	2
Nov. 20, 2005	Larry Johnson, Kansas City vs. Houston	36	211	2
Oct. 30, 2005	Tiki Barber, N.Y. Giants vs. Washington	24	206	1
Nov. 28, 2004	Rudi Johnson, Cincinnati vs. Cleveland	26	202	2
Nov. 21, 2004	Edgerrin James, Indianapolis vs. Chicago	23	204	1
Dec. 28, 2003	Ahman Green, Green Bay vs. Denver	20	218	2
Dec. 28, 2003	LaDainian Tomlinson, San Diego vs. Oakland	31	243	2
Dec. 21, 2003	Jamal Lewis, Baltimore vs. Cleveland	22	205	2
Dec. 7, 2003	Clinton Portis, Denver vs. Kansas City	22	218	5
Oct. 19, 2003	LaDainian Tomlinson, San Diego vs. Cleveland	26	200	1
Sept. 14, 2003	Jamal Lewis, Baltimore vs. Cleveland	30	295	2
Dec. 29, 2002	*Clinton Portis, Denver vs. Arizona	24	228	2
Dec. 28, 2002	Tiki Barber, N.Y. Giants vs. Philadelphia	32	203	0
Dec. 9, 2002	Ricky Williams, Miami vs. Chicago	31	216	2
Dec. 1, 2002	LaDainian Tomlinson, San Diego vs. Denver	37	220	3
Dec. 1, 2002	Ricky Williams, Miami vs. Buffalo	27	228	2
Sept. 29, 2002	LaDainian Tomlinson, San Diego vs. New England	27	217	2
Dec. 23, 2001	Marshall Faulk, St. Louis vs. Carolina	30	202	2
Nov. 11, 2001	Shaun Alexander, Seattle vs. Oakland	35	266	3
Dec. 24, 2000	Marshall Faulk, St. Louis vs. New Orleans	32	220	2
Dec. 3, 2000	Corey Dillon, Cincinnati vs. Arizona	35	216	1
Dec. 3, 2000	Warrick Dunn, Tampa Bay vs. Dallas	22	210	2
Dec. 3, 2000	*Mike Anderson, Denver vs. New Orleans	37	251	4
Dec. 3, 2000	Curtis Martin, N.Y. Jets vs. Indianapolis	30	203	1
Nov. 19, 2000	Fred Taylor, Jacksonville vs. Pittsburgh	30	234	3
Oct. 22, 2000	Corey Dillon, Cincinnati vs. Denver	22	278	2
Oct. 15, 2000	Marshall Faulk, St. Louis vs. Atlanta	25	208	1
Oct. 15, 2000	Edgerrin James, Indianapolis vs. Seattle	38	219	3
Sept. 24, 2000	Charlie Garner, San Francisco vs. Dallas	36	201	1
Sept. 3, 2000	Duce Staley, Philadelphia vs. Dallas	26	201	1
Nov. 22, 1998	Priest Holmes, Baltimore vs. Cincinnati	36	227	1
Oct. 11, 1998	Terrell Davis, Denver vs. Seattle	30	208	1
Dec. 4, 1997	*Corey Dillon, Cincinnati vs. Tennessee	39	246	4
Nov. 23, 1997	Barry Sanders, Detroit vs. Indianapolis	24	216	2
Oct. 26, 1997	Terrell Davis, Denver vs. Buffalo (OT)	42	207	1
Oct. 19, 1997	Napoleon Kaufman, Oakland vs. Denver	28	227	1
Oct. 12, 1997	Barry Sanders, Detroit vs. Tampa Bay	24	215	2
Sept. 21, 1997	Terrell Davis, Denver vs. Cincinnati	27	215	1
Aug. 31, 1997	Eddie George, Tennessee vs. Oakland (OT)	35	216	1
Sept. 22, 1996	LeShon Johnson, Arizona vs. New Orleans	21	214	2
Nov. 13, 1994	Barry Sanders, Detroit vs. Tampa Bay	26	237	0
Dec. 12, 1993	*Jerome Bettis, L.A. Rams vs. New Orleans	28	212	1
Oct. 31, 1993	Emmitt Smith, Dallas vs. Philadelphia	30	237	1
Nov. 24, 1991	Barry Sanders, Detroit vs. Minnesota	23	220	4
Dec. 23, 1990	James Brooks, Cincinnati vs. Houston	20	201	1
Oct. 14, 1990	Barry Word, Kansas City vs. Detroit	18	200	2
Sept. 24, 1990	Thurman Thomas, Buffalo vs. N.Y. Jets	18	214	0
Dec. 24, 1989	Greg Bell, L.A. Rams vs. New England	26	210	1
Sept. 24, 1989	Greg Bell, L.A. Rams vs. Green Bay	28	221	2
Sept. 17, 1989	Gerald Riggs, Washington vs. Philadelphia	29	221	1
Dec. 18, 1988	Gary Anderson, San Diego vs. Kansas City	34	217	1
Nov. 30, 1987	*Bo Jackson, L.A. Raiders vs. Seattle	18	221	2
Nov. 15, 1987	Charles White, L.A. Rams vs. St. Louis	34	213	1

Date	Player, Team, Opponent	Att.	Yards	TD
Dec. 7, 1986	Rueben Mayes, New Orleans vs. Miami	28	203	2
Oct. 5, 1986	Eric Dickerson, L.A. Rams vs. Tampa Bay (OT)	30	207	2
Dec. 21, 1985	George Rogers, Washington vs. St. Louis	34	206	1
Dec. 21, 1985	Joe Morris, N.Y. Giants vs. Pittsburgh	36	202	3
Dec. 9, 1984	Eric Dickerson, L.A. Rams vs. Houston	27	215	2
Nov. 18, 1984	*Greg Bell, Buffalo vs. Dallas	27	206	1
Nov. 4, 1984	Eric Dickerson, L.A. Rams vs. St. Louis	21	208	0
Sept. 2, 1984	Gerald Riggs, Atlanta vs. New Orleans	35	202	2
Nov. 27, 1983	*Curt Warner, Seattle vs. Kansas City (OT)	32	207	3
Nov. 6, 1983	James Wilder, Tampa Bay vs. Minnesota	31	219	1
Sept. 18, 1983	Tony Collins, New England vs. N.Y. Jets	23	212	3
Sept. 4, 1983	George Rogers, New Orleans vs. St. Louis	24	206	2
Dec. 21, 1980	Earl Campbell, Houston vs. Minnesota	29	203	1
Nov. 16, 1980	Earl Campbell, Houston vs. Chicago	31	206	0
Oct. 26, 1980	Earl Campbell, Houston vs. Cincinnati	27	202	2
Oct. 19, 1980	Earl Campbell, Houston vs. Tampa Bay	33	203	0
Nov. 26, 1978	*Terry Miller, Buffalo vs. N.Y. Giants	21	208	2
Dec. 4, 1977	*Tony Dorsett, Dallas vs. Philadelphia	23	206	2
Nov. 20, 1977	Walter Payton, Chicago vs. Minnesota	40	275	1
Oct. 30, 1977	Walter Payton, Chicago vs. Green Bay	23	205	2
Dec. 5, 1976	O.J. Simpson, Buffalo vs. Miami	24	203	1
Nov. 25, 1976	O.J. Simpson, Buffalo vs. Detroit	29	273	2
Oct. 24, 1976	Chuck Foreman, Minnesota vs. Philadelphia	28	200	2
Dec. 14, 1975	Greg Pruitt, Cleveland vs. Kansas City	26	214	3
Sept. 28, 1975	O.J. Simpson, Buffalo vs. Pittsburgh	28	227	1
Dec. 16, 1973	O.J. Simpson, Buffalo vs. N.Y. Jets	34	200	1
Dec. 9, 1973	O.J. Simpson, Buffalo vs. New England	22	219	1
Sept. 16, 1973	O.J. Simpson, Buffalo vs. New England	29	250	2
Dec. 5, 1971	Willie Ellison, Los Angeles vs. New Orleans	26	247	1
Dec. 20, 1970	John (Frenchy) Fuqua, Pittsburgh vs. Philadelphia	20	218	2
Nov. 3, 1968	Gale Sayers, Chicago vs. Green Bay	24	205	0
Oct. 30, 1966	Jim Nance, Boston vs. Oakland	38	208	2
Oct. 10, 1964	John Henry Johnson, Pittsburgh vs. Cleveland	30	200	3
Dec. 8, 1963	Cookie Gilchrist, Buffalo vs. N.Y. Jets	36	243	5
Nov. 3, 1963	Jim Brown, Cleveland vs. Philadelphia	28	223	1
Oct. 20, 1963	Clem Daniels, Oakland vs. N.Y. Jets	27	200	2
Sept. 22, 1963	Jim Brown, Cleveland vs. Dallas	20	232	2
Dec. 10, 1961	Billy Cannon, Houston vs. N.Y. Titans	25	216	3
Nov. 19, 1961	Jim Brown, Cleveland vs. Philadelphia	34	237	4
Dec. 18, 1960	John David Crow, St. Louis vs. Pittsburgh	24	203	0
Nov. 15, 1959	Bobby Mitchell, Cleveland vs. Washington	14	232	3
Nov. 24, 1957	*Jim Brown, Cleveland vs. Los Angeles	31	237	4
Dec. 16, 1956	*Tom Wilson, Los Angeles vs. Green Bay	23	223	0
Nov. 22, 1953	Dan Towler, Los Angeles vs. Baltimore	14	205	1
Nov. 12, 1950	Gene Roberts, N.Y. Giants vs. Chi. Cardinals	26	218	2
Nov. 27, 1949	Steve Van Buren, Philadelphia vs. Pittsburgh	27	205	0
Oct. 8, 1933	Cliff Battles, Boston vs. N.Y. Giants	16	215	1

*First season of professional football.

TIMES 200 OR MORE

121 times by 76 players…Simpson 6; Barber 5; Brown, Campbell, Sanders, Tomlinson 4; Bell, Davis, Dickerson, Dillon, Faulk, Lewis 3; Alexander, Gore, James, L. Johnson, Parker, Payton, Peterson, Portis, Riggs, Rogers, Turner, Williams 2.

4,000 YARDS PASSING IN A SEASON

Year	Player, Team	Att.	Comp.	Pct.	Yards	TD	Int.
2010	Philip Rivers, San Diego[3]	541	357	66.0	4,710	30	13
	Peyton Manning, Indianapolis[11]	679	450	66.3	4,700	33	17
	Drew Brees, New Orleans[5]	658	448	68.1	4,620	33	22
	Matt Schaub, Houston[2]	574	365	63.6	4,370	24	12
	Eli Manning, N.Y. Giants[2]	539	339	62.9	4,002	31	25
2009	Matt Schaub, Houston	583	396	67.9	4,770	29	15
	Peyton Manning, Indianapolis[10]	571	393	68.8	4,500	33	16
	Tony Romo, Dallas[2]	550	347	63.1	4,483	26	9
	Aaron Rodgers, Green Bay[2]	541	350	64.7	4,434	30	7
	Tom Brady, New England[3]	565	371	65.7	4,398	28	13
	Drew Brees, New Orleans[4]	514	363	70.6	4,388	34	11
	Ben Roethlisberger, Pittsburgh	506	337	66.6	4,328	26	12
	Philip Rivers, San Diego[2]	486	317	65.2	4,254	28	9

Year	Player, Team	Att.	Comp.	Pct.	Yards	TD	Int.
	Brett Favre, Minnesota[6]	531	363	68.4	4,202	33	7
	Eli Manning, N.Y. Giants	509	317	62.3	4,021	27	14
2008	Drew Brees, New Orleans[3]	635	413	65.0	5,069	34	17
	Kurt Warner, Arizona[3]	598	401	67.1	4,583	30	14
	Jay Cutler, Denver	616	384	62.3	4,526	25	18
	Aaron Rodgers, Green Bay	536	341	63.6	4,038	28	13
	Philip Rivers, San Diego	478	312	65.3	4,009	34	11
	Peyton Manning, Indianapolis[9]	555	371	66.8	4,002	27	12
2007	Tom Brady, New England[2]	578	398	68.9	4,806	50	8
	Drew Brees, New Orleans[2]	652	440	67.5	4,423	28	18
	Tony Romo, Dallas	520	335	64.4	4,211	36	19
	Brett Favre, Green Bay[5]	535	356	66.5	4,155	28	15
	Carson Palmer, Cincinnati[2]	575	373	64.9	4,131	26	20
	Jon Kitna, Detroit[2]	561	355	63.3	4,068	18	20
	Peyton Manning, Indianapolis[8]	515	337	65.4	4,040	31	14
2006	Drew Brees, New Orleans	554	356	64.3	4,418	26	11
	Peyton Manning, Indianapolis[7]	557	362	65.0	4,397	31	9
	Marc Bulger, St. Louis	588	370	62.9	4,301	24	8
	Jon Kitna, Detroit	596	372	62.4	4,208	21	22
	Carson Palmer, Cincinnati	520	324	62.3	4,035	28	13
2005	Tom Brady, New England	530	334	63.0	4,110	26	14
	Trent Green, Kansas City[3]	507	317	62.5	4,014	17	10
2004	Daunte Culpepper, Minnesota	548	379	69.2	4,717	39	11
	Trent Green, Kansas City[2]	556	369	66.4	4,591	27	17
	Peyton Manning, Indianapolis[6]	497	336	67.6	4,557	49	10
	Jake Plummer, Denver	521	303	58.2	4,089	27	20
	Brett Favre, Green Bay[4]	540	346	64.1	4,088	30	17
2003	Peyton Manning, Indianapolis[5]	566	379	67.0	4,267	29	10
	Trent Green, Kansas City	523	330	63.1	4,039	24	12
2002	Rich Gannon, Oakland	618	418	67.6	4,689	26	10
	Drew Bledsoe, Buffalo[3]	610	375	61.5	4,359	24	15
	Peyton Manning, Indianapolis[4]	591	392	66.3	4,200	27	19
	Kerry Collins, N.Y. Giants	545	335	61.5	4,073	19	14
2001	Kurt Warner, St. Louis[2]	546	375	68.7	4,830	36	22
	Peyton Manning, Indianapolis[3]	547	343	62.7	4,131	26	23
2000	Peyton Manning, Indianapolis[2]	571	357	62.5	4,413	33	15
	Jeff Garcia, San Francisco	561	355	63.3	4,278	31	10
	Elvis Grbac, Kansas City	547	326	59.6	4,169	28	14
1999	Steve Beuerlein, Carolina	571	343	60.1	4,436	36	15
	Kurt Warner, St. Louis	499	325	65.1	4,353	41	13
	Peyton Manning, Indianapolis	533	331	62.1	4,135	26	15
	Brett Favre, Green Bay[3]	595	341	57.3	4,091	22	23
	Brad Johnson, Washington	519	316	60.9	4,005	24	13
1998	Brett Favre, Green Bay[2]	551	347	63.0	4,212	31	23
	Steve Young, San Francisco[2]	517	322	62.3	4,170	36	12
1996	Mark Brunell, Jacksonville	557	353	63.4	4,367	19	20
	Vinny Testaverde, Baltimore	549	325	59.2	4,177	33	19
	Drew Bledsoe, New England[2]	623	373	59.9	4,086	27	15
1995	Brett Favre, Green Bay	570	359	63.0	4,413	38	13
	Scott Mitchell, Detroit	583	346	59.3	4,338	32	12
	Warren Moon, Minnesota[4]	606	377	62.2	4,228	33	14
	Jeff George, Atlanta	557	336	60.3	4,143	24	11
1994	Drew Bledsoe, New England	691	400	57.9	4,555	25	27
	Dan Marino, Miami[6]	615	385	62.6	4,453	30	17
	Warren Moon, Minnesota[3]	601	371	61.7	4,264	18	19
1993	John Elway, Denver	551	348	63.2	4,030	25	10
	Steve Young, San Francisco	462	314	68.0	4,023	29	16
1992	Dan Marino, Miami[5]	554	330	59.6	4,116	24	16
1991	Warren Moon, Houston[2]	655	404	61.7	4,690	23	21
1990	Warren Moon, Houston	584	362	62.0	4,689	33	13
1989	Don Majkowski, Green Bay	599	353	58.9	4,318	27	20
	Jim Everett, L.A. Rams	518	304	58.7	4,310	29	17
1988	Dan Marino, Miami[4]	606	354	58.4	4,434	28	23
1986	Dan Marino, Miami[3]	623	378	60.7	4,746	44	23
	Jay Schroeder, Washington	541	276	51.0	4,109	22	22
1985	Dan Marino, Miami[2]	567	336	59.3	4,137	30	21
1984	Dan Marino, Miami	564	362	64.2	5,084	48	17
	Neil Lomax, St. Louis	560	345	61.6	4,614	28	16
	Phil Simms, N.Y. Giants	533	286	53.7	4,044	22	18

Year	Player, Team	Att.	Comp.	Pct.	Yards	TD	Int.
1983	Lynn Dickey, Green Bay	484	289	59.7	4,458	32	29
	Bill Kenney, Kansas City	603	346	57.4	4,348	24	18
1981	Dan Fouts, San Diego[3]	609	360	59.1	4,802	33	17
1980	Dan Fouts, San Diego[2]	589	348	59.1	4,715	30	24
	Brian Sipe, Cleveland	554	337	60.8	4,132	30	14
1979	Dan Fouts, San Diego	530	332	62.6	4,082	24	24
1967	Joe Namath, N.Y. Jets	491	258	52.5	4,007	26	28

400 YARDS PASSING IN A GAME

Date	Player, Team, Opponent	Att.	Comp.	Yards	TD
Dec. 26, 2010	Aaron Rodgers, Green Bay vs. N.Y. Giants	37	25	404	4
Nov. 14, 2010	Matt Cassel, Kansas City vs. Denver	53	33	469	4
Nov. 7, 2010	Brett Favre, Minnesota vs. Arizona (OT)	47	36	446	2
Oct. 24, 2010	Carson Palmer, Cincinnati vs. Atlanta	50	36	412	3
Oct. 10, 2010	Tony Romo, Dallas vs. Tennessee	46	31	406	3
Oct. 10, 2010	Philip Rivers, San Diego vs. Oakland	42	27	431	2
Sept. 26, 2010	Kyle Orton, Denver vs. Indianapolis	57	37	476	1
Sept. 26, 2010	Philip Rivers, San Diego vs. Seattle	53	29	455	2
Sept. 19, 2010	Matt Schaub, Houston vs. Washington	52	38	497	3
Sept. 19, 2010	Donovan McNabb, Washington vs. Houston	38	28	426	1
Sept. 12, 2010	Peyton Manning, Indianapolis vs. Houston	57	40	433	3
Jan. 3, 2010	Kyle Orton, Denver vs. Kansas City	56	32	431	1
Dec. 20, 2009	Ben Roethlisberger, Pittsburgh vs. Green Bay	46	29	503	3
Dec. 6, 2009	Drew Brees, New Orleans vs. Washington (OT)	49	35	419	2
Nov. 22, 2009	Matthew Stafford, Detroit vs. Cleveland	43	26	422	5
Nov. 15, 2009	Donovan McNabb, Philadelphia vs. San Diego	55	35	450	2
Oct. 18, 2009	Ben Roethlisberger, Pittsburgh vs. Cleveland	35	23	417	2
Sept. 20, 2009	Philip Rivers, San Diego vs. Baltimore	45	25	436	2
Dec. 7, 2008	Matt Schaub, Houston vs. Green Bay	42	28	414	2
Nov. 23, 2008	Matt Cassel, New England vs. Miami	43	30	415	3
Nov. 13, 2008	Matt Cassel, New England vs. N.Y. Jets (OT)	51	30	400	3
Nov. 9, 2008	Drew Brees, New Orleans vs. Atlanta	58	31	422	2
Nov. 6, 2008	Jay Cutler, Denver vs. Cleveland	42	24	447	3
Sept. 28, 2008	Kurt Warner, Arizona vs. N.Y. Jets	57	40	472	2
Sept. 21, 2008	Drew Brees, New Orleans vs. Denver	48	39	421	1
Sept. 21, 2008	Brian Griese, Tampa Bay vs. Chicago (OT)	67	38	407	2
Nov. 25, 2007	Kurt Warner, Arizona vs. San Francisco (OT)	48	34	484	2
Nov. 4, 2007	Drew Brees, New Orleans vs. Jacksonville	49	35	445	3
Sept. 23, 2007	Jon Kitna, Detroit vs. Philadelphia	46	29	446	2
Sept. 16, 2007	Carson Palmer, Cincinnati vs. Cleveland	50	33	401	6
Dec. 10, 2006	Chris Weinke, Carolina vs. N.Y. Giants	61	34	423	1
Nov. 26, 2006	Matt Leinart, Arizona vs. Minnesota	51	31	405	1
Nov. 19, 2006	Drew Brees, New Orleans vs. Cincinnati	52	37	510	2
Nov. 12, 2006	Carson Palmer, Cincinnati vs. San Diego	42	31	440	3
Nov. 5, 2006	Ben Roethlisberger, Pittsburgh vs. Denver	54	38	433	1
Oct. 22, 2006	Joey Harrington, Miami vs. Green Bay	62	33	414	2
Sept. 17, 2006	Peyton Manning, Indianapolis vs. Houston	38	26	400	3
Oct. 2, 2005	Marc Bulger, St. Louis vs. N.Y. Giants	62	40	442	2
Jan. 2, 2005	Marc Bulger, St. Louis vs. N.Y. Jets (OT)	39	29	450	3
Dec. 19, 2004	Daunte Culpepper, Minnesota vs. Detroit	35	25	404	3
Dec. 19, 2004	Billy Volek, Tennessee vs. Oakland	60	40	492	4
Dec. 13, 2004	Billy Volek, Tennessee vs. Kansas City	43	29	426	4
Dec. 6, 2004	Matt Hasselbeck, Seattle vs. Dallas	40	28	414	3
Dec. 5, 2004	Peyton Manning, Indianapolis vs. Tennessee	33	25	425	3
Dec. 5, 2004	Donovan McNabb, Philadelphia vs. Green Bay	43	32	464	5
Nov. 29, 2004	Marc Bulger, St. Louis vs. Green Bay	53	35	448	2
Nov. 28, 2004	Kelly Holcomb, Cleveland vs. Cincinnati	39	30	413	5
Oct. 31, 2004	Peyton Manning, Indianapolis vs. Kansas City	44	25	472	5
Oct. 31, 2004	Jake Plummer, Denver vs. Atlanta	55	31	499	4
Oct. 17, 2004	Daunte Culpepper, Minnesota vs. New Orleans	37	26	425	5
Oct. 10, 2004	Tim Rattay, San Francisco vs. Arizona (OT)	57	38	417	2
Nov. 16, 2003	Peyton Manning, Indianapolis vs. N.Y. Jets	36	27	401	1
Oct. 12, 2003	Trent Green, Kansas City vs. Green Bay (OT)	45	27	400	3
Oct. 12, 2003	Steve McNair, Tennessee vs. Houston	27	18	421	3
Dec. 29, 2002	Matt Hasselbeck, Seattle vs. San Diego (OT)	53	36	449	2
Dec. 1, 2002	Matt Hasselbeck, Seattle vs. San Francisco	55	30	427	3
Nov. 10, 2002	Marc Bulger, St. Louis vs. San Diego	48	36	453	4
Nov. 10, 2002	Tommy Maddox, Pittsburgh vs. Atlanta (OT)	41	28	473	4

Date	Player, Team, Opponent	Att.	Comp.	Yards	TD
Oct. 6, 2002	Drew Bledsoe, Buffalo vs. Oakland	53	32	417	2
Sept. 22, 2002	Tom Brady, New England vs. Kansas City (OT)	54	39	410	4
Sept. 15, 2002	Drew Bledsoe, Buffalo vs. Minnesota (OT)	49	35	463	3
Sept. 15, 2002	Rich Gannon, Oakland vs. Pittsburgh	64	43	403	1
Dec. 30, 2001	Jon Kitna, Cincinnati vs. Pittsburgh	68	35	411	2
Dec. 23, 2001	Chris Chandler, Atlanta vs. Buffalo	40	28	431	2
Nov. 18, 2001	Charlie Batch, Detroit vs. Arizona	62	36	436	3
Nov. 18, 2001	Kurt Warner, St. Louis vs. New England	42	30	401	3
Sept. 23, 2001	Peyton Manning, Indianapolis vs. Buffalo	29	23	421	4
Dec. 24, 2000	Vinny Testaverde, N.Y. Jets vs. Baltimore	69	36	481	2
Dec. 17, 2000	Jeff Garcia, San Francisco vs. Chicago	44	36	402	2
Dec. 3, 2000	Aaron Brooks, New Orleans vs. Denver	48	30	441	2
Nov. 19, 2000	Gus Frerotte, Denver vs. San Diego	58	36	462	5
Nov. 5, 2000	Elvis Grbac, Kansas City vs. Oakland	53	39	504	2
Nov. 5, 2000	Trent Green, St. Louis vs. Carolina	42	29	431	2
Sept. 25, 2000	Peyton Manning, Indianapolis vs. Jacksonville	36	23	440	4
Sept. 4, 2000	Kurt Warner, St. Louis vs. Denver	35	25	441	3
Dec. 26, 1999	Brad Johnson, Washington vs. San Francisco (OT)	47	32	471	2
Dec. 5, 1999	Jeff Garcia, San Francisco vs. Cincinnati	49	33	437	3
Nov. 28, 1999	Jim Harbaugh, San Diego vs. Minnesota	39	25	404	1
Nov. 14, 1999	Jim Miller, Chicago vs. Minnesota (OT)	48	34	422	3
Sept. 26, 1999	Peyton Manning, Indianapolis vs. San Diego	54	29	404	2
Dec. 6, 1998	Vinny Testaverde, N.Y. Jets vs. Seattle	63	42	418	2
Dec. 6, 1998	John Elway, Denver vs. Kansas City	32	22	400	2
Nov. 26, 1998	Troy Aikman, Dallas vs. Minnesota	57	34	455	1
Nov. 23, 1998	Drew Bledsoe, New England vs. Miami	54	28	423	2
Nov. 15, 1998	Jake Plummer, Arizona vs. Dallas	56	31	465	3
Oct. 5, 1998	Randall Cunningham, Minnesota vs. Green Bay	32	20	442	4
Sept. 6, 1998	Glenn Foley, N.Y. Jets vs. San Francisco (OT)	58	30	415	3
Nov. 2, 1997	Tony Banks, St. Louis vs. Atlanta	34	23	401	2
Oct. 26, 1997	Warren Moon, Seattle vs. Oakland	44	28	409	5
Nov. 10, 1996	Boomer Esiason, Arizona vs. Washington (OT)	59	35	522	3
Nov. 3, 1996	Drew Bledsoe, New England vs. Miami	41	30	419	3
Oct. 27, 1996	Vinny Testaverde, Baltimore vs. St. Louis (OT)	51	31	429	3
Oct. 20, 1996	Mark Brunell, Jacksonville vs. St. Louis	52	37	421	0
Sept. 22, 1996	Mark Brunell, Jacksonville vs. New England (OT)	39	23	432	3
Dec. 18, 1995	Steve Young, San Francisco vs. Minnesota	49	30	425	3
Nov. 26, 1995	Dave Krieg, Arizona vs. Atlanta (OT)	43	27	413	4
Nov. 23, 1995	Scott Mitchell, Detroit vs. Minnesota	45	30	410	4
Oct. 1, 1995	Dan Marino, Miami vs. Cincinnati	48	33	450	2
Nov. 20, 1994	Warren Moon, Minnesota vs. N.Y. Jets	50	33	400	2
Nov. 13, 1994	Drew Bledsoe, New England vs. Minnesota (OT)	70	45	426	3
Nov. 6, 1994	Warren Moon, Minnesota vs. New Orleans	57	33	420	3
Sept. 25, 1994	Dan Marino, Miami vs. Minnesota	54	29	431	3
Sept. 4, 1994	Dan Marino, Miami vs. New England (OT)	42	23	473	5
Sept. 4, 1994	Drew Bledsoe, New England vs. Miami (OT)	51	32	421	4
Dec. 19, 1993	Steve Beuerlein, Phoenix vs. Seattle	53	34	431	3
Dec. 5, 1993	Brett Favre, Green Bay vs. Chicago	54	36	402	2
Nov. 28, 1993	Steve Young, San Francisco vs. L.A. Rams	32	26	462	4
Oct. 31, 1993	Jeff Hostetler, L.A. Raiders vs. San Diego	32	20	424	2
Sept. 13, 1992	Steve Young, San Francisco vs. Buffalo	37	26	449	3
Sept. 13, 1992	Jim Kelly, Buffalo vs. San Francisco	33	22	403	3
Nov. 10, 1991	Warren Moon, Houston vs. Dallas (OT)	56	41	432	0
Nov. 10, 1991	Mark Rypien, Washington vs. Atlanta	31	16	442	6
Oct. 13, 1991	Warren Moon, Houston vs. N.Y. Jets	50	35	423	2
Dec. 16, 1990	Warren Moon, Houston vs. Kansas City	45	27	527	3
Nov. 4, 1990	Joe Montana, San Francisco vs. Green Bay	40	25	411	3
Oct. 14, 1990	Joe Montana, San Francisco vs. Atlanta	49	32	476	6
Oct. 7, 1990	Boomer Esiason, Cincinnati vs. L.A. Rams (OT)	45	31	490	3
Dec. 23, 1989	Warren Moon, Houston vs. Cleveland	51	32	414	2
Dec. 11, 1989	Joe Montana, San Francisco vs. L.A. Rams	42	30	458	3
Nov. 26, 1989	Jim Everett, L.A. Rams vs. New Orleans (OT)	51	29	454	1
Nov. 26, 1989	Mark Rypien, Washington vs. Chicago	47	30	401	4
Oct. 2, 1989	Randall Cunningham, Philadelphia vs. Chicago	62	32	401	1
Sept. 24, 1989	Joe Montana, San Francisco vs. Philadelphia	34	25	428	5
Sept. 24, 1989	Dan Marino, Miami vs. N.Y. Jets	55	33	427	3
Sept. 17, 1989	Randall Cunningham, Philadelphia vs. Washington	46	34	447	5
Dec. 18, 1988	Dave Krieg, Seattle vs. L.A. Raiders	32	19	410	4

Date	Player, Team, Opponent	Att.	Comp.	Yards	TD
Dec. 12, 1988	Dan Marino, Miami vs. Cleveland	50	30	404	4
Oct. 23, 1988	Dan Marino, Miami vs. N.Y. Jets	60	35	521	3
Oct. 16, 1988	Vinny Testaverde, Tampa Bay vs. Indianapolis	42	25	469	2
Sept. 11, 1988	Doug Williams, Washington vs. Pittsburgh	52	30	430	2
Nov. 29, 1987	Tom Ramsey, New England vs. Philadelphia	53	34	402	3
Nov. 22, 1987	Boomer Esiason, Cincinnati vs. Pittsburgh	53	30	409	0
Sept. 20, 1987	Neil Lomax, St. Louis vs. San Diego	61	32	457	3
Dec. 21, 1986	Boomer Esiason, Cincinnati vs. N.Y. Jets	30	23	425	5
Dec. 14, 1986	Dan Marino, Miami vs. L.A. Rams (OT)	46	29	403	5
Nov. 23, 1986	Bernie Kosar, Cleveland vs. Pittsburgh (OT)	46	28	414	2
Nov. 17, 1986	Joe Montana, San Francisco vs. Washington	60	33	441	0
Nov. 16, 1986	Dan Marino, Miami vs. Buffalo	54	39	404	4
Nov. 10, 1986	Bernie Kosar, Cleveland vs. Miami	50	32	401	0
Nov. 2, 1986	Tommy Kramer, Minnesota vs. Washington (OT)	35	20	490	4
Nov. 2, 1986	Ken O'Brien, N.Y. Jets vs. Seattle	32	26	431	4
Oct. 27, 1986	Jay Schroeder, Washington vs. N.Y. Giants	40	22	420	1
Oct. 12, 1986	Steve Grogan, New England vs. N.Y. Jets	42	23	401	3
Sept. 21, 1986	Ken O'Brien, N.Y. Jets vs. Miami (OT)	43	29	479	4
Sept. 21, 1986	Dan Marino, Miami vs. N.Y. Jets (OT)	50	30	448	6
Sept. 21, 1986	Tony Eason, New England vs. Seattle	45	26	414	3
Dec. 20, 1985	John Elway, Denver vs. Seattle	42	24	432	1
Nov. 10, 1985	Dan Fouts, San Diego vs. L.A. Raiders (OT)	41	26	436	4
Oct. 13, 1985	Phil Simms, N.Y. Giants vs. Cincinnati	62	40	513	1
Oct. 13, 1985	Dave Krieg, Seattle vs. Atlanta	51	33	405	4
Oct. 6, 1985	Phil Simms, N.Y. Giants vs. Dallas	36	18	432	3
Oct. 6, 1985	Joe Montana, San Francisco vs. Atlanta	57	37	429	5
Sept. 19, 1985	Tommy Kramer, Minnesota vs. Chicago	55	28	436	3
Sept. 15, 1985	Dan Fouts, San Diego vs. Seattle	43	29	440	4
Dec. 16, 1984	Neil Lomax, St. Louis vs. Washington	46	37	468	2
Dec. 9, 1984	Dan Marino, Miami vs. Indianapolis	41	29	404	4
Dec. 2, 1984	Dan Marino, Miami vs. L.A. Raiders	57	35	470	4
Nov. 25, 1984	Dave Krieg, Seattle vs. Denver	44	30	406	3
Nov. 4, 1984	Dan Marino, Miami vs. N.Y. Jets	42	23	422	2
Oct. 21, 1984	Dan Fouts, San Diego vs. L.A. Raiders	45	24	410	3
Sept. 30, 1984	Dan Marino, Miami vs. St. Louis	36	24	429	3
Sept. 2, 1984	Phil Simms, N.Y. Giants vs. Philadelphia	30	23	409	4
Dec. 11, 1983	Bill Kenney, Kansas City vs. San Diego	41	31	411	4
Nov. 20, 1983	Dave Krieg, Seattle vs. Denver	42	31	418	3
Oct. 9, 1983	Joe Ferguson, Buffalo vs. Miami (OT)	55	38	419	5
Oct. 2, 1983	Joe Theismann, Washington vs. L.A. Raiders	39	23	417	3
Sept. 25, 1983	Richard Todd, N.Y. Jets vs. L.A. Rams (OT)	50	37	446	2
Dec. 26, 1982	Vince Ferragamo, L.A. Rams vs. Chicago	46	30	509	3
Dec. 20, 1982	Dan Fouts, San Diego vs. Cincinnati	40	25	435	1
Dec. 20, 1982	Ken Anderson, Cincinnati vs. San Diego	56	40	416	2
Dec. 11, 1982	Dan Fouts, San Diego vs. San Francisco	48	33	444	5
Nov. 21, 1982	Joe Montana, San Francisco vs. St. Louis	39	26	408	3
Nov. 15, 1981	Steve Bartkowski, Atlanta vs. Pittsburgh	50	33	416	2
Oct. 25, 1981	Brian Sipe, Cleveland vs. Baltimore	41	30	444	4
Oct. 25, 1981	David Woodley, Miami vs. Dallas	37	21	408	3
Oct. 11, 1981	Tommy Kramer, Minnesota vs. San Diego	43	27	444	4
Dec. 14, 1980	Tommy Kramer, Minnesota vs. Cleveland	49	38	456	4
Nov. 16, 1980	Doug Williams, Tampa Bay vs. Minnesota	55	30	486	4
Oct. 19, 1980	Dan Fouts, San Diego vs. N.Y. Giants	41	26	444	3
Oct. 12, 1980	Lynn Dickey, Green Bay vs. Tampa Bay (OT)	51	35	418	1
Sept. 21, 1980	Richard Todd, N.Y. Jets vs. San Francisco	60	42	447	3
Oct. 3, 1976	James Harris, Los Angeles vs. Miami	29	17	436	2
Nov. 17, 1975	Ken Anderson, Cincinnati vs. Buffalo	46	30	447	2
Nov. 18, 1974	Charley Johnson, Denver vs. Kansas City	42	28	445	2
Dec. 11, 1972	Joe Namath, N.Y. Jets vs. Oakland	46	25	403	1
Sept. 24, 1972	Joe Namath, N.Y. Jets vs. Baltimore	28	15	496	6
Dec. 21, 1969	Don Horn, Green Bay vs. St. Louis	31	22	410	5
Sept. 28, 1969	Joe Kapp, Minnesota vs. Baltimore	43	28	449	7
Sept. 9, 1968	Pete Beathard, Houston vs. Kansas City	48	23	413	2
Nov. 26, 1967	Sonny Jurgensen, Washington vs. Cleveland	50	32	418	3
Oct. 1, 1967	Joe Namath, N.Y. Jets vs. Miami	39	23	415	3
Sept. 17, 1967	Johnny Unitas, Baltimore vs. Atlanta	32	22	401	2
Nov. 13, 1966	Don Meredith, Dallas vs. Washington	29	21	406	2
Nov. 28, 1965	Sonny Jurgensen, Washington vs. Dallas	43	26	411	3

Date	Player	Att	Comp	Yards	TD
Oct. 24, 1965	Fran Tarkenton, Minnesota vs. San Francisco	35	21	407	3
Nov. 1, 1964	Len Dawson, Kansas City vs. Denver	38	23	435	6
Oct. 25, 1964	Cotton Davidson, Oakland vs. Denver	36	23	427	5
Oct. 16, 1964	Babe Parilli, Boston vs. Oakland	47	25	422	4
Dec. 22, 1963	Tom Flores, Oakland vs. Houston	29	17	407	6
Nov. 17, 1963	Norm Snead, Washington vs. Pittsburgh	40	23	424	2
Nov. 10, 1963	Don Meredith, Dallas vs. San Francisco	48	30	460	3
Oct. 13, 1963	Charley Johnson, St. Louis vs. Pittsburgh	41	20	428	2
Dec. 16, 1962	Sonny Jurgensen, Philadelphia vs. St. Louis	34	15	419	5
Nov. 18, 1962	Bill Wade, Chicago vs. Dall. Cowboys	46	28	466	2
Oct. 28, 1962	Y.A. Tittle, N.Y. Giants vs. Washington	39	27	505	7
Sept. 15, 1962	Frank Tripucka, Denver vs. Buffalo	56	29	447	2
Dec. 17, 1961	Sonny Jurgensen, Philadelphia vs. Detroit	42	27	403	3
Nov. 19, 1961	George Blanda, Houston vs. N.Y. Titans	32	20	418	7
Oct. 29, 1961	George Blanda, Houston vs. Buffalo	32	18	464	4
Oct. 29, 1961	Sonny Jurgensen, Philadelphia vs. Washington	41	27	436	3
Oct. 13, 1961	Jacky Lee, Houston vs. Boston	41	27	457	2
Dec. 13, 1958	Bobby Layne, Pittsburgh vs. Chi. Cardinals	49	23	409	2
Nov. 8, 1953	Bobby Thomason, Philadelphia vs. N.Y. Giants	44	22	437	4
Oct. 4, 1952	Otto Graham, Cleveland vs. Pittsburgh	49	21	401	3
Sept. 28, 1951	Norm Van Brocklin, Los Angeles vs. N.Y. Yanks	41	27	554	5
Dec. 11, 1949	Johnny Lujack, Chi. Bears vs. Chi. Cardinals	39	24	468	6
Oct. 31, 1948	Sammy Baugh, Washington vs. Boston	24	17	446	4
Oct. 31, 1948	Jim Hardy, Los Angeles vs. Chi. Cardinals	53	28	406	3
Nov. 14, 1943	Sid Luckman, Chi. Bears vs. N.Y. Giants	32	21	433	7

TIMES 400 OR MORE

219 times by 110 players...Marino 13; P. Manning 8; Montana, Moon 7; Bledsoe, Fouts 6; Brees, Jurgensen, Krieg 5; Bulger, Esiason, Kramer, Testaverde, Warner 4; Cassel, Cunningham, Hasselbeck, McNabb, Namath, Palmer, Rivers, Roethlisberger, Simms, Young 3; Anderson, Blanda, Brunell, Culpepper, Elway, Favre, Garcia, Green, C. Johnson, Kitna, Kosar, Lomax, Meredith, O'Brien, Orton, Plummer, Rypien, Schaub, Todd, Volek, D. Williams 2.

100 PASS RECEPTIONS IN A SEASON

Year	Player, Team	No.	Yards	Avg.	Long	TD
2010	Roddy White, Atlanta	115	1,389	12.1	46	10
	Reggie Wayne, Indianapolis[3]	111	1,355	12.2	50	6
2009	Wes Welker, New England[3]	123	1,348	11.0	58	4
	Steve Smith, N.Y. Giants	107	1,220	11.4	51	7
	Andre Johnson, Houston[3]	101	1,569	15.5	72	9
	Brandon Marshall, Denver[3]	101	1,120	11.1	75	10
	Dallas Clark, Indianapolis	100	1,106	11.1	80	10
	Reggie Wayne, Indianapolis[2]	100	1,264	12.6	65	10
2008	Andre Johnson, Houston[2]	115	1,575	13.7	65	8
	Wes Welker, New England[2]	111	1,165	10.5	64	3
	Brandon Marshall, Denver[2]	104	1,265	12.2	47	6
2007	T.J. Houshmandzadeh, Cincinnati	112	1,143	10.2	42	12
	Wes Welker, New England	112	1,175	10.5	42	8
	Reggie Wayne, Indianapolis	104	1,510	14.5	64	10
	Derrick Mason, Baltimore	103	1,087	10.6	79	5
	Brandon Marshall, Denver	102	1,325	13.0	68	7
	Larry Fitzgerald, Arizona[2]	100	1,409	14.1	48	10
2006	Andre Johnson, Houston	103	1,147	11.1	53	5
2005	Larry Fitzgerald, Arizona	103	1,409	13.7	47	10
	Steve Smith, Carolina	103	1,563	15.2	80	12
	Anquan Boldin, Arizona[2]	102	1,402	13.7	54	7
	Torry Holt, St. Louis[2]	102	1,331	13.0	44	9
2004	Tony Gonzalez, Kansas City	102	1,258	12.3	32	7
2003	Torry Holt, St. Louis	117	1,696	14.5	48	12
	Randy Moss, Minnesota[2]	111	1,632	14.7	72	17
	*Anquan Boldin, Arizona	101	1,377	13.6	71	8
	LaDainian Tomlinson, San Diego	100	725	7.3	73	4
2002	Marvin Harrison, Indianapolis[4]	143	1,722	12.0	69	11
	Hines Ward, Pittsburgh	112	1,329	11.9	72	12
	Randy Moss, Minnesota	106	1,347	12.7	60	7
	Eric Moulds, Buffalo	100	1,292	12.9	70	10
	Terrell Owens, San Francisco	100	1,300	13.0	76	13
2001	Rod Smith, Denver[2]	113	1,343	11.9	65	11
	Jimmy Smith, Jacksonville[2]	112	1,373	12.3	35	8

Year	Player, Team	No.	Yards	Avg.	Long	TD
	Marvin Harrison, Indianapolis[3]	109	1,524	14.0	68	15
	Keyshawn Johnson, Tampa Bay	106	1,266	11.9	47	1
	Troy Brown, New England	101	1,199	11.9	60	5
	Marty Booker, Chicago	100	1,071	10.7	66	8
2000	Marvin Harrison, Indianapolis[2]	102	1,413	13.9	78	14
	Muhsin Muhammad, Carolina	102	1,183	11.6	36	6
	Ed McCaffrey, Denver	101	1,317	13.0	61	9
	Rod Smith, Denver	100	1,602	16.0	49	8
1999	Jimmy Smith, Jacksonville	116	1,636	14.1	62	6
	Marvin Harrison, Indianapolis	115	1,663	14.5	57	12
1997	Tim Brown, Oakland	104	1,408	13.5	59	5
	Herman Moore, Detroit[3]	104	1,293	12.4	79	8
1996	Jerry Rice, San Francisco[4]	108	1,254	11.6	39	8
	Herman Moore, Detroit[2]	106	1,296	12.2	50	9
	Carl Pickens, Cincinnati	100	1,180	11.8	61	12
1995	Herman Moore, Detroit	123	1,686	13.7	69	14
	Jerry Rice, San Francisco[3]	122	1,848	15.1	81	15
	Cris Carter, Minnesota[2]	122	1,371	11.2	60	17
	Isaac Bruce, St. Louis	119	1,781	15.0	72	13
	Michael Irvin, Dallas	111	1,603	14.4	50	10
	Brett Perriman, Detroit	108	1,488	13.8	91	9
	Eric Metcalf, Atlanta	104	1,189	11.4	62	8
	Robert Brooks, Green Bay	102	1,497	14.7	99	13
	Larry Centers, Arizona	101	962	9.5	32	2
1994	Cris Carter, Minnesota	122	1,256	10.3	65	7
	Jerry Rice, San Francisco[2]	112	1,499	13.4	69	13
	Terance Mathis, Atlanta	111	1,342	12.1	81	11
1993	Sterling Sharpe, Green Bay[2]	112	1,274	11.4	54	11
1992	Sterling Sharpe, Green Bay	108	1,461	13.5	76	13
1991	Haywood Jeffires, Houston	100	1,181	11.8	44	7
1990	Jerry Rice, San Francisco	100	1,502	15.0	64	13
1984	Art Monk, Washington	106	1,372	12.9	72	7
1964	Charley Hennigan, Houston	101	1,546	15.3	53	8
1961	Lionel Taylor, Denver	100	1,176	11.8	52	4

*First season of professional football.

1,000 YARDS PASS RECEIVING IN A SEASON

Year	Player, Team	No.	Yards	Avg.	Long	TD
2010	Brandon Lloyd, Denver	77	1,448	18.8	71	11
	Roddy White, Atlanta[4]	115	1,389	12.1	46	10
	Reggie Wayne, Indianapolis[7]	111	1,355	12.2	50	6
	Greg Jennings, Green Bay[3]	76	1,265	16.6	86	12
	Mike Wallace, Pittsburgh	60	1,257	20.9	56	10
	Andre Johnson, Houston[5]	86	1,216	14.1	60	8
	Dwayne Bowe, Kansas City[2]	72	1,162	16.1	75	15
	Larry Fitzgerald, Arizona[5]	90	1,137	12.6	41	6
	Calvin Johnson, Detroit[2]	77	1,120	14.6	87	12
	Santana Moss, Washington[4]	93	1,115	12.0	56	6
	Steve Johnson, Buffalo	82	1,073	13.1	45	10
	DeSean Jackson, Philadelphia[2]	47	1,056	22.5	91	6
	Hakeem Nicks, N.Y. Giants	79	1,052	13.3	46	11
	Miles Austin, Dallas[2]	69	1,041	15.1	69	7
	Marques Colston, New Orleans[4]	84	1,023	12.2	43	7
	Brandon Marshall, Miami[4]	86	1,014	11.8	46	3
	Jason Witten, Dallas[3]	94	1,002	10.7	33	9
2009	Andre Johnson, Houston[4]	101	1,569	15.5	72	9
	Wes Welker, New England[3]	123	1,348	11.0	58	4
	Miles Austin, Dallas	81	1,320	16.3	60	11
	Sidney Rice, Minnesota	83	1,321	15.8	63	8
	Randy Moss, New England[10]	83	1,264	15.2	71	13
	Reggie Wayne, Indianapolis[6]	100	1,264	12.6	65	10
	Santonio Holmes, Pittsburgh	79	1,248	15.8	57	5
	Steve Smith, N.Y. Giants	107	1,220	11.4	51	7
	Vincent Jackson, San Diego[2]	68	1,167	17.2	55	9
	Hines Ward, Pittsburgh[6]	95	1,167	12.3	54	6
	Antonio Gates, San Diego[2]	79	1,157	14.6	56	8
	DeSean Jackson, Philadelphia	62	1,156	18.6	71	9
	Roddy White, Atlanta[3]	85	1,153	13.6	90	11
	Brandon Marshall, Denver[3]	101	1,120	11.1	75	10
	Greg Jennings, Green Bay[2]	68	1,113	16.4	83	4

Year	Player, Team	No.	Yards	Avg.	Long	TD
	Dallas Clark, Indianapolis	100	1,106	11.1	80	10
	Larry Fitzgerald, Arizona[4]	97	1,092	11.3	34	13
	Marques Colston, New Orleans[3]	70	1,074	15.3	68	9
	Donald Driver, Green Bay[7]	70	1,061	15.2	71	6
	Chad Ochocinco, Cincinnati[7]	72	1,047	14.5	50	9
	Jason Witten, Dallas[2]	94	1,030	11.0	69	2
	Derrick Mason, Baltimore[8]	73	1,028	14.1	72	7
	Anquan Boldin, Arizona[5]	84	1,024	12.2	44	4
2008	Andre Johnson, Houston[3]	115	1,575	13.7	65	8
	Larry Fitzgerald, Arizona[3]	96	1,431	14.9	78	12
	Steve Smith, Carolina[5]	78	1,421	18.2	65	6
	Roddy White, Atlanta[2]	88	1,382	15.7	70	7
	Calvin Johnson, Detroit	78	1,331	17.1	96	12
	Greg Jennings, Green Bay	80	1,292	16.1	63	9
	Brandon Marshall, Denver[2]	104	1,265	12.2	47	6
	Antonio Bryant, Tampa Bay[2]	83	1,248	15.0	71	7
	Wes Welker, New England[2]	111	1,165	10.5	64	3
	Reggie Wayne, Indianapolis[5]	82	1,145	14.0	65	6
	Vincent Jackson, San Diego	59	1,098	18.6	60	7
	Tony Gonzalez, Kansas City[4]	96	1,058	11.0	35	10
	Terrell Owens, Dallas[9]	69	1,052	15.2	75	10
	Santana Moss, Washington[3]	79	1,044	13.2	67	6
	Hines Ward, Pittsburgh[5]	81	1,043	12.9	49	7
	Anquan Boldin, Arizona[4]	89	1,038	11.7	79	11
	Derrick Mason, Baltimore[7]	80	1,037	13.0	54	5
	Dwayne Bowe, Kansas City	86	1,022	11.9	36	7
	Lee Evans, Buffalo[2]	63	1,017	16.1	87	3
	Donald Driver, Green Bay[6]	74	1,012	13.7	71	5
	Randy Moss, New England[9]	69	1,008	14.6	76	11
	Steve Breaston, Arizona	77	1,006	13.1	58	3
2007	Reggie Wayne, Indianapolis[4]	104	1,510	14.5	64	10
	Randy Moss, New England[8]	98	1,493	15.2	65	23
	Chad Ochocinco, Cincinnati[6]	93	1,440	15.5	70	8
	Larry Fitzgerald, Arizona[2]	100	1,409	14.1	48	10
	Terrell Owens, Dallas[8]	81	1,355	16.7	52	15
	Brandon Marshall, Denver	102	1,325	13.0	68	7
	Braylon Edwards, Cleveland	80	1,289	16.1	78	16
	Marques Colston, New Orleans[2]	98	1,202	12.3	45	11
	Roddy White, Atlanta	83	1,202	14.5	69	6
	Torry Holt, St. Louis[8]	93	1,189	12.8	40	7
	Wes Welker, New England	112	1,175	10.5	42	8
	Tony Gonzalez, Kansas City[3]	99	1,172	11.8	31	5
	Bobby Engram, Seattle	94	1,147	12.2	49	6
	Jason Witten, Dallas	96	1,145	11.9	53	7
	T.J. Houshmandzadeh, Cincinnati[2]	112	1,143	10.2	42	12
	Jerricho Cotchery, N.Y. Jets	82	1,130	13.8	50	2
	Kevin Curtis, Philadelphia	77	1,110	14.4	75	6
	Kellen Winslow, Cleveland	82	1,106	13.5	49	5
	Derrick Mason, Baltimore[6]	103	1,087	10.6	79	5
	Donald Driver, Green Bay[5]	82	1,048	12.8	47	2
	Plaxico Burress, N.Y. Giants[4]	70	1,025	14.6	60	12
	Joey Galloway, Tampa Bay[6]	57	1,014	17.8	69	6
	Steve Smith, Carolina[4]	87	1,002	11.5	74	7
2006	Chad Ochocinco, Cincinnati[5]	87	1,369	15.7	74	7
	Marvin Harrison, Indianapolis[8]	95	1,366	14.4	68	12
	Reggie Wayne, Indianapolis[3]	86	1,310	15.2	51	9
	Roy Williams, Detroit	82	1,310	16.0	60	7
	Donald Driver, Green Bay[4]	92	1,295	14.1	82	8
	Lee Evans, Buffalo	82	1,292	15.8	83	8
	Anquan Boldin, Arizona[3]	83	1,203	14.5	64	4
	Torry Holt, St. Louis[7]	93	1,188	12.8	67	10
	Terrell Owens, Dallas[7]	85	1,180	13.9	56	13
	Steve Smith, Carolina[3]	83	1,166	14.1	72	8
	Andre Johnson, Houston[2]	103	1,147	11.1	53	5
	Isaac Bruce, St. Louis[8]	74	1,098	14.8	45	3
	Laveranues Coles, N.Y. Jets[2]	91	1,098	12.1	58	6
	Mike Furrey, Detroit	98	1,086	11.1	31	6
	Javon Walker, Denver[2]	69	1,084	15.7	83	8
	T.J. Houshmandzadeh, Cincinnati	90	1,081	12.0	40	9

Year	Player, Team	No.	Yards	Avg.	Long	TD
	Joey Galloway, Tampa Bay[5]	62	1,057	17.1	64	7
	Terry Glenn, Dallas[4]	70	1,047	15.0	54	6
	*Marques Colston, New Orleans	70	1,038	14.8	86	8
2005	Steve Smith, Carolina[2]	103	1,563	15.2	80	12
	Santana Moss, Washington[2]	84	1,483	17.7	78	9
	Chad Ochocinco, Cincinnati[4]	97	1,432	14.8	70	9
	Larry Fitzgerald, Arizona	103	1,409	13.7	47	10
	Anquan Boldin, Arizona[2]	102	1,402	13.7	54	7
	Torry Holt, St. Louis[6]	102	1,331	13.0	44	9
	Joey Galloway, Tampa Bay[4]	83	1,287	15.5	80	10
	Donald Driver, Green Bay[3]	86	1,221	14.2	59	5
	Plaxico Burress, N.Y. Giants[3]	76	1,214	16.0	78	7
	Marvin Harrison, Indianapolis[7]	82	1,146	14.0	80	12
	Terry Glenn, Dallas[3]	62	1,136	18.3	71	7
	Chris Chambers, Miami	82	1,118	13.6	77	11
	Rod Smith, Denver[8]	85	1,105	13.0	72	6
	Eddie Kennison, Kansas City[2]	68	1,102	16.2	55	5
	Antonio Gates, San Diego	89	1,101	12.4	38	10
	Derrick Mason, Baltimore[5]	86	1,073	12.5	39	3
	Reggie Wayne, Indianapolis[2]	83	1,055	12.7	66	5
	Jimmy Smith, Jacksonville[9]	70	1,023	14.6	45	6
	Antonio Bryant, Cleveland	69	1,009	14.6	54	4
	Randy Moss, Oakland[7]	60	1,005	16.8	79	8
2004	Muhsin Muhammad, Carolina[3]	93	1,405	15.1	51	16
	Joe Horn, New Orleans[4]	94	1,399	14.9	57	11
	Javon Walker, Green Bay	89	1,382	15.5	79	12
	Torry Holt, St. Louis[5]	94	1,372	14.6	75	10
	Isaac Bruce, St. Louis[7]	89	1,292	14.5	56	6
	Chad Ochocinco, Cincinnati[3]	95	1,274	13.4	53	9
	Tony Gonzalez, Kansas City[2]	102	1,258	12.3	32	7
	Drew Bennett, Tennessee	80	1,247	15.6	48	11
	Reggie Wayne, Indianapolis	77	1,210	15.7	71	12
	Donald Driver, Green Bay[2]	84	1,208	14.4	50	9
	Terrell Owens, Philadelphia[6]	77	1,200	15.6	59	14
	Darrell Jackson, Seattle[3]	87	1,199	13.8	56	7
	*Michael Clayton, Tampa Bay	80	1,193	14.9	75	7
	Jimmy Smith, Jacksonville[8]	74	1,172	15.8	65	6
	Derrick Mason, Tennessee[4]	96	1,168	12.2	37	7
	Rod Smith, Denver[7]	79	1,144	14.5	85	7
	Andre Johnson, Houston	79	1,142	14.5	54	6
	Marvin Harrison, Indianapolis[6]	86	1,113	12.9	59	15
	Eddie Kennison, Kansas City	62	1,086	17.5	70	8
	Ashley Lelie, Denver	54	1,084	20.1	58	7
	Brandon Stokley, Indianapolis	68	1,077	15.8	69	10
	Eric Moulds, Buffalo[4]	88	1,043	11.9	49	5
	Nate Burleson, Minnesota	68	1,006	14.8	68	9
	Hines Ward, Pittsburgh[4]	80	1,004	12.6	58	4
2003	Torry Holt, St. Louis[4]	117	1,696	14.5	48	12
	Randy Moss, Minnesota[6]	111	1,632	14.7	72	17
	*Anquan Boldin, Arizona	101	1,377	13.6	71	8
	Chad Ochocinco, Cincinnati[2]	90	1,355	15.1	82	10
	Derrick Mason, Tennessee[3]	95	1,303	13.7	50	8
	Marvin Harrison, Indianapolis[5]	94	1,272	13.5	79	10
	Laveranues Coles, Washington[2]	82	1,204	14.7	64	6
	Keenan McCardell, Tampa Bay[5]	84	1,174	14.0	76	8
	Hines Ward, Pittsburgh[3]	95	1,163	12.2	50	10
	Darrell Jackson, Seattle[2]	68	1,137	16.7	80	9
	Steve Smith, Carolina	88	1,110	12.6	67	7
	Santana Moss, N.Y. Jets	74	1,105	14.9	65	10
	Terrell Owens, San Francisco[5]	80	1,102	13.8	75	9
	Amani Toomer, N.Y. Giants[5]	63	1,057	16.8	77	5
2002	Marvin Harrison, Indianapolis[4]	143	1,722	12.0	69	11
	Randy Moss, Minnesota[5]	106	1,347	12.7	60	7
	Amani Toomer, N.Y. Giants[4]	82	1,343	16.4	82	8
	Hines Ward, Pittsburgh[2]	112	1,329	11.9	72	12
	Plaxico Burress, Pittsburgh[2]	78	1,325	17.0	62	7
	Joe Horn, New Orleans[3]	88	1,312	14.9	63	7
	Torry Holt, St. Louis[3]	91	1,302	14.3	58	4
	Terrell Owens, San Francisco[4]	100	1,300	13.0	76	13

Year	Player, Team	No.	Yards	Avg.	Long	TD
	Eric Moulds, Buffalo[3]	100	1,292	12.9	70	10
	Laveranues Coles, N.Y. Jets	89	1,264	14.2	43	5
	Peerless Price, Buffalo	94	1,252	13.3	73	9
	Koren Robinson, Seattle	78	1,240	15.9	83	5
	Jerry Rice, Oakland[14]	92	1,211	13.2	75	7
	Marty Booker, Chicago[2]	97	1,189	12.3	54	6
	Chad Ochocinco, Cincinnati	69	1,166	16.9	72	5
	Keyshawn Johnson, Tampa Bay[4]	76	1,088	14.3	76	5
	Isaac Bruce, St. Louis[6]	79	1,075	13.6	34	7
	Donald Driver, Green Bay	70	1,064	15.2	85	9
	Jimmy Smith, Jacksonville[7]	80	1,027	12.8	47	7
	Rod Smith, Denver[6]	89	1,027	11.5	46	5
	Derrick Mason, Tennessee[2]	79	1,012	12.8	40	5
	Rod Gardner, Washington	71	1,006	14.2	43	8
2001	David Boston, Arizona[2]	98	1,598	16.3	61	8
	Marvin Harrison, Indianapolis[3]	109	1,524	14.0	68	15
	Terrell Owens, San Francisco[3]	93	1,412	15.2	60	16
	Jimmy Smith, Jacksonville[6]	112	1,373	12.3	35	8
	Torry Holt, St. Louis[2]	81	1,363	16.8	51	7
	Rod Smith, Denver[5]	113	1,343	11.9	65	11
	Keyshawn Johnson, Tampa Bay[3]	106	1,266	11.9	47	1
	Joe Horn, New Orleans[2]	83	1,265	15.2	56	9
	Randy Moss, Minnesota[4]	82	1,233	15.0	73	10
	Troy Brown, New England	101	1,199	11.9	60	5
	Tim Brown, Oakland[9]	91	1,165	12.8	46	9
	Johnnie Morton, Detroit[4]	77	1,154	15.0	76	4
	Jerry Rice, Oakland[13]	83	1,139	13.7	40	9
	Derrick Mason, Tennessee	73	1,128	15.5	71	9
	Curtis Conway, San Diego[3]	71	1,125	15.8	72	6
	Keenan McCardell, Jacksonville[4]	93	1,110	11.9	45	6
	Isaac Bruce, St. Louis[5]	64	1,106	17.3	51	6
	Kevin Johnson, Cleveland	84	1,097	13.1	55	9
	Darrell Jackson, Seattle	70	1,081	15.4	64	8
	Marty Booker, Chicago	100	1,071	10.7	66	8
	Qadry Ismail, Baltimore[2]	74	1,059	14.3	77	7
	Amani Toomer, N.Y. Giants[3]	72	1,054	14.6	60	5
	Willie Jackson, New Orleans	81	1,046	12.9	63	5
	Plaxico Burress, Pittsburgh	66	1,008	15.3	43	6
	Hines Ward, Pittsburgh	94	1,003	10.7	34	4
2000	Torry Holt, St. Louis	82	1,635	19.9	85	6
	Rod Smith, Denver[4]	100	1,602	16.0	49	8
	Isaac Bruce, St. Louis[4]	87	1,471	16.9	78	9
	Terrell Owens, San Francisco[2]	97	1,451	15.0	69	13
	Randy Moss, Minnesota[3]	77	1,437	18.7	78	15
	Marvin Harrison, Indianapolis[2]	102	1,413	13.9	78	14
	Derrick Alexander, Kansas City[3]	78	1,391	17.8	81	10
	Joe Horn, New Orleans	94	1,340	14.3	52	8
	Eric Moulds, Buffalo[2]	94	1,326	14.1	52	5
	Ed McCaffrey, Denver[3]	101	1,317	13.0	61	9
	Cris Carter, Minnesota[8]	96	1,274	13.3	53	9
	Jimmy Smith, Jacksonville[5]	91	1,213	13.3	65	8
	Keenan McCardell, Jacksonville[3]	94	1,207	12.8	67	5
	Tony Gonzalez, Kansas City	93	1,203	12.9	39	9
	Muhsin Muhammad, Carolina[2]	102	1,183	11.6	36	6
	David Boston, Arizona	71	1,156	16.3	70	7
	Tim Brown, Oakland[8]	76	1,128	14.8	45	11
	Amani Toomer, N.Y. Giants[2]	78	1,094	14.0	54	7
1999	Marvin Harrison, Indianapolis	115	1,663	14.5	57	12
	Jimmy Smith, Jacksonville[4]	116	1,636	14.1	62	6
	Randy Moss, Minnesota[2]	80	1,413	17.7	67	11
	Marcus Robinson, Chicago	84	1,400	16.7	80	9
	Tim Brown, Oakland[7]	90	1,344	14.9	47	6
	Germane Crowell, Detroit	81	1,338	16.5	77	7
	Muhsin Muhammad, Carolina	96	1,253	13.1	60	8
	Cris Carter, Minnesota[7]	90	1,241	13.8	68	13
	Michael Westbrook, Washington	65	1,191	18.3	65	9
	Amani Toomer, N.Y. Giants	79	1,183	15.0	80	6
	Keyshawn Johnson, N.Y. Jets[2]	89	1,170	13.2	65	8
	Isaac Bruce, St. Louis[3]	77	1,165	15.1	60	12

Year	Player, Team	No.	Yards	Avg.	Long	TD
	Terry Glenn, New England[2]	69	1,147	16.6	67	4
	Albert Connell, Washington	62	1,132	18.3	62	7
	Johnnie Morton, Detroit[3]	80	1,129	14.1	48	5
	Qadry Ismail, Baltimore	68	1,105	16.3	76	6
	Raghib Ismail, Dallas[2]	80	1,097	13.7	76	6
	Patrick Jeffers, Carolina	63	1,082	17.2	88	12
	Antonio Freeman, Green Bay[3]	74	1,074	14.5	51	6
	Bill Schroeder, Green Bay	74	1,051	14.2	51	5
	Marshall Faulk, St. Louis	87	1,048	12.1	57	5
	Tony Martin, Miami[4]	67	1,037	15.5	69	5
	Darnay Scott, Cincinnati	68	1,022	15.0	76	7
	Rod Smith, Denver[3]	79	1,020	12.9	71	4
	Ed McCaffrey, Denver[2]	71	1,018	14.3	78	7
	Terance Mathis, Atlanta[4]	81	1,016	12.5	52	6
1998	Antonio Freeman, Green Bay[2]	84	1,424	17.0	84	14
	Eric Moulds, Buffalo	67	1,368	20.4	84	9
	*Randy Moss, Minnesota	69	1,313	19.0	61	17
	Rod Smith, Denver[2]	86	1,222	14.2	58	6
	Jimmy Smith, Jacksonville[3]	78	1,182	15.2	72	8
	Tony Martin, Atlanta[3]	66	1,181	17.9	62	6
	Jerry Rice, San Francisco[12]	82	1,157	14.1	75	9
	Frank Sanders, Arizona[2]	89	1,145	12.9	42	3
	Terance Mathis, Atlanta[3]	64	1,136	17.8	78	11
	Keyshawn Johnson, N.Y. Jets	83	1,131	13.6	41	10
	Terrell Owens, San Francisco	67	1,097	16.4	79	14
	Wayne Chrebet, N.Y. Jets	75	1,083	14.4	63	8
	Michael Irvin, Dallas[7]	74	1,057	14.3	51	1
	Ed McCaffrey, Denver	64	1,053	16.5	48	10
	O.J. McDuffie, Miami	90	1,050	11.7	61	7
	Joey Galloway, Seattle[3]	65	1,047	16.1	81	10
	Johnnie Morton, Detroit[2]	69	1,028	14.9	98	2
	Raghib Ismail, Carolina	69	1,024	14.8	62	8
	Carl Pickens, Cincinnati[4]	82	1,023	12.5	67	5
	Tim Brown, Oakland[6]	81	1,012	12.5	49	9
	Cris Carter, Minnesota[6]	78	1,011	13.0	54	12
1997	Rob Moore, Arizona[3]	97	1,584	16.3	47	8
	Tim Brown, Oakland[5]	104	1,408	13.5	59	5
	Yancey Thigpen, Pittsburgh[2]	79	1,398	17.7	69	7
	Jimmy Smith, Jacksonville[2]	82	1,324	16.1	75	4
	Irving Fryar, Philadelphia[5]	86	1,316	15.3	72	6
	Herman Moore, Detroit[4]	104	1,293	12.4	79	8
	Antonio Freeman, Green Bay	81	1,243	15.3	58	12
	Michael Irvin, Dallas[6]	75	1,180	15.7	55	9
	Rod Smith, Denver	70	1,180	16.9	78	12
	Keenan McCardell, Jacksonville[2]	85	1,164	13.7	60	5
	Jake Reed, Minnesota[4]	68	1,138	16.7	56	6
	Shannon Sharpe, Denver[3]	72	1,107	15.4	68	3
	Andre Rison, Kansas City[5]	72	1,092	15.2	45	7
	Cris Carter, Minnesota[5]	89	1,069	12.0	43	13
	Johnnie Morton, Detroit	80	1,057	13.2	73	6
	Joey Galloway, Seattle[2]	72	1,049	14.6	53	12
	Frank Sanders, Arizona	75	1,017	13.6	70	4
	Robert Brooks, Green Bay[2]	60	1,010	16.8	48	7
	Derrick Alexander, Baltimore[2]	65	1,009	15.5	92	9
1996	Isaac Bruce, St. Louis[2]	84	1,338	15.9	70	7
	Jake Reed, Minnesota[3]	72	1,320	18.3	82	7
	Herman Moore, Detroit[3]	106	1,296	12.2	50	9
	Jerry Rice, San Francisco[11]	108	1,254	11.6	39	8
	Jimmy Smith, Jacksonville	83	1,244	15.0	62	7
	Michael Jackson, Baltimore	76	1,201	15.8	86	14
	Irving Fryar, Philadelphia[4]	88	1,195	13.6	42	11
	Carl Pickens, Cincinnati[3]	100	1,180	11.8	61	12
	Tony Martin, San Diego[2]	85	1,171	13.8	55	14
	Cris Carter, Minnesota[4]	96	1,163	12.1	43	10
	*Terry Glenn, New England	90	1,132	12.6	37	6
	Keenan McCardell, Jacksonville	85	1,129	13.3	52	3
	Tim Brown, Oakland[4]	90	1,104	12.3	42	9
	Derrick Alexander, Baltimore	62	1,099	17.7	64	9
	Shannon Sharpe, Denver[2]	80	1,062	13.3	51	10

Year	Player, Team	No.	Yards	Avg.	Long	TD
	Curtis Conway, Chicago[2]	81	1,049	13.0	58	7
	Andre Reed, Buffalo[4]	66	1,036	15.7	67	6
	Brett Perriman, Detroit[2]	94	1,021	10.9	44	5
	Rob Moore, Arizona[2]	58	1,016	17.5	69	4
	Henry Ellard, Washington[7]	52	1,014	19.5	51	2
	Charles Johnson, Pittsburgh	60	1,008	16.8	70	3
1995	Jerry Rice, San Francisco[10]	122	1,848	15.1	81	15
	Isaac Bruce, St. Louis	119	1,781	15.0	72	13
	Herman Moore, Detroit[2]	123	1,686	13.7	69	14
	Michael Irvin, Dallas[5]	111	1,603	14.4	50	10
	Robert Brooks, Green Bay	102	1,497	14.7	99	13
	Brett Perriman, Detroit	108	1,488	13.8	91	9
	Cris Carter, Minnesota[3]	122	1,371	11.2	60	17
	Tim Brown, Oakland[3]	89	1,342	15.1	80	10
	Yancey Thigpen, Pittsburgh	85	1,307	15.4	43	5
	Jeff Graham, Chicago	82	1,301	15.9	51	4
	Carl Pickens, Cincinnati[2]	99	1,234	12.5	68	17
	Tony Martin, San Diego	90	1,224	13.6	51	6
	Eric Metcalf, Atlanta	104	1,189	11.4	62	8
	Jake Reed, Minnesota[2]	72	1,167	16.2	55	9
	Quinn Early, New Orleans	81	1,087	13.4	70	8
	Anthony Miller, Denver[5]	59	1,079	18.3	62	14
	Bert Emanuel, Atlanta	74	1,039	14.0	52	5
	*Joey Galloway, Seattle	67	1,039	15.5	59	7
	Terance Mathis, Atlanta[2]	78	1,039	13.3	54	9
	Curtis Conway, Chicago	62	1,037	16.7	76	12
	Henry Ellard, Washington[6]	56	1,005	17.9	59	5
	Mark Carrier, Carolina[2]	66	1,002	15.2	66	3
	Brian Blades, Seattle[4]	77	1,001	13.0	49	4
1994	Jerry Rice, San Francisco[9]	112	1,499	13.4	69	13
	Henry Ellard, Washington[5]	74	1,397	18.9	73	6
	Terance Mathis, Atlanta	111	1,342	12.1	81	11
	Tim Brown, L.A. Raiders[2]	89	1,309	14.7	77	9
	Andre Reed, Buffalo[2]	90	1,303	14.5	83	8
	Irving Fryar, Miami[3]	73	1,270	17.4	54	7
	Cris Carter, Minnesota[2]	122	1,256	10.3	65	7
	Michael Irvin, Dallas[4]	79	1,241	15.7	65	6
	Jake Reed, Minnesota	85	1,175	13.8	59	4
	Ben Coates, New England	96	1,174	12.2	62	7
	Herman Moore, Detroit	72	1,173	16.3	51	11
	Fred Barnett, Philadelphia[2]	78	1,127	14.4	54	5
	Carl Pickens, Cincinnati	71	1,127	15.9	70	11
	Sterling Sharpe, Green Bay[4]	94	1,119	11.9	49	18
	Anthony Miller, Denver[4]	60	1,107	18.5	76	5
	Andre Rison, Atlanta[3]	81	1,088	13.4	69	8
	Brian Blades, Seattle[3]	81	1,088	13.4	45	4
	Rob Moore, N.Y. Jets	78	1,010	12.9	41	6
	Shannon Sharpe, Denver	87	1,010	11.6	44	4
1993	Jerry Rice, San Francisco[8]	98	1,503	15.3	80	15
	Michael Irvin, Dallas[3]	88	1,330	15.1	61	7
	Sterling Sharpe, Green Bay[4]	112	1,274	11.4	54	11
	Andre Rison, Atlanta[3]	86	1,242	14.4	53	15
	Tim Brown, L.A. Raiders	80	1,180	14.8	71	7
	Anthony Miller, San Diego[3]	84	1,162	13.8	66	7
	Cris Carter, Minnesota	86	1,071	12.5	58	9
	Reggie Langhorne, Indianapolis	85	1,038	12.2	72	3
	Irving Fryar, Miami[2]	64	1,010	15.8	65	5
1992	Sterling Sharpe, Green Bay[3]	108	1,461	13.5	76	13
	Michael Irvin, Dallas[2]	78	1,396	17.9	87	7
	Jerry Rice, San Francisco[7]	84	1,201	14.3	80	10
	Andre Rison, Atlanta[2]	93	1,119	12.0	71	11
	Fred Barnett, Philadelphia	67	1,083	16.2	71	6
	Anthony Miller, San Diego[2]	72	1,060	14.7	67	7
	Eric Martin, New Orleans[3]	68	1,041	15.3	52	5
1991	Michael Irvin, Dallas	93	1,523	16.4	66	8
	Gary Clark, Washington[5]	70	1,340	19.1	82	10
	Jerry Rice, San Francisco[6]	80	1,206	15.1	73	14
	Haywood Jeffires, Houston[2]	100	1,181	11.8	44	7
	Michael Haynes, Atlanta	50	1,122	22.4	80	11

Year	Player, Team	No.	Yards	Avg.	Long	TD
	Andre Reed, Buffalo[2]..............81		1,113	13.7	55	10
	Drew Hill, Houston[5]..............90		1,109	12.3	61	4
	Mark Duper, Miami[4]..............70		1,085	15.5	43	5
	James Lofton, Buffalo[6]..............57		1,072	18.8	77	8
	Mark Clayton, Miami[5]..............70		1,053	15.0	43	12
	Henry Ellard, L.A. Rams[4]..............64		1,052	16.4	38	3
	Art Monk, Washington[5]..............71		1,049	14.8	64	8
	Irving Fryar, New England..............68		1,014	14.9	56	3
	John Taylor, San Francisco[2]..............64		1,011	15.8	97	9
	Brian Blades, Seattle[2]..............70		1,003	14.3	52	2
1990	Jerry Rice, San Francisco[5]..............100		1,502	15.0	64	13
	Henry Ellard, L.A. Rams[3]..............76		1,294	17.0	50	4
	Andre Rison, Atlanta..............82		1,208	14.7	75	10
	Gary Clark, Washington[4]..............75		1,112	14.8	53	8
	Sterling Sharpe, Green Bay[2]..............67		1,105	16.5	76	6
	Flipper Anderson, L.A. Rams[2]..............51		1,097	21.5	55	4
	Haywood Jeffires, Houston..............74		1,048	14.2	87	8
	Stephone Paige, Kansas City..............65		1,021	15.7	86	5
	Drew Hill, Houston[4]..............74		1,019	13.8	57	5
	Anthony Carter, Minnesota[3]..............70		1,008	14.4	56	8
1989	Jerry Rice, San Francisco[4]..............82		1,483	18.1	68	17
	Sterling Sharpe, Green Bay..............90		1,423	15.8	79	12
	Mark Carrier, Tampa Bay..............86		1,422	16.5	78	9
	Henry Ellard, L.A. Rams[2]..............70		1,382	19.7	53	8
	Andre Reed, Buffalo..............88		1,312	14.9	78	9
	Anthony Miller, San Diego..............75		1,252	16.7	69	10
	Webster Slaughter, Cleveland..............65		1,236	19.0	97	6
	Gary Clark, Washington[3]..............79		1,229	15.6	80	9
	Tim McGee, Cincinnati..............65		1,211	18.6	74	8
	Art Monk, Washington[4]..............86		1,186	13.8	60	8
	Flipper Anderson, L.A. Rams..............44		1,146	26.0	78	5
	Ricky Sanders, Washington[2]..............80		1,138	14.2	68	4
	Vance Johnson, Denver..............76		1,095	14.4	69	7
	Richard Johnson, Detroit..............70		1,091	15.6	75	8
	Eric Martin, New Orleans[2]..............68		1,090	16.0	53	8
	John Taylor, San Francisco..............60		1,077	18.0	95	10
	Mervyn Fernandez, L.A. Raiders..............57		1,069	18.8	75	9
	Anthony Carter, Minnesota[2]..............65		1,066	16.4	50	4
	Brian Blades, Seattle..............77		1,063	13.8	60	5
	Mark Clayton, Miami[4]..............64		1,011	15.8	78	9
1988	Henry Ellard, L.A. Rams..............86		1,414	16.4	68	10
	Jerry Rice, San Francisco[3]..............64		1,306	20.4	96	9
	Eddie Brown, Cincinnati..............53		1,273	24.0	86	9
	Anthony Carter, Minnesota..............72		1,225	17.0	67	6
	Ricky Sanders, Washington..............73		1,148	15.7	55	12
	Drew Hill, Houston[3]..............72		1,141	15.8	57	10
	Mark Clayton, Miami[3]..............86		1,129	13.1	45	14
	Roy Green, Phoenix[3]..............68		1,097	16.1	52	7
	Eric Martin, New Orleans..............85		1,083	12.7	40	7
	Al Toon, N.Y. Jets[2]..............93		1,067	11.5	42	5
	Bruce Hill, Tampa Bay..............58		1,040	17.9	42	9
	Lionel Manuel, N.Y. Giants..............65		1,029	15.8	46	4
1987	J.T. Smith, St. Louis[2]..............91		1,117	12.3	38	8
	Jerry Rice, San Francisco[2]..............65		1,078	16.6	57	22
	Gary Clark, Washington[2]..............56		1,066	19.0	84	7
	Carlos Carson, Kansas City[3]..............55		1,044	19.0	81	7
1986	Jerry Rice, San Francisco..............86		1,570	18.3	66	15
	Stanley Morgan, New England[3]..............84		1,491	17.8	44	10
	Mark Duper, Miami[3]..............67		1,313	19.6	85	11
	Gary Clark, Washington..............74		1,265	17.1	55	7
	Al Toon, N.Y. Jets..............85		1,176	13.8	62	8
	Todd Christensen, L.A. Raiders[3]..............95		1,153	12.1	35	8
	Mark Clayton, Miami[2]..............60		1,150	19.2	68	10
	*Bill Brooks, Indianapolis..............65		1,131	17.4	84	8
	Drew Hill, Houston[2]..............65		1,112	17.1	81	5
	Steve Largent, Seattle[8]..............70		1,070	15.3	38	9
	Art Monk, Washington[3]..............73		1,068	14.6	69	4
	*Ernest Givins, Houston..............61		1,062	17.4	60	3
	Cris Collinsworth, Cincinnati[4]..............62		1,024	16.5	46	10

Year	Player, Team	No.	Yards	Avg.	Long	TD
	Wesley Walker, N.Y. Jets[2]	49	1,016	20.7	83	12
	J.T. Smith, St. Louis	80	1,014	12.7	45	6
	Mark Bavaro, N.Y. Giants	66	1,001	15.2	41	4
1985	Steve Largent, Seattle[7]	79	1,287	16.3	43	6
	Mike Quick, Philadelphia[3]	73	1,247	17.1	99	11
	Art Monk, Washington[2]	91	1,226	13.5	53	2
	Wes Chandler, San Diego[4]	67	1,199	17.9	75	10
	Drew Hill, Houston	64	1,169	18.3	57	9
	James Lofton, Green Bay[5]	69	1,153	16.7	56	4
	Louis Lipps, Pittsburgh	59	1,134	19.2	51	12
	Cris Collinsworth, Cincinnati[3]	65	1,125	17.3	71	5
	Tony Hill, Dallas[3]	74	1,113	15.0	53	7
	Lionel James, San Diego	86	1,027	11.9	67	6
	Roger Craig, San Francisco	92	1,016	11.0	73	6
1984	Roy Green, St. Louis[2]	78	1,555	19.9	83	12
	John Stallworth, Pittsburgh[3]	80	1,395	17.4	51	11
	Mark Clayton, Miami	73	1,389	19.0	65	18
	Art Monk, Washington	106	1,372	12.9	72	7
	James Lofton, Green Bay[4]	62	1,361	22.0	79	7
	Mark Duper, Miami[2]	71	1,306	18.4	80	8
	Steve Watson, Denver[3]	69	1,170	17.0	73	7
	Steve Largent, Seattle[6]	74	1,164	15.7	65	12
	Tim Smith, Houston[2]	69	1,141	16.5	75	4
	Stacey Bailey, Atlanta	67	1,138	17.0	61	6
	Carlos Carson, Kansas City[2]	57	1,078	18.9	57	4
	Mike Quick, Philadelphia[2]	61	1,052	17.2	90	9
	Todd Christensen, L.A. Raiders[2]	80	1,007	12.6	38	7
	Kevin House, Tampa Bay[2]	76	1,005	13.2	55	5
	Ozzie Newsome, Cleveland[2]	89	1,001	11.2	52	5
1983	Mike Quick, Philadelphia	69	1,409	20.4	83	13
	Carlos Carson, Kansas City	80	1,351	16.9	50	7
	James Lofton, Green Bay[3]	58	1,300	22.4	74	8
	Todd Christensen, L.A. Raiders	92	1,247	13.6	45	12
	Roy Green, St. Louis	78	1,227	15.7	71	14
	Charlie Brown, Washington	78	1,225	15.7	75	8
	Tim Smith, Houston	83	1,176	14.2	47	6
	Kellen Winslow, San Diego[3]	88	1,172	13.3	46	8
	Earnest Gray, N.Y. Giants	78	1,139	14.6	62	5
	Steve Watson, Denver[2]	59	1,133	19.2	78	5
	Cris Collinsworth, Cincinnati[2]	66	1,130	17.1	63	5
	Steve Largent, Seattle[5]	72	1,074	14.9	46	11
	Mark Duper, Miami	51	1,003	19.7	85	10
1982	Wes Chandler, San Diego[3]	49	1,032	21.1	66	9
1981	Alfred Jenkins, Atlanta[2]	70	1,358	19.4	67	13
	James Lofton, Green Bay[2]	71	1,294	18.2	75	8
	Steve Watson, Denver	60	1,244	20.7	95	13
	Frank Lewis, Buffalo[2]	70	1,244	17.8	33	4
	Steve Largent, Seattle[4]	75	1,224	16.3	57	9
	Charlie Joiner, San Diego[4]	70	1,188	17.0	57	7
	Kevin House, Tampa Bay	56	1,176	21.0	84	9
	Wes Chandler, New Orleans/San Diego[2]	69	1,142	16.6	51	6
	Dwight Clark, San Francisco	85	1,105	13.0	78	4
	John Stallworth, Pittsburgh[2]	63	1,098	17.4	55	5
	Kellen Winslow, San Diego[2]	88	1,075	12.2	67	10
	Pat Tilley, St. Louis	66	1,040	15.8	75	3
	Stanley Morgan, New England[2]	44	1,029	23.4	76	6
	Harold Carmichael, Philadelphia[3]	61	1,028	16.9	85	6
	Freddie Scott, Detroit	53	1,022	19.3	48	5
	*Cris Collinsworth, Cincinnati	67	1,009	15.1	74	8
	Joe Senser, Minnesota	79	1,004	12.7	53	8
	Ozzie Newsome, Cleveland	69	1,002	14.5	62	6
	Sammy White, Minnesota	66	1,001	15.2	53	3
1980	John Jefferson, San Diego[3]	82	1,340	16.3	58	13
	Kellen Winslow, San Diego	89	1,290	14.5	65	9
	James Lofton, Green Bay	71	1,226	17.3	47	4
	Charlie Joiner, San Diego[3]	71	1,132	15.9	51	4
	Ahmad Rashad, Minnesota[2]	69	1,095	15.9	76	5
	Steve Largent, Seattle[3]	66	1,064	16.1	67	6
	Tony Hill, Dallas[2]	60	1,055	17.6	58	8

Year	Player, Team	No.	Yards	Avg.	Long	TD
	Alfred Jenkins, Atlanta	57	1,026	18.0	57	6
1979	Steve Largent, Seattle[2]	66	1,237	18.7	55	9
	John Stallworth, Pittsburgh	70	1,183	16.9	65	8
	Ahmad Rashad, Minnesota	80	1,156	14.5	52	9
	John Jefferson, San Diego[2]	61	1,090	17.9	65	10
	Frank Lewis, Buffalo	54	1,082	20.0	55	2
	Wes Chandler, New Orleans	65	1,069	16.4	85	6
	Tony Hill, Dallas	60	1,062	17.7	75	10
	Drew Pearson, Dallas[2]	55	1,026	18.7	56	8
	Wallace Francis, Atlanta	74	1,013	13.7	42	8
	Harold Jackson, New England[3]	45	1,013	22.5	59	7
	Charlie Joiner, San Diego[2]	72	1,008	14.0	39	4
	Stanley Morgan, New England	44	1,002	22.8	63	12
1978	Wesley Walker, N.Y. Jets	48	1,169	24.4	77	8
	Steve Largent, Seattle	71	1,168	16.5	57	8
	Harold Carmichael, Philadelphia[2]	55	1,072	19.5	56	8
	*John Jefferson, San Diego	56	1,001	17.9	46	13
1976	Roger Carr, Baltimore	43	1,112	25.9	79	11
	Cliff Branch, Oakland[2]	46	1,111	24.2	88	12
	Charlie Joiner, San Diego	50	1,056	21.1	81	7
1975	Ken Burrough, Houston	53	1,063	20.1	77	8
1974	Cliff Branch, Oakland	60	1,092	18.2	67	13
	Drew Pearson, Dallas	62	1,087	17.5	50	2
1973	Harold Carmichael, Philadelphia	67	1,116	16.7	73	9
1972	Harold Jackson, Philadelphia[2]	62	1,048	16.9	77	4
	John Gilliam, Minnesota	47	1,035	22.0	66	7
1971	Otis Taylor, Kansas City[2]	57	1,110	19.5	82	7
1970	Gene Washington, San Francisco	53	1,100	20.8	79	12
	Marlin Briscoe, Buffalo	57	1,036	18.2	48	8
	Dick Gordon, Chicago	71	1,026	14.5	69	13
	Gary Garrison, San Diego[2]	44	1,006	22.9	67	12
1969	Warren Wells, Oakland[2]	47	1,260	26.8	80	14
	Harold Jackson, Philadelphia	65	1,116	17.2	65	9
	Roy Jefferson, Pittsburgh[2]	67	1,079	16.1	63	9
	Dan Abramowicz, New Orleans	73	1,015	13.9	49	7
	Lance Alworth, San Diego[7]	64	1,003	15.7	76	4
1968	Lance Alworth, San Diego[6]	68	1,312	19.3	80	10
	Don Maynard, N.Y. Jets[6]	57	1,297	22.8	87	10
	George Sauer, N.Y. Jets[3]	66	1,141	17.3	43	3
	Warren Wells, Oakland	53	1,137	21.5	94	11
	Gary Garrison, San Diego	52	1,103	21.2	84	10
	Roy Jefferson, Pittsburgh	58	1,074	18.5	62	11
	Paul Warfield, Cleveland	50	1,067	21.3	65	12
	Homer Jones, N.Y. Giants[3]	45	1,057	23.5	84	7
	Fred Biletnikoff, Oakland	61	1,037	17.0	82	6
	Lance Rentzel, Dallas	54	1,009	18.7	65	6
1967	Don Maynard, N.Y. Jets[5]	71	1,434	20.2	75	10
	Ben Hawkins, Philadelphia	59	1,265	21.4	87	10
	Homer Jones, N.Y. Giants[2]	49	1,209	24.7	70	13
	Jackie Smith, St. Louis	56	1,205	21.5	76	9
	George Sauer, N.Y. Jets[2]	75	1,189	15.9	61	6
	Lance Alworth, San Diego[5]	52	1,010	19.4	71	9
1966	Lance Alworth, San Diego[4]	73	1,383	18.9	78	13
	Otis Taylor, Kansas City	58	1,297	22.4	89	8
	Pat Studstill, Detroit	67	1,266	18.9	99	5
	Bob Hayes, Dallas[2]	64	1,232	19.3	95	13
	Charlie Frazier, Houston	57	1,129	19.8	79	12
	Charley Taylor, Washington	72	1,119	15.5	86	12
	George Sauer, N.Y. Jets	63	1,081	17.2	77	5
	Homer Jones, N.Y. Giants	48	1,044	21.8	98	8
	Art Powell, Oakland[5]	53	1,026	19.4	46	11
1965	Lance Alworth, San Diego[3]	69	1,602	23.2	85	14
	Dave Parks, San Francisco	80	1,344	16.8	53	12
	Don Maynard, N.Y. Jets[3]	68	1,218	17.9	56	14
	Pete Retzlaff, Philadelphia	66	1,190	18.0	78	10
	Lionel Taylor, Denver[4]	85	1,131	13.3	63	6
	Tommy McDonald, Los Angeles[3]	67	1,036	15.5	51	9
	*Bob Hayes, Dallas	46	1,003	21.8	82	12

Year	Player	No.	Yards	Avg	Long	TD
1964	Charley Hennigan, Houston[3]	101	1,546	15.3	53	8
	Art Powell, Oakland[4]	76	1,361	17.9	77	11
	Lance Alworth, San Diego[2]	61	1,235	20.2	82	13[2]
	Johnny Morris, Chicago	93	1,200	12.9	63	10
	Elbert Dubenion, Buffalo	42	1,139	27.1	72	10
	Terry Barr, Detroit[2]	57	1,030	18.1	58	9
1963	Bobby Mitchell, Washington[2]	69	1,436	20.8	99	7
	Art Powell, Oakland[3]	73	1,304	17.9	85	16
	Buddy Dial, Pittsburgh[2]	60	1,295	21.6	83	9
	Lance Alworth, San Diego	61	1,205	19.8	85	11
	Del Shofner, N.Y. Giants[4]	64	1,181	18.5	70	9
	Lionel Taylor, Denver[3]	78	1,101	14.1	72	10
	Terry Barr, Detroit	66	1,086	16.5	75	13
	Charley Hennigan, Houston[2]	61	1,051	17.2	83	10
	Sonny Randle, St. Louis[2]	51	1,014	19.9	68	12
	Bake Turner, N.Y. Jets	71	1,009	14.2	53	6
1962	Bobby Mitchell, Washington	72	1,384	19.2	81	11
	Sonny Randle, St. Louis	63	1,158	18.4	86	7
	Tommy McDonald, Philadelphia[2]	58	1,146	19.8	60	10
	Del Shofner, N.Y. Giants[3]	53	1,133	21.4	69	12
	Art Powell, N.Y. Titans[2]	64	1,130	17.7	80	8
	Frank Clarke, Dall. Cowboys	47	1,043	22.2	66	14
	Don Maynard, N.Y. Titans[2]	56	1,041	18.6	86	8
1961	Charley Hennigan, Houston	82	1,746	21.3	80	12
	Lionel Taylor, Denver[2]	100	1,176	11.8	52	4
	Bill Groman, Houston[2]	50	1,175	23.5	80	17
	Tommy McDonald, Philadelphia	64	1,144	17.9	66	13
	Del Shofner, N.Y. Giants[2]	68	1,125	16.5	46	11
	Jim Phillips, Los Angeles	78	1,092	14.0	69	5
	*Mike Ditka, Chicago	56	1,076	19.2	76	12
	Dave Kocourek, San Diego	55	1,055	19.2	76	4
	Buddy Dial, Pittsburgh	53	1,047	19.8	88	12
	R.C. Owens, San Francisco	55	1,032	18.8	54	5
1960	*Bill Groman, Houston	72	1,473	20.5	92	12
	Raymond Berry, Baltimore	74	1,298	17.5	70	10
	Don Maynard, N.Y. Titans	72	1,265	17.6	65	6
	Lionel Taylor, Denver	92	1,235	13.4	80	12
	Art Powell, N.Y. Titans	69	1,167	16.9	76	14
1958	Del Shofner, Los Angeles	51	1,097	21.5	92	8
1956	Bill Howton, Green Bay[2]	55	1,188	21.6	66	12
	Harlon Hill, Chi. Bears[2]	47	1,128	24.0	79	11
1954	Bob Boyd, Los Angeles	53	1,212	22.9	80	6
	*Harlon Hill, Chi. Bears	45	1,124	25.0	76	12
1953	Pete Pihos, Philadelphia	63	1,049	16.7	59	10
1952	*Bill Howton, Green Bay	53	1,231	23.2	90	13
1951	Elroy (Crazylegs) Hirsch, Los Angeles	66	1,495	22.7	91	17
1950	Tom Fears, Los Angeles[2]	84	1,116	13.3	53	7
	Cloyce Box, Detroit	50	1,009	20.2	82	11
1949	Bob Mann, Detroit	66	1,014	15.4	64	4
	Tom Fears, Los Angeles	77	1,013	13.2	51	9
1945	Jim Benton, Cleveland	45	1,067	23.7	84	8
1942	Don Hutson, Green Bay	74	1,211	16.4	73	17

*First season of professional football.

250 YARDS PASS RECEIVING IN A GAME

Date	Player, Team, Opponent	No.	Yards	TD
Oct. 11, 2009	Miles Austin, Dallas vs. Kansas City (OT)	10	250	2
Nov. 19, 2006	Lee Evans, Buffalo vs. Houston	11	265	2
Nov. 12, 2006	Chad Ochocinco, Cincinnati vs. San Diego	11	260	2
Nov. 10, 2002	Plaxico Burress, Pittsburgh vs. Atlanta (OT)	9	253	2
Dec. 17, 2000	Terrell Owens, San Francisco vs. Chicago	20	283	1
Sept. 10, 2000	Jimmy Smith, Jacksonville vs. Baltimore	15	291	3
Dec. 12, 1999	Qadry Ismail, Baltimore vs. Pittsburgh	6	258	3
Dec. 18, 1995	Jerry Rice, San Francisco vs. Minnesota	14	289	3
Dec. 11, 1989	John Taylor, San Francisco vs. L.A. Rams	11	286	2
Nov. 26, 1989	Flipper Anderson, L.A. Rams vs. New Orleans (OT)	15	336	1
Oct. 18, 1987	Steve Largent, Seattle vs. Detroit	15	261	3
Oct. 4, 1987	Anthony Allen, Washington vs. St. Louis	7	255	3
Dec. 22, 1985	Stephone Paige, Kansas City vs. San Diego	8	309	2
Dec. 20, 1982	Wes Chandler, San Diego vs. Cincinnati	10	260	2

Date	Player, Team, Opponent	No.	Yards	TD
Sept. 23, 1979	*Jerry Butler, Buffalo vs. N.Y. Jets	10	255	4
Nov. 4, 1962	Sonny Randle, St. Louis vs. N.Y. Giants	16	256	1
Oct. 28, 1962	Del Shofner, N.Y. Giants vs. Washington	11	269	1
Oct. 13, 1961	Charley Hennigan, Houston vs. Boston	13	272	1
Oct. 21, 1956	Billy Howton, Green Bay vs. Los Angeles	7	257	2
Dec. 3, 1950	Cloyce Box, Detroit vs. Baltimore	12	302	4
Nov. 22, 1945	Jim Benton, Cleveland vs. Detroit	10	303	1

*First season of professional football.

2,000 COMBINED NET YARDS GAINED IN A SEASON

Year	Player, Team	Rushing Att.-Yds.	Pass Rec.	Punt Ret.	Kickoff Ret.	Fum. Ret.	Total Yds.
2010	Danny Amendola, St. Louis[2]	7-81	85-689	40-452	50-1,142	0-0	182-2,364
	Arian Foster, Houston	327-1,616	66-604	0-0	0-0	1-0	394-2,221
	Darren Sproles, San Diego[3]	50-267	59-520	24-166	51-1,257	0-0	184-2,210
2009	Fred Jackson, Buffalo	237-1,062	46-371	6-69	41-1,014	0-0	330-2,516
	Josh Cribbs, Cleveland[2]	55-381	20-135	38-452	56-1,542	2-0	171-2,510
	Chris Johnson, Tennessee	358-2,006	50-503	0-0	0-0	1-0	409-2,509
	Jamaal Charles, Kansas City	190-1,120	40-297	0-0	36-925	3-0	269-2,342
	Darren Sproles, San Diego[2]	93-343	45-497	26-183	54-1,300	1-0	219-2,323
	Danny Amendola, St. Louis	3-2	43-326	31-360	66-1,618	1-0	144-2,302
	*Percy Harvin, Minnesota	15-135	60-790	0-0	42-1,156	0-0	117-2,081
	Ray Rice, Baltimore	254-1,339	78-702	0-0	0-0	1-2	333-2,043
2008	Leon Washington, N.Y. Jets[2]	76-448	47-355	29-303	48-1,231	4-(-5)	204-2,332
	Darren Sproles, San Diego	61-330	29-342	22-249	53-1,376	1-(-2)	166-2,295
	Jerious Norwood, Atlanta[2]	95-489	36-338	0-0	51-1,311	0-0	182-2,138
2007	Josh Cribbs, Cleveland	9-61	3-37	30-405	59-1,809	2-0	103-2,312
	Jerious Norwood, Atlanta	103-613	28-277	0-0	52-1,317	0-0	183-2,207
	Brian Westbrook, Philadelphia	278-1,333	90-771	4-79	0-0	0-0	372-2,183
	*Ted Ginn Jr., Miami	4-3	34-420	24-230	63-1,433	2-(-9)	127-2,077
	Leon Washington, N.Y. Jets	71-353	36-213	20-183	47-1,291	1-0	175-2,040
	*Adrian Peterson, Minnesota	238-1,341	19-268	0-0	16-412	3-0	276-2,014
	Maurice Jones-Drew, Jacksonville[2]	167-768	40-407	3-28	31-811	0-0	241-2,014
2006	Steven Jackson, St. Louis	346-1,528	90,806	0-0	0-0	2-0	438-2,334
	LaDainian Tomlinson, San Diego[3]	348-1,815	56-508	0-0	0-0	1-0	405-2,323
	*Maurice Jones-Drew, Jacksonville	166-941	46-436	1-13	31-860	0-0	244-2,250
	Larry Johnson, Kansas City[2]	416-1,789	41-410	0-0	0-0	1-0	458-2,199
	Frank Gore, San Francisco	312-1,695	61-485	0-0	0-0	0-0	373-2,180
	Wes Welker, Miami[2]	0-0	67-687	41-378	48-1,064	1-0	157-2,129
	Tiki Barber, N.Y. Giants[4]	327-1,662	58-465	0-0	0-0	1-0	386-2,127
	Chris Carr, Oakland	0-0	0-0	35-216	69-1,762	1-0	106-2,078
2005	Tiki Barber, N.Y. Giants[3]	357-1,860	54-530	0-0	0-0	1-0	412-2,390
	Dante Hall, Kansas City[4]	7-11	34-436	42-276	65-1,560	2-0	150-2,283
	Wes Welker, Miami	1-5	29-434	43-390	61-1,379	4-0	138-2,208
	Larry Johnson, Kansas City	336-1,750	33-343	0-0	0-0	3-0	372-2,093
2004	Dante Hall, Kansas City[3]	8-56	25-230	23-232	68-1,718	0-0	124-2,236
	Tiki Barber, N.Y. Giants[2]	322-1,518	52-578	0-0	0-0	2-0	376-2,096
	Edgerrin James, Indianapolis[3]	334-1,548	51-483	0-0	0-0	1-0	386-2,031
2003	Dante Hall, Kansas City[2]	16-73	40-423	29-472	57-1,478	0-0	142-2,446
	LaDainian Tomlinson, San Diego[2]	313-1,645	100-725	0-0	0-0	2-0	415-2,370
	Jamal Lewis, Baltimore	387-2,066	26-205	0-0	0-0	1-0	414-2,271
	Ahman Green, Green Bay	355-1,883	50-367	0-0	0-0	2-0	407-2,250
	Deuce McAllister, New Orleans	351-1,641	69-516	0-0	0-0	3-(-3)	423-2,154
	Priest Holmes, Kansas City[3]	320-1,420	74-690	0-0	0-0	0-0	394-2,110
2002	Michael Lewis, New Orleans	1-15	8-200	44-625	70-1,807	2-0	125-2,647
	Priest Holmes, Kansas City[2]	313-1,615	70-672	0-0	0-0	0-0	383-2,287
	Ricky Williams, Miami	383-1,853	47-363	0-0	0-0	1-0	431-2,216
	LaDainian Tomlinson, San Diego	372-1,683	79-489	0-0	0-0	0-0	451-2,172
	Dante Hall, Kansas City	11-54	20-322	29-390	57-1,354	1-0	118-2,120
2001	Priest Holmes, Kansas City	327-1,555	62-614	0-0	0-0	0-0	389-2,169
	Marshall Faulk, St. Louis[4]	260-1,382	83-765	0-0	0-0	2-0	345-2,147
	Derrick Mason, Tennessee[2]	0-0	73-1,128	20-128	34-748	1-0	128-2,004
2000	Derrick Mason, Tennessee	1-1	63-895	51-662	42-1,132	1-0	158-2,690
	MarTay Jenkins, Arizona	1-(-4)	17-219	1-1	82-2,186	0-0	101-2,402
	Edgerrin James, Indianapolis[2]	387-1,709	63-594	0-0	0-0	0-0	450-2,303
	Marshall Faulk, St. Louis[3]	253-1,359	81-830	0-0	1-18	2-0	337-2,207
	Tiki Barber, N.Y. Giants	213-1,006	70-719	39-332	1-28	5-0	328-2,085
1999	Marshall Faulk, St. Louis[2]	253-1,381	87-1,048	0-0	0-0	0-0	340-2,429

Year	Player, Team	Rushing Att.-Yds.	Pass Rec.	Punt Ret.	Kickoff Ret.	Fum. Ret.	Total Yds.
	*Edgerrin James, Indianapolis	369-1,553	62-586	0-0	0-0	2-0	433-2,139
	*Terrence Wilkins, Indianapolis	1-2	42-565	41-388	51-1,134	1-0	136-2,089
	Glyn Milburn, Chicago[2]	16-102	20-151	30-346	61-1,426	2-0	129-2,025
1998	Brian Mitchell, Washington[4]	39-208	44-306	44-506	59-1,337	0-0	186-2,357
	Marshall Faulk, Indianapolis	324-1,319	86-908	0-0	0-0	2-13	412-2,240
	Terrell Davis, Denver[2]	392-2,008	25-217	0-0	0-0	1-0	418-2,225
	Jamal Anderson, Atlanta	410-1,846	27-319	0-0	0-0	1-0	438-2,165
	Garrison Hearst, San Francisco	310-1,570	39-535	0-0	0-0	1-0	350-2,105
1997	Barry Sanders, Detroit[2]	335-2,053	33-305	0-0	0-0	1-0	369-2,358
	Kevin Williams, Arizona	1-(-2)	20-273	40-462	59-1,458	1-0	121-2,191
	Brian Mitchell, Washington[3]	23-107	36-438	38-442	47-1,094	0-0	144-2,081
	Terrell Davis, Denver	369-1,750	42-287	0-0	0-0	2-(-7)	413-2,030
	Jermaine Lewis, Baltimore	3-35	42-648	28-437	41-905	2-0	116-2,025
1995	Brian Mitchell, Washington[2]	46-301	38-324	25-315	55-1,408	0-0	164-2,348
	Emmitt Smith, Dallas[2]	377-1,773	62-375	0-0	0-0	0-0	439-2,148
	Glyn Milburn, Denver	49-266	22-191	31-354	47-1,269	0-0	149-2,080
	Ernie Mills, Pittsburgh	5-39	39-679	0-0	54-1,306	0-0	98-2,024
1994	Brian Mitchell, Washington	78-311	26-236	32-452	58-1,478	0-0	194-2,477
	Barry Sanders, Detroit	331-1,883	44-283	0-0	0-0	0-0	375-2,166
1992	Thurman Thomas, Buffalo[2]	312-1,487	58-626	0-0	0-0	1-0	371-2,113
	Emmitt Smith, Dallas	373-1,713	59-335	0-0	0-0	1-0	433-2,048
	Barry Foster, Pittsburgh	390-1,690	36-344	0-0	0-0	2-(-20)	428-2,014
1991	Thurman Thomas, Buffalo	288-1,407	62-631	0-0	0-0	0-0	350-2,038
1990	Herschel Walker, Minnesota[2]	184-770	35-315	0-0	44-966	4-0	267-2,051
1988	*Tim Brown, L.A. Raiders	14-50	43-725	49-444	41-1,098	7-0	154-2,317
	Roger Craig, San Francisco[2]	310-1,502	76-534	0-0	2-32	2-0	390-2,068
	Eric Dickerson, Indianapolis[4]	388-1,659	36-377	0-0	0-0	1-0	425-2,036
	Herschel Walker, Dallas	361-1,514	53-505	0-0	0-0	3-0	417-2,019
1986	Eric Dickerson, L.A. Rams[3]	404-1,821	26-205	0-0	0-0	2-0	432-2,026
	Gary Anderson, San Diego	127-442	80-871	25-227	24-482	2-0	258-2,022
1985	Lionel James, San Diego	105-516	86-1,027	25-213	36-779	1-0	253-2,535
	Marcus Allen, L.A. Raiders	380-1,759	67-555	0-0	0-0	2-(-6)	449-2,308
	Roger Craig, San Francisco	214-1,050	92-1,016	0-0	0-0	1-0	306-2,066
	Walter Payton, Chicago[4]	324-1,551	49-483	0-0	0-0	1-0	374-2,034
1984	Eric Dickerson, L.A. Rams[2]	379-2,105	21-139	0-0	0-0	4-15	404-2,259
	James Wilder, Tampa Bay	407-1,544	85-685	0-0	0-0	4-0	496-2,229
	Walter Payton, Chicago[3]	381-1,684	45-368	0-0	0-0	1-0	427-2,052
1983	*Eric Dickerson, L.A. Rams	390-1,808	51-404	0-0	0-0	1-0	442-2,212
	William Andrews, Atlanta[2]	331-1,567	59-609	0-0	0-0	2-0	392-2,176
	Walter Payton, Chicago[2]	314-1,421	53-607	0-0	0-0	2-0	369-2,028
1981	*James Brooks, San Diego	109-525	46-329	22-290	40-949	2-0	219-2,093
	William Andrews, Atlanta	289-1,301	81-735	0-0	0-0	0-0	370-2,036
1980	Bruce Harper, N.Y. Jets[2]	45-126	50-634	28-242	49-1,070	3-0	175-2,072
1979	Wilbert Montgomery, Philadelphia	338-1,512	41-494	0-0	1-6	2-0	382-2,012
1978	Bruce Harper, N.Y. Jets	58-303	13-196	30-378	55-1,280	1-0	157-2,157
1977	Walter Payton, Chicago	339-1,852	27-269	0-0	2-95	5-0	373-2,216
	Terry Metcalf, St. Louis[3]	149-739	34-403	14-108	32-772	1-0	230-2,022
1975	Terry Metcalf, St. Louis[2]	165-816	43-378	23-285	35-960	2-23	268-2,462
	O.J. Simpson, Buffalo[2]	329-1,817	28-426	0-0	0-0	1-0	358-2,243
1974	Mack Herron, New England	231-824	38-474	35-517	28-629	3-0	335-2,444
	Otis Armstrong, Denver	263-1,407	38-405	0-0	16-386	1-0	318-2,198
	Terry Metcalf, St. Louis	152-718	50-377	26-340	20-623	7-0	255-2,058
1973	O.J. Simpson, Buffalo	332-2,003	6-70	0-0	0-0	0-0	338-2,073
1966	Gale Sayers, Chicago[2]	229-1,231	34-447	6-44	23-718	3-0	295-2,440
	Leroy Kelly, Cleveland	209-1,141	32-366	13-104	19-403	0-0	273-2,014
1965	*Gale Sayers, Chicago	166-867	29-507	16-238	21-660	4-0	236-2,272
1963	Timmy Brown, Philadelphia[2]	192-841	36-487	16-152	33-945	2-3	279-2,428
	Jim Brown, Cleveland	291-1,863	24-268	0-0	0-0	0-0	315-2,131
1962	Timmy Brown, Philadelphia	137-545	52-849	6-81	30-831	4-0	229-2,306
	Dick Christy, N.Y. Titans	114-535	62-538	15-250	38-824	2-0	231-2,147
1961	Billy Cannon, Houston	200-948	43-586	9-70	18-439	2-0	272-2,043
1960	*Abner Haynes, Dallas Texans	156-875	55-576	14-215	19-434	4-0	248-2,100

*First season of professional football.

300 COMBINED NET YARDS GAINED IN A GAME

Date	Player, Team, Opponent	No.	Yards	TD
Nov. 28, 2010	*Jacoby Ford, Oakland vs. Miami	12	329	2
Nov. 7, 2010	*Jacoby Ford, Oakland vs. Kansas City (OT)	10	306	1

Date	Player, Team, Opponent	No.	Yards	TD
Dec. 20, 2009	Josh Cribbs, Cleveland vs. Kansas City	14	316	2
Oct. 18, 2009	Domenik Hixon, N.Y. Giants vs. New Orleans	12	303	0
Sept. 28, 2008	Steve Breaston, Arizona vs. N.Y. Jets	19	324	0
Sept. 14, 2008	Darren Sproles, San Diego vs. Denver	14	317	2
Nov. 18, 2007	Josh Cribbs, Cleveland vs. Baltimore (OT)	12	309	0
Nov. 4, 2007	*Adrian Peterson, Minnesota vs. San Diego	31	315	3
Oct. 14, 2007	*Adrian Peterson, Minnesota vs. Chicago	25	361	3
Sept. 30, 2007	Devin Hester, Chicago vs. Detroit	13	317	1
Dec. 10, 2006	*Maurice Jones-Drew, Jacksonville vs. Indianapolis	19	303	3
Dec. 14, 2003	Derrick Mason, Tennessee vs. Buffalo	21	302	0
Nov. 16, 2003	Jonathan Carter, N.Y. Jets vs. Indianapolis	7	304	2
Dec. 8, 2002	Steve Smith, Carolina vs. Cincinnati	9	313	3
Nov. 24, 2002	Priest Holmes, Kansas City vs. Seattle	30	307	3
Oct. 13, 2002	Michael Lewis, New Orleans vs. Washington	8	356	2
Dec. 24, 1999	Jason Tucker, Dallas vs. New Orleans	13	331	1
Dec. 7, 1997	Jermaine Lewis, Baltimore vs. Seattle	10	308	3
Dec. 25, 1995	Kevin Williams, Dallas vs. Arizona	16	307	2
Dec. 10, 1995	Glyn Milburn, Denver vs. Seattle	33	404	0
Oct. 23, 1994	Tyrone Hughes, New Orleans vs. L.A. Rams	11	347	2
Dec. 11, 1989	John Taylor, San Francisco vs. L.A. Rams	14	321	2
Nov. 26, 1989	Flipper Anderson, L.A. Rams vs. New Orleans (OT)	15	336	1
Nov. 28, 1988	*Tim Brown, L.A. Raiders vs. Seattle	12	306	1
Dec. 22, 1985	Stephone Paige, Kansas City vs. San Diego	8	309	2
Nov. 10, 1985	Lionel James, San Diego vs. L.A. Raiders (OT)	23	345	0
Sept. 22, 1985	Lionel James, San Diego vs. Cincinnati	20	316	2
Dec. 21, 1975	*Walter Payton, Chicago vs. New Orleans	32	300	1
Nov. 23, 1975	Greg Pruitt, Cleveland vs. Cincinnati	28	304	2
Nov. 1, 1970	Eugene (Mercury) Morris, Miami vs. Baltimore	17	302	0
Oct. 4, 1970	O.J. Simpson, Buffalo vs. N.Y. Jets	26	303	2
Dec. 6, 1969	Jerry LeVias, Houston vs. N.Y. Jets	18	329	1
Nov. 2, 1969	Travis Williams, Green Bay vs. Pittsburgh	11	314	3
Dec. 18, 1966	Gale Sayers, Chicago vs. Minnesota	20	339	2
Dec. 12, 1965	*Gale Sayers, Chicago vs. San Francisco	17	336	6
Nov. 17, 1963	Gary Ballman, Pittsburgh vs. Washington	12	320	2
Dec. 16, 1962	Timmy Brown, Philadelphia vs. St. Louis	19	341	2
Dec. 10, 1961	Billy Cannon, Houston vs. N.Y. Titans	32	373	5
Nov. 19, 1961	Jim Brown, Cleveland vs. Philadelphia	38	313	4
Dec. 3, 1950	Cloyce Box, Detroit vs. Baltimore	13	302	4
Oct. 29, 1950	Wally Triplett, Detroit vs. Los Angeles	11	331	1
Nov. 22, 1945	Jim Benton, Cleveland vs. Detroit	10	303	1

*First season of professional football.

2,000 SCRIMMAGE YARDS GAINED IN A SEASON

Year	Player, Team	Att.	Rushing Yards	Receptions	Receiving Yards	Scrimm. Yards
2010	Arian Foster, Houston	327	1,616	66	604	2,220
2009	Chris Johnson, Tennessee	358	2,006	50	503	2,509
	Ray Rice, Baltimore	254	1,339	78	702	2,041
2007	Brian Westbrook, Philadelphia	278	1,333	90	771	2,104
2006	Steven Jackson, St. Louis	346	1,528	90	806	2,334
	LaDainian Tomlinson, San Diego[3]	348	1,815	56	508	2,323
	Larry Johnson, Kansas City[2]	416	1,789	41	410	2,199
	Frank Gore, San Francisco	312	1,695	61	485	2,180
	Tiki Barber, N.Y. Giants[3]	327	1,662	58	465	2,127
2005	Tiki Barber, N.Y. Giants[2]	357	1,860	54	530	2,390
	Larry Johnson, Kansas City	336	1,750	33	343	2,093
2004	Tiki Barber, N.Y. Giants	322	1,518	52	578	2,096
	Edgerrin James, Indianapolis[3]	334	1,548	51	483	2,031
2003	LaDainian Tomlinson, San Diego[2]	313	1,645	100	725	2,370
	Jamal Lewis, Baltimore	387	2,066	26	205	2,271
	Ahman Green, Green Bay	355	1,883	50	367	2,250
	Deuce McAllister, New Orleans	351	1,641	69	516	2,157
	Priest Holmes, Kansas City[3]	320	1,420	74	690	2,110
2002	Priest Holmes, Kansas City[2]	313	1,615	70	672	2,287
	Ricky Williams, Miami	383	1,853	47	363	2,216
	LaDainian Tomlinson, San Diego	372	1,683	79	489	2,172
2001	Priest Holmes, Kansas City	327	1,555	62	614	2,169
	Marshall Faulk, St. Louis[4]	260	1,382	83	765	2,147
2000	Edgerrin James, Indianapolis[2]	387	1,709	63	594	2,303
	Marshall Faulk, St. Louis[3]	253	1,359	81	830	2,189

Year	Player, Team	Att.	Rushing Yards	Receptions	Receiving Yards	Scrimm. Yards
1999	Marshall Faulk, St. Louis[2]	253	1,381	87	1,048	2,429
	*Edgerrin James, Indianapolis	369	1,553	62	586	2,139
1998	Marshall Faulk, Indianapolis	324	1,319	86	908	2,227
	Terrell Davis, Denver[2]	392	2,008	25	217	2,225
	Jamal Anderson, Atlanta	410	1,846	27	319	2,165
	Garrison Hearst, San Francisco	310	1,570	39	535	2,105
1997	Barry Sanders, Detroit[2]	335	2,053	33	305	2,358
	Terrell Davis, Denver	369	1,750	42	287	2,037
1995	Emmitt Smith, Dallas[2]	377	1,773	62	375	2,148
1994	Barry Sanders, Detroit	331	1,883	44	283	2,166
1992	Thurman Thomas, Buffalo[2]	312	1,487	58	626	2,113
	Emmitt Smith, Dallas	373	1,713	59	335	2,048
	Barry Foster, Pittsburgh	390	1,690	36	344	2,034
1991	Thurman Thomas, Buffalo	288	1,407	62	631	2,038
1988	Roger Craig, San Francisco[2]	310	1,502	76	534	2,036
	Eric Dickerson, Indianapolis[4]	388	1,659	36	377	2,036
	Herschel Walker, Dallas	361	1,514	53	505	2,019
1986	Eric Dickerson, L.A. Rams[3]	404	1,821	26	205	2,026
1985	Marcus Allen, L.A. Raiders	380	1,759	67	555	2,314
	Roger Craig, San Francisco	214	1,050	92	1,016	2,066
	Walter Payton, Chicago[4]	324	1,551	49	483	2,034
1984	Eric Dickerson, L. A. Rams[2]	379	2,105	21	139	2,244
	James Wilder, Tampa Bay	407	1,544	85	685	2,229
	Walter Payton, Chicago[3]	381	1,684	45	368	2,052
1983	*Eric Dickerson, L.A. Rams	390	1,808	51	404	2,212
	William Andrews, Atlanta[2]	331	1,567	59	609	2,176
	Walter Payton, Chicago[2]	314	1,421	53	607	2,028
1981	William Andrews, Atlanta	289	1,301	81	735	2,036
1979	Wilbert Montgomery, Philadelphia	338	1,512	41	494	2,006
1977	Walter Payton, Chicago	339	1,852	27	269	2,121
1975	O.J. Simpson, Buffalo[2]	329	1,817	28	426	2,243
1973	O.J. Simpson, Buffalo	332	2,003	6	70	2,073
1963	Jim Brown, Cleveland	291	1,863	24	268	2,131

First season of professional football.

300 SCRIMMAGE YARDS GAINED IN A GAME

Date	Player, Team, Opponent	Att.	Yards	TD
Nov. 4, 2007	*Adrian Peterson, Minnesota vs. San Diego	31	315	3
Nov. 24, 2002	Priest Holmes, Kansas City vs. Seattle	30	307	3
Nov. 26, 1989	Flipper Anderson, L.A. Rams vs. New Orleans (OT)	15	336	1
Dec. 22, 1985	Stephone Paige, Kansas City vs. San Diego	8	309	2
Dec. 10, 1961	Billy Cannon, Houston vs. N.Y. Titans	30	330	5
Dec. 3, 1950	Cloyce Box, Detroit vs. Baltimore	12	302	4
Nov. 22, 1945	Jim Benton, Cleveland vs. Detroit	10	303	1

First season of professional football.

TOP 20 SCORERS

Player	Years	TD	FG	PAT	TP
1. Morten Andersen	25	0	565	849	2,544
2. Gary Anderson	23	0	538	820	2,434
3. John Carney	23	0	478	628	2,062
4. Matt Stover	19	0	471	591	2,004
5. George Blanda	26	9	335	943	2,002
6. Jason Elam	17	0	436	675	1,983
7. Jason Hanson	19	0	439	573	1,890
8. John Kasay	19	0	433	524	1,823
9. Norm Johnson	18	0	366	638	1,736
10. Nick Lowery	18	0	383	562	1,711
11. Jan Stenerud	19	0	373	580	1,699
12. Adam Vinatieri	15	0	364	565	1,659
13. Eddie Murray	19	0	352	538	1,594
14. Al Del Greco	17	0	347	543	1,584
15. Ryan Longwell	14	0	339	566	1,583
16. Steve Christie	15	0	336	468	1,476
17. Pat Leahy	18	0	304	558	1,470
18. Jim Turner	16	1	304	521	1,439
19. Matt Bahr	17	0	300	522	1,422
20. Olindo Mare	14	0	328	436	1,420

TOP 20 TOUCHDOWN SCORERS

Player	Years	Rush	Rec.	Total Returns	TD
1. Jerry Rice	20	10	197	1	208
2. Emmitt Smith	15	164	11	0	175
3. LaDainian Tomlinson	10	144	15	0	159
4. Terrell Owens	15	3	153	0	156
5. Randy Moss	13	0	153	1	154
6. Marcus Allen	16	123	21	1	145
7. Marshall Faulk	12	100	36	0	136
8. Cris Carter	16	0	130	1	131
9. Marvin Harrison	13	0	128	0	128
10. Jim Brown	9	106	20	0	126
11. Walter Payton	13	110	15	0	125
12. John Riggins	14	104	12	0	116
13. Lenny Moore	12	63	48	2	113
14. Shaun Alexander	9	100	12	0	112
15. Barry Sanders	10	99	10	0	109
16. Tim Brown	17	1	100	4	105
Don Hutson	11	3	99	3	105
18. Steve Largent	14	1	100	0	101
19. Franco Harris	13	91	9	0	100
Curtis Martin	11	90	10	0	100

TOP 20 RUSHERS

Player	Years	Att.	Yards	Avg.	Long	TD
1. Emmitt Smith	15	4,409	18,355	4.2	75	164
2. Walter Payton	13	3,838	16,726	4.4	76	110
3. Barry Sanders	10	3,062	15,269	5.0	85	99
4. Curtis Martin	11	3,518	14,101	4.0	70	90
5. Jerome Bettis	13	3,479	13,662	3.9	71	91
6. LaDainian Tomlinson	10	3,099	13,404	4.3	85	144
7. Eric Dickerson	11	2,996	13,259	4.4	85	90
8. Tony Dorsett	12	2,936	12,739	4.3	99	77
9. Jim Brown	9	2,359	12,312	5.2	80	106
10. Marshall Faulk	12	2,836	12,279	4.3	71	100
11. Edgerrin James	11	3,028	12,246	4.0	72	80
12. Marcus Allen	16	3,022	12,243	4.1	61	123
13. Franco Harris	13	2,949	12,120	4.1	75	91
14. Thurman Thomas	13	2,877	12,074	4.2	80	65
15. Fred Taylor	13	2,534	11,695	4.6	80	66
16. John Riggins	14	2,916	11,352	3.9	66	104
17. Corey Dillon	10	2,618	11,241	4.3	96	82
18. O.J. Simpson	11	2,404	11,236	4.7	94	61
19. Warrick Dunn	12	2,669	10,967	4.1	90	49
20. Ricky Watters	10	2,622	10,643	4.1	57	78

TOP 20 LEADERS IN PASSES COMPLETED

1.	Brett Favre	6,300
2.	Dan Marino	4,967
3.	Peyton Manning	4,682
4.	John Elway	4,123
5.	Warren Moon	3,988
6.	Drew Bledsoe	3,839
7.	Vinny Testaverde	3,787
8.	Fran Tarkenton	3,686
9.	Kerry Collins	3,439
10.	Joe Montana	3,409
11.	Dan Fouts	3,297
12.	Drew Brees	3,145
13.	Dave Krieg	3,105
14.	Donovan McNabb	3,076
15.	Tom Brady	2,996
16.	Boomer Esiason	2,969
17.	Troy Aikman	2,898
18.	Steve DeBerg	2,874
	Jim Kelly	2,874
20.	Jim Everett	2,841

TOP 20 LEADERS IN PASSING YARDS

1.	Brett Favre	71,838
2.	Dan Marino	61,361
3.	Peyton Manning	54,828
4.	John Elway	51,475
5.	Warren Moon	49,325
6.	Fran Tarkenton	47,003
7.	Vinny Testaverde	46,233
8.	Drew Bledsoe	44,611
9.	Dan Fouts	43,040
10.	Joe Montana	40,551
11.	Kerry Collins	40,441
12.	Johnny Unitas	40,239
13.	Dave Krieg	38,147
14.	Boomer Esiason	37,920
15.	Donovan McNabb	36,250
16.	Jim Kelly	35,467
17.	Drew Brees	35,266
18.	Jim Everett	34,837
19.	Tom Brady	34,744
20.	Jim Hart	34,665

TOP 20 LEADERS IN TOUCHDOWN PASSES

1.	Brett Favre	508
2.	Dan Marino	420
3.	Peyton Manning	399
4.	Fran Tarkenton	342
5.	John Elway	300
6.	Warren Moon	291
7.	Johnny Unitas	290
8.	Vinny Testaverde	275
9.	Joe Montana	273
10.	Dave Krieg	261
	Tom Brady	261
12.	Sonny Jurgensen	255
13.	Dan Fouts	254
14.	Drew Bledsoe	251
15.	Boomer Esiason	247
16.	John Hadl	244
17.	Len Dawson	239
18.	Jim Kelly	237
19.	George Blanda	236
20.	Drew Brees	235

TOP 20 LEADERS IN RECEPTION YARDS

1.	Jerry Rice	22,895
2.	Terrell Owens	15,934
3.	Isaac Bruce	15,208
4.	Tim Brown	14,934
5.	Randy Moss	14,858
6.	Marvin Harrison	14,580
7.	James Lofton	14,004
8.	Cris Carter	13,899
9.	Henry Ellard	13,777
10.	Torry Holt	13,382
11.	Andre Reed	13,198
12.	Steve Largent	13,089
13.	Irving Fryar	12,785
14.	Art Monk	12,721
15.	Tony Gonzalez	12,463
16.	Jimmy Smith	12,287
17.	Charlie Joiner	12,146
18.	Michael Irvin	11,904
19.	Derrick Mason	11,891
20.	Don Maynard	11,834

TOP 20 COMBINED YARDS GAINED

	Player	Years	Tot.	Rush.	Rec.	Int. Ret.	Punt Ret.	Kickoff Ret.	Fumble Ret.
1.	Jerry Rice	20	23,546	645	22,895	0	0	6	0
2.	Brian Mitchell	14	23,330	1,967	2,336	0	4,999	14,014	14
3.	Walter Payton	13	21,803	16,726	4,538	0	0	539	0
4.	Emmitt Smith	15	21,583	18,355	3,224	0	0	0	4
5.	Tim Brown	17	19,682	190	14,934	0	3,320	1,235	3
6.	Marshall Faulk	12	19,190	12,279	6,875	0	0	18	18
7.	Barry Sanders	10	18,308	15,269	2,921	0	0	118	0
8.	Herschel Walker	12	18,168	8,225	4,859	0	0	5,084	0
9.	LaDainian Tomlinson	10	17,727	13,404	4,323	0	0	0	0
10.	Marcus Allen	16	17,648	12,243	5,411	0	0	0	-6
11.	Curtis Martin	11	17,430	14,101	3,329	0	0	0	0
12.	Tiki Barber	10	17,359	10,449	5,183	0	1,181	544	2
13.	Eric Metcalf	13	17,230	2,392	5,572	0	3,453	5,813	0
14.	Derrick Mason	14	16,980	3	11,891	0	1,590	3,496	0
15.	Thurman Thomas	13	16,532	12,074	4,458	0	0	0	0
16.	Tony Dorsett	12	16,347	12,739	3,554	0	0	0	54
17.	Terrell Owens	15	16,276	251	15,934	0	0	78	13
18.	Henry Ellard	16	15,718	50	13,777	0	1,527	364	0
19.	Warrick Dunn	12	15,665	10,967	4,339	0	48	310	1
20.	Edgerrin James	11	15,610	12,246	3,364	0	0	0	0

TOP 20 YARDS FROM SCRIMMAGE

	Player	Years	Scrimmage Yards	Rushing Yards	Receiving Yards
1.	Jerry Rice	20	23,540	645	22,895
2.	Emmitt Smith	15	21,579	18,355	3,224
3.	Walter Payton	13	21,264	16,726	4,538
4.	Marshall Faulk	12	19,154	12,279	6,875
5.	Barry Sanders	10	18,190	15,269	2,921
6.	LaDainian Tomlinson	10	17,727	13,404	4,323
7.	Marcus Allen	16	17,654	12,243	5,411
8.	Curtis Martin	11	17,430	14,101	3,329
9.	Thurman Thomas	13	16,532	12,074	4,458
10.	Tony Dorsett	12	16,293	12,739	3,554
11.	Terrell Owens	15	16,185	251	15,934
12.	Tiki Barber	10	15,632	10,449	5,183
13.	Edgerrin James	11	15,610	12,246	3,364
14.	Eric Dickerson	11	15,396	13,259	2,137
15.	Isaac Bruce	16	15,347	139	15,208
16.	Warrick Dunn	12	15,306	10,967	4,339
17.	Tim Brown	17	15,124	190	14,934
18.	Jerome Bettis	13	15,111	13,662	1,449
19.	Randy Moss	15	15,017	159	14,858
20.	Ricky Watters	10	14,891	10,643	4,248

TOP 20 PASSERS

	Player	Years	Att.	Comp.	Pct. Comp.	Yards	Avg. Gain	TD	Pct. TD	Int.	Pct. Int.	Rating
1.	Aaron Rodgers	6	1,611	1,038	64.4	12,723	7.90	87	5.4	32	2.0	98.4
2.	Philip Rivers	7	2,455	1,564	63.7	19,661	8.01	136	5.5	58	2.4	97.2
3.	Steve Young	15	4,149	2,667	64.3	33,124	7.98	232	5.6	107	2.6	96.8
4.	Tony Romo	7	2,070	1,326	64.1	16,650	8.04	118	5.7	62	3.0	95.5
5.	Tom Brady	11	4,710	2,996	63.6	34,744	7.38	261	5.5	103	2.2	95.2
6.	Peyton Manning	13	7,210	4,682	64.9	54,828	7.60	399	5.5	198	2.7	94.9
7.	Kurt Warner	12	4,070	2,666	65.5	32,344	7.95	208	5.1	128	3.1	93.7
8.	Ben Roethlisberger	7	2,800	1,766	63.1	22,502	8.04	144	5.1	86	3.1	92.5
9.	Joe Montana	15	5,391	3,409	63.2	40,551	7.52	273	5.1	139	2.6	92.3
10.	Drew Brees	10	4,822	3,145	65.2	35,266	7.31	235	4.9	132	2.7	91.7
11.	Matt Schaub	7	1,987	1,288	64.8	15,457	7.78	83	4.2	52	2.6	91.5
12.	Chad Pennington	11	2,471	1,632	66.0	17,823	7.21	102	4.1	64	2.6	90.1
13.	Daunte Culpepper	11	3,199	2,016	63.0	24,153	7.55	149	4.7	106	3.3	87.8
14.	Jeff Garcia	11	3,676	2,264	61.6	25,537	6.95	161	4.4	83	2.3	87.5
15.	Carson Palmer	7	3,217	2,024	62.9	22,694	7.05	154	4.8	100	3.1	86.9
16.	Dan Marino	17	8,358	4,967	59.4	61,361	7.34	420	5.0	252	3.0	86.4
17.	Trent Green	11	3,740	2,266	60.6	28,475	7.61	162	4.3	114	3.0	86.0
18.	Brett Favre	20	10,169	6,300	62.0	71,838	7.06	508	5.0	336	3.3	86.0
19.	David Garrard	9	2,281	1,406	61.6	16,003	7.02	89	3.9	54	2.4	85.8
20.	Donovan McNabb	12	5,374	3,076	58.9	36,250	6.95	230	4.4	115	2.2	85.7

1,500 or more attempts. The passing ratings are based on performance standards established for completion percentage, interception percentage, touchdown percentage, and average gain. Please consult page 312 for more information.

OUTSTANDING PERFORMERS

TOP 20 PASS RECEIVERS

Player	Years	No.	Yards	Avg.	Long	TD
1. Jerry Rice	20	1,549	22,895	14.8	96	197
2. Marvin Harrison	13	1,102	14,580	13.2	80	128
3. Cris Carter	16	1,101	13,899	12.6	80	130
4. Tim Brown	17	1,094	14,934	13.7	80	100
5. Terrell Owens	15	1,078	15,934	14.8	98	153
6. Tony Gonzalez	14	1,069	12,463	11.7	73	88
7. Isaac Bruce	16	1,024	15,208	14.9	80	91
8. Randy Moss	13	954	14,858	15.6	82	153
Hines Ward	13	954	11,702	12.3	85	83
10. Andre Reed	16	951	13,198	13.9	83	87
11. Art Monk	16	940	12,721	13.5	79	68
12. Derrick Mason	14	924	11,891	12.9	79	66
13. Torry Holt	11	920	13,382	14.5	85	74
14. Keenan McCardell	16	883	11,373	12.9	76	63
15. Jimmy Smith	12	862	12,287	14.3	75	67
16. Muhsin Muhammad	14	860	11,438	13.3	72	62
17. Irving Fryar	17	851	12,785	15.0	80	84
18. Rod Smith	12	849	11,389	13.4	85	68
19. Larry Centers	14	827	6,797	8.2	54	28
20. Steve Largent	14	819	13,089	16.0	74	100

TOP 20 INTERCEPTORS

Player	Years	No.	Yards	Avg.	Long	TD
1. Paul Krause	16	81	1,185	14.6	81	3
2. Emlen Tunnell	14	79	1,282	16.2	55	4
3. Rod Woodson	17	71	1,483	20.9	98	12
4. Dick (Night Train) Lane	14	68	1,207	17.8	80	5
5. Ken Riley	15	65	596	9.2	66	5
6. Ronnie Lott	14	63	730	11.6	83	5
Darren Sharper	14	63	1,412	22.4	99	11
7. Dave Brown	15	62	698	11.3	90	5
Dick LeBeau	14	62	762	12.3	70	3
9. Emmitt Thomas	13	58	937	16.2	73	5
10. Mel Blount	14	57	736	12.9	52	2
Bobby Boyd	9	57	994	17.4	74	4
Eugene Robinson	16	57	762	13.4	49	1
Johnny Robinson	12	57	741	13.0	57	1
Everson Walls	13	57	504	8.8	40	1
15. Lem Barney	11	56	1,077	19.2	71	7
Pat Fischer	17	56	941	16.8	69	4
17. Aeneas Williams	14	55	807	14.7	65	9
18. Eric Allen	14	54	826	15.3	94	8
Willie Brown	16	54	472	8.7	45	2
Darrell Green	20	54	621	11.5	83	6
Ed Reed	9	54	1,438	26.6	107	6

TOP 20 PUNTERS (MINIMUM 250 PUNTS)

Player	Years	No.	Yards	Avg.	Long	Blk.
1. Shane Lechler	11	855	40,429	47.3	73	3
2. Donnie Jones	7	543	24,727	45.5	80	2
3. Mat McBriar	7	436	19,827	45.5	75	2
4. Andy Lee	7	645	29,099	45.1	82	2
5. Sammy Baugh	16	338	15,245	45.1	85	9
6. Brandon Fields	4	299	13,417	44.9	71	2
7. Tommy Davis	11	511	22,833	44.7	82	2
8. Jon Ryan	5	388	17,282	44.5	72	3
9. Mike Scifres	8	445	19,810	44.5	71	5
10. Yale Lary	11	503	22,279	44.3	74	4
11. Ben Graham	6	429	18,966	44.2	69	2
12. Chris Kluwe	6	474	20,929	44.2	70	1
13. Dustin Colquitt	6	485	21,410	44.1	81	3
14. Todd Sauerbrun	13	889	39,208	44.1	73	9
15. Bob Scarpitto	8	283	12,408	43.8	87	4
16. Horace Gillom	7	385	16,872	43.8	80	5
17. Jerry Norton	11	358	15,671	43.8	78	2
18. Sam Koch	5	402	17,587	43.7	74	2
19. Dave Lewis	4	285	12,447	43.7	63	0
20. Greg Montgomery	9	524	22,831	43.6	77	8

TOP 20 KICKOFF RETURNERS (MINIMUM 75 RETURNS)

Player	Years	No.	Yards	Avg.	Long	TD
1. Gale Sayers	7	91	2,781	30.6	103	6
2. Lynn Chandnois	7	92	2,720	29.6	93	3
3. Abe Woodson	9	193	5,538	28.7	105	5
4. Buddy Young	6	90	2,514	27.9	104	2
5. Travis Williams	5	102	2,801	27.5	105	6
6. Joe Arenas	7	139	3,798	27.3	96	1
7. Clifton Smith	3	75	2,038	27.2	97	1
8. Clarence Davis	8	79	2,140	27.1	76	0
9. Danieal Manning	5	101	2,711	26.8	83	1
10. Steve Van Buren	8	76	2,030	26.7	98	3
11. Lenny Lyles	12	81	2,161	26.7	103	3
12. Mercury Morris	8	111	2,947	26.5	105	3
13. Ellis Hobbs	6	141	3,739	26.5	108	3
14. Stefan Logan	2	110	2,914	26.5	105	1
15. Bobby Jancik	6	158	4,185	26.5	61	0
16. Mel Renfro	14	85	2,246	26.4	100	2
17. Bobby Mitchell	14	102	2,690	26.4	98	5
18. Terrence McGee	8	207	5,450	26.3	104	5
19. Eric Weems	4	89	2,333	26.2	102	1
20. Ollie Matson	14	143	3,746	26.2	105	6

TOP 20 PUNT RETURNERS (MINIMUM 75 RETURNS)

Player	Years	No.	Yards	Avg.	Long	TD
1. George McAfee	8	112	1,431	12.8	74	2
2. Jack Christiansen	8	85	1,084	12.8	89	8
3. Claude Gibson	5	110	1,381	12.6	85	3
4. Devin Hester	5	178	2,200	12.4	89	10
5. Bill Dudley	9	124	1,515	12.2	96	3
6. Rick Upchurch	9	248	3,008	12.1	92	8
7. Roscoe Parrish	6	130	1,576	12.1	82	3
8. Desmond Howard	11	244	2,895	11.9	95	8
9. Billy Johnson	14	282	3,317	11.8	87	6
10. Mack Herron	3	84	982	11.7	66	0
11. Billy Thompson	13	157	1,814	11.6	60	0
12. Darrien Gordon	9	314	3,601	11.5	94	6
13. Santana Moss	10	112	1,268	11.3	80	3
14. Henry Ellard	16	135	1,527	11.3	83	4
15. Rodger Bird	3	94	1,063	11.3	78	0
16. Bosh Pritchard	6	95	1,072	11.3	81	2
17. DeSean Jackson	3	99	1,112	11.2	85	4
18. Terry Metcalf	6	84	936	11.1	69	1
19. Bob Hayes	11	104	1,158	11.1	90	3
20. Jermaine Lewis	9	295	3,282	11.1	89	6

TOP 20 LEADERS IN SACKS

Player	*Years	No.
1. Bruce Smith	19	200.0
2. Reggie White	15	198.0
3. Kevin Greene	15	160.0
4. Chris Doleman	15	150.5
5. Michael Strahan	15	141.5
6. Richard Dent	15	137.5
John Randle	14	137.5
8. Leslie O'Neal	13	132.5
Jason Taylor	14	132.5
Lawrence Taylor	12	132.5
11. Rickey Jackson	14	128.0
12. Derrick Thomas	11	126.5
13. Simeon Rice	12	122.0
14. Clyde Simmons	15	121.5
15. Sean Jones	13	113.0
16. Greg Townsend	13	109.5
17. Pat Swilling	12	107.5
18. Trace Armstrong	15	106.0
19. Kevin Carter	14	104.5
Neil Smith	13	104.5

*Years played since 1982 when sacks became an official statistic.

POSTSEASON LEADERS

TOP 10 POSTSEASON RUSHERS

Player	Att.	Yards	Avg.	Long	TD
1. Emmitt Smith	349	1,586	4.5	65	19
2. Franco Harris	400	1,556	3.9	50	16
3. Thurman Thomas	339	1,442	4.3	40	16
4. Tony Dorsett	302	1,383	4.6	53	9
5. Marcus Allen	267	1,347	5.0	74	11
6. Terrell Davis	204	1,140	5.6	62	12
7. John Riggins	251	996	4.0	43	12
8. Larry Csonka	225	891	4.0	49	9
9. Chuck Foreman	229	860	3.8	62	7
10. Edgerrin James	218	852	3.9	34	6

TOP 10 POSTSEASON PASSERS

Player	Att.	Comp.	Pct. Comp.	Yards	Avg. Gain	TD	Pct. TD	Int.	Pct. Int.	Rating
1. Aaron Rodgers	174	118	67.8	1,517	8.72	13	7.5	3	1.7	112.6
2. Bart Starr	213	130	61.0	1,753	8.23	15	7.0	3	1.4	104.8
3. Kurt Warner	462	307	66.5	3,952	8.55	31	6.7	14	3.0	102.8
4. Drew Brees	285	189	66.3	2,052	7.20	15	5.3	2	0.7	102.0
5. Joe Montana	734	460	62.7	5,772	7.86	45	6.1	21	2.9	95.6
6. Mark Sanchez	157	95	60.5	1,155	7.36	9	5.7	3	1.9	94.3
7. Ken Anderson	166	110	66.3	1,321	7.96	9	5.4	6	3.6	93.5
8. Joe Theismann	211	128	60.7	1,782	8.45	11	5.2	7	3.3	91.4
9. Peyton Manning	718	453	63.1	5,389	7.51	29	4.0	19	2.6	88.4
10. Troy Aikman	502	320	63.7	3,849	7.67	23	4.6	17	3.4	88.3

TOP 10 POSTSEASON PASS RECEIVERS

Player	No.	Yards	Avg.	Long	TD
1. Jerry Rice	151	2,245	14.9	72	22
2. Hines Ward	88	1,181	13.4	45	10
3. Michael Irvin	87	1,315	15.1	53	8
4. Andre Reed	85	1,229	14.5	72	9
5. Reggie Wayne	83	1,128	13.6	72	9
6. Thurman Thomas	76	672	8.8	27	5
7. Cliff Branch	73	1,289	17.7	72	5
8. Fred Biletnikoff	70	1,167	16.7	57	10
9. Art Monk	69	1,062	15.4	48	7
10. Drew Pearson	67	1,105	16.5	83	8

TOP 10 POSTSEASON INTERCEPTION LEADERS

Player	Interceptions
1. Ronnie Lott	9
Bill Simpson	9
Charlie Waters	9
4. Lester Hayes	8
5. Willie Brown	7
Rodney Harrison	7
Ed Reed	7
Asante Samuel	7
Dennis Thurman	7
9. Bobby Bryant	6
Eric Davis	6
Glen Edwards	6
Darrell Green	6
Cliff Harris	6
Ty Law	6
Vernon Perry	6
Aeneas Williams	6

TOP 10 POSTSEASON SACK LEADERS

Player	Sacks
1. Willie McGinest	16.0
2. Bruce Smith	14.5
3. Reggie White	12.0
4. Charles Haley	11.0
LaMarr Woodley	11.0
6. Richard Dent	10.5
7. Trace Armstrong	10.0
Charles Mann	10.0
Terrell Suggs	10.0
Tony Tolbert	10.0

Sacks became an official statistic in 1982.

ANNUAL SCORING LEADERS

Year	Player, Team	TD	FG	PAT	TP
2010	David Akers, Philadelphia, NFC	0	32	47	143
	Sebastian Janikowski, Oakland, AFC	0	33	43	142
2009	Nate Kaeding, San Diego, AFC	0	32	50	146
	David Akers, Philadelphia, NFC	0	32	43	139
2008	Stephen Gostkowski, New England, AFC	0	36	40	148
	David Akers, Philadelphia, NFC	0	33	45	144
2007	*Mason Crosby, Green Bay, NFC	0	31	48	141
	Randy Moss, New England, AFC	23	0	0	138
2006	LaDainian Tomlinson, AFC	31	0	0	186
	Robbie Gould, Chicago, NFC	0	32	47	143
2005	Shaun Alexander, Seattle, NFC	28	0	0	168
	Shayne Graham, Cincinnati, AFC	0	28	47	131
2004	Adam Vinatieri, New England, AFC	0	31	48	141
	David Akers, Philadelphia, NFC	0	27	41	122
2003	Jeff Wilkins, St. Louis, NFC	0	39	46	163
	Priest Holmes, Kansas City, AFC	27	0	0	162
2002	Priest Holmes, Kansas City, AFC	24	0	0	144
	Jay Feely, Atlanta, NFC	0	32	42	138
2001	Marshall Faulk, St. Louis, NFC	21	0	0	#128
	Mike Vanderjagt, Indianapolis, AFC	0	28	41	125
2000	Marshall Faulk, St. Louis, NFC	26	0	0	##160
	Matt Stover, Baltimore, AFC	0	35	30	135
1999	Mike Vanderjagt, Indianapolis, AFC	0	34	43	145
	Jeff Wilkins, St. Louis, NFC	0	20	64	124
1998	Gary Anderson, Minnesota, NFC	0	35	59	164
	Steve Christie, Buffalo, AFC	0	33	41	140
1997	Mike Hollis, Jacksonville, AFC	0	31	41	134
	Richie Cunningham, Dallas, NFC	0	34	24	126
1996	John Kasay, Carolina, NFC	0	37	34	145
	Cary Blanchard, Indianapolis, AFC	0	36	27	135
1995	Emmitt Smith, Dallas, NFC	25	0	0	150
	Norm Johnson, Pittsburgh, AFC	0	34	39	141
1994	John Carney, San Diego, AFC	0	34	33	135
	Fuad Reveiz, Minnesota, NFC	0	34	30	132
1993	Jeff Jaeger, L.A. Raiders, AFC	0	35	27	132
	Jason Hanson, Detroit, NFC	0	34	28	130
1992	Pete Stoyanovich, Miami, AFC	0	30	34	124
	Morten Andersen, New Orleans, NFC	0	29	33	120
	Chip Lohmiller, Washington, NFC	0	30	30	120
1991	Chip Lohmiller, Washington, NFC	0	31	56	149
	Pete Stoyanovich, Miami, AFC	0	31	28	121
1990	Nick Lowery, Kansas City, AFC	0	34	37	139
	Chip Lohmiller, Washington, NFC	0	30	41	131
1989	Mike Cofer, San Francisco, NFC	0	29	49	136
	*David Treadwell, Denver, AFC	0	27	39	120
1988	Scott Norwood, Buffalo, AFC	0	32	33	129
	Mike Cofer, San Francisco, NFC	0	27	40	121
1987	Jerry Rice, San Francisco, NFC	23	0	0	138
	Jim Breech, Cincinnati, AFC	0	24	25	97
1986	Tony Franklin, New England, AFC	0	32	44	140
	Kevin Butler, Chicago, NFC	0	28	36	120
1985	*Kevin Butler, Chicago, NFC	0	31	51	144
	Gary Anderson, Pittsburgh, AFC	0	33	40	139
1984	Ray Wersching, San Francisco, NFC	0	25	56	131
	Gary Anderson, Pittsburgh, AFC	0	24	45	117
1983	Mark Moseley, Washington, NFC	0	33	62	161
	Gary Anderson, Pittsburgh, AFC	0	27	38	119
1982	*Marcus Allen, L.A. Raiders, AFC	14	0	0	84
	Wendell Tyler, L.A. Rams, NFC	13	0	0	78
1981	Ed Murray, Detroit, NFC	0	25	46	121
	Rafael Septien, Dallas, NFC	0	27	40	121
	Jim Breech, Cincinnati, AFC	0	22	49	115
	Nick Lowery, Kansas City, AFC	0	26	37	115
1980	John Smith, New England, AFC	0	26	51	129
	*Ed Murray, Detroit, NFC	0	27	35	116
1979	John Smith, New England, AFC	0	23	46	115
	Mark Moseley, Washington, NFC	0	25	39	114

Year	Player, Team	TD	FG	PAT	TP
1978	*Frank Corral, Los Angeles, NFC	0	29	31	118
	Pat Leahy, N.Y. Jets, AFC	0	22	41	107
1977	Errol Mann, Oakland, AFC	0	20	39	99
	Walter Payton, Chicago, NFC	16	0	0	96
1976	Toni Linhart, Baltimore, AFC	0	20	49	109
	Mark Moseley, Washington, NFC	0	22	31	97
1975	O.J. Simpson, Buffalo, AFC	23	0	0	138
	Chuck Foreman, Minnesota, NFC	22	0	0	132
1974	Chester Marcol, Green Bay, NFC	0	25	19	94
	Roy Gerela, Pittsburgh, AFC	0	20	33	93
1973	David Ray, Los Angeles, NFC	0	30	40	130
	Roy Gerela, Pittsburgh, AFC	0	29	36	123
1972	*Chester Marcol, Green Bay, NFC	0	33	29	128
	Bobby Howfield, N.Y. Jets, AFC	0	27	40	121
1971	Garo Yepremian, Miami, AFC	0	28	33	117
	Curt Knight, Washington, NFC	0	29	27	114
1970	Fred Cox, Minnesota, NFC	0	30	35	125
	Jan Stenerud, Kansas City, AFC	0	30	26	116
1969	Jim Turner, N.Y. Jets, AFL	0	32	33	129
	Fred Cox, Minnesota, NFL	0	26	43	121
1968	Jim Turner, N.Y. Jets, AFL	0	34	43	145
	Leroy Kelly, Cleveland, NFL	20	0	0	120
1967	Jim Bakken, St. Louis, NFL	0	27	36	117
	George Blanda, Oakland, AFL	0	20	56	116
1966	Gino Cappelletti, Boston, AFL	6	16	35	119
	Bruce Gossett, Los Angeles, NFL	0	28	29	113
1965	*Gale Sayers, Chicago, NFL	22	0	0	132
	Gino Cappelletti, Boston, AFL	9	17	27	132
1964	Gino Cappelletti, Boston, AFL	7	25	36	#155
	Lenny Moore, Baltimore, NFL	20	0	0	120
1963	Gino Cappelletti, Boston, AFL	2	22	35	113
	Don Chandler, N.Y. Giants, NFL	0	18	52	106
1962	Gene Mingo, Denver, AFL	4	27	32	137
	Jim Taylor, Green Bay, NFL	19	0	0	114
1961	Gino Cappelletti, Boston, AFL	8	17	48	147
	Paul Hornung, Green Bay, NFL	10	15	41	146
1960	Paul Hornung, Green Bay, NFL	15	15	41	176
	*Gene Mingo, Denver, AFL	6	18	33	123
1959	Paul Hornung, Green Bay	7	7	31	94
1958	Jim Brown, Cleveland	18	0	0	108
1957	Sam Baker, Washington	1	14	29	77
	Lou Groza, Cleveland	0	15	32	77
1956	Bobby Layne, Detroit	5	12	33	99
1955	Doak Walker, Detroit	7	9	27	96
1954	Bobby Walston, Philadelphia	11	4	36	114
1953	Gordy Soltau, San Francisco	6	10	48	114
1952	Gordy Soltau, San Francisco	7	6	34	94
1951	Elroy (Crazylegs) Hirsch, Los Angeles	17	0	0	102
1950	*Doak Walker, Detroit	11	8	38	128
1949	Pat Harder, Chi. Cardinals	8	3	45	102
	Gene Roberts, N.Y. Giants	17	0	0	102
1948	Pat Harder, Chi. Cardinals	6	7	53	110
1947	Pat Harder, Chi. Cardinals	7	7	39	102
1946	Ted Fritsch, Green Bay	10	9	13	100
1945	Steve Van Buren, Philadelphia	18	0	2	110
1944	Don Hutson, Green Bay	9	0	31	85
1943	Don Hutson, Green Bay	12	3	36	117
1942	Don Hutson, Green Bay	17	1	33	138
1941	Don Hutson, Green Bay	12	1	20	95
1940	Don Hutson, Green Bay	7	0	15	57
1939	Andy Farkas, Washington	11	0	2	68
1938	Clarke Hinkle, Green Bay	7	3	7	58
1937	Jack Manders, Chi. Bears	5	8	15	69
1936	Earl (Dutch) Clark, Detroit	7	4	19	73
1935	Earl (Dutch) Clark, Detroit	6	1	16	55
1934	Jack Manders, Chi. Bears	3	10	31	79
1933	Ken Strong, N.Y. Giants	6	5	13	64
	Glenn Presnell, Portsmouth	6	6	10	64
1932	Earl (Dutch) Clark, Portsmouth	6	3	10	55

*First season of professional football.

#Cappelletti's total and Faulk's total in 2001 include a two-point conversion.
##Faulk's total in 2000 includes 2 two-point conversions.

ANNUAL TOUCHDOWN LEADERS

Year	Player, Team	TD	Rush	Pass	Ret.
2010	Arian Foster, Houston, AFC	18	16	2	0
	Adrian Peterson, Minnesota, NFC	13	12	1	0
2009	Adrian Peterson, Minnesota, NFC	18	18	0	0
	Chris Johnson, Tennessee, AFC	16	14	2	0
	Maurice Jones-Drew, Jacksonville, AFC	16	15	1	0
2008	DeAngelo Williams, Carolina, NFC	20	18	2	0
	Thomas Jones, N.Y. Jets, AFC	15	13	2	0
	LenDale White, Tennessee, AFC	15	15	0	0
2007	Randy Moss, New England, AFC	23	0	23	0
	Terrell Owens, Dallas, NFC	15	0	15	0
2006	LaDainian Tomlinson, San Diego, AFC	31	28	3	0
	Marion Barber, Dallas, NFC	16	14	2	0
	Steven Jackson, St. Louis, NFC	16	13	3	0
2005	Shaun Alexander, Seattle, NFC	28	27	1	0
	Larry Johnson, Kansas City, AFC	21	20	1	0
2004	Shaun Alexander, Seattle, NFC	20	16	4	0
	LaDainian Tomlinson, San Diego, AFC	18	17	1	0
2003	Priest Holmes, Kansas City, AFC	27	27	0	0
	Ahman Green, Green Bay, NFC	20	15	5	0
2002	Priest Holmes, Kansas City, AFC	24	21	3	0
	Shaun Alexander, Seattle, NFC	18	16	2	0
2001	Marshall Faulk, St. Louis, NFC	21	12	9	0
	Shaun Alexander, Seattle, AFC	16	14	2	0
2000	Marshall Faulk, St. Louis, NFC	26	18	8	0
	Edgerrin James, Indianapolis, AFC	18	13	5	0
1999	Stephen Davis, Washington, NFC	17	17	0	0
	*Edgerrin James, Indianapolis, AFC	17	13	4	0
1998	Terrell Davis, Denver, AFC	23	21	2	0
	*Randy Moss, Minnesota, NFC	17	0	17	0
1997	Karim Abdul-Jabbar, Miami, AFC	16	15	1	0
	Barry Sanders, Detroit, NFC	14	11	3	0
1996	Terry Allen, Washington, NFC	21	21	0	0
	Curtis Martin, New England, AFC	17	14	3	0
1995	Emmitt Smith, Dallas, NFC	25	25	0	0
	Carl Pickens, Cincinnati, AFC	17	0	17	0
1994	Emmitt Smith, Dallas, NFC	22	21	1	0
	*Marshall Faulk, Indianapolis, AFC	12	11	1	0
	Natrone Means, San Diego, AFC	12	12	0	0
1993	Jerry Rice, San Francisco, NFC	16	1	15	0
	Marcus Allen, Kansas City, AFC	15	12	3	0
1992	Emmitt Smith, Dallas, NFC	19	18	1	0
	Thurman Thomas, Buffalo, AFC	12	9	3	0
1991	Barry Sanders, Detroit, NFC	17	16	1	0
	Mark Clayton, Miami, AFC	12	0	12	0
	Thurman Thomas, Buffalo, AFC	12	7	5	0
1990	Barry Sanders, Detroit, NFC	16	13	3	0
	Derrick Fenner, Seattle, AFC	15	14	1	0
1989	Dalton Hilliard, New Orleans, NFC	18	13	5	0
	Christian Okoye, Kansas City, AFC	12	12	0	0
	Thurman Thomas, Buffalo, AFC	12	6	6	0
1988	Greg Bell, L.A. Rams, NFC	18	16	2	0
	Eric Dickerson, Indianapolis, AFC	15	14	1	0
	*Ickey Woods, Cincinnati, AFC	15	15	0	0
1987	Jerry Rice, San Francisco, NFC	23	1	22	0
	Johnny Hector, N.Y. Jets, AFC	11	11	0	0
1986	George Rogers, Washington, NFC	18	18	0	0
	Sammy Winder, Denver, AFC	14	9	5	0
1985	Joe Morris, N.Y. Giants, NFC	21	21	0	0
	Louis Lipps, Pittsburgh, AFC	15	1	12	2
1984	Marcus Allen, L.A. Raiders, AFC	18	13	5	0
	Mark Clayton, Miami, AFC	18	0	18	0
	Eric Dickerson, L.A. Rams, NFC	14	14	0	0
	John Riggins, Washington, NFC	14	14	0	0
1983	John Riggins, Washington, NFC	24	24	0	0
	Pete Johnson, Cincinnati, AFC	14	14	0	0
	*Curt Warner, Seattle, AFC	14	13	1	0

Year	Player, Team	TD	Rush	Pass	Ret.
1982	*Marcus Allen, L.A. Raiders, AFC	14	11	3	0
	Wendell Tyler, L.A. Rams, NFC	13	9	4	0
1981	Chuck Muncie, San Diego, AFC	19	19	0	0
	Wendell Tyler, Los Angeles, NFC	17	12	5	0
1980	*Billy Sims, Detroit, NFC	16	13	3	0
	Earl Campbell, Houston, AFC	13	13	0	0
	*Curtis Dickey, Baltimore, AFC	13	11	2	0
	John Jefferson, San Diego, AFC	13	0	13	0
1979	Earl Campbell, Houston, AFC	19	19	0	0
	Walter Payton, Chicago, NFC	16	14	2	0
1978	David Sims, Seattle, AFC	15	14	1	0
	Terdell Middleton, Green Bay, NFC	12	11	1	0
1977	Walter Payton, Chicago, NFC	16	14	2	0
	Nat Moore, Miami, AFC	13	1	12	0
1976	Chuck Foreman, Minnesota, NFC	14	13	1	0
	Franco Harris, Pittsburgh, AFC	14	14	0	0
1975	O.J. Simpson, Buffalo, AFC	23	16	7	0
	Chuck Foreman, Minnesota, NFC	22	13	9	0
1974	Chuck Foreman, Minnesota, NFC	15	9	6	0
	Cliff Branch, Oakland, AFC	13	0	13	0
1973	Larry Brown, Washington, NFC	14	8	6	0
	Floyd Little, Denver, AFC	13	12	1	0
1972	Emerson Boozer, N.Y. Jets, AFC	14	11	3	0
	Ron Johnson, N.Y. Giants, NFC	14	9	5	0
1971	Duane Thomas, Dallas, NFC	13	11	2	0
	Leroy Kelly, Cleveland, AFC	12	10	2	0
1970	Dick Gordon, Chicago, NFC	13	0	13	0
	MacArthur Lane, St. Louis, NFC	13	11	2	0
	Gary Garrison, San Diego, AFC	12	0	12	0
1969	Warren Wells, Oakland, AFL	14	0	14	0
	Tom Matte, Baltimore, NFL	13	11	2	0
	Lance Rentzel, Dallas, NFL	13	0	12	1
1968	Leroy Kelly, Cleveland, NFL	20	16	4	0
	Warren Wells, Oakland, AFL	12	1	11	0
1967	Homer Jones, N.Y. Giants, NFL	14	1	13	0
	Emerson Boozer, N.Y. Jets, AFL	13	10	3	0
1966	Leroy Kelly, Cleveland, NFL	16	15	1	0
	Dan Reeves, Dallas, NFL	16	8	8	0
	Lance Alworth, San Diego, AFL	13	0	13	0
1965	*Gale Sayers, Chicago, NFL	22	14	6	2
	Lance Alworth, San Diego, AFL	14	0	14	0
	Don Maynard, N.Y. Jets, AFL	14	0	14	0
1964	Lenny Moore, Baltimore, NFL	20	16	3	1
	Lance Alworth, San Diego, AFL	15	2	13	0
1963	Art Powell, Oakland, AFL	16	0	16	0
	Jim Brown, Cleveland, NFL	15	12	3	0
1962	Abner Haynes, Dallas, AFL	19	13	6	0
	Jim Taylor, Green Bay, NFL	19	19	0	0
1961	Bill Groman, Houston, AFL	18	1	17	0
	Jim Taylor, Green Bay, NFL	16	15	1	0
1960	Paul Hornung, Green Bay, NFL	15	13	2	0
	Sonny Randle, St. Louis, NFL	15	0	15	0
	Art Powell, N.Y. Titans, AFL	14	0	14	0
1959	Raymond Berry, Baltimore	14	0	14	0
	Jim Brown, Cleveland	14	14	0	0
1958	Jim Brown, Cleveland	18	17	1	0
1957	Lenny Moore, Baltimore	11	3	7	1
1956	Rick Casares, Chi. Bears	14	12	2	0
1955	*Alan Ameche, Baltimore	9	9	0	0
	Harlon Hill, Chi. Bears	9	0	9	0
1954	*Harlon Hill, Chi. Bears	12	0	12	0
1953	Joseph Perry, San Francisco	13	10	3	0
1952	Cloyce Box, Detroit	15	0	15	0
1951	Elroy (Crazylegs) Hirsch, Los Angeles	17	0	17	0
1950	Bob Shaw, Chi. Cardinals	12	0	12	0
1949	Gene Roberts, N.Y. Giants	17	9	8	0
1948	Mal Kutner, Chi. Cardinals	15	1	14	0
1947	Steve Van Buren, Philadelphia	14	13	0	1
1946	Ted Fritsch, Green Bay	10	9	1	0

Year	Player, Team	TD	Rush	Pass	Ret.
1945	Steve Van Buren, Philadelphia	18	15	2	1
1944	Don Hutson, Green Bay	9	0	9	0
	Bill Paschal, N.Y. Giants	9	9	0	0
1943	Don Hutson, Green Bay	12	0	11	1
	*Bill Paschal, N.Y. Giants	12	10	2	0
1942	Don Hutson, Green Bay	17	0	17	0
1941	Don Hutson, Green Bay	12	2	10	0
	George McAfee, Chi. Bears	12	6	3	3
1940	John Drake, Cleveland	9	9	0	0
	Richard Todd, Washington	9	4	4	1
1939	Andrew Farkas, Washington	11	5	5	1
1938	Don Hutson, Green Bay	9	0	9	0
1937	Cliff Battles, Washington	7	5	1	1
	Clarke Hinkle, Green Bay	7	5	2	0
	Don Hutson, Green Bay	7	0	7	0
1936	Don Hutson, Green Bay	9	0	8	1
1935	*Don Hutson, Green Bay	7	0	6	1
1934	*Beattie Feathers, Chi. Bears	9	8	1	0
1933	*Charlie (Buckets) Goldenberg, Green Bay	7	4	1	2
	John (Shipwreck) Kelly, Brooklyn	7	2	3	2
	*Elvin (Kink) Richards, N.Y. Giants	7	4	3	0
1932	Earl (Dutch) Clark, Portsmouth	6	3	3	0
	Red Grange, Chi. Bears	6	3	3	0

*First season of professional football.

ANNUAL LEADERS—MOST FIELD GOALS MADE

Year	Player, Team	Att.	Made	Pct.
2010	Josh Brown, St. Louis, NFC	39	33	84.6
	Sebastian Janikowski, Oakland, AFC	41	33	80.5
2009	Nate Kaeding, San Diego, AFC	35	32	91.4
	David Akers, Philadelphia, NFC	37	32	86.5
2008	Stephen Gostkowski, New England, AFC	40	36	90.0
	John Carney, N.Y. Giants, NFC	38	35	92.1
2007	Rob Bironas, Tennessee, AFC	39	35	89.7
	*Mason Crosby, Green Bay, NFC	39	31	79.5
	Robbie Gould, Chicago, NFC	36	31	86.1
2006	Robbie Gould, Chicago, NFC	36	32	88.9
	Jeff Wilkins, St. Louis, NFC	37	32	86.5
	Matt Stover, Baltimore, AFC	30	28	93.3
2005	Neil Rackers, Arizona, NFC	42	40	95.2
	Matt Stover, Baltimore, AFC	34	30	88.2
2004	Adam Vinatieri, New England, AFC	33	31	93.9
	David Akers, Philadelphia, NFC	32	27	84.4
2003	Jeff Wilkins, St. Louis, NFC	42	39	92.9
	Mike Vanderjagt, Indianapolis, AFC	37	37	100.0
2002	Jay Feely, Atlanta, NFC	40	32	80.0
	Martin Gramatica, Tampa Bay, NFC	39	32	82.1
	Adam Vinatieri, New England, AFC	30	27	90.0
2001	Jason Elam, Denver, AFC	36	31	86.1
	*Jay Feely, Atlanta, NFC	37	29	78.4
2000	Matt Stover, Baltimore, AFC	39	35	89.7
	Ryan Longwell, Green Bay, NFC	38	33	86.8
1999	Olindo Mare, Miami, AFC	46	39	84.8
	*Martin Gramatica, Tampa Bay, NFC	32	27	84.4
1998	Al Del Greco, Tennessee, AFC	39	36	92.3
	Gary Anderson, Minnesota, NFC	35	35	100.0
1997	Richie Cunningham, Dallas, NFC	37	34	91.9
	Cary Blanchard, Indianapolis, AFC	41	32	78.1
1996	John Kasay, Carolina, NFC	45	37	82.2
	Cary Blanchard, Indianapolis, AFC	40	36	90.0
1995	Norm Johnson, Pittsburgh, AFC	41	34	82.9
	Morten Andersen, Atlanta, NFC	37	31	83.8
1994	John Carney, San Diego, AFC	38	34	89.5
	Fuad Reveiz, Minnesota, NFC	39	34	87.2
1993	Jeff Jaeger, L.A. Raiders, AFC	44	35	79.5
	Jason Hanson, Detroit, NFC	43	34	79.1
1992	Pete Stoyanovich, Miami, AFC	37	30	81.1
	Chip Lohmiller, Washington, NFC	40	30	75.0

Year	Player, Team	Att.	Made	Pct.
1991	Pete Stoyanovich, Miami, AFC	37	31	83.8
	Chip Lohmiller, Washington, NFC	43	31	72.1
1990	Nick Lowery, Kansas City, AFC	37	34	91.9
	Chip Lohmiller, Washington, NFC	40	30	75.0
1989	Rich Karlis, Minnesota, NFC	39	31	79.5
	*David Treadwell, Denver, AFC	33	27	81.8
1988	Scott Norwood, Buffalo, AFC	37	32	86.5
	Mike Cofer, San Francisco, NFC	38	27	71.1
1987	Morten Andersen, New Orleans, NFC	36	28	77.8
	Dean Biasucci, Indianapolis, AFC	27	24	88.9
	Jim Breech, Cincinnati, AFC	30	24	80.0
1986	Tony Franklin, New England, AFC	41	32	78.0
	Kevin Butler, Chicago, NFC	41	28	68.3
1985	Gary Anderson, Pittsburgh, AFC	42	33	78.6
	Morten Andersen, New Orleans, NFC	35	31	88.6
	*Kevin Butler, Chicago, NFC	37	31	83.8
1984	*Paul McFadden, Philadelphia, NFC	37	30	81.1
	Gary Anderson, Pittsburgh, AFC	32	24	75.0
	Matt Bahr, Cleveland, AFC	32	24	75.0
1983	*Ali-Haji-Sheikh, N.Y. Giants, NFC	42	35	83.3
	*Raul Allegre, Baltimore, AFC	35	30	85.7
1982	Mark Moseley, Washington, NFC	21	20	95.2
	Nick Lowery, Kansas City, AFC	24	19	79.2
1981	Rafael Septien, Dallas, NFC	35	27	77.1
	Nick Lowery, Kansas City, AFC	36	26	72.2
1980	*Ed Murray, Detroit, NFC	42	27	64.3
	John Smith, New England, AFC	34	26	76.5
	Fred Steinfort, Denver, AFC	34	26	76.5
1979	Mark Moseley, Washington, NFC	33	25	75.8
	John Smith, New England, AFC	33	23	69.7
1978	*Frank Corral, Los Angeles, NFC	43	29	67.4
	Pat Leahy, N.Y. Jets, AFC	30	22	73.3
1977	Mark Moseley, Washington, NFC	37	21	56.8
	Errol Mann, Oakland, AFC	28	20	71.4
1976	Mark Moseley, Washington, NFC	34	22	64.7
	Jan Stenerud, Kansas City, AFC	38	21	55.3
1975	Jan Stenerud, Kansas City, AFC	32	22	68.8
	Toni Fritsch, Dallas, NFC	35	22	62.9
1974	Chester Marcol, Green Bay, NFC	39	25	64.1
	Roy Gerela, Pittsburgh, AFC	29	20	69.0
1973	David Ray, Los Angeles, NFC	47	30	63.8
	Roy Gerela, Pittsburgh, AFC	43	29	67.4
1972	*Chester Marcol, Green Bay, NFC	48	33	68.8
	Roy Gerela, Pittsburgh, AFC	41	28	68.3
1971	Curt Knight, Washington, NFC	49	29	59.2
	Garo Yepremian, Miami, AFC	40	28	70.0
1970	Jan Stenerud, Kansas City, AFC	42	30	71.4
	Fred Cox, Minnesota, NFC	46	30	65.2
1969	Jim Turner, N.Y. Jets, AFL	47	32	68.1
	Fred Cox, Minnesota, NFL	37	26	70.3
1968	Jim Turner, N.Y. Jets, AFL	46	34	73.9
	Mac Percival, Chicago, NFL	36	25	69.4
1967	Jim Bakken, St. Louis, NFL	39	27	69.2
	Jan Stenerud, Kansas City, AFL	36	21	58.3
1966	Bruce Gossett, Los Angeles, NFL	49	28	57.1
	Mike Mercer, Oakland-Kansas City, AFL	30	21	70.0
1965	Pete Gogolak, Buffalo, AFL	46	28	60.9
	Fred Cox, Minnesota, NFL	35	23	65.7
1964	Jim Bakken, St. Louis, NFL	38	25	65.8
	Gino Cappelletti, Boston, AFL	39	25	64.1
1963	Jim Martin, Baltimore, NFL	39	24	61.5
	Gino Cappelletti, Boston, AFL	38	22	57.9
1962	Gene Mingo, Denver, AFL	39	27	69.2
	Lou Michaels, Pittsburgh, NFL	42	26	61.9
1961	Steve Myhra, Baltimore, NFL	39	21	53.8
	Gino Cappelletti, Boston, AFL	32	17	53.1
1960	Tommy Davis, San Francisco, NFL	32	19	59.4
	*Gene Mingo, Denver, AFL	28	18	64.3

Year	Player, Team	Att.	Made	Pct.
1959	Pat Summerall, N.Y. Giants	29	20	69.0
1958	Paige Cothren, Los Angeles	25	14	56.0
	*Tom Miner, Pittsburgh	28	14	50.0
1957	Lou Groza, Cleveland	22	15	68.2
1956	Sam Baker, Washington	25	17	68.0
1955	Fred Cone, Green Bay	24	16	66.7
1954	Lou Groza, Cleveland	24	16	66.7
1953	Lou Groza, Cleveland	26	23	88.5
1952	Lou Groza, Cleveland	33	19	57.6
1951	Bob Waterfield, Los Angeles	23	13	56.5
1950	Lou Groza, Cleveland	19	13	68.4
1949	Cliff Patton, Philadelphia	18	9	50.0
	Bob Waterfield, Los Angeles	16	9	56.3
1948	Cliff Patton, Philadelphia	12	8	66.7
1947	Ward Cuff, Green Bay	16	7	43.8
	Pat Harder, Chi. Cardinals	10	7	70.0
	Bob Waterfield, Los Angeles	16	7	43.8
1946	Ted Fritsch, Green Bay	17	9	52.9
1945	Joe Aguirre, Washington	13	7	53.8
1944	Ken Strong, N.Y. Giants	12	6	50.0
1943	Ward Cuff, N.Y. Giants	9	3	33.3
	Don Hutson, Green Bay	5	3	60.0
1942	Bill Daddio, Chi. Cardinals	10	5	50.0
1941	Clarke Hinkle, Green Bay	14	6	42.9
1940	Clarke Hinkle, Green Bay	14	9	64.3
1939	Ward Cuff, N.Y. Giants	16	7	43.8
1938	Ward Cuff, N.Y. Giants	9	5	55.6
	Ralph Kercheval, Brooklyn	13	5	38.5
1937	Jack Manders, Chi. Bears		8	
1936	Jack Manders, Chi. Bears		7	
	Armand Niccolai, Pittsburgh		7	
1935	Armand Niccolai, Pittsburgh		6	
	Bill Smith, Chi. Cardinals		6	
1934	Jack Manders, Chi. Bears		10	
1933	*Jack Manders, Chi. Bears		6	
	Glenn Presnell, Portsmouth		6	
1932	Earl (Dutch) Clark, Portsmouth		3	

*First season of professional football.

ANNUAL RUSHING LEADERS

Year	Player, Team	Att.	Yards	Avg.	TD
2010	Arian Foster, Houston, AFC	327	1,616	4.9	16
	Michael Turner, Atlanta, NFC	334	1,371	4.1	12
2009	Chris Johnson, Tennessee, AFC	358	2,006	5.6	14
	Steven Jackson, St. Louis, NFC	324	1,416	4.4	4
2008	Adrian Peterson, Minnesota, NFC	363	1,760	4.9	10
	Thomas Jones, N.Y. Jets, AFC	290	1,312	4.5	13
2007	LaDainian Tomlinson, San Diego, AFC	315	1,474	4.7	15
	*Adrian Peterson, Minnesota, NFC	238	1,341	5.6	12
2006	LaDainian Tomlinson, San Diego, AFC	348	1,815	5.2	28
	Frank Gore, San Francisco, NFC	312	1,695	5.4	8
2005	Shaun Alexander, Seattle, NFC	370	1,880	5.1	27
	Larry Johnson, Kansas City, AFC	336	1,750	5.2	20
2004	Curtis Martin, N.Y. Jets, AFC	371	1,697	4.6	12
	Shaun Alexander, Seattle, NFC	353	1,696	4.8	16
2003	Jamal Lewis, Baltimore, AFC	387	2,066	5.3	14
	Ahman Green, Green Bay, NFC	355	1,883	5.3	15
2002	Ricky Williams, Miami, AFC	383	1,853	4.8	16
	Deuce McAllister, New Orleans, NFC	325	1,388	4.3	13
2001	Priest Holmes, Kansas City, AFC	327	1,555	4.8	8
	Stephen Davis, Washington, NFC	356	1,432	4.0	5
2000	Edgerrin James, Indianapolis, AFC	387	1,709	4.4	13
	Robert Smith, Minnesota, NFC	295	1,521	5.2	7
1999	*Edgerrin James, Indianapolis, AFC	369	1,553	4.2	13
	Stephen Davis, Washington, NFC	290	1,405	4.8	17
1998	Terrell Davis, Denver, AFC	392	2,008	5.1	21
	Jamal Anderson, Atlanta, NFC	410	1,846	4.5	14
1997	Barry Sanders, Detroit, NFC	335	2,053	6.1	11
	Terrell Davis, Denver, AFC	369	1,750	4.7	15

Year	Player, Team	Att.	Yards	Avg.	TD
1996	Barry Sanders, Detroit, NFC	307	1,553	5.1	11
	Terrell Davis, Denver, AFC	345	1,538	4.5	13
1995	Emmitt Smith, Dallas, NFC	377	1,773	4.7	25
	*Curtis Martin, New England, AFC	368	1,487	4.0	14
1994	Barry Sanders, Detroit, NFC	331	1,883	5.7	7
	Chris Warren, Seattle, AFC	333	1,545	4.6	9
1993	Emmitt Smith, Dallas, NFC	283	1,486	5.3	9
	Thurman Thomas, Buffalo, AFC	355	1,315	3.7	6
1992	Emmitt Smith, Dallas, NFC	373	1,713	4.6	18
	Barry Foster, Pittsburgh, AFC	390	1,690	4.3	11
1991	Emmitt Smith, Dallas, NFC	365	1,563	4.3	12
	Thurman Thomas, Buffalo, AFC	288	1,407	4.9	7
1990	Barry Sanders, Detroit, NFC	255	1,304	5.1	13
	Thurman Thomas, Buffalo, AFC	271	1,297	4.8	11
1989	Christian Okoye, Kansas City, AFC	370	1,480	4.0	12
	*Barry Sanders, Detroit, NFC	280	1,470	5.3	14
1988	Eric Dickerson, Indianapolis, AFC	388	1,659	4.3	14
	Herschel Walker, Dallas, NFC	361	1,514	4.2	5
1987	Charles White, L.A. Rams, NFC	324	1,374	4.2	11
	Eric Dickerson, Indianapolis, AFC	223	1,011	4.5	5
1986	Eric Dickerson, L.A. Rams, NFC	404	1,821	4.5	11
	Curt Warner, Seattle, AFC	319	1,481	4.6	13
1985	Marcus Allen, L.A. Raiders, AFC	380	1,759	4.6	11
	Gerald Riggs, Atlanta, NFC	397	1,719	4.3	10
1984	Eric Dickerson, L.A. Rams, NFC	379	2,105	5.6	14
	Earnest Jackson, San Diego, AFC	296	1,179	4.0	8
1983	*Eric Dickerson, L.A. Rams, NFC	390	1,808	4.6	18
	*Curt Warner, Seattle, AFC	335	1,449	4.3	13
1982	Freeman McNeil, N.Y. Jets, AFC	151	786	5.2	6
	Tony Dorsett, Dallas, NFC	177	745	4.2	5
1981	*George Rogers, New Orleans, NFC	378	1,674	4.4	13
	Earl Campbell, Houston, AFC	361	1,376	3.8	10
1980	Earl Campbell, Houston, AFC	373	1,934	5.2	13
	Walter Payton, Chicago, NFC	317	1,460	4.6	6
1979	Earl Campbell, Houston, AFC	368	1,697	4.6	19
	Walter Payton, Chicago, NFC	369	1,610	4.4	14
1978	*Earl Campbell, Houston, AFC	302	1,450	4.8	13
	Walter Payton, Chicago, NFC	333	1,395	4.2	11
1977	Walter Payton, Chicago, NFC	339	1,852	5.5	14
	Mark van Eeghen, Oakland, AFC	324	1,273	3.9	7
1976	O.J. Simpson, Buffalo, AFC	290	1,503	5.2	8
	Walter Payton, Chicago, NFC	311	1,390	4.5	13
1975	O.J. Simpson, Buffalo, AFC	329	1,817	5.5	16
	Jim Otis, St. Louis, NFC	269	1,076	4.0	5
1974	Otis Armstrong, Denver, AFC	263	1,407	5.3	9
	Lawrence McCutcheon, Los Angeles, NFC	236	1,109	4.7	3
1973	O.J. Simpson, Buffalo, AFC	332	2,003	6.0	12
	John Brockington, Green Bay, NFC	265	1,144	4.3	3
1972	O.J. Simpson, Buffalo, AFC	292	1,251	4.3	6
	Larry Brown, Washington, NFC	285	1,216	4.3	8
1971	Floyd Little, Denver, AFC	284	1,133	4.0	6
	*John Brockington, Green Bay, NFC	216	1,105	5.1	4
1970	Larry Brown, Washington, NFC	237	1,125	4.7	5
	Floyd Little, Denver, AFC	209	901	4.3	3
1969	Gale Sayers, Chicago, NFL	236	1,032	4.4	8
	Dickie Post, San Diego, AFL	182	873	4.8	6
1968	Leroy Kelly, Cleveland, NFL	248	1,239	5.0	16
	*Paul Robinson, Cincinnati, AFL	238	1,023	4.3	8
1967	Jim Nance, Boston, AFL	269	1,216	4.5	7
	Leroy Kelly, Cleveland, NFL	235	1,205	5.1	11
1966	Jim Nance, Boston, AFL	299	1,458	4.9	11
	Gale Sayers, Chicago, NFL	229	1,231	5.4	8
1965	Jim Brown, Cleveland, NFL	289	1,544	5.3	17
	Paul Lowe, San Diego, AFL	222	1,121	5.0	7
1964	Jim Brown, Cleveland, NFL	280	1,446	5.2	7
	Cookie Gilchrist, Buffalo, AFL	230	981	4.3	6
1963	Jim Brown, Cleveland, NFL	291	1,863	6.4	12
	Clem Daniels, Oakland, AFL	215	1,099	5.1	3

Year	Player, Team	Att.	Yards	Avg.	TD
1962	Jim Taylor, Green Bay, NFL	272	1,474	5.4	19
	Cookie Gilchrist, Buffalo, AFL	214	1,096	5.1	13
1961	Jim Brown, Cleveland, NFL	305	1,408	4.6	8
	Billy Cannon, Houston, AFL	200	948	4.7	6
1960	Jim Brown, Cleveland, NFL	215	1,257	5.8	9
	*Abner Haynes, Dall. Texans, AFL	156	875	5.6	9
1959	Jim Brown, Cleveland	290	1,329	4.6	14
1958	Jim Brown, Cleveland	257	1,527	5.9	17
1957	*Jim Brown, Cleveland	202	942	4.7	9
1956	Rick Casares, Chi. Bears	234	1,126	4.8	12
1955	*Alan Ameche, Baltimore	213	961	4.5	9
1954	Joe Perry, San Francisco	173	1,049	6.1	8
1953	Joe Perry, San Francisco	192	1,018	5.3	10
1952	Dan Towler, Los Angeles	156	894	5.7	10
1951	Eddie Price, N.Y. Giants	271	971	3.6	7
1950	Marion Motley, Cleveland	140	810	5.8	3
1949	Steve Van Buren, Philadelphia	263	1,146	4.4	11
1948	Steve Van Buren, Philadelphia	201	945	4.7	10
1947	Steve Van Buren, Philadelphia	217	1,008	4.6	13
1946	Bill Dudley, Pittsburgh	146	604	4.1	3
1945	Steve Van Buren, Philadelphia	143	832	5.8	15
1944	Bill Paschal, N.Y. Giants	196	737	3.8	9
1943	*Bill Paschal, N.Y. Giants	147	572	3.9	10
1942	*Bill Dudley, Pittsburgh	162	696	4.3	5
1941	Clarence (Pug) Manders, Brooklyn	111	486	4.4	5
1940	Byron (Whizzer) White, Detroit	146	514	3.5	5
1939	*Bill Osmanski, Chicago	121	699	5.8	7
1938	*Byron (Whizzer) White, Pittsburgh	152	567	3.7	4
1937	Cliff Battles, Washington	216	874	4.0	5
1936	*Alphonse (Tuffy) Leemans, N.Y. Giants	206	830	4.0	2
1935	Doug Russell, Chi. Cardinals	140	499	3.6	0
1934	*Beattie Feathers, Chi. Bears	119	1,004	8.4	8
1933	Jim Musick, Boston	173	809	4.7	5
1932	*Cliff Battles, Boston	148	576	3.9	3

*First season of professional football.

ANNUAL PASSING LEADERS

(Current rating system implemented in 1973)

Year	Player, Team	Att.	Comp.	Yards	TD	Int.	Rating
2010	Tom Brady, New England, AFC	492	324	3,900	36	4	111.0
	Aaron Rodgers, Green Bay, NFC	475	312	3,922	28	11	101.2
2009	Drew Brees, New Orleans, NFC	514	363	4,388	34	11	109.6
	Philip Rivers, San Diego, AFC	486	317	4,254	28	9	104.4
2008	Philip Rivers, San Diego, AFC	478	312	4,009	34	11	105.5
	Kurt Warner, Arizona, NFC	598	401	4,583	30	14	96.9
2007	Tom Brady, New England, AFC	578	398	4,806	50	8	117.2
	Tony Romo, Dallas, NFC	520	335	4,211	36	19	97.4
2006	Peyton Manning, Indianapolis, AFC	557	362	4,397	31	9	101.0
	Drew Brees, New Orleans, NFC	554	356	4,418	26	11	96.2
2005	Peyton Manning, Indianapolis, AFC	453	305	3,747	28	10	104.1
	Matt Hasselbeck, Seattle, NFC	449	294	3,459	24	9	98.2
2004	Peyton Manning, Indianapolis, AFC	497	336	4,557	49	10	121.1
	Daunte Culpepper, Minnesota, NFC	548	379	4,717	39	11	110.9
2003	Steve McNair, Tennessee, AFC	400	250	3,215	24	7	100.4
	Daunte Culpepper, Minnesota, NFC	454	295	3,479	25	11	96.4
2002	Chad Pennington, N.Y. Jets, AFC	399	275	3,120	22	6	104.2
	Brad Johnson, Tampa Bay, NFC	451	281	3,049	22	6	92.9
2001	Kurt Warner, St. Louis, NFC	546	375	4,830	36	22	101.4
	Rich Gannon, Oakland, AFC	549	361	3,828	27	9	95.5
2000	Brian Griese, Denver, AFC	336	216	2,688	19	4	102.9
	Trent Green, St. Louis, NFC	240	145	2,063	16	5	101.8
1999	Kurt Warner, St. Louis, NFC	499	325	4,353	41	13	109.2
	Peyton Manning, Indianapolis, AFC	533	331	4,135	26	15	90.7
1998	Randall Cunningham, Minnesota, NFC	425	259	3,704	34	10	106.0
	Vinny Testaverde, N.Y. Jets, AFC	421	259	3,256	29	7	101.6
1997	Steve Young, San Francisco, NFC	356	241	3,029	19	6	104.7
	Mark Brunell, Jacksonville, AFC	435	264	3,281	18	7	91.2
1996	Steve Young, San Francisco NFC	316	214	2,410	14	6	97.2
	John Elway, Denver, AFC	466	287	3,328	26	14	89.2

Year	Player, Team	Att.	Comp.	Yards	TD	Int.	Rating
1995	Jim Harbaugh, Indianapolis, AFC	314	200	2,575	17	5	100.7
	Brett Favre, Green Bay, NFC	570	359	4,413	38	13	99.5
1994	Steve Young, San Francisco, NFC	461	324	3,969	35	10	112.8
	Dan Marino, Miami, AFC	615	385	4,453	30	17	89.2
1993	Steve Young, San Francisco, NFC	462	314	4,023	29	16	101.5
	John Elway, Denver, AFC	551	348	4,030	25	10	92.8
1992	Steve Young, San Francisco, NFC	402	268	3,465	25	7	107.0
	Warren Moon, Houston, AFC	346	224	2,521	18	12	89.3
1991	Steve Young, San Francisco, NFC	279	180	2,517	17	8	101.8
	Jim Kelly, Buffalo, AFC	474	304	3,844	33	17	97.6
1990	Jim Kelly, Buffalo, AFC	346	219	2,829	24	9	101.2
	Phil Simms, N.Y. Giants, NFC	311	184	2,284	15	4	92.7
1989	Joe Montana, San Francisco, NFC	386	271	3,521	26	8	112.4
	Boomer Esiason, Cincinnati, AFC	455	258	3,525	28	11	92.1
1988	Boomer Esiason, Cincinnati, AFC	388	223	3,572	28	14	97.4
	Wade Wilson, Minnesota, NFC	332	204	2,746	15	9	91.5
1987	Joe Montana, San Francisco, NFC	398	266	3,054	31	13	102.1
	Bernie Kosar, Cleveland, AFC	389	241	3,033	22	9	95.4
1986	Tommy Kramer, Minnesota, NFC	372	208	3,000	24	10	92.6
	Dan Marino, Miami, AFC	623	378	4,746	44	23	92.5
1985	Ken O'Brien, N.Y. Jets, AFC	488	297	3,888	25	8	96.2
	Joe Montana, San Francisco, NFC	494	303	3,653	27	13	91.3
1984	Dan Marino, Miami, AFC	564	362	5,084	48	17	108.9
	Joe Montana, San Francisco, NFC	432	279	3,630	28	10	102.9
1983	Steve Bartkowski, Atlanta, NFC	432	274	3,167	22	5	97.6
	*Dan Marino, Miami, AFC	296	173	2,210	20	6	96.0
1982	Ken Anderson, Cincinnati, AFC	309	218	2,495	12	9	95.3
	Joe Theismann, Washington, NFC	252	161	2,033	13	9	91.3
1981	Ken Anderson, Cincinnati, AFC	479	300	3,754	29	10	98.4
	Joe Montana, San Francisco, NFC	488	311	3,565	19	12	88.4
1980	Brian Sipe, Cleveland, AFC	554	337	4,132	30	14	91.4
	Ron Jaworski, Philadelphia, NFC	451	257	3,529	27	12	91.0
1979	Roger Staubach, Dallas, NFC	461	267	3,586	27	11	92.3
	Dan Fouts, San Diego, AFC	530	332	4,082	24	24	82.6
1978	Roger Staubach, Dallas, NFC	413	231	3,190	25	16	84.9
	Terry Bradshaw, Pittsburgh, AFC	368	207	2,915	28	20	84.7
1977	Bob Griese, Miami, AFC	307	180	2,252	22	13	87.8
	Roger Staubach, Dallas, NFC	361	210	2,620	18	9	87.0
1976	Ken Stabler, Oakland, AFC	291	194	2,737	27	17	103.4
	James Harris, Los Angeles, NFC	158	91	1,460	8	6	89.6
1975	Ken Anderson, Cincinnati, AFC	377	228	3,169	21	11	93.9
	Fran Tarkenton, Minnesota, NFC	425	273	2,994	25	13	91.8
1974	Ken Anderson, Cincinnati, AFC	328	213	2,667	18	10	95.7
	Sonny Jurgensen, Washington, NFC	167	107	1,185	11	5	94.5
1973	Roger Staubach, Dallas, NFC	286	179	2,428	23	15	94.6
	Ken Stabler, Oakland, AFC	260	163	1,997	14	10	88.3
1972	Norm Snead, N.Y. Giants, NFC	325	196	2,307	17	12	
	Earl Morrall, Miami, AFC	150	83	1,360	11	7	
1971	Roger Staubach, Dallas, NFC	211	126	1,882	15	4	
	Bob Griese, Miami, AFC	263	145	2,089	19	9	
1970	John Brodie, San Francisco, NFC	378	223	2,941	24	10	
	Daryle Lamonica, Oakland, AFC	356	179	2,516	22	15	
1969	Sonny Jurgensen, Washington, NFL	442	274	3,102	22	15	
	*Greg Cook, Cincinnati, AFL	197	106	1,854	15	11	
1968	Len Dawson, Kansas City, AFL	224	131	2,109	17	9	
	Earl Morrall, Baltimore, NFL	317	182	2,909	26	17	
1967	Sonny Jurgensen, Washington, NFL	508	288	3,747	31	16	
	Daryle Lamonica, Oakland, AFL	425	220	3,228	30	20	
1966	Bart Starr, Green Bay, NFL	251	156	2,257	14	3	
	Len Dawson, Kansas City, AFL	284	159	2,527	26	10	
1965	Rudy Bukich, Chicago, NFL	312	176	2,641	20	9	
	John Hadl, San Diego, AFL	348	174	2,798	20	21	
1964	Len Dawson, Kansas City, AFL	354	199	2,879	30	18	
	Bart Starr, Green Bay, NFL	272	163	2,144	15	4	
1963	Y.A. Tittle, N.Y. Giants, NFL	367	221	3,145	36	14	
	Tobin Rote, San Diego, AFL	286	170	2,510	20	17	
1962	Len Dawson, Dallas Texans, AFL	310	189	2,759	29	17	
	Bart Starr, Green Bay, NFL	285	178	2,438	12	9	

Year	Player, Team	Att.	Comp.	Yards	TD	Int.	Rating
1961	George Blanda, Houston, AFL	362	187	3,330	36	22	
	Milt Plum, Cleveland, NFL	302	177	2,416	18	10	
1960	Milt Plum, Cleveland, NFL	250	151	2,297	21	5	
	Jack Kemp, L.A. Chargers, AFL	406	211	3,018	20	25	
1959	Charlie Conerly, N.Y. Giants	194	113	1,706	14	4	
1958	Eddie LeBaron, Washington	145	79	1,365	11	10	
1957	Tommy O'Connell, Cleveland	110	63	1,229	9	8	
1956	Ed Brown, Chicago Bears	168	96	1,667	11	12	
1955	Otto Graham, Cleveland	185	98	1,721	15	8	
1954	Norm Van Brocklin, Los Angeles	260	139	2,637	13	21	
1953	Otto Graham, Cleveland	258	167	2,722	11	9	
1952	Norm Van Brocklin, Los Angeles	205	113	1,736	14	17	
1951	Bob Waterfield, Los Angeles	176	88	1,566	13	10	
1950	Norm Van Brocklin, Los Angeles	233	127	2,061	18	14	
1949	Sammy Baugh, Washington	255	145	1,903	18	14	
1948	Tommy Thompson, Philadelphia	246	141	1,965	25	11	
1947	Sammy Baugh, Washington	354	210	2,938	25	15	
1946	Bob Waterfield, Los Angeles	251	127	1,747	18	17	
1945	Sammy Baugh, Washington	182	128	1,669	11	4	
	Sid Luckman, Chicago Bears	217	117	1,725	14	10	
1944	Frank Filchock, Washington	147	84	1,139	13	9	
1943	Sammy Baugh, Washington	239	133	1,754	23	19	
1942	Cecil Isbell, Green Bay	268	146	2,021	24	14	
1941	Cecil Isbell, Green Bay	206	117	1,479	15	11	
1940	Sammy Baugh, Washington	177	111	1,367	12	10	
1939	*Parker Hall, Cleveland	208	106	1,227	9	13	
1938	Ed Danowski, N.Y. Giants	129	70	848	7	8	
1937	*Sammy Baugh, Washington	171	81	1,127	8	14	
1936	Arnie Herber, Green Bay	173	77	1,239	11	13	
1935	Ed Danowski, N.Y. Giants	113	57	794	10	9	
1934	Arnie Herber, Green Bay	115	42	799	8	12	
1933	*Harry Newman, N.Y. Giants	136	53	973	11	17	
1932	Arnie Herber, Green Bay	101	37	639	9	9	

*First season of professional football.

ANNUAL PASSING TOUCHDOWN LEADERS

Year	Player, Team	TD
2010	Tom Brady, New England, AFC	36
	Drew Brees, New Orleans, NFC	33
2009	Drew Brees, New Orleans, NFC	34
	Peyton Manning, Indianapolis, AFC	33
2008	Drew Brees, New Orleans, NFC	34
	Philip Rivers, San Diego, AFC	34
2007	Tom Brady, New England, AFC	50
	Tony Romo, Dallas, NFC	36
2006	Peyton Manning, Indianapolis, AFC	31
	Drew Brees, New Orleans, NFC	26
2005	Carson Palmer, Cincinnati, AFC	32
	Jake Delhomme, Carolina, NFC	24
	Matt Hasselbeck, Seattle, NFC	24
	Eli Manning, N.Y. Giants, NFC	24
2004	Peyton Manning, Indianapolis, AFC	49
	Daunte Culpepper, Minnesota, NFC	39
2003	Brett Favre, Green Bay, NFC	32
	Peyton Manning, Indianapolis, AFC	29
2002	Tom Brady, New England, AFC	28
	Aaron Brooks, New Orleans, NFC	27
	Brett Favre, Green Bay, NFC	27
2001	Kurt Warner, St. Louis, NFC	36
	Rich Gannon, Oakland, AFC	27
2000	Daunte Culpepper, Minnesota, NFC	33
	Peyton Manning, Indianapolis, AFC	33
1999	Kurt Warner, St. Louis, NFC	41
	Peyton Manning, Indianapolis, AFC	26
1998	Steve Young, San Francisco, NFC	36
	Vinny Testaverde, N.Y. Jets, AFC	29
1997	Brett Favre, Green Bay, NFC	35
	Jeff George, Oakland, AFC	29
1996	Brett Favre, Green Bay, NFC	39
	Vinny Testaverde, Baltimore, AFC	33

Year	Player, Team	TD
1995	Brett Favre, Green Bay, NFC	38
	Jeff Blake, Cincinnati, AFC	28
1994	Steve Young, San Francisco, NFC	35
	Dan Marino, Miami, AFC	30
1993	Steve Young, San Francisco, NFC	29
	John Elway, Denver, AFC	25
1992	Steve Young, San Francisco, NFC	25
	Dan Marino, Miami, AFC	24
1991	Jim Kelly, Buffalo, AFC	33
	Mark Rypien, Washington, NFC	28
1990	Warren Moon, Houston, AFC	33
	Randall Cunningham, Philadelphia, NFC	30
1989	Jim Everett, L.A. Rams, NFC	29
	Boomer Esiason, Cincinnati, AFC	28
1988	Jim Everett, L.A. Rams, NFC	31
	Boomer Esiason, Cincinnati, AFC	28
	Dan Marino, Miami, AFC	28
1987	Joe Montana, San Francisco, NFC	31
	Dan Marino, Miami, AFC	26
1986	Dan Marino, Miami, AFC	44
	Tommy Kramer, Minnesota, NFC	24
1985	Dan Marino, Miami, AFC	30
	Joe Montana, San Francisco, NFC	27
1984	Dan Marino, Miami, AFC	48
	Neil Lomax, St. Louis, NFC	28
	Joe Montana, San Francisco, NFC	28
1983	Lynn Dickey, Green Bay, NFC	32
	Joe Ferguson, Buffalo, AFC	26
	Brian Sipe, Cleveland, AFC	26
1982	Terry Bradshaw, Pittsburgh, AFC	17
	Dan Fouts, San Diego, AFC	17
	Joe Montana, San Francisco, NFC	17

Year	Player, Team	TD
1981	Dan Fouts, San Diego, AFC	33
	Steve Bartkowski, Atlanta, NFC	30
1980	Steve Bartkowski, Atlanta, NFC	31
	Dan Fouts, San Diego, AFC	30
	Brian Sipe, Cleveland, AFC	30
1979	Steve Grogan, New England, AFC	28
	Brian Sipe, Cleveland, AFC	28
	Roger Staubach, Dallas, NFC	27
1978	Terry Bradshaw, Pittsburgh, AFC	28
	Roger Staubach, Dallas, NFC	25
	Fran Tarkenton, Minnesota, NFC	25
1977	Bob Griese, Miami, AFC	22
	Ron Jaworski, Philadelphia, NFC	18
	Roger Staubach, Dallas, NFC	18
1976	Ken Stabler, Oakland, AFC	27
	Jim Hart, St. Louis, NFC	18
1975	Joe Ferguson, Buffalo, AFC	25
	Fran Tarkenton, Minnesota, NFC	25
1974	Ken Stabler, Oakland, AFC	26
	Jim Hart, St. Louis, NFC	20
1973	Roman Gabriel, Philadelphia, NFC	23
	Roger Staubach, Dallas, NFC	23
	Charley Johnson, Denver, AFC	20
1972	Billy Kilmer, Washington, NFC	19
	Joe Namath, N.Y. Jets, AFC	19
1971	John Hadl, San Diego, AFC	21
	John Brodie, San Francisco, NFC	18
1970	John Brodie, San Francisco, NFC	24
	John Hadl, San Diego, AFC	22
	Daryle Lamonica, Oakland, AFC	22
1969	Daryle Lamonica, Oakland, AFL	34
	Roman Gabriel, Los Angeles, NFL	24
1968	John Hadl, San Diego, AFL	27
	Earl Morrall, Baltimore, NFL	26
1967	Sonny Jurgensen, Washington, NFL	31
	Daryle Lamonica, Oakland, AFL	30
1966	Frank Ryan, Cleveland, NFL	29
	Len Dawson, Kansas City, AFL	26
1965	John Brodie, San Francisco, NFL	30
	Len Dawson, Kansas City, AFL	21
1964	Babe Parilli, Boston, AFL	31
	Frank Ryan, Cleveland, NFL	25

Year	Player, Team	TD
1963	Y.A. Tittle, N.Y. Giants, NFL	36
	Len Dawson, Kansas City, AFL	26
1962	Y.A. Tittle, N.Y. Giants, NFL	33
	Len Dawson, Dallas, AFL	29
1961	George Blanda, Houston, AFL	36
	Sonny Jurgensen, Philadelphia, NFL	32
1960	Al Dorow, N.Y. Titans, AFL	26
	Johnny Unitas, Baltimore, NFL	25
1959	Johnny Unitas, Baltimore	32
1958	Johnny Unitas, Baltimore	19
1957	Johnny Unitas, Baltimore	24
1956	Tobin Rote, Green Bay	18
1955	Tobin Rote, Green Bay	17
	Y.A. Tittle, San Francisco	17
1954	Adrian Burk, Philadelphia	23
1953	Robert Thomason, Philadelphia	21
1952	Jim Finks, Pittsburgh	20
	Otto Graham, Cleveland	20
1951	Bobby Layne, Detroit	26
1950	George Ratterman, N.Y. Yanks	22
1949	Johnny Lujack, Chi. Bears	23
1948	Tommy Thompson, Philadelphia	25
1947	Sammy Baugh, Washington	25
1946	Sid Luckman, Chi. Bears	17
	Bob Waterfield, Los Angeles	17
1945	Sid Luckman, Chi. Bears	14
	*Bob Waterfield, Cleveland	14
1944	Frank Filchock, Washington	13
1943	Sid Luckman, Chi. Bears	28
1942	Cecil Isbell, Green Bay	24
1941	Cecil Isbell, Green Bay	15
1940	Sammy Baugh, Washington	12
1939	Frank Filchock, Washington	11
1938	Bob Monnett, Green Bay	9
1937	Bernie Masterson, Chi. Bears	9
1936	Arnie Herber, Green Bay	11
1935	Ed Danowski, N.Y. Giants	10
1934	Arnie Herber, Green Bay	8
1933	*Harry Newman, N.Y. Giants	11
1932	Arnie Herber, Green Bay	9

*First season of professional football.

ANNUAL PASS RECEIVING LEADERS

Year	Player, Team	No.	Yards	Avg.	TD
2010	Roddy White, Atlanta, NFC	115	1,389	12.1	10
	Reggie Wayne, Indianapolis, AFC	111	1,355	12.2	6
2009	Wes Welker, New England, AFC	123	1,348	11.0	4
	Steve Smith, N.Y. Giants, NFC	107	1,220	11.4	7
2008	Andre Johnson, Houston, AFC	115	1,575	13.7	8
	Larry Fitzgerald, Arizona, NFC	96	1,431	14.9	12
2007	T.J. Houshmandzadeh, Cincinnati, AFC	112	1,143	10.2	12
	Wes Welker, New England, AFC	112	1,175	10.5	8
	Larry Fitzgerald, Arizona, NFC	100	1,409	14.1	10
2006	Andre Johnson, Houston, AFC	103	1,147	11.1	5
	Mike Furrey, Detroit, NFC	98	1,086	11.1	6
2005	Steve Smith, Carolina, NFC	103	1,563	15.2	12
	Larry Fitzgerald, Arizona, NFC	103	1,409	13.7	10
	Chad Ochocinco, Cincinnati, AFC	97	1,432	14.8	9
2004	Tony Gonzalez, Kansas City, AFC	102	1,258	12.3	7
	Joe Horn, New Orleans, NFC	94	1,399	14.9	11
	Torry Holt, St. Louis, NFC	94	1,372	14.6	10
2003	Torry Holt, St. Louis, NFC	117	1,696	14.5	12
	LaDainian Tomlinson, San Diego, AFC	100	725	7.3	4
2002	Marvin Harrison, Indianapolis, AFC	143	1,722	12.0	11
	Randy Moss, Minnesota, NFC	106	1,347	12.7	7
2001	Rod Smith, Denver, AFC	113	1,343	11.9	11
	Keyshawn Johnson, Tampa Bay, NFC	106	1,266	11.9	1
2000	Marvin Harrison, Indianapolis, AFC	102	1,413	13.9	14
	Muhsin Muhammad, Carolina, NFC	102	1,183	11.6	6

Year	Player, Team	No.	Yards	Avg.	TD
1999	Jimmy Smith, Jacksonville, AFC	116	1,636	14.1	6
	Muhsin Muhammad, Carolina, NFC	96	1,253	13.1	8
1998	O.J. McDuffie, Miami, AFC	90	1,050	11.7	7
	Frank Sanders, Arizona, NFC	89	1,145	12.9	3
1997	Tim Brown, Oakland, AFC	104	1,408	13.5	5
	Herman Moore, Detroit, NFC	104	1,293	12.4	8
1996	Jerry Rice, San Francisco, NFC	108	1,254	11.6	8
	Carl Pickens, Cincinnati, AFC	100	1,180	11.8	12
1995	Herman Moore, Detroit, NFC	123	1,686	13.7	14
	Carl Pickens, Cincinnati, AFC	99	1,234	12.5	17
1994	Cris Carter, Minnesota, NFC	122	1,256	10.3	7
	Ben Coates, New England, AFC	96	1,174	12.2	7
1993	Sterling Sharpe, Green Bay, NFC	112	1,274	11.4	11
	Reggie Langhorne, Indianapolis, AFC	85	1,038	12.2	3
1992	Sterling Sharpe, Green Bay, NFC	108	1,461	13.5	13
	Haywood Jeffires, Houston, AFC	90	913	10.1	9
1991	Haywood Jeffires, Houston, AFC	100	1,181	11.8	7
	Michael Irvin, Dallas, NFC	93	1,523	16.4	8
1990	Jerry Rice, San Francisco, NFC	100	1,502	15.0	13
	Haywood Jeffires, Houston, AFC	74	1,048	14.2	8
	Drew Hill, Houston, AFC	74	1,019	13.8	5
1989	Sterling Sharpe, Green Bay, NFC	90	1,423	15.8	12
	Andre Reed, Buffalo, AFC	88	1,312	14.9	9
1988	Al Toon, N.Y. Jets, AFC	93	1,067	11.5	5
	Henry Ellard, L.A. Rams, NFC	86	1,414	16.4	10
1987	J.T. Smith, St. Louis, NFC	91	1,117	12.3	8
	Al Toon, N.Y. Jets, AFC	68	976	14.4	5
1986	Todd Christensen, L.A. Raiders, AFC	95	1,153	12.1	8
	Jerry Rice, San Francisco, NFC	86	1,570	18.3	15
1985	Roger Craig, San Francisco, NFC	92	1,016	11.0	6
	Lionel James, San Diego, AFC	86	1,027	11.9	6
1984	Art Monk, Washington, NFC	106	1,372	12.9	7
	Ozzie Newsome, Cleveland, AFC	89	1,001	11.2	5
1983	Todd Christensen, L.A. Raiders, AFC	92	1,247	13.6	12
	Roy Green, St. Louis, NFC	78	1,227	15.7	14
	Charlie Brown, Washington, NFC	78	1,225	15.7	8
	Earnest Gray, N.Y. Giants, NFC	78	1,139	14.6	5
1982	Dwight Clark, San Francisco, NFC	60	913	15.2	5
	Kellen Winslow, San Diego, AFC	54	721	13.4	6
1981	Kellen Winslow, San Diego, AFC	88	1,075	12.2	10
	Dwight Clark, San Francisco, NFC	85	1,105	13.0	4
1980	Kellen Winslow, San Diego, AFC	89	1,290	14.5	9
	*Earl Cooper, San Francisco, NFC	83	567	6.8	4
1979	Joe Washington, Baltimore, AFC	82	750	9.1	3
	Ahmad Rashad, Minnesota, NFC	80	1,156	14.5	9
1978	Rickey Young, Minnesota, NFC	88	704	8.0	5
	Steve Largent, Seattle, AFC	71	1,168	16.5	8
1977	Lydell Mitchell, Baltimore, AFC	71	620	8.7	4
	Ahmad Rashad, Minnesota, NFC	51	681	13.4	2
1976	MacArthur Lane, Kansas City, AFC	66	686	10.4	1
	Drew Pearson, Dallas, NFC	58	806	13.9	6
1975	Chuck Foreman, Minnesota, NFC	73	691	9.5	9
	Reggie Rucker, Cleveland, AFC	60	770	12.8	3
	Lydell Mitchell, Baltimore, AFC	60	544	9.1	4
1974	Lydell Mitchell, Baltimore, AFC	72	544	7.6	2
	Charles Young, Philadelphia, NFC	63	696	11.0	3
1973	Harold Carmichael, Philadelphia, NFC	67	1,116	16.7	9
	Fred Willis, Houston, AFC	57	371	6.5	1
1972	Harold Jackson, Philadelphia, NFC	62	1,048	16.9	4
	Fred Biletnikoff, Oakland, AFC	58	802	13.8	7
1971	Fred Biletnikoff, Oakland, AFC	61	929	15.2	9
	Bob Tucker, N.Y. Giants, NFC	59	791	13.4	4
1970	Dick Gordon, Chicago, NFC	71	1,026	14.5	13
	Marlin Briscoe, Buffalo, AFC	57	1,036	18.2	8
1969	Dan Abramowicz, New Orleans, NFL	73	1,015	13.9	7
	Lance Alworth, San Diego, AFL	64	1,003	15.7	4
1968	Clifton McNeil, San Francisco, NFL	71	994	14.0	7
	Lance Alworth, San Diego, AFL	68	1,312	19.3	10

Year	Player, Team	No.	Yards	Avg.	TD
1967	George Sauer, N.Y. Jets, AFL	75	1,189	15.9	6
	Charley Taylor, Washington, NFL	70	990	14.1	9
1966	Lance Alworth, San Diego, AFL	73	1,383	18.9	13
	Charley Taylor, Washington, NFL	72	1,119	15.5	12
1965	Lionel Taylor, Denver, AFL	85	1,131	13.3	6
	Dave Parks, San Francisco, NFL	80	1,344	16.8	12
1964	Charley Hennigan, Houston, AFL	101	1,546	15.3	8
	Johnny Morris, Chicago, NFL	93	1,200	12.9	10
1963	Lionel Taylor, Denver, AFL	78	1,101	14.1	10
	Bobby Joe Conrad, St. Louis, NFL	73	967	13.2	10
1962	Lionel Taylor, Denver, AFL	77	908	11.8	4
	Bobby Mitchell, Washington, NFL	72	1,384	19.2	11
1961	Lionel Taylor, Denver, AFL	100	1,176	11.8	4
	Jim (Red) Phillips, Los Angeles, NFL	78	1,092	14.0	5
1960	Lionel Taylor, Denver, AFL	92	1,235	13.4	12
	Raymond Berry, Baltimore, NFL	74	1,298	17.5	10
1959	Raymond Berry, Baltimore	66	959	14.5	14
1958	Raymond Berry, Baltimore	56	794	14.2	9
	Pete Retzlaff, Philadelphia	56	766	13.7	2
1957	Billy Wilson, San Francisco	52	757	14.6	6
1956	Billy Wilson, San Francisco	60	889	14.8	5
1955	Pete Pihos, Philadelphia	62	864	13.9	7
1954	Pete Pihos, Philadelphia	60	872	14.5	10
	Billy Wilson, San Francisco	60	830	13.8	5
1953	Pete Pihos, Philadelphia	63	1,049	16.7	10
1952	Mac Speedie, Cleveland	62	911	14.7	5
1951	Elroy (Crazylegs) Hirsch, Los Angeles	66	1,495	22.7	17
1950	Tom Fears, Los Angeles	84	1,116	13.3	7
1949	Tom Fears, Los Angeles	77	1,013	13.2	9
1948	*Tom Fears, Los Angeles	51	698	13.7	4
1947	Jim Keane, Chi. Bears	64	910	14.2	10
1946	Jim Benton, Los Angeles	63	981	15.6	6
1945	Don Hutson, Green Bay	47	834	17.7	9
1944	Don Hutson, Green Bay	58	866	14.9	9
1943	Don Hutson, Green Bay	47	776	16.5	11
1942	Don Hutson, Green Bay	74	1,211	16.4	17
1941	Don Hutson, Green Bay	58	738	12.7	10
1940	*Don Looney, Philadelphia	58	707	12.2	4
1939	Don Hutson, Green Bay	34	846	24.9	6
1938	Gaynell Tinsley, Chi. Cardinals	41	516	12.6	1
1937	Don Hutson, Green Bay	41	552	13.5	7
1936	Don Hutson, Green Bay	34	536	15.8	8
1935	*Tod Goodwin, N.Y. Giants	26	432	16.6	4
1934	Joe Carter, Philadelphia	16	238	14.9	4
	Morris (Red) Badgro, N.Y. Giants	16	206	12.9	1
1933	John (Shipwreck) Kelly, Brooklyn	22	246	11.2	3
1932	Ray Flaherty, N.Y. Giants	21	350	16.7	3

*First season of professional football.

ANNUAL PASS RECEIVING LEADERS (YARDS)

Year	Player, Team	No.	Yards	Avg.	TD
2010	Brandon Lloyd, Denver, AFC	77	1,448	18.8	11
	Roddy White, Atlanta, NFC	115	1,389	12.1	10
2009	Andre Johnson, Houston, AFC	101	1,569	15.5	9
	Miles Austin, Dallas, NFC	81	1,320	16.3	11
2008	Andre Johnson, Houston, AFC	115	1,575	13.7	8
	Larry Fitzgerald, Arizona, NFC	96	1,431	14.9	12
2007	Reggie Wayne, Indianapolis, AFC	104	1,510	14.5	10
	Larry Fitzgerald, Arizona, NFC	100	1,409	14.1	10
2006	Chad Ochocinco, Cincinnati, AFC	87	1,369	15.7	7
	Roy Williams, Detroit, NFC	82	1,310	16.0	7
2005	Steve Smith, Carolina, NFC	103	1,563	15.2	12
	Chad Ochocinco, Cincinnati, AFC	97	1,432	14.8	9
2004	Muhsin Muhammad, Carolina, NFC	93	1,405	15.1	16
	Chad Ochocinco, Cincinnati, AFC	95	1,274	13.4	9
2003	Torry Holt, St. Louis, NFC	117	1,696	14.5	12
	Chad Ochocinco, Cincinnati, AFC	90	1,355	15.1	10
2002	Marvin Harrison, Indianapolis, AFC	143	1,722	12.0	11
	Randy Moss, Minnesota, NFC	106	1,347	12.7	7

Year	Player, Team	No.	Yards	Avg.	TD
2001	David Boston, Arizona, NFC	98	1,598	16.3	8
	Marvin Harrison, Indianapolis, AFC	109	1,524	14.0	15
2000	Torry Holt, St. Louis, NFC	82	1,635	19.9	6
	Rod Smith, Denver, AFC	100	1,602	16.0	8
1999	Marvin Harrison, Indianapolis, AFC	115	1,663	14.5	12
	Randy Moss, Minnesota, NFC	80	1,413	17.7	11
1998	Antonio Freeman, Green Bay, NFC	84	1,424	17.0	14
	Eric Moulds, Buffalo, AFC	67	1,368	20.4	9
1997	Rob Moore, Arizona, NFC	97	1,584	16.3	8
	Tim Brown, Oakland, AFC	104	1,408	13.5	5
1996	Isaac Bruce, St. Louis, NFC	84	1,338	15.9	7
	Jimmy Smith, Jacksonville, AFC	83	1,244	15.0	7
1995	Jerry Rice, San Francisco, NFC	122	1,848	15.1	15
	Tim Brown, Oakland, AFC	89	1,342	15.1	10
1994	Jerry Rice, San Francisco, NFC	112	1,499	13.4	13
	Tim Brown, L.A. Raiders, AFC	89	1,309	14.7	9
1993	Jerry Rice, San Francisco, NFC	98	1,503	15.3	15
	Tim Brown, L.A. Raiders, AFC	80	1,180	14.8	7
1992	Sterling Sharpe, Green Bay, NFC	108	1,461	13.5	13
	Anthony Miller, San Diego, AFC	72	1,060	14.7	7
1991	Michael Irvin, Dallas, NFC	93	1,523	16.4	8
	Haywood Jeffires, Houston, AFC	100	1,181	11.8	7
1990	Jerry Rice, San Francisco, NFC	100	1,502	15.0	13
	Haywood Jeffires, Houston, AFC	74	1,048	14.2	8
1989	Jerry Rice, San Francisco, NFC	82	1,483	18.1	17
	Andre Reed, Buffalo, AFC	88	1,312	14.9	9
1988	Henry Ellard, L.A. Rams, NFC	86	1,414	16.4	10
	Eddie Brown, Cincinnati, AFC	53	1,273	24.0	9
1987	J.T. Smith, St. Louis, NFC	91	1,117	12.3	8
	Carlos Carson, Kansas City, AFC	55	1,044	19.0	7
1986	Jerry Rice, San Francisco, NFC	86	1,570	18.3	15
	Stanley Morgan, New England, AFC	84	1,491	17.8	10
1985	Steve Largent, Seattle, AFC	79	1,287	16.3	6
	Mike Quick, Philadelphia, NFC	73	1,247	17.1	11
1984	Roy Green, St. Louis, NFC	78	1,555	19.9	12
	John Stallworth, Pittsburgh, AFC	80	1,395	17.4	11
1983	Mike Quick, Philadelphia, NFC	69	1,409	20.4	13
	Carlos Carson, Kansas City, AFC	80	1,351	16.9	7
1982	Wes Chandler, San Diego, AFC	49	1,032	21.1	9
	Dwight Clark, San Francisco, NFC	60	913	15.2	5
1981	Alfred Jenkins, Atlanta, NFC	70	1,358	19.4	13
	Frank Lewis, Buffalo, AFC	70	1,244	17.8	4
	Steve Watson, Denver, AFC	60	1,244	20.7	13
1980	John Jefferson, San Diego, AFC	82	1,340	16.3	13
	James Lofton, Green Bay, NFC	71	1,226	17.3	4
1979	Steve Largent, Seattle, AFC	66	1,237	18.7	9
	Ahmad Rashad, Minnesota, NFC	80	1,156	14.5	9
1978	Wesley Walker, N.Y. Jets, AFC	48	1,169	24.4	8
	Harold Carmichael, Philadelphia, NFC	55	1,072	19.5	8
1977	Drew Pearson, Dallas, NFC	48	870	18.1	2
	Ken Burrough, Houston, AFC	43	816	19.0	8
1976	Roger Carr, Baltimore, AFC	43	1,112	25.9	11
	*Sammy White, Minnesota, NFC	51	906	17.8	10
1975	Ken Burrough, Houston, AFC	53	1,063	20.1	8
	Mel Gray, St. Louis, NFC	48	926	19.3	11
1974	Cliff Branch, Oakland, AFC	60	1,092	18.2	13
	Drew Pearson, Dallas, NFC	62	1,087	17.5	2
1973	Harold Carmichael, Philadelphia, NFC	67	1,116	16.7	9
	*Isaac Curtis, Cincinnati, AFC	45	843	18.7	9
1972	Harold Jackson, Philadelphia, NFC	62	1,048	16.9	4
	Rich Caster, N.Y. Jets, AFC	39	833	21.4	10
1971	Otis Taylor, Kansas City, AFC	57	1,110	19.5	7
	Gene Washington, San Francisco, NFC	46	884	19.2	4
1970	Gene Washington, San Francisco, NFC	53	1,100	20.8	12
	Marlin Briscoe, Buffalo, AFC	57	1,036	18.2	8
1969	Warren Wells, Oakland, AFL	47	1,260	26.8	14
	Harold Jackson, Philadelphia, NFL	65	1,116	17.2	9
1968	Lance Alworth, San Diego, AFL	68	1,312	19.3	10
	Roy Jefferson, Pittsburgh, NFL	58	1,074	18.5	11

Year	Player, Team	No.	Yards	Avg.	TD
1967	Don Maynard, N.Y. Jets, AFL	71	1,434	20.3	10
	Ben Hawkins, Philadelphia, NFL	59	1,265	21.4	10
1966	Lance Alworth, San Diego, AFL	73	1,383	18.9	13
	Pat Studstill, Detroit, NFL	67	1,266	18.9	5
1965	Lance Alworth, San Diego, AFL	69	1,602	23.2	14
	Dave Parks, San Francisco, NFL	80	1,344	16.8	12
1964	Charley Hennigan, Houston, AFL	101	1,546	15.3	8
	Johnny Morris, Chicago, NFL	93	1,200	12.9	10
1963	Bobby Mitchell, Washington, NFL	69	1,436	20.8	7
	Art Powell, Oakland, AFL	73	1,304	17.8	16
1962	Bobby Mitchell, Washington, NFL	72	1,384	19.2	11
	Art Powell, N.Y. Titans, AFL	64	1,130	17.6	8
1961	Charley Hennigan, Houston, AFL	82	1,746	21.3	12
	Tommy McDonald, Philadelphia, NFL	64	1,144	17.9	13
1960	*Bill Groman, Houston, AFL	72	1,473	20.5	12
	Raymond Berry, Baltimore, NFL	74	1,298	17.5	10
1959	Raymond Berry, Baltimore	66	959	14.5	14
1958	Del Shofner, Los Angeles	51	1,097	21.5	8
1957	Raymond Berry, Baltimore	47	800	17.0	6
1956	Billy Howton, Green Bay	55	1,188	21.6	12
1955	Pete Pihos, Philadelphia	62	864	13.9	7
1954	Bob Boyd, Los Angeles	53	1,212	22.9	6
1953	Pete Pihos, Philadelphia	63	1,049	16.7	10
1952	*Billy Howton, Green Bay	53	1,231	23.2	13
1951	Elroy (Crazylegs) Hirsch, Los Angeles	66	1,495	22.7	17
1950	Tom Fears, Los Angeles	84	1,116	13.3	7
1949	Bob Mann, Detroit	66	1,014	15.4	4
1948	Mal Kutner, Chi. Cardinals	41	943	23.0	14
1947	Mal Kutner, Chi. Cardinals	43	944	21.9	7
1946	Jim Benton, Los Angeles	63	981	15.5	6
1945	Jim Benton, Cleveland	45	1,067	23.7	8
1944	Don Hutson, Green Bay	58	866	14.6	9
1943	Don Hutson, Green Bay	47	776	16.5	11
1942	Don Hutson, Green Bay	74	1,211	16.4	17
1941	Don Hutson, Green Bay	58	738	12.7	10
1940	*Don Looney, Philadelphia	58	707	12.2	4
1939	Don Hutson, Green Bay	34	846	24.9	6
1938	Don Hutson, Green Bay	32	548	17.1	9
1937	*Gaynell Tinsley, Chi. Cardinals	36	675	18.8	5
1936	Don Hutson, Green Bay	34	526	15.5	8
1935	Charley Malone, Boston	22	433	19.7	2
1934	Harry Ebding, Detroit	9	257	28.6	2
1933	*Paul Moss, Pittsburgh	18	383	21.3	2
1932	Johnny (Blood) McNally, Green Bay	19	326	17.2	3

First season of professional football.

ANNUAL PUNT RETURN LEADERS

Year	Player, Team	No.	Yards	Avg.	Long	TD
2010	Devin Hester, Chicago, NFC	33	564	17.1	89	3
	Julian Edelman, New England, AFC	21	321	15.3	94	1
2009	DeSean Jackson, Philadelphia, NFC	29	441	15.2	85	2
	Wes Welker, New England, AFC	27	338	12.5	69	0
2008	Roscoe Parrish, Buffalo, AFC	21	322	15.3	63	1
	*Clifton Smith, Tampa Bay, NFC	23	324	14.1	70	1
2007	Roscoe Parrish, Buffalo, AFC	27	440	16.3	74	1
	Devin Hester, Chicago, NFC	42	651	15.5	89	4
2006	Adam Jones, Tennessee, AFC	34	440	12.9	90	3
	*Devin Hester, Chicago, NFC	47	600	12.8	84	3
2005	Reno Mahe, Philadelphia, NFC	21	269	12.8	44	0
	B.J. Sams, Baltimore, AFC	33	401	12.2	51	0
2004	Eddie Drummond, Detroit, NFC	24	316	13.2	83	2
	Dennis Northcutt, Cleveland, AFC	36	432	12.0	44	0
2003	Dante Hall, Kansas City, AFC	29	472	16.3	93	2
	Brian Westbrook, Philadelphia, NFC	20	306	15.3	84	2
2002	Jimmy Williams, San Francisco, NFC	20	336	16.8	89	1
	Santana Moss, N.Y. Jets, AFC	25	413	16.5	63	2
2001	Troy Brown, New England, AFC	29	413	14.2	85	2
	Darrien Gordon, Atlanta, NFC	31	437	14.1	74	0

Year	Player, Team	No.	Yards	Avg.	Long	TD
2000	Jermaine Lewis, Baltimore, AFC	36	578	16.1	89	2
	Az-Zahir Hakim, St. Louis, NFC	32	489	15.3	86	1
1999	*Charlie Rogers, Seattle, AFC	22	318	14.5	94	1
	*Mac Cody, Arizona, NFC	32	373	11.7	31	0
1998	Deion Sanders, Dallas, NFC	24	375	15.6	69	2
	Reggie Barlow, Jacksonville, AFC	43	555	12.9	85	1
1997	Jermaine Lewis, Baltimore, AFC	28	437	15.6	89	2
	David Palmer, Minnesota, NFC	34	444	13.1	57	0
1996	Desmond Howard, Green Bay, NFC	58	875	15.1	92	3
	Darrien Gordon, San Diego, AFC	36	537	14.9	81	1
1995	David Palmer, Minnesota, NFC	26	342	13.2	74	1
	Andre Coleman, San Diego, AFC	28	326	11.6	88	1
1994	Brian Mitchell, Washington, NFC	32	452	14.1	78	2
	Darrien Gordon, San Diego, AFC	36	475	13.2	90	2
1993	*Tyrone Hughes, New Orleans, NFC	37	503	13.6	83	2
	Eric Metcalf, Cleveland, AFC	36	464	12.9	91	2
1992	Johnny Bailey, Phoenix, NFC	20	263	13.2	65	0
	Rod Woodson, Pittsburgh, AFC	32	364	11.4	80	1
1991	Mel Gray, Detroit, NFC	25	385	15.4	78	1
	Rod Woodson, Pittsburgh, AFC	28	320	11.4	40	0
1990	Clarence Verdin, Indianapolis, AFC	31	396	12.8	36	0
	*Johnny Bailey, Chicago, NFC	36	399	11.1	95	1
1989	Walter Stanley, Detroit, NFC	36	490	13.0	74	0
	Clarence Verdin, Indianapolis, AFC	23	296	12.9	49	1
1988	John Taylor, San Francisco, NFC	44	556	12.6	95	2
	JoJo Townsell, N.Y. Jets, AFC	35	409	11.7	59	1
1987	Mel Gray, New Orleans, NFC	24	352	14.7	80	0
	Bobby Joe Edmonds, Seattle, AFC	20	251	12.6	40	0
1986	*Bobby Joe Edmonds, Seattle, AFC	34	419	12.3	75	1
	*Vai Sikahema, St. Louis, NFC	43	522	12.1	71	2
1985	Irving Fryar, New England, AFC	37	520	14.1	85	2
	Henry Ellard, L.A. Rams, NFC	37	501	13.5	80	1
1984	Mike Martin, Cincinnati, AFC	24	376	15.7	55	0
	Henry Ellard, L.A. Rams, NFC	30	403	13.4	83	2
1983	*Henry Ellard, L.A. Rams, NFC	16	217	13.6	72	1
	Kirk Springs, N.Y. Jets, AFC	23	287	12.5	76	1
1982	Rick Upchurch, Denver, AFC	15	242	16.1	78	2
	Billy Johnson, Atlanta, NFC	24	273	11.4	71	0
1981	LeRoy Irvin, Los Angeles, NFC	46	615	13.4	84	3
	*James Brooks, San Diego, AFC	22	290	13.2	42	0
1980	J.T. Smith, Kansas City, AFC	40	581	14.5	75	2
	*Kenny Johnson, Atlanta, NFC	23	281	12.2	56	0
1979	John Sciarra, Philadelphia, NFC	16	182	11.4	38	0
	*Tony Nathan, Miami, AFC	28	306	10.9	86	1
1978	Rick Upchurch, Denver, AFC	36	493	13.7	75	1
	Jackie Wallace, Los Angeles, NFC	52	618	11.9	58	0
1977	Billy Johnson, Houston, AFC	35	539	15.4	87	2
	Larry Marshall, Philadelphia, NFC	46	489	10.6	48	0
1976	Rick Upchurch, Denver, AFC	39	536	13.7	92	4
	Eddie Brown, Washington, NFC	48	646	13.5	71	1
1975	Billy Johnson, Houston, AFC	40	612	15.3	83	3
	Terry Metcalf, St. Louis, NFC	23	285	12.4	69	1
1974	Lemar Parrish, Cincinnati, AFC	18	338	18.8	90	2
	Dick Jauron, Detroit, NFC	17	286	16.8	58	0
1973	Bruce Taylor, San Francisco, NFC	15	207	13.8	61	0
	Ron Smith, San Diego, AFC	27	352	13.0	84	2
1972	Ken Ellis, Green Bay, NFC	14	215	15.4	80	1
	Chris Farasopoulos, N.Y. Jets, AFC	17	179	10.5	65	1
1971	Les (Speedy) Duncan, Washington, NFC	22	233	10.6	33	0
	Leroy Kelly, Cleveland, AFC	30	292	9.7	74	0
1970	Ed Podolak, Kansas City, AFC	23	311	13.5	60	0
	*Bruce Taylor, San Francisco, NFC	43	516	12.0	76	0
1969	Alvin Haymond, Los Angeles, NFL	33	435	13.2	52	0
	*Bill Thompson, Denver, AFL	25	288	11.5	40	0
1968	Bob Hayes, Dallas, NFL	15	312	20.8	90	2
	Noland Smith, Kansas City, AFL	18	270	15.0	80	1
1967	Floyd Little, Denver, AFL	16	270	16.9	72	1
	Ben Davis, Cleveland, NFL	18	229	12.7	52	1

Year	Player, Team	No.	Yards	Avg.	Long	TD
1966	Les (Speedy) Duncan, San Diego, AFL	18	238	13.2	81	1
	Johnny Roland, St. Louis, NFL	20	221	11.1	86	1
1965	Leroy Kelly, Cleveland, NFL	17	265	15.6	67	2
	Les (Speedy) Duncan, San Diego, AFL	30	464	15.5	66	2
1964	Bobby Jancik, Houston, AFL	12	220	18.3	82	1
	Tommy Watkins, Detroit, NFL	16	238	14.9	68	2
1963	Dick James, Washington, NFL	16	214	13.4	39	0
	Claude (Hoot) Gibson, Oakland, AFL	26	307	11.8	85	2
1962	Dick Christy, N.Y. Titans, AFL	15	250	16.7	73	2
	Pat Studstill, Detroit, NFL	29	457	15.8	44	0
1961	Dick Christy, N.Y. Titans, AFL	18	383	21.3	70	2
	Willie Wood, Green Bay, NFL	14	225	16.1	72	2
1960	*Abner Haynes, Dall. Texans, AFL	14	215	15.4	46	0
	Abe Woodson, San Francisco, NFL	13	174	13.4	48	0
1959	Johnny Morris, Chi. Bears	14	171	12.2	78	1
1958	Jon Arnett, Los Angeles	18	223	12.4	58	0
1957	Bert Zagers, Washington	14	217	15.5	76	2
1956	Ken Konz, Cleveland	13	187	14.4	65	1
1955	Ollie Matson, Chi. Cardinals	13	245	18.8	78	2
1954	*Veryl Switzer, Green Bay	24	306	12.8	93	1
1953	Charley Trippi, Chi. Cardinals	21	239	11.4	38	0
1952	Jack Christiansen, Detroit	15	322	21.5	79	2
1951	Claude (Buddy) Young, N.Y. Yanks	12	231	19.3	79	1
1950	*Herb Rich, Baltimore	12	276	23.0	86	1
1949	Verda (Vitamin T) Smith, Los Angeles	27	427	15.8	85	1
1948	George McAfee, Chi. Bears	30	417	13.9	60	1
1947	*Walt Slater, Pittsburgh	28	435	15.5	33	0
1946	Bill Dudley, Pittsburgh	27	385	14.3	52	0
1945	*Dave Ryan, Detroit	15	220	14.7	56	0
1944	*Steve Van Buren, Philadelphia	15	230	15.3	55	1
1943	Andy Farkas, Washington	15	168	11.2	33	0
1942	Merlyn Condit, Brooklyn	21	210	10.0	23	0
1941	Byron (Whizzer) White, Detroit	19	262	13.8	64	0

*First season of professional football.

ANNUAL KICKOFF RETURN LEADERS

Year	Player, Team	No.	Yards	Avg.	Long	TD
2010	*David Reed, Baltimore, AFC	21	616	29.3	103	1
	Eric Weems, Atlanta, NFC	40	1,100	27.5	102	1
2009	Clifton Smith, Tampa Bay, NFC	31	902	29.1	83	0
	Josh Cribbs, Cleveland, AFC	56	1,542	27.5	103	3
2008	Danieal Manning, Chicago, NFC	36	1,070	29.7	83	1
	Ellis Hobbs, New England, AFC	45	1,281	28.5	95	1
2007	Josh Cribbs, Cleveland, AFC	59	1,809	30.7	100	2
	*Aundrae Allison, Minnesota, NFC	20	574	28.7	104	1
2006	Justin Miller, N.Y. Jets, AFC	46	1,304	28.3	103	2
	*Devin Hester, Chicago, NFC	20	528	26.4	96	2
2005	Terrence McGee, Buffalo, AFC	46	1,391	30.2	99	1
	Koren Robinson, Minnesota, NFC	47	1,221	26.0	86	1
2004	Willie Ponder, N.Y. Giants, NFC	36	967	26.9	91	1
	Terrence McGee, Buffalo, AFC	52	1,370	26.3	104	3
2003	Jerry Azumah, Chicago, NFC	41	1,191	29.0	89	2
	*Bethel Johnson, New England, AFC	30	847	28.2	92	1
2002	MarTay Jenkins, Arizona, NFC	20	559	28.0	95	1
	Kevin Faulk, New England, AFC	26	725	27.9	87	2
2001	Ronney Jenkins, San Diego, AFC	58	1,541	26.6	93	2
	*Steve Smith, Carolina, NFC	56	1,431	25.6	99	2
2000	*Darrick Vaughn, Atlanta, NFC	39	1,082	27.7	100	3
	Derrick Mason, Tennessee, AFC	42	1,132	27.0	66	0
1999	Tony Horne, St. Louis, NFC	30	892	29.7	101	2
	Tremain Mack, Cincinnati, AFC	51	1,382	27.1	99	1
1998	*Terry Fair, Detroit, NFC	51	1,428	28.0	105	2
	Corey Harris, Baltimore, AFC	35	965	27.6	95	1
1997	Michael Bates, Carolina, NFC	47	1,281	27.3	56	0
	Aaron Glenn, N.Y. Jets, AFC	28	741	26.5	96	1
1996	Michael Bates, Carolina, NFC	33	998	30.2	93	1
	Tamarick Vanover, Kansas City, AFC	33	854	25.9	97	1
1995	Ron Carpenter, N.Y. Jets, AFC	20	553	27.7	58	0
	Brian Mitchell, Washington, NFC	55	1,408	25.6	59	0

Year	Player, Team	No.	Yards	Avg.	Long	TD
1994	Mel Gray, Detroit, NFC	45	1,276	28.4	102	3
	Randy Baldwin, Cleveland, AFC	28	753	26.9	85	1
1993	Robert Brooks, Green Bay, NFC	23	611	26.6	95	1
	*Raghib Ismail, L.A. Raiders, AFC	25	605	24.2	66	0
1992	Jon Vaughn, New England, AFC	20	564	28.2	100	1
	Deion Sanders, Atlanta, NFC	40	1,067	26.7	99	2
1991	Mel Gray, Detroit, NFC	36	929	25.8	71	0
	Nate Lewis, San Diego, AFC	23	578	25.1	95	1
1990	Kevin Clark, Denver, AFC	20	505	25.3	75	0
	David Meggett, N.Y. Giants, NFC	21	492	23.4	58	0
1989	Rod Woodson, Pittsburgh, AFC	36	982	27.3	84	1
	Mel Gray, Detroit, NFC	24	640	26.7	57	0
1988	*Tim Brown, L.A. Raiders, AFC	41	1,098	26.8	97	1
	Donnie Elder, Tampa Bay, NFC	34	772	22.7	51	0
1987	Sylvester Stamps, Atlanta, NFC	24	660	27.5	97	1
	Paul Palmer, Kansas City, AFC	38	923	24.3	95	2
1986	Dennis Gentry, Chicago, NFC	20	576	28.8	91	1
	Lupe Sanchez, Pittsburgh, AFC	25	591	23.6	64	0
1985	Ron Brown, L.A. Rams, NFC	28	918	32.8	98	3
	Glen Young, Cleveland, AFC	35	898	25.7	63	0
1984	*Bobby Humphery, N.Y. Jets, AFC	22	675	30.7	97	1
	Barry Redden, L.A. Rams, NFC	23	530	23.0	40	0
1983	Fulton Walker, Miami, AFC	36	962	26.7	78	0
	Darrin Nelson, Minnesota, NFC	18	445	24.7	50	0
1982	*Mike Mosley, Buffalo, AFC	18	487	27.1	66	0
	Alvin Hall, Detroit, NFC	16	426	26.6	96	1
1981	Mike Nelms, Washington, NFC	37	1,099	29.7	84	0
	Carl Roaches, Houston, AFC	28	769	27.5	96	1
1980	Horace Ivory, New England, AFC	36	992	27.6	98	1
	Rich Mauti, New Orleans, NFC	31	798	25.7	52	0
1979	Larry Brunson, Oakland, AFC	17	441	25.9	89	0
	Jimmy Edwards, Minnesota, NFC	44	1,103	25.1	83	0
1978	Steve Odom, Green Bay, NFC	25	677	27.1	95	1
	*Keith Wright, Cleveland, AFC	30	789	26.3	86	0
1977	*Raymond Clayborn, New England, AFC	28	869	31.0	101	3
	*Wilbert Montgomery, Philadelphia, NFC	23	619	26.9	99	1
1976	*Duriel Harris, Miami, AFC	17	559	32.9	69	0
	Cullen Bryant, Los Angeles, NFC	16	459	28.7	90	1
1975	*Walter Payton, Chicago, NFC	14	444	31.7	70	0
	Harold Hart, Oakland, AFC	17	518	30.5	102	1
1974	Terry Metcalf, St. Louis, NFC	20	623	31.2	94	1
	Greg Pruitt, Cleveland, AFC	22	606	27.5	88	1
1973	Carl Garrett, Chicago, NFC	16	486	30.4	67	0
	*Wallace Francis, Buffalo, AFC	23	687	29.9	101	2
1972	Ron Smith, Chicago, NFC	30	924	30.8	94	1
	*Bruce Laird, Baltimore, AFC	29	843	29.1	73	0
1971	Travis Williams, Los Angeles, NFC	25	743	29.7	105	1
	Eugene (Mercury) Morris, Miami, AFC	15	423	28.2	94	1
1970	Jim Duncan, Baltimore, AFC	20	707	35.4	99	1
	Cecil Turner, Chicago, NFC	23	752	32.7	96	4
1969	Bobby Williams, Detroit, NFL	17	563	33.1	96	1
	*Bill Thompson, Denver, AFL	18	513	28.5	63	0
1968	Preston Pearson, Baltimore, NFL	15	527	35.1	102	2
	*George Atkinson, Oakland, AFL	32	802	25.1	60	0
1967	*Travis Williams, Green Bay, NFL	18	739	41.1	104	4
	*Zeke Moore, Houston, AFL	14	405	28.9	92	1
1966	Gale Sayers, Chicago, NFL	23	718	31.2	93	2
	*Goldie Sellers, Denver, AFL	19	541	28.5	100	2
1965	Tommy Watkins, Detroit, NFL	17	584	34.4	94	0
	Abner Haynes, Denver, AFL	34	901	26.5	60	0
1964	*Clarence Childs, N.Y. Giants, NFL	34	987	29.0	100	1
	Bo Roberson, Oakland, AFL	36	975	27.1	59	0
1963	Abe Woodson, San Francisco, NFL	29	935	32.2	103	3
	Bobby Jancik, Houston, AFL	45	1,317	29.3	53	0
1962	Abe Woodson, San Francisco, NFL	37	1,157	31.3	79	0
	*Bobby Jancik, Houston, AFL	24	826	30.3	61	0
1961	Dick Bass, Los Angeles, NFL	23	698	30.3	64	0
	*Dave Grayson, Dall. Texans, AFL	16	453	28.3	73	0

Year	Player, Team	No.	Yards	Avg.	Long	TD
1960	*Tom Moore, Green Bay, NFL	12	397	33.1	84	0
	Ken Hall, Houston, AFL	19	594	31.3	104	1
1959	Abe Woodson, San Francisco	13	382	29.4	105	1
1958	Ollie Matson, Chi. Cardinals	14	497	35.5	101	2
1957	*Jon Arnett, Los Angeles	18	504	28.0	98	1
1956	*Tom Wilson, Los Angeles	15	477	31.8	103	1
1955	Al Carmichael, Green Bay	14	418	29.9	100	1
1954	Billy Reynolds, Cleveland	14	413	29.5	51	0
1953	Joe Arenas, San Francisco	16	551	34.4	82	0
1952	Lynn Chandnois, Pittsburgh	17	599	35.2	93	2
1951	Lynn Chandnois, Pittsburgh	12	390	32.5	55	0
1950	Verda (Vitamin T) Smith, Los Angeles	22	742	33.7	97	3
1949	*Don Doll, Detroit	21	536	25.5	56	0
1948	*Joe Scott, N.Y. Giants	20	569	28.5	99	1
1947	Eddie Saenz, Washington	29	797	27.5	94	2
1946	Abe Karnofsky, Boston	21	599	28.5	97	1
1945	Steve Van Buren, Philadelphia	13	373	28.7	98	1
1944	Bob Thurbon, Card.-Pitt.	12	291	24.3	55	0
1943	Ken Heineman, Brooklyn	16	444	27.8	69	0
1942	Marshall Goldberg, Chi. Cardinals	15	393	26.2	95	1
1941	Marshall Goldberg, Chi. Cardinals	12	290	24.2	41	0

*First season of professional football.

ANNUAL INTERCEPTION LEADERS

Year	Player, Team	No.	Yards	TD
2010	Ed Reed, Baltimore, AFC	8	183	0
	Asante Samuel, Philadelphia, NFC	7	70	0
2009	*Jairus Byrd, Buffalo, AFC	9	118	0
	Asante Samuel, Philadelphia, NFC	9	117	0
	Darren Sharper, New Orleans, NFC	9	376	3
	Charles Woodson, Green Bay, NFC	9	179	3
2008	Ed Reed, Baltimore, AFC	9	264	2
	Nick Collins, Green Bay, NFC	7	295	3
	Charles Woodson, Green Bay, NFC	7	169	2
2007	Antonio Cromartie, San Diego, AFC	10	144	1
	O.J. Atogwe, St. Louis, NFC	8	125	1
2006	Champ Bailey, Denver, AFC	10	162	1
	Asante Samuel, New England, AFC	10	120	0
	Walt Harris, San Francisco, NFC	8	84	1
	Charles Woodson, Green Bay, NFC	8	61	1
2005	Ty Law, N.Y. Jets, AFC	10	195	1
	Deltha O'Neal, Cincinnati, AFC	10	103	0
	Darren Sharper, Minnesota, NFC	9	276	2
2004	Ed Reed, Baltimore, AFC	9	358	1
	Ken Lucas, Seattle, NFC	6	46	1
	*Chris Gamble, Carolina, NFC	6	15	0
2003	Tony Parrish, San Francisco, NFC	9	202	0
	Brian Russell, Minnesota, NFC	9	185	0
	Ed Reed, Baltimore, AFC	7	132	1
	Marcus Coleman, Houston, AFC	7	95	0
	Patrick Surtain, Miami, AFC	7	59	0
2002	Rod Woodson, Oakland, AFC	8	225	2
	Brian Kelly, Tampa Bay, NFC	8	68	0
2001	*Anthony Henry, Cleveland, AFC	10	177	1
	Ronde Barber, Tampa Bay, NFC	10	86	1
2000	Darren Sharper, Green Bay, NFC	9	109	0
	Samari Rolle, Tennessee, AFC	7	140	1
	Brian Walker, Miami, AFC	7	80	0
1999	Rod Woodson, Baltimore, AFC	7	195	2
	Sam Madison, Miami, AFC	7	164	1
	James Hasty, Kansas City, AFC	7	98	2
	Donnie Abraham, Tampa Bay, NFC	7	115	2
	Troy Vincent, Philadelphia, NFC	7	91	0
1998	Ty Law, New England, AFC	9	133	1
	Kwamie Lassiter, Arizona, NFC	8	80	0
1997	Ryan McNeil, St. Louis, NFC	9	127	1
	Mark McMillian, Kansas City, AFC	8	274	3
	Darryl Williams, Seattle, AFC	8	172	1
1996	Tyrone Braxton, Denver, AFC	9	128	1
	Keith Lyle, St. Louis, NFC	9	152	0
1995	*Orlando Thomas, Minnesota, NFC	9	108	1
	Willie Williams, Pittsburgh, AFC	7	122	1
1994	Eric Turner, Cleveland, AFC	9	199	1
	Aeneas Williams, Arizona, NFC	9	89	0
1993	Eugene Robinson, Seattle, AFC	9	80	0
	Nate Odomes, Buffalo, AFC	9	65	0
	Deion Sanders, Atlanta, NFC	7	91	0
1992	Henry Jones, Buffalo, AFC	8	263	2
	Audray McMillian, Minnesota, NFC	8	157	2
1991	Ronnie Lott, L.A. Raiders, AFC	8	52	0
	Ray Crockett, Detroit, NFC	6	141	1
	Deion Sanders, Atlanta, NFC	6	119	1
	*Aeneas Williams, Phoenix, NFC	6	60	0
	Tim McKyer, Atlanta, NFC	6	24	0
1990	*Mark Carrier, Chicago, NFC	10	39	0
	Richard Johnson, Houston, AFC	8	100	1
1989	Felix Wright, Cleveland, AFC	9	91	1
	Eric Allen, Philadelphia, NFC	8	38	0
1988	Scott Case, Atlanta, NFC	10	47	0
	Erik McMillan, N.Y. Jets, AFC	8	168	2
1987	Barry Wilburn, Washington, NFC	9	135	1
	Mike Prior, Indianapolis, AFC	6	57	0
	Mark Kelso, Buffalo, AFC	6	25	0
	Keith Bostic, Houston, AFC	6	-14	0
1986	Ronnie Lott, San Francisco, NFC	10	134	1
	Deron Cherry, Kansas City, AFC	9	150	0
1985	Everson Walls, Dallas, NFC	9	31	0
	Albert Lewis, Kansas City, AFC	8	59	0
	Eugene Daniel, Indianapolis, AFC	8	53	0
1984	Ken Easley, Seattle, AFC	10	126	2
	*Tom Flynn, Green Bay, NFC	9	106	0
1983	Mark Murphy, Washington, NFC	9	127	0
	Ken Riley, Cincinnati, AFC	8	89	2
	Vann McElroy, L.A. Raiders, AFC	8	68	0
1982	Everson Walls, Dallas, NFC	7	61	0
	Ken Riley, Cincinnati, AFC	5	88	1
	Bobby Jackson, N.Y. Jets, AFC	5	84	1
	Dwayne Woodruff, Pittsburgh, AFC	5	53	0
	Donnie Shell, Pittsburgh, AFC	5	27	0
1981	*Everson Walls, Dallas, NFC	11	133	0
	John Harris, Seattle, AFC	10	155	2

Year	Player, Team	No.	Yards	TD
1980	Lester Hayes, Oakland, AFC	13	273	1
	Nolan Cromwell, Los Angeles, NFC	8	140	1
1979	Mike Reinfeldt, Houston, AFC	12	205	0
	Lemar Parrish, Washington, NFC	9	65	0
1978	Thom Darden, Cleveland, AFC	10	200	0
	Ken Stone, St. Louis, NFC	9	139	0
	Willie Buchanon, Green Bay, NFC	9	93	1
1977	Lyle Blackwood, Baltimore, AFC	10	163	0
	Rolland Lawrence, Atlanta, NFC	7	138	0
1976	Monte Jackson, Los Angeles, NFC	10	173	3
	Ken Riley, Cincinnati, AFC	9	141	1
1975	Mel Blount, Pittsburgh, AFC	11	121	0
	Paul Krause, Minnesota, NFC	10	201	0
1974	Emmitt Thomas, Kansas City, AFC	12	214	2
	Ray Brown, Atlanta, NFC	8	164	1
1973	Dick Anderson, Miami, AFC	8	163	2
	Mike Wagner, Pittsburgh, AFC	8	134	0
	Bobby Bryant, Minnesota, NFC	7	105	1
1972	Bill Bradley, Philadelphia, NFC	9	73	0
	Mike Sensibaugh, Kansas City, AFC	8	65	0
1971	Bill Bradley, Philadelphia, NFC	11	248	0
	Ken Houston, Houston, AFC	9	220	4
1970	Johnny Robinson, Kansas City, AFC	10	155	0
	Dick LeBeau, Detroit, NFC	9	96	0
1969	Mel Renfro, Dallas, NFL	10	118	0
	Emmitt Thomas, Kansas City, AFL	9	146	1
1968	Dave Grayson, Oakland, AFL	10	195	1
	Willie Williams, N.Y. Giants, NFL	10	103	0
1967	Miller Farr, Houston, AFL	10	264	3
	*Lem Barney, Detroit, NFL	10	232	3
	Tom Janik, Buffalo, AFL	10	222	2
	Dave Whitsell, New Orleans, NFL	10	178	2
	Dick Westmoreland, Miami, AFL	10	127	1
1966	Larry Wilson, St. Louis, NFL	10	180	2
	Johnny Robinson, Kansas City, AFL	10	136	1
	Bobby Hunt, Kansas City, AFL	10	113	0
1965	W.K. Hicks, Houston, AFL	9	156	0
	Bobby Boyd, Baltimore, NFL	9	78	1
1964	Dainard Paulson, N.Y. Jets, AFL	12	157	1
	*Paul Krause, Washington, NFL	12	140	1
1963	Fred Glick, Houston, AFL	12	180	1
	Dick Lynch, N.Y. Giants, NFL	9	251	3
	Roosevelt Taylor, Chicago, NFL	9	172	1
1962	Lee Riley, N.Y. Titans, AFL	11	122	0
	Willie Wood, Green Bay, NFL	9	132	1
1961	Billy Atkins, Buffalo, AFL	10	158	1
	Dick Lynch, N.Y. Giants, NFL	9	60	0
1960	*Austin (Goose) Gonsoulin, Denver, AFL	11	98	0
	Dave Baker, San Francisco, NFL	10	96	0
	Jerry Norton, St. Louis, NFL	10	96	0
1959	Dean Derby, Pittsburgh	7	127	0
	Milt Davis, Baltimore	7	119	1
	Don Shinnick, Baltimore	7	70	1
1958	Jim Patton, N.Y. Giants	11	183	0
1957	Milt Davis, Baltimore	10	219	2
	Jack Christiansen, Detroit	10	137	1
	Jack Butler, Pittsburgh	10	85	0
1956	Linden Crow, Chi. Cardinals	11	170	0
1955	Will Sherman, Los Angeles	11	101	0
1954	Dick (Night Train) Lane, Chi. Cardinals	10	181	0
1953	Jack Christiansen, Detroit	12	238	1
1952	*Dick (Night Train) Lane, Los Angeles	14	298	2
1951	Otto Schnellbacher, N.Y. Giants	11	194	2
1950	Orban (Spec) Sanders, N.Y. Yanks	13	199	0
1949	Bob Nussbaumer, Chi. Cardinals	12	157	0
1948	*Dan Sandifer, Washington	13	258	2
1947	Frank Reagan, N.Y. Giants	10	203	0
	Frank Seno, Boston	10	100	0
1946	Bill Dudley, Pittsburgh	10	242	1

Year	Player, Team	No.	Yards	TD
1945	Roy Zimmerman, Philadelphia	7	90	0
1944	*Howard Livingston, N.Y. Giants	9	172	1
1943	Sammy Baugh, Washington	11	112	0
1942	Clyde (Bulldog) Turner, Chi. Bears	8	96	1
1941	Marshall Goldberg, Chi. Cardinals	7	54	0
	*Art Jones, Pittsburgh	7	35	0
1940	Clarence (Ace) Parker, Brooklyn	6	146	1
	Kent Ryan, Detroit	6	65	0
	Don Hutson, Green Bay	6	24	0

*First season of professional football.

ANNUAL PUNTING LEADERS

Year	Player, Team	No.	Avg.	Long
2010	Shane Lechler, Oakland, AFC	77	47.0	68
	Mat McBriar, Dallas, NFC	65	47.9	65
2009	Shane Lechler, Oakland, AFC	96	51.1	70
	Andy Lee, San Francisco, NFC	99	47.6	64
2008	Donnie Jones, St. Louis, NFC	82	50.0	68
	Shane Lechler, Oakland, AFC	90	48.8	70
2007	Shane Lechler, Oakland, AFC	73	49.1	70
	Andy Lee, San Francisco, NFC	105	47.3	74
2006	Mat McBriar, Dallas, NFC	56	48.2	75
	Shane Lechler, Oakland, AFC	77	47.5	67
2005	Brian Moorman, Buffalo, AFC	71	45.7	68
	Josh Bidwell, Tampa Bay, NFC	90	45.6	61
2004	Shane Lechler, Oakland, AFC	73	46.7	67
	Tom Tupa, Washington, NFC	103	44.1	61
2003	Shane Lechler, Oakland, AFC	96	46.9	73
	Todd Sauerbrun, Carolina, NFC	77	44.6	64
2002	Todd Sauerbrun, Carolina, NFC	104	45.5	67
	Chris Hanson, Jacksonville, AFC	81	44.2	64
2001	Todd Sauerbrun, Carolina, NFC	93	47.5	73
	Shane Lechler, Oakland, AFC	73	46.2	65
2000	Darren Bennett, San Diego, AFC	92	46.2	66
	Mitch Berger, Minnesota, NFC	62	44.7	60
1999	Tom Rouen, Denver, AFC	84	46.5	65
	Mitch Berger, Minnesota, NFC	61	45.4	65
1998	Craig Hentrich, Tennessee, AFC	69	47.2	71
	Mark Royals, New Orleans, NFC	88	45.6	64
1997	Mark Royals, New Orleans, NFC	88	45.9	66
	Tom Tupa, New England, AFC	78	45.8	73
1996	John Kidd, Miami, AFC	78	46.3	63
	Matt Turk, Washington, NFC	75	45.1	63
1995	Rick Tuten, Seattle, AFC	83	45.0	73
	Sean Landeta, St. Louis, NFC	83	44.3	63
1994	Sean Landeta, L.A. Rams, NFC	78	44.8	62
	Jeff Gossett, L.A. Raiders, AFC	77	43.9	65
1993	Greg Montgomery, Houston, AFC	54	45.6	77
	Jim Arnold, Detroit, NFC	72	44.5	68
1992	Greg Montgomery, Houston, AFC	53	46.9	66
	Harry Newsome, Minnesota, NFC	72	45.0	84
1991	Reggie Roby, Miami, AFC	54	45.7	64
	Harry Newsome, Minnesota, AFC	68	45.5	65
1990	Mike Horan, Denver, AFC	58	44.4	67
	Sean Landeta, N.Y. Giants, NFC	75	44.1	61
1989	Rich Camarillo, Phoenix, NFC	76	43.4	58
	Greg Montgomery, Houston, AFC	56	43.3	63
1988	Harry Newsome, Pittsburgh, AFC	65	45.4	62
	Jim Arnold, Detroit, NFC	97	42.4	69
1987	Rick Donnelly, Atlanta, NFC	61	44.0	62
	Ralf Mojsiejenko, San Diego, AFC	67	42.9	57
1986	Rohn Stark, Indianapolis, AFC	76	45.2	63
	Sean Landeta, N.Y. Giants, NFC	79	44.8	61
1985	Rohn Stark, Indianapolis, AFC	78	45.9	68
	*Rick Donnelly, Atlanta, NFC	59	43.6	68
1984	Jim Arnold, Kansas City, AFC	98	44.9	63
	*Brian Hansen, New Orleans, NFC	69	43.8	66
1983	Rohn Stark, Baltimore, AFC	91	45.3	68
	Frank Garcia, Tampa Bay, NFC	95	42.2	64

Year	Player, Team	No.	Avg.	Long
1982	Luke Prestridge, Denver, AFC	45	45.0	65
	Carl Birdsong, St. Louis, NFC	54	43.8	65
1981	Pat McInally, Cincinnati, AFC	72	45.4	62
	Tom Skladany, Detroit, NFC	64	43.5	74
1980	Dave Jennings, N.Y. Giants, NFC	94	44.8	63
	Luke Prestridge, Denver, AFC	70	43.9	57
1979	*Bob Grupp, Kansas City, AFC	89	43.6	74
	Dave Jennings, N.Y. Giants, NFC	104	42.7	72
1978	Pat McInally, Cincinnati, AFC	91	43.1	65
	*Tom Skladany, Detroit, NFC	86	42.5	63
1977	Ray Guy, Oakland, AFC	59	43.3	74
	Tom Blanchard, New Orleans, NFC	82	42.4	66
1976	Marv Bateman, Buffalo, AFC	86	42.8	78
	John James, Atlanta, NFC	101	42.1	67
1975	Ray Guy, Oakland, AFC	68	43.8	64
	Herman Weaver, Detroit, NFC	80	42.0	61
1974	Ray Guy, Oakland, AFC	74	42.2	66
	Tom Blanchard, New Orleans, NFC	88	42.1	71
1973	Jerrel Wilson, Kansas City, AFC	80	45.5	68
	*Tom Wittum, San Francisco, NFC	79	43.7	62
1972	Jerrel Wilson, Kansas City, AFC	66	44.8	69
	Dave Chapple, Los Angeles, NFC	53	44.2	70
1971	Dave Lewis, Cincinnati, AFC	72	44.8	56
	Tom McNeill, Philadelphia, NFC	73	42.0	64
1970	Dave Lewis, Cincinnati, AFC	79	46.2	63
	*Julian Fagan, New Orleans, NFC	77	42.5	64
1969	David Lee, Baltimore, NFL	57	45.3	66
	Dennis Partee, San Diego, AFL	71	44.6	62
1968	Jerrel Wilson, Kansas City, AFL	63	45.1	70
	Billy Lothridge, Atlanta, NFL	75	44.3	70
1967	Bob Scarpitto, Denver, AFL	105	44.9	73
	Billy Lothridge, Atlanta, NFL	87	43.7	62
1966	Bob Scarpitto, Denver, AFL	76	45.8	70
	*David Lee, Baltimore, NFL	49	45.6	64
1965	Gary Collins, Cleveland, NFL	65	46.7	71
	Jerrel Wilson, Kansas City, AFL	69	45.4	64
1964	Bobby Walden, Minnesota, NFL	72	46.4	73
	Jim Fraser, Denver, AFL	73	44.2	67
1963	Yale Lary, Detroit, NFL	35	48.9	73
	Jim Fraser, Denver, AFL	81	44.4	66
1962	Tommy Davis, San Francisco, NFL	48	45.6	82
	Jim Fraser, Denver, AFL	55	43.6	75
1961	Yale Lary, Detroit, NFL	52	48.4	71
	Billy Atkins, Buffalo, AFL	85	44.5	70
1960	Jerry Norton, St. Louis, NFL	39	45.6	62
	*Paul Maguire, L.A. Chargers, AFL	43	40.5	61
1959	Yale Lary, Detroit	45	47.1	67
1958	Sam Baker, Washington	48	45.4	64
1957	Don Chandler, N.Y. Giants	60	44.6	61
1956	Norm Van Brocklin, Los Angeles	48	43.1	72
1955	Norm Van Brocklin, Los Angeles	60	44.6	61
1954	Pat Brady, Pittsburgh	66	43.2	72
1953	Pat Brady, Pittsburgh	80	46.9	64
1952	Horace Gillom, Cleveland	61	45.7	73
1951	Horace Gillom, Cleveland	73	45.5	66
1950	*Fred (Curly) Morrison, Chi. Bears	57	43.3	65
1949	*Mike Boyda, N.Y. Bulldogs	56	44.2	61
1948	Joe Muha, Philadelphia	57	47.3	82
1947	Jack Jacobs, Green Bay	57	43.5	74
1946	Roy McKay, Green Bay	64	42.7	64
1945	Roy McKay, Green Bay	44	41.2	73
1944	Frank Sinkwich, Detroit	45	41.0	73
1943	Sammy Baugh, Washington	50	45.9	81
1942	Sammy Baugh, Washington	37	48.2	74
1941	Sammy Baugh, Washington	30	48.7	75
1940	Sammy Baugh, Washington	35	51.4	85
1939	*Parker Hall, Cleveland	58	40.8	80

*First season of professional football.

ANNUAL LEADERS IN SACKS (SINCE 1982)

Year	Player, Team	Sacks
2010	DeMarcus Ware, Dallas, NFC	15.5
	Tamba Hali, Kansas City, AFC	14.5
2009	Elvis Dumervil, Denver, AFC	17.0
	Jared Allen, Minnesota, NFC	14.5
2008	DeMarcus Ware, Dallas, NFC	20.0
	Joey Porter, Miami, AFC	17.5
2007	Jared Allen, Kansas City, AFC	15.5
	Patrick Kerney, Seattle, NFC	14.5
2006	Shawne Merriman, San Diego, AFC	17.0
	Aaron Kampman, Green Bay, NFC	15.5
2005	Derrick Burgess, Oakland, AFC	16.0
	Osi Umenyiora, N.Y. Giants, NFC	14.5
2004	Dwight Freeney, Indianapolis, AFC	16.0
	Bertrand Berry, Arizona, NFC	14.5
2003	Michael Strahan, N.Y. Giants, NFC	18.5
	Adewale Ogunleye, Miami, AFC	15.0
2002	Jason Taylor, Miami, AFC	18.5
	Simeon Rice, Tampa Bay, NFC	15.5
2001	Michael Strahan, N.Y. Giants, NFC	22.5
	Peter Boulware, Baltimore, AFC	15.0
2000	La'Roi Glover, New Orleans, NFC	17.0
	Trace Armstrong, Miami, AFC	16.5
1999	Kevin Carter, St. Louis, NFC	17.0
	*Jevon Kearse, Tennessee, AFC	14.5
1998	Michael Sinclair, Seattle, AFC	16.5
	Reggie White, Green Bay, NFC	16.0
1997	John Randle, Minnesota, NFC	15.5
	Bruce Smith, Buffalo, AFC	14.0
1996	Kevin Greene, Carolina, NFC	14.5
	Michael McCrary, Seattle, AFC	13.5
	Bruce Smith, Buffalo, AFC	13.5
1995	Bryce Paup, Buffalo, AFC	17.5
	William Fuller, Philadelphia, NFC	13.0
	Wayne Martin, New Orleans, NFC	13.0
1994	Kevin Greene, Pittsburgh, AFC	14.0
	Ken Harvey, Washington, NFC	13.5
	John Randle, Minnesota, NFC	13.5
1993	Neil Smith, Kansas City, AFC	15.0
	Renaldo Turnbull, New Orleans, NFC	13.0
	Reggie White, Green Bay, NFC	13.0
1992	Clyde Simmons, Philadelphia, NFC	19.0
	Leslie O'Neal, San Diego, AFC	17.0
1991	Pat Swilling, New Orleans, NFC	17.0
	William Fuller, Houston, AFC	15.0
1990	Derrick Thomas, Kansas City, AFC	20.0
	Charles Haley, San Francisco, NFC	16.0
1989	Chris Doleman, Minnesota, NFC	21.0
	Lee Williams, San Diego, AFC	14.0
1988	Reggie White, Philadelphia, NFC	18.0
	Greg Townsend, L.A. Raiders, AFC	11.5
1987	Reggie White, Philadelphia, NFC	21.0
	Andre Tippett, New England, AFC	12.5
1986	Lawrence Taylor, N.Y. Giants, NFC	20.5
	Sean Jones, L.A. Raiders, AFC	15.5
1985	Richard Dent, Chicago, NFC	17.0
	Andre Tippett, New England, AFC	16.5
1984	Mark Gastineau, N.Y. Jets, AFC	22.0
	Richard Dent, Chicago, NFC	17.5
1983	Mark Gastineau, N.Y. Jets, AFC	19.0
	Fred Dean, San Francisco, NFC	17.5
1982	Doug Martin, Minnesota, NFC	11.5
	Jesse Baker, Houston, AFC	7.5

*First season of professional football.

POINTS SCORED

Year	Team	Points
2010	New England, AFC	518
	Philadelphia, NFC	439

Year	Team	Points
2009	New Orleans, NFC	510
	San Diego, AFC	454
2008	New Orleans, NFC	463
	San Diego, AFC	439
2007	New England, AFC	589
	Dallas, NFC	455
2006	San Diego, AFC	492
	Chicago, NFC	427
2005	Seattle, NFC	452
	Indianapolis, AFC	439
2004	Indianapolis, AFC	522
	Green Bay, NFC	424
2003	Kansas City, AFC	484
	St. Louis, NFC	447
2002	Kansas City, AFC	467
	New Orleans, NFC	432
2001	St. Louis, NFC	503
	Indianapolis, AFC	413
2000	St. Louis, NFC	540
	Denver, AFC	485
1999	St. Louis, NFC	526
	Indianapolis, AFC	423
1998	Minnesota, NFC	556
	Denver, AFC	501
1997	Denver, AFC	472
	Green Bay, NFC	422
1996	Green Bay, NFC	456
	New England, AFC	418
1995	San Francisco, NFC	457
	Pittsburgh, AFC	407
1994	San Francisco, NFC	505
	Miami, AFC	389
1993	San Francisco, NFC	473
	Denver, AFC	373
1992	San Francisco, NFC	431
	Buffalo, AFC	381
1991	Washington, NFC	485
	Buffalo, AFC	458
1990	Buffalo, AFC	428
	Philadelphia, NFC	396
1989	San Francisco, NFC	442
	Buffalo, AFC	409
1988	Cincinnati, AFC	448
	L.A. Rams, NFC	407
1987	San Francisco, NFC	459
	Cleveland, AFC	390
1986	Miami, AFC	430
	Minnesota, NFC	398
1985	San Diego, AFC	467
	Chicago, NFC	456
1984	Miami, AFC	513
	San Francisco, NFC	475
1983	Washington, NFC	541
	L.A. Raiders, AFC	442
1982	San Diego, AFC	288
	Dallas, NFC	226
	Green Bay, NFC	226
1981	San Diego, AFC	478
	Atlanta, NFC	426
1980	Dallas, NFC	454
	New England, AFC	441
1979	Pittsburgh, AFC	416
	Dallas, NFC	371
1978	Dallas, NFC	384
	Miami, AFC	372
1977	Oakland, AFC	351
	Dallas, NFC	345
1976	Baltimore, AFC	417
	Los Angeles, NFC	351
1975	Buffalo, AFC	420
	Minnesota, NFC	377

Year	Team	Points
1974	Oakland, AFC	355
	Washington, NFC	320
1973	Los Angeles, NFC	388
	Denver, AFC	354
1972	Miami, AFC	385
	San Francisco, NFC	353
1971	Dallas, NFC	406
	Oakland, AFC	344
1970	San Francisco, NFC	352
	Baltimore, AFC	321
1969	Minnesota, NFL	379
	Oakland, AFL	377
1968	Oakland, AFL	453
	Dallas, NFL	431
1967	Oakland, AFL	468
	Los Angeles, NFL	398
1966	Kansas City, AFL	448
	Dallas, NFL	445
1965	San Francisco, NFL	421
	San Diego, AFL	340
1964	Baltimore, NFL	428
	Buffalo, AFL	400
1963	N.Y. Giants, NFL	448
	San Diego, AFL	399
1962	Green Bay, NFL	415
	Dall. Texans, AFL	389
1961	Houston, AFL	513
	Green Bay, NFL	391
1960	N.Y. Titans, AFL	382
	Cleveland, NFL	362
1959	Baltimore	374
1958	Baltimore	381
1957	Los Angeles	307
1956	Chi. Bears	363
1955	Cleveland	349
1954	Detroit	337
1953	San Francisco	372
1952	Los Angeles	349
1951	Los Angeles	392
1950	Los Angeles	466
1949	Philadelphia	364
1948	Chi. Cardinals	395
1947	Chi. Bears	363
1946	Chi. Bears	289
1945	Philadelphia	272
1944	Philadelphia	267
1943	Chi. Bears	303
1942	Chi. Bears	376
1941	Chi. Bears	396
1940	Washington	245
1939	Chi. Bears	298
1938	Green Bay	223
1937	Green Bay	220
1936	Green Bay	248
1935	Chi. Bears	192
1934	Chi. Bears	286
1933	N.Y. Giants	244
1932	Chi. Bears	160

TOTAL YARDS GAINED

Year	Team	Yards
2010	San Diego, AFC	6,329
	Philadelphia, NFC	6,230
2009	New Orleans, NFC	6,461
	New England, AFC	6,357
2008	New Orleans, NFC	6,571
	Denver, AFC	6,333
2007	New England, AFC	6,580
	Green Bay, NFC	5,931
2006	New Orleans, NFC	6,264
	Indianapolis, AFC	6,070

Year	Team	Yards
2005	Kansas City, AFC	6,192
	Seattle, NFC	5,915
2004	Kansas City, AFC	6,695
	Green Bay, NFC	6,357
2003	Minnesota, NFC	6,294
	Kansas City, AFC	5,910
2002	Oakland, AFC	6,237
	Minnesota, NFC	6,192
2001	St. Louis, NFC	6,690
	Indianapolis, AFC	5,955
2000	St. Louis, NFC	7,075
	Denver, AFC	6,554
1999	St. Louis, NFC	6,412
	Indianapolis, AFC	5,726
1998	San Francisco, NFC	6,800
	Denver, AFC	6,092
1997	Denver, AFC	5,872
	Detroit, NFC	5,798
1996	Denver, AFC	5,791
	Philadelphia, NFC	5,627
1995	Detroit, NFC	6,113
	Denver, AFC	6,040
1994	Miami, AFC	6,078
	San Francisco, NFC	6,060
1993	San Francisco, NFC	6,435
	Miami, AFC	5,812
1992	San Francisco, NFC	6,195
	Buffalo, AFC	5,893
1991	Buffalo, AFC	6,252
	San Francisco, NFC	5,858
1990	Houston, AFC	6,222
	San Francisco, NFC	5,895
1989	San Francisco, NFC	6,268
	Cincinnati, AFC	6,101
1988	Cincinnati, AFC	6,057
	San Francisco, NFC	5,900
1987	San Francisco, NFC	5,987
	Denver, AFC	5,624
1986	Cincinnati, AFC	6,490
	San Francisco, NFC	6,082
1985	San Diego, AFC	6,535
	San Francisco, NFC	5,920
1984	Miami, AFC	6,936
	San Francisco, NFC	6,366
1983	San Diego, AFC	6,197
	Green Bay, NFC	6,172
1982	San Diego, AFC	4,048
	San Francisco, NFC	3,242
1981	San Diego, AFC	6,744
	Detroit, NFC	5,933
1980	San Diego, AFC	6,410
	Los Angeles, NFC	6,006
1979	Pittsburgh, AFC	6,258
	Dallas, NFC	5,968
1978	New England, AFC	5,965
	Dallas, NFC	5,959
1977	Dallas, NFC	4,812
	Oakland, AFC	4,736
1976	Baltimore, AFC	5,236
	St. Louis, NFC	5,136
1975	Buffalo, AFC	5,467
	Dallas, NFC	5,025
1974	Dallas, NFC	4,983
	Oakland, AFC	4,718
1973	Los Angeles, NFC	4,906
	Oakland, AFC	4,773
1972	Miami, AFC	5,036
	N.Y. Giants, NFC	4,483
1971	Dallas, NFC	5,035
	San Diego, AFC	4,738
1970	Oakland, AFC	4,829

Year	Team	Yards
	San Francisco, NFC	4,503
1969	Dallas, NFL	5,122
	Oakland, AFL	5,036
1968	Oakland, AFL	5,696
	Dallas, NFL	5,117
1967	N.Y. Jets, AFL	5,152
	Baltimore, NFL	5,008
1966	Dallas, NFL	5,145
	Kansas City, AFL	5,114
1965	San Francisco, NFL	5,270
	San Diego, AFL	5,188
1964	Buffalo, AFL	5,206
	Baltimore, NFL	4,779
1963	San Diego, AFL	5,153
	N.Y. Giants, NFL	5,024
1962	N.Y. Giants, NFL	5,005
	Houston, AFL	4,971
1961	Houston, AFL	6,288
	Philadelphia, NFL	5,112
1960	Houston, AFL	4,936
	Baltimore, NFL	4,245
1959	Baltimore	4,458
1958	Baltimore	4,539
1957	Los Angeles	4,143
1956	Chi. Bears	4,537
1955	Chi. Bears	4,316
1954	Los Angeles	5,187
1953	Philadelphia	4,811
1952	Cleveland	4,352
1951	Los Angeles	5,506
1950	Los Angeles	5,420
1949	Chi. Bears	4,873
1948	Chi. Cardinals	4,705
1947	Chi. Bears	5,053
1946	Los Angeles	3,793
1945	Washington	3,549
1944	Chi. Bears	3,239
1943	Chi. Bears	4,045
1942	Chi. Bears	3,900
1941	Chi. Bears	4,265
1940	Green Bay	3,400
1939	Chi. Bears	3,988
1938	Green Bay	3,037
1937	Green Bay	3,201
1936	Detroit	3,703
1935	Chi. Bears	3,454
1934	Chi. Bears	3,900
1933	N.Y. Giants	2,973
1932	Chi. Bears	2,755

YARDS RUSHING

Year	Team	Yards
2010	Kansas City, AFC	2,627
	Philadelphia, NFC	2,324
2009	N.Y. Jets, AFC	2,756
	Carolina, NFC	2,498
2008	N.Y. Giants, NFC	2,518
	Baltimore, AFC	2,376
2007	Minnesota, NFC	2,634
	Jacksonville, AFC	2,391
2006	Atlanta, NFC	2,939
	San Diego, AFC	2,578
2005	Atlanta, NFC	2,546
	Denver, AFC	2,539
2004	Atlanta, NFC	2,672
	Pittsburgh, AFC	2,464
2003	Baltimore, AFC	2,674
	Green Bay, NFC	2,558
2002	Minnesota, NFC	2,507
	Miami, AFC	2,502

Year	Team	Yards	Year	Team	Yards
2001	Pittsburgh, AFC	2,774	1966	Kansas City, AFL	2,274
	San Francisco, NFC	2,244		Cleveland, NFL	2,166
2000	Oakland, AFC	2,470	1965	Cleveland, NFL	2,331
	Minnesota, NFC	2,129		San Diego, AFL	2,085
1999	San Francisco, NFC	2,095	1964	Green Bay, NFL	2,276
	Jacksonville, AFC	2,091		Buffalo, AFL	2,040
1998	San Francisco, NFC	2,544	1963	Cleveland, NFL	2,639
	Denver, AFC	2,468		San Diego, AFL	2,203
1997	Pittsburgh, AFC	2,479	1962	Buffalo, AFL	2,480
	Detroit, NFC	2,464		Green Bay, NFL	2,460
1996	Denver, AFC	2,362	1961	Green Bay, NFL	2,350
	Washington, NFC	1,910		Dall. Texans, AFL	2,189
1995	Kansas City, AFC	2,222	1960	St. Louis, NFL	2,356
	Dallas, NFC	2,201		Oakland, AFL	2,056
1994	Pittsburgh, AFC	2,180	1959	Cleveland	2,149
	Detroit, NFC	2,080	1958	Cleveland	2,526
1993	N.Y. Giants, NFC	2,210	1957	Los Angeles	2,142
	Seattle, AFC	2,015	1956	Chi. Bears	2,468
1992	Buffalo, AFC	2,436	1955	Chi. Bears	2,388
	Philadelphia, NFC	2,388	1954	San Francisco	2,498
1991	Buffalo, AFC	2,381	1953	San Francisco	2,230
	Minnesota, NFC	2,201	1952	San Francisco	1,905
1990	Philadelphia, NFC	2,556	1951	Chi. Bears	2,408
	San Diego, AFC	2,257	1950	N.Y. Giants	2,336
1989	Cincinnati, AFC	2,483	1949	Philadelphia	2,607
	Chicago, NFC	2,287	1948	Chi. Cardinals	2,560
1988	Cincinnati, AFC	2,710	1947	Los Angeles	2,171
	San Francisco, NFC	2,523	1946	Green Bay	1,765
1987	San Francisco, NFC	2,237	1945	Cleveland	1,714
	L.A. Raiders, AFC	2,197	1944	Philadelphia	1,661
1986	Chicago, NFC	2,700	1943	Phil-Pitt	1,730
	Cincinnati, AFC	2,533	1942	Chi. Bears	1,881
1985	Chicago, NFC	2,761	1941	Chi. Bears	2,203
	Indianapolis, AFC	2,439	1940	Chi. Bears	1,818
1984	Chicago, NFC	2,974	1939	Chi. Bears	2,043
	N.Y. Jets, AFC	2,189	1938	Detroit	1,893
1983	Chicago, NFC	2,727	1937	Detroit	2,074
	Baltimore, AFC	2,695	1936	Detroit	2,885
1982	Buffalo, AFC	1,371	1935	Chi. Bears	2,096
	Dallas, NFC	1,313	1934	Chi. Bears	2,847
1981	Detroit, NFC	2,795	1933	Boston	2,260
	Kansas City, AFC	2,633	1932	Chi. Bears	1,770
1980	Los Angeles, NFC	2,799			
	Houston, AFC	2,635			

YARDS PASSING

Leadership in this category has been based on net yards since 1952.

Year	Team	Yards
1979	N.Y. Jets, AFC	2,646
	St. Louis, NFC	2,582
1978	New England, AFC	3,165
	Dallas, NFC	2,783
1977	Chicago, NFC	2,811
	Oakland, AFC	2,627
1976	Pittsburgh, AFC	2,971
	Los Angeles, NFC	2,528
1975	Buffalo, AFC	2,974
	Dallas, NFC	2,432
1974	Dallas, NFC	2,454
	Pittsburgh, AFC	2,417
1973	Buffalo, AFC	3,088
	Los Angeles, NFC	2,925
1972	Miami, AFC	2,960
	Chicago, NFC	2,360
1971	Miami, AFC	2,429
	Detroit, NFC	2,376
1970	Dallas, NFC	2,300
	Miami, AFC	2,082
1969	Dallas, NFL	2,276
	Kansas City, AFL	2,220
1968	Chicago, NFL	2,377
	Kansas City, AFL	2,227
1967	Cleveland, NFL	2,139
	Houston, AFL	2,122

Year	Team	Yards
2010	San Diego, AFC	4,746
	New Orleans, NFC	4,636
2009	Houston, AFC	4,654
	New Orleans, NFC	4,355
2008	New Orleans, NFC	4,977
	Denver, AFC	4,471
2007	New England, AFC	4,731
	Green Bay, NFC	4,334
2006	New Orleans, NFC	4,503
	Indianapolis, AFC	4,308
2005	Arizona, NFC	4,437
	New England, AFC	4,120
2004	Indianapolis, AFC	4,623
	Minnesota, NFC	4,516
2003	Indianapolis, AFC	4,179
	St. Louis, NFC	3,961
2002	Oakland, AFC	4,475
	St. Louis, NFC	4,154
2001	St. Louis, NFC	4,663
	Indianapolis, AFC	3,989
2000	St. Louis, NFC	5,232
	Indianapolis, AFC	4,282
1999	St. Louis, NFC	4,353
	Indianapolis, AFC	4,066

Year	Team	Yards
1998	Minnesota, NFC	4,328
	N.Y. Jets, AFC	3,836
1997	Seattle, AFC	3,959
	Green Bay, NFC	3,705
1996	Jacksonville, AFC	4,110
	Philadelphia, NFC	3,745
1995	San Francisco, NFC	4,608
	Miami, AFC	4,210
1994	New England, AFC	4,444
	Minnesota, NFC	4,324
1993	Miami, AFC	4,353
	San Francisco, NFC	4,302
1992	Houston, AFC	4,029
	San Francisco, NFC	3,880
1991	Houston, AFC	4,621
	San Francisco, NFC	3,997
1990	Houston, AFC	4,805
	San Francisco, NFC	4,177
1989	Washington, NFC	4,349
	Miami, AFC	4,216
1988	Miami, AFC	4,516
	Washington, NFC	4,136
1987	Miami, AFC	3,876
	San Francisco, NFC	3,750
1986	Miami, AFC	4,779
	San Francisco, NFC	4,096
1985	San Diego, AFC	4,870
	Dallas, NFC	3,861
1984	Miami, AFC	5,018
	St. Louis, NFC	4,257
1983	San Diego, AFC	4,661
	Green Bay, NFC	4,365
1982	San Diego, AFC	2,927
	San Francisco, NFC	2,502
1981	San Diego, AFC	4,739
	Minnesota, NFC	4,333
1980	San Diego, AFC	4,531
	Minnesota, NFC	3,688
1979	San Diego, AFC	3,915
	San Francisco, NFC	3,641
1978	San Diego, AFC	3,375
	Minnesota, NFC	3,243
1977	Buffalo, AFC	2,530
	St. Louis, NFC	2,499
1976	Baltimore, AFC	2,933
	Minnesota, NFC	2,855
1975	Cincinnati, AFC	3,241
	Washington, NFC	2,917
1974	Washington, NFC	2,978
	Cincinnati, AFC	2,804
1973	Philadelphia, NFC	2,998
	Denver, AFC	2,519
1972	N.Y. Jets, AFC	2,777
	San Francisco, NFC	2,735
1971	San Diego, AFC	3,134
	Dallas, NFC	2,786
1970	San Francisco, NFC	2,923
	Oakland, AFC	2,865
1969	Oakland, AFL	3,271
	San Francisco, NFL	3,158
1968	San Diego, AFL	3,623
	Dallas, NFL	3,026
1967	N.Y. Jets, AFL	3,845
	Washington, NFL	3,730
1966	N.Y. Jets, AFL	3,464
	Dallas, NFL	3,023
1965	San Francisco, NFL	3,487
	San Diego, AFL	3,103
1964	Houston, AFL	3,527
	Chicago, NFL	2,841

Year	Team	Points
1963	Baltimore, NFL	3,296
	Houston, AFL	3,222
1962	Denver, AFL	3,404
	Philadelphia, NFL	3,385
1961	Houston, AFL	4,392
	Philadelphia, NFL	3,605
1960	Houston, AFL	3,203
	Baltimore, NFL	2,956
1959	Baltimore	2,753
1958	Pittsburgh	2,752
1957	Baltimore	2,388
1956	Los Angeles	2,419
1955	Philadelphia	2,472
1954	Chi. Bears	3,104
1953	Philadelphia	3,089
1952	Cleveland	2,566
1951	Los Angeles	3,296
1950	Los Angeles	3,709
1949	Chi. Bears	3,055
1948	Washington	2,861
1947	Washington	3,336
1946	Los Angeles	2,080
1945	Chi. Bears	1,857
1944	Washington	2,021
1943	Chi. Bears	2,310
1942	Green Bay	2,407
1941	Chi. Bears	2,002
1940	Washington	1,887
1939	Chi. Bears	1,965
1938	Washington	1,536
1937	Green Bay	1,398
1936	Green Bay	1,629
1935	Green Bay	1,449
1934	Green Bay	1,165
1933	N.Y. Giants	1,348
1932	Chi. Bears	1,013

FEWEST POINTS ALLOWED

Year	Team	Points
2010	Pittsburgh, AFC	232
	Green Bay, NFC	240
2009	N.Y. Jets, AFC	236
	Dallas, NFC	250
2008	Pittsburgh, AFC	223
	Philadelphia, NFC	289
2007	Indianapolis, AFC	262
	Tampa Bay, NFC	270
2006	Baltimore, AFC	201
	Chicago, NFC	255
2005	Chicago, NFC	202
	Indianapolis, AFC	247
2004	Pittsburgh, AFC	251
	Philadelphia, NFC	260
2003	New England, AFC	238
	Dallas, NFC	260
2002	Tampa Bay, NFC	196
	Miami, AFC	301
2001	Chicago, NFC	203
	Pittsburgh, AFC	212
2000	Baltimore, AFC	165
	Philadelphia, NFC	245
1999	Jacksonville, AFC	217
	Tampa Bay, NFC	235
1998	Miami, AFC	265
	Dallas, NFC	275
1997	Kansas City, AFC	232
	Tampa Bay, NFC	263
1996	Green Bay, NFC	210
	Pittsburgh, AFC	257
1995	Kansas City, AFC	241
	San Francisco, NFC	258

Year	Team	Points
1994	Cleveland, AFC	204
	Dallas, NFC	248
1993	N.Y. Giants, NFC	205
	Houston, AFC	238
1992	New Orleans, NFC	202
	Pittsburgh, AFC	225
1991	New Orleans, NFC	211
	Denver, AFC	235
1990	N.Y. Giants, NFC	211
	Pittsburgh, AFC	240
1989	Denver, AFC	226
	N.Y. Giants, NFC	252
1988	Chicago, NFC	215
	Buffalo, AFC	237
1987	Indianapolis, AFC	238
	San Francisco, NFC	253
1986	Chicago, NFC	187
	Seattle, AFC	293
1985	Chicago, NFC	198
	N.Y. Jets, AFC	264
1984	San Francisco, NFC	227
	Denver, AFC	241
1983	Miami, AFC	250
	Detroit, NFC	286
1982	Washington, NFC	128
	Miami, AFC	131
1981	Philadelphia, NFC	221
	Miami, AFC	275
1980	Philadelphia, NFC	222
	Houston, AFC	251
1979	Tampa Bay, NFC	237
	San Diego, AFC	246
1970	Pittsburgh, AFC	195
	Dallas, NFC	208
1977	Atlanta, NFC	129
	Denver, AFC	148
1976	Pittsburgh, AFC	138
	Minnesota, NFC	176
1975	Los Angeles, NFC	135
	Pittsburgh, AFC	162
1974	Los Angeles, NFC	181
	Pittsburgh, AFC	189
1973	Miami, AFC	150
	Minnesota, NFC	168
1972	Miami, AFC	171
	Washington, NFC	218
1971	Minnesota, NFC	139
	Baltimore, AFC	140
1970	Minnesota, NFC	143
	Miami, AFC	228
1969	Minnesota, NFL	133
	Kansas City, AFL	177
1968	Baltimore, NFL	144
	Kansas City, AFL	170
1967	Los Angeles, NFL	196
	Houston, AFL	199
1966	Green Bay, NFL	163
	Buffalo, AFL	255
1965	Green Bay, NFL	224
	Buffalo, AFL	226
1964	Baltimore, NFL	225
	Buffalo, AFL	242
1963	Chicago, NFL	144
	San Diego, AFL	255
1962	Green Bay, NFL	148
	Dall. Texans, AFL	233
1961	San Diego, AFL	219
	N.Y. Giants, NFL	220
1960	San Francisco, NFL	205
	Dall. Texans, AFL	253

Year	Team	Yards
1959	N.Y. Giants	170
1958	N.Y. Giants	183
1957	Cleveland	172
1956	Cleveland	177
1955	Cleveland	218
1954	Cleveland	162
1953	Cleveland	162
1952	Detroit	192
1951	Cleveland	152
1950	Philadelphia	141
1949	Philadelphia	134
1948	Chi. Bears	151
1947	Green Bay	210
1946	Pittsburgh	117
1945	Washington	121
1944	N.Y. Giants	75
1943	Washington	137
1942	Chi. Bears	84
1941	N.Y. Giants	114
1940	Brooklyn	120
1939	N.Y. Giants	85
1938	N.Y. Giants	79
1937	Chi. Bears	100
1936	Chi. Bears	94
1935	Green Bay	96
	N.Y. Giants	96
1934	Detroit	59
1933	Brooklyn	54
1932	Chi. Bears	44

FEWEST TOTAL YARDS ALLOWED

Year	Team	Yards
2010	San Diego, AFC	4,345
	New Orleans, NFC	4,900
2009	N.Y. Jets, AFC	4,037
	Green Bay, NFC	4,551
2008	Pittsburgh, AFC	3,795
	Philadelphia, NFC	4,389
2007	Pittsburgh, AFC	4,202
	Tampa Bay, NFC	4,454
2006	Baltimore, AFC	4,225
	Chicago, NFC	4,706
2005	Tampa Bay, NFC	4,444
	Pittsburgh, AFC	4,544
2004	Pittsburgh, AFC	4,134
	Washington, NFC	4,281
2003	Dallas, NFC	4,056
	Buffalo, AFC	4,313
2002	Tampa Bay, NFC	4,044
	Miami, AFC	4,656
2001	Pittsburgh, AFC	4,137
	St. Louis, NFC	4,471
2000	Tennessee, AFC	3,813
	Washington, NFC	4,474
1999	Buffalo, AFC	4,045
	Tampa Bay, NFC	4,280
1998	San Diego, AFC	4,208
	Tampa Bay, NFC	4,345
1997	San Francisco, NFC	4,013
	Denver, AFC	4,671
1996	Green Bay, NFC	4,156
	Pittsburgh, AFC	4,362
1995	San Francisco, NFC	4,398
	Kansas City, AFC	4,549
1994	Dallas, NFC	4,313
	Pittsburgh, AFC	4,326
1993	Minnesota, NFC	4,406
	Pittsburgh, AFC	4,531
1992	Dallas, NFC	3,931
	Houston, AFC	4,211

Year	Team	Yards
1991	Philadelphia, NFC	3,549
	Denver, AFC	4,549
1990	Pittsburgh, AFC	4,115
	N.Y. Giants, NFC	4,206
1989	Minnesota, NFC	4,184
	Kansas City, AFC	4,293
1988	Minnesota, NFC	4,091
	Buffalo, AFC	4,578
1987	San Francisco, NFC	4,095
	Cleveland, AFC	4,264
1986	Chicago, NFC	4,130
	L.A. Raiders, AFC	4,804
1985	Chicago, NFC	4,135
	L.A. Raiders, AFC	4,603
1984	Chicago, NFC	3,863
	Cleveland, AFC	4,641
1983	Cincinnati, AFC	4,327
	New Orleans, NFC	4,691
1982	Miami, AFC	2,312
	Tampa Bay, NFC	2,442
1981	Philadelphia, NFC	4,447
	N.Y. Jets, AFC	4,871
1980	Buffalo, AFC	4,101
	Philadelphia, NFC	4,443
1979	Tampa Bay, NFC	3,949
	Pittsburgh, AFC	4,270
1978	Los Angeles, NFC	3,893
	Pittsburgh, AFC	4,168
1977	Dallas, NFC	3,213
	New England, AFC	3,638
1976	Pittsburgh, AFC	3,323
	San Francisco, NFC	3,562
1975	Minnesota, NFC	3,153
	Oakland, AFC	3,629
1974	Pittsburgh, AFC	3,074
	Washington, NFC	3,285
1973	Los Angeles, NFC	2,951
	Oakland, AFC	3,160
1972	Miami, AFC	3,297
	Green Bay, NFC	3,474
1971	Baltimore, AFC	2,852
	Minnesota, NFC	3,406
1970	Minnesota, NFC	2,803
	N.Y. Jets, AFC	3,655
1969	Minnesota, NFL	2,720
	Kansas City, AFL	3,163
1968	Los Angeles, NFL	3,118
	N.Y. Jets, AFL	3,363
1967	Oakland, AFL	3,294
	Green Bay, NFL	3,300
1966	St. Louis, NFL	3,492
	Oakland, AFL	3,910
1965	San Diego, AFL	3,262
	Detroit, NFL	3,557
1964	Green Bay, NFL	3,179
	Buffalo, AFL	3,878
1963	Chicago, NFL	3,176
	Boston, AFL	3,834
1962	Detroit, NFL	3,217
	Dall. Texans, AFL	3,951
1961	San Diego, AFL	3,726
	Baltimore, NFL	3,782
1960	St. Louis, NFL	3,029
	Buffalo, AFL	3,866
1959	N.Y. Giants	2,843
1958	Chi. Bears	3,066
1957	Pittsburgh	2,791
1956	N.Y. Giants	3,081
1955	Cleveland	2,841
1954	Cleveland	2,658
1953	Philadelphia	2,998

Year	Team	Yards
1952	Cleveland	3,075
1951	N.Y. Giants	3,250
1950	Cleveland	3,154
1949	Philadelphia	2,831
1948	Chi. Bears	2,931
1947	Green Bay	3,396
1946	Washington	2,451
1945	Philadelphia	2,073
1944	Philadelphia	1,943
1943	Chi. Bears	2,262
1942	Chi. Bears	1,703
1941	N.Y. Giants	2,368
1940	N.Y. Giants	2,219
1939	Washington	2,116
1938	N.Y. Giants	2,029
1937	Washington	2,123
1936	Boston	2,181
1935	Boston	1,996
1934	Chi. Cardinals	1,539
1933	Brooklyn	1,789

FEWEST RUSHING YARDS ALLOWED

Year	Team	Yards
2010	Pittsburgh, AFC	1,004
	Chicago, NFC	1,441
2009	Green Bay, NFC	1,333
	Pittsburgh, AFC	1,438
2008	Minnesota, NFC	1,230
	Pittsburgh, AFC	1,284
2007	Minnesota, NFC	1,185
	Baltimore, AFC	1,268
2006	Minnesota, NFC	985
	Baltimore, AFC	1,214
2005	San Diego, AFC	1,349
	Carolina, NFC	1,465
2004	Pittsburgh, AFC	1,299
	Washington, NFC	1,304
2003	Tennessee, AFC	1,295
	Dallas, NFC	1,425
2002	Pittsburgh, AFC	1,375
	Tampa Bay, NFC	1,554
2001	Pittsburgh, AFC	1,195
	Chicago, NFC	1,313
2000	Baltimore, AFC	970
	N.Y. Giants, NFC	1,156
1999	St. Louis, NFC	1,189
	Baltimore, AFC	1,231
1998	San Diego, AFC	1,140
	Atlanta, NFC	1,203
1997	Pittsburgh, AFC	1,318
	San Francisco, NFC	1,366
1996	Denver, AFC	1,331
	Green Bay, NFC	1,416
1995	San Francisco, NFC	1,061
	Pittsburgh, AFC	1,321
1994	Minnesota, NFC	1,090
	San Diego, AFC	1,404
1993	Houston, AFC	1,273
	Minnesota, NFC	1,536
1992	Dallas, NFC	1,244
	Buffalo, AFC	1,395
	San Diego, AFC	1,395
1991	Philadelphia, NFC	1,136
	N.Y. Jets, AFC	1,442
1990	Philadelphia, NFC	1,169
	San Diego, AFC	1,515
1989	New Orleans, NFC	1,326
	Denver, AFC	1,580
1988	Chicago, NFC	1,326
	Houston, AFC	1,592

Year	Team	Yards
1987	Chicago, NFC	1,413
	Cleveland, AFC	1,433
1986	N.Y. Giants, NFC	1,284
	Denver, AFC	1,651
1985	Chicago, NFC	1,319
	N.Y. Jets, AFC	1,516
1984	Chicago, NFC	1,377
	Pittsburgh, AFC	1,617
1983	Washington, NFC	1,289
	Cincinnati, AFC	1,499
1982	Pittsburgh, AFC	762
	Detroit, NFC	854
1981	Detroit, NFC	1,623
	Kansas City, AFC	1,747
1980	Detroit, NFC	1,599
	Cincinnati, AFC	1,680
1979	Denver, AFC	1,693
	Tampa Bay, NFC	1,873
1978	Dallas, NFC	1,721
	Pittsburgh, AFC	1,774
1977	Denver, AFC	1,531
	Dallas, NFC	1,651
1976	Pittsburgh, AFC	1,457
	Los Angeles, NFC	1,564
1975	Minnesota, NFC	1,532
	Houston, AFC	1,680
1974	Los Angeles, NFC	1,302
	New England, AFC	1,587
1973	Los Angeles, NFC	1,270
	Oakland, AFC	1,470
1972	Dallas, NFC	1,515
	Miami, AFC	1,548
1971	Baltimore, AFC	1,113
	Dallas, NFC	1,144
1970	Detroit, NFC	1,152
	N.Y. Jets, AFC	1,283
1969	Dallas, NFL	1,050
	Kansas City, AFL	1,091
1968	Dallas, NFL	1,195
	N.Y. Jets, AFL	1,195
1967	Dallas, NFL	1,081
	Oakland, AFL	1,129
1966	Buffalo, AFL	1,051
	Dallas, NFL	1,176
1965	San Diego, AFL	1,094
	Los Angeles, NFL	1,409
1964	Buffalo, AFL	913
	Los Angeles, NFL	1,501
1963	Boston, AFL	1,107
	Chicago, NFL	1,442
1962	Detroit, NFL	1,231
	Dall. Texans, AFL	1,250
1961	Boston, AFL	1,041
	Pittsburgh, NFL	1,463
1960	St. Louis, NFL	1,212
	Dall. Texans, AFL	1,338
1959	N.Y. Giants	1,261
1958	Baltimore	1,291
1957	Baltimore	1,174
1956	N.Y. Giants	1,443
1955	Cleveland	1,189
1954	Cleveland	1,050
1953	Philadelphia	1,117
1952	Detroit	1,145
1951	N.Y. Giants	913
1950	Detroit	1,367
1949	Chi. Bears	1,196
1948	Philadelphia	1,209
1947	Philadelphia	1,329
1946	Chi. Bears	1,060
1945	Philadelphia	817

Year	Team	Yards
1944	Philadelphia	558
1943	Phil-Pitt	793
1942	Chi. Bears	519
1941	Washington	1,042
1940	N.Y. Giants	977
1939	Chi. Bears	812
1938	Detroit	1,081
1937	Chi. Bears	933
1936	Boston	1,148
1935	Boston	998
1934	Chi. Cardinals	954
1933	Brooklyn	964

FEWEST PASSING YARDS ALLOWED

Leadership in this category has been based on net yards since 1952.

Year	Team	Yards
2010	San Diego, AFC	2,845
	New Orleans, NFC	3,103
2009	N.Y. Jets, AFC	2,459
	Carolina, NFC	3,056
2008	Pittsburgh, AFC	2,511
	Philadelphia, NFC	2,913
2007	Tampa Bay, NFC	2,728
	Indianapolis, AFC	2,764
2006	Oakland, AFC	2,413
	New Orleans, NFC	2,854
2005	Green Bay, NFC	2,680
	N.Y. Jets, AFC	2,755
2004	Tampa Bay, NFC	2,579
	Miami, AFC	2,592
2003	Dallas, NFC	2,631
	Buffalo, AFC	2,707
2002	Tampa Bay, NFC	2,490
	Indianapolis, AFC	2,917
2001	Miami, AFC	2,829
	Philadelphia, NFC	2,864
2000	Tennessee, AFC	2,423
	Washington, NFC	2,621
1999	Buffalo, AFC	2,675
	Tampa Bay, NFC	2,873
1998	Philadelphia, NFC	2,720
	Oakland, AFC	2,876
1997	Dallas, NFC	2,522
	Indianapolis, AFC	2,820
1996	Green Bay, NFC	2,740
	Pittsburgh, AFC	2,947
1995	N.Y. Jets, AFC	2,740
	Philadelphia, NFC	2,816
1994	Dallas, NFC	2,752
	Houston, AFC	2,795
1993	New Orleans, NFC	2,606
	Cincinnati, AFC	2,798
1992	New Orleans, NFC	2,470
	Kansas City, AFC	2,537
1991	Philadelphia, NFC	2,413
	Denver, AFC	2,755
1990	Pittsburgh, AFC	2,500
	Dallas, NFC	2,639
1989	Minnesota, NFC	2,501
	Kansas City, AFC	2,527
1988	Kansas City, AFC	2,434
	Minnesota, NFC	2,489
1987	San Francisco, NFC	2,484
	L.A. Raiders, AFC	2,727
1986	St. Louis, NFC	2,637
	New England, AFC	2,978
1985	Washington, NFC	2,746
	Pittsburgh, AFC	2,783
1984	New Orleans, NFC	2,453
	Cleveland, AFC	2,696

Year	Team	Yards	Year	Team	Yards
1983	New Orleans, NFC	2,691	1936	Philadelphia	853
	Cincinnati, AFC	2,828	1935	Chi. Cardinals	793
1982	Miami, AFC	1,027	1934	Philadelphia	545
	Tampa Bay, NFC	1,384	1933	Portsmouth	558
1981	Philadelphia, NFC	2,696			
	Buffalo, AFC	2,870			
1980	Washington, NFC	2,171			
	Buffalo, AFC	2,282			
1979	Tampa Bay, NFC	2,076			
	Buffalo, AFC	2,530			
1978	Buffalo, AFC	1,960			
	Los Angeles, NFC	2,048			
1977	Atlanta, NFC	1,384			
	San Diego, AFC	1,725			
1976	Minnesota, NFC	1,575			
	Cincinnati, AFC	1,758			
1975	Minnesota, NFC	1,621			
	Cincinnati, AFC	1,729			
1974	Pittsburgh, AFC	1,466			
	Atlanta, NFC	1,572			
1973	Miami, AFC	1,290			
	Atlanta, NFC	1,430			
1972	Minnesota, NFC	1,699			
	Cleveland, AFC	1,736			
1971	Atlanta, NFC	1,638			
	Baltimore, AFC	1,739			
1970	Minnesota, NFC	1,438			
	Kansas City, AFC	2,010			
1969	Minnesota, NFL	1,631			
	Kansas City, AFL	2,072			
1968	Houston, AFL	1,671			
	Green Bay, NFL	1,796			
1967	Green Bay, NFL	1,377			
	Buffalo, AFL	1,825			
1966	Green Bay, NFL	1,959			
	Oakland, AFL	2,118			
1965	Green Bay, NFL	1,981			
	San Diego, AFL	2,168			
1964	Green Bay, NFL	1,647			
	San Diego, AFL	2,518			
1963	Chicago, NFL	1,734			
	Oakland, AFL	2,589			
1962	Green Bay, NFL	1,746			
	Oakland, AFL	2,306			
1961	Baltimore, NFL	1,913			
	San Diego, AFL	2,363			
1960	Chicago, NFL	1,388			
	Buffalo, AFL	2,124			
1959	N.Y. Giants	1,582			
1958	Chi. Bears	1,769			
1957	Cleveland	1,300			
1956	Cleveland	1,103			
1955	Pittsburgh	1,295			
1954	Cleveland	1,608			
1953	Washington	1,751			
1952	Washington	1,580			
1951	Pittsburgh	1,687			
1950	Cleveland	1,581			
1949	Philadelphia	1,607			
1948	Green Bay	1,626			
1947	Green Bay	1,790			
1946	Pittsburgh	939			
1945	Washington	1,121			
1944	Chi. Bears	1,052			
1943	Chi. Bears	980			
1942	Washington	1,093			
1941	Pittsburgh	1,168			
1940	Philadelphia	1,012			
1939	Washington	1,116			
1938	Chi. Bears	897			
1937	Detroit	804			

Compiled by Elias Sports Bureau

Super Bowl I, 1/15/67	Super Bowl XXIV, 1/28/90
Super Bowl II, 1/14/68	Super Bowl XXV, 1/27/91
Super Bowl III, 1/12/69	Super Bowl XXVI, 1/26/92
Super Bowl IV, 1/11/70	Super Bowl XXVII, 1/31/93
Super Bowl V, 1/17/71	Super Bowl XXVIII, 1/30/94
Super Bowl VI, 1/16/72	Super Bowl XXIX, 1/29/95
Super Bowl VII, 1/14/73	Super Bowl XXX, 1/28/96
Super Bowl VIII, 1/13/74	Super Bowl XXXI, 1/26/97
Super Bowl IX, 1/12/75	Super Bowl XXXII, 1/25/98
Super Bowl X, 1/18/76	Super Bowl XXXIII, 1/31/99
Super Bowl XI, 1/9/77	Super Bowl XXXIV, 1/30/00
Super Bowl XII, 1/15/78	Super Bowl XXXV, 1/28/01
Super Bowl XIII, 1/21/79	Super Bowl XXXVI, 2/3/02
Super Bowl XIV, 1/20/80	Super Bowl XXXVII, 1/26/03
Super Bowl XV, 1/25/81	Super Bowl XXXVIII, 2/1/04
Super Bowl XVI, 1/24/82	Super Bowl XXXIX, 2/6/05
Super Bowl XVII, 1/30/83	Super Bowl XL, 2/5/06
Super Bowl XVIII, 1/22/84	Super Bowl XLI, 2/4/07
Super Bowl XIX, 1/20/85	Super Bowl XLII, 2/3/08
Super Bowl XX, 1/26/86	Super Bowl XLIII, 2/1/09
Super Bowl XXI, 1/25/87	Super Bowl XLIV, 2/7/10
Super Bowl XXII, 1/31/88	Super Bowl XLV, 2/6/11
Super Bowl XXIII, 1/22/89	

INDIVIDUAL RECORDS

SERVICE
Most Games
- 6   Mike Lodish, Buffalo, XXV-XXVIII; Denver, XXXII-XXXIII
- 5   Marv Fleming, Green Bay, I-II; Miami, VI-VIII
-     Larry Cole, Dallas, V-VI, X, XII-XIII
-     Cliff Harris, Dallas, V-VI, X, XII-XIII
-     Charles Haley, San Francisco, XXIII-XXIV; Dallas, XXVII-XXVIII, XXX
-     D.D. Lewis, Dallas, V-VI, X, XII-XIII
-     Preston Pearson, Baltimore, III; Pittsburgh, IX; Dallas, X, XII-XIII
-     Charlie Waters, Dallas, V-VI, X, XII-XIII
-     Rayfield Wright, Dallas, V-VI, X, XII-XIII
-     Cornelius Bennett, Buffalo, XXV-XXVIII; Atlanta, XXXIII
-     John Elway, Denver, XXI-XXII, XXIV, XXXII-XXXIII
-     Glenn Parker, Buffalo, XXV-XXVIII; N.Y. Giants, XXXV
-     Bill Romanowski, San Francisco, XXIII-XXIV; Denver, XXXII-XXXIII; Oakland, XXXVII
-     Adam Vinatieri, New England, XXXI, XXXVI, XXXVIII, XXXIX; Indianapolis, XLI
-     Tedy Bruschi, New England, XXXI, XXXVI, XXXVIII-XXXIX, XLII
- 4   By many players

Most Games, Winning Team
- 5   Charles Haley, San Francisco, XXIII-XXIV; Dallas, XXVII-XXVIII, XXX
- 4   By many players

Most Games, Coach
- 6   Don Shula, Baltimore, III; Miami, VI-VIII, XVII, XIX
- 5   Tom Landry, Dallas, V-VI, X, XII-XIII
- 4   Bud Grant, Minnesota, IV, VIII-IX, XI
-     Chuck Noll, Pittsburgh, IX-X, XIII-XIV
-     Joe Gibbs, Washington, XVII-XVIII, XXII, XXVI
-     Marv Levy, Buffalo, XXV-XXVIII
-     Dan Reeves, Denver, XXI-XXII, XXIV; Atlanta, XXXIII
-     Bill Belichick, New England, XXXVI, XXXVIII-XXXIX, XLII

Most Games, Winning Team, Coach
- 4   Chuck Noll, Pittsburgh, IX-X, XIII-XIV
- 3   Bill Walsh, San Francisco, XVI, XIX, XXIII
-     Joe Gibbs, Washington, XVII, XXII, XXVI
-     Bill Belichick, New England, XXXVI, XXXVIII-XXXIX
- 2   Vince Lombardi, Green Bay, I-II
-     Tom Landry, Dallas, VI, XII

-     Don Shula, Miami, VII-VIII
-     Tom Flores, Oakland, XV; L.A. Raiders, XVIII
-     Bill Parcells, N.Y. Giants, XXI, XXV
-     Jimmy Johnson, Dallas, XXVII-XXVIII
-     George Seifert, San Francisco, XXIV, XXIX
-     Mike Shanahan, Denver, XXXII-XXXIII

Most Games, Losing Team, Coach
- 4   Bud Grant, Minnesota, IV, VIII-IX, XI
-     Don Shula, Baltimore, III; Miami, VI, XVII, XIX
-     Marv Levy, Buffalo, XXV-XXVIII
-     Dan Reeves, Denver, XXI-XXII, XXIV; Atlanta, XXXIII
- 3   Tom Landry, Dallas, V, X, XIII

SCORING
POINTS
Most Points, Career
- 48   Jerry Rice, San Francisco-Oakland, 4 games (8-td)
- 34   Adam Vinatieri, New England-Indianapolis, 5 games (7-fg, 13-xp)
- 30   Emmitt Smith, Dallas, 3 games (5-td)

Most Points, Game
- 18   Roger Craig, San Francisco vs. Miami, XIX (3-td)
-     Jerry Rice, San Francisco vs. Denver, XXIV (3-td); vs. San Diego, XXIX (3-td)
-     Ricky Watters, San Francisco vs. San Diego, XXIX (3-td)
-     Terrell Davis, Denver vs. Green Bay, XXXII (3-td)
- 15   Don Chandler, Green Bay vs. Oakland, II (3-pat, 4-fg)
- 14   Ray Wersching, San Francisco vs. Cincinnati, XVI (2-pat, 4-fg)
-     Kevin Butler, Chicago vs. New England, XX (5-pat, 3-fg)

TOUCHDOWNS
Most Touchdowns, Career
- 8   Jerry Rice, San Francisco-Oakland, 4 games (8-p)
- 5   Emmitt Smith, Dallas, 3 games (5-r)
- 4   Franco Harris, Pittsburgh, 4 games (4-r)
-     Roger Craig, San Francisco, 3 games (2-r, 2-p)
-     Thurman Thomas, Buffalo, 4 games (4-r)
-     John Elway, Denver, 5 games (4-r)

Most Touchdowns, Game
- 3   Roger Craig, San Francisco vs. Miami, XIX (1-r, 2-p)
-     Jerry Rice, San Francisco. vs. Denver, XXIV (3-p); vs. San Diego, XXIX (3-p)
-     Ricky Watters, San Francisco vs. San Diego, XXIX (1-r, 2-p)
-     Terrell Davis, Denver vs. Green Bay, XXXII (3-r)
- 2   Max McGee, Green Bay vs. Kansas City, I (2-p)
-     Elijah Pitts, Green Bay vs. Kansas City, I (2-r)
-     Bill Miller, Oakland vs. Green Bay, II (2-p)
-     Larry Csonka, Miami vs. Minnesota, VIII (2-r)
-     Pete Banaszak, Oakland vs. Minnesota, XI (2-r)
-     John Stallworth, Pittsburgh vs. Dallas, XIII (2-p)
-     Franco Harris, Pittsburgh vs. Los Angeles, XIV (2-r)
-     Cliff Branch, Oakland vs. Philadelphia, XV (2-p)
-     Dan Ross, Cincinnati vs. San Francisco, XVI (2-p)
-     Marcus Allen, L.A. Raiders vs. Washington, XVIII (2-r)
-     Jim McMahon, Chicago vs. New England, XX (2-r)
-     Ricky Sanders, Washington vs. Denver, XXII (2-p)
-     Timmy Smith, Washington vs. Denver, XXII (2-r)
-     Tom Rathman, San Francisco vs. Denver, XXIV (2-r)
-     Gerald Riggs, Washington vs. Buffalo, XXVI (2-r)
-     Michael Irvin, Dallas vs. Buffalo, XXVII (2-p)
-     Emmitt Smith, Dallas vs. Buffalo, XXVIII (2-r)
-     Emmitt Smith, Dallas vs. Pittsburgh, XXX (2-r)
-     Antonio Freeman, Green Bay vs. Denver, XXXII (2-p)
-     Howard Griffith, Denver vs. Atlanta, XXXIII (2-r)
-     Eddie George, Tennessee vs. St. Louis, XXXIV (2-r)
-     Keenan McCardell, Tampa Bay vs. Oakland, XXXVII (2-r)

Dwight Smith, Tampa Bay vs. Oakland, XXXVII (2-ret)
Larry Fitzgerald, Arizona vs. Pittsburgh, XLIII (2-p)
Greg Jennings, Green Bay vs. Pittsburgh, XLV (2-p)

POINTS AFTER TOUCHDOWN
Most (One-Point) Points After Touchdown, Career
13 Adam Vinatieri, New England-Indianapolis, 5 games (13 att)
9 Mike Cofer, San Francisco, 2 games (10 att)
8 Don Chandler, Green Bay, 2 games (8 att)
Roy Gerela, Pittsburgh, 3 games (9 att)
Chris Bahr, Oakland-L.A. Raiders, 2 games (8 att)
Jason Elam, Denver, 2 games (8 att)

Most (One-Point) Points After Touchdown, Game
7 Mike Cofer, San Francisco vs. Denver, XXIV (8 att)
Lin Elliott, Dallas vs. Buffalo, XXVII (7 att)
Doug Brien, San Francisco vs. San Diego, XXIX (7 att)
6 Ali Hají-Sheikh, Washington vs. Denver, XXII (6 att)
Martin Gramatica, Tampa Bay vs. Oakland, XXXVII (6 att)
5 Don Chandler, Green Bay vs. Kansas City, I (5 att)
Roy Gerela, Pittsburgh vs. Dallas, XIII (5 att)
Chris Bahr, L.A. Raiders vs. Washington, XVIII (5 att)
Ray Wersching, San Francisco vs. Miami, XIX (5 att)
Kevin Butler, Chicago vs. New England, XX (5 att)

Most Two-Point Conversions, Game
1 Mark Seay, San Diego vs. San Francisco, XXIX
Alfred Pupunu, San Diego vs. San Francisco, XXIX
Mark Chmura, Green Bay vs. New England, XXXI
Kevin Faulk, New England vs. Carolina, XXXVIII
Lance Moore, New Orleans vs. Indianapolis, XLIV
Antwaan Randle El, Pittsburgh vs. Green Bay, XLV

FIELD GOALS
Field Goals Attempted, Career
10 Adam Vinatieri, New England-Indianapolis, 5 games
6 Jim Turner, N.Y. Jets-Denver, 2 games
Roy Gerela, Pittsburgh, 3 games
Rich Karlis, Denver, 2 games
Jeff Wilkins, St. Louis, 2 games
5 Efren Herrera, Dallas, 1 game
Ray Wersching, San Francisco, 2 games
Jason Elam, Denver, 2 games
Matt Stover, Baltimore-Indianapolis, 2 games

Most Field Goals Attempted, Game
5 Jim Turner, N.Y. Jets vs. Baltimore, III
Efren Herrera, Dallas vs. Denver, XII
4 Don Chandler, Green Bay vs. Oakland, II
Roy Gerela, Pittsburgh vs. Dallas, X
Ray Wersching, San Francisco vs. Cincinnati, XVI
Rich Karlis, Denver vs. N.Y. Giants, XXI
Mike Cofer, San Francisco vs. Cincinnati, XXIII
Jason Elam, Denver vs. Atlanta, XXXIII
Jeff Wilkins, St. Louis vs. Tennessee, XXXIV
Adam Vinatieri, Indianapolis vs. Chicago, XLI

Most Field Goals, Career
7 Adam Vinatieri, New England-Indianapolis, 5 games (10 att)
5 Ray Wersching, San Francisco, 2 games (5 att)
4 Don Chandler, Green Bay, 2 games (4 att)
Jim Turner, N.Y. Jets-Denver, 2 games (6 att)
Uwe von Schamann, Miami, 2 games (4 att)
Jeff Wilkins, St. Louis, 2 games (6 att)

Most Field Goals, Game
4 Don Chandler, Green Bay vs. Oakland, II
Ray Wersching, San Francisco vs. Cincinnati, XVI
3 Jim Turner, N.Y. Jets vs. Baltimore, III
Jan Stenerud, Kansas City vs. Minnesota, IV
Uwe von Schamann, Miami vs. San Francisco, XIX
Kevin Butler, Chicago vs. New England, XX
Jim Breech, Cincinnati vs. San Francisco, XXIII

Chip Lohmiller, Washington vs. Buffalo, XXVI
Eddie Murray, Dallas vs. Buffalo, XXVIII
Jeff Wilkins, St. Louis vs. Tennessee, XXXIV
Adam Vinatieri, Indianapolis vs. Chicago, XLI
Garrett Hartley, New Orleans vs. Indianapolis, XLIV

Longest Field Goal
54 Steve Christie, Buffalo vs. Dallas, XXVIII
51 Jason Elam, Denver vs. Green Bay, XXXII
50 Jeff Wilkins, St. Louis vs. New England, XXXVI
John Kasay, Carolina vs. New England, XXXVIII

SAFETIES
Most Safeties, Game
1 Dwight White, Pittsburgh vs. Minnesota, IX
Reggie Harrison, Pittsburgh vs. Dallas, X
Henry Waechter, Chicago vs. New England, XX
George Martin, N.Y. Giants vs. Denver, XXI
Bruce Smith, Buffalo vs. N.Y. Giants, XXV

RUSHING
ATTEMPTS
Most Attempts, Career
101 Franco Harris, Pittsburgh, 4 games
70 Emmitt Smith, Dallas, 3 games
64 John Riggins, Washington, 2 games

Most Attempts, Game
38 John Riggins, Washington vs. Miami, XVII
34 Franco Harris, Pittsburgh vs. Minnesota, IX
33 Larry Csonka, Miami vs. Minnesota, VIII

YARDS GAINED
Most Yards Gained, Career
354 Franco Harris, Pittsburgh, 4 games
297 Larry Csonka, Miami, 3 games
289 Emmitt Smith, Dallas, 3 games

Most Yards Gained, Game
204 Timmy Smith, Washington vs. Denver, XXII
191 Marcus Allen, L.A. Raiders vs. Washington, XVIII
166 John Riggins, Washington vs. Miami, XVII

Longest Run From Scrimmage
75 Willie Parker, Pittsburgh vs. Seattle, XL (TD)
74 Marcus Allen, L.A. Raiders vs. Washington, XVIII (TD)
58 Tom Matte, Baltimore vs. N.Y. Jets, III
Timmy Smith, Washington vs. Denver, XXII (TD)

AVERAGE GAIN
Highest Average Gain, Career (20 attempts)
9.6 Marcus Allen, L.A. Raiders, 1 game (20-191)
9.3 Timmy Smith, Washington, 1 game (22-204)
5.4 Dominic Rhodes, Indianapolis, 1 game (21-113)

Highest Average Gain, Game (10 attempts)
10.5 Tom Matte, Baltimore vs. N.Y. Jets, III (11-116)
9.6 Marcus Allen, L.A. Raiders vs. Washington, XVIII (20-191)
9.3 Willie Parker, Pittsburgh vs. Seattle, XL (10-93)

TOUCHDOWNS
Most Touchdowns, Career
5 Emmitt Smith, Dallas, 3 games
4 Franco Harris, Pittsburgh, 4 games
Thurman Thomas, Buffalo, 4 games
John Elway, Denver, 5 games
3 Terrell Davis, Denver, 2 games

Most Touchdowns, Game
3 Terrell Davis, Denver vs. Green Bay, XXXII
2 Elijah Pitts, Green Bay vs. Kansas City, I
Larry Csonka, Miami vs. Minnesota, VIII
Pete Banaszak, Oakland vs. Minnesota, XI
Franco Harris, Pittsburgh vs. Los Angeles, XIV
Marcus Allen, L.A. Raiders vs. Washington, XVIII
Jim McMahon, Chicago vs. New England, XX

Timmy Smith, Washington vs. Denver, XXII
Tom Rathman, San Francisco vs. Denver, XXIV
Gerald Riggs, Washington vs. Buffalo, XXVI
Emmitt Smith, Dallas vs. Buffalo, XXVIII
Emmitt Smith, Dallas vs. Pittsburgh, XXX
Howard Griffith, Denver vs. Atlanta, XXXIII
Eddie George, Tennessee vs. St. Louis, XXXIV

PASSING
PASSER RATING
Highest Passer Rating, Career (40 attempts)
- 127.8 Joe Montana, San Francisco, 4 games
- 122.8 Jim Plunkett, Oakland-L.A. Raiders, 2 games
- 112.8 Terry Bradshaw, Pittsburgh, 4 games

ATTEMPTS
Most Passes Attempted, Career
- 156 Tom Brady, New England, 4 games
- 152 John Elway, Denver, 5 games
- 145 Jim Kelly, Buffalo, 4 games

Most Passes Attempted, Game
- 58 Jim Kelly, Buffalo vs. Washington, XXVI
- 51 Donovan McNabb, Philadelphia vs. New England, XXXIX
- 50 Dan Marino, Miami vs. San Francisco, XIX
  Jim Kelly, Buffalo vs. Dallas, XXVIII

COMPLETIONS
Most Passes Completed, Career
- 100 Tom Brady, New England, 4 games
- 83 Joe Montana, San Francisco, 4 games
  Kurt Warner, St. Louis-Arizona, 3 games
- 81 Jim Kelly, Buffalo, 4 games

Most Passes Completed, Game
- 32 Tom Brady, New England vs. Carolina, XXXVIII
  Drew Brees, New Orleans vs. Indianapolis, XLIV
- 31 Jim Kelly, Buffalo vs. Dallas, XXVIII
  Kurt Warner, Arizona vs. Pittsburgh, XLIII
  Peyton Manning, Indianapolis vs. New Orleans, XLIV
- 30 Donovan McNabb, Philadelphia vs. New England, XXXIX

Most Consecutive Completions, Game
- 13 Joe Montana, San Francisco vs. Denver, XXIV
- 10 Phil Simms, N.Y. Giants vs. Denver, XXI
  Troy Aikman, Dallas vs. Pittsburgh, XXX
  Kurt Warner, Arizona vs. Pittsburgh, XLIII
  Drew Brees, New Orleans vs. Indianapolis, XLIV
- 9 Jim Kelly, Buffalo vs. Dallas, XXVIII
  Neil O'Donnell, Pittsburgh vs. Dallas, XXX
  Steve McNair, Tennessee vs. St. Louis, XXXIV
  Peyton Manning, Indianapolis vs. Chicago, XLI

COMPLETION PERCENTAGE
Highest Completion Percentage, Career (40 attempts)
- 70.0 Troy Aikman, Dallas, 3 games, (80-56)
- 68.0 Joe Montana, San Francisco, 4 games (122-83)
- 67.5 Peyton Manning, Indianapolis, 2 games (83-56)

Highest Completion Percentage, Game (20 attempts)
- 88.0 Phil Simms, N.Y. Giants vs. Denver, XXI (25-22)
- 82.1 Drew Brees, New Orleans vs. Indianapolis, XLIV (39-32)
- 75.9 Joe Montana, San Francisco vs. Denver, XXIV (29-22)

YARDS GAINED
Most Yards Gained, Career
- 1,156 Kurt Warner, St. Louis-Arizona, 3 games
- 1,142 Joe Montana, San Francisco, 4 games
- 1,128 John Elway, Denver, 5 games

Most Yards Gained, Game
- 414 Kurt Warner, St. Louis vs. Tennessee, XXXIV
- 377 Kurt Warner, Arizona vs. Pittsburgh, XLIII

365 Kurt Warner, St. Louis vs. New England, XXXVI

Longest Pass Completion
- 85 Jake Delhomme (to Muhammad), Carolina vs. New England, XXXVIII (TD)
- 81 Brett Favre (to Freeman), Green Bay vs. New England, XXXI (TD)
- 80 Jim Plunkett (to King), Oakland vs. Philadelphia, XV (TD)
  Doug Williams (to Sanders), Washington vs. Denver, XXII (TD)
  John Elway (to R. Smith), Denver vs. Atlanta, XXXIII (TD)

AVERAGE GAIN
Highest Average Gain, Career (40 attempts)
- 11.10 Terry Bradshaw, Pittsburgh, 4 games (84-932)
- 9.62 Bart Starr, Green Bay, 2 games (47-452)
- 9.41 Jim Plunkett, Oakland-L.A. Raiders, 2 games (46-433)

Highest Average Gain, Game (20 attempts)
- 14.71 Terry Bradshaw, Pittsburgh vs. Los Angeles, XIV (21-309)
- 12.80 Jim McMahon, Chicago vs. New England, XX (20-256)
- 12.43 Jim Plunkett, Oakland vs. Philadelphia, XV (21-261)

TOUCHDOWNS
Most Touchdown Passes, Career
- 11 Joe Montana, San Francisco, 4 games
- 9 Terry Bradshaw, Pittsburgh, 4 games
- 8 Roger Staubach, Dallas, 4 games

Most Touchdown Passes, Game
- 6 Steve Young, San Francisco vs. San Diego, XXIX
- 5 Joe Montana, San Francisco vs. Denver, XXIV
- 4 Terry Bradshaw, Pittsburgh vs. Dallas, XIII
  Doug Williams, Washington vs. Denver, XXII
  Troy Aikman, Dallas vs. Buffalo, XXVII

HAD INTERCEPTED
Lowest Percentage, Passes Had Intercepted, Career (40 attempts)
- 0.00 Jim Plunkett, Oakland-L.A. Raiders, 2 games (46-0)
  Joe Montana, San Francisco, 4 games (122-0)
- 0.64 Tom Brady, New England, 4 games (156-1)
- 1.25 Troy Aikman, Dallas, 3 games (80-1)

Most Attempts, Without Interception, Game
- 48 Tom Brady, New England vs. N.Y. Giants, XLII
- 45 Kurt Warner, St. Louis vs. Tennessee, XXXIV
- 39 Drew Brees, New Orleans vs. Indianapolis, XLIV
  Aaron Rodgers, Green Bay vs. Pittsburgh, XLV

Most Passes Had Intercepted, Career
- 8 John Elway, Denver, 5 games
- 7 Craig Morton, Dallas-Denver, 2 games
  Jim Kelly, Buffalo, 4 games
- 6 Fran Tarkenton, Minnesota, 3 games

Most Passes Had Intercepted, Game
- 5 Rich Gannon, Oakland vs. Tampa Bay, XXXVII
- 4 Craig Morton, Denver vs. Dallas, XII
  Jim Kelly, Buffalo vs. Washington, XXVI
  Drew Bledsoe, New England vs. Green Bay, XXXI
  Kerry Collins, N.Y. Giants vs. Baltimore, XXXV
- 3 By 11 players

PASS RECEIVING
RECEPTIONS
Most Receptions, Career
- 33 Jerry Rice, San Francisco-Oakland, 4 games
- 27 Andre Reed, Buffalo, 4 games
- 21 Deion Branch, New England, 2 games

Most Receptions, Game
- 11 Dan Ross, Cincinnati vs. San Francisco, XVI
  Jerry Rice, San Francisco vs. Cincinnati, XXIII
  Deion Branch, New England vs. Philadelphia, XXXIX
  Wes Welker, New England vs. N.Y. Giants, XLII

   10 Tony Nathan, Miami vs. San Francisco, XIX
       Jerry Rice, San Francisco vs. San Diego, XXIX
       Andre Hastings, Pittsburgh vs. Dallas, XXX
       Deion Branch, New England vs. Carolina, XXXVIII
       Joseph Addai, Indianapolis vs. Chicago, XLI
    9 Ricky Sanders, Washington vs. Denver, XXII
       Antonio Freeman, Green Bay vs. Denver, XXXII
       Terrell Owens, Philadelphia vs. New England, XXXIX
       Santonio Holmes, Pittsburgh vs. Arizona, XLIII
       Jordy Nelson, Green Bay vs. Pittsburgh, XLV
       Mike Wallace, Pittsburgh vs. Green Bay, XLV

YARDS GAINED
Most Yards Gained, Career
   589 Jerry Rice, San Francisco-Oakland, 4 games
   364 Lynn Swann, Pittsburgh, 4 games
   323 Andre Reed, Buffalo, 4 games
Most Yards Gained, Game
   215 Jerry Rice, San Francisco vs. Cincinnati, XXIII
   193 Ricky Sanders, Washington vs. Denver, XXII
   162 Isaac Bruce, St. Louis vs. Tennessee, XXXIV
Longest Reception
   85 Muhsin Muhammad (from Delhomme), Carolina vs.
      New England, XXXVIII
   81 Antonio Freeman (from Favre), Green Bay vs.
      New England, XXXI (TD)
   80 Kenny King (from Plunkett), Oakland vs.
      Philadelphia, XV (TD)
      Ricky Sanders (from Williams), Washington vs.
      Denver, XXII (TD)
      Rod Smith (from Elway), Denver vs. Atlanta, XXXIII

AVERAGE GAIN
Highest Average Gain, Career (8 receptions)
  24.4 John Stallworth, Pittsburgh, 4 games (11-268)
  23.4 Ricky Sanders, Washington, 2 games (10-234)
  22.8 Lynn Swann, Pittsburgh, 4 games (16-364)
Highest Average Gain, Game (3 receptions)
  40.33 John Stallworth, Pittsburgh vs. Los Angeles, XIV
       (3-121)
  40.25 Lynn Swann, Pittsburgh vs. Dallas, X (4-161)
  38.33 John Stallworth, Pittsburgh vs. Dallas, XIII (3-115)

TOUCHDOWNS
Most Touchdowns, Career
    8 Jerry Rice, San Francisco-Oakland, 4 games
    3 John Stallworth, Pittsburgh, 4 games
      Lynn Swann, Pittsburgh, 4 games
      Cliff Branch, Oakland-L.A. Raiders, 3 games
      Antonio Freeman, Green Bay, 2 games
    2 Max McGee, Green Bay, 2 games
      Bill Miller, Oakland, 1 game
      Butch Johnson, Dallas, 2 games
      Dan Ross, Cincinnati, 1 game
      Roger Craig, San Francisco, 3 games
      Ricky Sanders, Washington, 2 games
      John Taylor, San Francisco, 3 games
      Gary Clark, Washington, 2 games
      Don Beebe, Buffalo-Green Bay, 4 games
      Michael Irvin, Dallas, 3 games
      Ricky Watters, San Francisco, 1 game
      Jay Novacek, Dallas, 3 games
      Keenan McCardell, Tampa Bay, 1 game
      Ricky Proehl, St. Louis-Carolina, 3 games
      David Givens, New England, 2 games
      Mike Vrabel, New England, 4 games
      Muhsin Muhammad, Carolina-Chicago, 2 games
      Larry Fitzgerald, Arizona, 1 game
      Greg Jennings, Green Bay, 1 game
      Hines Ward, Pittsburgh, 3 games

Most Touchdowns, Game
    3 Jerry Rice, San Francisco vs. Denver, XXIV; vs.
      San Diego, XXIX
    2 Max McGee, Green Bay vs. Kansas City, I
      Bill Miller, Oakland vs. Green Bay, II
      John Stallworth, Pittsburgh vs. Dallas, XIII
      Cliff Branch, Oakland vs. Philadelphia, XV
      Dan Ross, Cincinnati vs. San Francisco, XVI
      Roger Craig, San Francisco vs. Miami, XIX
      Ricky Sanders, Washington vs. Denver, XXII
      Michael Irvin, Dallas vs. Buffalo, XXVII
      Ricky Watters, San Francisco vs. San Diego, XXIX
      Antonio Freeman, Green Bay vs. Denver, XXXII
      Keenan McCardell, Tampa Bay vs. Oakland, XXXVII
      Larry Fitzgerald, Arizona vs. Pittsburgh, XLIII
      Greg Jennings, Green Bay vs. Pittsburgh, XLV

INTERCEPTIONS BY
Most Interceptions By, Career
    3 Chuck Howley, Dallas, 2 games
      Rod Martin, Oakland-L.A. Raiders, 2 games
      Larry Brown, Dallas, 3 games
    2 Randy Beverly, N.Y. Jets, 1 game
      Jake Scott, Miami, 3 games
      Mike Wagner, Pittsburgh, 3 games
      Mel Blount, Pittsburgh, 4 games
      Eric Wright, San Francisco, 4 games
      Barry Wilburn, Washington, 1 game
      Brad Edwards, Washington, 1 game
      Thomas Everett, Dallas, 2 games
      James Washington, Dallas, 2 games
      Darrien Gordon, San Diego-Denver-Oakland,
        4 games
      Dexter Jackson, Tampa Bay, 1 game
      Dwight Smith, Tampa Bay, 1 game
      Rodney Harrison, San Diego-New England, 4 games
Most Interceptions By, Game
    3 Rod Martin, Oakland vs. Philadelphia, XV
    2 Randy Beverly, N.Y. Jets vs. Baltimore, III
      Chuck Howley, Dallas vs. Baltimore, V
      Jake Scott, Miami vs. Washington, VII
      Barry Wilburn, Washington vs. Denver, XXII
      Brad Edwards, Washington vs. Buffalo, XXVI
      Thomas Everett, Dallas vs. Buffalo, XXVII
      Larry Brown, Dallas vs. Pittsburgh, XXX
      Darrien Gordon, Denver vs. Atlanta, XXXIII
      Dexter Jackson, Tampa Bay vs. Oakland, XXXVII
      Dwight Smith, Tampa Bay vs. Oakland, XXXVII
      Rodney Harrison, New England vs. Philadelphia,
        XXXIX

YARDS GAINED
Most Yards Gained, Career
   108 Darrien Gordon, San Diego-Denver-Oakland,
       4 games
   100 James Harrison, Pittsburgh, 2 games
    94 Dwight Smith, Tampa Bay, 1 game
Most Yards Gained, Game
   108 Darrien Gordon, Denver vs. Atlanta, XXXIII
   100 James Harrison, Pittsburgh vs. Arizona, XLIII
    94 Dwight Smith, Tampa Bay vs. Oakland, XXXVII
Longest Return
   100 James Harrison, Pittsburgh vs. Arizona, XLIII (TD)
    76 Kelly Herndon, Seattle vs. Pittsburgh, XL
    75 Willie Brown, Oakland vs. Minnesota, XI (TD)

TOUCHDOWNS
Most Touchdowns, Game
    2 Dwight Smith, Tampa Bay vs. Oakland, XXXVII
    1 Herb Adderley, Green Bay vs. Oakland, II
      Willie Brown, Oakland vs. Minnesota, XI

Jack Squirek, L.A. Raiders vs. Washington, XVIII
Reggie Phillips, Chicago vs. New England, XX
Duane Starks, Baltimore vs. N.Y. Giants, XXXV
Ty Law, New England vs. St. Louis, XXXVI
Derrick Brooks, Tampa Bay vs. Oakland, XXXVII
Kelvin Hayden, Indianapolis vs. Chicago, XLI
James Harrison, Pittsburgh vs. Arizona, XLIII
Tracy Porter, New Orleans vs. Indianapolis, XLIV
Nick Collins, Green Bay vs. Pittsburgh, XLV

PUNTING
Most Punts, Career
17 Mike Eischeid, Oakland-Minnesota, 3 games
    Mike Horan, Denver-St. Louis, 4 games
16 Brad Maynard, N.Y. Giants-Chicago, 2 games
15 Larry Seiple, Miami, 3 games
Most Punts, Game
11 Brad Maynard, N.Y. Giants vs. Baltimore, XXXV
10 Kyle Richardson, Baltimore vs. N.Y. Giants, XXXV
 9 Ron Widby, Dallas vs. Baltimore, V
Longest Punt
63 Lee Johnson, Cincinnati vs. San Francisco, XXIII
62 Rich Camarillo, New England vs. Chicago, XX
61 Jerrel Wilson, Kansas City vs. Green Bay, I

AVERAGE YARDAGE
Highest Average, Punting, Career (10 punts)
46.5 Jerrel Wilson, Kansas City, 2 games (11-511)
43.8 Tom Rouen, Denver-Seattle, 3 games (11-482)
43.0 Kyle Richardson, Baltimore, 1 game (10-430)
     Tom Tupa, New England-Tampa Bay, 2 games
     (12-516)
Highest Average, Punting, Game (4 punts)
50.2 Tom Rouen, Seattle vs. Pittsburgh, XL (6-301)
48.8 Bryan Wagner, San Diego vs. San Francisco, XXIX
     (4-195)
48.7 Chris Gardocki, Pittsburgh vs. Seattle, XL (6-292)

PUNT RETURNS
Most Punt Returns, Career
8 Troy Brown, New England, 3 games
6 Willie Wood, Green Bay, 2 games
  Jake Scott, Miami, 3 games
  Theo Bell, Pittsburgh, 2 games
  Mike Nelms, Washington, 1 game
  John Taylor, San Francisco, 3 games
  Desmond Howard, Green Bay, 1 game
  David Meggett, N.Y. Giants-New England, 2 games
  Darrien Gordon, San Diego-Denver-Oakland,
  4 games
5 Dana McLemore, San Francisco, 1 game
Most Punt Returns, Game
6 Mike Nelms, Washington vs. Miami, XVII
  Desmond Howard, Green Bay vs. New England, XXXI
5 Willie Wood, Green Bay vs. Oakland, II
  Dana McLemore, San Francisco vs. Miami, XIX
4 By 10 players
Most Fair Catches, Game
4 Jermaine Lewis, Baltimore vs. N.Y. Giants, XXXV
  Karl Williams, Tampa Bay vs. Oakland, XXXVII
3 Ron Gardin, Baltimore vs. Dallas, V
  Golden Richards, Dallas vs. Pittsburgh, X
  Greg Pruitt, L.A. Raiders vs. Washington, XVIII
  Al Edwards, Buffalo vs. N.Y. Giants, XXV
  David Meggett, N.Y. Giants vs. Buffalo, XXV

YARDS GAINED
Most Yards Gained, Career
94 John Taylor, San Francisco, 3 games
90 Desmond Howard, Green Bay, 1 game
67 David Meggett, N.Y. Giants-New England, 2 games

Most Yards Gained, Game
90 Desmond Howard, Green Bay vs. New England, XXXI
56 John Taylor, San Francisco vs. Cincinnati, XXIII
52 Mike Nelms, Washington vs. Miami, XXII
Longest Return
45 John Taylor, San Francisco vs. Cincinnati, XXIII
34 Darrell Green, Washington vs. L.A. Raiders, XVIII
   Desmond Howard, Green Bay vs. New England, XXXI
   Jermaine Lewis, Baltimore vs. N.Y. Giants, XXXV
   Steve Breaston, Arizona vs. Pittsburgh, XLIII
32 Desmond Howard, Green Bay vs. New England, XXXI

AVERAGE YARDAGE
Highest Average, Career (4 returns)
15.7 John Taylor, San Francisco, 3 games (6-94)
15.0 Desmond Howard, Green Bay, 1 game (6-90)
11.2 David Meggett, N.Y. Giants-New England, 2 games
     (6-67)
Highest Average, Game (3 returns)
18.7 John Taylor, San Francisco vs. Cincinnati, XXIII (3-56)
15.0 Desmond Howard, Green Bay vs. New England, XXXI
     (6-90)
14.0 Terrence Wilkins, Indianapolis vs. Chicago, XLI
     (3-42)

TOUCHDOWNS
Most Touchdowns, Game
    None

KICKOFF RETURNS
Most Kickoff Returns, Career
10 Ken Bell, Denver, 3 games
 8 Larry Anderson, Pittsburgh, 2 games
   Fulton Walker, Miami, 2 games
   Andre Coleman, San Diego, 1 game
   Marcus Knight, Oakland, 1 game
 7 Preston Pearson, Baltimore-Pittsburgh-Dallas, 5 games
   Stephen Starring, New England, 1 game
   David Meggett, N.Y. Giants-New England, 2 games
Most Kickoff Returns, Game
 8 Andre Coleman, San Diego vs. San Francisco, XXIX
   Marcus Knight, Oakland vs. Tampa Bay, XXXVII
 7 Stephen Starring, New England vs. Chicago, XX
 6 Darren Carrington, Denver vs. San Francisco, XXIV
   Antonio Freeman, Green Bay vs. Denver, XXXII
   Ron Dixon, N.Y. Giants vs. Baltimore, XXXV

YARDS GAINED
Most Yards Gained, Career
283 Fulton Walker, Miami, 2 games
244 Andre Coleman, San Diego, 1 game
210 Tim Dwight, Atlanta, 1 game
Most Yards Gained, Game
244 Andre Coleman, San Diego vs. San Francisco, XXIX
210 Tim Dwight, Atlanta vs. Denver, XXXIII
190 Fulton Walker, Miami vs. Washington, XVII
Longest Return
99 Desmond Howard, Green Bay vs. New England, XXXI
   (TD)
98 Fulton Walker, Miami vs. Washington, XVII (TD)
   Andre Coleman, San Diego vs. San Francisco, XXIX
   (TD)
97 Ron Dixon, N.Y. Giants vs. Baltimore, XXXV (TD)

AVERAGE YARDAGE
Highest Average, Career (4 returns)
42.0 Tim Dwight, Atlanta, 1 game (5-210)
38.5 Desmond Howard, Green Bay, 1 game (4-154)
35.4 Fulton Walker, Miami, 2 games (8-283)
Highest Average, Game (3 returns)
47.5 Fulton Walker, Miami vs. Washington, XVII (4-190)

42.0 Tim Dwight, Atlanta vs. Denver, XXXIII (5-210)
38.5 Desmond Howard, Green Bay vs. New England, XXXI
(4-154)

TOUCHDOWNS
Most Touchdowns, Game
1 Fulton Walker, Miami vs. Washington, XVII
Stanford Jennings, Cincinnati vs. San Francisco, XXIII
Andre Coleman, San Diego vs. San Francisco, XXIX
Desmond Howard, Green Bay vs. New England, XXXI
Tim Dwight, Atlanta vs. Denver, XXXIII
Ron Dixon, N.Y. Giants vs. Baltimore, XXXV
Jermaine Lewis, Baltimore vs. N.Y. Giants, XXXV
Devin Hester, Chicago vs. Indianapolis, XLI

FUMBLES
Most Fumbles, Career
5 Roger Staubach, Dallas, 4 games
4 Jim Kelly, Buffalo, 4 games
Kurt Warner, St. Louis-Arizona, 3 games
3 Franco Harris, Pittsburgh, 4 games
Terry Bradshaw, Pittsburgh, 4 games
John Elway, Denver, 5 games
Frank Reich, Buffalo, 4 games
Thurman Thomas, Buffalo, 4 games
Most Fumbles, Game
3 Roger Staubach, Dallas vs. Pittsburgh, X
Jim Kelly, Buffalo vs. Washington, XXVI
Frank Reich, Buffalo vs. Dallas, XXVII
2 Franco Harris, Pittsburgh vs. Minnesota, IX
Butch Johnson, Dallas vs. Denver, XII
Terry Bradshaw, Pittsburgh vs. Dallas, XIII
Joe Montana, San Francisco vs. Cincinnati, XXIII
John Elway, Denver vs. San Francisco, XXIV
Thurman Thomas, Buffalo vs. Dallas, XXVIII
Rex Grossman, Chicago vs. Indianapolis, XLI
Eli Manning, N.Y. Giants vs. New England, XLII
Kurt Warner, Arizona vs. Pittsburgh, XLIII

RECOVERIES
Most Fumbles Recovered, Career
2 Jake Scott, Miami, 3 games (1 own, 1 opp)
Fran Tarkenton, Minnesota, 3 games (2 own)
Franco Harris, Pittsburgh, 4 games (2 own)
Roger Staubach, Dallas, 4 games (2 own)
Bobby Walden, Pittsburgh, 2 games (2 own)
John Fitzgerald, Dallas, 4 games (2 own)
Randy Hughes, Dallas, 3 games (2 opp)
Butch Johnson, Dallas, 2 games (2 own)
Mike Singletary, Chicago, 1 game (2 opp)
John Elway, Denver, 5 games (2 own)
Jimmie Jones, Dallas, 2 games (2 opp)
Kenneth Davis, Buffalo, 4 games (2 own)
Kurt Warner, St. Louis-Arizona, 3 games (2 own)
Most Fumbles Recovered, Game
2 Jake Scott, Miami vs. Minnesota, VIII (1 own, 1 opp)
Roger Staubach, Dallas vs. Pittsburgh, X (2 own)
Randy Hughes, Dallas vs. Denver, XII (2 opp)
Butch Johnson, Dallas vs. Denver, XII (2 own)
Mike Singletary, Chicago vs. New England, XX (2 opp)
Jimmie Jones, Dallas vs. Buffalo, XXVII (2 opp)

YARDS GAINED
Most Yards Gained, Game
64 Leon Lett, Dallas vs. Buffalo, XXVII (opp)
49 Mike Bass, Washington vs. Miami, VII (opp)
46 James Washington, Dallas vs. Buffalo, XXVIII (opp)
Longest Return
64 Leon Lett, Dallas vs. Buffalo, XXVII
49 Mike Bass, Washington vs. Miami, VII (TD)

46 James Washington, Dallas vs. Buffalo, XXVIII (TD)

TOUCHDOWNS
Most Touchdowns, Game
1 Mike Bass, Washington vs. Miami, VII (opp 49 yds)
Mike Hegman, Dallas vs. Pittsburgh, XIII (opp 37 yds)
Jimmie Jones, Dallas vs. Buffalo, XXVII (opp 2 yds)
Ken Norton, Dallas vs. Buffalo, XXVII (opp 9 yds)
James Washington, Dallas vs. Buffalo, XXVIII
(opp 46 yds)

COMBINED NET YARDS GAINED
(Rushing, receiving, interception returns, punt returns, kickoff
returns, and fumble returns)
ATTEMPTS
Most Attempts, Career
108 Franco Harris, Pittsburgh, 4 games
81 Emmitt Smith, Dallas, 3 games
72 Roger Craig, San Francisco, 3 games
Thurman Thomas, Buffalo, 4 games
Most Attempts, Game
39 John Riggins, Washington vs. Miami, XVII
35 Franco Harris, Pittsburgh vs. Minnesota, IX
34 Matt Snell, N.Y. Jets vs. Baltimore, III
Emmitt Smith, Dallas vs. Buffalo, XXVIII

YARDS GAINED
Most Yards Gained, Career
604 Jerry Rice, San Francisco-Oakland, 4 games
468 Franco Harris, Pittsburgh, 4 games
410 Roger Craig, San Francisco, 3 games
Most Yards Gained, Game
244 Andre Coleman, San Diego vs. San Francisco, XXIX
Desmond Howard, Green Bay vs. New England, XXXI
235 Ricky Sanders, Washington vs. Denver, XXII
230 Antonio Freeman, Green Bay vs. Denver, XXXII

SACKS
Sacks have been compiled since XVII.
Most Sacks, Career
4.5 Charles Haley, San Francisco-Dallas, 5 games
3.0 Danny Stubbs, San Francisco, 2 games
Leonard Marshall, N.Y. Giants, 2 games
Jeff Wright, Buffalo, 4 games
Reggie White, Green Bay, 2 games
Willie McGinest, New England, 4 games
Tedy Bruschi, New England, 5 games
Mike Vrabel, New England, 4 games
Darnell Dockett, Arizona, 1 game
LaMarr Woodley, Pittsburgh, 2 games
2.5 Dexter Manley, Washington, 3 games
Michael Strahan, N.Y. Giants, 2 games
Most Sacks, Game
3.0 Reggie White, Green Bay vs. New England, XXXI
Darnell Dockett, Arizona vs. Pittsburgh, XLIII
2.0 Dwaine Board, San Francisco vs. Miami, XIX
Dennis Owens, New England vs. Chicago, XX
Otis Wilson, Chicago vs. New England, XX
Leonard Marshall, N.Y. Giants vs. Denver, XXI
Alvin Walton, Washington vs. Denver, XXII
Charles Haley, San Francisco vs. Cincinnati, XXIII
Danny Stubbs, San Francisco vs. Denver, XXIV
Jeff Wright, Buffalo vs. Dallas, XXVIII
Raylee Johnson, San Diego vs. San Francisco, XXIX
Chad Hennings, Dallas vs. Pittsburgh, XXX
Tedy Bruschi, New England vs. Green Bay, XXXI
Michael McCrary, Baltimore vs. N.Y. Giants, XXXV
Simeon Rice, Tampa Bay vs. Oakland, XXXVII
Mike Vrabel, New England vs. Carolina, XXXVIII
Adalius Thomas, New England vs. N.Y. Giants, XLII
Justin Tuck, N.Y. Giants vs. New England, XLII

LaMarr Woodley, Pittsburgh vs. Arizona, XLIII

TEAM RECORDS

GAMES, VICTORIES, DEFEATS
Most Games
- 8 Dallas, V-VI, X, XII-XIII, XXVII-XXVIII, XXX
  Pittsburgh, IX-X, XIII-XIV, XXX, XL, XLIII, XLV
- 6 Denver, XII, XXI-XXII, XXIV, XXXII-XXXIII
  New England, XX, XXXI, XXXVI, XXXVIII-XXXIX, XLII
- 5 Miami, VI-VIII, XVII, XIX
  Washington, VII, XVII-XVIII, XXII, XXVI
  San Francisco, XVI, XIX, XXIII-XXIV, XXIX
  Oakland/L.A. Raiders, II, XI, XV, XVIII, XXXVII
  Green Bay, I-II, XXXI-XXXII, XLV

Most Consecutive Games
- 4 Buffalo, XXV-XXVIII
- 3 Miami, VI-VIII
- 2 Green Bay, I-II; XXXI-XXXII
  Dallas, V-VI; XII-XIII; XXVII-XXVIII
  Minnesota, VIII-IX
  Pittsburgh, IX-X; XIII-XIV
  Washington, XVII-XVIII
  Denver, XXI-XXII; XXXII-XXXIII
  San Francisco, XXIII-XXIV
  New England, XXXVIII-XXXIX

Most Games Won
- 6 Pittsburgh, IX-X, XIII-XIV, XL, XLIII
- 5 San Francisco, XVI, XIX, XXIII-XXIV, XXIX
  Dallas, VI, XII, XXVII-XXVIII, XXX
- 4 Green Bay, I-II, XXXI, XLV

Most Consecutive Games Won
- 2 Green Bay, I-II
  Miami, VII-VIII
  Pittsburgh, IX-X, XIII-XIV
  San Francisco, XXIII-XXIV
  Dallas, XXVII-XXVIII
  Denver, XXXII-XXXIII
  New England, XXXVIII-XXXIX

Most Games Lost
- 4 Minnesota, IV, VIII-IX, XI
  Denver, XII, XXI-XXII, XXIV
  Buffalo, XXV-XXVIII
- 3 Dallas, V, X, XIII
  Miami, VI, XVII, XIX
  New England, XX, XXXI, XLII
- 2 Washington, VII, XVIII
  Cincinnati, XVI, XXII
  L.A./St. Louis Rams, XIV, XXXVI
  Oakland/L.A. Raiders, II, XXXVII
  Philadelphia, XV, XXXIX
  Baltimore/Indianapolis, III, XLIV
  Pittsburgh, XXX, XLV

Most Consecutive Games Lost
- 4 Buffalo, XXV-XXVIII
- 2 Minnesota, VIII-IX
  Denver, XXI-XXII

SCORING
Most Points, Game
- 55 San Francisco vs. Denver, XXIV
- 52 Dallas vs. Buffalo, XXVII
- 49 San Francisco vs. San Diego, XXIX

Fewest Points, Game
- 3 Miami vs. Dallas, VI
- 6 Minnesota vs. Pittsburgh, IX
- 7 By five teams

Most Points, Both Teams, Game
- 75 San Francisco (49) vs. San Diego (26), XXIX
- 69 Dallas (52) vs. Buffalo (17), XXVII
  Tampa Bay (48) vs. Oakland (21), XXXVII

- 66 Pittsburgh (35) vs. Dallas (31), XIII

Fewest Points, Both Teams, Game
- 21 Washington (7) vs. Miami (14), VII
- 22 Minnesota (6) vs. Pittsburgh (16), IX
- 23 Baltimore (7) vs. N.Y. Jets (16), III

Largest Margin of Victory, Game
- 45 San Francisco vs. Denver, XXIV (55-10)
- 36 Chicago vs. New England, XX (46-10)
- 35 Dallas vs. Buffalo, XXVII (52-17)

Most Points, Each Half
- 1st: 35 Washington vs. Denver, XXII
- 2nd: 30 N.Y. Giants vs. Denver, XXI

Most Points, Each Quarter
- 1st: 14 Miami vs. Minnesota, VIII
  Oakland vs. Philadelphia, XV
  Dallas vs. Buffalo, XXVII
  San Francisco vs. San Diego, XXIX
  New England vs. Green Bay, XXXI
  Chicago vs. Indianapolis, XLI
  Green Bay vs. Pittsburgh, XLV
- 2nd: 35 Washington vs. Denver, XXII
- 3rd: 21 Chicago vs. New England, XX
- 4th: 21 Dallas vs. Buffalo, XXVII

Most Points, Both Teams, Each Half
- 1st: 45 Washington (35) vs. Denver (10), XXII
- 2nd: 46 Tampa Bay (28) vs. Oakland (18), XXXVII

Fewest Points, Both Teams, Each Half
- 1st: 2 Minnesota (0) vs. Pittsburgh (2), IX
- 2nd: 7 Miami (0) vs. Washington (7), VII
  Denver (0) vs. Washington (7), XXII

Most Points, Both Teams, Each Quarter
- 1st: 24 New England (14) vs. Green Bay (10), XXXI
- 2nd: 35 Washington (35) vs. Denver (0), XXII
- 3rd: 24 Washington (14) vs. Buffalo (10), XXVI
- 4th: 37 Carolina (19) vs. New England (18), XXXVIII

TOUCHDOWNS
Most Touchdowns, Game
- 8 San Francisco vs. Denver, XXIV
- 7 Dallas vs. Buffalo, XXVII
  San Francisco vs. San Diego, XXIX
- 6 Washington vs. Denver, XXII
  Tampa Bay vs. Oakland, XXXVII

Fewest Touchdowns, Game
- 0 Miami vs. Dallas, VI
- 1 By 19 teams

Most Touchdowns, Both Teams, Game
- 10 San Francisco (7) vs. San Diego (3), XXIX
- 9 Pittsburgh (5) vs. Dallas (4), XIII
  San Francisco (8) vs. Denver (1), XXIV
  Dallas (7) vs. Buffalo (2), XXVII
  Tampa Bay (6) vs. Oakland (3), XXXVII
- 8 Carolina (4) vs. New England (4), XXXVIII

Fewest Touchdowns, Both Teams, Game
- 2 Baltimore (1) vs. N.Y. Jets (1), III
- 3 In six games

POINTS AFTER TOUCHDOWN
Most (One-Point) Points After Touchdown, Game
- 7 San Francisco vs. Denver, XXIV
  Dallas vs. Buffalo, XXVII
  San Francisco vs. San Diego, XXIX
- 6 Washington vs. Denver, XXII
  Tampa Bay vs. Oakland, XXXVII
- 5 Green Bay vs. Kansas City, I
  Pittsburgh vs. Dallas, XIII
  L.A. Raiders vs. Washington, XVIII
  San Francisco vs. Miami, XIX
  Chicago vs. New England, XX

Most (One-Point) Points After Touchdown, Both Teams, Game
- 9 Pittsburgh (5) vs. Dallas (4), XIII

Dallas (7) vs. Buffalo (2), XXVII
8   San Francisco (7) vs. Denver (1), XXIV
    San Francisco (7) vs. San Diego (1), XXIX
7   Washington (6) vs. Denver (1), XXII
    Washington (4) vs. Buffalo (3), XXVI
    Denver (4) vs. Green Bay (3), XXXII

Fewest (One-Point) Points After Touchdown, Both Teams, Game
2   Baltimore (1) vs. N.Y. Jets (1), III
    Baltimore (1) vs. Dallas (1), V
    Minnesota (0) vs. Pittsburgh (2), IX

Most Two-Point Conversions, Game
2   San Diego vs. San Francisco, XXIX

Most Two-Point Conversions, Both Teams, Game
2   San Diego (2) vs. San Francisco (0), XXIX

FIELD GOALS

Most Field Goals Attempted, Game
5   N.Y. Jets vs. Baltimore, III
    Dallas vs. Denver, XII
4   Green Bay vs. Oakland, II
    Pittsburgh vs. Dallas, XX
    San Francisco vs. Cincinnati, XVI; XXIII
    Denver vs. N.Y. Giants, XXI
    Denver vs. Atlanta, XXXIII
    St. Louis vs. Tennessee, XXXIV
    Indianapolis vs. Chicago, XLI

Most Field Goals Attempted, Both Teams, Game
7   N.Y. Jets (5) vs. Baltimore (2), III
    San Francisco (4) vs. Cincinnati (3), XXIII
    St. Louis (4) vs. Tennessee (3), XXXIV
    Denver (4) vs. Atlanta (3), XXXIII
6   Dallas (5) vs. Denver (1), XII
5   Green Bay (4) vs. Oakland (1), II
    Pittsburgh (4) vs. Dallas (1), X
    Oakland (3) vs. Philadelphia (2), XV
    Denver (4) vs. N.Y. Giants (1), XXI
    Dallas (3) vs. Buffalo (2), XXVIII
    Indianapolis (4) vs. Chicago (1), XLI
    New Orleans (3) vs. Indianapolis (2), XLIV

Fewest Field Goals Attempted, Both Teams, Game
1   Minnesota (0) vs. Miami (1), VIII
    San Francisco (0) vs. Denver (1), XXIV
    Philadelphia (0) vs. New England (1), XXXIX
    New England (0) vs. N.Y. Giants (1), XLII
2   Green Bay (0) vs. Kansas City (2), I
    Miami (1) vs. Washington (1), VII
    Minnesota (1) vs. Pittsburgh (1), IX
    Dallas (1) vs. Pittsburgh (1), XIII
    Dallas (1) vs. Buffalo (1), XXVII
    San Diego (1) vs. San Francisco (1), XXIX
    Denver (1) vs. Green Bay (1), XXXII
    Arizona (0) vs. Pittsburgh (2), XLIII

Most Field Goals, Game
4   Green Bay vs. Oakland, II
    San Francisco vs. Cincinnati, XVI
3   N.Y. Jets vs. Baltimore, III
    Kansas City vs. Minnesota, IV
    Miami vs. San Francisco, XIX
    Chicago vs. New England, XX
    Cincinnati vs. San Francisco, XXIII
    Washington vs. Buffalo, XXVI
    Dallas vs. Buffalo, XXVIII
    St. Louis vs. Tennessee, XXXIV
    Indianapolis vs. Chicago, XLI
    New Orleans vs. Indianapolis, XLIV

Most Field Goals, Both Teams, Game
5   Cincinnati (3) vs. San Francisco (2), XXIII
    Dallas (3) vs. Buffalo (2), XXVIII
4   Green Bay (4) vs. Oakland (0), II
    San Francisco (4) vs. Cincinnati (0), XVI
    Miami (3) vs. San Francisco (1), XIX

Chicago (3) vs. New England (1), XX
Washington (3) vs. Buffalo (1), XXVI
Atlanta (2) vs. Denver (2), XXXIII
St. Louis (3) vs. Tennessee (1), XXXIV
Indianapolis (3) vs. Chicago (1), XLI
New Orleans (3) vs. Indianapolis (1), XLIV
3   In 13 games

Fewest Field Goals, Both Teams, Game
0   Miami vs. Washington, VII
    Pittsburgh vs. Minnesota, IX
1   Green Bay (0) vs. Kansas City (1), I
    Minnesota (0) vs. Miami (1), VIII
    Pittsburgh (0) vs. Dallas (1), XIII
    Washington (0) vs. Denver (1), XXII
    San Francisco (0) vs. Denver (1), XXIV
    San Francisco (0) vs. San Diego (1), XXIX
    Philadelphia (0) vs. New England (1), XXXIX
    Pittsburgh (0) vs. Seattle (1), XLI
    New England (0) vs. N.Y. Giants (1), XLII

SAFETIES

Most Safeties, Game
1   Pittsburgh vs. Minnesota, IX; vs. Dallas, X
    Chicago vs. New England, XX
    N.Y. Giants vs. Denver, XXI
    Buffalo vs. N.Y. Giants, XXV
    Arizona vs. Pittsburgh, XLIII

FIRST DOWNS

Most First Downs, Game
31 San Francisco vs. Miami, XIX
29 New England vs. Carolina, XXXVIII
28 San Francisco vs. Denver, XXIV
    San Francisco vs. San Diego, XXIX

Fewest First Downs, Game
9   Minnesota vs. Pittsburgh, IX
    Miami vs. Washington, XVII
10 Dallas vs. Baltimore, V
    Miami vs. Dallas, VI
11 Denver vs. Dallas, XII
    N.Y. Giants vs. Baltimore, XXXV
    Oakland vs. Tampa Bay, XXXVII
    Chicago vs. Indianapolis, XLI

Most First Downs, Both Teams, Game
50 San Francisco (31) vs. Miami (19), XIX
    Tennessee (27) vs. St. Louis (23), XXXIV
49 Buffalo (25) vs. Washington (24), XXVI
48 San Francisco (28) vs. San Diego (20), XXIX

Fewest First Downs, Both Teams, Game
24 Dallas (10) vs. Baltimore (14), V
    N.Y. Giants (11) vs. Baltimore (13), XXXV
26 Minnesota (9) vs. Pittsburgh (17), IX
27 Pittsburgh (13) vs. Dallas (14), X

RUSHING

Most First Downs, Rushing, Game
16 San Francisco vs. Miami, XIX
15 Dallas vs. Miami, VI
14 Washington vs. Miami, XVII
    San Francisco vs. Denver, XXIV
    Denver vs. Green Bay, XXXII

Fewest First Downs, Rushing, Game
1   New England vs. Chicago, XX
    St. Louis vs. Tennessee, XXXIV
    Oakland vs. Tampa Bay, XXXVII
2   Minnesota vs. Kansas City, IV; vs. Pittsburgh, IX;
        vs. Oakland, XI
    Pittsburgh vs. Dallas, XIII
    Miami vs. San Francisco, XIX
    N.Y. Giants vs. Baltimore, XXXV
    Arizona vs. Pittsburgh, XLIII

3 Miami vs. Dallas, VI
 Philadelphia vs. Oakland, XV
 New England vs. Green Bay, XXXI
 Carolina vs. New England, XXXVIII
 Chicago vs. Indianapolis, XLII
 New England vs. N.Y. Giants, XLII
 New Orleans vs. Indianapolis, XLIV

Most First Downs, Rushing, Both Teams, Game
21 Washington (14) vs. Miami (7), XVII
19 Washington (13) vs. Denver (6), XXII
 San Francisco (14) vs. Denver (5), XXIV
18 Dallas (15) vs. Miami (3), VI
 Miami (13) vs. Minnesota (5), VIII
 San Francisco (16) vs. Miami (2), XIX
 N.Y. Giants (10) vs. Buffalo (8), XXV
 Denver (14) vs. Green Bay (4), XXXII

Fewest First Downs, Rushing, Both Teams, Game
6 Arizona (2) vs. Pittsburgh (4), XLIII
7 Oakland (1) vs. Tampa Bay (6), XXXVIII
 New England (3) vs. N.Y. Giants (4), XLII
8 Baltimore (4) vs. Dallas (4), V
 Pittsburgh (2) vs. Dallas (6), XIII
 N.Y. Giants (2) vs. Baltimore (6), XXXV

PASSING
Most First Downs, Passing, Game
20 Arizona vs. Pittsburgh, XLIII
19 New England vs. Carolina, XXXVIII
18 Buffalo vs. Washington, XXVI
 St. Louis vs. Tennessee, XXXIV
 Philadelphia vs. New England, XXXIX

Fewest First Downs, Passing, Game
1 Denver vs. Dallas, XII
2 Miami vs. Washington, XVII
4 Miami vs. Minnesota, VIII

Most First Downs, Passing, Both Teams, Game
32 Miami (17) vs. San Francisco (15), XIX
 Philadelphia (18) vs. New England (14), XXXIX
 Arizona (20) vs. Pittsburgh (12), XLIII
 Indianapolis (16) vs. New Orleans (16), XLIV
31 San Francisco (17) vs. San Diego (14), XXIX
 St. Louis (18) vs. Tennessee (13), XXXIV
 New England (19) vs. Carolina (12), XXXVIII
30 Buffalo (18) vs. Washington (12), XXVI
 New England (17) vs. N.Y. Giants (13), XLII

Fewest First Downs, Passing, Both Teams, Game
9 Denver (1) vs. Dallas (8), XII
10 Minnesota (5) vs. Pittsburgh (5), IX
11 Dallas (5) vs. Baltimore (6), V
 Miami (2) vs. Washington (9), XVII

PENALTY
Most First Downs, Penalty, Game
4 Baltimore vs. Dallas, V
 Miami vs. Minnesota, VIII
 Cincinnati vs. San Francisco, XVI
 Buffalo vs. Dallas, XXVII
 St. Louis vs. Tennessee, XXXIV
 Pittsburgh vs. Arizona, XLIII
3 Kansas City vs. Minnesota, IV
 Minnesota vs. Oakland, XI
 Buffalo vs. Washington, XXVI
 Green Bay vs. Denver, XXXII
 N.Y. Giants vs. Baltimore, XXXV
 St. Louis vs. New England, XXXVI
 Tampa Bay vs. Oakland, XXXVII
 New England vs. Carolina, XXXVIII

Most First Downs, Penalty, Both Teams, Game
6 Cincinnati (4) vs. San Francisco (2), XVI
 St. Louis (4) vs. Tennessee (2), XXXIV
5 Baltimore (4) vs. Dallas (1), V

Miami (4) vs. Minnesota (1), VIII
 Buffalo (3) vs. Washington (2), XXVI
 Green Bay (3) vs. Denver (2), XXXII
 New England (3) vs. Carolina (2), XXXVIII
 Pittsburgh (4) vs. Arizona (1), XLIII
4 Kansas City (3) vs. Minnesota (1), IV
 Buffalo (4) vs. Dallas (0), XXVII
 N.Y. Giants (3) vs. Baltimore (1), XXXV
 St. Louis (3) vs. New England (1), XXXVI
 Tampa Bay (3) vs. Oakland (1), XXXVII

Fewest First Downs, Penalty, Both Teams, Game
0 Dallas vs. Miami, VI
 Miami vs. Washington, VII
 Dallas vs. Pittsburgh, X
 Miami vs. San Francisco, XIX
 Pittsburgh vs. Seattle, XL
 Green Bay vs. Pittsburgh, XLV
1 Green Bay (0) vs. Kansas City (1), I
 Miami (0) vs. Washington (1), XVII
 Cincinnati (0) vs. San Francisco (1), XXIII
 San Francisco (0) vs. Denver (1), XXIV
 Dallas (0) vs. Buffalo (1), XXVIII
 Dallas (0) vs. Pittsburgh (1), XXX
 Denver (0) vs. Atlanta (1), XXXIII
 Chicago (0) vs. Indianapolis (1), XLI

NET YARDS GAINED RUSHING AND PASSING
Most Yards Gained, Game
602 Washington vs. Denver, XXII
537 San Francisco vs. Miami, XIX
481 New England vs. Carolina, XXXVIII

Fewest Yards Gained, Game
119 Minnesota vs. Pittsburgh, IX
123 New England vs. Chicago, XX
152 N.Y. Giants vs. Baltimore, XXXV

Most Yards Gained, Both Teams, Game
929 Washington (602) vs. Denver (327), XXII
868 New England (481) vs. Carolina (387), XXXVIII
851 San Francisco (537) vs. Miami (314), XIX

Fewest Yards Gained, Both Teams, Game
396 N.Y. Giants (152) vs. Baltimore (244), XXXV
452 Minnesota (119) vs. Pittsburgh (333), IX
481 Washington (228) vs. Miami (253), VII
 Denver (156) vs. Dallas (325), XII

RUSHING
ATTEMPTS
Most Attempts, Game
57 Pittsburgh vs. Minnesota, IX
53 Miami vs. Minnesota, VIII
52 Oakland vs. Minnesota, XI
 Washington vs. Miami, XVII

Fewest Attempts, Game
9 Miami vs. San Francisco, XIX
11 New England vs. Chicago, XX
 Oakland vs. Tampa Bay, XXXVII
12 Arizona vs. Pittsburgh, XLIII

Most Attempts, Both Teams, Game
81 Washington (52) vs. Miami (29), XVII
78 Pittsburgh (57) vs. Minnesota (21), IX
 Oakland (52) vs. Minnesota (26), XI
77 Miami (53) vs. Minnesota (24), VIII
 Pittsburgh (46) vs. Dallas (31), X

Fewest Attempts, Both Teams, Game
36 Green Bay (13) vs. Pittsburgh (23), XLV
37 Arizona (12) vs. Pittsburgh (25), XLIII
 New Orleans (18) vs. Indianapolis (19), XLIV
42 New England (16) vs. N.Y. Giants (26), XLII

YARDS GAINED

Most Yards Gained, Game
- 280 Washington vs. Denver, XXII
- 276 Washington vs. Miami, XVII
- 266 Oakland vs. Minnesota, XI

Fewest Yards Gained, Game
- 7 New England vs. Chicago, XX
- 17 Minnesota vs. Pittsburgh, IX
- 19 Oakland vs. Tampa Bay, XXXVII

Most Yards Gained, Both Teams, Game
- 377 Washington (280) vs. Denver (97), XXII
- 372 Washington (276) vs. Miami (96), XVII
- 338 N.Y. Giants (172) vs. Buffalo (166), XXV

Fewest Yards Gained, Both Teams, Game
- 91 Arizona (33) vs. Pittsburgh (58), XLIII
- 136 New England (45) vs. N.Y. Giants (91), XLII
- 150 New Orleans (51) vs. Indianapolis (99), XLIV

AVERAGE GAIN

Highest Average Gain, Game
- 7.00 L.A. Raiders vs. Washington, XVIII (33-231)
  Washington vs. Denver, XXII (40-280)
- 6.64 Buffalo vs. N.Y. Giants, XXV (25-166)
- 6.22 Baltimore vs. N.Y. Jets, III (23-143)

Lowest Average Gain, Game
- 0.64 New England vs. Chicago, XX (11-7)
- 0.81 Minnesota vs. Pittsburgh, IX (21-17)
- 1.73 Oakland vs. Tampa Bay, XXXVII (11-19)

TOUCHDOWNS

Most Touchdowns, Game
- 4 Chicago vs. New England, XX
  Denver vs. Green Bay, XXXII
- 3 Green Bay vs. Kansas City, I
  Miami vs. Minnesota, VIII
  San Francisco vs. Denver, XXIV
  Denver vs. Atlanta, XXXIII
- 2 Oakland vs. Minnesota, XI
  Pittsburgh vs. Los Angeles, XIV
  L.A. Raiders vs. Washington, XVIII
  San Francisco vs. Miami, XIX
  N.Y. Giants vs. Denver, XXI
  Washington vs. Denver, XXII; vs. Buffalo, XXVI
  Buffalo vs. N.Y. Giants, XXV
  Dallas vs. Buffalo, XXVIII; vs. Pittsburgh, XXX
  Tennessee vs. St. Louis, XXXIV
  Pittsburgh vs. Seattle, XL

Fewest Touchdowns, Game
- 0 By 31 teams

Most Touchdowns, Both Teams, Game
- 4 Miami (3) vs. Minnesota (1), VIII
  Chicago (4) vs. New England (0), XX
  San Francisco (3) vs. Denver (1), XXIV
  Denver (4) vs. Green Bay (0), XXXII
- 3 In nine games

Fewest Touchdowns, Both Teams, Game
- 0 Pittsburgh vs. Dallas, X
  Oakland vs. Philadelphia, XV
  Cincinnati vs. San Francisco, XXIII
- 1 In 16 games

PASSING

ATTEMPTS

Most Passes Attempted, Game
- 59 Buffalo vs. Washington, XXVI
- 55 San Diego vs. San Francisco, XXIX
- 51 Philadelphia vs. New England, XXXIX

Fewest Passes Attempted, Game
- 7 Miami vs. Minnesota, VIII
- 11 Miami vs. Washington, VII
- 14 Pittsburgh vs. Minnesota, IX

Most Passes Attempted, Both Teams, Game
- 93 San Diego (55) vs. San Francisco (38), XXIX
- 92 Buffalo (59) vs. Washington (33), XXVI
- 85 Miami (50) vs. San Francisco (35), XIX

Fewest Passes Attempted, Both Teams, Game
- 35 Miami (7) vs. Minnesota (28), VIII
- 39 Miami (11) vs. Washington (28), VII
- 40 Pittsburgh (14) vs. Minnesota (26), IX
  Miami (17) vs. Washington (23), XVII

COMPLETIONS

Most Passes Completed, Game
- 32 New England vs. Carolina, XXXVIII
  New Orleans vs. Indianapolis, XLIV
- 31 Buffalo vs. Dallas, XXVIII
  Arizona vs. Pittsburgh, XLIII
  Indianapolis vs. New Orleans, XLIV
- 30 Philadelphia vs. New England, XXXIX

Fewest Passes Completed, Game
- 4 Miami vs. Washington, XVII
- 6 Miami vs. Minnesota, VIII
- 8 Miami vs. Washington, VII
  Denver vs. Dallas, XII

Most Passes Completed, Both Teams, Game
- 63 New Orleans (32) vs. Indianapolis (31), XLIV
- 53 Miami (29) vs. San Francisco (24), XIX
  Philadelphia (30) vs. New England (23), XXXIX
- 52 San Diego (27) vs. San Francisco (25), XXIX
  Arizona (31) vs. Pittsburgh (21), XLIII

Fewest Passes Completed, Both Teams, Game
- 19 Miami (4) vs. Washington (15), XVII
- 20 Pittsburgh (9) vs. Minnesota (11), IX
- 22 Miami (8) vs. Washington (14), VII

COMPLETION PERCENTAGE

Highest Completion Percentage, Game (20 attempts)
- 88.0 N.Y. Giants vs. Denver, XXI (25-22)
- 82.1 New Orleans vs. Indianapolis, XLIV (39-32)
- 75.0 San Francisco vs. Denver, XXIV (32-24)

Lowest Completion Percentage, Game (20 attempts)
- 32.0 Denver vs. Dallas, XII (25-8)
- 37.9 Denver vs. San Francisco, XXIV (29-11)
- 38.5 Denver vs. Washington, XXII (39-15)
  N.Y. Giants vs. Baltimore, XXXV (39-15)

YARDS GAINED

Most Yards Gained, Game
- 407 St. Louis vs. Tennessee, XXXIV
- 374 Arizona vs. Pittsburgh, XLIII
- 354 New England vs. Carolina, XXXVIII

Fewest Yards Gained, Game
- 35 Denver vs. Dallas, XII
- 63 Miami vs. Minnesota, VIII
- 69 Miami vs. Washington, VII

Most Yards Gained, Both Teams, Game
- 649 New England (354) vs. Carolina (295), XXXVIII
- 615 San Francisco (326) vs. Miami (289), XIX
  St. Louis (407) vs. Tennessee (208), XXXIV
- 614 Indianapolis (333) vs. New Orleans (281), XLIV

Fewest Yards Gained, Both Teams, Game
- 156 Miami (69) vs. Washington (87), VII
- 186 Pittsburgh (84) vs. Minnesota (102), IX
- 204 Miami (80) vs. Washington (124), XVII

TIMES SACKED

Most Times Sacked, Game
- 7 Dallas vs. Pittsburgh, X
  New England vs. Chicago, XX
- 6 Kansas City vs. Green Bay, I
  Washington vs. L.A. Raiders, XVIII
  Denver vs. San Francisco, XXIV

5   Dallas vs. Denver, XII; vs. Pittsburgh, XIII
Cincinnati vs. San Francisco, XVI; XXIII
Denver vs. Washington, XXII
Buffalo vs. Washington, XXVI
Green Bay vs. New England, XXXI
New England vs. Green Bay, XXXI
Oakland vs. Tampa Bay, XXXVIII
New England vs. N.Y. Giants, XLII

Fewest Times Sacked, Game

0   Baltimore vs. N.Y. Jets, III; vs. Dallas, V
Minnesota vs. Pittsburgh, IX
Pittsburgh vs. Los Angeles, XIV
Philadelphia vs. Oakland, XV
Washington vs. Buffalo, XXVI
Denver vs. Green Bay, XXXII; vs. Atlanta, XXXIII
Tampa Bay vs. Oakland, XXXVII
New England vs. Carolina, XXXVIII
Indianapolis vs. New Orleans, XLIV

1   By 18 teams

Most Times Sacked, Both Teams, Game

10   New England (7) vs. Chicago (3), XX
Green Bay (5) vs. New England (5), XXXI

9   Kansas City (6) vs. Green Bay (3), I
Dallas (7) vs. Pittsburgh (2), X
Dallas (5) vs. Denver (4), XII
Dallas (5) vs. Pittsburgh (4), XIII
Cincinnati (5) vs. San Francisco (4), XXIII

8   Washington (6) vs. L.A. Raiders (2), XVIII
New England (5) vs. N.Y. Giants (3), XLII

Fewest Times Sacked, Both Teams, Game

1   Philadelphia (0) vs. Oakland (1), XV
Denver (0) vs. Green Bay (1), XXXII
Indianapolis (0) vs. New Orleans (1), XLIV

2   Baltimore (0) vs. N.Y. Jets (2), III
Baltimore (0) vs. Dallas (2), V
Minnesota (0) vs. Pittsburgh (2), IX
Denver (0) vs. Atlanta (2), XXXIII
Chicago (1) vs. Indianapolis (1), XLI

3   In five games

TOUCHDOWNS

Most Touchdowns, Game

6   San Francisco vs. San Diego, XXIX
5   San Francisco vs. Denver, XXIV
4   Pittsburgh vs. Dallas, XIII
Washington vs. Denver, XXII
Dallas vs. Buffalo, XXVII

Fewest Touchdowns, Game

0   By 19 teams

Most Touchdowns, Both Teams, Game

7   Pittsburgh (4) vs. Dallas (3), XIII
San Francisco (6) vs. San Diego (1), XXIX
6   Carolina (3) vs. New England (3), XXXVIII
5   Washington (4) vs. Denver (1), XXII
San Francisco (5) vs. Denver (0), XXIV
Dallas (4) vs. Buffalo (1), XXVII
Philadelphia (3) vs. New England (2), XXXIX
Green Bay (3) vs. Pittsburgh (2), XLV

Fewest Touchdowns, Both Teams, Game

0   N.Y. Jets vs. Baltimore, III
Miami vs. Minnesota, VIII
Buffalo vs. Dallas, XXVIII
1   In seven games

INTERCEPTIONS BY

Most Interceptions By, Game

5   Tampa Bay vs. Oakland, XXXVII
4   N.Y. Jets vs. Baltimore, III
Dallas vs. Denver, XII
Washington vs. Buffalo, XXVI
Dallas vs. Buffalo, XXVII

Green Bay vs. New England, XXXI
Baltimore vs. N.Y. Giants, XXXV

3   By 13 teams

Most Interceptions By, Both Teams, Game

6   Baltimore (3) vs. Dallas (3), V
Tampa Bay (5) vs. Oakland (1), XXXVII
5   Washington (4) vs. Buffalo (1), XXVI
4   In 10 games

Fewest Interceptions By, Both Teams, Game

0   Buffalo vs. N.Y. Giants, XXV
St. Louis vs. Tennessee, XXXIV
1   Oakland (0) vs. Green Bay (1), II
Miami (0) vs. Dallas (1), VI
Minnesota (0) vs. Miami (1), VIII
N.Y. Giants (0) vs. Denver (1), XXI
Cincinnati (0) vs. San Francisco (1), XXIII
New England (0) vs. Carolina (1), XXXVIII
N.Y. Giants (0) vs. New England (1), XLII
Indianapolis (0) vs. New Orleans (1), XLIV

YARDS GAINED

Most Yards Gained, Game

172   Tampa Bay vs. Oakland, XXXVII
136   Denver vs. Atlanta, XXXIII
100   Pittsburgh vs. Arizona, XLIII

Most Yards Gained, Both Teams, Game

184   Tampa Bay (172) vs. Oakland (12), XXXVII
137   Denver (136) vs. Atlanta (1), XXXIII
100   Seattle (76) vs. Pittsburgh (24), XL
Indianapolis (94) vs. Chicago (6), XLI

TOUCHDOWNS

Most Touchdowns, Game

3   Tampa Bay vs. Oakland, XXXVII
1   Green Bay vs. Oakland, II
Oakland vs. Minnesota, XI
L.A. Raiders vs. Washington, XVIII
Chicago vs. New England, XX
Baltimore vs. N.Y. Giants, XXXV
New England vs. St. Louis, XXXVI
Indianapolis vs. Chicago, XLI
Pittsburgh vs. Arizona, XLIII
New Orleans vs. Indianapolis, XLIV
Green Bay vs. Pittsburgh, XLV

PUNTING

Most Punts, Game

11   N.Y. Giants vs. Baltimore, XXXV
10   Baltimore vs. N.Y. Giants, XXXV
9   Dallas vs. Baltimore, V

Fewest Punts, Game

1   Atlanta vs. Denver, XXXIII
Denver vs. Atlanta, XXXIII
2   Pittsburgh vs. Los Angeles, XIV
Denver vs. N.Y. Giants, XXI
St. Louis vs. Tennessee, XXXIV
Indianapolis vs. New Orleans, XLIV
New Orleans vs. Indianapolis, XLIV
3   By 13 teams

Most Punts, Both Teams, Game

21   N.Y. Giants (11) vs. Baltimore (10), XXXV
15   Washington (8) vs. L.A. Raiders (7), XVIII
New England (8) vs. Green Bay (7), XXXI
13   Dallas (9) vs. Baltimore (4), V
Pittsburgh (7) vs. Minnesota (6), IX

Fewest Punts, Both Teams, Game

2   Atlanta (1) vs. Denver (1), XXXIII
4   Indianapolis (2) vs. New Orleans (2), XLIV
5   Denver (2) vs. N.Y. Giants (3), XXI
St. Louis (2) vs. Tennessee (3), XXXIV

AVERAGE YARDAGE
Highest Average, Game (4 punts)
- 50.17 Seattle vs. Pittsburgh, XL (6-301)
- 48.75 San Diego vs. San Francisco, XXIX (4-195)
- 48.67 Pittsburgh vs. Seattle, XL (6-292)

Lowest Average, Game (4 punts)
- 31.00 Tampa Bay vs. Oakland, XXXVII (5-155)
- 31.20 Washington vs. Miami, VII (5-156)
- 32.38 Washington vs. L.A. Raiders, XVIII (8-259)

PUNT RETURNS
Most Punt Returns, Game
- 6 Washington vs. Miami, XVII
     Green Bay vs. New England, XXXI
- 5 By seven teams

Fewest Punt Returns, Game
- 0 Minnesota vs. Miami, VIII
     Buffalo vs. N.Y. Giants, XXV
     Washington vs. Buffalo, XXVI
     Denver vs. Green Bay, XXXII
     Green Bay vs. Denver, XXXII
     Atlanta vs. Denver, XXXIII
     Denver vs. Atlanta, XXXIII
- 1 By 24 teams

Most Punt Returns, Both Teams, Game
- 10 Green Bay (6) vs. New England (4), XXXI
- 9 Pittsburgh (5) vs. Minnesota (4), IX
- 8 Green Bay (5) vs. Oakland (3), II
     Baltimore (5) vs. Dallas (3), V
     Washington (6) vs. Miami (2), XVII
     N.Y. Giants (5) vs. Baltimore (3), XXXV

Fewest Punt Returns, Both Teams, Game
- 0 Denver vs. Green Bay, XXXII
     Atlanta vs. Denver, XXXIII
- 2 Dallas (1) vs. Miami (1), VI
     Denver (1) vs. N.Y. Giants (1), XXI
     Buffalo (0) vs. N.Y. Giants (2), XXV
     Buffalo (1) vs. Dallas (1), XXVIII
     Indianapolis (1) vs. New Orleans (1), XLIV
- 3 Kansas City (1) vs. Minnesota (2), IV
     Minnesota (0) vs. Miami (3), VIII
     Washington (1) vs. Denver (2), XXII
     Washington (0) vs. Buffalo (3), XXVI
     Dallas (1) vs. Pittsburgh (2), XXX
     Tennessee (1) vs. St. Louis (2), XXXIV

YARDS GAINED
Most Yards Gained, Game
- 90 Green Bay vs. New England, XXXI
- 56 San Francisco vs. Cincinnati, XXIII
- 52 Washington vs. Miami, XVII

Fewest Yards Gained, Game
- −1 Dallas vs. Miami, VI
     Tennessee vs. St. Louis, XXXIV
- 0 By 14 teams

Most Yards Gained, Both Teams, Game
- 120 Green Bay (90) vs. New England (30), XXXI
- 80 N.Y. Giants (46) vs. Baltimore (34), XXXV
- 74 Washington (52) vs. Miami (22), XVII

Fewest Yards Gained, Both Teams, Game
- 0 Denver vs. Green Bay, XXXII
     Atlanta vs. Denver, XXXIII
- 4 Indianapolis (0) vs. New Orleans (4), XLIV
- 5 Green Bay (0) vs. Pittsburgh (5), XLV

AVERAGE RETURN
Highest Average, Game (3 returns)
- 18.7 San Francisco vs. Cincinnati, XXIII (3-56)
- 15.0 Green Bay vs. New England, XXXI (6-90)
- 14.0 Indianapolis vs. Chicago, XLI (3-42)

TOUCHDOWNS
Most Touchdowns, Game
- None

KICKOFF RETURNS
Most Kickoff Returns, Game
- 9 Denver vs. San Francisco, XXIV
     Oakland vs. Tampa Bay, XXXVII
- 8 San Diego vs. San Francisco, XXIX
- 7 By eight teams

Fewest Kickoff Returns, Game
- 1 N.Y. Jets vs. Baltimore, III
     L.A. Raiders vs. Washington, XVIII
     Washington vs. Buffalo, XXVI
- 2 By 10 teams

Most Kickoff Returns, Both Teams, Game
- 13 Oakland (9) vs. Tampa Bay (4), XXXVII
- 12 Denver (9) vs. San Francisco (3), XXIV
     San Diego (8) vs. San Francisco (4), XXIX
- 11 Los Angeles (6) vs. Pittsburgh (5), XIV
     Miami (7) vs. San Francisco (4), XIX
     New England (7) vs. Chicago (4), XX
     Green Bay (6) vs. Denver (5), XXXII

Fewest Kickoff Returns, Both Teams, Game
- 5 N.Y. Jets (1) vs. Baltimore (4), III
     Miami (2) vs. Washington (3), VII
     Washington (1) vs. Buffalo (4), XXVI
- 6 In five games

YARDS GAINED
Most Yards Gained, Game
- 244 San Diego vs. San Francisco, XXIX
- 227 Atlanta vs. Denver, XXXIII
- 222 Miami vs. Washington, XVII

Fewest Yards Gained, Game
- 16 Washington vs. Buffalo, XXVI
- 17 L.A. Raiders vs. Washington, XVIII
- 25 N.Y. Jets vs. Baltimore, III

Most Yards Gained, Both Teams, Game
- 292 San Diego (244) vs. San Francisco (48), XXIX
- 289 Green Bay (154) vs. New England (135), XXXI
- 281 N.Y. Giants (170) vs. Baltimore (111), XXXV

Fewest Yards Gained, Both Teams, Game
- 78 Miami (33) vs. Washington (45), VII
- 82 Pittsburgh (32) vs. Minnesota (50), IX
- 92 San Francisco (40) vs. Cincinnati (52), XVI

AVERAGE GAIN
Highest Average, Game (3 returns)
- 44.0 Cincinnati vs. San Francisco, XXIII (3-132)
- 38.5 Green Bay vs. New England, XXXI (4-154)
- 37.0 Miami vs. Washington, XVII (6-222)

TOUCHDOWNS
Most Touchdowns, Game
- 1 Miami vs. Washington, XVII
     Cincinnati vs. San Francisco, XXIII
     San Diego vs. San Francisco, XXIX
     Green Bay vs. New England, XXXI
     Atlanta vs. Denver, XXXIII
     Baltimore vs. N.Y. Giants, XXXV
     N.Y. Giants vs. Baltimore, XXXV
     Chicago vs. Indianapolis, XLI

Most Touchdowns, Both Teams, Game
- 2 Baltimore (1) vs. N.Y. Giants (1), XXXV

PENALTIES
Most Penalties, Game
- 12 Dallas vs. Denver, XII
     Carolina vs. New England, XXXVIII
- 11 Arizona vs. Pittsburgh, XLIII

10 Dallas vs. Baltimore, V

Fewest Penalties, Game

0 Miami vs. Dallas, VI
Pittsburgh vs. Dallas, X
Denver vs. San Francisco, XXIV
Atlanta vs. Denver, XXXIII
1 Green Bay vs. Oakland, II
Miami vs. Minnesota, VIII; vs. San Francisco, XIX
Buffalo vs. Dallas, XXVIII
2 By six teams

Most Penalties, Both Teams, Game

20 Dallas (12) vs. Denver (8), XII
Carolina (12) vs. New England (8), XXXVIII
18 Arizona (11) vs. Pittsburgh (7), XLIII
16 Cincinnati (8) vs. San Francisco (8), XVI
Green Bay (9) vs. Denver (7), XXXII

Fewest Penalties, Both Teams, Game

2 Pittsburgh (0) vs. Dallas (2), X
3 Miami (0) vs. Dallas (3), VI
Miami (1) vs. San Francisco (2), XIX
4 Denver (0) vs. San Francisco (4), XXIV
Atlanta (0) vs. Denver (4), XXXIII

YARDS PENALIZED

Most Yards Penalized, Game

133 Dallas vs. Baltimore, X
122 Pittsburgh vs. Minnesota, IX
106 Arizona vs. Pittsburgh, XLIII

Fewest Yards Penalized, Game

0 Miami vs. Dallas, VI
Pittsburgh vs. Dallas, X
Denver vs. San Francisco, XXIV
Atlanta vs. Denver, XXXIII
4 Miami vs. Minnesota, VIII
10 Miami vs. San Francisco, XIX
San Francisco vs. Miami, XIX
Buffalo vs. Dallas, XXVIII

Most Yards Penalized, Both Teams, Game

164 Dallas (133) vs. Baltimore (31), V
162 Arizona (106) vs. Pittsburgh (56), XLIII
154 Dallas (94) vs. Denver (60), XII

Fewest Yards Penalized, Both Teams, Game

15 Miami (0) vs. Dallas (15), VI
20 Pittsburgh (0) vs. Dallas (20), X
Miami (10) vs. San Francisco (10), XIX
38 Denver (0) vs. San Francisco (38), XXIV

FUMBLES

Most Fumbles, Game

8 Buffalo vs. Dallas, XXVII
6 Dallas vs. Denver, XII
Buffalo vs. Washington, XXVI
5 Baltimore vs. Dallas, V

Fewest Fumbles, Game

0 By 22 teams

Most Fumbles, Both Teams, Game

12 Buffalo (8) vs. Dallas (4), XXVII
10 Dallas (6) vs. Denver (4), XII
8 Dallas (4) vs. Pittsburgh (4), X

Fewest Fumbles, Both Teams, Game

0 Los Angeles vs. Pittsburgh, XIV
Green Bay vs. New England, XXXI
Pittsburgh vs. Seattle, XL
Indianapolis vs. New Orleans, XLIV
1 Oakland (0) vs. Minnesota (1), XI
Oakland (0) vs. Philadelphia (1), XV
Denver (0) vs. Washington (1), XXII
N.Y. Giants (0) vs. Buffalo (1), XXV
Denver (0) vs. Atlanta (1), XXXIII
2 In 10 games

Most Fumbles Lost, Game

5 Buffalo vs. Dallas, XXVII
4 Baltimore vs. Dallas, V
Denver vs. Dallas, XII
New England vs. Chicago, XX
3 Chicago vs. Indianapolis, XLI

Most Fumbles Lost, Both Teams, Game

7 Buffalo (5) vs. Dallas (2), XXVII
6 Denver (4) vs. Dallas (2), XII
New England (4) vs. Chicago (2), XX
5 Baltimore (4) vs. Dallas (1), V
Chicago (3) vs. Indianapolis (2), XLI

Fewest Fumbles Lost, Both Teams, Game

0 Green Bay vs. Kansas City, I
Dallas vs. Pittsburgh, X
Los Angeles vs. Pittsburgh, XIV
Denver vs. N.Y. Giants, XXI; vs. Washington, XXII
Buffalo vs. N.Y. Giants, XXV
San Diego vs. San Francisco, XXIX
Dallas vs. Pittsburgh, XXX
Green Bay vs. New England, XXXI
St. Louis vs. Tennessee, XXXIV
Oakland vs. Tampa Bay, XXXVII
Pittsburgh vs. Seattle, XL
Indianapolis vs. New Orleans, XLIV

Most Fumbles Recovered, Game

8 Dallas vs. Denver, XII (4 own, 4 opp.)
6 Dallas vs. Buffalo, XXVII (1 own, 5 opp.)
5 Chicago vs. New England, XX (1 own, 4 opp.)

TURNOVERS

(Number of times losing the ball on interceptions and fumbles.)

Most Turnovers, Game

9 Buffalo vs. Dallas, XXVII
8 Denver vs. Dallas, XII
7 Baltimore vs. Dallas, V

Fewest Turnovers, Game

0 Green Bay vs. Oakland, II
Miami vs. Minnesota, VIII
Pittsburgh vs. Dallas, X
Oakland vs. Minnesota, XI; vs. Philadelphia, XV
N.Y. Giants vs. Denver, XXI; vs. Buffalo, XXV
San Francisco vs. Denver, XXIV; vs. San Diego, XXIX
Buffalo vs. N.Y. Giants, XXV
Dallas vs. Pittsburgh, XXX
Green Bay vs. New England, XXXI
St. Louis vs. Tennessee, XXXIV
Tennessee vs. St. Louis, XXXIV
Baltimore vs. N.Y. Giants, XXXV
New England vs. St. Louis, XXXVI
New Orleans vs. Indianapolis, XLIV
Green Bay vs. Pittsburgh, XLV
1 By many teams

Most Turnovers, Both Teams, Game

11 Baltimore (7) vs. Dallas (4), V
Buffalo (9) vs. Dallas (2), XXVII
10 Denver (8) vs. Dallas (2), XII
8 New England (6) vs. Chicago (2), XX
Chicago (5) vs. Indianapolis (3), XLI

Fewest Turnovers, Both Teams, Game

0 Buffalo vs. N.Y. Giants, XXV
St. Louis vs. Tennessee, XXXIV
1 N.Y. Giants (0) vs. Denver (1), XXI
New Orleans (0) vs. Indianapolis (1), XLIV
2 Green Bay (1) vs. Kansas City (1), I
Miami (0) vs. Minnesota (2), VIII
Cincinnati (1) vs. San Francisco (1), XXIII
Carolina (1) vs. New England (1), XXXVIII
New England (1) vs. N.Y. Giants (1), XLII

Compiled by Elias Sports Bureau

Throughout this all-time postseason record section, the following abbreviations are used to indicate various levels of postseason games:

SB   Super Bowl (1966 to date)

AFC   AFC Championship Game (1970 to date) or AFL Championship Game (1960-69)

NFC   NFC Championship Game (1970 to date) or NFL Championship Game (1933-69)

AFC-D AFC Divisional Playoff Game (1970 to date), AFC Second-Round Playoff Game (1982), AFL Inter-Divisional Playoff Game (1969), or special playoff game to break tie for AFL Division Championship (1963, 1968)

NFC-D NFC Divisional Playoff Game (1970 to date), NFC Second-Round Playoff Game (1982), NFL Conference Championship Game (1967-69), or special playoff game to break tie for NFL Division or Conference Championship (1941, 1943, 1947, 1950, 1952, 1957, 1958, 1965)

AFC-FR AFC First-Round Playoff Game (1978 to date)

NFC-FR NFC First-Round Playoff Game (1978 to date)

Year indicates season in which game took place and does not necessarily reflect calendar year.

POSTSEASON GAME COMPOSITE STANDINGS

	W	L	PCT.	PTS.	OP
Green Bay Packers	29	16	.644	1,116	893
Pittsburgh Steelers	33	20	.623	1,260	1,094
Baltimore Ravens	9	6	.600	292	202
Carolina Panthers	6	4	.600	219	203
San Francisco 49ers	25	17	.595	1,044	853
New England Patriots#	21	15	.583	765	727
Oakland Raiders**	25	18	.581	1,028	797
Washington Redskins*	23	17	.575	819	707
Dallas Cowboys	33	25	.569	1,355	1,098
Denver Broncos	17	15	.531	694	794
Miami Dolphins	20	20	.500	789	875
Indianapolis Colts***	19	20	.487	785	786
Philadelphia Eagles	19	20	.487	757	720
Chicago Bears	17	18	.486	751	726
Buffalo Bills	14	15	.483	681	658
New York Jets	12	13	.480	510	508
Arizona Cardinals††††	6	7	.462	305	361
Jacksonville Jaguars	5	6	.455	262	288
New York Giants	20	24	.455	763	833
St. Louis Rams††	19	24	.442	770	944
Tennessee Titans†	14	19	.424	579	762
Minnesota Vikings	19	26	.422	900	1,017
Seattle Seahawks	8	11	.421	421	438
New Orleans Saints	5	7	.417	287	348
Detroit Lions	7	10	.412	365	404
Tampa Bay Buccaneers	6	9	.400	230	279
San Diego Chargers†††	10	16	.385	488	592
Atlanta Falcons	6	10	.375	343	409
Kansas City Chiefs****	8	14	.364	347	475
Cincinnati Bengals	5	9	.357	277	312
Cleveland Browns	11	20	.355	629	728

    *   *One game played when franchise was in Boston (lost 21-6).*

   ** *12 games played when franchise was in Los Angeles (won 6, lost 6, 268 points scored, 224 points allowed).*

  *** *15 games played when franchise was in Baltimore (won 8, lost 7, 264 points scored, 262 points allowed).*

 **** *One game played when franchise was Dallas Texans (won 20-17).*

    # *Two games played when franchise was in Boston (won 26-8, lost 51-10).*

    † *22 games played when franchise was in Houston and known as the Oilers (won 9, lost 13, 371 points scored, 533 points allowed).*

   †† *One game played when franchise was in Cleveland (won 15-14), 32 games played when franchise was in*

Los Angeles (won 12, lost 20, 486 points scored, 683 points allowed).

 ††† *One game played when franchise was in Los Angeles (lost 24-16).*

†††† *Two games played when franchise was in Chicago (won 28-21, lost 7-0), three games played when franchise was in St. Louis (lost 30-14, lost 35-23, lost 41-16).*

INDIVIDUAL RECORDS

SERVICE

Most Games, Career

  29 Jerry Rice, San Francisco-Oakland-Seattle (SB 4, NFC 6, AFC 1, NFC-D 11, AFC-D 2, NFC-FR 4, AFC-FR 1)

  27 D.D. Lewis, Dallas (SB 5, NFC 9, NFC-D 12, NFC-FR 1)

  26 Larry Cole, Dallas (SB 5, NFC 8, NFC-D 12, NFC-FR 1)
      Bill Romanowski, San Francisco-Philadelphia-Denver-Oakland (SB 5, NFC 5, AFC 3, NFC-D 6, AFC-D 4, NFC-FR 1, AFC-FR 2)

Most Games, Head Coach

  36 Tom Landry, Dallas
      Don Shula, Baltimore-Miami

  24 Chuck Noll, Pittsburgh
      Mike Holmgren, Green Bay-Seattle
      Joe Gibbs, Washington

  22 Bud Grant, Minnesota

Most Championships Won, Head Coach

   6 George Halas, Chicago
      Curly Lambeau, Green Bay

   5 Vince Lombardi, Green Bay

   4 Guy Chamberlin, Canton Bulldogs-Cleveland Bulldogs-Frankford Yellow Jackets
      Chuck Noll, Pittsburgh

Most Games Won, Head Coach

  20 Tom Landry, Dallas

  19 Don Shula, Baltimore-Miami

  17 Joe Gibbs, Washington

Most Games Lost, Head Coach

  17 Don Shula, Baltimore-Miami

  16 Tom Landry, Dallas

  13 Marty Schottenheimer, Cleveland-Kansas City-San Diego

SCORING

POINTS

Most Points, Career

 177 Adam Vinatieri, New England-Indianapolis, 23 games (51-pat, 42-fg)

 153 Gary Anderson, Pittsburgh-Philadelphia-San Francisco-Minnesota-Tennessee, 22 games (57-pat, 32-fg)

 134 David Akers, Philadelphia, 19 games (41-pat, 31-fg)

Most Points, Game

  30 Ricky Watters, NFC-D: San Francisco vs. N.Y. Giants, 1993 (5-td)

  19 Pat Harder, NFC-D: Detroit vs. Los Angeles, 1952 (2-td, 4-pat, 1-fg)
      Paul Hornung, NFC: Green Bay vs. N.Y. Giants, 1961 (1-td, 4-pat, 3-fg)

  18 By many players

Most Consecutive Games Scoring

  24 Adam Vinatieri, New England-Indianapolis, 1996-98, 2001, 2003-08, 2010 (current)

  19 George Blanda, Chi. Bears-Houston-Oakland, 1956-1975
      David Akers, Philadelphia, 2000-06, 2008-2010 (current)

  16 Norm Johnson, Seattle-Atlanta-Pittsburgh, 1983-84, 1987-88, 1991, 1995-97
      Matt Stover, Cleveland-Baltimore-Indianapolis, 1994, 2000-01, 2003, 2006, 2008-09

TOUCHDOWNS

Most Touchdowns, Career

  22 Jerry Rice, San Francisco-Oakland-Seattle, 29 games (22-p)

21 Thurman Thomas, Buffalo, 21 games (16-r, 5-p)
Emmitt Smith, Dallas, 17 games (19-r, 2-p)
17 Franco Harris, Pittsburgh, 19 games (16-r, 1-p)

Most Touchdowns, Game
5 Ricky Watters, NFC-D: San Francisco vs. N.Y. Giants, 1993 (5-r)
3 Andy Farkas, NFC-D: Washington vs. N.Y. Giants, 1943 (3-r)
Tom Fears, NFC-D: Los Angeles vs. Chi. Bears, 1950 (3-p)
Otto Graham, NFC: Cleveland vs. Detroit, 1954 (3-r)
Gary Collins, NFC: Cleveland vs. Baltimore, 1964 (3-p)
Craig Baynham, NFC-D: Dallas vs. Cleveland, 1967 (2-r, 1-p)
Fred Biletnikoff, AFC-D: Oakland vs. Kansas City, 1968 (3-p)
Tom Matte, NFC: Baltimore vs. Cleveland, 1968 (3-r)
Larry Schreiber, NFC-D: San Francisco vs. Dallas, 1972 (3-r)
Larry Csonka, AFC: Miami vs. Oakland, 1973 (3-r)
Franco Harris, AFC-D: Pittsburgh vs. Buffalo, 1974 (3-r)
Preston Pearson, NFC: Dallas vs. Los Angeles, 1975 (3-p)
Dave Casper, AFC-D: Oakland vs. Baltimore, 1977 (ot) (3-p)
Alvin Garrett, NFC-FR: Washington vs. Detroit, 1982 (3-p)
John Riggins, NFC-D: Washington vs. L.A. Rams, 1983 (3-r)
Roger Craig, SB: San Francisco vs. Miami, 1984 (1-r, 2-p)
Jerry Rice, NFC-D: San Francisco vs. Minnesota, 1988 (3-p)
Jerry Rice, SB: San Francisco vs. Denver, 1989 (3-p)
Kenneth Davis, AFC: Buffalo vs. L.A. Raiders, 1990 (3-r)
Andre Reed, AFC-FR: Buffalo vs. Houston, 1992 (ot) (3-p)
Sterling Sharpe, NFC-FR: Green Bay vs. Detroit, 1993 (3-p)
Napoleon McCallum, AFC-FR: L.A. Raiders vs. Denver, 1993 (3-r)
Thurman Thomas, AFC: Buffalo vs. Kansas City, 1993 (3-r)
William Floyd, NFC-D: San Francisco vs. Chicago, 1994 (3-r)
Ricky Watters, SB: San Francisco vs. San Diego, 1994 (1-r, 2-p)
Jerry Rice, SB: San Francisco vs. San Diego, 1994 (3-p)
Emmitt Smith, NFC: Dallas vs. Green Bay, 1995 (3-r)
Curtis Martin, AFC-D: New England vs. Pittsburgh, 1996 (3-r)
Terrell Davis, SB: Denver vs. Green Bay, 1997 (3-r)
Mario Bates, NFC-D: Arizona vs. Minnesota, 1998 (3-r)
Leroy Hoard, NFC-D: Minnesota vs. Arizona, 1998 (2-r, 1-p)
Willie Jackson, NFC-FR: New Orleans vs. St. Louis, 2000 (3-p)
Amani Toomer, NFC-FR: N.Y. Giants vs. San Francisco, 2002 (3-p)
Shaun Alexander, NFC-FR: Seattle vs. Green Bay, 2003 (ot) (3-r)
Ryan Grant, NFC-D: Green Bay vs. Seattle, 2007 (3-r)
Larry Fitzgerald, NFC: Arizona vs. Philadelphia, 2008 (3-p)
Sidney Rice, NFC-D: Minnesota vs. Dallas, 2009 (3-p)
Adrian Peterson, NFC: Minnesota vs. New Orleans, 2009 (3-r)

Most Consecutive Games Scoring Touchdowns
9 Thurman Thomas, Buffalo, 1992-98
8 John Stallworth, Pittsburgh, 1978-1983
Emmitt Smith, Dallas, 1993-96
7 John Riggins, Washington, 1982-84
Marcus Allen, L.A. Raiders, 1982-85
Terrell Davis, Denver, 1996-98
David Givens, New England, 2003-05

POINTS AFTER TOUCHDOWN
Most (One-Point) Points After Touchdown, Career
57 Gary Anderson, Pittsburgh-Philadelphia-San Francisco-Minnesota-Tennessee, 22 games (57 att)
52 Adam Vinatieri, New England-Indianapolis, 24 games (52 att)
49 George Blanda, Chi. Bears-Houston-Oakland, 19 games (49 att)

Most (One-Point) Points After Touchdown, Game
8 Lou Groza, NFC: Cleveland vs. Detroit, 1954 (8 att)
Jim Martin, NFC: Detroit vs. Cleveland, 1957 (8 att)

George Blanda, AFC-D: Oakland vs. Houston, 1969 (8 att)
Mike Hollis, AFC-D: Jacksonville vs. Miami, 1999 (8 att)
7 Danny Villanueva, NFC-D: Dallas vs. Cleveland, 1967 (7 att)
Raul Allegre, NFC-D: N.Y. Giants vs. San Francisco, 1986 (7 att)
Mike Cofer, SB: San Francisco vs. Denver, 1989 (8 att)
Lin Elliott, SB: Dallas vs. Buffalo, 1992 (7 att)
Doug Brien, SB: San Francisco vs. San Diego, 1994 (7 att)
Gary Anderson, NFC-FR: Philadelphia vs. Detroit, 1995 (7 att)
Jeff Wilkins, NFC-D: St. Louis vs. Minnesota, 1999 (7 att)
Mike Vanderjagt, AFC-FR: Indianapolis vs. Denver, 2004 (7 att)
6 George Blair, AFC: San Diego vs. Boston, 1963 (6 att)
Mark Moseley, NFC-D: Washington vs. L.A. Rams, 1983 (6 att)
Uwe von Schamann, AFC: Miami vs. Pittsburgh, 1984 (6 att)
Ali Haji-Sheikh, SB: Washington vs. Denver, 1987 (6 att)
Scott Norwood, AFC: Buffalo vs. L.A. Raiders, 1990 (7 att)
Jeff Jaeger, AFC-FR: L.A. Raiders vs. Denver, 1993 (6 att)
Jason Elam, AFC-D: Denver vs. Jacksonville, 1997 (6 att)
Jeff Wilkins, NFC-D: St. Louis vs. Green Bay, 2001 (6 att)
Martin Gramatica, SB: Tampa Bay vs. Oakland, 2002 (6 att)
Jay Feely, NFC-D: Atlanta vs. St. Louis, 2004 (6 att)
Mason Crosby, NFC-D: Green Bay vs. Seattle, 2007 (6 att)
Neil Rackers, NFC-FR: Arizona vs. Green Bay, 2009 (ot) (6 att)
Mason Crosby, NFC-FR: Green Bay vs. Arizona, 2009 (ot) (6 att)
Garrett Hartley, NFC-D: New Orleans vs. Arizona, 2009 (6 att)
Mason Crosby, NFC-D: Green Bay vs. Atlanta, 2010 (6 att)

Most (Kicking) Points After Touchdown, No Misses, Career
57 Gary Anderson, Pittsburgh-Philadelphia-San Francisco-Minnesota-Tennessee, 22 games
52 Adam Vinatieri, New England-Indianapolis, 24 games
49 George Blanda, Chi. Bears-Houston-Oakland, 19 games

Most Two-Point Conversions, Career
2 Terrell Owens, San Francisco-Philadelphia-Dallas, 12 games
Kevin Faulk, New England, 18 games

Most Two-Point Conversions, Game
2 Terrell Owens, NFC-FR: San Francisco vs. N.Y. Giants, 2002

FIELD GOALS
Most Field Goals Attempted, Career
54 Adam Vinatieri, New England-Indianapolis, 24 games
40 Gary Anderson, Pittsburgh-Philadelphia-San Francisco-Minnesota-Tennessee, 22 games
39 George Blanda, Chi. Bears-Houston-Oakland, 19 games

Most Field Goals Attempted, Game
6 George Blanda, AFC: Oakland vs. Houston, 1967
David Ray, NFC-D: Los Angeles vs. Dallas, 1973
Mark Moseley, AFC-D: Cleveland vs. N.Y. Jets, 1986 (ot)
Matt Bahr, NFC: N.Y. Giants vs. San Francisco, 1990
Steve Christie, AFC: Buffalo vs. Miami, 1992
Jeff Wilkins, NFC-D: St. Louis vs. Carolina, 2003 (2 ot)
5 By many players

Most Field Goals, Career
45 Adam Vinatieri, New England-Indianapolis, 24 games
32 Gary Anderson, Pittsburgh-Philadelphia-San Francisco-Minnesota-Tennessee, 22 games
31 David Akers, Philadelphia, 19 games

Most Field Goals, Game
5 Chuck Nelson, NFC-D: Minnesota vs. San Francisco, 1987
Matt Bahr, NFC: N.Y. Giants vs. San Francisco, 1990
Steve Christie, AFC: Buffalo vs. Miami, 1992
Brad Daluiso, NFC-FR: N.Y. Giants vs. Minnesota, 1997
John Kasay, NFC-FR: Carolina vs. Dallas, 2003
Jeff Wilkins, NFC-D: St. Louis vs. Carolina, 2003 (2 ot)
Adam Vinatieri, AFC: New England vs. Indianapolis, 2003
Adam Vinatieri, AFC-D: Indianapolis vs. Baltimore, 2006
4 Gino Cappelletti, AFC-D: Boston vs. Buffalo, 1963

George Blanda, AFC: Oakland vs. Houston, 1967
Don Chandler, SB: Green Bay vs. Oakland, 1967
Curt Knight, NFC: Washington vs. Dallas, 1972
George Blanda, AFC-D: Oakland vs. Pittsburgh, 1973
Ray Wersching, SB: San Francisco vs. Cincinnati, 1981
Tony Franklin, AFC-FR: New England vs. N.Y. Jets, 1985
Jess Atkinson, NFC-FR: Washington vs. L.A. Rams, 1986
Luis Zendejas, NFC-D: Philadelphia vs. Chicago, 1988
Gary Anderson, AFC-FR: Pittsburgh vs. Houston, 1989 (ot)
Norm Johnson, AFC-D: Pittsburgh vs. Buffalo, 1995
Chris Boniol, NFC-FR: Dallas vs. Minnesota, 1996
John Kasay, NFC-D: Carolina vs. Dallas, 1996
Mike Hollis, AFC-D: Jacksonville vs. New England, 1998
Al Del Greco, AFC-D: Tennessee vs. Indianapolis, 1999
David Akers, NFC-D: Philadelphia vs. Chicago, 2001
Nate Kaeding, AFC-D: San Diego vs. New England, 2007
David Akers, NFC-FR: Philadelphia vs. Minnesota, 2008
Neil Rackers, NFC-D: Arizona vs. Carolina, 2008
3   By many players

Most Consecutive Games Scoring Field Goals
13   Toni Fritsch, Dallas-Houston, 1972-79
12   Adam Vinatieri, New England, 1997-2004
11   Jason Elam, Denver-Atlanta, 1997-2000, 2003-05, 2008 (current)

Most Consecutive Field Goals
19   David Akers, Philadelphia, 2000-04, 2006, 2008
16   Gary Anderson, Pittsburgh-Philadelphia, 1989-1995
     Matt Stover, Baltimore, 2001, 2003, 2006, 2008; Indianapolis, 2009
15   Rafael Septien, Dallas, 1978-1982

Longest Field Goal
58   Pete Stoyanovich, AFC-FR: Miami vs. Kansas City, 1990
55   Jeff Wilkins, NFC-D: St. Louis vs. Atlanta, 2004
54   Ed Murray, NFC-D: Detroit vs. San Francisco, 1983
     Steve Christie, SB: Buffalo vs. Dallas, 1993
     John Carney, AFC-FR: San Diego vs. Indianapolis, 1995

Highest Field Goal Percentage, Career (10 field goals)
92.9   Martín Gramatica, Tampa Bay-Indianapolis-Dallas, 9 games (14-13)
91.3   John Kasay, Carolina, 10 games (23-21)
90.9   Chuck Nelson, L.A. Rams-Minnesota, 6 games (11-10)

SAFETIES
Most Safeties, Game
1   Bill Willis, NFC-D: Cleveland vs. N.Y. Giants, 1950
    Carl Eller, NFC-D: Minnesota vs. Los Angeles, 1969
    George Andrie, NFC-D: Dallas vs. Detroit, 1970
    Alan Page, NFC-D: Minnesota vs. Dallas, 1971
    Dwight White, SB: Pittsburgh vs. Minnesota, 1974
    Reggie Harrison, SB: Pittsburgh vs. Dallas, 1975
    Jim Jensen, NFC-D: Dallas vs. Los Angeles, 1976
    Ted Washington, AFC: Houston vs. Pittsburgh, 1978
    Randy White, NFC-D: Dallas vs. Los Angeles, 1979
    Henry Waechter, SB: Chicago vs. New England, 1985
    Rulon Jones, AFC-FR: Denver vs. New England, 1986
    George Martin, SB: N.Y. Giants vs. Denver, 1986
    D.D. Hoggard, AFC: Cleveland vs. Denver, 1987
    Bruce Smith, SB: Buffalo vs. N.Y. Giants, 1990
    Reggie White, NFC-D: Philadelphia vs. New Orleans, 1992
    Willie Clay, NFC-FR: Detroit vs. Green Bay, 1994
    Carnell Lake, AFC-D: Pittsburgh vs. Cleveland, 1994
    Reuben Davis, AFC-D: San Diego vs. Miami, 1994
    Jevon Kearse, AFC-FR: Tennessee vs. Buffalo, 1999
    Brady Smith, NFC-D: Atlanta vs. St. Louis, 2004
    Antonio Smith, NFC-FR: Arizona vs. Atlanta, 2008
    Mike DeVito, AFC: N.Y. Jets vs. Pittsburgh, 2010

RUSHING
ATTEMPTS
Most Attempts, Career
400   Franco Harris, Pittsburgh, 19 games
349   Emmitt Smith, Dallas, 17 games

339   Thurman Thomas, Buffalo, 21 games
Most Attempts, Game
40   Lamar Smith, AFC-FR: Miami vs. Indianapolis, 2000 (ot)
38   Ricky Bell, NFC-D: Tampa Bay vs. Philadelphia, 1979
     John Riggins, SB: Washington vs. Miami, 1982
37   Lawrence McCutcheon, NFC-D: Los Angeles vs. St. Louis, 1975
     John Riggins, NFC-D: Washington vs. Minnesota, 1982

YARDS GAINED
Most Yards Gained, Career
1,586   Emmitt Smith, Dallas, 17 games
1,556   Franco Harris, Pittsburgh, 19 games
1,442   Thurman Thomas, Buffalo, 21 games
Most Yards Gained, Game
248   Eric Dickerson, NFC-D: L.A. Rams vs. Dallas, 1985
209   Lamar Smith, AFC-FR: Miami vs. Indianapolis, 2000 (ot)
206   Keith Lincoln, AFC: San Diego vs. Boston, 1963
Most Games, 100 or More Yards Rushing, Career
7   Emmitt Smith, Dallas, 17 games
    Terrell Davis, Denver, 8 games
6   John Riggins, Washington, 9 games
    Thurman Thomas, Buffalo, 21 games
5   Franco Harris, Pittsburgh, 19 games
    Marcus Allen, L.A. Raiders-Kansas City, 16 games
Most Consecutive Games, 100 or More Yards Rushing
7   Terrell Davis, Denver, 1997-98
6   John Riggins, Washington, 1982-83
4   Thurman Thomas, Buffalo, 1990-91
Longest Run From Scrimmage
90   Fred Taylor, AFC-D: Jacksonville vs. Miami, 1999 (TD)
83   Ray Rice, AFC-FR: Baltimore vs. New England, 2009 (TD)
80   Roger Craig, NFC-D: San Francisco vs. Minnesota, 1988 (TD)
     Charlie Garner, AFC-FR: Oakland vs. N.Y. Jets, 2001 (TD)

AVERAGE GAIN
Highest Average Gain, Career (100 attempts)
5.59   Terrell Davis, Denver, 8 games (204-1,140)
5.04   Marcus Allen, L.A. Raiders-Kansas City, 16 games (267-1,347)
4.89   Eric Dickerson, L.A. Rams-Indianapolis, 7 games (148-724)
Highest Average Gain, Game (10 attempts)
15.90   Elmer Angsman, NFC: Chi. Cardinals vs. Philadelphia, 1947 (10-159)
15.85   Keith Lincoln, AFC: San Diego vs. Boston, 1963 (13-206)
11.31   Zack Crockett, AFC-FR: Indianapolis vs. San Diego, 1995 (13-147)

TOUCHDOWNS
Most Touchdowns, Career
19   Emmitt Smith, Dallas, 17 games
16   Franco Harris, Pittsburgh, 19 games
     Thurman Thomas, Buffalo, 21 games
12   John Riggins, Washington, 9 games
     Terrell Davis, Denver, 8 games
Most Touchdowns, Game
5   Ricky Watters, NFC-D: San Francisco vs. N.Y. Giants, 1993
3   Andy Farkas, NFC-D: Washington vs. N.Y. Giants, 1943
    Otto Graham, NFC: Cleveland vs. Detroit, 1954
    Tom Matte, NFC: Baltimore vs. Cleveland, 1968
    Larry Schreiber, NFC-D: San Francisco vs. Dallas, 1972
    Larry Csonka, AFC: Miami vs. Oakland, 1973
    Franco Harris, AFC-D: Pittsburgh vs. Buffalo, 1974
    John Riggins, NFC-D: Washington vs. L.A. Rams, 1983
    Kenneth Davis, AFC: Buffalo vs. L.A. Raiders, 1990
    Napoleon McCallum, AFC-FR: L.A. Raiders vs. Denver, 1993
    Thurman Thomas, AFC: Buffalo vs. Kansas City, 1993
    William Floyd, NFC-D: San Francisco vs. Chicago, 1994
    Emmitt Smith, NFC: Dallas vs. Green Bay, 1995
    Curtis Martin, AFC-D: New England vs. Pittsburgh, 1996
    Terrell Davis, SB: Denver vs. Green Bay, 1997
    Mario Bates, NFC-D: Arizona vs. Minnesota, 1998

Shaun Alexander, NFC-FR: Seattle vs. Green Bay, 2003 (ot)
Ryan Grant, NFC-D: Green Bay vs. Seattle, 2007
Adrian Peterson, NFC: Minnesota vs. New Orleans, 2009 (ot)

Most Consecutive Games Rushing for Touchdowns
- 8 Emmitt Smith, Dallas, 1993-96
  Thurman Thomas, Buffalo, 1992-98
- 7 John Riggins, Washington, 1982-84
  Terrell Davis, Denver, 1996-98
- 5 Franco Harris, Pittsburgh, 1974-75
  Franco Harris, Pittsburgh, 1977-79
  Curtis Martin, New England-N.Y. Jets, 1996-98
  Jerome Bettis, Pittsburgh, 2004-05

PASSING
PASSER RATING
Highest Passer Rating, Career (150 attempts)
- 112.6 Aaron Rodgers, Green Bay, 6 games
- 104.8 Bart Starr, Green Bay, 10 games
- 102.8 Kurt Warner, St. Louis-Arizona, 11 games

ATTEMPTS
Most Passes Attempted, Career
- 791 Brett Favre, Green Bay-Minnesota, 24 games
- 734 Joe Montana, San Francisco-Kansas City, 23 games
- 718 Peyton Manning, Indianapolis, 19 games

Most Passes Attempted, Game
- 65 Steve Young, NFC-D: San Francisco vs. Green Bay, 1995
- 64 Bernie Kosar, AFC-D: Cleveland vs. N.Y. Jets, 1986 (ot)
  Dan Marino, AFC-FR: Miami vs. Buffalo, 1995
- 60 Drew Brees, NFC-FR: New Orleans vs. Seattle, 2010

COMPLETIONS
Most Passes Completed, Career
- 481 Brett Favre, Green Bay-Minnesota, 24 games
- 460 Joe Montana, San Francisco-Kansas City, 23 games
- 453 Peyton Manning, Indianapolis, 19 games

Most Passes Completed, Game
- 39 Drew Brees, NFC-FR: New Orleans vs. Seattle, 2010
- 36 Warren Moon, AFC-FR: Houston vs. Buffalo, 1992 (ot)
- 33 Dan Fouts, AFC-D: San Diego vs. Miami, 1981 (ot)
  Bernie Kosar, AFC-D: Cleveland vs. N.Y. Jets, 1986 (ot)
  Dan Marino, AFC-FR: Miami vs. Buffalo, 1995
  Peyton Manning, AFC-D: Indianapolis vs. San Diego, 2007

COMPLETION PERCENTAGE
Highest Completion Percentage, Career (150 attempts)
- 67.8 Aaron Rodgers, Green Bay, 6 games (174-118)
- 66.5 Kurt Warner, St. Louis-Arizona, 13 games (462-307)
- 66.3 Drew Brees, San Diego-New Orleans, 7 games (285-189)

Highest Completion Percentage, Game (15 completions)
- 92.9 Tom Brady, AFC-D: New England vs. Jacksonville, 2007 (28-26)
- 88.0 Phil Simms, SB: N.Y. Giants vs. Denver, 1986 (25-22)
- 87.9 Kurt Warner, NFC-FR: Arizona vs. Green Bay, 2009 (ot) (33-29)

YARDS GAINED
Most Yards Gained, Career
- 5,855 Brett Favre, Green Bay-Minnesota, 24 games
- 5,772 Joe Montana, San Francisco-Kansas City, 23 games
- 5,389 Peyton Manning, Indianapolis, 19 games

Most Yards Gained, Game
- 489 Bernie Kosar, AFC-D: Cleveland vs. N.Y. Jets, 1986 (ot)
- 458 Peyton Manning, AFC-FR: Indianapolis vs. Denver, 2004
- 433 Dan Fouts, AFC-D: San Diego vs. Miami, 1981 (ot)

Most Games, 300 or More Yards Passing, Career
- 8 Peyton Manning, Indianapolis, 19 games
- 6 Joe Montana, San Francisco-Kansas City, 23 games
  Kurt Warner, St. Louis-Arizona, 13 games
- 5 Dan Fouts, San Diego, 7 games

Most Consecutive Games, 300 or More Yards Passing
- 4 Dan Fouts, San Diego, 1979-1981
- 3 Jim Kelly, Buffalo, 1989-1990
  Warren Moon, Houston, 1991-93
- 2 Daryle Lamonica, Oakland, 1968
  Ken Anderson, Cincinnati, 1981-82
  Terry Bradshaw, Pittsburgh, 1979-1982
  Joe Montana, San Francisco, 1983-84
  Dan Marino, Miami, 1984
  Troy Aikman, Dallas, 1994
  Steve Young, San Francisco, 1994-95
  Kurt Warner, St. Louis, 1999-2000
  Peyton Manning, Indianapolis, 2003
  Marc Bulger, St. Louis, 2003-04
  Matt Hasselbeck, Seattle, 2003-04
  Peyton Manning, Indianapolis, 2007-08
  Donovan McNabb, Philadelphia, 2004, 2008
  Kurt Warner, Arizona, 2008-09
  Peyton Manning, Indianapolis, 2009

Longest Pass Completion
- 96 Trent Dilfer (to Sharpe), AFC: Baltimore vs. Oakland, 2000 (TD)
- 94 Troy Aikman (to Harper), NFC-D: Dallas vs. Green Bay, 1994 (TD)
- 93 Daryle Lamonica (to Dubenion), AFC-D: Buffalo vs. Boston, 1963 (TD)

AVERAGE GAIN
Highest Average Gain, Career (150 attempts)
- 8.72 Aaron Rodgers, Green Bay, 6 games (174-1,517)
- 8.55 Kurt Warner, St. Louis-Arizona, 13 games (462-3,952)
- 8.45 Joe Theismann, Washington, 10 games (211-1,782)

Highest Average Gain, Game (20 attempts)
- 14.71 Terry Bradshaw, SB: Pittsburgh vs. Los Angeles, 1979 (21-309)
- 14.50 Peyton Manning, AFC-FR: Indianapolis vs. Denver, 2003 (26-377)
- 13.88 Peyton Manning, AFC-FR: Indianapolis vs. Denver, 2004 (33-458)

TOUCHDOWNS
Most Touchdown Passes, Career
- 45 Joe Montana, San Francisco-Kansas City, 23 games
- 44 Brett Favre, Green Bay-Minnesota, 24 games
- 32 Dan Marino, Miami, 18 games

Most Touchdown Passes, Game
- 6 Daryle Lamonica, AFC-D: Oakland vs. Houston, 1969
  Steve Young, SB: San Francisco vs. San Diego, 1994
- 5 Sid Luckman, NFC: Chi. Bears vs. Washington, 1943
  Daryle Lamonica, AFC-D: Oakland vs. Kansas City, 1968
  Joe Montana, CD: San Francisco vs. Denver, 1989
  Kurt Warner, NFC-D: St. Louis vs. Minnesota, 1999
  Kerry Collins, NFC: N.Y. Giants vs. Minnesota, 2000
  Peyton Manning, AFC-FR: Indianapolis vs. Denver, 2003
  Kurt Warner, NFC-FR: Arizona vs. Green Bay, 2009 (ot)
- 4 Otto Graham, NFC: Cleveland vs. Los Angeles, 1950
  Tobin Rote, NFC: Detroit vs. Cleveland, 1957
  Bart Starr, NFC: Green Bay vs. Dallas, 1966
  Ken Stabler, AFC-D: Oakland vs. Miami, 1974
  Roger Staubach, NFC: Dallas vs. Los Angeles, 1975
  Terry Bradshaw, SB: Pittsburgh vs. Dallas, 1978
  Don Strock, AFC-D: Miami vs. San Diego, 1981 (ot)
  Lynn Dickey, NFC-FR: Green Bay vs. St. Louis, 1982
  Dan Marino, AFC: Miami vs. Pittsburgh, 1984
  Phil Simms, NFC-D: N.Y. Giants vs. San Francisco, 1986
  Doug Williams, SB: Washington vs. Denver, 1987
  Jim Kelly, AFC-D: Buffalo vs. Cleveland, 1989
  Joe Montana, NFC-D: San Francisco vs. Minnesota, 1989
  Warren Moon, AFC-FR: Houston vs. Buffalo, 1992 (ot)
  Frank Reich, AFC-FR: Buffalo vs. Houston, 1992 (ot)
  Troy Aikman, SB: Dallas vs. Buffalo, 1992
  Jeff George, NFC-D: Minnesota vs. St. Louis, 1999
  Aaron Brooks, NFC-FR: New Orleans vs. St. Louis, 2000
  Kerry Collins, NFC-FR: N.Y. Giants vs. San Francisco, 2002

Peyton Manning, AFC-FR: Indianapolis vs. Denver, 2004
Daunte Culpepper, NFC-FR: Minnesota vs. Green Bay, 2004
Kurt Warner, NFC: Arizona vs. Philadelphia, 2008
Aaron Rodgers, NFC-FR: Green Bay vs. Arizona, 2009 (ot)
Brett Favre, NFC-D: Minnesota vs. Dallas, 2009
Matt Hasselbeck, NFC-FR: Seattle vs. New Orleans, 2010

Most Consecutive Games, Touchdown Passes
20   Brett Favre, Green Bay-Minnesota, 1995-2009 (current)
17   Tom Brady, New England, 2001-2010 (current)
13   Dan Marino, Miami, 1983-1995

HAD INTERCEPTED
Lowest Percentage, Passes Had Intercepted, Career (150 attempts)
0.70   Drew Brees, San Diego-New Orleans, 7 games (285-2)
1.41   Bart Starr, Green Bay, 10 games (213-3)
1.72   Aaron Rodgers, Green Bay, 6 games (174-3)
Most Attempts Without Interception, Game
60   Drew Brees, NFC-FR: New Orleans vs. Seattle, 2010
54   Neil O'Donnell, AFC: Pittsburgh vs. San Diego, 1994
48   Warren Moon, AFC-FR: Houston vs. Pittsburgh, 1989 (ot)
     Randall Cunningham, NFC: Minnesota vs. Atlanta, 1998 (ot)
     Tom Brady, SB: New England vs. N.Y. Giants, 2007
Most Passes Had Intercepted, Career
30   Brett Favre, Green Bay-Minnesota, 24 games
28   Jim Kelly, Buffalo, 17 games
26   Terry Bradshaw, Pittsburgh, 19 games
Most Passes Had Intercepted, Game
6   Frank Filchock, NFC: N.Y. Giants vs. Chi. Bears, 1946
    Bobby Layne, NFC: Detroit vs. Cleveland, 1954
    Norm Van Brocklin, NFC: Los Angeles vs. Cleveland, 1955
    Brett Favre, NFC-D: Green Bay vs. St. Louis, 2001
5   Frank Filchock, NFC: Washington vs. Chi. Bears, 1940
    George Blanda, AFC: Houston vs. San Diego, 1961
    George Blanda, AFC: Houston vs. Dall. Texans, 1962 (ot)
    Y.A. Tittle, NFC: N.Y. Giants vs. Chicago, 1963
    Mike Phipps, AFC-D: Cleveland vs. Miami, 1972
    Dan Pastorini, AFC: Houston vs. Pittsburgh, 1978
    Dan Fouts, AFC-D: San Diego vs. Houston, 1979
    Tommy Kramer, NFC-D: Minnesota vs. Philadelphia, 1980
    Dan Fouts, AFC-D: San Diego vs. Miami, 1982
    Richard Todd, AFC: N.Y. Jets vs. Miami, 1982
    Gary Danielson, NFC-D: Detroit vs. San Francisco, 1983
    Jay Schroeder, AFC: L.A. Raiders vs. Buffalo, 1990
    Rich Gannon, SB: Oakland vs. Tampa Bay, 2002
    Jake Delhomme, NFC-D: Carolina vs. Arizona, 2008
4   By many players

PASS RECEIVING
RECEPTIONS
Most Receptions, Career
151   Jerry Rice, San Francisco-Oakland-Seattle, 29 games
88   Hines Ward, Pittsburgh, 17 games
87   Michael Irvin, Dallas, 16 games
Most Receptions, Game
13   Kellen Winslow, AFC-D: San Diego vs. Miami, 1981 (ot)
     Thurman Thomas, AFC-D: Buffalo vs. Cleveland, 1989
     Shannon Sharpe, AFC-FR: Denver vs. L.A. Raiders, 1993
     Chad Morton, NFC-D: New Orleans vs. Minnesota, 2000
12   Raymond Berry, NFC: Baltimore vs. N.Y. Giants, 1958
     Michael Irvin, NFC: Dallas vs. San Francisco, 1994
     Darrell Jackson, NFC-FR: Seattle vs. St. Louis, 2004
     Steve Smith, NFC-D: Carolina vs. Chicago, 2005
11   Dante Lavelli, NFC: Cleveland vs. Los Angeles, 1950
     Dan Ross, SB: Cincinnati vs. San Francisco, 1981
     Franco Harris, AFC-FR: Pittsburgh vs. San Diego, 1982
     Steve Watson, AFC-D: Denver vs. Pittsburgh, 1984
     John L. Williams, AFC-D: Seattle vs. Cincinnati, 1988
     Jerry Rice, SB: San Francisco vs. Cincinnati, 1988
     Ernest Givins, AFC-FR: Houston vs. Pittsburgh, 1989 (ot)
     Amp Lee, NFC-D: Minnesota vs. Chicago, 1994
     Jay Novacek, NFC-D: Dallas vs. Green Bay, 1994
     O.J. McDuffie, AFC-D: Miami vs. Buffalo, 1995

Jerry Rice, NFC-D: San Francisco vs. Green Bay, 1995
Hines Ward, AFC-FR: Pittsburgh vs. Cleveland, 2002
Deion Branch, SB: New England vs. Philadelphia, 2004
Plaxico Burress, NFC: N.Y. Giants vs. Green Bay, 2007 (ot)
Wes Welker, SB: New England vs. N.Y. Giants, 2007
Roddy White, NFC-FR: Atlanta vs. Arizona, 2008
Pierre Garcon, AFC: Indianapolis vs. N.Y. Jets, 2009

Most Consecutive Games, Pass Receptions
28   Jerry Rice, San Francisco-Oakland, 1985-2002
22   Drew Pearson, Dallas, 1973-1983
18   Paul Warfield, Cleveland-Miami, 1964-1974
     Cliff Branch, Oakland/L.A. Raiders, 1974-1983
     Thurman Thomas, Buffalo, 1989-1998
     Shannon Sharpe, Denver-Baltimore-Denver, 1991-2003

YARDS GAINED
Most Yards Gained, Career
2,245   Jerry Rice, San Francisco-Oakland-Seattle, 29 games
1,315   Michael Irvin, Dallas, 16 games
1,289   Cliff Branch, Oakland/L.A. Raiders, 22 games
Most Yards Gained, Game
240   Eric Moulds, AFC-FR: Buffalo vs. Miami, 1998
227   Anthony Carter, NFC-D: Minnesota vs. San Francisco, 1987
221   Reggie Wayne, AFC-FR: Indianapolis vs. Denver, 2004
Most Games, 100 or More Yards Receiving, Career
8   Jerry Rice, San Francisco-Oakland-Seattle, 29 games
6   Michael Irvin, Dallas, 16 games
5   John Stallworth, Pittsburgh, 18 games
    Andre Reed, Buffalo, 21 games
    Hines Ward, Pittsburgh, 17 games
Most Consecutive Games, 100 or More Yards Receiving, Career
4   Larry Fitzgerald, Arizona, 2008
3   Tom Fears, Los Angeles, 1950-51
    Jerry Rice, San Francisco, 1988-89
    Randy Moss, Minnesota, 1999-2000
2   By many players
Longest Reception
96   Shannon Sharpe (from Dilfer), AFC: Baltimore vs. Oakland, 2000 (TD)
94   Alvin Harper (from Aikman), NFC-D: Dallas vs. Green Bay, 1994 (TD)
93   Elbert Dubenion (from Lamonica), AFC-D: Buffalo vs. Boston, 1963 (TD)

AVERAGE GAIN
Highest Average Gain, Career (20 receptions)
27.3   Alvin Harper, Dallas, 10 games (24-655)
23.7   Willie Gault, Chicago-L.A. Raiders, 12 games (21-497)
22.8   Harold Jackson, L.A. Rams-New England-Minnesota-Seattle, 14 games (24-548)
Highest Average Gain, Game (3 receptions)
46.3   Harold Jackson, NFC: Los Angeles vs. Minnesota, 1974 (3-139)
42.7   Billy Cannon, AFC: Houston vs. L.A. Chargers, 1960 (3-128)
42.0   Lenny Moore, NFC: Baltimore vs. N.Y. Giants, 1959 (3-126)

TOUCHDOWNS
Most Touchdowns, Career
22   Jerry Rice, San Francisco-Oakland-Seattle, 29 games
12   John Stallworth, Pittsburgh, 18 games
10   Fred Biletnikoff, Oakland, 19 games
     Antonio Freeman, Green Bay-Philadelphia-Green Bay, 16 games
     Randy Moss, Minnesota-New England, 12 games
     Hines Ward, Pittsburgh, 17 games
Most Touchdowns, Game
3   Tom Fears, NFC-D: Los Angeles vs. Chi. Bears, 1950
    Gary Collins, NFC: Cleveland vs. Baltimore, 1964
    Fred Biletnikoff, AFC-D: Oakland vs. Kansas City, 1968
    Preston Pearson, NFC: Dallas vs. Los Angeles, 1975
    Dave Casper, AFC-D: Oakland vs. Baltimore, 1977 (ot)
    Alvin Garrett, NFC-FR: Washington vs. Detroit, 1982
    Jerry Rice, NFC-D: San Francisco vs. Minnesota, 1988

Jerry Rice, SB: San Francisco vs. Denver, 1989
Andre Reed, AFC-FR: Buffalo vs. Houston, 1992 (ot)
Sterling Sharpe, NFC-FR: Green Bay vs. Detroit, 1993
Jerry Rice, SB: San Francisco vs. San Diego, 1994
Willie Jackson, NFC-FR: New Orleans vs. St. Louis, 2000
Amani Toomer, NFC-FR: N.Y. Giants vs. San Francisco, 2002
Larry Fitzgerald, NFC: Arizona vs. Philadelphia, 2008
Sidney Rice, NFC-D: Minnesota vs. Dallas, 2009

Most Consecutive Games, Touchdown Passes Caught
8   John Stallworth, Pittsburgh, 1978-1983
7   David Givens, New England, 2003-05)
5   James Lofton, Green Bay-Buffalo, 1982-1990
    Randy Moss, Minnesota, 1998-2000
    Antonio Freeman, Green Bay, 1997-2001
    Hines Ward, Pittsburgh, 2002-05
    Larry Fitzgerald, Arizona, 2008-09

INTERCEPTIONS BY
Most Interceptions, Career
9   Charlie Waters, Dallas, 25 games
    Bill Simpson, Los Angeles-Buffalo, 11 games
    Ronnie Lott, San Francisco-L.A. Raiders, 20 games
8   Lester Hayes, Oakland/L.A. Raiders, 13 games
7   Willie Brown, Oakland, 17 games
    Dennis Thurman, Dallas, 14 games
    Rodney Harrison, San Diego-New England, 13 games
    Asante Samuel, New England-Philadelphia, 19 games
    Ed Reed, Baltimore, 9 games

Most Interceptions, Game
4   Vernon Perry, AFC-D: Houston vs. San Diego, 1979
3   Joe Laws, NFC: Green Bay vs. N.Y. Giants, 1944
    Charlie Waters, NFC-D: Dallas vs. Chicago, 1977
    Rod Martin, SB: Oakland vs. Philadelphia, 1980
    Dennis Thurman, NFC-D: Dallas vs. Green Bay, 1982
    A.J. Duhe, AFC: Miami vs. N.Y. Jets, 1982
    Ty Law, AFC: New England vs. Indianapolis, 2003
    Ricky Manning Jr., NFC: Carolina vs. Philadelphia, 2003
2   By many players

Most Consecutive Games, Interceptions
4   Aeneas Williams, Arizona-St. Louis, 1998-2001
    Rodney Harrison, New England, 2004, 2007
3   By many players. Last time:
        Ed Reed, Baltimore, 2006, 2008

YARDS GAINED
Most Yards Gained, Career
227 Asante Samuel, New England-Philadelphia, 19 games
196 Willie Brown, Oakland, 17 games
187 Ronnie Lott, San Francisco-L.A. Raiders, 20 games

Most Yards Gained, Game
108 Darrien Gordon, SB: Denver vs. Atlanta, 1998
101 George Teague, NFC-FR: Green Bay vs. Detroit, 1993
100 Champ Bailey, AFC-D: Denver vs. New England, 2005
     James Harrison, SB: Pittsburgh vs. Arizona, 2008

Longest Return
101 George Teague, NFC-FR: Green Bay vs. Detroit, 1993 (TD)
100 Champ Bailey, AFC-D: Denver vs. New England, 2005
     James Harrison, SB: Pittsburgh vs. Arizona, 2008 (TD)
98   Darrol Ray, AFC-FR: N.Y. Jets vs. Cincinnati, 1982 (TD)

TOUCHDOWNS
Most Touchdowns, Career
4   Asante Samuel, New England-Philadelphia, 19 games
3   Willie Brown, Oakland, 17 games
2   Lester Hayes, Oakland/L.A. Raiders, 13 games
    Ronnie Lott, San Francisco-L.A. Raiders, 20 games
    Darrell Green, Washington, 18 games
    Melvin Jenkins, Seattle-Detroit, 5 games
    George Teague, Green Bay-Dallas-Miami-Dallas, 12 games
    Aeneas Williams, Arizona-St. Louis, 6 games
    Dwight Smith, Tampa Bay, 4 games

Most Touchdowns, Game
2   Aeneas Williams, NFC-D: St. Louis vs. Green Bay, 2001
    Dwight Smith, SB: Tampa Bay vs. Oakland, 2002
1   By many players

PUNTING
Most Punts, Career
111 Ray Guy, Oakland/L.A. Raiders, 22 games
101 Craig Hentrich, Green Bay-Tennessee, 22 games
84   Danny White, Dallas, 18 games
     Sean Landeta, N.Y. Giants-Tampa Bay-Green Bay-
        Philadelphia-St. Louis, 18 games

Most Punts, Game
14   Dave Jennings, AFC-D: N.Y. Jets vs. Cleveland, 1986 (ot)
12   David Lee, AFC-D: Baltimore vs. Oakland, 1977 (ot)
11   Ken Strong, NFC: N.Y. Giants vs. Chi. Bears, 1933
     Jim Norton, AFC: Houston vs. Oakland, 1967
     Ode Burrell, AFC-D: Houston vs. Oakland, 1969
     Dale Hatcher, NFC: L.A. Rams vs. Chicago, 1985
     Brad Maynard, SB: N.Y. Giants vs. Baltimore, 2000

Longest Punt
76   Ed Danowski, NFC: N.Y. Giants vs. Detroit, 1935
     Mike Horan, AFC: Denver vs. Buffalo, 1991
72   Charlie Conerly, NFC-D: N.Y. Giants vs. Cleveland, 1950
     Yale Lary, NFC: Detroit vs. Cleveland, 1953
71   Ray Guy, AFC: Oakland vs. San Diego, 1980

AVERAGE YARDAGE
Highest Average, Career (25 punts)
44.5   Rich Camarillo, New England, 6 games (35-1,559)
44.44 Todd Sauerbrun, Carolina-Denver-New England, 9 games
       (43-1,911)
44.38 Mike Scifres, San Diego, 8 games (42-1,864)

Highest Average, Game (4 punts)
56.0   Ray Guy, AFC: Oakland vs. San Diego, 1980 (4-224)
53.8   Sam Koch, AFC-D: Baltimore vs. Pittsburgh, 2010
       (4-215)
53.3   Craig Hentrich, AFC-D: Tennessee vs. Baltimore, 2008
       (4-213)

PUNT RETURNS
Most Punt Returns, Career
34   David Meggett, N.Y. Giants-New England-N.Y. Jets,
        13 games
     Brian Mitchell, Washington-Philadelphia, 16 games
33   Troy Brown, New England, 20 games
26   Antwaan Randle El, Pittsburgh-Washington, 12 games

Most Punt Returns, Game
7   Ron Gardin, AFC-D: Baltimore vs. Cincinnati, 1970
    Carl Roaches, AFC-D: Houston vs. Oakland, 1980
    Gerald McNeil, AFC-D: Cleveland vs. N.Y. Jets, 1986 (ot)
    Phil McConkey, NFC-D: N.Y. Giants vs. San Francisco,
       1986
    David Meggett, AFC-D: New England vs. Pittsburgh, 1996
    Reggie Barlow, AFC-FR: Jacksonville vs. New England,
       1998
6   George McAfee, NFC-D: Chi. Bears vs. Los Angeles, 1950
    Eddie Brown, NFC-D: Washington vs. Minnesota, 1976
    Theo Bell, AFC: Pittsburgh vs. Houston, 1978
    Eddie Brown, NFC: Los Angeles vs. Tampa Bay, 1979
    John Sciarra, NFC: Philadelphia vs. Dallas, 1980
    Kurt Sohn, AFC: N.Y. Jets vs. Miami, 1982
    Mike Nelms, SB: Washington vs. Miami, 1982
    Anthony Carter, NFC-FR: Minnesota vs. New Orleans,
       1987
    Desmond Howard, SB: Green Bay vs. New England, 1996
    Nate Jacquet, AFC-FR: Miami vs. Seattle, 1999
    Derrick Mason, AFC-FR: Tennessee vs. Baltimore, 2003
    Antonio Chatman, AFC-D: Green Bay vs. Philadelphia,
       2003
    Nate Burleson, NFC-FR: Seattle vs. Washington, 2007
    Jim Leonhard, AFC: Baltimore vs. Pittsburgh, 2008

5   By many players

YARDS GAINED
Most Yards Gained, Career
339   Brian Mitchell, Washington-Philadelphia, 16 games
315   Troy Brown, New England, 20 games
312   David Meggett, N.Y. Giants-New England-N.Y. Jets,
        13 games
Most Yards Gained, Game
152   Allen Rossum, NFC-D: Atlanta vs. St. Louis, 2004
143   Anthony Carter, NFC-FR: Minnesota vs. New Orleans,
        1987
141   Bob Hayes, NFC-D: Dallas vs. Cleveland, 1967
Longest Return
88   Jermaine Lewis, AFC-D: Baltimore vs. Pittsburgh, 2001
        (TD)
84   Anthony Carter, NFC-FR: Minnesota vs. New Orleans, 1987
        (TD)
83   Reggie Bush, NFC-D: New Orleans vs. Arizona, 2009 (TD)

AVERAGE YARDAGE
Highest Average, Career (10 returns)
23.9   Allen Rossum, Green Bay-Atlanta, 6 games (10-239)
15.3   Robert Brooks, Green Bay, 11 games (14-214)
15.2   Anthony Carter, Minnesota-Detroit, 9 games (17-259)
Highest Average Gain, Game (3 returns)
50.7   Allen Rossum, NFC-D: Atlanta vs. St. Louis, 2004 (3-152)
47.0   Bob Hayes, NFC-D: Dallas vs. Cleveland, 1967 (3-141)
36.3   Reggie Bush, NFC-D: New Orleans vs. Arizona, 2009
        (3-109)

TOUCHDOWNS
Most Touchdowns
1   Hugh Gallarneau, NFC-D: Chicago Bears vs. Green Bay,
      1941
    Bosh Pritchard, NFC-D: Philadelphia vs. Pittsburgh, 1947
    Charley Trippi, NFC: Chicago Cardinals vs. Philadelphia,
      1947
    Verda (Vitamin T) Smith, NFC-D: Los Angeles vs. Detroit,
      1952
    George (Butch) Byrd, AFC: Buffalo vs. San Diego, 1965
    Golden Richards, NFC: Dallas vs. Minnesota, 1973
    Wes Chandler, AFC-D: San Diego vs. Miami, 1981 (ot)
    Shaun Gayle, NFC-D: Chicago vs. N.Y. Giants, 1985
    Anthony Carter, NFC-FR: Minnesota vs. New Orleans, 1987
    Darrell Green, NFC-D: Washington vs. Chicago, 1987
    Antonio Freeman, NFC-FR: Green Bay vs. Atlanta, 1995
    Desmond Howard, NFC-D: Green Bay vs. San Francisco,
      1996
    Jermaine Lewis, AFC-D: Baltimore vs. Pittsburgh, 2001
    Troy Brown, AFC: New England vs. Pittsburgh, 2001
    Antwaan Randle El, AFC-FR: Pittsburgh vs. Cleveland,
      2002
    Santana Moss, AFC-D: N.Y. Jets vs. Pittsburgh, 2004 (ot)
    Allen Rossum, NFC-D: Atlanta vs. St. Louis, 2004
    Steve Smith, NFC: Carolina vs. Seattle, 2005
    Santonio Holmes, AFC: Pittsburgh vs. San Diego, 2008
    Reggie Bush, NFC-D: New Orleans vs. Arizona, 2009

KICKOFF RETURNS
Most Kickoff Returns, Career
36   Brian Mitchell, Washington-Philadelphia, 16 games
31   Kevin Williams, Dallas-Buffalo, 12 games
29   Fulton Walker, Miami-L.A. Raiders, 10 games
Most Kickoff Returns, Game
8   Marc Logan, AFC-D: Miami vs. Buffalo, 1990
    Andre Coleman, SB: San Diego vs. San Francisco, 1994
    Marcus Knight, SB: Oakland vs. Tampa Bay, 2002
7   Don Bingham, NFC: Chi. Bears vs. N.Y. Giants, 1956
    Reggie Brown, NFC-FR: Atlanta vs. Minnesota, 1982
    David Verser, AFC-FR: Cincinnati vs. N.Y. Jets, 1982
    Del Rodgers, NFC-D: Green Bay vs. Dallas, 1982

Henry Ellard, NFC-D: L.A. Rams vs. Washington, 1983
Stephen Starring, SB: New England vs. Chicago, 1985
Darick Holmes, AFC-D: Buffalo vs. Pittsburgh, 1995
Antonio Freeman, NFC: Green Bay vs. Dallas, 1995
Roell Preston, NFC-FR: Green Bay vs. San Francisco,
  1998
Robert Tate, NFC-D: Minnesota vs. St. Louis, 1999
Fred McAfee, NFC-D: New Orleans vs. Minnesota, 2000
Michael Bates, NFC-FR: Dallas vs. Carolina, 2003
Dante Hall, AFC-D: Kansas City vs. Indianapolis, 2003
Michael Lewis, NFC: New Orleans vs. Chicago, 2006
6   By many players

YARDS GAINED
Most Yards Gained, Career
875   Brian Mitchell, Washington-Philadelphia, 16 games
677   Fulton Walker, Miami-L.A. Raiders, 10 games
632   Kevin Williams, Dallas-Buffalo, 12 games
Most Yards Gained, Game
244   Andre Coleman, SB: San Diego vs. San Francisco, 1994
220   Ellis Hobbs, AFC: New England vs. Indianapolis, 2006
210   Tim Dwight, SB: Atlanta vs. Denver, 1998
Longest Return
102   Eric Weems, NFC-D: Atlanta vs. Green Bay, 2010 (TD)
100   Brian Mitchell, NFC-D: Washington vs. Tampa Bay, 1999
        (TD)
99   Desmond Howard, SB: Green Bay vs. New England, 1996
        (TD)

AVERAGE YARDAGE
Highest Average, Career (10 returns)
30.1   Carl Garrett, Oakland, 5 games (16-481)
30.0   Reggie Barlow, Jacksonville, 8 games (12-360)
29.2   Chad Morton, New Orleans-N.Y. Jets-N.Y. Giants, 6 games
        (14-409)
Highest Average, Game (3 returns)
56.7   Les (Speedy) Duncan, NFC-D: Washington vs. San Francisco,
        1971 (3-170)
51.3   Ed Podolak, AFC-D: Kansas City vs. Miami, 1971 (ot)
        (3-154)
49.0   Les (Speedy) Duncan, AFC: San Diego vs. Buffalo, 1964
        (3-147)

TOUCHDOWNS
Most Touchdowns, Career
2   Ron Dixon, N.Y. Giants, 4 games
1   By many players
Most Touchdowns, Game
1   Vic Washington, NFC-D: San Francisco vs. Dallas, 1972
    Nat Moore, AFC-D: Miami vs. Oakland, 1974
    Marshall Johnson, AFC-D: Baltimore vs. Oakland, 1977
      (ot)
    Fulton Walker, SB: Miami vs. Washington, 1982
    Stanford Jennings, SB: Cincinnati vs. San Francisco, 1988
    Eric Metcalf, AFC-D: Cleveland vs. Buffalo, 1989
    Andre Coleman, SB: San Diego vs. San Francisco, 1994
    Desmond Howard, SB: Green Bay vs. New England, 1996
    Chuck Levy, NFC: San Francisco vs. Green Bay, 1997
    Tim Dwight, SB: Atlanta vs. Denver, 1998
    Kevin Dyson, AFC-FR: Tennessee vs. Buffalo, 1999
    Charlie Rogers, AFC-FR: Seattle vs. Miami, 1999
    Brian Mitchell, NFC-D: Washington vs. Tampa Bay, 1999
    Tony Horne, NFC-D: St. Louis vs. Minnesota, 1999
    Derrick Mason, AFC: Tennessee vs. Jacksonville, 1999
    Ron Dixon, NFC-D: N.Y. Giants vs. Philadelphia, 2000;
      SB: N.Y. Giants vs. Baltimore, 2000
    Jermaine Lewis, SB: Baltimore vs. N.Y. Giants, 2000
    Dante Hall, AFC-D: Kansas City vs. Indianapolis, 2003
    Miles Austin, NFC-FR: Dallas vs. Seattle, 2006
    Devin Hester, SB: Chicago vs. Indianapolis, 2006
    Eric Weems, NFC-D: Atlanta vs. Green Bay, 2010

FUMBLES
Most Fumbles, Career
16	Warren Moon, Houston-Minnesota, 10 games
14	John Elway, Denver, 22 games
	Donovan McNabb, Philadelphia, 16 games
13	Tony Dorsett, Dallas, 17 games

Most Fumbles, Game
5	Warren Moon, AFC-D: Houston vs. Kansas City, 1993
4	Brian Sipe, AFC: Cleveland vs. Oakland, 1980
	Randall Cunningham, NFC-FR: Minnesota vs. N.Y. Giants, 1997
3	By many players

RECOVERIES
Most Own Fumbles Recovered, Career
8	Warren Moon, Houston-Minnesota, 10 games
7	John Elway, Denver, 22 games
6	Jim Kelly, Buffalo, 17 games

Most Opponents' Fumbles Recovered, Career
4	Cliff Harris, Dallas, 21 games
	Harvey Martin, Dallas, 22 games
	Ted Hendricks, Baltimore-Oakland/L.A. Raiders, 21 games
	Alvin Walton, Washington, 9 games
	Monte Coleman, Washington, 21 games
	Dave Thomas, Dallas-Jacksonville-N.Y. Giants, 13 games
3	Paul Krause, Minnesota, 19 games
	Jack Lambert, Pittsburgh, 18 games
	Fred Dryer, Los Angeles, 14 games
	Charlie Waters, Dallas, 25 games
	Jack Ham, Pittsburgh, 16 games
	Mike Hegman, Dallas, 16 games
	Tom Jackson, Denver, 10 games
	Rich Milot, Washington, 13 games
	Mike Singletary, Chicago, 12 games
	Darryl Grant, Washington, 16 games
	Wes Hopkins, Philadelphia, 3 games
	Wilber Marshall, Chicago-Washington, 15 games
	Tyrone Braxton, Denver-Miami-Denver, 19 games
	Neil Smith, Kansas City-Denver, 16 games
	Tony Brackens, Jacksonville, 7 games
	Phil Hansen, Buffalo, 14 games
	Carnell Lake, Pittsburgh-Jacksonville-Baltimore, 17 games
	Jason Gildon, Pittsburgh, 13 games
	Tedy Bruschi, New England, 22 games
	Jim Leonhard, Baltimore-N.Y. Jets, 6 games
2	By many players

Most Fumbles Recovered, Game, Own and Opponents'
3	Jack Lambert, AFC: Pittsburgh vs. Oakland, 1975 (3 opp)
	Ron Jaworski, NFC-FR: Philadelphia vs. N.Y. Giants, 1981 (3 own)
	Devin Hester, NFC-D: Chicago vs. Seattle, 2006 (3-own)
2	By many players

YARDS GAINED
Longest Return
93	Andy Russell, AFC-D: Pittsburgh vs. Baltimore, 1975 (opp, TD)
79	Neil Smith, AFC-D: Denver vs. Miami, 1998 (opp, TD)
64	Leon Lett, SB: Dallas vs. Buffalo, 1992 (opp)

TOUCHDOWNS
Most Touchdowns
1	By many players

COMBINED NET YARDS GAINED
Rushing, receiving, interception returns, punt returns, kickoff returns, and fumble returns.

ATTEMPTS
Most Attempts, Career
454	Franco Harris, Pittsburgh, 19 games
417	Thurman Thomas, Buffalo, 21 games
397	Emmitt Smith, Dallas, 17 games

Most Attempts, Game
43	Lamar Smith, AFC-FR: Miami vs. Indianapolis, 2000 (ot)
42	Curtis Martin, AFC-D: N.Y. Jets vs. Jacksonville, 1998
40	Lawrence McCutcheon, NFC-D: Los Angeles vs. St. Louis, 1975

YARDS GAINED
Most Yards Gained, Career
2,289	Jerry Rice, San Francisco-Oakland-Seattle, 29 games
2,124	Thurman Thomas, Buffalo, 21 games
2,060	Franco Harris, Pittsburgh, 19 games

Most Yards Gained, Game
350	Ed Podolak, AFC-D: Kansas City vs. Miami, 1971 (ot)
329	Keith Lincoln, AFC: San Diego vs. Boston, 1963
328	Darren Sproles, AFC-FR: San Diego vs. Indianapolis, 2008 (ot)

SACKS
Sacks have been compiled since 1982.
Most Sacks, Career
16.0	Willie McGinest, New England, 18 games
14.5	Bruce Smith, Buffalo, 20 games
12.0	Reggie White, Philadelphia-Green Bay, 19 games

Most Sacks, Game
4.5	Willie McGinest, AFC-FR: New England vs. Jacksonville, 2005
3.5	Rich Milot, NFC-D: Washington vs. Chicago, 1984
	Richard Dent, NFC-D: Chicago vs. N.Y. Giants, 1985
3.0	Richard Dent, NFC-D: Chicago vs. Washington, 1984
	Garin Veris, AFC-FR: New England vs. N.Y. Jets, 1985
	Gary Jeter, NFC-D: L.A. Rams vs. Dallas, 1985
	Carl Hairston, AFC-D: Cleveland vs. N.Y. Jets, 1986 (ot)
	Charles Mann, NFC-D: Washington vs. Chicago, 1987
	Kevin Greene, NFC-FR: L.A. Rams vs. Minnesota, 1988
	Greg Townsend, AFC-D: L.A. Raiders vs. Cincinnati, 1990
	Wilber Marshall, NFC: Washington vs. Detroit, 1991
	Fred Stokes, NFC-FR: Washington vs. Minnesota, 1992
	Pierce Holt, NFC-D: San Francisco vs. Washington, 1992
	Tony Casillas, NFC: Dallas vs. San Francisco, 1992
	Gerald Williams, AFC-FR: Pittsburgh vs. Kansas City, 1993
	Chad Brown, AFC-FR: Pittsburgh vs. Indianapolis, 1996
	Reggie White, SB: Green Bay vs. New England, 1996
	Warren Sapp, NFC-D: Tampa Bay vs. Green Bay, 1997
	Trace Armstrong, AFC-FR: Miami vs. Seattle, 1999
	Michael McCrary, AFC-FR: Baltimore vs. Denver, 2000
	Willie McGinest, AFC-D: New England vs. Tennessee, 2003
	Darnell Dockett, SB: Arizona vs. Pittsburgh, 2008
	Ray Edwards, NFC-D: Minnesota vs. Dallas, 2009
	James Harrison, AFC-D: Pittsburgh vs. Baltimore, 2010
	Terrell Suggs, AFC-D: Baltimore vs. Pittsburgh, 2010

TEAM RECORDS

CHAMPIONSHIPS
Most Seasons League Champion
13	Green Bay, 1929-1931, 1936, 1939, 1944, 1961-62, 1965-67, 1996, 2010
9	Chi. Bears, 1921, 1932-33, 1940-41, 1943, 1946, 1963, 1985
7	N.Y. Giants, 1927, 1934, 1938, 1956, 1986, 1990, 2007

Most Consecutive Seasons League Champion
3	Green Bay, 1929-1931

Green Bay, 1965-67
2 Canton, 1922-23
Chi. Bears, 1932-33
Chi. Bears, 1940-41
Philadelphia, 1948-49
Detroit, 1952-53
Cleveland, 1954-55
Baltimore, 1958-59
Houston, 1960-61
Green Bay, 1961-62
Buffalo, 1964-65
Miami, 1972-73
Pittsburgh, 1974-75
Pittsburgh, 1978-79
San Francisco, 1988-89
Dallas, 1992-93
Denver, 1997-98
New England, 2003-04

GAMES, VICTORIES, DEFEATS

Most Seasons Participating in Postseason Games
30 N.Y. Giants, 1933-35, 1938-39, 1941, 1943-44, 1946,
1950, 1956, 1958-59, 1961-63, 1981, 1984-86,
1989-1990, 1993, 1997, 2000, 2005-08
Dallas, 1966-1973, 1975-1983, 1985, 1991-96, 1998-99,
2003, 2006-07, 2009
27 Cleveland/L.A./St. Louis Rams, 1945, 1949-1952, 1955,
1967, 1969, 1973-1980, 1983-86, 1988-89,
1999-2001, 2003-04
26 Minnesota, 1968-1971, 1973-78, 1980, 1982, 1987-89,
1992-94, 1996-2000, 2004, 2008-09
Green Bay, 1936, 1938-39, 1941, 1944, 1960-62,
1965-67, 1972, 1982, 1993-98, 2001-04, 2007,
2009-2010
Pittsburgh, 1947, 1972-79, 1982-84, 1989, 1992-97,
2001-02, 2004-05, 2007-08, 2010

Most Consecutive Seasons Participating in Postseason Games
9 Dallas, 1975-1983
Indianapolis, 2002-2010 (current)
8 Dallas, 1966-1973
Pittsburgh, 1972-79
Los Angeles, 1973-1980
San Francisco, 1983-1990
7 Houston, 1987-1993
San Francisco, 1992-98

Most Games
58 Dallas, 1966-1973, 1975-1983, 1985, 1991-96, 1998-99,
2003, 2006-07, 2009
53 Pittsburgh, 1947, 1972-79, 1982-84, 1989, 1992-97,
2001-02, 2004-05, 2007-08, 2010
45 Minnesota, 1968-1971, 1973-78, 1980, 1982, 1987-89,
1992-94, 1996-2000, 2004, 2008-09
Green Bay, 1936, 1938-39, 1941, 1944, 1960-62,
1965-67, 1972, 1982, 1993-98, 2001-04, 2007,
2009-2010

Most Games Won
33 Dallas, 1967, 1970-73, 1975, 1977-78, 1980-82,
1991-96, 2009
Pittsburgh, 1972, 1974-76, 1978-79, 1984, 1989,
1994-97, 2001-02, 2004-05, 2008, 2010
29 Green Bay, 1936, 1939, 1944, 1961-62, 1965-67, 1982,
1993-97, 2001, 2003, 2007, 2010
25 Oakland/L.A. Raiders, 1967-1970, 1973-77, 1980,
1982-83, 1990, 1993, 2000-02
San Francisco, 1970-71, 1981, 1983-84, 1988-1990,
1992-94, 1996-98, 2002

Most Consecutive Games Won
10 New England, 2001, 2003-05
9 Green Bay, 1961-62, 1965-67
7 Pittsburgh, 1974-76
San Francisco, 1988-1990
Dallas, 1992-94

Denver, 1997-98
Most Games Lost
26 Minnesota, 1968-1971, 1973-78, 1980, 1982, 1987-89,
1992-94, 1996-2000, 2004, 2008-09
25 Dallas, 1966-1970, 1972-73, 1975-76, 1978-1983, 1985,
1991, 1994, 1996, 1998-99, 2003, 2006-07, 2009
24 L.A./St. Louis Rams, 1949-1950, 1952, 1955, 1967,
1969, 1973-1980, 1983-86, 1988-89, 2000-01,
2003-04
N.Y. Giants, 1933, 1935, 1939, 1941, 1943-44, 1946,
1950, 1958-59, 1961-63, 1981, 1984-85, 1989,
1993, 1997, 2000, 2002, 2005-06, 2008

Most Consecutive Games Lost
7 Kansas City, 1993-95, 1997, 2003, 2006, 2010 (current)
6 N.Y. Giants, 1939, 1941, 1943-44, 1946, 1950
Cleveland, 1969, 1971-72, 1980, 1982, 1985
Minnesota, 1988-89, 1992-94, 1996
Detroit, 1991, 1993-95, 1997, 1999 (current)
Seattle, 1984, 1987-88, 1999, 2003-04
Dallas, 1996, 1998-99, 2003, 2006-07
5 N.Y. Giants, 1958-59, 1961-63
Los Angeles, 1952, 1955, 1967, 1969, 1973
Denver, 1977-79, 1983-84
Baltimore/Indianapolis, 1971, 1975-77, 1987
Philadelphia, 1980-81, 1988-1990
Indianapolis, 1995-96, 1999-2000, 2002

SCORING

Most Points, Game
73 NFC: Chi. Bears vs. Washington, 1940
62 AFC-D: Jacksonville vs. Miami, 1999
59 NFC: Detroit vs. Cleveland, 1957
Most Points, Both Teams, Game
96 NFC-FR: Arizona (51) vs. Green Bay (45), 2009
95 NFC-FR: Philadelphia (58) vs. Detroit (37), 1995
86 NFC-D: St. Louis (49) vs. Minnesota (37), 1999
Fewest Points, Both Teams, Game
5 NFC-D: Detroit (0) vs. Dallas (5), 1970
7 NFC: Chi. Cardinals (0) vs. Philadelphia (7), 1948
9 NFC: Tampa Bay (0) vs. Los Angeles (9), 1979
Largest Margin of Victory, Game
73 NFC: Chi. Bears vs. Washington, 1940 (73-0)
55 AFC-D: Jacksonville vs. Miami, 1999 (62-7)
49 AFC-D: Oakland vs. Houston, 1969 (56-7)
Most Points, Shutout Victory, Game
73 NFC: Chi. Bears vs. Washington, 1940
41 NFC: N.Y. Giants vs. Minnesota, 2000
AFC-FR: N.Y. Jets vs. Indianapolis, 2002
38 NFC-D: Dallas vs. Tampa Bay, 1981
Most Points Overcome to Win Game
32 AFC-FR: Buffalo vs. Houston, 1992 (trailed 3-35,
won 41-38) (ot)
24 NFC-FR: San Francisco vs. N.Y. Giants, 2002 (trailed
14-38, won 39-38)
20 NFC-D: Detroit vs. San Francisco, 1957 (trailed 7-27,
won 31-27)
Most Points, Each Half
1st: 41 AFC: Buffalo vs. L.A. Raiders, 1990
AFC-D: Jacksonville vs. Miami, 1999
38 NFC-D: Washington vs. L.A. Rams, 1983
NFC-FR: Philadelphia vs. Detroit, 1995
35 NFC: Cleveland vs. Detroit, 1954
AFC-D: Oakland vs. Houston, 1969
SB: Washington vs. Denver, 1987
AFC-FR: Indianapolis vs. Denver, 2004
NFC-D: New Orleans vs. Arizona, 2009
2nd: 45 NFC: Chi. Bears vs. Washington, 1940
35 AFC-FR: Buffalo vs. Houston, 1992
NFC-D: St. Louis vs. Minnesota, 1999
NFC-FR: Green Bay vs. Arizona, 2009
32 AFC: Indianapolis vs. New England, 2006

Most Points, Each Quarter

1st:	28	AFC-D: Oakland vs. Houston, 1969
	24	AFC-D: San Diego vs. Miami, 1981
		AFC-D: Jacksonville vs. Miami, 1999
		AFC-D: Baltimore vs. New England, 2009
	21	NFC: Chi. Bears vs. Washington, 1940
		AFC: San Diego vs. Boston, 1963
		AFC-D: Oakland vs. Kansas City, 1968
		AFC: Oakland vs. San Diego, 1980
		AFC: Buffalo vs. L.A. Raiders, 1990
		NFC: San Francisco vs. Dallas, 1994
		NFC-D: New Orleans vs. Arizona, 2009
2nd:	35	SB: Washington vs. Denver, 1987
	31	NFC-FR: Philadelphia vs. Detroit, 1995
	28	NFC-D: Green Bay vs. Atlanta, 2010
3rd:	28	AFC-FR: Buffalo vs. Houston, 1992
	26	NFC: Chi. Bears vs. Washington, 1940
	21	NFC-D: Dallas vs. Cleveland, 1967
		NFC-D: Dallas vs. Tampa Bay, 1981
		AFC-D: L.A. Raiders vs. Pittsburgh, 1983
		SB: Chicago vs. New England, 1985
		NFC-D: N.Y. Giants vs. San Francisco, 1986
		AFC: Cleveland vs. Denver, 1987
		AFC: Cleveland vs. Denver, 1989
		NFC-D: St. Louis vs. Minnesota, 1999
4th:	27	NFC: N.Y. Giants vs. Chi. Bears, 1934
	26	NFC-FR: Philadelphia vs. New Orleans, 1992
	24	NFC: Baltimore vs. N.Y. Giants, 1959
OT:	6	NFC: Baltimore vs. N.Y. Giants, 1958
		AFC-D: Oakland vs. Baltimore, 1977
		NFC-D: L.A. Rams vs. N.Y. Giants, 1989
		AFC-FR: Miami vs. Indianapolis, 2000
		NFC-FR: Green Bay vs. Seattle, 2003
		NFC-D: Carolina vs. St. Louis, 2003
		AFC-FR: San Diego vs. Indianapolis, 2008
		NFC-FR: Arizona vs. Green Bay, 2009

TOUCHDOWNS

Most Touchdowns, Game

11	NFC: Chi. Bears vs. Washington, 1940
8	NFC: Cleveland vs. Detroit, 1954
	NFC: Detroit vs. Cleveland, 1957
	AFC-D: Oakland vs. Houston, 1969
	SB: San Francisco vs. Denver, 1989
	AFC-D: Jacksonville vs. Miami, 1999
7	AFC: San Diego vs. Boston, 1963
	NFC-D: Dallas vs. Cleveland, 1967
	NFC-D: N.Y. Giants vs. San Francisco, 1986
	AFC: Buffalo vs. L.A. Raiders, 1990
	SB: Dallas vs. Buffalo, 1992
	SB: San Francisco vs. San Diego, 1994
	NFC-FR: Philadelphia vs. Detroit, 1995
	NFC-D: St. Louis vs. Minnesota, 1999
	AFC-FR: Indianapolis vs. Denver, 2004
	NFC-FR: Arizona vs. Green Bay, 2009 (ot)

Most Touchdowns, Both Teams, Game

13	NFC-FR: Arizona (7) vs. Green Bay (6), 2009 (ot)
12	NFC-FR: Philadelphia (7) vs. Detroit (5), 1995
	NFC-D: St. Louis (7) vs. Minnesota (5), 1999
11	NFC: Chi. Bears (11) vs. Washington (0), 1940

Fewest Touchdowns, Both Teams, Game

0	NFC-D: N.Y. Giants vs. Cleveland, 1950
	NFC-D: Dallas vs. Detroit, 1970
	NFC: Los Angeles vs. Tampa Bay, 1979
	AFC-D: Baltimore vs. Indianapolis, 2006
1	NFC: Chi. Cardinals (0) vs. Philadelphia (1), 1948
	NFC: Cleveland (0) vs. N.Y. Giants (1), 1958
	AFC: San Diego (0) vs. Houston (1), 1961
	AFC-D: N.Y. Jets (0) vs. Kansas City (1), 1969
	NFC-D: Green Bay (0) vs. Washington (1), 1972
	NFC-FR: New Orleans (0) vs. Chicago (1), 1990
	NFC: N.Y. Giants (0) vs. San Francisco (1), 1990

	AFC-FR: L.A. Raiders (0) vs. Kansas City (1), 1991
	AFC-D: New England (0) vs. Pittsburgh (1), 1997
	NFC: Tampa Bay (0) vs. St. Louis (1), 1999
	AFC: Oakland (0) vs. Baltimore (1), 2000
2	In many games

POINTS AFTER TOUCHDOWN

Most (One-Point) Points After Touchdown, Game

8	NFC: Cleveland vs. Detroit, 1954
	NFC: Detroit vs. Cleveland, 1957
	AFC-D: Oakland vs. Houston, 1969
	AFC-D: Jacksonville vs. Miami, 1999
7	NFC: Chi. Bears vs. Washington, 1940
	NFC-D: Dallas vs. Cleveland, 1967
	NFC-D: N.Y. Giants vs. San Francisco, 1986
	SB: San Francisco vs. Denver, 1989
	SB: Dallas vs. Buffalo, 1992
	SB: San Francisco vs. San Diego, 1994
	NFC-FR: Philadelphia vs. Detroit, 1995
	NFC-D: St. Louis vs. Minnesota, 1999
	AFC-FR: Indianapolis vs. Denver, 2004
6	AFC: San Diego vs. Boston, 1963
	NFC-D: Washington vs. L.A. Rams, 1983
	AFC: Miami vs. Pittsburgh, 1984
	SB: Washington vs. Denver, 1987
	AFC: Buffalo vs. L.A. Raiders, 1990
	AFC-FR: L.A. Raiders vs. Denver, 1993
	AFC-FR: Denver vs. Jacksonville, 1997
	NFC-D: St. Louis vs. Green Bay, 2001
	SB: Tampa Bay vs. Oakland, 2002
	NFC: Atlanta vs. St. Louis, 2004)
	NFC-FR: Green Bay vs. Seattle, 2007
	NFC-FR: Arizona vs. Green Bay, 2009 (ot)
	NFC-FR: Green Bay vs. Arizona, 2009 (ot)
	NFC-D: New Orleans vs. Arizona, 2009
	NFC-D: Green Bay vs. Atlanta, 2010

Most (One-Point) Points After Touchdown, Both Teams, Game

12	NFC-FR: Arizona (6) vs. Green Bay (6), 2009
10	NFC: Detroit (8) vs. Cleveland (2), 1957
	AFC-D: Miami (5) vs. San Diego (5), 1981 (ot)
	AFC: Miami (6) vs. Pittsburgh (4), 1984
	AFC-FR: Buffalo (5) vs. Houston (5), 1992 (ot)
	NFC-FR: Philadelphia (7) vs. Detroit (3), 1995
	AFC-FR: Indianapolis (7) vs. Denver (3), 2004
9	In many games

Fewest (One-Point) Points After Touchdown, Both Teams, Game

0	NFC-D: N.Y. Giants vs. Cleveland, 1950
	NFC-D: Dallas vs. Detroit, 1970
	NFC: Los Angeles vs. Tampa Bay, 1979
	NFC: St. Louis vs. Tampa Bay, 1999
	AFC-D: Baltimore vs. Indianapolis, 2006

Most Two-Point Conversions, Game

2	SB: San Diego vs. San Francisco, 1994
	NFC-FR: Detroit vs. Philadelphia, 1995
	NFC-FR: San Francisco vs.. N.Y. Giants, 2002
1	By many teams

FIELD GOALS

Most Field Goals, Game

5	NFC-D: Minnesota vs. San Francisco, 1987
	NFC: N.Y. Giants vs. San Francisco, 1990
	AFC: Buffalo vs. Miami, 1992
	NFC-FR: N.Y. Giants vs. Minnesota, 1997
	NFC-FR: Carolina vs. Dallas, 2003
	NFC-D: St. Louis vs. Carolina, 2003 (2 ot)
	AFC: New England vs. Indianapolis, 2003
	AFC-D: Indianapolis vs. Baltimore, 2006
4	AFC-D: Boston vs. Buffalo, 1963
	AFC: Oakland vs. Houston, 1967
	SB: Green Bay vs. Oakland, 1967
	NFC: Washington vs. Dallas, 1972
	AFC-D: Oakland vs. Pittsburgh, 1973

SB: San Francisco vs. Cincinnati, 1981
AFC-FR: New England vs. N.Y. Jets, 1985
NFC-FR: Washington vs. L.A. Rams, 1986
NFC-D: Philadelphia vs. Chicago, 1988
AFC-FR: Pittsburgh vs. Houston, 1989 (ot)
AFC-D: Pittsburgh vs. Buffalo, 1995
NFC-FR: Dallas vs. Minnesota, 1996
NFC-D: Carolina vs. Dallas, 1996
AFC-FR: Jacksonville vs. New England, 1998
AFC-D: Tennessee vs. Indianapolis, 1999
NFC-D: Philadelphia vs. Chicago, 2001
AFC: San Diego vs. New England, 2007
NFC-FR: Philadelphia vs. Minnesota, 2008
NFC-D: Arizona vs. Carolina, 2008
3 By many teams

Most Field Goals, Both Teams, Game
8 NFC-FR: N.Y. Giants (5) vs. Minnesota (3), 1997
   NFC-D: St. Louis (5) vs. Carolina (3), 2003 (2 ot)
7 AFC-FR: Pittsburgh (4) vs. Houston (3), 1989 (ot)
   NFC: N.Y. Giants (5) vs. San Francisco (2), 1990
   NFC-D: Carolina (4) vs. Dallas (3), 1996
   AFC-D: Tennessee (4) vs. Indianapolis (3), 1999
   AFC-D: Indianapolis (5) vs. Baltimore (2), 2006
6 NFC-D: Minnesota (5) vs. San Francisco (1), 1987
   NFC-D: Philadelphia (4) vs. Chicago (2), 1988
   AFC: Buffalo (5) vs. Miami (1), 1992
   NFC-FR: Carolina (5) vs. Dallas (1), 2003
   AFC-FR: New England (3) vs. N.Y. Jets (3), 2006
   NFC-D: N.Y. Giants (3) vs. Philadelphia (3), 2008

Most Field Goals Attempted, Game
6 AFC: Oakland vs. Houston, 1967
   NFC-D: Los Angeles vs. Dallas, 1973
   AFC-D: Cleveland vs. N.Y. Jets, 1986 (ot)
   NFC: N.Y. Giants vs. San Francisco, 1990
   AFC: Buffalo vs. Miami, 1992
   NFC-D: St. Louis vs. Carolina, 2003 (2 ot)
5 By many teams

Most Field Goals Attempted, Both Teams, Game
11 NFC-D: St. Louis (6) vs. Carolina (5), 2003 (2 ot)
9 NFC-D: Philadelphia (5) vs. Chicago (4), 1988
   NFC-FR: N.Y. Giants (5) vs. Minnesota (4), 1997
8 NFC-D: Los Angeles (6) vs. Dallas (2), 1973
   NFC-D: Detroit (5) vs. San Francisco (3), 1983
   AFC-D: Cleveland (6) vs. N.Y. Jets (2), 1986 (ot)
   NFC-D: Minnesota (5) vs. San Francisco (3), 1987
   AFC-FR: Houston (4) vs. Pittsburgh (4), 1989 (ot)
   NFC-FR: Chicago (4) vs. New Orleans (4), 1990
   NFC: N.Y. Giants (6) vs. San Francisco (2), 1990
   NFC-D: N.Y. Giants (5) vs. Philadelphia (3), 2008

SAFETIES
Most Safeties, Game
1 By many teams
Most Safeties, Both Teams, Game
1 In many games

FIRST DOWNS
Most First Downs, Game
34 AFC-D: San Diego vs. Miami, 1981 (ot)
33 AFC-D: Cleveland vs. N.Y. Jets, 1986 (ot)
32 AFC: Indianapolis vs. New England, 2006
    NFC-FR: Green Bay vs. Arizona, 2009 (ot)
    NFC-FR: New Orleans vs. Seattle, 2010

Fewest First Downs, Game
6 NFC: N.Y. Giants vs. Green Bay, 1961
   AFC-D: Baltimore vs. Tennessee, 2000
7 NFC: Green Bay vs. Boston, 1936
   NFC-D: Pittsburgh vs. Philadelphia, 1947
   NFC: Chi. Cardinals vs. Philadelphia, 1948
   NFC: Los Angeles vs. Philadelphia, 1949
   NFC-D: Cleveland vs. N.Y. Giants, 1958
   AFC-D: Cincinnati vs. Baltimore, 1970

NFC-D: Detroit vs. Dallas, 1970
NFC: Tampa Bay vs. Los Angeles, 1979
AFC-D: Baltimore vs. Pittsburgh, 2001
AFC-FR: Kansas City vs. Indianapolis, 2006
8 By many teams

Most First Downs, Both Teams, Game
62 NFC-FR: Green Bay (32) vs. Arizona (30), 2009 (ot)
59 AFC-D: San Diego (34) vs. Miami (25), 1981 (ot)
55 AFC-FR: San Diego (29) vs. Pittsburgh (26), 1982

Fewest First Downs, Both Teams, Game
15 NFC: Green Bay (7) vs. Boston (8), 1936
19 NFC: N.Y. Giants (9) vs. Green Bay (10), 1939
    NFC: Washington (9) vs. Chi. Bears (10), 1942
20 NFC-D: Cleveland (9) vs. N.Y. Giants (11), 1950

RUSHING
Most First Downs, Rushing, Game
19 NFC-FR: Dallas vs. Los Angeles, 1980
18 AFC-D: Miami vs. Cincinnati, 1973
    AFC: Miami vs. Oakland, 1973
    AFC-D: Pittsburgh vs. Buffalo, 1974
    AFC-FR: Buffalo vs. Miami, 1995
    AFC-FR: Denver vs. Jacksonville, 1997
17 AFC-D: Cincinnati vs. Seattle, 1988
    AFC: Buffalo vs. Kansas City, 1993

Fewest First Downs, Rushing, Game
0 NFC: Los Angeles vs. Philadelphia, 1949
   AFC-D: Buffalo vs. Boston, 1963
   AFC: Oakland vs. Pittsburgh, 1974
   NFC-FR: New Orleans vs. Minnesota, 1987
   NFC: L.A. Rams vs. San Francisco, 1989
   NFC-D: Chicago vs. N.Y. Giants, 1990
   AFC-FR: Indianapolis vs. Pittsburgh, 1996
   AFC-FR: Seattle vs. Miami, 1999
   AFC-D: Miami vs. Jacksonville, 1999
   AFC-D: Miami vs. Oakland, 2000
   AFC-D: Baltimore vs. Pittsburgh, 2001
   AFC-D: Indianapolis vs. New England, 2004
   NFC-FR: Philadelphia vs. Dallas, 2009
1 By many teams

Most First Downs, Rushing, Both Teams, Game
26 AFC: Buffalo (14) vs. L.A. Raiders (12), 1990
25 NFC-FR: Dallas (19) vs. Los Angeles (6), 1980
23 NFC: Cleveland (15) vs. Detroit (8), 1952
    AFC-D: Miami (18) vs. Cincinnati (5), 1973
    AFC-D: Pittsburgh (18) vs. Buffalo (5), 1974
    AFC-FR: Buffalo (18) vs. Miami (5), 1995

Fewest First Downs, Rushing, Both Teams, Game
2 NFC-FR: New Orleans (1) vs. St. Louis (1), 2000
5 AFC-D: Buffalo (0) vs. Boston (5), 1963
   NFC-D: Washington (1) vs. Tampa Bay (4), 1999
   AFC-FR: Cleveland (2) vs. Pittsburgh (3), 2002
   AFC-D: Baltimore (2) vs. Indianapolis (3), 2009
6 NFC: Green Bay (2) vs. Boston (4), 1936
   NFC-D: Baltimore (2) vs. Minnesota (4), 1968
   AFC-D: Houston (1) vs. Oakland (5), 1969
   AFC-FR: N.Y. Jets (1) vs. Houston (5), 1991
   AFC-FR: Denver (1) vs. Baltimore (5), 2000
   AFC: Pittsburgh (1) vs. Baltimore (5), 2008
   SB: Arizona (2) vs. Pittsburgh (4), 2008

PASSING
Most First Downs, Passing, Game
24 AFC-FR: Pittsburgh vs. Cleveland, 2002
22 NFC-FR: New Orleans vs. Seattle, 2010
21 AFC-D: Miami vs. San Diego, 1981 (ot)
    AFC-D: San Diego vs. Miami, 1981 (ot)
    AFC-D: Cleveland vs. N.Y. Jets, 1986 (ot)
    NFC-D: Philadelphia vs. Chicago, 1988
    AFC-D: Indianapolis vs. San Diego, 2007
    NFC-FR: Arizona vs. Green Bay, 2009 (ot)

Fewest First Downs, Passing, Game
  0 NFC: Philadelphia vs. Chi. Cardinals, 1948
  1 NFC-D: N.Y. Giants vs. Washington, 1943
     NFC: Cleveland vs. Detroit, 1953
     SB: Denver vs. Dallas, 1977
  2 By many teams

Most First Downs, Passing, Both Teams, Game
  42 AFC-D: Miami (21) vs. San Diego (21), 1981 (ot)
     AFC-FR: Pittsburgh (24) vs. Cleveland (18), 2002
  38 AFC-FR: Pittsburgh (19) vs. San Diego (19), 1982
     NFC-D: Minnesota (20) vs. St. Louis (18), 1999
     NFC-FR: Arizona (21) vs. Green Bay (17), 2009 (ot)
  36 NFC: Minnesota (19) vs. Atlanta (17), 1998 (ot)

Fewest First Downs, Passing, Both Teams, Game
  2 NFC: Philadelphia (0) vs. Chi. Cardinals (2), 1948
  4 NFC-D: Cleveland (2) vs. N.Y. Giants (2), 1950
  5 NFC: Detroit (2) vs. N.Y. Giants (3), 1935
     NFC: Green Bay (2) vs. N.Y. Giants (3), 1939

PENALTY
Most First Downs, Penalty, Game
  7 AFC-D: New England vs. Oakland, 1976
     AFC: Tennessee vs. Oakland, 2002
  6 AFC-D: Cleveland vs. N.Y. Jets, 1986 (ot)
     NFC-D: Chicago vs. Carolina, 2005
     NFC-FR: Green Bay vs. Arizona, 2009 (ot)
  5 AFC-FR: Cleveland vs. L. A. Raiders, 1982
     NFC-D: San Francisco vs. Minnesota, 1997
     AFC-FR: Miami vs. Buffalo, 1998
     NFC-D: Arizona vs. Minnesota, 1998
     AFC: Pittsburgh vs. New England, 2001
     AFC-D: Pittsburgh vs. Tennessee, 2002 (ot)
     AFC-FR: Cincinnati vs. N.Y. Jets, 2009

Most First Downs, Penalty, Both Teams, Game
  10 AFC: Tennessee (7) vs. Oakland (3), 2002
  9 AFC-D: New England (7) vs. Oakland (2), 1976
  8 AFC-FR: Atlanta (4) vs. Minnesota (4), 1982
     AFC-FR: Miami (5) vs. Buffalo (3), 1998
     NFC-FR: Dallas (4) vs. Philadelphia (4), 2009
     NFC-FR: Green Bay (6) vs. Arizona (2), 2009 (ot)

NET YARDS GAINED RUSHING AND PASSING
Most Yards Gained, Game
  610 AFC: San Diego vs. Boston, 1963
  602 SB: Washington vs. Denver, 1987
  569 AFC: Miami vs. Pittsburgh, 1984

Fewest Yards Gained, Game
  86 NFC-D: Cleveland vs. N.Y. Giants, 1958
  99 NFC: Chi. Cardinals vs. Philadelphia, 1948
  112 NFC-D: N.Y. Giants vs. Washington, 1943

Most Yards Gained, Both Teams, Game
  1,038 AFC-FR: Buffalo (536) vs. Miami (502), 1995
  1,036 AFC-D: San Diego (564) vs. Miami (472), 1981 (ot)
  1,024 AFC: Miami (569) vs. Pittsburgh (455), 1984
       NFC-FR: Arizona (531) vs. Green Bay (493), 2009 (ot)

Fewest Yards Gained, Both Teams, Game
  331 NFC: Chi. Cardinals (99) vs. Philadelphia (232), 1948
  332 NFC-D: N.Y. Giants (150) vs. Cleveland (182), 1950
  336 NFC: Boston (116) vs. Green Bay (220), 1936

RUSHING
ATTEMPTS
Most Attempts, Game
  65 NFC: Detroit vs. N.Y. Giants, 1935
  61 NFC: Philadelphia vs. Los Angeles, 1949
  59 AFC: New England vs. Miami, 1985

Fewest Attempts, Game
  8 AFC-D: Miami vs. San Diego, 1994
  9 SB: Miami vs. San Francisco, 1984
     NFC: Minnesota vs. N.Y. Giants, 2000
  10 NFC: L.A. Rams vs. San Francisco, 1989
     NFC-FR: Atlanta vs. Green Bay, 1995

     NFC-FR: Detroit vs. Washington, 1999

Most Attempts, Both Teams, Game
  109 NFC: Detroit (65) vs. N.Y. Giants (44), 1935
  97 AFC-D: Baltimore (50) vs. Oakland (47), 1977 (ot)
  91 NFC: Philadelphia (57) vs. Chi. Cardinals (34), 1948

Fewest Attempts, Both Teams, Game
  32 AFC-D: Houston (14) vs. Kansas City (18), 1993
  36 SB: Green Bay (13) vs. Pittsburgh (23), 2010
  37 SB: Arizona (12) vs. Pittsburgh (25), 2008
     SB: New Orleans (18) vs. Indianapolis (19), 2009

YARDS GAINED
Most Yards Gained, Game
  382 NFC: Chi. Bears vs. Washington, 1940
  341 AFC-FR: Buffalo vs. Miami, 1995
  338 NFC-FR: Dallas vs. Los Angeles, 1980

Fewest Yards Gained, Game
  – 4 NFC-FR: Detroit vs. Green Bay, 1994
  7 AFC-D: Buffalo vs. Boston, 1963
    SB: New England vs. Chicago, 1985
  14 AFC-D: Miami vs. Denver, 1998
     AFC: N.Y. Jets vs. Denver, 1998

Most Yards Gained, Both Teams, Game
  430 NFC-FR: Dallas (338) vs. Los Angeles (92), 1980
  426 NFC: Cleveland (227) vs. Detroit (199), 1952
  411 AFC-FR: Buffalo (341) vs. Miami (70), 1995

Fewest Yards Gained, Both Teams, Game
  77 NFC-FR: Detroit (–4) vs. Green Bay (81), 1994
  84 NFC-FR: St. Louis (34) vs. New Orleans (50), 2000
  90 AFC-D: Buffalo (7) vs. Boston (83), 1963
     NFC-D: Tampa Bay (44) vs. Washington (46), 1999

AVERAGE GAIN
Highest Average Gain, Game
  9.94 AFC: San Diego vs. Boston, 1963 (32-318)
  9.29 NFC-D: Green Bay vs. Dallas, 1982 (17-158)
  8.18 NFC-D: Atlanta vs. St. Louis, 2004 (40-327)

Lowest Average Gain, Game
  – 0.27 NFC-FR: Detroit vs. Green Bay, 1994 (15-(– 4))
  0.58 AFC-D: Buffalo vs. Boston, 1963 (12-7)
  0.64 SB: New England vs. Chicago, 1985 (11-7)

TOUCHDOWNS
Most Touchdowns, Game
  7 NFC: Chi. Bears vs. Washington, 1940
  6 NFC-D: San Francisco vs. N.Y. Giants, 1993
  5 NFC: Cleveland vs. Detroit, 1954
    NFC-D: San Francisco vs. Chicago, 1994
    AFC-FR: Pittsburgh vs. Indianapolis, 1996
    AFC-FR: Denver vs. Jacksonville, 1997

Most Touchdowns, Both Teams, Game
  7 NFC: Chi. Bears (7) vs. Washington (0), 1940
  6 NFC: Cleveland (5) vs. Detroit (1), 1954
    NFC-D: San Francisco (6) vs. N.Y. Giants (0), 1993
    NFC-D: San Francisco (5) vs. Chicago (1), 1994
    AFC-FR: Denver (5) vs. Jacksonville (1), 1997
  5 NFC: Chi. Cardinals (3) vs. Philadelphia (2), 1947
    AFC: San Diego (4) vs. Boston (1), 1963
    AFC-D: Cincinnati (3) vs. Buffalo (2), 1981
    AFC-FR: Pittsburgh (5) vs. Indianapolis (0), 1996
    NFC-D: Arizona (3) vs. Minnesota (2), 1998
    NFC-FR: Seattle (3) vs. Green Bay (2), 2003 (ot)

PASSING
ATTEMPTS
Most Attempts, Game
  66 AFC-FR: Miami vs. Buffalo, 1995
  65 AFC-D: Cleveland vs. N.Y. Jets, 1986 (ot)
     NFC-D: San Francisco vs. Green Bay, 1995
  61 NFC-FR: Minnesota vs. Chicago, 1994

Fewest Attempts, Game
  5 NFC: Detroit vs. N.Y. Giants, 1935

6   AFC: Miami vs. Oakland, 1973
7   SB: Miami vs. Minnesota, 1973

Most Attempts, Both Teams, Game

102   AFC-D: San Diego (54) vs. Miami (48), 1981 (ot)
96   AFC: N.Y. Jets (49) vs. Oakland (47), 1968
95   AFC-D: Cleveland (65) vs. N.Y. Jets (30), 1986 (ot)
      NFC-FR: New Orleans (60) vs. Seattle (35), 2010

Fewest Attempts, Both Teams, Game

18   NFC: Detroit (5) vs. N.Y. Giants (13), 1935
23   NFC: Chi. Cardinals (11) vs. Philadelphia (12), 1948
24   NFC-D: Cleveland (9) vs. N.Y. Giants (15), 1950

COMPLETIONS

Most Completions, Game

39   NFC-FR: New Orleans vs. Seattle, 2010
36   AFC-FR: Houston vs. Buffalo, 1992 (ot)
34   AFC-D: Cleveland vs. N.Y. Jets, 1986 (ot)
      AFC-FR: Miami vs. Buffalo, 1995

Fewest Completions, Game

2   NFC: Detroit vs. N.Y. Giants, 1935
   NFC: Philadelphia vs. Chi. Cardinals, 1948
3   NFC: N.Y. Giants vs. Chi. Bears, 1941
   NFC: Green Bay vs. N.Y. Giants, 1944
   NFC: Chi. Cardinals vs. Philadelphia, 1947
   NFC: Chi. Cardinals vs. Philadelphia, 1948
   NFC-D: Cleveland vs. N.Y. Giants, 1950
   NFC-D: N.Y. Giants vs. Cleveland, 1950
   NFC: Cleveland vs. Detroit, 1953
   AFC: Miami vs. Oakland, 1973
4   NFC: N.Y. Giants vs. Detroit, 1935
   NFC-D: N.Y. Giants vs. Washington, 1943
   NFC-D: Pittsburgh vs. Philadelphia, 1947
   NFC-D: Dallas vs. Detroit, 1970
   AFC: Miami vs. Baltimore, 1971
   SB: Miami vs. Washington, 1982
   AFC-FR: Seattle vs. L.A. Raiders, 1984
   AFC-FR: Baltimore vs. New England, 2009

Most Completions, Both Teams, Game

64   AFC-D: San Diego (33) vs. Miami (31), 1981 (ot)
63   SB: New Orleans (32) vs. Indianapolis (31), 2009
61   NFC-FR: New Orleans (39) vs. Seattle (22), 2010

Fewest Completions, Both Teams, Game

5   NFC: Philadelphia (2) vs. Chi. Cardinals (3), 1948
6   NFC: Detroit (2) vs. N.Y. Giants (4), 1935
   NFC-D: Cleveland (3) vs. N.Y. Giants (3), 1950
11   NFC: Green Bay (3) vs. N.Y. Giants (8), 1944
   NFC-D: Dallas (4) vs. Detroit (7), 1970

COMPLETION PERCENTAGE

Highest Completion Percentage, Game (20 attempts)

92.9   AFC-D: New England vs. Jacksonville, 2007 (28-26)
88.0   SB: N.Y. Giants vs. Denver, 1986 (25-22)
87.9   NFC-FR: Arizona vs. Green Bay, 2009 (33-29) (ot)

Lowest Completion Percentage, Game (20 attempts)

18.5   NFC: Tampa Bay vs. Los Angeles, 1979 (27-5)
20.0   NFC-D: N.Y. Giants vs. Washington, 1943 (20-4)
25.8   NFC: Chi. Bears vs. Washington, 1937 (31-8)

YARDS GAINED

Most Yards Gained, Game

483   AFC-D: Cleveland vs. N.Y. Jets, 1986 (ot)
454   AFC-FR: Indianapolis vs. Denver, 2004
435   AFC: Miami vs. Pittsburgh, 1984

Fewest Yards Gained, Game

3   NFC: Chi. Cardinals vs. Philadelphia, 1948
7   NFC: Philadelphia vs. Chi. Cardinals, 1948
9   NFC-D: N.Y. Giants vs. Cleveland, 1950
   NFC: Cleveland vs. Detroit, 1953

Most Yards Gained, Both Teams, Game

809   AFC-D: San Diego (415) vs. Miami (394), 1981 (ot)
779   NFC-FR: Green Bay (404) vs. Arizona (375), 2009 (ot)
762   NFC-D: Minnesota (388) vs. St. Louis (374), 1999

Fewest Yards Gained, Both Teams, Game

10   NFC: Chi. Cardinals (3) vs. Philadelphia (7), 1948
38   NFC-D: N.Y. Giants (9) vs. Cleveland (29), 1950
102   NFC-D: Dallas (22) vs. Detroit (80), 1970

TIMES SACKED

Most Times Sacked, Game

9   AFC: Kansas City vs. Buffalo, 1966
   NFC: Chicago vs. San Francisco, 1984
   AFC-D: N.Y. Jets vs. Cleveland, 1986 (ot)
   AFC-D: Houston vs. Kansas City, 1993
8   NFC: Green Bay vs. Dallas, 1967
   NFC: Minnesota vs. Washington, 1987
   NFC-D: Philadelphia vs. Green Bay, 2003 (ot)
7   NFC-D: Dallas vs. Los Angeles, 1973
   SB: Dallas vs. Pittsburgh, 1975
   AFC-FR: Houston vs. Oakland, 1980
   NFC-D: Washington vs. Chicago, 1984
   SB: New England vs. Chicago, 1985
   AFC-FR: Kansas City vs. San Diego, 1992
   AFC-D: Pittsburgh vs. Buffalo, 1992

Most Times Sacked, Both Teams, Game

13   AFC: Kansas City (9) vs. Buffalo (4), 1966
   AFC-D: N.Y. Jets (9) vs. Cleveland (4), 1986 (ot)
12   NFC-D: Dallas (7) vs. Los Angeles (5), 1973
   NFC-D: Washington (7) vs. Chicago (5), 1984
   NFC: Chicago (9) vs. San Francisco (3), 1984
   AFC-FR: Kansas City (7) vs. San Diego (5), 1992
11   AFC-D: Houston (9) vs. Kansas City (2), 1993
   AFC-D: Pittsburgh (6) vs. Baltimore (5), 2010

Fewest Times Sacked, Both Teams, Game

0   AFC-D: Buffalo vs. Pittsburgh, 1974
   AFC-FR: Pittsburgh vs. San Diego, 1982
   AFC: Miami vs. Pittsburgh, 1984
   AFC-D: Buffalo vs. Miami, 1990
   AFC-D: Denver vs. Houston, 1991
   AFC-FR: Buffalo vs. Miami, 1995
   AFC: Indianapolis vs. Tennessee, 1999
   AFC: Indianapolis vs. San Diego, 2007
   NFC-D: N.Y. Giants vs. Philadelphia, 2008
1   In many games

TOUCHDOWNS

Most Touchdowns, Game

6   AFC-D: Oakland vs. Houston, 1969
   SB: San Francisco vs. San Diego, 1994
5   NFC: Chi. Bears vs. Washington, 1943
   NFC: Detroit vs. Cleveland, 1957
   AFC-D: Oakland vs. Kansas City, 1968
   SB: San Francisco vs. Denver, 1989
   NFC-D: St. Louis vs. Minnesota, 1999
   NFC: N.Y. Giants vs. Minnesota, 2000
   AFC-FR: Indianapolis vs. Denver, 2003
   NFC-FR: Arizona vs. Green Bay, 2009 (ot)
4   By many teams

Most Touchdowns, Both Teams, Game

9   NFC-D: St. Louis (5) vs. Minnesota (4), 1999
   NFC-FR: Arizona (5) vs. Green Bay (4), 2009 (ot)
8   AFC-FR: Buffalo (4) vs. Houston (4), 1992 (ot)
7   NFC: Chi. Bears (5) vs. Washington (2), 1943
   AFC-D: Oakland (6) vs. Houston (1), 1969
   SB: Pittsburgh (4) vs. Dallas (3), 1978
   AFC-D: Miami (4) vs. San Diego (3), 1981 (ot)
   AFC: Miami (4) vs. Pittsburgh (3), 1984
   AFC-D: Buffalo (4) vs. Cleveland (3), 1989
   SB: San Francisco (6) vs. San Diego (1), 1994
   NFC-FR: Detroit (4) vs. Philadelphia (3), 1995
   NFC-FR: New Orleans (4) vs. St. Louis (3), 2000
   NFC-FR: N.Y. Giants (4) vs. San Francisco (3), 2002
   NFC: Arizona (4) vs. Philadelphia (3), 2008

INTERCEPTIONS BY
Most Interceptions By, Game
- 8 NFC: Chi. Bears vs. Washington, 1940
- 7 NFC: Cleveland vs. Los Angeles, 1955
- 6 NFC: Green Bay vs. N.Y. Giants, 1939
  - NFC: Chi. Bears vs. N.Y. Giants, 1946
  - NFC: Cleveland vs. Detroit, 1954
  - AFC: San Diego vs. Houston, 1961
  - AFC: Buffalo vs. L.A. Raiders, 1990
  - NFC-FR: Philadelphia vs. Detroit, 1995
  - NFC-D: St. Louis vs. Green Bay, 2001

Most Interceptions By, Both Teams, Game
- 10 NFC: Cleveland (7) vs. Los Angeles (3), 1955
  - AFC: San Diego (6) vs. Houston (4), 1961
- 9 NFC: Green Bay (6) vs. N.Y. Giants (3), 1939
- 8 NFC: Chi. Bears (8) vs. Washington (0), 1940
  - NFC: Chi. Bears (6) vs. N.Y. Giants (2), 1946
  - NFC: Cleveland (6) vs. Detroit (2), 1954
  - AFC-FR: Buffalo (4) vs. N.Y. Jets (4), 1981
  - AFC: Miami (5) vs. N.Y. Jets (3), 1982

YARDS GAINED
Most Yards Gained, Game
- 172 SB: Tampa Bay vs. Oakland, 2002
- 161 NFC-D: St. Louis vs. Green Bay, 2001
- 138 AFC-FR: N.Y. Jets vs. Cincinnati, 1982

Most Yards Gained, Both Teams, Game
- 184 SB: Tampa Bay (172) vs. Oakland (12), 2002
- 161 NFC-D: St. Louis (161) vs. Green Bay (0), 2001
- 149 NFC: Cleveland (103) vs. Los Angeles (46), 1955

TOUCHDOWNS
Most Touchdowns, Game
- 3 NFC: Chi. Bears vs. Washington, 1940
  - NFC-D: St. Louis vs. Green Bay, 2001
  - SB: Tampa Bay vs. Oakland, 2002
- 2 NFC-D: Los Angeles vs. St. Louis, 1975
  - NFC-FR: Philadelphia vs. Detroit, 1995)
  - NFC-FR: Seattle vs. Washington, 2007
- 1 In many games

Most Touchdowns, Both Teams, Game
- 3 NFC: Chi. Bears (3) vs. Washington (0), 1940
  - NFC-D: St. Louis (3) vs. Green Bay (0), 2001
  - SB: Tampa Bay (3) vs. Oakland (0), 2002
- 2 NFC-D: Los Angeles (2) vs. St. Louis (0), 1975
  - NFC-D: Dallas (1) vs. Green Bay (1), 1982
  - NFC-D: Minnesota (1) vs. San Francisco (1), 1987
  - NFC-FR: Detroit (1) vs. Green Bay (1), 1993
  - NFC-FR: Philadelphia (2) vs. Detroit (0), 1995
  - AFC-FR: Buffalo (1) vs. Jacksonville (1), 1996)
  - NFC-FR: Seattle (2) vs. Washington (0), 2007
- 1 In many games

PUNTING
Most Punts, Game
- 14 AFC-D: N.Y. Jets vs. Cleveland, 1986 (ot)
- 13 NFC: N.Y. Giants vs. Chi. Bears, 1933
  - AFC-D: Baltimore vs. Oakland, 1977 (ot)
- 11 AFC: Houston vs. Oakland, 1967
  - AFC-D: Houston vs. Oakland, 1969
  - NFC: L.A. Rams vs. Chicago, 1985
  - SB: N.Y. Giants vs. Baltimore, 2000

Fewest Punts, Game
- 0 NFC-FR: St. Louis vs. Green Bay, 1982
  - AFC-FR: N.Y. Jets vs. Cincinnati, 1982
  - AFC-FR: Indianapolis vs. Denver, 2003
  - AFC-D: Kansas City vs. Indianapolis, 2003
  - AFC-D: Indianapolis vs. Kansas City, 2003
  - NFC-D: Green Bay vs. Atlanta, 2010
- 1 By many teams

Most Punts, Both Teams, Game
- 23 NFC: N.Y. Giants (13) vs. Chi. Bears (10), 1933
- 22 AFC-D: N.Y. Jets (14) vs. Cleveland (8), 1986 (ot)
- 21 AFC-D: Baltimore (13) vs. Oakland (8), 1977 (ot)
  - NFC: L.A. Rams (11) vs. Chicago (10), 1985
  - SB: N.Y. Giants (11) vs. Baltimore (10), 2000

Fewest Punts, Both Teams, Game
- 0 AFC-D: Kansas City vs. Indianapolis, 2003
- 1 NFC-FR: St. Louis (0) vs. Green Bay (1), 1982
- 2 AFC-FR: N.Y. Jets (0) vs. Cincinnati (2), 1982
  - SB: Atlanta (1) vs. Denver (1), 1998
  - AFC-FR: Indianapolis (0) vs. Denver (2), 2003
  - AFC-D: New England (1) vs. Jacksonville (1), 2007
  - NFC-FR: Arizona (1) vs. Green Bay (1), 2009 (ot)

AVERAGE YARDAGE
Highest Average, Punting, Game (4 punts)
- 56.0 AFC: Oakland vs. San Diego, 1980
- 53.8 AFC-D: Baltimore vs. Pittsburgh, 2010
- 53.3 AFC-D: Tennessee vs. Baltimore, 2008

Lowest Average, Punting, Game (4 punts)
- 24.9 NFC: Washington vs. Chi. Bears, 1937
- 25.3 AFC-FR: Pittsburgh vs. Houston, 1989
- 25.5 NFC: Green Bay vs. N.Y. Giants, 1962

PUNT RETURNS
Most Punt Returns, Game
- 8 NFC: Green Bay vs. N.Y. Giants, 1944
- 7 By many teams

Most Punt Returns, Both Teams, Game
- 13 AFC-FR: Houston (7) vs. Oakland (6), 1980
- 12 AFC-D: New England (7) vs. Pittsburgh (5), 1996
- 11 NFC: Green Bay (8) vs. N.Y. Giants (3), 1944
  - NFC-D: Green Bay (6) vs. Baltimore (5), 1965
  - AFC-FR: Jacksonville (7) vs. New England (4), 1998
  - AFC: Baltimore (6) vs. Pittsburgh (5), 2008

Fewest Punt Returns, Both Teams, Game
- 0 NFC: Chi. Bears vs. N.Y. Giants, 1941
  - AFC: Boston vs. San Diego, 1963
  - NFC-FR: Green Bay vs. St. Louis, 1982
  - AFC-FR: Houston vs. N.Y. Jets, 1991
  - AFC-D: Denver vs. Houston, 1991
  - NFC-D: San Francisco vs. Washington, 1992
  - SB: Denver vs. Green Bay, 1997
  - SB: Atlanta vs. Denver, 1998
  - AFC-FR: Oakland vs. N.Y. Jets, 2001
  - AFC-D: N.Y. Jets vs. Oakland, 2002
  - AFC-FR: Denver vs. Indianapolis, 2003
  - NFC-D: Carolina vs. St. Louis, 2003
  - AFC-D: Indianapolis vs. Kansas City, 2003
  - AFC-FR: Kansas City vs. Baltimore, 2010
  - NFC-D: Atlanta vs. Green Bay, 2010
- 1 In many games

YARDS GAINED
Most Yards Gained, Game
- 155 NFC-D: Dallas vs. Cleveland, 1967
- 152 NFC-D: Atlanta vs. St. Louis, 2004
- 150 NFC: Chi. Cardinals vs. Philadelphia, 1947

Fewest Yards Gained, Game
- −10 NFC: Green Bay vs. Cleveland, 1965
- −9 NFC: Dallas vs. Green Bay, 1966
  - AFC-D: Kansas City vs. Oakland, 1968
- −7 NFC-D: San Francisco vs. Atlanta, 1998

Most Yards Gained, Both Teams, Game
- 166 NFC-D: Dallas (155) vs. Cleveland (11), 1967
  - AFC-D: Baltimore (99) vs. Pittsburgh (67), 2001
- 160 NFC: Chi. Cardinals (150) vs. Philadelphia (10), 1947
- 152 NFC-D: Atlanta (152) vs. St. Louis (0), 2004

Fewest Yards Gained, Both Teams, Game
- −9 NFC: Dallas (−9) vs. Green Bay (0), 1966
- −6 AFC-D: Miami (−5) vs. Oakland (−1), 1970
- −3 NFC-D: San Francisco (−5) vs. Dallas (2), 1972

TOUCHDOWNS
Most Touchdowns, Game
- 1 By 20 teams

KICKOFF RETURNS
Most Kickoff Returns, Game
- 10 NFC-D: L.A. Rams vs. Washington, 1983
- NFC-FR: Detroit vs. Philadelphia, 1995
- 9 NFC: Chi. Bears vs. N.Y. Giants, 1956
  - AFC: Boston vs. San Diego, 1963
  - AFC: Houston vs. Oakland, 1967
  - SB: Denver vs. San Francisco, 1989
  - AFC-D: Miami vs. Buffalo, 1990
  - AFC: L.A. Raiders vs. Buffalo, 1990
  - AFC-D: Miami vs. Jacksonville, 1999
  - SB: Oakland vs. Tampa Bay, 2002
- 8 By many teams

Most Kickoff Returns, Both Teams, Game
- 15 AFC-D: Miami (9) vs. Buffalo (6), 1990
- 14 NFC-FR: Detroit (10) vs. Philadelphia (4), 1995
- 13 NFC-D: Green Bay (7) vs. Dallas (6), 1982
  - NFC-FR: Green Bay (7) vs. San Francisco (6), 1998
  - AFC-FR: N.Y. Jets (8) vs. Oakland (5), 2001
  - NFC-FR: San Francisco (7) vs. N.Y. Giants (6), 2002
  - AFC-D: Tennessee (7) vs. Pittsburgh (6), 2002
  - SB: Oakland (9) vs. Tampa Bay (4), 2002
  - NFC-FR: Seattle (7) vs. Green Bay (6), 2003 (ot)
  - AFC-D: Kansas City (7) vs. Indianapolis (6), 2003
  - AFC: Pittsburgh (8) vs. New England (5), 2004
  - AFC: New England (8) vs. Indianapolis (5), 2006

Fewest Kickoff Returns, Both Teams, Game
- 1 NFC: Green Bay (0) vs. Boston (1), 1936
  - AFC-FR: San Diego (0) vs. Kansas City (1), 1992
- 2 NFC-D: Los Angeles (0) vs. Chi. Bears (2), 1950
  - AFC: Houston (0) vs. San Diego (2), 1961
  - AFC-D: Oakland (1) vs. Pittsburgh (1), 1972
  - AFC-D: N.Y. Jets (0) vs. L.A. Raiders (2), 1982
  - AFC: Miami (1) vs. N.Y. Jets (1), 1982
  - NFC: N.Y. Giants (0) vs. Washington (2), 1986
- 3 In many games

YARDS GAINED
Most Yards Gained, Game
- 244 SB: San Diego vs. San Francisco, 1994
- 232 NFC-D: Atlanta vs. Green Bay, 2010
- 231 AFC: New England vs. Indianapolis, 2006

Most Yards Gained, Both Teams, Game
- 379 AFC-D: Baltimore (193) vs. Oakland (186), 1977 (ot)
- 348 NFC-D: Minnesota (174) vs. St. Louis (174), 1999
- 323 AFC-D: New England (231) vs. Indianapolis (92), 2006

Fewest Yards Gained, Both Teams, Game
- 5 AFC-FR: San Diego (0) vs. Kansas City (5), 1992
- 15 NFC: N.Y. Giants (0) vs. Washington (15), 1986
- 31 NFC-D: Los Angeles (0) vs. Chi. Bears (31), 1950

TOUCHDOWNS
Most Touchdowns, Game
- 1 NFC-D: San Francisco vs. Dallas, 1972
  - AFC-D: Miami vs. Oakland, 1974
  - AFC-D: Baltimore vs. Oakland, 1977 (ot)
  - SB: Miami vs. Washington, 1982
  - SB: Cincinnati vs. San Francisco, 1988
  - AFC-D: Cleveland vs. Buffalo, 1989
  - SB: San Diego vs. San Francisco, 1994
  - SB: Green Bay vs. New England, 1996
  - NFC: San Francisco vs. Green Bay, 1997
  - SB: Atlanta vs. Denver, 1998
  - AFC-FR: Tennessee vs. Buffalo, 1999
  - AFC-FR: Seattle vs. Miami, 1999
  - NFC-D: Washington vs. Tampa Bay, 1999
  - NFC-D: St. Louis vs. Minnesota, 1999
  - AFC: Tennessee vs. Jacksonville, 1999

- NFC-D: N.Y. Giants vs. Philadelphia, 2000
- SB: Baltimore vs. N.Y. Giants, 2000
- SB: N.Y. Giants vs. Baltimore, 2000
- AFC-D: Kansas City vs. Indianapolis, 2003
- NFC-FR: Dallas vs. Seattle, 2006
- SB: Chicago vs. Indianapolis, 2006
- NFC-D: Atlanta vs. Green Bay, 2010

Most Touchdowns, Both Teams, Game
- 2 SB: Baltimore (1) vs. N.Y. Giants (1), 2000

PENALTIES
Most Penalties, Game
- 17 AFC-FR: L.A. Raiders vs. Denver, 1993
- 14 AFC-FR: Oakland vs. Houston, 1980
  - NFC-D: San Francisco vs. N.Y. Giants, 1981
  - AFC: Oakland vs. Tennessee, 2002
  - NFC-FR: Dallas vs. Philadelphia, 2009
- 13 AFC-FR: Houston vs. Cleveland, 1988
  - AFC-D: Houston vs. Denver, 1991
  - NFC-D: Arizona vs. Minnesota, 1998
  - NFC-D: Carolina vs. St. Louis, 2003 (2 ot)

Fewest Penalties, Game
- 0 NFC: Philadelphia vs. Green Bay, 1960
  - NFC-D: Detroit vs. Dallas, 1970
  - AFC-D: Miami vs. Oakland, 1970
  - SB: Miami vs. Dallas, 1971
  - NFC-D: Washington vs. Minnesota, 1973
  - SB: Pittsburgh vs. Dallas, 1975
  - NFC: San Francisco vs. Chicago, 1988
  - SB: Denver vs. San Francisco, 1989
  - AFC-D: L.A. Raiders vs. Cincinnati, 1990
  - AFC-D: Miami vs. San Diego, 1992
  - SB: Atlanta vs. Denver, 1998
  - AFC-FR: N.Y. Jets vs. Oakland, 2001
  - NFC-FR: Carolina vs. Dallas, 2003
- 1 By many teams

Most Penalties, Both Teams, Game
- 27 AFC-FR: L.A. Raiders (17) vs. Denver (10), 1993
- 23 NFC-FR: Dallas (14) vs. Philadelphia (9), 2009
- 22 AFC-FR: Oakland (14) vs. Houston (8), 1980
  - NFC-D: San Francisco (14) vs. N.Y. Giants (8), 1981
  - AFC-FR: Houston (13) vs. Cleveland (9), 1988
  - NFC-D: Arizona (13) vs. Minnesota (9), 1998

Fewest Penalties, Both Teams, Game
- 1 AFC-D: L.A. Raiders (0) vs. Cincinnati (1), 1990
- 2 NFC: Washington (1) vs. Chi. Bears (1), 1937
  - NFC-D: Washington (0) vs. Minnesota (2), 1973
  - SB: Pittsburgh (0) vs. Dallas (2), 1975
  - NFC-FR: Carolina (0) vs. Dallas (2), 2003
- 3 AFC: Miami (1) vs. Baltimore (2), 1971
  - NFC: San Francisco (1) vs. Dallas (2), 1971
  - SB: Miami (0) vs. Dallas (3), 1971
  - AFC-D: Pittsburgh (1) vs. Oakland (2), 1972
  - AFC-D: Miami (1) vs. Cincinnati (2), 1973
  - SB: Miami (1) vs. San Francisco (2), 1984
  - NFC: San Francisco (0) vs. Chicago (3), 1988
  - AFC: New England (1) vs. Pittsburgh (2), 2004
  - AFC: San Diego (1) vs. New England (2), 2007

YARDS PENALIZED
Most Yards Penalized, Game
- 145 NFC-D: San Francisco vs. N.Y. Giants, 1981
- 133 SB: Dallas vs. Baltimore, 1970
- 130 AFC-FR: L.A. Raiders vs. Denver, 1993

Fewest Yards Penalized, Game
- 0 By many teams

Most Yards Penalized, Both Teams, Game
- 228 NFC-FR: Philadelphia (116) vs. Dallas (112), 2009
- 227 AFC-FR: L.A. Raiders (130) vs. Denver (97), 1993
- 206 NFC-D: San Francisco (145) vs. N.Y. Giants (61), 1981

Fewest Yards Penalized, Both Teams, Game
- 5 AFC-D: L.A. Raiders (0) vs. Cincinnati (5), 1990

9   NFC-D: Washington (0) vs. Minnesota (9), 1973
11   NFC-FR: Carolina (0) vs. Dallas (11), 2003

FUMBLES
Most Fumbles, Game
8   SB: Buffalo vs. Dallas, 1992
7   AFC-D: Houston vs. Kansas City, 1993
6   By 13 teams

Most Fumbles, Both Teams, Game
12   AFC: Houston (6) vs. Pittsburgh (6), 1978
    SB: Buffalo (8) vs. Dallas (4), 1992
10   NFC: Chi. Bears (5) vs. N.Y. Giants (5), 1934
    SB: Dallas (6) vs. Denver (4), 1977
    AFC: Jacksonville (5) vs. Tennessee (5), 1999
9   NFC-D: San Francisco (6) vs. Detroit (3), 1957
    NFC-D: San Francisco (5) vs. Dallas (4), 1972
    NFC: Dallas (5) vs. Philadelphia (4), 1980
    NFC: Minnesota (6) vs. New Orleans (3), 2009 (OT)

Most Fumbles Lost, Game
5   SB: Buffalo vs. Dallas, 1992
    AFC-D: Miami vs. Jacksonville, 1999
4   NFC: N.Y. Giants vs. Baltimore, 1958 (ot)
    AFC: Kansas City vs. Oakland, 1969
    SB: Baltimore vs. Dallas, 1970
    AFC: Pittsburgh vs. Oakland, 1975
    SB: Denver vs. Dallas, 1977
    AFC: Houston vs. Pittsburgh, 1978
    AFC: Miami vs. New England, 1985
    SB: New England vs. Chicago, 1985
    NFC-FR: L.A. Rams vs. Washington, 1986
    NFC-FR: Minnesota vs. Dallas, 1996
    AFC-FR: Buffalo vs. Miami, 1998
    AFC: N.Y. Jets vs. Denver, 1998
    AFC: Jacksonville vs. Tennessee, 1999
3   By many teams

Fewest Fumbles, Both Teams, Game
0   NFC: Green Bay vs. Cleveland, 1965
    AFC-D: Houston vs. San Diego, 1979
    NFC-D: Dallas vs. Los Angeles, 1979
    SD: Los Angeles vs. Pittsburgh, 1979
    AFC-D: Buffalo vs. Cincinnati, 1981
    NFC: Minnesota vs. Washington, 1987
    NFC-D: San Francisco vs. Washington, 1990
    NFC: Dallas vs. Green Bay, 1995
    AFC-D: New England vs. Pittsburgh, 1996
    SB: Green Bay vs. New England, 1996
    AFC-FR: Miami vs. Seattle, 1999
    AFC-FR: Miami vs. Indianapolis, 2000 (ot)
    AFC-D: Baltimore vs. Tennessee, 2000
    SB: Pittsburgh vs. Seattle, 2005
    SB: Indianapolis vs. New Orleans, 2009
1   In many games

RECOVERIES
Most Total Fumbles Recovered, Game
8   SB: Dallas vs. Denver, 1977 (4 own, 4 opp)
7   NFC: Chi. Bears vs. N.Y. Giants, 1934 (5 own, 2 opp)
    NFC-D: San Francisco vs. Detroit, 1957 (4 own, 3 opp)
    NFC-D: San Francisco vs. Dallas, 1972 (4 own, 3 opp)
    AFC: Pittsburgh vs. Houston, 1978 (3 own, 4 opp)
6   AFC: Houston vs. San Diego, 1961 (4 own, 2 opp)
    AFC-D: Cleveland vs. Baltimore, 1971 (4 own, 2 opp)
    AFC-D: Cleveland vs. Oakland, 1980 (5 own, 1 opp)
    NFC: Philadelphia vs. Dallas, 1980 (3 own, 3 opp)
    SB: Dallas vs. Buffalo, 1992 (1 own, 5 opp)
    NFC-D: Green Bay vs. San Francisco, 1996
       (4 own, 2 opp)
    AFC: Denver vs. N.Y. Jets, 1998 (2 own, 4 opp)
    AFC: Tennessee vs. Jacksonville, 1999 (2 own, 4 opp)

Most Own Fumbles Recovered, Game
5   NFC: Chi. Bears vs. N.Y. Giants, 1934
    AFC-D: Cleveland vs. Oakland, 1980

4   By many teams

TOUCHDOWNS
Most Touchdowns, Game
2   SB: Dallas vs. Buffalo, 1992

TURNOVERS
Numbers of times losing the ball on interceptions and fumbles.
Most Turnovers, Game
9   NFC: Washington vs. Chi. Bears, 1940
    NFC: Detroit vs. Cleveland, 1954
    AFC: Houston vs. Pittsburgh, 1978
    SB: Buffalo vs. Dallas, 1992
8   NFC: N.Y. Giants vs. Chi. Bears, 1946
    NFC: Los Angeles vs. Cleveland, 1955
    NFC: Cleveland vs. Detroit, 1957
    SB: Denver vs. Dallas, 1977
    NFC-D: Minnesota vs. Philadelphia, 1980
    NFC-D: Green Bay vs. St. Louis, 2001
7   In many games

Fewest Turnovers, Game
0   By many teams

Most Turnovers, Both Teams, Game
14   AFC: Houston (9) vs. Pittsburgh (5), 1978
13   NFC: Detroit (9) vs. Cleveland (4), 1954
    AFC: Houston (7) vs. San Diego (6), 1961
12   AFC: Pittsburgh (7) vs. Oakland (5), 1975

Fewest Turnovers, Both Teams, Game
0   SB: Buffalo vs. N.Y. Giants, 1990
    AFC-FR: Kansas City vs. Pittsburgh, 1993 (ot)
    NFC-FR: Detroit vs. Green Bay, 1994
    AFC-FR: Denver vs. Jacksonville, 1996
    SB: St. Louis vs. Tennessee, 1999
1   AFC-D: Baltimore (0) vs. Cincinnati (1), 1970
    AFC-D: Pittsburgh (0) vs. Buffalo (1), 1974
    AFC: Oakland (0) vs. Pittsburgh (1), 1976
    NFC-D: Minnesota (0) vs. Washington (1), 1982
    NFC-D: Chicago (0) vs. N.Y. Giants (1), 1985
    SB: N.Y. Giants (0) vs. Denver (1), 1986
    NFC: Washington (0) vs. Minnesota (1), 1987
    AFC-D: Cincinnati (0) vs. L.A. Raiders (1), 1990
    NFC: N.Y. Giants (0) vs. San Francisco (1), 1990
    NFC-FR: N.Y. Giants (0) vs. Minnesota (1), 1993
    AFC-FR: L.A. Raiders (0) vs. Denver (1), 1993
    NFC: Dallas (0) vs. San Francisco (1), 1993
    AFC: Indianapolis (0) vs. Pittsburgh (1), 1995
    NFC-D: San Francisco (0) vs. Minnesota (1), 1997
    AFC-D: Indianapolis (0) vs. Tennessee (1), 1999
    AFC-FR: Baltimore (0) vs. Denver (1), 2000
    AFC-D: Baltimore (0) vs. Tennessee (1), 2000
    AFC-D: Oakland (0) vs. New England (1), 2001
    NFC-FR: Green Bay (0) vs. Seattle (1), 2003 (ot)
    AFC-D: Indianapolis (0) vs. Kansas City (1), 2003
    AFC-FR: N.Y. Jets (0) vs. San Diego (1), 2004 (ot)
    NFC: Philadelphia (0) vs. Atlanta (1), 2004
    NFC-FR: Philadelphia (0) vs. N.Y. Giants (1), 2006
    NFC-D: Philadelphia (0) vs. New Orleans (1), 2006
    NFC-D: N.Y. Giants (0) vs. Dallas (1), 2007
    SB: New Orleans (0) vs. Indianapolis (1), 2009
    AFC-FR: Indianapolis (0) vs. N.Y. Jets (1), 2010
    NFC-D: Seattle (0) vs. Chicago (1), 2010
    AFC-D: N.Y. Jets (0) vs. New England (1), 2010
2   In many games

Includes records of AFC-NFC Pro Bowls, 1971-2010
Compiled by Elias Sports Bureau

INDIVIDUAL RECORDS

SERVICE
Most Games
- 12   Randall McDaniel, Minnesota 1990-2000; Tampa Bay 2001
      Will Shields, Kansas City, 1996-2007
- 11   *Reggie White, Philadelphia, 1987-1993; Green Bay, 1994, 1996-97, 1999
      Junior Seau, San Diego, 1992-2002
      Rod Woodson, Pittsburgh, 1990-95, 1997; Baltimore, 2000-02; Oakland, 2003
- 10   Lawrence Taylor, N.Y. Giants, 1982-1991
      Ronnie Lott, San Francisco, 1982-85, 1987-1991; L.A. Raiders 1992
      Mike Singletary, Chicago, 1984-1993
      **Bruce Matthews, Houston, 1989-1995, 1997; Tennessee, 2000, 2002
      ***Jerry Rice, San Francisco, 1987-88, 1990-94, 1996, 1999; Oakland, 2003
      Champ Bailey, Washington, 2001-04; Denver, 2005-08, 2010-11
      ****Tony Gonzalez, Kansas City, 2000-01, 2003-09; Atlanta, 2011
      ****Peyton Manning, Indianapolis, 2000-01, 2003-09, 2011

*Also selected, but did not play, in two additional games
**Also selected, but did not play, in four additional games
***Also selected, but did not play, in three additional games
****Also selected, but did not play, in one additional game

SCORING
POINTS
Most Points, Career
- 52   David Akers, Philadelphia, 2002-03, 2005, 2010-11 (19-pat, 11-fg)
- 45   Morten Andersen, New Orleans, 1986-89, 1991, 1993; Atlanta, 1996 (15-pat, 10-fg)
- 36   Tony Gonzalez, Kansas City, 2000-01, 2003-09; Atlanta, 2011 (6-td)

Most Points, Game
- 18   John Brockington, Green Bay, 1973 (3-td)
      Mike Alstott, Tampa Bay, 2000 (3-td)
      Jimmy Smith, Jacksonville, 2000 (3-td)
      Shaun Alexander, Seattle, 2004 (3-td)
- 15   Garo Yepremian, Miami, 1974 (5-fg)
      Jason Hanson, Detroit, 2000 (6-pat, 3-fg)
- 14   Jan Stenerud, Kansas City, 1972 (2-pat, 4-fg)

TOUCHDOWNS
Most Touchdowns, Career
- 6   Tony Gonzalez, Kansas City, 2000-01, 2003-09; Atlanta, 2011 (6-p)
- 5   Jimmy Smith, Jacksonville, 1998-2001 (5-p)
     Marvin Harrison, Indianapolis, 2000-06 (5-p)
- 4   Mike Alstott, Tampa Bay, 1998-2003 (3-r, 1-p)
     Hines Ward, Pittsburgh, 2002-05 (3-p, 1-ret)
     Terrell Owens, San Francisco, 2001-04; Dallas, 2008 (4-p)
     Larry Fitzgerald, Arizona, 2006, 2008-09, 2011 (4-p)
     Adrian Peterson, Minnesota, 2008-2011 (4-r)

Most Touchdowns, Game
- 3   John Brockington, Green Bay, 1973 (2-r, 1-p)
     Mike Alstott, Tampa Bay, 2000 (3-r)
     Jimmy Smith, Jacksonville, 2000 (3-p)
     Shaun Alexander, Seattle, 2004 (2-r, 1-p)
- 2   Mel Renfro, Dallas, 1971 (2-ret)

Earl Campbell, Houston, 1980 (2-r)
Chuck Muncie, New Orleans, 1980 (2-r)
William Andrews, Atlanta, 1984 (2-p)
Herschel Walker, Dallas, 1989 (2-r)
Johnny Johnson, Phoenix, 1991 (2-r)
Eric Green, Pittsburgh, 1995 (2-p)
Marvin Harrison, Indianapolis, 2001 (2-p)
Ricky Williams, Miami, 2003 (2-r)
Hines Ward, Pittsburgh, 2005 (1-p, 1-ret)
T.J. Houshmandzadeh, Cincinnati, 2008 (2-p)
Terrell Owens, Dallas, 2008 (2-p)
Adrian Peterson, Minnesota, 2008 (2-r)
Larry Fitzgerald, Arizona, 2009 (2-p)
DeSean Jackson, Philadelphia, 2010 (2-p)
Montell Owens, Jacksonville, 2011 (1-p, 1-ret)

POINTS AFTER TOUCHDOWN
Most Points After Touchdown, Career
- 19   David Akers, Philadelphia, 2002-03, 2005, 2010-11 (19 att)
- 15   Morten Andersen, New Orleans, 1986-89, 1991, 1993; Atlanta, 1996 (15 att)
- 11   Adam Vinatieri, New England, 2003, 2005 (11 att)

Most Points After Touchdown, Game
- 7   Mike Vanderjagt, Indianapolis, 2004 (7 att)
    David Akers, Philadelphia, 2011 (7 att)
- 6   Ali Haji-Sheikh, N.Y. Giants, 1984 (6 att)
    Jason Hanson, Detroit, 2000 (6 att)
    Adam Vinatieri, New England, 2003 (6 att)
    Nick Folk, Dallas, 2008 (6 att)
- 5   John Carney, San Diego, 1995 (5 att)
    Matt Stover, Baltimore, 2001 (5 att)
    Jason Elam, Denver, 2002 (5 att)
    Jeff Wilkins, St. Louis, 2004 (5 att)
    Adam Vinatieri, New England, 2005 (5 att)
    Dan Carpenter, Miami, 2010 (5 att)
    Billy Cundiff, Baltimore, 2011 (5 att)

FIELD GOALS
Most Field Goals Attempted, Career
- 18   Morten Andersen, New Orleans, 1986-89, 1991, 1993; Atlanta, 1996
- 15   Jan Stenerud, Kansas City, 1971-72, 1976; Minnesota, 1985
- 13   David Akers, Philadelphia, 2002-03, 2005, 2010-11

Most Field Goals Attempted, Game
- 6   Jan Stenerud, Kansas City, 1972
    Eddie Murray, Detroit, 1981
    Mark Moseley, Washington, 1983
- 5   Garo Yepremian, Miami, 1974
- 4   Jan Stenerud, Kansas City, 1976
    Nick Lowery, Kansas City, 1991, 1993
    Morten Andersen, New Orleans, 1993
    Cary Blanchard, Indianapolis, 1997
    John Kasay, Carolina, 1997
    David Akers, Philadelphia, 2002
    Jeff Wilkins, St. Louis, 2004

Most Field Goals, Career
- 11   David Akers, Philadelphia, 2002-03, 2005, 2010-11
- 10   Morten Andersen, New Orleans, 1986-89, 1991, 1993; Atlanta, 1996
- 8   Jan Stenerud, Kansas City, 1971-72, 1976; Minnesota, 1985

Most Field Goals, Game
- 5   Garo Yepremian, Miami, 1974 (5 att)
- 4   Jan Stenerud, Kansas City, 1972 (6 att)
    Eddie Murray, Detroit, 1981 (6 att)
- 3   Nick Lowery, Kansas City, 1991 (4 att)
    Nick Lowery, Kansas City, 1993 (4 att)
    Jason Elam, Denver, 1999 (3 att)

Jason Hanson, Detroit, 2000 (3 att)
David Akers, Philadelphia, 2002 (4 att)
Neil Rackers, Arizona, 2006 (3 att)
Rob Bironas, Tennessee, 2008 (3 att)
John Carney, N.Y. Giants, 2009 (3 att)

Longest Field Goal
- 53   David Akers, Philadelphia, 2003
- 51   Morten Andersen, New Orleans, 1989
      Jason Hanson, Detroit, 2000
- 49   Fuad Reveiz, Minnesota, 1995
      David Akers, Philadelphia, 2002

SAFETIES
Most Safeties, Game
- 1   Art Still, Kansas City, 1983
     Mark Gastineau, N.Y. Jets, 1985
     Greg Townsend, L.A. Raiders, 1992

RUSHING
ATTEMPTS
Most Attempts, Career
- 81   Walter Payton, Chicago, 1977-1981, 1984-87
- 68   O.J. Simpson, Buffalo, 1973-77
- 66   Barry Sanders, Detroit, 1990-93, 1995-98

Most Attempts, Game
- 19   O.J. Simpson, Buffalo, 1974
- 17   Marv Hubbard, Oakland, 1974
- 16   O.J. Simpson, Buffalo, 1973
     Marcus Allen, L.A. Raiders, 1986
     Adrian Peterson, Minnesota, 2008

YARDS GAINED
Most Yards Gained, Career
- 368   Walter Payton, Chicago, 1977-1981, 1984-87
- 356   O.J. Simpson, Buffalo, 1973-77
- 274   Adrian Peterson, 2008-2011

Most Yards Gained, Game
- 180   Marshall Faulk, Indianapolis, 1995
- 129   Adrian Peterson, Minnesota, 2008
- 127   Chris Warren, Seattle, 1995

Longest Run From Scrimmage
- 49   Marshall Faulk, Indianapolis, 1995 (TD)
- 41   Lawrence McCutcheon, Los Angeles, 1976
     Natrone Means, San Diego, 1995
     Marshall Faulk, Indianapolis, 1995
- 39   Chris Warren, Seattle, 1994
     Priest Holmes, Kansas City, 2002
     Adrian Peterson, Minnesota, 2008

AVERAGE GAIN
Highest Average Gain, Career (20 attempts)
- 9.36   Chris Warren, Seattle, 1994-96, (25-234)
- 6.68   Adrian Peterson, Minnesota, 2008-2011 (41-274)
- 6.45   Marshall Faulk, Indianapolis, 1995-96, 1999;
       St. Louis, 2000, 2002-03 (42-271)

Highest Average Gain, Game (10 attempts)
- 13.85   Marshall Faulk, Indianapolis, 1995 (13-180)
- 9.07   Chris Warren, Seattle, 1995 (14-127)
- 8.06   Adrian Peterson, Minnesota 2008 (16-129)

TOUCHDOWNS
Most Touchdowns, Career
- 4   Adrian Peterson, Minnesota, 2008-2011
- 3   Earl Campbell, Houston, 1979-1982, 1984
    Chuck Muncie, New Orleans, 1980; San Diego, 1982-83
    Mike Alstott, Tampa Bay, 1998-2003
- 2   John Brockington, Green Bay, 1972-74
    O.J. Simpson, Buffalo, 1973-77
    Walter Payton, Chicago, 1977-1981, 1984-87

Marcus Allen, L.A. Raiders, 1983, 1985-86, 1988;
    Kansas City, 1994
Herschel Walker, Dallas, 1988-89
Johnny Johnson, Phoenix, 1991
Barry Sanders, Detroit, 1990-93, 1995-98
Curtis Martin, New England, 1996-97; N.Y. Jets, 1999, 2002
Ricky Williams, Miami, 2003
Shaun Alexander, Seattle, 2004-06
LaDainian Tomlinson, San Diego, 2003, 2005-07
Steven Jackson, St. Louis, 2007, 2011

Most Touchdowns, Game
- 3   Mike Alstott, Tampa Bay, 2000
- 2   John Brockington, Green Bay, 1973
    Earl Campbell, Houston, 1980
    Chuck Muncie, New Orleans, 1980
    Herschel Walker, Dallas, 1989
    Johnny Johnson, Phoenix, 1991
    Ricky Williams, Miami, 2003
    Shaun Alexander, Seattle, 2004
    Adrian Peterson, Minnesota, 2008

PASSING
ATTEMPTS
Most Attempts, Career
- 184   Peyton Manning, Indianapolis, 2000-01, 2003-09, 2011
- 120   Dan Fouts, San Diego, 1980-84, 1986
- 101   Steve Young, San Francisco, 1993-96, 1998-99

Most Attempts, Game
- 41   Peyton Manning, Indianapolis, 2004
- 32   Bill Kenney, Kansas City, 1984
    Steve Young, San Francisco, 1993
- 30   Dan Fouts, San Diego, 1983

COMPLETIONS
Most Completions, Career
- 109   Peyton Manning, Indianapolis, 2000-01, 2003-09, 2011
- 63   Dan Fouts, San Diego, 1980-84, 1986
- 48   Steve Young, San Francisco, 1993-96, 1998-99

Most Completions, Game
- 22   Peyton Manning, Indianapolis, 2004
- 21   Joe Theismann, Washington, 1984
- 18   Steve Young, San Francisco, 1993

COMPLETION PERCENTAGE
Highest Completion Percentage, Career (40 attempts)
- 68.9   Joe Theismann, Washington, 1983-84 (45-31)
- 67.9   Rich Gannon, Oakland, 2000-03 (53-36)
- 64.4   Jim Kelly, Buffalo, 1988, 1991-92 (45-29)

Highest Completion Percentage, Game (10 attempts)
- 90.0   Archie Manning, New Orleans, 1980 (10-9)
- 85.7   Rich Gannon, Oakland, 2001 (14-12)
- 80.0   Rich Gannon, Oakland, 2002 (10-8)
     Jeff Garcia, Tampa Bay, 2008 (10-8)

YARDS GAINED
Most Yards Gained, Career
- 1,508   Peyton Manning, Indianapolis, 2000-01, 2003-09, 2011
- 890   Dan Fouts, San Diego, 1980-84, 1986
- 614   Steve Young, San Francisco, 1993-96, 1998-99

Most Yards Gained, Game
- 342   Peyton Manning, Indianapolis, 2004
- 274   Dan Fouts, San Diego, 1983
- 270   Peyton Manning, Indianapolis, 2000

Longest Completion
- 93   Jeff Blake, Cincinnati (to Thigpen, Pittsburgh), 1996 (TD)

90 Steve McNair, Tennessee (to Johnson, Cincinnati), 2004 (TD)
80 Mark Brunell, Jacksonville (to Brown, Oakland), 1997 (TD)

AVERAGE GAIN
Highest Average Gain, Career (40 attempts)
8.20 Peyton Manning, Indianapolis, 2000-01, 2003-09 (184-1,508)
8.19 Rich Gannon, Oakland, 2000-03 (53-434)
8.12 Brett Favre, Green Bay, 1993-94, 1996-97 (57-463)
Highest Average Gain, Game (10 attempts)
15.27 Randall Cunningham, Philadelphia, 1991 (11-168)
13.70 Rich Gannon, Oakland, 2002 (10-137)
13.07 David Garrard, Jacksonville, 2010 (14-183)

TOUCHDOWNS
Most Touchdowns, Career
14 Peyton Manning, Indianapolis, 2000-01, 2003-09, 2011
7 Rich Gannon, Oakland, 2000-03
4 Steve Young, San Francisco, 1993-96, 1998-99
   Marc Bulger, St. Louis, 2004, 2007
   Donovan McNabb, Philadelphia, 2001-03, 2005, 2010
Most Touchdowns, Game
4 Marc Bulger, St. Louis, 2004
3 Joe Theismann, Washington, 1984
   Phil Simms, N.Y. Giants, 1986
   Peyton Manning, Indianapolis, 2004
   Peyton Manning, Indianapolis, 2005
2 James Harris, Los Angeles, 1975
   Mike Boryla, Philadelphia, 1976
   Ken Anderson, Cincinnati, 1977
   Jim Kelly, Buffalo, 1991
   Mark Rypien, Washington, 1992
   Steve Young, San Francisco, 1998
   Peyton Manning, Indianapolis, 2000
   Rich Gannon, Oakland, 2001
   Peyton Manning, Indianapolis, 2001
   Rich Gannon, Oakland, 2002
   Donovan McNabb, Philadelphia, 2002
   Rich Gannon, Oakland, 2003
   Brad Johnson, Tampa Bay, 2003
   Carson Palmer, Cincinnati, 2007
   Tony Romo, Dallas, 2008
   Aaron Rodgers, Green Bay, 2010
   Matt Schaub, Houston, 2010
   Matt Cassel, Kansas City, 2011
   Matt Ryan, Atlanta, 2011
   Philip Rivers, San Diego, 2011

HAD INTERCEPTED
Most Passes Had Intercepted, Career
9 Peyton Manning, Indianapolis, 2000-01, 2003-09, 2011
8 Dan Fouts, San Diego, 1980-84, 1986
6 Jim Hart, St. Louis, 1975-78
   Donovan McNabb, Philadelphia, 2001-03, 2005, 2010
Most Passes Had Intercepted, Game
5 Jim Hart, St. Louis, 1977
4 Ken Stabler, Oakland, 1974
3 Dan Fouts, San Diego, 1986
   Mark Rypien, Washington, 1990
   Steve Young, San Francisco, 1993
   Jim Harbaugh, Indianapolis, 1996
   Vinny Testaverde, N.Y. Jets, 1999
   Jeff Garcia, San Francisco, 2003
   Peyton Manning, Indianapolis, 2006

Most Attempts, Without Interception, Game
27 Joe Theismann, Washington, 1984
    Phil Simms, N.Y. Giants, 1986
26 John Brodie, San Francisco, 1971
    Danny White, Dallas, 1983
23 Dave Krieg, Seattle, 1990

PERCENTAGE, PASSES HAD INTERCEPTED
Lowest Percentage, Passes Had Intercepted, Career (40 attempts)
0.00 Joe Theismann, Washington, 1983-84 (45-0)
1.89 Rich Gannon, Oakland, 2000-03 (53-1)
2.13 Dave Krieg, Seattle, 1985, 1989-1990 (47-1)

PASS RECEIVING
RECEPTIONS
Most Receptions, Career
42 Tony Gonzalez, Kansas City, 2000-01, 2003-09; Atlanta, 2011
37 Jerry Rice, San Francisco, 1987-88, 1990-94, 1996, 1999; Oakland, 2003
30 Marvin Harrison, Indianapolis, 2000-06
Most Receptions, Game
9 Randy Moss, Minnesota, 2000
8 Steve Largent, Seattle, 1986
   Michael Irvin, Dallas, 1992
   Andre Rison, Atlanta, 1993
   Jimmy Smith, Jacksonville, 2000
   Marvin Harrison, Indianapolis, 2001
   Terrell Owens, San Francisco, 2002
   Steve Smith, Carolina, 2006
   Terrell Owens, Dallas, 2008
   Roddy White, Atlanta, 2010
7 John Stallworth, Pittsburgh, 1983
   Jerry Rice, San Francisco, 1992
   Isaac Bruce, St. Louis, 1997
   Keyshawn Johnson, N.Y. Jets, 1999
   Randy Moss, Minnesota, 1999
   Warrick Dunn, Tampa Bay, 2001
   Torry Holt, St. Louis, 2001
   Torry Holt, St. Louis, 2004
   Vincent Jackson, San Diego, 2010

YARDS GAINED
Most Yards Gained, Career
632 Tony Gonzalez, Kansas City, 2000-01, 2003-09; Atlanta, 2011
495 Jerry Rice, San Francisco, 1987-88, 1990-94, 1996, 1999; Oakland, 2003
462 Marvin Harrison, Indianapolis, 2000-06
Most Yards Gained, Game
212 Randy Moss, Minnesota, 2000
156 Chad Ochocinco, Cincinnati, 2004
137 Tim Brown, Oakland, 1997
     Reggie Wayne, Indianapolis, 2007
Longest Reception
93 Yancey Thigpen, Pittsburgh (from Blake, Cincinnati), 1996 (TD)
90 Chad Ochocinco, Cincinnati (from McNair, Tennessee), 2004 (TD)
80 Tim Brown, Oakland (from Brunell, Jacksonville), 1997 (TD)

TOUCHDOWNS
Most Touchdowns, Career
6 Tony Gonzalez, Kansas City, 2000-01, 2003-09; Atlanta, 2011
5 Jimmy Smith, Jacksonville, 1998-2001
   Marvin Harrison, Indianapolis, 2000-06
4 Terrell Owens, San Francisco, 2001-04; Dallas, 2008

Larry Fitzgerald, Arizona, 2006, 2008-09, 2011

Most Touchdowns, Game
- 3 Jimmy Smith, Jacksonville, 2000
- 2 William Andrews, Atlanta, 1984
  Eric Green, Pittsburgh, 1995
  Marvin Harrison, Indianapolis, 2001
  T.J. Houshmandzadeh, Cincinnati, 2008
  Terrell Owens, Dallas, 2008
  Larry Fitzgerald, Arizona, 2009
  DeSean Jackson, Philadelphia, 2010

INTERCEPTIONS BY
Most Interceptions By, Career
- 4 Everson Walls, Dallas, 1982-84, 1986
  Deion Sanders, Atlanta, 1992-94; San Francisco, 1995; Dallas, 1999
  Champ Bailey, Washington, 2001-04; Denver, 2005-08, 2011
- 3 Ken Houston, Houston, 1971-73; Washington, 1974-79
  Jack Lambert, Pittsburgh, 1976-1984
  Ted Hendricks, Baltimore, 1972-74; Green Bay, 1975; Oakland, 1981-82; L.A. Raiders, 1983-84
  Mike Haynes, New England, 1978-1981, 1983; L.A. Raiders, 1985-87
  Ty Law, New England, 1999, 2002-04; N.Y. Jets, 2006
  Brian Dawkins, Philadelphia, 2000, 2002-03, 2005-06, 2009; Denver, 2010
- 2 By 21 players

Most Interceptions By, Game
- 2 Mel Blount, Pittsburgh, 1977
  Everson Walls, Dallas, 1982, 1983
  LeRoy Irvin, L.A. Rams, 1986
  David Fulcher, Cincinnati, 1990
  Brian Dawkins, Philadelphia, 2000
  Rod Woodson, Oakland, 2003
  Ed Reed, Baltimore, 2007
  Antonio Cromartie, San Diego, 2008

YARDS GAINED
Most Yards Gained, Career
- 147 Ty Law, New England, 1999, 2002-04; N.Y. Jets, 2006
- 103 Deion Sanders, Atlanta, 1992-94; San Francisco, 1995; Dallas, 1999
- 88 Rod Woodson, Pittsburgh, 1990-95, 1997; Baltimore, 2000-02; Oakland, 2003

Most Yards Gained, Game
- 87 Deion Sanders, Dallas, 1999
- 77 Antonio Cromartie, San Diego, 2008
- 73 Rod Woodson, Pittsburgh, 1994

Longest Gain
- 87 Deion Sanders, Dallas, 1999
- 73 Rod Woodson, Pittsburgh, 1994 (lateral)
- 67 Ty Law, New England, 1999 (TD)

TOUCHDOWNS
Most Touchdowns, Career
- 2 Ty Law, New England, 1999, 2002-04; N.Y. Jets, 2006
  Derrick Brooks, Tampa Bay, 1998-2001, 2003, 2006-07
- 1 By many

Most Touchdowns, Game
- 1 Bobby Bell, Kansas City, 1973
  Nolan Cromwell, L.A. Rams, 1984
  Joey Browner, Minnesota, 1986
  Jerry Gray, L.A. Rams, 1990
  Mike Johnson, Cleveland, 1990
  Junior Seau, San Diego, 1993

Ken Harvey, Washington, 1996
Ashley Ambrose, Cincinnati, 1997
Ty Law, New England, 1999
Derrick Brooks, Tampa Bay, 2000
Aeneas Williams, Arizona, 2000
Ray Lewis, Baltimore, 2002
Ty Law, New England, 2003
Dre' Bly, Detroit, 2004
Derrick Brooks, Tampa Bay, 2006
Jon Beason, Carolina, 2011

PUNTING
Most Punts, Career
- 33 Ray Guy, Oakland, 1974-79, 1981
- 23 Rohn Stark, Indianapolis, 1986-87, 1991, 1993
- 22 Reggie Roby, Miami, 1985, 1990; Washington, 1995

Most Punts, Game
- 10 Reggie Roby, Miami, 1985
- 9 Tom Wittum, San Francisco, 1974
  Rohn Stark, Indianapolis, 1987
- 8 Jerrel Wilson, Kansas City, 1971
  Tom Skladany, Detroit, 1982
  Reggie Roby, Washington, 1995

Longest Punt
- 73 Shane Lechler, Oakland, 2002
- 70 Shane Lechler, Oakland, 2002
  Mat McBriar, Dallas, 2011
- 65 Shane Lechler, Oakland, 2009

AVERAGE YARDAGE
Highest Average, Career (10 punts)
- 51.58 Shane Lechler, Oakland, 2002, 2005, 2008-2011 (12-619)
- 47.30 Jeff Feagles, Arizona, 1996; N.Y. Giants, 2009 (10-473)
- 46.73 Reggie Roby, Miami, 1985, 1990; Washington, 1995 (22-1,028)

Highest Average, Game (4 punts)
- 60.75 Shane Lechler, Oakland, 2002 (4-243)
- 55.50 Darren Bennett, San Diego, 1996 (4-222)
- 52.00 Matt Turk, Washington, 1999 (4-208)

PUNT RETURNS
Most Punt Returns, Career
- 13 Rick Upchurch, Denver, 1977, 1979-1980, 1983
- 11 Vai Sikahema, St. Louis, 1987-88
  Eric Metcalf, Cleveland 1994-95; San Diego 1998
- 10 Mike Nelms, Washington, 1981-83

Most Punt Returns, Game
- 7 Vai Sikahema, St. Louis, 1987
- 6 Henry Ellard, L.A. Rams, 1985
  Gerald McNeil, Cleveland, 1988
  Eric Metcalf, Cleveland, 1995
- 5 Rick Upchurch, Denver, 1980
  Mike Nelms, Washington, 1981
  Carl Roaches, Houston, 1982
  Johnny Bailey, Phoenix, 1993

Most Fair Catches, Game
- 2 Jerry Logan, Baltimore, 1971
  Dick Anderson, Miami, 1974
  Henry Ellard, L.A. Rams, 1985
  Isaac Bruce, St. Louis, 1997
  Desmond Howard, Detroit, 2001

YARDS GAINED
Most Yards Gained, Career
- 183 Billy Johnson, Houston, 1976, 1978; Atlanta, 1984
- 138 Mel Renfro, Dallas, 1971-72, 1974
  Rick Upchurch, Denver, 1977, 1979-1980, 1983
- 135 Eric Metcalf, Cleveland, 1994-95; San Diego 1998

Most Yards Gained, Game
159   Billy Johnson, Houston, 1976
138   Mel Renfro, Dallas, 1971
117   Wally Henry, Philadelphia, 1980
Longest Punt Return
90   Billy Johnson, Houston, 1976 (TD)
86   Wally Henry, Philadelphia, 1980 (TD)
82   Mel Renfro, Dallas, 1971 (TD)

AVERAGE YARDAGE
Highest Average, Career (4 returns)
22.88   Billy Johnson, Houston, 1976, 1978; Atlanta, 1984
       (8-183)
21.50   Tony Green, Washington, 1979 (4-86)
15.67   David Meggett, N.Y. Giants, 1990; New England, 1997
Highest Average, Game (3 returns)
39.75   Billy Johnson, Houston, 1976 (4-159)
39.00   Wally Henry, Philadelphia, 1980 (3-117)
21.50   Tony Green, Washington, 1979 (4-86)

TOUCHDOWNS
Most Touchdowns, Game
2   Mel Renfro, Dallas, 1971
1   Billy Johnson, Houston, 1976
     Wally Henry, Philadelphia, 1980

KICKOFF RETURNS
Most Kickoff Returns, Career
17   Michael Bates, Carolina, 1997-2001
14   Mel Gray, Detroit, 1991-92, 1995
     Devin Hester, Chicago, 2007-08, 2011
13   Josh Cribbs, Cleveland, 2008, 2010
Most Kickoff Returns, Game
9   Marc Mariani, Tennessee, 2011
8   Derrick Mason, Tennessee, 2004
7   Mel Gray, Detroit, 1995
    Jerry Azumah, Chicago, 2004
    Josh Cribbs, Cleveland, 2010

YARDS GAINED
Most Yards Gained, Career
488   Michael Bates, Carolina, 1997-2001
373   Josh Cribbs, Cleveland, 2008, 2010
362   Devin Hester, Chicago, 2007-08, 2011
Most Yards Gained, Game
326   Marc Mariani, Tennessee, 2011
228   Jerry Azumah, Chicago, 2004
217   Michael Lewis, New Orleans, 2003
Longest Kickoff Return
66   Michael Bates, Carolina, 2000
62   Greg Pruitt, L.A. Raiders, 1984
61   Eugene (Mercury) Morris, Miami, 1972

AVERAGE YARDAGE
Highest Average, Career (4 returns)
43.40   Michael Lewis, New Orleans, 2003 (5-217)
36.22   Marc Mariani, Tennessee, 2011 (9-326)
35.00   Les (Speedy) Duncan, Washington, 1972 (5-175)
Highest Average, Game (3 returns)
43.40   Michael Lewis, New Orleans, 2003 (5-217)
42.67   Clifton Smith, Tampa Bay, 2009 (3-128)
42.00   Michael Bates, Carolina, 2000 (4-168)

TOUCHDOWNS
Most Touchdowns, Game
1   Hines Ward, Pittsburgh, 2005

FUMBLES
Most Fumbles, Career
6   Dan Fouts, San Diego, 1980-84, 1986

4   Lawrence McCutcheon, Los Angeles, 1974-78
    Franco Harris, Pittsburgh, 1973-76, 1978-1981
    Jay Schroeder, Washington, 1987
    Vai Sikahema, St. Louis, 1987-88
    Trent Green, Kansas City, 2004, 2006
3   By 9 players
Most Fumbles, Game
4   Jay Schroeder, Washington, 1987
    Trent Green, Kansas City, 2004
3   Dan Fouts, San Diego, 1982
    Vai Sikahema, St. Louis, 1987
2   By 19 players

RECOVERIES
Most Fumbles Recovered, Career
3   Harold Jackson, Philadelphia, 1973; Los Angeles,
     1974, 1976, 1978 (3-own)
    Dan Fouts, San Diego, 1980-84, 1986 (3-own)
    Randy White, Dallas, 1978, 1980-86 (3-opp)
    Trent Green, Kansas City, 2004, 2006 (3-own)
    Peyton Manning, Indianapolis,
     2000-01, 2003-09, 2011 (3-own)
2   By many players
Most Fumbles Recovered, Game
3   Trent Green, Kansas City, 2004 (3-own)
2   Dick Anderson, Miami, 1974 (1-own, 1-opp)
    Harold Jackson, Los Angeles, 1974 (2-own)
    Dan Fouts, San Diego, 1982 (2-own)
    Joey Browner, Minnesota, 1990 (2-opp)
    Jessie Armstead, N.Y. Giants, 1999 (1-own, 1-opp)
    Steve Beuerlein, Carolina, 2000 (2-own)

YARDAGE
Longest Fumble Return
83   Art Still, Kansas City, 1985 (TD, opp)
70   Adalius Thomas, Baltimore, 2007 (TD, opp)
51   Phil Villapiano, Oakland, 1974 (opp)

TOUCHDOWNS
Most Touchdowns, Game
1   Art Still, Kansas City, 1985
    Keith Millard, Minnesota, 1990
    Adalius Thomas, Baltimore, 2007
    DeAngelo Hall, Washington, 2011
    Montell Owens, Jacksonville, 2011

SACKS
Sacks have been compiled since 1983.
Most Sacks, Career
9.5   Reggie White, Philadelphia, 1987-1993; Green Bay,
     1994, 1996-97, 1999
9.0   Howie Long, L.A. Raiders, 1984-88, 1990, 1993-1994
7.5   Bruce Smith, Buffalo, 1988-1991, 1995-96, 1998-99
Most Sacks, Game
4   Mark Gastineau, N.Y. Jets, 1985
    Reggie White, Philadelphia, 1987
3   Richard Dent, Chicago, 1985
    Bruce Smith, Buffalo, 1991
2.5   Bruce Smith, Buffalo, 1998

Rules

2011 NFL ROSTER OF OFFICIALS

Carl Johnson, Vice President of Officiating
Ed Coukart, Supervisor of Officials
Neely Dunn, Supervisor of Officials

Johnny Grier, Supervisor of Officials
Gary Slaughter, Supervisor of Officials
Bill Vinovich, Supervisor of Officials

No.	Name	Position	College
20	Anderson, Barry	Field Judge	North Carolina State
66	Anderson, Walt	Referee	Texas
108	Arthur, Gary	Line Judge	Wright State
26	Baltz, Mark	Head Linesman	Ohio
72	Banks, Michael	Side Judge	Illinois State
55	Barnes, Tom	Line Judge	Minnesota
56	Baynes, Allen	Side Judge	Auburn
59	Baynes, Rusty	Line Judge	Auburn-Montgomery
32	Bergman, Jeff	Line Judge	Robert Morris
91	Bergman, Jerry	Head Linesman	Robert Morris
34	Blakeman, Clete	Referee	Nebraska
23	Boger, Jerome	Referee	Morehouse College
18	Boston, Byron	Line Judge	Austin
74	Bowers, Derick	Head Linesman	East Central
98	Bradley, Greg	Head Linesman	Tennessee
31	Brown, Chad	Umpire	East Texas State
43	Brown, Terry	Field Judge	Tennessee-Knoxville
11	Bryan, Fred	Umpire	Northern Iowa
86	Buchanan, Jimmy	Field Judge	South Carolina State
134	Camp, Ed	Head Linesman	William Paterson
126	Carey, Don	Back Judge	California-Riverside
94	Carey, Mike	Referee	Santa Clara
39	Carlsen, Don	Side Judge	Cal State-Chico
60	Cavaletto, Gary	Field Judge	Hancock
41	Cheek, Boris	Field Judge	Morgan State
51	Cheffers, Carl	Referee	California-Irvine
95	Coleman, James	Side Judge	Arkansas
65	Coleman, Walt	Referee	Arkansas
99	Corrente, Tony	Referee	Cal State-Fullerton
70	Dawson, Scott	Umpire	Virginia Tech
58	DeBell, Jimmy	Side Judge	SUNY-Brockport
53	DeFelice, Garth	Umpire	San Diego State
6	Dornan, Kirk	Back Judge	Central Washington
27	Dyer, Lee	Back Judge	Tennessee-Chattanooga
3	Edwards, Scott	Field Judge	Alabama
81	Ellison, Roy	Umpire	Savannah State
61	Ferguson, Keith	Back Judge	San Jose State
64	Ferrell, Dan	Umpire	Cal State-Fullerton
71	Fowler, Ruben	Umpire	Huston-Tillotson
133	Freeman, Steve	Back Judge	Mississippi State
80	Gautreaux, Greg	Field Judge	S.W. Louisiana
19	Green, Scott	Referee	Delaware
49	Hall, Rich	Umpire	Arizona
40	Hannah, Butch	Umpire	Middle Tennessee State
125	Hayes, Laird	Side Judge	Princeton
54	Hayward, George	Head Linesman	Missouri Western
93	Helverson, Scott	Back Judge	Iowa
29	Hill, Adrian	Line Judge	Buffalo
97	Hill, Tom	Side Judge	Carson Newman
28	Hittner, Mark	Head Linesman	Pittsburg State
85	Hochuli, Ed	Referee	Texas-El Paso
82	Horton, Buddy	Field Judge	Oregon State
37	Howey, Jim	Field Judge	Erskine College
35	Hussey, John	Line Judge	Idaho State
76	Jenkins, Darrell	Umpire	San Jose State
121	King, Paul	Umpire	Nicholls State
103	Lamberth, Jeff	Side Judge	Texas A&M
73	Larrew, Joe	Side Judge	St. Louis
127	Leavy, Bill	Referee	San Jose State
130	Lewis, Darryll	Line Judge	Dartmouth
89	Lucivansky, Jon	Field Judge	Minnesota
106	Mackie, Wayne	Head Linesman	Colgate
52	Mapp, Julian	Head Linesman	Grambling State
107	Marinucci, Ron	Line Judge	Glassboro State
77	McAulay, Terry	Referee	Louisiana State

No.	Name	Position	College
5	McGrath, John	Head Linesman	Kentucky
8	McKenzie, Dana	Head Linesman	Toledo
110	McKinnely, Phil	Head Linesman	UCLA
48	Mello, Jim	Head Linesman	Northeastern
118	Meslow, David	Field Judge	Augsburg College
78	Meyer, Greg	Side Judge	Texas Christian
115	Michalek, Tony	Umpire	Indiana
111	Miles, Terrence	Back Judge	Arizona State
135	Morelli, Pete	Referee	St. Mary's
124	Paganelli, Carl	Umpire	Michigan State
105	Paganelli, Dino	Back Judge	Aquinas College
46	Paganelli, Perry	Back Judge	Hope College
87	Parham, Keith	Side Judge	Howard
132	Parry, John	Referee	Purdue
15	Patterson, Rick	Side Judge	Wofford
79	Payne, Kent	Head Linesman	Nebraska Wesleyan
9	Perlman, Mark	Line Judge	Salem
10	Phares, Ron	Line Judge	Virginia Tech
47	Podraza, Tim	Line Judge	Nebraska
109	Prioleau, Dyrol	Field Judge	Johnson C. Smith
30	Prukop, Todd	Back Judge	Cal State-Fullerton
63	Quirk, Jim	Field Judge	Middlebury
83	Reels, Richard	Back Judge	Chicago State
44	Rice, Jeff	Umpire	Northwestern
57	Riveron, Alberto	Referee	Miami
128	Rose, Larry	Side Judge	Florida
67	Rosenbaum, Doug	Field Judge	Illinois Wesleyan
129	Schuster, Bill	Umpire	Alfred
45	Seeman, Jeff	Line Judge	Minnesota
2	Smith, Billy	Back Judge	East Carolina
90	Spanier, Mike	Line Judge	St. Cloud State
24	Stabile, Tom	Head Linesman	Slippery Rock
12	Steed, Greg	Back Judge	Howard
88	Steenson, Scott	Field Judge	North Texas
84	Steinkerchner, Mark	Line Judge	Akron
22	Stelljes, Steve	Head Linesman	Friends
68	Stephan, Tom	Line Judge	Pittsburg State
114	Steratore, Gene	Referee	Kent State
112	Steratore, Tony	Back Judge	California
102	Stritesky, Bruce	Umpire	Embry Riddle
100	Symonette, Tom	Line Judge	Florida
62	Torbert, Ronald	Side Judge	Michigan State
42	Triplette, Jeff	Referee	Wake Forest
75	Vernatchi, Rob	Back Judge	California-Riverside
36	Veteri, Tony	Head Linesman	Manhattan College
25	Waggoner, Bob	Field Judge	Juniata College
96	Wash, Undrey	Umpire	Texas-Arlington
7	Washington, Keith	Side Judge	Virginia Military Institute
116	Weatherford, Mike	Side Judge	Oklahoma State
50	Weir, Mike	Field Judge	Missouri
119	Wilson, Greg	Back Judge	USC
14	Winter, Ron	Referee	Michigan State
4	Wrolstad, Craig	Field Judge	Washington
16	Wyant, David	Side Judge	Virginia
38	Yette, Greg	Back Judge	Howard
33	Zimmer, Steve	Field Judge	Hofstra

Roster as of May 2011

NUMERICAL ROSTER

No.	Name	Position
2	Billy Smith	BJ
3	Scott Edwards	FJ
4	Craig Wrolstad	FJ
5	John McGrath	HL
6	Kirk Dornan	BJ
7	Keith Washington	SJ
8	Dana McKenzie	HL
9	Mark Perlman	LJ
10	Ron Phares	LJ
11	Fred Bryan	U
12	Greg Steed	BJ
14	Ron Winter	R
15	Rick Patterson	SJ
16	David Wyant	SJ
18	Byron Boston	LJ
19	Scott Green	R
20	Barry Anderson	FJ
22	Steve Stelljes	HL
23	Jerome Boger	R
24	Tom Stabile	HL
25	Bob Waggoner	FJ
26	Mark Baltz	HL
27	Lee Dyer	BJ
28	Mark Hittner	HL
29	Adrian Hill	LJ
30	Todd Prukop	BJ
31	Chad Brown	U
32	Jeff Bergman	LJ
33	Steve Zimmer	FJ
34	Clete Blakeman	R
35	John Hussey	LJ
36	Tony Veteri	HL
37	Jim Howey	FJ
38	Greg Yette	BJ
39	Don Carlsen	SJ
40	Butch Hannah	U
41	Boris Cheek	FJ
42	Jeff Triplette	R
43	Terry Brown	FJ
44	Jeff Rice	U
45	Jeff Seeman	LJ
46	Perry Paganelli	BJ
47	Tim Podraza	LJ
48	Jim Mello	HL
49	Rich Hall	U
50	Mike Weir	FJ
51	Carl Cheffers	R
52	Julian Mapp	HL
53	Garth DeFelice	U
54	George Hayward	HL
55	Tom Barnes	LJ
56	Allen Baynes	SJ
57	Alberto Riveron	R
58	Jimmy DeBell	SJ
59	Rusty Baynes	LJ
60	Gary Cavaletto	FJ
61	Keith Ferguson	BJ
62	Ronald Torbert	SJ
63	Jim Quirk	FJ
64	Dan Ferrell	U
65	Walt Coleman	R
66	Walt Anderson	R
67	Doug Rosenbaum	FJ
68	Tom Stephan	LJ
70	Scott Dawson	U
71	Ruben Fowler	U
72	Michael Banks	SJ
73	Joe Larrew	SJ

No.	Name	Position
74	Derick Bowers	HL
75	Rob Vernatchi	BJ
76	Darrell Jenkins	U
77	Terry McAulay	R
78	Greg Meyer	SJ
79	Kent Payne	HL
80	Greg Gautreaux	FJ
81	Roy Ellison	U
82	Buddy Horton	FJ
83	Richard Reels	BJ
84	Mark Steinkerchner	LJ
85	Ed Hochuli	R
86	Jimmy Buchanan	FJ
87	Keith Parham	SJ
88	Scott Steenson	FJ
89	Jon Lucivansky	FJ
90	Mike Spanier	LJ
91	Jerry Bergman	HL
93	Scott Helverson	BJ
94	Mike Carey	R
95	James Coleman	SJ
96	Undrey Wash	U
97	Tom Hill	SJ
98	Greg Bradley	HL
99	Tony Corrente	R
100	Tom Symonette	LJ
102	Bruce Stritesky	U
103	Jeff Lamberth	SJ
105	Dino Paganelli	BJ
106	Wayne Mackie	HL
107	Ron Marinucci	LJ
108	Gary Arthur	LJ
109	Dyrol Prioleau	FJ
110	Phil McKinnely	HL
111	Terrence Miles	BJ
112	Tony Steratore	BJ
114	Gene Steratore	R
115	Tony Michalek	U
116	Mike Weatherford	SJ
118	David Meslow	FJ
119	Greg Wilson	BJ
121	Paul King	U
124	Carl Paganelli	U
125	Laird Hayes	SJ
126	Don Carey	BJ
127	Bill Leavy	R
128	Larry Rose	SJ
129	Bill Schuster	U
130	Darryll Lewis	LJ
132	John Parry	R
133	Steve Freeman	BJ
134	Ed Camp	HL
135	Pete Morelli	R

Roster as of May 2011

OFFICIALS

2011 OFFICIALS AT A GLANCE
REFEREES

Walt Anderson, No. **66,** Texas, college officiating coordinator, retired dentist, 16th year.
Clete Blakeman, No. **34,** Nebraska, attorney, 4th year.
Jerome Boger, No. **23,** Morehouse College, commercial insurance underwriter, 8th year.
Mike Carey, No. **94,** Santa Clara, owner, skiing accessories, 22nd year.
Carl Cheffers, No. **51,** California-Irvine, sales manager, 12th year.
Walt Coleman, No. **65,** Arkansas, manager dairy processor, 23rd year.
Tony Corrente, No. **99,** Cal State-Fullerton, educator, 17th year.
Scott Green, No. **19,** Delaware, president, government support services, 21st year.
Ed Hochuli, No. **85,** Texas-El Paso, attorney, 22nd year.
Bill Leavy, No. **127,** San Jose State, retired firefighter, 17th year.
Terry McAulay, No. **77,** Louisiana State, college officiating coordinator, 14th year.
Pete Morelli, No. **135,** St. Mary's, high school principal, 15th year.
John Parry, No. **132,** Purdue, financial advisor, 12th year.
Alberto Riveron, No. **57,** Miami, sales, commercial restaurant equipment, 8th year.
Gene Steratore, No. **114,** Kent State, co-owner, supply company, 9th year.
Jeff Triplette, No. **42,** Wake Forest, restructuring consultant, 16th year.
Ron Winter, No. **14,** Michigan State, university professor, 17th year.

UMPIRES

Chad Brown, No. **31,** East Texas State, executive manager of facilities/student affairs administration, 20th year.
Fred Bryan, No. **11,** Northern Iowa, superintendent, juvenile correctional facility, 3rd year.
Scott Dawson, No. **70,** Virginia Tech, president/owner, commercial construction company, 17th year.
Garth DeFelice, No. **53,** San Diego State, distribution center manager, beverage company, 14th year.
Roy Ellison, No. **81,** Savannah State, technical staff member, 9th year.
Dan Ferrell, No. **64,** Cal State-Fullerton, director, parts logistics, 9th year.
Ruben Fowler, No. **71,** Huston-Tillotson, retired firefighter, 6th year.
Rich Hall, No. **49,** Arizona, custom cabinetry, 8th year.
Butch Hannah, No. **40,** Middle Tennessee State, retired federal probation officer, 13th year.
Darrell Jenkins, No. **76,** San Jose State, retired, 10th year.
Paul King, No. **121,** Nicholls State, teacher, 3rd year.
Tony Michalek, No. **115,** Indiana, USA Football officiating director, 10th year.
Carl Paganelli, No. **124,** Michigan State, federal probation officer, 13th year.
Jeff Rice, No. **44,** Northwestern, attorney, 17th year.
Bill Schuster, No. **129,** Alfred, insurance broker, 12th year.
Bruce Stritesky, No. **102,** Embry Riddle, airline pilot, 6th year.
Undrey Wash, No. **96,** Texas-Arlington, claims controller, 12th year.

HEAD LINESMEN

Mark Baltz, No. **26,** Ohio, sales consultant, 23rd year.
Jerry Bergman, No. **91,** Robert Morris, sales executive, 10th year.
Derick Bowers, No. **74,** East Central, sales representative, 9th year.
Greg Bradley, No. **98,** Tennessee, chemical engineer, 3rd year.
Ed Camp, No. **134,** William Paterson, physical education teacher, 12th year.
George Hayward, No. **54,** Missouri Western, vice-president and manager, warehouse company, 21st year.
Mark Hittner, No. **28,** Pittsburg State, investment broker, 15th year.
Wayne Mackie, No. **106,** Colgate, director of housing, 5th year.
Julian Mapp, No. **52,** Grambling State, project leader, 3rd year.
John McGrath, No. **5,** Kentucky, vice president of sales, 10th year.
Dana McKenzie, No. **8,** Toledo, claims adjuster, 4th year.
Phil McKinnely, No. **110,** UCLA, inventory control, 9th year.
Jim Mello, No. **48,** Northeastern, facilities manager, 8th year.
Kent Payne, No. **79,** Nebraska Wesleyan, teacher, 8th year.
Tom Stabile, No. **24,** Slippery Rock, secondary educational administrator, 17th year.
Steve Stelljes, No. **22,** Friends, business planning manager, 10th year.
Tony Veteri, No. **36,** Manhattan College, physical education teacher, 20th year.

LINE JUDGES

Gary Arthur, No. **108,** Wright State, president, commercial printing company, 15th year.
Tom Barnes, No. **55,** Minnesota, manufacturing representative, 26th year.
Rusty Baynes, No. **59,** Auburn-Montgomery, general manager, safety services, 2nd year.
Jeff Bergman, No. **32,** Robert Morris, president and chief executive officer, medical services, 20th year.
Byron Boston, No. **18,** Austin, tax consultant, 17th year.
Adrian Hill, No. **29,** Buffalo, software engineer, 2nd year.
John Hussey, No. **35,** Idaho State, sales representative, retail logistics group, 10th year.
Darryll Lewis, No. **130,** Dartmouth, associate professor, 13th year.
Ron Marinucci, No. **107,** Glassboro State, vice president, novelty cone company, 15th year.
Mark Perlman, No. **9,** Salem, teacher, 11th year.
Ron Phares, No. **10,** Virginia Tech, president, construction company, 27th year.
Tim Podraza, No. **47,** Nebraska, banker, 4th year.
Jeff Seeman, No. **45,** Minnesota, brokerage sales, 10th year.
Mike Spanier, No. **90,** St. Cloud State, middle school principal, 13th year.
Mark Steinkerchner, No. **84,** Akron, vice-president, 18th year.
Tom Stephan, No. **68,** Pittsburg State, president and CEO, 13th year.
Tom Symonette, No. **100,** Florida, certified public accountant, 8th year.

Roster as of May 2011

FIELD JUDGES

Barry Anderson, No. **20,** North Carolina State, builder/developer, 5th year.
Terry Brown, No. **43,** Tennessee, probation supervisor, 6th year.
Jimmy Buchanan, No. **86,** South Carolina State, insurance agent, 3rd year.
Gary Cavaletto, No. **60,** Hancock, general manager, agricultural operations, 9th year.
Boris Cheek, No. **41,** Morgan State, director of operations and management, 16th year.
Scott Edwards, No. **3,** Alabama, environmental engineer, 13th year.
Greg Gautreaux, No. **80,** S.W. Louisiana, athletic programs manager, 10th year.
Buddy Horton, No. **82,** Oregon State, water service worker, 13th year.
Jim Howey, No. **37,** Erskine College, director of adult education, 13th year.
Jon Lucivansky, No. **89,** Minnesota, high school associate principal, 3rd year.
David Meslow, No. **118,** Augsburg College, marketing manager, 1st year.
Dyrol Prioleau, No. **109,** Johnson C. Smith, manager, law firm, 5th year.
Jim Quirk, No. **63,** Middlebury, financial advisor, 2nd year.
Doug Rosenbaum, No. **67,** Illinois Wesleyan, financial consultant, 11th year.
Scott Steenson, No. **88,** North Texas, commercial real estate broker, 21st year.
Bob Waggoner, No. **25,** Juniata College, probation officer, 15th year.
Mike Weir, No. **50,** Missouri, owner, sporting goods store, 10th year.
Craig Wrolstad, No. **4,** Washington, athletic director, 9th year.
Steve Zimmer, No. **33,** Hofstra, attorney, 15th year.

SIDE JUDGES

Michael Banks, No. **72,** Illinois State, carpenter foreman, 10th year.
Allen Baynes, No. **56,** Auburn, realtor, 4th year.
Don Carlsen, No. **39,** Cal State-Chico, retired county school superintendent, 23rd year.
James Coleman, No. **95,** Arkansas, electrical engineer, 7th year.
Jimmy DeBell, No. **58,** SUNY-Brockport, high school teacher, 3rd year.
Laird Hayes, No. **125,** Princeton, professor, physical education & athletics, 17th year.
Tom Hill, No. **07,** Caroon Newman, teacher, 13th year.
Jeff Lamberth, No. **103,** Texas A&M, attorney, 10th year.
Joe Larrew, No. **73,** St. Louis, attorney, 10th year.
Greg Meyer, No. **78,** Texas Christian, banker, 10th year.
Keith Parham, No. **87,** Howard, advertising operations manager, 1st year.
Rick Patterson, No. **15,** Wofford, banker, 16th year.
Larry Rose, No. **128,** Florida, financial planner, 15th year.
Ronald Torbert, No. **62,** Michigan State, attorney, 2nd year.
Keith Washington, No. **7,** Virginia Military Institute, program financial analyst, 4th year.
Mike Weatherford, No. **116,** Oklahoma State, energy trader, 10th year.
David Wyant, No. **16,** Virginia, consulting engineer, 21st year.

BACK JUDGES

Don Carey, No. **126,** California-Riverside, contract manager, 17th year.
Kirk Dornan, No. **6,** Central Washington, purchasing manager, 18th year.
Lee Dyer, No. **27,** Tennessee-Chattanooga, sales manager, 9th year.
Keith Ferguson, No. **61,** San Jose State, sales, 12th year.
Steve Freeman, No. **133,** Mississippi State, custom home builder, 11th year.
Scott Helverson, No. **93,** Iowa, sales, printing and promotions, 9th year.
Terrence Miles, No. **111,** Arizona State, quality control manager, 4th year.
Dino Paganelli, No. **105,** Aquinas College, educator, 6th year.
Perry Paganelli, No. **46,** Hope College, retired high school administrator, 14th year.
Todd Prukop, No. **30,** Cal State-Fullerton, medical sales representative, 3rd year.
Richard Reels, No. **83,** Chicago State, director of security, court services, 19th year.
Billy Smith, No. **2,** East Carolina, retired federal government, 18th year.
Greg Steed, No. **12,** Howard, computer systems analyst, 9th year.
Tony Steratore, No. **112,** California, PA., co-owner, supply company, 12th year.
Rob Vernatchi, No. **75,** California-Riverside, enforcement investigator, 8th year.
Greg Wilson, No. **119,** USC, law enforcement, 4th year.
Greg Yette, No. **38,** Howard, defense contractor, 2nd year.

Roster as of May 2011

1

**TOUCHDOWN, FIELD GOAL,
or SUCCESSFUL TRY**
Both arms extended above head.

2

SAFETY
Palms together above head.

3

FIRST DOWN
Arm pointed toward defensive
team's goal.

4

**DEAD BALL or
NEUTRAL ZONE ESTABLISHED**
One arm above head
with an open hand.
With fist closed: **Fourth Down.**

5

**BALL ILLEGALLY
TOUCHED, KICKED,
or BATTED**
Fingertips tap both shoulders.

6

TIME OUT
Hands crisscrossed above head.
Same signal followed by placing one
hand on top of cap: **Referee's Time Out.**
Same signal followed by arm swung at
side: **Touchback.**

7

**NO TIME OUT or
TIME IN WITH WHISTLE**
Full arm circled to
simulate moving clock.

8

**DELAY OF GAME
or EXCESS TIME OUT**
Folded arms.

9

**FALSE START,
ILLEGAL FORMATION, or
KICKOFF or SAFETY KICK
OUT OF BOUNDS or
KICKING TEAM PLAYER
VOLUNTARILY OUT OF BOUNDS
DURING A PUNT**
Forearms rotated over and over
in front of body.

10

PERSONAL FOUL
One wrist striking the other above head.
Same signal followed by swinging leg:
Roughing the Kicker.
Same signal followed by raised arm
swinging forward:
Roughing the Passer.
Same signal followed by grasping
facemask: **Major Facemask.**

11

HOLDING
Grasping one wrist,
the fist clenched,
in front of chest.

12

**ILLEGAL USE OF HANDS,
ARMS, or BODY**
Grasping one wrist,
the hand open and facing
forward, in front of chest.

13

**PENALTY REFUSED,
INCOMPLETE
PASS, PLAY OVER, or
MISSED FIELD GOAL or
EXTRA POINT**
Hands shifted in horizontal plane.

14

**PASS JUGGLED INBOUNDS AND
CAUGHT OUT OF BOUNDS**
Hands up and down in front of chest
(following incomplete pass signal).

15

ILLEGAL FORWARD PASS
One hand waved behind back
followed by loss of down
signal (23), when appropriate.

16

**INTENTIONAL
GROUNDING OF PASS**
Parallel arms waved in a diagonal
plane across body. Followed by loss of
down signal (23).

17

**INTERFERENCE WITH FORWARD
PASS or FAIR CATCH**
Hands open
and extended forward from
shoulders with hands vertical.

18

INVALID FAIR-CATCH SIGNAL
One hand waved above head.

19

**INELIGIBLE RECEIVER
or INELIGIBLE
MEMBER OF KICKING TEAM
DOWNFIELD**
Right hand touching top of cap.

20

ILLEGAL CONTACT
One open hand extended forward.

21

**OFFSIDE, ENCROACHMENT, or
NEUTRAL ZONE INFRACTION**
Hands on hips.

22

ILLEGAL MOTION AT SNAP
Horizontal arc with one hand.

23

LOSS OF DOWN
Both hands held behind head.

24

**INTERLOCKING
INTERFERENCE, PUSHING, or
HELPING RUNNER**
Pushing movement of hands
to front with arms downward.

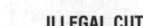

25

**TOUCHING A FORWARD
PASS or SCRIMMAGE KICK**
Diagonal motion of
one hand across another.

26

**UNSPORTSMANLIKE
CONDUCT**
Arms outstretched,
palms down.

27

ILLEGAL CUT
Hand striking front of thigh.
ILLEGAL BLOCK BELOW THE WAIST
One hand striking front of thigh
preceded by personal-foul signal (10).
CHOP BLOCK
Both hands striking side of thighs
preceded by personal-foul signal (10).
CLIPPING
One hand striking back of calf
preceded by personal-foul signal (10).

28

ILLEGAL CRACKBACK
Strike of an
open right hand
against the right mid-thigh
preceded by personal foul
signal (10).

29

PLAYER DISQUALIFIED
Ejection signal.

30

TRIPPING
Repeated action of right foot
in back of left heel.

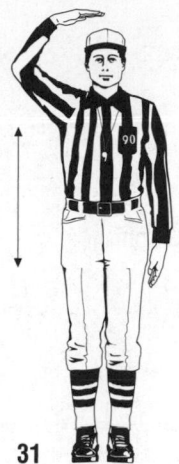

31

**UNCATCHABLE
FORWARD PASS**
Palm of right hand held
parallel to ground above head
and moved back and forth.

32

**TWELVE MEN IN OFFENSIVE HUDDLE
or TOO MANY MEN
ON THE FIELD**
Both hands on top of head.

33

FACEMASK
Grasping facemask with one
hand.

34

ILLEGAL SHIFT
Horizontal arcs with two hands.

35

**RESET PLAY CLOCK–
25 SECONDS**
Pump one arm vertically.

36

**RESET PLAY CLOCK–
40 SECONDS**
Pump two arms vertically.

280 Park Avenue, New York, New York 10017 (212) 450-2000

NFL Internet Network: www.NFL.com

Commissioner: Roger Goodell

Executive Vice President/Football Operations: Ray Anderson

Executive Vice President of Media/
  President and Chief Executive Officer of NFL Network: Steve Bornstein

Executive Vice President of NFL Ventures and Business Operations: Eric Grubman

Executive Vice President of Communications and Public Affairs: Paul Hicks

Executive Vice President/League Counsel: Jeff Pash